Oxford Dictionary of
National Biography

Volume 53

Oxford Dictionary of National Biography

IN ASSOCIATION WITH

The British Academy

From the earliest times to the year 2000

Edited by
H. C. G. Matthew
and
Brian Harrison

Volume 53
Strang–Taylor

OXFORD
UNIVERSITY PRESS

OXFORD

UNIVERSITY PRESS

Great Clarendon Street, Oxford OX2 6DP

Oxford University Press is a department of the University of Oxford.
It furthers the University's objective of excellence in research, scholarship,
and education by publishing worldwide in

Oxford New York

Auckland Bangkok Buenos Aires Cape Town
Chennai Dar es Salaam Delhi Hong Kong Istanbul Karachi
Kolkata Kuala Lumpur Madrid Melbourne Mexico City Mumbai Nairobi
São Paulo Shanghai Taipei Tokyo Toronto

Oxford is a registered trade mark of Oxford University Press
in the UK and in certain other countries

Published in the United States
by Oxford University Press Inc., New York

British Library Cataloguing in Publication Data
Data available

Library of Congress Cataloging in Publication Data
Data available: for details see volume 1, p. iv

ISBN 0-19-861403-9 (this volume)
ISBN 0-19-861411-X (set of sixty volumes)

Text captured by Alliance Phototypesetters, Pondicherry
Illustrations reproduced and archived by
Alliance Graphics Ltd, UK
Typeset in OUP Swift by Interactive Sciences Limited, Gloucester
Printed in Great Britain on acid-free paper by
Butler and Tanner Ltd,
Frome, Somerset

LIST OF ABBREVIATIONS

1 General abbreviations

AB	bachelor of arts
ABC	Australian Broadcasting Corporation
ABC TV	ABC Television
act.	active
A$	Australian dollar
AD	*anno domini*
AFC	Air Force Cross
AIDS	acquired immune deficiency syndrome
AK	Alaska
AL	Alabama
A level	advanced level [examination]
ALS	associate of the Linnean Society
AM	master of arts
AMICE	associate member of the Institution of Civil Engineers
ANZAC	Australian and New Zealand Army Corps
appx *pl.* appxs	appendix(es)
AR	Arkansas
ARA	associate of the Royal Academy
ARCA	associate of the Royal College of Art
ARCM	associate of the Royal College of Music
ARCO	associate of the Royal College of Organists
ARIBA	associate of the Royal Institute of British Architects
ARP	air-raid precautions
ARRC	associate of the Royal Red Cross
ARSA	associate of the Royal Scottish Academy
art.	article / item
ASC	Army Service Corps
Asch	Austrian Schilling
ASDIC	Antisubmarine Detection Investigation Committee
ATS	Auxiliary Territorial Service
ATV	Associated Television
Aug	August
AZ	Arizona
b.	born
BA	bachelor of arts
BA (Admin.)	bachelor of arts (administration)
BAFTA	British Academy of Film and Television Arts
BAO	bachelor of arts in obstetrics
bap.	baptized
BBC	British Broadcasting Corporation / Company
BC	before Christ
BCE	before the common (*or* Christian) era
BCE	bachelor of civil engineering
BCG	bacillus of Calmette and Guérin [inoculation against tuberculosis]
BCh	bachelor of surgery
BChir	bachelor of surgery
BCL	bachelor of civil law
BCnL	bachelor of canon law
BCom	bachelor of commerce
BD	bachelor of divinity
BEd	bachelor of education
BEng	bachelor of engineering
bk *pl.* bks	book(s)
BL	bachelor of law / letters / literature
BLitt	bachelor of letters
BM	bachelor of medicine
BMus	bachelor of music
BP	before present
BP	British Petroleum
Bros.	Brothers
BS	(1) bachelor of science; (2) bachelor of surgery; (3) British standard
BSc	bachelor of science
BSc (Econ.)	bachelor of science (economics)
BSc (Eng.)	bachelor of science (engineering)
bt	baronet
BTh	bachelor of theology
bur.	buried
C.	command [identifier for published parliamentary papers]
c.	*circa*
c.	*capitulum pl. capitula*: chapter(s)
CA	California
Cantab.	Cantabrigiensis
cap.	*capitulum pl. capitula*: chapter(s)
CB	companion of the Bath
CBE	commander of the Order of the British Empire
CBS	Columbia Broadcasting System
cc	cubic centimetres
C$	Canadian dollar
CD	compact disc
Cd	command [identifier for published parliamentary papers]
CE	Common (*or* Christian) Era
cent.	century
cf.	compare
CH	Companion of Honour
chap.	chapter
ChB	bachelor of surgery
CI	Imperial Order of the Crown of India
CIA	Central Intelligence Agency
CID	Criminal Investigation Department
CIE	companion of the Order of the Indian Empire
Cie	Compagnie
CLit	companion of literature
CM	master of surgery
cm	centimetre(s)

Cmd	command [identifier for published parliamentary papers]
CMG	companion of the Order of St Michael and St George
Cmnd	command [identifier for published parliamentary papers]
CO	Colorado
Co.	company
co.	county
col. *pl.* cols.	column(s)
Corp.	corporation
CSE	certificate of secondary education
CSI	companion of the Order of the Star of India
CT	Connecticut
CVO	commander of the Royal Victorian Order
cwt	hundredweight
$	(American) dollar
d.	(1) penny (pence); (2) died
DBE	dame commander of the Order of the British Empire
DCH	diploma in child health
DCh	doctor of surgery
DCL	doctor of civil law
DCnL	doctor of canon law
DCVO	dame commander of the Royal Victorian Order
DD	doctor of divinity
DE	Delaware
Dec	December
dem.	demolished
DEng	doctor of engineering
des.	destroyed
DFC	Distinguished Flying Cross
DipEd	diploma in education
DipPsych	diploma in psychiatry
diss.	dissertation
DL	deputy lieutenant
DLitt	doctor of letters
DLittCelt	doctor of Celtic letters
DM	(1) Deutschmark; (2) doctor of medicine; (3) doctor of musical arts
DMus	doctor of music
DNA	dioxyribonucleic acid
doc.	document
DOL	doctor of oriental learning
DPH	diploma in public health
DPhil	doctor of philosophy
DPM	diploma in psychological medicine
DSC	Distinguished Service Cross
DSc	doctor of science
DSc (Econ.)	doctor of science (economics)
DSc (Eng.)	doctor of science (engineering)
DSM	Distinguished Service Medal
DSO	companion of the Distinguished Service Order
DSocSc	doctor of social science
DTech	doctor of technology
DTh	doctor of theology
DTM	diploma in tropical medicine
DTMH	diploma in tropical medicine and hygiene
DU	doctor of the university
DUniv	doctor of the university
dwt	pennyweight
EC	European Community
ed. *pl.* eds.	edited / edited by / editor(s)
Edin.	Edinburgh
edn	edition
EEC	European Economic Community
EFTA	European Free Trade Association
EICS	East India Company Service
EMI	Electrical and Musical Industries (Ltd)
Eng.	English
enl.	enlarged
ENSA	Entertainments National Service Association
ep. *pl.* epp.	*epistola(e)*
ESP	extra-sensory perception
esp.	especially
esq.	esquire
est.	estimate / estimated
EU	European Union
ex	sold by (*lit.* out of)
excl.	excludes / excluding
exh.	exhibited
exh. cat.	exhibition catalogue
f. *pl.* ff.	following [pages]
FA	Football Association
FACP	fellow of the American College of Physicians
facs.	facsimile
FANY	First Aid Nursing Yeomanry
FBA	fellow of the British Academy
FBI	Federation of British Industries
FCS	fellow of the Chemical Society
Feb	February
FEng	fellow of the Fellowship of Engineering
FFCM	fellow of the Faculty of Community Medicine
FGS	fellow of the Geological Society
fig.	figure
FIMechE	fellow of the Institution of Mechanical Engineers
FL	Florida
fl.	*floruit*
FLS	fellow of the Linnean Society
FM	frequency modulation
fol. *pl.* fols.	folio(s)
Fr	French francs
Fr.	French
FRAeS	fellow of the Royal Aeronautical Society
FRAI	fellow of the Royal Anthropological Institute
FRAM	fellow of the Royal Academy of Music
FRAS	(1) fellow of the Royal Asiatic Society; (2) fellow of the Royal Astronomical Society
FRCM	fellow of the Royal College of Music
FRCO	fellow of the Royal College of Organists
FRCOG	fellow of the Royal College of Obstetricians and Gynaecologists
FRCP(C)	fellow of the Royal College of Physicians of Canada
FRCP (Edin.)	fellow of the Royal College of Physicians of Edinburgh
FRCP (Lond.)	fellow of the Royal College of Physicians of London
FRCPath	fellow of the Royal College of Pathologists
FRCPsych	fellow of the Royal College of Psychiatrists
FRCS	fellow of the Royal College of Surgeons
FRGS	fellow of the Royal Geographical Society
FRIBA	fellow of the Royal Institute of British Architects
FRICS	fellow of the Royal Institute of Chartered Surveyors
FRS	fellow of the Royal Society
FRSA	fellow of the Royal Society of Arts

FRSCM	fellow of the Royal School of Church Music		ISO	companion of the Imperial Service Order
FRSE	fellow of the Royal Society of Edinburgh		It.	Italian
FRSL	fellow of the Royal Society of Literature		ITA	Independent Television Authority
FSA	fellow of the Society of Antiquaries		ITV	Independent Television
ft	foot *pl.* feet		Jan	January
FTCL	fellow of Trinity College of Music, London		JP	justice of the peace
ft-lb per min.	foot-pounds per minute [unit of horsepower]		jun.	junior
FZS	fellow of the Zoological Society		KB	knight of the Order of the Bath
GA	Georgia		KBE	knight commander of the Order of the British Empire
GBE	knight or dame grand cross of the Order of the British Empire		KC	king's counsel
GCB	knight grand cross of the Order of the Bath		kcal	kilocalorie
GCE	general certificate of education		KCB	knight commander of the Order of the Bath
GCH	knight grand cross of the Royal Guelphic Order		KCH	knight commander of the Royal Guelphic Order
GCHQ	government communications headquarters		KCIE	knight commander of the Order of the Indian Empire
GCIE	knight grand commander of the Order of the Indian Empire		KCMG	knight commander of the Order of St Michael and St George
GCMG	knight or dame grand cross of the Order of St Michael and St George		KCSI	knight commander of the Order of the Star of India
GCSE	general certificate of secondary education		KCVO	knight commander of the Royal Victorian Order
GCSI	knight grand commander of the Order of the Star of India		keV	kilo-electron-volt
GCStJ	bailiff or dame grand cross of the order of St John of Jerusalem		KG	knight of the Order of the Garter
			KGB	[Soviet committee of state security]
GCVO	knight or dame grand cross of the Royal Victorian Order		KH	knight of the Royal Guelphic Order
			KLM	Koninklijke Luchtvaart Maatschappij (Royal Dutch Air Lines)
GEC	General Electric Company			
Ger.	German		km	kilometre(s)
GI	government (*or* general) issue		KP	knight of the Order of St Patrick
GMT	Greenwich mean time		KS	Kansas
GP	general practitioner		KT	knight of the Order of the Thistle
GPU	[Soviet special police unit]		kt	knight
GSO	general staff officer		KY	Kentucky
Heb.	Hebrew		£	pound(s) sterling
HEICS	Honourable East India Company Service		£E	Egyptian pound
HI	Hawaii		L	lira *pl.* lire
HIV	human immunodeficiency virus		l. *pl.* ll.	line(s)
HK$	Hong Kong dollar		LA	Lousiana
HM	his / her majesty('s)		LAA	light anti-aircraft
HMAS	his / her majesty's Australian ship		LAH	licentiate of the Apothecaries' Hall, Dublin
HMNZS	his / her majesty's New Zealand ship		Lat.	Latin
HMS	his / her majesty's ship		lb	pound(s), unit of weight
HMSO	His / Her Majesty's Stationery Office		LDS	licence in dental surgery
HMV	His Master's Voice		*lit.*	literally
Hon.	Honourable		LittB	bachelor of letters
hp	horsepower		LittD	doctor of letters
hr	hour(s)		LKQCPI	licentiate of the King and Queen's College of Physicians, Ireland
HRH	his / her royal highness			
HTV	Harlech Television		LLA	lady literate in arts
IA	Iowa		LLB	bachelor of laws
ibid.	*ibidem*: in the same place		LLD	doctor of laws
ICI	Imperial Chemical Industries (Ltd)		LLM	master of laws
ID	Idaho		LM	licentiate in midwifery
IL	Illinois		LP	long-playing record
illus.	illustration		LRAM	licentiate of the Royal Academy of Music
illustr.	illustrated		LRCP	licentiate of the Royal College of Physicians
IN	Indiana		LRCPS (Glasgow)	licentiate of the Royal College of Physicians and Surgeons of Glasgow
in.	inch(es)			
Inc.	Incorporated		LRCS	licentiate of the Royal College of Surgeons
incl.	includes / including		LSA	licentiate of the Society of Apothecaries
IOU	I owe you		LSD	lysergic acid diethylamide
IQ	intelligence quotient		LVO	lieutenant of the Royal Victorian Order
Ir£	Irish pound		M. *pl.* MM.	Monsieur *pl.* Messieurs
IRA	Irish Republican Army		m	metre(s)

m. *pl.* mm.	membrane(s)	ND	North Dakota
MA	(1) Massachusetts; (2) master of arts	n.d.	no date
MAI	master of engineering	NE	Nebraska
MB	bachelor of medicine	*nem. con.*	*nemine contradicente*: unanimously
MBA	master of business administration	new ser.	new series
MBE	member of the Order of the British Empire	NH	New Hampshire
MC	Military Cross	NHS	National Health Service
MCC	Marylebone Cricket Club	NJ	New Jersey
MCh	master of surgery	NKVD	[Soviet people's commissariat for internal affairs]
MChir	master of surgery		
MCom	master of commerce	NM	New Mexico
MD	(1) doctor of medicine; (2) Maryland	nm	nanometre(s)
MDMA	methylenedioxymethamphetamine	no. *pl.* nos.	number(s)
ME	Maine	Nov	November
MEd	master of education	n.p.	no place [of publication]
MEng	master of engineering	NS	new style
MEP	member of the European parliament	NV	Nevada
MG	Morris Garages	NY	New York
MGM	Metro-Goldwyn-Mayer	NZBS	New Zealand Broadcasting Service
Mgr	Monsignor	OBE	officer of the Order of the British Empire
MI	(1) Michigan; (2) military intelligence	obit.	obituary
MI1c	[secret intelligence department]	Oct	October
MI5	[military intelligence department]	OCTU	officer cadets training unit
MI6	[secret intelligence department]	OECD	Organization for Economic Co-operation and Development
MI9	[secret escape service]		
MICE	member of the Institution of Civil Engineers	OEEC	Organization for European Economic Co-operation
MIEE	member of the Institution of Electrical Engineers		
		OFM	order of Friars Minor [Franciscans]
min.	minute(s)	OFMCap	Ordine Frati Minori Cappucini: member of the Capuchin order
Mk	mark		
ML	(1) licentiate of medicine; (2) master of laws	OH	Ohio
MLitt	master of letters	OK	Oklahoma
Mlle	Mademoiselle	O level	ordinary level [examination]
mm	millimetre(s)	OM	Order of Merit
Mme	Madame	OP	order of Preachers [Dominicans]
MN	Minnesota	op. *pl.* opp.	opus *pl.* opera
MO	Missouri	OPEC	Organization of Petroleum Exporting Countries
MOH	medical officer of health	OR	Oregon
MP	member of parliament	orig.	original
m.p.h.	miles per hour	OS	old style
MPhil	master of philosophy	OSB	Order of St Benedict
MRCP	member of the Royal College of Physicians	OTC	Officers' Training Corps
MRCS	member of the Royal College of Surgeons	OWS	Old Watercolour Society
MRCVS	member of the Royal College of Veterinary Surgeons	Oxon.	Oxoniensis
		p. *pl.* pp.	page(s)
MRIA	member of the Royal Irish Academy	PA	Pennsylvania
MS	(1) master of science; (2) Mississippi	p.a.	per annum
MS *pl.* MSS	manuscript(s)	para.	paragraph
MSc	master of science	PAYE	pay as you earn
MSc (Econ.)	master of science (economics)	pbk *pl.* pbks	paperback(s)
MT	Montana	*per.*	[during the] period
MusB	bachelor of music	PhD	doctor of philosophy
MusBac	bachelor of music	pl.	(1) plate(s); (2) plural
MusD	doctor of music	priv. coll.	private collection
MV	motor vessel	pt *pl.* pts	part(s)
MVO	member of the Royal Victorian Order	pubd	published
n. *pl.* nn.	note(s)	PVC	polyvinyl chloride
NAAFI	Navy, Army, and Air Force Institutes	q. *pl.* qq.	(1) question(s); (2) quire(s)
NASA	National Aeronautics and Space Administration	QC	queen's counsel
NATO	North Atlantic Treaty Organization	R	rand
NBC	National Broadcasting Corporation	R.	Rex / Regina
NC	North Carolina	*r*	recto
NCO	non-commissioned officer	r.	reigned / ruled
		RA	Royal Academy / Royal Academician

RAC	Royal Automobile Club		Skr	Swedish krona
RAF	Royal Air Force		Span.	Spanish
RAFVR	Royal Air Force Volunteer Reserve		SPCK	Society for Promoting Christian Knowledge
RAM	[member of the] Royal Academy of Music		SS	(1) Santissimi; (2) Schutzstaffel; (3) steam ship
RAMC	Royal Army Medical Corps		STB	bachelor of theology
RCA	Royal College of Art		STD	doctor of theology
RCNC	Royal Corps of Naval Constructors		STM	master of theology
RCOG	Royal College of Obstetricians and Gynaecologists		STP	doctor of theology
RDI	royal designer for industry		*supp.*	supposedly
RE	Royal Engineers		suppl. *pl.* suppls.	supplement(s)
repr. *pl.* reprs.	reprint(s) / reprinted		s.v.	*sub verbo* / *sub voce*: under the word / heading
repro.	reproduced		SY	steam yacht
rev.	revised / revised by / reviser / revision		TA	Territorial Army
Revd	Reverend		TASS	[Soviet news agency]
RHA	Royal Hibernian Academy		TB	tuberculosis (*lit.* tubercle bacillus)
RI	(1) Rhode Island; (2) Royal Institute of Painters in Water-Colours		TD	(1) *teachtaí dála* (member of the Dáil); (2) territorial decoration
RIBA	Royal Institute of British Architects		TN	Tennessee
RIN	Royal Indian Navy		TNT	trinitrotoluene
RM	Reichsmark		trans.	translated / translated by / translation / translator
RMS	Royal Mail steamer		TT	tourist trophy
RN	Royal Navy		TUC	Trades Union Congress
RNA	ribonucleic acid		TX	Texas
RNAS	Royal Naval Air Service		U-boat	*Unterseeboot*: submarine
RNR	Royal Naval Reserve		Ufa	Universum-Film AG
RNVR	Royal Naval Volunteer Reserve		UMIST	University of Manchester Institute of Science and Technology
RO	Record Office		UN	United Nations
r.p.m.	revolutions per minute		UNESCO	United Nations Educational, Scientific, and Cultural Organization
RRS	royal research ship		UNICEF	United Nations International Children's Emergency Fund
Rs	rupees		unpubd	unpublished
RSA	(1) Royal Scottish Academician; (2) Royal Society of Arts		USS	United States ship
RSPCA	Royal Society for the Prevention of Cruelty to Animals		UT	Utah
Rt Hon.	Right Honourable		*v*	verso
Rt Revd	Right Reverend		v.	versus
RUC	Royal Ulster Constabulary		VA	Virginia
Russ.	Russian		VAD	Voluntary Aid Detachment
RWS	Royal Watercolour Society		VC	Victoria Cross
S4C	Sianel Pedwar Cymru		VE-day	victory in Europe day
s.	shilling(s)		Ven.	Venerable
s.a.	*sub anno*: under the year		VJ-day	victory over Japan day
SABC	South African Broadcasting Corporation		vol. *pl.* vols.	volume(s)
SAS	Special Air Service		VT	Vermont
SC	South Carolina		WA	Washington [state]
ScD	doctor of science		WAAC	Women's Auxiliary Army Corps
S$	Singapore dollar		WAAF	Women's Auxiliary Air Force
SD	South Dakota		WEA	Workers' Educational Association
sec.	second(s)		WHO	World Health Organization
sel.	selected		WI	Wisconsin
sen.	senior		WRAF	Women's Royal Air Force
Sept	September		WRNS	Women's Royal Naval Service
ser.	series		WV	West Virginia
SHAPE	supreme headquarters allied powers, Europe		WVS	Women's Voluntary Service
SIDRO	Société Internationale d'Énergie Hydro-Électrique		WY	Wyoming
sig. *pl.* sigs.	signature(s)		¥	yen
sing.	singular		YMCA	Young Men's Christian Association
SIS	Secret Intelligence Service		YWCA	Young Women's Christian Association
SJ	Society of Jesus			

2 Institution abbreviations

All Souls Oxf.	All Souls College, Oxford
AM Oxf.	Ashmolean Museum, Oxford
Balliol Oxf.	Balliol College, Oxford
BBC WAC	BBC Written Archives Centre, Reading
Beds. & Luton ARS	Bedfordshire and Luton Archives and Record Service, Bedford
Berks. RO	Berkshire Record Office, Reading
BFI	British Film Institute, London
BFI NFTVA	British Film Institute, London, National Film and Television Archive
BGS	British Geological Survey, Keyworth, Nottingham
Birm. CA	Birmingham Central Library, Birmingham City Archives
Birm. CL	Birmingham Central Library
BL	British Library, London
BL NSA	British Library, London, National Sound Archive
BL OIOC	British Library, London, Oriental and India Office Collections
BLPES	London School of Economics and Political Science, British Library of Political and Economic Science
BM	British Museum, London
Bodl. Oxf.	Bodleian Library, Oxford
Bodl. RH	Bodleian Library of Commonwealth and African Studies at Rhodes House, Oxford
Borth. Inst.	Borthwick Institute of Historical Research, University of York
Boston PL	Boston Public Library, Massachusetts
Bristol RO	Bristol Record Office
Bucks. RLSS	Buckinghamshire Records and Local Studies Service, Aylesbury
CAC Cam.	Churchill College, Cambridge, Churchill Archives Centre
Cambs. AS	Cambridgeshire Archive Service
CCC Cam.	Corpus Christi College, Cambridge
CCC Oxf.	Corpus Christi College, Oxford
Ches. & Chester ALSS	Cheshire and Chester Archives and Local Studies Service
Christ Church Oxf.	Christ Church, Oxford
Christies	Christies, London
City Westm. AC	City of Westminster Archives Centre, London
CKS	Centre for Kentish Studies, Maidstone
CLRO	Corporation of London Records Office
Coll. Arms	College of Arms, London
Col. U.	Columbia University, New York
Cornwall RO	Cornwall Record Office, Truro
Courtauld Inst.	Courtauld Institute of Art, London
CUL	Cambridge University Library
Cumbria AS	Cumbria Archive Service
Derbys. RO	Derbyshire Record Office, Matlock
Devon RO	Devon Record Office, Exeter
Dorset RO	Dorset Record Office, Dorchester
Duke U.	Duke University, Durham, North Carolina
Duke U., Perkins L.	Duke University, Durham, North Carolina, William R. Perkins Library
Durham Cath. CL	Durham Cathedral, chapter library
Durham RO	Durham Record Office
DWL	Dr Williams's Library, London
Essex RO	Essex Record Office
E. Sussex RO	East Sussex Record Office, Lewes
Eton	Eton College, Berkshire
FM Cam.	Fitzwilliam Museum, Cambridge
Folger	Folger Shakespeare Library, Washington, DC
Garr. Club	Garrick Club, London
Girton Cam.	Girton College, Cambridge
GL	Guildhall Library, London
Glos. RO	Gloucestershire Record Office, Gloucester
Gon. & Caius Cam.	Gonville and Caius College, Cambridge
Gov. Art Coll.	Government Art Collection
GS Lond.	Geological Society of London
Hants. RO	Hampshire Record Office, Winchester
Harris Man. Oxf.	Harris Manchester College, Oxford
Harvard TC	Harvard Theatre Collection, Harvard University, Cambridge, Massachusetts, Nathan Marsh Pusey Library
Harvard U.	Harvard University, Cambridge, Massachusetts
Harvard U., Houghton L.	Harvard University, Cambridge, Massachusetts, Houghton Library
Herefs. RO	Herefordshire Record Office, Hereford
Herts. ALS	Hertfordshire Archives and Local Studies, Hertford
Hist. Soc. Penn.	Historical Society of Pennsylvania, Philadelphia
HLRO	House of Lords Record Office, London
Hult. Arch.	Hulton Archive, London and New York
Hunt. L.	Huntington Library, San Marino, California
ICL	Imperial College, London
Inst. CE	Institution of Civil Engineers, London
Inst. EE	Institution of Electrical Engineers, London
IWM	Imperial War Museum, London
IWM FVA	Imperial War Museum, London, Film and Video Archive
IWM SA	Imperial War Museum, London, Sound Archive
JRL	John Rylands University Library of Manchester
King's AC Cam.	King's College Archives Centre, Cambridge
King's Cam.	King's College, Cambridge
King's Lond.	King's College, London
King's Lond., Liddell Hart C.	King's College, London, Liddell Hart Centre for Military Archives
Lancs. RO	Lancashire Record Office, Preston
L. Cong.	Library of Congress, Washington, DC
Leics. RO	Leicestershire, Leicester, and Rutland Record Office, Leicester
Lincs. Arch.	Lincolnshire Archives, Lincoln
Linn. Soc.	Linnean Society of London
LMA	London Metropolitan Archives
LPL	Lambeth Palace, London
Lpool RO	Liverpool Record Office and Local Studies Service
LUL	London University Library
Magd. Cam.	Magdalene College, Cambridge
Magd. Oxf.	Magdalen College, Oxford
Man. City Gall.	Manchester City Galleries
Man. CL	Manchester Central Library
Mass. Hist. Soc.	Massachusetts Historical Society, Boston
Merton Oxf.	Merton College, Oxford
MHS Oxf.	Museum of the History of Science, Oxford
Mitchell L., Glas.	Mitchell Library, Glasgow
Mitchell L., NSW	State Library of New South Wales, Sydney, Mitchell Library
Morgan L.	Pierpont Morgan Library, New York
NA Canada	National Archives of Canada, Ottawa
NA Ire.	National Archives of Ireland, Dublin
NAM	National Army Museum, London
NA Scot.	National Archives of Scotland, Edinburgh
News Int. RO	News International Record Office, London
NG Ire.	National Gallery of Ireland, Dublin

NG Scot.	National Gallery of Scotland, Edinburgh	Suffolk RO	Suffolk Record Office
NHM	Natural History Museum, London	Surrey HC	Surrey History Centre, Woking
NL Aus.	National Library of Australia, Canberra	TCD	Trinity College, Dublin
NL Ire.	National Library of Ireland, Dublin	Trinity Cam.	Trinity College, Cambridge
NL NZ	National Library of New Zealand, Wellington	U. Aberdeen	University of Aberdeen
NL NZ, Turnbull L.	National Library of New Zealand, Wellington, Alexander Turnbull Library	U. Birm.	University of Birmingham
		U. Birm. L.	University of Birmingham Library
NL Scot.	National Library of Scotland, Edinburgh	U. Cal.	University of California
NL Wales	National Library of Wales, Aberystwyth	U. Cam.	University of Cambridge
NMG Wales	National Museum and Gallery of Wales, Cardiff	UCL	University College, London
NMM	National Maritime Museum, London	U. Durham	University of Durham
Norfolk RO	Norfolk Record Office, Norwich	U. Durham L.	University of Durham Library
Northants. RO	Northamptonshire Record Office, Northampton	U. Edin.	University of Edinburgh
		U. Edin., New Coll.	University of Edinburgh, New College
Northumbd RO	Northumberland Record Office	U. Edin., New Coll. L.	University of Edinburgh, New College Library
Notts. Arch.	Nottinghamshire Archives, Nottingham		
NPG	National Portrait Gallery, London	U. Edin. L.	University of Edinburgh Library
NRA	National Archives, London, Historical Manuscripts Commission, National Register of Archives	U. Glas.	University of Glasgow
		U. Glas. L.	University of Glasgow Library
		U. Hull	University of Hull
Nuffield Oxf.	Nuffield College, Oxford	U. Hull, Brynmor Jones L.	University of Hull, Brynmor Jones Library
N. Yorks. CRO	North Yorkshire County Record Office, Northallerton		
		U. Leeds	University of Leeds
NYPL	New York Public Library	U. Leeds, Brotherton L.	University of Leeds, Brotherton Library
Oxf. UA	Oxford University Archives		
Oxf. U. Mus. NH	Oxford University Museum of Natural History	U. Lond.	University of London
Oxon. RO	Oxfordshire Record Office, Oxford	U. Lpool	University of Liverpool
Pembroke Cam.	Pembroke College, Cambridge	U. Lpool L.	University of Liverpool Library
PRO	National Archives, London, Public Record Office	U. Mich.	University of Michigan, Ann Arbor
		U. Mich., Clements L.	University of Michigan, Ann Arbor, William L. Clements Library
PRO NIre.	Public Record Office for Northern Ireland, Belfast		
		U. Newcastle	University of Newcastle upon Tyne
Pusey Oxf.	Pusey House, Oxford	U. Newcastle, Robinson L.	University of Newcastle upon Tyne, Robinson Library
RA	Royal Academy of Arts, London		
Ransom HRC	Harry Ransom Humanities Research Center, University of Texas, Austin	U. Nott.	University of Nottingham
		U. Nott. L.	University of Nottingham Library
RAS	Royal Astronomical Society, London	U. Oxf.	University of Oxford
RBG Kew	Royal Botanic Gardens, Kew, London	U. Reading	University of Reading
RCP Lond.	Royal College of Physicians of London	U. Reading L.	University of Reading Library
RCS Eng.	Royal College of Surgeons of England, London	U. St Andr.	University of St Andrews
RGS	Royal Geographical Society, London	U. St Andr. L.	University of St Andrews Library
RIBA	Royal Institute of British Architects, London	U. Southampton	University of Southampton
RIBA BAL	Royal Institute of British Architects, London, British Architectural Library	U. Southampton L.	University of Southampton Library
		U. Sussex	University of Sussex, Brighton
Royal Arch.	Royal Archives, Windsor Castle, Berkshire [by gracious permission of her majesty the queen]	U. Texas	University of Texas, Austin
		U. Wales	University of Wales
		U. Warwick Mod. RC	University of Warwick, Coventry, Modern Records Centre
Royal Irish Acad.	Royal Irish Academy, Dublin		
Royal Scot. Acad.	Royal Scottish Academy, Edinburgh	V&A	Victoria and Albert Museum, London
RS	Royal Society, London	V&A NAL	Victoria and Albert Museum, London, National Art Library
RSA	Royal Society of Arts, London		
RS Friends, Lond.	Religious Society of Friends, London	Warks. CRO	Warwickshire County Record Office, Warwick
St Ant. Oxf.	St Antony's College, Oxford	Wellcome L.	Wellcome Library for the History and Understanding of Medicine, London
St John Cam.	St John's College, Cambridge		
S. Antiquaries, Lond.	Society of Antiquaries of London		
		Westm. DA	Westminster Diocesan Archives, London
Sci. Mus.	Science Museum, London	Wilts. & Swindon RO	Wiltshire and Swindon Record Office, Trowbridge
Scot. NPG	Scottish National Portrait Gallery, Edinburgh		
Scott Polar RI	University of Cambridge, Scott Polar Research Institute	Worcs. RO	Worcestershire Record Office, Worcester
		W. Sussex RO	West Sussex Record Office, Chichester
Sheff. Arch.	Sheffield Archives	W. Yorks. AS	West Yorkshire Archive Service
Shrops. RRC	Shropshire Records and Research Centre, Shrewsbury	Yale U.	Yale University, New Haven, Connecticut
		Yale U., Beinecke L.	Yale University, New Haven, Connecticut, Beinecke Rare Book and Manuscript Library
SOAS	School of Oriental and African Studies, London		
Som. ARS	Somerset Archive and Record Service, Taunton	Yale U. CBA	Yale University, New Haven, Connecticut, Yale Center for British Art
Staffs. RO	Staffordshire Record Office, Stafford		

3 Bibliographic abbreviations

Adams, *Drama* — W. D. Adams, *A dictionary of the drama*, 1: *A–G* (1904); 2: *H–Z* (1956) [vol. 2 microfilm only]

AFM — J O'Donovan, ed. and trans., *Annala rioghachta Eireann / Annals of the kingdom of Ireland by the four masters*, 7 vols. (1848–51); 2nd edn (1856); 3rd edn (1990)

Allibone, *Dict.* — S. A. Allibone, *A critical dictionary of English literature and British and American authors*, 3 vols. (1859–71); suppl. by J. F. Kirk, 2 vols. (1891)

ANB — J. A. Garraty and M. C. Carnes, eds., *American national biography*, 24 vols. (1999)

Anderson, *Scot. nat.* — W. Anderson, *The Scottish nation, or, The surnames, families, literature, honours, and biographical history of the people of Scotland*, 3 vols. (1859–63)

Ann. mon. — H. R. Luard, ed., *Annales monastici*, 5 vols., Rolls Series, 36 (1864–9)

Ann. Ulster — S. Mac Airt and G. Mac Niocaill, eds., *Annals of Ulster (to AD 1131)* (1983)

APC — *Acts of the privy council of England*, new ser., 46 vols. (1890–1964)

APS — *The acts of the parliaments of Scotland*, 12 vols. in 13 (1814–75)

Arber, *Regs. Stationers* — F. Arber, ed., *A transcript of the registers of the Company of Stationers of London, 1554–1640 AD*, 5 vols. (1875–94)

ArchR — *Architectural Review*

ASC — D. Whitelock, D. C. Douglas, and S. I. Tucker, ed. and trans., *The Anglo-Saxon Chronicle: a revised translation* (1961)

AS chart. — P. H. Sawyer, *Anglo-Saxon charters: an annotated list and bibliography*, Royal Historical Society Guides and Handbooks (1968)

AusDB — D. Pike and others, eds., *Australian dictionary of biography*, 16 vols. (1966–2002)

Baker, *Serjeants* — J. H. Baker, *The order of serjeants at law*, SeldS, suppl. ser., 5 (1984)

Bale, *Cat.* — J. Bale, *Scriptorum illustrium Maioris Brytannie, quam nunc Angliam et Scotiam vocant: catalogus*, 2 vols. in 1 (Basel, 1557–9); facs. edn (1971)

Bale, *Index* — J. Bale, *Index Britanniae scriptorum*, ed. R. L. Poole and M. Bateson (1902); facs. edn (1990)

BBCS — *Bulletin of the Board of Celtic Studies*

BDMBR — J. O. Baylen and N. J. Gossman, eds., *Biographical dictionary of modern British radicals*, 3 vols. in 4 (1979–88)

Bede, *Hist. eccl.* — *Bede's Ecclesiastical history of the English people*, ed. and trans. B. Colgrave and R. A. B. Mynors, OMT (1969); repr. (1991)

Bénézit, *Dict.* — E. Bénézit, *Dictionnaire critique et documentaire des peintres, sculpteurs, dessinateurs et graveurs*, 3 vols. (Paris, 1911–23); new edn, 8 vols. (1948–66), repr. (1966); 3rd edn, rev. and enl., 10 vols. (1976); 4th edn, 14 vols. (1999)

BIHR — *Bulletin of the Institute of Historical Research*

Birch, *Seals* — W. de Birch, *Catalogue of seals in the department of manuscripts in the British Museum*, 6 vols. (1887–1900)

Bishop Burnet's History — *Bishop Burnet's History of his own time*, ed. M. J. Routh, 2nd edn, 6 vols. (1833)

Blackwood — *Blackwood's [Edinburgh] Magazine*, 328 vols. (1817–1980)

Blain, Clements & Grundy, *Feminist comp.* — V. Blain, P. Clements, and I. Grundy, eds., *The feminist companion to literature in English* (1990)

BL cat. — *The British Library general catalogue of printed books* [in 360 vols. with suppls., also CD-ROM and online]

BMJ — *British Medical Journal*

Boase & Courtney, *Bibl. Corn.* — G. C. Boase and W. P. Courtney, *Bibliotheca Cornubiensis: a catalogue of the writings … of Cornishmen*, 3 vols. (1874–82)

Boase, *Mod. Eng. biog.* — F. Boase, *Modern English biography: containing many thousand concise memoirs of persons who have died since the year 1850*, 6 vols. (privately printed, Truro, 1892–1921); repr. (1965)

Boswell, *Life* — *Boswell's Life of Johnson: together with Journal of a tour to the Hebrides and Johnson's Diary of a journey into north Wales*, ed. G. B. Hill, enl. edn, rev. L. F. Powell, 6 vols. (1934–50); 2nd edn (1964); repr. (1971)

Brown & Stratton, *Brit. mus.* — J. D. Brown and S. S. Stratton, *British musical biography* (1897)

Bryan, *Painters* — M. Bryan, *A biographical and critical dictionary of painters and engravers*, 2 vols. (1816); new edn, ed. G. Stanley (1849); new edn, ed. R. E. Graves and W. Armstrong, 2 vols. (1886–9); [4th edn], ed. G. C. Williamson, 5 vols. (1903–5) [various reprs.]

Burke, *Gen. GB* — J. Burke, *A genealogical and heraldic history of the commoners of Great Britain and Ireland*, 4 vols. (1833–8); new edn as *A genealogical and heraldic dictionary of the landed gentry of Great Britain and Ireland*, 3 vols. [1843–9] [many later edns]

Burke, *Gen. Ire.* — J. B. Burke, *A genealogical and heraldic history of the landed gentry of Ireland* (1899); 2nd edn (1904); 3rd edn (1912); 4th edn (1958); 5th edn as *Burke's Irish family records* (1976)

Burke, *Peerage* — J. Burke, *A general [later edns A genealogical] and heraldic dictionary of the peerage and baronetage of the United Kingdom* [later edns *the British empire*] (1829–)

Burney, *Hist. mus.* — C. Burney, *A general history of music, from the earliest ages to the present period*, 4 vols. (1776–89)

Burtchaell & Sadleir, *Alum. Dubl.* — G. D. Burtchaell and T. U. Sadleir, *Alumni Dublinenses: a register of the students, graduates, and provosts of Trinity College* (1924); [2nd edn], with suppl., in 2 pts (1935)

Calamy rev. — A. G. Matthews, *Calamy revised* (1934); repr. (1988)

CCI — *Calendar of confirmations and inventories granted and given up in the several commissariots of Scotland* (1876–)

CClR — *Calendar of the close rolls preserved in the Public Record Office*, 47 vols. (1892–1963)

CDS — J. Bain, ed., *Calendar of documents relating to Scotland*, 4 vols., PRO (1881–8); suppl. vol. 5, ed. G. G. Simpson and J. D. Galbraith [1986]

CEPR letters — W. H. Bliss, C. Johnson, and J. Twemlow, eds., *Calendar of entries in the papal registers relating to Great Britain and Ireland: papal letters* (1893–)

CGPLA — *Calendars of the grants of probate and letters of administration* [in 4 ser.: *England & Wales, Northern Ireland, Ireland*, and *Éire*]

Chambers, *Scots.* — R. Chambers, ed., *A biographical dictionary of eminent Scotsmen*, 4 vols. (1832–5)

Chancery records — chancery records pubd by the PRO

Chancery records (RC) — chancery records pubd by the Record Commissions

CIPM	*Calendar of inquisitions post mortem*, [20 vols.], PRO (1904–); also *Henry VII*, 3 vols. (1898–1955)
Clarendon, *Hist. rebellion*	E. Hyde, earl of Clarendon, *The history of the rebellion and civil wars in England*, 6 vols. (1888); repr. (1958) and (1992)
Cobbett, *Parl. hist.*	W. Cobbett and J. Wright, eds., *Cobbett's Parliamentary history of England*, 36 vols. (1806–1820)
Colvin, *Archs.*	H. Colvin, *A biographical dictionary of British architects, 1600–1840*, 3rd edn (1995)
Cooper, *Ath. Cantab.*	C. H. Cooper and T. Cooper, *Athenae Cantabrigienses*, 3 vols. (1858–1913); repr. (1967)
CPR	*Calendar of the patent rolls preserved in the Public Record Office* (1891–)
Crockford	*Crockford's Clerical Directory*
CS	Camden Society
CSP	*Calendar of state papers* [in 11 ser.: domestic, Scotland, Scottish series, Ireland, colonial, Commonwealth, foreign, Spain [at Simancas], Rome, Milan, and Venice]
CYS	Canterbury and York Society
DAB	*Dictionary of American biography*, 21 vols. (1928–36), repr. in 11 vols. (1964); 10 suppls. (1944–96)
DBB	D. J. Jeremy, ed., *Dictionary of business biography*, 5 vols. (1984–6)
DCB	G. W. Brown and others, *Dictionary of Canadian biography*, [14 vols.] (1966–)
Debrett's Peerage	*Debrett's Peerage* (1803–) [sometimes *Debrett's Illustrated peerage*]
Desmond, *Botanists*	R. Desmond, *Dictionary of British and Irish botanists and horticulturists* (1977); rev. edn (1994)
Dir. Brit. archs.	A. Felstead, J. Franklin, and L. Pinfield, eds., *Directory of British architects, 1834–1900* (1993); 2nd edn, ed. A. Brodie and others, 2 vols. (2001)
DLB	J. M. Bellamy and J. Saville, eds., *Dictionary of labour biography*, [10 vols.] (1972–)
DLitB	Dictionary of Literary Biography
DNB	*Dictionary of national biography*, 63 vols. (1885–1900), suppl., 3 vols. (1901); repr. in 22 vols. (1908–9); 10 further suppls. (1912–96); *Missing persons* (1993)
DNZB	W. H. Oliver and C. Orange, eds., *The dictionary of New Zealand biography*, 5 vols. (1990–2000)
DSAB	W. J. de Kock and others, eds., *Dictionary of South African biography*, 5 vols. (1968–87)
DSB	C. C. Gillispie and F. L. Holmes, eds., *Dictionary of scientific biography*, 16 vols. (1970–80); repr. in 8 vols. (1981); 2 vol. suppl. (1990)
DSBB	A. Slaven and S. Checkland, eds., *Dictionary of Scottish business biography, 1860–1960*, 2 vols. (1986–90)
DSCHT	N. M. de S. Cameron and others, eds., *Dictionary of Scottish church history and theology* (1993)
Dugdale, *Monasticon*	W. Dugdale, *Monasticon Anglicanum*, 3 vols. (1655–72); 2nd edn, 3 vols. (1661–82); new edn, ed. J. Caley, J. Ellis, and B. Bandinel, 6 vols. in 8 pts (1817–30); repr. (1846) and (1970)
DWB	J. E. Lloyd and others, eds., *Dictionary of Welsh biography down to 1940* (1959) [Eng. trans. of *Y bywgraffiadur Cymreig hyd 1940*, 2nd edn (1954)]
EdinR	*Edinburgh Review, or, Critical Journal*
EETS	Early English Text Society
Emden, *Cam.*	A. B. Emden, *A biographical register of the University of Cambridge to 1500* (1963)
Emden, *Oxf.*	A. B. Emden, *A biographical register of the University of Oxford to AD 1500*, 3 vols. (1957–9); also *A biographical register of the University of Oxford, AD 1501 to 1540* (1974)
EngHR	*English Historical Review*
Engraved Brit. ports.	F. M. O'Donoghue and H. M. Hake, *Catalogue of engraved British portraits preserved in the department of prints and drawings in the British Museum*, 6 vols. (1908–25)
ER	The English Reports, 178 vols. (1900–32)
ESTC	*English short title catalogue, 1475–1800* [CD-ROM and online]
Evelyn, *Diary*	*The diary of John Evelyn*, ed. E. S. De Beer, 6 vols. (1955); repr. (2000)
Farington, *Diary*	*The diary of Joseph Farington*, ed. K. Garlick and others, 17 vols. (1978–98)
Fasti Angl. (Hardy)	J. Le Neve, *Fasti ecclesiae Anglicanae*, ed. T. D. Hardy, 3 vols. (1854)
Fasti Angl., 1066–1300	[J. Le Neve], *Fasti ecclesiae Anglicanae, 1066–1300*, ed. D. E. Greenway and J. S. Barrow, [8 vols.] (1968–)
Fasti Angl., 1300–1541	[J. Le Neve], *Fasti ecclesiae Anglicanae, 1300–1541*, 12 vols. (1962–7)
Fasti Angl., 1541–1857	[J. Le Neve], *Fasti ecclesiae Anglicanae, 1541–1857*, ed. J. M. Horn, D. M. Smith, and D. S. Bailey, [9 vols.] (1969–)
Fasti Scot.	H. Scott, *Fasti ecclesiae Scoticanae*, 3 vols. in 6 (1871); new edn, [11 vols.] (1915–)
FO List	*Foreign Office List*
Fortescue, *Brit. army*	J. W. Fortescue, *A history of the British army*, 13 vols. (1899–1930)
Foss, *Judges*	E. Foss, *The judges of England*, 9 vols. (1848–64); repr. (1966)
Foster, *Alum. Oxon.*	J. Foster, ed., *Alumni Oxonienses: the members of the University of Oxford, 1715–1886*, 4 vols. (1887–8); later edn (1891); also *Alumni Oxonienses … 1500–1714*, 4 vols. (1891–2); 8 vol. repr. (1968) and (2000)
Fuller, *Worthies*	T. Fuller, *The history of the worthies of England*, 4 pts (1662); new edn, 2 vols., ed. J. Nichols (1811); new edn, 3 vols., ed. P. A. Nuttall (1840); repr. (1965)
GEC, *Baronetage*	G. E. Cokayne, *Complete baronetage*, 6 vols. (1900–09); repr. (1983) [microprint]
GEC, *Peerage*	G. E. C. [G. E. Cokayne], *The complete peerage of England, Scotland, Ireland, Great Britain, and the United Kingdom*, 8 vols. (1887–98); new edn, ed. V. Gibbs and others, 14 vols. in 15 (1910–98); microprint repr. (1982) and (1987)
Genest, *Eng. stage*	J. Genest, *Some account of the English stage from the Restoration in 1660 to 1830*, 10 vols. (1832); repr. [New York, 1965]
Gillow, *Lit. biog. hist.*	J. Gillow, *A literary and biographical history or bibliographical dictionary of the English Catholics, from the breach with Rome, in 1534, to the present time*, 5 vols. [1885–1902]; repr. (1961); repr. with preface by C. Gillow (1999)
Gir. Camb. opera	*Giraldi Cambrensis opera*, ed. J. S. Brewer, J. F. Dimock, and G. F. Warner, 8 vols., Rolls Series, 21 (1861–91)
GJ	*Geographical Journal*

Gladstone, *Diaries* — *The Gladstone diaries: with cabinet minutes and prime-ministerial correspondence*, ed. M. R. D. Foot and H. C. G. Matthew, 14 vols. (1968–94)

GM — *Gentleman's Magazine*

Graves, *Artists* — A. Graves, ed., *A dictionary of artists who have exhibited works in the principal London exhibitions of oil paintings from 1760 to 1880* (1884); new edn (1895); 3rd edn (1901); facs. edn (1969); repr. [1970], (1973), and (1984)

Graves, *Brit. Inst.* — A. Graves, *The British Institution, 1806–1867: a complete dictionary of contributors and their work from the foundation of the institution* (1875); facs. edn (1908); repr. (1969)

Graves, *RA exhibitors* — A. Graves, *The Royal Academy of Arts: a complete dictionary of contributors and their work from its foundation in 1769 to 1904*, 8 vols. (1905–6); repr. in 4 vols. (1970) and (1972)

Graves, *Soc. Artists* — A. Graves, *The Society of Artists of Great Britain, 1760–1791, the Free Society of Artists, 1761–1783: a complete dictionary* (1907); facs. edn (1969)

Greaves & Zaller, *BDBR* — R. L. Greaves and R. Zaller, eds., *Biographical dictionary of British radicals in the seventeenth century*, 3 vols. (1982–4)

Grove, *Dict. mus.* — G. Grove, ed., *A dictionary of music and musicians*, 5 vols. (1878–90); 2nd edn, ed. J. A. Fuller Maitland (1904–10); 3rd edn, ed. H. C. Colles (1927); 4th edn with suppl. (1940); 5th edn, ed. E. Blom, 9 vols. (1954); suppl. (1961) [see also *New Grove*]

Hall, *Dramatic ports.* — L. A. Hall, *Catalogue of dramatic portraits in the theatre collection of the Harvard College library*, 4 vols. (1930–34)

Hansard — *Hansard's parliamentary debates*, ser. 1–5 (1803–)

Highfill, Burnim & Langhans, *BDA* — P. H. Highfill, K. A. Burnim, and E. A. Langhans, *A biographical dictionary of actors, actresses, musicians, dancers, managers, and other stage personnel in London, 1660–1800*, 16 vols. (1973–93)

Hist. U. Oxf. — T. H. Aston, ed., *The history of the University of Oxford*, 8 vols. (1984–2000) [1: *The early Oxford schools*, ed. J. I. Catto (1984); 2: *Late medieval Oxford*, ed. J. I. Catto and R. Evans (1992); 3: *The collegiate university*, ed. J. McConica (1986); 4: *Seventeenth-century Oxford*, ed. N. Tyacke (1997); 5: *The eighteenth century*, ed. L. S. Sutherland and L. G. Mitchell (1986); 6–7: *Nineteenth-century Oxford*, ed. M. G. Brock and M. C. Curthoys (1997–2000); 8: *The twentieth century*, ed. B. Harrison (2000)]

HJ — *Historical Journal*

HMC — Historical Manuscripts Commission

Holdsworth, *Eng. law* — W. S. Holdsworth, *A history of English law*, ed. A. L. Goodhart and H. L. Hanbury, 17 vols. (1903–72)

HoP, *Commons* — *The history of parliament: the House of Commons* [*1386–1421*, ed. J. S. Roskell, L. Clark, and C. Rawcliffe, 4 vols. (1992); *1509–1558*, ed. S. T. Bindoff, 3 vols. (1982); *1558–1603*, ed. P. W. Hasler, 3 vols. (1981); *1660–1690*, ed. B. D. Henning, 3 vols. (1983); *1690–1715*, ed. D. W. Hayton, E. Cruickshanks, and S. Handley, 5 vols. (2002); *1715–1754*, ed. R. Sedgwick, 2 vols. (1970); *1754–1790*, ed. L. Namier and J. Brooke, 3 vols. (1964), repr. (1985); *1790–1820*, ed. R. G. Thorne, 5 vols. (1986); in draft (used with permission): *1422–1504*, *1604–1629*, *1640–1660*, and *1820–1832*]

IGI — *International Genealogical Index*, Church of Jesus Christ of the Latterday Saints

ILN — *Illustrated London News*

IMC — Irish Manuscripts Commission

Irving, *Scots.* — J. Irving, ed., *The book of Scotsmen eminent for achievements in arms and arts, church and state, law, legislation and literature, commerce, science, travel and philanthropy* (1881)

JCS — *Journal of the Chemical Society*

JHC — *Journals of the House of Commons*

JHL — *Journals of the House of Lords*

John of Worcester, *Chron.* — *The chronicle of John of Worcester*, ed. R. R. Darlington and P. McGurk, trans. J. Bray and P. McGurk, 3 vols., OMT (1995–) [vol. 1 forthcoming]

Keeler, *Long Parliament* — M. F. Keeler, *The Long Parliament, 1640–1641: a biographical study of its members* (1954)

Kelly, *Handbk* — *The upper ten thousand: an alphabetical list of all members of noble families*, 3 vols. (1875–7); continued as *Kelly's handbook of the upper ten thousand for 1878* [1879], 2 vols. (1878–9); continued as *Kelly's handbook to the titled, landed and official classes*, 94 vols. (1880–1973)

LondG — *London Gazette*

LP Henry VIII — J. S. Brewer, J. Gairdner, and R. H. Brodie, eds., *Letters and papers, foreign and domestic, of the reign of Henry VIII*, 23 vols. in 38 (1862–1932); repr. (1965)

Mallalieu, *Watercolour artists* — H. L. Mallalieu, *The dictionary of British watercolour artists up to 1820*, 3 vols. (1976–90); vol. 1, 2nd edn (1986)

Memoirs FRS — *Biographical Memoirs of Fellows of the Royal Society*

MGH — Monumenta Germaniae Historica

MT — *Musical Times*

Munk, *Roll* — W. Munk, *The roll of the Royal College of Physicians of London*, 2 vols. (1861); 2nd edn, 3 vols. (1878)

N&Q — *Notes and Queries*

New Grove — S. Sadie, ed., *The new Grove dictionary of music and musicians*, 20 vols. (1980); 2nd edn, 29 vols. (2001) [also online edn; see also Grove, *Dict. mus.*]

Nichols, *Illustrations* — J. Nichols and J. B. Nichols, *Illustrations of the literary history of the eighteenth century*, 8 vols. (1817–58)

Nichols, *Lit. anecdotes* — J. Nichols, *Literary anecdotes of the eighteenth century*, 9 vols. (1812–16); facs. edn (1966)

Obits. FRS — *Obituary Notices of Fellows of the Royal Society*

O'Byrne, *Naval biog. dict.* — W. R. O'Byrne, *A naval biographical dictionary* (1849); repr. (1990); [2nd edn], 2 vols. (1861)

OHS — Oxford Historical Society

Old Westminsters — *The record of Old Westminsters*, 1–2, ed. G. F. R. Barker and A. H. Stenning (1928); suppl. 1, ed. J. B. Whitmore and G. R. Y. Radcliffe [1938]; 3, ed. J. B. Whitmore, G. R. Y. Radcliffe, and D. C. Simpson (1963); suppl. 2, ed. F. E. Pagan (1978); 4, ed. F. E. Pagan and H. E. Pagan (1992)

OMT — Oxford Medieval Texts

Ordericus Vitalis, *Eccl. hist.* — *The ecclesiastical history of Orderic Vitalis*, ed. and trans. M. Chibnall, 6 vols., OMT (1969–80); repr. (1990)

Paris, *Chron.* — *Matthaei Parisiensis, monachi sancti Albani, chronica majora*, ed. H. R. Luard, Rolls Series, 7 vols. (1872–83)

Parl. papers — *Parliamentary papers* (1801–)

PBA — *Proceedings of the British Academy*

Pepys, *Diary* — The diary of Samuel Pepys, ed. R. Latham and W. Matthews, 11 vols. (1970–83); repr. (1995) and (2000)

Pevsner — N. Pevsner and others, Buildings of England series

PICE — *Proceedings of the Institution of Civil Engineers*

Pipe rolls — *The great roll of the pipe for . . .*, PRSoc. (1884–)

PRO — Public Record Office

PRS — *Proceedings of the Royal Society of London*

PRSoc. — Pipe Roll Society

PTRS — *Philosophical Transactions of the Royal Society*

QR — *Quarterly Review*

RC — Record Commissions

Redgrave, *Artists* — S. Redgrave, A dictionary of artists of the English school (1874); rev. edn (1878); repr. (1970)

Reg. Oxf. — C. W. Boase and A. Clark, eds., Register of the University of Oxford, 5 vols., OHS, 1, 10–12, 14 (1885–9)

Reg. PCS — J. H. Burton and others, eds., The register of the privy council of Scotland, 1st ser., 14 vols. (1877–98); 2nd ser., 8 vols. (1899–1908); 3rd ser., [16 vols.] (1908–70)

Reg. RAN — H. W. C. Davis and others, eds., Regesta regum Anglo-Normannorum, 1066–1154, 4 vols. (1913–69)

RIBA Journal — Journal of the Royal Institute of British Architects [later RIBA Journal]

RotP — J. Strachey, ed., Rotuli parliamentorum ut et petitiones, et placita in parliamento, 6 vols. (1767–77)

RotS — D. Macpherson, J. Caley, and W. Illingworth, eds., Rotuli Scotiae in Turri Londinensi et in domo capitulari Westmonasteriensi asservati, 2 vols., RC, 14 (1814–19)

RS — Record(s) Society

Rymer, *Foedera* — T. Rymer and R. Sanderson, eds., Foedera, conventiones, literae et cuiuscunque generis acta publica inter reges Angliae et alios quosvis imperatores, reges, pontifices, principes, vel communitates, 20 vols. (1704–35); 2nd edn, 20 vols. (1726–35); 3rd edn, 10 vols. (1739–45); facs. edn (1967); new edn, ed. A. Clarke, J. Caley, and F. Holbrooke, 4 vols., RC, 50 (1816–30)

Sainty, *Judges* — J. Sainty, ed., The judges of England, 1272–1990, SeldS, suppl. ser., 10 (1993)

Sainty, *King's counsel* — J. Sainty, ed., A list of English law officers and king's counsel, SeldS, suppl. ser., 7 (1987)

SCH — Studies in Church History

Scots peerage — J. B. Paul, ed. The Scots peerage, founded on Wood's edition of Sir Robert Douglas's Peerage of Scotland, containing an historical and genealogical account of the nobility of that kingdom, 9 vols. (1904–14)

SeldS — Selden Society

SHR — *Scottish Historical Review*

State trials — T. B. Howell and T. J. Howell, eds., Cobbett's Complete collection of state trials, 34 vols. (1809–28)

STC, 1475–1640 — A. W. Pollard, G. R. Redgrave, and others, eds., A short-title catalogue of . . . English books . . . 1475–1640 (1926); 2nd edn, ed. W. A. Jackson, F. S. Ferguson, and K. F. Pantzer, 3 vols. (1976–91) [see also Wing, STC]

STS — Scottish Text Society

SurtS — Surtees Society

Symeon of Durham, *Opera* — Symeonis monachi opera omnia, ed. T. Arnold, 2 vols., Rolls Series, 75 (1882–5); repr. (1965)

Tanner, *Bibl. Brit.-Hib.* — T. Tanner, Bibliotheca Britannico-Hibernica, ed. D. Wilkins (1748); repr. (1963)

Thieme & Becker, *Allgemeines Lexikon* — U. Thieme, F. Becker, and H. Vollmer, eds., Allgemeines Lexikon der bildenden Künstler von der Antike bis zur Gegenwart, 37 vols. (Leipzig, 1907–50); repr. (1961–5), (1983), and (1992)

Thurloe, *State papers* — A collection of the state papers of John Thurloe, ed. T. Birch, 7 vols. (1742)

TLS — *Times Literary Supplement*

Tout, *Admin. hist.* — T. F. Tout, Chapters in the administrative history of mediaeval England: the wardrobe, the chamber, and the small seals, 6 vols. (1920–33); repr. (1967)

TRHS — *Transactions of the Royal Historical Society*

VCH — H. A. Doubleday and others, eds., The Victoria history of the counties of England, [88 vols.] (1900–)

Venn, *Alum. Cant.* — J. Venn and J. A. Venn, Alumni Cantabrigienses: a biographical list of all known students, graduates, and holders of office at the University of Cambridge, from the earliest times to 1900, 10 vols. (1922–54); repr. in 2 vols. (1974–8)

Vertue, *Note books* — [G. Vertue], Note books, ed. K. Esdaile, earl of Ilchester, and H. M. Hake, 6 vols., Walpole Society, 18, 20, 22, 24, 26, 30 (1930–55)

VF — *Vanity Fair*

Walford, *County families* — E. Walford, The county families of the United Kingdom, or, Royal manual of the titled and untitled aristocracy of Great Britain and Ireland (1860)

Walker rev. — A. G. Matthews, Walker revised: being a revision of John Walker's Sufferings of the clergy during the grand rebellion, 1642–60 (1948); repr. (1988)

Walpole, *Corr.* — The Yale edition of Horace Walpole's correspondence, ed. W. S. Lewis, 48 vols. (1937–83)

Ward, *Men of the reign* — T. H. Ward, ed., Men of the reign: a biographical dictionary of eminent persons of British and colonial birth who have died during the reign of Queen Victoria (1885); repr. (Graz, 1968)

Waterhouse, *18c painters* — E. Waterhouse, The dictionary of 18th century painters in oils and crayons (1981); repr. as British 18th century painters in oils and crayons (1991), vol. 2 of Dictionary of British art

Watt, *Bibl. Brit.* — R. Watt, Bibliotheca Britannica, or, A general index to British and foreign literature, 4 vols. (1824) [many reprs.]

Wellesley index — W. E. Houghton, ed., The Wellesley index to Victorian periodicals, 1824–1900, 5 vols. (1966–89); new edn (1999) [CD-ROM]

Wing, *STC* — D. Wing, ed., Short-title catalogue of . . . English books . . . 1641–1700, 3 vols. (1945–51); 2nd edn (1972–88); rev. and enl. edn, ed. J. J. Morrison, C. W. Nelson, and M. Seccombe, 4 vols. (1994–8) [see also STC, 1475–1640]

Wisden — *John Wisden's Cricketer's Almanack*

Wood, *Ath. Oxon.* — A. Wood, Athenae Oxonienses . . . to which are added the Fasti, 2 vols. (1691–2); 2nd edn (1721); new edn, 4 vols., ed. P. Bliss (1813–20); repr. (1967) and (1969)

Wood, *Vic. painters* — C. Wood, Dictionary of Victorian painters (1971); 2nd edn (1978); 3rd edn as Victorian painters, 2 vols. (1995), vol. 4 of Dictionary of British art

WW — *Who's who* (1849–)

WWBMP — M. Stenton and S. Lees, eds., Who's who of British members of parliament, 4 vols. (1976–81)

WWW — *Who was who* (1929–)

Strang [*née* Carr]**, Barbara Mary Hope**, Lady Strang (1925–1982), English language scholar, born on 20 April 1925 at 18 Belvedere Road, Penge, London, was the only child of Frederick Albert Carr, of Wimbledon, and his wife, Amy Maud Wood. Her father was an engineer who suffered unemployment in the 1930s. She grew up in Shirley in Surrey, and was educated at Coloma Convent of the Ladies of Mary, Croydon, which early in the war was evacuated to Wales. She entered King's College, London, in 1942, and spent a year in Bristol until the college returned to the Strand. At King's she was introduced to the Anglican liturgy, which had a lasting influence. She obtained her BA degree in 1945, and then her MA in 1947 with an extended study of the historic Kentish dialects, under the direction of Professor C. L. Wrenn.

Barbara Carr was assistant lecturer at Westfield College, University of London, from 1947 to 1950, and then lecturer at King's College, Newcastle (then part of the University of Durham), from 1950 to 1963. There she met Colin Strang (*b.* 1922), then a lecturer in philosophy, whom she married on 21 April 1955. He was the son of Sir William *Strang, head of the Foreign Office, who had been created Baron Strang of Stonesfield in 1954, and on his death in 1978 Colin inherited the title as second Baron Strang. They had one child, a daughter, Caroline Jane (*b.* 1957).

Strang's first major publication was *Modern English Structure* (1962), which showed her 'unique integration of descriptive and historical approaches' (Nixon and Honey, xii). It rapidly became a standard work, and met its declared aim of being 'useful to elementary students without offending against the standards of professional linguists' (Strang, *Modern English Structure*, introduction) and communicating with 'students whose central interests lie elsewhere' (ibid.). Compared with older works it is less narrowly restricted to phonology and morphology, and does justice to new developments in the study of sentence patterns, the noun and verb phrase, 'kernel' structures, and transformations. It is based on copious examples of actual usage, insists on the primacy of speech, and brings out the role of language in everyday life. It effectively succeeds in its intention of cultivating 'humane, sensible and scholarly attitudes to language' (ibid., conclusion).

In 1964 Strang was appointed professor of English language and general linguistics at the University of Newcastle upon Tyne, the first chair of its kind in England, just as she was one of the first women to hold such a post. In her inaugural lecture, 'Metaphors and models', she noted that 'in linguistics the nineteenth century was dominantly concerned with the study of history, characteristically advanced by the study of metaphors', whereas 'the twentieth century has been dominantly concerned with the study of structure, increasingly advanced by means of models'. Her own scholarship combined these two approaches and, in a period marked by many new developments in linguistics, she and her department quickly gained an international reputation and attracted visitors from far afield. One of her closest associates was Professor Randolph Quirk, who had known her since they were students together.

Strang next published *A History of English* (1970), the fruit of twenty years' deep learning. This took account of the international spread of English and adopted the novel procedure of working back from contemporary English, with its advantage of being within the reader's experience, to the older periods of the language. Her later research topics included the linguistic analysis of such writers as Swift, Spenser, Shakespeare, and John Clare, and she was instrumental in forming the Tyneside Linguistic Survey. She contributed to, among other periodicals, *Transactions of the Philological Society*, *Durham*, *Notes and Queries*, *English Studies Today*, and *Lingua*.

Strang was also active in administration and was a member of the University Grants Committee (1947–50), and the Hong Kong university and polytechnic grants committee from 1981. Colleagues found her always helpful, and many students benefited from postgraduate funding privately supported by herself and her husband. Her recreations included horsemanship, which replaced her childhood liking for ballet. On 11 April 1982 she was suddenly struck down by a cerebral haemorrhage, and died the next day, aged fifty-six, at her home, Station House, Angerton, Morpeth. The funeral was at the West Road crematorium, Newcastle upon Tyne. Her husband and daughter survived her.

Randolph Quirk, who knew her for thirty-five years, wrote of her that 'she combined a rare and precious set of qualities. Sparkling intellect and originality. Profound moral strength. Unshakable dedication to the most demanding standards of scholarship. Generosity. Loyalty. And sense of fun' (Nixon and Honey, foreword).

JOHN D. HAIGH

Sources G. Nixon and J. Honey, eds., *An historic tongue: studies in English linguistics in memory of Barbara Strang* (1988) · *WWW, 1981–90* · T. McArthur, ed., *The Oxford companion to the English language* (1992) · Burke, *Peerage* (1999) · B. Strang, 'Metaphors and models: an inaugural lecture', 12 Oct 1964, U. Newcastle · B. Strang, *Modern English structure*, 2nd edn (1968) · B. Strang, *A history of English* (1970) · *Debrett's People of today* (2000) · CGPLA Eng. & Wales (1982) · d. cert.
Likenesses photograph, repro. in Nixon and Honey, eds., *An historic tongue*
Wealth at death £222,932: probate, 21 June 1982, CGPLA Eng. & Wales

Strang, John (1583/4–1654), university principal, was born at Irvine, Ayrshire, the son of William Strang (1545/6–1588), the minister there, and his wife, Agnes, sister of Alexander Borthwick of Nether Lenagher, Edinburghshire. Upon his father's death his mother married Robert Wilkie (*d.* 1601), minister of Kilmarnock, and Strang was educated at the local grammar school. About 1596 Strang was sent to the University of St Andrews, under the guidance of principal Wilkie, a relation of his stepfather. He graduated MA in 1600. Subsequently he became a regent of St Leonard's College, St Andrews. Following ordination, he was admitted as minister of Erroll, in the presbytery of Perth, on 10 April 1614, on the recommendation of the professors at St Andrews and of Arthur Henderson, then minister of Leuchars, one of his tasks being to counter the Catholicism of Francis Hay, ninth earl of Erroll. On 29 July 1616 he received a DD from St Andrews. In 1617 he took part in the disputations before James VI during the king's visit to Scotland. In the Perth assembly of 1618 he voted against the five articles, but this did not prevent his nomination in 1619 to the high commission appointed to ensure their implementation. However, Strang did not attend the commission's meetings. In 1620 he refused the offer of a church in Edinburgh. While at Erroll, Strang married Janet (1589?–1627), daughter of William Hay of Barra and widow of James Smyth, minister of Erroll; they had two daughters.

Before his death, James VI offered Strang the post of principal of Glasgow University and professor of divinity. Strang wished to secure the support of the former principal, Robert Boyd, who was intriguing to get his place back, but even without that he accepted and was admitted on 21 February 1626. The new position suited him better than the ministry, for he was reputed to be a poor preacher. In Glasgow, possibly on 9 September 1627, he married Agnes Fleming. They had one son (who died in 1651, aged twenty-two) and two daughters. At Glasgow, Strang became a promoter of new buildings, including the inner court of the college in the High Street.

In July 1637 Strang was a notable opponent of Charles I's liturgical innovations. Robert Baillie, who in 1656 married Strang's daughter Helen (d. 1679), later wrote that Strang's 'first concurrence did a great deal of good to further that universal refusal of the [Prayer] Book which followed' (Baillie, 1.28–9). However, Strang was reluctant to subscribe the covenant in February 1638 without qualifying it

> so far as that confession was not prejudicial to the king's authority, the office of episcopal government itself, and that power which is given bishops by lawful assemblies and parliaments, and in so far as we are bound to withstand all innovations in the worship of God, contrary to his written word, and the Confession of Faith of the Church of Scotland. (ibid., 1.66–9)

In the event, in July 1638 Archibald Johnston of Wariston persuaded Strang to take the covenant as it stood.

When Charles I withdrew the liturgy and canons, Strang supported the king's commissioner, James Hamilton, marquess of Hamilton, even sending him arguments opposing Johnston's protestation of 22 September 1638. In it he argued that the king's concessions were sufficient and that the king's covenant should be signed, although his desire for anonymity prevented its publication. Strang's views were valued, as he was perceived by Walter Balcangell as the 'learnedest Covenanter in Scotland' (Baillie, 1.476), and he supported peace in the church rather than theological purity. At the Glasgow assembly in November 1638 Strang was persuaded to disown his own protestation, against lay elders sitting in the assembly or voting in presbyteries, much to Hamilton's chagrin. However, when Hamilton departed from the assembly, so did Strang, and he then faced demands that he be summoned back. These were defeated and Strang continued to represent the university at general assemblies.

Strang's second wife died in January 1641 and he married Ann Stewart (d. 1649) in Glasgow, possibly on 9 December 1641. In 1643 Baillie recounted Strang's busy lifestyle, which included his university work and 'a charge beside would kill an ox' (Baillie, 2.71). The discovery after the battle of Naseby of Strang's correspondence with Archbishop William Laud and his unpublished treatise of 1638 placed him on the defensive. In 1646 the general assembly appointed commissioners to examine his views, particularly the charge that he inclined to the teachings of the Dutch theologian Moise Amyraut. The commissioners found him orthodox after Strang had signed a paper assenting to the decisions of the Synod of Dort. This was duly reported back to the general assembly in August 1647. Almost at the same date, Baillie was describing him as 'among the best scholars of the Reformed Church' (ibid., 3.5–6).

Strang's third wife died in June 1649. He was eventually forced to retire from Glasgow, after a visitation from the estates of the kingdom, and the general assembly accepted his supplication to retire on 19 April 1650. He was awarded a pension of 1000 merks, together with a testimonial of his orthodoxy, and lived in retirement in the college until 1653. He died while on a visit to Edinburgh on 20 June 1654, aged seventy, and was buried on 22 June at Greyfriars. He was survived by four daughters. Two of his works appeared posthumously, *De voluntate et actionibus Dei circa peccatum* (Amsterdam, 1657) and *De interpretatione et perfectione scripturae, una cum opusculis de sabbato* (Rotterdam, 1663), treating respectively sin and the sabbath.

STUART HANDLEY

Sources *Fasti Scot.*, new edn, 4.206; 7.394 · H. M. B. Reid, *The divinity principals in the University of Glasgow, 1545–1654* (1917), 252–301 · Chambers, *Scots.* (1855), 7.331–6 · IGI [Erroll parish register] · P. Donald, *An uncounselled king: Charles I and the Scottish troubles, 1637–1641* (1990), pp. 103–4 · G. D. Henderson, *Religious life in seventeenth century Scotland* (1937) · *The letters and journals of Robert Baillie*, ed. D. Laing, 3 vols. (1841–2) · *Diary of Sir Archibald Johnston of Wariston*, 1, ed. G. M. Paul, Scottish History Society, 61 (1911)

Strang, John (1795–1863), author and statistician, was born on 10 February 1795 in Charlotte Street, Dowanhill, just beyond the then western boundary of Glasgow, the son of John Strang (d. 1809/10), a wine merchant in the city. His mother's maiden name was McGilp, but nothing else is known about her. He received a liberal education at Dr Boyd's school and at Glasgow grammar school, and became proficient in both French and German; he learned Italian later in life. His father died when he was fourteen, and he subsequently inherited the business of John Strang & Co. and lived above the shop in Stockwell Street. Strang appears to have had little enthusiasm for the wine trade and gave up the shop before he moved to live in Woodside Place, probably in 1834. As a man of independent means, he was able to devote his energies to literature and the arts. In December 1842 he married Elizabeth, daughter of William Anderson, a distinguished Glasgow physician. There were no children from the marriage.

In 1817 Strang visited France and Germany, and he retained a love for foreign travel throughout his life. He began to translate stories and poems from the French and the German for British periodicals, and published a life of

Theodore Karl Koerner and (under the pseudonym Richard Holcruff) a book of translations of the works of other German writers. In 1831 he returned to the continent and wrote *Germany in 1831* (1836), a well-received two-volume work in which he set out to investigate the Teutonic character. He became a regular contributor to the *Scots Times* (1826–31) and a literary critic for *The Scotsman* (1832–3). In 1832 he became the editor of *The Day*, a short-lived daily literary paper published in Glasgow, to which he contributed articles and poems.

Strang was an accomplished artist, and took a keen interest in local architecture. It is said that it was while sketching features of Glasgow that he became interested in the creation of an imposing 'garden cemetery' to adorn the city. In 1831 he wrote a pamphlet, *Necropolis Glasguensis*, advocating the scheme and publicized his idea in letters to newspapers and through his social contacts. The Merchants House undertook the task of laying out the necropolis, modelled on the graveyard of Père Lachaise in Paris, in the Fir Park (which it owned) near Glasgow Cathedral. It opened in 1833 and it has remained one of the city's best-known landmarks.

After the demise of *The Day* Strang embarked on a career in civic affairs. In 1834 he was appointed Glasgow's city chamberlain, and served in that office for twenty-nine years. He won great respect for his sound management of the municipal finances, and was praised as a writer on social and economic affairs. His annual reports on the social and economic statistics of Glasgow, and a series of articles on statistics relating to the city's industries, public health, and living conditions published in *The Journal of the Statistical Society of London* were considered to be highly advanced for the day. Many of the articles were subsequently published in *The Economic and Social Statistics of Glasgow and the West of Scotland* (1851–61).

Strang's most popular book was *Glasgow and its Clubs* (1855), an entertaining history of the city, its people, and social life, which appeared in two subsequent editions (1857 and 1864) and has been mined for anecdote and fact by generations of journalists and historians of the city. In 1843 the University of Glasgow conferred on him the honorary degree of LLD, in recognition of his public service and of his literary work. On his retirement as city chamberlain in 1863 the citizens of Glasgow presented him with a cheque for £4600 as a token of their gratitude for his services.

Strang died on 8 December 1863 at Woodside Place, Glasgow. He was buried in the necropolis which was inspired by his vision on 14 December. He was survived by his wife. He was one of Glasgow's greatest public servants, and his painstaking work in compiling social and economic statistics for the city provided valuable data for social reformers and advocates of municipal improvement schemes. He was also one of Glasgow's leading men of letters, with *Glasgow and its Clubs* as his most popular and enduring work.   T. W. BAYNE, *rev.* IAIN F. RUSSELL

Sources *Glasgow Herald* (9 Dec 1863), 4 · *Memoirs and portraits of 100 Glasgow men*, 2 (1886), 305 · *Old Glasgow Club Transactions*, 1 (1907), 161 [in GUL Special Collection] · *Glasgow Herald* (15 Dec 1863), 2 · *Glasgow Citizen* (12 Dec 1863) · J. Strang, memoir, *Glasgow and its clubs*, 3rd edn (1864) · J. Strang, 'Notes on my own life, 1795–1804', Mitchell L., Glas., MS 105
Archives Mitchell L., Glas., corresp.; papers incl. section of autobiography | Mitchell L., Glas., Strathclyde Regional Archives, city chamberlain's MSS, 1834–63
Likenesses portrait, repro. in *Memoirs and portraits of 100 Glasgow men*

Strang, William (1859–1921), painter and printmaker, was born at Dumbarton, on 13 February 1859, the younger of the two sons of Peter Strang, a builder, of Dumbarton, and his wife, Janet Denny. He attended Dumbarton Academy and entered the Slade School of Art at the age of seventeen. He was to remain in London for the rest of his life. In 1875 Alphonse Legros succeeded Edward Poynter as Slade professor of fine art at University College, London, and his influence was to be deep and lasting on Strang's art. Under Legros, Strang took up etching and, although he continued to paint, printmaking dominated his œuvre until the turn of the century. It was as an etcher of imaginative compositions, in which homeliness and realism, often imbued with a macabre or fantastic element, were subdued to fine design and severe drawing, that he first made a name. He signed his prints 'W Strang'. The illustrations to *Death and the Ploughman's Wife* (1888) and *The Earth Fiend* (1892), two ballads written by himself, and those to *The Pilgrim's Progress* (1885) contain some of the best of his earlier etchings.

Strang's strong personal interest in social issues grew alongside the rapid development of organized socialism in the 1880s and 1890s. His print *The Socialists* (1891) shows the artist among the people, listening intently to the impassioned orator. His membership of the Art Workers' Guild in 1895 and close association with C. R. Ashbee and the Essex House Press established his commitment within its natural artistic and professional context. In 1885 he married Agnes McSymon, the daughter of David Rogerson JP, provost of Dumbarton; they had four sons (two of whom, Ian and David, were also printmakers) and one daughter.

Among Strang's numerous single plates the portraits are especially good, though these were to be surpassed as the artist acquired more confident mastery and a broader style, tending to exchange the use of acid for dry point or mezzotint. The best of the later portraits are masterpieces of their kind. Among later sets of etchings are the illustrations to *The Ancient Mariner* (1896), Kipling's *Short Stories* (1900), and *Don Quixote* (1902). A catalogue of Strang's etched work, published in 1906, with supplements (1912 and 1923), contains small reproductions of all his plates, 747 altogether. He designed and cut one of the largest woodcuts ever made, *The Plough*, which measures almost 5 by 6 feet. The impression in the Victoria and Albert Museum is dated 1899 and was published and sold by the Art for Schools Association, Bloomsbury.

During the latter part of his life Strang etched less and painted more, and much of his time was given also to portrait drawings executed in a style founded on the Holbein drawings at Windsor. He undertook a great number of these, and his sitters, many of the most distinguished people of his time, included Sir Lawrence Alma-Tadema (1908), Lord Kitchener (1910), the young Edward, prince of Wales (1909), and Thomas Hardy; his etching of the novelist became in the late twentieth century something of an icon. As a painter Strang experimented in many styles, but at his best was highly original. *Bank Holiday* (1912), in the Tate collection, and the *Portrait of a Lady* (Vita Sackville-West, 1918), at Glasgow, are good examples of his clean, bright colour and rigorous drawing. The Tate collection also holds two self-portraits (1912, 1919) and one landscape. The British Museum has 136 of the etchings, and an important collection of Strang's graphic work is in the Art Gallery and Museum in Glasgow.

Strang was elected ARA in 1906, RA (as an engraver) in 1921, and president of the International Society of Sculptors, Painters, and Gravers in 1918. He was of medium height and strongly built. Outspoken and combative in argument, he delighted in good company, conversation, and fun. He often travelled on the continent, and visited the United States. He produced many self-portraits, etched, drawn, and painted, in a variety of guises. He died suddenly of heart failure at the Brinklea Private Hotel, Bournemouth, on 12 April 1921.

Strang has suffered for being 'unclassifiable' in the history of early twentieth-century British art. An exhibition of his work, held in 1981 in Sheffield, Glasgow, and the National Portrait Gallery, went some way to re-establish the reputation of this most singular of image makers. He was an artist who combined a febrile imagination with formidable technical ability and a penetrating eye with a mordant wit, perhaps most clearly evident in his *Bal Suzette* (1913).

LAURENCE BINYON, *rev.* ANNE L. GOODCHILD

Sources L. Binyon, *William Strang: catalogue of his etched work*, 2 vols. (1912–23) • [H. Furst], 'William Strang, his place in art', *Colour*, 5 (1916), 58–60 • P. Athill, *William Strang, RA (1859–1921)* (1981) [exhibition catalogue, Sheffield, Glasgow, and London, 6 Dec 1980 – 28 June 1981] • D. Strang, ed., *William Strang RA: catalogue raisonné of the printed work of William Strang* (1962) • CGPLA Eng. & Wales (1921)

Likenesses W. Strang, self-portrait, black lead drawing, 1895, BM • W. Strang, self-portrait, chalk drawing, 1902, BM • G. Frampton, bronze bust, c.1903, RA • T. & R. Annan & Sons, photogravure, c.1907, NPG • W. Strang, self-portrait, oils, 1912–19, Tate collection • W. Strang, self-portrait, oils, 1917, NPG • W. Strang, self-portrait, oils, 1919, FM Cam. • W. Rothenstein, lithograph, BM, NPG • W. Strang, self-portrait, etchings, BM, NPG • W. Strang, self-portrait, oils, Scot. NPG • photograph, NPG

Wealth at death £5219 6s. 6d.: probate, 8 June 1921, *CGPLA Eng. & Wales*

Strang, William, first Baron Strang (1893–1978), diplomatist, was born on 2 January 1893 in Rainham, Essex, the eldest of eight sons (seven surviving: there were no daughters) of James Strang (1864–1951), farmer, of Rainham Lodge, Rainham, Essex, and his wife, Margaret (1870–1957), daughter of William Steven, farmer, of Temples, Eaglesham, Renfrewshire. Both parents were of Scottish lowland descent. Strang was educated at Palmer's School, Grays, Essex, and at University College, London, from where he graduated with an honours degree in English

William Strang, first Baron Strang (1893–1978), by Bassano, 1947

language and literature in 1912. While there he won the Quain essay prize, and with the proceeds he spent a year at the Sorbonne (University of Paris). On the eve of the First World War he joined the University of London Officers' Training Corps, and he served throughout the war, with the 4th battalion of the Worcestershire regiment and then on the headquarters staff of the 29th division. He ended the war as a captain and was made MBE in 1918.

Following demobilization Strang considered an academic career, and accepted a post as lecturer in English at the University of Hong Kong. However, he decided to enter the competition for the diplomatic service. He was successful, joined the service in September 1919, and a week later was posted to Belgrade as third secretary. Promoted second secretary in December 1920, he acted as chargé d'affaires in the summer of 1921 and again in spring 1922. Meanwhile, on 1 March 1920 he married Elsie Wynne Jones (d. 1974), daughter of Josiah Edward Jones, of Addiscombe, Welsh district manager of the Joint City and Midland Bank Ltd. They had a daughter, Jean (b. 1921), and a son, Colin (b. 1922).

Strang returned to the Foreign Office in September 1922, and for the next eight years served in the northern department, dealing primarily with Soviet affairs. He was attached to the secretariat of the Anglo-Soviet conference in 1924, and was promoted first secretary in November 1925. In July 1930 he was appointed acting counsellor in Moscow, where he remained until October 1933, being promoted full counsellor and appointed CMG in 1932. In his last six months in Moscow he received considerable acclaim for his handling of the Metropolitan-Vickers engineers' trial, at one point shutting himself in Sokolniki prison with two of the prisoners until the Russians carried out their promise to release them.

On his return to London, Strang was made head first of the League of Nations section (1933–7) and then of the central department, dealing with German affairs (1937–9). He accompanied Neville Chamberlain to his ill-fated meetings with Hitler at Berchtesgaden, Godesberg, and Munich. While increasingly sceptical of the policies that have come to be known as appeasement, he nevertheless worked loyally for Chamberlain, and the foreign secretary Viscount Halifax, when Sir Alexander Cadogan was the permanent under-secretary. He was appointed CB in 1939.

In 1939, after the failure of Chamberlain's Munich agreement, Hitler invaded Czechoslovakia and then turned his attention to Poland. Strang was sent to Moscow from June to August 1939 to try, with French diplomats, to negotiate a tripartite alliance with Stalin to stop the further expansion of the Nazi Reich, and to consolidate the recent British unilateral guarantee to Poland. The failure to secure a treaty with the Soviet Union at this critical moment has been called 'the greatest set-back for British diplomacy in the twentieth century' (Taylor, 157). Stalin and Hitler instead signed the Nazi–Soviet pact, in which Poland was to be partitioned and the Baltic states would be annexed by the Soviet Union. The negotiation in Moscow naturally attracted widespread attention, and criticisms were later made that Strang was too junior to have undertaken such a significant mission for Britain, although he was in fact working under the eye of the British ambassador, Sir William Seeds. The Soviet foreign minister, Vyacheslav Molotov, later told Strang that both sides were at fault in the failure to reach agreement in 1939, a view with which Strang largely concurred, although he thought that Stalin was probably negotiating not entirely in good faith, and with an increasing expectation that Hitler might tempt him with a better offer of a sphere of influence in eastern Europe. When Hitler invaded Poland, Britain was committed to war, and after the collapse of the Nazi–Soviet pact in 1941 the British and the Americans formed the grand alliance with the Soviet Union, an alliance forged on necessity, not trust.

The war marked the second distinct phase of Strang's career. Promoted assistant under-secretary of state in September 1939, for four years he oversaw relations with occupied Europe, and in particular with the governments-in-exile in London. He admired the prime minister, Winston Churchill, and the foreign secretary, Anthony Eden, who were now both at the height of their prestige. He accompanied Eden to the Moscow conference in 1943, which laid the foundation for the United Nations Organization and the European Advisory Commission (EAC). He was appointed British representative on the EAC with the personal rank of ambassador in November 1943, being knighted (KCMG) the same month. For the next two years he worked closely with the Soviet ambassador, Fyodor

Gusev, and the American ambassador, John Winant. Over 100 informal and twenty formal meetings of the EAC were held in London between 1944 and June 1945, and plans for the surrender terms to be imposed on Germany and for the occupation and control of Germany, Berlin, and Austria were agreed. Strang helped to ensure that Britain would secure the north-west zone of occupation of Germany, with its rich industrial resources.

The post-war period saw the third phase of Strang's career as a senior diplomat. Peace brought with it immense problems of economic and political reconstruction, and urgent decisions on the correct future policy for Britain. Despite the creation of the United Nations Organization, meaningful co-operation with the Soviet Union seemed increasingly unlikely. The cold war system, shaped by Marshall aid, the Berlin blockade, the founding of the North Atlantic Treaty Organization (NATO), and the creation of a democratic West Germany, characterized the first post-war decade. For Britain intergovernmental co-operation to create European economic institutions (the Organization for European Economic Co-operation: OEEC), political and security institutions (the Brussels treaty, the Council of Europe), and the building of an American-led Western community (especially through NATO) were the hallmarks of British policy.

Between the defeat of Germany and early 1949 Strang was concerned with the reconstruction of the British-occupied zone in Germany, first as political adviser to Field Marshal Montgomery, commander-in-chief of the British army of occupation, and then (from November 1947) as joint permanent under-secretary in the Foreign Office, in charge of the German section. The defeated Germany had been divided into four zones—American, British, French, and Soviet—but Strang soon realized that the deteriorating international position meant that four-power co-operation as envisaged in the Potsdam treaty of August 1945 was impossible, and that the British would have to encourage the rapid restoration of the political and economic life of the British zone, in co-operation with the United States. He played an important part in ensuring that the Americans took a leading diplomatic and economic role during this difficult period. He was promoted KCB in 1948.

Strang was appointed permanent under-secretary of the Foreign Office in February 1949. He was in charge of the Foreign Office during the Korean War (1950–53), at the time of the Colombo plan (1950), the defection of Guy Burgess and Donald Maclean (1951), and the changeover of power in the Soviet Union after the death of Stalin (1953), and during Churchill's controversial efforts at summitry. In the early 1950s Britain decided against participation in European supranational organizations, in particular in the European Coal and Steel Community but also in the proposed European Defence Community. These decisions reflected a general consensus between ministers and officials about Britain's role in the world, and, in retrospect, epitomized Britain's constant reluctance to go 'beyond the point of no return', as Strang put it, towards the federation of Europe. Britain's global reach, as typified by its

Commonwealth commitments, its valued relationship with the United States, nuclear weapons, and the Atlantic alliance, remained the first priorities.

Strang took a deep interest in the organization and role of the Foreign Office, an issue which became increasingly important as, by the 1950s, it came under constant attack from sections of the press as well as from the Treasury, and needed to restructure and modernize to perform well in a rapidly changing world. Under Eden's 1943 Foreign Service Act Strang streamlined the Foreign Office and diplomatic service, although he retained conservative views on women's employment in the service, and a preference for confidential diplomacy over extensive public discussion on foreign policy. He also established the permanent under-secretary's committee (PUSC) in 1949 to develop a coherent body of opinion on world affairs, and to think strategically about general questions of foreign policy. The committee produced several influential reports about Britain's role in the post-war world. Strang retired from the Foreign Office in November 1953. He was promoted GCMG in 1950 and GCB in 1953, and created Baron Strang of Stonesfield, in the county of Oxfordshire, in 1954.

Strang was very active in his retirement. He took his duties in the House of Lords seriously, becoming deputy speaker in 1962, and speaking out several times against British membership of the European Economic Community. He had been made a fellow of University College, London, in 1946, and was awarded an honorary doctorate by London University in 1954. He was chairman of the National Parks Commission (1954–66) and the Food Hygiene Advisory Council (1955–71), and a member of the Nature Conservancy Council (1954–66). He was an effective and highly respected chairman of the council of the Royal Institute of International Affairs (1958–65). He gardened in his property in Oxfordshire, and read widely, starting with, as he recalled, Proust's *À la recherche du temps perdu*. He wrote extensively and with clarity about the structure, character, and working of the Foreign Office and the practice of diplomacy, suggesting that the successful professional diplomat required ability, hard work, patience, and the capacity to keep his mouth shut, however tempting it was to shine in conversation. He also produced a memoir, *Home and Abroad* (1956), and a history, *Britain in World Affairs: Henry VIII to Elizabeth II* (1961).

Tall, slim, and moustached, and with the analytical mind of a mathematician, Strang was persistent rather than pugnacious, modest, deeply loyal, and highly disciplined. He was much appreciated by his political masters, particularly Churchill, Eden, and Bevin, and also had a reputation for kindness to junior members of the Foreign Office. However, he attracted an unusually large volume of comment during his career as a civil servant. This related in part to his background outside Oxford and Cambridge—he was cruelly labelled a suburban diplomat. There was also contemporary and later criticism of his role in the failure of the 1939 negotiations; his work on the EAC, not least because of the western powers' failure to secure adequate access routes through the Soviet zone into Berlin; his pliancy to Churchill's personal diplomacy

in the early 1950s; and his administrative reforms in the Foreign Office, which resulted in its massive expansion.

Strang died in hospital in Newcastle on 27 May 1978. He was survived by his daughter and son, his wife having predeceased him in 1974. His son, Colin, professor of philosophy at the University of Newcastle, succeeded him as second baron. ANNE DEIGHTON

Sources W. Strang, *Home and abroad* (1956) · Churchill College, Cambridge, Strang papers · R. Ovendale, 'William Strang and the permanent under-secretary's committee', *British officials and British foreign policy, 1945–50*, ed. J. Zametica (1990) · L. Woodward, *British foreign policy in the Second World War* (1976) · F. Roberts, *Dealing with dictators* (1991) · A. Bullock, *The life and times of Ernest Bevin*, 3 (1983) · E. Dell, *The Schuman plan and the abdication of British leadership in Europe* (1995) · A. Eden, *Facing the dictators* (1962) · Lord Vansittart, *The mist procession* (1958) · T. Sharp, *The wartime alliance and the zonal division of Germany* (1975) · A. Deighton, *The impossible peace: Britain, the division of Germany, and the origins of the cold war, 1945–1947* (1990) · J. W. Young, *Winston Churchill's last campaign: Britain and the cold war, 1951–1955* (1996) · J. W. Young, ed., *The foreign policy of Churchill's peacetime administration, 1951–1955* (1988) · A. J. P. Taylor, *Englishmen and others* (1956) · *The Times* (29 May 1978) · DNB · WWW, *1971–80* · Burke, *Peerage* · FO List

Archives CAC Cam., corresp. and papers · UCL, student papers, etc. | CAC Cam., corresp. with A. V. Hill · CUL, corresp. with Sir Samuel Hoare · U. Birm. L., corresp. with Lord Avon | FILM IWM FVA, documentary footage

Likenesses Bassano, photograph, 1947, NPG [*see illus.*] · photograph, repro. in *The Times*

Wealth at death £71,928: probate, 3 Aug 1978, CGPLA Eng. & Wales

Strange, Alexander (1818–1876), army officer and scientist, the fifth son and youngest of twelve children born to Thomas Andrew Lumisden *Strange (1756–1841) and his second wife, Louisa (1788–1862), daughter of Sir William Burroughs, baronet, was born in London on 27 April 1818. He entered Harrow School in September 1831, but left in 1834, aged sixteen, for India, on receiving a commission in the 7th Madras light cavalry (22 June 1834). He was promoted lieutenant on 10 May 1837. In India his flair for mechanics and invention was noted and, after studying at the Simla observatory, he was appointed on the recommendation of Andrew Waugh, in 1847, second assistant to the great trigonometrical survey of India. He was employed on the Karachi longitudinal series, extending from the Sironj base in central India to Karachi, and crossing the Thar Desert north of the Rann of Cutch. He began work in 1850 as first assistant to Captain Renny Tailyour, but after the first season Tailyour withdrew and Strange took chief command of a task which proved onerous because of the absence of building materials and the need to provision 200 men in the desert. The triangulation of the section was completed on 22 April 1853. The series was 668 miles long, consisted of 173 principal triangles, and covered an area of 20,323 square miles: Strange performed the task with great skill and rapidity. After this work was ended, Strange, as astronomical assistant, joined the surveyor-general, Sir Andrew Waugh, at Attock to help measure a verificatory base-line. In 1855 he joined the surveyor-general's headquarters office, and in 1856 was placed in charge of the triangulation southwards from Calcutta to Madras, along the east coast. In 1859 he was promoted major, and, in accordance with the regulations, retired from the survey. He received the special thanks of the government of India.

Strange returned to England in January 1861 and retired from the army in December of that year with the rank of lieutenant-colonel. In England he persuaded the government to establish a central department for the inspection of scientific instruments for use in India, and was appointed to organize it, gaining the office of inspector in 1862. Hitherto the government's system for the construction of scientific instruments for official use had been to keep a stock of patterns, invite tenders for copying them, and accept the lowest, thus preventing any chance of improvement in the instruments, and affording no guarantee of their quality. Strange abolished the patterns, encouraged invention, ensured competition as to price by employing at least two makers for each class of instrument, and enforced strict supervision. A marked improvement in design and workmanship was soon evident, and his first decennial report showed that the cost of the new system was only about 0.028 per cent of the outlay on the works where the instruments were employed. For the trigonometrical survey he himself designed and superintended the construction by Troughton and Simms of a great theodolite, two zenith-sectors designed to give the maximum power for the minimum weight, and two 5 foot transit instruments for the determination of longitude. The instruments were tested in an observatory which he designed at the Indian store depot at Lambeth. His design and testing procedures proved so effective that the speed and accuracy of Indian survey work increased markedly.

Strange was elected a fellow of the Royal Geographical and Royal Astronomical societies in 1861, and of the Royal Society on 2 June 1864. He took an active part in their proceedings. He served on the council of the Royal Astronomical Society from 1863 to 1867, and as foreign secretary from 1868 to 1873. He contributed several papers to the society's journals. He was on the council of the Royal Society from 1867 to 1869. He used his influence in scientific circles to argue for government support for scientific research and his advocacy was instrumental in the appointment in 1870 of the royal commission on this question.

Strange was a good public speaker, a capable artist, and a good violinist. He died at 97 Onslow Square, London, on 9 March 1876 of 'Indian fever' and a feeble heart. His wife, Adelaide, daughter of the Revd William Davies, probably predeceased him. They had three daughters, including Julia Fanny, his sole executor, and a son, Alexander Burroughs, a civil engineer in Madras.

Strange was a perceptive scientist, one of the few, for example, to recognize the importance of Babbage's calculating machines and the extent to which intellectual advance depended on the manufacture of precision equipment. His experience in the army led him to believe that science could achieve most if pursued collaboratively in well-organized departments with government support. He urged on government the duty of devising a coherent scientific policy, shaped by scientists. Dismissing the idea

that local initiatives, individual enterprise, or the Royal Society (a private body) should or could undertake such strategic planning, he argued that a great scientific council, a standing commission modelled on the Council of India, should be appointed to advise government, under a minister for science. The state should support basic scientific research by well-paid, full-time researchers in government laboratories. Applied science should be fostered in industrial centres. A science museum should be set up to encourage good instrument design. Strange was not the first or the only scientist to urge a consistent government policy for science, but he was at the time its most forceful advocate. He was opposed by those who feared that increased government involvement would hamper individual scientists' freedom, that a council of science would leave the Royal Society without a purpose, and that the concentration of science in government institutes would undermine the universities. Others, like Richard Strachey, a friend of Strange's who shared his Indian background, supported his ideas. The royal commission of 1870 adopted most of Strange's ideas, but its fundamental recommendations were not implemented in his lifetime, or in the subsequent century.

CHARLES TROTTER, *rev.* ELIZABETH BAIGENT

Sources J. G. Crowther, *Statesmen of science* (1965) • *The Times* (20 March 1876) • C. R. Markham, *A memoir on the Indian surveys*, 2nd edn (1878) • R. V. Jones, 'Science and the state', *The Advancement of Science*, 20 (1964), 393–405 • 'Royal commission on scientific instruction and the advancement of science', *Parl. papers* (1872–5) [reports 1–8] • D. S. L. Cardwell, *The organisation of science in England* (1957) • *Nature*, 13 (1875–6), 408–9 • *CGPLA Eng. & Wales* (1876) • d. cert.
Likenesses engraving, repro. in Crowther, *Statesmen of science*, facing p. 240 • wood-engraving, NPG; repro. in *ILN* (1 April 1876)
Wealth at death under £4000: probate, 13 Nov 1876, *CGPLA Eng. & Wales*

Strange, Frederick (1810x18–1854), natural history collector, was probably born at Aylsham, Norfolk, between 1810 and 1818. His parentage is unknown, although Strange is an ancient Norfolk surname. In 1836 he left England, probably as a crew member of the *Cygnet*, to become one of the first European settlers of South Australia. At first he was engaged in fishing, but in 1838 accompanied the explorer Charles Sturt (1795–1869) on surveys, and in 1839 was attendant to the surveyor T. Bowes Strangways on his expedition to the north of Adelaide. On this trip a small saltwater creek was named Strange's Creek. In 1839 Strange again accompanied Sturt, on his expedition with Governor Gawler to the Murray River. He also met John Gould, the English ornithologist, and this meeting may have inspired him to become a professional natural history collector.

By 1840 Strange had moved to New South Wales, where he became mate of the coastal steamer *Tamar*, based at Gosford. About this time he married Rosa Prince, of Sydney; they had four (possibly five) children between 1841 and 1853. By May 1843 Strange had moved to Sydney, becoming a full-time collector and dealer in natural history specimens. The following year he met Gould's collector, John Gilbert, and John MacGillivray, naturalist of HMS *Fly*. Both men seem to have stayed with Strange at this time, and henceforth Strange appears to have acted as their agent. Later in 1844 (and also in 1847, 1850, and 1851), Strange collected at Moreton Bay, near Brisbane.

Between May and September 1845 Strange made a trip back to Adelaide, apparently as an agent for a Mr Newman. On his return to Sydney, he sent many requests for employment to John Gould, accompanied by glowing testimonials; Strange correctly assumed that Gilbert had perished on the Leichhardt expedition from Moreton Bay to Port Essington (1844–6). Gould did briefly use Strange's services, but the partnership broke up amid much acrimony; Strange apparently drew money on both Gould and the Australian Museum's curator, George Bennett, and in 1848 Gould complained that Strange's latest collection had arrived back in England in bad condition. The final straw came when Strange flooded the market with molluscs, sending identical shells to the two most senior experts in Britain, Hugh Cuming and George Sowerby.

In 1848 Strange went to New Zealand on HMS *Acheron*'s surveying voyage under John Lort Stokes; the ship arrived back in Sydney in November 1849. In 1852 Strange visited England with his family, arriving with a large natural history collection; they had returned to Sydney by March 1853. In 1854 he entered into a trading venture to the islands off north-east Australia, leaving Sydney in the *Vision* in September 1854. On 15 October Strange's party was attacked by Aborigines on the Second Percy Island, of the Capricorn group; Strange and three others were killed.

Frederick Strange, despite difficulties with literacy (his grammar and spelling were both extremely eccentric) and money management, was an able man in the field and collected much of scientific importance. Among the many new forms which he discovered were the yellow-footed rock-wallaby *Petrogale xanthopus*, the plains wanderer, *Pedionomus torquatus*, and the superb blue wren, *Malurus cyaneus cyanochlamys*.   CLEMENCY THORNE FISHER

Sources H. M. Whittell, 'Frederick Strange', *Australian Zoologist*, 11/2 (1947), 96–114 · C. T. Fisher, 'The importance of early Victorian natural historians in the discovery and interpretation of the Australian fauna, with special reference to John Gilbert', PhD diss., Liverpool Polytechnic, 1992 · NHM, Gould archive
Archives Mitchell L., NSW, documents and letters | Academy of Natural Sciences, Philadelphia, bird and mammal specimens · Liverpool Museum, bird and mammal specimens · NHM, Gould archive · NHM, bird and mammal specimens · U. Cam., Museum of Zoology, bird and mammal specimens
Likenesses J. H. Maiden, photograph, repro. in Whittell, 'Frederick Strange' · portrait, Carnegie Mellon University, Pittsburgh, Hunt Botanical Library

Strange, Sir John (*bap.* 1696, *d.* 1754), judge, was baptized at St Bride's, Fleet Street, London, on 8 September 1696, the eldest son of John Strange of Fleet Street, London, and his second wife, Mary Plaistowe. He was admitted a student at the Middle Temple on 11 July 1712, and later commenced pupillage in the busy practice of Charles Salkeld, a solicitor of Brook Street, Holborn, where Thomas Parker (later chief baron of the exchequer), Philip Yorke (later Lord Chancellor Hardwicke), and Robert Jocelyn (later lord chancellor of Ireland) had all trained. One of his tasks

was to carry his master's papers to Westminster Hall, and in 1717 he witnessed Sir Joseph Jekyll's first appearance as master of the rolls, hardly suspecting that twenty years later he himself would be invited to succeed Jekyll in the office.

At this early stage in his career Strange was already beginning to compile notes and transcripts of various cases in the Westminster courts which were to form the basis of his posthumously published *Reports*. On 27 October 1718 he was called to the bar, and by 1722 was appearing as junior counsel for the crown. At St Bride's on 14 May 1722 he married Susan (1700/01–1747), daughter and coheir of Edward Strong of Greenwich, and a large family of two sons and nine daughters (two daughters dying young) followed. His second son was the natural philosopher John *Strange. In 1725 he was employed as defence counsel in the impeachment of Lord Chancellor Macclesfield, but though he maintained a commendable reputation at the bar it was not until 9 February 1736 that he became a king's counsel and thus marked out for future advancement. In the same year the Middle Temple elected him a bencher.

On 28 January 1737 Strange was appointed to Sir Robert Walpole's ministry as solicitor-general, and less than a fortnight later was brought into parliament for West Looe, Cornwall. As one of the crown's chief law officers in the Commons he was soon drawn into important work in assisting the government's bill against the provost and city of Edinburgh following the murder of Captain Porteous the previous year, and on 9 June he gave a lengthy summary to the house of the evidence against the provost. On the death of the master of the rolls, Sir Joseph Jekyll, on 19 August 1738, he was immediately invited to succeed by his old friend from student days Philip Yorke, now Lord Chancellor Hardwicke. Strange reluctantly declined, protesting his lack of experience in chancery jurisdiction but also expressing concern that the profits might be insufficient to support his large family. In November 1739 he was elected recorder of London by the court of aldermen, and on 12 May 1740 was knighted at Whitehall with his senior colleague Dudley Ryder, the attorney-general. He stood down at West Looe in the election of May 1741, but in January 1742 was returned at a by-election for Totnes, Devon, and continued to sit for the borough until his death. At the end of March 1742 he was one of the small handful of 'old corps' whig supporters elected to the secret committee to inquire into Walpole's conduct, but in spite of having supported the former minister on all previous occasions Strange's attitudes subsequently fell in line with those of the inquiry, and in May he voted in the Commons in favour of an (unsuccessful) opposition bill indemnifying such witnesses as chose to give evidence against Walpole.

It may have been later embarrassment for this act that caused Strange suddenly to resign all his legal appointments in November. A piece of satirical verse on his resignation entitled *The Causidicade* which appeared a few months later in 1743 insinuated darker reasons, speculating that Strange had resigned 'foreseeing approaching disgrace', but Strange himself, in his *Reports*, explained that he had done so 'having received a considerable addition to my fortune and some degree of ease and retirement being judged proper for my health' (Strange, 1176). His recent display of anti-Walpolian sentiment was not held against him, for on 27 November 1742 George II granted him precedence after the attorney-general for life. Strange continued to practise as a barrister but confined himself to morning sittings of the court of king's bench. His most important case work in these years came in the aftermath of the Jacobite rising; in 1746 he was one of the counsel for the crown at the trials of the rebels Francis Townley and Lord Balmerino, and in March 1747 acted as a manager of the impeachment of Lord Lovat, summing up the evidence against the peer in an hour-long speech.

In March 1750, after more than thirty years at the bar, Strange was prevailed upon by Hardwicke to accept judicial office as master of the rolls, and on 17 March, a week after his appointment took effect, he was sworn of the privy council. At the general election in the spring of 1754 he expressed indifference to retaining a parliamentary seat, but his mind was changed on hearing from the duke of Newcastle, the incoming first lord of the Treasury, the king's observation that it was essential the master of the rolls should have a seat in parliament. He died, however, on 18 May, a month after being re-elected at Totnes, and was buried next to his wife in the churchyard at Leyton, Essex, near the manor house which for many years had been his country residence. Newcastle extolled 'his many excellent public qualities and most amiable private ones' (Foss, *Judges*, 169).

Before his death Strange had been preparing his collection of reports for publication. Because of his willingness to lend his notes to judges there had been many opportunities for copies of this material, unscrupulously obtained, to pass into the hands of legal hacks. It included summaries and arguments of cases where no judgment had been made. It was Strange's chief concern, therefore, to have ready a definitive compilation of reports of adjudged cases that could be published in the event of any pirating of his work. Accordingly, when some of Strange's case notes did indeed appear shortly after his death under the title of *A Collection of Select Cases Relating to Evidence, by a Late Barrister-at-Law*, his executors acted swiftly to suppress it, and in 1755 his eldest son published the reports as authentically selected, dedicating them to Lord Hardwicke. Reprinted in second and third editions in 1782 and 1795, Strange's reports endured in their usefulness for the rest of the century and after.   A. A. HANHAM

Sources HoP, *Commons, 1715–54*, 2.451–2 · HoP, *Commons, 1754–90*, 3.491 · Foss, *Judges*, 8.166–9 · Holdsworth, *Eng. law*, 12.86, 130–32 · Sainty, *King's counsel*, 65, 92, 277 · Sainty, *Judges*, 151 · H. A. C. Sturgess, ed., *Register of admissions to the Honourable Society of the Middle Temple, from the fifteenth century to the year 1944*, 1 (1949), 270 · P. C. Yorke, *The life and correspondence of Philip Yorke, earl of Hardwicke*, 1 (1913), 584; 2 (1913), 429, 564 · Walpole, *Corr.*, 17.384, 429; 18.118 · *IGI* · J. Strange, *Reports of adjudged cases in the courts of chancery, kings bench, common pleas and exchequer*, 2 vols. (1755), 1176 · *N&Q*, 8th ser., 1 (1892), 450–51 · D. Lysons, *The environs of London*, 4 (1796), 168–9 · will, 1754, PRO, PROB 11/809/179

Archives BL, papers relating to trials following the Jacobite rising, Egerton MS 2000
Likenesses J. Houbraken, line engraving, BM, NPG; repro. in Strange, *Reports of adjudged cases* · oils, Harvard U., law school
Wealth at death approx. £10,000, much in bank stock, to seven surviving children; plus estate at Leyton Grange, Essex, and lands at Mapsbury, Hertfordshire: will, 1754, PRO, PROB 11/809/179

Strange, John (1732–1799), natural philosopher and diplomat, was born in Barnet, Middlesex, and baptized at St Andrew's, Holborn, on 10 March 1732, the second son of Sir John *Strange (*bap.* 1696, *d.* 1754), master of the rolls, and his wife, Susan Strong (1700/01–1747), the eldest daughter of Edward Strong of Greenwich. He was educated privately and at Clare College, Cambridge, where he graduated BA in 1753 and proceeded MA in 1755. Following his father's death in 1754 he supervised the publishing of his *Reports of Adjudged Cases* (1755). On inheriting considerable wealth, he travelled extensively in the south of France, the Tyrol, and Italy. He lived near Pisa for much of the time between 1757 and 1764 and entered the circle of Tuscan antiquaries and men of science. His relationship with the physician and natural historian Tozzetti in particular 'certainly had a role in deepening and strengthening his interest in geology and palaeontology' (Ciancio, 125). Botany was a prime area of interest, strongly supplemented by the natural history of the earth, especially conchology, palaeontology, and physical geography, with particular emphasis on method in geology, linking observation, examination, and description with theory. He also stressed the invaluable use of maps and illustrations. He became a member of several learned institutions such as the Bologna Academy of Sciences, the Botanical Society of Florence, the Royal Academy of Montpellier, and the Academia Leopoldina Curiosorum Naturae of Leipzig. About 1760 Strange married Mary Ann Gould (*d.* 1783), daughter of Davidge Gould of Sharpham Park, near Street in Somerset, and Honora Hockman of Buckland Baron, Devon. Her brother was Sir Henry *Gould (1710–1794). She died in Venice on 3 May 1783. They seemingly had no children.

For his contributions to geology Strange was elected a fellow of the Royal Society in April 1766; soon thereafter he was elected a fellow of the Society of Antiquaries for his contributions to archaeology. After spending the summer of 1768 in south Wales, he contributed 'An account of Roman remains in and near the city of Brecknock' to the first number of *Archaeologia* (1770). In 1771 he made an archaeological tour in northern Italy. As a result of meeting Abbé Fortis in Padua, he made several communications to the Society of Antiquaries on the Roman inscriptions and antiquities of Dalmatia and Istria, a region then little known in western Europe. In addition to further communications to *Archaeologia*, he contributed several papers to the *Philosophical Transactions* of the Royal Society, including accounts of 'The origin of natural paper found near Cortona in Tuscany' (59, 1769), 'Some specimens of sponges from Italy' (60, 1770), which included plates made from his own drawings, 'A curious Giant's causeway … newly discovered in the Euganean hills, near Padua' (65, 1775), and 'The tides in the Adriatic' (67, 1777). Such papers earned him an international reputation among scientists and antiquarians. The first-cited 'was also valuable for the accurate observations on microscopy it contained. Favourable reactions appeared in many learned journals stressing the erudition and skills of its author' (Ciancio, 124). Strange was playing a key role in the promotion of intellectual relations between Britain and the continent, particularly Italy, and corresponded with notable men of science such as Arduino, Bonnet, Caldani, and von Haller. His surviving correspondence reveals him as an important intermediary, especially regarding natural history, and as someone who was additionally thereby breaking down barriers between social ranks. A number of his papers were also published in Italy (in *Opuscoli scelti sulle scienze*) and in Switzerland (in Weber's *Mineralogische Beschreibungen*). He also contributed to the formation of private antiquarian collections which had significance for Britain. In England between 1765 and 1771 he had also had the opportunity to meet famous foreign visitors to London; he participated in public lectures on conchology by Emanuel Mendes da Costa; and he made notable geological observations as he travelled through numerous counties.

In Italy from the spring of 1771 Strange spent a year in the Veneto studying extinct volcanoes. He undertook geological studies in Switzerland in spring 1772 and France in spring 1773. In November 1773, thanks largely to Lord Bute, for whom he had lately acted as an unofficial collector of Italian drawings and rare books, he was appointed British resident minister in Venice. In post from autumn 1774, his official duties left him with far less time to pursue his antiquarian interests. He therefore supervised local naturalists, who surveyed notable areas of the region, and he paid Abbé Fortis and Girolamo Festari to carry out research in geology in particular but also in other disciplines. And from 1779 Strange kept Sir Joseph Banks, president of the Royal Society, informed of new developments in Italian science—one letter in particular, of March 1783, gave fulsome details of learned periodicals edited in Italy since the start of the century. Through the 1780s Strange ensured that the best of Italian scientific literature reached London. In addition to patronizing local studies, and hosting weekly *conversazioni* at the residency, Strange also reported regularly to London on the difficult and ever changing local political scene.

Strange ceased to act as resident in August 1786, and left Venice, with a 'leave of absence' from the king, in October. He settled at Ridge, near South Mimms in Hertfordshire. He did not officially resign his post until August 1789. About 1788 he was elected a member of the council of the Royal Society, but poor health prevented his regular participation in weekly evening meetings at Banks's house. He possibly returned to Italy to arrange the transportation of the valuable collections he had formed there—of books, manuscripts and antiquities, and of pictures, especially by Venetian masters. He had also commissioned engravings of many pictures in his collection. In London he was apparently unable to raise much interest or money when he sought to sell some pictures, possibly to defray the costs of his expensive years in Venice.

In July 1793 Strange was made an honorary DCL at Oxford. He died at Ridge on 19 March 1799. By his will he directed that all his collections should be sold. The pictures were sold by private contract, the natural history cabinets by King, and the prints, drawings, busts, coins, medals, bronzes, and antiquities by Christies. There was published in 1800 *Fossils, remains of animals and vegetables, minerals, recent shells, &c. catalogue of the … museum of … J. Strange*. The library, the catalogue of which (*Bibliotheca Strangeiana*) was compiled by Samuel Paterson and published in 1801, was sold by Leigh and Sotheby over a period of twenty-nine days in March–April of that year.

ROBERT SHARP

Sources *A calendar of the correspondence of John Strange, FRS (1732–1799)*, ed. L. Ciancio (1995) · L. Ciancio, 'The correspondence of a "virtuoso" of the late Enlightenment: John Strange and the relationship between British and Italian naturalists', *Archives of Natural History*, 22 (1995), 119–29 · G. R. De Beer, 'John Strange', *Notes and Records of the Royal Society*, 9 (1951–2), 96–108 · *GM*, 1st ser., 69 (1799), 348 · *DNB* · J. Ingamells, ed., *A dictionary of British and Irish travellers in Italy, 1701–1800* (1997), 902 ff. · *IGI*

Archives BL, corresp. and papers, King's MSS 290–294 · BL, corresp., literary MSS and papers, Add. MSS 19309–19315, 23729–23730, 60537; Egerton MSS 1969–1970, 1981, 2001–2002, 2233 · Bodl. Oxf., corresp., notes, and papers relating to antiquities of South Wales · U. Cam., Sedgwick Museum of Earth Sciences, geological notes | Bürgerbibliothek, Bern, letters to Albrecht von Haller · Bibliothèque Publique et Universitaire, Geneva, corresp. with Charles Bonnet · BL, letters to Sir Robert Keith, Add. MSS 35508–35536 · BL, letters to Thomas Martyn, Add. MS 33349 · RBG Kew, letters to Sir Joseph Banks

Strange, (Thomas) Lumisden (1808–1884), judge and theological writer, was born at Landon's Gardens, Poonamallee Road, Madras, on 4 January 1808, the eldest son of Sir Thomas Andrew Lumisden *Strange (1756–1841), first chief justice of Madras, and his second wife, Louisa (1788–1862), youngest daughter of Sir William Burroughs, bt, judge of the supreme court of Calcutta, of Castle Bagshaw, co. Cavan. Sent to England aged four, Strange (known to his family as Lumisden), was educated at Dr Pearson's school (1814?–18) at East Sheen, Surrey, Westminster School (1818–22), and the Revd G. K. Rusden's school at Leith Hill, near Dorking (1822–4). From 1824 to 1826 he attended the East India Company's college at Haileybury, his father having procured for him a writership in the Madras civil service. He arrived in Madras in June 1827.

Strange's Indian career was to consist entirely of judicial work. His first substantial appointment was as assistant judge of Tellicherry, Malabar, in June 1831. In 1834, worn down by fever, he obtained eighteen months' furlough and spent it travelling in Persia and across the Caspian Sea, often in oriental disguise. Increasingly fluent in Persian, he questioned Muslims and Jews he met about their religious rituals and the seriousness with which they observed them. His account of these travels in his unpublished autobiography, 'The Incidents of a Life', of 1870 suggests that it was this contact with people of other religions that set him thinking about the rituals and proofs of his own faith.

Strange returned to his duties at Tellicherry early in 1836, but his health had not fully mended, and in March 1839 he sailed for England. On board ship he met Mary Rose (Minnie; 1815–1847), widow of Captain William Hodgson of the Bengal artillery, whom he married at Iver, Buckinghamshire, on 1 January 1840. She was the daughter of Captain Samuel Tickell of the 8th Bengal native infantry, and a direct descendant of the poet Thomas Tickell (1685–1740).

In 1845 Strange was appointed civil and sessions judge of Bellary. In the following year Minnie sickened, and on 4 January 1847, Strange's birthday, she died. Despairing at her loss, Strange sent their three children to England and then himself lapsed back into ill health. This time, however, he obtained relief by homoeopathic remedies, and thereafter he ran an unofficial homoeopathic dispensary for anyone who sought his assistance. In 1851 his experience in Malabar was acknowledged when he was sent to investigate the unrest among the Moplahs, Muslim cultivators and fishermen of Arab descent who periodically chafed at the financial and cultural ascendancy assumed by their Hindu landlords.

In 1852 Strange was appointed puisne judge of the *sadr diwani* and *sadr faujdari adalat*, whereupon he moved to Madras. There on 4 April 1856 he married Emily Burn (*b.* 1837), eldest daughter of Major-General Peter James Begbie of the Madras army; they had four children. In 1859 Strange was appointed a commissioner for inquiring into Madras's system of judicature, and in 1862 he became a judge of the new high court of Madras. In 1863 he retired and arrived back in England in May. In the course of his career he had published a short *Manual of Hindoo Law* (1856; 2nd edn, 1863), taking his father's work as a basis, and *A Letter to the Governor of Fort St George on Judicial Reform* (1860).

Strange's other publications were numerous. India had sparked his interest in religious subjects, and in 1852 he had published *The Light of Prophecy* and *Observations on Mr. Elliott's Horae Apocalypticae*. Subsequently he was so impressed by observing a supposed convert at the gallows proclaim his faith to be in the Hindu god Rama, and not Christ, that, on his examining Christian evidence, his own faith in Christianity broke down. He remained, however, an ardent theist. He explained his position in *How I Became and Ceased to be a Christian* and other pamphlets for the series published between 1872 and 1875 by Thomas Scott (1808–1878); these were afterwards collected and issued as *Contributions to a Series of Controversial Writings* (1881). Larger works by Strange were: *The Bible: is it the Word of God?* (1871); *The Legends of the Old Testament Traced to their Apparent Primitive Sources* (1874); *The Sources and Development of Christianity* (1875); and *What is Christianity?* (1880). His *Development of Creation on the Earth* (1874) shows him to have been a keen researcher in botany and geology. He was a conscientious student and wrote in an eloquent, if not brilliant, style. He continued, after the loss of his Christian faith, to advocate good conduct and practical piety, and at the close of his autobiography—written at the request of his wife

Emmy—he thanked a gracious God for having blessed his life.

Strange died at 22 Farquhar Road, Upper Norwood, Surrey, on 3 September 1884. He was survived by his second wife.   J. B. KATZ

Sources *Old Westminsters*, 1.890–91 · *BL cat.* · catalogues, Bodl. Oxf. · T. L. Strange, 'Incidents of a life', BL OIOC, MS Eur. D 358 · Madras ecclesiastical records, BL OIOC, N/2/3, fol. 64; N/2/36, fol. 182; N/2/42, fol. 168 · writers' petitions, BL OIOC, J/1/39, fols. 266–72 · *The Times* (9 Sept 1884), 1 · *CGPLA Eng. & Wales* (1884)
Archives BL OIOC, MS autobiography, MS Eur. D 358
Wealth at death £624 14s. 3d.: probate, 4 Oct 1884, *CGPLA Eng. & Wales*

Strange, Richard (*c.*1611–1682), Jesuit, born in Northumberland, attended the English College at St Omer, and entered the Society of Jesus in 1631. He subsequently attended the college at Liège, where he was ordained priest about 1640. After teaching classics in the college at St Omer he was sent to the Durham district in 1644, and about 1651 was removed to the London mission, where he worked for many years. In 1671 he was appointed rector of the house of the English Jesuits at Ghent. It was while he was there that his principal work, *The life and gests of S. Thomas Cantilupe, bishop of Hereford and sometime lord chancellor of England* (Ghent, 1674), was published, as was *Of Adoration in Spirit and Truth* (1673), his translation of a work by John Nieremberg. In 1674 he was declared provincial superior of the English Jesuits and held that office for three years. His name figured in Titus Oates's list of Jesuits accused of plotting against the king, and also in Peter Hamerton's account of the adventures of priests and others hunted as the result of Oates's accusations. Having escaped to the continent in 1679 Strange became an adviser to John Warner, the provincial superior from 1679 to 1683. He died at the college in St Omer on 7 April 1682 and was buried there.

THOMPSON COOPER, *rev.* GEOFFREY HOLT

Sources H. Foley, ed., *Records of the English province of the Society of Jesus*, 5 (1879), 743 · T. M. McCoog, *English and Welsh Jesuits, 1555–1650*, 2, Catholic RS, 75 (1995), 305 · G. Oliver, *Collections towards illustrating the biography of the Scotch, English and Irish members, SJ* (1838), 183 · A. de Backer and others, *Bibliothèque de la Compagnie de Jésus*, new edn, 7, ed. C. Sommervogel (Brussels, 1896), 1619 · N. Southwell [N. Bacon], *Bibliotheca scriptorum societatis Jesu* (1676), 719 · C. Dodd [H. Tootell], *The church history of England, from the year 1500, to the year 1688*, 3 (1742), 313 · G. Holt, *St Omers and Bruges colleges, 1593–1773: a biographical dictionary*, Catholic RS, 69 (1979), 252 · A. F. Allison and D. M. Rogers, eds., *The contemporary printed literature of the English Counter-Reformation between 1558 and 1640*, 2 vols. (1989–94) · T. H. Clancy, *English Catholic books, 1641–1700: a bibliography*, rev. edn (1996) · Archives of the British Province of the Society of Jesus, London

Strange, Sir Robert (1725–1792), line-engraver, was the eldest son of David Strange, of Kirkwall in the Orkneys, and his second wife, Jane, *née* Scollay. In 1736, after a brief flirtation with the law, he was apprenticed to the engraver Richard Cooper in Edinburgh. Strange completed his apprenticeship in 1742, having worked on anatomical plates of bones for the folio edition of Bernard Albinus's *Tables of the Skeleton and Muscles of the Human Body*, projected by Cooper and the surgeon Alexander Monro, and

Sir Robert Strange (1725–1792), by Jean-Baptiste Greuze, *c*.1760

engraved plates to illustrate Monro's articles in *Medical Essays*. No signed plates survive, but as an apprentice Strange's work would normally have passed as Cooper's. In the early 1740s he fell in love with Isabella Lumisden (1721/2–1808), whose brother became private secretary to James Francis Edward Stuart. During the Jacobite rising of 1745 Strange joined Prince Charles Edward's lifeguard at her desire, designed Jacobite currency, and was with the prince at Culloden. He married Isabella Lumisden clandestinely in 1747. A daughter, Mary Bruce, was baptized in March 1748. After the Act of Grace, Strange went briefly to Rouen, a centre for exiled Jacobites, where he won a prize for drawing. He then went to work for Jacques Philippe Le Bas in Paris, dining with him for the first time on 19 June 1749.

In 1750 the historian George Vertue noted that Strange was about to move from Paris to London and then that he was about to publish a print after Carl Vanloo. Strange took lodgings with a pewterer in Parliament Street, Westminster, where he was joined by Isabella and Mary, and from where he began to publish and to deal in prints. One of his first advertised works was a specimen plate for William Hunter's projected 'Anatomy of the pregnant uterus'. He imported prints from Rome through his brother-in-law Andrew Lumisden and Piranesi, and from Paris through Le Bas and others. In 1753 James III stood godfather to his eldest son, James Charles Stuart Strange. But Strange had also begun to make his peace with the Hanoverian regime: his third publication, *Cleopatra* (1753), after Guido Reni, was dedicated to the widowed princess of Wales. Three more prints from paintings from the Royal Collection (*The Three Children of Charles I*, after Van Dyck, *St Agnes*, after Domenchino, and *Views Attired by the Graces*, after Guido) were published in 1758 and 1760. Lumisden wrote: 'I know your prudence will make the best use of what has happened without giving anyone just reason to say that a change of fortune has produced in you

a change of sentiment' (Dennistoun, 1.246). In 1754 Strange moved to Henrietta Street, Covent Garden.

Travels in Europe That same year Strange visited Paris, unearthed Dorigny's famous copperplates of Raphael's *Transfiguration* and its companion, and, back in London, printed a new edition. With Lumisden's help he began to lay plans to travel to Italy to make drawings of fine paintings for publication and to buy paintings for profit. His itinerary had been mapped and his targets identified when, in 1758, Allan Ramsay asked Strange to engrave his portraits of the prince of Wales and of Lord Bute. Strange was embarrassed. Not wishing to offend either his Jacobite or his Hanoverian patrons, he tried to refuse politely, citing his plans to travel and to base a career on historical engravings rather than portraiture. The prince's miserly offer, conveyed by Sir William Chambers, of 100 guineas for work that would occupy at least two years failed to alter Strange's determination. But he was unnerved when Ramsay told him that the prince had taken his refusal very badly and that Lord Bute had said, 'it is a thing we are determined never to forgive' (Dennistoun, 1.274). The courtiers let it be known that they were convinced that Strange had refused for political reasons. Strange tried to justify himself to Bute but was denied access, and, he later wrote, 'reports were spread greatly to my disadvantage' (Strange, *Inquiry*, 13), doing immediate damage to his current subscription. Now departure for the continent was expedient, and, after exhibiting twelve prints and ten drawings in May 1760, Strange left for Paris *en route* for Rome, using a passport through France (then at war with Britain) organized by Lumisden. During his absence his wife managed his business and marketed his prints from their house.

At Paris in August Strange visited an old acquaintance, the famous German engraver Johann Georg Wille, who gave him letters of recommendation to Johann Joachim Winckelmann and Anton Raphael Mengs. Horace Walpole had recommended Strange to Horace Mann in Florence as 'a very first-rate artist, and by far our best … tho you will not approve of his politics' (Dennistoun, 1.277). He was warmly welcomed in Rome, and was made a member of the academies of Florence and Naples. Strange's first seventeen plates had won him an international reputation as an engraver of the first rank. Indeed, an article published in the leading German-language review journal in 1762 considered him 'indisputably the greatest master that Britain has ever produced' (*Bibliothek der schönen Wissenschaften und der freyen Künste*, 7, 1762, 369). From Naples, Strange went on in 1763 to Parma, where he dined with the first minister, du Tillot, and was made a professor of the academy. He continued to Bologna, where Winckelmann admired his drawings, but there he found that George III's librarian, Richard Dalton, had hired a promising Italian, Francesco Bartolozzi, to make drawings of the paintings that Strange intended to publish. Strange obtained revenge by buying for Sir Lawrence Dundas a painting that Dalton had drawn for approval and potential purchase by the king. But he perceived a new threat in his talented rival. He determined to engrave the painting to invite direct comparison with Bartolozzi. 'You may be sure I wish in every shape for an opportunity to appear in the same subjects with Bartolozzi', he wrote to Lumisden, 'his plates being intended for England and, [I] have reason to believe, himself also' (Dennistoun, 2.10). Strange then presented himself for acceptance by the Academy of St Luke in Rome and by the Royal Academy at Paris as a painter, on the strength of his drawings. Thus fortified with marks of continental respect he returned to London in time for the 1765 exhibition, having just been made a fellow of the newly incorporated Society of Artists. He set up a new home at 14 Castle Street, Leicester Fields.

Building a reputation Now Strange found further evidence that the clique of artists in favour with Lord Bute and the king were still determined to obstruct his smooth passage to celebrity and prosperity. He exhibited and published two prints after Raphael's *Justice* and *Meekness* in the Vatican. For some time he had been nervous about 'that ugly creature the ostridge' in *Justice*, which, he worried, 'will make a ridiculous appearance, and may be an object of derision to those who are fond of cavilling, though it may bear the name of Raphael' (Dennistoun, 2.25). His fears proved well founded. A few days after publication there appeared in the *Public Advertiser* 'a long and elaborate performance taking to pieces these prints, in order to depreciate them in the esteem of the public' (ibid., 2.29). Criticism centred on the ostrich. Strange was in no doubt that the vituperative remarks came from Chambers or Dalton or one of their associates among the courtier directors of the Society of Artists. He then tried to exhibit the Italian drawings that Winckelmann had considered 'the most beautiful that I have ever seen in my life' (*Bibliothek der schönen Wissenschaften und der freyen Künste*, 11, 1764, 369), only to find them rejected by the same directors. He helped to oust the offending directors in 1768, but discovered that they had already laid plans to found a royal academy. Strange himself was a director from 1768 to 1773. The new academy excluded engravers from membership and, to add insult to injury, accepted Bartolozzi as a painter on the strength of his drawings. Strange, with a degree of vanity perhaps, judged these measures to be aimed at him personally.

Ironically, Strange's own instincts were of an academic kind. 'It is only by studying and meditating upon the works of the Italian masters that we can reasonably expect to form a true taste, and to defend ourselves against the destructive and capricious sorcery of fashion', he wrote in *A Descriptive Catalogue of a Collection of Pictures* (pp. ii–iii). This was published in 1769 to accompany his exhibition of paintings that he had bought and drawings that he had made in Italy. These imports that he exhibited and sold included some fine and valuable paintings, such as the *Landscape with a Snake* by Poussin, bought by Sir William Watkins Wynne in 1773. Strange's knowledge of the Italian schools made him a valued expert adviser to a circle of collectors, including Sir Lawrence Dundas and William Hunter.

Meanwhile Strange exhibited with the Society of Artists from 1768 until its financial crisis in 1775. With Stubbs,

Mortimer, Paine, Pine, and Woollett, he wrote *The conduct of the Royal Academicians, while members of the Incorporated Society of Artists of Great Britain* (1771) and followed this up with a more personal account, *An Inquiry into the Rise and Establishment of the Royal Academy of Arts* (1775). After the society collapsed Strange moved to the rue d'Enfer, Paris, and spent the next five years in France.

Royal patronage Strange returned to London in 1780 and bought a house at 52 Great Queen Street, Lincoln's Inn Fields; he insured the contents for the substantial sum of £2800, a figure raised to £3400 a year later. Soon after his return, Benjamin West effected a rapprochement with the king. Strange engraved a portrait of Charles I from the French royal collection, and in 1784 he was presented to the king and queen of France. As a companion he was allowed to engrave a portrait of Charles's queen, Henrietta Maria, from the British Royal Collection, and, from the same source, West's *Apotheosis of Prince Alfred and Prince Octavius*. He took the painting to Paris to work on it and was knighted in 1787 when he presented the result to George III. After an illness in 1788 Strange decided to destroy his plates to prevent their exploitation, but was persuaded not to as their continued existence—they were then valued at £10,000—provided insurance for his family. Strange died in London on 5 July 1792.

Strange engraved with unusual clarity and delicacy and produced some beautiful prints, especially those after Titian, Correggio, and Van Dyck. His self-righteousness and his flair for self-publicity invited hostile attention, but not all of the criticism directed at him was fair. He was, for instance, accused of employing French journeymen on the mechanical parts of his plates, which was true, but all engravers used assistants. Strange's only crime was that his were French. If his work had a flaw, it was that he was not particularly good at conveying the distinctive styles of different masters that he translated. He was survived by two daughters, Mary and Katherine, and three sons, all of whom had careers in India. James went out with a writership in the East India Company to Madras, but subsequently became a banker in London; Thomas went to Canada as a lawyer, was also knighted by George III, and became the first professional recorder of Madras; Robert was an officer first in the Indian navy, then in the army. Sir Robert's vivacious widow, Isabella, retired to East Acton and died on 28 February 1808.   TIMOTHY CLAYTON

Sources J. Dennistoun, *Memoir of Sir Robert Strange, knight, engraver, member of several foreign academies of design; and of his brother-in-law Andrew Lumisden, private secretary to the Stuart princes and author of The antiquities of Rome*, 2 vols. (1855) · R. Strange and others, *The conduct of the Royal Academicians, while members of the Incorporated Society of Artists of Great Britain* (1771) · R. Strange, *An inquiry into the rise and establishment of the Royal Academy of Arts* (1775) · *Bibliothek der schönen Wissenschaften und der freyen Künste*, ed. C. F. Weisse, 7 (1762), 369 · R. Strange, *A descriptive catalogue of a collection of pictures, selected from the Roman, Florentine, Lombard, Venetian, Neapolitan, Flemish, French and Spanish schools* (1769) · SA papers, RA · H. Smailes, 'The price of friendship? Romney and Sir Robert Strange', *Transactions of the Romney Society*, 3 (1998), 12–17 · J. C. Füssli, *Raisonirendes Verzeichniss der vornehmsten Kupferstecher und ihrer Werke* (1771)

Archives NL Scot., corresp. and papers | NL Scot., letters from him and his wife to Sir William Forbes
Likenesses J. S. Webster, oils, 1750, Scot. NPG · J.-B. Greuze, drawing, c.1760, National Museums of Scotland [see illus.] · R. Strange, copper-plate engraving (after Greuze), Scot. NPG

Strange, Roger. *See* Lestrange, Sir Roger (*d*. 1311).

Strange [*married names* Merritt, Selly], **Susan** (1923–1998), scholar of international relations, was born on 9 June 1923 at Langton Matravers, Swanage, Dorset, one of the two children of Lieutenant-Colonel Louis Arbon Strange (1891–1966), a legendary First World War flying ace and later a director of Spartan Aircraft, and his wife, Marjorie, *née* Beath. She was educated at the Royal School, Bath, the Université de Caen, and the London School of Economics, which had been evacuated to Cambridge; she graduated in 1943 with a first-class degree in economics. She married Denis McVicar Merritt (1909/10–1993), a doctor, on 5 September 1942: they had one son and one daughter. After her divorce in 1955 she married, on 14 December that year, Clifford (Cliff) Selly (*b*. 1922/3), a journalist on *The Observer* and later a farmer, and had three more sons and another daughter. She retained her maiden name for professional purposes.

Strange's first job, from 1944 to 1946, was as an editorial assistant on *The Economist*. From there she moved to *The Observer*, which sent her to Washington, where she was the youngest White House correspondent by many years. After a period in New York as United Nations correspondent for *The Observer*, she returned to London in 1949 as lecturer in international relations at University College, London, while continuing as economic correspondent and an editorial writer for *The Observer* until 1957. In 1965 she was appointed to a research fellowship at the Royal Institute of International Affairs at Chatham House, and later became director of the transnational relations project. She published her first important book on international finance, *Sterling and British Policy*, in 1971; in this she looked at the implications of the introduction of flexible exchange rates. In 1974 she was a founder of the British International Studies Association.

Strange's most important contribution to international relations as a field of study lay in her promotion of international political economy (IPE), the study of the influence of the activities of states on markets, as an academic discipline. In her paper 'International politics and international economics: a case of mutual neglect', published in *International Affairs* in 1970, she lamented the widening gulf between the study of international economics and the study of international politics, urging economists and political theorists to work together, and she more than anyone else was responsible for setting up graduate programmes in the subject in British universities. After holding a German Marshall Fund fellowship at the London School of Economics (LSE) from 1976 to 1978, she was appointed Montague Burton professor of international relations there in 1978, a chair she held until 1988; at the LSE in 1984 she set up the first graduate programme in IPE in the United Kingdom.

The International Politics of Surplus Capacity: Competition for Market Shares in the World Recession (1981) was followed by *Casino Capitalism* (1986) and *States and Markets* (1988; 2nd edn, 1994), the latter a very successful textbook of international political economy, translated into several languages. After her retirement from the LSE, Strange spent five years in Florence as professor of international relations at the European University Institute, where with John Stopford of the London Business School she published *Rival States, Rival Firms: Competition for World Market Shares* (1991): this won the George Terry award for the advancement of knowledge in management studies. She was strongly critical of what she regarded as the irresponsible policies of the United States, which in her view were damaging the world economy. (Her husband Cliff wrote an influential attack on industrial farming, and in particular US agricultural and agricultural trade policies, *Ill Fares the Land*, 1972.) After 1989 she hoped that the world powers would see the end of the cold war as an opportunity for devoting more economic and political resources to the better management of world problems.

Strange's final post, which she held from 1993, was the chair of international relations at the University of Warwick, where she built up the graduate programme in IPE. Her election in 1995 as president of the American International Studies Association, only the second non-American to hold the position, was an indication of the high regard in which she was held. Thanks to her, the University of Warwick won a large grant from the Economic and Social Research Council to fund an international centre for the study of globalization. In 1996 she published *The Retreat of the State: the Diffusion of Power in the World Economy*, and her last book, *Mad Money* (1998), came out two weeks before her death. She died on 25 October 1998 in Florence Nightingale House, Aylesbury, Buckinghamshire, and was survived by her husband, Cliff.

ANNE PIMLOTT BAKER

Sources R. Morgan and others, eds., *New diplomacy in the post-cold war world: essays for Susan Strange* (1993) · *The Guardian* (14 Nov 1998) · *The Times* (24 Nov 1998) · *The Independent* (9 Dec 1998) · b. cert. · m. cert. · d. cert. · WW
Likenesses photograph, repro. in Morgan and others, *New diplomacy*, frontispiece · photograph, repro. in *The Guardian* · photograph, repro. in *The Times* · photograph, repro. in *The Independent*

Strange, Sir Thomas Andrew Lumisden (1756–1841), judge in India and writer, was born on 30 November 1756 at Henrietta Street, Covent Garden, London, the fourth of the nine children of Sir Robert *Strange (1725–1792), engraver, of Kirkwall in the Orkneys, and Isabella (1721/2–1808), daughter of William Lumisden, of Cushnie, Aberdeenshire. His mother's family were staunch Jacobites: his maternal uncle Andrew *Lumisden was private secretary to Charles Edward Stuart in Rome. After developing a friendship with Lumisden while they were both in Rome, Strange's father enrolled in the Jacobite life guards during the rising of 1745. Andrew Strange's colonial career depended heavily on his family's Scottish connections.

Strange was admitted to Westminster School on 3 March 1769, and was awarded a king's scholarship in the following year. He was elected to Christ Church, Oxford, where he matriculated on 1 June 1774, graduating BA (1778) and MA (1782). Strange entered Lincoln's Inn in 1776, where he came under the patronage of the lord chief justice Lord Mansfield, a friend of his mother's. He was called to the bar in November 1787, and was appointed chief justice of Halifax, Nova Scotia, two years later, a position he obtained through Mansfield. He remained there for seven years, during which time he gained a reputation for conciliation in the debate between Nova Scotia's house of assembly and the council. Gradually Strange became weary of the conduct of Governor John Wentworth, and he left for England in July 1796.

In this year Strange's elder brother James sought leave of absence for the young judge, intending that Strange should enter parliament. But on his return he preferred to continue his imperial legal career. He was offered the position of recorder and president of the mayor's court in Madras by Sir Lawrence Dundas. While at Ramsgate in the summer of 1797, Andrew Lumisden introduced Strange to Jane Cecilia Anstruther (d. 1799), whose brother was a barrister in Madras. Jane and Thomas were married on 1 September 1797. Immediately before leaving, on 14 March 1798, Strange was knighted.

Under the charter enacted in Madras on 26 December 1800, the Madras mayor's court was re-created as the supreme court of Madras, with a chief justice and two puisne judges. Strange was immediately appointed chief justice of the court, a position he occupied until 1816. While in Madras Strange pursued an interest in the antiquities and architecture of ancient India, collecting drawings of south Indian temples. In 1801, at the height of British fear that the French would invade India via Egypt, two volunteer militias were organized in Madras. One was headed by the governor, Lord Clive; the other was commanded by Strange.

In 1799 Strange's wife, Jane, died in childbirth. Four years later he took leave to return to England. While in Nova Scotia he had intended to make a tour of the United States of America, but had been prevented from doing so by the war with France. In 1803 he revived his interest in travel to the United States, and departed Madras on an American ship bound for New York via St Helena. His aims were once again frustrated by war. News of the renewal of hostilities between France and Britain reached St Helena soon after Strange's arrival there in June 1803. Believing the passage to America too dangerous, and after waiting four months on the island for a convoy large enough to return to Britain, Strange sailed on a vessel bound for London. Soon after his return to Madras on 27 August 1806 Strange met his second wife, Louisa Burroughs (1788–1862), daughter of the Calcutta judge Sir William Burroughs. Within days they were engaged, and married at the chapel of Fort St George on 11 October 1806.

In his professional life Strange was concerned with what he believed was the 'uncertainty' of Indian law. Having jurisdiction only within the city of Madras's boundaries, both the mayor's court and its successor, the supreme court, applied English law to most civil and criminal causes. However, for disputes between Indian litigants that concerned inheritance, succession, and contract the judges based their decrees on the verdict of Indian legal officials employed to produce opinions according to Hindu and Muslim law. Strange's concern was that the opinions of the court's Hindu pandits in particular were vague and contradictory. Pre-colonial property disputes had been arbitrated by various authorities, who usually attempted to find an accommodation between the parties. Hindu or Muslim law texts offered moral and political guidance to the ruler; they did not lay down definite rules or procedures with which to try disputes. However, like most of his contemporaries, Strange believed that a common Hindu law had existed in pre-colonial India. Accordingly, he believed that the contradictory, inconsistent character of the legal opinions which his Indian officers gave him were a sign of the degenerate state of Hindu law. Such uncertainty, he argued, militated against the security of property in the province.

On retiring from the bench in 1816, Strange published a selection of translated Hindu legal opinions which he had compiled while a judge. The three-volume *Notes of Cases, in the Court of the Recorder and Supreme Court of Judiciary at Madras* was intended as a manual for those adjudicating causes which did not turn on 'local circumstances' or English law. The text was intended to meet the perceived problem of south Indian legal uncertainty. However, in his second publication—*Elements of Hindu Law*, published from London in 1826—Strange went further in attempting to reconstruct the supposed 'principles' of Hindu law from the opinions of pandits and the translations of ancient Sanskrit texts available at the time. In doing so, he was one of the first British officials to offer a coherent and systematic account of supposedly 'ancient' Hindu jurisprudence. Until the 1860s *Elements of Hindu Law* was regarded by most judicial officials as the only authoritative account of Hindu jurisprudence. The editor of the third edition of the text suggested that 'The Indian Courts are still governed as authoritatively by Sir Thomas Strange, as the old Philosophers were by Plato and Aristotle' (J. D. Mayne, introduction, T. Strange, *Hindu Law*, 3rd edn, 1864, xxv). Strange's work played an important part in the colonial transformation of Indian jurisprudence. His *Elements of Hindu Law* played a key role in the process in which the flexible idioms of pre-colonial judicial practice were replaced by textualized, prescriptive sanctions that had the same status as the enactments of a legislature.

On his return from Madras, Strange travelled widely around Britain and on the continent. His son (Thomas) Lumisden *Strange described him as 'grave and studious' (Strange, 41) in contrast to his more vivacious brother James. Strange and his second wife, Louisa, had twelve children, three of whom (Thomas Lumisden, Alexander *Strange, and William Robert Strange) also had careers in the East India Company's service. Strange spent the last years of his life living in Harley Street, London, but died after a protracted illness at St Leonards in Sussex on 16 July 1841. He was survived by his wife, who died on 2 January 1862.

JON E. WILSON

Sources *DNB* · T. L. Strange, 'Incidents of a life', BL OIOC, MS Eur. D 358 · *Old Westminsters* · *Annual Register* (1841) · J. J. Higginbotham, *Men whom India has known: biographies of eminent Indian characters*, 8 pts (1870–71) · J. Dawson Mayne, *A treatise on Hindu law and usage* (1878) · F. E. P., ed., *Marriages at Fort St George, Madras* (1907) · D. F. Chard, 'Strange, Sir Thomas Andrew Lumisden', *DCB*, vol. 7 · St Helena factory records, May–Sept 1803, BL OIOC, G/32/66
Archives NL Scot., corresp., mainly with William Graham of Airth · NL Wales, corresp. with Lord Clive
Likenesses B. West, oils, 1799, Scot. NPG · C. Turner, mezzotint, 1820, BL OIOC · T. Lawrence, oils, Madras High Court, India · M. A. Shee, oils, Christ Church Oxf. · B. West, oils, Nova Scotia High Court · ivory miniature, Scot. NPG

Stranger, Hannah (*fl.* 1656–1671), Quaker missionary, was the wife of John Stranger, combmaker of London. Hannah was one of the women who, with Martha Simmonds, challenged Francis Howgill and Edward Hubberthorne at London Friends' meetings in the summer of 1656, interrupting the meetings by singing. She and her husband were among the group who travelled to Exeter in October 1656 to secure Nayler's release from gaol. With Nayler, Martha and Thomas Simmonds, Dorcas Erbury, and three others they journeyed through Wells and Glastonbury, arriving in Bristol on 24 October. Hannah and Martha Simmonds walked on either side of Nayler's horse, holding the bridle, singing with their companions 'Holy, holy, holy, Lord God of Israel'. They were arrested, imprisoned, and questioned by Bristol magistrates before being sent to London in November for Nayler's trial.

Letters from Hannah, found on Nayler at the time of his arrest, were given as evidence of his blasphemy. Writing to Nayler from London (16 September 1656) Hannah had described him as 'Thou everlasting son of righteousnesse and Prince of Peace' (Deacon, 6). Another letter addressed him as 'Oh thou fairest of ten thousand, thou only begotten son of God', and its references to his 'Spouse' were taken to imply an improper relationship with Martha Simmonds (Farmer, 7). Particularly damaging was a postscript by John Stranger: 'Thy name is no more to be called James but Jesus.' On examination Hannah said that she had acted at the Lord's command. Like her husband, she avoided compounding the misunderstanding of their actions by refusing to answer questions about Nayler's being called Jesus. Thomas Cole, keeper of Newgate prison in Bristol, testified to the idolatrous behaviour of the women towards Nayler during their confinement, describing their kneeling before him. When Nayler was punished on 27 December the women sat at the foot of the pillory. Hannah wrote a section of Martha Simmonds's *O England, thy Time is Come* (1656/7?) beginning 'Consider I beseech you how clearly the Scripture is fulfilled in our dayes', speaking elliptically of Nayler's sufferings and proclaiming the coming of the Lord (Simmonds, 6).

Ostracized by Friends, some of the group persisted in their protests while others, including Hannah, sought reconciliation. In 1666, after her second marriage, to Henry Salter, with whom she had two sons in 1667 and 1668, she was received by Bristol Friends and at a meeting on 2 November 1669 submitted a written testimony of contrition for her former actions. In 1671 she and Martha Fisher

went at Fox's request to the king to ask for Margaret Fell's liberty. That her reputation was still sensitive is indicated by Ellwood's deletion of her name in his edition of Fox's journal, replacing it with 'another Woman-Friend' (Penney, 2.169). Her later life is undocumented, though she has been identified as a property-owning widow in Tokaney, Delaware, in 1678–9. MAUREEN BELL

Sources J. Deacon, *The grand impostor examined* (1656) · R. Farmer, *Sathan inthron'd in his chair of pestilence* (1657) · L. Damrosch, *The sorrows of the Quaker Jesus: James Nayler and the puritan crackdown on the free spirit* (1996) · K. L. Carroll, 'Martha Simmonds, a Quaker enigma', *Journal of the Friends' Historical Society*, 53 (1972–5), 31–52 · M. Simmonds, *O England, thy time is come* [n.d., *c.*1656–1657] · N. Penney, ed., *'The first publishers of truth': being early records, now first printed, of the introduction of Quakerism into the counties of England and Wales* (1907) · M. Bell, G. Parfitt, and S. Shepherd, *A biographical dictionary of English women writers, 1580–1720* (1990)

Strangeways, Henry (*d.* 1562), pirate, was a Dorset seafarer of obscure parentage. The ballad which commemorated his death stated that 'of birth he was born base, Although of worshipful Kyn' (Birch, 42), and tradition ties him to the family of Sir Giles Strangeways (*d.* 1546) of Melbury Sampford, Dorset. Characterized by contemporaries as wild in his youth, he first appeared in 1549 as a member of John Thompson's pirate crew at Cork. In the summer of 1552 Strangeways (Stranguishe), now captain of a ship owned by Miles Grey, allegedly captured several Spanish vessels of the Biscayan fleet and an English ship. Some of the proceeds were stored in Portland Castle, then commanded by Captain George Strangeways. He fled the realm by January of 1553 in the company of the pirates Peter and Thomas Killigrew. The pirates haunted the southern Irish coast, escaped capture by the two Royal Navy ships dispatched from Portsmouth, and arrived in France, where diplomatic efforts to extradite him in the final months of Edward VI's reign were futile.

On 23 March 1554 a London chronicler reported the arrival at the English court from France of 'Strangwyshe the Rover', with two vessels laden with munitions of war (J. G. Nichols, ed., *The Chronicle of Queen Jane, and of Two Years of Queen Mary*, CS, old ser., 48, 1850, 68). Strangeways submitted himself to the queen's mercy, and he was left unprosecuted until 27 February 1555, when an attempt to have him arrested, for unknown reasons, miscarried. However, he was in the Tower of London by 10 November 1555, when he was transferred to the Marshalsea prison. He secured his life and liberty, allegedly by buying the favour of the ladies of the queen's privy chamber. In May 1557 and again in January 1558 the crown attempted to enlist Strangeways as a naval captain in the Anglo-French war, but the result is uncertain. In August 1557 he settled out of court Spanish claims of piracy against him totalling £4000 in damages. By 1559 he was resident at Dorchester, Dorset.

In early 1559 Strangeways, 'beinge poore and in greate debt' (PRO, HCA 1/35, fol. 6), was engaged by William Wilford, merchant of London, and John Strange, gentleman of Chesterton, Gloucestershire, to command an expedition intended to capture the Portuguese fortress of Mina in equatorial west Africa. The plan acquired the support of some of the London merchants who had promoted English commercial voyages to Guinea under Edward and Mary. The privy council on 29 April 1559 publicly forbade Strangeways from putting to sea in a warlike state, following a Spanish protest that the intended target was Madeira. However, no less a person than the lord admiral, Edward, Lord Clinton, had invested in the voyage and had assigned to Strangeways naval artillery, munitions, armour, and victuals. It is uncertain whether the expedition had the secret approval of the crown. Strangeways and Wilford departed Plymouth on board the *Salamander* about Whitsuntide (14 May), intending to equip at La Rochelle. But while off Plymouth the *Salamander* encountered a fleet of Spanish hulks and, perhaps accidentally, sank one. Turning to open piracy in the channel approaches, Strangeways over the ensuing weeks captured four Spanish and Portuguese prizes, several richly laden. Apprehended off La Rochelle on 24 July by Sir Thomas Cotton's squadron, Strangeways and eighty of his men were taken to London on 13 August. Arraigned on 22 September at Southwark, Strangeways and sixty-six followers were sentenced to death. However, the order was stayed and most of the crewmen were released in December on condition that they serve with the English forces in Scotland. All prominent supporters of the expedition escaped prosecution. Strangeways remained in prison until pardoned on 18 December 1560. Sir Nicholas Throckmorton, who had interceded with the queen on the rover's behalf in September 1559, recommended his usefulness at sea on several occasions. Finally, in 1562 Strangeways was sent, or allowed to proceed, to the Irish coast to harry Biscayan fishermen.

The Newhaven campaign of 1562 brought to Strangeways an appointment as a captain, new-found respectability, and heroic stature. Arriving at Le Havre on 4 October with Cuthbert Vaughan, he was made a commander of the relief force of English and Huguenot soldiers dispatched on 8 October to Rouen. Strangeways was given the task of taking the reinforcements up the River Seine and through the French lines. Commanding the oared naval vessels *Brigadine* and *Flower de Luce* he took the brunt of the assault at the armed barricade constructed at Caudebec by the Italian engineer Barthelmy Campi. Although most of the English soldiers under Thomas Leighton and Henry Killigrew reached Rouen, both naval vessels were captured with heavy losses. Strangeways, mortally wounded, escaped in a small boat and died in Rouen. His captured sailors were executed by the French as pirates. Rouen fell to the French on 26 October.

Strangeways appears to have died intestate. Information on his personal life is scanty. In death he was celebrated in William Birch's ballad of 1563 as a valiant fighter of mean estate who had pledged to forsake piracy and serve only his queen and God.   J. D. ALSOP

Sources W. Birch, 'A new ballade of the worthy service of late doen by Maister Strangwiye in Fraunce, and of his death', *Old ballads, from early printed copies*, ed. J. P. Collier (1840), 42–5 · F. J. Levy, 'The strange life and death of Captain Henry Stranguishe', *Mariner's Mirror*, 48 (1962), 133–7 · P. Forbes, *A full view of the public transactions in the reign of Queen Elizabeth*, 2 vols. (1740–41), vol. 1, pp. 150, 166, 240; vol. 2, pp. 85–90, 98, 101–3, 162, 168, 186 · high court of the admiralty criminal depositions, PRO, HCA 1/35, fols. 2–55 · PRO, HCA 1/38, fols. 94–95v · PRO, HCA 1/36, fol. 321 · PRO, SP 70/5, fols. 425, 435; 70/7, fol. 691; 70/43, fol. 731 · M. A. S. Hume, ed., *Calendar of letters and state papers relating to English affairs, preserved principally in the archives of Simancas*, 1, PRO (1892), 1558–67 61, 63, 92–3 · R. G. Marsden, ed., *Select pleas in the court of admiralty*, 2, SeldS, 11 (1897), 84–6, 110 · *The diary of Henry Machyn, citizen and merchant-taylor of London, from AD 1550 to AD 1563*, ed. J. G. Nichols, CS, 42 (1848), 206, 212–13 · *Calendar of the manuscripts of the most hon. the marquis of Salisbury*, 1, HMC, 9 (1883), 489–90 · APC, 1552–4, 203, 222, 230, 236, 245, 268; 1554–6, 100, 138, 191; 1556–8, 140–41, 320, 340 · PRO, SP 11/13/9 · *CSP for.*, 1547–53, 242, 280 · A. C. Miller, *Sir Henry Killigrew, Elizabethan soldier and diplomat* (1963), 83–5 · account of treasurer of the navy, 1559–60, PRO, E 351/2197 · will, PRO, PROB 11/31, fols. 193v–198v [Sir Giles Strangeways] · T. Glasgow, 'The navy in the French wars of Mary and Elizabeth I [pt 2]', *Mariner's Mirror*, 54 (1968), 281–96, esp. 284–6 · VCH Dorset, 2.199–200

Likenesses G. Flicke, oils, 1554, NPG; repro. in *The Connoisseur*, 45 (1916), 163–5 · H. Strangeways, self-portrait, repro. in K. Hearn, ed., *Dynasties: painting in Tudor and Jacobean England, 1530–1630* (1995), 120 [exhibition catalogue, Tate Gallery, London, 12 Oct 1995–7 Jan 1996]

Strangeways, Sir James. *See* Strangways, Sir James (*c.*1410–1480).

Strangford. For this title name *see* Smythe, Percy Clinton Sydney, sixth Viscount Strangford (1780–1855); Smythe, George Augustus Frederick Percy Sydney, seventh Viscount Strangford (1818–1857); Smythe, Percy Ellen Algernon Frederick William Sydney, eighth Viscount Strangford (1825–1869); Smythe, Emily Anne, Viscountess Strangford (*bap.* 1826, *d.* 1887).

Strangman, James (*c.*1555–1595/6?), antiquary, was the second son of William Strangman (*d.* 1573) of Hadleigh, Essex, and his wife, Mary (*fl. c.*1550–1580), daughter of Sir Thomas Barnardiston, of Kedington, Suffolk. The Strangmans held other lands in Essex and were settled at Hadleigh by the fourteenth century. James matriculated as a pensioner of Peterhouse, Cambridge, in 1572, but is not known to have graduated. That he attended university when his elder brother, Bartholomew, like other members of the family, was entered at Lincoln's Inn in London suggests that he may have been intended for the church. If so he struck an independent line, and seems to have established himself in the capital, devoting himself to historical studies.

Strangman's life is obscure and was apparently short: he was alive in 1592, and is said to have died in 1595 or 1596. He seems not to have held public office, but he had access to the public records and to other archives and read them closely. In a letter which he drafted to George Boleyn, dean of Lichfield, seeking permission to work in the cathedral library, he described himself as a lover of antiquities and as hoping particularly to find chronicles and histories. His chief interest was probably in the history of Essex, but contemporary references to his work show that he took note of other material and was generous with his findings.

He was a member of the Elizabethan Society of Antiquaries in 1591. He communicated notes on manors in Buckinghamshire and Oxfordshire to Robert Glover, Somerset herald, and he told the Pembrokeshire antiquary George Owen of a reference to Kemes in the red book of the exchequer. He probably owned Old Hall manuscript (BL, Add. MS 57950), a major compendium of medieval music, at some time in his career.

Strangman was apparently the first antiquary to study Essex. Nathanael Salmon (1675–1742) and Philip Morant (1700–1770) both acknowledged indebtedness to him, the former acclaiming him as 'a great Collector of Antiquities for this County' (Salmon, 360). Strangman clearly understood the importance of public records as a source of local history. It seems likely that the bulk of his manuscripts, of which only a few examples remain, were later incorporated with those of Thomas Jekyll (1570–1653); these then passed through the hands of William Holman to Salmon and Morant. Those successors all respected him as a pioneer.   G. H. MARTIN

Sources P. Morant, *The history and antiquities of the county of Essex*, 1 (1763) · N. Salmon, *History and antiquities of Essex* (1739–42) · H. W. King, 'James Strangman, esq. of Hadleigh, an eminent Essex antiquary of the time of Queen Elizabeth and James I', *Transactions of the Essex Archaeological Society*, 2 (1863), 139–46 · H. W. King, 'The Strangman pedigree', *Transactions of the Essex Archaeological Society*, 3 (1865), 95–103, 116 · M. McKisack, *Medieval history in the Tudor age* (1971) · J. Venn and J. A. Venn, eds., *The book of matriculations and degrees … in the University of Cambridge from 1544 to 1659* (1913) · Venn, *Alum. Cant.*, 1/4.173 · M. Bent, 'The Old Hall MS: a palaeographical study', PhD diss., U. Cam., 1968 · F. G. Emmison, ed., *Feet of fines for Essex*, 6: *1581–1603* (1993)
Archives BL, genealogical and historical collections relating to Essex, Add. MS 5937; Ct Vitel F xii 142 · Bodl. Oxf., genealogical and heraldic collections | BL, Cotton MSS

Stranguage, William. *See* Udall, William (*fl. c.*1595–1636).

Strangways, Arthur Henry Fox (1859–1948), music critic and editor, was born on 14 September 1859 in Norwich, the eldest son of Captain (later Colonel) Walter Aston Fox Strangways, of the Royal Artillery (1832–1885), and his wife, Harriet Elizabeth (*d.* 1903), the second daughter of John Edward Buller, of Enfield. He was educated at Wellington College and Balliol College, Oxford, where he gained a third class in *literae humaniores* in 1882, then for the next two years he studied music, especially the piano, at the Berlin Hochschule für Musik.

Fox Strangways became a schoolmaster first at Dulwich College (1884–6), then at Wellington (1887–1910). In 1893 he was also appointed organist and master of music, but relinquished this post on becoming a housemaster in 1901. During this time he wrote the *Wellington College German Grammar*, and also paid his first visit to India. On his retirement from Wellington he revisited India, where his fieldwork and researches resulted in *The Music of Hindostan* (1914, reissued 1965), which continued to hold its place as an authoritative work at the end of the twentieth century. On his return to England in 1911 he wrote occasional criticisms of concerts for *The Times* and shortly afterwards joined the staff, writing regularly in the absence on war service of his senior colleague, but by far his junior in

years, H. C. Colles. In 1925 he joined the staff of *The Observer* as music critic, where he remained until the outbreak of war in 1939. A selection from his weekly articles edited by Steuart Wilson was published in 1936 under the title *Music Observed*. He was an important contributor to the third edition of *Grove's Dictionary of Music and Musicians* (1927), which Colles edited. In 1933 he wrote, in collaboration with Maud Karpeles, the life of his friend and colleague, the founder of the English Folk Dance Society, Cecil Sharp.

Fox Strangways's main contribution to music journalism was the establishment of *Music and Letters*, a quarterly review appearing first in January 1920, of which he was sole proprietor as well as editor. The avowed objects were that music was 'a subject of rational enquiry like any other' and that it was not needful to be 'so busy with ideas as to be careless of words'. In this spirit he continued the journal until the end of 1936, when it was rescued from disappearance by Richard Capell. In the earlier years of the journal Fox Strangways had interested himself in printing translations into English of German lieder, most of which were his own versions. In 1924 he published *Schubert's Songs Translated*, in 1928 a similar volume of Schumann, and later a small album of Brahms, all in collaboration with Wilson. After his retirement to Devon in 1939, he completed single-handedly the translation of all the songs of Brahms, Hugo Wolf, and Richard Strauss, and most of the songs of Liszt. The typescripts were deposited in the BBC Music Library in 1947. He also planned and partly completed an anthology of English verse never previously set to music, for students without literary experience.

Fox Strangways brought to music journalism an intellect trained to exact observation and expression. Although he lacked sympathy with all forms of fiction, he had a strong vein of poetry and Romanticism in his nature and a deep appreciation of the profounder emotions which music could arouse. He was a man of wide interests, which in his earlier years included hunting. He died unmarried on 2 May 1948 at his home, The Lodge, Dinton, near Salisbury.   STEUART WILSON, *rev.* JOHN WARRACK

Sources *New Grove* · B. Maine, *Behold these Daniels* (1928) · E. Blom and others, 'A. H. Fox Strangways (1859–1948)', *Music and Letters*, 29 (1948), 229–37 · F. Howes, 'A. H. Fox Strangways', *Music and Letters*, 50 (1969), 9–14 · Burke, *Peerage*
Archives BL NSA
Likenesses W. Rothenstein, pencil drawing, 1915, U. Hull; related drawing, *NPG*
Wealth at death £1588 3s. 2d.: probate, 12 June 1948, *CGPLA Eng. & Wales*

Strangways, Giles (1615–1675), politician, was born on 3 June 1615 in Melbury Sampford, Dorset, and baptized there on 15 June, the second but eldest surviving son of Sir John *Strangways (1584–1666) and his first wife, Grace (1583–1652), daughter of Sir George Trenchard of Wolveton, Dorset. Of his six brothers and sisters only Howard, the wife of Sir Lewis Dyve, and James, a colonel of foot in the civil war, lived to maturity. His ancestors had established themselves in Dorset in the fifteenth century, and between 1529 and 1713 the parliamentary representation of the county was held by successive members of the family. His father, who sat in nine parliaments for Dorset or Weymouth, was prominent as an opponent of the court in the 1620s and as a royalist in the civil war. Giles was educated at Wadham College, Oxford, 1629–32, and Sir Francis Wortley later wrote of him: 'What study e'er he undertakes, to master it he's able' (*DNB*). On returning from travel in France he married Susanna, daughter of Thomas Edwards, a London mercer and marine insurer, with a portion of £10,000. Three of their children died young, but three sons survived to sit in parliament and three daughters to marry into minor gentry families.

Strangways represented Weymouth (with his father) in the Short Parliament (1640) and Bridport in its successor, and as a student of mathematics he was chiefly occupied in counting votes for the nascent royalist party in the Commons. After the outbreak of civil war he left Westminster to raise a cavalry regiment for the king. Taken prisoner with his brother-in-law at the fall of Sherborne Castle (1645) he spent nearly three years in the Tower with Wortley and other leading cavaliers until his father paid the maximum delinquency fine of £10,000. Strangways later presented Charles II with £100 in gold when the fleeing monarch visited Melbury Sampford after military defeat at Worcester. He was also listed by a contemporary among those who acted 'very zealously to advance the king's business' in the west (Smith, 284). His involvement in royalist conspiracy during the interregnum did not exceed the bounds of prudence, however.

From 1661 Strangways sat in the Cavalier Parliament for Dorset, and was in opposition under both the Clarendon administration and, after 1667, the cabal, in which his local rival, Anthony Ashley Cooper, held high office. But his stalwart churchmanship brought him an honorary DCL from his old university in 1665, when he probably seconded the Five Mile Bill against dissenting ministers. He succeeded to the Melbury estate with an annual value of at least £5000 in 1666.

Election defeats at the hands of Ashley (now earl of Shaftesbury and lord chancellor) in 1673 put Strangways into 'a great rage' (HoP, *Commons, 1660–90*, 3.496) and brought him to the fore in parliamentary debates. He attacked with equal vigour the indulgence shown to dissenters and Roman Catholics, the French alliance, and the venality of placemen. Sir William Temple described his principal aims as being to 'secure the business of religion [and] break the war with Holland' (ibid.). After the disruption of the cabal, he was honoured by the Royal Society with a fellowship (1673) and by admission to Gray's Inn (1674). To him was also ascribed the chief credit for the failure to carry the impeachment of Danby, whose policies at the head of the new administration, both at home and abroad, harmonized with his own.

Strangways possessed real ability as a politician and was a prominent personality in the Commons. On secular matters he was far-sighted in his approval of neutrality between the French and the Dutch, and in proposing re-election as a requirement for members accepting office. Yet Andrew Marvell, who had applauded his single-handed resistance during a debate on the excise in 1666, later described him as 'a flagrant Churchman' (*Poems and Letters*, 2.320), and rejoiced at his death before he could embark on renewed persecution of dissenters. For after a number of outrageous demands for office Strangways was eventually rewarded with a seat on the privy council, but held it for less than a month before he died of apoplexy on 20 July 1675 at Melbury Sampford, where he was buried.

JOHN FERRIS

Sources J. P. Ferris, 'Strangways, Giles', HoP, *Commons, 1660–90*, 3.495–7 · J. Hutchins, *The history and antiquities of the county of Dorset*, 3rd edn, ed. W. Shipp and J. W. Hodson, 2 (1863), 566, 662–5 · A. R. Bayley, *The great civil war in Dorset, 1642–1660* (1910) · R. North, *Examen* (1740), 56 · *JHC* · A. Grey, ed., *Debates of the House of Commons, from the year 1667 to the year 1694*, 10 vols. (1763) · *The poems and letters of Andrew Marvell*, ed. H. M. Margoliouth, 2nd edn, 2 (1952), 320–21 · K. G. Feiling, *History of the tory party* (1924) · O. Airy, ed., *Essex papers*, CS, new ser., 47 (1890) · P. Seaward, *The Cavalier Parliament and the reconstruction of the old regime, 1661–1667* (1988) · Keeler, *Long Parliament* · D. L. Smith, *Constitutional royalism and the search for settlement, c. 1640–1649* (1994)
Archives Dorset RO, earl of Ilchester's papers, D124
Likenesses J. Roettiers, medal sculpture, 1661, repro. in *Notes and Queries for Somerset and Dorset*, 13 (1912) · C. Turner, mezzotint, pubd 1811 (after D. Loggan), BM, NPG

Strangways, Giles Stephen Holland Fox-, sixth earl of **Ilchester** (1874–1959), landowner and historian, was born on 31 May 1874 at his father's town house in Belgrave Square, London. The elder son of the fifth earl, Henry Edward Fox-Strangways (1847–1905), and his wife, Lady Mary Eleanor Anne Dawson (1852–1928), daughter of the first earl of Dartrey, he was descended from Stephen Fox, first earl of Ilchester (1704–1776), who added the name of Strangways and whose younger brother, Henry, first Baron Holland, was the father of the statesman Charles James Fox. As a boy, the heir to considerable estates in the west country and to Holland House, Kensington, London, he combined personal charm, aristocratic bearing, and an addiction to outdoor activities with a wilfulness which prevented him from distinguishing himself in his studies at Eton College and led to his leaving Christ Church, Oxford, without proceeding to a degree. He married in 1902 Lady Helen Mary Theresa Vane-Tempest-Stewart (*d.* 1956), the daughter of Charles Stewart Vane-Tempest-*Stewart, sixth marquess of Londonderry (1852–1915), and his wife, Theresa Susey Helen Vane-Tempest-*Stewart, *née* Lady Theresa Chetwynd-Talbot (1856–1919) [*see under* Stewart, Charles Stewart Vane-Tempest-]. They had two sons and two daughters. He succeeded to the earldom in 1905.

Ilchester's latent scholarly instincts came into play only after brief service as an officer in the Coldstream Guards, service which he resumed, as a king's messenger, in the First World War. He was made a member of the Légion d'honneur in 1918 and OBE in 1919. The greater part of Ilchester's middle life, except during the war, was devoted to the management of his estates at Melbury and Abbotsbury, in Dorset, to breeding racehorses (he was a pillar of the Jockey Club) and other country pursuits, and to the

Giles Stephen Holland Fox-Strangways, sixth earl of Ilchester (1874–1959), by Walter Stoneman, 1922

study of the history of his family. The last of these interests culminated in the publication in 1937 of his two most important works, *The Home of the Hollands, 1605–1820* and *Chronicles of Holland House, 1820–1900*. Holland House, so named after Henry Rich, the weathercock first earl of Holland and Baron Kensington, had been acquired by Henry Fox in the mid-eighteenth century and for a hundred years was a political, social, and literary focus of the whig aristocracy. Ilchester's narrative of its fortunes, derived from extensive family archives, is in some measure also a narrative of those of the whigs. With its 54 acres of park, Holland House was the last of the great country estates in London. The building was in large part destroyed in an air raid in 1940, but its valuable collection of documents, pictures, and *objets d'art* had been removed to safety. In 1951 the estate passed from the possession of the Fox family into that of the London county council.

The other books written or edited by Lord Ilchester, the first two over his courtesy title of Baron Stavordale, were all also based on Holland House papers. They were: in collaboration with his mother, *The Life and Letters of Lady Sarah Lennox* (2 vols., 1901); *Further Memoirs of the Whig Party* by the third Lord Holland (1905); Elizabeth, Lady Holland's *Journal* (2 vols., 1908) and her *Spanish Journal* (1910); *Letters to Henry Fox, Lord Holland* (Roxburghe Club, 1915); *Henry Fox, First Lord Holland, his Family and Relations* (2 vols., 1920); *The Journal of Henry Edward Fox, Fourth Lord Holland* (1923); in collaboration with Elizabeth Langford-Brooke, *Correspondence of Catherine the Great with Sir Charles Hanbury-Williams* and a life of Hanbury-Williams (1928); *Elizabeth Lady Holland to her Son* (1946); and *Lord Hervey and his Friends* (1950). Ilchester also did notable work for the Walpole Society on the notebooks of the eighteenth-century antiquary George Vertue. Oxford University recognized his distinction as a historian by conferring on him an honorary D.Litt. in 1949. He was promoted GBE in 1950.

Only comparatively late in life did Ilchester become a public figure. He delayed his maiden speech in the House of Lords for more than a quarter of a century: speaking on behalf of the British Museum of which he had become a trustee in 1931, he moved for papers on the extermination of muskrat and nutria. Most of his rare interventions in debates, all well informed and plainly argued, were inspired either by the museum or by the National Portrait Gallery (of which he was a trustee from 1922, chairman from 1940), or by bodies such as the British Field Sports Society. The subjects included the protection of wild birds (a matter of close concern to the owner of the swannery at Abbotsbury), the necessity for gin-traps ('I have lived all my life in a rabbit country'), and the pollution of the sea by waste oil. In his last speech in his eighty-fourth year he urged the appointment to the portrait gallery of elderly, rather than youthful, trustees.

Ilchester owed his position as a trustee of national institutions, and as chairman or president of the Royal Commission on Historical Monuments, Royal Literary Fund, London Library, Walpole Society, Roxburghe Club, and other bodies, in part to his unobtrusive scholarship, but also to integrity, assiduity, and tact. As a committee man he could on occasion carry tenacity of principle to the point of obstinacy; but he earned the gratitude of the officers of the institutions over which he presided by the firmness with which he fought their battles, and he was noted for his courtesy to junior staff. The same courtesy, grave and somewhat aloof, marked his relations with his tenantry. He took an active interest in the local affairs of his county, of which he was a deputy lieutenant, then vice-lieutenant. He is credited with having countered a move to grass over parts of the Cerne Giant with a proposal to form a society for the preservation of similar ancient monuments. Over 6 feet tall and of massive build, he was quiet in both movement and speech. Although reserved in manner in public, he was essentially clubbable and displayed an engaging frivolity among his chosen friends in the Society of Antiquaries.

Ilchester died in London at 31 Queen's Gate, Kensington, on 29 October 1959 and was succeeded by his elder son, Edward Henry Charles James (1905–1964), who had lost both his sons during his father's lifetime. Ilchester's younger son died unmarried in 1961, and on the death of the elder the earldom passed to a cousin, Walter Angelo Fox-Strangways.   SIMON NOWELL-SMITH, *rev.*

Sources *The Times* (30 Oct 1959) · *The Times* (3 Nov 1959) · *The Times* (16 Nov 1959) · personal knowledge (1981) · private information (1981) · GEC, *Peerage* · WWW · *CGPLA Eng. & Wales* (1959) · *CGPLA Eng. & Wales* (1960)

Archives BL, corresp. and notes, Add. MSS 51370–51372 | CUL, corresp. with Sir Samuel Hare · Durham RO, letters to Lady Londonderry

Likenesses W. Stoneman, photograph, 1922, NPG [*see illus.*] · J. Gunn, group portrait, oils, *c*.1954–1959 (*Society of Dilettanti conversation piece*), Society of Dilettanti, London · J. Gunn, oils, *c*.1954–1959, Althorp House, Northamptonshire · F. Dodd, group portrait, drawing (with family); formerly in family possession, 1971 · G. Philpot, group portrait, painting (with family); formerly in family possession, 1971

Wealth at death none: probate limited to settled land, 19 Nov 1959, *CGPLA Eng. & Wales* · £195,239 10s. 8d.: probate save and except settled land, 4 Jan 1960, *CGPLA Eng. & Wales*

Strangways, Sir James (*c*.1410–1480), administrator and speaker of the House of Commons, was the son of James Strangways (*d*. 1443) of West Harlsey in the North Riding of Yorkshire, a lawyer who became a puisne justice of common pleas, and his wife, Joan Orell. The younger Strangways had by 1431 made an advantageous marriage to Elizabeth (1417–*c*.1460), daughter of Philip Darcy and his wife, Eleanor, daughter of Henry *Fitzhugh, third Baron Fitzhugh; she was the granddaughter of John, Lord Darcy of Knaith, and was connected with a number of the leading families of north-east England. As well as lands in several counties she brought her husband antiquated financial claims upon the crown, which her husband would devote much time to attempting to realize. It is unlikely that the younger James was the Strangways who entered Lincoln's Inn in 1444. Instead he appears to have depended for advancement upon the patronage of Richard Neville, earl of Salisbury (*d*. 1460), by whom he was retained and whom he served as an executor. Following a number of local posts Strangways became sheriff of Yorkshire in 1445–6; by now he had been knighted. In 1449 he was elected to parliament as a knight of the shire for Yorkshire. Through his marriage he acquired substantial properties in Northumberland, which doubtless explains why later in the same year he was among the commissioners appointed to treat for a truce with Scotland, and was then made a conservator of that truce—many similar commissions were to follow.

His being at Westminster enabled Strangways to pursue the Darcy claims against the crown in the exchequer, though with little success. Although he retained close links with the Nevilles, he was also employed by the crown. In the early 1450s he served on a number of commissions, national and local, to assess or receive taxes and loans, while in November 1451 he became a JP for the North Riding. In 1452 he became sheriff of Yorkshire for a second time. In 1454, during the duke of York's first protectorate, Strangways was appointed to a commission to act against disorder in the North Riding. In the following year, despite his Neville affiliations, he probably avoided involvement in the first battle of St Albans. But although he escaped attainder by the Coventry parliament of November 1459, he was suspect enough to Queen Margaret's regime to be removed as a JP in June 1460.

After the Yorkist victory at Northampton on 10 July 1460 Strangways was quickly reappointed to the commission of the peace for the North Riding, and was also elected to parliament. After surviving active involvement in the battle of Wakefield (30 December) he seems to have participated in Edward IV's Towton campaign of March 1461. Returned to parliament later that year Strangways was elected speaker, though his allegiance remained Neville rather than Yorkist. He made a lengthy speech advocating Henry VI's deposition and Edward IV's coronation, and was rewarded with a grant of 200 marks. Though possibly returned to the parliament of 1463 he also took part between 1462 and 1464 in operations directed by John Neville, Lord Montagu (*d*. 1471), against rebels in the north. Edward IV still trusted Strangways sufficiently for him to

become sheriff of Yorkshire again in November 1468. The following twelve months saw growing disorder and finally outright rebellion in that county. Strangways managed to avoid giving offence to either the Nevilles or the king, and in spite of his connections with the former he prudently left involvement in their revolts of 1469 to his younger son, Robert. Indeed, he was dismissed from the county bench by the readeption government of 1470–71, and reappointed in 1472 by Edward IV, who also added a special exemption in Strangways's favour to the Act of Resumption of 1473. In 1474 he took part for the last time in negotiations for a truce with Scotland.

Strangways died shortly before 20 August 1480. His first wife had died about 1460, and between 1463 and 1468 he had married Elizabeth Bulmer, *née* Eure, who died in March 1482. His eldest son and heir, Sir Richard Strangways, who died in 1488, married Elizabeth, daughter of William Neville, earl of Kent (*d*. 1463); their son James Strangways, who was sheriff of Yorkshire in 1492–3 and 1508–9, has sometimes been confused with his grandfather.

JULIAN LOCK

Sources J. S. Roskell, 'Sir James Strangeways of West Harlsey and Whorlton', *Yorkshire Archaeological Journal*, 39 (1956–8), 455–82; repr. in *Parliament and politics in late medieval England*, 2 (1981), 279–306 · J. S. Roskell, *The Commons and their speakers in English parliaments, 1376–1523* (1965) · R. A. Griffiths, *The reign of King Henry VI: the exercise of royal authority, 1422–1461* (1981) · *CPR, 1232–1509* · A. J. Pollard, 'The northern retainers of Richard Nevill, earl of Salisbury', *Northern History*, 11 (1976), 52–69 · Sainty, *Judges* · W. P. Baildon, ed., *The records of the Honorable Society of Lincoln's Inn: admissions*, 1 (1896)

Strangways, Sir John (1584–1666), politician, was the third, but eventually the eldest surviving, son of John Strangways (*d*. 1593) and Dorothy Thynne (*d*. 1592). He matriculated from Queen's College, Oxford, in 1601 and was admitted to the Middle Temple on 4 January 1611, by which time he was already a knight. Before 1607 he married Grace Trenchard (1583–1652). He became sheriff of Dorset in 1612–13, and served as a justice of the peace. In 1623 he succeeded his elder brother in possession of the family estates at Chirk Castle and Melbury Sampford in Dorset. He represented Dorset in the Addled Parliament of 1614, and sat in all the parliaments of the 1620s, for Dorset (1621, 1624, 1628–9) and in 1625 and 1626 for Weymouth and Melcombe Regis; by then he was established as a protégé of John Digby, earl of Bristol.

Strangways emerged in these parliaments as one of the duke of Buckingham's strongest critics. He opposed the Spanish war and in 1626 supported the duke's impeachment. On 5 June 1626 he responded to Dudley Carleton's threat that the king might turn to 'new counsels' by asserting that:

> all kings that are not tyrants or perjured, will keep themselves within the bounds of the laws of the[ir] own kingdoms, and those that counsel them to other ways are vipers fitting to be cast out, and pests of the commonwealth. (Bidwell and Jansson, 3.370)

He refused to pay the forced loan and was temporarily imprisoned and removed from the commission of the peace as a result. He became increasingly concerned that royal policies threatened the rule of law, and reportedly declared on 1 May 1628 that 'what has been acted to the prejudice of the liberties of the subject of late, had it been in former ages, had been sufficient to have shaken the frame and foundation of the kingdom' (Keeler, *Long Parliament*; Bidwell, 3.197).

Strangways's relations with the crown remained touchy during Charles I's personal rule. In 1634 the king firmly rejected his request to keep Christmas in London and ordered him to return to Dorset. It is uncertain whether he paid ship money, but in 1637 he and three others were tried before Star Chamber for transporting a total of £200,000 in gold out of England. He ignored the king's request for a contribution to the campaigns against the Scottish covenanters.

Strangways was returned for Weymouth and Melcombe Regis to both the Short and Long parliaments. In April 1640 he argued vigorously that redress of grievances should precede any grant of supply. He also objected to the Laudian altar policy, primarily on the characteristic grounds that he regarded it as contrary to law. However, once the Laudians had been removed, he strongly defended the existing institutions and liturgy of the Church of England. When, on 9 February 1641, the Commons debated the London root-and-branch petition, he insisted that 'if wee made a paritie in the church wee must at last come to a paritie in the Commonwealth. And that the Bishops weere one of the three estates of the kingdome and had voice in Parliament' (*Journal*, ed. Notestein, 339–40).

Like many other moderate royalists, Strangways's attachment to the established church and to the rule of law led him, during the summer and autumn of 1641, to regard Charles I as less of a hazard than his fiercest critics. In September Sir Edward Nicholas identified Strangways as one of the king's supporters in the Commons. By the end of the year the anti-episcopal demonstrators milling outside the Palace of Westminster listed him among 'persons disaffected to the kingdom' (Clarendon, *Hist. rebellion*, 1.464), and on 29 November, trying to enter the Commons, he found himself 'encompassed with above 200 sworded and staved' who demanded that he 'give his vote against Bishopps' (S. D'Ewes, *The Journal of Sir Simonds D'Ewes from the Final Recess of the Long Parliament to the Withdrawal of King Charles from London*, ed. W. H. Coates, 1942, 214).

On 19 May 1642 Strangways acted as teller against the houses' demand that the king be 'bound by his oath to pass such bills as shall be presented unto him by both Houses of Parliament for the good of the kingdom' (*JHC*, 2.580), but the proposed clause was carried by 103 votes to 61. On 9 July he acted as teller against a proposal to raise an army of 10,000 volunteers, and when this proposal was carried by 125 votes to 45 he promptly withdrew to his home in Dorset.

Strangways was among the first royalists to be disabled, on 6 September 1642. He sat in the Oxford Parliament which assembled in January 1644, and he was consistently one of the royalists specifically exempted from any pardon in successive parliamentarian propositions. On 28 July 1644 the committee for the advance of money imposed a fine of £4000 on him. In October 1645 he was taken prisoner and eventually, in March 1648, he was allowed to compound for a fine of £10,000, in return for which he and his son Giles *Strangways (1615–1675) were pardoned for their delinquency and the sequestration was taken off their estates.

While imprisoned in the Tower, Strangways wrote a commonplace book and some verses that throw much light on his beliefs. As with many other royalists, the central elements of his outlook were a commitment to the established church, complete with non-Laudian episcopacy, and a belief in royal authority operating within the rule of law. He defended 'Church goverment' as 'an hedge or wall about the doctrine of religion: a curbe to licentious courses', and he opposed 'the extirpation of prelacie out of the Church of England' (Beinecke Library, Yale University, Osborn MS b. 304, 35, 75). He insisted that:

> we of the Kings partie doe detest monopolyes and Shippe Monie and all the greivances of the people as much as any men living: we doe well know that our estates, lives and fames are preserved by the lawes; and that the King is bound by his lawes: we love p[ar]laments.   (ibid., 47)

Just as his commitment to the rule of law had led him to oppose royal policies of the later 1620s, so it now prompted him to deplore the way in which the parliamentarians flouted legal propriety in order to win the war.

In May 1648, having paid £5000 and secured the rest, Strangways's sequestration was discharged and he was released from the Tower. He returned at once to Melbury Sampford, where his property had suffered considerable damage during the years of civil war. In October 1649 he told Sir Simonds D'Ewes, a distant relative with whom he shared a love for antiquarianism, that 'the greatest part' of his collection of 'old evidences' had been 'either burnt or plundered' (S. D'Ewes, *The Autobiography and Correspondence of Sir Simonds D'Ewes, Bart.*, ed. J. O. Halliwell, 2 vols., 1845, 2.317). He apparently lived very quietly throughout the interregnum, and when Charles II visited Melbury Sampford during his flight after the battle of Worcester it fell to Strangways's son Giles to give him £100 in gold and to apologize for his inability to provide the monarch with a boat. The family's political loyalties, although covert, remained firm.

Strangways's first wife died in 1652 and on 8 June 1653 he married Judith Edwards (*d.* in or after 1670). He apparently played no part in Penruddock's rising but he was nevertheless among the Dorset gentry imprisoned in Dorchester gaol following it. He appeared before Major-General Desborough in December 1655. He pleaded 'his integrity', but after the major-general 'dealt very plainly and indeed roundly' with him he finally agreed to pay the decimation tax and was released (Thurloe, *State papers*, 4.336–7). Thereafter he apparently lived in retirement at Melbury Sampford until the Restoration.

On 14 May 1660 Strangways presided over the Restoration ceremonies at Sherborne, and in the celebrations which followed he 'rode along the streets, encourag[ing] and commend[ing] the people of Sherborne for their hearty and constant loyalty to the King' (*Mercurius Publicus*, no. 21, 17–24 May 1660, 329, 331). The following month Strangways and his son Giles were among the signatories of a declaration of thanksgiving from the nobility and gentry of Dorset which was presented to the king at Whitehall. Subsequently he sat for Weymouth and Melcombe Regis in the Cavalier Parliament. Between May 1661 and May 1663 he was named to a total of thirty-two committees, but thereafter he seems to have played no active part in the parliament. He died on 30 December 1666 at Melbury Sampford, where he was buried.

DAVID L. SMITH

Sources Dorset RO, Fox-Strangways (earls of Ilchester) papers, MS D 124 · J. Strangways, commonplace book, Yale U., Beinecke L., Osborn MS b. 304 · Keeler, *Long Parliament*, 353–4 · R. C. Johnson and others, eds., *Proceedings in parliament, 1628*, 6 vols. (1977–83) · W. B. Bidwell and M. Jansson, eds., *Proceedings in parliament, 1626*, 4 vols. (1991–6) · *The journal of Sir Simonds D'Ewes from the beginning of the Long Parliament to the opening of the trial of the earl of Strafford*, ed. W. Notestein (1923) · W. H. Coates, A. Steele Young, and V. F. Snow, eds., *The private journals of the Long Parliament*, 3 vols. (1982–92) · *JHC*, 2–8 (1640–67) · state papers domestic, Charles I, PRO, SP 16 · committee for compounding papers, PRO, SP 23 · J. Hutchins, *The history and antiquities of the county of Dorset*, 3rd edn, ed. W. Shipp and J. W. Hodson, 4 vols. (1861–74) · D. L. Smith, *Constitutional royalism and the search for settlement, c. 1640–1649* (1994) · D. Underdown, *A freeborn people: politics and the nation in seventeenth-century England* (1996) · A. R. Bayley, *The great civil war in Dorset, 1642–1660* (1910)
Archives Dorset RO, corresp. · Yale U., Beinecke L., commonplace book, incl. poems
Likenesses portrait, 1663, Wadham College, Oxford · portrait, Melbury House, Dorset
Wealth at death given a composition fine of £10,000 in 1648: M. A. E. Green, ed., *Calendar of the proceedings of the committee for compounding*, 1 vol. in 5 (1889–92), 3.1828

Stratford. For this title name *see* Canning, Stratford, Viscount Stratford de Redcliffe (1786–1880).

Stratford, Edmund. *See* Lechmere, Edmund (c.1586–1640).

Stratford, Edward Augustus, second earl of Aldborough (1733/4–1801), politician, was the eldest son of the fourteen children of John Stratford (1697–1777), MP for Baltinglass, and his wife, Martha (1706–1796), daughter and coheir of Benjamin O'Neale, archdeacon of Leighlin, co. Carlow. His father was the grandson of Robert Stratford, who came to Ireland before 1660, and is said to have sprung from a younger branch of the Stratfords of Warwickshire. John Stratford was created baron of Baltinglass on 21 May 1763, Viscount Aldborough on 22 July 1776, and Viscount Amiens and earl of Aldborough on 19 February 1777, shortly before his death on 29 June 1777. Edward was educated at Dr Thompson's school in Leixlip before entering Trinity College, Dublin, in December 1751, aged seventeen.

Stratford was widely known for his ability and eccentricity, which caused him to be termed the 'Irish Stanhope'. He was elected MP for the family borough of Baltinglass in the Irish House of Commons at a by-election in 1759 and represented the seat until 1768, when he travelled to England. He was an ardent whig, and was elected member for Taunton to the British parliament in 1774, but was unseated with his colleague Nathaniel Webb, on petition, on 16 March 1775, for bribery and corrupt practices. He was returned for Baltinglass again in 1775 and held the seat until his father's death. On 29 May 1777, while still Viscount Amiens, he was elected a member of the Royal Society. On 3 July 1777 the University of Oxford conferred on him the honorary degree of DCL. He built Stratford Place in London and Aldborough House in Dublin, and in Ireland he founded the town of Stratford upon Slaney and greatly improved the borough of Baltinglass. On 29 July 1765 he married Barbara Herbert (1742–1785), only daughter and heir of Nicholas Herbert (d. 1775) of Great Glemham, Suffolk, and his wife, Anne North, and granddaughter of Thomas Herbert, eighth earl of Pembroke. Following her death on 11 April 1785 he married on 24 May 1787 Anne Elizabeth Henniker (d. 1802), only daughter of Sir John Henniker (1724–1803) and his wife, Anne (d. 1792). She brought him a fortune of £50,000 and considerable expectations, which enabled him to free his estates from encumbrances. There were no children from either marriage.

Aldborough had a consciousness of his recently acquired rank and of what he believed was due to it. The family was probably Cromwellian in origin but he tried to claim an earlier lineage: the Amiens title was supposed to reflect his unsubstantiated descent from one of William the Conqueror's barons. On 15 October 1778 he wrote to Lord Lieutenant Buckinghamshire, who did not personally reply to his letter, that 'noblemen will not like being classed with the canaile' (*Lothian MSS*, 338), and he appears to have regarded the governorship of the county of Wicklow as a personal fiefdom, saying that he understood that his brother was only his locum tenens. He demanded that the government appoint him immediately as he understood from the secretary's office that there were blank commissions ready to be filled up 'as soon as your Lordship pleased to give the orders' (ibid., 340). He even considered proceeding against his brother in the court of king's bench for disturbing instead of preserving the peace and good order of the county. The government bent to his wishes and appointed him governor of co. Wicklow in December 1778. He was an enthusiastic volunteer and in 1784 was one of the volunteer generals. He was the author of *An Essay on the True Interests of the Empire*, published in Dublin in 1783, and he voted in favour of the union with England in 1800.

Aldborough quarrelled with his brothers *inter alia* over the representation of the family borough of Baltinglass, but he died before the commissioners on 3 July 1801 made their determination over the compensation for the disfranchisement of the borough. One of his brothers, the Revd Francis Paul Stratford, was still unsuccessfully petitioning the commissioners as late as 1 October 1801. A result of these quarrels was his alienation from his immediate heirs of such property as previous settlements permitted. As a parliamentary speaker he was considered by a contemporary to be 'tolerable but his manner is pompous' and 'both in public and private life, [he] has been uniformly conspicuous' (*Public Characters of 1798–1799*). Perhaps his most conspicuous action was to conduct an ongoing vendetta against Lord Chancellor Fitzgibbon, which started with his criticism of Fitzgibbon's prosecution of the brutal and reckless George Robert Fitzgerald, and came to a climax when he published an inflammatory pamphlet, in consequence of which Fitzgibbon, now Lord Clare, successfully prosecuted him for libel. Aldborough was fined and briefly imprisoned in Newgate but he was released on 29 March 1798 after a display of contrition and an apology.

Aldborough died on 2 January 1801 at Belan in co. Kildare, and was buried that month in the vault of St Thomas's Church, Dublin. After his death his widow married George Powell in December 1801 and died on 14 July 1802. As Lord Aldborough died without children, his title and estates descended to his brother, John Stratford.

E. I. CARLYLE, *rev.* E. M. JOHNSTON-LIIK

Sources E. M. Johnston-Liik, *History of the Irish parliament, 1692–1800*, 6 vols. (2002) • PRO NIre., Aldborough MSS, T 3300/13 • PRO NIre., Verner / Wingfield MSS, D 2538 • Aldborough's Almanac 1792, NL Ire., MS 19144 • GEC, *Peerage* • *Report on the manuscripts of the marquess of Lothian*, HMC, 62 (1905), 338, 340 • HoP, *Commons, 1754–90* • 'Minutes of evidence taken before the select committee on the Baltinglass election', *Parliamentary Papers Ireland* (1783), 4, 47–8, 59 • J. O'Brien and D. Guinness, *Dublin: a grand tour* (1994), 137 • A. P. W. Malcomson, *The pursuit of the heiress: aristocratic marriage in Ireland, 1750–1820* (1982), 1, 3, 44 • A. C. Kavanaugh, *John Fitzgibbon, earl of Clare* (1997), 186–97 • *N&Q*, 2nd ser., 8 (1859), 376, 424 • J. L. J. Hughes, ed., *Patentee officers in Ireland, 1173–1826, including high sheriffs, 1661–1684 and 1761–1816*, IMC (1960) • Burtchaell & Sadleir, *Alum. Dubl.* • *Public characters of 1798–1799*, 3rd edn (1801)
Archives NL Ire., corresp., diaries, and papers • PRO NIre. | BL, corresp. with earl of Liverpool, Add. MSS 38211–38214; 38306–38308, *passim* • PRO NIre., Verner/Wingfield MSS • Sheff. Arch., corresp. with second Earl Fitzwilliam
Likenesses attrib. M. Brown, oils, Oriental Club, London • S. Einslie, mezzotint (after T. Gainsborough), BM • F. Wheatley, group portrait, oils (*The Irish House of Commons, 1780*), Leeds City Art Galleries, Lotherton Hall, West Yorkshire • F. Wheatley, group portrait, oils, Waddesdon Manor, Buckinghamshire • plaster medallion (after J. Tassie), Scot. NPG • portrait, repro. in G. M. Saubruit, 'Aldborough—an extinct Irish earldom', *Journal of the Kildare Arch. Soc.*, 16, 11 • portrait?, NG Ire.?
Wealth at death boasted of over £9600 from estates, 1794; wife's income est. almost £13,000 in 1792: Malcomson, *Pursuit of the heiress*, 1, 44

Stratford, Esmé Cecil Wingfield- (1882–1971), historian, was born on 20 September 1882, elder son of Brigadier-General C. V. Wingfield-Stratford and his wife, Rosalind Isabel, daughter of the Revd Hon. E. V. Bligh and Lady Isabel Bligh. Unhappy as an oppidan at Eton College (1893–1900), he came into his own intellectually at King's College, Cambridge, from which he matriculated in 1900. This was thanks in part to the help of the historian Oscar Browning, an Eton connection who made it possible for him to transfer from mathematics to history, in which he achieved a first class in 1904. This was followed by a research studentship at the London School of Economics. His description of the LSE in its early years under the shadow of the Webbs in his autobiographical essay *Before the Lamps Went out*, published in 1946, shows his capacity for a vivid evocation of an institution's atmosphere as well as of the other delights available to a presentable young man in Edwardian London. His work at the LSE on

what became the first volume of his *History of British Patriotism* (1913) led to his election in 1907 to a fellowship at King's College, Cambridge, which he retained until 1913. In the same year he was awarded the degree of DScEcon by the University of London. In 1915 he married Barbara Elizabeth, daughter of Lieutenant-Colonel H. L. Errington and the Hon. Mrs Errington.

After war service in India, Wingfield-Stratford sought no further academic preferment but with the advantage of an independent income settled down to a very productive life as historian and author, dividing his time between his home at Berkhamsted and London, where he could follow his many interests in the theatre, music and the arts. He also developed a taste for foreign travel. When he published his last book, *Beyond Empire*, in 1964 he could point to about forty volumes bearing his name, including—besides histories—polemical works, fiction, and poetry. Routledge was his chief publisher.

Wingfield-Stratford's first substantial work was *The History of English Patriotism* (2 vols., 1913), a theme to which he several times returned. The most lasting of his books remains *The History of British Civilization* (2 vols., 1928) which stands comparison with the better-known one-volume histories of England by G. M. Trevelyan and Keith Feiling. Trevelyan (thanked in the preface along with Eileen Power) was one of a number of professional historians, which also included R. H. Tawney and J. L. and Barbara Hammond, who were his neighbours in the country and provided companions for long walks during which historical issues provided the staple of conversation.

The 'aggressiveness of temper and the somewhat rhetorical extravagance of mind' noted by the *Times* obituarist did not prevent Wingfield-Stratford from treating with respect and inspiring younger walking companions such as the future historian Peter Quennell (then a schoolboy) who was to write of him:

> he was all of a piece, his physical build which was wonderfully large and expansive, his high ambitions and boisterous enthusiasms which were on the same gargantuan scale, even his fierce prejudices which lay scattered like rolled-up hedgehogs along the paths of his conversation.
> (P. Quennell, letter to *The Times*, 27 Feb 1971)

Walking was only one aspect of a life of physical endeavour both in field sports and on the cricket field—not for nothing were the Constitutional and the MCC the two clubs listed in Wingfield-Stratford's *Who's Who* entry. It was also part of his particular approach to history; the evidence of landscape and buildings was not seen by him as inferior to that of archives and literature. It may be that this helps to explain the difficulty of fitting him into any ideological classification. He was intensely patriotic as befitted someone with a military ancestry on both sides devoted in particular to England's free institutions. Yet he was at the same time strongly opposed to the imperialism which was so prominent a feature of the political scene in his early years. He saw tragedy in England's relationship with Ireland and in the conflict with the Boers. This aspect of his thought was fully apparent in his series of volumes on the Victorian age and its aftermath which occupied him in the 1930s.

Wingfield-Stratford's devotion to parliamentary institutions is rather hard to reconcile with one of his heroes being Charles I, 'a personality as human as Cromwell and certainly not less lovable'. He marked the tricentenary of the king's execution with a book, *Charles, King of England, 1600–1637* (1949), the first in another trilogy. He saw Charles as a man of principle while Pym and his friends in the parliamentary opposition were mere 'conspirators'. Charles's eleven years of personal rule evoked a bout of nostalgia: 'not for generations was England to know such peaceful prosperity or a government so mild in its incidence and—in the best sense—national in its aims'. Yet he still felt that it was a good thing that it had not lasted since that might have prevented 'the continuity of development that has evolved a commonwealth of free nations from the seeds of the old Common Law'. But 'Pym and his associates had turned traitor to representative government and paved the way for the nearest approach England has had to the Totalitarian tyranny'.

Whether writing of the seventeenth or the nineteenth centuries or the middle ages, Wingfield-Stratford treated figures of the past as though he had known them individually. Nor was his patriotism insular; he was fully aware of the manifold links between Britain's civilization and that of its European neighbours—not least in the religious dimension, despite the fact that he was not himself a churchgoer. His unconventional dress and lilting upper-class voice, which became familiar to his neighbours when he acted as an air raid warden in the Second World War, made him something of an oddity. For him rural England and the London of his youth—evoked in *The Victorian Aftermath, 1901–1914* (1933) and other books—were better than what later decades had made them and 1914 was indeed when the lights went out. While no foe to innovation in the arts, the political and social consequences of the new technologies gave him little comfort where society and politics were concerned. Wingfield-Stratford died of heart failure on 20 February 1971 at his home, The Oaks, Cross Oak Road, Berkhamsted, Hertfordshire, survived by his wife and daughter.   MAX BELOFF

Sources WWW · *The Times* (23 Feb 1971) · *Record* [King's College, Cambridge] (1971) · E. C. Wingfield-Stratford, *Before the lamps went out* (1946) · d. cert.
Archives King's AC Cam., letters to Oscar Browning · King's Lond., Liddell Hart C., corresp. with Sir B. H. Liddell Hart
Wealth at death £51,104: probate, 23 March 1971, *CGPLA Eng. & Wales*

Stratford, John (*c*.1275–1348), administrator and archbishop of Canterbury, was probably born at Stratford upon Avon into a prosperous burgher family.

Family background and early career The name of John's father was Robert, as was that of his brother—a future bishop of Chichester [see Stratford, Robert (*d*. 1362)]. His mother was called Isabel. Robert senior has been identified as 'Master' Robert, co-founder and first master of the hospital of St Cross within the town, but in view of the title *magister* and the celibate status required, this appears

John Stratford (*c*.1275–1348), tomb effigy

unlikely. The family was related to the Hattons, important men in the town, Ralph Hatton 'of Stratford', the future bishop of London (*d*. 1354), being John's nephew. Nothing definite is known of Stratford's schooling. He studied at Oxford, though not, as Anthony Wood claims, at Merton. By 1312 he was entitled doctor of civil law. He entered the service of Worcester Priory, but initially his beneficial progress was slow. However, by 1317 he was rector of Holy Trinity, Stratford, and acting as official of Bishop John Dalderby of Lincoln (*d*. 1320), whose executor he became. From Lincoln he migrated to Canterbury, and the service of Archbishop Walter Reynolds (*d*. 1327). He was dean of the court of arches in the early 1320s, by which time he held a useful portfolio of benefices, including canonries at Lichfield, Lincoln, and York, as well as the archdeaconry of Lincoln.

Stratford first attended a royal council in 1317 at Clarendon. With other clerks trained in law, he was summoned to the parliaments that met at York in 1318, 1319, and 1320—assemblies concerned with the implementation of the treaty of Leake, with Thomas of Lancaster's claim to the stewardship of the royal household, and with the ordinances. In 1320 he accompanied Edward II and Queen Isabella to Amiens, for the performance of homage for Aquitaine, and at the end of 1321 he travelled to Avignon, on an abortive mission to secure the see of Coventry and

Lichfield for Robert Baldock (*d.* 1327). Following a brief appearance at York he returned to the curia, where he remained for about a year engaged on a variety of business: the relaxation of oaths (perhaps those committing the government to the ordinances?), the foundation of the Dominican priory at Kings Langley, where Piers Gaveston was buried, and the diversion of a papal tenth to the king.

Bishop and diplomat under Edward II Fortuitously Stratford was still abroad in April 1323 when the wealthy bishopric of Winchester fell vacant, through Rigaud d'Assier's death at the curia. Edward II sent letters in favour of Baldock, which Stratford delivered, but the nominee was *persona non grata* with Pope John XXII (*r.* 1316–34), who by bulls dated 20 June 1323 provided the king's envoy instead. He was consecrated six days later by Bertrand, cardinal-bishop of Tusculum. The king was furious at this outcome and on Stratford's return he was interrogated by Chief Justice Geoffrey Scrope (*d.* 1340) and Master Robert Ayleston, keeper of the privy seal, who forced him to answer to an indenture of nine articles concerning his conduct of royal business. But eventually, after he had renounced any prejudicial articles in his provisory bull and consented to receive the Winchester temporalities as an act of Edward's special grace, Stratford was permitted to take the oath of fealty. At the same time he was forced to enter into a recognizance of £10,000, an obligation that was not cancelled until after Edward's abdication.

By mid-July 1324 the king's irritation had abated—he needed his erstwhile envoy to secure the support of the pope with respect to Aquitaine and Scotland. Pope John for his part was eager to act as 'impartial mediator' between the English and French kings, and to divert their martial energy to a crusade. Stratford became a member of an important embassy dispatched in 1324 to the French court, the first of four continental missions in which he played a major role. Unfortunately the so-called war of St Sardos precipitated a further crisis and in March 1325 Isabella herself was sent to France in an attempt to come to terms with her brother Charles IV. Stratford was one of those who advocated the move and he visited her at Poissy towards the end of the month. Later in the year he was nominated a guardian of the king's son, Edward, earl of Chester, whom he accompanied to France to perform homage at the Bois de Vincennes for the duchy of Aquitaine, which his allegedly ailing father had transferred to him. Towards the end of October Stratford embarked on his final mission of the reign in an attempt to persuade the queen to rejoin her husband. Following his return via Dover on 18 November he probably reported on his lack of success at the Westminster parliament then in session—despite a note in his register claiming that matters were 'successfully performed'.

The deposition of Edward II The lull in diplomatic employment enabled Stratford to carry out the primary visitation of his diocese, which began with an examination of the cathedral priory on 3 February 1326. He was at Southwark when Queen Isabella's force landed in September, and he joined other bishops at St Mary Overie and at Lambeth to decide on a common course of action. He volunteered to act as an emissary to the queen if Bishop Hamo Hethe (*d.* 1352) would accompany him. Shortly thereafter he joined Isabella, and was with the insurgents at Bristol on 26 October when the young Edward was recognized as *custos* of the realm. On 6 November he was appointed deputy treasurer and is said to have celebrated Christmas at Wallingford with the queen. He was a member of the delegation sent to Kenilworth to persuade Edward II to abdicate—an occasion reported by his 'nephew' Thomas Laurence de la More (Moore), who was in his entourage. He appeared at the London Guildhall to make a contribution to the rebuilding of the chapel. Stratford resigned the office of deputy treasurer on 28 January 1327 and assisted at Edward III's coronation on 1 February.

Following the cancellation of his recognizances he resumed his diplomatic career, travelling from Dover to Wissant on 10 March and on the last day of the month sealing a treaty with France at Paris. A member of the adolescent Edward III's council, he soon became estranged from the 'court party' of Isabella and Mortimer, and acted as Henry of Lancaster's mouthpiece at the Salisbury parliament of 1328, subsequently being forced to defend himself from a charge of contempt for leaving the assembly without licence. Allegedly he barely escaped with his life. He continued to be associated with the Lancastrian 'party' until Mortimer's fall in 1330, but was careful to dissociate himself from the former king's companions and the supposed plot of the earl of Kent.

Chancellor of England With Edward III's personal rule Stratford came into his own, being appointed chancellor on 28 November 1330, an office he retained until September 1334, though during that time, when he was frequently engaged in royal affairs in various parts of the kingdom or abroad, his brother Robert, in conjunction with others, was regularly placed in charge of the seal. In April 1331 Stratford joined Edward's small flotilla, which sailed for France to enable the king to meet the French monarch and to confirm his act of homage—a policy that was later to be criticized and imputed to Stratford. Towards the end of May he was engaged—in the king's presence—in resolving the dispute between the monks and townsmen of Bury St Edmunds. While in the area he also endeavoured to settle the grievances of the citizens of Great Yarmouth.

Stratford opened the Westminster parliaments of September 1331 and March 1332, and in December of 1331 and in April and May of the following year was again involved in negotiations with the French king. By December 1332 he had fallen ill and was obliged to appoint proctors for the parliament at York. On account of the Scottish situation the centre of political activity moved during 1333 to York. In consequence Stratford was in the north until 23 September. On 3 November, following the death of Simon Mepham, he was postulated as archbishop of Canterbury. This coincided with Edward's wishes, but Stratford judiciously awaited the issue of papal bulls of provision. These were issued on 26 November, after which he was enthroned at Canterbury on 9 December.

Stratford departed almost immediately on a mission to Paris, but on his return in January he set about the visitation of his diocese. Early in February he examined the monks of Canterbury Cathedral priory, but shortly afterwards he again left for the north, where on 6 June 1335 he was reappointed chancellor in the house of the Minorites at York. This time he retained the office until 24 March 1337 when it passed first to his brother Robert, and then to Richard Bintworth, bishop of London. He remained either at York or on the Scottish borders until February 1336. In mid-March he held a convocation at St Paul's and attended the Westminster parliament.

Following the mysterious death in September 1336 of the king's younger brother, John of Eltham, Stratford returned to London from Bothwell and celebrated a requiem mass at Westminster Abbey, where the young warrior was buried. He was preoccupied with national affairs at home until 1338, when he embarked with the mediating cardinals and Bishop Richard Bury of Durham (d. 1345) for further talks in France. Meanwhile Edward, intent on establishing continental alliances against France, travelled to meet the emperor at Koblenz. During January and February 1339 Stratford was in the Low Countries, gleaning information about French plans. In May, at Antwerp, he acted as a guarantor of the king's debts and of his agreement with the Bardi. At Marcoing he was named principal councillor of Edward, the young duke of Cornwall—the future Black Prince.

On Bintworth's death the great seal was handed to Stratford at Lambeth on 8 December 1339. Edward was determined to sail to the continent from Orwell Haven where Stratford sought to dissuade him from what he considered a rash enterprise. He surrendered the great seal on 28 April 1340, but this merely passed to his brother Robert. In the event Edward was initially victorious in the sea battle of Sluys (24 June 1340), but lack of resources forced him to conclude the truce of Espléchin (25 September) and on the night of 29–30 November he landed secretly at Tower Steps. Extremely angry, he felt himself betrayed by the 'false ministers' in charge of government at home, chief among them Stratford. They had failed to provide him with the sinews of war. A protracted crisis ensued.

The crisis of 1340–1341 Nicholas, Lord Cantilupe (d. 1355) was dispatched to Canterbury where he claimed that the archbishop was responsible for the payment of merchants in Louvain and directed him to go there, but meanwhile to appear before the king. Stratford demurred, fearing for his safety. His response was pointedly delivered in his cathedral on the feast of the passion of St Thomas (29 December 1340). In an emotional address he lamented his involvement in temporal affairs and requested his hearers to forgive him. There were, he claimed, men at the king's side who hated him, and who had been responsible for the arrest of chancery clerks, justices, and knights in defiance of Magna Carta, and had even defamed him as a traitor. He solemnly pronounced the sentences of excommunication incurred *ipso facto* by all guilty parties by reason of the

canons of the councils of Oxford (1222), Reading (1279), and Lambeth (1281). This was followed up on 31 December by his letter *Sacrosancta ecclesia*, a spirited defence of ecclesiastical liberty which was circulated to the comprovincial bishops by Ralph Stratford (Hatton), dean of the province. He also wrote a pastoral letter to the king, citing the example of Rehoboam, who had abandoned the council of older and wiser men, and reminding Edward of his coronation oath.

Unimpressed, Edward sent Ralph Stafford (d. 1372), steward of his household, who cited the archbishop to appear in London to answer for his conduct of the nation's affairs. Stratford pointed out that he brought no safe conduct and on 28 January complained to the new chancellor, Robert Bourchier (d. 1349), that the levy of 1340 of every ninth lamb, sheaf, and fleece, was being unlawfully demanded from the clergy, who in the same year had promised the king a tenth, on condition of their being exempted from any tax granted by parliament. Two other letters were sent to the bishops of the province, one of them reiterating the argument expressed to Bourchier, the other deploring the exactions from the clergy and the abandonment of the rule of law. The king's response was to issue in February 1341 the *Libellus famosus*, a wideranging and uninhibited attack on the archbishop. Its authorship is unknown, although—without evidence—it has been attributed to Adam Orleton, bishop of Winchester (d. 1345). Stratford's riposte, his *Excusaciones*, issued in March, constitutes a model of dispassionate reasoning, prefaced by a traditional statement of political philosophy. The tone throughout is that of an elder statesman addressing a wayward young monarch misled by evil counsellors, men responsible for the ill-considered, inaccurate, and disgraceful *Libellus*. In a strong defence of the integrity of his administration he provides a factual point by point rebuttal. He had, he claimed, received scant reward for his efforts and provided no favours. In short, he claimed, the *Libellus* was a sad reflection on the malicious persons who had concocted it. He was willing to defend his conduct in the appropriate place—parliament. This prompted a brief riposte, *Cicatrix cordium superbia*, which was the final salvo in the pamphlet war.

At that point the archbishop emerged from his selfimposed seclusion to attend the parliament summoned to Westminster for 23 April 1341. On reaching the great hall of the palace of Westminster, Stratford's way was barred by Ralph Stafford and John Darcy, the king's chamberlain. He was diverted to the exchequer to answer the demands upon him there—the alleged non-payment of wool for the ninth. The case was to be adjourned from session to session without result. He then joined the other bishops in the Painted Chamber, but when he attempted to enter parliament he was prevented, together with his relatives, the bishops of London and Chichester. His fearlessness in the face of threats suggests that he courted martyrdom, but the king's agents were not so foolish as to provide the occasion. Despite the attempts of William Kilsby (d. 1346)—the keeper of the privy seal and Stratford's most consistent opponent—and of Darcy to foment popular antagonism, more moderate counsels prevailed. Twelve peers, including four bishops, were deputed to investigate the charges against the archbishop and on 2 May he offered once again to purge himself. On the following day after a strong delegation of bishops, earls, and others had interceded with the king, he was readmitted to favour.

A more formal reconciliation is said to have taken place on 23 October in Westminster Hall, when Stratford responded to the most damaging of the articles alleged against him. In 1343 Edward ordered the annulment of Stratford's 'arraignment' as contrary to reason, and as late as 1346 letters patent declared him blameless of the articles from which he had been 'deservedly excused'. His political career was now largely over, but between 1342 and his death he continued to exert influence as an elder statesman, even being dubbed *dux regis* by Dene (Haines, *John Stratford*, 359). In June 1348 he fell ill at Maidstone. He died on 23 August at his manor of Mayfield, according to 'Birchington' in an aura of sanctity, and was buried in his cathedral on 9 September where his alabaster effigy, somewhat damaged, lies on a fine canopied tomb, in a prominent position on the south side of the choir next to Prior Eastry's screen—as he had requested in his will.

Ecclesiastical career and reputation Stratford's Canterbury register has not survived, but a large number of his *acta* can be gleaned from other sources. He was a notable legislator, drawing up detailed ordinances for the conduct of the court of Canterbury in 1342, while three sets of provincial constitutions, issued between 1341 and 1343, are attributed to him. The first set was clearly a draft, the second is particularly concerned with ecclesiastical administration and discipline, while the third was designed to preserve church liberties and deals with areas of friction between laymen and ecclesiastics. He was a notable benefactor to the hospital of St Thomas the Martyr at Canterbury, known as Eastbridge Hospital, but his efforts were principally directed towards his native Stratford, where he founded a chantry college with the same dedication. The initial foundation (1331) was for a warden, subwarden, and three priests, but in 1336 an augmentation allowed for a further eight priests, though whether the full complement was ever achieved is uncertain. He secured the appropriation of the parish church to the foundation and a papal bull of confirmation was issued in 1345.

Opinion is divided as to Stratford's character, intentions, and stature—he has been compared unfavourably with his predecessors John Pecham (d. 1292) and Robert Winchelsey (d. 1313). But it was partly due to his moderation and legal training that the change of monarch was accomplished so smoothly in 1326–7. He certainly had a concern for what have been called 'Lancastrian' principles, in particular the importance of parliament. During the regime of Isabella and Mortimer he hazarded his career, perhaps his life, to maintain them. Without question he was a staunch defender of the liberties of the English church. The fourth of the statutes of 1340, conceded by Edward III under constraint of circumstances, he circulated triumphantly as a 'charter of liberties'. His clerical

petitions of May 1341 were incorporated in modified form into statutes of that date, which were summarily revoked by the king a few months later as contrary to English law and his own prerogative. That he was ambitious is self-evident, but it would be indefensible to argue that he had no underlying convictions. Although he had laboured long in the cause of peace, by 1337 he was forced to accept the inevitability of war with France, though not at the price of oppression at home. Even then he was not prepared to organize opposition to Edward III, doubtless because he had no desire to renew the civil strife of the previous reign. He may have been guilty of pride (*superbia*), as the frustrated king alleged, but he was not a foolish man. His reasoned defence in 1340–41 taught Edward a lesson he had the good sense never to forget.

ROY MARTIN HAINES

Sources A. C. Ducarel, 'Fragmenta sequentia registrorum Simonis de Mepeham et Johannis de Stratford', BL, Add. MS 6066 · registers D, G, H, I, L, Q, Canterbury Cathedral, archives · audience court books A36 III, IV, Canterbury Cathedral, archives · copy of Stratford's will, Chartae Antiquae W.219, Canterbury Cathedral, archives · *Libellus Famosus*, Exeter Cathedral library, MS. 2227 · sermons attributed to Stratford, Hereford Cathedral library, MS P.5 XII · 'Stephen Birchington', LPL, Historia de Archiepiscopis, MS 99 [H. Warton, ed., 'Vitae', *Anglia Sacra* 1 (1691), 19–41] · J. Stratford, bishop's register, Hants. RO, Winchester diocesan records · register of John Dalderby 1–2 (Regs. 2–3), Lincs. Arch. · R. M. Haines, *Archbishop John Stratford: political revolutionary and champion of the liberties of the English church*, Pontifical Institute of Medieval Studies: Texts and Studies, 76 (1986) · R. M. Haines, 'An English archbishop and the Cerberus of War', *The church and war*, ed. W. J. Sheils, SCH, 20 (1983), 153–70 · R. M. Haines, 'Some sermons at Hereford attributed to Archbishop John Stratford', *Journal of Ecclesiastical History*, 34 (1983), 425–37 · R. M. Haines, 'Conflict in government: archbishops versus kings, 1279–1348', *Aspects of late medieval government and society*, ed. J. G. Rowe (1986), 213–45 · R. M. Haines, *The church and politics in fourteenth-century England: the career of Adam Orleton, c. 1275–1345*, Cambridge Studies in Medieval Life and Thought, 3rd ser., 10 (1978) · G. T. Lapsley, 'Archbishop Stratford and the parliamentary crisis of 1341', *Crown, community and parliament*, ed. H. M. Cam and G. Barraclough (1951), 231–72 · B. Wilkinson, 'The protest of the earls of Arundel and Surrey in the crisis of 1341', *EngHR*, 46 (1931), 177–93, esp. 181–93 · Emden, *Oxf.*

Archives Canterbury Cathedral, archives · Hants. RO, register, episcopal manorial records · Hereford Cathedral library, sermons, MS P.5 XII

Likenesses engraving, repro. in W. Somner, *The antiquities of Canterbury*, 2 vols. (1640), vol. 2, facing p. 33 · engraving, repro. in J. Dart, *The history and antiquities of the cathedral church of Canterbury* (1726), facing p. 144 · portrait, repro. in C. A. Stothard, *The monumental effigies of Great Britain* (1876), 82 · tomb effigy, Canterbury Cathedral [see illus.]

Wealth at death £6509 14s. 4d.: will, Haines, *Archbishop*, 512–13; Chartae Antiquae W.219, Canterbury Cathedral, archives

Stratford, John (b. 1582?, d. in or after 1634), merchant and entrepreneur, came of ancient gentry stock. He was the seventh son of John Stratford and his wife, Margaret, daughter of William Tracy of Toddington and Stanway, in Gloucestershire. John and Margaret had eight sons and one daughter, and in the early years of their marriage lived at Paynes Place, Bushley, Worcestershire. Margaret died at Bushley, leaving a nuncupative will dated 10 October 1621. Their son John Stratford became a London salter, being apprenticed to Peter Robinson, and marrying his daughter Joan at Cheshunt, Hertfordshire, on 20 April 1602. There were two sons and five daughters of this marriage, all born between 1603 and 1615 and baptized at St Matthew's Church, Friday Street, London.

Stratford traded first in Cheshire cheese and woollen hose, sent from the country by Robinson's chapmen, but then switched to rough flax, linen yarn, wheat, and rye, bought from Eastland (Baltic) merchants in exchange for English broadcloth. He entered into partnership with John Hopkins, a fellow apprentice, who also married one of Robinson's daughters. When, through a second marriage, Hopkins became a kinsman of one Vickares, a woollen draper, Hopkins took over the broadcloth trade and Stratford concentrated on the flax trade, in partnership with three others, his half-brother Ralph, Thomas Lane, married to a third daughter of Robinson, and Humphrey Thornbury. They prospered and employed many poor in and near London to dress flax, until the Netherlanders brought in dressed flax.

Then business diminished, and the partners persuaded Stratford to live off his Prescott estate in Gloucestershire. He began to grow tobacco, raising some capital from Abraham Burrell, but Henry Somerscales was his main partner, for Somerscales had learned in the Netherlands how to cultivate tobacco, and took responsibility for the sale of the matured crop. Each lease of land involved separate partnerships, usually sharing the costs and profits equally. Lessees included Thomas Lorenge of Cleeve and John Ligon of Beauchamp Court, Worcestershire, each being promised inflated rents of £5 and more per acre for four years. Stratford employed many poor, spending £1400 on labour in one year, and taking trouble to conceal planting procedures from prying eyes. The first crop was sown in February 1619, on 100 acres, but a proclamation banned tobacco growing on 30 December. He attempted to cancel his leases, and much litigation followed, but he failed to escape his obligations, and became deeply indebted.

At the same time Stratford was engaged with his half-brother Ralph in soap-boiling in London, and dealt in tallow, potash, soap-ash, and oil. An appeal to the privy council in 1623 prompted their recommendation that his creditors forbear, for one year, later extended, to press for payment. He paid off some debts in sheep, and by growing flax at Winchcombe and Cockbury on 40 acres, employing 800 poor. He also experimented with linen manufacture. He urged the growing of flax and hemp as a state policy, and more ploughing of pasture to make work. The date and place of his death are unknown; a lawsuit implies that Stratford was still living in 1634, but he predeceased his wife, who died at Cheshunt, Hertfordshire. Her will was proved on 1 May 1654, and the administration of the estate of a John Stratford of Monmouth was granted to his wife Joan in 1638.   JOAN THIRSK, rev.

Sources J. Thirsk, *Economic policy and projects: the development of a consumer society in early modern England* (1978) · *CSP dom.* · *APC, 1621–1623*, 347; *1623–1625*, 113–15; *1653–1654*, 168 · lawsuits in chancery, court of requests, court of exchequer, Req. 2, Bdle 308/45; C2, Jas 1, S3/11 · state papers, PRO, SP 14/180/79 · state papers, PRO, SP 16/57/28 · state papers, PRO, SP 16/57/14 II, III · J. Thirsk, 'Projects for gentlemen, jobs for the poor', *The rural economy of England* (1984), 287–307 · private information (2004) [G. M. Stratford] · admon, PRO, PROB 6/161, fol. 237v

Stratford, Nicholas (*bap.* 1633, *d.* 1707), bishop of Chester, was baptized on 8 September 1633 in Hemel Hempstead, Hertfordshire, the son of Nicholas Stratford, variously described as a draper or shoemaker, and Anne, his wife. He matriculated as a commoner at Trinity College, Oxford, on 29 July 1651, becoming a scholar on 17 June 1652. He graduated BA on 25 January 1654, proceeded MA on 20 June 1656, and became a probationer fellow of his college on 4 June 1656 and fellow on 20 June 1657. On 29 November 1664 he proceeded BD and on 9 July 1673 was created DD. He was incorporated at Cambridge in 1663.

In August 1667 Stratford was appointed by the crown as warden of the collegiate and parish church of Manchester by the interest of John Dolben, bishop of Rochester. By about this time he had married the daughter and coheir of Stephen Luddington, archdeacon of Stow and Dolben's nephew. They had two sons and two daughters. Stratford accumulated several other preferments: prebendary of Lincoln (1670); rector of Llansanffraid-ym-Mechain, Montgomeryshire (1672); chaplain-in-ordinary to the king (1673); dean of St Asaph (1674), and later rector of Llanrwst, Denbighshire.

As warden Stratford lived close to his church and began vigorously to restore church practices abandoned during the interregnum. Communion was to be received kneeling at the altar rails; the chaplains were to wear surplices for baptisms, churchings, weddings, and funerals; antiphonal singing and chanting in the choir were restored. Incumbents in the parish were to attend strictly to their cures, keep the church registers, render account of fees, and observe prayer book rubrics. The college fellows were encouraged to reside, chaplains' stipends improved, and the college's affairs were carefully administered. Stratford gave much to the poor and encouraged charitable giving by others.

Stratford upheld the divine right of kings and implemented observance of the political occasional services in the prayer book, including a sermon on Charles the martyr on 30 January. Despite his apparently severe political and religious opinions, however, Stratford had the reputation of being conciliatory and forbearing towards dissenters, probably in hopes of reconciling them to the Church of England. The leading Manchester presbyterian minister, Henry Newcome, thought Stratford on his appointment as warden 'likely to be a mercy to this place. A good man, of a sweet temper, brave scholar … and one that … seems to resolve to settle in the place and to reside. This was thought then, and then it was so' (*Autobiography*, 1.167). Although Newcome's subsequent comments on Stratford were frequently equivocal, the warden appears to have helped Newcome's clergyman son to obtain a Cheshire living. Stratford's relatively conciliatory attitude to dissent and his disquiet at Roman Catholic influence at court is alleged by local historians to have exposed him to attack from extremists and precipitated his departure

Nicholas Stratford (*bap.* 1633, *d.* 1707), by unknown artist, *c.*1700

from Manchester. In 1683 he was nominated vicar of St Mary Aldermanbury, London, by its parishioners. Richard Wroe, lobbying the bishop of Chester for the succession to the wardenship, wrote in June that Stratford had left Manchester 'and in such manner as the people think he will not return again' (*Palatine Note-Book*, 2.3–4). On 2 April 1684 Wroe was presented to the wardenship following Stratford's resignation. In the dedicatory epistle addressed to 'my worthy and beloved friends, the inhabitants of Manchester and Salford', prefaced to his *Dissuasive from Revenge* (1684) it is perhaps significant that Stratford pleaded for a spirit of charity, while upholding the duty of obedience to rulers. He nevertheless claimed that he had not left Manchester 'for any unkindness to me on your part, nor out of any low or mercenary respect on mine'.

Stratford remained at Aldermanbury until the revolution of 1688. Alienated by James II's favouring of Roman Catholics, Stratford supported the accession of William and Mary and was appointed bishop of Chester on 15 September 1689 along with the rich living of Wigan, Chester being a notoriously impoverished see. His upholding of Anglican order together with conciliation of dissent was shown by his membership of the committee for the abortive scheme to revise the prayer book with a view to comprehension of Presbyterians within the established church.

As bishop of Chester, Stratford once again demonstrated his administrative and pastoral abilities. Of his immediate predecessors as bishop John Pearson had been increasingly incapacitated by illness from the late 1670s, while Pearson's successor, Thomas Cartwright, caused scandal by his outspoken advocacy of James II's political

and ecclesiastical policies and fled with his master. A zealous pastor, constantly in residence, Stratford was well fitted to deal with a difficult diocese containing large parishes, numerous more or less independent chapelries, nonjuring clergy, and dissenters. He complained of poor parish conditions due to inadequate curates and the lack of visitations for thirteen years. He was keen to improve the quality of the clergy with regular visitations from 1691 and his *Charge* that year showed what he expected: study, catechizing, regular communions, public baptisms, preparation for confirmation, reduction of clandestine marriages. He was an active administrator, presiding regularly in the diocesan court and gathering round him a body of high-church tory officials, including his chancellor and archdeacons. Under his immediate successors the Cheshire clergy became notorious for their real or alleged Jacobitism especially when George I's ministers opposed promotion for tory clergy. Stratford's son William (1671–1729), archdeacon of Richmond and canon of Christ Church, Oxford, was a more extreme man than his father. Stratford did not rely simply on formal discipline to improve the church's performance. He was a member of the SPCK, founded in 1699 to improve piety and education as the best means for strengthening the church and combating dissent. Assisted by Dean Fogg of Chester, Stratford supported the societies for the reformation of manners (suspect to many high-churchmen for their co-operation between churchmen and dissenters) and monthly lectures to promote morality.

Stratford's publications included pamphlets (notably against Roman Catholicism), sermons, and visitation charges. In character he was described by a Manchester colleague as 'very laborious and extraordinary charitable, affable and humble in his place and generally beloved', as well as practical in business (Raines, 143). Surviving portraits of him in his sixties give him a benevolent and intelligent appearance. Stratford died of a stroke in Westminster on 12 February 1707 and was buried in Chester Cathedral on 20 February. He died intestate but on his son's recommendation part of his money went to support a blue coat school for thirty-five poor boys in Chester. The school buildings have survived but the school was closed in 1949.   HENRY D. RACK

Sources F. R. Raines, *The rectors of Manchester, and the wardens of the collegiate church of that town*, ed. [J. E. Bailey], 2 vols., Chetham Society, new ser., 5–6 (1885), 139–47 · VCH *Cheshire*, 3.36–49 · G. T. O. Bridgeman, *The history of the church and manor of Wigan, in the county of Lancaster*, 3, Chetham Society, new ser., 17 (1889), 578–601 · S. Hibbert and W. R. Whatton, *History of the foundations in Manchester of Christ's College, Chetham's Hospital and the free grammar school*, 4 vols. (1828–48), vol. 2, pp. 5–20 · *Palatine Note-Book*, 2 (1882), 3–4 · *The diary and correspondence of Dr John Worthington*, ed. J. Crossley, 2/1, Chetham Society, 36 (1855), 114, 244, 325 · *The autobiography of Henry Newcome*, ed. R. Parkinson, 1, Chetham Society, 26 (1852), 167–8, 180–81; 2, Chetham Society, 27 (1852), 211–13 · *The manuscripts of Lord Kenyon*, HMC, 35 (1894), 245–6, 263, 270–71, 274–5, 417–18 · J. Walsh and others, eds., *The Church of England, c.1689–c.1833* (1993), 173–7, 189–90 · R. V. H. Burne, *Chester Cathedral: from its founding by Henry VIII to the accession of Queen Victoria* (1958), 171–2 · *CSP dom.*, 1683–4, 355 · Foster, *Alum. Oxon.* · N. Stratford, *A dissuasive* *from revenge* (1684) · *The bishop of Chester's charge in his primary visitation at Chester, May 5, 1691* (1692)

Archives Bodl. Oxf., corresp.

Likenesses oils, *c.*1700, Bishop's House, Chester [*see illus.*] · attrib. M. Dahl, oils, *c.*1705; formerly, priv. coll., in 1898 · Thomson, engraving, 1830, repro. in Hibbert and Whatton, *History*

Wealth at death legacy of £100 to Blue Coat School, Chester: Burne, *Chester Cathedral*, 171

Stratford [Hatton], **Ralph** (*c.*1300–1354), bishop of London, was perhaps the son of Thomas Hatton—so called from a place near Stratford upon Avon—and of a sister of bishops John *Stratford and Robert *Stratford. John's will describes him as *cognatus*, but the *Historia Roffensis* states that the archbishop was his uncle. He was regent MA at Oxford in 1329, and was delegate of the university for the confirmation of the chancellor's election in 1332, when he is termed BCL. In that year he was at Bologna, maintained, in accordance with the papal bull *Cum ex eo* under which he was licensed to pursue his studies, from the rectory of Mapledurham, Hampshire, to which John Stratford had collated him in 1329. By 1340 he was doctor of canon and civil law, perhaps of Bologna.

Academic qualifications, status as a king's clerk (so described in 1332), and the prominence of his uncles ensured Ralph Stratford's promotion to a succession of benefices. In 1332 he had papal provision to a canonry of York, while in 1333 he secured Erchesfont prebend in St Mary's Abbey, Winchester, exchanging it two years later for that of Blewbury in Salisbury Cathedral, which he resigned on his provision as treasurer (1336). He was to present a silver-gilt image of Our Lady to that cathedral. There followed royal presentation to a canonry and prebend at St Paul's, where the chapter elected him bishop on 26 January 1340. The king signified his assent three days later. The temporalities were restored on 13 February and consecration followed on 12 March at Canterbury. John Stratford, archbishop of Canterbury since 1333 and clearly influential in this promotion, officiated as consecrator.

Ralph Stratford and his uncle Robert gave loyal support to Archbishop Stratford in his conflict with Edward III in 1340–41. As dean of the province of Canterbury, Ralph became responsible for circulating his uncle's letter *Sacrosancta ecclesia* in defence of ecclesiastical liberties. When the archbishop was refused entry to parliament in April 1341, Ralph and Robert accompanied him to the Painted Chamber in the palace of Westminster, while on 3 May the two kinsmen were named members of one of the committees that four days later presented proposals, subsequently embodied in a statute, for constitutional reform and the preservation of ecclesiastical liberties.

Despite his part in the crisis of 1340–41 Ralph Stratford was not long out of royal favour. In 1342 he was empowered to treat with the king's continental allies and also with the French king. In 1345 he was a member of Lionel of Antwerp's council of regency during Edward III's absence in Flanders in July, and in November of that year he was appointed to treat with the papal envoy about relations with France. But after the archbishop's death in 1348 he took little part in public affairs, although, according to

the chronicler Baker, in 1350 the king nominated him, together with Bishop William Bateman of Norwich (*d.* 1355), for the cardinalate.

Apart from joint political action there are other signs that Ralph Stratford was on good terms with his uncle John Stratford, who in his will left him Guido de Baysio's *Rosarium*, a copy of the *Speculum judiciale* purchased in Bologna, and an enamelled cup—a present from Ralph. He fell ill in October 1348, and was relieved of the onus of administering his uncle's will. Four years later he arranged for the construction of suitable premises to house the chaplains of the late archbishop's college of St Thomas the Martyr at Stratford, buildings that were still standing in Leland's time. Ralph Stratford's episcopal register has not survived. According to Stow's *Survey*, in 1348, during the black death, he bought a croft named No Man's Land as a burial-ground—later Pardon churchyard—and built a chapel there, the adjoining land becoming the site of the London Charterhouse. But this has been questioned by the historian of the Charterhouse for lack of supporting evidence. Stratford died at Stepney, on 7 or 17 April 1354, and on the 28th his uncle Robert, bishop of Chichester, granted forty days' indulgence to those who prayed for his soul. He was buried in St Paul's Cathedral.

ROY MARTIN HAINES

Sources F. C. Wellstood, ed., *Calendar of medieval records belonging to the mayor and corporation of Stratford-upon-Avon*, typescript, 1941 · Shakespeare Birthplace Trust RO, Stratford upon Avon, BRT 1/2/217,/223 · Shakespeare Birthplace Trust RO, Stratford upon Avon, BRT 1 /3/161,/167–8,/217 · Canterbury D & C, register L fol. 86v · Canterbury D & C, register Q. fols. 211v–212v · Winchester Register Stratford, fols. 116r, 117r · Worcester Register Montacute, fol. 52r · *Historia Roffensis*, BL, MS Cotton Faustina B.v, fol. 88r · Vatican transcripts, transcript of Andrea Sapiti's register, PRO, 31/9/17 · exchequer, lord treasurer's remembrance, pipe roll enrolled accounts, PRO, E. 372/187/48 · Charter Roll witnesses (C.53), Round Room list 25/50, PRO [typescript] · Rymer, *Foedera* · *Chancery records* (RC) · Emden, *Oxf.* · Le Neve, *Fasti*, 1.31; 3.19, 37; 5.2 · *Chronicon Galfridi le Baker de Swynebroke*, ed. E. M. Thompson (1889) · T. Fisher, *A series of ancient allegorical, historical, and legendary paintings in frescoes which were discovered at Stratford upon Avon* (1838), pl. 9 no. 7 · M. Richter, ed., *Canterbury professions*, CYS, 67 (1973), no. 286, pp. 102–3 · *Hemingby's register*, ed. H. M. Chew, Wiltshire Archaeological and Natural History Society, Records Branch, 18 (1963) · R. M. Haines, *Archbishop John Stratford: political revolutionary and champion of the liberties of the English church*, Pontifical Institute of Medieval Studies: Texts and Studies, 76 (1986) · J. Stow, *A survay of London*, rev. edn (1603) · E. M. Thompson, *The Carthusian order in England* (1930) · G. Hennessy, *Novum repertorium ecclesiasticum parochiale Londinense, or, London diocesan clergy succession from the earliest time to the year 1898* (1898)

Stratford, Robert (*c.*1292–1362), administrator and bishop of Chichester, was the son of Robert and Isabel Stratford, the younger brother of Archbishop John *Stratford (*d.* 1348), and the uncle of Bishop Ralph *Stratford (*d.* 1354). Their family took its name from Stratford upon Avon, Warwickshire. Robert was probably born in the 1290s, since he was ordained deacon in 1318, granted letters dimissory for the priesthood in the same year, and assumed his first benefice, Overbury rectory, Worcester diocese, in October 1317. He studied at Oxford where he was MA by 1330—when he was licensed to have an oratory in his lodgings—and scholar in theology by May 1335, when his election as chancellor of the university was confirmed by the diocesan, Bishop Henry Burghersh (*d*. 1340). Despite non-residence and promotion as royal chancellor he retained his university office, the first example of a practice common in the following century, but he had vacated it by November 1338. He successfully suppressed the rival university established at Stamford in 1333–4, and in 1336 secured royal confirmation of university privileges. In March 1345 he was commissioned to inquire into student obstruction of royal justices investigating disorders in Oxford.

Inevitably Stratford's career was intertwined with that of his brother. Thus he was granted leave of absence from his rectory of Stratford upon Avon—for which he had exchanged Overbury—to attend John Stratford when the latter was archdeacon of Lincoln. He was abroad with him in 1320 and acted as his steward and vicar-general (appointed on 2 December 1324) on his promotion to the see of Winchester. He was made a papal chaplain on 7 February 1332. Fraternal influence, papal provision, and royal presentation helped Robert Stratford to secure a succession of canonries, though not without opposition. A canon of Wells and prebendary of Yatton in 1328, his position was still in dispute six years later when he was provided to the deanery there. This too was subject to litigation in the curia and he probably withdrew his claim following papal reservation to him, at the king's instance, of the archdeaconry of Canterbury (1334). Meanwhile by royal grant he had succeeded his brother as canon of Salisbury and prebendary of Charminster and Bere. As bishop of Winchester his brother was instrumental in securing for him prebends in Wherwell and Romsey abbeys. In 1330 he became prebendary of Aylesbury in Lincoln Cathedral, and also received canonries at St Paul's, London, and at Chichester, where he was elected bishop in mid-August 1337. The temporalities were restored on 21 September and he was consecrated on 30 November at Canterbury, bishops Orleton of Winchester (perhaps his consecrator), Wyville of Salisbury, and Hethe of Rochester being present. Shortly afterwards he was among those who escorted cardinals Gomez and Montfavèz to London. During the archbishop's absence abroad in 1338–9 he acted as his vicar-general and convened convocation.

Stratford's episcopal register is not extant, but scattered *acta* have survived. He visited his chapter in 1337 and 1345 and in an attempt to solve a jurisdictional conflict between himself as bishop and the dean and chapter of Chichester he asked for his brother's arbitration. Both parties agreed to abide by the award, which was eventually delivered in 1340. However, its terms were resented by the dean and chapter, and a bull of 1355, known only from a later copy of an exemplification of 1478, purports to render it void.

Keeper of the great seal on his brother's behalf in 1331, 1332, and 1335, Robert Stratford was appointed chancellor of the exchequer on 16 October 1331, and held the office until 1334. He was chancellor of England between 24 March and 6 July 1338 and between 20 June and 1 December 1340, when the king abruptly dismissed both him and treasurer Roger Northburgh (*d*. 1358). According to a version of *The Brut* chronicle Edward threatened to detain them in the Tower of London, but they were released after Robert had expounded the canonical dangers of such procedure. He supported his brother against the king's charge that the archbishop had failed to provide the sinews of war, and with him and their nephew, the bishop of London, was temporarily excluded from the parliament of April 1341. Robert and Ralph Stratford were both members of the committees whose proposals for reform, subsequently enacted in a statute, ended the political crisis of that year. In May 1343 Robert Stratford was engaged in negotiations at Avignon and in 1345 was a member of the council of Lionel of Antwerp, guardian of the realm during the king's absence.

Stratford co-operated in the foundation of his brother's chantry college of St Thomas at Stratford upon Avon, secured grants of toll for paving the town during the 1330s, and assisted the Guild of the Holy Cross there. On the archbishop's death in 1348 he became his sole executor and was involved with his burial arrangements. He made his will and died at his manor of Aldingbourne in Sussex on 9 April 1362. Probate was granted on the 26th. His recumbent effigy lies in the south choir aisle of Chichester Cathedral.   ROY MARTIN HAINES

Sources F. C. Wellstood, ed., *Calendar of medieval records belonging to the mayor and corporation of Stratford-on-Avon*, typescript, 1941 · BRT 1/3/16, R's indulgence on behalf of Ralph Hatton de Stratford · Canterbury D. & C., acquittance as executor of his brother, Reg. G., fol. 115v · Canterbury D. & C., commission to act in prior's election, Reg. L., fols. 72v, 104v · Canterbury D. & C., notice of will and probate, register Islip, fol. 185r · Canterbury D. & C., acquittance for R's executors, register Islip, fol. 207v · Winchester Reg. Stratford, fol. 9r · *Historia Roffensis*, BL, Cotton MS Faustina B.v, fol. 81r · BL, Royal MS 12 D. xi, fol. 13r–v · Vatican transcripts, PRO, 31/9/17A, fols. 23v–r [transcript of Andrea Sapiti's register] · Charter Roll witnesses (C53), Round Room list 25/50 (typescript), PRO · Chancery, parliament and council proceedings, fragment of process before king and council against Robert de Stratford (1340–41), C.49/46/11 · (Brut chronicle), LPL, MS 99, fol. 50v · (Vitae Arch. Cant.), LPL, MS 99, fol. 137r · Lincoln Reg. Burghersh 5, fols. 162v, 170r · composition between bp. and city of Chichester, W. Sussex RO, Cap. 1/17/46 · register K or Swayne's Book, W. Sussex RO, Cap. 1/12/2, 170–90 · W. Sussex RO, Ep. VI/1/2 (Liber B), fol. 38r–v · W. Sussex RO, Ep. VI/1/4 (Liber E), fols. 163r–4r, 171v, 194r–8r, 209v · W. Sussex RO, Ep. VI/1/6 (Liber Y), fols. 116r–v(59), 235v(178) · Emden, *Oxf.* · *Fasti Angl.*, rev. edn, vols. 1, 3–5, 7–8 · *Calendar of the charter rolls*, 6 vols., PRO (1903–27), vol. 4, pp. 374–6, 439–42, 447–8, 454–5 · *Chancery records* (RC) · Rymer, *Foedera* · M. Richter, ed., *Canterbury professions*, CYS, 67 (1973), no. 283 · C. A. Swainson, *The history and constitution of a cathedral of the old foundation … the cathedral of Chichester* (1880) · Tout, *Admin. hist.* · R. M. Haines, *Ecclesia Anglicana: studies in the English church of the later middle ages* (1989), chap. 7 · R. M. Haines, *Archbishop John Stratford: political revolutionary and champion of the liberties of the English church*, Pontifical Institute of Medieval Studies: Texts and Studies, 76 (1986) · M. E. C. Walcott, 'The bishops of Chichester', *Sussex Archaeological Collections*, 28 (1878), 11–58

Archives W. Sussex RO, acta · W. Sussex RO, Cap. 1/17/46

Likenesses effigy, Chichester Cathedral

Stratford, William Samuel (1789x91–1853), naval officer and astronomer, was, according to one source, born on 31

May 1790, the eldest son of William Stratford of Farncote, Gloucestershire. He was educated at Hanwell Heath Academy, Middlesex, and Mr Oard's school, London. He entered the navy in February 1806 on the *Pompée*, flagship first of Sir William Sidney Smith and afterwards of Vice-Admiral Stanhope, and was in her at the defence of Gaeta, the reduction of Capri, the passage of the Dardanelles, the destruction of a Turkish squadron off Point Pesquies, and the bombardment of Copenhagen in September 1807. In March 1808 he was again with Smith in the *Foudroyant*, and sailed for the coast of Brazil. From 1809 to 1815 he served in the North Sea, as master's mate in the *Theseus*, and on 14 March 1815 was promoted lieutenant. At the peace he was placed on half pay and had no further service afloat.

Thereafter Stratford devoted himself to the study of astronomy. He was elected to the Astronomical Society in 1825 and served as its secretary from February 1826 until February 1831; he was elected vice-president of the newly named Royal Astronomical Society in 1834, 1835, and 1849. On 11 April 1827 he received the silver medal of the society for his co-operation with Francis Baily in the compilation of a catalogue of 2881 fixed stars, printed as an appendix to volume 2 of the *Memoirs of the Royal Astronomical Society* (1826).

In 1830 the Admiralty sought the society's opinion on proposed changes in the *Nautical Almanac* and Stratford was one of the committee of the society to whom it was referred. On 22 April 1831 he was appointed superintendent of the *Nautical Almanac*, a post he held until his death, introducing many improvements and supervising the production of issues from that for 1834 to that for 1856. On 7 June 1832 he was elected FRS. He was the author of *An Index to the Stars in the Catalogue of the Royal Astronomical Society* (1831). In 1845, following the death of Francis Baily, Stratford completed the printing and notes of a catalogue of stars for the British Association for the Advancement of Science. He published ephemerides of comets Halley (1835), Encke (1838–9), and Faye (1851) and many shorter papers.

Stratford was married and had at least one child; his wife, Martha, survived him by barely a month, dying on 22 April 1853. Stratford died at his home, 6 Notting Hill Square, London, on 29 March 1853.

J. K. LAUGHTON, *rev.* DEREK HOWSE

Sources *Monthly Notices of the Royal Astronomical Society*, 14 (1853–4), 115–16 · *GM*, 2nd ser., 39 (1853), 656 · G. A. Wilkins, 'The expanding role of HM nautical almanac office, 1818–1975', *Vistas in Astronomy*, 20 (1976), 239 · RAS, fellowship records · *Annual Register* (1853) · O'Byrne, *Naval biog. dict.* · Boase, *Mod. Eng. biog.* · *The record of the Royal Society of London*, 4th edn (1940) · d. cert.
Archives CUL, papers relating to Halley's comet · RAS, papers | CUL, corresp. with Sir George Airy · Ransom HRC, letters to Sir John Herschel · RAS, letters to RAS · RS, corresp. with Sir John Herschel · RS, letters to Sir John Lubbock

Strath, Sir William (1906–1975), civil servant, was born on 16 November 1906 at 213 Connel Park, New Cumnock, Ayrshire, the only child of John Glennie Strath, police constable, and his wife, Elizabeth Mair. He was educated first at Girvan high school and subsequently at the University of Glasgow, where he graduated in 1928 with first-class honours in Latin and Greek. He took the examination for tax inspectors, entering the Inland Revenue in 1929, and moved to the Air Ministry, London, in 1938. He married on 23 December 1938 Vera Lucy Brown (*b.* 1904/5), a schoolteacher, daughter of Arthur Edgcombe Brown, analytical chemist. They had no children.

From 1940 until the end of the war Strath served in the newly formed Ministry of Aircraft Production, where he came to the attention of Edwin Plowden, who was by 1944 the chief executive of the department. After two years at the Ministry of Supply (1945–7) he joined Plowden again in the central economic planning staff under Stafford Cripps. There he played an able and responsible part, taking the chair at meetings of the investment programmes committee. This committee was set up at the end of 1947 to keep investment plans under review and total investment within the limits of what could be afforded without inflation, while apportioning the total between various claimants. This was initially a very rough-and-ready process, as no one could say with confidence whether the total level of investment in Britain was rising or falling. He also took part on occasion in arrangements for drafting the economic survey—the nearest the Labour government got to a plan.

Strath remained with the central economic planning staff, latterly in the Treasury, from 1947 to 1955, serving as a member of the Treasury staff from 1948 and as a member of the Economic Planning Board from 1949. In 1955 he rejoined Plowden, by that time chairman of the Atomic Energy Authority, as a full-time member of the authority, exercising in due course the duties of a managing director. In 1959 he returned briefly to the civil service as permanent secretary successively of the ministries of Supply and of Aviation, and received a knighthood (KCB). In 1961 he became managing director of Tube Investments, of which Plowden was chairman, and in the following year took over from Plowden the chairmanship of British Aluminium, in which Tube Investments held a controlling interest. In 1968 he became deputy chairman of Tube Investments, continuing in a non-executive capacity as deputy chairman after retiring from executive duties.

Strath's later years with British Aluminium included an unfortunate attempt to build an aluminium smelter at Invergordon after 1967 (on the basis of what the government represented as cheap electricity, using nuclear power from an advanced gas-cooled reactor). However, the potential of the reactor had not been adequately developed and it proved to be a highly expensive source of power. The aluminium which was intended to provide relief to the balance of payments by saving imports proved to be a costly failure, and put an end to British Aluminium as an independent company after his death.

Strath was a man of attractive personality, an able and judicious chairman, sensible, and perceptive. He was good-looking and well-built, an enthusiastic mountaineer and golfer. He took an interest in relations between industry and Whitehall, having held high office in both, and was active in the affairs of the Confederation of British

Industry. He died suddenly on 8 May 1975 at Flat 20/23, 37/38 St James's Place, Westminster, and was survived by his wife.   ALEC CAIRNCROSS

Sources *The Times* (10 May 1975) · *WWW* · B. W. E. Alford, R. Lowe, and N. Rollings, *Economic planning, 1943–51: a guide to documents in the Public Record Office* (1992) · b. cert. · m. cert. · d. cert.
Wealth at death £95,176: probate, 16 June 1975, *CGPLA Eng. & Wales*

Strathallan. For this title name *see* Drummond, William, first viscount of Strathallan (c.1617–1688); Drummond, William, fourth viscount of Strathallan (1690–1746).

Strathalmond. For this title name *see* Fraser, William Milligan, first Baron Strathalmond (1888–1970).

Strathbogie, David, **styled tenth earl of Atholl** (*d.* 1326), magnate and soldier, was the son and heir of John of *Strathbogie, ninth earl of Atholl (c.1260–1306), and Marjory, daughter of *Donald, sixth earl of Mar (*d.* in or after 1297). He was the nephew of Robert Bruce, whose first wife, Isabel, was Marjory's sister. Earl John was executed in 1306 for supporting Bruce; the earldom was granted by Edward I to his son-in-law, Ralph de Monthermer, who was at that time earl of Gloucester. However, the young Strathbogie, who was married to Joan, the daughter of the John *Comyn of Badenoch slain by Bruce in 1306, recovered his patrimony, for 10,000 marks, when he submitted to Edward in May 1307. He was then involved in the hunt for his uncle, reputedly hiding on the west coast of Scotland, from the English base at Ayr. His good service was noted by Edward II in 1308, contrary to Barbour's assertion that Atholl remained in King Robert's service. By Christmas 1307 he had left Ayr to join his wife's relative the earl of Buchan and Sir John Mowbray, as they prepared to meet Bruce's army in the north-east. This eventually resulted in the defeat of Buchan's force at Inverurie in the spring of 1308; the Comyns were now effectively expelled from Scotland for good.

In 1311 Atholl was sent to relieve the English garrison holding Robert's own castle of Loch Doon, which was under pressure from the Scots. He then moved up to Dundee. In 1312 he went to Roxburgh on Edward II's affairs, but may have made overtures to his uncle. While in August that year he attended a parliament in London, three months later he was present at another parliament in Inverness, witnessing the confirmation of the Scottish–Norwegian treaty. King Robert's acceptance of his nephew extended so far as to make Atholl constable of Scotland in place of one of his most loyal supporters, Sir Gilbert Hay of Erroll. The earl initially repaid this trust and played a distinguished part in the capture of Perth. According to Barbour, though, Atholl fell out badly with the king's brother Edward, who allegedly seduced the earl's sister, Isabel, but refused to marry her. If so, Atholl exacted a very full revenge, attacking the Scottish store at Cambuskenneth immediately before Bannockburn, and killing its commander, Sir William Airth. He thus became the first Scottish earl to be forfeited since the twelfth century; the lands of the earldom were given to Sir Neil Campbell, who married the king's sister Mary on her release

from English prison later that year. Malcolm, earl of Lennox, and Sir Adam Gordon (*d.* 1328) also benefited from Atholl's defection, as did Sir Gilbert Hay, who was restored to the constableship.

Back in England, Sir David Strathbogie was 'rewarded' with three manors in Norfolk; he also regained the castle of Chilham, Kent, which had belonged to his father, in 1321 for his good service on the borders. He moved higher in Edward II's service in 1325, when he was sent on a mission to Aquitaine. On his return he was given his wife's share of the inheritance of her uncle Aymer de Valence, earl of Pembroke. Strathbogie died about 28 December 1326, predeceased by his wife, Joan Comyn, before 24 July 1326. Their eldest son, David, succeeded as the exiled earl of Atholl. The couple had another three children, Aymer, Isabella, and Maria.

David Strathbogie, styled eleventh earl of Atholl (1309–1335), was born on 1 February 1309 and baptized in the church of St Nicholas in Newcastle. Edward III allowed him entry to his inheritance in July 1327, when only eighteen, and he took part in the Weardale campaign of that year. He had considerable estates in England, as well as a claim to the Scottish earldom of Atholl and half of the lands of his maternal grandfather, John Comyn of Badenoch. In 1330 he was also granted the castle and manor of Odogh in Ireland, inherited from his great-uncle Aymer de Valence.

As one of the 'disinherited' Strathbogie played a key role, with Sir Henry de Beaumont, in Edward III's seizure of power in 1330 from Queen Isabella and Roger Mortimer. He was thus part of the young king's inner circle. Though his claims in Scotland were not officially recognized by the English government, he was allowed to pay court to Edward Balliol when the latter arrived in England in 1331, and he took part in Balliol's invasion of Scotland in 1332. He and Beaumont effectively acted as Edward III's agents with Balliol, particularly in the matter of the transfer of the counties of southern Scotland to the English king agreed in 1333 and enacted on 12 June 1334. Strathbogie was well rewarded by Balliol for his constant service, receiving Robert Stewart's lands and office. However, relations between the disinherited leaders and the Scottish king disintegrated during Balliol's parliament of February 1334 over the claim of Sir Alexander Moubray to the inheritance of his brother Philip. The quarrel came to an end only when Moubray deserted Balliol.

Having made great efforts to win over Stewart's men in the west, Strathbogie then went north to claim his inheritance there. John Randolph, earl of Moray, pursued him into Lochaber and eventually forced him and his men to swear allegiance to David II. That done, Strathbogie was allowed to serve as King David's lieutenant in the north, which office he performed faithfully; but a dispute arose over the control of former Comyn lands, and Strathbogie, by winning over the young Robert Stewart, caused so much dissension between Stewart and Randolph (both of whom were guardians) that a parliament in April 1335 achieved nothing. With the arrival of an English army at Perth in August Strathbogie changed sides again, still retaining his office of lieutenant. In October Balliol appointed him guardian of Scotland north of the Forth, and he acted in that office with growing ruthlessness, in his determination to root out the supporters of David II. His siege of Kildrummy Castle in Mar, held by Christian Bruce, attracted the attention of her husband, the new guardian, Sir Andrew Murray. Murray brought a force north to relieve the castle, and Strathbogie moved into the forest of Culblean to meet him. A surprise attack from the rear on 30 November 1335 brought victory to Murray, and Strathbogie was killed, fighting to the end. Strathbogie married Katherine, daughter of Sir Henry de Beaumont. She was left stranded in Lochindorb after her husband's death, but defended herself successfully against the Scots until 1336 when Edward III himself brought an English force to her rescue. She died in 1368. The couple had one son, David, who was aged three at his father's death.

FIONA WATSON

Sources *Scots peerage*, 1.428–32 · G. W. S. Barrow, *Robert Bruce and the community of the realm of Scotland*, 3rd edn (1988) · G. W. S. Barrow and others, eds., *Regesta regum Scottorum*, 5, ed. A. A. M. Duncan (1988) · *CDS*, vols. 2, 5 · *RotS*, vol. 1 · *Scalacronica, by Sir Thomas Gray of Heton, knight: a chronical of England and Scotland from AD MLXVI to AD MCCCLXII*, ed. J. Stevenson, Maitland Club, 40 (1836), 140 · J. Barbour, *The Bruce*, ed. W. W. Skeat, 2 vols., STS, 31–3 (1894) · *APS*, 1.461–3 · R. Nicholson, *Edward III and the Scots: the formative years of a military career, 1327–1335* (1965)

Strathbogie, David, styled eleventh earl of Atholl (1309–1335). *See under* Strathbogie, David, styled tenth earl of Atholl (d. 1326).

Strathbogie, John of, ninth earl of Atholl (c.1260–1306), magnate, was the son of David of Strathbogie, earl of Atholl, who died on crusade at Tunis in 1270 and who was the grandson of David Hastings, a previous holder of the earldom, and his wife, Forueleth. David of Strathbogie married, as his second wife, Isabella Chilham, heir to lands in Kent and Dover and a granddaughter of Richard, a bastard of King John of England. Their son, John, a minor at his father's death, was placed under the care of his mother's second husband, Alexander de Balliol of Cavers. He appears to have reached his majority by 1284, when he began to take part in affairs of state.

Despite being a Bruce supporter during the Great Cause, Atholl was present when John, king of Scots (John de Balliol) did homage to Edward I in 1292, and he ratified the treaty with France in February 1296. A month later he invaded England under the earl of Buchan, and shortly afterwards was captured at Dunbar. Atholl gained release from the Tower of London in 1297 by serving with Edward in Flanders. On his return to Scotland, he may have fought in the battle of Falkirk on the patriotic side; he was certainly with the Scots in 1299, taking part in a raid on the south-east of the country and the meeting of the Scottish political community at Peebles. In February 1300, as sheriff of Aberdeen, he attended the justiciar's court held by John Comyn, earl of Buchan, although Buchan's younger brother, Sir Alexander Comyn, claimed to be sheriff of Aberdeen for King Edward. Atholl had an interest in north-east Scotland through his estates of Stratha'an and Strathbogie. A few months later he attended the parliament at Rutherglen, siding with the bishop of St Andrews against John Comyn the younger of Badenoch, during an argument between the two.

The earl probably submitted to Edward during the latter's campaign in north-east Scotland in 1303, and was appointed warden and justiciar north of the Forth on 29 March 1304. His deputy was the earl of Strathearn. In that office he complained to the king about the power invested in his old enemy, Sir Alexander Comyn, who now held four castles in the area; Edward duly reduced them to two. Atholl also presided over a case involving his deputy, Strathearn, concerned, ironically, with the activities of the patriotic government of which he had been part. In 1305 he was ordered to find a site for a new castle that Edward was intending to build 'in a good place beyond the Forth' (*CDS*, vol. 2, no. 1722). Around July he complained to the king about the insufficiency of his fee; although Edward attempted to deal with his complaints, the earl, like others before and after him, was left with doubts as to the value of English service.

Despite remaining at Berwick immediately after the murder of John Comyn in February 1306, Atholl joined Robert Bruce, his former brother-in-law, in time for the latter's inauguration at Scone; he was one of only three earls present. It is possible that he was responsible for the presence there of Isabel, countess of Buchan. After the battle of Methven he was given charge of the queen and of his own niece, Marjory Bruce, taking them from Kildrummy to the sanctuary at Tain, where they were later captured. Atholl himself was seized after being shipwrecked in the Moray Firth in August 1306. Taken to London, on 7 November 1306 he was hanged on a gallows 30 feet higher than usual (in deference to his English royal blood), then decapitated and burnt.

Although engaged to a daughter of Sir William Soulis in 1286, Atholl certainly married Marjory, daughter of *Donald, sixth earl of Mar, and sister of Isabel, the first wife of Robert Bruce, earl of Carrick (later Robert I). Their son, David *Strathbogie, became earl of Atholl on his father's death, but he was in English hands at that time. Having been sent to defend Dundee Castle, Earl David submitted to King Robert with the rest of the English garrison in 1312 and was made constable of Scotland. He deserted the Scots on the eve of the battle of Bannockburn, apparently because Edward Bruce had seduced his sister, and remained on the English side thereafter.

FIONA WATSON

Sources *Scots peerage*, vol. 1 · *CDS*, vols. 1–5 · G. W. S. Barrow, *Robert Bruce and the community of the realm of Scotland*, 3rd edn (1988) · *APS*, 1124–1423 · W. Gibson-Clark, ed., *Facsimiles of national manuscripts of Scotland*, 2 (1870) · C. Innes and P. Chalmers, eds., *Liber s. Thome de Aberbrothoc*, 2 vols., Bannatyne Club, 86 (1848–56), vol. 1, p. 86 · A. A. M. Duncan, *Scottish Genealogist*, 7/2 (1960), 2–10 · E. L. G. Stones, *Anglo-Scottish relations, 1174–1328: some selected documents* (1970)

Strathcarron. For this title name *see* Macpherson, (James) Ian, first Baron Strathcarron (1880–1937).

Strathclyde. For this title name *see* Ure, Alexander, first Baron Strathclyde (1853–1928).

Strathcona and Mount Royal. For this title name *see* Smith, Donald Alexander, first Baron Strathcona and Mount Royal (1820–1914).

Strathearn. For this title name *see* individual entries under Strathearn; *see also* Murray, Maurice, earl of Strathearn (*d.* 1346); Stewart, David, first earl of Strathearn and first earl of Caithness (*b.* in or after 1357?, *d.* 1386?); Graham, Patrick, second earl of Strathearn (*d.* 1413) [*see under* Graham family (*per. c.*1250–1513)]; Stewart, Walter, earl of Atholl, first earl of Caithness, and earl of Strathearn (early 1360s–1437); Graham, Malise, third earl of Strathearn and first earl of Menteith (1406x13–1490).

Strathearn, Malise, **sixth earl of Strathearn** (*b. c.*1261, *d.* in or before **1317**), magnate, was descended from a native Celtic family of considerable antiquity, whose members began to be styled earls of Strathearn in the early twelfth century. The best known of the early earls was Gilbert (*fl.* 1171–1223) who, together with his wife, Matilda d'Aubigny, in 1198 founded a priory of Austin canons at Inchaffray; it became an abbey in 1220 or 1221.

The sixth earl of Strathearn was born *c.*1261, the son of Malise, the fifth earl, and the latter's wife, Matilda, daughter of Gilbert, earl of Orkney and Caithness. He became an important figure on the political stage during the wars of independence, and ultimately lost his title and lands as a consequence of the turmoil of that period. In 1284 he was one of thirty-nine magnates who accepted Alexander III's granddaughter, Margaret, the Maid of Norway, as heir-presumptive to the throne of Scotland. In 1290 he attended the parliament at Birgham which made arrangements for the marriage of the Maid to the prince of Wales, and he attested the treaty of Salisbury which confirmed those marriage plans some months later. In June 1291 he was one of the auditors for John de Balliol in the competition for the Scottish crown, and a month later he swore fealty to Edward I as lord superior of Scotland. He was also present in Berwick in the autumn of 1292, throughout the final stages of the proceedings of the Great Cause, and thereafter he threw in his lot with the Scots in their opposition to Edward I. In July 1295 he was present in the parliament held at Stirling which wrested the exercise of power from the hands of King John, subsequently acting as one of a council of twelve who assumed governance of Scotland in place of the deposed king, setting his seal to the confirmation of the Scoto-French treaty negotiated as one of the first acts of the new council. In the spring of 1296 he took part in an expedition to Carlisle.

Strathearn submitted to the English king after the conquest of Scotland in 1296. He was restored to his possessions, but was compelled to send two of his sons to the Tower as hostages for his good behaviour. Reverting temporarily to the Scottish cause in the years 1297–1303, he was once again in the allegiance of Edward I in 1303, and for the next three years served the English king, though not very energetically. Earl Malise's political troubles began in earnest in the summer of 1306 when he was taken prisoner by the English, probably soon after the battle of Methven in June, and sent to confinement in Rochester Castle. The following summer he was permitted to present a memorial to the English council explaining his alleged support of the rebel Robert Bruce. He claimed that in March 1306 he had been captured and compelled under pain of death to perform homage to Bruce, but in spite of his protestations of loyalty the earl remained in custody. He was sent to York Castle in November 1307 and his son and heir was detained as a hostage. The earl was not finally released until November 1308, and forbidden until 1310 to return to Scotland, subsequently receiving a pension and gifts from the English king. Strathearn demonstrated his ultimate loyalty by joining the English garrison in Perth in 1312, where he helped to defend the town against assault by King Robert in 1313. Ironically, his heir fought on the side of the Scots at this siege, and the old earl was taken captive there by his son. Although his life was spared by Bruce, he was compelled to resign his earldom in favour of his son.

Strathearn married Agnes, possibly a member of the Comyn family, and probably the same countess of Strathearn who, according to Fordun, was accused in the parliament of 1320 of having taken part in the conspiracy to assassinate King Robert. They had four children. The sixth earl was dead by 1317 (when his eldest son, and successor, Malise, was noted as having been 'in the king's peace') and he was buried in Inchaffray Abbey.

Malise Strathearn, seventh earl of Strathearn (1275x80–1328x30), succeeded his father as earl soon after the siege of Perth of 1313. Unlike his father he remained firmly committed to the Scottish patriotic cause. In 1320 he was one of eight earls and over thirty barons whose seals were appended to the declaration of Arbroath, a petition addressed to the pope in which the independence of Scotland was vigorously asserted. He was not implicated in the conspiracy of that year to assassinate Robert Bruce, though his mother, Agnes, was condemned and convicted. Little is known of his career. The last certain mention of him occurs in a royal charter of 28 July 1328, and he was dead by 1329 or 1330, when his son and heir, another Malise, succeeded to the title of earl of Orkney and Caithness (through his great-grandmother Matilda), as well as of Strathearn. The seventh earl married twice. The identity of his first wife is unknown, but she was the mother of his two children, Malise, the eighth earl, and Maria. His second wife was Joanna, daughter of Sir John Menteith, who survived her husband by many years, and eventually became countess of Strathearn again, by marriage to a subsequent earl, Maurice Murray of Drumsagard.

The accounts of previous historians of Strathearn have hopelessly confused the later history of the native earldom. It was the eighth earl who fought on the Scottish side at the battle of Halidon Hill in 1333, but later resigned his earldom into the hands of Edward Balliol. In June 1344 he was tried before David II in a parliament held at Scone and, although acquitted of treasonable intent, was never restored to the earldom of Strathearn. That title had been granted in 1343 to Maurice Murray of Drumsagard, with whom it remained until 1346.   CYNTHIA J. NEVILLE

Sources C. J. Neville, 'The earls of Strathearn from the twelfth to the mid-fourteenth century, with an edition of their written acts', PhD diss., U. Aberdeen, 1983 · C. J. Neville, 'The political allegiance of the earls of Strathearn during the war of independence', SHR, 65 (1986), 133–53 · CDS, vols. 1–4 · J. Stevenson, ed., Documents illustrative of the history of Scotland, 2 vols. (1870) · F. Palgrave, ed., Documents and records illustrating the history of Scotland (1837) · J. Barbour, The Bruce, ed. A. A. M. Duncan (1997) · Johannis de Fordun Chronica gentis Scotorum / John of Fordun's Chronicle of the Scottish nation, ed. W. F. Skene, trans. F. J. H. Skene, 2 vols. (1871–2) · Johannis de Fordun Scotichronicon, cum supplementis … Walteri Boweri, ed. W. Goodall, 2 vols. (1759) · W. Bower, Scotichronicon, ed. D. E. R. Watt and others, new edn, 9 vols. (1987–98), vol. 6 · GEC, Peerage, new edn, 12.385
Archives Condie, Mackenzie and Co. (Kinnoull Trustees), Perth, Dupplin Muniments | NA Scot., GD 24 (Abercairny Muniments), GD 90 (Yule Collection), GD 220 (Muniments of the duke of Montrose), GD 248 (Seafield Grant Charters), RH 6 (Register House Charters) · Blair Atholl, Perthshire, Athole Charters (Muniments of the duke of Atholl)

Strathearn, Malise, seventh earl of Strathearn (1275×80–1328×30). See under Strathearn, Malise, sixth earl of Strathearn (b. c.1261, d. in or before 1317).

Strathern, Christine. See Morrison, Agnes Brysson Inglis (1903–1986).

Strathmore and Kinghorne. For this title name see Lyon, Patrick, third earl of Strathmore and Kinghorne (1643?–1695); Lyon, John, ninth earl of Strathmore and Kinghorne (1737–1776) [see under Bowes, Mary Eleanor, countess of Strathmore and Kinghorne (1749–1800)]; Bowes, Mary Eleanor, countess of Strathmore and Kinghorne (1749–1800); Lyon, Claude George Bowes-, fourteenth earl of Strathmore and Kinghorne in the peerage of Scotland, and first earl of Strathmore and Kinghorne in the peerage of the United Kingdom (1855–1944).

Strathnairn. For this title name see Rose, Hugh Henry, Baron Strathnairn (1801–1885).

Straton, (Mary) Isabella Charlet- (1838–1918), mountaineer, was born, possibly in Wales, with the name Mary Isabella Straton. She walked in the Pyrenees and Alps in the 1860s and began climbing with Emmeline Lewis-Lloyd in the 1870s. They made the first female ascent of Monte Viso in 1870, and the first ascent of Aiguille du Moine in 1871. Jean-Estéril Charlet (1839–1925) was her guide on these and all of her later climbs. Before becoming a guide, Charlet had worked as a shepherd and carpenter. Isabella may have first met him at Lewis-Lloyd's home in Nantgwyllt, Wales, where he had been brought to work for a year as a groom. Although Lewis-Lloyd stopped climbing in 1873, Straton returned to the Alps to climb with Charlet. Their ascents included a 3761 metre peak in the Triolet chain in 1875 that he named Pointe Isabella. She made four ascents of Mont Blanc, including the first winter ascent on 31 January 1876, which made her a celebrity. During the ascent they endured an accident to a porter and a violent storm in which all of her fingers were frostbitten. After restoring circulation to her fingers, they

reached the summit and returned to Chamonix after four days and three nights on the mountain.

They married on 29 November 1876, took the surname Charlet-Straton, and lived in a house that Jean built in the hamlet of Les Frasserands, near Argentière in Haute Savoie. She continued to receive her private income, once reputed to be worth £4000 a year. He continued to climb and was well known for his ascent of the Petit Dru in 1879 and for developing new methods of abseiling that were universally adopted. In 1881 they made the first ascent of a beautiful peak in the Aiguilles Rouges, which they christened Pointe de la Persévérance in remembrance of the perseverance that they had shown before they had dared to confess their affection for one another. They had three sons, one of whom, Robert, was killed in action in 1915. Isabella had been devoted to him, and contemporaries reported that she never recovered from his death. After an illness she died on 12 April 1918 at La Roche-sur-Foron, Haute Savoie, where she and her husband often spent the winter. She was buried in the cemetery at Argentière.

PETER H. HANSEN

Sources Alpine Journal, 32 (1918–19), 262–5 · La Montagne, 14 (1918), 69–71 · La Montagne, 22 (1926), 59–60 · R. W. Clark, Victorian mountaineers (1953) · D. Chaubet, Histoire de la compagnie des guides de Chamonix (1994) · C. Williams, Women on the rope (1973) · The Times (2 May 1876)
Likenesses photographs, c.1870–1879, repro. in Clark, Victorian mountaineers · photograph, c.1875, repro. in Alpine Journal, 243
Wealth at death £2733: probate, 27 June 1919, CGPLA Eng. & Wales

Straton, Norman Dumenil John (1840–1918), bishop of Newcastle, was born on 4 November 1840 at Somersal Herbert, Derbyshire, the only son of the Revd George William Straton (1825–1891), rector of Somersal Herbert, and his wife, Elinor Katherine, eldest daughter of Richard Norman of Melton Mowbray. Straton had aristocratic ancestry: his father was grandson of the first earl of Roden; his mother was the granddaughter of the fourth duke of Rutland. He was first educated at a preparatory school in Leicester. He later attended Trinity College, Cambridge (1859–63). Straton took orders in 1865, serving briefly (1865–6) as curate of Market Drayton, Shropshire. He was soon appointed vicar of Kirkby-Wharfe, his ministry there (1866–75) beginning a long period of association with Yorkshire. Straton embraced his father's ecclesiastical outlook, being a lifelong adherent of the evangelical party within the Church of England. On 20 February 1873 he married a widow, Emily Jane Baines, daughter of J. R. Pease, of Hesslewood, Hull. A woman of simple faith Emily became a hard-working bishop's wife. She died on 21 April 1916. They had no children.

Straton's first great appointment was to the vicarage of Wakefield (1875), which he owed to the evangelical bishop of Ripon, Robert Bickersteth. Here Straton first became widely known as a vigorous exponent of Anglican evangelicalism. In his advocacy of militant protestant principles, he was both unintellectual and anti-intellectual. Like many late Victorian evangelicals he appealed to the plain common sense and prejudice of the average English layman. His time at Wakefield was successful, nevertheless. Straton evinced an uncommon talent for organization and fund-raising, his work as a secretary of the endowment fund for the proposed bishopric of Wakefield being outstanding. In 1883 he was made a rural dean. The first bishop of Wakefield, William Walsham How, was appointed in 1888. In the same year the new bishop appointed Straton archdeacon of Wakefield. The relationship between the two men was strained, however. Walsham How was a high-churchman, and for four years he and Straton worked uneasily together.

In 1892, persuaded by Lord Abergavenny, Lord Salisbury appointed Straton bishop of Sodor and Man. The island diocese was the most evangelical in the Church of England, and provided an agreeable working environment for Straton. His administrative talents were here put to good use. In 1893 he set up a sustentation fund to raise the minimum stipend of each parish to £200. In 1895 he pushed through the Manx parliament, Tynwald, the Church Act, an important piece of legislation founding a dean and chapter. The failure of Dumbell's Bank in 1900 led Straton to organize a clergy relief fund. He continued to involve himself in protestant controversy, making frequent visits to the mainland. During the anti-ritualist campaign beginning in the late 1890s he was severely critical of other bishops' failure to deal with lawless clergy. The strangest turn of Straton's career came in 1907 when Sir Henry Campbell-Bannerman appointed him bishop of Newcastle. The promotion of a 66-year-old tory by the Liberal prime minister was remarkable enough. Straton's elevation to a young diocese with a developing Anglo-Catholic character made the appointment very injudicious. Campbell-Bannerman in effect gave way to anti-ritualist pressure for an evangelical appointment. Predictably Straton was not a success at Newcastle. His talent for financial administration was well employed, the indebtedness of the diocese being erased and foundations laid for a securer future. But Straton's outspoken protestantism generated ill feeling, as did his mainly evangelical appointments. Few were sorry when he retired to Tunbridge Wells in September 1915. He died on 5 April 1918 at Bishopscourt, Broadwater Down, Tunbridge Wells. His funeral was held at Tunbridge Wells on 9 April 1918.

Like many men of fixed outlook Straton was essentially a shy and sensitive man, his vulnerability being covered up by his uncompromising protestantism. Much loved by close friends, the private man remained unknown to most people. Opponents saw only harshness in him, an impression accentuated by his unattractive, nasal voice. It was as an efficient administrator and fund-raiser that he achieved his successes. I. T. FOSTER

Sources The Times (6 April 1918), 9 · Record (11 April 1918), 234 · Crockford · Venn, Alum. Cant. · Men and women of the time (1899)
Archives Northumbd RO, Newcastle upon Tyne, Newcastle diocesan records
Likenesses line drawing, repro. in ILN, 100 (1892), 38 · photographs, Manx Museum library, Isle of Man
Wealth at death £22,542 17s. 3d.: probate, 17 July 1918, CGPLA Eng. & Wales

Stratton, Adam of (d. 1292x4), administrator and moneylender, was the son of Thomas de Argoges (or Arwillis) of Stratton St Margaret, Wiltshire. Of his early life, nothing is known. The first firm evidence of Adam occurs in 1256, by when he was already a royal clerk attached to the exchequer. Stratton St Margaret was a dependency of Sevenhampton, a manor held by the Redvers earls of Devon as hereditary chamberlains of the exchequer. It seems likely, therefore, that it was to the influence of the Redvers family that Stratton owed his early career at the exchequer. After 1257, when the seventh earl came of age following a long minority, Stratton's association with the Redvers family was almost continuous. Between 1260 and 1262 he acted as the earl's attorney at the royal court, and in the latter year as an executor of his will. Soon afterwards he entered the service of Isabella de Forz, countess of Aumale and sister to the seventh earl of Devon, whom he served in various capacities until 1286.

Throughout his career Stratton's primary sphere of activity lay at the exchequer. In 1262 he became the weigher of the receipt, an office he acquired from its hereditary holder, John of Windsor, and which in 1265 he granted, for life, to his brother William of Stratton, who held it until 1290. In 1266 he also secured grants of 6d. a day for life from the king for his two other brothers, Henry and Thomas, who were clerics. By the mid-1260s Stratton himself had become the chamberlain of the receipt, and thus the deputy of Isabella de Forz, now the hereditary chamberlain of the exchequer in succession to her brother. In 1276, however, Isabella granted him, in fee, her own chamberlainship of the exchequer, along with its appurtenant manor of Sevenhampton, which he held until his fall in 1290. In addition he also acquired possession, in fee, of half the ushership of the receipt, which he also held until 1290.

In addition to his duties at the exchequer Stratton was involved, from the late 1250s, with the supervision of the king's works at Westminster Abbey and Palace. Between 1264 and 1272 he was officially keeper of the Westminster works, though he may have been acting as keeper for some time before this. More than his work at the exchequer, it was probably his association with Westminster that brought him into contact with Henry III, and produced for him the continuing stream of royal gifts and grants of ecclesiastical livings that he enjoyed during the last years of the old king's reign. These gifts continued under Edward I. By 1290 his ecclesiastical income alone was reckoned by Bartholomew Cotton to amount to £1000 per annum.

Stratton's enormous wealth was certainly due in part to his clerical offices, but primarily it was the product of his moneylending, and of his related trafficking in Jewish debts and in the mortgaged estates which guaranteed them. His position and privileges as an exchequer clerk were of considerable advantage to him in this business, which earned him an unsavoury reputation for sharp practice and dishonesty. It is not possible to determine exactly when he began his career as a moneylender, but he was already well established in it by 1260. It was probably as a result of his moneylending, indeed, that Stratton acquired his position as the weigher of the receipt in 1262. By 1271 he had also begun to lend money in partnership with the Riccardi of Lucca, Italian moneylenders and wool merchants with whom he would thereafter be closely involved.

Typical of Stratton's methods as a moneylender were the loans he made to Bermondsey Priory, which eventually brought about his downfall. The priory's debts to him began in the 1260s, but they mounted dramatically after 1271, when the prior granted him an annuity of £40 to settle the house's existing debts, and agreed to a penalty charge of £1 a day for late payment of the annuity. Further loans soon followed, some involving penalty and interest charges of 900 per cent per annum. By 1288, when Bermondsey presented its complaints against him to the king, Stratton held five of the priory's manors, all of its advowsons, and yet was still owed debts of £6000.

Stratton's direct involvement with the management of the countess of Aumale's estates appears to have begun in 1274; it was probably as a reward for reorganizing her financial administration that in 1276 Isabella gave him her chamberlainship of the exchequer in fee. Between 1277 and 1286 Stratton was clearly Isabella's chief financial official, receiving, disbursing, and transferring the revenues of her estates from his London base with the help of the Riccardi. In 1279, while acting in Isabella's service, he was accused before parliament by the abbot of Quarr (Isle of Wight) of fraudulently removing the seal from an abbey charter. More allegations of dishonest conduct emerged when the king suspended him from his offices at the exchequer, and appointed special justices to hear all additional complaints against him. But despite overwhelming evidence of his guilt, Stratton was declared innocent of all charges and restored to his offices at the exchequer. In return he paid a 4000 mark bribe to the king through the Riccardi.

In 1289 Stratton did not escape so lightly. Bermondsey's complaints reached the king in Gascony in 1288. When Edward returned to England in late 1289, Stratton was deprived of his exchequer offices and put on trial for felony. Lurid tales of sorcery circulated about him, but the charges of which he was actually convicted in 1290 are not known. His secular property was confiscated, including cash found in his house to the value of £12,666 17s. 7d., but he retained his ecclesiastical revenues, and his friends were able to purchase the king's pardon for him by a fine of 500 marks. In early 1291, however, Stratton was again on trial for felony, this time accused of forging charters, and was once again committed to the Tower of London. Convicted near the end of 1292, he was dead by 14 August 1294, whether by execution or natural causes is nowhere recorded.   ROBERT C. STACEY

Sources *Chancery records* · N. Denholm-Young, *Seignorial administration in England* (1937) · R. W. Kaeuper, *Bankers to the crown: the Riccardi of Lucca and Edward I* (1973) · R. H. Bowers, 'From rolls to riches: king's clerks and moneylending in thirteenth century England', *Speculum*, 58 (1983), 60–71 · P. A. Brand, 'Edward I and the judges: the "state trials" of 1289–1293', *Thirteenth century England*: *proceedings of the Newcastle upon Tyne conference* [Newcastle upon Tyne 1985], ed. P. R. Coss and S. D. Lloyd, 1 (1986), 31–40 · M. Prestwich, *Edward I* (1988) · T. Madox, *The history and antiquities of the exchequer of the kings of England*, 2nd edn, 2 vols. (1769) · I. Abrahams, H. P. Stokes, and H. Loewe, eds., *Starrs and Jewish charters preserved in the British Museum*, 3 vols. (1930–32) · H. M. Colvin, ed., *Building accounts of King Henry III* (1971) · *Bartholomaei de Cotton … Historia Anglicana*, ed. H. R. Luard, Rolls Series, 16 (1859) · M. W. Farr, ed., *Accounts and surveys of the Wiltshire lands of Adam de Stratton*, Wiltshire Archaeological and Natural History Society, Records Branch, 14 (1959)

Archives PRO, special collections, ministers' accounts, SC 6

Wealth at death in 1290 house was said to have contained £12,666 17s. 7d.: Denholm-Young, *Seignorial administration*, 83–4

Stratton, Frederick John Marrian (1881–1960), astrophysicist, was born on 16 October 1881 in Birmingham, the eighth and youngest child of Stephen Samuel Stratton, professor of music, and his wife, Mary Jane Marrian. He was educated at King Edward's Grammar School, at Mason College, and at Gonville and Caius College, Cambridge. He was third wrangler in the mathematical tripos of 1904, Isaac Newton student in 1905, and a Smith's prizeman in 1906, the year in which he was elected a fellow of his college. Until 1914 he was a mathematics lecturer at his college and also assistant director of the Solar Physics Observatory under H. F. Newall. His early publications in astronomy covered a wide range, including celestial mechanics, but the outburst of the star Nova Geminorum (1912) focused his attention on novae, which proved to be a problem of lifelong interest.

A few years earlier Stratton had organized a signal company in the Cambridge University Officers' Training Corps to pioneer the military use of wireless telegraphy, then in its infancy. The group of young enthusiasts he collected at that time was also remarkable for a wide range of very distinguished careers in later life. On the outbreak of war in 1914 Stratton was with Newall in the Crimea, where they were preparing to observe the total solar eclipse of 21 August. Leaving immediately he hurried back to England, and joined the signal service, Royal Engineers. He served in France, reaching the rank of brevet lieutenant-colonel and being appointed to the DSO and awarded the Légion d'honneur.

The war over, Stratton returned to Caius, first as tutor, then as senior tutor, to face what was a difficult time of readjustment for the university, as for Britain as a whole. It was a job for which his personality and experience admirably suited him and which he carried out with much success. He continued to give lectures on astronomy, among them one of the first general courses on astrophysics to be given in Britain, which later appeared in book form, *Astronomical Physics* (1925). He contributed an article on novae to the *Handbuch der Astrophysik* (1928). He also found time to go to Sumatra for the 1926 total solar eclipse where, with C. R. Davidson, he made important observations of the spectrum of the sun's chromosphere.

On Newall's retirement in 1928 Stratton was appointed professor of astrophysics and director of the Solar Physics Observatory, relinquishing his tutorship at Caius. He held this post until 1947, although his tenure was interrupted, first by a serious illness in 1931, and later much more extensively by the war. He organized three more eclipse expeditions, to Siam, Canada, and Japan, but was dogged by bad luck with the weather. Only in Japan in 1936 were results of any scientific value obtainable, and even then success was only partial, the sun being covered by a cloud almost at the instant when totality commenced. However, members of his team made good measurements of wavelengths in the spectrum from near the edge of the sun's disc, settling a technical point then of some interest, and obtained photographs of the chromospheric spectrum, study of which stimulated a good deal of later work.

In 1934 Nova Herculis appeared, one of the most interesting stars of its kind, and despite the inadequate equipment of the observatory at Cambridge, Stratton and his staff during the next few months obtained a remarkable record of the changes in its spectrum. Work on this absorbed much of his energies for several years, culminating in the production with W. H. Manning of the *Atlas of Spectra of Nova Herculis 1934* (1939), using material made available from all over the world. It is still one of the most complete records of a nova outburst.

In 1939 Stratton was bitterly disappointed to be refused for active service at the age of fifty-seven. Eventually he spent the war travelling extensively, in Canada, Australia, India, and elsewhere, on duties for the Royal Corps of Signals. Thereafter he had only two more years as professor of astrophysics, and in the disorganized post-war conditions he realized that he could do little. He did, however, complete an interesting *History of the Cambridge Observatories* (1949). After his retirement he was deputy scientific adviser to the army council for two years and continued to serve on innumerable committees.

To celebrate his seventieth birthday some of his pupils undertook, with A. Beer as editor, to produce what was to have been a *Festschrift*, but which expanded, as more and more of his friends came to hear of it, into two large volumes, *Vistas in Astronomy* (1955–6). The publication quite outgrew its original purpose and several later volumes were produced.

Stratton's official posts formed only a part of his activities. In 1925–35 he was general secretary of the International Astronomical Union and did much to foster what was one of the earliest and most successful of the international scientific unions. He was also general secretary of the International Council of Scientific Unions from 1937 to 1952, and general secretary of the British Association, 1930–35. He was elected a fellow of the Royal Society in 1947. He was president of the Royal Astronomical Society (1933–5), treasurer (1923–7), and its foreign secretary (1945–55). He helped to found the Society for Visiting Scientists and was its honorary secretary, 1948–55. He was president of Gonville and Caius College in 1946–8 and at the time of his death was the senior fellow. He was president of the Society for Psychical Research in 1953–5.

For more than fifty years Stratton was chairman of the Unitarian church at Cambridge. He was ever active on behalf of ex-servicemen's societies and causes and in the early thirties he gave much help to refugee scientists from central Europe. To his many friends and acquaintances he was variously known as Professor, Colonel, Tubby, or Chubby. Short and rotund, until his last years he lived life at the double. He thought fast, talked fast (so that even close friends sometimes had difficulty in following him), decided fast, and in his younger days moved fast. He allowed himself fewer hours for sleep than most. Despite his great sociableness and much hospitality, few people knew him really well, in part because he tended to keep a life of wide interests and activities in watertight compartments.

Stratton's chief contributions to science and learning were through help and encouragement to younger men, and not merely in Britain alone. As president of commission 38 of the International Astronomical Union his activities in this direction continued until a few days before his death. A bachelor, he was accurately described as a man of tremendous principle; he also bubbled with good humour and was of outstanding generosity and modesty. Stratton died at the Evelyn Nursing Home, Cambridge, on 2 September 1960.   R. O. REDMAN, *rev.*

Sources *Vistas in Astronomy*, 1 (1955) · *Nature*, 188 (1960), 450–51 · *Quarterly Journal of the Royal Astronomical Society*, 2 (1961) · J. Chadwick, *Memoirs FRS*, 7 (1961), 281–93 · personal knowledge (1971) · *CGPLA Eng. & Wales* (1961)
Archives Royal Observatory Library, Edinburgh, corresp. relating to Nova Herculis | CAC Cam., corresp. with A. V. Hill · RAS Library, letters to John Reynolds
Likenesses W. Stoneman, photograph, 1953, NPG · O. Birley, oils, Gon. & Caius Cam. · photographs, RS · portrait, repro. in Chadwick, *Memoirs FRS*, facing p. 281
Wealth at death £12,662 10s. 9d.: probate, 17 Jan 1961, *CGPLA Eng. & Wales*

Stratton, John Proudfoot (1830–1895), surgeon and civil servant, son of David Stratton, a solicitor in Perth, was born in the parish of Caputh, near Dunkeld, Perthshire, on 2 July 1830. He was educated in his native town and afterwards at North Shields, where he became an apprentice to Dr Ingham in 1840. He was admitted a licentiate of the Royal College of Surgeons of Edinburgh in 1851, and graduated BM and MD at the University of Aberdeen in 1852 and 1855, respectively. At Aberdeen he gained either a medal or a first class in every subject of study. In May 1852 he was awarded a bursary from the East India Company.

After holding various posts in the Indian Medical Service (IMS) (Bombay) from 1852 onwards, Stratton was appointed in December 1854 residency surgeon in Baroda, where he took an active part in founding the Maharaja Gaikwar's hospital and in vaccinating the local population. In May 1857 he was, in addition to his medical post, appointed to act as assistant resident. He performed his duties with ability during the uprising, and received the thanks of the resident, Sir Richmond Campbell Shakespear. After Shakespear's departure for England, Stratton acted as resident until the arrival of Colonel Wallace. In 1859 he was selected to take political charge of Bundelkhand, a district embracing several minor states which were experiencing unrest. Stratton's services were again acknowledged by the government, while the East India

Company marked its appreciation by awarding him extra pay. Stratton married Georgina Anne Anderson on 12 April 1859. They had six children.

In 1862 Stratton was appointed commissioner and sessions judge for Bundelkhand and Baghelkhand, and he was promoted in June 1864 from political assistant to political agent; from May to July 1876 he was officiating resident. On 4 March 1881 he was appointed officiating resident in Mewar, and in July he was posted to the western states of Rajputana; on 27 January 1882 he moved to Jaipur in the eastern states. In 1885 he retired from the service, being under fifty-five years of age and following the rule, with the rank of brigade surgeon.

Stratton served Britain well in his capacity of political agent. He obtained from the local rulers free remission of transit duties and he established the Bundelkhand Rajkumar College for their sons. He also organized the building of hill roads and instituted vaccination in central India.

Stratton died on 8 August 1895 at his home, 51 Nevern Square, South Kensington, London, and was buried in Brookwood cemetery. His wife survived him.

D'A. POWER, *rev.* JEFFREY S. REZNICK

Sources *The Times* (16 Aug 1895) · private information (1898) · *CGPLA Eng. & Wales* (1895)
Wealth at death £9946 8s. 1d.: administration, 3 Sept 1895, *CGPLA Eng. & Wales*

Straub, Marianne (1909–1994), textile designer, was born on 23 September 1909 in Amriswil, Thurgau, Switzerland, the second of four daughters of Carl Straub (1871–1927), textile yarn merchant, and his wife, Cécile Kappeler (1881–1973). Despite her father's business Straub's interest in textiles developed independently, while she lived in a tubercular ward from the age of three and a half to eight. There she developed her acute memory for pattern, texture, and colour. At fifteen she decided to study textiles and, after boarding-school in Celerina, in 1928 she entered the Zürich Kunstgewerbeschule. The three-year course began with a general art training; the two remaining years were devoted to hand-weaving under the tutelage of Heinz Otto Hürlimann, who had studied at the Bauhaus in 1920–21. In her final year Straub additionally studied stage design with the sculptor Ernst Gubler; the freedom in the use of light, texture, and colour was a revelation, and greatly influenced her further work.

Committed to designing affordable cloths, and therefore seeking power-loom training, Straub found that both Swiss textile colleges barred women. Having briefly had her own studio, through family contacts she spent six months as a technician's assistant in Maurer's Weberei, an Amriswil domestic textiles mill, and came to hear of Bradford Technical College, to which she was admitted, as Mr Straub, for the academic year 1932–3. There she passed the textile industry's city and guilds' exam in weaving mechanisms, normally taken after three years of study. The only woman attending at the time, and the third in the history of the college, it was at Bradford that Straub displayed her facility for cloth construction and visualization of fabrics *in situ*. She took these skills to Gospels, Ethel

Marianne Straub (1909–1994), by Geoffrey Ireland

Mairet's hand-weaving studio-workshop in Ditchling, Sussex, where for nine months she was introduced to hand-spinning and natural dyeing, and in return developed new cloths for Gospels. Returning frequently thereafter, her position as daughter of the house introduced her to the English arts and crafts tradition and involved her in the management of Gospels' contents from Mairet's death in 1952 until 1977, when these became a founding collection of the Crafts Study Centre, Surrey Institute of Art and Design, University College, Farnham, of which Straub remained a trustee until 1992.

Uniquely placed to link craft and manufacture, Straub's belief that standards in industry could be raised by the production of hand-woven prototypes was demonstrated by her impact as the peripatetic designer (March 1934–February 1937) for the seventy-two Welsh woollen mills supported by the Rural Industries Bureau; as the head designer (March 1937–April 1950) and managing director (1947–50) of Helios, an independent subsidiary of Barlow and Jones Ltd, Lancashire; as a designer (May 1950–November 1970) for Warner & Sons Ltd, Braintree; and as a freelance designer (December 1970–*c*.1986). Her tweeds aided the survival of several Welsh mills; Helios's ranges were among the first reasonably priced avant-garde retail fabrics and were known for innovative use of yarns; Straub's designs for Warner's wholesale trade met exacting functional standards. Yet despite demanding briefs and changing tastes, throughout these years she sustained the creation of innovative yet subtle cloths characterized by the exploitation of both the essence and the restrictions of the materials, machines, and markets for which she designed.

Having initially also designed dress fabrics, Straub's *œuvre* was furnishing fabrics, for which she hand-wove at least 4000 trials. She did much to establish cloths of richly blended hues as the statement of choice by architects and interior designers. Straub's combinations of yarn types and her manipulation of warp spacing and weave structures fed the mid-century appetite for understated tone-

and-texture fabrics; upholstery cloths contributed to the success of furniture makers such as Ercolani, Heals, Parker Knoll, Ernest Race Ltd, and Gordon Russell Ltd, while co-ordinated woven fabrics, casement cloths, and blankets underpinned the reputation of Tamesa, London, from 1964 to 1985. Too numerous to recount are the ships, aeroplanes, trains, and hospitals, the public, collegiate, and government buildings that contained her cloths; their ubiquity is epitomized by a woollen moquette designed in 1964 and still in use in some London tubes and buses in 2000.

Straub's exacting standards, her readiness to experiment, and her enduring fascination with textiles made her sought after, particularly as an educational adviser, examiner, and lecturer; between 1947 and 1992 she taught part-time at the Central School (1956–64), at Hornsey (1964–8), and at the Royal College of Art (1968–74), and she visited numerous other colleges. Her influence was widespread and brought her several honours, including election as a royal designer for industry (1972), receipt of the first Textile Institute design medal (1972), the Crafts Council's best crafts book of the year award (1977) for *Hand Weaving and Cloth Design*, and an OBE (1985). By that time she was known for her exceptional empathy with students, borne out by her impressive memory for their interests and later careers. Many also admired the ready humour and energy that suggested a seemingly effortless disregard for her tuberculosis-withered right leg, a lifelong disability that gave her small frame an ungainly gait but never stopped her either travelling widely (including, for the World Bank in 1979, an investigative trip to Mali that resulted in the formation of a co-operative in Segou to support local weavers) or getting under a loom to put it right.

In 1992 Straub retired to Berlingen, Switzerland, where she died, unmarried, of heart failure on 8 November 1994; she was buried at Romanshorn a week later. In 1997 she was credited with 'over fifty years of nourishing, even battling for, the integrity of cloth and the creativity of those who wish to make it well' (Schoeser, 'Marianne Straub', 94).   MARY SCHOESER

Sources M. Schoeser, *Marianne Straub* (1984) · M. Schoeser, 'Marianne Straub', *Pioneers of modern craft*, ed. M. Coatts (1997), 83–94 · private information (2004) [E. Hoffmann-Straub]
Archives Warner Fabrics, Milton Keynes, archives, weaving notes, hand-woven prototypes, and power-woven cloths · Whitworth Art Gallery, Manchester, MSS, samples (Helios fabrics)
Likenesses G. Ireland, photograph, NPG [*see illus.*] · photograph, repro. in *The Times* (24 Nov 1984)

Straubenzee, Sir Charles Thomas Van (1812–1892), army officer, second son of Major Thomas Van Straubenzee (1782–1843), Royal Artillery, of Spennithorne Hall, Yorkshire, and his wife, Maria (d. January 1871), youngest daughter of Major Henry Bowen of the 2nd Royal Veteran battalion, was born in Malta on 17 February 1812. His great-grandfather, Philip William Casimir Van Straubenzee (d. 1765), captain in the Dutch guards, came to England about 1745, was naturalized by act of parliament (28 March 1759), and married Jane, only daughter of Cholmely

Turner of Kirkleatham, Yorkshire, and Jane, granddaughter and sole heir of Sir Henry Marwood, baronet, of Buskby Hall, Yorkshire. He had a younger brother, General A. Van Straubenzee, who was governor of Zutphen in 1798. His third son, Charles Spencer, married a granddaughter of Sir George Vane of Raby, and had seven sons in the British army and navy; of these, the eldest, Henry, succeeded a great-uncle as head of the family and in the property of Spennithorne, North Riding of Yorkshire; and the seventh was the father of Charles Thomas Van Straubenzee.

Van Straubenzee was commissioned ensign in the Ceylon Rifles on 28 August 1828, and arrived in Ceylon in June 1829. He was promoted lieutenant in the 39th foot on 22 February 1833. He joined it at Bangalore in India (Mysore), and on 17 March 1834 marched with it in the expedition under Brigadier-General Patrick Lindesay against Coorg. Mercara, the capital, was found undefended, and occupied on 6 April, the raja surrendering on 10 April, when Van Straubenzee returned with the 39th to Bangalore.

Van Straubenzee was promoted to a company in the 39th foot on 10 March 1837, and in November he went to England on furlough. He married, on 18 November 1841, Charlotte Louisa (d. 28 Nov 1900), youngest daughter of General John Luther Richardson HEICS, of the family of Lord Cramond; they had no children, and she survived her husband. In June 1842 he joined the 39th at Agra. In October 1842 he joined the army of reserve assembled at Ferozepore on the return of the troops from Afghanistan. On 27 August 1843 he was promoted regimental major, and in the autumn the 39th joined the army of exercise assembled at Agra because of the situation at Gwalior. Early in December he marched with it under Sir Hugh Gough against Sindhia. He distinguished himself at the battle of Maharajpur on 29 December, when the 39th, supported by the 56th native infantry, drove the enemy from their guns into the village, the scene of a bloody conflict; later the 39th with a charge captured the entrenched main position at Chouda, when the commanding officer of the regiment was desperately wounded, and Van Straubenzee, succeeding to the temporary command, brought it out of action after capturing two enemy standards. Van Straubenzee was mentioned in dispatches, and promoted brevet lieutenant-colonel on 30 April 1844.

On 30 August 1844 Van Straubenzee exchanged into the 13th Prince Albert's light infantry, and, returning to England with it in July 1845, was quartered at Walmer. He took part in the ceremony of presentation of new colours by Prince Albert on 13 August 1846 at Portsmouth. On 28 August he exchanged into the 3rd Buffs and accompanied them to Ireland in October. In April 1851 he embarked with the battalion for Malta, and on 11 November was promoted regimental lieutenant-colonel to command it. On 20 June 1854 he was promoted brevet colonel.

On 12 November Van Straubenzee took the 3rd to Piraeus in connection with the war with Russia. He was made a colonel on the staff on 15 November to command the British contingent in Greece. He remained at Piraeus until 23 March 1855, when the 3rd were relieved by the 91st, and he returned with them to Malta. The British minister at Athens wrote to Lord Clarendon on 4 April 1855, praising the conduct of the Buffs at Piraeus.

On 14 April Van Straubenzee sailed with his battalion for the Crimea, and joined the division of Sir Colin Campbell. On 11 May he was made brigadier-general. His brigade, consisting of the Buffs, the 31st, and the 72nd, was posted to the right attack, and he commanded it in the fight at the Quarries on 7 June. On 30 July he was appointed to command the 1st brigade of the light division, and took part in both assaults on the Redan, was wounded in that of 8 September, and was mentioned in dispatches. He returned home in July 1856. He was made a CB, military division, and an officer of the Légion d'honneur; he also received the Mejidiye (third class), and he was promoted temporary major-general on 24 July 1856. On 29 July he was appointed to command the infantry brigade at Dublin.

On 20 September 1857 Van Straubenzee was gazetted to the command of a brigade in the expedition to China under Lieutenant-General Thomas Ashburnham, having already sailed in June for Hong Kong. Many of the troops intended for China were diverted to India because of the Indian mutiny, and in November Ashburnham and his staff also left Hong Kong for India, leaving Van Straubenzee in command of the British land forces in China. In December the available troops from the garrison of Hong Kong were conveyed by the fleet to the Canton River, and the island of Hainan was occupied. Van Straubenzee arrived on 22 December, and the attack on Canton by the allied British and French naval and military forces began with a bombardment on 28 December; on 5 January 1858 the city was taken. On 19 June Van Straubenzee was made a KCB (military division). He was promoted major-general on the establishment on 11 August 1859. On 15 April 1860 he was compelled by ill health to resign his command, and returned to England.

On 7 April 1862 Van Straubenzee took up the command of a division of the Bombay army at Ahmadabad. He was appointed colonel of the 47th foot on 31 May 1865. In this year he was temporarily in command of the Bombay army, pending the arrival of Sir Robert Cornelis Napier. He returned to England on 16 February 1866, was transferred to the colonelcy of the 39th foot on 8 December 1867, and was promoted to be lieutenant-general on 27 March 1868.

On 3 June 1872 Van Straubenzee was appointed governor and commander-in-chief at Malta, and was promoted general on 29 April 1875. He was governor of Malta for six years, and was made a GCB (military division) on 29 May 1875. He returned to England in June 1878, retired from the army on 1 July 1881, and settled at Bath. He died at his home, 100 Sydney Place, Bath, on 10 August 1892, and was buried in the Bathwick cemetery, Bath.

R. H. VETCH, rev. ROGER T. STEARN

Sources War office records, PRO · dispatches, *LondG* · R. Cannon, ed., *Historical record of the thirty-ninth, or the Dorsetshire regiment of foot* (1853) · R. Cannon, ed., *Historical record of the third regiment of foot, or the buffs* (1839) · W. H. Russell, *The British expedition to the Crimea* (1858) · S. Lane-Poole, *Life of Sir Harry Parkes* (1894) · Burke, *Gen. GB* (1914) · private information (1899) · Boase, *Mod. Eng. biog.* · P. Moon, *The British conquest and dominion of India* (1989) · A. D. Lambert, *The Crimean War: British grand strategy, 1853–56* (1990) · C. Hibbert, *The dragon wakes: China and the West, 1793–1911* (1970) · Kelly, *Handbk* (1891) · S. Wolpert, *A new history of India* (1993) · Burke, *Peerage* (1889)

Archives NAM, papers | Bodl. Oxf., corresp. with Lord Kimberley

Likenesses engraving, repro. in *ILN*, 32 (1858), 508

Wealth at death £9780 0s. 1d.: probate, 19 Sept 1892, *CGPLA Eng. & Wales*

Strauss, George Russell, Baron Strauss (1901–1993), politician, was born in London on 18 July 1901, the younger son of Arthur Strauss (1847–1920), tin merchant and Conservative MP for the Camborne division of Cornwall, and later for North Paddington, and his wife, Minna, née Cohen. He attended Rugby School, suffering the anti-semitism then meted out to Jewish boys. Following his father's death in 1920 he decided to join the family firm rather than go to university. When he married Patricia Frances Elizabeth O'Flynn (1907/8–1987), daughter of Patrick Frank O'Flynn, a merchant, on 21 March 1932 he was able to take her to his elegant inherited home on 'millionaire's row', 1 Kensington Palace Gardens. By then he was already an experienced Labour politician, having represented impoverished North Lambeth from 1925 to 1931 on the old London county council—being elected at twenty-four—and Lambeth North from 1929 to 1931 in parliament. He linked the two together by serving Herbert Morrison as his parliamentary private secretary from 1929 to 1931. He returned to the London county council as councillor for South-East Southwark, 1932–46, and to parliament as the MP for Lambeth North, 1934–50, and for Lambeth, Vauxhall, 1950–79. He had been a protégé of Herbert Morrison. But during the 1930s, like many Jewish intellectuals who felt the threat of Nazism, he moved to the left, joining Sir Stafford Cripps and Aneurin Bevan in their efforts to form an anti-fascist alliance stretching from the Communists to the Liberals. In 1937 they launched the left-wing weekly *Tribune*, for which he wrote and provided funds. They were expelled from the Labour Party in 1939, but were shortly readmitted.

When Labour swept into power in 1945 Strauss was named parliamentary secretary for transport. In 1947 he was promoted minister of supply and made a privy councillor, outside the cabinet. He skilfully steered through the nationalization of iron and steel, one of the most controversial measures of the Attlee government. After Labour left office in 1951 he and John Strachey played a key role in bridging the gap between the pro-Americans, led by Hugh Gaitskell, and the leftish 'Bevanites', led by Aneurin Bevan, who resisted American pressure to speed Britain's rearmament. In 1957 he protested to paymaster-general Reginald Maudling that the London Electricity Board was disposing of scrap cable at below its value. When Maudling contacted the board they threatened to sue Strauss for libel. He retorted, unsuccessfully, that a letter from an MP to a minister should be covered by parliamentary privilege; nevertheless, the threatened libel action was not proceeded with. He also argued with Richard Crossman over whether the Labour cabinet had approved the decision to manufacture an A-bomb. In fact, Attlee had never submitted the question to full cabinet and had released his decision through an obscure written answer. Nevertheless, Strauss correctly argued that the right question had never been asked or answered in parliament. His last parliamentary achievement was to secure in 1968 the abolition of theatre censorship. He was father of the house from 1974 to 1979.

In 1979 Strauss became a life peer, Baron Strauss of Vauxhall, having served forty-six years as MP for Lambeth North and Vauxhall and twenty years on the London county council. In 1987 his wife, Patricia, with whom he had had two sons and a daughter, died. On 11 August the same year, at eighty-six, he married Benita Eleonora Mary Armstrong (b. 1906/7), daughter of the merchant banker Joseph Jaeger, a successful sculptor and Strauss's longtime companion, and mother of a son and a daughter. He died of hepatitis and cancer at his home, 1 Palace Green, Kensington, London, on 5 June 1993. He was survived by his second wife.   ANDREW ROTH

Sources *Parliamentary Profile*, files, Open University · *WWW*, 1991–5 · *The Times* (7 June 1993) · *The Independent* (9 June 1993) · *The Independent* (6 July 1993) · m. certs. · d. cert.
Archives CAC Cam., unpublished autobiography |SOUND BL NSA, performance recording
Likenesses photograph, repro. in *The Times* · photograph, repro. in *The Independent* (9 June 1993)
Wealth at death £2,309,838: probate, 11 Aug 1993, *CGPLA Eng. & Wales*

Strauss, Gustave Louis Maurice (c.1807–1887), writer, was born at Trois Rivières in Lower Canada. Although a British subject, he asserted that he had 'a strange mixture of Italian, French, German, and Sarmatian blood' in his veins. In 1812 his father moved to Europe, and about 1816 settled at Linden, near Hanover. Gustave was educated at the Klosterschule in Magdeburg, at the University of Berlin (where he took the degree of doctor of philosophy), and at the Montpellier school of medicine.

In 1832 Strauss visited Great Britain in the company of Legros, a wealthy Marseillais, who wished to inspect the industrial establishments of the country. He returned to Germany in 1833 to share in the liberal demonstrations against the government. Afterwards he succeeded in escaping to France, although the Prussian government sequestrated his property, which was not returned to him until 1840.

In 1833 Strauss went to Algiers as assistant surgeon to the French army. At first he was attached to the Foreign Legion, but in 1834 his connection with it was severed. After some years' service his health broke down, and he returned to France, only to be banished in 1839 for supposed complicity in a revolutionary plot. He then went to London, where he turned his hand to a variety of callings, including those of chemist, politician, cook, journalist, tutor, playwright, surgeon, author, and linguist. At this time he produced a *German Reader* (1852), a *German Grammar* (1852), and a *French Grammar* (1853). He also published

some works on Islam, including *Moslem and Frank* (1854) and *Mahometism: an Historical Sketch* (2nd edn, 1857). He was also the first editor of *The Grocer* (1862), a weekly trade circular. Strauss was well known in London as the Old Bohemian, and was one of the founders of the Savage Club in 1857.

In 1865 Strauss published *The Old Ledger: a Novel*, which was described by *The Athenaeum* as 'vulgar, profane, and indelicate'. In consequence he brought an action against that journal, which was settled by mutual consent. *The Athenaeum*, however, repeated the original criticism on 7 April 1866, and Strauss brought a second action. In this his plea for free literary expression was met by a demand for equal latitude in criticism; the jury returned a verdict in favour of *The Athenaeum*.

In later life Strauss's circumstances became straitened, and through Gladstone's intervention he received a bounty from the civil list. In 1879 he was admitted into the Charterhouse as a poor brother, but after a short residence he applied for an outdoor pension, which was granted by the governors. His memoir, *Reminiscences of an Old Bohemian* (1882), 'liberally mingled' fact and fiction (*Life and Adventures of George Augustus Sala*, 124); it was followed by the perhaps more aptly titled *Stories of an Old Bohemian* (1883). Strauss also contributed to a wide range of periodicals, including *The Lancet* and the *Morning Advertiser*. Strauss died unmarried, on 2 September 1887, at Teddington.

E. I. CARLYLE, rev. MEGAN A. STEPHAN

Sources *The Athenaeum* (17 Sept 1887), 374 · *The Times* (14 Sept 1887), 3 · *The life and adventures of George Augustus Sala*, 2 vols. (1895); repr. in 1 vol. (1896), 123–4, 223, 225–32 · Allibone, *Dict.* · BL cat., [CD-ROM] · Boase, *Mod. Eng. biog.*
Likenesses R. T., wood-engraving (after photograph by Fradelle and Young), NPG; repro. in *ILN* (17 Sept 1887)

Strauss, Henry George, Baron Conesford (1892–1974), lawyer and politician, was born at 19 Pembridge Gardens, Kensington, London, on 24 June 1892, the only son of Alphonse Henry Strauss, general merchant, and his wife, Hedwig Aschrott. He won scholarships both to Rugby School and to Christ Church, Oxford. He was junior treasurer of the Oxford Union in 1914, and he obtained first classes in both classical honour moderations (1913) and *literae humaniores* (1915). He enlisted in 1914, but was discharged on medical grounds, and served in the Ministry of Munitions, the Board of Trade, and the Ministry of Food until he was called to the bar by the Inner Temple in 1919.

Although he never enjoyed a substantial practice at the bar, Strauss had the good fortune to be in chambers headed by Walter Monckton, which also contained several of the most talented young members of the bar, several of them destined for high judicial preferment. This experience gave him a deep reverence for the law and a passionate devotion to the rights of the citizen under the law. He also became friends with and was much influenced by A. P. Herbert. One of the results of this was a lifelong enthusiasm for the purity of the English language, and a dislike of those who misused it.

Strauss entered the House of Commons at the general election of 1935 as Conservative member for Norwich. He had little sympathy with the appeasement policy then prevailing, but as a very junior member was in no position to influence it. He performed efficiently, and likeably, the duties of parliamentary private secretary to the attorney-general, Sir Thomas Inskip. But in 1942 Winston Churchill appointed him joint parliamentary secretary at the Ministry of Works and Buildings, under Sir Wyndham Portal. In 1943 he was transferred to the new Ministry of Town and Country Planning, and played a large part in seeing through the Commons the controversial, and in the event unfortunate, Town and Country Planning Act.

In 1945 Strauss performed the most characteristically courageous and honourable action of his life. Although his departmental duties involved no concern with foreign affairs, he felt so strongly about the Yalta agreement, and what he regarded as its betrayal of the Poles, that he resigned his office and left the government. He lost his seat at Norwich in the Labour landslide election of 1945, but returned to the House of Commons in March 1946 as the result of a by-election in the Combined English Universities seat. He also took silk in 1946 and in the same year published *Trade Unions and the Law*. When the Attlee government abolished the university seats Strauss returned to Norwich and was re-elected as member for Norwich South at the 1950 election. He held this seat until he was created a peer in 1955.

In October 1951, on the return of the Conservatives to power, Churchill, who characteristically did not hold Strauss's Yalta resignation against him, appointed him parliamentary secretary to the Board of Trade. He was seventeen years older than Peter Thorneycroft, the president of the Board of Trade, and had no experience of business life or of an economic department. He did not fit in well in the department, although he did his full share of work for it in the House of Commons and at the innumerable functions of a social character which trade associations organize and which are the bane of ministers in this type of ministry. Indeed Strauss, only half humorously, used to accuse Thorneycroft of having had made a special stamp embossed 'Refer to Parliamentary Secretary' which he used to apply remorselessly to invitations to trade lunches. And the trade associations got good value, for Strauss was a witty and polished speaker. Sometimes, however, his wit was not wholly understood or appreciated by those attending functions organized by the less sophisticated trades. In the House of Commons, though handicapped by a somewhat high-pitched voice, he could argue the departmental case with precision and elegance. He retained even in the utilitarian milieu of the Board of Trade his passion for the right use of the English language. His colleagues appreciated this, and sometimes exploited it. On one occasion a hard-pressed financial secretary to the Treasury beside whom Strauss was sitting on the Treasury bench used a clumsy cliché, and by way of recovery added, 'if I may quote my honourable and learned friend the parliamentary secretary to the Board of Trade'. A high-pitched 'Good God' echoed through the chamber, and an amused House of Commons was distracted from an awkward point.

In 1955 Strauss was one of a number of able men whose qualities did not appeal to the incoming prime minister, Sir Anthony Eden. He went to the House of Lords as Baron Conesford. The atmosphere of the upper house, courteous, civilized, tolerant of eccentricity, suited him from the start. He attained a standing and popularity there greater than he had had in the Commons. In April 1964 he was elected chairman of the Association of Independent Unionist Peers, the body which includes all back-bench Conservative peers, and is broadly the equivalent of the 1922 committee in the House of Commons. He retained this office until July 1970, and made a considerable mark on the evolving character of the House of Lords.

Strauss married on 29 January 1927 Anne Sadelbia Mary, the daughter of John Bowyer Nichols FSA, of Lawford Hall, Manningtree. She was artistically talented, and her calm personality provided an ideal foil for Harry's excitable liveliness. Their life in their lovely house at 25 Cheyne Walk was peaceful and happy. They had, however, no children. They adopted, when very young, a boy and a girl whom they brought up as their own, the boy following Strauss to Rugby School.

Conesford died at home in London on 28 August 1974, and the barony became extinct; he was survived by his wife. Although his health had been clearly failing for some time, the fact that he was eighty-two came as a surprise to many friends. For, as one of them wrote at the time, 'he did not grow old gracefully; he simply didn't grow old at all'. He retained to the end his gift for friendship, his wit, and his enjoyment of social life among congenial friends. He was a much valued member of many dining clubs, able to enliven any gathering. This he combined with integrity and lack of malice. He was president of the Architecture Club and in 1965 became honorary FRIBA. In 1969 he became honorary bencher.

BOYD-CARPENTER, *rev.*

Sources *The Times* (30 Aug 1974) · *The Times* (6 Sept 1974) · personal knowledge (1986) · private information (1986) · b. cert. · *CGPLA Eng. & Wales* (1975)

Archives priv. coll., MSS | Welwyn Garden City Central Library, corresp. with Frederic Osborn

Wealth at death £44,986: probate, 11 March 1975, *CGPLA Eng. & Wales*

Streat, Sir (Edward) Raymond (1897–1979), cotton trade administrator, was born on 7 February 1897 at 2 Brunswick Terrace, Prestwich, Lancashire, the fifth of the six children of Edward Streat (1856–1918), a commercial traveller, and his first wife, Helen (Nellie) Wallis (1859–1908). His father, who was born in Chaddleworth, near Newbury, Berkshire, and went to Manchester at an early age to find work, was a Wesleyan Methodist of sincere convictions, an ardent freemason, and an active member of the local Liberal Party; his mother was a cultured woman. Streat attended Manchester grammar school; although a good student, he left in 1913 to become an office boy. Several months later, not yet eighteen years old, he enlisted in the 10th Manchester regiment, against his father's wishes. He had been a 'delicate' child but he survived the First World War, having seen active service in France, where he was

Sir (Edward) Raymond Streat (1897–1979), by Elliott & Fry, 1947

slightly wounded. Looking back, he commented that 'really it was the experiences as an infantry officer which broadened my social armoury' (*Lancashire and Whitehall*, 1.xiii).

Manchester chamber of commerce After being demobilized as a captain in early 1919, Streat became secretary to the director of a Manchester insurance firm. Six months later, out of 600 applicants, he was made assistant secretary to the Manchester chamber of commerce; following the death of the secretary, the board of directors, in January 1920, by a margin of one vote, appointed Streat secretary. It was a bold appointment: he was only twenty-two years old, and he became the highest-ranking permanent paid official of the richest, the largest, and probably the most influential chamber of commerce in the country. Without any member of his family having any connection with the cotton industry, he found himself secretary of an organization dominated by merchants in the cotton trade. He remained at the chamber for twenty years until in 1940 he was appointed chairman of the Cotton Board, a position he held until 1957. He married on 16 March 1921 Doris Davies (1896–1976), a friend from his school days, the daughter of Amos Davies, a manufacturer; they had three sons—Basil, Tony (who died from wounds during the Second World War), and Christopher—and established their home at Wilmslow, Cheshire.

For thirty-eight years Streat was at the centre of the cotton industry's attempts to cope with the drastic decline of its trade. No one else played such a leading part in Lancashire's struggle to find a workable solution over so long a period. Neither a businessman nor a civil servant, Streat belonged to a relatively new occupational group, the professional secretary. His duty as secretary of the Manchester chamber of commerce was to record the proceedings of meetings, but, with his energy, vision, charm, and tact, he exercised initiative in administration and played an active role in the formation of the chamber's policy and in negotiations. He built up the staff from half a dozen in 1920 to fifty in 1939; he trained assistant secretaries who went on to become secretaries of other chambers of commerce; he wrote the annual report and the presidents' speeches; he edited the chamber's magazine, the *Monthly Record*; he contributed articles to newspapers; and he served as a link between the chamber and other Lancashire organizations. He was also a link between the chamber and the international chamber of commerce, and served as a member of its delegation to the World Economic Conference held at Geneva in 1927 under the auspices of the League of Nations. He built up personal contacts with civil servants, MPs, and key figures, gaining a reputation for providing an authoritative briefing paper quickly, and he came to play an intermediary role, taking proposals and counter-proposals from one group to another, and earned an accolade as 'a tennis ball with a decided spin of its own' (*Lancashire and Whitehall*, 1.531). He contributed innovative ideas such as that for the Lancashire Industrial Development Council, which, from its inaugural meeting in 1931, worked to bring new industries into Lancashire.

During the interwar years the troubles of the cotton trade overshadowed the chamber's other activities. Because many of the industry's difficulties revolved around the loss of export markets and questions of tariffs, quotas, and trade agreements, the chamber became the principal voice of the cotton trade, wielding considerable influence. India presented the most complex problems. In the early 1930s Streat was among those who believed it was useless for Lancashire to seek safeguards in the Government of India Bill. In 1933 he was a member of the British textile mission to India led by Sir William Clare Lees, and he formulated the compromise which led to an agreement. He was a central witness in the Privileges Affair of 1934. In 1935 he was a member of the delegation which presented Lancashire's case before the Indian tariff board and obtained a reduction of duties on most British cotton goods. He was also part of the delegation representing Lancashire's interest in negotiations in India that eventually resulted in the Anglo-Indian trade agreement of 1939. By the 1930s, however, Japanese competition was taking more of Lancashire's trade than was being blocked by Indian tariffs. Streat played a central role in long negotiations which in 1934 led the British government to impose a system of quotas, restricting imports of Japanese goods throughout colonial markets, and doing more than anything else to slow down the contraction of Lancashire's export trade. In addition he was particularly active in urging the reluctant Board of Trade to use the protective tariff brought in by the Import Duties Act, 1932, as a bargaining counter in renegotiating trade agreements to

Lancashire's advantage as the world moved from multilateral to bilateral trade relations.

The reduced demand for exports after 1920 left Lancashire with the problem of how, in a horizontally divided industry, to adjust industrial capacity and reduce equipment and labour to match the new conditions. In 1925 the sectional organizations joined to form the Joint Committee of Cotton Trade Organizations, which included representative employers, merchants, and trade unionists; Streat served as its honorary secretary.

Cotton Board chairman Streat's appointment as chairman of the Cotton Board in June 1940 evolved out of his broad experience with the problems of the export trade in cotton goods and his work at the Export Council, which he served as secretary on loan from the chamber from February 1940. The Cotton Board was not a government department but a statutory body, financed by a levy on the industry. Based in Manchester, it consisted of eleven members drawn from employers and trade unionists in the different sections of the industry, appointed by the president of the Board of Trade with an independent chairman. As chairman, and with his authority strengthened by a knighthood in 1942, Streat pushed ahead plans to promote exports until the advent of lend-lease subordinated exports to the needs of the war economy. The board rationed the remaining export trade, organized the concentration of the finishing section, planned and operated a scheme for the care and maintenance of the closed mills and their reopening at the end of the war, and established the 'utility scheme' supplying standard cotton cloths to meet civilian needs. Also, implementing an idea of Streat's, it set up the Colour, Design and Style Centre, which worked to bring manufacturers and designers together to raise the standard of design.

From 1942 Streat was particularly active in discussions of post-war plans for industry, and he attended the Nuffield College weekend conferences on post-war reconstruction. A Wesleyan turned Anglican, he was among the Manchester business and university leaders who publicly supported the archbishop of Canterbury's 'religion and life campaign', which affirmed Christian principles as the basis for economic and political action after the war. Furthermore in 1943 he wrote the *Report* of the Cotton Board's Post-war Reconstruction Committee. The Industrial Organization and Development Act, 1947, empowered the Board of Trade to set up 'industrial development councils' modelled on the Cotton Board for various industries. Under the act, a new Cotton Board took over the assets and activities of the existing board, and Streat continued as chairman.

At the end of the war the cotton industry had lost 40 per cent of its operatives and the reopening mills faced a sellers' market without sufficient labour. The board promoted measures to reorganize the industry and increase productivity, as well as to attract workers and increase exports. Aware of the threat of Japanese competition, Streat worked for a voluntary agreement among textile-exporting countries to share the shrinking world trade in cotton goods. He travelled to the USA twice in 1949 to secure the collaboration of American manufacturers and went to Japan and India in 1950 for talks with government representatives and industrialists. After 1952 large-scale duty-free imports from India, Hong Kong, and eventually Pakistan shook the confidence of the Lancashire industry. Despite protests and deputations, including one to Churchill in 1955, Streat and the Cotton Board were unable to alter government policy, and in 1957, lacking a sympathetic policy from the government, and with continuing sectional conflict, Streat decided to step down as chairman at the age of sixty.

University administrator Although the lucrative directorships Streat hoped for did not materialize he was able to bring his skills and experience to bear during a period of unprecedented growth and change in universities. In 1957 he succeeded Ernest Simon as chairman of the council of Manchester University. He had been associated with the university since his election to the court of governors in 1938. He was elected to the council in 1943 and became treasurer in 1951; he helped work out the financial partnership between the government and university that supported the Jodrell Bank telescope (where a tree was planted in his memory after his death). While his time in the cotton industry had been characterized by an atmosphere of decline, Streat's eight-year tenure as chairman of Manchester University council were years of expansion, ample finance, and ready implementation of new ideas. He guided the university through the Robbins report of 1962, student revolts, and a new charter. His contributions were recognized with an honorary LLD in 1963. Outside Manchester he was visiting fellow of Nuffield College, Oxford, from 1944 and an honorary fellow from 1959.

While chairman of the Cotton Board, Streat had served a number of related organizations, particularly those concerned with the application of science to industry and technical education. He was a member of the advisory council of the Department of Scientific and Industrial Research (1942–7); president of the Association of Technical Institutions (1944–5); a member of the General Advisory Council of the BBC (1947–52); and president of the Textile Institute (1948–51). Later he served on the North Western Electricity Consultative Council (1960–68). Weekend rounds of golf and family summer holidays provided most of his recreation. He was a lively companion and a renowned organizer of games at family parties. People who knew him before the war in particular spoke of his extrovert high spirits and the irresistible attraction of his personality. After 1940 the heavy burden of the jobs he carried out and the anxiety and doubt, both national and personal, dampened his spirits, but he kept his resilience and his broad and generous way of thought. He died at the Churchill Hospital in Oxford on 13 September 1979 and was cremated at Oxford crematorium on 20 September.   MARGUERITE W. DUPREE

Sources *Lancashire and Whitehall: the diary of Sir Raymond Streat*, ed. M. Dupree, 2 vols. (1987) • M. W. Dupree, 'Streat, Sir Edward Raymond', *DBB* • M. W. Dupree, 'Foreign competition and the interwar period', *The Lancashire cotton industry: a history since 1700*, ed. M. B. Rose (1996) • M. W. Dupree, 'The cotton industry: a middle way between nationalisation and self-government?', *The 1945 labour government and the private sector*, ed. J. Tomlinson, H. Mercer, and N. Rollings (1992), 137–61 • M. W. Dupree, 'Fighting against fate: the cotton industry and the government during the 1930s', *Textile History*, 21 (1990), 101–17 • M. W. Dupree, 'Struggling with destiny: the cotton industry, overseas trade policy and the cotton board, 1940–1959', *Business History*, 32/4 (1990), 106–28 • R. Robson, *The cotton industry in Britain* (1957) • M. W. Kirby, 'The Lancashire cotton industry in the inter-war years: a study of organisational change', *Business History*, 16 (1974), 145–59 • J. Singleton, 'The decline of the British cotton industry since 1940', *The Lancashire cotton industry: a history since 1700*, ed. M. B. Rose (1996), 296–324 • E. L. Hargreaves and M. M. Gowing, *Civil industry and trade* (1952) • J. Bamberg, 'The rationalization of the British cotton industry in the interwar years', *Textile History*, 19 (1988), 83–102 • B. Chatterji, *Trade, tariffs, and empire: Lancashire and British policy in India, 1919–1939* (1992) • C. A. Wurm, *Business, politics and international relations: steel, cotton and international cartels in British politics, 1924–1939*, trans. P. Salmon (1993) • A. J. Robertson, 'Lancashire and the rise of Japan, 1910–1937', *International competition and strategic response in the textile industries since 1870*, ed. M. B. Rose (1991), 87–105 • S. E. Finer, *Anonymous empire: a study of the lobby in Great Britain*, 2nd edn (1966) • J. Singleton, *Lancashire on the scrapheap: the cotton industry, 1945–70* (1991) • Board of Trade, *Working party report: cotton* (1946) • G. W. Furness, 'The cotton and rayon textile industry', *The structure of British industry: a symposium*, ed. D. Burn, 2 (1958), 184–221 • C. Bridge, 'Churchill, Hoare, Derby and the committee of privileges, April to June 1934', *HJ*, 22 (1979), 215–27 • S. C. Ghosh, 'Pressure and privilege: the Manchester chamber of commerce and the Indian problem, 1930–34', *Parliamentary Affairs*, 18 (1965), 201–15 • M. Gilbert, *Winston S. Churchill*, 5: *1922–1939* (1976) • P. D. Henderson, 'Development councils: an industrial experiment', *The British economy, 1945–1950*, ed. G. D. N. Worswick and P. H. Ady (1952) • B. Lovell, *The story of Jodrell Bank* (1968) • *Monthly Record* [Manchester chamber of commerce] (1925–40) • A. Redford and others, *Manchester merchants and foreign trade*, ed. A. Redford, 2: *1850–1939* (1956) • C. Miles, *Lancashire textiles: a case study of industrial change* (1968) • L. H. C. Tippett, *A portrait of the Lancashire textile industry* (1969) • *Daily Telegraph* (17 Sept 1979) • *Manchester Guardian* (15 Sept 1979) [northern edn only] • *The Times* (17 Dec 1979) • G. Kenyon, 'Address at the memorial service for Sir Raymond Streat', 15 Oct 1979 • J. Bamberg, 'The government, the banks and the Lancashire cotton industry, 1918–1934', PhD diss., U. Cam., 1984 • H. J. Goodwin, 'The politics of the Manchester chamber of commerce, 1921–1951', PhD diss., University of Manchester, 1982 • Hugh Dalton, diary, BLPES, Dalton MSS • Man. CL, Manchester chamber of commerce MSS, M8/3/8, fol. 219; M8/2/16, fol. 51 • PRO, Cotton Board minutes, 1939–52, BT64/1006, BT175/1–6 • JRL, Streat MSS

Archives JRL • NRA, corresp., diaries, and papers | BLPES, diary of Hugh Dalton • JRL, letters to *Manchester Guardian* | SOUND JRL, Streat MSS, taped interviews about aspects of his life between Sir Raymond Streat and the editor of his diary, Dr Marguerite Dupree, 1977–9

Likenesses cartoon, 1931, repro. in *Manchester chamber of commerce, official handbook 1931–2* • Elliott & Fry, photograph, 1947, NPG [*see illus.*] • photographs, JRL, Streat MSS • photographs, priv. coll.

Wealth at death £73,109: probate, 17 Jan 1980, *CGPLA Eng. & Wales*

Streat, William (1599/1600–1666x9), Church of England clergyman, was the son of John Streete, merchant, of Dartmouth, Devon. Having entered Exeter College, Oxford, early in 1617, he matriculated on 8 May 1621 aged twenty-one, graduated BA on 31 January 1622, and proceeded MA on 10 June 1624. He was ordained and became rector first, in 1630, of St Edmund on the Bridge, Exeter, and then, in 1632, of South Pool, Devon.

According to Anthony Wood, after 1641 Streat sided with the presbyterians, and 'preached very bitterly' against Charles I and the royalists, 'blasting them with the name of Bloody papists'. Later he 'became a desperate enemy to, and continually preached against' the exiled Charles II, spreading from his pulpit satirical propaganda from parliamentarian newspapers and pamphlets (Wood, *Ath. Oxon.*, 3.728). Yet his only publication, *The dividing of the hooff, or, Seeming-contradictions throughout sacred scriptures, distinguish'd, resolv'd and apply'd* (1654), while it acknowledges the power of 'his Highness' (Cromwell), placed by God as a steward, and looks forward to the thousand-year rule of the saints, regrets the storms and madness among God's people, 'our spirituall divisions in points of religion'. A substantial 496-page work, it attempts to reconcile 295 ostensibly contradictory texts from the Old and New testaments. Appealing to the conciliatory tradition of John Jewel and William Perkins, it seeks to 'cast out that evill spirit of contradiction among professors of the Gospel' and 'to bring a poor creature into Gods chamber of presence' (Streat, dedications).

Streat remained at South Pool, and conformed in 1662. At an unknown date he had married Amy, and in his will, drawn up on 14 June 1666, he named four of their sons, Robert, Joseph, William, and John, and a daughter Sarah, and mentioned five other children, dividing among them property in Dartmouth and a lease in South Allington. He died some time before 7 December 1669, when probate was granted to his executors William and John Streete.

VIVIENNE LARMINIE

Sources Foster, *Alum. Oxon.* • Wood, *Ath. Oxon.*, new edn, 3.728 • PRO, PROB 11/331, fol. 165 • W. Streat, *The dividing of the hooff, or, Seeming-contradictions throughout sacred scriptures, distinguish'd, resolv'd and apply'd* (1654)

Wealth at death property in Dartmouth

Streater, John (c.1620–1677), soldier, printer, and political pamphleteer, was born in Lewes, Sussex, the son of William Streater, tailor. He had at least two brothers: Aaron, who called himself a divine and a physician; and Thomas, who in 1644 signed on with John as a stationer's apprentice. At an unknown date he married Susan (d. in or after 1677), and had at least one son, Joseph.

Streater began an apprenticeship with the London stationer Robert Hoskins in 1635. He did not have time to complete his service before the outbreak of the civil war. He joined the parliamentary army early, and fought at Newbury and Edgehill. Wounded, he returned to the capital to become a printer in his own right, gaining his freedom in June 1644. But he was soon back in the army again. He was probably at St Albans during the regicide. Subsequently he was sent to Ireland as a fortifications engineer and later quartermaster-general, where he remained for three years. It is likely that the distinctive political ideas that he published in the 1650s found their inspiration in debates during this time.

Streater returned to London in 1653, just before Cromwell forcibly dissolved the Rump Parliament. He thought this a disastrous act, aimed at elevating an army interest and eventually at making Cromwell himself 'absolute Lord of his Country'. In response Streater circulated doubts among his fellow officers, proposing a six-month parliament elected by the citizenry according to their 'inalienable Rights' (Streater, *Secret Reasons*). From then on he became a prolific pamphleteer, returning to his trade to circulate strikingly sophisticated arguments for a republic. The first of these tracts was *A Glympse of that Jewel, Judicial, Just Preserving Libertie*. Apparently written while he was still in Ireland, it advocated a classical republicanism in which the commonwealth would be composed of heroic citizens duty-bound to understand the laws and liberties of their nation, which must be circulated in the vernacular and in print. Parliaments would be short-term affairs, with office-holders limited to terms of a year. His idea was that, with such limits in place, officials would serve the public rather than any private interest. When 'reasons of state' were open to and judged by all, harmony would prevail. The result would be a nation whose prowess rivalled that of the ancient Roman republic.

During the whole of Cromwell's ascendancy Streater remained a consistent irritant. He was cashiered for *A Glympse*, and soon found himself in gaol for issuing a periodical, *The Grand Politick Informer* (no copies of this are now known). He remained interned until the collapse of Barebone's Parliament, despite an energetic and articulate campaign to be released. As soon as he was at large again he resumed his innovative use of publishing in parts as a way of avoiding suppression. His idea was to create newsbooks that, when bound together, added up to political treatises. The two principal examples were *Observations … upon Aristotles First Book of Political Government* and *A Politick Commentary on the Life of Caius Julius Caesar* (both 1654). Each provided grounds for opposing (and, Streater unsubtly hinted, assassinating) a military 'tyrant'. Like his other works, they espoused a republican commonwealth, but in more sustained terms. *Observations* in particular added up to an impressive argument for a form of government 'according to nature', in which all citizens would participate. Drawing on a wide range of authorities, Streater argued that states were akin to organisms, in that they must either grow or wither, and depended on circulations in order to flourish. On this basis he built a complex republican system notable for its thoroughgoing portrait not just of political structures, but of republican virtues in action, especially those arising from public knowledge. He clearly shared convictions not only with the Milton of *Areopagitica* but with James Harrington, whose *Oceana* Streater printed clandestinely in 1656. And the same concerns were also evident in other books he printed, which shared a conviction of the importance of knowledge and its circulation akin to that of Samuel Hartlib. Streater even seems to have embarked at one point with Giles Calvert on a scheme to publish all of Jakob Boehme's works in English.

Streater returned to military service in 1659 with the revival of the Rump. During this climactic year he continued to publish republican arguments (especially in *Government Described*). And he made his endorsement of Harringtonian ideas plain, arguing that 'that a Commonwealth may be Governed as Mr. Harrington describeth, is certain; nay, England it self' (*A Shield*, 17–18). But the leader he hoped would institute such a polity, Charles Fleetwood, did not think likewise, and Streater found himself watching once more in dismay as the military dismissed the Rump. But this time he resolved on defiance. He hatched a plot to seize the Tower of London and declare for parliament. The plan was betrayed, but Streater then joined the similarly disgruntled Admiral John Lawson, who sailed his fleet up the Thames while Streater handled the printing of a manifesto. With Monck approaching from the north and Lawson from the east, the army command decided to yield, and the Rump returned once more, with Streater reinstated as its official printer. Subsequently, as the revived assembly edged towards a restoration of the monarchy, Streater reluctantly acquiesced. In the spring of 1660 he and his men faced down the last hope of the military republicans, John Lambert, at the evocative field of Edgehill, thus ending the final challenge to Restoration.

From 1660 onwards Streater remained a printer. He built up probably the largest private printing house in the country, at one stage having five presses. Overall he seems to have accommodated himself to the new dispensation surprisingly readily. Indeed, he now presented his printing for parliament during the transition as service to the king, and was rewarded for this service, remarkably, with a blanket exemption from the new Press Act. Yet at the same time he was embarking on his most ambitious enterprise of all.

Throughout his confrontations with Cromwell, Streater had sought to publish law books. Besides being profitable, the practice coincided with his republican ideals. Now he forged an alliance with Richard Atkyns, an ex-cavalier seeking a patent on such works. For a decade and a half they mounted a campaign to secure the patent—a campaign that called into doubt the entire customary basis of the London book trade, and pioneered structures of collective publishing that would survive to become basic to the eighteenth-century trade.

Atkyns and Streater argued that the Stationers' Company laid claim to an unjustified autonomy from royal oversight. The result was a trade dedicated to books that were trivial, poorly produced, and even seditious. In particular, the company's register system for copyrights implicitly denied the crown's ability to grant patents. So they proposed replacing this system with one dominated by gentlemen patentees, who would adhere to higher standards. In short, Streater and Atkyns sought to make the everyday world of the book trade into an extension of the Restoration state. Their case found a ready audience among a political class convinced of the role of print in fomenting the civil war, and but for the revolution of 1688 would have succeeded. Yet Streater did not live to see its outcome. Financially exhausted, he was imprisoned again, this time for debt. For once he could not extricate himself, and he died in gaol in London in 1677. He was survived by his wife and their son, Joseph, who together carried on his printing business after his death.

ADRIAN JOHNS

Sources [J. Streater], *Observations historical, political and philosophical, upon Aristotles first book of political government* (1654) • J. Streater, *Secret reasons of state* (1659) • J. Streater, *A glympse of that jewel, judicial, just preserving libertie* (1653) • [J. Streater], *A politick commentary on the life of Caius Julius Caesar* (1654) • [J. Streater], *Clavis ad Aperiendum Carceris Ostia* (1654) • R. Atkyns, *The original and growth of printing* (1664) • J. S. [J. Streater], *Government described* (1659) • [R. Atkyns and J. Streater], *The king's grant of privilege for sole printing common-law-books, defended* (1669) • N. Smith, 'Popular republicanism in the 1650s: John Streater's "Heroick Mechanicks"', *Milton and republicanism*, ed. D. Armitage, A. Himy, and Q. Skinner (1995) • A. Johns, *The nature of the book: print and knowledge in the making* (1998) • J. S. [J. Streater], *A shield against the Parthian dart* (1659) • J. S. [J. Streater], *A further continuance of the grand politick informer* (1653) • J. Streater, *A letter sent to his excellency the Lord Fleetwood* (1659) • J. Feather, 'The publication of James Harrington's *Commonwealth of Oceana*', *The Library*, 5th ser., 32 (1977), 262–8
Archives PRO, state papers, domestic • PRO, Chancery papers • Worcester College, Oxford, letters to George Monck • Worshipful Company of Stationers and Newspapermakers, London, archives

Streater, Robert (1624–1679), painter, was born in Covent Garden, London, the son of a painter. He allegedly trained abroad with one Du Moulin but was in England by 1658, where he specialized in large-scale architectural and decorative paintings. Appointed sergeant-painter by Charles II in 1660, he worked from 1664 to 1672 on the decoration of royal carriages and of the queen's barges.

Streater excelled in the use of perspective and foreshortening. George Vertue called him:

> a compleat Master therein, as also in other Arts of Etching, Graving, and his works of Architecture and Perspective, not a line but is true to the Rules of Art and Symmetry (and in all kind of Paintings—see Streeters most exact & rare Landskips in Oyl. (Vertue, *Note books*, 4.31)

In 1660 William Russell, seventh earl of Bedford, bought a Streater landscape for his bedroom. The artist's only known topographical landscape is his *View of Boscobel, with the Royal Oak* (c.1660?; Royal Collection), attributed to Streater, along with six other works, four of them landscapes, in *A Catalogue of the Collection of Pictures, etc. Belonging to King James the Second* (1758).

Streater was noted for his illusionistic painted 'perspectives' (decorations). In 1664 Evelyn described one, painted in the court of Mr Povey's house in Lincoln's Inn Fields, as 'indeede excellent, with the Vasas [vases] in Imitation of *Porphyrie*; & fountaine' (Evelyn, 3.375, 1 July 1664). On 1 February 1669 Samuel Pepys visited 'Mr. Streater, the famous history-painter', finding the architect Christopher Wren and 'other virtuosos looking upon the paintings he is making of the new theatre at Oxford' (Pepys, 9.434). This was Streater's ceiling painting for Wren's Sheldonian Theatre, Oxford, a spectacular allegory painted in oil on canvas. Streater depicted a red awning (like those thought to have been used in the ancient Roman theatres that inspired Wren's architecture) being rolled back to reveal *Truth Descending on the Arts and Sciences* and *Envy, Rapine and Ignorance Overcome by Minerva, Hercules and Mercury*. The ceiling's allegorical figures were listed by Robert Whitehall in his poem *Urania, or, A description of the painting of the top of the theater at Oxford as the artist laid his design* (1669); they include Mosaical Law, the Gospel, History, Divine Poesy, Mathematics, Astronomy, Geography, Architecture, Rhetoric, Law, Justice, Physic, Logic, Printing, and Truth, and the poem concludes:

> That future ages must confess they owe
> to Streeter more than Michael Angelo.

Streater also painted a *Last Judgment*, in the chapel at All Souls College, Oxford, in 1661–5 (repainted by Sir James Thornhill but recorded in Ackermann's *History of Oxford*, 1814). He worked for Wren on thirteen City churches in London but little remains of his work apart from the Sheldonian ceiling, an altarpiece for the church of St Benet Fink, panels of Moses and of Aaron, and a ceiling at St Michael Cornhill, London (reused at the Old Rectory, Great Waldingfield, Sudbury, in Gloucestershire). His ceilings for Whitehall Palace, London, and scenery for Dryden's *Conquest of Granada* at the Whitehall Theatre were destroyed by fire. In 1672 Evelyn recorded Sir Robert Clayton's dining-room decorations (later removed to Marden, near Godstone, Surrey): 'the history of the Gyants War, incomparably done by Mr. Streeter, but the figures are too near the eye' (Evelyn, 4.625). Evelyn saw fine works by Streater in 1679 at Mr Boone's (or Bohun's) house, Lee Place, Blackheath (pulled down in 1825).

Streater also painted portraits, including *Sir Francis Prujean, M.D.* (1662; Royal College of Physicians, London). He was commissioned by the second earl of Chesterfield to paint *Mucius Scaevola* and *Rinaldo*, and according to Vertue painted a small *Jupiter upon the Rock*. His works, sold cheaply at auction following the death of his son on 13 December 1711, included a portrait of the actor Lacy, paintings of animals, still lifes, *Isaac and Rebecca*, *Abraham Sacrificing Isaac*, *The Nativity*, *The Vision of Jacob*, *St. Mary Magdalen*, and an architectural subject (for a fuller list see Vertue, *Note books*, 2.70).

A gifted engraver, Streater engraved a self-portrait for Horace Walpole's *Anecdotes of Painting*, etched *View of the Battle of Naseby*, and designed a frontispiece and plates for Sir Robert Stapylton's *Satires of Juvenal* (1660), etched by Wenceslaus Hollar. His art collection included a sketch by Rubens of two children, for the Whitehall ceiling; an oil sketch by Sir Peter Lely for a *Holy Family*; H. van Steenwyck's *St Peter in Prison*; a large *St Sebastian* by Van Dyck; a *Hercules and Dejanira* by Benedetto Gennari; a 'limning' by Lankrinck; and almost thirty still-life subjects by 'Vanzoon'—perhaps the Flemish flower-painter Jan Frans van Son (1658–c.1718), husband of Streater's cousin.

Streater died in 1679, following an operation for 'the stone' by a surgeon summoned from Paris by Charles II. He was succeeded as sergeant-painter by his son Robert. His brother Thomas married the daughter of Remigius van Leemput.   ANNE THACKRAY

Sources T. Borenius, *Burlington Magazine*, 84 (1944), 2–12 • E. Waterhouse, *Painting in Britain, 1530–1790* (1953), 3–4, 79, 87 • [B. Buckeridge], 'An essay towards an English school of painting', in R. de Piles, *The art of painting, with the lives and characters of above 300 of the most eminent painters*, 3rd edn (1754), 354–439, esp. 420–21 • Pepys, *Diary*, 9.434 • Evelyn, *Diary*, 3.375–6, 569–70, 625–6; 4.51–2, 288 • Vertue, *Note books*, vols. 1–4 • T. Wilson and C. Whistler, 'The Sheldonian Theatre', *Apollo*, 145 (May 1997), 20–22 • H. Walpole,

Anecdotes of painting in England: with some account of the principal artists, ed. R. N. Wornum, new edn, 3 vols. (1888), vol. 2, pp. 83–7 · P. Hetherington, 'The altarpiece for Wren's church of St Benet Fink: an addition to the œuvre of Robert Streater', *Apollo*, 142 (July 1995), 44–6 · K. E. Campbell, 'Church of St Michael Cornhill: the post-great fire records', *London Topographical Record*, 27 (1995), 135–47 · E. H. Gombrich, *Art history and the social sciences* (1975) [Romanes lecture, Oxford, 1973] · J. Summerson, *The Sheldonian in its time* (1964) · H. M. Colvin, *The Sheldonian Theatre and the Divinity School* (1964)

Likenesses A. Bannerman, line engraving (after R. Streater), BM, NPG; repro. in Walpole, *Anecdotes* · R. Streater, self-portrait; formerly priv. coll. · portrait (Robert Streater?), repro. in Borenius, *Burlington Magazine*, pl. 5A

Streatfeild, Lucy Anne Evelyn Deane (1865–1950), factory inspector and social worker, was born at Madras, India, on 31 July 1865, and was baptized there on the following day, the daughter of Lieutenant-Colonel Bonar Millett Deane (1834–1881) and his wife, the Hon. Lucy Boscawen, a sister of the sixth Viscount Falmouth. Her father served in India and South Africa, and was killed at Laing's Neck on 28 January 1881 during the First South African War. Her mother died in March 1886.

In the 1890s Lucy Deane trained as a health worker and lecturer for the National Health Society, a charitable body established to provide some professional training for those working in a largely amateur, altruistic service. In 1893 she and Rose Squire (1861–1938) were appointed by the vestry of St Mary Abbots in Kensington as sanitary inspectors of workshops and factories that employed women. Both were subsequently appointed as factory inspectors by the Home Office, Deane in 1894 and Squire in 1895. The work of the early women's inspectorate, headed by May Abraham (later Tennant), was arduous: they faced antagonism from employers and in many cases from workers, as well as from their male colleagues. The women travelled long distances throughout Britain and Ireland, on public transport or by bicycle, often without revealing the nature of their work to protect the women whose working conditions they were investigating. In Ireland, where Deane undertook several periods of duty, she was particularly angered by the truck system, noting that even the priests would not support the workers and that there was 'utter disregard for law and justice, terrible tales of the corruption of the magistrates' (Deane Streatfeild MSS, business diaries, 9 Nov 1897). In 1900 there were only seven women factory inspectors, and Lucy Deane was in charge of 4000 workshops (including the court dressmakers') in west London alone (*Manchester Guardian*, 13 July 1900, 5).

In 1901 Deane was one of the six women appointed by the British government to report on conditions in the South African concentration camps (the committee of inquiry into the Second South African War concentration camps, chaired by Millicent Fawcett), approaching the work in much the same way as she did that of factory inspection. In letters to her sister, Hyacinthe Mary (*d.* 1903), an inspector of domestic science and one of the first women inspectors in the education department, she gave a detailed account of the committee's travels in South Africa, and sometimes complained about the unprofessional methods of her colleagues. Although she usually got on well with her companions, she described herself as 'one against five' because she disagreed with them on so many points (Deane Streatfeild MSS, letter to Hyacinthe Deane, 23 Dec 1901). It was largely at her insistence that the committee's report included criticisms of the operation of the camps system.

In 1906 Deane resigned from the factory inspectorate because of ill health, and moved from London to Westerham in Kent, where she lived until her death. On 16 March 1911 she married Granville Edward Stewart Streatfeild (1868/9–1947), an architect; they had no children. She remained an active voluntary worker. She was the first woman organizing officer for the National Health Insurance Commission, and organized infant welfare centres in London; she was also a member of various trade boards. In 1912, she was one of the two women (the other was E. S. Haldane) appointed to the royal commission on the civil service. She supported female suffrage, and lectured for the National Union of Women's Suffrage Societies. In 1913 she was one of the organizers of the women's suffrage pilgrimage from Westerham and district, which joined the union's rally of about 50,000 people held in Hyde Park on 26 July 1913.

During the First World War, Lucy Deane Streatfeild was a member of the executive committee of the Women's Land Army in Kent. She was a member of the War Office appeals committee, which adjudicated on separation allowances for soldiers' and sailors' dependants, and of a special arbitration tribunal to settle disputes over wages and conditions in munitions works. In 1918 she was appointed chairman of a committee of inquiry into the conduct of members of the Women's Army Auxiliary Corps in France, and was appointed CBE.

After the war Deane Streatfeild was one of the first women JPs (appointed in 1920), and a member of Kent county council. She was a leading member of the Women's Institute and was one of the founders of the Westerham branch, of which she became the president. She was an enthusiastic producer of amateur theatre and mounted village productions of several Shakespeare plays. She was a member of the University Women's Club and of the National Union of Working Women. She published a number of articles on aspects of factory work and industrial legislation. She died on 3 July 1950 at her home, Cottage on the Hill, Westerham, Kent, and was buried at Westerham on 7 July. She was remembered by her contemporaries as a lively and inspiring colleague with a strong social conscience—an impression confirmed by the account of her work left in her business diaries.

ELAINE HARRISON

Sources letters, business diaries, memoir by V. Markham, BLPES, Deane Streatfeild MSS · private information (2004) [M. Wright] · Madras baptisms, BL OIOC, Z/N 66 · m. cert. · d. cert. · Burke, *Peerage* (1889) · M. D. McFeely, *Lady inspectors: the campaign for a better workplace, 1893–1921* (1988) · *The Times* (26 July 1913) · *The Times* (28 July 1913) · *ILN*, 149 (1881) · O. Fleming, 'Granville Streatfeild', *RIBA Journal*, 55 (1947–8), 228–9 · *CGPLA Eng. & Wales* (1950)

Archives BLPES, diaries and papers

Likenesses photograph, BLPES
Wealth at death £7667 8s. 8d.—save and except settled land: probate, 1950, *CGPLA Eng. & Wales* • £1600—limited to settled land: probate, 1950, *CGPLA Eng. & Wales*

Streatfeild, (Mary) Noel (1895–1986), children's writer, was born on 24 December 1895 in Frant, Sussex, the second child and second daughter in the family of five daughters (the second youngest of whom died at the age of two) and one son of William Champion Streatfeild (1865–1929), an Anglican vicar, and his wife, Janet Mary, daughter of Henry Venn, vicar of Walmer. She grew up in Amberley, St Leonards, and Eastbourne, where her father was vicar (he later became suffragan bishop of Lewes). In the first part of her autobiography she describes overhearing her mother's friends identify her as 'the plain one'. That, and the genteel poverty in which they lived, made her fiercely resentful and in later years it was noticeable what an important part clothes played in her plots and her own life; she was always elegant. She was educated at the Hastings and St Leonard's Ladies' College in St Leonards and Laleham School in Eastbourne. In 1916 she went to work in Woolwich arsenal, but became ill. In 1919 she joined the (Royal) Academy of Dramatic Art in London. She had moderate success as an *ingénue* playing in repertory, reviews, and pantomime. She also went on tour in South Africa, Rhodesia, New Zealand, and Australia. When her father died in 1929 she returned home and decided to adopt a more stable career, choosing to be a writer.

Noel Streatfeild's first efforts were three fairy stories published in a children's magazine and a novel, *The Whicharts* (1931), based on children's misunderstanding of the prayer 'Our Father which art …'. Its success encouraged her to write five other novels, including *I Ordered a Table for Six* (1942), which anticipated the bomb which destroyed the Café Royal a year later. It was about this time, after her agent suggested she try writing for children, that she rather unenthusiastically produced *Ballet Shoes* (1936), which became a runaway success, and which caused her to have no further worries about money.

Almost by accident Noel Streatfeild had found the perfect ingredients for a children's book. Into it she had put all her accumulated backstage knowledge of the theatre and of her sister's ballet training, as well as their childhood struggles with hardship and a genuine picture of family life. *Tennis Shoes* (1937) incorporated the advice given to her by John Galsworthy, in the first fan letter she received, 'always remember to know at least three times as much as you are going to put on paper'. Her third book, *The Circus is Coming* (1938), was the result of nearly a year spent travelling with a family circus and won her the Library Association's Carnegie medal.

On the outbreak of the Second World War, Noel Streatfeild trained as an air raid warden and joined the Women's Voluntary Service, running a canteen service in London for people in the Deptford shelters. In her spare time, she prettified London by scattering flower seeds on bomb sites. In 1941 her London flat was bombed and she lost almost everything. She nevertheless wrote four more children's books during the war, including *Party Frock*

(Mary) Noel Streatfeild (1895–1986), by Lewis Baumer, exh. RA 1926

(1946). After the war she spent some time in Hollywood, from which came *The Painted Garden* (1949). In 1951 *White Boots*, a story about skating, appeared. She began to share a flat at 51A Elizabeth Street, London, with a friend, Margot Grey.

Noel Streatfeild believed that every detail in her books should be factually correct and she also developed her characters convincingly. Her writing for young readers had a reassuring warmth, or 'heart' as she described it, and almost all her stories were centred on families. The family background and rules of behaviour between parents and siblings had a warm quality which made them both fascinating and believable.

In all Noel Streatfeild wrote sixty-four books, all but seventeen for children, always drawing on her own experience to make them as authentic as possible. Many of them were broadcast on radio or television; it was the BBC which introduced her Bell family to radio; the serials were broadcast from 1949 to 1953. *The Growing Summer* (1966) was a television serial set in Ireland, and *Thursday's Child* (1970) was also serialized. She wrote her autobiography in three volumes, and a life of another renowned writer of children's books, Edith Nesbit (*Magic and the Magician*, 1958). She was generous in encouraging young writers and replied kindly to every child who wrote to her. She was also indefatigable in her response to schools and libraries, never treating this as a duty, but taking the trouble to make her visits as exciting and glamorous as possible. On the days when she visited the yearly exhibition of the Puffin Club (the children's branch of Penguin Books, which published her work), huge queues formed to get her autograph. Mothers came with their daughters, bringing their own battered copies of *Ballet Shoes* to be signed. She was appointed OBE in 1983.

Noel Streatfeild was a tall woman, with a fine carriage. She often wore a mink coat, and her lovely hands were regularly manicured with rich red nail polish. She was physically somewhat clumsy, with a rather loud, commanding voice. She never married. She died on 11 September 1986 in a nursing home, Vicarage Gate House, Vicarage Gate, London, after a stroke. Her funeral was held at St Michael's Church, Chester Square, London, on 22 September 1986.   KAYE WEBB, *rev.*

Sources N. Streatfeild, *A vicarage family* (1963) • N. Streatfeild, *Away from the vicarage* (1965) • N. Streatfeild, *Beyond the vicarage* (1971) • A. Bull, *Noel Streatfeild: a biography* (1984) • B. K. Wilson, *Noel Streatfeild* (1961) • personal knowledge (1996) • *The Times* (12 Sept 1986) • *WWW, 1981–90* • Burke, *Gen. GB*
Archives BBC WAC • Bodl. Oxf. • LMA • University of Bristol | U. Reading, George Bell and Sons MSS | SOUND BL NSA
Likenesses L. Baumer, oils, exh. RA 1926, NPG [*see illus.*]
Wealth at death £42,018: resworn probate, 11 May 1987, *CGPLA Eng. & Wales* (1986)

Streatfeild, Sophia (*bap.* 1755, *d.* 1835), beauty, was baptized on 9 May 1755 at St Anne's, Soho, London, the elder daughter of Henry Streatfeild (1706–1762), of Chiddingstone, Kent, and his wife, Anne Sidney (1732–1812), natural daughter of Jocelyne Sidney, seventh earl of Leicester (*d.* 1743). She was tutored in Latin and Greek by Dr Arthur Collier (1707–1777), lawyer and classicist. An earlier student of his was Hester Lynch Salusbury (later Thrale), whose diary, *Thraliana*, gives the fullest account of Sophia Streatfeild. Hester Thrale met her in Brighton in 1777 and described her on 19 May 1778:

> Her Face is eminently pretty, her Carriage elegant, her Heart affectionate, and her Mind cultivated. There is above all this an attractive Sweetness in her Manner, which claims & promises to repay one's Confidence, & which drew from me the secret of my keeping a Thraliana to deposit all kinds of Nonsense in.   (Thrale, 323)

Sophia Streatfeild's classical learning aroused Hester Thrale's jealousy, yet little is known of it; the single extant example of her scholarship is a letter to Hester Thrale that bristles with references to, and quotations from, ancient Greek authors. Samuel Johnson acknowledged her knowledge of Greek, though he did not rate her intelligence. At her death her library contained forty-three volumes of Greek literature.

Hester Thrale had further occasion to be jealous of Sophia Streatfeild, as her husband, Henry Thrale, was much taken with her. As early as December 1778 she wrote in a footnote, 'I see my Husband is in love with her' (Thrale, 348, n. 1). Not long thereafter, under 10 January 1779, she wrote:

> M[r] Thrale has fallen in Love *really & seriously* with Sophy Streatfeild—but there is no wonder in that: She is very pretty, very gentle, soft & insinuating; hangs about him, dances round him, cries when She parts from him, squeezes his Hand slyly, & with her sweet Eyes full of Tears looks so fondly in his Face—& all for *Love of me* as She pretends; that I can hardly sometimes help laughing in her Face.   (ibid., 356)

Hester Thrale repeatedly refers to her husband's obsession with Sophia, and also records other amorous conquests of hers. Her favourite in May 1781 was William Vyse, of Lichfield, yet she was rumoured to have considered Lord Loughborough as a suitor. In the previous autumn she had dazzled Beilby Porteus, bishop of Chester and for fifteen years a married man. According to Hester Thrale, 'She shewed me a Letter from him that was as tender, and had all the *Tokens* upon it as strong as I ever remember to have seen 'em' (ibid., 761). The last of Sophia's conquests to be named was Dr Charles Burney: 'he is *now* the reigning Favourite, and she spares neither Pains nor Caresses, to turn that poor Man's head, much to the Vexation of his Family' (ibid., 523). In exasperation Hester Thrale summed up Sophia Streatfeild's character thus:

> a Young Coquet whose sole Employment in this World seems to have been winning Men's hearts on purpose to fling them away. How She contrives to keep Bishops, & Brewers, & Doctors, & Directors of the East India Company all in her Chains so—& almost all at a Time would amaze a wiser Person than me.   (ibid., 523)

Sophia Streatfeild died, unmarried, on 30 November 1835 and was buried in her native Chiddingstone, Kent, where there is a memorial tablet to her in the church. Her library was sold by W. H. Robinson Ltd. Edward Burney's drawings of the characters from *Evelina*, by his cousin Fanny Burney, supposedly depict Sophia Streatfeild as Evelina.   ARTHUR SHERBO

Sources *Thraliana: the diary of Mrs. Hester Lynch Thrale (later Mrs. Piozzi), 1776–1809*, ed. K. C. Balderston, 2nd edn, 2 vols. (1951) • *The letters of Samuel Johnson*, ed. B. Redford, 5 vols. (1992–4) • *Diary and letters of Madame D'Arblay (1778–1840)*, ed. C. Barrett and A. Dobson, 6 vols. (1904–5) • IGI

Streatfeild, Thomas (1777–1848), topographer and antiquary, was born on 5 January 1777. He was the eldest son of Sandeforth Streatfeild (*bap.* 1750, *d.* 1809) of Long Ditton, Surrey (descended from the Streatfeilds of Chiddingstone, Kent), who was a partner, first in the house of Brandram & Co., and then in that of Sir Samuel Fludyer & Co. His mother was Frances, daughter of Thomas Hussey, of Ashford, Kent. He matriculated from Oriel College, Oxford, on 19 May 1795 and graduated BA in 1799.

Christmases at Long Ditton at that time were enlivened by some two-act comedies of manners which Streatfeild wrote and which were performed by friends and relatives in the laundry, temporarily converted to use as a theatre. At least two survive from those days, *Ton and Antiquity* (1798) and *The Road to Ridicule* (1799), as well as a slim volume of *Prologues and Epilogues* (1799).

In early life Streatfeild was curate at Long Ditton to the Revd William Pennicott (*d.* 1811), and his talents received early encouragement from his father, whose funeral sermon he preached and later had published. He was at that time also chaplain to the duke of Kent, and became subsequently curate of Tatsfield, in Surrey, retaining the post until, in 1842, ill health compelled him to retire. On 8 October 1800 Streatfeild married Harriet, daughter and coheir of Alexander Champion, of Wandsworth, who brought with her a considerable fortune. They had five sons and three daughters, before she died on 10 November 1814. In 1822 he established his family on an estate of 40 acres at Chart's Edge, Westerham, where he had a house built to his own design, and on 30 September 1823 he married again. His second wife was Clare, widow of Henry Woodgate, of Spring Grove, and daughter of the Revd Thomas Harvey, rector of Cowden; they had three sons and two daughters.

Streatfeild was elected a fellow of the Society of Antiquaries on 4 June 1812, and was for many years employed in forming collections, chiefly genealogical and biographical, in illustration of the history of Kent. A number of drawings (many by himself) and engravings for this projected work were also made, but Streatfeild was able to publish no more of it than *Excerpta Cantiana* (1836), a 23-page prospectus for the work, which it was proposed to bring out in ten parts. Streatfeild appears to have taken a strenuous part in the general election of 1837, and shortly afterwards to have suffered a stroke. After his death his fifty-two volumes of notes and manuscript materials for the proposed history were left to his collaborator, the Revd Lambert Blackwell Larking, in the hope that the latter would be able to bring the project to fruition. In the event only one instalment of the work was to be published, in 1886, under the editorship of H. H. Drake, with the title *Hasted's History of Kent: Corrected, Enlarged, and Continued to the Present Time, from the Manuscripts of the Late Rev T. Streatfeild, and the Late Rev L. B. Larking, Part 1: The Hundred of Blackheath*. The Streatfeild manuscript collections are now in the British Library.

Otherwise Streatfeild published little. Of several verse tragedies which he wrote later in life only *The Bridal of Armagnac* (1823) was published. *Lympsfield and its Environs*, a short series of drawings made in the vicinity of this Surrey village, was given in manuscript to a bazaar, and subsequently published by a local printer in 1838. Streatfeild died at Chart's Edge on 17 May 1848, and was buried at Chiddingstone. SHIRLEY BURGOYNE BLACK

Sources L. B. Larking, 'The late Rev. Thomas Streatfeild of Chart's Edge', *Archaeologia Cantiana*, 3 (1860), 137–44 · H. H. Drake, introduction, in *Hasted's history of Kent: corrected, enlarged, and continued to the present time*, ed. H. H. Drake (1886) · J. M. Kuist, *The Nichols file of the Gentleman's Magazine: attributions of authorship and other documentation in editorial papers at the Folger Library* (1982) · Burke, *Gen. GB* (1886) · Foster, *Alum. Oxon.* · Streatfeild MSS, BL, Add. MSS 33878–33929 · *DNB*
Archives BL, Add. MSS 33878–33929, 34103–34106, Add. ch 36460–36991
Likenesses B. Clark, engraving, 1881 (after oils by H. Smith), repro. in *The hundred of Blackheath* (1886), part 1 of Drake, ed., *Hasted's history of Kent: corrected, enlarged, and continued to the present time*, frontispiece · H. L. Smith, lithograph, BM

Strecche, John (*fl.* 1407–1425), Augustinian canon, historian, and antiquary, of St Mary's Priory, Kenilworth, was in 1407 presented to the custody of the *cellula* of Broke in Rutland, a cell of Kenilworth. He resigned this office in 1425 and returned to his mother house. He was a compiler and copier of texts as well as author of a chronicle and of other texts, and two volumes survive that were probably compiled by him. BL, Add. MS 38665 contains five Latin works in his hand, and he was probably author of three of them: verses against the Augustinian friars; a *Cronica cuisdam amici veritatis in argumentum fundacionis canonicorum regularium ordinis sancti Augustii*, which forms a reply to the work of an Augustinian friar claiming priority for his order over that of the Augustinian canons; and a treatise on the thirty different colours or kinds of rhyming verse, with examples. Two further texts, the *Liber Catonis* and Aesop's fables, are in his hand. The remaining texts, which include materials on the Augustinian canons (a list of houses and a chronicle of their general chapters between 1325 and 1350), are not in Strecche's hand.

BL, Add. MS 35295 contains a mixture of his own compositions along with other works of romance and history. The *Historia Trojana* of Guido delle Colonne and the *Historia regum Britanniae* of Geoffrey of Monmouth are in the hand of John Aston, but Strecche's appears as corrector, and the opening poem on the fall of Troy is in his hand. Strecche was the author and scribe of the *Historia regum omnium Anglorum* which concludes the volume. This is divided into five books, preceded by a brief history of England from Brutus to 827 and the story of Albina and her sisters. The first book deals with the early Saxon kings, the second with Alfred and his successors, the third with the Danish kings, and the fourth with kings from the Norman conquest to the usurpation of Henry IV. The fifth book devotes three folios to Henry IV and twenty-four to Henry V, the latter being by far the longest section in the work, and historiographically the most important. It was compiled shortly after 1422, and deals mainly with the French war in typically patriotic tone, including the story of the dauphin's gift of tennis balls, which is also found in Thomas Elmham's *Liber metricus*. The desire to eulogize Henry led Strecche to omit any reference to the king's supposedly riotous youth and to misrepresent certain events in the war, playing down, for instance, the defeat at Baugé in 1421. Although its approach is sometimes anecdotal, the chronicle does include details not found elsewhere, providing the fullest account by any early commentator of Henry's brief visit to England in 1421, during which, as on several previous occasions, the king visited Kenilworth. Strecche has set short pieces of verse by himself and by others throughout his *Historia*, and there are frequent references in the text to the priory of Kenilworth. His compilations and compositions provide a useful example of the intellectual tastes and activities of an early fifteenth-century canon. ANNE CURRY

Sources BL, Add. MSS 35295, 38665 · 'The chronicle of John Strecche for the reign of Henry V, 1414–1422', ed. F. Taylor, *Bulletin of the John Rylands University Library*, 16 (1932), 137–87 · A. Gransden, *Historical writing in England*, 2 (1982) · *VCH Rutland* · A. H. Thompson, ed., *Visitations of religious houses in the diocese of Lincoln*, 1, CYS, 17 (1915) · J. H. Wylie and W. T. Waugh, eds., *The reign of Henry the Fifth*, 3 vols. (1914–29)
Archives BL, Add. MSS 35295, 38665

Street, Arthur George (1892–1966), farmer and author, was born at Wilton, near Salisbury, on 7 April 1892. The fifth of six children, he was the youngest son of Henry Street (*d.* 1917) and his wife, Sarah Anne, *née* Butt, tenant farmers of the earl of Pembroke. At the age of fifteen he left Dauntsey's School, near Devizes, to assist his father on Ditchampton Farm, Wilton. It was a large mixed holding consisting originally of two separate farms encompassing about 700 acres, over 400 acres of which were arable. In addition there were two milking herds, a breeding flock of pedigree Hampshire Down sheep, and a staff of more than twenty men.

In 1911, following a rift with his father, Street emigrated to Canada to work on a large arable farm in north-west Manitoba, though he returned to Britain to enlist as a soldier in the First World War. His application, however, was rejected because of a congenital malformation of the feet which had prevented him from walking until the age of seven. He remained in Britain, working with his father until the latter's death in 1917, then at Michaelmas 1918 took over the tenancy of the farm at nearly double the previous rent. On 3 July that same year he married Vera Florence (*b.* 1896/7), the daughter of Francis Foyle, the foreman of the local felt mill.

During the short-lived post-war boom Street, like many other farmers, benefited from inflated prices for agricultural produce, enabling him to farm the holding along traditional labour-intensive lines and to indulge in extravagant leisure activities, including hunting, shooting, and tennis parties. The collapse of prices after 1921, accompanied by the birth of his daughter Pamela, compelled him to rationalize his lifestyle and farming methods. In an attempt to remain solvent he terminated the tenancy on part of his farm at Michaelmas 1928, having converted the remaining fields to grass. He established an outdoor dairy herd and, in the following year, began to retail milk himself, canvassing for customers in the nearby city of Salisbury.

In 1929, having read what he regarded as an incompetent farming review, Street tried his own hand at writing. Much to his amazement, his article was published in the *Daily Mail*. This experience heralded a lifelong career as an agricultural journalist. In 1931, encouraged by the novelist Edith Olivier, he began work on an autobiographical account which he called *Farmer's Glory*. A large proportion of the book was written in longhand, late at night in bed after haymaking in the summer of 1931. Each chapter was planned as he travelled on his milk round in the early morning, and on wet days he would type up what he had composed and correct it. This highly successful text, published in 1932, can aptly be described as a countryman's credo, written from reminiscences of his own life. It was his first among more than thirty novels and cameos of country life. None of the later novels was quite as popular, although *Strawberry Roan* (1932) was made into a film. Among his other books were *The Endless Furrow* (1934), *The Gentlemen of the Party* (1936), *Harvest by Lamplight* (1943), *Hitler's Whistle* (1943), *Holdfast* (1946), and *Shameful Harvest* (1952), a novel dedicated to George Walden, who had been killed while being evicted from his farm by the local war

agricultural executive committee. His last two books, *Johnny Cowslip* and *Fish and Chips*, were published in 1964.

In 1932 Street made his first broadcast, establishing himself as a popular commentator on current affairs in general and on agriculture in particular. His outspoken, common-sense approach enabled him to become a regular contributor to a number of radio programmes. By this time, despite being a working farmer and honorary secretary of the local hunt, he was a prolific writer of articles and sketches for publications such as *The Countryman*, *The Star*, *Evening News*, *Sunday Dispatch*, *News Chronicle*, *Radio Times*, and *Salisbury Times*. In 1935 he started writing what he was to be best remembered for: a regular column for the *Farmer's Weekly*, which he continued without interruption for thirty years. In 1937, at the invitation of the Canadian government, Street embarked upon an extensive tour of Canada and America, lecturing on agriculture.

During the Second World War, Street assisted the ministry of information in making wartime films and was credited as scriptwriter for *The Great Harvest* (1942), in addition to commentating on *Spring Offensive* (1941) and *Simple Fruit Pruning* (1944). In 1949 he became a member of the team for the new radio programme *Any Questions*, visiting towns in the south and west of England. The sound advice that he espoused on the show made him a popular contributor, enhancing his national reputation.

Arthur Street was tall and burly, with a ruddy complexion and a head of thick black hair cut short. In religion an eclectic Anglican and in politics a high tory, he combined compassion with intolerance, jostling generosity with pugnacity. The maze of human motive interested him, but he did not presume to explore it deeply. Jung he sampled *cum grano salis*; Freud with a sceptical chuckle. His novels therefore were never more than tales. As an interpreter of country life, and especially of farming technique, he ranked with the best of his contemporaries. Sir Arthur Bryant admired his 'beautiful, direct and Cobbett-like English' (Street, 8). Sometimes he achieved true poetry—as in what was undoubtedly his best book, *Farmer's Glory*. His rural reminiscences have been enriched rather than outdated over the years since they recall commonplace events which rapidly became rarities. Although it was radically transformed during his lifetime, his writings encapsulate the rural scene and type of society that prevailed before the agricultural intensification and agribusinesses of the post-1950s.

In 1951 Street moved to Mill Farm on the opposite side of the Wylye valley at South Newton, which, like Ditchampton, he rented from the earl of Pembroke. During his later years he suffered a stroke, although he continued to write his weekly column for the *Farmer's Weekly*. After a long illness he died in Salisbury Infirmary on 21 July 1966. He was cremated in Salisbury on 23 July.

J. H. B. Peel, *rev.* John Martin

Sources P. Street, *My father A. G. Street* (1969) · *The Times* (22 July 1966) · *Daily Telegraph* (22 July 1966) · *Farmer's Weekly* (29 July 1966) · *Salisbury Journal* (28 July 1966) · J. Martin, *The development of modern agriculture: British farming since 1931* (2000) · m. cert.

Archives NRA, papers | FILM BFI NFTVA | SOUND BL NSA

Likenesses photograph, repro. in Street, *My father* • photograph, repro. in *Salisbury Journal* (28 July 1966), 10 • photograph, repro. in *The Times*, 14 • photographs, repro. in *Farmer's Weekly* (1940–66)
Wealth at death £42,166: probate, 14 Sept 1966, CGPLA Eng. & Wales

Street, Sir Arthur William (1892–1951), civil servant, was born on 16 May 1892 at Cowes, Isle of Wight, the son of William Charles Street, a licensed victualler, and his wife, Minnie Clark. He was educated at the county school, Sandown. At the age of fifteen he went to London to start in the civil service as a boy clerk. Street was determined to improve his position by further study at King's College, London, and by 1914 he had become an established second division clerk at the Board of Agriculture and Fisheries.

During the First World War Street served with the Inns of Court regiment, the Hampshire regiment, and the machine-gun corps. He fought on various fronts—mainly in the Middle East—was wounded, mentioned in dispatches, awarded the Military Cross, and attained the rank of major. In 1915 Street married Denise, daughter of Jules Mantanus, a Belgian businessman; they had three sons and a daughter. She died in 1924 and in 1926 Street married her sister, Angèle Eléanore Théodorine Mantanus.

On his return to his old department in 1919, Street became private secretary to Lord Lee of Fareham, who was so impressed with Street's ability that he took him with him to the Admiralty when he became first lord in February 1921. In 1922 Street returned to the Ministry of Agriculture as a principal, and he became secretary to the Linlithgow committee on the distribution and prices of agricultural produce. The report of the committee, presented in November 1923, 'diagnosed the main ills of British agriculture' and 'led to the outstanding developments in agricultural policy that were to unfold in the next fifteen years; it initiated the Street era for British agriculture' (*Public Administration*, 304). Street headed a small, newly created marketing department, which issued reports on co-operative marketing in other countries and on the marketing in the United Kingdom of agricultural commodities. These reports bore fruit in agriculture marketing acts in the thirties. The legislation afforded some protection for the producers, but on condition that they organized themselves more efficiently, and it created new administrative machinery for these purposes in the form of marketing boards independent of the government.

Throughout the thirties Street moved up rapidly in the Ministry of Agriculture and Fisheries, serving as second secretary in 1936–8. He was fast gaining a reputation in Whitehall and beyond as a leading civil servant, who combined an intense devotion to duty with an ability to formulate proposals on which ministers could make decisions on policy. Though much of his career was concerned with extending the sphere of administrative control in British life, Street was a strong individualist who believed that adversity could be overcome by hard work and organization:

> The path to economic salvation lay in individual effort. He repudiated the 'feather-bed' as an economic symbol for the age. Those who need help should be given it, but the best form of help is to show people how they can do without it. (*Public Administration*, 305)

In 1938 Street was transferred to the Air Ministry, becoming permanent under-secretary of state and a member of the Air Council in 1939. This was a difficult change. The role of the permanent head of a service department is less clear-cut than in a civil department. The Air Council in Street's day consisted of the minister, his parliamentary secretary, the leading service officers, and one civil servant. Moreover, the Air Ministry was, perhaps, the most difficult of service departments. A war was imminent which for the first time in history would be extensively fought in the air. The air marshals who formed the Air Council believed passionately in the importance of the Royal Air Force and they considered it Street's function to find the resources they deemed necessary for expansion. But Street, as accounting officer to the Air Ministry, was responsible for its expenditure and it was his duty, therefore, from time to time, to ask questions which the air marshals might dislike. Moreover, as a newcomer he had to work doubly hard to master the unfamiliar facts of a rapidly expanding department.

Street took to his task very carefully. He was concerned not to overplay his hand, and in consequence spoke little on the Air Council. When he did intervene, though, it was with real authority. By intensive hard work and with his remarkable ability for working with other people, he convinced his fellow members of the Air Council that he had the interests of the Royal Air Force as much at heart as anyone. The air marshals found in Street an adviser and a friend to whom they could bring their problems with the full confidence that they would obtain guidance and inspiration.

Before the war broke out in 1939 Street completed one congenial task in the field of civil aviation: he took a leading part in preparing the British Overseas Airways Act in 1939. This important legislation laid the basis for the advances in British civil aviation that would come after the war.

During the war Street did not spare himself. He worked far into the night, and slept at his office. His influence on the department was profound: he always found time to attend to the personal problems of his staff. His own tragedy was the death of his youngest son, one of the fifty RAF officers shot while attempting to escape from Stalag Luft III. Street learned of this news while at his desk, reading through the Foreign Office telegrams that first told of the incident. In spite of his own grief, he began at once the task of writing letters to the relatives of those killed.

At the end of the war Street took charge of a new office to supervise the British elements of the Allied Control Commission for Germany and Austria. But in July 1946 he was called to his last great task—the deputy chairmanship of the National Coal Board, which in January 1947 took over the coalmining industry of Great Britain.

Street's task at the coal board was herculean: he had to create an organization to replace 800 colliery companies and he had to do it quickly. The nationalization act of 1946 left the board to devise its own organization. The coalmining industry was run down after the war: coal was in very short supply and in February 1947 there was the worst fuel crisis in British history. There was also the intensely human and long-standing problem of relations with the miners, who were prone to regard their employers with suspicion. Again Street did not spare himself and gradually the organization took root. The early difficulties experienced by the nationalized coal industry led to criticism of the coal board, which inevitably reflected on its deputy chairman. In some quarters Street was regarded as living proof that civil servants made poor managers of nationalized industries. In fact his prestige and experience brought vital stability and order to the coal board in its early years when it was grappling with complex problems of organization and production. It should have been no surprise that Street, worn out with his incessant labours, died in London on 24 February 1951 on his way to St Mary Abbots Hospital, Kensington. He was survived by his second wife. Had he lived, he would have succeeded Lord Hyndley as chairman.

Street was a large man with a commanding presence and personality. Although he could appear brusque and gruff, his powers of persuasion were legendary, yet he rarely seemed to argue. He was always good company, and his interest, enthusiasm, and capacity for work swept along all who met him. A man of great vision and a designer of large policies, he could yet lavish tremendous, somewhat excessive, pains on matters of detail. Among his wide circle of friends were men of affairs and leaders of thought, not only in Britain but also abroad, especially in France and the dominions. Not the least of his achievements was his interest in and influence on the group of young administrative officers in the Air Ministry, many of whom subsequently rose to high positions in other departments.

In 1924 Street was appointed CIE (he had been joint secretary with Findlater Stewart of the royal commission on superior civil services in India); in 1933 he was appointed CMG after the Ottawa conference; in 1935 he was appointed CB, in 1941 advanced to KCB, and in 1946 to GCB; in 1938 he had been appointed KBE. He was also a commander of the Légion d'honneur and held other foreign decorations.   REUBEN KELF-COHEN, *rev.* MARK POTTLE

Sources *Public Administration*, 29 (1951), 301–15 · W. Ashworth and M. Pegg, *The nationalized industry: 1946–1982* (1986), vol. 5 of *The history of the British coal industry* (1984–93) · *The Times* (10 Dec 1948) · *The Times* (21 Dec 1948) · *The Times* (30 Dec 1948) · *The Times* (26 Feb 1951) · private information (1971) · *CGPLA Eng. & Wales* (1951)
Likenesses H. Coster, photographs, 1930–39, NPG · W. Stoneman, photographs, 1938, NPG · H. Carr, oils, 1942, IWM · photograph, repro. in *Public Administration*
Wealth at death £8420 7s. 0d.: probate, 12 June 1951, *CGPLA Eng. & Wales*

Street, Fanny (1877–1962), educationist, was born at North Street, Wilton, near Salisbury, on 21 November 1877, the eldest of the six children of Henry Street (*d.* 1917), who was described as a working baker, grocer, and farmer (Powell, 21), and his wife, Sarah Anne Butt, an elementary schoolteacher. Arthur George *Street was her brother. She was educated at Wilton Elementary School, where she became a pupil teacher. She then entered Salisbury Diocesan Training College before moving to Whitelands Training College, Chelsea, and then returning to Salisbury to become a lecturer in history for three years. In 1905, recognizing that she needed a degree, she sat the London intermediate exam, relinquished her teaching position, and became a student at Royal Holloway College, University of London. She was awarded a scholarship in addition to the prestigious Martin Holloway prize, an annual award for the best and most efficient student in respect of academic and intellectual distinction. She graduated with a first-class honours degree in medieval and modern history.

Street was a junior lecturer at Whitelands before becoming, in 1907, mistress of method and head of staff at Barnard's Cross, an extension of Salisbury Training College. In 1911 she returned to Royal Holloway College as staff lecturer in history, and completed her MA in 1915. There she joined a group of scholars, including Helen Cam, who undertook original research; her own work was on the borough of Sarum. Academic life, she later said, was her 'first experience of real democracy' (*The Times*), and she was a leading figure in the campaign by former students to secure the representation of women on Royal Holloway College's governing body. Following a High Court judgment in 1909 the college's foundation deed was amended in 1912 to allow women to become governors. In national politics Street supported the constitutional suffragist movement, and once women gained the vote she became an active member of the Labour Party.

From 1917 until the end of the First World War, Street was an assistant administrative officer at the Ministry of Food. In 1919, in her role as organizing secretary of the Teachers' Christian Union, she became a member of a group considering the educational opportunities for working women. The outcome was a plan to establish a residential working women's college under the auspices of the Young Women's Christian Association. At the end of the year a suburban, double-fronted house called The Holt, in Beckenham, Kent, was acquired on a six-year lease. In 1920 Street became principal of the first residential working women's college, which was intended to be the women's counterpart of Ruskin College, Oxford. She was responsible for developing the college from its beginning, at Beckenham with eleven students, through to its eventual move to Surbiton, when the local council adopted the name Hillcroft College to associate it by analogy with the existing Fircroft and Avoncroft colleges. By Easter 1933, when Street retired, 252 students had passed through the college. Her retirement was a response to the constant strain of trying to deal with the college's financially precarious position, coupled with the problems of securing grants or bursaries for the students. Initially she went to France to recuperate for several months, and then returned to England to live in Chelsea with Miss Margaret Powell. She continued to be a member of the college council until 1936.

In 1933 Street became a governor of Royal Holloway College, as a representative of the old students' association, of which she was secretary. From 1944 to 1945 she was acting principal of the college while a new principal was sought. By then she was over sixty-six, and the domestic rules that she sought to impose on the students were regarded by some as outmoded. She played an important part, however, in fusing the college into a more homogeneous community, following its previous phase of internal divisions. Following her second retirement she continued to live in Chelsea. For many years she was a leading figure in the British Federation of University Women.

Throughout her life Street was acclaimed for her outstanding gifts as an able administrator—a practical, down-to-earth teacher, never the remote or absent-minded intellectual. She was interested in doing practical things, but though a renowned cook she never learnt to drive a car. Her powerful and independent mind—a trait that she shared with her brother—reflected her family upbringing on her parents' tenanted farm in Wiltshire. Her religious convictions were expressed in *The Faith of a Teacher*, published by the Student Christian Union in 1924; her pamphlet *Our Political Responsibility* (1922) urged the duty of Christians to participate in politics. She died, unmarried, at Stoneycrest Nursing Home, Hindhead, Surrey, on 20 March 1962.   JOHN MARTIN

Sources H. Cam, *The Times* (24 March 1962), 10 · *WWW, 1961–70* · M. Powell, *The history of Hillcroft College* (1964) · C. Bingham, *The history of Royal Holloway College* (1987) · P. Street, *My father A. G. Street* (1969) · *CGPLA Eng. & Wales* (1962) · b. cert.

Likenesses photograph, *c*.1944–1945, repro. in Bingham, *History of Royal Holloway*, following p. 256 · photograph, repro. in Powell, *History of Hillcroft*, facing p. 1

Wealth at death £10,508 19s.: probate, 30 May 1962, *CGPLA Eng. & Wales*

Street, George Edmund (1824–1881), architect and architectural theorist, was born on 20 June 1824 at Woodford, Essex, the third son of Thomas Henry Street (*d*. 1840), solicitor, and his second wife, Mary Anne Millington (*d*. 1851). A principal shaper of the architectural style later called 'High Victorian', he was also one of the most thoughtful architectural writers of his day.

Education Street attended schools in Mitcham and Camberwell until the age of fifteen, when his father retired and moved the family to Devon. There he took painting lessons and explored the local architectural antiquities with his brother Thomas, but despite his artistic and antiquarian leanings he found his first employment back in the family law office in London. After this brief professional detour and his father's death, Street was articled to Owen Carter of Winchester, an enthusiastic antiquarian and a competent but unremarkable architect who produced both classical and Gothic designs. Street was Carter's pupil for two years and his assistant for a third, before moving to London in 1844, when he found a place in the office of George Gilbert Scott.

Street was a craggily handsome man with a powerful intellect, and a brilliant draughtsman, whose special forte was the fluid pen-and-ink perspective. In Scott's office in the late 1840s these talents were fully appreciated, as

George Edmund Street (1824–1881), by Lock & Whitfield, pubd 1878

work went ahead simultaneously on numerous large projects. Street's fellow assistants were George Frederick Bodley and William White, destined to share with him the artistic leadership of their generation; for them the purist Gothic revival, championed by Augustus Welby Northmore Pugin and the Ecclesiological Society, was rapidly falling into disfavour. Together they worked on the great Nicholaikirche for Hamburg, where Scott dared to use German precedents, and on stark, big-boned churches for Alderney and St John's, Newfoundland, which turned their backs on the soft forms of English Decorated Gothic which were still preferred by Gothic revival purists. It was in Scott's office that the more confident eclecticism and the powerful visual language of High Victorian architecture were born.

Early works Street played an important role in this swift reshaping of architectural taste. Some of his first independent work, executed in Cornwall while he was still employed by Scott, was conservatively Puginian. For example, the little church of St Peter at Treverbyn, Cornwall, of 1848–50, is gentle and picturesque in composition and faithful to the precedents of English Decorated Gothic. But another early work in Cornwall, St Mary at Biscovey of 1847–8, is Early English in detail and already forthright—almost primitive—in spirit, with details borrowed from heretofore neglected Cornish exemplars. Its freedom and vigour herald High Victorianism.

In 1849 Street established his own practice, first in London and then in Wallingford Street, Wantage, Berkshire, as his early Cornish connections were supplanted by more important ties to the diocese of Oxford. He served as

Oxford diocesan architect from 1850 until his death, enjoying the patronage and friendship of Bishop Samuel Wilberforce. On 17 June 1852 Street married Mariquita (Marique) Proctor (*d.* 1874), and that year moved to Beaumont Street, Oxford; then, having begun to establish a national reputation, he returned to London, renting a house at 33 Montague Place, in 1856. (He maintained his principal residence in London for the rest of his life, moving to 51 Russell Square in 1862 and to a great house at 14 Cavendish Place in 1870.)

Street's designs and writing of the first dozen years of his practice, in Oxford and London, defined the character of High Victorian architecture. In responding to mid-Victorian needs, his work became increasingly secular and urban, and although church-building remained the mainstay of his practice and his own high-church beliefs were unwavering, the religious symbolism that had so fully invested the work of earlier Gothic revivalists now diminished. Moreover, Street rejected the narrow historical and geographical confines within which Pugin and the Ecclesiological Society had bound the Gothic revival. He embraced eclecticism, and he viewed architectural history as an always dynamic system in which elements from different places and periods were transformed by a process of perpetual modernization that he and his contemporaries called 'development', a term he apparently borrowed from contemporary theology.

Street was a strenuous logician who, more effectively than any other architect of his generation, explained the rationale and *modus operandi* of eclectic design. He first laid out his philosophical position in three seminal articles in *The Ecclesiologist* in 1850–53. Later publications reiterated the same themes while supplying a wealth of information about Gothic architecture on the continent, thereby providing the material with which eclecticism could be put into practice. Street travelled widely, traversing France, Germany, and the Low Countries and following the footsteps of John Ruskin to northern Italy—all in the early 1850s. He reported on these travels with lectures and publications. Numerous articles on France and Germany appeared in *The Ecclesiologist* in 1854–9, and his influential book on northern Italian Gothic, which reiterated his position on architectural eclecticism and widened the appreciation of Ruskin's views, came out in 1855. A second book, on Spanish Gothic, was published in 1865. Both books were revised for second editions.

Street put his ideas to work in creating scores of quintessentially High Victorian buildings whose vigour and monumentality responded to the visual challenges of the mid-nineteenth-century environment. In his early works in Oxfordshire, such as the Wantage vicarage (1849–50) and the theological college in Cuddesdon (1852–4), the growing energy of his style seems to emerge almost unbidden from the local vernacular. But in later designs and especially after his move to London in 1856, foreign precedents are tellingly employed, including Italian polychromy, muscular French stonework, the Baltic's adroit use of brick. The church and accompanying school, vicarage, and houses of All Saints, Boyne Hill, Berkshire (1854–

65), blaze with quasi-Italian colour, and his best-known early work, St James-the-Less, Westminster (1859–61), is a powerful urban church which combines a French apsidal plan and plate tracery, a campanile and polychromy of Italian origin, and a north German sensitivity to the monumental potential of brickwork and the making of space for worship.

Major works In his early use of polychromy Street was only a half step behind William Butterfield, whose church of All Saints, Margaret Street, in London (1849–59), was the first large embodiment of the fashion. But by virtue of his publications and more outgoing personality, Street overshadowed Butterfield and his accomplishments. Moreover, Street's use of colour soon declined, and the power of most of his mature works came from a fondness for the simple and muscular forms of early French Gothic, a taste which he shared with the rather eccentric William Burges, whom, like Butterfield, Street tended to outshine. Street's 'Early French' appears in his design for the Lille Cathedral competition of 1855–6 (where it is combined with polychromatic brick). He was placed second in that contest, and he fared similarly in the competition for the Crimean Memorial Church (Constantinople, 1856), in which he entered another Early French proposal. The executed Constantinople church of 1863–8, for which Street ultimately received the commission, is an exceedingly powerful variation on the same theme. Perhaps his masterpiece in this vein is the church of Sts Philip and James, Oxford (1858–65), whose mighty ashlar forms are only barely constrained by the equal might of Street's intelligent eye. Other notable exemplars are the churches of St John the Evangelist, Whitwell on the Hill (North Riding, Yorkshire, 1858–60), St John the Evangelist, Howsham (East Riding, Yorkshire, 1859–60), and All Saints, Denstone (Staffordshire, 1860–62).

In addition to pioneering the bold and characteristic—but ultimately exhausting—vocabulary of High Victorian architecture, Street was also one of the first to test alternatives. All Saints' Church in Brightwalton, Berkshire (1862–3), turns the clock back to the gentle picturesque of the English Middle Pointed, and Street's precociousness in reverting to such forms is underscored by the fact that between 1852 and 1862 he trained or employed three of the leading designers of the new 'Queen Anne' generation: Philip Webb, William Morris, and Richard Norman Shaw. The filiation is nowhere more visible than in Shaw's bravura sketching style. Perfectly suited to rendering the gentle picturesque character of his buildings—and coincidentally readily reproduced by the new photolithographic process used by the architectural magazines—Shaw's technique descended directly from Street's.

Street's greatest commission, the Royal Courts of Justice in London, was designed during the time when High Victorian tastes were waning. The competition design of 1866–7 is a last, brilliant effort at High Victorian stylistic synthesis, Early French in its power, but specifically intended to unite—through skilful 'development'—the irregular vigour of Gothic with the quasi-classical symmetry and monumentality appropriate for a public building. (Street's contemporary neo-Byzantine entry in the competition for an extension to the National Gallery took the quest for Gothic–classical synthesis even further.) The long series of revised schemes for the law courts increasingly displayed the unabashed picturesque that Shaw and his contemporaries had begun to make fashionable. The final design (1870–82) is a curious mixture of strong, High Victorian detail and irregular, almost relaxed, composition. It was approved in the teeth of Liberal opposition only because Street had won the support of William Ewart Gladstone, the prime minister, himself a high-churchman and Gothic enthusiast.

Later works Other later works reflect more explicitly the desiderata of late Victorian architecture. The High Victorian conviction that art was served by transnational and transtemporal interbreeding had waned, and Street's own home, Holmdale, at Holmbury St Mary (Surrey, 1873–6), is a relatively pure Old English half-timbered manor, with obvious debts to Shaw. Foreign precedents were now treated more circumspectly and usually restricted to special circumstances, notably the very Italian design for St Paul's American Church, Rome (1872–6).

Large projects of great prestige joined the law courts in keeping Street's office fully occupied through the last years of his life. These included the nave and towered west façade for Bristol Cathedral (1867–88) and an almost total reconstruction of Christ Church, Dublin (1868–78).

The vastness of these projects did not deter Street from maintaining an unusually high degree of artistic control over all of them, unlike some of his contemporaries. His astonishing rapidity of drawing and his unmatched combination of artistic originality and historical knowledge enabled him to keep ahead of his assistants. Seemingly tireless, Street continued to travel abroad every year, but his morale was sapped by the bureaucratic wranglings necessitated by his larger commissions, especially the Royal Courts of Justice. He was also cruelly injured by the death in 1874 of Marique, his wife of twenty-two years, and his eight-week second marriage, to Jessie Holland (a friend of his first wife), whom he married on 11 January 1876, ended tragically in her death from an illness contracted during their wedding trip to Italy in March that year.

Street received all the honours of his profession. He was elected an associate of the Royal Academy in 1866 and a full member in 1871. In 1874 he was awarded the gold medal of the Royal Institute of British Architects (RIBA), which he loyally accepted after Ruskin turned it down to chastise architects for their restoration practices, and in 1881, the year of his death, he served both as president of RIBA and as professor of architecture at the Royal Academy. As president of RIBA he stood up for the artists in the dispute that was growing between those who viewed architecture as an art and those who judged it to be a profession, and his Royal Academy lectures were the last to

essay the arduous High Victorian task of reconciling the architecture of the middle ages and life of the nineteenth century.

Street died at his home, 14 Cavendish Place, London, on 18 December 1881, after suffering two strokes. His death at the age of fifty-seven was surely hastened by the physical and emotional strain of work, and his greatest commission, the law courts, was opened a year after his death. Street was buried on 29 December in Westminster Abbey, near his old friend and former employer Sir Gilbert Scott, and beneath a brass designed by George Frederick Bodley, with whom he had worked in Scott's office. His only son, Arthur Edmund Street (d. 1938), oversaw the completion of many of his works.   DAVID B. BROWNLEE

Sources A. E. Street, *Memoir of George Edmund Street* (1888) · P. Joyce, 'The architecture of George Edmund Street, RA', *George Edmund Street in Yorkshire*, ed. J. Hutchinson (1981), 5–14 · D. B. Brownlee, *The law courts: the architecture of George Edmund Street* (1984) · D. B. Brownlee, 'The first High Victorians: British architectural theory in the 1840s', *Architectura*, 15 (1985), 33–46 · H.-R. Hitchcock, 'G. E. Street in the 1850s', *Journal of the Society of Architectural Historians*, 19 (1960), 145–71 · J. N. Summerson, 'Two London churches', *Victorian architecture: four studies in evaluation* (1970), 47–76 · J. N. Summerson, 'A Victorian competition', *Victorian architecture: four studies in evaluation* (1970), 77–117 · M. H. Port, 'The new law courts competition, 1866–67', *Architectural History*, 11 (1968), 75–93 · N. Jackson, 'The un-Englishness of G. E. Street's church of St James-the-Less', *Architectural History*, 23 (1980), 86–94 · G. G. King, ed., *George Edmund Street: unpublished notes and reprinted papers* (1916) · G. E. Street, *Brick and marble architecture in the middle ages: notes on tours in the north of Italy* (1855) · G. E. Street, *Some account of Gothic architecture in Spain* (1865) · CGPLA Eng. & Wales (1882)
Archives PRO, drawings and MSS · RA, drawings and MSS · V&A, drawings and MSS | BL, letters to W. E. Gladstone, Add. MSS 44404–44786, *passim* · Bodl. Oxf., letters to F. G. Stephens
Likenesses H. H. Armstead, statue and memorial, 1886, Royal Courts of Justice, London · H. H. Armstead, bust, RIBA · Lock & Whitfield, woodburytype photograph, NPG; repro. in *Men of mark* (1878) [see illus.] · photographs, repro. in Street, *Memoir of George Edmund Street* · prints, NPG · wood-engraving (after photograph), BM, NPG; repro. in *ILN* (14 Jan 1882)
Wealth at death £55,136 13s. 6d.: probate, 28 March 1882, CGPLA Eng. & Wales

Street, Harry (1919–1984), jurist, was born on 17 June 1919 at 23 Station Road, Kersley, near Bolton, Lancashire, the only child of Alfred Street (1890–1947), builder, and his wife, Lilian, *née* Livesey (1891–1936/7), teacher. He was educated at Farnworth grammar school from 1930 to 1935 and Manchester University from 1935 to 1938. He graduated LLB with first class honours in law in 1938, was articled in Bolton, and qualified, with distinction, as a solicitor in 1940. He served in the Royal Air Force (flight lieutenant) as a navigator from 1942 to 1946, when he became a lecturer in the faculty of law at Manchester. He married Muriel Helene Swain (b. 1920) in 1947; they had two sons and a daughter, all of whom became solicitors. In 1947–8 he held a Commonwealth Fund fellowship at Columbia University. On his return to Manchester he added, in 1951, a PhD to his LLM and was made senior lecturer. From 1952 to 1956 he was professor and head of the department of law at the University of Nottingham. He then returned to a chair at Manchester which he held until his death. He was visiting professor at Harvard law school in 1957–8.

Street achieved great distinction as a writer and made an exceptional reputation as a law teacher. He was one of the few successful English practitioners of the 'case method' or Socratic method which he had observed with admiration at Columbia: this consists in teaching not by lecturing but by putting questions in class to law students on material that they are required to prepare in advance. This rigorous method of instruction had a profound effect on his students, more fully appreciated in retrospect than at the time—an experience, one said years later, more terrifying than appearing before any High Court judge.

Much of Street's writing was of a pioneering nature. *The Principles of Administrative Law* (1951; 5th edn, 1973, with J. A. G. Griffith) was the first textbook in a neglected subject which now features prominently in all law schools. *A Comparative Study of Governmental Liability* (1953), a product of Street's work at Columbia with Walter Gellhorn, revealed the need for reform of the civil liability of the state. *Freedom, the Individual and Law* (1963; 7th edn, 1993, ed. Geoffrey Robertson) was the first comprehensive survey of the state of civil liberties in England. Its publishers fairly claim that it has been a watchdog over fundamental freedoms. *Principles of the Law of Damages* (1962), another original work, had much influence on later writing. At Nottingham he wrote a textbook, *The Law of Torts* (1956; 10th edn, 1997, ed. Margaret Brazier), with an approach different from that of the established classics, with which it still competes successfully. Glanville Williams hailed it as the first to be arranged in the right teaching order, beginning with specific torts and leaving general principles to the end. It stressed the interest of the plaintiff rather than the conduct of the defendant. In 1968 Street delivered the annual Hamlyn lectures, published as *Justice in the Welfare State* (2nd edn, 1975), at the University of Liverpool. He also wrote *Law Relating to Nuclear Energy* (1966, with F. R. Frame) and *Road Accidents* (1968, with D. W. Elliott).

Street rendered substantial public service. He was chairman of the committee on racial discrimination in 1967 and of the royal commission on the Fiji electoral system in 1975–6. He was a member of the royal commission on the constitution from 1969 to 1973 and the Monopolies and Mergers Commission between 1973 and 1980.

Friendly and unassuming, Street was well liked by colleagues and students. He was generous in recognizing merit but blunt in condemning what he saw as shoddy or inadequate—as some authors of the many books he reviewed would ruefully testify. He was a great popularizer of the law: consultant editor of the Reader's Digest *You and Your Rights* and Granada Television's *This is Your Right*. He put theory into practice, once invoking the medieval remedy for cattle-trespass, 'distress damage feasant', against a corporation bus which had crashed into his father's garden.

Street was elected FBA in 1968, and made CBE in 1978 and honorary LLD of the University of Southampton in 1974. He died of a heart attack on 20 April 1984, while walking on Force Crag, Braithwaite, in the Lake District. His remains were cremated at Stockport crematorium on 26 April.   J. C. SMITH

Sources J. C. Smith, 'Harry Street, 1919–1984', *PBA*, 72 (1986), 473–90 · *CGPLA Eng. & Wales* (1984) · *WWW* · private information (2004) · H. Street, 'The university law teacher', *Journal of the Society of Public Teachers of Law*, 14 (1979), 243–52 · b. cert. · d. cert.
Archives JRL, papers | SOUND BL NSA, performance recording
Likenesses photograph, 1957, U. Nott., department of law · photograph, repro. in Smith, 'Harry Street', pl. 29
Wealth at death £293,281: probate, 17 Aug 1984, *CGPLA Eng. & Wales*

Street, (Cecil) John Charles [*pseuds.* John Rhode, Miles Burton] (1884–1964), army officer and writer of detective stories, was born in Gibraltar on 3 May 1884, the son of General John Alfred Street CB (1822–1889) and his wife, the daughter of the Revd James Holroyd. At the time of Cecil's birth his father was colonel of the 2nd battalion, the Cameronians (Scottish Rifles), stationed in Cawnpore, Bengal. Educated at Wellington College and the Royal Military Academy, Woolwich (1901–3), he was commissioned into the Royal Garrison Artillery in July 1903; he served with 23 company at Fort Grange (the western land defences of Portsmouth harbour) and afterwards with 16 company at Clarence barracks in Portsmouth. He resigned his commission on 24 March 1906, one month after marrying Hyacinth Maud (*d.* 1949) of Fareham, Hampshire, daughter of Major John Denis Kirwan RA.

Following the outbreak of the First World War, Street rejoined the Royal Artillery as a lieutenant in the special reserve in September 1914. He served on the western front, taking part in the ill-fated battle of Loos in September 1915, and, as an acting major, he was awarded the MC in January 1918. At the end of the war he was listed as being at the War Office and 'employed at the Ministry of Labour' but was possibly serving as an intelligence officer in Ireland. He was made OBE (military division) in January 1919 and left the army in 1920.

While on the western front in 1916, using the pseudonym F.O.O. (field observation officer), Street wrote two books on the Royal Artillery, both of which were well received. *With the Guns* (covering the battle of Loos) was described by *The Times* as 'a remarkable contribution to the literature of the war' while the *Pall Mall Gazette* considered it 'one of the best war books that have appeared'. *The Making of a Gunner*, which appeared later in 1916, included a severe indictment of the 'priesthood' of older officers of the Royal Garrison Artillery who 'utterly discouraged any attempt on their part to experiment with guns on wheels … the Coast Defences lost all sight of what would be their true role in time of war and lapsed into a condition of torpid complacency.' Such views perhaps explain his resignation of his commission a decade earlier.

Street's first foray into fiction was his 1917 semi-autobiographical novel *The Worldly Hope*, again by F.O.O. It was the story of a lieutenant of the Royal Garrison Artillery (special reserve) who arrived in France six weeks before the battle of Loos as senior subaltern to a siege battery. On leaving the army Street continued writing by specializing in strategic and current affairs. In 1921, now writing as I.O. (intelligence officer), he published *The Administration of Ireland, 1920* and a year later, under his own name, he published *Ireland in 1921*. As I.O. he also published *G.Q.G.—French Headquarters, 1915–1918*, a translation from the French of a work by Jean de Pierrefeu. Under his own name he wrote *Hungary and Democracy* (1923) and *East of Prague* (1924); he then criticized French behaviour following the peace treaties in *The Treachery of France* (1924). A biography of Rufus Isaacs, *Lord Reading*, appeared under Street's own name in 1928.

In 1925 Street published his first detective story, *The Paddington Mystery*, using the pseudonym John Rhode, and in that identity he quickly became one of the leading authors in the golden age of English detective fiction. By 1928 he was also writing other detective and mystery stories using the pseudonym Miles Burton. Thereafter his output was prodigious: in the thirty years from 1930 he published a new detective novel every three months. John Rhode's private detective was the scientist Dr Priestley who advised and assisted Inspector, later Superintendent, Jimmy Waghorn of Scotland Yard, while Miles Burton's detective was Inspector Arnold, who was ably assisted by the inspired amateur sleuth Desmond Merrion. Street's popularity with readers who wanted a challenging plot or mystery continued long after his death although leading critics, particularly H. R. F. Keating, considered his books 'dull', with both 'ingenuity of plot and cardboardity of character' (Keating, *Bedside Companion to Crime*, 223).

In the early 1930s Street was, with Dorothy L. Sayers, Agatha Christie, Freeman Wills Crofts, and others, an active member of the select Detection Club whose members funded their Gerrard Street premises and their ceremonial club dinners by publishing books with chapters written serially by different members. As John Rhode, Street contributed to their compilations *The Floating Admiral* (1931) and *Ask a Policeman* (1933). He contributed a study of the 1860 Constance Kent case to the Detection Club's true crime collection *The Anatomy of Murder* (1936), having, in 1928, written up the Kent case in the Famous Trials series. In all, from 1925 to 1960 nearly eighty books appeared under the name of John Rhode and another sixty-five under that of Miles Burton. As John Rhode he also edited collections of detective short stories.

John Street was a generous but intensely private person who seldom spoke of his past, even to friends. In spite of his popular literary success he shunned publicity and, in his final years, became somewhat reclusive. Although internationally known as the author of the John Rhode books, his authorship of those by Miles Burton was not common knowledge in his lifetime. He lived in Somerset, Norfolk, and then Suffolk, often locating his stories in those areas and frequently using local place names for his supporting characters. His first wife, Hyacinth, died in 1949 and later that year on 9 November, aged sixty-five, he married Eileen Annette Waller (1894/5–1967), the daughter of John Waller, a civil engineer. There were no children

of either marriage. In the 1950s Street and his new wife moved to Seaford on the Sussex coast to live near Eileen's relatives. Street himself died of arterial thrombosis on 8 December 1964 at the Leaf Hospital, Eastbourne, and, in accordance with his wishes, was cremated.

ROBIN WOOLVEN

Sources *Army List* (1903–6) · *Army List* (1914–20) · *Royal Artillery List* (1903–6) · *Royal Artillery List* (1914–20) · *LondG* (1 Jan 1918) · *LondG* (3 Jan 1919) · H. R. F. Keating, *Whodunit?* (1982) · H. R. F. Keating, *The bedside companion to crime* (1989) · H. Haycraft, ed., *The art of the mystery story* (1946); 2nd edn, with new introduction by R. W. Winks (1992) · H. Haycraft, *Murder for pleasure: the life and times of the detective story* (1941) · private information (2004) [P. Ibbotson of Westbourne, Bournemouth; Michael Lane, cousin and executor of Eileen Street] · *The Times* (2 Jan 1965), 13 · d. cert. · B. Benstock and T. F. Staley, eds., *British mystery writers, 1920–1939*, DLitB, 77 (1989) · Royal Military Academy, Woolwich, Royal Military Academy records · m. cert. [Hyacinth Maud Kirwan] · m. cert. [Eileen Annette Waller] · will, 9 Nov 1949 · codicil, 13 July 1961 · census returns, 1901
Archives Wheaton College, Illinois, Marion E. Wade Center, corresp. with D. L. Sayers
Likenesses photograph, repro. in Haycraft, *Murder for pleasure* · portrait, repro. in J. Rhode, *The House on Tollard Ridge*, Penguin edn (Sept 1940)
Wealth at death £36,605 15s.—gross, on which £9808 13s. was paid in tax: probate, 23 Feb 1965, *CGPLA Eng. & Wales*

Street, Peter (*bap.* 1553, *d.* 1609), builder, was baptized on 1 July 1553 at St Stephen, Coleman Street, close to Guildhall, the fourth-born child of John Street (*d.* 1563), a citizen of London and joiner, and his wife, Margaret; she was apparently the only child of Thomas Bullasse, a citizen and freeman of the Merchant Taylors, one of the leading livery companies, and his wife, Edith. The Streets were married at St Stephen's on 16 May 1546, and eight children were born between 1548 and 1563, of whom Peter was the only one to survive to adulthood: three of his sisters, and his father, succumbed to the plague in the autumn of 1563. On 15 August 1569 Peter's mother became the second wife of William Marryot (Marrett), a citizen and brewer.

On 25 March 1570 Street was apprenticed for an eight-year term to William Brittaine of the Carpenters' Company. In the following year he was taken over by Robert Maskall, a very prominent freeman of the company, who had perhaps noted a marked talent. He was made free on 26 March 1577. The Carpenters' Company, consisting of craftsmen in wood, was of major importance before the great fire of 1666: its handsome coat of arms dates from 1466, and its charter from 1477—much earlier than those of a number of more famous companies. Successive Carpenters' halls have stood just within the north wall of the City, between Moorgate and Bishopsgate, and in the parish of All Hallows, London Wall.

Street's career prospered, and by 6 August 1581 he was able to acquire a company house adjoining the hall, formerly occupied by his late master, putting down the substantial sum of £10 for a twenty-one-year lease, and paying annual rent of 40s.; in 1584 he also leased one of the company's gardens. He married a woman called Elizabeth (*d.* 1613), and their first child, John (1584–1620), was baptized at St Stephen's on 22 March 1584.

Street took more than twenty apprentices during his career, many of them from various English counties and at least two from Wales; some left before completing their terms, but he made six free of the City. In September 1586 (September marked the start of the company year) he was elected to the livery, and in 1598 he was appointed second warden. The court minute book for September 1594 to September 1600, covering the most momentous period of his life, is missing, but it is clear that company members did not take kindly to his preoccupation with the Theatre in 1598–9, the Globe on Bankside in 1599, and the Fortune in Finsbury in 1600. In 1608 they accused him (somewhat unfairly) of having neglected company business for years and seeking to 'take his ease'.

In the 1590s the Burbage family was facing a crisis: the ground landlord of the Theatre in Shoreditch was refusing to renew the original twenty-one-year lease of 1576; and James Burbage, supported by his sons, laid out £600 for part of the former monastic property in Black-friars, intending to convert it to a playing-place. He moved from Shoreditch to live in the precinct, and Street, whom he had no doubt contracted to carry out the conversion, acquired the lease of a house and wood wharf in Bride-well, on the other side of the Fleet close to its confluence with the Thames, and linked to Blackfriars by a wooden footbridge. This emerges from a court of requests suit of 1596–7, in the course of which Street describes himself as an ordinary servant in Queen Elizabeth's household. He states that it is 'a great ease' for him to be able to 'bringe his Tymber and Frames' from 'the Countrie [Berkshire, where prefabrication was done] by water to his owne house' in London (REQ 2/91/57).

The conversion work was almost completed by November 1596. But the lord chamberlain, Lord Hunsdon, a sympathetic patron of Shakespeare's company, had died in the previous July, and the whole Blackfriars project was finally blocked by influential residents of the precinct. At this critical time James Burbage died, probably at the end of January 1597. His sons were now faced with the prospect of having no playing-place. Eventually they found a plot in Southwark; Cuthbert commissioned Street and his men to dismantle the Theatre and use the timbers to build the Globe, and the enterprise began at the end of December 1598.

In January 1600 Street began work for Henslowe and Edward Alleyn on the Fortune, on a site just north of the present Barbican Centre: the contract—which Street initialled 'P S'—is for a square instead of polygonal building, incorporating features of the Globe.

Street seems to have been a man of quick temper. The Carpenters' court minutes of 26 July 1608 state that he had verbally abused the master and wardens several times, had refused to attend the meeting, and had been committed to prison. However, the aldermen, meeting at Guildhall on the same day, found that the freedom of the City granted to Street and his six apprentices had not been recorded: they ordered an entry to be made, and a copy given to Street, and his son was made a freeman by patrimony on 3 August.

In that month the King's Men moved into the Black-friars theatre, and presumably Street was commissioned to adapt it. But he died, in Blackfriars, in May 1609, and was buried at St Bride's on the 13th: 'Peter Streat, Carpenter'. The court of Bridewell Hospital, meeting on the funeral day, appointed his son John to succeed him as their carpenter. Peter's widow, Mistress Street, was buried on 7 April 1613. Street's two open-air theatres were destroyed by fire, the Globe in 1613 and the Fortune in 1621.

MARY EDMOND

Sources M. Edmond, 'Peter Street, 1553–1609: builder of playhouses', *Shakespeare Survey*, 45 (1993), 101–14 · M. Edmond, 'The builder of the Rose Theatre', *Theatre Notebook*, 44 (1990), 50–54 · Carpenters' court minute books, GL, 4329 · wardens' account books, GL, 4326 · B. Marsh, J. Ainsworth, and A. M. Millard, eds., *Records of the Worshipful Company of Carpenters*, 7 vols. (1913–68) · J. Ridley, *A history of the Carpenters' Company* (1995) · parish register, St Stephen Coleman Street, 1 July 1553, GL, MSS 4448, 4449/1 [baptism] · parish register, St Bride's, Fleet Street, 13 May 1609, GL, MS 6538 [burial] · Bridewell Hospital court minutes, 1609, GL, MS 513, vol. 5, fol. 347 · Carpenters' court minutes, 26 July 1608, GL, MS 4329/3, fols. 167–167v · repertories of the court of aldermen, CLRO, fol. 258 · GL, MS 9172, fol. 177 [Thomas Bullasse] · GL, MS 9168/16, fol. 87v [Thomas Bullasse] · PRO, PROB 6/10, fol. 87 [John Street] · *Henslowe's diary*, ed. R. A. Foakes and R. T. Rickert (1961) · A. Gurr, 'Money or audiences: the impact of Shakespeare's Globe', *Theatre Notebook*, 42 (1988), 3–14

Street, Sir Thomas (*bap.* **1625**, *d.* **1696**), judge, was baptized on 13 October 1625 at St Andrew's, Worcester, the son of George Street (*d.* 1643) of Worcester, brewer, and Elizabeth (*d.* 1644), daughter of Thomas Andrews of Barnshall, Upton upon Severn, Worcestershire. He was one of sixteen children, though only he and three others survived. He entered Lincoln College, Oxford, on 22 April 1642, but returned to Worcester without a degree early in 1645 after the death of his father, a former Worcester mayor and ship money collector. He was briefly imprisoned by parliamentarian forces at this time.

Street entered the Inner Temple on 22 November 1646, and lived intermittently with his brother John at his family's Worcester home, The Friary, until 1650. During this period he married Maria (*d.* 1668), daughter of John Wightwick, serjeant-at-law, of Tamworth; they had three sons, all of whom studied at Oxford, and two daughters.

Street was called to the bar on 24 November 1653, and began a law practice that kept him closely engaged with the city of his birth. In January 1659 Worcester sent him to parliament for the first time, but a petition from some of the inhabitants soon followed him there, condemning Street as 'a person who had been in arms, and a common swearer, [and who] was chosen by the profane rabble and cavaliers' (*Diary of Thomas Burton*, 3.70). The Commons investigated the charges, which Street answered by denying that he had fought for the king, though he admitted that he had worn a sword while in the company of royalist soldiers in 1645. Little more came of the accusations and Street was again chosen at Worcester to sit in the convention in 1660 and for the parliament seated in 1661. In the Commons Street's greatest efforts were reserved for Worcestershire interests: he served on committees or spoke for bills concerned with the county's salt and cloth industries, with Severn fishing, and with uniting parishes in Droitwich, whose recorder Street had become by 1664.

By then Street's legal career was on the rise, beginning with his work for the cathedral chapter in Worcester, for which he handled various issues ranging from estate management to a defence of the cathedral in respect of fee farm rents owed to the queen mother since the 1640s. Street should not be confused with a younger cousin of the same name who served as Worcester's mayor in 1667–8 and as justice of the peace the following year; it was probably this cousin who acted briefly as Worcester's town clerk in 1668. In November 1669 Street became a bencher of the Inner Temple, and on 2 October 1672 Worcester corporation unanimously made him the city's recorder.

Throughout the 1660s and 1670s Street was outspoken in parliament against protestant dissenters, and he was increasingly seen as a supporter of court policies. In December 1667 he defended Chief Justice Sir John Kelyng from charges in the Commons that he mistreated jurors. By now Street himself was a judge in Wales; in 1677 he became chief justice for south Wales and a serjeant-at-law, and in October 1678 a king's serjeant.

Worcester returned Street to both parliaments in 1679 together with Sir Francis Winnington, who now moved against court interests as surely as Street supported them. Street's loyalty was rewarded on 21 April 1681 when he was sworn a baron of the court of exchequer; the king knighted him in June. His loyalty and his concern with the politics of his home city converged in late 1681 when, probably owing to his influence, the first *quo warranto* was brought against one of England's urban corporations. This was a direct attack on twenty-six of his foes in Worcester, all of them notable for supporting Winnington, who became their most ardent defender in court. In 1683 the court's judgment ousted and fined all twenty-six, marking an important legal and political triumph for Street. In May 1683 he resigned as recorder of Worcester, probably because he was so heavily committed in London; in July the reconstituted city corporation voted him its thanks for his help in the *quo warranto* proceedings.

In 1683 Street sat in judgment in the Old Bailey with Sir Francis Pemberton in the trial of the Rye House Plot conspirators, though in the following year some noted how lenient he was toward Quakers at the Northampton assizes. On 29 October 1684 he became a justice of common pleas but in June 1686, in the crucial case of *Godden* v. *Hales*, he was the only judge to declare against the royal dispensing power—a sign of judicial independence that incorrectly convinced some that he would be turned off the bench. Later authors charged that Street gave his decision in collusion with the crown in order to give an appearance of judicial integrity to proceedings in the case. No contemporary evidence exists to support this claim, and Street's memorial in Worcester Cathedral includes this decision among his signal accomplishments. On 16 September 1686 Street married Penelope (*d.* 1696), the daughter of Sir Rowland Berkeley of Cotheridge, Worcestershire.

After the revolution of 1688 William of Orange refused to see Street, and he lost his place on the bench. He retired to Cotheridge and Worcester. He died at one of those two places on 8 March 1696 and was buried in the south cloister of Worcester Cathedral, having left a modest estate to his grandchildren. PAUL D. HALLIDAY

Sources HoP, *Commons, 1660–90*, 3.501–2 · W. R. Buchanan-Dunlop, 'The family of Street, and The Friary, Worcester', *Transactions of the Worcestershire Archaeological Society*, new ser., 24 (1947), 40–54 · Foss, *Judges*, 7.273–7 · Worcester Cathedral Library, MS classes A, B, and D · corporation chamber order book, Worcester, Worcs. RO · will, PRO, PROB 11/435, fols. 173v–175r · *VCH Worcestershire* · N. Luttrell, *A brief historical relation of state affairs from September 1678 to April 1714*, 6 vols. (1857) · *The correspondence of Henry Hyde, earl of Clarendon, and of his brother Laurence Hyde, earl of Rochester*, ed. S. W. Singer, 2 vols. (1828) · *The autobiography of Sir John Bramston*, ed. [Lord Braybrooke], CS, 32 (1845) · A. Grey, ed., *Debates of the House of Commons, from the year 1667 to the year 1694*, 10 vols. (1763) · *Diary of Thomas Burton*, ed. J. T. Rutt, 4 vols. (1828) · *CSP dom.*, 1660–61; 1687–9 · *Calendar of the manuscripts of the marquess of Ormonde*, new ser., 8 vols., HMC, 36 (1902–20), vol. 8 · Foster, *Alum. Oxon.* · Sainty, *Judges* · W. A. Shaw, ed., *Calendar of treasury books*, 2, PRO (1905)

Archives Worcester Cathedral, corresp. with dean and chapter of Worcester

Likenesses R. White, line engraving, 1688, BM, NPG · J. Instan, oils?, 1829 (after R. White), S. Antiquaries, Lond. · oils (after R. White), Inner Temple, London · oils, Harvard U., law school

Wealth at death lands in Worcestershire: will, PRO, PROB 11/435, fols. 173v–175r

Streete, Thomas (1621–1689), astronomer and astrologer, was born on 5 March 1621 in Cork. As an ensign in Colonel Kingsmill's regiment under Inchiquin, he fought for the king at Tredagh and Dublin, and was twice captured. After the Restoration, Streete lived in London, initially at the New Buildings on Tower Hill, and later in Popping Court, near Fleet Street. There are no records of his having had any formal schooling. He was employed by Elias Ashmole, first as a clerk and then, in 1667, as deputy comptroller in the Excise Office for London, Middlesex, and Surrey. The post was renewed in 1671. For this Streete earned £150 per annum.

Despite his humble background and somewhat marginal status, Streete's abilities were acknowledged by the most eminent natural philosophers of the day. He was an early and committed heliocentrist, whose principal work was *Astronomia Carolina: a New Theorie of Coelestial Motions* (1661); a work of computational astronomy, with extensive tables of planetary positions and motions, this became a standard textbook used well into the eighteenth century. It was consulted, as were Streete's ephemerides, by Newton, Flamsteed, and Halley, while Ashmole—and undoubtedly others—also used it to cast horoscopes. *Astronomia Carolina* was the first printed text in English to discuss Kepler's first and third laws of planetary motion (alongside Streete's own version of Kepler's second law). Streete followed this up with *An Appendix to Astronomia Carolina* (1664), dedicated to Ashmole, and *The Description and Use of the Planetary Systeme* (1674), as well as a running defence of his work in pamphlets countering the attacks of another self-taught astronomer, the astrologer and mathematician Vincent Wing.

Although he was never invited to join the charmed circle of the Royal Society, Streete's abilities were recognized by its leading members. His attempt to solve the notoriously difficult problem of ascertaining longitude at sea won the commendation of Lord Brouncker, John Wilkins, John Pell, and Sir Jonas Moore in a testimonial attesting that Streete 'hath attained a greater Exactitude in the Discovery of true Longitude by the motion of the Moon then hath yet been Extant' (Josten, 3.1080). He viewed a lunar eclipse with Edmond Halley in 1675, and was invited by Robert Hooke to observe Mercury's transit of the sun at Gresham College in October 1677; it is probable that there were other such occasions for which no record survives. After Streete's death Halley edited a second edition of *Astronomia Carolina*, with an appendix, in 1710.

Streete was both an autodidact and a respected natural philosopher at a time when the two still commonly went together. As with other such men, including Vincent Wing and Jeremy Shakerley, astronomy and astrology shared his attention. Thus, for example, in the dedication of *Astronomia Carolina*, he related the coronation of Charles II to the 'rare and most remarkable Appearance of Mercury in the sun' (its transit of the sun). This was no mere rhetorical conceit; the belief in a correspondence between the natural and the social was still widely held even among the readership of a specialized work such as *Astronomia Carolina*.

More specifically, the hopes raised by exciting new discoveries and theories in astronomy seemed to Streete to apply equally to astrology, as the application of such new knowledge to human affairs. As early as 1652 Streete produced *A Double Ephemeris for the year … 1653: Geocentricall and Heliocentricall*; this set of tables along with those of his friend and fellow researcher Joshua Childrey were the first of their kind. Both of Streete's tables were explicitly intended for use by astrologers for the improvement of their art, as well as to convince doubting astronomers. He defended both geocentric and heliocentric aspects (that is, angular relationships between the planets), arguing that 'long continued and infallible experiments do also confirm the same, both in the Change of Weather, and things of near concernment unto us'. However, as befitted a careful natural philosopher who was also a royalist writing in 1652, he added, 'Let honest Astrologers be cautious … and modest in their Predictions. So will I' (Streete, *Double Ephemeris*, dedication).

Streete wrote other ephemerides, 'with Astrological Observations thereon', for 1663 and finally 1683. He died in Westminster on 17 August 1689 and was buried in Westminster New Chapel.   PATRICK CURRY

Sources W. Applebaum, 'Streete, Thomas', *DSB* · Elias Ashmole (1617–1692): his autobiographical and historical notes, ed. C. H. Josten, 5 vols. (1966 [i.e. 1967]) · E. G. R. Taylor, *The mathematical practitioners of Tudor and Stuart England* (1954), 225–6 · B. S. Capp, *Astrology and the popular press: English almanacs, 1500–1800* (1979) · T. Streete, *A double ephemeris for the year … 1653* [1652] · Bodl. Oxf., Ashmole MS 183, p. 367; p. 426, fol. 292

Streeter, Burnett Hillman (1874–1937), biblical scholar, was born at Croydon on 17 November 1874, the only son of John Soper Streeter, solicitor, and his wife, Marion Walker. He was educated at King's College School in London, and from 1893, when he went up to Oxford with a classical scholarship at Queen's College, his life was that of a typical Oxford don. Queen's College claimed practically the whole of his academic loyalty: he became successively fellow, dean, and praelector (1905), chaplain (1928), and provost (1933). The only break was from 1899 to 1905, when he was fellow and dean of Pembroke College, Oxford. In 1910 he married Irene Louisa (*d.* 1937), daughter of Captain Edward Cuthbert Brookes Rawlinson, formerly of the Bengal cavalry, and then living at Slough. The marriage was childless.

Streeter's academic career was brilliant, with a first class in classical moderations (1895), *literae humaniores* (1897), and theology (1898), and a series of theological prizes and scholarships. It was his work at this time that laid the foundation of his studies in the New Testament, but he himself would probably have regarded the philosophy of religion as his main interest, viewing the various fields into which his inquiring mind was led as all subsidiary to the one central theme of the interpretation and presentation of religion in the modern world. The background of this was his intense concern and care for people. Although never of strong physique he rowed for his college as an undergraduate, and throughout his life retained an interest both in rowing and in undergraduates which was very closely linked in his mind with his academic work. His numerous writings were, in almost every case, conceived and written with the student world in view.

It was this pastoral and human interest which led Streeter to be ordained in 1899, despite the fact that his faith had always something of the character of a quest. He was more than once attacked as a modernist (especially after his contribution to *Foundations: a Statement of Christian Belief in Terms of Modern Thought* in 1912) but the obvious sincerity of his religion and its practical applicability to human problems were a sufficient answer, and the attacks were never pressed far. He was, indeed, a regular speaker and a most popular figure at Student Christian Movement conferences. This same interest in movements of thought and the search for a vital answer to the problems of life led him to undertake lengthy visits abroad. He made two long tours in China and Japan, lecturing both there and in India, and he visited the United States of America several times.

Streeter was one of the most distinguished New Testament scholars of his day, and a man beloved and respected by many generations of Oxford undergraduates. But apart from his Oxford life few honours came his way, although he was a member for nearly fifteen years (1922–37) of the archbishops' commission on doctrine in the Church of England, and was also appointed to a canonry in Hereford Cathedral, which he held from 1915 to 1934. This latter office led to the writing of one of his most interesting and most learned books, *The Chained Library* (1931), a study that revealed his astonishing power of assimilating large masses of detail about a subject quite remote from those which had already made him famous. He was elected a fellow of the British Academy in 1925 and an honorary fellow of Pembroke College in 1933. He was Dean Ireland's professor of exegesis from 1932 to 1933, and received the honorary degree of DD from the universities of Edinburgh, Durham, and Manchester.

Probably Streeter's best work was that on the New Testament, which attracted worldwide attention. He entered the front rank of scholars with his essay in the Oxford *Studies in the Synoptic Problem* (1911). This gave weight to the case for the priority of St Mark's gospel and the existence of Q. It was followed in 1924 by *The Four Gospels: a Study of Origins*, which, in its day, was an authoritative treatment of the problems of New Testament criticism. In particular he developed two new hypotheses of great importance: he argued in favour of an early Caesarean text of the gospels and of an original source behind St Luke's gospel in its present form. The great value of his work lies in its entirely first-hand character. Whether he was dealing with chained libraries or with the gospels and the manuscripts, he went direct to the sources and owed very little to the work of other scholars.

Streeter's other writings, some of which had a very large circulation, were in part essays in apologetics and the philosophy of religion—such as *Reality: a New Correlation of Science and Religion* (1926) and his Bampton lectures, *The Buddha and the Christ* (1932)—and in part contributions to composite volumes of essays. The earliest of the latter, and that which caused the most stir, was *Foundations*, a work which, when it was published, seemed to some critics alarmingly modernist, a judgement which time has reversed. A modern authority has indeed characterized Streeter, and other British biblical scholars, as 'of immense biblical and patristic learning but of rather little sustained theological skill' (Hastings, 231).

In his closing years, after he had become provost of Queen's and a scholar with a worldwide reputation, Streeter joined, with Mrs Streeter, in the work of the movement founded by Dr Frank N. D. Buchman which was widely known as the Oxford Group. It was as they were returning on 10 September 1937 from Switzerland, where Streeter had spent a long convalescence with some of the Oxford Group's members, that their aeroplane crashed into a mountain at Waldweide, Waldenburg, near Basel, in a fog, and he and his wife were killed.

L. W. GRENSTED, rev. ROBERT BROWN

Sources *The Times* (13 Sept 1937) · *Queen's College Record* (Nov 1937) · *Oxford* (winter 1937) · private information (1949) · personal knowledge (1949) · F. L. Cross, ed., *Oxford dictionary of the Christian church*, 3rd edn, ed. E. A. Livingstone (1997) · P. Hinchliff, *God and history: aspects of British theology, 1875–1914* (1992) · A. Hastings, *A history of English Christianity, 1920–1990*, 3rd edn (1991) · *CGPLA Eng. & Wales* (1938)
Archives Bodl. Oxf., corresp. and papers relating to chained libraries · Queen's College, Oxford, theological notes | BL, corresp. with Macmillans, Add. MSS 55102–55105

Likenesses P. Macdonald, photograph, *c.*1900–1905, Pembroke College, Oxford · D. Harmood Banner, oils, 1929, Queen's College, Oxford · Draw, caricature drawing, Queen's College, Oxford
Wealth at death £24,669 5*s.* 1*d.*: probate, 10 Feb 1938, *CGPLA Eng. & Wales*

Stretes, Guillim. *See* Scrots, Guillim (*fl.* 1537–1553).

Stretton, Hesba. *See* Smith, Sarah (1832–1911).

Stretton [Eyrik], **Robert** (*d.* 1385), bishop of Coventry and Lichfield, came from Leicestershire. Usually surnamed Stretton, from his presumed birthplace at Stretton Magna, Leicestershire, his family name was apparently Eyrik. However, suggestions of links with the later Eyricks of Houghton are unsubstantiated. He possibly inherited lands at Stretton, as he held the manor in the 1370s. In 1378 he named his parents as Robert (son of John) and Joan, and also identified two brothers (Sir William, a knight, and John, a cleric) and a sister (Atheline), who were all dead. Although these too are named Stretton, John is also called John Eyrik, and the dissolution certificate for his chantry calls the bishop 'Robert Heyrick'.

Of Stretton's education and upbringing nothing is known. He is occasionally called master, but no specific degree is identified (the tradition that he was a doctor of laws and an auditor of the *Rota Romana* is mistaken). He began his ecclesiastical career as a dependent of Edward, the Black Prince (*d.* 1376), for whom he was successively clerk, almoner (by March 1347), and confessor (by May 1349). He already held the rectory of Wigston, Leicestershire, when he was granted an expectative to a Chichester canonry in 1343. As a result of petitions to the pope and his connections with the Black Prince, he later acquired canonries and prebends at Lincoln, Gnosall, London, and Salisbury, and in St Asaph and Llandaff, and the rectory of Llanbadarn Fawr in the diocese of St David's. (A papal bull in 1360 said that he was a canon of Lichfield when elected bishop, but this seems to be incorrect.)

Stretton appears in secular employment as a king's clerk from 1350. In 1347 he was nominated as an envoy in abortive negotiations for a marriage between the prince of Wales and a daughter of the king of Portugal, and in 1355 was among those mandated by the pope to avert hostilities between the Black Prince and the count of Ponthieu. In 1350 he obtained a mortmain licence to found a chantry at Stretton, but this was not immediately implemented.

Following Bishop Roger Northburgh's death in November 1358 Stretton was elected bishop of Coventry and Lichfield, presumably with royal and princely support. Royal assent was granted on 21 January 1359, but the appointment then stalled, for two years. According to the fourteenth-century *Vitae archiepiscoporum Cantuariensium* (variously embroidered by later historians) Stretton was summoned to Avignon to have his literacy assessed, and was rejected. Following pressure from the prince of Wales the pope commissioned the archbishop of Canterbury and the bishop of Rochester to hold a further examination. This tale cannot be adequately corroborated. The final papal bull of 22 April 1360 states that Stretton was elected in ignorance of a papal reservation of the see, and had gone to Avignon to argue his case. The cardinals had judged him a fit candidate and there was no outstanding provision, so the decision on confirmation and provision was left to Canterbury and Rochester, unless Archbishop Simon Islip (d. 1366) deputed the bishop of London to act for him. Because of pressure of business Islip did just that. There is no sign of reluctance or opposition. In any event, Stretton was consecrated on 27 September 1360. His profession of obedience to Canterbury was read for him, for unstated reasons, although he did subscribe personally. Given his career and qualifications, illiteracy seems inconceivable, but it is possible that he was already afflicted by the deterioration of his eyesight which was later to deprive him of all vision, and which may also explain, at least in part, the quiet course of his later career.

Stretton's governance of his see was relatively straightforward and efficient. There are occasional hints of discord between himself and the Lichfield Cathedral chapter; but in general relations were amicable. In 1369 his anniversary was established within the cathedral, at the altar of St Andrew. The pope presumably thought that he retained influence with Edward III, as in 1371 he was asked to intercede to secure the admission of cardinals Simon Langham (d. 1376) and Jean de Dormans to England. In 1378 he arranged for the shrine of St Ceadda (Chad) to be moved to a new location. His pontificate had occasional dramatic incidents. When he visited Repton Priory in 1364, the townspeople invaded the priory compound, and blockaded the bishop and his household in the buildings. They were released only with assistance. Unsurprisingly Stretton fulminated excommunication and interdict against the perpetrators. From 1376 (if not earlier) he was consistently absent from parliament, possibly because of declining health. In September 1378 he finally established the chantry at Stretton Magna originally envisaged in 1350. (The tradition that he augmented another chantry at Stretton-on-Dunsmore, Staffordshire, is based on a misunderstanding.) He had become totally blind by 7 September 1381, and the prior and convent of Canterbury (sede vacante) ordered him to appoint a coadjutor for the see. He died at Haywood in Staffordshire, one of his episcopal residences, on 28 March 1385, and was buried in St Andrew's Chapel in Lichfield Cathedral. His relatively uninformative will, with few specific bequests, was drawn up on 19 March and probated on 10 April. What was probably his tomb was described and depicted by later antiquaries, but no longer survives.   R. N. SWANSON

Sources W. G. D. Fletcher, 'Robert de Stretton, bishop of Coventry and Lichfield, 1360 to 1385', *Associated Architectural Societies' Reports and Papers*, 19 (1887–8), 198–208 · *Chancery records* (RC) · W. H. Bliss, ed., *Calendar of entries in the papal registers relating to Great Britain and Ireland: petitions to the pope* (1896) · [H. Wharton], ed., *Anglia sacra*, 2 vols. (1691) · register of Archbishop Islip, LPL · Lincs. Arch., Reg. 12 · M. C. B. Dawes, ed., *Register of Edward, the Black Prince*, 4 vols., PRO (1930–33) · R. A. Wilson, ed., *The registers … of the bishops of Coventry and Lichfield: being the second register of Bishop Robert de Stretton*, 4–5 (1905–7) · Bodl. Oxf., MS Ashmole 794 · S. Shaw, *The history and antiquities of Staffordshire*, 1 (1798)

Archives Joint RO, Lichfield, episcopal registers, B/A/1/4–5; administrative papers
Likenesses tomb [now destroyed], repro. in Shaw, *History and antiquities of Staffordshire*
Wealth at death see will, Fletcher, 'Robert de Stretton'

Strevens, Peter Derek (1922–1989), linguistic scholar and applied linguist, was born on 31 August 1922 in the Norfolk and Norwich Hospital, Norwich, the elder son and first of three children of William Strevens (1893–1982), master mariner of Trinity House, and his wife, Dorothy Lydia (1895–1983), daughter of John William Henry McCarthy of Ramsgate, Kent.

Strevens was educated at Ackworth School, Pontefract, from 1936 to 1938 and served in the Friends' Ambulance Unit in the Second World War from 1940 to 1945. He then studied French with subsidiary German at University College, London (BA honours with upper second in 1948); this was followed by a Rhosten scholarship to research into Portuguese phonetics for a year. On 1 June 1946 he married Gwyneth Moore (1924–2002), daughter of Harold Moore, of Birmingham, at the Friends' meeting-house in Bull Street. Their son Jason was born in 1951 in Accra after Strevens began his career at the University College of the Gold Coast, as lecturer in phonetics from 1949 to 1956. He moved to Edinburgh University, where from 1957 to 1961 he was a major influence on the innovative postgraduate applied linguistics course being developed there.

From 1961 to 1964 Strevens held the chair in contemporary English at the University of Leeds, and for the following ten years the first British chair with the designation 'applied linguistics' at the University of Essex, where he set up the second major postgraduate programme in this field. From 1966 to 1970 he was secretary of the International Association of Applied Linguistics, and from 1972 to 1975 the second chairman of the British Association for Applied Linguistics. Frustrated by the amount of committee work in British universities, he moved to the private sector, becoming director-general of the Bell Educational Trust in Cambridge (where he was a fellow of Wolfson College) from 1978 to 1988, and combined this with chairing the International Association of Teachers of English as a Foreign Language from 1983 to 1987. In 1988 he was distinguished visiting professor in the humanities at Eastern Michigan University, and at the time of his death was professor at the University of Illinois.

Following Strevens's return to Britain from Africa, he played a key role in developing and defining the new discipline of applied linguistics across the world. The book he co-wrote with Edinburgh colleagues Angus McIntosh and Michael Halliday, *The Linguistic Sciences and Language Teaching* (1964), was the most influential of its generation in defining a scientific, but by no means mechanistic, foundation for teaching foreign languages. In the 1960s boom in language interest, reflected both in the emergence of markets for English in the developing world and the concern for European languages as the European Common Market defined itself, this book became the centrepiece of reading lists at postgraduate level. The masters course at Essex was the first in applied linguistics in Britain, and for many years graduates from there and from his earlier base, Edinburgh, were the major British leaders in the field, both at home and overseas. At the same time he recognized that effective applied linguistics could not be tied to the burgeoning market for teachers of English as a foreign language: particularly in the period before leaving Essex, he collaborated with her majesty's inspectorate for schools and with other agencies in developing a research base for the teaching of modern languages in Britain. As his publications show, throughout his career he was a major leader in widening the scope of applied linguistic research beyond a concern solely for language teaching.

Strevens published influential books on phonetics, the theory of language teaching, and teacher education, and was also concerned, through a series edited for Oxford University Press, to establish greater awareness of the history of language teaching. He collaborated in the development of Seaspeak (1984), international English for maritime communication, which was established as the international language of the sea. His *Who's Who* recreations were travel and the sea, so that his extensive work for the British Council and other international bodies arose directly from his personal enthusiasms and interests. At the same time he was highly professional. When the post-oil-crisis demand for English in many parts of the world led to a market in which there was much scope for sharp practice and over-enthusiastic promotion of shoddy products, he constantly worked to ensure that systematic analysis, serious research, and a well-educated teaching force supported the expansion of English teaching. Thus his shift from university to private sector work made sense, for it enabled him to address the professional needs of the increasingly powerful private language schools, and to counter the risks of over-aggressive marketing in a field where maintenance of professional standards was essential.

Above all else, though, Strevens charmed his colleagues and audiences. No one was better at facilitating rich professional contacts. He supported colleagues and students alike, and was constantly called upon in situations where personal relationships might be difficult to manage. When the long-standing organizer and founder of the International Association of Teachers of English as a Foreign Language, Dr W. R. Lee, had to be persuaded that change was needed in the association, Peter Strevens proved an ideal successor, incorporating his predecessor in the activities of the association while ensuring that it addressed the needs of new generations of teachers. His belief that all teachers and scholars needed personal support as well as academic criticism contributed to the affection he earned throughout the language-teaching professions. But he was not simply a promoter of great skill, for his lucid writing made many language teachers more aware of the principles they were unconsciously using. His clear and elegant manner of speaking, clarity of thinking, and outstanding committee skills ensured that social relations between diverse cultures, people of diverse

levels of sophistication and education, and diverse linguistic groups would always be positive. An outstanding command of French, particularly, and a wide-ranging mind enabled him to cross boundaries within Europe as much as in the British Commonwealth where so many of his students had worked. He died suddenly of a heart condition in Tokyo, Japan, on 3 November 1989.

CHRISTOPHER BRUMFIT

Sources WWW, 1981–90 · *The Times* (16 Nov 1989) · *The Guardian* (15 Nov 1989) · *The Independent* (14 Nov 1989) · *The Independent* (28 Nov 1989) · private information (2004) [Gwyneth Strevens, widow; colleagues in universities and British Council] · *British Association for Applied Linguistics Newsletter*, 35 (spring 1990) · T. McArthur, ed., *The Oxford companion to the English language* (1992), 912–13, 989–90 · b. cert. · *CGPLA Eng. & Wales* (1990)
Archives U. Lond., Institute of Education, collection
Wealth at death under £100,000: probate, 1990, *CGPLA Eng. & Wales*

Strickland, Agnes (1796–1874), historian, was born on 19 August 1796, in north-west Kent, near London, the second eldest of the six surviving daughters and two sons of Thomas Strickland (1758–1818), a shipping agent and dock manager, and his second wife, Elizabeth Homer (1772–1864). Her sisters were **Elizabeth Strickland** (1794–1875); Sarah; **Jane Margaret Strickland** (1800–1888), born on 18 April 1800, also in north-west Kent, Catharine Parr *Traill (1802–1899); and Susanna *Moodie (1803–1885). All her female siblings except Sarah Strickland became authors, as did too her brother **Samuel Strickland** (1805–1867). The Stricklands were descended from Yorkshire farmers, but a more romantic family tradition connected them to the Stricklands of Sizergh Castle.

Education and early authorship With her elder sister, Elizabeth, who was born on 17 November 1794, also in north-west Kent, Agnes Strickland was educated by her father; he believed that girls should be educated 'upon the same plan as boys because … it strengthened the female mind' (Pope-Hennessy, 5). He taught them Latin and mathematics, and made them write abstracts of the books they had read; Agnes's reading included Shakespeare, Pope, Thoyras-Rapin's *History of England*, and Plutarch's *Lives*. The family was brought up in London and East Anglia, but by 1808 Thomas Strickland had made enough money to buy Reydon Hall, an Elizabethan mansion near Southwold in Suffolk. In the summer, the girls hunted for wild flowers in the surrounding countryside, and shells on the local beach; in winter, they took to writing stories. Part of the year was spent in Norwich, where they used the free library and joined the cultivated circle surrounding the Taylor family.

'Extravagantly fond of poetry' (Pope-Hennessy, 6), Agnes Strickland wrote a good deal of juvenile verse imitative of Walter Scott, while Elizabeth preferred to express herself in historical essays. Agnes's *Monody* on the death of Princess Charlotte appeared in the *Norwich Mercury*; rather ominously for her career as a poet, she read her *Worcester Field, or, The Cavalier*, a poem in four cantos, to her father two days before his death. This event obliged

Agnes Strickland (1796–1874), by John Hayes, 1846

the family, now settled entirely at Reydon, to earn livings: five of the girls took to writing children's stories. Agnes Strickland's efforts included *The Use of Sight* (1824) and *The Rival Crusoes* (1826).

The two eldest sisters, despite shared interests, differed in appearance and character. Agnes, with a plump, rosy face and silky black hair, was the more sociable and talkative: one of her sisters later recalled that 'possessed of an excellent temper, great flow of eloquence, and playful repartee, her descriptive powers never seemed to flag' (*Susanna Moodie*, 313). By contrast, Elizabeth, slim and pale-faced with aquiline features, was reserved, intensely studious, and independent, 'possessing the governing powers in no ordinary degree' and with a temper 'warm to faultiness' (Strickland, 384). They began to spend some of the year in London attempting to establish careers as professional writers. In the drawing-room of one cousin, who was the wife of the architect Thomas Leverton, they made important literary contacts, meeting the poet Thomas Campbell, Robert Southey, Charles Lamb, and William Jerdan, editor of the *Literary Gazette*. Most significant among these contacts were women of letters: these included Louisa Costello, Barbara Hofland, and the Porter sisters (who became close friends of the Stricklands). Such women offered encouragement, role models, and potential access to work on the keepsakes and annuals which were a major outlet for minor littérateurs in the early to mid-nineteenth century (Agnes was a contributor to and sometime editor of *Fisher's Juvenile Scrapbook*). A friendship with the poet Letitia Landon, however, did not advance

Agnes's career; the disappointed aspirate printed by subscription *Worcester Field* (1826) and *The Seven Ages of Woman* (1827). Despite their lack of originality they served as publicity for future work. An imitation of Byron, her poem *Demetrius: a Tale of Modern Greece* appeared in 1833: inspired by the struggle of the Greeks against the Turks, it was her last poetical fling. She had now begun to write a historical romance entitled *The Pilgrims of Walsingham* (1835), a sixteenth-century version of the *Canterbury Tales* in which a party of pilgrims including Henry VII, Charles V, and Wolsey each narrate a tale as they travel to the shrine. It was a mediocre production, despite favourable reviews, and seems to have convinced Agnes that fiction was not her forte. Meanwhile Elizabeth Strickland had considerably advanced her career: a contact with Lady Morgan had led to employment by the publisher Henry Colburn, founder and financier of several periodicals including the *New Monthly Magazine* and *The Athenaeum*. By 1830 she had become editor of the *Court Journal*, which covered court and society news, fashion, cultural events, racing, and other similar events.

Embarking on the *Lives of the Queens of England*, 1830–1840
In the early 1830s the Strickland family was largely dispersed: both Strickland brothers were already living abroad, one in Canada, one in the West Indies; in 1832 Catharine Parr Traill and Susanna Moodie emigrated to Canada with their new husbands; the domestically minded Sarah had married Robert Childs, partner in the dissenting publishing firm of that name, while Jane stayed at home with her mother, a labour for which Agnes piously opined she would not 'lose [her] heavenly reward' (Strickland, 300). The two eldest sisters were moving towards a new field of authorship, popular history: they had decided to collaborate on a series of biographies of the queens of England. By the early 1830s Agnes and Elizabeth Strickland were devoting part of the morning to reading historical manuscripts in the British Museum Library, with instruction in palaeography from the staff. Agnes was in contact with antiquaries and scholars, including Harris Nicolas, Cuthbert Sharp, Joseph Hunter, and the French historian and government minister Guizot. Though firmly protestant herself, she also formed links with prominent Catholic families in her endeavour to understand the pre-Reformation world. The *Lives of the Queens of England* (1840–48) owed much to the Catholic priest John Lingard's *History of England* (1819–30), one of the few full national histories available in the 1830s, and Henry and Philip Howard of Corby Castle both lent her manuscripts.

'Facts not opinions' was the motto adopted by the sisters, and their manuscript research was both pioneering and intensive. As the sisters began work on the Tudor queens for the fourth volume, it became necessary to gain access to the state paper office: initially refused permission by the home secretary, Lord John Russell, they finally gained permits from Lord Normanby with the help of Henry Howard and Sir George Strickland; later they obtained permits for the rolls office from Sir Francis Palgrave. While Elizabeth wrote twelve of the pre-1485 biographies and Agnes only seven, an agreement between the two sisters obliged Agnes to conduct all correspondence, both scholarly and business, and her name alone appeared on the title-pages of all their publications. While Elizabeth lived in relative seclusion in Bayswater, Agnes attended the parties, salons, and country houses to which the *Lives* gained them entrée. Agnes, however, did not prove an effective woman of business: when she was ill and the publisher Colburn was pressing for the third volume of the *Lives*, Elizabeth intervened and secured a new and better agreement for £150 per volume.

Agnes Strickland's enthusiasm for female royalty was not limited to deceased queens. She had earlier persuaded a Catholic friend, Lady Bedingfeld, to approach Queen Adelaide with an almanac of her verses, which was dedicated to the queen. In 1836 she viewed Princess Victoria returning from a drawing-room; in 1837 she somehow obtained an invitation to the coronation. When the queen became engaged in 1840, Colburn commissioned her to write an account of Victoria's life from her birth to her wedding, offering to provide press cuttings and other materials himself. Agnes accepted, and both she and Colburn networked vigorously to obtain a ticket for her to the queen's wedding, which was gained only the evening before the ceremony. Shortly afterwards, the two-volume *Victoria from Birth to Bridal* appeared. The book presented Victoria in a very favourable light, but the queen herself was critical, disputing many matters of fact with an emphatic 'not true' in the margin. Allegedly, most of the edition, although already on sale, was subsequently pulped; copies of the work are certainly very rare.

Travel and celebrity, 1840–1847 As the sisters prepared the fourth volume of the *Lives* in 1840, Agnes took advantage of her increasing celebrity to tour country houses in the north and west of England that had links with the Tudor queens. She was accompanied by Elizabeth; their tour started with a visit to Middle Hall in Gloucestershire, the home of the bibliophile Sir Thomas Phillipps, who often helped her in her research. They then proceeded to Sizergh Castle, where Agnes excitedly explored the rooms in which she imagined Katherine Parr to have resided and found documents relating to the exiled court of James II and Mary of Modena, where the Stricklands had featured. They toured the surrounding Lake District, before proceeding to Corby Castle, the home of the Howards. During the succeeding winter Agnes took a break from the *Lives* to polish up an old story for publication as *Alda: the British Captive*: it was reviewed dismissively in *The Athenaeum* but the *Gentleman's Magazine* was more generous. The fifth volume of the *Lives*—containing the biographies of Katherine Parr by Agnes and of Mary Tudor by Elizabeth—attracted more critical attention: there, back to back, were a highly laudatory portrait of the proto-protestant last wife of Henry VIII (by Agnes) and a radical and sympathetic reinterpretation of the Catholic queen Mary Tudor (by Elizabeth). Accused of papistry (by dint of her sole authorial credit), Agnes increased her attendance at church and

made greater efforts with Sunday school teaching in Reydon to dispel the rumours.

From before the publication of the *Lives*, Agnes and Elizabeth Strickland had been translating and collating the letters of Mary, queen of Scots. With the publication of Prince Lobanov's selection of her letters from Russian archives came the impetus to publish their own translations. Agnes's friend Jane Porter was then staying with her brother, Sir Robert Ker Porter, in St Petersburg, and she offered to obtain transcripts of all of the Scottish queen's letters in the imperial library there. Initially issued in a supplementary volume to the first edition of 1842, they subsequently appeared in chronological order in later editions. Agnes Strickland spent most of 1842 and part of 1843 writing the life of Elizabeth I; the first volume of this biography was well received. In summer 1843 Agnes with her widowed sister Sarah Childs undertook a tour of the Lake District; here Sarah met her second husband, a local clergyman, and Agnes explored the historical sights and visited Wordsworth at Rydal Mount. After a few days at Corby Castle, they travelled on to Scotland to visit Edinburgh and the Crauford family at Craufordland Castle. They returned in mid-November to Reydon, where Agnes proof-read the second section of Elizabeth I's life, which was to appear in the same volume with Elizabeth Strickland's life of Anne of Denmark.

In April 1844 the elder Strickland sisters set off for a visit to France to conduct research into the lives of Henrietta of France and Mary of Modena. The sisters embarked from Southampton for Le Havre, and a boat down the Seine. They stayed at Rouen where they visited the cathedral of Notre-Dame for an evening service and stayed to view the tombs. The vicar of the cathedral, who showed them some fine illuminated manuscripts, took them on to the church of St Ouen. During their stay they also visited the cathedral library and the church of St Maclou. On Easter Saturday they took the train to Paris and attended Easter morning mass at Notre-Dame. On Easter Monday the Strickland sisters travelled to St Germain-en-Laye, to research the Stuarts in exile. After a short illness on Agnes's part, the sisters paid a visit to Guizot, then premier of France, who provided them with a general letter of introduction to the officials in charge of the Paris archives. The sisters at once began work in the well-catalogued Archives du Royaume and the Archives du Ministère des Affaires Etrangères. A visit to Jules Michelet was more than just pleasure, as he produced documents relating to Queen Henrietta for Elizabeth and three bundles of letters from Mary of Modena for Agnes. The sisters visited the Scots College, where they inspected many Jacobite relics, and the nearby Augustinian convent of English ladies, where the abbess proved to be a fount of Stuart trivia. Agnes Strickland also attended many social events, including the British embassy ball and the salon of Lady Elgin, widow of the collector of the marbles. Both sisters saw the famous actress Rachel act in *Cinna*, as Elizabeth preferred to confine herself to public entertainments and seances—she had a lifelong though sceptical interest in spiritualism. The sisters visited Dieppe and Eu before sailing back to Southampton after three months abroad.

Agnes Strickland's increasing celebrity was also reflected in her London life. Staying with the Mackinnon family at 4 Hyde Park Place in summer 1844 (Elizabeth went to Reydon), Agnes spent her evenings attending the social functions of a London season, while working at the British Museum in the mornings and resting in the afternoons. At such events she met the duke of Wellington and the exiled kings of Portugal and Spain; she also made a series of close friendships with aristocratic men and women, friendships of both sentimental and practical value, as many of these new acquaintances opened their country houses, archives, and picture galleries to her. Despite these enjoyments, the eighth volume of the *Lives* was published in autumn 1844; the ninth volume, containing the first part of Agnes's biography of Mary of Modena, followed in 1845, as too the over-lengthy second instalment of Mary's life in the tenth volume. In this biography the keenly Jacobite Agnes produced the first English account of the life of James II's queen, and she was unable to resist including many details from the original documentation discovered in France.

In 1846 the flattering portrait of Agnes by John Hayes was exhibited at the Royal Academy, and the *Lives* was an inspiration for artists of historical genre in the 1840s and 1850s. But other attributes of celebrity were less pleasing: begging letters and plagiarism by other writers afflicted the Stricklands. Agnes exacted a polite apology from Lord Campbell, whom she held to have plagiarized her life of Eleanor of Provence in his *Lives of the Lord Chancellors* (1845–7). In July 1847 the *Edinburgh Review* published a lengthy article attacking the Stuart volumes of the *Lives*. The writer was C. M. S. Phillipps. He berated Agnes rather for her treatment of Stuart kings than Stuart queens, condemning both her tory and monarchist views and her moral judgments as falling short of the 'masculine gravity and impartiality' which the historian ought to exercise. Attacks came too from both evangelicals and Roman Catholics.

Writing the *Lives of the Queens of Scotland*, 1847–1853 Undeterred by these controversies, Agnes Strickland now suggested a comprehensive series of lives of the Scottish queens, which would allow her to write a biography of her beloved Mary, queen of Scots. Fearing that most of the research in medieval records would fall upon her, now that Agnes's social life was so full, Elizabeth opposed this suggestion. The sisters finally agreed to open the new series with the life of Margaret Tudor, wife of James IV, by Elizabeth. She was also to undertake the biographies of Elizabeth, queen of Bohemia, and Sophia, electress of Hanover, while Agnes was to write the lives of the two wives of James V and her heroine, Mary Stewart. Accordingly, Agnes spent summer 1847 at Chatsworth, Hardwick Hall, and Bolsover Castle, all properties belonging to the helpful duke of Devonshire; in spring 1848 she was busy working in the British Museum and the state paper office. Other projects were also under way: Colburn called for a

revised edition of the *Lives*, with illustrations, and Elizabeth undertook most of the work for this. Meanwhile Agnes prepared her magazine poetry for publication under the title *Historic Scenes and Poetic Fancies* (1850), for which Colburn paid her £100: it also offered her the chance to take Macaulay to task for accusing Mary of Modena of selling prisoners from the Monmouth campaign into slavery in the West Indies.

While Agnes toured Scotland in 1850 (she visited Edinburgh and the surrounding area every year until 1855), her high-ranking friends assiduously drew her attention to portraits of Mary, queen of Scots, and showed her watches, rosaries, gloves, and other items which had belonged to the Scottish queen. She attended a young friend's wedding, at which she learnt to reel dance, and met Lord Ashley, later Lord Shaftesbury, the philanthropist, with whom she had little in common; nevertheless, she wrote him a set of verses, *The Factory Child*, to be sold on behalf of children in factories. Archibald Alison, the historian and diehard tory politician, was a more congenial acquaintance: he attentively listened to her enthusiastic conversation on her work, reviewed *The Queens of Scotland* favourably in *Blackwood's Magazine*, and described her with affectionate mockery in his *Autobiography*.

In spring 1850 Agnes Strickland opened negotiations with Colburn, with the first volume of *The Queens of Scotland* prepared for the press. When he refused her terms, she offered the series to William Blackwood, the Edinburgh publisher, who accepted it. Two volumes were published in the same year. Agnes saw them through the press, working meantime in Edinburgh libraries and continuing to visit Scottish friends as she approached 'the crowning labour of my life' (Pope-Hennessy, 213), the biography of Mary, queen of Scots. Later she returned to England, staying with friends and spending Christmas at Reydon, before continuing her work in London in the new year. Here she met Macaulay at a dinner party: the two argued over James II and William III, and Agnes opined that the great historian was 'vulgar, pompous and unprepossessing' (ibid., 223).

In 1852 Agnes was visited by her brother Samuel, who by this time had been twice widowed and was a farmer and leading citizen of Lakefield, Canada. It was Agnes who persuaded him to write an account of his experiences there, *Twenty-Seven Years in Canada West* (1853; repr. 1970). While in England, Samuel met Katherine Rackham, who became his third wife in 1855. They returned to Lakefield, where Samuel died on 3 January 1867.

Later publications: bachelors and bishops, 1855–1864 In 1854 Jane Margaret Strickland, Agnes's devoted sister, had published her school history, *Rome, Regal and Republican*, the proceeds of which allowed her to buy a cottage in Southwold. This was followed in 1856 by *Adonijah: a Tale of the Jewish Dispersion*, the crudely sensationalist story of a Jewish captive who becomes a slave in a Roman family, converts a vestal virgin to Judaism, and finally becomes a Christian: it reflects her broad knowledge of ancient history and her ability to spin a thumping good (if unlikely) yarn. In the same year Elizabeth Strickland was obliged to move out of her Bayswater cottage; she purchased a small villa, Abbot's Lodge, at Tilford, near Farnham, Surrey, where she lived for the rest of her life. Agnes sometimes stayed there but Elizabeth's hot temper could cloud a visit. On one occasion Agnes wrote home that she was 'not in health for her hurricanes' (Pope-Hennessy, 241–2) and had been obliged to leave after a quarrel on the third day of her stay. Other events in Agnes's life at the time included a protest against an incorrect tax assessment for 1856–7 (she regarded herself as something of a national benefactor, and was therefore liable to regard any tax demand as iniquitous), and a refusal to support a petition against the Married Women's Property Act: Agnes piously viewed these grievances as 'part and parcel of the penalties entailed by Eve's transgression' (Pope-Hennessy, 243). Other events of the late 1850s included a budding friendship with the recently widowed duchess of Somerset and involvement in the British Association.

From 1858 to 1860 Agnes Strickland spent much time cultivating her social circle. In 1858 she toured the west of England, before visiting Wales and paying a flying visit to Scotland. Winter was spent writing at Reydon. An Ipswich publisher suggested a volume on the three bachelor kings of England (William Rufus, Edward V, Edward VI); the subject appealed to the two lifelong spinsters. Elizabeth offered to deal with Edward V and to see to the illustrations. In spring 1859 Agnes returned to London; later in the year she stayed with the Howards at Corby and the Broughams at Brougham. After staying with her sister at Ulverston, she moved to Aberdeen to attend a meeting of the British Association. In 1860 she again spent the season in London, before staying at Stanford Hall, Rugby, and Althorp, where she delighted in the magnificent library and collection of portraits. On a visit to the Northamptonshire county lunatic asylum, she met the pastoral poet John Clare, an inmate there. While at Althorp, she also met a more congenial man of letters, Whyte Melville, with whom she shared a passion for Mary Stewart.

In 1861 *The Bachelor Kings of England* was published, to lukewarm reviews. Agnes sent a presentation copy to the prince of Wales, then at the Curragh in Ireland; in return, she received an invitation to the mayor of Dublin's ball in honour of the heir to the throne. Despite being sixty-five, Agnes attended the ball, and afterwards dined at the viceregal lodge and visited several Irish country houses. After the London season of 1862 she again went on a round of country house visits, including Sudeley Castle and Rousham; from the latter, she was able to make trips to the Bodleian Library to carry out research for her new book on the senior clerics who refused to swear allegiance to William and Mary, *The Lives of the Seven Bishops* (1866). Handing over two of the bishops to Elizabeth, she wrote the remaining five herself, warming in particular to William Sancroft, a Suffolk man, and Thomas Ken. She also worked on a school abridgement of the *Lives*.

Later years and death, 1864–1888 After Mrs Strickland's death in 1864, at ninety-two, the sisters were obliged to sell Reydon. In March 1865 Agnes took up residence in Park Lane Cottage, Southwold, which she leased from Jane; Jane herself was to live in a smaller annexe. In 1864 Agnes published *Alethea Woodville*, a novel written some thirty years before under the more intriguing title *How Will it End?* In June 1865 she visited Oxford for the commemoration, where the undergraduates greeted her with cheers of 'the queens!' Agnes and Elizabeth visited the Tower of London together that summer before Agnes returned to Southwold to spend time in the company of her Suffolk friends, Sir John and Lady Blois. Agnes was unwell in 1866, but soon recovered when back in the midst of London social life. She attended a drawing-room before visiting the Dillons at Dytchley.

Agnes Strickland spent most of 1867 at work in the British Museum on a new book, although she did tour Wales, staying with (among others) Lady Llanover. The two sisters were planning *The Tudor Princesses* (1868): the idea was Elizabeth's, and it was she who undertook Mary Tudor, and Lady Jane Grey and her sisters. Agnes wrote the lives of Lady Eleanor Brandon and Lady Margaret Clifford—neither of whom interested her much—and Lady Arabella Stuart. Elizabeth's references to the Archives de France show that the book had long been brewing in her mind: Mary Tudor's Suffolk connections clearly appealed to her. In 1869 Agnes—who, unlike Elizabeth, was more attached to the Stuarts than to the Tudors—undertook a historical work by herself, a study of the three daughters of Charles I and the youngest daughter of James II. The Dutch connections of the dynasty presented problems: with introductions and information provided by Archbishop Tait and the Lambeth Palace librarian, Wayland Kershaw, she resolved to visit the Netherlands and examine the libraries of The Hague. Despite initial apprehensions at undertaking a trip abroad alone at seventy-three, she enjoyed the visit: she saw the sights, was presented to the queen of Holland, and was given much assistance by the royal librarian, Mr Campbell. After a brief tour of the Rhine she returned to England and Southwold to complete the work; Jane helped revise the proofs, but Elizabeth refused even this assistance. At seventy-five she preferred the quiet of her Tilford home, where she entertained supporters of Kossuth and attended the occasional seance. *The Stuart Princesses* (1872) was completed in March 1870; Agnes then settled down to the task of compressing her life of Mary, queen of Scots, into two volumes, which were published by Bell and Daldy in 1872.

After 1870 Agnes Strickland began to spend more time at home at Southwold: she took an interest in local affairs, writing a life of St Edmund, to whom the local church was dedicated, to raise money for charitable purposes. In this year she also received a civil-list pension of £100 in recognition of her services to literature. In 1871 she attended the Scott commemoration festival in Edinburgh and then stayed with her sister Sarah at Ulverston. While staying at Crouch End in 1872, she fell downstairs and broke her right leg in several places; later she had a stroke. She recovered temporarily, but died in Park Lane Cottage, Southwold, on 13 July 1874; she was buried in the churchyard of St Edmund, Southwold. Elizabeth Strickland died on 30 April 1875 at Abbot's Lodge, Tilford, and was buried in the churchyard at Tilford. Jane wrote a biography of Agnes, published in 1887; she died at Park Lane Cottage on 14 June of the following year and was buried beside the sister to whom she was so devoted. A lifelong spinster, Jane seems to have been a rather lonely figure: in the late 1860s her sister Catharine Parr Traill wrote of her that 'with talents of no mean order, beauty of person, and religious principles', she had 'never obtained the real tender love of any human being' (*Selected Correspondence*, 174). Less charitably, Susanna Moodie opined that 'in most families there is one, that always is a trial and who gets their own way by merely insisting upon it' (*Susanna Moodie*, 286).

Assessment and reputation During her lifetime Agnes Strickland enjoyed considerable celebrity as the historian of the queens and cultivated a circle of aristocratic and literary friends, while her sister Elizabeth chose to remain outside the limelight. The *Lives of the Queens of England* and—to a lesser extent—the *Lives of the Queens of Scotland* were among the most popular of all Victorian historical publications, and remain important landmarks in the development of the biographical genre. By the beginning of the twentieth century the reputation of Agnes Strickland was much eclipsed, although those who produce biographies of the queens of England—from the writers of articles for the *Dictionary of National Biography* to scholars reinterpreting the careers of figures such as Anne Boleyn and Eleanor of Aquitaine in the 1990s—have found themselves obliged to turn to the Stricklands' seminal accounts. Most major public libraries continue to carry an edition of the *Lives*, among other encyclopaedic works, and the later twentieth century saw a revival of academic interest in the elder Strickland sisters as female historians and historians of women. They were undoubtedly key figures in the development of writing on women's history, playing a role in creating a tradition of female worthies which can be seen as the first step towards fuller scholarly investigation. While a range of contemporary women writers—including Anna Jameson, Lucy Aikin, Louisa Costello, Hannah Lawrance, Mrs Matthew Hall, and Emily Holt—were writing the biographies of royal and aristocratic women and court histories, the Stricklands were undoubtedly the most prominent and influential figures in their field of study. Womanist rather than feminist, they interpreted their subjects through the medium of Victorian domestic ideology: the queens are valued as much for their domestic and private virtues as for their public characters, and were intended as exemplars for a predominantly female readership. But this did not prevent challenging reinterpretations—such as Elizabeth's treatment of Mary I and Agnes's of Mary, queen of Scots—or the underlying suggestion of dissatisfaction with 'masculine' approaches to history which ignored social, cultural, and domestic issues.

In their interest in this more 'picturesque' approach to the past—one which challenged the philosophical tradition of the eighteenth century—the Stricklands were by no means at odds with their age, which saw the rise of the historical novel under the authorship of Walter Scott. However, unlike some of their rivals they were also influenced by the antiquarian tendency of picturesque history writing: they wrote queenly lives based on full and original documentation, pursuing research in archives in both Britain and France. It was in Mary Anne Everett Green, the author of *The Lives of the Princesses of England* and a historian equally devoted to record research, that they were to find their most satisfactory disciple. Her employment in the Public Record Office—an acceptance as a professional historian—makes her a bridge between the Stricklands and the next generation of women historians—which included Kate Norgate, Lucy Toulmin Smith, and Alice Stopford Green—who were themselves precursors of the women social and economic historians in the early twentieth century such as Alice Clark and Eileen Power.

ROSEMARY MITCHELL

Sources U. Pope-Hennessy, *Agnes Strickland: biographer of the queens of England, 1796–1874* (1940) · J. M. Strickland, *The life of Agnes Strickland* (1887) · C. Ballstadt, 'The literary history of the Strickland family', PhD diss., 1965? · R. A. Maitzen, *Picturing the past: English history in text and image, 1830–1870* (2000) · R. A. Maitzen, *Gender, genre, and Victorian history writing* (1998) · A. Laurence, 'Women historians and documentary research: Lucy Aikin, Agnes Strickland, Mary Anne Everett Green, and Lucy Toulmin Smith', *Women, scholarship and criticism*, ed. J. Bellamy, A. Laurence, and G. Perry (2000), 125–41 · Bodl. Oxf., MSS Phillipps-Robinson · C. P. Traill, *Pearls and pebbles* (1894) · R. A. Mitchell, 'The busy daughters of Clio: women writers of history from 1820 to 1880', *Women's History Review*, 7/1 (1998), 107–34 · R. A. Mitchell, 'A stitch in time? Women, needlework, and the making of history in Victorian Britain', *Journal of Victorian Culture*, 1/2 (autumn 1996), 185–202 · M. Delorme, 'Facts not opinions: Agnes Strickland', *History Today*, 38 (1988), 45–50 · B. G. Smith, 'The contribution of women to modern historiography in Great Britain, France and the United States, 1750–1940', *American Historical Review*, 89 (1984) · U. Reading L., Bell archives · J. Sutherland, 'Henry Colburn, publisher', *Publishing History*, 19 (1986), 59–84 · C. Campbell Orr, 'Agnes Strickland, historian of women, and the Langham Place Group', delivered at the Age of Equipoise conference, Trinity and All Saints College, Leeds, July 1996, priv. coll. · R. A. Mitchell, 'The exemplification of medieval queens in nineteenth-century Britain', *Heroic reputations and exemplary lives*, ed. G. Cubitt and A. Warren (2000), 157–77 · *Susanna Moodie: letters of a lifetime*, ed. C. Ballstadt, E. Hopkins, and M. A. Peterman (1985) · *I bless you in my heart: selected correspondence of Catharine Parr Traill*, ed. C. Ballstadt, E. Hopkins, and M. A. Peterman (1996) · *DNB* · C. McCandless Thomas, 'Strickland, Samuel', *DCB*

Archives Bodl. Oxf., corresp. with Sir T. Phillipps · Glos. RO, corresp. · Herts. ALS, letters to E. B. Lytton · Lincs. Arch., letters to Charles Tennyson D'Eyncourt · NL Scot., corresp. with Blackwoods · priv. coll., NRA, letters to Philip Henry Howard · Suffolk RO, Ipswich, corresp. and papers · Suffolk RO, Lowestoft, historical corresp. · U. Edin. L., letters to James Halliwell-Phillipps · U. Reading L., letters to George Bell and Sons | National Library of Canada, Patrick Hamilton Ewing collection of Moodie-Strickland-Vickers-Ewing family papers

Likenesses C. L. Gow, chalk drawing, 1846, NPG · J. Hayes, oils, 1846, NPG [*see illus.*] · engraving, *c.*1860–1879, repro. in Strickland, *Life*, frontispiece · Southwell Bros., carte-de-visite, NPG · miniature (aged between fifteen and twenty), repro. in Pope-Hennessy, *Agnes Strickland*, facing p. 20; priv. coll. · photograph, repro. in Pope-Hennessy, *Agnes Strickland*, facing p. 268

Wealth at death under £3000: probate, 4 Dec 1874, *CGPLA Eng. & Wales* · under £3000—Elizabeth Strickland: probate, 22 May 1875,

CGPLA Eng. & Wales • £2048 9s. 5d.—Jane Margaret Strickland: probate, 24 July 1888, *CGPLA Eng. & Wales*

Strickland, Catharine Parr. *See* Traill, Catharine Parr (1802–1899).

Strickland, Elizabeth (1794–1875). *See under* Strickland, Agnes (1796–1874).

Strickland, Gerald Paul Joseph Cajetan Carmel Antony Martin, Baron Strickland (1861–1940), prime minister of Malta, was born in Malta on 24 May 1861, the eldest son of Commander Walter Strickland (1824–1868), of the Royal Navy, and Donna Maria Aloysia Paula Bonici-Monpalao (1834–1907), daughter of Cavaliere Peter Paul Bonici of Malta, and niece and heir of Sir Nicholas Sceberras Bologna, fifth Count della Catena in Malta, whom Strickland succeeded as sixth count in 1875. He was educated away from Malta at St Mary's College, Oscott, near Birmingham, Warwickshire, and at the Jesuit College of Mondragone, outside Rome. He also became a law student at Trinity College, Cambridge, and was president of the union, graduating in 1887. In that year he was called to the bar at the Inner Temple. However, the island continued to exert a strong attraction on Strickland, and he influenced the Maltese political scene from 1886 to 1902, and again from 1918 until his death. The Maltese had sought protection from Napoleon's army in 1800 and in 1814 the Maltese islands came under the British crown.

At the age of twenty-one Strickland set out on a two-year tour around the world, and it was in Australia that he conceived the far-reaching idea of emigration to that country of Maltese nationals, to relieve the over-populated island of Malta. While still a student he was advising Fortunato Mizzi, the leader of the Partito Nazionale—who was married to an Italian wife, and consequently a supporter of the Italian language—on equality between the Maltese and British people. In 1886 he was elected a member of the Maltese council of government. The following year saw Strickland and Mizzi's collaboration in the framing of a new constitution, and both men gained seats in a new legislature. This constitution (known as the Strickland–Mizzi constitution) marked Malta's entry into the field of representative government after nearly a century of British rule. In 1888 Strickland acted as unpaid assistant secretary of Malta after relinquishing his seat in the council of government.

With his boundless energy and foresight Strickland became chief secretary in 1889, responsible for the civil administration of the Maltese government, lieutenant-governor in all but name. The same year he organized the committee which succeeded in stamping out a serious epidemic of cholera in Malta, introduced many reforms, created the Royal regiment of militia, initiated drainage and electricity works and the construction of the breakwater across the Grand Harbour at Valletta, and, always suspicious of the Italian connection, secured for parents the right of choice of English as a second language in the schools, of which he built twenty-six. In 1892 Strickland persuaded the government to take over the Malta Railway which was slowly deteriorating as a private enterprise. For

another five years he struggled to obtain authority from the council for its expansion, including an underground tunnel into Valletta, which would have helped the defence of Malta in the Second World War. If all his improvements had been carried out the country villages would have advanced and developed. He was appointed CMG in 1889.

Though Strickland and Mizzi had waged their joint campaign in 1887 on the promise of never substituting English for Italian, Strickland felt no allegiance to this party by 1889 as chief secretary, and Mizzi's hopes of having a strong Italian-speaking Englishman on the electoral bench faded. No break between the two men happened immediately, but it laid the groundwork for a violent split when one favoured the English language and the other remained pro-Italian. By 1899 Strickland was pointing out to Mizzi that he was printing articles in his paper *La Gazzetta di Malta* calculated to excite disloyalty between various classes of her majesty's subjects, and as a member of the Maltese bar and an elected member of the council of government he had taken an oath of allegiance to the queen. By 1901 the co-founders of the constitution of 1887 were in a head-on struggle against each other's official existence.

In 1890 Strickland married Lady Edeline (1870–1918), eldest daughter of Reginald Windsor Sackville, seventh Earl De La Warr. This must have influenced his determination to become a servant of the crown, and his bias towards the English language. They had two sons who died in infancy, and six daughters. The fourth daughter died as an infant; five survived him. In 1896 he acquired Sizergh Castle in Westmorland as his English estate and thereafter divided his time between that and Villa Bologna in Malta.

In 1895 Joseph Chamberlain had become colonial secretary in Salisbury's tory government. Fearing that the language question in Malta might drive the Italians towards Germany, Strickland revoked the planned measures against Italian in the law courts which, combined with Mizzi's increasingly violent vendetta against him, made Strickland's position untenable. In 1902, therefore, he accepted the governorship of the Leeward Islands, where he revived the ailing economy by fostering co-operative sugar refineries and cotton growing.

In 1904 Strickland was promoted to Tasmania, and in 1909 he became governor of Western Australia, followed by further promotion in 1913 as governor of the state of New South Wales, though the Orange faction were fiercely against his Catholic religion, which Strickland discreetly observed all his life. He was appointed GCMG the same year. Inevitably a clash came with Holman's Labor Party and Strickland was recalled. In 1917 Strickland, and a mortally ill Lady Edeline, returned with their family to Malta. Lady Edeline died the following year.

Strickland was now a mature and experienced politician and when his daughter, Mabel, appealed to him to concentrate on Malta's political destiny, and anticipating a growing danger from Italy, he launched a powerful journalistic campaign in the *Malta Herald*. In 1921 he founded

Il-Progress and, with Mabel's assistance, an English supplement in February 1922; these were merged into the *Times of Malta Weekly* in English, with *Il-Progress* in Maltese. In September 1928 *Ix-Xemz* ('The Sun') and *Id-Dehen* ('The Understanding') were founded and in May 1930 *Il-Berqa* ('The Lightning') appeared. The first two were terminated during a religious strife.

In 1921 Strickland formed his Anglo-Maltese Party. During two legislatures from 1921 to 1927 he was leader of the opposition, and in 1927 he assumed office as prime minister, and minister of justice. In 1924 in England he was returned as Conservative member of parliament for the Lancaster division where he used his platform in Westminster to speak almost exclusively for Malta. Possibly for this reason in 1928 he was created Baron Strickland of Sizergh Castle.

In 1926 Strickland married for the second time; his wife was Margaret (1867–1949), fourth daughter of Edward Hulton (1838–1904), of Ashton-on-Mersey, Cheshire, the owner of vast newspaper interests. Her brother was Sir Edward Hulton. Lady Strickland founded St Edward's College in January 1929 for Catholic boys, and settled £5000 a year on her husband. She recreated the garden at Villa Bologna and was known for her many charitable works. She was created DBE in 1937, and was also dame of grace of the order of St John of Jerusalem.

In Malta the priest–politicians and pro-Nationalist clergy vilified Strickland, exerting a strong political influence against him. Strickland, often with immoderate language, fought against them with all the aggression at his command and in 1930 narrowly escaped assassination. When Strickland failed to get approval for his first budget he had to get an amendment of the Amery–Milner constitution (set up in 1921) to gain his majority.

Strickland's war with the church came to its climax in 1930 when there were imminent elections. The Maltese and Gozitan bishops intervened in the electoral process with a notorious 'Mortal Sin' pastoral letter refusing absolution to anyone who voted for Strickland. A royal commission was set up in 1932 and recommended a return to the Amery–Milner constitution, in spite of which the pastoral letter was reimposed. Strickland, at his most patriotic, made a public apology, but even so the Nationalist Party had a resounding victory.

With Malta reverting to crown colony rule Strickland strove for a restoration of representative government, and fought a long series of *ultra vires* legal battles for the restoration of the peoples' liberties, which were partially obtained in 1936 and 1939.

As the Second World War threatened, Strickland, with his unflagging vision, designed undercliff hangers and submarine pens, but to Malta's cost was ignored by the country's defenders. He had been among the first to raise the alarm to the threat of fascism, and he helped to defend Malta and its people when the island became the last bastion of freedom.

Dominating, aggressive, and a pugnacious fighter in public, in his private life he was charming, genial, and excellent company. Inventor, politician, loyal husband, a strict, high-principled, but caring father, a true patriot both to the British empire and above all to Malta, he was a man before his time. Strickland died in Malta at the Villa Bologna on 22 August 1940, and was buried the following day at the cathedral, Mdina.   JOAN CARNWATH

Sources J. Alexander, *Mabel Strickland* (1996) · *DNB* · private information (2004) · H. Smith and A. Koster, *Lord Strickland: servant of the crown* (1983) · *CGPLA Eng. & Wales* (1941)
Archives Bodl. RH, corresp. and papers relating to Malta · Sizergh Castle, Westmorland | Bodl. Oxf., corresp. with Lewis Harcourt · NL Aus., corresp. with Viscount Novar · U. Southampton, Mountbatten MSS
Likenesses E. Caruana, oils, Villa Parisio, Malta · Hay, lithograph, NPG; repro. in *VF* (4 May 1893) · A. Sciortino, statue, Upper Barracoa Gardens, Valletta, Malta · C. Thorp, oils, Sizergh Castle, Kendal, Cumbria
Wealth at death £15,516 16s. 11d. — effects in England: administration with will, 21 Jan 1941, *CGPLA Eng. & Wales*

Strickland, Hugh Edwin (1811–1853), natural historian and geologist, was born on 2 March 1811 at Reighton in the East Riding of Yorkshire, the second son of Henry Eustatius Strickland (1777–1865) and his wife, Mary, daughter of the inventor Edmund *Cartwright. He was the grandson of Sir George Strickland, baronet, of Boynton, Yorkshire. At the time of his birth his father held a large farm in the neighbourhood of Reighton, but the family later moved south, to the Cotswold region. Strickland was educated at home until 1827, when he was sent to Thomas Arnold's school at Laleham, south-west of London. There he was so advanced in mathematics that a special tutor was engaged for him. He matriculated at Oriel College, Oxford, in the spring of 1828, and began his studies early in 1829, taking a third-class degree in classics in 1832.

While an undergraduate, Strickland attended William Buckland's lectures on geology and John Kidd's lectures on anatomy. He also developed his skills as a naturalist, scrutinizing the geological features of the Vale of Evesham, where his family then lived, and of the Isle of Wight and the region around Paris, which he visited during university vacations. After he left Oxford, natural history became his main pursuit. He began to publish articles in the general areas that would continue to preoccupy him throughout his career: geological description, ornithology, and problems of classification and nomenclature.

Strickland was encouraged in his geological work, and introduced into the national network of élite amateur naturalists, by Sir Roderick Murchison, with whom he became friendly at this period. Freed by his family's wealth from financial concerns, he expanded his practical experience of the natural world through travel. In 1835–6 he accompanied William John Hamilton on a tour through southern Europe to Asia Minor. Back in Britain, he continued his researches both at home and on a summer journey through Scotland and Orkney in 1837. He travelled with his father, who shared his scientific and intellectual interests.

As Strickland was emerging as an active and prolific contributor to the community of naturalists, he made his first serious attempt to marry. But when, in 1839, he asked Sir Thomas Phillipps for permission to court his daughter, he

Hugh Edwin Strickland (1811–1853), by Thomas Herbert Maguire (after Francis William Wilkins, 1837)

was first asked to pay Sir Thomas's debts, as well as a large amount of cash. His father's more conventional offer of a marriage settlement of £40,000 was rejected with anger and threats. It took the family and their solicitor half a year to extricate themselves. In the end, Strickland found his wife, as most of his other satisfactions, through natural history. He met Sir William Jardine, bt, at the British Association for the Advancement of Science meeting at Glasgow in 1840, having previously corresponded with him on ornithological topics. On 23 July 1845 he married Jardine's second daughter, Catherine Dorcas Maule, and they set out on a wedding tour to Sweden, stopping on the way to visit museums and scientists in the Netherlands and Germany.

The stream of articles that began in the mid-1830s continued into the 1840s. It consisted mostly of solid work in ornithology and geology: descriptions of formations or species. Strickland's most substantial work of this type was a monographic study of *The Dodo and its Kindred*, published in 1848, in which he provided the history and external description, while his co-author, A. G. Melville, analysed the anatomy. In addition, he revised and expanded the Ray Society's edition of Louis Agassiz's *Bibliographia zoologiae et geologiae*, in four volumes (1848–54). At the time of his death he was working on *Ornithological Synonyms*, a compendium of scientific names for bird species. The first volume, on the Accipitres, was posthumously published in 1855, under the editorship of his widow and her father.

Strickland was a member of a committee appointed at the British Association meeting at Plymouth in 1841 to draft rules that would govern zoological nomenclature. He was largely responsible for its report, which, after a little acrimonious discussion, was adopted at the British Association meeting at Manchester in 1842. The proposed rules were widely praised, but had little immediate effect, either at home or abroad.

During the 1840s Strickland kept up his scientific ties with Oxford, and in 1850 he became deputy reader in geology at the university, filling the gap left by Buckland's deteriorating mental condition. He offered three courses of twelve to fifteen lectures: one in 1850, one in 1851, and one in 1853. His classes were small, but he took his responsibilities seriously, leading his students on field trips. In 1852 he published a pamphlet entitled *On Geology in Relation to the Studies of the University of Oxford*, a contribution to the then ongoing debate over the role of natural science in the university curriculum. Apparently conceding that physical science was ultimately inferior to moral science, he felt that it nevertheless merited a prominent place in the university curriculum, because of its religious, material, and cultural benefits to students. His educational commitments also extended beyond the scholarly community. He was active in the Natural History Society of Worcester and the Tewkesbury Mechanics' Institute, and he helped to found the Cotteswold Naturalists' Field Club. He was elected a fellow of the Royal Society in 1852.

Strickland's death made him a martyr both to science and to progress, and attracted more attention than any of his quieter accomplishments. He had often examined the geological strata exposed by railway cuttings. On 14 September 1853, after that year's meeting of the British Association at Hull, he went to inspect a new section on the Manchester, Sheffield, and Lincolnshire Railway at Clarborough, near Retford. Because he had not waited to get a pass from the stationmaster, no one knew that he was on the line. He was working on a rock face near a sharp curve, and when he stepped backwards to avoid a coal train, he was instantly killed by a passenger train coming in the other direction. His death was widely reported and much lamented. He was buried at the priory church of St Mary, Deerhurst, Gloucestershire. His widow donated his osteological collection to the Hastings Museum at Worcester, but finding a satisfactory home for his most important collection, the approximately six thousand bird skins that he had accumulated, posed a problem. They were initially given to Oxford, to be stored safely until the new University Museum was completed. But when Mrs Strickland viewed the collection on display in 1861, she was extremely displeased, and after protracted negotiations, the collection was redonated to the University of Cambridge in 1867.

HARRIET RITVO

Sources Glos. RO, Strickland (Apperley) papers · nomenclature MSS, U. Cam., Museum of Zoology, Hugh E. Strickland collection · W. Jardine, *Memoirs of Hugh Edwin Strickland* (1858) [incl. H. E. Strickland, 'Chronological list of writings'] · O. Salvin, *A catalogue of a collection of birds formed by the late Hugh Edwin Strickland* (1882) · C. L. Shadwell, *Registrum Orielense*, 2 (1902)

Archives American Philosophical Society, Philadelphia, corresp. · Glos. RO, corresp. and papers · NHM, diaries, journals, and sketchbook · U. Cam., Museum of Zoology, corresp. and

papers • U. Cam., Sedgwick Museum of Earth Sciences, catalogue of fossil collection • Zoological Society of London, ornithological papers | GS Lond., letters to Sir R. I. Murchison
Likenesses portrait, 1837, repro. in Jardine, *Memoirs of Hugh Edwin Strickland* • photograph, 1853, repro. in Jardine, *Memoirs of Hugh Edwin Strickland* • T. H. Maguire, lithograph (after F. W. Wilkins, 1837), NPG [*see illus.*] • engraving, RS
Wealth at death personal and scientific property, incl. large collection of bird skins

Strickland, Jane Margaret (1800–1888). *See under* Strickland, Agnes (1796–1874).

Strickland, John (*bap.* 1601?, *d.* 1670), clergyman and ejected minister, was probably the John Strickland who was baptized on 11 March 1601 at Kendal, Westmorland, son of James Strickland of Kendal and his wife, Mary Hodgson. He matriculated from Queen's College, Oxford, on 15 May 1618, graduated BA on 9 December 1622, and proceeded MA on 25 June 1625. His early promise was noted by William Seymour, earl of Hertford and later duke of Somerset, to whom he became chaplain. In 1631 he was nominated assistant to John White at Dorchester, Dorset, and in the following year, during which he also proceeded BD, Sir John Horner presented him to the rectory of Pudimore Milton, Somerset. Anthony Wood cited a sermon given by Strickland at Southampton in June 1643, invoking divine support against the 'Antichrist [who] hath drawn his Sword against thy Christ; and if our Enemies prevail, thou wilt lose thine Honour' (Dugdale, 567), as evidence that Strickland 'prayed several times blasphemously' (Wood, 3.910), but Edmund Calamy, by contrast, judged him 'a great divine, and generally esteemed', who 'was eminent for expounding the scriptures, and an excellent casuist' (*Nonconformist's Memorial*, 3.372).

A member of the Westminster assembly from October 1643, Strickland was shortly afterwards appointed minister of St Peter-le-Poer, London, in place of the sequestered Richard Holdsworth, and might also have been presented to St Martin-in-the-Fields. He preached a number of fast sermons before the Commons, 'exciting the Members thereof to proceed in their blessed cause' (Wood, 3.910). Four of these were published in 1644 and 1645—*A Discovery of Peace*, *God's Work of Mercy in Sion's Misery*, *Immanuel, or, The Church Triumphing in God with Us*, and *Mercy Rejoycing Against Judgement*. He also became an assistant to the ecclesiastical commissioners for Wiltshire.

Strickland was removed from St Peter-le-Poer in January 1647 and, after losing the mastership of St Nicholas's Hospital, East Harnham, Wiltshire, to which he had been appointed in February 1646, unsuccessfully petitioned for a living at Lancaster, though some authorities cite him as officiating there from November 1647. His interest in the north is evidenced by his signing orders for placing a minister at St Mary's, Carlisle, and urging the Commons 'to have a care how they plant the towns of Cumberland and Northumberland with able preachers' (Nightingale, 2.939). In 1656 he was presented to Kendal by Trinity College, Cambridge, but, although denounced by a local Quaker for demanding a stipend of £180, it is again unlikely that he officiated.

By this time Strickland's principal living was at St Edmund's, Salisbury, but he was evidently a peripatetic preacher, for Thomas Mason, former prebendary of Salisbury, occasionally preached there in his absence. With Byfield and Humphrey Chambers, among others, Strickland wrote the *Apology for the Ministers of the County of Wiltshire* (1654) in answer to a tract which had condemned them for opposing the election to parliament of the republican Edmund Ludlow. After he was ejected from St Edmund's in 1662, Strickland formed his own congregation in the town, in contravention of the Five Mile Act, and is also known to have preached in Tisbury, Wiltshire, and in Dorchester, in the company of Adoniram Byfield and the congregationalist minister Peter Ince. In his will, made on 5 October 1670, Strickland left tenements in Alford, Somerset, and the greater part of his library, manuscripts, and sermons to his wife, Susan, a daughter of Sir Thomas Piggot, while his sons-in-law, the nonconformist ministers Thomas Rosewell and William Gough, were bequeathed works by St Augustine as well as his seven-volume edition of the Bible; he also left land in Wiltshire, Buckinghamshire, and Westmorland. He died on 23 October 1670 immediately after preaching to his congregation, and was buried in the churchyard of St Edmund's two days later.   HENRY LANCASTER

Sources *Calamy rev.*, 467–8 • *The nonconformist's memorial … originally written by … Edmund Calamy*, ed. S. Palmer, [3rd edn], 3 (1803), 372 • Wood, *Ath. Oxon.*, new edn, 3.910 • G. L. Turner, *Original records of early nonconformity under persecution and indulgence*, 3 (1914), 1063, 1066 • W. A. Shaw, *A history of the English church during the civil wars and under the Commonwealth, 1640–1660*, 2 vols. (1900) • *Walker rev.*, 43, 51, 377 • BL, Add. MS 4276, fol. 166 • Foster, *Alum. Oxon.* • T. Fuller, *The church history of Britain*, ed. J. S. Brewer, new edn, 6 vols. (1845), vol. 4, p. 248 • *IGI* • B. Nightingale, *The ejected of 1662 in Cumberland and Westmorland: their predecessors and successors*, 2 vols. (1911) • F. Nicholson and E. Axon, *The older nonconformity in Kendal* (1915) • will, PRO, PROB 11/335, fol. 223v • H. Lancaster, 'Nonconformity in Restoration Wiltshire, 1660–1689', PhD diss., University of Bristol, 1995 • W. Dugdale, *A short view of the late troubles in England* (1681)
Wealth at death land in Somerset, Wiltshire, Westmorland, and Buckinghamshire: will, 1670, PRO, PROB 11/335, fol. 223v

Strickland, Mannock John (1683–1744), counsellor and lawyer, was born on 23 August 1683 at Thornton Bridge, Yorkshire, the fifth of the ten children of Robert Strickland (1639–1709), vice-chamberlain and treasurer to Queen Mary of Modena, and his wife, Bridget (*d.* 1736), fourth daughter of Sir Francis Mannock of Gifford's Hall, Stoke by Nayland, Suffolk, and his wife, Mary Heneage.

Strickland went with his parents into exile in France with the court of James II in 1688 and received a Roman Catholic education at the English College at Douai, and from 1700 to 1703 at the English College at St Omer. Returning to England, he was admitted to Gray's Inn in January 1704, becoming a pupil of Henry Eyre (*c.*1667–1719) until 1709, and gradually taking over and then inheriting his practice. Strickland practised at Gray's Inn until his admission on 9 February 1733 to Lincoln's Inn, where he was based until his death. He was the leading Roman Catholic conveyancer and legal adviser of his day (preceding the better-known Matthew Duane), although not, as often stated, the first practising Catholic solicitor.

As a Roman Catholic, Strickland was technically debarred from sustaining lawsuits, but he was able to operate a full range of legal services through an alliance from 1726 with Henry Rogers Trubshaw (d. c.1770), a non-Catholic clerk who was also a solicitor and undertook any necessary litigation. His active legal practice was condoned in 1732 by Sir Robert Walpole in instructions for the Derwentwater estate settlement. He had two main patrons, William Herbert, second marquess of Powis (c.1665–1745), and Robert, eighth Baron Petre (1713–1742), and their families, as well as a wide clientele of English Roman Catholic gentry, with a sprinkling of nobility and of commoners. His work consisted of the provision of a full range of legal and financial services, professional advice, and estates administration to his clients, with the principal aim of circumventing the disadvantages for Catholics of penal legislation, and ensuring the successful transmission of their estates. His services were in demand for the drafting of settlements, conveyances, and wills, and he was a broker and lender for mortgages and loans. He provided expert legal advice and management and accounting services to his clients, and acted as trustee and agent during minorities, most notably that of Lord Petre, for whom he reclaimed the substantial forfeited marriage portion of Petre's wife, Anna Maria, daughter of the executed Jacobite third earl of Derwentwater.

Although he travelled infrequently to the continent, Strickland acted as agent to four foreign English convents: the English Benedictines at Dunkirk (home of his sister Catherine and of his mother following the death of Mary of Modena), the Benedictine nuns in Brussels, the Augustinian canonesses of St Monica's, Louvain, and the Dominicans of Spellekens (the Pin-House), Brussels. All were key centres for the promotion of Jacobitism; through them Strickland was a safe and regular channel for Jacobite intelligence, and a committed and highly discreet agent for the cause.

Strickland was as widely criticized for his 'magnificence' of style as lauded for his excellent legal services; his portrait shows a proud and handsome man, fashionably dressed and wearing a full brown wig. He suffered severely from gout and bouts of ill health. In October 1719 Strickland married Mary (d. 1750), third of the five children of John Wright, goldsmith, of Henrietta Street, Covent Garden, Middlesex, and of Kelvedon Hatch, Essex, and his wife, Eugenia Trinder. They had ten children; four of the six survivors to adulthood entered religious orders, and one the West Indies trade. From 1719 he rented a house at 4 Queen Square, Bloomsbury, London, and occasionally leased another in Isleworth, Middlesex.

In active practice until his death at 4 Queen Square on 19 November 1744, Strickland was buried in St Nicholas's Old Church, Kelvedon Hatch. He died intestate, with no successor to his practice; his complete business papers constitute a rare survival from the period. His wife, who was also his administrator, died on 4 March 1750.

RICHARD G. WILLIAMS

Sources R. G. Williams, 'Mannock Strickland, 1683–1744: life and professional career of a Jacobite lawyer', PhD diss., U. Lond., 1999 · H. Hornyold, *Genealogical memoirs of the family of Strickland of Sizergh: being a brief account of the family and its branches* (1928) · L. P. Wenham, *Roger Strickland of Richmond: a Jacobite gentleman, 1680–1749* (1982) · Mapledurham House, Mapledurham, Oxfordshire, Blount MSS, Mannock Strickland papers · N. Yorks. CRO, Scrope papers · G. Holt, *St Omers and Bruges colleges, 1593–1773: a biographical dictionary*, Catholic RS, 69 (1979) · H. Phillips, *Mid-Georgian London: a topographical and social survey of central and western London about 1750* (1964)
Archives Mapledurham House, Oxfordshire, business and personal papers | BL, Caryll MSS
Likenesses school of J. Closterman, oils, 1730?, Mapledurham House, Oxfordshire
Wealth at death see inventories and administration accounts, Mapledurham House, Oxfordshire, Blount MSS

Strickland, Sir Roger (*bap.* **1640**, *d.* **1717**), naval officer and Jacobite sympathizer, was baptized on 2 February 1640 at Kendal, the second son of Walter Strickland (d. 1670×77) of Nateby Hall, Garstang, Lancashire, and his wife, Anne Croft (d. 1665×80). Walter Strickland was a member of a junior line of the Stricklands of Sizergh Castle, Westmorland, and fought for the king in the civil wars, compounding for delinquency in 1652. Roger entered the navy after the Restoration, becoming lieutenant of the *Sapphire* on 27 November 1661 and serving aboard her until the following July. He was then successively lieutenant of the *Crown* and the *Providence* prior to the outbreak of the Second Anglo-Dutch War, serving in the same post aboard the *Rainbow* from April to September 1665. He fought in her in the admiral's division of the White squadron (commanded by Prince Rupert) at the battle of Lowestoft on 3 June 1665. Strickland was lieutenant of the hired ship *Hamburg Merchant* late in 1665 before gaining his first command, the former Spanish prize *Santa Maria*, on 16 March 1666. Although his ship missed the Four Days' Battle in June, Strickland commanded her at the St James's day fight on 25 July, forming part of the Blue squadron, and remained aboard her until 5 December. He held no command in 1667, but commanded the *Success* in 1668–9, the *Kent* in 1670–71, and the *Antelope* briefly in January and February 1672. He took command of the *Plymouth*, of 58 guns, on 11 March 1672. At the battle of Sole Bay on 28 May, Strickland's ship formed part of the rear-admiral of the blue's division, and gained distinction by retaking the second-rate *Henry*, which had been captured by the Dutch; because of the death in the battle of the *Henry*'s captain, Francis Digby, Strickland was moved into her on 8 June. Later in the year Strickland was knighted for his gallantry at Sole Bay. He took command of the *Mary* on 19 September 1672 and continued in her until March 1674. He fought in all three battles of the 1673 campaign, being singled out by Rupert for his conduct at the first battle of Schooneveld (28 May) and the Texel (11 August). Following the end of the war, he went to the Mediterranean to join the campaigns under Sir John Narbrough against the north African corsairs, commanding successively the *Dragon* (September 1674 to November 1677), the *Centurion* (November to December 1677), the *Mary* again (December 1677 to January 1679), and the *Bristol* (January to September 1679).

Strickland took part in a number of actions against the corsairs, notably the capture of a 40-gun Algerine vessel on 1 April 1678. He was appointed rear-admiral of the Mediterranean Fleet on 19 February 1678, but after his return to England in 1679 he retired from the service—albeit reluctantly, as he regularly but unsuccessfully solicited for plum commands during the years 1680–84.

Strickland bought an estate at Thornton Bridge, Yorkshire, from his cousin Sir Thomas Strickland MP in 1680, and in the following year inherited an estate at Catterick from his aunt Mary, widow of Richard Brathwaite. In 1681 he was also appointed deputy governor of Southsea Castle, thereby continuing his parallel career in the army which had begun when he became a captain in Prince Rupert's regiment in 1672, subsequently joining Lord Widdrington's regiment in 1673. In 1682 Strickland took over Sir Thomas's farm of the salt duties, and in 1684 leased the estates of a number of Lancashire recusants. This action was at best ironic, at worst distinctly suspicious, as Strickland's own religious beliefs had already been called into question during the Popish Plot, and many of his close relations remained openly Catholic. His brother was a member of the household of James, duke of York, becoming vice-chamberlain to Queen Mary of Modena when James became king, and James himself had been active in promoting Strickland's interests during the early 1680s. Within four days of his accession, James recalled Sir Roger to the navy, giving him command of the *Bristol* to convey the new ambassador to Constantinople—duty which precluded his active attendance in parliament, to which he was elected as MP for Aldborough in March 1685. Although Strickland's career was also being promoted at this time by his friend George Legge, Lord Dartmouth, it owed little to one of Dartmouth's other close associates, the Admiralty secretary Samuel Pepys, who clashed often and bitterly with Strickland during 1685–6, most notably over the latter's insistence on flying a special flag of distinction at all times and on other points of precedence, which Sir Roger always guarded jealously. Strickland's public conversion to Catholicism in the winter of 1686–7 greatly strengthened his position: he became vice-admiral of the fleet going to the Mediterranean in July 1687, rising to the prestigious post of rear-admiral of England on 30 December. He used his new position to advance the careers of his co-religionists in the navy, and in the summer of 1688 was appointed to command the fleet guarding against Dutch naval preparations. His tactless introduction of Catholic priests onto the ships inspired a mutiny which James II had to quell in person, and when the fleet was expanded in September, Strickland was effectively demoted to rear-admiral, albeit under his friend Dartmouth. The fleet's failure to prevent William of Orange's invasion effectively ended Strickland's career. He resigned his commission on 13 December 1688, writing shortly afterwards that 'his heart and eyes are … full of grief and tears' (*Dartmouth MSS*, 1.238). Strickland soon followed James to France, serving in the Irish campaign of 1689 and aboard the French fleet in 1690; his name was included in a bill of attainder in 1689,

but was struck out through lack of evidence, although his estates were subsequently confiscated in any case. He lived in exile at St Germain, where he died on 8 August 1717, having never married. He was buried in St Germain church the following day. The sequestration of his estates almost thirty years before, and the disputed legality of that action, led to prolonged litigation between and among his heirs and those who claimed various reversions on his lands.

J. D. DAVIES

Sources H. Hornyold, *Genealogical memoirs of the family of Strickland of Sizergh* (1928) • PRO, ADM MSS • Magd. Cam., Pepys Library • J. D. Davies, 'James II, William of Orange, and the admirals', *By force or by default? The revolution of 1688–1689*, ed. E. Cruickshanks (1989), 82–108 • J. D. Davies, *Gentlemen and tarpaulins: the officers and men of the Restoration navy* (1991) • *The manuscripts of the earl of Dartmouth*, 3 vols., HMC, 20 (1887–96), vol. 1, pp. 3, 238 • W. A. Shaw, ed., *Calendar of treasury books*, 7, PRO (1916); 9 (1931); 10 (1935); 31 (1957) • C. Dalton, ed., *English army lists and commission registers, 1661–1714*, 1 (1892), 122, 160, 191 • HoP, *Commons, 1660–90*, 3.503–4
Archives Magd. Cam., corresp. with Samuel Pepys

Strickland, Samuel (1805–1867). *See under* Strickland, Agnes (1796–1874).

Strickland, Thomas John Francis (*c*.1682–1740), Roman Catholic bishop of Namur and diplomatist, was the fourth son of Sir Thomas Strickland (1621–1694) of Sizergh, Westmorland, and his wife, Winifred *Strickland, *née* Trentham (1645–1725). He spent his early years at the family seat of Sizergh Castle, where he was educated by Thomas Shepherd, who served as his personal tutor. However, following the collapse of King James II's regime his parents fled to France, and it was not until April 1689 that the necessary passes were obtained that enabled him to follow them into exile. On 18 April 1689 Strickland was stopped by the authorities at Dover, together with another of his siblings and his tutor, on the suspicion of Jacobitism. Fortunately, they were allowed to take ship after producing their letters of safe conduct and arrived at the court of St Germain without further incident or mishap.

After being raised in the household of the fallen Stuarts, Strickland was admitted into St Gregory's College, Paris, at his own expense, on 9 January 1703 to study for the priesthood. Thereafter, his educational career would seem to have been both lengthy and chequered. He appears to have studied at St Sulpice in Paris from April 1704 onwards before returning to St Gregory's in October 1711. He took the degree of doctor of divinity at the Sorbonne in 1712, and left St Gregory's following his ordination as a priest on 2 April 1712. He tended a side chapel in the church of St Sulpice for some months before returning to England—and Sizergh—in 1713. It is probable that he used his time to travel through the northern counties, taking soundings—and gathering intelligence—from the leading recusant families, and his resulting notes formed the basis of his *Memoir on the State of the English Mission*. This work, written in French in 1714, was submitted by him to the papal internuncio in Flanders, and was subsequently forwarded to the office of the propaganda in Rome.

Having thus come to the notice of the hierarchy of the

church, Strickland was noted as being 'ardently ambitious of the episcopal dignity for himself' (Brady, 3.154), and in 1716 he lobbied hard for his own appointment as co-adjutor to Bishop Bonaventure Giffard of the London district, who was then seventy-four years of age. In this he was supported by John Talbot Stonor, a friend from St Gregory's who had become bishop of Thespiae and vicar apostolic of the midland district that year. It is clear that Strickland had already broken, decisively, with the Jacobite movement that had nurtured him, and it would seem highly likely that it was primarily political considerations that motivated the storm of criticism and complaint that greeted his candidature for the post. Bishop Giffard provided evidence of his own continuing health and competency, while his ally Bishop George Witham appealed to Rome against: 'Strickland ... [who] was possessed of less capacity than any of the persons who had been ... proposed for the office of Vicar Apostolic in England, especially as he was very young and had but recently been introduced into England' (Hornyold, 151). Stonor himself said that he thought Strickland vain and lacking in judgement, and that he could 'neither keep his own counsel nor anybody's else' (Duffy, 351). In the face of such strong feeling and bitter censure Strickland's candidature collapsed.

Strickland had, however, gained a powerful patron in the form of Thomas Howard, eighth duke of Norfolk. Norfolk began negotiations with the papacy in 1716 in order to obtain the pope's support for an oath that would allow English Catholics to swear allegiance to George I, and thereby prepare the ground for the removal of some at least of their civil disabilities. Strickland put pressure on the papal nuncio at Brussels, and succeeded in obtaining a preliminary agreement by which English Catholics would be able to swear allegiance to George I, provided the oath made no mention of the papal dispensing and disposing powers. Strickland also visited Hanover, where he gained the support of George I for the proposed oath. Norfolk sent Strickland on a mission to Rome, where he arrived by Easter 1717, in order to secure papal approval for the scheme. Strickland proved himself to be an intelligent, highly articulate, and socially adept envoy. He won verbal agreement for the desired change in church policy, but his actions also brought him the undying enmity of the Jacobites. Unfortunately, even though the church authorities had committed themselves verbally to the agreement, Strickland's appeals that the decision should be set down in writing and published as a decree were rejected by the church, which did not want to alienate the Jacobites. Consequently, on his arrival in Flanders to inform the nuncio of the pontiff's tacit recognition of the protestant succession, he found his credibility substantially weakened.

Strickland's efforts were still supported by Norfolk, Stonor, and other leading English Catholics, and in spring 1718 he travelled to Paris. There, he contacted John Dalrymple, second earl of Stair, British minister to France, and presented a short memorial to him outlining the plight of English Catholics and arguing that, in return for toleration, they might be persuaded formally to renounce their support for the beleaguered Jacobite cause and be usefully employed within the British governmental structure. Such an offer proved extremely attractive, and Lord Stair was quick to recommend Strickland as 'a sensible, good-natured man, who seems concerned for the good and quiet of his country and for the good of the Roman Catholics themselves' (Hornyold, 152).

In order to drive a wedge more firmly between English Catholics and the exiled Jacobites, Strickland returned to England in July 1718 and composed and published an anonymous pamphlet purporting to be *A letter from a gentleman at R[ome] dated September 15, 1718, to a friend at L[ondon]*. In it he presented an unflattering portrait of James Francis Edward, the Pretender, as a religious bigot and as the unwitting pawn of the 'perfectly Despotic' John Erskine, twenty-third or sixth earl of Mar. The pair were shown presiding over their tattered and threadbare court at Urbino, unable to pay the wages of their followers and ridiculing the attempts of the English Jacobites to win back the throne for them. Only Scotsmen, 'my Lord M[ar]'s Kindred and Creatures', were to be valued, and the first effect of a new restoration was confidently predicted to be the 'Inundation of S[cots] without Merit [into England], greedy of Money ... fancying that all our Treasure will be little enough to reward them' (Strickland, 5–6). Following the pamphlet's appearance Strickland received death threats and had his appointment as the vicar-general of Meaux blocked at the behest of Mary of Modena, the Pretender's mother. General Arthur Dillon considered Strickland, as the author of the 'scurrilous, malicious English epistle, which is handed about here ... capable of everything base and unworthy' (Hornyold, 153), while the earl of Mar—predictably—branded his critic as 'a little, conceited, empty, meddling prig' (*Stuart Papers*, 7.493). For his part, the Pretender could only pity Dr Strickland's 'poor mother' (ibid., 7.544–5), who still continued in her devotion to his flagging cause.

Strickland returned to Paris by September 1718. The British government was keen to protect its ally, and to see that he was properly rewarded for his services and promoted to high office within the Catholic church. Consequently, vigorous appeals were made to Philippe, duke of Orléans, the regent of France, in order to settle a suitable benefice upon Strickland. The vacant abbey of St Pierre de Preaux in Normandy—which carried with it a stipend of between 12,000 and 15,000 livres—was granted to him on 25 August 1718.

Having been presented to the regent, and thanked him for the gift of the abbey, Strickland travelled to Vienna in January 1719 with a formal diplomatic commission from George I. He was to engineer an alliance between the pope and the emperor, and destroy the influence of Jacobite agents at the imperial court. The emperor would then persuade the pope to give final approval to the proposed oath of allegiance. On 8 February 1719 he was confidently writing to secretary of state James Craggs of his great success with Charles VI. He left Vienna in March, and in June judged it safe to return to England. He took lodgings in London, and formulated a series of proposals—with the approval of Craggs and the British government—which aimed to secure Catholic toleration in return for the acknowledgement of the protestant succession, the severing of all communications with the Pretender, and the removal of the office and title of protector of England from the pro-Jacobite Cardinal Gualterio, at the court of Rome. However, resistance to his plans was strong among many leading English Catholics, who found Strickland self-serving and arrogant. Strickland advised Craggs to arrest Bishop Giffard, Gilbert Talbot, thirteenth earl of Shrewsbury (a Jesuit), and other Catholics in order to leave the way clear for negotiations with more moderate and amenable figures. Some arrests were made, and Strickland met Norfolk on 7 July, but an impasse had been reached over the refusal of the government to allow Catholics to take the oath of allegiance alongside an oath to uphold the authority of the pope. In addition, the ministry of which Strickland had become an agent was perceived as weak. It was opposed in the Commons by Robert Walpole, widely expected to return to power, who employed strongly anti-Catholic rhetoric and who could not be expected to maintain any agreement made on the Catholic question. Strickland's reliance on the authority of the emperor also unsettled English Catholics, as it seemed to confirm protestant allegations that they were subjects of a foreign prince. The negotiations broke up without the issue of Jacobitism ever having been adequately addressed by Norfolk, and Strickland's proposals were comprehensively rejected by his co-religionists. Saddened and gravely dismayed, Strickland left England. The British government continued to regard him as the English Catholics' principal negotiator, but further efforts to revive the allegiance proposals proved fruitless. The return of Walpole to power in 1721 and the revelation of the Jacobite plot of Francis Atterbury, bishop of Rochester, ended hopes that the English Catholics would be able to reach an accommodation with the British government.

Strickland had by then settled at the court of the exiled king of Poland, Stanisław Leszczyński, at Bar, in Lorraine. He was later to claim that he had obtained a cardinal's hat from Stanisław, but had chosen to resign it upon a point of conscience. More probably, Stanisław had nominated Strickland as a cardinal after coming under sustained pressure from the British government, and Strickland had then sold the nomination to the emperor for a lump sum and the promise of his support in securing the bishopric of Namur. With the full backing of Charles VI, Strickland was proposed as the new bishop of Namur in 1725, and was finally consecrated by the archbishop of Malines on Sunday 28 February 1728. He made his entry into his cathedral at Namur on the eve of Pentecost, and celebrated his first pontifical mass the next day, 16 May 1728.

Strickland's taste for diplomatic intrigue had not deserted him. He visited Rome and Vienna in 1733 in an attempt to gather intelligence on the Jacobite exiles domiciled there. His desire to become a cardinal looked like finally being realized as the British government championed his appointment with the Austrians and as he won

the trust and friendship of the empress. However, in deciding to carry the prospect of a military alliance between Britain and the imperial court back to Whitehall, at the behest of Charles VI, he at last overreached himself. He returned to London in autumn 1734 disguised as a Mr Mosley, where he attempted to promote the alliance and urged a declaration of war with France. He impressed both George II and Queen Caroline during a private interview, and attempted to form a war party about William Stanhope, Baron Harrington, which might have been capable of replacing Sir Robert Walpole's ministry. However, Walpole's spies had 'dogged and traced him to every place he had frequented from his first coming to England, [and] soon found what he drove at' (Hervey, 2.395). Consequently Walpole was able to destroy utterly Strickland's credit with the king and queen by pointing out that the bishop—'though now near three-score'—had been repeatedly observed going out 'late at night on foot, and wrapped up in a red rug riding coat' (ibid.) to an infamous local brothel. At the same time Walpole posted dispatches to the emperor alleging that Strickland was in correspondence with his domestic and foreign foes, while Harrington suddenly withdrew from his advocacy of the bishop's embassy, swayed by information from one of his own clients that Strickland not only aimed to have a cardinal's hat but also aimed: '[as] his principle ambition … to slip himself, by one means or other, into some share of the ministry' (Coxe, 3.177). With his reputation as a diplomat effectively destroyed, Strickland was firmly but 'civilly dismissed' (ibid., 2.444) and returned to France.

Ensconced at his see of Namur, Strickland proved to be—even by the admission of his enemies—a popular, diligent, and wholly competent administrator. He enlarged the cathedral, endowed a seminary, and built a large episcopal palace. However, having distinguished himself as an enthusiastic patron of artists, musicians, and sculptors, he suddenly fell ill towards the end of 1739 and retired to Louvain in a forlorn attempt to regain his failing health. He died at Louvain quickly and peacefully on 14 January 1740 NS, and his body was brought back to lie in state at the episcopal palace at Namur. He was buried in the vaults of his own cathedral on the evening of 16 January 1740, but no stone or inscription was ever raised to honour and perpetuate his memory.

Reviled as an 'inveterate wire-puller' (Scott, 191), Strickland was said to have been possessed of 'an artful and intriguing … manner' (Hervey, 1.392) and to have 'passed his whole life in gluttony, drunkenness, and the most infamous debauchery' (Coxe, 1.443). Yet he won a reputation for fairness and financial probity while at Namur, and genuinely sought to improve the political condition of the English Catholics by dissociating them from Jacobitism in return for a guarantee of civil and legal rights from the Hanoverian British government.   JOHN CALLOW

Sources H. Hornyold, *Genealogical memoirs of the family of Strickland of Sizergh* (1928) • [T. Strickland], *A letter from a gentleman at R[ome] dated September 15, 1718, to a friend at L[ondon]* (1718) • D. Scott, *The Stricklands of Sizergh* (1908) • Gillow, *Lit. biog. hist.*, vol. 5 • *CSP dom., 1689–90* • *Calendar of the Stuart papers belonging to his majesty the king,* preserved at Windsor Castle, 7 vols., HMC, 56 (1902–23), vols. 3, 5, 7 · W. M. Brady, *The episcopal succession in England, Scotland, and Ireland, AD 1400 to 1875*, 3 (1877) · *Annals and correspondence of the viscount and the first and second earls of Stair*, ed. J. M. Graham, 2 vols. (1875) · J. Hervey, *Memoirs of the reign of George the Second*, ed. J. W. Croker, 2 vols. (1848) · J. Bossy, *The English Catholic community, 1570–1850* (1975) · W. Coxe, *Memoirs of the life and administration of Sir Robert Walpole, earl of Orford*, 3 vols. (1798) · G. Brenan and E. P. Statham, *The house of Howard*, 2 vols. (1907) · *N&Q*, 2 (1850), 198, 237, 270 · 'True copy of the paper put into the hands of the R[oman] Catholicks', c.1719, BL, Add. MS 28252, fols. 94–95 · 'Answer to the aforesaid proposals', c.1719, BL, Add. MS 28252, fols. 96–7 · E. Duffy, '"Englishmen in Vaine": Roman Catholic allegiance to George I', *Religion and national identity*, ed. S. Mews, SCH, 18 (1982), 345–65 · E. H. Burton, ed., 'The register book of St Gregory's College, Paris, 1667–1786', *Miscellanea, XI*, Catholic RS, 19 (1917), 93–160 · J. Ingamells, ed., *A dictionary of British and Irish travellers in Italy, 1701–1800* (1997) · G. O. Gürtler, 'Homo Politicus or Homo Religiosus?', *Transactions of the Cumberland and Westmorland Antiquarian and Archaeological Society*, 89 (1989), 207–31 · G. O. Gürtler, 'Thomas J. F. Strickland of Sizergh', *Transactions of the Cumberland and Westmorland Antiquarian and Archaeological Society*, 90 (1990), 217–34 · G. O. Gürtler, 'Under the shadow of high diplomacy', *Transactions of the Cumberland and Westmorland Antiquarian and Archaeological Society*, 94 (1994), 143–69

Archives BL, Italian corresp. relating to Strickland, Add. MSS 20311, fols. 291, 295; 20313, fols. 112, 149 · BL, letters to Lord Sunderland, Add. MSS 61547, fols. 211–214b; 6162, fols. 199–208b · BL, recommendation for Strickland, Add. MS 61612, fol. 138

Likenesses A.-S. Belle, oils, c.1703, Sizergh Castle, Cumbria; repro. in Hornyold, *Genealogical memoirs*, 158 · J. Vanderbank, oils, 1724 (middle-aged), Sizergh Castle, Cumbria; repro. in Hornyold, *Genealogical memoirs*, 158 · J. Faber junior, mezzotint (after J. Vanderbank, 1724), BM; NPG · oils, Namur episcopal palace · pastels

Strickland, Walter, appointed Lord Strickland under the protectorate (1598?–1671), politician and diplomatist, was the second son of Walter Strickland (d. 1636) of Boynton, Yorkshire, and Frances (d. 1636), daughter of Peter Wentworth of Lillingstone Lovel, Oxfordshire, and niece of Sir Francis Walsingham. Sir William *Strickland was his elder brother. Walter Strickland was admitted to Gray's Inn on 10 August 1618, and matriculated at Queens' College, Cambridge, at Easter 1619. He married Anne Morgan (d. 1688), daughter of Sir Charles Morgan (d. 1595), governor of Bergen-op-Zoom, and widow of Sir Lewis Morgan. Until 1642 merely a Yorkshire JP, his selection as parliamentary ambassador to the United Provinces that October appears to have been primarily due to his wife's Dutch connections. Resident at The Hague on a salary of £400 p.a., he initially protested at Henrietta Maria's attempt to raise funds there and thereafter sought to counter the influence of her Orange relatives on Dutch attitudes to parliament, and reported on royalists hiring Dutch ships. He received a £500 gift from parliament for his efforts in July 1645, and was recruited to the Long Parliament to fill a vacancy at Minehead.

The king's execution made the Commonwealth a pariah, but the states of Holland commenced commercial negotiations and parliament sent Isaac Dorislaus to assist Strickland. Dorislaus's assassination by royalists on 2 May 1649 emphasized the danger Strickland was in, but he stayed on, though royalist revival in Scotland caused the states general of the United Provinces to delay receiving him. He persuaded the states of Holland to protest at this delay, regarding their goodwill as 'a foundation to cut off for ever the hopes of [England's] greatest enemies'. Even so, he had to act on the council of state's resolution of 21 June 1650 to recall him on account of his having been snubbed while assuring Holland of parliament's continuing goodwill. He reported to parliament on 7 August, receiving their thanks. Hopes of the Dutch revived after William II provoked a confrontation with Holland and then suddenly died in October. To exploit this, parliament sent Strickland back on 23 January with a new colleague, Oliver St John, to press for the closest possible alliance with the resurgent republicans. Harassed by the royalists, their attempt to focus the talks on royalist rebels' activities in the United Provinces met with vague replies. The Dutch would expel only active rebels, and proposed that English shipping be allowed to trade in Dutch areas of the West Indies and America, the fleets to act against pirates, and each to have free access to the other's harbours. The preponderance of the Dutch mercantile marine gave them the advantage, and they rejected attempts to impound Princess Mary's property to reimburse victims of Dutch licensed royalist pirates. Amid continuing deadlock the English left on 18 June; both sides were inflexible but it may be that St John favoured breakdown from the start, in association with those MPs who prompted retaliation to the failed negotiations with the Navigation Acts.

Strickland had been a commissioner for the assessment in Yorkshire since 1649, and in 1652 he took up the same post in his wife's home county, Glamorgan. A member of the council of state since 13 February 1651, he was now eclipsed by the warmongers in Dutch policy but represented the council's opinion on scandalous ministers to parliament in July. His wife, calling herself Lady Morgan, made an independent visit to Holland in June 1652, no doubt to promote English interests with her relatives. Strickland acquired the manor of Flamborough, Yorkshire, under sequestration from Sir Henry Griffith, in 1650 for £4800, £2000 of it from his wife. In January 1652 he asked parliament to confirm that he could acquire full title by paying off £500 outstanding on the mortgage, which the committee for advance of money arranged.

Milton considered Strickland a close ally of Cromwell in 1652, and he was one of those he consulted after the expulsion of the Rump in 1653. He continued on councils of state and acquired Whitehall lodgings, and the army selected him to sit for Yorkshire in the Barebones Parliament. As an experienced diplomat he joined their committee for foreign affairs and was one of the council's negotiators with the Dutch over the ending of the First Anglo-Dutch War (1652–4). Cromwell, handling negotiations, insisted on considering federation despite Dutch opposition. Where Strickland believed in alliance with the Dutch republicans against the house of Orange, Cromwell unnecessarily insisted that the latter be formally excluded from power and thus delayed the settlement. Meanwhile Strickland represented the council case against John Lilburne to parliament, and signed the assembly's renunciation of its powers on 12 December 1653 with other moderates.

The second oldest, but a very active, member of Cromwell's council, Strickland sat in the protectorate parliaments for the East Riding in 1654 and Newark in 1656, and handled some Yorkshire business for the council, as when judges questioned the legality of Cromwell's treason laws during royalists' trials in 1655. In foreign affairs he supported alliance with France, being appointed to negotiate with its ambassadors in April 1654. Conversely, as an opponent of alliance with Sweden he was detailed in January 1656 to join the more sympathetic Whitelocke to negotiate the Swedish treaty. He was firm in insisting that all goods which could be used for military purposes, particularly guns, should be declared contraband for export to possible enemies. He took part in commercial negotiations with the Dutch ambassador Nieupoort in 1656, and assisted the committee to give aid to persecuted Piedmontese and Polish protestants.

A tolerant pragmatist in religion, Strickland condemned parliamentary eagerness to prosecute the Quaker 'prophet' Nayler in 1656, declaring, 'which sticks with me the most is the nearness of his opinion to that which is a most glorious truth, that the spirit is personally in us'. He preferred Quakers to be prosecuted for 'plainly explained' offences and heresy to be visible and easier to discover, and assisted the readmission of the Jews. He also took a ceremonial role from 1654 as commander of Cromwell's foot guards, and was jeered at by republicans for importing Dutch ceremonial. He was summoned to Cromwell's 'other house' in 1657, taking his seat as Walter, Lord Strickland, on 20 January 1658.

Strickland moved towards the generals' party in Cromwell's council, and after the latter's death supported them against Richard Cromwell. Consequently he was admitted to the army-dominated committee of safety in October 1659, also retaining a seat in the restored Rump and on local commissions for assessment and the militia. He took no part in resisting the Restoration and was not prosecuted. Retiring to Flamborough, he wrote a 'History of persecution' defending the protestant sects. He died on 1 November 1671 and was buried in Flamborough church where a memorial was later erected. A shrewd and pragmatic politician and foreign affairs expert to both the Long Parliament and Cromwell, he was ultimately overruled by both on his main area of expertise.

TIMOTHY VENNING

Sources JHC, 3 (1642–4) · JHC, 4 (1644–6) · JHC, 5 (1646–8) · JHC, 6 (1648–51) · VCH Yorkshire East Riding, vol. 2 · Venn, Alum. Cant. · J. Foster, The register of admissions to Gray's Inn, 1521–1889, together with the register of marriages in Gray's Inn chapel, 1695–1754 (privately printed, London, 1889) · CSP dom., 1649–54 · The diary of Bulstrode Whitelocke, 1605–1675, ed. R. Spalding, British Academy, Records of Social and Economic History, new ser., 13 (1990) · Index of wills, administrations, and probate acts, in the York registry, AD 1666 to 1672, Yorkshire Archaeological Society, Record Series, 60 (1920) · Dugdale's visitation of Yorkshire, with additions, ed. J. W. Clay, 3 (1917) · S. R. Gardiner, History of the great civil war, 1642–1649, new edn, 1 (1893); 4 (1893); facs. repr. (1987) · S. R. Gardiner, History of the Commonwealth and protectorate, 1649–1656, new edn, 4 vols. (1989), vols. 1, 3 · B. Whitelocke, Memorials of English affairs, new edn, 4 vols. (1853), vol. 4 · J. H. Matthews, ed., Cardiff records: being materials for a history of the county borough from the earliest times, 6 vols. (1898–1911), vol. 2 · C. H. Firth and R. S. Rait, eds., Acts and ordinances of the interregnum, 1642–1660, 3 vols. (1911) · T. Venning, Cromwellian foreign policy (1995); repr. (1996) · D. Underdown, Pride's Purge: politics in the puritan revolution (1971) · T. Allen, A new and complete history of the county of York, 6 vols. (1828–31) · GEC, Peerage · GEC, Baronetage

Archives PRO, documents relating to ambassadorial career and legal cases | Bodl. Oxf., journal of Strickland–St John embassy, MS Rawl. C 129 · Bodl. Oxf., letters to council of state, MSS Rawl. A2 187, 206, 255 · Yale U., Beinecke L., letters to J. Pym

Wealth at death manor of Flamborough, Yorkshire (purchased for £4800 in 1650); property owned in borough of Cardiff; 2¾ burgages in 1666: CSP dom., 1650–51, 1652; Matthews, ed., Cardiff records; VCH Yorkshire East Riding, vol. 2

Strickland, William (d. 1419), bishop of Carlisle, was probably a member of the Westmorland family of Strickland of Sizergh; however, it has also been suggested that he was the son of John Strickland of Great Strickland and his wife, Joan de Vaux. Educated at Oxford University, he was styled clerk by 1362, and magister by 1369. Presumably while still in minor orders he married Alice Warcop, with whom he had a daughter, Margaret, who married first Sir John Derwentwater and second Sir Robert *Lowther [see under Lowther family]—the latter was Strickland's principal executor. Recorded as notary public in 1366, by 1368 he was rector of Stapleton in Cumberland, even though he was not ordained to the priesthood until 1381. In the meantime he had entered the service of Bishop Thomas Appleby of Carlisle, on whose behalf he was a mainpernor in 1374, whose proctor he was in parliament in January 1377, and for whom he collected the issues of a clerical subsidy in 1383. He was rewarded by being presented successively to the valuable livings of Rothbury, Northumberland, in 1380 and Horncastle, Lincolnshire, in 1388. He also had connections with the regionally powerful families of Clifford and Percy, acting as a feoffee in the foundation of a Percy chantry in Cockermouth Castle in 1399. Early in 1396 the canons of Carlisle Cathedral elected Strickland their bishop in succession to Appleby, but the election was quashed by the pope. Strickland had come to have lands and interests in and round Penrith, in the south of Cumberland. In 1395 he founded a chantry in St Andrew's Church in that town, and was also responsible for substantial improvements to the town's water supply. In 1399, following a licence to crenellate of two years earlier, he was reported to be 'making a fortalice at Penrith on the March of Scotland, for fortifying that town and the whole adjacent country' (CPR, 1396–9, 480).

Before 8 December 1399, following Thomas Merk's deprivation, Strickland was elected, and on 24 December papally provided, to the see of Carlisle. Henry IV, who had been willing to grant Strickland custody of the temporalities on 18 February, then made difficulties over his installation as a means of putting pressure on the pope to withdraw ecclesiastical immunity from Merk, following the latter's involvement in the conspiracy of January 1400. Nevertheless Strickland was consecrated bishop at Cawood Castle by Archbishop Scrope of York on 15 August 1400, and received full restitution of the temporalities on 15 November. Strickland was occasionally involved in secular affairs. He was appointed a commissioner in 1401 to treat for peace with the Scots, and in 1402 to arrest those declaring Richard II was still alive, while in December 1406 he was one of the bishops who sealed the act entailing the crown on the descendants of Henry IV. He also attended parliament in February 1413. But in spite of the disappearance of his register (extant in 1606 but lost since then), it is clear that he was principally concerned with the administration of his diocese. Much of his activity was conventional in form. But, in a region badly ravaged by war, Strickland attended to the episcopal finances, and reorganized the division of the revenues of St Nicholas's Church, Newcastle, to his own advantage while reducing the vicar's share. No doubt he needed the extra money for building. Tradition ascribed to him the construction of Strickland's Tower at the north-east corner of the inner court of the bishop's palace of Rose Castle, his usual residence, and a major contribution to the rebuilding of Carlisle Cathedral, in progress since a devastating fire in 1292. The tower and north transept, and the canons' stalls in the choir, are attributed to him, an attribution given greater likelihood by the papal indulgence issued in 1410 'for the completion and conservation of the church of Carlisle' (*CEPR letters*, 1404–1415, 220). In his will, dated 25 May 1419, Strickland left 100 marks for masses for his soul, and £10 for distribution to the poor at his funeral. He died on 30 August following, and was buried in Carlisle Cathedral, as he had requested in his will. His obit was still being commemorated there over a century later.

HENRY SUMMERSON

Sources C. M. L. Bouch, *Prelates and people of the lake counties: a history of the diocese of Carlisle, 1133–1933* (1948) · J. Wilson, *Rose Castle* (1912) · *Fasti Angl., 1300–1541*, [York] · Emden, *Oxf.* · *Chancery records* (RC) · [J. Raine], ed., *Testamenta Eboracensia*, 3, SurtS, 45 (1865), 60–61 · *CEPR letters*, vols. 5–6 · N. H. Nicolas, ed., *Proceedings and ordinances of the privy council of England*, 7 vols., RC, 26 (1834–7) · H. Summerson, *Medieval Carlisle: the city and the borders from the late eleventh to the mid-sixteenth century*, 2 vols., Cumberland and Westmorland Antiquarian and Archaeological Society, extra ser., 25 (1993) · special collections, parliamentary proxies, PRO, SC10/31/1533 · P. A. Wilson, 'The parentage of Bishop Strickland', *Transactions of the Cumberland and Westmorland Antiquarian and Archaeological Society*, [new ser.,] 82 (1982), 91–6
Wealth at death £176 13s. 4d.—bequests: Raine, ed., *Testamenta Eboracensia*, 3.60–61

Strickland, William (*d.* 1598), member of parliament, was the son of Roger Strickland and his wife, Mary Appleton. He married Elizabeth, daughter of Sir William Strickland of Westmorland, and had two sons and three daughters. Described as 'founder of the house of Strickland of Boynton' (*VCH Yorkshire, North Riding*, 2.475), he or his heir, Walter, built Boynton Hall, near Bridlington, Yorkshire. Strickland steadily accumulated estates in Yorkshire, including the manors of Auburn, Coneysthorpe, Hildenley, and Wintringham, and lands in Bridlington and Easton. As a substantial country gentleman, described in 1564 as one of the 'favorers of Religion' (Bateson, 71), he was appointed to various commissions in the province of York (concerning sedition, recusancy, and heresy) and, in

the East Riding, as justice of the peace (from 1559), a commissioner of sewers, and, in 1572, one of those responsible for raising cavalry and foot soldiers.

Strickland also represented Scarborough in four Elizabethan parliaments. There is no surviving record of his activity there in 1559 or 1563–1566/7. In 1571, however, he was prominent as one of those seeking further reformation in the Elizabethan church. On 6 April, Strickland, described by an anonymous diarist as 'a grave and auncient man of greate zeale, and not perhapps (as hee himself thought) unlearned' (Hartley, 1.200), informed the house that a fellow member, Thomas Norton, held a newly published copy of the unadopted Edwardian revision of the canon law, the *Reformatio legum*, and required him to produce it. He also complained of shortcomings in the prayer book and the quality of the clergy. Norton duly produced the *Reformatio legum*, and a committee, including Strickland, was appointed to confer with the bishops about it. Next day he called upon Norton to deliver a series of reform measures, known as the ABC bills. On 14 April he introduced his own bill to reform the prayer book. He was resisted by members of the privy council, which summoned him to its presence during the Easter recess and sequestered him from parliament. On 20 April this provoked an animated Commons debate about the liberties of the house. Next day Strickland was restored to his place there and promptly named to the committee on the bill for coming to church. He was also appointed to committees for bills concerning priests in disguise, maintenance of navigation, corrupt presentations, and tillage. Strickland's role in this parliament has been a subject of extended historical debate. He was for long seen as a leading figure in a reforming protestant (or puritan) party which launched an organized parliamentary campaign in 1571. Although this is no longer accepted, he was clearly working with Norton, John Foxe (who wrote the preface for the new edition of the *Reformatio*), and others to effect further reformation within the English church.

Perhaps his experience in 1571, or simply advancing years, taught Strickland discretion. Whatever the explanation, his parliamentary performance in 1584–5 was circumspect, largely confined to membership of committees to scrutinize, amend, or add to a variety of bills: the observance of the sabbath; fraudulent conveyances; unlawful marriage licences; excessive fees in ecclesiastical courts; and continuance of statutes. However, while he may have been publicly cautious, with only one recorded—and uncontroversial—speech, he was still dedicated to religious reformation, as most of these bills indicate. Furthermore, the seemingly innocuous Continuance Bill, which extended the life of acts with a limited time-span, included the Maintenance of Navigation Act and its controversial fish day clause. This statutory designation of Wednesday as a compulsory fish day smacked of Catholic practice and offended godly protestants. On 6 March, Strickland offered a proviso to the continuance of statutes committee, to which, five days later, he was appointed. When the Continuance Bill came out of committee, the fish day clause had gone. One can only speculate on Strickland's precise role. It was his last parliament. He remained a dutiful Yorkshire country gentleman until his death in 1598.   MICHAEL A. R. GRAVES

Sources T. E. Hartley, ed., *Proceedings in the parliaments of Elizabeth I*, 1–2 (1981–95) • *JHC*, 1 (1547–1628) • S. D'Ewes, ed., *The journals of all the parliaments during the reign of Queen Elizabeth, both of the House of Lords and House of Commons* (1682) • HoP, *Commons, 1558–1603* • *VCH Yorkshire East Riding*, vol. 2 • *VCH Yorkshire North Riding*, vol. 2 • *CSP dom.*, 1547–80 • *CPR*, 1560–75 • M. A. R. Graves, *Thomas Norton: the parliament man* (1994) • J. E. Neale, *Elizabeth I and her parliaments*, 2 vols. (1953–7) • T. S. Freeman, '"The Reformation of the Church in this Parliament": Thomas Norton, John Foxe and the parliament of 1571', *Parliamentary History*, 16 (1997), 131–47 • J. Strype, *Annals of the Reformation and establishment of religion … during Queen Elizabeth's happy reign*, new edn, 4 vols. (1824) • BL, Lansdowne MSS • M. Bateson, ed., 'A collection of original letters from the bishops to the privy council, 1564', *Camden miscellany, IX*, CS, new ser., 53 (1893)

Strickland, Sir William, first baronet, appointed Lord Strickland under the protectorate (*c.*1596–1673), politician, was born at Boynton, near Bridlington, Yorkshire, the eldest son of the antiquary Walter Strickland (*d.* 1636) of Boynton and his wife, Frances (*d.* 1636), daughter of Peter Wentworth of Lillingstone Lovell, Oxfordshire, and his second wife, Elizabeth. His grandfathers, William Strickland and Peter Wentworth, were leading Elizabethan exponents of further reformation for the church and he has been described as 'a third generation Puritan' (Cliffe, *Puritan Gentry*, 12). He matriculated at Queens' College, Cambridge, at Easter 1614 and was admitted to Gray's Inn on 21 May 1617. On 18 June 1622 he married his first wife, Margaret (*c.*1604–1629), daughter of Sir Richard Cholmley of Whitby and his first wife, Susanna, daughter of John Legard of Ganton. The couple had four daughters but no sons; she died in 1629 and was buried at Whitby. Strickland was knighted on 24 June 1630 and married again on 3 May 1631. His second wife was Lady Frances Finch (*d.* 1663), eldest daughter of Thomas Finch, first earl of Winchilsea, and Cicely, daughter of John Wentworth of Gosfield, Essex. Strickland served as a JP in the North and East ridings and was MP for Hedon during the Long Parliament of 1640–53. He signed the Yorkshire petition presented to the king on 30 July 1640 and later took the protestation. The king created him baronet, of Boynton, on 30 July 1641, but he nevertheless embraced the parliamentary cause. He was an active committeeman at Westminster and his younger brother Walter *Strickland (1598?–1671) was parliament's agent in the Netherlands. On 22 February 1643 a royalist convoy containing Queen Henrietta Maria came ashore at Bridlington and plundered Boynton Hall, as reported to parliament by Sir John Hotham on 9 March: 'Sir William hath lost above 4,000*l.* in his goods and all his evidence seized upon' (*Portland MSS*, 1.102).

In 1644 Strickland served on the key parliamentary committees for demolishing superstitious monuments and for preparing the directory of public worship. Siding with the presbyterians in 1647, he remained in parliament during the speaker's absence. He was not excluded by Pride's Purge on 6 December 1648, but temporarily withdrew to avoid involvement in the regicide. Edmund Ludlow asserted that Strickland carried the news to London of Cromwell's victory at Dunbar on 3 September 1650. Strickland was MP for the East Riding in the protectorate parliaments of 1654–5 and 1656. He spoke out against the 'horrid blasphemy' of the Quaker James Nayler, but was opposed to his execution until after the sentence of imprisonment had been passed. Debating the Quaker problem on 18 December 1656, he orated: 'They are a growing evil and the greatest that ever was … all levellers against magistracy and propriety' (*Diary of Thomas Burton*, 1.131, 169, 220). He condemned tithe refusers, warning parliament on 24 April 1657: 'Nothing is so like to blast your settlement, as a land tax' (ibid., 2.24). Elevated to Cromwell's House of Lords as William, Lord Strickland, on 10 December 1657, he later served Richard Cromwell as a privy councillor. He sat in the restored Rump Parliament of 1659, but withdrew after the excluded members returned.

Although Strickland profited substantially from his interregnum offices and his purchase of confiscated royalist estates in the 1650s, at the Restoration he was unmolested and retired from public life. Having inherited nine manors from his father, by the 1670s he was among the ten richest East Riding landowners, holding estates at Boynton, Flamborough, and Hildenley worth up to £2000 a year. He wore visibly puritan attire and remained an important patron of the godly: 'a public professor of religion, and one that openly owned it, and that to the uttermost of his power sheltered and protected the strictest professors thereof' (Morrice MSS, vol. 3). He died at Boynton on 12 September 1673 and was buried there on 16 September. His only son, Thomas (1638–1684), succeeded him as second baronet.   ANDREW J. HOPPER

Sources GEC, *Baronetage* • GEC, *Peerage*, new edn • Keeler, *Long Parliament* • Greaves & Zaller, *BDBR* • *Diary of Thomas Burton*, ed. J. T. Rutt, 4 vols. (1828), vols. 1–2 • J. T. Cliffe, *The puritan gentry: the great puritan families of early Stuart England* (1984) • J. T. Cliffe, *Puritans in conflict: the puritan gentry during and after the civil wars* (1988) • B. English, *The great landowners of East Yorkshire, 1530–1910* (1990) • Venn, *Alum. Cant.* • J. D. Legard, *The Legards of Anlaby and Ganton* (1926) • *The manuscripts of his grace the duke of Portland*, 10 vols., HMC, 29 (1891–1931), vol. 1 • DWL, Morrice MSS, vol. 3 • J. Foster, ed., *Pedigrees of the county families of Yorkshire*, 3 vols. (1874) • *Dugdale's visitation of Yorkshire, with additions*, ed. J. W. Clay, 3 vols. (1899–1917) • parish registers, Boynton, East Riding of Yorkshire Archives Service, Beverley, CB/CMB/141 [burial] • will, Borth. Inst., PROB Reg. 54, fol. 287 • W. W. Bean, *The parliamentary representation of the six northern counties of England* (1890) • *CSP dom.*, 1640
Archives priv. coll., family MSS | BL, Egerton MS 2645, fols. 241, 243 • DWL, Morrice MSS, vol. 3 • East Riding of Yorkshire Archives Service, Beverley, Boynton parish registers, CB/CMB/141
Likenesses portrait, Boynton Hall, Yorkshire; repro. in Legard, *Legards of Anlaby and Ganton*, facing p. 198
Wealth at death approx. £1500–£2000 p.a. from landed Yorkshire estates (incl. Boynton, Flamborough, and Hildenley): Keeler, *Long Parliament*, 355; English, *Great landowners*, 25, 46

Strickland [née Trentham], **Winifred**, Lady Strickland (1645–1725), Jacobite courtier, was born at Rocester Priory, Staffordshire, in May 1645 and baptized at Rocester on 19 May. She was the daughter of Sir Christopher Trentham (*d. c.*1649×51), of Rocester Priory, and Winifred, daughter of John Biddulph, of Biddulph, Staffordshire. Following the death of her father, a Catholic royalist, she was brought up by her mother and her second husband, Roger King, a barrister. In 1674 she married Sir Thomas Strickland (1621–1694), of Sizergh, Westmorland, a Catholic widower with two married daughters. The couple had five sons, four of whom survived childhood: Walter (1675–1715), Robert (c.1678–1715), Roger (1680–1704), and Thomas *Strickland (c.1682–1740), who became bishop of Namur.

The Stricklands of Sizergh had incurred substantial debts and sought the patronage of the Catholic James II. It was probably Lady Strickland's success in raising four healthy sons that most recommended them. In June 1688 she was present at the birth of James, prince of Wales, and appointed to be the child's under-governess. In the following month Sir Thomas was sworn of the privy council. During the revolution of 1688–9 Lady Strickland and her husband remained loyal to the king and queen. On the night of 9–10 December 1688 she and a few other servants secretly left Whitehall Palace and accompanied Mary of Modena and the prince of Wales in a small open boat to France. Sir Thomas joined them there soon afterwards, and the couple then lived at the exiled Jacobite court at St Germain-en-Laye.

Lady Strickland was fully occupied with bringing up the prince but Sir Thomas, though a privy councillor, had no active employment and was suffering from ill health, so in October 1692 the queen allowed her to resign her post as under-governess and retire with her husband to the English convent of Poor Clares at Rouen, where her half-brother (Roger King) happened to be the chaplain. Lady Strickland was away from St Germain until January 1694, when Sir Thomas died at Rouen. She was then recalled to be governess to the prince until he was entrusted to a governor on reaching the age of seven, in June 1695. It is unlikely that she had any lasting influence on the prince, although it is clear from James's later correspondence that he continued to hold her in high regard.

Lady Strickland courageously returned to England in the autumn of 1695 and remained there for about four and a half years. Before leaving for France her husband had placed Sizergh in trust with a family servant, so that when the estates of Jacobites employed at St Germain were confiscated in 1696 Sizergh remained secure. Lady Strickland had connections at Gray's Inn, where she placed her son Robert as a student, and in 1697 initiated legal action for the recovery of the family's property. Before returning to St Germain in 1700 she had achieved this, and also had consolidated its finances by persuading her sons Roger and Thomas to hand over their inheritances to their eldest brother, Walter, and make what careers they could in France. In a deed of December 1699 Lady Strickland gave Walter everything she possessed in England, except for a small annuity. She left the country for the last time in the spring of 1700 and was appointed a bedchamber woman to the queen at St Germain. She was in the second rank of household servants, below the ladies of the bedchamber, and does not seem to have had any involvement in the politics of the exiled court. On the other hand she was one of the earliest Jacobite patrons of the painter Alexis-Simon Belle, from whom she commissioned portraits of her sons Roger and Thomas as early as 1703.

The outbreak of the War of the Spanish Succession in 1702, during which Lady Strickland's son Roger died at Toulon, prevented any contact between the two halves of her family until 1713, when visits were resumed. She saw her son Walter again at the English convent of Poor Clares at Rouen, where he died in October 1715. Four months earlier his brother Robert had died in England. Her youngest son, Thomas, having entered the church, she probably hoped to use her influence with Mary of Modena and her husband to further his career in the interests of the Jacobite cause. To her great disappointment, though he became an abbot he deserted the Stuarts, preferring to secure the patronage of the new French regent, the duc d'Orléans, and his ally George I. Lady Strickland remained in Mary's service until the latter's death, in May 1718. The following month she left St Germain; she passed the remaining years of her life with her half-brother at the convent at Rouen where her husband and eldest son lay buried. She died there on 17 April 1725 and was buried with them the following day.

Lady Strickland is mainly remembered today because she assembled the most important private collection of portraits and other relics of the exiled Stuarts in France. It is not clear when the Stuart portraits came into her possession but as they were neither mentioned in the queen's will nor listed among the items given away after her death it is most likely that they were a gift from Mary. Lady Strickland bequeathed her collection to her grandson; most of it subsequently remained at Sizergh Castle.

EDWARD CORP

Sources E. Corp, 'The Strickland family', *Sizergh Castle*, National Trust Guidebook (2001), 40–56 · H. Hornyold, *Strickland of Sizergh* (1928) · *The letter book of Lewis Sabran*, ed. G. Holt, Catholic RS, 62 (1971)
Likenesses W. Wissing, oils, 1687, Sizergh Castle, Cumbria
Wealth at death see will, Hornyold, *Strickland*, 147–8

Striguil. For this title name *see* Clare, Richard fitz Gilbert de, second earl of Pembroke [earl of Striguil] (c.1130–1176).

Strijdom, Johannes Gerhardus (1893–1958), prime minister of South Africa, born on 14 July 1893 at the farm Klipfontein, near Willowmore, Cape Colony, was the second son in the family of ten children of Petrus Gerhardus Strijdom (1867–1932), farmer, and his wife, Ellen Elizabeth Nortier (1871–1938). After attending the Franschhoek high school, he proceeded to Victoria College (later Stellenbosch University), and in 1912 graduated BA. Following a spell of ostrich farming, he moved to Pretoria, joining the public service in 1914. After the outbreak of the First World War he served in South-West Africa, first in an ambulance unit and subsequently as a scout. After his discharge in August 1915 he joined a firm of Pretoria attorneys, obtained his LLB degree, and in 1918 was admitted to the bar. On 14 January 1931 Strijdom married Susan, daughter of the Revd W. J. de Klerk; they had a son and a daughter. A marriage in 1918 to Margaretha van Hulsteijn (1897–1970), the actress Marda Vanne, daughter of Sir

Willem van Hulsteijn, a former member of parliament, was dissolved.

Strijdom moved to Nylstroom in northern Transvaal to practise as an attorney. There he entered politics, becoming secretary for the Waterberg division of the National Party of J. B. M. Hertzog. An enthusiastic farmer, Strijdom also served as secretary to the Waterberg Agricultural Union (1923–9). In the general election of 1929 he was returned to parliament as the member for Waterberg, the constituency which he continued to represent until his death. Starting out as a typical upholder of Afrikaans language rights, Strijdom by 1934 had advanced to the more extreme stance of advocating a 'Christian-nationalist' Afrikaner republic outside the Commonwealth.

Although Strijdom, like D. F. Malan, the Cape Nationalist leader, stood as a coalitionist in the general election of 1933, he joined Malan in the following year in denouncing the fusion of parties, led respectively by Hertzog and J. C. Smuts, as a betrayal of Nationalist principles. Following the formation of the 'Purified' National Party, Strijdom for most of the period up to 1940 was its only parliamentary representative from Transvaal, and became its leader in that province, 'the lion of the north'. As chairman of the company publishing the Nationalist newspaper *Die Transvaler*, he was assisted in building up the party by its editor, H. F. Verwoerd, subsequently his successor as prime minister.

After Hertzog's defeat in parliament and resignation over the war issue, Strijdom became joint leader in Transvaal, with General J. C. G. Kemp, of the Herenigde (Reunited) Nasionale Party (HNP), formed in 1940. An avowed antisemite, Strijdom secured the adoption by the HNP in Transvaal of the clause in its constitution that excluded Jews from membership. Opposing any compromise over the republican aim, Strijdom believed that a German victory might furnish an opportunity to achieve it. He refused to endorse Hertzog's unequivocal undertaking to guarantee English-speaking rights. Insistent nevertheless that the republic should be achieved by constitutional means, Strijdom also attacked national socialism as an ideology foreign to South Africa. He supported Malan in successfully resisting (as the general election of 1943 demonstrated) the claims of extra-parliamentary movements, in particular the *Ossewa Brandwag*, to challenge the HNP as the political voice of the Afrikaner *volk*. An outspoken protagonist of white *baasskap* ('supremacy'), Strijdom provided a major input into the party political programme that was implemented as the policy of apartheid when the Nationalists came to power in 1948.

Strijdom received the relatively minor portfolio of lands (and later also irrigation) in Malan's cabinet. He tackled his departmental work with vigour and succeeded in raising his prestige in the party. Malan, upon retiring in 1954, intended to advise the governor-general to invite N. C. Havenga, the minister of finance, to succeed him; but Strijdom's supporters, representing the radical element in the party and especially strong in the Transvaal, insisted that the parliamentary caucus elect the new party leader and prime minister. Strijdom's unanimous election was ensured by Havenga's withdrawal.

In the four years of his premiership Strijdom, who now accepted that the republic could not be established by a simple majority in parliament, continued to pursue his republican goal. Legislation in 1957 secured that South Africa would have one national flag and anthem. The most controversial issue of his premiership derived from the struggle to remove the Cape coloured voters from the common roll. Through the enlargement of the senate Strijdom in 1956 obtained the necessary two-thirds majority of both houses, and the appeal court upheld the government by validating the Senate Act. Strijdom, who suffered poor health throughout his premiership, became ill shortly before the general election of 1958. He recovered sufficiently to participate in the campaign, but afterwards his condition deteriorated. Suffering from a heart ailment, he died at Volkshospitaal, Cape Town, on 24 August 1958, survived by his wife. He was buried on 30 August at Heroes' Acre old cemetery in Pretoria.

As a *volksleier*, Strijdom commanded the almost unqualified devotion of many of his followers. His personal appeal and integrity, his accessibility, and his active membership of the Dutch Reformed church all played their part. To his opponents, however, his steadfastness and his blunt oratory typified the intransigent *Broederbonder*, pursuing a narrow and exclusive Afrikaner cause.

N. G. GARSON

Sources J. L. Basson, *J. G. Strijdom: sy politieke loopbaan van 1929 tot 1948* (1980) · A. P. J. van Rensburg, 'Strijdom, Johannes Gerhardus', *DSAB* · P. J. Furlong, *Between crown and swastika: the impact of the radical right on the Afrikaner nationalist movement in the fascist era* (1991) · D. O'Meara, *Forty lost years: the apartheid state and the politics of the national party* (1996) · G. M. Carter, *The politics of inequality: South Africa since 1948* (1958) · H. B. Thom, *D. F. Malan* (1980) · O. Geyser and A. H. Marais, eds., *Die nasionale party*, 3: *Die eerste bewindsjare, 1924–1934*, ed. P. W. Coetzer and J. H. le Roux (1982) · O. Geyser and A. H. Marais, eds., *Die nasionale party*, 4: *Die 'Gesuiwerde' nasionale party, 1934–1940*, ed. P. W. Coetzer and J. H. le Roux (1986) · B. M. Schoeman, *Van Malan tot Verwoerd* (1973) · A. N. Pelzer, 'Strijdom, Johannes Gerhardus', *Standard encyclopaedia of southern Africa*, ed. D. J. Potgieter, 10 (1974), 326–7 · G. Coetsee, *Hans Strijdom: lewensloop en beleid van Suid-Afrika se vyfde premier* (1958) · J. M. Strydom, *J. G. Strijdom: sy lewe en stryd* (1965) · *Sunday Times* [Johannesburg] (24 Aug 1958) · *Die Burger* [Cape Town] (25 Aug 1958)
Archives National Archives of South Africa, Pretoria, private collection | FILM BFI NFTVA, documentary footage
Likenesses group photograph, 1956, Hult. Arch. · D. de Jager, statue, 1972, Nylstroom, Transvaal · C. Steynberg and D. de Jager, monument, 1972, Strijdom Square (formerly Market Square), Pretoria · J. A. Labuschagne, Nylstroom granite bust, Paardekraal, near Krugersdorp, Transvaal · C. Steynberg, bronze bust, houses of parliament, Cape Town · C. Steynberg, bronze bust, Heroes' Acre, Pretoria · photographs, repro. in Basson, *J. G. Strijdom* · photographs, repro. in Strydom, *J. G. Strijdom*

Stringer, Mabel Emily (1868–1958), golfer and journalist, was born on 25 September 1868 at The Elms, New Romney, Kent, the eldest of the seven children of Henry Stringer (1838?–1912), a solicitor, and his wife, Harriet, formerly Walker (b. 1845?). Her girlhood impression of the game to which she was to devote her life was that it was a 'particularly stupid' and 'dull' pursuit, which could not compare with her favoured pastimes of 'cricket, pole-jumping, bird-nesting, catapult-shooting, hunting, and the like!' (Stringer, 13). In 1887 a men's golf club was established at Littlestone, close to where she grew up, and on the links there she discovered her love for the game, playing alone in the afternoons with a cleek, a heavy mashie, and a putter. When Littlestone Ladies' Club was established in 1891 she became its first captain, a post she held until 1896.

The ladies' links at Littlestone consisted of nine holes right along the shore, facetiously dubbed the 'hen run', but they were seldom used as the women enjoyed unrestricted access to the men's links. The women were not, however, given similar access to the men's clubhouse, and had to make do with two empty rooms in an unoccupied coastguard cottage, onto which was tacked a tiny dressing-room of corrugated iron. This state of social apartheid was relaxed each Christmas, when there was a mixed foursome competition, after which the ladies were given tea in the men's clubhouse. The invitation, though, came on the strict understanding that the visitors were 'on no account to go in by the front entrance!' (Stringer, 14). Years later, when the conditions enjoyed by women golfers seemed luxurious by comparison, Stringer reflected nostalgically on the 'wretched little tin tabernacle' (ibid., 25) at Littlestone. But she felt no similar emotional attachment to the older style of dress, and wondered how women had managed to play at all in 'the outrageous garments' decreed by Victorian and Edwardian fashion: 'The golfing girl of to-day should indeed be grateful that she need not play golf in a sailor hat, a high stiff collar, a voluminous skirt and petticoats, a motor-veil, or a wide skirt with leather binding' (ibid., 29).

In 1894 Littlestone was chosen as the venue for the second (British) ladies' championship and Stringer made her championship début on her home course. She subsequently entered every year, until illness forced her absence in 1901. She also missed the championships of 1904 and 1905, when she pursued employment as a lady's companion, but she competed in her final championship in 1907. Although she never advanced very far in championships, she was a first-rate golfer, and joint holder of the women's course record at Littlestone. Lung trouble denied her a place on the England team to face Scotland in 1902, but she represented her country in the international cup held that year.

The 1894 ladies' championship brought about Stringer's first meeting with Isette Pearson, a founder and honorary secretary of the Ladies' Golf Union (LGU). Pearson visited Littlestone in advance of the championship to view the course, and Stringer was asked to entertain her. A lifelong friendship began, which deepened Stringer's own involvement with the union. She represented Kent on its council for more than twenty years, and briefly deputized for Pearson when the latter was ill, serving as assistant honorary secretary. A great enthusiast for and instigator of county golf, Stringer was also involved in establishing a proper handicap system for women golfers, a regulated system that put the much looser male equivalent to

shame and which she considered 'the greatest achievement' of the LGU (Stringer, 175).

Stringer had helped to produce the early yearbooks of the LGU, and in 1903 she was asked by a national newspaper to cover a tournament in place of its regular correspondent, who was ill. This was her start in golf journalism and being 'almost the only woman in this particular work' she found regular employment. By the spring of 1906 she was making, by her own estimate, 'a fairly good living' from writing, and decided to make it her profession. Thereafter she covered the important championships for the British and foreign press, writing for a range of publications from dailies to periodicals. Her reports were then more likely to be placed in the social columns of newspapers rather than on the sports pages, but by the time that she had retired in 1924 this had changed; she had played an important part in establishing women's golf as a recognized sport, with its own news value. Her descriptions of the major tournaments, and of those who played in them, stimulated public interest and encouraged new players. She was present at all the ladies' championships from 1908 to 1923, and witnessed the débuts of many great golfers, notably Cecil Leitch at St Andrews in 1908. Stringer regarded the 1908 championship as 'the most epoch-making' because of the venue:

> not only did our presence there indicate that any prejudices against women's intrusion on men's *rights* had been overcome, but the subsequent happenings of the week clearly showed that we had justified our right to play over the ground where other women had played three hundred years before.   (Stringer, 164)

In 1914 J. S. Wood, co-proprietor and chairman of *The Gentlewoman*, to which Stringer had long been a contributor, approached her with the idea of an English girls' golf championship. Together they organized a match-play event for sixteen qualifiers. The large number of entries for the inaugural championship that year was testimony to the potential of the event, though it had to be cancelled after the outbreak of war. When in 1919 Stringer became editor of the sports pages of *The Gentlewoman*, she revived the plan, and the first girls' championship was played that year at Stoke Poges, home of the event until 1938. The tournament was an immediate success, combining a friendly atmosphere with fine competition. Stringer was the driving force behind it, making sure that the organization ran smoothly and that the girls and their anxious relatives were kept happy.

It was Cecil Leitch who famously christened Stringer 'Auntie Mabel', and by mid-century Auntie Mabel was already 'a mythical person to the moderns' (Wilson, 108). A mentor to young players, those 'nieces' to whom she dedicated her book of *Golfing Reminiscences* (1924), Stringer was closely involved in the founding of several important women's golfing societies, and on her retirement in 1924 seven associations raised a special collection of £160 as a token of their esteem: she used the money to install electric lighting in her simple cottage in Kent. Many women had reason to be grateful for what she had achieved in her sixty years' involvement with the game of golf. A competitor in the second ladies' championship in 1894, she lived to witness the great home triumph in the ninth Curtis cup match at Prince's, Sandwich, in 1956. She never married, and died at her home, 26 Herschell Square, Walmer, Kent, on 10 February 1958.   MARK POTTLE

Sources E. Wilson, *A gallery of women golfers* (1961) · R. Milton, *A history of ladies' golf in Sussex* (1993) · *The Times* (13 Feb 1958) · R. Cossey, *Golfing ladies: five centuries of golf in Great Britain and Ireland* (1984) · M. E. Stringer, *Golfing reminiscences* (1924) · census returns, 1881 · b. cert. · d. cert.
Likenesses photograph, repro. in Stringer, *Golfing reminiscences*, frontispiece
Wealth at death £3071 5s. 11d.: probate, 17 April 1958, *CGPLA Eng. & Wales*

Stringer, Moses (*d.* 1714), chemical physician and master of mines, was one of the eleven children of Richard Stringer of Loughborough, Leicestershire. He practised paramedically before leaving the Newcastle under Lyme area in 1690 and obtaining a medical licence at Chester in July 1691. Stringer was admitted a member of the Society of Mineral and Battery Works in December 1692 and of the Society of Mines Royal in June 1693. After studying chemistry and medicine under Benjamin Woodroffe, principal of Gloucester Hall, Oxford (later refounded as Worcester College), in 1692, he taught chemistry and experimental philosophy there until about 1696, by which time he was working at his refineries in the High Peak, Derbyshire.

In March 1698 Stringer was settled in the Strand, London, and he published a congratulatory poem to Peter the Great on the tsar's arrival in England, together with accounts from the *Protestant Mercury* of his dramatic cure of a person bitten by a viper and his spectacular experiments with metals and minerals for the tsar at the Deptford manor house belonging to John Evelyn. In his 1699 pamphlet, *English and Welsh Mines and Minerals Discovered*, 'M. S.' advocated to the House of Commons the employment of the poor for profitable mining. The following year he moved to Hugh's Court, Blackfriars, considerably extending the premises with a large laboratory and foundry.

In 1701 the Admiralty ordered a squadron to the West Indies, commanded by John Benbow, to carry out the first recorded naval therapeutic trials of two chemical medicines invented by Stringer to combat scurvy and fevers. Admiral Sir Cloudesley Shovell may also have used them in the Mediterranean. Three editions of Stringer's tract, *Variety of Surprising Experiments* (1703, 1705, and 1707), supplemented by three published open letters to Woodroffe (in 1704 and 1707), evince his skill in devising these and other chemico-mineral medicines along Paracelsian lines.

State Papers and other sources indicate that Stringer ran a large foundry business, owned ships for exporting and importing metals and ordnance, and planned to set up a company for colonizing West Indian islands. The societies of Mines Royal and of Mineral and Battery Works, incorporated in 1568, had become virtually moribund by 1695.

Stringer, whose book *Opera mineralia explicata* ('By M. S., M. D.', 1713) presents a detailed history of the societies, played a decisive part in preserving their records, salvaged by Sir Isaac Newton, and in renewing their rights and charters. They amalgamated under him as mineral master general in 1709–10. He persuaded the bishop of London to be a governor and Newton to become a deputy governor. Sir Christopher Wren helped build a new meeting-room above Stringer's laboratory in Blackfriars. Robert Boyle was one of several distinguished members of the societies.

Stringer's titles of chemist and physician to King William and chemist, physician, and mineralist to Queen Anne in some of his publications were probably honorary designations. A controversial character, he was incarcerated in the Fleet prison on three occasions. In January 1713 Stringer issued an advertisement to scotch rumours of his death occasioned by the demise of the empiric William Salmon in Blackfriars.

Stringer was married by 1692. He and his wife, Mary, had at least seven children. He died intestate at Blackfriars in 1714.   JOHN H. APPLEBY, *rev.*

Sources J. H. Appleby, 'Moses Stringer, *fl.* 1695–1713: iatrochemist and mineral master general', *Ambix*, 34 (1987), 31–45 · L. Loewenson, 'People Peter the Great met in England: Moses Stringer, chymist and physician', *Slavonic and East European Review*, 37 (1958–9), 459–68 · W. Rees, *Industry before the industrial revolution*, 2 (1968), 658–65 · Register of the Mineral and Battery Works, 1620–1713, BL, Loan MS 16/2 · Register of the Mines Royal, 1654–April 1709, BL, Loan MS 16/3

Stringfellow, John (1799–1883), bobbin manufacturer and aeronautical engineer, was born in Attercliffe, near Sheffield, on 6 December 1799, the son of William Stringfellow, cutler, and his wife, Martha. His father was a man of wide scientific interests from whom he inherited a considerable degree of mechanical aptitude and ingenuity.

At an early age Stringfellow was apprenticed to the lace trade in Nottingham, but about 1820 moved to Chard in Somerset, a centre of lace making, and was so successful that within a few years he had established his own business as a manufacturer of bobbins and bobbin carriages. Thus provided with a steady income, he was able to devote much of his time to aeronautical experiments and other scientific pursuits.

In 1831 and again in 1832 Stringfellow launched hot-air balloons at local festivals, one of which flew a distance of more than 4 miles, but even at that time his goal was powered flight with fixed-wing aeroplanes. The idea was developed in discussions with another manufacturer of lace-making machinery who had moved to Chard in the late 1830s, William Samuel Henson (1812–1888), and was inspired by the aeronautical writings and experiments of Sir George Cayley. Henson and Stringfellow began testing various wing forms in model gliders, and by 1840 had evolved their projected full-size passenger-carrying flying machine or 'aerial steam carriage', which Henson patented in April 1843.

A 20 foot wingspan model powered by a steam engine, of Henson origin but much improved by Stringfellow, was tested in 1845 but could not sustain itself in the air. Henson then abandoned his aeronautical ambitions altogether. Stringfellow persevered on his own, however, and built another 10 foot model powered by a smaller steam engine of his own design. More than one witness recalled that it gained height steadily after being launched on several occasions in 1848, and Stringfellow himself certainly considered that he had demonstrated with it the possibility of powered flight.

Stringfellow then built a number of other model aeroplanes and engines before entering a model steam-powered triplane and a model steam engine in the aeronautical exhibition at Crystal Palace in June 1868. His steam engine was awarded a prize of £100 by the Royal Aeronautical Society for having the greatest power-to-weight ratio of all the fifteen engines exhibited, but unfortunately the triplane could never be tested in the still-air conditions to which it was suited, and so never proved itself to be, if indeed it was, a practical flying machine.

Stringfellow was an outstanding designer and builder of small lightweight steam engines, but his model aeroplanes suffered from the twin disadvantages of being too large to be fully tested indoors, and not stable enough to be tested out of doors. It is remarkable, however, that his fixed-wing propeller-driven models showed the way ahead so clearly at a time when most other proposals for aerial machines involved flapping wings or unlikely applications of the helicopter principle.

In the late 1850s Stringfellow took up the new art of photography, becoming so proficient that he advertised himself as a professional portrait photographer, with a studio in Chard High Street. He was elected a member of the Royal Aeronautical Society in 1868, and with his prize money erected a building 70 feet long in which to continue his experiments, but his sight began to fail and he was unable to make any further progress. He patented in 1870 a wheeled apparatus for affording protection from bullets and other missiles, but did not succeed in selling it to any of Europe's warring armies.

On 24 February 1827 Stringfellow married Hannah Keetch, said to have been born in Newfoundland. Their surviving family consisted of six sons and four daughters. Stringfellow died in High Street, Chard, on 13 December 1883.   RONALD M. BIRSE, rev.

Sources M. J. B. Davy, *Henson and Stringfellow: their work in aeronautics … 1840–1868* (1931) · C. H. Gibbs-Smith, *Aviation: an historical survey from its origins to the end of World War II*, 2nd edn (1985) · H. Penrose, *An ancient air: a biography of John Stringfellow of Chard, the Victorian aeronautical pioneer* (1988) · d. cert.
Archives Royal Aeronautical Society, London, papers
Wealth at death £863 9s. 1d.: probate, 10 March 1884, *CGPLA Eng. & Wales*

Strode [Stroud], **Sir George** (1583–1663), royalist administrator, was the second son of William Strode, landowner, of Shepton Mallet, Somerset, and Elizabeth, daughter and heir of Geoffrey Upton of Warminster in the same county. William Strode was grandnephew of Richard Whiting, the last abbot of Glastonbury. George Strode came to London and entered trade, and on 11 February 1615 married, at

Sir George Strode (1583–1663), by unknown artist

All Hallows Church, Lombard Street, Rebecca, daughter and coheir of Alderman Nicholas Crisp, first cousin to Sir Nicholas Crisp. They had fourteen children. Rebecca (d. 1645) was sister-in-law to Sir Abraham Reynardson, lord mayor of London in 1648, and Sir Thomas Cullum, sheriff of London in 1646.

Strode shared the royalist opinions of his connections, and, like them, suffered in the cause. At the outbreak of hostilities Strode took service in the infantry and was knighted on 30 July 1641. For his role in organizing the infamous 1642 Kentish petition, parliament ordered his arrest. Bail was posted by Sir Nicholas Crisp and Strode's friend, the royalist William Russell. He then joined the king at Oxford and was appointed a commissioner of the ordnance about July. He conducted the artillery train at the battle of Edgehill on 23 October 1642 and was badly wounded, a fact alluded to in his epitaph. Thereafter he remained at Oxford, his activities as ordnance commissioner vital to the royalist war effort.

By 1636 Strode owned the estate of Squeries in Kent, which he purchased from the Beresfords, and later he had to compound for it with the parliamentary commissioners. In 1646 Marylebone Park, a property of the crown, was granted by letters patent of Charles I, dated Oxford, 6 May, to Strode and fellow ordnance commissioner John Wandesford as security for a debt of £2318 11s. 9d., for supplying arms and ammunition. These claims were disregarded by the parliamentary party when in power, and the park was sold for the benefit of Colonel Thomas Harrison's dragoons. At the Restoration, Strode and Wandesford were reinstated, and held the park, with the exception of one portion, until their debt was discharged.

Late in the war, perhaps shortly after Rebecca died in October 1645, Strode went abroad, and there 'in these sad distracted times, when I was inforced to eat my bread in forein parts', as he wrote, he solaced himself by translating a work by Cristofero da Fonseca, which appeared in 1652, under the title *Theion enōtikon: a Discourse of Holy Love, by which the Soul is United unto God*, 'done into English with much Variation and some Addition by Sr George Strode, Knight'. Early in 1649 he returned to England and submitted to the committee for compounding, who fined him half his estate. Despite his composition, he remained on the fringes of royalist conspiracy in the early 1650s. He sold Squeries in 1650.

At the Restoration, he settled once more in London. His will, in which he declared his adherence to that 'orthodox religion, professed in this our Church of England' which has 'flourished here for some years past, to the honour and glory of Almighty God and the Admonition of the neighbouring nations' (will, PRO, PROB 11/311, sig. 76), was dated 24 August 1661, confirmed on 5 February following, and proved on 3 June 1663. Strode was buried in St James's Church, Clerkenwell, on the previous day; the entry in the registers of the church described him as 'that worthy Benefactour to Church and Poore' (Hovenden, 351). One of his sons, Sir Nicholas Strode, knighted on 27 June 1660, was an examiner in chancery; and another, Colonel John Strode, was in 1661 in personal attendance on Charles II, who appointed him governor of Dover Castle. One of the daughters, Anne, married successively Ellis, eldest son of Sir Nicholas Crisp, and Nicholas, eldest son of Abraham Reynardson.

G. G. M-G. Cullum, *rev.* Sarah E. Trombley

Sources Clarendon, *Hist. rebellion* • P. Clark, *English provincial society from the Reformation to the revolution* (1977) • D. Underdown, *Royalist conspiracy in England, 1649–1660* (1960) • M. A. E. Green, ed., *Calendar of the proceedings of the committee for compounding … 1643–1660*, 5 vols., PRO (1889–92); repr. (1967), vol. 3 • will, PRO, PROB 11/311, sig. 76 • C. de Fonseca, *Theion enōtikon: a discourse of holy love, by which the soul is united unto God*, ed. and trans. G. Strode (1652) [Sp. orig.] • J. Stowe, *Survey of London* (1956) • D. Lysons, *Environs of London* (1989) • J. Collinson, *History and antiquities of the county of Somerset* (1792) • G. W. G. Leveson Gower, *Parochial history of Westerham* (1883) • I. Roy, ed., *The royalist ordnance papers, 1642–1646*, 2 vols., Oxfordshire RS, 43, 49 (1964–75) • M. Toynbee, ed., *The papers of Captain Henry Stevens, waggon-master-general to King Charles I*, Oxfordshire RS, 42 (1962) • R. Hovenden, ed., *A true register of all the christenings, mariages, and burialles in the parish of St James, Clarkenwell, from … 1551 (to 1754)*, 4, Harleian Society, register section, 17 (1891) • J. J. Howard, ed., *Miscellanea genealogica et heraldica*, 2nd ser., 4 (1892), 184

Likenesses Bocquet, pubd 1810 (after G. Glover, 1652) • G. Glover, line engraving, BM, NPG; repro. in Strode, *Discourse of holy love* • W. Richardson (after G. Glover, 1652) • oils, NPG [*see illus.*]

Strode, Ralph (*d.* 1387), scholastic philosopher and lawyer, is of unknown origins. His name is first found in the records for 1359 and 1360 of Merton College, Oxford (a college predominantly but not entirely of southerners), where he was then fellow. The bursar's roll for 1361 is missing, and he might still have been a fellow then. He had evidently become acquainted with John Wyclif (*d.*

1384) while at Oxford, a fact of which Wyclif reminded him at the time of a theological controversy in which they took opposite sides. This could place Strode there as early as 1355, the earliest date at which Wyclif might have entered Merton, although since Wyclif was master of Balliol from 1360, their later meeting would have been almost inevitable. No more specific details of Strode's life are known before his election as common serjeant or pleader—effectively public prosecutor—of the city of London, on 25 November 1373, an office he held until 1382.

In London, Strode occupied a mansion over Aldersgate from 27 October 1375 to 4 May 1386, when he received an annuity of 4 marks in compensation for his life tenancy. During his period of office he had further dealings with former Merton colleagues. In 1374, jointly with Wyclif, he acted as surety for a former fellow of the college, Master Richard Benger, then rector of Donington, Berkshire. Three years later he likewise acted jointly with the former fellow Master Robert Rygge on behalf of John Bloxham, warden of the college, in a dispute between the king and the college over the ownership of land in Oxford. In 1381, with his neighbour and friend the poet Geoffrey Chaucer (*d.* 1400), he went surety for John Hende, a merchant destined to become mayor of London after Strode's death.

The pattern of Strode's career has led some to argue that the philosopher and lawyer were two persons of the same name. One argument is that the lawyer was married—he was survived by a wife, Emma, a son Ralph, and possibly a daughter Margery. If the scholar Strode had quit Merton for London, and was not a religious, marriage was not out of order. The more common argument for two Strodes is that no one man of the time would have had such diverse professional interests, but there are many contemporaries whose lives show this to be simply untrue. As common serjeant he would have needed knowledge normally only procured in the London inns of court, and in view of the large lacuna in his known career it would be foolish to suggest that the schoolman could not have acquired that readily enough.

About 1385 Chaucer dedicated his *Troilus and Criseyde*—where he treats skilfully of the problem of free will and predestination—to the poet John Gower and the scholar Strode:

> O moral Gower, this book I directe
> To the, and to the, philosophical Strode,
> To vouchen sauf, ther nede is, to correcte,
> Of youre benignites and zeles goode.
> (G. Chaucer, *Troilus and Criseyde*, v. 1857–9)

Chaucer uses the word 'philosophical' of academic philosophy, often natural philosophy. The Merton connections of the lawyer Strode whom Chaucer knew, and the epithet 'philosophical' that here suggests a university man of some standing, in juxtaposition to a reference to another friend as 'moral', all speak for the identity of lawyer and Mertonian.

It was in connection with Wyclif's *De civili dominio* that Strode took issue with this increasingly controversial schoolman, the *flos Oxonie*. Strode's own side of the seemingly amicable debate was set down in a work that a college document calls simply *Positiones contra Wiclevum*, known only through Wyclif's replies, since printed as *Responsiones ad decem questiones magistri R. Strode* and *Responsiones ad argumenta Radulphi Strode*. Strode rejected Wyclif's view of predestination, believing that it implied that man cannot act freely, and so cannot have responsibility or indeed hope of salvation. In ecclesiastical matters he took a pragmatic position: harmony and concord in the church was so important as to demand a moderate toleration of abuses. While his own views are known only through the veil of Wyclif's texts, it is clear that Strode experienced many of the ecclesiastical and political uncertainties of the age.

While Chaucer brought Strode's name to the notice of his fellow countrymen, his own scholastic writings earned him a reputation in Italy. This was largely brought about by the Augustinian friar Paulo da Venezia (d. 1429), who spent at least three years in Oxford after 1390, before returning to teach at Padua. Later commentaries on Strode were written by such Paduans as Paolo da Pergola and Gaetano da Thiene, students of Paulo; and when the sixteenth-century writer Matteo Bossi wished to contrast scholasticism with ancient philosophy, he said he seemed to hear not Plato, Aristotle, and Theophrastus but 'your Burleys, Pauls of Venice, or Strodi' (Thorndike, 238). Strode's *Logica* was written in or not long after 1359. It comprises six parts, which were often copied as independent works. The sections on *Consequentiae* and *Obligationes* were required texts in the University of Padua and several other universities in the fifteenth and sixteenth centuries. Both were printed in several editions. The earlier parts were *De arte logica*, *De principiis logicalibus*, and *De suppositionibus*, while *De insolubilibus* ended the series, if not in Strode's intentions, at least in the sole surviving manuscript of the complete collection. At many points he echoed other Mertonians. He paraphrased Bradwardine's survey (1321-4) of the literature of insolubles, for example, and showed an awareness of the arguments of Swineshead, Heytesbury, Fland, and Billingham. He followed Bradwardine on the question of whether an individual says anything at all in uttering an insoluble like the self-referential paradox 'I am lying'. (Both argued that to say this was not to say nothing, for those words were being spoken.) He did not hide his admiration for Bradwardine, whom he described as the 'prince of the modern philosophers of nature … who was the first to hit upon something worthwhile concerning insolubles' (Ashworth and Spade, 38). On obligations, the rules of disputation that according to Heytesbury must be used to provide a context for insolubles, Strode disagreed on various points with him, and with Swineshead too. In his text on consequences he took the same line as Ockham had done, and treated them as what would now be known as material consequences, that is, not necessarily involving a relationship between the logical forms of antecedent and consequent. He spoke of consequences as inferences, valid or invalid, but was also capable of treating them as true or false, as though they were propositions.

Although Merton College was a centre of activity in natural philosophy and astronomy, Strode has left no writings on either subject. A fifteenth-century note, added to a manuscript copy of Chaucer's treatise on the astrolabe, claims that he wrote it for his son who was at the time under the tutelage of the most noble philosopher Master N. Strode. Some have chosen to read the initial as an 'R'. The only value of this note is that it might hint very distantly at a tradition that Strode put Chaucer in touch with Oxford astronomy. A marginal note in the *Catalogus vetus* of Merton College describes Strode (with the Christian name added later as 'Rad.') in these words: 'nobilis poeta fuit et versificavit librum elegiacum vocatum *Fantasma Radulphi*' (*Pearl*, xlvi–xlix). Israel Gollancz took this to be a reference to the poem *Pearl*, an unwarranted claim, although the identity of *Pearl's* author—someone who wrote in a west midlands dialect—is still far from certain.

Strode died in London in 1387, judging by a record of his will, now lost. J. D. NORTH

Sources Emden, *Oxf.*, 3.1807-8 • M. M. Crow and C. C. Olsen, eds., *Chaucer life-records* (1966), 281-4 • A. Maierú, ed., *English logic in Italy in the 14th and 15th centuries* (1982) • J. D. North, *Chaucer's universe* (1988), 85 • H. B. Workman, *John Wyclif*, 2 (1926), 125-9 • G. C. Brodrick, *Memorials of Merton College*, OHS, 4 (1885), 214 • E. P. Kuhl, 'Chaucer and Aldgate', *PMLA*, 39 (1924), 101-22 • H. T. Riley, ed., *Memorials of London and London life in the XIIIth, XIVth, and XVth centuries* (1868), 388 • L. Thorndike, *Science and thought in the fifteenth century* (1967) • P. V. Spade and E. J. Ashworth, 'Logic in late medieval Oxford', *Hist. U. Oxf. 2: Late med. Oxf.*, 35-64 • *Pearl*, ed. I. Gollancz (1921)
Archives Bibliotheca Amploniana, Erfurt, Q255 • Bodl. Oxf., Canon. misc. 219 • Cabildo, Toledo, 94-28 • Merton Oxf., *Catalogus vetus*

Strode, Thomas (d. 1697), mathematician, son of Thomas Strode of Shepton Mallet, Somerset, was probably born about 1626. He matriculated at University College, Oxford, on 1 July 1642. After remaining there about two years, he travelled in France with his tutor, Abraham Woodhead. On his return he taught in London, having been ejected from Oxford. He settled at Maperton, Somerset, and corresponded regularly with James Gregory.

Strode is best known for his work on dialling, presented in *A New and Easie Method to the Art of Dyalling* (1688), but he also wrote on arithmetic and conic sections. He died at Maperton in 1697. He should not be confused with another Thomas Strode (1628-1699), also from Shepton Mallet, who was the son of Sir John Strode and his second wife, Anne, daughter of Sir John Wyndham of Orchard. He was called to the bar at the Inner Temple in 1657 and became serjeant-at-law in 1677. He died on 4 February 1699 and was buried at Beaminster.

E. I. CARLYLE, *rev.* H. K. HIGTON

Sources E. G. R. Taylor, *The mathematical practitioners of Tudor and Stuart England* (1954) • Wood, *Ath. Oxon.* • Foster, *Alum. Oxon.* • J. Hutchins, *The history and antiquities of the county of Dorset*, 3rd edn, ed. W. Shipp and J. W. Hodson, 4 vols. (1861-74)

Strode, Sir William (1562-1637), politician, was born on 5 March 1562, the only child of Richard Strode (1528-1581), landowner, of Newnham, near Plymouth, Devon, and his wife, Frances Cromwell (d. 1563), daughter of Gregory, second Baron Cromwell. He was admitted to the Inner Temple in 1580, and avoided the penalties of wardship by marrying, on 15 July 1581, less than a month before his father's death, Mary (d. 1619), daughter of Thomas Southcote, landowner and tinner, of Bovey Tracey, Devon.

Strode was a JP for his county from the early 1590s and served as sheriff in 1593–4. His ancestors had regularly sat for Plympton, the borough neighbouring the family seat of Newnham, since 1437, but in 1597 he became the first of the family to represent the county. He left no mark on this parliament, but he was knighted in 1598 and became surveyor of crown lands in Devon upon his father-in-law's resignation. He commanded the local stannary regiment during the threatened Spanish invasions.

Strode continued to sit in the next seven parliaments. In 1604 he complained that the king had been misinformed about proceedings in the House of Commons. No friend to the ecclesiastical hierarchy and a strong Calvinist, who in his home county actively supported the ministry of the militant rector of Modbury, Samuel Hieron, and later maintained weekly lecturers, Strode was named to most committees of puritan intent. On supply, he habitually favoured parsimony, not refusal, and in the interests of free speech preferred debate in committee, with the speaker out of the chair. Although he showed little inclination to comply with the government over purveyance, wardship, and union with Scotland, he was actively helpful with several private bills promoted on behalf of the earl of Salisbury, the king's chief minister. Bishop Cotton of Exeter complained that 'Sir William Strode's canvass against the ecclesiastical commission in Devon' gained strength from the 'favourable respect' in which he was held by the earl (Salisbury MSS, 18.297). In 1610 he initially supported the great contract to put government finance on a sounder footing and reduce unparliamentary taxation. His 'diligent attendance and good service to the House' were noted in the Commons' Journal (JHC, 1547–1628, 350).

As recorder of Plymouth, Strode represented the borough in 1614, showing increased concern over commercial matters, especially the attempt of the Londoners to monopolize trade with France and Spain, and the imposition of customs duties by the crown. Predictably he was outraged by the speech of Bishop Richard Neile (once Salisbury's chaplain) describing the spirit of the lower house as undutiful and seditious. Plymouth corporation voted Strode £20 for his services in parliament and 'for assisting the town in withstanding the patent for packing and salting of fish' (Worth, 152), but he was replaced as recorder before the next election by a lawyer.

Sitting again for his family borough in 1621, Strode set out his position on taxation: 'I would help the King, and yet look to the country', which was suffering a severe depression (Notestein, Relf, and Simpson, 2.90). He admonished his fellow landlords to abate rents during the depression and to forbear from imposing taxes that chiefly hit the poor. He took a strong line against monopolies among other barriers to freedom of trade. Although an investor in the Virginia Company, however, he advocated a total ban on tobacco imports. He was troubled by the increase in petty crime in Devon, and introduced a bill to reduce those offenders unable to pay fines to slavery for eight years, at the end of which he hoped they would have acquired such skills and habits of industry as would enable them to earn an honest living.

Strode had been without a patron at court since Salisbury's death in 1612, but by 1624, when he again represented his county in parliament, he had become a client of the duke of Buckingham. He expressed satisfaction with the duke's rambling account of his conduct in Madrid, 'If any man can take exception, reason to take consideration; but now no reason … to stay it' (JHC, 1547–1628, 721). He supported the absurdly inadequate estimates of the cost of war, and was even prepared to defer the presentation of grievances. In 1625 Bishop John Williams described him as 'never out of my lord duke's chamber and bosom' (J. Hacket, Scrinia reserata, 1695, pt 2, 18), and in 1626 he acted as teller against his patron's impeachment. This was the last parliament in which he sat, and for the election of 1628 he gave his interest at Plympton to another of the duke's clients, Sir James Bagg. Meanwhile, at home in Devon during these years of war Strode, living near Plymouth with the problems of disorder and martial law raised by the presence of mutinous and ill-paid troops, had been active as a magistrate and deputy lieutenant.

Lady Strode was buried on 24 February 1619, leaving a grown-up family of three sons and seven daughters. The eldest son, Sir Richard, married a sister of Sir Walter Erle and later became a Baptist; the second son, William *Strode (bap. 1594, d. 1645), achieved prominence as one of Sir John Eliot's allies in the session of 1629 and as one of the five members in 1642. The daughters all married into prominent Devon families, two of them marrying baronets and four of them knights; the eldest daughter, Mary, married Sir George *Chudleigh, a neighbour to the Strodes who shared Sir William's puritanism, and Elizabeth married a son of the diarist Walter Yonge. On 31 March 1624 Strode married his second wife, Dennes, daughter of Stephen Vosper of Liskeard, Cornwall. She died childless, and was buried on 16 September 1635.

Under the personal rule of Charles I, Strode continued to be consulted over local matters. In 1632, now aged seventy, he was unsuccessful in his attempt to resign from the county bench and deputy lieutenancy. In January 1634 his brother justices reported that although his 'extreme sickness' had prevented him from attending their meetings, yet he had been 'very careful and forward' in implementing the Book of Orders in his division (Wolffe, 67). His last public action was a protest against ship money. He died on 27 June 1637 and was buried alongside his two 'most loving and religious wives' at St Mary's Church, Plympton, the following day (will). An epitaph composed by his son William speaks of his religion, integrity, public justice, generous hospitality, and upright and successful management of his affairs.

JOHN FERRIS

Sources T. M. Venning, 'Strode, Sir William', HoP, *Commons, 1604–29* [draft] · P. W. Hasler, 'Strode, William II', HoP, *Commons, 1558–1603* · W. Notestein, *The House of Commons, 1604–1610* (1971) · J. L. Vivian, ed., *The visitations of the county of Devon, comprising the herald's visitations of 1531, 1564, and 1620* (privately printed, Exeter, [1895]) · *JHC*, 1 (1547–1628) · *CSP dom.*, 1598–1601; 1625–36 · M. Jansson, ed., *Proceedings in parliament, 1614 (House of Commons)* (1988) · J. Prince, *Danmonii orientales illustres, or, The worthies of Devon*, 2nd edn (1810) · R. N. Worth, *Calendar of the Plymouth municipal records* (1893) · W. Notestein, F. H. Relf, and H. Simpson, eds., *Commons debates, 1621*, 7 vols. (1935) · M. Wolffe, *Gentry leaders in peace and war: the gentry governors of Devon in the early seventeenth century* (1997) · will, PRO, PROB 11/176, sig. 18 · R. Lockyer, *Buckingham: the life and political career of George Villiers, first duke of Buckingham, 1592–1628* (1981) · *Calendar of the manuscripts of the most hon. the marquess of Salisbury*, 18, HMC, 9 (1940)

Wealth at death see will, PRO, PROB 11/176, sig. 18

Strode, William (*bap.* 1594, *d.* 1645), politician, was baptized on 6 November 1594 at Bovey Tracey, Devon, the second son of Sir William *Strode (1562–1637), politician, of Newnham in the same county, and his first wife, Mary (*d.* 1619), daughter of Thomas Southcote of Bovey Tracey, Devon. In 1614 Strode was admitted to the Inner Temple and on 9 May 1617 he matriculated from Exeter College, Oxford; he graduated BA on 20 June 1619.

In the last parliament of James I and in the earliest three parliaments called by Charles I, Strode represented Bere Alston in Devon. An energetic critic of the Caroline regime, in 1625 he favoured proceedings against Richard Montagu and in 1628 supported the petition of right and spoke in the remonstrance debate, linking perceived foreign and domestic threats to the English state. He apparently favoured the war with Spain. A close ally of Sir John Eliot in the Commons in 1629, he was concerned with religion and constitutionally provocative in asserting the position of parliament. On 2 March, when the speaker tried to adjourn the house and refused to put Eliot's resolutions to the vote, Strode played a major part in the disorderly scene which followed. He did not content himself with pointedly reminding the speaker that he was only the servant of the house, but called on all those who desired Eliot's declaration to be read to signify their assent by standing up. He explained:

> I desire the same, that we may not be turned off like scattered sheep, as we were at the end of the last session, and have a scorn put on us in print; but that we may leave something behind us. (Gardiner, 7.69)

The next day Strode was summoned before the privy council. As he declined to come, he was arrested in the country. With Eliot and other imprisoned MPs he was a committed recalcitrant in the major state case of 1629–30 which influenced Charles I's retreat to personal rule. When proceeded against in Star Chamber (proceedings which eventually lapsed) he repudiated the jurisdiction of the court and refused to answer outside parliament for words spoken within it. With five of the other prisoners he sued for *habeas corpus*, seeking bail, on 6 May 1629.

In a test case for the petition of right, Charles subverted the law in preventing the prisoners from being brought to court to be bailed, lodging them in the Tower. In October, Strode was one of those refusing bail linked to a good behaviour bond designed to rationalize their arbitrary imprisonment. He remained incarcerated in various prisons until January 1640, when released in a conciliatory gesture prior to the meeting of the Short Parliament. The Long Parliament later voted the proceedings against him a breach of privilege, awarding £500 compensation, and in 1667 both houses upheld these resolutions.

Strode was returned for Bere Alston to the two parliaments elected in 1640, where his militancy was surely related to bitterness at his imprisonment. His sufferings gave him a position in Pym's group which his abilities would not have entitled him to claim, and though one of the most active MPs in the Long Parliament he was a fellow traveller rather than a prime mover among the agitators. His boldness and freedom of speech soon made him notorious. Clarendon terms him 'one of the fiercest men of the party', and 'one of those Ephori who most avowed the curbing and suppressing of majesty' (Clarendon, *Hist. rebellion*, 2.86; 4.32). D'Ewes describes him as a 'firebrand', a 'notable profaner of the scriptures', and one with 'too hot a tongue' (J. Forster, *Arrest of the Five Members by Charles the First*, 1860, 220).

Strode's prominent pursuit of Long Parliament business reflected his 'godly' and anti-episcopal religious views, his assertion of parliamentary authority over prerogative, and his political friendship for the Scots. He was one of the managers of Strafford's impeachment, and was so bitter that he proposed that the earl should not be allowed counsel to speak for him. He spoke against Lord Keeper Finch, recalling his actions as speaker of the house in 1629, and was zealous for the protestation, but arguably his most important constitutional act was the introduction of the bill for annual parliaments—eventually the Triennial Act. His speech in favour of the Scots was part of the manoeuvring which brought about the end of the projected settlement of early 1641.

In the second session of the Long Parliament, Strode was again provocative. On 23 October 1641 he seconded the motion against evil counsellors, and demanded that parliament have a negative voice in all ministerial appointments, and on 28 October he moved for revival of the committee for the grand remonstrance. In late November he moved that the kingdom be put in a posture of defence, thus foreshadowing the Militia Bill.

To his activity rather than his influence Strode's inclusion among the five members impeached by Charles I was due: Clarendon describes both him and Heselrig as 'persons of too low an account and esteem' to be joined with Pym and Hampden (Clarendon, *Hist. rebellion*, 4.192). The articles of impeachment were presented on 3 January 1642, and on the following day the king came to the house in person to arrest the members. A pamphlet printed at the time gives a speech which Strode is said to have delivered in his vindication on 3 January, but there can be little doubt that it is a forgery. According to D'Ewes, it was difficult to persuade him to leave the house even when the king's approach was announced.

> Mr William Strode, the last of the five, being a young man and unmarried, could not be persuaded by his friends for a

pretty while to go out; but said that, knowing himself to be innocent, he would stay in the house, though he sealed his innocency with his blood at the door ... nay when no persuasions could prevail with the said Mr Strode, Sir Walter Erle, his entire friend, was fain to take him by the cloak and pull him out of his place and so get him out of the House. (Sanford, 464)

After his impeachment Strode was naturally the more embittered against the king, and appears to have been resigned to war in early 1642. When the civil war began he became one of the chief opponents of attempts at accommodation with Charles. He was present at the battle of Edgehill, and was sent up by Essex (with whom he was politically connected) to give a narrative of it to parliament. In the speech which he made to the corporation of London on 27 October 1642 Strode gave a short account of the fight, specially praising the regiments 'that were ignominiously reproached by the name of Roundheads', whose courage had restored the fortune of the day (Cobbett, *Parl. hist.*, 11.479). In 1643 his house in Devon was plundered by Sir Ralph Hopton's troops, and the Commons introduced an ordinance for indemnifying him out of Hopton's estate.

Strode remained prominent among the Commons leadership, being a target of Waller's plot (June 1643), and when Pym was buried in Westminster Abbey, Strode was one of his bearers (13 December 1643). In May 1644 he reintroduced the ordinance to renew the powers of the committee of both kingdoms. He was also active against Archbishop Laud, and on 28 November 1644 was employed by the Commons to press the Lords to agree to the ordinance for the archbishop's execution. He is said to have threatened the peers that the mob of the city would force them to pass it if they delayed. *Mercurius Aulicus*, commenting on the incident, accused Strode of making 'all the bloody motions'. On 31 January 1645 he was added to the assembly of divines.

Strode died of a fever at Tottenham on 9 September 1645. On 10 September the house ordered that he should have a public funeral and be buried in Westminster Abbey. Whitelocke, who attended the funeral on 22 September, described him as a constant servant to the parliament, just and courteous. Gaspar Hickes, who preached the funeral sermon, dwelt on the disinterestedness of Strode, stated that he spent or lost all he had in the public service, and asserted that his speeches were characterized by a 'solid vehemence and a piercing acuteness' (Hickes). Hickes's estimate of Strode's use of his estate was, however, overly optimistic. His will disposed of significant amounts of cash, valuable plate, horses, a house, and various property rights, manors, and advowsons, the chief beneficiary being his executor, Sir Edward Barkham, baronet. The benefits of the will were to be paid within two years of his death and the end of the wars in England: perhaps a measure to protect his property from further plunder without compensation. At the Restoration, Strode's remains were disinterred by a warrant dated 9 September 1661.

Strode's historical significance lies chiefly in his being a link between the political crises of the 1620s and 1640s, in the combination of his gentry background with religious and constitutional radicalism, and in the role he played in driving the Long Parliament into conflict and war. His character was marked by energy, honesty, passionate commitment, and lack of compromise. Strode was the uncle of the poet William Strode. He is also sometimes confused with William Strode (1589?–1666) of Barrington, near Ilchester, a colonel in parliament's service and a member of the Long Parliament expelled at Pride's Purge.   C. H. FIRTH, *rev.* L. J. REEVE

Sources M. Jansson and W. B. Bidwell, eds., *Proceedings in parliament, 1625* (1987) · W. Notestein and F. H. Relf, eds., *Commons debates for 1629* (1921) · *The journal of Sir Symonds D'Ewes: from the first recess of the Long Parliament to the withdrawal of King Charles from London / edited by Willson Havelock Coates*, ed. W. H. Coates (1942) · Clarendon, *Hist. rebellion* · L. J. Reeve, *Charles I and the road to personal rule* (1989) · L. J. Reeve, 'The legal status of the petition of right', *HJ*, 29 (1986), 257–77 · L. J. Reeve, 'The arguments in king's bench in 1629 concerning the imprisonment of John Selden and other members of the House of Commons', *Journal of British Studies*, 25 (1986), 264–87 · C. Russell, *Parliaments and English politics, 1621–1629* (1979) · C. Russell, *The causes of the English civil war* (1990) · C. Russell, *The fall of the British monarchies, 1637–1642* (1991) · S. R. Gardiner, *History of England from the accession of James I to the outbreak of the civil war*, 10 vols. (1883–4) · *State trials* · *The journal of Thomas Juxon*, ed. K. Lindley and D. Scott, CS, 5th ser., 13 (1999) · *The Short Parliament (1640) diary of Sir Thomas Aston*, ed. J. D. Maltby, CS, 4th ser., 35 (1988) · *The works of the most reverend father in God, William Laud*, ed. J. Bliss and W. Scott, 7 vols. (1847–60) · *Devon Notes and Queries*, 4 (1906–7) · J. L. Chester, ed., *The marriage, baptismal, and burial registers of the collegiate church or abbey of St Peter, Westminster*, Harleian Society, 10 (1876) · Foster, *Alum. Oxon.* · *The letters and journals of Robert Baillie*, ed. D. Laing, 3 vols. (1841–2) · J. Bruce, ed., *Verney papers: notes of proceedings in the Long Parliament*, CS, 31 (1845) · H. A. Hamilton, ed., *The notebook of Sir John Northcote* (1877) · Cobbett, *Parl. hist.* · B. Whitelocke, *Memorials of English affairs*, new edn, 4 vols. (1853) · G. Hickes, *The life and death of David: a sermon preached at the funeral of William Strode* (1645) · J. Forster, *Sir John Eliot: a biography*, 2 vols. (1864) · J. Sanford, *Studies and illustrations of the great rebellion* (1858) · A. Fletcher, *The outbreak of the English civil war* (1981) · H. Hulme, *The life of Sir John Eliot* (1957) · R. E. Ruigh, *The parliament of 1624: politics and foreign policy* (1971) · T. Cogswell, *The blessed revolution: English politics and the coming of war, 1621–1624* (1989) · H. Trevor-Roper, *Archbishop Laud, 1573–1645*, 3rd edn (1988) · V. A. Rowe, *Sir Henry Vane the younger: a study in political and administrative history* (1970) · IGI · PRO, PROB 11/194, fols. 18r–19r · P. Crawford, *Denzil Holles, 1598–1680: a study of his political career* (1979) · V. Snow, *Essex the rebel: the life of Robert Devereux, the third earl of Essex, 1591–1646* (1970) · D. Brunton and D. H. Pennington, *Members of the Long Parliament* (1954) · P. Zagorin, *The court and the country: the beginnings of the English revolution of the mid-seventeenth century* (1970) · C. Holmes, *The eastern association in the English civil war* (1974)

Archives PRO, state papers domestic, Charles I, SP 16

Wealth at death apparent substantial gentry wealth—approx. £600 cash bequests; plus house in Tavistock; plate; also one sixth of the manor of Mevy Walkhampton with attached properties; also various manors at Taynton in Devon: will, PRO, PROB 11/194, fols. 18r–19r

Strode, William (1601?–1645), poet and playwright, was baptized at Shaugh Prior, near Plymouth, Devon, on 11 January 1603, probably aged one (a brother was baptized three months later, a sister in 1599); he was the son of Philip Strode (d. 1605), fourth son of Sir William Strode of Newnham, near Plymouth, and Wilmot (d. after 1620), daughter of William Houghton of Houghton Towers,

Lancashire. Left fatherless at an early age, he owed his education at home, and later as a king's scholar at Westminster School, to relatives who had been impressed by his scholastic aptitude. Although his mother quickly remarried, Strode's middle-aged first cousin at Newnham, another Sir William Strode (father of the poet's namesake, the parliamentarian), probably took responsibility for him. In 1617 Strode entered Christ Church, Oxford, where he soon made his mark as a poet, contributing Latin verses to university publications from 1619 onwards. Having graduated BA in 1621 he remained at Christ Church, and was awarded MA in 1624 and BD in 1631; on 6 July 1638 he proceeded DD.

Throughout the 1620s Strode's English poems—lyrics, elegies, and occasional pieces both serious and comic—circulated widely in the university and beyond. The charming 'I saw faire Cloris walke alone' is his best known piece. Answer-poems, parodies, ballads, and songs form a noticeable part of his corpus; 'A Devonshire Song' uses dialect for comic effect; several elegies were written for memorial monuments. His light-hearted colloquial pieces explain his friendship with Richard Corbett, poet and dean of Christ Church, though other poems, including his best elegies, show him as less boisterous and more devout.

His ordination as deacon is unrecorded but he was priested in December 1628 and acquired a reputation as a 'most florid' preacher (Wood, *Ath. Oxon.*, new edn, 1817, 3.151). Of his three extant sermons only *On Death and the Resurrection* (1644) is now genuinely moving; these topics often inspired Strode's best work. During Corbett's tenure of the see of Oxford (1628–32) Strode became his chaplain. In 1629 he was made proctor; the same year his eloquence earned him the post of public orator, thus bringing him into contact with Laud, then chancellor of the university. Pressure of work or an altered social scene may explain subsequent changes in Strode's writing habits; the output of his English poems decreased and, while many earlier poems appear in manuscript collections (in some considerable numbers) and printed miscellanies, later ones, except 'The Townes New Teacher' (a vigorous attack on Puritan preachers), hardly circulated at all.

Corbett's translation to Norwich brought Strode no benefits, although they remained friends. Advancement came through the king who, in 1635, perhaps at Laud's instigation, annexed to the post of public orator the next Christ Church canonry to fall vacant. The royal visit to Oxford in 1636 offered further opportunities; not only did Strode deliver the welcoming speech but his *Floating Island* was one of three plays performed on this occasion. Probably Laud, organizing the visit, commissioned Strode to mould public opinion; the play is political satire, allegorically attacking Burton, Bastwick, and Prynne, whom Laud arraigned in the Star Chamber shortly afterwards. The plot, later seen as prophetic, turned on rebellion and restoration. Unfortunately Strode was no playwright. Music by Henry Lawes and scenery by Inigo Jones could not redeem the piece; one spectator called it fitter for scholars than a court, another thought it the worst he had ever

seen except for one at Cambridge; women in the audience found it misogynist. Unsurprisingly no rewards followed, but Henry Burton, fulminating from his London pulpit against Strode's 'scurrilous Enterlude', held it responsible for increasing plague 'and very bad weather withall' (H. Burton, *For God and the King*, 1636, 49–50).

The Christ Church canonry, however, became Strode's on 1 July 1638. Now free to marry, he chose the daughter of a prebendary of Canterbury connected to two bishops. Mary Simpson (*d.* 1648) was seventeen or eighteen, Strode in his forties, when they married on 17 July 1642. A daughter, Jane, was born fourteen months later. His income augmented by several livings, Strode could have expected a comfortable life, had not public events intervened.

In February 1641, as subdean, Strode had headed the college's list of subscribers to the protestation; the following July he regretfully acknowledged Laud's resignation of the chancellorship. Soon afterwards his wife's connection Bishop Skinner was imprisoned. Strode himself was summoned before a parliamentary committee to account for the fulsome style of earlier official letters to Laud, but not charged. When war broke out his Devon family, with whom he had maintained good relations, was heavily involved on the parliament side. He himself remained at Oxford, apparently arranging his poems for publication, a project interrupted by his death on 10 March 1645; the fact that he died intestate suggests that the event was sudden and unexpected. He was buried in Christ Church Cathedral on 13 March; his grave is unmarked. His widow died on 6 February 1648.

A mild, reasonable, humorous man, by inclination charitable and tolerant, Strode found such attitudes increasingly difficult to maintain as the Puritan threat grew. Posthumous publication of *The Floating Island* (1655) and *A Sermon at a Visitation* (1660) shows him remembered and valued as a royalist propagandist. In troubled times and without the aid of print he was soon forgotten as a poet, contemporary reputation notwithstanding. Bertram Dobell's edition of his poetical works (1907) received little notice; but Strode's lyric gift is genuine, if minor, and his personality attractive. A fuller edition of his works (based on the holograph in Corpus Christi College, Oxford, MS 325) was produced in 1966 (Forey), and in recent years the growing interest in manuscript verse of the early seventeenth century has led to increased and deserved attention for this rewarding poet. MARGARET FOREY

Sources M. Forey, 'A critical edition of the poetical works of William Strode, excluding *The floating island*', BLitt diss., U. Oxf., 1966 · Christ Church Cathedral, Oxford, transcript of registers, Bodl. Oxf., MS Top. Oxon. c. 169 · R. Hovenden, ed., *The register booke of christeninges, marriages, and burials within the precinct of the cathedrall and metropoliticall church of Christe of Canterburie*, Harleian Society, register section, 2 (1878) · J. R. Elliott and J. Buttrey, 'The royal plays at Christ Church in 1636: a new document', *Theatre Research International*, 10 (1985), 93–107 · letter of administration, PRO, PROB 6/23, 1D 26676 · J. L. Vivian, ed., *The visitations of the county of Devon, comprising the herald's visitations of 1531, 1564, and 1620* (privately printed, Exeter, [1895]) · J. L. Vivian, ed., *The visitations of Cornwall, comprising the herald's visitations of 1530, 1573, and 1620* (1887) · J. Welch, *The list of the queen's scholars of St Peter's College, Westminster*, ed. [C. B. Phillimore], new edn (1852) · Wood, *Ath. Oxon.: Fasti*

(1815) • *The life and times of Anthony Wood*, ed. A. Clark, 1, OHS, 19 (1891)
Wealth at death see administration, PRO, PROB 6/23

Strong [*née* Sellers], **Eugénie** (1860–1943), archaeologist and art historian, was born in London on 25 March 1860, the elder daughter of Frederick William Sellers (*d.* 1877), a wineseller, and his wife, Anna Oates (*d.* 1871). Her maternal great-grandfather was the baron du Cluseau, of the Château de Clerant in Périgord (Dordogne). She had a cosmopolitan education, first at Valladolid in Spain, then in France at the convent of the Sisters of St Paul at Dourdan, and finally at Girton College, Cambridge, where she obtained a third-class degree in the classical tripos in 1882.

After a year spent teaching at St Leonard's School in St Andrews, Sellers moved to London to study classical archaeology. Her archaeological mentor was Sir Charles Newton of the British Museum. In London she participated in amateur theatricals and moved in the artistic circles of Frederic, Lord Leighton, Edward Burne Jones, and Lawrence Alma Tadema. She gave university extension lectures and demonstrations on Greek art at the British Museum and in 1890–91 she became the first female student at the British School in Athens. In 1891 she published an English translation of Carl Schuchardt's account of Heinrich Schliemann's excavations at Troy. Sellers then studied for some years in Germany, mainly in Munich with Adolf Fürtwangler and Ludwig Traube. In 1895 she published an English translation of Fürtwangler's *Meisterwerke der griechischen Plastik*; however, the major publication of her Munich years was a historical introduction and commentary to *The Elder Pliny's Chapters on the History of Art* (1896) with a translation of the Latin text by her Girton colleague Katharine Jex-Blake. This work represents the start of a shift in her research interests, away from Greek and towards Hellenistic and Roman art. Her final choice of Roman archaeology as her major field of scholarly activity was strengthened by her 1900 translation, with preface, of Franz Wickhoff's study of the miniatures in the Vienna codex of the book of Genesis, published as *Roman Art*.

On 11 December 1897 Sellers married Sandford Arthur *Strong (1863–1904), an oriental scholar and art historian, the librarian to the duke of Devonshire and keeper of the collections at Chatsworth House; they had no children. After her husband's death in 1904 she was appointed his successor as librarian at Chatsworth and continued in that position until the death of the eighth duke of Devonshire in 1908. In 1907 she published *Roman Sculpture from Augustus to Constantine*, her most significant and enduring contribution to scholarship. This remarkable pioneering work helped secure recognition for Roman art as a subject worthy of attention on its own merits, not as a mere appendix to Greek art. It helped secure her appointment in 1909 as assistant director of the British School at Rome. Thomas Ashby was the director. She lived in Rome until her death.

From 1909 to 1925 Eugénie Strong helped make the British School a major scholarly and cultural centre in Rome. She was honoured with invitations to give the Charles Eliot Norton lectures of the Archaeological Institute of America in 1913 and the Rhind lectures in Edinburgh in 1920. Although Strong and Ashby were internationally respected as classical archaeologists, personality and policy disagreements led to the controversial decision to terminate both of their contracts in 1925. Strong took a flat on the via Balbo near the basilica of Santa Maria Maggiore, which became the locus not only of her continued scholarly activity but also of her weekly salons that drew together scholars, students, and distinguished persons of all types and nationalities. She had throughout her life an exceptional gift for friendship and her close acquaintances included many of the most important scholarly and cultural figures of her age.

Strong's research remained focused on Roman art and archaeology. In 1923 she published *La scultura romana*, a revised Italian edition of her 1907 work on Roman sculpture. Her two-volume *Art in Ancient Rome from the Earliest Times to Justinian* appeared in 1929. She was invited to contribute two chapters, 'The art of the Roman republic' and 'The art of the Augustan age', to the *Cambridge Ancient History*. Her research stressed the range of Roman accomplishment in both Italy and the provinces, and indigenous creativity rather than external Greek influences. Her enthusiasm for 'Romanita' led her to sympathize with the archaeological policies and activities of Mussolini.

Strong early developed a special interest in Roman religion. Her *Apotheosis and After Life* (1915) developed out of her Norton lectures in America. In that and other works she stressed the importance of religious symbolism in Roman art. It also reflected her own spiritual development. In 1917 she reaffirmed her Roman Catholic faith. She combined her spirituality and interest in the later art and history of Rome in her intellectual work. She was one of the first English scholars to treat Gianlorenzo Bernini and the baroque with sympathy and respect. In 1923 she published *La chiesa nuova*, a guide to the church of Santa Maria in Vallicella, and at her death in 1943 she had completed a manuscript on the history of the Vatican palace, which was never published.

Strong received many honours in her lifetime. In 1910 she was made a life research fellow of Girton College, she was appointed CBE in 1927, and she was awarded the Serena medal for Italian studies by the British Academy in 1938. She received honorary degrees from the universities of St Andrews and Manchester. In Italy she was elected to the Accademia dei Lincei, the Pontificia Accademia Romana di Archeologia, and the Society of the Arcadians, and received the gold medal of the city of Rome in 1938. She elected to stay in Rome when the Second World War started, and she died there, in the Polidori Nursing Home, on 16 September 1943, and was buried in the campo Verano cemetery, Rome.

J. M. C. TOYNBEE, *rev.* STEPHEN L. DYSON

Sources S. L. Dyson, *Portrait of an archaeologist: Eugénie Strong from Victoria to Mussolini* [forthcoming] • G. S. Thompson, *Mrs Arthur Strong, a memoir* (1949) • M. Praz, 'La Signore Strong', *La Casa della Fama* (Milan, 1952) • N. C. Jolliffe, *Cambridge Review* (20 Nov 1943) •

L. Curtius, *Rendiconti della Pontificia Accademia Romana di Archeologia*, 21 (1943–6), 29–32 • J. M. C. Toynbee, *Antiquaries Journal*, 23 (1943), 188–9 • T. P. Wiseman, *A short history of the British School at Rome* (1990) • G. Richtes, *American Journal of Archaeology*, 2nd ser., 48 (1944), 79–81 • M. Beard, *The invention of Jane Harrison* (2000) • *The Times* (21 Sept 1943) • m. cert. • *CGPLA Eng. & Wales* (1945)

Archives Girton Cam., diaries, working papers, and corresp. | BLPES, letters to Violet Markham • Bodl. Oxf., corresp. with Sir J. L. Myres • British School at Rome, archives • Harvard University Center for Italian Renaissance Studies, near Florence, Italy, letters to Bernard Berenson and Mary Berenson • King's Cam., letters to Roger Fry

Likenesses C. Phillott, oils, 1890, Girton Cam. • D. Evans, bronze head sculpture, Girton Cam. • photograph, Girton Cam.

Wealth at death £4748 15*s*. 5*d*. — effects in England: administration, 2 June 1945, *CGPLA Eng. & Wales*

Strong, John (*c*.1654–1693). *See under* Holditch, Abraham (*bap.* 1639, *d.* 1678).

Strong, Sir Kenneth William Dobson (1900–1982), army and intelligence officer, was born in Montrose, Scotland, on 9 September 1900, the only son among the four children of John Strong, rector of Montrose Academy and subsequently professor of education at Leeds University, and his wife, Ethel May, daughter of A. Knapton Dobson. Strong was educated at Montrose Academy, Glenalmond, and the Royal Military College, Sandhurst. He was commissioned into the Royal Scots Fusiliers in July 1920. After being an intelligence staff officer in Germany, he was defence security officer, Malta and Gibraltar, and then assistant military attaché, Berlin (January 1938 – August 1939). He was then promoted lieutenant-colonel and GSO1 in MI14 (German section, War Office), a position he held until April 1941, and next he commanded the 4th battalion, 5th Royal Scots Fusiliers, until January 1942. He was then brigadier general staff (intelligence) home forces until appointed brigadier general staff (intelligence), allied forces headquarters Algiers, on 11 March 1943. He was promoted major-general in December 1943.

Strong had a distinguished career in intelligence and became fluent in three foreign languages, particularly German. But the turning-point in his career was his appointment as General Dwight Eisenhower's chief of intelligence in March 1943. This appointment came about as a result of the failure of intelligence before the Kasserine pass débâcle and subsequent changes among the senior staff at allied forces headquarters. Strong brought a new and much needed discipline and direction to the intelligence services in north Africa. He became a firm friend and confidant of Eisenhower and of his chief of staff, Walter Bedell Smith—a friendship which lasted for life.

The Tunisian campaign ended in May 1943. After he helped to plan the Sicily landings Strong's next important role was to accompany Bedell Smith to the Italian armistice negotiations, with the Italian General Castellano, in Lisbon in mid-August 1943. The armistice was signed in Sicily on 3 September by Bedell Smith, with Strong taking an important part in the ceremony and the events preceding it.

Strong then suffered a major disappointment. At the Cairo conference in November 1943 Eisenhower was appointed to take charge of the allied invasion of north-west Europe. Eisenhower wished to take Strong back to London with him as his chief of intelligence, but the British chiefs of staff prevented his transfer on the ground of not wishing to denude allied forces headquarters, though Strong always felt that he was too closely identified with the Americans for the War Office's liking. Eisenhower finally appealed to Winston Churchill, and as a result Strong returned to London to join Supreme Headquarters, Allied Expeditionary Force, on 19 May 1944. He was therefore present at and participated in the historic decision to invade Normandy on 6 June 1944.

Strong's close association with Eisenhower and Bedell Smith did not always endear him to General Bernard Montgomery and the War Office. He was not immune from some of the British sniping at Eisenhower's methods and decisions. This was particularly true at the time of the German offensive in the Ardennes (December 1944 – January 1945). That the German attack was not foreseen subjected the intelligence staff in general and Strong in particular to a good deal of criticism. Strong did much soul-searching to try to discover if he had missed a vital clue, but the real culprit was lack of air reconnaissance due to bad weather and low cloud. Blame does not attach to Strong and his senior staff.

By 20 December an extremely serious situation had arisen, with the Germans advancing towards the River Meuse. Had they reached the Meuse, they would have driven a wedge through the centre of General Omar Bradley's command, separating his divisions in the north from those in the south. Consequently, Generals Whiteley and Strong felt compelled to recommend to Bedell Smith that the American First Army—Bradley's northern force—be put under Montgomery's command. It says much for the standing of these two British generals that they had the courage to make this very unpopular recommendation and Eisenhower had the wisdom to accept it. In the event the German offensive was halted, but relations between Montgomery and Generals Bradley and George Patton, never good, went through a bad patch. Relations were not improved by the suggestion emanating from London that there be one ground forces commander, who should be Montgomery.

Montgomery's counter-attack, spearheaded by the US First Army, was launched on 3 January 1945. The capture of the Remagen bridgehead and the crossing of the Rhine by both Bradley and Montgomery brought the end of the war finally into sight. Strong played a leading part in organizing the surrender ceremony in Rheims on 7 May. He was always mindful of the signing of the armistice by the Germans in 1918, which was done in such a way as to permit the German army to claim that it had never been defeated in the field. Strong urged Eisenhower to ensure that this error should not be repeated. Strong participated in the arrest of Wilhelm Keitel and other senior officers at Flensburg and also in the final surrender ceremony at Karlshorst, Berlin, on 8 May.

Supreme Headquarters Allied Expeditionary Force, was

disbanded shortly after the German surrender, and Strong had reached another turning-point in his career. His first inclination was to continue his military career, which would have meant commanding a brigade, but as Montgomery was about to become chief of the Imperial General Staff this would probably have been unwise. The post of director-general of MI5 was mooted, but in the end he accepted the appointment of director-general of the political intelligence department of the Foreign Office. This was an interim assignment, as the department was a wartime organization and was being run down. Strong was then appointed director of the joint intelligence bureau—a job to which he was well suited and of which he made an outstanding success. He retired from the army in May 1947 to become a civil servant. In 1964 there was a reorganization of the intelligence services and Strong became director-general of intelligence, Ministry of Defence—a post he held until his final retirement on 9 May 1966.

Strong subsequently pursued a career in the City as a director of the Eagle Star Insurance Co., Philip Hill Investment Trust, and other companies. He wrote *Intelligence at the Top* (1968) and *Men of Intelligence* (1970). He was appointed OBE (1942) and CB (1945), was knighted in 1952, and became KBE (1966). He was also an officer of the legion of merit (USA) and an officer of the Légion d'honneur, had the croix de guerre with palms (France), and belonged to the order of the Red Banner (USSR).

In 1979 Strong married Brita Charlotta, widow of John Horridge, master of the Supreme Court (King's Bench Division), and daughter of E. S. Persson, engineer, of Malung, Sweden. They had no children. Strong died on 11 January 1982 at his home, 25 Kepplestone Staveley Road, Eastbourne.   KENNETH KEITH, *rev.*

Sources K. Strong, *Intelligence at the top* (1968) · K. Strong, *Men of intelligence* (1970) · *The Times* (13 Jan 1982) · personal knowledge (2004) · *CGPLA Eng. & Wales* (1982)
Archives IWM, corresp. with Eisenhower [microfilm] · IWM, papers relating to his appointment as Eisenhower's senior intelligence officer · King's Lond., Liddell Hart C., corresp. with Sir B. H. Liddell Hart
Wealth at death £360,579: probate, 1982, *CGPLA Eng. & Wales*

Strong, Leonard Alfred George (1896–1958), writer, was born on 8 March 1896 at 7 Hartley Villas, Compton Gifford, Devon, the only son of Leonard Ernest Strong, manager in a chemical works (he eventually became director of Fisons), and his wife, Marion Jane, daughter of Alfred Mongan, a lawyer's clerk in Dublin. His mother was Irish, and his father was half-English and half-Irish.

Leonard Strong's early years affected him profoundly, and his childhood Irish and Devon memories often feature in his later writings. He was a child of delicate health, and was first educated at Hoe preparatory school, from which he won an open scholarship to Brighton College. The obscure spinal trouble from which he suffered kept him from sport, except swimming, and may explain the later emphasis in his writings on the uneasy relationship between physical strength and brutality. In 1915, four years after his admission at Brighton, he was awarded an

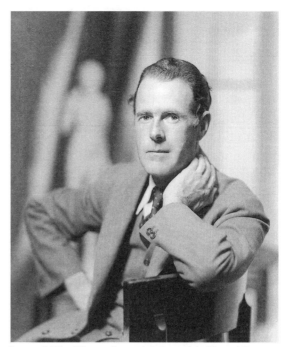

Leonard Alfred George Strong (1896–1958), by Howard Coster, 1937

open classical scholarship to Wadham College, Oxford, but illness interrupted his education, and kept him from active service in the First World War. In 1917 he became an assistant master at Summer Fields School, a classical preparatory school in north Oxford. He returned to Wadham in 1919 to take a pass degree in classics and English, graduating BA in 1920. He went back to Summer Fields and remained a master there until 1930, varying his teaching with interludes as a theatrical cartoonist and actor. All this time he was also actively engaged in writing.

Strong had begun to send contributions to editors as early as 1915. At Oxford he wrote for undergraduate journals, and in 1921 he began to devote himself more and more to freelance writing, deriving many of his subjects from his teaching experiences. *Dublin Days* (1921) and *The Lowery Road* (1923), his first two volumes of poetry, demonstrate his achievement as a lyric poet of epigrammatic conciseness, tenderness, and wit, although his reputation as a poet has not survived. On 29 July 1926 he married Dorothea Sylvia Tryce (b. 1904/5), the younger daughter of Hubert Brinton, assistant master at Eton College. They had one son, Patrick Strong.

Strong's first published novel, *Dewer Rides* (1929), a story of Dartmoor, was such a success that he gave up schoolmastering in 1930, and devoted himself to writing. He produced a volume of short stories, *The English Captain* (1929), and gradually built up a substantial readership for his novels, which included *The Jealous Ghost* (1930); *The Garden* (1931), a largely autobiographical novel; *The Brothers* (1932), a tale of highland fishermen; *Corporal Tune* (1934); and *The Seven Arms* (1935). Ireland served as a setting for some of his best novels. *The Open Sky* (1939) deals with an aspiring writer in an island off the west coast of Ireland; *The Bay* (1941), like the earlier novel *Sea Wall* (1933), is set in Dublin; and in *The Director* (1944), 'Hollywood comes to Ireland and its impact on the simple values of Irish peasant life gave Strong an occasion for some of his most perceptive characterization' (*The Times*, 19 Aug 1958). This last novel he later adapted for the stage, and it was performed at the Gate Theatre, Dublin. He also continued to write short fiction—*Travellers* (1945) was awarded the James Tait Black memorial prize, and *Darling Tom* (1952) showed him in turn as a master of comedy and sentiment, of the macabre, the fearful, and the ironic.

Throughout his career as a writer of fiction, Strong was also active in publishing circles. He acted as a reviewer for *The Spectator* for two years, and was a literary adviser to Thomas Nelson for four years. He became a director of Methuens in 1938, and served as such until his death. He was also a member of the Irish Academy of Letters, a fellow of the Royal Society of Literature, and for many years honorary treasurer of the Society of Authors. But he continued to prove to be an incredibly versatile writer, increasingly willing to turn his hand to anything that came along. He became a zealous spectator and defender of boxing, on which he wrote *Shake Hands and Come Out Fighting* (1939). He was also a biographer of some merit, producing *The Minstrel Boy* (1937), a biography of Thomas Moore; *John McCormack: the Story of a Singer* (1941); and *Dr Quicksilver* (1955), a biography of the eighteenth-century physician Thomas Dover. His literary criticism, best seen in his study of James Joyce, *The Sacred River* (1949), and in *Personal Remarks* (1953), demonstrates 'an honest independence of judgement, a keen sense of a good biographical anecdote, and (suddenly combining these two) a fresh … insight of the subject' (*The Times*, 23 Aug 1958). In 1953 Strong produced a book of practical advice for the aspiring writer, entitled *The Writer's Trade*. He also compiled anthologies and wrote one-act plays, books for children, schoolbooks, detective stories, radio and television scripts, and even titles as diverse as *The Story of Sugar* (1954) and *The Rolling Road* (1956), a study of travel in Britain and the development of public transport. His collected poems, *The Body's Imperfection*, appeared in 1957. Although Strong may be criticized as something of a 'literary chameleon', and although this attitude to writing, which he did not deny, deprived him of a certain single-mindedness, even in his fiction, he may be remembered by his early novels and his short stories.

Strong was also an accomplished amateur singer and actor. He had early been involved in broadcasting, producing a series of talks under the title *The Enjoyment of Novels* for the BBC in 1933. He was an impressive lecturer and became an inspiring teacher of drama and voice production, notably at the Central School of Speech and Drama. He was also the author of a book on the speaking of English, *A Tongue in Your Head* (1945). As an adjudicator in amateur dramatics, he travelled all over the country. He always had time for young actors and writers, one of whom wrote to *The Times* after his obituary appeared with

this additional tribute: 'He gave us clear and patient criticism, sound advice, and the most kindly encouragement—all in his rare spare time' (*The Times*, 26 Aug 1958). Strong was of medium height and pleasant looks. Contradictory as he could appear in his writings, he was personally a man of most engaging modesty, charm, and humour.

Leonard Strong died of a heart attack following surgery on 17 August 1958, at the Royal Surrey County Hospital in Guildford, Surrey; he was survived by his wife. His autobiography of his early life, *Green Memory*, was published posthumously, in 1961.

DEREK HUDSON, *rev.* M. CLARE LOUGHLIN-CHOW

Sources b. cert. · m. cert. · d. cert. · *The Times* (19 Aug 1958) · *The Times* (23 Aug 1958) · *The Times* (26 Aug 1958) · L. Mégroz, *Five novelist poets of today* (1933) · *WWW* · S. A. Moseley, *Who's who in broadcasting* (1933) · F. A. Marteau, *Who's who in press, publicity, printing* (1939) · L. A. G. Strong, *Green memory* (1961) · D. C. Browning, *Everyman's dictionary of literary biography, English and American*, 3rd edn (1962) · personal knowledge (1971) · private information (1971) · *CGPLA Eng. & Wales* (1958)
Archives Ransom HRC, corresp. and literary papers · U. Edin. L., corresp. and papers | BL, corresp. with Society of Authors, Add. MSS 56825–56826 · NL Ire., letters to F. R. Higgins · TCD, letters to Seumas O'Sullivan · U. Reading L., letters to L. Mégroz
Likenesses H. Coster, photographs, 1930–39, NPG [*see illus.*] · N. Lewis, pencil and wash drawing, 1932, NPG · H. Gerson, photograph, 1955, NPG · D. Low, pencil sketches, NPG
Wealth at death £14,967 3s. 11d.: probate, 27 Nov 1958, *CGPLA Eng. & Wales*

Strong, Patience. *See* Cushing, Winifred Emma (1907–1990).

Strong [*née* Thorogood], **Rebecca** (1843–1944), nurse, was born on 23 August 1843 at the Blue Boar inn, High Street, Aldgate, London, the daughter of John Thorogood (1785–1870), the innkeeper, and his wife, Mary Westell (1804–1854). On 19 July 1863 Rebecca Thorogood married Andrew Robert Strong (1841–1865), a mathematical instrument maker and son of Andrew Robert William Strong, a wholesale rag merchant. A daughter, Annie Ellen, was born in 1864 and a year later Rebecca was widowed. When her daughter was three Rebecca entered the Nightingale Training School, St Thomas's Hospital, London, and started her career as a nurse. As it was necessary for nurses to live in the nurses' home, both during training and when qualified, Strong's daughter was brought up by her family.

The Nightingale school, which had opened in 1860, was still in an experimental stage and after one year's practical work in the wards of St Thomas's, with some lectures, Strong was sent to Winchester Hospital and then to the new British army hospital at Netley, Southampton. In 1874, when her contract with the Nightingale school was completed, Strong applied and was appointed as matron of the Dundee Royal Infirmary. With the support of the managers she raised the standard of nursing and improved the nurses' working conditions. Her reputation reached Glasgow and, in 1879, she was appointed matron of the Glasgow Royal Infirmary, the largest voluntary hospital in Scotland. Strong was shocked by the poor standard of nursing at Glasgow and insisted that all the ward sisters attend medical lectures and pass an examination. Strong had decided that nurses could no longer be properly trained on the wards alone; with recent developments in medicine they needed theoretical lectures if they were to carry out their duties intelligently. William *Macewen (1848–1924), surgeon to the Royal Infirmary, had been one of the first to adopt Lister's antiseptic methods and was at the forefront of brain surgery. Although Macewen encouraged Strong to develop the nurses' education, he demanded a continuous supply of good nurses for his wards. Lack of sufficient accommodation limited the number of nurses available and when the infirmary managers repeatedly refused to provide more Strong resigned from her position in 1885.

For five years Strong ran her own private nursing home in Glasgow. During this time she and Macewen developed their ideas on the education of nurses. Then in 1891, Strong was asked to return to the Glasgow Royal Infirmary as matron, and thus they were given the opportunity to put their ideas into practice. The new training scheme started in 1893 and included several features which became standard for nurse training schemes in the twentieth century. It pioneered the block system by dividing the nurses' training into blocks of lectures, followed by blocks of practical ward work. It introduced compulsory theoretical instruction and examination before probationary nurses entered the wards. It set an educational standard for entry to training and it elevated nurses' education to the medical college, placing nurses on a par with medical students. Strong and Macewen both paid tribute to the contribution that the other had made to their achievements. The collaboration between them was rare and it advanced the development of brain surgery and the development of nurses' education.

Strong was a friend of Mrs Bedford Fenwick, the leader of the campaign for state registration, and they shared the view that nurses' education should be established at a university level, with postgraduate opportunities. They also shared ideas on the value of international contacts with professional women and Strong was an enthusiastic supporter of the International Council of Nurses, founded by Bedford Fenwick in 1899. She attended meetings of the council in Europe and North America until she was in her eighties. Strong was also a member of the various professional nursing organizations of the time, the Royal British Nurses' Association, and the Matrons Council, and was a vice-president of the National Council of Nurses of Great Britain and Ireland. In 1909 Strong and Macewen formed the Scottish Nurses Association and she later became president and represented the association on the committee of the Society for the State Registration of Nurses. The next ten years was a period of great professional development for nurses with the impact of the First World War, the establishment of the College of Nursing, and the passing of the Nurses' Registration Acts. Strong, like Bedford Fenwick, did not support the College of Nursing, and they were disappointed with the educational standards set by the new statutory bodies, the general nursing councils for England and Wales, Scotland, and Ireland.

Strong retired from the Glasgow Royal Infirmary in 1907 and moved to England to live with her sister. In 1912, following her sister's death, she returned to Scotland to live in St Fillans on the shores of Loch Earn, Perthshire. In 1886 her daughter had married the minister of the German protestant church in Glasgow, Adolf Geyer, and was settled there with five children. Strong did not approve of her son-in-law; she referred to him as 'that Austrian gypsy' and did not speak to him for over thirty years. However, she contributed financially to the upkeep and education of her grandchildren.

In her retirement Strong supported initiatives which promoted nurses' educational and professional standards, among them the Scottish Nurses Club in Glasgow and the Glasgow Royal Infirmary Nurses' League. She was still very fit and enjoyed travelling and mountain climbing. She was appointed OBE in 1938, and at the Glasgow Royal Infirmary the work of Macewen and Strong was commemorated by the annual presentation of two medals to the best nurses. In Britain her reputation is less than in North America, where nurse education was developed in universities as early as the 1920s. In 1941 she moved to Chester to live with her great-nephew. Her hundredth birthday was celebrated in the nursing press, and the BBC broadcast a message from Strong to younger nurses. She died on 24 April 1944 at Heathfield, Vicars Cross, Christleton, Cheshire, and her funeral took place in Liverpool, where she was cremated.

SUSAN MCGANN

Sources R. Strong, *Education in nursing: an address given in London in 1895* (privately printed, Edinburgh, 1927) · R. Strong, *Reminiscences* (privately printed, Edinburgh, 1935) · R. Strong, *Hints to beginners in the work of nursing* (privately printed, Glasgow, 1882) · Glasgow Royal Infirmary managers' committee minutes, 1871–1908, Mitchell L., Glas., Greater Glasgow health board archives, GHB14/1/14–21 · miscellaneous papers relating to Rebecca Strong, 1894–1942, Mitchell L., Glas., Greater Glasgow health board archives, GHB14/6/97 · register of nurses, 1902–42, Mitchell L., Glas., Greater Glasgow health board archives, GHB14/10/1 · collection of pamphlets, cuttings, correspondence, and photographs relating to Rebecca Strong, 1893–1967, Mitchell L., Glas., Greater Glasgow health board archives, GHB35/1/9 · corresp. between Macewen and Strong, 1882–4, Royal College of Physicians and Surgeons of Glasgow, William Macewen collection, RCPSG 10 · corresp. between Macewen family and Strong, 1942–3, Royal College of Physicians and Surgeons of Glasgow, William Macewen collection, RCPSG 10 · Z. Cope, *Six disciples of Florence Nightingale* [n.d., c.1961] · H. J. C. Gibson, *Dundee Royal Infirmary, 1798–1948* (1948) · R. Hallowes, 'Rebecca Strong', *Nursing Mirror* (25 Nov 1955) · J. E. Gordon, 'Mrs Rebecca Strong: pioneer and centenarian, 1843–1944', *Midwife, Health Visitor and Community Nurse*, 11 (Dec 1975) · *Nursing Times* (6 May 1944) · *Nursing Mirror* (6 May 1944) · b. cert. · m. cert. · d. cert. · private information (2004) · S. McGann, *The battle of the nurses: a study of eight women who influenced the development of professional nursing, 1880–1930* (1992)

Archives Mitchell L., Glas., Greater Glasgow health board archives · Royal College of Nursing Archives, Edinburgh, archives, pamphlets · Royal College of Physicians and Surgeons of Glasgow, corresp. with Macewen | SOUND BL NSA, 'A talk by a lady 100 years old who served under Florence Nightingale', 20 Aug 1943, BBC Sound Archive no. 6477

Strong, Sir Samuel Henry (1825–1909), judge in Canada, was born on 13 August 1825 at Poole, Dorset, the son of the Revd Samuel Spratt Strong DD LLD and Jane Elizabeth, the daughter of the miniature painter Thomas Gosse and the sister of Philip Henry Gosse. In 1836 the Revd Strong emigrated to Canada, and eventually settled with his family in Bytown (later Ottawa), where Samuel Strong became associated with the lawyer Augustus Keefer. He was called to the bar in Hilary term 1849, and worked initially with Henry Eccles in a practice that was heavily centred on the court of chancery. Having established the foundations of his practice, Strong served from December 1856 to December 1859 as a commissioner for consolidating the public general statutes of Upper Canada. In 1860 he became a bencher of the Law Society of Upper Canada, and three years later was named QC.

As a friend and legal adviser of prime minister John A. Macdonald, Strong drafted the earliest legislative proposal for the supreme court of Canada. Although nothing immediately came of this initiative, for his various efforts on behalf of Macdonald's federal administration, and in recognition of his formidable legal talent, he was appointed vice-chancellor of Ontario on 27 December 1869. In 1871 he agreed to serve on a committee examining the relationship between Ontario's courts of common law and equity. This inquiry was soon dissolved and the government proceeded with the fusion of law and equity, culminating in the Ontario Judicature Act of 1881.

Strong left the chancery bench in the spring of 1874 and on 17 June was sworn in as justice of the court of error and appeal, where he served only briefly before being named as one of the initial members of the new supreme court of Canada. The *Canada Law Journal* (1875) described him as 'a man of great talent and learning, and … one of the best civil law jurists in Canada' (pp. 265–6).

On the general issue of provincial sovereignty, Strong, despite his connections with Macdonald, declined to associate himself with supreme court colleagues who severely criticized provincial rights. In one contest between the realms of federal and provincial authority, concerning timber licences on native lands in northern Ontario, Strong forcefully displayed his analytical powers. The *St Catherine's Milling case* also had the effect of restricting the legal claims of aboriginal peoples to their homelands, with Strong's judgment now better known for advancing the concept of usufructuary rights which the judicial committee of the privy council later employed to describe the subordinate nature of native interests. The doctrine recognized aboriginal interests in the use of natural resources such as game on lands owned by others. Yet his firm and principled dissent from the supreme court's finding on the question of federal versus provincial ownership is noteworthy for its broader observations on governmental relations with aboriginal peoples. In the interpretation of section 91(24) of the British North America Act

dealing with 'lands reserved for the Indians', Strong insisted upon the importance of 'recourse to external aids derived from the surrounding circumstances and the history of the subject matter dealt with' (*St Catherine's Milling Company* v. *R.*). He specifically affirmed the continuing force of the royal proclamation of 1763, including the procedural requirements it imposed on surrenders of native lands, which he considered to remain unaffected by the subsequent passage of the Quebec Act.

Throughout the 1890s sensitive and controversial cases affecting religious minorities and provincial rights continued to come before the supreme court. In *Barrett* v. *The City of Winnipeg*, the court recognized the prejudice to the Roman Catholic and Franco-Manitoban community in the province's Public Schools Act and struck down the legislation. Here Strong was part of a unanimous decision—subsequently reversed by the privy council—in which the Canadian judges protected minority rights to denominational schools. Yet in a few short years Strong, who became chief justice in 1892, joined the majority in a reference decision that denied to Manitoba's Catholic community a right of appeal to the federal cabinet and declared the federal parliament to be without authority to pass remedial educational legislation. Strong's acceptance of this position has been explained as a consequence of his close associations with members of the federal Conservative Party and a desire to save the government from the divisive dilemma of remedial legislation. He was knighted in January 1893.

When the contentious subject of provincial legislation prohibiting the liquor trade came before the supreme court of Canada in 1895, Strong's judgments accommodated provincial aspirations, for he construed the scope of the municipal institutions power in section 92(8) of the British North America Act broadly. He also appeared more willing than several of his colleagues to accept concurrency: 'it appears to me that there are in the Dominion and the provinces respectively several and distinct powers authorizing each, within its own sphere, to enact the same legislation on this subject of prohibitory liquor laws restraining sale by retail' (*Huson* v. *South Norwich*, 1895).

Contemporary assessments of Strong's technical legal skills and analytical capability were extremely positive. Whatever his intellectual merits, his performance on the bench does not suggest a high level of organizational capability, and he has often been criticized for a tendency to offer short oral judgments not properly followed up with an elaboration of reasons. He continued as chief justice until 1902, when he stepped down to chair a commission for the consolidation of Canadian statutes. In the same year he chaired an arbitration panel established to resolve a minor dispute between the United States and San Salvador.

Strong had once been sharply critical of the judicial committee of the privy council, but in 1897 he became the first Canadian judge appointed to the committee, and served until his death, on 31 August 1909 in Ottawa. He was buried in Beechwood cemetery in the city.

Robert Laird Borden, later recalling his own days at the bar as well as the experience of other contemporaries, referred to Strong's 'pre-eminent intellectual qualities' but described him as a man 'of violent and bullying temperament', possessed of an 'evil temper' and sometimes given to truculency. Borden's assessment is apt: 'Neither as puisne judge nor as Chief Justice did his usefulness, in reasonable degree, approach the standard of his ability, learning and experience' (*Memoirs*, 26–7).

Elizabeth Charlotte Cane, who married Strong in 1850, survived him, along with his two daughters, Mrs H. Gourlay and Mrs L. Lyon. JAMIE BENIDICKSON

Sources G. Bale, 'Law, politics and the Manitoba school question: supreme court and privy council', *Canadian Bar Review*, 63 (1985), 461 · *Barrett v. the city of Winnipeg*, Supreme Court Reports, 19 (1891), 374 · R. L. Borden, *Robert Laird Borden: his memoirs* (1938), 26–7 · J. Pope, *Correspondence of Sir John Macdonald* (1921) · 'Re certain statutes of the province of Manitoba relating to education', *Reports of the Supreme Court of Canada*, 22 (1894), 577 · P. Romney, *Mr Attorney: the attorney general for Ontario in court, cabinet and legislature, 1791–1899* (1986) · *St Catherine's Milling Company v. the Queen*, Supreme Court Reports, 13, p. 577 · J. G. Snell and F. Vaughan, *The supreme court of Canada: history of the institution* (1985) · 'The chief justice of Canada', *Canadian Law Times*, 13 (1893), 50 · 'The honourable Sir Samuel Henry Strong', *The Canadian Green Bag*, 1/1 (Jan 1895), 1 · 'The late Sir Henry Strong', *Canadian Law Times*, 29 (1909), 1044
Likenesses oils, Supreme Court, Ottawa

Strong, Sandford Arthur (1863–1904), orientalist and art historian, born in London on 10 April 1863, was the second son of Thomas Banks Strong, of the War Office, and his wife, Anna, *née* Lawson, a Hebrew scholar. His elder brother was Thomas Banks *Strong. In 1877 he entered St Paul's School, London, as a foundation scholar, but remained there for little more than a year. His next two years were passed as a clerk at Lloyd's, though during this time he also attended classes at King's College, London. In 1881 he matriculated at Cambridge, with a Hutchinson studentship at St John's College. He graduated in 1884, with a third class in part one of the classical tripos, being placed in the second class in part two the following year. He proceeded MA in 1890.

Even in his undergraduate days Strong was inclined towards oriental studies, and on the recommendation of Professor Edward Byles Cowell he worked at Sanskrit with Cecil Bendall. However, he received little encouragement at Cambridge and moved to Oxford towards the end of 1885. There he was employed as subkeeper and librarian of the Indian Institute, and came to know Max Müller, Archibald Sayce, and Adolf Neubauer. Neubauer advised him to visit the continent, and gave him letters of introduction to Ernest Renan and James Darmesteter at Paris. Both were deeply impressed with his attainments, and their testimonials are quoted at length in Lord Balcarres's memoir; he also studied with Schrader at Berlin. Despite his qualifications Strong did not quickly find recognition or remunerative employment on his return to England. To Sanskrit he added Pali, to Arabic he added Persian and Assyrian, and he made some progress in hieroglyphics and Chinese. On all of these he wrote in learned publications, and he also contributed reviews to *The Athenaeum*

and *The Academy*. He produced editions of the *Maha-Bodhi-Vamsa* for the Pali Text Society (1891), and of the *Futah al-Habashah* or *Conquest of Abyssinia* (1894) for the Royal Asiatic Society's monographs. But he failed in his candidature for the chair of Arabic at Cambridge, made vacant by the death of Robertson Smith in 1894. He was, however, appointed professor of Arabic at University College, London, in 1895 and held this office, largely nominal, until his death.

In the same year a new career suddenly opened before Strong. Sidney Colvin introduced him to the duke of Devonshire, who was then in need of a librarian to succeed Sir James Lacaita. Installed at Chatsworth in 1895, Strong was as much interested in the historic collection of pictures and other works of art there as in the books in the library. He now showed what the scientific training of a scholar could accomplish in a new field, which was in fact the return to an old love. As a boy he had been taught drawing by Albert Varley, who gave him a copy of Pilkington's *Dictionary of Painters*, and he had acquainted himself with the styles of the different masters in the National Gallery. The discoveries he made at Chatsworth, and no doubt also his personal charm, opened to him other collections—the duke of Portland's at Welbeck, where he also acted for a time as librarian, the earl of Pembroke's at Wilton, and Lord Wantage's at Lockinge. Between 1900 and 1904 he published descriptions of these artistic and literary treasures.

On 11 December 1897 Strong married the distinguished classical archaeologist Eugénie Sellers [see Strong, Eugénie (1860–1943)]; they had no children. Also in 1897 he was appointed librarian at the House of Lords, where he compiled two catalogues, one of the general library and one of the law books. This appointment, while it did not interrupt his studies or his tenure of office at Chatsworth, introduced him to another sphere of interest, where he made himself equally at home. He became absorbed in politics and even dreamed that his ideal career would be in colonial government. But his health was never robust, and he had strained what physical vigour he possessed. After a lingering illness, he died at 7 Queen Anne Street, London, on 18 January 1904, and was buried in Brompton cemetery. At his death he was working on the Arabic text of Ibn Arabshah's *History of Yakmak, Sultan of Egypt*. A full bibliography of his works was included in the 1905 publication of his *Critical Studies and Fragments*. The Arthur Strong Oriental Library at University College, London, was formed around a nucleus which consisted of the books given in his memory by his widow, and it contained the bust by Countess Feodora Gleichen (1894), presented by a group of his friends. The collection was later redistributed in the library, some of the oriental books being transferred to the library of the new School of Oriental Studies after its foundation in 1916.

J. S. COTTON, *rev.* J. B. KATZ

Sources Lord Balcarres, 'Memoir', in S. A. Strong, *Critical studies and fragments* (1905), 1–25 · *The Times* (19 Jan 1904) · Lord Reay, *Journal of the Royal Asiatic Society of Great Britain and Ireland* (1904), 379–

80 · M. E. Lowndes, *A distinguished librarian* (June 1905) · private information (2004) · *CGPLA Eng. & Wales* (1904)
Archives Girton Cam., Eugénie Strong MSS, corresp. with Eugénie Strong
Likenesses F. G. M. Gleichen, clay model for a bust, 1894, repro. in Balcarres, 'Memoir', pl. xxiii · A. Legros, silverpoint drawing, 1896, FM Cam. · A. Legros, silverpoint drawing, 1897, FM Cam. · C. Holroyd, pencil drawing, 1904, NPG · Miss Caswall-Smith, photograph (aged thirty-nine), repro. in Balcarres, 'Memoir', frontispiece
Wealth at death £983 3s. 4d.: probate, 7 March 1904, *CGPLA Eng. & Wales*

Strong, Thomas Banks (1861–1944), dean of Christ Church and bishop of Oxford, was born on 24 October 1861 in London, the eldest of three sons and one daughter of Thomas Banks Strong, a clerk in the War Office, and his wife, Anna Lawson, a Hebrew scholar. The orientalist Sandford Arthur *Strong was his younger brother. His other brother, Rowland, was a journalist, acting as a correspondent to the *Pall Mall Gazette*, and his sister, Mary K. C. Strong, taught Greek, mathematics, and psychology.

Strong went to Westminster School in 1873, gaining an exhibition in the following year. In 1879 he matriculated as a junior student on the Westminster foundation at Christ Church, Oxford. He gained a first class in classical moderations in 1881 and a second class in *literae humaniores* in 1883. He graduated BA in 1883 and MA in 1886. Strong was ordained deacon on 20 September 1885 and priest on 19 September 1886 by Bishop Mackarness of Oxford. He offered a BD thesis, 'The doctrine of the real presence', in 1899, and graduated DD in 1902.

In 1884 Strong was appointed to a lecturership at Christ Church, and in 1888, after a slight delay attributed to the unease of the dean (H. G. Liddell) about his high-church leanings and somewhat casual manner, was elected to a studentship. He was identified as one of a group of young clerical tutors who did not share the pessimism of Liddon about the prospects for promoting religion and morality in the secularized university. An inspiring tutor, he got to know his pupils closely, taking them on reading parties during the vacations. In 1892 he became junior censor and later became senior censor, roles to which he brought a detached tolerance and a flair for administration. In 1901, on the recommendation of the outgoing dean, Francis Paget, and an honorary student, Sir Michael Hicks Beach, Strong became dean of Christ Church. Unmarried and sometimes socially awkward, Strong was an unconventional choice, but his public shyness and reserve disguised a gift for friendship and humour on a private level. He was happiest among the young men who were his students, and had a phenomenal memory for their names and backgrounds. During the First World War he corresponded with a large number of former pupils on active service.

Strong also took a keen interest in the cathedral choir. He was himself a gifted musician and composer, and was a reader of musical proofs, as well as a delegate, for the university press. He could have stayed at Christ Church as a musician rather than a lecturer, having been recommended as cathedral organist by Sir John Stainer to Dean Liddell. Strong also had an eye for musical talent, giving

Thomas Banks Strong (1861–1944), by Sir William Orpen, 1923

personal and financial support to the young composer William Walton. Strong's commitment was recognized by the award of an honorary DMus in 1917.

Strong did not marry nor, with few exceptions, did he seek the company of women. His few female friends were women with whom he shared intellectual interests, such as his sister, Mary, whom he asked to read drafts of his Bampton lectures, and Dean Church's daughter, with whom he collaborated on the *Oxford Hymnbook* (1925). He acted as chair of the council and visitor to Lady Margaret Hall, Oxford, but was not generally a friend to women's education in the university; however, following their admission to the university he thought it illogical not to admit women to degrees.

In 1907, as chairman of the Oxford University extension delegacy, Strong presided over a committee comprising seven university nominees and seven representatives of the Workers' Educational Association, led by the trade unionist David Shackleton, to review the university's extramural work. Their report, largely drafted by A. E. Zimmern and R. H. Tawney, but polished by Strong himself, *Oxford and Working-Class Education* (1908; 2nd edn, 1909; new edn, 1987), was an important landmark in the development of adult education. Strong served as vice-chancellor of the university between 1913 and 1917. It was here that his skills as an administrator were fully exploited. In 1914, on the outbreak of war, he formed a small *ad hoc*, and strictly unconstitutional, committee for interviewing candidates for commissions, thus bypassing the university delegacy for military instruction, and in doing so dealt with more than 2000 candidates before the end of the vacation. With the departure of most of his colleagues and undergraduates, Strong was left as acting treasurer of Christ Church, and also as the university's representative in negotiations with the government. His war work was rewarded with a GBE in 1918. In 1919 he became a member of the royal commission on Oxford and Cambridge chaired by H. H. Asquith, who considered that Strong, together with the master of Gonville and Caius

College, Cambridge, Hugh Kerr Anderson, contributed most to the commission's work. In 1923 Strong became one of eleven statutory commissioners appointed to carry out the recommendations of the commission of inquiry.

Strong was a high-churchman, but he disliked ritualism and enthusiasm, believing that the Anglican church should encompass a wide range of views and parties. As a writer Strong showed breadth of learning rather than originality. His Bampton lectures, delivered in 1895 and published as *Christian Ethics* (1896), were considered his best work, while his most widely known was the *Manual of Theology* (1892). He also published on the authority of the church. Strong was not a contributor to *Lux mundi*, but joined the group regularly in their meetings at Longworth.

It was known that Strong would have liked the see of Durham, having been examining chaplain to bishops Lightfoot and Westcott, where he had been awarded an honorary DD in 1913. However, that appointment went to Herbert Hensley Henson, and Strong was instead consecrated bishop of Ripon at York on 24 August 1920. Strong was not perhaps suited to being a bishop, given his distaste for ceremony and his lack of eloquence as a preacher. Nevertheless, he was at home in the urban environment of Leeds, where he took an active interest in the emergence of Leeds University, which in turn recognized him with an honorary LittD in 1922. He became involved in the music of Ripon Cathedral and also in making diocesan administration more effective.

In 1925 Strong translated to Oxford. The return to the scene of his past successes was difficult, as he himself recognized: 'At Oxford the college rotated round me. Here I have to rotate round the parishes' (Anson, 68). Strong was not equipped to deal with a vast rural diocese. His shyness and dislike of public ceremony were compounded by increasing age and ill health. The office did however bring Strong back into contact with the young through Cuddesdon College, whose ordinands he regularly entertained.

Strong was not a conspicuous figure in convocation, except in relation to prayer book revision, with which he was closely involved for over twenty years. It was work that exploited his skills as a committee man and his ability to master a subject. Although not personally dissatisfied with the prayer book, he recognized the necessity of adapting to modern needs in order to preserve unity and uniformity in the same way that, as dean of Christ Church, he had modified cathedral services to make them more attractive to undergraduates. He gave general support to the new Book of Common Prayer (1928) and questioned parliament's authority to reject the church's proposed reform.

Strong resigned as bishop of Oxford in September 1937. In retirement he lived with his sister in Kensington, spending much of his time at his club, the Athenaeum. During later life he suffered from increasing memory loss and during the Second World War he moved to Collingham Gardens Nursing Home, where he died on 8 June 1944. His funeral was held at St Jude's, Kensington. A Strong Memorial Fund was set up to mirror an exhibition fund Strong himself had set up when leaving Christ Church with the aim of helping a member of the choir school continue their education at a public school. Sir William Orpen's portrait (1923) strikingly holds its own in Christ Church Hall.   ELLIE CLEWLOW

Sources H. Anson, *T. B. Strong: bishop, musician, dean, vice-chancellor* (1949) · *DNB* · C. M. Blagden, *Well remembered* (1953) · *The Guardian* (16 June 1944) · *Church Times* (7 Dec 1945) · *Annual Report* [Christ Church, Oxford] (1943–4) · *Oxford Magazine* (15 June 1944) · J. F. A. Mason, 'Christ Church under three deans', *Hist. U. Oxf. 7: 19th-cent. Oxf. pt 2* · J. Prest, 'The Asquith commission', *Hist. U. Oxf. 8: 20th cent.*, 27–43 · J. C. Masterman, *On the chariot wheel: an autobiography* (1975) · *The Strong Memorial Fund* (1944)

Archives Christ Church Oxf. · Christ Church Oxf., archives · Oxford University Press, corresp. and papers mostly relating to revised prayer book | BL, corresp. with Albert Mansbridge, Add. MSS 65255A–65255B · Bodl. Oxf., Fisher MSS · Borth. Inst., corresp. with second Viscount Halifax · Hatfield House, Hertfordshire, Salisbury MSS · Oxon. RO, Oxford diocesan records

Likenesses W. Rothenstein, pencil drawing, 1916, NPG · W. Rothenstein, pencil drawing, 1916, Christ Church Oxf.; repro. in Anson, *T. B. Strong* · W. Orpen, oils, 1923, Christ Church Oxf. [*see illus.*] · Bassano, photograph (as bishop of Oxford), Christ Church Oxf., Strong MSS · T.E. Cox, photograph (as bishop of Oxford), NPG · J. Russell, photograph, Christ Church Oxf., Strong MSS · J. Wheatley, chalk and watercolour drawing, Athenaeum Club, London · photograph, Christ Church Oxf., Common Room album, p. 7

Wealth at death £11,871 3s. 9d.: probate, 2 Aug 1944, *CGPLA Eng. & Wales*

Strong, William (*d.* 1654), Independent minister, was probably a native of Dorset (and possibly the son of Timothy Strong), although Durham and Abbots Langley, Hertfordshire, have also been given as his birthplace by his modern biographers. He was educated, as of Dorset, at the University of Cambridge. Early in 1631 he graduated BA from St Catharine's College and on 28 February he was elected a fellow; he proceeded MA in 1634. It appears that even at this early age Strong had embraced the puritan stance in his religious beliefs as well as in his attitude towards church polity, for at a hearing in July 1634 he was alleged to have said that Archbishop William Laud had sinned against the Holy Ghost and, perhaps more subversively, that there would soon be no bishops in England. Consequently he was suspended that year from his fellowship at St Catharine's, deprived of his degrees, and banished from the university.

In 1640 Strong became the rector of Moor Crichel, near Wimborne, Dorset, but he fled to London in 1643 when the royalist forces obtained ascendancy in the county. In London Strong received a warm reception at the parish of St Dunstan-in-the-West, Fleet Street, and soon became a lecturer there. On 13 June 1644 the vestry ordered that the churchwarden 'shall lend Mr Strong £30 to be deducted £6 a quarter from his lecture' (London, Guildhall Library, MS 3016/1, fol. 241), and a year later, on 7 July 1645, the vestry again resolved that 'care might be taken by the vestrymen to provide soe for Mr Strong that they might not lose the benefit of his ministry' (ibid., fol. 263). He had a cordial relationship with the vicar, Andrew Perne, and upon Perne's resignation the House of Commons appointed Strong to be the minister of the parish, on 14 October 1647.

In the meantime Strong had rapidly become a prominent divine at Westminster as well as in the City. He was to preach frequently before the houses of parliament and the civic leaders of London; some of his sermons were separately published. In 1645 he was appointed one of the seven preachers at Westminster Abbey to have morning exercises in place of the traditional daily service. Later in the year, upon the death of Edward Peale of Dorset, Strong was chosen in his stead as a member of the Westminster assembly of divines. He appeared in the assembly on 13 January 1646 and took the protestation, and on 16 January he took the solemn league and covenant and subscribed. In August 1648 he was appointed a trier of ministers for the twelfth classis in the province of London under the new presbyterian church government. He was likewise a weekday lecturer at St Margaret's, Westminster, in 1649. It appears that as late as 1648, when he was appointed a trier and preached before the lord mayor and aldermen at St Paul's a sermon published as *The Vengeance of the Temple* (1648), there was no sign that Strong had become an Independent. However, in the middle of 1650, he drafted, according to Thomas Bakewell in his *A Plea for Mr Strong's Church-Members*, eight articles, all of which are clearly the fundamental tenets of Independency or congregationalism, and imposed them upon his parishioners to subscribe; and 'til they do it, he is resolved to debar them from the Lords Table, if not wholly forsake them' (Bakewell). Apparently Strong attempted to turn the parochial church into an Independent congregation. It was probably as a result of this conflict that he left St Dunstan-in-the-West and gathered his Independent church at Westminster Abbey; its members elected him their pastor on 9 December 1650. Subsequently, in the early 1650s, Strong became a leading Independent divine in church affairs. On 2 January 1651, at the desire of Oliver Cromwell, Sir Henry Vane conferred with him concerning his going to Scotland, undoubtedly as chaplain to the English army, and on 29 July 1652 he was one of the Independent ministers called to a meeting at Cromwell's house in the Cockpit about sending godly persons to preach the gospel in Ireland. Earlier in the latter year he had joined other Independent divines in presenting to the Rump Parliament their proposals for the propagation of the gospel, which were, in effect, an Independent design for religious settlement; on 20 March 1654, when the Independent church polity had been finally established, he was appointed one of the commissioners for the approbation of public preachers, commonly known as triers, under the Cromwellian protectorate.

In spite of the fact that Strong eventually embraced the Independent church polity, he was a moderate and perhaps even a conservative man in his religious thought. Unlike his radical Independent brethren such as John Goodwin, he unequivocally upheld the power and authority of the magistracy not only in civil affairs but also in matters of religion. It was the ordinance of God, Strong would argue, that 'there should be a Magistracie; they are called the *shields of the earth*'; for as 'it is not good there should be an Anarchie', magistrates were necessary 'to restrain men of giddy spirits, who are like the *children of Belial* without a Yoke' (*XXXI Select Sermons*, 1656, 386). He complained that 'it is woful liberty, a liberty of sinning' that some men now 'call all into question' and 'cry down instituted worship' as 'but forms' (ibid., 246, 250); and he maintained that 'a bounding of mens spirits by the word is not bounding of the spirit' (ibid., 629). It is true that like many of his puritan brethren Strong was profoundly affected by Christian eschatology and at times of political crisis spoke in apocalyptic language. He even attempted to determine the time of the coming of Christ's kingdom. However, he was not reluctant to denounce the radical claims of the Fifth Monarchy Men. If 'the Kingdoms of the earth shall become the kingdom of the Lord and his Christ', Strong asked, 'then what need have you to be disquieted because some of your inferiour injudicious mistaken ends be not brought about' (ibid., 679)? In early November 1653, when the Fifth Monarchy Men in and out of the Barebones Parliament attempted to destroy what they called the Antichristian national ministry, Strong told the London magistrates in his *A Voice from Heaven Calling the People to Perfect Separation* (1653) that 'I do never fear Antichrist more then when he professes to fight under Christ's banner', and he appealed to the citizens of London: '*Let all those that fear God* unite *against this common adversary*' (*A Voice from Heaven*, foreword and p. 26).

Strong died suddenly in late June 1654 and was buried in Westminster Abbey on 4 July. His funeral sermon was preached by the presbyterian divine Obadiah Sedgwick. He was survived by his wife, Damaris, to whom was granted administration of his estate on 22 August, and some children whose names are not known. A William Strong of Dorset, admitted pensioner at Emmanuel College, Cambridge, on 3 July 1652, was perhaps his son. After Strong's death his works were published from his notes transcribed by Elizabeth, Lady Carr (afterwards wife of Nathaniel Rich). It was said that Strong had left 'all his notes under a Character of his own devising' and that it was impossible for any one to publish anything 'by his own notes', but his widow protested that Strong had used the characters of the stenographer John Willis, only adding 'here and there some of his own, sufficiently known to, and understood by that person of honour … to whom he committed his notes' (Strong). Following the Restoration his remains were disinterred in 1661 and thrown into a pit in the churchyard of St Margaret's, Westminster.

TAI LIU

Sources T. Bakewell, *A plea for Mr. Strong's church-members* (1650) • O. Sedgwick, *Elisha his lamentation, upon the sudden translation of Elijah* (1656) • D. Strong, *Having seen a paper printed*, [1655], BL, E 861/2 [A defence of the authenticity of the posthumous publications of William Strong] • vestry minutes, St Dunstan-in-the-West, GL, MS 3016/1 • Venn, *Alum. Cant.* • *DNB* • J. Boseley, *The ministers of the Abbey Independent Church* (1911) • A. F. Mitchell and J. Struthers, eds., *Minutes of the sessions of the Westminster assembly of divines* (1874) • J. Twigg, *The University of Cambridge and the English Revolution, 1625–1688* (1990) • B. W. Ball, *A great expectation: eschatological thought in English protestantism to 1660* (1975) • administration, PRO, PROB 6/28, fol. 118v

Strother, Edward (1675–1737), physician, born at Alnwick, Northumberland, was the son of Edward Strother, physician, who was admitted extra-licentiate of the Royal College of Physicians on 1 October 1700, and afterwards practised at Alnwick. On 24 August 1695 the younger Strother was admitted pensioner of Christ's College, Cambridge, but left without a degree. On 8 May 1720 he graduated MD at the University of Utrecht, and on 3 April 1721 he was admitted a licentiate of the Royal College of Physicians. He probably married Mary Allenton at Durham on 15 January 1697. He died on 13 April 1737 at his house near Soho Square, London.

He was the author of a number of medical works, in particular making detailed comments on the problems and use of 'Jesuits' bark', cinchona, in fever, and on the treatment of smallpox.   E. I. CARLYLE, *rev.* PATRICK WALLIS

Sources Venn, *Alum. Cant.* · Munk, *Roll* · *GM*, 1st ser., 7 (1737), 253 · A. Boyer, *The political state of Great Britain*, 53 (1737), 432 · *Album studiosorum academiae Rheno-Traiectinae MDCXXXVI–MDCCCLXXXVI: accedunt nomina curatorum et professorum per eadem secula* (Utrecht, 1886), col. 121

Stroudley, William (1833–1889), mechanical engineer, was born in Sandford, Oxfordshire, on 6 March 1833, one of three sons of William Stroudley, machinist in a local paper mill, and his wife, Anne. After education at a primary school he commenced work with his father at a paper mill and then, again with his father, at a Birmingham printing works. In 1847 he was apprenticed to John Inshaw, who had a small engineering business in Birmingham. His engineering training continued from 1853 to 1854 under Daniel Gooch, locomotive superintendent of the Great Western railway. He completed his training in 1855 on the Great Northern railway at Peterborough and became locomotive shed foreman. In 1861 he was appointed manager of the Cowlairs works of the Edinburgh and Glasgow (later North British) railway and in 1865 locomotive superintendent of the newly formed Highland railway at Inverness, where he rebuilt existing locomotives to make them more suitable for use over its heavily graded lines.

In 1870 Stroudley was appointed locomotive and carriage superintendent of the London, Brighton, and South Coast railway at a time when its locomotives, rolling-stock, and workshops were in poor condition. He rapidly set about building new and well-equipped workshops at Brighton and introduced new and more powerful locomotives for main-line and suburban passenger and freight services. All were of excellent design and construction and of elegant outline, enhanced by their bright yellow livery. His new passenger carriages were also impressive, with polished mahogany bodies. He was a pioneer in the introduction of train electric lighting, applied to a Pullman car only two years after the invention of the incandescent lamp by Thomas Edison in 1879. He was also responsible for the design of marine engines for the company's cross-channel steamers and patented a successful design for paddle wheels.

Stroudley was an active member of the institutions of Civil and Mechanical Engineers and in 1884 was awarded the George Stephenson medal and Telford premium for his outstanding paper 'The construction of locomotive engines'. Previously, in 1878, one of his Terrier class 0-6-0 tank locomotives was awarded a gold medal at the Paris Exhibition, and in 1889 his Gladstone class locomotive of 0-4-2 type received a similar award. After the exhibition this locomotive took part in high-speed trials with a number of French locomotives. The locomotive *Gladstone* is preserved in the National Railway Museum, York.

While he was a firm disciplinarian Stroudley had the reputation of being scrupulously fair in dealing with his men, by whom he was much respected. He encouraged their interest and enthusiasm by allocating locomotives to individual drivers, whose names were painted in gold letters in the driving cab. He was short-sighted, broad, and stocky, with a dapper appearance.

Stroudley was married twice, first about 1860 to an unknown person who died in 1865, and second in 1877 to Elise Lumley Brewer, from a family engaged in finance. There were no children. Stroudley died from pneumonia at the Hotel Terminus, rue St Lazare, Paris, on 20 December 1889, following a severe chill after the testing of his locomotive. He was buried in the extramural cemetery in Brighton, where his wife was also later interred.

GEORGE W. CARPENTER, *rev.*

Sources *PICE*, 99 (1889–90), 365–72 · H. J. Campbell Cornwell, *William Stroudley, craftsman of steam* (1968) · C. Hamilton Ellis, 'Famous locomotive engineers', *Locomotive, Railway Carriage and Wagon Review* (15 May 1937) · *CGPLA Eng. & Wales* (1890)
Wealth at death £44,053 19s. 2d.: probate, Feb 1890, *CGPLA Eng. & Wales*

Strudwick, Ethel (1880–1954), headmistress, was born on 3 April 1880 at 14 Edith Villas, Fulham, London, the only child of John Melhuish Strudwick (1849–1937), artist, and his wife, Harriet Reed. Her father was one of the Pre-Raphaelites, and Ethel as a child met several of the group. She was educated at Queen Elizabeth's School, West Kensington, where she was a star pupil whom her teachers had 'to praise sufficiently without sounding fulsome' (Hughes, 175). She won the coveted Reed scholarship to Bedford College, London, and graduated with honours in classics in 1900. After two years as a classics mistress at the Laurels School, Rugby, she returned to Bedford College, where she graduated MA with distinction (1904), taught classics (1903–13), and became head of the Latin department (1909).

In 1913 Strudwick was appointed headmistress of the City of London School for Girls in succession to Alice Blagrave, so embarking on the first of two headships whose tenure embraced the social changes from before the First World War until after the second. Almost immediately she was plunged into the problems of running a school in wartime. Her pupils were encouraged to make garments for the troops, work on the land, and raise money for the Red Cross. After the war she created a physics laboratory and introduced social work by the school in south London. Under her influence many of her pupils secured important posts in the new career opportunities available for women.

Out of forty-six candidates Ethel Strudwick was appointed high mistress of St Paul's Girls' School in Brook Green, London, in 1927. For the second time she succeeded a founder head (her predecessor, Frances Gray, having been appointed in 1903) and was faced with the task of preserving young but cherished traditions while moving forward. She herself taught a half timetable and, as at both Bedford College and the City of London School, generations of pupils were inspired by the lucidity and clarity of her teaching, enthralled by her diction, and absorbed by her scholarship, whether in the classics, literature, or the scriptures.

As high mistress Strudwick immediately initiated a programme to build a new science block, which was opened in 1933, 'the last word in equipment and comfort', she told parents at speech day (St Paul's School for Girls, Strudwick box). Her philosophy of education found expression in a volume of essays by headmistresses, published in 1937, in which she wrote that 'schools exist to show how many possibilities there are, not to tie upon young shoulders precisely the same little packet of knowledge to take out into the world' (*The Head Mistress Speaks*, 113). Schools were to her not so much workshops as places of mutual trust and fellowship.

In 1939 the imminent prospect of war raised various options for the school's immediate future. Strudwick decided on an evacuation policy involving 183 girls going to Wycombe Abbey School in Buckinghamshire, where they spent the winter of 1939–40. A small but influential lobby wished the school to go to Canada. At the height of the invasion crisis in May 1940, the high mistress canvassed parents, who voted by 155 to 44 to return to Brook Green—though by the autumn term pupil numbers had shrunk to sixty-five. For the second time in her career Strudwick balanced the needs of education and the demands of war. She sought, with some difficulty, to get girls involved in work on the land, took her own share (with staff and pupils over sixteen) in fire-watching, taught in the air raid shelter, and stood 'as a bulwark against all that was uncertain, hazardous and fearful' (Harrison, 26). The exercise of authority—whether in war or peace—seemed to come to her effortlessly, and burdens were carried serenely.

School numbers quickly rose to 300 and at the end of the war Strudwick could tell the governors that not a day passed without parental 'letters begging for admission for their daughters' (St Paul's School for Girls, archives, report to governors, 30 May 1945). When she retired in 1948 she was hailed as one who had 'brought to her profession distinction and greatness' (*Paulina*, 2).

Strudwick was already a public figure, for whom retirement meant simply more time to give to her various interests. She had been on the senate of the University of London since 1921 (and remained so until 1952) and a trustee of the London Museum since 1934. From 1931 to 1933 she was president of the Association of Headmistresses and in 1937 she became the first president of the British Federation of Business and Professional Women. She was a governor of four educational institutions and became, in 1948, a member of the council of the Girls' Public Day School Trust.

Ethel Strudwick was no militant feminist; as a young woman she had 'silently disapproved from the Embankment' (Harrison, 14) of her suffragette friends marching to the Albert Hall. But she contributed to the cause by demonstrating the highest professionalism, setting a model for women's careers after the first 'heroic' phase of the foundation of modern day schools for girls. Unlike many of the pioneers of the girls' school movement, she had herself undergone a formal schooling, and she set out to make this an enriching experience for later generations. Her devotion to liberalism was fundamental to her outlook: *liberalis* in her commitment to the concept of freedom, justice, and educational opportunities for all, and Liberal in her political affiliation. She served from 1943 on the Liberal Party council and, in 1949, became president of the Women's Liberal Federation, campaigning in the general election of 1950. Yet this tall, possibly austere, figure with a profound sense of obligation to society was not without humour. She could collapse in 'gusts of uncontrollable laughter' (Harrison, 33) in the theatre (to which she allegedly went on 1600 occasions), act in staff reviews, and struggle to conceal her mirth when rebuking a pupil for some misdemeanour. Leisure times found her walking with friends as much as 30 miles a day in the Lake District or the Dolomites. She claimed no aptitude for domestic chores but rejoiced when a Paulina commented that her education at St Paul's had given her something to think about when she did the washing up.

Ethel Strudwick's work was recognized when she was appointed OBE in 1936 (Edward VIII's only honours list) and advanced to CBE in 1948. She died at her home, 15 Leinster Avenue, Mortlake, Surrey, on 15 August 1954, and was cremated at Mortlake crematorium five days later. There was a memorial service in St Paul's Cathedral; 'a great lady and a great leader' (Harrison, 40), declared the preacher.   GERALD M. D. HOWAT

Sources K. C. Harrison, ed., *Ethel Strudwick* (1955) • H. Bailes, *Once a Paulina* (2000) • J. Carden, ed., *Daughters of the city: a history of the City of London School for Girls founded by William Ward* (1996) • M. G. Hirschfield, ed., *St Paul's Girls' School, 1904–54* (1954) • *Paulina* [St Paul's School for Girls magazine], 124 (1948), 2 • *The Times* (16 Aug 1954) • *The Times* (23 Aug 1954) • M. V. Hughes, *A London girl of the eighties* (1936); repr. as *A London girl of the 1880s* (1978) • St Paul's School for Girls, Brook Green, London, archives, Strudwick box
Archives City of London School for Girls, papers • St Paul's School for Girls, Brook Green, London, papers; reports to governors
Likenesses J. Gunn, oils, 1950, St Paul's School for Girls, Brook Green, London
Wealth at death £3188 6s. 1d.: probate, 27 Oct 1954, *CGPLA Eng. & Wales*

Struther, Jan. See Placzek, Joyce Anstruther (1901–1953).

Struthers, John (1776–1853), poet and anthologist, was born at Longcalderwood, East Kilbride, Lanarkshire, on 18 July 1776, the second son and fourth child of William Struthers, shoemaker, and his wife, Elizabeth Scott. Joanna Baillie and her family, then resident at Longcalderwood, took an interest in him as a child. After working as cow-herd and farm-servant until the age of fifteen, he learned the trade of shoemaking in Glasgow, and settled at Long-calderwood in 1793 to work for Glasgow employers.

Struthers married on 24 July 1798 despite some opposition from his wife's family. In 1801 they settled in Glasgow, where he worked at his trade until 1819. During this time, he continued to read and write extensively, and through Joanna Baillie, he came to know Walter Scott, who helped Struthers in negotiations with Constable the publisher.

In 1803 Struthers published 'Anticipation', a successful war ode, prompted by rumours of Napoleon's impending invasion. His most popular poem, 'The Poor Man's Sabbath', appeared in 1804. Although digressive and diffuse, the poem is written in fluent Spenserian stanza, and expresses a passionate love of nature and rural life; 'The Peasant's Death' was published as a companion piece to it in 1806. In 1811 'The Winter Day' appeared, followed in 1814 by *Poems, Moral and Religious*. In addition to poetry, Struthers published anonymously an *Essay on the State of the Labouring Poor, with some Hints for its Improvement*, in 1816. About the same date he edited, with a biographical preface, *Selections from the Poems of William Muir*. A pamphlet entitled *Tekel*, sharply criticizing voluntaryism, is another undated product of this period.

Struthers's wife died of consumption in April 1818, and was followed within two weeks by their youngest daughter, and within a few months by their eldest son. 'The Plough', written in Spenserian stanza, was nevertheless published in that year. His first marriage had been a love match; his second, to Cecilia Morton (1787/8–1847) on 27 September 1819, was entered upon for his family's requirements. He and his second wife were to add six children to this family in their twenty-eight-year marriage. In 1819 Struthers also published *The Harp of Caledonia*, a good collection of Scottish songs in three volumes, with a supplementary essay on Scottish songwriters, compiled with the aid of Scott and Joanna Baillie. A similar anthology called *The British Minstrel* appeared in two volumes in 1821.

Having gained a literary reputation, Struthers reluctantly abandoned shoemaking to become editorial reader for Glasgow-based publishers. During this career Struthers produced in two volumes a *History of Scotland from the Union* (1827), and was engaged on a third volume at his death. In 1833 Struthers was appointed librarian of Stirling's Public Library, Glasgow, a position he held for about fifteen years. In 1836 he published his fine descriptive poem 'Dychmont'. Besides numerous pamphlets, Struthers wrote many of the lives in Chambers's *Biographical Dictionary of Eminent Scotsmen*, and contributed to the *Christian Instructor*. His collected poems—in two volumes—with a useful autobiography—appeared in 1850. Struthers died in Glasgow on 30 July 1853, his second wife having predeceased him on 22 August 1847. Struthers Crescent in East Kilbride is named after him.

T. W. BAYNE, *rev.* DOUGLAS BROWN

Sources J. G. Lockhart, *Memoirs of the life of Sir Walter Scott*, 7 vols. (1837–8) · Anderson, *Scot. nat.* · J. Struthers, *The poetical works of John Struthers, with autobiography*, 1 (1850) · *GM*, 2nd ser., 40 (1853), 318–19 · Chambers, *Scots.* (1835) · m. reg. Scot.

Struthers, Sir John (1823–1899), anatomist and medical reformer, second son of Alexander Struthers, a wealthy flax mill owner, and his wife, Mary Reid, was born at Brucefield, Dunfermline, Fife, on 21 February 1823, and was educated privately. His two brothers qualified in medicine: James (1821–1891) practised in Leith, and Alexander (1830–1855) died at Scutari during the Crimean campaign while serving as an assistant surgeon. John Struthers studied medicine at Edinburgh University, where he was admitted successively a licentiate and a fellow of the College of Surgeons and a doctor of medicine of the university in 1845. On 22 October 1847 the College of Surgeons certified him to teach anatomy in an extramural school; Struthers substituted for Professor John Goodsir during his illness in the winter of 1853–4.

In 1854 Struthers was appointed one of the assistant surgeons to the Edinburgh Royal Infirmary and was later full surgeon, an office he resigned in 1863 when he was appointed to the chair of anatomy at Aberdeen. The University of Aberdeen had begun a new existence on 15 September 1860 by the fusion of Marischal and King's colleges. Divinity and arts were taught at King's in Old Aberdeen and law and medicine in Simpson's building in Aberdeen itself. The accommodation, however, was meagre, and the students were few when Struthers began his work. Under the provisions of the Universities (Scotland) Act of 1858 the buildings of Aberdeen University were maintained by the board of works. Struthers made good use of this to have extensive new accommodation constructed for his anatomy department. This was at a time when the Royal Infirmary generally was being greatly enlarged and was well known for its clinical teaching. Struthers built up a museum of anatomy and established a university medal and prize in the subject in 1891; by the time he retired to Edinburgh in 1889 the number of students had more than doubled and the museum was almost unequalled.

Struthers was a skilled anatomist, and one of the earliest advocates in Scotland of the Darwinian hypothesis of natural selection. Aberdeen students were noted for championing Darwinism; even the keeper of the anatomy room was an out-and-out evolutionist. Struthers taught anatomy from a comparative perspective and his lectures were illustrated with his extensive collection of specimens that demonstrated Darwinian evolution. He was a keen dissector and a firm believer in practical work in all aspects of medical education.

In Edinburgh, Struthers became chairman of the board of directors of Leith Hospital and was elected a manager of the Edinburgh Royal Infirmary. He was a member and president of the Royal Physical Society, and a member of the board of management of the Royal Dispensary, Edinburgh. In 1885 the University of Glasgow conferred upon him the honorary degree of LLD. He was president of the

Sir John Struthers (1823–1899), by Sir George Reid, 1892

Royal College of Surgeons of Edinburgh from 1895 to 1897. He was knighted in 1898.

On 5 August 1857 Struthers married Christina Margaret, daughter of James Alexander, surgeon, of Wooler, Northumberland. Struthers and his wife were both champions of the cause of admission of women to the Scottish universities. They had five sons and four daughters. Three of his sons qualified in medicine. Two predeceased him; the youngest, John William Struthers (1874–1959), was a general surgeon in Edinburgh and president of the Royal College of Surgeons of Edinburgh from 1941 to 1943. Struthers died on 24 February 1899 at his home, 15 George Square, Edinburgh, and was buried on the 27th in Warriston cemetery, Edinburgh. He was survived by his wife.

Struthers's most valuable scientific works are papers on the supracondyloid process and on the anatomy of whales. Whaling was an important local industry, and from time to time whole carcasses were washed up on the shore of eastern Scotland. Their dissection provided Struthers with the opportunity to elucidate and demonstrate an example of mammalian adaptation to life in the sea.

Struthers had a long interest in the reform of the medical curriculum. As a member of the General Medical Council from 1883 to 1891 and particularly as chairman of the education committee he sought to introduce measures to increase practical and clinical teaching and to ensure a rational ordering of the subjects of the medical course. This culminated in the extension of the medical course to five years in 1892. At Aberdeen he pressed for a compulsory pathology course and a chair of pathology. In the early 1870s he had encouraged students to nominate T. H. Huxley as university rector knowing that Huxley shared his belief in the need for curricular reform.

CAROLYN PENNINGTON

Sources W. L. Mackenzie, 'The professor of anatomy, 1863–1889', *Aurora borealis academica: Aberdeen University appreciations, 1860–1889*, ed. P. J. A. [P. J. Anderson] (1899), 237–48 • R. D. Anderson, *Education and opportunity in Victorian Scotland: schools and universities* (1983) • C. Pennington, *The modernisation of medical teaching at Aberdeen in the nineteenth century* (1994) • L. Moore, *Bajanellas and Semilinas: Aberdeen University and the education of women, 1860–1920* (1991) • A. Keith, 'Anatomy in Scotland during the lifetime of Sir John Struthers', *Edinburgh Medical Journal*, 3rd ser., 8 (1912), 7–33 • J. Struthers, *References to papers in anatomy: human and comparative* (1889) [incl. bibliography] • *Aberdeen Journal* (25 Feb 1899) • *The Scotsman* (25 Feb 1899) • *The Times* (25 Feb 1899) • *BMJ* (4 March 1899), 561–3 • *The Lancet* (4 March 1899) • A. L. Gillespie, *Edinburgh Medical Journal*, new ser., 5 (1899), 433–4 • communion roll, Old Machar parish, 1861–70, St Machar Cathedral, Old Aberdeen, Muniment Room • parish register (baptism), 23 March 1823, Dunfermline, Fife • d. cert. • CCI (1899)

Archives Royal College of Surgeons, Edinburgh, corresp. and papers • U. Edin. L., corresp. and papers | U. Aberdeen L.

Likenesses photograph, 1886, repro. in Keith, 'Anatomy in Scotland during the lifetime of Sir John Struthers' • G. Reid, oils, 1892, Royal College of Surgeons, Edinburgh; copy, Marischal College, U. Aberdeen [*see illus.*] • M. Wane, photograph, U. Aberdeen

Wealth at death £8255 15s. 3d.: confirmation, 1 April 1899, CCI

Struthers, Sir John (1857–1925), educationist and civil servant, was born in Adelphi Street, Glasgow, on 19 January 1857, the eldest son of Robert Struthers, provision merchant, and his wife, Agnes Muir. He was one of a large family, and was practically adopted and brought up by his father's sister in Renfrewshire, who was married but childless. Struthers was educated at the parish school at Mearns, Renfrewshire, where he served for five years as a pupil teacher. Thence he went to the Church of Scotland Training College, Glasgow, and, combining his course at the college with a university course, he took his degree at Glasgow University with first-class honours in mental philosophy and a second class in classics. In 1881 he won an exhibition at Worcester College, Oxford, where he obtained a second class in classical moderations (1883) and a first class in *literae humaniores* (1885). In 1886 he was appointed an inspector of schools in Scotland; he developed a special interest in technical and manual education, and in 1898 he was transferred to the London office of the Scotch education department following its takeover of the Scottish work of the Department of Science and Art. He became assistant secretary of the department in 1900, and in 1904 succeeded Sir Henry Craik as secretary, retiring in 1921.

Even before Craik's retirement, Struthers had a strong influence on the making of policy. Following the Scottish Education Act of 1901, which made fourteen the effective school-leaving age, the framework of Scottish education was reshaped by a series of departmental minutes and circulars. These were criticized by many defenders of Scottish traditions because they sharpened the distinction between secondary and elementary education, on lines of social efficiency and vocational differentiation, and meant the withdrawal of advanced teaching from many rural schools; but Struthers made only small concessions to this criticism. His work in this period included the reorganization of technical education by the development of evening continuation classes and 'central institutions', a comprehensive overhaul of teacher training which involved the transfer of colleges from the churches to the state, and the consolidation of the system of central grants to schools in the Scottish Education Act of 1908.

The 1908 act also extended the provision of bursaries for

Sir John Struthers (1857–1925), by Maurice Greiffenhagen, 1922

secondary education, gave powers to school boards to provide school meals, and instituted a system of school medical inspection; powers to provide medical treatment were added in 1913. Struthers was responsible for the detailed execution of these policies, and for the wartime planning which led to the Scottish Education Act of 1918. This was notable for substituting county education authorities for school boards, and for the compromise with the Catholic and Episcopal churches, negotiated by Struthers, which brought their schools under education authority control. The provisions of the act for raising the leaving age to fifteen, and for compulsory continuation classes above that age, were, however, to remain unfulfilled because of financial constraints. Some aspects of Struthers's later policies were controversial, notably 'Circular 44' of 1921, which maintained the divide between advanced elementary education and secondary schools proper.

Struthers was a member of the royal commission on manual and practical instruction in Ireland (1898); of the committee on physical deterioration for England and Wales (1904); of the committee on local and imperial taxation (1912); and of the joint board of insurance commissioners (1912). He was an active trustee of the Carnegie Library Trust and a member of the executive committee of the Central Library for Students.

In 1912 Struthers married Jessie Mary Gertrude (*d.* in or after 1939), daughter of Julian Hill, of Dean's Yard, Westminster, nephew of Sir Rowland Hill; they had no children. He was created CB in 1902 and KCB in 1910, and given the honorary degree of LLD by Aberdeen University in 1905. He died at his house, 31 Sloane Gardens, London, on 25 October 1925.   R. D. ANDERSON

Sources A. Morgan, *Makers of Scottish education* (1929), 231–41 · *The Times* (26 Oct 1925) · *Glasgow Herald* (26 Oct 1925) · *Glasgow Herald* (29 Oct 1925) · private information (1937) · *CGPLA Eng. & Wales* (1926) · *DNB* · *WW*
Likenesses M. Greiffenhagen, oils, 1922, Scot. NPG · M. Greiffenhagen, oils, 1922, NPG [*see illus.*]
Wealth at death £18,464 11s. 11d.: resworn probate, 14 Jan 1926, *CGPLA Eng. & Wales*

Struthers, William (*c.*1578–1633), Church of Scotland minister, was probably the son of William Struthers, exhorter (preacher) at Stonehouse, in Hamilton presbytery, Lanarkshire (1562), then reader at Glasgow and exhorter at Kirkintilloch, Dunbartonshire (1569). He graduated MA from Glasgow in 1599 and a William Struthers was recorded in 1602 as an 'expectant' (waiting for a vacant charge) in Berwickshire. Two years later he was on the weekly exercise of doctrine in Glasgow presbytery and, in March 1607, he became minister of Kirkintilloch. In 1612 he was translated to Glasgow Cathedral and then to St Giles, Edinburgh, in 1614, where he was to spend the rest of his life.

In August 1616, at the general assembly at Aberdeen, Struthers was appointed to committees 'to answeir the books and pamphletts sett out by Papists' (Calderwood, 7.225) and to draw up canons from the acts of general assemblies. In May 1617, during James VI's visit, he preached in the royal chapel at Holyrood, using the English liturgy. In June, when a number of ministers were in Edinburgh to oppose attempts by the king to have royal supremacy recognized by parliament, Struthers and his colleague Peter Hewatt drafted formal protests. Although Hewatt's version was preferred, the final version incorporated some of Struthers's work and his was the fourth of fifty-five signatures appended. This led to his deprivation by the court of high commission but, admitting fault on his knees before the king, he was pardoned, although later that summer he was a defence witness in David Calderwood's trial before the bishops.

Struthers upheld the liturgical innovations known as the five articles of Perth and, on Christmas day 1618, preached to a depleted congregation (celebration of the five days of the Christian year being one of the articles). In January 1619 he preached bitterly against those who had absented themselves, saying 'Ye must receive instruction from us [the ministers] and not we from you' (Calderwood, 7.344). Those with whom he had opposed the crown in 1617 now saw him as a traitor, confirmed by his appointment in 1619 to the court of high commission. He actively supported kneeling to receive communion (another of the five articles) and, at Easter 1620, he took bread from the hand of a woman who was about to put it in her own mouth. He began, however, to develop misgivings about the innovations. In 1621 he declared that 'The Five Articles which have bredd this rent in the kirk are come from Papists' (Calderwood, 7.461), while in a letter of 1630 to the earl of Airth, he wrote of 'this poore kirk, wich is rent so grivouslie for ceremonies'. The letter was intended for royal eyes. With striking frankness Struthers described episcopacy and the five articles as 'two woundes' under which the kirk 'layes groning' and warned of 'a dissipatione of the churche' if a third wound were inflicted. He expressed confidence, however, that Charles would make no 'further novatione' (*Historical Works of Balfour*, 2.181).

When, in 1626, Edinburgh was formally split into four parishes Struthers took the north-west quarter as minister of the High Kirk. He published a number of works in later life. *A Resolution for Death* (Edinburgh, 1628) contrasted the mortality of the body and the immortality of the soul. *Scotland's Warning, or, A Treatise of Fasting* (Edinburgh, 1628) was addressed to the ministry and argued that fasting and repentance were the only answers for Scotland, assailed with sin and Catholicism. *Christian Observations and Resolutions* (Edinburgh, 1628) dealt with how to lead a Christian life, salvation, and the operation of God's spirit. *A Looking Glasse for Princes and People* (Edinburgh, 1632) was dedicated to Charles I in thanksgiving for the birth of his son, the future Charles II. It addressed the duties of monarchs and their subjects in a tone suggesting that Struthers felt he had gone too far in his criticisms of the state of the kirk in his letter to the earl of Airth in 1630. It asserted that kings are limited only by God and mortality, that ecclesiastical councils exist only to offer advice to monarchs, and that the clergy should have authority only in doctrine and the conduct of worship. *True Happines, or, King Davids Choice* (Edinburgh, 1633) argued that true happiness was to be achieved only through worship of and obedience to God. Published posthumously was *The Grievances Given in by the Ministers before the Parliament Holden in June 1633* (Edinburgh, 1635), presumably to demonstrate that even one regarded as 'a conformitane' had misgivings about royal policy.

At the erection of the diocese of Edinburgh in 1633 Struthers was appointed dean of Edinburgh, but he died on 9 November of that year and was buried, according to his will, 'among my deir childrene in the gray freir kirkyaird' (Edinburgh commissary court records, CC8/8/57, fols. 164–8). He was survived by his wife, Elizabeth Robertoun (*d.* February 1641). He left 6000 merks (£4000 Scots) to the universities of Glasgow and Edinburgh to provide each with bursaries for two theology students from the poor of those cities or from ministers' families.

ALAN R. MACDONALD

Sources T. Thomson, ed., *Acts and proceedings of the general assemblies of the Kirk of Scotland*, 3 pts, Bannatyne Club, 81 (1839–45) · Edinburgh commissary court records, register of testaments, NA Scot., CC8/8/57–60 · *Fasti Scot.*, new edn, vols. 1, 3 · D. Calderwood, *The history of the Kirk of Scotland*, ed. T. Thomson and D. Laing, 8 vols., Wodrow Society, 7 (1842–9) · *The historical works of Sir James Balfour*, ed. J. Haig, 4 vols. (1824–5)
Wealth at death £15,933 6s. 8d. Scots: NA Scot., Edinburgh commissary court records, register of testaments, CC8/8/57, fols. 164–8

Strutt, Edward, first Baron Belper (1801–1880), politician, born at his parents' home at St Helen's House, Derby, on 26 October 1801, was the only son of William *Strutt (1756–1830) [*see under* Strutt, Jedediah] and his wife, Barbara (1761–1804), daughter of Thomas Evans, also of Derby. His grandfather was Jedediah *Strutt, a cotton spinner and inventor. He was educated at Trinity College,

Cambridge, where he graduated BA in 1823 and proceeded MA in 1826. He was president of the Cambridge Union Society and, after graduating, settled in London in order to study law (he attended the lectures of John Austin). He never took an active part in the affairs of the family firm (W. G. and J. Strutt), of which he was a partner. On 10 May 1823 he was admitted to Lincoln's Inn, and on 13 June 1825 to the Inner Temple, but he was not called to the bar. He married on 28 March 1837 Amelia Harriet, youngest daughter of William *Otter, bishop of Chichester. They had four sons and four daughters.

Strutt shared his father's interest in science, but devoted his leisure, while a law student in London, mainly to a study of social and economic questions. He became close to Jeremy Bentham (a friend of his father) and to James and John Stuart Mill, and under their influence his political views took shape. Strutt was not a doctrinaire philosophical radical, but his Benthamism ensured that he later refused to join the Anti-Corn Law League, owing to its 'sectional interest'. On 31 July 1830 he was returned as a liberal for the borough of Derby but his parliamentary impact as a radical was minimal, although he did become a privy councillor in 1845. He retained his seat until 1847, when his election, with that of his fellow member the Hon. Frederick Leveson-Gower, was declared void on petition on account of bribery practised by their agents (*Hansard 3*, 98, 402–14). On 16 July 1851 he was returned for Arundel in Sussex. That seat he exchanged in July 1852 for Nottingham, which he represented until his elevation to the peerage. From 1846 to 1848 he was chief commissioner of railways; in 1850 he became high sheriff for Nottinghamshire; and in December 1852 he became chancellor of the duchy of Lancaster in Aberdeen's coalition government, but resigned in June 1854 in favour of Earl Granville.

On 29 August 1856 Strutt was created Baron Belper of Belper in Derbyshire, an early instance of a family being elevated to the peerage whose wealth had been made in industry. In 1862 he received the honorary degree of LLD from Cambridge University. In 1864 he was nominated lord lieutenant of Nottinghamshire, and in 1871 he succeeded George Grote as president of University College, London, an office he held until 1879. He was also chairman of quarter sessions for the county of Nottingham for many years, and was highly regarded in that capacity, particularly by the legal profession.

Belper became a recognized authority on questions of free trade, law reform, and education and earned the respect of many eminent contemporaries, including Macaulay, John Romilly, McCulloch, John and Charles Austen, George Grote, and Charles Buller. In his later life he also developed an interest in science and literature. He was elected a fellow of the Royal Society on 22 March 1860, and to fellowships of the Geological Society and the Zoological Society. From 1879 to his death he was also a vice-president of the Sunday Society. He died on 30 June 1880 at his house, 75 Eaton Square, London. He was succeeded, as second Baron Belper, by his son Henry Strutt (1840–1914).

E. I. CARLYLE, *rev.* MATTHEW LEE

Sources *Men of the time* · Venn, *Alum. Cant.* · GEC, *Peerage* · W. Thomas, *The philosophic radicals: nine studies in theory and practice, 1817–1841* (1979) · H. L. Malchow, *Agitators and promoters in the age of Gladstone and Disraeli: a biographical dictionary* (1983) · *The Times* (1 July 1880) · *PRS*, 31 (1880–81), 75 · Walford, *County families* (1880) · *CGPLA Eng. & Wales* (1880)
Archives Derby Central Library · Notts. Arch., corresp. and papers | Derby Local Studies Library, Derby, letter to his father
Wealth at death under £180,000: resworn probate, July 1881, *CGPLA Eng. & Wales* (1880)

Strutt, Edward Gerald (1854–1930), agriculturist, the fifth son of John James Strutt, second Baron Rayleigh, and his wife, Clara Elizabeth La Touche, eldest daughter of Captain Richard Vicars RE, was born at his father's country estate, Terling Place, Witham, Essex, on 10 April 1854. He was educated at Winchester College and at Trinity College, Cambridge, before being articled to Rawlence and Squarey, land agents, of Salisbury. In 1876, at the request of his eldest brother, John William *Strutt, third Baron Rayleigh, he became responsible for the management of the family's Essex estates. At this stage most of the farms were let to tenants, which enabled Strutt to carry out the administration of the estate while completing his training. In 1878 he married Maria Louisa (1854–1938), daughter of John Joliffe Tufnell, of Langleys, Essex. They had five sons, two of whom died in infancy, and three daughters.

In 1877 Strutt, in partnership with Charles Parker, a friend of his childhood, established the London firm of Strutt and Parker, land agents and surveyors. Initially its main role was that of land agent for the Lincolnshire and Essex estates of Guy's Hospital, London. Under Strutt's administration the estate income for the hospital virtually doubled. In 1919 he negotiated the sale of the Lincolnshire estates to the Board of Agriculture and Fisheries, for the establishment of smallholdings. An annuity was accepted in preference to a cash payment, and the hospital received £5000 per annum by the transaction.

In the meantime, the number of tenants on the Rayleigh estates had declined, following a succession of bad harvests and the disastrous fall of wheat prices from 1878 onwards. Being unable to find suitable replacements it became necessary to take the land in hand. This encouraged Strutt to investigate alternative ways of farming the land. His solution was the adoption of large-scale arable and dairy farming, utilizing lucerne and other rotational grasses to supplement the limited amount of pasture. Strutt's system depended on carefully kept records of milk yield, which were initiated in 1883. Better feeding coupled with the culling of the less productive animals enabled milk production per cow to be more than doubled. From 1896 the use of the tuberculin test was progressively extended, and the reacting cows, which at first comprised at least 50 per cent of the whole number, were eliminated. The old cow-houses were replaced by new ones of hygienic construction, and other exacting standards of hygiene were introduced. In 1928, towards the end of Strutt's career, there was on the Rayleigh estate a herd of 850 cows which won the championship for clean milk production in England.

Strutt was also instrumental in developing an extensive milk-retailing organization in London which became known as Lord Rayleigh's Dairies Ltd, taking milk from the Rayleigh estate which was still predominantly arable. In order to enhance the profitability of the estate, Strutt helped to pioneer a detailed system of cost accounting, enabling the profit or loss on each enterprise to be ascertained. This was complemented with the introduction of a profit-sharing scheme for his employees.

In outlining these management practices in his presidential address to the Surveyors Institution on 11 November 1912, Strutt used the occasion to expound his views on agricultural policy. He advocated in particular an increase in the arable acreage, the extension of smallholdings, more agricultural education and research, and government assistance in building rural cottages. He was particularly keen to emphasize his opposition to any form of legislation which might jeopardize long-term capital investment into the agricultural sector.

During the First World War, Strutt played a key role in determining the government's agricultural policy. In 1915 when the submarine menace began to imperil food imports he was appointed a member of Lord Milner's food production committee. In the following year he also became a member of Lord Selbourne's committee, looking ahead to post-war agricultural policy. Following the appointment of Rowland Prothero (Lord Ernle) as minister of agriculture, Strutt was made 'agricultural adviser' and became influential in framing the Corn Production Act of 1917, which compelled farmers to plough up grassland. In recognition of his wartime services he was made a Companion of Honour in 1917. After the war he campaigned in support of a minimum wage for agricultural labourers and he also tried, without success, to persuade the government not to repeal the legislation guaranteeing minimum corn prices.

Strutt served on the royal commission on Oxford and Cambridge universities (1920–22) and on the royal commission on tariffs (1923) chaired by Lord Milner. In addition he played a significant role in promoting the development of the sugar-beet industry.

As an agriculturist Strutt was primarily interested in practical rather than academic issues. In this he was a notable success. In 1876 he had farmed the untenanted part of the estate which amounted to 1000 acres; by the time of his death the land under his administration had increased to 25,000 acres. Not all of this expansion can be attributed to Strutt himself; the incorporation of the estate as Strutt and Parker (Farms) Ltd also facilitated the process.

Strutt was less well known than his elder brother Lord Rayleigh; he had, however, the same ability for attention to detail and he also resembled him in appearance. He was of medium height with a fair complexion and rather rugged features. Up to the age of fifty he took a keen interest in hunting, but otherwise his work was his main interest and pleasure. He was a very sympathetic person in his dealings with people, though inefficiency or slackness made him angry. He died at his home, Whitelands, Hatfield Peverel, on 8 March 1930. The large attendance at his funeral at All Saints' parish church, in Terling, where he was buried on the 13th, was a tribute to the affection in which he was regarded in the locality, and his memorial plaque described him as 'a man of heart and greatly loved'.   RAYLEIGH, *rev.* JOHN MARTIN

Sources *The Times* (11 March 1930) · *The Times* (13 March 1930) · Lord Ernle [R. E. P. Ernle], *In the nineteenth century and after* (1931) · H. R. Haggard, *Rural England*, 1 (1932) · S. W. Gavin, *Ninety years of farming* (1967) · *Essex Weekly News* (14 March 1930) · Venn, *Alum. Cant.* · *CGPLA Eng. & Wales* (1930) · d. cert. · *The Times* (21 May 1938)
Likenesses F. Watt, portrait; formerly in family possession, 1937 · photograph (after unknown portrait), repro. in Gavin, *Ninety years of farming*
Wealth at death £170,636: probate, 12 April 1930, *CGPLA Eng. & Wales*

Strutt [*née* Woollat], **Elizabeth** (1729–1774), wife and business associate of Jedediah Strutt, was born at Findern, near Derby, of an established family. The Woollats were members of the Findern congregation of Ebenezer Latham (1688?–1754), then proprietor of a large nonconformist academy, and they may have boarded its pupils; certainly in the early 1740s they provided lodgings for Jedediah *Strutt (1726–1797).

In 1745 Latham moved his academy to Derby, and then, if not before, Elizabeth became his servant. In 1749 she moved to London, to work for Dr George Benson (1699–1762), newly appointed pastor to a dissenting congregation at Crutched Friars, and late of Birmingham, where Elizabeth probably met him. At home or in service she acquired an education, a love of learning, and her faith. Her relationship with Benson seems to have been as much companion as servant, and through his household she was introduced to London's nonconformist community. Her connections with the midlands were maintained. From 1745 she and Strutt had an episodic relationship, conducted through correspondence, which survived her cooling, and brought, in 1755, a proposal of marriage. After an exchange of personality assessments, she accepted, despite Benson's reluctance to let her go, and the imputation of friends that she was marrying beneath herself. She may have been influenced by Strutt's prospects, a recent inheritance having allowed him to commence farming.

Elizabeth and Strutt were married on 25 September 1755 in Blackwell parish church. They had five children, William *Strutt (1756–1830) [*see under* Strutt, Jedediah], Elizabeth (b. 1758), Martha (b. 1760), George Benson (b. 1761), and Joseph *Strutt (1765–1844) [*see under* Strutt, Jedediah]. From 1756 Elizabeth, fully engaged in family tasks, was to play a crucial part in the establishment of a business that was, by the 1790s, one of the country's largest industrial enterprises. While Jedediah and her brother William built up a hosiery business in east Derbyshire, Elizabeth, in 1757, visited London in an effort to obtain finance from Benson. Though he was unable to comply—he left 'Elizabeth Strutt, formerly faithful servant' £40 in his will—the nonconformist contacts she sought out were to provide the connections and advice essential to the exploitation of her husband's 'Derby rib machine' and the enterprise's success. Although she was never a legal partner, Elizabeth was fully engaged with the business; from

1762, when the family moved to St Mary's Gate, Derby, she regularly saw to the workings of the warehouse. The Strutts had a house at Cromford, where Jedediah's partner, Richard Arkwright, and their associates developed the factory spinning of cotton. The thrust of the Strutts' correspondence suggests she would have been consulted about Jedediah's decision to join with Arkwright; a letter of 1774 shows her fully informed about the warehousing and marketing of the partners' cotton stuffs. Despite family commitments, she continued to support Jedediah in his business; her death, on 11 May 1774, occurred in London, where she had joined her husband, then lobbying parliament over duties on calicos. She was buried on 15 May at the dissenting burial-ground at Bunhill Fields. Elizabeth Strutt was survived by her husband and children. Outstanding figures, they, as much as the business to which she contributed, were her legacy.   J. J. MASON

Sources R. S. Fitton and A. P. Wadsworth, *The Strutts and the Arkwrights, 1758–1830: a study of the early factory system* (1958) · W. Felkin, *A history of the machine-wrought hosiery and lace manufactures* (1867) · J. C. Cox, *Memorials of old Derbyshire* (1907) · C. L. Hacker, 'William Strutt of Derby (1756–1830)', *Journal of the Derbyshire Archaeological and Natural History Society*, 80 (1960), 49–70 · 'Benson, George', *DNB*
Archives Derby Central Library

Strutt [*other married name* Byron], **Elizabeth** (*fl.* 1805–1863), writer, was possibly the daughter of a lawyer named Thomas Frost. Little is known about her early life. She was first married to John Byron (1780–1805), a Hull physician, who died aged twenty-five. Elizabeth's early works as Mrs Byron include *Drelincourt and Rodalvi, or, Memoirs of Two Noble Families: a Novel* (1807), a three-volume tale of tragic love set in England and Florence. In the preface Byron states:

> To amuse without injuring, and to instruct without offending, is the highest aim of the following pages … The approbation of the wise and good is … always valuable, and they must be undeserving of it, who are insensible of its worth.

The style is reminiscent of Ann Radcliffe's late eighteenth-century romances, and her protagonists demonstrate sensibility worthy of Radcliffe's heroines. Byron was anxious to instruct as well as delight her readers, and her texts are all concerned with morality and virtue. Her epistolary novel *Anti-Delphine* (1806), for example, is a response to Germaine de Staël's tragic tale of adulterous love. Predictably, in Byron's version the suffering wife uses patience and virtue to reclaim her husband, who has been seduced. *The Borderers* (1812), another historical romance in an international setting, takes place in the fourteenth century and includes various transformations: a knight who becomes a hermit, Moorish women who convert to Christianity, and a girl who dresses as a page. Other novels, such as *Genevieve, or, The Orphan's Visit* (1818) and the later *Chances and Changes: a Domestic Story* (1835), combine the romance plot with overtly moral themes, and conclude with the marriages of the scrupulously virtuous heroines to their worthy suitors.

By 1818 Elizabeth Byron had married the artist Jacob

George *Strutt (1784–1867), with whom she travelled through France, Italy, and Switzerland. As a consequence she wrote European travel guides: *A Spinster's Tour in France, the States of Genoa etc. During the Year 1827* (1828), *Six Weeks on the Loire with a Peep into La Vendee* (1833), and *Domestic Residence in Switzerland* (1842). Aimed primarily at the unaccompanied female traveller, these include practical advice on choosing hotels. Her travel books are straightforward accounts, providing insight into the character of Strutt herself, who comes across as refined and possessed of a keen eye for the beauties of the landscape.

Elizabeth Strutt also wrote devotional works. Like some of her moral novels, her religious texts testify to her orthodox Christianity and keen sense of morality. *The Book of the Fathers* (1837) is a kind of dictionary of eminent church leaders, while the preface of *The young Christian's companion, or, Manual of devotion for the use of schools and young persons* (1830) makes clear Strutt's pedagogical aims:

> The object in the following selection has been to produce a form of prayer, and of devotional exercises, concise enough to insure the attention of the young, and sufficiently impressive to excite the reverence of their hearts, toward the Divine being, whom they are too commonly accustomed to approach with the mere worship of their lips.

The Hermit of Dumpton Cave (1823) is a biography of a modern hermit, Joseph Groome Peptit, and is subtitled 'devotedness to God, and usefulness to man', while *The Feminine Soul* (1857) presents a heartfelt argument for spiritual equality between the sexes. *The Curate and the Rector* (1859) satirizes the Reverend Mr Plufty.

Though little is known about Strutt's life after her residence in Switzerland, a public notice of 1863 announced that she was to receive a modest government pension, in recognition of her poverty in advanced age and after almost sixty years of literary life. She was one of the nineteenth century's most prolific women of letters.

EMMA PLASKITT

Sources Blain, Clements & Grundy, *Feminist comp.*, 1041–2 · J. Robinson, *Wayward women: a guide to women travellers* (1990)

Strutt, Jacob George (1784–1867), landscape painter and etcher, studied in London, and was a contributor to the Royal Academy, British Institution, and the Society of British Artists, Suffolk Street, between 1819 and 1858. For a few years he practised portrait painting, but from 1824 to 1831 he exhibited studies of forest scenery and was best-known for two sets of etchings published at this time— 'Sylva Britannica', or, Portraits of Forest Trees Distinguished for their Antiquity in 1822 (reissued in 1838) and 'Deliciae sylvarum', or, Grand and Romantic Forest Scenery in England and Scotland in 1828. By 1818 he was married to the writer Elizabeth Byron [see Strutt, Elizabeth (*fl.* 1805–1863)]. He had at least one daughter, Alice Elizabeth. About 1831 Strutt went abroad and, after residing for a time at Lausanne, settled in Rome. From there, he sent to the Royal Academy *The Ancient Forum, Rome* (exh. 1845) and *Tasso's Oak, Rome* (exh. 1851); in 1851 he returned to England. In 1858 he exhibited

a view of the Roman campagna, but then his name disappears from exhibition catalogues. He died in 1867. Strutt's portraits of the Revd William Marsh and Philander Chase DD were engraved by J. Young and C. Turner.

F. M. O'DONOGHUE, *rev.* EMILY M. WEEKS

Sources Redgrave, *Artists* · Graves, *RA exhibitors* · Wood, *Vic. painters*, 3rd edn

Strutt, Jedediah (1726–1797), inventor and cotton manufacturer, was born on 26 July 1726, at South Normanton, near Alfreton, Derbyshire, the second of the three sons of William Strutt, a small farmer and maltster, and his wife, Martha, the daughter of Joseph Statham, a yeoman. At the age of fourteen Strutt was apprenticed to Ralph Massey, a wheelwright, at Findern, a village near Derby, and boarded with the Woollats, members of the nonconformist congregation of Ebenezer Latham. Here, if not earlier—the Strutts might have been members of Alfreton's dissenting community—he acquired his love of books and a tendency towards reflection, and met his future wife, Elizabeth Woollat [see Strutt, Elizabeth]. Jedediah left his master in 1747 and, working as a journeyman wheelwright, moved to Belgrave, near Leicester, then to Leicester itself.

In 1754 Strutt inherited an uncle's farm stock and became a farmer wheelwright at Newton, near Blackwell, and on 25 September 1755 he married Elizabeth (1729–1774). About this time he became interested in the hosiery trade. He perfected a device, the 'rude and imperfect idea' of one Roper, 'an indolent fellow', brought to him by his wife's brother William Woollat, which could be attached to the front of the knitting frame to manufacture ribbed stockings. With Woollat and Elizabeth, he commenced a putting-out business around Blackwell. Woollat's and Elizabeth's nonconformist and London links established the necessary business and financial connections. In 1758 Strutt and Woollat entered a partnership with the Derby hosiers and dissenters John Bloodworth and Thomas Stamford—the two were replaced in 1762 by the wealthy Nottingham hosier and dissenter Samuel Need—and applied for patents in 1758 and 1759. The Strutts prospered; in 1762 Strutt was made a freeman of Nottingham, and the family moved to St Mary's Gate, Derby. Strutt's elder brother Joseph, with whom he took out a patent for a stove in 1770, lived in London and took no part in the business, but brother William joined the concern. The 'Derby rib machine' brought Strutt acquaintance with the Society of Arts, and, through a successfully countered challenge to his patent in 1765, experience of the London courts of law. Business success and frugality provided the means to consider other ventures.

In 1769, through Need, Strutt was introduced to Richard *Arkwright (1732–1792) and his partners, then newly arrived in Nottingham and requiring finance. For £500 Strutt and Need each took one-fifth of the partnership of Richard Arkwright & Co., set up to exploit Arkwright's patent. Tradition assigns Strutt a part in improving the machine, but his influence was probably more general. The yarn was first used for stockings, and it was Strutt and

Need who, manufacturing calicos at Derby, identified the natural vent. Strutt handled the negotiations for the reduction of excise duties on calico in 1774—his wife died that May while on a visit to him in London—and in 1782 he joined Arkwright in defence of the latter's 1769 patent. Though relations with Arkwright could be tense—in 1774 Strutt's eldest son, William [see below], wrote, 'he wants you out'—Strutt remained in the partnership until 1782, a year after Need's death. He participated in the mill-building programme and enjoyed the fruits of the new industry's rapid growth. The exact terms of the firm's expansion are not known, but perhaps Strutt himself financed the model factory communities at Belper and Milford, for, after the partnership's dissolution, these, and a calico factory at Derby, constituted the core of his own cotton empire. Samuel Slater, an ex-apprentice of Strutt's at Milford, was, in the 1790s, instrumental in introducing the new system of manufacture in the United States.

Strutt and his wife delighted in the commonplace and the upbringing of their five children. His sons, and for a time his daughters, worked in the business as they came of age. George Benson came to manage the mills and estates, Joseph [see below] the commercial side, and William the technical aspects. Jedediah's second marriage in 1781 or 1782 to Anne, the widow of George Daniels, a yeoman of Belper, strained relations with the children, and, increasingly, their education, their originality, and, to Strutt, the extravagance of their social life set them apart. His later life was split between his mansion, Milford House, and Derby; in 1795 he bought Exeter House, Derby, and, after a 'lingering illness', died there, on 7 May 1797, aged seventy. He was buried in the Unitarian chapel at Belper.

His eldest son, **William Strutt** (1756–1830), cotton manufacturer, born on 20 July 1756 at Newton, near Alfreton, Derbyshire, was educated at private schools. Although he entered the business at the age of fourteen, he continued to study and read widely throughout his life. Reconstruction and extension of the mills—the brothers traded as W. G. and J. Strutt—enabled William to demonstrate his skills: as an architect of fireproof buildings, and as an engineer of water power and transmission, of textile machinery, and of heating. His 'cockle' warm-air system was believed to be the most efficient for non-steam factories, and his design for the Derby Infirmary's heating and ventilation system was later copied by others. Strutt's original mind and achievements brought his election to the Royal Society in 1817. The Strutt brothers and their sister Elizabeth were sought out by society, and Strutt could count among his friends Erasmus Darwin (whom he helped to establish the Derby Philosophical Society and succeeded as president in 1802), R. L. and Maria Edgeworth (on whose drafts he commented), Coleridge (who described Strutt as 'a man of stern aspect, but strong, very strong abilities'), Tom Moore, the engineer Charles Sylvester, Samuel and Jeremy Bentham, and Robert Owen. Strutt was a major benefactor of Derby and its built and social infrastructure. Even so, his ownership of the manor of

Kingston in Nottinghamshire and a house in Leicestershire suggests that, like many of his generation, he found land attractive. On 12 January 1793 he married Barbara (1761–1804), the daughter of Thomas Evans of Darley Dale, a banker, industrialist, and early factory master. They had five daughters and one son, Edward *Strutt, first Lord Belper (1801–1880). Strutt died at Derby on 29 December 1830, and was buried in the Unitarian chapel at Friar Gate. In 1813 the fortune of the Strutt brothers had been estimated at £1 million.

Strutt's youngest son, **Joseph Strutt** (1765–1844), cotton manufacturer and philanthropist, was baptized at Friar Gate Presbyterian Chapel, Derby, on 19 September 1765. He was the only member of the family to be educated at the Derby School. On 5 January 1793 he married Isabella (1769–1802), 'sweet minded … lovely, handsome, beautiful', according to Coleridge (Collected Letters, ed. Griggs, 1.306), the daughter of Archibald Douglas of Swaybrook, Derbyshire; they had two sons and three daughters. He shared his family's politics and Unitarianism—in 1817 he supported the accused in the Derby treason trials—and many of his brother's friends, and was similarly public-spirited. With William he established a Lancasterian school in Derby and in 1824–5 a mechanics' institute; in 1835 he was first mayor of the reformed borough. He opened his house, St Peter's, with its paintings and statues, to the public, and in 1840 gave to the people of Derby an 11 acre arboretum planned by J. C. Loudon. He died on 13 January 1844 at Derby, leaving the bulk of his estate to his sole surviving child, Isabella, the wife of John Howard Galton and the mother of Sir Douglas Galton (1822–1899).

J. J. MASON

Sources R. S. Fitton and A. P. Wadsworth, The Strutts and the Arkwrights, 1758–1830: a study of the early factory system (1958) • W. Felkin, A history of the machine-wrought hosiery and lace manufactures (1867) • J. C. Cox, Memorials of old Derbyshire (1907) • C. L. Hacker, 'William Strutt of Derby (1756–1830)', Journal of the Derbyshire Archaeological and Natural History Society, 80 (1960), 49–70 • J. Tann, The development of the factory (1970) • H. R. Johnson and A. W. Skempton, 'William Strutt's cotton mills, 1793–1812', Transactions [Newcomen Society], 30 (1955–7), 179–205 • C. Sylvester, The philosophy of domestic economy (1819) • Derby Mercury (12 Jan 1831) • Derby Mercury (24 Jan 1844) • A catalogue of paintings and drawings, marbles, bronzes, ivories, alabasters and plaster busts and figures, china ornaments, etc. etc., in the collection of Joseph Strutt, Derby (1827) • J. C. Loudon, The Derby arboretum … and … a copy of the address … by … Joseph Strutt Esq. … when it was opened to the public (1840) • Modern mayors of Derby (1909) • W. J. Piper, 'Joseph Strutt', Derby Evening Telegraph (4 Sept 1952) • Collected letters of Samuel Taylor Coleridge, ed. E. L. Griggs, 1 (1956), 306

Archives Derby Public Library • Derbys. RO • FM Cam. • Inst. EE

Likenesses J. Wright, oils, c.1790, Derby Museum and Art Gallery; repro. in B. Nicolson, Joseph Wright of Derby (1968), 163 • Chantrey, bust (William Strutt), Derby Museum and Art Gallery • Reinagle, oils (William Strutt), Derby Museum and Art Gallery • portrait (William Strutt), repro. in Hacker, 'William Strutt of Derby', facing p. 56 • portrait (Joseph Strutt), Council House, Derby • portrait (Joseph Strutt; after statue), repro. in Derby Evening Telegraph (4 Sept 1952) • statue (Joseph Strutt), arboretum, Derby

Wealth at death £160,000—Joseph Strutt: will, PRO, PROB 11/1992

Strutt, John William, third Baron Rayleigh (1842–1919), experimental and mathematical physicist, was born at

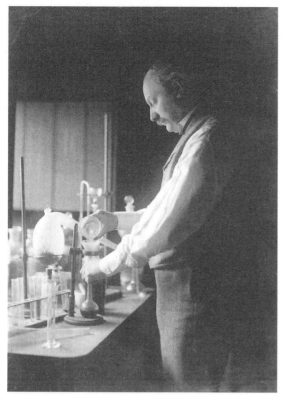

John William Strutt, third Baron Rayleigh (1842–1919), by
Frederick Hollyer, c.1888

Langford Grove, Maldon, Essex, on 12 November 1842, the
eldest son of John James Strutt, second Baron Rayleigh (d.
1873), and his wife, Clara Elizabeth La Touche, eldest
daughter of Captain Richard Vicars RE and sister of the
Crimean War hero Hedley Shafto Johnstone Vicars.

Education and marriage Strutt started his education at
Eton at the age of ten, but ill health prevented him from
completing even the first year, having spent most of his
time in the school sanatorium. After three years at a private school at Wimbledon he went to Harrow School in
1855, but stayed for less than a year. In the autumn of 1857
he was put under the care of the Revd George Townsend
Warner, who took pupils at Torquay—a place which
proved more congenial for his health and where he stayed
for four years. His first attempt to enter Trinity College,
Cambridge, on a scholarship was unsuccessful. In October
1861 he entered the college as a fellow commoner. He
started his preparation for the mathematical tripos under
Dr E. J. Routh of Peterhouse. He took a course in chemical
analysis with G. D. Liveing and attended the lectures of Sir
George Gabriel Stokes, Lucasian professor of mathematics. Strutt had been very much interested in photography
and four months before the tripos examination he had
been awarded the Sheepshanks exhibition in astronomy.
In January 1865 he became senior wrangler. Strutt
impressed the examiners with the lucidity of his answers
in the examination. In 1865 he received the first Smith's
prize, and he was elected a fellow of Trinity College in the

next year. Right after his graduation Strutt—unlike many
graduates who chose to visit European universities—went
to the United States. After his return he purchased his first
equipment and started his experimental investigations at
the family seat, Terling Place, Witham, Essex. This was the
origin of a unique laboratory where Strutt for the rest of
his life carried out ingenious experiments with very simple equipment.

In 1871 Strutt resigned his fellowship to marry Evelyn
Georgiana Mary (d. 1934), the daughter of James Maitland
Balfour of Whittingehame, East Lothian, and the sister of
an undergraduate friend, Arthur James *Balfour, later earl
of Balfour and prime minister. The year after his marriage
Strutt had a severe attack of rheumatic fever and following his doctors' recommendations he spent a winter in
Egypt. Shortly after his return his father died, in June 1873,
and he succeeded as third Baron Rayleigh at Terling Place.
In the same year he was elected a fellow of the Royal Society. The prevailing economic depression in agriculture
forced Strutt to devote a considerable part of his time to
the management of his estate. He was especially interested in experimenting with artificial fertilizers, and was
among the first to use nitrate of soda. After 1876 he left the
entire management of the land to his younger brother,
Edward *Strutt.

Psychical research Rayleigh's involvement with psychical
research started in the early 1870s. William Crookes's
investigations had stimulated him to develop an interest
in such phenomena. His sister-in-law Eleanor Balfour,
who collaborated with him in his capillarity studies and
who later assisted him in his researches at the Cavendish,
and her husband, Professor Henry Sidgwick, were actively
engaged with the study of psychical phenomena. In 1882
they were all among the founding members of the Society
for Psychical Research. Rayleigh was a council member
and vice-president throughout the 1880s and 1890s, and,
in fact, one of his last public appearances was to deliver
the presidential address of the society in 1919. He declared
that he had 'no definite conclusions to announce' (Strutt,
380) and that nothing had occurred to shake him from
'forty five years of hesitation' (Strutt, 391). Despite his
long involvement with the society he never became a convinced follower. Religious considerations should be also
taken into account in assessing Rayleigh's involvement in
psychical research for so many years. He was a devout and
practising Christian and on more than one occasion he
had stressed that it was absurd to adopt definite claims of
faith over science or vice versa. Rayleigh was also among
the first members of the Synthetic Society, founded in
1896, whose members sought a 'new synthesis of religious
positions and convictions' (Oppenheim, 127). He held
strong Conservative and Unionist opinions. The prospect
of a political career did not attract him. He seconded the
address in the House of Lords in 1875, and on rare occasions intervened in debate.

Acoustics and optics, 1871–1879 Nearly three-quarters of
Rayleigh's papers dealt with problems in acoustics and

optics. His long paper on the theory of resonance published in 1871 was based on similar work on the sensations of tone done by Helmholtz, and the extensions Rayleigh suggested were the beginnings of his eventually becoming the leading authority on sound. In the same year Rayleigh proposed a solution of one of the most intriguing problems in optics: why the colour of the sky is blue. Rayleigh used the elastic solid theory of light and not Maxwell's recently introduced theory, and proved that the scattering of light by small particles was a function of the inverse fourth power of the wavelength of the incident light. His early work in optics was not confined to theoretical considerations alone. In the laboratory at Terling he attempted to manufacture diffraction gratings by photographic means. These experiments, whose practical results were initially quite poor, led to the study of the resolving power of gratings. One of the important results of these researches was the proof that the resolving power of a plane transparent grating is equal to the product of the order of the spectrum and the total number of lines in the grating. This work was continued with a series of fundamental researches on the optical properties of the spectroscope, an instrument that in the late 1870s was becoming increasingly important in the study of the solar spectrum as well as of the spectra of the chemical elements. In 1872, during his winter in Egypt, Strutt started his *Theory of Sound* (1877) which for many years was the standard textbook.

Cavendish professor, 1879–1884 Rayleigh was to have been the first Cavendish professor of experimental physics at Cambridge in 1871 if James Clerk Maxwell had refused the chair. When Maxwell died in 1879 Sir William Thomson (later Lord Kelvin), at that time professor of natural philosophy at the University of Glasgow, was proposed to be the person to succeed him. Thomson did not want to leave Glasgow and the post was offered to Rayleigh, who accepted in December. Though he preferred to continue his researches at Terling the strains from the continuing agricultural depression played their role in his accepting the post. Rayleigh lectured on such varied subjects as colour vision, scattering, sound, electricity, magnetization, and the density of gases. He systematized laboratory instruction in elementary physics and this, in the coming years, became the basis for physics education in many other institutions of higher education. Above all, Rayleigh's stay at Cambridge was marked by the intricate research programme he initiated with the help of his assistants Richard Glazebrook and William Napier Shaw. This was the redetermination of the absolute units of the ohm, the ampere, and the volt. The British Association for the Advancement of Science (BAAS) had set up a committee for the determination of electrical units in 1863 and work to this effect had already been performed by Maxwell. The accuracy of the measurements, however, was doubted, and Rayleigh developed much more precise equipment than Maxwell's and organized the work, which demanded remarkable patience and painstaking care for its completion. Eleanor Sidgwick was an important collaborator at Terling, where much of the work was

done. The investigation was completed in 1884 and the results stood the test of time remarkably well. The undertaking of such work had been encouraged by similar endeavours in France and Germany, and recognized the needs of industry. It was during Rayleigh's presidency of the BAAS in 1884 that the association held its annual meeting for the first time outside the United Kingdom, in Montreal. Rayleigh did not wish to extend his tenure at Cambridge and he resigned at the end of 1884. Terling Place remained his scientific headquarters for the rest of his life. George Gordon, an instrument maker at Cambridge, was employed to help him there. Rayleigh stayed at Terling even during his relatively demanding commitments in London.

Natural philosopher, 1887–1905 As well as his involvement with the BAAS Rayleigh served as the professor of natural philosophy at the Royal Institution of Great Britain from 1887 to 1905 and as the secretary of the Royal Society from 1885 to 1896 after the resignation of G. G. Stokes. Neither post required continuous residence in London. At the Royal Institution he was called on to deliver a number of lectures on topics of his own research interests or on topics of a more general interest. During his tenure at the Royal Society he discovered and publicized the memoir in which J. J. Waterston in 1846 had anticipated some of the important features of the kinetic theory of gases.

During the 1880s and up to the mid-1890s Rayleigh published papers on optical and acoustical radiation, electromagnetism, general mechanical theorems, vibrations of elastic media, capillarity, thermodynamics, filtration of waves in periodic structures, interference and scattering of light, the telephone and its technical problems, and on the measurement of the minimum audible intensity of sound. Rayleigh, in his work on scattering by small objects, obtained approximations for isolated scatterers, periodic structures, gratings, rough surfaces, and random media. He contributed on more or less every class of scattering problems. He generalized the reciprocal idea introduced by Helmholtz which was eventually used for the calibration of transducers. He was also the first to work out the coupling of circuits.

Argon Few discoveries have been as dramatic as the discovery of argon in the atmosphere by Lord Rayleigh and William Ramsay, professor of chemistry at University College, London. The discovery of argon involved a bitter public dispute concerning the legitimacy of a chemical element whose most important characteristic was its inertness, and which forced the chemists to reassess the very notion of a chemical element.

Rayleigh's measurements for the exact determination of the densities of gases had started in 1882 in Cambridge and were continued until 1888. It was a programme aimed to test Prout's hypothesis by finding the atomic weights of gases and observing the extent to which they were multiples of the atomic weight of hydrogen. By 1892 Rayleigh had found a curious discrepancy. In a letter to *Nature* he noted the difference in density between physical nitrogen—derived by absorbing oxygen, carbon dioxide, and moisture from atmospheric air—and chemical nitrogen—derived from ammonia. It had been found that physical nitrogen was heavier than chemical nitrogen by about a thousandth. Further improvements showed that chemical nitrogen was about 0.5 per cent lighter than physical nitrogen. The first alternative Rayleigh entertained was that atmospheric nitrogen was too heavy because of the imperfect removal of oxygen from the atmospheric air, or chemical nitrogen was too light because when it was removed from ammonia it was contaminated with gases which were lighter than nitrogen. Further experiments by Rayleigh excluded both possibilities, and by the beginning of 1894 Rayleigh was convinced that the atmosphere contained a new, and hitherto unknown, constituent.

To isolate this substance Rayleigh used sparking and the addition of oxygen to oxidize nitrogen. Ramsay proposed another method of isolation and made use of heated magnesium which absorbed the nitrogen. Rayleigh and Ramsay were working independently until they joined forces at the beginning of August 1894. Rayleigh presented the first preliminary results during the meeting of the BAAS at Oxford on 13 August 1894. They continued their exhaustive experiments and the tiny samples they sent to William Crookes and Arthur Schuster for spectroscopic analysis provided additional evidence which confirmed the new element.

On 6 December 1894 James Dewar, in a talk at the Chemical Society, claimed that the assumed new substance was a triatomic form of nitrogen. Letters were written to *The Times* criticizing Rayleigh's and Ramsay's work, especially their unwillingness to make public the details of their investigations. Rayleigh and Ramsay kept the details private until they were absolutely certain about the new element because they wished to receive (which they did) the Smithsonian Hodgkins prize for discoveries associated with the atmosphere. The final announcement was made at a meeting of the Royal Society at University College, London, on 31 January 1895, less than a week after Lord Kelvin in his presidential address to the Royal Society had referred to the discovery of the new constituent as the greatest scientific event of the year. Lord Kelvin chaired the meeting to which the councils of both the Chemical and the Physical Society were invited. There were 800 people present when Ramsay read the paper. Rayleigh's comment at the end was quite characteristic: 'I am not without experience of experimental difficulties, but certainly I have never encountered them in anything like so severe and aggravating a form as in this investigation' (Rucker, 337).

The discovery of argon brought the 1904 Nobel prize for physics to Rayleigh, and the prize for chemistry to William Ramsay. Rayleigh had been proposed to the Nobel committee by Lord Kelvin in the same year that Rayleigh had proposed Kelvin for the prize.

Late research and public service In the 1890s Rayleigh became interested in the problem of the complete radiation law, which was closely related to the distribution of energy in the spectrum of black body radiation. Though aware of the problems that electromagnetic theory, thermodynamics, and statistical mechanics were facing at the end of the nineteenth century, his convictions lay with classical physics and on its ability eventually to deal with such deadlocks. Rayleigh never attacked the quantum hypothesis or the relativistic view, but neither did he ever express any enthusiasm or show any sign of adopting the newly emerging non-classical framework. Surely his derivation of what came later to be called the Rayleigh–Jeans radiation law (published in 1900, a few months before Planck's famous paper on the distribution law) provided ample ground for entertaining such hopes, since the statistical principle of equipartition of energy among resonators appeared to work so well for long wavelengths as to raise hopes that a future solution about the short wavelengths would come from the same core of ideas. About 1895 Rayleigh became deeply interested in physical optics, work which won him the Rumford medal.

From 1896 to 1911 Rayleigh was the chief scientific adviser to Trinity House, which maintained the fog warnings and lighthouses around the English coast, and he was involved in the design of foghorns. He was also the chairman of the explosives committee of the War Office, and chief gas examiner of the London gas supply. Through his brother-in-law Balfour, Rayleigh had considerable influence. This was decisive against fierce resistance when he was vice-chairman of the Treasury committee which reported in favour of the formation of the National Laboratory, and then was appointed president of its first executive committee in 1900. Rayleigh was one of the first members of the new Order of Merit when it was established in 1902. After receiving the Nobel prize in 1904 he donated its cash award to Cambridge University to improve the Cavendish Laboratory and the university library. From 1905 to 1908 he served as president of the Royal Society. He also became a privy councillor in 1905. From 1908 to 1919 he served as chancellor of Cambridge University. In 1909 he was appointed president of the special government advisory committee on aeronautics, an appointment which led to his devoting much time to problems of aviation. He was the recipient of thirteen honorary degrees and held honorary memberships in, or received special awards from, over fifty learned societies. Edward VII is said to have accosted him at a social gathering with: 'Well, Lord Rayleigh, discovering something I suppose?' (Fulford, 21).

Rayleigh died at Terling Place on 30 June 1919. 'An unerring leader in the advancement of natural knowledge' is the inscription on his memorial in Westminster Abbey. Of his three sons the eldest, Robert John *Strutt, became a professor of physics at Imperial College, London, and succeeded to the barony.

The last notes Rayleigh jotted at the end of his pocket book are very characteristic of his lifelong interests with everyday problems: 'Difficulties: Why are winds high in winter?; Why is damp cold so disagreeable?; Sun stroke and heat stroke; Snow blindness; Ironing of clothes to make them flat'. KOSTAS GAVROGLU

Sources R. T. A. Glazebrook, *History of the Cavendish Laboratory, 1871–1910* (1910) · J. N. Howard, 'John William Strutt, third Baron Rayleigh', *Applied Optics*, 3 (1964), 1091–1101 · J. N. Howard, 'The optics papers of John W. Strutt, third Baron Rayleigh', *Applied Optics*, 3 (1964) · J. N. Howard, ed., *The Rayleigh Archives dedication*, United States Air Force Research Laboratories Special Reports, 63 (1967) · R. B. Lindsay, *Men of physics: Lord Rayleigh: the man and his work* (1970) · J. Oppenheim, *The other world: spiritualism and psychical research in England, 1850–1914* (1985) · C. R. Strutt, *The Strutt family of Terling, 1650–1873* (1939) · R. J. Strutt, *Life of John William Strutt, third Baron Rayleigh*, enl. edn (1968) · R. Fulford, 'The king', *Edwardian England, 1901–1914*, ed. S. Nowell-Smith (1964) · A. Rucker, *Nature*, 51 (1894–5), 337 · *DNB* · *DSB* · Lord Rayleigh [J. W. Strutt], *Scientific papers*, 6 vols. [1964] · d. cert.

Archives Air Force Research Laboratories, Cambridge, Massachusetts, corresp. and papers · JRL, notes on offprints · NRA, priv. coll., corresp. and papers · Royal Institution of Great Britain, London, notebook and letters | BL, letters to Macmillans, Add. MS 55220 · CUL, letters to Lord Kelvin · CUL, letters to Sir George Stokes · CUL, letters to Sir Joseph Thomson · ICL, college archives, letters to Silvanus Thompson · King's AC Cam., letters to Oscar Browning · MHS Oxf., corresp. with Frederick Jervis Smith · NA Scot., corresp. with Arthur Balfour · Royal Institution of Great Britain, London, Dewar MSS · Trinity Cam., corresp. with Sir Joseph John Thomson · UCL, letters to Sir Oliver Lodge · UCL, letters to Sir William Ramsay

Likenesses P. Burne-Jones, oils, 1888, Trinity Cam. · F. Hollyer, photograph, *c*.1888, V&A [*see illus.*] · H. von Herkomer, oils, 1911?, Examination School, Cambridge · G. Reid, oils, exh. RA 1911, RS · W. Rothenstein, crayon and pencil drawing, 1916, NPG · W. Stoneman, photograph, 1917, NPG · F. T. D. [F. T. Dalton], caricature, chromolithograph, NPG; repro. in *VF* (21 Dec 1899) · E. Glazebrook, photograph, NPG · photographs, repro. in Lord Rayleigh [J. W. Strutt], *Collected papers* (1964)

Wealth at death £172,972 16*s*. 11*d*.: probate, 25 Feb 1920, *CGPLA Eng. & Wales*

Strutt, Joseph (1749–1802), antiquary and engraver, was born on 27 October 1749 at Springfield Mill, near Chelmsford, Essex, the youngest of five children of Thomas Strutt (*d*. 1751), a wealthy miller, and his wife, Elizabeth (1727–1780), daughter of John Ingold, also a miller, of Woodham Walter, near Maldon. Only one brother, John, survived beyond infancy. Thomas Strutt died of smallpox when Joseph was not yet two. Joseph was educated at King Edward VI School, Chelmsford, and in 1764 was apprenticed to the engraver William Wynne Ryland, and moved to the latter's workshop in London. On 30 January 1769 he entered the newly established Royal Academy Schools, and in the first of the school's annual competitions, held in that year, took a silver medal for a drawing from the antique. Two years later, in December 1771, he won the gold medal for two oil paintings on classical themes. Despite these early successes and the fact that he exhibited work at the Royal Academy during the 1780s Strutt cannot claim any real distinction as a painter, for his real achievements lay in his work as an antiquary.

Strutt's first employment was with Foote Gower, the Essex antiquary, who commissioned him to complete a series of engravings of Roman antiquities. Through Gower he was introduced to Richard Gough, who was almost certainly responsible for securing him access to the British Museum in 1771. There he became acquainted with the collections of manuscripts and illuminated books, and conceived a series of antiquarian works drawing primarily on these visual sources that was to represent the majority of his subsequent published output. The

first, *The Regal and Ecclesiastical Antiquities of England* (1773), owed its initial inspiration to Montfaucon's *Monuments de la monarchie française*, and was the first book of its kind to be published in England. It was essentially a series of engraved portraits, illustrative of the English monarchs, drawn entirely from contemporary sources. Its aim, according to the preface, was to encourage artists to be more accurate in their representation of historic dress. In the same year Louis Dutens published the first of his three volumes on ancient coins, with engravings by Strutt, but by this time Strutt was devoting himself almost entirely to antiquarian subjects. His next work, *Horda-Angel-Cynnan: the Manners and Customs, Arms and Habits of the Inhabitants of England*, published in three volumes between 1774 and 1776, drew on an even wider range of manuscript sources—from the British Museum, Lambeth Palace Library, the Bodleian Library, and Oxford and Cambridge college libraries.

Both these early publications were well received in most quarters, which encouraged Strutt to venture upon a third publication, *The Chronicle of England*, a more ambitious work, with fewer engravings, intended as a work of reference rather than a narrative history. Six volumes had been initially projected but only the first two were published (1777–8). Together they covered the history of England from the Roman period to the end of the Saxon heptarchy. Strutt drew heavily on illustrated manuscript sources again, but the *Chronicle* inevitably contained much material similar to that of his earlier volumes. It also suffered from competition with other historical publications, in particular Robert Henry's *History of Great Britain* (1771–93), which laid a similar emphasis on manners and customs. Reviewers were also critical of the style in which it was written.

While engaged on these projects in the early 1770s Strutt resided partly in London and partly in Chelmsford, but following his marriage, on 16 August 1774, to Ann Blower (1754–1778) of Bocking, Essex, he took a house in Duke Street, Portland Place, London. Three children were born to the couple: two sons, Joseph and William Thomas [*see below*], and a daughter, Elizabeth Ann, born on 24 August 1778. Ann Strutt died on 15 September 1778, soon after giving birth to her daughter, who survived her mother by only a few months. The following year Strutt published, anonymously, a short elegiac poem to his wife's memory.

Following the death of his wife and the disappointing reception to the *Chronicle* Strutt appears to have abandoned his literary and antiquarian researches to engage in more lucrative work; he exhibited nine paintings at the Royal Academy between 1778 and 1785 and produced several of his best stipple engravings—using the style introduced into England from the continent by his master, Ryland. After the death of his brother, John, an eminent physician in Westminster, in 1784 Strutt shared his home with his widowed sister-in-law until he retired, to Bacon's farm, Bramfield, Hertfordshire, in 1790. In 1785–6 he published the two volumes of his *Biographical Dictionary of Engravers*, a historical account of the art of engraving and of engravers from the earliest time to his own day that has remained the basis of all later studies of a similar kind. He continued to produce engravings, including thirteen, after designs by Thomas Stothard, for John Bradford's edition of *The Pilgrim's Progress* (published 1792). He also established a day-school and Sunday school in the nearby village of Tewin, where the local manor house, Queenhoo Hall, served as the inspiration for his posthumously published historical novel of the same name.

In 1795, with his health and finances slightly improved, Strutt returned to London and resumed his antiquarian researches. From this time onwards he undertook almost no engraving work that was not intended to illustrate his own books. *A Complete View of the Dresses and Habits of the People of England* was published by subscription in two volumes (1796 and 1799); this was the first detailed, illustrated, and properly sourced history of dress in England. It was followed in 1801 by *The Sports and Pastimes of the People of England* (1801). Both volumes concentrated chiefly on the medieval period. Strutt's antiquarian learning was considerably more advanced by this time but his emphasis was always on the engravings as the primary source of information in a period that was so notoriously barren of literary sources.

Strutt next conceived the idea of using his antiquarian knowledge to write a historical novel set in the reign of Henry VI, but did not live to complete it. After his death the unfinished manuscript was acquired by the publisher John Murray, who asked Walter Scott to prepare it for publication. Scott added a final chapter, bringing it to a rather abrupt and inelegant conclusion, and the book was eventually published in 1808. Intended by Strutt as a lively means of conveying information about the past, *Queen-Hoo Hall: a Romance of Ancient Times* is unsuccessful as a work of fiction; it lacks a coherent plot and the language is deliberately archaic. However, it sheds valuable light on the author's life, as it is substantially autobiographical, and was later acknowledged by Scott to have been influential in inspiring him to complete *Waverley*.

Strutt died, of an inflammation of the bowel, on 16 October 1802 at his home in Charles Street, Hatton Garden, London, and was buried on 20 October in the churchyard of St Andrew's, Holborn. When alterations were later made to the Farringdon Street viaduct his remains were disinterred and transferred to the city cemetery in Ilford, Essex. He did not die a rich man. By his own account he managed his financial affairs badly. His antiquarian works were unremunerative in his own lifetime and there seems little doubt that, had he pursued a career in engraving exclusively, he might have enjoyed greater affluence. He suffered from chronic asthma for much of his life and became increasingly corpulent, as is evident from a late portrait of him by Ozias Humphry in the National Portrait Gallery (no. 323).

Strutt may justifiably be regarded as the first serious historian of dress in England, and his pioneering works of scholarship were heavily drawn upon by nineteenth-century costume historians. Unlike many of his contemporaries, who doubted the reliability of artistic sources as

historical evidence, he employed a comparative analysis of the manuscripts, showing that they were reliable indicators of changes not just in matters of dress but also of the 'manners and customs' of the time. He was one of the first to realize the potential value of visual material as a historical source rather than as simply serving an illustrative purpose. He showed an early appreciation of the intrinsic merit of medieval art and was unusual in producing near-facsimile engraved reproductions of the originals. Antiquaries such as Richard Gough were critical of his antiquarian scholarship but appreciated the quality of his engravings. In his own lifetime *Manners and Customs* was probably the most successful of his antiquarian works (there were two subsequent editions, in 1779 and 1793) but *Sports and Customs* has enjoyed greater longevity and has been frequently reprinted, one edition appearing in 1973.

Strutt left two sons. The elder, **Joseph Strutt** (1775–1833), was born on 28 May 1775. He was apprenticed to the printer John Nichols and later became librarian to the duke of Northumberland. He edited some of his father's posthumous works and contributed a biographical memoir of his life to Nichols's *Literary Anecdotes of the Eighteenth Century* (1812). He died on 12 November 1833 at Isleworth, Middlesex, leaving a widow and a large family.

Strutt's younger son, **William Thomas Strutt** (1777–1850), was born on 7 March 1777. He held a position in the Bank of England but was also a miniature painter of some repute. He died on 22 February 1850, leaving several sons, two of whom, Arthur and William, were also painters.

JENNIFER HARRIS

Sources W. Strutt, *A memoir of the life of Joseph Strutt (1749–1802)* (1896) · Nichols, *Lit. anecdotes*, 5.665–86 · R. M. Christy, 'Joseph Strutt, author, artist, engraver & antiquary, 1749–1802: a biography', 1912, BL [unpublished typewritten manuscript] · B. L. Haigh, 'A consideration of the antiquarian and literary works of Joseph Strutt, with a typescript of a hitherto unedited manuscript novel', PhD diss., U. Lond., 1984 · 'Memoranda relating to Joseph Strutt the engraver, collected from his own papers', Bodl. Oxf., MS Douce, fol. 10 · F. Gower and R. Gough, correspondence, BL, Add. MS 22936 · *IGI* · *DNB*

Archives BL, memoranda books, Egerton MSS 888 · Norfolk RO, corresp. | BL, letters to John Strutt, Add. MS 38091 · Lpool RO, letters to William Roscoe · NL Scot., drafts and notes for Emma Darcy

Likenesses O. Humphry, pastel, 1790–99, NPG · group portrait, line engraving, pubd 1798 (after *Sketches taken at Print Sales* by P. Sandby), BM · J. Jackson, pen-and-ink drawing (after Biggs), NPG · pencil drawing (after O. Humphry)

Strutt, Joseph (1765–1844). *See under* Strutt, Jedediah (1726–1797).

Strutt, Joseph (1775–1833). *See under* Strutt, Joseph (1749–1802).

Strutt, Robert John, fourth Baron Rayleigh (1875–1947), experimental physicist, was born on 28 August 1875 at the family home, Terling Place, Essex, the eldest of the four sons of the renowned physicist John William *Strutt, third Baron Rayleigh (1842–1919), and his wife, Evelyn Georgiana Mary (d. 1934), daughter of James Maitland Balfour, of Whittingehame, East Lothian, the sister of the first and second earls of Balfour, F. M. Balfour, and Eleanor Mildred Sidgwick. Strutt was a shy and aloof boy, a characteristic which never quite left him even when he had won renown by his discoveries, although he had self-assurance and a kindly humour. Though his temperament might have led him to withdraw from the world of affairs he fulfilled both his scientific responsibilities and those of his estate.

Strutt was at Eton College from 1889 to 1894; he won the college science prize and entered Trinity College, Cambridge, in October 1894 initially to read mathematics, but changing after two terms to natural sciences. He graduated with a first class in both parts of the natural sciences tripos in 1897 and 1898 respectively. He shared with Henry Dale the award of a Coutts Trotter studentship in 1898. Soon after graduating Strutt began to publish results of experimental work carried out under the influence of J. J. Thomson in the Cavendish Laboratory. He was a highly skilled experimentalist (Thomson considered him better than his father), mastering both lathe turning and glass-blowing. He was also an amateur conjuror. He was a fellow of Trinity, 1900–06.

In 1905 Strutt married Lady Mary Hilda Clements, second daughter of the fourth earl of Leitrim, bringing him into contact with the Irish Unionist cause. The couple had two daughters and three sons. The eldest daughter, born in 1906, died of diphtheria in 1910. In 1908 Strutt was appointed professor of physics at the Imperial College of Science and Technology, South Kensington, London, remaining until he succeeded to the title of Baron Rayleigh on the death of his father in 1919, and being appointed emeritus professor in 1920. He was chairman of the governing body of the college from 1936 until his death. His first wife died in 1919, only a few weeks before the death of his father. In 1920 he married Kathleen Alice Cuthbert OBE, widow of Captain James Harold Cuthbert DSO, Scots Guards, of Beaufront Castle, Northumberland, and eldest daughter of John Coppin Straker of Stagshaw House, Northumberland. Lady Rayleigh had three sons and one daughter from her first marriage and she and Rayleigh had one son. The family circle was therefore a large one.

Rayleigh continued his scientific work in his private laboratory at Terling, where his habits were regular. He would spend the morning in the laboratory; take some exercise in the afternoon, often swimming or gardening with his family; read to the children after tea; and return to the laboratory from 6 p.m. until dinner time. A fire in the laboratory in 1930 provided the opportunity to install a glass dome for observing the night sky. Rayleigh was an experimental philosopher who, like Henry Cavendish, worked independently out of pure curiosity. His work was carried out entirely by himself (he had one laboratory assistant, R. Thompson, who came to him as a boy in 1908 and remained with him throughout); much of it was done in his private laboratory at Terling Place. He was a prolific and skilful investigator with wide-ranging interests. His papers number over 300, of which 113 were published in the *Proceedings of the Royal Society*: far more than those of

any other fellow in the same period. His most important contributions were his investigations into the age of minerals and rocks by measurements of their radioactivity and helium content, his discovery of active nitrogen, and his studies of the resonance and fluorescence of metallic vapours excited by electric discharges. In 1916 he and his colleague, Alfred Fowler, were the first to prove the existence of ozone in the atmosphere, and Strutt proceeded to show that it was mainly located in the higher regions. A number of other subjects came under his investigation: electrical discharges *in vacuo*, the Becquerel rays, optical contact, the green flash at sunset, the glow of phosphorus, iridescent colours in nature, the bending of marble and glass, and the formation of pebbles, pallasites, and red sandstones. His work on the helium content of rocks was pioneering research and led to a great extension of the estimate of Lord Kelvin of the age of the earth, and a closer accord with geological evidence.

The value of Rayleigh's unpublished data on the light of the night sky to later researchers led to the acquisition of many of his, and his father's, laboratory notebooks by the United States Air Force Cambridge Research Laboratories. He was the first to distinguish between two types of light in the night sky, the aurora seen in polar regions and the airglow observable all over the earth; his posthumous nickname was 'the Airglow Rayleigh'. In 1929 he succeeded in measuring the intensity of the light from the night sky, and the photometric unit for sky brightness, the rayleigh, is named after him. Rayleigh was very methodical in his ways, and his papers are a model of lucidity. He was author of one of the earliest books on radioactivity—*The Becquerel Rays and the Properties of Radium* (1904). He also wrote two admirable biographies, one of his father (1924) and the other of Sir J. J. Thomson (1942), and a number of other obituaries of distinguished men of science.

Rayleigh was elected FRS in 1905, serving twice on the council before becoming the society's foreign secretary from 1929 to 1934. He received the Rumford medal in 1920. He was chairman of the executive committee of the National Physical Laboratory (1932–9), president of the Physical Society of London (1934–6), and joint president of the International Congress of Physics held in London in 1934. He went to South Africa in 1929 as president of the mathematics and physics section of the British Association and was president of the association in 1938 at the meeting in Cambridge. He was president of the Royal Institution from 1945 until his death, delivering the Friday evening discourse eight times through his life.

Rayleigh received honorary degrees from the universities of Dublin (ScD, 1913), Durham (DSc, 1929), and Edinburgh (LLD, 1933). He served on the advisory council of the Department of Scientific and Industrial Research (1929–34). Among other public duties he was a trustee of the Beit memorial fellowships (1928–46), a fellow of Eton College (1935–45), and a justice of the peace for Essex. He was president of the Central Council of Milk Recording Societies (1939). He took active interest in the debates in the House of Lords and spoke on several occasions on matters relating to science.

During the Second World War, Rayleigh, personally, took X-ray apparatus to Farnham and took photographs for the patients, an initiative which soon led him to X-ray work with the Royal Army Medical Corps. Like his father he was interested in the physical aspects of psychical phenomena. His outlook was consistently that of a man of science on all matters. He died of a heart attack at his home in Essex on 13 December 1947. He was survived by his second wife. A. C. EGERTON, rev. ISOBEL FALCONER

Sources A. C. Egerton, *Obits. FRS*, 6 (1948–9), 503–38 [incl. bibliography] · G. Strutt, 'Robert John Strutt, fourth Baron Rayleigh', *Applied Optics*, 3 (1964), 1105–12 · J. N. Howard, ed., *The Rayleigh Archives dedication*, United States Air Force Research Laboratories Special Reports, 63 (1967) · R. J. Strutt, *Life of John William Strutt, third Baron Rayleigh*, enl. edn (1968)
Archives Air Force Research Laboratories, Cambridge, Massachusetts, notebooks · BGS, corresp. · ICL, college archives, corresp. relating to Imperial College | BL, corresp. with T. D. N. Besterman, Add. MS 57729 · California Institute of Technology, Pasadena, archives, corresp. with G. E. Hale · CUL, Society for Psychical Research, corresp. with Sir Oliver Lodge · CUL, Rutherford MSS, Add. MS 7653 R20–25 · Nuffield Oxf., corresp. with Lord Cherwell · TCD, corresp. with John Joly
Likenesses W. Stoneman, photographs, 1918–43, NPG · H. Coster, photographs, 1930–39, NPG · M. Fisher, oils, Terling Place, Essex · A. John, drawing; in possession of the family, 1959 · photograph, repro. in Egerton, *Obits. FRS* · two photographs, RS
Wealth at death £232,850 6s. 3d.—save and except settled land: probate, 3 Nov 1948, *CGPLA Eng. & Wales* · £29,188 14s.—limited to settled land: probate, 31 May 1949, *CGPLA Eng. & Wales*

Strutt, William (1756–1830). *See under* Strutt, Jedediah (1726–1797).

Strutt, William Goodday (*bap.* 1762, *d.* 1848), army officer, was baptized at Springfield, Essex, on 26 February 1762, the third son of John Strutt (1727–1816) MP, of Terling Place, Whitham, Essex, and his wife, Anne (1732–1814), the daughter of the Revd William Goodday of Maldon, rector of Strelly, Nottinghamshire. He also had an elder sister. After attending Felsted School and a Mr Lochée's military academy, he entered the army, joining his regiment, the 61st, at Minorca. In 1799 he was promoted lieutenant, and later was appointed to a company in the 91st, with whom he took part in the defence of St Lucia. In 1782, having exchanged into the 97th, he served at the siege of Gibraltar. He purchased a majority in the 60th regiment in 1783 and, being placed on half pay, visited several German courts to observe their military organization. In 1787 he went with his regiment to the West Indies. He purchased a lieutenant-colonelcy in 1790 and was removed in 1792 to the 54th. In 1793 he saw much hard fighting in Flanders. On his return he was sent to St Vincent, where he was promoted brigadier-general in 1795. In January 1796, with two hundred men, he attacked a force of twelve hundred, was wounded three times, and had to have his right leg amputated above the knee. After returning to England in 1796 he received the governorship of Stirling Castle, a sinecure, on 23 February, but afterwards served on the staff in Ireland. The loss of his leg and attendant poor health obliged him to cease active service, although on 23 June 1798 he was promoted major-general. On 13 May 1800 he was given another sinecure,

that of governor of Quebec. He never visited that city, though he held the post until his death.

In retirement Strutt spent much time at Southend, Essex, and was one of the prime movers in the building of Southend pier, the longest in the world, and of the nearby church of St John the Baptist. He died unmarried at his home, Tofts, Little Baddow, Essex, on 5 February 1848 and was buried in the family vault at Terling.

MILLER CHRISTY, *rev.* ELIZABETH BAIGENT

Sources *Public characters*, 10 vols. (1799–1809) · C. R. Strutt, *The Strutt family of Terling, 1650–1873* (1939) · *GM*, 2nd ser., 29 (1848), 661–2 · *Essex Herald* (8 Feb 1848) · 'Holden, Joseph', 'Strutt, John', 'Strutt, William Goodday', HoP, *Commons* · *Annual Register* (1848), 90
Archives BL, corresp. with D. Dundas, Add. MS 46703
Likenesses watercolour, 1835, repro. in Strutt, *Strutt family of Terling*, facing p. 62

Strutt, William Thomas (1777–1850). *See under* Strutt, Joseph (1749–1802).

Strype, John (1643–1737), historian and biographer, the youngest son of John Strype or Jan van Strijp (*d.* 1648) and his wife, Hester (*d.* 1665), daughter of Daniel Bonnel, was born in November 1643 at his father's house in Strype's Yard (now Stripe Street), off Petticoat Lane, London. In a letter to Dr Knight of 19 January 1729 Strype explained that his father and his ancestors had been 'great sufferers for religion' in their home town of 's-Hertogenbosch, Brabant, and had found it necessary to 'fly for shelter to England' (*GM*, 61/1, 1791, 223). In London the elder Strype had been apprenticed to his uncle Abraham in the Drapers' Company, took his freedom, was naturalized, and set up his own business as a silk throwster, becoming master of the short-lived Silk Throwsters' Company. Hester's grandfather had also fled from Brabant and had settled in Norwich. The Flemish and English branches of the Strype family kept in touch over the years.

Young John grew up in a family with strong nonconformist links on both sides, and after his father's death he came under the influence of his brother-in-law, the presbyterian minister John Johnson. He went to St Paul's School in 1657. On 29 March 1662 he was admitted as a pensioner to Jesus College, Cambridge, holding a Pauline scholarship of £10 p.a. until 1666. However, when in the autumn of 1662 his tutor Edmund Hough refused to subscribe the Act of Uniformity and was ejected from his fellowship, Strype's family thought it best to remove him. With Johnson's help he migrated to St Catharine's College, from where he graduated BA early in 1666. That autumn, in accordance with his late father's wish, he was ordained in London. He proceeded MA in 1669.

Parish duties In 1669, after a brief period as curate of the poor parish of Theydon Bois, he was licensed in November as priest and curate of Low Leyton, Essex, and instituted as vicar in 1674, a position which he held for the rest of his life. In 1678 he moved into a new house erected at vestry expense and in 1681 married Susannah, daughter of Edward Lowe of Oxfordshire. Two of their four daughters survived infancy: Susannah (*b.* 1686), who later married James Crawforth, and Hester (1687–1711). In later years he

John Strype (1643–1737), by George Vertue, pubd 1733

contributed to and oversaw substantial repairs to the church.

Strype had welcomed the Restoration, but like many clergymen he found his loyalty to a Roman Catholic monarch tested too far when James II issued his declaration of indulgence in April 1687. After consulting local colleagues Strype disobeyed the instruction to read it in his church. After the revolution of 1688 he was rewarded for his loyalty to the protestant establishment and to the new regime by a lectureship at Hackney, held from 1689 to 1724. His earlier support for Henry Compton, bishop of London, led to his institution as rural dean of Barking, and in 1711 Archbishop Tenison added the sinecure rectory of West Tarring, Sussex, to which Strype journeyed annually to preach. Strype's income derived from rents of the property inherited from his father, from his own writing, and from boarding and educating children. He was instrumental in establishing a free school in Low Leyton using money from a local benefactor; the first students arrived in 1711 and Strype, as one of the trustees, kept a close eye on progress.

As rural dean Strype was expected to acquaint clergymen with the bishop's orders and to supervise enforcement of his directives. Before parliamentary elections he had to instruct clergymen to exert their influence in favour of the designated candidates for Essex; in this role, and to a lesser extent as minister, he moved among whig churchmen and other influential figures, thus becoming involved in contemporary political and ecclesiastical controversies.

Biographical works Strype's principal pursuits were the collection of sixteenth-century family papers and other documents, and the writing of histories. At the start of his *Life of … Sir John Cheke* he wrote 'my inclinations (I know not how) have carried me now for many years to search more curiously into the Affairs of that Age' (p. 3) but it seems probable that he had been inspired ever since his college years, his first scholarly work being an edition of the works of John Lightfoot (1684), who had been master while he was at St Catharine's, prefaced by a biography derived from papers given to him by Lightfoot's son-in-law. In 1700 he published *Some Genuine Remains of John Lightfoot*. His other study outside the sixteenth century was a biography of his cousin James Bonnell, accountant-general of Ireland, in 1703.

Throughout his life at Low Leyton, Strype crossed the River Lea into London each week to meet and converse with his antiquarian friends and to call on his contacts in the book trade. He drew on sources in the state paper office, the pre-fire Cotton Library, the Petyt manuscripts now in the Inner Temple, Lambeth Palace Library, and Archbishop Parker's papers at Corpus Christi, Cambridge. More valuable documents and records came from the descendants of his subjects, others from fellow antiquarians who assisted him by visiting distant libraries and transcribing documents for him. He was generous in return, but declined to share his information with those whose views displeased him.

Strype's major source was, however, Sir William Hickes of Ruckholt, Essex, great-grandson of Sir Michael Hickes, secretary to William Cecil, Lord Burghley. Sir William had inherited the majority of the family manuscripts and, 'through a combination of circumstance and chicanery' (Zinberg, 126–7) Strype obtained and kept the entire collection. An arrangement was made that Hickes would give part of these manuscripts to Strype and lend the remainder to the publisher Richard Chiswell, to be transcribed and edited by Strype for publication and ultimately returned to Hickes. Strype duly sent his annotated manuscripts to Chiswell, who then decided that the project would be too costly. He cancelled the publication and refused the £50 commission agreed to Strype. But in 1699 Hickes was declared insane and as the Hickes relatives were unaware of the agreement Strype kept everything, seeking later to justify his actions in his will. The papers of the martyrologist John Foxe were lent to Strype in the 1680s by William Willys of Hackney, executor to one of Foxe's descendants, and Strype retained them after the death in 1701 of Foxe's last descendant. They were included when Robert Harley bought some of Strype's collection, paying what he regarded as an exorbitant price.

Strype was fifty when his first biography, *Memorials of Thomas Cranmer* (1694), appeared, to be followed by *The Life of the Learned Sir Thomas Smith* (1698), *Historical Collections of* the *Life and Acts of John Aylmer, Lord Bishop of London* (1701), and other narratives and biographies of the Tudor period. His *Life of the Learned Sir John Cheke* (1705) was a major study, demonstrating a deep appreciation of Cheke's life and his importance, based on a commanding knowledge of a wide range of original sources.

Strype's *History of the Life and Acts of Edmund Grindal*, published in 1710, achieved excellent sales, having been brought forward to take advantage of the controversy stirred up the previous year by Henry Sacheverell, who had published a sermon fiercely denouncing the prelates of his own day under cover of an attack on Grindal. It was followed by Strype's best-known work, *The Life and Acts of Matthew Parker, Archbishop of Canterbury* (1711). These ecclesiastical biographies were didactic in purpose and intended to defend the reputation of the Church of England against criticism from those who denied that it was a true church and others who objected to its relationship to the state.

Meanwhile, in the three volumes of his *Ecclesiastical Memorials* (1721) he covered the reigns of Henry VIII, Edward VI, and Mary Tudor; in the four volumes of *Annals of the Reformation* (1709–31) the reign of Elizabeth. The *Memorials* are probably his most important work because subsequent historians have focused their attention on those documents which Strype chose to include. His chronological range is remarkable, and the quality of his transcriptions generally good for its day. Strype also annotated the section on Mary Tudor for White Kennet's *Complete History of England*, and published six of his own sermons delivered between 1689 and 1729.

The *Survey of London* Strype was approached by the publishers Richard Chiswell and Thomas Horne to provide yet another revised version of John Stow's much admired *Survey of London* (1598). An agreement was drawn up whereby Strype would receive 43 guineas, his expenses, and six bound copies of the finished work. The *Survey* had been repeatedly revised and enlarged in order to keep up with the changing aspect of the post-fire city, now much expanded and altered in its religion and other ways. Strype immediately set about transcribing documents from the London archives and in 1703 Awnsham Churchill joined the agreement as senior partner, and Strype's payment was increased to £103. There was co-operation from the city livery companies and the clergy, urged on by Bishop Henry Compton, and also from the librarians of Lambeth Palace and the Tower. Among the many private individuals who offered help were the Yorkshire antiquary Ralph Thoresby, who had been in correspondence for some years before his first visit to Strype on 22 January 1709, and Humphrey Wanley, librarian to the Harleian collection in which Stow's manuscript now reposed. Although Strype had arranged most of the work by 1707, and the engravings had been prepared, it was set aside after the publication of Edward Hatton's *New View of London* in 1708, which seemed to cover much the same ground and was considerably smaller and cheaper. Strype forfeited £71 of his fee, and perhaps had no one to blame but himself as he had allowed work on his biographies to take

up much of his time. Finally, once the defects of Hatton's book were acknowledged another agreement in November 1716 led to the *Survey*'s publication at the end of 1720. Strype made no changes beyond inserting some current information on titled people, lord mayors, and city charities.

Unlike its predecessors Strype's *Survey* did not aim to be a pocket guide, with its listings and tables of figures (although he included the obligatory and now outdated list of carriers), but rather an updated edition of a celebrated Elizabethan text. It filled two folio volumes, embellished with high quality engravings and ward maps, and cost 6 guineas. The print run was probably more than 500 copies; it was reprinted in 1754. Strype included what he believed to have been Stow's entire original text, which had by this time been conflated with the 1618 and 1633 additions of Anthony Munday. His own additions, where he had identified gaps in Stow's narrative and where the passage of time demanded them, were clearly identified as such in the margins. Inevitably his own protestant convictions and his abhorrence of popery led him to be selective and even emphatic in the space allocated to the provision of almshouses and other charitable donations, and in the details of sermons and services held within the city. Political events, such as the defeat of the Armada, the civil war, the Jacobite period, and the return to an assured protestantism all called for judgemental comment. Strype was however one of three editorial voices writing in the first person and the present tense. To quote Merritt, 'By this stage the *Survey* has a multiple personality, switching with little warning from nostalgic Elizabethan antiquary [Stow] to triumphalist Jacobean pageant-master [Munday] to diligent post-Restoration recorder of events [Strype] and back again' (Merritt, 87).

Later years In 1720 Wanley was alerted by reports that Strype had suffered a stroke, and he arranged for John Wyat, a bookseller of St Paul's Churchyard, to keep a discreet eye on Strype's health and collections. Wanley's foresight was rewarded with a substantial collection of manuscripts now in the Harleian collection in the British Library; his own correspondence with Strype is in Cambridge University Library.

In the event Strype outlived his wife and daughters. A visitor to the Low Leyton parsonage in March 1733 found him busy in his study, 'turned ninety, yet very brisk and well, with only a decay of sight and memory' (letter, Samuel Knight to Zacharias Grey, 24 March 1733; Nichols, *Illustrations*, 4.327). He continued to collect and copy materials in the last years of his life, but by 1733 acknowledged that failing eyesight prevented him from bringing his projected lives of Lord Burghley and John Foxe to the press. In his later years Strype lived at Hackney, Middlesex, with his granddaughter Susannah, who was married to Thomas Harris, a surgeon. He died at Hackney on 11 December 1737 and was buried at Leyton, having composed his own Latin epitaph.

Strype had made money by his writings; he also had an income from his freehold property in and around Strype's Yard, which had come through his late wife's jointure,

86167

plus two houses near Well Close, his stock in the Bank of England, and his East India Company bonds. In his will, written in 1732, he left almost everything to Susannah and Thomas Harris, apart from several charitable donations to the poor of those parishes with which he had been connected. He also gave his version of why Sir William Hickes's papers were still in his keeping, explaining that the bookseller Richard Chiswell had passed them over to assess their suitability for printing, but that Chiswell had died before this had been accomplished and without having paid Strype the agreed £50 for his work. He identified bundles of papers that should now be passed to Chiswell's son.

Posthumous reputation Writing in 1975 Cargill Thompson remarked that 'even today ... the twenty-five volumes of his works in the Clarendon Press reissues of the 1820s are still a standard source for the study of English church history' (p. 237), and his biographies of Cheke, Cranmer, Parker, and Grindal are consulted both for what he has to say about his subjects and for his quotation or transcription of sources. Yet by providing valuable transcriptions of manuscripts now lost or never printed elsewhere Strype has inevitably channelled the interests of historians who in recent times have begun to remark on his neglect of chronology, his want of critical sense, and his transcriptions which were often silently abridged or poorly referenced. Strype followed the contemporary practice of arranging his materials by year, writing in the form of annals. His habit of gathering and including irrelevant material, together with his lack of critical analysis of his sources, were in keeping with the historiographical practice of his time.

Strype himself believed that his works had made a major contribution to existing historical knowledge, that they were in no way derivative, but filled the gaps in ecclesiastical histories of the sixteenth century. He intended that his readers would learn about the nature of the Reformation, how it had come about and its participating figures, thereby uniting protestants at home and abroad in a better understanding. He regularly protested his own honesty as a sincere lover of truth, preferring, as he often claimed, to go as near the fountainhead as possible to draw his material, and to leave the original wording of his sources, including original documents in his appendices, to convince his readers. But his claim to be unbiased was naïve in that he ignored the bias arising by his selection of sources.   G. H. Martin and Anita McConnell

Sources C. Zinberg, 'John Strype and the sixteenth-century portrait of an Anglican historian', PhD diss., University of Chicago, 1968 • J. F. Merritt, 'The reshaping of Stow's *Survey*: Munday, Strype, and the protestant city', *Imagining early modern London*, ed. J. F. Merritt (2001), 52–88 • 'Extracts from Mr John Strype's letters to the Rev. Tho. Baker', *GM*, 1st ser., 61 (1791), 223 • will, PRO, PROB 11/686, sig. 287 • J. J. Morrison, 'Strype's Stow, the 1720 edition of "A survey of London"', *London Journal*, 3 (1977), 40–54 • [J. Hunter], ed., *Letters of eminent men, addressed to Ralph Thoresby*, 2 vols. (1832) • W. D. J. Cargill Thompson, 'John Strype as a source for the study of sixteenth-century English church history', *The materials, sources and methods of ecclesiastical history*, ed. D. Baker, SCH, 11 (1975), 237–47

Archives BL, Harley MSS 416–426, 427–428, 431, 433–435, 590, 6202, 6995–6998, 7002 • BL, collections and papers, Lansdowne MSS 93/28, 114–116, 119–122, 388–389, 446, 819, 1045, 1055, 1195–1197 • BL, corresp., Add. MSS 5831, 5836, 5840, 5852–5853, 5866 • CUL, corresp., Add. MSS 1–10, 2508 | Essex RO, Chelmsford, corresp. with William Holman

Likenesses G. Vertue, line engraving (after unknown artist), BM, NPG; repro. in Strype, *Ecclesiastical memoirs* (1733) [*see illus.*]

Strzelecki, Sir Paul Edmund de (1797–1873), explorer in Australia, was born on 20 July 1797 at Gluszyna, near Poznań, in (Prussian) Poland, the son of Francis Strzelecki, of a family of Polish knights which can be traced back to 1391, and his wife, Anna, *née* Raczynski. Between 1810 and 1814 he was educated probably at the Piarist Fathers college, Warsaw. He became the plenipotentiary of Prince Francis Sapieha's estates, but following a legal dispute an embittered Strzelecki left his native country, never to return. Being a Polish nobleman or *szlachcic* he was often referred to as 'the Count', although he did not use the title himself. He was in England from 1831 until 1834 and then travelled extensively through North and South America, where he engaged in geological and mineralogical investigations as well as recording his chemical analyses of soils and of wheat growing.

In 1838 Strzelecki visited the Marquesas, Hawaii (where he made a scientific appraisal of the crater of Kilauea), Tahiti, and New Zealand before arriving in Sydney on 25 April 1839. It was Strzelecki's aim, and his achievement, to formulate a *Physical Description of New South Wales and Van Diemen's Land*. His book of that title was published in London in 1845, the result of research throughout the colony over a period of four years in which he walked thousands of miles pursuing his subject. At the same time he produced a giant geological map of the area of his travels.

Strzelecki's first excursion was westward over the Blue Mountains. During September to November 1839 he visited Mount Hay and its vicinity and the country further west to Bathurst and the Wellington caves. In these travels he discovered the first authenticated specimens of silver and gold. One of his letters records that, when he handed specimens of the gold to Sir George Gipps, the governor of New South Wales—'specimens both representing the metal as attached to the rock, and as disintegrated from it'—the governor considered its discovery more a mineralogical curiosity than an economic asset. He entreated Strzelecki not to say anything about its existence, for fear of creating an 'unnecessary perturbation' in the colony.

Strzelecki's second excursion was to the area south of the Monaro, still blank on the map. He joined with James McArthur (the son of Hannibal McArthur) to explore it—both men sharing the expenses. Strzelecki left Sydney on 22 December 1839. On 2 March 1840, from Hannibal McArthur's station Ellerslie, west of Tumut, the combined party set off to the south. A side excursion took Strzelecki and McArthur, on 12 March 1840, to the roof of Australia, and Strzelecki to its highest point. He named it and the massif Mount Kosciusko after the Polish patriot Tadeusz Kosciuszko. The party then journeyed into the area Strzelecki named Gippsland. The portion between the Tambo and Macalister rivers had been probed by Angus McMillan

Sir Paul Edmund de Strzelecki (1797–1873), by unknown photographer

weeks before, but Strzelecki broke new ground through rugged country from the Macalister to Western Port, the last section through the Strzelecki Ranges causing the party considerable distress.

On reaching Melbourne the results of the exploration were announced and, after recuperating, Strzelecki left for Van Diemen's Land on 10 July 1840. There he was well looked after by Governor Sir John Franklin and his wife, Jane. He spent two years exploring the island to great scientific effect, making three excursions and cruises to adjoining areas before returning to New South Wales in October 1842. Following a further excursion from Port Stephens, he left Sydney on 22 April 1843 to arrive in London on 24 October 1843, after visiting the Orient and Egypt.

A naturalized British subject from November 1845, Strzelecki received many honours—the founder's medal of the Royal Geographical Society on 25 May 1846, a CB on 21 November 1848, FRGS in May 1853, FRS in June 1853, the honorary degree of DCL from the University of Oxford on 20 June 1860, and KCMG on 30 June 1869. He was a friend of Florence Nightingale, Lord Sidney Herbert, Antony Panizzi, and W. E. Gladstone. Some of his fame rested on philanthropical work of this later period, including that as central agent of the British Relief Fund formed for the great famine in Ireland in 1846–9. He is honoured too by some dozen geographical names, including the Strzelecki Ranges in Victoria and the Strzelecki Peaks on Flinders Island, off Tasmania. He died of cancer at his home, 23 Savile Row, London, on 6 October 1873 and was buried in Kensal Green cemetery.   ALAN E. J. ANDREWS

Sources L. Paszkowski, 'Sir Paul Edmund Strzelecki: explorer and scientist', *Poles in Australia and Oceania, 1790–1940* (1987) [Polish orig., *Polacy w Australii i Oceanii, 1790–1940* (Sydney, 1962)] · L. Paszkowski, *Sir Paul Edmund de Strzelecki: reflections on his life* (Melbourne, 1997) · P. E. de Strzelecki, *Physical description of New South Wales and Van Diemen's Land* (1845) · A. E. J. Andrews, 'Kosciusko ascended', *Kosciusko: the mountain in history* (Canberra, 1991) · A. E. J. Andrews, 'A flower and a giant map', *Kosciusko: the mountain in history* (Canberra, 1991) · D. F. Branagan, 'Strzelecki's geological map of southeastern Australia: an eclectic synthesis', *Historical Records of Australian Science*, 6 (1984–7), 375–92 · A. E. J. Andrews, 'Strzelecki's ascent of Mount Kosciusko: another view', *Royal Australian Historical Society Journal and Proceedings*, 74 (1988), 159–66 · A. E. J. Andrews, 'Strzelecki's route 1840 from the Murray River to Melbourne', *Royal Australian Historical Society Journal and Proceedings*, 77 (1992), 50–62 · W. L. Havard, 'Sir Paul Edmund de Strzelecki', *Royal Australian Historical Society Journal and Proceedings*, 26 (1940), 20–97 · G. Rawson, *The Count: Paul Edmund Strzelecki; explorer and scientist* (1953) · L. Paszkowski, *Social background of Sir Paul Strzelecki and Joseph Conrad* (1980) · W. Slabczynski, *Pawel Edmund Strzelecki: Pisma Wybrane* (1960) · Gladstone, *Diaries* · DNB

Archives BGS, geological map of New South Wales · Mitchell L., NSW · State Library of Victoria, Melbourne | BL, corresp. with W. E. Gladstone, Add MSS 44385–44440 · LUL, corresp. with Lord Overstone

Likenesses photograph, State Library of Victoria, Melbourne, La Trobe picture collection · photograph, Mitchell L., NSW [*see illus.*]

Wealth at death under £10,000: probate, 15 Oct 1873, *CGPLA Eng. & Wales*

Stuart. *See also* Steuart, Stewart.

Stuart. For this title name *see* individual entries under Stuart; *see also* Wortley, Charles Beilby Stuart-, Baron Stuart of Wortley (1851–1926) [*see under* Wortley, James Archibald Stuart-, first Baron Wharncliffe (1776–1845)].

Stuart, (Herbert) Akroyd [Ackroyd] (1864–1927), mechanical engineer, was born at 37 Victoria Street, Halifax, Yorkshire, on 28 January 1864, the second of six children of Charles Stuart, a pattern maker, and his wife, Ann, daughter of Jonathan Ackroyd, a worsted cloth weaver of Luddenden near Halifax. His father was born in Paisley, near Glasgow, but was working in Halifax by 1858.

At the age of twelve Stuart was sent to St Bartholomew's Grammar School in Newbury, Berkshire. Shortly afterwards the family moved to Fenny Stratford, where his father had acquired the Bletchley ironworks, manufacturing steam engines and boilers. On leaving school Stuart joined his father as an engineering apprentice, and also worked for a time in the mechanical engineering laboratories of the City and Guilds Technical College in Finsbury, London. His father had installed a Spiel petroleum engine to drive some of the machinery in his workshops, and Stuart was inspired to work on the problem of developing an internal combustion engine that would run on heavier (and safer) grades of fuel oil. He took out his first two engine patents in 1886, and having progressively improved the design to give more complete combustion and avoid pre-ignition, in 1890 he was granted two patents for a hot-bulb oil engine, two years before Rudolf Diesel's first English patent for his compression-ignition oil engine. A small number of Stuart's engines had already been built and tested in Bletchley by 1890, on one occasion by the chief engineer of Richard Hornsby & Sons of Grantham, who soon afterwards became the sole licensees, manufacturers, and developers of the Hornsby–Akroyd oil engine.

The engine was very simple, efficient, and reliable in operation, with the minor disadvantage that the vaporizer required preheating for a few minutes before the engine could be started; when running, it retained sufficient heat to ignite the injected fuel. Essentially slow running and of limited horsepower, the majority of the many thousands of engines made by Hornsby between 1892 and 1922 were used as stationary engines for agricultural and general workshop purposes. They were also used to power the first oil-engined tractor and the first practical oil-engined locomotive, both in 1896. A 20 hp Hornsby–Akroyd engine powered the world's first caterpillar tractor in 1905, but later attempts to match the development of the high-speed diesel engine were unsuccessful.

Stuart was elected a member of the Institution of Mechanical Engineers in 1901. A few years previously he had emigrated to Australia, where he involved himself in the design and manufacture of the Akroyd patent downdraught gas producer. He evidently resented the fact that the name 'diesel' had come to be applied to virtually every type of oil engine, hot-bulb (ignition) as well as compression-ignition, and in 1923 he asked the institution to declare that henceforth the word diesel should only be used to describe oil engines operating on the compression-ignition principle, hot-bulb engines to be known as akroyds. The institution, however, did not feel able to recommend such a change after the word diesel had been in universal use for so long.

Stuart died in Claremont, Western Australia, on 19 February 1927, a disappointed if not embittered man, and in his will directed that all his papers should be burned. His body was brought home and buried in the Akroyd cemetery, Halifax. RONALD M. BIRSE, *rev.*

Sources *Institution of Mechanical Engineers: Proceedings* (1927), 577 · R. Wailes, 'The early history of Akroyd Stuart's oil engine', *Transactions* [Newcomen Society], 48 (1976–7), 103–110 · private information (1993) · L. Day and I. McNeil, eds., *Biographical dictionary of the history of technology* (1996)

Stuart, Alexander (1673?–1742), physician and natural philosopher, was probably born in the north-east of Scotland, possibly in Aberdeen. Practically nothing is known of his early life. One of his name graduated MA from Marischal College, Aberdeen, in 1691. By 1698 he was practising as a surgeon–apothecary, although where is not known. In 1701 he followed the path of many other Scots surgeons and signed on as a ship's surgeon. He was on the trader *London* from 1701 to 1704 and on the *Europe* from 1704 to 1707.

While at sea Stuart corresponded with Hans Sloane (who may have been responsible for his getting a place), sending him natural history specimens. A few of Stuart's reports appeared in the *Philosophical Transactions*. Stuart also kept detailed journals of his surgical cases on the *Europe*. After a brief sojourn in Ireland in 1708 he settled for a time in London, where he continued to practise as a surgeon. The following year, with the sponsorship of Sloane and Sir David Hamilton, one of the queen's physicians, Stuart entered medical school at the University of Leiden, where he matriculated on 14 December 1709, aged thirty-six. While at Leiden Stuart continued his lifelong habit of compiling notebooks of medical cases and prescriptions. He greatly admired Boerhaave, his professor at Leiden, and kept Sloane informed of his activities. He graduated MD on 22 June 1711 with a dissertation 'De structura et motu musculari'. The study of muscular motion continued to be of interest and he returned to it as a topic of research later in life.

Upon completing his Leiden degree Stuart travelled to Flanders for a time to serve with the British army, but by 1712 he was back in London and pursuing a medical career. In the highly competitive London environment he made at first slow progress, earning only £100 in 1713; a decade later he would earn that much in a month. On 30 November 1714 he was elected to the Royal Society, and in December 1719 he was named first practising physician for the new Westminster Hospital. In June 1720 he took the examination for the licence of the Royal College of Physicians of London, and was admitted a licentiate on 25 June.

Stuart was an early advocate of inoculation for smallpox, conducting several trials among his patients in 1725. William Douglass's 1722 anti-inoculation pamphlet, *The Abuses and Scandals of some Late Pamphlets in Favour of Inoculation of the Small Pox* was addressed to Stuart. In 1728 Stuart was awarded the MD from Cambridge, *comitiis regiae*, and named one of Queen Caroline's physicians-in-ordinary. The Royal College of Physicians admitted him as a fellow on 2 September 1728, and he served as censor in 1732 and 1741. In October 1733 he led the secession from the Westminster Hospital in a dispute over a new site; he and his colleagues founded St George's Hospital, where he served until 9 July 1736.

Despite his apparent success as a practitioner Stuart was continually in financial difficulties. He borrowed money to invest in the South Sea Bubble in the early 1720s and lost heavily, and in 1727 was forced to the expedient of turning over his assets to his wife with the exception of his manuscripts, which he hoped to sell to pay off some of his debts. He had married Susannah, whose surname was probably Wishaw, in January 1726; she owned property in the parish of St Paul's, Covent Garden. The union was apparently childless.

In the late 1720s Stuart resumed the research in physiology he had begun two decades earlier, and contributed several papers to the *Philosophical Transactions* on the role of bile in digestion and on the existence of the nervous fluid. He was invited to give the first Croonian lecture on muscular motion at the Royal Society in 1738, and in the same year he published a revised version of his MD thesis on that topic which won a prize from the Academy of Bordeaux. Stuart was also a foreign member of the French Academy of Sciences. The Royal Society awarded him its Copley medal in 1740 in recognition of his research on muscles, and he delivered the Croonian lecture again in 1740 and 1741. Against the prevailing emphasis on waves and ethers, Stuart, following his mentor, Boerhaave, and also his fellow Scot, Archibald Pitcairne, argued in favour of a more strictly mechanical system to explain muscular motion and nervous activity. He supported this concept of vascular hydraulics with an extensive series of experiments and observations. These included microscopic examination, injection of vessels, and comparison of the structure of blood vessels and nerves. He demonstrated his principle of muscular motion with a decapitated frog; pushing with a probe on its exposed spinal column made its legs twitch, an indication, said Stuart, that the nervous fluid was pushed into the muscles. The spinal frog experiment was important to later studies of reflex action by Whytt and Haller, although they did not agree with Stuart's theories.

Stuart died on 15 September 1742. His will, written only a month before his death, chronicles his continuing indebtedness; he still owed money to the people he had borrowed from in 1720. He assigned Henry Baker and Hugh Fraser, chaplain of St George's Hospital, as executors and asked Baker to oversee the publication by subscription of his remaining scientific papers in the hope that this would help pay his debts. However, Baker and Fraser refused to act as executors, and it was left to Susannah Stuart to sell her husband's manuscripts for very small sums. William Hunter eventually acquired several of them and they are among the Hunterian MSS at the University of Glasgow. ANITA GUERRINI

Sources G. Peachey, *History of St. George's Hospital* (1914) · U. Glas. L., Hunter MSS · BL, Sloane MSS 4038–4040, 4042, 4045, 4056 · R. W. Innes Smith, *English-speaking students of medicine at the University of Leyden* (1932) · private information (2004) [Helen Brock] · will, PRO, PROB 11/723, sig. 23 · Munk, *Roll*

Archives RCP Lond. | BL, corresp., Sloane MSS 4038–4040, 4042, 4045–4056 · U. Glas. L., Hunter MSS

Wealth at death owed at least £3000 from loans made at time of South Sea Bubble in 1720: will, PRO, PROB 11/723, sig. 23

Stuart, Sir Alexander [Alick] (1824–1886), merchant and politician in Australia, was born on 21 March 1824 in Edinburgh, one of the nine children of Alexander Stuart, writer to the signet, and his wife, Mary, née McKnight. Alick, as he was known, was educated at Edinburgh Academy (1832–5) and at the city's university (1837). Having embarked on a commercial career, he went into a merchant's office in Glasgow, then to Belfast as manager of the North of Ireland Linen Mills, and in 1845 joined Carr Tagore & Co. in Calcutta, India. Finding the climate there debilitating, he moved to New Zealand in 1850, visited New South Wales, and spent some time on the Victorian goldfields. He eventually settled in Sydney, where he became assistant secretary to the Bank of New South Wales in December 1852; in 1854 he was made secretary and inspector. On 10 November 1853, at Narellan, he married Christiana Eliza (d. 1889), the daughter of John Wood RN.

Stuart's abilities attracted the notice of the head of the firm of Robert Towns & Co., which he joined in 1855 as a partner (senior partner from 1873), and he soon became prominent in commercial circles. He was a director of the Bank of New South Wales (for seventeen years between 1855 and 1879) and of a number of insurance and mining companies, and a committee member of the Sydney chamber of commerce; he invested heavily in Queensland pastoral stations.

Although he had been brought up as a member of the Episcopal Church of Scotland, in Sydney Stuart served on the diocesan, provincial, and general synods of the Church of England, sat on the cathedral chapter, and was a trustee of church lands. In the 1870s he championed the retention of state aid to denominational schools and

helped to form the Church of England Defence Association. Having been asked by Bishop Frederick Barker to stand for parliament, in December 1874 he entered the legislative assembly for East Sydney. A free-trader, he was slow to action, but dogged, and proved an effective debater. From 8 February 1876 until the ministry fell on 21 March 1877 he was treasurer in the cabinet of Sir John Robertson. He was re-elected for East Sydney, but resigned in March 1879, when he was appointed agent-general for the colony in London. Unable to unravel his own and Towns & Co.'s financial difficulties, he did not take up the post. Having managed to avoid bankruptcy (partly through the Coal Cliff Coal Company), at the general election of 1880 he was returned for Illawarra. In 1882 he became leader of the opposition, defeating the Parkes–Robertson ministry on the Land Bill of 1882. The government lost at the polls, and on 5 January 1883 Stuart became premier. He at once appointed a commission of inquiry into the land laws, and in October brought in a land bill to control the indiscriminate selection and sale of crown land, to give some security of tenure to squatters, and to establish local land boards and courts. This was discussed with heat and acrimony during the record thirteen-month session and eventually passed into law in October 1884. Stuart had established the Aborigines protection board in 1883 and carried an act (1883) to regulate the civil service. He supported the annexation of eastern New Guinea by Queensland in 1884 and presided over the intercolonial convention which established the ineffective federal council of Australasia.

Unable to delegate and 'imprudently industrious', Stuart had a sudden stroke early in 1885; after holidaying in New Zealand he resumed office in May and was made KCMG in June, but he was so enfeebled that on 6 October 1885 he retired. He was nominated to the legislative council, and later in the year went to London as executive commissioner for the colony for the Indian and Colonial Exhibition of 1886; but he died of typhoid fever on 16 June 1886 at 52 Stanhope Gardens, Kensington, after the opening of the exhibition. His wife, son, and a daughter survived him. He was buried at Christ Church, Roxeth, near Harrow. MARTHA RUTLEDGE

Sources *AusDB* · Alexander Stuart, letters, Mitchell L., NSW, MS 1279 · Robert Towns & Co., Parkes, Loftus, Cowper MSS, Mitchell L., NSW · Shepherd Smith–Donald Lernach MSS, Westpac Archives, Sydney · R. F. Holder, *Bank of New South Wales: a history*, 1 (1970) · Church of England diocese of Sydney, votes and proceedings of Synod (1866–84) · *Sydney Morning Herald* (18 June 1886) · *The Times* (17 June 1886) · *The Times* (21 June 1886) · *Daily Telegraph* [Sydney] (23 Sept 1884), 6 · Colonial Office papers, PRO, 201/*581 f52, *588 f45, 597–603, *passim*, *598, *f52, *f358 · [T. Henderson and P. F. Hamilton-Grierson], eds., *The Edinburgh Academy register* (1914) · parish register (births and marriages), Edinburgh, 1824 · marriage register · d. cert.

Wealth at death £83,546 13s. 2d.—assets: probate, New South Wales · £160: probate, 1 Feb 1887, *CGPLA Eng. & Wales*

Stuart, Alexander John Mackenzie, Baron Mackenzie-Stuart (1924–2000), lawyer and judge, was born at 37 Queen's Road, Aberdeen, on 18 November 1924. He was the only son and elder child of Alexander Mackenzie Stuart KC (d. c.1934) and his wife, Amy Margaret Dean (d.

c.1980). His father was professor of Scots law in the University of Aberdeen, and author of *Law of Trusts* (1932), a standard textbook on trust law in Scotland. Jack, as he was always known, went to Fettes College, and in 1942 joined the Royal Engineers. After an engineering course at Sidney Sussex College, Cambridge, he saw service in northern Europe and then Burma, with a further period dismantling mines in England. In 1947 he returned to Sidney Sussex to read law, obtaining first-class honours. He then took an LLB degree (with distinction) at the University of Edinburgh, and was called to the Scottish bar in 1951. Soon thereafter, on 7 August 1952, he married Anne Burtholme Millar (*b.* 1930), a fellow graduate in law, who was to play an important role in his professional career—most significantly (as he said in his preface to his 1977 Hamlyn lectures) in 'keeping my interest in the law of the Communities alive at a time when it seemed of remote concern to the practising lawyer in the United Kingdom'.

The practising bar in Scotland in 1951 was very small. However, the new post-war generation was outstandingly able. Tradition and necessity alike demanded that an advocate accepted work of all kinds. This non-specialist approach suited Mackenzie Stuart's character: he was naturally open-minded, with a commitment to justice and underlying principles, not to causes or sides. It also suited his talents: he was meticulous and scholarly, but always realistic. Along with his friendliness and charm, his abilities brought a wide-ranging practice.

Even a generalist's practice will become concentrated on certain areas. Mackenzie Stuart found himself increasingly engaged in the fields of tax and estate duty, trusts, and commercial work. None the less he kept a large reparation and planning practice. What was missing, to his regret, was criminal work. On becoming a judge, he claimed that he only found his way into the high court in Glasgow, where he had never appeared as counsel, because the circuit judge was still greeted with trumpets.

In 1970 the regard in which Mackenzie Stuart was held by the bar was expressed in his election as keeper of the Advocates' Library. In 1971 he was appointed to the part-time judicial post of sheriff principal of Aberdeen, Kincardine, and Banff. Less formally, his position in the practising profession was significant. He had been an outstanding 'devil-master' to a series of intrants to the bar. And after he took silk in 1963 his influence spread to every junior advocate lucky enough to be instructed with him. The custom of using one's home as chambers for consultations always gave scope for informal after-hours contact. But at the Mackenzie Stuarts' there was a welcome to devils and juniors which earned both Jack and Anne an affection and influence which were unrivalled.

In June 1972, Mackenzie Stuart was appointed to the Scottish bench, with the judicial title of Lord Mackenzie Stuart. That would have come in the normal course of events—but the course of events in 1972 was not normal. The appointment was simply a precursor to his next move. Having acceded to the EEC, Britain needed a judge and an advocate-general for the European Court of Justice. That one or other should be from Scotland was seen as important, if not self-evident, in Scotland. The point seemed less clear to the political and legal hierarchy in England, but it was conceded. Mackenzie Stuart was rapidly identified as the appropriate Scot. Initially he was to have the apparently more junior post of advocate-general. Views altered belatedly. He was to be the judge. After resigning his briefly held seat on the Scottish bench, he took up his European post in January 1973.

National sensitivities apart, it probably mattered little which of the United Kingdom jurisdictions was represented, or how. But Mackenzie Stuart's typically Scottish regard for principle, and his natural acceptance that different systems may have shared aims, were advantageous in the first British judge to join a court which, if multifarious, was also long-established, collegiate, and decidedly 'continental'.

Interest in community law had been fostered in Edinburgh by Professor J. D. B. Mitchell. Both Mackenzie Stuart and his wife had become involved in this important but unfashionable endeavour. Their wider interest in Europe, and in particular France, also lay behind Mackenzie Stuart's appointment. But his French was not really fluent, and his knowledge of community law included little that was directly applicable. Moreover, there were in effect two jobs to be done. In addition to the direct burdens of casework, there was the vital but delicate task of winning respect for British legal approaches to procedure and substance, and enabling the court to draw upon these. That Mackenzie Stuart, with J.-P. Warner QC as advocate-general, was able slowly to effect this change was a crucial, and very personal, achievement. Its full extent was revealed most clearly in 1984, when he was elected president of the court.

Mackenzie Stuart remained as president until 1988. With new member states, the court had grown; its workload and backlog were becoming overwhelming. However, both the replacement of the inadequate court buildings, and the creation of a new court of first instance, had been achieved. Both were crucial, and both substantially due to the president's own labours.

On retirement Mackenzie Stuart received a peerage (and, in his title, a hyphen) as Baron Mackenzie-Stuart of Dean. He had already been elected an honorary fellow of Sidney Sussex, and an honorary bencher of the Middle Temple and of King's Inns, Dublin. He had received honorary doctorates from the universities of Stirling, Exeter, Edinburgh, Glasgow, Aberdeen, Cambridge, and Birmingham. A fine portrait by Alberto Morrocco RSA was commissioned by the Faculty of Advocates in 1988, and is in the faculty's collection in Parliament House in Edinburgh. Among other honours he received the grand cross of the Luxembourg Grand Ducal Ordre de la Couronne de Chêne. In 1989 he was awarded the Prix Bech for services to Europe.

In 1975 Mackenzie Stuart had delivered the British Academy's Maccabaean lecture, 'The "non-contractual" liability of the European Economic Community', and in 1977 the twenty-ninth series of Hamlyn lectures, published as

The European Communities and the Rule of Law. In his retirement he was in demand for arbitration work, but continued also to share and spread his own enthusiastic understanding of European affairs.

After moving to Luxembourg, the Mackenzie Stuarts acquired a property near Les Vans, in the Ardèche, where over the years they created a beautiful house and garden, a much loved second home. There and in Edinburgh, Mackenzie Stuart after his retirement pursued his lifelong recreation of studying and collecting French drawings and paintings, and happily completed *A French King at Holyrood* (1995), an absorbing account of the periods spent by Charles X in Edinburgh, both as comte d'Artois and subsequently after his abdication.

Baron Mackenzie-Stuart died in St Columba's Hospice, Edinburgh, on 1 April 2000. He was survived by Lady Mackenzie-Stuart and the four daughters of their marriage.   WILLIAM D. PROSSER

Sources personal knowledge (2004) · private information (2004) [Lady Mackenzie-Stuart] · *WW* · *The Independent* (10 April 2000) · *The Times* (5 April 2000) · *The Scotsman* (6 April 2000) · *Daily Telegraph* (6 April 2000) · b. cert. · d. cert.
Likenesses A. Morrocco, drawing, European Court of Justice, Luxembourg · A. Morrocco, oils, Faculty of Advocates, Parliament House, Edinburgh

Stuart [Stewart], **Andrew** [Anders] (*c*.1570–1640), army officer and diplomat in the Swedish service, was born in Scotland, the son of John Stewart of Ochiltree, a soldier who served in the escort of Mary, queen of Scots, and Agneta Forbes. Andrew's brother John (Hans) *Stuart had also migrated to Sweden and gained distinction as a gentleman of the bedchamber at the court of Karl IX in 1604 and inspector-general of all foreign troops in Swedish service by 1609. Their genealogy is interesting in that no John Stewart of Ochiltree can be traced in the Scottish peerage. However, Andrew's godfather was Andrew *Stewart, second Lord Ochiltree, who signed a letter proving Hans Stuart's nobility in 1585. This was accompanied by an open letter from James VI of Scotland that referred to Hans as 'our dear relative'. These documents allowed Hans Stuart to use the same coat of arms as James Stuart, earl of Arran, the second son of Lord Ochiltree, suggesting a relationship which remains elusive.

Andrew Stuart emigrated to Sweden and became a gentleman of the bedchamber at the court of Duke Karl of Södermanland (later King Karl IX) by 1592. He was known in Sweden as Anders the elder to distinguish him from his nephew, who also served in the Swedish army. In reward for his military services Andrew the elder received land in 1599 from Karl IX in Ledingelunda (or Lagerlund), part of the parish of Kärna in Sweden. During this period he also married Elisabet Anrep, daughter of Adolf Anrep and Gertrud von Nieroth, although the exact date remains unclear.

At the beginning of 1600 Stuart became a commander of the Swedish forces at Fellin in Livland and by 1602 he was serving as governor of Dorpat. His administrative duties continued when in 1604 he assumed responsibility for the Norra Möre region of Kalmar. He later received further

lands in Starsäter (renamed Stuartsäter) in Vists parish and Lida in Kvillinge parish.

Stuart continued to serve in the army and became colonel in chief for the Östgöta infantry in 1605. However, he continued to pursue work outside his military life. During the Kalmar War between Sweden and Denmark–Norway (1611–13), Stewart joined the Swedish diplomatic service and acted as their envoy to Russia in 1611. During this period Stuart also maintained contact with the court of James VI and I. Perhaps more surprising is that Stuart also had indirect communication with Christian IV of Denmark–Norway through a Scottish nobleman in Danish service, Andrew Sinclair, governor of the newly conquered Swedish fortress of Kalmar.

Stuart's functions in later life included service in the Swedish fleet. He is recorded as having become a vice-admiral in the fleet of the riksamiral (state admiral) in 1621. He also continued to hold posts on land, acting as master of the court to Pfalzgreve Johan Casimir in 1633. Anders Stuart died on 27 December 1640, apparently from natural causes, and was buried in Vists parish church in Sweden. Together Anders and his wife, Elisabet, had three sons and two daughters: Carl (*c*.1600–1637), Johan Adolf (1603–1666), Anders (d. 1637), Christina (1600–1648), and Catharina (1622–1699). The sons all engaged in Swedish military service and both daughters also married soldiers.   STEVE MURDOCH

Sources J. Berg and B. Lagercrantz, *Scots in Sweden* (1962), 20–21 · C. F. Bricka and J. A. Fridericia, eds., *Kong Christian den fjerdes egenhaendige breve*, 1: *1589–1625* (Copenhagen, 1887–9), 63–5 · G. Elgenstierna, *Den introducerade svenska adelns ättartavlor med tillägg och rättelser*, 9 vols. (1925–36), vol. 7 · T. Fischer, *The Scots in Sweden* (1907), 176 · A. Zettersten, *Svenska flottans historia åren, 1522–1634* (1890)

Stuart, Andrew (1725–1801), lawyer and politician, probably born at Torrance in Lanarkshire, was the second son of Archibald Stuart (d. 1767) of Torrance and Elizabeth, daughter of Sir Andrew Myreton of Gogar. Educated at Edinburgh high school, in 1746 he was apprenticed in his father's law practice, and became a writer to the signet in 1759. An urbane member of the Select Society and the Poker Club, he participated in the intellectual life of Enlightenment Edinburgh, counting David Hume and George Dempster as friends.

Through his Lanarkshire connection Stuart became in 1758 a guardian to the young James, seventh duke of Hamilton, and promoted his claim to the Douglas estates. Having named Hamilton as his heir, the duke of Douglas altered the succession in favour of Archibald Stewart, son of Lady Jane Douglas and her husband, Colonel John Stewart, whom he declared to be his nephew and heir in 1761. Stuart's challenge to this provision failed in the court of session in 1762. Undaunted, he painstakingly gathered evidence in France, the Netherlands, and Germany to prove that Lady Jane Douglas had not given birth to the boy when living in France. During his visits to Paris he impressed the *philosophes*. His proofs convinced the court to decide the succession in the duke of Hamilton's favour in July 1767. During the subsequent appeal to the House of

Lords in January 1769, Stuart and the opposing counsel, Edward Thurlow (later Lord Thurlow) fought a bloodless duel. In February, in a sensational reversal of the court of session's decision in the Douglas cause, Lord Camden, lord chancellor, and Lord Mansfield, lord chief justice, attacked Stuart's integrity as a lawyer. Hume believed he had conducted the contentious case with 'singular Integrity and Ability' (*Letters*, 2.199).

After this débâcle Stuart's friends supported him financially, especially by purchasing the office of king's remembrancer in May 1770, which he held jointly from 1771 until his resignation in 1786. Meanwhile he contested the 1768 election in Lanarkshire for the duke of Hamilton's interest, which he bolstered with the votes of the Lanarkshire estates he helped to purchase for Sir George Colebrooke. In return for favouring Colebrooke's nominee in the Linlithgow burghs election in 1771, he was nominated to the East India Company's commission of inquiry in 1772, only for it to be cancelled. Stuart revenged himself on Lord Mansfield with a savage, privately distributed polemic, *Letters to Lord Mansfield* (1773), which alleged Mansfield's bias towards the Douglas claim. The *Letters* was widely admired, although Samuel Johnson compared it to 'the wailings of a dog that had been licked' (*Ominous Years*, 305).

Stuart held that the vindication of his honour was worth the price it shortly cost him of a place he desired on the Bengal supreme council. Lord North wished to help, but the king demurred, so Stuart obligingly withdrew from the contest. He was already highly effective in the legal transactions regarding freehold votes and the negotiations which underpinned the political interests of his friends and patrons, undertaking frequent journeys for the purpose. On 28 October 1774 he won the Lanarkshire seat. Stuart became a member of Henry Dundas's 'Scotch ministry' and his close ally, sharing with him the office of keeper of the signet from March 1777. When Dundas was rewarded with the sole keepership in 1779, he insisted that Stuart be compensated with a place on the Board of Trade (6 July 1779), and the promise of the lucrative keepership of the register of sasines, which he gained in 1781. His offices and meticulously managed business made him wealthy, allowing him to spend lavishly, especially on his coaches. Boswell, no admirer, noted his 'awkward, stammering vanity' (*Applause of the Jury*, 21).

In 1775 Stuart secured a place in the East India Company for his brother James *Stuart (*d.* 1793), and after his suspension in 1777 Stuart published several letters to the directors of the company and the secretary at war, eloquently justifying his brother's arrest of Lord Pigot, the governor of Madras. He was a regular and assiduous attendee at the Board of Trade. During 1783 he remained friendly with North after his resignation and joined his friends in the coalition, rather than follow Dundas into opposition. Honourably resisting pleas to return to the Dundas interest at the election in 1784, he stood aside to concentrate on his legal and personal business. Before leaving parliament he assisted his brother-in-law Thomas Cochrane, eighth earl of Dundonald, concerning his salt manufacture patent, but as the earl mostly ignored his advice Stuart despaired of mitigating the financially disastrous effects of his scientific enthusiasms.

From 1787 Stuart researched the claims of John Stewart, seventh earl of Galloway, to the chiefship of the Stewarts, at Galloway's request. During 1789 he made discoveries in the Vatican archives concerning the marriages of Robert II, and while in Paris he professed to admire the 'ardent spirit of liberty' (Thorne, 5.306). At his friend Sir William Pulteney's invitation, on 19 July 1790 Stuart re-entered parliament for Pulteney's pocket borough of Weymouth and Melcombe Regis. On 9 October 1790 Stuart married Margaret, daughter of Sir William Stirling of Ardoch, who bore three daughters. In 1796 he inherited the estate of Torrance in Lanarkshire from his brother, and in 1797 the estate of Sir John Stuart of Castlemilk.

Stuart's assiduous research in public and private records in London, Edinburgh, and elsewhere convinced him that the Galloway claim was faulty. In his *Genealogical History of the Stewarts* (1798) he contended that with the failure of the Stewart royal line, the chiefship of the Stewarts would fall to the Stuarts of Castlemilk, coolly defending his claim in 1799. That year he recommended to Henry Dundas that the government relieve the hardships of Henry Stuart, Cardinal York. Andrew Stuart died at his home in Lower Grosvenor Street, London, on 18 May 1801.   TRISTRAM CLARKE

Sources E. Haden-Guest, 'Stuart, Andrew', HoP, *Commons, 1754–90* • R. G. Thorne, 'Stuart, Andrew', HoP, *Commons, 1790–1820* • *DNB* • Stuart MSS, 1746–1801, NL Scot., MSS 5331, 5373, 5379, 5390, 5392, 5394–5396, 5400, 5402, 8325 • *The letters of David Hume*, ed. J. Y. T. Greig, 2 vols. (1932) • *Boswell: the ominous years, 1774–1776*, ed. C. Ryskamp and F. A. Pottle (1963), vol. 8 of *The Yale editions of the private papers of James Boswell*, trade edn (1950–89) • *Boswell: the applause of the jury, 1782–1785*, ed. I. S. Lustig and F. A. Pottle (1981), vol. 12 of *The Yale editions of the private papers of James Boswell*, trade edn (1950–89) • M. Fry, *The Dundas despotism* (1992) • L. de la Torre, *The heir of Douglas* (1953) • A. Stuart, *Genealogical history of the Stewarts* (1798) • Edinburgh commissary court register of testaments, NA Scot., CC8/8/133, fols. 137–50

Archives NL Scot., corresp. and papers • U. Edin. L., corresp. and papers | Lennoxlove House, East Lothian, Hamilton MSS • NA Scot., corresp. and papers relating to the Douglas cause • U. Edin., Laing MSS

Likenesses J. Reynolds, oils, repro. in de la Torre, *Heir of Douglas* • T. Watson, mezzotint (after J. Reynolds), BM, NPG

Wealth at death £600 in moveable goods and outstanding debts owed to him by one debtor: Edinburgh commissary court register of testaments, NA Scot., CC8/8/133, fols. 137–150

Stuart [married name Seymour], **Lady Arabella** [Arbella] (**1575–1615**), noblewoman and royal kinswoman, was the daughter of Charles Stuart, earl of Lennox (1555/6–1576), and his wife, Elizabeth (1554?–1582), daughter of Sir William *Cavendish and his third wife, Elizabeth, *née* Hardwick (from 1567 or 1568, by her fourth marriage, Elizabeth *Talbot, countess of Shrewsbury). Arabella was probably born at Lennox House, the Hackney home of her paternal grandmother, Margaret *Douglas, dowager countess of Lennox. Arabella's parents had met and married in late 1574; she was born by 10 November 1575, when Countess Margaret wrote to the baby's aunt, Mary, queen of Scots,

Lady Arabella Stuart (1575–1615), by John Whittakers senior, 1619

thanking her 'for your good remembrance and bounty to our little daughter' (*CSP Scot.*, 1574–80, 202). After Lady Arabella's father died of tuberculosis in April 1576, his earldom went to a male relative, and when old Lady Lennox died in 1578, her English properties passed to Elizabeth I. Arabella's income had vanished, but she remained of great significance dynastically. She was the first cousin of James VI of Scotland while her grandmother, Lady Lennox, had been Elizabeth's first cousin. The scarcity of royal relatives brought Arabella very close to the thrones of both Scotland and England. Indeed, there were those who argued that she should be Elizabeth's heir if the queen remained childless, since James VI had not been born in England.

After her mother's death in January 1582 Arabella Stuart was brought up in Derbyshire by her maternal grandmother, the formidable Bess of Hardwick. A clever child, she studied Latin, Italian, French, Spanish, Greek, and Hebrew, while Bess and Mary, queen of Scots, a prisoner in the charge of Bess's husband, made strenuous but vain attempts to obtain the Lennox earldom for her. There was, however, another means of securing Arabella's future.

Given her dynastic importance, she was obviously a highly desirable bride, and in 1583 or 1584 Bess arranged her betrothal to Robert, Lord Denbigh, three-year-old son of Robert Dudley, earl of Leicester. When he died in 1584, Arabella was spoken of as a possible bride for James VI himself. Nothing came of that idea, nor was her suggested marriage to Rainutio Farnese, son of the duke of Parma, taken forward. Indeed, as the months went by, it became evident that Elizabeth I had no desire to see Arabella marry and have children, possible rivals for her own throne.

In 1588 Lady Arabella Stuart became one of Elizabeth's ladies in waiting, but when she was seen chatting in a friendly fashion with the queen's favourite, the earl of Essex, she was sent home in disgrace. A portrait of her painted at about that time shows an elaborately dressed girl with reddish fair hair, a heart-shaped face, large, bright, dark blue eyes, and a neat little mouth. She returned to her studies, but as the years went by, she found life in her grandmother's household increasingly restrictive. After a series of bitter quarrels with Bess, she decided to escape. In December 1602 she sent a message to Edward Seymour, first earl of Hertford, telling him that her friends accepted his suggestion that she should marry his grandson and namesake Edward Seymour.

Historians ever since have marvelled at Arabella's lack of judgement in involving herself with the Seymours, the very family with whom she should not have had any dealings. They, too, had a claim to the English throne and Elizabeth would suspect a plot against herself. Hertford instantly denied any involvement and the queen sent Sir Henry Brouncker to question Arabella. He concluded that she was simply attempting to draw attention to her unhappy situation and no action was taken against her. When she announced in January 1603 that she had a secret lover, refused to eat and drink, and finally divulged his identity as the already married James VI, Cecil wrote across the back of one of her agitated letters, 'I think that she hath some vapours on her brain' (Durant, 108).

With the death of Elizabeth I in March 1603, Arabella Stuart's position improved, for on his arrival in England James VI was disposed to be sympathetic to her. Soon afterwards there was an alarming episode when Henry Brooke, Lord Cobham, was discovered plotting to murder James and Cecil, with the notion of marrying Arabella to Thomas Grey, fifteenth Baron Grey of Wilton, and placing her on the throne instead. Cecil knew that Arabella had not been implicated, however, and said so at Cobham's trial. She had received only one letter from the accused man, had laughed at it, and had passed it on to the king. Soon after this James invited her to court, increased her pension, and made her carver to his queen, Anne of Denmark. Arabella was contemptuous of the childish pastimes of the court ladies and viewed politics with deep cynicism, but gladly accepted the further revenues that came her way. In 1605 she was godmother to the queen's new daughter, Mary, and that same year escaped any involvement in the Gunpowder Plot, which aimed at assassinating James and replacing him on the throne with his daughter, Elizabeth.

In 1607 the Venetian ambassador noted that the king's nearest relative, Madam Arabella, was 'not very beautiful but highly accomplished, for besides being of the most refined manners, she speaks fluently Latin, Italian, French, Spanish, reads Greek and Hebrew and is always studying' (Durant, 156). Most of Arabella's time continued to be spent at court, although she did visit Hardwick after her grandmother's death in 1608 and that summer purchased a house in the Blackfriars, presumably as a quiet refuge for herself. After an attack of smallpox that Christmas, she made another journey north to take the waters at Buxton, and visited various friends and relatives in the area. Perhaps this serious illness made her conscious of the fact that time was passing, and she began to hope that the king would now find her a husband. When she realized that he was no more willing to marry her off than Elizabeth had been, she looked once more to the forbidden Seymour family as a means of forcing the royal hand.

At four o'clock in the morning of 22 June 1610 in her apartments at Greenwich Palace, 35-year-old Lady Arabella Stuart married 22-year-old William *Seymour (1587–1660), another grandson of the earl of Hertford. Young, impressionable, and eager to find a means of supporting himself, he had been flattered by her attention and they had both ignored the king's warnings that they must have nothing to do with each other. Seventeen days later the marriage was discovered, the unfortunate bridegroom was sent to the Tower of London, and Arabella was held in Sir Thomas Parry's house in Lambeth. Even so, she managed to visit William, and in September she had what may have been a miscarriage. The king immediately decided to banish her to Durham. Illness delayed her departure and two days before she was finally due to set out for the north, she disguised herself as a man and escaped. When William failed to appear at their intended rendezvous at Blackwall, Arabella's anxious servants urged her aboard the ship hired to take them to France. In the hope that William would catch up with them, Arabella insisted that they linger in the Channel, with the result that they were overtaken by an English naval vessel and intercepted. Arabella was taken to the Tower of London. Meanwhile William, although delayed, had managed to escape, boarded another vessel, and arrived safely at Ostend.

In the Tower, Lady Arabella Seymour fell ill. All her pleas for release were ignored, and she finally died on 25 September 1615, after a long and chronic sickness exacerbated by her refusal to eat. She was buried in Westminster Abbey two days later. A highly strung, unworldly intellectual, Arabella does not seem to have aimed at the English crown but, taught since her earliest days that she was royal in all but title, she expected her status to be secured by an appropriate marriage. When successive monarchs refused to allow her what she considered to be her rightful destiny, she desperately sought the very means of escape most likely to bring disaster upon herself.

ROSALIND K. MARSHALL

Sources D. N. Durant, *Arbella Stuart, a rival to the queen* (1978) · G. P. V. Akrigg, *Jacobean pageant: the court of King James I* (1962), 113–24 · E. Cooper, *The life and letters of Lady Arabella Stuart*, 2 vols. (1866) · E. T. Bradley, *Arabella Stuart*, 2 vols. (1889) · *Scots peerage*, 5.354–5 · A. Fraser, *Mary, queen of Scots*, 266, 450, 463–4, 466, 554 · GEC, *Peerage*
Archives BL, corresp. relating to time at court, Harley MSS 6986, 7003 · Longleat House, Wiltshire, Seymour MSS, vol. xxii | Chatsworth House, Derbyshire, Cavendish account books, Hardwick MSS 7–9, 23, 29, Hardwick Drawers 143–145, 367 · Folger, Cavendish/Talbot letters · Longleat House, Wiltshire, Talbot letters
Likenesses oils, 1577 (aged twenty-three months), Hardwick Hall, Derbyshire, negative, Courtauld Inst. · CVM, oils, 1589, Hardwick Hall, Derbyshire · oils, *c*.1605, Gov. Art Coll. · J. Whittakers senior, line engraving, 1619, BM, NPG [*see illus.*] · J. Cochran, engravings (after P. van Somer), Scot. NPG · attrib. J. de Critz the elder, oils, North Carolina Museum of Art, Raleigh · T. A. Dean, engraving (after P. van Somer), Scot. NPG · M. Gheeraerts, oils, Scot. NPG · I. Oliver, miniature, Rijksmuseum, Amsterdam · P. Oliver, miniature, Royal Collection · oils (after M. Gheeraerts), Longleat House, Wiltshire

Stuart, Bérault [Bernard Stuart or Stewart] (1452/3–1508), soldier and diplomat, was the son of John *Stewart (*d. c*.1469), seigneur d'Aubigny (Aubigny-sur-Nère, near Bourges) [*see under* Stewart, Sir John, of Darnley], and of Béatrice, daughter of Bérault, seigneur d'Apchier. His grandfather, John *Stewart of Darnley, had disembarked at La Rochelle in October 1419 at the head of a contingent of Scotsmen, in support of Charles, then regent of the kingdom of France: in 1423 Charles, having become king, gave him the *seigneurie* of Aubigny. John Stewart of Darnley was constable of the Scottish army in France from 1421 to 1429: in the latter year he received from the king the right to quarter his arms with those of France.

Bérault Stuart was a man-at-arms in the regular Scottish company in 1469. In 1483 he received command of a company of 100 lances, and in the same year was appointed castellan of the castle of the Bois de Vincennes. He was sent to Scotland in 1484 to announce the accession of Charles VII (*d.* 1498) to James III (*d.* 1488) and added his signature to the treaty renewing the 'auld alliance'. In 1485 he was placed at the head of the French mercenaries who fought on the side of Henry Tudor at the battle of Bosworth. He acted as *bailli* of Berry from 1487 to 1498, and became seigneur d'Aubigny on the death of his father. For most of his life he styled himself counsellor and chamberlain of the king of France. In 1491 he was charged with setting free Louis, duke of Orléans (the future Louis XII), until then held prisoner by Charles VIII. The annual pension which he received from the king rose to 3000 livres tournois in the years 1491, 1492, and 1493. Also in 1491 he went to Milan on a diplomatic mission to Lodovico Sforza (*d.* 1510); he was with Ferdinand of Aragon at the taking of Granada in 1492. From that year to 1508 he was captain of Harfleur and of Montivilliers. He became a knight of the order of St Michel in 1492. In the following year he was appointed captain of Charles VIII's Scottish guard, a post he retained until his death. In 1494 he married Anne de Maumont, daughter of Jean d'Alençon, bastard of Jean (II), duke of Alençon: from this marriage was born Anne, who became the wife of Robert Stewart, future marshal of France and seigneur d'Aubigny. In the same year, several months before the beginning of his expedition to Italy, Charles VIII sent Stuart on a mission to Milan, Ferrara, Mantua, Florence, and Rome. He conducted a campaign in the Romagna, then rejoined Charles's army and made his entry into Florence on 15 November 1494. Stuart took part in the conquest of Calabria. Charles made him grand constable of the kingdom of Naples, and in this capacity he found himself entrusted with the defence of Calabria against the Aragonese. With his Swiss troops he defeated King Ferdinand and Gonzalve de Cordoba at Seminara on 21 June 1495, but he was soon on the defensive and was forced to leave the kingdom of Naples with his army and return to France in 1497. In consideration of his distinguished service Charles VIII granted him a reward of 12,000 livres tournois. His pension at this time was 1800 livres tournois.

Stuart remained in favour with Charles's successor, Louis XII (d. 1515), who by 1500 had increased his pension to 4000 livres tournois. He conducted a campaign against Lodovico Sforza in northern Italy in 1499, and in 1500 he was named one of the governors of Milan. In the following year he was entrusted by the king with a new expedition against the kingdom of Naples; he took the city of Capua by assault and entered Naples. Fighting against the Spanish continued in 1502, when he won a victory at Terranova, but the following year he was defeated at Seminara on 21 April. He was taken prisoner on the capitulation of Rocca Angistola and incarcerated in the Castel Nuovo at Naples, but was freed following the suspension of hostilities. He then returned to France, where he evidently retained the sovereign's favour. He took part in the expedition against Genoa in 1507. Having fallen ill at Savona he received a visit from Ferdinand of Aragon, who paid homage to his legendary courage. In 1508 he decided to make a pilgrimage to the sanctuary of St Ninian at Whithorn in Scotland. Louis XII charged him on that occasion with an embassy to the Scottish king, James IV (d. 1513), intended principally to renew the 'auld alliance'. Having passed through London in great pomp on 21 March, he reached Scotland. He and the Scottish king, who dubbed him 'father of war', exchanged gifts, notably of horses. To celebrate his arrival William Dunbar (d. 1530) wrote a ballad in which he was compared to Achilles, Hector, Hannibal, and Arthur, and lauded as the 'most strong, incomparable knyght, the fame of the armys and the floure of vassalage' (Dunbar, 109). Stuart finally left on his pilgrimage, but he fell ill and died at Corstorphine, near Edinburgh. In his will, dated 8 June, he asked to be buried in the house of the Observant Franciscans in Edinburgh, while his heart was to be sent to St Ninian's. James IV wrote a letter of condolence to Queen Anne of France, while Dunbar composed an elegy on him addressed to Louis XII.

In the course of his final embassy Stuart dictated to his secretary and household chaplain Étienne le Jeune, a native of Aubigny, a treatise on the art of war that borrowed its essentials from the work of a French captain, Robert de Balsac, composed some years earlier, but Stuart added a number of details on the basis of his military experience in the kingdom of Naples. Philippe de Commines wrote of him: 'Monseigneur d'Aubigny, of the Scottish nation, good and wise and honourable knight' (Commines, 3.136). In fact he was at once both a good diplomat and an experienced war captain, though for the greater part of his life he suffered from gout, which often forced him to interrupt his activities. Of all his merits the chronicler Jean d'Auton praises in particular his reconnaissance of terrain: 'In the matter of war he was the master of all others in spying out the countryside and dealing with ambushes' (Auton, 2.265). His arms were a quartered escutcheon, the first and fourth quarters azure, three fleurs-de-lis or, the second and third a fess checky azure and argent. There is a medal of him by the engraver Nicolò Spinelli. In a manuscript that belonged to him (*Le livre du gouvernement des princes*, a French translation of Giles of Rome's *De regimine principum*; Paris, Bibliothèque de l'Arsenal, MS 6328), a miniature represents him in armour, haughty, mounted on a barded horse, and brandishing in his right hand his baton of command.

Philippe Contamine

Sources E. de Comminges, ed., *Traité sur l'art de la guerre de Bérault Stuart, seigneur d'Aubigny* (1976) · P. Contamine, 'The war literature of the late middle ages: the treatises of Robert de Balsac and Béraud Stuart, lord of Aubigny', *War, literature and politics in the late middle ages*, ed. C. T. Allmand (1976), 102–21 · E. Cust, *Some accounts of the Stuarts of Aubigny in France, 1422–1672* (1891) · Billiond, 'Aubigny, Béraud Stuart', *Dictionnaire de biographie française*, ed. J. Balteau and others, 4 (Paris, 1948), 179–80 · J. d'Auton, *Chroniques de Louis XII*, ed. R. de Maulde La Clavière, 4 vols (1889–95) · W. Forbes-Leith, *The Scots men-at-arms and life-guards in France*, 2 vols. (1882) · Y. Labande-Mailfert, *Charles VIII et son milieu, 1470–1498: la jeunesse au pouvoir* (Paris, 1975) · P. Contamine, 'Scottish soldiers in France in the second half of the fifteenth century: mercenaries, immigrants or Frenchmen in the making?', *The Scottish soldiers abroad, 1297–1967*, ed. G. G. Simpson (1992), 16–30 · W. Dunbar, *Poems*, ed. J. Kinsley, repr. (1979) · P. de Commines, *Mémoires*, ed. J. Colmette and G. Durville, 3 (1925)
Archives Bibliothèque Nationale, Paris, MSS Fr. 2070, 20003 · Bibliothèque Nationale, Paris, PO 2731 · Château de la Verrerie, Aubigny-sur-Nère, Cher · Marquis of Bute's Library, Rothesay, MS F 21
Likenesses N. Spinelli, engraved medal, repro. in Comminges, ed., *Traité sur l'art de la guerre* · portrait, Mountstuart, Isle of Bute, marquess of Bute MSS, fol. 2r · portrait, Bibliothèque de l'Arsenal, Paris, 5062, fol. 1r

Stuart, Lord Bernard, styled earl of Lichfield (1622–1645), royalist army officer, was born on 28 December 1622, the youngest of ten children of Esmé *Stuart, third duke of Lennox (1579?–1624), and his wife, Katherine (c.1592–1637), only daughter and heir of Gervase Clifton, Lord Clifton of Leighton Bromswold, Huntingdonshire. After her father's death in 1618 Stuart's mother became Baroness Clifton in her own right. James *Stuart, fourth duke of Lennox and first duke of Richmond, was his eldest brother.

Stuart was brought up under the direction of appointees of the king, with distinct revenue assigned for his maintenance. He was created MA at Cambridge University in 1637. On 30 January 1639 he obtained a licence to travel abroad for three years with his elder brother John. It was probably before they went abroad that Van Dyck painted a double portrait of the brothers, a painting greatly admired by Thomas Gainsborough who came across it in 1785. He produced a full-scale copy of the work and a head-and-shoulders study of Lord Bernard.

Stuart was knighted at York on 18 April 1642 by his kinsman Charles I. On the outbreak of the civil war he was appointed captain of the King's Own life guards. This troop attracted so many 'persons of honour and quality' and was so dazzlingly equipped that it was known as the 'show troop'. It formed, Clarendon recorded:

> so gallant a body, that upon a very modest computation the estate and revenue of that single troop might justly be valued at least equal to all theirs who then voted in both Houses under the name of the Lords and Commons of Parliament, and so made and maintained that war. (Clarendon, *Hist. rebellion*, 2.348)

Stuart and the king's life guard of cavalry were given permission to serve in the front rank of Prince Rupert's cavalry at the battle of Edgehill on 23 October 1642. Stuart himself left a brief account of the battle (Davies, 38–9), in which his brother George Stuart, Lord D'Aubigny, was killed. Stuart was with Rupert when he retook Lichfield on 20 April 1643. Stuart fought at the battle of Newbury on 19–20 September 1643. On 29 June 1644, at the head of the life guards, he supported Thomas Wentworth, earl of Cleveland, in his charge against Sir William Waller's parliamentarian troops at Cropredy Bridge, Oxfordshire. He was among the last to remain at Charles I's side at the devastating defeat at Naseby on 14 June 1645, while they vainly attempted to 'prevail with those shattered and frightened troops either to give or stand one charge more' (*Ormonde MSS*, new ser., 2.386–7). In July Stuart attended the king at Raglan Castle where the marquess of Worcester ensured that they gained a brief respite from the war.

Before Naseby the king had designated Stuart as Baron Stuart of Newbury and earl of Lichfield, but the money to pay the necessary fees had been lost in the battle and its aftermath. Sir Edward Nicholas consequently wrote to the king recommending him to command the patent to pass the seals without any fee being paid. Before this could be done, however, Stuart fell in battle. He accompanied the king on his march to relieve Chester, and entered the town with the king on 23 September. While most of the cavalry quartered 3 miles from the city the king's life guard and Lord Gerard's troops remained with Charles. The next day, while Sir Marmaduke Langdale engaged the parliamentarian forces on Rowton Heath, Stuart led a sally out of the city. For a time he was successful, but he was eventually driven back. Although there were few casualties in the rout that followed, Stuart himself was killed, in view of the town and the king, 'who from one of the towers of the wall, saw his troops defeated' (*Diary of Sir Henry Slingsby*, 66).

Stuart's death was 'such a loss', Lord Digby told the marquess of Ormond, 'as a victory would scarce repair' (Carte, 1.92–3). 'He was', Clarendon wrote, 'a very faultless young man, of a most gentle, courteous, and affable nature, and of a spirit and courage invincible; whose loss all men

exceedingly lamented, and the King bore it with extraordinary grief' (Clarendon, *Hist. rebellion*, 4.115–16). The royalist memorialist claimed that Stuart said of the hazards of war, 'That a small courage might serve a man to engage for that cause; the ruine whereof no courage would serve him to survive' (Lloyd, 329).

Stuart died unmarried. Richard Johnson, his master of horse, obtained a licence from parliament to bury his lord in October. He was buried with his fallen brothers, George and John (who had been mortally wounded at the battle of Cheriton on 29 March 1644) in Christ Church Cathedral, Oxford, where the date is recorded (possibly wrongly) as 11 March 1646.   E. I. CARLYLE, *rev.* S. L. SADLER

Sources Clarendon, *Hist. rebellion* · GEC, *Peerage* · *Calendar of the manuscripts of the marquess of Ormonde*, new ser., 8 vols., HMC, 36 (1902–20), vol. 2, pp. 386–7 · *The manuscripts of his grace the duke of Portland*, 10 vols., HMC, 29 (1891–1931), vol. 1, p. 282 · *Seventh report*, HMC, 6 (1879) · *CSP dom.*, 1623–5, 488; 1638–9, 378; 1645–7, 110–11 · *Scots peerage*, 5.358–9 · *The king's forces totally routed, 29 Sept 1645*, BL, E303/18 [Thomason tract], 9 · *A letter from Poyntz* (30 Sept 1945) [Thomason tract] · F. Whortley, *Characters and elegies* (1646) · *A list of officers claiming to the sixty thousand pounds granted by his sacred majesty for the relief of his truly loyal and indigent party* (1663), cols. 86, 126 · D. Lloyd, *Memoires of the lives … of those … personages that suffered … for the protestant religion* (1668), 329, 351 · R. Simms, *Bibliotheca Staffordiensis* (1894), 440 · *The letter books of Sir Samuel Luke, 1644–45*, ed. H. G. Tibbutt, Bedfordshire Historical RS, 42 (1963), 255 · P. Warwick, *Memoires of the reign of Charles I* (1701), 288, 302 · E. Walker, *Historical discourses* (1707), 75, 132, 140 · *A collection of original letters and papers, concerning the affairs of England from the year 1641 to 1660. Found among the duke of Ormonde's papers*, ed. T. Carte, 1 (1739), 91–3 · *England's black tribunal* (1765) · *The diary of Sir Henry Slingsby, bart.*, ed. D. Parsons (1836), 65–6 · E. Warburton, *Memoirs of Prince Rupert and the cavaliers*, 3 vols. (1849), vol. 3, pp. 103–4 · Venn, *Alum. Cant.* · C. V. Wedgwood, *The king's war* (1966), 128, 147, 434, 464 · S. R. Gardiner, *History of the great civil war, 1642–1649*, new edn, 4 vols. (1901–5), vol. 2, p. 345 · P. R. Newman, *Royalist officers in England and Wales, 1642–1660: a biographical dictionary* (1981), 363 · *Subject catalogue of paintings in public collections*, 2 vols. (1989–90), vol. 1, p. 1149 · G. Davies, 'The battle of Edgehill', *EngHR*, 36 (1921), 30–45 · C. Brown and others, *Van Dyck, 1599–1641* (1999) [exhibition catalogue, Koninklijk Museum voor Schone Kunsten, Antwerp, 15 May – 15 Aug 1999, and RA, 11 Sept – 10 Dec 1999]

Likenesses Van Dyck, double portrait, oils, *c*.1639 (with Lord John), National Gallery, London · T. Gainsborough, oils (after Van Dyck), Art Museum, St Louis, Missouri · J. McArdall, engraving (with Lord John; after Van Dyck) · R. Thomas, double portrait, engraving (with Lord John; after Van Dyck) · Vertue, engraving, portraits, Bodl. Oxf.

Stuart, Sir Campbell Arthur (1885–1972), newspaper manager, was born in Montreal, Canada, on 5 July 1885, the youngest son of Ernest Henry Stuart, stockbroker, and his wife, (Letitia) Mary S. Brydges, daughter of Charles John Brydges, head of the Grand Trunk Railway. He was educated at private schools. Throughout his life Canada, England, and America formed a triangle of allegiances. He was proud to trace his ancestry back to emigrants from Buckinghamshire to New York in 1715; proud that others had, as United Empire loyalists, emigrated to Canada as a result of the war of independence; and proud that in Canada they had filled posts of distinction. Three of his forebears had been chief justices. No matter what other interests he had at various times of his life, these associations were chords he struck time and again.

In 1915–16 Stuart raised in Quebec province an Irish Canadian battalion, half protestant and half Roman Catholic, to fight in France. He then marched it through protestant and Roman Catholic cities in Ireland, falsifying forebodings of trouble. His description in his autobiography, *Opportunity Knocks Once* (1952), of how he went about getting ecclesiastical approval for this is revealing of his pertinacity. It led Sir Robert Borden, then prime minister of Canada, to send the 31-year-old Stuart to see Pope Benedict XV and interest him in French Canada's part in the war. The speed with which he obtained his audience with the pontiff astonished Vatican officials.

A short spell in 1917 as an assistant military attaché at the British embassy in Washington was not a success. He was happier as military secretary to Lord Northcliffe's British war mission in New York. From there he moved with Northcliffe to a propaganda post in London. His *Secrets of Crewe House*, dealing with this work, was a pioneer book when it was published in 1920. He ended the war as a lieutenant-colonel in the Canadian army, having been mentioned in dispatches.

Northcliffe claimed Campbell Stuart was his find, and that he had 'made' him. This was not so. Stuart was assured of an influential future in Canada before he met Northcliffe. A choice of careers was open to him. Lord Atholstan, who owned the *Montreal Star*, had asked Stuart to join him, with the promise he would own the paper on Atholstan's death. He could have entered Canadian politics. What Northcliffe did was to move Stuart's life from Canada to England. When Stuart was about to return to Canada to be demobilized in 1920 Northcliffe offered him the managing directorship of *The Times*, including supervision of the editorial staff and the news services. Northcliffe also made him managing editor of the *Daily Mail* (1921). 'Campbell is the only person I have yet found who understands the harmonising of my newspapers', Northcliffe said (*The Times*, 15 Sept 1972). He acted as 'a buffer between Northcliffe and the "editorial troglodytes" of *The Times*' (ibid.).

As Northcliffe became increasingly irresponsible Stuart protected both papers with courage. He played a leading part in the battle for the ownership of *The Times* that followed Northcliffe's death, favouring John Jacob Astor, who acquired a controlling interest in 1922. It was not Stuart, however, who first thought of Astor as the ideal proprietor of the paper. The credit for that must go to Bruce Richmond, editor of the *Times Literary Supplement*. Stuart's managerial role in the paper ceased in 1923 with the reinstatement of G. Geoffrey Dawson as editor of *The Times* by the new owners; but he remained an active director of the newspaper for thirty-seven years thereafter, only stepping down in 1960.

In addition, Stuart filled a succession of roles in imperial and Commonwealth communications from 1923 to 1945. He was deputy director of propaganda in enemy countries at the end of the First World War and briefly (1939–40) director at the beginning of the Second World War. All these activities were overshadowed by the many projects he helped bring to fruition. Those he was closely involved in

included the King George's Jubilee Trust, of which he was treasurer, 1935–47, the Hudson's Bay Record Society (chairman, 1938–59), and the committee to erect a memorial to General Wolfe at Greenwich (1930). He was a moving spirit in the erection of the statue of President Franklin Roosevelt in Grosvenor Square, London, from 1946 to 1948. An important figure in the Canadian History Society, and of its French counterpart, to do justice to Quebec, he was also chairman of the Pilgrims from 1948 to 1958.

Although a lifelong bachelor Stuart entertained widely, assisted by his mother, who acted as hostess. 'His tall, lean figure and eager, expressive face, quick to break into smiles, were familiar in Embassies and drawing-rooms in Mayfair and in Montreal, Cape Town and other centres of the old Empire' (*The Times*, 15 Sept 1972). At dinner parties at his seventeenth-century Highgate house, The Grove, he brought together leading figures from the worlds of journalism, diplomacy, and business. He undoubtedly did things in style. When he gave a lunch to form the French Canadian History Society he held it at Versailles, and insured at Lloyd's the palace and all its contents for twenty-four hours to make this possible.

Stuart was appointed KBE in 1918 and GCMG in 1939, and he held honorary LLDs from Melbourne University (1942) and William and Mary College, Virginia (1938). He died on 14 September 1972 at The Grove.

WILLIAM HALEY, rev. ROBERT BROWN

Sources C. Stuart, *Opportunity knocks once* (1952) · personal knowledge (1986) · *The Times* (15 Sept 1972) · *WWW* · D. Wilson, *The Astors, 1763–1992: landscape with millionaires* (1993) · [S. Morison and others], *The history of The Times*, 3 (1947) · [S. Morison and others], *The history of The Times*, 4 (1952) · I. McDonald, *The history of The Times*, 5 (1984) · S. E. Koss, *The rise and fall of the political press in Britain*, 2 vols. (1981–4) · R. Pound and G. Harmsworth, *Northcliffe* (1959)
Archives CUL, corresp. and papers relating to imperial communications · IWM, corresp. and papers relating to department of enemy propaganda · NA Canada, corresp. and MS of *Days with the Times* · News Int. RO, papers relating to work for *The Times* | BL, corresp. with Lord Northcliffe, Add. MSS 62240–62242 · Lpool RO, corresp. with seventeenth earl of Derby
Likenesses W. Stoneman, photograph, 1921, NPG · M. Codner, oils

Stuart, Charles, sixth duke of Lennox and third duke of Richmond (1639–1672), courtier and ambassador, was born in London on 7 March 1639, the only son of George Stuart, seigneur d'Aubigny (1618–1642), and Lady Katherine Howard (d. 1650) [see Stuart, Katherine], daughter of Theophilus *Howard, second earl of Suffolk. His early childhood and youthful development were both defined and seriously marred by the upheavals of the English civil wars. His father was mortally wounded at the battle of Edgehill on 23 October 1642, while his mother was subsequently imprisoned for smuggling royalist correspondence. On 10 December 1645, owing to the death in action of his father's younger brother, Lord Bernard *Stuart (1622–1645), he was designated Baron Stuart of Newbury and earl of Lichfield, titles which had been intended for his uncle but were never officially recognized by the Long

Parliament, or by the Commonwealth and the protectorate governments.

By late 1648 Lichfield's mother had married Sir James *Livingston, created Viscount Newburgh that September, but following her premature death in exile at The Hague he became the ward of his second cousin, General Charles Fleetwood, who recommended him to John Thurloe, in September 1654, as 'a very hopefull young gentleman' (Cust, 111). However, he appears to have had little love for the republican form of government, and later attempts to incorporate him within the framework of a new Cromwellian, aristocratic élite failed dramatically. Consequently, at the first available opportunity, in January 1658 he sailed for France. Together with his governor and manservant, he took up residence in Paris at the house of his uncle Ludovic Stuart, tenth seigneur d'Aubigny, and was there acknowledged as 'a forward and witty' youth by one of Thurloe's informants operating in the city (Thurloe, State papers, 6.782). In August 1659 he took part in Sir George Booth's abortive royalist rising and was punished by the council of state, by the sequestration of his goods and estates.

The Restoration transformed Lichfield's fortunes and in May 1660 he returned to England with Charles II, attending the king upon his triumphant entry into London. The premature death of his cousin Esmé Stuart (1649–1660), on 10 August 1660, further strengthened his position at court, as he inherited the dukedoms of Richmond and Lennox, together with a whole swathe of Scottish offices and titles, which included the posts of hereditary great chamberlain and great admiral of Scotland, and keeper of Dumbarton Castle. His appointments as lord lieutenant of Dorset, in 1660, and as gentleman of the royal bedchamber and knight of the Order of the Garter, in 1661, only served further to underline his growing political importance. By the summer of 1660 he had contracted what was to be a brief first marriage to Elizabeth (1643/4–1661), widow of Charles Cavendish, styled Viscount Mansfield (d. 1659), and daughter of Richard Rogers of Bryanston, Dorset, who brought large estates in the county. She died in childbed on 21 April 1661. On 31 March 1662 Richmond married Margaret (d. 1666/7), widow of William Lewis of Bletchington, Oxfordshire, and daughter of Lawrence Banaster of Papenham, Buckinghamshire.

In 1662 Richmond set off to join the administration in Scotland of John Middleton, earl of Middleton, and was sworn of the newly expanded privy council in August, alongside his stepfather, who had been created earl of Newburgh in 1660. However, while he successfully reasserted his customary rites as the lord of Dumbarton Castle, combated encroachments on his jurisdiction of the Admiralty, and—during the Anglo-Dutch wars—licensed a significant number of privateers to raid against foreign merchantmen, he showed little interest in the workings of the Scottish privy council and only occasionally attended its meetings. It was the need to destroy the formidable power base of John Maitland, earl of Lauderdale, through a reform in the workings of the Edinburgh parliament and the institution of a secret ballot for its

members, which had initially motivated Richmond's entry into Scottish politics. Unfortunately, in pushing for a dozen rival members to be expelled from the parliament, Richmond's party had seriously overreached themselves and he, in particular, earned himself the antipathy and mistrust of his king.

On his return to London, Richmond fought a duel with Colonel Russell over the honour of a lady of the court. As a result, on 30 March 1665 both gentlemen were arrested and sent to the Tower of London; Richmond was released from custody on 21 April. However, honours, sinecures, and titles continued to come his way, as he was created baron of Cobham on 28 May 1666, took command of a regiment of horse known as the 'select militia' in July 1666, and became de jure Lord Clifton of Leighton Bromswold on 4 July 1667. Following the death of his second wife in late December 1666 or the first few days of January 1667, he embarked upon a relationship with his kinswoman Frances Teresa *Stuart (1647–1702), who had until that time been mistress to the king. According to Edmund Ludlow, Richmond was no more than an unwitting dupe in the plans of the lord chancellor, the earl of Clarendon, to prevent Charles II from divorcing the queen and marrying Frances, in order to ensure the succession. However, it would appear that this was a genuine love match and there is little reason to suppose that Richmond either rushed into marriage 'as the most certain way he could take to advance himself' with Clarendon, or as a favour to the king in order to lessen the scandal surrounding the fate of his former mistress (Memoirs of Edmund Ludlow, 3 vols., 1698–9, 2.407; Pepys, 8.120). Indeed, rather than forwarding his career, his marriage to Frances—which was concluded in a private ceremony, at the end of March 1667—threatened to ruin it. Charles II was furious at the couple's elopement to Kent, and forbade them to return to court. This order was rescinded only in August 1668, when Frances, her beauty tarnished by an attack of smallpox, was permitted to return to their home at the Bowling Green, in Whitehall Palace.

In the meantime, the continuing attrition brought about by the Second Anglo-Dutch War had seen Richmond going down to Dorset, in order to prepare the county to resist invasion. When, amid constant rumours of the sighting of a large Dutch fleet, on 6 July 1667 the alarm was given that forty hostile ships were sailing towards Weymouth, Richmond was quick to lead his troop of horse and the county militia in a reconnaissance mission along the coast. However, though the duke's soldiers 'were soon in posture, with a cheerful heart to engage the enemy, had there been occasion' (CSP dom., 1667, 271), it was to prove a false alarm. Arriving in Lyme on 13 July 1667 Richmond was 'handsomely received' by the mayor, who ordered two companies of musketeers to fire a salute in his honour (CSP dom., 1667, 291). In May 1668 he was commissioned as lord lieutenant of Kent and in August he reviewed the county militia outside the walls of Canterbury. Nevertheless, the threat of a Dutch invasion continued to trouble Richmond's mind and he took steps to protect his own private property, demanding—and evidently receiving—from the Ordnance office: '2 brass three-pounders, with carriages, shot and stones … for defence of his house at Cobham, Kent' (BL, Add. MS 21951, fol. 5; *CSP dom.*, *1670*, 634).

Although his uncle Ludovic Stuart had died on 3 November 1665, it was not until 31 December 1668 that Richmond was finally recognized by the French authorities as the eleventh seigneur d'Aubigny. In order to make good his claim, he visited his lands at Aubigny in spring 1669, and evidently took pleasure in his stay, ordering twenty horses to be shipped across the channel for his personal use. He returned to England in November 1669 and on 11 March 1670 was permitted to do homage to Louis XIV, by proxy, in return for the confirmation of his rights.

With his position at court effectively compromised, Richmond now began to look for a diplomatic appointment in order to restore his ebbing fortunes and lobbied, unsuccessfully, to be sent as an ambassador to the Italian princes. During his visit to France in 1669 he had left it to his friend Sir Anthony Ashley Cooper to press for him to be sent to Poland as an extraordinary ambassador, in order to monitor the forthcoming elections for king that were to be held there. Even though this appointment was similarly refused, Richmond immediately embarked upon another fruitless campaign to press his candidacy as lord chamberlain, even while the current incumbent, the earl of Manchester, was still sickening.

Once again scandal was to cling to Richmond's name, as after a formal reception at Lincoln's Inn Hall in late 1671 he headed off into the night with the dukes of Monmouth, Albemarle, and Rochester towards a rough and disreputable area of the city. All had been drinking and made such a clamour that, as they approached Whetstone Park, the parish constables were alerted and sent to quieten them down. Swords were drawn and a scuffle followed in which an unfortunate officer was killed in spite of his anguished pleas for mercy. Facing a trial for murder, Richmond, Monmouth, and Albemarle were saved from the justice of the courts only by the intervention of the king, who was forced to offer a general amnesty for felons in order to remove the capital charges laid against them.

Increasingly appearing to be a liability at court, in February 1672 Richmond had his desire for a diplomatic posting at last realized with his appointment as ambassador to Denmark. At the same time, he was created lord high admiral of Scotland and continued to issue letters of marque to privateer captains. After setting out for Denmark in late April 1672 aboard the frigate *Portland*, Richmond experienced extremely bad weather. Although the crossing was destined to take almost six weeks, with his ship being forced repeatedly to turn for home, the duke was still able to pursue a Dutch merchantman that had unwittingly strayed into his path. However, he refused to allow the commander of the frigate to take possession of the vessel and instead, at the last minute, invoking his powers as lord high admiral of Scotland, he commandeered an English fishing boat and commissioned its crew, together with his own servants, to act as privateers.

Consequently, he ensured that the Dutch vessel and its valuable cargo of salt would be judged as his own prize before the Admiralty court and not as the property of the king of England, as would otherwise have been the case.

Determined to live in splendour, Richmond ordered furs to keep out the Scandinavian cold, as well as ample provisions and tobacco. However, despite the allowance of £2500 given to him 'for his equipage and transport' and his receipt of a grant of £100 a week 'for his entertainment' as ambassador to Denmark, he still managed to run up debts of over £1500 within a few months of his arrival (BL, Add. MS 21948, fol. 289, Add. MS 21950, fol. 423, Add. MS 21951, fol. 40; *CSP dom.*, *1671–2*, 25). Boredom was, no doubt, to blame for this. He constantly grumbled that Copenhagen was a damp city, that the Danes were a dull people, and that their women were singularly unprepossessing. Leaving the day-to-day business of the embassy to his deputy, Thomas Henshaw, he fell to self-pity and lamented that: 'Neaver man was so weary of a place as I am of this, it being I thinke the least diverteing of any that I ever came in' (Hartman, 197). Consequently, the arrival of an English frigate in the sound off the coast of Helsingør (Elsinore) in December 1672 offered him the possibility of both companionship and much needed entertainment. Despite thick snow and freezing temperatures, he left his lodgings on 12 December and rowed out to join the ship's captain on board. After a hearty dinner, during which he drank at least two bottles of wine, he took his leave of his host. However, being 'a little merry' he missed 'a step on the side of the ship … that should have eased him down, fell betwixt the ship and the boat, and sank straight' to the bottom like a stone. It would appear, despite Captain Taylor's later report, that the sailors did manage to locate his body and were able to resuscitate him. Unfortunately, by that time he had contracted a chill due to the icy waters and went into violent convulsions during his coach journey back to his lodgings. He died the same day in his rooms, on the outskirts of Helsingør.

Richmond's brains and bowels were removed and interred within the precincts of the Dutch church at Helsingør, but there was a long delay in transferring his body back for burial in England. His servants had great difficulty in finding a lead coffin to lay him in, and it soon transpired that King Christian V's offer of a ship to bear the corpse home had been made only as a kindly overture, and one which had never meant to be accepted by Charles II's government. As a result, almost a year passed before a new Danish ship, its sails and hull especially painted black as a sign of respect, was dispatched for this doleful mission. The body was landed at Gravesend in early September 1673 before being transferred by barge up the Thames and finally laid to rest in Henry VII's chapel in Westminster Abbey on 20 September 1673.

Even the elegists plying their trade in the streets of London failed to find any inspiration in the duke's life and could manage only a lacklustre tribute to 'Richmond's loss'. These doggerel verses are chiefly notable for their failure to make any solid claims for his possession of any virtues or abilities whatsoever. Rather, while 'Britain's

Genius' shed icicle tears over his death, he was seen to have 'left … all his Services on score', ultimately: 'Unsum'd, Deny'd by Fate, to make them more' (*An Elegie on his Grace the Illustrious Charles Stuart*, 1). Although both Samuel Pepys and Captain Guy of the *Portland* remarked upon the 'good nature' he showed to his subordinates in the naval establishment, Count Grammont thoroughly castigated him as a brute and a debauchee, who managed to cut only an 'indifferent figure at court' (*CSP dom.*, 1671–2, 369; Hamilton, 240; Pepys, 9.302). While Grammont should be considered to be a deeply biased source, Richmond would seem to have been a graceless and often quick-tempered individual, who had no understanding of the value of money and only limited political acumen. Having inherited estates already burdened by the debts of the civil war years, and despite frequent and very considerable grants from the crown, he continued to add to his financial difficulties through his penchant for gambling and horse-racing. His account books reveal not only the substantial costs incurred by his extensive refurbishment of Cobham House, but also that those bills that he did receive were usually left unpaid for a considerable length of time. His first two wives were considerable heiresses, but both died childless and his relations with Margaret were marked by a series of personal, financial, and legal disputes. Frances Teresa Stuart survived Richmond by almost thirty years, dying in relative obscurity on 15 October 1702.

JOHN CALLOW

Sources corresp. and papers, 1644–72, BL, Add. MSS 21947–21951 · *An elegie on his grace the illustrious Charles Stuart, duke of Richmond and Lenox* (1673) · GEC, *Peerage* · Evelyn, *Diary*, vols. 3–4 · J. Greenstreet, 'Will of Frances, countess of Kildare … Frances Stuart … and Charles Stuart, last duke of Richmond and Lenox', *Genealogical tracts* (1877) · Pepys, *Diary*, vols. 1, 6, 8–9 · C. H. Hartmann, *La Belle Stuart: memoirs of court and society in the times of Frances Theresa Stuart, duchess of Richmond and Lenox* (1924) · *Fifth report*, HMC, 4 (1876) · E. Cust [Lady Brownlow], *Some account of the Stuarts of Aubigny in France, 1422–1672* (1891) · J. N. P. Watson, *Captain-general and rebel chief: the life of James, duke of Monmouth* (1979) · R. Hutton, *Charles the Second: king of England, Scotland and Ireland* (1989) · A. Hamilton, *Memoirs of the count de Grammont*, ed. and trans. H. Walpole and Mrs Jameson (1911) · *Bishop Burnet's History*, vols. 1–2 · *The memoirs of Edmund Ludlow*, ed. C. H. Firth, 2 vols. (1894) · will, PRO, C108/53 [copy]

Archives BL, bills and papers relating to debts, inventory, Egerton MS 2435 · BL, corresp. and papers, Add. MSS 21947–21951 · BL, Egerton MS 3382, fols. 160–80 · BL, notice of birth and death, Sloane MS 1708, fol. 121 · BL, swearing-in as gentleman of bedchamber, Sloane MS 856, fol. 30 · PRO, estate papers, accounts, etc., C 108/9–10 53–55 161 · U. Edin. L., financial papers | BL, petition to Charles II, Add. MS 23134, fol. 44 · BL, corresp. with Henry Coventry, Add. MS 25117 · BL, letters to Lauderdale, Add. MS 23127, fol. 74, Add. MS 351125, fol. 163 · Bristol RO, letters to Sir Hugh Smyth

Likenesses P. Lely, oils, c.1663–1667, priv. coll. · E. Scriven, stipple, pubd 1810, NPG

Wealth at death estates in Donegal, Gravesend, Westcliffe, Watton in Yorkshire, Kirkby Moreside and Nunnington, Yorkshire; Ravensworth, Yorkshire; Brayles in Warwickshire; Witham in Essex; also tenements in the Duke's Yard, St Martin's in the Fields, London: BL Add. MS 21951, fols. 25–6 [inventories of Cobham and Whitehall properties], fol. 28 (other goods), fols. 29–31 [undated inventory], fol. 37 [estate records and deaths]. J. Greenstreet, 'Will of Frances, countess of Kildare … Frances Stuart … and Charles Stuart, last duke of Richmond and Lenox', *Genealogical tracts* (1877)

Stuart, Sir Charles (1753–1801), army officer, the fourth son of John *Stuart, third earl of Bute (1713–1792), politician, and his wife, Mary (1718–1794), the daughter of Lady Mary Wortley *Montagu and Edward Wortley *Montagu, was born at Kenwood House, London, in January 1753. His siblings included John *Stuart, first marquess of Bute, William *Stuart, archbishop of Armagh, and Lady Louisa *Stuart. He grew to be a strikingly handsome man, as appears in his portrait by George Romney. After schooling at home and at Dr Graffiani's academy in Kensington, he entered the army in 1768 as an ensign in the 37th foot; he purchased a lieutenancy in the 7th foot in 1770 and a captaincy in the 37th foot in 1773. He served with distinction in the war in America from 1775 to 1779 and was promoted lieutenant-colonel of the 26th foot (Cameronians) in 1777. During his service in America he returned twice to England in 1778. On the first occasion, on 19 April he married Anne Louisa (1757–1841), the second daughter and coheir of Lord Vere Bertie, MP, and his wife, Anne Casey. They had two sons, of whom the elder, Charles *Stuart, became Baron Stuart de Rothesay. On the second occasion he was commissioned to inform the ministry of the army's plans. He was deeply critical of the conduct of the war by the army command and by Lord George Germain, the secretary of state, and he left America for good at the end of 1779, convinced that the American theatre of war was one 'where there is no honour to be obtained' (*A Prime Minister and his Son*, 162). Despite his criticisms of the high command, he won the confidence of General George Clinton, who offered him the post of adjutant-general and continued to correspond with him until the end of the war.

Stuart failed to obtain further military employment, probably because his father had become *persona non grata* with the king, and so he travelled extensively in Europe and sought, though without success, appointment to a diplomatic post abroad. His fierce pride and fiery temper, against which his father continually warned him, scarcely qualified him for the life of a diplomat. He was elected to parliament three times, for Bossiney in 1776, Ayr burghs in 1790, and Poole in 1796, but he took little part in parliamentary life. After his father's death in 1792 and Britain's declaration of war against France in 1793, George III agreed to his re-employment in the army. In April 1794 he was given command of the army in Corsica and with Nelson's help drove the French from Calvi, their last remaining stronghold on the island. His energy and bravery during the siege won him the admiration of Sir John Moore, who served as his second in command. Unfortunately he quarrelled with Admiral Lord Hood, who commanded the Mediterranean Fleet, over the conduct of the siege, and later with Sir Gilbert Elliot, viceroy of Corsica. His unwillingness to take orders from a civilian (albeit a viceroy), his siding with the Corsican patriot General Pasquale Paoli in disputes with Elliot, and his conviction that Corsica could be ruled only by a military man led to his resignation of his command in February 1795.

In January 1797 Stuart was given command of a force

sent to Portugal at the urgent request of the Portuguese government, threatened with invasion by France and Spain. There he succeeded in transforming his army, made up partly of foreign troops who lacked discipline and motivation, into a very effective force. The foreign regiments later fought in Egypt and there 'displayed a steadiness and resolution which spoke volumes for what Charles Stuart's influence had done' (Atkinson, 138). In 1798 he received a commission to capture Minorca from the Spanish with a force of 3000 men drawn mostly from Gibraltar. His appointment received the approval of the British admiral Lord St Vincent, who told the secretary of state that Stuart was 'the best general you have … no man can manage Frenchmen so well and the British will go to hell for him' (*A Prime Minister and his Son*, 284). He succeeded in capturing Minorca from a numerically superior enemy in November 1798 without the loss of a single man. In recognition he was created knight of the Bath and governor of Minorca. He radically reformed the island's administration, bringing about changes described by a French historian as 'the most important ever effected in a country which had not been ceded by treaty' (Lameire, 703).

While in Minorca Stuart responded at once to a plea by Nelson to send troops to Messina to preserve Sicily from a French invasion. Nelson had the highest opinion of Stuart, whom he described as an officer who 'by his abilities would make a bad army into a good one' (*Dispatches and Letters*, 3.226). Stuart accompanied two regiments to Messina and then paid a fleeting visit to Malta, where the French still held out in Valletta. He reported to Pitt that, contrary to the views of other senior officers, Valletta could be reduced only by continuing with the naval blockade. Ill health compelled him to return to England, where he was immediately offered command of an army in the Mediterranean, to operate in Italy in conjunction with the Austrians. Disagreements with the duke of York, the commander-in-chief, and with government ministers over the size and composition of this army, and over the ministry's commitment to allow a Russian garrison into Malta when the French garrison eventually surrendered, resulted in his resignation in April 1800. He was then offered the important post of commander-in-chief of the army in Ireland, but before he could accept it he died, on 25 March 1801, at his home, the Thatched House, Richmond Park, Surrey. He was buried in the family vault at Petersham. There is a monument to him by Nollekens in Westminster Abbey.

Stuart was a brilliant and courageous soldier but a difficult subordinate. Fortescue has described him as a man of rare talent both as administrator and commander, 'the greatest of all the British officers of the period', and to be compared with Wellington (Fortescue, *Brit. army*, 4, 2.77). But Stuart was too arrogant, too contemptuous of the views of politicians, and too liable to quarrel with other commanders, whether naval or military, to have done the work that Wellington was later to do in Spain and Portugal. As the duke of York told George III on Stuart's resignation in 1800: 'I can only regret that Sir Charles Stuart's unfortunate jealousy of temper and impatience of controul from any superior authority preclude the possibility of taking advantage of his otherwise excellent talents' (*Correspondence of George III*, 3.337).

DESMOND GREGORY

Sources *A prime minister and his son: from the correspondence of the 3rd earl of Bute and of Lt-General the Hon. Sir Charles Stuart*, ed. Mrs E. S. Wortley (1925) · Fortescue, *Brit. army* · D. Gregory, *The ungovernable rock: a history of the Anglo–Corsican kingdom and its role in Britain's Mediterranean strategy during the revolutionary war (1793–1797)* (1985) · D. Gregory, *Minorca the illusory prize: a history of the British occupations of Minorca between 1708 and 1802* (1990) · D. Gregory, *Sicily the insecure base: a history of the British occupation of Sicily, 1806–1815* (1988) · D. Gregory, *Malta, Britain and the European powers, 1793–1815* (1996) · *The diary of Sir John Moore*, ed. J. F. Maurice, 2 vols. (1904) · *The dispatches and letters of Vice-Admiral Lord Viscount Nelson*, ed. N. H. Nicolas, 7 vols. (1844–6) · *Life and letters of Sir Gilbert Elliot, first earl of Minto, from 1751 to 1806*, ed. countess of Minto [E. E. E. Elliot-Murray-Kynynmound], 2 (1874) · Burke, *Peerage* (1976) · *GM*, 1st ser., 71 (1801), 374 · I. Lameire, *Les occupations militaires de l'île de Minorque pendant les guerres de l'ancien droit* (1908) · *The later correspondence of George III*, ed. A. Aspinall, 5 vols. (1962–70) · E. Haden-Guest, 'Stuart, Hon. Charles', HoP, *Commons* · C. T. Atkinson, 'Foreign regiments in the British army, 1793–1802, part 5: the Mediterranean and southern Europe', *Journal of the Society for Army Historical Research*, 22 (1943–4), 132–42

Archives NL Scot., corresp. | BL, letters to William Huskisson, Add. MSS 38736 · BL, corresp. with first earl of Liverpool, Add. MSS 38210–38227, 38307–38310 · NL Scot., papers of Sir Gilbert Elliot, first Earl Minto, M 35, 116, 1707, 11138 · NL Scot., corresp. with Sir Thomas Graham, MSS 3597–3625 · NMM, corresp. with Lord Minto, EU/103, 149, 152, 153 · PRO, Foreign Office records, FO 20/6, 25; FO 63/23, 24, 25, 28 · PRO, War Office records, WO 1/217, 218, 220, 291, 296, 297, 302 · U. Mich., Clements L., corresp. with Sir Henry Clinton

Likenesses J. Grozer, mezzotint, pubd 1794 (after G. Romney), BM, NPG · G. Romney, oils, Hunterian Museum and Art Gallery, Glasgow · plaster medallion (after J. Tassie), Scot. NPG

Stuart, Charles [called Hindoo Stuart] (**1757/8–1828**), art collector and author, was born in Galway, Ireland, and was reputedly the son of Thomas Smyth (*d.* 1785), MP for Limerick (1776–85). Stuart's will indicates that he had siblings, Eliza, John, and Thomas Stuart, but given his alleged parentage how he came to be known as Charles Stuart remains a mystery. He grew up in the Irish countryside and his later literary works indicate that he was well educated. By 1777, at nineteen, Stuart had sailed for India, having enlisted as a cadet in the East India Company army. In 1780 he was adjutant and between 1784 and 1794 quartermaster to the first European regiment of the Bengal army.

There are no reports that Stuart engaged in any significant military battles, but he rose steadily through the ranks after transferring to the Bengal native infantry in 1798, eventually becoming a major-general in 1814. Throughout his military career Stuart was an avid student of Indian languages, literature, and religion, and had occasion to be in far greater contact with Indians than was the norm. He travelled extensively and began to collect stone sculptures of Hindu deities as well as manuscripts, paintings, and other *objets d'art*. It has been said that he had an Indian concubine who predeceased him, and he referred to his native servants as his 'family'. There are also reports that he practised Hindu rituals publicly, including daily worship at the Ganges and offering puja to idols. Stuart retained two Brahmin priests in the care of his statues, according to local custom. He became well known in India as 'Hindoo Stuart', a man of great charity, eccentricity, and daring.

In 1798, under the pseudonym 'A Bengal Officer', Stuart began his writing career with a treatise entitled *Observations and Remarks on the Dress, Discipline, etc., of the Military*. He had strong opinions about how the Indian sepoy army ought to be run and had interests in instituting reform. However, by 1804 Stuart was suffering from poor health and returned to Britain for five years on furlough. After visiting his family in Ireland he travelled to England where he became involved in a political controversy which arose following the Vellore mutiny in 1806 over the extent to which Christian missionary work in India should be restricted. Charles Stuart, maintaining the pseudonym 'A Bengal Officer', joined two contemporaries, Thomas Twining and Major John Scott-Waring, on the side against Christian missionizing through the publication of two pamphlets known as *Vindication of the Hindoos*. These essays provided a passionate defence of Hinduism as a fine, long-standing moral religious system, in which Stuart argued that the Indians did not need Christianity. As a result, Stuart aroused the ire of pro-Christian movements who believed in British moral superiority, and was dismissed as an 'infidel'.

After publishing another pamphlet on the subject of female apparel, *The Ladies' Monitor*, Stuart returned to India and resumed his career in the Bengal army. By 1813 he attempted to implement some of his opinions and reforms by publishing orders to change the uniforms and hairstyles of the native soldiers under his command. This met with severe reprimand by his military superiors and a transfer to a new command. A friend reported that Major Stuart was very much broken afterwards. Nevertheless he continued to exercise his passion for Indian art, especially stone sculpture, and amassed a comprehensive collection which he eventually displayed for public view in his home in Calcutta.

Stuart died at home, Chowringhee, Calcutta, after a brief illness on 31 March 1828 and was buried with Christian rites on the following day in South Park Street cemetery, Calcutta. A tomb resembling a Hindu shrine, embellished with stone sculptures from his collection, was erected over the grave site. Prior to his death Stuart had arranged for the art collection to be shipped to England and sold for the benefit of his estate. Having died a bachelor, he left a sizeable bequest to his numerous native servants, while the bulk of his estate went to his kindred in Ireland.

More importantly Charles Stuart's legacy was to be found in his singular appreciation of Indian culture. His life story did not end with his death in 1828. His art collection can be appreciated today at the British Museum, where it became known as the Bridge collection. His writings indicate that he was a visionary far in advance of his times. It is not known why he chose to publish anonymously and, as a result, a controversy arose over the true identity of the author of the two *Vindication* pamphlets, as well as *The Ladies' Monitor*. It is possible that his position in the military or his irregular birth circumstances caused him to refrain from putting his name to his writings.

Over time, some writers ascribed these works to Major Scott-Waring; however, modern research and documentary evidence reveals 'A Bengal Officer' to be Charles Stuart. He deserves to be recognized as a vigorous freethinker and activist for social reform. Stuart dared to challenge the prevailing belief in British supremacy and superiority and met with great disapproval as a result. Nevertheless he was a man who stood his ground and lived his life by the courage of his convictions.   LIZ WOODS

Sources V. C. P. Hodson, *List of officers of the Bengal army, 1758–1834*, 4 vols. (1927–47) · will, BL OIOC, IOR L/AG/34/29/43, 213–24 · 'Major Gen. Chas. Stuart', *Asiatic Journal*, 26 (1828) · GM, 1st ser., 100/1 (1830), 470 · Bengal secret consultations, 17 Dec 1813, BL OIOC, IOR P/Secr./253 · J. Fisch, 'A solitary vindicator of the Hindus: the life and writings of General Charles Stuart', *Journal of the Royal Asiatic Society of Great Britain and Ireland* (1985), 35–57 · R. Chanda, 'Hindoo Stuart — a forgotten worthy and his tomb', *Bengal: Past and Present*, 50 (1935), 52–5 [Calcutta] · E. Cotton, 'Hindoo Stuart', *Bengal: Past and Present*, 46 (1933), 32–3 [Calcutta] · D. Kopf, *British orientalism and the Bengal renaissance* (Berkeley, California, 1969) · M. Willis, 'Sculpture of India', *A. W. Franks: nineteenth-century collections and the British Museum*, ed. M. Caygill (1997), 250–61 · H. Pearse, *The Hearseys: five generations of an Anglo-Indian family* (1905) · J. Fisch, 'A pamphlet war on Christian missions in India, 1807–1809', *Journal of Asian History*, 19 (1985), 22–70 [Wiesbaden] · E. Woods, unpublished paper to the British Library re: authorship of *Vindication of the Hindoos* and *The ladies' monitor*, 2001
Archives BL OIOC, Bengal secret consultations, IOR P/Secr./253, 17 Dec 1813 · BM, Bridge collection
Wealth at death £15,000 · 8300 Rupees · many bequests of a year's wages (amount not specified): proved, 28 Aug 1828, Charles Stuart's will — BL OIOC IOR L/AG/34/29/43

Stuart, Charles, Baron Stuart de Rothesay (1779–1845), diplomatist, was born on 2 January 1779, the elder son of Sir Charles *Stuart (1753–1801) and his wife, Anne Louisa (1757–1841), younger daughter of Lord Vere Bertie and his wife, Anne. His father was the fourth and favourite son of the prime minister John *Stuart, third earl of Bute.

Stuart was educated at Eton College (1787–95), Christ Church, Oxford (1797–8), and the University of Glasgow (1798–9); he was admitted to Lincoln's Inn on 6 November 1797 and may have read for the bar in 1800–01. He entered the diplomatic service in 1801. Appointments as secretary of legation at Vienna (1801–4) and secretary of embassy at St Petersburg (1804–8) were followed by a liaison and intelligence-gathering assignment with the provincial juntas in French-occupied Spain (1808–10). As minister at Lisbon (1810–14) he made himself indispensable to Wellington, and he was made a member of the Portuguese regency council. During the 'hundred days' (1815), he was ambassador at the courts of both the king of the Netherlands and Louis XVIII of France, who was in exile in Ghent. He was rewarded with a knighthood in 1812 and the GCB on 2 January 1815.

On 6 February 1816 Stuart married Lady Elizabeth Margaret (1789–1867), third daughter of Philip *Yorke, third

Charles Stuart, Baron Stuart de Rothesay (1779–1845), by Sir George Hayter, 1830

earl of Hardwicke. The marriage was one of convenience—Sir Charles was reported by Lady Granville to have 'no thoughts of parting with a French actress whom he keeps' (Surtees, 95)—but seems to have been happy none the less, and produced two remarkable daughters, Charlotte (1817–1861), later Lady Canning [*see* Canning, Charlotte], and Louisa Anne (1818–1891), later Lady Waterford [*see* Beresford, Louisa Anne], whose beauty belied their parentage, as both Sir Charles and Lady Stuart were plain.

In 1815 Stuart became ambassador at Paris, where he remained until 1824. His greatest diplomatic achievement was the treaty by which Brazil became independent of Portugal, negotiated on a joint Anglo-Portuguese special mission in 1825. He was reappointed as ambassador to France in 1828, and was created Baron Stuart de Rothesay of the Isle of Bute on 22 January that year. He was in Paris in 1830, at the time of the July revolution, and was rebuked by his government for not giving them sufficient warning. The foreign secretary, Lord Aberdeen, told him, 'This is a time when a little more exertion may reasonably be expected' (Aberdeen to Stuart, 31 July 1830; BL, Add. MSS). What Aberdeen meant by this was that he should keep them informed, but Stuart plunged into a frenzy of activity, which gravely embarrassed his government. Although instructed to maintain neutrality, he told the duke of Orléans (the future King Louis Philippe) that his claims were unlikely to be accepted by the great powers and became deeply involved in a plot to ensure that the succession passed to Charles X's grandson the duke of Bordeaux. When he learned of it the British prime minister, the duke of Wellington, was furious and pointed out that

Britain might be accused of promoting civil war in France. Aberdeen did not, as Wellington wished, recall Stuart but warned him that he might be publicly disavowed. Stuart indignantly replied that he had suppressed all mention of the matter in his official dispatches and he presumed that his private letters were not liable to be 'brought forward' (Stuart to Aberdeen, 23 Aug 1830; BL, Add. MS 43085). The matter did not leak out and no trace remains in the Foreign Office files.

Paris was an important centre for collectors at this time, and Stuart made extensive purchases, sometimes also acting as agent for George IV. He built Highcliffe Castle at Christchurch, Hampshire, a rare example of the romantic and picturesque style of architecture, and furnished it with his Parisian acquisitions. The whig government removed Stuart from Paris in 1831 and he was not employed again until Sir Robert Peel's government sent him to St Petersburg in 1841. He was already a sick man. In April 1842 the Russian chancellor, Count Nesselrode, called him 'un cadavre ambulant' (W. Hamilton to earl of Aberdeen, 6 April 1842; BL, Add. MS 43142). In July 1843 he had a stroke, which left him unable to conduct business. He evidently suffered from what is now called cerebrovascular disease. Although he tried to conceal his condition, his resignation was forced in March 1844. Stuart died at Highcliffe on 6 November 1845 from a series of strokes. He was buried a week later in St Mark's Church, Highcliffe, and his title became extinct.

ROBERT A. FRANKLIN

Sources R. A. Franklin, *Lord Stuart de Rothesay* (1993) · S. Medlam, *The Bettine, Lady Abingdon collection* (1996) · GEC, *Peerage*, new edn, vol. 12/1 · S. T. Bindoff and others, eds., *British diplomatic representatives, 1789–1852*, CS, 3rd ser., 50 (1934) · V. Stuart Wortley, *Highcliffe and the Stuarts* (1927) · *The dispatches of … the duke of Wellington … from 1799 to 1818*, ed. J. Gurwood, 13 vols. in 12 (1834–9) · L. Bethall, 'The independence of Brazil', *Cambridge history of Latin America*, 3, ed. L. Bethall (1985), 157–96 · private information (1986) · d. cert. · V. Surtees, *A second self: the letters of Harriet Granville, 1810–1845* (1990)

Archives Bodl. Oxf., travel journal · Indiana University, Bloomington, Lilly Library, corresp. and papers relating to Brazil · NL Scot., corresp. and papers · PRO, corresp. with Foreign Office · U. Edin. L., corresp. · University of Chicago Library, corresp. · University of Minnesota, Minneapolis, corresp. and papers | All Souls Oxf., letters to Sir Charles Richard Vaughan · BL, corresp. with Sir William A'Court, Add. MSS 41512–41513 · BL, corresp. with Lord Aberdeen, Add. MSS 43082–43085, 43097–43101 · BL, corresp. with Lord Bathurst, loan 57 · BL, dispatches to Lord Castlereagh, etc., Add. MS 31236 · BL, corresp. with second earl of Liverpool, Add. MSS 3825–3826, 38411, 38578, *passim* · BL, letters to Sir John Moore, Add. MS 57541 · Bucks. RLSS, letters to Lord Hobart · PRO, corresp. with Stafford Canning, FO 352 · PRO, corresp. with Lord Granville, PRO 30/29 · PRO NIre., corresp. with Lord Castlereagh, D3030 · U. Durham L., corresp. with Earl Grey · U. Nott. L., letters to Lord William Bentinck

Likenesses D. Foyatier, marble bust, 1823, Gov. Art Coll. · C. Landseer, sketch, 1825, repro. in C. Guinle de Paula Machado, ed., *Sketchbook containing studies made in Brazil, 1825–26, and associated documents* (1972) · oils, 1825–6, Gov. Art Coll. · F. Gérard, oils, 1828–31, V&A · G. Hayter, oils, 1830, Gov. Art Coll. [*see illus.*] · J. de Frey, engraving (after G. Hayter, 1830), NPG

Wealth at death under £30,000: GEC, *Peerage*

Stuart, Charles Edward. *See* Charles Edward (1720–1788).

Stuart, Charles Edward (1799?–1880). *See under* Stuart, John Sobieski Stolberg (1795?–1872).

Stuart, Daniel (1766–1846), newspaper proprietor and journalist, was born on 16 November 1766 in Edinburgh. Both his father and his grandfather were reputed to have been active Jacobites. In 1778 he went to London to join his elder brothers, Peter [*see below*] and Charles, who were already established in the print trade there. The three set up home in Charlotte Street, Portland Place, with their two sisters, Catherine and Elizabeth.

By 1788 Daniel Stuart was listed as the printer of the *Morning Post*. In 1795 he bought the paper for the relatively small sum of £600, after its circulation had fallen to about 350 copies per day. Under Stuart's leadership the *Morning Post* appears to have flourished. He claimed to have increased sales to more than 4500 by 1803. In this year he reportedly sold it owing to ill health for £25,000. Before this temporary interruption to his career Stuart had absorbed another newspaper, *The Telegraph*, into his fledgeling business empire, and attempted to buy the ailing *Gazetteer* in 1797.

During the early 1790s Stuart became deputy secretary of the Society of the Friends of the People, a group which campaigned for parliamentary reform. In 1794 his pamphlet *Peace and Reform, Against War and Corruption* appeared. The work, which was dedicated to the society, attacked Arthur Young's warning against following the example of the French revolutionaries, defended the revolution, and proposed a programme of parliamentary reform in Britain. In 1796 the *Morning Post* serialized Thomas Paine's *Decline and Fall of the English System of Finance*. The paper received harsh criticism from the pro-establishment newspaper the *Anti-Jacobin*. Stuart's brother-in-law was the philosopher Sir James *Mackintosh (1765–1832), honorary secretary of the Society of the Friends of the People, whom his sister Catherine had secretly married in 1789. Mackintosh wrote regularly for the *Morning Post*. Other contributors to the paper included Coleridge, Southey, Godwin, Lamb, and John Thelwell.

In 1800 or 1801 Stuart purchased *The Courier* with T. G. Street. Although they held an equal number of shares, Street was described as the sole editor. In 1815 Crabb Robinson claimed that Stuart had long since ceased to have anything to do with the management of the paper, but simply took his share of the profits and looked over the accounts. However, Coleridge appears to have attributed much of the paper's political tone to Stuart. During the Napoleonic wars *The Courier* was fiercely patriotic, its conservatism providing a sharp contrast to the radical edge which the *Post* had displayed. Coleridge, in a letter to Stuart which reveals the *Courier*'s importance, asserted that the paper greatly contributed to Napoleon's defeat by ensuring public support for the government's war efforts:

> It is far, very far, from hyperbole to affirm, that you did more against the French scheme of Continental domination, than the Duke of Wellington has done; or rather Wellington could neither have been supplied by the Ministers, nor the Ministers supported by the Nation, but for the tone first given, and then constantly kept up, by the plain, unministerial, anti-opposition, anti-jacobin, anti-gallican, anti-Napoleonic spirit of your writings, aided by the colloquial good style, and evident good sense, in which as acting on an immense mass of knowledge of existing men and existing circumstances, you are superior to any man I ever met with in my life time. (Coleridge, 2.660)

Canning claimed that, unknown to Stuart, Street was given as much as £2000 to support the Perceval ministry in *The Courier*. Stuart himself maintained that neither he nor the paper had ever taken such bribes. He wrote to J. Benjafield in 1811:

> I often hear of persons, and sometimes meet them, who assert that they can prove I receive a regular salary from the ministry for the support *The Courier* gives them, though I never received a shilling from any minister, or for any such consideration. (Benjafield, iv)

A letter from Canning to Huskisson in 1809 states that Stuart was still writing for the paper and that Street and Stuart were divided politically, with Stuart opposed to *The Courier*'s attacks on Canning. In 1823 Stuart still owned a third share of *The Courier* but appears to have fallen out with William Mudford, who became editor in 1817, again over politics. Stuart refused to back Mudford in his denial that he was in the pay of the French government.

Stuart married Mary Napier in 1813, and they went on to have three sons. The following year he bought a house in Harley Street, having made a large fortune from his newspaper ventures. In 1817 he successfully pursued a case for libel against Daniel Lovell, the proprietor of *The Statesman*, who had accused him of embezzling money from the funds of the Society of the Friends of the People. In the same year Stuart purchased Wykeham Park, a 300 acre estate near Banbury. Here he spent half of each year, becoming an active magistrate, a deputy lieutenant, and in 1823 serving as high sheriff. He died in his London home on 25 August 1846. His demise has been partly attributed to the shock of his eldest son's death in 1842, which brought about a long illness culminating in a fatal bout of dysentery. Although he had been involved in a public argument with the executors of Coleridge's estate concerning his alleged mistreatment of the poet, Charles Lamb said of Stuart that 'He ever appeared to us one of the finest tempered of Editors' (Lamb, 212).

Daniel's brother **Peter Stuart** (*b. c.*1760, *d.* in or after 1812), newspaper proprietor, purchased *The Oracle* in 1794, reputedly for as little as £80 since the circulation was only 800 a day. He had previously started the *Morning Star*, the first daily evening paper in London. In 1805 *The Oracle* was accused of publishing a libel on the House of Commons, following the publication of an article about Lord Melville. Peter Stuart was forced to appear at the house to apologise. In 1812 he asked the prince of Wales for a sinecure in return for a pamphlet written in his support, entitled *Thoughts on the State of the Country*. This request was granted, apparently after Stuart threatened the prince with negative publicity. HANNAH BARKER

Sources A. Aspinall, *Politics and the press, c.1780–1850* (1949) · M. Stuart, ed., *Letters from the Lake poets* (1889) · J. Benjafield, *Statement of facts* (1813) · W. Hindle, *The Morning Post, 1772–1937: portrait of*

a newspaper (1937), 65–85 • BM, Huskisson MSS, Add. MS 38737 • PRO, Stamp Office records, AO 31950–80 • A. Andrews, *The history of British journalism*, 2 (1859), 25–7 • *Letters of Samuel Taylor Coleridge*, ed. E. H. Coleridge, 2 (1895), 660 • *GM*, 2nd ser., 27 (1847), 90–91 • C. Lamb, *Essays of Elia*, [new edn] (1835), 212

Archives BL, corresp., Add MS 34046
Likenesses J. Partridge, oils, Scot. NPG

Stuart, Lord **Dudley Coutts** (1803–1854), politician, was born on 11 January 1803 in South Audley Street, London, the only son of John Stuart, first marquess of Bute (1744–1814), and his second wife, Frances (*d.* 1832), daughter of Thomas Coutts, a banker. Although Dudley and his sister Frances (1801–1859) were the only children of this couple, Stuart had no chance of succession to his father's title, as John Stuart had ten children with his first wife, seven sons among them. At least three of Stuart's half-brothers had sat in parliament and that fact—together with the memory of the career of their grandfather John Stuart, third earl of Bute—had certainly some influence on the atmosphere in which he was brought up. Among his youthful associates were Dudley Ryder, Lord Sandon, and Lord Holland's son Henry Edward Fox. He was also steered towards public activity by his beloved mother, who superintended his education. His home tutor was the Revd Edmund Mortlock, and they travelled in Italy. Charles Dickens's *Uncommercial Traveller* paper, 'The Italian Prisoner', is a romanticized account of how Stuart secured the release of a political prisoner about this time.

In 1820 Stuart became a member of Christ's College, Cambridge. Three years later (1823) he graduated MA. Soon after that, in 1824 and to the consternation of many of his relatives and friends, he married Napoleon's niece Christina Alexandrina Egypta (1798–1847), daughter of Lucien Bonaparte, prince of Canino. They married at Rome, in secret, and according to Roman Catholic rites. On 21 May 1826 they went through an Anglican ceremony in Florence. The reappearance in 1827 of Christina's first husband, a Swede, Count Aasvid de Possé—who had been reported dead—was an inconvenience: one that required a papal dispensation for an annulment, which was granted the following year. Despite the birth of a son—Paul Amadeus Francis (1825–1889)—the Stuarts' marriage proved a failure. By 1840 Lady Stuart had left their only child with her husband and moved to Rome. She died there on 19 May 1847.

In the meantime, Stuart was elected to the House of Commons as the Liberal member for Arundel (1830). He was re-elected in 1831, 1832, and 1835. The greatest influence on Stuart's views was his uncle, and first political mentor, Sir Francis Burdett. Drawn by his example, Lord Dudley joined the group of the Reform Bill supporters. His parliamentary maiden speech was made in favour of the bill, on 7 March 1831.

In 1832 Stuart became acquainted with a few participants of the suppressed Polish uprising of 1830–31, who had emigrated to western Europe. Three of them, Prince Adam Czartoryski, Julian Ursyn Niemcewicz, and Count Wladyslaw Zamoyski, soon became intimate friends. Czartoryski especially, a former minister of Emperor Alexander I and in 1830–31 one of the leaders of the Polish national government, made a deep impression on Stuart. The fascination of the prince's personality, newly discovered family connections with him, and Stuart's approbation of Czartoryski's political opinions, gave a stimulus to his activities on behalf of the Poles.

There were two main aspects of this activity. As early as 1833 Stuart became the leading organizer of the action to provide help for hundreds of Polish refugees who had arrived in England. He was supported by the members of the London Literary Association of the Friends of Poland (LAFP), established by Thomas Campbell in 1832. In 1833, accepting the post of one of its vice-presidents, Lord Dudley became *spiritus movens* of the association, far more active than the nominal president, Thomas Wentworth Beaumont. After Beaumont's death in 1848 Stuart took over his function and performed it until 1854. Under his guidance LAFP organized many public subscriptions for the relief of the Poles. In 1834, as a result of Stuart's motion, the House of Commons voted an annual grant for the Polish exiles of £10,000. LAFP distributed the grant—which was renewed every year at a different amount—until 1838, when the Treasury took over the task.

The engagement of Lord Dudley in affording the relief for the Poles was as strong as his support for their political claims. He was convinced that restoration of Poland would not only be an act of justice, but it also would help to eliminate a menace to British interests caused by Russian expansion in the Middle East. Until 1837 he expressed these opinions mostly in parliament, where he was supported by Sir Stratford Canning, Joseph Hume, Robert Cutlar Fergusson, David Urquhart, and several other politicians. Debates initiated by them played a considerable role in stirring up the anti-Russian feelings in England. But theories about the growing danger from Russia and the necessity of supporting Turkey had also their eloquent opponents at that time. One of them was Richard Cobden, who regarded the British Russophobes as false prophets and dangerous warmongers.

In 1837 Stuart was defeated at Arundel by Lord Fitzalan. For the next decade he could only give some informal inspiration to parliamentary debates on Poland. Pro-Polish agitation was meanwhile led by him at public meetings, in private conversations, and through the press and other publications, which included *Speech of Lord Dudley Stuart on the policy of Russia delivered in the House of Commons, Friday, February 19, 1836* (1836), *An appeal of the Literary Association of the Friends of Poland to the inhabitants of Great Britain and Ireland in behalf of the Polish refugees* (1840), and the *Speech of Lord Dudley Stuart in the House of Commons on the 16th of May, 1848 with official and other documents relating to the insurrection in Posen and the bombardment of Cracow* (1848). He also facilitated the contacts between British officials and the Poles and backed up Czartoryski's political undertakings.

At the general election of 1847 Stuart returned to Westminster, via the metropolitan borough of Marylebone. He was re-elected in 1852, and kept the seat until his death. In the spring of 1848, with continental Europe in turmoil,

Lord Dudley shared the opinion that the restoration of Poland was very close. He tried to gain active support in Whitehall for that idea but with no positive results. Once hopes for Poland had vanished, he started to organize help for Hungarians, who were fighting for independence. After the suppression of the Hungarian uprising (1849) he was among those who insisted on firm British action in defence of several thousand emigrants who took refuge in Turkey and whose extradition was demanded by eastern powers.

From 1850 Stuart's public activity declined. Yet his contacts with the Poles were not suspended: in 1853 and 1854 he spent a few weeks in Turkey, inducing local authorities to form Polish military units and to use these against Russia. In the autumn of 1854 he went to Sweden where, in conversations with King Oscar I and his advisers, he sought approval of the idea of the restoration of Poland and encouraged the Swedes to take part in the war. All of these activities broke off suddenly. Stuart died in Stockholm on 17 November 1854 of pneumonia, which followed a typhoid fever. His body was returned to England and he was buried in All Saints parish church, Hertford, on 16 December 1854. *Burke's Peerage* (1857), a publication not easily moved to elegy, recorded that his death was 'deeply lamented'.   KRZYSZTOF MARCHLEWICZ

Sources Lord D. C. Stuart, Polish matters, Harrowby MSS Trust, Sandon Hall, Staffordshire · Biblioteka Ksiazat Czartoryskich, Cracow, Poland, Hotel Lambert Archives · Biblioteka Polska, Paris, France, documents and records of the Committee of the Polish Emigration in England · Biblioteka Polskiej Akademii Nauk, Cracow, Poland, S. E. Koźmian MSS · *GM*, 2nd ser., 43 (1855), 79–81 · *Report of the annual meeting of the Literary Association of the Friends of Poland* (1833–59) · *Speech of Lord Dudley Stuart on the policy of Russia delivered in the House of Commons, Friday, February 19, 1836* (1836) · *Appeal of the Literary Association of the Friends of Poland to the inhabitants of Great Britain and Ireland in behalf of the Polish refugees* (1840) · *Address of the Literary Association of the Friends of Poland to the people of Great Britain and Ireland* (1846) · *Speech of Lord Dudley Stuart in the House of Commons on the 16th of May, 1848 with official and other documents relating to the insurrection in Posen and the bombardment of Cracow* (1848) · *An address of condolence on the death of the Rt Hon. Lord Dudley Coutts Stuart, M.P., president of the Literary Association of the Friends of Poland, delivered by Lieut. Charles Szulczewski, secretary of the association, at a meeting of the Polish exiles held at Sussex Chambers, Duke Street, St James's, on 29th November, 1854* (1854) · Venn, *Alum. Cant.* · Burke, *Peerage* (1857) · H. J. Spencer, 'Stuart, Lord Dudley Coutts', HoP, *Commons, 1820–32* [draft] · K. Marchlewicz, *Polonofil doskonaly: propolska dzialalnosc charytatywna i polityczna lorda Dudleya Couttsa Stuarta, 1803–1854* (Poznan, 2001)

Archives Sandon Hall, Staffordshire, Harrowby MSS Trust, corresp. and papers, particularly relating to Polish affairs | Biblioteka Jagiellońska, Cracow, Poland, P. Falkenhagen-Zaleski papers, letters to P. Falkenhagen-Zaleski, MS 3774 II · Biblioteka Ksiazat Czartoryskich, Cracow, Poland, Hotel Lambert Archives, corresp. with A. J. Czartoryski, MSS 5473 II, 5474 II, 5475 IV, 5517 III, 5518 I, 5519 I · Biblioteka Ksiazat Czartoryskich, Cracow, Poland, Hotel Lambert Archives, letters to W. Zamoyski, MS 6959 III · Biblioteka Polska, Paris, France, documents and records of the Committee of Polish Emigration in England, corresp. with the committee, MSS 591, 592, 596 · Biblioteka Polskiej Akademii Nauk, Cracow, Poland, S. E. Koźmian MSS, letters to S. E. Koźmian, MS 2210, vol. 14 · Biblioteka Polskiej Akademii Nauk, Kórnik, Poland, W. Zamoyski and L. Niedźwiecki MSS, documents relating to the activities of D. Stuart and the Literary Association of the Friends of Poland, MSS 2476–2477 · BL, letters to Lord Holland, Add. MSS 52015–52016 · LPL, corresp. with John Lee · U. Southampton L., corresp. with Lord Palmerston

Likenesses G. Hayter, oils, 1830–34 · Count D'Orsay, lithograph, 1839, Biblioteka Polskiej Akademii Nauk [Polish Academy of Sciences library], Cracow, T. Lenartowicz papers, MS 2029, p. 191 · oils, 1846–54, probably Polish National Lodge No. 534, London; repro. in M. Danilewicz, 'Nostrove vashia: Nieznana karta dziejów wolnomularstwa polskiego w Anglii', *Wiadomości* (11 Feb 1962) · A. Oleszczyński, line engraving, 1855 (after G. Hayter), BM; repro. in M. Handelsman, *Adam Czartoryski*, vol. II, no. 3 · commemorative medal, 1859, priv. coll. · G. Hayter, group portrait, oils (*The House of Commons, 1833*), NPG · Ploszczynski, group portrait, lithograph (after C. Compton, *Banquet given by the reformers of Marylebone, 1st Dec 1847*), BM · portrait, repro. in *ILN* (1843–9)

Stuart [Stewart], **Esmé**, **first duke of Lennox** (*c.*1542–1583), courtier and magnate, was born in France, the only child of John Stewart or Stuart (*d.* 1567), fifth seigneur d'Aubigny, and his wife, Anne de La Queulle (*d.* 1579), fourth daughter and coheir of François, seigneur de La Queulle, and his wife, Anne de Rohan. John Stewart, a Scot, had been adopted at an early age by the maréchal d'Aubigny, who had made him his heir, and he had spent his life in France.

Background and arrival in Scotland Brought up by his mother at La Verrerie, near Aubigny, Esmé Stuart succeeded his father as seigneur d'Aubigny in 1567, and in 1572 married Catherine de Balsac (*d. c.*1631), youngest daughter of Guillaume de Balsac, seigneur d'Entragues. Slim, with a neatly trimmed red beard, mild-mannered and affable, Aubigny was sent by the French in 1576 as an envoy to the Low Countries, and then went to England on a diplomatic mission, where he was reported to be in dispute with representatives of the infant Lady Arabella Stuart (as the name was usually spelt in England) over their competing claims to her dead father's earldom of Lennox.

Although to all appearance a Frenchman, Aubigny remained conscious of his Scottish origins. Not only was he in line for the Lennox titles and estates, he was also a descendant of James II, king of Scots, and he had been first cousin of James VI's murdered father, Lord Darnley. In the end the Lennox earldom was granted to his elderly uncle, Robert Stewart, bishop of Caithness, and when Robert married for the first time seven months later Aubigny would have been aware that if his uncle now had sons—an unlikely prospect—then their claims would supersede his. A sudden message from Scotland inviting him to visit his father's native land therefore arrived at a propitious moment. A journey north would allow him to establish his own position, and in any case the invitation apparently came from the king himself and could not be refused. Moreover, the leaders of the Hamilton family, hereditary enemies of the Lennox Stewarts, had recently been accused of the murder of two earlier regents of Scotland, James Stewart, earl of Moray, and Aubigny's uncle Matthew, fourth earl of Lennox. The downfall of Lord John and Lord Claud Hamilton seemed assured, and

Aubigny could hope to benefit, not least because the main issue between the two families was their quarrel as to who had the senior position in the Scottish succession, both being descended from daughters of James II.

In September 1579 Aubigny therefore took leave of his wife and five young children and set out for Scotland. He was seen off at Dieppe by the French courtiers, led by the duc de Guise, and a few days later he landed at Leith and made his way to Holyroodhouse, where he presented himself to James VI. By 10 October Nicholas Errington, the English envoy, was writing to tell Walsingham that, 'Touching M. d'Aubigny, it appears that the king is much delighted with his company' (*CSP Scot.*, *1574–81*, 355). The newcomer had been given the fairest and nearest lodging to the royal apartments in Holyroodhouse. It seemed that he would spend the winter in Scotland and there was talk of his wife's coming to join him.

Rise to prominence The young king was entranced with his charming, sophisticated 37-year-old cousin. Starved as he had been of affection throughout his childhood, James revelled in Aubigny's kindly attention. Here at last was a relative of his own, sensitive, cultured, and perceptive, who treated him as an adult, discussing theology and politics and poetry with him, respecting his views, and nurturing his self-confidence. James was overjoyed. Not everyone was so delighted with Aubigny's arrival, however, for it was widely believed that he had come as a Roman Catholic agent of the duc de Guise, to scheme for the overthrow of protestantism and the return of Mary, queen of Scots. James ignored the rumours, however, and after the Hamiltons were forfeited in November 1579 he made Aubigny commendator of Arbroath Abbey, a lucrative position previously occupied by Lord John Hamilton. On 5 March 1580 Aubigny was granted the earldom of Lennox, which his uncle had been persuaded to resign in his favour. By 13 September he was being mentioned as keeper of Dumbarton Castle, and on 11 October he was nominated chamberlain and first gentleman of the royal chamber.

Sir James Melville of Halhill believed that Lennox was 'of nature upright, just and gentle, but lacked experience in the state of the country' (*Memoirs*, 107), commenting that he would have been 'tolerable, if he had happened upon as honest counsellors as he was well inclined himself' (ibid., 27–8). As it was, Lennox turned to James Stewart, later earl of Arran, who had been eagerly cultivating his friendship. Together they outmanoeuvred the increasingly unpopular fourth earl of Morton, formerly regent, and on 31 December 1580, at Lennox's prompting, Stewart accused Morton before the privy council of having participated in the murder of Lord Darnley. Morton was arrested and imprisoned. For the next twenty months, Lennox and Stewart governed Scotland.

Lennox and the young king now set about trying to silence the alarmist rumours about the earl's supposed intentions. On 28 January 1581 James signed the negative confession, a strongly worded document condemning 'the Roman Antichrist' and all the doctrines of the Catholic church, and Lennox let it be known that he had converted to protestantism. His conversion appears to have been genuine and, if he had ever entertained the ambition of restoring Queen Mary to the throne, his views were modified by his growing loyalty to her son. When the duc de Guise early in 1581 put forward Mary's plan for an 'association', whereby she and James VI would rule Scotland jointly, Lennox's mildly encouraging response nevertheless included the insistence that James should retain his title as king. Any scheme for Mary's release would have to be led by Guise himself, Lennox said.

Duke of Lennox Under Lennox's administration parliament set up a commission to improve the stipends of ministers, but this too failed to reassure the ultra-protestants. They noted with alarm the appointment of some of Mary's former supporters to the privy council in the aftermath of Morton's execution on 2 June 1581, but regardless of his subjects' misgivings James continued to shower gifts upon his favourite. On 5 June Lennox was granted the lordship and regality of Dalkeith, Aberdour, and other properties which had belonged to Morton, and on 5 August 1581 at an elaborate ceremony in Holyroodhouse he was created duke of Lennox, earl of Darnley, and lord of Aubigny, Tarboltoun, and Dalkeith, the only duke in Scotland. By now he and Stewart, then earl of Arran, were rivals rather than friends, with Arran protesting volubly against Lennox's right to bear the crown at the meeting of parliament in October. Presumably Arran's jealousy had been intensified by the knowledge that the king intended to have Lennox recognized as his heir during that session of parliament, but ecclesiastical opposition became so vehement that James had to abandon this plan.

The privy council had split into two separate factions. Arran and his sympathizers met at Holyrood, while Lennox and his supporters held their discussions at Dalkeith. Arran gave people to understand that he and his colleague were at odds because he was trying to prevent Lennox from plotting against protestantism, but their differences in fact had far more to do with their competing desires to control access to the king. To an extent matters were smoothed over on 2 December after Arran agreed to resign his office as captain of the royal guard, leaving Lennox in sole charge of the royal household. However, rumours of Lennox's involvement in Roman Catholic plots were still circulating. The situation was made worse when his administration refused to accept the condemnation of episcopacy by the general assembly of the Church of Scotland, and its arrangement for Robert Montgomerie to be appointed to the vacant see of Glasgow. Furious, the presbytery of Edinburgh excommunicated Montgomerie, but Lennox had the excommunication annulled by royal prerogative.

Fall from power Early in 1582 Lennox was secretly visited by two Jesuits, William Crichton and William Holt, who invited him to take command of an army to be raised by Philip II for the invasion of England, with the aim of freeing Queen Mary and placing her on the English throne.

Rumours about this scheme were rife and on 12 July the king was forced to issue a proclamation denouncing current allegations that Lennox was a 'deviser' of 'the erecting of papistrie' and reiterating that the duke had 'sworne in the presence of God, approved with the holie action of the Lord's Table' to maintain protestantism and was 'readie to seale the samine with his blood' (Calderwood, 3.783).

These denials were in vain, and on 22 August 1582, in the Ruthven raid, a group of ultra-protestant notables, including former adherents of Regent Morton, seized the king in protest at Lennox's regime and the extravagant expenditure of the recently enlarged royal household. Led by the earl of Gowrie the Ruthven raiders took the government into their own hands for the next ten months. Arran attempted to ride to the king's rescue, but he was imprisoned, while Lennox was ordered to leave the country. Plunged into despair Lennox rode to Dumbarton where it was said that he was 'so far appalled and cast down as there appeared in him little courage or resolution' (Willson, 45). He knew his enemies were saying that he had been plotting to betray the king, and his greatest fear was that James had believed them and had personally ordered his banishment. Desperately, he wrote him a series of letters, but received no reply, for the king was in no position to respond.

Eventually Lennox rode back to Dalkeith. On 18 December he sent James another long letter, declaring that 'whatever might happen to me, I shall alwayes be your very faithful servant ... in spite of all you will be always my true master, and he alone in this world whom my heart is resolved to serve' (CSP Scot., 1581–3, 223). That same day he rode for London, where he had an audience with Elizabeth I. She later told James VI in a letter about her conversation with Lennox, 'whom at the first we did roundly charge with such matters whereof we thought him culpable' (ibid., 251). Lennox next crossed the channel and was reunited with his family. He continued to send urgent letters to James, but early in February he fell seriously ill, in Paris. According to Calderwood he was suffering from 'a dissenterie, or excoriatioun of the inward parts, engendred of melancholie, wherewith was joyned gonorrhea' (Calderwood, 3.715). The attentions of the leading French doctors failed to save him, and as he lay dying he declared again that he was a protestant. He wished to be buried at Aubigny, he said, but he wanted his embalmed heart to be sent to James and commended his young children to the king. He died on 26 May 1583.

News of Lennox's death became known in Scotland on 4 June, and James could scarcely believe it. His distress was compounded when Aubigny's final letter to him arrived a few days later. That autumn the king wrote a long vernacular poem mourning the loss of his friend. 'Ane Metaphoricall Invention of a Tragedie called Phoenix' tells the moving tale of a beautiful and exotic phoenix, which makes its way from Arabia to Scotland where it is tamed by the king. The other birds, envious, attack it and, in spite of the monarch's efforts to protect it, it eventually flies away and dies in a foreign land:

... now begin
My woes: her death makes lyfe to grief in me.
(Bergeron, 34)

Whether the duke's embalmed heart ever came to Scotland remains unknown, but in November Lennox's elder son, Ludovick (or Louis) *Stuart (or Stewart), arrived at James's invitation, and the king subsequently arranged the betrothal of Lennox's three daughters to Scottish noblemen. Lennox's widow lived until about 1631.

The king and his cousin According to one of James VI's biographers, the duke of Lennox 'possessed such genius for intrigue and deception that contemporaries and posterity alike have been baffled as to his true intentions' (Willson, 32). Nineteenth- and early twentieth-century historians were in no doubt as to Lennox's duplicitous motives in coming to Scotland, accepting that he was intent on subverting the protestant religion and restoring Queen Mary. More recent writers have been inclined to believe that he was prompted rather by self-interest and the desire to establish his claim to the throne. His brief intervention in Scottish affairs lasted for only three years, but his influence on the young James VI was considerable. The nature of their relationship has been the subject of much speculation, and from the start there have been allegations that Lennox introduced James not only to French poetry but also to homosexuality. According to one Scottish chronicler, 'His majesty having conceived an inward affection to the Lord d'Aubigny, entered in great familiarity and quiet purposes with him', while the church ministers accused the duke of setting out 'to draw the king to carnal lust' (ibid., 36).

'I have such extreme regret that I desire to die rather than to live, fearing that that has been the occasion of your no longer loving me', Lennox had told James in his last letter (CSP Scot., 1581–3, 223). However, it would be a mistake to read too much into the often extravagant language of the sixteenth-century courtier. Lennox's evident affection for his lonely young cousin brought him a glittering career, but there is no cause to think that he deliberately exploited the king's adolescent sexuality for his own benefit. Whatever James's later sexual preferences, it is not unusual for a young adolescent to hero-worship a handsome and accomplished older man, and it may be that, closely related by blood as they were, they shared a genuine sense of affinity. It was undeniably a personal tragedy for them both when their mutually rewarding friendship evoked the bitter enmity of the Scottish courtiers and led to their final separation.

ROSALIND K. MARSHALL

Sources CSP Scot., 1574–85 · J. Goodare and M. Lynch, eds., The reign of James VI (2000) · E. C. Cust, Some account of the Stuarts of Aubigny in France (1891) · D. M. Bergeron, Royal family, royal lovers: King James of England and Scotland (1991) · M. Lee, Great Britain's Solomon: James VI and I in his three kingdoms (1990) · W. Fraser, The Lennox (1874), 2.319 · G. R. Hewitt, Scotland under Morton (1982) · G. Donaldson, Scotland: James V to James VII (1965), 172–3, 175–8, 187–8 · J. H. Willson, King James VI and I (1956) · J. Fergusson, The man behind Macbeth and other studies (1969) · The memoirs of Sir James Melville of Halhill, ed. G. Donaldson (1969) · G. Donaldson and R. S. Morpeth, Who's who in Scottish history (1973) · G. P. V. Akrigg, Jacobean pageant: the court of

King James I (1962) · R. Ashton, *James I by his contemporaries* (1969), 106–8 · D. Calderwood, *The history of the Kirk of Scotland*, ed. T. Thomson and D. Laing, 8 vols., Wodrow Society, 7 (1842–9), vol. 3, p. 783 · GEC, *Peerage*, 7.602–4

Likenesses F. Quesnel, drawing, Bibliothèque Nationale, Paris · P. Roberts, engraving (after unknown artist), repro. in J. Pinkerton, *Iconographia Scotica* (1797) · oils, Scot. NPG · oils, Longleat House, Wiltshire · oils, Paxton House, Scottish borders; registered with Scot. NPG, neg. H7032

Stuart, Esmé, **third duke of Lennox** (1579?–1624), nobleman, was the second son of Esmé *Stuart (c.1542–1583), seigneur d'Aubigny and first duke of Lennox, and Catherine de Balsac d'Entragues (d. c.1631). The family was a junior branch of the Scottish royal dynasty that had established itself in France in the fifteenth century. In 1579 the elder Esmé travelled to Edinburgh from the French court and quickly became the favourite of James VI, who in 1580 created him duke of Lennox. Driven from power in 1582, Lennox returned to France and died the next year. His eldest son, Ludovick *Stuart, who became second duke of Lennox, was sent to be raised at the Scottish court, while the younger Esmé remained in France as seigneur d'Aubigny. Aubigny attended the University of Bourges, did homage to Henry IV on April 8 1600, and served in the ceremonial guard of the *cent gentilhommes* at the French court.

By 1603 Aubigny had moved to Edinburgh, probably in the company of Lennox, who served as James's ambassador to Paris in 1601. Both brothers followed the king to London in 1603, where they were appointed gentlemen of the newly constituted royal bedchamber. Over the next several years Aubigny was one of the leading recipients of James's bounty, receiving concealed crown lands worth £1000 a year, cash gifts of £18,000, and other rewards. In 1609 the king arranged Aubigny's marriage with Katherine (c.1592–1637), only daughter and heir of Gervase, Lord Clifton of Leighton Bromswold, Huntingdonshire; they had nine children. Their eldest son, James *Stuart, was born in 1612, and their youngest child, Lord Bernard *Stuart, in 1622. During 1619 Aubigny was raised to the English peerage as earl of March and appointed joint lord lieutenant of Huntingdonshire. He became third duke of Lennox on his brother's death, which occurred on 16 February 1624, and knight of the Garter on 22 April the same year, but died of a spotted fever at the house of Sir Christopher Hatton in Kirby, Northamptonshire, on 30 July. He was buried on 6 August in Westminster Abbey.

R. MALCOLM SMUTS

Sources GEC, *Peerage* · E. Cust, *Some account of the Stuarts of Aubigny, France* (1891) · N. Cuddy, 'The revival of the entourage: the bedchamber of James I, 1603–1625', *The English court: from the Wars of the Roses to the civil war*, ed. D. R. Starkey and others (1987), 173–225 · *CSP dom.* · L. Stone, *The crisis of the aristocracy, 1558–1641* (1965) · W. Forbes-Leith, *The Scots men-at-arms and life-guards in France*, 2 vols. (1882) · *The letters of John Chamberlain*, ed. N. E. McClure, 2 vols. (1939) · State Papers Domestic, reign of James I, PRO, SP 14 [scattered references]

Likenesses oils, 1590, Scot. NPG · eleventh earl of Buchan, pencil and chalk drawing (after a portrait), Scot. NPG · F. Quesnel?, crayon drawing, Bibliothèque Nationale, Paris · oils, Longleat, Wiltshire

Stuart [née Howard; *married name* Prannell], **Frances**, **duchess of Lennox and Richmond** [*other married name* Frances Seymour, countess of Hertford] (1578–1639), noblewoman, was born at Lychet, Dorset, on 27 July 1578, between nine and ten at night, the only child of Mabel Burton (1540–1580) with her husband, Thomas, first Viscount Howard of Bindon (1520–1582).

Orphaned at age three, Frances was made a ward of her cousin Thomas, Baron Howard de Walden (later created earl of Suffolk). A dowerless maid, she had no resource but her beauty, royal extraction, and well-connected relatives whereby to secure a marriage settlement. At age thirteen she was wedded to a wealthy young vintner of London and Hertford, Henry Prannell (d. 1599), eldest son and heir of Henry Prannell (d. 1588), a London alderman. The couple's marriage was celebrated by Jo. M. with a tract called *Phillipes Venus* (1591); but William Cecil, Lord Burghley, who was obliged to keep a watchful eye on the queen's Howard cousins, was incensed: he had personally intended, under Elizabeth's direction, to arrange a match for the maid. Henry Prannell's letter of apology to Cecil (8 February 1592) is preserved among the Burghley papers. The young couple appear to have escaped further censure; but Thomas Mountforde, the prebendary of Westminster who performed the ceremony, was suspended for three years by Archbishop Whitgift.

Beginning in May 1597 Mrs Prannell regularly visited Dr Simon Forman, a London physician and astrologer of mixed fame, to learn whether her husband would return from sea, and if not, whether she might marry her 'love', Henry Wriothesley, the earl of Southampton; also, to learn by giving water (in July and August) whether she were pregnant. Forman predicted that Frances would 'change her estat 3 times', and found that the stars shone favourably on her desired match, despite her 'woman enimie', Elizabeth Vernon (Bodl. Oxf., MS Ashmole 226). Upon returning home, Henry Prannell was honoured with Leon Battista Alberti's *Hecatonphila: the Arte of Love* (1598, registered 20 December 1597) in an anonymous translation by Anthony Munday. In Munday's treatment, dedicated to Henry, Frances is transparently figured as 'Hecatonphila', the mistress of one hundred loves, yet an affectionate and faithful wife during her husband's absence, Penelope-like.

Henry Prannell died on 10 December 1599 at his house in Hertfordshire, leaving behind a beautiful and wealthy 21-year-old widow who inherited all. Southampton in the meantime had secretly married Elizabeth Vernon and suffered disgrace. In December 1600, when the widow Prannell ended her mourning, she was besieged by suitors, among whom was Edward *Seymour (1539?–1621), the 61-year-old earl of Hertford, whose second wife (another Frances Howard) had died in May 1598 and who offered the young lady a jointure of more than £4000 upon his decease. On Dr Forman's advice Mrs Prannell accepted Hertford's suit, and on 27 May 1601 married him, at Hertford House on Canon Row.

Among the rejected suitors were Sir William Woodhouse, Sir William Evers, and Sir George *Rodney, the last

Frances Stuart, duchess of Lennox and Richmond (1578–1639), by Francis Delaram, in or before 1621

of whom lost his wits upon news of Mrs Prannell's marriage. Following the couple to their Wiltshire estate, Rodney wrote the countess a woebegone 'Elegia', using blood for ink, in which he threatened suicide. In her 'Answer', a witty verse-epistle of 160 lines, the countess draws on various literary sources, including Munday's *Hecatonphila* and Shakespeare's *As You Like It*, to mock Rodney's Petrarchan posturing:

> No, no, I never yet could hear one prove
> That there was ever any died for love.
> (Seymour, ll. 139–40)

Upon receipt of this, Rodney wrote a farewell note and slit his throat.

Defeating Dr Forman's prognosis, Hertford lived for another twenty years, by which time Lady Seymour was past childbearing age. It was an unhappy marriage. Fiercely jealous, resentful of his bride's popularity at court, the earl kept his lady in the country, allowing her much freedom to hunt rabbits in the warrens of Old Sarum (owned by Robert Cecil, the countess's most powerful friend and ally), but only rare visits to London. Hertford died on 6 April 1621, at the age of almost eighty-two, and was buried in Salisbury Cathedral.

Wilson reports that while the earl was yet living, the countess was courted by Ludovick *Stuart, duke of Lennox (1574–1624), who visited her wearing 'odd disguises'. That she sometimes deceived her jealous husband concerning her friendships is evident from her correspondence with the earl of Salisbury. Only a few weeks after the earl's death, Countess Frances was secretly married to the duke, and henceforth maintained great pomp, not so much as attending chapel without a stately procession. In 1623 the Stuarts were made duchess and duke of Richmond as well as of Lennox.

Ludovick Stuart died in bed, in London, on 16 February 1624. The earl of Southampton followed nine months later, in Holland. The duchess, who grieved for both, continued a widow until her death, by report vowing not to remarry unless it should be to the king. On 8 October 1639 she died at Exeter House in the Strand, aged sixty-one, contented and very rich. She is interred beside her third husband in Henry VII's Chapel in Westminster Abbey, in a stately monument erected for herself and the duke under her direction and at her own expense.

Frances Howard's stellar rise from penniless orphan to merchant's wife, countess, duchess, double duchess, and would-be queen of England, and her alleged vanity and avarice, were a theme of Jacobean wags, including the letter-writer John Chamberlain, who makes frequent mention of this 'Diana of the Ephesians' (*Letters of John Chamberlain*, 2.499). Wilson reports that:

> When she was Countess of *Hertford*, and found admirers about her, She would often discourse of her two Grandfathers, the *Dukes* of *Norfolk* and *Buckingham*; recounting the time since one of her *Grand-Fathers* did this, the other did that. But if the Earl her husband came in presence, she would quickly desist; for when he found her in those *Exaltations*, to take her down, he would say, Frank, Frank, *How long is it since thou wert Maried to* Prannel? which would damp the Wings of her *Spirit*.   (Wilson, 259)

Not easily subdued, the Countess Frances appears on strong evidence to be the anonymous writer who replied to the misogynist Joseph Swetnam in 1617 with a pamphlet called *Ester hath hang'd Haman … written by Ester Sowernam, neither maide, wife, nor widdowe, yet really all, and therefore experienced to defend all.* Biographical facts, vocabulary, prosody, and source material converge on the countess as sole author of the pamphlet by *Sowernam. (The unnamed 'gentleman' who introduced 'Ester' to Rachel Speght's *Muzzle for Melastomus* (1617) may be the countess's friend, Dr Mountforde, whose wife was Rachel Speght's godmother.)

Biographical commentary on Frances Stuart has had a sharply disdainful edge, with innuendo that swells by the nineteenth century into unfounded allegations that she repeatedly swindled the royal family and killed her own husbands as they slept. But her letters reveal her to be an amiable, witty, and honourable lady, a shrewd businesswoman but generous in dispensing praise and material gifts.

> And can we then be blamed (if, being harmed
> By sad experience) we be strongly armed

With resolution to defend our wrongs
Against the perjured falsehood of your tongues?
(Seymour, ll. 59–62)

DONALD W. FOSTER

Sources *The letters of John Chamberlain*, ed. N. E. McClure, 2 vols. (1939) · A. Wilson, 'The dutches of Richmonds legend', *The history of Great Britain: being the life and reign of King James the First* (1653), 258 · S. Forman, journals and notebooks, Bodl. Oxf., MSS Ashmole 226 (1597); 208 (1600); 411 (1601); 802 (Dec 1601), 298–9 · d. cert., Dec 1599, Coll. Arms, I.16 [Henry Prannell], fol. 69 · D. W. Foster, '"Against the perjured falsehood of your tongues": Frances Howard on the course of love', *English Literary Renaissance*, 24 (1994), 72–103 · *Calendar of the manuscripts of the marquis of Bath preserved at Longleat, Wiltshire*, 5 vols., HMC, 58 (1904–80), vol. 4 · *Calendar of the manuscripts of the most hon. the marquis of Salisbury*, 24 vols., HMC, 9 (1883–1976), vols. 18, 21–2 · *Report on the manuscripts of Lord De L'Isle and Dudley*, 6, HMC, 77 (1966) · F. Seymour, 'The answer of the countess of Hertford', Bodl. Oxf., MS Rawl. poet. 160 [lines 1–115 only], fols. 118v–119v · F. Seymour, 'The answer of the countess of Hertford', Bodl. Oxf., MS Ashmole 38, fols. 34v–36r · F. Seymour, 'The answer of the countess of Hertford', BL, Sloane MS 1446, fols. 32r–36r · will, 10 June 1597, PRO, PROB 11/94, sig. 93 [H. Prannell] · H. Prannell, letter from Henry Prannell to William Cecil, Lord Burghley, 8 Feb 1592, BL, Lansdowne MS LXIX, art. 52, fol. 117 [transcription in Ellis, *Orig. lett.*, 3rd ser., 4.91–5] · marriage licence, Edward Seymour, earl of Hertford, and Mrs Frances Prannel (disp. 29 May 1601), 27 May 1601, Dean and Chapter, Westminster · *CSP dom.*, 1591–4; 1603–10; 1611–18 · GEC, *Peerage*, new edn, 6.505–7 · *APC*, 1630–1631, 293–4, 353–4 · A. L. Rowse, *Sex and society in Shakespeare's age* (New York, 1974), 226–33

Likenesses F. Delaram, engraving, in or before 1621, NPG [*see illus.*] · N. Hilliard, portrait · portrait, repro. in Rowse, *Sex and society* · portrait, repro. in F. G. Waldron, *The biographical mirror*, 3.14 · portrait, repro. in E. Lodge, *Illustrious personages of Great Britain* (1850)

Wealth at death said to be the richest woman in England at time of death

Stuart [Stewart], **Frances Teresa**, duchess of Lennox and Richmond [*called* La Belle Stuart] (**1647–1702**), courtier, was born on 8 July 1647, the eldest daughter of Walter Stewart or Stuart (*d*. in or before 1657), politician, and his wife, Sophia (1610/11?–1702), daughter of Sir George *Carew and widow of Richard Nevill of Newton St Loo, Somerset. Her father was the third son of Walter *Stewart, first Lord Blantyre, was elected MP for Monmouth Boroughs in 1624 and 1625, and seems to have joined Queen Henrietta Maria's exiled court in Paris after 1649. Her mother, who as maid of honour to Henrietta Maria had been noted for her beauty and skill in dancing, acted as a dresser to the queen in France, an appointment confirmed after the Restoration. Frances was educated as a Catholic in France, while her half-brother, George Nevill, remained in England 'well fixed in the protestant religion' (*Diary of Bulstrode Whitelocke*, 466), married in 1657 Mary, daughter of Bulstrode Whitelocke, and was the father of George Nevill, thirteenth Baron Abergavenny.

The young Frances Stuart was a favourite of Henrietta Maria and also acquired the approbation of the duchess of Orléans, who wrote to her brother Charles II on 4 January 1662 that 'she is the prettiest girl in the world and the most fitted to adorn a court' (Hartmann, 11). With such

Frances Teresa Stuart, duchess of Lennox and Richmond (1647–1702), by Samuel Cooper, *c*.1663–4

connections it is unsurprising that she secured an appointment as maid of honour to Charles II's new queen, Catherine of Braganza. Louis XIV 'would fain have had her mother, who is one of the most cunning women in the world, to let her stay in France' (Baillon, *Henriette-Anne*, 80), but contented himself with giving her an expensive farewell present. She arrived in England early in 1662 and made an immediate impression, one observer noting in February 1662, 'beautiful Mrs Stuart is here so admired and so rich in clothes and jewels, she is the only blazing star' (*Various Collections*, 8.65). Although little else is known her of during 1662, she was undoubtedly in waiting on Queen Catherine, who arrived in England in May, and her appointment as maid of honour was formalized in June 1663. Early in 1663, when she was still only fifteen years old, the king began to take notice of her. Possibly spotting a dangerous rival in the making, Barbara Villiers, Lady Castlemaine, the king's mistress, befriended Frances, but could do little to distract Charles from pursuing the latest beautiful addition to his court.

By June 1663 the marquis de Ruvigny was reporting to Louis XIV:

> no one doubts but that Miss Stuart has taken her [Lady Castlemaine's] place. She did not partake of communion at Whitsun, which is an assured mark of their [Frances's and the king's] recent understanding, so the best Catholics inform me. (Hartmann, 38–9)

Frances, however, did not become the king's mistress, nor did she become a pawn in court politics. In the summer and autumn of 1663 various politicians, most notably Sir Henry Bennet (later earl of Arlington), the duke of Buckingham, and the earl of Bristol, tried to use her to influence the king but she was either too 'cunning' (Pepys, *Diary*, 4.366), or too 'infantile' (Grammont in Pepys, *Diary*, 4.37–8n.)—opinion was divided—to be of much use as a political operator. Her chosen amusements were blindman's buff, hunt the slipper, and card-building rather than political intrigue. Such was the king's infatuation with what Samuel Pepys called 'her sweet eye, little Roman nose, and excellent taille' (Pepys, *Diary*, 4.230) that there were rumours that the king intended to marry her. The queen, however, recovered from a near fatal illness she had suffered late in 1663, and Charles II consistently refused suggestions that he divorce Catherine.

Charles continued to pursue Frances, who maintained her position at court. In July 1665 Courtin observed: 'she is the rising sun, and in truth too incomparably more beautiful than the other [Castlemaine]' (Hartmann, 82). By November 1665 it was reported that the duke of York, too, had fallen in love with her. Her fame as one of the most beautiful women of the court increased: in 1667 she was the model for John Roettier's figure of *Britannia, seated at the foot of a rock with the legend 'Favente Deo' in the medal entitled 'The peace of Breda', and in a similar guise in the unfinished 'Naval victories' medal, with the legend 'Quatuor maria vindico'. Pepys noted on a visit to his goldsmith on 25 February 1667, 'the king's new medal, where in little there is Mrs Stewards face' (Pepys, *Diary*, 8.83). Edmund Waller and Andrew Marvell both wrote verses referring to the medal and Frances's role as Britannia, though twentieth-century scholarship has questioned the connection. Subsequently the design by Roettier was used on the reverse side of the copper coinage introduced in 1672.

In March 1667, according to John Evelyn's later account, Frances 'could no longer continue at court without prostituting herself to the king, whom she had long kept off' (Hartmann, 115). An attractive suitor appeared in the guise of Charles *Stuart, third duke of Richmond, sixth duke of Lennox, and eleventh seigneur d'Aubigny (1639–1672), courtier, whose second wife had died in January 1667. Richmond was distantly related to the king, who affected to agree to a match as long as Richmond made a suitable settlement on Frances. Perhaps suspecting that the king would not in the end allow her to marry, Frances left London secretly and married Richmond about 30 March 1667. The couple returned to London soon afterwards and lodged with Frances's mother at Somerset House in order to gauge the king's reaction. Charles was furious, the earl of Lauderdale writing that he had never seen Charles 'more offended than he is at the duke and all concerned' (Seaward, 321), a reaction not assuaged when Frances returned his presents of jewellery. In response Frances and her husband retired to Cobham Hall in Kent. The secret marriage and the king's reaction to it have even

been used to explain the downfall of the earl of Clarendon, whose supposed fault was to encourage the Richmond match in order to ensure that Charles remained married to his barren queen and thus protected the claims of his own grandchildren, princesses Mary and Anne, to the throne. It seems more likely that at most it was one further instance of Clarendon's alienating the king.

The duchess of Richmond remained unreconciled to the king until, while again in residence in Somerset House, she contracted smallpox in March 1668. There were fears for her beauty, but as Charles wrote to his sister in May 1668, 'she is not much marked with the smallpox, and I must confess this last affliction made me pardon all that is past' (Hartmann, 154). The only after-effect of her illness appears to have been some residual eye trouble. She duly returned to court, and on 6 July 1668 Pepys reported that the previous week she had been sworn a lady of the bedchamber to the queen. The duke and duchess moved into new Whitehall lodgings in the Bowling Green. Back at court Frances was still favoured by the king, which gave some alarm to his new mistress, Louise de Kéroualle, duchess of Portsmouth. Although, according to Baron Dartmouth, the king told her husband in 1671 that Frances had surrendered to him after her marriage, she never sought the position of acknowledged royal mistress.

The duke of Richmond was appointed ambassador to Denmark in February 1672, and following his departure the duchess was left with power of attorney to receive the money due from his grant of duties on the aulnage and the payments due for his embassy. She also, in contrast to the frivolity of her younger days and indeed her spendthrift husband, applied herself to running the Richmond estates with prudence and good judgement. Richmond did not return from his diplomatic posting, dying near Elsinore in Denmark on 12 December 1672. The Richmonds had no children, and the titles and estates of Lennox and Richmond reverted to the crown, although the king with characteristic generosity allowed the duchess the use of the Lennox estate for her life. The next duke of Richmond was the son of Louise de Kéroualle and Charles II, who was created a duke in 1675. In 1677 Frances resigned her claims on the Aubigny estate in France to Charles for a pension of £1000 per annum, and about the same time sold her life interest in Cobham Hall to her sister-in-law Lady Catherine O'Brien, thereby ending the bone of contention between them.

Frances lived quietly at court attending the queen, and was evidently concerned to maintain her reputation as a respectable widow, in 1678 demanding and obtaining an apology from the rakish young courtier John Grobham Howe after he falsely claimed to have had an affair with her. She continued at court until 1688, although she was not present at the birth of the prince of Wales. Thereafter perhaps prudence and ill health dictated her retirement. Nevertheless, she defended tenaciously her right to collect the aulnage, petitioning parliament in 1692, 1693, and 1700 when legislation threatened to extinguish her rights. However, her pension from the crown fell into arrears in

1690. She attended the coronation of Queen Anne in April 1702.

Frances died on 15 October 1702 and was buried on 22 October next to her husband in Westminster Abbey. Boyer recorded that 'she was a Roman Catholic and very devout in her way' (Boyer, 1–2.231). Details of her will became public very soon after her death. She left legacies of £500 and £300 per annum to her mother, who died at the end of 1702. She left her sister, the Jacobite Sophia *Bulkeley, who was married to the exiled Lord Bulkeley, £1000, and £500 apiece to her sister's six children, including 'La Belle Nanette', wife of the duke of Berwick. However, after being 'advised I cannot safely do the same in respect of their being in France and other circumstances attending them', she gave them seven years to return to England and 'be taken into the favour and protection of the crown and discharged and freed from the offences against the same' in order to claim the money (will). She also made the unusual request, which was honoured, that an effigy be made of her 'as well done in wax as can bee' (ibid.), dressed in her coronation robes and coronet, and set up under glass near the tomb of the second duke and duchess of Richmond in Westminster Abbey. Most of her estate was left in trust to the earl of Rochester, Alexander Stewart, fifth Lord Blantyre (d. 1704), Sir William Whitelocke, and James Gray (her gentleman of horse), to be laid out on the purchase of a Scottish estate to be named Lennoxlove, which was to be settled on Walter Stuart, son of Lord Blantyre.   STUART HANDLEY

Sources GEC, Peerage, new edn · C. H. Hartmann, La Belle Stuart: memoirs of court and society in the times of Frances Teresa Stuart, duchess of Richmond and Lennox (1924) · BL, Sloane MS 1708, fol. 121 · Pepys, Diary (1970–83) · Bishop Burnet's History · R. Hutton, Charles the Second: king of England, Scotland and Ireland (1989) · CSP dom., 1666–73 · P. Seaward, The Cavalier Parliament and the reconstruction of the old regime, 1661–1667 (1989) · will, PRO, PROB 11/466, sig. 166 · E. Hawkins, Medallic illustrations of the history of Great Britain, ed. A. W. Franks and H. A. Grueber, 2 vols. (1885) · D. Rowland, An historical and genealogical account of the noble family of Nevill, particularly the house of Abergavenny (1830) · The diary of Bulstrode Whitelocke, 1605–1675, ed. R. Spalding, British Academy, Records of Social and Economic History, new ser., 13 (1990) · C. Macleod and J. M. Alexander, eds., Painted ladies: women at the court of Charles II (2001) [exhibition catalogue, NPG, 11 Oct 2001–6 Jan 2002; Yale U. CBA, 25 Jan – 17 March 2002] · IGI · The manuscripts of the House of Lords, 4 vols., HMC, 17 (1887–94), vol. 3 · Report on manuscripts in various collections, 8 vols., HMC, 55 (1901–14), vol. 8 · The manuscripts of S. H. Le Fleming, HMC, 25 (1890), 8 · J. L. Chester, ed., The marriage, baptismal, and burial registers of the collegiate church or abbey of St Peter, Westminster, Harleian Society, 10 (1876) · A. Boyer, The history of the reign of Queen Anne digested into annals, vols. 1 and 2 (1703) · C. de Baillon, Henriette-Marie de France: reine d'Angleterre. Étude historique (Paris, 1877) · le comte de Baillon, Henriette-Anne d'Angleterre, duchesse d'Orléans, sa vie at sa correspondance avec son frère Charles II (1886)

Archives PRO, estate papers, C 104/46 | BL, Add. MSS 21947–21948

Likenesses P. Lely, oils, c.1662, Royal Collection · S. Cooper, miniature, c.1663–1664, Royal Collection [see illus.] · S. Cooper, miniature, c.1664, Mauritshuis, The Hague, Netherlands · J. Huysmans, oils, 1664, Royal Collection · J. Roettier, silver medal, c.1677, BM; modern copy, NPG · H. Gascar, oils, c.1678, Goodwood House, West Sussex · P. Lely?, oils, c.1678–1680, Museum of Fine Arts, Budapest, Hungary · W. Wissing and J. vander Vaart, oils, 1687, NPG · G. Kneller?, oils, Goodwood House, West Sussex; copy, Royal Collection · funeral effigy, Westminster Abbey, London

Stuart, (Henry) Francis Montgomery (1902–2000), novelist and poet, was born on 29 April 1902 at Rostrevor, Stagpole Street, Townsville, Queensland, Australia, the only child of Henry Irwin Stuart (1853–1902), sheep farmer and landowner, and Elizabeth Barbara Isabel (Lily) Montgomery (1875–1959). His parents, who were both Irish, had sailed for Australia shortly after marrying in Antrim in 1900. Henry Stuart committed suicide while in a lunatic asylum in August 1902, and his wife returned to Antrim with their infant son, who was known as Harry during his childhood, changing to Francis when he became an adult and a writer. Stuart was educated at day schools in Dublin before he was sent to Bilton Grange in 1912, in preparation for Rugby School, which he entered in 1916. There he read poetry widely, greeted the Russian Revolution with delight, and was regarded as academically a failure. He returned to Dublin in 1918, abandoning his hopes of entering Trinity College when he met the beautiful 24-year-old Iseult Gonne (1894–1954) [see Stuart, Iseult], daughter of Maud Gonne MacBride [see Gonne, (Edith) Maud]. The couple eloped and, after pressure from both families, married reluctantly on 4 April 1920, after Stuart, who had been raised a protestant, had converted to Roman Catholicism. The marriage, Stuart complained, suffered from the constant interference of Iseult's mother and her admirer W. B. Yeats. Maud Gonne, herself a victim of a violent marriage, invited Yeats to be the arbiter in her daughter's relationship, alleging that Stuart was physically cruel to Iseult, starved her, and kept her short of money. The relationship was tempestuous, but Iseult herself denied physical cruelty, and Stuart believed that the charges were invented in a deliberate effort to undermine the marriage (Elborn, 39–46). Apparently unconcerned, but overwhelmed by depression, Stuart refused to mourn the death of his eight-month-old daughter in 1921, which further contributed to his deteriorating marriage.

In August 1922 Stuart was imprisoned for republican activities during the civil war, and his first collection of poems, *We Have Kept the Faith*, was published in January 1924, within weeks of his release. It won the Irish Royal Academy prize. A son, Ion, was born two years later. The Stuarts lived in temporary accommodations until 1929, when Iseult's mother made them a gift of Laragh Castle, Glendalough, co. Wicklow. Stuart ran a poultry farm and that same year published *Mystics and Mysticism*. His first novel, *Women and God* (1931), portrayed the conflict between materialism and spiritual values and was a failure, as were nine of the eleven other novels he wrote before the war. Only *The Coloured Dome* (1932) and *Pigeon Irish* (1933) were of value, and the progressive decline in the quality of his writing paralleled the breakdown of his marriage. In all his novels from the first to the last, Stuart saw the female as a mystical being, who would reconcile the sexual with the spiritual, and bring a sense of personal redemption to his male protagonists, who were often guilty of a crime. Stuart spent much of the 1930s between

Dublin and London, drinking, horse-racing, and woman-izing. A daughter, Kay, was born in May 1931 and there were unsubstantiated rumours—vehemently repudiated by the Gonnes—that the child's real father was Yeats, who praised Stuart's fiction ('If luck comes to his aid he will be our great writer'), but considered him a 'dunce' in marriage (Elborn, 91–2, 79).

Although Stuart learned the circumstances of his father's death only in later years, Henry Stuart had featured as an archetype of the outcast in his son's fiction. Determined to place *himself* outside society, Stuart left his wife and family in 1940 to teach literature at Berlin University. He wanted to see Hitler at first hand, considering him to be a 'Samson … who would tear down the whole political and social system in England and Ireland' (*The Guardian*). In 1942 he accepted an invitation by the German foreign office to broadcast to Ireland; the talks that he gave were not so much pro-Nazi as anti-British (transcript, 16 Dec 1942, 6 Jan 1943). He left Berlin in 1944 with a student, Gertrude Meissner (1915–1986), who had been his lover for two years, and was arrested by the occupying French at Dornbirn, Austria, in 1945. He was imprisoned for eight months, during which he was transferred to Freiburg. He was released without charge in 1946 and remained in Freiburg for three years. The novels he wrote about his experiences in the war, *The Pillar of Cloud* (1948) and *Redemption* (1949), were critically acclaimed. After two years in Paris, he and Meissner came to London, where on 28 April 1954, after Iseult's death the previous month, they were married. Stuart renamed Gertrude Madeleine, after Mary Magdalene. This was a natural development of the philosophy that he propagated in his fiction and wished to expound in his own life. His first and third wives refused to be moulded by him, but Madeleine was so devoted to Stuart that she was happy to enact the role of his 'ideal' woman.

Stuart's desire to return to Ireland was hampered by the poor sales of the six novels he wrote during a five-year period, but in 1959 he and his wife moved to The Reask, Dunshaughlin, Meath, where he spent several years working on a novel eventually published in 1971 as *Black List Section H*. Exploring the themes of personal and spiritual redemption, with particular reference to Stuart's own life, the book is regarded as his masterpiece. In 1975 he bought a house at 14 Highfield Park, Dublin, where he wrote five further novels, which belong to his third period of decline. The last, *A Compendium of Lovers*, was published in 1991. He also published two further volumes of poetry and *The Abandoned Snail Shell* (1987), a philosophical essay about the nature of reality, written to commemorate Madeleine, who had died in 1986. On 28 December 1987 he married the artist Finola Graham (*b.* 1946). Controversy over Stuart's past was renewed in 1996 when, amid protests, he was elected *Saoi* ('wise man'), the highest Irish award for writers, which had also been given to Stuart's friend Samuel Beckett. The following year he successfully sued the *Irish Times* which had accused him of anti-semitism.

Stuart spent the last two years of his life at his wife's home at Fanore, Clare, and died of heart disease on 2 February 2000 in the nearby St Joseph's Hospital at Ennis. He was interred in St Patrick's churchyard, Fanore, on 5 February at a funeral attended by representatives of the president and the Taoiseach. His cat, which had died suddenly, was concealed in his coffin and buried with him.

Stuart was described by his publisher Victor Gollancz as 'the handsomest man I have ever met' (*Daily Telegraph*). He was over 6 feet tall and attracted women throughout his long life. In old age he remained lean; his severe circus clown face, with light blue eyes, was crowned by an upturned bowl of white hair. Despite a life of turmoil and controversy, he was ordered in his habits. In company he was often silent for several hours, but could be an amusing conversationalist. Stuart's selfishness, in regard to Iseult Gonne and Finola Graham, and the egotism of portraying his fictional heroes as versions of himself, were tempered by genuine humility. He refused to apologize for his past and never compromised his search for truth as he saw it. 'His legacy', as Colm Tóibín noted, 'is likely to remain difficult' (*London Review of Books*).

GEOFFREY ELBORN

Sources G. Elborn, *Francis Stuart: a life* (1991) · M. Stuart, *Manna in the morning* (1984) · J. H. Natterstad, *Francis Stuart* (1974) · *Daily Telegraph* (3 Feb 2000) · *Yeats' poems*, ed. A. N. Jeffares (1989) · *The letters of W. B. Yeats*, ed. A. Wade (1954) · *London Review of Books* (14 Jan 2001) · broadcasts, PRO NIre., CAB 9CD/207BBCMR [transcript] · *The Guardian* (29 April 1999) · *The Independent* (3 Feb 2000) · personal knowledge (2004) · b. cert. · m. certs. · d. cert.

Archives NL Ire., corresp. and papers · Southern Illinois University, Carbondale, Morris Library, corresp. and literary MSS · University of Ulster, Coleraine, books, corresp., diaries, and papers | King's Lond., Liddell Hart C., corresp. with Sir B. H. Liddell Hart · NL Ire., letters to Joseph O'Neill · Southern Illinois University, Carbondale, Morris Library, Geoffrey Elborn collection, papers | FILM BFI NFTVA, Channel 4 documentary

Likenesses E. McGuire, oils, 1974, Hugh Lane Municipal Gallery of Modern Art, Dublin · F. Graham, portrait, mixed media, 1989, priv. coll. · J. Crabtree, portrait, mixed media, repro. in F. Stuart, *Black list section H* (1996)

Stuart, Gilbert (1743–1786), historian and political writer, was born in the Old College Buildings, Edinburgh, on 9 November 1743, the eldest of six children of George Stuart (*bap.* 1711, *d.* 1793), professor of humanity, and Jean Duncanson (*b.* 1712, *d.* in or before 1793) of Gearsheath in Dunbartonshire. Distinct from much writing of his day, Stuart's works are characterized by their intensity of personal feeling and their oppositional rhetoric. Journalism was his main source of income, but historical writing was his true calling. Excessive drinking shortened his life and brought upon him the opprobrium of critics in his own lifetime and ever since, but alcohol made him a 'boon companion' (*GM*, 1786, 716) and warmed a pen that naturally tended towards extremes.

Stuart grew up among the professors and students at Edinburgh University, where he attended lectures, but did not take a degree. As a young man, he worked in the university library, which his father had been cataloguing since 1747, and about 1766 began a legal apprenticeship. The novelist Henry Mackenzie, a fellow apprentice, recalled that 'Gilbert sat up too late, and drank too much to be often there' (*Anecdotes and Egotisms*, 174). Stuart was not inclined towards the law as a profession, seeing in it only the 'sordid prospect of future gain' (*Monthly Review*, 47.362). During this time he wrote *An Historical Dissertation Concerning the Antiquity of the English Constitution*. Published in 1768, the work summarizes the history of English liberty from the time of the first Britons to the Norman invasion. Implicit in this whiggish perspective was a challenge to David Hume, whose *History of England* had put a relativist historiographical agenda at the forefront of the debate on the nature of British liberty. In this ambitious attempt to synthesize the conjectural method of such writers as Kames and Adam Ferguson with the controversial approach of his relative Thomas Ruddiman, Stuart applied the legal scholarship of Montesquieu and John Dalrymple.

Stuart's attempt to purchase the chair of public law at Edinburgh University on the strength of his first book and his father's influence proved unsuccessful. All he could obtain was an honorary LLD in November 1768, from which time he was known as 'Dr Stuart' (Edinburgh University, senate minutes). As other employment opportunities in Scotland did not materialize, he set off for London's Grub Street. Thomas Somerville referred to frequent drunken gatherings in London over which Stuart was 'assigned oracular authority' and at which 'contempt was expressed for the most esteemed authors living'. While Somerville condemned Stuart's profligate habits, he also acknowledged his 'transcendent intellectual talents' and his 'facility and quickness in composing—the more extraordinary because his style has so much the appearance of art and elaboration' (Somerville, 149).

As a periodical writer Stuart contributed mainly to the *London Magazine* and the *Monthly Review*. For Ralph Griffiths's *Monthly* he wrote reviews and notices for nearly 250 books during his career. In Stuart's best reviews the polite surface of eighteenth-century criticism gives way to a dynamic, sometimes personal, commentary. By employing the vocabulary of controversy as a rhetorical tool, he engaged his reader and charged his text with emotion, making his reviews writing to be read for entertainment as well as a vehicle for judging literature.

The most important association Stuart formed in London was with the bookseller–publisher John Murray. Stuart read prospective publications and for a six-month period in 1770 edited Murray's *Repository*, a short-lived monthly composed mainly of articles on Junius and John Wilkes. Stuart's talent for translation was also promoted by the publisher. He received nearly £30 for translating a quarter of Millot's *Éléments de l'histoire d'Angleterre*, and completed the whole of Delolme's *Constitution de l'Angleterre*.

Several other projects engaged Stuart during his first stay in London. After preparing for the press Rolt's short *History of the Isle of Man* (1772), he began his own comprehensive Manx history and obtained the patronage of the third duke of Atholl, whose family had lost their sovereignty over the island in 1765. When the duke decided

against publication in March 1773, Stuart was compensated with just 50 guineas, an event which sorely disappointed him. (The manuscript is preserved in the Manx Museum Library at Douglas.) Another unrealized project was a biography of Tobias Smollett. A cousin of the novelist, James Smollett of Bonhill, had agreed to supply Stuart with original material and to introduce him to the widow and sister, but these relatives proved to be unco-operative and the biography never materialized. Yet another work was a history of Edinburgh which was advertised in the press but never appeared (*Caledonian Mercury*, 27 Nov 1773). A final publication initiated by Stuart before returning to Edinburgh in the autumn of 1773 was his introduction and notes to the second edition of Francis Sullivan's *Lectures on the Constitution and Laws of England* (1776), largely a reworking of the themes in the earlier *English Constitution*.

With the printer William Smellie, Stuart established the *Edinburgh Magazine and Review*. This monthly work—published from November 1773 to August 1776—became a lively forum for the expression of religious, political, and literary opinion. In the history of Scottish literary criticism it stands between the short-lived *Edinburgh Review* of 1755–6 and the successful journal of the same name founded by Francis Jeffrey and others in 1802. It suffered from the provincialism of the former and anticipated the audacious style of the latter. Pride in Scottish achievement and the boldness to criticize whatever or whomever he found objectionable formed the central elements of Stuart's journalistic method. Among those attacked were the Revd Robert Henry and Lord Monboddo, whose *Origin and Progress of Language* was so maligned that many readers cancelled their magazine subscriptions. While generally aligned with the moderate party of the Scottish church, the periodical was too often guided by Stuart's personal animosities and provincial concerns to retain either patronage or, ultimately, a wide audience.

When the *Edinburgh Magazine and Review* folded, Stuart returned to historical writing. The *View of Society in Europe* (1778), regarded as his most important historical work, went into several editions and was translated into German in 1779 and French in 1789. The concept of property, as it developed from an object of communal to private interest, formed the framework from which Stuart considered such topics as the roles of the sexes, the place of religion, and the state of manners in medieval European society. In part Stuart wrote the *View of Society* in opposition to the introductory volume of William Robertson's popular *History of Charles V*. Where Robertson emphasized the gradual improvement of society, Stuart marked out the gradual corruption of feudal institutions, pessimistically attributing this decline to man's inability to alter his destiny. A more direct challenge to Robertson continued in Stuart's next work, *Observations Concerning the Public Law and the Constitutional History of Scotland* (1779). Stuart attributed his failure to obtain a university chair in 1778 to Robertson and spared nothing in criticizing his successful *History of Scotland*. Stuart's opposition to Catholic relief legislation, which Robertson advocated, also fuelled an attack which continued, though less overtly, in Stuart's *History of* the *Establishment of the Reformation of Religion in Scotland* (1780). In this work and its sequel, *The History of Scotland from the Establishment of the Reformation till the Death of Queen Mary* (1782), Stuart altered his style from a conjectural to a more popular narrative model, but one with a difference. Where many contemporary historians emphasized the systematic, the rational, and the pragmatic, Stuart believed that a more sentimental, immediate, and intentional approach could better re-create historical verisimilitude. His compelling portrayal of Mary, queen of Scots, as a victim of both English oppression and self-interested Scottish alliances won him considerable acclaim, particularly south of the border, and the *History* was soon reprinted and translated.

Despite this success Stuart received little remuneration from his *History*, or indeed from any of his major works. In 1783 he returned to London once again to take up his pen as a critic and political writer. Initially he returned to the *Monthly Review* and assisted Murray with his newly established *English Review*. But in 1785 the leaders of the opposition—Fox, Burke, and Sheridan—asked him to edit the *Political Herald*, in which he orchestrated a vehement attack on William Pitt and his Scottish minister Henry Dundas. However, his tenure as a leading political writer was short-lived. By the spring of 1786 illness, aggravated by dissolute habits, prevented Stuart from working. During the summer his condition grew critical: fluid settled on his lungs, and his body swelled painfully. In late July on a ship to Scotland he sat on deck watching some gambolling seals. 'Tell me', he inquired of the captain, 'upon what diet do these creatures feed?' To the answer 'Salmon and saltwater', Stuart replied, 'Very good meat but very bad drink' (*Annual Biography*, 2.101). A few weeks later, on 13 August 1786, he died, unmarried, at his parents' home in Fisherrow, Musselburgh. He was buried the following day at the nearby Inveresk churchyard.

The *Gentleman's Magazine* concluded its obituary by dismissing Stuart as 'a martyr to intemperance' (*GM*, 1786, 716). Nearly 100 years later Allibone called him a 'sot, grumbler, scold and literary Ishmaelite' (Allibone, *Dict.*, 2.2292). Nevertheless a number of Stuart's contemporaries, while acknowledging his personal failings, were more balanced in their judgements: Godwin in the *Political Herald* remarked: 'If ever any man defended or opposed measures from the genuine sentiments of his heart, it was doctor Stuart' (*Political Herald, and Review*, 1786, 3281). Boswell wrote: 'His bluntness did not please me, though his strong mind did' (*Ominous Years*, 305). John Murray, who knew him best, concluded: 'He was the greatest enemy to himself. He could not endure to be thought subject to human infirmities' (John Murray to John Millar, 7 Sept 1786, John Murray Archive, London). WILLIAM ZACHS

Sources W. Zachs, *Without regard to good manners: a biography of Gilbert Stuart, 1743–1786* (1992) • R. Kerr, *Memoirs of the life, writings and correspondence of William Smellie*, 2 vols. (1811) • [I. D'Israeli], *Calamities of authors*, 2 (1812), 49–74 • B. C. Nangle, *The Monthly Review, first series, 1749–1789: indexes of contributors and articles* (1934) • *The anecdotes and egotisms of Henry Mackenzie, 1745–1831*, ed. H. W. Thompson (1927) • T. Somerville, *My own life and times, 1741–1814*, ed. W. Lee (1861) • *Boswell: the applause of the jury, 1782–1785*, ed. I. S. Lustig and F. A. Pottle (1981), vol. 12 of *The Yale editions of the private papers of James Boswell*, trade edn (1950–89) • Allibone, *Dict.* • *Annual Biography and Obituary*, 2 (1818) • old parish records, Edinburgh • old parish records, Dumbarton • matriculation rolls, U. Edin. L., special collections division, university archives • *GM*, 1st ser., 56 (1786), 716

Archives Blair Castle, Perthshire, MSS • John Murray, London, archive, MSS • Manx Museum Library, Isle of Man, MSS | Bodl. Oxf., Hughenden papers • Bodl. Oxf., letters to John Murray • Edinburgh City Archives, town council minutes • NL Scot., Minto papers • U. Edin. L., special collections division, matriculation rolls of Edinburgh University • U. Edin. L., special collections division, senate minutes

Likenesses J. Donaldson, graphite miniature on paper, 1780, John Murray Archive, London; repro. in Zachs, *Without regard to good manners* • J. K. Sherwin, engraving (after J. Donaldson, 1780), repro. in G. Stuart, *The history of the establishment of the Reformation of religion in Scotland* (1780), frontispiece • line engraving (aged thirty-five; after J. Donaldson), BM, NPG; repro. in *European Magazine* (1780)

Stuart, Gilbert Charles (1755–1828), portrait painter, was born on 3 December 1755 near Saunderstown, Rhode Island, USA, the youngest of the three children of Gilbert Stewart, later Stuart (*c*.1718–1793), inventor and snuff-mill operator, and Elizabeth (*d*. after 1810), daughter of Albro Anthony. The artist's father, the son of a Presbyterian minister from Perth, was supposedly present at the battle of Culloden and it has been suggested that his emigration in the late 1740s was to avoid persecution. Stuart's maternal grandfather, of English descent, was a landowner and disciple of Bishop Berkeley. Stuart spent his youth in Newport as a charity scholar at the parochial school of Trinity Church, founded by Berkeley, where he received a liberal education. His aptitude for drawing caused him in 1769 to be taken on as an assistant and pupil of the Scottish portraitist Cosmo Alexander, then working in Newport, eventually sailing with him to Scotland *c*.1772. Alexander died shortly after their arrival and accounts differ as to whether Stuart then studied at the University of Glasgow; he was back in Newport by 1774, where he attempted to make a living painting portraits. Those that survive are stiff in manner. At some point after his return from Scotland Stuart saw the work of Copley, and realized that he needed to be in London in order to succeed as an artist. He arrived in London late in 1775 with little money and few prospects. By December 1776 Stuart was living on one meal a day and finally wrote for assistance to Benjamin West, who hired him to finish portraits and as a drapery painter for half a guinea a week.

Stuart's exposure to West's successful studio and practice caused his work to improve dramatically and he exhibited a portrait (now unidentified) in the Royal Academy exhibition of 1777. His work took on a new sophistication that owed as much to the work of George Romney and Gainsborough as it did to West's. Stuart remained 'wretchedly poor' according to the painter John Trumbull (Evans, 128, n. 19), but he exhibited portraits again at the Royal Academy in 1779. In 1781 he received published reviews for the first time and painted his celebrated portrait of William Grant ice skating (National Gallery of Art, Washington), which was extremely well received, both as

Gilbert Charles Stuart (1755–1828), self-portrait, c.1788

a good likeness and as an inventive composition. Despite his success at the Royal Academy in 1782, Stuart exhibited at the Incorporated Society of Artists only in 1783, not at all in 1784, sent three pictures to the Royal Academy in 1785, and never exhibited again in Britain. John Boydell commissioned him to paint fifteen portraits of his associates, which included Reynolds (National Gallery of Art, Washington) and the engraver William Woollett (Tate collection), and which Boydell displayed in his gallery along with John Singleton Copley's *Death of Major Peirson*. Lord Percy, later second duke of Northumberland, who had served in America during the American War of Independence, commissioned at least three pictures from Stuart in 1783–7 (all priv. coll.). Stuart gained a reputation for exceptional likenesses, in which he was aided by the use of life masks. Stuart moved to fashionable (and expensive) lodgings in New Burlington Street, London, in 1784. On 10 May 1786 he married Charlotte Coates (1767/8–1845), with whom he had twelve children (one of whom published the first accounts of her father's life); they lived prodigally and Thomas Lawrence recalled that Stuart was imprisoned for debt. In 1787 Stuart moved to Dublin, accepting a commission from Charles Manners, fourth duke of Rutland, to paint his portrait as viceroy of Ireland. He returned to London at least twice but, having received several commissions in Ireland and considering his financial troubles in England, settled there. He was again imprisoned for debt in 1789, and in 1793 returned to what had become the United States.

Stuart worked in New York until early 1795, when he moved to the American capital, Philadelphia. In London he had received commissions from Americans as early as 1784, and on his repatriation he used these connections to obtain an introduction to George Washington, whom he painted for the first time early in 1795 (the 'Vaughan' portrait; National Gallery of Art, Washington, DC). A second sitting about March 1796 produced the unfinished 'Athenaeum' portrait (National Portrait Gallery, Washington, DC, and Museum of Fine Arts, Boston) which, engraved in reverse, is the iconic image of Washington seen on the United States $1 bill. The Athenaeum portrait was the preparatory study for the full-length 'Lansdowne' portrait, commissioned as a gift to William Petty, the first marquess of Lansdowne, and for which Washington sat one further time in April 1796 (National Portrait Gallery, Washington, DC). Stuart kept the Athenaeum portrait (and a similarly unfinished pendant of Mrs Washington) and used it as the model for over 100 autograph replicas.

Stuart always intended to return to London but his chronic insolvency meant that he could not raise the fare and he remained in the United States for the rest of his life. He followed the seat of government from Philadelphia to the new District of Columbia in 1803, and moved finally, in 1805, to Boston, where he lived at 101 Essex Street. Stuart painted most of the important figures of the early republic including much of Philadelphia and Boston society. His American-period portraits are flashier in execution than the subtle portraits of his London years, are of consistently high quality, and influenced portrait painting in America late into the nineteenth century. Throughout his life Stuart was known for his intelligence; he was well-read, cultured, and had a good sense of humour. However, in addition to gout and asthma, he suffered from fluctuations in mood and extended periods of lethargy and inactivity; a recent biographer suggested he displayed symptoms of manic depression (Evans, 118). The left side of his face and part of his left arm were paralysed in 1825. He died on 9 July 1828 at his home in Boston, and was buried in the central burial-ground on Boston Common. JOHN WILSON

Sources D. Evans, *The genius of Gilbert Stuart* (Princeton, NJ, 1999) · W. T. Whitley, *Gilbert Stuart* (Cambridge, Massachusetts, 1932) · C. M. Mount, *Gilbert Stuart: a biography* (New York, 1964) · W. Dunlap, *History of the rise and progress of the arts of design in the United States*, 3 vols. (New York, 1834); F. W. Bayley and C. E. Goodspeed, eds., new edn, 2 vols. (Boston, 1918) [written by a personal acquaintance] · D. Meschutt, 'Stuart, Gilbert', *ANB* · G. C. Mason, *The life and works of Gilbert Stuart* (1879) [written with the assistance of Jane Stuart] · J. Stuart, 'The Stuart portraits of Washington', *Scribner's Monthly*, 12/3 (July 1876), 367–74 · J. Stuart, 'The youth of Gilbert Stuart', *Scribner's Monthly*, 13/5 (March 1877), 640–46 · J. Stuart, 'Anecdotes of Gilbert Stuart', *Scribner's Monthly*, 14/3 (July 1877), 376–82 · Graves, *RA exhibitors*, 7 (1906), 295–6

Archives Harvard U., medical school, Waterhouse papers, 'Autobiography' and 'Memoirs' · Pickering House, Salem, Massachusetts, Henry Pickering interviews

Likenesses G. C. Stuart, self-portrait, oils, c.1785, Tate collection · G. C. Stuart, self-portrait, oils, c.1788, Redwood Library and Athenaeum, Newport, Rhode Island [see illus.] · J. H. I. Browere, bust, 1825, Redwood Library and Athenaeum, Newport, Rhode Island · J. Neagle, oils, 1825, Boston Museum of Fine Arts, Boston · C. W.

Peale, oils, New York Historical Society · G. C. Stuart, self-portrait, sketch, Metropolitan Museum of Art, New York · B. West, pen and wash drawing, BM

Wealth at death see inventory, Boston New Court House Archives and Records Preservation, Supreme Judicial Court

Stuart, Henry Benedict. *See* Henry Benedict (1725–1807).

Stuart, Henry Windsor Villiers (1827–1895), politician, born on 13 September 1827, was the only son of Henry Villiers Stuart, first Baron Stuart de Decies (1803–1874). His mother was Theresia Pauline Ott, of Vienna (*d.* 1867), said to have been married to his father in 1826, but the marriage was never legally recognized. On his father's death Stuart claimed the barony and was shocked to find no proof of his parents' marriage was accepted. However, he succeeded to his father's estates. Stuart was educated at University College, Durham, graduating in 1850. He was ordained the same year, and appointed vicar of Bulkington, Warwickshire, in 1854, and of Napton on the Hill, Southam, Warwickshire, in 1855. On 3 August 1865 he married Mary, second daughter of Ambrose Power, archdeacon of Lismore, and his wife, Susan Thacker of Ballymelish; they had five sons and four daughters.

From 1871 to 1874 Stuart was vice-lieutenant of co. Waterford, and, on his father's death in the latter year, succeeded to the property of Dromana near Cappoquin in that county. In 1873 he surrendered his holy orders and successfully contested co. Waterford for parliament as a Liberal, holding the seat until 1885. At the general election of 1885 he contested East Cork as a Unionist, but was defeated.

Stuart travelled extensively, and published many accounts of his wanderings, notably *Adventures amid the Equatorial Forests and Rivers of South America* (1891). He was in South America in 1858, in Jamaica in 1881, and he made several journeys through Egypt, and published various works on ancient and modern Egypt. After the English occupation of Egypt he was attached to Lord Dufferin's mission of reconstruction, and in the spring of 1883 was commissioned to investigate the condition of the country. His work received the special recognition of Lord Dufferin, and his reports were published as a parliamentary blue book (*Parl. papers*, 1883, 83, C 3554). He took a keen interest in Egyptian exploration, and was a member of the Society of Biblical Archaeology. He was also a member of the committee of the Royal Literary Fund.

Stuart was drowned on 12 October 1895 off Villierstown quay on the River Blackwater, near his residence at Dromana, having slipped while entering a boat.

J. R. MacDonald, rev. H. C. G. Matthew

Sources GEC, *Peerage* · *The Times* (14 Oct 1895) · Burke, *Gen. Ire.*
Archives BL, letters to W. E. Gladstone, Add. MSS 44434–44516, *passim* · NL Ire., corresp. and papers · NRA, priv. coll.
Likenesses R. J. Lane, lithograph, BM · portrait?, repro. in *ILN*, 107 (1895), 487
Wealth at death £82,301 14s. 3d.: probate, 22 April 1896, CGPLA Eng. & Wales

Stuart, Hindoo. *See* Stuart, Charles (1757/8–1828).

Stuart [*née* Gonne], **Iseult Lucille Germaine** (1894–1954), writer and friend of W. B. Yeats, was born in Paris on 6 August 1894, the daughter of (Edith) Maud *Gonne (1866–1953), Irish nationalist, and her lover the Boulangist politician Lucien Millevoye (1850–1918). Iseult's conception had been planned to replace Maud Gonne and Millevoye's first child, Georges, who died in 1891. They had intercourse in the crypt of the child's tomb in Samois-sur-Seine, Fontainebleau, hoping to reincarnate him. Iseult Gonne was brought up and educated in France and was a Francophone. Her existence was concealed from Maud Gonne's English and Irish friends, except her sister Kathleen Pilcher, her cousin May Gonne, and, after 1898, W. B. Yeats. Iseult could not address Maud Gonne as her mother, so called her Amour, which she later revised to Moura; Iseult herself was known as Bellotte and Millevoye as le Loup. The inhibitions forced on her by illegitimacy and her mother's prolonged absences from their various Paris residences contributed to Iseult's insecurity, so that when a child she asked her mother whether she would ever be as intelligent and interesting as the family dogs. Iseult Gonne later suffered from depression.

In February 1903 Maud Gonne married the Irish nationalist John *MacBride (1868–1916): the marriage rapidly deteriorated, but in January 1904 a son, Seán (Seaghan) *MacBride (1904–1988), the Irish revolutionary and Nobel peace prize winner, was born. In 1904 John MacBride made several sexual assaults on Iseult, a trauma which further distorted her life: she told her mother of MacBride's 'eyes of an assassin' (*Gonne–Yeats Letters*, 232). Maud Gonne fought a bitterly contested divorce case in 1905–6. A judicial separation followed by which Maud Gonne gained custody of Seaghan. Iseult was fond of her half-brother, whom she called Bichon.

Iseult Gonne made remarkable cultural strides, with Homer her preferred reading in 1908 and Aquinas in 1910, although this co-existed with a fantasy life in which she was Sir Maurice, and her cat Minoulouche her page. Yeats stayed regularly at Maud Gonne's country house in Colleville, Normandy, and became Iseult's Uncle Willie. In her first surviving letter to him she describes herself as 'a wild gutter cat' (26 Dec 1910, priv. coll.). She had contact with the Millevoye and Gonne families, staying with her aunt Kathleen, whose daughter Thora became a close friend.

By 1913 Iseult Gonne's beauty had begun to attract proposals: she was over 6 feet tall with brown hair and brown eyes. In 1914 she decided to learn Bengali, prompted by her admiration for Rabindranath Tagore, whom she had met in 1913. She and her teacher, Divabrata Mukerjee, hoped to translate Tagore but fell in love. The outbreak of war ended the affair. By 1915 Maud Gonne identified Iseult's fatal weakness: 'She has written some strange & very beautiful fragments of her own … but … she never has the will to finish anything—she is destroying her health by endless smoking … and she is unhappy and bored' (*Gonne–Yeats Letters*, 356).

In 1915 Iseult Gonne worked as a nurse and as a secretary. After the Easter rising of 1916 and the execution of MacBride, Iseult and Maud Gonne travelled to London. Yeats introduced her to London society and then travelled back with her to Colleville, staying for the summer, writing 'Easter 1916', proposing for the last time to Maud Gonne and then to Iseult. She had proposed to him in 1910, but he had told her that she had too much Mars in her horoscope. Yeats respected Iseult Gonne's intellect and in 1916 she introduced him to the work of Péguy and Claudel, writers whose mystical Catholicism strongly influenced her. Although she rejected Yeats's proposals she 'encouraged him'; Yeats refused to procrastinate and in mid-September 1917 asked her 'Yes, or No?' and she answered 'No' (Ellmann MSS). On 20 October 1917 Yeats married Georgie Hyde Lees while still infatuated with Iseult Gonne. He told Iseult of 'his trouble': her reply, saying that she prayed for him and would share his joy when told 'All is well' cannot have helped (26 Oct 1917, priv. coll.). But for George Yeats's rapidly mobilized spirit communications, the marriage would have been wrecked. Iseult Gonne remained a major presence in these communications, although one spirit warned Yeats of her indolence and obstinacy.

Iseult Gonne was devastated by the death of her father on 25 March 1918, telling her mother that her eyes were sore with crying. After working as a librarian at the School of Oriental Studies, she became secretary to Ezra Pound's *Little Review* and had a brief affair with him late in 1918, while her mother was imprisoned in Holloway gaol. Pound was sufficiently in love with Iseult to offer to leave his wife, Dorothy, for her, and he later thought of calling his daughter with Olga Rudge Iseult. She was also romantically attached to her cousin Toby Pilcher. After Maud Gonne's release in November 1918 the family returned to Dublin.

In 1919 Iseult Gonne met Francis *Stuart (1902–2000), a poet and later novelist of Ulster descent. She saw him as a spiritual child of Yeats and their relationship as a grail quest. After three months in London early in 1920, they married on 4 April 1920 in Dublin. Allegedly Stuart (Grim) treated Iseult (Mini) appallingly, starving her, beating her, and burning her clothes. By August 1920 they had separated but became reconciled. A daughter, Dolores, was born in Dublin on 25 March 1921 and died of meningitis on 24 July 1921, devastating Iseult. Yeats commented that a race of tragic women would now die out.

The marriage stabilized. Iseult broadened her husband's reading and typed his manuscripts. She also published two of her own prose reflections in *To-Morrow* (August–September 1924): one, 'The Kingdom Slow to Come' shows the influence of Joachim of Fiore. A son, Ian, was born on 5 October 1926 and a daughter, Katherine (known as Kay; *d.* 1993), on 25 May 1931. In 1928 Maud Gonne bought Laragh Castle, a castellated blockhouse built in 1798, near Glendalough, co. Wicklow, for the Stuarts. Iseult's life was restricted—Stuart spent much time and money in Dublin and London—and she tolerated this with detachment. Her consolations were her children and gardening. An account of the marriage, insidiously antagonistic to Iseult, is given in Stuart's *Black List, Section H* (1971).

In 1939 Stuart lectured in Germany and accepted a position at Berlin University. In May 1940 Hermann Goertz, an Abwehr agent, was parachuted into Ireland and came to Laragh Castle, on Stuart's advice. Iseult—apolitical but with German friends—helped Goertz. She was arrested on 23 May, imprisoned, tried in camera, and acquitted on 1 July. From 1942 to 1944 Stuart broadcast for *Ireland-Redaktion*; his family listened to the talks and Iseult hoped that he would return to Ireland, despite his relationship with Gertrud (Madeleine) Meissner.

In the 1940s Iseult worked on a religious anthology (unfinished). At the end of her life she shared Laragh Castle with her son and his wife, Imogen. Maud Gonne died in April 1953; Iseult was not acknowledged as a daughter in her mother's will. Iseult Stuart died at Laragh on 22 March 1954 from a coronary thrombosis—her heart condition exacerbated by neglect—and was buried in Glendalough cemetery on 24 March.

Her trajectory was summed up by Yeats:

> A girl that knew all Dante once
> Lived to bear children to a dunce.
> ('Why should not Old Men be Mad')

She is the subject of poems by Yeats including 'To a Child Dancing in the Wind', 'Two Years Later', 'Men Improve with the Years', 'The Living Beauty', 'To a Young Beauty', 'To a Young Girl', 'Michael Robartes and the Dancer', 'Owen Aherne and his Dancers', and 'The Death of the Hare'. She is also a pervasive presence in novels by Francis Stuart.   DEIRDRE TOOMEY

Sources private information (2004) [Anna MacBride White] · MacBride family papers · *The Gonne–Yeats letters, 1893–1938*, ed. A. MacBride White and A. N. Jeffares (1992) · letters from Iseult Stuart to Francis Stuart, University of Ulster at Coleraine · letters from Iseult Stuart to Francis Stuart, Southern Illinois University · G. Elborn, *Francis Stuart: a life* (1990) · F. Stuart, *Black list, section H* (1971) · letters from Iseult Gonne to W. B. Yeats, 26 Dec 1910 and 26 Oct 1917, priv. coll. · Ellmann MSS, University of Tulsa · W. B. Yeats, *Poems*, ed. A. N. Jeffares (1996), 443 · d. cert.
Archives priv. coll., MSS · Southern Illinois University, Carbondale, letters · University of Ulster, Coleraine, letters |SOUND BL NSA, London, recording, speaking about Yeats
Likenesses M. Gonne, drawing, 1905, priv. coll. · AE [G. Russell], pastels, NG Ire. · photographs, priv. coll.

Stuart, James, fourth duke of Lennox and first duke of Richmond (1612–1655), nobleman, was born at Blackfriars, London, on 6 April 1612, the eldest son of Esmé *Stuart, third duke of Lennox (1579?–1624), and Katherine Clifton (*c*.1592–1637). Lord Bernard *Stuart was his younger brother. A cousin of James VI and I and of Charles I, he had a claim to the Scottish but not the English throne. King James was a sponsor at his baptism, and became his guardian at his father's death in 1624. Created an MA of the University of Cambridge by royal mandate in 1624, and in receipt of a royal pension of £1400 a year, Lennox became a gentleman of the bedchamber in April 1625. Knighted in June 1630, he was created an English privy councillor on 28 July 1633 and a knight of the Garter the following November; during the summer of that same year he accompanied Charles I to his Scottish coronation.

Lennox married Lady Mary Villiers [*see* Villiers, Mary,

James Stuart, fourth duke of Lennox and first duke of Richmond (1612–1655), by Sir Anthony Van Dyck, c.1633–7

duchess of Lennox and Richmond], only daughter of George *Villiers, first duke of Buckingham, on 3 August 1637, and her £20,000 dowry relieved him of financial worries until the mid-1640s. He was also appointed to several local English offices, notably lord lieutenant of Hampshire in May 1635, keeper of Richmond park in 1638, and lord warden of the Cinque Ports in June 1640. His Scottish lands were small and unprofitable, but he owned extensive estates in England. His country seat was at Cobham Hall in Kent, and he also possessed scattered lands in Norfolk, Lincolnshire, Nottinghamshire, Bedfordshire, Huntingdonshire, Hampshire, Berkshire, Gloucestershire, and Wiltshire.

Lennox was deeply loyal to the crown: Clarendon later wrote of his 'unspotted fidelity' and 'entire resignation of himself to the King' (Clarendon, 1.76, 2.528). In the autumn of 1637, when Lennox visited Scotland for his mother's funeral, the covenanters hoped that he would represent their case to the king, but Lennox's instinctive response to complaints about Caroline policy was the tactful assurance 'that the King was misinformed' (Letters and Journals of Robert Baillie, 1.302). Although he apparently questioned the wisdom of war with the Scots, his loyalty to the crown was unshakeable. He opposed Strafford's

attainder during the spring of 1641. That summer he accompanied Charles to Scotland, but was not permitted to sit in the Scottish parliament until he had taken the covenant. On 17 September he was named to the Scottish privy council. He was created duke of Richmond on 8 August 1641, and early the following December was appointed lord steward of the king's household.

Lennox's position in the Lords was fatally compromised on 26 January 1642, when he 'put the question whether we shall adjourn the Parliament for six months' (The Private Journals of the Long Parliament, ed. W. H. Coates, A. S. Young, and V. F. Snow, 3 vols., 1982–92, 1.195). This provoked an outcry in both houses and some members of the Commons demanded his impeachment for threatening parliament's sitting. In the event, Lennox was required only to 'make an humble submission and acknowledgement' that he had spoken 'inconsiderately and inadvisedly', although twenty-two peers (including Warwick, Essex, Wharton, Pembroke, and Brooke) protested that this was 'not a sufficient punishment' (JHL, 4.543). On 2 February Lennox was given leave, and he never attended the Lords again. By April he had joined the king at Hull.

During the civil wars Lennox regularly acted as one of the king's commissioners in peace talks with the houses. In December 1644 he and the earl of Southampton acted as go-betweens in the negotiations that set up the treaty of Uxbridge. Lennox, together with the earls of Southampton, Hertford, and Lindsey, made a final desperate attempt to reach agreement with the parliamentarian army at Woodstock in April 1646, but this went wrong and led to his brief imprisonment in Warwick Castle. The committee for compounding assessed him at £9810 on 15 December 1646; he compounded and received letters of discharge in May 1647. Lennox remained close to Charles I and he was among a select group of advisers whom the king summoned to attend him during the summer and autumn of 1647. Charles appointed him one of his commissioners at the treaty of Newport between September and December 1648. Lennox attended Charles during his trial and execution and was one of the royalist peers present at the king's funeral.

According to Sir Edward Walker, 'after the murther of the King, [Lennox] retyred unto his house at Cobham Hall in Kent, seldome ever appearing abroad' (Bodl. Oxf., MS Ashmole 1110, fol. 167r). He resolutely refused to get involved in any conspiracies against the republic, despite the approaches of several royalist activists. Although he had declined to assist the royalist campaigns of 1650–51, he was summoned before the committee of examinations in May 1651. His request to be excused from taking the engagement reinforced the council of state's suspicions about his loyalties, and he was bailed on a bond for £10,000, with two sureties for £5000 each. The following October, he was again summoned before the council, but responded by sending a doctor's certificate affirming that he was too ill to attend. A further summons in December 1651 was again declined on grounds of ill health. His final years were dogged by illness, and according to Robert Baillie, by the summer of 1654 the duke was living in Kent as quietly 'as a man buried' (*Letters and Journals of Robert Baillie*, 3.249). Lennox died at Cobham Hall on 30 March 1655, and was buried on 18 April in Henry VII's chapel at Westminster Abbey.

Lennox's widow suffered growing hardship in the later 1650s: the timber at Cobham Hall was plundered for Cromwell's navy, and by 1658 the family had sold off most of its Scottish lands. She seems to have lived very quietly, and in the summer of 1658 moved to Paris where she spent the rest of the interregnum. She lived until November 1685, but their only son and heir, Esmé, fifth duke of Lennox and second duke of Richmond, died in Paris in 1660.   DAVID L. SMITH

Sources state papers domestic, Charles I, PRO, SP 16 · committee for compounding papers, PRO, SP 23 · council of state papers, PRO, SP 25 · *The letters and journals of Robert Baillie*, ed. D. Laing, 3 vols. (1841–2) · Clarendon, *Hist. rebellion* · *Scots peerage* · *JHL*, 4–10 (1628–48) · D. L. Smith, *Constitutional royalism and the search for settlement, c. 1640–1649* (1994) · *DNB* · GEC, *Peerage*, new edn · J. E. Doyle, *The official baronage of England*, 2 (1886), 472–3; 3 (1886), 121–5 · *The historical works of Sir James Balfour*, ed. J. Haig, 4 vols. (1824–5) · Bodl. Oxf., MS Ashmole 1110, fol. 167r
Archives Medway Archives and Local Studies Centre, Rochester, Kent, letters and papers | NRA, priv. coll., corresp. with first earl of Traquair
Likenesses A. Van Dyck, oils, c.1633–1637, Kenwood, London · A. Van Dyck, oils, c.1633–1637, Louvre, Paris · A. Van Dyck, oils, c.1633–1637, Metropolitan Museum of Art, New York [see illus.] · A. Van Dyck, oils, c.1633–1637, Buccleuch estate, Selkirk; version, Clarendon collection (on loan to Plymouth Art Gallery) · R. Dunkarton, mezzotint (after A. Van Dyck), NPG · attrib. T. Russel, oils, NPG · A. Van Dyck, oils, Wilton House, Wiltshire
Wealth at death annual income was £3000 in 1637: *DNB*

Stuart, James [*called* Athenian Stuart] (**1713–1788**), painter and architect, was born in Creed Lane, Ludgate Street, London, the eldest son of a Scottish mariner who died when he was a boy, leaving the family with insufficient financial support.

Italy and Greece 1742–1754 Stuart found early employment with Lewis Goupy, a well-known fan painter, at the same time as studying mathematics, geometry, and anatomy, and teaching himself Greek and Latin. After his mother's death, with his brother and sister in employment, he was able to fulfil his long-held ambition of continuing his artistic training in Rome. In 1742, aged twenty-nine, he set off on foot to Rome, where he remained for eight years, acquiring a reputation as a connoisseur of art, continuing his study of Greek and Latin at the Collegio di Propaganda Fide, and mastering the art of engraving. As a result, he produced an illustrated account of the Egyptian obelisk found in the Campus Martius, which he published in A. M. Bandini's *De obelisco Caesaris Augusti* (1750).

In April 1748 Stuart and Nicholas Revett (1720–1804), the wealthy son of a Suffolk squire, together with the painter and dealer Gavin Hamilton and the architect Robert Brettingham the younger, visited Naples, where they first formed an ambition of measuring the buildings of Athens. Though lip-service had been paid since the Renaissance to Greece as the fountainhead of Western civilization, almost no one had ever bothered to go to Athens to

James Stuart (1713–1788), self-portrait, c.1730

investigate the surviving buildings, though it was, admittedly, very difficult of access.

In Rome in 1750 Stuart and Revett met Robert Wood, a scholar who had visited Greece in the 1740s, and his colleague James Dawkins, who had inherited a Jamaican fortune in 1744. Wood and Dawkins were about to travel to the Levant, where their investigations led to the publication of their well-organized and popular archaeological study *The Ruins of Palmyra* (1753). Having received financial support from Dawkins, as well as valuable professional advice from Wood, Stuart and Revett left Rome for Athens in 1750. They were delayed in Venice, where Sir James Gray procured their election to the Society of Dilettanti, whose members subscribed to their proposed publication. From Venice they travelled to Pola in Istria, where they made the first accurate drawings of the two Roman temples, triumphal arch, and amphitheatre, described by Stuart as 'built in the most exquisite taste of the Augustan Age' (Wiebenson, 80). Their reconstruction of the Corinthian temple of Rome and Augustus at Pola was used by Sir James Gray's brother Colonel George Gray as the model for a proposed clubhouse for the Society of Dilettanti in Cavendish Square in 1753. This serves to remind us that neither Stuart and Revett, nor the Society of Dilettanti, was limited to the exclusive study and promotion of Greek architecture.

Between leaving Pola in November 1750 and departing for Greece in January 1751 Stuart and Revett issued in Venice a manuscript called 'Proposal for publishing a new accurate description of the antiquities, &c. in the province of Attica'. In a later printed version of this, they claimed that 'Artists who aim at perfection, must be more pleased and better instructed, the nearer they approach the Fountain-Head of their art' (*The Antiquities of Athens*, 1, 1762, v n.), thus expressing the belief of the eighteenth-century Enlightenment in the return to first principles and in the creative link between the study of archaeology and the practice of art and architecture.

In March 1751 Stuart and Revett finally arrived in Athens where opportunities for investigating the major monuments of the Acropolis were restricted by the presence of the Turkish garrison on its southern ridge. Everywhere they aroused suspicion and were taken for spies. Stuart was eventually forced to leave Athens in September 1753 during the riots that took place following the death of Osman, chief of the black eunuchs. Stuart was involved in a violent quarrel in which he knocked down a Greek official, and on a similar occasion was nearly murdered by a gang of Turkish cut-throats. He travelled from Athens to Salonica, where he was joined in January 1754 by Revett, with whom he revisited the Aegean Islands, including Delos, but an outbreak of plague prevented them from returning to Athens to continue their studies. They returned in October 1754 to London, where they prepared their drawings for publication, meanwhile living in the house of James Dawkins.

The antiquities of Athens Europe awaited with interest, but Winckelmann, in particular, expressed signs of impatience because their first volume was not published until 1762. *The Antiquities of Athens Measured and Delineated by James Stuart, F.R.S. and F.S.A., and Nicholas Revett, Painters and Architects*, dedicated to George III, consisted of Revett's measured drawings with a text and attractive topographical views by Stuart, which began as coloured gouaches but were reproduced as black and white engravings. The delay had led to disagreement between the two men, as a result of which Stuart bought out Revett's financial interest before publication, though their joint names appeared on the title-pages of all the volumes.

The reason for the delay was not only Stuart's laziness, but his decision at the last moment to undertake a substantial revision of the text by correcting the errors in Julien-David Leroy's *Les ruines des plus beaux monuments de la Grèce* (1758), the first scholarly illustrated account of the buildings of fifth-century Athens. This delay also had the unfortunate result of making him forgo his plan to return to Athens to make a detailed study of the buildings on the Acropolis. Stuart's main quarrel with Leroy, whose book had, to his annoyance, deprived him of the distinction of being the first to publish an accurate survey of Greek architecture, was that Leroy had misidentified a portico or stoa in Athens as a fragment of the temple of Olympian Zeus, the Olympeion. We now know that this building was part of the library of Hadrian, and it is significant that, with the exception of the temple on the Ilissus, all but one of the six buildings in the first volume of *The Antiquities of Athens* were not Greek but comparatively minor monuments of either the Hellenistic or Roman periods.

Stuart, indeed, seemed to feel that everything in Greece was Greek. He thus explained that the third volume would include:

> buildings erected after the time that Athens became subject to the Romans. For though deprived of its liberty, and greatly fallen from its ancient splendour, it was still a respectable City, to which the principal men of Rome sent their Sons for education; it still produced Artists, and had a taste for magnificence. (*The Antiquities of Athens*, 2, 1787, advertisement)

He also attempted to explain the modesty and late date of the buildings in the first volume by claiming that, in the event of there being no demand from the public for further volumes, then at least they 'might find in it something interesting on the different Grecian modes of decorating Buildings' (ibid.). Stuart has sometimes been credited with producing a manifesto for an architectural style based exclusively on that of classical Greece; certainly he became known in his lifetime as Athenian Stuart. However, neither his books nor his buildings really bear this out: his aim was not to replace the Roman orders but to extend them. His eight years in Rome tend to be neglected because of his famous but briefer stay in Athens. The view of Stuart as an architect with an exclusively Greek mission was largely formed at the peak of the nineteenth-century Greek revival, when its promoters, architects such as Robert Smirke and William Wilkins, were anxious to create a respectable ancestry for the movement.

In 1770 Leroy produced a second edition of his *Les ruines des plus beaux monuments de la Grèce*, in which he, in turn, criticized Stuart and Revett's first volume for having as its sole aim the provision of exact measurements, and for the fact that, in Stuart's gouache views, the monuments were obscured by lesser objects. Stuart had certainly opened himself to criticism by his stress on 'the different methods of decorating buildings', which implied that he was concerned with enlarging the existing stock of decorative motifs rather than initiating a radical architectural form. Leroy was, however, somewhat unfair to Stuart, who did promote a serious, culturally contingent interpretation of Greece in which work carried out 'while the Athenians were a free people' (*The Antiquities of Athens*, 2, 1787, advertisement), particularly in the time of Pericles, was seen as necessarily superior to that produced when they were subjugated by Rome.

Early architectural commissions On his return from Greece, Stuart was showered with commissions from members of the Society of Dilettanti, although he seemed to lack the application to bring them all to a successful conclusion. In 1758 he was appointed surveyor of Greenwich Hospital, a post worth £200 a year for which he was indebted to the recommendation of his future patron Lord Anson. In 1763 he became painter to the Society of Dilettanti, who instructed him in that year to paint portraits of James and Henry Dawkins; having failed to produce them by 1768, he was forced to relinquish his post to Reynolds. In 1764 he succeeded Hogarth as sergeant painter in the office of works, and exhibited for several years at the Free Society of Artists, showing mainly water-colour drawings of Athens.

An important early monument was the garden temple which Stuart designed in 1758 for George Lyttelton, the first Baron Lyttelton at Hagley Park, Worcestershire, as a miniature echo of the Theseion in Athens. Executed in 1759, it was the first since the ancient world to incorporate the fluted baseless columns of the Greek Doric order. Stressing its role as a picturesque object in the landscape, Lord Lyttelton wrote to the bluestocking Mrs Montagu, 'Stuart is going to embellish one of the Hills with a true attick building, a portico of six pillars, which will make a fine effect to my new house and command a most beautiful view of the country' (Blunt, 2.150).

This theme recurred at Shugborough, the Staffordshire estate of Thomas Anson, a founder member of the Society of Dilettanti in 1732, who inherited a fortune in 1762 from his elder brother Admiral Lord Anson, the naval hero. With the help, first of Thomas Wright, and then of Stuart from about 1761 to 1771, the Anson brothers turned the park into an Enlightenment vision of world architecture, reflecting the taste of the eighteenth century for the monuments of different cultures, east and west. Gardens such as Shugborough, Hagley, Stowe, and Stourhead became a kind of memory theatre, reflecting intellectual and cultural voyages. With its Greek, Gothic, Roman, and Chinese buildings, Shugborough was, indeed, a visual parallel to the actual circumnavigation of the globe undertaken by Admiral Anson. The buildings included a version of the choragic monument of Lysicrates in Athens, Stuart's favourite building, although it was not of the fifth century BC, but a whimsical ornamental folly of the late fourth century. Its fanciful quality perhaps made it seem appropriate for imitation as a modern garden folly. Stuart also provided versions of two other monuments in Athens, the Tower of the Winds and Hadrian's Arch, the latter erected by Hadrian as a demonstration of his devotion to ancient Athenian culture.

Nathaniel Curzon, created Baron Scarsdale in 1761, and subscriber to the first volume of *The Antiquities of Athens*, consulted Stuart about 1757 concerning the design of interiors in which to display his collection of paintings and sculpture at Kedleston Hall, Derbyshire. Stuart produced attractive coloured drawings for interiors, including Greek tripods as painted wall decoration, as incense burners on chimney-pieces, as candelabra in front of mirrors, and in friezes above doors. He based these on his restoration of the metal tripod on the choragic monument of Lysicrates. Adam, who saw the drawings in December 1758, described them as 'so excessively & so ridiculously bad, that … they move pity rather than contempt' (Clerk of Penicuik MS 4854, NA Scot.). None the less, when he supplanted Stuart at Kedleston about 1760, he borrowed much from Stuart's designs.

Wimbledon Park and Spencer House (from 1758) Viscount Spencer, also a subscriber to *The Antiquities of Athens*, created Earl Spencer in 1765 and elected a member of the Society of Dilettanti in the same year, employed Stuart to provide fashionable new interiors at the family house, Wimbledon Park, Surrey (c.1758; dem.), following his marriage in 1756. At the same time, he began to build, from designs by the Palladian architect John Vardy, Spencer House, a magnificent town mansion in Green Park with a decorative programme celebrating themes of love and marriage. Vardy was dismissed in September 1758 on the suggestion of Colonel George Gray, founding member and secretary of the Society of Dilettanti, who had been asked by Spencer to supervise the design for the house. Gray brought in Stuart to make the house more authentically classical. In the Great Room, Stuart designed a chimney-piece incorporating a figured frieze based on that of the choragic monument of Lysicrates with its dancing Bacchantes. More remarkably, in both the Great Room and adjacent Painted Room, he exercised total control, designing the architectural joinery such as dados and door frames, the chimney-pieces, picture frames, seat furniture, pier glasses, and tables, mostly in a version of the contemporary French *goût grec* manner.

One of the richest rooms in eighteenth-century England, the Painted Room shows the inadequacy of his description as Athenian Stuart, for during his eight years in Rome he had clearly absorbed the ancient Roman grotesque or arabesque type of decoration which had been revived in Renaissance Italy by Raphael and Vasari. None the less, the jealous Adam said of Stuart's ceilings at Spencer House, 'they may be Greek to the teeth but by God they are not handsome' (J. Fleming, *Robert Adam and his Circle*, 1962, 258). The bay at the south end of the Painted Room is separated by a screen of Corinthian columns inspired by the temple of Antoninus and Faustina in Rome, but carrying a Greek anthemion frieze based on the Erechtheion on the Acropolis. Between the columns stood Stuart's torchères, nearly 7 feet high and important as some of the earliest furniture decorated with painted panels in a manner later developed by Adam. Painted with Pompeian winged figures of Victory, the stands are surmounted by winged griffins supporting ormolu tripods with candle sconces and a central incense burner, inspired by the tripod on the choragic monument of Lysicrates, but recalling the ancient Roman practice of burning incense during dinner parties. Stuart's sofas, designed to fit into the curve of the apse, are also neo-antique, with winged lions inspired by those on Hellenistic marble thrones.

Work at Spencer House proceeded with Stuart's characteristic slowness, though partly because of his other commissions, such as Holdernesse House (later Londonderry House; dem.) and Lichfield House. His work from about 1760 to 1765 at Holdernesse House was carried out for the fourth earl of Holdernesse, who belonged to the Society of Dilettanti, the members of which frequently met in it. It contained ceilings inspired by plates in Wood's *The Ruins of Palmyra*, as does Lichfield House, St James's Square, which Stuart built in 1764–6 for Thomas Anson of Shugborough. With the first stone-fronted façade in the square, its composition is purely Palladian, yet it sports immaculate Greek Ionic capitals which are life-size copies of those on the Erechtheion, though Stuart did not include the rich frieze which surmounts them in the original.

Portman Square (from 1775) In 1775 Stuart was commissioned by Mrs Montagu to build her a free-standing mansion in Portman Square which, despite its dull façade, attracted so much interest that she arranged for it to be opened to the public by ticket. Excited by Stuart's Athenian reputation, visitors saw what they wanted to see; the poet James 'Hermes' Harris exclaimed, 'I have seen an edifice which for the time made me imagine I was at Athens, in a house of Pericles, built by Phidias' (Blunt, 2.100). However, the interiors were Adamesque, thus showing that Stuart's rivalry with Adam had ended in victory for Adam, for Stuart had failed to produce a style of his own. Mrs Montagu praised the house in 1780 as 'so convenient and cheerful as a place of retirement, so ample for the devoirs of Society, and so calculated for Assemblies that it will suit all one's humours, and adapt itself to all one's purposes' (ibid., 2.103). This is in harmony with the eighteenth-century belief in the creation of appropriate character in architecture, with interior design and furniture expressing the personality of the patron. Stuart responded by providing the house with a unique plan in which a group of five intercommunicating rooms for entertaining opened off the main staircase, with a virtually separate apartment for Mrs Montagu at the south end with her own staircase. Stuart's indolence and drinking habits had made him unreliable by the late 1780s; the interior of the ballroom, recalling that in an Italian palazzo, was executed after his death from designs by Joseph Bonomi in 1789–90.

Other works In his capacity as surveyor of Greenwich Hospital, Stuart replaced the chapel, built in the 1730s by Thomas Ripley, after its destruction by fire in 1779. His assistant William Newton, author of the first English translation of Vitruvius, claimed that he had designed most of it himself, which seems unlikely, although he completed it in 1788 after Stuart's death. The plasterwork has a rich succulence going beyond fifth-century Athens towards the freedom of Palmyra, with a crispness and stiffness about the details which seem characteristically Stuartian. Although the chapel is prettily coloured, Stuart seems to have been unaware of the importance of polychromy in Greek architecture: he certainly noted a trace of colour on the frieze of the Ionic temple on the River Ilissus in Athens in the first volume of The Antiquities of Athens, but drew no conclusions from this. It was only after about 1810 that scholars began to suppose that polychromy may have been integral to the design of Greek architecture.

Stuart was elected a fellow of the Royal Society and of the Society of Antiquaries, and long remained active in the affairs of the Society of Dilettanti. As well as his architectural practice, limited chiefly to sophisticated interiors and garden buildings, he designed furniture, medals, and numerous monuments. Mostly executed by Peter Scheemakers and his son Thomas, his monuments include those in Westminster Abbey to the third Viscount Howe (d. 1758) and to Admiral Charles Watson (d. 1775). One of the finest is that of 1766 to the first earl of Hardwicke, at Wimpole church, Cambridgeshire, incorporating a handsome Grecian Minerva.

The second volume of The Antiquities of Athens, dated 1787 but not published until January 1790, was published by Stuart's widow, Elizabeth, with help from William Newton. Stuart had also left materials for the third volume, which appeared in 1795 under the editorship of the architect Willey Reveley, who included in it a lengthy defence of Greek architecture from the sharp criticisms of it by Sir William Chambers. With this volume the series as envisaged by Stuart and Revett may be said to have been concluded. However, in 1816 a fourth volume of miscellaneous drawings, principally of the Roman antiquities at Pola, but including valuable plates of the Parthenon sculpture, was issued by Josiah Taylor, the architectural publisher who had acquired Stuart's papers about 1809. It contained a memoir of Stuart by Joseph Woods (1776–1864), a scholar and minor Greek revival architect. A final supplementary volume appeared in 1830 under the distinguished editorship of C. R. Cockerell (1788–1863) as The Antiquities of Athens and other Places of Greece, Sicily etc.

Private life and death Stuart was twice married, on the first occasion to someone variously described as his housekeeper and as a 'Grecian lady', and on the second, at the age of sixty-seven, to a woman of twenty named Elizabeth, with whom he had five children, of whom three survived him. He had been 'very infirm for some years preceding his death, [and] left his papers in great confusion and disorder' (The Antiquities of Athens, 2, 1787, iii). By the 1780s he 'regularly frequented a public-house on the north side of Leicester-fields, of the sign of the feathers', while 'his face declared him to be fond of what is called friendly society' (J. T. Smith, Nollekens and his Times, 1929, 27). His rather idle existence was sustained by a private fortune, for, according to a contemporary report, 'Athens Stuart, unexpectedly to most people, has died possessed of much property, chiefly on mortgage on new buildings in Marybone' (The World, 22 Feb 1788). His death had taken place suddenly on 2 February 1788 at his house on the south side of Leicester Square, London. He was buried in the crypt of St Martin-in-the-Fields.

Conclusion Stuart exercised a wide influence on British architects, though they tended to ignore his advice to follow the principles not the details of Greek architecture. James Wyatt produced an inspired version of the Tower of the Winds at Athens at the Radcliffe Observatory, Oxford (1776–94), but early nineteenth-century architects such as Robert Smirke, John Foster, and William and Henry William Inwood incorporated into their buildings replicas of works such as the choragic monument of Lysicrates, based on plates in The Antiquities of Athens. John Soane frequently put the baseless Greek Doric order, whether fluted or unfluted, to powerful effect, while William Wilkins, at Grange Park, Hampshire (1809), provided the most complete templar house ever erected in Britain.

James Elmes, whose St John's Chapel, Chichester, Sussex (1812–13), was an early use of the Lysicrates model for a church tower, claimed boldly in 1847 that, 'No event that ever occurred in the history of architecture in England, and thence throughout all Europe, produced so sudden, decided, and beneficial effect as did the works of James Stuart' (*Civil Engineers' and Architects' Journal*, 10, 1847, 338–9). If this interpretation cannot exactly be sustained today, it is significant for revealing how Stuart was regarded at the time; his reputation has, moreover, remained high.   DAVID WATKIN

Sources *GM*, 1st ser., 58 (1788), 95–6, 181, 216–8 · *GM*, 1st ser., 79 (1809), 596–7 · *European Magazine and London Review*, 13 (1788), 68, 143, 284 · D. Watkin, *Athenian Stuart: pioneer of the Greek revival* (1982) · [W. Papworth], ed., *The dictionary of architecture*, 11 vols. (1853–92) · L. Cust and S. Colvin, eds., *History of the Society of Dilettanti* (1898) · L. Lawrence [Lewis], 'The architects of the chapel at Greenwich Hospital', *Art Bulletin*, 29 (1947), 260–67 · L. Lawrence [Lewis], 'Greece and Rome at Greenwich', *ArchR*, 109 (1951), 17–24 · J. Landy, 'Stuart and Revett: pioneer archaeologists', *Archaeology*, 9 (Dec 1956), 252–9 · *The parish of St James, Westminster*, 1, Survey of London, 29–30 (1960) · P. Thornton and J. Hardy, 'The Spencer furniture at Althorp [pt 2]: James Stuart's neo-classical furniture from Spencer House', *Apollo*, 87 (1968), 440–51 · D. Wiebenson, *Sources of Greek revival architecture* (1969) · M. Richardson, ed., *Catalogue of the drawings collection of the Royal Institute of British Architects: S* (1976) · J. Harris, 'Newly acquired drawings by James Stuart in the British Architectural Library', *Architectural History*, 22 (1979), 72–7 · E. Harris and N. Savage, *British architectural books and writers, 1556–1785* (1990), 439–50 · J. Friedman, *Spencer House: chronicle of a great London mansion* (1993) · Colvin, *Archs.* · G. Worsley, *Classical architecture in Britain: the heroic age* (1994) · W. Papworth, 'William Newton and the chapel of Greenwich Hospital', *Journal of Proceedings of the Royal Institute of British Architects*, new ser., 7 (1890–91), 417–20 · E. Chancellor, *The private palaces of London, past and present* (1908) · *Mrs Montagu, 'Queen of the Blues': her letters and friendships from 1762 to 1800*, ed. R. Blunt, 2 vols. (1923) · L. Lawrence, 'Stuart and Revett: their literary and architectural careers', *Journal of the Warburg Institute*, 2 (1938), 128–46 · E. Croft-Murray, 'A drawing by "Athenian" Stuart for the Painted Room at Spencer House', *British Museum Quarterly*, 21 (1957–9), 14–15 · E. Croft-Murray, *Decorative painting in England, 1537–1837*, 2 vols. (1962–70) · J. Harris, *A catalogue of British drawings for architecture, decoration, sculpture and landscape gardening, 1550–1900, in American collections* (1972) · J. M. Crook, *The Greek revival: neo-classical attitudes in British architecture, 1760–1870* (1972) · N. Goodison, 'Mr Stuart's tripod', *Burlington Magazine*, 114 (1972), 695–705 · J. Hayward and H. Hayward, 'Kedleston Hall, Derbyshire', *Country Life*, 163 (1978), 262–6 · L. Harris, *Robert Adam and Kedleston: the making of a neo-classical masterpiece*, ed. G. Jackson-Stops (c.1987) · I. Roscoe, 'James "Athenian" Stuart and the Scheemakers family: a lucrative partnership between architect and sculptors', *Apollo*, 126 (1987), 178–84 · M. Hopkinson, 'A portrait by James "Athenian" Stuart', *Burlington Magazine*, 131 (1990), 794–5 · G. Worsley, 'Out from Adam's shadow', *Country Life* (14 May 1992), 100–03 · G. Worsley, 'Spencer House [pt 1]', *Country Life* (24 Dec 1992) · G. Worsley, 'Spencer House [pt 2]', *Country Life* (31 Dec 1992)

Archives BL, notebook relating to visit to Athens, Add. MS 62088 · BL, papers relating to publication of antiquities of Athens · BM · Morgan L. · NMM

Likenesses J. Stuart, self-portrait, drawing, c.1730, BAL RIBA [*see illus.*] · attrib. P. Jean, miniature, c.1779, NPG · S. W. Reynolds, etching, pubd 1785 (after J. Reynolds), BM · J. Basire, line engraving, BM; repro. in *Rudiments of ancient architecture*, 2nd edn (1794), frontispiece · J. Henning?, oils (after G. Dance), V&A · C. Knight, stipple (after death mask), BM, NPG; repro. in J. Stuart, *The antiquities of Athens*, 3 vols. (1762–94) · J. Wedgwood, medallion, Scot. NPG

Wealth at death considerable: *The World* (22 Feb 1788)

Stuart, James (d. 1793), army officer, was the third and youngest son among the seven children of Archibald Stuart (d. 1767) of Torrance, Lanarkshire, and his wife, Elizabeth, daughter of Sir Andrew Myreton, baronet, of Gogar. Andrew *Stuart (1725–1801), lawyer, was an elder brother. James Stuart was first in the Dutch service, where he reached the rank of captain. He became lieutenant in the 58th regiment of the British army on 5 May 1756, and first saw active service in 1758 at the siege of Louisbourg in Nova Scotia, under Lord Amherst. On 20 October of the same year he was promoted captain in the 83rd regiment, and major on 7 December 1759. In 1761 he was present with Colonel Morgan's regiment at the reduction of Belle Île. During the course of that expedition he acted as quartermaster-general, and in consequence obtained the brevet rank of lieutenant-colonel. From Belle Île Stuart went to the West Indies, where he served in the operations against Martinique and on the death of Colonel Morgan took command of the regiment. After the conquest of Martinique (February 1762) his regiment was ordered to join the expedition against Havana, where Stuart greatly distinguished himself by his conduct in the assault on the castle of Morro, the capture of which determined the success of the expedition. He returned home, and on 20 September 1763 married Lady Margaret, daughter of Hugh Hume, third earl of Marchmont, and his wife, Anne Western. They had no children before her early death on 7 January 1765.

In 1775 Stuart received permission to enter the service of the East India Company as second in command on the Coromandel coast, with the rank of colonel. On his arrival he found serious differences existing between the council of the Madras presidency and the governor, Lord Pigot. Stuart followed the orders of the council in trying to restore the raja of Tanjore to lands dubiously transferred to the nawab of Arcot, whose debts were the main cause of the trouble. The affair degenerated into confusion, in the course of which Stuart arrested Pigot on 23 August 1776 and allowed the dissident councillors to assume power in Madras. After news of the arrest reached Britain, Pigot was reinstated but immediately recalled, while Stuart was suspended by the company directors from the office of commander-in-chief to which he had succeeded with the rank of brigadier-general in December 1776. Although he repeatedly demanded a trial, he could not, despite peremptory orders from Britain, succeed in obtaining a court martial until December 1780, when he was honourably acquitted and by order of the directors received the arrears of his pay from the time of his suspension. On 11 January 1781 he was restored to the chief command in Madras by order of the governor and council. He returned to Madras in that year and, under Sir Eyre Coote, on 1 July took part in the battle of Porto Novo, in which he distinguished himself by his able handling of the second line of the British force. In the battle of Polillur, on 27 August, he lost a leg to a cannon shot. He was promoted major-general on 19 October, and on the return of Sir Eyre Coote to Bengal in January 1782 took command of the forces in Madras. The governor, Lord Macartney, however, would not allow him the freedom of action which Eyre Coote had enjoyed, and on the death of Haidar Ali on 7 December 1782 urged Stuart immediately to attack the Mysore army. Stuart declared his forces were not ready, and made no active movement for two months. While besieging Cuddalore he was suspended from the command by the Madras government, was placed in strict confinement in Madras, and then sent back to Britain. Resenting 'his Lordship's personal conduct to him', Stuart called out Lord Macartney, and on 8 June 1786 they fought a duel in Hyde Park. Owing to the loss of his leg, Stuart was 'under the necessity from the first of putting his back to a tree' (*GM*, 523), but succeeded in severely wounding his opponent. Unsatisfied by the outcome, both participants threatened to resume the duel, until the king indicated his wish that the matter be taken no further. On 8 February 1792 Stuart was appointed colonel of the 31st foot. He died a year later, on 2 February 1793. E. I. CARLYLE, *rev.* MICHAEL FRY

Sources A. Stuart, *Genealogical history of the Stewarts* (1798) · M. Wilks, *Historical sketches of the south of India, in an attempt to trace the history of Mysoor*, 3 vols. (1810–17) · A. Stuart, *Letters to the directors of the East India Company, and the Right Hon Lord Amherst, from Andrew Stuart, Esq, in the years 1777, 1778 and 1781; on the subject of certain events in India and of Gen. Stuart's conduct in his majesty's service and in that of the East India Company* (1782?) · A. Stuart, *A letter to the honourable the directors of the East India Company, from Andrew Stuart esq; respecting the conduct of Brigadier-General James Stuart, at Madras* (1778) · *N&Q*, 8th ser., 9 (1896), 170, 258 · HoP, *Commons, 1790–1820* · *Scots peerage* · *GM*, 1st ser., 56 (1786), 523 · *The later correspondence of George III*, ed. A. Aspinall, 5 vols. (1962–70), vol. 1, p. 229
Archives National Archives of India, New Delhi, official papers · NL Scot., accounts, corresp., notebooks, and papers | BL OIOC, corresp. as commander-in-chief, Madras · Bodl. Oxf., corresp. with Lord Macartney · NL Scot., corresp. with Andrew Stuart
Likenesses C. H. Hodges, mezzotint, pubd 1789 (after G. Romney), BM · G. Romney, oils, 1832, Scot. NPG

Stuart, James (1741–1815), army officer, was born on 2 March 1741 at Blairhall, Perthshire, the third son of John Stuart of Blairhall and his wife, Lady Anne (1703–1783), daughter of Francis Stuart, seventh earl of Moray. He was educated at the schools at Culross and Dunfermline, and in 1757 went to Edinburgh to study law. Abandoning the law, he entered the army on 1 October 1761 as ensign in the 64th foot, became lieutenant on 7 December 1764, and captain on 12 January 1770. He served in the American War of Independence, and attained the rank of major in the 78th foot on 18 December 1777.

In 1782 Stuart arrived with his regiment in India, where he was appointed lieutenant-colonel on 14 February, and to the local rank of colonel on 13 June following. He took part in Sir Eyre Coote's campaign against Haidar Ali of Mysore, and was present at the siege of Cuddalore, when he commanded the attack on the right of the main position in the assault of 13 July 1782. In the campaign of 1790, under General Sir William Medows, against Tipu Sultan of Mysore, he reduced the fortresses of Dindigul and Palghat. He served under Cornwallis through the campaigns of 1791–2, was placed in immediate charge of the siege of

Seringapatam, and commanded the centre column in the assault of 6 February 1792. On 8 August he was promoted colonel on his appointment as aide-de-camp to the king, and, after a visit to England, returned to Madras in 1794. On 26 February 1795 he was appointed major-general, and in the same year took command of the expedition which captured the Dutch possessions in Ceylon. These were secured in 1796. Stuart then became commander-in-chief of the forces in Madras. On 2 March 1797 he was appointed colonel of the 82nd regiment of foot, and on 23 October 1798 colonel of the 72nd regiment of foot. In the following year, in the last war against Tipu, he commanded the Bombay army which occupied Coorg and repulsed Tipu at Seedaseer (6 March). On 15 March he joined Major-General George Harris before Seringapatam, and took charge of the operations on the northern side of the city. After its capture Stuart, with several other officers, received the thanks of both houses of parliament. In 1801 he was appointed commander-in-chief of the Madras army; on 29 April 1802 he attained the rank of lieutenant-general, and in the following year took part in the Second Anglo-Maratha War, Major-General Wellesley being under his orders. In 1805 he returned to England in bad health; he was promoted general on 1 January 1812. Stuart died in London at Charles Street, Berkeley Square, on 29 April 1815, and was buried in a vault in St James's Chapel, Hampstead Road, London. MICHAEL FRY

Sources Burke, *Gen. GB* · *Scots peerage* · *N&Q*, 8th ser., 9 (1896), 170, 258 · *N&Q*, 8th ser., 11 (1897), 91 · M. Wilks, *Historical sketches of the south of India, in an attempt to trace the history of Mysoor*, 3 vols. (1810–17) · *GM*, 1st ser., 85/1 (1815), 475 · N. B. Leslie, *The succession of colonels of the British army from 1660 to the present day* (1974) · DNB
Archives BL, corresp. with Lord Wellesley, Add. MSS 13768–13769 · BL OIOC, corresp. as commander-in-chief, Bombay and Madras · Cleveland Public Library, Ohio, letters to Clive and Wellesley · NL Scot., corresp. with Alexander Walker · U. Southampton L., corresp. with Arthur Wellesley
Likenesses T. Hickey, drawing, 1799, Stratfield Saye, Hampshire · G. Clint, mezzotint, pubd 1802 (after T. Lawrence), BM · pen-and-ink drawing, NPG

Stuart, James (1764–1842), historian and journalist, son of Benjamin Stuart of co. Antrim, was born in Armagh. He was educated at the Royal School, Armagh, and in January 1784 entered Trinity College, Dublin, where he was taught by Dr George Miller. He graduated BA in the spring term of 1789, and enrolled as a student in the Middle Temple in January 1790 but he was never called to the bar. In 1811 he published *Poems on Various Subjects*, some of which are on places near Armagh, some on his friends, none of more than occasional interest. In 1812 he became the first editor of the *Newry Telegraph*, and from 1815 to 1819 also edited the *Newry Magazine*. Here he wrote *Historical Memoirs of the City of Armagh for a Period of 1,373 Years*, which was published in 1819. The book combines a short history of Ireland with a history of Armagh. Stuart also included a skilful denunciation of Edward Ledwich's view that St Patrick never existed.

Stuart went to live in Belfast in 1821 and became editor of the *News Letter*. Some theological letters by him, which first appeared in this journal, were published in 1825 as

The Protestant Layman. In 1827 he founded and edited the *Guardian and Constitutional Advocate*, but ill health soon forced him to give it up. He married Mary Ogle; they had no children. Stuart died in September 1842 in Belfast.

NORMAN MOORE, *rev.* MARIE-LOUISE LEGG

Sources H. A. C. Sturgess, ed., *Register of admissions to the Honourable Society of the Middle Temple, from the fifteenth century to the year 1944*, 2 (1949) · D. MacCartney, 'The writing of history in Ireland, 1800–30', *Irish Historical Studies*, 10 (1956–7), 347–62, esp. 349 · F. C. Crossle, *Notes on the literary history of Newry* (1897)

Stuart, James (1775–1849), landowner, politician, and factory inspector, was the eldest son of Dr Charles Stuart (1745/6–1826), of Dunearn in Fife, and Mary, the daughter of the Revd Dr John *Erskine. His father was minister of Cramond, on the Firth of Forth, and later a physician in Edinburgh who, after graduating MD from the University of Edinburgh in 1781, established the Anabaptist community in the city. His son James attended Edinburgh high school from 1785 to 1789 before studying at Edinburgh University from 1790 to 1797. James Stuart was apprenticed to Hugh Robertson, writer to the signet, and became a member of the Society of Writers to the Signet in 1798. On 29 April 1802 he married Eleanor Anna, only daughter of Dr Robert Moubray, of Cockairnie, Fife. They had no children.

Although Stuart was collector of the widows' fund of the Society of Writers to the Signet from 1818 to 1828, his main interest was in farming his estates in Fife, particularly in breeding large beef cattle. He played an active role in county affairs as deputy lieutenant and justice of the peace; but his outspoken whig sympathies upset the tory gentry. In December 1815, when a new commission of the peace was issued for Fife, the lord lieutenant, the earl of Morton, tried to exclude him. However Stuart's whig supporters petitioned successfully for his reappointment. He was also deeply involved in the very fraught Edinburgh politics of the period, speaking out clearly against the tory-controlled town council. The strength of his opinions and the forcefulness of his onslaughts, often accompanied by threats of physical violence, against tory opponents earned him a certain notoriety throughout Scotland. However, he was a complex man with intellectual interests, particularly in collecting antiquarian books. During the 'radical war' of 1820, he was reprimanded by the earl of Morton for drilling a troop of Fife yeomanry against orders. Stuart took exception and resigned his commission in a fit of pique, but not before engaging Morton in lengthy correspondence which he later published as a political tract.

In December 1820 some Edinburgh tories, irritated by attacks from the whig press, established a newspaper, *The Beacon*, printed by Duncan Stevenson. The first issue, which appeared in January 1821, contained unwarranted criticisms of the whigs. On 28 July 1821, the Saturday after the coronation of George IV, *The Beacon* accused Stuart of supporting the queen. Furious, Stuart demanded the name of the author from Stevenson, who, thoroughly scared, went into hiding. Stuart caught and horsewhipped him in Parliament Square on 15 August. Both Stevenson

and Stuart published lengthy tracts justifying their behaviour. Subsequently *The Beacon* libelled Stuart's friend and fellow whig John Gibson of Ingleston. In the ensuing trial it emerged that Stevenson was supported by many leading tories, including the lord advocate, Sir William Rae. On learning this news Stuart challenged Rae to a duel unless he disavowed his connection with the newspaper. When Rae gave way, Gibson challenged Sir Walter Scott, another of Stevenson's backers. In October 1821 the tory-controlled *Glasgow Sentinel* published a scurrilous poem about the whigs which contained the couplet:

> There's a stot feeder Stuart,
> Kent for the fat-cow art.

Stuart took exception to this and other articles in which his name appeared and again demanded to know the name of the author, even apparently going in disguise to Glasgow to negotiate with the erstwhile partner of the publisher, William Murray Borthwick, who had been declared bankrupt. He persuaded him to give him the name of the author. On learning it was Sir Alexander Boswell of Auchinleck, Stuart issued yet another of the challenges to a duel. He and Boswell were arrested in Edinburgh that night and bound over to keep the peace, so the duel was fought in Fife, on 26 March 1822. Boswell was seriously injured and died the next day. Stuart fled to France, but gave himself up to stand trial for murder. Amid intense public interest, he was found not guilty.

After his acquittal Stuart took less part in politics, continuing to live in Edinburgh and Fife and devoting much of his time to gardening. In 1828 he became bankrupt, describing himself in the proceedings as a 'Writer to the Signet and Banker'. All his effects, including his enormous collection of books, were sold in an auction that extended over fourteen days. He was forced to resign as collector of the widows' fund and went to America. After his return in 1831 he published an account of his travels, *Three Years in North America* (1833). A best-seller, the book was controversial, supporting the view in the United States about the poor conduct of the British troops during the campaign of 1814–15, particularly of their destruction of the White House and of the congressional library. The British commanders, Sir John Lambert and Major Pringle, reacted angrily in the press and in pamphlets to these accusations.

In the early 1830s Stuart became editor of the London whig *Courier* newspaper. He tried to improve circulation by publishing a weekly review supplement. His political sympathies were rewarded in 1833, when he was invited to become a member of the factory commission and to report on the employment of children in factories in Scotland and Ulster—an office for which he seems to have had no qualifications except an ability to write reports and his friendship with Leonard Horner. When Horner changed his responsibilities in 1836, Stuart succeeded him as factory inspector for the north of England and Scotland, a post he held for the remainder of his life. The job involved extensive travel and correspondence. Judging from his annual reports, Stuart was a conscientious inspector and like Horner went out of his way to help factory owners comply with the regulations.

In later life Stuart became a devoted disciple of the phrenologist George Combe. He died on 3 November 1849 at his home, 4 Boyne Terrace, Kensington, London.

MICHAEL S. MOSS

Sources Catalogue of the library of David Constable … sold with the library of James Stuart (1828) [sale catalogue, D. Speare, Edinburgh, 19 Nov 1828] • 'Report … inquiring into the employment of children in factories', Parl. papers (1833), vol. 20, no. 450; vol. 21, no. 519; (1834), vols. 19, 20.253, no. 167 [royal commission] • correspondence with G. Combe on phrenology, NL Scot. • Memorials of his time, by Henry Cockburn, new edn, ed. H. A. Cockburn (1909) • Correspondence between James Stuart esq, younger of Dunearn and the lord advocate, William Rae (1821) • Correspondence between James Stuart esq. younger of Dunearn and the earl of Morton … relative to Mr Stuart's resignation of his commission in the royal Fifeshire yeomanry cavalry (1821) • A full report of the trial of James Stuart younger of Dunearn before the high court of justiciary, 10 June 1822 (1822) • d. cert.

Archives BL, corresp. with M. Napier, Add. MSS 34613–34626 • NL Scot., corresp. with George Combe • UCL, letters to James Brougham

Likenesses D. Macnee, oils, Scot. NPG

Stuart, Sir James, first baronet (1780–1853), lawyer and politician in Canada, was born on 2 March 1780 at Fort Hunter, New York, the third son of John *Stuart (1741–1811), Church of England curate there, and his wife, Jane (1747–1821), the daughter of George Okill of Philadelphia. The son of a loyalist, Stuart moved to Canada with his parents as an infant in 1781. A gifted lad, he later received a strong conservative education at King's College, Windsor, Nova Scotia. He was only fourteen when he entered the office of John Reid, the protonotary of the court of king's bench at Montreal, to study for the law; in 1798 he moved to Quebec and became a pupil of Jonathan Sewell, then attorney-general of Lower Canada. Two years later the lieutenant-governor, Sir Robert Shore Milnes, appointed Stuart his personal secretary. Stuart was called to the bar in 1801, and on 1 August 1805 was appointed by Milnes solicitor-general for the province, whereupon he returned to Montreal and quickly built a prosperous private practice.

In 1808 Stuart entered the house of assembly as a member for Montreal East. After a disagreement with the governor, Sir James Henry Craig, and having been passed over for the post of attorney-general, he joined the nationalist opposition Canadian party, which dominated the assembly. In 1809 he was dismissed by Craig from the solicitor-generalship. He then devoted himself to private practice and to politics. During the administration of Governor Sir George Prevost he constantly opposed the government and became leader of the Canadian party in the assembly. In 1813 he inspired a motion adopted by the assembly to inquire into the conduct of the chief justices Jonathan Sewell and James Monk. He renewed his attacks in 1814, leading to an attempt, ultimately unsuccessful, to impeach them. Stuart's relentless pursuit of this matter, as late as 1817, finally alienated even his best friends in the Canadian party. Frustrated and embittered, he withdrew

from the assembly that year. On 14 March 1818 he married Elizabeth (1795–1849), the daughter of Alexander Robertson of Montreal; they had at least three sons and a daughter.

In December 1822 Stuart was once more brought to the fore, this time at the head of the British party, by a movement for the union of Upper and Lower Canada. He drafted a petition from supporters in Montreal, and was sent to London by the unionists to advocate their cause. There in 1824 he published Observations on the proposed union of the provinces of Upper and Lower Canada under one legislature, as well as a critique of a federalist plan proposed by Sewell. He attracted the attention of the colonial secretary, Lord Bathurst, and on 31 January 1825 was appointed attorney-general for Lower Canada. That year he stood for election to the assembly as member for William Henry (Sorel), but only on the insistence of Governor Lord Dalhousie, who assigned him the unenviable task of defending the executive's policies there. After being elected he became the house's constant target of irony from the former allies of the patriote party, led by Louis-Joseph Papineau. For his service Stuart was appointed by Dalhousie to the executive council on 6 July 1827. Following the dissolution of parliament that year he lost to Dr Wolfred Nelson by two votes in new elections, which led to charges of abuse of power on his part, and eventually, in 1831, to a demand by the assembly for his impeachment; this resulted in March in his suspension by Governor Lord Aylmer from the office of attorney-general. Stuart sailed to England that year to defend himself. Lord Goderich, the colonial secretary, absolved Stuart on this and other charges levelled by the assembly, but, in a controversial decision, dismissed him in November 1832 on other grounds. Stuart persuaded Goderich's successor, Lord Stanley, that Goderich had been unfair, but failed to obtain a reversal, and, after bitterly declining the offer of the chief justiceship of Newfoundland, he returned to Canada in 1834 and resumed his practice at Quebec, with a success which was proof of general confidence.

In the political storm which led up to the rebellions of 1837–8, Stuart took no part; but on 2 April 1838 Governor Sir John Colborne appointed him to the governor's special council. Its members, including Stuart, were all replaced two months later by Lord Durham, who, however, on 22 October 1838 appointed him chief justice of Lower Canada in succession to his former master and rival, Sewell, to compensate for his earlier dismissal as attorney-general. Stuart at once became active politically, encouraged by his reappointment in November 1839 to the special council, over which he presided until shortly before its dissolution in February 1841. He prepared the ordinance establishing register offices in Lower Canada, and was one of Governor Lord Sydenham's chief advisers in framing the Act of Union of 1841. Subsequently he promoted the grant of corporations to Quebec and Montreal, and the institution of municipalities throughout the province. He was created a baronet on 5 May 1841.

On the union of the Canadas (10 February 1841), Stuart

became chief justice of Canada, and for the rest of his career he devoted himself to his judicial duties. He was a talented, practical lawyer, knowledgeable in, but largely antipathetic towards, the colony's French civil law. In politics he was conservative and British-orientated but fundamentally self-serving and opportunistic, as demonstrated by his flirtation with the Canadian party. In personality he was ambitious, unlikeable, arrogant, sensitive, and often bitter and frustrated. He died at Quebec on 14 July 1853, and was buried at Holy Trinity Cathedral in the city on 16 July.

JAMES H. LAMBERT

Sources E. Kolish, 'Stuart, Sir James', *DCB*, vol. 8 · A. H. Young, *The Revd John Stuart, D.D., U.E.L. of Kingston, U.C. and his family: a genealogical study* (1920) · E. Kolish, *Nationalismes et conflits de droit: le débat du droit privé au Québec, 1760–1840* (1994) · E. Kolish and J. H. Lambert, 'The attempted impeachment of the Lower Canadian chief justices, 1814–15', *Canadian state trials series, the early period, 1608–1837*, ed. M. Greenwood and B. Wright, Canadian state trials series, 1 (1996), 450–86 · G. E. Giguère, 'Les biens de Saint-Sulpice et "the Attorney General Stuart's opinion respecting the seminary of Montreal"', *Revue d'Histoire de l'Amérique Française*, 24 (1970–71), 45–77 · Christ Church Cathedral, Montreal, register, marriages (1818) · Holy Trinity Cathedral, Quebec, register, burials (1853)

Archives NA Canada | NA Canada, Neilson, Papineau MSS · PRO, CO 42

Stuart, James (1843–1913), educational reformer and politician, was born in Balgonie, Fife, on 2 January 1843, the eldest child of James Gordon Stuart, mill owner, and his wife, Catherine, daughter of David *Booth, lexicographer, of Newburgh, Fife. He had seven brothers, three of whom died in childhood, and one sister. He was educated at Madras College in St Andrews, and at St Andrews University, where he graduated BA in 1861 (he was awarded an honorary LLD in 1875). In 1862 he won a minor scholarship to Trinity College, Cambridge, and he graduated third wrangler in 1866. Elected a fellow of Trinity in 1866, he became an assistant tutor in 1867.

Stuart was aware of the 'vast masses who desire education', as he put it in his 'On the work of the universities in higher education' (*Transactions of the National Association for the Promotion of Social Science 1871*, 1872, 373), and in addition to his college duties he organized intercollegiate lectures and courses of university extension lectures. From 1867 he gave a series of lectures in the north of England, the most successful of the several initiatives of Josephine Butler's North of England Council for Promoting the Higher Education of Women. From 1873 to 1876 he was the first secretary of the local lectures syndicate in Cambridge, and he materially assisted similar developments by an Oxford committee and by the London Society for the Extension of University Education. He should not, as has sometimes been the case, be seen as sole originator of university extension, but he was certainly its most prominent early activist. In 1875 he was elected the first professor of mechanism and applied mechanics at Cambridge and planned the mechanical science tripos. Practical training cut across Cambridge's theoretical tradition, and Stuart's approach and his radical politics led to criticism. He resigned his chair in 1889 when his tripos proposals were rejected and his department's existence threatened.

In 1882 Stuart unsuccessfully contested one of the Cambridge University seats, standing as a Liberal; he was strongly opposed by the clergy. He was elected for Hackney in 1884 and represented Hoxton from 1885 to 1900, when he was defeated. He was MP for Sunderland from 1906 until 1910, when he was again defeated. He continued his association with Josephine Butler by assisting in the campaign for the repeal of the Contagious Diseases Acts, and was a vigorous advocate of female suffrage and of reform of the House of Lords. He was an energetic editor of the *Star* and *Morning Leader* from 1890 to 1898. To his acute disappointment, especially in 1892, he was never offered office by a Liberal prime minister, but he served on several royal commissions. He was an alderman of the London county council from 1889 to 1898 and an elected councillor (for Haggerston ward) from 1901 to 1907. He was sworn of the privy council in 1909.

In 1890 Stuart married Laura Elizabeth, daughter of Jeremiah James *Colman (1830–1898), the mustard manufacturer [*see under* Colman family (*per.* 1814–1898)], and his wife, Caroline *Colman, *née* Cozens-Hardy [*see under* Colman family (*per.* 1814–1898)]; they had no children. They moved on the fringes of the circle around Gladstone, staying at Hawarden Castle and organizing prime ministerial visits to Norfolk. When his father-in-law died unexpectedly in 1898, Stuart moved to Norfolk and managed the firm. He died at his home, Carrow Abbey, Norwich, on 13 October 1913. His widow founded an extramural lectureship at Cambridge in his memory; Stuart House, to which she contributed, was for many years the home of the Cambridge Board of Extramural Studies. Stuart's was a fragmented public career: he achieved some eminence in several capacities, but distinction only as an educational reformer in the early part of his public life.

H. C. G. MATTHEW

Sources J. Stuart, *Reminiscences* (1911) · T. J. N. Hilken, *Engineering at Cambridge University, 1783–1965* (1967) · E. Welch, *The peripatetic university* (1973) · L. Goldman, *Dons and workers: Oxford and adult education since 1850* (1995) · Gladstone, *Diaries* · E. J. Bristow, *Vice and vigilance* (1977)

Archives CUL, corresp., texts of lectures and other papers relating to the university extension | BL, letters to W. E. Gladstone, Add. MSS 44468–44789, *passim* · King's AC Cam., letters to Oscar Browning

Likenesses F. Hollyer, photograph, repro. in Stuart, *Reminiscences* · lithograph, repro. in *VF* (1899)

Wealth at death £36,756 4s. 7d.: probate, 22 Dec 1913, *CGPLA Eng. & Wales*

Stuart, James Francis Edward. *See* James Francis Edward (1688–1766).

Stuart, James Gray, first Viscount Stuart of Findhorn (1897–1971), politician, was born at 2 Belford Park, Edinburgh, on 9 February 1897, the third son and third of the four children of Morton Gray Stuart, seventeenth earl of Moray (1855–1930), and his wife, Edith Douglas Palmer (c.1869–1945). He was educated at Eton College and intended for Cambridge but went from school to war in 1914. He was soldiering in France with the 1st battalion Royal Scots when only eighteen, after being commissioned into the 3rd battalion, and was invalided home in

James Gray Stuart, first Viscount Stuart of Findhorn (1897–1971), by Walter Stoneman, 1943

1915. He returned to the front with the 2nd battalion in 1916 and by 1918 was brigade major (15th infantry brigade) with the Military Cross and bar. He was mentioned in dispatches.

On demobilization Stuart spent a year studying law in Edinburgh for the Scottish bar but found this uncongenial. From 1920 to 1921 he was first equerry in waiting to Prince Albert, later George VI, and introduced the prince to his future queen, Lady Elizabeth Bowes-Lyon. She came from the same Scottish aristocratic background as Stuart and had previously seemed, though not necessarily to her, a possible bride for him.

Stuart himself found a wife in the court circle—Lady Rachel Cavendish (1902–1977), fourth daughter of Victor Christian William *Cavendish, ninth duke of Devonshire. Stuart met her shortly after her return from Canada, where her father had been governor-general and her sister, Lady Dorothy, had settled on matrimony with Harold Macmillan, aide-de-camp and future prime minister. The Stuarts, who married on 4 August 1923, had two sons and a daughter.

Stuart, made MVO for service as equerry, tentatively ventured into oil, learning the industry's ways in Oklahoma during 1922–3, but on returning to Scotland was invited to be parliamentary Conservative candidate for Moray and Nairn. It was no family seat, not even usually Unionist but Liberal, latterly held by a Lloyd Georgian with Conservative votes. His father, however, urged or instructed him to 'have a shot' (Stuart, 2). Stuart, whose turn of phrase was often more expressive and pungent than epigrammatic, despite the elegance and wit of his autobiography, reputedly reacted to winning the seat at the general election of 1923 by saying: 'This is bloody ridiculous'. But he held the seat for thirty-six years until 1959.

Stuart's apprenticeship in parliament was undistinguished. It was twelve years, during which he also worked in stockbroking, before he became Scottish whip, although slowness of promotion was partly due to claims on office of the Conservatives' National Government allies. As whip, Stuart developed gifts for persuasion, polite intimidation, cajoling, and listening, and in 1937 became deputy chief Conservative whip. He also began, amid some turbulence, his dealings with Winston Churchill, who had by then moved from party rebellion on India towards opposition to appeasement.

Stuart became Conservative chief whip at the beginning of 1941 (and joint chief government whip in the coalition, working alongside the chief Labour whip), his predecessor David Margesson having been posted by Churchill to the War Office in December 1940. Although he had enemies, notably Lord Beaverbrook, and Churchill may have required persuasion from Brendan Bracken to ratify the promotion, Stuart was more successful and popular than Margesson, 'his character perfectly suiting the job', according to Lord Home, his friend and later ministerial colleague (DNB). He did not fuss, assumed a casual air of indifference, showed the gregarious side of his nature, won a reputation for firmness and fairness, and was acknowledged to be a good parliamentary business manager. He also developed an important political and personal relationship with Churchill, although in the judgement of John Colville's Downing Street staff (Colville, 2.431), the wartime premier respected him rather than particularly liked him. However, Churchill 'always listened to his sound political advice', as both prime minister and party leader.

During the wartime electoral truce, Stuart faced the difficulty of keeping Conservative MPs in line at a time when the leadership took little interest in party matters, and there was a resulting lack of a constructive Conservative policy. As sole chief whip during Churchill's brief caretaker government in 1945, he disagreed with Churchill's negative tactics during the general election campaign and shared in the shock of the party's landslide defeat. His complex relationship with Churchill was strained when, in July 1947, a cabal of senior Conservatives designated him as messenger to suggest that their leader might 'seek peace in retirement' (Stuart, 146). The interaction between the two men was nevertheless a constructive, productive one which Home in his foreword to Stuart's autobiography called 'an intimate relationship of mutual understanding and affection'.

Stuart retired as chief whip in 1948, after antrum trouble required an operation, which was the official reason given for his departure, though it was probably brought about by his being named as co-respondent in a divorce case (Headlam Diaries, 567, 571, 20 Jan 1949, 1 Feb

1949). When Churchill returned to power in 1951 their relationship gave Stuart an option on the Scottish Office, to the exclusion of Walter Elliot, a more articulate, popular, and urban politician and the most prominent Scot in shadow cabinet and Conservative campaigning. Stuart had already in 1950 been appointed by Churchill to the new post of Scottish party chairman, also chairing the Scottish Unionist MPs' committee.

As secretary of state, Stuart had to cope with a legacy of Scottish discontents after Labour's hard line in face of demands for less centralization and some kind of Scottish self-government. Churchill's brief for Scottish ministers was: 'Go and quell those turbulent Scots and don't come back till you've done it' (Home, 105). Stuart's appointment, pressed on him by Churchill, aroused little enthusiasm and one of Attlee's Scottish team called him a 'bloody fool' for taking it (Stuart, 164). But despite his unspectacular style it was a spectacular success.

In 1955 the Conservatives (still 'Unionist' in title) won a narrow absolute majority in Scotland in seats and popular vote, while the Scottish discontents and home-rule movement had subsided. Although this Scottish mood reflected short-term economic conditions, and was to change as heavy industries declined, Stuart had substantially contributed to it. He was a team leader who was also a team player, greatly helped by persuading Churchill to allow him Lord Home as vice-captain (minister of state working mainly and highly visibly in Scotland). The Scottish Office responded to someone with influence in the cabinet and strong on reaching decisions, for example on the go-ahead for the Forth road bridge. He was good at assessing options, respected civil-service briefs when well prepared, and did not intrude much ideology into administration. Even allowing for civil servants' inclination to classify as a 'good Secretary of State' someone who took advice well, he thrived in office and presided over an era of good feeling in Scottish life and politics, on relatively amiable terms not only with the opposition in parliament but with Labour-dominated local authorities. However, he confessed: 'I do not think I have ever suffered or enjoyed the friendship of a Liberal' (Stuart, 161).

Stuart practised what his party had preached, though he also secured the backing of the royal commission on the government of Scotland which the Conservatives set up in 1951. This was that administrative devolution to Edinburgh (extended to roads and electricity), relaxation of wartime and post-war controls, and close contact between government and Scottish business, farming, local authorities, and interest groups would weaken the demand for major constitutional change. He was a pragmatic Conservative in social and economic matters who did not ask to see the distant scene, and underestimated the potential for Scottish nationalism, even eventually in his own constituency.

Stuart did commit himself in 1950, writing to the home-rule leader John MacCormick on behalf of Scottish tory MPs, to accepting that 'if the Scottish people were ultimately to decide in favour of a Scottish Parliament nothing could gainsay them' (MacCormick, 139), but his policies and tactics were shaped to prevent the issue being pursued. This remained the Conservative line until electoral disaster in 1997, except for an interlude when Edward Heath and Home contemplated limited legislative devolution. But Stuart went with many trends which Thatcherite Conservatism later found abhorrent, such as the redevelopment of urban Scotland with limited scope for private house building, the creation of vast council housing estates, and an apparently irreversible move towards comprehensive education. However, it was after his retirement, under his brother-in-law Macmillan, that the Scottish Office became most firmly attached to regional economic incentives to encourage industrial developments unable to survive in a freer and globalizing market economy. Much was done under Stuart's regime, however, to encourage diversification of Scottish industry.

Stuart remained at the Scottish Office, under Eden as well as Churchill, until 1957, though unhappy with Eden's leadership and the ignominious Suez climb-down. He retained good looks, trim appearance, and apparent vigour, but pleaded the need for a less arduous life, as well as the avoidance of even the appearance of nepotism, as reasons for retirement when his brother-in-law Macmillan formed a government. He remained as MP and Scottish party chairman, a post which he did not allow to tax his powers, until 1959. He then became, in November 1959, Viscount Stuart of Findhorn, the village where he had his constituency home.

Stuart summed himself up as taking 'things as they came', with chance playing a large part in his life (Stuart, 1). Unlike many politicians he was honest in claiming that he was not driven by ambition. Home noted an inclination to vanity in personal matters, but also wrote: 'He was apparently detached, work-shy, and bored with life: nothing could have been more misleading' (Home, 103). Beneath 'the apparently lackadaisical veneer he had a strong will which it was unwise to test too often' (*DNB*). For much of his career Stuart divided his time among homes in Findhorn, London, and Salisbury, but in retirement lived mainly near Salisbury. He was made CH in 1957. He died in Salisbury Infirmary on 20 February 1971.

R. D. KERNOHAN

Sources J. Stuart, *Within the fringe* (1967) · Lord Home, *The way the wind blows* (1976) · *DNB* · D. Milne, *The Scottish office* (1957) · J. M. MacCormick, *The flag in the wind* (1955) · R. Galbraith, *Without quarter* (1995) · J. Colville, *The fringe of power: the Downing Street diaries*, 2 vols. (1985) · J. S. Gibson, *The thistle and the crown: a history of the Scottish office* (1985) · *The Times* (22 Feb 1971) · *The Scotsman* (22 Feb 1971) · J. Ramsden, *The age of Churchill and Eden, 1940–1957* (1995) · J. Ramsden, *The winds of change: Macmillan to Heath, 1957–1975* (1996) · *Parliament and politics in the age of Churchill and Attlee: the Headlam diaries, 1935–1951*, ed. S. Ball, CS, 5th ser., 14 (1999) · Burke, *Peerage*
Archives NRA Scotland, priv. coll., corresp. and papers
Likenesses W. Stoneman, photograph, 1943, NPG [*see illus.*] · D. H. Anderson, oils, 1957, Gov. Art Coll.; repro. in Gibson, *The thistle and the crown*, 123 · photograph, c.1960, repro. in Stuart, *Within the fringe*, cover and frontispiece; probably priv. coll.
Wealth at death no value given: confirmation sealed in London, 9 Sept 1971, CGPLA Eng. & Wales

Stuart, Jane (*c*.1654–1742), the alleged natural daughter of James II, was, according to an oral tradition first set down thirty years after her death by Samuel Peckover, a prominent Cambridgeshire Quaker, born in Paris, the daughter of James, duke of York [see James II and VII], then in exile, and an unnamed maid of honour to Queen Henrietta Maria, and to have lived at the English court from the Restoration to 1688 without, apparently, any contemporary ever noticing her. The legend of the royal Quaker was lent credence because of James's friendship with William Penn and his generosity to Quakers. What is known about Jane is that she lived in a cellar in Wisbech, earning her living by reaping in the fields in the summer and spinning wool and flax in the winter. She was a mystery to her neighbours, whose curiosity was aroused when she was found reading the New Testament in Greek.

After the 1688 revolution, when she moved to Wisbech, Jane Stuart is reputed to have evaded questions from the government about the birth of the prince of Wales, whom she had nursed, but this was the last thing William III would have wanted to enquire into. Although several Quakers visited James II at St Germain, there is no record of her ever being there. During the rising of 1715 she was reported as having hired a chaise to take her to Scotland to see her half-brother James III (James Francis Edward). Yet she never visited her 'family' at St Germain; nor did James II, a tender father to his natural children, ever mention her. There is no connection between Jane Stuart and a namesake, a widow, who claimed to be a great-granddaughter of James I. Jane Stuart died in Wisbech on 12 September 1742 and was buried in the Quaker burial-ground there. She was unmarried.

EVELINE CRUICKSHANKS

Sources F. J. Gardiner, *History of Wisbech* (1898), 263–4 · M. R. Brailsford, *Quaker women, 1650–1690* (1915) · N. Penney, 'Jane Stuart', *N&Q*, 12th ser., 6 (1920), 21–3 · N. Rouffiac, 'Un épisode de la présence britannique en France: les Jacobites à Paris et Saint-Germain-en-Laye, 1688–1715', diss., École des Chartres, 1991 · *The manuscripts of his grace the duke of Portland*, 10 vols., HMC, 29 (1891–1931), vol. 10, p. 29

Stuart, Janet Erskine (1857–1914), Roman Catholic nun, was born at the rectory, Cottesmore, Rutland, on 11 November 1857, the last of six children born to Godfrey Andrew Stuart (d. 1889), rector of Cottesmore and canon of Peterborough, and his second wife, Mary Penelope Noel (d. 1859). When she was just over a year old her mother died, and Stuart found a substitute mother in her half-sister, Theodosia, who died of tuberculosis nineteen years later.

Stuart was educated at home by a succession of Swiss and German governesses. One of these, the daughter of Rinz von Bürger, a prominent theologian, introduced Stuart to contemporary German philosophy and theology. Such reading led her to religious scepticism, but she nevertheless played the part of the rector's daughter. She taught Sunday school and took a keen interest in the local tenantry, acquiring a thorough knowledge of livestock and botany.

At the age of twenty Stuart made the acquaintance of her Noel relatives, who had inherited the Gainsborough title and moved to nearby Exton Manor. This family had recently converted to Roman Catholicism and Stuart developed a strong attraction to the dogma and liturgy of the Catholic church. Through the Noels she met Elizabeth Ross, who in turn introduced her to the Jesuit Peter Gallwey. On 6 March 1879 she was received into the Roman Catholic church at the Jesuit Church of the Immaculate Conception (Farm Street) in London. For the next three years she made her home in London with Elizabeth Ross, travelling often and enjoying hunting and fishing. A turning point came in July 1882 when Stuart made a retreat under Father Gallwey at the Convent of the Sacred Heart, Roehampton. Two months later she entered the Society of the Sacred Heart, receiving the habit on 13 November 1882 and pronouncing vows two years later.

Stuart's ability singled her out from the start, and while still a novice she was called upon to act as secretary to Mother Mabel Digby, vicaress of the English houses. Though still engaged in her own spiritual and intellectual formation Stuart began to teach in the school and soon gave classes to her fellow sisters in the juniorate. She was also sent to the mother house in Paris to make her probation and profession two years before the customary time. On her return to Roehampton in February 1889 Stuart was appointed councillor, and was given charge of the noviciate in 1892. In August 1894, when Mother Digby was elected assistant-general (and nine months later superior-general of the Society), Stuart replaced her as vicaress and superior at Roehampton. In 1898 she accompanied Mother Digby on a visitation of the North American houses of the society and three years later was sent as visitor to the Latin American houses.

Concern for the individual characterized both Mother Stuart's educational philosophy and her exercise of religious authority. As novice mistress she impressed upon her charges the necessity of personal development. In an age which favoured cutting novices to a pattern she abhorred copies, even of the best models. To a novice who was modelling herself rather too self-consciously on a canonized Jesuit, Stuart said 'Drop John Berchmans, sister, and be yourself' (Monahan, 81). Eager to further the educational values of the Society, Mother Stuart devoted much effort to developing Sacred Heart schools and colleges in England. She summed up her educational philosophy in *The Education of Catholic Girls*, published by Longman in 1911, and in her study *The Society of the Sacred Heart*, which went to press just after her death. Two volumes of essays and one of poetry were also published posthumously, and her *Life and Letters*, edited by Mother Maud Monahan, went through sixteen impressions.

Following Mother Digby's death in May 1911, Stuart was elected mother-general. During the four years which remained to her she visited almost every house of the Sacred Heart Society, not only those in Europe and the Americas but also houses in Australia and New Zealand, as well as those more recently established in China and Japan. Reports of her visits make it clear that she was greeted with enthusiasm by her sisters. Her journeyings produced a voluminous travel correspondence. Keenly observant, nothing escaped her pen: astronomical and climatic changes, exotic flora and fauna, local customs and peoples are all described with verve and wit.

Stuart's generalate was all too short; arriving back at the mother house at Ixelles in July 1914 it was apparent that she was seriously ill. Soon after the start of the First World War the general administration of the society left Belgium for Roehampton, and it was there, after unsuccessful surgery for cancer, that she died on 21 October 1914 and was buried on 30 October. ANSELM NYE

Sources M. Monahan, *Life and letters of Janet Erskine Stuart* (1922) · M. H. Quinlan, *Mabel Digby, Janet Erskine Stuart: superiors general of the Society of the Sacred Heart, 1895–1914* (1984) · M. Williams, *The Society of the Sacred Heart: the history of a spirit* (1978)
Archives NRA, corresp. and papers · Society of the Sacred Heart, London, provincial archives
Likenesses photographs, Society of the Sacred Heart, London, provincial archives

Stuart, John, of Darnley. *See* Stewart, Sir John, of Darnley (*c*.1380–1429).

Stuart [Stewart], **John** [Hans] (*b.* before **1550**, *d.* **1618**), army officer in the Swedish service, was born in Scotland, the eldest son of John Stewart of Ochiltree and his wife, Agneta Forbes, the daughter of Robert Forbes and Anna Sinclair. It seems clear that his family was in some way related to that of the Stewart lords Ochiltree, but an exact connection has proved impossible to establish. John Stuart's father is believed to have accompanied Mary, queen of Scots, to France in the 1550s, serving there as a colonel for François II before returning to Scotland in 1560; Stuart himself probably gained his education in France, and visited Germany and other European countries on his travels. Before 1564 he was back in Scotland, as that year he sailed from Edinburgh towards Danzig. However, his ship was captured by Danes, who were embroiled in the Nordic Seven Years' War against Sweden, and Stuart was imprisoned in Varberg on suspicion of wanting to enter Swedish military service. Varberg was seized by Swedish forces in August, and all the Scottish troops in the Danish army were forcibly placed under Swedish command. Stuart was then stripped of his moneys by Swedish troops and moved to a prison in Uppsala, presumably as the Swedes were not certain about his status. It was through the efforts of other Scottish officers already in Swedish service that he was finally released.

It is not certain exactly when Stuart decided to stay in Sweden, where he was known as Hans, although he is recorded as master of horse of Erik XIV, who reigned from 1560 to 1568. He then entered the service of the duke of Södermanland, king of Sweden as Karl IX from 1599 to 1611. Similarly it is unknown when Stuart married Brita Eriksdotter (*d.* 1622), both of whose parents were of noble Swedish stock. As was required of foreigners aspiring to marry into the Swedish nobility, Stuart provided evidence of his noble origins in a letter to Johan III and his brother Duke Karl dated 12 October 1579 and signed by Earl Collins of Ergadie (Colin Campbell, sixth earl of Argyll), the chancellor of Scotland, Earl Robert Stuart of Levenox (Robert Stewart, earl of Lennox), and Andrew Stuart of Ochiltree (perhaps his brother). Stuart obtained another letter, dated 14 June 1585, from James VI, allowing him to use the Ochiltree coat of arms at the request of James Stewart, earl of Arran. Duke Karl had already endowed Stuart with land in Södermanland in 1579, which he exchanged for land in Hedenlunda in 1582; in 1610 he obtained rights of inheritance for himself, his wife, and his male descendants. Hedenlunda remained the Stewart family seat in Sweden for the next two centuries.

In 1604 Stuart was a gentleman of the chamber of Karl IX, and he soon became the colonel of a regiment he had raised himself in Scotland. By 1609 he was not only the quartermaster-general and the war commissioner-general, but also the muster-general of all the foreign soldiers in Sweden. He was sent to Russia as an envoy during the Swedish campaign there of 1609–10, but after that little is known of him until his death in Sweden in October 1618. He had five children, four of whom survived him. Both of his sons, Anders the younger and David, became gentlemen of the chamber of Gustavus Adolphus. Stuart's wife died in March 1622 and they were both buried in Vadsbro church. Stuart's brother Andrew (Anders) *Stuart (*c*.1570–1640) also entered Swedish service and became a colonel. They were the first Stewarts known to have emigrated to Sweden in the sixteenth century.

A. N. L. GROSJEAN

Sources G. Elgenstierna, *Den introducerade svenska adelns ättartavlor med tillägg och rättelser*, 9 vols. (1925–36), vol. 8 · J. Berg and B. Lagercrantz, *Scots in Sweden* (1962) · T. A. Fischer [E. L. Fischer], *The Scots in Sweden* (1907) · CSP for., 1547–53 · GEC, *Peerage*, new edn, vol. 10 · *Scots peerage*, vol. 6
Wealth at death property in Sweden

Stuart, John, third earl of Bute (**1713–1792**), prime minister, was born at Parliament Square, Edinburgh, on 25 May 1713, the elder son of James, second earl of Bute (1689/90–1723), and his wife, Lady Anne Campbell (1692–1736), only daughter of Archibald, first duke of Argyll. His paternal grandfather, Sir James Stuart (1651–1723), represented Buteshire in the Scottish parliament from 1685 to 1693, when he had to vacate his seat, having failed to take the oath of allegiance to William III. He was re-elected in 1702, and in the same year became a member of Queen Anne's privy council. On 14 April 1703 he was created earl of Bute, viscount of Kingarth, and Lord Mount Stuart, Cumra, and Inchmarnock. He was also named one of the commissioners to consider union with England, but eventually opposed the measure, and absented himself from the stormy parliamentary session of 1706 when the Union was debated and carried. He died at Bath on 4 June 1710. His son, the second earl, was born in 1689 or 1690. He was lord lieutenant of county Bute from 1715 and served as lord of the bedchamber from 1721 until his death, at only thirty-three, on 28 January 1723. John Stuart succeeded to his father's titles and lands in January 1723, under the guardianship of his Campbell uncles, the duke of Argyll and the earl of Ilay, who were both strong supporters of the Hanoverian succession. A great bibliophile, Ilay strongly influenced his nephew in passing on his interest in astronomy, mechanics, and natural history.

John Stuart, third earl of Bute (1713–1792), by Sir Joshua Reynolds, 1773

Early years In 1724 Bute was sent to Eton College, where he remained until 1728. He then studied civil law at the University of Leiden, and received his degree in 1732. He returned to Scotland and spent the next four years at Mount Stuart, his ancestral home on the Isle of Bute, where he attended to domestic affairs and the improvement of his estates. On 24 August 1736 he married Mary Wortley Montagu (1718–1794), only daughter of Edward Wortley Montagu of Wortley, Yorkshire, and his wife, Lady Mary Wortley *Montagu, née Pierrepont, the eldest daughter of the first duke of Kingston. The marriage ultimately brought the immense Wortley estates into the Bute family, and was by all accounts a happy union. Lady Bute seems to have been a woman of prudence, loyalty, and tact, greatly devoted to her husband and family. The couple had five sons and six daughters, of whom perhaps the most accomplished was the eldest child, John *Stuart, first marquess of Bute, politician and diplomatist, who succeeded to the earldom on the death of his father (1792) and was advanced to the marquessate of Bute on 21 March 1796. Two other sons, James Archibald Stuart (1747–1818) and Frederick Stuart (1751–1802), played minor roles in British politics; a fourth, Charles *Stuart, pursued a distinguished military and diplomatic career, while their last son, William *Stuart, was archbishop of Armagh. All their daughters contracted marriages except the youngest, Louisa *Stuart, a poet, who died on 4 August 1851, at the age of ninety-four.

In August 1737, through the influence of his uncles, Bute was elected a Scottish representative peer, but he appeared only occasionally in the House of Lords and took no part in the debate. In the same year he was appointed one of the commissioners of police for Scotland, and on 10 July 1738 was invested with the Order of the Thistle. Having failed to secure re-election in the parliament of 1741, he retired for five years to the Isle of Bute, where he devoted his time to reading, agriculture, and his lifelong passion, the study of botany.

The Leicester House period Soon after the outbreak of the Jacobite rising Bute moved to London, and in 1747 made the chance acquaintance of Frederick, prince of Wales. It was an encounter that proved to be the major turning point in his life. He became a favourite at Leicester House, the prince's London residence and centre of opposition politics, and on 16 October 1750 was appointed by Frederick one of the lords of his bedchamber. Upon the prince's premature death in 1751 Bute remained the confidant of his widow, Princess Augusta. Their friendship subsequently led to his appointment as tutor and principal adviser to her son, the future George III. In this capacity Bute not only directed the prince's formal education but also gained his respect and confidence, becoming, in George's own words, 'his dearest friend' (Letters … to Lord Bute, 6).

This relationship developed rapidly. The impressionable young man's emotional dependence upon his mentor ensured a ready acceptance of Bute's personal ideals and political principles, portrayed in written assignments that combined formal instruction in history, constitutional theory, and finance with ambitious plans for future governmental reform. To instruct George in the principles of the constitution Bute is said to have obtained from William Blackstone a major portion of the manuscript of the Commentaries on the Laws of England, the first volume of which was not published until 1765. Elaborated further in daily letters, their ideas comprised a blend of traditional Leicester House themes and 'country' party precepts—a composite, idealistic political creed advocating an isolationist foreign policy, the abolition of party distinctions, the purging of corruption, and the enhancement of monarchial control over policy and patronage. These ideas, however conventional an opposition ideology, were taken seriously by Bute and his pupil, and emerged as their shared vision of Britain's future, to be implemented whenever George ascended the throne. Their relationship would thus profoundly affect the reconfiguration of politics commonly associated with George III's early reign.

Bute first became active in the political world following the death of Henry Pelham in 1754. On behalf of Leicester House he enlisted the support of William Pitt in opposition to the Fox–Newcastle connection, and together Bute and Pitt formed an alliance based on a common hostility to George II's pro-Hanoverian policy in the face of impending war with France. This arrangement unravelled during 1757, as Pitt joined forces with Newcastle, acquired the position of secretary of state, and then reversed his stand on the German war and continental subsidies. Pitt's actions, taken without the approval of his former political allies, severely offended Bute and the prince, and created a rift between the Great Commoner and Leicester House that was never repaired. Bute, though without formal political office, had meanwhile emerged as one of the leading public figures in the kingdom. Both the advanced age and uncertain health of George II made the prince and *ipso facto* Bute principal figures in all future political calculations. Important individuals both within and outside the confines of Leicester House looked to Bute for patronage, asked for his intervention at the highest levels, and sought his advice on their strategies for political advancement. His unquestioned dominance at the prince's court secured him the position of groom of the stole (5 November 1756), and he was widely considered a prime candidate for high office once Prince George became king.

Bute and George III The long-awaited moment arrived with the death of George II on 25 October 1760. The event wrought an immediate change in Bute's situation: within two days of George III's accession he was sworn of the privy council, and on 25 March 1761 he received the seals as secretary of state for the northern department and a cabinet seat. These appointments were made to the manifest displeasure of Pitt and other senior ministers, who questioned his ability, feared his ambitions, and resented his influence with the king. On 3 April 1761 Lady Bute was created Baroness Mount Stuart of Wortley in the peerage of Great Britain; in May Bute himself was elected a Scottish representative peer and the following month was appointed ranger of Richmond Park.

From the outset Bute's rapid elevation created confusion, strife, and misunderstandings not warranted by the actual course of events. Despite a new atmosphere at court, existing arrangements continued. Newcastle retained control of Treasury affairs, Pitt's management of the war proceeded unchanged, and the main contours of Britain's overall military/diplomatic strategy remained intact. Moreover, Bute proved to be a competent secretary of state, performing his duties with a diligence and efficiency that surprised many. As events were to show, Bute had a sound understanding of European developments and was quite capable of pursuing coherent policies with intelligence and resolution. He swiftly acquired self-confidence once in office and won both the respect and the loyalty of his subordinates, among them the veteran under-secretary Edward Weston, with whose collaboration he greatly enhanced departmental efficiency. He also made a good impression on the foreign envoys in London as being industrious, perceptive, and capable—qualities considerably greater than his historical reputation suggests.

Indeed, during the important Anglo-French peace negotiations in the summer of 1761, it was Bute rather than Pitt who proved the decisive force in devising the proposals submitted to France and maintaining the political unity that made effective negotiations possible. Bute sided with Pitt on most of the key issues but could not sanction his proposal for a pre-emptive strike against Spain, which was then joined to France in alliance. This refusal hastened the cabinet crisis leading to Pitt's resignation on 5 October 1761, the first important turning point of the new reign.

Bute after Pitt's retreat Pitt's departure from office was not politically coerced: unable to compromise or share power, he defied united cabinet opinion and so made his retention impossible. Nevertheless, popular perception considered him a victim of court intrigue. The result was a highly volatile situation in which the remaining ministers, and Bute especially, came in for bitter press attacks and popular protest. Bute attempted to calm tensions by continuing Pitt's military policies and by pursuing firm measures against Spain, a policy that resulted in Spain's open defiance and Britain's consequent declaration of war. Simultaneously, in response to growing war weariness, Bute secretly renewed the lapsed negotiations with France and, concerned about the financial implications of conflict with Spain, gradually curtailed Britain's European commitments. This resulted in the progressive dissolution of the Anglo-Prussian wartime alliance, dating from 1757, a breach traditionally considered instrumental in the nation's prolonged post-war diplomatic isolation.

What ultimately fostered this outcome, more than Anglo-Prussian antagonism, was the emergence of new alliance patterns that seriously diminished Britain's diplomatic options and influence after 1763. International diplomacy in the 1760s no longer revolved around France's diminishing threat to European security but around emerging issues in the eastern half of the continent: the Polish question and Austro-Russian relations with the Turks. These developments undermined the traditional basis of British foreign policy, which was to manipulate European powers into anti-French coalitions by exploiting the dangers of France's unrestrained preponderance. Prussia's primary aim following the war was to secure the alliance of Russia, and once she had achieved this (by 1764) agreement with Britain became both unnecessary and a liability, since it could only involve Prussia in Anglo-French disputes, issues that did not concern her. Hence Frederick the Great's coolness towards Britain after the Seven Years' War owed more to reasons of state—the desire to avoid needless and costly complications—than lingering resentment at his dealings with Lord Bute, as his rebuff of even Pitt's overtures in 1766 was to demonstrate.

From this perspective Bute's diplomacy was effective in difficult circumstances. There has been increasing recognition that on many diplomatic issues Bute merely brought to successful completion those policies previously initiated by the Newcastle–Pitt administration. Even in the military realm Bute's leadership in retaining and supporting the essential elements of Pitt's wartime strategy yielded further triumphs, including the capture of St Lucia, Martinique, and Havana, the key to Spain's

West Indian possessions. This suggests that the contrast between Bute's ministry and that of his immediate predecessors was less drastic than has often been assumed, an important conclusion with wide implications for Bute's historical status.

Nevertheless, Bute's severance of the connection with Prussia, part of his anti-continental orientation, fostered deep divisions within the cabinet over the general direction of government policy and culminated on 26 May 1762 in Newcastle's resignation as first lord of the Treasury. The following day Bute succeeded him and was invested with the Garter, having previously resigned the Order of the Thistle.

Bute as prime minister Now the head of government, Bute accelerated the pending negotiations with France. These were tortuous and plagued with endless complications. On three issues—the future of St Lucia, the possibility of a separate peace without Spain, and the question of compensation for Havana—he encountered bitter resistance from his cabinet colleagues which required all his authority combined with royal intervention to overcome. Uncertain of the ability of George Grenville, the leader of the Commons, to defend the peace, Bute had him transferred to the Admiralty and replaced with the able but unscrupulous Henry Fox, who could secure the required parliamentary support. He then appointed the duke of Bedford as special ambassador to Paris with instructions to finalize deliberations. The resulting preliminaries were signed at Fontainebleau on 3 November 1762.

Although the terms of peace were vehemently attacked by Pitt as inadequate, most historians now agree that the treaty, considered by Bute himself to be his major achievement, was an honourable, advantageous settlement: rich compensation for Britain's global victories and a serious blow to French power. George III called it 'a noble peace' and the consensus of political opinion concurred. The preliminaries passed in both the Lords and the Commons by decisive majorities, and received formal ratification on 10 February 1763. What opposition there was to the peace derived primarily from personal antagonism towards Bute by political rivals who fanned public hostility against him and his policies. This steadily gathered momentum until by the spring Bute was the most unpopular man in the country. Maligned, insulted, and manhandled wherever he went, he suffered threats of assassination, incurred the wrath of brilliant polemicists such as John Wilkes and Charles Churchill, and was lampooned in over 400 prints and broadsheets. In addition, Bute's emblem, the 'jackboot', was regularly burned alongside that of his reputed lover, the 'pettycoat', Princess Augusta.

The uproar was compounded by the unfortunate proposal from Sir Francis Dashwood, Bute's chancellor of the exchequer, for a cider tax, the collection and enforcement of which would have threatened personal liberty through the intrusion of inquisitorial officials into private dwellings. The measure was portrayed by Bute's opponents as part of an odious scheme to introduce a 'general excise' similar to that envisaged by Walpole in 1733. Despite its intense unpopularity, Bute ably defended the bill in the House of Lords and it received royal approval on 1 April 1763.

Eight days later, physically ill, weary of politics and politicians, and unnerved by the savage attacks against him, Bute resigned from office, and recommended George Grenville as his successor. The king reluctantly accepted the decision but, retaining confidence in his favourite, continued to seek Bute's advice on important political matters over the next few years: the overtures towards Pitt and the Bedford connection in August 1763, the Stamp Act, the Regency Bill, and probably the negotiation with the opposition in early 1767. Inevitably this gave rise to the notion of 'secret influence', the belief prevalent well into the nineteenth century that even in retirement Bute directed the wheels of government from behind the scenes. As a powerful and persuasive theme the myth of Bute's secret influence provided many with an explanation for the incessant political convulsions of the 1760s, and eventually broadened into an all-encompassing conspiracy theory that defined the ideology and manoeuvres of leading opposition groups well into the age of Lord North.

Hence successive administrations attributed their misfortunes to Bute's covert machinations and persistently demanded that the king cease to consult his favourite on public affairs; indeed, the Grenvillites made this a condition of their continuation in office. In response to these feelings Bute agreed to leave London in September 1763. He resigned his last post, of keeper of the privy purse, and withdrew to Luton Hoo, the country home in Bedfordshire that he had purchased the year before. There he appears to have kept up a correspondence with the king, though gradually their contacts lessened as the latter acquired more experience and self-confidence. When, in the summer of 1766, George III formed an alliance with Pitt that excluded Bute and most of his friends, the earl wrote a bitter letter of reproach that effectively ended their relationship, and thereby Bute's intervention in matters of state.

Later years Aside from travelling for three years through Italy (1769–71), Bute spent the remainder of his life at Christchurch, Hampshire, where in 1771 he built a villa, Highcliffe, overlooking the Needles and the Isle of Wight. There, in melancholy grandeur, he conducted his botanical studies, collected prints, books, and scientific instruments, and devoted himself to the patronage of literature, science, and the arts. He was by now one of the richest men in Britain, having acquired immense wealth upon the death of his father-in-law, Edward Wortley Montagu, in 1761. The sole inheritor, Lady Bute, was left a life interest in the Wortley estates in west Yorkshire worth £17,000 per annum, while her personal fortune was estimated at over £1 million. This wealth enabled Bute to play a leading role in promoting the intellectual life of his day.

Of note is Bute's enlightened patronage of several of Scotland's leading universities and colleges. At Edinburgh he established the chair of rhetoric and *belles-lettres*, appointed John Hope, an accomplished scholar known for his taxonomic studies, to the professorship of botany and materia medica, and secured the new regius chair of natural history for David Skene, a distinguished Aberdeen botanist. He was also active in establishing the Royal Botanical Garden at Edinburgh, and at Glasgow he secured John Miller as the regius professor of civil law and supported William Leechman as professor of ecclesiastical history. In 1786 Bute donated his private scientific library of 1300 volumes to Marischal College, Aberdeen (of which he was chancellor), made additions to the college's museum, and supplied money to improve its observatory together with telescopes and other instruments of the highest quality. These gifts were to be of prime importance in the emergence of Aberdeen as a centre of practical astronomy and medical education.

Bute was a patron of literary merit; his beneficiaries included Samuel Johnson, Tobias Smollett, Thomas Sheridan, and John Home. The painter Allan Ramsay, the architect Robert Adam, and the historian William Robertson were others who benefited from his generosity. He recruited the likes of John Shebbeare, Philip Francis, Arthur Murphy, and David Mallet to defend the peace negotiations in the press. Contrary to widespread belief at the time, Bute did not show undue partiality to Scots but dispensed his patronage according to proven ability rather than national or personal considerations.

A gifted scholar himself, deeply interested in floriculture, Bute published—at the cost of some £12,000—a splendid nine-volume work, *Botanical Tables Containing the Families of British Plants* (1785), which contained 654 hand-coloured plates. Another privately printed work, *The Tabular Distribution of British Plants*, in two parts—the first containing the genera, the second the species—is sometimes attributed to him. Two of the groups classified by Linnaeus and Sir William Jones, *Stewartia* and *Butea*, were named after him, and Albrecht von Haller's valuable *Bibliotheca botanica* (1771) and John Hill's *Vegetable System* (1759–75) were inscribed to him. Other authors who dedicated botanical works to him included William Curtis, George Edwards, and Samuel Pullein. His best-known role in botany, however, was in connection with the development of the Royal Botanic Gardens at Kew, which were first laid out as a private garden by Frederick, prince of Wales, in 1730, and then after his death were remodelled into a botanical centre by Princess Augusta with Bute's assistance. In 1755 Bute leased a house on Kew Green, expanded to accommodate his botanical library, from where he supervised the garden alterations. Sir William Chambers was commissioned to design new buildings, including the orangery, the pagoda, and numerous temples. In 1759 Bute appointed William Aiton head gardener, and charged him with establishing the herbaceous plant garden on the Linnaean system. Bute closely co-ordinated these operations, as well as procuring trees and plants through his contacts from around the world. In this work he created the foundation on which his successor Sir Joseph Banks would subsequently build.

Bute's place in the history of science is further consolidated by his enlightened patronage of such noted figures as the anatomist William Hunter, the naturalist John Strange, and the mineralogist Peter Woulfe. There is ample evidence of Bute's active interest in mineralogy, and of a sound acquaintance with current theories of the earth and the experimental arrangement of minerals based on chemical analysis. It was due to the depth, seriousness, and durability of his commitment to virtually all aspects of natural history that, for his contemporaries, Bute stood out among other noble patrons and amateur scholars, and as such should be remembered by posterity.

Bute died at South Audley Street, London, on 10 March 1792, from complications following a fall at Highcliffe, and was buried on 2 April at Rothesay on the island of Bute. He was survived by his wife, who died at Isleworth, Middlesex, on 6 November 1794, aged seventy-six.

Historical standing and importance Traditionally an elusive and misunderstood figure, Bute has gradually received recognition for his contribution to British politics as well as his achievements as a patron of artistic, literary, and academic merit. His reputation now is that of a hardworking, competent statesman with a genuine concern for king and country that commands admiration.

Bute's importance derived largely from factors beyond his control, namely the interaction of domestic and external developments that would eventually reshape the pattern of British politics and institutions. It was his misfortune that he assumed office amid the crisis conditions of war and following the accession of a new king whose quest for enhanced executive power proved politically destabilizing. It created bitter conflict with a political establishment devoted to the status quo and quick to raise the alarm over an apparent constitutional crisis in which Bute became the central focus. Enjoying power and status through court favour alone, Bute was a disturbing presence for the ruling élite: disliked and distrusted, he fostered ministerial instability as those directing government policy had to confront the threat to their political security he represented.

Personifying the changing agenda implicit in George III's accession—that of ending party distinctions and reasserting royal independence—Bute undermined the whig oligarchy by challenging the premises on which this hegemony was based. As a royal favourite, opposition to whom the king considered a personal affront, Bute embodied an unacceptable form of politics, which in its erosion of the distinction between king and minister was to some reminiscent of tory notions of personal monarchy. Determined to preserve this distinction, the crown's opponents observed constitutional propriety and maintained that it was Bute, not the king, who was responsible for a system of government that disregarded the precepts of political responsibility. In this way, regardless of the facts of the case, Bute became a political scapegoat, held culpable for the conflicts between George III and the country's political leaders. Moreover, his nationality—Scots then being much disliked in England—made Bute a prime focus for disparate social and economic grievances, which enabled the opposition to mobilize public hostility against him, and to add popular disapprobation to their own indictment of his political involvement.

From these conflicts there emerged new political alignments and doctrines, culminating in the evolution of an organized party system and the concomitant legitimization of opposition. The constitutional questions explored in this process—notably those of ministerial responsibility and the parameters of royal power—expanded into an evolving public debate, which resulted in important innovations in contemporary political arguments that were of crucial significance for the long-term development of the British constitution. The widespread controversy surrounding Bute's career provided a focus for a variety of social and political discontents, which in turn fostered the growth of extra-parliamentary radicalism dedicated to political change and reform. The importance of Bute to the historian, then, lies partly in the fact that he was a potent if unwilling catalyst of these developments.

The discordant currents introduced by Bute's appearance on the political scene were further intensified through his initiatives in the sphere of foreign policy and diplomacy. Here the earl's negative reputation stems mainly from the shift, successfully executed during the years 1761 to 1763, away from his predecessor's continental interventionism. Unlike politicians solidly committed to a system in Europe with strong attachments to particular powers, Bute took a more prudent line on the necessity of alliances, the desirability of particular allies, and the expenditures and concessions involved in securing or retaining an alliance. This explains his opposition to anything that might have favoured Hanover, long a contentious issue politically, with the result that after 1760 British diplomacy was far less affected by European commitments than it was before the Seven Years' War. Thus Bute personifies what has been called a tory or country view of international relations—a view traditionally hostile to continental connections but strongly favouring maritime and colonial objectives. Whatever its ideological roots, this policy was shaped in large measure by Bute's sensitivity to domestic pressures and the need to reconcile diplomatic imperatives with fiscal exigencies and parliamentary requirements.

The desire to harmonize the conflicting needs of government economy and American security similarly prompted the Bute administration to impose the cost of postwar defence upon the colonists. This was a decision that led to an imperial crisis that ended in revolution but was probably inevitable given the state of British finances in 1763 and the Bourbons' known plans for revenge. Bute's awareness of the transitory nature of peace, and the appreciation that an enlarged empire demanded new fiscal and protective provisions, was a sound response to altered realities, though one much criticized by historians. Such criticism, as with so many aspects of his career, was invariably influenced by the long-standing controversies over the reign of George III, another example of the extent to which partisan dimensions have shaped Bute's historical reputation.

Ultimately, however, Bute is more than a symbol of the aberrations conventionally associated with George III's early reign. Though brief and turbulent, his tenure as secretary of state and as prime minister was not without success. While his plans for political reform remained unfulfilled, Bute showed himself generally capable of leading a ministry in time of domestic stress and international conflict. For all his limitations, he implemented a coherent political strategy, one that consolidated Britain's imperial achievement and projected a minimalist continental policy at a time of intensifying national concern over the financial consequences of war. Altogether, he was a responsible, cautious minister who maintained his concentration on the most important issues and had a clear sense of political priorities.

This accomplishment commands all the more respect when one remembers Bute's psychological aversion to governing and the multitude of problems that confronted him from the outset. As with Pitt, his political woes can be ascribed in part to his personality. Although an affectionate friend and devoted family man, in public he appeared invariably cold, distant, and haughty, probably more from shyness than arrogance. Happiest in scholarly seclusion, Bute was ill at ease and insecure on the political stage. His entire ministerial career is the tragic story of a man called into politics in middle age to assume a position he initially feared and eventually came to detest. His limitations, ultimately, were not ones of achievement as of personality and will—an inability to kindle enthusiasm among his colleagues and the public at large, and failure to convince others that he was an effective minister.

The lack of support from cabinet colleagues, his personal unpopularity, bitter factionalism within the whig ranks, a hostile press, and an inherently complex political situation might all have unsettled a more experienced minister. That Bute's concern for king and country prompted him to struggle on reveals qualities of courage, dedication, and loyalty not always associated with the trade of politics. 'I follow one uniform system', he wrote to Henry Fox shortly before his resignation, 'and that is founded on the strictest honour, faith and duty' (BL, Add. MS 51379, fol. 160). It is no mean epitaph for any public figure.

KARL WOLFGANG SCHWEIZER

Sources DNB · K. W. Schweizer, ed., *Lord Bute: essays in re-interpretation* (1988) · K. W. Schweizer, *Frederick the Great, William Pitt and Lord Bute* (1991) · *The Devonshire diary: memoranda on state of affairs, 1759–1762*, ed. P. D. Brown and K. W. Schweizer, CS, 4th ser., 27 (1982) · J. Brewer, *Party ideology and popular politics at the accession of George III* (1976) · J. McKelvey, *George III and Lord Bute: the Leicester House years* (1973) · *Letters from George III to Lord Bute, 1756–1766*, ed. R. Sedgwick (1939) · R. A. Downie, *Bute and the Cumbraes* (1934) · J. Reid, *History of the county of Bute* (1864) · GEC, *Peerage* · H. Butterfield, *George III and the historians* (1957) · J. A. Lovat-Fraser, *John Stuart, earl of Bute* (1912) · L. B. Namier, *England in the age of the American revolution*, 2nd edn (1963) · *A prime minister and his son: from the correspondence of the 3rd earl of Bute and of Lt-General the Hon. Sir Charles Stuart*, ed. Mrs E. S. Wortley (1925) · J. Brooke, *King George III* (1972) · J. Bullion, *A great and necessary measure: George Grenville and the genesis of the Stamp Act, 1763–1765* (1982) · J. Brewer, 'The misfortunes of Lord Bute: a case study in eighteenth century political argument and public opinion', *HJ*, 16 (1973), 3–43 · J. Brewer, 'The faces of

Lord Bute: a visual contribution to Anglo-American political ideology', *Perspectives in American History*, 6 (1972), 95–116 • K. W. Schweizer, 'William Pitt, Lord Bute and the peace negotiations with France, May–September 1761', *Albion*, 13 (1981), 262–75 • J. Bullion, 'Security and economy: the Bute administration's plans for the American army and revenue, 1762–1763', *William and Mary Quarterly*, 45 (1988), 499–509 • K. W. Schweizer and J. Bullion, 'The vote of credit controversy: 1762', *British Journal for Eighteenth-Century Studies*, 15 (1992), 175–88 • J. Bullion and K. W. Schweizer, 'The use of private papers of politicians in the study of policy formulation during the 18th century: the Bute papers as a case study', *Archives*, 22/93–5 (1995–6), 34–44 • K. W. Schweizer, 'The Bedford motion and House of Lords debate, 5 Feb. 1762', *Parliamentary History*, 5 (1986), 107–23 • A. Valentine, *The British establishment, 1760–1784: an eighteenth-century biographical dictionary*, 2 (1970), 838–9 • D. Englefield and others, eds., *Facts about British prime ministers* (1995), 31 • R. A. Austen-Leigh, ed., *The Eton College register, 1698–1752* (1927), 57 • E. Peacock, *Index to English speaking students who have graduated at Leyden University* (1883), 16 • Mount Stuart Trust, Isle of Bute, Bute MSS • Bute letter-books, BL, Add. MS 36797 • register, Bute corresp., BL, Add. MS 36796 • Holland House MSS, Add. MSS 51375–51398 • BL, Hardwicke MSS, Add. MSS 35352–35368 • BL, Mitchell MSS, Add. MSS 6804–6836 • Chatsworth House, Derbyshire, Devonshire MSS • Bodl. Oxf., North MSS • Hockworthy House, Wellington, Somerset, Oswald MSS • Royal Arch. • Woburn Abbey, Bedfordshire, Bedford MSS • Yale U., Lewis Walpole Library, Weston MSS • Hunt. L., Stowe papers • BL, Newcastle MSS, Add. MSS 32713–32735; 32857–32869

Archives BL, letter-books, Add. MS 36796–36797 • BL, register, corresp., Add. MS 36796 • Bodl. Oxf., papers relating to royal household and foreign policy • CUL, account book • CUL, travel journal and essays on travel writing • CUL, travel writings • Mount Stuart Trust Archive, Isle of Bute, corresp. • NRA, letter-book • Yale U., Farmington, Lewis Walpole Library, drafts relating to Berlin | BL, corresp. with duke of Bedford and earl of Liverpool, Add. MSS 38191–38222, 38304–38310, 38458, 38566, *passim* • BL, corresp. with George Grenville, Add. MS 57809 • BL, letters to earl of Hardwicke, etc., Add. MSS 35423–36123, *passim* • BL, letters to Lord Holland, Add. MS 51379 • BL, letters to S. Martin, Add. MSS 41354, 41357 • BL, Mitchell MSS, Add. MSS 6804–6836 • BL, corresp. with duke of Newcastle, etc., Add. MSS 32684–32992 • Bodl. Oxf., letters to Lord Guilford • Bodl. Oxf., corresp. with Lord Macartney • Chatsworth House, Derbyshire, letters to duke of Devonshire • Hunt. L., letters to earl of London • NA Scot., corresp. with Charles Erskine • NL Scot., letters to Mure family • NRA, priv. coll., letters to Lord Shelburne • U. Nott. L., letters to Lord Lincoln • U. Nott. L., corresp. with duke of Newcastle • Yale U., Beinecke L., corresp. with James Boswell

Likenesses J. Hall, line engraving, 1757 (after A. Ramsay), BM; repro. in T. Smollett, *A complete history of England*, 4 vols. (1757–8) • A. Ramsay, oils, 1758, NG Scot. • J. Reynolds, oils, 1763, NPG • L. Sullivan, miniature on ivory, 1767, V&A • J. Reynolds, oils, 1773, NPG [*see illus.*] • Kirkwood, line engraving (after A. Ramsay), NPG • R. Purcell, mezzotint (after A. Ramsay), BM, NPG • A. Ramsay, chalk drawing, NG Scot. • attrib. A. Ramsay, oils, Scot. NPG • line engraving (after unknown artist), NPG

Stuart, John (1718–1779), colonial official and merchant, was born in Inverness on 25 September 1718, the son of John Stuart, merchant and magistrate of Inverness, and his second wife, Christian MacLeod. After an initial education in the Inverness grammar school, Stuart left at the age of seventeen for London to work in a merchant house, moving between London and San Lucar de Barrameda, Andalusia. When war between Britain and Spain erupted, he joined Commodore George Anson's expedition, which set sail in 1740 to harass Spanish shipping in the Americas.

During his brief naval career he served as a clerk and as a ship's purser and rose to the rank of midshipman.

In 1748 Stuart moved to South Carolina, like many Scots at the time, and established himself in Charles Town as a business partner of Patrick Reid, a fellow Scot whom Stuart had met in England in 1746. Soon after his arrival he married Sarah, with whom he had three daughters and one son. The business did not fare well, and when Reid died in April 1754 he left Stuart with heavy debts, which forced him into bankruptcy and near destitution within a year. During this time and the years that followed—during which Stuart repaid his creditors—he established himself in Charles Town society, serving in a number of public offices including St Philip's parish firemaster (1752) and assemblyman for St Helena parish (1754–6), and joined social organizations such as the Charles Town Library Society and the Charles Town grand lodge of free and accepted masons.

When the French and Indian war erupted, Stuart was commissioned a captain in the South Carolina provincial militia. His first task was to recruit a company to assist in the construction of Fort Loudoun in the neighbouring Overhill Cherokee country (subsequently Tennessee), which was intended to offer protection to Britain's American Indian allies while their warriors were away campaigning. At the fort Stuart built upon the good relations he had developed with the Cherokee as a trader, and ultimately took charge of arranging for the local women to provide provisions for the fort's garrison. Cherokee–British relations rapidly deteriorated after the fort's completion as young warriors on their return from campaigning took to plundering backcountry colonial farms, and white frontiersmen took Cherokee scalps and attempted to pass them as enemy Creek scalps in order to claim the hefty bounties being offered by the colonial governments. In 1759 full-scale war erupted, and in early 1760 Stuart and his company were sent to bolster Fort Loudoun's garrison. Although the British claimed victory, the war was inconclusive. Each summer a combination of British regulars, allied American Indians, and colonial militia would invade the Cherokee territory and destroy as many crops and towns as possible; meanwhile the Cherokee would avoid the advancing troops and instead raid the frontier and cut off supplies to existing forts. At Fort Loudoun the garrison was besieged for nine months in 1760 before starvation forced surrender. The troops were promised safe passage but were massacred within a few miles of the fort. Stuart was one of the few survivors, and owed his life to Attakullakulla (Little Carpenter), a prominent, tea-drinking Cherokee leader who had visited Britain and was a long-standing supporter of a British–Cherokee friendship.

Following his safe return to Charles Town, Stuart's prominence in handling American Indian relations grew. With the backing of South Carolina governor Thomas Boone and Attakullakulla, Stuart was chosen to replace the generally inactive, and shortly afterwards deceased, Edmund Atkin as the British Indian superintendent for Indian affairs for the southern district. Created in 1756, the two superintendents were part of the British programme to assert a centralized diplomatic and military authority in order to achieve victory in North America. The superintendents and their staffs answered directly to the British commander-in-chief in America and to the secretaries of state, thus bypassing any colonial authorities. After defeating the French and their American Indian allies, the superintendencies, like many elements of the British military establishment, remained in peacetime North America. During the French and Indian wars the British government had been shocked at how well the American Indians fought, disappointed that so many sided with France over Britain, and frustrated with how ineffective the bickering colonial governments had been in remedying the situation. Stuart and his northern counterpart, Sir William Johnson, were charged with the task of maintaining a peaceful frontier and ensuring American Indian grievances were addressed before a war broke out that would disrupt the all-important recovering economies of colonial America.

The primary American Indian grievances were the invasion of their lands by white settlers and the abuses of white traders who took advantage of American Indian dependence on a number of European goods, particularly firearms and gunpowder. The complaint about encroachment was addressed initially by the royal proclamation of 1763, which was intended to guide expansion away from major American Indian nations in the interior. Stuart's task was to enforce the proclamation by mediating border treaties between the colonial governments and the American Indians and by evicting illegal settlers. The British answer to trade grievances was regulation. Traders were expected to be licensed, and trade was to be conducted only at specified locations where, in theory, the superintendents or a member of their staffs could monitor activities. Stuart went to work immediately, organizing a massive congress in Augusta, Georgia, in November 1763 at which the southern colonial governors met with delegations from the various neighbouring American Indian nations. This was the first of a series of congresses that ultimately led to one of the most peaceful decades on the colonial American frontier and the establishment of a western border. Stuart's favoured tools in these negotiations were gifts. More than mere bribes, abundant gifts bestowed on favourably disposed leaders ensured that these men, who would in turn spread the wealth to their own supporters within their communities, would rise to power. At the Augusta conference alone, Stuart distributed gifts that included 1077 guns, 2300 shirts, 500 brass pans, 576 hatchets, 79 looking glasses, 36,500 gun flints, 190 saddles, 798 bridles, and an abundance of gunpowder (PRO, CO 5/65, part 2, fol. 74). He sent the bill to the secretary of state.

Although initially willing to pay handsomely for results, the British government became increasingly apprehensive of such administrative costs in America as its postwar efforts to compel the colonists to share in some of the costs met alarming resistance. By 1768 the superintendents' budgets had been drastically slashed, forcing Stuart

to release much of his staff and cease lavish gift-giving. By this point the British government had abandoned any hopes of an imperially regulated American Indian trade. Enforcing the borders was an equally lost cause, as frontier garrisons were redeployed to the riotous colonial cities. By the early 1770s the British had effectively given up, and Stuart was placed on a shoestring budget.

When the American War of Independence broke out in 1775, the British reaped the rewards of Stuart's work. The vast majority of American Indian leaders in his district either sided with the British or declared their neutrality. Stuart received unprecedented financial resources to secure continued Indian support, but the tide of American patriotism proved too strong. Hampered by British war leaders who were unfamiliar with Indian affairs, an increasingly desperate British government, and American Indian leaders who were wary of remaining allied to a collapsing British authority, Stuart was forced out of the Carolinas and then Georgia. As the interior order he helped to construct collapsed around him, he took refuge in the loyalist-dominated Floridas, dying in Pensacola on 21 March 1779.   TROY O. BICKHAM

Sources U. Mich., Clements L., Thomas Gage MSS · U. Mich., Clements L., Shelburne papers · U. Mich., Clements L., Sir Henry Clinton papers · PRO, Colonial Office papers, ser. 5 · J. R. Alden, *John Stuart and the southern colonial frontier: a study of Indian relations, war, trade, and land problems in the southern wilderness, 1754–1775* (1944) · K. E. H. Braund, *Deerskins and duffels: Creek Indian trade with Anglo-America, 1685–1815* (1993) · T. Hatley, *The dividing paths: Cherokees and South Carolinians through the era of revolution* (1993) · H. L. Shaw, *British administration of the southern Indians, 1756–1783* (1931) · J. R. Snapp, *John Stuart and the struggle for empire on the southern frontier* (1996) · J. H. O'Donnell III, 'Stuart, John', *ANB* · J. M. Sosin, *Whitehall and the wilderness: the middle west in British colonial policy, 1760–1775* (1961)
Archives PRO, corresp., PRO 30/55 | BL, corresp. with Frederick Haldimand, etc., Add. MSS 21671–21672 · PRO, Colonial Office ser. 5 · U. Mich., Clements L., corresp. with Thomas Cage · U. Mich., Clements L., Sir Henry Clinton papers · U. Mich., Clements L., Shelburne papers
Wealth at death substantial lands and trading interests in southern mainland colonies, but these were under threat by American Revolution

Stuart, John (1741–1811), Church of England clergyman and missionary, was born on 24 February 1741 in Paxton township, Lancaster county, Pennsylvania, the eldest son of Andrew Stuart (c.1699–1774), a native of co. Tyrone, Ireland, and a successful farmer, and his wife, Mary (1707–1772), daughter of Robert Dinwiddie and his wife, Elizabeth Cumming. John Stuart's uncle, Robert *Dinwiddie (1692–1770), was lieutenant-governor of Virginia in 1751–8. Stuart was raised in a devout Presbyterian family in rural Pennsylvania. As a student at the College of Philadelphia (later the University of Pennsylvania), where he graduated BA 1763, MA 1770, and DD *honoris causa* 1799, he came under the influence of the Revd Dr William Smith and converted to Anglicanism. Stuart spent seven years teaching in Lancaster county. In 1770 he was ordained in London and appointed by the Society for the Propagation of the Gospel in Foreign Parts (SPG) as missionary to the British and Mohawk Anglican congregations at Fort

Hunter, New York. On 12 October 1775 he married Jane Okill (1747–1821), the daughter of a wealthy Anglican family in Philadelphia. Sir James *Stuart, first baronet (1780–1853), was their son.

The American War of Independence soon threatened the comfortable life the Stuarts and their young children enjoyed at Fort Hunter. As an Anglican clergyman Stuart was automatically suspected of British sympathies. The family eventually retreated to Schenectady, New York, and in 1780 joined the loyalist exodus north to Montreal. For the next four years Stuart served there as a military chaplain, schoolteacher, sometime assistant clergyman, and spiritual adviser to the Mohawk nation.

In the summer of 1785 the Stuarts relocated permanently in Cataraqui (later Kingston), where Lake Ontario flows into the St Lawrence River. Their loyalty to the crown had cost them at least £1200 in property losses; they had been able to take only a few personal possessions and several black slaves inherited from the Okills. When he settled in Cataraqui Stuart was determined to recreate the gracious life denied him by the war. Securing financial independence (he eventually acquired 7000 acres of land) and a place among Kingston's emerging élite became overriding preoccupations. Stuart's eight children were sent to the best schools in Montreal, Nova Scotia, Schenectady, and even to Harvard University. Although they caused him considerable heartache, several went on to play leading roles in the development of Upper and Lower Canada.

Stuart's professional duties were initially onerous. An employee of the SPG and the only resident clergyman in Kingston, he acted as garrison chaplain, conducted religious services in a barrack room for the general population, established a school, and served as its master for three years. Intermittently he travelled on horseback to outlying settlements and ministered to the Mohawk at Tyendinaga on the Bay of Quinte. He also held the post of chaplain to the legislative council of Upper Canada from 1792 to 1807. Not until 1792 was Stuart able to construct his first church, named for George III and England's patron saint. His congregation, although it included some of Kingston's most prominent citizens, remained small and never contributed towards his maintenance. He thought of himself as 'a Centinel at the Out-Post' (Blackwell and Stanley, 175), defending his communion against encroachments from Methodists and Roman Catholics. Although a staunch loyalist, Stuart kept up his American connections, especially with his former classmate William White, first Protestant Episcopal bishop of the diocese of Pennsylvania (1787–1836).

In late September 1787 a clerical reinforcement arrived from the SPG. The Revd John Langhorn, the first British Anglican missionary in Upper Canada, proved, however, a mixed blessing. Langhorn took over Stuart's mission to the west of Kingston, a wilderness of some 40 square miles. Although the two men's careers ran parallel for almost a quarter century, they had very different visions of Anglicanism. A strict high-churchman from northern England, Langhorn quickly became embroiled in conflicts with Presbyterians, Methodists, and the numerous other denominations in his parish. Always the cynical realist whose bitter American experience had taught him the wisdom of following 'the peaceable course' (Blackwell and Stanley, 176), Stuart had the irksome task of adjudicating between Langhorn and his adversaries.

Stuart and Langhorn eventually made their peace. When Stuart died on 15 August 1811 at the age of seventy, it was Langhorn, and not his eldest son, the Revd George Okill Stuart (1776–1862), who officiated at the interment which took place at St George's burial-ground on 17 August. John Strachan (1778–1867), another Presbyterian convert to Anglicanism, who became the first bishop of Toronto and continued to champion Stuart's loyalist vision of Anglicanism right into the year of confederation, eulogized the elder Stuart as 'the father of the Episcopal Church in this Province' (Strachan, 29).

JOHN D. BLACKWELL and LAURIE C. C. STANLEY-BLACKWELL

Sources P. Banfield, 'To the love of peace & ease: John Stuart's later career', *St. George's Cathedral: two hundred years of community*, ed. D. Swainson (1991), 149–63; 290–91 • E. Bellasis, *Westmorland church notes* (1888), 1.262 • J. D. Blackwell and L. C. C. Stanley, 'Two Anglican images: John Stuart and John Langhorn', *St George's Cathedral: two hundred years of community*, ed. D. Swainson (1991), 167–87, 291–4 • W. Canniff, *History of the settlement of Upper Canada* (1869) • J. R. Carruthers, 'The little gentleman: the Reverend John Stuart and the inconvenience of revolution', MA diss., Queen's University at Kingston, 1975 • J. C. Hodgson, *A history of Northumberland*, 6 (1902) • T. R. Millman, 'Stuart, John', *DCB* • P. L. Northcott, 'The financial problems of the Reverend John Stuart', *Historic Kingston*, 13 (1965), 27–40 • M. A. O'Dell, 'Launching loyalist children: the Stuart family of early Kingston', MA diss., Queen's University at Kingston, 1984 • R. A. Preston, ed., *Kingston before the war of 1812: a collection of documents* (1959) • G. F. G. Stanley, 'John Stuart: father of the Anglican church in Upper Canada', *Journal of the Canadian Church Historical Society*, 3/6 (1956–9), 1–13 • J. Strachan, *Sermon on the death of the Rev. John Stuart* (1811) • [J. Stuart], *The parish register of Kingston, Upper Canada, 1785–1811*, ed. A. H. Young (1921) • E. Thomas, 'Missionary to the Mohawks: John Stuart's early career', *St. George's Cathedral: two hundred years of community*, ed. D. Swainson (1991), 133–46; 288–90 • L. Turner, *Ernestown: rural spaces, urban places* (1993) • A. H. Young, *The Revd. John Stuart, D. D., U. E. L. of Kingston, U. C., and his family: a genealogical study* (1920)
Archives Anglican Church of Canada, Diocese of Ontario Archives, Kingston, Ontario • Public Archives of Ontario, Toronto
Likenesses portrait, repro. in D. Swainson, ed., *St George's Cathedral*

Stuart, John (1743–1821), Gaelic scholar and botanist, was born at the manse, Killin, Perthshire, on 31 July 1743, the son of James Stuart (1700–1789), a minister in the Church of Scotland, and Elizabeth Drummond. Educated at Edinburgh University, he was licensed by the city's presbytery on 27 February 1771, presented to the parish of Arrochar, Dunbartonshire, by Sir James Colquhoun in October 1773, and ordained on 12 May 1774. He was translated to Weem, Perthshire, on 26 May 1776, and to Luss, Dunbartonshire, on 1 July 1777.

Stuart was one of the leading Gaelic scholars of his time. His father had published a Gaelic translation of the New Testament for the Society in Scotland for the Propagation of Christian Knowledge in 1767 and was engaged with a translation of the Old Testament at the time of his death.

Stuart supervised the completion of the first two volumes of his father's work and himself made the translation of the remaining Old Testament books, which were published as volume 3 of the whole in 1801. On 24 July 1792 he married Susan Macintyre (1768–1846), the daughter of Joseph Macintyre, minister of Glenorchy. They had four children, including Joseph, who later became minister at Kingarth, Isle of Bute. In 1795 Stuart was awarded the degree of DD by Glasgow University and in 1796 he published a second, revised, edition of his father's translation of the New Testament.

Stuart's valuable services earned him the thanks of the general assembly of the Church of Scotland on 28 May 1819, and a gift of £1000 from the lords of the Treasury in the following year. Aside from his interest in the Gaelic language, Stuart was also a devoted student of botany and lichenology, and identified many of Perthshire's rare alpine plants. He died on 24 May 1821 at Luss, where he was also buried. He was survived by his wife, who died on 7 July 1846.

GEORGE STRONACH, rev. RODERICK MACLEOD

Sources D. W. MacKenzie, *The worthy translator* (1992) · *Fasti Scot.* · D. MacKinnon, *The Gaelic Bible and psalter: being the story of the translation of the scriptures into Scottish Gaelic* (1930), 56, 59, 65, 71, 76 · D. E. Meek, 'The Gaelic Bible', *The Bible in Scottish life and literature*, ed. D. F. Wright, I. Campbell, and J. S. Gibson (1988), 9–23
Archives Warks. CRO, letters to Thomas Pennant

Stuart, John, **first marquess of Bute** (1744–1814), diplomatist, was born at Mount Stuart on the Isle of Bute, Scotland, on 30 June 1744, the eldest of the eight surviving children of John *Stuart, third earl of Bute (1713–1792), prime minister, and his wife, Mary Wortley Montagu (1718–1794), who was created Baroness Mount Stuart in 1761. His siblings included Sir Charles *Stuart (1753–1801), William *Stuart, archbishop of Armagh, and Lady Louisa *Stuart. He was educated at Harrow School and Winchester College and was privately tutored by the Revd James Bladen at Oxford; he was later an honorary DCL of Oxford University in 1793. His grand tour (1761–5), from which he returned tall and handsome, included studies in the Netherlands and Geneva and travels in Italy together with James Boswell. He successfully courted a wealthy heiress, Charlotte Jane (1746–1800), daughter of Herbert Hickman Windsor, second Viscount Windsor and Baron Mountjoy (*bap.* 1707, *d.* 1758), and Alice Clavering (*bap.* 1705, *d.* 1776). They married at St John's Chapel, Hanover Square, London, on 12 November 1766; four of their seven sons and one of two daughters survived infancy.

Following the deaths of his wife's parents the Windsor estates in south Wales passed to Stuart, who restored Cardiff Castle and was created Baron Cardiff on 20 May 1776. He vacated his seat in the Commons for Bossiney, which he had held on his mother's interest since 1766. Following his father politically he supported successive ministries after Rockingham's, but was miffed by Lord North's indifference towards him. Even North's support did not avail him to carry the Scottish Militia Bill in 1776. In the Lords he was a firm supporter of war with the American colonies, but he was critical of civil list provisions, and his

speeches in support of the ministry tailed off after 1778. He served as lord lieutenant of Glamorgan from 1772 to 1793, and again from 1794, together with the lord lieutenancy of Bute, until his death, and raised a company for the war in America. Sworn of the privy council on 4 August 1779, he proceeded to Turin as envoy, styled Lord Mountstuart, for three years. Appointed auditor of the imprest in 1781, he received £7000 a year compensation for its abolition in 1785. He was named ambassador to Spain in 1783, but did not take up his post until 1795–6, by which time he had succeeded his parents to their titles, in 1792 and 1794, and changed his politics when he joined Portland in defecting to Pitt in 1794. He had previously supported the coalition ministry of 1783 as a Portland whig and continued in opposition after Pitt came to power, a position which alienated the king's favour. A mortgage on Luton Park prejudiced his inheritance and he attempted to regain the king's favour in 1792–3. His diplomatic service in Spain and support of the ministry from 1794 onwards led to his creation as first marquess of Bute on 27 February 1796, before Spain's alliance with France brought him home.

In 1798 Bute renounced diplomacy and petitioned unsuccessfully for the position of lord steward. He failed to receive the Garter in 1799. A fellow of the Society of Antiquaries from 1776 he became a fellow of the Royal Society in 1799 and, in 1800, a trustee of the British Museum. His wife died suddenly of apoplexy on 28 January 1800 and Bute married, on 17 September 1800, Frances (1772/3–1832), daughter and coheir of Thomas Coutts, banker, and his first wife, Susan Starkie; they had a son and a daughter. Bute reverted to political opposition and joined the prince of Wales, who made him one of his councillors of state in 1800. He died at Geneva on 16 November 1814, and was buried on 20 December in the Bute vault at Roath, Cardiff.

ROLAND THORNE

Sources E. Haden-Guest, 'Stuart, John, Lord Mountstuart', HoP, *Commons, 1754–90*, 3.502–3 · GEC, *Peerage*, new edn, 2.443 · Cobbett, *Parl. hist.*, vols. 18–20 · *The later correspondence of George III*, ed. A. Aspinall, 5 vols. (1962–70), vol. 1, p. 749; vol. 2, pp. 834, 894, 1378; vol. 3, pp. 1676, 1918 · *GM*, 1st ser., 85/1 (1815), 651–2 · *GM*, 1st ser., 84/2 (1814), 606 · D. B. Horn, ed., *British diplomatic representatives, 1689–1789*, CS, 3rd ser., 46 (1932), 126, 137 · S. T. Bindoff and others, eds., *British diplomatic representatives, 1789–1852*, CS, 3rd ser., 50 (1934), 140–41 · *Boyle's Court Directory* (1793–1811)
Archives Beds. & Luton ARS, corresp. and papers relating to local and estate matters · BL, corresp. and papers, Add. MSS 36799–36806, 36808–36814, 37080–37085, 38774 · BL, diplomatic MSS, Add. MSS 35517–35531, 36801–36813, 37080–37085, 38216, 38308, 38774 · Cardiff RO · JRL, corresp. and papers · NL Scot., journal of tour of western isles · NL Wales · Royal Library, Windsor, Berkshire, letters · Rothesay, MSS | Beds. & Luton ARS, letters to William Stuart · BL, corresp. with Lord Grenville, Add. MS 59026 · BL, corresp. with Sir Robert Keith, Add. MSS 35517–35531, *passim* · NA Scot., corresp. relating to curatory of earl of Dumfries · NL Scot., corresp. with Robert Liston · PRO, Chatham MSS, letters to Pitt, 30/8/118 · U. Nott. L., letters to duke of Portland · U. Wales, Bangor, letters to Richard Littlehales · Yale U., Beinecke L., corresp. with James Boswell
Likenesses J. E. Liotard, oils, *c.*1774 · J. R. Smith, engraving, 1774 (after J. E. Liotard, *c.*1774) · E. Fisher, engraving, 1777 (after J. Reynolds, *c.*1777) · J. Reynolds, oils, *c.*1777 · W. Baillie, engraving, 1779 (after N. Hone, *c.*1779) · N. Hone, oils, *c.*1779 · E. Fisher, engraving,

1783 (after J. Reynolds, c.1777) · J. C. Ibberson, group portrait, 1789, Cardiff Castle · T. Gainsborough, oils, c.1791 · C. Watson, engraving, 1791 (after T. Gainsborough) · F. Bartolozzi, engraving (after G. Romney) · G. Romney, oils, Cardiff Castle
Wealth at death estates in Scotland, England, and Wales

Stuart, Sir John (1761–1815), army officer, son of Colonel John Stuart (1718–1779) and his wife, Sarah Fenwick of Charles Town, South Carolina, was born in Georgia. His father was superintendent of Indian affairs for the southern department. A prominent loyalist in the American War of Independence, he died at Pensacola, Florida. At the end of the war his property was confiscated by the American government.

Young Stuart was educated at Westminster School and obtained a commission as ensign in the 3rd foot guards on 7 August 1778. He took part in the War of Independence, serving under Lord Cornwallis in the Carolinas; he was dangerously wounded in the battle of Guilford on 15 March 1781. On 6 November 1782 he was promoted lieutenant in the 3rd foot guards and captain in the army.

Ten years later, following the outbreak of war with revolutionary France, Stuart went with his regiment to Flanders as part of the force commanded by the duke of York (March 1793). On 25 April he was promoted to be captain in the 3rd foot guards and lieutenant-colonel in the army. His regiment formed part of the guards brigade which distinguished itself at Famars, Valenciennes, and Linselles. It also took part in the siege of Dunkirk, abandoned in October, and shared in the victory of Lannoy, won on 28 October; it then went into winter quarters. When hostilities resumed the following spring Stuart commanded his battalion in the assault on Landrecies and in subsequent battles around Tournai and Tourcoing. After the British army was forced to fall back on the line of the Waal, Stuart's battalion held Nijmegen until forced out on 9 November. He accompanied it in its retreat in the winter of 1794–5 and its evacuation from Bremen on 14 April 1795.

Stuart was promoted brevet-colonel on 1 May 1796. On 30 November he was appointed to a command, with the rank of brigadier-general, in a force sent to Portugal under command of Sir Charles Stuart. He stayed with it until he joined an expedition to Minorca, again commanded by Sir Charles Stuart, in November 1798, being gazetted brigadier-general on the 10th of that month. When Minorca's garrison surrendered on 15 November it included 1000 ex-Austrian prisoners (mostly Germans and Swiss). They were enlisted into a regiment known as 'the Minorca' (renamed in 1801 'the Queen's Germans') and Stuart was given command of it.

Stuart accompanied Sir Ralph Abercromby's force to Egypt in 1801, in command of the 5th brigade. This consisted of three foreign regiments, including the Minorca. It distinguished itself in the battle on 21 March fought on the plain of Alexandria. Its repulse of a cavalry charge ensured a British victory and received a commendation in general orders. The campaign over, Stuart was sent on a political mission to Constantinople and then returned to Egypt to command the troops left in Alexandria. He

received the order of the Crescent from the sultan of Turkey for his services. He was promoted major-general with effect from 29 April 1802 and returned to England in that year.

On 17 October 1803 Stuart was appointed to command a brigade in the force stationed on the coast of Kent against a threatened French invasion. He held the command until 24 March 1805 when he accompanied Lieutenant-General Sir James Craig, who had been given command of all British land forces in the Mediterranean. The expedition, 5000 strong, which arrived at Malta on 18 July, was destined to assist the kingdom of Naples, in conjunction with a Russian force, with the aim of driving the French from Italy. Both forces landed in the Bay of Naples on 21 November 1805. Overall command was given to the Russian general Lacy, but Napoleon's victory at Austerlitz caused the tsar to order Lacy to re-embark his troops and return to Corfu. Craig, seeing no point in remaining, obeyed his instructions to safeguard Sicily, where he took his force in January 1806. It disembarked at Messina on 17 February, when the king of Naples allowed it to land, he and his family having fled to Palermo.

In April 1806 Craig, on grounds of ill health, resigned his command, which passed by seniority to Stuart. Stuart's naval counterpart, Vice-Admiral Sir Sydney Smith, reinforced the Neapolitan garrison at Gaeta, which still held out against the French, and captured the island of Capri, off Naples. Stuart supported the admiral's action by sending a regiment under Colonel Lowe to relieve the naval garrison of Capri. Stuart was allowed by King Ferdinand to raise a corps of Sicilian fencibles, clothed and paid by the British, organize a flotilla of Sicilian gunboats to protect the straits of Messina, and take command of the coastal area stretching from Milazzo to Cape Passaro.

Learning that the French forces in Lower Calabria that threatened Sicily with invasion were seriously depleted on account of the continuing siege of Gaeta, Stuart decided to strike a surprise blow. His aim was to drive the French from the province, destroying their batteries and magazines. With a force of 5200 men he landed in the Bay of Santa Eufemia on 30 June 1806. General Reynier did not wait to be attacked but unwisely abandoned a strong position below the town of San Pietro di Maida. The battle that ensued was won by the British, though Stuart was scarcely responsible, the victory being entirely due to the action of his subordinates and the skill and bravery of his troops. Yet Stuart got all the credit for it, receiving the thanks of both houses of parliament and a pension of £1000 a year for life. He was made a knight of the Bath, created count of Maida by King Ferdinand, and received from the City of London its freedom and a sword of honour.

Reynier's army had been shattered, but Stuart was unable to pursue it to destruction. His troops were exhausted by the great heat and he lacked the necessary transport and cavalry. In any case his primary task remained the defence of Sicily and he had embarked on the operation without ministerial authorization. Stuart was a cautious general and, having overseen the capture of Scylla, which commanded the narrowest part of the straits, and placed a garrison in both it and Reggio, he was content to return to Messina.

Relations between Stuart and Sydney Smith, both vain men and both competing for the favour of Ferdinand's queen, were worsened when Stuart learned that Sydney Smith had been given viceregal powers in Calabria. There the admiral gave every encouragement to the local people to revolt. Stuart had issued a proclamation urging the Calabresi to join him, but once aware of their brutal treatment of prisoners of war, and that their primary interest was to wage class war in pursuit of plunder, he made public his disapproval, and Sydney Smith's viceregal commission was cancelled.

Stuart returned to Sicily to discover that command of land forces in the Mediterranean had passed to General Henry Fox, who had already arrived at Messina. On learning that Fox's second in command was to be Lieutenant-General Sir John Moore, expected shortly with strong reinforcements, Stuart decided to resign. He had no wish to be subordinate to a man of whom he was bitterly jealous, Moore having won at Alexandria the fame to which Stuart felt himself entitled.

Nevertheless, on 11 February 1808 Stuart was again sent to the Mediterranean to assume command of the land forces there, Fox having resigned and Moore posted to another assignment. On 25 April Stuart was promoted to the rank of lieutenant-general. On arrival in Sicily he was confronted with the prospect of a serious French invasion attempt now that Joachim Murat was ruling in Naples. When the latter captured Capri in October 1808 morale in Sicily was badly affected. Stuart was partly to blame for the loss, having reinforced the island's garrison with an unreliable foreign regiment which surrendered to the French with little fight.

In 1809 Stuart was placed in a difficult situation by the British government: told first to send away regiments to Spain, in support of Wellesley's peninsular campaign, and then, when Austria re-entered the war, urged to make a major military diversion aimed at freeing the whole of Italy. In May he embarked a force numbering upwards of 11,000, but delayed sailing until 11 June. This delay caused great discontent among his subordinate officers with whom he was already very unpopular, but was caused by Stuart's extreme caution. He had learned of Austrian defeats in Bavaria and the withdrawal of their forces from northern Italy. When the expedition eventually sailed it was delayed by calm weather and arrived in the Bay of Naples only on 24 June. There it captured, with little resistance, the islands of Ischia and Procida. Stuart's further hesitation about what to do next afforded Murat the opportunity of concentrating his troops round Naples and making an assault on the city unwise. Urged by Admiral Collingwood to land his force on the Roman coast, from which French troops had been withdrawn, Stuart waited until too late. News of Napoleon's victory at Wagram and Collingwood's warning that the British fleet could not ensure the safety of the convoy if a French squadron escaped from Toulon, caused him to abandon the enterprise and withdraw at once to Sicily. This action embittered his relations with Palermo—ones that were already under great strain.

Three months later, under pressure from Collingwood, Stuart dispatched a force of 1700 to capture four Ionian islands. Lord Liverpool, the war minister, approved Stuart's action if it protected Sicily better, but insisted that the islands' garrisons be reduced. In March 1810 Stuart was ordered to send four regiments to Gibraltar in exchange for three raw and sickly battalions, but he declined to obey the order. It was clear that Murat was preparing an invasion of Sicily. On remonstrating with London about the dangers Sicily was facing, not least the feared treachery of Ferdinand's queen and the court's refusal to allow him a unified command of British and Sicilians, Stuart was permitted to retain his regiments. He was told, however, that once the danger was past he must obey the original order.

Murat's abortive attempt at invasion took place on the night of 17 September. Thirty-five hundred French troops landed on the Sicilian coast 7 miles to the south of Messina. They were successfully repulsed by the British troops and Sicilian peasants. The major attack across the straits of Messina never took place as the French commanders, on Napoleon's orders, refused to run the risk of defeat. Though Murat removed the bulk of his forces Stuart felt sure the danger remained. Liverpool was unconvinced and renewed the order to send away troops. Stuart thereupon resigned on 16 October 1810. His resignation was accepted in April 1811. Despite his strained relations with the Sicilian court, the king offered him, on his departure, the order of knighthood of San Germano—an honour he decided to refuse, in view of the delicacy of his position.

Having returned to England Stuart was appointed lieutenant-governor of Grenada. On 10 June 1813 he was given command of the western district but resigned on grounds of ill health on 24 June 1814. He was an outspoken critic of flogging in the army. On 3 January 1815 he was made a military knight grand cross in the Order of the Bath. He died at Clifton on 1 April 1815 and was buried in the south aisle of Bristol Cathedral on the 13th. A small marble slab marks the spot. DESMOND GREGORY

Sources R. Cannon, ed., *Historical record of the twentieth, or the east Devonshire, regiment of foot* (1848) · J. G. Wilson and J. Fiske, eds., *Appleton's cyclopaedia of American biography*, 5 (1888), 730 · H. Bunbury, *Narratives of some passages in the great war with France (1799–1810)*, [new edn] (1927) · P. Mackesy, *The war for America, 1775–1783* (1964) · P. Mackesy, *The war in the Mediterranean, 1803–1810* (1957) · P. Mackesy, *British victory in Egypt, 1801: the end of Napoleon's conquest* (1995) · Fortescue, *Brit. army*, vols. 4–5, 7 · A. H. Burne, *The noble duke of York* (1949) · W. H. Flayhart III, *Counterpoint to Trafalgar: the Anglo Russian invasion of Naples, 1805–1806* (1992) · D. Gregory, *Sicily the insecure base: a history of the British occupation of Sicily, 1806–1815* (1988) · D. Gregory, *Napoleon's jailer: Lt Gen. Sir Hudson Lowe, a life* (1996) · R. Muir, *Britain and the defeat of Napoleon, 1807–1815* (1996) · M. Finley, *The most monstrous of wars: the Napoleonic guerrilla war in southern Italy, 1806–1811* (1994) · *The diary of Sir John Moore*, ed. J. F. Maurice, 2 (1904) · H. M. M. Acton, *The Bourbons of Naples, 1734–1825* (1956) · *Annual Register* (1806–15) · *GM*, 1st ser., 76–85 (1806–15) · J. Philippart, ed., *The royal military calendar*, 1 (1815) · J. H. O'Donnell

III, 'Stuart, John', *ANB* · *Old Westminsters* · P. J. Haythornthwaite, *The armies of Wellington* (1994) · *Army List* (1782–1815) · PRO, W01/308, 5–7

Archives BL, corresp. with Sir James Willoughby Gordon, Add. MS 49494, *passim* · BL, corresp. with Sir Hudson Lowe, Add. MSS 20107–20115, 20662–20891, *passim* · NL Scot., corresp. with Hugh Eliot · PRO, Foreign Office records, FO 20 · PRO, War Office records, WO 1 and WO 6

Likenesses A. Cardon, stipple, pubd 1806, BM, NPG · W. Wood, portrait

Stuart, John (1813–1877), archivist and genealogist, was born in November 1813 at Forgue, Aberdeenshire, where his father had a small farm. He was educated at Aberdeen University, and in 1836 became a member of the Aberdeen Society of Advocates. In 1853 he was appointed one of the official searchers of records in the Register House, Edinburgh, and in 1873 became principal keeper of the register of deeds at £400 p.a. In 1854 he was appointed secretary of the Society of Scottish Antiquaries, and from that time he became the guiding spirit of the association. In 1839, along with Joseph Robertson (1810–1866) and Cosmo Innes, he set on foot the Spalding Club, of which he acted as secretary until the close of its operations in 1870. Of the thirty-eight quarto volumes issued by the club, fourteen were produced under Stuart's editorship. Prominent among these were the two large folios entitled *The Sculptured Stones of Scotland*, published in 1856 and 1867, and important in their day. Another of the Spalding volumes was *The Book of Deer*, published in 1869, a reproduction by Stuart of a manuscript copy of the gospels which belonged to the abbey of Deer—of great historical and linguistic value, especially with regard to the Celtic history of Scotland. Among the other works which Stuart prepared for publication by the Spalding Club were the three volumes of *Miscellanies* published in 1841, 1842, and 1849; *Extracts from the Presbytery Book of Strathbogie, 1631–54*, published in 1843; *Extracts from the Council Register of Aberdeen, 1398–1625*, two volumes, issued in 1844–9; *Memorialls of the Trubles in Scotland and England from 1624 to 1645*, printed in 1850–51; and *Notices of the Spalding Club*, prepared in 1871 as a record of its labours. At the final meeting, on 23 December 1870, Stuart was presented by the club with a piece of plate and his portrait, the work of George Reid.

Stuart contributed largely to the *Transactions of the Society of Antiquaries of Scotland* (of which he was principal secretary), especially on the subject of Scottish crannogs. For the society he edited two volumes of ancient cartularies, entitled *Records of the Isle of May* (1868) and *Records of the Monastery of Kinloss* (1872).

Of Stuart's researches among old family records there remains the *Registrum de Panmure*, in two quarto volumes, printed by the earl of Dalhousie in 1874. At the instance of the historical records commission Stuart examined the charter chests of the Scottish nobility and furnished reports. Among the records at Dunrobin Castle he discovered the original dispensation for the marriage of Bothwell and Lady Jane Gordon. This find gave Stuart the opportunity of discussing, as he did in his volume, *A Lost Chapter in the History of Mary Queen of Scots* (1874), the law and practice of Scotland relating to marriage dispensations in Roman Catholic times.

For the Burgh Records Society Stuart edited two volumes of *Extracts from the Burgh Records of Aberdeen, 1625–1747*, and he also edited an edition of *Archaeological Essays of the Late Sir J. Y. Simpson* (1872). In 1866 the University of Aberdeen conferred on him the degree of LLD. He was elected an honorary member of the Archaeological Institute and of the Society of Antiquaries of Zürich and the Assemblea di Storia Patria in Palermo.

Stuart was twice married; no details about his first wife are known. He died at Crescent Villa, Ambleside, on 19 July 1877 and was survived by his second wife, Jane Stewart Ogilvie, and two daughters from his first marriage.

GEORGE STRONACH, *rev.* H. C. G. MATTHEW

Sources *The Scotsman* (21 July 1877) · Irving, *Scots.* · D. Stevenson and W. B. Stevenson, *Scottish texts and calendars* (1987) · *Proceedings of the Society of Antiquaries of Scotland*, 12 (1876–8), 362–4 · A. S. Bell, ed., *The Scottish antiquarian tradition* (1981) · *CCI* (1877) · d. cert.
Archives PRO, corresp. as an HMC inspector
Likenesses G. Reid, portrait, *c.*1870 · portrait, repro. in *Proceedings of the Society of Antiquaries of Scotland*, following p. 363
Wealth at death £13,014 0s. 10d.: probate, 27 Nov 1877, *CCI* · £4171 7s. 9d.: additional estate, 10 June 1878, *CCI*

Stuart, John Crichton-, second marquess of Bute (1793–1848), landowner and industrialist, was born on 10 August 1793 at Dumfries House, Ayrshire, the eldest son (there were no daughters) of John Stuart, Viscount Mountstuart (1767–1794), of Mountstuart House, Isle of Bute, and his wife, Elizabeth Penelope (1767–1797), the younger daughter of Patrick Macdowal Crichton, sixth earl of Dumfries. Lord Mountstuart, who predeceased his father, was the eldest of the eleven children of John Stuart, first marquess of Bute. The youngest John Stuart inherited the titles and the estates of his maternal grandfather on the death of the sixth earl of Dumfries in 1803 and those of his paternal grandfather on the death of the first marquess of Bute in 1814. On 26 August 1805 he took the arms and the name of Crichton.

Following the death of his mother in 1797, John Stuart (styled Viscount Mountstuart from his father's death) spent his boyhood in the various houses of his paternal grandfather. He was educated at Eton College and at Christ's College, Cambridge (MA, 1812), where he was strongly influenced by his tutor, John Kaye, later the bishop of Lincoln. Between 1809 and 1814 he travelled extensively, making the acquaintance of Madame de Staël, Louis Philippe, and Napoleon. On 29 July 1818, at St George, Hanover Square, London, he married Maria, daughter and coheir of George Augustus *North, third earl of Guilford [*see under* North, Frederick, second earl of Guilford]. Maria died childless on 11 September 1841. On 10 April 1845, at Loudoun Castle, Ayrshire, he married Sophia Frederica Christina (1809–1859), daughter of Francis Rawdon *Hastings, first marquess of Hastings, and his wife, Flora, *suo jure* countess of Loudoun. They had one son.

John Crichton-Stuart, second marquess of Bute (1793–1848), by Sir Henry Raeburn, exh. RA 1821

Bute's fame rests upon his achievements as a landowner. He owned over 100,000 acres; most of his property was situated in the counties of Bute, Ayr, and Wigtown, but he was also a major proprietor in Glamorgan, where the Cardiff Castle estate, originally granted in the sixteenth century to William Herbert, earl of Pembroke, had passed to his grandfather through marriage. He spent his adult life in a circuit of his estates, staying in turn at Mountstuart House, Dumfries House, Newcastle upon Tyne, Luton Hoo in Bedfordshire, and Cardiff Castle. (During the lifetime of his first wife he had also had estate responsibilities at Banbury in Oxfordshire and Kirtling in Cambridgeshire.) A passionate improver, his vast correspondence chronicles his attempts to develop his estates and to improve the lot of their inhabitants.

Bute's most significant contribution to estate development came in Glamorgan, where the Cardiff Castle estate included almost all the land of the ancient borough together with manorial rights over the valleys of the central part of the south Wales coalfield. He was the landlord of the Dowlais ironworks, in the 1840s the largest ironworks in the world, and his paltry returns from the Dowlais lease caused him to drive a hard bargain with those seeking the coal of his estate. As a result his son, John, third marquess of Bute, was by the late nineteenth century the largest individual receiver of mineral royalties in Britain. In order to prove the commercial value of his coal reserves in the Rhondda valley, the second marquess initiated steps to show that the steam coal of the valley lay at exploitable depths, an act which led to the astounding growth of the Rhondda.

Bute's main contribution to the development of the south Wales coalfield was his construction of a masonry dock at Cardiff; opened in 1839, it was the first of the five Bute docks, docks which would in the late-nineteenth century be handling more coal than any other port in the world. Cardiff, which in 1801 was twenty-fifth in size among the towns of Wales, expanded rapidly in the wake of the dock development, and the marquess paid assiduous attention to the layout of new streets and the design of frontages. By the 1870s Cardiff had become the largest town in Wales and the marquess was being hailed as its 'creator'.

An intensely dutiful, rather dour man, Bute was plagued by eye troubles and as a result he shunned fashionable society. He was a friend of Arthur Wellesley, first duke of Wellington, and his views on issues such as Catholic emancipation, parliamentary reform, and the corn laws closely mirrored those of the duke. An ardent champion of the established church, both English and Scottish, he was nevertheless a tireless advocate of the relief of the disabilities of the Jews.

Bute served as lord lieutenant of the counties of Glamorgan and Bute from 1815 until his death. He was also colonel of the Glamorgan militia and high steward of Banbury. His honours included FRS (1818), DCL (Oxford, 1834), LLD (Cambridge, 1835), FSA (1838), and KT (1843). He was high commissioner to the general assembly of the Church of Scotland in 1842–6, a period which coincided with the disruption crisis.

Bute died at Cardiff Castle on 18 March 1848 and was buried alongside his first wife at Kirtling in Cambridgeshire. He was succeeded as third marquess by his son, John Patrick Crichton-*Stuart (1847–1900).

JOHN DAVIES, *rev.*

Sources J. Davies, *Cardiff and the marquesses of Bute* (1981) • Boase, *Mod. Eng. biog.* • Burke, *Peerage* (1999) • GEC, *Peerage*, new edn **Archives** Beds. & Luton ARS, corresp. and papers mainly relating to estate business • Cardiff Central Library, corresp. and papers • Glamorgan RO, Cardiff • Mount Stuart, Isle of Bute, corresp. and papers • NL Wales, corresp. and papers | BL, corresp. with Sir Robert Peel, Add. MSS 40419–40567, *passim* • NL Scot., corresp. with John Lee • U. Southampton L., letters to first duke of Wellington **Likenesses** by or after J. Miers, bronzed silhouette in ink on plaster, 1809, Scot. NPG • H. Raeburn, portrait, exh. RA 1821, priv. coll. [*see illus.*] • A. R. Venables, portrait, 1852 • portrait, Cardiff Castle • portrait, Mountstuart House, Isle of Bute

Stuart, John Crichton-, fourth marquess of Bute (1881–1947), architectural patron and conservationist, was born at Chiswick House, Middlesex, on 20 June 1881, the eldest of the four children of John Patrick Crichton-*Stuart, third marquess of Bute (1847–1900), and his wife, Gwendolen Mary Anne Fitzalan-Howard (1854–1932). He attended

Harrow School for one term only, in 1897, but although he went to Oxford in 1901 to be privately tutored, he did not enter Christ Church as intended, as did his brothers Ninian and Colum. He was styled by the courtesy title earl of Dumfries until his succession to the marquessate in 1900, while still a minor. Interested in art and architecture as well as Scottish history, Bute travelled extensively and often alone in Asia and Africa before he married, on 6 July 1905, Augusta Mary Monica (1880–1947), the daughter of Sir Alan Henry Bellingham, fourth baronet; they had seven children. Although in poor health with a weak heart, he was the only peer to enlist as a private during the First World War, when he served with observation balloons. Like his father, Bute was a devout Roman Catholic; also like his father, he was a munificent builder and was actively concerned with the preservation of the historic buildings of Scotland.

When Bute came of age in 1902 he was able to resume several of the building projects interrupted by his father's death. He continued with the restoration of the Old Place of Mochrum, Wigtownshire, and work at Dumfries House, designed by Robert Adam, in both cases using his father's architect, Robert Weir Schultz—as he did on new projects of his own, notably St Andrew's chapel in Westminster Cathedral (1910–15). He also commissioned Roman Catholic churches in Troon and Rothesay from Reginald Fairlie and built hotels in Gibraltar and Tangier (as he had a particular affection for Morocco). In the 1930s he purchased and restored Acheson House in Edinburgh, Lamb's House in Leith, and Loudon Hall in Ayr. Angered by demolitions in Fife, he founded the Friends of Falkland to front his purchase of threatened buildings in the historic royal burgh. Bute was also instrumental in the restoration of Caerphilly Castle in Wales, and in 1938 sold most of his family's estate in Cardiff in one of the largest property transactions ever carried out in Britain.

In 1920, fearful of 'a bloody revolution or general strike' (letter to Lord Colum Crichton-Stuart, 28 May 1919, Mount Stuart Trust archives), Bute offered Mount Stuart, his Gothic revival seat on the Isle of Bute, for sale for re-erection elsewhere. While his father had been immersed in medievalism, the fourth marquess—possibly mindful of the house by Robert Adam at Luton owned by the prime minister Bute—developed a contrary taste for classical architecture and became concerned with the preservation of Georgian Edinburgh. Probably the last nobleman to own a town house in the city, in 1903 he bought 5 Charlotte Square, and subsequently he acquired and restored the neighbouring three houses in the grand terrace designed by Adam. His actions inspired the Edinburgh town planning (Charlotte Square) scheme order of 1930, and, as Ian Gow has concluded, 'it is impossible to underestimate the importance of Charlotte Square in the subsequent history of the Scottish Conservation Movement' (Gow, 98).

Bute supported the foundation of the National Trust for Scotland in 1931, and in 1936 the trust distributed as a pamphlet his speech condemning the demolition of old houses merely because they failed to meet current official standards. Bute was 'heart and soul in the developing movement of the time for the preservation of Scottish architecture and of Scottish history in stone' (*Glasgow Herald*, 26 April 1947) and instigated a survey for the Department of Health by the architect Ian Lindsay of old houses throughout Scotland. He was therefore the obvious choice in 1941 for chairman of the new Scottish records committee (now the National Monuments Record of Scotland), although when first invited by Lord Reith, minister of works, he responded that there was no point to the proposed record unless it had powers to protect historic buildings, as 'the average Scottish Local Authority posed a no less serious threat to ancient buildings than the *Luftwaffe*' (*National Monuments Record of Scotland Jubilee*, ix).

Bute was anxious to preserve the coastline of the Clyde estuary from development and was also interested in preserving the traditional crafts of Scotland. In 1912 he founded the Dovecot Studios of the Edinburgh Tapestry Company in fulfilment of a project first mooted by the third marquess. A shy man, retiring and secretive, the fourth marquess was a less flamboyant and conspicuous figure than his father; nevertheless, he was determined and effective, although 'it would be difficult to name all the minor works which he undertook, and … he worked so quietly, that much may never be known of what he did, for he often acted through others' (*Glasgow Herald*, 26 April 1947). Bute was made a knight of the Order of the Thistle in 1922. Like several members of his family, he died of cancer comparatively young, on 25 April 1947, after a long illness. He was buried in the Shore chapel at Mount Stuart.

GAVIN STAMP

Sources *Glasgow Herald* (26 April 1947) · *The Scotsman* (26 April 1947) · Mount Stuart Trust, Isle of Bute, Bute MSS · G. Stamp, *Robert Weir Schultz, architect, and his work for the marquess of Bute* (1981) · *National Monuments Record of Scotland jubilee: a guide to the collections* (1991) · personal knowledge (2004) · private information (2004) [Andrew McLean, archivist] · Burke, *Peerage* (1939) · J. W. Moir, *Harrow School register, 1885–1949* (1951) · I. Gow, 'Charlotte Square Buteified', *The architecture of Scottish cities: essays in honour of David Walker*, ed. D. Mays and D. Walker (1997)

Archives Mount Stuart Trust, Isle of Bute, archives | NL Scot., corresp. with William Skeoch Cumming

Likenesses portrait, *c*.1902, Mount Stuart House, Rothesay, Isle of Bute · S. Cumming, portrait, 1908, Mount Stuart House, Rothesay, Isle of Bute

Stuart, John Crichton-, sixth marquess of Bute (1933–1993), benefactor and patron of the arts, was born at 10 Charles Street, Mayfair, London, at 9.50 a.m. on 27 February 1933, fifteen minutes before his twin brother, David; they were the two eldest among the four children of John Crichton-Stuart, fifth marquess of Bute (1907–1956), and his wife, Lady Eileen Beatrice Forbes (1912–1993), younger daughter of Bernard Arthur William Patrick Hastings Forbes, eighth earl of Granard. As a member of a prominent Roman Catholic family, Lord Cardiff, as John was known before becoming earl of Dumfries on the death of John Crichton *Stuart, the fourth marquess, in 1947, was educated at Ampleforth College. After national service in the Scots Guards he went to Trinity College, Cambridge, where he read history and attended the Slade lectures in art history given by Nikolaus Pevsner. He succeeded to the marquessate on the death of his father in 1956 and was immediately faced with a heavy burden of death duties. One consequence of this was the sale of family property in Cardiff to the corporation and, in 1969, the transfer of the Robert Adam houses bought by his grandfather on the north side of Charlotte Square, Edinburgh, to the National Trust for Scotland: 6 Charlotte Square became the official residence of the secretary of state for Scotland.

In addition to serving on Bute county council and as lord lieutenant of Bute and, subsequently, of Argyll and Bute, and chairing several charities—all 'tasks befitting his station, rather than his character' (Drummond, 23)—John Bute contributed much to the artistic life of Scotland and towards preserving its artistic treasures. He did so first as chairman and then vice-president and president of the National Trust for Scotland after 1969, as a trustee of the National Galleries of Scotland (1980–87), and as chairman of the Historic Buildings Council for Scotland (1983–8). In all these and other roles he commanded respect by his assured mastery of the business in hand. Tam Dalyell observed that

> In the second half of the century, when the notion of public service is somehow going out of fashion, Bute was one of the aristocrats who stuck to the age-old tradition whereby those who inherited wealth believed that privilege brought with it responsibilities to the nation or local community. (The Independent, 22 July 1993)

Like his grandfather and his great-grandfather the third marquess, whom he resembled physically as well as in a certain dandyism in dress, Bute achieved much by stealth and through influence: 'If criticism were to be levelled, it would have to be that he played his cards very close to his chest, and did not always inform his committee members of the options before they were presented with a *fait accompli*' (The Independent, 22 July 1993). Conscious of his position and of his predecessors' work in both commissioning new architecture and in preserving historic buildings, he was unable himself to build on such a scale, although he loved architecture; nevertheless, he was able to patronize modern design in enterprises he supported, notably the Dovecot Studios of the Edinburgh Tapestry Company. This concern was also evident in the livery of his estates on Bute, in which he took a close and constructive interest, and in the industries he promoted on the island to attempt to stem the haemorrhage of its population. In 1992 he was made a fellow of the Royal Society of Edinburgh.

Although assured in his many public roles, Bute was withdrawn and essentially shy in private. In middle age he seemed melancholy and lonely, especially after the premature death of his twin brother and that of his beloved daughter Caroline in a road accident in 1984. He had married (Beatrice) Nicola Grace Weld-Forester (b. 1933), only daughter of Lieutenant-Commander W. B. C. Weld-Forester RN, on 19 April 1955 but this ended in divorce in 1977. On 12 November in the following year he married Jennifer Home-Rigg (b. 1933), a wine merchant, the former wife of Gerald Percy and the daughter of J. B. Home-Rigg of Plaston, South Africa, who brought him much happiness and encouraged him to restore and enhance Mount Stuart, the vast and lugubrious Gothic revival house on Bute designed by Sir Robert Rowand Anderson for his great-grandfather.

John Bute's last important contribution to the artistic life of Scotland was to chair the trustees of the National Museums of Scotland after 1985. In this role he was the guiding force behind the commissioning of the new building for the Museum of Scotland in Edinburgh; when the prince of Wales attempted to undermine the architectural competition because he disliked the winning design (by Benson and Forsyth), Bute ensured that the project proceeded regardless. At the laying of the foundation-stone in April 1993 Bute gave an 'excellent oration' despite being by then disfigured by cancer of the throat. Tam Dalyell recalled how, 'conversing with everybody afterwards, there was not a trace of self-pity. It was a courageous and supremely dignified curtain call' (The Independent, 22 July 1993). Bute died at Mount Stuart on 21 July 1993 and was buried at Shore Chapel there. His eldest son, John Colum Crichton-Stuart (b. 1961), succeeded to the marquessate.

GAVIN STAMP

Sources M. Drummond, ed., *John Bute: an informal portrait* (1996) · *The Independent* (22 July 1993) · *The Independent* (26 July 1993) · *The Times* (23 July 1993) · WWW · Burke, *Peerage* · b. cert. · m. cert. [Jennifer Home-Rigg] · d. cert.
Likenesses photograph, repro. in *The Independent* (22 July 1993) · photograph, repro. in *The Independent* (26 July 1993) · photograph, repro. in *The Times*

Stuart, John Ferdinand Smyth (1745–1814), army officer and author, claimed to be descended through both parents from James *Scott, the duke of Monmouth. According to his own doubtful statement, his father, Wentworth Smyth, was son of the duke and Lady Henrietta Maria, daughter of Thomas, Lord Wentworth. After Monmouth's execution, Wentworth Smyth is said to have been adopted by Colonel Smyth, Monmouth's aide-de-camp, who made him his heir. Wentworth Smyth took part in the Jacobite risings of 1715 and 1745, and was killed in the highlands at some later date. His reputed wife, Maria Julia Dalziel, who was said to be John Ferdinand's mother, was represented to be the granddaughter of General James Crofts, Monmouth's natural son.

John Ferdinand Smyth, who in 1793 adopted the name of Stuart, studied medicine at Edinburgh University. He then emigrated to America and settled near Williamsburg, Virginia, where he practised medicine. At the outbreak of the American War of Independence he was among the few loyalists in the area, and on 15 October 1775 he abandoned his home. He served in several loyalist regiments with the rank of captain, distinguishing himself, according to his own account, by his zeal and activity. He was taken prisoner on several occasions, and was once kept in irons for eighteen months. At the close of the war he moved to England with a compensatory pension of £300 p.a. In 1784, on some insinuations secretly made against him to the commissioners for American claims, his income was suspended and never restored. Extreme poverty resulted in his accepting the position of barrackmaster. He made strenuous representations to government, and in 1795 demanded justice from William Pitt peremptorily.

Smyth's *Tour in the United States of America* appeared in London in 1784. An account of his travels and military service in America, the work was well reviewed despite, or perhaps because of, his harsh critique of rural American society. Forever enchanted by the Jacobite cause, he also wrote *Destiny and Fortitude: an Heroic Poem on the Misfortunes of the House of Stuart* (1808), to which he attached his own family history.

In 1795 Smyth was persuaded to accompany Admiral Sir Hugh Cloberry Christian to the West Indies, where he was shipwrecked three times and was present at the capture of St Lucia. He later returned to England and was killed by a carriage at the corner of Southampton Street, London, on 20 December 1814. He was survived by his wife, two sons, and a daughter, details of whom are unknown.

E. I. CARLYLE, rev. TROY O. BICKHAM

Sources *The case of Ferdinand Smyth Stuart* (1807) · J. F. S. Stuart, *A letter to Lord Henry Petty on coercive vaccination* (1807) · J. F. S. Stuart, *Destiny and fortitude: an heroic poem on the misfortunes of the house of Stuart* (1808) · *N&Q*, 2nd ser., 8 (1859), 495 · *N&Q*, 2nd ser., 9 (1860), 232, 334

Stuart, John McDouall (1815–1866), land surveyor and explorer in Australia, was born in Rectory Lane, Dysart, Fife, on 7 September 1815, the fourth of the seven (possibly nine) children and third (or fifth) son of William Stuart, a customs officer and retired army captain, and his wife, Mary, *née* McDouall. Educated at Edinburgh, first privately and later at the Scottish Naval and Military Academy, he emigrated to South Australia, where he arrived in January 1839. Working first as a government and later as a private surveyor, he quickly acquired considerable skills as a bushman. On 12 August 1844 he joined Charles Sturt's expedition to explore central Australia and, following the death of James Poole, was appointed second in command. From this experience Stuart learned a great deal about travel in arid Australia and the difficulties of large cumbersome expeditions. Between 1846 and 1858 he practised land surveying and as a land agent surveyed runs and discovered new pastures for James Chambers, a horse breeder, pastoralist, and financier, and William Finke, who became the principal backers for all six of Stuart's expeditions into the interior.

The first of these (14 May – 16 August 1858) was a three-man expedition prospecting for new pasture country to the west of Lake Torrens and south of Lake Eyre, when Stuart found and named Chambers (now Stuart) Creek on the south-western side of Lake Eyre South. Stuart reported finding 40,000 square miles of new territory, of which around one-third, he claimed, suitable for grazing. His achievements were drawn to the attention of Sir Roderick Murchison, president of the Royal Geographical Society, by the governor of South Australia, Sir Richard MacDonnell. Stuart was rewarded when MacDonnell

named the Stuart range after him and gave him a rent-free lease of 1000 square miles around Chambers Creek.

Stuart next led a four-man expedition (2 April – 3 July 1859) north to discover and name Peake Creek and Neales River, draining into the western shore of northern Lake Eyre. This was followed almost immediately by a third expedition, which left Adelaide on 22 August. With a party of five, which included English-born William Kekwick, his faithful and resourceful second in command, Stuart spent the next five months surveying some 8000 square miles of pastoral prospects as well as looking for gold to the west of Lake Eyre. Sighting the lake's northern shore, he realized that a way was open to solve the mystery of the inland sea, fix the position of the centre of Australia (which Sturt had failed to do), and find a route for the proposed overland telegraph line connecting Australia to London via India.

With the way open, Stuart, Kekwick, and others left Chambers Creek on 2 March 1860, heading for the centre. They discovered and named the Finke River and the MacDonnell range before arriving on 21 April at the spot which Stuart considered to be the centre. After building a cairn and raising the 'British flag', the party pushed on until, on 26 June, 800 miles beyond Stuart's previous furthest, they were faced with Aboriginal hostility. Nearly starving, Stuart, suffering from scurvy and almost blind, ordered a retreat at Attack Creek, just north of Tennant Creek.

Stuart reached Adelaide on 7 October 1860 to find the South Australian government hurriedly organizing another attempt to cross the continent to beat the Victorian party led by Burke and Wills. Stuart's party consisted of Kekwick as second in command and ten others. Stuart's fifth expedition started from Chambers Creek on 1 January 1861 and crossed Attack Creek in April. However, by 12 July the party was so short-rationed and worn out that Stuart had again to retreat. On reaching Adelaide on 23 September 1861 he received the Royal Geographical Society's patron's medal, its highest award, for his previous exploits.

Stuart was almost immediately provided with a widely supported new expedition, with Kekwick as second in command, F. G. Waterhouse as government-appointed botanist, twelve men, and seventy-one horses. Although Stuart, by now a confirmed alcoholic and the second oldest and least fit, had the misfortune to have a horse break his hand, and was held up, the party left Chambers Creek on 8 January 1862, reached the centre on 12 March 1862, and, on 24 July, after bursting through a thick belt of scrub, arrived at the Indian Ocean at the mouth of what Stuart mistakenly thought was the Adelaide River. Consequent doubt as to whether Stuart had in fact crossed the continent remained until his marker was found at the mouth of the nearby Mary River in 1883.

After immense hardship, the abandonment of all but the bare essentials, and with Stuart suffering from scurvy, the party finally reached Adelaide on 17 December 1862. He was awarded £2000 (later increased by a further £1000), of which he was allowed only the interest, and his party

£1500 between them. Stuart later received a watch from the Royal Geographical Society.

With his health broken by the combined effects of alcohol and the privations of being almost constantly in the field from May 1858 to December 1862, Stuart left for England in April 1864. He died, unmarried, on 5 June 1866 in London at 9 Notting Hill Square. He was buried at Kensal Green cemetery on the 9th. Stuart was a superb bushman, capable of surviving and to a certain extent living off the land in Australia's arid and near waterless interior. His very considerable exploits are to be compared with those of such other practical surveyor-explorers as Augustus and Frank Gregory and Alec and John Forrest. His track to the north settled the route of the overland telegraph and his perhaps too favourable account of the country to the north did much to encourage the South Australian government in its successful bid for the incorporation of the Northern Territory. His modesty, indomitable spirit, determination, and practical achievements place him among the greatest of Australian explorers.

MARTYN WEBB

Sources M. S. Webster, *John McDouall Stuart* (1958) · I. Mudie, *The heroic journey of John McDouall Stuart* (1968) · E. H. J. Feeken, G. E. E. Feeken, and O. H. K. Spate, *The discovery and exploration of Australia* (1970) · G. McLaren, 'The development of the traditions of scientific research and bushmanship in nineteenth-century Australia', Ph.D. thesis, Curtin University of Technology, Western Australia, 1994 · *Explorations in Australia: the journals of John McDouall Stuart during the years 1858, 1859, 1860, 1861 & 1862 when he fixed the centre of the continent and successfully crossed it from sea to sea*, ed. W. Hardman (1865) · B. Treadgill, *South Australian land exploration, 1856 to 1880*, 2 vols. (1922) · A. Carter, *John McDouall Stuart: an annotated bibliography of works held in the library of the Royal Geographical Society of Australasia (South Australian branch) Inc. relating to John McDouall Stuart* (1991) **Archives** RGS, papers and journals relating to Australian exploration · State Library of South Australia, Adelaide **Likenesses** oils (after photograph), State Library of South Australia, Adelaide, Royal Geographical Society of Australasia (South Australia) library · portraits, State Library of South Australia, Adelaide, Royal Geographical Society of Australasia (South Australia) library · portraits, repro. in Mudie, *Heroic journey of John McDouall Stuart* · portraits, repro. in Webster, *John McDouall Stuart* · statue, town centre, Adelaide, Australia **Wealth at death** under £3000: probate, 22 June 1866, *CGPLA Eng. & Wales*

Stuart, John Patrick Crichton-, third marquess of Bute

(1847–1900), civic benefactor and patron of architecture, was born at Mount Stuart, Isle of Bute, Scotland, on 12 September 1847. He was the only child of John Crichton-*Stuart, second marquess (1793–1848), and his second wife, Sophia Frederica Christina (1809–1859), daughter of Francis *Hastings, first marquess of Hastings, and Flora, in her own right countess of Loudoun. His father died in 1848, and he was orphaned in 1859 by the death of his mother; he became a ward in chancery in 1861. He was educated at Harrow School and Christ Church, Oxford, where he matriculated in 1865. A man of scholarly interests from an early age, his guiding passion was his reverence for ancient institutions. The Presbyterian religion in which he had been brought up was one of

John Patrick Crichton-Stuart, third marquess of Bute (1847–1900), by Thomas Rodger [in the robes of rector of St Andrews University]

the first casualties of his medievalism. At Oxford he studied the forms of eastern and western Christianity, Judaism, Islam, and Buddhism, and shortly after reaching his majority, he was received into the Roman Catholic church at the chapel of the Sisters of Notre Dame, Southwark, on 8 December 1868. His conversion caused a great sensation, and the incident is believed to have inspired the plot of Disraeli's novel *Lothair*. His Catholicism was reinforced by his marriage on 16 April 1872 to the Hon. Gwendolen Mary Anne (1854–1932), eldest daughter of Edward Howard, first Baron Howard of Glossop [see Howard, Edward George Fitzalan-], from an old Catholic family. They had three sons and a daughter.

On coming of age Bute acquired control of his Scottish and Welsh estates, and the tremendous wealth which they generated. Under his ownership the Cardiff docks (which his father had begun building) were completed, contributing substantially to the prosperity of that city. He sought to re-establish the political dominance of his family in south Wales, but much authority had been lost during his long minority. His connections with the city were strong: he was twice mayor in the 1890s, and president of University College, Cardiff. He was proud of his Scottish heritage, and maintained a close identification with that country. His conviction of the superiority of ancient institutions led him to advocate home rule for Scotland, although in all other respects his political views were conservative. He wrote extensively on Scottish history and institutions, and became a benefactor of the universities of St Andrews and Glasgow, providing the former with a chair of anatomy, a medical hall, and a students' union building, and a hall of residence for the latter. He was twice elected rector of St Andrews University, serving in that office between 1892 and 1898.

Bute travelled extensively, particularly in the Middle East, and made a systematic study of the languages of the countries he visited. In 1882 he published a translation of the Coptic morning service, and in 1891 a study of the language of Tenerife. His greatest literary project, begun within two years of his conversion, was an English translation of a pre-Reformation breviary, published in 1879 in two volumes. He went on to translate the services for many of the major festivals, and was closely involved in the preparation of a *proprium sanctorum* for Scotland. He was greatly interested in all questions relating to liturgy, ritual, and church architecture. In addition to his own work, he was a great patron of scholars working on matters relating to the church, and many important texts, such as Sir William Fraser's edition of *Registrum monasterii S. Marie de Cambuskenneth, AD 1147–1535* (1872) and works on Irish saints, the Friars Preachers of Ayr, and the *Itinerary of Edward I* (1901) edited by Gough, were issued at his expense.

Above all, Bute was a great patron of architecture. His collaboration with William Burges in the rebuilding of Cardiff Castle and the recreation of Castell Coch provided two of the masterpieces of the Gothic revival. The intensity of the colours, the extent of the decorative detail, and the specially designed furnishings gave these distinctive buildings a lasting interest; the symbolic schemes which guided the decoration were devised by Bute, and put into effect by the architect, 'soul-inspiring Burges'. In the Gothic style Bute's medievalism and Catholicism found aesthetic expression. Mount Stuart on the Isle of Bute was rebuilt in Florentine style, after a disastrous fire in 1877, by Sir Robert Rowand Anderson under Bute's direction. His interest in building extended to archaeology and the restoration of ancient monuments: among other sites, he was responsible for the excavations of the houses of the Greyfriars and Blackfriars in Cardiff, and of Whithorn Priory in Galloway, and for carrying out restoration work at Rothesay and Falkland castles, and St Andrew's Priory, and for beginning the restoration of Caerphilly Castle.

In the 1890s, Bute developed an interest in spiritualism and the investigation of psychic phenomena; he subsidized an enquiry into second sight in the Scottish highlands conducted by Ada Goodrich-Freer, and, in 1899, with the same lady published a book concerning the alleged haunting of Ballechin House in Perthshire. He purchased the *Scottish Review*, and from 1882 until his death he contributed to it frequently, the range of his articles reflecting the variety of his interests, from 'Ancient Celtic Latin hymns' to 'The Bayreuth festival', from translations of Turgenev to 'Parliament in Scotland'. A natural scholar, Bute took little active part in the political life of the nation. His profound medievalism gave him a feudal outlook, while his sense of the duties of wealth and position was reinforced by his Catholicism.

In August 1899 Bute had an apoplectic attack, from which he in great measure recovered. The following October, while at his residence Dumfries House, he experienced another seizure, and died the following day, 9 October 1900. He was buried in the chapel at Mount Stuart, and, in accordance with his instructions, his heart was buried on the Mount of Olives at Jerusalem on 13 November 1900.   K. D. REYNOLDS

Sources GEC, *Peerage* · J. Davies, *Cardiff and the marquesses of Bute* (1981) · J. Davies, 'Aristocratic town makers and the coal metropolis: the marquesses of Bute and Cardiff, 1776–1947', *Patricians, power and politics in nineteenth-century towns*, ed. D. Cannadine (1982) · J. M. Crook, *William Burges and the high Victorian dream* (1981) · J. M. Crook, 'Patron extraordinary: John, marquess of Bute', *Victorian South Wales*, ed. P. Howell (1970) · *The Times* (11 Oct 1900)
Archives Cardiff Central Library · Glamorgan RO, Cardiff | BL, letters to W. E. Gladstone, Add. MSS 44511–44520 · CUL, letters to B. F. Westcott, Add. MSS 8316/1/16–45 · NL Scot., corresp. with Lord Rosebery
Likenesses H. von Herkomer, portrait, 1892, Cardiff Castle · E. T. Haynes, portrait, 1895, U. St Andr. · E. T. Haynes, portrait, 1898, Rothesay Town Council Chamber · W. G. Boss, drawing, Scot. NPG · T. Rodger, photograph, NPG [*see illus.*]
Wealth at death £1,142,246 10s. 4d.: c.1901, Scotland

Stuart, John Sobieski Stolberg [*real name* John Carter Allen] (1795?–1872), and **Charles Edward Stuart** [*real name* Charles Manning Allen] (1799?–1880), impostors, were brothers who claimed to be the heirs of Charles Edward Stuart, the Young Chevalier. Mystery surrounds the places and dates of their births, and they sought to surround their ancestry with similar obfuscation. Their father was Thomas Gatehouse Allen (*d.* 1839), a lieutenant in the Royal Navy, and their mother was Katherine Matilda, daughter of the clergyman and antiquary Owen *Manning, of Godalming, Surrey. Their pretensions were based on the belief that Thomas Gatehouse Allen was not the son of his supposed father, Admiral John Carter Allen, but was in fact the legitimate son of the Young Chevalier and his wife, born in Italy and fostered by the admiral.

There is no reliable account of the youth and education of the brothers; by their own account, they discovered the 'truth' of their birth in 1811, and promptly offered their services to Napoleon, fighting at Dresden and Leipzig in 1813, and again at Waterloo, where they claimed to have been personally decorated by Napoleon. The date of their first appearance in Scotland is unknown, but they were certainly there with their father in 1822 at the time of George IV's visit to Edinburgh. They threw themselves fervently into the acquisition of Scottish culture, and Scotticized their name first to Allan, then to Hay Allan, and then to Hay, encouraging the belief that they were related to the last Hay earl of Erroll. They gained the patronage of the earl of Moray, and spent much time in Darnaway Forest, where they became expert deer-hunters (the source of their 1848 volume, *The Lay of the Deer Forest, with Sketches of Olden and Modern Hunting*), and were frequent guests at the homes of many highland chiefs. In 1822 a volume of romantic poetry, *The Bridal of Caolchairn*, was published under the name of John Hay Allen. On 9 October 1822, Charles married Anna (1787–1862), daughter of the Hon. John Beresford, MP for co. Waterford, and widow of Charles Gardiner; they had a son and three daughters. John married, on 29 October 1845, Georgiana (*d.* 1888), eldest daughter of Edward Kendall of Cheltenham. They had no children; and, indeed, there is some doubt as to their ever having resided together.

In 1829, the brothers' careers entered a new phase, with the revelation to the antiquary and novelist Sir Thomas Dick Lauder of their possession of what purported to be a late fifteenth-century manuscript, entitled the *Vestiarium Scoticum, or, The Garde-Robe of Scotland*, depicting the clan tartans of Scottish families. They refused to show the 'original' of the manuscript (which, had it been genuine, would have lent substance to the claims then current as to the antiquity of the use of clan tartans), and it was dismissed by Sir Walter Scott as fraudulent. The brothers withdrew to Eilean Aigas, a hunting lodge on an island in the Beauly River in Inverness-shire, the grant of which they had obtained from their new patron, Lord Lovat. They declared themselves to be Roman Catholics and adopted the final version of their names, an unambiguous declaration of their belief in their Stuart ancestry and claims. They set up a miniature court on their island: Elizabeth Grant of Rothiemurchus recalled that 'for several years they actually *reigned* in the north country' (Strachey, 369).

In 1842, the brothers published their manuscript in a limited edition of fifty, and in 1844 produced another volume, *The Costume of the Clans*, which has been described as 'a monumental work', in which they set out to demonstrate that the Catholic, Celtic Scotland of the middle ages had been part of a sophisticated and rich culture; as Hugh Trevor-Roper has demonstrated, they saw themselves as living embodiments of the revival not just of highland dress, but of an entire, vanished civilization. *The Costume of the Clans* was a work of immense scholarship, drawing on a wide variety of disciplines and arcane sources; it was, none the less, 'shot through with pure fantasy and barefaced forgery' (Trevor-Roper, 36).

The brothers followed this publication with a volume of romantic short stories, *Tales of the Century, or, Sketches of the Romance of History between the Years 1746 and 1846* (1847), in which they made their most explicit claim to royal blood, through historical fictions which the reader was intended to read as thinly disguised historical facts. Far from having the desired effect, the pretensions of the brothers and their earlier work on the clans of Scotland were subjected to a devastating anonymous attack in the *Quarterly Review* (in fact written by Professor George Skene of Glasgow), which exposed the weaknesses, flaws, and fantasies of the *Vestiarium*. Despite the attempts at rebuttal by the brothers, their reputation and scholarship were compromised, and the household at Eilean Aigas finally broke up. The family moved to the continent, where they lived principally at Prague and Pressburg for the next twenty

years, and where their pretensions to royal blood continued to be entertained. In 1868, very poor but maintaining their illusions, the Stuarts returned to London, where they were well-known figures in the British Library reading rooms, where a table was reserved for them. Their pens, paper-knives, paperweights, and other paraphernalia were surmounted with miniature gold coronets.

John Sobieski Stuart, who had assumed the title of Count d'Albanie on the death of his father in 1839, died at 52 Stanley Street, Hanover Square, London, on 13 February 1872. His brother then assumed the Albanie title, and continued to defend the family claims, dying on board the steamer *Rainbow* at Pauillac, near Bordeaux, on 25 December 1880. Of Charles Stuart's children, the son, Charles Edward Lewis Casimir (1824–1882), served in the Austrian cavalry and married Lady Alice Hay, youngest daughter of the seventeenth earl of Erroll, and died without children. Of the daughters, the eldest, Marie (1823–1873), died unmarried; Louisa Sobieska (1827?–1897) married Edouard von Platt of the Austrian imperial bodyguard and had a son; Clementina (1830?–1894) became a Passionist nun and died at a convent at Bolton, Lancashire. The Stuarts also had a sister, Catherine, who married Count Charles Ferdinand de Lancastro, and whose only son (also Charles Ferdinand), served in Mexico with the Austrian army, but died in London in 1873. The claims to direct male descent from the Young Chevalier thus ended with the death of Charles Edward Lewis Casimir Stuart in 1882.   K. D. REYNOLDS

Sources H. Trevor-Roper, 'The invention of tradition: the highland tradition of Scotland', in E. Hobsbawn and T. Ranger, *The invention of tradition* (1983) · review, QR, 81 (1847), 57–85 · N&Q, 5th ser., 8 (1877), 92 · *Memoirs of a highland lady: the autobiography of Elizabeth Grant of Rothiemurchus*, ed. J. M. Strachey (1898) · DNB · Burke, *Peerage* · CGPLA Eng. & Wales (1881) [Charles Edward Stuart]
Archives NL Scot., corresp. and papers | NL Scot., letters to Blackwoods; letters to Robert Chambers
Likenesses W. C. Ross, portrait, Beaufort Castle
Wealth at death under £2000—Charles Edward Stuart: Scottish certificate on English probate, 24 Jan 1881, CCI

Stuart, Sir John Theodosius Burnett- (1875–1958), army officer, was born in Cirencester on 14 March 1875, the eldest of the four sons of Eustace Robertson Burnett-Stuart, a soldier, of Dens and Crichie, Aberdeenshire, and his wife, Carlotta Jane, daughter of J. Lambert of Cottingham, Yorkshire. He was educated at Repton School and at the Royal Military College, Sandhurst. He was commissioned in the rifle brigade in 1895 and served with the Tochi field force on the north-west frontier of India (1897–8). He subsequently served in the Second South African War (1899–1902), where he was mentioned in dispatches and was awarded the DSO. Promoted captain, Burnett-Stuart served with the 4th battalion of his regiment in Egypt. He graduated from the staff college in 1904 and was posted to the War Office in the directorate of military operations. In the same year he married Nina, only daughter of Major A. A. C. Hibbert Nelson; they had one son and two daughters. In 1910 he was seconded to the New Zealand military forces as director of organization but two years later returned to Britain as instructor GSO2 at Staff College, Camberley.

During the First World War, Jock Stuart, the name by which Burnett-Stuart was familiarly known, held several staff appointments. He was promoted brigadier-general and made brigadier-general, general staff, of 7th corps under Sir Thomas Snow in February 1916. In the final two years of the war Burnett-Stuart gained a reputation as a talented military strategist and a progressive. In the battle of Cambrai in November 1917 the 7th corps was on the flank of the main attack and played no part in the assault. Burnett-Stuart warned that a German counter-offensive was being mounted, but his warnings were ignored. Thus the German counterstroke penetrated deep into the sector held by the 7th corps, but was eventually halted. A month later Burnett-Stuart was promoted major-general and made deputy adjutant-general at general headquarters, a post he held until the end of the war. Before the war ended he demonstrated his vision of a modern fighting force by supporting the army's director of training, Major-General Sir Charles Bonham-Carter, in his drive to ensure that British soldiers were physically fit enough to take part in a modern war.

In 1920 Burnett-Stuart was sent to India to command the Madras district and was in charge of suppressing the Malabar rising of 1921. Two years later he returned to Britain to be director of military operations and intelligence in the War Office. In 1926 he was given command of the 3rd division in the southern command, with A. P. (later Earl) Wavell as his GSO1. The following year Burnett-Stuart was appointed director of the first experimental mechanized force, which was assembled on Salisbury Plain. He pointed out that the infantry would not be capable of keeping pace with the rest of the force in battle unless they were mounted in armoured cross-country vehicles. During the First World War Burnett-Stuart had been sceptical about the use of tanks, but during the early 1920s he changed his mind. He urged the War Office to allow the appointment of men with modern mechanical expertise to assist him. He wanted 'enthusiastic experts and visionaries' (*DNB*) to aid him. One such was Colonel J. F. C. Fuller, chosen to command the new force, who was the outstanding advocate of the need for a highly mobile, mechanized army. However, after exercises in 1928, a decision was taken to disband the armoured force in order to concentrate on the mechanization of infantry and cavalry units.

From 1931 to 1934 Burnett-Stuart commanded the British troops in Egypt and there began to advocate the possible use of mechanized forces in desert warfare. He was promoted general in 1934 and returned to the southern command (holding that post until April 1938). He was horrified to find how bad the condition of the army was on his return from Egypt: 'the ranks are more depleted than ever, the equipment and armament practically unchanged' (Bond, 53). At this time he became the outstanding advocate of a policy of 'limited liability' towards a military commitment to the continent, and was scornful of the capacity of a British expeditionary force to play an effective role in a European war. The proper purpose of the army, he argued, was to guard the empire and form an imperial reserve. Burnett-Stuart 'boldly and perhaps recklessly as far as his own career was concerned, disseminated these views among his fellow-officers'. He also made them public in several letters to *The Times* in November 1938 (Bond, 216).

In 1936 Burnett-Stuart was considered as a successor to Sir Archibald Montgomery-Massingberd as chief of the Imperial General Staff, but he had clashed too often with the latter and was passed over. Although his military career finally stalled, Burnett-Stuart was a colourful figure. In 1936 he admitted that he did not enjoy peacetime soldiering very much: 'what I really like is poetry and shooting partridges, and heraldry, and dry fly fishing' (Bond, 53). In a perceptive but critical assessment published in 1971, B. H. Liddell Hart noted that he was 'a man of sparkling mind, lively imagination, and long if variable vision. He had an impish turn of mind, which handicapped his career but which, together with his informality of manner, made him beloved by his subordinates' (*DNB*). Burnett-Stuart was appointed CB (1917), KCB (1932), and GCB (1937), CMG (1916) and KBE (1923). He died at his home, Avington Park near Winchester, on 6 October 1958, and was buried there on 11 October 1958. Recent studies have demonstrated that, although a fine soldier and a perceptive advocate of the use of armoured forces, Burnett-Stuart possessed a curious mixture of progressive and reactionary traits. He was undoubtedly frustrated by the conservatism of senior officers and the scaling down of Britain's military capability. The paradox was that although he and Liddell Hart 'were prophetically perceptive in pressing for a highly mobile, mechanised Army', they nevertheless 'opposed the European commitment which alone could have justified the creation of such an élite force' (Bond, 338).   GAYNOR JOHNSON

Sources H. R. Winton, *To change an army: General Sir John Burnett-Stuart and British armoured doctrine, 1927–1938* (1988) · B. Bond, *British military policy between the two world wars* (1980) · S. P. Mackenzie, *Citizenship education in the British army, 1914–1950* (1992) · B. Holden Reid, *Studies in British military thought: debates with Fuller and Liddell Hart* (1998) · B. H. Liddell Hart, *The memoirs of Captain Liddell Hart*, 1 (1965) · M. Howard, ed., *The theory and practice of war* (1965) · B. H. Liddell Hart, *The tanks: the history of the royal tank regiment and its predecessors*, 1 (1959) · *The Times* (7 Oct 1958)
Archives King's Lond., Liddell Hart C., papers · NRA, priv. coll., papers relating to work in Madras and Egypt · priv. coll., papers | King's Lond., Liddell Hart C., corresp. with Sir B. H. Liddell Hart
Likenesses W. Stoneman, photograph, 1920, NPG · D. Styles, portrait, priv. coll.
Wealth at death £10,662 3s. 5d.: confirmation, 11 May 1959, *CCI*

Stuart [*née* Howard], **Katherine**, **Lady Aubigny** [*other married name* Katherine Livingston, Viscountess Newburgh] (*d.* **1650**), conspirator, was the daughter of Theophilus *Howard, second earl of Suffolk (1584–1640), and Lady Elizabeth Home (*c.*1599–1633), daughter of George Home, earl of Dunbar. Nothing is known of her early years or education. In May 1638 she married secretly Lord George Stuart, ninth seigneur d'Aubigny (1618–1642), fourth son of Esmé Stuart, third duke of Lennox (1579?–1624), and brother of James Stuart, fourth duke of Lennox and first

Katherine Stuart, Lady Aubigny (d. 1650), by Sir Anthony Van Dyck, c.1638

duke of Richmond (1612–1655), the close confidant of Charles I. The marriage was against the wishes of her parents and of the king, who was guardian to the Stuart brothers; it is commemorated in a sumptuous Van Dyck portrait of Lord Aubigny (now in the National Portrait Gallery), with the motto, 'Love is stronger than I am'. The couple had a son, Charles *Stuart (1639–1672), later sixth duke of Lennox and third duke of Richmond, and a daughter, Katherine, was also born before the civil war.

George Stuart was killed at the battle of Edgehill in October 1642, and his young widow became a noted member of the royal court at Oxford. In May 1643 she took advantage of permission granted her by parliament to come to London to deal with her husband's affairs, and was entrusted with a commission of array signed by the king in March which aimed at raising forces among royalist sympathizers in the city. This plot, known as the Waller plot after the poet Edmund Waller, another intermediary between Oxford and London, was betrayed, and some of the obscurer figures involved were hanged by parliament. Lady Aubigny claimed the protection of the French ambassador, by virtue of her husband's French title, but was none the less imprisoned in the Tower for some months. By May 1645 she was in Bristol, from where she wrote a sad letter to Lord Digby, asking him to help her in the king's favour. In the summer of 1647 the House of Lords dealt on several occasions with the claims of Katherine and her children by Aubigny to various customs farms granted by James I to the younger sons of Esmé, third duke of Lennox. Perhaps through the influence of her brother

James *Howard, third earl of Suffolk, a presbyterian peer, extensive rights were confirmed to Katherine.

By late 1648 Katherine had married her second husband, the Scottish gentleman of the bedchamber to the king James *Livingston, Viscount Newburgh (1621/2–1670). In December 1648 Charles I spent a night at the Newburghs' house in Bagshot, Surrey, on his way from the Isle of Wight to Windsor, and the couple seem to have made some attempt to secure the king's escape. Their plans were foiled by the precautions of Major-General Thomas Harrison, but they were able to pass messages from Charles to his exiled queen. It is intriguing that the rights of Katherine and her Stuart children inherited from Esmé, third duke of Lennox, were still being sympathetically considered by parliament's revenue committee in mid-January 1649. Perhaps some on the parliament side would have welcomed the king's escape. However, following the regicide the Newburghs joined other royalist exiles at The Hague, where Katherine attempted to mediate between the Scottish connections of both her husbands and English councillors such as Edward Hyde. She died at The Hague in 1650 and was survived by her husband, who was created earl of Newburgh in 1660, and their daughter Elizabeth; her son Charles from her first marriage succeeded his cousin Esmé Stuart as sixth duke of Lennox and third duke of Richmond in 1660.

Katherine's death was a blow to the royalist cause. Hyde's affection for this inveterate intriguer is evident in his History of the Rebellion: 'a woman of a very great wit, and most trusted and conversant in those intrigues which at that time could be best managed and carried on by ladies' (Clarendon, Hist. rebellion, 5.19–20). On the other hand, the alarm which she (and perhaps all female conspirators) aroused in the parliament is revealed in a broadside recording parliament's 'Miraculous preservations' from 'manifold plots, conspiracies, contrivances and attempts of forraigne and homebred treacherous enemies', which has a full-length portrait of Lady Aubigny (holding the infamous commission of array) surrounded by smaller pictures of Strafford, Digby, Rupert, and Montrose.

ANN HUGHES

Sources Clarendon, Hist. rebellion · DNB [Stuart, Esmé; Stuart, Lord Bernard; Howard, Theophilus; Stuart, James, fourth duke of Lennox and first duke of Richmond] · C. V. Wedgwood, The trial of Charles I (1964) · England's monument of mercies (1646) [includes a portrait] · JHL, 4–10 (1628–48) · CSP dom., addenda, 1625–49 · letter to earl of Digby, BL, Sloane MS 1519, fol. 86 · order of the revenue committee, Bodl. Oxf., MS Nalson 15, fol. 291 · S. R. Gardiner, History of the great civil war, 1642–1649, new edn, 1 (1893) · IGI · C. V. Wedgwood, The king's war, 1641–1647 (1958) · GEC, Peerage, new edn, 9.511–14; 12/1.466–7
Likenesses A. Van Dyck, portrait, c.1638, National Gallery of Art, Washington DC [see illus.] · woodcut, repro. in England's monument of mercies

Stuart, Leslie. See Barrett, Thomas Augustine (1863?–1928).

Stuart, Louisa. See Louisa, styled countess of Albany (1752–1824).

Stuart, Lady Louisa (1757–1851), author, was born on 12 August 1757, the youngest of the eleven children of George III's prime minister, John Stuart, third earl of Bute (1713–1792). Her mother, Mary (1718–1794), to whom she was greatly attached, was the daughter of Edward Wortley Montagu of Wortley and his wife, Lady Mary Wortley *Montagu. The presence of this grandmother was a notable element in her rich dynastic background, with its royal blood and its interlocking Stuarts, Scotts, and Campbells, but a 'tainted' one too, as she confided in a letter (*Letters … to Miss Louisa Clinton*, 2.354). No such suggestion figures in her important 'Introductory anecdotes', concerning Lady Mary, which was published anonymously in 1837. By the age of ten she had begun to take after her grandmother, having embarked upon a French novel and planned a Roman play, and she was to feel threatened by brothers who teased her for her sensibility and learning. 'Such are men', she once sighed, with reference to the brother of her closest female friend, Frances Scott, eventually Lady Douglas (Miller, 29). Louisa's own brothers included John *Stuart, first marquess of Bute, Sir Charles *Stuart (1753–1801), and William *Stuart, archbishop of Armagh.

In 1763 Lady Louisa's father retired from a bruising experience of political life to the grandeur and seclusion of Luton Hoo and the pursuit of botany. He is understood to have forbidden her marriage to a second cousin, the distinguished soldier William Medows, who campaigned against Tipu Sultan in the Carnatic and took part in the seizure of Seringapatam. She was thought to have worn mourning clothes at his death in 1813.

Lady Louisa Stuart was a gifted writer who hoped, for reasons of caste, never to see her name in print, and it was not until the 1890s that writings of hers were published under her name. Her memoirs and letters are addressed in the main to women—friends and relatives. One of her correspondents was Walter Scott, who, while no immediate relation to these Scotts of Dalkeith Palace, nevertheless saw himself as feudally bound to their dukes of Buccleuch. Scott valued her taste and talent, together with her far descent (Lockhart's *Life of Scott* contains several of her letters). Conscious of his poetry, and of that of Pope and Samuel Johnson, she wrote a number of poems of her own—among them elegant, sententious fables, and a ballad about cannibal brothers and an ill-starred woman who marries for money.

Stuart's accounts of Lady Douglas and of Lady Mary Coke are magnificent pieces of writing. The first is an evocation of her friend—a granddaughter of John, second duke of Argyll, and a pattern of afflicted virtue. Frances had to suffer the aversion of her mother, Lady Dalkeith, and was to be shielded from it by her mother's second husband, the brilliant and unstable politician Charles Townsend, whose customs duties hastened the loss of the American colonies. George III (Miller, 42) was said to have thought him the worst man in the world. Stuart sees him in a sympathetic light, while relating that a dangerous intimacy developed between Frances and her stepfather,

and that she had to flee the stressful south of England for the palace of Dalkeith in order to marry her 'safe man' (ibid., 38), in the person of Archibald, Lord Douglas, the claimant in the celebrated lawsuit over the right to the Douglas estates.

The memoir of Lady Mary Coke, dated 1827, also presents—this time in comic vein—a pattern of afflicted virtue. She is seen as a tragedy queen, as a woman subject to paranoid delusions, but as also subject to house arrest at the hands of a brutal husband. Later she was to suffer the imaginary machinations of the empress Maria Theresa; she believed herself, reported Horace Walpole, to have been robbed of a passage by sea from Ostend to England by a codicil in the empress queen's will. Lady Mary was her own woman:

> The dry rot that broke out in her house was totally different in its nature from the dry-rot at her next neighbour's; and in case of a cold, or a sore throat, woe to the apothecary who ventured to quicken her pulse and excite her ire by tendering that established consolation, 'It is going about, madam, I assure you; I suppose I have now twenty patients with just the same symptoms as your ladyship's.'
> (*Selections*, 60)

She was also a survivor. Those who 'fairly love a grievance', Stuart writes, may be able to support real evils better than imaginary ones. 'As heroic sufferers they are in their proper element' (*Selections*, 64).

Stuart is a writer who is able to produce a compelling aphorism—'the injurer never forgives'—while also, in mid-passage, casting doubt on it (*Lady Mary Wortley Montagu: Essays*, 56). 'Most people addicted to romancing', she declared, 'are their own heroes'. Like Walter Scott, she was herself capable of romancing, while remaining a disapprover of the addiction. A 'leaning towards the romantic' is linked with possession of 'wit, genius or imagination' (Stuart, *Memoire of Lady Douglas*, 37, 56). The loss of the man she might have married is likely to have affected her own romantic leanings and yearnings, this shrewd woman's castles in the air. Her shrewdness is disclosed in the ability to contradict herself to interesting effect, and she can sometimes appear to believe in a spirit of contradiction inherent in the order of things. Her inconsistencies include a fidelity to the old order in matters of politics and government, and an aversion to the mob, accompanied by a regard for unadorned human worth, which could make her resistant to family pride and anxious about Sir Walter's regard for rank and lineage. A chronicler of the patrician bluestockings of her time, she was both for and against the emancipation of women.

Stuart was to settle at 108 Gloucester Place, Marylebone, from which she would go rambling round Regent's Park. She spoke in 1837 of the 'quiet hole' in which she had spent her days (*Lady Mary Wortley Montagu: Essays*, 55), but can be accounted a highly sociable recluse. There she sat in her studious closet, bent over her books, deploring the Reform Bill, listening to the excitements and unreason of a bellowing John Bull, writing about her Lady Marys, and destroying, it was said, many of her manuscripts. But her days were also spent counselling, conversing, corresponding, and on progresses from one great house to another. She is the least-known, but by no means the least, of the good writers of her long lifetime. She died unmarried at the age of ninety-four on 4 August 1851 at her London home.   KARL MILLER

Sources L. Stuart, *Memoire of Frances, Lady Douglas*, ed. J. Rubenstein (1985) · L. Stuart, 'Introductory anecdotes', in *The letters and works of Lady Mary Wortley Montagu*, ed. Lord Wharncliffe, rev. edn, with a memoir by W. M. Thomas, 2 vols. (1887) · L. Stuart, 'Anecdotes', in *Lady Mary Wortley Montagu: essays and poems and 'Simplicity: a comedy'*, ed. R. Halsband and I. Grundy (1977) · Mrs G. Clark, ed., *Gleanings from an old portfolio*, 3 vols. (1895–8) · *Lady Louisa Stuart: selections from her manuscripts*, ed. J. Home (1899) · *Letters of Lady Louisa Stuart to Miss Louisa Clinton*, ed. J. Home, 2 vols. (1901–3) · *A prime minister and his son: from the correspondence of the 3rd earl of Bute and of Lt-General the Hon. Sir Charles Stuart*, ed. Mrs E. S. Wortley (1925) · *The letters of Lady Louisa Stuart*, ed. R. B. Johnson (1926) · *Notes by Lady Louisa Stuart on 'George Selwyn and his contemporaries' by John Heneage Jesse*, ed. W. S. Lewis (1928) · S. Buchan, *Lady Louisa Stuart: her memories and portraits* (1932) · K. Miller, *Authors* (1989)
Archives Bodl. Oxf., corresp. and papers · NRA, priv. coll. | NL Scot., corresp. with Sir Walter Scott
Likenesses Zoffany, double portrait, 1770 (with her sisters), repro. in Miller, *Authors*, cover · J. Hayter, chalk sketch, 1837, priv. coll. · G. Hayter, oil sketch, 1851; formerly priv. coll. · Mrs Mee, portrait (as a young woman), repro. in Home, ed., *Lady Louisa Stuart: selections*

Stuart [Stewart], **Ludovick, second duke of Lennox and duke of Richmond** (1574–1624), courtier, was born in France on 29 September 1574, the eldest son of Esmé *Stuart, sixth seigneur d'Aubigny and first duke of Lennox (c.1542–1583), and his wife, Catherine de Balsac d'Entragues (d. c.1631). He spent his early years in France but shortly after the death of his father on 26 May 1583 he was summoned to Scotland by his cousin James VI. Having surrendered his seigneurie of Aubigny to his younger brother Esmé *Stuart (1579?–1624), he was on 31 July confirmed by the king in his father's titles of duke of Lennox and Earl Darnley and in his offices and estates. As a symbolic gesture, acknowledging Lennox's place in the Scottish succession as heir to the throne (a position disputed by the Hamilton family, especially in the later 1580s), the duke carried the crown to the opening session of the parliament of May 1584; he bore it again at the opening of the 1587 parliament. The duke was placed in the care of John Graham, third earl of Montrose, and the king showed a continued interest in his education by appointing the well-regarded Dr Gilbert Moncrieff as his tutor.

Lennox continued to receive regular demonstrations of royal favour: in November 1583 he was made a gentleman of the bedchamber and great chamberlain for life; in July 1583 he received the lordships of Dalkeith (formerly belonging to Regent Morton), Methven, and Balquidder along with the teinds of the archbishopric of Glasgow (administered by his great-uncle Robert *Stewart, earl of March and, formerly, earl of Lennox (1522/3–1586)); and on 21 August 1586 he was granted the priory of St Andrews *in commendam*. In 1589 Lennox was considered 'a chyld of age, yet for his yeres wyese and wary, yea wyly' (*CSP Scot.*, vol. 10, no. 311). In spite of his youth, the duke began to

Ludovick Stuart, second duke of Lennox and duke of Richmond (1574–1624), by Paul van Somer, c.1620

engage in political affairs—as a privy councillor, and along with most of the rest of the Scottish nobility, he was granted a commission to pursue Jesuits and Catholics during the height of the Armada crisis in July 1588 and a number of days later he was given specific responsibility for guarding Dumbarton Castle and the Clyde approaches. Lennox was closely allied to the court party of George Gordon, sixth earl of Huntly, throughout the 1580s, but in 1589 he was active in support of the king against the Brig o' Dee rebels. From October of that year, when James VI was absent from Scotland for a period of eight months to get married, Lennox acted as governor of the kingdom and president of the privy council, with the assistance of Francis Stewart, first earl of Bothwell, in Edinburgh and John Hamilton (subsequently marquess of Hamilton) on the border. The period of Lennox's governorship was notably peaceful with little disruption on the border and a conscious governmental effort to settle ongoing feuds between fractious noblemen, such as the northern earls of Moray and Huntly. On 20 April 1591 Lennox married Lady Sophia (d. 1592), daughter of William *Ruthven, first earl of Gowrie (c.1543–1584), with whom he had been having secret relations for some time: the day before the wedding, Lennox had forcibly removed Sophia from the protective custody of Wemyss Castle where she had been placed by James VI—to the king's annoyance. The marriage was brief and childless.

Lennox's relations with his Stewart kin were complicated. He had been a willing part of a corporeal 'Stewart faction' formed during the king's absence in 1590 and had allied with Bothwell and John Stewart, earl of Atholl, in actions against the chancellor, John Maitland of Thirlestane, with whom he was regularly at odds. Above all, however, Lennox was loyal to his monarch and consequently returned to the king's chamber more swiftly than other members of the nobility during disputes. Lennox was credited as having the greatest influence over the king of any of the nobility, to the extent that a number of English agents attempted to discredit him or counteract his influence.

As chamberlain, Lennox was closely involved in court function and ceremonial and in May 1590 was at the forefront of the celebrations surrounding Queen Anne's arrival in Scotland and her coronation and ceremonial entry into the Scottish capital. In June 1590, less than two months after the king's return to Scotland, Lennox's growing stature was recognized when he replaced Francis, earl of Bothwell, as first gentleman of the bedchamber—much to the frustration of the older man. Lennox benefited greatly from the disgrace of Bothwell (especially following allegations of the earl's involvement in witchcraft at North Berwick in April 1591), receiving the office of high admiral and large estates on the border and in Lothian. He also secured valuable links within the court after the marriage of two of his sisters to prominent noblemen, Henrietta to George Gordon, sixth earl of Huntly (1588), and Marie to John Erskine, eighteenth or second earl of Mar (1592), although the proposed marriage of his third sister, Gabrielle, to Hugh Montgomerie, fifth earl of Eglinton (1598), did not take place and she retired to a French nunnery at Glatigny.

Lennox's former associations with the disgraced Bothwell soon led to allegations that the duke was collaborating with his kinsman, and was merely administering the earl's extensive estates on behalf of Francis Stewart's family. Although denied, these allegations resurfaced in the aftermath of the murder of James Stewart, earl of Moray, in February 1592, which Lennox was eager to avenge. Politically, Lennox found it expedient to re-associate himself with the Stewart faction and he was more willing to favour Bothwell openly. He obtained a grant of the ward of the young James Stewart, third earl of Moray (the murdered earl's son), and in June 1593 Bothwell was able to gain access to King James at Holyrood through the duke's stables. Along with the earls of Atholl and Mar and Alexander Lindsay, first Lord Spynie, Lennox interceded with the monarch to effect Bothwell's recovery of favour. Aware of James's unhappiness, however, Lennox again was one of the first to desert the earl and return to his monarch's side.

Lennox was active at James's side during the armed expedition against the rebel northern lords that followed the battle of Glenlivet in 1594. After the king returned south, Lennox was given a commission of lieutenancy over the north of Scotland to ensure its continuing quiet and was able to persuade Huntly and Erroll to leave Scotland for voluntary exile; he was also largely credited with persuading the king to demonstrate a lenient attitude to Huntly and his companions. The duke was granted the administration of the rebel earl's estates but, as formerly, he permitted the wives of the exiled lords to enjoy the profits of their lands. On 7 July 1598 he was given a lieutenancy over the island of Lewis and on 9 July 1599 this was extended to the whole highlands and islands. The highland west was the focus of Lennox's territorial holdings and this led to heated confrontations with the earls of Argyll and Mar in 1601 over the participation of Scottish troops in Irish warfare.

In 1598, probably on 3 September, Lennox had married Jean (d. 1610), daughter of Sir Mathew Campbell of Loudon and widow of Robert Montgomerie, master of Eglinton. The duke and duchess of Lennox had two children—a boy (d. 1602x7) and a girl, Lady Elizabeth (d. 1607x24)—but were not suited to each other. By 1605 Lennox wished to divorce his wife and in September 1607 she was declared a rebel at the duke's petition for keeping his daughter from him and for mistreating her.

As an accomplished horseman, Lennox was a regular hunting companion of the king and in 1594, at the baptism celebrations for Prince Henry Frederick, was accomplished enough to win the prize for running at the ring and glove. He was present on a hunt with James when the king heard of the events that culminated in the Gowrie conspiracy of August 1600, and was active in backing his monarch against his former brother-in-law John Ruthven, third earl of Gowrie, who died during the confrontation. On 1 July 1601 he was sent as ambassador to France, ostensibly to renew the auld alliance, which had been in abeyance since 1560. Owing to Henri IV's opposition to this, Lennox was unsuccessful but on his return journey to Scotland he visited the English court, where he was entertained by Elizabeth for three weeks according to his position as the only non-royal duke in either Scotland or England at this time.

Lennox next returned to England in April 1603, in the company of James VI upon his accession to the English throne. The duke was appointed to the English privy council and was created first gentleman of the king's English bedchamber before James even reached his new capital. Although for the remainder of his life he was based at the English court, he rarely attended the privy council and, increasingly, his offices were more honorific than functional. Shortly after James's entry to London, Lennox returned to Scotland to remove Prince Henry Frederick from the care of the earl of Mar and place him in the care of Queen Anne, prior to their journey south to London. On 18 June 1603 he was naturalized as an English citizen, and on 23 July he was installed with Prince Henry and Mar as a knight of the Garter.

Lennox continued to accumulate honours in England: on 6 August he was granted the manors of Settrington, Temple-Newsam, and Wensleydale in Yorkshire along with a pension of £600 a year. These lands had been part of the Lennox holdings in England held by Matthew *Stewart, earl of Lennox and Lord Darnley (d. 1571), and his countess while in English exile and had been unsuccessfully sought by James from Elizabeth through much of the 1580s and 1590s. In 1604 Lennox was again sent to the French court as ambassador for the king—on his tomb he was called 'Captain of the Scots Gens d'Arms' in France. On 31 August 1605 he was created MA of Oxford University, following a visit there in attendance upon James VI and I. In September 1605 he was appointed king's aulnager (inspector of woollen cloth) and on 13 August 1606, on the forfeiture of Lord Cobham, he received a grant of the manor of Cobham in Kent. At the funeral of Henry, prince of Wales, in 1612 Lennox was one of the principal supporters of Prince Charles, the chief mourner. In February 1613 he accompanied James's eldest daughter, Elizabeth, on the journey with her husband to the Palatinate and then continued to France as ambassador. Following his return, he was on 6 October created earl of Richmond in the peerage of England and Baron Settrington. In 1614 he was named deputy Earl Marischal, and in November 1616 he became lord high steward of the royal household. In the intervening period, Lennox had been part of the commission of inquiry for the trial of Robert Carr, earl of Somerset, and his wife for the alleged poisoning of Sir Thomas Overbury and in October 1616 he had also officiated at the celebration surrounding the creation of Prince Charles as prince of Wales. In 1618 he was made king's aulnager in Ireland, in November 1620 he was appointed lord lieutenant of the county of Kent, and from May to July 1621 he was joint commissioner for the great seal.

Periodically, Lennox had returned to Scotland, as for example in July 1607, when he had been named high commissioner to the Scottish parliament in James's place. In 1617 he accompanied King James on his one return visit to the kingdom of his birth. Sitting in the Scottish parliament by heritage, in 1621 he voted in favour of the reforms of worship introduced in the unpopular five articles of Perth. Throughout much of his life, Lennox had been accused of lukewarm adherence to protestant doctrine. His close family were all Catholic and he was openly suspected of Catholicism on a number of occasions. Following the marriage of his sister to Huntly, these suspicions had grown in frequency and the duke had been excommunicated by the Church of Scotland; when absolution finally came in 1616 it was from the archbishop of Canterbury. For much of his later life, however, Lennox avoided serious political or religious confrontation as he was more content to play the role of courtier than administrator.

On 16 June 1621 Lennox married his third wife, Frances (1578–1639) [see Stuart, Frances, duchess of Lennox and Richmond], daughter of Thomas Howard, Viscount Howard of Bindon, and widow successively of Henry Prannell and Edward *Seymour, first earl of Hertford (1539?–1621).

On 17 August 1623 he was created duke of Richmond and earl of Newcastle upon Tyne in the peerage of England. He died on 16 February 1624, suddenly, in bed at his home in the parish of St Andrew's, Holborn, from 'a fit of apoplexy' (Crawfurd, 335). He left no legitimate heirs but an illegitimate son, Sir John Stewart of Methven, was keeper of Dumbarton Castle in the early 1620s. Parliament, which had been due to open that day, was postponed. On 19 April, with great ceremony, his body was borne from Ely House in Holborn to Westminster Abbey where he was buried, in King Henry VII's chapel, in a magnificent tomb, raised by his wife. His English titles became extinct; his Scottish titles descended to his brother Esmé.

ROB MACPHERSON

Sources CSP Scot. • G. Crawfurd, *The lives and characters, of the officers of the crown, and of the state in Scotland* (1726) • *Scots peerage* • GEC, *Peerage*, new edn • [T. Thomson], ed., *The historie and life of King James the Sext*, Bannatyne Club, 13 (1825) • *Reg. PCS*, 1st ser. • *Reg. PCS*, 2nd ser. • *APS* • D. Calderwood, *The history of the Kirk of Scotland*, ed. T. Thomson and D. Laing, 8 vols., Wodrow Society, 7 (1842–9) • J. Spottiswood, *The history of the Church of Scotland*, ed. M. Napier and M. Russell, 3 vols., Bannatyne Club, 93 (1850) • D. Moysie, *Memoirs of the affairs of Scotland, 1577–1603*, ed. J. Dennistoun, Bannatyne Club, 39 (1830) • NA Scot., Lennox papers, GD 220/6/2003/3, 6
Archives NA Scot., Lennox papers, Montrose muniments, GD 220/6
Likenesses I. Oliver, portrait, c.1605, NPG • P. van Somer, oils, c.1620, NPG [see illus.] • S. de Passe, line engraving (after unknown artist), NPG • pen and ink and wash drawing, NPG

Stuart, Maria Clementina. See Clementina (1702–1735).

Stuart, Muriel. See Irwin, Muriel Stuart (1885–1967).

Stuart, Peter (b. c.1760, d. in or after 1812). See under Stuart, Daniel (1766–1846).

Stuart, Robert. See Stewart, Robert (c.1470–1544).

Stuart, Robert (1812–1848), historian, eldest son of William Stuart, was born on 21 January 1812 in Glasgow, where his father was a merchant. When he was about a year old, because of his father's absence abroad on business, he was placed with his maternal grandfather, George Meliss, resident near Perth, and was strongly influenced by his grandmother, a descendant of the Stewarts of Invernahyle. In 1819 he joined his parents at Nice, thereafter accompanying them to Gibraltar. In 1821 he was sent to a boarding-school near Perth, and in 1825 his parents returned to Glasgow, where he settled with them and attended school.

The business depression of 1826 led Stuart's father to become a bookseller and publisher, with his son as assistant. In 1836 he turned to some new enterprise, and Stuart undertook the business himself and married; his wife's name is not known. He wrote Byronic verses for his father's *Literary Rambler* and edited his own *Scottish Monthly Magazine*, issued during 1836. In 1841 his friend John Buchanan of Glasgow showed him inscribed altars and other memorials of the Roman occupation of Scotland and expressed surprise that authors should have neglected such a fascinating subject. The result was Stuart's chief work, *Caledonia Romana: Roman Antiquities in Scotland*

(1845), a work well regarded in its day, which ran to a post-humous second edition, with a memoir by David Thomson (1852). In 1848 Stuart published an antiquarian study of Glasgow. He died in Glasgow of cholera on 23 December 1848, and was survived by his wife and family.

T. W. Bayne, *rev.* H. C. G. Matthew

Sources R. Stuart, *Caledonia Romana*, 2nd edn with memoir by David Thomson (1852)

Stuart, William (1755–1822), Church of Ireland archbishop of Armagh, was born on 15 March 1755, the fifth son of John *Stuart, third earl of Bute (1713–1792), prime minister, and Mary Wortley Montagu (1718–1794), only daughter of Edward Wortley *Montagu and Lady Mary Wortley *Montagu. His siblings included John *Stuart, first marquess of Bute, Sir Charles *Stuart (1753–1801), and Lady Louisa *Stuart. He was educated at Winchester College and St John's College, Cambridge, where he graduated MA in 1774. Shortly after being ordained in 1779 he was appointed vicar of Luton, Bedfordshire. He was made DD in 1789 and in the same year became a canon of Christ Church, Oxford. In 1793 he was appointed bishop of St David's and in December 1800 he became archbishop of Armagh and primate of all Ireland. On 3 May 1796 at St George's, Hanover Square, he married Sophia Margaret Juliana Penn (*d.* 1847), the daughter of Thomas *Penn (1702–1775), colonial politician, and Lady Juliana Fermor.

Stuart's correspondence with his fellow archbishop and confidant Charles Brodrick of Cashel shows him to have been a stern and somewhat intemperate critic of many of his fellow bishops. He wrote that Bishop Stopford of Cork showed a 'total incapacity to attend to the duties of his diocese' (Brodrick MSS, 3 June 1805), that Bishop Knox of Derry was 'the mere echo of the Castle' (ibid., 10 April 1805), and that William Magee, while doing damage in the episcopal college, could do little as a bishop (ibid., 29 March 1813). He maintained that the educational interests of the Church of Ireland were endangered, 'so ignorant are some of their lordships' (ibid., 3 Feb 1808), while the English bishops showed little interest in Irish affairs (ibid., 1 Oct 1805). His strictures against the church's performance in general embraced in particular its neglect of education, for which in large measure he blamed lack of clerical zeal. He criticized the high incidence of non-residence among the clergy, and on unsubstantiated moral grounds objected (unavailingly) to the translation into his province of Bishop George de la Poer Beresford, a member of a family that was highly influential in church and state. Being virtually independent of political patronage, he used his high office to institute reforms, especially through the resources of the board of first fruits. He was a diligent chairman of the Irish board of education inquiry, which issued fourteen important reports between 1809 and 1813. Stuart died of accidental poisoning at his London home at Hill Street, Berkeley Square, on 6 May 1822 and was buried at Luton Park, Bedfordshire.

Kenneth Milne

Sources M. MacDonagh, *The viceroy's post-bag* (1904) · A. R. Acheson, *A history of the Church of Ireland, 1691–1996* (1997) · A. Ford, J. McGuire, and K. Milne, eds., *As by law established: the Church of Ireland since the Reformation* (1995) · K. Milne, *The Irish charter schools, 1730–1830* (1997) · J. B. Leslie, *Armagh clergy and parishes* (1911) · NL Ire., Brodrick MSS · Beds. & Luton ARS, Stuart MSS · *The Times* (8–10 May 1822) · *DNB* · GEC, *Peerage*

Archives Beds. & Luton ARS, corresp. and papers | BL, corresp. with third Lord Hardwicke, Add. MSS 35731–35763 · NL Ire., Brodrick MSS

Likenesses S. W. Reynolds, mezzotint, pubd 1816 (after portrait by W. Owen), BM, NG Ire. · F. Chantrey, figure on monument, 1826, Armagh Cathedral · F. Chantrey, marble bust, 1826, V&A; plaster cast, AM Oxf. · attrib. A. Buck, pastel, Ulster Museum, Belfast; repro. in W. A. Maguire, ed., *Up in arms: the 1798 rebellion in Ireland* (1998), 26 [exhibition catalogue, Ulster Museum, Belfast, 3 April – 31 Aug 1998]

Stubbe [Stubbes, Stubbs], **Henry** (1632–1676), author and physician, was born on 28 February 1632 at Partney, Lincolnshire, the son of Henry *Stubbes (1605/6–1678), rector of the parish, and Mary Purefoy. They may not have been married at Henry's birth as, when he died intestate, it was said his estate was confiscated, he 'being a Bastard' (Bodl. Oxf., MS Aubrey 12, fol. 327). Be that as it may, the 'anabaptistically inclined' rector was soon ejected, and thereafter moved his family to Tredagh, Ireland, where—as a critic of the younger Stubbe quipped years later—he found employment as 'beadle of the beggars, as being well acquainted with the executive part of power at the carts-tail' (Wood, *Ath. Oxon.*, 3.1068).

Early life and education Following the outbreak of the Irish rising in 1641 the boy and a sibling were whisked by their mother to safety in England. They settled in London, where Mary's skill in needlework procured her a 'comfortable subsistence', enabling her to enrol Henry at Westminster School in 1642. A most precocious linguist, Stubbe quickly attracted the attention of the headmaster, Richard Busby, who, in turn, recommended the boy to Sir Henry Vane; he, after supporting the youth at Westminster, secured him a scholarship at Christ Church, Oxford, in 1649. There Stubbe quickly distinguished himself, not only for his scholarly attainments—he habitually performed his exercises in Greek—but for 'shewing himself too forward, pragmatical and conceited (being well stock'd with impudence at school)'. Indeed, Stubbe's sharp tongue and conceit often caused him to be 'kick'd and beaten' by his fellow students and, on one occasion at least, publicly whipped in the college's refectory (Wood, *Ath. Oxon.*, 3.1068). In later life Stubbe also claimed that it was he who had carried the engagement to Oxford in 1650, and again he who had saved several royalist fellows of Christ Church and Queen's from expulsion.

Political pamphleteer While still an undergraduate Stubbe embarked on a literary career with his publication in 1651 of *Horae subsecivae* and *Miscellanea epigrammata*—respectively, Greek paraphrases of two biblical stories and a translation into Greek of poems by, among others, Thomas Randolph and Richard Crashaw. After graduating BA in July 1653 Stubbe served with the parliamentary army in Scotland for two years before returning to Oxford to proceed MA in December 1656. A few weeks later he was appointed deputy keeper of the Bodleian Library thanks to the support of the Independent John Owen, dean of Christ Church, whom Stubbe assisted in polemics against the presbyterians. By early 1656 Stubbe had also befriended Thomas Hobbes, and vigorously championed his campaign against John Wallis, the Savilian professor of geometry, by attacking Wallis's linguistic competency. Stubbe also began preparing a Latin translation of Hobbes's *Leviathan*, but never completed it. At the same time, however, Stubbe was careful to deny, privately as well as publicly, charges of Hobbism. In 1658 Stubbe's crusade against Wallis became more personal, following the latter's contestable election as keeper of the Oxford archives. Stubbe vented his disapprobation by publishing *The Savilian Professor's Case Stated* but, following John Wilkins's appeal to Cromwell, was forced on 5 May by vice-chancellor John Conant to recant publicly.

By mid-1659 Stubbe was conscripted by Sir Henry Vane into heavy political and religious pamphleteering. His first effort appeared in May, *The Common-Wealth of Israel*, a short critique of William Prynne's *The Re-publicans and other Spurious Good Old Cause … Anatomized*. The following month Stubbe published the first edition of *A Light Shining out of Darkness*, an incendiary attack on the presbyterians and the universities, a much augmented version of which appeared in November, and included a defence of the Quakers. In September Stubbe published *An Essay in Defence of the Good Old Cause*, which forcefully promoted Vane's limited vision of republicanism as well as controverted the authority of government over religious matters. To the treatise was appended *Malice Rebuked*, an intemperate assault on Richard Baxter, who had maligned Vane the previous year. (Stubbe had already attacked Baxter a couple of months earlier in *A Vindication of … Sir Henry Vane, from the Lies and Calumnies of Mr. Richard Baxter*.) In *An Essay in Defence of the Good Old Cause*, Stubbe, like Vane earlier, was quite flattering about Harrington's republican model despite disagreeing on the nature of citizenry in the political nation. Indeed, Stubbe 'was ready to cry out as if [*Oceana*] were the pattern in the mount' (Wood, *Ath. Oxon.*, 3.1121). Yet following Harrington's critique of Vane's élitist vision of government Stubbe turned quite censorious. In mid-October he published *A Letter to an Officer of the Army Concerning a Select Senate* and, within days of the publication in January 1660 of Harrington's *Rota*, Stubbe produced his satirical *The Rota, or, News from the Common-Wealths-Mens Club*. Stubbe capped his campaign against Harrington two months later with *The Common-Wealth of Oceana Put into the Ballance, and Found too Light*.

Thus ended Stubbe's first foray into political pamphleteering. His considerable skills were fully appreciated, even feared, at the time, judging by Thomason's inscribing on his copy of *A Letter to an Officer of the Army* that the author was 'A dangerous fellow; Sir Henry Vanes Advisor' and the complaint launched in parliament against him in February 1660 that it was Stubbe who had 'palliated in print Sir Henry Vane's wickedness' (Wood, *Life and Times*, 1.303). Quite possibly, however, Stubbe was carried away with his zeal. If one of Baxter's correspondents can be believed, certain of Vane's friends were far from pleased

with Stubbe's 'Edge and Bitterness' (*Reliquiae Baxterianae*, 4.93). Certainly his political activity and anti-university writings—not only *A Light Shining out of Darkness* but the biting raillery at the expense of the Oxford scientific club and certain members of Christ Church published in June 1659 in *Sundry Things from Several Hands Concerning the University of Oxford*—provided ample ammunition to his enemies at Oxford. In late 1659 the presbyterian Edward Reynolds was reinstalled as dean of Christ Church and within four months managed to deprive Stubbe not only of his studentship at Christ Church, but of his sublibrarianship as well. Reynolds's own departure from Oxford shortly thereafter may have enabled Stubbe to remain at Christ Church but the Restoration visitors of the university ejected him in early August on the grounds that he was 'unduely brought in' as a student as well as for the 'many complaints of his carryadge' (Varley, 17).

Physician and critic of the Royal Society Stubbe now turned to practising medicine. Thanks to the recommendation of Sir Alexander Frazier, principal physician to Charles II, he obtained in early 1662 the office of king's physician to Jamaica and was granted £200 for expenses. By then he had made his peace with the restored monarchy and church, having taken the oath of allegiance and having subscribed to the articles of the Church of England several months earlier. Prior to his departure Stubbe also presented the king with *The Indian Nectar, or, A Discourse Concerning Chocolata*, where his conformity was made public. The Caribbean climate did not agree with Stubbe, however, and he returned to England by autumn 1664. Having failed to obtain the position of physician for seamen in Yarmouth and adjacent ports Stubbe took up medical practice in and around Warwick, numbering Edward, Lord Conway, and his family at Ragley Hall among his patients. Such an association brought him in early 1666 to encounter Valentine Greatrakes, 'the Stroker', who demonstrated his highly publicized cures of scrofula at Ragley Hall and elsewhere in England. Stubbe's semi-naturalistic explanation of Greatrakes's powers, which was dedicated to Thomas Willis and addressed to Robert Boyle, was published later that year as *The Miraculous Conformist*.

In 1669 Stubbe launched a massive attack on the Royal Society. Already peeved at the underhanded treatment that (he believed) greeted the observations on Jamaica which he had sent the society, Stubbe was provoked by the vehemence with which Thomas Sprat's *History of the Royal Society* (1667) and, even more, Joseph Glanvill's *Plus ultra* (1668) advocated the cause of the nascent society. Not only did Stubbe believe that the protagonists' claims regarding the utility of science were vastly exaggerated, but he was convinced that their inflammatory rhetoric seriously threatened the humanist culture of the universities, the erudite foundations upon which protestantism rested, as well as the medical profession. And as he failed to effect privately the society's disavowal of Sprat's and Glanvill's writings Stubbe issued in rapid succession in 1670 four treatises—*A Censure upon Certaine Passages Contained in the 'History of the Royall Society'*; *The 'Plus Ultra' Reduced to a Non-Plus*; *Legends no histories, or, A specimen of some animadversions* upon the 'History of the Royal Society'; and *Campanella Revived, or, An Enquiry into the History of the Royal Society*—all excoriating the aims and work of the society as well as the learning of its propagandists. Glanvill and other members of the society quickly responded, eliciting further rejoinders from Stubbe, who, in the meantime, had inadvertently become implicated in a controversy between the College of Physicians and the London apothecaries, and was attacked first by the physician Christopher Merrett and then the iatrochemist George Thompson. Stubbe responded in 1671 with *An Epistolary Discourse Concerning Phlebotomy* and *The Lord Bacons Relation of the Sweating-Sickness Examined*.

Final publications and death The controversy became increasingly abusive. Stubbe's passion soon alienated even those members of the Royal Society and the College of Physicians who were initially well disposed toward his campaign, and strong pressure was put on him to desist. Perhaps the impending Third Anglo-Dutch War contributed to such pressure as Stubbe's patron, Secretary of State Arlington, wished to conscript the gifted controversialist to bolster the English cause. Thus began Stubbe's second career of political pamphleteer. In June 1672 he published *A Justification of the Present War Against the United Netherlands*, to which he added early in 1673 *A Further Justification of the Present War Against the United Netherlands*. In addition, *Rosemary & Bayes, or, Animadversions upon a Treatise called, 'The Rehearsall Trans-Prosed'*, published the previous year—and satirizing both Andrew Marvell's and Samuel Parker's position on ecclesiastical policy—was another offshoot of his work on behalf of the government. A further contribution to the religious debate, 'An enquiry into the supremacy spiritual of the kings of England, occasioned by a proviso in the late act of parliament against conventicles' (PRO, SP 29/275/220), appears to have been refused publication. Stubbe was handsomely rewarded for his efforts. He was paid £200 and, on 19 October 1673, was granted the reversion of the office of secretary of Jamaica. Ironically, eleven days later a warrant was issued for Stubbe's arrest, 'for seditious discourses and printing and publishing unlicensed papers' (PRO, SP 44/40, fol. 127). The reference was to his *Paris Gazette*, a broadside enumerating historical precedents for the annulment of marriages by proxy—against the background of a portrait of James, duke of York—which was published shortly after parliament convened on 20 October and hotly debated the marriage of James and Mary of Modena. Stubbe procured his release with another work of propaganda, a translation of Jacques Godefroy's *The History of the United Provinces of Achaia*, in which the ultimate destruction of Achaia was used to foretell the analogous fate of the Dutch.

Once again Stubbe resumed his medical practice. It was also then that he wrote *An Account of the Rise and Progress of Mahometanism*, which expanded upon Edward Pococke's tolerant and historicized view of Islam to include the prophet Muhammad as well. The work remained unpublished until the twentieth century, though it enjoyed a limited manuscript circulation. Late in the evening on 12 July 1676, while riding from Bath to Bristol to attend a patient, and 'his head being then intoxicated with bibbing, but more with talking, and snuffing of powder' (Wood, *Ath. Oxon.*, 3.1082), Stubbe drowned in a shallow river 2 miles from Bath. He was buried two days later in St Peter's and St Paul's Church in Bath, with his old adversary Joseph Glanvill preaching an indifferent funeral sermon. The fate of his papers appears to have concerned the government, for his study was immediately sealed and the bishop of London was expected 'to appoint a person to inspect the papers for dangerous papers state and church' (*CSP dom.*, 1676–7, 310–11). Anthony Wood, who knew Stubbe well, best characterized this truly erudite and enigmatic person:

> as he was so admirably well qualified with several sorts of learning and generous spirit, so he was very unhappy in this, that he was extream rash and imprudent, and wanted common discretion to manage his parts … Had he been endowed with common sobriety and discretion, and not have made himself and his learning mercenary and cheap to every ordinary and ignorant fellow, he would have been admired by all, and might have pick'd and chus'd his preferment. But all these things being wanting, he became a ridicule, and undervalued by sober and knowing scholars and others too.   (Wood, *Ath. Oxon.*, 3.1071–2)

MORDECHAI FEINGOLD

Sources *Reliquiae Baxterianae, or, Mr Richard Baxter's narrative of the most memorable passages of his life and times*, ed. M. Sylvester, 1 vol. in 3 pts (1696) • Wood, *Ath. Oxon.*, new edn, 3.1067–83 • A. Wood, *The history and antiquities of the University of Oxford*, ed. J. Gutch, 2 vols. in 3 pts (1792–6), vol. 3, pp. 682–3 • *Calamy rev.*, 468–9 • F. J. Varley, ed., 'The Restoration visitation of the University of Oxford and its colleges', *Camden miscellany, XVIII*, CS, 3rd ser., 79 (1948), 17 • *Complete prose works of John Milton*, ed. D. Wolfe, 8 vols. in 10 (1953–82), vol. 7, pp. 55–7, 82–3, 126–8 • P. M. Holt, *A seventeenth-century defender of Islam: Henry Stubbe (1632–76) and his book* (1972) • O. Nicastro, ed., *Lettere di Henry Stubbe a Thomas Hobbes (8 luglio 1656–6 maggio 1657)* (Siena, 1973) • C. Webster, *The great instauration: science, medicine and reform, 1626–1660* (1975), 172–7 • N. H. Steneck, 'Greatrakes the Stroker: the interpretation of historians', *Isis*, 73 (1982), 161–77 • J. R. Jacob, *Henry Stubbe, radical protestantism and the early Enlightenment* Cambridge (1983) • H. J. Cook, 'Physicians and the new philosophy: Henry Stubbe and the virtuosi-physicians', *The medical revolution of the seventeenth century*, ed. R. French and A. Wear (1989), 246–71 • *The correspondence of Thomas Hobbes*, ed. N. Malcolm, 2 vols. (1994), esp. vol. 2, pp. 899–902 • *Report on the manuscripts of the late Reginald Rawdon Hastings*, 4 vols., HMC, 78 (1928–47) • Bodl. Oxf., MS Aubrey 12, fol. 327 • Bodl. Oxf., MS Savile 104, fol. 1 • PRO, SP 44/40, fols. 124, 127 • *CSP dom.*, 1676–7, 310–11

Archives BL, catalogue of library, Sloane MS 35 • PRO, 'An enquiry into the supremacy spiritual of the kings of England', SP 29/275/220 • RS, account of Jamaica, early letters S1.89–91 | BL, letters to Thomas Hobbes, Add. MS 32553

Wealth at death estate value approx. £800 (mostly books): HMC, *Hastings*, 2.385

Stubbe [Stubbs], **John** (*c.*1541–1590), religious writer, was born possibly in Norfolk, the eldest of three sons and four daughters of John Stubbe (*fl.* 1541–1554), a country gentleman of Buxton, and his wife, Elizabeth (*fl.* 1540–1590). Nothing is known of his education until he matriculated at Trinity College, Cambridge, as a pensioner on 12 November 1555. At Cambridge he was tutored by George Blythe, and knew both Vincent Skinner and Michael

Hickes; all three men were later to be secretaries to William Cecil, Lord Burghley. Stubbe graduated BA on 31 January 1561 and entered Lincoln's Inn on 7 November 1562, where he was later joined by Skinner and Hickes (admitted 1565), William Lambarde, Ralph Rokeby, and others. His *A Discourse … Conteyning the Life and Death of John Calvin* appeared in print two years later.

Stubbe's time at Lincoln's Inn was formative. With Skinner, Hickes, Rokeby, and others he formed a close-knit group of protestants; some friendships lasted until Stubbe's death. Witnessing the suspensions of a number of London clergymen by Archbishop Parker after the vestarian controversy (1565–6), this group increasingly identified with those, like John Field and Thomas Wilcox, who demanded further reforms to the religious settlement of 1559, particularly the eradication of such practices as the wearing of surplices and kneeling at communion. In 1569 Skinner dedicated his translation of Gonsalvius, *A discovery and playne declaration of sundry subtill practises of the holye inquisition of Spayne*, to Parker in laudatory terms. But, though there is no firm evidence, it is thought that five years later Stubbe, Skinner, and Hickes may have collaborated in a vituperative attack on Parker entitled *The Life of the 70. Archbishopp off Canterbury. Englished*, a translation of the final chapter of *De antiquitate Britannicae ecclesiae* with polemical and satirical marginal notes. Much of the criticism levelled against the archbishop concerned Parker's hostility to the moderate puritans' concerns and the defence of episcopacy in *De antiquitate Britannicae ecclesiae*. Though Stubbe was moving among prominent puritans at this time—his sister Alice married Thomas Cartwright in 1578—typographical evidence suggests *The Life* was produced independently, and was not part of a larger propaganda campaign. It is significant that it was printed in Zürich by Christoph Froschauer, not by Michael Shirat (Heidelberg), who printed a number of important protestant works by Thomas Cartwright and Walter Travers at this time.

Stubbe was called to the bar on 2 February 1572 (along with Sir Thomas Egerton) and may have practised. He was appointed steward for the reader's dinner at Lincoln's Inn in August 1578—a senior post—though this may have been recognition of long residence: it was alleged that he wrote *The Discoverie of a Gaping Gulf* at the inn. Some time between 1575 and 1579 Stubbe married Anne, daughter of Aubrey Vere and widow of Christopher Sharnborne of Norfolk. They had three children: two sons—Edmund and Francis—and a daughter who later married Francis Sharnborne; the eldest child was born before 1579. Stubbe's brother Francis married Anne, sister of Sir Edward Coke; she corresponded with Cartwright on the issue of separatism in 1590.

In August 1579 Stubbe wrote *The Discoverie of a Gaping Gulf*, objecting to Elizabeth's proposed marriage with the duke of Anjou. He attacked the marriage on the grounds that it was against God's law for a protestant to marry a Catholic; he also answered in detail all the points the earl of Sussex had made in support of the marriage, both in a letter to Elizabeth in August 1578 and in a later memorandum. It has been argued that Leicester or Walsingham supplied Stubbe with Sussex's arguments to engineer popular opposition to the match; this was certainly what Elizabeth thought. It is difficult to trace close connections between either man and Stubbe, but the book was printed by Hugh Singleton, who also printed the first edition of Edmund Spenser's *The Shepheardes Calendar*. Spenser was a member of Leicester's household at this time, and his poem, too, was critical of the marriage.

Elizabeth was incensed by *A Gaping Gulf*: Stubbe had no claim to offer counsel, his criticism of Anjou was vituperative, and he openly questioned her commitment to protestantism. On 27 September 1579 a royal proclamation was issued prohibiting the circulation of the book. On 13 October Stubbe, Singleton, and William Page (secretary to the earl of Bedford and an MP who had attempted to distribute fifty copies to Sir Richard Grenville in the west country) were arrested. Elizabeth wanted to hang them by royal prerogative but agreed to their trial for felony. The jury refused to convict, and they were charged with conspiring to excite sedition under 1 & 2 Philip & Mary c. 3 and retried in queen's bench. The use of this statute was criticized by Robert Monson, a judge of common pleas and member of Lincoln's Inn; he was imprisoned and removed from the bench when he refused to retract. The three men were sentenced to have their right hands cut off and to be imprisoned, though it appears that Singleton was pardoned because of his age: he was about eighty. The sentence was carried out at the market place in Westminster, with surgeons present to prevent them bleeding to death. Camden's eye-witness account, also printed by Harington and circulated in manuscript, recounts Stubbe's speech on the scaffold: he asserted his loyalty and asked the crowd to pray that God would give him strength to endure the punishment. After his hand was chopped off (it took three blows) he managed to cry out 'God save the queen' before he fainted and was carried away. The crowd watched in absolute silence—either, Camden believed, in horror of the punishment and pity for Stubbe, or out of hatred of the marriage. Stubbe subsequently signed his name 'John Stubbe, scaeva' ('the left-handed').

Stubbe remained in the Tower until 1581, the year in which parliament passed the Act against Seditious Words and Rumours Uttered against the Queen's Most Excellent Majesty. Though designed as an anti-Catholic measure, opposition in the Commons appears to have been stimulated by fears that it could be used against protestants, like Stubbe. The following year, Stubbe's *Christian Meditations upon Eight Psalms* (dedicated to Lady Anne Bacon) was printed at Bacon House by Christopher Barker. In 1585 he became steward of Great Yarmouth and, four years later, its MP. In parliament he sat on four committees (including privileges and the subsidy) and drew up a draft petition against the use of the *ex officio* oath against puritan ministers. The circumstances surrounding the petition are unclear, but it appears to have been part of an attempt to initiate religious reform at the end of the session after earlier attempts had failed. However, there does not appear to have been time to present either it or another petition to Elizabeth. In 1587 Burghley commissioned him to reply to Cardinal Allen's attack on Burghley's own *Execution of Justice*, a treatise defending the regime's proceedings against Edmund Campion; there is no evidence, however, that Stubbe's work was published. At the same time, Stubbe was appointed an associate of the bench at Lincoln's Inn, an honorary benchership which enabled him to advise on the running of the inn. From 1585 he was also employed as secretary to Lord Willoughby de Eresby, and may have resided at Willoughby's house at the Barbican while Willoughby was abroad. He acted as a channel of communication between Willoughby and Burghley on Dutch affairs, as well as overseeing Willoughby's household and financial affairs. He also accompanied Lady Willoughby to the Low Countries in 1588.

After the dissolution of parliament in 1589, Stubbe went to France with the English force, where he died in February the following year; his will, written in haste before his departure for France, was proved on 27 June 1590. Stubbe left the wardship of their son and most of his property and possessions to his 'faithfull and righte well deserving' wife. Some things (including a gold ring engraved 'Mortall') were left to his mother, and he released his brother, Edmond, from a debt of £60. The promised schedule of legacies to kin and friends does not appear to have been made. He testified that he 'lyved and do dye the true man and most loyall Subjecte of her most excellente majestie', beseeching Elizabeth to show her grace and favour to his widow (PROB 11/75, fols. 313–314). His burial, on the seashore near Havre de Grace, was witnessed by three nephews of his old friend Ralph Rokeby.

NATALIE MEARS

Sources John Stubbs's 'gaping gulf' with letters and other relevant documents, ed. L. E. Berry (1968) · W. T. MacCaffrey, *Queen Elizabeth and the making of policy, 1572–1588* (1981) · BL, Lansdowne MSS, vols. 10, 12, 13, 18, 21, 23, 25, 31, 33, 36, 54, 61, 69, 107 · state papers domestic (Elizabeth), PRO · BL, Add. MS 4810, fols. 136–137 · BL, Add. MS 15891, fols. 8–9, 28v–29 · PRO, KB27, KB29 · Fitzwilliam (Milton) political III, Northants. RO · Folger, Folger MS V.b.142 · Grimsthorpe, Lincolnshire, Ancaster MSS · PRO, PROB 11/75, fols. 313–314 · K. Barnes, 'John Stubbe, 1579: the French ambassador's account', *Historical Research*, 64 (1991), 421–6 · J. Strype, *The history of the life and acts of the most reverend father in God Edmund Grindal*, new edn (1821) · J. Strype, *Historical collections of the life and acts of … John Aylmer*, new edn (1821) · W. Camden, *Annales, or, The historie of the most renowned and victorious Princesse Elizabeth*, trans. R. N. [R. Norton], 3rd edn (1635) · HoP, *Commons, 1558–1603* · J. Harington, *Nugæ antiquæ*, ed. T. Park and H. Harington, 1 (1801) · A. Johnson, 'Books printed at Heidelberg for Thomas Cartwright', *The Library*, 5th ser., 2 (1947–8), 284–6 · R. Rokeby, 'Oeconomia Rokebiorum', *A history of Richmondshire, in the North Riding of the county of York*, ed. T. D. Whitaker, 1 (1823), 158–80 · Venn, *Alum. Cant.* · J. B. Heath, *Some account of the Worshipful Company of Grocers of the city of London*, 3rd edn (privately printed, London, 1869) · C. J. Palmer, *The history of Great Yarmouth* (1856) · J. D. Alsop and W. M. Stevens, 'William Lambarde and the Elizabethan polity', *Studies in Medieval and Renaissance History*, new ser., 8 (1986), 231–65 · P. Collinson, *The Elizabethan puritan movement* (1967) · R. M. Fisher, 'The Reformation in microcosm? Benchers at the inns of court, 1530–1580', *Parergon*, new ser., 6 (1988), 33–61 · W. R. Prest, *The inns of court under Elizabeth I and the early Stuarts, 1590–1640* (1972) · R. M. Fisher, 'Privy council coercion and religious conformity at the inns of court', *Recusant History*, 15 (1979–81), 305–24 · *Report on the manuscripts of the earl of Ancaster*, HMC, 66 (1907)

Archives BL, Lansdowne MSS · BL, Add. MSS · Folger, Folger MS V.b.142 · Northants. RO, Fitzwilliam (Milton) political MSS · PRO, state papers domestic [Elizabeth] · PRO, king's bench, coram rege rolls (KB 27); controllment rolls (KB 29) · Grimsthorpe, Lincolnshire, Ancaster MSS

Wealth at death his will suggests he had debts: PRO, PROB 11/75, fols. 313–14

Stubbes [Stubbs], **Henry** (1605/6–1678), clergyman and ejected minister, was the son of Henry Stubbes of Bitton, Gloucestershire. He matriculated from Magdalen Hall, Oxford, on 16 April 1624, aged eighteen, graduated BA on 27 January 1628, and proceeded MA in June or July 1630. Within eighteen months he became rector of Partney, Lincolnshire; about this time he married Mary Purefoy, but it is not clear whether this was before or after the birth of their son, Henry *Stubbe (1632–1676), at Partney on 28 February 1632. 'Being anabaptistically inclined', according to Anthony Wood, Stubbes was later compelled to leave his rectory; taking his family to Ireland, he found employment as a 'beadle of the beggars' (Wood, *Ath. Oxon.*, 3.1067).

The Irish rising of 1641 induced Mistress Stubbes, and presumably within a short time Stubbes himself, to return to England. His movements over the next few years are unknown, but by July 1647 he was vicar of St Philip and St Jacob, Bristol, and in 1648 he signed the *Testimony* of the Somerset ministers. He then became vicar of Chew Magna in that county. By September 1652 he was one of the ministers of St Cuthbert, Wells, where in 1654 he assisted the commission of triers and ejectors in the work of regulating the ministry. He lectured at St Philip, Bristol, every month in 1658.

At the Restoration, Stubbes was still at St Cuthbert, Wells, but he left when the sequestered minister was restored and served as assistant minister to Joseph Woodward at Dursley, Gloucestershire, until August 1662, when he was again ejected. On 20 November the presbyterian but conformist MP John Birch sympathetically promised Stubbes a £5 a year allowance while he remained in need. Over the next decade he appeared throughout London, establishing his reputation as a learned and energetic preacher, but he retained links with the west country: in 1669 he preached in five Wiltshire parishes, including Chippenham, and at Winsham, Somerset. Fellow ministers who later celebrated his life reminded his congregations that 'We have often known him to continue five or six hours together in Preaching, chiefly in prayer on fasting-days', and that he had accomplished this 'without impertinencies, tautologies, tedious repetitions, or any crude, raw, rude, and nauseating expressions' (Vincent and others, 6). Richard Baxter, who recorded meeting him on 13 May 1671, noted his unusually charitable attitude towards other ministers. On 2 April 1672 he was licensed as a presbyterian minister at his house in Jewin Street, London, but in or before 1675 he left the city. His farewell sermon to his congregation, published as *A Disswasive from*

Conformity to the World, as also God's Severity Against Impenitent Sinners (1675), was a call to repentance and holy living in the mode of many contemporary devotional works.

Stubbes's last charge was in Gloucestershire. John Prichett, who had been consecrated bishop of Gloucester in November 1672, awarded Stubbes the long-vacant vicarage of Horsley, not far from Dursley, at a salary of £8 a year. Here he 'preached for some years … in peace' and 'used part of the Liturgy' (Baxter, 27), despite the criticism of some who thought this an unacceptable compromise. His *Conscience the Best Friend upon Earth* (1677) bears out his fellow ministers' emphasis on his 'constant secret Devotions, his dayly prayers with his Wife, and in his Family' (Vincent and others, 5) and his careful catechizing, and Baxter's observations on his peaceableness and humility: 'His studies, and parts, and labours lay not in the Critical or Controversial way' and he did not make 'himself of a sect or faction, nor Preacht for this party against that, except for Christ's party against the Devils' (Baxter, 25–6).

While on a preaching visit to London in the summer of 1678 Stubbes was taken ill with fever and dysentery. He died on 7 July and was buried at Bunhill; two funeral sermons were delivered, one on a Sunday by Thomas Watson, the other on a weekday by Richard Baxter. His will, drawn up on 31 May and proved on 5 September, was sprinkled with biblical references and contained prayers for his kin, congregation, fellow ministers, and country. He left property at Dundry, Somerset, and Uley, Gloucestershire, and money to the poor of several Gloucestershire parishes for books and teaching poor children to read. He was survived by his second wife, Dorothy, three sons (Robert, Samuel, and John), and a daughter (Dorothy); his eldest son and namesake had drowned two years earlier.

CARL B. ESTABROOK

Sources *Calamy rev.*, 468–9 · Foster, *Alum. Oxon.* · R. Baxter, *A sermon preached at the funeral … of Mr Henry Stubbs* (1678) · T. Vincent and others, *The death of ministers improved* (1678) · *Calendar of the correspondence of Richard Baxter*, ed. N. H. Keeble and G. F. Nuttall, 2 vols. (1991) · Wood, *Ath. Oxon.*, new edn, 3.1255 · PRO, PROB 11/357, sig. 103
Archives York Minster Library, York Minster archives, diary
Likenesses line engraving, NPG

Stubbes, Katherine (1570/71–1590). *See under* Stubbes, Philip (*b. c.*1555, *d.* in or after 1610).

Stubbes [Stubbs], **Philip** (*b. c.*1555, *d.* in or after **1610**), pamphleteer, is likely to have been born in the reign of Mary I. A native of Cheshire, his family may have come from the Congleton area, where the surname was common and where, before 1586, he seems to have owned a tenement. Although he styled himself 'gentleman' in his published works, it is unclear if this was merely literary and social pretension. Suggestions that he was related to John Stubbs, author of *The Discoverie of a Gaping Gulf* (1579), are probably mistaken (Wood, *Ath. Oxon.*, 1.646). Stubbes was a pious youth, and 'in his minority' had apparently been employed as a lay reader in his local parish church (*Works of Thomas Nashe*, 3.357). According to Anthony Wood, he was educated initially at Cambridge, but 'having a restless and hot head, left that university, rambled thro'

several parts of the nation, and settled for a time in Oxon, particularly … in Gloster Hall' (Wood, *Ath. Oxon.*, 1.645). However, his name occurs in the records of neither institution and elsewhere he is said to have been 'nourst up onely at Grammer schoole' (*Cuthbert Cunny-catcher*, sig. C4v).

Stubbes's career as a semi-professional author seems to have begun in the 1580s and by the end of that decade Gabriel Harvey and Thomas Nashe reputed him one of the 'common Pamfletters of London' (*Works of Gabriel Harvey*, 2.280) and grouped him with William Elderton, Thomas Deloney, and other ballad-mongers who plied their pens to eke out a living. His first publication was a broadside ballad about the divine judgment which had befallen a habitual swearer from Boothby in Lincolnshire; this was reprinted in 1581 with a secondary cautionary tale relating to one Joan Bowser of Donington, Leicestershire (*Two Wunderfull and Rare Examples*, 1581). A list of witnesses to the latter incident survives in BL, Lansdowne MS 819, fol. 87r. Religious and moralistic in character, Stubbes's other works are equally typical of the output of the hack writers of the capital. They include a metrical jeremiad entitled *A View of Vanitie, and Allarum to England, or, Retrait from Sinne* (1582, now lost), a jingoistic account of *The Intended Treason of Doctor Parrie* ([1585]), a fiercely anti-Catholic attack upon *The Theater of the Popes Monarchie* (1585), and two tiny volumes of meditations and prayers, *The Rosarie of Christian Praiers and Meditations* (1583, also no longer extant) and *A Perfect Pathway to Felicitie* (1592).

Stubbes's best-known book is *The Anatomie of Abuses* (1583), a colourful diatribe against contemporary fashions, customs, and pastimes which called for a speedy 'reformation of maners and amendement of lyfe' (sig. ¶4v) in order to avert a visitation of providential wrath. This took the form of a highly readable dialogue between Philoponus and Spudeus about the 'verie famous Ilande called Ailgna' (title-page), a device which allowed Stubbes to indulge in a rich, quasi-anthropological description of late sixteenth-century English society. The instant success of this book (four editions of which were published before 1595), induced him to produce a sequel subtitled *The Display of Corruptions*, a taxonomical analysis of the vices of various professions and estates. The uncompromising assault upon dancing, May games, plays, wakes, and other popular recreations which Stubbes launched in the first part of the *Anatomie* earned him an enduring reputation as a puritan spoilsport and killjoy. Cuthbert Cunny-catcher (perhaps Robert Greene) and Thomas Nashe accused him of being a 'holy brother' and 'privy Martinist' (*Cuthbert Cunny-catcher*, sig. C4v; *Works of Thomas Nashe*, 3.358) but their remarks were made in the context of the scurrilous literary squabbles unleashed by the Marprelate controversy of 1588–9, and cannot be taken at face value. Stubbes was certainly no presbyterian: he staunchly defended the established church and the office of bishop and sharply reproved 'precisians' and separatists. It is difficult to fathom the depth of his piety and it seems likely that he was motivated by a combination of financial necessity, ambition, and religious zeal.

The dedications to his works suggest that Stubbes moved in a variety of circles: Mr and Mrs William Milward bore 'the whole charges' of printing his *Perfect Pathway* (sig. ¶4r), and he acknowledged that he had received 'bountifull remuneration' from the suspected Catholic Philip Howard, earl of Arundel, to whom he presented both parts of his *Anatomie* (*The Second Part of the Anatomie of Abuses, Conteining The Display of Corruptions*, 1583, sig. A4r). The Latin verses on the 'Papist Bloodsuckers or Leeches' by Stubbes which prefaced the 1583 edition of John Foxe's *Actes and Monuments* imply more than a passing acquaintance with the martyrologist. In September of 1586 Stubbes, described as 'Gentleman, of St Mary at Hill, London' (Foster, 1300), was licensed to marry Katherine Emmes of the same parish, with whom he moved to Burton upon Trent, Staffordshire. Her untimely death at the age of nineteen led Stubbes to write a best-selling biography of his godly bride, *A Christal Glasse for Christian Women* (1591). At least twenty-eight impressions of this pamphlet appeared to 1664 and, an excellent example of the protestant *ars moriendi*, it became one of the most popular chapbooks of the late seventeenth century.

By 1593 Stubbes was once again living in London, from whence he set out on a three-month tour of England on horseback to acquaint himself with 'the maners and dispositions of the people' and to inspect schools, almshouses, highways, and other monuments erected by private benefactors. This journey, which was undertaken 'partly for my private pleasure and recreation' and 'partly for avoidance of the plague', supplied Stubbes with the material for his *Motive to Good Workes*, published in that same year, a lengthy lament for the passing of an age of charity and hospitality in which he documented the decay of churches and many other public amenities. On 8 November of that year he was 'lodging by Cheape side' (Stubbes, *Motive to Good Workes*, sigs. A3v, A6r). He appears to have been alive in 1610, when a revised version of his *Perfect Pathway* was republished, incorporating fifteen additional prayers. Thereafter he cannot be traced.

Katherine Stubbes [*née* Emmes] (1570/71–1590) was the daughter of a Dutch woman whose maiden name is unknown and William Emmes, cordwainer of the parish of St Dunstan-in-the-West and a freeman of the city of London. The youngest but one of six children, she inherited property on the death of her father late in 1583 and at the age of fifteen was married to Philip Stubbes. The contemporary suggestion that Stubbes cynically insinuated himself into the young heiress's affections is unsubstantiated and probably slanderous. According to her husband's pious account of her life, Katherine was 'a perfect paterne of true Christianitie' and 'a mirrour of womanhood'. Modest, virtuous, and an avid reader of the scriptures, she prophesied her own death from postnatal complications following the birth of a son, and passed away after making 'a most heavenly confession' of the protestant faith and struggling heroically against the temptations of Satan (Stubbes, *Christal Glasse*, sigs. A2r and title-page). It is difficult to disentangle the historical person Katherine Stubbes from the paragon she became in a text heavily conditioned by generic convention. The parish registers of St Modwen's, Burton upon Trent, confirm the baptism of John Stubbes on 17 November 1590 and the burial of Katherine on 14 December.

ALEXANDRA WALSHAM

Sources P. S. Gent [P. Stubbes], *A christal glasse for Christian women* (1591) · P. Stubbes, *A motive to good workes* (1593) · *The works of Thomas Nashe*, ed. R. B. McKerrow, 5 vols. (1904–10); repr. with corrections and notes by F. P. Wilson (1958) · *The works of Gabriel Harvey*, ed. A. B. Grosart, 3 vols. (1884–5) · Cuthbert Cunny-catcher [Robert Greene (?)], *The defence of conny catching* (1592) · Wood, *Ath. Oxon.*, new edn, 1.645–7 · 'Forewords', *Phillip Stubbes's 'Anatomy of abuses' in England in Shakspere's youth, A.D.1583*, ed. F. J. Furnivall, 2 pts, New Shakspere Society, ser. 6, 4, 12 (1877–82) · parish register, Burton upon Trent, St Modwen, Staffs. RO, F4219/1/1 [baptism, burial] · A. Maunsell, *The first part of the catalogue of English printed bookes* (1595) · J. L. Chester and J. Foster, eds., *London marriage licences, 1521–1869* (1887) · T. P. W. Pearson, 'The life and works of Phillip Stubbes', MA diss., Queen Mary College, London, 1958 · A. Walsham, '"A Glose of Godlines": Philip Stubbes, Elizabethan Grub Street, and the invention of puritanism', *Belief and practice in Reformation England*, ed. S. Wabuda and C. Litzenberger (1998), 177–206

Stubblefield, Sir (Cyril) James (1901–1999), palaeontologist and geologist, was born on 6 September 1901 at 8 Melbourn Place, Cambridge, the only son and younger child of James Stubblefield (1853–1925), gardener, and his wife, Jane Goodier (1861–1941). Jane Stubblefield was particularly anxious that her son should have an education that she and her husband had missed. From the higher grade school, Cambridge, which he attended from 1907 to 1912, Stubblefield went by scholarship to the Perse School, Cambridge. There he developed an interest in collecting biological specimens and in geology. Science teaching was somewhat disrupted by the war, and after matriculation in 1918 Stubblefield became a junior chemist in a factory. He accepted advice to move to London to continue his education at evening classes, enrolling at the Southwestern Polytechnic Institute (later Chelsea College, of which he eventually was to become a governor). There he took his London intermediate science examination and studied for the royal scholarship, which he obtained in 1921 together with the university scholarship. These took him to Imperial College, London, where he graduated ARCS and (separately) BSc in 1923, both with first class honours in geology.

Stubblefield was appointed departmental demonstrator in geology at Imperial College in 1923. With his lifelong friend O. M. B. Bulman, whom he had met at Chelsea and who had also proceeded to Imperial College, he began research into early Palaeozoic rocks and their faunas in Shropshire, under Professor W. W. Watts. Stubblefield and Bulman were awarded their PhDs in 1925. Jointly they were awarded the Daniel Pidgeon fund of the Geological Society, also in 1925. With J. W. Evans, Stubblefield edited the *Handbook of the Geology of Great Britain* (1929), a highly successful work of great detail for which he was ideally suited. Stubblefield's earlier palaeontological work revealed his interest in the trilobites, the three-lobed arthropods that were prolific in Palaeozoic seas. Especially important were his demonstrations of the development (ontogeny) of the larval stages of trilobites, settling a long-

Sir (Cyril) James Stubblefield (1901–1999), by Elliott & Fry, 1953

debated argument, and papers on the classification of trilobites.

In 1928 Stubblefield was appointed to the Geological Survey and Museum of Practical Geology in London. Initially assigned to fieldwork in the Dorking district, he was soon moved to fill a vacancy in the palaeontology department. His room in the Jermyn Street headquarters was redolent of history: its window was etched with the name of a former chemist to the Geological Survey, Lyon Playfair, and it had later been occupied by T. H. Huxley, naturalist to the Museum of Practical Geology. In the Geological Survey and Museum Stubblefield was involved in numerous studies of Lower Palaeozoic fossils, of Shrewsbury and elsewhere, followed by Carboniferous studies of the coalfields of south Wales and Kent, and other rocks in Cumberland. In preparation for the move of the Geological Museum and headquarters of the Geological Survey from Jermyn Street to South Kensington, which took place in 1934–5, there was an increasing amount of detailed planning and the curation of over one million specimens. Stubblefield was deeply involved in the palaeontological aspects. Meanwhile, on 11 June 1932 he had married, at St Cuthbert's Church, Philbeach Gardens, London, (Emily) Muriel Elizabeth Yakchee (b. 1908), daughter of Leonard Randolph Yakchee, of the port commissioners, Calcutta. They had two sons, Peter Jackson (b. 1935) and Rodney George (b. 1937).

Stubblefield served as secretary of the Palaeontographical Society from 1934 to 1948, and subsequently as president and trustee. He was also the compiler for many years of the trilobite section of *Zoological Record*. He served on the council of the Geological Society, becoming vice-president (twice), president in 1958–60, and a senior fellow in 1974. While president he received a formal approach from the Netherlands to consider and submit to the long-established International Geological Congress a proposal to form an international union of geological sciences. With great skill this was eventually brought about. From the society he received the Murchison fund, the Bigsby medal (1945), and the Murchison medal (1951). By the time of his death he was easily the most senior honorary member of the Geological Society Club (from which the society had originally developed). Elected to it in 1937, he had probably the longest membership in the club's history, from its establishment in the early years of the nineteenth century. He received his London DSc in 1942, and was elected FRS in 1944, an event celebrated fifty years later by a luncheon given by the Royal Society.

Stubblefield was promoted to chief palaeontologist of the Geological Survey and Museum in 1947, assistant director in 1953, and director in 1960, a position he held until his retirement in 1966. During his directorship fundamental changes were taking place in the organization of British science, affecting the Geological Survey and Museum as much as any institution. Its parent government department, the Department of Scientific and Industrial Research (DSIR), was dissolved in 1965 and new research councils were established. Stubblefield was asked whether the Geological Survey and Museum should be transferred to the Science Research Council, but agreed instead to its transfer to the Natural Environment Research Council. It was a decision about which he subsequently had increasing doubts. He was also involved in the amalgamation of the home and Overseas Geological Surveys, to form the Institute of Geological Sciences (later renamed the British Geological Survey), of which joint organization he became the first director.

Stubblefield was knighted in 1965. His contributions to Carboniferous palaeontology were recognized by his presidency of the Sixth International Congress of Carboniferous Geology and Stratigraphy in 1967. He received many academic honours, and was elected to many foreign and British scientific bodies. His eightieth birthday was marked by a collection of papers in his honour in the *Geological Magazine*. A trilobite genus, *Stubblefieldia*, was named in his honour, as were sixteen other fossil species.

The nickname Stubbie, by which Stubblefield was affectionately and widely known, was appropriate in view of the short stub of pencil that was never far from his hand for correcting and improving any manuscript that came within reach. He was a man of small physical stature, whose scientific ability and integrity were legendary; these were matched by his courtesy and kindliness. He achieved a position of pre-eminence in his field by immensely hard and continuous work, and by having an excellent memory and superb eye for detail, whether of a fossil or of a manuscript, aided by his living to the age of ninety-eight. He died at the Georgian House Nursing Home, Lyncroft Gardens, Ealing, London, on 23 October

1999, and was cremated at Breakspear crematorium, Ruislip, on 1 November; a service was held at St Stephen's Church, Ealing. He was survived by his wife, Muriel, and their two sons.   PETER A. SABINE

Sources BGS, Stubblefield MSS · M. A. Calver, 'Palaeozoic studies in honour of Sir James Stubblefield', *Geological Magazine*, 118 (1981) · H. B. Whittington, *Memoirs FRS*, 47 (2001) · *Geological Society annual review, 1999* (2000), 35 · *Daily Telegraph* (8 Nov 1999) · *The Guardian* (11 Nov 1999) · *The Times* (10 Dec 1999) · *WWW* · personal knowledge (2004) · private information (2004) [Austin P. Stubblefield] · b. cert. · d. cert.
Archives BGS · NHM, palaeontology collection
Likenesses Elliott & Fry, photograph, 1953, NPG [*see illus.*] · probably by W. Bird, photograph, RS · photograph, repro. in *Daily Telegraph* · photograph, repro. in *The Guardian* · photograph, repro. in *The Times* · portrait, BGS · prints, priv. coll.
Wealth at death £224,208—gross; £221,824—net: probate, 20 Jan 2000, *CGPLA Eng. & Wales*

Stubbs, George (1724–1806), painter, engraver, and anatomist, was born in Liverpool on 25 August 1724 and baptized there at Our Lady and St Nicholas on 31 August, the eldest of six children (not all surviving infancy) of John Stubbs (*d.* 1741), currier, of Dale Street, Liverpool, and his wife, Mary (*d. c.*1756), formerly Mary Laithwait, widow.

Early life Biographical information about Stubbs is sparse. Almost the only source for his first thirty-five years is the rambling, inexact 'Memoir' ('particulars of the life of Mr. Stubbs'), jotted down by Ozias Humphry RA from conversations with Stubbs between about 1794 and 1797, when Stubbs was over seventy. Quotations here not otherwise identified are from this 'Memoir'. Humphry relates that Stubbs began to draw at the age of five, and that his interest in anatomy began at the age of eight, when Dr Holt, a neighbour, lent him 'bones & prepared subjects'.

Stubbs worked in his father's currier's shop until he was fifteen or sixteen, when his father agreed that he could learn to paint, if he could find a good master. Hamlet Winstanley, the Lancashire painter and engraver then working for the tenth earl of Derby copying paintings at Knowsley Hall (just outside Liverpool), agreed to take Stubbs on as assistant; but Stubbs quickly rebelled, because he was allowed no choice over which pictures to copy, and disliked the whole idea of copying. He left Winstanley, 'vowing he wou'd for the future look into Nature for himself and consult *and study her only*'. So ended (in 1741?) Stubbs's first and only experience of tuition in painting.

From about 1741 to 1744 (or until the age of about twenty) Stubbs lived in Liverpool with his mother (widowed in 1741), teaching himself to paint, dissecting small animals, and perhaps helping to settle his father's estate, which may have included several small properties which passed to Stubbs (Farington notes that at Stubbs's death he owned 'two or three small Houses at Liverpool' (Farington, *Diary*, 8.2854). Later he worked in Wigan, Leeds, and York, painting portraits. The earliest work by Stubbs so far known is the double portrait of *Sir Henry and Lady Nelthorpe*, of Barton upon Humber, north Lincolnshire (priv. coll.), painted about 1744–5 (a date inferred from the fact that Sir Henry Nelthorpe died in June 1746).

George Stubbs (1724–1806), self-portrait, 1781

Painted on a fairly large scale, this has a robust quality which prevails over some weaknesses of observation. Stubbs was to retain some connection with the Nelthorpes for nearly fifty years.

From about 1745 to 1751 Stubbs concentrated on the study of human anatomy at York County Hospital, his principal instructor being the surgeon Charles Atkinson (*fl.* 1740–1783), who procured the first human cadaver for Stubbs to dissect. Stubbs's combined drawing and dissecting skills prompted Dr John Burton (1710–1771) to ask him to design and etch eighteen plates ('Foetus's Wombs infant Children &c &c') for his *Essay towards a Complete New System of Midwifery*. With no previous experience of printmaking, Stubbs had to teach himself how to etch, using 'a common sewing-needle stuck in a Skewer … and Gravers … borrowed of a clock-maker'. Some of the plates illustrate Stubbs's own dissections of the body of a woman who had died in childbirth, 'brought to York by Stubbs's pupils where it was conceal'd in a Garret and all the necessary dissections made'. Probably this episode occasioned the 'vile renown' for which Stubbs was remembered in York over thirty years later (Sir Thomas Frankland to Sir Joseph Banks, 12 March 1786, *The Banks Letters*, ed. Warren R. Dawson, 1958, 343–4). Dr Burton's book was published in 1751. Aware of the imperfections of his plates, Stubbs did not sign them, and they appear anonymously. In York, about 1746, Stubbs painted the portrait of *George Fothergill* (Ferens Art Gallery, Kingston upon Hull). After York, Stubbs spent about two years (1751–3?) 'in Hull', according to Humphry, but perhaps based rather with the Nelthorpes at Barton upon Humber (6 miles by ferry from Hull).

Visit to Italy, 1754 Probably in the spring of 1754 Stubbs embarked for Italy, perhaps at his own expense, perhaps subsidized by Lady Nelthorpe. He was in Rome by Easter 1754, lodging in the piazza di Spagna. His residence there, noted in the local census or *Stato delle anime* (Ingamells, 912, n. 1) is, after Stubbs's baptism, the first officially documented fact in Stubbs's career. He was in Rome at the same time as William Chambers, Thomas Jenkins, Matthew Brettingham, Richard Wilson, Hamilton (perhaps Gavin Hamilton), and Simon Vierpyl, but told Humphry that on visits 'to consider the pictures in Rome [he] always found himself differing from them in opinion'. Stubbs later told Humphry that he 'copied nothing' while in Rome (a statement to be considered later). His stay appears to have been short. Recollecting it to Humphry some forty years later, he claimed that his motive for going to Italy was 'to convince himself that nature was & is always superior to art whether Greek or Roman, & having renew'd this conviction he immediately resolved upon returning home'. He may have been back in Liverpool a year or so before Christmas 1755, the date he inscribed on the back of a portrait of *James Stanley* (Walker Art Gallery, Liverpool).

The anatomy of the horse Stubbs's driving ambition in the early 1750s was to study the anatomy of the horse. He had discussed this project with Charles Atkinson and others at York, hoping to enlist their help, but they were unable to join him. In or about 1756 Stubbs returned to Barton upon Humber to paint a portrait of Lady Nelthorpe's young son, *Sir John Nelthorpe* (priv. coll.). Presumably he discussed his project with Lady Nelthorpe, who may have arranged for him to work in a farmhouse in the village of Horkstow, a few miles from Barton upon Humber.

Stubbs's work at Horkstow occupied him for about eighteen months. He dissected many horses, working on them one by one, first bleeding them to death by the jugular vein, then injecting the veins and arteries with wax-like substances to preserve their shape. Having fixed iron hooks in the farmhouse ceiling, he rigged up tackle from which (with drawings in mind) he could suspend a horse in a seemingly natural attitude, its hooves resting upon a plank. He then dissected each horse until it was no longer 'fit for use'; each lasted on average six to seven weeks.

At each stage of dissection Stubbs made drawings, of which forty-two survive. Most are working drawings made directly in front of the cadaver; eighteen are immaculately finished drawings, designed to be engraved for publication. Once in the collection of Sir Edwin Landseer RA, the forty-two drawings were bequeathed by his brother Charles Landseer RA to the Royal Academy, and were used for teaching in the Royal Academy Schools.

In this arduous work at Horkstow Stubbs's only assistant was Mary Spencer (d. 1817), according to Humphry 'the posthumous child of Captain Spencer of the Guinea Trade'. Born like Stubbs in Liverpool (at an unknown date:

Fountain suggests 1741), she remained with him throughout his life and was his sole legatee. Almost everything about their relationship is obscure. Humphry first refers to her as Stubbs's 'Female Relation & Friend', then inserts 'his Aunt'; edited transcripts made by William Upcott alter this to 'Niece', then to 'Aunt' and again to 'Niece'. Mary Spencer is now assumed to have been Stubbs's common-law wife. Possibly either Stubbs or Mary Spencer had contracted an early, failed marriage which prevented a marriage of their own. Probably Mary Spencer was the mother of three of Stubbs's children, George (almost certainly the son later known as George Townly *Stubbs), whose baptism on 26 February 1748 NS is recorded in the registers of St Helen's Church, York (information traced by David Alexander), Charles Edward, also born in York, and Mary, whose burial in Liverpool on 18 September 1759 is recorded in the registers of St Peter's, Liverpool; for both these children the father's name is entered as 'George Stubbs, Limner', but the mother's name is not recorded. Mary Spencer is named as the mother (and George Stubbs as the father) of Richard Stubbs, born in London on 16 August 1791, named as 'Richard Spencer Stubbs', and as a legatee in the first draft of Stubbs's will (1794), but not baptized until 18 November 1811, five years after his father's death (St Marylebone register of baptisms). A Robert Stubbs, apprenticed to the engraver William Austin in 1761, was described as 'Relat. of the celebrated Horse Painter' when he won a premium from the Society of Arts in 1766; but the nature of his relationship to George Stubbs remains unknown.

Probably in 1759 (exasperatingly, Humphry writes 'in 1758 1759 176–', Stubbs moved south to London, hoping to commission a professional engraver to etch his drawings of the anatomy of the horse for publication. Finding nobody willing to undertake such subject matter, he decided to etch the plates himself, although from 1759 he was inundated with commissions for paintings. Working 'early in the Morning & in the Evening and sometimes very late at Night' (Humphry), he achieved austerely elegant plates that combine 'scientific exactitude with a harmonious beauty of placing and balance' (Godfrey, *Printmaking in Britain*, 57). After six years they were ready for publication, with forty-seven pages of detailed letterpress, as a bound book. Its title-page reads: *The anatomy of the horse. Including a particular description of the bones, cartilages, muscles. fascias, ligaments, nerves, arteries, veins, and glands. In eighteen tables, all done from nature. By George Stubbs, painter. London: Printed by J. Purser, for the author, 1766.* The 'eighteen tables' or plates begin with views of the skeleton of the horse from the side, front, and back, followed by views from similar angles of different stages of dissection; many are accompanied by key plates.

Stubbs's title-page description of himself as 'George Stubbs, painter' stresses his purpose in undertaking his research. As a painter he wanted fully to understand what lay beneath a horse's skin, and how muscles and veins, schematized by earlier horse painters, actually functioned. When the Dutch anatomist Petrus Camper wrote in 1771 praising the book and hoping that Stubbs would proceed with further investigation into the horse's anatomy, Stubbs replied:

> What you have seen is all I meant to do, it being as much as I thought necessary for the study of Painting … I looked very little into the internal parts of a Horse, my search there being only a matter of curiosity. (letter of 17 Oct 1771, Egerton, *Stubbs, 1724–1806*, 31)

Making a reputation in the 1760s In London Stubbs evidently showed his *Anatomy of the Horse* drawings to various noblemen who were keenly interested in breeding and racing horses. Most of them were quick to recognize that Stubbs's work had an accuracy (or 'truthfulness to nature') lacking in earlier horse painters such as James Seymour and John Wootton. The lead in commissioning Stubbs's work was taken by the third duke of Richmond, who in 1759 invited Stubbs to Goodwood to paint three large scenes: *The Third Duke of Richmond and the Charlton Hunt*, *Henry Fox and the Earl of Albemarle Shooting at Goodwood*, and *The Duchess of Richmond and Lady Louisa Lennox Watching the Duke's Racehorses at Exercise*, perhaps about 1760 (all three paintings remain at Goodwood House, Sussex).

Commissions rapidly followed from Viscount Spencer, Lord Grosvenor, the marquess of Rockingham, Viscount Bolingbroke, the dukes of Ancaster, Grafton, and Portland, and Viscount Torrington (probably in that order). Collectively their patronage helped to make Stubbs's name and to give him the confidence, in June 1763, to buy a leasehold property in London at 24 Somerset Street (adjoining the later Portman Square), his home for the rest of his life.

Stubbs's first works for such patrons were portraits of single horses with grooms or jockeys, such as *A Stallion Called Romulus* (priv. coll.), the first work Stubbs exhibited, in 1761. Other examples include *Lustre* (c.1760–62; Yale U. CBA, Paul Mellon collection), *Molly Long Legs* (1762; Walker Art Gallery, Liverpool), and *Tristram Shandy* (exh. 1762; priv. coll.). Underlying these was the knowledge gained in the near-solitary years of dissecting and drawing the anatomy of the horse; but in painting horses from life Stubbs depicted them in natural settings of almost spring-like freshness, in which trees, skies, broad-leaved plants, and flowers all play their part. Between 1762 and 1777 Stubbs devised ten variations on the theme *Brood Mares and Foals*. These subjects—brood mares which had perhaps already produced winners, and long-legged foals destined (with luck) for future successes—particularly appealed to breeders of thoroughbred horses, whether or not they depicted horses from their own stud farms.

The most eminent (and most discerning) of Stubbs's early patrons was the second marquess of Rockingham. Twice prime minister (in 1765 and 1782), Rockingham found private pleasure in his stud farms and strings of racehorses. Between 1762 and 1766 Stubbs painted about twelve pictures for him, ranging from a picture of his racehorse, *Bay Malton Ridden* ['at Speed'] *by John Singleton* (priv. coll.), to a frieze-like portrait, *Five Staghounds*, seen against a hilly background (priv. coll.). Accounts survive for most of them (see Constantine). Three of Stubbs's paintings for

Rockingham—*Whistlejacket*, the magnificent near life-size portrait of a rearing stallion (National Gallery, London), *Mares and Foals*, probably the first of those subjects, paid for in August 1762, and *Whistlejacket and Two Other Stallions with Simon Cobb the Groom* (also of 1762; the latter two both priv. coll.)—break with convention in having only plain backgrounds. This was almost certainly Rockingham's decision. A collector of sculpture, he evidently perceived that the finest of Stubbs's paintings of his horses would be seen to best advantage, like his classical statues, against plain backgrounds.

Stubbs's talents blossomed during the 1760s, a decade described by Taylor as 'in scope and productiveness … the most fecund time of his life' (Taylor, *Stubbs*, 13). His ability to combine landscape, horses, and figures in complex and inventive designs is demonstrated in such works as *The Grosvenor Hunt*, dated 1762 (priv. coll.), with its virtuoso painting of hounds splashing through water, and *Gimcrack on Newmarket Heath, with a Trainer, Jockey and Stable-Lad* (priv. coll.; version, Jockey Club, Newmarket), in which the squat shape of one of the brick rubbing-down houses at Newmarket confers a permanent sense of place upon the passing event of a win for Lord Bolingbroke's horse; that motif recurs in some of the finest of Stubbs's racehorse and jockey portraits, such as *Turf* (Yale U. CBA, Paul Mellon collection) and *Gimcrack* (Fitzwilliam Museum, Cambridge), both dating from about 1756. *Setting out from Southill* (c.1765–8; priv. coll.) depicts hunt servants, fresh-faced in the morning air, riding out from a Bedfordshire village. Stubbs's servants, grooms, and jockeys are invariably drawn from life; he regards them with a sensitive and uncondescending eye.

Exhibiting at the Society of Artists From 1761 to 1774 Stubbs exhibited annually at the Society of Artists. Of the thirty-five or so works which he showed there, only about one-third (including five versions of *Mares and Foals*) were portraits of his patrons' well-bred horses. The range of his portraiture of people was demonstrated by the four *Shooting* paintings (exh. singly, 1767–70; Yale U. CBA, Paul Mellon collection) and by *A Conversation* (exh. 1770), almost certainly the group portrait now known as *The Milbanke and Melbourne Families* (National Gallery, London). He also showed a few classical subjects: two versions of *Phaeton and the Horses of the Sun* (exh. 1762; National Trust collection, Saltram House, Devon, and exh. 1764, untraced), and two episodes from the labours of Hercules, *Hercules and Achelous* (exh. 1770) and *The Centaur, Nessus, and Dejanira* (exh. 1772), both seemingly lost. But about half Stubbs's exhibits at the Society of Artists depicted encounters between wild animals.

The 'lion and horse' theme From the early 1760s Stubbs was preoccupied with the idea of a wild horse, existing precariously in a state of nature, where it was the prey of a lion (See Taylor, 'George Stubbs: "The lion and horse theme"'). Stubbs returned repeatedly to this theme, developing it into episodes: the horse first frightened at seeing the lion; recoiling in terror at the lion's approach; attacked by the lion springing onto his back; finally forced to the ground to be devoured by the lion.

Stubbs exhibited his first two paintings on this theme in 1763: *A Horse and Lion* (described by Horace Walpole as 'The horse rising up, greatly frightened' (Graves, *Soc. Artists*, 249) and *Its Companion*. If correctly identified as the pair now in the Tate collection (T1192 and T02058), then the second picture, which shows the horse forced to the ground before being devoured by the lion, virtually proves that Stubbs's initial inspiration for the whole theme was the pre-Hellenic sculpture of a lion devouring a horse which he could have seen in the Palazzo dei Conservatori on his visit to Rome in 1754. Conceivably, Stubbs's later insistence to Humphry that he copied nothing while he was in Rome relates only to painted works. Later 'lion and horse' paintings include *Horse Attacked by a Lion* (c.1765; National Gallery of Victoria, Melbourne), *White Horse Frightened by a Lion* (1770; Walker Art Gallery, Liverpool), and *White Horse Attacked by a Lion* (1770; Yale U. CBA). He also depicted the subject in enamel and in his own prints.

Stubbs painted (and exhibited) other imaginary encounters between wild animals; these encounters were usually savage, such as that in the *Lion and Stag* (several versions, the finest exh. 1766; priv. coll.), but sometimes peaceable, such as that in the *Lion and Lioness* (one of several versions is in the collection of the Boston Museum of Fine Arts). Such subjects appealed to few of Stubbs's Newmarket-oriented patrons; but the marquess of Rockingham commissioned two vast paintings, *Horse Attacked by a Lion* (paid for in 1762) and *Lion Attacking a Stag* (c.1764?), which hung in his London house (both now Yale U. CBA, Paul Mellon collection). James Barry, writing about 1764, described Stubbs's wild animal subjects as 'pictures that must rouse and agitate the most inattentive: he is now painting a lion panting and out of breath lying with his paws over a stag he has run down: it is inimitable' (*Works of James Barry*, 1.23). Most people would have known these and other subjects in the form of engravings after Stubbs, which were produced in steadily increasing numbers, from fourteen in 1770 to some sixty by 1780 to ninety or so by 1791 (see Lennox-Boyd, Dixon, and Clayton, esp. 22–3).

Stubbs portrayed many specific wild animals. Barry's description of his 'tyger lying in his den large as life, appearing as it were disturbed and listening' (*Works of James Barry*, 1.23) is of *A Tigress* (priv. coll.), a creature presented by Lord Clive, governor of Bengal, to the duke of Marlborough, and painted by Stubbs in the menagerie in Blenheim Park. *Cheetah with Two Indian Attendants and a Stag* (exh. 1765; City of Manchester Art Galleries) is a superbly painted image of the abortive encounter staged in Windsor Great Park between a cheetah presented to George III and a stag (from which the cheetah fled).

Because of his accuracy Stubbs was frequently asked to portray newly imported animals. His *Zebra* depicted the first zebra seen in England; presented to Queen Charlotte in 1762, it was installed in the royal menagerie at Buckingham Gate, where Stubbs took its likeness with an exact eye for conformation and markings (Yale U. CBA, Paul Mellon collection). For Sir Joseph Banks he painted (from a stuffed skin) *The Kongouro from New Holland*, 1770 (priv. coll.), and also the *Dingo*. He undertook various commissions for William and John Hunter (brothers, surgeons, anatomists, and picture collectors). For William Hunter he painted the *Nylghau* from India (c.1769), the *Moose* presented to the duke of Richmond by the governor-general of Canada (dated 1770), and the *Blackbuck* (c.1770–78; all Hunterian Art Gallery, University of Glasgow). When lecturing on the nylghau to the Royal Society, William Hunter had Stubbs's painting beside him, remarking that 'Whoever looks at the picture … can never be at a loss to know the nyl-ghau, wherever he may happen to meet with it' (*Philosophical Transactions of the Royal Society*, 61, 1771, 21). For John Hunter Stubbs painted the *Male Drill and Albino Male Papio Hamadryas* (c.1770–75), the *Yak* (1791), and *Rhinoceros* (c.1790–92; all Royal College of Surgeons, Hunterian Museum, Glasgow; version of *Yak*, priv. coll.). To such acute observations should be added the lithe but almost palpably nervous *Monkey* (exh. 1775; priv. coll.). Stubbs's interest in animals however small is evident in three meticulous pencil drawings of *Marmaduke Tunstall's Mouse Lemur* (1773; BM).

Relationship with the Royal Academy In the Society of Artists, to which he was elected in 1765, Stubbs had served as a director (1765–74), treasurer (1768–72), and president (October 1772 – October 1773); but in 1775 he (like others before him) left the declining society to exhibit with the more prestigious Royal Academy, founded in 1768. He exhibited at the Royal Academy (irregularly) until 1803; but his relationship with the academy soured early. Having been elected an associate of the Royal Academy in 1780, on 13 February 1781 he was provisionally elected royal academician, with the usual condition (stipulated in the academy's instrument of foundation) that an RA-elect must deposit a diploma work before receiving the diploma entitling him to the status of royal academician. Stubbs refused to deposit a work, alleging that the request for it was a 'new rule' aimed specifically against him. He seems not to have consulted royal academicians who had complied with the rule, such as his friend Richard Cosway (RA 1770) or Philippe Jacques de Loutherbourg, voted RA-elect on the same day as himself. Instead, Stubbs formed 'an *unconquerable resolution*' not to deposit a picture. Given over a year to comply with the rule, he still refused to do so; consequently, his provisional election as royal academician was annulled, and never repeated.

In the late 1760s Stubbs began to experiment with enamel painting, an art practised by his day only by miniaturists and decorators of small objects. His chief purpose appears to have been to re-create key images in his work in the unchanging, virtually indestructible form of enamel. Preparing enamel paints involves grinding particles of colourless glass with selected metallic oxides; in the heat of a furnace the glass fuses with and gains colour from the oxides. Humphry relates that Stubbs spent 'near two years with great expense' experimenting with chemical compounds 'of the Colour they were required to be when the pictures were fired'. The resulting paints could be brushed onto solid, non-inflammable supports which carried the work through a furnace to be fired. From about 1769 to 1775 Stubbs used copper supports.

The first enamel Stubbs exhibited was *Lion Attacking a Horse*, on copper, dated 1769 (exh. 1770; Tate collection); technically faultless, it concentrated all the drama of the subject into the small octagonal space of 24.3 x 28.2 cm. Others followed, including *Horse and Lion*, dated 1770 (priv. coll.), exhibited in 1771 with *Lion and Lioness* (Yale U. CBA). This stage culminated with Stubbs's largest enamel painting in copper, the oval *Phaeton and the Horses of the Sun* (38.5 x 46 cm), dated 1775 (priv. coll.), with which Stubbs posed for Ozias Humphry's portrait of about 1777 (watercolour, NPG).

Wanting larger supports for his enamels, Stubbs approached the manufacturers of ceramics. Mrs Coade's Artificial Stone Manufactory could not help, but Josiah Wedgwood, after much experiment, developed a special earthenware body which could sustain a thin, flat shape in firing. By May 1779 Wedgwood was supplying Stubbs with large oval ceramic tablets, about 72.5 x 94.5 cm, later increasing the size to about 77 x 105 cm (see Emmerson). Seventeen paintings by Stubbs on Wedgwood tablets are known, mostly fired in Wedgwood's enamel kiln at Greek Street, Soho, London. They include portraits of *Josiah Wedgwood* and his wife, *Sarah Wedgwood* (Wedgwood Museum, Barlaston, Staffordshire), each dated 1780, painted in part payment for Wedgwood's tablets.

For the first five years after Stubbs's transfer to the Royal Academy, his exhibits had all been oils. In 1781 he exhibited *Two Horses in Enamel* (now known as 'Horses Fighting'; Yale U. CBA, Paul Mellon collection) on a large oval Wedgwood tablet. In the following year five of his seven exhibits at the Royal Academy were in enamel on similar tablets, including *Portrait of an Artist* (a self-portrait with brush and palette, NPG), *Portrait of a young lady [Isabella Saltonstall] in the character of Una, from Spenser's 'Faerie queen'* (Fitzwilliam Museum, Cambridge), and *The Farmer's Wife and the Raven* (Lady Lever Art Gallery, Port Sunlight).

To most royal academicians Stubbs's enamels were an unwelcome intrusion into the display of oil paintings, from which they differed in tone, texture, and shape; nor did they resemble the small jewel-like work allowable in the exhibited work of professional enamellists. In the hang of 1782 Stubbs's enamels were skied. Indignant, Stubbs showed nothing whatever at the Royal Academy for the next three years. He continued occasionally to work in enamel, as in *Self Portrait on a White Hunter* (1782) and *Equestrian Portrait of Warren Hastings* (1791) (each priv. coll.), and the harvesting scenes of 1794–5 which are among his greatest achievements in enamel (see below). He exhibited again at the Royal Academy from 1786 to 1791 and, after a gap of eight years, from 1799 to 1803; but he sent no more works in enamel to the academy.

Though absorbing a great deal of his time, Stubbs's enamel paintings constitute only a small part of his output. Most of his work continued to be in oil, but whereas he had formerly applied oil paint to canvas quite thickly

and crisply, after 1769 the experience of painting in enamel on smooth, hard supports inclined him often to paint on wooden panels; and when doing so, he continually experimented by mixing his oils with pine resin, beeswax, non-drying oils, and fats, producing a very thin paint film. While many of his panels have survived in good condition, others have suffered from past restorers' incomprehension of Stubbs's experimental and sometimes faulty techniques (see Shepherd, in Egerton, *Stubbs, 1724–1806*, 20–21).

Work of the 1770s and 1780s Few of Stubbs's first noble patrons continued to commission his work, apart from Earl Spencer and Lord Grosvenor, for each of whom he worked in the 1770s. But new patrons appeared, including gentlemen in the shires who wanted portraits of their hunters and hacks. For John Musters of Colwick Hall, Nottinghamshire, Stubbs painted a notable group of subjects in 1776-7, including *John and Sophia Musters Riding at Colwick Hall* and *Thomas Smith, Huntsman of the Brocklesby Hounds*, depicted with his elderly father, the former huntsman (both priv. coll.). For Thomas Foley, Charles James Fox's racing associate, he painted *Pumpkin with a Stable-Lad* (1774; Yale U. CBA, Paul Mellon collection), with the same freshness of observation as anything he had painted in the 1760s. Revisiting Lincolnshire in 1776, Stubbs painted *Sir John Nelthorpe Shooting with his Pointers in Barton Field* (priv. coll.), and for some unknown patron he painted the exquisite *Phaeton with a Pair of Cream Ponies in Charge of a Stable-Lad* (c.1780–85; Yale U. CBA, Paul Mellon collection).

Single portraits of dogs (and a few hounds) enter Stubbs's repertory in the early 1770s, proving popular enough to inspire many commissions. Two of the four paintings with which Stubbs made his début at the Royal Academy in 1775 were portraits of dogs: *A Spanish Dog, Belonging to Mr Cosway* (referring to Richard Cosway RA; priv. coll.), and Earl Spencer's *Mouton, a 'Pomeranian' Dog* (priv. coll.). Most of his later dog portraits were exhibited merely as *Portrait of a Dog*, making it difficult to know whether some of Stubbs's most endearing dog portraits, such as *White Poodle in a Punt* (National Gallery of Art, Washington, Paul Mellon Bequest) or *King Charles Spaniel* (priv. coll.) were exhibited. Stubbs's dog portraits are closely observed, sometimes more light-heartedly than his horse portraits; but what chiefly distinguishes them is Stubbs's sense of design. In almost every case the compact build of the dog (compared with that of long-legged horses) allows the body of the subject to occupy most of the pictorial space. Two portraits of foxhounds painted on a return visit to Lincolnshire in 1792 show Stubbs's powers of design at their finest: these are *Ringwood, a Brocklesby Foxhound* (priv. coll.) and *A Couple of Foxhounds* (Tate collection).

Haymakers and Reapers, 1785 In 1786 Stubbs marked his return to the Royal Academy (after the fracas over his enamel exhibits) by showing *Haymakers* and *Reapers* (both Tate collection). In oil on panel, each dated 1785, they are among his most lyrical works. The subject matter is hardly original; their distinction lies rather in the rhythmic designs—perfected from versions of 1783 (Bearsted collection, Upton House, Bearsted, Warwickshire)—by which Stubbs graces his subjects without falsifying their naturalism. Stubbs sent *Haymakers* and *Reapers* to the 1787 exhibition of the Society for Promoting Painting and Design in Liverpool. His personal vote of confidence in his subjects was to translate them into enamel. In 1794–5 he re-created *Haymakers* and *Reapers* in enamel, on the largest of all his Wedgwood tablets. The enamel of *Reapers*, dated 1795, is in the collection of the Yale Center for British Art. *Haymakers*, dated 1795, and a related subject, *Haymaking*, dated 1794, are both in the Lady Lever Art Gallery, Port Sunlight.

Stubbs as a printmaker In printed *Proposals* issued on 24 September 1788, Stubbs invited subscriptions for engravings of *Haymakers* and *Reapers* (duly published in 1791). In small print at the foot of his *Proposals* he briefly listed fifteen prints which 'may also be had' at his house (evidently they were not for sale in printsellers' shops). The earliest of these are two quite large line engravings, *A Horse Frightened by a Lion* and *Leopards at Play*, dated 1777 and 1780 respectively. These (and later prints such as *Labourers* and *The Farmer's Wife and the Raven*) echo the imagery of subjects already painted; yet they are not reproductive engravings, but re-creations of those subjects, in different moods. A group of prints with the publication line 1 May 1788 may well have been made over the previous decade, before Stubbs was ready to launch his engraved work. Three small engravings of single foxhounds, each of which appears as a detail in the large *Charlton Hunt* painting of 1759, are probably derived from pencil studies preserved in Stubbs's studio. Stubbs continually experimented with engraving techniques; Godfrey observes that 'He gives the impression of an artist stooped over a copper plate with a small battery of tools beside him, the function of each being diverted to original and unexpected use as it came to hand' (Godfrey, 'George Stubbs', 115). Altogether Stubbs made eighteen prints (*The Death of the Doe*, published in 1804, may be largely G. T. Stubbs's work). Stubbs is among the greatest and most original printmakers in British art. His prints have an intense, deeply felt quality, particularly telling on the small scale of the *Foxhound* prints, or the *Sleeping Leopard*, published in 1791.

Commissions in the 1790s George III had shown no interest in Stubbs's work, but the prince of Wales commissioned fifteen works between 1790 and 1793 (one now lost; the others remain in the Royal Collection). Stubbs's portrait of the prince riding in Hyde Park is dated 1791. Outstanding in this group are *The Prince of Wales's Phaeton*, *Soldiers of the 10th Light Dragoons*, and *William Anderson with Two Saddle-Horses*, each dated 1793 and each painted with the same brilliance of invention he had shown in the 1760s. Piecemeal payments were still being made for the group in 1805.

In 1790 Stubbs became involved with a project to publish a *Review of the Turf from the Year 1750 to the Completion of the Work*. It was planned that Stubbs would paint at least 145 portraits of racehorses: George Townly Stubbs would engrave them, and the engravings would be published, with letterpress, in forty-five numbers. By January 1794 Stubbs had completed sixteen paintings (some of them replicas of earlier works); these were displayed in the so-called Turf Gallery in Conduit Street, London, where subscriptions for the *Review* were invited. George Townly Stubbs completed fourteen engravings. Only two numbers of the *Review* were published before the project failed at the end of 1794. For Stubbs this meant the loss of years of promised income; reputedly, £9000 had been deposited in a bank for him to draw on as he progressed with the work. The initiator of the project requested anonymity, and remains unidentified.

At the age of seventy-six Stubbs produced two of his greatest and most meditative works. Each is dated 1800, and each was painted for a new patron. Sir Henry Vane-Tempest, second baronet, wanted a portrait of his racehorse Hambletonian to commemorate his recent win at Newmarket. On one of the largest canvases he had ever painted, Stubbs set down a monumental image of the exhausted racehorse. With a rubbing-down house at Newmarket just sufficiently visible to establish a sense of place, Hambletonian is rubbed down by a stable-lad, while an impassive trainer at his head holds his reins. Stubbs had to sue Vane-Tempest (successfully) for payment of 300 guineas for the picture. Exhibited at the Royal Academy in 1800 as *Hambletonian, Rubbing Down*, it is now in the collection of Mount Stewart, co. Down, Northern Ireland.

Thomas Villiers, second earl of Clarendon, of The Grove, Watford, was the last patron to commission Stubbs's work in quantity (perhaps ten varied subjects, including racehorses, spaniels, and an Indian bull). One painting in this group is mysteriously elevated from the rest by its mood of grave, almost elegiac poetry: set in a darkening wood, it depicts Freeman, the earl of Clarendon's gamekeeper, with a dying doe and a hound. Stubbs exhibited it at the Royal Academy in 1801, with the title *A Park Scene at The Grove* (Yale U. CBA, Paul Mellon collection).

A Comparative Anatomical Exposition Stubbs's last project, begun at the age of seventy-one in 1795, was *A comparative anatomical exposition of the structure of the human body with that of a tiger and a common fowl*. Humphry observed in July 1796 that 'at 72 Stubbs is forming Plans with as much resolution as might be expected at 40' (Farington, *Diary*, 2.597). A 'common fowl' was easily obtained, and Pidcock's menagerie supplied the body of a tiger; but procuring a human cadaver was more difficult. Here Stubbs may have had help from Henry Cline, one of his occasional visitors and an anatomy lecturer at St Thomas's Hospital, which could legitimately receive the bodies of executed criminals for dissection.

Stubbs made 125 drawings for his *Comparative Anatomical Exposition* (Yale U. CBA). Some are highly finished, others mere tracings for working purposes. As with *The Anatomy of the Horse*, Stubbs did not probe deeper than the musculoskeletal system. Chiefly he was engaged in comparing the structure of his three subjects. He demonstrated this compellingly in finished profile drawings of the man, tiger, and fowl, standing and running, partly dissected and in skeletal form. The value of his work lies chiefly in his ability to draw what he saw, with accuracy and detachment, demonstrating 'a superbly coordinated empirical hand and eye flourishing at the end of a rational era' (Ober, 992). Between 1804 and 1806 Stubbs engraved and published three numbers of the *Comparative Anatomical Exposition*, each with five plates (and a separately issued letterpress). He had hoped to publish six numbers.

Stubbs had seemed ageless and tireless; but in January 1804 George Dance, who had drawn a profile pencil portrait of him in 1794 (RA), was shocked to observe the change in Stubbs's appearance: 'so aged—so in-jawed and shrunk in his person' (Farington, *Diary*, 6.2225). Stubbs died on 10 July 1806 at his home, 24 Somerset Street, London. He was buried in St Marylebone on 18 July. Farington heard 'that when Stubbs died there was no money in the house', that 'His House was mortgaged to a Lady a friend of his', and that 'He owed Her money besides' (ibid., 6 June 1807, 3060). The 'Lady', an entirely well-meaning benefactor, was Isabella Saltonstall (*b*. 1765/6), whom Stubbs had portrayed as a child with her parents in a *Conversation Piece* dated 1769 (priv. coll.), and later as *Una, from Spenser's 'Faerie Queene'* (mentioned above). Stubbs had made a will in 1794, leaving his property to Mary Spencer, George Townly Stubbs, and Richard Spencer Stubbs. On the day of his death he made a new will, leaving everything to Mary Spencer and appointing Mary Spencer and Isabella Saltonstall joint executors. By then suffering 'violent spasms', he was unable to sign it, but after attestations by witnesses, it was accepted for probate.

The sale of the contents of Stubbs's studio was conducted by Peter Coxe on 26–7 May 1807. No fully annotated copy of the sale catalogue has been traced; but evidently many lots were bought in by Isabella Saltonstall. As Farington reported, she

> had advanced to Stubbs a considerable Sum of money and Had a Bond of Security which gave Her a claim to His pictures &c. These were sold the last week & the prices were kept up by Her agents & many articles were bought in. It is understood that after Her debt is paid there will be little left. (Farington, *Diary*, 8.3056, 3 June 1807)

The eventual fate of most of the works acquired for Isabella Saltonstall remains a mystery. In particular, many sketchbooks and preliminary drawings which might have offered insights into Stubbs's working methods have disappeared. There are other serious gaps in documentation of Stubbs's work. A methodical man, he is likely to have kept accounts and 'sitters' books' for his varied subjects; and Humphry mentions that he kept memoranda of his experiments with enamels. All these have vanished. But what will survive is the work itself which, in the words of E. K. Waterhouse, embraces not only paintings of horses, but 'man, the whole animal kingdom, and nature' (Waterhouse, 207).   JUDY EGERTON

Sources O. Humphry, 'Memoir, or, Particulars of the life of Mr Stubbs', Liverpool Central Library, Picton Collection [with two edited MS transcripts made by William Upcott]; Upcott's 2nd transcript, with notes added by Mary Spencer, published in N. Hall, ed., *Fearful symmetry: George Stubbs, painter of the English Enlightenment*

(2000), 200–12 [exhibition catalogue, Hall and Knight, New York] · B. Taylor, *Stubbs* (1971) · B. Taylor, 'George Stubbs: "The lion and horse theme"', *Burlington Magazine*, 107 (1965), 81–6 · B. Taylor, *The prints of George Stubbs* (1969) · B. Tattershall, *Stubbs and Wedgwood* (1974) [exhibition catalogue, Tate Gallery, London; incl. intro. by B. Taylor] · B. Taylor, *Stubbs in the 1760s* (1970) [exhibition catalogue, Agnews, London] · J. Egerton, *George Stubbs, 1724–1806* (1984) [exhibition catalogue, Tate Gallery, London, and New Haven, Connecticut] · J. Egerton, *George Stubbs: anatomist and animal painter* (1976) [exhibition catalogue, Tate Gallery, London] · R. Emmerson, 'Stubbs and Wedgwood: new evidence from the oven books', *Apollo*, 150 (Aug 1999), 50–55 · C. Lennox-Boyd, R. Dixon, and T. Clayton, *George Stubbs: the complete engraved works* (1989) · H. F. Constantine, 'Lord Rockingham and Stubbs: some new documents', *Burlington Magazine*, 95 (1953), 236–8 · W. Gilbey, *Life of George Stubbs R.A.* (1898) · R. B. Fountain, *Some speculations on the private life of George Stubbs, 1724–1806* (1984) · J. Ingamells, ed., *A dictionary of British and Irish travellers in Italy, 1701–1800* (1997) · Graves, *Soc. Artists* · will, PRO, PROB 11/1447, fol. 37r–v · E. Waterhouse, *Painting in Britain, 1530–1790* (1953); 2nd edn (1962), 207 · R. T. Godfrey, *Printmaking in Britain: a general history from its beginnings to the present day* (1978) · *The works of James Barry*, 2 vols. (1809) · T. Godfrey, 'George Stubbs as a printmaker', *Print Collector's Newsletter*, 13/4 (Sept–Oct 1982), 113–16 · W. B. Ober, 'George Stubbs: mirror up to nature', *New York State Journal of Medicine*, 70/8 (April 1970), 985–92

Likenesses O. Humphry, portrait study, chalk, 1777, Trustees of the Right Hon. Olive, Countess Fitzwilliam's Settlement · G. Stubbs, self-portrait, enamel on china tablet, 1781, Lady Lever Art Gallery, Port Sunlight · G. Stubbs, self-portrait, enamel on Wedgwood plaque, 1781, NPG [*see illus.*] · G. Dance, pencil and chalk drawing, 1794, RA · Bretherton, etching (after T. Orde), BM, NPG · O. Humphry, pastels, Walker Art Gallery, Liverpool · O. Humphry, watercolour, NPG · G. Stubbs, self-portrait, plumbago, Yale U. CBA

Wealth at death believed to be small

Stubbs, George Townly (*bap.* 1748, *d.* 1815?), engraver and printseller, was probably the son of George *Stubbs (1724–1806), painter. His baptism on 26 February 1748 NS is recorded in the registers of St Helen's Church, York (information traced by David Alexander). His mother may have been Mary Spencer (*d.* 1817), who is now identified as George's common-law wife, although the birth of Richard Spencer Stubbs to George Stubbs and Mary Spencer in 1791 suggests that this is doubtful. More likely, the name Towny (as it appears on his prints) or Townley might have been the surname of his mother. His first mezzotints, *The Lion and Stag* and *The Horse & Lion*, were published by John Wesson in 1770 and he was probably the 'gentleman' who exhibited *A Lion Devouring a Stag; Mezzotinto* with the Society of Artists in that year. In 1771 he exhibited a drawing as 'Mr George Stubbs junior'. He scraped a number of mezzotints after George Stubbs's paintings in the 1770s and began to publish on his own account in 1776.

In the early 1780s George Townly Stubbs collaborated with the drawing-master and engraver Charles White and the gem-engraver and caricaturist James Wickstead on a series of stipple engravings, some of which had humorous subjects. He was bankrupted in 1785. Stylistic evidence suggests that he might have been the engraver of some caricatures about the prince of Wales's romance with Mrs Fitzherbert that were published in 1786. In 1788 he produced two large mezzotints of high quality, *Horses Fighting* and *Bulls Fighting*, after paintings by George Stubbs and during the next decade he returned to interpreting

George Stubbs's work, employing either stipple or sophisticated combinations of tools. During the 1790s he was the manager of the Turf Gallery in Conduit Street, off New Bond Street, and he may have written the text of a *Review of the Turf*. As originally proposed this ambitious project was to have encompassed 'the history of every horse of note, with various anecdotes on the most remarkable races', and it was to have been 'embellished with upwards of one hundred and twenty prints, engraved in the best manner from original portraits of the most famous racers, painted by Mr. Stubbs at an immense expence and solely for the above work' (Lennox-Boyd and others, 43). The enterprise collapsed in 1796 after only fourteen horses had been engraved by George Townly Stubbs. From the inception of this project he styled himself 'engraver to the prince of Wales' and there was a strong implication that this most unreliable of patrons may have promised to underwrite the enterprise. The prints were published by 'Messrs Stubbs' and it is conceivable that George Townly Stubbs was himself the mysterious Mr Turf upon whose backing they relied. During the 1790s Stubbs also engraved sets of prints after designs by Edward Penny and Anthony van Assen and published some landscapes by Thomas Morris. He maintained a print shop on Marylebone High Street from at least 1793 to 1800. His latest publications were a series of heads expressing passions after Henry Singleton and William Frederick Wells issued in summer 1800. After this date George Townly Stubbs may have lived by painting or dealing in paintings. He is said to have died in 1815 and this notion is supported by the republication by other publishers of some of his prints in that year.

TIMOTHY CLAYTON

Sources C. Lennox-Boyd, R. Dixon, and T. Clayton, *George Stubbs: the complete engraved works* (1989) · W. Gilbey, *Life of George Stubbs, R.A.* (1898) · D. Snelgrove, *British sporting and animal prints, 1658–1874* (1981) · F. Siltzer, *The story of British sporting prints*, 2nd edn (1929) · Graves, *Soc. Artists* · A. Ledgard, 'Mr Stubbs' views of the passions', *Print Collector's Newsletter*, 16 (March–April 1985), 1–4

Stubbs, Henry. *See* Stubbes, Henry (1605/6–1678); Stubbe, Henry (1632–1676).

Stubbs, John. *See* Stubbe, John (c.1541–1590).

Stubbs, John (c.1618–1675), Quaker minister, was probably born in Durham, though details of his parentage are unknown. He married Elizabeth Stubbs, and both became Quakers at the same time. According to George Fox's description, Stubbs was 'a poore man haveing a wife & four Children [sic]' (*Journal of George Fox*, 2.49). Only two of these children can be identified: they are named in the Swarthmore manuscripts as Sarah and Lydia. Stubbs worked in a variety of jobs: if all the contemporary records are to be believed he was a soldier, a schoolmaster, and a husbandman.

Stubbs was a Baptist serving in the army at the time when the Quaker leader, George Fox, secured his conversion in 1653. Fox, who was then imprisoned at Carlisle, remembers Stubbs's conversion in his *Journal*, and the two were clearly good friends. Stubbs's travels and sufferings after he became a Friend were extensive, even by early

Quaker terms. He joined a movement whose charismatic ministers felt the 'call' to publish their ideas both in England and abroad; Stubbs, however, went further than most.

Stubbs's ministry began on home soil before encompassing Europe and the New World. From his northern base Stubbs moved southwards; he was travelling with William Caton in Kent when the couple were charged with vagrancy, placed in the stocks, and whipped. From being one of the first Quakers in Kent in 1655, Stubbs went on to contribute to the expansion of Quakerism in London, Colchester (1655), Scotland (1655), and Ireland (1656 and 1669): he was attacked in Coldbeck and imprisoned at Cork, but elsewhere appears to have escaped any serious injury. George Fox's recollection of Stubbs's journeys in 'Holland, Ireland, Scotland, Legarne, Rome, Aegypt, America' shows that these foreign travels left a strong impression on the minds of others (*Journal of George Fox*, 1.141).

Stubbs made a brief journey to the continent with William Caton in 1655 (he had returned by August 1656). This international ministry was at first focused on establishing a Quaker community in the Netherlands, and Stubbs's residence in 1657 continued this work. In 1658, with Samuel Fisher, Stubbs's continental evangelism reached Italy, where pamphlets were distributed. Stubbs then became part of one of the Quakers' most ambitious ministries: beginning in the Netherlands he and two other Friends tried to travel to China via Alexandria. However, they were banished from Egypt and so Stubbs travelled on through Europe. During the 1660s Stubbs's ministry was mostly based in England—he was in Lancaster prison until November 1664, which led to his petitioning Charles II for clemency. His final overseas ministry occurred in 1671, when a group including George Fox travelled throughout the North American colonies.

Stubbs died in London of consumption on 31 July 1675, and was buried at Chequer Alley, London. Fox commemorated the 'wise' Stubbs's 'many sufferings', remarking that he was 'a notable Minister of the Gospel of Christ' (Lodge, 52).

CATIE GILL

Sources 'Biographical memoirs', 1854, RS Friends, Lond., MS vol. 213 · J. Besse, *A collection of the sufferings of the people called Quakers*, 2 vols. (1753) · W. C. Braithwaite, *The beginnings of Quakerism*, ed. H. J. Cadbury, 2nd edn (1955); repr. (1981) · 'Dictionary of Quaker biography', RS Friends, Lond. [card index] · N. Penney, *First publishers of truth* (1907) · *The journal of George Fox*, ed. N. Penney, 2 vols. (1911) · Quaker register of births, marriages, and burials, RS Friends, Lond. · J. Smith, *A descriptive catalogue of Friends' books*, 2 vols. (1867) · RS Friends, Lond., Swarthmore papers · R. Lodge, *Several living testimonies given forth by divers Friends* (1891)
Archives RS Friends, Lond., Swarthmore papers

Stubbs, Philip. *See* Stubbes, Philip (b. c.1555, d. in or after 1610).

Stubbs, Philip (1665–1738), archdeacon of St Albans and educationist, was born on 2 October 1665 in the parish of St Andrew Undershaft, London, the son of Philip Stubbs, vintner, and his wife, Elizabeth Hillier. Having been a pupil at Merchant Taylors' School, London, from 1678 to

Philip Stubbs (1665–1738), by John Faber junior, 1722 (after Thomas Murray, 1713)

1682, he matriculated at Oxford as a commoner of Wadham College on 13 March 1683. He was made a scholar of the college on 26 September 1684, and graduated BA on 20 October 1686, proceeding MA on 15 June 1689 and BD on 3 July 1722. He was elected a fellow on 1 July 1691, moderator *novae classis* in 1688, and subdean in 1691. He was repetitioner of the Easter sermons in 1691. After ordination in 1688 he became a curate in the united parishes of St Benet Gracechurch and St Leonard, Shoreditch. From 1691 he was successively chaplain to Robert Grove, bishop of Chichester, and George, earl of Huntington.

In 1694 he became rector of Woolwich; at that time developments associated with the royal dockyard were changing the area from a fishing village to a town. There he married in 1696 Mary (1664–1759), daughter of John Willis, rector of West Horndon, Essex. They had two surviving sons and one daughter. The concern he showed for the sailors probably led to his becoming the first chaplain of Greenwich Hospital for disabled seamen, and he simultaneously held other clerical posts. On leaving Woolwich in 1699 he became rector of St Alphage, London Wall, and in 1705 also of St James Garlickhythe in London. He relinquished these parishes in 1715 when he became archdeacon of St Albans; later he became rector of Launton, Oxfordshire (1719 until his death). He was elected FRS on 30 November 1703 and took an active interest in literature and archaeology. His responsibilities at Greenwich Hospital and the annual visit to his archdeaconry meant that he was absent from Launton for half the year and he employed a curate at the full rate of £40 a year.

Richard Steele recalled the care he devoted to public worship:

While being at St James's Garlick-Hill church I heard the service read so distinctly, so emphatically and so fervently that it was next to an impossibility not to be attentive. ... The rector of this parish at that time was Mr Philip Stubbs, afterwards archdeacon of St Albans, whose excellent manner of performing the service was long remembered by the parishioners. (*The Spectator*, no. 147, 18 Aug 1711)

Stubbs was also renowned as a preacher. He published many individual sermons and addresses, and in 1704 a collected volume. In one published sermon on Revelation 20: 13, the *Sea-Assize*, which had been preached at Greenwich and Woolwich on Advent Sunday, 28 November 1708, in memory of Prince George of Denmark, Stubbs was designated 'Chaplain of HM Navy in Ordinary and of her Royal Hospital for Seamen at Greenwich'; another sermon, *God's Dominion over the Seas and the Seaman's Duty* (1701), preached at Longreach, Essex, on the *Royal Sovereign*, went to three editions and was translated into French for French seamen who were prisoners of war. He was an early supporter of the Society for the Propagation of the Gospel (SPG), and compiled its first report in 1703. The society gave him a special vote of thanks and chose him to preach the sermon in St Paul's Cathedral on Trinity Sunday, 1711, the day the queen had appointed for SPG collections to be taken in the city churches. This sermon was afterwards published under the title *The Divine Mission of Gospel Ministers* (1711).

As an incumbent Stubbs cared for poor children. He was an early member of the Society for Promoting Christian Knowledge, supporting its encouragement of charity schools. He established such schools in his London parishes, at St Alphage, London Wall, and St James Garlickhythe, and in Bicester, near his Launton parish, and he also paid £2 a year to Bicester grammar school to support two boys from Launton.

Archdeacon Stubbs died at Greenwich Hospital on 13 September 1738 and was buried in the hospital's old cemetery. His tombstone survives there in the mausoleum.

LEONARD W. COWIE

Sources R. B. Gardiner, ed., *The registers of Wadham College, Oxford*, 2 vols. (1889–95) · Foster, *Alum. Oxon.* · Mrs E. P. Hart, ed., *Merchant Taylors' School register, 1561–1934*, 2 vols. (1936) · E. McClure, *Minutes of the SPCK* (1888) · H. P. Thompson, *Into all lands* (1951) · P. Newell, *Greenwich Hospital, 1692–1983* (1984) · D. Lysons, *The environs of London*, 2nd edn, 2 vols. in 4 (1811) · Wood, *Ath. Oxon.*, 2nd edn · W. D. Cooper, 'St James Garlickhithe', *Transactions of the London and Middlesex Archaeological Society*, 3 (1865–59), 392–403 · P. C. Carter, *History of the church and parish of St Alphage, London Wall* (1925) · *The Spectator* (18 Aug 1711)

Archives Bodl. Oxf., essays, MS Eng. th. c. 63 · Wadham College, Oxford, MSS collection

Likenesses J. Faber senior, mezzotint, 1708 (after his earlier work), BM · T. Murray, portrait, 1713 · J. Faber junior, mezzotint, 1722 (after T. Murray, 1713), NPG, BL, 32. 351, f. 17 [*see illus.*]

Stubbs, Sir Reginald Edward (1876–1947), colonial governor, was born on 13 October 1876 in Oxford, the youngest of the five sons of William *Stubbs (1825–1901), regius professor of modern history at Oxford, who became bishop of Chester and then of Oxford. His mother was Catherine Dellar (*b.* 1838) of Navestock, who had worked as the headmistress of the village school there. He attended Radley College, from where he won an exhibition to Corpus Christi College, Oxford. Stubbs, noted for his acid wit, demonstrated his superior academic ability by taking a first class in both classical moderations (1897) and *literae humaniores* (1899).

In January 1900 Stubbs entered the Colonial Office and worked in the Eastern department, where he monitored developments in the Straits settlements, the Federated Malay States, Hong Kong, and Ceylon. In 1910–11 Stubbs, who eventually became a first-class clerk in the Colonial Office, went on an official fact-finding tour of Malaya and Hong Kong. Apart from his official duties, he pursued some academic interests. In 1906, for example, he edited the second edition of *The Mediterranean and Eastern Colonies*, volume 1 of Sir Charles Prestwood's *Historical Geography of the British Colonies*; in addition, he served as the joint editor of the *Colonial Office List* (1910–12). In 1909 Stubbs married Winefrid Marjory, daughter of the London physician and member of parliament Frederick Womack. The couple had two sons and a daughter. Lady Stubbs (CBE, 1919) became known for her social and charitable work in the colonies where her husband served.

After a thirteen-year career in Whitehall, Stubbs became colonial secretary of Ceylon (1913–19). This was an unusual career move, as in those days there was little, if any, interchange between the staff of the Colonial Office and the colonial service overseas. He remained in Ceylon throughout the First World War and so consolidated his reputation that, in 1919, he received the unprecedentedly quick promotion to the governorship of Hong Kong. Despite boycotts and troubles on the mainland affecting Hong Kong, he served with success for the full term of six years. In 1926 he was transferred as captain-general and governor-in-chief to Jamaica, where he remained for six years.

Largely because of Stubbs's outspoken and direct manner, his colonial service career was not without controversy. While governor of Hong Kong, for example, he frequently clashed with Foreign Office officials because of the latter's determination to control policy in the colony. One of the more serious incidents occurred when he sided with the provincial government of Canton (Guangzhou) against Peking (Beijing) in a dispute over the distribution of customs revenues. In Jamaica, the largest of the British Antillean colonies, Stubbs helped to ensure that progress towards the implementation of a new constitution and universal adult suffrage proceeded at a rational pace, much to the chagrin of some Jamaican nationalists.

Within weeks of being appointed governor of Cyprus in 1932 Stubbs alienated many Cypriots by increasing his legal powers to suppress seditious behaviour among individuals who advocated *Enosis* (union between Greece and Cyprus). In 1933 he moved to Ceylon as governor and during his four years there he resisted demands by a group of Sinhalese ministers of the Ceylon state council to amend the Donoughmore constitution to facilitate the emergence of complete responsible government. In Stubbs's view such a step was premature, as the island's Tamil and Muslim communities opposed what they considered to be an attempt by the Sinhalese ministers to erode their political rights.

Despite Stubbs's pugnacious and sometimes quarrelsome personality, many of his critics readily acknowledged that he was highly efficient and extremely dedicated to his work. As a result, he received numerous awards for his many accomplishments: he was made CMG (1914), KCMG (1919), and GCMG (1928), was appointed to the Japanese order of the Rising Sun, first class (1921), and received the honorary degree of LLD from Hong Kong University (1926). He was elected an honorary fellow of Corpus Christi College, Oxford, in 1926.

In 1937 Stubbs retired on pension and settled at Commonwood, Bearsted, Kent; he remained active, however, in public affairs. In 1938 he became a member of the West India royal commission, which resulted in the establishment of the West Indian Welfare Fund with an annual budget of £1 million and the creation of administrative offices to stimulate the region's social and economic development. In 1941 Stubbs agreed to serve as chairman of the northern appellate tribunal for conscientious objectors. A lover of animals, especially of Siamese cats, he was a fellow of the Zoological Society. On 7 December 1947 Stubbs died of heart failure at Bearsted in Kent. He was survived by his wife. THOMAS PAUL OFCANSKY

Sources DNB • P. Arnold, *Cyprus challenge* (1956) • K. M. De Silva, *A history of Sri Lanka* (1981) • H. A. J. Hulugalle, *British governors of Ceylon* (1963) • F. Welsh, *A history of Hong Kong*, rev. edn (1997) • J. A. Williamson, *A short history of British expansion*, vol. 2 (1958) • Zeylanicus, *Ceylon: between orient and occident* (1970) • CGPLA Eng. & Wales (1948)
Likenesses double portrait, photograph, 1920 (with Lady Stubbs), NPG • W. Stoneman, photograph, c.1935, NPG • photograph, repro. in Hulugalle, *British governors of Ceylon*
Wealth at death £34,558 3s. 10d.: probate, 23 March 1948, CGPLA Eng. & Wales

Stubbs, Thomas (*fl.* 1343–1381), Dominican friar and supposed chronicler, is described by John Bale as the author of the continuation of the chronicle of the archbishops of York known as *Chronica pontificum ecclesiae Eboracensis*; but there is no contemporary ascription to him, nor is he mentioned in any of the extant manuscripts, and the authorship remains undecided. The continuation in question extends from the time of Henry Murdac (1147–53) to the pontificates of William Zouche (d. 1352) and John Thoresby (d. 1373), and it is possible, from more detailed comments made in the chronicle on archbishops Melton (1317–40) and Zouche, that the writer had personal knowledge of them, or at least knew members of their entourage. An edition of the chronicle by James Raine was published in the Rolls Series in 1886.

The available information about Stubbs is very slight. Bale states that he was a Yorkshireman, but so far research has failed to produce any confirmatory evidence. The first detail there is records his ordination to the priesthood in Durham Cathedral on 20 December 1343 by Richard, titular bishop Bisaciensis, acting as the suffragan of the bishop of Durham. There were two Dominican convents in the diocese of Durham, one at Bamburgh, the other at Newcastle, and presumably Stubbs was a member of one of these convents at the time of his ordination. Earlier confusion over a Franciscan friar of the same name is the result of a misreading of the Durham ordination register by the editor of the chronicle continuation. Stubbs was in the Oxford Dominican convent by 1354–5, but a reference to him as being a member of the order's convent in York in the late 1350s is given without any source (*VCH Yorkshire*, 3.285) and more recent research on the mendicants in the York diocese has failed to locate him there. The latest reference found to him is in early 1381, when he was appointed one of the nine executors of the will of Thomas Hatfield, bishop of Durham (1345–81), in a list headed by his fellow Dominican John Gilbert, bishop of Hereford (1375–89). In the bishop's will Stubbs is described as *sacrae paginae professor*, showing that he had attained the degree of doctor of theology. Bale, John Leland, and John Pits ascribe to Stubbs the following theological works, in addition to the continuation of the York chronicle: *Statutum contra impugnantes ecclesiasticas constitutiones*; *De stipendiis praedicatoribus verbi debitis*; *De perfectione vitae solitariae*; *De arte moriendi*; *Meditationes quaedam pro consolatione contemplativorum*; *In revelaciones Brigidae*; *De misericordia Dei*; *Super cantica canticorum*; *Sermones de sanctis*; *Sermones de tempore*; *Officium completum cum missa de nomine Jesu*; *Officium de beata Anna*; *De poenis peregrinationis huius vitae*. None of these can now be identified.

DAVID M. SMITH

Sources J. Raine, ed., *The historians of the church of York and its archbishops*, 2, Rolls Series, 71 (1886), 388–421 · J. Taylor, *Medieval historical writing in Yorkshire* (1961) · J. Taylor, *English historical literature in the fourteenth century* (1987) · Emden, *Oxf.*, 3.xliii · A. B. Emden, *A survey of Dominicans in England* (1967) · [J. Raine], ed., *Testamenta Eboracensia*, 1, SurtS, 4 (1836) · 'Registrum palatinum Dunelmense': the register of Richard de Kellawe, lord palatine and bishop of Durham, ed. T. D. Hardy, 4 vols., Rolls Series, 62 (1873–8) · G. D. Jones, 'The relationship of the mendicant orders in Yorkshire to the archbishops of York', MA diss., University of York, 1987 · *VCH Yorkshire*, vol. 3

Stubbs, William (1825–1901), historian and bishop of Oxford, the eldest child of the two sons and four daughters of William Morley Stubbs (1800–1842), solicitor of Knaresborough, Yorkshire, and Mary Ann (1803–1884), daughter of William Henlock, was born in High Street, Knaresborough, on 21 June 1825. He could trace his Yorkshire yeoman descent through sixteen generations to another William Stubbs mentioned in 1359; his ancestry mattered to him and for his view of English history. From 1832 Stubbs attended a small private school in his native town, where he laid the foundation of his knowledge of languages, studying Latin, Greek, French, German, and—unusually—Old English, all of which were taught by the proprietor, a Mr. Cartwright. He went on to Ripon grammar school (in 1839), where he received an extremely thorough classical education; the study of Roman history extended to the work of Niebuhr. There he was fortunate in attracting the attention of Bishop Charles Thomas Longley (later archbishop of Canterbury), who secured for him a servitorship at Christ Church, Oxford, in 1844. The death of his father in 1842 left his mother impoverished and with six children. As a servitor Stubbs gained a university education at small expense but had to accept a position of low status; this normally implied an element of

William Stubbs (1825–1901), by Sir Hubert von Herkomer, 1885

social exclusion in the college, which does not, however, seem markedly to have affected him. He took his opportunities and gained a first-class degree in classics and a third in mathematics in 1848. His interest in English medieval history had already been aroused in Knaresborough, where his father had taught him to read old documents and he had worked on medieval records in the court house of Knaresborough Castle. Although Oxford made no provision for the formal study of medieval history Stubbs was able to pursue this interest in Christ Church Library, which contained most of the essential works. His religious opinions were much influenced by E. B. Pusey, and although brought up in an evangelical ambience, he became a lifelong high-churchman, but by no means a ritualist. Immediately after taking his degree he was elected to a fellowship at Trinity College.

Early parochial and historical work In 1850 Stubbs was ordained priest and presented to the Trinity living of Navestock, Essex, vacating his fellowship. There he succeeded James Ford, a local historian and bibliographer of some note. That Ford left £2000 to endow an Oxford professorship in English history (which ultimately endowed the Ford lectures) is a reminder of how far the roots of the revolution in historical studies, in which Stubbs played so large a part, were local and English. For sixteen years Stubbs worked as a diligent parish priest at Navestock, adding to his pastoral activities administrative duties as a poor-law guardian and inspector of diocesan schools. He supplemented his income by taking occasional resident private pupils, the most remarkable being A. C. Swinburne. On 20 June 1859 he married Catherine (b. 1838), daughter of John Dellar of Navestock; she had been the village schoolmistress. Five sons, including the colonial governor Sir Reginald Edward *Stubbs, and one daughter survived childhood.

It was at Navestock that Stubbs's learning and reputation were largely founded. His first published work on history was *Registrum sacrum Anglicanum* (1858) which sought to establish the episcopal succession in all the English sees from the earliest times. It was based on ten years' enquiry into printed and manuscript sources, including visits to diocesan registries to consult episcopal registers. Far in advance of any predecessors, it is the foundation of all later work. In 1861 he published *De inventione sanctae crucis*, a late twelfth-century tract chiefly concerned with the history of the collegiate church at Waltham, Essex. At the same time he began to contribute to historical periodicals: some of his early work of this kind was notably mature and original. His papers on the early history of Peterborough and of Worcester, for instance, reveal a remarkable knowledge and judgement in the use of Anglo-Saxon charters, including materials at that time unpublished. These papers were delivered in 1861 and 1862, and published in the *Proceedings* of the Archaeological Institute. In 1862 his old patron, now Archbishop Longley, made him librarian of the Lambeth Library. The duties were light and could be discharged by twice-weekly railway visits to London, allowing him to enjoy his easy access to a major library.

Stubbs and the Rolls Series In 1863 Stubbs was commissioned to edit *Chronicles and Memorials of Richard I* for the Rolls Series. This series had been inaugurated in 1857 to publish 'Chronicles and Memorials of Great Britain and Ireland during the Middle Ages'. The two volumes of his work published in 1864 and 1865 were the first of nineteen which he was to contribute to the series; his last contribution being the *Gesta regum* and *Historia novella* of William of Malmesbury, published in 1887–9. Stubbs's work was well paid: he received some £6600 all told for his volumes. As an editor, he made available good texts of sources previously poorly edited, if at all. The great majority of his editions, if outmoded, have not yet been superseded. The generous spirit in which the Rolls Series was conceived permitted him very long introductions, up to 100 pages or more. His are outstanding in scope and value. On points relating to his texts he could display minute learning: for example, the two pages he devoted to the possible origins of Ralph de Diceto's name. But he took the opportunity to spread himself much more widely. Sometimes he investigated a historical episode in detail: a good (rather moving) instance is his account in his introduction to Diceto of the last days of Henry II. In such passages his lively narrative command displays almost Macaulayesque qualities, hardly to be found in the *Constitutional History*. Often he paints on a much larger canvas. Thus the introduction to the second volume of *Chronicles and Memorials of Richard I* (*Epistolae Cantuarienses*) contains a substantial account of the history of monasticism in England, and that to *Memorials of St Dunstan* (1874) provides a detailed account of English monastic reform in the tenth century. The introduction to the *Chronicle* of Roger of Howden (4 vols., 1868–71)

provides a full general account of the reign of Henry II. Secure in judgement, eloquent in conviction, Stubbs's introductions to the Rolls Series have their deficiencies. He made little use of unpublished record material and seems indeed to have had relatively little sense of the wealth of the Public Record Office. He could have made more use of the published pipe rolls, although he wrote the preface to the Pipe Roll Society's edition of that for 1165–6 (1888). Finance was not his forte; nor was law, although he could make a passing observation, for example on the continuing influence of Anglo-Saxon law, which anticipates modern research. Very occasionally his rhetoric sinks to fustian, and his style of judging men of the past 'at the bar of history' has dated greatly and can jar. But his introductions put the study of large tracts of English history (above all, between the mid-twelfth century and the early thirteenth) on evidenced foundations on which all later scholars have built.

Regius professor of history at Oxford To learning Stubbs joined ambition. In 1862 he was a candidate for the Chichele chair of modern history of Oxford; in 1863 for the professorship of ecclesiastical history there; in 1865 for the principal librarianship of the British Museum. All in vain. But on 2 August 1866 Lord Derby offered him the regius professorship of modern history at Oxford. Stubbs was not the most obvious candidate: both E. A. Freeman and J. A. Froude had published more, were better known and more experienced. Nevertheless, Stubbs was moving towards closer friendship and intellectual contact with the two most significant English medievalists of the day, Freeman and J. R. Green, and had already examined in the Oxford school of history and law. The government was particularly anxious to appoint a regius professor whose views would contrast with those of the radical Goldwin Smith, newly resigned. The appointment seems to have been left largely in the hands of Lord Carnarvon, the colonial secretary, who, as high steward of the university, was in touch with its affairs. Carnarvon consulted his former tutor H. L. Mansel, Waynflete professor of moral and metaphysical philosophy, who had been involved in public controversy with Goldwin Smith and who was nominated towards the end of 1866 to the chair of ecclesiastical history, which some had expected to be given to Stubbs. Mansel wrote to recommend Stubbs: he did not know him personally, nor did he mention any of his works, but he characterized him as 'a good churchman', 'trustworthy', 'the nearest approach to a Conservative of all the candidates of whom I have heard'. But if Stubbs's appointment was largely determined on political grounds it proved fully justified on others. In the eighteen years in which he held the chair, he consolidated his position as the leading medieval historian, one might say the leading historian, in the country.

This was a time of determinative transition in the position of historical study at Oxford and in British higher education generally. Although the Oxford regius chair of modern history had been established in 1724, its significance was minor because no degree syllabus included modern (that is, post-ancient) history. In 1850 a joint degree in law and history was established, but it was of no more than marginal significance until the system was reformed in 1864. A crucial change came with the establishment of an independent degree in modern history in 1872. Within a generation modern history became the largest school in the university.

As professor, Stubbs lectured with great care, chiefly on English and German medieval history. Many of his lectures were published: one volume in his lifetime (*Seventeen Lectures on the Study of Medieval and Modern History and Kindred Subjects*, 3rd edn, 1900); posthumously there appeared one on English history, two on German history, and one on European history extending into the seventeenth century. His lectures, particularly those on European history, could have a brisk, opinionated tone, considerably more strident than that almost universally adopted in the *Constitutional History*. He expressed vigorous judgements on whole countries: 'French ambition has brought infinitely more misery upon Europe than all the repressive policy of Austria in all the years of her influence'. Stubbs had considerable sympathy with Habsburg rulers whom he felt to have been unjustly treated by Robertson and by Motley. He could be sweeping on whole centuries—for example, his comment that 'the best men of the sixteenth century were men of impulse rather than principle'.

Stubbs's relationship to the new school of modern history was not altogether happy. His personal influence (as contrasted with that of his books) on the new systems for examination and teaching of history was modest. His lectures were ill-attended, and he was marginalized, to an extent deliberately, by the college tutors, whose offerings were nearer to the level of what undergraduates felt they required. Stubbs resented the thinness of his audiences and complained that the system of historical education at Oxford was too much directed towards pupils' classification in the final examination. At the same time his personal influence on and help to historians were important. Although, as regius professor, Stubbs was a fellow of Oriel College, he had a special connection with Balliol, where he acted as chaplain from 1876. He was, somewhat surprisingly granted the differences in their religious and other views, on friendly terms with Benjamin Jowett and from 1870 he lived in Kettel Hall in Broad Street, virtually next door to Balliol. He taught a number of Balliol undergraduates as personal pupils, among whom were future historians of the highest distinction, in particular J. H. Round, C. H. Firth, R. L. Poole, and T. F. Tout.

Select Charters **and** The Constitutional History of England
Stubbs's commanding influence at various levels of historical study came, above all, from four volumes: *Select charters and other illustrations of English constitutional history from the earliest times to the reign of Edward I* (1870), and *The Constitutional History of England in its Origins and Development*, volumes 1 (1873), 2 (1875), and 3 (1878). The *Select Charters* is a collection of documents and excerpts beginning with passages from Caesar and Tacitus. It concludes with the reign of Edward I, although it includes the tract *Modus tenendi parliamentum*, which Stubbs thought to be of the

mid-fourteenth century, but is now known to be somewhat earlier. (In the second edition of 1874, he appended a handful of seventeenth-century documents.)

The *Select Charters* is most carefully disposed: an introduction of some fifty pages outlines the early constitutional history of England, and the chapters are chronologically arranged, each with a general introduction. All major documents are preceded by a commentary. Stubbs's introduction is programmatic: it is, he says, 'of the greatest importance' that English constitutional history 'should become a recognised part of a regular English education'. 'It is not creditable to us as an educated people' that students while well acquainted with the 'state machinery' of Athens and of Rome should be ignorant 'of the corresponding institutions of our own forefathers' which 'have exercised on the civilised world an influence not inferior certainly to that of the Classical nations'. So he commended 'this little book to the good offices of teachers, and to the tender mercies of pupils'. (The humour here is characteristic: Stubbs was a very humorous man—although this is hardly evident from the *Constitutional History*—and was given to writing comic verses.)

The *Constitutional History* was the keystone of Stubbs's achievement. Its first words are: 'The History of Institutions cannot be mastered,—can scarcely be approached—, without an effort'. This recommendation (as he saw it) misleads if it conveys an impression that Stubbs was concerned only with institutional history in a narrow sense. He saw English constitutional history in quasi-organic and teleological terms; as he put it in the preface to the *Select Charters*, it was: 'the examination of a distinct growth from a well-defined germ to full maturity … a growth whose life and developing power lies deep in the very nature of the people'. He continued: 'It is not then the collection of a multitude of facts and views, but the piecing of the links of a perfect chain'.

Thus the *Constitutional History* is not only a tremendous manual, but a major work of interpretation; almost a statement of faith. Considered simply as a manual its virtues are great: it is founded on wide learning, strongest on the twelfth century, not so strong on the early Anglo-Saxon period, where it begins, or on the fifteenth century, where it ends. It rests very largely on original sources: its extensive annotation includes references to secondary authorities only occasionally, except in relation to the earliest period where Stubbs depended greatly on German work, particularly that of Georg Waitz. No such comprehensive and learned a work on English medieval history had been written before. It was not only epoch making, but orderly: among Stubbs's gifts was that of organized exposition. His alternation of the descriptive and the analytic, his combination of narrative and interpretation were masterly. Massive though it is, the *Constitutional History* is an easy book to use. A characteristically handy device is the separate numbering of each paragraph; the numbering of the paragraphs remained consistent from edition to edition: all references below to the *Constitutional History* are by paragraph numbers.

The *Select Charters* and *Constitutional History* very soon became major educational instruments in growing under-graduate schools of history. As the Oxford honour school of modern history developed, much stress was laid on the study of constitutional history, felt to give 'a strength and dignity to the School which it might otherwise lack' (Slee, 91). Constitutional history was difficult and complicated, required the study of original texts, and was a barrier against descent into mere discourse. The work of Stubbs was deeply valued at Oxford and also at Cambridge (the only other university in the late nineteenth and early twentieth centuries with a large history school). J. R. Tanner described the study of history at Cambridge about 1880: 'The lecturer lectured on Stubbs; the commentator elucidated him; the crammer boiled him down. Within those covers was to be found the final word on every controversy and in this faith the student moved serene' (F. W. Maitland and others, *The Teaching of History*, 1901, 54). The great influence could reach into schools. G. M. Trevelyan, writing of his time at Harrow in the early 1890s, recalled that he was set to read Stubbs as 'a strict regimen of the modern type of scientific history at its best' to supplement the 'sweet cake' of Gibbon, Macaulay, and Carlyle. He analysed Stubbs 'in three massive notebooks' (G. M. Trevelyan, *An Autobiography and other Essays*, 1949, 12). The influence of Stubbs on the university study of history was not only strong, but long; it was ultimately thanks to Stubbs that as late as 1968 all twenty-five of the British universities founded before 1949 required undergraduate historians to study English medieval history.

The main line of thought in the *Constitutional History* is a devoted, teleological interpretation of the English state. For Stubbs the origins of the English constitution, of English liberties, lie in Germany as described by Tacitus. He saw the organization of Anglo-Saxon England as containing crucial elements which continued the liberties of early Germany, not least in the quasi-representative or popular courts of hundred and shire which survived the impact (drastic but in major ways beneficial) of the Norman conquest. Under the Angevins the administrative and legal systems were developed in ways intimately connected with arrangements and ideas which came from the Anglo-Saxon and early German pasts. The nation had begun 'to realise its unity and identity' (*Constitutional History*, para. 134): Magna Carta, argued Stubbs, was 'the first act of a corporate life that had reached full consciousness' (ibid., para. 155). The reigns of Henry III and Edward I were determinative: under the former, the effect of civil war was that 'England was reclaimed for the English' (ibid., para. 229), while under his son came the crucial development of parliament—a national representative institution intimately connected with the local representative institutions which had preserved German freedom. By 1307 parliament was established in 'definiteness and completeness' (ibid., para. 455). Stubbs regarded the later middle ages as a somewhat unhappy period for England, marred by the misadventure of premature constitutionalism under the Lancastrians. But the Tudors restored order and in the seventeenth century constitutional liberty

revived, 'rising as it were from the dead'; from then, it survived and flourished into Stubbs's own day.

In perspective Stubbs's *Constitutional History* is necessarily a period piece, though aptly described by Professor J. W. Burrow as 'one of the great books of the nineteenth century ... the most perfectly realised embodiment of English Burkean ideas' (Burrow, 300). A leading example of nineteenth-century historicism, it was dominated by such concepts as that of the historically determined individuality of the nation and of the importance of the development of a nation's self-consciousness. The origins of such views are diverse and take us from Burke and Coleridge to Germany. Stubbs was greatly indebted to German historians as guides and models, not least to the *Verfassungsgeschichte* of Georg Waitz. Stubbs's competence in German and involvement with German historical scholarship were a counterpart to Pusey's determination to master German theological learning. (One of Stubbs's first published works was a translation (and continuation) of Mosheim's *Ecclesiastical History*, 1863.) Among English historians Stubbs may not unfairly be regarded as sharing some of the views of what has been characterized as the 'liberal Anglican' school of historicist historians, prominent among whom was Thomas Arnold. Not all Arnold's views, let alone the adjective 'liberal', could have been congenial to Stubbs. However, his interpretation is distinctly Arnoldian, in its repeated emphasis on the analogy (or by diffuse implication, something more than analogy) between the progress of the life of a nation and that of an individual. On some specific points Stubbs's views were precisely Arnold's: he too saw 'Lancastrian constitutionalism' as, to use Arnold's term, 'a false Spring'.

Stubbs's historical work extended even beyond the Rolls Series and constitutional history. He undertook (in co-operation with A. W. Haddan) an edition of materials relating to the pre-Reformation councils of the churches of Britain and Ireland. The whole projected work was never completed; but Stubbs's volume (3), *Councils and Ecclesiastical Documents Covering the History of the Anglo-Saxon Church*, published in 1878, was and is an invaluable collection (Stubbs characteristically extended it well beyond merely conciliar documents). His devotion to work such as that involved in the preparation of this volume is a reminder of the intimate relationship between his position as a churchman and as a historian. The continuity of the Church of England, through its medieval past to apostolic times, was of fundamental importance to him. It was largely in connection with his work for *Councils and Ecclesiastical Documents* that he wrote approximately 400 lives of Anglo-Saxons for the *Dictionary of Christian Biography* between 1877 and 1887. He also contributed to the *Dictionary of Christian Antiquities* (1875–80).

The success of the *Constitutional History* is indicated by its having reached its ninth edition before Stubbs's death, while the *Select Charters* reached its eighth (the additions or corrections made by him in successive editions of his works were by no means extensive). Stubbs's reputation extended far: he received honorary doctorates from Heidelberg, Cambridge, Edinburgh, Oxford, and Dublin, membership of the Bavarian, Prussian, and Irish academies, and of the Académie des Sciences Morales et Politiques of the Institut de France. The most outstanding foreign honour was his appointment in 1897 to the Prussian order of merit: one of the thirty foreign members of its division chosen for distinction in the arts or sciences. Stubbs was consistently anti-French, regarding France as originally and essentially absolutist. Thus it is the more remarkable that not only was a French translation of the *Constitutional History* published between 1907 and 1927, but it was accompanied by a series of studies supplementary to Stubbs (the translation and many of the studies were among the earliest works of Georges Lefebvre).

Other activities Though a professor, Stubbs by no means abandoned the activities and career of a clergyman. From 1875 to 1879 he held the Oriel College living of Cholderton, Wiltshire, residing there during the long vacations, while a curate officiated at other times. (An important consideration here must have been that while he had been appointed to the regius chair at an annual salary of £350, Cholderton was worth £300; Crockford, 1870.) In 1878 he was tempted to accept the living of the university church of St Mary. In 1879 Disraeli made him a canon of St Paul's, an appropriate (and remunerative) distinction for a scholar who had three years before, in the introduction to his edition of the works of Diceto, provided an outstanding account of St Paul's in the late twelfth century. So Stubbs became a member of a most distinguished chapter, regularly performed his turn of duty in the cathedral and lived in London for part of the year at no. 1 Amen Court, where he found a quantity of long-forgotten muniments in the garret.

In 1881–3 Stubbs's eminence both as a churchman and as a historian was brought out by the prominent role he played as a member of the royal commission on ecclesiastical courts. Its subject was of the first importance in the great ecclesiastical conflicts of the day. Stubbs, who attended all the commission's sittings, sought to maintain a firm distinction between, on the one hand, the authority of the state, which included the power to endow or disendow and to exercise coercive jurisdiction, and, on the other, the spiritual authority of the church. He contributed five appendices to the commission's report and in these investigated major elements in the history of ecclesiastical authority and jurisdiction in England. He contended that the medieval English church had enjoyed a substantial degree of independence from papal authority. A major issue here was that, in historical terms, royal authority over the church, not least as expressed in the judicial authority of the privy council, derived from Henry VIII's legislation to replace the powers of the pope. Stubbs's views were powerfully controverted by F. W. Maitland in papers subsequently published as *Roman Canon Law in the Church of England* (1898). Once again Stubbs had been deeply concerned with the historic Catholic continuity of the Church of England with its medieval past. When he prepared the text of *Tractatus de veritate conceptionis beatissimae virginis* by Cardinal de Torquemada for Pusey's edition (1869) it was not with strictly historical

intent but, rather, to assist in an effort to deter the coming Vatican Council from moving Roman Catholic doctrine too far from that of the Church of England.

Bishop of Chester and then of Oxford Thus Stubbs's acceptance in 1884 of Gladstone's offer of the see of Chester was not a divergence from the main path of his life, even though it marked almost the end of his career as a historian. He was an active bishop, unwearying in visiting his parishes. Part of Chester diocese was industrialized, populous, and under-churched, and Stubbs immediately launched an appeal for the creation of nine new parishes, each with church, school, and vicarage, and for fifteen mission rooms. The estimated cost was £84,000, of which the bishop contributed £1000 (he was believed to give away half his episcopal income for such purposes). The appeal was largely successful, and in general, Stubbs played a prominent part in local affairs. At this time he was also highly regarded in the central affairs of the Church of England: in 1886, at the request of the archbishop of Canterbury, E. W. Benson, he drew up a paper on the possibility of establishing a national synod. He was also largely responsible for the encyclical letter issued by the Lambeth conference of 1888.

Stubbs's distinction and justified reputation for sound judgement explain his translation, by Lord Salisbury, to the see of Oxford in 1888. Bishops of Oxford were felt to require special qualities because of the presence of the university and not least because of the ambiguous position of Christ Church and of its dean. Stubbs was well qualified to relate to the university; in due course he became a curator of the Bodleian Library, a delegate of the university press, and a member of the board of the faculty of modern history. His episcopal activity was hindered by his being required to live in the palace at Cuddesdon. Doubtless with an episcopal income of £3000 annually (increased to £5000 on the death of his predecessor in 1889) the cost of living in quite high style at Cuddesdon cannot have troubled him seriously. But the inconvenience did: the diocese was a large one with 645 parishes, and Cuddesdon was not on a railway. Stubbs attempted, in vain, to have the episcopal residence moved. His pupil and friend T. F. Tout wrote in his account of Stubbs, in the *Dictionary of National Biography*, that at this period of his life

> Age … began to tell upon him, and he found his routine work increasingly laborious and irksome, and his clergy did not appreciate his attempts to distinguish between his strictly episcopal functions, which he rigidly discharged, and the conventional duties which modern bishops are expected to fulfil and for which he did not conceal his distaste.

His episcopal policy and stance were aptly expressed in his ordination addresses and visitation charges, many of which were published:

> In all these addresses can be seen his ardent faith, his strong sense of personal religion, his kindly tolerance, his strenuous maintenance of the ancient ways in all matters of dogma and church usage and his increasing dislike of all ecclesiastical innovations.   (*DNB*)

In 1889 Stubbs unwillingly agreed to be one of the assessors at the trial before Archbishop Benson of Edmund King, bishop of Lincoln, for ritualistic practices. He felt that the archbishop was acting *ultra vires* and was glad of King's acquittal on nearly all matters of substance. His administrative burdens were lightened by the appointment of a suffragan bishop of Reading in 1889.

Last years, and reputation Stubbs's health began to fail early in 1898. He discharged his last public duty on 3 February 1901 when (presumably in his capacity of chancellor of the Order of the Garter) he preached at Windsor a sermon before Edward VII and Wilhelm II of Germany, in memory of Queen Victoria, who had died on 22 January. Stubbs died on 22 April 1901 at Cuddesdon, where he was buried on 25 April in the churchyard. He was survived by his wife. Stubbs's gifts were great. Not least were his extraordinary powers of work. 'I will work', he said, 'while there is day', and so he did. He was a very fast reader and writer and 'worked with extraordinary rapidity, accuracy, and sureness' (*DNB*). A foundation of his achievement was an ordered life, helpfully caricatured in an account he gave of his rules: 'Never do anything underhand, never get your feet wet, go to bed at ten'. 'He disliked dinner-parties, smoking, late hours, and committees. He conscientiously discharged every duty that lay straight before him, but he did not spend too much time in doing so' (ibid.). Unwillingness to fritter time probably accounts for his reluctance to write reviews; he claimed to have written only one.

Stubbs was a commanding figure who bridged changing worlds of action and attitude. His primary devotion to the Christian religion and to the Church of England related strongly to his view of English history: as a historian he saw the united English nation as a great agent for good in this world, and its unity as in large measure the creation of the Christian church. He was very much a thinker of his day in his belief in what he called (in his oration for Queen Victoria) the 'vitalizing, sympathizing tone and instinct of nationalism', expressing the hope that a nationalism of the whole empire might be created. He played a crucial part in the establishment of modern history as a professional study and a major means of education; yet the historian's professionalism of his kind differed from that of later generations: he sought justice in judgement, they freedom from value judgements. Yet the power of his works was such that he set much of the agenda of research on medieval England for two or more generations and his influence could be denounced as banefully pervasive so late as 1963 (by H. G. Richardson and G. O. Sayles, *The Governance of Mediaeval England from the Conquest to Magna Carta*).   J. CAMPBELL

Sources *DNB* · W. H. Hutton, *William Stubbs* (1906) · J. W. Burrow, *A liberal descent: Victorian historians and the English past* (1981) · J. G. Edwards, *William Stubbs* (1952) · H. M. Cam, 'Stubbs seventy years after', *Cambridge Historical Journal*, 9 (1947–9), 129–47 · J. Kenyon, *The history men: the historical profession in England since the Renaissance* (1983) · J. Campbell, *Stubbs and the English state* (1989) · R. Jann, *The art and science of Victorian history* (1985) · H. G. Richardson and G. O. Sayles, *The governance of medieval England from the conquest to the Magna Carta* (1963) · F. Collins, ed., *Genealogical history of the family of the late Bishop William Stubbs compiled by himself*, Yorkshire Archaeological Society Record Series, 55 (1915) · P. R. H. Slee, *Learning and a liberal education: the study of modern history in the universities of Oxford, Cambridge and Manchester, 1800–1914* (1986) · F. W. Maitland, 'William Stubbs, bishop of Oxford', *EngHR*, 16 (1901), 417–26 · N. J. Williams, 'Stubbs's appointment as regius professor', *BIHR*, 33 (1960), 121–5

Archives LPL, corresp. and papers | BL, letters to W. E. Gladstone and related papers, Add. MSS 44469–44702, *passim* · Bodl. Oxf., letters to E. A. Freeman · Borth. Inst., undergraduate notebooks · LPL, corresp. with E. W. Benson · LPL, corresp. with A. C. Tait · LPL, corresp. with Frederick Temple · Society of the Most Holy Trinity, Ascot, letters to Edward Pusey

Likenesses H. Aitchison, chalk drawing, 1884, NPG · H. von Herkomer, oils, 1885, Bodl. Oxf. [*see illus.*] · C. W. Furse, oils, 1892, Trinity College, Oxford · photograph, NPG

Stubs, Peter (1756–1806), toolmaker and innkeeper, was born on 15 June 1756 at the White Bear inn, Bridge Street, Warrington, Lancashire, the only child of John Stubs (1736–1757), a currier, of Warrington, and his wife, Mary, daughter of Peter Johnson, yeoman, of Orford, near Warrington. In the second half of the eighteenth century south-west Lancashire was renowned as an area of small metal trades. If these trades had a centre, it was probably Warrington, and it was here that, as a very young man, Stubs established a small workshop as a filesmith. In 1777 he married Mary (1758–1821), daughter of Thomas Sutton of Warrington.

By 1788 Stubs had acquired the tenancy of the White Bear inn, where the file-making business was continued upon an expanded scale. The combination of innkeeping and file making was not wholly accidental, for the dregs of the beer barrels were utilized to form a paste which, when spread into the teeth of the files, gave them greater durability and strength. In 1802 Stubs set up new workshops and warehouses in Scotland Road, Warrington, and it was with this particular manufactory that the legendary quality of his files became most closely identified. Files with the initials P. S. stamped on their heel became treasured among craftsmen: it was not just the superiority of the steel from which they were made, but the perfection with which they were cut and finished. Many orders came to him through personal recommendation and by the 1780s his files were being sold as far afield as London. Later they were finding markets with wholesalers and ironmongers in towns and cities up and down the country. They were also being sold in America. Invariably, though, it was the machine workers of Lancashire and other centres of the industrial revolution who were Stubs's largest customers, for machine making was still then largely a manual rather than a mechanical process. The high standard of his product was vividly attested by the way the P. S. stamp was illegally used by other filesmiths, particularly in Sheffield. Indeed, so serious did this counterfeiting problem become that Stubs was forced to publish a caution to filesmiths in a Sheffield newspaper in 1805. By the early nineteenth century, Stubs's annual profits were estimated at £700, no mean figure by the standards of the day. Alongside his business as an innkeeper and in brewing, he acquired property in Warrington and in 1799 became part owner of a vessel plying the Baltic trade. He was the father of eighteen children and was generous in his dealings with them. He was also given to generous support and hospitality more widely and hence was some way removed from the austere nonconformity which characterized some of his industrialist contemporaries. He died at his home on 28 February 1806 and was buried in Warrington parish churchyard. He was survived by his wife and thirteen of his children.

What is known about Stubs as an industrialist derives from the continuity of the firm he founded for well over a century after his own death and from the concomitant survival of a mass of records relating to it. This archive subsequently came to the notice of T. S. Ashton, who recognized it as affording a unique insight into the trades which supplied the tools of the machine age. What Ashton saw was an industrial sector in transition. In the first decade or so of the firm's existence Stubs was as much merchant as industrialist in that he relied quite heavily on outworkers who combined their craft with farming. As time went by, however, he increasingly gave direct employment to filesmiths and sought ways to induce outworkers to move to Warrington. In the marketing of his product he initially used factors or middlemen. He also capitalized on trading contacts arising from his need for steel castings from which to make files and also for the supply of barley for malt for his brewing business. Later, though, middlemen were more and more replaced by direct dealing with retailers, assisted by the firm's own travellers, of whom Peter's son John became one. The measure of Ashton's insight into this single, small firm owed much to the survival of the correspondence records with the firm's clients and suppliers.   Michael Freeman

Sources T. S. Ashton, *An eighteenth-century industrialist* (1939) · T. S. Ashton, 'The domestic system in the early Lancashire tool trade', *Economic History*, 1 (1926–9), 131–40 · T. S. Ashton, 'The records of a pin manufactory, 1814–22', *Economica*, 5 (1925), 281–92 · L. S. Presnell, *Studies in the industrial revolution* (1960) · records of Peter Stubs Ltd of Warrington, Man. CL
Archives Man. CL, records of Peter Stubs Ltd of Warrington; records of Stubs, Wood & Co. of Warrington
Wealth at death £150 annuity to widow; £200 each to thirteen surviving children; superintendence of business to son John and co-trustees: Ashton, *Eighteenth-century industrialist*

Stuckey family (*per. c.*1770–1845), bankers and merchants, came to prominence with **Samuel George Stuckey** (1740–1812). Born in April 1740 at Langport, Somerset, he was the youngest of the five children of George Stuckey (1697–1774), merchant, and his wife, Elizabeth (1699–1752), daughter of Lawrence Tuttiett of Stoke St Gregory, Somerset. Stuckey had an elder brother and three sisters.

Samuel's father, who was three times portreeve, or mayor, of Langport, was responsible for developing a flourishing mercantile firm that traded in a wide range of commodities including corn, timber, and salt. Samuel, together with his elder brother, George, greatly developed the family firm and established beyond doubt the name of Stuckey in the business and commercial life of the county of Somerset. On 20 August 1764 he married Sarah (1741–1812), daughter of Robert Jennings of Cerne Abbas, Dorset. Together they had one son and five daughters.

About 1770, Samuel Stuckey began to provide a banking

Vincent Stuckey (1771–1845), by Maxim Gauci (after Eden Upton Eddis)

function in parallel with his trading activities; and the origin of Stuckey's Bank, which was to grow into one of the country's premier provincial banking companies, is traced to this date. The banking activities of the firm grew quickly, and agents were soon appointed in London and Bristol. In 1800 Samuel took his brother, George, into the bank, and the latter's son Vincent joined in 1801. By 1806 banking business had so increased that Samuel chose to separate the bank from the rest of the family business, and officially founded the Langport Bank in that year. By bringing in three additional partners, together with his brother George, Samuel Stuckey was able to increase the bank's capital, enabling the establishment of branches at Bridgwater and Bristol. From 1807, however, Samuel Stuckey's health was failing and he relinquished many of his direct interests in the bank. He died on 13 February 1812 at Langport and was buried there shortly after, at All Saints' Church.

The key figure in the subsequent development of the bank was Samuel's nephew **Vincent Stuckey** (1771–1845). Born on 24 March 1771 at Langport, Somerset, he was the youngest of the eight children of George Stuckey (1731–1807), banker and merchant, and his wife, Edith (1742–1793), daughter of Thomas Beedal, of Langport, Somerset. He had four brothers and three sisters, though he was the only surviving son. His father, George, Samuel Stuckey's elder brother, was widely known in Langport and its environs, not only as a prominent member of the bank and merchant house, but as mayor of the town on no fewer than four occasions.

At an early age Vincent Stuckey showed himself to be of

enterprising spirit when, probably about 1790, he presented himself to Lady Chatham, a neighbour and family friend, and asked if she would give him an introduction to her son the prime minister. Armed with a letter from Lady Chatham, Stuckey obtained from William Pitt (1759–1806) a clerkship in the Treasury. He was soon appointed to the department of bills of exchange and owing to rapid growth in its business was in almost daily contact with Pitt himself. He was also private secretary to William Huskisson, then secretary to the Treasury. Despite such promising beginnings to a public career, Stuckey resigned from the Treasury in 1801 and returned to the family business at Langport, a decision connected with his marriage on 16 April 1801 to his first cousin Julia (1781–1861), the youngest daughter of his uncle Samuel. By 1807 he was made a partner in the bank, though with the death of his father, George, and his uncle Samuel in increasingly poor health, Vincent Stuckey became *de facto* head of the firm; with Samuel's death in 1812 he became senior partner.

The Bank of England's monopoly of joint-stock banking meant country banks in England and Wales were limited until 1826 to private partnerships of no more than six persons, which clearly limited their capitalization and branch development. Stuckey was fortunate that in 1810 he came into a considerable fortune through a bequest from an old friend, which provided him with capital for the establishment of additional branches at Taunton and Wells, together with an agency at Illminster. In 1825 Thomas Watson Bagehot, Vincent's brother-in-law, became a partner, and this further cemented links between the two patriarchal Langport families. In the following year Stuckey's nephew, the great Victorian banker, economist, and writer Walter *Bagehot was born at the Bank House, Langport, and he was later to become closely involved in the management of its affairs.

Following the financial crisis of 1825–6, when eighty private banks failed in London and the country, the government rescinded the Bank of England's monopoly of joint-stock organization, which had stood since 1708. Stuckey was the first private banker to take advantage of the new legislation, by converting the Langport Bank to Stuckey's Banking Company in 1826. By reacting so quickly to the new opportunities, Stuckey displayed his genius as a banker. None the less, even after conversion Stuckey's Bank remained essentially a partnership, with Stuckey himself exercising the shrewd judgement and personal authority characteristic of his private banking days. The bank retained its distinctive regional focus, with further branches being confined to the Somerset and Bristol region. Such caution was perhaps best captured in his oft-quoted phrase 'bankers are mortal, but banks should never die' (Stuckey).

Stuckey was widely regarded as the leading country banker of his generation, an opinion confirmed by the quality of his testimonies to the frequent parliamentary inquiries on banking and currency questions in the early nineteenth century. Thus, despite leaving the Treasury in 1801, he remained influential in government circles and was particularly close to Sir Robert Peel: he acted as Peel's adviser and confidant during the long debates on currency reform which culminated in the Bank Charter Act of 1844.

Though heavily involved in the management of the bank, Stuckey continued to expand the family's mercantile and shipping business, in close partnership with the Bagehots. He inherited the salt interests of his late father and uncle, including an estate with salt pans at Droitwich, Worcestershire. Much involved in the social and political life of Langport and the county, he was mayor of the town on three occasions—in 1810, 1823, and 1833—and served as a magistrate, churchwarden, and trustee of the local grammar school. He was also made a deputy lieutenant and, in 1822, high sheriff of Somerset. A robust and hearty figure, a memoir recalls how

> Vincent Stuckey kept a pack of hounds in Whatley, and dwelt in patriarchal style among his people—hospitable, free-handed, and popular. He might be seen at times seated under the great elm on the Hill fronting the west door of the church and chatting with his neighbours. He used to tell how in his Treasury days he had shot snipe in the muddy fields between St. James's Park and Sloane Street (his home), now called Belgravia. (Ross, 355)

Stuckey's great longing for a son was unfulfilled and indeed his family life was marred by tragedy; of ten children born to the couple only two daughters survived to adulthood. Hereditary defects intensified by the marriage of first cousins were possibly to blame. Vincent Stuckey died at Langport on 8 May 1845 and was buried there shortly afterwards in All Saints' Church. After his death, his wife, Julia, maintained a close interest in the affairs of the bank until she died, on 15 February 1861. Their considerable fortune was passed to Vincent Stuckey Wood, second son of their daughter Julia Wood, who had died in 1832. The younger Vincent took the name and arms of Stuckey in 1861 and subsequently became the third chairman of Stuckey's Banking Company between 1876 and 1900.

IAIN S. BLACK

Sources T. E. Gregory, *The Westminster Bank through a century*, 1 (1936), 144–57 · P. T. Saunders, *Stuckey's Bank* (1928) · D. M. Ross, *Langport and its church* (1911) · V. Stuckey, *Thoughts on the improvement of the system of country banking: in a letter to Lord Viscount Althorp* (1834) · L. S. Pressnell, *Country banking in the industrial revolution* (1956) · E. I. Barrington, *Life of Walter Bagehot* (1914) · I. S. Black, 'Money, information and space: banking in early-nineteenth-century England and Wales', *Journal of Historical Geography*, 21 (1995), 398–412 · records of Stuckey's Bank, Royal Bank of Scotland Group, London · d. cert. [Vincent Stuckey]

Archives Royal Bank of Scotland Group, London, records of Stuckey's Bank

Likenesses E. U. Eddis, portrait (Vincent Stuckey), Royal Bank of Scotland Group, London · M. Gauci, engraving (Vincent Stuckey; after E. U. Eddis), NPG [*see illus.*] · oils (Vincent Stuckey), Royal Bank of Scotland Group, London

Wealth at death £60,000—Samuel Stuckey: PRO, death duty registers, IR26/559, fol. 123 · £90,000—Vincent Stuckey: PRO, death duty registers, IR26/1722, fol. 689

Stuckey, Samuel George (1740–1812). *See under* Stuckey family (*per. c.*1770–1845).

Stuckey, Vincent (1771–1845). *See under* Stuckey family (*per. c.*1770–1845).

Stucley, Sir Lewis (1574/5–1620), local politician, was the son and heir of John Stucley (c.1551–1611) of Affeton, Devon, and Frances (d. in or before 1597), second daughter of Sir John St Leger of Annery. He had two sisters and one brother and four stepsisters and one stepbrother. He matriculated at Broadgates Hall, Oxford, in 1589 aged fourteen and became a student at the Middle Temple in 1592. In 1596 he married Frances (b. 1571), eldest daughter of Anthony Monk of Potheridge; they had five sons and one daughter. Stucley was knighted on 23 July 1603. He did not succeed his father on the bench, possibly because of straitened financial circumstances as he sold his manor of East Worlington in 1614 and that of Thelbridge in 1616. In 1617 he was appointed guardian of Thomas Rolfe, son of Pocahontas and John Rolfe. He purchased the potentially profitable office of vice-admiral of Devon for £600 shortly before Sir Walter Ralegh returned to Plymouth in the *Destiny* in 1618. This gave him considerable powers over ships entering Devon ports and his deputy had already arrested the *Destiny* when Stucley received orders, dated 12 June, from the lord admiral, to arrest Ralegh. This was followed by an order from the secretary of the council to bring Ralegh before them, 'in fair Manner, and, as his Health would give Leave, by easy Journies to London' (*Harleian Miscellany*, 3.25). It is on his actions in fulfilling this order that his claim to fame, or perhaps more truly infamy, rests.

The report on Ralegh's demeanour states that he attempted to escape to France before he was under guard and that 'it was not any Train laid for him by Sir Lewis Stukeley, … as was voiced, to move or tempt him to an Escape' (*Harleian Miscellany*, 3.25). While Ralegh remained free in Plymouth, Stucley was active selling tobacco from the *Destiny* and paying off the mariners. This meant that he, Ralegh, and attendants, including Manourie, a French physician, had only got as far as John Drake's house in east Devon by 25 July when Stucley received a council letter rebuking him for his delays and ordering him to bring Sir Walter speedily before them. The party left immediately and reached Salisbury on 27 July. Ralegh admitted, on the scaffold, that he feigned illness at Salisbury. Stucley was taken in by this and sought further medical advice which led to their remaining at Salisbury until 1 August and provided the grounds for Ralegh's being allowed to go to his London house, rather than to the Tower. These delays gave Ralegh the opportunity to prepare his escape. Stucley discovered this intention at Andover and increased the guards on Ralegh, who therefore drew him into his plans for escape. Stucley may have been tempted by financial offers to co-operate but he claimed that he had only done so to unmask Ralegh's intentions, which he betrayed and so caused Ralegh's arrest in the act of escaping and his immediate transfer to the Tower. His duplicity, condemned in Ralegh's speech on the scaffold, turned Sir Lewis into Sir Judas. He received additional obloquy because of his supposed relationship to Ralegh, which depended on his being a nephew of Sir Richard Grenville, who termed Ralegh 'cousin', although there was no blood relationship.

Stucley remained in London, giving information against Ralegh, writing his 'Apology' and preparing his 'Petition' which was actually written by Leonell *Sharpe. He received £965 6s. 3d. for his services and expenses. His greatest use to the king was as an acceptable target for national discontent at Ralegh's execution. Stucley's reputation suffered further damage when he and his son, Hugh, were imprisoned for clipping coin in January 1619. He was pardoned for this, presumably for his services to the king, but continued to be so vilified that he retired to the island of Lundy where he is reputed to have died, raving mad, in 1620. He was buried at South Molton.

MARY WOLFFE

Sources T. N. Brushfield, 'Raleghana VII: three state documents relating to the arrest and execution of Sir Walter Ralegh in 1618', *Report and Transactions of the Devonshire Association*, 37 (1905), 284–324; 38 (1906), 416–90 · 'A declaration of the demeanour and carriage of Sir Walter Raleigh', *The Harleian miscellany*, ed. W. Oldys, 3 (1745), 17–31 · J. L. Vivian, ed., *The visitations of the county of Devon, comprising the herald's visitations of 1531, 1564, and 1620* (privately printed, Exeter, [1895]), 568, 722 · N. L. Williams, *Sir Walter Raleigh* (1962), 258–62 · R. G. Marsden, 'The vice-admirals of the coast [pt 1]', *EngHR*, 22 (1907), 468–77 · *CSP dom.*, 1611–23 · *APC, 1617–19* · S. R. Gardiner, *History of England from the accession of James I to the outbreak of the civil war*, 3 (1883); repr. (1965) · J. C. Tingay, calendar of deeds enrolled in the county of Devon, Devon RO [transcript], fols. 584, 600 · *DNB* · Foster, *Alum. Oxon.*

Stucley, Thomas (c.1520–1578), soldier, was the third of five sons of Sir Hugh Stucley (c.1495–1559) of Affeton Castle, West Worlington, Devon, and his wife, Jane, second daughter of Sir Lewis Pollard. His family was important locally (his father served as sheriff of the county) and had connections with the wider world of Tudor politics. There were contemporary reports that Thomas was an illegitimate son of Henry VIII. He probably attended one of the inns of court, before embarking on a military career. In 1545 he was serving as a soldier in Berwick Castle, and from 1547 he was paid as standard-bearer at Boulogne the substantial sum of 6s. 8d. a day. He was a standard-bearer again on the Scottish borders in 1550 and in May of that year he helped escort the marquis de Maine, a French hostage held in England, when he travelled to Scotland. He accompanied Robert Dudley on an embassy to Henri II at Amboise in April 1551. Stucley was associated with the disgraced duke of Somerset, and this placed him under suspicion with the regime of the duke of Northumberland. Thus on 21 November 1551 the privy council ordered Stucley's arrest, and he fled to France; it was also useful for him to be abroad at this time to escape his creditors.

French and Habsburg service, 1551–1557 In France Stucley entered royal service, and probably played a part in the siege of Metz. He returned to England in August 1552, bearing a letter of recommendation addressed to Edward VI from Henri II. As he delivered the letter Stucley claimed that he had been sent by Henri as a spy, to help the French, who planned to attack Calais and then launch an invasion of England. The English government did not know what to make of this, but after consulting the ambassador in France, who mentioned it to the French king, decided it was a fabrication. In any case the government wished to improve relations with France, so Stucley was put in the Tower of London, where he remained until Mary I released him on 6 August 1553.

Freed from prison Stucley served as a volunteer in the armies of Queen Mary's allies. He was at Brussels in December 1553, and in February 1554 he fought with the emperor's forces at St Omer. He wrote to the queen from St Omer offering her his services and those of his band of soldiers, perhaps to help maintain order at the time of Wyatt's rebellion; he also sent the English government a letter from the French king to his ambassador in England which had been intercepted and might be of value to English security. His military aid not being required in England, Stucley is next found working for Philibert, duke of Savoy, to whom he had been recommended the previous year by Queen Mary. This involved playing a part in the successful military campaigns that Savoy led on behalf of the Habsburgs against the French in Picardy. The duke of Savoy came to England in December 1554, and Stucley accompanied him. He took the precaution of writing to the queen before arriving in England in order to receive a safe conduct to prevent his arrest for debt.

Stucley probably married during this visit. His wife was an heiress, Anne Curtis, granddaughter of the wealthy pewterer Sir Thomas Curtis who later became lord mayor of London. This was clearly a sensible marriage in the light of Stucley's debts. But it did not prevent him getting into financial trouble: in May 1555 the sheriffs of Devon and Cheshire were ordered by the privy council to arrest him on the charge of coining false money. Stucley fled the country, leaving his bride to deal with the difficulties that ensued, and resumed his work for the duke of Savoy. It was probably as part of the English contingent under Lord Pembroke and Lord Dudley that he fought in the great victory over France at St Quentin on 10 August 1557. For a gentleman soldier of the Tudor age this was a highly significant personal achievement.

Maritime activities, 1557–1565 Having returned to England, Stucley began the first of his maritime exploits. He acted, it seems, as a privateer, attacking French shipping, a legitimate enterprise once England was at war with France, and one that his Devon connections made easy for him to pursue. But the line between privateering and piracy was thin; there is a suggestion that he had already engaged in attacks on the French before war was declared. On 30 May 1558 he was summoned before the council on the charge of plundering Spanish ships. The court of admiralty, however, found that there was insufficient evidence for Stucley to answer. It is perhaps significant in this connection that Mary employed Stucley late in 1558 to attend a visiting Spanish admiral, the marqués de Saria, when he was at Dartmouth, which suggests that he retained the confidence of the queen, and that the naval dignitaries of her Spanish allies were not averse to him.

Family matters engaged Stucley's attentions in the succeeding months. In 1558 he seized the house of his niece's deceased husband, Serjeant Prideaux, in order to secure the property of his great-nephew, whose wardship he had been granted, partly as a result of a letter of support from

the Spanish admiral to the queen. This led to a reprimand from the privy council. The death of his wife's grandfather in November 1559 provided him with much needed cash, which he was not slow to spend. Stucley accommodated himself to the accession of the protestant Queen Elizabeth with little difficulty, and for the first years of her reign he enjoyed her favour. He was engaged in local militia duties in Berkshire in 1560, at a time when war with France and Scotland seemed imminent, and he received very good reports from his superiors for his hard work. In the following year he was a captain in Berwick. In the winter of 1561–2 he helped to entertain Shane O'Neill, the Irish leader, on a visit to England; O'Neill wrote to the queen strongly commending him. In 1562 reports show Stucley to be a supporter of Lord Robert Dudley, engaged in intrigues on his behalf to thwart the possible marriage between Elizabeth and Erik, prince of Sweden.

On 23 June 1563, a fortnight after staging a naval pageant on the Thames for the queen, Stucley sailed off with a small fleet financed jointly by the queen and himself, in the company of the French explorer Jean Ribaut. The expedition was said to be bound for Florida, from which Ribaut had recently returned, although this was probably no more than a cover for the real intention which was to prey on French shipping. Before leaving London Stucley paid a mysterious visit to the Spanish ambassador, apologizing in advance for anything he might do on the voyage to the prejudice of the king of Spain: the ambassador did not know whether to trust Stucley or not. He almost certainly never crossed the Atlantic, but for over a year he attacked shipping off the coast of France and Spain, using ports in Ireland and Devon as bases, and taking time off in between to visit London. He did not discriminate very carefully between enemy and neutral shipping, and attacked two French ships while they were in a Galician port, which drew justifiable complaints from Spain. The queen decided to put a stop to Stucley's adventures and to the piracy of others based in Ireland, largely in order to repair relations with France, and at Michaelmas 1564 gave a commission to Sir Peter Carew, a cousin of Stucley's, to fit out two ships in order to apprehend pirates in the Irish seas. A ship crewed by Stucley's men was taken by Carew in Cork Haven in the spring of 1565, by which time Stucley had himself surrendered to the English authorities in Ireland. He was then sent back to England, and held for a while in ward. Although there was a case entered against him in the court of admiralty and a list of offences drawn up, he was discharged for lack of evidence. He visited the Spanish ambassador to apologize.

In Ireland, 1565–1570 In view of O'Neill's friendship with Stucley, Cecil sensibly agreed to send him to assist the lord deputy of Ireland, Sir Henry Sidney, who was preparing to send an embassy to O'Neill. This deputation, which finally departed from Dublin with Stucley early in 1566, was intended to persuade O'Neill to come to meet the lord deputy in the pale to negotiate a peace treaty in person. At the same time Stucley and his companions were to sound out O'Neill's true intentions and feelings. As Sidney reported to Cecil, the embassy failed to persuade O'Neill it was safe to come to Dublin, but Stucley and his companions were made aware of O'Neill's dangerous anti-English ambitions. Sidney was most pleased with Stucley's conduct in this matter and for the next four years tried to support his efforts to recover his credit with Elizabeth and make a career for himself in Ireland. In March 1566, with Sidney's strong support, Stucley wrote asking to be permitted to buy from Sir Nicholas Bagenal for the sum of Ir£3000 the important office of marshal of Ireland, and some valuable estates in northern Ireland close to O'Neill's territory. According to Sidney, Stucley hoped to settle in Ireland and was planning to marry the earl of Worcester's sister, his first wife having died about 1564. This scheme did not succeed, but he did marry a rich Irish widow, Elizabeth Peppard, *née* Popley, about 1566. The queen, however, utterly refused to consider his promotion, and reminded Sidney that Stucley was still out of favour and had a case pending against him in the admiralty court, and therefore should not be given any position of trust in Ireland.

Following this set-back Stucley returned to England, but in 1567 he was back in Ireland, attempting to buy the office of seneschal of Wexford and other positions and lands from Sir Nicholas Heron. He faced the same opposition from Elizabeth in this as he had done before, and she ordered Heron to be reinstated. Heron's death meant that Stucley was able to prevent the complete failure of these schemes for two years, although in 1567 he ceded the barony of Odrone to his old adversary Sir Peter Carew. Despite Sidney's support, Stucley was eventually forced, by the summer of 1569, to relinquish the rest of his claim to Nicholas White, sent from England to take Heron's place. White arrived in Dublin and had Stucley committed to prison, charged with obstructing his rights but also with using coarse language against the queen and supporting Irish rebels. Stucley was in Dublin Castle for eighteen weeks, and then released for lack of evidence. Being ousted a second time seems to have been decisive in shifting Stucley, increasingly ambiguous over the last few years, into a position of open disloyalty to the queen.

Flight to Spain, 1570 The years 1569–70 were very difficult for the Elizabethan regime, with rebellion in northern England, the publication of the papal bull of excommunication, and hostility from Catholic Spain. These wider opportunities for sedition chimed in with Stucley's personal grudges, a yearning for more adventure, and probably also a long-felt sympathy for the old religion. Released in October 1569 and still enjoying the friendship of Sidney, Stucley began to prepare a vessel for his departure from Ireland, claiming that he would sail for England. While these preparations were proceeding, he sounded out both the Spanish and French ambassadors. He then set out for Spain, arriving at Viviero on 24 April 1570. He was favourably received in Madrid, where Jane, the English-born duchess of Feria, and her husband provided him with influential support. This charming old soldier, with his eight-year-old son, William, was soon very much at home at the Spanish court. He was given a pension and a house in a nearby village, was enrolled as a knight of the order of Calatrava, and was generally addressed as duke of

Ireland. But Stucley faced difficulties in persuading Philip II to equip an expedition to Ireland. Throughout most of the 1570s the king was attempting to improve relations with England. In any case, Irish exiles in Europe were dubious about Stucley and had their own schemes which they hoped to sell to the Spanish. Nevertheless Philip's caution and hospitality meant that he would never completely dismiss Stucley. From the perspective of the English government he was a real threat once in exile, and Elizabeth used a number of diplomatic channels to try to remove his Spanish support. There were repeated rumours in London in the 1570s that he was about to launch an attack on Ireland.

In April 1571, having received no real promises of Spanish support, Stucley left for Rome to enlist aid there and was again very well received. It was typical of Stucley that he should have played a part, while waiting for his Irish plans to mature, as captain of three galleys in the great victory of the Spanish over the Turks at Lepanto in October 1571. He then returned to Spain, and continued to urge Philip II to use his triumphant naval forces to attack England. In early 1572 he was in Paris, then back in Spain, where he made his base, by now something of a hero. In 1575 there were rumours that he was once more in England, but he was certainly in Rome in autumn and winter that year, when the pope granted him the right to sell indulgences commemorating the jubilee to raise cash for his English enterprise. In 1576 he made the pilgrimage to Loreto. By this time Stucley had received promises in Rome and Madrid of support for a limited expedition to Ireland of the sort that he eventually led two years later. In 1577, however, these plans were shelved, and he travelled twice to Flanders from Rome, where the new Spanish governor and his former companion-in-arms, Don John of Austria, was contemplating a major invasion of England, and there seemed a real chance of Spanish support.

The battle of Alcazar, 1578 The death of Don John put an end to any real prospect of a Spanish invasion of Ireland or England, and Rome was now Stucley's only hope. The pope was enthusiastic, but had little to offer in terms of major military support. The situation was complicated by divisions among the exiled English Catholics in Rome, many of whom distrusted Stucley, as did Irish Catholic exiles. However, it was at last settled that the scheme first agreed by Stucley and Pope Gregory XIII in 1576 was to be implemented, and Stucley seemed now to have the support of James fitz Maurice Fitzgerald, the leading Irish exile. The pope and Philip II provided enough money to equip a force of perhaps 700 English and Irish exiles, Italian bandits, and sundry soldiers, some press-ganged by Stucley himself. He set off from Civita Vecchia in February 1578 in the *San Juan* of Genoa, a ship of 800 tons, which after a minor mutiny among the crew arrived by easy stages at Lisbon in May. Here King Sebastian, who was desperate, despite all his advisers, to attack the Moors of north Africa, persuaded Stucley to join him in that enterprise, in clear contravention of his papal instructions and despite the strong opposition of the papal nuncio in Lisbon. Stucley had his reasons for being thus diverted from his Irish course: his ship was leaky, and Sebastian had told him that when they had defeated the Moors they would sail together in a Portuguese fleet to Ireland. Stucley had far more military skill than Sebastian, and when they had crossed into Africa and he saw the size of the Moorish forces ranged against them, he advised against immediate fighting. Having been overruled by the foolhardy king he fought bravely at the battle of Alcazar on 4 August 1578. He was killed early in the battle, with both legs shot off by a cannon, and the Portuguese expedition was overwhelmed by the vastly superior Moorish cavalry.

Stucley's life became a subject for balladeers and dramatists, who saw him as a hero whose martial reputation was enhanced by his notoriety. The duke of Northumberland said of him as early as 1552: 'I dare say there is not in Italy or Christendom a better soldier of his time' (*CSP dom.*, *1547–53*, 713). He was certainly a brave and intelligent soldier, but he was also devious and he loved the limelight. Burghley accused him of 'the highest degree of vain-glory, prodigality, falsehood, and vile and filthy conversation of life … altogether without faith, conscience, or religion' (Simpson, 136). Yet before he went to Spain his record had not been worse than that of a number of his flamboyant contemporaries. It is a mystery why Elizabeth withdrew her favour so comprehensively in 1566, when Stucley had the support in Ireland of the deputy, and indeed at that stage the support of the future Lord Burghley, and when he was clearly the sort of tough frontiersman required to help subdue the island. But her decision was the turning point in Stucley's career, and its apparent unfairness helps to justify his move into open treason in 1570. Whether Elizabeth's suspicions and Stucley's intemperate response to them really did stem from a belief that he was her half-brother is an interesting and unanswerable question.   PETER HOLMES

Sources DNB · R. Simpson, *The school of Shakespeare*, 1 (1878), 1–268 · J. Izon, *Sir Thomas Stucley* (1956) · E. W. Bovill, *The battle of Alcazar* (1952), 79–82, 86–7, 104, 110, 118–19, 142, 149 · J. C. Levinson, ed., *The famous history of the life and death of Captain Thomas Stukeley* (1979) · A. Munday, *The English Roman life*, ed. P. J. Ayers (1980), 17–19 · T. Westcote, *A view of Devonshire in MDCXXX, with a pedigree of most of its gentry*, ed. G. Oliver and P. Jones (1845), 271–3, 585–6 · J. L. Vivian, ed., *The visitations of the county of Devon, comprising the herald's visitations of 1531, 1564, and 1620* (privately printed, Exeter, [1895]), 721 · CSP for., 1547–53, 92, 218, 221; 1553–8, 36, 55, 126, 146, 406; 1559–60, 323 (7); 1561–2, 117, 998; 1562, 380 (2), 381, 439 (7), 440; 1563, 572, 731, 745, 851, 966, 1487; 1564–5, 633, 879, 1137; 1569–71, index; 1572–4, index; 1575–7, index; 1577–8, index; 1578–9, 21, 31, 37, 47, 49; 1579–80, 336, 474 · CSP dom., 1547–53, 713, 716, 750, 811; 1553–8, 815, 823; 1547–1601, with addenda, 1566–79 · CSP Rome, 1558–71; 1572–8 · CSP Venice, 1558–80, 464–5 · M. A. S. Hume, ed., *Calendar of letters and state papers relating to English affairs, preserved principally in the archives of Simancas*, 4 vols., PRO (1892–9), 1558–79 · LP Henry VIII, 20/1, no. 828; 21/1, no. 499 · CSP Ire., 1558–85 · Report of the Deputy Keeper of the Public Records in Ireland, 22 (1890), appx 6 [index of fiants, index] · APC, 1547–50, 356, 396, 412; 1550–52, 26, 48, 278, 285, 391, 422; 1552–4, 142, 312; 1554–6, 125, 131, 152, 259; 1556–8, 320, 340, 414; 1558–70, 8, 216, 234, 261; 1575–7, 51, 54; 1577–81, 236, 245, 257 · J. Morrin, ed., *Calendar of the patent and close rolls of chancery in Ireland, of the reigns of Henry VIII, Edward VI, Mary, and Elizabeth*, 2 (1862), 47 · J. S. Brewer and W. Bullen, eds., *Calendar of the Carew manuscripts*, 1: 1515–1574, PRO (1867), 369, 383 · J. S. Brewer and W. Bullen, eds., *Calendar of the Carew manuscripts*, 2: 1575–1588, PRO (1868), 137, 308, 349 · Calendar *of the manuscripts of the most hon. the marquis of Salisbury*, 1, HMC, 9 (1883), 273, 401, 539, 553; 2 (1888), 20, 41, 97, 100, 124, 152, 173, 177; 13 (1915), 29 · *The manuscripts of Charles Haliday … Acts of the privy council in Ireland, 1556–1571*, HMC, 40 (1897), 232, 271 · Report on the *manuscripts of Lord De L'Isle and Dudley*, 6 vols., HMC, 77 (1925–66), vol. 1, pp. 400, 412; vol. 2, pp. 9, 75, 83–4, 86 · J. H. Pollen, *The English Catholics in the reign of Queen Elizabeth* (1920), index · M. V. Ronan, *The Reformation in Ireland under Elizabeth, 1558–1580* (1930), index · Literary remains of King Edward the Sixth, ed. J. G. Nichols, 2, Roxburghe Club, 75 (1857), 266, 455, 457, 462, 540, 542, 593 · H. Sydney and others, *Letters and memorials of state*, ed. A. Collins, 1 (1746), 38–9, 233–4, 256–7, 262–3, 270 · R. Bagwell, *Ireland under the Tudors*, 3 vols. (1885–90), vol. 2, pp. 103–5, 196–206, 225–7, 239, 248; vol. 3, pp. 1–2, 5–7, 117 · J. Maclean, *The life and times of Sir Peter Carew* (1857), 75, 77, 84, 190, 192, 199, 203, 210
Likenesses drawing, *Picture Post* Library

Studd, Charles Thomas (1860–1931), cricketer and missionary, was born in Spratton, Northamptonshire, on 2 December 1860, the third of the six sons (with one daughter) of Edward Studd (1819–1877), indigo planter in India, later of Tidworth House, Wiltshire, and his second wife, Dorothy (Dora) Sophia (d. 1923), daughter of John Thomas, Calcutta merchant, of Bletsoe, Bedfordshire; there were four children of the first marriage. He was educated at Eton College and at Trinity College, Cambridge, where he took a pass degree and graduated BA in 1883. Like his elder brothers, J. E. Kynaston *Studd (later first baronet) and G. B. Studd, he played cricket for Eton and Cambridge. The three brothers captained Cambridge University from 1882 to 1884, with C. T. captain in 1883. He was a superb all-rounder, famous at the age of twenty-one for his century when Cambridge beat the Australians by six wickets in a celebrated match of 1882. That year he played for England at the Oval when Australia won by 7 runs. He was among the top all-rounders in England in 1882 and became only the second player (after W. G. Grace) to achieve the 'double' of 1000 runs and 100 wickets. In 1882–3 he went to Australia with the MCC team which recovered the 'Ashes'.

A dedicated rather than a born cricketer, Studd trained himself to supremacy. He used a longer bat than was usual, had the typical upright stance of the top amateurs of the day, and had a hard wrist stroke, with which he scored rapidly. He bowled slightly above medium pace, round-arm, his best performance being eight wickets for 40 runs for Cambridge University against Middlesex, the county he later played for. In his brief career in first-class cricket he made 4391 runs (average 30.49) and took 441 wickets (average 17.36).

By 1884 C. T. Studd was a household name. The sensation therefore was immense when he abandoned cricket, and a life of wealth and ease, to go as a missionary to China. In 1875 his father had heard the American evangelist D. L. Moody in London, and had sold his racehorses and devoted himself to personal evangelism. His three cricketing sons became committed Christians while still at Eton but after his father's death C. T. lost his fervour, until January 1884, after he had believed that his brother G. B. was dying. C. T. threw himself into Christian activity with the same discipline and dedication he had given to cricket, and determined to join another well-known Cambridge

Charles Thomas
Studd (1860–1931),
by unknown
photographer

athlete, the oarsman Stanley Smith, in the then little-known China Inland Mission led by J. Hudson Taylor. Five of their friends followed their example and volunteered, making the celebrated 'Cambridge seven' who left for China in 1885.

Studd spent nine years as a pioneer missionary in north China. In 1887 he gave away his fortune and 'lived by faith' (and, indeed, on the generosity of his family). On 7 April the following year, while in China, he married another missionary, Priscilla Livingstone (1864/5–1929), daughter of William Stewart, flax merchant, of Lisburn, Ireland. They had four daughters (two sons died in infancy). In 1894 he was invalided home and never completely recovered his health. In 1896–8 he toured North American universities. Though not a natural speaker his pithy style, backed by his fame and renunciation, strengthened the student volunteer missionary movement.

From 1900 to 1906 the Studds served in India. In 1908, in Liverpool, C. T. saw a poster—'Cannibals want missionaries'—the first step in an extraordinary saga which led him, against medical and family advice, to found the Heart of Africa mission in the Congo. In 1913 Studd and his daughter Edith's young fiancé, Alfred Buxton, a descendant of the emancipator Sir Thomas Fowell Buxton, bicycled across east Africa to a populous region untouched by Christianity. In the next years Studd and a small band of young people overcame difficulties to found a flourishing church, the start of a new pioneer mission, the Worldwide Evangelization Crusade (1919).

Studd's personality and methods became increasingly controversial; his autocratic leadership caused dismissals and resignations, and his determination to continue despite declining health led to dependence on morphine. Yet when he died in Ibambi, Belgian Congo, on 16 July 1931, 2000 Africans attended his funeral there in torrential rain.   JOHN POLLOCK

Sources N. Grubb, *C. T. Studd, cricketer and pioneer* (1933) · J. C. Pollock, *The Cambridge seven* (1955) · E. Buxton, *Reluctant missionary* (1968) · E. Vincent, *C. T. Studd and Priscilla* (1988) · T. B. Walters, *Charles T. Studd: cricketer and missionary* (1930) · K. White, *C. T. Studd: cricketer and crusader* (1985) · J. T. Erskine, *Millionaire for God: the story of C. T. Studd* (1968) · G. F. Timpson, *Kings and commoners: studies in British idealism* (1936) · private information (2004) · b. cert. · m. cert. · Burke, *Peerage* · Venn, *Alum. Cant.* · *CGPLA Eng. & Wales* (1932)

Likenesses three photographs, c.1884–c.1906, repro. in Grubb, *C. T. Studd*, frontispiece, facing pp. 48, 128 · photograph, repro. in Walters, *Charles T. Studd*, frontispiece [*see illus.*]

Wealth at death £4713 4s. 6d.: probate, 12 March 1932, *CGPLA Eng. & Wales*

Studd, Sir (John Edward) Kynaston, first baronet (1858–1944), local politician and college head, was born on 26 July 1858 at Netheravon, Wiltshire, the eldest in the family of six sons and one daughter of Edward Studd (1819–1877) of Tidworth House, Marlborough, Wiltshire, an indigo planter in Bihar, and his second wife, Dorothy Sophia (d. 1923), daughter of John Thomas, a Calcutta merchant, of Bletsoe, Bedfordshire. His father, a master of foxhounds and racehorse owner, underwent an evangelical conversion after attending D. L. Moody's mission in 1875 and renounced his worldly ways. His three elder sons experienced conversion in the following year. Kynaston, who entered Eton College in 1872, left the school in 1877 to enter a London firm of tea traders in preparation for joining the family firm of J. Thomas & Co. But Moody invited him to train as a medical missionary and he gave up the City to enter Trinity College, Cambridge, in 1880. Two of his younger brothers, George Brown Studd and Charles Thomas *Studd, were already in residence at the university, and the three formed a notable cricketing partnership, gaining 'blues' and playing in the Cambridge side which beat the Australians in 1882.

As president of the Cambridge Inter-Collegiate Christian Union, Studd organized Moody and Sankey's mission to Cambridge in November 1882; his prestige as a university sportsman (he captained the cricket eleven in 1884) helped to overcome much initial opposition from among students. He graduated BA in 1884 and on 10 December 1884 married Hilda (d. 1921), daughter of Sir Thomas William Brograve Proctor-Beauchamp, fourth baronet. They had four sons and a daughter. In the following year, at Moody's invitation, he visited the USA to assist the mission to college students. On his return to England he was asked by Quintin Hogg, one of a group of Etonians undertaking evangelistic work in London, to join in pioneering the Regent Street Polytechnic, which combined technical and other educational work with social and sporting facilities. Studd accepted, and thenceforward became Hogg's lieutenant. He was honorary secretary from 1885, vice-president in 1901, and, on Hogg's death in 1903, president of the polytechnic. He held the office until his death.

Studd was also a keen freemason, being junior grand warden in 1929, president of the board of benevolence, and provincial grand master for Cambridgeshire from 1934. As a volunteer, he was commandant of the West London volunteer corps, and, with the rank of major, a member of the general purposes committee of the Territorial

Forces Association from its inception until 1936. For his services during the war of 1914–18, in which his second son, Revd Lionel Fairfax Studd, was killed, he was appointed OBE in 1919.

It is remarkable that one who had deliberately turned his back on a business career should have become lord mayor of London. Studd entered upon civic life at the encouragement of members of the polytechnic, which received financial support from City parochial charities. It was not until he was well advanced in middle age that he joined a City company, the Fruiterers, and later the Merchant Taylors. He stood as a candidate for the shrievalty, and was elected senior sheriff in 1922. During his year of office he succeeded Sir William Treloar as alderman of Farringdon Without. On 18 June 1924, following the death of his first wife, he married Princess Alexandra, daughter of Prince Pavel Lieven, grand master of ceremonies at the imperial court of Russia. In 1928 he was elected lord mayor, and entered on a mayoralty marked by his splendid entertainment of Fuad II, king of Egypt, an official visit to Amsterdam where he received the gold medal of the city, and a dinner at the Mansion House for many of the leading cricketers of the day. Studd was knighted in 1923 and created a baronet in 1929. In the same year he received the honorary degree of LLD from the University of Cambridge. He was president of the Old Etonian Association from 1929 to 1930. In 1930 he was elected president of the Marylebone Cricket Club. Studd died at his home, 67 Harley Street, London, on 14 January 1944, survived by his wife.   B. STUDD, rev. M. C. CURTHOYS

Sources *The Times* (15 Jan 1944), 6 · private information (1959) · personal knowledge (1959) · E. M. Wood, *The polytechnic and its founder Quintin Hogg*, rev. edn (1932) · Burke, *Peerage* · J. C. Pollock, *Moody without Sankey* (1963)

Likenesses Miles & Kaye, photograph, c.1928, repro. in Wood, *The polytechnic and its founder*, facing p. 290 · A. Burton, oils, exh. RA 1929, University of Westminster · photograph, repro. in *The Times*

Wealth at death £49,002 17s. 10d.: probate, 7 June 1944, CGPLA Eng. & Wales

Studholme, Marie [*real name* Caroline Maria Lupton] (1872–1930), actress, was born on 10 September 1872 (commonly misreported as 1875) in Stonehall, Eccleshill, Bradford, the only child of Joseph Ludholme Lupton, auctioneer, and his wife, Emma Greaves. Raised locally, by her paternal grandparents in Baildon and her father's half-sister Mrs Frank Rhodes in Shipley, she received her secondary education at Salt's Girls' School on the Saltaire mill estate. Despite family objections to the theatre, school productions piqued her interest in the stage.

After joining her mother in London, Caroline Lupton first appeared under her professional name, Marie Studholme, at the Lyric in 1891. After other minor roles at the Criterion she played at the Shaftesbury in 1893 in *Morocco Bound*, an early musical comedy, in the same year marrying the cast member Gilbert Porteous and attracting the attention of George Edwardes, who hired her for the famous chorus line in *A Gaiety Girl* at the Prince of Wales. Though quickly graduating from the chorus, the blonde

Marie Studholme was permanently identified as 'a gaiety girl', the epitome of modern glamour and a ready subject for the ubiquitous new picture postcard and illustrated press, making her one of the most photographed beauties of her day.

Studholme remained in steady employment with Edwardes, the principal promoter of musical comedy. Though not a regular first-choice lead in new productions, she frequently took over from the original star or played major roles with Edwardes's number-one touring company. In the 1890s she understudied Letty Lind at Daly's, assuming her role in *An Artist's Model* in its transfer to New York in 1895, and returning to Broadway in a revival of *In Town* in 1897. In 1899 she succeeded Marie Tempest in the title role of *San Toy* on its provincial tour. Having taken over from Valerie Lloyd in *The Messenger Boy* at the Gaiety in 1900, Studholme enjoyed great personal success with the wartime hit song 'When the boys come home once more'. She created original roles as Dora Selby in *The Toreador* in 1901 and Cicely Marchmont in *The School Girl* in 1903. Studholme was not tall, and continued to specialize in *ingénue* or juvenile roles, playing Alice in a West End revival of *Alice in Wonderland* in 1906. Returning to musical comedy, she undertook further provincial tours, notably a lengthy engagement as *Miss Hook of Holland* between 1907 and 1909, and played in South Africa during 1910–11. Thereafter little was seen of her until 1913 when she followed other stars from legitimate theatre onto the music-hall stage, appearing in a sketch, 'Her Ladyship', at London's Wood Green Empire and touring in variety. She enjoyed her greatest popularity in the provinces and was besieged by home-town fans at the opening of Bradford's Alhambra music-hall in 1914. She retired in 1915.

Divorced from Porteous, Studholme married Harold Giles Borrett in September 1908 following a long secret engagement in approximation of the cross-class romance of the Earl and the Girl. Borrett, son of Major General Herbert Charles Borrett, took to the stage under an assumed name to court Marie, daughter of small-business people. In the 1920s, with no offspring of their own, the couple adopted two children, Peter and Jill. A convert to Christian Science, Studholme lived quietly in retirement in Hampstead and a riverside bungalow at Laleham; a council block, Studholme Court, was later built on the site of the garden of her former Hampstead home. The face that launched 1000 postcards reportedly charged 6d. to autograph them, the proceeds going to animal and theatrical charities in which she was long active.

Marie Studholme was known and remembered for what was described as her typically English beauty. Boosted by the new power of the mass-produced celebrity image, she took advantage of expanded opportunities for women on the popular stage and the growing respectability of a theatrical career. If unexceptional in dramatic talent, she had an appealing stage presence, projecting the warmth and generosity that made her genuinely well liked by fellow professionals of all ranks. She died at her London home, Croftway, 298 Finchley Road, Hampstead, on 10 March

1930 from rheumatic fever and was buried in St Marylebone cemetery, East Finchley. She was survived by her second husband. PETER BAILEY

Sources biographical and production files, Theatre Museum, London • NYPL for the Performing Arts, Billy Rose Theatre collection • R. Waters, 'Marie Studholme', *Picture Postcard Annual* (1994), 14–17 • K. Gänzl, *The encyclopedia of the musical theatre*, 2nd edn, 3 vols. (2001) • K. Gänzl, *The British musical theatre*, 1 (1986) • *New York Times* (29 Dec 1895) • *New York Times* (7 Sept 1897) • *Daily Chronicle* (12 Sept 1908) • *Bradford Telegraph and Argus* (10 March 1930) • *Bradford Telegraph and Argus* (13 March 1930) • *The Era* (12 March 1930) • *Hampstead Gazette* (14 March 1930) • *Hampstead and Highgate Express* (15 March 1930) • *Shipley Times and Express* (15 March 1930) • *The Stage* (13 March 1930) • *The Times* (11 March 1930) • *Yorkshire Observer* (14 March 1930) • *Yorkshire Observer* (8 May 1930) • B. Hunt and J. Parker, eds., *The green room book, or, Who's who on the stage* (1906–9) • *Who's who in the theatre* • A. Reeve, *Take it for a fact* (1954) • E. Short, *Fifty years of vaudeville* (1946) • b. cert. • d. cert. • census returns, 1881
Likenesses postcards, Theatre Museum, London • press illustrations, Theatre Museum, London
Wealth at death £58,303 14s. 11d.: probate, 1930, *Yorkshire Observer* (8 May 1930); *CGPLA Eng. & Wales*

Studley, John (*c.*1545–1590?), translator, was born of a Dorset family and was educated at Westminster School, where he was both one of the original queen's scholars elected on the 1560 foundation and, in 1561, the first to be elected to Trinity College, Cambridge. He graduated BA in 1566 and became a minor fellow on 8 September 1567 and a major fellow on 7 April 1570, the year in which he proceeded MA. In college politics Studley adhered firmly to the puritan party, and followed Thomas Cartwright, the Lady Margaret professor of divinity, in opposing the rule of the master, John Whitgift, who was chiefly responsible for new university statutes aimed against puritans. In 1572 Studley's signature appears as one of 164 declaring opposition to these statutes, and on 1 February 1573 he was convened before the heads of colleges on a charge of nonconformity; he vacated his fellowship at the end of that year. As a rebellious fellow Studley probably also shared in the disfavour with which Whitgift regarded the new Westminster foundation scholars.

Studley's years at Trinity were otherwise occupied by his translation of four of Seneca's tragedies: the *Agamemnon* and *Medea*, published in 1566 by Thomas Colwell (the former being the earlier work, with prefatory verses asking the reader's indulgence on account of Studley's youth and inexperience); the *Hippolytus*, which was entered in 1567 in the Stationers' register by Henry Denham, although no copy survives; and the *Hercules Oeteus*, first printed in Thomas Newton's 1581 collected edition entitled *Seneca, his Tenne Tragedies, Translated into Englysh*, along with the other three. Studley's translating style was popular and colloquial, the verse heavy if exuberant and tending to obscure the sharp detonations of the original, with no apparent effort to reproduce an epigrammatic style; the restrictively archaic 'fourteener' metre was employed. Studley treated his original text freely, inserting into the *Medea* a new chorus of his own emphasizing Jason's inconstancy in love, and adding an entire scene to the *Agamemnon* re-narrating the death of Cassandra, the imprisonment of Electra, and the flight of Orestes. These additions,

however imperfect, are an early example of breaking away from the prescribed letter of the text, while the move towards moral order and social reintegration in the translations is, if un-Senecan, an expression of contemporary taste.

Studley also wrote Latin verses addressed to Sir William Cecil (the dedicatee of his *Agamemnon*) and Latin elegies marking the death of Nicholas Carr, professor of Greek at Cambridge, which were printed with the latter's Latin translation of Demosthenes in 1571. These demonstrate Studley's close involvement with elements of a mid-century Cambridge literary humanism which, through personal contacts, linked many of the classical scholars of the day. In 1574 Studley published a translation 'with sondrye additions' of Bale's *Acta pontificum Romanorum* as *The pageant of the popes, conteyning the lyves of all the bishops of Rome from the beginninge of them to the yeare 1555*, dedicated to Thomas Radcliffe, earl of Sussex (title-page). This work, not to the taste of later scholarly orthodoxy, was dismissed by Thomas Warton as a misapplication of the time and talents of one 'qualified for better studies' (Warton, 4.272).

Little is known of Studley's later career. He married Maria Baskervill of Nethwood, Thornbury, Herefordshire, and they had a son and a daughter. He seems to have been a member of Barnard's Inn, London, and is said to have crossed to Flanders where he held a command under Prince Maurice, and died at the siege of Breda (1590), although no contemporary authority places him there.

Opinion of the literary merit of Studley's translations has differed; C. S. Lewis thought them 'execrable … the metre is a torment to the ear, the language at once artless and unnatural' (Lewis, 256) yet T. S. Eliot found in them 'poetic charm … with occasional flashes of real beauty' (Newton, 1.vi). Perhaps his most lasting literary bequest was unintentional; it was in Studley's translation of 'Tacitae Stygis' as 'Stygian Puddle glum' (ibid., 1.158) that Lewis, despite his revulsion, found the name for one of his most memorable Narnian characters. T. P. J. EDLIN

Sources E. M. Spearing, ed., *John Studley's translations of Seneca's 'Agamemnon' and 'Medea'* (1913) • T. Newton, ed., *Seneca: his tenne tragedies*, 2 vols. (1927) [with an introduction by T. S. Eliot] • H. B. Lathrop, *Translations from the classics into English from Caxton to Chapman, 1477–1620* (1967) • C. S. Lewis, *English literature in the sixteenth century, excluding drama* (1954) • J. W. Binns, *Intellectual culture in Elizabethan and Jacobean England: the Latin writings of the age* (1990) • T. Warton, *The history of English poetry*, new edn, ed. W. C. Hazlitt, 4 vols. (1871), vol. 4 • Cooper, *Ath. Cantab.*, 2.100; 3.117 • *Old Westminsters* • *DNB*

Stukeley, William (1687–1765), antiquary and natural philosopher, was born on 7 November 1687 in Holbeach, Lincolnshire, the eldest son in the family of four boys and one girl of John Stukeley (*d.* 1705), attorney, and his wife, Frances Bullen (*d.* 1707), daughter of Robert Bullen of Weston, Lincolnshire (whom Stukeley erroneously believed to be of the family of Anne Boleyn).

Education and admission to the learned societies Stukeley showed an early interest in and skill for map making and drawing, and was educated from the age of five under

William Stukeley (1687–1765), by John Smith, 1721 (after Sir Godfrey Kneller, 1720–21)

Edward Kelsall at the Free School, Holbeach. In 1700 he left school and was apprenticed as a clerk in his father's law firm in Holbeach, occasionally travelling with him to the law courts in London. But he was more interested in books, natural philosophy, and antiquities than the law, and in 1703 he was admitted as a student at Bene't College (the nickname at that time for Corpus Christi College), Cambridge, where he studied medicine. There he showed a keen interest in botany, Newtonian natural philosophy, and astronomy; he designed and built an early form of orrery with his friend Stephen Hales. Although his studies were interrupted by the death of both his father and his uncle in 1705 and subsequent financial difficulties, he left Cambridge in 1708 after graduating as bachelor of medicine, and moved to London, where he lived at his father's former lodgings in Staples Inn. There he studied anatomy in Chancery Lane, and medicine under Dr Richard Mead at St Thomas's Hospital, Southwark. In 1710 he moved to Boston, Lincolnshire, where he practised as a physician, and was made a freeman of the town in 1713. During his time in Boston he joined the Gentlemen's Society of Spalding, and became a close friend of its founder, Maurice Johnson.

In 1717 Stukeley left Boston and returned to London, where he would live at a house in Ormond Street until 1726. These ten years were intellectually and socially the most interesting in his long life, for his friends included such prominent figures as Richard Mead, Hans Sloane, Edmond Halley, William Whiston, and Martin Folkes, as well as aristocrats such as the earl of Pembroke and the earl of Winchilsea. A major influence, though, was the friendship he made with Sir Isaac Newton, who was by

then president of the Royal Society. Stukeley became a fellow of the Royal Society on 20 March 1718, was elected to its council, and stood creditably as a candidate for Halley's successor as secretary in November 1721. On a number of occasions Stukeley visited and conversed alone with Newton, during which time they discussed various subjects, including astronomy, physiology, and chronological history. On one of these visits, as they sat in his garden drinking tea, Newton informed Stukeley that his speculations upon the theory of gravitation had been 'occasion'd by the fall of an apple, as he sat in a contemplative mood. Why sh[oul]d it not go sideways, or upwards? but constantly to the earths center?' (Royal Society of London, Stukeley MS 142 fols. 15–16). This was the earliest record of this now famous anecdote. Stukeley was greatly influenced by Newtonian natural philosophy, and wrote and presented papers at the Royal Society defending the religious orthodoxy of the new science, for instance showing that fossils were evidence of a universal deluge. He also supported and expanded upon Newton's belief that the ancients had recognized the heliocentric nature of the universe and had understood the inverse-square rule of gravity.

In 1719 Stukeley travelled to Cambridge and took the degree of MD on 7 July, and on 30 September 1720 he was admitted a fellow of the Royal College of Physicians, where he gave the Goulstonian lecture in 1722. This was later published as *Of the Spleen, its Description and History, Uses and Diseases* (1722), and included as an appendix the report of the dissection of an elephant Stukeley had made with Sir Hans Sloane. In 1720 'curiosity led him to be initiated into the mysterys of Masonry, suspecting it to be the remains of the mysterys of the antients' (*Family Memoirs of the Rev. William Stukeley*, 1.267), and on 27 December 1721 he was constituted as a grand master. He was also a founder member of the re-established Society of Antiquaries in January 1718, and was appointed as the society's first secretary. His manuscript histories of the society were later used by the antiquary Richard Gough. At this time he made two of his closest lifelong friendships, with the antiquarian brothers Roger and Samuel Gale, who travelled to Avebury in Wiltshire with him in 1719. He also travelled the length of Hadrian's Wall with Roger Gale in 1725 and in November 1757 brought the destruction of the wall by the government's military road builders to the attention of the Society of Antiquaries. He regularly attended meetings of both the Society of Antiquaries and the Royal Society, where he presented papers and 'curious' objects, often antiquarian or philosophical material resulting from the annual perambulations around the English counties that he had been making since 1711. These journeys and observations resulted in his second major publication, *Itinerarium curiosum, or, An account of the antiquitys and remarkable curiositys in nature or art, observ'd in travels thro' Great Brittan, illustrated with copper prints: centuria 1* (1724). A second volume, *Centuria II*, was published posthumously in London in 1776.

In July 1722 Stukeley became involved with a group of friends in the foundation of a new antiquarian club, the Society of Roman Knights, devoted to the classical rather than medieval or 'gothic' past that dominated the interests of the Society of Antiquaries. Stukeley declared that its aim was 'to adorn & preserve the truly noble Monuments of the Romans in Britain, & the truley great & stupendous works of our British Ancestors …' (Bodl. Oxf., MS Eng. misc. c.401 fol. 19). The society's proposed members included Lord Pembroke and Lord Winchilsea, Samuel Buck, Martin Folkes, Roger and Samuel Gale, Alexander Gordon, and Maurice Johnson. In a novel development for an eighteenth-century learned society, Stukeley's first wife, Frances, was also later admitted, so becoming the first woman to belong to an English antiquarian society. The members all assumed nicknames for themselves taken from the Roman or Celtic past. Stukeley took the name of Chyndonax, supposedly a Gaulish druid, and his and his friends' use of this pseudonym would out-survive the short-lived society.

Medicine, marriage, and ordination In 1726 Stukeley left London to pursue a medical practice in Grantham, Lincolnshire, a decision seemingly based on his natural affection for the countryside and concern for his health, for he suffered periodically from gout, a new remedy for which affliction he later promoted in his *Of the Gout* (1735). He had some involvement in local politics, and supported the whig cause, dining on occasion with Robert Walpole. While in Grantham he gathered biographical material on Isaac Newton, who had grown up in the town. Much of this material focused on Newton's childhood, and thus has been of particular interest to Newtonian scholars. In Grantham he met Frances Williamson (1696/7–1737), daughter of Robert Williamson of Allington, Lincolnshire, and they married in 1728. They had three daughters before Frances died in 1737.

It was Stukeley's desire for a more settled life that allowed him to continue his researches into the history of religion, and this, together with the encouragement of his friend William Wake, archbishop of Canterbury, led to his ordination in the Church of England on 20 July 1729. In 1730 he moved to his living of All Saints', Stamford. The demands of this ecclesiastical position were neither as onerous nor as unpredictable as those of medicine, and he was able to pursue his twin interests of gardening (he landscaped and planted in the gardens of all his homes), and reading and writing on religious antiquities.

Stone circles While a brief glance through his bibliography of works shows that Stukeley published variously and extensively over much of his adult life, his principal publishing achievement was two monographs on the ancient stone circles of Stonehenge and Avebury in Wiltshire: *Stonehenge: a Temple Restor'd to the British Druids* (1740) and *Abury: a Temple of the British Druids* (1743). These volumes resulted from the extensive fieldwork—including notes, sketches, drawings, and measurements—that he had made at both sites during the summers between 1718 and 1724. As early as 1724 he had proposed the publication of four books on the history and religion of the ancient Celts, but it was only these two volumes which ever appeared in print, under the collective title of *Patriarchal*

Christianity, or, A chronological history of the origin and progress of true religion, and of idolatry. The likely cause of the delay in publication was financial as much as scholarly: in terms of sales *Itinerarium curiosum* had not been a success, for illustrated books were expensive to produce, and Stukeley subsequently held a low opinion of publishers. But his second marriage, in 1739, to Elizabeth Gale (1687–1757), sister of Roger and Samuel and daughter of the antiquary Thomas *Gale (1635/6–1702), dean of York, and Barbara Pepys (d. 1689), included a sizeable wedding portion (£10,000) and gave him the financial wherewithal to support his publications without worrying about earnings.

Stukeley's *Abury* and *Stonehenge* are both remarkable for the detail of their illustrations, and the new discoveries he made at the sites. At Stonehenge he was the first to discover and name the neighbouring earthwork avenue and cursus, to identify the stones' astronomical alignment, and he coined the word 'trilithon' to describe their unique construction. At Avebury he made important and extensive surveys of the stone circles and avenues at a time when they were being destroyed for building materials, and identified the site as a 'dracontium' or serpent-temple. This imaginative but erroneous interpretation—based upon Egyptian hieroglyphs of a snake passing through a circle—was to remain influential through the nineteenth century. It was John Aubrey who had first suggested that the stone circles abundant in the British Isles had been built by the ancient British priests the druids, but it was the publications of Stukeley, and his Cornish correspondent William Borlase, which established the popular association of stone temples with druids in the public imagination. Some of his theories on patriarchal British druids influenced the work of William Blake, especially his *Jerusalem*. But at a time when other contemporary writers were suggesting Roman, Danish, or even Anglo-Saxon builders for these antiquities, Stukeley's argument was by no means as naïve as some later historians have implied. He was well read in contemporary authors on the history of religion, and he intended his work to combat deism and Arianism, both heterodoxies circulating in England in the first half of the century. His writing reveals the influence of writers such as Gerard Vossius, Athanasius Kircher, Ralph Cudworth, and Bishop Edward Stillingfleet, although his own religious beliefs and historical arguments often came close to the natural religion he aimed to counter. An important friendship at this time was with William Warburton, bishop of Gloucester and author of the influential anti-deistic tract *The Divine Legation of Moses*. Stukeley continued to publish works on British antiquities in his three-volume series *Palaeographica Britannica* (1743, 1746, 1752), the first volume of which contained his account of the Royston cave, discovered in 1742.

The Brazen Nose Society Stukeley particularly enjoyed the company of those who shared his intellectual interests, and while loathing the bustle and pollution of London, he missed the fraternity of like minds which it offered. In an attempt to overcome this isolation, in the summer of 1736 he founded a literary and antiquarian society in Stamford.

In 1334 the town had briefly been the refuge of a group of secessionist scholars from Oxford who brought with them the brass knocker which gave its name to Brasenose College. The original knocker remained in the town until 1890 and Stukeley utilized this piece of local history, naming his new club the Brazen Nose Society. Modelled on the Gentlemen's Society of Spalding, its purpose was to provide 'a weekly conference for the promoting of useful learning sacred & civil, [and] the knowledg of antiquitys & nature' (Bodl. Oxf., MS Eng. misc. e.122). Stukeley set about making the first attempt to interpret Stamford's topographical history, and his society's meetings included a demonstration of 'Philosophical experiments' with an air-pump, a microscope, and a magic lantern by William Whiston, the disgraced former Lucasian professor of mathematics at Cambridge. Although at one point there were up to thirty members, the society soon lapsed, and an attempted revival in 1745 was unsuccessful. In 1738 Stukeley also established a clergyman's book club in the town, 'with [the] intent of making it a Vertuoso Club, but it prov'd absolutely abortive: for they had no taste for anything but wine & tobacco' (Bodl. Oxf., MS Eng. misc. e.128 fol. 4). Despite the 'solitude' he complained of in Stamford, he was able to spend his winters in London, and on 11 December 1741 he participated in Lord Sandwich's foundation of the Egyptian Society at the Lebeck's Head tavern, Chandos Street (*Family Memoirs of the Rev. William Stukeley*, 1.470). Unfortunately, this society was also short-lived, but Stukeley made there a close and influential new friend and patron, John Montagu, second duke of Montagu. He became a regular visitor to Montagu's country seat at Boughton, Northamptonshire.

Final years and reputation In November 1747 Montagu offered Stukeley the living of St George the Martyr in Queen Square, Bloomsbury, which, given his frustration with Stamford's provinciality, he accepted. He spent the final years of his life in London, where once more he was able regularly to attend the meetings of the Royal Society and the Society of Antiquaries. It was these final years which did most to cloud Stukeley's reputation, when as an old man he enthused about his patriarchal druids, warranting him his self-appointed nickname the Arch Druid. But he continued to be interested in natural philosophical subjects, and attempted to explain the earthquake that shook London in the spring of 1750 through the medium of electricity. His essay *The Philosophy of Earthquakes, Natural and Religious* (1750) was based on papers he read at the Royal Society (which were also reprinted in the *Philosophical Transactions*, vol. 46) and a sermon given at his church. In the essay Stukeley noted his debt to Benjamin Franklin's recent experiments with lightning, which had been communicated to the Royal Society. Horace Walpole recorded in his correspondence how 'One Stukeley, a parson, has accounted for it [the earthquake], and I think prettily, by electricity. But that is the fashionable cause, and everything is resolved into electrical appearances' (H. Walpole, *Correspondence*, ed. W. S. Lewis, 20, 1960, 154).

In 1747 Stukeley received a letter from a young Englishman named Charles Bertram, resident in Copenhagen, informing him of his discovery of a medieval copy of a previously unknown Roman map and itinerary of Britain, allegedly made by a fourteenth-century monk of Westminster. Stuart Piggott has described this episode as 'one of the most audacious and successful literary forgeries of the eighteenth century' (Piggott, *William Stukeley: an Eighteenth-Century Antiquary*, 127). Although Stukeley attempted to purchase the (non-existent) manuscript of *De situ Britanniae* for the newly opened British Museum, the amicable correspondence between him and Bertram did lead to the publication of Stukeley's *An Account of Richard of Cirencester, Monk of Westminster, and of his Works* (1757) and Bertram's *Britannicarum gentium historiae antiquae scriptores tres* (1757, including authentic works by Gildas and Nennius). Bertram's forgery as disseminated in these two books was a great success, and *De situ* was considered an authentic source for Roman Britain (it was even used in part by Edward Gibbon). The forgery was not fully discredited until 1869. Although Stukeley was an unfortunate dupe in this episode, his nineteenth-century reputation suffered additionally from his defence in 1763 of the Scottish poet James Macpherson. Macpherson had published three collections of poems purporting to be authentic translations of the work of an ancient Gaelic poet, Ossian. Although the poems were hugely popular throughout Europe, Samuel Johnson declared his scepticism and opinion was divided on the extent of their authenticity.

On 27 February 1765 Stukeley suffered 'a stroke of the palsy' at his rectory in Queen Square, and after lying in a coma for three days he died there on 3 March 1765. He was buried in an unmarked grave in East Ham churchyard, Essex. Stukeley was a warm-hearted and generous man who valued intellectual curiosity and personal piety over the temporal riches which, as a well-connected London physician in the 1720s, could have been his. Often, and probably unfairly, considered an eccentric, he was reluctant to practise the circumspection necessary in the study of prehistory, to temper his imagination, or to take the more cautionary advice of friends. However, his unstinted enthusiasm, dedication, and keen eye merited him his position as the father of British field archaeology.

DAVID BOYD HAYCOCK

Sources D. B. Haycock, *William Stukeley: science, archaeology and religion in eighteenth-century England* (2002) · S. Piggott, *William Stukeley: an eighteenth-century antiquary*, rev. edn (1985) · Bodl. Oxf., MSS Stukeley · S. Piggott, 'William Stukeley: new facts and an old forgery', *Antiquity*, 60 (1986), 115–22 · *The family memoirs of the Rev. William Stukeley*, ed. W. C. Lukis, 3 vols., SurtS, 73, 76, 80 (1882–7)

Archives BL, notebooks and papers relating to numismatics, Add. MSS 45570–45573 · BL, notebooks relating to Crowland Abbey · Bodl. Oxf., corresp., journals, drawings, and papers; account of Roman wall in Northumberland; copies of inscriptions; annotated copy of Edmund Gibson's edition of Camden's *Britannia*; account of Chertsey · Cardiff Central Library · CCC Cam., notebooks and papers · CUL, scheme for constructing a new royal palace behind Buckingham Palace · Devizes Museum, Wiltshire, notes and commonplace book · Freemasons' Hall, London · NL Scot., catalogue of Richard Topham's library · NL Wales, MSS relating to medallic history · NRA, priv. coll., drawings and papers · NRA, priv. coll., notes and drawings · RCP Lond. · RS ·

S. Antiquaries, Lond., commonplace book and antiquarian papers · Wellcome L., papers relating to Druids, Hebrew antiquities, astrology · Wiltshire Archaeological and Natural History Society, commonplace book; notes on medical subjects; notes relating to the Druids and British coins | BL, letters to Sir Hans Sloane · NA Scot., corresp. with Sir John Clerk · Spalding Gentlemen's Society, Spalding, Lincolnshire

Likenesses R. Collins, oils, 1720–29, S. Antiquaries, Lond. · G. Kneller, pen-and-ink sketch, 1721, NPG · J. Smith, mezzotint, 1721 (after G. Kneller, 1720–21), BM, NPG [*see illus.*] · G. Vandergucht, drawing, 1722, Bodl. Oxf. · W. Stukeley, self-portrait, drawing, 1726, Bodl. Oxf. · W. Stukeley, self-portrait, pen-and-ink, 1727, AM Oxf., Hope collection · bronze medallion, 1765, Salisbury and South Wiltshire Museum · W. Stukeley, self-portrait, drawing, BM · G. Vandergucht, engraving, repro. in W. Stukeley, *Stonehenge* (1740), frontispiece · etching (after unknown artist), NPG · oils, Lydiard Mansion, borough of Thamesdown, Wiltshire

Wealth at death large house with land, servants, and horses in Kentish Town

Stump, Samuel John (*c*.1783–1863), miniature and landscape painter, of whose parents, birthplace or early education nothing is known, studied at the Royal Academy Schools in London and exhibited at the academy from 1802 to 1845, sending mainly miniatures as well as a few oil portraits and landscape views. He exhibited miniatures with the Oil and Watercolour Society during its brief existence from 1813 to 1820, and showed landscapes of England, Italy, and Switzerland with the British Institution up to 1849. He was also a member of the Sketching Society.

Stump had a large theatrical clientele, and his portraits of stage celebrities—some of them in character—were numerous. His portraits of Lady Audley, Mrs Gulston, the collector Richard Miles, George Frederick Cooke, Harriot Mellon and Louisa Brunton, and others were engraved, some of them by himself in stipple. Stump died in 1863.

EMILY M. WEEKS

Sources DNB · Wood, *Vic. painters*, 3rd edn · Redgrave, *Artists* · Graves, *Artists* · J. L. Roget, *A history of the 'Old Water-Colour' Society*, 2 vols. (1891)

Likenesses J. Partridge, group portrait, pen and ink, and wash (*A meeting of the sketching society*), BM · S. J. Stump, self-portrait, miniature, Guildhall Art Gallery, London

Stumpe, William (*c*.1497–1552), clothier, of Malmesbury, Wiltshire, was probably the son of a weaver of North Nibley, Gloucestershire. From obscure origins he rose to be the best-known Wiltshire clothier of his day, famous in the 1540s for his use of the buildings of Malmesbury Abbey as industrial workshops. Well before the dissolution of the monasteries Stumpe had settled in Malmesbury; by 1524 he was one of the town's richest inhabitants. He was elected MP for Malmesbury in 1529, and again in 1547, and may well have served in intervening parliaments for which the names of the members for Malmesbury are unknown.

In 1536, when the court of augmentations was established to deal with the lands acquired by the crown through the dissolution of the smaller monasteries, Stumpe was appointed a receiver for north Wales, with a generous travelling allowance besides his salary of £20

p.a. In 1538 he was named a justice of the peace for Wiltshire, an appointment he retained until his death, and in March 1539, during an invasion scare, he helped to muster able men in Malmesbury and elsewhere in the county. On the surrender of the abbey to the king's commissioners in December 1539, the buildings assigned 'to remain undefaced' were given into the custody of its former steward, Sir Edward Baynton, but all those 'deemed to be superfluous' were committed to Stumpe as Baynton's deputy: they included the church, cloister, chapter house, dormitory, frater, and infirmary. Stumpe was instrumental in saving the nave of the church for use by the townspeople as their parish church. In 1541 Thomas Cranmer issued a licence for the conversion, which ensured the survival of at least part of the great abbey.

Indirectly, the town probably also gained from Stumpe's decision to install broad looms in other parts of the abbey buildings. John Leland, visiting Malmesbury in the early 1540s, reported that 3000 cloths were being made there every year. (The city of Oxford in 1546 negotiated with Stumpe for a similar use of Osney Abbey, hoping to provide work for 2000 people, but nothing came of this project.) Finally, in 1544 Stumpe consolidated his interest in the property by paying over £1500 for a royal grant to himself and his heirs of the whole site of the abbey. By the end of the decade he was living in a new house built within the precinct.

Stumpe was married three times. His first wife was Joyce, daughter of James Berkeley of Bradley, Gloucestershire; there were two sons of the marriage, the elder born in 1519. He married secondly, in or after 1533, Tibbilda, widow of William Billing, and thirdly, in 1551, Katherine (or Catherine), widow of Richard Mody, who survived him with the infant son of the marriage. Stumpe was named sheriff of Wiltshire in November 1551, but died on 22 July 1552, during his term of office. His second son succeeded him as a clothier, his eldest son, Sir James, having already moved into the ranks of the landed gentry.

HELEN MILLER, *rev.*

Sources HoP, *Commons, 1509–58*, 3.403–5 · H. Brakspear, 'Malmesbury Abbey', *Wiltshire Archaeological and Natural History Magazine*, 38 (1913–14), 458–497 · 'William Stump of Malmesbury, his descendants and relatives', *Wiltshire Notes and Queries*, 8 (1914–16), 385–95

Sturch, William (1753–1838), ironmonger and theological writer, was born at Newport, Isle of Wight, on 9 February 1753, the son of John Sturch (*d*. 1794), General Baptist minister of the Pyle Street congregation in Newport, and his wife, Mary. His great-grandfather William Sturch (*d*. 1728) was a General Baptist minister in London, and his grandfather John Sturch was General Baptist minister at Crediton, Devon, and author of *A Compendium of Truths* (1731) and a sermon on persecution (1736). His father published several sermons and *A View of the Isle of Wight* (1778), which passed through numerous editions, and was translated into German by C. A. Wichman in 1781. One of William's sisters married John Potticary (1763–1820), who was Benjamin Disraeli's first schoolmaster.

Sturch worked as an ironmonger in London, where he was one of the original members of the Unitarian chapel opened by Theophilus Lindsey at Essex Street, the Strand, in 1774. In 1799 he published anonymously *Apeleutherus, or, An Effort to Attain Intellectual Freedom*, which consists of three essays on public worship, religious education, and Christianity as a supernatural communication. In 1819 it was expanded and reprinted with a dedication to Thomas Belsham. Sturch wrote one or two pamphlets in controversy with conservative Unitarians, and was a frequent contributor to the *Monthly Repository*. He published also a pamphlet on Roman Catholic emancipation entitled *The Grievances of Ireland* (1826). He met and possibly knew the Roman Catholic barrister Charles Butler, and Henry Montgomery, founder of the Remonstrant Synod of Ulster.

Sturch died at York Terrace, Regent's Park, London, on 8 September 1838, aged eighty-five, leaving a widow, Elisabeth (1759/60–1841), and family. He was buried in the graveyard of the New Gravel Pit Chapel, Hackney. His second daughter, Elisabeth Jesser (1789–1866), married John Reid (1776–1822) and founded Bedford College, London, in October 1849 [see Reid, Elisabeth Jesser].

ALEXANDER GORDON, rev. EMMA MAJOR

Sources *Christian Reformer, or, Unitarian Magazine and Review*, 5 (1838), 740 • A. Taylor, *History of the English General Baptists*, 2: *The new connection of General Baptists* (1818), 93 • R. B. Aspland, *Memoir of the life, works and correspondence of the Rev. Robert Aspland* (1850), 106, 154, 557 • *The Inquirer* (7 April 1866), 221 • *The Inquirer* (5 May 1866), 284 • IGI • tombstones of William and Elisabeth Sturch, New Gravel Pit Chapel graveyard, Hackney, London • private information (1898) • ESTC

Sturdee, Sir Frederick Charles Doveton, first baronet (1859–1925), naval officer, was born at Charlton, Kent, on 9 June 1859, the eldest son of Captain Frederick Rannie Sturdee RN (d. 6 Jan 1885) and his wife, Anna Frances (d. 20 April 1889), daughter of Colonel Charles Hodson, of Oakbank, St Helena. He attended the Royal Naval School, New Cross, in 1870 and entered the *Britannia* as a naval cadet in July 1871. He passed out first and after going to sea as a midshipman in July 1873 served until 1878 in the channel squadron and on the East India station. After promotion to sub-lieutenant in June 1878 he was for nearly two years at Portsmouth in the gunnery school ship *Excellent* for courses and examinations, which he passed with distinction. He was promoted lieutenant in May 1880. From February 1881 to September 1882 he was in the *Hecla* on the Mediterranean station and took part in the operations at Alexandria in 1882.

Sturdee married on 23 September 1882 Marion Adela (d. 9 Dec 1940), daughter of William John Andrews, of Fortis Green, Middlesex. They had two children, Rear-Admiral Lionel Arthur Doveton, second baronet (1884–1970), at whose death the baronetcy became extinct, and Margaret Adela, who married Vice-Admiral Cecil Minet Staveley.

From September 1882 to December 1885 Sturdee was in the *Vernon* torpedo school, and made his mark as a brilliant torpedo officer. For the next three and a half years he served as torpedo lieutenant in the *Bellerophon*, Lord Clanwilliam's flagship on the North American and West Indies station. From 1889 to 1893 he was on the staff of the *Vernon* and was continuously in command of torpedo

boats: he gained more experience of these than any other lieutenant. He was promoted commander in June 1893, and then served at the Admiralty for four years in the naval ordnance department as a torpedo specialist. He was awarded the gold medal of the Royal United Service Institution for an essay in 1894, having won it previously as a lieutenant. Despite his early career as a technical specialist, Sturdee considered himself something of an intellectual, but he lacked the flexibility of mind, logical rigour, and application to meet the specification. He would not take advice, and refused to see the flaws in his argument. In November 1897 he went for two years in command of the *Porpoise* on the Australian station, and took command of the British force in Samoa in the summer of 1899 at the time of the trouble between Germany and the United States. For his services in handling a delicate international situation Sturdee was created CMG and promoted captain. He then returned to the Admiralty as assistant director of naval intelligence until October 1902, when he again went to sea and commanded successive cruisers in home waters until, in May 1905, he became chief of staff to Lord Charles Beresford, commander-in-chief of the Mediterranean Fleet. Sturdee continued with Beresford on the latter's transfer to the command of the Channel Fleet in 1907; he had been created CVO in 1906. During this period he was a leading member of the 'syndicate of discontent' that opposed the policies of the first sea lord, Sir John Fisher. Fisher despised Sturdee, who returned the feeling with interest. Sturdee's last year before promotion to flag rank in September 1908 was spent in command of the battleship *New Zealand* in the Channel Fleet. In 1910 he commanded the 1st battle squadron for a year, and after presiding over the submarine committee at the Admiralty in 1911, was again employed afloat in command of cruiser squadrons, being the senior cruiser admiral in the Home Fleet, until his promotion to vice-admiral in December 1913. He had been created KCB in the previous June.

In July 1914, immediately before the outbreak of the First World War, Sturdee relieved Admiral Sir Henry Jackson as chief of the war staff under Prince Louis of Battenberg, first sea lord. He was widely regarded as a failure in this post, and bore the largest share of responsibility for the destruction of the cruiser squadron under Sir Christopher Cradock at Coronel on 1 November 1914. This disaster made it urgently necessary to deal with Admiral von Spee's German cruisers; and, when Lord Fisher succeeded Prince Louis as first sea lord, he decided that Sturdee should be appointed commander-in-chief in the south Atlantic and south Pacific. Sturdee reached Port Stanley in the Falkland Islands on the evening of 7 December 1914, and von Spee's squadron was sighted the next morning. The decisive victory of the Falkland Islands followed, in which Sturdee with two battle cruisers, five cruisers, and one armed merchant cruiser annihilated the German squadron of two armoured cruisers, three light cruisers, and two colliers; only one light cruiser escaped. He was rewarded by a baronetcy on 19 January 1916.

Early in 1915 Sturdee hoisted his flag in the *Benbow* in

command of the 4th battle squadron of the Grand Fleet, which he commanded at Jutland (31 May 1916). In the honours after the battle he was promoted KCMG, and he remained in command of the 4th battle squadron until February 1918, despite being above the new commander-in-chief, Sir David Beatty, on the navy list. He was promoted admiral in May 1917. During his period in the Grand Fleet he devoted much time and thought to fleet tactics and to tactical and strategical exercises. He then became commander-in-chief at the Nore until 1921, when he was promoted admiral of the fleet and GCB. At the end of the war he received the thanks of parliament and a grant of £10,000. Soon after ceasing active service he succeeded Lord Milford Haven (Prince Louis of Battenberg) as president of the Society for Nautical Research, and devoted himself to the restoration of the *Victory*. He had achieved this before he died at his residence, Wargrave House, Camberley, Surrey, on 7 May 1925.

Sturdee was an able naval officer, and an effective squadron commander. Despite being an indefatigable student of his profession, however, he never grasped the higher demands of war, and failed as chief of the war staff. His victory at the Falkland Islands was both fortunate and ironic.   V. W. BADDELEY, rev. ANDREW LAMBERT

Sources A. J. Marder, *From the Dreadnought to Scapa Flow: the Royal Navy in the Fisher era, 1904–1919*, 5 vols. (1961–70) · R. F. MacKay, *Fisher of Kilverstone* (1973) · G. M. Bennett, *Charlie B: a biography of Admiral Lord Beresford of Metemmeh and Curraghmore* (1968) · E. N. Poland, *The torpedomen: HMS Vernon's story, 1872–1986* (1993) · WWW · Burke, *Peerage* (1967)
Archives CAC Cam., corresp. and papers · NMM, corresp. relating to HMS Implacable | NMM, Lord Charles Beresford MS · NMM, Reginald Custance MS | FILM BFI NFTVA, documentary footage
Likenesses F. Dodd, charcoal and watercolour drawing, 1917, IWM · W. Stoneman, photograph, 1917, NPG · G. Philpot, oils, 1918, IWM · A. S. Cope, group portrait, oils (*Naval officers of World War I, 1914–18*), NPG; study, NMM · photographs, repro. in Marder, *From the dreadnought to Scapa Flow* · photographs, repro. in Bennett, *Charlie B*
Wealth at death £15,535 17s. 7d.: probate, 30 Sept 1925, CGPLA Eng. & Wales

Sturge, Eliza Mary (1842–1905), women's activist, was born on 14 November 1842 in Frederick Street, Edgbaston, the daughter of Charles Sturge (1800–1888), corn factor and sometime mayor of Birmingham, and his wife, Mary Darby, *née* Dickinson. As such, she was a member of the dynasty of midlands Quaker philanthropists: Joseph *Sturge was her uncle, and Sophia *Sturge (1795–1845), the Birmingham anti-slavery activist, her aunt.

Brought up in a reforming atmosphere, Eliza Sturge dedicated her life to liberal causes, in particular 'asserting the right of women to work, side by side with men, for the public good' (*Englishwoman's Review*, 122). In 1869 she took up the cause of women's suffrage with fervour, becoming secretary and then vice-president of the Birmingham branch of the Women's Suffrage Association. She became an active suffrage lecturer, on one occasion moving the resolution in favour of women's suffrage in opposition to her family friend John Bright. One of her speeches, given at a meeting in Birmingham town hall on 6 December

1872, was published (as *On Women's Suffrage*). The speech ranged over the inability of politicians to suggest practical methods of making a living for women reduced to poverty, the failure of the Liberal Associations to take up the cause of women's suffrage, the undervaluing of women's work and activities, and the demeaning practices of chivalry ('I set a low value upon the surface forms of politeness which we are supposed to receive in lieu of a vote'). Sturge highlighted the fact that class, not gender, frequently dictated the treatment meted out to women, and that women were blamed for being the product of a social and educational system designed to restrict their intellectual and spiritual development ('if [men] will not allow room for the virtues of independence, they must be content with the vices of dependence'). Her rousing conclusion asserted 'You may say we have liberty of conscience; liberty of conscience without liberty of action is a mockery'.

In 1873 Eliza Sturge was adopted by the Birmingham Liberal caucus as a candidate for the school board elections; she came third, behind Joseph Chamberlain and George Dixon, and served on the board until 1876. The first woman elected to the Birmingham school board, her work has been assessed as 'highly competent' (Hollis, 140), but she was 'rendered virtually voiceless and invisible' at meetings of the board which were dominated by her male Liberal colleagues. She stepped down in 1876 to pursue her interests in the suffrage movement and in temperance reform. She retained an interest in education, however, and from 1902 served on the Worcestershire education committee. In later years she lived at 28 Bank Hill, Bewdley. Eliza Sturge died from cancer of the breast and lungs on 24 November 1905 at 45 Hagley Road, Edgbaston, the home of her niece, Dr Mary Darby Sturge, who certified her death and was the sole beneficiary of her will.

K. D. REYNOLDS

Sources *Englishwoman's Review*, 38 (1906), 122–3 · P. Hollis, *Ladies elect: women in English local government, 1865–1914* (1987) · Boase, *Mod. Eng. biog.* · b. cert. · d. cert. · CGPLA Eng. & Wales (1905) · will, proved, London, 21 Dec 1905
Wealth at death £2424 4s. 4d.: probate, 21 Dec 1905, CGPLA Eng. & Wales

Sturge, Emily (1847–1892), campaigner for women's education and suffrage, was born on 20 April 1847 at Highbury Villa, Cotham New Road, Cotham, Bristol, the eldest of the eleven children of William *Sturge (1820–1905) and his wife, Charlotte Allen Sturge (1817–1891). Four of her sisters were also involved to a greater and lesser extent in the movement for women's education. The Sturge family were prominent members of the Society of Friends and were linked by marriage and descent to a number of Quaker families. Emily was a great-niece of the Quaker Ann(e) Knight who had campaigned for women's right to vote in the 1840s, and in the memoir of Emily (1892) Charlotte Sturge wrote that Ann Knight 'would have rejoiced to see how far her desires have been fulfilled and will probably be yet further carried out' (Goodbody, 50).

William Sturge was a partner in the family business of surveying which prospered in the nineteenth century. In 1864 the family moved into Chilliswood (later part of the

Emily Sturge (1847–1892), by unknown photographer

University of Bristol) in Cotham, and the third daughter, Elizabeth, lived there until her death in 1944 at the age of ninety-four. The house was a centre for visiting lecturers and for drawing-room meetings during the suffrage campaigns of the 1870s. Emily was described by her Aunt Matilda as 'shy and sensitive in infancy' (E. Sturge, 79), and this developed into a deep reserve which gave the impression of aloofness. She was also 'a woman of considerable personal attractions, a little above the middle height, with good features, a fine bearing, and magnificent hair, which gave a certain distinction to her appearance' (ibid., 84). In early life she broke away from the evangelicalism of her upbringing, and experienced periods of religious doubt, though she continued to attend Friends' meetings all her life. Her sister Elizabeth said that 'we—her sisters—hardly knew how much strong feeling her rather cold and distant manner covered until, after her death, her private memoranda revealed it' (ibid., 79). In one of these memoranda Emily wonders

> how it is that I come to be where I am—how it has come about that I am absorbed in the practical work of life. If the line of least resistance had not lain in this direction I could have lived the student's life. (Goodbody, 44)

After attending schools at Weston-super-Mare and then Frenchay, near Bristol, Emily's own education was cut short at the age of about fourteen, and thereafter she was largely self-taught. In contemplating the life of a student Emily may have been envying her younger sisters Mary Charlotte, known as Carta (1852–1929), and Caroline

(1861–1922), who attended the University College which opened at Bristol in 1876. Carta went on to study at Newnham College, Cambridge, gaining the moral science tripos in 1887, and Caroline qualified as a doctor at London University. One of Emily's brothers, William Allen Sturge (1850–1919), was also medically qualified and married to Dr Emily Bovell, one of the seven female medical students expelled from Edinburgh University during the Sophie Jex-Blake struggle for women's access to medical training in the early 1870s.

The 'practical work' of Emily Sturge's brief life was almost wholly concerned with promoting women's suffrage and women's education. From 1878 until her death she was honorary secretary of the west of England branch of the National Society for Women's Suffrage. The West of England Suffrage Society had been formed in Bristol in 1868 at the home of Matthew Davenport Hill, whose daughter Florence was a founding member. Emily Sturge was a member by 1872–3, and from the 1870s until about 1885 she was involved in travelling to public meetings, giving public speeches, and campaigning through the Liberal Party to obtain women's franchise by electoral reform. She was a member of the Bristol Women's Liberal Association, formed about 1880 alongside similar branches formed in other Quaker strongholds, whereby parliamentary and municipal candidates were asked to state their views of women's suffrage. Women were not enfranchised by Gladstone's 1884–5 reforms and Emily Sturge moved across to support the Liberal Unionists in the home rule split. She was a member of the committee of the West Bristol Temperance Society.

Emily Sturge was elected as a Liberal to the Bristol school board in January 1880. School boards were the first form of elected body open to women, and Emily succeeded Helena Richardson as the second woman member, having come second in the poll at the age of thirty-two. She had experience of teaching in a Friends' Sunday school, and took an interest in an elementary school for girls run by the British and Foreign School Society. During her membership of the board she campaigned for free school meals, established as 'penny dinners' in 1884; was involved in the setting up of evening schools, chairing the evening school committee from 1886; and was concerned to ensure equal access for women and girls to technical instruction and to promote the training and status of women teachers.

Emily Sturge achieved the latter aim through the new University College, founded in 1876. The college was a direct result of the Clifton Association for Promoting Higher Education for Women, formed in Bristol in 1868. The association founded the Lectures for Ladies in the 1860s, which were attended by the Sturge sisters and are described by Elizabeth Sturge in her *Reminiscences* (1928). The new University College, to become the University of Bristol in 1909, was open to both men and women, except for the medical school. In its early years money was a problem and Emily Sturge organized a successful fund-raising campaign in the late 1880s. She helped to establish a day training school for women teachers at the University College, which opened in October 1892: Marion Pease, a graduate of the new University College and a member of another key Bristol Quaker family, the Frys, was appointed the first mistress of method.

Emily Sturge was also involved in setting up at Bristol a school of cookery to train domestic science teachers, using moneys set aside by the technical instruction committee of the town council, and derived from the Technical Instruction Act of 1889 and the Local Taxation (Customs and Excise) Act of 1890. Unlike the school boards, town councils were still restricted to men, and following receipt of a memorial from 'certain ladies' in October 1891, Emily Sturge, who wanted grants for technical education to benefit girls as well as boys, was invited to assist with the formation of the school of cookery. It was to open in September 1893. Emily Sturge was re-elected to the Bristol school board in January 1892 shortly before her death at her home, Chilliswood, Tyndall's Park, Cotham, Bristol, on 3 June 1892, from injuries sustained after being thrown from her horse. She was buried in the Quaker burial-ground at Friars Meeting-House, Rosemary Street, Bristol.

ELIZABETH BIRD

Sources M. Goodbody, *Five daughters in search of learning: the Sturge family, 1820–1944* (privately printed, Bristol, 1986) · E. Sturge, *Reminiscences of my life: and some account of the children of William and Charlotte Sturge and of the Sturge family of Bristol* (privately printed, Bristol, 1928) · M. Sturge, *Emily Sturge: a portrait in outline* (1892) · *Englishwoman's Review*, 23 (1892), 191–4 · M. Pease, 'Some reminiscences of University College, Bristol', 1942, University of Bristol Library, Special Collections, DM 563 W219 · J. B. Thomas, 'University College, Bristol: pioneering teacher training for women', *History of Education*, 17 (1988), 55–70 · H. E. Meller, *Leisure and the changing city, 1870–1914* (1976) · E. Malos, 'Bristol women in action, 1839–1919: the right to vote and the right to earn a living', *Bristol's other history*, ed. I. Bild (1983), 97–128 · J. Hannam, '"An enlarged sphere of usefulness": the Bristol women's movement c.1860–1914', *The making of modern Bristol*, ed. M. Dresser and P. Ollerenshaw (1996), 184–209 · S. J. Tanner, *How the women's suffrage movement was founded in Bristol 50 years ago* (1918) · A. M. Beddoe, *The early years of the women's suffrage movement* (1911) · R. Fulford, *Votes for women: the story of a struggle* (1957) · technical instruction committee minutes, 1891–1903, Bristol RO, Bristol school board minutes, TC/03/1–2 · birth record of Society of Friends, Bristol RO · d. cert.
Likenesses photograph, repro. in Sturge, *Reminiscences of my life*, facing p. 79 · photograph, Women's Library, London [see illus.]
Wealth at death £218 19s. 2d.: administration, 15 July 1892, CGPLA Eng. & Wales

Sturge, Emily Bovell (1840–1885). *See under* Edinburgh Seven (*act.* 1869–1873).

Sturge [*née* Dickinson], **Hannah** (1816–1896), philanthropist, was born on 30 December 1816, the ninth of the eleven children of Barnard Dickinson (1781–1852), ironmaster, and Ann Darby (1779–1840), daughter of Abraham *Darby (1750–1789), ironmaster of Coalbrookdale, and his wife, Rebecca. The Dickinsons and Darbys were members of the Society of Friends (Quakers) and both Barnard and Ann were formally recorded as ministers, a status which recognized qualities of inspiration and leadership. In 1831 Barnard Dickinson retired from business to devote himself to

the Society's religious life and administration; his daughter was brought up in this atmosphere of entrepreneurial values and strenuous piety.

In 1846 Joseph *Sturge (1793–1859), a widower twenty-three years her senior, proposed to Hannah, and the couple were married on 14 October of that year at the Coalbrookdale Quaker meeting-house. Hannah's sister, Mary Darby Dickinson, had married Joseph's younger brother, Charles, and close ties had developed between the two families. For the rest of her life Hannah Sturge lived at 64 Wheeley's Road, Sturge's home in the fashionable Birmingham suburb of Edgbaston. There were five children of the marriage, one son and four daughters: Joseph, Sophia *Sturge (1849–1936), Priscilla, Eliza, and Hannah.

Hannah Sturge played a significant part in her husband's public life. Joseph and Charles Sturge were partners in a grain importing company, a highly speculative venture which was saved from bankruptcy during a crisis by the £1800 she had inherited from her father. This ensured the continued flow of wealth without which Joseph could not have sustained his activities as one of the best known Quaker philanthropists and reformers of his day. Hannah also played a useful supportive role as hostess in a busy household visited by many people prominent in public life, including Richard Cobden, John Bright, and Harriet Beecher Stowe. She acquired a sympathy for a variety of reforms, and after Joseph's death in 1859 she continued to promote his work, gaining a reputation in her own right as 'one of the most benevolent and philanthropic ladies in Birmingham' (*Birmingham Daily Mail*, 21 Oct 1896). One of her visitors in 1865 was delighted by the 'atmosphere of benevolent thought and action' (Mackie, 2.70) that prevailed under her roof. In addition to her work for the poor, at various times she was active in the Ladies' Temperance Association, the Ladies' Negro's Friend Society, the anti-slavery Free Produce Committee, a committee to promote the education of girls in Jamaica, the Infirm and Aged Women's Society, and the juvenile reformatory movement. She played a less active role in the Society of Friends than her parents, taking only an occasional part in the work of the Quaker women's committees in Warwickshire. Joseph Sturge died while their children were young, but Hannah brought them up in accordance with his wishes, and two of them, Joseph and Sophia, carried his ideals and work into the 1930s. She also compiled a publication entitled *Tracts and Hymns Selected for Children* (1857), which was intended to provide her children and others with religious and moral materials 'suitable for them to commit to memory'. The volume was republished almost unchanged in 1896.

In her prime Hannah Sturge was a tall, fine woman with high colour and brown hair, but in later life she was described as fat. She had a mind of her own, and, as Charles Sturge disapprovingly noted, Joseph admitted that he could do little to control 'her doings'. She was remembered during her declining years as 'eccentric, morbid, warm hearted, very nervous' (Sturge). On 19 October 1896 Hannah died at her home at 64 Wheeley's Road 'while she was engaged in one of those acts of unobtrusive kindness in which she found so much pleasure' (*The Friend*). The cause of death was registered as bronchitis and heart failure. She was interred on 24 October in the Quaker burial-ground at Coalbrookdale. She is best seen as a product of the early nineteenth-century religious revival, fulfilling roles as wife, mother, widow, and philanthropist within the conventions appropriate to middle-class Quaker women of her day.   ALEX TYRRELL

Sources 'Dictionary of Quaker biography', RS Friends, Lond. [card index] · digest of deaths, 1837–1961, RS Friends, Lond. · *The Friend*, new ser., 36 (30 Oct 1896) · *Birmingham Daily Mail* (21 Oct 1896) · *CGPLA Eng. & Wales* (1896) · M. D. Sturge, ed., 'Record of family faculties', 1884, priv. coll. · W. R. Hughes, *Sophia Sturge: a memoir* (1940) · A. Tyrrell, *Joseph Sturge and the 'moral radical party' in early Victorian Britain* (c.1987) · C. Midgley, *Women against slavery: the British campaigns, 1780–1870* (1992) · A. Tyrrell, '"Woman's mission" and pressure group politics in Britain, 1825–60', *Bulletin of the John Rylands University Library*, 63 (1980–81), 194–230 · J. B. Mackie, *The life and work of Duncan McLaren*, 2 vols. (1888) · *Annual Monitor* (1853), 103–13 · d. cert.
Likenesses group portrait, photograph, 1850–59 (with her family), repro. in Hughes, *Sophia Sturge* · group portrait, photograph (as an elderly woman; with her children), Friends' Meeting House, Birmingham; repro. in W. A. Cadbury, *The Society of Friends, Bull Street, Birmingham* (1956)
Wealth at death £781 4s. 8d.: probate, 11 Dec 1896, *CGPLA Eng. & Wales*

Sturge, Joseph (1793–1859), philanthropist, son of Joseph Sturge (1763–1817), a farmer and grazier, and his wife, Mary Marshall (d. 1819) of Alcester, Warwickshire, was born at Elberton, Gloucestershire, on 2 August 1793. He was the fourth of twelve children: six boys and six girls. After a year at Thornbury day school and three years at the Quaker boarding-school at Sidcot, Sturge at fourteen commenced farming with his father. Afterwards he farmed on his own account. The Sturges were members of the Society of Friends, and at the age of nineteen, when Joseph followed the family's pacifist beliefs and refused to find a proxy or to serve in the militia, he watched his flock of sheep driven off to be sold to cover the delinquency. In 1814 he settled at Bewdley as a corn factor, but did not make money. In 1822 he moved to Birmingham, where he lived for the rest of his life. There, in partnership with his brother Charles Sturge (1801–1888), who was associated with him in many of his later philanthropic acts, he created one of the largest grain-importing businesses in Britain. With other family members he invested in railways and in the new docks at Gloucester. Leaving the conduct of the business to Charles, he devoted himself after 1831 to philanthropy and public life. On 29 April 1834 he married Eliza, only daughter of James *Cropper, the philanthropist. She died in 1835. He married again on 14 October 1846; his second wife was Hannah [see Sturge, Hannah (1816–1896)], daughter of Barnard Dickinson of Coalbrookdale, Shropshire, with whom he had a son and four daughters.

From the 1820s Sturge warmly espoused the anti-slavery cause in collaboration with his younger sister Sophia *Sturge (1795–1845). He soon became dissatisfied with T. F. Buxton and the leaders of the movement, who favoured a policy of gradual emancipation. In 1831 he was one of the

Joseph Sturge (1793–1859), by Jerry Barrett, 1855

founders of the agency committee of the Anti-Slavery Society, whose programme was entire and immediate emancipation. Sturge and his friends engaged lecturers, who travelled through Britain and Ireland arousing popular interest. They were disappointed by the measure of emancipation passed by the government on 28 August 1833, granting compensation to slave owners and substituting a temporary system of unpaid apprenticeship for slavery. Between November 1836 and April 1837 Sturge visited the West Indies gathering evidence to demonstrate the flaws of the apprenticeship system. On his return he published *The West Indies in 1837* (1838), the first edition of which rapidly sold, and gave evidence for seven days before a committee of the House of Commons. He travelled round Britain, hoping, as one of his friends explained, to bring 'the battering ram of public opinion' to bear on parliament and the West Indian planter interest. He was successful, and in 1838 the apprenticeship system was terminated.

Sturge and his friends subsequently sent large sums of money to Jamaica in support of schools, missionaries, and a scheme for settling former slaves in 'free townships'. He founded the British and Foreign Anti-Slavery Society in 1839, and organized international anti-slavery conventions in 1840 and 1843. In 1841 he travelled through the United States with the poet J. G. Whittier, to observe the condition of the slaves there, and on his return published *A Visit to the United States in 1841* (1842). Towards the end of his life he bought an estate on the island of Montserrat to prove the economic viability of free labour if efficiently and humanely managed.

Meanwhile political agitation in England was rising.

One of the first members of the Anti-Corn Law League, Sturge was reproached by the *Free Trader* for deserting repeal when, in 1842, he launched a campaign for 'complete suffrage', hoping to secure the co-operation of the league and the Chartist movement under his leadership. He was encouraged by the support he received from Edward Miall and middle-class nonconformists as well as from some of the Chartists, including A. G. O'Neill and Henry Vincent, but the league leaders refused to participate, and the movement faded away after it was opposed by William Lovett and Feargus O'Connor at a conference in Birmingham in December 1842. Sturge unsuccessfully contested parliamentary elections at Nottingham in 1842, Birmingham in 1844, and Leeds in 1847 on platforms that included 'complete suffrage'.

For several years after the mid-1840s Sturge was one of the leaders of a movement for 'people diplomacy', which attempted to create an international public opinion in favour of arbitration as a means of avoiding war. Together with Richard Cobden, Henry Richard, Elihu Burritt, and others, he organized peace congresses at Brussels, Paris, Frankfurt, London, Manchester, and Edinburgh. In 1850 he visited Schleswig-Holstein and Copenhagen with the object of inducing the governments of Schleswig-Holstein and Denmark to submit their dispute to arbitration. In January 1854 he was appointed one of the deputation from the Society of Friends to visit the tsar of Russia in an attempt to avert the Crimean War. Largely through Sturge's support, the *Morning Star* was launched in 1856 as an organ for the advocacy of non-intervention and arbitration. In 1856 he visited Finland to arrange for distribution of funds from the Friends towards relieving the famine caused by the British fleet's destruction of private property during the war. Sturge died suddenly after a heart attack at Edgbaston, near Birmingham, on 14 May 1859, as he was preparing to attend the annual meeting of the Peace Society, of which he was president. He was buried in the graveyard of the Bull Street meeting-house, Birmingham.

A man of stocky build, with a prominent forehead, brown hair, blue eyes, and benevolent features, Sturge was often admired for the energy with which he pursued his good causes. Two of his children, Joseph and Sophia *Sturge (1849–1936), continued his philanthropic and reforming work into the twentieth century.

Sturge's range of interests as a philanthropist and reformer was very wide: anti-slavery, peace, free trade, suffrage extension, infant schools and Sunday schools, reformatories, spelling reform, teetotalism, hydropathy, and public parks. He was one of the street commissioners of Birmingham during the 1820s, and from 1838 to 1840 he was an alderman of the newly created Birmingham town council. The mainspring of his actions was a sense of Christian duty derived from his Quakerism. He was also influenced by his association with radical nonconformists who shared his antipathy for the aristocratic Anglican élite which dominated British political life. He has been seen as one of the many wealthy Quakers who attempted to alleviate the problems of the age by their philanthropy.

He has also been described as one of the best examples of a group of reformers who called themselves 'moral radicals' and strove to impart a religiously based idealism to the emergent Liberal Party of the mid-nineteenth century.   ALEX TYRRELL

Sources A. Tyrrell, *Joseph Sturge and the 'moral radical party' in early Victorian Britain* (c.1987) · H. Richard, *Memoirs of Joseph Sturge* (1864) · *Birmingham Journal* (1830–59) · Bodl. RH, Anti-Slavery Society MSS · *The Friend*, 1–18 (1843–60) · *British Emancipator* (1838–40) · *British and Foreign Anti-Slavery reporter* (1840–60) · *Herald of Peace* (1819–59) · *Nonconformist* (1841–59) · J. Sturge and T. Harvey, *The West Indies in 1837* (1838) · J. Sturge, *A visit to the United States in 1841* (1842) · J. Sturge and T. Harvey, *Report of a visit to Finland, in the autumn of 1856* (1856)
Archives BL, corresp., Add. MSS 43722–43723, 43845, 50131 · Bodl. RH, corresp., journal relating to involvement with the Anti-Slavery Society · Boston PL, letters and papers · priv. coll., family MSS | BL, corresp. with Richard Cobden, Add. MS 43656 · BL, Sturge MSS · Hunt. L., letters to Thomas Clarkson · L. Cong., papers of Lewis Tappan · St John Cam., letters (among papers of Thomas Clarkson) · U. Lond., Brougham corresp. · W. Sussex RO, corresp. with Richard Cobden
Likenesses B. R. Haydon, group portrait, oils, 1841 (*The Anti-Slavery Society convention, 1840*), NPG · J. Barrett, oils, 1855, Birmingham Museums and Art Gallery [*see illus.*] · woodcut, pubd 1859, NPG; repro. in *British Workman* (July 1859) · M. Gauci, lithograph (after R. Rippingille), BM · D. J. Pound, stipple and line engraving (after photograph by Whitlock), BM, NPG · J. Thomas, marble statue, Five Ways, Birmingham · marble bas-relief, William Knibb Memorial Baptist Church, Falmouth, Jamaica
Wealth at death under £60,000: probate, 26 May 1859, *CGPLA Eng. & Wales*

Sturge, Matilda (1829–1903), Quaker minister and essayist, was born on 29 May 1829 at Wilson Street, St Paul's, Bristol, the sixth of eight children of Jacob Player Sturge (1793–1857), surveyor, and Sarah (1789–1867), daughter of William Stephens and his wife, Ann Dawe. She was born into the quietist tradition of Quakerism, and her parents maintained restrictions on dress, speech, and entertainment while other Quakers were relaxing them. Their home was 'somewhat austere' (Sturge, 192). Apparently she was educated at home, where her father encouraged a love of knowledge and a taste for good literature but banned frivolous activities such as the reading of drama. She may have attended university extension lectures for ladies in Bristol about 1868.

Matilda Sturge's essays on a variety of topics, including religion, biography, history, and social issues such as temperance and the position of women, were published in Quaker periodicals over a span of thirty years. Her writings on women, such as Mary Carpenter, Pandita Ramabai, and Sister Dora Pattison, establish her women subjects as diverse, varied, and important contributors to social and religious life. She published a collection of her essays and two memorials in the tradition of Quaker life writing, one on Emily Sturge (1847–1892), her niece and a prominent feminist, and the other on her friend Ann Hunt, Quaker minister.

Sturge was an active and energetic member of her local monthly meeting of the Society of Friends at Bristol. Beginning as a teacher in the First Day School in Bristol, she ultimately became superintendent of the Sunday

School for Girls. The first day school movement was an early form of adult education. She also ran a mothers' meeting of ninety working-class women over many years. She was recognized as a minister in 1880, was clerk of her local women's monthly meeting, and became assistant clerk to the national women's yearly meeting in 1883. She made a strong impression when she spoke at meeting: 'she took care never to exceed the message which she believed was given her or to speak without it' (*The Friend*, 17 July 1903, 476). She was also a member of the rather controversial home mission committee, established in 1882 to gain a more official and permanent basis within the Society of Friends for the home mission movement, a Quaker evangelical outreach to the poor.

Sturge's nieces were active in the women's movement, but she focused her energies upon Quaker organizations. Although Quakers believed in the spiritual equality of women and men, women members of the Society of Friends had to work to gain equality in its governing councils. With others from the Bristol and Somerset quarterly meeting, where women and men had enjoyed a virtual equality for some time, Matilda worked to extend this to the national level in the 1880s. In 1895, after a debate in which Matilda commented that women 'only knew what went on by gossip in the yard', formal equality was extended to women (*The Friend*, 1895, 382).

A consideration of Matilda Sturge urges a revision of the view that British Quakerism of the era was increasingly sharply divided between the older evangelicals and the younger liberal reformers. In both her practice and some of her writing, she seems to have remained liberal in theology while also deeply involved in aspects of the evangelical project and ready at times to defend evangelicalism. The liberals prevailed at the Manchester conference of 1895, called to consider the state of the society. But Matilda's crucial role at the Manchester conference—her paper, the first to be presented, set the tone of the whole meeting—suggests the inadequacy of interpretations focused upon a struggle between two generations of men.

She was short in stature, 'homely in person', lively and clever although sensitive to criticism. Matilda Sturge died from heart failure and pneumonia at a sister's house, Southleigh, Winscombe, near Sidcot, Somerset, on 13 June 1903 and was buried near by on 18 June 1903.

MARGARET ALLEN

Sources M. Allen, 'Matilda Sturge: "Renaissance woman"', *Women's History Review*, 7 (1998), 209–26 • E. Sturge, *Reminiscences of my life: and some account of the children of William and Charlotte Sturge and of the Sturge family of Bristol* (privately printed, Bristol, 1928) • *The Friend*, new ser., 43 (1903), 476 • *The Friend*, new ser., 35 (1895), 382 • 'Dictionary of Quaker biography', RS Friends, Lond. [card index] • d. cert.
Likenesses photograph, repro. in *The Friend*, new ser., 43 (1903)
Wealth at death £8687 6s. 5d.: resworn probate, 4 Aug 1903, CGPLA Eng. & Wales

Sturge, Sophia (1795–1845), slavery abolitionist, was born at Elberton, Gloucestershire, on 17 August 1795, the fifth of the twelve children of Joseph Sturge (1763–1817), grazier, and Mary Marshall (d. 1819), only child of Thomas Marshall, steward of the marquess of Hertford. The two families had been members of the Society of Friends since the seventeenth century, and Sophia was brought up to observe the Quaker values of the day.

A chronic invalid—she described herself as a victim of disease and medicine from infancy—Sophia Sturge was educated at a school in Wellington, an experience that she remembered as 'not the happiest of my life' (S. Sturge to John Sturge, 23 June 1829, Sturge family MSS). In the straitened circumstances of a large family her mother took a strong line against superfluous educational subjects and denied her the drawing and French lessons that she requested. The brothers and sisters subsequently compensated as best they could for their narrow education, and their correspondence shows them to have been a circle of autodidacts eagerly exchanging ideas on the literature and events of the day: Sophia Sturge's letters refer to the *Edinburgh Review* and writers including Walter Scott and Lord Byron. During the political furore arising from George IV's attempts to divorce Queen Caroline, she wrote of her wish to see only moderate reform lest the cry of liberty might lead on to disorder and despotism.

In 1815 Sophia Sturge joined her brother Joseph *Sturge (1793–1859) at Bewdley as his housekeeper. For a time she was also the bookkeeper of the partnership J. and C. Sturge, which he had set up with one of their brothers after their move to Birmingham. From their earliest days her 'great love' for Joseph was evident (Mary Sturge to Thomas Marshall, 8 Dec 1803, Marshall MSS), and on her deathbed she spoke of her idolatry of him. His marriage to Eliza Cropper in 1834 was a breaking of 'tender bonds' for her (S. Sturge to Mary Darby Sturge [1834?], Sturge family MSS), when she was displaced from his household and unhappily took employment as a governess; but on Eliza's death in 1835 she resumed her position in his home, 64 Wheeley's Road, Edgbaston, where she remained for the rest of her life.

Like many women Quakers of that era Sophia Sturge had a formidable personality; her obituary in *The Pilot* described her as a woman with a 'vigorous intellect and understanding universally well informed'. As his secretary and confidante she was one of the mainstays of Joseph Sturge's public life as a reformer, and he deferred to her opinions. Although she was alarmed by his discussions with Feargus O'Connor and other militant Chartists in 1842, her views were radical enough to endorse his support of complete suffrage.

For an invalid Sophia Sturge was surprisingly active in many benevolent projects. She was one of the founders of the Birmingham Ladies Society for the Relief of Negro Slaves, which was virtually the headquarters of a nationwide campaign by women during the 1820s. At a time when the male abolitionists could not decide between immediate and gradual emancipation, women campaigners opted for the former and organized a boycott of slave-produced sugar. Many years later Joseph remembered his sister calling on some 3000 families in Birmingham to seek their support. When the slaves were set free, as secretary of the Birmingham Ladies Negro's Friend

Society, Sophia Sturge tried to help them to adjust to the conditions of freedom; in 1844, for example, a school for which she had raised funds was opened in Jamaica. Sympathizing with the American anti-slavery movement, she became a friend and correspondent of Lewis Tappan, one of the leaders.

Sophia Sturge died on 6 June 1845 at 64 Wheeley's Road, Edgbaston, attended by Joseph throughout her last illness. Medical advice opined that she had died of lung disease. She was interred in the burial-ground of the Bull Street Friends' meeting-house, Birmingham, on 11 June 1845. Her death was the occasion of J. G. Whittier's poem, 'To my Friend on the Death of his Sister'. Quakerism, strongly influenced by evangelical ideals, was the mainspring of her life, enabling her to fulfil roles as a supportive sister and anti-slavery campaigner in her own right.

ALEX TYRRELL

Sources priv. coll., Sturge family MSS · Oxon. RO, Marshall MSS, XVII/I/I · *The Pilot* (14 June 1845) · minute book of the Ladies Society for the Relief of Negro Slaves, Birmingham Public Library · 'Joseph Sturge's account of his sister Sophia's last illness, 1845', priv. coll. · P. Burlingham, 'Reminiscences of her early days', priv. coll. · *Birmingham Journal* (7 May 1853) · quarterly meeting of Gloucestershire and Wiltshire, Wilts. & Swindon RO [births] · *Edwin Octavius Tregelles: civil engineer and minister of the gospel*, ed. S. E. Fox (1892), 224

Archives Oxon. RO · priv. coll., family MSS | Oxon. RO, Marshall MSS, XVII/I/I

Wealth at death bequests of £800–£1000

Sturge, Sophia (1849–1936), peace campaigner, was born in Birmingham, on 5 January 1849, the second of the five children of Joseph *Sturge (1793–1859), corn merchant, and his second wife, Hannah *Sturge (1816–1896), daughter of Barnard Dickinson, ironmaster of Coalbrookdale, and his wife, Ann. The two families were members of the Society of Friends. Joseph Sturge was a well-known philanthropist, and Sophia was brought up in an atmosphere of strenuous piety and community service. After her education at home by governesses she embarked on a lifelong career of philanthropy and reform. At a time when women were claiming a share in public life she served as president of the Young British Women's Temperance Association and as a member of the Women's Liberal Social Council. From the 1860s she supported the women's suffrage campaign. Deeply moved by the sufferings of the Irish people, she sympathized with Irish home rule and went to Connemara in 1888, where, with financial assistance from some Quakers, she set up a basket-making industry in the village of Letterfrack. She lived there for seven years, pursuing this venture with great energy. Subsequently, in Ireland and the Scottish highlands, she attempted to set up cottage industries for making toys. As an authority on handicrafts she was consulted by the congested districts boards in Scotland and Ireland. Hoping to diminish unemployment and urban destitution in England, she was also associated with the land settlement schemes of Joseph Fels, an American philanthropist.

Sophia Sturge's sympathies recognized no frontiers: from her parents she had inherited business-cum-philanthropic interests in the Caribbean island of Montserrat, and in her own right she supported reforms promoted by the early Indian National Congress. By the turn of the century world peace had become her chief interest. A strong believer in international arbitration, she attended peace conferences in Boston and Stockholm in 1904 and 1910. She opposed the Second South African War and assisted Norman Angell's peace campaign. In July and August 1914 she worked strenuously for the Neutrality League which attempted to keep Britain out of the First World War. Putting the strength of her convictions to severe tests during the war years, she not only pressed for a negotiated peace but also assisted enemy aliens in Britain through the Friends Emergency Committee and attempted to ameliorate the harsh treatment of conscientious objectors. After the war she went to the Netherlands where she helped German children to recuperate from their hardships. During the 1920s she promoted peace by participating in the conferences of the Union of Democratic Control and by travelling throughout Britain to address schoolchildren. Her published works were primarily directed to young people in the hope of fostering international understanding: they included books on Germany, the Netherlands, Denmark, and Norway; a tale called *The Patriot* (1909); and *The Children of Hunger*, a collection of children's letters from Germany and Austria written in the aftermath of the First World War.

Sophia Sturge never married; she lived in the parental home at Wheeleys Road, Edgbaston, until her mother's death, when, with her brother and sisters, she moved to 318 Hagley Road, Edgbaston. Later she moved to nearby Frederick Road. She lived frugally, but her home was always a base for her public life where she entertained local and international visitors. Vehement, even importunate, in pursuit of her good causes, she cultivated an impressive presentation of self. She was remembered as a 'beautiful tall lady' (Hughes 181) who dressed in a blue cloak (the colour of peace) with flowing draperies in the style of Elizabeth Fry. Her attitude to Quakerism was ambivalent: loyal to her parents' example, as a young woman she was none the less alienated by what she saw as restrictive Quaker customs and became a member of the Church of England. However, she resumed her Quakerism before her death. She died on 17 January 1936 at 39 Frederick Road and was buried on 21 January at Lodge Hill cemetery, Selly Oak, Birmingham. The registered cause of death was dermatitis herpetiformis and chronic rheumatism.

ALEX TYRRELL

Sources W. R. Hughes, *Sophia Sturge: a memoir* (1940) · monthly meeting minutes, North Division, Warwickshire, Leicestershire and Rutland, 1839–50, Society of Friends, Birmingham, Bull Street Meeting House · *The Times* (18 Jan 1936) · *The Times* (24 Jan 1936) · b. cert. · d. cert. · A. Tyrrell, *Joseph Sturge and the 'moral radical party' in early Victorian Britain* (c.1987) · E. Isichei, *Victorian Quakers* (1970) · J. Liddington, *The long road to Greenham: feminism and anti-militarism in Britain since 1820* (1989) · P. Kilroy, *The story of Connemara* (1989)

Likenesses photographs, repro. in Hughes, *Sophia Sturge*

Wealth at death £7595 18s. 4d.: probate, 22 Feb 1936, CGPLA Eng. & Wales

Sturge, William (1820–1905), surveyor and land agent, was born on 21 August 1820 in Bristol, the eldest of four sons and four daughters of Jacob Player Sturge (1793–1857), of Y. and J. P. Sturge, surveyors and land agents of Bristol, and his wife, Sarah (1789–1867), daughter of William and Ann Stephens of Bridport. His father was a cousin of Joseph Sturge (1793–1859), philanthropist. William Sturge, of a Quaker family, attended schools at Sidcot near Winscombe, Somerset, and at Fishponds, Bristol. He married Charlotte Allen (1817–1891) of Stoke Newington in June 1846; they had eleven children. A son, William, was responsible for the Sturge flint collection presented to the British Museum; his daughter, Emily *Sturge, became a campaigner for women's education and suffrage.

On leaving school in 1836 Sturge entered the family firm of Y. and J. P. Sturge of Bristol, which was run by his uncle, Young Sturge, who had opened the Bristol office, and his father, Jacob Player Sturge. The business had been started in 1760 by John Player of Stoke Gifford, who was joined by his nephew Jacob Player Sturge, father of Young and Jacob Player. William Sturge became a partner in 1842, and head of the firm at his father's death in 1857. The practice was named J. P. Sturge & Sons after Young's death in 1844. Sturge's brothers Walter and Robert, the latter a member of the Institution of Surveyors, became junior partners. During Sturge's association with the practice, until 1905, it was situated in Bristol at 1 Broad Street and 34 and 33 Corn Street respectively. It merged with King & Co. of London in 1992 to become King Sturge & Co. of London and Bristol, with other UK and European offices.

Sturge was involved in surveying and mapping land in connection with the Enclosure and Tithe Commutation Acts, with railways, and with Bristol residential developments. He was appointed surveyor to the Bristol Water Works Company in 1846 and was arbitrator or witness in many compensation cases concerning land purchase for railways in the west of England and south Wales; one particular case concerned the local board of health and the Great Western Railway Company in 1870. In 1847–8 he was responsible for purchasing land for the Bristol and Exeter, and the Wilts., Somerset, and Weymouth railways. He followed his uncle and father respectively as land steward to the corporation of Bristol in 1857, a post he held until 1905. He was appointed to survey the city of Bristol for assessment of the borough rate in 1860 and 1870, and he advised the Somerset county rate committee on the county rate in 1865 and undertook this for Glamorgan in 1875. Under the Extraordinary Tithe Act of 1888 Sturge was appointed assistant commissioner. He trained land agents and surveyors, and he and his brother Robert founded the Bristol branch of the Surveyors' Institution.

A founder member of the Institution of Surveyors (later the Surveyors' Institution, followed by the Royal Institution of Chartered Surveyors) Sturge was a member of the council in 1868, and served as president from 1878–80. He presented ten papers at the institution between 1868 and 1899. These were published subsequently in the *Transactions*, and included his presidential addresses (1878–9), 'The education of the surveyor' (1868), 'Tithes and tithe commutation' (1871), 'The Rating Act' (1874), and 'The burdens on real property and land' (1894). He continued to write on the subject of rating in *Professional Notes* (1904), when he was over eighty years old. He was also author of several personal memoirs, as well as *A Report on the Farming of Somersetshire*, an entry for a Royal Society of Agriculture competition in 1851.

Sturge died from heart failure at his home, Chilliswood, Tyndall's Park Road, Bristol, on 26 March 1905. His obituary in the *Transactions of the Surveyors' Institution* (1905) described his calm judgement and keen practical insight, as well as his scrupulous honesty, 'almost painfully keen to do justice to all parties'. He was serious but with a 'quiet restrained humour', and gentle, but with a 'flame of wrath ready to burn fiercely should occasion demand it'. His publications showed concern about the agricultural depression, the conditions of farm labourers, and the future of agriculture and of his own profession. His main interests were business, religion, and family; he was a member of the Religious Society of Friends throughout his life.   JENNY WEST

Sources *Transactions of the Surveyors' Institution*, 37 (1904–5), 585–92 · E. Sturge, *Reminiscences of my life: and some account of the children of William and Charlotte Sturge and of the Sturge family of Bristol* (privately printed, Bristol, 1928) · M. C. Sturge, *Some little Quakers in their nursery*, 2nd edn (1929) · A. Bradley, *J. P. Sturge & Sons: 225 anniversary* (privately printed, Bristol, [1985]) · 'Bi-centenary of J. P. Sturge & Sons', *Bristol Chamber of Commerce Monthly Journal*, 35 (1961), 53–77 · J. P. Sturge & Sons, *The ports of the Bristol channel* (1893), 195 · *The Times* (28 March 1905)
Archives Bristol RO | Royal Institution of Chartered Surveyors, council minutes of the Institution of Surveyors
Likenesses drawing; copy, King Sturge & Co., Bristol
Wealth at death £155,256 6s.: probate, 1 May 1905, *CGPLA Eng. & Wales*

Sturgeon, Henry (*c*.1781–1814), army officer, was admitted to the Royal Military Academy, Woolwich, as a cadet in May 1795, was commissioned as second lieutenant, Royal Artillery on 1 January 1796, and became lieutenant on 21 August 1797. He served in Pulteney's expedition to Ferrol in 1800, and in the expedition to Egypt, and was wounded in the battle of Alexandria on 13 March 1801. On 25 June 1803 he was transferred to the Royal Staff Corps with the rank of captain, and became major in it on 1 June 1809.

Sturgeon served throughout the war in the Peninsula, always showing himself 'a clever fellow', as Wellington described him. At Ciudad Rodrigo in 1812 his exertions and ability were conspicuous from the start of the siege. He reconnoitered the breaches before the assault, and guided a column which was told off, at his suggestion, to make a demonstration on the right of the main breach. The column subsequently joined the attack on that breach. Sturgeon was specially mentioned in Wellington's dispatch, both for his services during the siege and for his construction of a bridge over the Agueda, which was an indispensable preliminary to it. He was made brevet lieutenant-colonel on 6 February 1812. He was again specially mentioned in the Salamanca dispatch, and was sent three months afterwards to erect a bridge at Almaraz.

During April 1813 Sturgeon was placed in charge of the corps of guides, and the post office and communications of the army. In February 1814 he took a prominent part in the bridging of the Adour, and was one of the officers praised by General Hope in his report for the zeal they showed in carrying out that bold project. The historian William Napier, who speaks of it as a 'stupendous undertaking, which must always rank among the prodigies of war', attributed its conception to Sturgeon. A few weeks afterwards, on 19 March, Sturgeon was killed by a bullet as he was riding through a vineyard during the action near Vic Bigorre, France.   E. M. LLOYD, rev. DAVID GATES

Sources W. F. P. Napier, *History of the war in the Peninsula and in the south of France*, rev. edn, 6 vols. (1876) · marquess of Londonderry [C. S. H. Vane-Tempest-Stewart], *Narrative of the Peninsular War, from 1808 to 1813*, 3rd edn, 2 vols. (1829) · F. Duncan, ed., *History of the royal regiment of artillery*, 2 vols. (1872–3) · W. Porter, *History of the corps of royal engineers*, 2 vols. (1889) · D. Gates, *The Spanish ulcer: a history of the Peninsular War* (1986) · R. Muir, *Britain and the defeat of Napoleon, 1807–1815* (1996)

William Sturgeon (1783–1850), by unknown engraver

Sturgeon, William (1783–1850), electrician and scientific lecturer, was born on 22 May 1783 at Whittington, Lancashire, near Kirkby Lonsdale, the only son of John Sturgeon, shoemaker, and his wife, Betsy Adcock (d. 1793), the daughter of a small shopkeeper. All accounts of his father, who had migrated from Dumfries, describe him as idle and a poacher, who obliged William to assist him with his nightly raids. Furthermore, it would appear that his father treated him harshly during the day. His mother died when he was ten, and three years later he was apprenticed, at the standard age, to a shoemaker, whose name is unknown, at Old Hutton, near Kendal. Sturgeon's lot did not improve, for his master exacted a slavish drudgery from him during the week, and on Sundays made him help with his cock-fighting activities. At the age of sixteen, apparently, Sturgeon stood up to him and thereafter was treated better. To what extent the Victorian texts on which this account is based are coloured by contemporary attitudes is hard to say, but it is clear that during this period Sturgeon gained sufficient mechanical skill to clean clocks and watches, and also acquired some musical proficiency.

Military life Sturgeon's experience as an apprentice decided him against becoming a journeyman shoemaker, and in 1802 he enlisted in the Westmorland militia, in which he served for two years, before joining the 2nd battalion of the Royal Artillery as a private and gunner. The Royal Artillery had a major base in Woolwich, and shortly after he had joined the regiment he married a widow, Mary Hutton, who kept a shoe shop there. They had three children, all of whom died in infancy, while Mary died in the 1820s. Despite serving during the final decade of the war against France, it would appear that Sturgeon was never on active service and spent some of his time in Newfoundland, where he was posted shortly after his marriage. He spent the frequent periods of inactivity of army

life in self-improvement. In this he was helped by a sergeant who lent him many books, and by the officers who, in exchange for Sturgeon's bootmaking services, overlooked the occasions on which he used a rushlight to read behind windows which had been covered with blankets. In these circumstances he worked at mathematics; learned some Greek and Latin, as well as French, German, and Italian; and studied optics and other branches of natural philosophy, as well as improving his mechanical skills, such as in lithography. It was while serving in Newfoundland that Sturgeon witnessed a terrific thunderstorm which developed his first interest in electrical phenomena.

Sturgeon left the army in 1820 and returned to his native north-west and to his trade of shoemaking. However, at the insistence of his wife, they soon returned to Woolwich. The Royal Military Academy at Woolwich, which trained gentleman cadets for the Royal Artillery and the Royal Engineers, had one of the largest concentrations of scientific men in the London area at that time. These included Peter Barlow (1776–1862), Samuel Hunter Christie (1784–1865), and Olinthus Gilbert Gregory (1774–1841), who all taught mathematics there, as well as James Marsh (1794–1846), who from at least 1822 occupied the very junior post of teaching practical chemistry. All of them had a strong interest in the subject of electromagnetism which stemmed from the initial discovery by Danish savant Hans Christian Oersted (1777–1851) in 1820, and then from the work of many others in the early 1820s, particularly André-Marie Ampère (1775–1836) in Paris and Michael Faraday (1791–1867) at the Royal Institution in London. Barlow, following Faraday's 1821 discovery of electromagnetic rotations, had invented a wheel that turned continuously on its axis; Christie observed that the rotation of iron altered its magnetic properties, but was pre-empted in publishing this result by Dominique François Jean Arago (1786–1853); Marsh assisted both Barlow and Christie with their work.

At Woolwich, using a lathe he had purchased, Sturgeon started constructing scientific instruments, and was able to sell some of them to instrument makers in London. Such work brought him into contact with the men of science in the academy—with them he helped found the Woolwich Literary Society—and these connections may well explain why his interests turned towards electromagnetism. His first papers, published in the *Philosophical Magazine*, were on thermoelectricity and magnetism. But in 1825 he was awarded the large silver medal of the Society of Arts for his 'Improved Electro-Magnetic Apparatus'. This included a description of what was the first electromagnet, though, according to James Prescott Joule (1818–1889), Sturgeon had made this device a couple of years earlier. In it a soft iron bar (in the form of a horseshoe) became magnetic when a current of electricity was passed through a coil of wire wound round it. In his submission to the society Sturgeon included supporting letters from Christie, Gregory, and Barlow praising his work highly.

Experimentalist At the end of 1824, through Barlow's influence, Sturgeon was appointed lecturer in experimental philosophy at the East India Company's military seminary at Addiscombe, near Croydon, though he continued to live in Woolwich and seems to have held other teaching positions in the vicinity which brought him a good living. He also lectured at the Adelaide Gallery, at the 'Laboratory of Science' in the Lowther Arcade, and to the Western Literary and Scientific Institution, all in central London. He continued publishing his experimental work in the *Philosophical Magazine*, though there was a gap of four years in his publications between 1827 and 1831. In 1832, however, he made the first electric motor which could be used for turning machinery. The gap in publication might be due to his need to earn an income or to the death of his first wife. It is not known exactly when she died, but on 19 September 1829 he married Mary Bromley (c.1790–1867) of Shrewsbury. They had one daughter who also died in infancy, and they then adopted his niece.

At some point Sturgeon managed to antagonize some influential members of the London scientific community, though not his original patrons at Woolwich. The American natural philosopher Joseph Henry (1797–1878) briefly recorded in the diary he kept during his tour of Europe in 1837 a conversation he had with Edward Solly (1819–1886) at the Royal Institution. Solly said that Humphry Davy (1778–1829) had passed a harsh comment on one of Sturgeon's experiments. This, according to Solly, was the origin of Sturgeon's dissatisfaction with the Royal Institution which was extended to Davy's successor, Faraday. As Henry put it: 'He [Sturgeon] and Mr Faraday are not on good terms' (*Papers of Joseph Henry*, 4.152), and this perhaps explains why Faraday never gave Sturgeon credit for inventing the electromagnet—something which puzzled a number of Faraday's biographers. Henry had already met Sturgeon on a visit to Woolwich, and

indeed had sought him out as he had been using some of Sturgeon's results in America. He 'found that he is a man of great industry has a strong mind but the want of early discipline has rendered him not as clear in his conceptions as an other course of education would have rendered him' (ibid., 3.202). A few weeks later Henry attended a lecture by Sturgeon, who 'is a very good experimenter but an indifferent lecturer. He does not use good language and is very obscure in his theoretical notions' (ibid., 3.307).

On 16 June 1836 Sturgeon offered his first paper to the Royal Society, on magnetic electric machines. Although it was read, it was refused publication in the *Philosophical Transactions*. This seems to have been a key event in Sturgeon's life. He never published anything again in the *Philosophical Magazine*, and offered only two further papers to the Royal Society, in 1845 and 1846, which received the same treatment as the first, despite being communicated by Christie, by then one of the secretaries of the society. Instead Sturgeon founded his own journal and a society devoted solely to electrical science.

Scientific editor and lecturer In October 1836 Sturgeon began the *Annals of Electricity*, which had among its subtitles *Guardian of Experimental Science*, presumably a reflection of Sturgeon's view of the scientific élite. Thus in the first issue Sturgeon included an open letter to Faraday in which he attacked the latter's views about the identity of various forms of electricity: 'the errors you have fallen into in your Voltaic experiments are too palpable to escape notice, even of the humblest enquirer' (*Annals of Electricity*, 1.60). Faraday took no notice, though he did dismiss Sturgeon's views in a private letter to Solly. This paper set the tone for much of Sturgeon's work published in the ten volumes of the *Annals of Electricity* that he produced in the following seven years. He referred to the papers of William Snow Harris (1791–1867) on lightning conductors as 'impotent productions' (5.53), and the work of John Frederic Daniell (1790–1845) on the constant battery also came in for criticism; this must have made for an interesting time at Addiscombe, where from 1836 Daniell taught chemistry and geology. In all Sturgeon published in the *Annals of Electricity* a third of his sixty-nine papers listed in the Royal Society's catalogue of nineteenth-century scientific papers. However, most of the journal was given over to publishing original papers by others, translations of continental work, and the republication of earlier papers on the subject of electricity.

Sturgeon was one of the main instigators in founding the London Electrical Society. He suggested, during a lecture in the Lowther Arcade, the desirability of establishing such a society, and a meeting to do so was held in the spring of 1837. The original membership did not include any fellows of the Royal Society, and in general the élite of the London scientific community ignored it. Sturgeon was an active member, and was frequently elected to chair the meetings of the society, which were held on Saturday evenings in the Adelaide Gallery. During the late 1830s and early 1840s the London Electrical Society published both *Proceedings* and *Transactions*, to which Sturgeon contributed a few papers. Following Sturgeon's departure in

1840, the society went through a bad patch, tried to keep going in 1841, but folded in 1843 as a result of a large debt caused by printing costs. The membership of the society, which never exceeded eighty, and its structure undoubtedly justified Henry's remark to Asa Gray (1810–1888) that 'Mr Sturgeon is at the head of the second rate philosophers of London' (*Papers of Joseph Henry*, 4.152).

In 1840 Sturgeon was invited to become superintendent of the Royal Victoria Gallery of Practical Science in Manchester. He resigned his positions in London and returned to the north-west. The institution, modelled on the Adelaide Gallery in London, had been founded the year before. Sturgeon was in overall charge for the direction of the institution, its courses of lectures, and its displays of apparatus. In March he commenced his course of lectures on electricity, and in June the exhibition gallery opened. That year he arranged for Joule (whom he already knew through his contributions to the *Annals of Electricity*) to lecture there. With Joule and some others, Sturgeon formed a small social and intellectual circle in Manchester during the 1840s. Joule had a very high opinion of Sturgeon, and expressed a different view from Henry as to his abilities: 'As a lecturer he was distinguished by his power of impressing the truths of science clearly and accurately on the minds of his auditory, and especially by the uniform success of his experimental illustrations' (Joule, 77). Part of what impressed Joule about Sturgeon was his religious beliefs which, as a member of the Church of England, he expressed in his lectures, for example in terms of the 'Great Creator' possibly using electricity to drive the rest of the universe.

The economic depression in the early 1840s meant that local support for the Victoria Gallery dried up and it closed in 1842, but not before Sturgeon was able to have his lectures published. Given Sturgeon's experience his appointment to the gallery was an ideal position for him, but with its closure he was put in desperate financial straits. His initial reaction was to found the Manchester Institute of Natural and Experimental Science in January 1843, but this failed after his course of lectures on mechanical philosophy. One of the consequences of these failures was that he was forced to cease publishing the *Annals of Electricity*, some of the expenses of which he seems to have incurred personally, and the final issue appeared in May 1843. He sought to replace this with the *Annals of Philosophical Discovery*, but this ran only to six issues, ending in December 1843. He earned some money by lecturing at the Mechanics' Institution and the Royal Manchester Institution. He was elected in 1844 to membership of the Manchester Literary and Philosophical Society, in the *Memoirs* of which he published a substantial paper on the magnetic properties of various matters, and six on various meteorological phenomena.

This decline in productivity over what had gone before can doubtless be ascribed to Sturgeon's need to earn a living. Ultimately he became an itinerant lecturer going round villages in the Manchester area, taking his apparatus in a cart. By May 1845 Joule, in the course of a letter to Faraday seeking support for Sturgeon, described him as living in 'great poverty and [having] no means of supporting his family beyond the precarious proceeds of his lectures' (*Correspondence*, letter 1738). Joule and others mounted a successful campaign to persuade the government to support Sturgeon. By the time Joule knew him Sturgeon was a conservative in politics, but nevertheless in 1847 the whig government of Lord John Russell (1792–1878) made a one-off payment of £200 from the Royal Bounty Fund, and in July 1849 granted him an annual civil-list pension of £50. The limited financial security thus assured permitted Sturgeon to undertake his last major task, collecting most of his papers into a handsome quarto volume of *Scientific Researches*, which was published in Bury in 1850.

Sturgeon never fully recovered from a severe attack of bronchitis which he suffered in 1847, and which forced him to move to Prestwich, Lancashire, for better air. At the end of November 1850 he caught a cold. He died on 8 December in Barnfield Terrace, Prestwich, and was buried in the churchyard there; a plaque commemorating him was later placed in the church at Kirkby Lonsdale. He was survived by his second wife, to whom the pension was transferred.   WILLIAM GEE, *rev.* FRANK A. J. L. JAMES

Sources W. W. H. Gee, *The Electrician* (13 Sept 1895), 632–5 · J. P. Joule, 'A short account of the life and writings of the late Mr. William Sturgeon', *Memoirs of the Literary and Philosophical Society of Manchester*, 2nd ser., 14 (1857), 53–83 · S. P. T. Thompson, *William Sturgeon, the electrician: a biographical note* (1891) · *The papers of Joseph Henry*, ed. N. Reingold and others, [8 vols.] (Washington, DC, 1972–), vols. 3–4 · I. R. Morus, *Frankenstein's children: electricity, exhibition and experiment in early-nineteenth-century London* (1998) · R. H. Kargon, *Science in Victorian Manchester* (1977) · *The correspondence of Michael Faraday*, ed. F. A. J. L. James, [4 vols.] (1991–) · d. cert.
Archives Manchester Literary and Philosophical Society, letters
Likenesses engraving, NPG [*see illus.*] · portrait, repro. in Gee, *The Electrician*

Sturges, Octavius (1833–1894), physician, eighth son of John Sturges, a merchant, and his wife, Elizabeth, of 35 Connaught Square, London, was born in London on 19 August 1833. After attending King's College School he obtained a commission in the East India Company's service, studied at Addiscombe, went to India in 1852, and in 1853 became a lieutenant in the Bombay artillery. He also saw service in Aden. Sturges described his experiences at Addiscombe and in India in a novel written in collaboration with a niece, Mary Sturges, entitled *In the Company's Service*, and published in 1883. Poor health forced Sturges to resign and he left India in 1857, and began to study medicine, for which he had always had a predilection, at St George's Hospital, London. In October 1858 he entered at Emmanuel College, Cambridge, and he graduated BA in 1862, MB in 1863, and MD in 1867. He was captain of the first university company of volunteers at Cambridge. He became a member of the Royal College of Physicians in 1863, and was elected a fellow in 1870.

Sturges was medical registrar at St George's Hospital from 1863 to 1865, and became assistant physician at the Westminster Hospital in 1868 and physician in 1875. He lectured there in a practical, terse, and vigorous fashion, successively on forensic medicine, materia medica, and medicine. Sturges was sceptical about the use of drugs and deplored the marketing and advertising of cures. He was elected assistant physician to the Hospital for Sick Children, Great Ormond Street, in 1873, and physician in 1884. At the time of his death he was senior physician both there and at the Westminster Hospital. He delivered the Lumleian lectures at the Royal College of Physicians on diseases of the heart in childhood, and was senior censor in the same year. Sturges, who practised from Wimpole Street, was considered by colleagues to be honest, genial, and sound in judgement. 'He never offended by self-assertion; indeed had he been more assertive he would probably have had a larger practice—and perhaps fewer friends' (The Lancet, 1127). Sturges published An Introduction to the Study of Clinical Medicine (1873), The Natural History and Relations of Pneumonia (1876), and Chorea and Whooping Cough (1877).

On the evening of 26 October 1894 Sturges was crossing Cavendish Square in London when he was knocked down by a hansom cab, 'the approach at which with India-rubber tyred wheels he had not heard being somewhat deaf' (BMJ, 1084). He died on 3 November 1894 and was buried in Kensal Green cemetery five days later, following a funeral service at St Andrew's, Wells Street, at which his brothers, Andrew Smith Sturges (1840–1909) and Edward Sturges (1832–1907), assisted the vicar. He was unmarried. Staff at Westminster Hospital later decided to remember Sturges by establishing provision for a memorial prize, an exhibition, or a scholarship.

NORMAN MOORE, rev. MICHAEL BEVAN

Sources The Lancet (10 Nov 1894), 1127–8 · BMJ (10 Nov 1894), 1084–5 · Venn, Alum. Cant. · personal knowledge (1898) · Munk, Roll · CGPLA Eng. & Wales (1894)

Wealth at death £18,024 19s. 3d.: probate, 7 Dec 1894, CGPLA Eng. & Wales

Sturgion, John (d. 1665), General Baptist preacher and pamphleteer, was a member of the General Baptist church of Edmund Chillenden that in June 1653 received permission to meet in the Stone Chapel of St Paul's Cathedral. Gilbert Mabbott's newsletter of 1 September 1655 described Sturgion as pastor of a church, but he was probably only a lay preacher in Chillenden's congregation. With Chillenden, Henry Danvers, and a dozen others, he issued Questions about Laying on of Hands in 1655, arguing against the necessity of this practice. The work provoked a substantive response from another General Baptist, John Griffith, entitled Gods Oracle & Christs Doctrine (1655). A member of Cromwell's life guard, Sturgion was arrested in late August 1655 as the suspected author and distributor of A Short Discovery of his Highness the Lord Protector's Intentions (1655), which charged Cromwell with planning to dismiss Baptist officers, defended the nominated assembly for espousing the Good Old Cause, and called on the army to defend liberty and property. The radical printer Richard Moone confessed that Sturgion had paid him 40s. to print 1000 copies, some 800 of which he delivered to Sturgion. Copies were disseminated in London and as far away as Wales. Interrogated on the 27th, Sturgion denied having

written the tract, commissioned Moone to print it, or discussed its contents with the life guards. Although he was never tried, he was cashiered and incarcerated for a number of months.

In the spring of 1656 Sturgion held public meetings every evening in Reading, where, according to Major-General William Goffe, many people came to hear him and others preach. Goffe admitted that Sturgion did not discuss public affairs. Later that year Sturgion joined nine other Baptists and Levellers, including John Wildman and William Howard, in offering to support Charles's restoration if he agreed to recall the Long Parliament, ratify the treaty of Newport, abolish tithes, bestow liberty of conscience, and support an amnesty act. Condemning Cromwell and his confederates as wicked and ambitious, they described the country as lost in a labyrinth, all legitimate authority having been trampled by the tyrannical Cromwell. According to Secretary Thurloe, Sturgion was engaged in Edward Sexby's plot to have Miles Sindercombe assassinate Cromwell, and when this scheme failed Sturgion fled to the Netherlands. Shortly after returning to England, Sturgion was arrested on 25 May 1657 for having imported approximately 380 copies of Killing No Murder, a call for Cromwell's assassination. Under examination he refused to confess where he had obtained the books. He apparently remained in prison without trial, and was transferred to the Tower in late January 1659 on suspicion of high treason; the Fifth Monarchists Thomas Venner and John Portman were among his fellow prisoners. Presumably because the government had insufficient evidence for a conviction, it released him the following month.

Sturgion's professions of loyalty to Charles were rewarded in July 1660 with an appointment as an exchequer messenger. Remaining loyal to his Baptist convictions, he responded to a proclamation against conventicles in January 1661 by writing A Plea for Toleration, printed by Simon Dover for Francis Smith in late March. Reminding Charles of his promise of liberty to tender consciences in the declaration of Breda, Sturgion stressed the futility of attempting to coerce people's beliefs, quoting liberally from Jeremy Taylor's The Liberty of Prophesying, and pledging to suffer patiently if persecuted. He may have been the John Sturgeon, grocer of St Margaret's, Westminster, arrested in the summer of 1662 for attending a conventicle. In October 1662 he resigned his exchequer office because of ill health. He died three years later. In his will, dated 30 August 1665 (and proved on 19 October), he described himself as a grocer of St Giles-in-the-Fields: he bequeathed most of his estate to his wife, Elizabeth, and to his children, John, Elizabeth, Benjamin, and Joseph. Throughout his career, his defining conviction was freedom of conscience.

RICHARD L. GREAVES

Sources Thurloe, State papers, 3.150–51; 738–40; 4.752; 6.311, 316–20; 7.598–9 · Clarendon, Hist. rebellion, 6.105–19 · CSP dom., 1658–59, 582; 1660–61, 144; 1661–2, 513 · E. B. Underhill, ed., Tracts on liberty of conscience and persecution, 1614–1661 (1848), 311–41 · The Clarke papers,

ed. C. H. Firth, 3, CS, new ser., 61 (1899), 51 • W. A. Shaw, ed., *Calendar of treasury books*, 1, PRO (1904), 443 • B. S. Capp, *The Fifth Monarchy Men: a study in seventeenth-century English millenarianism* (1972) • J. C. Jeaffreson, ed., *Middlesex county records*, 4 vols. (1886–92), vol. 3, pp. 324–5 • J. Griffith, *Gods oracle & Christs doctrine* (1655) • J. More, *Lost ordinance* (1654) • GL, MS 9171/32, fol. 294r–v
Archives Bodl. Oxf., Rawlinson MSS, A29, fol. 268

Sturgis, Julian Russell (1848–1904), novelist, was born at Boston, Massachusetts, USA, on 21 October 1848, the fourth son of Russell Sturgis (1805–1883) of Boston, a merchant and lawyer, and his second wife, Juliet Overing Boit (*d. c.*1883). His younger brother, Howard Overing Sturgis (1855–1920), was also a writer. When Julian was seven months old he was brought to England, a country which he adopted as his own though much of his childhood was also spent in Italy. He was educated in Dame Evan's house at Eton College from 1862 to 1867 and matriculated at Balliol College, Oxford, on 27 January 1868, graduating BA in 1872 and taking a second class in the final classical school. His first sketch, 'The Philosopher's Baby', appeared in *Blackwood's Edinburgh Magazine* in 1874, and he proceeded MA in 1875. His intellectual interest at university lay in classics, but he preferred dabbling in drama and was a notable athlete, being captain of the school football eleven and rowing in his college boat. He became a barrister of the Inner Temple in 1876, and a naturalized British subject in January 1877.

Over the next two years Sturgis travelled extensively throughout the world and embarked on his career as a novelist, specializing in light comedies, mostly set at Eton or Oxford. His first, the chatty *John-a-Dreams* (1878), was followed in 1879 by *An Accomplished Gentleman*, and in 1880 by *Little Comedies*, dialogues in dramatic form containing some of his most dazzling and characteristic writing. *Comedies New and Old* and *Dick's Wandering* appeared in 1882.

On 8 November 1883 Sturgis married, at St Patrick's Cathedral in Armagh, Ireland, Mary Maud, daughter of Colonel Marcus de la Poer Beresford, and granddaughter of Captain Robert Blakeney, whose memoirs Sturgis edited. Their marriage, which was a very happy one, produced three sons, including Mark Beresford Russell Grant-*Sturgis. Possessed of an ample fortune which he had inherited from his father who died in 1883, having just retired as senior partner of Barings, Sturgis divided his time between London and the country, first at Elvington, near Dover, and then at Compton, near Guildford, where he built a house, Wancote. He continued to write, producing novels such as *My Friends and I* (1884), *John Maidment* (1885), *Thraldom* (1887), *The Comedy of a Country House* (1889), and *The Folly of Pen Harrington* (1897). He also attempted verse in *Count Julian: a Spanish Tragedy* (1893) and *A Book of Song* (1894), and wrote the librettos for Goring Thomas's *Nadeshda* (1885), Sir Arthur Sullivan's *Ivanhoe* (1891), and Sir Charles Villiers Stanford's *Much Ado about Nothing* (1901), which was published in the same year as his best novel, *Stephen Calinari*.

Sturgis died on 13 April 1904 at 16 Hans Road, Knightsbridge, his London residence, after a long illness; his wife survived him. He was cremated at Woking and was buried in the cemetery at Compton. He was a man of singular charm of character, the reticence which distinguishes his writings being laid aside in social circles. His novels show a peculiar and sympathetic insight into the minds of young men, while his style, at times allusive and elliptical, is influenced by Walter Pater and George Meredith, the latter of whom was greatly admired by Sturgis and was a personal friend.

ELIZABETH LEE, *rev.* KATHARINE CHUBBUCK

Sources J. Sutherland, 'Sturgis, Julian Russell', *The Longman companion to Victorian fiction* (1988) • J. R. Sturgis, *From the books and papers of Russell Sturgis* (1893) • P. Lubbock and A. C. Benson, 'Julian Russell Sturgis', *Monthly Review*, 46 (July 1904) • R. L. Wolff, *Nineteenth-century fiction: a bibliographical catalogue based on the collection formed by Robert Lee Wolff*, 4 (1985), 177–9 • J. R. Sturgis, ed., *A boy in the Peninsular War* (1899) • *Foster, Alum. Oxon.* • *The Times* (17 April 1904) • *The Times* (18 April 1904) • *CGPLA Eng. & Wales* (1904)
Archives NL Scot., corresp. with Blackwoods and verses
Wealth at death £79,435 16s.: probate, 8 June 1904, *CGPLA Eng. & Wales*

Sturgis, Sir Mark Beresford Russell Grant- (1884–1949), civil servant in Ireland, was born at 17 Carlton House Terrace, London, on 10 July 1884, the son of Julian Russell *Sturgis (1848–1904), barrister and novelist, and his wife, Mary Maud, daughter of Colonel Marcus de la Poer Beresford. Educated at Eton College, he came from a landed and literary background. He was assistant private secretary to Herbert Asquith when chancellor of the exchequer (1906–8), and private secretary to him as prime minister (1908–10). He served as a special commissioner of income tax in 1910. On 9 July 1914 he married Lady Rachel Montagu Stuart-Wortley (1894–1968), daughter of the second Earl Wharncliffe of Wortley, Yorkshire. They had two sons (one of whom was killed on active service in 1944) and one daughter.

Sturgis was chairman of the treasury selection board (1919–20). Early in 1920—during the Anglo-Irish War (1919–21)—he was appointed to the British administration in Dublin Castle as part of a new team installed by Lloyd George's government, with Sir Hamar Greenwood as chief secretary. He was listed as private secretary to the under-secretary (Sir John Anderson), though he was originally selected as joint assistant under-secretary with his colleague Alfred 'Andy' Cope. As Anderson's principal assistant he was his point of liaison with the viceroy's aide, Richard Wyndham-Quin (later Viscount Dunraven). More important he became the chronicler of events from the vantage point of the castle through his five volumes of diaries, kept from July 1920 to January 1922. A selection from these was published as *The Last Days of Dublin Castle* (1999), edited by Michael Hopkinson. This 'vivid and breezy' account is informed throughout by 'an appealingly cynical view of humanity in general and those he describes as "bigwigs" in particular' (Hopkinson, introduction, Sturgis, *Last Days*, 9). He was, according to one historian, 'an amiable man and dashing huntsman, who brought a rare quality of gaiety to the dismal surroundings of the Castle' (Townshend, 80).

Although a supporter of the union Sturgis was against force being used to maintain it, and believed that the prime minister should make a generous offer of self-government. 'The Irish aren't fit to govern themselves', he once declared, adding the crucial rider 'but I'll be damned if the English aren't either—or even the Welsh' (Sturgis, diary, 20 Aug 1920; Sturgis, *Last Days*, 17). He was critical of reprisals by crown forces and found fault with the cabinet for turning a blind eye. He saw correctly that these merely diminished support for government policy, and feared that agents of the crown would prove impossible to control, deploring the prevalence of 'so much talk as if we had nothing to do but beat an enemy' (Sturgis, *Last Days*, 100). Yet he was in no way sympathetic to Sinn Féin or to Irish nationalism in general, though he did differentiate between its shades: concerning the Irish self-government bill of 1920, he noted the hostility of 'the whole of Irish public opinion, reasonable or unreasonable' (ibid., 2). His own preferred solution was twofold: an offer of dominion status and the placement of British police and army under the same command. He advised Lloyd George that martial law would succeed in Ireland only if a 'take it or leave it' settlement was offered first, to put the onus of war onto Sinn Féin if it was refused.

When the truce was arranged on 11 July 1921, for which he gave the primary credit to his colleague Cope, Sturgis observed that the Irish had weakened their bargaining position by agreeing to meet on British turf in London. With respect to the partition of Ireland he recorded that Sir James Craig, the leader of the northern unionists, had told him that he was going to sit on Ulster 'like a rock' and let the prime minister and Sinn Féin arrive at a settlement for the south. For Sturgis, as for many of his colleagues in the administration, northern unionism was a closed book, and he contrived never to visit Belfast. He played no part in the negotiations preceding the Anglo-Irish treaty, the successful conclusion of which he ascribed to the leadership skills of Lloyd George. This was 'another milestone', he wrote, 'but if Ireland—or England—expects that the golden age is dawning I hope they won't be too roughly disillusioned. It is a huge gamble and we are groping in the dark' (Sturgis, *Last Days*, 227). His diary ends shortly afterwards, on 20 January 1922, with a reference to the discovery of a cupboard full of valuable documents on British–Irish relations 'and few later than 1870' (Sturgis, *Last Days*, 228); many of these have since been damaged or lost.

From March 1922 Sturgis was assistant under-secretary of state for Irish services, effectively succeeding both his former superiors Sir Hamar Greenwood and Sir John Anderson, under the aegis of the Colonial Office in London. He had previously contemplated a return to the capital with some distaste: 'here one is up the neck in intrigue plot and counterplot with a small spice of danger, all mixed up with the life of something like the big country house in the old days' (6 November 1920: Sturgis, *Last Days*, 68). Refusing to 'live like moles' in the castle, he and his wife had continued to enjoy visits to the theatre, horse-racing, and polo during their time in Dublin, (Sturgis, *Last Days*, 20). He was awarded a KCB in 1923 and left his post

the following year, finishing his career at the treasury, latterly as presiding special commissioner of income tax. He took the additional surname of Grant in 1935 on inheriting the Hillersdon estate near Cullompton, Devon, and died on 29 April 1949 at 99 Cromwell Road, South Kensington, London.

Sturgis's diary remains an invaluable inside source on the Dublin Castle administration, filling many gaps in official records by revealing informal relationships and the influences of ministers and civil servants upon one another. They give some support to the notion that the vacillation of Greenwood's administration left many important decisions to civil servants. His commentary on the most important participants in this climactic episode is witty and wry, and reveals much of the character of Sturgis, a man whose 'insouciant air', according to Warren Fisher, hid 'a shrewd judgement' (Sturgis, *Last Days*, 7).

MARTIN F. SEEDORF

Sources M. Sturgis, *The last days of Dublin Castle*, ed. M. Hopkinson (Dublin, 1999) · M. Hopkinson, introduction, in M. Sturgis, *The last days of Dublin Castle*, ed. M. Hopkinson (1999) · M. Sturgis, diaries, 1920–22, PRO · *WWW, 1941–50* · J. McColgan, *British policy and the Irish administration, 1920–22* (1983) · J. W. Wheeler Bennett, *John Anderson, Viscount Waverley* (1967) · M. F. Seedorf, 'The Lloyd George government and the Anglo-Irish War, 1919–21', PhD diss., University of Washington, Seattle, 1974 · M. F. Seedorf, 'Defending reprisals: Sir Hamar Greenwood and the "troubles", 1920–21', *Eire-Ireland*, 25 (winter 1990), 77–92 · T. Jones, *Whitehall diary*, 3: *Ireland, 1918–25* (1971) · S. Lawlor, *Britain and Ireland, 1914–1923* (1983) · F. Pakenham, *Peace by ordeal* (1935) · K. O. Morgan, *Consensus and disunity: the Lloyd George coalition government, 1918–1922* (1979) · Burke, *Peerage* (1957) · C. Townshend, *The British campaign in Ireland, 1919–1925* (1975) · b. cert. · d. cert.

Archives PRO, diaries, PRO 30/59 | HLRO, Lloyd George papers · HLRO, Bonar Law papers · PRO, Colonial Office records, Sir John Anderson papers · PRO, Cabinet papers

Likenesses photograph, 1920, repro. in Sturgis, *Last days*, jacket · photograph, NL Ire.; repro. in Sturgis, *Last days*, facing p. 151

Wealth at death £28,540 7s. 8d.—save and except settled land: probate, 25 Aug 1949, *CGPLA Eng. & Wales* · £110,623 13s. 7d.—limited to settled land: further grant, 4 April 1951, *CGPLA Eng. & Wales*

Sturmey, (John James) Henry (1857–1930), cycle and automobile writer and promoter, was born at Norton-sub-Hamdon, Somerset, on 28 February 1857, the son of Henry Gundry Sturmey, a master mariner and merchant navy captain, and his wife, Mary Ann Trask. He was educated at Melcombe Regis School and Weymouth College. His first career as a schoolmaster, in mathematics and science, soon mingled with, and ultimately gave way to, his passion for cycling. This enthusiasm initially took the form of touring, attempts to sell bicycles made to his own specification, and the compilation and publication of a handbook for bicyclists. By 1879 he was a 'chief consul' of the infant Bicycle Touring Club, which became the Cyclists Touring Club in 1883. After Sturmey had published the first edition of the '*Indispensable' Bicyclist's Handbook* (1877), he established contact with William Iliffe, of a Coventry family printing firm, a meeting which was to be a significant event for both.

Sturmey suggested a new weekly periodical, the '*Cyclist,*

to replace *Bicycle World*, which Iliffes already printed. Sturmey edited the new periodical and Iliffes published the next edition of Sturmey's *Handbook*. Another of Sturmey's technical interests gave rise to a new periodical in 1888, *Photography* (later *Amateur Photographer*). Seven years later his intense interest in another technical innovation, the horseless carriage, resulted in the launch of another Iliffe periodical which Sturmey edited, *Autocar*. (While 'autocar' did not gain currency, except as the title of a successful and long-lived periodical, the term 'cyclist' did. It seems that it is to Sturmey's choice of this title that the word which entered common parlance is owed.) In the view of one of the contributors to a booklet commemorating Sturmey's life and work, *Autocar* in 1930 still bore the imprint of his personality and it was 'hardly an exaggeration to say as much of technical journals generally' (*H. S. Some Tributes*, 3). Sturmey also began a quarterly periodical, *Flying*, but this proved to be before its time.

The extension of Sturmey's interests from the cycle to the automobile paralleled the evolution of part of the motor industry from cycle manufacture. Sturmey invested heavily in the Great Horseless Carriage Company, one of the numerous companies promoted by the inventor turned financier, H. J. Lawson (1852–1925), whom Sturmey succeeded as chairman of the Daimler Motor Company. In October 1897 Sturmey successfully drove from John o' Groats to Land's End in a Daimler with Mulliner body, which he had designed. Three years later, in November 1900, Sturmey became an early victim of a motor accident, when he was seriously injured in a Dawson car in which he was a passenger. After a slow recovery, he broke with Iliffe in 1901, as a result of the latter's belief that Sturmey's editorial position was incompatible with his active involvement in the motor industry.

Sturmey then began the import of the American Duryea car, having visited the principal American motor manufacturers in 1899. In 1902 Sturmey set up the British Duryea Company, which built under licence in Coventry for a few years, utilizing a Rugby-made engine. The Duryea was a light runabout in the American buggy style. It was popular for a time, but the Duryea brothers split up and an enduring marque did not emerge from their pioneering efforts. St John Nixon described the Duryea, with its tiller steering, as very unconventional, and was also somewhat dismissive of Sturmey, describing his reputation as a 'high authority' on motor vehicles as 'largely unjustified' (St John Nixon, 127). Sturmey Motors Ltd made the Napier-Parsons light van for one year, 1907, before inaugurating the Lotis marque of cars and commercial vehicles. The range included taxicabs and lasted from 1908 to 1911. The collapse of Lotis has been attributed to the failure of the Brazilian importer for whom a car for the Brazilian market had been produced. It appears that Sturmey failed to benefit from his own insights, for in 1902 he had identified lack of capital resources as one of the reasons why British manufacturers had failed to make headway.

His break with Iliffe did not mean the end of Sturmey's involvement in motoring journalism, for he became a major contributor to *Autocar's* rival, *Motor*, which was launched in 1903. His contribution to cycling continued indirectly through the Sturmey-Archer three-speed hub gear. This device had a complex background. Although manufactured by Frank Bowden's Three-Speed Gear Syndicate from 1903, numerous initiatives were involved. It owed something to Sturmey, but in practical terms probably more to the mechanic William Reilly, whose designs were patented in the name of a colleague, James Archer, to avoid a restrictive contract Reilly had entered into with the Hub Two-Speed Gear Company Ltd. The gear was used in an experimental light car that Sturmey built in 1900 and was subsequently used for motor cycles for a few years, but found its appropriate application in the cycle. Sturmey appears to have had no significant involvement with the syndicate after 1904, when he sold it his foreign patent rights.

By the time Lotis collapsed, Sturmey was in middle age. His American contacts were further made use of in the establishment of Bramco Ltd (whose name was derived from 'British American components'), a business importing car components from the USA. Sturmey remained in his adopted city of Coventry, a tall and by all accounts somewhat forbidding figure, with an air of authority unrelieved by humour, at least in the company of strangers. He was said to have taken little part in the civic and social life of the city, but he 'had a penchant for expressing his very decided views upon a wide range of subjects' in letters to the press (*Midland Daily Telegraph*, 9 Jan 1930). In the 1920s Sturmey returned to the topic of cycle gears, advocating in the cycling press the hub as opposed to the bracket gear. With John Peart, a Coventry engineer, he took out a patent (118, 178 of 1922) for the first five-speed hub gear, but failed to interest a manufacturer.

Sturmey never married, and died at his Coventry home, Quarry Close, St Nicholas Street, on 8 January 1930. His funeral at St Nicholas Church, Radford, Coventry, was attended by the Iliffes and staff members of Bramco Ltd, but the local press remarked that otherwise the motor and cycle industries were scarcely represented.

RICHARD A. STOREY

Sources *H. S. Some tributes: in memoriam Henry Sturmey, 1857–1930* (1930?) · *The Times* (10 Jan 1930) · T. Hadland, *The Sturmey-Archer story* (1987) · S. Taylor, 'Inventing the wheel', *Autocar* (2 Nov 1994), 30–31 · K. Richardson and C. N. O'Gallagher, *The British motor industry, 1896–1939* (1977) · K. Richardson, *Twentieth-century Coventry* (1972) · St J. C. Nixon, *The antique automobile* (1956) · G. N. Georgano, ed., *The complete encyclopedia of motorcars*, 2nd edn (1973) · G. N. Georgano, ed., *The complete encyclopedia of commercial vehicles* (1979) · b. cert. · d. cert. · CGPLA Eng. & Wales (1930)

Wealth at death £650: probate, 10 April 1930, CGPLA Eng. & Wales

Sturmy, Robert (d. 1458), merchant, was probably a native of Bristol, but nothing is known of his parentage, though a brother, John is recorded. His wife, Ellen, to whom he was married before 1438, and who traded as feme sole, survived him and was still alive in 1466. They had no children. Sturmy served as bailiff in Bristol in 1442–3, as sheriff in 1451–2, and as mayor in 1453–4. His first entry into the records, however, concerns trade. Apparently acting as a factor for the Londoners John Nanskilly, draper, and Stephen Titmersh, mercer, he imported dyestuffs and oil into London in 1433. As an independent merchant, Sturmy initially concentrated his activities—not atypically for a Bristol merchant—on Ireland and Gascony. But later his horizons expanded: imports of dyestuffs, fruit, and paper to London and Southampton between 1447 and 1457 indicate contacts with Italy and Spain, and this is confirmed by his exporting wool to Pisa in 1456. As an extension of his commercial activities in the Mediterranean, Sturmy transported pilgrims to Jerusalem (1445) and Santiago de Compostela (1451). All these activities were dwarfed, however, by the expedition to the Mediterranean that Sturmy mounted in 1457–8. On 8 February 1457 he obtained a licence to export thither tin, lead, wool, and cloth, worth some £37,000, via Bristol and Weymouth, and his will, dated 27 June 1457, bore witness to his high hopes: it contained legacies of at least £173 12s. but these were to more than double (to £372 8s. 8d.) if his three ships returned safely to port.

Commercial enterprise on this scale was far beyond the powers of any one merchant, and Sturmy managed to persuade not only a number of London and Bristol merchants, but also John, Lord Stourton (d. 1462), and Richard, duke of York (d. 1460), to invest in his expedition. At first all went well: the ships called at Pisa in September 1457 and Naples in the autumn, but once they embarked on their return voyage, via Rhodes and Candia (Crete), they were attacked off Malta by the Genoese freebooter Giuliano Gattilusio on 10 June 1458. Sturmy was killed, but his partner, the Bristol merchant John Heyton, managed to escape, collect depositions from local authorities, and make his way back to England, where on 30 October 1458 he charged the Genoese merchants in England with collusion in the attack. The ensuing council trial confirmed the dimensions of the expedition, and also demonstrated Sturmy's real purpose. Of the total of £18,166 13s. 4d. in damages claimed, sweet eastern Mediterranean wines, Turkish carpets, oriental fine cloth—velvet, damask, satin—and spices ranked prominently, but Sturmy's true objective is revealed by the claim for the loss of 152 tons of alum worth £3040. Europe's supplies of alum, a mordant required to fix dyes in fine cloth, had been cut off for the time being by the Turkish conquest of Asia Minor in 1453 and prices had soared. The monopoly of the alum trade previously enjoyed by the Genoese *maona* of Chios (a Genoa-based company which had gained control of the administration of the island) was inevitably endangered, and Bristol and London merchants, heavily committed to exporting west-country cloth made of fine Cotswold wool, suffered. Sturmy seized the opportunity to deal directly with the Turks, buy up alum, and break the Genoese monopoly. Their commercial position gravely imperilled, the Genoese fitted out Gattilusio's corsairs in March and April 1458 and dispatched him to scuttle Sturmy's commercial ambitions. As an Aegean freebooter and a partner in the *maona*, Gattilusio was the ideal agent for such an enterprise, and indeed he did manage to capture Sturmy's ships

and cargoes. The long-term consequences were, however, grave. Genoese merchants in England were arrested and their goods sequestered, and on 25 July 1459 the council condemned them to pay damages to the value of £6000 to Sturmy's English investors. Sturmy himself had perished in Gattilusio's attack, and his will was proved on 12 December 1458. STUART JENKS

Sources S. Jenks, 'Robert Sturmys Handelsexpedition in den Mittelmeerraum (1457/8) mit einer Edition des Kronratsprozessprotokolls und verwandter Aktenstücke', *Vera lex historiae: Studien zu mittelalterlichen Quellen*, ed. S. Jenks and others (1993), 305–72 · E. M. Carus-Wilson, ed., *The overseas trade of Bristol in the later middle ages*, Bristol RS, 7 (1937) · J. Heers, 'Les Génois en Angleterre: la crise de 1458–1466', *Studi in onore di Armando Sapori*, 2 (1957), 807–32 · E. M. Carus-Wilson, 'The overseas trade of Bristol in the fifteenth century', *Medieval merchant venturers: collected papers*, 2nd edn (1967), 1–97 · E. M. Carus-Wilson, 'The merchant adventurers of Bristol in the fifteenth century', *TRHS*, 4th ser., 11 (1928), 61–82 · F. W. P. Hicks, 'Robert Sturmy, of Bristol', *Transactions of the Bristol and Gloucestershire Archaeological Society*, 60 (1938), 169–79 · PRO, C1/9/81; C244/102/206

Sturmy, Samuel (1633–1669), writer on seamanship, was born on 5 November 1633 in Gloucester, the son of a glover; the names of his parents are unknown, although the name of Sturmy was of some antiquity in the region. According to his own account, Sturmy was apprenticed to a Bristol sailmaker and then commanded ships sailing out of Bristol, mainly to Virginia and the West Indies. He later found employment in the customs service, acquired a house at Pill, on the Avon below Bristol, and achieved some status as a burgess of the city and possibly a member of the Society of Merchant Venturers, several of whom he counted among his friends alongside two well-known mathematical teachers, William Leybourn and Henry Phillippes. In 1668 the Royal Society published his observations on magnetic variation and, in answer to the society's earlier questionnaire, his detailed account of the tides at Hungrode, near Bristol, including the phenomenon of the Severn bore, data which Isaac Newton made use of in his *Principia*.

The fruits of Sturmy's experience formed the substance of his *Mariner's Magazine, or, Sturmy's Mathematical and Practical Arts* (1669). The aim of this veritable encyclopaedia was to provide his three brothers, his sons, and other young seamen with all they needed to know, even if their mathematical knowledge was restricted to arithmetic. In fact it ranged far beyond the necessities of compass, tides, variation, and working the ship, containing, as displayed on its title-page:

> The description and use of the scale of scales … the art of navigation … a discourse on the practick part of navigation … a new way of surveying of land … the art of gauging all sorts of vessels … the art of gunnery … astronomy … the art of dialling … whereunto is annexed, an abridgement of the penalties and forfeitures … relating to the customs and navigation.

To this Sturmy added a compendium of fortification, contributed by the Bristol teacher of mathematics Philip Staynred, and a set of Briggs's log tables, amplified by

Sturmy himself. The principal dedicatee was Charles II, other sections being dedicated to his patron Sir John Shaw, bt, farmer of customs, and, among others, the Society of Merchant Venturers, who on 11 November 1667 voted Sturmy £10 as a gratuity; another £10 was voted on 15 July 1669. Sadly Sturmy did not live to see the success of his book, which went into a revised fourth edition in 1700.

The *Magazine* was written in lively fashion, in the sections on seamanship the usual commands and responses being set out as dialogue between captain and crew (parts of this were lifted verbatim by Jonathan Swift for *Gulliver's Travels*). The mathematical chapters were illustrated with small diagrams, and fine engravings were provided from which the seaman could cut out and mount his own instruments; there was also a three-layer volvelle to enable him to calculate tides. Sturmy was one of several writers on navigation who advertised Walter Hayes of London as a competent scientific instrument maker.

On 2 July 1669 Sturmy went to explore an old lead mine working known as Pen-Park-Hole, in company with a former miner. They descended two shafts by means of ropes, nearly 200 feet in all, emerging in a vast lofty cavern, through which flowed a broad deep river. According to the miner, this river rose and fell with the tide, which Sturmy did not believe, as the water was fresh; they spent several hours exploring below ground without seeing any change in water level. Four days later Sturmy was seized with a violent headache, which developed into a fever, from which he died soon afterwards at his home in St George's, Bristol. A memorial plaque was erected in the church of St George, Easton in Gordano, but he does not appear to have been buried there.   ANITA MCCONNELL

Sources C. E. Kenney, *The quadrant and the quill* (1947) · R. C. Anderson, 'Some cases of cribbing', *Mariner's Mirror*, 8 (1922), 344–5 · C. J. Batten, 'Literary responses to the eighteenth-century voyages', *Background to discovery*, ed. D. Howse (1990), 153 · R. Southwell, 'A description of Pen-Park-Hole in Glocestershire', *PTRS*, 13 (1683), 2–6 · P. McGrath, ed., *Records relating to the Society of Merchant Venturers of the city of Bristol in the seventeenth century*, Bristol RS, 17 (1951) · E. G. R. Taylor, *The mathematical practitioners of Tudor and Stuart England* (1954), 242

Likenesses engraving, 1669, repro. in S. Sturmy, *Mariner's magazine* (1669), frontispiece

Sturt, Charles (1795–1869), soldier and explorer in Australia, was born on 28 April 1795 at Chunar-Ghur, Bengal, India, the eldest of the eight surviving sons and third of the thirteen children of Thomas Lenox Napier Sturt (1767–1837), an East India Company judge from a genteel but not well-to-do Dorset family, and his wife, Jannette, *née* Wilson (1772–1835). He was sent at the age of five to relatives at Middlewich in England, and was educated at Astbury, Cheshire (1802–10), Harrow School (1810–12), and Little Shelford, near Cambridge (1812–13). His father could not afford to send him to university, but on 9 September 1813 an aunt obtained him a commission as ensign in the 39th regiment. He served at Weymouth, and from June 1814 in the war against the USA. With his regiment he returned to

Charles Sturt (1795–1869), by John Michael Crossland, *c.*1853 [replica]

Europe in August 1815, entered Paris, and for three years was with the army of occupation in northern France. For eight years from late 1818 he was on garrison duty in Ireland, helping to quell the 'Whiteboy' riots; he was promoted lieutenant in 1823 and captain in 1825. In December 1826 he sailed with a detachment of his regiment in the *Mariner* in charge of convicts for New South Wales, and arrived in Sydney on 23 May 1827. Governor Ralph Darling sent him briefly to King George's Sound in Western Australia and to Port Macquarie in New South Wales, and then made him military secretary and garrison brigade major. In November 1827 Darling appointed him to lead an expedition into the interior, to seek pastoral land and to trace a presumed inland river system.

With three soldiers and eight convicts, Sturt left Sydney on 10 November 1828, and at Bathurst joined his second in command, Hamilton Hume, an expert explorer who taught him much bushcraft and Aboriginal protocol. The party followed the Macquarie River until it terminated in extensive marshes: while Hume charted their limits, Sturt explored north-west of the Bogan River. The combined party then followed the Bogan, and on 2 February 1829 came upon a river which Sturt called the Darling. In the searing heat of a drought summer, the river's only water came from salt springs, and after following it down for a week Sturt was obliged to turn back. He picked up and followed the Castlereagh until it joined the Darling, then returned, reaching Sydney on 27 April 1829. He noted no good land, but in the Darling he had found Australia's longest river, and shown that all the western streams north of the Lachlan flowed into it.

In Sydney Sturt applied to lead an expedition to trace the Darling, if possible to a sea which he supposed existed inland. Instead Darling sent him to follow the Murrumbidgee. The governor discounted the notion of an inland sea, but told his superiors in England that a navigable river and good land would attract settlers. He assigned a ship to meet Sturt at Lake Alexandrina, on Australia's southern coast. With three soldiers, nine convicts, an Aborigine, and George *Macleay [see under Macleay, Alexander] as companion, Sturt left Sydney on 3 November 1829, picked up the Murrumbidgee, in a month passed the limit of its white settlement, and in another reached its confluence with the Lachlan. On 7 January 1830 he launched a boat and with seven companions sailed downstream, reaching another river on 14 January. Sturt later named it the Murray, after Sir George Murray, secretary of state for the colonies. On 23 January the party encountered a river which Sturt rightly took to be the Darling, then sailed down the Murray to reach on 12 February its shallow outlet to the sea beyond Lake Alexandrina. The ship had gone. Weary and short of food, the party sailed upriver until 17 February, then rowed almost 900 miles to help on the Murrumbidgee. Sturt reached Sydney on 25 May. For the rest of his life he suffered frequent illness.

In August 1830 Sturt was posted as officer commanding troops at the convict garrison on Norfolk Island, and helped quell a convict uprising there, but illness forced him in July 1831 to hand over command. In January 1832 he returned to Sydney and the following April he sailed for England. On the voyage he became blind, and although treatment partly recovered his sight he was obliged to sell his commission and renounce his military entitlements; he quitted the army on 19 July 1833, and in return received 5000 acres in New South Wales. In 1833 his *Two Expeditions into the Interior of New South Wales* (2 vols.) was published.

On 20 September 1834 Sturt married, at Dover, Charlotte Christiana (1801–1887), the daughter of Colonel William Sheppey Greene of the India service, a family friend. The couple sailed for Sydney in October. Sturt selected his land grant at Ginninderra, near present-day Canberra, and bought 1950 acres closer to Sydney, near Mittagong, where the Sturts lived for two years. In 1837 he bought a further 1000 acres west of Sydney, and moved there, but he was not a good manager, and in May 1838 financial difficulties obliged him to attempt a journey overlanding stock to the new settlement at Adelaide. He followed the Hume, proving it to be the Murray, but because of delays ran short of supplies. The trek was a financial failure. Sturt's report of good country seen in 1829–30 had favourably influenced the selection of the site for South Australia, and in Adelaide he was welcomed. On 8 November 1838 South Australia's governor, George Gawler, offered him the position of surveyor-general. He accepted, sold his New South Wales interests, and on 2 April 1839 brought his wife and two sons to Adelaide. In 1840 the

family settled at the Reed Beds, later the Adelaide suburb of Grange, named after the Sturts' house.

In September 1839 Sturt's time as surveyor-general was unexpectedly terminated when Lieutenant Edward Frome arrived from England with the appointment. Sturt became assistant commissioner of lands and acting registrar-general, and then on 29 August 1842 registrar-general. On 1 January 1843 his salary was cut by a third, and on 25 January he volunteered to spend two years searching for an inland sea in central Australia. He was instructed merely to penetrate to the centre of the continent, and in August 1844 led sixteen men from Adelaide up the Murray and Darling rivers into what became the north-west corner of New South Wales. He struck drought, and on 27 January 1845 was forced to shelter at Depot Glen. Shriven by heat and stricken by scurvy, which killed his second in command, James Poole, his party was stranded until rain fell in July. Sturt then sent a third of his men back to Adelaide, and probed north-west to Eyre Creek on the edge of the Simpson Desert, and north along Cooper's Creek. Heat, stone, and sand finally forced him back, and he returned to Adelaide on 19 January 1846. He had reached within 150 miles of the centre. There was no inland sea.

In his absence, and while still registrar-general, on 28 September 1845 Sturt was appointed colonial treasurer, but on 8 May 1847 took his family on leave to England. In 1849 he published his *Narrative of an Expedition into Central Australia* (2 vols.), and that August returned to Adelaide, where he was made colonial secretary. His health and sight failing, he resigned as from 31 December 1851, and on 19 March 1853 left Australia with his family for England. In retirement at Cheltenham, he kept an interest in Australian affairs, and applied unsuccessfully for the governorship of Victoria in 1855 and of Queensland in 1858. He died at his home, 19 Clarence Square, Cheltenham, on 16 June 1869 and was buried at Prestbury on 22 June. He had been nominated a KCMG: his wife was allowed to use the title Lady Sturt. He left two sons and a daughter; his youngest son died of cholera in India on 29 May 1864.

Sturt was tall and slim, with brown hair and blue eyes. He made lifelong friends easily, and was distant but considerate towards his men, even under the most trying conditions evoking great loyalty from them. He was exceptional in his ability to befriend and learn from the Aborigines. Yet he seems never to have attained a good sense of Australia's topography, and his judgement as an explorer was questionable: he kept his dream of an inland sea after his own work proved that it did not exist. He was no bushman, and in 1845 particularly he took foolhardy risks. He took a boat on all his expeditions, but never overcame a habit of heading into the arid interior in summer, commonly in a drought year. Feeling that he was not properly rewarded for his exertions, he wrote in 1841 to the Colonial Office criticizing George Grey's appointment as governor of South Australia, and proposing himself. Grey responded by cutting Sturt's salary and prospects. His financial judgement too was poor: he squandered his land grants, and Macleay had to help pay for his funeral.

The results of Sturt's explorations were uninspiring: he found dry country which he rated poorly, then a river system without a navigable outlet to the sea, and finally desert. Yet his endurance and his courage became a model for generations of Australian schoolchildren, and he remains among the best known and most liked of Australian land explorers. In four states natural features, streets, buildings, suburbs, and a university are named after him. More monuments honour him than any Australian explorer. Perhaps the most fitting is that in the centre of Adelaide: there his bronzed figure stands high on a pedestal, straining forward, eyes shaded against the bright sun, searching still for the green land and great reward he never found.

BILL GAMMAGE

Sources N. G. Sturt, *Life of Charles Sturt* (1899) • *DNB* • *AusDB* • J. H. L Cumpston, *Charles Sturt: his life and journeys of exploration* (1951) • C. Sargent, 'Sturt's military service', *Sabretache* [Sydney, New South Wales, Australia], 21 (July–Sept 1990) • K. Swan and M. Carnegie, *In step with Sturt* (1979) • M. Langley, *Sturt of the Murray* (1969) • C. Sturt, *Two expeditions into the interior of southern Australia, during the years 1828, 1829, 1830 and 1831*, 2 vols. (1833) • C. Sturt, *Narrative of an expedition into central Australia during the years 1844, 5 and 6*, 2 vols. (1849) • C. Sturt, *An account of a journey to south Australia, 1838* (1990) • C. Sturt, *The Mount Bryan expedition, 1839* (1982) • C. Sturt, *Journal of the central Australian expedition, 1844–5* (1984) • C. Sturt, *Proceedings of an expedition into the interior of New Holland 1829 and 1830* (1989) • *Four letters from Charles Sturt on a proposed exploration of the Australian continent … 1843 and 1844* (1988) • D. G. Brock, *To the desert with Sturt: a diary of the 1844 expedition* (1975) • E. Stokes, *To the inland sea: Charles Sturt's expedition, 1844–45* (1984) • E. Beale, *Sturt: the chipped idol* (1979) • B. Gammage, 'Sturt's noble stream', *Journeys into history*, ed. G. Davison (1990), 113–23 • B. Gammage, *Narrandera shire* (1986)
Archives Auckland Public Library, corresp. • Bodl. RH, corresp., journals, and papers • Mitchell L., NSW • NRA, priv. coll., corresp. and journal • RGS, letters and memoranda relating to North Australia Expedition • State Library of South Australia, Adelaide, Mortlock Library • State Library of South Australia, Adelaide, corresp. and papers | estate office, Crichel, Crichel MSS
Likenesses J. M. Crossland, oils, 1847, Art Gallery of South Australia, Adelaide • J. M. Crossland, oils, second version, *c*.1853, NPG [*see illus.*] • Koberwein, crayon sketch (in old age), Cheltenham Art Gallery and Museum • C. Sumners, bust, Art Gallery of South Australia, Adelaide
Wealth at death under £1500: administration, 9 July 1869, *CGPLA Eng. & Wales*

Sturt, George [*pseud.* George Bourne] (**1863–1927**), author, the younger son of Francis Sturt (1823–1884) and his wife, Ellen, daughter of William Smith, was born at Farnham, Surrey, on 18 June 1863. His grandfather and then his father had owned the wheelwright's shop in East Street from 1810 and the firm itself had existed there since 1706. Sturt attended Farnham grammar school from 1876, and in 1879 he became a junior teacher there until his father's death in 1884, when he resigned to take over the wheelwright's shop. He was thus plunged into onerous business responsibilities just at the time his intellectual interests were widening and he was beginning to think of himself as a writer. Sturt left a graphic account of his early life in *A Small Boy in the Sixties* (1927).

In the late 1880s Sturt published several articles in *The Commonweal*, the periodical of the Socialist League which

was financed by William Morris. His socialist sympathies were constant but never uncritical, as evidenced by his doubts about Fabianism. His beliefs often clashed uneasily with his role as an employer of labour himself. In 1891–2 Sturt met Arnold Bennett and their close friendship was crucial for his literary work. Bennett helped him to publish his first book, *A Year's Exile* (1898), a novel, and, more important, encouraged him to continue his journal. Sturt read widely at this time and Ruskin—'to whom I owe it that I am a Socialist' (*The Commonweal*, 20 April 1889)—and Thoreau, Emerson, and Pater all influenced his writing. His view of William Cobbett, another Farnham man, was more guarded. In 1891 he took a partner in the firm to make more time for literary work though he continued to be active in the wheelwright's shop. By his own admission, Sturt was never a competent craftsman himself but he understood the work from observation and did undertake such duties as choosing and ordering wood. In the autumn of 1891 he moved to Vine Cottage in The Bourne, near Farnham, where he lived until his death.

Sturt continued to write (but not publish) fiction, but in 1901 he found his true vein with *The Bettesworth Book*, a vivid record of the life and talk of an old villager, Frederick Grover, who was his gardener. Edward Thomas called this book 'a near approach to perfection'. It was followed by *Memoirs of a Surrey Labourer* (1907) and *Lucy Bettesworth* (1913). The Bettesworth books give a uniquely precise picture of rural life that ranges from the comic to the harrowing, sympathetic without sentimentality, in prose as clear as a window pane. Sturt's feeling for rustic character recalls Thomas Hardy, but he is free of Hardy's tendency to caricature. In 1912 the appearance of *Change in the Village*, his classic study of the profound changes at work in rural England, established his reputation. It is notable both for its detail and its grasp of large social trends. It may overstate the effects of the enclosures but it contains much that cannot be found elsewhere. Sturt sometimes regrets the old order but he eschews nostalgia, hoping for a more enriching life for the people in the future. In 1910 he published *The Ascending Effort*, an essay on aesthetics and social issues which shows his continuing engagement with 'progressive' thought. But his main concern was always with 'the folk' and the continuity of common life rather than with individual 'culture' (a notion he distrusted). He is one of the rare writers who can evoke the intelligence and imagination that go into manual work.

Despite increasingly poor health Sturt still oversaw the firm, now fighting a losing battle against the motor car, but in 1916 he suffered a severe stroke and he eventually sold out in 1920. By then paralysis, with his lifelong asthma, often confined him to Vine Cottage, where he was cared for by his sisters, Mary and Susan, who lived with him. Yet he remained productive: *William Smith, Potter and Farmer* (1920) and *A Farmer's Life* (1922) describe his maternal ancestors from Farnborough and a more ancient England that always moved him, for all his dislike of modern nationalism. Both books are mellower and more wistful than *Change in the Village*.

In 1923 Sturt published his best-known book, *The Wheelwright's Shop*, a record both of the wheelwright's craft and of the momentous change from handwork to the machine age. It describes in detail how a wheel was made, but it is in no way a manual, and is equally concerned with the farm wagon as a thing of beauty. For Sturt, the workers' skill and the product of their work form a single process. The book, like all his books, speaks of a vanishing world that was once common, but it is also practical and realistic. Like *A Small Boy in the Sixties* it appeared under his own name.

Sturt himself thought his 'best book' was his journal, which he kept until just before he died. It ranges from anecdotes and conversations to virtually self-contained essays. He drew frequently on it for his books. It was perhaps in his journals that he came nearest to expressing the idea of 'the folk' that underlies all his work. Some early extracts from them were published in 1941 by Geoffrey Grigson, and in 1967 E. D. Mackerness brought out a much larger selection. This is indispensable, although it still omits some important material.

Sturt's books had moderate success in his lifetime, and *Change in the Village* and *The Wheelwright's Shop* have, in E. P. Thompson's phrase, 'classic distinction' (E. P. Thompson, ix). After his death, his work tended to be presented as a plea for 'the organic community' (ibid., xiv), a notion that misses the complexity of his own sense of the strengths and weaknesses of rural life. Because his writing impinges on many fields, from craft and history to literature and cultural criticism, its readership has been fragmented and he is less widely known than he deserves to be. Among those he has influenced may be mentioned Edward Thomas, F. R. Leavis, Raymond Williams, and Richard Hoggart. But he will be fully appreciated only when he is read not only for historical reasons but as the master of English prose where he is at his best.

Sturt died on 4 February 1927 at Vine Cottage and was buried in Green Lane cemetery, Farnham. He was unmarried; his brother, Frank, and sister Susan survived him.

DAVID GERVAIS

Sources *The journals of George Sturt, 1890–1927*, ed. E. D. Mackerness, 2 vols. (1967) · G. Sturt, *A small boy in the sixties* (1927) · G. Grigson, ed., *The journals of George Sturt, 1890–1902* (1941) · F. R. Leavis and D. Thompson, *Culture and environment* (1933) · W. J. Keith, *The rural tradition* (1975) · D. Thompson, 'A cure for amnesia', *Scrutiny*, 2 (June 1933), 2–11 · G. Day, *Re-reading Leavis* (1996), 63–74 · E. P. Thompson, 'Foreword', in G. Sturt, *The wheelwright's shop* (1993) · R. Hoggart, *Townscape with figures: Farnham, portrait of an English town* (1994) · D. Gervais, *Literary Englands* (1993), 102–32 · b. cert. · d. cert.
Archives BL, journals, Add. MSS 43359–43374, 43466–43467, 43690–43693 · Museum of Farnham, MSS, cuttings, photographs · priv. colls. · Ransom HRC, corresp. and papers · University of British Columbia Library, literary MSS | NYPL, Berg collection, letters to Arnold Bennett
Likenesses memorial tablet, 1937, St Andrew's Church, Farnham · W. H. Allen, charcoal and pastel drawings, Hampshire County Council Museum Service, Winchester, Hampshire · photographs, Farnham Museum
Wealth at death £2682 1s. 9d.: probate, 25 April 1927, *CGPLA Eng. & Wales*

Sturt, Henry Cecil (1863–1946), philosopher, was born on 14 June 1863 in Sheen Vale, Mortlake, Surrey, the son of Henry Sturt, a surgeon, and Mary Elizabeth Sturt, *née* Terry. In 1882 he won a Hastings exhibition scholarship to Queen's College, Oxford, where he took a first class in *literae humaniores* and a second class in modern history, and graduated BA in 1888. After graduation he moved to London to work as a librarian at the British Museum; he returned to Oxford in 1898 to devote his life to philosophy and there he remained until his death. On 27 June 1895 he married Florence Miriam May (*b.* 1866/7). They had a daughter and two sons.

In the absence of a university or college position, Sturt was obliged to support his philosophical interests by other means: he ran a school from 1900 to 1914 to prepare candidates for the civil service examination. During the First World War and in the years immediately following, he taught philosophy at various universities, notably St Andrew's and University College of North Wales, as a replacement for instructors called to war work. He was occasionally substitute professor of moral philosophy at Aberdeen. From 1925 to 1931 he tutored non-collegiate students in philosophy at Oxford. None the less, he was a familiar figure in university philosophical circles. He was a founding member of the Oxford Philosophical Society and acted as its secretary from 1898 to 1908. The adherents of the society, most notably F. C. S. Schiller and Sturt, sought to replace absolute idealism, which remained a formidable presence at Oxford, with a new system of thought, termed personal idealism. This position, which bore a strong resemblance to the pragmatism of the American philosopher William James, was outlined in a volume of essays—*Personal Idealism* (1902)—which Sturt edited.

In his most notable and widely read publication, *Idola theatri: a criticism of Oxford thought and thinkers from the standpoint of personal idealism* (1906), Sturt developed a comprehensive assault on the philosophical idealism of T. H. Green, F. H. Bradley, and B. Bosanquet. He charged them with failing to translate the underlying spirituality which they posited into an immediate, practical, and personal philosophy. Regarding their thought as too other-worldly, he sought to advance 'personal idealism', in which individual will or striving is treated as the central fact of human experience. While Sturt was influenced by the British idealists' critique of naturalism, he believed that Green, Bradley, and Bosanquet had not understood how evolutionary science, particularly such theories as natural selection, might illuminate philosophical inquiry. Sturt attempted to use evolutionary science to explain the increasingly pivotal place of individual will in social development. But *Idola theatri* was primarily a critical work and, though he faulted idealists for failing to provide a constructive philosophy, he made little effort here to formulate an alternative system. *The Principle of Understanding* (1915), a study of logic from the perspective of personal idealism, attempted to establish an alternative to absolute idealism, but Sturt was unable to clarify an underlying confusion between truth and the knowledge of truth; his account of cognition did not persuade many readers. In *The Idea of a Free Church* (1909) Sturt advocated the formation of a new national religion which would promulgate a patriotic creed. Contemporaries were troubled by the fascist overtones in this book and in his other writings published in the 1930s. In *Socialism and Character* (1922) Sturt extended his more abstract discussions of individual will to defend socialism on the grounds that socialism would foster the development of moral citizenship. Accordingly, he advocated the redistribution of wealth, nationalization of industry, reform of family life, and elevation of the status of women. Sturt also urged the establishment of a strong nation state and maintained that competition among nations was more conducive to progress than co-operation. He regarded the 'vigorous nations of the North' as the 'hope for Humanity'; he later dissociated his position from the fascism of Hitler and Mussolini.

Sturt was elected to the Aristotelian Society in 1893, and also served as secretary for the Mind Association from its inception in 1900 until 1921; he audited its accounts from 1925 to 1941, and thereafter acted as its treasurer until his death. The initial success of the association, which was to play an important role in the professionalization of philosophy, was attributed in part to Sturt's labours. He remained active in the association: at the age of eighty-three he still attended the annual meeting to present the accounts; and he was making entries in its accounts until the day before his death. A fine swimmer, Sturt earned praise for diving twenty times into the Cherwell River in an unsuccessful attempt to rescue a drowning person. Until his eighty-second year he regularly frequented Parsons' Pleasure, a popular swimming venue on the Cherwell.

Though Sturt failed to command a strong following for personal idealism and though his tentative reflections on a radical empiricism were overshadowed by the new linguistic philosophers, he affords a useful vantage point on early twentieth-century philosophical developments. His writings reflect the growing disenchantment, from the 1890s, of earlier adherents of idealism. In his review of *Personal Idealism*, William James pointed out the need for 'a more commanding and all-round statement in classical style of personal idealism' (*Mind*, 12, 1903), but neither Sturt nor Schiller produced such a statement and they never commanded the following in Britain that William James did. Sturt was increasingly out of line with the growing professionalization of the discipline of philosophy. His work attracted reviews that regretted the absence of sustained argument and the preponderance of imprecisions. Following cerebral thrombosis, Henry Cecil Sturt died on 13 December 1946 at his home at 55 Park Town, Oxford. He was cremated in Headington four days later.   S. M. DEN OTTER

Sources C. C. J. Webb, *Mind*, new ser., 56 (1947), 185–7 · *Oxford Times* (20 Dec 1946) · W. James, 'Review of *Personal idealism*', *Mind*, new ser., 12 (1903), 93–7 · Foster, *Alum. Oxon.* · b. cert. · m. cert. · d. cert.

Wealth at death £690 11*s.* 3*d.*: administration with will, 31 Aug 1948, *CGPLA Eng. & Wales*

Sturt, Henry Gerard, first Baron Alington (1825–1904), racehorse owner and politician, was born on 16 May 1825, the eldest son of Henry Charles Sturt (1795–1866) of Crichel, Dorset, and MP for that county, and his wife, Charlotte Penelope (*d.* 1879), third daughter of Richard Brudenell, sixth earl of Cardigan. Educated at Eton College, he matriculated from Christ Church, Oxford, in 1843. He was Conservative MP from 1847 to 1856 for Dorchester, and from 1856 to 1876 for the county of Dorset. He was raised to the peerage on 15 January 1876 as Baron Alington, a title borne by maternal ancestors in both the English and Irish peerages but which had become extinct. His estates amounted to some 17,500 acres.

Sturt's name first appeared in the list of winning owners on the turf in 1849, and he was elected to the Jockey Club the following year. The colours he registered were 'light blue, white cap', which had formerly belonged to Lord George Bentinck. Almost throughout his career on the turf he preferred to race in partnership. His first confederate was Mr H. Curzon, with whom he owned a filly called Kate. Underestimating her potential, they sold her as a two-year-old in 1851, and the following year had the mortification of seeing her win the One Thousand Guineas. However, a later partnership with Sir Frederic Johnstone, beginning in 1868, brought Sturt six classic wins, most notably Common's victories in the Derby, St Leger, and Two Thousand Guineas in 1891. It is said that Sturt and Sir Frederic had an important influence on the prince of Wales's decision to take up racing. In 1876 he was privy to the details of Lord and Lady Aylesford's separation, and was party to what Queen Victoria considered an 'unpardonable' approach to the princess of Wales by Lord Randolph Churchill who wished to pressurize the prince of Wales into preventing Lord Aylesford from seeking a divorce.

Sturt was a shrewd, genial, and witty man. He married on 10 September 1853 Lady Augusta (*d.* 1888), eldest daughter of George Charles *Bingham, third earl of Lucan. They had one son and five daughters. After her death he married, on 10 February 1892, Evelyn Henrietta, daughter of Henry Blundell Leigh, but had no further children. He died at his home, Crichel, near Wimborne, Dorset, on 17 February 1904, and was buried there. His will bequeathed a set of waistcoat buttons to King Edward VII and £100 to Queen Alexandra.

EDWARD MOORHOUSE, *rev.* WRAY VAMPLEW

Sources R. Mortimer, R. Onslow, and P. Willett, *Biographical encyclopedia of British flat racing* (1978) · W. Day and A. J. Day, *The racehorse in training* (1925) · *The Sportsman* (19 Feb 1904) · *The Times* (19 Feb 1904) · *The Field* (19 Feb 1904) · G. Plumptre, *The fast set: the world of Edwardian racing* (1985) · GEC, *Peerage* · R. S. Churchill, *Winston S. Churchill*, 1: *Youth, 1874–1900* (1966) · *CGPLA Eng. & Wales* (1904)
Archives estate office, Crichel, Wimborne, Dorset, family and estate papers
Likenesses J. Brown, stipple, BM; repro. in *Bailey's Magazine* (1869) · Graves, portrait, Crichel, Wimborne, Dorset · Spy [L. Ward], chromolithograph caricature, NPG; repro. in *VF* (8 July 1876)

Wealth at death £43,751 13s. 2d.: probate, 27 July 1904, *CGPLA Eng. & Wales*

Sturt, John (1658–1730), engraver, was born in London on 6 April 1658 of unknown parentage. In 1674 he was apprenticed to Robert White, the most distinguished pupil of David Loggan. Like most engravers of the time, he derived his staple income by working as a book illustrator, and in the course of a long and industrious life he executed the plates for many important works, including Francis Bragge's *Passion of our Saviour* (1694), Samuel Wesley's *History of the Old and New Testament in Verse* (1704), Gerard Audran's *Perspective of the Human Body*, Andrea Pozzo's *Rules and Examples of Perspective*, dedicated to Queen Anne, with 105 plates (1707), Charles Perrault's *Treatise on the Five Orders of Architecture* (1708), Laurence Howell's *View of the Pontificate* (1712), Hamond's *Historical Narrative of the Whole Bible* (1727), and an edition of Bunyan's *The Pilgrim's Progress* (1728). Sturt was particularly celebrated for his skill as a writing engraver, and he engraved several of the works of the calligrapher John Ayres, most notably *A Tutor to Penmanship, or, The Writing Master* (1698), adding—as he frequently did—a frontispiece portrait of the author. He specialized in miniature work, and it was said that he could engrave the creed on a silver penny, a claim amply reinforced by his best-known works: engraved versions of the Book of Common Prayer and of Laurence Howell's *The Orthodox Communicant*, published respectively by subscription in 1717 and 1721. The first of these books, executed on 188 silver plates adorned with borders and vignettes, had a frontispiece portrait of King George I, the lines for which were composed of the creed, the Lord's prayer, the ten commandments, a prayer for the royal family, and Psalm 21, all inscribed in minute characters. Yet Sturt could also work on a large scale, and in 1692 he produced a notable engraving of *Britannia*, the royal first capital ship of England, printed on four sheets after drawings by William van de Velde. Many other drawings, particularly for book-plates, were prepared for Sturt by Bernard Lens the younger, with whom he opened a drawing school in St Paul's Churchyard about 1697.

Sturt later moved to Aldersgate Street, where he was established by 1707. From 1712 until his death he was on good terms with George Vertue, to whom he provided information about other engravers and artists, including John Payne and Willem Wissing. Despite failing health, he continued to work until the end of his life, being last employed on plates for the *Selectus diplomatum et numismatum thesaurus*, projected by James Anderson of Edinburgh. 'Worn out with age and … drove to great difficulties to live' (Vertue, *Note books*, 3.44), he declined to take advantage of efforts made on his behalf to secure him a place in the Charterhouse, and he died, in debt, in the parish of St Botolph, Aldersgate, in August 1730. He was buried at St Botolph on 13 August. From the evidence of his will he was a widower, but nothing is known of his wife or any child.   RICHARD SHARP

Sources Vertue, *Note books* · Thieme & Becker, *Allgemeines Lexikon* · T. Clayton, *The English print, 1688–1802* (1997) · A. Griffiths and R. A. Gerard, *The print in Stuart Britain, 1603–1689* (1998) [exhibition catalogue, BM, 8 May – 20 Sept 1998] · *Engraved Brit. ports.*
Likenesses W. Humphrey, mezzotint, pubd 1874 (after W. Faithorne), BM, NPG · Barrett, line engraving, BM, NPG; repro. in H. Walpole, ed., *A catalogue of engravers* (1794)
Wealth at death probably died very poor: will, PRO, PROB 6/107, fol. 20v; Vertue, *Note books*

Stury, Sir Richard (c.1327–1395). *See under* Lollard knights (act. c.1380–c.1414).

Stutchbury, Samuel (1798–1859), naturalist and geologist, was born in London on 15 January 1798, the third child and second son of Joseph Sidney Stutchbury (1769–1810), gauging instrument maker, and his wife, Hannah, née Smith (1776–1820x29). Although he had little formal education, in 1820 Stutchbury became assistant to William Clift, conservator of the Hunterian Museum of the Royal College of Surgeons. That same year, he married, on 2 August, Hannah Louise Barnard; a daughter, Louise, was born in 1822.

In 1825 Stutchbury became zoologist to the Pacific Pearl Fishery Company's expedition to the Tuamotu archipelago. His journal contains pertinent observations on the natural history and social conditions of the places visited and accounts of diving and pearling, and he made extensive collections of shells and native artefacts. Between 1827 and 1830 he was a dealer in natural-history specimens, associated with his brother, Henry Rome Stutchbury (1796–1853). In 1831 Stutchbury became curator at the Bristol Institution, where he published significant papers on conchology and palaeontology and made the museum one of the best in Europe. He also carried out geological surveys of the mines of the duchy of Cornwall and others, and was involved in the early work of the first director of the Geological Survey of Great Britain, Henry De la Beche.

In 1850 Stutchbury resigned from his curatorship to become mineral surveyor of New South Wales, provoking the hostility of Revd William Clarke (1798–1878), who had also applied for the position and who believed Stutchbury to be a mere museum curator, unqualified for field work. Following his appointment, Stutchbury spent five years mapping 80,000 square kilometres of eastern Australia (including part of what is now Queensland), virtually unaided. In the frenzy of gold-rush fever his work received little acknowledgement by officials at the time. He returned to Bristol in ill health in 1855, and undertook consulting work until his death, at 3 Park Street, Bristol, on 12 February 1859. He was buried on 17 February at Arnos Vale cemetery in Bristol.

Stutchbury had excellent powers of observation and a good critical sense, both of which made him a fine scientist, and his work has stood the test of time. He was not an aggressive person or of high social status, and he had little ambition for public notice, so he tended to be overshadowed by contemporaries such as Richard Owen (1804–1892), Charles Darwin (1809–1882), for whom he provided barnacles, and Charles Lyell (1797–1875), who used his information on the Pacific islands and coral reefs.

Samuel Stutchbury (1798–1859), by unknown engraver, pubd 1852 (after Marshall Claxton)

Stutchbury became an associate of the Linnean Society in 1821, a fellow of the Geological Society of London in 1841, and he was an honorary member of a number of European scientific bodies. Somewhat portly and with an open countenance, his friendly co-operation and his knowledge were greatly appreciated by a wide range of scientists, who honoured him in the scientific names of a number of fossil and recent organisms.

D. F. BRANAGAN

Sources D. F. Branagan, 'Samuel Stutchbury and his manuscripts', *In search of New Zealand's scientific heritage*, ed. M. E. Hoare and L. G. Bell, Royal Society of New Zealand Bulletin, 21 (1984), 7–15 · M. D. Crane, 'Samuel Stutchbury (1798–1859), naturalist and geologist', *Notes & Records of the Royal Society of London*, 37/2 (March 1983), 189–200 · D. F. Branagan, 'Samuel Stutchbury: a natural history voyage to the Pacific, 1825–27 and its consequences', *Archives of Natural History*, 20/1 (1993), 69–91 · D. F. Branagan, 'Samuel Stutchbury and the Australian Museum', *Records of the Australian Museum*, supplement 15 (1992), 99–110 · D. F. Branagan, 'Samuel Stutchbury and Reverend W. B. Clarke, not quite equal and opposite', *100 years of Australian scientific explorations*, ed. P. J. Stanbury (1975), 89–98 · H. Stuchbery, A. Stuchbery, and R. Stuchbury, 'Stotesburie: these are our people' (private publication [H. Stuchbery], Ringwood, Victoria, Australia, 1981) · S. Stutchbury, 'Pacific Voyage Journals', NL NZ, Turnbull L. · S. Stutchbury, diary, Mitchell L., NSW [New South Wales, 1850s] · S. Stutchbury, reports, Mitchell L., NSW [1850s] · S. Stutchbury, reports, state archives of New South Wales [1850s] · S. Stutchbury, curator's reports, Bristol Library, Bristol [1830s–50] · S. Stutchbury, mining reports, duchy of Cornwall archives, London · Stutchbury MSS, priv. coll. · *CGPLA Eng. & Wales* (1859) · m. cert. · d. cert.
Archives NHM, corresp. with Sir Richard Owen and William Cliff
Likenesses monochrome, Mitchell L., NSW · pen sketch (after M. Claxton), NPG; repro. in *ILN* (3 July 1852) [*see illus.*]
Wealth at death under £450: probate, 13 May 1859, *CGPLA Eng. & Wales*

Stuteville, Robert (III) de (d. 1183), baron, was the son of Robert (II) de Stuteville and Erneburga, of unknown parentage. Robert (III) was probably a second son, whose elder brother, Nicholas, inherited the family's Norman lands and some English estates. Besides Nicholas, Robert (III) had brothers named William, Roger, and John, and a sister, who married Robert d'Eyville. He probably also had a brother Osmund and a sister Burga. Some time before 1138 Stuteville recovered some of the English lands forfeited by his grandfather, Robert (I) de Stuteville, for his support of Robert Curthose, duke of Normandy, though the majority of those lands remained in the hands of the Mowbray family, to which they had been granted by Henry I. In 1138 Stuteville was one of the English leaders at the battle of the Standard. At some point in Stephen's reign he issued coinage at the mint in York, and in the same reign, according to a set of miracle stories, he held two clerics for ransom in a practice that was all too common during the anarchy.

Early in Henry II's reign a settlement was made between Stuteville and Roger (I) de Mowbray over the lands forfeited by Robert (I) de Stuteville, whereby Mowbray granted Stuteville a valuable manor and ten knights' fees, though in 1166 Stuteville held only one new and eight old fees from Mowbray; he also held eight old fees and one-eighth of a new fee directly of the king in that year. Stuteville attested a number of charters of Henry II, performed various tasks in the royal government, including acting as a justice on eyre, and served as sheriff of Yorkshire from 1170 to 1175. During the revolt against Henry II in 1173–4 Stuteville and his brothers and sons were notable supporters of the king; his brother Roger, sheriff of Northumberland from 1170 to 1185, was particularly active. In 1174 Stuteville was one of the leaders of the army that captured William the Lion, king of Scots.

Stuteville gave land to Meaux and Pipewell abbeys and probably founded Keldholme Priory. He married Helewise, whose family is unknown. He had five sons, named William, Nicholas, Osmund, Eustace, and Robert, a daughter Burga, who married William de Vescy, and probably a second daughter, named Helewise, who made several important marriages. Stuteville died in 1183 and was succeeded by his eldest son, William de *Stuteville.

HUGH M. THOMAS

Sources W. Farrer and others, eds., *Early Yorkshire charters*, 12 vols. (1914–65), vol. 9 · *Pipe rolls* · *Chronica magistri Rogeri de Hovedene*, ed. W. Stubbs, 4 vols., Rolls Series, 51 (1868–71) · W. Stubbs, ed., *Gesta regis Henrici secundi Benedicti abbatis: the chronicle of the reigns of Henry II and Richard I, AD 1169–1192*, 2 vols., Rolls Series, 49 (1867) · *Chancery records* (RC) · J. H. Round, ed., *Rotuli de dominabus et pueris et puellis de XII comitatibus* (1185), PRSoc., 35 (1913), 2

Stuteville, William de (d. 1203), baron, was the eldest son of Robert (III) de *Stuteville (d. 1183) and his wife, Helewise. He first appears in the records in 1173, when he received custody of Knaresborough, Aldborough, and other manors. Like his father and uncle Roger de Stuteville he was an important royalist during the revolt of 1173–4. In 1174 he was put in charge of a castle built at Topcliffe to oppose the rebel forces of Roger (I) de Mowbray, and later that year he was one of the leaders of the force that captured William the Lion, king of Scots. He was made custodian of Roxburgh Castle in 1177.

Late in Henry II's reign Stuteville began his occasional service as a royal justice and he went on to serve the governments of both Richard and John in a variety of tasks. At the beginning of Richard I's reign he was sheriff of Northumberland for half a year (1189–90) and in 1191 he served as sheriff of Lincolnshire for a short time. During Richard's absence on crusade he was a strong supporter of William de Longchamp until the latter's fall. In 1193, during John's rebellion, Stuteville helped Geoffrey, archbishop of York, to fortify the castle at Doncaster, but refused to help him besiege one of John's castles, saying that he was John's man. This notable piece of equivocation paid off once John came to the throne, for Stuteville, with the help of a number of large proffers became sheriff of Northumberland (1199–1200), Yorkshire (1200–02), Westmorland (1200–02), and Cumberland (1199–1203), and obtained custody of various royal boroughs, castles, and manors.

Stuteville received rich rewards for his services to the crown. Henry II granted to him Knaresborough and Aldborough, which he already held in custody, for the service of three knights, probably in July 1175. Later he was granted important custodies and privileges and in 1201 King John gave him the Forest of Milburn in Westmorland. John's favour may also have enabled him to renew the old family claim against the Mowbrays, and in a new compromise in 1201 he received nine additional knight's fees and another valuable manor. William was a benefactor of Fountains Abbey and Keldholme Priory, but was remembered at Meaux Abbey for seizing his father's benefactions and causing the monks trouble. In the lives of St Robert of Knaresborough he was depicted as a villainous persecutor of the saint who had a change of heart after a terrifying dream.

Stuteville was married to Bertha, a niece or granddaughter of Ranulf de Glanville, but it is possible that he had another (unrecorded) wife who was the mother of his son and heir, Robert. He also had an illegitimate daughter. Stuteville died in 1203 and was probably buried at Fountains Abbey.   HUGH M. THOMAS

Sources W. Farrer and others, eds., *Early Yorkshire charters*, 12 vols. (1914–65), vols. 1, 9 · *Pipe rolls* · *Chronica magistri Rogeri de Hovedene*, ed. W. Stubbs, 4 vols., Rolls Series, 51 (1868–71) · W. Stubbs, ed., *Gesta regis Henrici secundi Benedicti abbatis: the chronicle of the reigns of Henry II and Richard I, AD 1169–1192*, 2 vols., Rolls Series, 49 (1867) · *Chancery records* (RC) · P. Grosjean, ed., 'Vitae S. Roberti Knaresburgensis', *Analecta Bollandiana*, 57 (1939), 364–400 · T. D. Hardy, ed., *Rotuli chartarum in Turri Londinensi asservati*, RC, 36 (1837), 108a

Style, William (*c.*1599–1679), law reporter and legal writer, was the first son of William Style of Beckenham (*d.* 1615), who was the grandson of Sir Humphrey Style, esquire of the body to Henry VIII, and his second wife, Mary, daughter of Sir Robert *Clarke, baron of the exchequer. He matriculated at Oxford in 1618, resided briefly in Brasenose College, was admitted to the Inner Temple in 1619, and was called to the bar in 1628. Although he was still living in chambers in Paper Buildings in the 1650s, he played little part in the formal life of the society and never became a bencher. This is rather surprising, given his interest in legal learning and the dedication of his *Modern*

William Style (*c.*1599–1679), by unknown artist, 1636

Reports 'more particularly and affectionately' to the members of his inn, where he had lived 'for so many years together … amidst so many learned men'. He does not seem to have been a prominent practitioner, and referred in the same place to his constant attendance for many years at the bar, 'with very litle profit either to others or my self' (Style, *Modern Reports*, dedication); indeed, he said he had earned little more than a 'little *quelque chose … pur fair bouillir la marmite*' (Style, *Practical Register*, preface).

Style collected a number of legal manuscripts, which contain his notes of the dates when he read them through in the 1630s and 1640s, one as late as 1671. The library came into the hands of Thomas Grey, second earl of Stamford (*d.* 1720), and many of the volumes were obtained by Sir Thomas Phillipps and dispersed at his sales; eight have come to light with notes by Style. One of the manuscripts contains notes, in Style's hand, of practice cases in the king's bench and upper bench, dated between 1646 and 1655, and these may have been the foundation of Style's *Practical Register*, first printed in 1657. This was a useful guide to modern practice decisions, collected at a time when the law reports were somewhat thin or non-existent, and it was reprinted in 1670, 1671, and 1694. The preface contains a strong warning against the dangers of law reform as espoused by the 'infatuated Spirits of this distempered Age'. A new edition by John Lilly appeared in 1707, with a continuation volume in 1710, after which it was known as Lilly's *Practical Register* (last edition 1745). Style's other original publication was *Narrationes modernae, or, Modern Reports* (1658), a collection of law reports in the king's bench and upper bench from 1648 to 1655, translated (with evident distaste) from law French into English, as required by legislation of 1650 (which Style castigated). The reports are unusual in that they were prepared for the press by the author, and they remain the principal source of case law from the time of Chief Justice Rolle, whom Style greatly admired, and his successor Glynne. Style lamented in his preface that 'the Press hath been very fertile in this our Age, and hath brought forth many, if not too many births of this nature. … This I am sure of, there is not a father alive to own many of them'. His own reports, however, were 'a lawfull Issue', and he claimed to have been as careful in penning his collection 'as was possible at a throngued Bar to do'. Conscious, it seems, of his failure at the bar, he hoped they would prove he had not neglected his calling or 'lived altogether a drone'. Style also published in 1640 an English translation, entitled *Contemplations, Signs and Groans of a Christian*, of a work by John Michael Dilherr.

Style married Elizabeth, daughter of William Dueling of Rochester, with whom he had two sons and two daughters. In 1659 he succeeded to the family estates at Langley in Beckenham, Kent, on the death of his elder half-brother Sir Humphrey Style, baronet, gentleman of the privy chamber and cup-bearer to Charles I. This no doubt put an end to any further legal aspirations. By this time, in any case, he thought death could not be far off, 'by reason of my declining years; but more especially in respect of the weak and crafty constitution of my Body much macerated by sharp, and tedious sicknesses' (Style, *Modern Reports*, dedication). When he made his will in 1673 he said he was somewhat more than seventy-three and was still complaining of 'an indifferent health … declyning age and decaying body'. He died on 7 December 1679 and was buried in the family vault in the south aisle of Beckenham church. His own eldest son, William, had predeceased him, and when his second son, Humphrey, later died without male issue Langley passed to the Elwill family.

J. H. Baker

Sources E. Hasted, *The history and topographical survey of the county of Kent*, 1 (1778), 85–7 · J. D. Cowley, *A bibliography of abridgments, digests, dictionaries and indexes of English law to the year 1800* (1932) · J. H. Baker, *English legal manuscripts in the United States of America: a descriptive list*, 1 (1985), no. 186 · J. H. Baker, *English legal manuscripts in the United States of America: a descriptive list*, 2 (1990), nos. 372, 485, 540, 653–5 · will, PRO, PROB 11/361, sig. 167 · private information (2004) [A. Taussig] · W. H. Cooke, ed., *Students admitted to the Inner Temple, 1547–1660* [1878] · F. A. Inderwick and R. A. Roberts, eds., *A calendar of the Inner Temple records*, 2 (1898), 168 · BL, Add. MS 38008
Likenesses oils, 1636, Tate collection [*see illus.*]

Sualo [St Sualo, Solus] (*d.* 794), hermit, was one of the pilgrim Anglo-Saxon religious who travelled to the continent in the eighth century. Knowledge of him depends on a life written between 839 and 842 by Ermanric (*d.* 874), a monk of Ellwangen who later became bishop of Passau. Ermanric wrote at the request of his friend Gundram, a monk of Fulda who administered Sualo's cell for that abbey, and claimed to derive his information from an old servant of Sualo. Ermanric's Latin style is poor, however, and his information often demonstrably defective. His mistake in thinking that Sualo's name could appropriately be equated with the Latin *solus*, meaning 'alone', is typical.

According to Ermanric, Sualo came to Germany in the wake of his master, Boniface, who ordained him priest. Before the latter's death in 754, Sualo undertook the life of a solitary: memory of his cell is preserved in the name of the village of Solnhofen, on the River Altmuhl some 10 miles west of Eichstätt, the see of Boniface's English appointee Willibald. Ermanric claims that his cell was bestowed on Sualo by Charlemagne. Twelfth-century sources report that Willibald's brother Winnebald, abbot of Heidenheim, gave Sualo other estates in the area. He passed all his property to Boniface's foundation of Fulda on his death in 794. His day is traditionally kept on 3 December.

Marios Costambeys

Sources A. Bauch, ed. and trans., *Quellen zur Geschichte der Diözese Eichstätt*, 2nd edn, 1: *Biographien der Gründungszeit* (Eichstätt, 1984) [incl. edn of Ermanric's *Vita Soli*] · W. Levison, *England and the continent in the eighth century* (1946) · Ermanric of Ellwangen, 'Vita Soli', [*Supplementa tomorum I–XII, pars III*], ed. O. Holder-Egger, MGH Scriptores [folio], 15/1 (Stuttgart, 1887), 151–63 · Adelbert of Heidenheim, 'Relatio, qua ratione … monasterium Heidenheimense ad ordinem Sancti Benedicti redierit', in *Jacobi Gretseri … opera omnia*, ed. J. Gretser, 10 (Regensburg, 1737), 805–29

Suárez de Figueroa, Gomez, first duke of Feria in the Spanish nobility (1520?–1571), diplomat, was the second son of Lorenzo Suárez de Figueroa, third count of Feria, and his wife, Catalina Fernandez de Córdoba. He came of a great landowning family in Extremadura in south-west Spain, and it was at Zafra in that region that he was born. He became fifth count of Feria on the death of his elder brother Pedro in 1551.

Feria's importance in English history lies in the fact that he was a favourite and confidant of Philip II, who held the crown matrimonial of England from 1554 to 1558. Feria was not regarded as particularly gifted, but he was loyal, personable, and without ambition. He was also transparently honest, and this seems to have been the quality that Philip most admired in him. He was regarded as second in influence only to the king's Portuguese secretary, Ruy Gomez da Silva. He came to England with the king for his marriage to Mary in July 1554, and was one of the handful of Spanish nobles who remained when the majority departed to the Low Countries in August and September. He left with Philip in August 1555, but returned on at least two occasions for confidential discussions with the English council, and also accompanied the king during his second visit, from March to July 1557. At the end of 1557 Feria was appointed Philip's resident representative in England, particularly to co-ordinate the war effort. The letters that he wrote to Philip during his seven-month stay (until July 1558) contain some of the most informative comments upon the latter part of Mary's reign. Feria was scathing about what he considered to be the apathy and incompetence of the English council, but equally frank when he considered that the king was not treating his English subjects justly. At some point between 6 and 23 June 1558 he visited Princess Elizabeth at Ashridge, with the king's approval but without the queen's knowledge. He described the outcome of these discussions as highly satisfactory, but reported them verbally to Philip on his return, and no record of their content survives.

The king sent Feria back to England early in November 1558, when the news of the queen's health had become alarming, with instructions to support Elizabeth's succession when Mary died, using his supposedly good relations with the new queen to handle the difficult transition. He stuck to this difficult task until May 1559, but in spite of his relative Anglophilia soon discovered that he had no sympathy with, or confidential contacts in, the new government. His only close political ally was John Boxall, Mary's principal secretary, who retired into private life after her death. Before his departure he had come to regard himself as a protector of the English Catholics. On 29 December 1558 he was married in London to Jane Dormer [see Suárez de Figueroa, Jane, duchess of Feria (1538–1612)], formerly a lady of Mary's privy chamber, against the wishes of both their families, and their household quickly became a refuge for those disaffected with the state of English religion. After his departure he and his wife continued to be leading patrons of the exiled Catholic community, and Feria did his best to influence Philip towards the overthrow of Elizabeth's government. The appointment of Guerau de Spes as ambassador to England in 1568 has been attributed to his influence, and he was a strong supporter of Ridolfi in 1571. Philip made him duke of Feria in September 1567, and understandably regarded him as something of an expert on English affairs. In 1566 and 1571 he offered his services as governor-general of the Netherlands, while in 1568 he went on a diplomatic mission to the Portuguese court at Lisbon. Feria died in the palace of the Escorial on 7 September 1571 and was buried in the monastery of San Jeronimo de Guisando there, but his remains were later transferred to the family mausoleum at Santa Clara de Zafra. His son Lorenzo, who was born at Malines on 6 September 1559, succeeded as second duke. He was employed as an ambassador by Philip III, and also served as viceroy of Sicily between 1602 and 1606.

DAVID LOADES

Sources *CSP Spain, 1554–8*, 12–13 · *CSP Venice, 1555–8* · H. Clifford, *The life of Jane Dormer, duchess of Feria*, ed. J. Stevenson (1887) · 'The count of Feria's dispatch to Philip II of 14th November 1558', ed. M. J. Rodríguez-Salgado and S. Adams, *Camden miscellany, XXVIII*, CS, 4th ser., 29 (1984) · M. J. Rodríguez-Salgado, *The changing face of empire: Charles V, Philip II, and Habsburg authority, 1551–1559* (1988) · D. Loades, *The reign of Mary Tudor: politics, government and religion in England, 1553–58*, 2nd edn (1991) · M. Fernandez Alvarez, *Tres embajadores de Felipe II en Inglaterra* (1951) · G. Bleiberg, ed., *Diccionario de historia de España*, 2nd edn, 3 vols. (1968–9)
Archives Archivo General, Simancas, Estado Inglaterra

Suárez de Figueroa [née Dormer], **Jane**, **duchess of Feria in the Spanish nobility** (1538–1612), noblewoman and courtier, was born at Heythrop in Oxfordshire on 6 January 1538, one of the two daughters of Sir William Dormer and his first wife, Mary Sidney. She was brought up by her maternal grandparents after her mother's death in 1542. She then lived with her grandmother Jane, *née* Newdigate, Lady Dormer, until admitted into the household of Princess Mary some five years later. As a child she played frequently with Edward VI at the instigation of her grandfather Sir William Sidney, Edward's chamberlain and tutor, but it was Mary Tudor's favour that proved fundamental to her rise. She was one of the nine ladies and maids who attended the queen at her coronation in September 1553 and thereafter received a number of gifts as one of the queen's 'welbeloved women'. Her kinship with some of the most important aristocratic families made her valuable, but it was her efficiency and trustworthiness that particularly appealed to the queen, who on her deathbed charged her to take her jewels to Elizabeth. There is also good evidence of her striking looks. According to a poet, 'Dormar is a darline and of suche lively hewe that who so fedes his eyes on her may sone her bewte vue' (BL, Cotton MS Titus A xxiv, fol. 83v). Her portrait was one of the examples of female beauty in Philip II's main picture gallery in Spain.

Gomez *Suarez de Figueroa, count (from 1567 duke) of Feria, met Jane in 1554 when he arrived with Philip II in England for the king's marriage to Queen Mary. Feria was the king's favourite at the time, and he remained a key political figure as well as a leading household official until his death in 1571. Despite strong opposition from his own family, but with the king's full support, Feria sued for Dormer's hand in 1558, lavishing jewels and gifts on Mary's courtiers. He remained committed to the match after Mary's death, although he knew that Elizabeth I would not favour her predecessor's servants any more than her faith. The wedding took place on 29 December 1558 and was the only high-ranking union between English and Spanish courtiers to result from the brief reign of Philip II in England.

The count of Feria left England in May 1559 and Jane followed in July, both taking a number of Catholic nobles and clergy with them. It was the beginning of a lifelong commitment to English and Irish Catholic exiles. They stayed briefly in the Low Countries, where she gave birth to their son Lorenzo on 28 September 1559. They departed in spring 1560, making a spectacular and princely progress through the Low Countries and France (where they met Mary Stewart) to Spain, where the monarchs officially welcomed them. Jane's grandmother, Lady Dormer, meanwhile established herself in Louvain, where her home became an important base for Elizabethan Catholic exiles. Once in Spain, the Feria household acted as a magnet for the English, Irish, and Scottish communities, whom they protected and aided. They devoted substantial personal resources to the endeavour, and were generous in hospitality and almsgiving. Feria put their political and military proposals at court, and promoted their suits for offices and pensions. Both spouses were ardent supporters of the Jesuits, whom Feria had tried to introduce into England in the 1550s, and were instrumental in helping to set up the Jesuit training colleges that were to change the face of English Catholicism. Owing to his long sojourn in England and the privileged information and contacts provided by his wife's kin, Feria became the most prominent adviser on English matters at the Spanish court. As a result, the activities of the Feria household were closely observed and discussed throughout Europe, especially by those eager to fathom Philip II's policy towards England.

It was the death in 1571 of both her husband (on 7 September) and her formidable grandmother that brought Jane, now duchess of Feria, into the limelight and made her the main object of attention for the increasingly divided Elizabethan exile community. Feria left her in a position of power as tutor to their sole surviving son and in control of his extensive estates during Lorenzo's minority. Philip II's favour to the family remained unshaken, and this enhanced her value within the Spanish court, where she was trusted to provide good information on Queen Elizabeth and was recognized as a leader of the exiles. Her importance at this juncture was increased by circumstance: clashes between Elizabeth and Philip II, reinforced by immense pressure from the papacy, persuaded the king on two occasions in 1570 and 1571 of the need for an aggressive campaign against England. But he encountered strong opposition from his advisers in the Low Countries and especially from the governor, the duke of Alba, who persuaded Philip II to pull back from the brink of war. Realizing the importance of neutralizing the opposition of the Low Countries, some English exiles petitioned Philip II to send Jane there. They belonged to the group most closely associated with Rome which had wanted an aggressive policy towards England since 1559. Some hoped she might even replace Alba as governor of the Low Countries. Philip II did not approve the plan. He wanted to come to an accord with Elizabeth, and for a time in 1576 he even ejected the exiles from the Low Countries. Yet he remained sympathetic and responsive to the petitions Jane and her longtime associate Sir Francis Englefield made for money and help for the exiles, and this made her a significant player in the patronage network of the Spanish court.

Although she had a firm character and above average intelligence, the duchess of Feria found herself at the centre of political intrigues whose complexity and international dimensions often eluded her. She remained closely associated with the 'Roman' exile contingent despite being approached by other individuals and factions, and it was they who most benefited from her regular information from England and Ireland. Throughout the 1570s Gregory XIII worked hard to secure Philip II's backing for an attack against Elizabeth as proposed by the adventurers Thomas Stucley and James fitz Maurice, and he encouraged his nuncios in Spain to make use of Jane's influence. She too approved these plans and tried to advance them by all means possible. In 1578 she even sold two statues of the Virgin, which had been rescued from St Paul's, to help them purchase arms and munitions. The papal nuncio believed, wrongly, that she had a secret understanding with her uncle Sir Henry Sidney for him to

defect from his command of Elizabeth's troops in Ireland and help fitz Maurice's invasion in 1579. A year later the remnants of the invasion force were trapped at Smerwick, surrounded by loyal and implacable Elizabethan troops. Jane forwarded their request for help to Philip II. This close association with papal policy towards England and the additional pressure she brought to bear on the king did not always endear her to the Spanish court, nor was her support of the various plots linked to Mary Stewart always approved of. While she remained a respected figure, she exerted no real influence over the king's policy. Nevertheless, to Elizabeth and her council she always appeared dangerous.

Significantly, we hear little of Jane in connection with the Armada campaign (1585–8). Her political role had been reduced since 1579, when Sir Francis Englefield settled in Spain and took over the business relating to patronage and pensions for the exiles. Shortly afterwards William Allen established strong, if not unchallenged, leadership over the exiles. Once Philip II decided to act against Elizabeth after 1585, the exiles had a direct line to the king and council without need for her intervention. But as soon as they realized that Philip II was wavering from his commitment to fight Elizabeth in 1590, the exiles once again turned their attention to the duchess of Feria, particularly because Lorenzo had no desire to play the Englishman in Philip's court or take up his parents' role in this respect. In the 1590s, her prominence reasserted, she became involved with such shady characters as Francis Dacre, whose dubious activities at the Spanish court discredited her for a time. Her sister Anne, Lady Hungerford, who had taken refuge in the Low Countries in 1571, also came under the baneful influence of one of the many factions among the exiles, and notably of the adventurer Thomas Morgan. In 1593, and at their instigation, Anne took up the campaign to persuade Philip II to send Jane to the Low Countries so that she might lead the exile community and threaten Elizabeth. Jane was enthusiastic, failing to appreciate that this scheme was primarily intended to reduce the influence of her friends and collaborators Englefield and Allen, and to agitate for an aggressive policy towards England which would not meet with approval at the Spanish court. The duke of Feria successfully countered these proposals. Although by 1593 he too was under the influence of an English exile, Thomas Fitzherbert, Feria was a senior official of Philip II whose primary aim was not to risk the honour or finances of his house or threaten its future by undermining his own career. He believed the plan would be disastrous for his mother, who would become the butt of vicious attacks by dissident exile factions, as Allen and Englefield had been. He doubted whether it would have a significant impact on Elizabeth and was aware that the office would be a serious drain on the family's resources. He dismissed as shady intriguers those who had advanced the proposal, not sparing his aunt Lady Hungerford. The king and council of state agreed with him. Lady Hungerford nevertheless continued for over two years to argue for Jane's appointment, and the duchess remained eager to take it up. Her son opposed it with even greater force, and as a result their relations were tense and sour for years.

This disappointment did not deter Jane from making further attempts to influence Philip II's English policy, and she continued to act on behalf of the exiles. In 1596 she presented the king with a document which Persons, Englefield, and the Jesuit Joseph Creswell also signed, requesting that Philip II should make a public declaration to the effect that his eldest daughter, Isabel, was the rightful claimant to the throne of England. In a separate document that year, largely drawn up by Persons, the king was also urged to set up a special mixed council for English affairs in the Low Countries; but significantly there was no suggestion that Jane should be there. Unwilling to exacerbate relations with England while his forces were stretched by the wars against the Dutch and French, Philip II rejected both requests. Thereafter Jane continued with her pious benefactions and good works towards the exiles, but was either less active or more circumspect in political matters. Even after the death of Allen and Englefield, it was evident that she would not be able to take their place at the helm of the exile community. Evidence remains of further, fitful activity: in 1600, for example, she wrote to James VI urging him to embrace Catholicism. It was James's accession to the English throne in 1603 that once again focused attention on her, but now as the shining symbol of the Anglo-Spanish amity that both courts were eager to re-establish. The papacy, as ever, missed no chances. In 1603–4 vague plans were hatched in Rome to send her as a lady-in-waiting to Queen Anne, and the question was raised by Lord Howard of Effingham on behalf of the queen when he visited Spain in May 1605. The duke of Feria vetoed the plan, believing that it would put his mother in an invidious position, since her presence at the English court would nurture the wildest expectations from the Catholics, and he did not believe that Philip III would help them. Although she outlived her son by five years, her failing health and the new alliance with England combined to keep her out of major international politics in the years before her death on 13 January 1612. She was buried on 26 January at the monastery of Santa Clara at Zafra.

M. J. RODRIGUEZ-SALGADO

Sources state papers, letters, etc., Archivo General de Simancas · *CSP for.*, 1558–74 · *CSP dom.*, 1547–1613 · H. Clifford, *The life of Jane Dormer, duchess of Feria*, ed. J. Stevenson (1887) · A. J. Loomie, *The Spanish Elizabethans* (1963) · M. Fernández Álvarez, *Tres embajadores de Felipe II en Inglaterra* (Madrid, 1951) · E. García Hernán, *Irlanda y el rey prudente* (Madrid, 2000) · *Patris Petri de Ribadeneira*, 2 vols. (Madrid, 1920–23) · 'The count of Feria's dispatch to Philip II of 14th November 1558', ed. M. J. Rodríguez-Salgado and S. Adams, *Camden miscellany, XXVIII*, CS, 4th ser., 29 (1984)
Archives Archivio Vaticano, Vatican City · Warks. CRO, original and copy documents | Secretaria de Estado Legajo, Archivo General de Simancas
Likenesses A. Sánchez-Coello, oils, c.1563, Rousham House, Oxfordshire · A. Mor, portrait

Suckling [*formerly* Fox], **Alfred Inigo** (1796–1856), antiquary, born on 31 January 1796, was the only son of Alexander Fox of Norwich and his wife, Anna Maria (*d.* 1848),

daughter of Robert Suckling of Woodton, Norfolk, and his wife, Susannah Webb, a descendant of Inigo Jones. The Suckling family, which included the poet Sir John Suckling and Nelson's uncle Maurice Suckling, had owned the Woodton-cum-Langhall estate since the fourteenth century and another at Barsham, Suffolk, since 1627. Alfred Inigo Fox matriculated at Pembroke College, Cambridge, in May 1814 and graduated LLB in 1824. On 31 January 1816 he married Lucia Clementina, eldest daughter of Samuel Clarke of Bergh Apton, Norfolk; they had ten children. When Robert Suckling's son Maurice William died without children on 1 December 1820, Alfred Inigo took the surname and arms of Suckling and succeeded to the estates. He was ordained at Norwich on 15 October 1820, but was unbeneficed until he took the family living of Barsham on 10 July 1839; he then held it until his death.

As his manuscript collections show, Suckling's antiquarian pursuits took him around East Anglia and into France. Apart from publishing selections from his famous poet forebear, with a biography in 1836, he devoted his energies to Suffolk and Essex topography. A competent topographical artist, as the originals in his manuscripts show, he drew most of the illustrations for his books, and many of his drawings were engraved on steel by Orlando Jewitt. His *Memorials of … Essex* first appeared, edited by the London publisher John Weale, in the latter's *Quarterly Papers on Architecture* for 1845. Suckling's monumental *History and Antiquities of Suffolk* began with a volume treating the hundreds of Wangford, and Lothingland and Mutford in 1846, over which he fell out with Weale. The second (1848) took readers no further than Leiston in Blything; it was published by the author for subscribers. It is said that the stock of the first volume was lost by fire; this would account for its being far rarer than the second. Had the project been completed, Suffolk would have had the worthy published history it still lacks.

Suckling died on 3 May 1856 at 40 Belmont Road, St Helier, Jersey. He was buried at St Helier.   J. M. BLATCHLY

Sources Burke, *Gen. GB* (1894) · Venn, *Alum. Cant.* · *Norfolk Chronicle* (10 May 1856) · *Norwich Mercury* (10 May 1856), 4 · *ILN* (17 May 1856) · *N&Q*, 4th ser., 2 (1868), 512 · *N&Q*, 4th ser., 8 (1871), 522 · D. Hipwell, *N&Q*, 8th ser., 12 (1897), 6 · *DNB*
Archives BL, antiquarian and heraldic collections, Add. MSS 18476–18491

Suckling, Sir John (*bap.* 1569, *d.* 1627). *See under* Suckling, Sir John (*bap.* 1609, *d.* 1641?).

Suckling, Sir John (*bap.* 1609, *d.* 1641?), poet, was born in his father's house, Goodfathers, in Whitton, Twickenham, Middlesex; and baptized at St Mary the Virgin, Twickenham, on 10 February 1609, the second child and elder son of the six children of **Sir John Suckling** (*bap.* 1569, *d.* 1627), secretary of state, and his first wife, Martha (1578–1613), daughter of Thomas Cranfield, London merchant, and his first wife, also named Martha.

Descended from ancestors resident in Norfolk and Suffolk for at least four centuries, the family claimed descent from Thomas Esthawe, the socling—presumably a man who held his lands by socage—who was 'admitted to certain copyholds of Langhall and Woodton', Norfolk, in

Sir John Suckling (*bap.* 1609, *d.* 1641?), by Sir Anthony Van Dyck, *c.*1637–8

1348. 'Suckling' became the family surname with the poet's great-grandfather, Richard, who was sheriff of Norwich, as was his grandfather Robert (1564), who was also mayor (1572) and MP (1571, 1586). The poet's uncle Edmund was dean of Norwich from 1614 to 1628. His father, the youngest of six sons, was at Gray's Inn and served five terms as MP (1601, 1614, 1623, 1625, and 1626). By 1602 he was secretary to the lord treasurer, became receiver of fines on alienations in 1604, was knighted in 1616, and in 1619 was appointed master of requests (by purchase). A serious competitor for the chancellorship of the exchequer in 1621, he became secretary of state in March 1622 and in August was appointed comptroller of the king's household (in consideration of £7000), an office he held until his death.

The poet's mother, Martha, was the sister of Lionel Cranfield, created earl of Middlesex in 1622 and, until his unjustified impeachment in 1624, lord treasurer of England. Aubrey heard that Suckling's 'witt came by the mother' (*Brief Lives*, 287), but it is doubtful that his father 'was but a dull fellow': his sonnet in *Coryats Crudities*

(1611)—to which Lionel Cranfield also contributed—is competent and apt for the context. Martha, the eldest child (*b.* 1605), remained on closer terms with the poet than his younger brother and sisters did, perhaps partly because their mother died when he was but four and a half. In March 1616 his father married Jane Hawkins (*née* Reve or Reeve), widow of Charles Hawkins, who would carry into the family of her third husband, Sir Edwyn Rich, knight, of Mulbarton, Norfolk, the estate of Roos Hall, Beccles, Suffolk, purchased in 1613, which was enfeoffed to her by pre-marriage contract and not purchased in reversion by the poet. With her also went the house in Dorset Court, Fleet Street, the leasing of which had been left to the poet.

Education, military service, and travel abroad, 1623–1632
Suckling's learning was not inconsiderable for a courtier, but was evidently not acquired systematically or in great earnest. Aubrey wondered whether Suckling had attended Westminster School, but the records are silent. On 2 July 1623 he matriculated at Trinity College, Cambridge, where he 'studied three or four yeares', Aubrey says, on the authority of his chief informant, Suckling's close friend Sir William Davenant. Like many other gentlemen, he seems not to have taken a degree. Admitted to Gray's Inn on 23 February 1627, he left almost at once—his father died on 27 March—and did not return, although he briefly studied mathematics and possibly fortifications at Leiden University, where he was admitted on 26 February 1630 and remained until May.

Of his earlier experience abroad Aubrey says that 'by 18 Suckling had well travelled France and Italie, and part of Germany, and … Spaine', which is otherwise undocumented. Certainly he saw military and hazardous diplomatic service on the continent more than once after 18 May 1627, when Edward, Lord Conway, sent him for cavalry service in the duke of Buckingham's expedition to the Île de Ré (for which the poet Robert Herrick was a chaplain). The expedition was a disaster with half the men lost, the last survivors leaving on 8 November. Two years later Suckling is listed among those who 'bore armes and trayled pikes at the Siege of the Busse' (that is, Den Bosch), which fell on 7 September 1629 (H. Hexham, *A Historicall Relation of the Famous Siege of the Busse*, 1630, sig. C6r); but he must have returned to England afterwards, because on 22 October he was licensed to proceed to the Low Countries to join Lord Wimbledon's regiment in the Dutch service. On the 30th he wrote his earliest surviving holograph letter at Gravesend, which dates his departure for 'those countryes which I am now to visit'. The four English regiments were discharged in November, and Suckling's wholly jocular letter of the 18th from Leiden (*Works*, vol. 1, letter no. 9) makes no reference to military action. On 5 May 1630 he wrote from Brussels that he had 'lately come out of a country' where most of the people 'would doe what Judas did for half the Money', and had arrived in one so poor that, if there were a Judas ready, 'yet would there want a man to furnish out the 30 peices of silver' (ibid., vol. 1, no. 11)—assertions not to be taken as derision in earnest: in these epistolary characters, the national stereotypes are *données* of the satirical genre.

By September 1630 Suckling was back in England and was knighted at Theobalds on the 19th. From early October 1631 until spring 1632 he accompanied Sir Henry Vane, Charles I's ambassador to Gustavus Adolphus, in Germany, whence he sent letters (nos. 5, 12–18) describing his travels and the progress of what became the Thirty Years' War (1618–48). He was undoubtedly at times in danger, but that he had 'run the hazard of three battels, five sieges, and as many skirmishes' seems a creative figment in David Lloyd's secular hagiography (Lloyd, 159). Leaving Frankfurt in 1632 with Vane's dispatch to the king, Suckling wrote briefly to Vane on his landing at Dover and in London had a private audience with the king. His report to Vane (2 May) blends matters of international state with court machinations, and notes of Gustavus Adolphus that if his successes continue 'wee shall heere feare him as too great or hee himself will bee more difficult. If hee bee lesse successfull, wee shall not conclude with him, as too weake' (*Works*, vol. 1, no. 19).

Suckling's relations with the immediate family of his uncle, Lionel Cranfield, first earl of Middlesex, were close and lifelong; in effect, they were his family. His letter from Gravesend identifies his first cousin Mary Cranfield (1610–1635) as probably his first love, and several of his printed letters to anonymous recipients were probably written to her. (Years later her younger half-sister Frances claimed to be 'the mistress and goddess in his poems', his 'Aglaura', but that was almost certainly one Mary Bulkeley. The scanty evidence outside Suckling's letters suggests that she was a young woman of uncommon abilities and charm, and as late as 1640 'Lord Sheffield said that he and his wife would prefer not to stay with Middlesex since Elizabeth could not bear the thought of the house without her sister' (Prestwich, 509). Mary Cranfield was apparently one of only two women to whom Suckling was able to remain devoted for any length of time.

Suckling at court, 1632–1637 Back in London, Suckling embarked upon a seven-year course of dedicated prodigality.

> He returned to England an extraordinary accomplished Gent., grew famous at Court for his readie sparkling witt, which was envyed, and he was … the Bull that was bayted. He was incomparably readie at repartying, and his Witt most sparkling when most sett-upon and provoked. (*Brief Lives*, 287)

His father's will withheld his inheritance—most of his father's properties in Suffolk, Lincoln, Middlesex, and London—until he was twenty-five (1634), but he nimbly maintained his extravagance by selling parts of his patrimony, borrowing, and gambling. 'He was the greatest gallant of his time', Aubrey wrote, 'and the greatest Gamester, both for Bowling and Cards, so that no shop-keeper would trust him for 6d.': one day he might be worth £200, the next half so much or 'sometimes *minus nihilo*'. He was also 'one of the best Bowlers of his time'; and he 'played at cards rarely well, and did use to practise by himselfe a-bed, and there studied how the best way of managing the cards could be'. He 'sent his Cards to all Gameing places in the countrey, which were marked with private markes of his; he gott twenty thousand pounds by this way' (*Brief Lives*, 287). He also 'invented the game of cribbidge', as all the circumstantial evidence affirms and none contradicts.

About October 1633 Suckling sought to marry a Derbyshire heiress: Anne, daughter of Sir Henry Willoughby, bt. Despite the king's support, father and daughter were opposed, and his efforts came to nothing then and worse a year later when he renewed them, his appetite whetted by gaming losses. A great hulking competitor, Sir John Digby, stopped his coach near Risley and, when Suckling refused to sign a disavowal of interest in her, 'falls upon him with a Cudgel, which being a yard long, he beat out upon him almost to an handfull, he never offering to draw his Sword' (*Earl of Strafforde's Letters and Dispatches*, 1.336–7). The better part of valour has something to commend it in such cases: Suckling was 'but a slight timberd man, and of midling stature; Sir John Digby was a proper person of great strength, and courage answerable, and yielded to be the best swordsman of his time' (*Brief Lives*, 288). Later that year Suckling and his associates assaulted Digby and his party outside the Blackfriars Theatre but ran off after one of Suckling's men was killed. 'Twas pitty', wrote Aubrey, 'that this accident brought the blemish of Cowardise to such an ingeniose young Sparke. Sir J. D. was such a Hero that there were very few but he would have served in like manner.' He adds that after this ''twas strange to see the envie and ill-nature of people to … deject one in disgrace; inhumane as well as un-christian' at an entertainment where the hostess, Lady Moray, showed a better nature:

> seeing Sir John out of Countenance, for whose worth she alwaies had a respect: 'Well', sayd shee, 'I am a merry wench, and will never forsake an old friend in disgrace, so come, sitt downe by me, Sir John' (said she), and seated him on her right hand, and countenanced him. This raised Sir John's dejected spirites that he threw his Reparties about the table with so much sparklingness and gentilenes of witt, to the admiration of them all. (*Brief Lives*, 288)

In 1635 Suckling sold the estate of Barsham, Suffolk, to his uncle Charles, but in September won £2000 from Randall MacDonnell, Viscount Dunluce, at ninepins played at Tunbridge Wells. And at an unspecified time he characteristically:

> made a magnificent entertainment in London for a great number of Ladies of Quality, all beauties and young, which cost him many hundreds of pounds, where were all the rarities that this part of the world could afford, and the last service of all was Silk Stockings and Garters, and … Gloves. (*Brief Lives*, 289)

He somehow found time also to be a family man. He helped his cousin, Martha, Lady Carey, arrange an advantageous marriage for her daughter Anne; and he firmly supported his sister Martha in her unfortunate first marriage—in 1635, to Sir George Southcot, twice her age and four times widowed. The marriage was already in trouble by 9 September 1635, when her brother gave marital advice to Sir George in the form of a falconry lesson:

Woman is a Hawk upon her wings: and if she be handsome, she is the more subject to go out at check … The Lure to which all stoop in this world, is either garnisht with pleasure or profit, and when you cannot throw her the one, you must be content to shew out the other.   (*Works*, vol. 1, no. 23)

When Sir George hanged himself on 9 October 1639, Suckling wrote to Martha that he 'would not have you so much as enquire whether it were with his garters or his Cloakbag strings, nor ingage your self to fresh sighs by hearing new relations'; and, thinking of the political storm already in progress, he concluded:

I assure you Christianity highly governs me in the minute in which I do not wish with all my heart that all the discontents in his Majesties three Kingdoms would find out this very way of satisfying themselves and the world.   (ibid., vol. 1, no. 44)

Suckling the writer First known as a gallant and gamester, Suckling became famous also as a writer. He somehow found time to write much, and often well, in a range of genres, his *œuvre* extending to seventy-eight poems (*c*.1624–1641); four plays, *The Sad One* (*c*.1632, unfinished), *Aglaura* (1637, rev. 1638), *The Goblins* (1638–1641), and *Brennoralt* (late 1639?); *An Account of Religion by Reason* (1637); several political tracts; and over fifty surviving letters, a few of literary genre and most of literary quality. His earliest known writings are religious poems written probably about 1624, when he was fifteen: St Thomas figures in two of these, and the concern with faith and doubt anticipates *An Account of Religion*.

The years 1637 and 1638 were Suckling's literary *anni mirabiles*. In 1637 he wrote the tragedy *Aglaura*, the *Account of Religion*, and 'The Wits' ('A Sessions of the Poets' in *Fragmenta aurea*, 1646), with its witty but also probing fictional contest between Davenant, Thomas Carew, Ben Jonson, and others; the queen is present, and Apollo the god of poetry himself is judge. No one has better expressed Suckling's character than himself in this poem in a genre of his own invention—the trial for the bays—imitated by many, including Dryden in his *Essay of Dramatic Poesy*.

Suckling next was call'd, but did not appear,
And strait one whisperd Apollo in's ear,
That of all men living he cared not for't,
He loved not the Muses so well as his sport;
And prized black eyes, or a lucky hit
At bowls, above all the Trophies of Wit.
('A sessions of the Poets', 73–8)

While 'The Wits' was being sung to the king on a hunting expedition to the New Forest in August 1637, only 60 miles away Suckling was writing his *Account of Religion* in Bath, where he had 'had a Cart-load of Bookes carried downe … 'Twas as pleasant a journey as ever men had; in the height of a long Peace and luxury, and in the Venison Season' (*Brief Lives*, 289)—the last such retreat for Suckling and many another, after 1638.

Suckling's other major poem, in the novel genre of rustic epithalamion, is 'A Ballade upon a Wedding' ('I tell thee *Dick*, where I have been'), written probably for the marriage of John, Lord Lovelace, and Lady Anne Wentworth on 11 July 1638. In this, a fashionable town wedding is described by a cottage rustic in country terms and perspective but also with sensitivity, perceptiveness, and a keen levelling humour, a sustained balancing act between dramatis personae and poet especially deft in conclusion: what the bride and groom did at bedtime:

who can tell?
But I beleeve it was no more
Than thou and I have done before
with *Bridget*, and with *Nell*.

In winter 1637–8 Suckling wrote commendatory poems for Davenant's *Madagascar* (1638) and for *Romulus and Tarquin* (2nd edn, 1638), the translation by Henry Carey, Lord Leppington, of a work by Malvezzi; published his *Aglaura*; and had dedicated to him Thomas Nabbes's comedy *Covent Garden* and Wye Saltonstall's translation of Ovid's *De Ponto. Aglaura* was staged at court and, shortly before 7 February 1638, at Blackfriars Theatre 'with much Applause'; 'Sutlin's Play cost three or four hundred pounds setting out, eight or ten Suits of new Cloaths he gave the Players; an unheard of Prodigality' (*Earl of Strafforde's Letters and Dispatches*, 2.150). His production featured innovations not only in costume but also in scenery, previously seen only in masques; thus began a stage tradition persisting through to the present day. On 3 April it was produced before the king and queen in the Cockpit Theatre with a new fifth act making it a tragicomedy, possibly at the king's suggestion. The whole, with all prologues and epilogues and both fifth acts, was printed at Suckling's expense 'to present to the quality' when it was 'acted at Court'. The lavish folio format naturally excited satirical derision, in three lampoons 'Upon *Aglaura* in Folio', Richard Brome's comparing the text with its wide margins to a child in the Great Bed of Ware.

Suckling's casually artful discourse in his writings must have been a function of his conversation as 'natural, easy Suckling' in life, in Millamant's immortal phrase in Congreve's *Way of the World* (IV.iv). He was successful as a lyric poet because of his gifts of perception and expression, and because of his smooth facility in verse. He wrote short lyrics not only because they were the classical form of Caroline court verse but also because they come more easily in a life lived to the hilt and at speed than do works of reflection and sustained effort. Suckling has been called a 'Son of Ben', which he was not. He is nearer Donne and Shakespeare. But his verse and dramatic dialogue are *sui generis*, virtual court and country conversation. Scenes begin *in medias res* and so do poems, in mid-reflection or in immediate response ('What noe more favours, not a Ribbon more?'). Most of the poems are quasi-dramatic, whether they are in couplets or in lyric stanzas; but some have the mark of meditation, often of an amorous kind:

That none beguiled be by times quick flowing
Lovers have in their heart a clock still going.
('Loves Clock')

His commendatory poems abound in sociability and wit. Then as now the quintessentially characteristic 'Constant Lover' ('Out upon it, I have lov'd / Three whole days together') and 'Why so pale and wan, fond lover?' were favourites of all who read and the many who copied them.

Years of the bishops' wars, 1638–1640 Suckling's thought and writing in 1637–8 show what he might have done if he had had the years and leisure to continue maturing, and England were in a condition to make this possible. On 20 November 1638 he joined Thomas Carew as a gentleman of the privy chamber extraordinary, but he had little time to enjoy the royal intimacies because discontents were growing apace in Scotland and Charles favoured a military expedition to the north. From 1638 he was back in the saddle again, for most of the rest of his life. 'Attached to the court, and to the King himself, with a romantic loyalty surprising in a sceptic' (Bruce, 311), he was one of the first to volunteer and 'raysed a Troope of 100 very handsome young proper men, whom he clad in white doublets and scarlett breeches, and scarlett Coates, hatts, and feathers, well horsed, and armed. They say 'twas one of the finest sights in those days' (*Brief Lives*, 289), with the cost of men and equipment said to be £12,000 (Lloyd, 159)—another ready target for lampooning, which came rapidly in 'Upon Sir John Suckling's Hundred Horse' ('I tell thee *Jack* thou'st given the King'), which also burlesques Suckling's 'Ballade upon a Wedding'.

In a letter to the earl of Middlesex written on 6 June at the camp west of Berwick (no. 40), Suckling describes in detail the fiasco of a battle not fought between the English and Scottish armies on 3 June near Kelso, about which additional lampoons exaggerated his personal part in the general retreat ordered by the general of the horse, the earl of Holland. The treaty of Berwick was signed on 18 June. About three months later Suckling wrote to the earl of Middlesex from London that he might stop at Milcote in Warwickshire to see him on his way to Wales 'to kisse Mrs Buckleys hands' (30 Sept 1639, *Works*, vol. 1, no. 43)—his sole use of the surname of his second and last love, his 'Aglaura' and 'Dear[est] Princess' (of letters 25–35), who was evidently Mary Bulkeley, of Baron Hill, Beaumaris, Anglesey. Suckling's acquaintance with her probably began no later than 1635, and he very likely kissed her hands for the last time on that visit, because she married a local squire not long after.

In early 1640 the Scottish covenanters' increasing assertiveness prompted the king to raise 40,000 men for another expedition to the north, and Suckling was commissioned captain of a troop of Carabiniers. On 30 April he was elected MP for Bramber, Sussex, in a by-election said by a complainant to have been won by 'undue means' (*Fourth Report*, HMC, House of Lords MSS, 25); no matter, because Charles dissolved parliament on 5 May. On the day Charles's army marched out of London, 20 August, the Scots crossed the Tweed at Coldstream and 'pushed steadily on' (Gardiner, 9.189). On the 28th Suckling was in the fight at Newburn Ford, near Newcastle, which rendered the second bishops' war as decisive a failure as the first for the king's men. In a credible Scottish report:

> our troups … did mak good, not onlie there first attempt, bot also put Schir Johne Suckling bak with his horss troups, being the prime of all England (whiche ar oppositis) to the retreat, took sum of his horssis, whereof one (being most excelent) was presentit to our Generall.

This was Sir Alexander Leslie, who had personally led the Scottish cavalry ('Sure newis from Newcastell'; *Works*, 1.li). Other reports said that Suckling's coach was captured, with £300 and clothing, and used by Leslie; that he was not at the place of battle; and that he had been killed. The general retreat began abruptly when 'the raw troops, never having before seen a gun fired in anger' and 'a shot struck to the ground some of the defenders of the nearest work … threw down their arms and fled' (Gardiner, 9.194).

Shortly after the opening of the Long Parliament (3 November) Suckling wrote *To Mr. Henry German* [Jermyn], *in the beginning of Parliament, 1640*, in which he advised the king on how to deal with the widespread popular disquiet, most notably by giving the people what they sought and more. From this time his direct service to the king was constant until his flight to France. In this period he incurred a debt of £50 and was owed a gaming debt of £100 by George Goring, colonel of the 1st brigade in the second bishops' war. He found time, too, to write a celebratory new year's (1641) poem to the king ('May no ill vapours cloud the skie'), 'almost the last outburst of Cavalier gaiety' (Bruce, 311); his very last poem was an informal epithalamion 'On my Lord Brohalls Wedding' (27 January 1641).

Last months, 1641 Suckling's fate was sealed by his participation in the second army plot, the bolder of two plots to bring the army to the aid of the king, though it remains uncertain just how much 'plot' there was and how much was a rhetorical construction by parliamentarians, especially Pym, as Clarendon thought, to force the king to sign the bill of attainder against the earl of Strafford—which he finally did on 10 May, resulting in the earl's beheading on the 12th. By March 1641 two groups were active on the king's side, the first including several MPs who were also army officers. The principals in the second group were Suckling, Goring, and Jermyn, whose purpose was first to secure command of the army. What the House of Commons called justice in seeking the death of Strafford probably 'inclined Charles to look to the army as a weapon which he might lawfully wield in order to secure Strafford as well as himself from irregular violence' (Gardiner, 9.315). On 29 March representatives of both groups met in Henry Percy's lodgings in Whitehall to discuss consolidating. Suckling was not admitted in spite of the pleading of Goring and Jermyn, and the attempt to combine failed through disagreement over Suckling's participation and, more importantly, over the command of the army. The king refused to entertain the proposals of either group.

The beginning of the end for Suckling came with Charles's conviction that Strafford could be saved only by force, for which Suckling and Captain Billingsley were raising the necessary troops. On Monday 3 May Suckling was called before a House of Commons committee to explain his recruiting, and his bringing sixty armed men to the White Horse tavern in Bread Street where they stayed 'all night, and are to meete againe this night'

(More's diary, BL, Harley MS 477, fols. 26*v*–27*r*). Arthur Brett wrote to the earl of Middlesex on 8 May that:

> his answeare was, that hee hadd undertaken the profession of a shouldier and that his fortunes call'd him to itt; having gott Leave from his Majesty to rayse a Regiment, hee was For Portiugale; receaveing commicions from the Embassador whereupon hee was dismist; nottwithstanding they found him faulty in his answeare, yett tooke noe notice,

but they quickly ascertained from the ambassador that there was no such project. 'The next morning being Thursday, hee was againe to appeare, Butt Harry Pearcye, Harry Jermaine William Davenant and him selfe all rann away. Which augeres they weare the wise and active agents in this treacherous imployment' (*Fourth Report*, HMC, Cranfield papers, 295). Brett's tone is disapproving, and this is the last mention of Suckling in the Cranfield papers. Suckling and Jermyn escaped to Portsmouth, where Goring was in command, and sailed for Dieppe in the royal pinnace *Roebuck* on 6 May.

When, how, and where Suckling died is uncertain. Thomas May wrote that on 6 May the conspirators fled to France, 'where *Suckling* not long after dyed' (T. May, *History of the Parliament of England*, 1647, sig. P2r); and in 1664 his family gave the date of his death as 7 May. The main accounts of his death are Alexander Pope's, William Oldys's (a variant of Pope's), and Aubrey's. According to Pope, in the night when Suckling reached Calais his servant drove a nail up into one of his boots before absconding with his money and papers; booted in haste and oblivious of pain, Suckling caught him 'two or three posts off', but 'the wound was so bad and so much inflamed that it flung him into a violent fever which ended his life in a very few days' (Spence, 1.190–91).

Suckling, however, reached Paris alive on 14 May, and the countess of Leicester wrote to the earl, probably before 18 June, that 'From Sukling we receave many visitts, who is good companie but much abaited in his mirthe' (*De L'Isle and Dudley MSS*, 403; Parker, 317)—the last mention of Suckling as alive in Paris. Henry Percy's treatment, when he finally arrived on 22 July, is probably typical of Suckling's and Jermyn's at about the same time: Percy 'arrived here … very weake and indisposed', and was taken in by the countess of Leicester,

> that he might be the better attended in his sicknes, but this morning [23 July] one comming from my Lord [the earl] … who landed yesterday at Diepe, brought letters by which his Lordship desires my lady not to receive him into her house, so that now he changes his lodging againe. (M. Battière from Paris, PRO, SP 78/111, fol. 63)

Suckling was possibly alive at that date, on which Sir Francis Windebank also wrote from Paris, to his son Thomas, to say that the House of Commons was stopping pensions due him, Jermyn, and Suckling (PRO, SP 16/482, no. 73; *CSP dom.*, 1641–3, 58).

An Elegie upon the Death of the Renowned Sir John Sutlin, written in February 1642 or earlier (*Catalogue of the Pamphlets*, 1.85), argues that Suckling was dead by early 1642 at the latest. According to Aubrey:

> after sometime, being come to the bottome of his Found, reflecting on the miserable and despicable condition he should be reduced to, having nothing left to maintaine him, he (having a convenience for that purpose, lyeing at an apothecarie's house in Paris) tooke poyson, which killed him miserably with vomiting. He was buryed in the Protestants Churchyard. (*Brief Lives*, 290)

The Revd Alfred Suckling wrote that 'family tradition confirms … [this] most revolting narration' (*Selections*, 48). The exact site of his burial is unknown. Suckling's name continued to be used in parliamentary proceedings, and *in absentia* he, Jermyn, and Percy were found guilty of high treason by a Commons committee on 13 August; but such notices constitute no evidence that Suckling was still alive.

The only authenticated original likeness is the full-length portrait by Sir Anthony Van Dyck painted probably in 1637–8, oil on canvas, 84¼ inches by 50⅜ (2.13 metres x 1.28), not signed or dated; but the attribution dates from the mid-seventeenth century and is generally accepted by art historians. Aubrey reports this as hanging at Lady Southcot's in Bishopsgate Street, and he may owe his description of Suckling to it:

> He was of middle stature and slight strength, brisque round eie, reddish fac't and red nose (ill-liver), his head not very big, his hayre a kind of sand colour, his beard turned-up naturally, so that he had a briske and gracefull looke. (*Brief Lives*, 289)

There is little ruddiness in the portrait, whether suppressed by Van Dyck or moralistically added by Aubrey. The portrait passed from Lady Southcot to her niece Anne Davis and, through her marriage to Sir Thomas Lee, first baronet, came into the possession of the Lee family of Hartwell, near Aylesbury, Buckinghamshire, from whom it was purchased by Henry Clay Frick for what is now the Frick Collection in New York city.

Significant details are the poet's holding a Shakespeare Folio open to *Hamlet*, and the motto on a rock he leans against, 'NE TE QUAESIVERIS EXTRA' ('seek not outside thyself'; Persius, *Satires*, i.7), which would seem to express his characteristic attitude of indifference to 'Apollo' and the critics (as in 'The Wits'), and his valuing the kind of independent judgement he exercises in his *Account of Religion*. The motto may also express Suckling's preference for Shakespeare the independent over the ancients and their imitators (such as Ben Jonson), his own indebtedness to Shakespeare in *Aglaura*, and even his 'tenderness towards his own Aglaura, Mary Bulkeley'.

Status and reputation Suckling made his mark as a poet, playwright, and belletrist, but he was a writer mainly by avocation, and by second nature. He was first and last a wit and a courtier to Charles I, being occupied mainly as a gentleman officer, socio-political observer, gamester, amorist, and marital fortune seeker—often impetuously and not always successfully. Rough times ended his life prematurely: heir at eighteen and prodigal as soon, he died at thirty-two in Paris, penniless and probably a suicide; the Commons judged him a traitor to parliament, to royalists he was a martyr before the king. His works circulated widely in manuscript during his lifetime and, published posthumously by Humphrey Mosely, were bought in large numbers and read with eagerness and admiration during the interregnum and after. Editions of *Fragmenta aurea*, the best and most important collection, were published in 1646, 1648, and 1658; and *The Last Remains of Sir John Suckling* appeared in 1659. His stature as a poet—and literary *arbiter deliciarum*—was at its highest during the Restoration, when the Hon. Edward Howard, sharing Dryden's high estimation, wrote that:

> Of all the Pens of the Ancients, I judge that of *Petronius Arbiter* to be in all kindes the most polite and ingenious, it being so familiarly applicable to the Natures and converse of men, … wherefore I … allow him their best general Writer, or Essayist. And with us, I know of none so near his parallel as the late *Sir John Suckling*, whose wit was every way at his command, proper and useful in Verse and Prose, equally gentile and pleasant: And I believe he has not too partial an esteem and memory, if allow'd the *Petronius* of his Age. (E. Howard, *Poems and Essays*, 1674, 48–9)

Multiple editions of Suckling's *Works* or *Poems* have been published in each of the past four centuries and are in print for the twenty-first. His reputation with readers and critics remained quite high until the last quarter of the twentieth century, when changes in the cultural, and especially academic, climate brought a chillier reception to Suckling and others whose monarchism and patriarchal traditionalism made them *personae non gratae* in a time when academic preference was for oppositional or subversive writers. It is perhaps helpful to view Suckling in a longer perspective than that of Caroline court culture or modern academic fashions. Although Suckling is not of the comparable stature of Catullus, Horace, and Ovid, their poetry and ethos provide a liberating context for viewing him, and not just because Catullus died young, Horace never married, and Ovid perished in exile, but because all four live in their poetry and all have the power to move our emotions memorably from beyond the grave with their distinctive *curiosa felicitas* in verse.

TOM CLAYTON

Sources *The works of Sir John Suckling*, ed. T. Clayton and L. A. Beaurline, 2 vols. (1971) · *Aubrey's Brief lives*, ed. O. L. Dick (1949); repr. (1957), 287–90 · H. Berry, *Sir John Suckling's poems and letters from manuscript* (1960) · M. Prestwich, *Cranfield: politics and profits under the early Stuarts* (1966) · G. Radcliffe, *The earl of Strafforde's letters and dispatches, with an essay towards his life*, ed. W. Knowler, [another edn], 2 vols. (1740) · *Selections from the works of Sir John Suckling*, ed. A. Suckling (1836) · K. van Strien, 'Sir John Suckling in Holland', *English Studies*, 78 (1995), 443–54 · M. P. Parker, 'Suckling in Paris', *N&Q*, 232 (1987), 316–18 · J. Spence, *Observations, anecdotes, and characters, of books and men*, ed. J. M. Osborn, new edn, 2 vols. (1966) · *Catalogue of the pamphlets … collected by George Thomason, 1640–1661*, 2 vols. (1908) · D. Bruce, 'The war poets of 1639: Carew, Suckling and Lovelace', *Contemporary Review*, 259 (1991), 309–14 · Clarendon, *Hist. rebellion*, vol. 1 · S. R. Gardiner, *History of England from the accession of James I to the outbreak of the civil war*, new edn, 9–10 (1899) · D. Lloyd, *Memoires of the lives … of those … personages that suffered … for the protestant religion* (1668) · J. F. Merritt, ed., *The political world of Thomas Wentworth, earl of Strafford, 1621–1641* (1996), esp. chaps. 10 and 11 · D. B. Haley, *Dryden and the problem of freedom: the republican aftermath, 1649–1680* (1997) · K. Sharpe, *The personal rule of Charles I* (1992) · T. Clayton, 'An historical study of the portraits of Sir John Suckling', *Journal of the Warburg and Courtauld Institutes*, 23 (1960), 105–26 · O. Sitwell, introduction, *Frick collection: an illustrated catalogue*, 1 (1949), 96–7 · M. Rogers, 'The meaning of Van Dyck's portrait of Sir John Suckling', *Burlington Magazine*, 120 (1978), 741–5 · A. K. Wheelock, 'Thomas Killigrew and William, Lord Crofts', in A. K. Wheelock and others, *Anthony Van Dyck* (1990), 313–14 [catalogue of *Anthony Van Dyck*, organized by the National Gallery of Art, Washington, DC, 11 Nov 1990–24 Feb 1991] · *Fourth report*, HMC, 3 (1874) · *CSP dom.*, 1635; 1640–41 · *Report on the manuscripts of Lord De L'Isle and Dudley*, 6 vols., HMC, 77 (1925–66) · *Seventh report*, HMC, 6 (1879) · More's diary, BL, Harley MS 477, fols. 26v–27r · PRO, SP 16/482, no. 73 · PRO, SP 78/111, fol. 63 · J. Spalding, 'Sure newis from Newcastell, and from the Scottish Army, 27th Aug, 1640', *Memorialls of the trubles in Scotland and England, AD 1624 – AD 1645*, ed. J. Stuart, 1, Spalding Club, [21] (1850), 335–6 · W. A. Shaw, *The knights of England*, 2 (1906) · Davy, 'Suffolk connections', 74, BL, Add. MS 19150, fols. 287–303 · J. Foster, *The register of admissions to Gray's Inn, 1521–1889, together with the register of marriages in Gray's Inn chapel, 1695–1754* (privately printed, London, 1889), 77 · F. Blomefield, *History of Norfolk*, 4 (1806), 308–9 · W. Bruce Bannerman, ed., *Registers of St Olave, Hart Street, London, 1563–1700* (1916), 261

Archives CKS, Cranfield Papers, corresp. with Cranfield and related material · PRO, State Papers, 16/482, 78/111

Likenesses D. Des Granges, unfinished miniature, 1630–70, Knole, Kent · A. Van Dyck, oils, *c*.1637–1638, Frick collection, New York [*see illus.*] · oils, *c*.1637–1645 (after A. Van Dyck), Knole, Kent · W. Marshall, engraving, 1646 (after Russell), repro. in Clayton, 'An historical study' · attrib. T. Russel, portrait, before 1646 (after A. Van Dyck), NPG · engraving, *c*.1659–1672 (after Marshall), repro. in Clayton, 'An historical study' · C. de Neve?, oils, in or before 1683 · oils, before 1709 (after unknown artist, 1600–1700), Roos Hall, Beccles, Suffolk · J. Whiteside, oils, *c*.1720 · E. Lee, portrait, 1738–1811 (after Van Dyck); Sothebys, 26 April 1938, lot 87 · G. Vertue, engraving, 1744 (after portrait at Knole), repro. in Clayton, 'An historical study' · engraving, 1755 (after Vertue), BM; repro. in *Biographical Magazine* (1794); copy, NPG; AM Oxf. · J. Hopwood, stipple, *c*.1790–1810 (after Vertue), BM; copy, NPG · C. Rivers, engraving, 1795 (after Vertue), repro. in Clayton, 'An historical study'; copy, BM; NPG · W. P. Sherlock, stipple, *c*.1800–1820 (after Vertue), BM; repro. in *TLS* (9 May 1942), 236; copy, NPG · J. Thomson, stipple and line engraving, 1835 (after portrait at Roos Hall, 1835), repro. in *Selections*, ed. Suckling, frontispiece · Annan and Swan, stipple and line engraving, 1892 (after Thomson), repro. in *The poems, plays, and other remains of Sir John Suckling*, ed. W. C. Hazlitt, 2 vols. (1892), frontispiece · J. Hoskins, miniature, repro. in A. B. Edwards, *The photographic historical portrait gallery* (1864); priv. coll. · A. Van Dyck, oils, second version, NPG · M. Vandergucht, engraving (after portrait at Roos Hall), repro. in *The works of Sir John Suckling* (1709) · M. Vandergucht, engraving (after W. Marshall), repro. in *The works of Sir John Suckling* (1719) · engraving (after Vertue, 1744), AM Oxf., BM, NPG · portrait (after Van Dyck), Barsham House, Beccles, Suffolk

Wealth at death exile in Paris; almost certainly penniless

Suckling, Maurice

Suckling, Maurice (1725–1778), naval officer and administrator, the second son of Maurice Suckling, prebendary of Westminster and rector of Barsham in Suffolk, and Anne Turner, daughter of Sir Charles Turner and niece of Robert Walpole, first earl of Orford, was born at Barsham rectory on 14 May 1725. Suckling's sister Catherine married Edmund Nelson and was the mother of Horatio *Nelson.

Having joined the navy Suckling passed for lieutenant on 8 March 1745 and was commissioned on the same day. Considering that he had not yet reached the age of twenty, this celerity confirms the strength of his patronage. In May 1747 Rear-Admiral John Byng, then commanding in the Mediterranean, took him as a lieutenant in his flagship, the *Boyne*. Although hostilities ended in 1748 Suckling remained employed at sea, serving from November in the *Gloucester*. On 3 January 1754 he was promoted master and commander and on 2 December 1755, soon before the official beginning of the Seven Years' War, he was posted to the *Dreadnought* (60 guns), as flag captain to Rear-Admiral George Townshend, bound for Jamaica.

In October 1757 he remained on the Jamaica station which was now commanded by Rear-Admiral Thomas Cotes. With two other ships of 60 and 64 guns respectively, the *Dreadnought* was detached under the orders of Captain Arthur Forrest to intercept a convoy about to sail homeward from Cap François. On 21 October—a date recalled forty-eight years later by Suckling's nephew and protégé Horatio as he prepared for battle off Cape Trafalgar—the comte de Kersaint brought out the convoy with an unexpectedly powerful escort comprising two 74-gun ships, a 64-gun ship, and four lesser warships. Forrest summoned his fellow captains to the quarterdeck of the *Augusta*. He said, 'Well, gentlemen, you see they are come out to engage us'. Suckling replied, 'I think it would be a pity to disappoint them' (Clowes, 3.165). Captain William Langdon agreed. There ensued a spirited action lasting two and a half hours. Although the three British ships inflicted markedly disproportionate casualties on Kersaint's squadron, they were all severely damaged aloft and could not prevent the convoy from making for France.

In 1761 Suckling returned to England to pay off the *Dreadnought*. The following year, when commanding the *Nassau* (64 guns), he served under Sir Edward Hawke in the Bay of Biscay, but in the aftermath of Hawke's great victory in November 1759 serious opposition was neither expected nor encountered. Peace having been signed in 1763, Suckling was mainly on half pay for the remainder of the decade. On 20 June 1764 he married his cousin Mary (d. 1766), daughter of Horatio, Lord Walpole of Walterton; they had no children.

In November 1770 a dispute with Spain, abetted by France, over the Falkland Islands, led to Suckling's being given command of the *Raisonnable* (64 guns), an almost new ship. The threatened war did not eventuate but meanwhile a newspaper report about the manning of the *Raisonnable* prompted the twelve-year-old Horatio Nelson to ask to join his uncle at sea. 'What has poor Horatio done', Suckling responded, 'who is so weak, that he above the rest should be sent to rough it out at sea? But let him come, and the first time we go into action, a cannon-ball may knock off his head, and provide for him at once' (Marcus, 87). In March 1771 Nelson joined the *Raisonnable* (rather surprisingly as a midshipman). As already indicated, his uncle's brave conduct on 21 October 1757 remained for him a source of inspiration until his own dying day.

In April 1771, the war scare having receded, Suckling was appointed to the *Triumph* (90 guns). She was then a guardship in the Medway but had many years of active service ahead of her. However, on 12 April 1775 Suckling was appointed to the important post of controller of the navy. Like his predecessor, Sir Hugh Palliser, Suckling was, by dint of ability and detailed naval knowledge, of fundamental value to Lord Sandwich in his extensive reform of naval administration. Although no exhaustive study has been made of Suckling's work as the leading member of

the Navy Board, he appears to have been assiduous and effective. However, by January 1777 ill health of a painful but otherwise uncertain nature began to affect him. The onset of the American crisis involved great logistical problems which were ably handled by Palliser (as a naval lord) and by the hard-working Suckling. From 18 May 1776 Suckling was an MP for the borough of Portsmouth. He died on 14 July 1778 and was buried in the chancel of Barsham Church.   RUDDOCK MACKAY

Sources DNB · N. A. M. Rodger, *The wooden world: an anatomy of the Georgian navy* (1986) · N. A. M. Rodger, *The insatiable earl: a life of John Montagu, fourth earl of Sandwich* (1993) · W. L. Clowes, *The Royal Navy: a history from the earliest times to the present*, 7 vols. (1897–1903); repr. (1996–7), vol. 3 · G. J. Marcus, *Heart of oak* (1975) · D. Syrett and R. L. DiNardo, *The commissioned sea officers of the Royal Navy, 1660–1815*, rev. edn, Occasional Publications of the Navy RS, 1 (1994) · *The Hawke papers: a selection, 1743–1771*, ed. R. F. Mackay, Navy RS, 129 (1990) · *The private papers of John, earl of Sandwich*, ed. G. R. Barnes and J. H. Owen, 1, Navy RS, 69 (1932) · B. Lavery, *The ship of the line*, 1 (1983) · M. M. Drummond, 'Suckling, Maurice', HoP, *Commons*
Archives NMM, Sandwich MSS · PRO, Admiralty MSS
Likenesses T. Bardwell, oils, 1764, NPG · W. Ridley, stipple, BM, NPG; repro. in *Naval Chronicle* (1805) · portrait (after portrait by Bardwell), repro. in Clowes, *Royal Navy*, vol. 3, p. 166
Wealth at death see will, PRO, PROB 11/1044, fol. 157

Sudbury, Simon (*c*.1316–1381), administrator and archbishop of Canterbury, was born at East Dereham in Norfolk, the second son of Nigel Thebaud and his wife, Elizabeth. His father was a wealthy merchant of woollen cloths and furs, who received an esquire's livery from Elizabeth de Burgh, Lady of Clare (d. 1360). Simon's elder brother, John, lived the life of a local gentleman of substance; he was a justice of the peace in both Essex and Suffolk, and represented Essex in parliament in 1360 and 1362. Nothing is known for certain of Sudbury's early career, nor is it known where he went to university, but his later patronage of Cambridge suggests that it was there that he studied civil law, incepting as doctor before 1344, when he was presented to his first benefice, the rectory of Wickhambrook, Suffolk. He received a second local living at Herringswell, Suffolk, from the abbot of Bury St Edmunds soon afterwards and, by 1345, had entered the service of William Bateman (d. 1355), bishop of Norwich. In this capacity Sudbury became involved in a bitter dispute between his two principal patrons, Bateman and the abbot of Bury St Edmunds, which led eventually to a royal order for the arrest and imprisonment of all those, including Sudbury, who had published a sentence of excommunication against one of the abbot's attorneys. Sudbury evaded arrest by flight, probably in the early summer of 1346, and retreated to the papal court at Avignon, where he continued to press Bateman's case.

Sudbury's talents as a practitioner of canon law (which he had presumably studied since 1344, as he was licentiate by February 1348), together with the uncharacteristically dramatic nature of his arrival at Avignon, soon brought him to papal attention. By July 1349 Sudbury was an auditor of the rota, a position he continued to hold for the next decade, and a string of papal provisions to English benefices followed: promoted to a canonry at Lincoln, with expectation of a prebend, in 1348, he was provided to

Simon Sudbury
(c.1316–1381), seal

even including the notoriously fractious cathedral chapter of St Paul's. His reputation among the laity is attested by the testimonial the citizens of London produced on his behalf in 1363, when Urban V (r. 1362–70) threatened to translate Sudbury from London to Worcester, as a rebuke for his failure to give more forcible support to William Lynn, bishop of Chichester, in the latter's dispute with the earl of Arundel: 'so gracious, so kind and so affable a pastor, by whose teaching and example in life we are being shaped, in a wonderful unity, to a pattern of wholesomeness and spirituality' (Corporation of London Research Office, Roll of Letters, 1, no. 211).

Sudbury also continued to give the king loyal service while at London. An occasional attender at council meetings from 1365, he was sent on three diplomatic missions to Calais and the Low Countries, all concerned with Edward III's attempt to marry his son Edmund to Marguerite de Male, heir to the county of Flanders, between July 1364 and November 1365. Such work brought him a growing reputation for reliability within the royal administration and ensured that, as the health of William Whittelsey, archbishop of Canterbury, steadily deteriorated in the early 1370s, it was increasingly to Sudbury that Edward III and his advisers looked for effective management of the English church. A frequent witness to royal charters from 1371, the bishop of London took the leading role in cajoling a recalcitrant convocation, angered by the anti-clerical stance of the parliamentary Commons and high levels of papal taxation, into granting substantial clerical subsidies in April 1371 and December 1373. On both occasions Sudbury addressed the assembly in English when expounding the need for a grant. He also resumed his diplomatic career—he was one of the king's representatives at the Anglo-French peace talks at Calais, sponsored by Gregory XI (r. 1370–78), in February 1372 and January 1373 and, once more, when negotiations resumed at Bruges in February 1375. By the time of Whittelsey's death in June 1374, therefore, Sudbury was the obvious and favoured candidate to succeed him at Canterbury. His elevation to the primacy was unusually delayed, however, first by the unexpected capitular election of Cardinal Simon Langham, and then by Gregory XI's successful tactic of deliberately delaying the provision in order to bring pressure to bear on the government to agree the imposition of a heavy papal subsidy on the English clergy. The bull translating Sudbury to Canterbury was finally issued on 4 May 1375.

a canonry at Hereford, with the prebend of Great Moreton, in the following year, and, in 1353, to the chancellorship of Salisbury. He later exchanged his Lincoln prebend of Nassington, the subject of continual litigation, for the prebend of Hentridge at Wells. Although such provisions created great resentment among the English clergy, they provided Sudbury with an income more adequate than exorbitant—in the region of 160 marks p.a. at its highest point.

Sudbury was never outlawed for his offences in 1345–6, and so needed no pardon, and the crown made no effort to prevent his being provided to benefices in England. But his formal rehabilitation with the authorities at home began only in 1356, when Innocent VI (r. 1352–62) sent him to urge Edward III to seek peace with the French through papal mediation. Although his mission proved entirely fruitless, it served to bring Sudbury to the attention of the king, who asked him to facilitate royal business at the curia in 1357 and named Sudbury as his proctor to give effect to the ecclesiastical sanctions in that year's treaty of Berwick between England and Scotland. Such services played their part in disposing Edward III to accept the pope's actions in 1361, when he quashed the capitular election of Simon Langham (d. 1376), the king's treasurer, as bishop of London, and on 22 October provided Sudbury to the vacant see instead—he was consecrated in St Paul's on 20 March 1362. Edward nevertheless retained the temporalities until 15 May 1362, when the new bishop of London made his oath of allegiance in person.

For the next ten years most of Sudbury's time and attention was devoted to the care of his new diocese. He was an active and popular diocesan, who made sparing use of suffragans and delegated only minor decisions to his vicars-general. Concerned to enforce clerical discipline, particularly over the issue of unlicensed absence from benefices, he nevertheless enjoyed good relations with his clergy,

The following years were stormy ones in the affairs of church and state, and the new archbishop's leadership was several times called into question. After a further period of residence at Bruges between October 1375 and April 1376, engaged in ultimately fruitless negotiations for a final Anglo-French peace treaty, Sudbury was immediately plunged into the political crisis of the Good Parliament (June 1376) on his return to England. He faced a restless convocation, which followed the example of the laity in successfully refusing to grant a subsidy, and was forced to engage in a bitter jurisdictional conflict with William Courtenay (d. 1396), bishop of London. The following spring Sudbury's decision to obey the royal order excluding William Wykeham (*d.* 1404), bishop of Winchester, from parliament and convocation led to accusations of excessive pliancy. The archbishop was eventually forced to admit Wykeham to convocation by the strength of clerical protest, led by Courtenay and Henry Despenser (*d.* 1406), bishop of Norwich. A further bone of contention between Wykeham and some of his diocesans, especially Courtenay, was the relative lenience of his attitude towards the academic publicist, John Wyclif. Although Sudbury published the papal bulls condemning eighteen of Wyclif's propositions on lordship in December 1377, and examined him personally at Lambeth in May 1378, the archbishop did not obey Gregory XI's orders to detain Wyclif in prison, and eventually allowed himself to be satisfied with the argument that although Wyclif's propositions 'sounded ill to the ear' (*Eulogium historiarum*, 3.348), they were nevertheless true.

In other respects, however, Sudbury's discharge of the pastoral duties of the primacy was conscientious and generally effective. His continued insistence on maintaining standards of clerical discipline is reflected in the two sets of provincial constitutions he issued in 1378, in his vigorous visitation of several of the major religious houses of the Canterbury diocese, and in the attempt at regulating the wages of chantry priests made in the ordinance *Effrenata generis* (October 1378). Following a violation of sanctuary at Westminster in the same year, Sudbury showed himself to be a firm defender of clerical privileges, and, in his management of convocation, he was generally successful in obtaining substantial sums in clerical taxation while reducing the *gravamina* attached to the grants to a minimum acceptable to the court.

Sudbury's involvement in affairs of state while archbishop was, initially, relatively slight. Although he was one of the nine persons named to attend the king's council during the Good Parliament, he played little direct part in government over the next three years. He seems to have been most valued as a persuasive spokesman, addressing parliament in June 1376 and October 1377. At Easter 1379, however, Sudbury was nominated as one of the committee of magnates appointed to 'examine the state of the king', and in January 1380, following the resignation of Sir Richard Scrope (*d.* 1403), he was appointed chancellor, possibly against his will. The archbishop responded with characteristic conscientiousness to this new and burdensome responsibility, and in November the Commons endorsed his administration by requesting that he and the other great officers of state remain in office. As chancellor, however, Sudbury bore formal responsibility for the imposition of the poll-tax granted at Northampton. As a result, he became one of the principal targets of the rebellious Commons in June 1381: when the Kentish rebels swarmed into Canterbury Cathedral on 10 June, they called on the monks to elect a new archbishop, telling them that Sudbury was a traitor who would be beheaded for his iniquity. Trapped in the Tower of London with the king throughout the crisis, Sudbury allegedly counselled against any concessions to the rebels. When Richard went

to parley at Mile End on 14 June, however, he promised the commons that action would be taken against any traitors around him. Acting on this authority, a group of rebels forced an entry to the Tower, dragged out Sudbury and the treasurer, Sir Robert Hales, and beheaded them on Tower Hill. Sudbury's body was left unburied for two days and his head, with an episcopal cap nailed to the skull, was impaled on a lance and displayed on London Bridge.

Simon Sudbury was buried in Canterbury Cathedral. He had been a notable benefactor to the fabric there, initiating the rebuilding of the nave and contributing at least £2000 to the project himself. He also paid for the reconstruction of the west gate at Canterbury and contributed to the cost of renovating the city walls, besides financing further building work at Chelmsford and Trinity Hall, Cambridge. At Sudbury he and his brother John in 1375 founded St Gregory's, a collegiate church of six chaplains, and endowed it with lands worth 40 marks p.a.

A conscientious and effective diocesan bishop, as archbishop of Canterbury Sudbury allied a watchful defence of specific ecclesiastical privileges to a general policy of close co-operation with the lay power. His alleged pliancy attracted some contemporary criticism, most notably from the chronicler Thomas Walsingham, but Sudbury's pragmatism had much to recommend it as a policy in the anti-clerical atmosphere of the 1370s. His natural disposition to conciliate and compromise proved an insufficient response, however, to the exceptional social and political problems of the era. With hindsight it is clear that Sudbury underestimated the appeal of John Wyclif's teachings and allowed the latter's followers vital time to develop as a sect, while the archbishop's lack of governmental experience, together with the pressure of his other duties, contributed to a fatal lack of precision in the terms of the poll-tax granted at Northampton. The industry and amiability that were the keynotes of Sudbury's character proved a less effective defence for the English church than the natural authority to command brought to the primacy by his aristocratic successors, William Courtenay and Thomas Arundel (*d.* 1414).

SIMON WALKER

Sources W. L. Warren, 'Simon of Sudbury, bishop of London and archbishop of Canterbury', DPhil diss., U. Oxf., 1956 · *Registrum Simonis de Sudbiria, diocesis Londoniensis, AD 1362–1375*, ed. R. C. Fowler, 2 vols., CYS, 34, 38 (1927–38) · register of Simon Sudbury, LPL · W. L. Warren, 'A reappraisal of Simon of Sudbury, bishop of London (1361–75) and archbishop of Canterbury (1375–81)', *Journal of Ecclesiastical History*, 10 (1959), 139–52 · *CEPR letters*, vols. 3–4 · W. H. Bliss, ed., *Calendar of entries in the papal registers relating to Great Britain and Ireland: petitions to the pope* (1896) · PRO [esp. exchequer, king's remembrancer, accounts various (E.101)] · D. Wilkins, ed., *Concilia Magnae Britanniae et Hiberniae*, 3 (1737) · Rymer, *Foedera* · *RotP* · [T. Walsingham], *Chronicon Angliae, ab anno Domini 1328 usque ad annum 1388*, ed. E. M. Thompson, Rolls Series, 64 (1874) · V. H. Galbraith, ed., *The Anonimalle chronicle, 1333 to 1381* (1927) · C. E. Woodruff, ed., *Sede vacante wills*, Kent Archaeological Society Records Branch, 3 (1914), 81 · Roll of Letters 1, Corporation of London Research Office, no. 211 · F. S. Haydon, ed., *Eulogium historiarum sive temporis*, 3 vols., Rolls Series, 9 (1858), vol. 3, p. 348 · *Chancery records*

Archives BL, Harley MSS, 335, 3705 · GL, MS 9351/2 · LPL, register | PRO, E 101
Likenesses seal, BL; Birch, *Seals*, 1226 [*see illus.*]
Wealth at death see will, Woodruff, ed., *Sede vacante wills*

Sudbury, William (*b.* after **1350**, *d.* **1415**), Benedictine monk and scholastic theologian, was the son of Henry Sudbury, a London skinner (*d.* 1381), and Margaret, his wife. Professed at Westminster Abbey in 1373, he was a deacon in 1376, and probably said his first mass in 1377. The decision to send him to Gloucester College, Oxford, in 1375, only two years after profession, suggests that he was well educated and considered by his superiors to be of exceptional promise. He proceeded BTh in 1382 but stayed at Oxford, though paying visits of varying duration to the monastery, until 1387. The inventory of the vestry which Sudbury, Richard Cirencester, and two others compiled in 1388 may owe its orderly division into parts and chapters, and its alphabetical index, to the skills of the newly returned scholastic. In 1392–3 he held the demanding offices of senior treasurer and warden of the foundation of Eleanor of Castile. These employments, however, now appear aberrations in a career devoted to intellectual pursuits and to the task of representing the monastery in the world, when situations might arise calling for a graduate's distinctive contribution. On one such occasion, in 1391–2, he appeared before the king at Windsor, to speak for the abbey's case in its long-running dispute with St Stephen's Chapel in the palace of Westminster.

Sudbury began his *Tabula super libros sancti Thome de Aquino* (BL, Royal MS 9 F. iv) at Oxford in 1382 and completed it, as he notes, after sixteen years' work in the cloister. Making tables (indexes) was a characteristic employment of scholars who possessed or had access to well-stocked libraries, and other works of this kind were attributed to Sudbury by Bale and Leland. His *Tractatus de sanguine Christi precioso* (Longleat House, Wiltshire, marquess of Bath MS 38, fols. 256v–308), proving that the relic of the precious blood of Christ given to Westminster Abbey by Henry III was genuine, is more original, serving to justify W. A. Pantin's opinion that he was 'perhaps the nearest to a constructive theologian' produced by Westminster (private information). This text survives in a late fifteenth-century manuscript with Westminster associations, and Sudbury was probably the author of the lengthy treatise on the privilege of sanctuary at Westminster that precedes it here (fols. 9–256). His treatise on the coronation regalia, which is addressed to Richard II and in which he argues that the regalia were used at Alfred's coronation by Leo IV, was included in Richard Cirencester's *Speculum historiale* and written for this purpose. There is a slender possibility, but no more, that Sudbury also wrote the Westminster continuation of the *Polychronicon* for the years 1381–94. William Sudbury died in 1415. His career, in which solid abilities, honed at considerable cost to his monastery in long years at the university, were subsequently deployed in the ponderous defence of its interests, with scarcely a glance beyond the narrow world they represented, may have had many parallels in the history of the Benedictine order in this period. BARBARA F. HARVEY

Sources private information (2004) [W. A. Pantin] · J. W. Legg, 'On an inventory of the vestry in Westminster Abbey, taken in 1388', *Archaeologia*, 52 (1890), 195–286 · E. H. Pearce, *The monks of Westminster* (1916) · L. C. Hector and B. F. Harvey, eds. and trans., *The Westminster chronicle, 1381–1394*, OMT (1982) · Emden, *Oxf.*, vol. 3 · R. R. Sharpe, ed., *Calendar of wills proved and enrolled in the court of husting, London, AD 1258 – AD 1688*, 2 (1890), 225 · B. F. Harvey, 'The monks of Westminster at the University of Oxford', *The reign of Richard II: essays in honour of May McKisack*, ed. F. R. H. Du Boulay and C. M. Barron (1971), 108–30 · N. Vincent, *The holy blood: King Henry III and the Westminster blood relic* (2001) · D. A. Carpenter, 'The burial of King Henry III, the regalia and royal ideology', in D. A. Carpenter, *The reign of Henry III* (1996), 427–61
Archives BL, Royal MS 9 F. iv · Longleat House, Wiltshire, marquess of Bath MS 38, fols. 256v–308

Sudeley. For this title name *see* individual entries under Sudeley; *see also* Boteler, Ralph, first Baron Sudeley (*c.*1394–1473).

Sudeley family (*per. c.***1050–1336**), barons in Gloucestershire, were descended from *Ralph (*d.* 1057), who was a nephew of Edward the Confessor, being the son of Drogo, count of Amiens and the Vexin, and his wife, Godgifu (Gode), a daughter of Æthelred II. Initially Ralph's earldom was probably that of the east midlands. But about 1052 he became earl of Hereford (which included Gloucestershire and probably Oxfordshire), and in that capacity took command of the defence of England against the Welsh. A heavy defeat in 1055 seems to have led to the loss of this earldom, and of the comital manors associated with it. However, Domesday Book records that Ralph had held lands at Sudeley and Toddington worth £40 per annum, and these, with other estates in other counties, were subsequently to be either inherited or recovered by his descendants. In 1066 Ralph's son **Harold of Sudeley** (*fl.* 1057–*c.*1100) was still a minor, in the custody of Queen Eadgyth. Lord of Sudeley in 1086, he profited from the Welsh campaigns of William Rufus's reign to re-establish himself in Herefordshire. Between 1086 and 1100 he was granted the castle of Ewyas Harold (which bears his name), along with Lydiard in Wiltshire and other lands formerly held by Alfred of Marlborough. To consolidate his hold upon Ewyas, in 1100 he founded a small Benedictine priory there, and he was also a substantial benefactor of St Peter's at Gloucester, as well as initiating a family tradition of patronage of the major Gloucestershire monastery at Winchcombe, to which he granted half a hide of land. With his wife, Matilda, allegedly a daughter of Earl Hugh of Chester (*d.* 1101), he had two sons. Normal practice in this period was for patrimonial estates to go to the eldest son, while the younger sons succeeded to whatever their father might have acquired. But in the case of the Sudeleys this practice was reversed. The elder son, Robert of Ewyas, inherited the estates in Herefordshire and Wiltshire which had been Alfred of Marlborough's, while the Gloucestershire lands went to the younger son, John.

John of Sudeley (*fl. c.*1100–*c.*1140) was probably on the fringes of court circles in the reign of Henry I. He married an unidentified sister of Henry de Tracy, lord of Barnstaple, and he appears to have been friendly with the Beaumonts, to whom he was related, and who were intermittently in favour with King Henry. However, although he gave his support to Stephen in the years immediately after the latter's accession, the landing of Matilda in England in 1139 caused Sudeley to reconsider his position, and he joined Robert of Gloucester. For this his lands were subjected to a terrible ravaging by the Beaumonts, and he lost control of Sudeley itself, at least for a time. A benefactor of Winchcombe, he also gave land at Greet and Gretton to the Templars. He had two sons, **Ralph** [i] **of Sudeley** (*d.* 1192) and William. The latter, who took his mother's name, surrendered his inheritance at Burton Dassett, Warwickshire, to his brother, probably in the 1130s or 1140s, and received in exchange the manor of Toddington, a few miles north of Sudeley. Ralph took little part in public affairs. A benefactor of Winchcombe, St Peter's at Gloucester, and the Templars, before December 1159 he founded a small Augustinian priory at Arbury, Warwickshire. His foundation charter shows that he was already married, to a woman named Emma, and had a son, Otuel (a name also found in the family of the earls of Chester), who succeeded when Ralph died, at what must have been an advanced age, in 1192.

Otuel of Sudeley (*d.* 1198) paid 20 marks' relief to enter upon his father's lands. In 1197 he was temporarily deprived of them, because the knight he had undertaken to provide for the king's army in Normandy was not found at his post, and had to pay £40 for repossession. Otuel may well have been too old to serve in person. Like previous Sudeleys, he was a benefactor to Winchcombe, bequeathing his body to the abbey for burial, along with lands in Greet to finance a light at the mass of the Blessed Virgin. He had married a woman named Margaret, but they had no recorded children, and when Otuel died in 1198 his successor was his younger brother, Ralph. **Sir Ralph** [ii] **of Sudeley** (*d.* in or before 1222) was fiscally more hardly dealt with than his brother had been, having to pay £160 for Otuel's lands (doubtless a more accurate reflection of the family's perceived wealth at this time than the relief of 1192), and also having to pay the latter's £40 fine. Having cleared his debts by 1201, he paid scutage in 1202 and 1203 at the rate of 10 marks for his three knights' fees, but in 1204 and 1205 at a rate twice as high. He appears to have served in the army mustered in Kent in 1212 to meet a threatened French invasion, but took no recorded part in the civil wars at the end of John's reign. A knight by *c.*1215, he was dead before 26 February 1222, when his heir was his son Ralph, born of his marriage to a woman named Isabella.

Sir Ralph [iii] **of Sudeley** (*d.* 1242) paid a relief of £100 for his father's lands, showing that they constituted a barony, as defined by clause 2 of Magna Carta. In 1225 he was ordered to assume knighthood. Unlike his immediate forebears, he took an active part in local administration, serving as a tax assessor and collector, a commissioner for the assize of arms, and a justice of assize and gaol delivery, all in Gloucestershire. At a national level, between 1239

and 1241 he served as a justice itinerant on the circuit of eyres in northern and central England headed by Robert of Lexinton. With his wife, Imenia, said to have been a member of the Corbet family, he had a son, Bartholomew, who was still a minor when Ralph died, early in 1242. Sir Ralph is recorded as litigating to secure his rights at Burton Dassett, and it may be a measure of his success in husbanding and augmenting his resources that after his death his widow undertook to pay 1000 marks for the wardship and marriage of his heir.

Sir Bartholomew of Sudeley (*d.* 1279/80) was still a minor in 1248, but had probably come of age by 8 September 1254, when he married Joan, daughter of William (III) de Beauchamp (*d.* 1269) of Elmley, hereditary sheriff of Worcestershire—a match which brought him the manor of Fairfield, and which also provides further evidence for the standing of the Sudeleys as a significant baronial family. Sudeley clearly remained close to Beauchamp, acting as an executor of his will, but in the 1260s he gained increasing favour at the royal court. In March 1264 he was summoned to the muster of the king's army at Oxford, and presumably served Henry III thereafter. In 1267 he was granted a market and fair at Burton Dassett, and free warren on his demesnes at Sudeley and at Chilvers Coton, Warwickshire. Two years later, on 9 July 1269, he was a party to the transactions which deprived Robert Ferrers, earl of Derby, of his lands, and transferred them to the king's second son, Edmund of Cornwall. In 1270, by now a knight, he became sheriff of Herefordshire, an office he held for four years. He received gifts of deer from both Henry III and Edward I. Sudeley's services to the latter were primarily fiscal, especially as a justice dealing with offences against the coinage and implementing measures against the Jews. But he received a variety of other commissions as well—for instance, inquiring into official malpractices in Warwickshire in March 1278. In November 1276 he was present at the meeting of the king's council at which action against Llywelyn was decided upon, and in the summer of 1278 was commissioned to take oaths for the keeping of the peace between the Welsh prince and the English king. At Michaelmas 1278 he was present at Westminster when the king of Scots did homage to Edward I. He was still active in November 1279, but had died by June 1280.

Bartholomew's son and heir, **John Sudeley**, first Lord Sudeley (*c.*1258–1336), was already of age at his father's death. Summoned to perform military service in Wales in 1282–3, he was a knight of the king's household in 1285, and received gifts of deer from Edward I in 1284 and again in 1290. In November 1287 he went to Wales on the king's order. He may, indeed, have found service to the crown an expensive privilege, for he ran heavily into debt, and had to raise money by borrowing from creditors who included Italian merchants and the abbot of Winchcombe. Nevertheless he served in Gascony in 1295 (when his ship was holed by a stone from a catapult as it approached Bordeaux), and again in 1298, and campaigned in Scotland in 1304 and 1307. By the latter date he had become the king's chamberlain. On 29 December 1299 he received a personal summons to parliament (regularly repeated thereafter), and as a result is regarded as having become Lord Sudeley, a title to which the descendants of his marriage to an unknown woman, who may have been a member of the Say family, subsequently succeeded. John Sudeley's elevation completed a unique genealogical process, which within the framework of eight generations of a single family linked the élite nobility of pre-Conquest England to the parliamentary baronage of the later middle ages.

SUDELEY

Sources *The Sudeleys, lords of Toddington*, Memorial Society (1987) · GEC, *Peerage*, new edn, 12/1.411–16 · Chancery records · Pipe rolls, 14 Henry II – 5 Henry III · D. Royce, ed., *Landboc, sive, Registrum de Winchelcumba*, 2 vols. (1892–1903) · E. Dent, *Annnals of Winchcombe and Sudeley* (1877) · E. Mason, ed., *The Beauchamp cartulary: charters, 1100–1268*, PRSoc., new ser., 43 (1980) · B. A. Lees, ed., *Records of the templars in England in the twelfth century: the inquest of 1185 with illustrative charters and documents*, British Academy, Records of Social and Economic History, 9 (1935) · Dugdale, *Monasticon*, new edn, 6/1.406–8 · F. Palgrave, ed., *The parliamentary writs and writs of military summons*, 1 (1827), pt 2, p. 852 · *The chronicle of John of Worcester, 1118–1140*, ed. J. R. H. Weaver (1908) · *CIPM*, 2, no. 347 · B. F. Byerly and C. R. Byerly, eds., *Records of the wardrobe and household, 1285–1286* (1977) · P. A. Clarke, *The English nobility under Edward the Confessor* (1994) · D. Crouch, *The Beaumont twins: the roots and branches of power in the twelfth century*, Cambridge Studies in Medieval Life and Thought, 4th ser., 1 (1986) · F. C. Wellstood, ed., *Warwickshire feet of fines*, 1 (1932) · *VCH Warwickshire*, vol. 5

Sudeley, Sir Bartholomew of (d. 1279/80). *See under* Sudeley family (*per.* c.1050–1336).

Sudeley, Harold of (*fl.* 1057–c.1100). *See under* Sudeley family (*per.* c.1050–1336).

Sudeley, John of (*fl.* c.1100–c.1140). *See under* Sudeley family (*per.* c.1050–1336).

Sudeley, John, first Lord Sudeley (c.1258–1336). *See under* Sudeley family (*per.* c.1050–1336).

Sudeley, Otuel of (d. 1198). *See under* Sudeley family (*per.* c.1050–1336).

Sudeley, Ralph of (d. 1192). *See under* Sudeley family (*per.* c.1050–1336).

Sudeley, Sir Ralph of (d. in or before 1222). *See under* Sudeley family (*per.* c.1050–1336).

Sudeley, Sir Ralph of (d. 1242). *See under* Sudeley family (*per.* c.1050–1336).

Sudell, Henry (1763/4–1856), cotton merchant and manufacturer, was baptized on 4 May 1764 at St Mary's Church, Blackburn, the only child of Henry Sudell, a merchant and cotton hand-loom manufacturer who died in 1763 before his son's birth, and his wife, Alice (1742–1823), the daughter of James and Margaret Livesey. Little is known of his early life, though from the late seventeenth century, if not earlier, his family had developed an interest in the emerging textile industry; his grandfather John Sudell was described in parish records as a yeoman and chapman. Sudell probably took charge of the family textile business on the death of his bachelor uncles, John and William, in 1785. At this time the production of all-cotton textile

goods was entering a far quicker phase of growth than hitherto. Operating as both a hand-loom manufacturer and merchant, Sudell evidently took full advantage of his opportunities, and the family business continued to prosper.

On 13 June 1796 Sudell married Maria (d. 1848), the daughter of Thomas Livesey of Burwell in Lincolnshire; they had four sons and four daughters, only three of whom survived him. The couple at first lived in Blackburn, but Sudell soon purchased land at Mellor, a mile or so to the west of the town. Here he built Woodfold Hall, an imposing classical-style mansion with a nine-bay frontage featuring a projecting, tetrastyle portico. The hall was set in extensive parklands and enclosed by a stone wall 4 miles in circumference. To a degree, Sudell led the life of a country gentleman; he stocked his grounds with deer and wildfowl and kept a pack of hounds for fox-hunting. He was known to make spectacular entries into town by carriage and four, the perfectly matched horses ridden by postilions dressed in crimson and gold livery.

Sudell survived the vicissitudes of the cotton trade during the late eighteenth and early nineteenth centuries and reputedly became a near millionaire. He preferred to remain an employer of hand-loom weavers rather than turning to power-loom weavers, and operated an extensive putting-out system from his warehouse in Ainsworth Street; he probably employed at least a thousand domestic weavers. According to George Burgess, sometime tutor to the Sudell family, Sudell's preference for hand weaving lay in his appreciation of the fortune the industry had brought him and his wish not to hurt the interests of the hand weavers he employed. Given the prominence Sudell attained as an employer, news of his insolvency in July 1827 inevitably brought great consternation. It may be that he was unable to recover from losses incurred during the acute depression of the previous year, but he is also thought to have lost heavily through speculative merchanting activity in German and American markets. At the first meeting of his creditors during the following month his debts were stated to have reached £131,793, more than twice the value of the assets available to discharge them. The gap was so wide partly because Sudell took the precaution of settling the major portion of his estate, including Woodfold Hall, on his family. He is presumed to have done this in the knowledge of the financial difficulties he faced, thus giving rise to concern about the propriety of his actions. When his creditors met for the second time, they issued a commission of bankruptcy against him.

Sudell's civic contributions were concerned mainly with charitable activity, though he formed a company of Blackburn volunteers in 1798 and became its captain. He had a reputation for generosity and for many years had an ox roasted in the town's market place at Christmas, when he distributed the beef to poor families, along with clothes and money. He also attended to the spiritual needs of his community. In 1788 he subscribed £4000, half the sum required, towards the building of St John's Church at Blackburn, and in 1827 he provided the site for St Mary's

Church at Mellor, as well as contributing to the endowment. Prior to the declaration of his insolvency Sudell and his family left Blackburn, never to return. He took up residence at Ashley House, Box, near Chippenham, Wiltshire, where he died on 30 January 1856, at the age of ninety-two.　　　　　　　　　　　　　　J. GEOFFREY TIMMINS

Sources G. C. Miller, *Blackburn: the evolution of a cotton town* (1951), 393–5 · W. A. Abram, *A history of Blackburn, town and parish* (1877), 403–5 · 'Some notes on the Sudell family of Blackburn', *Blackburn Times* (15 Sept 1906) · J. G. Shaw, *Bits of old Blackburn* (1889), chap. 3 · M. Rothwell, *A guide to the industrial archaeology of Blackburn*, 1: *The textile industry* (1985), 12 · 'State of trade', *Blackburn Mail* (8 Aug 1827) · 'Mr Sudell's affairs', *Blackburn Mail* (15 Aug 1827) · 'The new church of St Mary at Mellor', *Blackburn Mail* (4 July 1827) · 'Select committtee on hand loom weavers', *Parl. papers* (1834), vol. 10, no. 556 · G. Timmins, *Blackburn: a pictorial history* (1993)

Sueter, Sir Murray Frazer (1872–1960), naval officer, was born in Alverstoke, Gosport, on 6 September 1872, the son of fleet paymaster John Thomas Sueter and his wife, Ellen Feild Lightbourn. He entered the *Britannia* as a naval cadet in 1886, served as a midshipman in the *Swiftsure*, flagship on the Pacific station, was promoted lieutenant in 1894, and appointed to the *Vernon* to qualify as a torpedo specialist in 1896. He commanded the destroyer *Fame* at the diamond jubilee naval review of 1897, and after a further two years' service on the staff of the *Vernon* was appointed in 1899 to the *Jupiter* for torpedo duties.

In 1902 Sueter received an appointment to the gunboat *Hazard*, at the time commanded by Reginald Bacon and recently commissioned as the first parent ship for submarines, of which the Holland boats were just entering for service as the navy's first submarines. While serving in the *Hazard*, Sueter distinguished himself by entering the battery compartment of the submarine A.1, after an explosion caused by a concentration of hydrogen, to assist in the rescue of injured men who would otherwise have been badly burnt. This period of service with the early submarines led to a lifelong interest in these vessels, and in 1907 Sueter published one of the first books of real merit on this subject under the title *The Evolution of the Submarine Boat, Mine and Torpedo*.

In 1903 Sueter married Elinor Mary de Winton (*d.* 1948), only daughter of Sir Andrew *Clarke; they had two daughters. In that year he was promoted commander and was appointed in 1904 to the Admiralty to serve as assistant to the director of naval ordnance. He returned to sea in 1906 to command the cruiser *Barham* in the Mediterranean, returning two years later to the naval ordnance department in the Admiralty. He was promoted captain in 1909.

The Admiralty at this time was considering the use of aircraft, especially airships, for reconnaissance duties with the fleet and in 1909 had placed contracts for the construction of a rigid airship to be named *Mayfly*. Sueter took a very keen interest in her construction and contributed many useful suggestions during her building. As a result he was appointed in 1910 to command the cruiser *Hermione* with the additional title of inspecting captain of airships. Unfortunately before her first flight the *Mayfly*'s back was broken while she was being manoeuvred out of her hangar in a high wind in 1911, an accident which for a

time put a stop to further airship development for the navy. In 1912 Sueter was brought back to the Admiralty to take over the new air department and much of the rapid development of the seaplane as a naval aircraft was due to his enthusiasm. Shortly before the outbreak of war in 1914, and largely on Sueter's suggestions, the naval wing broke away from its parent body, the Royal Flying Corps, to become the Royal Naval Air Service (RNAS). For his work on the development of naval flying Sueter was appointed CB in 1914.

Sueter was promoted commodore second class shortly after the outbreak of war and, still as director of the air department, was largely instrumental in the rapid build-up of the RNAS to a full war strength. In this he was encouraged by Winston Churchill, the first lord, and by Lord Fisher, recalled as first sea lord in October 1914. Sueter, who had continued with some success to press for airship development, was very largely responsible for the design and rapid production of small non-rigid airships designed to search out U-boats operating in British coastal waters. In all, some 200 of these were built and proved of great value particularly when convoy was adopted later in the war. Sueter also interested himself in the development of torpedo-carrying aircraft, and, working with Lieutenant Douglas Hyde-Thomson, it was he who initiated the design which was adopted in the navy. An early success when a Turkish supply ship was sunk by an air-launched torpedo in the sea of Marmara in 1915 not only vindicated Sueter's ingenuity and foresight but proved to be the first step in the development of one of the navy's most powerful weapons.

In 1915 Sueter turned his inventive mind to new avenues of service for the RNAS and advanced the idea of providing armoured cars for the defence of airfields established abroad. During the early months these cars did useful work in Flanders and northern France but as the war settled into its static phase of trench warfare their value declined. Two squadrons of these armoured cars were sent abroad, one to Russia under Commander Oliver Locker-Lampson and one to Egypt under the second duke of Westminster. Sueter's restless brain, not content with the armoured car design, concentrated on means of giving it a cross-country capability by fitting it with caterpillar tracks. From this advance it was a short step to the development of the tank.

With the appointment of an officer of flag rank in September 1915 as fifth sea lord with responsibility for naval aviation, Sueter was made superintendent of aircraft construction with full responsibility for the *matériel* side of all naval aircraft. At the same time he was promoted commodore first class. But in 1917, after some differences of opinion with the Board of Admiralty, he was sent to southern Italy to command the RNAS units there. Later in the year Sueter wrote a letter to George V on the subject of recognition of his work, and that of two other officers associated with him, in initiating the idea of tanks. This was passed to the Admiralty in the normal manner and roused considerable resentment. Sueter was informed that he had incurred their lordships' severe displeasure and relieved of his command. He returned to England in January 1918 and despite his protests no further employment was found for him. He was placed on the retired list early in 1920 and shortly afterwards the Admiralty obtained a special order in council to promote him to rear-admiral.

Sueter was gifted with a restless brain which he used skilfully and effectively to suggest means of overcoming difficulties, both technical and professional. He was always outspoken, and intolerant of official lethargy in any matter in which he took an interest. It was this intolerance, allied to a headstrong character, which brought to an end a naval career of considerable future promise.

After the war Sueter did much useful work in the development of the empire air mail postal services, and he received the thanks of three successive postmasters-general for his assistance in organizing these services. In 1921 he was elected an independent member of parliament for Hertford, remaining a member as a Conservative until the general election of 1945. He was knighted in 1934. In 1928 he wrote *Airmen or Noahs*, largely autobiographical but also attacking current concepts of naval and military warfare and advocating the development of independent air power. It was followed in 1937 by *The Evolution of the Tank*.

Sueter died at his home, The Howe, Watlington, Oxfordshire, on 3 February 1960.   PETER KEMP, rev.

Sources *The Times* (5 Feb 1960) · WWW · *CGPLA Eng. & Wales* (1960) · M. F. Sueter, *Airmen or Noahs: fair play for our airmen: the great "neon" air myth exposed* (1928) · WWBMP
Archives Royal Air Force Museum, Hendon, department of research and information services, papers | King's Lond., Liddell Hart C., corresp. with Sir B. H. Liddell Hart | FILM IWM FVA, news footage | SOUND IWM SA, oral history interview
Likenesses W. R. Flint, oils, 1928, NMM
Wealth at death £5265 8s. 5d.: probate, 31 Aug 1960, *CGPLA Eng. & Wales*

Suetonius Paullinus, Gaius (*fl. c.*AD 40–69), Roman governor of Britain, almost certainly derived from the town of Pisaurum (Pesaro), on the Adriatic coast of Italy. Nothing else is known about his family, except that a man of the same names as himself, consul in AD 66, may be assumed to be his son (the famous biographer of the Caesars, Gaius Suetonius Tranquillus, is not known to have been related to Paullinus).

Paullinus first came to notice at the beginning of the 40s. He was one of the Roman generals, with the rank of ex-praetor, who pacified the Moorish rising provoked by the annexation of the north African kingdom of Mauretania. Paullinus was the first Roman commander ever to cross the summit of the Atlas Mountains. He may have owed his selection for this expedition to the prefect of the praetorian guard, Arrecinus Clemens, a native of Pisaurum. Paullinus must have held the consulship in the 40s, but nothing further is known of his career until his appointment to Britain in AD 58. This followed the unexpected death in the province of the governor Quintus Veranius, who had begun a forward policy after some years of quiescence under the intervening governor, Didius Gallus. In AD 58 and 59, taking up the challenge implied in the testament of Veranius, who had claimed that 'he

could have conquered the rest of Britain if he had had another two years' (Tacitus, *Annals*, xiv.29), Paullinus subjugated and garrisoned much of Wales. There remained the island of Mona (Anglesey), the stronghold of the druids, whose influence over the Britons made it an inevitable target. Paullinus had the best part of two legions, the fourteenth and the twentieth, under his command; the other two, IX Hispana and II Augusta, were left guarding the north-east and south-west of the province respectively. No sooner had the island been occupied and the sacred groves cut down than Paullinus received news of Boudicca's uprising.

A combination of factors had provoked the great rebellion. Prasutagus, client ruler of the Iceni of what is now East Anglia, had died shortly before and his kingdom was incorporated into the province. In the process the imperial procurator (chief financial administrator), the knight Decianus Catus, acted very harshly, and Prasutagus's widow, Boudicca, and her daughters were maltreated. The land-grabbing activities of the veteran colonists at Camulodunum (Colchester) had also caused deep resentment and the Temple of Claudius in the *colonia* (chartered town for the settlement of veterans) was regarded, according to Tacitus, as 'a citadel of eternal domination' (Tacitus, *Annals*, xiv.31). Cassius Dio mentions that the wealthy Seneca, still a leading adviser of the emperor Nero, had suddenly called in loans made to the Britons, which would certainly have caused hardship among the British élite. Finally, the assault on the druid 'holy island' may well have stirred the religious feelings of the Britons. At all events, the rising won widespread support, with Boudicca as its figurehead. Camulodunum was stormed and largely destroyed. The procurator Catus, with only a few hundred soldiers at his disposal, was unable to defend the town and fled across the channel to Gaul, while the legate of the IX Hispana, Petillius Cerialis, who brought his troops south (presumably from the legionary base at Longthorpe, near Peterborough), was routed, with heavy casualties. Cerialis himself escaped with his cavalry. Paullinus had meanwhile marched rapidly south, but, although he reached London, he decided that it could not be defended and withdrew into the midlands. London and Verulamium (St Albans) were both destroyed, with heavy loss of life. It was later claimed by Cassius Dio that 'eighty thousand Romans' died at the hands of the rebels, and that some of the captives were sacrificed in bestial fashion 'in the grove of Andate' (Cassius Dio, *Roman History*, lxii. 1, 7).

With the fourteenth legion, part of the twentieth, and some auxiliary regiments, Paullinus had about 10,000 men when he met the rebel army, probably in the midlands, close to the Roman road now called Watling Street, where he won a famous victory. 'A little less than eighty thousand Britons' were said by Tacitus to have fallen, as against only 400 on the Roman side (Tacitus, *Annals*, xiv.37). Boudicca took her own life, as did a senior Roman officer, Poenius Postumus, who had been too frightened to bring the II Augusta from its base in south-west Britain to help. The scale of the destruction caused by the rebels and the report by the procurator Catus of the sack of

Camulodunum had evidently led Nero to contemplate abandoning Britain. It must have seemed like a repetition of the great disaster in Germany in AD 9, when the loss of three legions resulted in the withdrawal from Germany east of the Rhine. As it was, the ninth legion had lost 2000 men, who had to be replaced by troops from the Rhineland, and eight new auxiliary infantry cohorts and two cavalry regiments, a further 5000 men, were also sent to Britain.

Paullinus followed his victory with repressive measures, which had the result of stoking up resistance. The new procurator, Julius Classicianus, protested to Rome that peace could not be achieved unless Paullinus was replaced. Nero sent a senior imperial freedman, Polyclitus, to inspect the situation. Paullinus was initially retained, but dismissed on a pretext not long afterwards, to be succeeded by one of the consuls of AD 61, Petronius Turpilianus, nephew of the first governor of Britain, Plautius. (Since Petronius was sent to Britain straight after his consulship, but in the year following the rebellion, it is clear that the rebellion and its suppression, although described by Tacitus under the year 61, must have occurred in 60.) However, Paullinus was by no means disgraced: a lead tessera from Rome with the emperor's name on one side and that of Paullinus, with victory symbols, on the reverse (Rostowzew, no. 230), suggests that Nero issued largesse to celebrate the victory. Further, Paullinus's presumed son was consul a few years later, in AD 66. The two legions which had defeated Boudicca were honoured with new titles, the fourteenth becoming Martia Victrix and the twentieth Valeria Victrix. Camulodunum was rebuilt with the new title *colonia Victricensis*, suggesting that veterans of these two legions were settled there. The last record of Paullinus comes from the 'year of the four emperors', AD 69, when, by now 'the oldest of the ex-consuls' (Tacitus, *Histories*, ii.37), he held high command for Otho in his unsuccessful campaign against Vitellius in northern Italy.   A. R. BIRLEY

Sources C. Tacitus, *The histories [and] the annals*, ed. and trans. C. H. Moore and J. Jackson, 4 vols. (1925–37), vols. 1–2 · Tacitus, *Agricola*, ed. and trans. M. Mutton (1914), 5, 14 · R. Syme, *Tacitus* (1958) · A. R. Birley, *The fasti of Roman Britain* (1981) · M. Rostowzew, *Tesserarum urbis Romae et suburbi plumbearum sylloge* (1903)

Suett, Richard (*bap.* **1755**, *d.* **1805**), actor and singer, was baptized on 29 July 1755 at St Luke's, Chelsea, the son of John Suett (*d.* 1783), a butcher and later an officer of St Paul's Cathedral, and his wife, Jane, probably the Jane Griffiths who married a John Suet at St George's, Hanover Square, on 24 March 1754. At the age of ten he allegedly became a member of the choir at Westminster Abbey, then under Benjamin Cooke, from whom he received his musical and classical education. Alternatively, Thomas Dibdin reports that Suett had been in the choir of St Paul's Cathedral under Robert Hudson. In 1769, when he was fourteen, he sang at Ranelagh (according to Oxberry, through an introduction to Charles Dibdin) with Charles Bannister, Dibdin, Sophia Baddeley, and Mrs Thompson. The following season, according to *The Thespian Dictionary*,

Richard Suett (*bap.* 1755, *d.* 1805), by Samuel De Wilde, in or before 1803

he made his first appearances in juvenile characters and allegedly sang at Foote's theatre in the Haymarket. He also sang at Marylebone Gardens and at Finch's Grotto Gardens in Southwark, although nothing can be authenticated until 1771, when he performed at the Grotto Gardens on 22 June and at the Haymarket on 24 July.

In autumn 1771 Suett was invited by Tate Wilkinson to join his company at York, where he remained for nine years, eventually earning the highest salary of any actor there. He made his first appearance with the company at Hull on 20 November 1771, singing 'Chloe's my myrtle and Jenny's my rose'. Wilkinson reported that Suett arrived at about the age of seventeen and was known from only one season at Ranelagh. 'Despite a most unpromising pair of legs', he continued, Suett was very successful and 'of very real importance to my little community before he left me' (Wilkinson, 116). When Suett was offered an engagement at Drury Lane in 1780, Wilkinson magnanimously tore up his contract and helped him negotiate the new engagement. While in the York company Suett met the dancer Louisa Margaretta West (1754–1832), when she and her brother were engaged in spring 1772. They married on 8 September 1781, but later separated. Wilkinson states somewhat ambiguously of Louisa that he is 'informed that she makes a good wife' and that, since leaving the stage to become Mrs Suett, 'she combs the lap-dog, scolds the servant (not her husband)—and it is her own fault if in every respect she is not a contented woman' (ibid., 1.183). She and Suett had two sons.

Suett made a successful Drury Lane début on 7 October

1780, as Ralph in Isaac Bickerstaff's *The Maid of the Mill*. A few nights later he played Squire Richard in *The Provok'd Husband* by John Vanbrugh and Colley Cibber. In November 1781 a comedy, *Dissipation*, by Miles Peter Andrews, was commanded by George III, at whose request Suett allegedly filled the role usually undertaken by William Parsons, who was indisposed. Henceforth he often substituted for Parsons when the latter was ill, not always to his advantage. In original parts, however, he had no rival. Among these were Moll Flaggon in John Burgoyne's *Lord of the Manor* (1780), Old Pickle in Bickerstaffe's *The Spoiled Child* (1790), Weazel in Richard Cumberland's *The Wheel of Fortune* (1795), Samson in George Colman the younger's *The Iron Chest* (1796), and Diego in Richard Brinsley Sheridan's *Pizarro* (1799), when he almost damned the play on its first night so that his part was subsequently cut. Away from Drury Lane, he reappeared briefly at the Haymarket on 16 September 1785 and on a regular basis through the summers from 1793 to 1803. Original roles there included Fustian in Colman the younger's *New Hay at the Old Market* (1795) and Lord Duberly in his *The Heir at Law* (1797). Among his Shakespearian roles were the Clowns in *Measure for Measure*, *The Winter's Tale*, and *Twelfth Night*, Touchstone, Launcelot Gobbo, Dogberry, Trinculo, Sir Andrew Aguecheek, Pistol (*Henry V*), Thurio, a Witch (*Macbeth*), and a Gravedigger (*Hamlet*).

Suett, says Charles Lamb, was the Robin Goodfellow of the stage: 'Shakespeare foresaw him, when he framed his fools and jesters. They have all the true Suett stamp, a loose and shambling gait, a slippery tongue' (Lamb, 186). Leigh Hunt called him 'the very personification of weak whimsicality … with a laugh like a peal of giggles' (Russell, 256), while Hazlitt, referring to a role he played in Prince Hoare's *My Grandmother*, called him 'the old croaker, the everlasting Dicky Gossip of the stage' (*London Magazine*, January 1820). According to Oxberry, Suett was 'to a certain extent, inimitable: he never premeditated anything—all he did was the immediate result of impulse and his clownish and simple assumptions were exquisite' (*Oxberry*, 3/45, 1825, 222-3). Suett was 'lamentably lank … when he walked in the street it appeared like an experiment—a sort of trial whether skin and bone could go alone' (newspaper clipping, New York Public Library). According to the *Candid and Impartial Strictures*, 'his figure is too thin for its height. His turned-in, tottering knees and lathy body, when performing old men, give us more an idea of an aged Spaniard than of any other character' (*Strictures*, 22). However, *The Thespian Dictionary* considered: 'his merit chiefly lies in old men and clownish servants, eccentric lovers or gallants'. Genest waspishly suggested that no part suited him better than the Drunken Porter in *Feudal Times*: 'in that part he was sure to be at home' (Genest, *Eng. stage*, 7.654). Indeed, he had a reputation for always being drunk when he played drunken parts. According to Oxberry he was 'sadly indolent and incorrect in his text, and pretty frequently mixed up his real with his assumed character (especially when drunk)' (*Oxberry*, 3/45, 1825, 223). The author of the *Strictures* complained

that he was 'too fond of distorting his features into grimace, and saying more than is set down for him'. Nevertheless, he praised him for his original method of delivering dialogue and found him 'a pleasant, entertaining comedian' (*Strictures*, 22). He was also acclaimed for his use of wigs and make-up to achieve his effects.

Charles Lamb wrote fondly of Suett:

> He came in to trouble all things with a welcome perplexity, himself no whit troubled for the matter. He was known, like Puck, by his note—*Ha! Ha! Ha!*—sometimes deepening to *Ho! Ho! Ho!* with an irresistible accession, derived, perhaps, remotely from his ecclesiastical education, foreign to his prototype of,—*O La!* Thousands of hearts yet respond to the chuckling *O La!* of Dicky Suett … Care, that troubles all the world, was forgotten in his composition. (Lamb, 185)

James Boaden claimed that 'few comedians have ever afforded more amusement than Suett … he was diverting to every description of audience' (Russell, 255). Talking after Suett's death of Cumberland's *Wheel of Fortune*, John Philip Kemble told Michael Kelly:

> Penruddock has lost a powerful ally in Suett; I have acted the part with many Weazels, and good ones too, but none of them could work up my passions to the pitch Suett did; he had a comical, impertinent way of thrusting his head into my face, which called forth all my irritable sensations. (Kelly, 84-5)

To O'Keeffe he was 'the most natural actor' (O'Keeffe, 2.300) of his time. He was also an accomplished musician who composed a number of original pieces; as a child he had an outstanding singing voice. His singing skills later 'rendered him valuable in opera, as he could blend harmony with humour' (Gilliland, 2.990), although Oxberry stated that his voice 'from frequent excesses deteriorated considerably, and it was never safe to trust him with any important musical duties' (*Oxberry*, 3/45, 1825, 221).

'Mr Suett's life', complained Oxberry, 'was a long tissue of irregularities, and we are sorry to record the disgraceful and disgusting fact of his actually living with two sisters at the same time and under the same roof' (*Oxberry*, 3/45, 1825, 221). It is unknown whether one of these sisters was the Lucy Wood mentioned in his will. A rather intemperate, scatological letter (undated) in Suett's hand in the Harvard Theatre Collection appears to refer to this. Suett, says John Genest, ruined himself by drinking. He recounts a story told him by a gentleman who visited the actor one morning at breakfast and found a bottle of rum and a bottle of brandy on the table. His society, adds Gilliland, was little courted by polite society 'from his partiality to tippling in low public houses' (Gilliland, 2.991). 'Mr Suett's ruin', said Oxberry, 'was low society. Any man that could sit and drink was his companion' (*Oxberry*, 3/45, 1825, 221). *The Records of a Stage Veteran* provides a less censorious view:

> men would rather record in my time the bright things or the merry stories that Suett uttered, than delight in expiating on his love of the lasses or the bottle. It was impossible to remain for any length of time angry with him; he had about him an unconsciousness of offending that disarmed you. (Russell, 255)

Ann Mathews also recalled that he was very popular with his fellow actors. His last performance was at Drury Lane on 10 June 1805, as Lampedo in John Tobin's *The Honeymoon*. He died on 6 July 1805, either at a public house in Denzell Street, Clare Market, or at his lodgings in Paradise Row. He had apparently suffered from an apoplectic fit about a fortnight previously. His funeral, on 15 July 1805 at St Paul's Cathedral, was attended by nearly all of the theatrical fraternity who were still in town.   JIM DAVIS

Sources T. Gilliland, *The dramatic mirror, containing the history of the stage from the earliest period, to the present time*, 2 vols. (1808) · T. Wilkinson, *The wandering patentee, or, A history of the Yorkshire theatres from 1770 to the present time*, 4 vols. (1795) · *GM*, 1st ser., 75 (1805), 684 · Genest, *Eng. stage*, vol. 7 · *The thespian dictionary, or, Dramatic biography of the present age*, 2nd edn (1805) · *Candid and impartial strictures on the performers* (1795) · *Oxberry's Dramatic Biography*, 3/45 (1825) · C. Lamb, 'On some of the old actors', *The essays of Elia*, [new edn] (1849) · W. Hazlitt, 'On play-going and on some of our old actors', *London Magazine*, 1 (1820) · W. C. Russell, *Representative actors* [1888] · J. O'Keeffe, *Recollections of the life of John O'Keeffe, written by himself*, 2 vols. (1826) · T. Dibdin, *The reminiscences of Thomas Dibdin*, 2 vols. (1827) · Mrs Mathews, *Tea-table talk, ennobled actresses, and other miscellanies*, 2 vols. (1857) · M. Kelly, *Reminiscences*, 2 vols. (1826) · Highfill, Burnim & Langhans, *BDA* · IGI

Archives Harvard TC, corresp.

Likenesses S. De Wilde, oils, *c*.1790, Theatre Museum, London · S. De Wilde, pencil and watercolour drawing, 1794, Garr. Club · S. De Wilde, oils, in or before 1803, Garr. Club [*see illus.*] · S. De Wilde, oils, *c*.1803, Theatre Museum, London · S. De Wilde, oils, AM Oxf. · S. De Wilde, two oil portraits, Garr. Club · J. Graham, oils, Theatre Museum, London · J. Graham, oils (as Bayes in Duke of Buckingham's *The rehearsal*), V&A · W. Loftis, watercolour drawings, Folger · J. Zoffany, portrait, priv. coll. · engravings, Harvard TC · engravings, Theatre Museum, London

Wealth at death £150: Highfill, Burnim & Langhans, *BDA*

Suffeld, Walter. *See* Suffield, Walter of (d. 1257).

Suffield. For this title name *see* Harbord, Edward, third Baron Suffield (1781–1835).

Suffield, Robert Rodolph (1821–1891), Roman Catholic priest and Unitarian minister, was born on 5 October 1821 at Vevey, Switzerland, younger son of George Suffield, member of an old Norfolk Catholic family, and his wife, Susan Tulley Bowen. He received lay baptism by a relative at Vevey but was later rebaptized at the Anglican church of St Peter Mancroft, in Norwich. His father, a disciple of Rousseau, had ceased Catholic practice and, accordingly, brought up his sons to develop independency of judgement.

Suffield was taught by private tutors; much of his secular and religious education seems to have been fated to be incomplete or interrupted. In 1841, as a nominal Anglican, he was admitted as a commoner at Peterhouse, Cambridge, but he spent less than two years there. Religious scruples and declining family prosperity may have determined his withdrawal. He had also been influenced by the Anglican Catholic revival and, possibly, a rekindling of pride in his old Catholic connections. By 1846 he was a practising Catholic, intending to enter the priesthood. After a brief stay at Ushaw College, where he had considered training, he moved in 1847 to the fashionable seminary of St Sulpice, Paris. One of his contemporaries there, with whom he remained sporadically in touch, was the future liberal Catholic Hyacinthe Loyson (1827–1912). The turmoil of the 1848 revolution drove him back to Britain, and after more than a year in Ireland among sympathetic relatives he enrolled at Ushaw later that year.

Suffield was ordained on 15 August 1850. A year of parish work completed, he joined a small community of secular mission priests based at St Ninian's, Wooler, in Northumberland. Their work took them throughout the country and revealed his remarkable gifts as a preacher. In 1858 he took vigorous charge of St Andrew's, Newcastle upon Tyne, where, an ardent supporter of the papacy, he reintroduced into England the collection of Peter's pence, abolished at the Reformation. He entered the Dominican novitiate at Woodchester in 1860. Here he was permitted to complete, with Father C. F. R. Palmer, a 880 page compendium of Catholic faith and practice, *The Crown of Jesus* (1862), which was published anonymously and sold thousands of copies. With other friars he established the priory at Kentish Town, London, but at the behest of the Dominican general he returned to duties at Woodchester in 1863. His burgeoning reputation as a talented priest was enhanced by his founding of the Perpetual Rosary Association that year. He continued its director until 1870 when, he estimated, there were 36,000 members. His mission preaching continued unabated.

However, during this decade of conflict over papal claims Suffield began to have radical doubts over the authority of the church. He withdrew in 1868, by permission, to a quiet pastoral post at Husbands Bosworth in Leicestershire. He was impressed during these years by the works of Unitarian writers such as the American preacher and reformer Theodore Parker (1810–1860), F. W. Newman, and Frances Power Cobbe. Unable to stifle his doubts, he wrote to James Martineau, a leading Unitarian minister and thinker, in May 1870. Martineau responded tactfully but firmly; with the latter's backing, an opening into Unitarian ministry was offered at Croydon, where a new church was planned. So, shortly after the decree of papal infallibility had been proclaimed in 1870, to the despair of J. H. Newman and Catholics generally the erstwhile friar became a Free Christian minister. The following year, on 7 December 1871, he married Madeline (d. 1918), daughter of Edward Bramley and a member of a prominent Sheffield Unitarian family; the couple had no children. During a busy, successful ministry Suffield built up the congregation and plunged into civic life and Liberal politics. Typically, he strove to get local authority funding for a public library and, failing, opened one at the church. He largely abstained from anti-Catholic polemics, with the exception of two pamphlets, *Five Letters on a Conversion to Roman Catholicism* (1873) and *The Vatican Decrees* (1874), which attracted the interest of W. E. Gladstone. The two men met and corresponded from 1874 to 1880, and on occasion thereafter, on ecclesial and theological issues and the Irish question—the last an abiding concern of Suffield. After a breakdown of health in 1877 he resigned his Croydon ministry, but felt sufficiently recovered to undertake the ministry at Reading from 1879 until 1888. As in

Croydon, he soon came to prominence in civic and political affairs. He died of cancer at Malvern Villa, Craven Road, Reading, on 13 November 1891. The funeral was held at Woking crematorium and his ashes were buried in the Reading churchyard. In 1990 his ashes, with those of his wife, were reburied at Underbank Chapel, Sheffield.

TONY CROSS

Sources [C. Hargrove], *The life of Robert Rodolph Suffield* (1893) · Croydon public library, 1 The Flyover, Croydon, Local History Collection, Croydon Unitarian Church Archives · Dominican Archives, 25 George Square, Edinburgh · *The letters and diaries of John Henry Newman*, ed. C. S. Dessain and others, [31 vols.] (1961–), vol. 25, pp. 83, 175, 180–85; vol. 31, p. 90, addenda · priv. coll., Reading Unitarian Church archives [photocopies in Harris Man. Oxf.] · BL, Gladstone MSS, Add. MS 44318, fols. 174–354 · *The Inquirer* (21 Nov 1891) · *The Inquirer* (28 Nov 1891) · J. Morris, *Religion and urban change: Croydon, 1840–1914* (1992), 155 · T. A. Walker, ed., *Admissions to Peterhouse or St Peter's College in the University of Cambridge* (1912), 474 · m. cert. · Gladstone, *Diaries* · private information (2004) [Revd Peter B. Godfrey] · T. Cross, 'Monstrous propositions of a Dominican: Rodolph Suffield and David Urquhart on the morality of war', *New Blackfriars*, 82 (Jan 2001), 23–34 · T. Cross, 'From friar to Free Christian', *Transactions of the Unitarian Historical Society*, 21 (1998), 296–301 · T. Cross, 'One of the advanced school—Robert Rodolph Suffield's Croydon ministry 1870–1877', *Transactions of the Unitarian Historical Society*, 22 (2001), 261–74
Archives BL, corresp. with W. E. Gladstone, Add. MS 44318 · McMaster University, Hamilton, Ontario, letters to Lord and Lady Amberley
Likenesses photograph in group, 1866, English Dominican Archive, Edinburgh, Carisbrooke Convent album · Messrs Farrer of Reading, photogravure photograph, repro. in Hargrove, *Life of Robert Rodolph Suffield*, frontispiece · photograph, repro. in *Reading Library and Scientific Society Report for 1914* (1915?), 12
Wealth at death £986 5s. 3d.: probate, 1 Jan 1892, CGPLA Eng. & Wales

Suffield [Calthorpe], **Walter of** (d. **1257**), bishop of Norwich, was probably born in Norfolk at Calthorpe (near Suffield), from which his alternative surname derived. He was probably educated at Oxford before moving to Paris, where he graduated DCnL and taught as regent master. He was in England again in 1240, when he acted as papal judge-delegate in a Suffolk case. After a complex dispute, when the government of Henry III opposed the papal translation of William of Raleigh from Norwich to Winchester, Suffield was eventually elected bishop of Norwich before 9 July 1244, when royal assent was given, the temporalities were restored on 17 July, and he was consecrated at Norwich on 26 February 1245.

In the summer of 1245 Suffield attended the first Council of Lyons. On 13 October 1247 he preached in Westminster Abbey at the translation of the relic of the holy blood. He attended parliament at London in February 1248, and in the following October obtained royal protection for a pilgrimage to St Gilles in southern France. During this journey he again visited the papal court, where he obtained a 'shameful privilege for extorting money in his diocese' (Paris, 5.80)—presumably confirmation of the custom, unique in England, whereby the bishop of Norwich received the first-fruits of vacant churches in his diocese. In 1251 he joined with other bishops in protesting against Archbishop Boniface's exercise of Canterbury's rights of provincial visitation; in January 1252 he was one of the arbitrators between the king and Simon de Montfort concerning the expenses of the latter in Gascony; and in 1253 he attended the great council at Westminster where general sentence of excommunication was pronounced against violators of the church's liberties.

Late in 1253 Suffield was commissioned to assess one tenth of ecclesiastical property throughout England, granted by the pope to the king for the Holy Land subsidy. The authorities regarded the resulting survey, known as the valuation of Norwich, as over-indulgent, and the collectors as having been lukewarm in their task. A new survey was ordered, but after bitter complaints from the clergy, this second valuation was abandoned and Suffield's survey remained in force until 1276.

Suffield was heavily influenced by two renowned English prelates, Edmund of Abingdon, archbishop of Canterbury (d. 1240) and Richard of Wyche, bishop of Chichester (d. 1253), both of whom were canonized and to whose cults Suffield became devoted. He himself proved to be an admirable diocesan bishop, and gained a posthumous reputation of his own for sanctity and miracles. It was noted that he sold many of his own assets to help the poor in a time of famine. At Norwich he founded in 1246 the 'Great' hospital of St Giles, for a master, brethren, and sisters living under a rule, resident poor men and scholars, and for the succour of the transient infirm poor. He was a benefactor of his monastic cathedral chapter, and was remembered by the community with affection, both for his gifts and for his addition to the cathedral of a magnificent lady chapel. He issued several diocesan statutes to supplement those promulgated by his immediate predecessor. It is, however, impossible to distinguish his legislation from that of his successor Simon of Walton, with the single exception of the statute relating to the disposal of tithes in the last testaments of rectors. Some one hundred *acta* are extant from his episcopate, and these reflect his concern to ensure the provision of effective pastoral ministry in the parishes of East Anglia, by the appointment of resident vicars with decent incomes and security of tenure. He also made the first detailed episcopal regulations in this region for chantry foundations. But his practical piety was relieved by his fondness for hunting; in 1253 he received royal licence for the chase through the forests of Essex, and he bequeathed a pack of hounds to the king.

Walter of Suffield died at Colchester on 19 May 1257 and was buried in his own cathedral. Among other bequests, he made provision for poor scholars at Oxford and left money to complete the ornamental work that he had begun at the tomb of St Edmund at Pontigny. His residual legatee was his nephew, William of Calthorpe.

CHRISTOPHER HARPER-BILL

Sources C. Harper-Bill, ed., *Norwich, 1245–1299*, English Episcopal Acta [forthcoming] · Paris, *Chron.*, vols. 4–6 · F. Blomefield and C. Parkin, *An essay towards a topographical history of the county of Norfolk*, [2nd edn], 11 vols. (1805–10), vol. 3, pp. 486–92 · W. E. Lunt, ed., *The valuation of Norwich* (1926) · H. W. Saunders, ed., *The first register of Norwich Cathedral priory*, Norfolk RS, 11 (1939)

Archives BL · BL, Cotton MS Faustina A. iii, fols. 11r–16v · BL, Cotton MS Titus A. viii, fols. 2r–5v · Norfolk RO
Likenesses seal
Wealth at death see will, Blomefield and Parkin, *An essay*

Suffolk. For this title name *see* Ufford, Robert, first earl of Suffolk (1298–1369); Pole, Michael de la, first earl of Suffolk (c.1330–1389); Ufford, William, second earl of Suffolk (c.1339–1382); Pole, Michael de la, second earl of Suffolk (1367/8–1415); Pole, Michael de la, third earl of Suffolk (c.1395–1415) [*see under* Pole, Michael de la, second earl of Suffolk (1367/8–1415)]; Pole, William de la, first duke of Suffolk (1396–1450); Chaucer, Alice, duchess of Suffolk (c.1404–1475); Pole, John de la, second duke of Suffolk (1442–1492); Pole, Edmund de la, eighth earl of Suffolk (1472?–1513); Brandon, Charles, first duke of Suffolk (c.1484–1545); Grey, Henry, duke of Suffolk (1517–1554); Grey, Frances, duchess of Suffolk (1517–1559); Bertie, Katherine, duchess of Suffolk (1519–1580); Howard, Thomas, first earl of Suffolk (1561–1626); Howard, Katherine, countess of Suffolk (b. in or after 1564, d. 1638); Howard, Theophilus, second earl of Suffolk (1584–1640); Howard, James, third earl of Suffolk (1619–1689); Howard, Susanna, countess of Suffolk (1627–1649); Howard, Henrietta, countess of Suffolk (c.1688–1767); Howard, Henry, twelfth earl of Suffolk and fifth earl of Berkshire (1739–1779).

Sugden, Edward Burtenshaw, Baron St Leonards (1781–1875), lord chancellor, was born on 12 February 1781, the second son of Richard Sugden, wig maker and hairdresser, of Duke Street, Westminster, and his wife, Charlotte Burtenshaw.

Early life and legal education: success as an author and barrister Sugden was precocious and largely self-educated, learning at home and at an unnoted private school, followed by time as an office boy and clerk in solicitors' offices. The details of his legal education are obscure. By one account, in 1802 Sugden was taking solicitors' business to one Mr Duval, an established conveyancing attorney, who happened to converse with him about a case and was struck by the young man's knowledge of the legal issues. Duval immediately took Sugden on as a pupil without fee. Sugden enrolled as a student member of Lincoln's Inn on 16 September 1802, and soon won a reputation for extraordinary devotion to the law. Campbell, a fellow student, relates that on meeting him at a dinner at their inn Sugden opened conversation by asking his opinion of the arcane doctrine of the *scintilla juris*. This fascination with the near-theological abstractions of English property law remained with Sugden for the whole of his career.

In 1802, at the age of twenty-one, Sugden produced his first work on property law, a *Brief Conversation with a Gentleman about to Buy or Sell Lands*, laid out as a series of letters. The quality of the exposition is striking, explaining basics of the common law and equity system with the utmost lucidity. No one had previously thought to write an accessible law book for the lay public on a particular legal subject, as opposed to encyclopaedic treatments. Building on this impressive début, in 1805 he published *Vendors and Purchasers of Estates*, a large-scale treatise which caused a

Edward Burtenshaw Sugden, Baron St Leonards (1781–1875), by Eden Upton Eddis, exh. RA 1853

sensation in the legal world. This book was a remarkable achievement considering Sugden's youth, the difficulty of the subject, and the fact that there were few enough modern law treatises to serve as models at this time. In a memoir written half a century later, Sugden recounted how his colleagues had tried to discourage him from this project:

> Nothing daunted, I laboured diligently, and, with the aid of Lincoln's-inn Library—for my own shelves were but scantily furnished—I at length finished the work in the original shape. My courage then failed me. The expense of publication was certain, and success, I thought, more than doubtful, and it was not without some difficulty that I could be persuaded to refrain from committing the manuscript to the flames.

The success of that book gave him enormous satisfaction, and as he said, 'was certainly the foundation of my early success in life' ('Preface' to *Vendors and Purchasers of Estates*, 13th edn, 1857, iii–iv). The work was regarded as authoritative; it shaped conveyancing practice and precedents and was cited in case law throughout the nineteenth and twentieth centuries. Demand for the book was extraordinary—two editions in the first year and twelve further editions issued under Sugden's hand up to 1862; and this brought him considerable royalties with advances of up to £4000 for the later editions. The book deserved its success: it provided sure guidance to a myriad of authorities in contract, property, and trusts law; it presented sophisticated civilian doctrines as well as common-law learning; and it displayed a practical understanding of the operation of land markets.

Sugden followed this early triumph with the equally impressive *Practical Treatise on Powers* (1808), dealing with the difficult subject of how an owner could control and delegate discretions to grant, dispose, and convey property, an essential part of trusts and land law. Sugden was most proud of this work, which also proved to be a durable classic, exerting influence on American as well as English law. The last edition under Sugden's authorship was the eighth edition of 1861. Also worthy of note was a scholarly modern edition of Gilbert's *Law of Uses and Trusts* prepared by Sugden in 1811, making accessible one of the great works of older equity jurisprudence. He later wrote three further specialist property texts, and expanded his first epistolary book of 1802 into a *Handy Book on Property Law* (1858), a work for a lay audience that was not only a long-running best-seller but was also cited in court—so much so, that Campbell quipped that he would support legislating the entire book as a property statute, but that its influence made this redundant. Sugden continued to address a non-specialist audience with a series of some twenty pamphlets, usually reprints of his speeches, on topical legal and political issues. In all his writings, Sugden ordered his materials with a thorough command of the sources, a firm rationalizing mind, and a trenchant and lucid, if not particularly artful, writing style. He maintained his treatises by interleaving all current legal materials into his own master copies, so that assistants could easily prepare further editions.

Sugden's stunning success as a legal writer in his twenties laid the foundation for his professional career as a barrister. It was said that no abstract of title could be sure unless Sugden had perused it in chambers. He was admitted as a full member of the bar after two years of practice on 23 November 1807. His swelling conveyancing practice led him to confine himself to court work from 1817, but he was soon swamped with briefs. Many of his arguments in the courts of chancery and king's bench on property issues were reproduced in the law reports. He was a master both of difficult legal concepts and of forensics and the rules of evidence, and his enormous skill and facility in presentation soon made him a favourite in court of Eldon and Lyndhurst. Eldon gave him the distinction of a silk gown in 1822, at a time when the station of king's counsel was still extremely rare; Sugden responded by dedicating later editions of his book on *Powers* to Eldon. He was elected a bencher of Lincoln's Inn in that year, and finally became its treasurer in 1836.

Political career As Sugden's legal career burgeoned he began to campaign for political and judicial advancement. He was a tory candidate for a notionally vacant parliamentary seat in Sussex in 1818, but withdrew from the poll when the popular incumbent withdrew his resignation. At the hustings in that election he was taunted for his origins as a barber's son. He replied 'Yes, I was, and still am, the son of a barber … but have risen to be a barrister …; if [my assailant] had been a barber's son, he would probably have remained a barber's son all his life.' He stood for the Sussex borough of Shoreham in 1826, but this adventure failed when he mishandled the issue of Catholic emancipation. In a letter to agents of the duke of Norfolk, the dominant magnate of the region, Sugden promised to vote for the lifting of Catholic disabilities, but he then made a campaign speech promising to vote against emancipation. His aristocratic sponsors were sufficiently irritated at this to release the earlier letter and withdraw all support, and with his credibility so undermined, Sugden came bottom of the poll. This was uncharacteristically maladroit conduct, however, and on 20 February 1828 Sugden fought and won a by-election for Weymouth, Dorset. He held the seat at the general election of August 1830, but then moved to the borough of St Mawes in Cornwall; in 1831 he moved again to a seat for the borough of Cambridge; and from 1837 to 1841 he held a seat for Ripon. It may be surmised that his party wanted Sugden in parliament as a proficient lawyer, but only later helped him to take a secure seat.

Sugden's political intuitions were strongly tory. His first speeches in the Commons vehemently defended the court of chancery against its detractors, a controversy he had first broached in a printed defence of chancery in 1825. Sugden's defence strained credulity, asserting that it was 'chiefly fraudulent trustees' and discontented suitors who had any reason to resent the dilatory chancery system. He was always a strong and partisan protestant and a relentless opponent of Irish separatism; in 1829 he argued that O'Connell should be excluded from the Commons following the County Clare by-election. Yet he pragmatically supported the duke of Wellington's Catholic Emancipation Act in the same year, despite his objections to admitting papists to government or state office. He was rewarded for his party loyalty by appointment as solicitor-general in June 1829, and was knighted. Though he left office with the fall of the government one year later in November 1830, he passed a number of minor but useful reforming statutes, mainly dealing with wills and estates, and also signalled an intention to reform chancery procedure and reduce sinecures, waste, and delay (Atkinson). Sugden continued to practise throughout this period, and by 1830 was counted the leading chancery barrister of his day.

Sugden was displeased by Brougham's elevation to the lord chancellorship in the new whig-led administration, and was dismayed by his radical plans for law reform, which he thought superficial and lacking understanding of the existing legal system. The two men's differences soon became personal as well as political. Sugden was angered by Brougham's lack of attention during chancery hearings and once rebuked him for reading state papers during argument in open court. Brougham soon retaliated by mocking Sugden's self-important rhetoric in the Commons: when Sugden declared to the house that he could not respect Fox's policies, Brougham jeered 'Poor Fox', and the house dissolved into mirth. Sugden responded by raising before the Commons the propriety of Brougham's appointment of his own brother to a legal sinecure that the lord chancellor had just pledged to abolish. Brougham lost all self-control and, after making a veiled attack on Sugden in the Lords, launched an intemperate and abusive attack on him outside parliament, calling him a 'bug' and a 'crawling reptile'. Sugden failed in trying to have Brougham reproved in the Commons, but finally settled accounts with a memorable quip at Brougham's expense: praising the chancellor's encyclopaedic knowledge of insects he then added: 'If the lord chancellor only knew a little law, he would know a little of everything.' Brougham realized that he had gone too far and privately apologized. Late in 1834 Brougham was prepared to offer Sugden either the legal moiety of the lord chancellorship (confining himself to political activity), or else a place on the exchequer bench. The offers led nowhere, but Sugden and Brougham became friends, and Sugden defended Brougham after his death against Campbell's depredations (*Misrepresentations in Campbell's Lives of Lyndhurst and Brougham Corrected by Lord St Leonards*, 1869).

Lord chancellor of Ireland and then Great Britain On Peel's accession to power in December 1834 Sugden was appointed lord chancellor of Ireland and was sworn as a privy councillor; but this tenure soon expired when Peel's government fell in April 1835. Sugden's appointment was at first resented by the Irish bar, but his judicial performance was so outstanding that he was quickly accepted. Back in opposition he spoke in favour of the jurisdiction of the court of queen's bench to decide the powers of the parliament over matters of privilege (debates on *Stockdale v. Hansard*, 17 June 1839, 7 February, 5 March 1840). In Peel's second administration he was restored to his former office and presided over Irish chancery from 3 October 1841 until July 1846. During this time he produced many fine judgments that were extensively reported, and produced a codification of chancery practice and procedure. He courted controversy in the partisan political role he took as chancellor; for example in 1843 he dismissed Irish nationalist magistrates as unworthy to hold commissions, and Wellington and Lyndhurst ratified his action in parliament against nationalist uproar. As chancellor he was officially guardian over lunatics, and he took this job seriously, assiduously visiting institutions with Phillip Crampton, a surgeon and the chief inspector of asylums. It was told that on one such visit Crampton was delayed, and when Sugden was found wandering around the asylum by himself declaring that he was the lord high chancellor making an inspection, the keeper had him restrained in a strait-jacket and locked in a cell. Sugden later claimed that Crampton had exaggerated the story for effect.

Sugden continued as an active member of the House of Commons throughout the 1830s and 1840s whether in public office or not, and he emerged as an articulate, independent-minded commentator on legal and constitutional matters, radical and reactionary by turn. He persistently advocated modernization of chancery procedure and the mechanisms for attesting and proving wills, but was dismissive of Campbell's attempts to move in the same directions. He opposed the Great Reform Bill of 1832 on the basis that £10 householders would prove venal and corrupt voters; for him politics were not the concern of the populace. He linked his opposition to the bill with an attack on the government's dealings with O'Connell and the nationalists in Ireland. He resisted reform of the usury laws on the basis that repeal would be 'a great mischief to

both the commercial and landed classes', while freely conceding 'the injurious effects' of those laws. He made detailed criticisms of Melbourne's proposals to augment the overstretched appellate judiciary, while accepting that the entire system of judicial review was tottering and close to collapse. In 1850 he attacked Dickens for his negative portrayal of chancery in *Bleak House*, and also made an inflammatory speech at Epsom condemning papal interference in British politics; but generally he confined himself to legal matters. Ultimately his political career was retarded by his arrogant manner; he was 'waspish, overbearing and impatient of contradiction' (Selborne, 1.374–5), and spoke to parliament in a pedantic and monotonous fashion, over-conscious of his superiority. He was certainly not a lawyer–politician of the calibre of Eldon or Brougham, though he matched them in self-esteem and confidence.

In 1852 Lord Derby formed a tory government and Sugden succeeded Truro as lord chancellor of Great Britain on 27 February, taking the title Baron St Leonards of Slaugham, Sussex, on 1 March. He took his seat on the woolsack on 4 March, becoming the first person to hold successively the great seals of Ireland and of Great Britain, and held the post until the fall of the administration in December of the same year. The profession was delighted by his appointment and Lincoln's Inn hall was packed to overflowing with crowds of attorneys gathering to celebrate the elevation of one of their own. Many reforms of chancery procedure during Sugden's tenure as Irish lord chancellor now pointed the way for reforms in England. He adopted many recommendations of the whig chancery commission chaired by Sir John Romilly, including abolition of the notorious masters in chancery, using public funds to retire the incumbents. He passed legislation clarifying the methods for stating and enforcing court orders and decrees, and extracting judgment debts from estates. He helped to start legal aid to the poor and tried to restrain improper or abusive use of court processes. He initiated codification of the criminal law and accepted the need for a separate court of appeal. However, he strongly resisted all attempts to professionalize the law lords, and he opposed the scheme to make Sir James Parke a life peer with voting powers in 1856 in order to buttress the Lords' legal capacities. He accepted that talented professionals should be ennobled as working peers, but insisted on an undiluted hereditary principle as a foundation of parliamentary as well as monarchical authority. He also insisted that the political and legal roles of the lord chancellor should not be divided. At the end of his career he joined in the long debates concerning the judicature reforms introduced to parliament in 1869 by Lord Hatherley. Sugden was deeply critical of the great judicature scheme to rationalize England's complex court system; yet as lord chancellor he had himself accelerated the evolution of the court system into its modern form.

Contributions to the development of law and equity Sugden excelled at technical reform of the detailed rules of property and trusts, the fields where his chief expertise lay. As solicitor-general and then as lord chancellor he passed laws relaxing the over-stringent formalities required to make a valid will (including the requirement that a will be signed at the bottom), controlling fraudulent devises, reducing chancery's wide contempt powers, and providing methods for equity courts to establish clear transferable titles of property owned or held by infants, lunatics, and married women, whether directly or through trustees and mortgagees. However, Sugden was sceptical of sweeping reforms to property law and rejected the ambitious programme of the real property commissioners. He powerfully resisted all attempts, such as those by James Humphreys, Campbell, and Brougham, to rationalize titles through a radical system of land registration, on the practical bases that registration would be expensive for smaller title-holders, and that the finality of the register would interfere with the fluidity of boundaries and exclude equitable claims. Sugden did support registration of commercial and judgment claims; he was a practical rather than ideological opponent of title registration. One notable achievement was an amendment in 1859 to the law of trusts (22 & 23 Vict. c.35) settling the arcane problem of how a legal estate could feed a contingent use under the mechanism created by the Statute of Uses. Sugden cleverly invoked the *scintilla juris* doctrine as a solution. This was law reform by the lawyers for the lawyers; fittingly it was Sugden's last piece of legislation initiated as lord chancellor and came to be known as Lord St Leonards's Act. (His legislative achievements are detailed in Holdsworth, 16, 1966, 52–4.) He refused reappointment as lord chancellor in 1858, and spent the balance of his career as an active peer and law lord, forming a dominant triumvirate with Brougham and Cranworth. Sugden sat in judicial hearings of the House of Lords and privy council regularly into his late eighties, and became a legendary figure of the Victorian legal age. He presided over hearings with enormous authority, presenting an erect and impassive mien and paying utmost attention to counsel. He was never seen to take notes, but would interrupt on occasion to quiz counsel intensely on their understanding of legal rules. He could be harsh and sarcastic to the ill-prepared, yet he enjoyed enormous respect from the profession. His judgments were shrewd and to the point, and almost always delivered extempore; his powers of memory and mental ordering did not desert him as he aged. His decisions were generally accepted as very sound, and only three of his Irish cases were reversed or overturned. He was sometimes in dissent in the Lords, as in *Spackman v. Evans* (1868), his last speech recorded in twenty-eight pages of close argument where he rejected a scheme of compromise of an insurance company's debts, emphasizing that directors should be bound stringently by objective notice of facts. The extempore style of his judgments rendered them somewhat orthodox, and he is rightly regarded as technically irreproachable but only rarely a creative or searching appellate judge. He made his mark in cases concerning trusts and estates, as could be expected, but also in commercial law and contract. In *Ex parte Hennessey* (1842) he laid the foundations for a new doctrine of equitable assignment of policies of assurance, based on consent rather than notice. In *Dyer v. Hey* (1852) he held that the heads of easement were not closed, and that common-law categories of land use were to be moulded to changing economic conditions. The doctrine of *bona fide* purchase was held to apply to defend the taker of an equitable as well as a legal estate in *Colyer v. Finch* (1856). In *Egerton v. Earl Brownlow* (1853) he gave a classical exposition of the law on limitation and constitution of trusts and also allowed a role for public policy in curbing obnoxious transactions. In that case a gift of a great estate was made conditionally on the grantee attaining noble rank; this limitation was held by the Lords to be void, against the opinion of the common-law judges. In the *Berkeley Peerage case* (1858) he gave a profound analysis of the nature of feudal titles, holding that a lesser interest such as a life estate in a territory could not bring with it a barony by tenure; his learning towered over that presented by his brother judges Campbell and Cranworth, and his speech was reprinted as a pamphlet and widely read. He held there was no copyright at common law in *Jeffreys v. Boosey* (1854, one of the major intellectual property decisions of the century); that ambiguities in an insurance policy were to be construed against the company, overtly to defend the customer (*Anderson v. Fitzgerald*, 1853); that directors could not take advantage of their own misfeasance (*Bargate v. Shortridge*, 1853); that a company's capacity is that of a natural person save that it must not act *ultra vires* beyond its incorporating act (*Eastern Counties Railway v. Hawkes*, 1855); and that a father must demonstrate the absence of undue influence where a son transfers property to him on attaining majority (*Savery v. King*, 1856). He dissented in *Jorden v. Money* (1854), holding that a statement of present intention could be actionable in misrepresentation as a statement of existing fact. The law of contract has since edged in this direction, as in the doctrine of estoppel *in pais*. *Lumley v. Wagner* (1852) is his most celebrated decision, where he applied an injunction to prevent Wagner, a young German opera singer, from performing at a rival house in breach of a prior contractual duty to sing for her employer Lumley. Damages would have been inadequate; an order specifically to perform was impossible according to liberal doctrines of free labour; confiscation of the profits of breach was too unorthodox; injunction was left as the best possible remedy. The case made a huge and often negative impact in labour law and intellectual property decisions; it is read to this day by every law student and its principle still hotly debated by lawyers seeking to define the nature of a promise of services. In another dissent he held that the law of God forbade common-law recognition of a marriage to a deceased wife's sister even if valid abroad (*Brook v. Brook*, 1861). At times the line between judging and legislating in the Lords could be slender: one of Sugden's last pieces of law making was the statutory scheme of compulsory labour arbitration he sponsored in 1867; it favoured the interests of employers and quickly failed (30 & 31 Vict. c.105).

Assessment Sugden was a quintessential lawyers' lawyer, a true heir of Lord Eldon. Unlike Eldon he was eager to make piecemeal improvements to rules and institutions where necessary, but opposed sweeping legal innovation, which he condemned as 'revolutionary'. His resistance to professionalization of the higher judiciary both as lord chancellor and as a senior judge helped keep the House of Lords in low esteem as a law tribunal for much of the mid-nineteenth century. Yet Sugden himself was utterly devoted to the technical and demanding vocation of the law, and moreover there was in him a vein of compassion and anger at injustice that prompted many radical and effective reformist measures. As lord chancellor he passed into law a major recasting of the lunacy statutes that greatly benefited the indigent insane, creating an elaborate parochial obligation of care and maintenance, subjecting asylums to close regulation by justices, and protecting the insane from arbitrary interference with their persons and property (16 & 17 Vict. cc.70, 96, 97). He was also sympathetic to the indebted poor and was hostile to mesne imprisonment of debtors, a self-defeating and vicious policy that he helped to curtail. As a barrister he would regularly visit Fleet Street and strive to help debtors personally by proffering legal advice and even discharging their debts from his own pocket. He claimed intellectual authorship of Romilly's acts of 1848–9 for the reform of encumbered Irish estates, though Romilly later asserted that he had drafted the policy as Liberal attorney-general without being aware of Sugden's advocacy of like policies to Peel and Russell. Taking his career as a whole, Sugden combined innate conservatism, naked ambition, and staunch defence of professional and inherited privilege with a pragmatic sense for improvement and a strong antipathy to cruel and outmoded practices. He represents many of the contradictions of his society and its legal-political order: he was at once a self-made professional of humble origins, a tory defender of privilege, a consummate technical lawyer and brilliant legal writer, a cautious and fluent judge, a narrow-minded opponent of broad legal change—and yet ultimately a responsible legal statesman and one of the most effective judges and law reformers of his age, a Coke for the Victorians.

Family and retirement In the latter part of his life Sugden lived at Thames Ditton on an estate named Boyle Farm, in a grand house overlooking the river, later converted into an old people's home. He entertained a wide circle of friends and colleagues there, and spent the rest of his time at a retreat at Slaugham, Sussex. He won many honours including the LLD from Cambridge (1835) and the DCL from Oxford (1853). He was high steward of Kingston upon Thames and deputy lieutenant of Sussex. He married Winifred, daughter of John Knapp, on 23 December 1808. They had seven daughters and seven sons, and she died on 19 May 1861. He lived on to near the age of ninety-four, and his last public appearance was in 1873 when he visited the local assize court in Surrey; he was immediately recognized and all stood to pay respect to the great ancient, 'the Nestor of the profession' (Cockburn, 7n.). He died, presumably of old age, on 29 January 1875, outliving not only his wife but also many of his children; it was his grandson Edward who inherited the title. Sugden was buried on 2 February before a large crowd of mourners at St Nicholas's Church adjacent to Boyle Farm, reunited with his wife beneath a modest slab of pink marble. There is an engraving of Sugden at Lincoln's Inn, made after a portrait of him by his daughter Charlotte, and showing his refined features to good effect.

There was one final posthumous episode occasioning much comment at the time, suggesting another piquant contradiction. Sugden, the great lawyer who had striven all his working life to simplify and encourage testation by property holders, was found at death to have left no discoverable will, but only six codicils. His servants seem to have stolen the will to see if legacies had been made for them. Charlotte Sugden, daughter and amanuensis, claimed that she could supply a firm outline of the missing will's contents; but *prima facie* Sugden had died intestate and his natural heir stood to inherit. A lawsuit was joined, and a great appeal court convened to hold that Miss Sugden's reliable extrinsic evidence could be admitted on the strong factual presumption that Lord St Leonards must have executed a will. It is said that Miss Sugden had frozen in the witness box, but that counsel freed her memory by pouring her a glass of water, the noise of which reminded her of her aged father's habit of serving sherry as he read his will to her every night before his death. The missing will was then proved by her testimony, even though she was an interested witness and even though there was no precedent for such a radical discarding of formality rules. It cannot be certain that Lord St Leonards would have approved of the result of this case, his final contribution to the law of England.

JOSHUA S. GETZLER

Sources E. Walford, *Law Times* (6 Feb 1875), 256–8 • 'Lord St Leonards', *Solicitors' Journal*, 19 (1874–5), 250–51 • Holdsworth, *Eng. law*, vols. 7, 11, 12, 14, 17 • E. Manson, *Builders of our law during the reign of Queen Victoria*, 2nd edn (1904), 108–15 • ER, vols. 41–4, 63–4 • W. B. Drury and R. R. Warren, *Reports of cases argued and determined in the high court of chancery, during the time of Lord Chancellor Sugden*, 1–4 (1843–6) • *Law reports* (1865) • G. H. Jones, 'Sugden, Edward Burtenshaw (Baron St Leonards)', *Biographical dictionary of the common law*, ed. A. W. B. Simpson (1984), 495–7 • 'Lord St Leonards', *Solicitors' Journal*, 19 (1874–5), 259–60 • 'Sugden v. Lord St Leonards', *Law Journal* (4 Dec 1875), 703–4 • 'Lord St Leonards and Lord Romilly', *Solicitors' Journal*, 13 (1868–9), 423–4 • review, *Legal Observer*, 11 (1835–6), 153–6 • J. F. Archbold, *The new statutes relating to lunacy, comprising the law relating to pauper lunatics … and … lunatic asylums* (1854) • J. Elmer, *Practice in lunacy* (1857) • S. Atkinson, ed., *Sir E. B. Sugden's Acts* (1830) • Foss, *Judges*, 9.267–70 • A. W. B. Simpson, 'The rise and fall of the legal treatise: legal principles and the forms of legal literature', *Legal theory and legal history: essays on the common law* (1987), 273–320 • A. W. B. Simpson, 'Legal science and legal absurdity: Jee v. Audley (1787)', *Leading cases in the common law* (1995), 76–99 • J. S. Anderson, *Lawyers and the making of English land law, 1832–1940* (1992) • B. Rudden, 'A code too soon: the 1826 property code of James Humphreys', *Essays in memory of Professor F. H. Lawson*, ed. P. Wallington and R. M. Merkin (1986), 101–16 • Lord Selborne, *Memorials, family and personal*, 1 (1890) • A. Cockburn, *Our judicial system* (1870) • *DNB* • GEC, *Peerage* • d. cert.

Archives Lincoln's Inn, London, legal opinions, papers | BL, corresp. with Sir Robert Peel, Add. MSS 40399–40601 • Bodl. Oxf., letters to Benjamin Disraeli • Cumbria AS, Carlisle, corresp. with Sir James Graham • LPL, letters to Baroness Burdett-Coutts • Lpool RO, letters to fourteenth earl of Derby • NL Scot., corresp. with

Blackwoods · NRA, priv. coll., letters to S. H. Walpole · Surrey HC, letters to Henry Goulburn

Likenesses E. U. Eddis, oils, exh. RA 1853, Lincoln's Inn, London [see illus.] · F. Holl, stipple, 1859 (after C. Sugden), NPG · E. Scriven, stipple (after J. Moore), BM, NPG; repro. in H. T. Ryall, *Portraits of eminent conservatives and statesmen* [1836] · T. Woolnoth, stipple (after C. Penny), BM, NPG · engraving (after C. Sugden), Lincoln's Inn, London

Wealth at death under £70,000: probate, 22 April 1876, *CGPLA Eng. & Wales* · £20,000: administration [ceased and expired], 26 Oct 1875, *CGPLA Eng. & Wales*

Sugden, Edward Charles (1902–1982), surgeon, was born on 24 July 1902 at 10 Vanbrugh Park Road West, Blackheath, the younger son and third and youngest child of Arthur Henry Sugden (1862–1947), a well-regarded official (1883–1926) of the Chinese maritime customs, and his wife, Edith Lilian Bush (1867–1936). He was great-grandson of Edward Burtenshaw *Sugden, first Baron St Leonards, and from 1972 was heir presumptive to his nephew, the fourth and last Baron St Leonards. After studying medicine at St Bartholomew's Hospital, London (Bart's), and at Cambridge University, he became a member of the Royal College of Surgeons (1929), licentiate of the Royal College of Physicians in London (1929), bachelor of medicine at Cambridge (1935), and member of the Royal College of Gynaecologists (1936).

In the early 1930s Sugden was a senior house surgeon at Bart's, and resident medical officer at the hospital for women in Soho Square and at Queen Charlotte's Maternity Hospital, London. Women's medicine was still in an 'era of savagery' (*The Times*, 19 Dec 1931, 12c), as Sir Henry McCardie declared in 1931 while presiding at the trial of a back-street abortionist accused of manslaughter. Information on contraception was cruelly refused and withheld from women. Abortion had been criminalized under English statutes of 1803, although abortions continued to be performed by physicians when they believed that continuation of the pregnancy would jeopardize the woman's physical or mental health. Sugden deplored the ignorance and brutality with which the law was often administered, and could not think it right that women should be forced to bear children against their will. He became junior partner in a medical practice headed by the elderly Henry Strawson Turner at 5 Half Moon Street, Mayfair, off Piccadilly, and (after wartime service as a major in the Royal Army Medical Corps) later developed his own practice at 4 Half Moon Street, providing the easy contraception and abortion to which he thought women were entitled. Until the reform of abortion laws in 1967 such operations were illegal unless two psychiatrists had certified that the woman's mental health was at risk. Sugden was adept at obtaining such certification. This process was costly, and thus discriminated against the poor, but if he liked a patient Sugden would perform her abortion at cost. Many society women consulted him: in consequence he became known as the Deb's Delight.

Sugden was a gregarious womanizer who because of his reputation as an abortionist had difficulty attracting women outside surgery hours. He took a Thames-side cottage at Wraysbury in Buckinghamshire, where he held parties with generous amounts of food and drink for all comers. Farouche individuals (property and antique dealers, minor show-business personalities, and good-time girls) attended these parties, which sometimes ended in orgies. In 1963 Sugden supplied the tablets with which Stephen Ward committed suicide. As there was a possibility that Ward's police persecutors intended to add a charge of procuring an abortion to the other trumpery charges aimed against him, his death perhaps relieved Sugden.

Natural history was a great interest of Sugden's: the walls of his Half Moon Street waiting-room were lined with glass cases containing live snakes, lizards, iguanas, and other reptiles. In old age he was a striking, white-haired man with sensual but perhaps somewhat melancholy features. Sugden died of lung cancer and general deterioration due to ageing, on 30 January 1982, at his home, 49 Arlington Road, Camden Town, London. A funeral service was held on 8 February at St Bartholomew-the-Less, West Smithfield, London. He was survived by his widow, Catherine Bernadette, whom he had married late in life. RICHARD DAVENPORT-HINES

Sources P. Knightley and C. Kennedy, *An affair of state: the Profumo case and the framing of Stephen Ward* (1987), 54–5, 244 · *Medical Register* · A. Jenkins, *Law for the rich* (1960) · J. Keown, *Abortion, doctors and the law* (1988) · b. cert. · *The Times* (19 Dec 1931) · *The Times* (4 Feb 1982) · *CGPLA Eng. & Wales* (1982) · d. cert. · Burke, *Peerage*

Likenesses photograph, 1963?, repro. in Knightley and Kennedy, *An affair of state*, pl. 35

Wealth at death £57,591: probate, 12 May 1982, *CGPLA Eng. & Wales*

Sugden, Sir (Theodore) Morris (1919–1984), physical chemist, was born on 31 December 1919, at Triangle, near Sowerby Bridge in Yorkshire, the only child of Frederick Morris Sugden, company secretary, and his wife, Florence Chadwick. He was educated at Sowerby Bridge and District secondary school, from which he won an open scholarship in natural sciences to Jesus College, Cambridge. After obtaining a first class in the preliminary examination in natural sciences in 1939, he decided to read part two (chemistry) which, because of the war, he took at the end of his second year in 1940, obtaining a first. After eighteen months' research into ionization potentials with W. C. Price, Sugden was transferred to war work, investigating methods of suppressing gun flash under R. G. W. Norrish.

These investigations led to the main themes of Sugden's post-war research which were studies of ionization of alkali and alkaline earth metals in flames, and the chemistry of flames. He showed that the apparently complex processes could be systematized in terms of equilibrium between some chemical species and an approach to equilibrium by others. His wartime work in the Ministry of Supply had also involved using the absorption of microwaves to study ionization in gun flash, and after the war he extended this to flames and to microwave spectroscopy. In 1945 he married Marian Florence, daughter of Ernest George Cotton, an export manager. The couple had one son, Andrew, who became an editor of scientific journals.

Following the war Sugden was elected to a Stokes studentship at Pembroke College (1945), was appointed a university demonstrator the following year, and in 1950 was promoted to the Humphrey Owen Jones lecturership. In 1957 he was elected a fellow of Queens' College, Cambridge, of which he became an honorary fellow in 1976, and in 1960 he was appointed to an *ad hominem* readership in physical chemistry, by which time he had built up a large research group in the department. He was elected FRS in 1963.

Sugden was a highly gifted pianist and would, when possible, practise for several hours a day, preferring the work of the romantic composers. He was also widely read, particularly in the history of thought and in economic theory, some of which he read in the original Italian. His cosmopolitan social circle, remarkable skills as a teacher, independence of spirit, slightly bohemian appearance, and disregard for punctuality made Sugden seem a natural part of the post-war Cambridge scene. Nevertheless, in 1963 he accepted the position of director of research at Shell's Thornton Research Centre in Cheshire. There he showed considerable skills in management, recruiting talented scientists and using their abilities to the full. He rose to be director of the centre in 1967, and in 1974 chief executive of Shell Research Limited.

In 1976 Sugden returned to Cambridge as master of Trinity Hall. He sat on many committees, being chairman of the faculty board of engineering and of the syndics of the University Press. He became a director and vice-president of the Combustion Institute (1974–82) and was president of the Faraday division and honorary treasurer of the Royal Society of Chemistry before becoming its president in 1978–9. From 1977 he also chaired the government advisory committee on nuclear safety, a responsibility which weighed heavily on his shoulders. He was also increasingly involved in the activities of the Royal Society, acting as physical secretary from 1979 until his death. In that post he took a strong interest in how far the society should advise the public as well as the government on scientific issues. He was appointed CBE in 1975, the year in which he received the Davy medal of the Royal Society, and knighted in 1983. He had honorary degrees from Bradford, Liverpool, Leeds, and York University, Toronto. His scientific output included over a hundred papers and a successful textbook on microwave spectroscopy with C. N. Kenney (1965).

Sugden was a keen rambler but he never learned to drive or ride a bike. While in Cheshire he developed a passion for gardening, which continued after his return to Cambridge. Indeed, shortly before his death he was to be seen constructing a Japanese garden outside his cottage near Elsworth. Sugden died on 3 January 1984 in Cambridge following a short illness; he was survived by his wife.   B. A. Thrush, *rev.*

Sources C. P. Quinn and B. A. Thrush, *Memoirs FRS*, 32 (1986), 569–96 · personal knowledge (1986) · private information (1986)
Archives CUL, corresp. with Peter Mitchell

Likenesses W. Bird, photograph, *c.*1964, RS
Wealth at death under £40,000: administration, 9 April 1984, *CGPLA Eng. & Wales*

Sugden, Samuel (1892–1950), chemist, was born on 21 February 1892 at 2 Arthington View, Hunslet, Leeds, the eldest son of Samuel Sugden, a master draper of Leeds who was connected with wool-trade journals, and his wife, Eliza Jane Broadbent. He was educated at Batley grammar school from where he went to the Royal College of Science in London in 1912. In 1914 he graduated with first-class honours as an associate.

Because of the outbreak of war Sugden abandoned plans to do research and took an industrial job, but in September 1915 he joined the Royal Army Medical Corps as a private soldier and served with the British expeditionary force. In June 1916 he was released to join the research department at the Royal Arsenal, Woolwich, working under Robert Robertson. He prospered there, but in April 1919 resigned to become a lecturer at Birkbeck College, London.

In 1924 Sugden published work on the 'parachor', a function of surface tension which could give information about the structure of molecules. This attracted much attention and thereafter his advancement was rapid: in 1928 he was appointed reader and in 1932 professor of physical chemistry at Birkbeck. He was elected FRS in 1934 and in 1937 he was appointed professor of chemistry at University College, London.

At the outbreak of the Second World War, Sugden immediately joined the Ministry of Supply and went to the chemical defence experimental station in Porton, near Salisbury. He became impatient with the pace of work there, and felt that gas warfare was unlikely to be used, and so he obtained a post as a superintendent of explosives research at the armament research department in 1942. But here, too, there were soon difficulties and in 1943 he resigned to become scientific adviser to the United States 8th army air force in Great Britain. Later that year he suffered a breakdown of health following a severe attack of influenza. In September 1944 he was able to return to his academic duties, but soon after the war ended he was stricken by chronic illness and did relatively little research thereafter.

Though Sugden did very useful work on molecular structure by other means, his main contributions came through his parachor. This proved to be an additive function of atomic constants with structural constants in addition. Unfortunately these constants could not be determined theoretically but only empirically, and eventually this proved to be an unsound basis. Nevertheless, because it came when the instrumental techniques of structural determination were in a rudimentary state or were nonexistent, Sugden's work was very stimulating and may have helped encourage the search for better methods. He published his major book, *The Parachor and Valency*, in 1930.

In 1926 Sugden married Eleanor, daughter of Thomas Dunlop of Glasgow. They had no children. Sugden died on

Samuel Sugden (1892–1950), by Walter Stoneman

20 October 1950 at the Epsom and Ewell Cottage Hospital near his home in West Hill Avenue, Epsom, Surrey; his wife survived him. L. E. SUTTON, *rev.*

Sources L. E. Sutton, *Obits. FRS*, 7 (1950–51), 493–503
Likenesses W. Stoneman, photograph, RS · W. Stoneman, photograph, NPG [*see illus.*]
Wealth at death £10,356 6s. 0d.: probate, 14 Dec 1950, *CGPLA Eng. & Wales*

Suibne (*d.* 772). *See under* Iona, abbots of (*act.* 563–927).

Suibne Menn mac Fiachnai (*d.* 628), high-king of Ireland, was the son of Fiachnae mac Feradaig and it is said that his wife was Rónat, daughter of Dúngalach, king of the Uí Thuirtri. He came of the branch of Cenél nEogain called after his grandfather Cenél Feradaig. The dominant branch had been Cenél Maic Ercae, which had supplied seven kings of Tara (the title of the high-kings of Ireland) in the sixth and early seventh centuries (including Mac Ercae himself) and Suibne's father was never king of Cenél nEogain. Suibne Menn's rise to power reversed this pattern, so that his descendants were the dominant branch for the rest of the seventh century. In the process, however, they had to prosecute a fierce kin feud with the rival branch of Cenél nEogain. Since Suibne Menn emerged as king of Cenél nEogain after the death of Áed Uaridnach, king of Tara, in 612, it is possible that his predecessor had allowed him—a potential troublemaker from a rival branch of the kindred—a measure of authority within Cenél nEogain in order to safeguard his base while he himself was active more widely as king of Tara.

Three years later, in 615, Suibne Menn seized the kingship of Tara by killing his predecessor, Máel Coba mac Áeda of Cenél Conaill. If the annals of Tigernach are correct in placing this battle among the Luigni, it probably occurred within the territories of the midland branch of that people and thus within what was the normal stamping ground of the southern Uí Néill, far from Suibne Menn's own base in the north. His rise to power was thus unusually rapid. The method by which he held on to power until 628 may have been by allying with the Uí Néill of Mide, themselves in feud with the Uí Néill of Brega to their east. The annals give Óengus mac Colmáin the title king of the Uí Néill at his death in 621; this is likely to be a title conceded by Suibne to his principal ally among the southern Uí Néill so as to assert Óengus's authority over the Uí Néill of Brega as well as of Mide. In 628, at the end of his reign, Suibne Menn was successful in defeating Domnall mac Áeda, the brother of Máel Coba, his victim and predecessor as king of Tara. In the same year, however, he was killed, perhaps by some form of surprise attack, by Congal Cáech, king of the Cruithni and of the province of Ulster. In the confused political situation after his death, Congal Cáech emerged as king of Tara only to be killed in 637 by his successor, Domnall mac Áeda.

T. M. CHARLES-EDWARDS

Sources W. Stokes, ed., 'The annals of Tigernach [8 pts]', *Revue Celtique*, 16 (1895), 374–419; 17 (1896), 6–33, 119–263, 337–420; 18 (1897), 9–59, 150–97, 267–303, 374–91; pubd sep. (1993) · K. Meyer, ed., 'The Laud genealogies and tribal histories', *Zeitschrift für Celtische Philologie*, 8 (1910–12), 291–338 · *Ann. Ulster* · G. Murphy, 'On the dates of two sources used in Thurneysen's *Heldensage*: 1. *Baile Chuind* and the date of *Cin Dromma Snechtai*', *Ériu*, 16 (1952), 145–56, esp. 145–51 · M. C. Dobbs, ed. and trans., 'The Ban-shenchus [3 pts]', *Revue Celtique*, 47 (1930), 283–339; 48 (1931), 163–234; 49 (1932), 437–89 · W. M. Hennessy, ed. and trans., *Chronicum Scotorum: a chronicle of Irish affairs*, Rolls Series, 46 (1866) · M. A. O'Brien, ed., *Corpus genealogiarum Hiberniae* (Dublin, 1962) · F. J. Byrne, *Irish kings and high-kings* (1973)

Suibne moccu Urthrí (*d.* 657). *See under* Iona, abbots of (*act.* 563–927).

Suidbert. *See* Swithberht (*d.* 713).

Sukuna, Josefa Lalabalavu Vaanialialia (1888–1958), chief of Lau and civil servant in Fiji, was born on 22 April 1888 in the village of Nanukuloa, Fiji, the eldest son of Ratu Jone Madraiwiwi (1859–1920) and Adi Litiana Maopa. Through his mother he was 'vasu levu' to Lau, meaning that he took precedence over all the chiefs of the province of Lau. By birth he was among the most exalted Fijian chiefs of his time.

Sukuna was educated by a private tutor, Charles Andrew, an Oxford graduate and retired Anglican priest, and at the age of fourteen was sent to New Zealand for secondary education. From 1903 to 1906 he attended Wanganui Collegiate School (an Anglican boarding-school), where he matriculated. Returning to Fiji, he was appointed to the Fijian civil service, alternating between clerical and teaching positions. His aspiration for higher education was encouraged by his father, and the expenses were met by a levy imposed by the great council of chiefs who wanted an educated spokesman to represent them.

Sukuna joined Wadham College, Oxford, in 1913. When the First World War broke out he was dismayed at the British refusal to accept him for military service, and in January 1915 joined the French Foreign Legion. For his exploits in action he was awarded the Croix de Guerre and the médaille militaire before being wounded in 1916. The British government then recalled him and sent him home to Fiji. He served briefly as acting assistant secretary for Fijian affairs. Eager to get back to the war, Sukuna raised a labour unit which he accompanied to France in 1917. Further clerical employment in Fiji followed in 1918 before he returned to Oxford in 1919, took his BA, and proceeded to study law at the Middle Temple. He was called to the bar in 1921 and returned to Fiji immediately.

Although his education, intellectual acumen, and leadership were acknowledged, Sukuna was passed over for responsibilities in favour of less qualified and less experienced administrative officers recruited from England. During the 1920s he was an aide-de-camp and served as chief assistant to the native land commission, a sensitive job involving the resolution of land tenure difficulties, a responsibility that made good use of his European education and his intimate knowledge of Fijian custom.

In 1928 Sukuna married Maraia Vosawale Tatawaqa (1903–1956). The marriage produced several children, who were all either stillborn or died in infancy. While still having responsibilities to the native land commission, Sukuna was appointed provincial commissioner for Lau (the scattered archipelago which forms the eastern boundary of Fiji) in 1932. In 1932 also he became a member of the Fijian legislative council. This was a nominated position representing the Fijian people on a council which still had an official majority. His appointment had been urged by the great council of chiefs for some years, but Sukuna was opposed to it on principle and routinely and unsuccessfully offered his resignation. He was even more opposed to suggestions by the representatives of the Indian and European settler communities for an unofficial majority and for elected members. Sukuna used his position to consistently advance the conservative view that Fijian interests were the first responsibility of government, and that Fijians should be governed by their own chiefs.

Personal successes in the late 1930s included selection as Tui Lau (that is, paramount chief of the Lau province) in 1938, appointment as a CBE, and promotion to administrative officer grade one in 1940, the highest level of the civil service. Nevertheless, throughout the 1930s he was exasperated at what he considered a bankrupt land and native policy which was predicated on the hope and expectation of the individualization of Fijian society through eroding ties between people and their chiefs, and through encouraging economic individualism. He argued that Fijian progress was retarded not by their traditional communalism but by lack of markets for their produce and the pricing policies of the major trading firms.

In 1940 Sukuna accomplished a reversal of policy with his Native Land Trust Bill. As a result he became chairman of the Native Lands Trust Board and chief reserves commissioner, which gave him extensive influence in Fijian affairs generally. In a companion move, though much delayed, he launched the Fijian Development Fund in 1950–51 to provide working capital for Fijian economic development, and to market Fijian produce more advantageously than through the commercial operations of the trading companies.

Sukuna's land reform and its implicit paternalism were endorsed by the governor, Sir Philip Mitchell, who arrived in 1942. During the Second World War Sukuna was the senior officer of the Fijian defence force with the rank of lieutenant-colonel, and worked energetically to recruit Fijians to fight in the Solomons campaign, which they did with distinction. This assertion of imperial loyalty and Fijian patriotism further commended Sukuna to the new governor. Mitchell was easily convinced by Sukuna's arguments that individualism did not suit the Fijian character. In 1943 he appointed Sukuna secretary for Fijian affairs, head of a separate department of government which had been abolished about twenty years before. The earlier colonial structure of indirect rule, with the Fijians governed by chiefs holding official administrative positions, was thus re-established. European district officers were relegated to general administrative tasks and the supervision of the Indian and European populations. Sukuna was knighted in 1946, and led the Fijian contingent in the victory parade in London.

Sukuna's ten-year period as secretary for Fijian affairs was the apogee of his public career during which he was virtually the paramount chief of Fiji. In this role he exercised enormous influence in Fijian life, much of it against proposals for political devolution and localization. He took a belatedly renewed interest in education for Fijians, although even here he was more pragmatic than liberal, seeing the educational needs of Fijians in terms of elementary and practical training rather than the élite education he had enjoyed.

Sukuna's wife died in 1956, and he subsequently married Maca Likutabua, an aristocrat from his own province of Lau. He retired as secretary of Fijian affairs in 1953, the year in which he was elevated to KCMG. He then served as speaker of the legislative council until 1958, retiring only a month before his death, which occurred on 30 May 1958 at sea, off Colombo *en route* for England on SS *Arcadia*. His body was flown back to Fiji and he was buried on 11 June in the chiefly cemetery at Tubou on the island of Lakeba.

Sukuna was mourned deeply by his people, by whom he was regarded with awe, affection, and respect as their pre-eminent chief. Sukuna's thorough assimilation of both Fijian and English cultures gave rise to paradoxes in his life. He was the first Fijian university graduate and barrister, but opened no pathway for others on the same route. His staunch defence of Fijian interests was matched by his devotion to European civilization and loyalty to Britain, both coinciding with his own social and political conservatism. His progressivism was firmly within the framework of Fijian culture. In retrospect his life seems to have been a rearguard action at a time when colonial leaders elsewhere were pressing for radical change.

I. C. CAMPBELL

Sources D. Scarr, *Ratu Sukuna: soldier, statesman, man of two worlds* (1980) · D. Scarr, ed., *Fiji, the three legged stool: selected writings of Ratu Sir Lala Sukuna* (1983) · B. V. Lal, *Broken waves: a history of the Fiji Islands in the twentieth century* (1992) · *Pacific Islands Monthly* (June 1958) · WWW, 1951–60

Sulcard (*fl. c.*1080), historian, was a monk of the Benedictine abbey of St Peter at Westminster. The unusual name may as well be Old English as Norman. Sulcard's only known work is an account of the history of the abbey, through many vicissitudes, from the building of the first church on the site (then known as Thorney Island) by a rich citizen of London and his wife, when Mellitus was bishop of London (604–17), to the dedication of the church built by Edward the Confessor (r. 1042–66) for the Benedictine community which was by then in possession. Sulcard probably entered the community in the 1050s. His interest in the history of the cathedral priory at Rochester may provide a clue to his immediate origin. In dedicating his work to Abbot Vitalis (r. 1076–85?), he describes it as a commemorative book (*codex memorialis*) about the monastery which Vitalis ruled. The now commonly accepted title, *Prologus de constructione Westmon* ('Prologue concerning the construction of Westminster'), is that given in an abbey cartulary into which it was copied c.1300 and where it does indeed serve as a prologue. This is the earlier of the two surviving copies of Sulcard's work.

Sulcard wrote mainly in order to promote the cult of St Peter, the patron saint of his monastery. His account of the miraculous dedication of the church on Thorney Island by St Peter in person no doubt represents the tradition current in the monastery when he wrote. But he was careful not to embellish the historical parts of his narrative with details invented for the purpose. Thus he did not claim to know the name of the rich citizen who built the church on Thorney Island. He used the anonymous life of King Edward, and so provides evidence that this work was in existence by, at latest, 1085. His own failure to attribute miracles to Edward indicates that the king was not yet revered as a saint at Westminster. According to a later tradition, which is probably reliable, Sulcard was buried in the abbey cloister, a prestigious site, suggesting that to be learned was to be exceptional in the community of this period. In the thirteenth century his bones were moved to the abbey's new chapter house. His work continued to be read, despite a shift of interest at Westminster from the cult of St Peter to that of Edward the Confessor, and in the fifteenth century John Flete made copious use of it in his own history of the abbey.

BARBARA F. HARVEY

Sources BL, Cotton MS Faustina A.iii, fols. 11r–16v · BL, Cotton MS Titus A.viii, fols. 2r–5v · B. W. Scholz, 'Sulcard of Westminster: *Prologus de construccione Westmonasterii*', *Traditio*, 20 (1964), 59–91 · F. Barlow, ed. and trans., *The life of King Edward who rests at Westminster*, 2nd edn, OMT (1992), xxxvi–xxxvii, xl–xli, 110–11 · J. Flete, *The history of Westminster Abbey*, ed. J. A. Robinson (1909), 3, 4–5, 40–43, 83 · E. H. Pearce, *The monks of Westminster* (1916), 40

Sulien [Sulgen, Sulgenus] (*c.*1012–1091), bishop of St David's, was born of a noble family at Llanbadarn Fawr in Ceredigion (Cardiganshire). He studied in monastic schools in Wales, Scotland (where he spent five years), and Ireland (where he spent ten), and then returned to his native district, where he soon made a reputation as a teacher.

In 1073, on the death of Bleiddudd, Sulien was chosen bishop of St David's, where he lived for twelve years. He resigned the office in 1078, but when his successor, Abraham, was killed in 1080, he was persuaded, against his will, to become bishop once again. In 1081 he received Gruffudd ap Cynan and Rhys ap Tewdwr before the battle of Mynydd Carn and probably William I when that monarch visited St David's in the same year. In 1085 he resigned a second time and abandoned public life to devote himself to Christ. He died on 31 December 1091. *Brut y tywysogyon* styles him 'the most learned of the Britons' and refers to his circle of disciples. There is some manuscript evidence of the literary activity fostered by his school. At his request, between 1085 and 1091, his son Ieuan made a copy of Augustine's *De trinitate*, which is extant in Corpus Christi College, Cambridge (MS 199); at the end in Latin is 'Ieuan's poem on the life and family of Sulien'. Sulien's sons were all leading clerics and scholars in Wales: *Rhigyfarch (1056/7–1099), Daniel (d. 1127), archdeacon of Powys, Ieuan (d. 1137), arch-priest of Llanbadarn, and Arthgen.

J. E. LLOYD, rev. NANCY EDWARDS

Sources M. Lapidge, 'The Welsh–Latin poetry of Sulien's family', *Studia Celtica*, 8–9 (1973–4), 68–106 · T. Jones, ed. and trans., *Brut y tywysogyon, or, The chronicle of the princes: Red Book of Hergest* (1955) · T. Jones, ed. and trans., *Brut y tywysogyon, or, The chronicle of the princes: Peniarth MS 20* (1952) · *Historia Gruffud vab Kenan / Gyda rhagymadrodd a nodiadau gan*, ed. D. S. Evans (1977) · J. E. Lloyd, 'Bishop Sulien and his family', *National Library of Wales Journal*, 2 (1941–2), 1–6 · N. K. Chadwick, 'Intellectual life in west Wales in the last days of the Celtic church', in N. K. Chadwick and others, *Studies in the early British church* (1958), 121–82 · J. C. Davies, ed., *Episcopal acts and cognate documents relating to Welsh dioceses, 1066–1272*, 2 vols., Historical Society of the Church in Wales, 1, 3–4 (1946–8) · J. L. Davies and D. P. Kirby, eds., *From the earliest times to the coming of the Normans*, Cardiganshire County History, 1 (1994) · J. E. Lloyd, *A history of Wales from the earliest times to the Edwardian conquest*, 3rd edn, 2 vols. (1939)

Sulivan, Sir Bartholomew James (1810–1890), naval officer and hydrographer, the eldest son of Rear-Admiral Thomas Ball *Sulivan (1780–1857) and his wife, Henrietta, daughter of Rear-Admiral Bartholomew *James, was born at Tregew, near Falmouth, on 18 November 1810. On 4 September 1823 he entered the Royal Naval College, Portsmouth, where he passed with distinction, and was appointed to the *Thetis*. In her, with Sir John Phillimore, and afterwards with Captain Arthur Batt Bingham, he remained until 1828, when the *Thetis* happened to come into Rio de Janeiro just as one of her former lieutenants, Robert Fitz-Roy, was promoted to command the *Beagle*. FitzRoy obtained leave for Sulivan to go with him. At the end of

Sir Bartholomew James Sulivan (1810–1890), by Maull & Fox

1829 Sulivan returned to England in the *North Star*, passed his examination on 29 December, and on 3 April 1830 was promoted lieutenant. In June 1831, at FitzRoy's request, he was again appointed to the *Beagle*, and remained in her during her famous voyage, forming a lifelong friendship with Charles Darwin. The *Beagle* returned to England in November 1836, and Sulivan had a year's rest, during which he married, in January 1837, Sophia, third daughter of Vice-Admiral James Young. They had a large family, the eldest of whom, James Young Falkland Sulivan, became a naval officer.

In December 1837 Sulivan was appointed to command the schooner *Pincher*, going out to the west coast of Africa; but a few weeks later he was moved to the *Arrow*, and sent to survey the Falkland Islands. His wife accompanied him, and the Christian name of Falkland, given to his eldest son, marked the belief of the family that he was the first British subject born in the islands. The *Arrow* came home in 1839, and on 14 May 1841 Sulivan was promoted to the rank of commander.

In April 1842 Sulivan was appointed to the brig *Philomel*, in which he was sent out to continue the survey of the Falklands during the summer months, and to return each winter to the River Plate. There, however, the disturbed state of the country rendered it necessary to consider the *Philomel* a warship rather than a surveying vessel, although such surveys of the river as were practicable were made, and proved afterwards of extreme value. In August 1845, when the English and French squadrons

were obliged to undertake hostile operations against Paraguay, the *Philomel* formed part of the squadron, under Captain Charles Hotham, which forced the passage of the Parana at Obligado on 20 November 1845. Sulivan acted as the pilot of the squadron, charting or correcting the charts of the river.

In the early spring of 1846 Sulivan returned to England, and in March was posted by a commission dated back to 15 November 1845. In 1847 he was appointed supernumerary to the *Victory* for surveying duties, and to organize the dockyard brigade, composed of the dockyard workmen, then enrolled and drilled as a sort of militia. At this time, too, he paid great attention to the formation of a naval reserve, his ideas on which were prominently brought forward ten years later. Towards the end of 1848, seeing no prospect of immediate employment, he obtained three years' leave, and went with his whole family to the Falkland Islands, where he remained until 1851. During his journey home in a merchant ship, the crew mutinied, and until they were starved into submission the captain, the mate, and Sulivan worked the ship.

When war with Russia seemed imminent early in 1854, Sulivan applied for a command; and although, on account of his lack of influence, he was denied a fleet command commensurate with his standing, he was selected as a fleet surveying officer by Sir Francis Beaufort, and appointed to command the small steam vessel *Lightning*, which was well suited to the difficult navigation of the Baltic, and more especially to the gulfs of Finland and Bothnia. During the 1854 campaign Sulivan worked closely with Sir Charles Napier, resurveying the areas in which the fleet was to operate, and improving the existing Russian charts. His work culminated in the capture of Bomarsund in August, and the development of plans for the next campaign. In 1855 he continued to act as effective chief of staff and planning adviser to the new commander-in-chief, Sir Richard Dundas. The destruction of Sveaborg in August 1855, following his plans, was a masterpiece of naval power projection. Returning home in the autumn, Sulivan provided the plans for a massive operation to capture Kronstadt in early 1856, and these were adopted by the Admiralty, playing a major role in bringing Russia to accept peace. His merits were acknowledged when his ship led the fleet at the great review of 23 April 1856.

On 5 July 1855 Sulivan was made a CB, and in December 1856 was appointed professional officer to the marine department of the Board of Trade, where he was responsible for navigation and harbour design. Despite his outstanding service he was denied the necessary sea time to remain on the active list, and on 3 December 1863 was placed on the retired list with the rank of rear-admiral. On his retirement from the Board of Trade in April 1865 he settled at Bournemouth. On 2 June 1869 he was made a KCB; he became vice-admiral on 1 April 1870 and admiral on 22 January 1877. He died of bronchitis at Bournemouth on 1 January 1890.

Sulivan was an outstanding officer; his combination of technical and maritime skill, strategic grasp, and organizational power earned him the admiration of all those who served with him. Throughout his career he was frequently concerned for his own mental health, but this appears to have been a response to overwork. Although his complete lack of political influence and personal wealth deprived him of further seagoing command, he was still being consulted by the Admiralty on possible Baltic operations in 1878.

J. K. LAUGHTON, *rev.* ANDREW LAMBERT

Sources H. N. Sulivan, ed., *Life and letters of Admiral Sir Bartholomew James Sulivan KCB, 1810–1890* (1896) · A. D. Lambert, *The Crimean War: British grand strategy, 1853–56* (1990) · A. Desmond and J. Moore, *Darwin* (1991) · P. H. Colomb, *Memoirs of Admiral the Right Honble. Sir Astley Cooper Key* (1898) · G. B. Earp, *Sir Charles Napier's campaign in the Baltic* (1856) · J. W. D. Dundas and C. Napier, *Russian war, 1854, Baltic and Black Sea: official correspondence*, ed. D. Bonner-Smith and A. C. Dewar, Navy RS, 83 (1943) · R. S. Dundas, *Russian war, 1855, Baltic: official correspondence*, ed. D. Bonner-Smith, Navy RS, 84 (1944) · A. Friendly, *Beaufort of the Admiralty* (1977) · G. S. Ritchie, *The Admiralty chart: British naval hydrography in the nineteenth century* (1967) · Burke, *Peerage* (1879) · *CGPLA Eng. & Wales* (1890)

Archives BL, Napier MSS · NA Scot., Dundas MSS · PRO, Admiralty MSS

Likenesses Maull & Fox, photograph, NPG [*see illus.*]

Wealth at death £10,613 19*s.* 9*d.*: probate, 3 March 1890, *CGPLA Eng. & Wales*

Sulivan, Laurence (*c.*1713–1786), director of the East India Company and politician, is thought to have been the illegitimate son of Philip O'Sullivan (*bap.* 1682, *d.* 1737) of co. Cork, Ireland. Nothing is known of his life until he went to India. By 1739 he is recorded as a private merchant in the East India Company's settlement of Bombay. He was appointed to the company's service in 1741. For the next twelve years he held various administrative posts in Bombay and became a member of the council for the settlement in 1752. Having accumulated a comfortable fortune, he returned to Britain in 1753 with his wife, Elizabeth Owen (*d.* 1782). Elizabeth is likely to have been the daughter of Edward Owen of the company's service; the couple had married in 1739, and had at least one surviving child, their son Stephen.

Although Sulivan bought an estate at Ponsbourne in Hertfordshire, he spent most of his time in London, living for many years in a house in Queen Square. In 1755 he was elected to the court of directors of the East India Company. From then until his death some thirty years later, except for an interval of six years between 1772 and 1778, Sulivan was more or less continuously a director. He had three spells as chairman and three as deputy chairman. At such times his domination of the company was virtually complete. He was accused of being 'dictator' over it (Bowen, 99). Even when he was not formally responsible for them, the company's affairs were the main interest of his life. His concern for the company led him to seek seats in parliament, first at Taunton (1762–8) and then at Ashburton (1768–74).

At any time in the eighteenth century management of the East India Company's complex concerns was a formidable task, but the years from the 1750s to the 1780s were a period of tumultuous upheavals. In addition to managing its trade, its directors had to sustain wars in Asia, to try to

devise means of governing newly conquered Indian provinces, and to cope with the demands of the national government and of parliament for an ever greater measure of control over the company. The difficulties which the directors faced were greatly exacerbated by constantly recurring struggles for power within the company itself. To gain and maintain his hold over the company Sulivan had to become a formidable politician, and he inevitably made many enemies. These tended to portray him as being concerned with little more than his own power. There can, however, be no doubt that he was devoted to what he considered to be the company's interests and to finding appropriate solutions to the unprecedented problems facing it.

Sulivan later wrote that his power over the company had been 'absolute' from 1757 to 1763 (letter to his son, 27 Feb 1778, Bodl. Oxf., MS Eng. hist. c 472, fol. 4). During that period he had co-operated closely with the government in the war against the French and in the subsequent peace. In 1763, however, his authority over the company was challenged by Robert, Baron Clive, the conqueror of Bengal. Their antagonism, which had much more to do with a clash of temperaments than with deep issues of principle, convulsed the company and drew national political factions into supporting one side or the other. In 1764 Sulivan was worsted. He staged a counter-attack, which brought him back into power in 1769, but at the price of a financial disaster from which he never recovered; money was borrowed to buy shares with which to create votes for the election of directors at a time when the value of the company's stock collapsed. In the early 1770s he promoted the career of Warren Hastings as a reforming governor of Bengal, but he was unable to prevent a major loss of the company's autonomy when the government took powers over it in the Regulating Act of 1773. The government of Lord North, which he had opposed in 1773, encouraged Sulivan to take on the management of the company yet again in 1780. He was engaged in a new round of organizing the company's war effort and parrying political threats to it virtually until the time of his death. By then his beloved company had survived and had even acquired an imperial role, which Sulivan had never envisaged. The price of survival had, however, involved a cession of power to the government, which he deplored.

In 1778 in a letter to his son Sulivan described himself as having once been 'wild, dissipated and favorite with both sexes'. After his marriage he had reformed, filling the day with unremitting attention to business and spending 'almost every evening of my life with my family'. In twenty-five years he had not been 'ten times in a tavern, eight times in a coffee house'. The happiness he believed that he enjoyed he attributed to 'method, regularity and constantly measuring our whole time in habitual but commendable pursuits' (Bodl. Oxf., MS Eng. hist. c.269). He died, probably in London, on 21 February 1786, and was buried at St George the Martyr, Queen Square, London.

P. J. MARSHALL

Sources L. S. Sutherland, 'Sulivan, Laurence', HoP, *Commons, 1754–90* · G. K. McGilvary, 'The early life and career of Laurence

Sulivan', MLitt diss., U. Edin., 1979 · Bodl. Oxf., MSS Sulivan, MSS Eng. hist. b. 190–91, c. 269–71, c. 471–2 · L. S. Sutherland, *The East India Company in eighteenth century politics* (1952) · J. G. Parker, 'The directors of the East India Company, 1754–1790', PhD diss., U. Edin., 1977 · *Bengal Past and Present*, 42 (1931), 159 · Bombay births, deaths and marriages, BL OIOC, N/3/1 · H. V. Bowen, *Revenue and reform: the Indian problem in British politics, 1757–73* (1991) · lists of Bombay company servants, BL OIOC, 0/6/37 · *GM*, 1st ser., 56 (1786), 143

Archives Bodl. Oxf., papers, MSS Eng. Hist. b. 190–91, c. 269–71, c. 471–2 | BL, Warren Hastings papers, Add. MSS 29132–29194, *passim* · BL OIOC, corresp. relating to India · PRO, letters to Sir Charles Wynham, PRO 30/47/20/2

Wealth at death fortune seems never to have recovered from the stock crash of 1769; owed c.£18,000 in 1772 and had mortgaged his estate; said to have lost £35,000 by the bankruptcy of Sir George Colebrooke in 1777: *Bengal Past and Present*, 18, 29; Sutherland, 'Sulivan, Laurence', 1.509; PRO, PROB 6/162, fol. 233

Sulivan, Thomas Ball (1780–1857), naval officer, born at Cawsand, Cornwall, on 5 January 1780, was entered on the books of the *Triumph*, flagship of Lord Hood, at Portsmouth in 1786. He was afterwards on the books of different ships on the home station until the outbreak of the war of 1793, when he went out to the Mediterranean, and was a midshipman of the *Southampton* when she captured the *Utile* on 9 June 1796. He was afterwards in the *Royal George*, flagship in the channel, and on 26 April 1797 he was promoted a lieutenant of the *Queen Charlotte*. In March 1798 he was appointed to the brig *Kite*, in which he continued seven years in the North Sea, the Baltic Sea, and the channel. In May 1798 he was in Sir Home Riggs Popham's expedition to destroy the locks on the Bruges Canal, and in September 1803 was at the bombardment of Granville. In May 1805 he was appointed to the *Brisk*, and on 26 December to the frigate *Anson* (Captain Charles Lydiard) on the Jamaica station. In the *Anson* he took part in the capture of the Spanish frigate *Pomona* on 23 August 1806, and again in the engagement with the *Foudroyant*, bearing the flag of Rear-Admiral Willaumez, on 15 September. On 1 January 1807 the *Anson* was one of the four frigates with Captain Charles Brisbane at the capture of Curaçao, and for his services then Sulivan was promoted commander on 23 February. He came home in the *Anson*, and was in her as a volunteer when she was lost, with Captain Lydiard and sixty men, in Mount's Bay on 27 December 1807. On 19 March 1808 Sulivan married Henrietta, youngest daughter of Rear-Admiral Bartholomew *James. They had fourteen children, four of whom entered the navy. Their eldest son was Sir Bartholomew James *Sulivan (1810–1890).

In January 1809 Sulivan was appointed chief agent of transports and sailed for the Peninsula with reinforcements. In November he was appointed to the *Eclipse* for a few months, and in February 1813 to the *Woolwich*, in which he escorted Sir James Lucas Yeo with troops and supplies to Canada for service on the Great Lakes. On 6 November 1813 the ship was wrecked in a hurricane on the north coast of Barbuda, but without loss of life. Sulivan was honourably acquitted by the subsequent court martial, and in the following February he was appointed to the troopship *Weser*, employed on the American coast, and commanded a division of boats at the destruction of the American flotilla in the Patuxent River on 22 August 1814. At the battle of Bladensburg he commanded a division of seamen, and for his services in the expedition was advanced to post rank on 19 October 1814. He was made a CB on 4 June 1815. After many years on half pay he was appointed in March 1836 to the *Talavera* (74 guns) at Portsmouth, and in November to the *Stag* (46 guns), in which he served as commodore on the South American station until spring 1841. On 31 October 1846 he was placed on the retired list, and died at his home, Flushing, near Falmouth, Cornwall, on 17 November 1857.

J. K. LAUGHTON, *rev.* ANDREW LAMBERT

Sources H. N. Sulivan, *Life of Admiral Sir B. J. Sulivan* (1896) · O'Byrne, *Naval biog. dict.* · private information (1898) · W. James, *The naval history of Great Britain, from the declaration of war by France, in February 1793, to the accession of George IV in January 1820*, 5 vols. (1822–4), vol. 4, pp. 113–15 · Boase, *Mod. Eng. biog.*

Sullivan, Alexander Martin (1829–1884), journalist and Irish nationalist, was born on 15 May 1829 at Bantry, co. Cork, the second of seven children of Daniel Sullivan, house painter, and his wife, Catherine, *née* Baylor, schoolmistress. He received an elementary education locally. Influenced by the impact on the region of the Great Famine of 1845–6, he joined the local confederate club. He (reportedly) set out for Tipperary in July 1848 to join an abortive protest in arms, only to be induced to return home by relatives who pursued him. Between June 1849 and November 1852 he was employed by the Bantry poorlaw union as a relief officer. He left for Dublin early in 1853, intent on a career in journalism.

Having been associated with the *Dublin Expositor*, the *Tipperary Leader*, and the *Liverpool Daily Post*, Sullivan joined a partnership that took over *The Nation* in 1855, and he emerged as the paper's sole proprietor and editor early in 1858. He began publication of the *Evening News* in January 1859, and the *Morning News* the following April. Both ceased publication in 1864; but his weeklies—the *Weekly News* (from 1860) as well as *The Nation*—flourished. *Zozimus*, a comic weekly, was published from the *Nation* office, as were papers for boys, *The Emerald* and *Young Ireland*. He used his newspapers to promote a broadly based constitutional movement to win some measure of self-government for Ireland, in which he hoped to play a leading role; success proved elusive.

On 30 October 1858 in a leading article in *The Nation* Sullivan repudiated the Phoenix Society, with whose supposedly clandestine activities his name had been falsely linked. When the government swooped on the conspirators, however, he became the chief promoter of a fund for their defence. The Fenian leader James Stephens, to whose (then anonymous) movement the 'Phoenix men' had been recruited, denounced him for 'felon-setting' (making the activities of nationalists known to the authorities). There followed a struggle between the two men for the allegiance of Irish nationalists, in which Sullivan proved no match for Stephens's unscrupulous but effective methods. Sullivan's political initiatives were largely gestural. The setting up of the National Brotherhood of St Patrick was a setback for his ambitions;

Stephens's hijacking of the MacManus funeral was a major defeat. The Fenians disrupted his meetings and he was attacked by their apologists. He exposed their machinations in three supplements in *The Nation* (19 April–3 May 1862), but in personalizing his charges he added to the rancour of contemporary politics. After the collapse of their rising, however, Sullivan defended the Fenians; *The Nation*'s contribution to the cult of the 'Manchester Martyrs'—notably 'God Save Ireland' and *Speeches from the Dock* (1867)—provided him with a way forward politically.

Sullivan was present at the meeting convened by Isaac Butt at the Bilton Hotel, Sackville Street, Dublin, on 19 May 1870, which adopted a resolution calling for the establishment of an Irish parliament with control over domestic affairs, and at the Home Government Association's first monthly meeting on 6 October. On the latter occasion he was elected to the association's executive council. *The Nation* was virtually the official organ of the movement in its early years. It supported home-rule candidates in the critical 1870–72 by-elections, and its editor supported them on the hustings. His lecture tours of Irish settlements in England and Scotland (and later America) were significant propaganda initiatives. From autumn 1873 *The Nation* became critical of the shortcomings of the Home Government Association, and Sullivan played a key part in the Rotunda conference of 18–21 November 1873, which launched the Home Rule League.

Sullivan was MP for Louth county, 1874–80, and for Meath county, 1880–82. He became an outstanding debater and won Gladstone's tribute to 'the eloquent member for Louth'. During his first year in parliament he contributed impressively on 20 March 1874 to Butt's amendment to the motion of an address in reply to the queen's speech and on 30 June to his home-rule motion, and he sought to advance the temperance cause. Butt's leadership proved lacklustre, however, and the commitment of a large minority of his followers did not impress Sullivan, an active moderate, let alone the emerging obstructionist wing. At the end of the 1876 session he criticized, in *The Nation*, Butt's management of the debate on his second home-rule motion, which Sullivan himself had wound up for the Irish side on 30 June. Elsewhere he drew attention to his leader's early career of 'debt, difficulty and dissipation'.

Although he was called to the Irish bar at the end of 1876, Sullivan chose to practise at the English bar, to which he received a 'special call' a year later, to enable him to combine a legal practice and a career at Westminster. On moving to London with his wife, Frances Genevieve, *née* Donovan (d. 29 Jan 1922), the Irish American whom he married on 27 April 1861, and their family (eventually three sons, including the younger Alexander Martin *Sullivan, and five daughters), he severed his connection with *The Nation*. During the 'obstruction' crisis (1877–8) he was slow to support Parnell, whose entry into public life he had sponsored, and came to be distrusted by both factions in the party. The mixed reviews of his best-selling

New Ireland (1877) underlined the difficulties of the moderates at a time of growing Anglo-Irish tension. As a man of order, he deplored the excesses of the land war (1879–82); but the government's decision to introduce coercion in advance of land legislation led him to join the obstructionists. During the forty-one hour sitting that began on 31 January 1881, he showed great procedural resourcefulness, and on 3 February he was among the thirty home-rulers suspended from the house.

Sullivan suffered a severe heart attack on 15 August 1881, a week before the 1881 Land Bill became law. He believed that the act 'got no fair play from the Land League', as he wrote in an expanded edition (1882) of *New Ireland*. He resigned his seat at the beginning of 1882, partly from ill health, but also because, as he wrote privately, he had come to believe that there was no longer a place in Irish politics for a person of his views. He died at Dartry Lodge, Upper Rathmines, Dublin, on 17 October 1884, and was buried in Glasnevin cemetery. He had been followed into nationalist politics by his brothers Timothy Daniel (1827–1914) and Donal (1838–1907). The brothers Sullivan, together with seven other MPs from their native region, came to be known as the Bantry band, a pejorative designation suggesting that they were not deficient in ambition.

Sullivan lacked the charisma and ruthlessness that enabled others to dominate the political scene: he was firmly in the second rank. He was representative of the mainstream of Irish Catholic nationalism, and reflected its ambivalence towards armed resistance and the composition of the nation. He welcomed 'priests in politics'—as long as they were on the right side. But he insisted that Irish nationalism should not be a purely Catholic preserve, and rebuked extreme clerical pretensions. On education he took an orthodox Catholic-nationalist line. Conventionally, too, he held Ireland's socio-economic ills to be mainly a function of foreign rule. His historical importance lies less in his political activism than in his role of ideologue. Historicism and moralism were key elements in his repertoire. His *Story of Ireland* (1867), *Nutshell History of Ireland* (1883), and related *Nation* publications, such as *Speeches from the Dock* (1867) and *The Story of England* (1872), deployed the past in the service of the present. He annexed Butt's cautious federalism to *The Story of Ireland*'s inspirational myth of a seamless liberation struggle, and so contributed to Parnellism. Similarly, *The Nation*'s stress on the virtues of an idealized pious Irish society, and its intense feeling of moral superiority over England, fuelled the cultural nationalism of later times, as did its promotion of the Irish language.   RAY MORAN

Sources R. Moran, 'Alexander Martin Sullivan (1829–1884) and Irish cultural nationalism', MA diss., University College, Cork, 1993 • T. D. Sullivan, *A. M. Sullivan* (1885) • *Speeches and addresses … by A. M. Sullivan*, ed. T. D. Sullivan (1881) • T. D. Sullivan, *Recollections of troubled times in Irish politics* (1905)
Archives NL Ire., W. Smith O'Brien MSS • University College, Dublin, Healy-O'Sullivan MSS
Likenesses T. Farrell, plaster death mask, NG Ire. • R. T., wood-engraving (after photograph by Russell & Sons), NPG; repro. in *ILN* (1 Nov 1884)

Wealth at death £2138 10s. 0d.: probate, 2 Dec 1884, *CGPLA Eng. & Wales* · £639: resealed probate, 23 Dec 1884, *CGPLA Ire.*

Sullivan, Alexander Martin (1871–1959), barrister, was born in Dublin on 14 January 1871, the second son of Alexander Martin *Sullivan (1829–1884), one of the founders of the Home Rule League and proprietor and editor of *The Nation*, and his wife, Frances Genevieve Donovan (d. 1922). The Sullivans were part of a network of families from west Cork, known as 'the Bantry band', some members of which played prominent parts in Irish public life.

Sullivan was educated at Ushaw College, Belvedere College, Trinity College, Dublin, and the King's Inns, Dublin. After working initially as a journalist, he was called to the Irish bar in 1892 and, having joined the Middle Temple, to the English bar in 1899. He was an outstandingly successful member of the Irish bar, becoming a king's counsel in 1908, and was further advanced to the position of king's serjeant in Ireland (1912), second serjeant in 1913, and first serjeant in 1920, being the last to hold that office. In 1900 Sullivan married Helen Kiely (d. 1952) of Brooklyn, New York; they had five sons and seven daughters.

Coming as he did from a nationalist background, Sullivan was, not surprisingly, a supporter of the Irish Parliamentary Party at Westminster. In the bitter factions which divided the party after the death of Charles Stewart Parnell in 1891, however, Sullivan was in a different camp from his cousin T. M. Healy, who had been Parnell's most virulent opponent after the split: in 1900 he joined the United Irish League which had been founded by William O'Brien, Healy's most vocal critic.

Sullivan was strongly opposed to the use of physical force in the struggle for Irish independence and had no sympathy with the Easter rising of 1916. However, he accepted the brief for the defence of one of the leaders, Sir Roger *Casement, whose trial was to prove the most controversial episode in his legal career. Casement, after resigning from the British colonial service, in which he had distinguished himself by exposing atrocities in the Belgian Congo and South America, became deeply involved in the Irish independence movement. He travelled to Germany shortly before the rising to obtain assistance and was arrested when he came ashore from a German submarine on the coast of co. Kerry. He was charged with high treason and it would appear that no member of the English criminal bar was willing to defend him. Despite his status at the Irish bar, Sullivan ranked as a junior counsel only in England and the attorney-general, F. E. Smith, who was leading the prosecution, suggested that Sullivan should be given silk in England, but this was rejected by the lord chancellor.

Before the trial began, Smith furnished the defence with the notorious 'black diaries' found in Casement's lodgings, recording numerous homosexual encounters and later the subject of intense controversy, following claims that they had been forged by British intelligence with a view to frustrating any campaign in England and the United States for the reprieve of Casement. Sullivan declined to look at them: they were apparently being produced with a view to enabling the defence to plead insanity, a strategy different from that which Sullivan had decided to adopt.

Sullivan elected for a purely legal defence at the trial which took place at the Old Bailey from 26 to 29 June 1916: he argued that the statute of Edward III under which Casement had been indicted applied only to treasonable activities within the king's realm. Sullivan broke down during his closing address to the jury, when he was interrupted by both Lord Chief Justice Reading, the presiding judge, and Smith, and he left the completion of his speech to his junior. Casement was found guilty by the jury and, after an unsuccessful appeal, again conducted by Sullivan, was hanged.

Sullivan's appearance for the crown in prosecutions during the period between 1919 and 1921 led to at least one attempt on his life. Following the establishment of the Irish Free State in 1922, he transferred to the English bar and became a bencher of the Middle Temple in 1925. He had a large practice, but retired from it in 1949 when Ireland left the Commonwealth, on the ground that he was now 'an alien'.

Sullivan enjoyed a high reputation among his contemporaries both at the English and Irish bars. He was a commanding figure, tall and with a neatly trimmed beard, and frequently displayed the courage of a great advocate, particularly in his clashes with the notoriously difficult Lord Chief Justice Hewart. Among his best-known cases was the libel action brought by Marie Stopes against Halliday Sutherland, whom Sullivan, himself a devout Roman Catholic, successfully represented. His most notorious client was W. C. Hobbs, the villain of the 'Mr A' case, for whom he appeared in his libel actions against various newspapers.

Towards the end of Sullivan's life the controversy over the Casement diaries erupted again. An English journalist in a book on Casement said that Sullivan had told him that Casement had effectively admitted to him (Sullivan) that he was a practising homosexual; Sullivan subsequently confirmed this in a newspaper letter. This led to a petition being presented to the benchers of the King's Inns to remove Sullivan from his position as an honorary bencher, on the ground that he had committed a serious breach of professional confidence. The benchers found that he had, but confined themselves to censuring him, whereupon Sullivan resigned. He died on 9 January 1959 at Beckenham, Kent. He published two books, consisting largely of legal reminiscences, *Old Ireland* (1927) and *The Last Serjeant* (1952).   RONAN KEANE

Sources A. M. Sullivan, *Old Ireland* (1927) [autobiography] · A. M. Sullivan, *The last serjeant: the memoirs of Serjeant A. M. Sullivan* (1952) · minutes of the benchers of the Honourable Society of King's Inns, Dublin, April/July 1956 · R. McColl, *Roger Casement: a new judgement* (1956), 231–5, 256–60, 283 · B. Inglis, *Roger Casement* (1973), 345–8, 353–7, 362–6, 440 · F. Callanan, *T. M. Healy* (1996), 472, 528 · *Irish Law Times and Solicitors' Journal* (17 Jan 1920); (31 Jan 1920) · *Irish Law Times and Solicitors' Journal* (31 Jan 1959), 31–2 · *Law Times* (23 Jan 1959), 43–4 · R. Sawyer, *Casement, the flawed hero* (1984) · *DNB* · *CGPLA Eng. & Wales* (1959)

Likenesses J. Lavery, group portrait, oils, 1916 (*The trial of Roger Casement, 1916*), King's Inns, Dublin; on loan from the Royal Courts of Justice, London · photograph, repro. in Sullivan, *Old Ireland*, frontispiece · photograph, repro. in Sullivan, *The last serjeant*, frontispiece · portrait, Middle Temple, London
Wealth at death £350 1s. 6d.: probate, 22 April 1959, *CGPLA Eng. & Wales*

Sullivan, Sir Arthur Seymour

Sullivan, Sir Arthur Seymour (1842–1900), composer and conductor, was born on 13 May 1842 at 8 Bolwell Terrace (now no longer standing), Lambeth, London, the son of Thomas Sullivan (1805–1866), a musician, and his wife, Mary Clementina, *née* Coghlan (1811–1882). His father's family was Irish: his paternal grandfather (also Thomas Sullivan) was born in co. Kerry and enlisted in the British army in 1806. That his maternal grandmother was Italian is probably sufficient to explain Sullivan's 'short and tight' appearance, 'with dark complexion and thick curly hair' as William Allingham described him in 1863. Suggestions of a part-Jewish origin are unsupported by any evidence.

Early years, education, and first steps in composition Sullivan's musical education was remarkable in that it came to him free. His talent procured for him a training of the highest class, such as would otherwise have been far beyond the resources of his lower-middle-class family. The first steps, however, arose within the family itself. From 1845 his father (who had been educated at the Royal Military Asylum for the children of soldiers) served as sergeant bandmaster at the Royal Military College, Sandhurst, where the boy 'learned to play every wind instrument, with which I formed not merely a passing acquaintance, but a real, lifelong intimate friendship' (A. Sullivan, 'In the days of my youth', *MAP* [periodical], 4 Feb 1899). At the same time he began the piano and at the age of eight composed an anthem, 'By the waters of Babylon'.

Perhaps through some private reciprocal arrangement, Sullivan was sent as a boarder to a London school kept by William Gordon Plees at 20 Albert Terrace, Bayswater. Once in London, the sight of the uniformed boys of the Chapel Royal marching to or from Sunday services at St James's Palace may have fired his ambition: at any rate it was on his own initiative that he and Plees called without notice on the patriarchal Sir George Smart, the titular organist and composer to the chapel. Smart directed his callers to the master of the choristers, Thomas Helmore, who was won over by the boy's exceptional singing voice. Admission was granted in April 1854 despite the fact that, at nearly twelve, Sullivan was older than most boys on entry.

Helmore, at whose house the boys lived and who tutored them in general as well as musical subjects, was an important figure in the Victorian high Anglican revival of church music. He proved an ideal nourisher of Sullivan's talent. While still living in Helmore's house Sullivan won the first competition for the newly endowed Mendelssohn scholarship to the Royal Academy of Music. At the academy his principal teachers were William Sterndale Bennett for piano and John Goss for composition. He

Sir Arthur Seymour Sullivan (1842–1900), by Sir John Everett Millais, 1888

was able to combine his choristership with academy studies until June 1857 when his voice broke and he had to leave the Chapel Royal. A new appointment for his father—as professor of the clarinet at the newly established Royal Military School of Music at Kneller Hall, Twickenham—led to the family's moving to a London home at 3 Ponsonby Street, Pimlico.

Sullivan's chief strength at the academy was discovered to be in composition. An (unnamed) overture performed on 13 July 1858 won commendation in the *Musical World*. His prowess had already prolonged the Mendelssohn scholarship for a second year; now a further extension allowed him two years of study at the Leipzig conservatory, the equal of that of Paris in providing musical training higher than London could boast. Ignaz Moscheles (friend of Beethoven and Mendelssohn) became Sullivan's personal mentor, Julius Rietz his principal teacher of composition, and Moscheles and Louis Plaidy his principal teachers of piano. He also learned the violin. Another talent developed: 'I come in for all the conducting now!' he wrote home enthusiastically in 1860 (H. Sullivan and N. Flower, *Sir Arthur Sullivan: his Life and Letters*, 1950, 27).

An overture, *The Feast of Roses* (after Thomas Moore's *Lalla Rookh*; Sullivan's score is now lost), was performed on 26 May 1860 at the end of Sullivan's second year at Leipzig and won favourable comment in the Leipzig press. He spent a further year in the city funded by private donations organized by his father and by the conservatory's exempting him from fees. For his graduation exercise (performed on 6 April 1861) he conducted his suite of incidental music to Shakespeare's *The Tempest*, much on the lines of Mendelssohn's to *A Midsummer Night's Dream*.

Throughout his Leipzig stay he wrote affectionately and with amusing descriptions to his family at home. His elder brother and only sibling, Frederic Thomas Sullivan (1837–1877), was made the butt of considerable chaff, extended to Frederic's future wife, Charlotte Louisa Lacy. His sense of family obligation remained strong throughout his life, though he never married: after his brother's early death Sullivan brought up Frederic and Charlotte's eldest son, Herbert, as his own. He remained closely bound to his mother (widowed in 1866), writing long, lively letters and frequently visiting her in the London suburb of Fulham where, on Frederic's death, she took up residence with Charlotte and the latter's seven younger children.

A reputation established On returning to London from Leipzig, Sullivan advertised in the *Musical World* to invite 'communications regarding pupils, etc.', and he also took an organist's post at St Michael's, Chester Square. The decisive step in a developing career, however, was a meeting with George Grove, secretary of the Crystal Palace and administrator of the Saturday orchestral concerts there—concerts which, under the baton of August Manns, provided London's liveliest exposure of new music alongside the classics.

At those concerts, on 5 April 1862, a revised version of the *Tempest* music was given, with linking narrative written by the critic Henry F. Chorley. The audience's enthusiasm was sealed by such press notices as Chorley's in *The Athenaeum* of 12 April ('Years on years have elapsed since we have heard a work by so young an artist so full of promise, so full of fancy, showing so much conscientiousness'). At a repeat performance the following Saturday, Chorley's friend Charles Dickens was present: he 'seized my hand with his iron grip' (recalled Sullivan), saying, 'I don't pretend to know much about music, but I do know that I have been listening to a very great work' (A. Sullivan, 'In the days of my youth', *MAP*, 4 Feb 1899).

The fame which gathered round a new-found genius (Sullivan was not yet twenty) was enhanced by a winning charm which gained him the friendship of Chorley and of the equally influential critic J. W. Davison of *The Times*, of Grove, and of Jenny Lind (now settled in London as the wife of the prominent conductor–pianist Otto Goldschmidt). Through Grove's position as secretary of the Society of Arts came a connection with the civil servant and promoter of the arts Henry Cole and with members of the royal family, including the prince of Wales, to whom 'by special permission' Sullivan dedicated *The Princess of Wales's March* to mark the prince's wedding in 1863. With the queen's youngest son, the duke of Edinburgh (an enthusiastic amateur violinist), a long-lasting friendship arose.

Sullivan was henceforth assured of work. A cantata, *Kenilworth*, with words by Chorley, for the Birmingham festival (8 September 1864) was the first of many destined for the periodical choral-based festivals at which new works

were prominently featured. Sir Michael Costa, the powerful music director of the Royal Opera at Covent Garden, gave Sullivan the position of organist (for those few operas requiring such participation), leading to the opportunity to compose a short ballet for production there on 16 May 1864, *L'île enchantée*. A cordial but not uncritical welcome was given to a symphony (Crystal Palace, 10 March 1866), a cello concerto for Alfredo Piatti (Crystal Palace, 24 November 1866), and the overtures *In Memoriam* (Norwich festival, 30 October 1866) and *Marmion* (Philharmonic Society, St James's Hall, London, 3 June 1867). In celebration of the prince of Wales's recovery from typhoid he wrote for the Crystal Place a brilliantly festive Te Deum involving not only soprano solo, chorus, and orchestra but a military band as well: an audience of 30,000 heard its first performance (1 May 1872).

Given the sparseness of orchestral concert series at the time, symphonic music could not provide a living; no more could such admirable, refined song settings as 'Orpheus with his lute'—one of a set of five Shakespearian songs (1863–4) which Sullivan had sold outright to the publisher for 5 guineas apiece. What could make money was the composition of ballads—songs written in a broader style for a broader public, paid on a royalty per copy sold. One such was 'Will he come?' (1865), with words by Adelaide A. Procter, from whose verse he later struck a goldmine with 'The Lost Chord' (1877), which sold a reputed 200,000 copies. Hymn tunes, commanding a fee at each new printing, could also earn handsomely. Sullivan wrote about fifty, of which 'St Gertrude' became hugely popular as the standard setting (though not the first setting) of S. Baring-Gould's 'Onward, Christian soldiers': it remains one of the best-known hymn tunes.

Chiefly, however, what raised Sullivan to riches (his income at its peak could match W. E. Gladstone's salary as prime minister) was the succession of works for the lighter musical stage which he began in 1866—not at first with W. S. *Gilbert, with whose name his was to be so firmly linked. In Sullivan's day these works were generally called 'comic operas'; most modern commentators find 'operettas' a more appropriate description.

Operettas and other stage work Offenbach's Paris operettas, greatly successful in London both in French and in translation, spurred emulation. It was for a double bill with Offenbach's *Les deux aveugles* that Sullivan composed *Cox and Box* (with a libretto by F. C. Burnand based on the admired one-act farce *Box and Cox* by John Maddison Morton). It first emerged in a private entertainment put on by the all-male Moray Minstrels on 26 May 1866, with piano accompaniment. A London stage production with orchestra followed (in a single benefit performance at the Adelphi, 11 May 1867). Soon afterwards, likewise in collaboration with Burnand, came *The Contrabandista, or, The Law of the Ladrones*, in two acts, produced on 18 December 1867 at St George's Hall under the management of Thomas German Reed. Next, as one of the works by which the actor–manager John Hollingshead kept 'the sacred lamp of burlesque' burning at the Gaiety Theatre, came *Thespis, or, The*

Gods Grown Old (26 December 1871). The text, which survives, was the work of W. S. Gilbert (their first collaboration); the music, save for fragments, is lost.

Meanwhile in 1867 Sullivan had visited Vienna in the company of George Grove, hunting and finding some long-buried treasures of Schubert's music. At the Birmingham festival on 21 August 1870 he brought out the best of his orchestral works, the curiously named *Overtura di ballo* (much later published as *Overture di ballo*). In 1871, as well as contributing the cantata *On Shore and Sea* to the ceremony which opened the Royal Albert Hall (29 March), he published a song cycle, *The Window, or, Songs of the Wrens*, to verses specially written by Tennyson. About this time he met Mary Frances (Fanny) Ronalds, *née* Carter (1839–1916), an American beauty separated but not divorced from her husband. A gifted amateur singer, prominent in society, she became—outside marriage—Sullivan's close companion for the rest of his life, though the sexual bond was to slacken in his latter years. They did not share a residence and the liaison was not publicly acknowledged.

Again invoking comparison with Offenbach (whose *La Périchole* was the main piece of the evening) Sullivan's one-act *Trial by Jury* to Gilbert's words was heard at the Royalty Theatre on 25 March 1875. Richard D'Oyly *Carte, a sub-manager on that occasion, thereafter formed his own production company, subsequently presenting all the full-length Gilbert and Sullivan pieces in a run of box-office successes unprecedented on the London stage. First, however, Sullivan collaborated with another librettist, Bolton Rowe (pseudonym of B. C. Stephenson), in a further one-acter, *The Zoo* (St James's Theatre, 5 June 1875).

The Gilbert–Sullivan–Carte productions began with *The Sorcerer* (Opera Comique, 17 November 1877) and continued with *HMS Pinafore, or, The Lass that Loved a Sailor* (Opera Comique, 25 May 1878). A wave of pirated performances of the latter in various American cities prompted Gilbert, Sullivan, and Carte to visit New York and launch *The Pirates of Penzance, or, The Slave of Duty* there at the Fifth Avenue Theatre on 31 December 1879. (A partial preview to establish British copyright was given on the previous day at Paignton, Devon.) *Patience, or, Bunthorne's Bride* followed at the Opera Comique on 23 April 1881. The Savoy Theatre, built by Carte, was the location of all the remaining first nights: *Iolanthe, or, The Peer and the Peri* (25 November 1882), *Princess Ida, or, Castle Adamant* (after Tennyson's *The Princess*, 5 January 1884), *The Mikado, or, The Town of Titipu* (14 May 1885), *Ruddygore* (altered to *Ruddigore*), *or, The Witch's Curse* (22 January 1887), *The Yeomen of the Guard, or, The Merryman and his Maid* (3 October 1888), *The Gondoliers, or, The King of Barataria* (7 December 1889), and (unsuccessful, rarely revived since) *Utopia Limited, or, The Flowers of Progress* (7 October 1893) and *The Grand Duke, or, The Statutory Duel* (7 May 1896).

Many of the scores were subjected to revision after the first night. But to a remarkable degree they maintain a fertility of musical invention which, while serving Gilbert's verbal ingenuities, has allowed the music its independent life: indeed, the scores were promptly and profitably adapted for dance music and marches. Though the middle

and later operettas show a progressive refinement of harmony, the essential musical style was present from the start. Invariable for the two-act works was the plan of construction: following the model of the Italian *opera buffa*, maximum musical complexity is reached in the 'first finale' (end of act 1)—a scheme carefully 'built in' by the texts Gilbert provided, with a climax of dramatic intrigue at the same point (so that technically the second act is a denouement).

Of Sullivan's operettas only the early *Trial by Jury* and *The Zoo* (both short) are set to music throughout, the others being interspersed with spoken dialogue. For the separate musical numbers (solos, ensembles up to octets, choruses) Sullivan calls deftly on a whole range of forms, even the simple verse-repeating song being capable of the subtlest inner construction. The contrast between 'The sun, whose rays are all ablaze' and 'Tit-willow' (both from *The Mikado*) may be cited. A virtual trademark of the scores is the 'counterpoint of characters' when two or more soloists (or the male and/or the female section of the chorus) deliver apparently separate tunes which then simultaneously combine: the dovetailing of the lovers' strains with the weather chatter of the women's chorus in *The Pirates of Penzance* is outstanding in both musical and comical effect.

Comic touches, however, are sometimes hidden for the delectation of connoisseurs: few listeners to the dilemma ensemble from *Trial by Jury* recognize a close parody of the second-act finale of Bellini's *La sonnambula*. More patently, the so-called madrigals in the operettas are a charming reflection of the composer's Chapel Royal training; the patter song as popularized by Rossini ('Figaro here, Figaro there') is extended in *Ruddigore* to a supremely comic patter trio. Influences from Handel to Bizet (*Carmen* was first given in 1875) are detectable enough, but Sullivan's achievement is to weave them all into such memorable identifications of Gilbert's characters. Orchestrations are unfailingly apt and should not really be called orchestrations at all: Sullivan generally composed directly into an orchestral score, leaving others to make the piano arrangement. The overtures of most (not all) of his operettas he left to be written by a musical assistant.

An expanding career Operetta was as yet only a sideline when, hailed by the magazine *The Orchestra* (February 1876) as 'the most conspicuous musician we have', Sullivan was appointed in 1876 as principal of London's new conservatory, the National Training School of Music (to merge later into the Royal College of Music). He worked there conscientiously but, one senses, not congenially, and resigned in 1880. In that year he became conductor of the Leeds triennial musical festival and directed there his cantatas *The Martyr of Antioch* (words by H. H. Milman, adapted by Gilbert, 15 October 1880) and *The Golden Legend* (words by Longfellow, adapted by Joseph Bennett, 16 October 1886). In 1882, following his mother's death, he moved to 1 Queen's Mansions, Victoria Street, London, which was to remain his home henceforth.

In 1883 Sullivan was knighted. The mid-1880s marked the apex of his multifold career, when *The Mikado* enjoyed the longest opening run of all the operettas (672 performances) and proved easily the most successful in continental Europe, both on tours by Carte's company and in German, Hungarian, Russian, and other translations. For three seasons from 1885 to 1887 Sullivan was conductor of the Philharmonic (later Royal Philharmonic) Society, the most prestigious provider of London's orchestral concerts. With Joseph Joachim among his distinguished soloists, his repertory and tastes remained conservative—mainly in the chronological range from Haydn and Mozart to Dvořák and Massenet, with some room for Wagner as represented by the *Ride of the Valkyries* and the overture to *Die Meistersinger*.

In 1885 Sullivan revisited the United States. He not only conducted *The Mikado* in New York, but also journeyed to California to see 'his' family—the younger children of his late brother Frederic, now bereaved a second time by the death of their mother Charlotte (she had married a second, shiftless husband and had emigrated to join her brother William Lacy in Los Angeles). Sullivan, who had contributed regularly to the children's upkeep, continued to do so after a joyous reunion which included a family trip to the Yosemite valley—an adventure vividly described in his diary.

While the public saw an ideal match between Gilbert's witty inventiveness and Sullivan's mellifluously varied music, the partnership was subject to hidden strains. The relationship between the affable, sociable composer and the aloof, authoritarian librettist never moved into personal intimacy. Sullivan felt chained by the rigour and rhyming of Gilbert's verse and the artificiality of his plots. The break that finally manifested itself in April 1890 in the 'carpet quarrel'—when Gilbert accused Carte of cheating on the division of profits by deducting an alleged £500 for front-of-house carpets from Gilbert and Sullivan's share, and Sullivan sided with Carte—masked long-simmering differences. So it was that an amazed public beheld W. S. Gilbert and Arthur Sullivan on opposite sides in a court of law (September 1890).

Convinced that success awaited him in 'grand opera', Sullivan had even told Carte in 1884 that he was resolved 'not to write any more Savoy pieces'. But the Savoy—that is, operetta—was a fountain of prosperity on which he could not turn his back. During the estrangement with Gilbert (1890–91), and even after a reconciliation a year later, Sullivan resorted to other librettists in order to keep up an output for Carte at the Savoy. He turned to Sydney Grundy for *Haddon Hall* (24 September 1892); to his old collaborator Burnand for *The Chieftain* (an expanded version of *The Contrabandista*, 12 December 1894); to A. W. Pinero and J. Comyns Carr for *The Beauty Stone* (28 May 1898); and finally to the young Basil Hood for *The Rose of Persia, or, The Story-Teller and the Slave* (29 November 1899) and for *The Emerald Isle, or, The Caves of Carig-Cleena* (27 April 1901, musically completed by Edward German). None endured.

Yet his artistic concentration on operetta, the profits of which gave assurance of a gilded life, seemed to rob Sullivan of the ability to innovate and consolidate elsewhere.

Apart from the *Macbeth* overture (originally for Henry Irving's production of the play at the Lyceum Theatre, 29 December 1888) not a single orchestral work of substance appeared after 1870. His long-awaited 'grand opera' emerged on 31 January 1891 as *Ivanhoe* (libretto, after Scott, by Julian Sturgis). It was magnificently launched by Carte, who built for it the Royal English Opera House (now the Palace Theatre) and optimistically presented it in an unbroken run, not in the usual mixed operatic repertory. *Ivanhoe* achieved 160 performances—remarkable enough, but insufficient to recover costs, obliging Carte to sell the theatre. It is a flawed and, as was immediately noticed, an old-fashioned work, broken into separate 'numbers' rather than welded into whole-act continuity.

A return after thirty-five years to the world of ballet came with an invitation from the Alhambra Theatre to mark Queen Victoria's diamond jubilee. The result, with some reuse of music from earlier compositions, was *Victoria and Merrie England* (25 May 1897). Sullivan must have been grateful for the commission, aware as he was of a diminishing annual income. But with a sense of obligation he handed to the Prince of Wales's Hospital Fund the profit of £200 he netted from the printing of a jubilee hymn, and likewise the proceeds from the sale of 75,000 copies of 'The Absent-Minded Beggar' (a rousing song setting of a text by Kipling, 1899, in support of the Second South African War) went entirely to forces' charities.

Sullivan's work as a conductor Only a few foreign-born musicians (Costa, Hallé, Henschel, Manns) could make a specialized career as a conductor in Britain before the 1890s. On the other hand the status of prominent composer was supposed to carry a competence as conductor too. Having been conductor of the (Royal) Amateur Orchestral Society, with the duke of Edinburgh as violinist–leader, Sullivan took professional footholds as conductor of the Glasgow Choral and Orchestral Union for two seasons during 1875 and 1876, and of the concerts in London at the newly founded Royal Aquarium and Summer and Winter Garden in 1876. His own compositions were welcomed when he conducted some of the Promenade Concerts which the catering firm of Gatti promoted at Covent Garden Theatre in 1878.

Sullivan's appointment to the Leeds triennial festival, however, gave scope for much more ambitious work. Nominally the programmes were the choice of the committee, but the conductor was chief professional adviser. Sullivan brought Beethoven's *Missa solemnis* (by no means a familiar work even to London audiences) to Leeds for the first time in 1883; in 1886 came Bach's mass in B minor in 'the most complete interpretation of Bach's sacred masterpiece ever heard in this country or, for that matter, in any other' (*Musical Times*, November 1886, 655). But though Sullivan might thus be praised for fidelity and conscientiousness, he was frequently found wanting in vigour of interpretation. Suffering recurrently from kidney disease, he was compelled (at least from the 1880s) to conduct seated. To the Viennese critic Eduard Hanslick, attending the Philharmonic concerts in London in 1886, Sullivan as conductor was 'a drowsy fellow', showing 'unequalled phlegm' in his commitment to the music and to the audience (*Musical Times*, September 1886, 518–20).

This was an extreme view, but Sullivan resigned his Philharmonic position after three seasons, complaining of sniping by London critics constantly comparing him with 'their god [Hans] Richter'. At Leeds, though a weakening of his physical power became evident, not until 1899 (a year before his death) was he persuaded by the committee to resign his festival appointment. The new style of conducting—not only of Richter, but of Arthur Nikisch and of the young Henry J. Wood—had made Sullivan's obsolete.

Personal characteristics and posthumous reputation In his own time Sullivan's features were almost as well known as those of royalty and prime ministers, thanks to the hundreds of line drawings (both faithful and caricatured) published in *Punch*, *The Graphic*, and other prominent organs of the press in connection with his work. Often the small, smiling Sullivan and the tall, severe Gilbert make a pair. Sullivan occasionally appears dandified, with monocle: so the cartoonist 'Ape' (Carlo Pellegrini) showed him as early as 1874, with baton drooping by his side in white-gloved hand, under the title *English Music* in the celebrated *Vanity Fair* series. Linley Sambourne's cartoon in *Punch* (30 October 1880) displayed Sullivan with upraised baton, using as conductor's rostrum the duke of Edinburgh's violin case: the progress from bandmaster's son to royal favourite was never more wittily encapsulated.

The personal charm which assisted that progress was unfeigned and was extended to children as well as colleagues. Ethel Smyth, a great admirer, found on meeting him (1890) 'such a blend of chaff and seriousness (the exact perfection of cadence there is in his work) that my one idea ever after was to see him whenever I could' (*Impressions that Remained*, 1920, 2.232). He kept in touch with the remoter as well as the closer members of his own family and embraced Fanny Ronalds's family as his own also, referring to her father as 'the guv'nor'. His genial humour, missing from the formal portrait painted by his friend John Millais (1888), emerges in the comment he recorded on an Edison cylinder in the same year: congratulating the inventor, he nevertheless declared himself terrified that 'so much hideous and bad music' would be put on record for ever.

Sullivan was not of systematic working habits. Sometimes a task was allowed to lie long unattended; at other times he was at his desk for most of a twenty-hour day. His willingness to let fate take its course—even when a deadline or a production schedule was imperilled—seems linked with his behaviour (as revealed in his diaries) as an obsessive gambler. He would visit London clubs, sometimes twice in a single day, to play cards at high stakes. On the French riviera, where he liked to rent a house for a period of sustained work away from casual callers, the tables of Monte Carlo were a lure.

Sullivan was an inveterate traveller, to Paris from early years, later often to Switzerland and Italy and also to Belgium, Germany, and Austria; to the Baltic in 1881 (as far as St Petersburg) as the shipboard guest of the duke of Edinburgh, by this time a rear-admiral; to Egypt in the same year with his friend Edward Dicey. While in the United States in 1879–80 he found time for a visit to Niagara Falls and also to Ottawa as house guest of Canada's governor-general, the marquess of Lorne, whose wife, Princess Louise, Queen Victoria's sixth child, had been Sullivan's dinner guest in London. In 1897 he followed other leading British musicians in making the pilgrimage to the Wagnerian shrine of the Bayreuth festival, attending *The Ring* and *Parsifal*, and liking little of what he saw and heard: 'What a curious mixture of sublimity and absolute puerile drivel are all these Wagner operas' (diary).

The death of a friend in a carriage accident moved Sullivan to devise (and in 1899 to patent) the Sullivan Safety Shaft, to minimize the likelihood of injury and damage from a runaway horse. But such practical ingenuity was not habitual: what generally diverted him from musical work was the pleasurable pursuit of the well-to-do social round, including attendance at the great race meetings. In summer he often rented a country house where he would entertain friends, and in London his hospitality was lavish. At his flat on 7 June 1885 a dinner party for twelve including the prince of Wales and the duke of Edinburgh was swelled after dinner by a further fifty-six guests, entertainment being provided by performers from the Savoy and elsewhere.

Sullivan's intimates included several members of the Anglo-Jewish banking families of Rothschild and Sassoon, the actor Squire Bancroft, and such musicians as Grove, Frederic Clay (who died early), and Joseph Barnby, who had been a fellow chorister at the Chapel Royal. With many friends, including his collaborators Francis Burnand and Joseph Bennett, he moved quickly to first-name terms—but never with Gilbert.

Dynastic connection gave Sullivan an acquaintance with members of the German as well as the British royal family. At Kiel in 1881 'Prince William' (the future Emperor Wilhelm II) saluted the composer by singing a snatch of *HMS Pinafore*; in Berlin six years later Wilhelm's younger sister Princess Victoria posed as Yum-Yum (*The Mikado*) at two private shows of tableaux vivants, with Sullivan himself at the piano. With Queen Victoria he formed a new, informal contact in 1897 when he played the harmonium at an Easter service while she was staying at a hotel at Cimiez, near Nice. Three visits to Windsor Castle followed, and the conferment in the Royal Victorian Order (1897). He had previously received the orders of the French Légion d'honneur (1878) and the Turkish order of the Mejidiye (1888), as well as honorary doctorates from Cambridge (1876) and Oxford (1879) and the fellowship of the Royal Academy of Music.

Sullivan had become the representative British musician, honoured and prominent, in later terminology an 'establishment' figure. His cantatas and hymn settings fulfilled his formal adherence to the Church of England. Neither his diaries nor his letters, however, show any sense of being strongly guided by religious faith; nor, on the other hand, do they hint at the agnostic soul-searching which pressed on so many of his intellectual contemporaries. He died in London on 22 November 1900 at his home, 1 Queen's Mansions, Victoria Street, Westminster (the death certificate specifies 'bronchitis, 21 days, cardiac failure', with no mention of his kidney disease), apparently in the presence only of his devoted valet and housekeeper, Louis Jaeger and Clotilde Raquet. Both were generously provided for in his will, which included bequests of manuscript scores to both the Royal Academy of Music and the Royal College of Music.

Sullivan had left instructions that he was to be buried in the family grave at Brompton cemetery. The grave had already been opened when burial was offered at St Paul's Cathedral, which took place on 27 November, preceded by another service at the Chapel Royal. The memorial plaque in the cathedral bears a sculptured effigy of Sullivan by William Goscombe John, as does the statue erected in the Embankment Gardens (close to the Savoy Theatre) bearing a quatrain chosen by Gilbert from *The Yeomen of the Guard*: 'Is life a boon? ...'

After his death, Sullivan and Gilbert's operettas retained public favour in performances by the D'Oyly Carte Opera Company, but his other music quickly lost favour. A single revival of *Ivanhoe* under the auspices of Beecham (but not conducted by him) in 1910 was poorly received. In 1907 the musical historian Ernest Walker not only attached the words 'disgraceful rubbish' to such songs as 'The Lost Chord' and 'The Sailor's Grave' but depreciated the artistic worth of his concert works, categorizing Sullivan as 'after all, the idle singer of an empty evening' (E. Walker, *A History of Music in England*, 3rd edn, 1952, 325)—an allusion to William Morris's self-deprecatory reference to the 'idle singer of an empty day'. A 'British musical renaissance' was increasingly postulated as having begun with the generation after Sullivan (Stanford, Parry, Mackenzie).

In the mid-1950s, after the label 'Victorian' had ceased to be generally derisive in musical contexts, a rehabilitation began. The acquisition (and later amplification) by the Pierpont Morgan Library, New York, of a magnificent Gilbert and Sullivan collection gave new scope for scholarship. From the 1970s the composer's diaries became publicly accessible, in part at that library, but mainly at Yale University. Following a pioneer recording (1968) of the symphony by the conductor Charles Groves, the compact disc era brought a surge in the exposure of Sullivan's music, even a reconstruction (by Charles Mackerras and David Mackie, 1986) of Sullivan's cello concerto, of which no complete score had survived.

The Sir Arthur Sullivan Society, founded in 1977, has assiduously promoted or assisted performances (including a complete recording of *Ivanhoe*, 1989) as well as publishing the results of research. From 1961, the British copyright of both Sullivan and Gilbert having expired, the joint stage works were reanimated in productions by major opera companies, and in the mid-1990s a British and an American firm independently began publication of the full scores of the Gilbert and Sullivan works in a critical detail hardly accorded to any comparable British composer save Elgar and Delius. The first book on Sullivan in any language other than English appeared (in German) in 1993.   ARTHUR JACOBS

Sources A. Jacobs, *Arthur Sullivan: a Victorian musician*, 2nd edn (1992) [incl. complete work list] • P. M. Young, *Sir Arthur Sullivan* (1971) • A. H. Lawrence, *Sir Arthur Sullivan: life-story, letters and reminiscences* (1899) • F. Cellier and C. Bridgeman, *Gilbert, Sullivan and D'Oyly Carte* (1914) • M. Saremba, *Arthur Sullivan: ein Komponistenleben in viktorianischen England* (Wilhelmshaven, 1993) • G. Dixon, *Index to the Sir Arthur Sullivan Society magazine* (1995) [incl. all pubns of the Society, 1977 onwards] • F. W. Wilson, *An introduction to the Gilbert and Sullivan operas from the collection of the Pierpont Morgan Library* (1989) • R. Allen and G. R. D'Luhy, *Sir Arthur Sullivan: composer and personage* (1975) [exhibition catalogue, Morgan L., 13 Feb – 20 April 1975] • P. H. Dillard, *How quaint the ways of paradox! An annotated Gilbert and Sullivan bibliography* (1991) • N. Temperley, ed., *Music in Britain: the romantic age, 1800–1914* (1981) • D. Eden, *Gilbert and Sullivan: the creative conflict* (1986) • A. Goodman, *Gilbert and Sullivan's London* (1988) • G. B. Shaw, *Shaw's music*, ed. D. H. Laurence (1981) • G. Hughes, *The music of Arthur Sullivan* (1960) • E. Blom, 'Sullivan, (Sir) Arthur (Seymour)', Grove, *Dict. mus.* (1954) • H. Klein, *Thirty years of musical life in London, 1870–1900* (1903) • B. W. Findon, *Sir Arthur Sullivan and his operas* (1908) • L. Baily, *The Gilbert and Sullivan book* (1952) • d. cert.

Archives Morgan L. • Royal Academy of Music, London, MSS • Sir Arthur Sullivan Society, Bishop Auckland, co. Durham, letters by Sullivan, his secretary and his executors, scores • Yale U., Beinecke L. | SOUND Edison cylinder recording

Likenesses Walery, photograph, 1885, NPG • J. E. Millais, oils, 1888, NPG [*see illus.*] • W. Goscombe John, bronze bas-relief, *c.*1902, St Paul's Cathedral, London • W. Goscombe John, marble bust, 1902, Royal College of Music, London • Ape [C. Pellegrini], chromolithograph caricature, NPG; repro. in *VF* (14 March 1874) • W. Goscombe John, bronze memorial bust, Embankment Gardens, London • London Stereoscopic Co., photograph, NPG, Watts Society • L. Sambourne, cartoon, repro. in *Punch* (30 Oct 1880) • Sarony, carte-de-visite, NPG • R. & E. Taylor, woodcut, NPG; repro. in *The Illustrated Review* (25 Oct 1873) • H. Watkins, carte-de-visite, NPG • photographs, Morgan L.

Wealth at death £56,536: resworn probate, 15 Jan 1902, *CGPLA Eng. & Wales* (1901)

Sullivan, (Thomas) Barry (1821–1891), actor, was born at Howard's Place, Birmingham, on 5 July 1821, one of three children. His mother was Mary Barry, the daughter of a Cork farmer; his father, Peter Sullivan, also from Cork, served as an infantryman in the 101st regiment. The family moved from Birmingham to Bristol, where the young Sullivan was educated by Jesuits at a day school attached to the church in Trenchard Street near their home. He was orphaned at the age of eight, but finished his education at the Stokes Croft endowed school before being apprenticed when he was fourteen to a lawyer. After W. C. Macready's visit to Bristol in 1834, Sullivan decided on a stage career and joined an itinerant company of players.

Sullivan began his stage noviciate at the age of sixteen in Cork, under Frank 'Schemer' Seymour, the manager of the Theatre Royal in George's Street, earning 15*s.* per week as a 'singing, walking gentleman' (Lawrence, 12). Rosencrantz, his first Shakespearian part, was performed on 14 June 1837 to the Hamlet of Charles Kean. He wanted to concentrate on straight roles, and left Seymour for the rival manager Collins, who had arrived in Cork in January 1838, with his Pavilion Theatre, which specialized in sensational melodrama. In 1839 Sullivan toured throughout

(Thomas) Barry Sullivan (1821–1891), by London
Stereoscopic Co.

Munster with his own 'fit-up' troupe, and in 1840 he was
re-engaged at the Theatre Royal, Cork, where Paumier
taught him elocution and fencing. In October 1841 he
played Duke Frederick in a production of *As You Like It*
which featured Ellen Tree and James Anderson, Macready's protégé, who encouraged Sullivan to try his luck
in Scotland.

After embarking on his apprenticeship in Scotland
under W. H. Murray, 'the wet-nurse *par excellence* of the histrionic child' (Lawrence, 17), Sullivan spent some time in
the prompter's box. He eventually made his début at the
Theatre Royal in Edinburgh on 24 November 1841, as Red
Rody in Isaac Pocock's *The Robber's Wife*. He was paid £1 10s.
per week to play 'seconds' to John Ryder (1814–1885), an
actor of 'heavy' parts, who received £2. At the end of the
1842–3 season Sullivan assumed Ryder's salary and parts
as principal heavy. On 4 July 1842, at St Cuthbert's in Princes Street, Sullivan married Mary Amory, without the
blessing of her father. It was Sullivan's day off, and the
couple spent the evening at the theatre. After his benefit,
on 30 May 1844, Sullivan, tired of playing important but
not principal parts, left Edinburgh for the Adelphi Theatre, Glasgow. He then joined the Theatre Royal, Aberdeen, becoming its leading man and stage-manager. He
managed the City Theatre in Glasgow for a short time,
and, from 1845 to 1847, the reopened Theatre Royal in
Aberdeen.

Sullivan's début in England was at Wakefield in March
1847, but shabby treatment soon led him to accept £5 per
week as leading man for Robert Roxby, the manager of the
Theatre Royal, Liverpool. He appeared there on 7 May as
Sir Edward Mortimer in Colman's *The Iron Chest*, making a
success of a part he disliked. He was then engaged by John
Knowles at the Theatre Royal, Manchester, where he
opened on 9 October 1847 as Stukely in Edward Moore's
The Gamester. On 25 October he appeared as Hamlet, bringing new readings and business to the role. On 26 November 1847 he was a hit as Robert Macaire. The next night he
gave his Henry VIII to Macready's Wolsey. Sullivan's star
was now in the ascendant. On 8 January 1848 he played
Long Tom Coffin in Edward Fitzball's *The Pilot*, and was
thought by some to have been a better stage sailor even
than the famous T. P. Cooke. Moreover, in January 1848
Sullivan appeared as Edgar to Macready's Lear and was
called to share the curtain with him. On 3 March 1848 he
played Claude Melnotte in Bulwer-Lytton's *The Lady of
Lyons* for the first time, and on 15 April he was Melnotte to
Fanny Kemble's Pauline. Sullivan quarrelled with Wal-
lack, his manager, over, among other things, the preferment of G. H. Lewes (a pretentious amateur) in principal
roles, and returned to Edinburgh, where Murray welcomed him back.

Back in Liverpool, where he was always popular, Sullivan played opposite Samuel Phelps, alternating Othello
and Iago, and Macbeth and Macduff, in addition to playing
Falconbridge to Phelps's King John, and supported Macready in his farewell performances, distinguishing himself as Othello. Sullivan's Macbeth was innovatory, for he
portrayed the thane and his lady as co-travellers in evil,
and introduced an invisible ghost of Banquo.

On 7 February 1852 Sullivan made his London début at
the Haymarket as Hamlet. The London critics welcomed
his absence of mannerism: there was nothing of Macready or the elder Kean about him. As intelligent in his
melancholy as he was playful in other moods, Sullivan's
was a thoughtful Hamlet who feigned his madness. His
Evelyn in Bulwer-Lytton's *Money* (24 March) prompted *The
Examiner* to recognize 'a graceful, unobtrusive, and intelligent actor, capable of real feeling and unaffected in his
expression of it' (Sillard, 1.234). He stayed at the Haymarket, playing mostly leading roles, until 15 July 1853,
when he gave the Earl of Rochester for his benefit in
Coyne's *Presented at Court*. By this time Sullivan had acted
110 times at the Haymarket, representing ten different
characters, six of which were original performances.

Following a tour of England and Ireland in 1854, and an
engagement at the St James's Theatre, London, Sullivan
returned to the Haymarket as Evelyn on 24 May 1855.
When Helen Faucit joined the company he played
Melnotte to her Pauline in *The Lady of Lyons* (May) and
Jaques to her Rosalind (June). He also created Franklyn,
the amorous hunchback in John Saunders's *Love's Martyrdom*, and, in July, Lord Norcliffe in John Heraud's *Wife or No
Wife*. Tempted to Drury Lane, on 8 October 1855 he created

Tihrak in Fitzball's exotic *Nitocrius*, but his Petruchio in *The Taming of the Shrew* (responding to the Shakespeare revivals of Phelps and the Keans) was not as successful as he would have liked. However, by 1857, in a production of *Richelieu* in Edinburgh that saw the young Henry Irving as Gaston, Sullivan in the title role was on the bills as 'the popular and celebrated tragedian' (Sillard, 270).

In May Sullivan returned to London, where he played at Sadler's Wells Theatre. His social acceptability is indicated by the number of clubs which claimed him. In 1858 the Reunion Club made him a life member. Later he was a founder member of the Arundel Club, and much later still (1874) a member of the Savage Club. After a provincial tour, he left for America accompanied by his fourteen-year-old son, Thomas, who later became his business manager. Sullivan made his New York début at the Broadway Theatre on 22 November 1858 in Hamlet, which was followed by Macbeth, Richard, Shylock, Claude Melnotte, Petruchio, and Don Caesar de Bazan. He was well received by the critics, who applauded his realistic portrayals (Sullivan eschewed rant), notably of Beverley in *The Gamester*. In Washington, on 11 December, he performed Hamlet, then returned to New York's Burton Street Theatre. In January 1859 he went to Boston, and from there to Philadelphia, where he appeared first as Richelieu. On 6 June 1859 Sullivan crossed into Canada and played in Halifax, Montreal, and Toronto. He then went to Chicago, St Louis, Baltimore, Richmond (Virginia), and New Orleans. He ended his seventeen-month tour of North America £8000 richer, and departed for Liverpool at the end of May 1860.

Sullivan was engaged at the St James's Theatre at £45 per night, alternately playing Hamlet, Richelieu, Macbeth, and Richard III. After engagements at the Standard and the Amphitheatre in Liverpool he went to Belfast, but returned to the Amphitheatre to play Claude Melnotte on 26 February. On 11 March he was seen in a new role: Henri Desart in F. C. Burnand's *The Isle of St Tropez*. In the autumn he toured again, heading north to play in Blackburn, Leeds, Edinburgh, and Liverpool, before leaving for Australia.

On 9 August 1862 Sullivan made his first appearance in Australia, at the Theatre Royal in Melbourne, playing Hamlet. Richard III followed on 21 August, and soon afterwards Beverley, Macbeth, Othello, Iago, Claude Melnotte, and Don Caesar. He then opened at the Princess's Theatre in *Money*, playing to overflowing houses. The following month he was at the Royal Victoria Theatre, Sydney, as Richelieu. On his return to Melbourne he became lessee and manager of the Theatre Royal, which he refitted. His *Richard III* was a remarkable production, and considered as spectacular as anything Kean had done in London. On 23 April 1864 Sullivan unveiled a statue of Shakespeare in front of the Victorian Public Library. In February 1866 he returned to Sydney for a month's engagement at the Prince of Wales Opera House, and on his way back to England he visited New Zealand, Queensland, Western Australia, and India.

Sullivan spent the 1866–7 winter season at Drury Lane, where he opened as Falconbridge in *King John*, with Phelps

in the title role, on 22 September. He was now commanding £60 per night. In October 1868 his Claude Melnotte was up against Charles Fechter's at the Lyceum, and succeeded in drawing great houses to Drury Lane. Yet another provincial tour ensued, which he cut short to play Cibber's Richard III at Drury Lane for £75 per night. He returned to his London address—Cambridge Terrace, Hyde Park—and on 18 February he performed before a capacity house, now at the height of his career. Sullivan became manager of the proverbially unlucky Holborn Theatre in May 1869. He opened with *Money*, playing Evelyn, and followed that with *The Gamester* and *The School for Scandal*; however, he incurred a loss of £8000, and closed on 16 January 1870, never to gain a firm footing in the metropolis again.

Sullivan embarked on another of his triumphal processions through the provinces. On 21 March 1870 he made his first appearance as Hamlet in Birmingham, and, on 18 April, his first appearance in Dublin, where his Hamlet was rapturously received. From 1870 to 1874 he played in the major cities in the United Kingdom. His tragic representations—Richard III, Macbeth, Hamlet, Othello, Beverley, and, of course, Claude Melnotte—were considered impressive portraits of human passion, with a realism the stage had not previously witnessed. His comic roles as Benedick and Charles Surface were inimical. After farewells in Birmingham, Manchester, Liverpool, and London, he embarked on his second American tour.

Sullivan spent nine months during the 1875–6 season playing in thirty-three cities and making $140,000, giving 250 performances of fifteen different plays. He began as Hamlet at Booth's Theatre in New York on 30 August 1875, facing stiff competition from E. L. Davenport. Of his Hamlet *Appleton's Journal* spoke of 'well-studied pictures' but 'no fire and no imagination' (Lawrence, 67). American tastes favoured his Richard III, Beverley, and Richelieu. He ended his American tour as Richard III in Providence, Rhode Island.

Sullivan spent the 1876–7 season at Drury Lane, and in 1877 returned to Ireland, where he was greeted in university circles as a champion of Shakespeare. When the Shakespeare Memorial Theatre at Stratford upon Avon opened, on 23 April 1879, he played Benedick in *Much Ado about Nothing* to the Beatrice of Helen Faucit. On the following evening he performed Hamlet for the 3061st time. He continued to receive handsome offers to return to Australia and America, but his health was starting to wane. A performance as Richard III at the Alexander Theatre, Liverpool, on 4 June 1887 was Sullivan's last appearance on the stage. He returned to his home near Brighton (46 Albany Villas, Hove) never to act again. He had suffered dizziness and headaches as early as 1880, when a tour had to be cancelled on doctor's orders, and barely a month after his last performance he suffered a 'paralysis of the brain' and was bedridden for the next three years; he was cared for at first by his family, and later by the nuns from the local convent. In the winter of 1890 he contracted influenza; he died at his home in Hove on 3 May 1891, in the presence of his wife, three daughters, and two sons. He was buried in Glasnevin cemetery in Dublin. On 28 June 1894 a statue of Sullivan as Hamlet by Sir Thomas Farrell was unveiled at the site of his grave.

Physically Sullivan was well qualified for the stage. He was considered tall (5 feet 9 inches) and well built, with dark curly locks, piercing blue eyes, and a face whose character had been etched by smallpox. He had a graceful figure and commanding look, which suited him to leading roles, especially of the grave and sardonic kind. Despite his early potential as a singer and stage Irishman, he devoted his career industriously and soberly to the maintenance of legitimate drama and Shakespeare. While general opinion placed Sullivan in the second rank of Shakespearian actors, Shaw declared him equal to the best. He was, according to Shaw, the last 'of the line of British Shakespearian star actors from Burbage and Betterton to Macready' (Leech and Craik, 138). Acknowledged early, and at the height of his career, for intelligent and realistic playing, in his latter days Sullivan was viewed as premeditated and mechanical. After his death the metropolitan press epitomized him as melodramatic, stagey, and artificial. Despite his London successes, Sullivan was always more popular in the provinces, Ireland, America, and Australia. He was not a fashionable actor, and was easily overlooked by influential theatre historiographers, in particular G. H. Lewes, whom he had slighted early in his career. Sullivan spent so much time out of London that he lost touch with, or chose to ignore, its theatre trends. Late in his career he tried quixotically to maintain the old star and stock company system, when the prevailing trend was for the ensemble, and 'cup and saucer' acting.

BARRY O'CONNOR

Sources R. M. Sillard, *Barry Sullivan and his contemporaries: a histrionic record*, 2 vols. (1901) · W. J. Lawrence, *Barry Sullivan: a biographical sketch* (1893) · C. E. Pascoe, ed., *The dramatic list*, 2nd edn (1880) · *The Times* (4 May 1891) · J. Coleman, *The Theatre*, 4th ser., 17 (1891), 279–84 · 'Death of Barry Sullivan', *The Era* (9 May 1891) · *The life and reminiscences of E. L. Blanchard, with notes from the diary of Wm. Blanchard*, ed. C. W. Scott and C. Howard, 2 vols. (1891) · R. Courtneidge, *I was an actor once* [1930] · G. C. D. Odell, *Shakespeare from Betterton to Irving*, 2 vols. (1920); repr. with introduction by R. H. Ball (1966) · H. Love, ed., *The Australian stage: a documentary history* (1984) · C. Leech, T. W. Craik, L. Potter, and others, eds., *The Revels history of drama in English*, 8 vols. (1975–83), vol. 6, p. 138 · m. cert.

Likenesses T. Farrell, statue, 1894 (as Hamlet), Glasnevin cemetery, Dublin · London Stereoscopic Co., photograph, priv. coll. [*see illus.*] · J. Moore, stipple and line engraving (as Hamlet; after daguerreotype), BM, NPG; repro. in Tallis, *Drawing-room table book* · H. O'Shea, portrait · W. & D. Downey, photograph (as Hamlet); repro. in Courtneidge, *I was an actor once*, 65 · line drawing, repro. in Lawrence, *Barry Sullivan*, title page · seven prints, Harvard TC

Wealth at death £25,441 17s. 1d.: probate, 19 June 1891, CGPLA Eng. & Wales

Sullivan, Clive (1943–1985), rugby player, was born at 49 Wimborne Street, Cardiff, on 9 April 1943, the second among the four children of Charles Henry Sullivan, an electrical engineer then serving in the Royal Air Force, and his wife, Doris Eileen, *née* Boston. He was educated at Moreland Road primary school at Splott, on the outskirts of Cardiff, and then, after the family moved to the Ely district of Cardiff, at the Herbert Thompson Secondary Modern School. The remarkable natural speed which was a family trait—his elder brother, Brian, ran for Great Britain—emerged at a local competition when Sullivan was five and a half years old and, in spite of being left at the start, beat seven-year-old rivals comfortably. He started playing rugby at secondary school and won selection once for Cardiff schools, but his progress was halted by a series of injuries. At the age of fourteen he was warned that he might never walk properly again, and gave up the game.

After leaving school Sullivan worked as a motor mechanic before joining the army early in 1961. He was posted to the Royal Corps of Signals at Catterick as a wireless operator. Picked for a rugby match, he chose to play because revealing his medical history would have led to being invalided out of the army, and found that he suffered no ill effects after scoring a long-distance try. A trial with Bradford Northern was unsuccessful, but the touch judge in the match recommended him to his home town club Hull. He made his début for them on 9 December 1961, when he scored three tries against Bramley, and signed as a professional the following day.

The 1960s and 1970s, in the words of one historian, 'virtually passed Hull by' (Proctor and Varley, 86), but Sullivan, 5 feet 11 inches and 12 and a half stone, described as 'running like a deer, daintily and precisely and with an effortless grace' (Latus, 104), became one of the most prolific try scorers in the game, his attacking qualities supplemented by being 'a master of the cover tackle ... likely to pop up in the most improbable positions in the field' (Gate, 158). Alan Kellett, a frequent opponent, said he was 'like a thoroughbred racehorse' (Latus, 96). Sullivan's first three seasons were restricted by army duties, including a spell in Cyprus, three knee operations, and a nearly fatal car crash in October 1963. He left the army in 1964. He made his début for Great Britain in 1967, when he scored two tries against France. His international career peaked in 1972, when he was chosen captain of Great Britain—the first black player to lead a British national team in any major sport—and led the squad that won the world cup, played in France. In the final against Australia he scored the first try, 'a length of the field try which will be talked about as long as the game endures' (Gate, 162), then made the vital break for the decisive second, scored by the hooker, Mick Stephenson.

Sullivan scored thirteen tries in seventeen matches (nine as captain) for Great Britain and seven in seventeen for Wales. His 250 tries for Hull were a club record. In 1974 he moved to local rivals Hull Kingston Rovers, where he won a championship medal in 1979. His 113 tries in six seasons made him the only player to score 100 tries for both Hull clubs. Appropriately his final game for Rovers was in the all-Humberside challenge cup final of 1980, when they beat Hull 10–5 at Wembley. He subsequently joined Oldham, and played a few matches while coach of Hull's A team, and Doncaster. His 406 tries ranked him seventh of all time when he retired. He was appointed MBE in 1974.

Sullivan married Rosalyn Patricia Byron (*b.* 1946) of

Welton, near Hull, on 10 October 1966. They had two children. Their son Anthony (*b.* 1968) emulated him as a fast, high-scoring winger in rugby league for Hull Kingston Rovers, St Helens, and Great Britain and rugby union for Cardiff and Wales. Clive Sullivan died of liver cancer on 8 October 1985 at Kingston General Hospital, Hull, and his body was cremated after a private funeral. He was commemorated in the naming of Clive Sullivan Way, the approach road to the Humber Bridge in Hull. His wife survived him.   HUW RICHARDS

Sources J. Latus, *Hard road to the top (the Clive Sullivan story)* (1973) · R. Gate, *Gone north: Welshmen in rugby league*, 2 (1988) · M. E. Ulyatt, *Hull Kingston Rovers: a centenary history* (1983) · M. E. Ulyatt, *Old faithful: a history of Hull football club, 1895–1987* (1988) · I. Proctor and A. Varley, *The rugby league directory* (1990) · E. Waring, *Eddie Waring on rugby league* (1981) · *Hull Daily Mail* (8–15 Oct 1985) · *The Rugby Leaguer* (24 Oct 1985) · P. Fitzpatrick, *The Guardian* (9 Oct 1985) · b. cert. · d. cert. · R. Fletcher, *The boulevard voices* (2000)
Archives FILM *This is your life*, 1972
Likenesses photographs, repro. in Latus, *Hard road to the top*

Sullivan, Sir Edward, first baronet (1822–1885), judge, was born at Mallow, co. Cork, on 10 July 1822. He was the eldest son of Edward Sullivan (1800–1867), and his wife, Anne Surflen (*d.* 1841), *née* Lynch, widow of John Surflen. His father was a local wine merchant who had realized a substantial fortune in business. Sullivan received his earliest education at Mallow School and later on was sent to the endowed Midleton School, an institution in which many distinguished Irishmen had been trained. In 1841 he entered Trinity College, Dublin, where he had a distinguished university career. He obtained first classical scholarship in 1843 and graduated BA in 1845. He was also elected auditor of the college historical society in 1845 and gained the gold medal for oratory. In 1846 he entered Lincoln's Inn, and after two years of preliminary study at chambers in London he was called to the Irish bar, where he joined the Munster circuit. He married, on 24 September 1850, Bessie Josephine, daughter of Robert Bailey of Cork; they had four sons and one daughter.

Sullivan's well-trained and richly stored mind, and his great readiness, indomitable tenacity, and fiery eloquence very quickly brought him into notice at the bar, and within ten years he was appointed a queen's counsel, in 1858. Two years later, during the viceroyalty of Lord Carlisle, he was appointed third serjeant-at-law. Sullivan was always known as 'the Little Serjeant', 'the Big Serjeant' being Serjeant Armstrong's sobriquet. In 1861 Sullivan was appointed law adviser to the crown and in 1865 he became for a brief period solicitor-general for Ireland in Lord Palmerston's last administration. In this capacity he was called upon to deal with the Fenian conspiracy. In 1865 he was elected Liberal MP for Mallow, though from 1866 to 1868, while his party was in opposition, he applied himself mainly to his profession. About this time he acted in conjunction with James Whiteside as leading counsel for the plaintiff in the cause célèbre, *Thelwell v. Yelverton*. The question at issue was whether Major Yelverton had legally married Teresa Longworth, which Yelverton denied, he wishing to marry another. Sullivan's masterly cross-examination of Yelverton, widely acknowledged to be a model of forensic advocacy, was most influential in winning the case and establishing the unfortunate lady's honour.

In December 1868, on the return of the Liberal Party to power, Sullivan became attorney-general for Ireland in Gladstone's first administration. Next to Gladstone he took the leading part in the conduct of the Irish Church Bill—which was to bring about the disestablishment of the Irish church—in the Commons. His services on this occasion, the debating ability he displayed in the stormy discussions which the bill provoked, and his knowledge and grasp of the details of a most intricate subject, raised him to a high place in the estimation of the House of Commons, and earned him the complete confidence of his leader. Later in 1869 he played an important part in formulating the Irish Land Bill. Sullivan retired from parliament in 1870 to succeed John Walsh as master of the rolls in Ireland. Until 1882 he was mainly engrossed by his judicial duties, but he was also an active member of the privy council. Sullivan exercised very great influence in the government of Ireland, and his assistance was of the utmost value during a particularly unsettled period in the country's history. Gladstone placed much reliance on his judgement and his knowledge of Ireland, and it was mainly at his instance that the important step of arresting Charles Stewart Parnell was adopted by the government in 1881.

In December 1881 Sullivan was created a baronet on Gladstone's recommendation, in recognition of his services both as a judge and as a confidential adviser of the servants of the crown in Ireland. In the same year he received an honorary DL degree from Trinity College, Dublin, and in 1883 the premature death of Hugh Law opened the way for his elevation to the Irish chancellorship. In this capacity he displayed governing qualities of the highest order, and during the troubled period of Lord Spencer's second viceroyalty he may be said to have been the mainspring of the Irish government in the measures taken to stamp out the 'Invincible' conspiracy. He enjoyed his office for a comparatively brief period, but at the time of his sudden death, at his house, 32 Fitzwilliam Place, Dublin, on 13 April 1885, his power was immense. He was buried near Dublin in Dean's Grange cemetery.

Sullivan was a man of varied accomplishments and scholarly tastes. An ardent and lifelong bibliophile, he had at his death amassed one of the most valuable private libraries in the kingdom. He was, of course, a sound classical scholar, but he was also a skilled linguist, familiar with German, French, Italian, and Spanish literature. He was in religion a protestant and in politics a Liberal, and he was a member of the Athenaeum and Reform clubs.

In the list of Irish chancellors of the nineteenth century Sullivan is one of the most eminent. But he was more distinguished as a statesman than as a judge. His thorough knowledge of Ireland, combined with the courage, firmness, and decision of his character, qualified him to be what during the period of his chancellorship he was—an active champion of law and order throughout the country. It is not to be forgotten, however, that he was also one of the finest barristers of his day, whose skill as a forensic advocate was virtually unparalleled in Irish legal history.

C. L. FALKINER, rev. NATHAN WELLS

Sources F. E. Ball, *The judges in Ireland, 1221–1921*, 2 (1926) • *Thom's directory* (1885) • E. Keane, P. Beryl Phair, and T. U. Sadleir, eds., *King's Inns admission papers, 1607–1867*, IMC (1982) • private information (1898) • M. Healy, *The old Munster circuit* (1948) • V. T. H. Delany, *Christopher Palles* (1960) • Burke, *Peerage* • E. D. Steele, *Irish land and British politics: tenant-right and nationality, 1865–1870* (1974) • Gladstone, *Diaries*
Archives BL, corresp. with W. E. Gladstone, Add. MSS 44417–44783 • Bodl. Oxf., Wodehouse MSS, corresp. with Lord Kimberley
Wealth at death £90,949 8s. 6d.: probate, 19 May 1885, CGPLA Ire.

Sullivan, Francis Stoughton (1715/16–1766), jurist, was born at Galway, the son of Francis Sullivan. He was educated at Waterford, under Dr Fell, before entering Trinity College, Dublin, on 25 January 1732, aged sixteen. Awarded a scholarship in 1734, he graduated BA in 1736 and was elected a fellow in 1738. His academic career continued to prosper and, having proceeded MA (1739) and LLB and LLD (1745), he was appointed regius professor of laws in 1750 and professor of feudal and English law in 1761. He enjoyed a very high reputation as a jurist and actively promoted the study of early Irish history in the university.

Sullivan died in Dublin in 1766. His only work, *An historical treatise on the feudal law, and the constitution and laws of England, with a commentary on Magna Charta*, was published posthumously in 1776 and reprinted several times. His son, **William Francis Sullivan** (1756–1830), was born in Dublin and educated there at Trinity College. Intended for the church, he instead entered the navy and served throughout the American War of Independence. He settled in England in 1783, where with his wife and daughter he took to the stage. In addition he wrote a farce, *The Rights of Man*, and published various poems and short stories. He died in 1830.

C. L. FALKINER, rev. S. J. SKEDD

Sources W. J. Stubbs, *The history of the University of Dublin* (1889) • Burtchaell & Sadleir, *Alum. Dubl.* • Allibone, *Dict.* • private information (1922) [E. J. Gwynn] • B. Ó'Cuív, 'Irish language and literature, 1691–1845', *A new history of Ireland*, ed. T. W. Moody and others, 4: *Eighteenth-century Ireland, 1691–1800* (1986), 374–419

Sullivan, James (1903–1977), rugby player, was born at 35 Elaine Street, Cardiff, on 2 December 1903, the son of Cornelius Sullivan, a labourer at an ironworks, and his wife, Mary Dobbin. He attended St Alban's School, Cardiff. He played for the Cardiff rugby union first fifteen when he was seventeen and remains the youngest player to have represented the Barbarians, at just seventeen years and twenty-six days old when he played against Newport on 28 December 1920. Within six months he had signed as a professional for Wigan for a fee of £750.

Sullivan made his rugby league début for Wigan against Widnes on 27 August 1921 and kicked five goals. Within five years he had landed more goals than any other player in rugby league's history. In 1928 he became the first man to amass 1000 goals and by the time he retired in 1946 his tally was 2867 goals, a record which is still intact. His aggregate of 6022 points is second only to Neil Fox's 6220.

Among Jim Sullivan's record-breaking feats, his twenty-two goals for Wigan against Flimby and Fothergill in a challenge cup-tie in 1925 remains unbroken in first-class rugby league. No player in the game's history has exceeded his 928 appearances. One of his most astounding achievements was to kick at least 100 goals in every season between 1921–2 and 1938–9, a feat not remotely paralleled. In 1922–3 he kicked 161 goals during the season to break Ben Gronow's record and in 1933–4 set a new record with 194 goals. That season he became the first man to top 400 points in a season.

In 1924 Sullivan was in the first Wigan team to lift the challenge cup when it defeated Oldham 21–4 at Rochdale. In 1929 he became the first player to score in a Wembley final and the first captain to lift the challenge cup there, when Wigan defeated Dewsbury 13–2. He won three peacetime championships with Wigan and played in nine Lancashire cup finals. He was made player–coach at Wigan in 1931 and made his last appearance for the club at Batley on 23 February 1946.

Tall and heavy, Sullivan presented a formidable problem to the opposition. Apart from his supreme ability as a goal-kicker, he possessed all the attributes necessary for a top-class full-back: uncanny positioning, enormous punting ability, fly-paper hands, and superb technique combined with devastating power in tackling. He is widely regarded as the finest full-back to have played the game. His skills were such that he was capped for Wales just eight days after his eighteenth birthday in 1921, before going on to win a record twenty-six Welsh caps, the last in 1939, when he kicked five goals in a 16–3 victory over England at Bradford. His sixty goals and 129 points remain records for Wales.

At test level Sullivan won twenty-five caps against Australia and New Zealand. On his test début against Australia at Sydney on 23 June 1924, he landed a goal from inside his own half with his first kick of the ball in the first few seconds of the match. The Australians had a holy dread of Sullivan's power with the boot, for his kicking often decided test matches against them. He played in five consecutive Ashes-winning series between 1924 and 1933, and went on three Lions tours (1924, 1928, and 1932), the last of them as captain. In 1936 he was selected as captain for a record fourth tour but declined for domestic reasons. He still holds the Great Britain records for appearances (fifteen), goals kicked (thirty-one), and points scored (sixty-two) in Ashes tests. In all international rugby league he stands supreme with sixty caps, having represented Wales, England, Great Britain, and Other Nationalities, in the course of which he amassed 160 goals and 329 points.

After retiring as a player Sullivan became a phenomenally successful coach. Between 1946 and 1952 he guided Wigan to four championships, two challenge cups, six Lancashire cups, and four Lancashire league titles. He then took over at St Helens, and led them to their first challenge cup victory in 1956 and to the championship in

1953 and 1959. A fine golfer, snooker player, and cricketer, Sullivan also played baseball at international level for Wales. He was variously a boilermaker, butcher, haulier, masseur, and rugby league columnist for the *News of the World*. His occupation was described as butcher when he married, on 24 November 1928 at St John's Roman Catholic Church, Wigan, Eva Linney Highton (*b*. 1903/4) of Wigan, the daughter of William Highton, a butcher. They had one child, Kevan. Sullivan died at the Royal Albert Edward Infirmary, Wigan, on 14 September 1977. His ashes were scattered on Wigan's ground, Central Park. His wife survived him.   ROBERT GATE

Sources R. Gate, *Gone north: Welshmen in rugby league*, 2 vols. (1986–8) · *News of the World* (27 Sept–18 Oct 1936) [Sullivan's career serialized] · b. cert. · m. cert. · d. cert.

Wealth at death £3348: probate, 8 Nov 1977, *CGPLA Eng. & Wales*

Sullivan, James Frank (1852–1936), cartoonist and writer, was born on 31 October 1852 at 40 Great Ormond Street, Queen Square, London, the son of James Sullivan, printer and stationer, and his wife, Harriett Crosbie.

Sullivan studied at the National Art Training School, South Kensington, where he drew from classical sculpture. He soon took a studio where he sketched 'enthusiastically and earnestly from the nude' (*Strand Magazine*, December 1895, 789). In his spare time the young, energetic artist walked, cycled, beagled, and sculled. He didn't think of becoming a cartoonist until 1871 when at the age of eighteen he was invited to contribute to *Fun*, the Liberal counterpart of the tory *Judy*, both cheaper rivals to *Punch*. Sullivan was 'for many years the incarnation of *Fun*' (Spielmann, 567) and he became 'the immortal depictor of the humours and amenities of "The British Workman"' (ibid.). Although *Fun* often depicted street life and the lower rungs of society its appeal was to a fast-expanding, upwardly mobile, politically aware lower middle-class readership.

Sullivan also contributed to other journals, among them *Black-and-White*, *Cassell's*, *Pearson's*, *Pick-Me-Up*, *Punch*, and the *Strand Magazine*. His flirtation with *Punch* began in 1893 and lasted three months when, according to Spielmann, his contributions 'incontinently ceased' (Spielmann, 561). He revisited *Punch* in 1905 for a similar, inexplicably brief period.

Early in his career Sullivan began to specialize in satirical strip cartoons, with printed text unrolling beneath each successive drawing rather than filling speech balloons as in American strips. He was a 'cartoonist of advanced radical ideas' (Hillier, 61) whose reputation too narrowly rests on *The British Working Man, by One who Doesn't Believe in Him*, a series first published in *Fun* and later collected in book form (1878). Some readers perceived the series as being more reactionary than radical. William Morris chanced on Sullivan's work on a railway bookstall:

> Morris readily admitted the essential justice of Sullivan's satire on shoddy workmanship, but in ambivalent terms that betray an awareness not shared by Sullivan, of the systematic oppression and alienation that took the pleasure—and quality—out of the old tradition of once-beautiful, honored and profitable craftsmanship. (Kunzle, 326)

That said, a botched job is a botched job, which was and is a suitable subject for humour. Although he often dealt with effect rather than cause many of Sullivan's subjects were essentially timeless: dishonesty, deceit, and greed.

> But are there not truly offenders
> In every sphere?

he wrote in his preface to *The British Tradesman, Including Grandmotherly Government and the Complete Builder-Landlord* (1880). In these satires Sullivan encompassed the sharp practices of builders, salesmen, and shopkeepers, as well as their customers of high and low degree. His commuters suffered still familiar discomforts: 'One carriage to each thousand passengers' (*The British Tradesman*, 42), while journalists pandered to the 'prevailing taste for the unnatural and the revolting' (*The British Working Man*, 61). Sullivan mistrusted politicians, although he would have liked to see women in parliament; he deplored 'grandmotherly government' long before the term 'nanny state' was coined, he took 'a jaundiced view of Victorian imperialism' (Hillier, 61), and attacked industrialists, landlords, and landowners. He protested against vandalism, foxhunting, and overcrowding in cities. In his funniest work (in his own estimation)—*The Great Water Joke* (1899)—he railed in verse and drawings against the greed and incompetence of the water company's monopoly. He capped Marie Corelli's novel of Britain's spiritual bankruptcy and corruption, *The Sorrows of Satan* (1895), with *Belial's Burdens* (1896), a still hilarious, parodic *tour de force*. He also wrote and illustrated books for children.

Sullivan's early, stilted, cross-hatched, unmistakably Victorian draughtsmanship did not always match the relaxed, joyously vituperative qualities of his writing. (The young H. M. Bateman was to find inspiration among the grotesqueries of Sullivan's imagination.) Occasionally, with mixed results, Sullivan attempted the decorative simplicity of art nouveau. As he matured his drawing became more relaxed, more conventional (and less interesting) but his freewheeling humour remained intact.

Surprisingly, given his qualities, Sullivan has no biographer and his background is elusive. Some standard reference works state that he was a brother of the distinguished illustrator Edmund J. Sullivan, but the claim is groundless. In a purportedly autobiographical item in the *Ludgate Monthly* (Sullivan, 'Black and white artists') Sullivan claimed he was the son of an elderly Devonshire village vicar who married a young, runaway farm girl. On his father's death—so the reader is led to believe—Sullivan, at age nine, helped keep his now penniless mother by working as an assistant 'screever' (a pavement artist) to a half-brother who had 'gone to the bad' but who eventually came to the good. He provided a clue to this nonsense by stating that both his grandfather (an undertaker 'in a small way of business') and his own father loved practical jokes. The lie is given to Sullivan's fantasizing by the mundane truths of his birth certificate. To present himself in such a fashion in that age of snobbery, in a serious middle-class magazine, reveals a wealth of self-assurance amounting to arrogance. A firmly drawn self-caricature accompanying the article depicts a tall, bearded figure grinning satanically.

Taken as a whole, Sullivan's works reflect a man whose wild imagination is buttressed by firm beliefs. He responded to news as many 'topical' cartoonists do: in a magazine article. In the *Magazine of Art* Sullivan, thinly disguised as Jones the satirist, claimed that while reading the morning paper he 'suddenly, violently rages and blares— a sign he has scented some abuse requiring correction' (Sullivan, 'Illustrated journalism', 420). To which he added, 'Again, [Jones] may decide that the idea would work out better in writing than in drawing; and again, better in verse than in prose; for he is equally good, or bad, at either of these three forms of development'. This simple pride in his various abilities is apparent elsewhere in Sullivan's writings. Undoubtedly he was pleased with himself. His strips, stories, and verse stood out from those of his contemporaries when social cartoons and comment, consisting almost exclusively of illustrated jokes, were remarkable for their lack of bite.

On 24 July 1877 Sullivan married Agnes Amelia Mullett of Chelsea, a marriage which lasted more than half a century and which survived until his death. In 1904, in his early fifties, Sullivan retired, settling in Chertsey among a large circle of friends. He pursued several interests: metalwork, illuminated manuscripts, wood-carving, and the painting of heraldic devices. According to his obituarist, he was able to indulge 'Antiquarian tastes by collecting armour, weapons and oak' (*The Times*, 7 May 1936). He died on 5 May 1936 at his home, Rosemead, Bridge Road, Chertsey, Surrey, aged eighty-three, leaving his widow a not inconsiderable estate valued at £13,289 15s. 3d.

JOHN JENSEN

Sources D. Kunzle, *The history of the comic strip*, 2 (1990) · *The Times* (7 May 1936) · *Surrey Advertiser and County Times* (9 May 1936) · 'Artists of the *Strand Magazine*', *Strand Magazine*, 10 (1895), 786–90 · F. Dolman, 'Our graphic humorists', *Strand Magazine*, 23 (1902), 76–88 · J. F. Sullivan, 'Illustrated journalism: the comic paper', *Magazine of Art*, 14 (1890–91), 416–20 · J. F. Sullivan, 'Black and white artists of to-day', *Ludgate Monthly*, 3 (April 1897), 584–7 · M. Bryant and S. Heneage, eds., *Dictionary of British cartoonists and caricaturists, 1730–1980* (1994) · B. Hillier, *Cartoons and caricatures* (1970) · b. cert. · m. cert. · d. cert. · M. H. Spielmann, *The history of 'Punch'* (1895)
Archives LUL, letters to Austin Dobson
Likenesses Elliott & Fry, photograph, repro. in Dolman, 'Our graphic humorists' · E. Passingham, photograph, repro. in 'Artists of the *Strand Magazine*' · J. F. Sullivan, self-portrait, caricature, repro. in Sullivan, 'Black and white artists of to-day'
Wealth at death £13,554 15s. 6d.—effects (resworn, £13,289 15s. 3d.): *Times*

Sullivan, John (1740–1795), revolutionary army officer and politician in America, was born on 17 February 1740 in Summersworth parish, New Hampshire, the third of six children of John Sullivan (who changed his name from Owen) (*b.* 1690), schoolmaster, and Margery Brown (*b.* 1714). For two years (1758–60) he studied law under Samuel Livermore at Portsmouth, and after being admitted to the bar practised in Berwick, Maine. In 1760 he married Lydia Remick Worster (*b.* 1738); they had six children, two of whom died in infancy. Sullivan moved to Durham, New Hampshire, in 1763; he was the first lawyer in the town,

and made no secret of his ambition and vanity. His clients accused him of provoking litigation, overcharging for services, and being too enthusiastic in collecting fees. Nevertheless he was an able lawyer and made a comfortable living for his family. In 1772 he was appointed a major in the New Hampshire militia by Governor John Wentworth. Two years later he joined the patriot cause and was elected to the New Hampshire provincial congress. In the autumn of 1774 he attended the first continental congress in Philadelphia.

After returning to New Hampshire, Sullivan rallied a group of citizens on 15 December to storm Castle William and Mary in Portsmouth harbour and seize 100 barrels of gunpowder. Next day, in a second raid, he captured sixty muskets and fifteen cannon. Elected to the second continental congress, he joined his fellow legislators on 10 May 1775 and was appointed a brigadier-general on 22 June. He reached the army besieging Boston on 10 July and led a successful skirmish against the British on 26 August. However, he bungled another operation against Bunker Hill on 29 December. While at Boston he urged politicians to declare independence and sent the New Hampshire committee of safety a scheme for a new state government. After the British evacuated Boston on 17 March 1776, he was ordered to join the northern army, which was retreating from Canada under General John Thomas. He reached the army at Chambly and assumed command when Thomas died of smallpox. On 16 June congress, concerned about his inexperience, replaced Sullivan with General Horatio Gates. Sullivan hastened to Philadelphia, where he complained bitterly to the legislators and threatened to resign, but President John Hancock dissuaded him.

Instead, Sullivan joined General George Washington's army in New York. On 9 August he was promoted major-general and eleven days later was ordered to Long Island to replace Nathanael Greene, who was ailing. In the battle of Long Island on 27 August he commanded American forces outside fortifications on Brooklyn Heights. Surprised by a British assault on his left, he was captured and carried aboard the flagship of Lord Howe, who persuaded him to convey peace terms to congress. The legislators, believing Sullivan to be 'Howe's decoy duck', peremptorily rejected the proposals. On 25 September he was exchanged for General Richard Prescott and rejoined Washington's army on Harlem Heights. Given command of a division, he took part in the American retreat from Manhattan to White Plains, New York. There he was ordered to join General Charles Lee at North Castle. When Lee was captured at Basking Ridge, New Jersey, on 13 December, Sullivan assumed command of Lee's troops and marched to join Washington in Pennsylvania. In the battle of Trenton on 26 December he successfully commanded the American right wing and on 3 January 1777 led his division to victory in the battle of Princeton. Suffering from stomach problems, he took leave for the winter and went home. There he spent his time grousing to Washington about various perceived slights.

In the spring of 1777 Sullivan returned to the main army and in May was given command of a division. He angered congress in July by complaining with other officers about the promotion of the Frenchman, Colonel Philippe du Coudray. On 22 August he led an unsuccessful expedition against Staten Island. In the battle of the Brandywine on 11 September he commanded an important part of the American line and was almost outflanked on his right. Although disaster was averted, his congressional foes advanced a proposal to suspend him from command while an inquiry was made into his failure at Staten Island. Delegate Thomas Burke of North Carolina also violently accused him of misconduct at the Brandywine. Washington refused to relieve Sullivan, and congress finally exonerated him. On 4 October, in the battle of Germantown, he led a column against the enemy and was defeated with the rest of the American army.

After spending the winter of 1777–8 at Valley Forge, Sullivan was ordered to take command of American forces in Rhode Island and expel the British from Newport. In August he besieged the town, relying upon a French fleet under Comte d'Estaing to deter a British squadron under Lord Howe from relieving the enemy by water. When a storm wrecked both fleets and d'Estaing withdrew to Boston for repairs, Sullivan was compelled to give up the siege. Retreating to the north end of Rhode Island, he was attacked by superior British forces on 29 August but repulsed them. That evening he withdrew his army to the mainland, where he spent the following winter complaining bitterly to Washington about what he regarded as d'Estaing's betrayal. In March 1779 he was ordered to lead an expedition against the Iroquois in western Pennsylvania and New York. Assembling his troops at Easton, Pennsylvania, he marched through the Wyoming valley, reaching Tioga on 10 August. Nine days later, after joining forces with General James Clinton, he proceeded slowly toward Newtown, razing American Indian villages and burning crops. On 29 August, at Newtown, he routed the Indians in a pitched battle, then destroyed villages and crops in the Finger Lakes region. By mid-October he was back in Easton.

Although Sullivan deemed his expedition a success, many in congress and the army declared that he had done little to curtail Indian raids on the frontier. The legislators, disgusted with both his military conduct and his complaints, appointed a committee to investigate his handling of the campaign. On 30 November 1779, before the committee could report, Sullivan resigned, citing poor health. Congress immediately accepted his resignation, although Washington expressed regret at the loss of his services. As a soldier, he had been hostile and overly sensitive towards his superiors, and he had manifested weaknesses as a battlefield commander. But he did not deserve all his bad reputation, for he was a brave, generous, and efficient officer.

After returning to New Hampshire, Sullivan reopened his law practice and was appointed by the state to settle a dispute with New York over possession of the New Hampshire grants. A born politician, he was elected to congress in 1780, serving for one year and promoting a stronger central government. He attended the New Hampshire constitutional convention in 1782 and was state attorney-general from 1782 to 1786. He served as speaker of the assembly in 1785. Elected president (governor) in 1786, he suppressed paper-money riots at Exeter and urged leniency towards loyalists; he was re-elected in 1787 and 1789. In 1788 he was again speaker of the assembly and also chairman of the state convention that ratified the constitution. Appointed judge of the federal district court of New Hampshire in 1789, he retained this office until his death, although he was incapacitated by alcoholism after 1792. He died on 23 January 1795 at Durham and was interred in the family burial plot there. He left an estate that was valued in excess of $4500, but his debts were almost as large.

PAUL DAVID NELSON

Sources C. P. Whittemore, *A general of the revolution: John Sullivan of New Hampshire* (1961) · *Letters and papers of Major-General John Sullivan, continental army*, ed. O. G. Hammond, New Hampshire Historical Society, *Collections*, 13–15 (1930–39) · C. P. Whittemore, 'John Sullivan: luckless Irishman', *George Washington's generals*, ed. G. A. Billias (1964), 137–62 · L. M. Waddell, 'Sullivan, John', *ANB* · S. Adams, 'John Sullivan', *New Hampshire: years of revolution*, ed. P. E. Randall (1976) · R. F. Upton, 'John Langdon and John Sullivan, a biographical essay', *New Hampshire: the state that made us a nation*, ed. W. M. Gardner, F. C. Mevers, and R. F. Upton (1989)
Archives Mass. Hist. Soc., MSS · New Hampshire Historical Society, Concord, MSS | L. Cong., George Washington MSS
Likenesses engraving, repro. in Whittemore, *General of the revolution*, frontispiece
Wealth at death $4582.33: Whittemore, *General of the revolution*, 225

Sullivan, John (1749–1839), East India Company servant and politician, was born on 7 April 1749 in Cork, co. Cork, the second of three sons of Benjamin Sullivan (1720–1767), clerk of the crown for the counties of Cork and Waterford, and Bridget (*d.* 1802), daughter of the Revd Paul Limric DD, of Scull, co. Cork. His brother Richard Joseph *Sullivan achieved note as a writer. Though of ancient Irish stock, Sullivan's family were members of the established church and supporters of the dominant protestant ascendancy.

After an early education in Ireland and England, Sullivan joined the East India Company at Madras as a writer in 1765, at the age of sixteen. This and later appointments came through the patronage of his powerful kinsman Laurence Sulivan, who was then deputy chairman of the company. Sullivan's progress through the company's merchant ranks was rapid and profitable at a time when British interests in south India were threatened by French forces and the military rulers of Mysore, Haidar Ali and his son Tipu Sultan. In 1774, as a junior merchant on the council of Masulipatam, Sullivan produced a study of local revenue systems entitled 'Observations respecting the Circar of Mazulipatam' (BL OIOC, Home Miscellaneous series, file 335 (1)) which established his claim for political service with the court of directors in London. The claim was recognized in 1781 with his appointment as resident at the court of Tanjore with responsibility for all the southern provinces of the Madras presidency. Sullivan's ambitious plan to subvert the threat from Mysore by a secret treaty with the deposed Hindu dynasty was pre-empted by an armistice with the French in 1783. In addition to his official duties at Tanjore, he acted privately to accumulate substantial profits from supplying grain to the Madras army: when he returned to England on leave in 1785 he had a considerable fortune, with which he purchased a country estate, Richings Lodge, near Iver, Buckinghamshire.

The key to Sullivan's future political success lay in his marriage on 23 May 1789 to Henrietta Anne Barbara (*bap.* 1762, *d.* 1828), second daughter of George *Hobart (1731–1804) of Nocton and Blyborough, Lincolnshire, who in 1793 succeeded his half-brother as third earl of Buckinghamshire. The couple had one son, John, before they were married and three further sons and five daughters. Through his marriage Sullivan was now closely linked to the fortunes of the Hobart family, who had their own considerable aspirations for power in India. Now resident in England, his role was to provide support at home for his brother-in-law Robert, Lord Hobart (later fourth earl of Buckinghamshire), who became governor of Madras in 1793 and sought the position of governor-general in India. William Pitt, the prime minister, recommended Sullivan, as a 'nabob of good fortune' and 'good character' (HoP, *Commons, 1790–1820*), to Lord Camelford for the parliamentary seat of Old Sarum in 1790, and he held it until standing down to become high sheriff of Buckinghamshire in 1797. About 1791 he spoke in the Commons in support of the former governor-general of Bengal, Warren Hastings, urging that Hastings's trial be stopped in view of the defendant's merits; Sullivan was one of twenty-two guests invited by Hastings to a celebration dinner following his acquittal in 1795. He argued his brother-in-law's case for compensation when Hobart was prematurely withdrawn from the governorship of Madras in 1798, and in 1795 published a volume entitled *Tracts upon India: Written in the Years 1779, 1780, and 1788 with Subsequent Observations*, which established his own political credentials as a specialist in Indian affairs. In January 1799 he persuaded Henry Dundas, the president of the Board of Control, to support Lord Wellesley's campaign against Tipu Sultan in Mysore.

Reward for supporting Hobart came with Sullivan's return to parliament as the member for Aldburgh, and his appointment as under-secretary for war and the colonies from May 1801 to 1804, when his brother-in-law was secretary of state. Sullivan became a privy councillor in 1805 and, after a brief period as commissioner on the Board of Control for Indian affairs (February 1806 to April 1807), rejoined the board in April 1812 to serve Hobart, now earl of Buckinghamshire, who was the president. There followed a marked deterioration in the relationship between the East India Company and the board, as Buckinghamshire, for the government, tried to impose his authority over the court of directors. Surprisingly, Sullivan survived as a commissioner when George Canning succeeded to the presidency after Buckinghamshire's death in a riding accident in 1816. Once again, Sullivan's experience and advocacy were decisive in persuading the board to accept the marquess of Hastings in his military action in 1818 against the dissident Maratha states and their associated bands of organized marauders, known as Pindaris. He also persuaded the board to support Sir Thomas Munro's individual and annual revenue assessment in the Madras presidency, known as ryotwar, in the debate over taxation (the company's principal source of income following the granting of a new charter in 1813).

Sullivan retired from the Board of Control in 1828, after seventeen years as a commissioner, just before his eightieth birthday. He died on 1 November 1839 at Richings Lodge and was survived by his son, John Augustus, principal-marshal of Jamaica.   NIGEL CHANCELLOR

Sources writers' petitions, BL OIOC, J/1/5, fols. 310–13 [1763–4] • 1780–85, BL OIOC, Home misc. • observations respecting the Circar of Mazulipatam in a letter from John Sullivan esq. to the court of directors of the East India Company, BL OIOC, V3226, Home misc. file 335 (1) • H. D. Love, *Vestiges of old Madras, 1640–1800*, 4 vols. (1913) • East India Company list of civil servants, BL OIOC • J. Sullivan, *Tracts upon India: written in the years 1779, 1780, and 1788* (1795) • HoP, *Commons, 1790–1820* • M. Wilks, *Historical sketches of the south of India, in an attempt to trace the history of Mysoor*, 3 vols. (1810–17), vol. 1, p. 378; vol. 2, pp. 488–90 • M. S. Rao, *Modern Mysore*, 1 (1936) • *GM*, 2nd ser., 13 (1840), 428 • Burke, *Gen. GB* (1837) • B. Stein, *Thomas Munro: the origins of the colonial state and his vision of empire* (1989) • A. J. Arbuthnot, *Major General Sir Thomas Munro, Bart., governor of Madras: selections of his minutes and other official writings* (1881) • H. H. Wilson, *A glossary of judicial and revenue terms* (1855) • C. H. Philips, *The East India Company, 1784–1834* (1940) • C. H. Aitchison, *A collection of treaties, engagements and sanads*, 9 (1929), 223 • Burke, *Peerage* (1939) • private information (2004)
Archives BL, letters to Warren Hastings and others, Add. MSS 29143–29189 • BL OIOC, observations respecting the Circar of Mazulipatam in a letter to the court of directors of the East India Company, V3226, Home misc. file 355 (1) • BL OIOC, political corresp. • BL OIOC, letters to Sir Thomas Munro • Bodl. Oxf., corresp. with Lord Macartney • Bucks. RLSS, letters to Lord Hobart
Likenesses W. Beechey, portrait, 1808, Hobart Town Hall, Hobart, Tasmania • W. W. Barney, mezzotint, 1809 (after W. Beechey) • J. Hagbolt, medal, 1830

Sullivan, John Patrick (1930–1993), classical scholar, was born on 13 July 1930 at the Royal Infirmary, Liverpool, the elder son and oldest of three children of Daniel Sullivan (*d.* 1952), a dock labourer, and his wife, Alice, *née* Long, who had worked in a cigarette factory before her marriage. Both parents were proud of their Irish roots. It was a close-knit family, and Sullivan was in constant touch with his siblings Denis and Patricia throughout his life. Though the family was poor, he received a sound preparatory education at St John's, the local parish school (1935–41). On the strength of high examination scores, he was admitted to St Francis Xavier's College, Liverpool (1941–9), where he was rigorously and with caning instructed in classics, as Horace had been drilled by Orbilius. Recognizing his talents in classics he put himself forward and in 1948 won an open scholarship to St John's College, Cambridge. (He was the first member of his family to go to university.) After a year's national service, during which he served in the rifle brigade and Royal Army Education Corps (1949–50), he entered St John's College in 1950. There he won numerous prizes and graduated with a starred double first in the classical tripos in 1953. Also at Cambridge he found friends among young creative writers, including Frederic Raphael; sought out established literary figures around

Cambridge such as E. M. Forster, F. R. Leavis, and Kingsley Amis; corresponded with Ezra Pound; and contributed poems to the *Cambridge Review*.

Sullivan began graduate studies in Greek philosophy at St John's College, Cambridge, in 1953, under Renford Bambrough. On 16 July 1954 he married Mary Frances (1920–2003), a radiographer, and daughter of Henry Rock, a hospital cook. Later that year he moved to Oxford to take up a junior research fellowship at Queen's College. In 1955 he was made fellow and tutor in classics at Lincoln College, and in 1956 university lecturer, both of which positions he held until 1961. During the Oxford years he acquired his own voice. Though he could debate with all the skill of a Jesuit-trained Platonist, he remained a gentle and engaging conversationalist. Early in the Oxford years he began to move away from Greek philosophy to Latin literature and to combine an interest in modern literary works with classics. From this point on his studies of Latin texts always included analyses of these same texts made by creative writers and translators. Translation as an art form and new interpretations of the works of Propertius (he and Wallace Robson visited Ezra Pound in his 'castle' in Italy), Petronius, and Martial became the non-exclusive focus of his intellect. After a time he felt that at Oxford he was not always among supporters of his style of classics. He was also not eager to prolong his marriage (which ended in divorce in 1962). In 1961 he accepted a visiting professorship (converted in 1963 into a full professorship) at the University of Texas in Austin, where scholars embraced creative translations and planned a new journal, *Arion*, in which they could explain their radical programme.

Sullivan's Texas years (1961–9) marked an exciting period in classics, not only in Austin but in North America generally. *Arion* was born in 1962, the product of several left-leaning American and Oxbridge classicists. One of Sullivan's goals as an editor of *Arion* was to bring classics out of its isolation and ever-dwindling importance within universities. *Arion* became the organ of radical classicists, championing creative translations, and in this greenhouse Sullivan wrote his *Ezra Pound and Sextus Propertius* (1965), a model of its genre. The theme had been suggested to him by T. S. Eliot. *Critical Essays on Roman Literature*, which he edited in two volumes in 1962–3, represented some of the ways in which anthropologists might approach classical literature. Such critical approaches won for Sullivan both admirers and detractors. In 1965 Penguin brought out his translation of Petronius's *Satyricon*, which for many years remained the standard text, and in 1968 he followed this with his most influential work, *The Satyricon of Petronius: a Literary Study* (again suggested by T. S. Eliot and published by Faber and Faber). Both old and young were caught up by its originality, based on a sound scholarly understanding of the text and an interpretation of an ancient narrative as a modern novel. But all was not joy in Texas: Sullivan's radical approaches in classics extended to politics, drugs, the Vietnam war, and lifestyles. On 6 April 1967 he married Judith Patrice (Judy) Eldridge. She moved with him to New York in 1969 when he became faculty professor of arts and letters at the State University of New York at Buffalo, but the marriage ended in divorce in 1972. Only with his third wife, Judith Lee (Judy) Godfrey, whom he met in Florida in 1972 and married on 21 April 1973, did he find lasting happiness.

Sullivan remained in New York until 1978, becoming provost of the faculty of arts and letters (1972–5) and editor of *Arethusa* (1971–5), for which he arranged a series of special issues on subjects of interest to him: politics, feminism, psychoanalysis, Marxism. In 1976 he returned one more time to his first love, when Cambridge University Press published his *Propertius: a Critical Introduction*. He undertook two major lecture series while at Buffalo: in 1976 the Martin lectures at Oberlin which resulted in *Literature and Politics in the Age of Nero* (1985), and in 1978 the Gray lectures at Cambridge which yielded *Martial: the Unexpected Classic* (1991).

The University of California at Santa Barbara was Sullivan's final academic home: he was professor of classics there from 1978 until his death. This was a particularly rich period for him: in addition to his numerous articles, he co-edited (with J. J. Peradotto) *Women in the Ancient World* (1984), (with P. Whigham) *Epigrams of Martial* (1987), (with A. J. Boyle) *Roman Poets of the Early Empire* (1991), (with I. J. F. de Jong) *Modern Critical Theory and Classical Literature* (1994), and (with A. J. Boyle) *Martial in English* (1996).

At conferences Sullivan was regularly surrounded by friends and young classicists, all talking quietly and laughing under a thick cloud of his cigarette smoke. He was a conversationalist in the style of past, more graceful times; his house was a centre of entertainment; he travelled widely and often, visiting friends and lecturing. A few small volumes of his verse were privately printed and show modest talent. He had no ear for music, no eye for flowers or trees, and disliked animals—though he sketched horses on restaurant napkins. Driving in an automobile with him was an act of courage. He was proud of his Irish heritage and his ability to turn his Liverpool accent on and off. He was an agnostic, as only a Jesuit-trained, Irish-descended classicist could be. At a classics conference after Christmas in New Orleans in 1992, he complained that he could not swallow, and on 9 April 1993 he died at his home in Palermo Drive, Santa Barbara, California, of oesophageal cancer. He was survived by his wife, Judy, who had looked after him in his final months.

GARETH SCHMELING

Sources *The Independent* (14 April 1993) · *The Times* (17 April 1993) · F. Raphael, 'Friendship', *Independent Magazine* (24 April 1993) · A. J. Boyle, 'John Patrick Sullivan', *Roman literature and ideology*, ed. A. J. Boyle (1995), 6–23 · personal knowledge (2004) · private information (2004) · b. cert. · m. cert. [Mary Frances Rock]
Likenesses C. Barger, coloured chalk, 1981, repro. in *The Independent*; priv. coll.

Sullivan, John William [Jacobite Sir John Sullivan] (*b. c.*1700, *d.* in or after 1752), Jacobite army officer, was born in co. Kerry; details of his parentage are unknown. He is said to have been descended from the O'Sullivans of Munster, but consistently spelled his name Sullivan. At the age of nine he was sent to France to study for the Catholic priesthood, but in 1721 he instead entered the French army under the patronage of Marshal Maillebois. Subsequently Sullivan served under Maillebois in Corsica, Italy, and on the Rhine, gaining considerable experience of irregular warfare and eventually becoming a captain on the general staff. On the strength of this useful experience the stoutly built professional soldier was offered a colonel's commission to act as military adviser to the Jacobite heir, Prince Charles Edward Stuart, in 1745. Shortly after the prince landed in Scotland, Sullivan's position was formalized by his appointment as adjutant-general and quartermaster-general in the Jacobite army. As such he was primarily responsible for drafting orders, and for drawing up the elaborate marching tables which enabled the prince's forces to move swiftly in dispersed columns and to evade the British army's attempts to intercept them. Unfortunately, however, he clashed from the first with Lord George Murray, one of the Jacobite lieutenant-generals, who afterwards accused him of incompetence and blamed him for much of what went wrong during the campaign. Sullivan's own account (not published until 1938) and a number of surviving regimental orderly books reveal the reverse to be the case. Sullivan was, in fact, a very capable and professional staff officer, but it cannot be denied that he went out of his way to be condescending towards Murray, whom he considered with good reason to be an impetuous amateur.

At the outset of the campaign Sullivan was involved in an attempt to capture Ruthven barracks, near Kingussie—successfully defended by another Irishman, Sergeant Terry Molloy, and just twelve men. He was rather more successful with his friend Donald Cameron of Lochiel in seizing Edinburgh by a *coup de main* on 16 September 1745. He was present at the battle of Prestonpans, but after reaching Manchester he grew increasingly pessimistic about the invasion of England. He did not take part in the crucial council of war at Derby, when the decision was taken to return to Scotland, but wholeheartedly supported it, and in his narrative is critical of the prince's behaviour at this time. At both the battles of Falkirk on 17 January 1746 and Culloden on 16 April he was in effective command of the Jacobite army, since both lieutenant-generals present simply acted as brigade commanders and the prince was no more than a passive spectator. Having escaped to the continent after Culloden, Sullivan was knighted for his services by the Jacobite King James VIII and III and again served on the French staff at the battle of Lauffeldt on 21 June 1747. Despite being very close to Prince Charles during the Jacobite rising and having been largely instrumental in arranging his rescue, Sullivan became estranged from the prince shortly afterwards. This was due to persistent rumours that Sullivan had shared Charles's mistress, Clementine *Walkinshaw (c.1720–1802), whom he had met at Falkirk in 1746. He is last heard of living in Cambrai in the summer of 1752.

The date of Sullivan's death is unknown, but he had married a Miss Fitzgerald and left a son, **Thomas Herbert Sullivan** (d. 1824), army officer, who was commissioned in the Franco-Irish regiment Walsh. In 1779 he served with a detachment of the regiment assigned as marines on board John Paul Jones's privateer *Bon Homme Richard*. He took part in the famous fight with the *Serapis* off Flamborough Head on 23 September 1779. Subsequently, however, he deserted to the British army and then transferred to the Dutch service, dying a major at The Hague in 1824. Thomas Sullivan's son John, employed in the American consular service, died in 1825.   STUART REID

Sources *DNB* · J. W. O'Sullivan, *1745 and after*, ed. A. Taylor and H. Taylor (1938) · J. C. O'Callaghan, *History of the Irish brigades in the service of France*, [new edn] (1870) · S. Reid, *1745: a military history of the last Jacobite rising* (1996) · David, Lord Elcho, *A short account of the affairs of Scotland in the years 1744, 1745, 1746*, ed. E. Charteris (1907)

Sullivan, Luke (c.1725–1771), engraver and miniature painter, was said to have been born in co. Louth, Ireland, and to have been the son of one of the duke of Beaufort's grooms. According to Joseph Strutt (writing in 1786) his skill as a draughtsman was recognized early, and he was placed as an apprentice with Thomas Major; in 1751 George Vertue recorded that Sullivan studied with Bernard Baron and helped him with his engraved portraits of the earl of Hardwicke in 1742 and Richard Mead in 1749. Sullivan's earliest signed engraving is a view of the battle of Culloden, after Augustin Heckel, dated 1746. Vertue claimed that by 1751 he had 'so far outdone his Master [Baron] or any other, that his reputation must be above all engravers here or abroad—and to the honour of this nation' (Vertue, 6.204).

In the 1750s Sullivan was associated with William Hogarth and engraved a number of his designs. According to John Ireland he was an unreliable assistant:

> while [Sullivan] was employed in engraving, Hogarth held out every possible inducement to his remaining at his house in Leicester Square night and day; for if once Luke quitted it, he was not visible for a month. It has been said … that for engraving [Hogarth's *March to Finchley*] he was paid only one hundred pounds. (Ireland, 3.343)

In 1759 Sullivan engraved a series of six country seats, published by John Tinney in collaboration with Thomas and John Bowles. From 1764 to 1770 he exhibited miniatures and watercolours at the Society of Artists, giving his address in 1764 as 'at Mr Mackenzie's, near Norris Street, in the Haymarket' and in successive years as 'at the Golden Lion, St Alban's Street'. On 9 January 1765 he was elected to the Society for the Encouragement of Arts, Manufactures, and Commerce as a 'miniature painter'. Sitters for his miniatures included such fashionable figures as the earl of Bute and the duchess of Lennox, but according to Strutt, 'being much addicted to women, his chief practice lay among the girls of the town' (Strutt, 347). According to J. T. Smith, writing in 1828, he was among the artists who frequented The Feathers in Leicester Fields and Old Slaughter's Coffee House in St Martin's Lane, but this may be an assumption based on the style of his work which shows the influence of artists in that circle. Smith recorded Sullivan's death (in March 1771) at the White Bear, Piccadilly, 'being too much attached to what are denominated the good things of this world, … in a miserable state of disease and poverty' (Smith, 2.212). He was buried at St James's, Piccadilly, on 27 March.

SHEILA O'CONNELL

Sources Vertue, *Note books*, 6.204 · Graves, *Soc. Artists* · Society for the Encouragement of Arts, Manufactures and Commerce, subscription books, RSA · J. Strutt, *A biographical dictionary, containing an historical account of all the engravers, from the earliest period of the art of engraving to the present time*, 2 vols. (1785–6) · J. Ireland, *Hogarth illustrated*, 2nd edn, 3 (1804), 343–4 · J. T. Smith, *Nollekens and his times*, 2 (1828), 212 · B. S. Long, *British miniaturists* (1929), 426 · R. Paulson, *Hogarth's graphic works*, 3rd edn (1989), 16, 141, 155–6, 192, 196 · parish register (burial), London, Piccadilly, St James's, 27 March 1771

Sullivan, Sir Richard Joseph, first baronet (1752–1806), writer, was born on 10 December 1752, the third son of Benjamin Sullivan (1720–1767) of Dromeragh, co. Cork, attorney at law and clerk of the crown for counties Cork and Waterford, and his wife, Bridget (*d.* 1802), daughter of Paul Limric (or Limrick) DD of Scull, co. Cork. His eldest brother, Sir Benjamin Sullivan (1747–1810), knighted on 17 February 1801, was from 1801 until his death puisne judge of the supreme court of judicature at Madras. The second brother, John *Sullivan (1749–1839), was under-secretary at war from 1801 to 1804, and married Henrietta Anne Barbara (*bap.* 1762, *d.* 1828), daughter of George Hobart, third earl of Buckinghamshire.

Through the influence of Laurence Sulivan, chairman of the East India Company, and probably his kinsman, Richard Joseph was early in life sent to India with his brother John. On his return to Europe in 1784 he made a tour through various parts of England, Scotland, and Wales. He was elected a fellow of the Society of Antiquaries on 9 June 1785 and a fellow of the Royal Society on 22 December following. On 3 December 1778 he had married Mary, the only surviving daughter of Thomas Lodge of Leeds; they had two daughters and six sons. She died on 24 December 1832.

On 29 January 1787, being then described as of Cleveland Row, St James's, London, Sullivan was elected MP for New Romney after Sir Edward Dering resigned. He was returned for the same constituency at the general election on 19 June 1790. He lost his seat in 1796, but on 5 July 1802 was elected, after a sharp contest, for Seaford, Sussex, another of the Cinque Ports. On 22 May 1804, on Pitt's return to office, Sullivan was created a baronet of the United Kingdom.

Sullivan's works include the anonymously published *Analysis of the political history of India. In which is considered the present situation of the East, and the connection of its several powers with the empire of Great Britain* (1779). Its second edition appeared with the author's name in 1784, and it was translated into German by M. C. Sprengel in 1787. Also drawing upon his experiences in India and his travels in Europe was *Philosophical rhapsodies: fragments of Akbur of Betlis; containing reflections on the laws, manners, customs, and religions of certain Asiatic, Afric, and European nations* (3 vols., 1784–5). His other travel inspired literature included: *Observations Made during a Tour through Parts of England, Scotland, and Wales* (1780; 2nd edn, 2 vols., London, 1785; reprinted in

Mavor's *British Tourists*; *Thoughts on the Early Ages of the Irish Nation and History …* (privately printed in 1789); and *A view of nature, in letters to a traveller among the Alps, with reflections on atheistical philosophy now exemplified in France* (6 vols., 1794; translated into German by E. B. G. Hebenstreit, 4 vols., 1795–1800). He also wrote *Thoughts on Martial Law, and on the Proceedings of General Courts Martial*, published anonymously in 1779, but revised and republished under his own name in 1784.

To Sullivan have been inaccurately assigned two anonymous pamphlets: *History of the administration of the leader in the Indian direction. Shewing by what great and noble efforts he has brought the company's affairs into their present happy situation* (1765?), and *A defence of Mr Sullivan's propositions (to serve as the basis of a negociation with government), with an answer to the objections against them, in a letter to the proprietors of East India stock* (1767). Sullivan died at his seat, Thames Ditton, Surrey, on 17 July 1806. His eldest son, Richard, having died in 1789, the title devolved on his second son, Henry (1785–1814), MP for the City of Lincoln (1812–14) and lieutenant-colonel of the Coldstream Guards. He died in battle at Toulouse on 14 April 1814. Sir Charles Sullivan (1789–1862), his younger brother, succeeded him as third baronet, entered the navy in February 1801, and eventually became admiral of the blue.

THOMPSON COOPER, rev. REBECCA MILLS

Sources will, PRO, PROB 11/1447, fols. 7–14 · Burke, *Peerage* (1896), 1385 · *GM*, 1st ser., 76 (1806), 687, 871, 896 · *GM*, 1st ser., 102/2 (1832), 656 · *GM*, 1st ser., 56 (1786), 45 · J. Foster, *The peerage, baronetage, and knightage of the British empire for 1881*, [pt 2] [1881] · [D. Rivers], *Literary memoirs of living authors of Great Britain*, 2 (1798), 287–8 · T. Thomson, *History of the Royal Society from its institution to the end of the eighteenth century* (1812), appx 4, p. lix · J. S. Crone, *A concise dictionary of Irish biography*, rev. edn (1937), 242 · Nichols, *Lit. anecdotes*, 9.51 · Watt, *Bibl. Brit.*, 2.88 · Allibone, *Dict.* · J. Watkins, *The universal biographical dictionary*, new edn (1821) · A. J. Webb, *A compendium of Irish biography* (1878)
Archives BL, corresp. with Warren Hastings, etc., Add. MSS 29138–29178, *passim*
Wealth at death valuable estates in Thames Ditton, Surrey; house and trappings, apparent value *c.*£25,000–30,000: will, PRO, PROB 11/1447, sig. 600

Sullivan, Robert (1800–1868), educational writer, son of Daniel Sullivan, a publican, was born in Holywood, co. Down, in January 1800. He was educated at the Belfast Academical Institution and at Trinity College, Dublin, where he graduated BA in 1829, MA in 1832, and LLB and LLD in 1850. On the introduction of national education in Ireland Sullivan was appointed an inspector of schools in 1832, under the national education commissioners. In 1838 he was appointed professor of English literature at the training department in Dublin, which trained teachers for the commission-controlled schools. From 1840 until his death he was professor and superintendent of training and model schools. He died at Clanrida Park, Kingstown (Dún Laoghaire), near Dublin, on 11 July 1868, and was buried at Holywood.

Sullivan was the author of numerous school textbooks published and printed by the national education commissioners. These were regarded as being of a high standard and were widely used in England as well as Ireland. His most important work was *A Dictionary of the English Language* (1847). He also wrote manuals of orthography, etymology, spelling, grammar, and geography.

E. I. CARLYLE, rev. C. A. CREFFIELD

Sources A. J. Webb, *A compendium of Irish biography* (1878) • Boase, *Mod. Eng. biog.* • D. J. O'Donoghue, *The poets of Ireland: a biographical dictionary with bibliographical particulars*, 1 vol. in 3 pts (1892–3), 238 • Allibone, *Dict.*

Wealth at death under £45,000: probate, 4 Sept 1868, *CGPLA Ire.*

Sullivan, Thomas Herbert (d. 1824). See under Sullivan, John William (b. c.1700, d. in or after 1752).

Sullivan, Timothy. See Ó Súilleabháin, Tadhg Gaelach (c.1715–c.1795).

Sullivan, William Francis (1756–1830). See under Sullivan, Francis Stoughton (1715/16–1766).

Sully, James (1842–1923), philosopher and psychologist, was born on 3 March 1842 at Salmon Parade, Bridgwater, Somerset, the eldest son of the eight children of James Wood Sully, a liberal Baptist merchant and shipowner, and his wife, Eliza Fender. In 1859, having attended various dame-schools in Bridgwater and also Taunton School, Sully was baptized and joined the family business. Planning to become a Baptist minister he studied at Regent's Park College in London from 1863 to 1866. However, his religious feelings ebbed and instead of taking holy orders he went to Göttingen, in Germany, to study under Lotze for an MA of the University of London; he was awarded the gold medal in 1868. Alexander Bain, who examined Sully, recommended him to John Morley as an assistant; in 1871, after a brief period as a classical tutor at the Baptist college in Pontypool, Sully became Morley's assistant at the *Fortnightly Review* and tutor to his stepson. Contributing philosophical and psychological essays to the *Fortnightly Review*, the *Contemporary Review*, the *Saturday Review*, the *Westminster Review*, the *Cornhill Magazine*, and to the ninth edition of the *Encyclopaedia Britannica* (including an article entitled 'Evolution', written with Thomas Huxley), Sully gained an entrée to 'the innermost circle of men of letters' (Sully, 135). Membership of the Savile Club also helped him to make literary and scientific acquaintances.

In the winter of 1871–2 Sully studied physiology in Berlin with Helmholtz and Dubois-Reymond. Sully's first book, *Sensation and Intuition* (1874), was compiled from his psychological articles. Between 1871 and 1901 he published about fifty articles on music, illusions, childhood, laughter, and German culture in general interest periodicals; most of these were subsequently elaborated in books, including *Pessimism* (1877), *Illusions* for the International Scientific Series (1881), *Studies of Childhood* (1895), and *An Essay on Laughter* (1902). He contributed regularly to the journal *Mind*.

On 3 October 1868 Sully married Sarah Ann Wood, with whom he had two children. Having left Pontypool the Sullys lived at Compton, not far from the Morleys, then in St John's Wood, near the Huxleys and Richard Garnett. In 1878 they settled in Hampstead; there Sully, who had suffered a nervous breakdown and bouts of insomnia in the previous five years, found refuge from the London noise, to which he devoted an article in the *Fortnightly Review* (1878) in a vain attempt to overcome his affliction through writing about it.

Until 1879 the Sully household relied mainly on an allowance from his father. After his father's bankruptcy, however, Sully, whose three applications for university chairs in philosophy proved unsuccessful, had to increase his journalistic output and to take on examining in philosophy for Cambridge University and Victoria University, Manchester, in addition to examining in logic and psychology for the University of London, which he began in 1878. He also started lecturing on the theory of education at the College of Preceptors and at the Maria Grey Training College. Having thus found a keen audience for his psychological researches he published three textbooks, which became set texts in British and American universities. Among the first systematic expositions of psychology in the English language his *Outlines of Psychology* (1884; new edn, 1892), *The Teacher's Handbook of Psychology* (1886; 5th edn, rewritten, 1909), and *The Human Mind* (1892) had a profound influence on the genre of the psychology textbook. In 1892 Sully was elected to the Grote chair of the philosophy of mind and logic at University College, London. In 1897 he was secretary to the organizing committee of the psychology laboratory but showed little interest in experimental work once the laboratory was established. W. H. R. Rivers came down from Cambridge to hold laboratory classes. Sully believed that experimental work was of limited relevance to the investigation of mental evolution and genetic psychology, on which he focused during the later years of his career.

Central to Sully's research was the study of children, which was facilitated by his involvement in the British Child Study Association, a federation of local child study societies comprising mainly teachers and parents, who keenly shared observations with Sully. Sully became 'the most influential figure in the Association, shaping its ideas and often presiding over its day-to-day business' (Wooldridge, 37). He held various offices in the London Child Study Society during the 1890s. Alongside teacher training, child study provided him with a context for defining the role of the professional psychologist in relation to amateur practitioners of the science, and for elaborating his views on the scientific method as a component of humanistic education. Sully's *Studies of Childhood* appeared in 1895. His writings on children drew on a wide range of sources and paid particular attention to children's early language and their games and fantasies (Wooldridge, 39).

Having retired from his chair in 1903 Sully, who was a keen traveller, spent much time touring the continent. He scaled down his writing activity, publishing only travel sketches and memoirs, including autobiography (1918), after his retirement. He died at 6 Montague Road, Richmond, Surrey, on 1 November 1923.

According to Adrian Wooldridge, Sully's 'distinctive approach to children ensured that the [British Child Study] Association was something more than just a branch of the American child study movement, while his position in the academic world provided an invaluable link between a movement of interested amateurs and the emerging profession of psychology' (Wooldridge, 37).

LYUBOV G. GURJEVA

Sources J. Sully, *My life and friends: a psychologist's memories* [1918] · L. S. Hearnshaw, *A short history of British psychology, 1840–1940* (1964), 132–6 · R. Thomson, *The Pelican history of psychology* (1968), 174–89 · A. Wooldridge, *Measuring the mind: education and psychology in England, c.1860–c.1990* (1994) · E. Block jun., 'James Sully, evolutionary psychology, and late Victorian Gothic fiction', *Victorian Studies*, 25 (1981–2), 443–67 · b. cert. · m. cert. · d. cert. · *CGPLA Eng. & Wales* (1923) · L. G. Gurjeva, 'James Sully and scientific psychology, 1870–1910', *Psychology in Britain: historical essays and personal reflections*, ed. G. C. Bunn, A. D. Lovie, and G. D. Richards (2001), 72–94
Archives UCL, corresp. and papers | King's AC Cam., letters to Oscar Browning · UCL, letters to Francis Galton
Likenesses Elliott & Fry, photograph, repro. in Sully, *My life and friends*, frontispiece
Wealth at death £4210 18s. 3d.: probate, 29 Dec 1923, *CGPLA Eng. & Wales*

Sumbel, Mary Stephens. *See* Wells, Mary Stephens (1762–1829).

Sumerled. *See* Somerled (*d.* 1164).

Summers, Charles (1825–1878), sculptor, was born at East Charlton, Somerset, on 27 July 1825, the son of George Summers, mason, and his wife, Ruth (*d. c.*1840x45). His brother Joseph attained success as a musician, being awarded the degree of doctor of music, despite his artisan background. Charles received little education but showed early talent for sketching portraits. As the family income was precarious he was sent to work in menial jobs from the age of eight, and the combination of his obvious talent and humble origins, together with an unaffected nature, later captured the imagination of many contemporaries. While employed at Weston-super-Mare erecting a monument he attracted the attention of the sculptor Henry Weekes, who took him, aged nineteen, into his studio and gave him his first lessons in modelling. Summers entered the Royal Academy Schools in 1850, having worked his way up through the lowliest and most basic positions in large sculptural studios. He also received lessons from Musgrave Lewthwaite Watson, after whose death he was employed in completing the immense group of Lord Eldon and Lord Stowell, now in the library of University College, Oxford. In 1850 he won the silver medal of the Royal Academy, and in 1851 the gold medal, for *Mercy Interceding for the Vanquished*. In the same year his *Boy with a Shell* won a bronze medal at the Great Exhibition. He also began to show at the Royal Academy's annual exhibition. About 1851 he married Augustine Ameot or Amiot.

Having been diagnosed with suspected tuberculosis Summers was advised to travel to Australia, and in 1852 he arrived in Melbourne, where he built a house. He took out a claim on the Tarnagulla goldfield but had no success and subsequently obtained employment as an architectural sculptor modelling the complex neo-rococo figurative decoration of the legislative council chamber in the Victorian houses of parliament then being built, working with William Scurry and John Simpson Mackennal. In the

next decade he became the most important sculptor in colonial Australia, monopolizing local sculptural commissions, and a high-profile public figure in Melbourne. As testimony to his status as a sculptor he attended civic masquerade balls dressed as Michelangelo and, more seriously, was appointed to official government positions such as that of chairman overseeing drawing instructors in the common schools (1864). The Victorian Intercolonial Exhibition of 1866 presented elaborate circular figurative bas-relief plaques by Summers as prizes. He was active in promoting and organizing the earliest artists' society in Melbourne, the Victorian Society of Fine Arts, which was founded in 1856. His range of cultural activities was not only a remarkable achievement at a personal level but documents a surprising level of cultural ambition in a colonial outpost.

Summers's sculptural practice encompassed portrait busts, prize medallions, and large free-standing sculptures, including the neo-classical group *The Sure Friend* (*c.*1863–1864, des.), which was used as a logo of the Australian Mutual Provident Society for the next century. His Shakespeare memorial (*c.*1863) is now known only through photographs, but his *River God Fountain* has been restored and reinstalled in Melbourne. His undoubted masterpiece was the memorial to the ill-fated explorers Robert O'Hara Burke and William John Wills, reputed to be the largest bronze hitherto cast in Australia. As he had never before worked in bronze and had to construct his own furnace his success was the more remarkable. His first designs, published in November 1861, showed a complex figurative group, with the explorers supported by a camel, surrounded by free-standing statues of Australian Aboriginal people and decorative bas-reliefs. A high degree of cultural erudition in both sculptor and audience was demonstrated by multiple quotations from ancient Greek and Roman sculpture, Michelangelo, and Donatello. The monument would have been notable even in metropolitan London, and curiously prefigured the elaborate memorial programmes of sculptures erected later in the decade honouring the prince consort. The simpler design, as completed, demonstrates the power of established precedent over mid-Victorian sculpture and yet, by adapting the style of Michelangelo and the high Renaissance to depict colonial explorers and their tragic folly, Summers produced a genuinely memorable work of art. Since its unveiling the memorial has changed position no fewer than five times, due to various capital works in central Melbourne, and has suffered the indignity of some dubious, officially sanctioned reworkings on the pedestal, including incorporation of a modernist fountain, as well as yards of silver foil during an 'art happening', but has now been restored to the format originally unveiled, if not to its original position. In 1862 Summers also produced an elaborate life-sized group of the explorers in wax for a Melbourne waxworks, which showed a more romantic emphasis upon emotional extremes than his usual classical reserve.

In 1867 Summers returned to England, then moved to Rome, where he established a studio that reputedly employed up to twenty assistants at the time of his death. He exhibited regularly at the Royal Academy, mostly portraiture with both Australian and British sitters. The majority of his works now in British public collections are portrait busts. At the Paris Exhibition of 1867 the government of the state of Victoria, Australia, showed a collection of heads cast by Summers from live models at the Coranderk Aboriginal Mission. They aroused great interest and Summers produced an edition of the work. A set of casts was acquired by the Jardin des Plantes, Paris, and other sets survive in the Museum of Victoria, Melbourne, and the British Museum. In 1876 he executed, in marble, life-size seated statues of Queen Victoria, the prince consort, and the prince and princess of Wales for the public library at Melbourne. The queen and prince consort were portrayed as they appeared c.1860, the prince and princess of Wales contemporary to the date of the commission by Sir William Clarke. These important works formed part of an impressive collection of Summers's sculptures, including portrait and ideal sculpture, held by the Victoria Public Library and the National Gallery of Victoria but all were later de-accessioned by the gallery, together with other Victorian and *beaux arts* sculpture after the Second World War. The royal figures survive, badly weathered, in various outdoor locations. Some of the portraits of Melbourne personages, including the flamboyant posthumous bust of the popular actor Gustavus Vaughan Brooke, are held by the State Library of Victoria, Melbourne.

Summers's best-known pupils were both somewhat unusual Victorian sculptors: Charles Stanford was serving a term in Pentridge prison, Coburg, Victoria, when he came to Summers's notice; Margaret Thomas was an early woman sculptor, painter, and art writer. Summers died, after an operation, on 24 November 1878 at Neuilly-sur-Seine, France, and was buried in the protestant cemetery in Rome. He left one son, Charles Francis Summers, a sculptor, who worked closely with the Italian neo-classical sculptors G. B. Lombardi and G. M. Benzoni. Works by C. F. Summers and Lombardi grace the sculpture pavilion (c.1866) at Ballarat Fine Art Gallery, Victoria.

C. A. HARRIS, rev. JULIET PEERS

Sources C. Downer, 'Noble savages, or, Ourselves writ strange? Idealism and empiricism in the Aboriginal sculptures of Charles Summers', *La Trobe Library Journal*, 11/43 (1989), 27–9 · J. Evans, *Charles Summers, 1825–1878* (1978) [exhibition catalogue, Woodspring Museum, Weston-super-Mare] · C. Downer, 'Heroic failure: Charles Summers' maquette for the Burke and Wills memorial', *Creating Australia: 200 years of Australian art*, ed. D. Thomas (1988) [exhibition catalogue, 'The Great Australian Art Exhibition', Brisbane and elsewhere, May 1988 – July 1989] · N. Hutchison, *Early Australian sculpture* (Ballarat, Australia, 1976) [exhibition catalogue, Ballarat Fine Art Gallery, Australia] · M. Thomas, *A hero of the workshop and a Somersetshire worthy, C. Summers* (1879) · A. Callaway, *Visual ephemera: theatrical art in 19th century Australia* (Sydney, 2000) · K. Scarlett, *Dictionary of Australian sculptors* (Melbourne, 1980) · G. Hayes, 'Melbourne's first monument: Charles Summers' Burke and Wills', *La Trobe Library Journal*, 11/42 (1988) · P. Mennell, *The dictionary of Australian biography: comprising notices of eminent colonists from the inauguration of responsible government down to the present time (1855–1892)* (1892) · *AusDB* · *CGPLA Eng. & Wales* (1878) · *Catalogue of the Victorian Industrial Society*, 8 (1858)

[exhibition catalogue] · *Sands and Macdougall's directory for Victoria* (1866)
Archives Royal Society of Victoria, Melbourne
Likenesses M. Thomas, oils, 1860–69, State Library of Victoria, Melbourne, La Trobe picture collection · M. Thomas, marble bust, 1880, Shire Hall, Somerset · engraving, State Library of Victoria, Melbourne; repro. in *Australasian Sketcher* (15 Feb 1879)
Wealth at death under £300—in England: probate, 9 Dec 1878, *CGPLA Eng. & Wales*

Summers, James (1828–1891), Sinologist and teacher of English in Japan, was born on 5 July 1828 at Bird Street, Lichfield, Staffordshire, the only son of Edward Summers, a plasterer, and his wife, Catherine. He was interested in languages from his youth and developed an interest in east Asia with the hope of entering the diplomatic or consular service. In 1848 he went to Hong Kong to teach at St Paul's School, and in 1849 he inadvertently instigated an unfortunate incident at Macao when he came across a Corpus Christi procession and, refusing to uncover his head, was arrested. His rescue from prison by Captain Henry Keppel RN resulted in one death and three casualties. This incident showed the stubborn and volatile character that persisted throughout his life.

Summers was appointed professor of Chinese at King's College, London, in 1852 and remained in post until 1873. In December 1853 he matriculated at Magdalen Hall, Oxford, but never took a degree. After taking holy orders in 1863 he held various positions, including a curacy at Hitchin church, Hertfordshire. He was the third professor of Chinese in Britain after Samuel Kidd at University College, London, and S. T. Fearon at King's College. Since his salary was minimal, he had to find other employment, and he worked for the India Office Library and the British Museum as an assistant. He took on the editorship of the *Chinese and Japanese Repository* (July 1863–December 1865) and *The Phoenix* (July 1870–June 1873) and published various articles on Japan, among them a series of 'Practical lessons in Japanese' in *The Phoenix*. His main books include *A Handbook of the Chinese Language, Part I and II, Grammar and Chrestomathy* (1863) and the *Descriptive catalogue of the Chinese, Japanese and Manchu books in the library of the India Office* (1872).

In 1873, when he was forty-five years old, Summers decided to give up teaching Chinese in England and to go to Japan with his family to teach English literature at the newly founded Kaisei Gakko (a forerunner of Japan's Imperial University). When the Iwakura mission from Japan was visiting Britain in 1872 Summers was offered a new post by Tomomi Iwakura (1825–1883), the leader of the mission. Before leaving for Japan he published in London in 1873 the *Taisei Shimbun*, one of the two earliest Japanese-language newspapers produced outside Japan, with Teisuke Minami (1847–1915); this is considered in Japan to have been one of Summers's most important contributions. As one of the early foreign employees for the Japanese government, Summers taught at the Kaisei Gakko (1873–6) and other early schools of English, as well as at the Sapporo School of Agriculture (1880–82). He was a pioneer of English literature in Japan and is particularly known as the person who introduced Shakespeare to the country.

After leaving Sapporo, Summers returned to Tokyo and bought a house at Tsukiji, the foreign settlement. In 1884 he opened 'Summers' school' at his house, which flourished and was attended by many well-known Japanese. The teachers at the school were himself and members of his family, and it was run mainly by his wife, Ellen, née Williams (1843–1907). Summers and his wife had nine children, five of whom were born in Japan. The second daughter, Lily (Ellen; 1865–1958), continued to work as a teacher of English in Japan until she died at the age of ninety-two. After settling at Tsukiji, Summers devoted much time to compiling dictionaries of Chinese characters; he distributed the specimen pages of two Chinese/Japanese–English dictionaries for subscription in 1884 but they were never published.

In 1890 Summers brought about the so-called Summers incident in Tokyo. When he met a procession escorting the empress dowager a lancer impatiently struck off his hat and injured him. Although the lancer was punished and an apology was made, some Japanese rebuked Summers for disrespect. Summers, fearing for his family's safety, returned to England. However, the incident had already died down when they returned to Tokyo four months later. Summers died of a stroke on 26 October 1891 at his residence, 33 Tsukiji, Tokyo, and was buried on 27 October in the foreigners' cemetery, Yokohama.

NOBORU KOYAMA

Sources N. Koyama, 'James Summers, 1828–91: early Sinologist and pioneer of Japanese newspapers in London and English literature in Japan', *Britain and Japan: biographical portraits*, 3, ed. J. E. Hoare (1999), 25–37 · L. Summers, 'Impressions of Japan in 1873: told by old foreign resident', *Nippon Times* (11–25 June 1951) · D. Twitchett, *Land tenure and the social order in T'ang and Sung China* (1962) · J. W. Norton-Kyshe, 'The case of Mr. Summers at Macao' and 'Result of Captain Keppel's rescue of Mr. Summers', *The history of the laws and courts of Hongkong*, 1 (1889), 244–8 · 'Attacks on foreigners in Japan', *The Times* (27 June 1890) · S. Adachi, 'Sao kenkyu no senkusha Samazu', *Gakuen* (Dec 1940), 55–78 · 'J. Samazu', *Kindai bungaku kenkyu sosho*, 2 (1959), 17–59 · M. Sasaki, 'J. Samazu', *Eigaku no reimei* (1975), 73–102 · T. Shigehisa, 'Nihon ni okeru Sao kenkyu no senku to shiteno Jamuzu Samazu', *Shomotsu Tembo* (Nov 1932), 318–24 · S. Shiga, 'Choro Jemusu Sammasu sensei o kokusu', *Kokkai Shimbun* (26 Oct 1891) · T. Inoue, 'Yo ga kioku ni zonsuru ni san no Eikokujin', *Taiyo*, 16/9 (1910), 145–9 · T. Tezuka, 'Tokyo-fu shiryo ni miru Samma Gakko', *Eigakushi no shuhen* (1968), 174–93 · Crockford (1865) · J. Summers, 'English in Japan', *Leisure Hour*, [23] (1874), 165 · Foster, *Alum. Oxon.*
Archives King's Lond.

Summers, Joseph (1903/4–1954), test pilot, was the son of John Richard Summers, a club manager. No birth certificate has been found; at the time of his marriage, on 4 September 1922, he gave his age as twenty-one, but on his death in 1954 his age was given as fifty. Nothing is known of his early life prior to his marriage, at a register office in Hull (where he was then living), to Dulcie Jeanette (b. 1896/7), daughter of Harry Frederick Belcher, a tax officer; they had one son and two daughters. At the time of his marriage his occupation was given as electrical engineer.

He then joined the Royal Air Force on a short-service commission, attending no. 2 flying training school at Duxford, where he learned to fly on Avro 504s and Sopwith Snipes. He passed out at Digby in 1924 and was posted to the crack 29 (fighter) squadron, where he flew Snipes and later Gloster Grebes. His outstanding flying ability was soon recognized, and after only six months he was posted as a test pilot to the Aircraft and Armament Experimental Establishment at Martlesham Heath, Suffolk, a rare distinction for a short-service officer. It was there that he acquired the name Mutt, by which he was known to a wide circle of friends and associates.

Summers was involved in testing a number of planes at Martlesham, including the Gloster Gamecock, Bristol Bulldog, Hawker Hornbill, and Avro Avenger. The first of his many narrow escapes came when he was testing the first dual-control version of the Grebe, normally a single-seater: the plane fell to within 150 feet of the ground in a flat spin before Summers managed to regain flying speed. On a later occasion he prepared to bale out of his Bulldog prototype as it fell from 10,000 to 2000 feet in an uncontrollable spin. As he began to clamber onto the centre section ready to jump, his body shape so altered the airflow that the plane went into a straight dive. By pushing the stick back with his foot he was able to flatten this out and climb back into the cockpit to land safely. The fuselage of the Bulldog type was subsequently lengthened after this incident, his last adventure with the Royal Air Force.

In 1929 Summers was appointed chief test pilot at Vickers (Aviation) Ltd, Weybridge, in succession to Tiny Scholefield, who had been killed during a test flight of the Vickers Vanguard the previous year. After Vickers acquired the Supermarine Aviation works at Southampton in 1930 Summers became for a time chief test pilot to both firms. It was an era in which prototype aircraft were sometimes produced at the rate of two a year, and in his new posts Summers quickly accumulated wide experience of first flights and prototype testing. He was an expert in assessing flight-handling capabilities and in communicating his impressions to the design teams. At Vickers he became an influential voice and gained the confidence of Rex Pierson, the chief designer, and Sir Robert McLean, the company chairman, as well as of Barnes Wallis, whose innovatory designs played a leading part in the future of the company.

The air force expansion programme of 1935 placed a heavy burden of experimental flying on Summers. On 19 June 1935 he made the first flight in the Vickers Wellesley bomber, the first of Barnes Wallis's geodetic structures, derived from work on the R100 airship. In that month he also flew the prototype of the twin-engined Wellington, the famous successor to the Wellesley. As the volume of test flying grew Summers sought a principal assistant, and found his man in a young RAF pilot, Jeffrey Quill. Quill held his new boss in awe, bracketing his name with the great figures of inter-war aviation: P. W. S. (George) Bulman, Sydney Camm, Rex Pierson, R. J. Mitchell, P. E. G. Sayer, and Cyril F. Uwins. It was Quill who flew Summers from Martlesham to Eastleigh on 6 March 1936 for the first flight of K5054—the prototype Supermarine Spitfire. The plane's blue-grey priming coats could not disguise its thoroughbred appearance, and after a 15 minute flight Summers landed and declared: 'I don't want anything touched' (Quill, 85). Quill has written that in Spitfire folklore this remark has been widely misinterpreted as meaning that Summers thought the plane perfect—'an obviously absurd and impractical notion' (ibid.). In fact Summers was indicating no more than that there were no immediate obstacles to further test flights. But by now Quill knew his chief well enough to see that he was 'obviously elated' (ibid., 86) with the Spitfire's performance, and after more test flying, much of it done by Quill, K5054 was handed to the RAF for evaluation on 26 May 1936.

To an outsider Summers's general approach to flying at Weybridge was 'casual and outwardly disorganized' (Quill, 156), and the greater volume of test flying after 1935 in particular exposed organizational deficiencies that he was temperamentally disinclined to correct. His strength was as a pilot rather than a manager, and he took on the bulk of the testing of the vast Vickers output during the war. He was also closely concerned with developing the special mines used by Guy Gibson's dambuster squadron. In Gibson's classic memoir *Enemy Coast Ahead* (1946) Summers appears as Mutt, who under conditions of great secrecy introduces Gibson to the scientist Jeff, a thinly disguised Barnes Wallis.

Summers's career was notable not least for its longevity, and in its last phase, after 1945, he made a series of important first flights, including the first pure-jet civil aircraft, the Nene-Viking, on 6 April 1948, and the first civil turbo-prop airliner, the Vickers Viscount, on 16 July 1948. He was determined before he retired to record the first flight of a four-jet V-bomber, and on a gusty day (18 May 1951) he took the prototype Vickers Valiant on its maiden journey.

Summers retired on 27 July 1951, the twenty-first anniversary of his first flight as a test pilot. Thick-set and of strong build, he remained to the end an individualist, one of the old school of 'knee-pad' test pilots whose judgement and horse sense added an important qualitative element to the increasingly quantitative business of experimental prototype flying. G. R. (Jock) Bryce, who succeeded him as chief test pilot at Vickers, recalled that on their first flight together, in the prototype Viscount 630, Summers began his pre-flight checks by relieving himself alongside the main wheels, telling his startled co-pilot: 'A bit of advice for you boy. Never fly with a full bladder, I know people who crashed with one and it killed them!' (Middleton, *Test Pilots*, 193). After he retired from flying Summers served as chief liaison officer at the Weybridge division of Vickers-Armstrongs Ltd (1951–2). He was awarded the CBE in 1953, having been appointed to the OBE in 1946. He died on 16 March 1954 at Beaumont House, Beaumont Street, St Marylebone, London, following an operation, survived by his wife, son, and two daughters. Summers was the brother of Wing Commander Maurice Summers, also a test pilot. MARK POTTLE

Sources D. Middleton, *Test pilots: the story of British test flying, 1903–1984* (1985) · D. Middleton, *Tests of character: epic flights by legendary test pilots* (1995) · G. Dorman, *British test pilots* (1950) · J. Quill, *Spitfire: a test pilot's story* (1996) · *Flight* (26 March 1954) · WWW · H. Penrose, *British aviation: the ominous skies, 1935–1939* (1980) · R. P. Hallion, *Designers and test pilots* (1983) · A. Brookes, *V force: the history of Britain's airborne deterrent* (1982) · *Aeroplane*, 86/2227 (26 March 1954) · G. Gibson, *Enemy coast ahead* (1946)

Summers, (Augustus) Montague [*name in religion* Alphonsus Joseph-Mary] (1880–1948), literary scholar, occultist, and eccentric, was born in Pembroke Lodge, Clifton, near Bristol, on 10 April 1880, the youngest of the seven children of Augustus William Summers, a wealthy banker, and his wife, Ellen Bush. He grew up in Tellisford House, Clifton Down, in the evangelical Anglican faith of his parents, and was educated in the extensive library of his home, at the Misses Lucas's academy, and, after his fourteenth year, as a day-boy at Clifton College. He entered Trinity College, Oxford, in 1899, and after a university career in which he attracted attention by his dandyism, wit, and unusual learning, went down in 1903 with a fourth-class degree in theology. He graduated BA in 1905 and MA in 1906. He attended Lichfield Theological College as a candidate for holy orders, and in 1908 he was ordained as deacon and appointed first to a curacy in Bath and then at Bitton in Bristol. Rumours of studies in Satanism and a charge of pederasty, of which he was acquitted, terminated this phase of his career.

On 19 July 1909 Summers was received into the Church of Rome and was granted the clerical tonsure on 28 December 1910; after this his clerical career became murky and remains so. He may have received minor orders as a deacon, but no record of his ordination has ever been found. During his lifetime, he was addressed as the Revd Montague Summers, celebrated mass in his own chapel and those of friends, adopted two names in religion, and invariably wore the dress pertaining to Roman priesthood; his appearance in soutane, buckled shoes, and shovel hat, later with an umbrella of the Sairey Gamp order, was familiar in London and Oxford. He became increasingly eccentric and was described as combining a manifest benignity with a whiff of the Widow Twankey. Some spoke of an aura of evil. It was charitably assumed by his friends that he was indeed a priest, and his devotion was never in question; his biographer Joseph Jerome (Father Broccard Sewell) records that all his life Summers wore the Carmelite scapular.

After religion Summers's great pursuit was the theatre, and it is as a scholar of the Restoration drama that he is remembered. As a child he and his siblings played seriously with a toy theatre. Until the death of his father (who left him a comfortable independence) he supported himself as a schoolmaster and during that time came under the influence of Henry Bullen of the Shakespeare Head Press. It was Bullen who encouraged Summers to produce his excellent edition of Villiers's *The Rehearsal* (1914) and *The Works of Aphra Behn* (6 vols., 1915). There followed *Restoration Comedies* (1921) and *Shakespeare Adaptations* (1921), opening up a neglected area of scholarship to which Summers made extensive additions with *The Complete Works of*

William Congreve (4 vols., 1923), *The Complete Works of William Wycherley* (4 vols., 1924), *The Complete Works of Thomas Otway* (3 vols., 1927), *The Complete Works of Thomas Shadwell* (3 vols., 1927), an edition of John Downes's *Roscius Anglicanus* (1928), and *Dryden, Dramatic Works* (6 vols., 1932).

These handsome books made available for the first time the substance of a period of English drama formerly neglected and dismissed by such critics as Macaulay as unmeritable and indecent. Summers's 'Introductions' may well be the finest things he ever wrote, being in Edmund Gosse's words, 'astonishingly full of marrowy information'. Although sometimes careless in detail, and although the wrongs suffered by his church obtrude needlessly here and there, the scope and depth of his knowledge is awesome.

Summers was a moving spirit in the founding of the Phoenix Theatre (1919–25), which presented much admired productions of Restoration plays hitherto unknown to playgoers, with casts of players of the first rank. Summers provided copious and excellent programme notes, and at rehearsal was a mine of information about the manner of performance. The Phoenix was succeeded by the Renaissance Theatre, which gave performances sporadically until 1928, Summers providing the same scholarly understructure. He was very popular with the theatre folk, and was devoted to them and their art.

In addition to his writing on the drama Summers published several volumes about demonology, witchcraft, vampires, and werewolves. They are enlightening reading even when the credulity of the reader does not match that of the writer. He also wrote a history of the Gothic novel in two volumes, *The Gothic Quest* (1938) and *A Gothic Bibliography* (1940).

Summers died suddenly at his home, 4 Dynevor Road, Richmond, on 10 August 1948, and was buried three days later in Richmond cemetery, garbed in his priest's vestments and with the coat of his dog, Tango. All his life Summers was a notable eccentric, and legends about him, benign and malign, are numerous.

ROBERTSON DAVIES

Sources M. Summers, *The galanty show: an autobiography* (1980) • J. Jerome [B. Sewell], *Montague Summers* (1965) • T. d'A. Smith, *A bibliography of the works of Montague Summers* (1964) • R. Davies, *High spirits* (1982)

Archives BL, Add. MSS 57772 | King's Cam., Dent MSS • U. Reading L., Jonathan Cape archives • U. Reading L., Chatto and Windus archive • U. Reading L., Hogarth Press MSS

Likenesses photograph, *c.*1925, repro. in Jerome, *Montague Summers*, frontispiece • photograph, repro. in M. Summers, *Essays in Petto* (1928), frontispiece

Wealth at death £10,464 14s. 1d.: probate, 30 Oct 1948, CGPLA Eng. & Wales

Summerskill, Edith Clara, Baroness Summerskill (1901–1980), medical practitioner and politician, was born on 19 April 1901 at Doughty Street, London, the youngest of three children and the youngest daughter of Dr William Summerskill MRCS LRCP (1866–1947) and his wife, Edith West. She was educated at Eltham Hill grammar school and then, from 1918, at King's College and

Edith Clara Summerskill, Baroness Summerskill (1901–1980), by Georges Maiteny, 1950s

Charing Cross Hospital, both in London, where she studied medicine. She qualified MRCS and LRCP in 1924. She thus followed in the footsteps of her doctor father, who had been, she claimed, a Gladstonian Liberal at a time when such political radicalism was rare among the medical profession: he had stood, unsuccessfully, as a candidate in a local by-election on the single issue of better public health provision. Her father was clearly a profound influence on Edith. She recalled that as a child she had accompanied him on home visits and that this early exposure to ill health and poverty, when combined with his radical politics and support for women's suffrage, was crucial in shaping her professional and political careers.

Summerskill married, on 7 August 1925, Edward Jeffrey Samuel (1895–1983), son of Edward Samuel of Llanelli, Carmarthenshire. They had met as medical students and went on to form a long-standing (1928–45) joint medical practice in north London, where her exposure to ill health and poverty reinforced her socialist beliefs and revealed what she saw as the inadequacies of the existing social services. Many years later she recalled attending her first confinement as a newly qualified doctor. Shocked at the sparse surroundings and the undernourishment of the mother, whose first child had rickets, she said 'In that room that night, I became a socialist' (*Strangers in the House*, Radio 4 programme, 10 Nov 1985). The marriage produced two children, Michael and Shirley. Edith retained, and both her son and her daughter used, the surname Summerskill. Shirley was to follow Edith into the medical profession and into parliament as a Labour member.

Summerskill was an early member of the Socialist Medical Association, an organization founded in 1930 and affiliated to the Labour Party the following year. Throughout the 1930s and 1940s, alongside other association members such as Esther Rickards, Somerville Hastings, and David Stark Murray, she put forward the case for a socialized health service, and it was she who came up with the idea of organizing social events both to raise money and to attract publicity to the organization. Such middle-class professionals, and especially women, were relatively rare in the Labour Party at this time, dominated as it was by male trade unionists. In the 1930s she was on the left of the party, and was among the few Labour MPs prepared publicly to welcome the hunger-marchers on their arrival in London. She was also active, through the 'National Women's Appeal for Food for Spain', in seeking support for the republican cause, and visited refugee camps for women and children in Spain.

As a feminist, Summerskill paid particular attention to women's social and political issues. In the 1930s she was outspoken in her attacks on the prevailing high rate of maternal mortality and urged that the interests of the expectant mother must always be prioritized by the maternity services. She was especially critical of negligent doctors and inadequate provision, pointing out that a significant proportion of deaths in childbirth resulted from preventable, and hence unnecessary, infections. Unsurprisingly, this was related to broader claims for a publicly funded and administered health care service. Summerskill was also an early member of the Married Women's Association, founded in 1938, and was for some years its president. The association sought equal relationships between men and women in marriage. One long-term consequence of its campaigning was Summerskill's successful private member's bill which became the 1964 Married Women's Property Act. All this reflected her own view that marriage should be a contract, albeit based on love, between two equals.

The 1930s saw the start of a career as an elected representative of the Labour Party which was to culminate in ministerial office and membership of the House of Lords. In 1934 Summerskill, rather unexpectedly, won a by-election to Middlesex county council and she represented the working-class Green Lanes division of Tottenham until 1941. Her by-election victory was won with the help of Ted Willis. At the time of her election Labour's electoral fortunes were at a low ebb nationally and such local government successes were important in boosting party morale in an era when locally elected bodies still had significant powers and still commanded widespread political loyalty.

Also in 1934 Summerskill was the Labour candidate in the Putney parliamentary by-election, where, although unsuccessful, she reduced the Conservative majority by some 18,000 votes. At the following year's general election she contested, amid controversy, the constituency of Bury. She was by now a well-known proponent of women's right to birth control, and personally acquainted with campaigners such as Marie Stopes. In Bury the Roman Catholic church, strongly represented in the local population, knew that Labour's political programme attracted many of the church's adherents. Summerskill was approached by members of the Catholic clergy who offered their support provided that she agreed never to give any woman advice on birth control techniques. This she declined to do, which resulted in a denunciation from the pulpit on the Sunday preceding the election. Whether or not this was the sole cause of her failure to win the election (the seat was retained by the Conservatives), Summerskill apparently felt that it was, and saw her treatment as highlighting an important difference between the conduct of politics in the north and in London. In any event, she later claimed that she never revisited Bury. In 1936 Summerskill was adopted as Labour candidate for the parliamentary constituency of West Fulham; she won the seat at a by-election in April 1938, and was returned in the general elections of 1945, 1950, and 1951. Her constituency was abolished following boundary reorganization, and from 1955 to 1961 she was MP for Warrington.

The coming of the Second World War further encouraged Summerskill's enthusiasm for social reform and, like many on the left, she urged the social reconstruction of Britain once the conflict was over. In October 1940, at the beginning of the blitz, she told fellow MPs that the wartime organization of health services, and the impact of the war itself, had greatly and irreversibly changed the provision and perception of health care. The clear implication was that there could be no return to the conditions of the inter-war years and that medical services must be socialized. In 1944 she became a member of Labour's national executive committee, a sign of her rising status, and served on it until 1958; she was party chairman in 1954–5.

After the 1945 general election Summerskill, a great admirer of Clement Attlee, received her first major post as parliamentary secretary at the Ministry of Food. This was always going to be a challenging position at a time of rationing and austerity—aspects of post-war life with which the British people were becoming increasingly disenchanted. Among her campaigns were those to make milk free from tuberculosis, an issue on which she could draw upon her medical knowledge; and to make the unappetisingly named fish snoek acceptable to the British public. She argued, with the rationalism of someone trained in medical science, that snoek was an excellent source of nutrition. She was not, however, successful in convincing her fellow citizens. This she in part attributed to the propaganda of the Housewives' League, which she saw as determinedly opposed to Labour government policies. Given these difficulties, she was surprised to be made a privy councillor in 1949, especially since she was not a member of the cabinet.

In 1950, and a further sign of Attlee's confidence in her, Summerskill became minister of national insurance in succession to Jim Griffiths. She had little time to settle in this post, however, before Labour's defeat at the 1951 general election. From 1951 until 1959 she served on Labour's shadow cabinet. In the late 1940s and 1950s she implacably opposed Aneurin Bevan and his supporters. While claiming that she personally liked Bevan—he had been a visitor to her home in the 1930s—and that he had been manipulated by his followers, she was none the less prepared to denounce him both within the Labour Party and publicly. She was one of the most vigorous advocates of his expulsion from the Parliamentary Labour Party in the mid-1950s. During the election campaign in 1951 Summerskill told an election rally that Bevan was not the architect of the National Health Service, only its midwife, and that credit for the service should be given to those, such as herself, who had campaigned for socialized medicine since the 1930s.

With Labour out of office, Summerskill devoted herself with her usual vigour and enthusiasm to a range of activities and causes. By the 1950s she had already travelled abroad for political reasons on a number of occasions—for example in a visit to the Soviet Union in the early 1930s, and as part of a parliamentary goodwill mission to Australia and New Zealand in 1944—and in 1954 was part of a national executive committee delegation to communist China. She was a prominent anti-boxing campaigner and in 1956 was one of the platform speakers at Labour's famous Trafalgar Square rally against the Suez War. Her involvement in the latter was part of a wider sympathy with Arab interests, on occasions promoted with a zeal which some of her colleagues found overwhelming. In February 1961 Summerskill was made a life peeress, but this was far from signalling the end of her active political life. Despite her reputation as being on the right of the Labour Party in the post-war era, she was publicly and forcefully sceptical about nuclear weapons and about the American intervention in Vietnam. She also campaigned during the 1960s for a reform of the law relating to homosexuality and for the legalization of abortion. In Harold Wilson's 1966 new year's honours list she was made a Companion of Honour.

Summerskill's views were manifested not only by her political actions but also in a range of articles and books. The latter included the publication, in 1957, of letters to her daughter, Shirley. This volume is of interest not least in its frank discussion, for the time, of both male and female sexuality, although Summerskill also made clear her disapproval of sexual promiscuity, particularly by women. In another letter Edith argued that politics should not be a career in itself. Rather, politicians should have other professional interests, a reflection and justification of the conduct of her own life. Such themes also emerged in her autobiography, *A Woman's World* (1967), which is an invaluable source of information about Edith's activities and attitudes, yet almost completely lacking in any serious self-reflection.

Edith Summerskill was throughout her adult life a committed feminist and member of the Labour Party. Her strong personality sometimes made enemies. Hugh Gaitskell wrote in his diaries that she was emotional, unintelligent, and governed in her political judgements almost entirely by personal experience. After one particularly bruising encounter Richard Crossman described Summerskill as a 'cantankerous bitch'. Such remarks, while revealing, should not be taken strictly at face value as they almost certainly reflect contemporary male attitudes towards ambitious and successful women. Summerskill was undoubtedly a significant figure in forging a successful political career, holding high office in both government and party, at a time when it remained relatively unusual for a woman to do so.

Summerskill's career, which embraced both politics and medicine as well as motherhood, must also be seen in the context of her social background. She was a product of the professional middle class and retained many of its attitudes and concerns. It is revealing that her admiration for Harold Wilson was based largely on his ability to appeal to this group and to represent the technocrats of the 1960s. Her social position might be seen as partially qualifying her feminism. She consistently argued for women's rights and for all women to take whatever opportunities were available to them in order to pursue careers traditionally dominated by men. Socialism and feminism were, for her, readily reconciled. Just as she pursued greater equality in the wider society, so within the home there should be 'real sharing … where the wife and husband are legal partners' (*House of Commons Debates*, 16 July 1943, col. 597). On the other hand, from childhood the households in which she lived were supported by domestic servants. After the birth of her own first child Summerskill relied heavily on the children's nurse, Agnes Wakeford. Edith recorded regretfully, and without irony, in her autobiography that service such as Wakeford's was latterly hard to come by, and that this in turn prevented many professional women from pursuing their careers after the birth of children. And although a supporter of much reforming legislation of the 1960s, she was none the less opposed to any easing of the divorce laws. Rather, what concerned her were equality within the institution of marriage and a recognition that motherhood in itself was a worthwhile and acceptable vocation.

After a long and active life and career, which might now be seen as containing certain contradictions, Edith Summerskill died at her home, Pond House, Millfield Lane, Highgate, London, on 4 February 1980.

JOHN STEWART

Sources E. Summerskill, *A woman's world* (1967) · *DNB* · J. Stewart, *The battle for health: a political history of the Socialist Medical Association, 1930–51* (1999) · O. Banks, *The biographical dictionary of British feminists*, 2 (1990) · R. H. S. Crossman, *The diaries of a cabinet minister*, 2 (1976) · *The diary of Hugh Gaitskell, 1945–1956*, ed. P. M. Williams (1983) · P. Brookes, *Women at Westminster: an account of women in the British parliament, 1918–1966* (1967) · W. D. Rubinstein, ed., *The biographical dictionary of life peers* (New York, 1991) · *CGPLA Eng. & Wales* (1980)

Archives U. Hull, Socialist Medical Association archive | FILM BFI NFTVA, documentary footage · BFI NFTVA, news footage · IWM FVA, actuality footage · IWM FVA, news footage | SOUND IWM SA, oral history interviews

Likenesses photographs, 1938–70, Hult. Arch. · G. Maiteny, photograph, 1950–59, NPG [*see illus.*]

Wealth at death £13,298: probate, 1 April 1980, *CGPLA Eng. & Wales*

Summerson, Sir John Newenham (1904–1992), museum curator and architectural historian, was born at Barnstead, Coniscliffe Road, Darlington, co. Durham, on 25 November 1904, the only surviving child of Samuel James Summerson (*d.* 1907) and Dorothea Worth Newenham (*d.* 1963), and the grandson of Thomas Summerson, the self-made founder of a railway works in Darlington. His mother belonged to a branch of an Anglo-Irish family of some distinction. His father, who worked in the family firm, died in 1907. His widow concentrated a small private income and all her love on her son.

After a lonely childhood moving with his mother round England and the continent Summerson spent contented years at a preparatory school at Riber Castle, near Matlock, the crazy architecture of which immediately appealed to him. At Harrow School from 1918 he was moderately happy, achieved little distinction in work or games, but became an organist of outstanding quality. Organs led to an interest in church architecture, and when P. C. Buck, the school's distinguished music master, dissuaded him from embarking on the limited life of a professional organist, he chose instead to train as an architect. In 1922 he enrolled in the Bartlett School at University College, London. Over the next eleven years it may have seemed that he had taken a wrong turning. He made little mark at the Bartlett, at a succession of architect's offices, or teaching at the College of Art in Edinburgh in 1929–30. He could not bring himself to hurt his mother by ceasing to live with her. A feeling of failure led, as he put it, to 'grinding and consuming unhappiness' (Summerson, typescript autobiography, chap. 5, p. 10). On the other hand in these years he made many friends, had the first of many affairs, travelled extensively in Europe visiting buildings old and new, became a campaigning member of the MARS (Modern Architectural Research) Group, and began to make a mark as an architectural journalist.

In 1934 Summerson steeled himself to the necessary but painful break with his mother. Meanwhile 10s. spent in 1933 on a folder of drawings from the bargain bin of a Bloomsbury shop had at last set him on the road to success. Identification of the drawings as by John Nash and Humphrey Repton encouraged him to embark on a biography of Nash. It was published in 1935 and was outstandingly successful. The declaration of war put work on a projected book on Georgian London to one side, while he concentrated his energies on founding what became the National Buildings Record, originally set up to record buildings threatened by bombardment. He became assistant director early in 1941. In 1945 he was appointed curator of Sir John Soane's Museum, and remained there until 1984. During his long curatorship he changed an agreeable, if largely inaccessible, curiosity into a small museum of international repute. Its inadequate private endowment was replaced by public funding, though it preserved independence under its own trustees, and it expanded into the adjacent no. 12, also designed by Soane, which was purchased in 1968. Summerson's conducted tour of the museum, open to all comers every Saturday afternoon, became famous. His first years at the museum

Sir John Newenham Summerson (1904–1992), by Stephen Hyde, 1984 [in the library of Sir John Soane's Museum]

saw the publication of a book of essays, *Heavenly Mansions* (1949), and of his two most important books: *Georgian London*, finally published in 1946, and *English Architecture, 1550–1850* (1953). Both went into numerous revised editions.

Summerson was knighted in 1958, received the Royal Institute of British Architects royal gold medal in 1976, and was created a Companion of Honour in 1987. He sat with distinction on many committees and public bodies. As chairman of the National Council for Diplomas in Art and Design he presided over a controversial reduction in the number and composition of art schools. Although he was an effective advocate of listing and state support for historic buildings, his commitment to contemporary architecture prevented him from ever becoming an out-and-out conservationist. He caused dismay in some quarters by supporting a new building in Dublin in 1961, and new designs by Mies van der Rohe and James Stirling in the City of London in 1984 and 1988, as of higher quality than the Georgian and Victorian buildings which they would replace. But after the mid-1950s he wrote little about contemporary architecture; a degree of disillusionment had set in. His posthumous reputation must rest less on his career as a public man or on his advocacy of the modern movement than on his brilliance as an architectural historian.

Summerson led the way in changing English architectural history from an agreeable recreation for practising architects to a serious academic discipline. Although he had no academic training, he acquired with impressive ease the skills of a professional historian. He was influenced by the continental art and architectural historians who had taken refuge in England, but was an innovator, not a disciple. *Georgian London* broke new ground in analysing the influence of landownership and building regulations on the architecture of a great city. *English Architecture,*

1550–1850 laid the foundations on which all subsequent architectural historians have built. Summerson saw 'curiosity' as his driving impulse; he had the gift of asking worthwhile and sometimes unexpected questions, finding convincing answers, and embodying them in prose of outstanding ease and distinction, enriched by the occasional memorable phrase.

Although Summerson produced no subsequent books of the stature of his two masterpieces, a steady output of articles, short books, reviews, lectures, and programmes on radio and television, all marked with the same distinction of thought and form, maintained his position at the head of his profession. In essays collected in *The Unromantic Castle* (1990) he documented the previously amorphous figure of John Thorpe, brilliantly reconstructed Wren's second design for St Paul's Cathedral, established the villa as one of the dominant types in Georgian architecture, and illuminated aspects of Soane and the Victorians. His short *The Classical Language of Architecture* (1964), written for a general readership, deservedly went into many editions and translations. His essay on Thorpe led to a catalogue of his drawings, published as volume 40 of the Walpole Society in 1966. Two meticulously researched volumes (1976, 1982) covering the period 1485–1660 in the *History of the King's Works* took up perhaps too much of his time. *The Life and Work of John Nash Architect* (1980) was a virtual rewriting of his first book. An unfinished and unpublished autobiography tails off after an illuminating account of his first forty years.

Tall, elegant, assured, courteous, and outstandingly handsome, Summerson was by no means as aloof or unapproachable as he could seem on first contact. To serious scholars he was unfailingly helpful. When relaxing with congenial friends he could be gay and delightful company. He had a soft spot for rakes and eccentrics, and many friends among artists, writers, and creative people. On 31 March 1938 he married Elizabeth Alison, daughter of H. R. Hepworth; she had trained as a dancer and was the sister of Barbara Hepworth, the sculptor. They had triplet sons, born in 1946. In the 1970s a long affair with the artist Nancy Culliford Spender (1909–2001), widow of Michael Spender and former wife of William Coldstream, nearly destroyed his marriage. He broke off the relationship, and lived peacefully with his wife until her death in 1991. By then he was in the advanced stages of Parkinson's disease. He died on 10 November 1992 at 1 Eton Villas, the house near Chalk Farm into which he and his family had moved in 1949.   MARK GIROUARD

Sources RIBA BAL, Summerson MSS [incl. typescript of unpublished autobiography] · H. Colvin, 'John Newenham Summerson, 1904–92', *PBA*, 90 (1996), 467–95 · *The Times* (12 Nov 1992) · *The Independent* (13 Nov 1992) · *The Independent* (17 Nov 1992) · *The Independent* (12 Dec 1992) · Burke, *Peerage* · *WWW* · personal knowledge (2004) · private information (2004) · b. cert. · d. cert.
Archives Durham RO, family corresp. and papers · RIBA, corresp., literary and research papers
Likenesses S. Hyde, photograph, 1984, NPG [*see illus.*] · N. Sharp, portrait, Sir John Soane's Museum, London · photograph, repro. in *The Times*

Wealth at death £1,428,688: probate, 4 March 1993, *CGPLA Eng. & Wales*

Sumner. For this title name *see* Hamilton, John Andrew, Viscount Sumner (1859–1934).

Sumner, Benedict Humphrey (1893–1951), historian, was born in London on 8 August 1893, the second of the three sons in a family of five children of (George) Heywood Maunoir *Sumner (1853–1940) and his wife, Agnes (*d.* 1939), daughter of William Benson, and a sister of Sir Frank *Benson, Godfrey Rathbone *Benson (Lord Charnwood), and William Arthur Smith *Benson. Heywood Sumner, a figure of patriarchal dignity and the son and grandson of bishops (his father was bishop of Guildford and his grandfather was C. R. Sumner, bishop of Winchester), forsook the episcopal tradition for art. He was a disciple of William Morris and a painter who in later life became a distinguished archaeologist. Nevertheless the Barchester atmosphere lingered in the Sumner household, and Heywood's mother [*see* Sumner, Mary Elizabeth], the founder of the Mothers' Union, made a deep impression on her five grandchildren.

Sumner went up to Balliol, his grandfather's college, as a Brackenbury scholar from Winchester College in 1912, but his career there was interrupted by the outbreak of war in 1914. After three gruelling years in France as an officer in the King's Royal Rifle Corps he was invalided home and transferred to the directorate of military intelligence at the War Office in 1917. Thence he passed to the peace conference, and from 1920 to 1922 served in the International Labour Office. In 1919 he had been elected to a fellowship at All Souls, and from Geneva he returned to Balliol in 1922 to serve as fellow (1925) and tutor in modern history for the next twenty years.

In this difficult period Sumner was a tower of strength in the life of the college. The effects of the war upon Oxford were profound and to many disquieting. The numbers of the college rose steeply; accommodation, staffing, and finance became major problems, and new schools were altering the traditional balance between the humanities and the sciences. The teaching load, too, was very heavy, and in this Sumner, despite the efforts of his colleagues, carried always more than his proper share. He displayed a prodigious capacity for work, an almost overdeveloped conscientiousness, and an unusual ability for assimilating facts. His own range was immense, and if he set both himself and his pupils an unattainable standard, his teaching always had a wide horizon.

In his scholarship Sumner engaged himself in two interrelated spheres of interest. The first was the history of modern diplomacy and international relations. He lectured extensively in this field and was closely concerned with the inception and development of the Institute of International Affairs at Chatham House. The other area of his expertise was altogether more original, though little regarded in the Oxford of his time: from his schooldays, when he had had the opportunity to begin learning the Russian language, Sumner was fired with a fascination for Russian history. Along with Bernard Pares he pioneered the academic study of that subject in Britain; along with R. W. Seton-Watson he did the same for the diplomatic history of Slavonic Europe. In scholarly terms Sumner was the greatest of the three.

Sumner characteristically published little until he had achieved full mastery of his materials. Then in 1937 there appeared his monumental study, *Russia and the Balkans, 1870–80*. This work remains unsurpassed for the extraordinary range of its sources, which embrace not only the diplomatic records, printed and manuscript, from all over Europe and the Russian memoir and analytical literature, but also all relevant work in south Slav languages and in Romanian. It is vividly and compellingly written, with telling vignettes of the personalities involved in the political and military imbroglio which culminated in the Congress of Berlin, as well as balanced judgements about the significance of Russia's Balkan ambitions in the last decades of tsarist autocracy.

V. H. Galbraith wrote of Sumner:

> The early years at Balliol were perhaps the happiest of Sumner's life. Tall and wiry, a great pipe smoker and a keen walker, he was the very centre of the teaching in modern history and 'Modern Greats'. He seemed to have endless reserves of strength and energy until, in the year 1931, a perforated appendix involved three major operations. He made an excellent recovery, but between 1939 and 1943 ... he came near to breaking down under the double strain of college work and a post with the foreign research and press department, organized by the Royal Institute of International Affairs, which was then located in Balliol College. There was another serious operation, due to ulcer trouble; and although he again made a good recovery, his health, as it proved, was permanently impaired. (*DNB*)

In 1944 Sumner was induced to leave Balliol to become professor of history at the University of Edinburgh. There he set himself to active lecturing on British and European history since the eighteenth century and delivered an inaugural on 'War and history'. But his tenure was cut short when he returned to Oxford in the course of the next year as warden of All Souls.

The war also redirected Sumner's learned work. The Raleigh lecture which he delivered before the British Academy in 1940, published in 1942 as *Tsardom and Imperialism in the Far East and Middle East, 1880–1914*, a suggestive examination of the shifting and contested priorities of Russian foreign policy in Asia, had to rest on a limited range of readily available sources. For this reason, presumably, Sumner turned to reflect on the Russian past as a whole. In 1944 there appeared his best-known book, *Survey of Russian History*. This imaginatively conceived and challenging work treats its story backwards, moving from the contemporary development of the Russian state, society, and economy into their ever more distant antecedents, and thus suggesting—what has only more recently become a commonplace—how far the Soviet Union was able to build on long-established continuities. The following year Sumner was elected to the British Academy.

Sumner threw himself not only into the task of building up All Souls after the war, but also into ensuring its co-operation with the university. In the period of reconstruction he was constantly on the alert that the college by its finance, by its elections, and not least by its hospitality, should make its maximum contribution, while retaining its distinctive character as a place of liaison between public and academic life. His efforts won general confidence, founded as they were upon the respect he enjoyed for his far-sighted and sober judgement; while within the college itself his consideration for each individual, and his private hospitality in the lodgings, which owed much to his sister Beatrix, made a lasting impression. But the work was very heavy, and he was drawn into endless committees, of which not the least onerous was the University Grants Committee. His health began to fail. He was often confined to bed for weeks on end, and there were further serious operations, all faced with the same imperturbability. He died in the Radcliffe Infirmary, Oxford, on 25 April 1951. He was unmarried. His important collection of books on Russian history passed to the Bodleian Library.

Sumner had produced two further significant works of scholarship, the fruit of his enhanced interest in earlier Russian history. *Peter the Great and the Ottoman Empire* (1949) achieved for the period 1700–25, in briefer compass, what his earlier *magnum opus* had done for the 1870s, thus underlining the important continuities in Russian policy towards south-east Europe. *Peter the Great and the Emergence of Russia* (1950), a shrewd short survey of the reign of that most commanding of tsars, continues to impress by its balanced and authoritative judgements. Sumner's papers (in Balliol College Library) consist mainly of notebooks which illustrate his meticulous working methods. They also include some materials evidently intended for publication, especially the almost complete typescript of a book designed 'to set out the development and application of Lenin's conception of revolution, as given by him in his writings and speeches'.

It was a sadness of Sumner's life that he could make so little direct contact with the country of his main academic concern. He paid only one short visit to Russia, in 1930; and his efforts to attract Russian scholars to Britain, especially through his involvement with the British national committee of the International Congress of Historical Sciences, proved abortive. He found compensation in a wide range of artistic and literary interests. Notable among these was his love of Shakespeare and of Dante, on whom he published two papers.

Sumner exerted great influence on his contemporaries. A commanding personality, he struck all, friends and pupils alike, as a good and a great man. His impenetrable reserve, although no bar to friendship, repelled intimacy, and only on the rarest occasions did he show by a sudden forthright judgement the strength of feeling that underlay his iron restraint. Even his friends were sometimes tempted to suppose hidden depths of repression behind such invariable moderation; but it seems more likely that he was a man moulded by the traditional religious influence of his childhood against which he never rebelled.

R. J. W. Evans

Sources DNB · C. Webster, 'Benedict Humphrey Sumner, 1893–1951', *PBA*, 37 (1951), 359–72 · Balliol Oxf., Sumner MSS · A. L. Rowse, *All Souls in my time* (1993), 129–54 · H. W. C. Davis, *A history of*

Balliol College, rev. R. H. C. Davis and R. Hunt (1963) · private information (2004)
Archives Balliol Oxf., papers | Bodl. Oxf., corresp. with L. G. Curtis
Likenesses W. Stoneman, photograph, 1950, NPG · A. John, unfinished drawing, All Souls Oxf. · D. Wynne, bronze bust, All Souls Oxf. · photograph, repro. in Webster, 'Benedict Humphrey Sumner', pl. 17
Wealth at death £15,938 5s. 10d.: probate, 14 Aug 1951, *CGPLA Eng. & Wales*

Sumner, Charles Richard (1790–1874), bishop of Winchester, born at Kenilworth on 22 November 1790, was the third son of the Revd Robert Sumner (1748–1802), vicar of Kenilworth and Stoneleigh, and his wife, Hannah (1756/7–1846), daughter of John Bird, alderman of London, and through her mother, Judith, niece of William Wilberforce. John Bird *Sumner, archbishop of Canterbury, was his eldest brother; the pair were second cousins to Samuel Wilberforce, whom Charles consecrated to the episcopacy. Sumner was educated by his father at home until June 1802, when he was sent as an oppidan to Eton College, a school with which his family was closely connected, his brother John being an assistant master. In 1804 he obtained a place on the foundation, and remained at Eton until 1809. While there he wrote a sensational novel, *The White Nun, or, The Black Bog of Dromore*, which he sold to a local bookseller. The Eton foundation was linked with that of King's College, Cambridge, but there were only two vacancies there during 1809–10. Having been elected Davis's scholar Sumner was entered at Trinity College, Cambridge, on 17 February 1810. He then went to Sedbergh for a few months to read mathematics with a popular tutor, John Dawson, after which he made a short tour in the Lakes, visiting Coleridge and Wordsworth. He matriculated on 13 November 1810, and was admitted scholar on 10 April 1812. He graduated BA in 1814 and MA in 1817. On 5 June 1814 he was ordained deacon, and on 2 March 1817 priest. At Cambridge he was the last secretary of the Speculative Society, afterwards merged with the union.

In the summer of 1814 Sumner accompanied, as their tutor, Lord Mount-Charles (who had been a fellow undergraduate at Trinity College) and Lord Francis Nathaniel Conyngham, the eldest and second sons of Marquess Conyngham, through Flanders and by the Rhine to Geneva. Here he unexpectedly met John Taylor Coleridge, who introduced them to J. P. Maunoir, a professor of surgery. The professor's wife was an English woman, and Sumner became engaged in January 1815 to the eldest of their three daughters, Jennie Fanny Barnabine (1794–1849). Rumour asserted that he took this step to forestall similar action on the part of the elder of his pupils, whose father secured Sumner's preferment in the church by way of showing his gratitude. During the winter of 1814–15 he obtained a building for an English congregation at Geneva and ministered to them over that winter and the next. On 24 January 1816 he married his fiancée at the English chapel of Geneva; they had four sons and three daughters. (Their son George Henry (1826–1909) married Mary Elizabeth Heywood [see Sumner, Mary Elizabeth], founder of

Charles Richard Sumner (1790–1874), by Sir Martin Archer Shee, 1833

the Mother's Union.) From September 1816 to 1821 Sumner served as curate of Highclere, Hampshire, and took pupils, Lord Albert Conyngham and Frederick Oakeley being among them. The latter, though later separated from Sumner by his conversion to Roman Catholicism, was never totally estranged.

In 1820 Sumner was introduced by the Conynghams to George IV at Brighton, where he dined with the king and talked with him afterwards for three hours. He made a favourable impression and in April of the following year George, without waiting for the approval of Lord Liverpool, the prime minister, announced to Sumner that he intended to promote him to a vacant canonry at Windsor. Liverpool refused to sanction the appointment, and an angry correspondence took place between king and minister, which ended in a compromise. The canonry was given to Dr James Stanier Clarke, and Sumner succeeded to all Clarke's appointments, which included the posts of historiographer to the crown, chaplain to the household at Carlton House, and librarian to the king. George IV also made him his private chaplain at Windsor, with a salary of £300 a year 'and a capital house … opposite the park gate' (Sumner, *Life*, 62). Other promotions followed in quick succession. From September 1821 to March 1822 Sumner was vicar of St Helen's, Abingdon; he held the second canonry in Worcester Cathedral from 11 March 1822 to 27 June 1825, and was then the second canon at Canterbury until 16 June 1827. He became chaplain-in-ordinary to the king on 8 January 1823, and deputy clerk of the closet on 25 March 1824. In January 1824 the new see of Jamaica was offered to him, but George IV refused to sanction his leaving England, asserting that he wished Sumner to be with him in the hour of death. In July 1825 Sumner took at Cambridge, by the king's command, the degree of DD. On 27 December 1824 he was with Lord Mount-Charles when he died at Nice.

On 21 May 1826 Sumner was consecrated at Lambeth as bishop of Llandaff, an office which he held with the deanery of St Paul's (from 25 April 1826) and the prebendal stall of Portpoole (from 27 April 1826). Within a year he made his first visitation of the diocese. When the rich bishopric of Winchester became vacant in 1827 by the death of George Pretyman Tomline (whom George III had never much liked), George IV hastened to bestow it upon Sumner, remarking that this time he had determined that the see should be filled by a gentleman. Sumner was confirmed in the possession of the bishopric on 12 December 1827, and next day was sworn in as prelate of the Order of the Garter. He was just thirty-seven years old when he became the head of this enormous diocese (which then included the archdeaconry of Surrey, and hence much of the metropolis south of the Thames), with its vast revenues and a castle of unsurpassed comfort for the bishop's use. He was the first bishop of Winchester to be enthroned. The strong tory views which Sumner held in early life moderated gradually. He voted for the Roman Catholic Relief Bill of 1829 (a step which he regretted later), with the result that he forfeited the affection of George IV, and R. J. Carr, bishop of Chichester, was summoned to attend the king's deathbed. Sumner strove strenuously to pacify rural discontent in 1830, but opposed the Reform Bill in 1832. One of Sumner's first acts as bishop of Winchester was to purchase with the funds and timber of the see a house for its bishop in St James's Square, London. Finding the contribution of his diocese to missionary causes almost nil, he instigated regular fundraising. In 1829 he began the practice of frequent visitation of his diocese, no visitation at all having been held since 1788. He pressed upon the clergy the necessity of providing schools for the poor, pleaded with landlords for the provision of better houses for their tenants, and protested against trading on Sundays. During his occupation of the bishopric he made ten visitations (there are said to have been only eleven in the entire previous history of the see), the last being in October and November 1867, and he twice issued a conspectus of the diocese (1854 and 1864). By 1867 there were 747 permanent or temporary churches in the diocese: 201 being new and additional, and 119 having been rebuilt since 1829. During the same period 312 churchyards and cemeteries were provided; the new districts, divided parishes, and ancient chapelries formed into separate benefices amounted to 210, and nearly every living was supplied with a parsonage-house. Sumner had proved himself a vigorous administrator, instituting the office of rural dean throughout the diocese. He was the first diocesan regularly to visit the Channel Islands. He was a determined supporter of diocesan education of teachers, a college for which was for a time maintained in his house at Wolvesey. If he had a fault it was in believing

that a secretary could never equal letters in his own hand.

Sumner's munificence and energy were remarkable; his revenues and his liberality were great. In 1837 he formed a church building society for the diocese, in 1845 he instituted a Southwark fund for schools and churches, and in 1860 he set up the Surrey Church Association. When the lease for lives of the Southwark Park estate lapsed in the summer of 1863, he refused to renew it, and sold his rights to the ecclesiastical commissioners for £13,270 and an annuity of £3200 during the term of his episcopate. The whole of this sum, both capital and income, he placed in the hands of the two archdeacons and the chancellor of the diocese for the purpose of augmenting poor benefices. It ultimately amounted to £34,900.

The religious views of Sumner were evangelical, and most of the preferments in his gift were conferred upon members of that party. But he bestowed considerable patronage upon Samuel Wilberforce, who succeeded him in the see, and he conferred a living on George Moberly, afterwards bishop of Salisbury. He spoke strongly against the Tracts for the Times in his charge of 1841 and disapproved of the appointment of Hampden to the see of Hereford. He was vehement against the 'papal aggression' crisis of 1850 when the Roman Catholic hierarchy in England was restored. He sought to prevent any action on the Gorham judgment on the part of his clergy which might lead to an abridgement of traditional liberty in the interpretation of the article on baptism, but fully sympathized with the agitation against *Essays and Reviews* in 1860–61 and against Colenso in 1863. He was also hostile to the recurrence of revivalism after the manner of Wesley and Whitefield in the church. He was attacked in 1854 as being hostile to the reform and lukewarm over the revival of convocation. Though he strongly opposed the establishment of the ecclesiastical commission he loyally aided in carrying out its designs, and from 1856 to 1864 was a member of its church estates committee. By 1865 he had concluded that his diocese should be divided, Surrey being granted a bishop of its own and not annexed to Rochester. On the opening day of the first Lambeth conference in 1867, Sumner took a leading part in a successful effort to redefine the episcopal declaration in an evangelical direction.

Sumner was favoured by Samuel Wilberforce as successor to his brother in the office of primate in 1862, but he was seized with a paralytic stroke on 4 March 1868. In August 1869 Sumner took advantage of a new act enabling bishops to resign their sees, and sent the prime minister his resignation. He took a smaller pension from the revenues of the see than he might have claimed, and an order in council continued to him the possession of Farnham Castle as his residence for life. He died there on 15 August 1874, and was buried on 21 August in the vault in the churchyard of Hale by the side of his wife, who had died at Farnham Castle on 3 September 1849.

Sumner edited and translated the Latin manuscript treatise of John Milton entitled *De doctrina Christiana*, which was discovered by Robert Lemon (1779–1835) in the state paper office in 1823. By the command of George IV it was published in two volumes in 1825. Macaulay highly praised the work in the *Edinburgh Review* in August 1825. The Latin version was reprinted at Brunswick in 1827 and the English rendering was reissued at Boston, USA, in 1825, in two volumes. Sumner also published many charges and sermons, as well as a volume entitled *The Ministerial Character of Christ Practically Considered* (1824). Sumner has been identified with Bishop Solway in Frances Trollope's novel *The Three Cousins* (1847), though probably erroneously.   W. P. COURTNEY, rev. W. R. WARD

Sources G. H. Sumner, *Life of Charles Richard Sumner* (1876) • A. R. Ashwell and R. G. Wilberforce, *Life of the right reverend Samuel Wilberforce … with selections from his diary and correspondence*, 3 vols. (1880–82) • C. R. Sumner, *Conspectus of the diocese of Winchester* (privately printed, Westminster, 1854) • C. R. Sumner, *Conspectus of the diocese of Winchester* (privately printed, London, 1864) • *The Times* (17 Aug 1874) • *The Times* (18 Aug 1874) • *The Times* (26 Aug 1874) • *The Times* (28 Aug 1874) • *The Guardian* (19 Aug 1874) • *The Guardian* (26 Aug 1874)
Archives BL, corresp. with Sir Robert Peel, Add. MSS 40361–40593, *passim* • Bodl. Oxf., letters, mainly to Samuel Wilberforce • LPL, corresp. with Charles Golightly • LPL, corresp. with A. C. Tait
Likenesses M. A. Shee, portrait, 1833, Wolvesey, Winchester, Hampshire [*see illus.*] • S. Cousins, mezzotint, 1834 (after M. A. Shee, 1833), BM, NPG • C. Baugniet, print drawn on stone, 1848 • C. Baugniet, lithograph, BM • D. J. Pound, stipple and line engraving (after photograph by Mayall), NPG • portrait; formerly at Eton, 1898 • portraits, Royal Collection
Wealth at death under £80,000: probate, 19 Sept 1874, *CGPLA Eng. & Wales*

Sumner, (George) Heywood Maunoir (1853–1940), artist and archaeologist, was born on 14 October 1853 in Old Alresford, Hampshire, the youngest of three children and only son of the Revd George Henry Sumner (1826–1909), rector of Alresford and later bishop of Guildford, and his wife, Mary Elizabeth *Sumner (1828–1921), the founder of the Mothers' Union and daughter of Thomas *Heywood, a Liverpool banker and antiquary. His other grandfather was Charles Richard *Sumner, bishop of Winchester. Sumner was educated at Eton College and at Christ Church, Oxford, where he read classics and then changed to modern history, being awarded second-class honours in 1874. Two years later he entered Lincoln's Inn and was called to the bar in 1879, but he never practised.

During this time Sumner shared lodgings with W. A. S. Benson, a metalwork designer and friend of William Morris. Sumner was thus introduced to the arts and crafts movement, and became a keen adherent for the next twenty years. In 1883 he married Agnes, daughter of William Benson, barrister, and sister of W. A. S. Benson, the actor–manager Sir Frank Benson, and the politician Godfrey Benson, first Baron Charnwood. They had three sons and two daughters. The middle son was Benedict Humphrey *Sumner, warden of All Souls College, Oxford. Sumner began his artistic career as an etcher and published two books of etchings—*The Itchen Valley* (1881) and *The Avon from Naseby to Tewkesbury* (1882). In 1883 a new edition of *The New Forest* by J. R. Wise was published containing twelve additional etchings by Sumner. These etchings were produced with a detailed traditional technique, but

during the next twenty years his style altered radically to one that verged on art nouveau. He illustrated editions of *Sintram and his Companions* (1883) and *Undine* (1888), both written by F. H. K. De La Motte Fouqué.

Sumner worked in a wide range of other media which included textiles, wallpapers, tapestries, tesserae, painted gesso, and stained glass. Sumner became the leading English exponent of the technique of sgraffito, a method of decorating walls by incising designs on coloured plaster; he decorated eleven churches and several private houses in this way. The first of these was his parents' house at 1 The Close, Winchester, in 1885; he also designed and executed St Paul's Church, Winchester (1902). His other churches included St Mary's, Llanfair Cilgedin, Monmouthshire (1888); St Agatha's, Landport, Portsmouth, Hampshire (1895); and All Saints, Ennismore Gardens in London (1897–1903) which also contains examples of Sumner's stained glass.

Sumner was associated with the Century Guild from 1884. From 1885 to 1888 and in 1894 he was a committee member of the Art Workers' Guild. With Walter Crane and W. A. S. Benson he organized the first arts and crafts exhibition in Crane Street in 1888.

At the turn of the century Sumner and his family moved out of London, and finally settled in 1904 at Cuckoo Hill near Fordingbridge in the New Forest. The house, the garden, and all the furnishings and fittings were designed by Sumner. His move to the New Forest and the forest itself were vividly described in his *The Book of Gorley* (1910). Probably disillusioned with the arts and crafts movement, Sumner turned to archaeology and during the next thirty years worked on sites in the area. His best-known excavations were those which he described in *Excavations in New Forest Roman Pottery Sites* (1927).

Sumner was a tall, strikingly handsome man with dark hair and a beard which turned white in old age. He died at Cuckoo Hill on 21 December 1940, one year after his wife. They are buried together in the churchyard at Ibsley, Hampshire.   JANE BARBOUR, rev.

Sources M. Coatts and E. Lewis, eds., *Heywood Sumner* (1988) • B. Cunliffe, ed., *Heywood Sumner's Wessex* (1985) • H. Sumner, *Cuckoo Hill, the book of Gorley* (1987) • *CGPLA Eng. & Wales* (1941)
Archives Alexander Keiller Museum, Avebury, corresp. • S. Antiquaries, Lond., history and archaeology of part of Cranborne Chase | Winchester Museums Service Historic Resources Centre, corresp. with J. P. Williams-Freeman and W. G. Wallace
Wealth at death £2453 6s. 8d.: probate, 20 March 1941, *CGPLA Eng. & Wales*

Sumner, Sir John (1856–1934), tea merchant, was born on 25 February 1856 at 97 High Street, Birmingham, the elder son of John Sumner (1824–1907), grocer and druggist of Birmingham and Coleshill, and his first wife, Ann (1825–1869), née Lees.

The family grocery and druggist business was founded in 1820 by William Sumner (*b. c.*1796) and passed in 1852 to his sons John (senior) and William. In 1863 John, author of *A Popular Treatise on Tea* (1863), took specific responsibility for the grocery trade, while his brother ran the adjacent chemist's and druggist's. Sumner was educated at a private school in Moseley before entering his father's business. In 1894 the business was transferred to Hutton House, 25/26 High Street, Birmingham, to premises built by the noted local antiquary and historian William Hutton. From there Sumner 'rescued' the Priory Stone, which he presented to Birmingham Museum. This episode aside, there was little to distinguish Sumner from the majority of successful provincial grocers of his day until in 1903 he began to packet and market the tips of tea leaves or 'fannings'.

Until then the market had been dominated by whole leaf tea, and these siftings had been thought to be of little or no commercial value, but Sumner successfully promoted them as a cure for indigestion and nervous disorders and sold them through chemists and grocers under the brand name 'Typhoo Tipps'. In 1905 he sold his retail business to finance the creation of Sumner's 'Typhoo' Tea Ltd, a private company which relied on financial backing from family members and from J. H. Brindley, founder and director of the Priory Tea and Coffee Company in Dale End, Birmingham.

Rapid expansion followed through the adoption of aggressive marketing of the brand and in 1909 Sumner visited Ceylon to secure supplies, establishing an agency to buy, blend, and ship tea ready for packaging in Birmingham. Until the early 1920s these tea imports were stored in bonded warehouses in London, Liverpool, Manchester, and Avonmouth, but between 1923 and 1925 new canalside packaging and storage facilities were developed in Birmingham enabling the firm to operate completely independently from the London tea market. By the early 1930s Typhoo was retailed from over 40,000 outlets, making it one of the most popular packet teas in Britain. When asked on one occasion to describe his business methods Sumner emphasized 'close personal supervision' in the early stages of his career, and 'absolute freedom from routine' with the confidence to delegate to 'the right type of man and woman' as the firm grew (*Worcester Daily Times*, 12 May 1934).

In 1926 Sumner passed control of the firm to his son and began to channel his energies into a wide range of charitable and public activities in Birmingham and the west midlands. In 1927 he founded the John Sumner Trust to promote works and objects of humanity, public utility, education, and research and to provide financial support for deserving persons not adequately provided for against infirmity and old age. This was followed in 1930 by the Colehaven Trust to finance the building in Coleshill of the Colehaven endowed homes for gentlewomen in reduced circumstances and failing health. He also took an active interest in the management of local hospitals, including the Birmingham nerve, children's, and general hospitals, Bromsgrove Cottage Hospital, and Worcester Royal Infirmary. He was a member of the Anti-Vivisection Society and, after retiring to Ham Court, Powick, near Worcester, joined Worcester Archaeological Society and became president of the Worcester branch of the National Citizens' Union.

Sumner married Martha Elizabeth, daughter of Richard Potter, farmer of Coleshill, on 22 August 1885; they had one son. Sumner retained an interest in country life throughout his life. In his younger days he hunted with South Staffordshire hounds; in retirement he pursued farming, topiary, landscape gardening, and forestry as hobbies. As a staunch Conservative, Sumner did much to support the party's cause in the west midlands and was rewarded with a knighthood in June 1932 in recognition of his philanthropic and political services.

Sumner died on 11 May 1934 at Ham Court, of prostate cancer. His funeral service at Powick parish church on 15 May was attended by representatives of the firm and all the organizations with which he had been associated. Cremation followed at Perry Barr, Birmingham, and his ashes were placed in the family vault in Coleshill cemetery. He was survived by his wife. His son, J. R. Hugh Sumner, succeeded him as chairman of the company; his nephew, Roland Sumner Kneale, became general manager.

MICHAEL WINSTANLEY

Sources K. Williams, *The story of Typhoo and the Birmingham tea industry* (1990) · *Worcester Daily Times* (12 May 1934) · *Coleshill Chronicle and Advertiser* (19 May 1934) · *The Grocer* (19 May 1934) · *The Times* (14 May 1934) · *The Times* (16 May 1934) · *The Grocer* (11 June 1932) · *Worcester Daily Times* (3 June 1932) · b. cert. · m. cert. · d. cert. · CGPLA Eng. & Wales (1934)
Archives Birm. CA, corresp. and papers | Bishopsgate Institute, London, corresp. with Hypatia Bradlaugh Bonner
Likenesses photograph (after oil portrait), repro. in Williams, *Story of Typhoo and the Birmingham tea industry* · photograph, repro. in *The Grocer* (11 June 1932), 59
Wealth at death £740,041 19s. 1d.: probate, 3 July 1934, CGPLA Eng. & Wales

Sumner, John Bird (1780–1862), archbishop of Canterbury, the eldest son of the Revd Robert Sumner (1748–1802) and Hannah Bird (1756/7–1846), and brother of Charles Richard *Sumner (1790–1874), bishop of Winchester, was born at Kenilworth on 25 February 1780. Here he received his early education, and then continued his studies at Eton College from 1791 to 1798 and proceeded to King's College, Cambridge, in 1798.

Cambridge and early career, 1798–1828 Sumner's years at Cambridge were marked by academic distinction: he was elected a scholar on 5 November 1798 and a fellow on 5 November 1801. In the second quarter of his residence at Cambridge he was nominated to a King's Betham scholarship, which he held until 1803. He won the Sir William Browne medal for a Latin ode in 1800, the subject being 'Mysorei tyranni mors'. To this accolade he added the Hulsean divinity prize in 1802. Like many others of his generation Sumner was touched by the influence of Charles Simeon (1759–1836), as was his brother Charles, and he left Cambridge a 'convinced' evangelical. Simeon's example had a lasting effect on Sumner's care for the poor during his later years at Eton College and on his strategy as a bishop of a northern diocese.

In 1802 Sumner returned to Eton as an assistant master. In 1803 he was made a deacon by John Douglas, bishop of

1820, when Bishop Shute Barrington (1734–1826) appointed him to the ninth prebendal stall in Durham Cathedral; in 1826 he succeeded to the more highly endowed fifth stall. From 1827 to 1848 he held the still more lucrative second stall. Apart from his periods of residence in Durham, Sumner lived out the life of a devoted evangelical pastor. He resided in his parish, held two services every Sunday, preached regularly, and attended himself to the occasional offices. His orthodox opinions, sound scholarship, and devotion to duty inevitably marked him out for elevation to the bench of bishops. His rise to the episcopate was also assisted by his younger brother, Charles, who tutored the children of the king's mistress, Marchioness Conyngham, and was himself appointed bishop of Winchester in 1827. In the same year Sumner declined an offer of the see of Sodor and Man, but in the following year he accepted the duke of Wellington's nomination to the bishopric of Chester. He was consecrated at Bishopthorpe on 14 September 1828; the second of the consecrators was his brother.

Chester, 1828–1848 Sumner's nineteen years at Chester, a diocese that included most of industrial Lancashire, were widely acclaimed as a model of leadership, pastoral care, and clear-sighted policy. His strategy for the diocese had four key aspects: the greater provision of church accommodation, especially for the poor; the encouragement and support of the clergy; the advocacy of lay visitors and lay helpers; and the provision of education. Sumner first mooted the possibility of lay workers as support for the clergy in his charge of 1829. 'Let the minister of a populous district', he wrote,

> using careful discrimination of character, select such as 'are worthy' and 'of good report' … [that] they may lessen his own labour by visiting and examining schools, by reading and praying with the infirm and aged, by consoling the fatherless and widows in their affliction.   (Sumner, *Charge*, 1829, 23)

Sumner promoted the building of churches by initiating and supporting church building societies, such as the Chester Diocesan Building Society, which he founded in 1843. In all, he consecrated 233 new churches. Unlike many earlier nineteenth-century prelates, Sumner saw one of his major roles as that of *pastor pastorum*. During his time in the diocese, 671 new day schools were built, and he was also a major influence in the founding of Chester Training College in January 1830. Inevitably he began to receive widespread public acclaim. On 5 May 1843 Sir Robert Peel spoke in the House of Commons of 'my admiration of the conduct of the Bishop of Chester who has effected so much improvement in the diocese which has the good fortune to be under his charge' (*Hansard 3*, 8, 1843, 1287).

Canterbury and church politics In 1848 Sumner was elevated to the archbishopric of Canterbury, a move which delighted Queen Victoria. A major factor in his appointment was his earlier refusal to sign the remonstrance organized by Samuel Wilberforce against the appointment of Renn Dickson Hampden to the see of Hereford in

John Bird Sumner (1780–1862), by Eden Upton Eddis, 1853

Salisbury, and priested in 1805. On 31 March 1803 he married Marianne (1780–1829), the daughter of George Robertson of Edinburgh, a captain in the navy, and sister of Thomas Campbell Robertson (1789–1863). Sumner took little part in the religious life of the school, but spent much of his spare time visiting the poor and ministering at the chapel of ease in New Windsor. Two of Sumner's most significant published works belong to the Eton period of his life: *Apostolic Preaching Considered in an Examination of St Paul's Epistles* (1815) and *A Treatise of the Records of Creation and the Moral Attributes of the Creator* (1816). Both these works won immediate acclaim: *Apostolic Preaching* was revised and reprinted in 1817 and eventually reached a ninth edition in 1850, from which a French translation was later made and printed in Paris in 1856, while the *Treatise* went through seven editions. In *Apostolic Preaching*, which is taken up with a detailed consideration of the great doctrines of the Christian faith, Sumner stressed that 'the doctrine of conversion must be preached plainly and directly'. The *Treatise on the Records of Creation* attracted more public attention, on account of its defence of a hierarchical class system and its view of Malthusian economic and social theories as acceptable Christian teaching.

These two works, published in successive years, brought Sumner into the public eye as a thoughtful writer and scholar. It came as no surprise, therefore, that in 1817 he was elected a fellow at Eton College. The following year the valuable college living of Mapledurham fell vacant and was duly offered to Sumner; he was instituted on 20 November 1818. He retained his college fellowship until

1847. Sumner's achiepiscopate was beset with controversies, which included the Gorham affair, the restoration of the Roman Catholic hierarchy, the revival of convocation, and the publication of *Essays and Reviews* (1860). Other issues of less national import included the Ecclesiastical Commission Bill and the beginnings of ritualism associated with the second phase of the Oxford Movement. Of all these matters the Gorham controversy was probably the most momentous. George Cornelius Gorham maintained against the opinion of his diocesan bishop, Henry Phillpotts of Exeter, that it was legitimate for a clergyman to hold that baptized infants were not automatically regenerate, eventually winning his case on appeal to the judicial committee of the privy council. Phillpotts then refused to institute Gorham to the living of Brampford Speke in his diocese, and even went so far as to issue a public pronouncement excommunicating Sumner and any who would undertake the institution on his behalf. Sumner wisely authorized the dean of arches to perform the necessary legal formalities. His diplomacy and *savoir-faire* were also apparent in lesser issues. In the matter of reviving convocation Sumner had been a strong opponent, fearing that it would open up a rift over liturgy and doctrine. When, in the event, the will of parliament was for the recall of convocation, Sumner acted with magnanimity, chairing the debates and speaking very occasionally. In the debates surrounding the Ecclesiastical Commission Bill, Sumner showed himself to be a man of business who wanted to ensure that the church's money and effects were properly managed. In all of these issues, despite his strong evangelical convictions, Sumner acted without prejudice to opponents or undue bias to friends, exercising a firm, gracious, and statesmanlike leadership.

As a parliamentarian Sumner took his duties very seriously. In 1829 he supported the Catholic Emancipation Bill, a measure which *The Record* declared to have been 'quickened by Jesuitical leaven' (26 Feb 1829). He voted for the Great Reform Bill of 1832 and the new Poor Law Bill of 1834, the provisions of which he helped to shape. He was also a keen supporter of the repeal of the corn laws in 1846. As archbishop he was a consistent opponent of the bill for removing Jewish disabilities and of that for legalizing marriage with a deceased wife's sister. He spoke in favour of Lord Cranworth's Divorce Bill of 1847 and argued on the basis of the Matthean exception clause that divorce should be permitted on the grounds of adultery.

An evangelical and publishing archbishop Throughout his long ministry Sumner was a 'moderate' rather than a 'Recordite' evangelical, eschewing the premillenarian fervour, biblical literalism, and ghetto mentality of evangelical extremists. Lastingly influenced by Simeon, he held to a faith which focused on evangelism, preaching Christ crucified: he himself frequently ministered at Clapham church, the evangelical Mecca, and was an ardent supporter and encourager of evangelical societies. He was prominent on the platforms and at the meetings of those societies which had their roots in Clapham, such as the Church Missionary Society, the British and Foreign Bible Society, and the Lord's Day Observance Society. The Church Pastoral Aid Society and the Society for Promoting Christian Knowledge also enjoyed his patronage. He remained staunchly opposed to Tractarianism, warning his clergy against a movement which he believed to be undermining the protestant church; he condemned the bad faith of ministers who, although successors of the sixteenth-century reformers, traduced their achievement. Sumner himself did not go uncriticized, his moderation being interpreted by Tractarians as ineffectuality: his second cousin Samuel Wilberforce and W. E. Gladstone, both high-churchmen, accused him of Erastianism, although Wilberforce's disparagement was clearly coloured by his disappointment at failing to secure the primacy in place of Sumner.

Sumner was one of the most fertile authors ever to hold the primacy, publishing more than forty volumes during his lifetime. His scholarly works belong to his earlier years at Eton and Mapledurham, while his more practical and pastoral writings arose out of his long episcopate. *Apostolic Preaching* and *A Treatise on the Records of Creation* were succeeded in 1824 by *The Evidence of Christianity Derived from its Nature and Reception*, in which Sumner maintained that the Christian faith would not have continued as a vital force were it not for its divine origin. A new edition of this work was produced in 1861 as a riposte to *Essays and Reviews*. *Sermons on the Principal Festivals of the Church with Three Sermons on Good Friday* followed in 1827, with a fourth edition published in 1831, and *Four Sermons on Subjects Relating to the Christian Ministry* was published in 1841. Here he complemented his Malthusian endorsement of poverty as a natural and honourable condition with an insistence on the Christian duty of charity incumbent on the privileged. In 1843 he published *Doctrine of Justification Briefly Stated*, which offered a defence of the Reformation principle of justification by faith in an effort to counteract the teaching of the Oxford Movement. Between 1831 and 1851 Sumner issued a series of volumes of 'practical expositions' on the four gospels, the Acts, Romans, and the other New Testament letters; many editions were sold. He contributed an article on the poor laws to the *Encyclopaedia Britannica* (suppl., 6, 1824) and to Charles Knight's serial *The Plain Englishman*. Many of his sermons, speeches, and charges were published as single volumes. Sumner was taken ill in May 1861, but recovered briefly. He died at Addington, Surrey, on 6 September 1862, and was buried with extreme simplicity in the churchyard there. Two sons and several daughters survived him.

Final years and assessment A tall, imposing figure, John Bird Sumner was an outgoing, gentle, and gracious individual, who was held in affection by the faithful of many religious complexions. He lived a disciplined and methodical existence, and as archbishop he regarded himself as the servant rather than the master of his people: no prince-archbishop, his conscientious performance of his duties and modest lifestyle established a pattern for his successors. His *Times* obituary celebrated him as 'a ripe scholar, a fluent writer, a sound divine, a not illiberal thinker with moderate views'. By contrast Randall Davidson, one of his successors, recognized his achievement in generous, rolling rhetoric: 'For fourteen memorable years, from 1848 to 1862, he upheld with sometimes courageous consistency the splendid evangelical principles of the best sort, whereof in his twenty years tenure of the see of Chester, he had been a firm exponent' (*Five Archbishops: a Sermon Preached on 14 September 1911*, 1911). It is true that Sumner sometimes found discretion the better part of valour: as Owen Chadwick has rightly said, he 'produced no watchwords, sounded no tocsin, marched along with the army and watched others command' (Chadwick, 453). But (at a time when the ship of faith was much tossed on the high seas) Sumner's temperate evangelicalism, his personal amiability, and his unassailable good character made him an unspectacular but appropriate archbishop for a church in no need of a colourful controversialist at its helm.   NIGEL SCOTLAND

Sources N. A. D. Scotland, *John Bird Sumner, evangelical archbishop* (1995) · A. M. C. Waterman, 'The ideological alliance of political economy and Christian theology, 1798–1833', *Journal of Ecclesiastical History*, 34 (1983), 231–44 · R. A. Soloway, *Prelates and people: ecclesiastical social thought in England, 1783–1852* (1969) · M. Fowler, *Some notable archbishops of Canterbury* (1895) · G. Sumner, *Life of R. C. Sumner DD, bishop of Winchester* (1872) · A. R. Ashwell and R. G. Wilberforce, *Life of the right reverend Samuel Wilberforce … with selections from his diary and correspondence*, 3 vols. (1880–82) · O. Chadwick, *The Victorian church*, 2nd edn, 1 (1971) · B. Hilton, *The age of atonement: the influence of evangelicalism on social and economic thought, 1795–1865* (1988) · ordination papers of John Douglas, bishop of Salisbury, Wilts. & Swindon RO, DI/14/125 · *The Times* (8 Sept 1862)
Archives Cumbria AS, Kendal, notebook of evangelical extracts; family papers · LPL, corresp. and papers | BL, corresp. with Lord Aberdeen, Add. MS 43195 · BL, corresp. with W. E. Gladstone, Add MSS 44358–44372, *passim* · BL, corresp. with Sir Robert Peel, Add. MSS 40532–40593 · Bodl. Oxf., letters to Samuel Wilberforce · Hunt. L., corresp. with E. H. Locker · LPL, corresp. with Charles Blomfield · LPL, letters to Henry Labouchere · LPL, corresp. with A. C. Tait · Oxon. RO, Mapledurham parish records · PRO, corresp. with Lord Ellenborough, PRO 30/12 · PRO, corresp. with Lord John Russell, PRO 30/22 · U. Durham L., corresp. with third Earl Grey
Likenesses G. Richmond, chalk drawing, 1849, NPG · E. U. Eddis, oils, *c*.1851, LPL · M. S. Carpenter, oils, *c*.1852, NPG · E. U. Eddis, portrait, 1853, King's Cam. [*see illus.*] · H. Weekes, marble sculpture, *c*.1862, Canterbury Cathedral · G. G. Adams, plaster bust, 1863, NPG · J. Phillip, group portrait, oils (*The marriage of the Princess Royal, 1858*), Royal Collection · portrait (after E. U. Eddis), King's Cam.
Wealth at death under £60,000: probate, 1 Oct 1862, *CGPLA Eng. & Wales*

Sumner [*née* Heywood], **Mary Elizabeth** (1828–1921), founder of the Mothers' Union, the daughter of Thomas *Heywood (1797–1866), antiquary, and his wife, Mary Elizabeth Barton (*d.* 1870), was born on 31 December 1828 at the Barton family home at Swinton near Manchester. In 1832 Thomas Heywood retired from the family bank to live as a country gentleman, purchasing the estate of Hope End, Colwall, Herefordshire, from the father of Elizabeth Barrett Browning, the poet. Mary and her elder brother and sister were taught literature, mathematics, and music by their parents, and were taken abroad to learn languages. Mary showed exceptional talent in music: her father bought her an organ and engaged an

Mary Elizabeth Sumner (1828–1921), by Elliott & Fry, pubd 1903

Italian singing teacher in Rome, who suggested that she pursue an operatic career. However, during this visit she met her future husband, George Henry Sumner (1826–1909), son of Charles Richard *Sumner, the bishop of Winchester, and soon himself to be ordained; the couple were married in Colwall church on 26 July 1848.

George and Mary Sumner lived first at Crawley, near Winchester, moving to Farnham Castle after the death of George's mother. Here, at the bishop's palace, two daughters were born. Soon afterwards George was appointed to the living of Old Alresford, where they remained for thirty-four years. In 1853 a son was born who would make his mark as the artist (George) Heywood Maunoir *Sumner (1853–1940). Mary Sumner worked in the parish and played the organ. The family were joined in their substantial rectory by Mary's widowed mother, whose influence partly inspired the meetings for women which Mary began to hold in 1876. At first her visitors were women of her own class; then, boldly crossing the social boundaries, she invited the 'cottage mothers', whose long working hours in the fields provoked her concern. At the first meeting all were addressed by the rector, and in this informal way the Mothers' Union was anticipated (meetings were also held for husbands on Sunday evenings).

With her children married, Mary Sumner at just past fifty was ready for a new challenge. Then her husband became archdeacon, entailing a move to Winchester Cathedral Close; further preferment came with his appointment as suffragan bishop of Guildford, but they still resided at 1 The Close. Relieved of parochial duties, Mary Sumner concentrated on her ideas for a network of mothers' groups which would help women deepen their spiritual lives through Bible reading, prayer, and fellowship. The groups would benefit both church and society, strengthening family life through material influence for good and providing a meeting-ground for women of different social classes.

Knowing of her aspirations, the bishop of Newcastle asked her to speak at a church congress at Portsmouth in 1885: this proved to be the foundation of the Mothers' Union proper. It was established initially in Winchester diocese, with Mary Sumner herself as an active chairperson; this position she held until the age of eighty, always chairing the monthly diocesan Mothers' Union meetings until 1910, and frequently addressing large meetings throughout the country thereafter. Many other branches were soon launched, often by competent clergy wives, and they drew their members from a wide social spectrum. Meetings were interdenominational, concentrating on devotional and practical topics. Mary Sumner became a well-known figure as the Mothers' Union spread to other dioceses and to the colonies. In her pamphlets, and in a journal which she co-edited with Charlotte Yonge, she dwelt on the subjects of Bible reading and prayer, although showing a considerable breadth of knowledge and an awareness of family problems.

The Edwardian period saw the heyday of Mary Sumner and her new movement: it was heavily patronized by royalty and titled ladies, who saw it as a bastion of respectability in an age of growing emancipation. For their diamond wedding in 1908 the Sumners were given a large triptych screen, painted and illuminated by women and signed by Queen Alexandra and other royal and aristocratic supporters (this now hangs in Mary Sumner House, the world-wide headquarters of the Mothers' Union).

After her husband's death in 1909 Mary Sumner continued to speak, write, and work for the movement, living at 1 The Close but often travelling alone to London by train. She frequently visited and entertained her numerous grandchildren. From her bedroom window she could see her husband's grave, where she finally joined him after her death at home on 9 August 1921. Her funeral service was attended by 4000 people, including representatives from Mothers' Union branches all over the country. It is true that she herself experienced few deprivations in her life, but sour comments about her affluence cannot conceal her vision, her understanding, and her dedicated commitment to her faith.   PAMELA JOHNSTON

Sources F. Hill, 'Mary Elizabeth Sumner', *Missing persons* · J. Coombs, *George and Mary Sumner: their life and times* (1965) · F. Hill, *Mission unlimited: the history of the Mothers' Union* (1988) · Hants. RO, Deposit 145M/85 · *Hampshire Chronicle* (1890–1919) · *Hampshire Chronicle* (13 Aug 1921) · J. Vaughan, *A short memoir of Mary Sumner, the founder of the Mothers' Union* (1921) · M. Porter, *Mary Sumner: her life and work* (1926) · O. Parker, *For the family's sake* (1976) · *Mothers in Council* (1891–1921) · b. cert. · m. cert.

Archives Hants. RO, Mothers' Union minute book
Likenesses Elliott & Fry, photograph, pubd 1903, NPG [*see illus.*] · photographs, Hants. RO
Wealth at death £8916 2s. 1d.: probate, 15 Nov 1921, CGPLA Eng. & Wales

Sumner, Robert Carey (1729–1771), schoolmaster, was born and baptized on 9 March 1729 at Windsor, the son of William and Sarah Sumner, and the grandson of a Bristol merchant. John Sumner (*d.* 1772), canon of Windsor and headmaster of Eton College from 1745 to 1754, was his uncle. He was educated at Eton College (1742–7) as a king's scholar and at King's College, Cambridge, where he was admitted a scholar on 18 December 1747. Having been elected a fellow on 28 December 1750 he graduated BA in 1752, and proceeded MA in 1755 and DD in 1768. He became assistant master at Eton in 1751 and master at Harrow in 1760. On 3 August 1760, at Eton, he married Susanna, the sister of his fellow pupil at Eton William Arden (*bap.* 1731, *d.* 1768); they had a son, John, who died young.

During his eleven years as headmaster of Harrow, Sumner raised the school's academic reputation while securing the patronage of an aristocratic and gentry clientele. Trained in the Eton system, he stretched his pupils intellectually—especially his most outstanding pupils, Samuel Parr (1747–1825) and William Jones (1746–1794)—and introduced them to a much wider range of classical authors and texts than was usually taught. He initiated monthly declamations on the Eton model so that the boys could practise the oratorical skills necessary for public life. Though discipline was firmly enforced in the school 'the democratic spirit somewhat prevailed', partly because the pupils were 'so well read under the tuition of their learned … master in Greek history' (Tyerman, 124). Harrow reaped the financial benefits of Sumner's skills as a master, for admissions reached an average of over 200 in the 1760s. Regarded by William Whately as 'the best schoolmaster in England' (ibid., 121), Sumner provided a model for his successors (such as Joseph Drury) and protégés (such as Parr) to emulate. He published only one work, a sermon, *Concio ad clerum* (1768). Always a heavy smoker and drinker, Sumner suffered a sudden stroke and died a few hours later on 12 September 1771, aged forty-two. He was buried in Harrow church.   S. J. SKEDD

Sources Venn, *Alum. Cant.* · R. A. Austen-Leigh, ed., *The Eton College register, 1698–1752* (1927) · C. Tyerman, *A history of Harrow School, 1324–1991* (2000) · *GM*, 1st ser., 30 (1760), 394; 95/1 (1825), 388 · will, PRO, PROB 11/971, sig. 389 · *DNB*

Sumter, Thomas (1734–1832), revolutionary army officer and politician in the United States of America, was born on 14 July or 14 August 1734 in the Preddy's Creek settlement of Hanover county, Virginia, near present-day Charlottesville. Second of four children born to William Sumter, farmer and mill owner, and his wife, Patience, Thomas had an elder brother, William, and two sisters, Patience and Anne. Little is known of William Sumter sen., who was supposedly of Welsh descent; he died early, but his wife lived long and became a famous midwife.

Thirsty for adventure, Thomas Sumter served with the

Thomas Sumter (1734–1832), by Rembrandt Peale, 1796

militia in the French and Indian War (1754–63). A sergeant by 1761, he gained reputation by carrying news of a treaty to the Overhill Cherokees in December and then chaperoning Chief Ostenaca and two other American Indians to London in 1762. He was arrested for debt in Virginia in 1763 but escaped to South Carolina to pursue his fortune. By 1765 he owned land, the next year a store, south of Nelson's Ferry on the Santee river, St John's parish. Sensitive about his humble birth, he married in 1767 the wealthy and disabled widow Mary Cantey Jameson (d. 1817), his elder by eleven years; the marriage lasted half a century and produced two children, Thomas jun., and Mary, who died in infancy.

His wife's lands and the Cantey connections north of the Santee in St Mark's parish, where he now moved, gave Sumter respectability; he was a justice of the peace by the eve of the American War of Independence. Elected a member of the first and second provincial congresses (1775–6), his political and military careers became inextricably mixed. In December 1775 he served as captain of militia and adjutant-general in the 'Snow campaign' against loyalist forces. Then the provincial congress created the 6th South Carolina regiment and named Sumter lieutenant-colonel and commandant, which gained him a role in the defence of Charles Town in June 1776. In the middle of the campaign against the Cherokees he became commander of the 6th South Carolina continentals (20 September 1776). Two days earlier he was elected to the new state's first general assembly and in October to the second (1776–8). Despite his promotion to colonel in 1777, two frustrating military campaigns into Georgia (1777–8)

led Sumter to resign his commission on 19 September 1778. On 30 November he was elected to the South Carolina house of representatives.

When British and German troops captured the army of the Southern Department at Charleston (12 May 1780), Sumter was the best-known military figure to resist the ensuing occupation. Like-minded men along the Catawba and Broad rivers admired this well-built man of modest stature and on 15 June elected him their militia general. John Rutledge, governor without a government, confirmed the commission on 6 October. Sumter and his adherents disrupted the occupation in a remarkable series of battles, among them Rocky Mount (30 July), Hanging Rock (6 August), Fishing Creek (18 August), Fishdam Ford (9 November), and Blackstocks (20 November). The commander of the British Legion, Banastre Tarleton, admired Sumter: 'This active partizan was thoroughly sensible, that the minds of men are influenced by enterprize, and that to keep undisciplined people together, it is necessary to employ them' (Tarleton, 94). Eleven days after Tarleton decimated Sumter's militia at Fishing Creek, Lord Cornwallis wrote: 'the indefatigable Sumpter is again in the field, and is beating up for recruits with the greatest assiduity' (Gregorie, *Sumter*, 103). At Blackstocks Sumter defeated Tarleton but suffered a serious wound that affected him both physically and mentally. If Sumter was not dead, Cornwallis wanted him eliminated: 'he certainly has been our greatest plague in this country' (Bass, 111).

Although the continental congress expressed thanks to Sumter on 13 January 1781, he clashed with its new commander of the Southern army, Nathanael Greene. Viewing militia essentially as auxiliary to regular troops, Greene treated Sumter as a sulker and pillager, not a seriously wounded man. Recruiting became difficult so Sumter instituted by fiat 'Sumter's law' to raise ten-month state regulars and pay them in captured slaves and booty. Avoiding subordination to Greene's army, Sumter eventually lost the respect of many of his own men after a bloody repulse at Shubrick's Plantation (17 July 1781). He then rode away from the war, returned in October, and departed again for a seat in the South Carolina senate in January 1782. His great military accomplishments a year behind him, he resigned his commission shortly thereafter. In 1783 South Carolina voted him its thanks and a gold medal, and in 1784 indemnity against lawsuits for his war actions.

Sumter served in the South Carolina house of representatives (1783–9). He founded the town of Stateburg, boosted it unsuccessfully for state capital, and gradually concentrated his business interests thereabouts. Economic losses probably led to his taking pro-paper money positions in the 1780s and possibly to his vote against ratifying the federal constitution. Nevertheless, he served as member of the US house of representatives (1789–93, 1797–1801) and of the US senate (1801–10) where he consistently voted against centralized government power. Near the end of his life he became an outright advocate of state nullification of federal laws.

An early nominal Baptist, Sumter became an Episcopalian and vestryman about 1788, but reverted to the Baptists after 1811. After his wife Mary's death in 1817 he lived for a time at his Bradford Springs plantation. In 1821 he turned over Home plantation to his son, Tom jun., and moved to South Mount plantation. He went broke attempting to help his son financially, but the legislature in 1827 excused his debt to the state bank during his lifetime. A humane man, Sumter raised two of Tom's illegitimate children as his own. He was generous to a fault and vigorous literally until his death. He pruned fruit trees at South Mount on 1 June 1832, went inside his house, and died. He was buried next to Mary in the Home plantation cemetery near Stateburg.   CLYDE R. FERGUSON

Sources A. K. Gregorie, *Thomas Sumter* (1931) · R. D. Bass, *Gamecock: the life and campaigns of General Thomas Sumter* (1961) · A. K. Gregorie, 'Sumter, Thomas', *DAB* · C. R. Ferguson, 'General Andrew Pickens', PhD diss., Duke U., 1960 · 'Official correspondence between … Sumter and … Greene … 1780 to 1783', *Year Book, City of Charleston, S.C.*, 1899 (1900), 3–135 · W. B. Edgar, N. L. Bailey, and A. Moore, eds., *Biographical directory of the South Carolina house of representatives*, 5 vols. (1974–92) · H. A. M. Smith, *An address delivered … at the unveiling of the monument to General Thomas Sumter … August 14, 1907* (1907) · J. S. Ames, 'Cantey family', *South Carolina Historical and Genealogical Magazine*, 11 (1910), 203–58 · Wisconsin State Historical Society, L. C. Draper collections, Thomas Sumter MSS, series VV [microfilm edn] · M. H. Harris, *History of Louisa County, Virginia* (1936) · B. Tarleton, *A history of the campaigns of 1780 and 1781* (1787) · C. R. Ferguson, 'Carolina and Georgia patriot and loyalist militia in action, 1778–1783', *Southern experience in the American revolution*, ed. J. Crowe and L. Tise (1978), 174–99 · W. Hemphill, W. A. Wates, and R. N. Olsberg, eds., *Journals of the general assembly and house of representatives, 1776–1780, State Records of South Carolina* (1970) · H. M. Ward, 'Sumter, Thomas', *ANB*
Archives L. Cong. · State Historical Society, Madison, Wisconsin | Duke U., Nathanael Greene Collection · L. Cong., Nathanael Greene letter-books · New York Historical Society, Horatio Gates MSS · U. Mich., Clements L., Nathanael Greene MSS
Likenesses R. Peale, oils, 1796, Independence National Historical Park, Philadelphia, Pennsylvania [*see illus.*] · H. Mitchell, oils, repro. in Gregorie, *Thomas Sumter* · C. W. Peale, oils, repro. in Gregorie, *Thomas Sumter* · W. S. Pendleton, lithograph (after portrait by H. Mitchell), repro. in Gregorie, *Thomas Sumter* · oils, Winterthur Museum, Delaware
Wealth at death Sumter was granted an indulgence by South Carolina legislature from the Bank of the State of South Carolina for a $35,000 debt in 1827; one of 'the most notorious of debtors' in this revolutionary generation: Gregorie, *Thomas Sumter*; Gregorie, 'Sumter, Thomas'; Bass, *Gamecock*; Bailey and Cooper, eds., *Biographical directory*

Sunderland. For this title name *see* Scrope, Emanuel, earl of Sunderland (1584–1630); Spencer, Dorothy, countess of Sunderland (1617–1684); Spencer, Henry, first earl of Sunderland (*bap.* 1620, *d.* 1643); Spencer, Robert, second earl of Sunderland (1641–1702); Spencer, Charles, third earl of Sunderland (1674/5–1722).

Sunderland [*née* Sykes], **Susan** (1819–1905), singer, was born on 30 April 1819 at Spring Gardens, Slead Syke, Brighouse, Yorkshire, the daughter of James Sykes (1782–1846), a gardener, and his wife, Hannah (1785–1855). After her marriage to Henry Sunderland (1817–1893), a Brighouse butcher and farmer, on 7 June 1838, she moved to the nearby Spring Terrace (later 24 Waterloo Road), Waring Green, Brighouse, which remained her home for the rest of her life. Notwithstanding her humble social background, her early employment in a textile mill, her lack of a formal musical education, and her domestic responsibilities as a wife and mother of six children, she emerged from the distinctive West Riding tradition of choral music to become an accomplished singer of oratorio and popular songs during the period 1834–64 in both London and the provinces. However, she neither sought nor achieved the international celebrity status of her contemporaries Clara Novello, Jenny Lind, and Thérèse Tietjens, who judged Susan Sunderland's voice to be the finest English voice she had heard.

Susan Sunderland received her earliest musical training from Luke Settle, a Brighouse blacksmith and later choirmaster of Brighouse parish church, who discovered her talents by accident in 1831; John Denham, choirmaster of the Bridge End Independent Chapel, Rastrick; and Daniel Sugden, who was associated with both the Halifax Choral Society and the Halifax Sunday School Jubilee Sings. She made her début at Deighton, an industrial hamlet near Huddersfield, in 1834, became a founder member of the Huddersfield Choral Society in 1836, and sang with the Halifax Choral Society, the Yorkshire Choral Union, and church and chapel choirs in Brighouse, Huddersfield, Rastrick, Southowram. She attracted the attention of royalty, earning the compliments of the prince consort and the duke of Cambridge at her London début at the Antient Concerts at the Hanover Square Rooms in 1842, and of Queen Victoria (who had reputedly been moved by her rendering of the national anthem at the opening of Leeds town hall in September 1858) at private performances at Buckingham Palace. Following a performance with the Sacred Harmonic Society at the Exeter Hall in December 1858, the *Times* critic maintained that, with the exception of Clara Novello, there was no contemporary English singer able to render the soprano music of *Messiah* 'so impressively'.

Invariably simply attired for concert performance in black silk or satin enhanced with a small coral brooch, Sunderland was endowed with an imposing stature and prodigious stamina, frequently walking miles to attend her Yorkshire engagements. Critics admired the flexibility of her voice, her moving interpretation of Handel's 'I know that my redeemer liveth', and her repertory of popular songs, including 'Home, sweet home'. Her appeal evidently transcended social barriers. She sang at the annual soirées of the Brighouse Mechanics' Institute and participated in glee evenings in taverns and public houses in the county of her birth, where she was known affectionately as the Calderdale Nightingale and the Yorkshire Queen of Song, and where tickets for her concerts were evidently raffled in the mills. At her farewell concert in Huddersfield in 1864, crowds unable to gain admission to the Philosophical Hall listened outside open windows in the street below. Large crowds later assembled at Brighouse town hall for her golden wedding celebration in 1888, when she was presented with an illuminated address and inscribed silver casket. Additional subscriptions collected on this occasion funded the establishment of the Mrs Sunderland Music Festival, which has been held annually in Huddersfield since 1889 (except in 1940).

After retiring at the height of her popularity at the age of forty-five, Sunderland taught privately. Widowed in 1893, she died aged eighty-six on 7 May 1905 and was buried on the 10th in Brighouse cemetery, where huge crowds, many of whom would have been too young to have heard her sing, assembled to witness the surviving members of her family (three of her children had predeceased her), local dignitaries, and the musical fraternity of Yorkshire paying their last respects to one of the county's most distinguished vocalists.   JOHN A. HARGREAVES

Sources *Brighouse Echo* (16 May 1905) · *Halifax Guardian* (13 May 1905) · J. A. Hargreaves, 'The Calderdale nightingale: Susan Sunderland, 1819–1905', *Transactions of the Halifax Antiquarian Society*, new ser., 6 (1998), 46–54 · J. H. Turner, *History of Brighouse, Rastrick and Hipperholme* (1893) · D. Russell, *Popular music in Britain, 1840–1941: a social history* (1987) · E. A. H. Haigh, ed., *Huddersfield: a most handsome town* (1992) · M. Kennedy, ed., *The concise Oxford dictionary of music*, 3rd edn (1980) · cuttings file, Halifax Courier Library · *Halifax Choral Society, 150th anniversary souvenir brochure* (1967) · W. Smith, ed., *Old Yorkshire*, new ser., 2 (1890), 235–8 · *Halifax Guardian* (1858–60) · private information (2004) · m. cert. · d. cert.
Likenesses photograph, 1888, repro. in *Brighouse Echo* · photograph, repro. in Turner, *History of Brighouse* · photograph (in later life), repro. in Turner, *History of Brighouse* · photograph, repro. in *Brighouse Echo*

Sunderlin. For this title name *see* Malone, Richard, Baron Sunderlin (1738–1816) [*see under* Malone, Edmund (1704–1774)].

Sundon. For this title name *see* Clayton, Charlotte, Lady Sundon (*c*.1679–1742).

Sundon, Charlotte Clayton. *See* Clayton, Charlotte, Lady Sundon (*c*.1679–1742).

Sunley, Bernard (1910–1964), property developer, was born on 4 November 1910 at 46 Jugela Street, Catford, London, the son of John Sunley and his wife, Emily Martha Gillies. He was educated at St Anne's School, Hanwell, Middlesex. He left school at the age of fourteen to help his father, who worked as a muck shifter with a pony and cart. Described in 1910 as a landscape gardener, by 1931 John Sunley was listed as a retired florist and fruiterer. Sunley himself made a brief move into the landscape gardening business, but earned his first fortune from earth moving, via Blackwood Hodge Ltd, a company of which he was chairman until his death. This firm also acted as agents for a number of motor vehicle-related products. Its clients included General Motors, Cummins Diesel, and Rolls-Royce.

On 18 November 1931 Sunley married Mary (*b*. 1910/11), daughter of William Goddard, a farmer from Southall; they had one son and two daughters. Like several other property developers, Sunley entered the property industry first as a contractor, establishing his building company, Bernard Sunley & Sons Ltd, in 1940. It became a wholly owned subsidiary of Bernard Sunley Investment Trust shortly before the latter company went public. During his thirties Sunley considered leaving business for a career in politics. He stood as Conservative candidate for Ealing West in 1945, but was defeated.

By this time, however, Sunley had already established the property development company which was to form the basis of his post-war fortune. Bernard Sunley Investment Trust Ltd was founded in 1944. Its development projects were to range from office blocks in the City and West End to flats, hotels, and shops in the Bahamas, and Sunley served as its chairman and managing director until his death. The company was publicly floated in 1959, with an issued capital of £1.5 million. In 1960 a further development company, Sunley Homes, was acquired as a subsidiary, to develop residential property.

Bernard Sunley Investment Trust developed close financial links with Eagle Star. In 1961 Eagle Star agreed to finance Bernard Sunley's property development programme by making £12 million available over a five-year period, to be secured by a twenty-year first mortgage debenture stock. At the same time Eagle Star purchased £4 million of Bernard Sunley Investment Trust's shares—one third of the company's equity—from existing shareholders. Eagle Star's chairman, Sir Brian Mountain, and one of its assistant general managers, H. J. A. Harbour, joined the company's board as part of this agreement.

Sunley ranked alongside the most successful property developers of the 1950s property boom; Bernard Sunley Investment Trust had assets of £33 million at the time of his death in 1964. While he is said to have become carried away by success towards the end of his life (Marriott, 38), Sunley remained proud of his working-class origins and was happy to recall his early days working as a muck shifter with his father. Edward Erdman recalled Sunley as 'a rumbustious character. Blunt and with little regard for convention' (Erdman, 120).

Sunley's recreations included golf, swimming, and horse-racing. One of his horses, Slippery Serpent, started as third favourite in the 1959 Grand National, but fell at the thirteenth fence and had to be destroyed. In addition to his property development activities, Sunley also served as a director of the Bank of Nova Scotia Trust Company (Bahamas) Ltd, from 1961, and as a member of the council of the Royal Society of St George. He was also well known for his many gifts to charity, and donated about £500,000 in the year before his death. The beneficiaries included a number of Oxford colleges.

Bernard Sunley suffered from obesity and hypertension and died of a heart attack at his home, 26 Harley Road, Hampstead, on 20 November 1964, at the age of fifty-four. Bernard Sunley Investment Trust was eventually taken over by Eagle Star in 1979, following an earlier bid in 1973 which was thwarted by referral to the Monopolies and Mergers Commission and the 1973–4 property crash. Sunley's personal estate was worth at least £5 million at the time of his death. Although Sunley's will stipulated that no funeral or committal or memorial service be held, a sum of up to £3500 was provided for a banquet to be held at Claridge's Hotel for his employees and business friends.   PETER SCOTT

Sources E. L. Erdman, *People and property* (1982) · *The Times* (23 Nov 1964) · *WWW* · O. Marriott, *The property boom* (1967) · B. P. White-house, *Partners in property* (1964) · 'Report on the proposed merger', *Parl. papers* (1974), 8.343, Cmnd 5641 [monopolies and merger commission; Eagle Star, Bernard Sunley, and Grovewood Securities] · b. cert. · m. cert. · d. cert. · *CGPLA Eng. & Wales* (1965) · will, proved London, 16 Feb 1965
Wealth at death £5,204,764: probate, 16 Feb 1965, *CGPLA Eng. & Wales*

Sunlight, Joseph (1889–1978), architect and property developer, was born in Novogrudock, Belorussia, then part of the Russian empire, on 2 January 1889 NS (20 December 1888 OS), the son of Israel Schimschlavitch, afterwards Sunlight (1864–1945), and his wife, Minnie (*d.* 1941). His father, like many Russian Jews, was anxious to evade conscription into the tsarist army and the family emigrated to Britain in 1890. Israel, who was a cotton merchant, and Joe became naturalized British subjects on 10 July 1900, adopting the surname of Sunlight, no doubt after Port Sunlight in Cheshire, but the family settled in Manchester.

Sunlight's was a classic rags-to-riches life story. For his education it seems that he was sent to London to private school in Kingston upon Thames. Unusually for a first-generation Jewish immigrant, he trained as an architect, in the office of William Purdey of Brazenose Street, Manchester. He began his apprenticeship in 1904 earning 3 s. a week. In 1907, at the age of eighteen, he had set up on his own at 4 St Ann's Square, 'and before he was 21 had designed and built more than 1000 houses in Prestwich' (*Manchester Evening News*, 18 April 1978). He himself boasted that 'By 1921 [he] could account for one million pounds sterling worth of buildings from [his] plans' ('Sunlight House AD 1929', Sunlight papers). Sunlight acted as architect–developer, buying up land, planning, designing, and building whole estates and then selling or letting the properties. He also built factories and warehouses in Cheetham, many of them for Jewish clients, immigrant entrepreneurs like himself. His best-known building in Manchester is Sunlight House, Quay Street, just off Deansgate in the city centre. At fourteen storeys and 135 feet, this art deco steel and concrete building clad in Portland stone was claimed to be the first skyscraper in the north of England when erected in 1932–3 as the headquarters of Sunlight's building empire. The original scheme was scaled down from thirty storeys after being blocked by the city council. After the Second World War (1948–9) he designed a 40-floor extension, intended by Sunlight to be Manchester's answer to New York's Rockefeller Center; but this was never built. A decade later Sunlight House, rented out as offices to the Ministry of Works, had fallen into a dilapidated condition. Sunlight was criticized as a bad landlord and for allegedly overcharging his tenants, and in 1959 the dispute with the ministry led to a court case. Very late in the 1990s the grade II listed landmark was renovated and adapted for reuse as shops and offices. Sunlight became a member of the Institute of Registered Architects on 31 January 1942 but, it seems, never bothered to apply to become an FRIBA.

At the age of twenty-four Sunlight won a limited competition, in which six architects participated, for South Manchester Synagogue, Wilbraham Road, Fallowfield (1913). This was his only known commission for a religious building. The synagogue was built in the style of a Turkish mosque with dome and minaret, in a simplified, almost cubist manner. Sunlight himself claimed to have used 'St Sophia of Constantinople' as his model, with the tower (which in execution had to be scaled down by 20 feet on grounds of economy) derived from Westminster Cathedral. In the estimation of the *British Architect* the whole gave 'a very satisfactory effect of an Eastern place of worship' (20 Feb 1914, 157–8). While exhibiting a mix of stylistic influences, there can be no argument over the fact that the construction of South Manchester Synagogue was innovative. Reinforced concrete was used for the 35 feet span of the dome and for the lattice girders carrying the gallery, thus dispensing with the need for column supports beneath, probably the earliest application of this technology to synagogue architecture in Britain. Always a great publicist, Sunlight made sure that his work was written up in the architectural press.

Sunlight had a brief political career, being elected Liberal MP for Shrewsbury in 1923—some achievement for a Russian-born Jew in a constituency with a staunchly conservative history and where his family origins had been made something of an election issue. In June 1924 he introduced a private member's bill to make all bricks a standard size. The ideal dimensions of a 'Sunlight brick' were 9 inches by 4 ½ inches by 3 ½ inches. He proposed that bricks used in all state-subsidized housing schemes conform to these specifications. The rationale was that the greater thickness would reduce the number of bricks required per unit, thus making building quicker and cheaper—with the unarticulated additional benefit of facilitating Sunlight's own speculative housing schemes. Unfortunately he faced practical opposition from builders and bricklayers as well as ideological objections to the increased state interference in the building trade that the measure represented. The bill passed by a single vote but was lost, along with Sunlight's seat, in 1924. A contemporary newspaper lampooned:

> You will never quicken housing
> By such childish little tricks
> As a Bill for making people
> Manufacture bigger bricks.
> No; what's wanted, Mr Sunlight,
> Is a measure which contains
> Some provision which will give our
> Union leaders *bigger brains*.
> (Sunlight's press cutting book, Sunlight papers, Portico Library, Manchester)

Sunlight's personality, like some of his buildings, was larger than life. He was fond of mythologizing his youth in Russia, where his family faced persecution and he himself on more than one occasion narrowly escaped premature death. He claimed to have survived being run over by a troika on a bridge at the age of two and subsequently being dropped into the river at the same spot. In Manchester his father, Israel, became well known as a committed

Zionist, promoter of Jewish education, and founder of the Holy Law Synagogue. Joe Sunlight professed his 'great love for the Jewish faith' imbued in him by his Hebrew teacher in Russia, 'which I have always retained' (will). Yet his lifestyle, especially after the Second World War, was that of a moneyed English gentleman. In addition to his London address at 14 Victoria Square, Belgravia, he owned a large mansion called Hallside in Chelford Road, Knutsford, Cheshire. His wife, Edith Forshaw (1913–2000), though she identified with her father-in-law's Zionist causes, came from a fairly humble Church of England background; her father was a motor engineer. Edith was nearly half Joe's age and they finally married in a register office in Brighton on 8 May 1940. Their only son, Ben Sunlight, the artist, had been born in Brighton in 1935; he died in 2002.

Sunlight died an eccentric millionaire at his home, Hallside, on 15 April 1978, and was remembered chiefly for Sunlight House and for his love of gambling and horseracing. He left £500 to the minister at Wilbraham Road 'in recognition of his having looked after the South Manchester Synagogue (which I consider as my monument) with such loving care for so many years' (will). He was buried on 17 April in the Jewish section of the southern cemetery, Barlow Moor Road, Manchester.   SHARMAN KADISH

Sources Portico Library, Manchester, Sunlight papers • architectural drawings, Manchester city architects' department • *Hansard* 5C (1924), 174.1949–54 • *British Architect* (20 Feb 1914) • *The Builder* (19 Feb 1926), 314 • *Manchester Evening News* (18 April 1978) • *Manchester Evening News* (18 April 1979) • *Daily Mail* (19 April 1979) • *Jewish Chronicle* (21 April 1978) • *Jewish Chronicle* (27 April 1979) • *Jewish Chronicle* (11 May 1979) • *Jewish Gazette* [Manchester] (14 Nov 1975) • *Jewish Telegraph* [Manchester] (28 Jan 1983) • *Building Design* (27 April 1979) • *Dir. Brit. archs.*, 2nd edn • *WWW*, 1971–80 • J. J. Parkinson-Bailey, *Manchester: an architectural history* (2000), 147 • will • collection of press cuttings on Sunlight House compiled and reprinted for the exhibition 'Ben Sunlight, brilliant Sunlight', May 2002, Portico Library, Manchester
Archives Portico Library, Manchester, papers • RIBA BAL
Likenesses P. W. Smith, oils, 1929?, South Manchester Synagogue • Bernieri?, oils, Portico Library, Manchester
Wealth at death £5,714,422: probate, 5 April 1979, *CGPLA Eng. & Wales*

Sunman, William. *See* Sonmans, William (*d.* 1708).

Surenne, John Thomas (1814–1878), organist and music teacher, born in London on 4 March 1814, was the son of Gabriel Surenne, a Frenchman, who moved to London in 1800, and settled in Edinburgh in 1817 as a teacher of French and professor of military history and antiquities in the Scottish Naval and Military Academy.

In 1831 Surenne, a pupil of Henri Herz, became organist at St Mark's Episcopal Chapel, Portobello, and in 1844 he was appointed organist at St George's Episcopal Chapel, Edinburgh. He became a popular and respected teacher of music and the composer of arrangements for the piano, psalm tunes, chants, and the catch 'Mister Speaker'. In 1851 he compiled *The Dance Music of Scotland*, which reached five editions; in 1852 *The Songs of Scotland*, without words; and in 1854 *The Songs of Ireland*. He was also associated with the music historian George Farquhar Graham in

the publication of the national music of Scotland in a volume entitled *The Scottish Episcopal Church Music Book*, and published a *Students' Manual of Classical Extracts for the Pianoforte*. He died at 2 Clarence Street, Edinburgh, on 3 February 1878. He and his wife, whose identity is unknown, had a family of at least two sons and five daughters.

L. M. MIDDLETON, *rev.* NILANJANA BANERJI

Sources Brown & Stratton, *Brit. mus.* • J. D. Brown, *Biographical dictionary of musicians: with a bibliography of English writings on music* (1886) • D. Baptie, *A handbook of musical biography* (1883) • D. Baptie, ed., *Musical Scotland, past and present: being a dictionary of Scottish musicians from about 1400 till the present time* (1894) • *The Scotsman* (4 Feb 1878) • *CCI* (1878) • private information (1898)
Wealth at death £423 6s. 8d.: inventory, 12 April 1878, *CCI*

Surfleet, William (*d.* 1466). *See under* Cressey, John (*d. c.*1450).

Surr [*née* Grabham], **Elizabeth** (*b.* 1825/6, *d.* in or after 1898), educational reformer, was born in Essex, the daughter of John Grabham, a doctor; little else is known of her early life. On 26 October 1852 she married Joseph Surr, a silk manufacturer and eminent City merchant, and with him had two sons and two daughters (including Jenny, Minnie, and Howard). A grandson was born in America in 1891.

An earnest evangelical churchwoman, Elizabeth entered public life in 1873 when she put herself forward as a candidate for the London school board. Campaigning on the ground that the education of girls required women's guidance and care, she favoured sound secular teaching and unsectarian Bible instruction, and was returned fourth in the poll for Finsbury; she was returned head of the poll in 1879. She gained a high public profile through her membership of the school board's special committee on incorrigible truants, which later became the industrial schools committee. A zealous advocate of the reform of industrial schools she focused the attention of the board on the cruelties practised by the superintendents of the Upton House School on the poor boys detained there, ensuring that they were exposed and stopped. With the support of Florence Fenwick Miller and Helen Taylor she was also largely responsible for exposing the treatment of boys incarcerated at St Paul's Industrial School, owned by Thomas Scrutton, chairman of the industrial schools committee. The allegations of cruelty and mismanagement included the reallocation of food intended for the boys to the governor, his family, and the rest of the staff, the provision of insufficient clothing and footwear (which resulted in severe cases of chilblains), and the use on boys of handcuffs and foot manacles.

The intervention of the home secretary, Sir William Harcourt, forced the board into an inquiry (1881), though the special committee appointed was so heavily biased in favour of Scrutton that Benjamin Lucraft, Henrietta Muller, and Edith Simcox (the last two having been elected to the board in 1879) refused to serve. Unable to escape the censure of public opinion, Scrutton resigned his position as chairman of the industrial schools committee and later his seat on the board. The home secretary decided to close the school down and issue a royal commission on reformatory and industrial schools, while acknowledging Elizabeth's role in a personal letter of thanks. Giving evidence to the commission in April 1883 Elizabeth held firm to the principle that institutional life is generally prejudicial to a child's moral and physical welfare. She supported the use of day industrial schools for all save the children of the profligate (who should be either boarded out, emigrated, or sent to farm schools), while stressing the need for a more efficient inspectorate, an end to the employment of former army personnel, and for the assimilation of institutions of this kind to family life.

Having seen her actions vindicated, Elizabeth decided not to stand for re-election in 1882 on grounds of ill health. Opinions varied as to the nature of her contribution to public life. Some lauded the women as the champions of the outcasts of the metropolis. Others followed Edward Lyulph Stanley in arguing that, as enemies of the board, the women were using the issue to discredit their opponents. Keen to acknowledge her contribution, Henrietta Muller confidently declared:

> Women like Mrs Elizabeth Surr, Mrs Charles of Paddington and Mrs Evans leave their mark on our day. They create a type—the hard-headed and large-hearted woman who has a keen scent for 'a job', who routs out dirty corners, is beloved by the people and detested by the official. (H. M. S., 4)

Elizabeth was known for her sense of humour. Thomas Gautrey recalled the occasion when, looking suspiciously on voluble talkers, she asked that the board-room clock be so placed as to be visible to the majority of members. Belief in the doctrine of effort to alleviate social injustice was central to her public work and informed her view of the agnostic Helen Taylor as the best Christian on the board. Operating in a spirit of friendship and mutual co-operation, it was she who sent a doctor to attend Florence Fenwick Miller following her haemorrhage after childbirth. Much later Helen Taylor provided emotional and financial support when Elizabeth's daughter Minnie was diagnosed as having breast cancer.

At the end of 1883 Elizabeth and her family emigrated to San Diego, California, where straitened financial circumstances told on her appearance as well as on her health. In 1891 she suffered a severe fall and it seems that Helen Taylor continued to help with gifts of money. Her writing may have provided a minimal income, since a fifth biblical tale for children was published in 1896. Of her other books, three were illustrated picture books on animal and bird life (she was a keen ornithologist) and the fourth a moralistic tale for children, *Good out of Evil* (1877). In 1898 her sons lost their ranch and Elizabeth wrote asking for Helen's help in finding a buyer for a painting to provide her with some independent means. The bond of feeling between the two women is evident and remains until the correspondence ends in October 1898; thereafter there is no record of her. JANE MARTIN

Sources *School Board Chronicle* (1876–82) · minutes of proceedings of the School Board for London, 1876–82 · *Englishwoman's Review* (15 Dec 1876) · *Englishwoman's Review* (15 Nov 1879) · correspondence, BLPES, Mill-Taylor MSS, vol. 23 · E. Hill, 'The late Miss Helen Taylor:

an appreciation', *Women and Progress* (8 Feb 1907) [Mill-Taylor special collection box 7] · H. M. S., 'Women as county-councillors', *Women's Penny Paper* (10 Nov 1888), 4 · T. Gautrey, *Lux mihi laus: school board memories* (1937) · 'Royal commission on reformatories and industrial schools', *Parl. papers* (1884), vol. 45, C. 3876 · m. cert. · census returns, 1881

Archives London School of Economics, Mill-Taylor special collection

Likenesses drawing (*A meeting of the London School Board*), repro. in *The Graphic* (8 July 1882)

Surr, Thomas Skinner (*bap.* 1770, *d.* 1847), novelist, baptized on 20 October 1770 at St Botolph, Aldersgate, London, was the son of John Surr, citizen and wheelwright, a grocer by trade, of the parish of St Botolph, and his wife, Elizabeth, sister of Thomas Skinner, lord mayor of London in 1794. Surr was admitted to Christ's Hospital on 18 June 1778, which he later commemorated in 'Christ's Hospital: a Poem' (1797). After his discharge on 7 November 1785 he became a clerk in the Bank of England, where he rose to the position of principal of the drawing office. It was his experience in the bank that led him to write *A Refutation of Certain Misrepresentations Relative to the Nature and Influence of Bank Notes and of the Stoppage of Specie at the Bank of England upon the Price of Provisions* (1801). He married Miss Griffiths, sister-in-law of Sir Richard Phillips (1767–1840).

Surr wrote several novels which contained portraits of well-known persons of his time. Best-known of these was *A Winter in London* (1806), which satirized Georgiana, duchess of Devonshire, in its characterization of the duchess of Belgrave as a well-meaning but ineffectual woman who is constantly being imposed upon by fraudsters. In one episode she is tricked into a bribe to prevent the publication of a libellous memoir and in another she tries to pawn some borrowed jewels, only to be robbed by the servant that she has sent to the jewellers. An inveterate gambler, the character was a gross distortion of the duchess of Devonshire, but it hit close to home in some respects. She consequently 'dreadfully hurt at the novel' (Foreman, 356), although the *Dictionary of National Biography*'s contention that it hastened her death is unsubstantiated. The work went through numerous editions and was translated into French by Madame de Terrasson de Sennevas. Surr also wrote *The Magic of Wealth* (1815) and *Richmond, or, Scenes in the Life of a Bow Street Officer* (1827). Several of his novels were translated into French and German. The allegation that Lord Lytton was indebted to Surr for the materials for his novel *Pelham* remains unproven. He died at Hammersmith on 15 February 1847.

E. I. CARLYLE, *rev.* M. CLARE LOUGHLIN-CHOW

Sources private information (1898) · *GM*, 2nd ser., 27 (1847), 448 · [J. Watkins and F. Shoberl], *A biographical dictionary of the living authors of Great Britain and Ireland* (1816) · *N&Q*, 5th ser., 7 (1877), 48, 174, 255, 339 · A. Foreman, *Georgiana, duchess of Devonshire* (1998) · IGI

Surrey. For this title name *see* Warenne, William (I) de, first earl of Surrey (*d.* 1088); Warenne, William (II) de, second earl of Surrey (*d.* 1138); Warenne, William (III) de, third earl of Surrey (*c.*1119–1148); William, earl of Surrey (*c.*1135–

1159); Warenne, Hamelin de, earl of Surrey (*d.* 1202); Warenne, Isabel de, *suo jure* countess of Surrey (*d.* 1203); Warenne, William (IV) de, fifth earl of Surrey (*d.* 1240); Warenne, John de, sixth earl of Surrey (1231–1304); Warenne, John de, seventh earl of Surrey (1286–1347); Fitzalan, Richard (II), third earl of Arundel and eighth earl of Surrey (*c.*1313–1376); Fitzalan, Richard (III), fourth earl of Arundel and ninth earl of Surrey (1346–1397); Holland, Thomas, sixth earl of Kent and duke of Surrey (*c.*1374–1400); Fitzalan, Thomas, fifth earl of Arundel and tenth earl of Surrey (1381–1415); Howard, Henry, styled earl of Surrey (1516/17–1547); Howard, Thomas, fourteenth earl of Arundel, fourth earl of Surrey, and first earl of Norfolk (1585–1646); Howard, Henry Frederick, fifteenth earl of Arundel, fifth earl of Surrey, and second earl of Norfolk (1608–1652).

Surrey and Sussex. For this title name *see* Warenne, John de, sixth earl of Surrey [earl of Surrey and Sussex] (1231–1304); Warenne, John de, seventh earl of Surrey [earl of Surrey and Sussex] (1286–1347).

Surridge, (Walter) Stuart (1917–1992), cricketer and manufacturer of sporting equipment, was born on 3 September 1917 at 29 Milton Road, Herne Hill, London, within 2 miles of the Oval, the second child in the family of two sons and one daughter of Percival Surridge (*d.* 1951), timber merchant and batmaker, and his wife, Edith Alice, *née* Clarkson, daughter of Frederick Clarkson, who ran a sand, ballast, and refuse-collecting business. With a father so closely connected with cricket, Surridge was given every encouragement to play the game himself, although by no means was he a natural exponent. Educated at Emmanuel School, Wandsworth, he became captain of the first cricket eleven there more through the robustness of his personality than outstanding success on the field of play. Being well over 6 feet tall and heavy-footed, he relied more on strength and ambition than refinement to become the cricketer he did.

Surridge was taken in hand first by Alan Peach, the Surrey coach, and then by A. R. Gover, Surrey's foremost fast bowler in the 1930s. They turned him into a useful outswing bowler, short of the top pace but confident, bustling, and not to be underrated. He was, to boot, a lusty hitter of the ball and a fearless and rapacious close fielder. Surridge had two seasons playing for Surrey's second eleven in his early twenties, but, with the Second World War intervening, he was past thirty by the time he won a place in their championship team. He spent the war on the land, farming being, in certain circumstances, a reserved occupation, and there being family land in Essex and Berkshire. For many years the farm in Essex was a main source of cricket bat willows. That Surridge did not join the forces was to be offered years later as a reason for his not being asked to captain the Gentlemen against the Players at Lord's, when it was still one of the great matches of the English season, though this was no more than conjecture. On 3 April 1943 he married Betty Patricia

(*b.* 1921/2), daughter of Alfred Spicer, fruiterer, of Upminster, Essex. There was one son of the marriage, also called Stuart.

The war over, Surridge joined his brother, Percy, in the family firm, an arrangement which enabled him to play as much cricket as he liked (this being good for business) and to take on, in 1952, the Surrey captaincy, the position from which he made his name. For two or three years Surrey had had the individual talent to do well but had wanted for firm leadership. It was, in fact, thirty-eight years since they had won the county championship outright, something they were to do in each of Surridge's five years in charge.

Surridge's style of captaincy was uncompromising, not to say aggressive, and his relationship with his players occasionally, sometimes audibly, confrontational, but never damagingly so. In P. B. H. (Peter) May he had in his side the best batsman in England, and on the Oval pitches of the 1950s Surrey's bowling attack, when at full strength, was the equal of any in the world. The so-called featherbed pitches of the 1930s, heavily tilted in the batsman's favour, had been replaced by something altogether rougher, on which A. V. (Alec) Bedser, J. C. Laker, P. J. Loader, and G. A. R. Lock, with Surridge himself and Bedser's twin E. A. (Eric) in support, brooked little opposition. In May 1956 Surrey became the first county side for forty-four years to beat an Australian touring team: indeed, they overwhelmed them, winning by ten wickets, in recognition of which the Australian captain, I. W. Johnson, presented Surridge, his opposite number, with his Australian cap.

'Attack all the time, whether batting, bowling, or fielding' was Surridge's doctrine. Although a lumbering giant, fielding at slip or at silly-point or in the leg trap, he held 58 catches in 1952 and 56 in 1955, totals that have seldom been surpassed—he had large hands and stood domineeringly close to the bat. Upon his retirement at the end of the 1956 season he had taken 506 wickets in first-class cricket at 28.89 runs apiece, scored 3882 runs at an average of 12.94, with a top score of 87, and held 375 catches.

Surridge was still working in the family business when he died suddenly, of a heart attack, at Tameside General Hospital, Ashton under Lyne, on 13 April 1992, thirty-six years after his retirement from the Surrey team. He had been on a visit to one of his company's factories in Glossop, Derbyshire, which made sports clothing. He had maintained close links with Surrey, becoming their president in 1982; and through keenness, perseverance, and opportunity he became a very good game shot. His son, Stuart, who also played for Surrey, carried on the family business. A memorial service was held at Southwark Cathedral on 16 June 1992.   JOHN WOODCOCK

Sources *The Times* (15 April 1992) · *The Independent* (18 April 1992) · personal knowledge (2004) · private information (2004) · b. cert. · m. cert. · d. cert.
Likenesses two photographs, 1952, Hult. Arch. · photograph, repro. in *The Times* · photograph, repro. in *The Independent*

Surtees, Robert (1779–1834), historian, was born in the South Bailey, Durham, on 1 April 1779, the only surviving child of Robert Surtees (d. 1802) of Mainsforth, near Bishop Middleham, co. Durham, and his wife and first cousin, Dorothy (d. 1797), the daughter and coheir of William Steele of Lamb Abbey, Kent, an East India Company director. He was educated from 1786 at Kepier grammar school, Houghton-le-Spring, under the Revd William Fleming, and later (1793) at Neasden, Middlesex, under Dr Bristow. He matriculated from Christ Church, Oxford, on 28 October 1796, and graduated BA in November 1800 and MA in 1803. At Oxford he was studious enough to be known as Greek Surtees and numbered among his college friends Arthur Hallam, Reginald Heber (a fellow pupil at Neasden), and Charles Kirkpatrick Sharpe. In 1800 he became a student of the Middle Temple, under a conveyancer with a north-country practice, but was not called to the bar. Surtees's father died in July 1802, and at the age of twenty-three the younger Robert inherited Mainsforth, where he was a conscientious squire and an improving landowner.

Surtees's antiquarian interests developed early, especially in numismatics and in the study of regional folklore. As an undergraduate he resolved to write the history of Durham, which he had the means and leisure, and scholarly training, to investigate thoroughly. He aimed at not only comprehensive documentary research but also the investigation of monuments and local topographical detail. He was assisted by the willingness of the dean and chapter of Durham to allow him access to their library and collections, and to their muniments, and the local nobility and gentry allowed comparable privileges to a fellow landowner. Poor health impeded his researches and his history was composed intermittently, but (having been first advertised on 14 April 1812) its first volume appeared in 1816, the second in 1820, the third in 1823, and the fourth posthumously (edited and much augmented by James Raine) as late as 1840. The work was well subscribed in the county but was an expensive enterprise for its author. Although other county histories were beginning to include geological and archaeological information, Surtees maintained the old genealogical tradition, and his pedigrees are well presented and generally reliable. In a county whose Victoria History is regrettably uncompleted, Surtees's History (which was reprinted in 1972) remains an essential resource at the end of the twentieth century. Surtees showed a partiality for historically evocative scenery and a creditable scepticism for the traditions of a vigorous local folklore, for which he sought documentary verifications wherever possible. Industrious and exact, the History is nevertheless enlivened by many light literary touches. Robert Southey, reviewing the work in the Quarterly Review, drew attention to this unexpected humorous trait, 'every now and then breaking out like a gleam of sunshine ... and exciting the reader to a smile when least expecting to be surprised' (Quarterly Review, 39, 1829, 361).

A shared taste for balladry and northern history put Surtees in touch with Walter Scott, with whom he corresponded frequently from 1806 onwards. Surtees's playful vein led him to send Scott a ballad of his own devising, 'The Death of Featherstonehaugh', accompanied by plausible annotations. It found its way into the notes on the first canto of Marmion, and Scott did not detect the imposture of this 'curious old ballad', which was also given a place in The Minstrelsy of the Scottish Border. The Scott–Surtees correspondence shows them deeply engaged in border lore and regional and Jacobite genealogy. They met for the first time at Mainsforth in March 1809. Correspondence between them in December 1810 and January 1811, on Jacobite verses, may have helped to steer Scott's thoughts in the direction of Waverley.

In March 1810 Scott, in a letter to Southey, described Surtees as 'an excellent antiquary, some of the rust of which study has clung to his manners', but good-hearted and excellent company (Letters, 2.342). Surtees was broadly built and grizzled, plainly dressed in drab gaiters, but, despite his solid appearance, humour was never far away. He was devoted to Mainsforth (which was demolished in 1962), and filled the house with books, charters, and transcripts, all in some disarray. He was generous in entertaining fellow antiquaries and in allowing them access to his collections. On 23 June 1807 he married Anne (d. 1868), the daughter of Ralph Robinson of Middle Herrington, co. Durham; they had no children.

Surtees died at Mainsforth on 11 February 1834, and was buried on the 15th in the churchyard of Bishop Middleham; a marble tablet designed by his friend the architect Edward Blore is in the church.

To meet the exigencies of succession Surtees's books and pictures were sold by Walker, a Durham auctioneer, at Mainsforth in December 1836 and January 1837. His manuscript collections, threatened with dispersal, were largely saved and a substantial group of sixty volumes survives in the dean and chapter library of Durham Cathedral. His coins were sold in London by Sothebys for more than £600. On 27 May 1834 Surtees's friends, led by the Revd James Raine, met in Durham and founded in his memory the Surtees Society, which still flourishes, for publishing documentary sources for the history of Northumbria.

ALAN BELL

Sources G. Taylor, *A brief memoir of Robert Surtees*, ed. J. Raine, new edn, SurtS, 24 (1852) · E. Birley, introduction, in R. Surtees, *The history and antiquities of the county palatine of Durham* (1972) · C. Sharp, 'Biographical notice', *Reprints of rare tracts and imprints of antient manuscripts ... printed at the press of M. A. Richardson*, 7 vols. (1843–9) · *The letters of Sir Walter Scott*, ed. H. J. C. Grierson and others, centenary edn, 12 vols. (1932–79)
Archives Borth. Inst. · Borth. Inst., notes for his history of Durham · Durham Cath. CL, antiquarian corresp., etc. · Durham RO, weather diary · Lambton Park, Chester-le-street, Durham, genealogical notes · NL Scot., corresp. · Northumbd RO, Newcastle upon Tyne, corresp. · U. Durham, guardbook of poems, ballads, corresp., and papers | Bodl. Oxf., pedigree of family of Anthony Wood · NL Scot., corresp. with Walter Scott · W. Yorks. AS, Leeds, Yorkshire Archaeological Society, letters to William Radcliffe
Likenesses silhouette, repro. in Taylor, *Memoir*

Surtees, Robert Smith (1805–1864), author, was born on 17 May 1805 at The Riding, Northumberland, the second son in the family of nine children (two of whom died young) of Anthony Surtees JP and his wife, Alice, sister of Christopher Blackett MP of Wylam. He was baptized at

Robert Smith Surtees (1805–1864), by unknown artist

Bywell St Andrew, Northumberland, on 29 August 1806 and grew up at Hamsterley Hall, co. Durham, which his father purchased about this date. For some years he was a boarder in a private school at Ovingham, Northumberland, and in 1818–19 he briefly attended Durham grammar school. In 1822 he was articled to R. A. Purvis, a solicitor in Newcastle upon Tyne. In May 1825 he was further articled to William Bell of Bow Churchyard in London, where he lived for a time at 27 Lincoln's Inn Fields. He was admitted to chancery in 1828 but it is doubtful whether he ever practised, and in 1835 he removed his name from the law list.

Surtees's social status was materially altered by the death in 1831 of his unmarried elder brother, Anthony. In 1836 he was invited to stand as Conservative candidate for Gateshead, where there was a split in the dominant Liberal Party, but, anticipating defeat in the general election of 1837, he withdrew before the poll. When his father died in March 1838 he inherited the Hamsterley estate and three years later, on 19 May 1841, at Bishopwearmouth, he married Elizabeth Jane, coheir of Addison Fenwick of Field House, co. Durham. They had three children: a son, Anthony (b. 1847), and two girls, Elizabeth Anne and Eleanor. In 1842 Surtees was appointed JP and deputy lieutenant for the county and for two years he held a commission in the Durham militia. In 1844 he joined the Northumberland Society for the Protection of Agriculture but after the repeal of the corn laws in 1846 he withdrew from his local Conservative association and declared his general support for Lord John Russell's whig-Liberal ministry. He declined

an invitation to become a parliamentary candidate in the interests of Lord Derby's government in 1852, even though he would not have been personally pledged to its protectionist principles. He was an active landowner, farming 250 acres and managing 700 acres of woodland; an agricultural reformer; and a conscientious magistrate and poor-law guardian. He served as high sheriff for co. Durham in 1856 and as deputy sheriff in 1859 and 1863.

Surtees's career as author, which he never publicly acknowledged (though he took little trouble to conceal it), began in his early days in London. In the 1820s he started and then destroyed a 'semi-sporting novel' but his first completed work was a largely legal treatise, *The Horseman's Manual* (1831), the only title which ever came out under his name. He was already contributing to the *Sporting Magazine* by this time and in 1830, when C. J. Apperley (Nimrod) withdrew from his position as hunting correspondent, Surtees was engaged as his successor, writing under the pseudonyms of Nim South and a Durham Sportsman. In 1831, after he had been refused a share in the management of the magazine, he started the *New Sporting Magazine* in association with his friend the art publisher Rudolph Ackermann, and took for himself the positions of editor and hunting correspondent.

In 1838 Surtees published in book form a collection of his magazine articles featuring Mr Jorrocks, the 'jolly, free-and-easy, fox-hunting grocer' (to use Surtees's own description), under the title of *Jorrocks's Jaunts and Jollities*. A longer, more rounded Jorrocks novel, *Handley Cross*, appeared in 1843 and another, *Hillingdon Hall*, in 1845. Then came two insipid productions, *The Analysis of the Hunting Field* (1846) and *Hawbuck Grange* (1847), both revolving around fox-hunting but lacking plot or strong characterization. His first moderate success came with *Mr Sponge's Sporting Tour* (1853). This was followed by two novels of a different type, *Ask Mamma* (1858) and *Plain or Ringlets?* (1860), in which the sporting interest is only part of a broader picture of provincial society. Although these contain interesting social detail and some memorable characters, they too suffer from having no strong central figure to hold the plot together. His last book, published posthumously in 1865, was *Mr Facey Romford's Hounds*, which Surtees himself regarded as a good sequel to *Mr Sponge* and which some critics consider his best novel.

Most of Surtees's novels were serialized in the *New Sporting Magazine*, *Bell's Life in London*, or the *New Monthly Magazine*, and were sometimes substantially revised and enlarged before appearing in book form. His last three, published by Bradbury and Evans, first came out in monthly parts. An unfinished and abandoned serialized novel, *Young Tom Hall*, fragmentary notes for a book of sporting and social recollections, and selections from his miscellaneous journalistic work, were published by E. D. Cuming between 1924 and 1929. A bibliography of his writings is in Frederick Watson's *Robert Smith Surtees* (new edn, 1991), published by the R. S. Surtees Society.

Surtees was a tall, lean man, over 6 feet, thin-featured and with high cheekbones and a cleft chin. Although he hunted all his life, he was not a good horseman. His interest was in the scientific skills of hunting, not in the fashionable hell-for-leather galloping across country, which he despised. Reticent and proud, he was quick to resent slights and persistent in his animosities, as he showed in his feud with Nimrod in the 1830s. 'I never push myself an inch forward,' he once remarked, 'but I damned well see that I'm never pushed an inch back.' He died of a heart attack in a hotel at 80 King's Road, Brighton, on the night of 16 March 1864 and was buried in Ebchester churchyard, co. Durham.

No notice of Surtees's death appeared in either the national or local newspapers, a reflection of his failure to secure public recognition as a serious or even respectable author. His books ran counter to the currents of his age in their lack of idealism, absence of sentimentality, and almost wilful flouting of conventional moralism. His leading male characters were coarse or shady; his leading ladies dashing and far from virtuous; his outlook on society satiric to the point of cynicism. One Victorian theory was that such readership as he enjoyed was due to the humour of John Leech's illustrations, a view perpetuated in the *Dictionary of National Biography*. Yet, paradoxically, the qualities that in his own time prevented an appreciation of his talents as a writer, preserved his books in a later age from the oblivion which befell many of his more famous contemporaries.

Surtees's range was limited, his style often clumsy and colloquial. Even in the better-constructed novels the plots are loose and discursive. Nevertheless, his sharp, authentic descriptions of the hunting field have retained their popularity among fox-hunters, for whom the sanitized (and in their day immeasurably better-selling) hunting novels of George Whyte-Melville have long lost their appeal. Among a wider public his mordant observations on men, women, and manners; his entertaining array of eccentrics, rakes, and rogues; his skill in the construction of lively dialogue (a matter over which he took great pains); his happy genius for unforgettable and quotable phrases; and above all, his supreme comic masterpiece, Jorrocks, have won him successive generations of devoted followers. Although his proper place among Victorian novelists is not easy to determine, his power as a creative artist was recognized, among professional writers, by Thackeray, Kipling, Arnold Bennett, and Siegfried Sassoon, and earned the tributes of laymen as distinguished and diverse as William Morris, Lord Rosebery, and Theodore Roosevelt.   NORMAN GASH

Sources *Robert Smith Surtees (creator of "Jorrocks") 1803–1864. By himself and E. D. Cuming* (1924) · F. Watson, *Robert Smith Surtees*, new edn (1991) · J. Welcome, *The sporting world of R. S. Surtees* (1982) · N. Gash, *Robert Surtees and early Victorian society* (1993) · L. Cooper, *R. S. Surtees* (1952) · A. Noakes, *Horses, hounds, and humans: R. S. Surtees* (1957) · R. S. Surtees, *Town and country papers*, ed. E. D. Cuming (1929) · A. Steel, *Jorrocks's England* (1932) · Nimrod [C. J. Apperley], *My life and times*, ed. E. D. Cuming (1927) · m. cert. · Burke, *Gen. GB* · d. cert.
Archives BL, notebooks, RP4379 [copies] · priv. coll., personal papers | Bodl. Oxf., letters to F. M. Evans
Likenesses G. Ross, portrait, *c*.1845, repro. in Watson, *Robert Smith Surtees* · G. D. Armour, portrait (*Surtees in old age*), repro. in Welcome, *Sporting world of R. S. Surtees* · photograph, repro. in Watson, *Robert Smith Surtees* · photograph, repro. in Noakes, *Horses, hounds and humans* · portrait, repro. in Watson, *Robert Smith Surtees*; formerly at Hamsterley Hall · portrait, repro. in Welcome, *Sporting world of R. S. Surtees*, facing p. 54 [*see illus.*]
Wealth at death under £3000: probate, 11 Oct 1864, *CGPLA Eng. & Wales*

Suschitzky, Edith. See Hart, Edith Tudor (1908–1973).

Sussex. For this title name *see* Radcliffe, Robert, first earl of Sussex (1482/3–1542); Radcliffe, Henry, second earl of Sussex (*c*.1507–1557) [*see under* Radcliffe, Robert, first earl of Sussex (1482/3–1542)]; Radcliffe, Thomas, third earl of Sussex (1526/7–1583); Radcliffe, Frances, countess of Sussex (1531?–1589); Radcliffe, Henry, fourth earl of Sussex (1533–1593); Radcliffe, Robert, fifth earl of Sussex (1573–1629); Radcliffe, Anne, countess of Sussex (*d*. 1579×82) [*see under* Radcliffe, Robert, first earl of Sussex (1482/3–1542)]; Savile, Thomas, first earl of Sussex (*bap*. 1590, *d*. 1657×9); Augustus Frederick, Prince, duke of Sussex (1773–1843).

Sutch, David Edward [*known as* Screaming Lord Sutch] **(1940–1999)**, rock singer and politician, was born on 10 November 1940 at New End Hospital, Hampstead, London, the son of William Joseph Sutch (*d*. 1941), police constable, and his wife, Annie Emily, *née* Smith (*d*. 1997). His father was killed in the blitz when Sutch was only ten months old and he was brought up single-handedly, in post-war poverty, by his mother, to whom he remained devoted until her death. Circumstances improved when they moved to Harrow, where Sutch took up window-cleaning before getting his break as one of the original 'long hairs' in the first days of rock and roll. By his own admission he could not sing or even read music, but he was a good 'shouter'. And although he never had any real hits on record, he was a born showman, who shrewdly put together an outrageous Gothic extravaganza based on his new persona, Screaming Lord Sutch, and his backing band, the Savages. Starting with his stepping out of a coffin and including setting his hair alight, the show had audiences all over the country screaming in horror, especially when Sutch threw live worms among them. Although the show gradually became more and more threadbare, he never varied it in thirty years.

Nevertheless it was as a politician—albeit an unlikely one—that Sutch really made his mark. He first stood for parliament for the National Teenage Party in 1963, campaigning for the voting age to be lowered to eighteen from twenty-one, and then against the prime minister, Harold Wilson, in 1966. After forming the Sod 'Em All and then the Go to Blazes parties he departed at the end of the 1970s to America, where he had a son, Tristan Lord Gwynne, with the American model Thann Rendessy. The relationship did not last and in 1983, back in Britain, his political career settled down when he formed the Monster Raving Loony Party (MRLP). His maniacal grin and trademark top hat and leopardskin jacket soon became standard fixtures at by-elections and in all he stood for parliament forty-one times.

Although he had originally entered politics partly to

David Edward Sutch (1940–1999), by unknown photographer, 1984

gain publicity, Sutch was a deeply moral person with a contempt for all politicians, whom he saw as motivated purely by self-interest. He really believed that, as an 'outsider', he represented those people, particularly at the bottom end of the social spectrum and among the young, who were so disillusioned by the process that they did not even bother to vote. To prick political pomposity he therefore put together an anarchical agenda of 'loonyism', based on the absurd slogan 'Vote for insanity, you know it makes sense'. Ever the patriot, he was to claim in a letter to *The Times* that this 'represented the true spirit of the British people'. Most MRLP policies were simply jokes made up as he went along, like demanding to know why there was only one Monopolies Commission, or proposing heated toilet seats for old-age pensioners. But Sutch always claimed proudly that he had been ahead in calling for commercial radio, a lowering of the voting age, pubs to be open all day, and passports for pets—all of which later came about.

The MRLP's political peaks came in the general elections of 1983 and 1987, when Sutch put together a 'rainbow alliance' of fringe candidates, but to his eternal regret it never fielded enough candidates to qualify for the party-political broadcast on television it so dearly craved. Even Sutch himself never came close to saving his deposit, although more than once he personally polled over 700 votes, and on several occasions succeeded at garnering more votes than one or other of the major parties. Only a few days after Sutch's party, in the Bootle by-election of May 1990, gained 418 votes to the Owenite Social Democrat candidate's 155 David Owen announced that the Social Democratic Party was being wound up. Yet, from first being regarded as a nuisance, Sutch gradually became the subject of increasing affection, from both the public and politicians, as a true British eccentric. This was reflected in his chaotic private life, where he was notorious for his forgetfulness and unpunctuality and never happier than when poking round street markets, beating the traders at their own banter while accumulating the bags of junk with which he gradually filled his house. Yet underneath the zany, madcap exterior there always lay a darker side, which manifested itself in deep periods of depression. This finally overcame him after his mother

had died, when, about to sell her house and embark on a new life with his recent fiancée, Yvonne Elwood, he found himself unable to make the break and instead hanged himself. He was found dead at his home, 10 Parkfield Road, South Harrow, Middlesex, on 16 June 1999; an inquest held on 31 August 1999 returned a verdict of suicide. He was buried at Harrow cemetery.

PETER CHIPPINDALE

Sources P. Chippindale, '*Life as Sutch*' (1991) • *The Times* (19 June 1999) • *The Guardian* (19 June 1999) • personal knowledge (2004) • private information (2004) • b. cert. • d. cert.
Likenesses photographs, *c*.1965–1992, Hult. Arch. [*see illus.*] • photograph, repro. in *The Times* • photograph, repro. in *The Guardian* • photographs, repro. in Chippindale, '*Life as Sutch*'
Wealth at death £402,899—gross; £399,405—net: probate, 21 March 2000, *CGPLA Eng. & Wales*

Sutcliff, John (1752–1814), Particular Baptist minister, was born on 9 August 1752 on a farm called Strait Hey, 2 miles east of Todmorden, West Riding of Yorkshire, the son of Daniel Sutcliff (*d.* 1794), farmer, and his wife, Hannah (*fl.* 1735–1773), who were ardent Baptists. In May 1769 Sutcliff was baptized as a professing Christian by John Fawcett, minister of Wainsgate Particular Baptist Church, West Riding of Yorkshire. For the next two years Fawcett acted as Sutcliff's academic tutor and spiritual mentor. A hunger for further academic study led to Sutcliff's going to Bristol Baptist Academy in January 1772. Under the tutelage of Hugh Evans, the principal of the academy, and his son Caleb, Sutcliff had an outstanding academic record. He left Bristol in May 1774. After brief preaching stints in Shrewsbury and Birmingham, in July 1775 he entered upon what would be his life's ministry, at the Particular Baptist church in Olney, Buckinghamshire.

Early on at Olney Sutcliff made the friendship of two other Particular Baptists, John Ryland and Andrew Fuller. These friendships would be an important factor in the revitalization of the Particular Baptist cause in late eighteenth-century England. It was also during the early days of his ministry at Olney that Sutcliff began to study in earnest the writings of the New England theologian Jonathan Edwards. In 1784, influenced by a treatise of Edwards on corporate prayer for spiritual revival, Sutcliff proposed to the Northamptonshire Association of Baptist Churches, of which the Olney church was a part, that monthly prayer meetings for revival be established. Some historians regard the subsequent renewal of the British Particular Baptist community as linked in part to these regular gatherings for prayer, which continued for the next forty years or so.

In 1792 Sutcliff helped found the Particular Baptist Missionary Society, which sent its first missionary, William Carey, out to Bengal, India, the following year. In 1796 Sutcliff married a member of his congregation, Jane Johnston (*d.* 1814), about whom very little is known. The late 1790s also saw Sutcliff initiate a parsonage seminary for prospective pastors and candidates of the missionary society. He acquired the house next to his, and between 1798 and 1814 trained upwards of thirty-two men.

Though well read in theological literature—his friend

Andrew Fuller once reckoned that he had 'one of the best libraries in this part of the country' ('Principles and prospects', 354)—Sutcliff published very little. Only one sermon, *Jealousy for the Lord of Hosts Illustrated* (1791), is extant, along with a catechism (1783) and a few circular letters published by the Northamptonshire Association. During his ministry at Olney the membership of the church nearly doubled. In the early years of his ministry it never exceeded sixty-one members; by the time of his death it stood at 100.

Sutcliff died on 22 June 1814, at 21 High Street, Olney, from heart failure. He was buried in the Particular Baptist church cemetery at Olney on 28 June; his funeral sermon, *Principles and Prospects of a Servant of Christ* (1814), which contains the earliest biographical sketch of his life and ministry, was preached by Andrew Fuller. His wife survived her husband by only a few weeks, and died on 3 September. MICHAEL A. G. HAYKIN

Sources 'Principles and prospects of a servant of Christ', *The complete works of the Rev. Andrew Fuller*, ed. A. G. Fuller, 1 (1845), 342–56 · M. A. G. Haykin, *One heart and one soul: John Sutcliff of Olney, his friends and his times* (1994)

Archives Regent's Park College, Oxford, papers | Bristol Baptist College, MSS · NL Wales, Isaac Mann collection · Rochester, New York, American Baptist Historical Society archives

Likenesses group portrait (Baptist ministers), repro. in *The Transactions of the Baptist Historical Society*, 1 (1908–9) · silhouette, repro. in *Baptist Magazine*, 7 (1815), 44

Wealth at death library sold for £100: Fuller, 'Principles and prospects'

Sutcliff, Rosemary (1920–1992), writer, was born on 14 December 1920 at West Clandon, Guildford, Surrey, the only surviving child of Lieutenant-Commander George Ernest Sutcliff RN and his wife, Nessie Elisabeth, *née* Lawton. (There had been an older daughter who died in infancy.) Before she was three she had contracted Still's disease, a form of juvenile arthritis, which was to cripple her for life and led to her spending much of her childhood in hospitals and to necessarily fitful schooling. Her early years were spent in the environs of naval dockyards—Malta, Sheerness, Chatham. But in 1931 her father retired from the navy (to rejoin it again at the outbreak of the Second World War) and the family went to live in Yarnscombe, north Devon, where they were to stay until the death of her mother, when she and her father moved to Walberton, near Arundel, Sussex. Childhood and adolescence were very lonely, and her dominating and possessive mother was her main companion. Such general education as she received finished when she was fourteen, after which she did a three-year course at Bideford Art School.

Most of Sutcliff's intellectual stimulus had come from books read aloud by her mother, so that she was to say in her monograph on Kipling (1960), 'I was able to enjoy books far in advance of those I could have coped with myself' (p. 32). It seems to have been Kipling who made the deepest impression. Remembering 'The King's Ankus' in *The Second Jungle Book*, a story of a vanished, once-proud city, she wrote that it 'battered me and tore at my heart strings with the tremendous sorrows of tragic saga' (p. 34).

Rosemary Sutcliff (1920–1992), by Harry Kerr, 1983

It was a theme that lay at the heart of many of her own books, and she also followed Kipling in his attention to atmospheric detail, of which she said that he 'could never visualize any incident without its attendant light and weather, season of the year and time of day' (p. 36). Phrases from the two Jungle books were to creep into unlikely places in her fiction. Bronze Age tribesmen and Roman soldiers wish each other 'good hunting', and speak of their juniors as 'cubs' or, more tenderly, 'cublings'.

After leaving art school Sutcliff was advised by her elders to take up miniature painting. Technically she was good; she exhibited at the Royal Academy and became a member of the Royal Society of Miniature Painters. But the medium cramped her and, needing a larger canvas, she secretly began to write. An early effort was called *Wild Sunrise*, a saga of the Roman invasion of Britain told from the British viewpoint. Its hero was called Cradoc, a name she was later to use in *The Eagle of the Ninth* and in *Sun Horse, Moon Horse*. (Her father's naval hero had been Admiral Sir Christopher Cradock, who went down with his flagship at the battle of Coronel in 1914.) *Wild Sunrise* disappeared, which was as well, she said in her memoir *Blue Remembered Hills* (1983), 'because so much of me was in it, naked and defenceless' (Sutcliff, 119). She was to return to Roman Britain often again in the books that made her name. She wrote a handful of novels about later periods, but was always most at ease with distant epochs where there were few historical records.

Sutcliff's first book, a retelling of Robin Hood legends, was published by Oxford University Press in 1950, the same year as *The Queen Elizabeth Story*, which, as she said herself, was 'too cosy and too sweet, as were the next two or three books to follow it' (Sutcliff, 140). *The Eagle of the Ninth* (1954) was an extraordinary step forward. It describes how a young Roman centurion serving in Britain, invalided out of the army, sets off north to try to recover the eagle standard lost when his father's legion had marched into the mists of Caledonia and had disappeared. He brings back the mutilated eagle, but the legion has been disgraced and dispersed and can never be revived. Though written for children, as was nearly all her fiction, Sutcliff did not shrink here from savage scenes of brutality, and these were to be an even more marked feature of later books. Her next book, *Outcast* (1955), saw the Roman empire from the viewpoint of an underdog, the galley slave who, eventually maddened by ill treatment, hurls himself at his tormentor 'with a black berserk fury that saw in him … the proud and heedless Legate on the poop, the men who had turned down their thumbs for a gladiator at the Colosseum, the whole pitiless might of Rome' (p. 145).

In this phase of Sutcliff's writing there were to be two more books about Roman Britain, both of them linked to *The Eagle of the Ninth*: *The Silver Branch* (1957) and *The Lantern Bearers* (1959). The latter won the Library Association's Carnegie medal in 1960. With its opening chapter showing the symbolic extinguishing of the Rutupiae light on the Kent shore as the last Romans leave Britain, and the subsequent account of the dark years that follow, it is one of her finest expositions of favourite themes—the evolution of history, light after apparent darkness, the invader who becomes the settled inhabitant, enmity transmuted into acceptance.

By 1962 Sutcliff's achievement made her one of the very few living subjects included by the Bodley Head in their series of monographs on children's writers. She had still thirty years of writing ahead of her and many books, some of distinction. Among her best were *The Mark of the Horse Lord* (1965), about a gladiator who wins his freedom and becomes leader of the horse people in western Scotland, and *Sun Horse, Moon Horse* (1977). This latter is a brilliantly devised scenario to account for the creation of the White Horse on the Berkshire Downs above Uffington. It includes a powerful evocation of ancient ritual and mysteries (primitive religion was one of her great interests). A final book, *Sword Song*, was transcribed by her cousin, Anthony Lawton, from a draft manuscript and, edited by Jill Black, was published posthumously in 1997. Like *The Shield Ring* (1956) it centres upon a Cumbrian community of Norsemen in the early tenth century, and ends with the implication that piracy and warfare there are fading into legend, and Christianity replacing pagan belief. Her large output also included five novels for adults, retellings of myths and legends, radio scripts, and a play.

Immobilized in a wheelchair (something she was not allowed in her mother's lifetime), Sutcliff had visited few of the localities she described with such passionate feeling, and her experience of life was of necessity vicarious and mainly through literature. Kipling was one influence she named; another may be identified as Dorothy Kathleen Broster, whose trilogy of novels about the Jacobite rising of 1745 was published in 1925–9. The emotional climate is very similar, featuring male loyalty and camaraderie (both writers tended to use women only as subsidiary characters), the enemy who becomes a friend, the hero-worship of a leader. (The resemblance is particularly marked in *Bonnie Dundee* (1983), a romantic story about John Graham of Claverhouse, the seventeenth-century Scottish royalist.)

Indomitable and cheerful, Sutcliff was a great enjoyer who could find amusement even in the vagaries of the various carers upon whom, after the death of her father, she wholly depended. Dogs played an important part in her life and feature in most of her books. From OBE in 1975 she was appointed CBE in 1992. She died on 23 July 1992 at St Richard's Hospital, Chichester.   GILLIAN AVERY

Sources R. Sutcliff, *Blue remembered hills* (1983) · M. Meek, *Rosemary Sutcliff* (1962) · T. Chevalier, ed., *Twentieth-century children's writers* (1989) · b. cert. · d. cert.
Archives priv. coll., MSS | U. Reading L., letters to the Bodley Head Ltd · University of Minnesota, Minneapolis, Kerlan Collection, MSS collection
Likenesses H. Kerr, photograph, 1983, News International Syndication, London [*see illus.*]
Wealth at death £493,167: probate, 1 Oct 1992, *CGPLA Eng. & Wales*

Sutcliffe, Alice (*fl.* 1624–1634), author, was probably the daughter of Luke Woodhouse, of Kimberley in Norfolk. Little is known about her early life, but she seems to have been attached to the household of Katherine, duchess of Buckingham, the widow of George Villiers, first duke of Buckingham, for she refers to the duchess as 'a *Mother*'. This association with the Buckingham faction makes it likely that Sutcliffe herself was either a Catholic or sympathetic to the Catholic cause, since the duchess of Buckingham was involved in the resurgence in Catholicism at court under the auspices of Queen Henrietta Maria. In addition, Sutcliffe specifically thanks the duchess of Buckingham and her sister for the '*Spirituall* blessings' they have bestowed upon her, and she concludes her carefully worded prose treatise with a prayer to God for knowledge of 'the Glory of the inheritance of his Saints'. Any open statement of Catholicism would, however, have been unwise.

It is likely that Sutcliffe, after leaving the Buckingham household, entered court, for by 1624 she was married to John Sutcliffe of Yorkshire, a squire to James I and subsequently groom of the privy chamber to Charles I. They had a daughter, Susan, of whom nothing else is known. The connection with the Buckingham group appears to have persisted after Sutcliffe's marriage, since her only recorded work, *Meditations of Man's Mortality, or, A Way to True Blessedness* (1634), includes dedications to Susan, countess of Denbigh, Buckingham's sister, to Philip Herbert, earl of Pembroke and Montgomery, whose son had married Buckingham's daughter, as well as to Katherine, the widowed duchess of Buckingham.

Meditations of Man's Mortality, or, A Way to True Blessedness comprises a biblical prose treatise and a spiritual poem. It sets out to warn the reader of the omnipresence of death, initially painting a darkly Gothic picture of human sin and damnation, but then turning in the final stanzas to welcome death as a way to salvation and eternal life. The poem demonstrates Sutcliffe's biblical knowledge as well as her classical learning, but she seems to be torn between openly demonstrating her literary skill, and disavowing expertise on the grounds of her sex. Thus, she denigrates her 'sex's' act' in writing, but simultaneously praises female intelligence:

Nor is there aught that lives in woman kind
Exceeding the rare prowess of her mind.

Similarly, while the poem attacks Eve as a 'Wicked woman' Sutcliffe is also able to defend her sex, 'courage woman'. This balancing act between defending women and accepting their vilification parallels that of the central theme of the poem: a fear and a welcoming of death, and of the religious subtext of Catholicism and protestantism. In each case Sutcliffe evades open confrontation between the opposing discourses, but the resulting tensions inevitably thread through the poetry, leaving the reader with a sense of unsettling ambiguity. Among the commendatory poems prefixed to *Man's Mortality* is one by Ben Jonson.

The date and place of Alice Sutcliffe's death are not known.   MARION WYNNE-DAVIES

Sources R. Hughey, 'Forgotten verses by Ben Jonson, George Wither, and others to Alice Sutcliffe', *Review of English Studies*, 10 (1934), 156–64 · M. Wynne-Davies, ed., *Women poets of the Renaissance* (1998) · G. Greer and others, eds., *Kissing the rod: an anthology of seventeenth-century women's verse* (1988) · K. Walker, *Women writers of the English Renaissance* (1996)

Sutcliffe, Charles Edward (1864–1939), football administrator, was born at 38 Parsonage Street, Burnley, Lancashire, on 8 July 1864, the second of the four sons of John Sutcliffe, solicitor's clerk and later solicitor, and his wife, Jane Pollard Brown. He followed his father and elder brother into the legal profession by joining the family firm in Burnley as a clerk at the beginning of the 1880s and qualified as a solicitor in July 1886. At about this time he married Annie (1867–1924), with whom he had two sons and a daughter. He became involved with organized football in his home town, first as a rugby half-back before changing along with the Burnley club to the more spectacular association game. He gave up playing around the mid-1880s but continued his involvement with the game as a member of Burnley's committee and then directorate.

After joining the Football League's list of referees in 1891 Sutcliffe, known as C. E. or Charlie, to his friends, quickly earned a reputation as an obstinate and controversial official. His actions often made him unpopular with spectators and club officials alike, as during a league match between Blackburn Rovers and Liverpool in 1896, when he disallowed six goals in succession, or on another occasion when he was alleged to have escaped from an angry crowd of spectators by leaving Sunderland's Roker Park dressed as a policeman. Notwithstanding his controversial reputation he was appointed to officiate in numerous international matches in the British Isles in addition to his league and cup appointments, although he was never chosen to referee the FA cup final.

Sutcliffe, however, earned his real reputation after he had finished refereeing, as an administrator associated closely with the development of the Football League. He was elected to the management committee of the league in 1898 and, with the exception of the 1902–3 season, stayed there for the rest of his life, becoming a vice-president in 1927, president in 1936, and a life member in 1938. He was the main architect of the league's rapid growth from a parochial clique of thirty-two clubs drawn mainly from the north and midlands of England at the turn of the century to a truly national body of eighty-eight clubs in four divisions by 1923, and worked tirelessly devising new legislative schemes in every area of the league's activities. One of his major legacies was his method for constructing the league's fixture list based on a complex system of charts and maps, which he bequeathed to his son Harold on his death.

As a stout defender of league interests in the committee room, the law court, and the press, Sutcliffe was the main advocate of the philosophy of mutual support, whereby the richer clubs within the league 'family' supported the poorer ones. For this reason he stood firm in the 1890s against the leaders of football's governing body, the Football Association, who wanted to remove the league's retain-and-transfer system and later established the legality of the system by representing the Aston Villa club during the Kingaby case of 1912. In addition, he almost single-handedly kept the league functioning during the First World War by persuading clubs, players, and officials to contribute to a central financial pool for the preservation of those in distress. Sutcliffe's legal expertise, allied to powerful oratorical skills, was instrumental to his success. However, he was not without his critics, many of whom found themselves the victim of his tongue or his pen. In particular, he waged a long battle through his weekly newspaper columns with the Players' Union and those professional footballers who he believed were intent on bankrupting clubs through lavish financial demands. Despite being a member of the FA council for many years, he also crossed swords regularly with the gentlemen amateurs of the governing body with whom he had little in common. He was blunt and uncompromising, a characteristic shared by many of the league administrators from 'the harder, Northern school' (Sharpe, 157).

A small, frail man, Sutcliffe's physical appearance belied his strong character and ceaseless energy. Alongside his numerous football activities, he was a practising solicitor in Rawtenstall and the Rossendale valley, Lancashire, whither he moved in 1901, and a regular at the local courts in criminal and industrial cases. He was also prominent in the public life of the area: he became a Liberal councillor in 1903 and an alderman two years later. He inherited from his parents a commitment to Methodism and was involved throughout his life as a worshipper and sometime preacher and Sunday school teacher. He was also a prominent member of the Burnley temperance movement in his early years. These moral values undoubtedly informed his attempts to keep the reputation of professional football 'clean' and free from the corrupt influence of drink and gambling. His abhorrence of gambling on football also led to his biggest miscalculation, when in February and March 1936 he devised a scheme on behalf of league clubs intended to ruin the pools companies by altering the published fixture list and revealing the rearranged fixtures only at the last minute. The scheme generated widespread opposition, forcing a quick league climb-down and leaving Sutcliffe to endure both private and public criticism from which he never properly recovered.

Following the death of his first wife Sutcliffe married Sarah Pickup (1862–1931), his former housekeeper, on 12 June 1926. He died at his home, 76 Burnley Road, Rawtenstall, Lancashire, on 11 January 1939 and was buried three days later at Rawtenstall cemetery.

MATTHEW TAYLOR

Sources S. Inglis, *League football and the men who made it: the official centenary of the Football League, 1888–1988* (1988), 103–11 · *Burnley Express* (14 Jan 1939) · *Rossendale Free Press* (14 Jan 1939) · I. Sharpe, *40 years in football* (1952) · C. E. Sutcliffe and F. Hargreaves, *History of the Lancashire football association, 1878–1928* (1928) · W. C. Cuff, 'Charles E. Sutcliffe: an appreciation', *The story of the Football League, 1888–1938*, ed. C. E. Sutcliffe and others (1938), 166–7 · M. Taylor, 'Proud Preston: a history of the Football League, 1900–1939', PhD diss., De Montfort University, 1997 · b. cert. · m. cert. · d. cert.
Archives Football Association Library, London · Football League archives, Lytham St Annes, Lancashire
Likenesses photograph, repro. in Sutcliffe and others, eds., *Story of the Football League* · photograph, repro. in Sutcliffe and Hargreaves, *History*, 59
Wealth at death £7874 3s. 6d.: probate, 13 Feb 1939, *CGPLA Eng. & Wales*

Sutcliffe, Francis Meadow [Frank] (1853–1941), photographer, was born on 6 October 1853 at Headingley, Leeds, Yorkshire, the eldest son of the painter Thomas Sutcliffe (1828–1871) and his wife, Sarah Lorentia Button (*d*. 1915). Thomas Sutcliffe attempted to establish a career as a watercolour painter selling to Yorkshire patrons, but he died young; after an elementary education at a dame-school, his son Frank tried to support the family by taking up the relatively new technology of photography. By this time the family was living on the Yorkshire coast near Whitby, a town with which Sutcliffe's name and work was to become inextricably linked.

Frank Sutcliffe was one of the first generation of practitioners to take on photography and to devote a lifetime to investigating its potential. His work demonstrates photography's role as a direct, expressive medium through which he was able to convey his vision of the life of ordinary people and the landscape in which he lived and worked. In this he was very different from many earlier photographers who had often been businessmen looking for new openings or painters seeking ways of making a living in a changing world. He resented the fact that he had to make his living as a portrait photographer, working first in Tunbridge Wells, Kent, and then for over half a century in Whitby. His father had brought him into contact with prominent men in the art world including John Ruskin, whom Sutcliffe visited and photographed at his home, Brantwood, in 1873. Throughout his career he nurtured higher ambitions, though he was also a shrewd and hard-working businessman and was routinely in touch with the successful commercial photographers of the day, such as Francis Frith. Thus Sutcliffe led a double life, taking portraits of holiday-makers during the summer season and producing photographs for himself which were exhibited and admired around the world. His work was shown at and won prizes in exhibitions from London

Francis Meadow Sutcliffe (1853–1941), by Irene Sutcliffe?

to Chicago and Tokyo; prints made from his negatives have been on sale to visitors to the Yorkshire coast, and more widely, for over 120 years.

Sutcliffe's business in his Skinner Street studio rooted him to Whitby and Eskdale, but what seemed to him initially to be a severe disadvantage actually proved an immense strength in his work. He left the most complete and revealing photographic record of a late Victorian town and the people who lived there. Not only was he a superb photographer, but he was known by everyone in the community, who co-operated with him in photographing the everyday life of the area, its fishing activities, and the changing seasons. His most famous photograph, entitled *Water Rats* and taken in 1886, shows the misty east side of Whitby, with young boys playing by a boat in the harbour water. There was some contemporary comment from locals concerning the indecency of photographing naked boys (who were, moreover, on the run from the truancy officer), but the image is hardly erotic. It is probably best interpreted as a realist image filtered through a high art lens: Sutcliffe was clearly experimenting with the traditional conventions of the academic nude in an attempt to illustrate how photography could reach to the level of art.

Sutcliffe's misty landscapes, with the sun breaking through the sea fret and figures in the foreground set against hazy backgrounds, were early examples of naturalistic photography of the kind promoted by P. H. Emerson. In both his photography and his writing, Sutcliffe showed an awareness of the techniques and the ideas of other visual artists, such as the French painter Jean-François Millet. His work embodied a sophisticated approach previously seen in painting, combined with the strength of the direct recording powers of the camera. His style and subject matter were much admired and much copied, and he was one of the photographers asked by Kodak to demonstrate the potential of their new snapshot cameras, including panoramic cameras.

Sutcliffe married a woman from a local family, Eliza Weatherill Duck (b. 1847/8), the daughter of a bootmaker, on 1 January 1875 and brought up one son and three daughters in Sleights, near Whitby, where he built himself a substantial house on the proceeds of his photographic business. A prolific writer on photographic subjects, he contributed to the *Amateur Photographer*, the *Photographic Journal*, and many other periodicals. For over twenty years he wrote a photography column in the *Yorkshire Weekly Post*. In 1922 he retired from photography to become the curator of the Whitby Museum, and in 1935 he was made an honorary fellow of the Royal Photographic Society. Frank Sutcliffe died at his home in Carr Hill Lane, Sleights, on 31 May 1941 and was buried in the churchyard at Aislaby, overlooking the Esk valley. His work is in the collection of the Whitby Literary and Philosophical Society in the Whitby Museum, and in national collections such as the National Museum of Photography, Film and Television in Bradford. MICHAEL HILEY

Sources M. Hiley, *Frank Sutcliffe, photographer of Whitby* (1974) · C. N. Armfield, 'Mr F. M. Sutcliffe', *Sun Artists* [ed. W. A. Boord], 8 (July 1891), 55 · H. Hood, 'Sutcliffe of Whitby', *British Journal of Photography* (5 Jan 1923), 4 · F. M. Sutcliffe, 'Introduction', *Whitby writers, 1867–1949*, ed. M. Keighley (1957) · *Frank Meadow Sutcliffe*, The Aperture History of Photography Series (1979) [introductory essay by M. Hiley] · I. Sutcliffe, 'Frank M. Sutcliffe, Hon. FRPS: some reminiscences', *Photographic Journal*, 82 (1942), 397–9 · b. cert. · m. cert.

Likenesses I. Sutcliffe?, photograph, Sutcliffe Gallery, Whitby [*see illus.*]

Wealth at death £3240 17s. 0d.: probate, 7 July 1941, *CGPLA Eng. & Wales*

Sutcliffe, Herbert William (1894–1978), cricketer, was born at Gabblegate, Summerbridge, near Hartwith, Yorkshire, on 24 November 1894, the second of three sons (there were no daughters) of William Sutcliffe (1864–1898), bobbin turner, journeyman, and later hotel proprietor, of Pateley Bridge, and his wife, Jane Elizabeth Bell (1867–1904). He was educated at Pudsey School in Pudsey, a town also associated with three other great Yorkshire cricketers, John Turnicliffe, Sir Leonard Hutton, and Raymond Illingworth.

Sutcliffe's father died when he was three and his mother when he was ten. His aunt Carrie, his father's sister, became his guardian. His appearance in first-class cricket was delayed by the First World War, during which he was commissioned in the Green Howards, then known as the Yorkshire regiment. At the age of twenty-four he was an immediate success as an opening batsman for Yorkshire in 1919, when he scored five centuries. He first played for England in 1924, and was at once a success against South

Herbert William Sutcliffe (1894–1978), by Bassano, 1932 [right, with Percy Holmes after scoring a world record first-wicket partnership of 555 against Essex]

Africa putting on 136 and 268 with Jack *Hobbs in his first two test matches. The following winter in Australia he had a triumphant series, making 734 runs at an average of 81, including two hundreds in the second test at Melbourne (176 and 127), despite which England were beaten. In a character sketch written in 1925 H. D. G. Leveson-Gower wrote: 'Many who through the plodding years of county cricket had known his name only as one among dozens which stood for efficiency, not for greatness, have now discovered in him a player … who has placed himself amongst the Immortals' (Leveson-Gower, 44). He was always at his best when the challenge was greatest, for England against Australia, or for Yorkshire against Lancashire, and his supreme skill was most famously demonstrated at the Oval in 1926 and at Melbourne in 1929, when he scored hundreds on pitches made treacherous by rain. His 161 in the second innings in the final test of 1926 was easily the highest score of the match and laid the foundation of the victory which restored the 'Ashes' to England after heavy defeats in the three previous series.

In his prime, from 1925 to 1932, Sutcliffe averaged over 50 in eight consecutive seasons and on four overseas tours, and from May 1931 to May 1933 he scored 7687 runs. On 15 and 16 June 1932 he and Percy Holmes broke the world record for an opening partnership, putting on 555 against Essex at Leyton, a record in first-class cricket which stood until 1977. Having attained the record, Sutcliffe deliberately threw away his wicket after making 313. He seldom showed such charity to bowlers.

The only cricketer to play through every season between the wars, scoring more than 1000 runs in each of those twenty-one summers, Sutcliffe made 3336 runs in 1932 alone, at an average of 74, hitting fourteen centuries in a wet season. By the time he retired from first-class cricket (effectively in 1939, although he played one more match in 1945) he had scored 50,138 runs at an average of 52, with 149 hundreds, 16 of them in tests. He had become a father figure to the young professionals of Yorkshire, who called him 'maestro'.

The partner in two famous opening pairs, with Percy Holmes for Yorkshire and Jack Hobbs for England, Sutcliffe's cricketing hallmarks were courage, calmness—even against the trickiest or fiercest bowling—concentration, and an exemplary technique. Everything about him, from his smoothed-down, carefully parted hair, to his perfectly white boots, was immaculate. Nothing worried him, or if it did he never showed it. If a ball beat his bat, he would show no reaction, whatever the provocation from the unfortunate bowler; if a spectator moved behind the sight-screen, Sutcliffe would stop the bowler in the middle of his run-up and with an imperious gesture wave the culprit, as Neville Cardus remarked, 'out of all decent society'.

Sutcliffe's right-handed batting method was strictly functional and simple, lacking the easy grace of Hobbs, yet not without its own artistic flourish. His attacking shots would finish with a late curve of the bat, like a writer adding the last touch to his signature. Moreover, though contemporaries rated Hobbs the greatest English batsman of his time, it was Sutcliffe who finished with the higher test batting average, a remarkable one of 60.73, the highest attained by any England player of any era who has scored more than 1500 test runs. With Hobbs he had a perfect understanding, each batsman entirely confident of the other's ability and judgement and each a speedy runner between the wickets. They shared twenty-six century opening partnerships and Sutcliffe shared seventy-four more with Holmes.

Jack Hobbs wrote of Sutcliffe:

> What I admired in Herbert was his thoroughness. Evidently, his motto is: 'what is worth doing is worth doing well'. As an illustration, he was, a few years ago, quite an ordinary speaker, but recently I heard him make a speech on a big occasion, and it was a wonderful bit of oratory. I felt very envious of him. (Hobbs, 207)

If Sutcliffe himself ever felt envy, he never showed it. Always assured, he was the sort, as R. C. Robertson-Glasgow remarked, who would rather miss a train than be seen to hurry. When Sutcliffe finally lost his place in the England side, during the series against South Africa in 1935, he was replaced by Denis Smith of Derbyshire. On being told of his replacement Sutcliffe remarked without expression: 'Who is Smith?' The story may be apocryphal, but it is indicative of the man's unshakeable poise.

As organized and determined in his private and business life as he was on the cricket field, Sutcliffe built up a very successful sports outfitting business in Yorkshire, bought a grand house on the hill at Pudsey for £2000 in the 1930s, and during the Second World War rose to the rank of major in the Royal Army Ordnance Corps, having spoken frequently before hostilities began in the cause of wider recruitment. He also spoke in aid of the Red Cross and organized cricket matches to raise money for them. He was an England cricket selector and also served on the Yorkshire County Cricket Club committee, on the royal commission on betting, lotteries, and gaming, and on the rugby league disciplinary committee. He was a high-ranking official in the London lodge of the freemasons. Deliberately turning his Yorkshire accent into one more associated with Oxford, he sent his children to private schools. Dogged by arthritis in later years he made a final appearance on the field at Headingley in a wheelchair in 1977, when he was honoured by a large crowd during the test match in which Geoffrey Boycott followed Sutcliffe and Len Hutton as the third Yorkshireman to score 100 first-class centuries. Hutton said of Sutcliffe: 'He was correct in all he did, on and off the field, but never so ambitious as to forget that he was playing in a team game.' Another contemporary, the Yorkshire off-spinner Ellis Robinson, told Sutcliffe's biographer, Alan Hill:

> He set a perfect example … one of his great attributes was … his guts. Many times I have seen him black and blue, after taking the brunt of the bowling on his body, rather than play the ball, thus resisting the chance of getting out. (Hill, 2)

On 21 September 1921, in the parish church of Pudsey, Sutcliffe married Emily (d. 1974), a bookkeeper, who had lived in the same street in Pudsey (Robin Lane) and was the daughter of William Pease, farmer; they had two sons and one daughter. One of their sons, W. H. H. (Billy) Sutcliffe (b. 1926), played for Yorkshire as an amateur and captained the side in 1956 and 1957: Herbert Sutcliffe had himself been offered the honour but, as a professional, refused it. Sutcliffe died at Beanlands Nursing Home, Colne Road, Crosshills, near Skipton, Yorkshire, on 22 January 1978. His funeral service took place at the United Reformed church, Otley—he was a lifelong Congregationalist—on 27 January 1978, his coffin being surmounted by a wreath in the shape of a cricket bat before cremation at Rawdon crematorium.   CHRISTOPHER MARTIN-JENKINS

Sources A. Hill, *Herbert Sutcliffe: cricket maestro* (1991) · J. B. Hobbs, *My life story* (1935) · R. C. Robertson-Glasgow, *Cricket prints* (1943) · N. Cardus, *Days in the sun* (1924) · H. D. G. Leveson-Gower, *Cricket personalities* (1925) · H. Sutcliffe, *For England and Yorkshire* (1935) · E. W. Swanton and M. Melford, eds., *The world of cricket* (1966) · C. Martin-Jenkins, *The complete who's who of test cricketers* (1980) · private information (2004) · *CGPLA Eng. & Wales* (1978)
Archives FILM BFI NFTVA, 'Heroic partnership', Topical Budget, 12 Feb 1925 · BFI NFTVA, documentary footage · BFI NFTVA, sports footage
Likenesses Bassano, vintage print, 1932, NPG [*see illus.*] · portraits, repro. in Hill, *Herbert Sutcliffe*
Wealth at death £40,580: probate, 5 May 1978, *CGPLA Eng. & Wales*

Sutcliffe, Matthew (1549/50–1629), dean of Exeter, was the second son of John Sutcliffe of Melroyd, Halifax, and his wife, Margaret Owlsworth of Ashley, Yorkshire. He had at least four brothers: Adam, Solomon, who went to Trinity College, Cambridge, in 1577 and died in 1609, Luke, admitted to Trinity in 1573, and John. Admitted to Peterhouse, Cambridge, on 10 November 1565, aged fifteen, Sutcliffe became a scholar at Trinity on 30 April 1568. He graduated BA there in 1571 and was admitted a minor fellow on 27 September 1572. He proceeded MA in 1574 and became a major fellow on 3 April that year. He studied law rather than divinity and was awarded the degree of LLD in 1581, two years after his college appointment as *lector mathematicus*. He was admitted an advocate at Doctors' Commons on 1 May 1582. His wife, Anne, daughter of John and Frances Bradley of Louth, Lincolnshire, outlived him, but their only child, Frances, predeceased him.

Sutcliffe's last stipend as a fellow of Trinity was paid at midsummer 1580, so it is likely that he either married or was ordained about this time. He rapidly received preferment in the church in south-west England, a region with which he is not known to have had previous links. On 30 January 1587 he was collated to the archdeaconry of Taunton and its associated prebend of Milverton, but the appointment does not appear to have taken effect. On 27 October 1588, however, he was made dean of Exeter and held this senior appointment for more than forty years, serving no fewer than five bishops. Archbishop Whitgift had granted him a dispensation on 10 March 1589 to continue to hold the vicarage of West Alvington, Devon, together with the deanery and a prebendal stall as well as another benefice, and eighteen months later, on 9 November 1590, he was instituted to the vicarage of Harberton. He further received the rectory of Newton Ferrers (27 December 1591), and that of Lezant (6 April 1594), a Cornish living formerly held by Bishop John Woolton, who assigned it to him. Early in 1590 John Herbert, dean of Wells, granted him the prebend of Buckland Dinham in that diocese.

As an apologist for the Church of England Sutcliffe is best remembered as an anti-Roman polemicist, both for his tracts, in which he took on the likes of Bellarmine, Suarez, and Gretser, and for the foundation of the college at Chelsea in 1610. His earlier publications, however, were written in response to presbyterianism. He was a staunch defender of ecclesiastical discipline and of holy orders from a conformist position, and attacked those who held more sectarian tenets. With the likes of Thomas Bilson, John Bridges, John Downame, George Carleton, and the later primate Richard Bancroft, he expressed, initially at least, an exalted opinion of episcopacy as *jure divino*. His first two known publications, written under the patronage of the earl of Bath in 1591, treat of ecclesiastical discipline in the wake of the Marprelate controversy, and attack those who would intrude novelty into church polity. They also display his legalistic frame of mind. His legal training came more fully into play with his fifth publication, *The Practise, Proceedings, & Lawes of Armes*, which he dedicated to the second earl of Essex in 1593, while for Robert Cecil he wrote *A Challenge Concerning the Romish Church* (1602). Fair copies of many of his books are among the working papers of his that constitute the fourteen manuscript volumes presented to Emmanuel College, Cambridge, by Nicholas Bernard, Cromwell's almoner, in 1657, after the suppression of Chelsea College. Several of the volumes include textual revisions by Sutcliffe and are marked up for the press: a number bear a clerical imprimatur or justification to print.

The theological corpus of Sutcliffe's polemical defence of the developing Anglican tradition forcefully anathematized the Roman church. In his *De Turcopapismo, hoc est, De Turcarum et papistarum adversus Christi ecclesiam et fidem conjuratione* of 1599 he claimed that papists were actually more dangerous than Muslims, and in 1606, in *A Briefe Examination of a Certaine … Disleal Petition*, he rejected the idea that the Church of Rome was the mother church that had only recently defaulted, a view that James I himself held. The latter text expanded ideas he had published as *De missa papistica* in the year of the king's accession, in controversy with Robert Bellarmine, and suggests a real contemporary fear that the new king might relax the proscriptions under which Catholics lived. Again and again Sutcliffe's writings display a neurotic fear of the power of Rome to subvert. They rarely progress beyond xenophobia and violent anti-Catholicism, though they also show that he had read widely. Although he never held a doctorate in divinity contemporaries often so styled him, suggesting the stature of his theological erudition and scholarship. Nor did time soften this hardline position; in 1626 he denounced Sir Tobie Matthew, the convert son of his namesake, the archbishop of York, in *The unmasking of a masse-monger, who in the counterfeit habit of S Augustine hath cunningly crept into the closets of many English ladies*.

Increasingly, however, Sutcliffe's teaching denounced another Trojan horse within English protestantism: 'Those false teachers alsoe among us that palliate popish-heresies, and under the name of Arminius, seeke to bring in poperie', anti-Calvinists who 'endeavour with all their little skill to reconcile darkness to light Antechrist to Christ heresie to the true Catholike faith' (PRO, PROB 11/156, fol. 271r). His last publication, written when he was well into his seventies and published anonymously, *A Briefe Censure upon an Appeale to Caesar* (1626), showed that he had lost none of his old-style Elizabethan rigour and fear of sects. In it he denounced Richard Montagu for acting like the lapsed protestant convert Marco Antonio de Dominis, insidiously trying 'to lessen controversies and compose matters between the Pope and us' (*A Briefe Censure*, 5). Bishop William Laud allegedly tried to have this publication seized in the press.

Sutcliffe seems to have used his leisured distance in Devon to stay away from the court and London. Whether he had at some point been disgraced at Elizabeth's court is not known. Until his project for a London college of preachers and increasing involvement in the colonial affairs of New England brought him more often to the Jacobean capital he seems to have dedicated himself to writing. If he had once served Elizabeth as a chaplain-in-ordinary, as has been suggested, there is no evidence that he was reappointed at the accession of James I. Whitgift did not enter him among the 'Names of such as were her late Majesties Chaplens and other persons likewise, Fitt to preache before his Majestie if occasion be offerred' (Westminster Abbey muniments, book 15, fol. 6). Although he may have entered the household of Prince Henry, to whom he later dedicated one of his tracts, he is not recorded among the Lenten preachers who ever preached before James, an appointment eagerly sought by many senior clergy as a route to higher office. In the summer of 1621 he was among those imprisoned for their outspoken protestant opposition to Prince Charles's proposed Spanish match. Writing in July 1621 the Devon MP Walter Yonge reported that Sutcliffe was censured 'for speaking against the Spanish Match, and saying the King showed no natural affection to leave his daughter in distress' (*Diary of Walter Yonge*, 41). He was suspended from his decanal functions for at least a year, since in July 1622 James exercised the dean's traditional patronage in appointing William Challoner to the vicarage of Braunton.

By the time of his death Sutcliffe had established Chelsea College and substantially endowed it with lands in the south-west and at Whitby. It was incorporated by charter as 'King James's College at Chelsey' on 8 May 1610. It was one practical outcome of the controversy over the oath of allegiance and the disputed place of Catholics in English society, being primarily designed for controversialists who, freed from the confines of an Oxbridge college, could be 'imployed to write, as occasion shall require, for maintaining the Religion professed in Our Kingdomes and confuting the Impugners thereof', as James I informed Archbishop Abbot in 1616 (Fuller, bk 10, p. 52). 'The Royal liberality of Dr Sutcliffe' was widely commemorated; 'though no prince by birth' he, like Araunah before him, who gave David land for the temple, had made it possible for the king to build (Darley, 20).

The college's charter stipulated that the crown was to appoint the provost and nineteen fellows, of whom all but two had to be theologians. James chose Sutcliffe as the first provost, and the fellows included John Overall, John Howson, John Boys, and Richard Field. There is little doubt that the project would not have been sustainable without the active support of Richard Bancroft and the king's notorious predilection for theological discourse. James laid the foundation stone of the college on 8 May 1609 and gave timber from the Great Park at Windsor for its building, as well as introducing a silver tax. An act of parliament provided a perpetual income for the college from a water system that supplied London. The building was never completed and only one side of the first quadrangle was standing at Sutcliffe's death; its importance lay in its becoming a virtual school for Jacobean bishops such as Robert Abbot, Martin Fotherby, Miles Smith, and Thomas Morton. That the college fell into disuse and was so readily put down by Oliver Cromwell may have been because it rivalled the ancient universities. Moreover Charles I lacked his father's theological appetite and had increasingly promoted fellows whom Sutcliffe would not have accepted as suitably 'well-affected and orthodox Bishops' (PRO, PROB 11/156, fol. 271*r*).

Sutcliffe had several proselytizing links with North America. He became a member of the council for Virginia on 9 March 1607 and of that for New England in 1620. In July 1624 he was appointed one of the commissioners to wind up the Virginia Company, 'the dissensions in which threaten its ruin', as Sir Francis Nethersole reported (PRO, SP 14/164/46). At his death Sutcliffe shared an interest in a Whitby-based ship, the *Great Neptune*, with Barnabas Gooch. In his will, drawn up on 4 October 1628, he left that interest, along with most of his property in Devon, to Chelsea College. He professed himself to be most assuredly God's:

being bought most dearly by the blood of our Saviour Christ Jesus whom I have by thy grace knowne beleeved & preached according to the talent given mee relyinge upon his grace and merritts And not upon Angells Saints or Creature or my owne merits workes or justice.

Much of the will, indeed, reads like a bilious tract for the times, with a bitter invective against 'the wicked decrees of the conventicle of Trent, Constance, Lateran and Nice under the Empresse Irene' as contrary to the doctrine of the Church of England. But he also made bequests to his wife, whom he named as his executor, and to four named grandchildren. Probate was granted on 24 November 1629. In requesting burial in Exeter Cathedral 'if I dye neere to that place' Sutcliffe specified that his interment was to take place 'without any solemnitie or monument'. His request appears to have been heeded, with the result that the exact date of his death is unrecorded.

NICHOLAS W. S. CRANFIELD

Sources Venn, *Alum. Cant.*, 1/4.186 · F. B. Troup, 'Biographical notes on Dr Matthew Sutcliffe', *Report and Transactions of the Devonshire Association*, 23 (1891), 171–96 · *Fasti Angl.* (Hardy) · will, PRO, PROB 11/156, fols. 270*v*–272*r* · W. Prynne, *Canterburies doome, or, The first part of a compleat history of the commitment, charge, tryall, condemnation, execution of William Laud, late arch-bishop of Canterbury* (1646) · muniments, Westminster Abbey, book 15, fols. 2, 6 · T. Fuller, *The church-history of Britain*, 11 pts in 1 (1655) · *Diary of Walter Yonge*, ed. G. Roberts, CS, 41 (1848) · J. Darley, *The glory of Chelsey College revived* (1662) · state papers domestic, Charles I, PRO, 14/164/46 · CCC Oxf., MS E 297, fol. 188 · *Fasti Angl., 1541–1857*, [Bath and Wells]
Wealth at death no value given: will, PRO, PROB 11/156, fols. 270*v*–272*r*

Sutcliffe, Reginald Cockcroft (1904–1991), meteorologist, was born on 16 November 1904 at Wrexham, north Wales, the third son in a family of four brothers of Ormerod Greenwood Sutcliffe (1870?–1928), manager of Wrexham Co-operative, and his wife, Jessie (*d.* 1942), daughter of Robert Cockcroft. Both parents were from Yorkshire, where they returned soon after Sutcliffe was born, his father becoming manager of the Co-operative at Cleckheaton, between Huddersfield and Bradford. After attending the local primary school, Sutcliffe won a scholarship to Whitcliffe Mount grammar school. He was a brilliant student, excelling in mathematics and physics, becoming head boy, and captaining the school at both football and cricket. From Whitcliffe he gained a scholarship to Leeds University, where he obtained first-class honours in mathematics and was among the best four students of his year. He continued his studies for a PhD in statistics under Professor Berwick, whom he later followed to University College, Bangor. He then joined the Meteorological Office in

Reginald Cockcroft Sutcliffe (1904–1991), by unknown photographer

1927 and served in a number of posts, including four years in Malta where he worked for a time with the distinguished Scandinavian meteorologist Tor Bergeron. In Malta he married, on 25 March 1929, Evelyn Williams (1908–1998), whom he had met at Bangor. They had two daughters.

After returning to Britain in 1932 Sutcliffe worked at a number of outstations and was to make a major impact upon meteorology with his renowned book *Meteorology for Aviators*, published in 1939. This became the standard meteorological text for Royal Air Force flight crews during the Second World War—and hence for senior captains of Britain's civil airlines afterwards. To the British aviator of this generation the terms 'meteorology' and 'Sutcliffe' were almost synonymous. His wartime career saw him forecasting for flying operations in northern France; being evacuated to Britain just before Dunkirk; returning to southern France to forecast for operations over northern Italy; and, with the final collapse, being one of the last British servicemen to escape via the sea route through Marseilles and Gibraltar. Perhaps his greatest contribution came at 3 group headquarters, Bomber Command, with his crucial role in forecasting for bombing operations over Germany. He also participated in the discussions on forecasts for D-day. At the end of the war he became chief meteorological officer to the British forces in Germany with rank of group captain, and played a vital part in rebuilding the German meteorological service.

Sutcliffe laid the foundations for his work on atmospheric dynamics before the war, publishing important papers during 1938–9 and somehow finding time to extend his thinking in 1942 with a fundamentally important paper written in collaboration with the little-known Belgian meteorologist O. Godart, whom he held in high regard. Vital to Sutcliffe's thinking was the use of pressure instead of height as vertical co-ordinate in the atmosphere, and his ideas attained operational usage at 3 group. His most famous publication, the seminal 'A contribution to the problem of development', appeared in the *Quarterly Journal of the Royal Meteorological Society* for 1947, during the post-war reconstruction period. He was now in the forefront of British, and indeed world, dynamical meteorologists. In subsequent reorganizations he became, in 1948, the first assistant director of forecasting research and, in 1957, the first director of research in the office's history. He was president of the Royal Meteorological Society from 1955 to 1957 and, in the wider field of the World Meteorological Organization, served as president of the commission for aerology from 1957 to 1961, president of the International Association for Meteorology and Atmospheric Physics from 1967 to 1971, and chairman of the WMO advisory committee from 1964 to 1968, making important contributions to the education and training programme. His election as a fellow of the Royal Society in 1957 was widely regarded as an indication that weather forecasting had advanced to the status of a true mathematical and physical science, and could henceforth be ranked with any other branch of geophysics.

Retirement from the Meteorological Office in 1965 did not end Sutcliffe's career. The paucity of tertiary level teaching of meteorology in Britain had always concerned him, and he now turned his attention to founding a new meteorological department at Reading University—a task he accomplished before finally retiring from working life in 1970, handing over the reins to Professor Robert Pearce. Sutcliffe contributed two books and well over eighty publications to the literature on meteorology. His many honours included appointment as OBE in 1942 and CB in 1961. He received the Buchan prize (1950) and Symons gold medal (1955) from the Royal Meteorological Society, being elected an honorary member in 1976, and receiving the Charles Chree medal from the Physical Society in 1959. Tall and distinguished, he was a stimulating and sometimes controversial companion whose world status was shown by his obtaining the International Meteorological Organization prize in 1963, and by his election to honorary membership of the American Meteorological Society in 1975. He died at Cadmore End, High Wycombe, Buckinghamshire, on 28 May 1991 and was buried at Halkyn churchyard, Holywell, Flintshire, overlooking the Dee estuary. He was survived by his wife and two daughters.

JIM BURTON

Sources H. Taba, 'The *Bulletin* interviews', *World Meteorological Organization Bulletin*, 30 (1981), 169–81 · Transcript of three interviews of Prof. R. C. Sutcliffe, 1983–85, Royal Meteorological Society, London, Meteorological Office Library · O. G. Sutton, 'Dr R. C. Sutcliffe, F.R.S.', *Meteorological Magazine*, 86 (1957), 129–30 · C. W. G. Daking, 'Presentation of the I.M.O. prize', *World Meteorological Organization Bulletin*, 12 (1963), 234–5 · O. G. Sutton, 'Retirement of Dr R. C. Sutcliffe', *Meteorological Magazine*, 94 (1965), 258–9 · *Whitcliffe Mount School* (1957), 159, 172, 178 · B. J. Mason, 'R. C. Sutcliffe – honorary member', *Bulletin of the American Meteorological Society*, 73 (April 1992) · J. S. Sawyer, *Memoirs FRS*, 38 (1992), 347–58 · R. Pearce, 'Reginald Cockcroft Sutcliffe', *World Meteorological Organization*, 40 (1991), 409 · *The Times* (29 May 1991) · *The Independent* (4 June 1991) · *WWW*, 1991–5 · personal knowledge (2004) · private information (2004) [Mrs Elin Bowes]

Archives Meteorological Office, Bracknell, Berkshire, National Meteorological Library | SOUND Meterological Office, Bracknell, Berkshire, National Meteorological Library

Likenesses photograph, repro. in *The Times* · photograph, repro. in *The Independent* · photograph, RS [*see illus.*]

Wealth at death under £125,000: probate, 20 Aug 1991, *CGPLA Eng. & Wales*

Sutcliffe, Thomas (1790?–1849), army officer, was the son of John Sutcliffe of Stansfield, parish of Halifax, Yorkshire, and great-grandson of John Kay of Bury, the inventor. He entered the Royal Navy and was on board the *Kingfisher* in the blockade of Corfu in 1809, and about that time fell into the enemy's hands, but managed to escape to Albania. He afterwards held a commission in the Royal Horse Guards, and was with the regiment at Waterloo, where he was severely wounded. In 1817 he was one of a group of adventurous Englishmen who went to aid the Colombians in their rebellion against Spain, and was appointed lieutenant-colonel of cavalry in the army of the republic. He was made a prisoner of war, and was detained at Havana.

After returning to England in 1821, Sutcliffe set out again for South America in August of the following year. He offered his services to the republic of Chile, and was appointed captain of cavalry. For sixteen years he remained in Chilean military service, and took part in the operations of the liberating army in Peru. In 1834 he was appointed political and military governor of the island of Juan Fernandez, then used as a convict station by Chile. He survived the earthquake there in February 1835, when he lost many of his possessions. Shortly afterwards an insurrection took place on the island, and Sutcliffe was recalled. Eventually, through a change of administration, he was cashiered in March 1838, and he returned to England in January 1839 with very slender means, heavy claims for arrears of pay remaining unsettled.

Sutcliffe then tried to earn money by writing. He published several books, among them *Sixteen Years in Chile and Peru, from 1822 to 1839* (1841). However, John Lord's *Memoir of John Kay* (1903) devoted an entire chapter to a systematic refutation of the errors and legends ascribed to Sutcliffe; apparently Sutcliffe was not a reliable witness. After living in the Manchester area, he moved to London about 1846, and died in poverty, of 'suffocation from ossification of the heart' (*GM*), in lodgings at 357 Strand on 22 April 1849, aged fifty-nine. C. W. SUTTON, *rev.* JAMES LUNT

Sources T. Sutcliffe, *The earthquake at Juan Fernandez, as it occurred in the year 1835* (1839) · T. Sutcliffe, *Sixteen years in Chile and Peru, from 1822 to 1839* (1841) · *GM*, 2nd ser., 32 (1849), 102 · G. L. M. Strauss, *Reminiscences of an old bohemian*, new edn (1883), 172 · M. G. Mulhall, *The English in South America* (1878), 246 · J. Lord, *Memoir of John Kay of Bury* (1903)

Suter, Fergus [Fergie] (1857–1916), footballer, the only son of David Suter, a journeyman stonemason, and his wife, Catherine (*née* Cooke), was born at 159 Shamrock Street, Glasgow, on 21 November 1857. He began his football career with Partick Thistle in 1878, but was attracted to Turton in Lancashire for he saw, like other Scottish players, the potential in the clubs of Lancashire and Yorkshire. He appeared for Turton Football Club in a local cup competition and was paid £3 for his service. This broke the rules but within twelve months he had joined the Darwen club.

Suter, like his father, was a stonemason by trade but when he performed his craft with Lancashire stone his hands and arms began to swell. Concentrating on football without financial payment was hard, so a benefit match between Darwen and Turton was played in the spring of 1879 to help him and a fellow Scot, Jimmy Love, to survive as the earliest 'professionals' in an amateur game. In a short period of time his captaincy of Darwen had revolutionized the side, and it was even challenging the supremacy of the top teams such as the Old Etonians.

To the disappointment of the fans and the officials Fergie Suter, as he was known, left Darwen for Blackburn Rovers in 1880. He found a normal employment at a cotton mill but resentment at his leaving Darwen culminated in a serious disturbance when he played against his old club before a crowd of 10,000 at Alexandra Meadows on 24 November 1880. Suter was deliberately fouled by a Darwen player and a large section of the crowd invaded the pitch, forcing Sam Ormerod, as the referee, to abandon the game.

The coming of Suter and his Scottish colleagues (known as the 'Scotch professors' on account of their technical proficiency) brought a new era to Blackburn Rovers. Within two years they were regarded as the outstanding team. Suter, a full-back, played a key role, as in the 1882 cup final, when they lost 1–0 to the Old Etonians. His magnificent exhibition on that occasion was so outstanding that the two MPs for Blackburn, W. E. Briggs and Sir William Coddington, entertained him and his colleagues to a dinner. Losing in the cup final again in 1883 to their neighbours Blackburn Olympics spurred Suter and his fellow players to a remarkable period when they won the cup final for three successive years: in 1884 beating Queen's Park, Glasgow, 2–1, in 1885 beating the same side 2–0, and in 1886 defeating West Bromwich Albion 2–0 at Derby after a goalless draw at the Oval. The 1886 final made football history as the first in which two professional clubs appeared: payments to players had been legalized that year largely through the efforts of Blackburn officials, in particular Dr E. S. Morley and T. B. Mitchell.

Suter was in a class of his own, rarely beaten in a tackle, always decisive with his clearances, effective in the air, and dependable at all times. Without his great defensive work his side would not have beaten West Bromwich Albion. He with Herbie Arthur (the goalkeeper) performed miracles, and ensured a special shield for his club from the Football Association (FA) for three consecutive FA cup victories. His playing days came to an end in 1888, the year his club was invited to be one of the founder members of the Football League. Suter's last appearance was on 22 December 1888 against West Bromwich Albion, when he deputized for Arthur in goal.

Like so many of the first generation of professionals, Suter in his retirement kept a public house, the County Arms, in his adopted town of Blackburn. He died of cancer at his home, 8 Seafield Road, North Shore, Blackpool, on 31 July 1916, leaving a widow, Martha. D. BEN REES

Sources H. Kay, *Things about Blackburn Rovers* (1948) · M. Jackman, *Blackburn Rovers: a complete record, 1875–1990* (1990) · A. Pawson, *100*

years of the FA Cup: the official centenary history (1972) • C. Francis, *History of the Blackburn Rovers football club, 1875–1925* (1925) • B. Butler, *The official history of the Football Association* (1991) • W. T. Dixon, *History of Turton football club and carnival sports handbook* (1909) • *Darwen News* (3 May 1879) • *Blackburn Standard* (6 Dec 1882) • b. cert. • CGPLA Eng. & Wales (1916) • d. cert.

Likenesses photographs, repro. in Kay, *Things about Blackburn Rovers* • photographs, repro. in Jackman, *Blackburn Rovers* • photographs, repro. in Francis, *History of the Blackburn Rovers football club*

Wealth at death £610 0s. 4d.: administration, 21 Sept 1916, CGPLA Eng. & Wales

Sutherland. For this title name *see* individual entries under Sutherland; *see also* Gordon, John, eleventh earl of Sutherland (1525–1567); Gordon, Jean, countess of Bothwell and Sutherland (*c*.1546–1629); Gordon, John, fourteenth earl of Sutherland (1609–1679); Gower, George Granville Leveson-, first duke of Sutherland (1758–1833); Gower, Elizabeth Leveson-, duchess of Sutherland and *suo jure* countess of Sutherland (1765–1839); Gower, Harriet Elizabeth Georgiana Leveson-, duchess of Sutherland (1806–1868); Gower, Millicent Fanny Sutherland-Leveson-, duchess of Sutherland (1867–1955).

Sutherland family (*per. c*.1200–*c*.1510), nobility, were descended from Hugh Freskin, who obtained the lands of Sutherland from William the Lion in 1196. Nineteenth-century scholarship, probably misled by the researches of Sir Robert Gordon (completed in 1630, published in 1813 as *A Genealogical History of the Earldom of Sutherland*) seriously confused the identities and numbers of the earls. Hugh's son William succeeded his father as lord of Sutherland, after 1214, and was created earl of Sutherland at some point between 1223 and 1245. He is said to have died in 1248. William's son, also William, had been infeft as second earl of Sutherland by 1263. He attended the convention at Birgham on 14 March 1290, and in July 1291 was nominated by Edward I to receive fealties to the English king at Inverness. Later he appears to have been actively hostile to the claims of Robert Bruce, possibly preferring the Balliol claim and regarding Bruce as a usurper, and he maintained this position until his death some time between April 1306 and September 1307.

William Sutherland, third earl of Sutherland (*c*.1286–1330), was under age when he succeeded his father, as John Ross, younger son of Earl William of Ross, held the young earl of Sutherland in ward, but his tutelage must have been near its end, as William was styled third earl of Sutherland by 16 March 1309 when he appeared at Robert I's first parliament held at St Andrews, having clearly abandoned his father's hostility to Bruce's kingship. He was also present at the parliament held in Arbroath in 1320, appending his seal to the letter to Pope John XXII known as the 'declaration of Arbroath'. He died before December 1330, apparently unmarried, and was succeeded by his brother.

Kenneth Sutherland, fourth earl of Sutherland (*d*. 1333), was styled earl on 7 December 1330, when he granted a writ to Reginald Moray of Culbin, renouncing all claim to Moray's possessions within the earldom of Sutherland. This agreement formed part of a formal alliance between the two families, which was sealed by the marriage of Reginald Moray's son, Gilbert, to Sutherland's daughter, Eustachia. After the death of Thomas Randolph, regent of Scotland, in 1332, Sutherland may have become active in opposing the following year's English invasion, for he was killed at the battle of Halidon Hill on 19 July 1333. He was married to Lady Mary, daughter of *Donald, sixth earl of Mar.

William Sutherland, fifth earl of Sutherland (*d*. 1370/71), who succeeded his father in 1333, is said by the Lanercost chronicle to have joined with the earls of Fife and Dunbar, in laying siege to the castle of Cupar in 1336, held at that time by William Bullock for the English. In 1340 he raided into England with the earl of March; they inflicted considerable damage, but suffered a defeat on their return journey at the hands of Sir Thomas Gray. In 1341 *David II returned to Scotland after spending nine years in France, and Sutherland clearly found considerable favour at court, sufficient to receive the king's sister Margaret in marriage, papal dispensation for the match being given at the end of 1342.

Sutherland's rising influence was such that the earldom of Sutherland was erected into a free regality on 10 October 1345, while on 4 November the barony of Cluny in Aberdeenshire was added to Sutherland's possessions. On 30 March 1346 he and his wife received a grant of the stronghold of Dunnottar in the Mearns, together with a special licence to build a fortalice upon the crag. In 1346 Sutherland joined the king's army which invaded England, but the campaign ended with the defeat of the Scots at the battle of Nevilles Cross, and with the capture of David II and of Sutherland himself. Sutherland is next recorded in June 1351, when he received a safe conduct to go to Newcastle to negotiate David II's ransom. In September his infant son John, born in 1346, was handed over as a hostage; John's important position as his royal uncle's nearest male heir enabled David II to return to Scotland for a few months. In 1357 Sutherland and his son were both handed over as hostages. The earl remained in England for more than ten years, while according to Walter Bower, the young John Sutherland died of plague at Lincoln on 8 September 1361, thus ending any Sutherland hopes of a royal succession.

David II made a number of grants to Sutherland, including the barony and castle of Urquhart, on 28 February 1359, apparently in exchange for thanages in Kincardineshire, while between 1360 and 1365 he received a number of grants from the exchequer, in addition to £80 paid by David II towards Sutherland's expenses in England. In terms of political influence, however, Sutherland's day was over, possibly because of the machinations of the faction led by Robert Stewart, whose members would have had readier access to the king while Sutherland was languishing in England. It may have been due to Stewart that David II was in no hurry to secure Sutherland's release. Sutherland had returned to Scotland by the time a grant was issued to him on 27 February 1370, but he must have died before June 1371, when the barony of Urquhart was back in royal hands. Following the death of his first wife, Margaret Bruce, possibly in 1346, Sutherland had married

Joanna Menteith by November 1347. With his second wife, Earl William had a son who succeeded him.

Robert Sutherland, sixth earl of Sutherland (*d.* in or before 1427?), who was formerly misnamed William and thought to have died perhaps in 1398, may have been still a minor in 1371, and Alexander Stewart, lord of Badenoch and younger son of Robert II, was administering the earldom of Sutherland as Robert's guardian by October 1372, conducting business from the chief Sutherland stronghold of Dunrobin in 1373–4. However, in 1384 the chronicler Froissart refers to Robert as welcoming a party of French knights to Scotland, and the same writer, despite inaccurately naming him John, credits Sutherland with leading the Scottish force which invaded north-west England in 1388. He first appears in government records on 2 November 1389, when he was present at the condemnation of his erstwhile guardian and then father-in-law, Alexander *Stewart, earl of Buchan. On 22 January 1401 Sutherland issued a grant from the castle of Dunrobin to his brother, Kenneth, but the rest of his career is rather obscure. The date of his death has been placed in 1442, but he was probably dead by 1427; the earl of Sutherland sent to England in that year as a hostage for James I's ransom seems less likely to have been Earl Robert than the latter's son John, born of Robert's marriage to Lady Margaret Stewart, daughter of Alexander, earl of Buchan.

John Sutherland, seventh earl of Sutherland (*d.* in or before 1460), wrongly identified as Robert in the nineteenth century, is mentioned by the chronicler Wyntoun as having been knighted by his uncle, Alexander Stewart, earl of Buchan, when the latter took a Scottish contingent to Flanders in 1408. He was sent to England as a hostage for James I's ransom in 1427, probably very soon after the death of his father, and he remained there for many years, confined in Pontefract Castle, where he married Margaret Baillie (*d.* 1509/10), probably a relative of one of his fellow hostages at Pontefract, Sir William Baillie of Hoprig and Lamington. Sutherland was still at Pontefract in July 1444, but had been released by May 1448, when he was at Dunrobin Castle, presenting a chaplain to the chapel of St Andrew at Golspie. On 29 April 1451 Sutherland and his wife received a crown charter of lands in the parish of Loth, Sutherland; the rents from these were reserved for their use during their lifetimes when, on 22 February 1456, Sutherland resigned his earldom into the hands of James II in favour of his son John. Three days later John was infeft in the lands of the earldom during his father's lifetime, by precept of sasine given by James II at Inverness. The reason for this move is unclear, but it may have been prompted by the earl's ill health. The seventh earl was dead by 1460, and was buried in the chapel of St Andrew at Golspie.

John Sutherland, eighth earl of Sutherland (*d.* 1508), was accused by Sir Robert Gordon, in his history of the family, of using his mother and relatives with great cruelty. He seems to have suffered from a form of mental illness, and in 1494 a brieve of idiotry was issued by James IV, which resulted in a declaration of Sutherland's inability to manage his affairs. He was placed under the tutelage of Sir James Dunbar of Cumnock, and died in 1508, when he was succeeded by his son John, who was to suffer from the same mental affliction. John was the son of the first of the eighth earl's three marriages; his mother may have been the daughter of Alexander Macdonald, lord of the Isles. There were no children of the eighth earl's two later marriages, to Fingole, widow of John Munro of Foulis (which probably ended in divorce), and to Catherine (surname unknown), who outlived him.

C. A. MᶜGLADDERY

Sources W. Fraser, ed., *The Sutherland book*, 3 vols. (1892), vols. 1, 3 · J. M. Thomson and others, eds., *Registrum magni sigilli regum Scotorum / The register of the great seal of Scotland*, 11 vols. (1882–1914), vol. 2 · G. Burnett and others, eds., *The exchequer rolls of Scotland*, 23 vols. (1878–1908), vols. 1, 13 · *APS*, 1124–1423 · *CDS*, vol. 4 · R. Gordon and G. Gordon, *A genealogical history of the earldom of Sutherland ... with a continuation to the year 1651* (1813) · J. R. N. Macphail, ed., *Highland papers*, 4 vols., Scottish History Society, 2nd ser., 5, 12, 20; 3rd ser., 22 (1914–34) · Rymer, *Foedera*, new edn, vol. 3 · C. Innes, ed., *Registrum episcopatus Moraviensis*, Bannatyne Club, 58 (1837) · *Scots peerage*, vol. 8 · S. I. Boardman, *The early Stewart kings: Robert II and Robert III, 1371–1406* (1996) · J. Stevenson, ed., *Chronicon de Lanercost, 1201–1346*, Bannatyne Club, 65 (1839)

Sutherland, Alexander (1852–1902), journalist in Australia, born at Wellcroft Place, Glasgow, on 26 March 1852, was the eldest son of George Sutherland, an artist, and his wife, Jane, the daughter of William Smith, of Galston, Ayrshire. Two brothers, George and William, gained some prominence, the former as a journalist and inventor and the latter as a mathematician and an original scientific enquirer. Alexander was educated in Glasgow until 1864, when the state of his father's health led to the whole family's emigrating to Sydney, Australia. At the age of fourteen he became a pupil teacher in the education department of New South Wales and studied for the arts course at Sydney University. In 1870 the family moved to Melbourne, where Sutherland taught at the Hawthorn grammar school during the day and worked at night for the arts course at Melbourne University. He entered the university in the first term of 1871 and graduated BA with distinction in 1874, sharing—with H. B. Higgins—the Shakespeare scholarship; he took his MA the following year. In 1879 he married Elizabeth Jane, the second daughter of Robert Dundas Ballantyne, controller-general of the convict settlement at Port Arthur, Tasmania. They had one son and three daughters.

On leaving the university Sutherland became mathematical master at Scotch College, Melbourne (1875–7), and principal of Carlton College, Melbourne (1877–92). In 1892 he retired to the seaside at Dromana in order to devote himself to work on *The Origin and Growth of the Moral Instinct*, which was published in London in 1898. The financial crisis of 1893, however, compelled him to take up journalism, and he became a major contributor to the *Melbourne Review*, of which he was a founder and for a time co-editor, *The Argus*, *The Australasian*, and other papers and periodicals. He made two unsuccessful attempts to enter politics, contesting Williamstown in 1897 in the Victorian legislature, and standing for South Melbourne in the federal parliament in 1901. In late 1898 he went to London as representative of the *South Australian Register*, and the following year he reported the sittings of the peace conference at The Hague. After his return to Australia and his 1901 electoral defeat he was appointed registrar of Melbourne University, and when the professor of English died in 1902, he became lecturer in that subject as well. But the double duty overtaxed him, and he died suddenly of heart disease at Adelaide on 9 August 1902. He was buried in Kew cemetery, Melbourne; his former pupils placed a tablet to his memory in Carlton College.

Sutherland was in the front rank of Australian men of letters. A stimulating teacher, he was equally successful in the preparation of many geographical textbooks. Apart from the *Moral Instinct*, his most significant works were *Victoria and its Metropolis* (1888) and his contributions to Andrew Garran's *Picturesque Atlas of Australasia* (1886). His *History of Australia from 1606 to 1876* (1877) (in which his brother George collaborated) sold more than 100,000 copies. He was a minor poet and a scientific investigator, and acted for some years as secretary of the Royal Society of Victoria. He also wrote biographies of Henry Kendall and Adam Lindsay Gordon, and memoirs of Sir Redmond Barry and Professor Edward Hearn.

CHEWTON ATCHLEY, rev. A. G. L. SHAW

Sources F. H. Northcott, 'Sutherland, Alexander', *AusDB*, vol. 6 · H. G. Turner, *Alexander Sutherland* (1908) · E. Scott, *A history of the University of Melbourne* (1936) · *The Argus* [Melbourne] (13 Aug 1902) · G. Blainey, *A centenary history of the University of Melbourne* (1957)
Likenesses G. Sutherland, sketch, *c*.1874, Colonial Office Library, London
Wealth at death £5959: probate, Victoria, Australia; Northcott, 'Sutherland, Alexander'

Sutherland, Angus (1848–1922), politician, was born in Helmsdale, Sutherland, the third son of William Sutherland, a crofter. Both of his grandfathers, also crofters, had suffered eviction. He was educated at Helmsdale parish school, where he became a pupil teacher in 1863, and entered Edinburgh Training College in 1868 and the University of Glasgow in 1872. He taught in Aberfeldy and later acted as the tutor to John Sinclair (Lord Pentland), secretary for Scotland from 1905 to 1912, before his appointment in 1876 as mathematics master at the Glasgow Academy.

During the 1870s Glasgow saw the development of many associations of émigré Gaels, among the most important being the Glasgow Highland Society. Sutherland was a member and in 1880 made a speech which was widely reported. In it he argued that 'Every Highlander is a born agitator because he has suffered directly or indirectly from landlordism' (*Oban Times*, 13 Nov 1880). His career as an agitator began in earnest in 1882 when, along with John Mackay, a wealthy highlander based in Hereford, he formed the Sutherland Highland Land Law Reform Association. At the general election of 1885 he unsuccessfully contested the county seat of Sutherland, standing as a crofters' candidate against the marquess of Stafford, the eldest son of the duke of Sutherland. The marquess, a Liberal, had been one of a group of inactive landowning MPs for highland constituencies and had

Angus Sutherland (1848–1922), by James Russell & Sons, 1887

held his seat without distinction since 1874. In 1884 Stafford began to take a greater interest in his constituency and he convened a mass meeting at Golspie in October which discussed franchise reform and the land issue. He became steadily more radical as the election of 1885 approached, even advocating the abolition of the House of Lords and currying favour with Free Church ministers. Thus, Stafford was well placed to fight off Sutherland's challenge.

Despite putting forward a Crofters Bill in the 1886 parliament Stafford chose not to contest the election of 1886 and Angus Sutherland became the MP for his native county, joining a group of crofters' MPs in parliament. In 1886 he advocated postponing the union between the Sutherland, Glasgow, and Edinburgh Highland Land Reform Associations: the Sutherland association to which he belonged was not a slavish follower of the urban elements of the crofters' movement. The Highland Land League, as the new organization was called, soon began to suffer from factionalism and Sutherland was blamed for some of the problems. A formal breach between the Highland Land League and Sutherland took place in 1888 as his opposition to the London control of the organization hardened.

During the 1890s Sutherland's career took a very different line from that of the other crofter MPs. From 1892 to 1895 he was a member of the royal commission (highlands and islands, 1892), chaired by David Brand. This commission had been established to discover the extent of land which could be added to crofters' holdings. However, it was dogged by acrimony among the members and the suspicion that it was meant as a delaying tactic by a government dominated by the Irish home rule issue. The commission itself was widely criticized and Sutherland was accused of being insufficiently favourable to the crofters' cause. He resigned his parliamentary seat in 1894 after accepting the chairmanship of the fishery board for Scotland, a position which brought with it membership of the congested districts board for Scotland. In this capacity

Sutherland advocated a hard line with crofters on the Kilmuir estate in the north of Skye who were unwilling to purchase their holdings after the estate had been acquired by the board in 1904. In 1906 he became a member of the royal commission on congestion in Ireland, and was made CB in 1907. Sutherland died, unmarried, at his home, 9 Forres Street, Edinburgh, on 16 January 1922. His nephew, Sir William Sutherland (1880–1949), was Liberal MP for Argyll from 1918 to 1924.   EWEN A. CAMERON

Sources I. M. M. MacPhail, *The crofters' war* (1989) · J. Hunter, *The making of the crofting community* (1970) · *Inverness Courier* (20 Jan 1922) · E. A. Cameron, *Land for the people* (1996) · *WWW* · D. W. Crowley, 'The "crofters' party", 1885–1892', *SHR*, 35 (1956), 110–26 · *WWBMP* · A. Newby, 'Shoulder to shoulder? Scottish and Irish land reformers in the highlands of Scotland, 1878–1894', PhD diss., U. Edin., 2001

Archives NA Scot., congested districts board files · NA Scot., fishery board for Scotland

Likenesses J. Russell & Sons, photograph, 1887, NPG [*see illus.*]

Wealth at death £17,886 5s. 5d.: confirmation, 4 April 1922, *CGPLA Eng. & Wales*

Sutherland, Sir Gordon Brims Black McIvor (1907–1980), physicist, was born on 8 April 1907 at Watten, Caithness, the youngest of seven children (of whom five survived) of Peter Sutherland, a teacher, of Dundee, and his wife, Eliza Hope, also a teacher, daughter of Alexander Morrison, grocer, of Dufftown, Banffshire. Sutherland attended Morgan Academy, Dundee, where he excelled in mathematics and science. He entered St Andrews University in 1924 and obtained two first-class honours degrees, the MA in mathematics (1928), and the BSc in physics (1929). He was attracted by the possibility of a university career, and moved with the aid of scholarships to Trinity College, Cambridge, where he worked with Ralph H. Fowler. As part of his introduction to research he was to draft a chapter on the specific heats of gases for the second edition of Fowler's well-known book, *Statistical Mechanics*.

At Cambridge Sutherland met Professor David M. Dennison, who was on leave from the University of Michigan. Dennison was a leading theorist on the vibrations and rotations of molecules, topics very close to those which Sutherland was reviewing in his chapter for Fowler. Sutherland decided that he would try to work with Dennison; his application for a Commonwealth fellowship was successful and he spent two rewarding years at Ann Arbor, becoming an experienced research scientist.

Having returned to Cambridge Sutherland resumed work on some of the molecules he had studied earlier, and collaborated with W. G. Penney, who was working theoretically on similar molecules. The positions of the atoms in the molecules of hydrogen peroxide, hydrazine, ozone, and nitrogen tetroxide were all determined by a combined study of their electronic structures, their vibrational motions, and their Raman spectra. While this work was in progress Sutherland was appointed in 1934 to the Stokes studentship of Pembroke College, Cambridge. He was elected a fellow of Pembroke College in 1935 and soon assembled a research group, well equipped in infra-red and Raman spectroscopy. He married, in 1936, Gunborg Elisabeth, elder daughter of Filip Wahlström, artist, of

Göteborg, Sweden. The marriage was a happy one, and they had three daughters.

Research was suspended on the outbreak of war in 1939, and Sutherland worked in London on bomb disposal. In 1941 a military need arose to determine rapidly the sources of the fuel mixtures being used by enemy aircraft. The group was reassembled at Cambridge and, in collaboration with others, analysed fuel recovered from destroyed enemy aircraft, and identified the main sources.

The return of British science to peacetime conditions was slow and difficult. Sutherland did well at Cambridge, becoming reader in spectroscopy in 1947, and when he received in 1949 an offer of a full professorship (of physics) at Ann Arbor he was uncertain what to do. He accepted but hoped he might some day return to Britain if a suitable opportunity arose. His work at Michigan was notable for some papers on crystalline polymers. The offer from Britain came in 1956, the directorship of the National Physical Laboratory (NPL).

The time Sutherland spent at NPL (1956–64) was a period of rapidly increasing prosperity in the western world. Sutherland believed that economic growth depended on science and under his energetic leadership the NPL grew in numbers and facilities. Particular emphasis was laid on the new basic physics division. However, by the 1960s constraints began to be imposed on the rising cost of science. Basic research was now to be conducted mainly in the universities or in specialist institutes. Sutherland was disappointed and, as at this moment he was offered the mastership of Emmanuel College, Cambridge, he accepted. Many improvements were made to the college during Sutherland's period as master (1964–77). New rooms were added and the library was completed. The master and his wife were noted for their hospitality. Sutherland presided easily and with dignity, showing his natural Scots courtesy, caution, and wit, qualities which were especially important during the student troubles of the late 1960s. Sutherland contributed to national and university science policy. He was mainly responsible for the first authoritative collection of statistics showing the large number of scientists emigrating from Britain to the United States, the so-called brain drain.

In appearance, Sutherland was a little over average height, strong but not heavy, with dark hair and wearing glasses. He enjoyed mountaineering, hockey, and golf; he had a keen sense of humour and relished stories about the careful Scot. Sutherland received many academic honours (including the honorary degrees of LLD of St Andrews in 1958 and DSc of Strathclyde in 1966) and many other awards and marks of distinction. He was elected FRS in 1949, knighted in 1960, and was a vice-president of the Royal Society in 1961–3. He died at Cambridge on 27 June 1980. He was survived by his wife. PENNEY, *rev.*

Sources N. Sheppard, *Memoirs FRS*, 28 (1982), 589–626 · *The Times* (28 June 1980), 16g [tribute] · *The Times* (13 Oct 1980), 14a [memorial service] · personal knowledge (1986) · *WWW* · *CGPLA Eng. & Wales* (1980)

Archives CUL, corresp. and papers | Bodl. Oxf., corresp. with C. A. Coulson

Likenesses photograph, repro. in Sheppard, *Memoirs FRS*

Wealth at death £17,115: probate, 26 Aug 1980, *CGPLA Eng. & Wales*

Sutherland, Graham Vivian (1903–1980), painter and printmaker, was born at 8 Pendle Road, Streatham, London, on 24 August 1903, the eldest of the three children of George Humphrey Vivian Sutherland (1873–1952), barrister and civil servant at the Board of Education, and his wife, Elsie Foster (1877–1957). His younger brother, (Carol) Humphrey Vivian *Sutherland (1908–1986), became a distinguished numismatist. The Sutherlands lived in south London, successively in Streatham, Merton Park, and Sutton. They also built a small holiday home in Rustington, Sussex, in 1913. Sutherland went as a day boy to Epsom College, Surrey, but only for two years: in 1919 he was sent as an engineering apprentice to the midland railway works, Derby, where one of his uncles was a senior engineer. But he had no talent for mathematics, and had developed a taste for drawing during a not very happy childhood. He persuaded his father to let him give up engineering, and in 1921 he entered Goldsmiths' College of Art in south London.

There Sutherland eventually specialized in etching, studying first under Malcolm Osborne and then Stanley Anderson; his closest friends, Paul Drury, Edward Bouverie Hoyton, and William Larkins, all later distinguished themselves in this medium. He came under the spell of the etchings and drawings of Samuel Palmer (1805–1881), then being rediscovered, and was subsequently befriended by F. L. Griggs, one of the best-known printmakers of that time and also a devotee of Palmer's work.

In October 1924 Sutherland had his first exhibition, at the Twenty-One Gallery near the Strand in London, a successful début which led to election the following year as an associate of the Royal Society of Painter–Etchers and Engravers. Shortly after leaving Goldsmiths' in the summer of 1926 he was appointed to teach engraving at the Chelsea School of Art in London. On 29 December 1927 he married a fellow student (of fashion), Kathleen Barry (1905–1991), a year after being received into the Roman Catholic church. A devoted and inseparable couple, they lived in Kent, first in Farningham, then Eynsford (1931), Sutton-at-Hone (1933), and finally Trottiscliffe, in a house leased in 1937 and purchased in 1945.

Sutherland's relatively remunerative career as a printmaker was abruptly ended in late 1929 by the collapse of the mainly American market, along with the New York stock exchange. While continuing to etch into the early 1930s, he switched to the teaching of composition and book illustration at Chelsea and became more involved in commercial work, encouraged by his friend Milner Gray, who later founded the Society of Industrial Artists and Designers. His designs ranged from glassware and ceramics to a notable series of posters for artistically enlightened companies such as Shell-Mex and the London transport board. He also turned to watercolours and oil paint.

The key moment in Sutherland's artistic life occurred in the spring of 1934, when he first visited Pembrokeshire on the recommendation of a friend. 'It was in this country

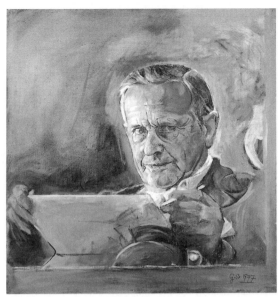

Graham Vivian Sutherland (1903–1980), self-portrait, 1977

that I began to learn painting', he wrote in a letter to a subsequent patron, Colin Anderson, which was later published as 'Welsh sketchbook' in *Horizon* magazine. 'It was in this area that I learned that landscape is not necessarily scenic, but that its parts have an individual figurative detachment ... the whole setting is one of exuberance—of darkness and light—of decay and life' (April 1942, 225–35). He spent each summer there until the war, revisited it during the war years, and then again regularly from 1967 onwards, his imagination rekindled by returning for a television film about his career.

Sutherland's increasingly bold paraphrases of Welsh landscape, painted in the studio from sketches of lanes, hills, roots, and other organic forms and 'bringing out the anonymous personality of these things', won acclaim at his first one-man show, arranged by an important new patron, Sir Kenneth Clark, at the Rosenberg and Helft Gallery in London in September 1938. As an official war artist, again at the invitation of Clark, he produced equally evocative work derived from studies of war devastation in Swansea and London's East End, and visits to Cornish tin mines, iron foundries, limestone quarries, and, in liberated France, marshalling yards near Paris and flying-bomb sites in Normandy. These experiences of human suffering were a form of preparation both for his later portraits and for his religious works. Combined with his lyrical landscapes, his war drawings established him as a leader of what came to be seen as the neo-romantic strain in contemporary British painting, inspiring painters as various as Keith Vaughan, Lucian Freud, and John Craxton.

In 1944 Sutherland was commissioned to paint a large-scale crucifixion for St Matthew's Church in Northampton: his first religious work and his first big figure study. Inspired in part by photographs from liberated German concentration camps and by Mathias Grünewald's Isenheim altarpiece (1512/1513–1515), it was completed in 1946 and remains arguably the most powerful and effective of all his religious works. Sutherland's preliminary studies of thorns marked a switch, influenced by the work of Picasso and Matisse, to more overtly realistic subject matter and a general lightening and brightening of style, if not often of mood. In the decade after the war he regularly visited France, became close to Francis Bacon, and was accepted as a leader of the avant-garde. Exhibitions in London and New York culminated in 1952 in a major showing at the Venice Biennale, the Musée d'Art Moderne in Paris, and—the following year, to a cooler critical reception—at the Tate Gallery in London.

For all his vulnerability, Sutherland was never afraid to tackle daunting new challenges. In 1952 he accepted a commission to design the huge tapestry *Christ in Glory* for the new Coventry Cathedral. In 1949 he had painted his first portrait, a startling full-length study of Somerset Maugham (Tate collection). This powerful work, widely acclaimed, was followed by a portrait of Maugham's neighbour on the Riviera, Lord Beaverbrook (1952, National Portrait Gallery, London), whose newspapers did much to make Sutherland famous in Britain—not least when an all-party parliamentary committee commissioned him to paint Sir Winston Churchill as a gift for the latter's eightieth birthday in 1954. The result, both praised and reviled by MPs, was detested by its subject for making him look old and, he claimed, half-witted. It was subsequently destroyed on Lady Churchill's orders, though sketches for it survive. Among the best of Sutherland's later portraits are those of his friend Edward Sackville-West (1954), Paul Sacher (1956), Princess Gourielli (Helena Rubinstein) (1957, Beaverbrook Art Gallery, Fredericton, New Brunswick, Canada), Prince von Fürstenberg (1959), Konrad Adenauer (1965, priv. coll.), and Lord Goodman (1973). Others lacked conviction and revealed his weaknesses as a draughtsman.

Sutherland toiled off and on for ten years over the Coventry Cathedral tapestry, visiting the weavers, Pinton Frères, at Felletin in central France, nine times to check progress as they worked from photographic enlargements of his cartoons or finished sketches. These had previously been approved by the cathedral authorities after much debate. Sutherland was embittered by the authorities' refusal to allow him to see the completed tapestry hung before its dispatch to Coventry: France's culture minister André Malraux had even offered the Sainte-Chapelle in Paris for such a display. It remains the most controversial as well as the largest single item in the rebuilt cathedral, its sheer size causing serious problems of sagging.

After a succession of London dealers had handled his work, Sutherland settled in 1959 with Marlborough Fine Art, then dominant in the contemporary art field. In the mid-1960s he formed a Swiss company to handle his affairs, and in the last ten years of his life became a tax exile, based mainly in the house near Menton which he had acquired in the mid-1950s and greatly enlarged. His chief patrons in those later years were across the nearby Italian border, following a successful retrospective in Turin in 1965. The Sutherlands habitually spent part of each summer in Venice, where they developed many friends, and it was in Venice that he painted one of his finest large oils, *Interior 1965*.

It was, furthermore, with an Italian film crew that Sutherland made his seminal return trip to Pembrokeshire in 1967, sparking an annual pilgrimage which inspired much of the work of his last twelve years: 'I thought I had exhausted what the countryside had to offer both as "vocabulary" & as inspiration. I was sadly mistaken', he commented (*Sutherland in Wales*, 1984, 6; Graham Sutherland Gallery, Picton Castle, exhibition catalogue). Some of this final output was destined for the Graham Sutherland Gallery at Picton Castle, Pembrokeshire, home of the Philipps family, which opened in 1976 and closed in October 1995, its contents passing to the National Museums and Galleries of Wales in Cardiff. In his last decade Sutherland reverted frequently to his original trade as printmaker, producing *inter alia* two notable series of technically advanced aquatints: The Bees (1977), and a Bestiary (1979) based on poems by Guillaume Apollinaire. Among the best of his somewhat uneven later paintings was *The Thicket* (1978), a tangle of mysterious natural forms in front of which he depicted himself sketching: a prophetic work, since organic growth, in the form of liver cancer, was soon to kill him. A fine self-portrait from 1977 is in the National Portrait Gallery, London.

Sutherland's was a complex personality. His charm was exceptional, a compound of wonderful manners, a very attractive, light, speaking voice, good looks, a flattering capacity to concentrate on his interlocutor, and an engaging if often feline sense of humour. Furthermore, he enjoyed good living: dressing and eating well, driving the latest Jaguar, having convivial evenings with stimulating friends; and he was astonishingly generous with his work. Yet his personality had a darker side, reflected in his painting. He could be devious. His perfectionism, carried to obsessional lengths, often alienated those professionally involved with him. For a man of socialist instincts, he was over-impressed by people of power, rank, and title; and he was over-sensitive to criticism and thus vulnerable to flattery. These tendencies were fostered by his relationship with his wife, Kathleen. She too was impressed by wealth and titles—and fiercely protective of her husband. He depended on her to stave off unwanted visitors or callers. She became his sometimes sharp-tongued Cerberus who enabled him to present a generally charming face to the outside world. As often with childless couples, theirs was an intensely close relationship.

It was typical of Sutherland's fallible judgement that he failed to see the dangers in having as his most fervent champion the flamboyant critic, collector, and art historian Douglas Cooper, who sought to build up Sutherland's reputation by denigrating that of virtually all his British contemporaries. Cooper's monograph on Sutherland, published in 1961, proclaimed its subject to be 'the most distinguished and the most original English artist of the mid-twentieth century' (*The Work of Graham Sutherland*, 1), one who had transcended the weaknesses and provincialism of the English school to emerge as a painter of international standing. In the early 1950s Sutherland and Cooper had been on the same attacking side in the row which convulsed the Tate Gallery's trustees, over the stewardship of various trusts. This led to Sutherland's resignation as a trustee in 1954. Twenty years later Cooper and the Sutherlands fell out, and Cooper later stated, in a letter to *The Times*, that he had never believed or claimed that Sutherland was, in the historical perspective, an artist of major stature. Sutherland needed an element of tension in his life: with Cooper, as with the Pembrokeshire landscape, he was forever on the brink of some drama.

The most consistent element in Sutherland's life, apart from the bastion of his marriage to Kathleen, was his devotion to his work. 'I am, I have to admit, a tireless worker—with regular hours', he said (*DNB*). Travel or staying with friends he considered a waste of time. He described his working methods with characteristic vividness. On his daily walks in search of material he reacted to certain things only as if in response to some internal need of the nerves:

> In the studio, I remember; it may be an hour ago or years, and I react afresh. The images dissolve; objects may lose their normal environment and relationship. Then they seem to be drawn together and redefined in the mind's eye in a new life and a new mould—there has been a substitution, a change. But I feel this to be valid only in so far as the process of digestion has preserved in the substance of my material—paint and canvas—the sensation of the original presence, in its new and permanent form. (ibid.)

He was obsessed by correspondences, 'between machines and organic forms, between organic forms and people, and of people with stones' (ibid.).

For all his celebrity in the last twenty-five years of his life, Sutherland remained insecure and in need of reassurance. Little enough of that came from British critics, and in his adoptive France, to his distress, his reputation was before long far eclipsed by that of his old friend Francis Bacon. Yet he was not without honours in his own country, and his work was widely admired abroad, especially in Germany and Italy. He was admitted to the Order of Merit before Henry Moore and their patron Kenneth Clark, in 1960; was made an honorary DLitt at Oxford in 1962; was elected an honorary fellow of the American Academy of Arts and Letters in 1972; became a Commandeur des Arts et Lettres in Paris and honorary fellow of the Accademia Nazionale di San Luca, Rome, in 1973. In 1974 he became the first artist to receive the Shakespeare prize in Hamburg.

Despite feeling increasingly unwell, Sutherland worked in Wales up to a few weeks before his death at the Royal Free Hospital in Hampstead, London, on 17 February 1980. He was buried near his home in Trottiscliffe, Kent. He was survived by his wife.   ROGER BERTHOUD

Sources R. Berthoud, *Graham Sutherland: a biography* (1982) · J. Hayes, *The art of Graham Sutherland* (1980) [incl. comprehensive bibliography] · *Graham Sutherland: correspondences: selected writings on art*, ed. J. Andrews (1982) · personal knowledge (2004) · *CGPLA Eng. & Wales* (1981) · *DNB* · b. cert.

Archives Tate collection, Tate Gallery archive, annotated exhibition catalogues [photocopies] · Tate collection, Tate Gallery archive, sketchbooks and fragments of sketchbooks · Tate collection, Tate Gallery archive, typescripts of an interview [photocopies] · V&A NAL, MSS and typescripts | HLRO, corresp. with Lord Beaverbrook · Tate collection, Tate Gallery archive, corresp. with Lord Clark · Tate collection, Tate Gallery archive, typescripts of two conversations with Andrew Revai · Tate collection, Tate Gallery archive, corresp. with Edward Sackville-West · V&A NAL, Forster Library, corresp. with Bernhard Baer · V&A NAL, letters to Felix Man · W. Sussex RO, letters to Walter Hussey and related papers | FILM London Weekend TV, *South Bank Show*, interview with Melvyn Bragg and Bryan Robertson, 1 April 1979

Likenesses G. V. Sutherland, self-portrait, pencil, 1945, NPG · G. V. Sutherland, self-portrait, pencil, c.1945–1946, NPG · photographs, 1954–77, Hult. Arch. · G. V. Sutherland, self-portrait, oils, 1977, NPG [*see illus.*] · J. Hedgecoe, platinum print, NPG

Wealth at death £77,885—in England and Wales: administration with will, 13 Feb 1981, *CGPLA Eng. & Wales*

Sutherland, Halliday Gibson (1882–1960), physician and writer, was born in Glasgow on 24 June 1882, the elder son of John Francis Sutherland, deputy commissioner for lunacy in Scotland, and his wife, Jane, daughter of John Mackay, a free-church minister in Caithness. After attending Glasgow high school and Merchiston Castle School, Edinburgh, he studied medicine at Edinburgh University, where he graduated MB, ChB in 1906 and MD with honours in 1908. As an undergraduate, Sutherland was a leading debater and prominent personality in Liberal politics, though in 1945 it was as a Labour candidate that he stood unsuccessfully for the Scottish universities.

Soon after graduation, Sutherland came under the influence of Robert William Philip, pioneer of modern anti-tuberculosis schemes, on whose model in 1911 Sutherland opened a tuberculosis dispensary in St Marylebone, London. It included the original feature of an open-air school, held in the bandstand of Regent's Park. He also produced a cinema film on tuberculosis which was probably the first film on health education in Britain. In 1911 Sutherland edited a remarkable compilation of tributes to Philip's work from pupils all over the world; the volume gained Philip a knighthood and secured official approval for his tuberculosis schemes, in which Sutherland played a leading part.

War service in the Royal Navy and the Royal Air Force interrupted Sutherland's career. He used the opportunity to write a textbook, *Pulmonary Tuberculosis* (1916). Although planned before the war, it was actually written when he was medical officer on the armed merchant-cruiser, *Empress of Britain*, which was stationed near the equator.

On returning to practise in London, Sutherland became physician to St Marylebone (later St Charles's) Hospital, Ladbroke Grove, and assistant physician to the Royal Chest Hospital. Between 1920 and 1925 he was deputy commissioner (tuberculosis) for the south-west of England, and he then joined the medical service of the London county council.

Sutherland's many-sided personality was now ripe for new expression. In 1920 Sutherland had married Muriel, daughter of John Frederick Fitzpatrick, the managing director of a City firm of oriental importers. They had five sons and one daughter. He had also become a Roman Catholic, and following the publication of Marie Stopes's *Married Love* (1918), which had made birth control a lively public issue, Sutherland plunged into controversy, attacking the practice on sociological and religious grounds. The subject was new and shocking, and Sutherland became an uninhibited and pungent critic. He asserted in *Birth Control, a Statement of Christian Doctrine* (1922) that it was truly amazing that this monstrous campaign of birth control should be tolerated by the home secretary, and that Charles Bradlaugh had been condemned to gaol for a less serious crime. Dr Stopes, herself no mean controversialist, sued him for libel. After prolonged litigation, Sutherland's defence to this action was upheld by the House of Lords (1924) and the case became a leading one in the English law of defamation. Sutherland's opponent described him as 'the most cocksure man in the British empire'. This self-confidence was both his strength and a limitation. He never had any doubts. He could produce an impressive argument, but it did not always seem convincing. In truth, he was more temperamentally fitted for law or politics than for medicine, in which his reputation never maintained the level of its brilliant beginning. In 1941 he became deputy medical officer of health for Coventry, and in 1943 he started the mass radiography centre in Birmingham which he directed until 1951. He also spent periods in general medical practice in north London.

In the meantime Sutherland had made his name as a writer, publishing in 1933 a very readable volume of reminiscences, *The Arches of the Years*, a title taken from 'The Hound of Heaven' by Francis Thompson. Enormously successful, it ran to thirty-two English editions, and was translated into eight languages. It was followed by further anecdotal autobiographies—*A Time to Keep* (1934), *In my Path* (1936), *Lapland Journey* (1938), *Hebridean Journey* (1939), *Southward Journey* (1942), *Spanish Journey* (1948), and *Irish Journey* (1956). Sutherland's great theme was himself. When describing his triumphs or misadventures, with doctors, with bullfighters, or in the law courts, his style is terse, emphatic, and very sympathetic. He explored no new pathways of human experience, but his idiosyncrasies and pugnacious judgements were highly entertaining.

Sutherland had red hair and blue eyes. He was thickset and not very tall. Touches of humour came through his ceremonious and resonant tones of voice in which there were echoes of the pulpit. He was indeed gifted with his mother's highland temperament and his grandfather's free-church fervour. Courage and provocative wit gained him friends but also enemies. Sutherland was made a knight commander of the order of Isabel the Catholic in 1954. He died at the Hospital of St John and St Elizabeth, St Marylebone, London, on 19 April 1960.

HARLEY WILLIAMS, rev.

Sources *The Times* (20 April 1960) · *BMJ* (30 April 1960), 1368–9 · *The Lancet* (30 April 1960), 984–5 · personal knowledge (1971) · probate, 1960
Archives BL, corresp. with Society of Authors, Add. MSS 63334
Likenesses oils, priv. coll.; in possession of the family in 1971
Wealth at death £3686 6s. 2d.: probate, 30 Aug 1960, CGPLA Eng. & Wales

Sutherland [*married name* Denman]**, Helen Christian** (1881–1965), collector and patron of the arts, was born on 24 February 1881 at 167 Cromwell Road, Kensington, London, the eldest of three children and the only daughter of Sir Thomas *Sutherland (1834–1922), shipowner and Liberal Unionist MP for Greenock, and his wife, Mary Alice Morris (d. 1920), daughter of the Revd John Macnaught. Thomas Sutherland was a cultured man who loved the theatre, travel, and literature—traits inherited by his daughter. She was educated at boarding-school in Barnet and afterwards at the Convent of the Assumption in Paris, whose frugality and order she loved. Though she appeared small and rather delicate, she even at an early age had a strong will and a desire for perfection.

On 11 February 1904 Sutherland married Richard Douglas Denman (b. 1876/7), and they set up home at Swan Walk, Chelsea. She occupied herself in voluntary work at the Lady Margaret Hall Settlement in Lambeth and in mixing among friends whom Denman introduced to her. The marriage failed and was annulled in 1913, after which she surrounded herself with their friends who included the Quaker Hodgkin family, and in particular Ellen and her husband, the archaeologist R. C. Bosanquet. Sutherland herself became a Quaker in 1914 or 1915. During the First World War she continued her social work, sheltering enemy aliens at a house in Vale Avenue.

On her mother's death in 1920, Sutherland, who had reverted to her maiden name, inherited a substantial fortune; her father left his own fortune to the King Edward's Hospital Fund when he died in 1922. She bought the lease on 4 Lowndes Square, London, and also rented a summer residence at Bamburgh Castle, Northumberland, to be near the Hodgkins and the Bosanquets. She also visited Paris, where she frequented exhibitions and began to buy pictures, including two by Courbet, several Persian miniatures, and works by Seurat and André Derain. In 1925 she was introduced to Ben and Winifred Nicholson by her friend the painter Constance Lane, and began to buy works by them and by Paul Nash, Duncan Grant, and the French sculptor Aristide Maillol.

In 1929 Sutherland leased Rock Hall, near Alnwick, Northumberland. She gave up Lowndes Square and rented a flat in Grosvenor Square as a base for her frequent visits to London. Rock Hall was beautifully decorated and hung with a growing collection of art works that she regarded 'not as a collection but singly as particular delights, fresh experiences, sometimes as experiments' (Gray, 19). In the introduction to an exhibition of her collection held at Abbott Hall Art Gallery, Kendal, in 1964 Helen Knapp observed that 'Miss Sutherland does not collect as other people do: each painting, each object seems rather to be drawn to her than she to it; and becomes part

Helen Christian Sutherland (1881–1965), by unknown photographer

of her and her ambience'. Her patronage of artists, both in purchasing works and in offering other forms of support, was a major contribution to contemporary art in the 1930s. She was clear in her likes and dislikes, and concentrated on the works of those whom she knew and admired, whether professional or amateur.

Many guests stayed at Rock Hall, including the painter David Jones, whom Sutherland met in 1929 through a fellow art lover, Jim Ede. She was a demanding hostess whose personal regime impressed Winifred Nicholson: 'She had a cold bath every morning, walked every day … about twenty miles, lived on nothing but apples, grapes, pineapple and a little lettuce'. But equally Sutherland impressed the painter because she 'carried with her a life of imagination, in which the most tangible objects were flowing streams, almost invisible new Moons, Chinese painters … the warbling of larks and wailing of curlews' (Checkland, 63). Politics and religion also played an important part in Sutherland's life: she rejoined the Church of England, though she later turned to Catholicism.

After the lease on Rock Hall ended Sutherland moved in 1939 to Cockley Moor, a Lakeland farmhouse above Ullswater. There, as in Northumberland, she involved herself in local issues and got to know local musicians and artists. In 1964, having become increasingly frail, she moved to a nursing home at Stoke Poges, in Buckinghamshire. She donated much of her library to Lancaster University and sold or gave away a large part of her collection, retaining just a few prized pieces, which she took with her. She died, of stomach cancer, on 29 April 1965 at Stoke Place Nursing Home. She bequeathed the remainder of her collection to Nicolete Gray. The importance of the works that Sutherland collected is reflected by their later acquisition by

such major galleries as the Tate; the British Museum; the Scottish Museum of Modern Art, Edinburgh; and Kettle's Yard, Cambridge.   CHERRIE TRELOGAN

Sources Helen Sutherland collection: a pioneer collection of the 1930's (1970) [exhibition catalogue, Hayward Gallery, London, Dec 1970 – Jan 1971, and Abbot Hall Art Gallery, Kendal, May 1971; incl. introductory material by N. Gray and R. Campbell] · V. Corbett, Helen Sutherland at Cockley Moor, 1939–1965: a rhythm, a rite and a ceremony (1996) [incl. introduction by N. Jones] · Helen Sutherland (1964) [exhibition catalogue, Abbot Hall Art Gallery, Kendal, 1964] · private information (2004) · S. J. Checkland, Ben Nicholson: the vicious circle of his life and art (2000) · b. cert. · m. cert.
Archives Kettle's Yard Archive · Lancaster University · Tate collection, corresp. and papers from the estate, loan
Likenesses photograph, 1996, repro. in Rhythm, a rite and a ceremony · photographs, Tate collection, Tate Gallery Archive [see illus.]
Wealth at death £217,734: probate, 29 June 1966, CGPLA Eng. & Wales

Sutherland, (Carol) Humphrey Vivian (1908–1986), classical scholar and numismatist, was born on 5 May 1908 at Merton Park in Surrey, the second of the three children of George Humphrey Vivian Sutherland (1873–1952) and his wife, Elsie (1877–1957), daughter of James Foster. He was known by his second name, Humphrey. His father spent his career in the Board of Education; Graham *Sutherland, the distinguished painter, was his elder brother.

Humphrey Sutherland was educated at Homefield preparatory school, Sutton, Surrey, and at Westminster School, where he was a king's scholar and, in his final year, captain of the school. A Westminster scholarship took him to Christ Church, Oxford, where he took a first in moderations, in 1929, and a second in Greats, in 1931. He worked briefly at the Hellenic Society's library in London before returning to Oxford in 1932, at the invitation of J. G. Milne, to work as a part-time assistant keeper in the newly founded Heberden coin room, in the Ashmolean Museum, at a salary of £200 a year. He began a lifetime's work in numismatics with no previous knowledge of coins.

In 1933 Sutherland married Monica Porter (d. 1982), a widow with three young children, and the family soon moved to Westfield House, Cumnor, where Humphrey and Monica Sutherland were to remain to the end of their lives; the garden there, and classical music, were Sutherland's particular delights. At work he quickly developed an expertise in Roman numismatics and won the Barclay Head prize for ancient numismatics in 1934; he published Romano-British Imitations of Bronze Coins of Claudius I in 1935 and Coinage and Currency in Roman Britain in 1937. During the Second World War he served with the fire service and took on additional teaching duties within the university and at St Edward's School, in Oxford, but his work at the Ashmolean continued. His swift response to the auction of Lord Grantley's collection secured, in 1944, the Crondall hoard of early Anglo-Saxon gold coins. Although the jewellery associated with this hoard had disappeared all the coins were acquired and these provided the basis for Sutherland's 1948 publication, Anglo-Saxon Gold Coinage in *the Light of the Crondall Hoard*, which remains an essential source on this topic. It was characteristic of the breadth of Sutherland's vision that he should have recognized the importance of such material outside his own specialization and moved so energetically to acquire it.

After the war Sutherland was elected a student of Christ Church and was appointed to a permanent and full-time assistant keepership at the Ashmolean. He also served as a university lecturer in numismatics from 1939 until his retirement and, in his college, as curator of pictures from 1947 to 1955 and from 1970 to 1975. He had a fine, aesthetic eye and a well-developed sense of style, which he employed to good advantage both in the coin room and in the Christ Church picture gallery. He also took care to ensure that his own appearance was never less than spruce, even dapper, which, combined with his polished and courteous manner and rather dashing Jaguar car, enabled him to cut a figure of considerable panache. Despite the minutely detailed and exacting standards of his scholarship Sutherland never allowed numismatics to seem dull. This may account for the great influence of his teaching; many of his pupils went on to museum and university posts with a greatly enhanced understanding of the importance of coins for the study of history.

Sutherland's assured and urbane style may also explain how he managed to carve out a growing share of the university's resources for the Heberden coin room. As an adjunct to the department of antiquities the coin room was staffed, in the 1930s, by 'a man and a boy', as Sutherland used to say. By the time of his appointment as keeper, in 1957, the coin room had achieved the status of an independent department in its own right, and when he retired, in 1975, the establishment consisted of five full-time academics, a part-time assistant, and two secretaries. The original coin room had expanded through the addition of a library, a teaching room, and a suite of offices.

If Sutherland's greatest work was the creation of a thriving department which was securely enough established to continue to flourish after his departure his scholarly publications also constituted an enduring legacy. In addition to hundreds of articles and reviews he published a number of longer works, including two volumes of the important Roman Imperial Coinage series: volume 1, *31 BC–AD 69* (1986), and volume 6, *From Diocletian's Reform (AD 294) to the Death of Maximinus (AD 313)* (1967). He also helped to edit this series and the *Numismatic Chronicle* as well as serving as president of the Royal Numismatic Society (1948–1953), of the International Numismatic Commission (1960–73), and as *consiglio* of the Centro Internazionale di Studi Numismatici in Naples (1966–73). He was honoured by all the leading European and American numismatic societies and in 1970 was created a CBE and elected a fellow of the British Academy. Sutherland died at his home, Westfield House, Cumnor, Oxford, on 14 May 1986, working to the end on the proofs of his *Roman History and Coinage, 44 BC–AD 69*.   N. J. MAYHEW

Sources R. A. G. Carson, 'Carol Humphrey Vivian Sutherland, 1908–1986', *PBA*, 72 (1986), 491–9 and pl. 30 · R. A. G. Carson and C. M. Kraay, eds., *Scripta nummaria Romana: essays presented to Humphrey Sutherland* (1978) · M. W. Brown and C. E. King, 'C. H. V. Sutherland', *Spink Numismatic Circular*, 94 (Sept 1986), 219–22 · archives, AM Oxf., Heberden coin room · *CGPLA Eng. & Wales* (1986)
Archives AM Oxf., collection
Likenesses photograph, *c.*1975, AM Oxf.
Wealth at death £254,617: probate, 22 July 1986, *CGPLA Eng. & Wales*

Sutherland, James (*c.*1638–1719), botanist, was probably born in Scotland. Of his early life little is known. According to Robert Sibbald, Sutherland was self-taught in botany and also in his knowledge of coins and medals. By the 1670s he had established a reputation as a botanist, and in July 1675 he was put in charge of the Edinburgh Physic Garden, which Sibbald and fellow physician Andrew Balfour had established near Holyroodhouse. In September 1676 the Edinburgh town council leased a site for the garden near Trinity Hospital to Sutherland for nineteen years, naming him 'intendant', with a salary of £20 per annum.

The intendant was expected to teach botany to medical students, a duty which Sutherland performed for many years without a specific title. He was an able gardener, and, according to Sibbald, an expert botanist and a good man of business. He built up a network of correspondents around the world—many of them his former students—who sent him seeds and plants. The *Hortus Kewensis* of 1789 credited Sutherland with the introduction of twelve new species to Great Britain, and he introduced many more new to Scotland, including the common larch. By the early 1680s the garden numbered over 2000 plants, which were described briefly by Sibbald in his *Scotia illustrata* (1684) and in detail by Sutherland in his *Hortus medicus Edinburgensis* (1683).

In the dedication to this work (addressed to George Drummond, lord provost of Edinburgh), Sutherland described how he acquired foreign plants and the purposes of the garden. The garden was organized according to Morison's classification. It was heavily damaged in 1689 during the siege of Edinburgh Castle, when the north loch was drained into its grounds, burying it in mud. Sutherland supervised the repair and renovation of the garden, continually petitioning the town council for funds.

In recognition of his efforts, the council appointed Sutherland to a new post as professor of botany in the University of Edinburgh in February 1695, which paid him his yearly £20 pension as well as an additional £10 for supervising the university garden. In June of the same year the Incorporation of Surgeon-Apothecaries engaged Sutherland to teach botany to its apprentices at a fee of 1 guinea per pupil, and to lead the masters four times a year in a 'publick herbarizing' (Cowan, 30). In the same year Sutherland established a third garden under his supervision at Holyroodhouse; this was a different garden from that originally established by Sibbald and Balfour.

Several letters from Sutherland to Hans Sloane and James Petiver detail Sutherland's collecting efforts as well as his sponsorship of students and apprentices. He sent many of them to London for further education or to obtain positions on ships. His letters also discuss medals and coins.

In August 1705 the town council accused Sutherland of neglecting his duties and reduced his pension to £5. The following spring Sutherland, by now in his late sixties, retired as intendant and professor, although he retained the office of king's botanist and (under a royal warrant of 1710) regius professor of botany for a further eight years. The warrant of 1710 granted him a pension of £50 per annum. In his retirement Sutherland continued his botanical work as well as his interests in numismatics and medals. His collection of coins was later acquired by the Edinburgh Society of Antiquaries. He apparently never married.

Sutherland died on 24 June 1719, aged over eighty. He was buried in Greyfriars churchyard in Edinburgh on 26 June. His will was not proved until 9 January 1730. He left his estate to Jean Bell, widow of James Halket, possibly the Edinburgh physician of that name.   ANITA GUERRINI

Sources J. M. Cowan, 'The history of the Royal Botanic Garden, Edinburgh', *Notes from the Royal Botanic Garden, Edinburgh*, 19/91 (1933), 1–62 · A. Bower, *The history of the University of Edinburgh*, 1 (1817), 362–84 · A. Grant, *The story of the University of Edinburgh during its first three hundred years*, 1 (1884), 217–29, 293–4, 317–19; 2 (1884), 378 · R. Sibbald, *Memoirs*, ed. F. P. Hett (1932) · inventory, NA Scot., CC8/8/92, pp. 275*v*–276*r*

Archives BL, corresp., Sloane MSS 4036, 4037, 4038, 4040, 4063, 4065

Wealth at death see inventory, NA Scot., CC 8/8/92, pp. 275*v*–276*r*

Sutherland, John, seventh earl of Sutherland (*d*. in or before **1460**). *See under* Sutherland family (*per. c.*1200–*c.*1510).

Sutherland, John, eighth earl of Sutherland (*d*. **1508**). *See under* Sutherland family (*per. c.*1200–*c.*1510).

Sutherland [*formerly* Gordon]**, John**, sixteenth earl of **Sutherland** (*bap.* **1661**, *d*. **1733**), army officer and politician, was baptized on 2 March 1661, the only son of George Gordon, fifteenth earl of Sutherland (1633–1703), and his wife, Jean (*d*. 1715), the daughter of the second earl of Wemyss and the widow of Archibald Douglas, earl of Angus. On 28 April 1680 he married Helen Cochrane (*d*. *c.*1690), the second daughter of William, Lord Cochrane, a son of the first earl of Dundonald. Her sister Jean was married to Viscount Dundee. The couple had a son and two daughters. As Lord Strathnaver (1679–1703), Gordon took an active part in public affairs, as commissioner of supply for Sutherland. In 1685 he raised a force of Sutherlanders to march against the expedition of the earl of Argyll. In 1689 he took up arms to support the revolution and William III, and in conjunction with Sir Thomas Livingstone, commander of the forces, wrote to Viscount Dundee (3 July 1689), offering to be his mediator with the king.

Strathnaver was appointed a privy councillor by William III, under whom he commanded a regiment of infantry in Flanders. On his father's death in 1703 he succeeded as earl of Sutherland, and on 11 July 1704 took the oaths and his seat as a lord of parliament. He attended all the parliaments between that date and the Act of Union of 1707, and made repeated efforts to obtain payment of arrears of pay due to his regiment. In 1703 he was appointed a privy councillor by Queen Anne. He supported the union between England and Scotland in parliament, and in 1706 was one of the commissioners for arranging its terms. He was a representative peer in the union parliament between 1707 and 1708 and from 1715 until his death. In 1715 he was appointed president of the board of trade and manufactures, and about the same time lord lieutenant of the eight northernmost counties of Scotland.

Sutherland's first wife had died about 1690. His second wife, Katherine, the widow of James Stuart, Lord Doune (the eldest son of the earl of Moray), was the daughter of Sir Lionel Tollemache and his wife, Elizabeth *Murray (*bap.* 1626, *d*. 1698), in her own right countess of Dysart and later duchess of Lauderdale. Katherine died about 1705, leaving no children. Sutherland married, thirdly, on 12 August 1727, Frances (*d*. 1732), the widow of Sir John Travell and the daughter of Sir Thomas Hodgson of Bramwith Hall, Yorkshire.

In 1715, when the Jacobite rising broke out under the leadership of the earl of Mar, Sutherland at once proceeded to his own district, raised forces which the government agreed to equip, and endeavoured to prevent the earl of Seaforth from joining Mar. A shipment of arms destined for Sutherland was captured by Jacobite forces at Burntisland in late September. However, on 5 October, with 900 men from his own estates and those of Lord Reay, Sutherland joined Colonel Robert Munro, who had collected 300 men at Alness. Seaforth raised 3000 highlanders, and on 9 October advanced towards Alness, causing Sutherland to retreat ignominiously to the Bonar River. Seaforth took possession of Inverness and then joined Mar for the battle of Sheriffmuir. Sutherland marched to recover Inverness, but was forestalled by Lord Lovat, who had invested the castle on about 10 November and recaptured the town when the Jacobite garrison slipped away on the night of 12 November. Annoyed at his absence from the capture, Sutherland criticized the failure to seize the garrison forces. He was unmollified by his promotion to lieutenant-general, and published in 1716 an account of events at Inverness, minimizing the role of others, including Lovat, who later published his own *Account of the Taking of Inverness*. The castle and town were held by government forces for the duration of the rising: when Seaforth, on returning to the highlands in December 1715, made plans in conjunction with the marquess of Huntly to retake Inverness, Sutherland marched forth with a superior force and obliged him to surrender. Huntly also surrendered shortly afterwards. The rising quelled, Sutherland went to London, where in June 1716 he was invested by George I with the Order of the Thistle and in September received an annual pension of £1200 in recognition of his services. In 1719 his men took part in the battle at Glensheil, which brought to a close the first Jacobite rising.

John Macky left a description of Sutherland:

He is a very honest man, a great assertor of the liberties of the people; hath a good rough sense, is open and free, a great lover of his bottle and of his friend; brave in his person, which he hath shewn in several duels; too familiar for his quality, and often keeps company below it; is a fat, fair-complexioned man, forty-five years old.   (*Memoirs of the Secret Services*, 201)

Sutherland died in Chelsea on 27 June 1733 and was buried at Dornoch in Sutherland. His son having died in 1720, his grandson, William, succeeded as seventeenth earl.

HENRY PATON, *rev.* JONATHAN SPAIN

Sources GEC, *Peerage* · *Scots peerage* · *Second report*, HMC, 1/2 (1871); repr. (1874), appx., pp. 177–80 · J. H. Burton, *History of Scotland from the revolution to the extinction of the last Jacobite insurrection (1689–1748)*, 2 vols. (1853) · J. Baynes, *The Jacobite rising of 1715* (1970) · *Memoirs of the secret services of John Macky*, ed. A. R. (1733) · W. Fraser, ed., *The chiefs of Grant*, 3 vols. (1883)
Archives NL Scot., corresp. and papers | NA Scot., letters to Sir William Bennet · NA Scot., letters to John Clerk · NA Scot., letters to duke of Montrose
Likenesses oils, Dunrobin Castle, Highland region

Sutherland, John (1808–1891), physician and promoter of sanitary science, the son of William Sutherland, a saddler, was born in Edinburgh in December 1808, and educated at Edinburgh high school. He became a licentiate of the Royal College of Surgeons of Edinburgh in 1827, and graduated MD at the university in 1831. After spending some time on the continent he practised for a short period in Liverpool. On 28 September 1839 he married Sarah Elizabeth, daughter of John Cowie, a merchant, of Wavertree, Lancashire. At Liverpool he edited *The Liverpool Health of Towns Advocate* in 1846 and the *Journal of Public Health and Monthly Record of Sanitary Improvement* from 1847 to 1848. In 1848, at the request of the earl of Carlisle, Sutherland entered public service as an inspector under the first Board of Health, where he was employed until 1855. He conducted several special inquiries, notably one into the cholera epidemic of 1848–9 (*Parl. papers*, 1850, 21, no. 1273; 1852, 20, no. 1523). He was the head of a commission sent overseas to inquire into the law and practice of burial, and he went to the Paris conference on quarantine law in 1851–2, when Louis Napoleon presented him with a gold medal.

In 1855 Sutherland was engaged at the Home Office in bringing into operation the act for abolishing intramural interments. He was also working for the reorganized General Board of Health when, at the request of Lord Palmerston and Lord Panmure, he became the head of the commission sent to the Crimea to inquire into the sanitary condition of the British soldiers. It was during this visit that he became a close friend of Florence Nightingale, whom he had met at the British army hospital in Scutari. On 25 August 1855 he returned to Britain for consultation, and was summoned to Balmoral to inform Queen Victoria of the steps that had been taken for the benefit of the troops.

Afterwards Sutherland took an active part in the preparation of the report of the royal commission on the health of the army, dated 1858, and also of the report entitled 'State of the army in India', dated 19 May 1863. Sutherland had been invited to take part in these commissions at Nightingale's request. The two had become close and

Sutherland became her personal physician. He was devoted to her and served on the commissions without remuneration. But he was also prone to a flippancy which Nightingale found irritating, having been likened on one occasion to an Amazon queen. Although she respected Sutherland's sanitary expertise, she seldom had a good word to say about him. He was apparently untidy, unpunctual, and frivolous, and she often told him so. Sutherland feared her displeasure so much that he often induced his wife to write to Nightingale on his behalf, begging forgiveness for his conduct or his failure to keep appointments. He described himself to her as 'one of your wives' (Smith, 290).

The reports of both commissions were of vast importance to the welfare of the soldiers, and most of Sutherland's recommendations were carried out. One of these was the appointment of the barrack and hospital improvement commission, with Sidney Herbert as president and Captain Douglas Galton, Dr Burrell of the army medical department, and Sutherland as members. This committee visited every barrack and hospital in the United Kingdom, and the sanitary arrangements of each were reported. Defects were brought to light and remedied, and the health of the troops consequently improved (*Parl. papers*, 1861, 16, no. 2839). Subsequently Sutherland and Galton visited and made reports on the Mediterranean stations, including the Ionian Islands (*Parl. papers*, 1863, 13, no. 3207).

In 1862 the barrack and hospital improvement commission was reconstituted with the quartermaster-general as president and Sutherland as a prominent member; it was renamed as the army sanitary committee in 1865. Two Indian officers were added, and all sanitary reports were submitted to the committee and suggestions for improving Indian stations prepared. Sutherland was also called upon to investigate cholera epidemics among British soldiers in Gibraltar and Malta in 1865, and in the following year was dispatched to Algeria, where he prepared a report on the health of the French army. He continued to serve on the army sanitary committee until his retirement on 30 June 1888, when he was appointed a medical superintending inspector-general of the Board of Health and of the Home Office.

While engaged by the army sanitary committee, Sutherland and Nightingale again joined forces successfully to oppose plans to close the army medical school, which had been established as a result of the report of the royal commission in 1858. It was argued that the education provided by the school was superfluous given that entrants into the Army Medical Services already possessed a thorough knowledge of their subject, but Sutherland insisted that the teaching of sanitation and other more specialized aspects of medicine was vital to the well-being and efficiency of the army.

Sutherland continued his work until a few years before his death, despite having grown completely deaf. He died at his home, Oakleigh, Alleyne Park, Camberwell, London, on 14 July 1891. His last words were for Nightingale:

'give her my love and blessing', he told his wife (Smith, 584). His body was buried on 20 July at Norwood cemetery. He was survived by his wife.

G. C. BOASE, *rev.* MARK HARRISON

Sources *The Lancet* (25 July 1891) · C. Woodham-Smith, *Florence Nightingale, 1820–1910* (1950) · *The Times* (24 July 1891) · A. R. Skelley, *The Victorian army at home: the recruitment and terms and conditions of the British regular, 1859–1899* (1977) · N. Cantlie, *A history of the army medical department*, 2 vols. (1974) · m. cert. · *CGPLA Eng. & Wales* (1891)

Archives BL, corresp. with Florence Nightingale and papers, Add. MSS 43394–43400, 45751–45758, 47714–47767 · UCL, corresp. with Sir Edwin Chadwick · Wellcome L., Royal Army Medical Corps muniment collection

Likenesses R. T., wood-engraving, NPG; repro. in *ILN* (1 Aug 1891) · portrait, repro. in *ILN* (24 July 1891)

Wealth at death £54,542 12s. 9d.: probate, 6 Aug 1891, *CGPLA Eng. & Wales*

Sutherland, Kenneth, fourth earl of Sutherland (*d.* 1333). *See under* Sutherland family (*per. c.*1200–*c.*1510).

Sutherland, Dame Lucy Stuart (1903–1980), historian and college head, was born in Geelong, Australia, on 21 June 1903, the only daughter (she had one brother who died young) of Alexander Charles Sutherland (1870–1941) and his wife, Margaret Mabel Goddard (1871–1950). Both her parents, Australians by birth, were graduates of the University of Melbourne, her father, a mining engineer, being descended from Scottish highland stock, and her mother (whose father had emigrated in 1865) from a family with City of London affiliations. She was brought up in South Africa, and educated at Roedean School, Johannesburg, and the University of the Witwatersrand, where she won a scholarship which enabled her to go to Oxford. After a first class in the honour school of modern history (1927), her Oxford college, Somerville, appointed her a tutor, and later elected her to an Oxford tutorial fellowship (1928–45). In 1926 she had been the first woman undergraduate to speak at the Oxford Union, winning applause for her opposition to the motion 'That the women's colleges … should be levelled to the ground'.

Three scholars, very different in their interests and approach, were to form Lucy Sutherland as a historian. At Witwatersrand she enjoyed much encouragement from Professor William N. Macmillan. The distinguished medievalist Maude Clarke, her tutor at Somerville, instilled into her the most rigorous scholarly standards. *The Structure of Politics at the Accession of George III* (1929) by Lewis Namier gave her the conceptual framework upon which rested her output of eighteenth-century history. During the 1930s she built up a growing reputation as a scholar, while her ability was increasingly recognized in her college and in the university.

When war came Lucy Sutherland felt herself increasingly restless in Oxford, and in 1941 accepted the offer of a principalship in the Board of Trade. She immediately proved a talented civil servant, rising by 1945 to the rank of assistant secretary. But though she found it hard to live without any time for her research, these years were of crucial significance in turning her from a somewhat shy Oxford don, who had not yet shed her 'colonial' accent, into a sophisticated woman of the world.

In 1945 both Somerville and Lady Margaret Hall were looking for a new principal; Lucy Sutherland was a frontrunner in both elections, withdrawing from that at Somerville when she perceived that her candidature was likely to split the college. Her appointment as principal of Lady Margaret Hall was to bring her great happiness. Brought up a Presbyterian, she had been confirmed into the Church of England in 1931, and found the Anglican ambience of the hall a congenial one. Her administrative talents were fully stretched by the problems of post-war Oxford, but she was soon recalled to outside responsibilities, including the chairmanship of the Board of Trade working party on the lace industry (1946), and membership of the committee of inquiry into the distribution and exhibition of cinematographic films (1949), the royal commission on taxation of profits and income (1951), the committee into grants for students (1958), and later the University Grants Committee (1964–9). She was actively engaged, in addition, with the administration of many educational bodies and was president of the Girls' Public Day School Trust.

But Lucy Sutherland's commitments outside Oxford never displaced her central interest in her college and university. During her time Lady Margaret Hall doubled in size; she took an intense interest in its new buildings. Its intellectual standing was her major concern, but she also enjoyed it greatly as a human community. In the university she became increasingly prominent; it gave her great pleasure to act as pro-vice-chancellor between 1961 and 1969, the first woman to do so. In these and many other spheres, she showed the same businesslike and financial capacity, always tempered by humanity and common sense. Her services to the university were marked by an honorary DCL (1972) after her retirement in 1971, when her college made her an honorary fellow. She had been made an honorary Oxford DLitt in 1955; her other honorary degrees included those from Cambridge (1963), Glasgow (1966), Kent (1967), Keele (1968), and Belfast (1970).

Lucy Sutherland's notable contribution to eighteenth-century studies was recognized by her election in 1954 to a fellowship of the British Academy, in the affairs of which she played a characteristically wise and active part. Three years later she was approached by the then prime minister, Harold Macmillan, to see whether, if offered to her, she would accept the regius chair of modern history. Since at Oxford the tenure of a college headship was not compatible with a professorial chair, she was faced with an acutely difficult choice, but decided eventually to remain at Lady Margaret Hall. Her interest in the East India Company remained constant all her life; her book on its part in eighteenth-century politics was published in 1952 and later reprinted. She also became an expert on the eighteenth-century City of London. Co-operation with other scholars came easily to her, as in the edition of volume 2 of *The Correspondence of Edmund Burke* (1960), and in the History of Parliament.

In the last decade of her life, when her sphere of interest

became the history of the University of Oxford in the eighteenth century, Lucy Sutherland found a perfect subject in which to exercise her intellectual energy and her ability to organize a team of willing contributors, besides making a noteworthy contribution to the understanding of the university in that period (her volume, *The Eighteenth Century*, appeared posthumously in 1986, co-edited by L. G. Mitchell). Although primarily a historian of institutions, she always had regard to the importance of ideas; her judgements were based on an exceptionally thorough examination of a mass of evidence, but she never lacked the courage to come to a conclusion about its import. She was an admirable tutor and supervisor of young historians.

Lucy Sutherland made and kept friends easily; among historians of her time she much enjoyed discussions with Lewis Namier and Richard Pares. She was a splendid conversationalist, and excellent company, as well as compassionate and generous. Of medium height, she was a dynamic personality, quick in her movements and often disconcertingly rapid in her speech and her response to situations. One of the outstanding women of her generation, she did a great deal, though always unobtrusively and wisely, to show how effectively women could take their part in academic and public life. She was appointed CBE in 1947 and DBE in 1969.

Lucy Sutherland died at her home, 59 Park Town, Oxford, on 20 August 1980. She was unmarried.

ANNE WHITEMAN, *rev.*

Sources A. Whiteman, 'Lucy Stuart Sutherland, 1903–1980', *PBA*, 69 (1983), 611–30 · priv. coll. · personal knowledge (2004) · *CGPLA Eng. & Wales* (1980)

Archives SOUND BL NSA, performance recording

Likenesses A. E. Gingel, oils (?), *c.*1934, Lady Margaret Hall, Oxford · R. Moynihan, oils, 1953, Lady Margaret Hall, Oxford · M. Sumner, oils, 1957, Lady Margaret Hall, Oxford · Bassano, photograph, repro. in Whiteman, 'Lucy Stuart Sutherland', p. 611

Wealth at death £248,847: probate, 30 Oct 1980, *CGPLA Eng. & Wales*

Sutherland, Mary Elizabeth (1895–1972), political organizer, was born on 30 November 1895 at Burnhead, Banchory-Ternan, some miles up the River Dee from Aberdeen. She was the second child and only daughter of Alexander Sutherland and Jessie (d. 1911), *née* Henderson. She had one younger brother. Her father was a farmworker and later a crofter at Nether Anguston, Peterculter, a few miles from Mary's birthplace. Here she grew up. She attended the local parish school, then won a bursary to the Girls' High School in Aberdeen. During her last years at school her mother was very ill with pulmonary tuberculosis and Mary had to combine schooling with assisting with nursing and housekeeping, travelling to Aberdeen daily. Her mother died in 1911. Her father was a radical, and she later wrote that her parish minister preached socialist sermons and that while still at school she 'found she was a Socialist' (*Clarion*, 6 June 1934).

Sutherland won a bursary to Aberdeen University in 1913. Initially she intended to take only an ordinary degree, but she won another bursary which enabled her to stay for a fourth year to take an honours MA in history. She

Mary Elizabeth Sutherland (1895–1972), by unknown photographer

graduated in 1917 and in the following year qualified as a teacher at Aberdeen Training College, where she helped to organize the trainee teachers who were demanding a minimum salary. She then taught for a year at Aberdeen Girls' High School.

From 1919 to 1920 Sutherland was assistant secretary to the departmental committee on women in agriculture in Scotland, and from February 1920 to November 1922 organizer for the Scottish Farm Servants' Union, founded in 1913. She travelled widely in Scotland, paying particular attention to the unionizing of women workers in agriculture. In 1922 she was a delegate to the meeting of the International Federation of Landworkers in Vienna. She edited her union's journal, the *Scottish Farm Servant*, and was also vice-chair of the Stirling Trades and Labour Council (1921–2). From January 1923 to January 1924 she was sub-editor on the weekly *Forward*, which gave extended coverage to Scottish Independent Labour Party matters.

In 1924 Mary Sutherland was appointed Labour Party women's organizer for Scotland, a position she held until 1932; she then became the national Labour Party chief woman officer, following the death of Dr Marion Phillips. This entailed advising and supervising women's sections of local Labour Party branches, arranging the annual women's conference of the Labour Party, and editing the monthly journal *Labour Woman*. Throughout her career as chief woman officer she was secretary to the standing joint committee of industrial women's organizations (SJC, from 1941 the national joint committee of working women's organizations, NJC), whose members were representatives of the trade unions and the Co-operative

Women's Guild as well as of the Labour Party. It campaigned and advised the national executive committee of the Labour Party on matters affecting women. In the 1930s these included factory legislation, family allowances, improved social services, especially for children, and a successful campaign for free school milk and the extension of free school meals. The SJC also supported the Indian nationalist movement and the extension of the franchise to Indian women. From 1934 to 1938, on behalf of the SJC and the International Council of Social Democratic Women, Mary Sutherland campaigned for the release in the USSR of the dissident Russian socialist Eva Broido. The failure of this campaign deepened Sutherland's hostility to communism and all left-wing extremism. From 1932 to 1939 she represented women in the British labour movement on the women's committee of the Labour and Socialist International.

During the Second World War Sutherland was a member of the Women's Consultative Committee which advised Ernest Bevin, the minister of labour, on matters affecting women workers. She was also a member of a Labour Party anti-German group, which argued that no German, even a Social Democrat, could ever again be entrusted with power. During and after the war she personally assisted refugees of various nationalities. At the end of the war she was active in the Fabian Women's Group while it was preparing its evidence to the royal commission on equal pay (1945–6), which she strongly favoured; the evidence stressed what little progress had been made in the previous thirty years. She was also active in an unsuccessful NJC campaign to stop the closure of wartime nurseries for young children.

In 1946 the Labour Party established the National Institute of Houseworkers to raise the status of domestic employment by training women who would become domestic workers in institutions such as hospitals and local authority home helps. Mary Sutherland was an active member of its board of directors during 1946–66 and believed strongly in the need to raise the status of domestic work. From 1947 to 1952 she was British representative on the United Nations Commission on the Status of Women. She stressed the importance of this commission to the International Council of Social Democratic Women, of which she was a member from 1955 and chair during 1959–61. She enjoyed travelling abroad and had many friends among women socialists in other countries. She supported British entry to the EEC. She opposed the Campaign for Nuclear Disarmament, which she regarded as left wing. In 1949 she was appointed CBE.

Sutherland retired as chief woman officer in December 1960. She received a less than effusive message of thanks at her last party conference in office, in October 1960, moved by Bessie Braddock MP, who pointed out that the tribute was needed because 'our Party would not exist at all if it were not for the valiant band of women supporters of the Party who do the work when everybody else is sometimes doing a lot of talking' (*Labour Party Conference Report*, 248). Sutherland had similarly defended the

women's sections of the party to the Women's Annual Conference in 1946 against 'a number of quaint notions of critics, who know nothing about their work, the idea for example that a Women's Section was a place where they went to drink tea!' Sutherland continued to be on the Women's Consultative Committee of the Ministry of Labour until 1965. Thereafter she retired from public life.

Throughout her career Mary Sutherland fought to improve the conditions of women, whether they worked for pay or worked unpaid in the home, and those of children. According to Dame Margaret Cole 'all who worked with her in one capacity or another ... retain a clear recollection of a vivid and warm though certainly not an uncritical personality'. She went on to recall the entertainment provided by Mary's stories, told in her native lowland Scots, even when her audiences sometimes failed to catch the full meaning of her broad Doric—'for she had a strong sense of humour' (*The Times*, 26 Oct 1972). A close Labour Party colleague, however, described her as 'moody to a serious degree', but at other times 'delightful' (*DLB*, 248). She was perhaps depressive, at least later in her career, and lonely in the male-dominated Labour Party headquarters. She was an excellent administrator and organizer, and was supportive of, and well regarded by, the women party organizers whom she supervised.

Sutherland wrote effectively, but in later life her public speaking was marred by a speech impediment which had not been evident when she was younger. She read widely. She did not marry. She lived in a succession of London flats, first in Highgate, then in West Kensington, then in Dolphin Square. The flats were always decorated in dark colours and she habitually dressed in brown. She loved London, but she suffered a stroke, followed by a traffic accident; hence she returned to Scotland to be near relatives. She spent her last years in another flat in the new town of East Kilbride near Glasgow. She died intestate, following a second stroke on 19 October 1972, at Hairmyres Hospital in East Kilbride. Her many books were divided between a local secondary school and Strathclyde University, but her papers were destroyed by her nephew; it is unknown whether this was at her request.

PAT THANE

Sources DLB · M. Cole, *The Times* (26 Oct 1972) · *The Times* (23 Oct 1972) · *WWW* · *Labour party conference report* (1960), 248 [retirement tribute by Bessie Braddock MP] · 'Mary Sutherland', *Labour Woman* (Jan 1961), 12–13
Archives Labour History Archive and Study Centre, Manchester, labour party archives | Ruskin College, Oxford, letters to James Middleton
Likenesses F. Mann, group photograph, 1939, Hult. Arch. · photograph, People's History Museum, Manchester [see illus.]

Sutherland, Norman Stuart (1927–1998), psychologist, was born on 26 March 1927 at 57 Hook Road, Surbiton, Surrey, the son of Norman MacLeod Sutherland, an export manager, and his wife, Cecilia Dickson, *née* Jackson. He was educated at King Edward's School, Birmingham, and Magdalen College, Oxford, where he took a first in classics in 1949. After national service he also took a first in the school of psychology, philosophy, and physiology, winning the John Locke prize in mental philosophy (1953). Fellowships at Magdalen (1954–8) and Merton College (1963–4) followed, and he was also a university lecturer in experimental psychology between 1960 and 1964. He spent two years in the USA as a visiting professor at the Massachusetts Institute of Technology (1961–2), where he worked with Noam Chomsky and advocated the cross-fertilization of experimental psychology and artificial intelligence. On 30 June 1956 he married José Louise Fogden (*b.* 1930/31), a secretary. They had two daughters.

From the mid-1950s to the mid-1960s Sutherland spent his summers at the zoological station in Naples, researching shape recognition in the common octopus under the guidance of the neurophysiologist J. Z. Young. Sutherland's research led to the publication of *Shape Discrimination in Animals* in 1959, which established his academic reputation in the field of visual perception. In 1964 he was appointed to head the laboratory of experimental psychology at the nascent University of Sussex, which under his leadership quickly became one of the most prestigious psychology departments in Britain. As a professor of an expanding department Sutherland worked hard, but his numerous administrative responsibilities left little time for either his own research or his family. However, he did publish *Mechanisms of Animal Discrimination and Learning* in 1971, co-authored with his former student N. J. Mackintosh.

In 1973 Sutherland suffered a sudden mental collapse characterized by extreme anxiety. He sought help from several psychoanalysts, but his background in experimental psychology and his natural impatience did not suit him to the role of analysand. He formed a highly critical view of psychoanalysis as a therapeutic approach to mental crisis.

A five-week voluntary stay in hospital provided Sutherland with the refuge for moderate recovery. He formed an alliance with a clinical psychologist trained in cognitive-behavioural therapy, which he found sensible and efficacious. However, following his discharge from hospital he entered a period of hypomania, characterized by lack of sleep, extreme optimism, and excessive spending. After four months of high spirits he descended again into depression. This cycle of euphoria in winter and depression in summer continued for several years. Long-term stability was aided by the prescription of lithium, which he took until the end of his life.

This experience, and Sutherland's recovery, formed the basis of *Breakdown: a Personal Crisis and a Medical Dilemma* (1976). Part memoir, part evaluation of the prevailing models and treatments of mental illness, the book was an extremely candid account of his own mental turmoil. By airing his own experience he hoped to educate the mentally healthy, reassure the mentally ill, and also describe the various therapeutic and medical options available to those in distress.

Sutherland's breakdown effectively ended his own original research, but he continued to oversee the department at Sussex (until his retirement in 1994), lecture (while flagrantly disregarding the university's no-smoking policy), and write numerous book reviews on a wide range of topics for *Nature*, the *Times Literary Supplement*, and a number of national broadsheets. He also indulged his creative ambitions. *Men Change too* (1987), his only published novel, was a thinly-veiled fictionalization of his own life as an academic and womanizer. He also wrote a libretto for a musical entitled 'The Vice-Chancellor', which was never staged. Simon Gray transformed *Breakdown* into a play, *Melon*, which ran in the West End and on Broadway. Sutherland later claimed that he did not identify the central character with himself.

In 1989 Macmillan published a 500-page *Dictionary of Psychology* written solely by Sutherland. In it his continued antipathy towards psychoanalysis found expression in his definition of a psychoanalyst as '[a] person who takes money from another on the pretence that it is for the other's own good'. His last book was *Irrationality: the Enemy Within* (1992), which drew on research in social psychology to show how people, including professionals with considerable training and experience, make irrational decisions.

A revised edition of *Breakdown* was published in 1998. In a postscript to the memoir Sutherland related the mild depressions that continued to plague him into his final years, though without the compensations of hypomania. He also expressed regret for the difficulties that his condition brought to his wife and children. He remained a bon viveur to the end. He died, of a heart attack, on 8 November 1998 at the Royal Sussex County Hospital, Brighton.

MARK J. SCHOFIELD

Sources *The Times* (25 Nov 1998) · *The Guardian* (19 Nov 1998), 22 · *The Independent* (18 Nov 1998), 6 · *Daily Telegraph* (12 Nov 1998), 33 · b. cert. · m. cert. · d. cert.
Archives UCL, corresp. with J. Z. Young

Sutherland, Robert, sixth earl of Sutherland (*d.* in or before 1427?). *See under* Sutherland family (*per. c.*1200–*c.*1510).

Sutherland, Robert Garioch [*pseud.* Robert Garioch] (**1909–1981**), poet and translator, was born on 9 May 1909 at 109 Bellevue Road, Edinburgh, the son of Robert Garioch Sutherland, a house painter, and his wife, Catherine (*née* Mathewson), a music teacher. He attended Edinburgh high school and then Edinburgh University (1927–31). On 26 January 1942 he married Margaret Lillie (1914/15–*c.*1979), a schoolteacher, in Edinburgh. They had at least one child, Ian. Conscripted in 1941, Sutherland served in the north African campaign with the Royal Signals, and was a prisoner of war in Italy and Germany from 1942 to 1945. Between 1946 and his retirement in 1964 he was a schoolteacher, first in London and Kent (until 1959) and thereafter in Edinburgh. With fellow poet Edwin Morgan he served as literary adviser to the cultural review *Scottish International* (1968–74). From 1971 to 1973 he was writer in residence at the University of Edinburgh, and was also employed as a 'lexicographer's orraman [odd-job man]' (Royle, 305)—his own description—on the *Dictionary of the*

Robert Garioch Sutherland (1909–1981), by Alexander Moffat, 1978

Older Scottish Tongue. He was a popular performer of his own poetry—written mainly in Scots—and participated in the readings circuit right up to his final months.

Sutherland based his idiom on the speech of his native city, but augmented his working vocabulary from his constant study of Scots language and literature; a particular mentor was the major poet Robert Fergusson (1750–1774), tragic in his life, comic (even caustic) in his work. In such poems as 'In Princes Street Gairdens' and 'A Wee Local Scandal' Sutherland deployed the reductive possibilities of Scots to puncture the pretensions of city councillors, academics, political dogmatists, and their like. Together with an often deadpan satirical wit, his adoption of the faux-naïf 'wee man' persona accounts for much of his popularity.

Sutherland found a kindred spirit in the nineteenth-century Italian poet Giuseppe Belli, who wrote scurrilous sonnets in the working-class dialect of Rome. In his Scots versions of Belli, always preserving the strict sonnet form, Sutherland was able to transpose this mockery of church and state to the Edinburgh streets. Indeed, it is in his consummate craftsmanship as a poet ('makar'—'maker' in Scots) that it can be discovered where his sympathies lie—

with the skilled tradesman and his unassuming, necessary, but increasingly redundant labours. In 'Perfect' Sutherland adopted the persona of a french polisher, drily lamenting how his craftsmanly standards are giving way to mass production.

Sutherland's most ambitious poetic projects were his 1959 translations from Latin into Scots of two tragedies, *Jephthah* and *The Baptist*, by the great Scottish humanist George Buchanan (1506–1582). Although he valued these translations above everything else he had attempted, they remain neglected in spite of their organ-voiced sonorities:

> I come frae the Thunderer's throne in Hevin,
> his airborne herald, til Israel's hame
> promised to Jacob's seed as the centre o pouer …
> ('Jephthah' and 'The Baptist', 1959)

The Masque of Edinburgh (1954) and *The Laird o Dreepdaily* (1983) are worthy of note as his two other forays into verse drama in Scots.

Buchanan also served as a sounding board for Sutherland's complaints against the realities of the teaching profession, and the disillusionment of the would-be writer and new university graduate who is forced to teach for a living:

> A kep and goun—what dae they maitter?
> a kep and bells wad suit him better.
> (*Complete Poetical Works*, 1983)

In a letter to a fellow makar J. K. Annand, Garioch simultaneously offers a *cri de coeur* and administers a gentle dig at the Scottish obsession with 'doubles', the Jekyll-and-Hyde co-existence of opposing qualities:

> But it is an awful strain, this Deacon Brodie sort of life,
> Sutherland by day and Garioch by night, school-mastering
> and making poetry being such different things, and yet both
> tiring you out in the same way, that's the damn thing about
> it.

(Deacon Brodie was an eighteenth-century figure who alternated between the roles of respectable citizen and elusive burglar.)

Sutherland's friends and fellow poets Hamish Henderson and Sorley MacLean were also veterans of north Africa. Sutherland typically eschewed the elegiac sweep of their war poetry in favour of a hard-headed prose account of his experiences as a prisoner of war. *Two Men and a Blanket* (1975), his only venture into sustained autobiography, records without self-pity or heroics the boring, basic level of existence in captivity. Prisoner-of-war camp was its own way of life:

> Where we had all started off equal, we began to have
> relatively rich and poor. The most successful businessman
> would run a gambling outfit of some kind and would
> combine this with their knowledge of the market to live
> pretty well. At the other end of the scale, somebody must
> have been going short, but nobody was going to worry about
> him. (Garioch, *Two Men and a Blanket*, 51)

Such mordant commentary does not mean that Sutherland was a confirmed misanthrope. During his writer's residency at Edinburgh University he gained a reputation for going out of his way to help aspiring poets, even advising them on where to place their work. He gave space to younger and little-known poets in his 1974 anthology, *Made in Scotland*. Towards the end of his life he expressed warm sympathy with the aims of the fledgeling Scottish Poetry Library Association. Sadly he did not live to see the library as an up-and-running reality.

Sutherland was much more than an 'Edinburgh' poet, but it is likely that his home-based work will continue to be his most read. In harking back to his childhood he does not allow his wit to give way to sentimentality. His 'Fi'baw in the Street' concerns any group of boys whose game is interrupted by the polis (police). The mellower 'Lesson' evokes the changes, both during and before Sutherland's lifetime, to the character of Edinburgh's port of Leith. Returning to the docks after many years, the poet is nostalgic but realistic; Leith is not better or worse, it is just different.

Sutherland died on 26 April 1981 at the Western General Hospital in Edinburgh. He had been predeceased by his wife, and was survived by at least one son, Ian.

TOM HUBBARD

Sources *A Garioch miscellany*, ed. R. Fulton (1986) · 'In memoriam Robert Garioch', *Chapman*, 31 (winter 1981–2) · 'Robert Garioch', R. Garioch [R. G. Sutherland], *The big music and other poems* (1971) · b. cert. · d. cert. · T. Royle, *The mainstream companion to Scottish literature* (1993) · J. B. Caird, 'Robert Garioch: a personal appreciation', *Scottish Literary Journal*, 10/2 (1983), 68–78 · R. Garioch [R. G. Sutherland], *Complete poetical works*, ed. R. Fulton (1983) · R. Garioch [R. G. Sutherland], *Two men and a blanket: memoirs of captivity* (1975) · R. Garioch [R. G. Sutherland], 'Early days in Edinburgh', *As I remember: ten Scottish authors recall how writing began for them*, ed. M. Lindsay (1979), 45–58
Archives NL Scot. | SOUND Scotsoun Productions, Glasgow, audio archive of Scottish poetry, incl. Garioch reading his own works [U. Glas., SCRAN project]
Likenesses photograph, 1971?, repro. in Garioch, *Big music* · A. Moffat, oils, 1978, Scot. NPG [*see illus.*] · A. Moffat, portraits, 1978–80, repro. in A. Moffat, J. Matthew, and C. Carrell, eds., *Seven poets* (1981), 6, 15, 26, 60 [exhibition catalogue] · J. A. Matthew, photograph, 1980, repro. in A. Moffat, J. Matthew, and C. Carrell, eds., *Seven poets* (1981), 66 [exhibition catalogue]
Wealth at death £73,327.89: confirmation, 29 Oct 1981, *CCI*

Sutherland, Sir Thomas (1834–1922), shipowner, was born at Aberdeen on 18 August 1834, the eldest of the four children of Robert Sutherland, glazier and house painter, and his wife, Christian, daughter of Thomas Webster, grocer. While still a child, he lost his father, brother, and a sister. In these circumstances, he, his widowed mother, and his surviving sister left their home to live with his maternal grandparents. The Websters sent him to Aberdeen grammar school (1844–7) where he was taught by a renowned classics master. With the ministry in view, he attended the Marischal College and Aberdeen University, but after one year (1848) he decided to make a career in commerce.

Sutherland's interest in shipping was fired by his uncle, an agent for the Aberdeen and Hull Ship Company and an acquaintance of James Allan, a fellow Aberdonian who started as a clerk in a Dublin shipping company and became a managing director in the Peninsular and Oriental Steam Navigation Company (P. & O.). In 1852 he moved to London, where Allan took him on as a junior clerk. Thus

Sir Thomas Sutherland (1834–1922), by Sir Benjamin Stone, 1897

began the service to which he devoted the whole of his business life.

In 1854 Sutherland was sent out to Bombay, but soon transferred to Hong Kong. He rapidly rose to superintendent of this important agency. Here he had ample scope to show his business talent. He started a company which built the first dock in Hong Kong and opened the first regular steamship line to Japan. The most significant of his undertakings, however, was the formation of the Hongkong and Shanghai Banking Corporation in 1864, the first bank in China. A director on its provisional board, then deputy chairman until he left Shanghai in 1866, he remained on the board until he departed from China to become an assistant manager in the London office of P. & O. in 1868.

From its inception in 1840, P. & O. was under contract to the government to carry mails to the East by the Red Sea route. This required two fleets separated by the overland passage through Egypt. For more than two decades P. & O. had a monopoly of eastern trade. In the 1860s, however, a technological revolution made P. & O.'s existing ships increasingly out of date. At the same time, the company suffered heavy losses in the aftermath of the American Civil War, management was in disarray, and the Suez canal was about to be opened. Sutherland found a company in crisis; he was to be the architect of recovery.

Over the next decade, Sutherland built an entirely new fleet, reorganized the company in England and abroad, paid its debts, and introduced modern methods of accounting. Although P. & O.'s monopoly vanished, he kept competitors at bay and retained P. & O.'s reputation as an élite and exclusive concern. His rise was meteoric: a managing director in 1872, he was chairman and managing director in 1881. Not yet forty-seven, he had charge of the largest and most successful shipping company in the world.

After Britain's occupation of Egypt in 1882 (in which P. & O. played a part), shipowners became impatient with France's overwhelming dominance in the Suez Canal. Britain used the canal more than any other nation, and P. & O. far more than any other single company. Grievances about the canal grew apace: dues and charges were exorbitant, the waterway was narrow and awkward, the passage slow and hazardous.

In 1883 Sutherland led a popular campaign for a second canal to be made with British money and British ownership. When parliament threw out Gladstone's remedial proposals, Sutherland took the lead again, inviting Charles de Lesseps, son of the famous Ferdinand, to come to P. & O.'s headquarters at 122 Leadenhall Street, London, to draw up, in private, an acceptable agenda for negotiation concerning the management of the Suez Canal. This accomplished, he chaired more than two weeks of argument between French representatives and several British shipowners.

Sutherland's diplomacy during the sessions, and his geniality when both parties repaired to the nearby Ship and Turtle for refreshment, contributed to a satisfactory outcome, the 'London programme'. This document conceded the main demands of the shipowners: a British committee based in London to deal with canal problems; seven British directors selected from the shipping and mercantile communities (three British officials were already on the board), giving Britain one third of a new total of directors on the canal company's board; dues to be reduced in stages; pilot charges scrapped; and improvement of the waterway begun forthwith. Sutherland was one of the new directors and in 1903 became one of three vice-presidents, an office he held until his death. His command of the French language, acquired when he was forty years of age, gave him an edge in the many business and social meetings he attended with his French and other continental colleagues.

Shipping was a cut-throat business. Sutherland acted ruthlessly if an intruder tried to poach P. & O.'s trade or a recalcitrant member of an existing arrangement fell out of line. But he preferred rings or conferences, and at the royal commission on shipping rings (1909) he asserted that they made for efficiency and peace, and were the best way to contain the fierce and unremitting competition all shipowners had to meet.

In 1889 unionization began to spread into unskilled dock labour. Like other shipowners, Sutherland abhorred this development and looked to the Shipping Federation, the shipowners' union that was forged in 1890 with his help, to counter strikes and encourage 'free' labour.

In 1884 Sutherland entered the House of Commons, (first as a Liberal, then as a Liberal Unionist) for Greenock, the shipbuilding constituency in which most of P. & O.'s ships were built. He joined the shipowners' parliamentary committee (1893), a lobby set up to protect the shipping interest, and often spoke in its defence. He sat on two royal commissions, one on ships' load lines (1882), the other on Ireland's financial relations with Britain (1893). He kept his seat in five general elections, but stood down because of increasing deafness in 1900. He was created a KCMG in 1891 and a GCMG in 1897, and became a knight of the order of St John and a member of the Légion d'honneur. He was appointed a deputy lieutenant for the City of London, and the University of Aberdeen honoured him with an LLD in 1892.

In 1880 Sutherland married Mary Alice Morris Macnaught (d. 1920), daughter of John Macnaught, vicar of Holy Trinity, Conduit Street, London. They had two sons and one daughter. Both sons were killed in action, one in the South African War, the other in the First World War. Their daughter, Helen Christian *Sutherland, became an important collector and patron of the arts. In his leisure interests, Sutherland was eclectic. For many years he was an ardent theatregoer. In the 1900s, transport by motor car gave him much pleasure. He travelled in Britain and Europe with family or friends in one or other of his cars, and was especially fond of his six-cylinder Darracq. Late in life, he became fascinated by aviation. He read, listened to music, and liked a round of golf. One of the best public speakers in the City, he was in constant demand for grand occasions and institutional dinners in the shipping world. At his country home, Coldharbour Wood at Liss, near Petersfield, in Hampshire, he was a generous host to large gatherings. He was known as Tom in the City.

Sutherland wanted to retire in his early seventies, but a successor of his stature was difficult to find. Not until 1914 was the right man available: this was James Lyte Mackay, Lord Inchcape (1852–1932), chairman of the British India Steam Navigation Company, with whom he had long and close relations. Inchcape agreed to merge his company with P. & O. and to chair both companies, each keeping its own identity.

In Sutherland's last year as P. & O.'s chairman, a French colleague saw him as big, ugly, old, ill, deaf, and autocratic, but the way his face sparkled with intelligence and 'good British humour' made up for the marks of old age. He stood highest among many clever shipowners at the peak of British maritime hegemony. He was proud to have been the custodian of P. & O., symbol of Britain's imperial strength over half the globe: Egypt, India, China, and Australia. Indeed, for over thirty years, Sutherland was himself a living symbol. He died on 1 January 1922 at his London residence, 7 Buckingham Gate, South Kensington.

FREDA HARCOURT

Sources 1865–1914, NMM, P. & O. archive · Aberdeen Grammar School Magazine, 25/1 (1921–2) · Aberdeen University Magazine, 20 (1902–3) · Fairplay's annual survey of shipping finance (1865–1914) · F. H. H. King, The history of the Hongkong and Shanghai Banking Corporation, 1 (1987) · The Times (27 April 1883), 4, 9–10 · Confidential prints, PRO, FO 423/10 · old parish register and census returns, 1851, General Register Office for Scotland, Edinburgh · m. cert. · CGPLA Eng. & Wales (1922)

Archives CUL, corresp. with Lord Hardinge · NMM, P. & O. archive
Likenesses J. H. Lorimer, oils, 1882, Scot. NPG · B. Stone, photograph, 1897, NPG [*see illus.*] · Spy [L. Ward], cartoon, *c.*1900, P. & O., London · Ape [C. Pellegrini], caricature, watercolour study, NPG; repro. in *VF* (22 Oct 1887) · J. S. Sargent, oils, P. & O., London · photographs, P. & O., London
Wealth at death £723,075 6s. 11d.: probate, 22 March 1922, *CGPLA Eng. & Wales*

Sutherland, William, third earl of Sutherland (*c.*1286–1330). *See under* Sutherland family (*per. c.*1200–*c.*1510).

Sutherland, William, fifth earl of Sutherland (*d.* 1370/71). *See under* Sutherland family (*per. c.*1200–*c.*1510).

Sutro, Alfred (1863–1933), playwright and translator, was born at 3 Dean Street, Finsbury Square, London, on 7 August 1863. He was the youngest son of the five children of Helena Cohen (1829/30–1891) and Sigismund Sutro MD (1815–1886), an authority on continental spas who emigrated from Bavaria to England as a young man and became naturalized, and the grandson of a German rabbi of Sephardi Jewish ancestry. Sutro was educated at the City of London School, Cheapside, under E. A. Abbott, at Asquith's School, and in Brussels. While still a boy he became a clerk in the City and at the age of twenty joined his elder brother Leopold in partnership as wholesale merchants in tea, coffee, and cheeses. It was while in this business that he made the acquaintance of Alexander Teixeira de Mattos, like Sutro a Sephardi Jew, and who likewise became a translator of Maurice Maeterlinck.

In 1894 Sutro married Esther Stella (Essie) Isaacs (1869–1934), daughter of Joseph Michael Isaacs, fruit broker and importer in Covent Garden, and Sarah, daughter of Daniel Davis. Esther was also the sister of Rufus Daniel Isaacs, first marquess of Reading, who had been an art student in Paris and exhibited at the Royal Academy, and who later became lord chief justice of England. Esther agreed to marry Sutro only on the condition that he abandon business and take up one of the arts. An avid theatregoer, Sutro agreed, and the couple moved to Paris. They enrolled in the Théâtre de L'Oeuvre, a society dedicated to the production of fine plays, where they befriended Maeterlinck and Henrik Ibsen. Sutro became instrumental in bringing the Théâtre to London, where its members performed Maeterlinck's *Pelléas et Mélisande* in 1895 with sets painted by the French impressionist Édouard Vuillard. It was received with acclaim by the critics William Archer and George Bernard Shaw.

After this experience, the Sutros were fast friends with Maeterlinck, who summered with them in a cottage in Dorset the same year. Soon after, Sutro's first play was produced, a joint adaptation with Arthur Bourchier of Alexandre Bisson's *Monsieur le directeur*, entitled *The Chili Widow*. The proceeds allowed the Sutros to become collectors of impressionist paintings by Vuillard and Vincent Van Gogh, and to attend various salons in London and Paris where they met Stephane Mallarmé, Paul Verlaine, Thomas Hardy, and George Meredith, with whom Sutro

unsuccessfully collaborated in converting his novel *The Egoist* into a drama. He also became close friends with W. Somerset Maugham, Arthur Symons, and W. B. Yeats. Sutro was, however, a more successful translator than original dramatist, publishing Maeterlinck's *La sagesse et la destinée* (as *Wisdom and Destiny*, 1897) and *La vie des abeilles* (as *The Life of the Bee*, 1901). The latter had in the first instance been dedicated to Sutro, for whose play *The Cave of Illusion* (1900) Maeterlinck wrote an introduction.

In fact it was not until 1902, with his 'duologues' *Women in Love*, that Sutro achieved any success in his own right. A series of eight one-acts devoted to female experiences, they were performed individually or together over the next fifteen years. But his main success came in 1904 with *The Walls of Jericho*, a dark comedy about a disillusioned millionaire and his heartless, aristocratic wife. Thenceforth Sutro was accounted one of the leading English dramatists, no year being complete for theatregoers without a new play from his pen—sometimes more than one. The best-known of these are *Mollentrave on Women* (1905), *The Fascinating Mr Vanderveldt* (1906), *John Glayde's Honour* and *The Desperate Duke* (both 1907), *The Perplexed Husband* (1911), and *The Marriage will not Take Place* (1917). During this time he also helped found The Dramatists' Club with Shaw and became a patron of the young D. H. Lawrence. One of the first things he did with his royalties was to send 100 guineas to poor parishes in the East End of London. Meanwhile Esther had become a fashionable painter, securing the patronage of Henry James and publishing a study of Nicolas Poussin.

Wartime did not diminish the Sutros' fame. Sutro joined the Artists' Rifles and served in the war trade intelligence department, for which he was made an officer in the Order of the British Empire in 1918. But although after the war he continued to produce plays, they were mostly light crowd-pleasers such as *Far above Rubies* (1924) and *The Desperate Lovers* (1927). He had been overtaken by a new school of dramatists led by Noël Coward, and when his last play, *Living Together* (1929), was so poorly received that even his nephew Edward Sutro criticized it, he not only swore to write no more plays but also had his nephew struck out of his will. Instead he composed a volume of reminiscences, *Celebrities and Simple Souls* (1933), 'dedicated to my wife'. He was only just able to read the warm reviews before becoming dangerously ill with a bronchial complaint in August 1933, and he died at his country home, The Gurdons, Witley, Surrey, on 11 September 1933. Esther Sutro survived her husband, but died the following year, on 3 December 1934. They had no children.

KATHARINE CHUBBUCK

Sources L. Sawin, *Alfred Sutro: a man with a heart* (1989) · A. Sutro, *Celebrities and simple souls* (1933) · A. Nicoll, *English drama, 1900–1930* (1973) · S. J. Kunitz and H. Haycraft, eds., *Twentieth century authors: a biographical dictionary of modern literature* (1942) · *WWW, 1941–50* · Boase, *Mod. Eng. biog.*, vol. 6 [Sigismund Sutro] · *The Times* (13 Sept 1933) · *Jewish Chronicle* (15 Sept 1933) · *DNB*
Archives BL · NRA, corresp. and literary papers · Yale U., Beinecke L. | BL, corresp. with Society of Authors, Add. MS 56827 · priv. coll.

Likenesses photograph, c.1910, repro. in Sawin, *Alfred Sutro* · photograph, 1930–39, repro. in Sawin, *Alfred Sutro* · double portrait, photograph, 1933 (with Essie), repro. in Sawin, *Alfred Sutro* · H. Furniss, pen-and-ink caricature, NPG

Wealth at death £34,670 2s. 2d.: probate, 2 Jan 1934, *CGPLA Eng. & Wales*

Sutton, Sir Bertine Entwisle (1886–1946), air force officer, was born in Kensington, London, on 17 December 1886, the son of the Revd Alfred Sutton (d. 1938), vicar of Bridekirk, Cockermouth, and his wife, Bertha Frances Entwisle, daughter of John Edward Walker. He was educated at Eton College and University College, Oxford, and while an undergraduate became one of the original members of the Oxford University mounted infantry. He graduated with a pass BA in 1908 and worked for a time in a solicitor's office in London before joining the publishing firm of Hutchinson.

Soon after the outbreak of war in 1914, Sutton became a private in the Inns of Court Officers' Training Corps. In the autumn of that year he was commissioned as second lieutenant in the Westmorland and Cumberland yeomanry and went to France. At the beginning of 1916 he was seconded to the Royal Flying Corps as an observer, and towards the end of that year gained his wings as a pilot. During his service in France with the army co-operation squadrons, one of which he commanded, he distinguished himself by carrying out many valuable reconnaissances and patrols at low altitudes, particularly during the third battle of Ypres. For this fine work, in the course of which he was wounded, he was awarded the MC in 1917 and later in the same year was appointed to the DSO for conspicuous gallantry and devotion to duty. The citation added that 'by his energy, skill, and courage he set a magnificent example to his squadron'.

Sutton ended the war as an acting lieutenant-colonel in the newly formed Royal Air Force, and in 1919 he was granted a permanent commission in that service as a squadron leader. In 1921 he attended the Staff College, Camberley, and in the following year he had the distinction of being selected as one of the five original instructors on the formation of the Royal Air Force Staff College, where he proved himself a born teacher. On one occasion he displayed the same example of courage as he had shown in the war. Practice parachute jumps from the air were being carried out and one parachute failed to open. The commanding officer of the station ordered the practices to stop, but Sutton, who was among those who saw the accident, asked for an aircraft to be kept in action, immediately put on parachute harness, and proceeded to make a successful jump. He married in 1928 Margaret Griselda, daughter of Alexander Dundas Ogilvy Wedderburn CBE KC and widow of Stuart Andros de la Rue, third son of Sir Thomas Andros de la Rue, first baronet. They had two sons.

In 1929 Sutton was appointed Royal Air Force instructor at the Imperial Defence College. Two and a half years later he was posted to India, where he commanded 1 group near the north-west frontier, and then served as senior air staff officer at air headquarters before returning to England in 1936 to command 22 army co-operation group. By 1937 he had attained the rank of air vice-marshal.

At the outbreak of war in 1939 Sutton was commanding 21 group, and two years later he returned to the Royal Air Force Staff College as commandant. Between 1942 and 1945, as an air marshal, he was a member of the Air Council, in the highly demanding post of air member for personnel. During this period, he faced numerous manning problems, not least a projected shortfall in aircrew which coincided with the army's demands for more troops to meet the force level required for D-day. In June 1945 he retired from the Royal Air Force. He was appointed OBE in 1919 and CB in 1939, and promoted KBE in 1942.

Sutton used to say that he was more interested in people than in anything else, and it was this characteristic, combined with his other gifts, which made him so fine a leader and so wise an administrator. Moreover, his innate friendliness, which did not diminish as he rose in rank, made him most popular with both officers and men. A penetrating mind lay behind his gaiety and keen sense of humour, and the easy charm which delighted his friends cloaked real firmness and determination which could, if the interests of the service demanded it, turn even to ruthlessness.

It was sometimes said of Sutton that he would have been equally successful as a don; and undoubtedly his love of literature and drama coloured his whole life. Though not interested in sports, he took pleasure in many open-air activities, and he shared with his father, who became an honorary canon of Carlisle, a deep affection for his native Cumberland. He was always happy walking the fells, hunting or riding, and fishing in the Derwent. He was not destined to enjoy for long his retirement in his happy home, Little Park Farm, Crookham Common, near Newbury, Berkshire, with his library, pictures, and garden. The strain of his arduous wartime duties had undermined his health, which was never robust, and he died there on 28 September 1946.

E. B. BEAUMAN, *rev.* CHRISTINA J. M. GOULTER

Sources air historical branch (RAF) records, London · private information (1959) · personal knowledge (1959) · *CGPLA Eng. & Wales* (1947)

Archives PRO, papers | FILM IWM FVA, actuality footage | SOUND BL NSA, current affairs recordings

Likenesses W. Stoneman, photograph, 1944, NPG

Wealth at death £29,614 8s. 1d.: probate, 25 Jan 1947, *CGPLA Eng. & Wales*

Sutton, Sir Charles (1775–1828), army officer, was born at Screveton, near Bingham, Nottinghamshire, the eldest son of Admiral Evelyn Sutton and his wife, daughter of Thomas Thoroton of Screveton. He was a nephew of Mary Thoroton, the wife of Charles Manners-*Sutton (1755–1828), archbishop of Canterbury.

Sutton entered the army as an ensign in the 3rd foot guards in July 1800 and in 1802 was promoted lieutenant and captain. He transferred to the 23rd foot in 1803, and was promoted major in 1807. After serving with Sir John Moore in his last campaign Sutton entered the Portuguese service. At the battle of Busaco on 27 September 1810 he commanded the 9th regiment and was mentioned in Wellington's dispatch. On 8 May 1811 he was in the hottest part of the action at Fuentes d'Oñoro in command of the light companies in Champelmond's Portuguese brigade. Two days later he was recommended for the brevet rank of lieutenant-colonel in the British army because of his distinction in the Portuguese service. He became lieutenant-colonel in his regiment in 1813.

At the siege of Badajoz Sutton was attached to the 3rd division under Thomas Picton, and he was present at Salamanca, Vitoria, and the later actions in the south of France. He was awarded a cross and three clasps. In 1814 he attained the rank of colonel in the Portuguese army and was made a knight of the order of the Tower and Sword. He was later promoted colonel in the British army, and was made KCB on 2 January 1815.

After the peace Sutton was appointed an inspecting field officer of the militia in the Ionian Islands, where Colonel Charles James Napier (1782–1853) was a colleague. On 26 March 1828, while on leave from Zante, he died suddenly of a stroke in the rectory of his uncle, the Revd Charles Thoroton, at Bottesford, near Belvoir, Leicestershire.

G. Le G. Norgate, rev. Gordon L. Teffeteller

Sources The dispatches of … the duke of Wellington … from 1799 to 1818, ed. J. Gurwood, 13 vols. in 12 (1834–9) · Army List · GM, 1st ser., 98/1 (1828), 368–9

Sutton, Charles Manners- (1755–1828), archbishop of Canterbury, was born Charles Manners on 14 February 1755, the fourth son of Lord George Manners (1723–1783), and his wife, Diana (d. 1767), daughter of Thomas Chaplin of Blankney, Lincolnshire; he was grandson of John, third duke of Rutland. In 1762 his father assumed the additional surname Sutton on inheriting the estates of his maternal grandfather, Robert *Sutton, second Baron Lexington. Educated at Charterhouse School, he then matriculated as a pensioner at Emmanuel College, Cambridge, on 1 March 1773; he graduated BA as fifteenth wrangler in 1777, his younger brother, Thomas Manners-*Sutton, being at the same time fifth wrangler. He proceeded MA in 1780 and DD in 1792. In 1785 he was presented to the rectory of Averham with Kelham, Nottinghamshire, and also to Whitwell, Derbyshire. Manners-Sutton married in 1778 Mary (d. 1832), daughter of Thomas Thoroton of Screveton, Nottinghamshire. They had two sons and ten daughters.

Preferment was rapid. Manners-Sutton became dean of Peterborough in 1791, in 1792 bishop of Norwich, and—because Norwich had a small income and was a large and expensive diocese—influence at court secured him the deaneries of Windsor and Wolverhampton in 1794, to be held in commendam. He and his wife became great favourites with George III and the royal family. In 1794 he was offered the archbishopric of Armagh, but he declined the appointment. At Norwich, Manners-Sutton was a conscientious and well-liked diocesan bishop. He was the first bishop of Norwich consistently to undertake all his ordinations in Norwich. He was hospitable and generous to charities. He dined with his clergy after his visitations and

treated them with wine, 'a bottle between two' (Diary of a Country Parson, 3.367). He separated confirmations from visitations. After a confirmation James Woodforde, rector of Weston Longueville, noted that his niece, 'Miss Woodforde [was] much pleased … with the Bishop's very agreeable and affable, as well as polite and sensible behaviour' (ibid., 4.141). In his visitations he demonstrated a keen interest in matters of contemporary concern to the church—the employment of curates; the administration of baptism, schools, and almshouses; and disputes over tithe payments—and he asked for

> any other Matters relating to your Parish of which it may be proper to give me Information, Or any proposal to make whereby the Glory of God and the Good of his Church may be promoted, and this Diocese better ordered, and ourselves mutually aiding and assisting each other in the Discharge of our respective Duties. (Visitation inquiries, 1801, Norwich RO, NDR VIS 39/17)

During the threat of French invasion in 1803 Manners-Sutton urged the clergy to warn the poor of the risks a French occupation might have for them, but he advised the clergy against joining militias or defensive corps. At Norwich, Manners-Sutton seems to have got into financial difficulties, despite the additional revenues of the deanery of Windsor, and he was criticized for extravagance.

On the death of Archbishop Moore in 1805 George III intervened personally with William Pitt to secure Manners-Sutton's translation to Canterbury, although Pitt wished to appoint his former tutor, Bishop Pretyman-Tomline of Lincoln. As archbishop Manners-Sutton played an active part in the policies of the traditional high-church party then ascendant in the church. He was himself a high-churchman: it was noted that at his primary visitation in Canterbury Cathedral in 1806 that he preached on the significance of confession and its history. Manners-Sutton played a central role in the series of initiatives and reforms to promote the church's mission in the period of dramatic social change brought about by population growth, urbanization, and industrialization. From at least 1809 he worked to secure government funds to build new churches to meet the needs of the rapidly expanding population. In the House of Lords he took an active part in the attempt to secure satisfactory legislation to provide adequate stipends for curates. With lay members of the Hackney Phalanx, notably Joshua Watson, and with the co-operation of the prime minister, the earl of Liverpool, he worked to secure the Additional Churches Act of 1818, which gave the Church of England £1 million to build new churches, although he was defeated by ministers in his wish that clergy should be in the majority on the subsequent commission for building new churches. He was one of the most regular attenders at the commission's committee meetings.

Manners-Sutton was also active with the Hackney Phalanx in reinvigorating existing voluntary bodies to promote the church's mission and in creating new bodies. The Society for the Promotion of Christian Knowledge was overhauled and Manners-Sutton played a significant part in the foundation of the National Society for Promoting the Education of the Poor in the Principles of the Established Church in 1811; he nearly always chaired the fortnightly meetings of the society's committee and he persuaded the prince regent to become patron of the society. The society provided a model for the church to act in a corporate capacity in the absence of the convocations, including all of the bishops as its vice-presidents, along with leading laymen. He was closely involved in the foundation of the Incorporated Church Building Society, of which he chaired the majority of meetings, to raise funds to provide grants for building and repairing churches to provide more seats in churches for the increasing population.

Manners-Sutton worked closely with the Hackney Phalanx to revive the Society for the Propagation of the Gospel and he was active in the campaign that secured the establishment of a bishop for India, being closely involved in recruiting Thomas Middleton, archdeacon of Huntingdon, and an associate of the phalanx, as first bishop of Calcutta. Manners-Sutton was also concerned with the extension of higher education. He contributed £1000 towards the endowment of King's College, London, and was instrumental in persuading George IV to give his name to the college; he also contributed towards the establishment of both St David's College, Lampeter, by Bishop Burgess of St David's and of King's College in Halifax, Nova Scotia. In 1814 he was appointed to preside over the German Relief Fund to administer a parliamentary grant of £100,000 for the relief of Germany during the winter of the final Napoleonic campaign, which—because of opposition to the grant in the light of needs for charity relief at home—needed to be a model of accurate accounting. Joshua Watson acted as administrator of the funds. In 1816 Manners-Sutton and Bishop Howley of London unsuccessfully attempted to revive the Association for the Relief of the Manufacturing and Labouring Poor, established in 1812, and in 1817 he briefly flirted with Robert Owen's plan to put the poor into 'Villages of Co-operation' where, after an initial capital grant from taxes, they would pay their own way while becoming useful, industrious, self-disciplined, and temperate.

Manners-Sutton may have been the initiator of a meritocratic revolution that reinvigorated the Church of England in the early nineteenth century. Although his own preferment was due to aristocratic patronage and royal favour, he, along with Bishop Howley of London, worked with Joshua Watson and his associates in the Hackney Phalanx to test the potential of able young graduates from middle-class backgrounds, making discriminate use of the extensive patronage available to archbishops of Canterbury and promoting the most promising candidates. His own chaplains provided able leaders for the next generation of high-churchmen: Christopher Wordsworth, subsequently master of Trinity College, Cambridge; George Cambridge, subsequently archdeacon of Middlesex; John Lonsdale, subsequently bishop of Lichfield; Charles Lloyd subsequently bishop of Oxford; Richard Mant, subsequently bishop of Down and Connor, and

Hugh James Rose, subsequently principal of King's College, London. Manners-Sutton was however, bitterly attacked by radical pamphleteers for alleged nepotism in his use of patronage. Manners-Sutton was regularly consulted by Lord Liverpool about the appointment of bishops. He was a key figure in the queen's council appointed to review George III's health and in the complex relations between the queen and the doctors caring for the king, whom the queen distrusted. He attracted public hostility for supporting the bill for George IV's divorce on the grounds that divorces 'were expressly declared by our Saviour himself' (Varley, 97). He was also involved in the negotiations over the modifications to the liturgy for George IV's coronation. At the end of his life Manners-Sutton opposed Roman Catholic emancipation, but favoured the repeal of the Test and Corporation Acts. At Canterbury he was reckoned to be generous in his charity and his hospitality, but he paid meticulous attention to the administration of the archiepiscopal estates, which included major developments at Dover and Deal. In 1808 he purchased Addington Place as a country seat for archbishops in succession to the palace at Croydon, which had been sold in 1780. He published two sermons in 1794 and 1797; *An Address to the Clergy of the Diocese of Norwich*, in 1803; and he contributed 'A description of five British species of orabanch' to the *Transactions* of the Linnean Society (vol. 4, 1797, 173). Archbishop Manners-Sutton died on 21 July 1828 at Lambeth Palace and was buried on 29 July at Addington parish church. His eldest son, Charles Manners-*Sutton, became speaker of the House of Commons and subsequently first Viscount Canterbury, and his second son was a colonel in the army. W. M. JACOB

Sources E. Churton, ed., *Memoir of Joshua Watson*, 2 vols. (1861) · E. A. Varley, *The last of the prince bishops: William Van Mildert and the high church movement of the early nineteenth century* (1992) · C. Dewey, *The passing of Barchester* (1991) · M. H. Port, *Six hundred new churches: a study of the church building commission, 1818–1856, and its church building activities* (1961) · H. J. Burgess, *Enterprise in education* (1958) · A. W. Rowden, *The primates of the four Georges* (1916) · R. A. Soloway, *Prelates and people: ecclesiastical social thought in England, 1783–1852* (1969) · *The diary of a country parson: the Reverend James Woodforde*, ed. J. Beresford, 3–4 (1927–9) · P. Collinson and others, eds., *A history of Canterbury Cathedral, 598–1982* (1995) · C. Manners-Sutton, *An address to the clergy of the diocese of Norwich* (1803) · Norfolk RO, NDR VIS 33a/13, VIS 39/13, ORR 4, VIS 39/17 · LPL, Manners-Sutton MSS · *DNB*

Archives LPL, corresp. and papers, incl. material relating to King's College, Nova Scotia · LPL, manuscript collection · Norfolk RO, account books | BL, corresp. with Lord Liverpool, Add. MSS 38248–38328, 38574–38575, *passim* · BL, corresp. with Sir Robert Peel, Add. MSS 40271–40390, *passim* · BL, letters to Lord Spencer

Likenesses J. Hoppner, oils, *c.*1794, Royal Collection · J. Hoppner?, oils, *c.*1795–1800, LPL · G. Hayter, group portrait, oils, 1820 (*The trial of Queen Caroline, 1820*), NPG · W. Holl, stipple, pubd 1828 (after T. Wagemann), BM, NPG · F. Chantrey, bust, AM Oxf. · F. Chantrey, pencil drawing, NPG · G. Hayter, drawing, NPG · Stephanoff, watercolour drawing, V&A · oils (after T. Lawrence), LPL · two oils, Bishop's House, Norwich

Sutton, Charles Manners-, first Viscount Canterbury

(**1780–1845**), speaker of the House of Commons, was born at Screveton, Nottinghamshire, on 29 January 1780, the eldest son of Charles Manners-*Sutton (1755–1828), later archbishop of Canterbury, and his wife, Mary (d. 1832), daughter of Thomas Thoroton of Screveton. He was educated at Eton College (1793–6) and Trinity College, Cambridge (1798–1802), where he took a BA degree as fourth junior optime in 1802 and an MA in 1805. Admitted to Lincoln's Inn on 19 May 1802, he was called to the bar in May 1806 and practised on the western circuit for several years.

Manners-Sutton's father, a grandson of the third duke of Rutland, who had been the royal choice as primate in 1805, provided him with a post worth over £600 a year, and in the general election of 1806 the Rutland electoral interest secured his return for Scarborough, a constituency he continued to represent until 1832. In London he joined the Alfred Club, then a cradle of rising young tory politicians like Palmerston, Robinson, and Peel. He made his first parliamentary speech in June 1808 on the Curates Residence Bill. On general issues he supported the Portland and Perceval administrations. His gentlemanly appearance and good voice impressed his contemporaries, and in October 1809 he was invited by Perceval, with royal approval, to take the office of judge-advocate-general.

Over the next eight years Manners-Sutton's interventions in debate were largely confined to his official business, including the periodic defence of flogging in the army against whig-Liberal criticism. He also spoke against parliamentary reform and concessions to Roman Catholics, and in April 1817 introduced a consolidating measure (57 Geo. III c. 99) on clerical residence and payment of curates. In June 1817 he was the ministerial candidate for the vacant speakership of the House of Commons, defeating his whig opponent, C. W. W. Wynn, by 312 votes to 150. While comparatively young for the office, he was older than two recent speakers, W. W. Grenville and Addington, at the time of their election. The chief criticism of his selection was his lack of knowledge of the forms and procedures of the house. However, he seems to have taken advice from his immediate predecessor, Charles Abbot, and his courteous and obliging manners soon established his authority in the House of Commons.

On 8 July 1811 Manners-Sutton married Lucy Maria Charlotte, eldest daughter of John Denison of Ossington, Nottinghamshire, with whom he had two sons, Charles John and John Henry Thomas Manners-*Sutton, and a daughter, Charlotte Matilda. His wife died on 7 December 1815 and he remained a widower until 6 December 1828, when he married Ellen (1791?–1845), widow of John Home-Purves and daughter of Edmund Power of Curragheen, co. Waterford, a hearty, lively Irishwoman (according to Thomas Moore) who contributed further to the popularity of his official entertainments (Dasent, 306). He retained his strong political views, and in 1827 refused Canning's offer of the Home Office because of their disagreement on the Catholic question. In May 1832, when attempts were being made, following Grey's resignation, to construct a tory reform ministry, he declined to enter a cabinet under Wellington. His resolution wavered, however, when his own name, as one of the rare Conservative politicians uncommitted on the parliamentary reform issue, was put forward for the premiership. At a meeting of senior tories at Apsley House on Sunday 13 May, he treated his future colleagues to an insufferably long and tedious exposition of his views and asked for more time to consider. Next day he wrote to Wellington to accept if no other arrangement seemed possible. His performance at the meeting, however, had disgusted everybody—the coarse and impatient Lyndhurst swore that he would have nothing to do with such 'a damned tiresome old bitch' (Greville Memoirs, 17 May 1832, 2.298)—and in any case events in the House of Commons that evening put a stop to any further talk of a tory ministry.

In July 1832, at the conclusion of the protracted and exhausting Reform Bill debates, Manners-Sutton expressed his wish to retire from the speaker's chair and was granted a life pension of £4000, with one of £3000 for his heir male. At the ensuing general election he was returned for the University of Cambridge; the whig ministry, unsure of its ability to control the remodelled House of Commons, at the end of December 1832 asked him in flattering terms to continue as speaker. He was accordingly re-elected in January 1833 as governmental candidate with a majority of 210 over E. J. Littleton, who had been put forward by disgruntled radicals. In August 1833, as a special mark of the cabinet's gratitude, he was given the GCB.

During Peel's Hundred Days (1834–5) in office, Manners-Sutton was again embroiled in the formation of a tory administration. After the destruction by fire of the old House of Commons (including his own official residence) in October 1834, he had been in communication with the king over the latter's embarrassing offer of temporary accommodation for the Commons in the grounds of Buckingham Palace. He also attended a few formal privy council meetings subsequent to the change of ministry. This led to partisan charges in the whig press of collusion with William IV in the dismissal in November of Melbourne's government. In the contested election for the speakership in the new parliament in February 1835 he was defeated by 316 votes to 306 by the whig candidate, James Abercromby, in an unprecedented mobilization of party strength, designed to test the stability of the new Conservative administration. He was able, however, to demonstrate that he had not been involved in the king's decision to change his ministers, nor advised a dissolution, nor assisted in the formation of Peel's ministry. In March 1835, on Peel's initiative, he was created Viscount Canterbury, a higher rank than was normally conferred on a retiring speaker. But he seldom spoke in the House of Lords, and after appointment to the high commission for Canadian claims in March 1835 he soon resigned on grounds of his wife's health.

Manners-Sutton was a tall, urbane man with a dignified bearing, though devoid of any great talents. He was short-sighted and, as speaker, occasionally affected, it was alleged, not to be able to recognize the faces or recall the names of whig members (Dasent, 309). Nevertheless, he earned a reputation for both equanimity and impartiality. The *Annual Register* summed up his outward qualities when it wrote in its obituary of his 'commanding presence, sonorous voice, and imperturbable temper' (*Annual Register*, 1845, 291). In handling the inexperienced and boisterous 1833 House of Commons he preferred, in his own metaphor, the snaffle rather than the curb, despite a certain laxity of discipline which resulted (*Greville Memoirs*, 5 Sept 1833; cf. Dasent, 305). He established a record as the only speaker to have been elected seven times, though his actual tenure of the chair was exceeded in length by Onslow and Shaw-Lefevre. He became a bencher of Lincoln's Inn in 1817, was given the degree of LLD by Cambridge University in 1824, and held the office of registrar of the court of faculties of the archbishop of Canterbury from 1827 to 1834.

On the night of 18 July 1845, while travelling by train between Slough and Paddington, Manners-Sutton suffered a stroke and died three days later, on 21 July 1845, at his younger son's house in Southwick Crescent, Paddington. His burial took place in the family vault at Addington, Surrey, on 28 July 1845. His wife, with whom he had a daughter, Frances Diana, survived him by only a few months, dying in November 1845. The title passed to his elder son, who died unmarried in 1869, and then to his younger son. NORMAN GASH

Sources GEC, *Peerage* · M. H. Port and R. G. Thorne, 'Manners Sutton, Charles', HoP, *Commons* · *Annual Register* (1845), 291 · *DNB* · *The Greville memoirs, 1814–1860*, ed. L. Strachey and R. Fulford, 8 vols. (1938) · *The Croker papers: the correspondence and diaries of … John Wilson Croker*, ed. L. J. Jennings, 3 vols. (1884) · *Political correspondence: Wellington*, ed. J. Brooke and J. Gandy, 1: *1833 – November 1834* (1975) · *Despatches, correspondence, and memoranda of Field Marshal Arthur, duke of Wellington*, ed. A. R. Wellesley, second duke of Wellington, 8 vols. (1867–80) · private information · A. I. Dasent, *The speakers of the House of Commons* (1911) · *A portion of the journal kept by Thomas Raikes esq. from 1831 to 1847: comprising reminiscences of social and political life in London and Paris during that period*, 4 vols. (1856–8) · *The Creevey papers*, ed. H. Maxwell, 3rd edn (1905); repr. (1923)
Archives NRA, priv. coll., corresp. and papers | Balliol Oxf., letters to Henry Jenkyns · BL, corresp. with Sir Robert Peel · U. Durham, corresp. with Charles, second Earl Grey · U. Southampton L., letters to first duke of Wellington
Likenesses T. Lawrence, oils, *c.*1810–1815, Niedersächsische Landesgalerie, Hanover · R. Dighton, caricature, etching, pubd 1821 (*Elegant manners*), NPG, V&A · J. Doyle, pencil and chalk caricature, 1830 (*Make way for the speaker*), BM · Count D'Orsay, pencil and chalk drawing, 1833, NPG · H. W. Pickersgill, oils, 1833, NPG · S. Cousins, engraving (after H. W. Pickersgill), repro. in Dasent, *Speakers of the House of Commons*, 304 · H. B. Hall, stipple (after A. E. Chalon), BM, NPG; repro. in H. T. Ryall, *Portraits of eminent conservatives and statesmen* (1836) · G. Hayter, group portrait, oils (*The House of Commons 1833*), NPG

Sutton, Christopher (*c.*1565–1629), Church of England clergyman and devotional writer, probably born in Hampshire, matriculated at Oxford from Hart Hall in March 1583, graduated from Lincoln College in 1586, and proceeded MA in 1589. In 1591 he became incumbent of Woodrising, Norfolk. Presented by his patron, Sir Robert

Southwell, to the vicarage of Rainham, Essex, in June 1597, he resigned a year later on his presentation by Alice Berney to Caston, Norfolk; this he held with Woodrising until 1618, when he was succeeded by John Sutton, probably the brother mentioned in his will.

Christopher Sutton was the author of three fervently devotional works, which enjoyed considerable popularity among contemporaries. Dedicated to Lady Elizabeth Southwell, Sir Robert's widow, *Disce mori: Learne to Die*, first published in 1600, invited 'the godly reader' and 'those whose hearts desire is, that Israel may be saved, … to enter into a serious remembrance of his ende'. Two years later this was complemented by *Disce vivere: learne to live … wherein is shewed that the life of Christe is and ought to be the most perfect patterne of direction to the life of a Christian*. In 1613 his *Godly Meditations upon the most Holy Sacrament of the Lord's Supper*, dedicated to Lady Elizabeth's younger daughters Lady Catherine Verney and Lady Frances Rodney, addressed 'that high mystery of human salvation'. It was a matter of faith, not of understanding, but Sutton was convinced that 'the more often a Christian doth repair to the Holy Communion, the greater is his perfection, and the nearer he doth come to the piety of ancient Christians' (*Godly Meditations*, 262). In his prose can be glimpsed the 'excellent and florid preaching' style to which Wood attributed his acquisition in April 1605 of a prebend in Westminster Abbey (Wood, *Ath. Oxon.*, 2.456), where in 1623 he delivered William Camden's funeral sermon.

Southwell family patronage continued to advance Sutton's career. He was already, from November 1612, rector of Much (or Murly) Bromley, Essex, and in 1623 Lady Elizabeth's son Sir Thomas presented him to the rectory of Cranworth, Norfolk; he held both benefices until his death. Meanwhile, in October 1618, he had become a prebendary of Lincoln, adding this to his Westminster stall. Having drawn up his will on 29 April 1629, he died within a few weeks (his will was proved on 27 July) and was buried, as he had requested, in Westminster Abbey. Reprints of his works continued after his death, and from the 1830s the enthusiasm of leaders of the Oxford Movement for a 'learned, eloquent and pious … younger brother in divine things [to Hooker]' (Sutton, *Disce mori*, iii–iv), led to a clutch of reissues by the Society for Promoting Christian Knowledge and a Welsh version of *Disce mori* (1852). John Henry Newman's 'Advertisement' prefacing the 1838 edition of *Godly Meditations* commended it as 'written in the devotional tone of Bishops Taylor and Ken', and warned the reader inclined to censure the language as 'too rapturous' to consider whether his own estimate of the sacred subject was not inadequate.

G. LE G. NORGATE, *rev.* VIVIENNE LARMINIE

Sources Wood, *Ath. Oxon.*, new edn, 2.456 · Foster, *Alum. Oxon.* · F. Blomefield and C. Parkin, *An essay towards a topographical history of the county of Norfolk*, [2nd edn], 11 vols. (1805–10), vol. 2, p. 283; vol. 10, pp. 202, 280 · C. Sutton, *Disce mori: learn to die* (1600); repr. (1839) · C. Sutton, *Disce vivere: learn to live* (1602); repr. (1847) · C. Sutton, *Godly meditations upon the most holy sacrament of the Lord's supper*

(1838) • *Fasti Angl.* (Hardy), 2.283; 3.358 • PRO, PROB 11/156, fol. 61 (67 Ridley) • catalogue, Bodl. Oxf. • BL cat.

Wealth at death modest property in Essex; also cattle and goods: will, PRO, PROB 11/156, fol. 61

Sutton, Daniel (1735–1819), smallpox inoculator, was born on 4 May 1735 in Kenton, Suffolk, the second of eight sons (there were also three daughters) of Robert *Sutton (*bap.* 1708, *d.* 1788), surgeon, apothecary, and inoculator, and his wife, Sarah Barker of Debenham. He trained under and worked for his father until about 1760. He then became an assistant to an Essex doctor, and returned to him late in 1762 or early in 1763. Disagreeing with him over the patients' preparatory period before inoculation, which he proposed to reduce from a month to eight or ten days, and recommending an open-air regime instead of confinement indoors following inoculation, Sutton left to set up his own practice at Ingatestone, Essex, in October 1763.

In his first year of independent practice Sutton earned 2000 guineas. He inoculated 923 people in the first twenty weeks of 1765 and by late September had three inoculation houses at Ingatestone for different classes of patients paying 6, 4, or 3 guineas. By the end of the year two inoculation houses had been opened in London and in conjunction with his father and brothers Sutton had begun setting up partnerships throughout the country with 'Eminent physicians and surgeons daily applying … to be appointed partners for particular counties, or for foreign parts'. The income of the practice in 1765 was £6300.

In May 1766 in Maldon, Essex, Sutton performed his first mass or general inoculation. In one day 487 inhabitants were inoculated, thereby curtailing an epidemic. About the same time he purchased Maisonette, a country house and grounds in Ingatestone. A few weeks later he appeared at Chelmsford summer assizes, charged with causing an epidemic then raging in the town. Since all the doctors in Chelmsford practised inoculation it was impossible to prove him responsible and Sutton declared the prosecution to have been founded on the envy and malice of his enemies in the medical profession. In July and August further successful general inoculations took place in Maidstone, Kent, and Ewell, Surrey. In 1766 Sutton personally inoculated 7816 people. The total number inoculated by him, his assistants, and partners in the three years 1764–6 amounted to almost 20,000 without, it was claimed, a single death directly attributable to the treatment.

Events continued to move rapidly. By 1767 Sutton's method was becoming known on the European mainland, where it was recommended by Sir John Pringle. In August 1767 Sutton was granted a coat of arms with the motto 'Safely, quickly and pleasantly'. He also married Rachel, widow of William Westley of Shepton Mallet, Somerset, and daughter of Simon and Frances Warlock of Antigua and Westminster. They were to have one son, Daniel, born in 1768, and a daughter, Frances. The inoculating business had now reached its zenith with forty-seven 'authorized' partnerships (including Sutton, his father, and six

brothers) in England, Ireland, Wales, the Netherlands, France, Jamaica, and Virginia in 1768.

By about 1769 Sutton began to be superseded as first-choice inoculator of the wealthy by Thomas Dimsdale. Having successfully demonstrated the safety of his method of treatment so that it was being adopted by inoculators throughout the country, Sutton had already unwittingly performed his greatest service in the fight against smallpox. At the time of his father's death in April 1788 he and his brothers were still 'very eminent in the practice', and in 1796 he published *The Inoculator*, in which he explained his method and displayed his contempt for the medical establishment. In his final years he witnessed the introduction of vaccination, in 1798, and the rejection of inoculation by the majority of doctors. He died in semi-obscurity at his London residence in Hart Street, Bloomsbury Square, in February 1819.   J. R. SMITH, *rev.*

Sources J. R. Smith, *The speckled monster* (1987) • *GM*, 1st ser., 89/1 (1819), 281

Sutton, Denys Miller (1917–1991), art critic and journal editor, was born on 10 August 1917 at Pyne House, 64 South Side, Clapham, London, the son of Edmund Miller Sutton, a jeweller's assistant, and Dulcie Laura Wheeler, an actress. He was educated at Uppingham School and Exeter College, Oxford, where he received a third class in English in 1939 and a BLitt. On 4 July 1940 he married Sonja Klibansky (*b.* 1915/16); they later had a daughter. In the same year he joined the Foreign Office research department, where he worked for five years, and in 1945 he served as secretary of the international commission for the restitution of cultural material. In the following year, he published an anthology, *Watteau's Les charmes de la vie*, and his first biography, *Matisse*. In 1948 he published *Picasso, Blue and Pink Periods* and became a fine arts specialist at UNESCO, resigning after a year because of political interference. The following year was spent enjoyably as a visiting lecturer at Yale University, with publications on *French Drawings of the 18th Century* and *American Painting*, followed by *Flemish Painting* in 1950. These were all popular treatments. After his first marriage was dissolved, he married Gertrud Koebke-Knudson in 1952; they had a son.

Sutton worked as an art critic for *Country Life* and the *Financial Times*, his articles for the latter being published as *Delights of a Dilettante* (1980); he was also a salesroom correspondent for the *Daily Telegraph*. He continued to write books, including *Artists in 17th Century Rome* with Denis Mahon (1955), and *Catalogue of the French, Spanish and German Schools in the Fitzwilliam Museum* with J. W. Goodison (1960), which were more academic works. His second marriage having ended in divorce, on 3 May 1960 he married his third and last wife Cynthia Leah Abrahams, *née* Sassoon (*b.* 1925/6). Three impressive biographies followed: *Toulouse-Lautrec* in 1962 and *Titian* and *The Art of Whistler* in 1963.

Sutton became the editor of the arts magazine *Apollo* in March 1962 and remained in that position for a quarter of a century, renowned for his attention to detail and his encyclopaedic knowledge of his field. The magazine, founded in 1925, was thin and dullish, but Sutton immediately expanded it, made it more attractive, and widened its scope to cover a range of contemporary issues, from the destruction of the English country house to the possible threat of capital gains tax to works of art. This enthusiastic personal vision attracted many prominent art historians, including Kenneth Clark, Graham Reynolds, Peter Thornton, and Ralph Edwards. Sutton, himself a prolific and elegant writer, filled many issues virtually alone, turning out four numbers on 'aspects of British collecting' and four on 'the world of Sacheverell Sitwell'. Entire issues were also devoted to museums throughout the world and their collections, and many museums used these as guides before they produced their own. He also wrote another, more impressive book on Whistler (1966), edited the *Letters of Roger Fry* (1973), and published a biography of Sickert (1976).

In addition to his editing and writing, Sutton organized some twenty exhibitions, including those on Bonnard at the Royal Academy in 1966 and on France in the eighteenth century at the Royal Academy in 1968; for the latter he collected and catalogued, with Cynthia's help, more than 1000 works of art. Other impressive exhibitions under his direction were two in Columbus, Ohio: 'British Art' in 1971 and 'Irish Art' in 1974. He also organized seven exhibitions in Tokyo, including those on Constable (1985), Whistler (1987), and Sargent (1989).

Sutton was a dapper figure with a closely trimmed beard. He had a gregarious personality with strong opinions, an explosive temper (especially to those who did not meet his high standards), and a delightful sense of humour. Despite his busy schedule, he spent an inordinate amount of time telephoning friends and enjoying life, often at the theatre. He became wealthy and was an astute collector of art. His colleague Brinsley Ford recalled him rushing from the office to his daily swim at the Royal Automobile Club in Pall Mall before lunching at Wheeler's restaurant on three dozen oysters washed down with Muscadet or Sancerre. He also remembered Sutton for his eager pursuit of women, creating the office joke that this drove some of his secretaries to a local nursing home, nicknamed the Sutton sanatorium.

Sutton faced a crisis in his last years, after being stricken in 1975 with cancer of the throat. After an operation to remove his larynx he began the tenacious effort of learning to use breath control to create a whispering speech. He received exceptional support from Cynthia. Colleagues were awed by his optimism, courage, and energy in those dark days as he continued to produce his magazine for another twelve years. In 1985, two years after surrendering the reins, he was made a CBE, and a year later produced his last biography, *Degas: Man and Work* (1986). He died on 25 January 1991 at his home, 22 Chelsea Park Gardens, London. His wife survived him.

JOHN D. WRIGHT

Sources *WWW*, 1991–5 • J. Pope-Hennessy, 'Denys Sutton's *Apollo*', *Apollo* (1987) • B. Ford, 'Denys Sutton, editor of *Apollo*, 1962–1987', *Apollo* (1987) • private information (2004) [D. Ekserdjian] • m. cert. [Sonja Klibansky] • m. cert. [Cynthia Leah Abrahams] • d. cert.

Archives U. Glas. L., corresp., papers, and literary MSS • U. Glas. L., further letters and papers • U. Glas. L., papers, mainly relating to *Apollo*
Wealth at death £9,110,811: probate, 11 July 1991, *CGPLA Eng. & Wales*

Sutton [Dudley], **Edward, fourth Baron Dudley** (c.1515–1586), soldier and landowner, was the son of John Sutton (Dudley), third baron (1496–1553), landowner, and his wife, Cecily (b. in or before 1501, d. 1554), daughter of Thomas *Grey, first marquess of Dorset (c.1455–1501), and his wife, Cicely. His date of birth is conjectural (the earliest reference to him is 1527), but derived from his father's age and Henry VIII's reference to him as 'young Dudley' in 1537. His education was not extensive; in 1554 he mentioned that he spoke no Spanish, and Latin 'but rudely', though he may have had some French (*CSP for.*, 1553–8, 85).

Early life, c.1515–1553 Sutton's early life was shaped by the dramatic collapse of his family's finances. His grandfather, Edward Sutton (Dudley), second Baron Dudley (c.1459–1532), enjoyed some favour under Henry, including the chamberlainship to Princess Mary from 1525 to 1528, but sold off a substantial portion of his estate in the later 1520s. The process was completed by his father. Soon after succeeding to the barony, the third Lord Dudley sold the remainder (including Dudley Castle in Worcestershire) to his cousin Sir John *Dudley (1504–1553) in circumstances that remain controversial, earning himself the celebrated sobriquet 'the quondam lord'. Together with his later notorious younger brother Henry *Sutton (Dudley) (d. 1564?), Edward Sutton sought service in the wars and, following an established family practice, adopted Dudley as his surname. He informed Edward Seymour, duke of Somerset, on 28 April 1549 that he had first served in Ireland 'sixteen years ago' [1533], but otherwise he is not encountered there until 1536, when his uncle Leonard *Grey, Viscount Graney (c.1490–1541), was appointed lord deputy (*Bath MSS*, 4.109). Henry VIII nominated him to the command of a foot company and he continued in Ireland until at least 1538. In 1541 he was granted a lease of the manor of Keyingham in Holderness, Yorkshire, a significant location given the Sutton claim of descent from the lords of Sutton in Holderness. In 1544, styled the king's servant, he received a new lease of Keyingham for life, for his 'promptness to serve against the king's enemies' (*LP Henry VIII*, 19/1.377). Although Dudley is not mentioned in any of the narratives, he undoubtedly took part in the Boulogne expedition of 1544, for in the following year he and his younger brother were prominent members of the garrison. In June 1546 he was appointed captain of the new outlying fort, nicknamed 'the Young Man', and made a member of the council of Boulogne.

In August 1547 Dudley joined the large contingent from the Boulogne garrison that his cousin William *Grey, thirteenth Baron Grey of Wilton (1508/9–1562), commanded in the Pinkie campaign. After Hume Castle (The Hirsel) surrendered to Somerset on his march back to England (21 September), Dudley was appointed its captain. The author William Patten styles him Sir Edward Dudley, but there is no evidence that he had been knighted by this point (Pollard, 142–3). In December 1548 Hume Castle was recaptured by the Scots, and Dudley was taken prisoner. Edward VI heard it was 'by night and treason by the Scots' (*Chronicle*, ed. Jordan, 12), but Dudley blamed his soldiers when appealing to Somerset for help with his ransom in April 1549. He was presumably released in one of the subsequent exchanges of prisoners, but thereafter nothing more is heard of him until 1551, when he was nominated to escort Mary of Guise on her return to Scotland.

Succeeds to the barony, 1553–1558 Although Dudley is not known to have played any significant role in the events of 1553, he enjoyed considerable favour in Mary I's reign—possibly owing to his grandfather's service to her, possibly because he was pitied as a member of the old aristocracy 'victimized' by John Dudley, duke of Northumberland. After succeeding to the barony on his father's death on 18 September 1553, he was made a KB at Mary's coronation on 2 October. It is not surprising to find him in a list of men to be rewarded for service against Sir Thomas Wyatt the younger in February 1554. In the following month he went to Spain as a member of the embassy led by Thomas Radcliffe, Viscount Fitzwalter, to obtain Philip's ratification of the marriage articles. Dudley was well received by Philip and later escorted his envoy to England. For these services he received first a life annuity of £66 13*s.* 4*d.* in May, and then on 4 November the lordship of Dudley Castle and other lands his father had lost to Northumberland. Although this was only a rump of the estate his grandfather had held in 1520, he was compensated with the manors of Budbrook and Balsall in Warwickshire and the lands of the former priory of Dudley, all of which had also belonged to Northumberland. At the same time his restoration was confirmed by a writ of summons to the parliament of November 1554 as Lord Dudley.

Two further grants had less happy consequences. On 5 February 1555 Dudley was appointed lieutenant of Hammes Castle in the Calais pale. His considerable experience as a garrison commander and his proven loyalty probably lay behind this decision, but the fact that his cousin Grey of Wilton commanded Guînes Castle, the most modernized fort in the pale, may not have been irrelevant. The function of Hammes Castle was to guard the upper reaches of the River Hammes and the turnpike between Calais and Guînes, but it was a small and old-fashioned work, defended primarily by the marshes that surrounded it. Early in 1556 Dudley married a gentlewoman of Mary's privy chamber, Katherine (*d.* 1566), daughter of John Bridges, first Baron Chandos, and his wife, Elizabeth. In anticipation of the marriage he received a new grant on 31 December 1555, which gave him several additional Staffordshire manors obtained by Northumberland from the third Baron Dudley. However, it also converted the tenure of his first grant into a complex of entails to him and his wife jointly and then their heirs, presumably to provide her with a jointure. This grant did not come cheap; he had to surrender his annuity, one of the manors of his first grant, and pay £666 13*s.* 4*d.* He later complained to Sir Robert *Dudley (1532/3–

1588) that overall the recovery of the family estate had cost him £5000.

Dudley's marriage was followed by the discovery of his brother's conspiracy (the 'Dudley plot'). Yet, although Mary interrogated Lady Dudley about Henry Dudley's motives, his collusion with the French does not appear to have compromised Lord Dudley's own position at Calais. In the siege of January 1558 Hammes was initially bypassed by the French when they invested Calais town. On 3 January Lord Dudley wrote to the lord deputy, Thomas Wentworth, second Lord Wentworth, for news, for he had heard 'muche shotte this night'. His men had held their own in local skirmishing, but he was concerned about his ammunition expenditure. This letter was intercepted and is now among the surviving papers of François de Lorraine, second duc de Guise (Paris, Bibliothèque Nationale, MS français 23191, fols. 41–3). On the 8th, the day after Wentworth capitulated, Dudley was summoned to surrender, but he was determined to make a fight of it, despite being short of men, food, and munitions. His eventual course of action was determined by his soldiers, who effectively mutinied on 22 January, after learning of the surrender of Guînes the previous day, and demanded that he evacuate Hammes. With difficulty he persuaded them to destroy the artillery and stores first and they then retired safely to Habsburg Flanders.

Career under Elizabeth I, 1558–1586 Although Dudley was not among those tried for the loss of Calais in 1559, and remained on lists of potential officers, this was the effective end of his military career. While granted a new annuity of £50 in July 1558, he was heavily in debt and was actually imprisoned for it in the previous month. By 1559 he was the father of a daughter, Anne (*d.* after 1584), and Dudley Castle needed extensive repairs to make it habitable. Elizabeth I's accession also saw a new influence on his life in the form of his cousin, Sir Robert Dudley, who was intent on regaining Northumberland's lands. In 1559 Sir Robert Dudley offered to purchase Budbrook, but Lord Dudley agreed only to sell Balsall, if Sir Robert Dudley would help him to break the entail of 1555. However, when Sir Robert Dudley later proposed an exchange of lands for Dudley Castle, Lord Dudley refused, 'as it is mine ancient inheritance … and next to God and the queen's majesty I am the poor head of this house' (Longleat, Dudley papers I, fols. 84, 108, 171). Nothing came of these negotiations initially, but his cousin was too valuable an ally to alienate. In 1567 he gave Robert Dudley (now earl of Leicester) a chimney-piece from Dudley Castle, dating presumably from Northumberland's rebuilding. He was even more concerned to break the entail, for during the 1560s his family circumstances changed. His wife Katherine died in April 1566, and he then married Jane (*d.* 1569), daughter of Edward Stanley, third earl of Derby, and his second wife, Dorothy. The couple had two sons, Edward (1567–1643), and John, who was born in November 1569. Lady Dudley died in December 1569, probably of the consequences of her pregnancy.

Dudley now wished to marry Mary (*d.* 1600), a maid of honour and daughter of the lord chamberlain of the household, William *Howard, first Baron Howard of Effingham, and his second wife, Margaret. She was also the sister of Leicester's then mistress Douglas *Sheffield, dowager Lady Sheffield (1542/3–1608), and this created an even closer bond between them. Dudley's third marriage probably took place in early 1571, with Leicester's active assistance, if Dudley's effusive letter of thanks for his obtaining for 'my very friend Mistress Howard leave to come unto me' is anything to go by (Longleat, Dudley papers II, fols. 289–90). Sheffield came to stay with her sister on at least one occasion in 1571–2, and it was at Dudley Castle that her putative first child with Leicester was born and died. A witness in the case of Sir Robert Dudley (1574–1649) later deposed that it was given out that the child was Lady Dudley's but she was too old. There are no known children of her marriage to Dudley.

Dudley was in attendance during Leicester's famous visit to Warwick in September 1571, sold him the manor of Balsall in 1572, and gave him his proxy for the parliaments of 1571, 1572, and 1584. Leicester's benevolence together with Lady Dudley's own relationship to the queen were probably responsible for Elizabeth's visit to Dudley Castle on 12 August during the famous Kenilworth progress of 1575, an occasion which the Dudleys intended to use to advance a suit. This was probably the old one for breaking the entail of 1555. In the end Leicester, William Cecil, Lord Burghley, and Sir Walter Mildmay acted as his feoffees to uses in a typically complex new settlement of his estates on his heir in 1579–81, probably related to Edward Dudley's marriage on 12 June 1581 to Theodosia (d. 1650), daughter of Sir John Harington of Exton and his wife Lucy.

Of Dudley's domestic life, only fragments survive. He employed musicians and, like other landowners in the future 'black country', engaged in proto-industrialization: a coalmine is mentioned in the grant of Dudley Castle of 1554 and he refers to his ironworks in his will. He was JP for Staffordshire and Worcestershire, and, with Edward Stafford, third Lord Stafford, and Thomas Paget, fourth Lord Paget, was considered one of the key figures in Staffordshire local government. His rustication was not complete; he and his wives appear to have visited London regularly. It was on one such visit in 1586 that he fell fatally ill and died in Westminster on 9 July, having made his last will the day before. At his own request, he was buried in St Margaret's, Westminster, where his parents lay, on 11 August. His wife was his executor, and his overseers Ambrose *Dudley, earl of Warwick (c.1530–1590), his brother-in-law Charles *Howard, second Lord Howard of Effingham (1536–1624), Henry Grey, first Lord Hunsdon, and his neighbour, Sir John Lyttelton. To them he leased his ironworks to pay off his debts. His command that his disastrously feckless heir not interfere with the will suggests an existing tension between them. Lady Dudley died on 21 August 1600 and was buried in St Margaret's two days later.

Dudley's will is businesslike in its phrasing and he has left no other evidence of a strong religious commitment either way. Throughout his life he walked a curious tightrope between the old aristocracy and the new élite. His daughter Anne married Francis *Throckmorton (1554–1584), but his heir's father-in-law, Harington of Exton, was a leading member of the protestant establishment in Warwickshire. If his standing with Mary's government was not jeopardized by his brother's conspiracy in 1555–6, he also survived implications of involvement in the conspiracy of his second wife's brothers (the 'Stanley plot') in 1571. His youthful poverty undoubtedly drove him to follow a more 'professional' military career than he might otherwise have done. Here he displayed competence, despite the misfortune of commanding two small isolated garrisons. Unlike his brother, he seems to have distanced himself from Northumberland, and relied instead on Henry VIII and on his Grey relations. Once he inherited the barony and was able to recover its lands, the future of the family estate became his chief concern. The benevolence of his cousin Leicester was a valuable means to that end. It was small reward for his efforts that his son, the fifth Lord Dudley, would destroy all his work.

SIMON ADAMS

Sources W. R. B. Robinson, 'Edward Sutton (d. 1532), Lord Dudley: a west midlands peer in national and local government under the early Tudors', *Staffordshire Studies*, 8 (1996), 50–65 · W. R. B. Robinson, 'Family and fortune: the domestic affairs of Edward Sutton (d. 1532), Lord Dudley', *Staffordshire Studies*, 10 (1998), 29–48 · H. S. Grazerbook, 'The barons of Dudley', *Collections for a history of Staffordshire*, William Salt Archaeological Society, 9/2 (1888), 1–152 · *Calendar of the manuscripts of the marquis of Bath preserved at Longleat, Wiltshire*, 5 vols., HMC, 58 (1904–80), vol. 4 · *State papers published under … Henry VIII*, vols. (1830–52), vol. 2 · *CSP Ire.*, 1509–73 · *LP Henry VIII*, vols. 19/1, 20/2, 21 · H. M. Colvin and others, eds., *The history of the king's works*, 3 (1975) · *CSP Scot.*, 1547–63 · J. Bain, ed., *The Hamilton papers*, 2 vols. (1892), vol. 2 · A. F. Pollard, ed., *Tudor tractors, 1532–1588* (1903), 53–157, 290–330 · *The chronicle and political papers of King Edward VI*, ed. W. K. Jordan (1966) · M. Merriman, *The rough wooings: Mary queen of Scots, 1542–1551* (2000) · *CSP for.*, 1547–58 · *APC*, 1542–1631 · *CSP dom.*, 1553–58 · *CPR*, 1553–82 · *CSP Spain*, 1554–8 · D. M. Loades, *Two Tudor conspiracies* (1965) · Bibliothèque Nationale, Paris, MS français 23191 [Bourdin MSS] · S. Adams, '"Because I am of that Countrye & Mynde to Plant myself there": Robert Dudley, earl of Leicester and the west midlands', *Leicester and the court: essays on Elizabethan politics* (2002), 310–73 · S. Adams, ed., *Household accounts and disbursement books of Robert Dudley, earl of Leicester, 1558–1561, 1584–1586*, CS, 6 (1995) · R. W. Kenny, *Elizabeth's admiral: the political career of Charles Howard, earl of Nottingham, 1536–1624* (1970) · correspondence with the earl of Leicester, depositions in the Sir Robert Dudley case, 1604–5, Longleat House, Wiltshire, Dudley MSS 1–2, box 6 · letter to the earl of Leicester, 1567, BL, Evelyn MS I · W. Dethick, 'Book of funerals of the nobility', 1586–1603, Coll. Arms · GEC, *Peerage*

Archives Bibliothèque Nationale, Paris, letter, MS français 23191, Bourdin MSS

Sutton, Sir (Oliver) Graham (1903–1977), meteorologist and mathematician, was born on 4 February 1903 at Cwmcarn, Monmouthshire, the second child in the family of three sons and one daughter of Oliver Sutton, headmaster of the local elementary school, and his wife, Rachel, daughter of William Rhydderch, haulage contractor, of Blaenau Gwent, Monmouthshire. Sutton was educated at the local elementary school, Pont-y-waun grammar school (1914–20), the University College of Wales, Aberystwyth (1920–23), and Jesus College, Oxford (1923–5). The early mathematical training of Sutton and his two brothers was initially guided by their headmaster father and was later continued at the grammar school, which had an established reputation in science and mathematics. At Aberystwyth, where, in 1923, he graduated with first-class honours in pure mathematics, his teachers included W. H. Young and G. A. Schott, and his postgraduate work at Oxford (for which he obtained the degree of BSc in 1925) was supervised by G. H. Hardy.

In 1926–8 Sutton was a lecturer at his former college in Aberystwyth. His interest in meteorology was stimulated by David Brunt, himself a graduate of Aberystwyth, and in 1928 Sutton joined the Meteorological Office as a professional assistant. Seconded by the office in 1929 to the Chemical Defence Experimental Station at Porton, for the next twelve years he worked on problems in atmospheric turbulence and diffusion. Security requirements restricted freedom of publication from Porton and it was not until the conclusion of the Second World War that open recognition of Sutton's major contributions became possible. His gift for lucid explanation, which stemmed naturally from his deep physical and mathematical understanding of complex problems, was widely recognized and in addition to his scientific papers he wrote many specialist and general books on meteorological and mathematical topics, a task which gave him great satisfaction.

In 1931 Sutton married Doris, daughter of Thomas Oswald Morgan, boot and shoe merchant with a business at Pontycymer, Glamorgan. They had two sons. Throughout his career Sutton displayed considerable ability in the organization of research and development, a quality which was well recognized by the various posts to which he was appointed during the war. At Porton he was, in turn, head of the meteorological section, superintendent of research (1942–3), and head of tank armament research (1943–5). When the war ended he was for a time chief superintendent of the Radar Research and Development Establishment at Malvern (1945–7).

In 1947 Sutton was appointed the first Bashforth professor of mathematical physics at the Military College of Science at Shrivenham. He stayed there until 1952. He greatly enjoyed this temporary return to academic life where, in addition to his teaching duties, he maintained his research activity. In these years he published the key papers which established his reputation. His early research work at Porton, which was also of great importance for the study of industrial air pollution, but which had been held back as a state secret, was now published in the *Quarterly Journal of the Royal Meteorological Society* (73, 1947, 257–76; 74, 1948, 13–30). The reception of these papers resulted in his becoming a key member, and later chairman, of the atmospheric pollution research committee of the government Department of Scientific and Industrial Research, and later in his membership of the Beaver committee which set the scene for the first Clean Air Act and for the formation of the Clean Air Council. In 1947 he also published two topical papers on the practical problem of the rise of smoke from factory chimneys; he later went on to write on atmospheric pollution in America, and on the atmospheric results of thermonuclear explosions. The Shrivenham period also saw the publication of his two main books, *Atmospheric Turbulence* (1949, 2nd edn 1955), and *Micrometeorology* (1953); as well as the first of his many popular science books, the Penguin volume on *The Science of Flight* (1948).

In 1953 Sutton returned to the Meteorological Office as its director-general. His period in office saw a complete reorganization of the office with a greater emphasis on research and centralization from a new headquarters building at Bracknell. He vigorously pressed forward with this reorganization and also with the development of mathematical methods and the use of electronic computers in weather forecasting. As part of the expansion on the research side he also established a section for high atmosphere research using the latest space research techniques. At the same time the public service aspects of the Meteorological Office were greatly extended. These included the establishment of weather centres open to the public, the provision of automatic telephone weather forecasts, and the extended use of television broadcasts of weather information.

Sutton was director-general of the Meteorological Office until 1965. During this period he openly recognized that his own career as a research scientist must be regarded as closed, but he continued with his non-specialist publications and maintained an interest in the research done by others. For the last three years of his career in government scientific administration (1965–8) he was chairman of the newly established Natural Environment Research Council, in the establishment of which he had played a leading part. The council's remit was to bring together the disparate environmental sciences as a unified group of disciplines, and in this Sutton was regarded as reasonably successful (though ironically his own science of meteorology remained outside the research council's aegis).

Sutton received many honours and awards, both national and international. He was president of the Royal Meteorological Society (1953–5), was awarded the society's Symons memorial gold medal in 1959, and was elected honorary fellow in 1976. He was also an honorary fellow of the American Meteorological Society and a gold medallist and fellow of the Society of Engineers. He was elected a fellow of the Royal Society in 1949, appointed CBE in 1950, and knighted in 1955. He received honorary degrees from the universities of Leeds (1956) and Wales (1961) and was an honorary fellow of Jesus College, Oxford (1958). For many years he was a leading figure in the World Meteorological Organization (WMO) and he received the WMO international medal and prize in 1968.

In his last years Sutton returned to Wales, to Swansea, and an interesting glimpse of his continued concern with organization is provided by the fact that the house he built for his retirement at Swansea was of identical design to the one he had earlier built at Bracknell. In this way all the furniture fitted perfectly and the upheaval of moving house was reduced to a minimum. He served as a JP at both Bracknell and Swansea. He also became a member of the council (and later vice-president) of his old college at Aberystwyth. He died at his home, 4 The Bryn, Sketty Green, near Swansea, on 26 May 1977.   W. J. G. BEYNON, *rev.*

Sources F. Pasquill, P. A. Sheppard, and R. C. Sutcliffe, *Memoirs FRS*, 24 (1978), 529–46 · private information (1986) · personal knowledge (1986)
Likenesses G. Argent, photograph, RS · W. Stoneman, photograph, RS; repro. in Pasquill, Sheppard, and Sutcliffe, *Memoirs FRS*, facing p. 529
Wealth at death £41,828: probate, 24 Aug 1977, *CGPLA Eng. & Wales*

Sutton [Dudley], **Henry** (*d.* 1564?), conspirator, was the third son of John Sutton (Dudley), third Baron Dudley (1496–1553), landowner, and his wife, Cecily (*d.* 1554), daughter of Thomas *Grey, first marquess of Dorset, and his wife, Cicely. His brother was Sir Edward *Sutton (Dudley). Nothing is known about his education but he made his career as a soldier and his early years were probably preoccupied with martial exercise. As was usual, his father styled himself Dudley and it is by this name that Henry Dudley is best known.

In 1547 Dudley entered crown service as captain of the guard at Boulogne with an annual salary of £80, a daily allowance of 4s., and a licence to import to England, tax-free, 500 tons of wood and wine. On completion of his first year's service at Boulogne, he received a bonus of £47 10s. 'for the Kinges secrete affaires' (*APC*, 1547–50). Dudley, like his father, was undisciplined in managing his own finances since, barely three years later, he first received a grant of £300, towards payment of his debts, and an annuity of £80 'till he be better provided' (*APC*, 1550–52, 98). Dudley was well-known as a protestant, which recommended him to the regime during Edward VI's reign. His suits were assisted by his kinsman, John *Dudley, earl of Warwick and duke of Northumberland, who headed the regency government.

In September 1550 Dudley was entrusted with the safe conduct of François de Vendôme, vîdame de Chartres, from France to Scotland and, on their return to France in January 1551, was charged with 'thatteigneng of knowledge' (*APC*, 1550–52, 203). He served the dual role of garrison commander and spy and was amply reimbursed for his troubles, receiving £120. Dudley and his men were recalled from France in March 1551, but he was in debt again and his debts were once more covered by the crown. On 25 May he was appointed captain of Guînes, and barely a year later was made vice-admiral of the English channel. Based in Portsmouth, his main duty was to protect English and Irish merchant vessels from pirates. In April 1552 he captured two Flemish pirate barges, charged their captains with the wilful sinking of an Irish vessel, and brought them to Dover to be prosecuted. On 28 July he was again sent to Guînes to protect it against a threatened attack from the French. Dudley was arrested at Guînes on 25 July 1553, because of his connections as cousin to Northumberland and to Sir Andrew Dudley [*see below*], and

was incarcerated in the Tower of London on 6 August. He was not tried and was released on 18 October.

A persistent debtor, in spring 1556 Dudley appears to have been outlawed as a result. He stated that 'he stood in debt for 1000 marks and therefore was driven to flee the realm' (*CSP for.*, 1553–8, 229). Both his grave financial predicaments and his disenchantment with the increasing Spanish influence on English politics during Mary I's reign motivated him to plot against the crown, together with John Throckmorton, Christopher Ashton, Sir Henry Killigrew, Sir Anthony Kingston, and Richard Uvedale. The conspirators planned 'to send the queen over to the king, [Philip of Spain], and to make the lady Elizabeth queen and marry the earl of Devon' (*CSP dom.*, 1553–8, 423). Having been promised a position in the French privy chamber, Dudley with Uvedale's help secretly embarked at Portsmouth and made for Le Havre, where he arrived with twenty-eight men on 31 March. Before his departure he is reported to have said:

> I am going now to France and mind to serve the French king for a while, to get a band of men, most of them English, 2000–3000 at least. When I see my time, I will come with them and land at Portsmouth and either banish this vile nation of Spaniards, or die for it.   (*CSP dom.*, 1553–8, 334)

Such forthrightness led to Dudley being declared a traitor on 4 April.

In late 1555 and early 1556 an English merchant and would-be government agent, Martin Dore, sought to learn more about Ashton and other conspirators in France by playing one against the other. He told Ashton that Dudley was 'a prowde man [and] not wyse' (Loades, *Two Tudor Conspiracies*, 160). It is unknown what effect this had. Whether Dore was actually involved in any conspiracy himself is uncertain, although the privy council was suspicious. On 8 April 1556, Mary's ambassador in France, Dr Nicholas Wotton, required Dudley's extradition, which Henri II denied, although he was ambivalent towards the English exiles. In November Dudley aided attacks on the English garrisons at Calais, Guînes, and Hammes (the commander of which was his brother Lord Dudley), and promised 'to deliver Calais to the king [of France]' (*CSP for.*, 1553–8, no. 284.6). Early in 1557 he used his knowledge of English garrisons to advise the French military on lines of attack but, despite raising money and men, any prospect of invading England collapsed with the arrest of sympathizers by the privy council. At the French court Dudley enjoyed a brief respite from the debts that had driven him from England, but in June 1559 was once again forced to seek influential creditors, finding them in Charles de Guise, archbishop of Rheims and second cardinal of Lorraine, and François de Lorraine Guise, duc de Guise. At the same time he made informal approaches about the possibility of returning to England. In November 1561 he was committed to the Châtelet for debt. It is likely that he made his way back to England before 1564, where he was supported by Northumberland's son, Robert *Dudley, earl of Leicester. He is said to have married Ashton's sister or daughter and he died soon after his return.

Sir Andrew Dudley (*c.*1507–1559), soldier, was the second of three sons of Edmund *Dudley (*c.*1462–1510), administrator, of Atherington, Sussex, and his second wife, Elizabeth (1482x4–1525/6), daughter of Edward Grey, third Viscount Lisle, and his first wife, Elizabeth, *suo jure* Baroness Lisle. His brothers were John Dudley, earl of Warwick and duke of Northumberland, and Jerome Dudley (*d.* in or after 1555). His early career is obscure but he was a servant of Thomas Howard, third duke of Norfolk, and an officer of the exchequer by 1540, equerry of the stable by 1544, and captain of the *Swallow* in 1545. His elder brother provided him with lands in the midlands and sought military patronage for him. Dudley was appointed admiral of the fleet with 'speceal charge of all the sayd shippes of warre at Harwich', on 27 February 1547 (PRO, SP 10/1/23, fol. 95*r*). He was knighted by Edward Seymour, duke of Somerset and lord protector to Edward VI, on 18 September, when charged with Thomas Seymour, Baron Seymour of Sudeley, the lord admiral, to hold Broughty Craig at the mouth of the River Tay, and was appointed a gentleman of the privy chamber in reward. On 24 October 1549 he was made one of the four knights in attendance on King Edward and, a fortnight later, joint keeper of the palace of Westminster. On 5 January 1551 he was appointed keeper of the king's jewels and robes at Westminster and replaced Sir John Wallop as captain of Guînes in July. These rewards were a consequence of his brother's preeminence.

In January 1552 Northumberland brought to the privy council's attention a dispute between William Willoughby, first Baron Willoughby of Parham, lord deputy of Calais, and Dudley, 'renewing unquietness between them and their retinues' (*CSP dom.*, 1547–53, no. 584). Northumberland also alerted the privy council to his brother's 'impoverishment there in guine [Guînes] wherby necessite [necessity] shall compell hym ether to departe or to be a cravor for succor' (PRO, SP 10/15/14, fol. 33*r*). On 6 October Willoughby and Dudley were recalled to England. Dudley had been charged with surveying Portsmouth and the Isle of Wight in May of that year, with a view to advise on strategic reinforcements of the sea defences there, and on 28 December Sir William Cecil, principal secretary, suggested to Northumberland that Dudley be appointed ambassador either to France or to Charles V. Dudley was created KG on 17 March 1553 and was elected MP for Oxfordshire that same month, assisting in carrying the king's train at the state opening of parliament. He was a wealthy man, with an annual income of £160 by August 1553. Dudley was betrothed to Lady Margaret Clifford, daughter of Henry Clifford, second earl of Cumberland, and his first wife, Eleanor, and cousin to Lady Jane Grey, with her own claim to the throne, but was prevented from marrying her by Edward's death on 6 July 1553.

In the same month Dudley assembled a group of some 500 men at Ware, Hertfordshire, in an attempt, with Northumberland, to place Jane Grey on the throne. He was arrested, brought to the Tower of London and, on 18 August, found guilty of treason and ordered to be hanged, drawn, and quartered at Tyburn. Sentence was suspended, he was released on 5 April 1555, and later that year was not only assigned an annual pension of £100 by the crown, but was also permitted to retain lands and goods, the ownership of which he had previously concealed in order to evade their forfeiture. This rehabilitation was part of a conscious effort by Philip of Spain to bring disgruntled former Edwardians in from the cold. Dudley lived quietly in his house on Tothill Street, London. On 21 July 1556 he made his will with his nephews, including Sir Ambrose *Dudley and Robert Dudley, earl of Leicester, as overseers, and died before 22 November 1559, when it was proved. He was probably buried in Westminster.

J. ANDREAS LÖWE

Sources APC, 1547–54 • CPR, 1547–55 • CSP for., 1553–8; 1558–9 • CSP dom., 1547–58 • D. M. Loades, *Two Tudor conspiracies* (1965) • *Literary remains of King Edward the Sixth*, ed. J. G. Nichols, 2 vols., Roxburghe Club, 75 (1857) • H. Sydney and others, *Letters and memorials of state*, ed. A. Collins, 2 vols. (1746) • HoP, *Commons, 1509–58* • A. Bryson, '"The speciall men in every shere": the Edwardian regime, 1547–1553', PhD diss., U. St Andr., 2001 • D. Loades, *John Dudley, duke of Northumberland, 1504–1553* (1996) • S. Adams, 'The Dudley clientèle, 1553–1563', *The Tudor nobility*, ed. G. W. Bernard (1992), 241–65

Wealth at death £160 per annum in August 1553, excluding money from land grants from John Poret, bishop of Winchester: PRO, LR 2/118; PRO, E 154/2/39

Sutton, Henry (*c.*1624–1665), maker of mathematical instruments, whose parentage is unknown and whose birth date depends upon the assumption that he was apprenticed at the age of fourteen, was bound to Thomas Browne, mathematical instrument maker, in the Joiners' Company on 18 August 1638. He was made free of the company in August 1648 and became a liveryman in 1657. He booked five apprentices in the company, one of whom, John Marke (free 1664), succeeded him.

Sutton, who lived and worked in Threadneedle Street behind the Royal Exchange, London, was quickly integrated into the circle of superior craftsmen, mathematical practitioners, and savants of mid-century London, which included men such as John Collins, Thomas Harvey, Samuel Morland, and Euclid Speidell. In the *Sector on a Quadrant* (1658), a work written by John Collins at Sutton's request, and of which the latter was joint publisher, Henry Sutton shares an advertisement for 'All manner of Mathematical Instruments, either for Sea or Land … in Wood or Brass' with William Sutton (free of the Joiners' Company 2 February 1656); as William's father was also a Henry, it is likely that they were related, as both may also have been to the instrument maker Baptist Sutton (*fl.* 1636–1653).

Sutton was a prolific maker, more than thirty of whose instruments are known to have survived, and he also exploited the possibilities of printing and publishing to advance his career. Many of his instruments were cheap, popular sundials printed on paper from copper plates which he had engraved, and he was noted for the accuracy of his scale division. On 6 December 1653 he was paid £20 2*s.* for instruments supplied for 'the service of the publique in Ireland', and in 1654 he provided the graph paper for Petty's 'down survey'. Sutton's first wife, Susan, was buried on 20 October 1658. He quickly married again on 22 February 1659, but his new wife, Jane, soon followed her predecessor to the grave. She was interred on 26 November 1659.

Instruments signed and dated by Sutton cover the whole of his active career from 1648 to 1664, and those known to have been made for clients such as Samuel Morland and William Rook attest to his contacts with the learned world. Sutton also maintained creative collaboration with other craftsmen, in particular with John Browne, son of Thomas Browne, Sutton's master, for whom he was joint publisher of two books, and with the clockmaker Samuel Knibb, cousin of the clockmakers Joseph and John Knibb. Sutton collaborated with Samuel Knibb in the making of Samuel Morland's trigonometrical machine of 1664, and John Knibb was apprenticed to William Sutton in the same year. Henry Sutton's connection with Morland can be shown to go back to the 1650s: some of the earliest examples of a perpetual calendar invented by Morland are to be found on quadrants by Sutton dated 1658. On 8 August 1663 Sutton, who, as John Collins had noted, was not without knowledge of the mathematical sciences, observed a lunar eclipse in company with Thomas Streete and Robert Anderson.

Sutton died of the plague and was buried at St Christopher-le-Stocks, London, on 21 September 1665, soon to be followed by his two surviving children. His early death robbed the scientific community of London of a highly talented craftsman who was clearly only just beginning to realize his full potential. In 1669, R. Morden reissued a single sheet *Description and Use of a Large Quadrant* by Sutton, and in the next century his quadrants could still be described by Edmund Stone as 'the finest divided instruments in the World, and the Regularity and Exactness of the vast Number of Circles drawn upon them is highly delightful to behold' (Bion, suppl.).

A. J. TURNER

Sources J. Collins, *The sector on a quadrant, or, A treatise containing the description and use of four several quadrants* (1658) • S. P. Rigaud and S. J. Rigaud, eds., *Correspondence of scientific men of the seventeenth century*, 2 vols. (1841) • Bodl. Oxf., MS Rawl. A. 208, fol. 457 • G. H. Gabb, 'The astrological astrolabe of Queen Elizabeth', *Archaeologia*, 86 (1937), 101–3 • W. Petty, *The history of the survey of Ireland: commonly called the down survey*, AD 1655–6, ed. T. A. Larcom (1851) • M. A. Crawforth, 'Instrument makers in the London guilds', *Annals of Science*, 44 (1987), 319–77 • E. G. R. Taylor, *The mathematical practitioners of Tudor and Stuart England* (1954) • N. Bion, *The construction and principal uses of mathematical instruments*, trans. E. Stone (1723) • parish records (burial), St Christopher-le-Stocks, London, 20 Oct 1658 [Susan Sutton] • parish records (burial), St Christopher-le-Stocks, London, 21 Sept 1665 [Henry Sutton]
Archives MHS Oxf. • Museo di Storia della Scienza, Florence • NMM • Sci. Mus. • U. Cam., Whipple Museum of the History of Science

Sutton, Henry Septimus (1825–1901), poet and journalist, born at Nottingham on 10 February 1825, was the seventh child of the seven sons and three daughters of Richard Sutton (1789–1856) of Nottingham, bookseller, printer, and proprietor of the *Nottingham Review*, and his wife, Sarah, daughter of Thomas Salt, farmer, of Stanton by Dale, Derbyshire. A sister, Eliza S. Oldham, was the author

of *The Haunted House* (1863) and *By the Trent* (1864). From childhood he spent his time among the books in his father's shop, and he acquired literary tastes at an early age. He was educated at a private school in Nottingham and at Leicester grammar school. A study of medicine was soon abandoned for literature and journalism, and he began his journalistic career at the *Nottingham Review*. Among early literary friends were his fellow townsman Philip James Bailey, and Coventry Patmore, with whom an intimacy was formed soon after the publication of Patmore's first volume of poems in 1844, and continued until Patmore's death in 1896.

Sutton, who was a vegetarian and total abstainer all his life, developed a strong vein of mysticism and had an active interest in social and religious problems, being especially influenced by the writing of Ralph Waldo Emerson. His first book, *The Evangel of Love* (1847), echoed Emerson and was welcomed by Patmore with friendly encouragement, while Emerson himself, to whom the book had been shown by J. Neuberg, Thomas Carlyle's friend and admirer, declared it to be 'worthy of George Herbert'. When Emerson visited Manchester in 1847 he invited Sutton to come from Nottingham to meet him, and a lifelong friendship began. Emerson visited Sutton at Nottingham the following year. (They met again in Manchester in 1872.) In 1849, on Emerson's recommendation, Alexander Ireland found journalistic employment in Manchester for Sutton at the *Manchester Examiner and Times*. In January 1850 he married Sarah Prickard (d. 1868); they had one son, Arthur James Sutton (d. 1880), a promising scholar, and a daughter. In 1853 Sutton became chief of the newspaper's reporting staff. Soon after, he met George MacDonald; they became lifelong friends and mutually influenced each other's spiritual development.

In 1848 Sutton's first work of poetry, a volume of mystical tone entitled *Clifton Grove Garland*, was published in Nottingham. In 1854 *Quinquenergia: Proposals for a New Practical Theology* appeared, including a series of simply phrased but subtly argued poems, *Rose's Diary*, on which his poetic reputation is based, and which was enthusiastically received. Emerson's friend Bronson Alcott, writing on 15 October 1854, detected in Sutton 'profound religious genius' (F. G. Sanborn and W. T. Harris, *A. Bronson Alcott*, 2, 1893, 484–5). Frances Power Cobbe and James Martineau rated the book very highly, and Francis Turner Palgrave included 'How beautiful it is to be alive' (from *Rose's Diary*) and two other of Sutton's poems in his *Golden Treasury of Sacred Poetry*. Carlyle, however, scornfully wondered that 'a lad in a provincial town' should have presumed to handle such themes (Espinasse, 160). However, he subsequently withdrew his poems on adopting the doctrines of Emanuel Swedenborg. In later years Sutton added other new poems to a collected edition of his poetry (1886), among them 'A Preacher's Soliloquy and Sermon', which reveals a genuine affinity with Herbert. *Rose's Diary*, with other poems, was reprinted in the Broadbent booklets as *A Sutton Treasury* (1899; 17,000 copies by 1909).

Meanwhile Sutton's journalistic work continued. He had joined the United Kingdom Alliance on its foundation at Manchester in 1853, and he was editor of its weekly journal, the *Alliance News*, from its inception in 1854 until 1898, contributing leading articles until his death. He was also editor from 1859 to 1869 of *Meliora*, a quarterly journal devoted to social and temperance reform. In May 1870 he married Mary Sophia Ewen (*d.* 1910); they had no children.

In 1857 Sutton had joined the Peter Street Society of Swedenborgians, which had a profound effect on him. He took an active part in Swedenborgian church and Sunday school work, was popular as a lay preacher, and zealously expounded Swedenborg's writings on somewhat original lines in *Outlines of the Doctrine of the Mind According to Emanuel Swedenborg* (1889) and *Five Essays for Students of the Divine Philosophy of Swedenborg* (1895), with a sixth essay, *Our Saviour's Triple Crown* (1898), and a seventh and last essay, *The Golden Age: pt. i. Man's Creation and Fall; pt. ii. Swedenborgian Phrenology* (1900).

Sutton was of delicate health and, despite his constant concern for public matters, had a retiring but most genial and affectionate disposition. He died at his home, 18 Yarburgh Street, Moss Side, Manchester, on 2 May 1901 and was buried at nearby Worsley. His second wife and his daughter survived him.

W. B. OWEN, rev. SAYONI BASU

Sources The Times (6 May 1901) · Allibone, Dict. · J. M. Wheeler, *A biographical dictionary of freethinkers of all ages and nations* (1889) · A. H. Miles, ed., *The poets and the poetry of the nineteenth century*, 12 (1907) · F. Espinasse, *Literary recollections and sketches* (1893) · New Church Magazine (June 1901), 271–86 · Alliance News (9 May 1901) · Manchester Guardian (3 May 1901) · Manchester City News (20 May 1899) · Manchester City News (27 May 1899)
Archives U. Nott. L., Hallward Library, corresp.
Likenesses E. Oldham, oils, priv. coll. · portrait, repro. in *Alliance News*
Wealth at death £1280 9s. 1d.: probate, 24 May 1901, CGPLA Eng. & Wales

Sutton, John (VI) [John Dudley], **first Baron Dudley** (1400–1487), courtier and diplomat, was born on 25 December 1400, the son of John (V) Sutton (*d.* 1406) and his wife, Constance Blount (*d.* 1432). The Suttons were the descendants of John, Lord Somery (*d.* 1308), through his elder daughter, Margaret, who had brought her husband, John (I) Sutton, half the barony of Dudley. However, none of the family was to bear a baronial title until 1440. The town of Dudley was in Worcestershire, but its castle lay in Staffordshire, and it was in the south-west of the latter county that the Sutton estates were concentrated. They also had important interests in Cheshire, centred upon the manor of Malpas. Following the death of his father, on 3 September 1406, John (VI) Sutton's inheritance was seriously depleted by the dower of his mother, who lived for another twenty-six years. This may help to explain his having taken service under the crown as a soldier by February 1418, well before he had attained his majority, when he attended Henry V to France as an esquire in the king's retinue. By 4 July 1419 he had been knighted. He served in France in 1421 with a small retinue, and in the following year he was given the honour of bearing the royal standard at the king's funeral. Sutton crossed the channel again in 1425 in the service of the duke of Exeter. On 23 March 1428 he was appointed royal lieutenant in Ireland, where he served with some success, probably because efforts were made to ensure that he was properly paid, until his resignation in 1430. In 1435 he was appointed constable of Clun Castle, Shropshire, and on 25 November 1437 lieutenant of Calais Castle; he remained in this post into the summer of 1442, despite the expiry of his indenture, at least partly to investigate the mismanagement of works on the town's defences.

In February 1440 Sutton was summoned to parliament as Lord Dudley; his was one of six peerages awarded to members of the royal household during the early 1440s. On his return to England, Dudley continued to enjoy the king's patronage: in October 1443 he was granted an annuity of £100, and in the following month he was appointed a royal councillor. His connections with Staffordshire and Cheshire led to his employment on the marches of Wales during 1443 and 1444. Increasingly, however, he was employed as a diplomat, a field in which he developed an expertise that doubtless proved highly serviceable once he became involved in national politics, enhancing the skills that enabled him to win acceptance from one regime after another, in a manner that made him one of fifteenth-century England's great political survivors. Having gained experience in negotiations with the Hanse in 1436, he served on embassies to France in 1439, 1441, and 1446; in 1447 he was involved in negotiations with a visiting French embassy, as well as diplomatic service in Aquitaine, Castile, and Brittany; while in 1449 he served on embassies to Burgundy and Prussia. His absences abroad may well have weakened his position at home; hence, perhaps, the apparent outbreak of poaching on his Staffordshire estates which led to Dudley's bringing a number of actions in the central courts in 1440–41. Nevertheless he played at least some part in the governance of the west midlands. In 1444, for instance, he acted as arbitrator in the bitter dispute between Sir Sampson Meverell of Throwley and Sir Ralph Basset of Blore.

In the 1440s Dudley had been involved in the unpopular diplomacy that led to the surrender of Maine to the French king. This, and his association with the duke of Suffolk's hated regime, led to the sacking of his London house by Jack Cade and his Kentish rebels during the revolt of 1450. Following the removal of Cade's forces from London, Dudley played an active part in harassing the rebels retreating into Kent; this led to his being indicted on seven counts in August by local jurors, during the commission of oyer and terminer sent to redress grievances. With the arrival in September of Duke Richard of York (whose councillor he had become) in north Wales, Dudley fled to Ludlow to seek his protection; while in the duke's custody he was tried for treason but was acquitted. He was similarly exempted by Henry VI from the list of twenty-nine individuals whose removal from the king's presence was demanded by parliament in November.

In November 1452 Dudley was reappointed to the royal council, and was appointed treasurer of the royal household on 27 March 1453. Although he retained this office during York's first protectorate, Dudley resigned on 3 December 1454, possibly in protest at the proposed reductions in the size of the royal household. On 23 May 1455 he fought on the king's side at the battle of St Albans, where he was captured, having been wounded in the face. York's subsequent attempts as protector to ease the political tension led him to incarcerate Dudley to prevent him making any further embarrassing accusations against the Yorkists; nevertheless he received a parliamentary summons on 26 June 1455, while still imprisoned in the Tower of London. Henry VI's resumption of power in February 1456 witnessed Dudley's return to prominence as one of the king's more regular councillors. On 28 January 1459 he was appointed steward of the lordship of Montgomery, and in the following month he succeeded Lord Stanley as chamberlain of north Wales, while on 23 April of that year he was admitted to the Order of the Garter. His military usefulness may in fact have been waning by this time (he was now in his late fifties), for on 25 July he was appointed one of the English delegates to the Congress of Mantua, summoned by the pope to organize resistance to the Turks. But the renewal of civil strife prevented Dudley's departure, and on 23 September, in his last appearance in defence of the Lancastrian crown, he was captured at the battle of Bloreheath, a conflict in which men from Cheshire were heavily engaged. Following the capture of Henry VI at the battle of Northampton on 10 July 1460, Dudley moved into the Yorkist camp. Despite his strong connections with the king's household, Duke Richard was willing to include Dudley in the new royal council, and in November 1460 was even prepared to use him on an embassy to France.

Dudley's astute change of loyalties to the house of York ensured him great personal gain and high favour under Edward IV: on 26 February 1462 he was pardoned all debts owed to the king; on 4 July 1465 he was granted an annuity of £100 from the customs of the port of Southampton; and on 18 February 1467 he was appointed joint constable of the Tower. His political realignment led to Dudley's exclusion during Henry VI's readeption not only from the parliamentary summons of 26 November 1470, but also from nomination to commissions of the peace. Following Edward IV's recovery of the throne, Dudley, in his capacity as constable of the Tower, defended London against the assault led by Thomas Neville, the Bastard of Fauconberg, on 14 May 1471, and later superintended the imprisonment of Margaret of Anjou. Now a trusted servant of the Yorkist crown, Dudley was chamberlain to the queen, and also steward of the duke of Clarence's Staffordshire estates. He was summoned to parliament in 1472-5, and was appointed to serve on commissions throughout the 1470s. During Edward IV's absence in France in 1475, he was appointed to the great council of England, having earlier been one of the commissioners chosen by parliament to receive the issues of the tax levied to finance the king's expedition; in 1477-8 he went on an embassy to France to negotiate the continuation of the peace treaty.

In 1483 Dudley appears to have been close to the events of Richard III's usurpation without being directly involved. Certainly he transferred his loyalties with what had become his accustomed ease, receiving by way of a reward the confirmation of his existing annuities, and on 30 March 1484 a further grant of £100 for his services against the rebellion of the duke of Buckingham. In the same month Dudley was also appointed steward of the Forest of Kinver, Staffordshire, and in December he was included in the commission of the peace for Staffordshire and in March 1485 that of oyer and terminer for Essex. Yet despite the favour he enjoyed with Richard III, Dudley did not attempt to bar Henry Tudor's march from Milford Haven: perhaps as a reward for his neutrality, Henry VII on 9 March 1486 gave him an annuity of £100, and three days later also granted him in tail male (albeit for a payment of 1000 marks) the Worcestershire manor of Northfield and Weobley, forfeited by Sir William Berkeley.

Lord Dudley died on 30 September 1487, and was buried in St James's Priory, Dudley, of which he was hereditary patron. In his will of 17 August (which he made under the name of John Dudley, knight, Lord Dudley), he directed that he should be buried beside his wife, Elizabeth, daughter of Sir John Berkeley and widow of Edward, Lord Charlton, whom he had married some time between 1421, when her first husband died, and 1431, and who died in 1478. He founded no chantry, but ordered that 1000 masses be said for his soul, and bequeathed 20 marks for distribution in alms. His eldest son, Edmund, having died on 6 July 1483, he was succeeded as Lord Dudley by Edmund's son Edward. His second son, another John, was probably the father of Henry VII's notorious councillor Edmund *Dudley. His third son, William *Dudley, became bishop of Durham. Oliver, the fourth son, was killed at the battle of Edgcote, on 25 July 1469. The first Lord Dudley also had three daughters, Margaret, Jane, and Eleanor.

HUGH COLLINS

Sources B. Williams, 'Richard III and the house of Dudley', *The Ricardian*, 8 (1988-90), 346-50 • I. D. Rowney, 'The Staffordshire political community, 1440-1500', PhD diss., University of Keele, 1981 • C. Carpenter, *Locality and polity: a study of Warwickshire landed society, 1401-1499* (1992) • H. E. L. Collins, 'The order of the Garter, 1348-1461: chivalry and politics in later medieval England', DPhil diss., U. Oxf., 1996 • J. Ferguson, *English diplomacy, 1422-1461* (1972) • R. A. Griffiths, *The reign of King Henry VI: the exercise of royal authority, 1422-1461* (1981) • C. Ross, *Edward IV*, new edn (1983) • J. Watts, *Henry VI and the politics of kingship* (1996) • P. A. Johnson, *Duke Richard of York, 1411-1460* (1988) • C. L. Scofield, *The life and reign of Edward the Fourth*, 2 vols. (1923) • I. M. W. Harvey, *Jack Cade's rebellion of 1450* (1991) • J. D. Milner, 'The order of the Garter in the reign of Henry VI, 1422-1461', MA diss., University of Manchester, 1972 • *Chancery records* • *CIPM*, 19, nos. 208, 351 • *CIPM, Henry VII*, 1, nos. 285, 288, 296 • H. S. Grazerbook, 'The barons of Dudley', *Collections for a history of Staffordshire*, William Salt Archaeological Society, 9/2 (1888), 1-152, esp. 64-71 • G. Wrottesley, ed., 'Extracts from the plea rolls of the reign of Henry VI', *Collections for a history of Staffordshire*, William Salt Archaeological Society, new ser., 3 (1900), 121-229, esp. 153, 158 • GEC, *Peerage*, new edn, 4.479-80 • R. Horrox and P. W. Hammond, eds., *British Library Harleian manuscript 433*, 4 vols. (1979-

83) · E. Matthew, 'The financing of the lordship of Ireland under Henry V and Henry VI', *Property and politics: essays in later medieval English history*, ed. T. Pollard (1984), 97–115 · M. A. Hicks, '*False, fleeting, perjur'd Clarence': George, duke of Clarence, 1449–78* (1980), 153 · M. Harvey, *England, Rome, and the papacy, 1417–1464* (1993) · *Reports … touching the dignity of a peer of the realm*, House of Lords, 5 vols. (1820–29) · Rymer, *Foedera*, 3rd edn · N. H. Nicolas, ed., *Proceedings and ordinances of the privy council of England*, 7 vols., RC, 26 (1834–7) · *The Paston letters, AD 1422–1509*, ed. J. Gairdner, new edn, 6 vols. (1904); repr. in 1 vol. (1983); repr. (1987) · *CPR* · *CClR* · *Calendar of the fine rolls*, 22 vols., PRO (1911–62)

Sutton, John

Sutton, John (*bap.* 1777, *d.* 1863), corn dealer and seedsman, was baptized at St Mary Somerset, London, on 1 June 1777, the fourth son in a family of six sons and four daughters of James Sutton (1744–1789), partner in Sutton and Winckworth, flour factors, and his wife, Anne Martha (1749–1789), daughter of John and Rachel Johnston, also of London. Both parents died prematurely in 1789, and the seven surviving children were brought up by the Winckworths. After apprenticeship in the firm, about 1800 John and his elder brother James moved to Reading, and ran some mills which they had inherited along the River Kennet. In 1806 John established a corn and meal business in King Street; three years later he married Sarah, daughter of Joseph Norris of Shinfield, near Reading. Three sons and three daughters survived infancy.

During the final decade of the Napoleonic wars, the brothers built up a thriving business. Then early in 1815 their Reading bank, Marsh and Deane, failed at the same time as a major customer in London to whom they regularly consigned substantial quantities of flour. They had very large overdrafts, which the commissioners of bankruptcy put intense pressure on them to repay. James, owing £1450, had to declare himself bankrupt, and died of drink in 1826. John apparently reached an accommodation with the commissioners for the £960 he owed and was able to continue trading on a modest scale. His only known portrait reveals the face, under an impressive stovepipe hat, of a man who has known genuine misfortune. During this critical period his second son, Martin Hope *Sutton (1815–1901), was born, the name Hope expressing his parents' aspiration for better times to come.

Owing to indifferent health and his wife's prolonged illness before she died in 1834, John Sutton was by 1827 barely capable of managing on his own. Martin therefore had to leave school at the age of twelve, and enter the firm. From 1829 onwards he took over the counting-house, and with the help of an outside loan—not paid off until 1841—he restored the finances. Aware that the corn trade had only a limited commercial future, Martin soon began to deal in the more profitable line of seeds. However, his father insisted that he must carry out all seed activities, as well as the study of botanic works, outside working hours, and only after a time allowed him to open accounts with London seed wholesalers. In 1836, when Martin was twenty-one, he became a partner.

While Martin was energetically building up all sides of

John Sutton (*bap.* 1777, *d.* 1863), by unknown photographer

the business, John Sutton was little more than an adviser and helper. His lethargy sprang from the result of his doctor's earlier advice—that he should fortify himself daily with strong drink. By 1838 he had become so forgetful, bilious, and irritable that Martin resolved to cure him of his addiction, distracting him by spending as much time with him as could be spared, and thereby restoring him to health. John Sutton finally retired in 1850.

John Sutton is of interest as typifying a provincial tradesman of the period: limited in his education but, by dint of reading, well up in history and public affairs, and, as a moderate whig, able to trace current political ills back to those ultimately responsible. Originally a Unitarian, he later worshipped in the established church, audibly and fervently joining in that part of the liturgy acceptable to him and ostentatiously silent when he disagreed.

A man of the utmost probity, John Sutton's family respected and feared rather than loved him. He had ambitions for his brighter children, training his eldest son for medicine and briefly apprenticing Martin to a surveyor. As he refused to entertain or be entertained, his three daughters never had the opportunity of marrying; after working hard in the early days, they were later condemned to idleness. They lived with him until he died at his home, Southampton Villa, Reading, on 31 May 1863. He was buried in Reading cemetery.   T. A. B. CORLEY

Sources A. B. Cheales, *MHS …: the life of Martin Hope Sutton of Reading* (1898) · T. A. B. Corley, 'The making of a Berkshire entrepreneur: Martin Hope Sutton of Reading, 1815–40', *Berkshire Archaeological Journal*, 74 (1991–3), 135–43 · priv. coll., manuscript diaries, business and personal, of M. H. Sutton · *Reading Mercury* (6 June 1863)

Archives priv. coll., diaries · U. Reading, Sutton & Sons Archives

Sutton, John (1919–1992), geologist, was born on 8 July 1919 at 100 Esmond Road, Acton, Middlesex, the son of Gerald John Sutton, mechanical engineer, and his wife, Kathleen Alice, *née* Richard, schoolteacher. His father was an engineer and inventor in the Victorian tradition, who was credited with the development of the gas water-heater and the motor lawnmower, and was one of the team of engineers assembled by Churchill during the Second World War with a general brief to invent unusual warlike devices. His mother was the daughter of a railway engineer and bridge builder in the Burmese government service. She was one of the first women to qualify for a classics degree at Oxford, but as women could not then be admitted she had to wait some years before she could graduate. Meanwhile she taught classics in girls' schools. She was appointed MBE in 1919 for wartime committee service. After attending Gunnersbury preparatory school, Middlesex, and the King's School, Worcester, Sutton went up to Imperial College, London, in 1937 to study general science, and later geology, but his degree was interrupted by war service. This took the form of the rather unexciting supervision of radar stations on the east coast, but he seized the opportunity to take up bird-watching, and to develop a general enthusiasm for nature which never left him.

After the war Sutton returned to Imperial College, graduating in 1946. He then joined the staff as a postgraduate researcher. There he met a fellow geology postgraduate, Janet Vida *Watson (1923–1985), daughter of David Meredith Seares Watson, professor of zoology. Sutton and Watson were given adjacent fieldwork areas in the northern highlands of Scotland. They forged a partnership which was to last for the whole of their careers. On 13 June 1949 they married at the register office in Hampstead; they had two daughters, both of whom died at birth. Sutton and Watson formed a brilliant team, their strength being in their difference, not their similarity. Sutton was the extrovert, the broad thinker, the ideas man. Watson was the careful fieldworker, the painstaking recorder of detail, and it was she who wrote the greater part of their joint papers, in which every sentence was carefully weighed and composed. This was a formidable combination.

The earliest Precambrian rocks had long been recognized as a difficult area. In all later geological series, from the Cambrian to the present, relationships can be established partly by fossils and partly by sedimentary sequences. But in the earliest rocks there are no fossils, and sedimentary relations are seldom seen. The rocks are mainly gneisses, altered from their original states by the processes of metamorphism. The contribution of Sutton and Watson was to show that relationships in the Precambrian are to be established in terms of metamorphic events, not stratigraphic sequences. They identified an older metamorphic episode, the Scourian, later shown to be about 2600 million years old, and a later, the Laxfordian, about 1700 million years old. This discovery opened up a new way of looking at Precambrian complexes, and a new technique for deciphering their geology. The methods which they pioneered were applied by others to basement rocks in many parts of the world.

The whole of Sutton's working life was spent at Imperial College, where he was appointed lecturer in the geology department in 1948, prior to completing his postgraduate research. He was promoted to reader in 1956, to professor of geology in 1958, and to head of department in 1964. He served a three-year period as dean of the Royal School of Mines in 1965–8 and again in 1974–7, and he left the geology department on his appointment as pro-rector in 1980. The rector at that time was Sir Brian Flowers, and he and Sutton formed a powerful administrative team. On his retirement in 1983 at the age of sixty-four he was confirmed as emeritus professor and fellow of Imperial College. He had been elected a fellow of the Royal Society in 1966 (vice-president, 1975–7).

One of Sutton's great virtues was his infectious enthusiasm, which inspired all he met, and he was inevitably drawn into committee work, administration, and science policy debates. He was president of the Geologists' Association 1966–8, and after serving for many years as external examiner he was a member of the council of the University of Rhodesia/Zimbabwe from 1976 to 1983. He gave a long period of service from 1964 to 1985 to the scholarships committee of the Royal Commission for the Exhibition of 1851, and he was a trustee of the Natural History Museum 1976–81. He was the first chairman of the Imperial College Centre for Environmental Technology, a cross-departmental research facility of which he was joint founder in 1977, and was president of the Remote Sensing Society 1977–84. From 1976 to 1979 he served as a council member of the Natural Environment Research Council (NERC), and he was involved in the fundamental changes which were made to the status of the geological survey, which for a hundred years had reported directly to a government minister, but which was now made subordinate to the NERC. The direct grant previously enjoyed by the survey was replaced at that time by the customer-contractor principle set out in the Rothschild Report of 1971.

Towards the end of his career Sutton made an important contribution when he was appointed by the Royal Society to develop a renewed relationship with the scientific community in China. This started with the visit of a party of six fellows to Beijing (Peking) in 1973; there were several other visits over the next few years, and student exchanges were followed by the establishment of joint research programmes. These efforts culminated in 1985 with the great Tibet geotraverse, in which a party of twenty-five geologists from many countries undertook an arduous ten-week traverse of the Tibet Himalayas, covering a distance of 600 miles, usually at over 10,000 feet above sea level.

Sutton's retirement was marred by the death in March 1985 of his first wife, Janet Watson. On 21 August 1985 he married (Millicent) Betty Middleton-Sandford (*b.* 1932), artist, daughter of James Middleton Honeychurch, master tailor. They enjoyed a period of country living in Cornwall and then Dorset, but this was cut short by illness, and Sutton died of cancer on 6 September 1992 at the Weymouth and District Hospital, Weymouth, Dorset. He was buried on 15 September 1992 at Martinstown parish church, a few miles west of Dorchester. He was survived by his second wife.   JOHN SPRING

Sources J. S. Spring, *Memoirs FRS*, 41 (1995), 441–56 · *The Times* (15 Sept 1992) · *WWW*, 1991–5 · b. cert. · m. certs · d. cert. · personal knowledge (2004) · private information (2004)
Archives GS Lond., corresp. with his wife (Janet Vida Watson) and papers · ICL, corresp. and papers
Likenesses W. Bird, photograph, repro. in Spring, *Memoirs FRS*, 440

Sutton, Sir John Bland- [*formerly* John Sutton], **first baronet** (1855–1936), surgeon, was born two months prematurely at Durants, Green Street, Enfield Highway, Middlesex, on 21 April 1855, the second of nine children and eldest son of Charles William Sutton, of Enfield Highway, farmer, stock slaughterer, market gardener, and amateur taxidermist, from whom he acquired that keen interest in natural history which is so apparent in his writings. His mother was Elizabeth, eldest daughter of Joseph Wadsworth, farmer, of Long Buckby, Northamptonshire. His second name was given him in memory of his maternal grandmother's family, and in 1899 he assumed by deed poll the prefix surname of Bland.

Sir John Bland-Sutton, first baronet (1855–1936), by Walter Stoneman, 1924

Bland-Sutton's parents were poor, and being originally intended for the profession of schoolmaster he qualified as a pupil teacher during his last two years at St James the Great elementary school at Enfield Highway and afterwards in London. However, his father's taxidermy had aroused his interest in anatomy and he determined to become a surgeon. By thrift and hard work he managed after four years to save enough money, with help from his mother's family, to pay the fees of a medical school. In 1878 he began work at Thomas Cooke's school of anatomy in Brunswick Square, the last of the private anatomical schools, and in the same year he paid 100 sovereigns to join the medical school of the Middlesex Hospital. His progress was rapid; he won prizes and scholarships, became a demonstrator of anatomy, and in 1881 was appointed prosector and pathologist to the Zoological Society, in which he retained a lifelong interest. Bland-Sutton's small physique and delicate health precluded sport. Instead, he worked. Between 1878 and 1886 he dissected 12,000 subjects, ranging from fish to humans, including some 800 stillborn foetuses. He devised a cure for rickets in lion cubs, and a diet for pregnant animals. The study of teeth, jaw-bones, and tusks, their evolution and diseases, was a special interest.

Bland-Sutton was admitted a member of the Royal College of Surgeons of England in 1881 and rented a house in Gordon Street where he took resident pupils. He was admitted a fellow of the college in 1884 and in 1886 was appointed assistant surgeon to the Middlesex Hospital, becoming surgeon nineteen years later (1905). In 1892 he

won the Jacksonian prize of the college, and in 1896 was appointed surgeon to the Chelsea Hospital for Women, a post which he held until 1911. This gave him the opportunity of developing his chief surgical interest, which had been aroused by the subject set for the Jacksonian prize, the surgery of the female generative organs. He was attracted to the abdominal 'valise', and during his career the abdominal surgeon graduated 'along the corridors of the female pelvis' (Gordon-Taylor, 239). Bland-Sutton became the master of techniques to remove pelvic tumours. He wore no cap or mask, 'such appanage he called surgical coquetry' (ibid., 244). Bland-Sutton speedily became known as the leading exponent of gynaecological surgery of the day, although his new methods were initially controversial. When, in 1890, he began to propose the partial removal of the uterus for the cure of fibroids, the Edinburgh obstetrician James Matthews Duncan accused him of being a 'criminal mutilator of women' (Moscucci, 173).

In 1886 Bland-Sutton married Agnes Hobbs (*d.* 1898), of Didcot. Their honeymoon was spent arranging the drawing-room as a museum. In 1899 he married as his second wife Edith Goff (*d.* 1943), youngest daughter of Henry Heather-Bigg. They lived from 1901 to 1929 at 47 Brook Street (now pulled down) and at the back of the house he built a remarkable hypostyle hall after the pattern of the Apadana (hall of honour) built by Darius at Susa, the roof of which was supported by thirty-two bull-columns of specially constructed enamelled bricks.

The amount of research work which Bland-Sutton

accomplished in his younger days was very great. Between 1882 and 1895 he made 152 communications to various medical societies dealing with comparative anatomy, comparative embryology, and comparative pathology. Of these the most noteworthy are *Ligaments, their Nature and Morphology*, expanded into a small book in 1887, and 'On odontomes' which formed the basis of subsequent work on the subject. He was an original and arresting writer, and his best-known book, *Tumours Innocent and Malignant* (1893), became a classic. Towards the close of his life he wrote an autobiography, *The Story of a Surgeon* (1930).

As a surgeon Bland-Sutton possessed brilliant dexterity of hand and the faculty of instant appreciation and decision, but most of all a splendid self-reliance which overrode all obstacles of place and circumstance. In his time this was an essential quality, and remains the first attribute of a really great surgeon.

Bland-Sutton's conviction that a wide knowledge of pathology is the hub of all medical teaching led him in 1913 to present to the Middlesex Hospital the Institute of Pathology which bears his name. His widow at her death in 1943 made bequests both to it and to the Royal College of Surgeons, the latter taking the form of a scholarship in memory of her husband.

Bland-Sutton was a small man with features strongly recalling Napoleon Bonaparte, to whom his mental make-up also bore a decided resemblance. He retained a strong cockney accent, and was terse and decisive in speech; his humour was puckish in quality and quite peculiar to himself, and his mind betrayed a genius of a very uncommon type. In his later years he entertained lavishly, but there was a certain aloofness about him and he had very few intimate friends; among these was Rudyard Kipling. He had the gift of bestowing inspiration on those who worked under him, for he invested all that he did with a halo of drama and romance. He was often discreetly generous to junior staff.

Bland-Sutton was knighted in 1912 and was created a baronet in 1925. He was first president of the Association of Surgeons (1919) and then of the Royal College of Surgeons of England (1923–6), and was Hunterian orator (1923). Many other honours, including numerous honorary degrees, were conferred on him. He was a prolific writer and lecturer. Bland-Sutton died at his home at 29 Hertford Street, Park Lane, London, on 20 December 1936, having had no children by either marriage. After a memorial service at Westminster Abbey, his ashes in a Burmese urn are at his request kept in the museum of the Pathology Institute where he taught 'over the dead in the hope of aiding the living' (Gordon-Taylor, 236).

VICTOR BONNEY, rev. ROGER HUTCHINS

Sources W. R. Bett, *Sir John Bland-Sutton, 1855–1936* (1956) • G. Gordon-Taylor, 'The Bland–Sutton centenary', *Annals of the Royal College of Surgeons of England*, 17 (1955), 236–50 • *BMJ* (26 Dec 1936), 1319 • *BMJ* (2–9 Jan 1937), 47–50, 102 • *WWW* • J. Bland-Sutton, *The story of a surgeon* (1930) • *The Times* (21 Dec 1936) • personal knowledge (1949) • *CGPLA Eng. & Wales* (1937) • O. Moscucci, *The science of woman: gynaecology and gender in England, 1800–1929* (1990)

Likenesses Elf, caricature, 1910, NPG; repro. in *VF* (3 Feb 1910) • G. Frampton, marble bust, *c*.1922, Middlesex Hospital, London,

Institute of Pathology • W. Stoneman, photograph, 1924, NPG [*see illus.*] • G. Belcher, drawing, 1925, Middlesex Hospital, London • J. Collier, oils, 1925, RCS Eng. • J. Collier, oils, before 1925, Royal Society of Medicine, London • Elliott & Fry, photograph, repro. in Bett, *Sir John Bland-Sutton*, frontispiece • Elliott & Fry, photograph, NPG; repro. in *The reign of George V*, vol. 2 • photograph, repro. in *BMJ*, 1 (1937), 47

Wealth at death £21,316 1s. 3d.: probate, 1 Feb 1937, *CGPLA Eng. & Wales*

Sutton, John Henry Thomas Manners-, third Viscount Canterbury (1814–1877), politician and colonial governor, the younger son of Charles Manners-*Sutton, first Viscount Canterbury (1780–1845), politician, and his first wife, Lucy Maria Charlotte (*d*. 1815), eldest daughter of John Denison of Ossington, Nottinghamshire, was born in Downing Street, London, on 27 May 1814. He was educated at Eton College and Trinity College, Cambridge, where he graduated MA in 1835. He gained a blue for cricket in 1836. He was admitted a student of Lincoln's Inn on 18 September 1835, but was never called to the bar, and took his name off the books of the society on 25 November 1853. He was registrar of the court of faculties from 1834 until his death. Standing as a Conservative, in September 1839 he defeated Thomas Milner-Gibson at a by-election for the borough of Cambridge, but was subsequently unseated for bribery (*JHC*, 45.293–4). At the general election in June 1841 he was again returned for Cambridge, and from September 1841 until June 1846 he was Peel's under-secretary for the Home Office, but took little part in debates. In 1847, he first withdrew as a candidate for Cambridge in the face of protectionist opposition, then stood, and was defeated by the Liberal candidate. He stood for Harwich unsuccessfully in 1848, and with this his career in the Commons—where he did not make the most of his opportunities—ended.

In 1851 Manners-Sutton published the Lexington Papers, which had been discovered at Kelham, Nottinghamshire, in the library of his cousin, John Henry Manners-Sutton, MP for Newark. On 1 July 1854 he was appointed lieutenant-governor of New Brunswick, a post which he retained until October 1861, when he was succeeded by Sir A. H. Gordon. He became governor of Trinidad on 24 June 1864, and on 19 May 1866 was promoted to the post of governor of Victoria, Australia. He was created KCB on 23 June, and assumed the office of governor on 15 August 1866. On the death of his elder brother, Charles John Manners-Sutton, in November 1869, he succeeded as third Viscount Canterbury. He resigned his post of governor of Victoria, where he had been very popular, in March 1873, and returned to England to his seat, Brooke House, Brooke, Norfolk. He played no significant role in the business of the House of Lords except to make occasional speeches on colonial affairs. He was created GCMG on 25 June 1873.

Manners-Sutton married, on 5 July 1838, Georgiana (*d*. 14 Sept 1899), youngest daughter of Charles Tompson of Witchingham Hall, Norfolk, and his wife, Juliana, *née* Kett. They had five sons—the eldest of whom, Henry Charles, succeeded to the title—and two daughters. Manners-Sutton died at his London home, 12 Queensberry Place, on 23 June 1877.   G. F. R. BARKER, *rev.* H. C. G. MATTHEW

Sources GEC, *Peerage* · *Annual Register* (1877) · Venn, *Alum. Cant.* · J. B. Conacher, *The Peelites and the party system* (1972) **Archives** Bodl. Oxf., corresp. with Lord Kimberley · U. Nott. L., letters to the duke of Newcastle **Likenesses** wood-engraving, repro. in *ILN* (7 July 1877) **Wealth at death** under £40,000: probate, 26 Sept 1877, *CGPLA Eng. & Wales*

Sutton, Joseph Hertford (1902–1992), headmaster, was born at 7 Lower Lune Street, Fleetwood, Lancashire, on 25 June 1902, the son of Joseph Sutton, fisherman, and his wife, Sarah Ellen Locock. Educated at Chaucer Road council school, Fleetwood, and Baine's Grammar School, Poulton-le-Fylde, he became a student teacher in September 1920. From 1926 to 1929 he read economics and political science at Manchester University and in 1929 gained a teacher's diploma at the same university. In rapid succession Sutton subsequently studied for a master's degree in education which was awarded in 1930 and an MA in 1932, at which time he was a member of convocation.

In 1938 Sutton was appointed headmaster of a school in Lancaster, built in 1907 as a council school but which in 1926, responding to a national trend to create an alternative to grammar school education, became a central school. It was his task to change its character yet again, to Greaves secondary modern school, in response to the Hadow report of 1926 and the move to tripartite organization after the 1944 Education Act. Its pupils were drawn from the 75 per cent of their age group who were not selected for grammar or technical schools after the eleven-plus examination. Under Sutton's headship Greaves School was identified by the inspectorate in 1956 as an exemplar of the secondary modern type of school (McCulloch, 101). His aims for the school were summed up in the memorable phrase that the school would prepare students 'both to live and get a living' (*The Greavesan*, July 1949). That he was free to develop his interpretation of the new type of school was due to lack of definition by the ministry and the powerful tradition in English education that curriculum decisions should be left to schools.

From 1953 Sutton was editor of the *Bulletin* of the Lancashire Association of Head Teachers of Secondary Modern Schools. He traced many of his initiatives as head teacher to the experience of running Greaves School in wartime when attendance was part-time and the school was shared with evacuees. In such circumstances the potential of the locality, particularly its rural life, had to be exploited for learning resources, and novel teaching styles were necessary. Concern about teaching quality gave him a career-long interest in teacher training. He had been influenced, among others, by the writing of Henri Bergson, which had led him to the view that education consisted not of facts only but the opening up of 'a more abundant life' (Association of Headmasters and Headmistresses of Lancashire County Secondary Modern Schools, *Bulletin*, 4, June 1956). He had come 'to the vital conclusion that the aims of the

school did not differ fundamentally from those of any other type of secondary school' (ibid.). Sutton rejected the implication of the Norwood report (1943) that there were three distinct types of child, and took as the starting point for the school the need to restore the self-esteem of those who, as a result of the selection process, might see themselves as failures. Confidence was encouraged by the introduction from 1949 of entry to first aid and agricultural competitions and learning musical instruments.

Because Sutton's vision of the secondary modern school grew out of the grammar school tradition, and as he recognized no difference between types of school other than acceptance of variations in ability, it was natural to find in the organization and rituals of Greaves School everything that represented a quality educational experience: houses, uniform, prefects, clubs, expeditions, sport, prizes, drama performances, and a school magazine. Had this been all, the school might have failed, but it was Sutton's considerable achievement to create within a traditional environment flexibility of organization designed to meet the needs of a wide range of abilities. Although disliking streaming, he felt it necessary to create express, practical, and remedial classes, the latter a significant innovation, and he frequently used setting for subject groups. The desire to emphasize the individuality of the children led him to introduce three years of general education, characterized by project work and individualized learning and an experiment with social studies, as he was determined that the school would not be regarded as a vocational school. In the senior forms work experience, liaison with further education, and the introduction of a pre-nursing course were notable features. Dreading that secondary modern schools should become stereotyped, he was reluctant to accept the trend to external examinations in modern schools and introduced them judiciously so that they would not distort the character of the curriculum.

The exceptional range of extra-curricular provision encouraged by Sutton at Greaves School included debating and essay-writing clubs which did well in county competitions, visits to theatres and places of interest, sporting activities, and expeditions abroad. Cumulatively they created a stimulating and relaxed environment. The blend of old and new is well seen in the practice of devolving to the head boy and girl responsibility for the writing and delivery on speech day of the head teacher's report. A school council contributed to the aim, which permeated the school, of preparing young people to be thoughtful and self-confident citizens. Close relationships with parents were emphasized.

Sutton, who was unmarried, retired in December 1965 and a year later the school amalgamated with Castle School to form the Central Lancaster high school. Sutton occupied his leisure in studying local history and in various community activities. He died at Ellel House retirement home, Galgate, Lancaster, on 15 September 1992 and was cremated at Morecambe on 21 September.

A. B. ROBERTSON

Sources *The Greavesan* (1949–65) [Lancs. RO, DDX 1282 acc. 5877] · *Bulletin* of the Lanchashire Association of Head Teachers of Secondary Modern Schools, Lancs. RO, DDX 1282/2–3 · log books of Greaves School, 1951–73, Lancs. RO, SMQ acc. 8634 · managers' minutes, Greaves School, 1945–57, Lancs. RO, CC/EXLA acc. 3394 box 194 · annual reports of headteachers, 1955–66, Lancs. RO, box 142 · *Lancaster Guardian* (2 Nov 1979) · *Lancaster Guardian* (25 Sept 1992) · Greaves School photograph albums, 1951–61, Lancs. RO, SMQ15, acc. 7935 · photograph of Sutton, 1965, Lancs. RO, SMQ 15, acc. 7935 · diary as a student teacher, Lancs. RO, DDX 553/2 · b. cert. · d. cert. · Greaves School farm projects, 1955, Lancs. RO, DDX 1282/5–6 · G. McCulloch, *Failing the ordinary child? The theory and practice of working-class secondary education* (1998)
Archives Lancs. RO, LEA collections
Likenesses photograph, repro. in *The Greavesan* (Sept 1963) · photographs, Lancs. RO
Wealth at death under £125,000: probate, 9 Nov 1992, *CGPLA Eng. & Wales*

Sutton, Katherine (*d.* 1376), abbess of Barking and supposed liturgical dramatist, owes her importance solely to a tantalizing reference in the Barking customary drawn up by Sibille Felton, abbess from 1394 to 1419, and presented to the abbey in 1404:

> the venerable lady Katherine de Sutton, who then had pastoral charge [of the abbey,] … with the unanimous consent of the sisters, ordained that, immediately after the third responsory of Matins on Easter day, the celebration of the Lord's Resurrection would take place, and that the procession would be established [ordered?] in this manner. (Tolhurst, 107)

There then follows an unusual piece of Latin liturgical drama, depicting the harrowing of hell, in which the nuns, representing the souls of the patriarchs in limbo, are led out of a side chapel by the officiating priest. Each carrying a palm and a candle, they go in triumphant procession to a side-altar, the 'sepulchre'. Here a crucifix-figure and a communion-host, concealed on Good Friday to represent the burial of Christ, are now 'raised', and the host carried in a monstrance to the main altar of the Holy Trinity, with appropriate liturgical antiphons being sung at each stage. Not only is this piece of drama an unusual variant of the *elevatio*, the symbolic raising of Christ's body on Easter morning which was a standard part of medieval church practice, but it affords a rare glimpse of a female, non-clerical experience of liturgy. On both counts the Barking 'Harrowing of Hell' has attracted much interest and Katherine Sutton has been hailed as the first known female dramatist in England. While this may be correct, the evidence is not conclusive and needs careful scrutiny.

Almost nothing is known about Katherine. The only other documents concerning her, the royal assent to her election as abbess on 15 March 1358, and the royal leave (date 16 April 1376) to elect a new abbess on her death, do not give her parentage, as such documents often do, nor is there any indication of her date of birth or date of profession as a nun. The lack of information about Katherine Sutton is therefore unusual for the head of an abbey of such powerful standing as Barking, which claimed to be the oldest community of women in England (after the destruction of other communities by the Danes), ranked as a royal foundation. Its abbess took precedence over other abbesses and was considered to hold her lands by barony. Despite impoverishment caused by repeated flooding of its lands along the Thames, at the dissolution Barking was found to be the third richest abbey of nuns in England.

Since many abbesses of Barking were princesses or members of the most powerful families in the country, the relative anonymity of Katherine Sutton requires explanation. She may have had family connections for which evidence does not survive, or may have been elected solely for her personal qualities of leadership. The existence of a previous abbess of the same surname, Yolande Sutton, could be purely coincidental, but suggests that there was an established family association with the abbey. These two abbesses might have come from the Suttons of Dudley Castle, Staffordshire, or from the Suttons of Cheshire, who were later among the founders of Brasenose College, Oxford. On the other hand, the entry in the customary suggests a forceful personality, and Sibille Felton mentions no one else among her recent predecessors.

When it comes to claiming Katherine Sutton as a dramatist, problems arise from the nature of the material. Liturgical drama, drawing most of its dialogue from pre-existing antiphons and scriptural texts, does not usually have named authors, however distinctive the play. In contrast, religious plays performed outside the liturgy, as entertainment rather than worship, are sometimes ascribed to individuals. In addition, the Barking play, although unique in itself, is but one elaboration on an antiphon about the harrowing of hell which formed a standard part of the *elevatio* right across western Europe. Furthermore, there seems to have been an established tradition of lively liturgical drama at Barking: in 1279 Archbishop Peckham had had to admonish the nuns about maintaining the decorum of their Holy Innocents' play, and some of their other rituals have unusual elaborations, such as the washing of the crucifix-figure in wine at its 'burial' on Good Friday. Against all this, there is the Barking customary's unique emphasis on Katherine's decrees about the Easter celebration. The text itself stresses her daring break with universal tradition in moving the *elevatio* from before to after matins. How much she contributed to the form of the *elevatio* itself depends on how much weight is given to the last phrase of the passage from the customary, how closely it may be linked with Katherine, and whether the Latin means that she ordained that the procession 'be ordered' or 'be established': the latter would suggest the setting up of a new piece of liturgical action. It can be said with confidence, however, that Katherine struck her contemporaries as a woman of notable energy and decisiveness, and that they associated her name, in whatever way, with an interesting and unusual piece of liturgical drama.

SANTHA BHATTACHARJI

Sources 'The Barking ordinal', University College, Oxford, MS 169 · J. B. L. Tolhurst, ed., *The ordinale and customary of the Benedictine nuns of Barking Abbey*, 1, HBS, 65 (1927), v–ix, 100–08; 2, HBS, 66 (1928), 346, 361 · *VCH Essex*, 2.115–19 · Dugdale, *Monasticon*, new edn, vol. 1 • K. Young, *The drama of the medieval church*, 2 vols. (1933), 1.149–77 • D. Knowles, C. N. L. Brooke, and V. C. M. London, eds., *The heads of religious houses, England and Wales*, 1: *940–1216* (1972) • S. Shaw, *The history and antiquities of Staffordshire*, 2 (1801), 138–46 • *CPR*, 1358–61, 26

Archives University College, Oxford, MS 169

Sutton, Katherine (*fl.* 1630–1663), prophetess, lived in England during her early life and subsequently emigrated to the Netherlands about 1659. Although nothing of her parents or of her origins is known, a broad outline of Sutton's life can be gathered from her spiritual autobiography, *A Christian Womans Experiences of the Glorious Working of God's Free Grace* (published in Rotterdam in 1663).

Sutton was a governess by profession, and in her youth she was drawn 'into a darck corner of the land' inhabited by 'many Papists', possibly Lancashire (Sutton, 2). She then married 'a man that was much in practical duties' with whom she had a number of children, at least two of which died prematurely (ibid., 3, 5–6, 10).

Sutton's life was marked both by intense religious experience and by robust journeying. She recalls marching 'many miles' through 'all weathers' to attend worthy sermons and, in her quest to join a suitable congregation, she relocated with her family at least once in England before travelling twice overseas. The first journey abroad may have been prompted by Archbishop Laud's reforms of church practices in the early 1630s: Sutton resolved to separate from 'such a way of worship' after 'Altars were reared up', following which 'the Lord carried mee over the Sea', she states, 'where I did injoy further and fuller communion with himself in his ordinances' (Sutton, 6–7, 10). By the late 1650s she had set sail for the Netherlands, suffering a shipwreck in which her writings (recalling 'thirty years experiences') were lost (ibid., 21–2).

The most remarkable aspect of Sutton's life lies in her gift for 'spiritual singing', first experienced while out walking in February 1655 (Sutton, 13–14; Smith, 5–6, 332–3). Filled with the spirit, Sutton suddenly found herself able to sing extempore verse prophecies predicting England's imminent destruction and claiming 'that God would afflict that nation' with war and other calamities for its 'sins'. At one point, Sutton 'had an opportunity to declare this to some that then were in high places': after disregarding her counsel, 'they were soon brought down and laid low' (Sutton, 14–16). Occurrences of such singing apparently intensified around 1658, immediately before Sutton's removal to the Netherlands. However, not all her songs prophesied national doom. Many of the inspired hymns were devotional in nature, as are those collected at the end of her account.

Doctrinally, Sutton's faith was broadly Calvinist or Reformed, asserting foremost that salvation is by 'grace' and not 'by workes of righteousness' or 'of our selves' (Sutton, 33). Denominationally, it seems that Sutton was a Baptist, having rejected early on 'the evil and falseness' of paedobaptist 'Christening' and being later 'baptized together' with other adult members of her church (Sutton, 7, 12). More specifically, she may have been associated with English Particular Baptists, as *A Christian Womans Experiences* includes a laudatory preface by the renowned Particular Baptist divine Hanserd Knollys.

MICHAEL DAVIES

Sources K. Sutton, *A Christian womans experiences of the glorious working of God's free grace* (1663) • M. Bell, G. Parfitt, and S. Shepherd, *A biographical dictionary of English women writers, 1580–1720* (1990), 187 • N. Smith, *Perfection proclaimed: language and literature in English radical religion, 1640–1660* (1989), 5–6, 332–3 • Blain, Clements & Grundy, *Feminist comp.*, 1049 • W. T. Whitley, ed., *A Baptist bibliography*, 2 vols. (1916–22) • E. Hobby, *Virtue of necessity: English women's writing, 1649–1688* (1988), 242 • P. Mack, *Visionary women: ecstatic prophecy in seventeenth-century England* (1992), 413–14 • 'Knollys, Hanserd (*c.*1599–1691)', Greaves & Zaller, *BDBR*, 2.160–62 • Wing, *STC*

Archives Bodl. Oxf., copy of Sutton's only published work (*A Christian womans experiences …*) • CUL, copy of Sutton's only published work (*A Christian womans experiences …*)

Sutton, Leslie Ernest (1906–1992), scientist and university teacher, was born on 22 June 1906 at 48 Newry Road, Isleworth, Middlesex, the only son of Edgar Sutton (1880–1972), a railway clerk, and his wife, Margaret Lilian Winifred, *née* Heard (1880–1965). The family later moved to 9 Southsea Avenue, Watford. Sutton's parents were supportive, but had fallen on hard times. Educated at Watford grammar school from 1918 to 1924, Sutton emerged as an outstanding student, leaving with a scholarship to Lincoln College, Oxford, to read chemistry; he obtained further support from a Hertfordshire county scholarship and a Kitchener memorial scholarship. At Lincoln, Sutton was by his own admission an unhappy loner. Acutely aware of his modest background and lack of social graces in relation to those of the typical undergraduate of that time, he buried himself in his work. He was lucky to have as his tutor N. V. Sidgwick, a major figure in Oxford chemistry. After gaining a first-class degree in 1928, he started his doctoral research with Sidgwick.

A key property of the chemical bond is its electrical polarity, and Sutton spent six months with Peter Debye in Leipzig in 1929, learning how to measure it. He soon became the leading experimentalist using this technique—then almost unique in its ability to reveal the shape of molecules, and he obtained his Oxford doctorate in 1932. That same year he became a junior research fellow at Magdalen College.

Perhaps the most formative year in Sutton's life was spent with Linus Pauling at the California Institute of Technology in 1933–4, as a Rockefeller Foundation fellow. Pauling was developing his ideas on the quantum mechanics of chemical bonding. Sutton not only grasped the implications for his own work, but also learned to measure molecular geometry using electron diffraction. After returning to Oxford he established an influential programme to relate molecular geometry to electronic structure, and in 1936 he became a tutor and fellow of Magdalen College. His work, recorded in nearly 150 scientific publications, was recognized by the award of British chemistry's most prestigious prizes, the Meldola medal (1932), the Harrison memorial prize (1935), and the Tilden lectureship (1940). He was elected fellow of the Royal Society in 1950, and became a reader in physical chemistry at Oxford in 1962. In 1973 he was made an honorary DSc of Salford University.

Sutton was reserved, but courteous, kindly, and unassuming. He experienced much personal grief. The war separated him from his American wife and their two young children, who were refugees in America. He had married Catharine Virginia Stock in Oxford on 4 August 1932, but she died on 3 February 1962, comparatively young, leaving three children: Virginia (b. 1936), Stephen (b. 1938), and Richard (b. 1945). Rachel Ann Long, née Batten, whom he married on 20 April 1963, and with whom he had two sons, Geoffrey (b. 1964) and Martin (b. 1967), developed multiple sclerosis within a few years, and their life together, before she died on 26 May 1987, was marred by the progress of the disease. This he bore with quiet dignity. Sutton was a religious man, regularly attending college chapel. His interest in music included much of the English choral repertory as well as organ music. He died at the John Radcliffe Hospital, Oxford, from heart failure on 31 October 1992, and was buried at St Andrew's Church, Headington, on 6 November 1992.

As a tutor and research supervisor Sutton inspired respect and loyalty. Always meticulously organized, he liked to keep in touch with eighty or so former research students. He ends a summary of his scientific work with the note:

> It is for others to judge my career, if they think that is worth doing; but I might quote a pithy comment by the late T. W. J. Taylor, Fellow of BNC, on my undergraduate efforts at practical organic chemistry. He wrote 'Trying at times; but tries all the time.' I am content for that to be my epitaph. (The Independent, 5 Nov 1992)

Sutton was a pioneer of the new principles of electronic structure and bonding that transformed chemistry between 1930 and 1950 and which are now universally accepted. As a fellow of Magdalen College for forty-one years he influenced generations of pupils, many of whom in their turn became influential in universities and institutes across the world. ROBERT DENNING

Sources personal records of fellows of the Royal Society · D. H. Wiffen, *Memoirs FRS*, 40 (1994), 369–82 · R. G. Denning, *The Independent* (5 Nov 1992) · b. cert. · m. certs. · d. cert.

Archives Bodl. Oxf., corresp. and papers | Bodl. Oxf., corresp. with C. A. Coulson · Lincoln College, Oxford, corresp. with N. V. Sidgwick

Wealth at death £202,904: probate, 1993, *CGPLA Eng. & Wales*

Sutton, Martin Hope (1815–1901), seed merchant, was born on 14 March 1815 at Reading, the second of three sons (there were also three daughters, as well as a further son and daughter who died young) of John *Sutton (bap. 1777, d. 1863), corn factor, and his wife, Sarah Norris (d. 1834). The name Hope was added because his father, in severe financial straits after the collapse of a Reading bank, welcomed the child's arrival as a hopeful sign for the future.

Although his elder brother was allowed to study medicine, after a brief education at Huntley's School and Greathead's School, Sutton at the age of twelve was obliged to join his father's business. As John Sutton's poor health

was exacerbated by a drink problem—which Martin's devoted efforts later cured—Martin had great responsibility at an early age. He realized that far better returns could be achieved from seeds than from dealing in corn, but his father refused to let him study botany or to deal in seeds during working hours, and he pursued these activities in his spare time. He nevertheless built up a network of seed growers from among local market-gardeners, and the corn side of the business was phased out after Martin Sutton was made partner in 1836, aged twenty-one. In 1840 turnover came to £1800 and profits to nearly £580.

Until then Sutton had sold mainly agricultural seeds, but he steadily enlarged his range to include flower seeds for the suburban and country gardens that were by then becoming popular. He also advertised vegetables and ornamental plants, at first in handbills, from 1832, and later in catalogues. The introduction of the penny post in 1840 allowed him to create a mail-order system: each year he sent out thousands of these catalogues, which contained order forms, and he executed the resulting orders by return of post. By then he had embarked on a typically persistent and laborious campaign to bring about the improvement of seed quality throughout the country, but not until 1869 was the Seeds Adulteration Act passed into law.

In his younger days Sutton was sociable and quite a dandy. Then he became converted to more sober ways by Charlotte Trendell (1818–1846), daughter of a Reading watchmaker, whom he married in 1844. A son and a daughter died soon after birth; Charlotte herself died of consumption in 1846, aged twenty-eight. Sutton was helped over his grief by months of exertion in fulfilling large government orders for Ireland after the outbreak of the great famine there, and by experiments to develop disease-resistant strains of potato. In 1848 he married Sophia Woodhead (d. 1894), daughter of William Warwick of nearby Whitley. They had five sons and four daughters.

During the 1850s annual sales rose from under £5000 to £35,000, and Sutton was asked to supply seeds to the royal gardens at Windsor, to give advice on crops in the home farm there, and to help with the laying out of the gardens at Osborne House, Queen Victoria's residence in the Isle of Wight. Thereafter he received a present from her each Christmas; he was also offered a knighthood, which he declined. His 'Royal Seed Establishment' received royal warrants from both the queen and from the prince of Wales (later Edward VII). In 1856 Sutton issued the first *Amateur's Guide in Horticulture*, in five parts, the last of which provided a 'calendar of operations' which enthusiasts could follow through the seasons. He wrote an article on laying down land for permanent pasture in the Royal Agricultural Society's journal for 1861.

Together with his younger brother Alfred, Sutton oversaw the steady growth of the firm, which in 1870 had sales of £75,000 and which he boasted was the largest retail seed firm in Britain. A few years later he raised this claim to the most considerable business of its kind in the world, by turnover and by the number of customers. In 1871 his eldest son, Martin John *Sutton, became a partner, and two other sons later joined the partnership of Sutton & Sons. As the father aged he fought a succession of running battles with his sons—never face-to-face but by the exchange of notes and memoranda—over issues such as the need to keep costs down and for them to pay ever more detailed attention to all aspects of the business. They in turn looked for some enjoyment out of their growing affluence, and fruitlessly campaigned for him to stand down; not until 1888 did he and Alfred retire, and Martin John Sutton become the senior partner. Turnover was then nearly £170,000 and profit £33,000. An equally sore point was the extent of Martin Sutton's charitable donations, which he increased from 5 per cent of his personal income in the mid-1840s to 20 per cent from the late 1860s onwards.

Sutton consistently refused to serve either as an MP or as a town councillor; instead he actively supported such religious bodies as the British and Foreign Bible Society, the Church Missionary Society, and the YMCA. As a young man he had been a Sunday school teacher and had thought of becoming a missionary; and he and Alfred subsidized the foundation of certain local schools. On the evangelical wing of the Church of England, he regularly met delegations and individuals of the same persuasion, and he freely handed out tracts that reflected his views.

A grandson by marriage characterized Sutton in his riper years as 'a direct-looking old gentleman with rather wide-set eyes, a bold and broad-based nose and patriarchal beard', easily mistaken for a nonconformist divine or even a street-corner evangelist (Bashford, 180). While entertaining dignitaries in his home, he was accompanied by a footman who placed over his shoulders different thicknesses of cloak according to the temperature. Sutton died at his home, Cintra Lodge, Whitley, Reading, on 4 October 1901. The distance he had travelled socially since his early corn-chandling days may be seen from the eloquent words uttered by a clergyman son at his funeral: 'And he died mourned by the whole town and his eighteen indoor and outdoor servants' (ibid., 200). He was buried at Reading cemetery.   T. A. B. CORLEY

Sources T. A. B. Corley, 'The making of a Berkshire entrepreneur: Martin Hope Sutton of Reading, 1815–40', *Berkshire Archaeological Journal*, 74 (1991–3), 135–43 · T. A. B. Corley, 'A Berkshire entrepreneur makes good: Martin Hope Sutton of Reading, 1840–71', *Berkshire Archaeological Journal*, 75 (1994–7), 103–10 · A. B. Cheales, *MHS …: the life of Martin Hope Sutton of Reading* (1898) · U. Reading, Rural History Centre, Suttons archive · private information · H. H. Bashford, *Lodgings for twelve* (1935), 179–205 [Harborough Bolton Sr] · *CGPLA Eng. & Wales* (1901)

Archives U. Reading, Rural History Centre, archives

Likenesses photograph, 1897, repro. in Cheales, *MHS*, 21

Wealth at death £91,220 15s. 4d.: probate, 19 Nov 1901, *CGPLA Eng. & Wales*

Sutton, Martin John (1850–1913), scientific agriculturist, was born in Reading on 25 October 1850, the eldest of five sons and four daughters of Martin Hope *Sutton (1815–1901), seed merchant, and his second wife, Sophia Woodhead Warwick (d. 1894), of Whitley, Berkshire. He was educated at Blackheath proprietary school, and joined Sutton

Martin John Sutton (1850–1913), by Henry Tanworth Wells, exh. RA 1900

& Sons, his father's seed firm, at the age of sixteen; he became a partner in 1871. Four years later, he married Emily Owen (d. 1911), daughter of Colonel Henry Fouquet. They had two sons and a daughter.

In the early 1870s Suttons claimed to be the largest seed firm in Europe, with sales in 1870–71 of £87,000 and a net profit of £17,000. By 1912–13 sales had risen to £270,000 and profits to £52,000. The firm prospered both through the care it took in testing seeds and through experimental work begun by Sutton's father, particularly on the improvement of the potato and of agricultural grasses. Sutton likewise carried out searching field trials in the firm's nursery grounds and on his own farms. He succeeded, with the help of the French botanist Vilmorin, in improving methods of seed selection, and he collaborated with John C. A. Voelcker in experiments on grasslands. His standard work, *Permanent and Temporary Pastures* (6th edn, 1902), was awarded a gold medal at the Paris Exhibition of 1900. He also successfully bred cattle, sheep, and horses.

All Sutton's professional successes were achieved against a background of indifferent health. From 1876 onwards he suffered bouts of rheumatism and fever, and his doctors insisted on lengthy spells of recuperation in warm climates. On their advice he lived outside Reading, leasing one local mansion after another and moving on every three or four years. These illnesses and his unsettled life probably sprang from difficult relations with his father, who constantly badgered him and his brothers over such matters as extravagance in all branches of the firm and the brothers' habit of spending to the limit of their incomes. Martin Hope Sutton retired in 1888 but continued to be a sore trial to his sons until he died in 1901.

Outside the firm, Martin John Sutton had many achievements to his name. He early joined the Royal Agricultural Society of England and was an active member of its council from 1883 to 1904. He never tired of stressing the need for systematic agricultural education, and was a mainstay of the national agricultural examination board. He was also a member of the Smithfield Club and the London Farmers' Club. For his services to agriculture he was made a fellow of the Linnean Society and a chevalier of the Légion d'honneur and of the ordre du mérite agricole.

Sutton was a conservative in politics, but he held independent views on such issues as temperance and religious education in elementary schools. He served as mayor of Reading in 1904 and as a member of Berkshire county council. A staunch evangelical, he sat for the diocese of Oxford in the Canterbury house of laymen. He generously supported religious, philanthropic, and educational institutions, most notably in Reading and its neighbourhood.

In appearance Sutton was tall, broad-shouldered, and stout, with prominent eyes and a closely trimmed beard. Except in height he resembled the prince of Wales (later Edward VII), adopting in company the prince's robust and genially autocratic air. He married in 1912 his second wife, Grace, eldest daughter of the African missionary Charles Thomas *Studd, then in her early twenties. Sutton died of heart failure at the Piccadilly Hotel, Regent Street, London, on 14 December 1913. He was buried at Sonning, Berkshire. In its obituary on 15 December 1913 *The Times* referred to him as 'one of the most prominent agriculturalists of his time'.   T. A. B. CORLEY

Sources *The Times* (15 Dec 1913) · *The Times* (31 Jan 1914) · *Berkshire Chronicle* (19 Dec 1913) · *Journal of the Royal Agricultural Society of England*, 75 (1914), 232 · *Nature*, 92 (1913–14), 456 · H. Bashford, *Lodgings for twelve* (1935) · private information (1927) · *WWW*, 1897–1915 · *CGPLA Eng. & Wales* (1914) · DNB
Archives U. Reading, Rural History Centre
Likenesses H. T. Wells, portrait, oils, exh. RA 1900, priv. coll. [*see illus.*]
Wealth at death £137,086 16s. 4d.: probate, 4 Feb 1914, *CGPLA Eng. & Wales*

Sutton [Lexinton], **Oliver** (c.1219–1299), bishop of Lincoln, was born into a family of small landowners taking its name from Sutton-on-Trent in Nottinghamshire. He was probably the son of Rowland Sutton, a minor royal servant, and Elizabeth of Lexinton, whose four brothers—Henry (d. 1258), Stephen of *Lexinton (d. 1258), Robert of *Lexinton (d. 1250), and John of *Lexinton (d. 1257)—all attained eminence in the service of church and crown. Oliver in his youth sometimes used the surname Lexinton, and may have been identical with the Oliver of Lexinton recorded as a canon of Lincoln in 1259. He and his brother Stephen entered the church, and the course of his ecclesiastical career suggests that he was born about 1219. It is clear that he spent much of his early life at the University of Oxford, where he became a regent master and rented his own hall of residence, called Deep Hall. By 1244 he held the living of Shelford, but he was still then teaching at Oxford. After 1270 he seems to have been drawn

back to Lincoln, where he obtained the prebend of Milton Manor, and in 1275 he was elected dean of the cathedral. In 1280, after the death of Richard of Gravesend, he was unanimously elected bishop.

Sutton was an excellent bishop—just, conscientious, and deeply devoted to his diocese, which he hardly ever left except when summoned to convocation or parliament. Throughout his life he was thorough and hard-working in his visitations, and ceased to travel round his very large diocese a fortnight only before his death. Although after 1297 his health was beginning to fail, he did not delegate his ordinations until the spring of 1299, and after he became bishop he never held office in the royal household or left England, though he maintained a permanent proctor at the papal curia. He was consecrated by Archbishop Pecham (d. 1292) on 19 May 1280. A month later there took place the greatest public ceremony of his episcopate, the translation of St Hugh to a new shrine at the east end of the cathedral, in the presence of all the notable people of England, headed by Edward I himself. In December 1290 Sutton officiated at the funeral of Queen Eleanor, and he was later appointed a papal judge-delegate in the matrimonial dispute between Edmund, earl of Cornwall (d. 1300), the king's cousin, and his wife, Margaret de Clare. In 1291 he served as a collector of the crusading tenth granted to Edward I—no crusade took place, but the king still took the money raised. In 1294 he took a leading part in opposing Edward I's demand for a war tax of a half of all clerical temporalities. But his suggestion that the clergy should offer one fifth of their temporalities in return for the repeal of the Statute of Mortmain (1279) seems to have pleased nobody. Two years later he followed Archbishop Winchelsey (d. 1313) in resisting royal demands for a clerical subsidy. As a result his temporalities were confiscated in 1297. But Sutton was now an elderly man, and very well liked in his diocese, and against the bishop's own will his friends were able to negotiate with the sheriff, who seized the appropriate amount of money and restored all the rest.

Sutton was remembered as a notable benefactor to his cathedral, and his relations with the canons were usually extremely friendly—he raised their daily commons from 8 to 12 pence, supplied a suitable collegiate house for the vicars-choral, charging his executors to finish building their kitchen and hall, and made extra provision for the choirboys. In his relations with Oxford University his attitude was that of a thoroughly benevolent conservative at a time when the chancellor and regent masters were intent on establishing their independence from diocesan control. In 1296 he supported the university's appeal to the pope for the *jus ubique docendi* which gave universal recognition to its degrees. But disputes arose from his determination to retain his rights as diocesan, especially with regard to appointments to the office of chancellor, the conduct of visitations, and appellate jurisdiction over the chancellor's court. In 1281, for instance, his efforts to make a formal visitation of the university met with determined resistance. Sutton complained that he had been treated 'injuriously and contemptuously' (Salter, 1.105), but he never managed to carry out a successful visitation, though he continued to try. Nevertheless he remained genuinely fond of Oxford, and when he confirmed Dervorguilla de Balliol's charter founding Balliol College, he praised it as 'a deed which redounds to the praise of God … and the honour of the said university' (Hill, 4.94–5).

As a diocesan Sutton showed himself to be especially careful, just, and humane. The letters in the surviving memoranda of his register give a clear impression of his work and personality. He was particularly careful to check the records of the elections of heads of religious houses, insisting on strict conformity to the proper forms; if there were any doubt, he quashed the election and appointed the candidate himself. He was also careful in following up cases of neglect or mismanagement in parish churches. Before licensing a private chapel or chantry he always investigated the relevant details, and he took great care in issuing testimonials and dispensations. He seems to have been personally concerned with his clergy, and showed especial kindness in appointing suitable coadjutors for those who were aged or ill. And he was no less conscientious in dealing with the affairs of the laity. Sutton's biographer and registrar, John *Schalby (d. 1333), who worked closely with him for nineteen years, praised Sutton as a man particularly charitable towards the poor, and careful of the welfare of the serfs on his estates, and quoted his confessor as saying, after the bishop's death, 'I cannot deny that he was a man most just, most steadfast and most pure' (*Book of John de Schalby*, 161). Oliver Sutton died peacefully, at a ripe old age, at his manor of Nettleham, on 13 November 1299, while his household clergy were singing matins in his room. On 21 November he was buried in his cathedral, his body being carried in by a company of the leading citizens. With him were laid his chalice and paten, together with his pastoral staff, which was carved with maple leaves and gilded. He wore his episcopal ring of gold set with rock crystal. He had already arranged for a perpetual chantry to be set up in his memory, and had left precise and highly characteristic instructions as to how it was to be organized and financed. One of the first acts of his successor, Bishop John Dalderby (d. 1320), was to issue an indulgence of forty days to all who should visit the tomb of Bishop Sutton and pray for his soul.

ROSALIND HILL

Sources R. M. T. Hill, ed., *The rolls and register of Bishop Oliver Sutton*, 8 vols., Lincoln RS, 39, 43, 48, 52, 60, 64, 69, 76 (1948–86) • John de Schalby, 'Lives of the bishops of Lincoln', *Gir. Camb. opera*, 7.193–216, esp. 208–12 • *Fasti Angl., 1066–1300*, [Lincoln] • *CPR, 1272–1307* • C. J. Holdsworth, ed., *Rufford charters*, 1, Thoroton Society Record Series, 29 (1972) • *The chronicle of Walter of Guisborough*, ed. H. Rothwell, CS, 3rd ser., 89 (1957) • *The book of John de Schalby: canon of Lincoln, 1299–1333, concerning the bishops of Lincoln and their acts*, trans. J. H. Srawley, another edn (1966) • W. Stubbs, ed., *Chronicles of the reigns of Edward I and Edward II*, 2 vols., Rolls Series, 76 (1882–3) • *Ann. mon.* • H. E. Salter, ed., *Mediaeval archives of the University of Oxford*, 1, OHS, 70 (1920), 105

Sutton, Sir Richard (c.1460–1524), college head, was born at Sutton, Cheshire, the younger son of Sir William Sutton, a wealthy landowner and master of the hospital at Burton Lazars, Leicestershire. Very little is known about his early life. He may have been educated at Macclesfield grammar school: in his will he asked for his obit to be commemorated there with *dirige* and masses. Probably from school he was sent to London to study at the inns of court. Certainly, by the end of the 1480s he was established in the city as a lawyer and a member of the Inner Temple. Sutton remained a leading figure in this community for almost fifty years. He was seven times governor of his inn between 1508 and 1522, and also chief governor from 1519 to 1520. Early in his career Sutton entered the service of the crown. From 1497 he was a judge in the court of requests, and in 1498 he was appointed legal assessor to the privy council. There is a tradition that he also became a member of Henry VII's council, but his name does not appear in any of the surviving conciliar records.

It was during this period that Sutton first formed the intention of founding a college at Oxford. Probably it was his involvement with the council that brought him together with his co-founder, William Smith, bishop of Lincoln, who was also a councillor. Before 1509 the pair had entered into a formal partnership. Sutton was to fund the project, acquiring a site and providing property for the endowment, while Smith was to consider the constitution of the college and devise its statutes. On 20 October 1508 Sutton acquired the lease of Brasenose Hall in School Street, Oxford, from the master and fellows of University College, to be used as the basis for the new college. There were few vacant sites in the overcrowded city, but Sutton's decision also reflected a personal connection with Brasenose Hall. It appears that several of his kinsmen had been members of the hall: a William Sutton was cautioner there in 1467 and 1483, and three other Suttons were among its membership when he acquired the lease in 1508. In June 1509 Sutton acquired a quarry at Headington to provide stone for the college, although the building may not have progressed far before he and Bishop Smith secured a charter of foundation from Henry VIII on 15 January 1512. Meanwhile he also began to transfer the income of some of his own estates to the college and to purchase new properties in Berkshire, Hampshire, Oxford, and the city of London to form part of its endowment.

Sutton was a successful and wealthy lawyer, but he was also a man of conspicuous piety and in the latter part of his career he diverted much of his energy towards his devotional interests. In the early stages of the work he attempted to recast the college at Oxford as a monastic foundation, but was prevented by a hostile Bishop Smith. Nevertheless, several of his grants of property to the college were made conditional on the performance of daily services by the principal and fellows, supported by a whole host of stipendiary priests and choristers.

In 1513 Sutton was appointed steward of Syon Abbey, Middlesex, and within a few years he had made the Bridgettine community his permanent residence. He became an intimate both of the abbess and of the scholar priest John Fewterer, and in his will provided for a priest to be employed there to teach girls intending to enter the nunnery. In 1519 he funded the publication of the *Orchard of*

Syon, an English devotional text based on the revelations of Catherine of Siena. According to the prologue, Sutton had discovered the manuscript of the text himself 'in a corner by it selfe' and had supervised the edition 'wyllynge … it shold come to lyghte that many relygous and devoute soules myght be releved and have comforte'. He also acquired several devotional books of his own at this time, among them a missal printed on vellum which includes a miniature of himself, depicted as an elderly man, kneeling in prayer and saying, 'of your charitie pray for the soule of Rycharde Sutton, the squier stuerd of Syon, Jhesus a mercy upon me'.

Sutton none the less remained a public figure of some importance. He was knighted, presumably for his political service, at an unknown date between 1519 and 1523. He also continued to be closely involved with Brasenose College, especially after the death of Bishop Smith in 1514. He acquired further estates and secured the benefactions of others, including Elizabeth Morley, a wealthy London gentlewoman. In 1522 Sutton also completed a revision of Smith's statutes at the request of the principal and fellows, presenting them at Syon to a deputation led by the bursar.

Sutton died in the summer of 1524. He made his will on 16 March and it was proved on 7 November. Although he provided for his burial at the Temple Church, it probably actually took place at Syon. He requested that his tombstone be inscribed with the Marian anthem 'Sub tuam protectionem confidimus'. He made no bequests to Brasenose College in his will except for a small legacy of 40s. to his nephew who was studying there.

JAMES G. CLARK

Sources R. Churton, *The lives of William Smyth, bishop of Lincoln and Sir Richard Sutton, knight, founders of Brasen Nose College* (1800) · [F. Madan], ed., *Brasenose College quatercentenary monographs*, 2 vols. in 3, OHS, 52–4 (1909) · VCH *Oxfordshire*, vol. 3 · PRO, PROB 11/21, fols. 209v–210v · F. A. Inderwick and R. A. Roberts, eds., *A calendar of the Inner Temple records*, 1 (1896) · PRO, Reg. 215.134

Likenesses stained-glass window, 1500–40, Brasenose College, Oxford · stone bust, *c.*1518, Brasenose College, Oxford · manuscript portrait, *c.*1520, Brasenose College, Oxford · oils, 1600–40, Brasenose College, Oxford · J. Faber senior, mezzotint (after unknown artist), BM, NPG · engraving, repro. in Churton, *Lives*

Sutton, Sir Richard, second baronet (1798–1855), sportsman, the only child of John Sutton (1770–1801) and his wife, Sophia Frances (*d.* 1844), daughter of Charles Chaplin, was born at Brant Broughton, Lincolnshire, on 16 December 1798. At his father's death he became heir to his grandfather, Sir Richard Sutton, who was created the first baronet in 1772, on retiring from the office of under-secretary of state. In 1802, at the age of four, Sutton succeeded his grandfather in the title and estates; the latter's enormous wealth, which accumulated during his long minority, made him one of the richest men in England, possessing extensive estates in Nottinghamshire, Norfolk, and Leicestershire as well as a large part of Mayfair, London's most expensive district. Sutton was educated at Westminster School (1812–13) and at Trinity College, Cambridge, where he matriculated in 1816, graduating MA in

1818. The day after he came of age, he married at St Peter's, Eastgate, Lincoln, on 17 December 1819, Mary Elizabeth (*d.* 1842), the daughter of Benjamin Burton of Burton Hall, co. Carlow, Ireland. They had seven sons and four daughters.

Like many men who inherited wealth at an early age, Sutton devoted himself to field sports. He soon decided that the family seat of Norwood Hall, Nottinghamshire, was unsuitable for a sporting base, and so he took Sudbrooke Hall, Lincolnshire, for a hunting residence, and Weeting Hall in Norfolk as a shooting box. He bought three neighbouring estates in Norfolk to ensure that nothing would interfere with the breeding and preservation of his game birds. A keen and successful shot, he rented large moors in Aberdeenshire for grouse-shooting and deer-stalking. Fox-hunting was his real passion. In 1822 he bought his first pack of foxhounds and succeeded Thomas Assheton Smith as master of the Burton hunt, in Lincolnshire, formerly the territory of his great friend George Osbaldeston. After a serious accident while hunting, Sutton moved to Lincoln for some time and there entertained so lavishly that he had a noticeable effect on the town's economy. He hunted the Burton country on six days each week in the season, until 1842, when he took the Cottesmore hunt in Rutland, where he stayed in great style for five seasons; he eventually departed in disgust, however, because the local farmers preserved game birds to the detriment of foxes.

In 1847 Sutton took over the prestigious Quorn hunt, and purchased Quorn Hall for £12,000; here he kept seventy-nine couples of hounds and a stud of seventy-eight hunters. He added the former Donington hunt country to his Quorn territory in order to reinstate the Quorn country to the area that Hugo Meynell had hunted in the late eighteenth century. There was no subscription taken for the expenses of the Quorn while he was the master, and he was generous enough to finance the Billesdon hunt from 1853 for his second son, Richard. It is estimated that he spent £300,000 on hunting during his lifetime. The advent of the railway made it possible for him to be one of the first people to travel from London to hunt in Leicestershire, and return to town the same day.

A good rider who liked difficult horses, even though he had several bad accidents, Sutton was also a talented flautist and read widely. He had no interest in politics, although he was asked to stand for parliament. He died suddenly, of angina pectoris, on 14 November 1855 at his London residence, Cambridge House, 94 Piccadilly, and was buried at Linford, Nottinghamshire, on 21 November. At auction his stud of horses was sold for £7300 and his seventy couples of hounds raised £1890.

IRIS M. MIDDLETON

Sources Burke, *Peerage* · GM, 2nd ser., 45 (1856), 80–82 · ILN (17 Nov 1855) · *The Times* (15 Nov 1855) · DNB · Venn, *Alum. Cant.* · *Old Westminsters*, 2.897 · *Annual Register* (1855) · *The Field* (24 Nov 1855) · *Leicester Journal* (16 Nov 1855) · VCH *Leicestershire*, 3.271–4 · will, 12 Dec 1855, PRO

Archives Notts. Arch., letter-book

Likenesses Graves, engraving (after portrait by F. Grant), repro. in ILN, 612

Sutton, Robert, first Baron Lexington (1594–1668), royalist nobleman, the eldest son of Sir William Sutton (*c*.1560–1611) of Averham, Nottinghamshire, and his wife, Susan, daughter of Thomas Cony of Basingthorpe, Lincolnshire, was born at Averham, on 21 December 1594. Sutton's family had acquired the manor of Averham in the thirteenth century by marriage to the daughter and heir of Lexington. His father was an Elizabethan courtier. Sutton attended Trinity College, Cambridge, from 1611 but did not graduate. He inherited an estate of about 2000 acres in rich farming country, and according to Thoroton, 'very much increased his patrimony' (*Thoroton's History*, 3.112). By 1640 he also had five smaller manors, and an income of £1700 a year. He was an active JP from 1627 to 1641, and a deputy lieutenant by 1638. His election as shire MP in 1624 and 1640 confirmed his place among the Nottinghamshire élite.

Sutton married three times. On 14 April 1616 he married Elizabeth Manners, daughter of Sir George Manners of Haddon Hall and sister of John *Manners, eighth earl of Rutland. His second marriage (after 16 April 1635) was to Anne, Lady Browne, daughter of Sir Guy Palmes of Lindley, Yorkshire, and widow of Sir Thomas Browne, baronet, of Walcott, Northamptonshire. His third took place after the Restoration, on 21 February 1661, when he married Mary St Leger (*d.* 1669), daughter of Sir Anthony St Leger, warden of the mint.

At the beginning of the Long Parliament Sutton sat on the committee to investigate ship money, and was prominent in offering security for loans to settle the war with Scotland. But as tensions grew between parliament and monarch, Sutton (like most Nottinghamshire gentry) favoured the king, though he found it difficult to assert this position against vigorous parliamentarian elements in the county and in London. On 15 December 1641 fellow MPs resisted his attempt to introduce a Nottinghamshire petition defending the church establishment against root and branch reform. He managed to present the petition but it was not actually read. The political aspect of his royalism appeared in the open letter which he endorsed in July 1642, with other leading Nottinghamshire landowners, rejecting parliament's claim to make law on its own authority, particularly in respect of the Militia Ordinance. He was suspended from parliament in September 1642.

Sutton executed the commission of array, and when war began joined the royalist garrison at Newark, near his estate. Although he was never in arms his contribution was vital, especially in underwriting the civic loan which sustained the garrison. He was also the channel of communication between Newark-on-Trent and the royalist headquarters at Oxford. In March 1644 he helped to arrange Prince Rupert's march to relieve the garrison. In November 1645 he was rewarded with the barony of Lexington (or Lexinton) of Averham (or Aram).

Lexington negotiated the surrender of Newark in April 1646. He then fell into the hands of General Fairfax, and subscribed the covenant to appease his captors. He compounded for his estates at the heavy fine of £5000. After many problems the estate was eventually cleared in June 1655. But later that year he found himself imprisoned for the debts he had incurred in paying the fine. He petitioned Cromwell to excuse him the decimation tax, claiming that he had alienated most of his estates, and his income was much reduced. Major-General Whalley advised against leniency, claiming that Sutton had shown none himself: 'He is in this country termed the devil of Newark, he exercised more cruelty than any, nay than all of that garrison against the parliament's soldiers when they fell into his power' (Thurloe, *State papers*, 4.364). Lexington's appeal was apparently turned down.

In the early stages of the Restoration Lexington exerted a moderating influence as one of the eminent royalists who publicly disclaimed any idea of revenge. But he then persistently sought legislation through the Lords to get the Newark loan repaid out of the estates of the Nottinghamshire parliamentarian John Hutchinson. This was rejected by the Commons. The loan was finally repaid by the Treasury in 1664.

Lexington died 'full of years' (Sutton, 3) on 11 October 1668 and was buried at Averham beside his second wife. In his will he reaffirmed his devotion to the episcopal establishment: 'which I look of as the most exact copy of the primitive church of all the churches of the world' (PRO, PROB 11/331, sig. 154). Lexington and his third wife had a son, Robert *Sutton, second Baron Lexington, and a daughter, Bridget. Other children who had died before, 'all my little ones', were to be set on the tomb which he ordered to be built for himself and his three wives (PRO, PROB 11/331, sig. 154). His widow died at Paris of a fever during the September following his death and was buried beside him.

GEORGE YERBY

Sources *Thoroton's history of Nottinghamshire*, ed. J. Throsby, 3 vols. (1797) · Thurloe, *State papers*, vol. 4 · L. Hutchinson, *Memoirs of the life of Colonel Hutchinson*, ed. J. Sutherland (1973) · A. C. Wood, *Nottinghamshire in the civil war* (1937) · H. M. Sutton, ed., *The Lexington papers* (1851) · Keeler, *Long Parliament* · *The journal of Sir Simonds D'Ewes from the beginning of the Long Parliament to the opening of the trial of the earl of Strafford*, ed. W. Notestein (1923) · *The journal of Sir Simonds D'Ewes from the first recess of the Long Parliament to the withdrawal of King Charles from London*, ed. W. H. Coates (1942) · G. Holles, *Memorials of the Holles family, 1493–1656*, ed. A. C. Wood, CS, 3rd ser., 55 (1937) · C. Brown, *Annals of Newark-upon-Trent* (1879) · H. H. Copnall, ed., *Nottingham county records* (1915) · Venn, *Alum. Cant.* · K. Feiling, *A history of the tory party, 1640–1714* (1924) · *CSP dom., 1642–88* · *JHC*, 1–5 (1547–1648) · GEC, *Peerage*, new edn, vol. 2 · PRO, PROB 11/331 · *Report on the manuscripts of the late Reginald Rawdon Hastings*, 4 vols., HMC, 78 (1928–47), vol. 2 · *The manuscripts of his grace the duke of Rutland*, 4 vols., HMC, 24 (1888–1905), vol. 2 · M. A. E. Green, ed., *Calendar of the proceedings of the committee for compounding … 1643–1660*, 5 vols., PRO (1889–92)

Sutton, Robert, second Baron Lexington (1661–1723), diplomatist, was born at Averham Park, near Newark, Nottinghamshire, the only son of Robert *Sutton, first Baron Lexington (1594–1668), and his third wife, Mary (*d.* 1669), the daughter of Sir Anthony St Leger. He succeeded as second baron while still a child, in October 1668, and in the following year his mother died. He held an army commission, which he resigned at the time of the *Godden v. Hales* case in June 1686. In the revolution of 1688 Lexington supported the cause of William of Orange and endorsed his joint rule with Mary, behaving thereafter as a court tory. In early June 1689 the king sent him on a mission to Brandenburg Prussia, where he stayed from July to November. He was charged with promoting a cordial alliance with the elector and securing closer co-operation among the northern allies. However, his task was made harder by William's unusual courtesies towards the envoy of the rival house of Hanover, and then by the breaking out of a damaging dispute over the succession to the duchy of Saxe-Lauenburgh, which threatened seriously to divide the allies. In June 1690 Lexington was made a commissioner of Admiralty. In mid-September 1691 he married Margaret (d. 1703), the daughter and heir of Sir Giles Hungerford of Coulston, Wiltshire, with a fortune said to be around £30,000.

Lexington was well regarded by the king, considered for high appointments, and on 17 March 1692 he was sworn of the privy council. In the rift between William and Princess Anne from 1692 to 1695 Lexington took the side of the king. In February 1693 he resigned his place as gentleman of horse to Anne's husband, the prince of Denmark, and a few days later was appointed William's great treasurer of the chamber, a place worth £2000 a year. In May he went as a volunteer to serve in Flanders. In early August he was sent by the king to Hamburg to join the Dutch pensionary Hop in mediating between the king of Denmark and the house of Lunenburg, which had seized the duchy of Saxe-Lauenburgh and fortified Ratzeburgh, on the Danish border. After many vexations a treaty to settle this destabilizing affair was signed, and Lexington left Hamburg in early October. Appointed a colonel of horse in January 1694, in early April he was named envoy-extraordinary to Vienna; he set off in late May and arrived in early December. Almost at once he displeased the king by making excessive claims for expenses. The Lexingtons' first child, William George, was born in Vienna in October 1697, and his godmother was the Electress Sophia of Hanover, with whom Lexington had corresponded since 1693. They remained on cordial terms until her death. Lexington was named as one of the commissaries in the negotiation of the treaty of Ryswick between May and September 1697, but to his great mortification he remained in Vienna until his final departure from his post in late December 1697. One colleague offered him advice that he may well have taken: 'Give me leave … to preach up to you patience, perseverance, and obedience; and remember we have to do with a Prince who will go his own way. Add a bottle to your ordinary dose' (George Stepney to Lexington, 30 Dec 1696 NS, Manners Sutton, 235). Lexington's own letters reveal a chronic kidney complaint: 'Since my last to you, I have been like to take a journey into t'other world by a fit of the stone; but, thank God, 'tis over, at least for this bout' (Lexington to William Blathwayt, 18 Dec 1697 NS, ibid., 324–5). Before quitting Vienna, he had made his cousin Sir Robert *Sutton (1671/2–1746) secretary of embassy, and left him in charge of affairs, though official recognition was not easily achieved. His patronage finally secured his cousin

the post of ambassador to Constantinople in December 1700.

Despite prolonged ill health, Lexington managed eventually to join the king in the Netherlands late in 1698. In June 1699 he was appointed a member of the council of trade and plantations, a post from which he was dismissed in May 1702 after the accession of Queen Anne. Though still often ill, he was a diligent member of the board, explored various schemes to promote industry and help the poor, and advised strongly against the Darien scheme as destructive to both trade and peace. Around this time he was also sinking trial coalmines on his Nottinghamshire property. His bedchamber post ended in 1702 with the death of King William, which he witnessed. In April the following year his wife, Margaret, died of breast cancer.

Lexington was out of public employment for most of Anne's reign, though one extant letter shows that he was exercising local patronage, despite a grave illness, during the winter of 1702–3. In 1710 he was one of the court-supporting tory lords who unexpectedly voted for Henry Sacheverell's acquittal. His next known public employment came in September 1712, when (after a gap of ten years) he was appointed ambassador-extraordinary and plenipotentiary to Madrid, to negotiate a peace with Spain. Viscount Bolingbroke, his patron in the appointment, urged him to rely in all commercial matters upon Manuel Manasses Gilligan. Lexington arrived in Madrid on 18 October 1712, though stricken in health once more. He relied on Gilligan to deputize for him and incurred the queen's displeasure by keeping him in Madrid when Gilligan's presence in Britain was 'of indispensable necessity' (Bolingbroke to Lexington, 7, 12 May, 5 July 1713, BL, Add. MS 46545, fols. 5–6, 11, 15). Pleading for a speedy recall, Lexington received the queen's formal revocation of his embassy on 13 July 1713, but the negotiations stretched on. He angered Anne by meekly forwarding to the duke of Savoy a Spanish treaty draft attempting to deny him Sicily: he should have torn it up, said Bolingbroke, in the presence of the Spanish ministers.

Autumn found Lexington still in Madrid and, as Bolingbroke heard, still 'afflicted with ye distemper which you have complain'd of ever since you was in Spain' (Bolingbroke to Lexington, 16 Sept 1713, BL, Add. MS 46545, fol. 43r). A greater blow had fallen on him in August, when his eldest child, William, fifteen years old, died in Madrid. As protestant graves in that city were often desecrated, William's body was shipped home, concealed in a bale of cloth, and interred with his mother in the family tomb at Kelham, the parish adjoining Averham and later the family's principal seat. Lexington eventually went home only in December 1713.

Two years later he was condemned by the committee of secrecy chaired by Robert Walpole for feebly surrendering the national interest in his negotiations and for abandoning Britain's Catalan allies, but no specific charges were brought against him.

Lexington was an able diplomatist without achieving anything particularly striking, and he never quite stood in the front rank of politics. John Macky described him as 'of good understanding, and very capable to be in the ministry; a well-bred gentleman and an agreeable companion, handsome, of a brown complexion' (*Memoirs of the Secret Services*, 101). He had important connections, including the powerful duke of Shrewsbury, and his failure to reach great office may have been due partly to his persistent bouts of the stone, so familiar to his friends. Shrewsbury, writing from Paris, sent compliments from his wife, who, 'to shew herself truly your cousin, has never had her health since she left England' (Shrewsbury to Lexington, 10 April 1713 NS, BL, Add. MS 46545, fol. 185r). Though Lexington's public career ended on his return from Madrid, his electoral influence was still considerable and brought him personal letters from both the duke of Newcastle and the king in the election year of 1722. He was offered some new honour (unspecified in the surviving letters) but refused it, gratefully but firmly: 'for indeed my Lord I did not think it would look well in the Eye of the World to be seeking new honours, when I am incapacitated to injoy even those that I have' (Lexington to Newcastle, 24 May 1722, BL, Add. MS 32686, fol. 217r). Lexington died on 19 September 1723 at Averham Park and was buried in St Wilfred's Church, Kelham, where classical marble effigies of him and his wife lie, unusually, back to back. His second child, Eleanora Margaretta, had died in 1715, and his estates were devised to his surviving daughter, Bridget, the wife of John Manners, third duke of Rutland. After her death in 1734 the estate passed to her second son, Lord Robert Manners, on condition that he adopt the name and arms of Sutton.   PHILIP WOODFINE

Sources DNB · N. Luttrell, *A brief historical relation of state affairs from September 1678 to April 1714*, 6 vols. (1857) · PRO, SP 104/194 · BL, Add. MSS 46557, 15572, 46525, 28900, 46538, 46542, 46545, 32686 · H. Manners Sutton, ed., *The Lexington papers, or, Some account of the courts of London and Vienna at the conclusion of the seventeenth century* (1851) · P. de Rapin-Thoyras, *The history of England*, 2nd edn, 4 vols. (1732–47) [with additional notes by N. Tindal] · Hunt. L., Huntington MS 44710 · *Memoirs of the secret services of John Macky*, ed. A. R. (1733) · *White's directory of Nottinghamshire* (1853) · B. Burke, *A genealogical history of the dormant, abeyant, forfeited and extinct peerages of the British empire*, new edn (1883) · GEC, *Peerage* · D. B. Horn, ed., *British diplomatic representatives, 1689–1789*, CS, 3rd ser., 46 (1932) · HoP, *Commons, 1715–54*

Archives BL, corresp. and papers, Add. MSS 46525–46559, 53816; Egerton MS 929 · Yale U., Beinecke L., diplomatic corresp. | BL, letters to William Blathwayt, Add. MS 9736 · BL, letters to Lord Carteret, Add. MS 22521 · BL, letters to John Ellis, Add. MSS 28882–28903 · BL, letters to George Stepney, Add. MS 7075 · CKS, corresp. with Alexander Stanhope · CKS, corresp. with Lord Stanhope · U. Nott. L., letters to earl of Portland

Likenesses W. Palmer, tomb effigy (with his wife), St Wilfred's Church, Kelham, Nottinghamshire

Sutton, Sir Robert (1671/2–1746), diplomatist and politician, was the elder son of Robert Sutton of Averham, Nottinghamshire, and his wife, Katherine, the daughter of the Revd William Sherborne of Pembridge, Herefordshire. He went to Trinity College, Oxford, in 1688 and the Middle Temple in 1691, the year in which he inherited property upon his father's death. Far from wealthy, he took deacon's orders and became chaplain to his cousin Robert Sutton, second Baron Lexington, the new ambassador to Vienna in 1694.

Sutton abandoned the church on being appointed secretary to the embassy at Vienna in 1697. As secretary and later resident he was responsible for English representation at Vienna in 1697–1700, although William III placed more reliance on his Dutch counterpart. Thanks to Lexington's influence, Sutton was appointed ambassador at Constantinople in December 1700. Having been knighted in 1701, he reached Constantinople in early 1702 and remained there until 1717. Sutton served with distinction: his assessment of Turkish policy was usually correct, and he knew Italian and Latin, the crucial languages in Constantinople.

In 1717 Sutton was appointed, with Abraham Stanyan, joint mediator at the Austro-Turkish peace congress at Passarowitz, a task he discharged ably the following year and for which he was well rewarded. His last diplomatic posting was as ambassador and plenipotentiary in Paris. He was appointed in April 1720, but had to be threatened with dismissal by James Craggs, the secretary of state, before he would go. He was in Paris from June 1720 until November 1721, but the ministry had little confidence in him and appointed first John, second Baron Carteret (later Earl Granville), as ambassador-extraordinary in January 1721, a post he did not take up, and second Sir Luke Schaub as ambassador the following month. Schaub had already served in Paris, and he acted jointly with Sutton from March 1721 until the latter's departure.

Aside from the fact that he was considered a very good ombre player, opinions of Sutton varied considerably. Described to the French government in April 1720 as very gallant, and able in both diplomacy and the sciences, he was nevertheless criticized by one of George I's diplomats, St Saphorin, for being too inclined to sharp practice.

Sutton had become wealthy as a result of his diplomatic career, and he was one of the successful whig candidates in the very expensive Nottinghamshire election in April 1722, after which he was sworn of the privy council. He acquired estates in Lincolnshire and Nottinghamshire, worth nearly £5000 a year, and houses in Grosvenor Square, London, and at Broughton, Lincolnshire. In 1724 he married Judith, the daughter of Benjamin Tichborne and the widow of Charles Spencer, third earl of Sunderland. Two sons survived infancy. Sutton was appointed KCB in 1725 and moved the address in 1726, the same year he became sub-governor of the Royal African Company.

In 1725 Sutton became a member of the committee of management of the Charitable Corporation. Active in increasing the authorized capital of this corporation, he made money by insider dealing in its shares and was involved in the scandal following disclosures of extensive frauds in 1732, in which he himself lost severely. He was expelled from the Commons as a result of giving false statements, but was returned unopposed in 1734 for Great Grimsby, a venal borough that had elected other disreputable financiers and in which Sutton owned considerable property. He remained MP until 1741, and did not stand again. He played no further part in politics or business, having ceased his connection with the African Company in 1732, and died on 13 August 1746.

JEREMY BLACK, rev.

Sources HoP, *Commons, 1715–54* · H. A. C. Sturgess, ed., *Register of admissions to the Honourable Society of the Middle Temple, from the fifteenth century to the year 1944*, 3 vols. (1949) · Foster, *Alum. Oxon.* · *The despatches of Sir Robert Sutton, ambassador in Constantinople, 1710–1714*, ed. A. N. Kurat (1953)
Archives BL, letters to Lord Carteret, Add. MSS 22521–22522 · BL, letters to John Ellis, Add. MSS 28898–28916, *passim* · NA Scot., letters to Lord Carteret · PRO, letters to Lord Carteret
Wealth at death house in Grosvenor Square, London; estates in Broughton, Lincolnshire and Nottinghamshire

Sutton, Robert (*bap.* **1708**, *d.* **1788**), surgeon, apothecary, and smallpox inoculator, was baptized in Kenton, Suffolk, on 12 February 1708, the son of Robert Sutton, gentleman. He was apprenticed in September 1726 to John Turner of Debenham, Suffolk, apothecary. In October 1731, shortly after completing his apprenticeship, he married Sarah Barker of Debenham. The first of their eight sons, Robert, was born in 1732 and in the same year Sutton returned to Kenton to start his own practice as surgeon and apothecary. There were also three daughters of the marriage.

Sutton then worked for many years as a country doctor, during which time his son Robert nearly died from smallpox inoculation performed by a 'surgeon of his acquaintance'. This experience determined Sutton 'to dedicate his thoughts solely to the Small-pox; to … investigate a means whereby … that distemper might be lessened and danger, if possible, prevented by inoculation'. Following a lengthy period of study he evolved a plan for inoculation. This he tested on a single patient in 1755. The results were favourable and there began a series of trials which 'convinced him that he had made some valuable discoveries'.

In the spring of 1757 Sutton opened an inoculation house staffed by nurses where patients stayed for one month. So successful was this venture that two further houses were opened in September. A fourth house was opened in the summer of 1758. By the autumn of 1760 he had agents in sixteen towns and villages in Suffolk, south Norfolk, and north-east Essex. In 1761, probably as the result of competition from a rival inoculator, Sutton reduced his top fee from 7 to 5 guineas, with easier terms 'for the … lower Class of People'.

By December 1761 the observations and modifications of several years' practical experience led Sutton to believe he had perfected his method. Earlier English inoculators had made deep cuts with the lancet and inserted large amounts of material from mature smallpox pustules, believing that protection was not obtainable unless the patient suffered a pronounced smallpox attack. As a later inoculator pointed out, 'little difference was perceived between the natural Smallpox, and that conveyed by inoculation'. This was rejected by Sutton, who reverted to the original Graeco-Turkish technique of superficial scarification using small amounts of lymph. Even more important was his use of lymph taken from a smallpox pustule in its early stage of development, rather than

from a mature pustule which was likely to be contaminated with a variety of organisms. The severity of symptoms in inoculees was thereby much reduced and the risk of a healthy patient's dying almost eliminated. In brief, the Suttonian method comprised treatment which was almost painless and relatively mild in its effects, while the greatly decreased number of pustules lessened disfigurement.

In the nine months from December 1761 to September 1762 Sutton performed a further 365 inoculations, all successfully. In the autumn of 1762 two inoculation houses were opened in Barrow, near Bury St Edmunds, under the control of his son Robert. About the same time his second son, Daniel *Sutton, who had been working as an assistant to an Essex doctor, joined the practice, which was then at its zenith. A disagreement over patients' preparation and post-operational recovery regime resulted in Daniel's leaving his father in 1763 to set up on his own at Ingatestone, Essex. Thereafter Sutton was overshadowed by his ambitious, avaricious, and energetic second son, who was to amass a fortune by publicizing and exploiting the Suttonian method of inoculation. Sutton died in 1788 and was buried on 13 April in Thetford, Norfolk.

J. R. SMITH, rev.

Sources J. R. Smith, *The speckled monster* (1987)

Sutton, Thomas (*fl.* **1274–1300**), Dominican friar and theologian, was ordained deacon on 20 September 1274 at Blyth in the York diocese. He may have been a fellow of Merton College, Oxford, *c.*1270, and was certainly a member of the Dominican convent in Oxford, perhaps by *c.*1282. He had a long career in the university, graduating bachelor and then, *c.*1284, doctor of theology as well as master *c.*1290. He was licensed to hear confessions in the Lincoln diocese on 11 October 1300, and it is likely that he is the Thomas Sutton who preached in Oxford on 23 November 1292, and on 1 March and 24 May 1293. He was perhaps still living in 1315, but the date of his death and the place of his burial are not known.

Sutton was one of the foremost early exponents and defenders at the University of Oxford of the teaching of Thomas Aquinas, the Dominican philosopher and theologian. Aquinas had incorporated into his philosophy many Aristotelian features, such as the notion that human knowledge starts from sense perception rather than with a divine illumination of the human mind in which 'seminal reasons' are implanted. Also controversial at Oxford at this time was the question whether man, being both body and soul, has both a corporeal and a spiritual form: Aquinas taught that in every corporeal being there is one substantial form. In 1277 Robert Kilwardby (*d.* 1279), the archbishop of Canterbury, himself a Dominican friar and former master at Oxford University, condemned a range of Aristotelian theses as well as Aquinas's novel doctrine of the unicity of forms. This condemnation was renewed in 1284 by Archbishop John Pecham (*d.* 1292), a Franciscan friar and former master at Oxford who also excommunicated an English Dominican master, Richard Knapwell, in 1286. At this time and in this climate Thomas Sutton emerged as a keen student and follower of Thomas Aquinas and as a notable thinker among the group of English Dominican Thomists who flourished in the last quarter of the thirteenth century. The group included Robert Winchelsey (*d.* 1313), Simon of Faversham, and Robert Orford. Thomas Sutton also participated in the quarrels between the Friars Preacher and the Friars Minor over the issue of poverty.

Sutton's writings are difficult to identify and to date, and some have in the past been confused with writings of Thomas Aquinas. He apparently wrote a continuation of the unfinished commentary of Aquinas on Aristotle's *Perihermeneias*, as well as a continuation of Aquinas's commentary on Aristotle's *De generatione et corruptione*. Another confusion is possibly with a Thomas the Englishman, whose *Liber propugnatorius* (*c.*1311) contains an attack upon Duns Scotus (*d.* 1308), the Franciscan master, who taught at Oxford during the 1290s. Thomas Sutton wrote *De esse et essentia* (in support of Aquinas, and against Henri de Gand) and probably also *Quaestiones super sententias*. He wrote *Quodlibeta* (between 1291 and 1301), and treatises opposing the doctrine of the plurality of forms.

DAVID LUSCOMBE, *rev.*

Sources W. Senko, 'Un traité inconnu *De esse et essentia*', *Archives d'Histoire Doctrinale et Littéraire du Moyen Âge*, 27 (1960), 229–66 · T. Sutton, *Quodlibeta*, ed. M. Schmaus and M. Gonzalez-Haba, Bayerische Akademie der Wissenschaften, 2 (1969) · T. Sutton, *Quaestiones ordinariae*, ed. J. Schneider, Bayerische Akademie der Wissenschaften, 3 (1977) · F. Ehrle, 'Thomas de Sutton, sein Leben, seine *Quodlibet* und seine *Quaestiones disputatae*', *Festschrift für G. von Hertling* (1913), 426–50 · F. Pelster, 'Thomas von Sutton O. Pr., ein Oxforder Verteidiger der thomistischen Lehre', *Zeitschrift für katholische Theologie*, 46 (1922), 212–54, 361–402 · F. Pelster, 'Thomas von Sutton und das Correctorium *Quare detraxisti*', *Mélanges Auguste Pelzer* (1947), 441–66 · Emden, *Oxf.*, 3.182–5 · F. E. Kelley, ed., *Expositionis D. Thomae Aquinatis in libros Aristotelis de generatione et corruptione continuatio per Thomam de Sutona* (1976) · P. O. Lewry, 'Two continuators of Aquinas: Robertus de Vulgarbia and Thomas Sutton on the *Perihermeneias* of Aristotle', *Mediaeval Studies*, 43 (1981), 58–130

Sutton, Thomas (1532–1611), founder of the London Charterhouse, was born, according to the inscription on his tomb, in 1532 at Knaith, Lincolnshire. His father was Richard Sutton, clerk to the sheriff of Lincoln, his mother Elisabeth Mering of South Collingham, from a gentry family in Nottinghamshire. His father's origin is obscure. After Thomas Sutton's death, the College of Arms assigned to him the blazon of the Suttons of Burton by Lincoln, but neither his father nor he are recorded in their pedigrees. By his nuncupative will, dated 27 July 1558, Richard Sutton left his lease of the manor of Cockerington to his son Thomas and divided the rest of his property between his widow and his son.

Early career Thomas Sutton's career, until his thirty-seventh year, is undocumented. There is no evidence to support claims that he entered military service. According to Henry Holland's *Heröologia Anglica* (1620), the earliest and only reliable secondary source, Sutton, after being educated locally as a gentleman, entered the service first of Thomas Howard, fourth duke of Norfolk, and then of Ambrose Dudley, earl of Warwick, and, through him, of

Thomas Sutton (1532–1611), by Renold Elstrack

his brother Robert Dudley, earl of Leicester; it was when he was 'in the highest favour' with Warwick (who was master-general of the ordnance), that he was appointed master of the ordnance in the north and sent to Berwick (Holland, 128). Letters patent date his appointment to 28 February 1570.

Documentary evidence supports this account. On 12 November 1569 the earl and countess of Warwick gave their well-beloved servant Thomas Sutton a pension of £3 6*s.* 8*d.* out of their manor of Walkington, Yorkshire (afterwards converted into a lease of the manor), and in the same year Warwick was clearly the agent who persuaded Richard Cox, bishop of Ely and an old protégé of the Dudleys, to grant to Sutton leases of the manors of Hadstock and Littlebury, near Saffron Walden in Essex. These two manors, together with Balsham in Cambridgeshire, granted by the same bishop shortly afterwards, were to be the nucleus of Sutton's ultimately extensive landed property. Finally, it was the same three noblemen named by Holland—Norfolk, Warwick, and Leicester—who pressed for Sutton's appointment in the north and warranted his sufficiency. Although Howards and Dudleys, the two greatest dynasties under the Tudors, did not agree on much, they agreed that in the sudden crisis in the north Sutton was the man required.

That crisis, the rising of the northern earls, posed a threat which the crown's forces in the region, hampered by incompetence and corruption, were ill-prepared to meet. It was Sutton's task to repair the damage. He joined the army of the earl of Sussex at Darlington and accompanied it as it pursued the rebels retreating from Durham into Scotland. Then he applied himself to his duties. In this he showed himself, as in all matters of business, active and efficient. However, as a servant of the Dudleys, and now especially of the earl of Leicester, he was regarded with suspicion by Leicester's great rival at court, Lord Burghley. He was warmly defended by the marshal of Berwick, Sir William Drury, who, in a letter which Sutton himself carried to London, assured Burghley that:

> in this town there is nothing that appertaineth to his office of the Ordnance but is in such readiness, so good a case, from time to time so well repaired, and with so little charge to Her Majesty, as since my being here I have not known the like. (PRO, SP 59/19)

The same report, he added, was made from all the strongholds and forts of the north.

Burghley was not entirely reassured. In May 1573 he ordered that Sutton's clerk, but not Sutton himself, should accompany the English army sent into Scotland against Queen Mary's remaining supporters. But Sutton defied the order, and in Edinburgh was placed in command of one of the five 'mounts' or artillery batteries surrounding the besieged castle—a post of great honour. In a letter from Edinburgh defending his action he challenged Burghley to explain his distrust. Burghley accepted the *fait accompli*. He knew that Leicester was behind Sutton, and it was not an issue on which to challenge the queen's favourite. He did not answer Sutton but remained vigilant and critical.

Opportunities in the north The defeat of the uprising not only ended the political threat to the Elizabethan government: it also ended the old order in the north and opened economic opportunities to new men who were waiting to exploit them. In this context Sutton was able to serve not only the crown but also his patrons and himself. On his arrival in the north he established himself at Alnwick, in lodgings found for him by Sir John Forster, the warden of the middle marches, in the house of a widow, Agnes Inskip, *née* Armorer (d. before 1611). Alnwick was a convenient centre for Sutton, being mid-way between the English garrison at Berwick and the queen's storehouse of arms at Newcastle upon Tyne. Sutton's relations with Forster were close: in 1570 he aspired to marry Forster's daughter and wrote to Leicester seeking his support. The suit failed, and Sutton consoled himself in the arms of Mrs Inskip. They had a son, Roger Sutton, whom he recognized and sent to school in Alnwick: afterwards he disposed of him in the army.

Sutton's services to his patron in the north elude the record. He made several journeys to London, to wait on Leicester 'at the court'. It may well be, since copper was an essential ingredient in brass cannon, that he was involved in the affairs of the recently established Mines Royal Company whose copper mine on the lands of the rebel earls

had been one of their grievances. Leicester was an original and principal shareholder in the company, as was his cousin John Dudley, now of Stoke Newington, whose elder brother Richard Dudley of Yanwath, Westmorland, was the collector of the queen's tenth of the copper. In his will Sutton mentions incidentally that he had secured for Leicester a loan of £400 from Alderman Lionel Duckett, the chief English entrepreneur of the company, in order to export copper to Spain.

Sutton's reward for his services is better documented. When Bishop Richard Pilkington of Durham died in 1577, his see was offered to Richard Barnes, bishop of Carlisle, on condition that he undertook to lease the episcopal manors of Whickham and Gateshead to the queen for seventy-nine years. Behind this move lay the influence of Sutton's patron Leicester, picking up an abortive project devised by his father John Dudley, duke of Northumberland, in 1553. When Leicester had thus acquired the lease, he passed it on—not, as his father had done, to the expectant corporation of Newcastle, but to Thomas Sutton. It gave Sutton control of the richest coalfields in Europe.

Having secured the lease—'the Grand Lease' as it was called—Sutton evidently intended to exploit the coalmines himself. But to do this successfully he needed access to the export trade to London, which was available only to the freemen of Newcastle. He therefore applied for election and mobilized all the support and influence that he could. The Newcastle merchants, however, were in no mood to gratify him. Having seen a coveted prize snatched from them by an interloper, they closed ranks. Sutton's only known supporter among the aldermen was Robert Dudley of Chopwell—one of the clan. Undeterred, Sutton attempted to operate the mines outside the ring. But the difficulties proved insuperable, and after five years he decided to accept defeat. Having improved the value of his property by securing a new lease—this time for ninety-nine years—he sold it to the leaders of the merchant oligarchy and left the north for ever, riding south (as his servant later deposed) with two horse-loads of money.

Money and property Meanwhile Sutton had similarly improved his property in the south: the three manors leased from the bishop of Ely. Once again the influence of his powerful patrons was brought in. This time the pressure was applied on his behalf by Leicester's former tutor at Cambridge, now secretary of state, the humanist scholar Sir Thomas Wilson. Bishop Cox, as usual, complied; but unexpected opposition came from Andrew Perne, dean of Ely (also Sutton's parson at Balsham), who obstinately refused to countersign the new lease. Wilson had to send no less than seven letters of steadily rising acrimony and scarcely veiled menace before Perne's nerve broke and Sutton's twenty-one year lease of Hadstock and Littlebury, and afterwards of Balsham, were replaced by new leases for seventy-nine years. The leases were granted to Wilson and by him sold to Sutton.

After his arrival at Littlebury, Sutton's first recorded act was his marriage. His wife, like so much else in his career, was supplied by his patrons. She was Elizabeth (d. 1602), daughter of John Gardiner of Grove Place, Chalfont St

Giles, Buckinghamshire, and widow of Leicester's cousin John Dudley of Stoke Newington. This John Dudley, who had become rich in the earl's service, had died in 1580. Marriage to his widow, evidently 'brokered' by the countess of Warwick, brought Sutton a new fortune, for John Dudley had left half his estate to his wife and the other half to their young child, Anne; Sutton thus obtained possession of the first half and administration and profits, during Anne's minority, of the second. After his marriage, which took place on 17 September 1582, he moved from Littlebury to his wife's house at Stoke Newington. From here, and from a London house which he leased at 'Broken Wharf' on the Thames, he carried on the business which filled the rest of his life: the management of his lands and moneylending.

Moneylending at interest, though denounced by moralists as 'usury' and declared illegal under Edward VI, had been legalized, at interest of 10 per cent, in 1570. Naturally acquisitive and parsimonious, Sutton was never without surplus cash to invest, and while in the north he had lent money to fellow officials and local gentry. Now, in London, he found a well-established mechanism of lending, devised by London merchants mainly for their own commercial purposes. But although he used this mechanism, Sutton never was, or sought to be, a London merchant. As at Newcastle, he was an outsider, operating alone.

At the same time he made a radical change in his investment policy. Hitherto he had invested exclusively in leases of church lands which, once acquired, he had improved. From 1585 onwards he sought only freehold land, acquired by purchase or in redemption of debt from lay landlords. In 1597–1600 he was able, since the see of Ely was vacant, to complete the process by purchasing from the crown the fee simple of his original leases—which still had over fifty years to run—of Hadstock, Littlebury, and Balsham. The purpose of this switch was obvious. Leases are wasting assets; but he was thinking in long terms. He had decided to endow not a dynasty—he had no interest in his family—but a permanent charity: in fact a hospital and a school.

Laying charitable foundations 'Hospitals' (i.e. almshouses) and schools had often been casualties of the radical phase of the English Reformation, having been dissolved with the chantries on which they depended, but under Elizabeth many were replaced by new foundations on a more secular base. Leicester's hospital at Warwick, endowed by his will and erected by his brother in 1586–90, may have suggested the idea to Sutton, for it was at that time that he began his preparations. In 1594, by a revocable deed in gift, he assigned his lands in Essex—his newly acquired freehold lands—to trustees to erect a hospital on his estate of Hallingbury Bouchers, and in December 1595 he drafted a will (preserved among the Charterhouse manuscripts) leaving £3000 to build it. The same will, having provided separately for his wife, expressed the hope that, 'out of devotion to God and the poor and love to me', she might renounce her legal right to a third of his lands in favour of his hospital. Her death on 17 June 1602 spared her this choice. She was buried at Stoke Newington in the

monumental wall-tomb set up for them both by her first husband, John Dudley.

After his wife's death Sutton left Stoke Newington and bought a house in Hackney, now identified as the Tan House: the nearby Sutton House preserves his memory. For business he now used rooms in Fleet Street above a draper's shop. There he kept his 'great iron chest', so heavy with gold pieces that a visiting client feared that it would break through the floor into the shop below.

Meanwhile Sutton went on lending money and acquiring land—he bought manors in Lincolnshire, Essex, Cambridgeshire, and Lancashire, along with a whole string of manors from Lord Compton in Wiltshire. He always kept one manor in hand for his own summer residence. In 1608 he acquired the particularly desirable estate of Castle Camps, Cambridgeshire, formerly the property of the spendthrift eighteenth earl of Oxford. It cost him a great deal of trouble, for it was encumbered with debts and lawsuits; but it became, for his last years, his favourite residence, where he lived simply with few servants and few visitors. By this time his wealth, though inconspicuous, was legendary—he was always known simply as 'rich Sutton'—and there was speculation about its destiny; but when asked, his only answer was that he held it in trust for the poor.

Others had other plans for its disposal. One of them, Queen Elizabeth's 'merry godson' Sir John Harington, being eager to commend himself to the new Stuart dynasty, devised a plan whereby Sutton, in exchange for a peerage, would declare the duke of York, afterwards Charles I, his heir. The plot did not succeed. The contrast between Harington's jolly letter to the earl of Salisbury, warranting the success of his ingenious stratagem, and Sutton's indignant repudiation of it, shows how completely Harington had mistaken his man.

'Sutton's Hospital' Quickened, perhaps, by this episode, Sutton turned his thoughts to his hospital which, so far, he had done nothing to realize. By 1608 the huge estate which he had acquired since 1594 had become disproportionate to a provincial hospital, but time was short and he had no alternative site in view. To be secure, he needed a parliamentary statute; but the first parliament of James I, which had been sitting since March 1604, might now be dissolved any day; and could Sutton, at seventy-six, expect to see another? Almost miraculously, he triumphed over all these difficulties. He got his statute, carefully drafted, ready in time, and saw it through parliament shortly before the dissolution; and although there had been no time to change the location of the hospital—the statute still placed it at Hallingbury Bouchers—a loophole had been left for a last-minute relocation. In the statute Sutton's original manors of Hadstock and Littlebury were expressly omitted from the endowment of the hospital.

The reason for this omission soon became clear. Thomas Howard, earl of Suffolk, was a friend of Sutton and a borrower in the lean Elizabethan days. Now he was high in favour at James's court, and was rebuilding, more grandly than ever, his country seat of Audley End at Saffron Walden. In order to round off the estate, he coveted these neighbouring manors. Sutton, who must have known this, seized his chance: he offered to sell the two manors to Suffolk in exchange for Suffolk's town house, 'the Charterhouse', the dissolved Carthusian monastery in London. The deal was struck. On 9 March 1611 Sutton bought the Charterhouse for £13,000; then, on 23 June, since parliament was no longer sitting, he obtained letters patent transferring the projected hospital to the new site; and in his will, drawn up in October 1611, he left to Suffolk an option to buy the two manors for £10,000. Financially Suffolk did well by the bargain, but Sutton got what he wanted: a collegiate 'hospital', already built, on a grand scale, and in London.

By its statute Sutton's hospital was to be called the Hospital of King James (in order to ensure royal support); it was to have a board of powerful governors already nominated by Sutton; and he himself was to be the first master, with monarchical power: only after his death would the governors take over. In October 1611, however, he was taken ill. On 12 December he died. But on paper at least his hospital was secure.

As he lay in his bed in his house at Hackney, Sutton's chief concern was for his will, lest it fall into wrong hands, for there were many who would be disappointed by it. It was brought to him in a black bag, together with the keys of his 'great iron chest'. A meticulous document of twenty-three pages, it distributed a substantial sum to various charitable causes, remembered the poor and the highways in all his parishes and the children of personal benefactors long deceased. £300 was left to his heir-at-law, his nephew Simon Baxter; trivial sums to a few relations on his mother's side; to his son Roger nothing. All the residue, some £50,000, was added to the huge endowment of the hospital. Any legatee who presumed to challenge his legacy was to receive nothing. Sutton had the will read out to his servants, and to visiting friends, and made them witness it. On his last day he had the black bag secreted in his bed with him. After his death it was fished out and carried to the probate office.

When Sutton's will was published, it aroused astonished admiration. The new hospital dwarfed all the London charities of the past century. The protestant clergy were jubilant: they hailed Sutton as a 'hero', a 'saint', 'the right Phoenix of charity', his foundation as 'the greatest gift that ever was given in England' (*The Charterhouse*, ESTC 5056); this surely, they said, would stop the mouths of the papists who declared protestantism the enemy of charity. For Sutton's body, lying embalmed in his house at Hackney, a magnificent funeral was prepared, to take place on 28 May. For its final resting place a huge monumental tomb was later erected in the chapel of the Charterhouse.

Sutton's relatives were less enthusiastic. Simon Baxter, spurning his legacy of £300, attempted to seize the Charterhouse by force. Repelled by the porter, he appealed to the king. Sir Francis Bacon, as solicitor-general, advised the king to decide the matter in council and to use Baxter's case to remodel 'this rude mass and chaos of a good deed' on Baconian principles (Spedding, 250). The case was referred to the courts, where Sir Edward Coke and the law prevailed, though Baxter was consoled by the free gift of a manor in Lancashire. Sir Francis Popham, who had married Sutton's stepdaughter in 1590, claimed—without evidence—that Sutton had robbed him of his wife's inheritance. Notoriously a vexatious litigant, he pursued the governors in vain until his death in 1644. Roger Sutton, now a discarded soldier in the obsolete garrison of Berwick, appealed to the king, who was shocked at his treatment and told the governors to do something about it. They did as little as they could. 'Divers poor kindred' from Nottinghamshire and Lincolnshire raised faint, unavailing voices. Having seen off all these attacks, the hospital survived intact, as Sutton had designed it, although in 1872 the school was separated from the almshouse and moved to Godalming, Surrey.

Sutton and his myth With the possible exception of a portrait now at Charterhouse School, all the known images of Sutton are posthumous. The fame which followed his death naturally prompted interest in his life, for which, however, material was hard to find. For his last thirty years he had been known only as a very rich and reclusive 'usurer'. For a national and religious icon, this would hardly do, and his biographers—mostly beneficiaries of his bounty with privileged access to his papers—preferred to avert their eyes from the evidence and deploy their imagination. So they produced the more edifying image of Sutton the valiant soldier who became a merchant prince, 'the chief and richest merchant in London' (Bearcroft, 11): who through his thirty agents abroad and his privateering exploits at sea contributed to victory in the great patriotic wars against Spain. Though criticism gradually eroded some details of this portrait, its substance held firm for three centuries. 'Usury'—except by an exasperated Jesuit in the heat of controversy—was never mentioned.

Remove the myth and Sutton is a duller man. A competent official in the north, a discreet and valued servant of more colourful noble patrons, punctilious and exact in business, he played a part in English economic history: in the transfer of the northern coal industry from clerical to mercantile control and in the lubrication of the market in lay estates. All this would have been forgotten but for his foundation of the Charterhouse: a charity so grandiose that it poses psychological questions to which the austerity and privacy of his personal life frustrate any confident answer.   HUGH TREVOR-ROPER

Sources LMA, Charterhouse papers · *CSP dom.*, 1547–1625 · *CSP for.*, 1558–96 · J. Bain, ed., *The border papers: calendar of letters and papers relating to the affairs of the borders of England and Scotland*, 2 vols. (1894–6) · H. H. [H. Holland], *Heröologia Anglica* (Arnhem, 1620) · *The Charterhouse with the last will and testament of T. Sutton esquire* (1614) · P. Bearcroft, *An historical account of Thomas Sutton esq and of his foundation in Charter-house* (1737) · J. U. Nef, *The rise of the British coal industry*, 2 vols. (1932) · W. K. Jordan, *The charities of London, 1480–1660* (1960) · H. Trevor-Roper, 'The bishopric of Durham and the capitalist reformation', *Durham University Journal*, 38 (1946); repr. in *Durham Research Review*, 18 (1967), 103–16 · N. R. Shipley, 'Thomas Sutton: Tudor-Stuart money-lender and philanthropist', PhD diss., Harvard U., 1967 · N. R. Shipley, 'Thomas Sutton: Tudor-Stuart money-lender', *Business History Review*, 50 (1976), 456–76 · R. Gardiner, *England's grievance discovered in relation to the coal trade*,

repr. (1796) • R. Welford, *History of Newcastle and Gateshead* (1884–7) •
G. S. Davies, *Charterhouse in London* (1922) • N. E. McClure, ed., *Letters
and epigrams of Sir John Harington* (1930) • *The letters and life of Francis
Bacon*, ed. J. Spedding, 7 vols. (1861–74), vol. 4 • *APC*
Archives BL, Lansdowne MSS • Lancs. RO, Clifton of Lytham MSS,
DD. CP. 592 • LMA, Charterhouse MSS • PRO, recognizances for
debt, LC4/192-6
Likenesses N. Stone and N. Johnson, tomb effigy, 1615, Charter-
house chapel, London • J. Faber junior, mezzotint, 1714 (after
unknown artist), NPG • R. Elstrack, line engraving, BM, NPG [*see
illus.*] • Passe, line engraving, BM, NPG; repro. in Holland,
Herōologia • oils, Charterhouse, London
Wealth at death over £50,000; £5000 p.a. in land

Sutton, Thomas (1584/5–1623), Church of England clergyman, was born of humble parents at Sutton Gill in the parish of Bampton, Westmorland. He matriculated as a servitor at Queen's College, Oxford, on 15 October 1602, aged
seventeen, was designated a taberdar (scholar), and graduated BA on 20 May 1606. After proceeding MA on 6 July
1609 he was elected a perpetual fellow of Queen's in 1611.
Following ordination he served as lecturer at St Helen's,
Abingdon, Berkshire, and minister of nearby Culham,
Oxfordshire. Having attained a reputation for his 'smooth
and edifying way of preaching' (Wood, *Ath. Oxon.*, 2.338),
Sutton was invited to speak at Paul's Cross, London, on 3
January 1613. Taking Micah 6: 2 as his text, he warned that
if ministers did not prevail, God would inflict suffering on
England, the nation which enjoyed the greatest grace. He
claimed that 'the Preachers voice is Gods voice' (p. 34) and
denounced the theatre, usury, adultery, and corrupt lawyers. Published in expanded form as *Englands Summons*
(1613), the sermon was dedicated in part to Henry Airey,
provost of Queen's. The attack on the theatre elicited a
protest from the actor Nathaniel Field, who argued that
the Bible does not condemn acting and that Sutton's criticism was disloyal because the king patronized the theatre.

On 22 February 1615 the vestry of St Saviour's, Southwark, elected Sutton their lecturer, a position he retained
until his death, untroubled by church courts because he
had no ecclesiastical living. He again preached at Paul's
Cross on 5 February 1616, this time on Revelation 3: 15–16.
Published as *Englands Second Summons* (1615 [i.e. 1616]), the
sermon, replete with learned citations as the predecessor
had been, called on magistrates to 'loppe and prune the
corrupt and rotten branches, that infect and pester the
Land, [and] to cut off the trayterous heads of Priests and
Jesuites' (*Englands First and Second Summons*, 1616, 187). Sutton proceeded BD on 15 May 1616 and DD on 12 May 1620.
By the time he received his doctorate he had married
Catherine, daughter of Francis Little the elder, of Abingdon, brewer and innkeeper. Their son, Thomas, matriculated at St Edmund Hall, Oxford, on 30 June 1637, aged
seventeen, and subsequently became a fellow of Corpus
Christi College, Oxford, from which parliamentary visitors ejected him in 1648.

In a sermon to judges at St Saviour's on 5 March 1621 Sutton warned against 'Catholicke vipers' (p. 15), urged jurors
and witnesses not to be intimidated by the powerful, and
exhorted magistrates to be courageous, deal honestly, and

detest covetousness. The sermon was published posthumously as *Jethroes Counsell to Moses* (1631). Another sermon,
published as *The Good Fight of Faith* (1624) with an epistle by
his brother-in-law, Francis Little the younger, was
preached to the Artillery Company on 19 June 1623. Calling on his audience to take up arms in the 'mysticall' war
against superstition and ignorance, he implored them to
pray that God would 'blowe away the swarms of AEgyptian
Wasps, and Locusts' that plagued England (p. 433). That
summer Sutton went back to Bampton to complete the
foundation of a free school for which he had raised funds
in London, but as he returned by sea from Newcastle he
drowned on 24 August 1623. A body believed to be his was
interred in the churchyard at Aldeburgh, Suffolk. The Jesuit Robert Drury, who reportedly gloated that the sea had
claimed Sutton because 'he was not worthy the earth
should receive him' (*Diary of Walter Yonge*, 70), himself was
killed when the Blackfriars hall in which he was preaching collapsed on 23 October 1623. Sutton's *Lectures upon the
Eleventh Chapter to the Romans*, published posthumously in
1631, included an epistle by John *Downham, who married Sutton's widow. Reflecting Sutton's Calvinist tenets,
the lectures deal with such topics as perseverance, assurance, reprobation, and idolatry. A portrait of Sutton is
included in a copper engraving, *The Christians Jewell* (1624),
that also contains depictions of Moses and Aaron, the ten
commandments, the Lord's prayer, and the creed. Sold by
Thomas Jenner to hang on the walls of protestant homes,
it capitalized on Sutton's reputation.

RICHARD L. GREAVES

Sources Wood, *Ath. Oxon.*, new edn, 2.338–9 • Foster, *Alum. Oxon.* •
P. S. Seaver, *The puritan lectureships: the politics of religious dissent,
1560–1662* (1970) • *CSP dom.*, 1611–18, 419 • *Diary of Walter Yonge*, ed.
G. Roberts, CS, 41 (1848) • Wood, *Ath. Oxon.: Fasti* (1820), 316, 334,
366, 381, 394 • T. Watt, *Cheap print and popular piety, 1550–1640*
(1991) • M. Burrows, ed., *The register of the visitors of the University of
Oxford, from AD 1647 to AD 1658*, CS, new ser., 29 (1881) • A. Walsham,
Providence in early modern England (1999)
Archives BL, Add. MS 28032, fol. 54v
Likenesses engraving, repro. in T. Sutton, *The Christians jewell*
(1624)

Sutton, Thomas (1767?–1835), medical writer, was born in
Staffordshire in 1766 or 1767. He studied medicine first in
London, then in Edinburgh, and finally at Leiden, where
he graduated MD on 19 June 1787. He was admitted a licentiate of the Royal College of Physicians, London, on 29
March 1790, and soon afterwards was appointed physician
to the army. Sutton later settled at Greenwich, where he
became consulting physician to the Kent Dispensary. As
the first modern British physician to advocate bleeding
and the reduction of inflammation in the treatment of
fever, Sutton was able to achieve a lowering of the mortality rate in such cases. He also discriminated between delirium tremens and the other diseases with which it had previously been confounded.

Sutton and his wife Elizabeth (*d.* 1836) had at least four
daughters, all of whom survived them; they also had a son
William (*b.* 1809), who obtained his MB in 1833 but who

then died while studying medicine in Paris, and Benjamin (*b.* 1811). Thomas Sutton died at Greenwich in the first half of 1835.   E. I. Carlyle, *rev.* Anita McConnell

Sources Munk, *Roll* · PRO, PROB 11/1848, sig. 386 · *British and Foreign Medical Review*, 1 (1836), 44 · *GM*, 2nd ser., 6 (1836), 555 · F. W. Kielhorn, 'Zurgeschichte des Alkoholismus: Pearson, Sutton, und das DT', *Suchgefahren*, 34 (1988), 111–14

Sutton, Thomas (1819–1875), photographic pioneer and writer, was born in Kensington on 22 September 1819, the son of Arthur White Sutton of Teddington, Middlesex. He was educated for six years at Newington Butts and then studied architecture for four years in London before becoming a pensioner (later scholar) of Gonville and Caius College, Cambridge, on 27 June 1842. He graduated with a first in the mathematical tripos in 1846 and became for some time a private tutor. On 8 June 1847 Sutton married Mary, third daughter of John Grace of Cheshire, and the couple set up home in a cottage at St Brelade's Bay in Jersey.

Although Sutton continued to take an interest in mathematics (in 1847 he published anonymously *Proofs of the Rules of Arithmetic* and *Elements of Statics*, a translation of the work by Louis Poinsot), he discovered his true vocation about 1850, when he attended a series of lectures on photography. In 1851, accompanied by his wife and infant son, he spent a year in Italy where 'the fit for calotyping came strong upon me' (Sutton, 414). On his return to England, Sutton devoted himself to the technical problems of printing stable images from paper negatives and, in September 1855, he started an 'Establishment for Permanent Positive Printing' on Jersey in partnership with the French inventor Louis Blanquart-Evrard. In January 1856 the partners (whose association lasted only two years) founded the journal *Photographic Notes*, which became for more than a decade a platform for Sutton's numerous inventions and for his often belligerent criticism of colleagues.

Although he remained an opponent of the collodion process long after its general adoption, Sutton pioneered a considerable range of photographic innovations. In 1859, for example, he suggested a gun camera for taking instantaneous images and in the same year he gave a paper to the British Institution on his invention of a triplet lens for architectural photography; in 1861 he patented his most original invention, a single-lens reflex camera.

In 1861 Sutton became lecturer in photography at King's College, London, but he resigned shortly afterwards because the post necessitated frequent journeys between Jersey and the mainland. His enthusiasms also found fictional expression, and in 1866 he published *Unconventional* (previously serialized as 'The Photographers' in *Photographic Notes*), in which much of the plot and dialogue turns on technical aspects of camerawork, and in which the heroine is at one point trapped in a château by a degenerate marquess who wishes her to pose for lubricious cartes-de-visite (she escapes by swimming the moat). Sutton's two other novels also exercised his hobby-horses: *St Agnes' Bay* (1864) advocates the desirability of swimming lessons for women and *Romance in a Yacht* (1867) champions yachting (and swimming) with buoyant fervour.

In 1867 Sutton moved to Redon in Brittany, where he remained until late in 1874, when he took up residence at Pwllheli in north Wales. He died very suddenly there after a seizure of stomach cramps on 19 March 1875.

Sutton's contribution to photography lay more in publicizing the new technology than in his own inventions. *Photographic Notes* provided a valuable forum for discussion and in 1858 Sutton compiled the first English *Dictionary of Photography*. Despite his combative public persona, Sutton appears to have been a genial figure, radiant with his enthusiasms, whom one visitor described as 'the frankest, the most intelligent, man I had ever seen' ('Reminiscences of a retired photographer IX', 111).

ROBERT DINGLEY

Sources J. Venn and others, eds., *Biographical history of Gonville and Caius College*, 1–2 (1897–8) · T. Sutton, 'Reminiscences of an old photographer', *British Journal of Photography* (30 Aug 1867), 413–14 · *British Journal of Photography* (26 March 1875), 147; (30 April 1875), 210–12 · H. Gernsheim, 'Cuthbert Bede (the Rev. Edward Bradley, 1827–1889), Robert Hunt FRS (1807–1887), and Thomas Sutton (1819–1875)', *One hundred years of photographic history: essays in honor of Beaumont Newhall*, ed. Van Deren Coke (1975), 59–67 · 'Scintilla', 'Reminiscences of a retired photographer IX', *British Journal of Photography* (19 March 1871), 110–11
Likenesses Anderson, engraving (after photograph by A. L. Henderson), repro. in *British Journal of Photography* (1875), 211

Sutton, Thomas Manners-, first Baron Manners of Foston (1756–1842), judge, was born Thomas Manners on 24 February 1756, the fifth son of Lord George Manners (1723–1783) and his first wife, Diana (*d.* 1767), daughter of Thomas Chaplin of Blankney, Lincolnshire. His paternal grandfather was John Manners, third duke of Rutland. In 1772 his father took the additional surname of Sutton on inheriting the estates of his maternal grandfather, Robert *Sutton, second Baron Lexington, from his elder brother Lord Robert Manners-Sutton. He was at Charterhouse School from 1769 and matriculated at Emmanuel College, Cambridge, on 1 March 1773. His elder brother Charles Manners-*Sutton, later archbishop of Canterbury, matriculated at Emmanuel on the same day. Thomas worked hard at Cambridge, graduating as fifth wrangler in 1777. While still an undergraduate he had entered Lincoln's Inn on 16 November 1775. He was called to the bar in November 1780, his years of 'diligence and application' as a law student having left him 'well qualified to practise his profession' (O'Flanagan, 338).

Despite his strong academic record and his family connections Manners-Sutton's progress at the bar was slow. Over the years however he built up a considerable chancery practice and obtained a number of minor judicial preferments. He was at various times a commissioner of bankrupts (1783–97), recorder of Grantham, temporal chancellor of the palatinate of Durham, and chief justice of Anglesey (from July 1797 until 1802), covering the north Wales circuit.

Manners-Sutton also ventured into politics, succeeding his brother John in the family seat of Newark in 1796, where he supported William Pitt the younger. His political career, rarely high-profile, was never permitted to interfere with his legal practice. He took silk on 2 July 1800 and was appointed a bencher of Lincoln's Inn on 16 July. At the same time Pitt appointed him solicitor-general to George, prince of Wales. In this latter capacity he addressed the Commons on 17 February 1802, asserting the prince's claims to those revenues from the duchy of Cornwall that had been collected during his minority. His subsequent motion for a committee to investigate the question was defeated but he had won the support of a large minority from both sides of the house and both Pitt and Charles James Fox praised his performance. In May 1802 he was appointed solicitor-general in Henry Addington's administration, although he made a point of obtaining Prince George's consent before accepting, and he was knighted on 19 May. He remained a confidant of the prince and continued to support him when matters affecting him were debated in the Commons.

Manners-Sutton's appointment to the solicitor-generalship did not increase his parliamentary profile but it did lead to his involvement in some cases of note. In February 1803 he took part in the prosecution for high treason of Colonel Edward Despard, who had attempted to seize the Tower of London and the Bank of England the previous November. Manners-Sutton displayed 'great legal astuteness' (O'Flanagan, 338) and much 'temperance and ability' (Foss, *Judges*, 372) in the prosecution and, though he was a chancery lawyer by training, his handling of the witnesses and his knowledge of crown law were extremely good. Also in February 1803 he played a small role in the prosecution of Jean-Gabriel Peltier for libelling Napoleon Bonaparte in his poem *Le 18 Brumaire an VIII*. On 4 November 1803 at Bentley Priory, Stanmore, he married Anne, daughter of Sir Joseph Copley, bt. She died suddenly on 5 August 1814 at Thomas's Hotel, Berkeley Square; they had no children.

On the retirement of Beaumont Hotham, Manners-Sutton was raised to the bench on 4 February 1805 as a baron of the exchequer, having resigned his Commons seat. He served in this role for two unremarkable years until, in April 1807, Spencer Perceval appointed him lord chancellor of Ireland. On 20 April 1807 he was elevated to the peerage as Baron Manners of Foston, Lincolnshire, and was sworn of the British and Irish privy councils on 22 April and 12 May respectively.

Lord Manners served as lord chancellor of Ireland for an unbroken period of twenty years, the second longest tenure of that office. As the senior Irish equity judge Manners performed quite adequately, although he was clearly not of the calibre of Eldon or Redesdale. Foss says that his decisions were held 'in high estimation' (Foss, *Judges*, 372) but he is probably best described as a workmanlike judge; he disposed swiftly of his cases, seeking always to do justice, 'not, indeed, deeply read, but evincing ability to understand and judgment to decide' (O'Flanagan, 339). One of his most important judicial decisions was that on *Commissioners of Donations* v. *Walsh* (1823), where he upheld as a valid charitable trust a bequest for masses in the will of Mrs Judith Rush. The decision has been regarded as the

root of modern Irish case law in this area and also indicated that Manners did not necessarily pursue his political opposition to Catholicism inside the courts.

Several nineteenth-century commentators politically opposed to Manners depicted him as a privileged oaf, unsuited to judicial office and owing his position solely to family connections. He certainly made some mistakes and was on occasion candidly aware of his limitations; in 1824, for instance, he confessed to having 'very little confidence' in his construction of a bequest by Viscount Powerscourt, and expressed the hope that the case might proceed to the House of Lords for further consideration (J. Comyn, *Irish at Law*, 1981, 80). Nevertheless he remained on the Irish woolsack for two decades, spanning a number of administrations, and, according to Oliver Burke, of his 4469 decisions only fourteen were reversed and seven modified. Many of Manners's judgments were published in the Irish law reports of the period, mostly in Ball and Beatty's chancery reports.

Manners's execution of his legal duties was fairly unremarkable, though by no means inadequate, but his presence as a politician and administrator was more keenly felt. His critics alleged that he 'entertained violent ascendancy principles' and 'cordially detested' both the Irish Roman Catholics and those protestants who supported Catholic emancipation (O'Flanagan, 352, 354–5). He reduced Catholic spheres of influence in so far as he could, dismissing numerous Catholics from the magistracy and refusing to appoint them to those few posts (such as commissioner of bankrupts) which, prior to emancipation, were open to them. It has been noted that 'emancipationists, be they Protestant or Catholic, were the objects of the Chancellor's pious detestation, and they were accordingly subjected to countless annoyances' (Burke, 197). It is questionable however whether Manners was quite so small-minded in this regard as his critics have claimed. One frequently recounted story concerns his refusal to recommend the grant of the honour of earls' children to the siblings of the young Joseph Leeson, fourth earl of Milltown. The story has it that Manners refused to assist because the children's mother had married Valentine Lawless, second Baron Cloncurry, a Catholic peer and ardent emancipationist. Manners strenuously denied such pettiness, and the fact that the grant was made to the Milltown children in 1817, as they approached maturity, when Earl Talbot replaced Lord Whitworth as viceroy, goes some way to supporting that denial.

Manners was assisted in both his legal and political roles by William Saurin, his attorney-general from 1807 to 1822 and himself an ardent anti-emancipationist. A contemporary writer observed:

> daily the business of the government of Ireland was done by the two legal functionaries of kindred spirits, as they regularly walked down every morning from Stephen's Green to the Four Courts … with arms linked and solemn steps, and bended brows, settling affairs of state.   (O'Flanagan, 354)

Neither would countenance the appointment of a Catholic to any position of influence and both insisted that only protestants of unquestionable ability would enjoy their patronage.

Manners also participated in the House of Lords, including the so-called trial of Queen Caroline in 1820. He raised a number of evidential points during the debates and on 4 November delivered a speech in which he opined that the queen's adultery had been fully established and that the divorce should be granted so as to make an example of her for the moral good of the country. In 1829 he argued strenuously against Catholic emancipation in the form of the Roman Catholic Relief Bill, although he subsequently confessed that he might have been wrong in voting against it, and hoped that it might calm the Irish situation and strengthen the government. In April of the same year however he spoke in support of the Qualification of Freeholders (Ireland) Bill, which disenfranchised the 40s. freeholders, many of whom were Catholic. These final assaults on Irish Catholicism marked the end of his participation in the Lords.

Manners finally retired from the Irish woolsack in November 1827. He would have retired earlier but stayed on at the request of George IV, who wanted him to remain until a 'proper Protestant successor' could be found (Kenny, 137). He returned to England immediately and spent most of his time at his country residence, Fornham Hall, near Bury St Edmunds. After his participation in the disenfranchisement and emancipation debates he retired from public life, living out a long retirement with his second wife, Jane (d. 1846), daughter of James Butler, ninth Baron Cahir, whom he had married at Baronscourt, near Newtownstewart, in co. Tyrone, on 28 October 1815.

Aside from his strong views on Catholic emancipation Manners was an attractive personality. On the bench he was 'attentive, decorous, gentlemanlike, [and] distinguished for his urbanity' (O'Flanagan, 339), although he disliked being challenged by counsel when he had made up his mind on a point. Even political adversaries had to admit that in private Manners was 'a perfect gentleman' (Curran, 10); he was 'dignified, courteous, just and generous' (ibid., 9), with strong moral instincts and a very perceptible charm, and despite the strength of his political views he invariably did not let them stand in the way of his friendships.

While he was lord chancellor Manners lived in considerable style in the mansion at 51 Stephen's Green East, Dublin (now the Office of Public Works). On Sundays he and Lady Manners would walk to St Peter's Church, preceded by their ten servants, walking two by two. Away from law and politics Manners was an enthusiastic shot and was often seen at Carton, seat of the duke of Leinster, or at Baronscourt, seat of the marquess of Abercorn, in his sporting attire—his chancellor's hat, which resembled a bishop's mitre, a green jacket, a scarlet waistcoat, silk breeches, and long black gaiters.

Manners died on 31 May 1842 at his London house in Brook Street and was buried at Kelham in Nottinghamshire. Manners and his second wife had one surviving child, John Thomas Manners-Sutton, second Baron Manners of Foston (1818–1864). Manners was very fond of his son and heir and occasionally brought him to court to sit with his father on the bench. His grandson John Thomas Manners, third Baron Manners of Foston (1852–1927), is remarkable for having ridden his own horses to victory in the 1882 Grand National and the 1882 Grand Military Gold Cup—the only two races that he ever rode in.

NATHAN WELLS

Sources J. R. O'Flanagan, *The lives of the lord chancellors and keepers of the great seals of Ireland*, 2 (1870) • GEC, *Peerage* • W. R. Williams, *The history of the great sessions in Wales, 1542–1830* (privately printed, Brecon, 1899) • M. H. Port, 'Manners Sutton, Thomas', HoP, *Commons, 1790–1820* • W. H. Curran, *Sketches of the Irish bar*, 2 (1855) • *Hansard 2* (1821), vol. 3; (1829), vol. 21 • Foss, *Judges*, vol. 8 • R. L. Sheil, *Sketches, legal and political*, ed. M. W. Savage, 1 (1855) • F. E. Ball, *The judges in Ireland, 1221–1921*, 2 (New York, 1927) • O. J. Burke, *The history of the lord chancellors of Ireland from AD 1186 to AD 1874* (1879) • Venn, *Alum. Cant.* • C. Kenny, 'Irish ambition and English preference in chancery appointments, 1827–1841', *Explorations in law and history*, ed. W. N. Osborough (1995), 133–76 • Sainty, *King's counsel* • Sainty, *Judges* • *State trials*, vol. 28 • V. B. L. Cloncurry, *Personal recollections of the life and times: with extracts from the correspondence of Valentine, Lord Cloncurry* (1849) • Burke, *Peerage* (1999) • J. C. Brady, *Religion and the law of charities in Ireland* (1976)

Archives Notts. Arch., election returns | BL, corresp. with Sir Robert Peel, Add. MSS 40206–40494, *passim*

Likenesses A. Cardon, stipple, pubd 1811 (after J. Comerford), BM, NPG • Irish school, group portrait, etching with watercolour, pubd 1811 (*A view of the Four Courts, Dublin*), NG Ire. • W. Burrell, oils, King's Inns, Dublin • J. Doyle, caricatures, BM

Wealth at death under £250,000: Port, 'Manners Sutton, Thomas'

Sutton, William Richard (1835×7–1900), entrepreneur and housing philanthropist, was born in Kennington, Lambeth, the youngest son of five children born to Frederick Wilson Sutton (1798–1852) and his wife, Mary Head Matts (1811–1866/7). His father was a partner in the stationery firm of Shepherd and Sutton, based in Foster Lane in the City of London. In 1851 Sutton was living with his family in Foster Lane, next door to the stationery firm. His grandmother headed the household and ran the adjacent Fountain inn, in which his father assisted as a barman. Sutton was educated at the City of London School between 1845 and 1850, when he left aged fourteen. After the death of his father in 1852, his eldest brother emigrated to New Zealand and Sutton moved with his sister Mary and their mother back to Mrs Sutton's birthplace in Merton, Surrey.

Sutton would seem to be an example of a self-made millionaire and according to an obituary showed signs of business ability early in his career (*City Press*). In the mid-1850s he established the business of Sutton & Co. Carriers from The Fountain inn, exploiting the inn's existing function as a receiving and distribution house for goods and parcels. The company expanded rapidly and the firm's head offices moved, first to Aldersgate Street and then in 1878 to purpose-built premises in Golden Lane. Sutton profited from using the railways to distribute large parcels at lower 'tonnage' rates than would have been due if the parcels' smaller constituent packages had been sent individually. The expansion of this business during the 1860s brought Sutton into conflict with the South Eastern and Great Western railway companies which tried to recover some of their 'lost' income through repeatedly imposing surcharges on Sutton's goods. After several years of litigation an appeal to the House of Lords ultimately settled the case in Sutton's favour in 1868. On the occasion of Sutton's legal success his employees presented him with a testimonial paying tribute to his 'energy, tact, forethought and straightforward dealing' (Butcher and Butcher, 9). A former employee recalled him as strict and honest, but rather humourless and sometimes hasty (ibid.). Nevertheless, his employees pledged their 'earnest co-operation' and by 1900 the carrying company possessed some 600 branches throughout the UK, the colonies, and elsewhere.

Important though Sutton & Co. Carriers was as the foundation of Sutton's business success, it was not the only source of the multi-million pound fortune which he amassed. Sutton's many property investments included a £200,000 scheme of office and factory development in the St Luke's area of the City of London and a variety of commercial and residential premises in London and Brighton. Other areas of investment included some eleven brewing, bottling, and distilling firms. Sutton was a founder, director, and major shareholder of two of these companies—the gin, whisky, and brandy distillery, Sutton, Carden & Co. based in Finsbury, and the New London Brewery which manufactured ale, port, and stout in its Kennington premises. Both firms were founded in the early 1880s and later diversified their operations to meet changes in demand by supplying wines, cordials, mineral waters, tea, coffee, and tobacco as well as acquiring hotels and inns.

Sutton married his first wife, Ann Eleanor (1836×8–1891), daughter of Thomas Archdeacon Lewis, on 15 October 1864. By 1871 the couple had moved to their new house, Sunnydene, West Hill, near Crystal Palace in Sydenham. Sutton appreciated fine design in his surroundings and commissioned J. F. Bentley, the architect of Westminster Cathedral, to design both his head office in Golden Lane and his house. Sutton also sponsored his brother-in-law, the organ builder Thomas Christopher Lewis, who was a friend of Bentley's. Lewis lived with the Suttons at Sunnydene and worked from business premises provided by Sutton, but there is no other evidence of links between Sutton and the wider artistic circles of his day.

In 1891 Ann Sutton died and four years later Sutton married again, on 14 December 1895. His second wife was Eliza Anna Venus White (d. 1937), widowed daughter of William Dobson, surgeon. Sutton had no children of his own, although both of his wives brought children with them to their marriages. Ann had an adopted daughter, Kate, and Eliza a son and two daughters. After the death of his first wife, Sutton withdrew from his business affairs for a few years due to ill health. Although he retained his house in London, he took up residence with his second wife in Hove, Sussex. In 1899 Sutton resumed his business activities which he continued to pursue until a few days before his death. On 20 May 1900 Sutton died, from bronchitis

and cardiac failure, at his Sussex home, 6 Adelaide Crescent, Hove. He was buried at Norwood cemetery, London, on 24 May.

Sutton's obituary in the *City Press* stressed his business prowess and noted that 'He took but little interest in public affairs' as he 'confined his attention mainly to his business' (23 May 1900). At his death, however, Sutton left the bulk of his estate to establish a trust for the provision of dwellings for the poor in London and other populous places in England. After a limited number of additional bequests were paid to his brother Charles, certain business associates, and his second wife, who lived until 1937, the assets left to found the trust were valued at over £2 million.

In 1913, when speaking of his brother's intentions, Charles Sutton said that he had had 'one great idea, and that was to crystallise the old proverb that prevention was better than cure. He believed that healthy homes and pure air and sanitation were better than all the hospitals that could be built' (*Liverpool Courier*, 24 Sept 1913). Despite having lived his life in a society which emphasized voluntary activity, there is no evidence of Sutton or his immediate family having been actively involved in philanthropy. He did, however, work in close proximity to well-known public figures and Sir Sydney Waterlow, lord mayor of London and founder of the Improved Industrial Dwellings Company, owned business premises adjacent to those of Sutton, Carden & Co. in Finsbury.

The trustees nominated by Sutton to establish his housing trust were his elder brother Charles, his solicitor, Charles Edward Tranter Lamb, and Thomas Watson, manager and inheritor of Sutton & Co. The task of realizing the estate and administering the trust was extremely onerous and difficult. The will was contested by some disinherited family members, while the prospect of so large a housing charity alarmed public authorities, the attorney-general, and other would-be administrators of the trust. They were concerned that so large a sum of money could have detrimental effects on existing labour and property markets if the provision of low-rented housing for the poor by the Sutton Dwellings Trust were not carefully controlled. Despite these administrative difficulties, however, the trust undertook its first building activities in 1907 and by 1919 had built 1783 dwellings on six estates in London, Bimingham, and Newcastle. It was not until 1927 that a scheme for the administration of the trust was finally agreed, by which time almost all of those directly associated with William Sutton and his trust had died. The trust had the largest endowment of all the philanthropic housing organizations and by 1939 had built nearly 8000 dwellings in fifteen towns and cities. The William Sutton Trust, as it is now known, still ranks among the largest housing associations in England.

PATRICIA L. GARSIDE and SUSANNAH MORRIS

Sources P. L. Garside and S. Morris, *Building a legacy: William Sutton and his housing trust* (1994) • H. Butcher and I. Butcher, *The Sutton housing trust: its foundation and history* (1982) • Kelly's Post Office London directory, 1864 • City of London directory, 1899 • Towners directory, Brighton, 1897–1900 • *Brighton Herald* (26 May 1900) • *City*

Press (23 May 1900) · census returns, 1851, 1861, 1871, 1881, 1891 · *English and Empire Digest* (1865) [section re Court of Exchequer] · m. certs. · d. cert. · *CGPLA Eng. & Wales* (1900) · City of London RO, register of pupils, City of London School, vol. 1 (1837–1860) 534 F
Archives LMA, Sutton Housing Trust, esp. executor's committee minutes, accession no. 2983
Likenesses oils, William Sutton Trust, Tring, Hertfordshire
Wealth at death £2,158,009 18*s.* 7*d.*: probate, 1900–1905, *CGPLA Eng. & Wales*

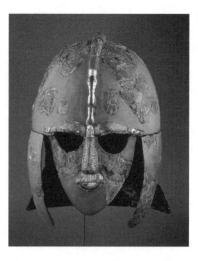

Sutton Hoo burial (early 7th cent.), parade helmet

Sutton Hoo burial (early 7th cent.) is named from the place where a king or aristocrat probably lay buried in the barrow known as mound 1. Sutton Hoo, in the extreme south-east of modern Suffolk, is situated on a high bluff on the left bank of the River Deben some 7 miles from the sea, from which in the past it could have been visible. It is necessary to say 'probably' because no indisputable human remains were found there, though this is almost certainly attributable to the action of acid soil. This person's burial is of primary importance for early medieval history because it was accompanied by an untouched and exceedingly rich funeral deposit. Barrows at Sutton Hoo have been recorded (and too often robbed) since 1601. Modern archaeological investigation began in 1938. In 1939 a magnificent ship burial was discovered in mound 1. Further excavations were undertaken in the late 1960s and (in association with a wide programme of enquiry) in 1986–92. Very nearly all finds are in the British Museum.

The man honoured in mound 1 was interred in a ship some 90 feet long. Although its wood had perished entirely, its rivets survive, and meticulous excavation of its impression in the sand has permitted detailed reconstruction of a big open vessel, rowed by forty oarsmen, in which a burial chamber had been constructed amidships. The king or aristocrat concerned had very rich personal accoutrements (including cloisonné gold and garnet shoulder-clasps, and a great golden buckle), weaponry (including a highly decorative parade helmet, chain mail, six spears of different types, and a unique 'axe-hammer' with an iron handle), silver and bronze vessels, objects of apparently great (but undoubtedly mysterious) significance (in particular a carved whetstone decoratively mounted in bronze), such domestic items as a cauldron with a suspension chain over 11 feet long, and the remains of textiles of many kinds.

Mound 1 is one of up to twenty barrows. Most are unexplored by modern techniques, but some contained rich burials disposed in differing ways and apparently belonging to the same chronological horizon as that in mound 1. Thus mound 3 contained the cremated remains of a man and a horse, with important objects of Mediterranean origin; mound 2 contained a boat burial organized differently from that of mound 1. Twenty-seven entirely different burials have been found outside the mounds. These are of men buried without grave goods (apart from one accompanied by what may have been a plough), many of whom had died violently. The radial disposition of twelve of these around mound 1 strengthens the supposition that the burial of the man commemorated was accompanied by human sacrifice, though the question arises as to how far these burials may be those of a later 'execution cemetery'.

The grandeur of some of the burials and the proximity of Sutton Hoo to a royal centre of authority at Rendlesham (4 miles north-east) indicate a connection between Sutton Hoo and the East Anglian royal house. It has been forcefully contended that mound 1 is the burial of King *Rædwald. Dating is crucial here and depends on the coins in the burial (thirty-seven Merovingian gold tremisses). These include few regal coins capable of exact dating; but the most modern research suggests that the earliest coins are later than 582 (or more probably 595) and that the latest could be as early as 613. Thus the deposit could have been made in the 620s or even a little earlier. These dates permit the possibility of the burial's being that of Rædwald, whose reign ended between 616 and 627. But there is only a *terminus post quem*; the written record for East Anglia is too meagre to give a secure framework; too few rich burials have survived to permit calibration of this one in a context in which a considerable number of men may have been powerfully rich, while not being kings as Rædwald was. It follows that, whatever Sutton Hoo's links to the East Anglian royal house, efforts towards specific identification must be inconclusive. A linked question is that of whether such an item as the grand, unused, mounted whetstone was (as has been suggested) 'regalia'. The most that can be said is that only a very important man could have owned such a thing and that it could have had numinous implications.

Sutton Hoo demonstrates a rich availability of techniques and complication of contacts and resonances. Arguments as to whether the ship could have had a sail and on the significance of its lacking a real keel relate to the question, at present insoluble, as to how specialized a craft it may have been, but do not alter the plain facts of its scale and the skill of its construction. The jewellery demonstrates highly sophisticated techniques: an example is that the cloisonné gold and garnet items have the garnets backed by gold foil stamped with most minutely regular patterns, such that the best explanation for the production of the required dies is the deployment of a jig apparatus, not otherwise known for some centuries. The textile fragments have a wide variety of complicated weaves.

A paradigm case of the range of relationships demonstrated is the elaborate parade helmet, with its mask and embossed figures. Such helmets are of a kind which the Romans imitated from their Sassanian (Persian) enemies in the earlier fourth century. Meaningfully close relations of the helmet (as with the shield) appear in Swedish burials at Vendel and Valsgärde of the seventh century and later; that these are also ship burials gives Sutton Hoo a dimension such as to suggest Swedish origins for the East Anglian dynasty. The largest silver dish bears a stamp dating it to the reign of the eastern Roman emperor Anastasius (r. 491–518). Other silver and bronze ware had come from the eastern Mediterranean much more recently. Three 'hanging bowls' were of Celtic origin. Some objects have Christian links: two silver spoons are inscribed respectively Saulos and Paulos in Greek lettering. The great gold buckle is probably a portable reliquary, to hang from, not fasten, a belt.

Thus, although it is impossible to know who the man commemorated in mound 1 at Sutton Hoo was, its contents and location tell a lot about him. He was probably connected with the East Anglian royal house. The maritime implications of his being buried in a ship accord with the possible implications of rich grave goods with connections extending from Sweden to Byzantium. Although he was accompanied by objects of Christian significance his burial may have been attended by human sacrifice. He was a man such that objects at his disposal reflected varied craftsmanship of the highest quality. Some of them indicate the continued influence on such a barbarian grandee of the external pomps of Rome.

The burial has been the subject of continuing close analysis and over-strenuous interpretation. Suggestions such as that it has to be regarded as a rearguard demonstration of grand pagan ritual are inconclusively interesting. The gift of the Sutton Hoo treasures to the nation by their owner, Edith May Pretty, was a great and inadequately recognized act of generosity.　　　　J. CAMPBELL

Sources R. Bruce-Mitford and others, *The Sutton Hoo ship burial*, 3 vols. in 4 (1975–83) · A. Care-Evans, *The Sutton Hoo ship burial* (1986) · C. B. Kendall and P. S. Wells, eds., *Voyage to the other world: the legacy of Sutton Hoo* (1992) · M. O. H. Carver, ed., *Sutton Hoo research committee bulletins, 1983–1993* (1993) · M. O. H. Carver, ed., *The age of Sutton Hoo: the seventh century in north-western Europe* (1992) · V. I. Evison, 'The body in the ship at Sutton Hoo', *Anglo-Saxon Studies in Archaeology and History*, 1 (1979), 121–38 · K. East, 'The Sutton Hoo ship burial: a case against the coffin', *Anglo-Saxon Studies in Archaeology and History*, 3 (1984), 79–84 · M. P. Pearson, R. van de Noort, and A. Woolf, 'Three men and a boat: Sutton Hoo and the East Saxon kingdom', *Anglo-Saxon England*, 22 (1993), 27–50 · I. Wood, 'The Franks and Sutton Hoo', *Peoples and places in northern Europe, 500–1600*, ed. I. Wood and N. Lund (1991), 1–14
Likenesses parade helmet, BM [*see illus.*]

Swaddon, William (1560x63–1623), Church of England clergyman, was the son of William Swaddon (d. 1607), a clothier of Calne, Wiltshire, and older brother of Robert, a

notorious swindler in Jacobean London. In 1576, when his age was recorded as thirteen, he went to Winchester College; from there he went on to New College, Oxford, which he entered as a scholar in 1580, graduating BA in 1584 and proceeding MA in 1588, BD in 1595 and DD in 1602. He acquired the rectories of Haselbury, Wiltshire, in 1593, and Great Horwood, Buckinghamshire, in 1594, and a canonry of Lincoln in 1595, without the help of his own or his wife's family, as he sourly recalled in his will. Indeed, although William inherited property in Calne from his father, his wife, Elizabeth, received no jointure on their marriage, which probably occurred in the 1590s; they were to have no children, and she outlived him. Further preferment came after Swaddon's appointment as chaplain to Anne of Denmark, who was probably responsible for securing him the archdeaconry of Worcester in August 1610 on the nomination of James I; three years later she failed in a bid to procure for him the wardenship of New College, Oxford. It was Swaddon who, on her death in 1619, composed the inscription on her monument in Westminster Abbey, and wrote some commemorative verses, *In obitum serenissimae principis, Annae* (1619), an English version of which was appended to the 1623 edition of William Camden's *Remaines Concerning Britain*.

In 1612 Swaddon was struck with a palsy, which he regarded as God's judgment on his ambition, and he determined thereafter 'to use well those preferments I have' (BL, Royal MS 18 C. v). Few details remain of his time as archdeacon of Worcester, beyond a conventional set of visitation articles issued in 1615. He resented, however, his exclusion from the cathedral chapter at Worcester and the manner in which chancellors had usurped the archdeacon's role as eyes and ears of the bishop. His general outlook might fairly be described as 'clericalist'. In 1621, still a royal chaplain, Swaddon presented 'Treatise of tythes' to the king, in which he defended, against the recent attacks published by John Selden, the status of tithes due by divine right and attacked lay influence over the clerical estate. The tract contains some autobiographical asides, and even advocated that clergy be elected to the House of Commons. Swaddon drew up his will, in which his age was given as fifty-nine, in January 1620. He died on 4 August 1623 and was buried, on his request, in the north aisle of Worcester Cathedral.

KENNETH FINCHAM

Sources BL, Royal MS 18 C. v. · PRO, PROB 11/142/110, 11/109/32 · Bodl. Oxf., MS Top. Oxon. b. 48 · *Articles to be enquired of ... within the archdeaconrie of Worcester* (1615) · BL, Lansdowne MS 984, fol. 18 · T. F. Kirby, *Winchester scholars: a list of the wardens, fellows, and scholars of ... Winchester College* (1888), 147 · Foster, *Alum. Oxon.* · *Fasti Angl., 1541–1857*, [Ely], 113 · W. Swaddon, 'Treatise of tythes', 1621 · A. F. Johnston and R. Tittler, '"To catch a thief" in Jacobean London', *The salt of common life ... essays presented to J. Ambrose Raftis*, ed. E. B. DeWindt (1995), 233–69
Archives BL, Royal MS 18 C.v
Wealth at death land and leases at Calne: will, PRO, PROB 11/142/110

Swadlin, Thomas (1599/1600–1670), Church of England clergyman, was born in Worcestershire. He matriculated from St John's College, Oxford, on 15 November 1616, aged sixteen, and graduated BA on 4 February 1619. For the next decade details of his life are unknown, but in 1628 or soon afterwards he was appointed curate of St Botolph, Aldgate, where he acquired some repute as a preacher. In or before 1632 he married Alice, whose other name is unknown. Between November 1632 and April 1640 they baptized four children, Susanna, John, Elizabeth, and Thomas. Swadlin's first published work, *Sermons, Meditations, and Prayers upon the Plague, 1636*, appeared in 1637.

In the months preceding the outbreak of the civil war trouble began brewing for Swadlin in the parish. On 29 February 1642 the House of Commons ordered him to admit John Simpson as a lecturer. A petition against Swadlin from his parishioners was formally received by the Commons on 1 August, though it had no immediate effect. But Swadlin was then denounced by one of his parishioners for a sermon that he had preached in defence of the king, and was imprisoned in Crosby House. He was examined by the lord mayor, and then moved to Gresham College. The total duration of his imprisonment on this occasion was from 29 October to 2 December. While at Gresham College, Swadlin defiantly prepared for publication his offending sermon and others under the title *The Soveraignes Desire Peace: the Subjects Dutie Obedience*; this eventually appeared in February 1643. The work was not extremist, endorsing the common royalist theory of mixed monarchy in which 'the Monarchie is bound by an Aristorcracie of Peeres, and Democracie of Commons and this mixture meeting in their command' (p. 10). The Commons ordered on 10 November 1642 that Swadlin be tried by martial law as a spy. At some point Swadlin's living was sequestrated and his wife and children turned out: he was the first signatory to a petition from sequestrated ministers seeking charity, which dates probably from 1643. Presumably this was produced during what seems to have been an extended period in captivity, as were *A Manual of Devotions* (1643) and *The Scriptures Vindicated from ... Cardinal Bellarmine* (1643). On 26 May 1643 the Lords ordered that Swadlin be moved from Gresham College to Norwich prison, then on 2 August the Commons ordered that he be moved from London House to Newgate.

By his own account after the Restoration, Swadlin was imprisoned a total of five times, but there was a brief interlude to his troubles in the mid-1640s, when, freed from imprisonment, he spent time with Charles I in Oxford. There he was created DD on 17 June 1646. During the 1640s Swadlin produced a number of political works. These included three further collections of political sermons castigating rebels in 1647. Swadlin also experimented with a variety of different forms of political writing in these years. Probably his most significant work was *The Soldiers Catechisme, Composed for the Kings Armie* (July 1645). This work was a response to Robert Ram's work of the same title produced for the parliamentary armies. Swadlin told the rank and file that whatever they did in obedience to the commands of their king they did blamelessly. In January 1646 Swadlin tried his hand at ventriloquy in *A Letter of an Independent to his Honoured Friend Mr Glyn*, written to suggest that the Independents were about

to support the king in return for a grant of liberty of conscience. He demonstrated his continuing anti-Catholicism in *The Jesuites the Chiefe, if not the onely State-Heretique* [1646] and produced a single number of the newsbook *Mercurius Academicus*, addressed from Oxford to the 'passive party' in April 1648. According to Wood he worked at this time as a schoolmaster in London. But after the regicide Swadlin again found himself in difficulty. He was held in custody on suspicion of having treasonable links with Charles I, being released on bail by order of the council on 9 January 1651. By his own later account Swadlin helped many royalists in distress and gave material assistance to enable two royal servants to attend Charles II and further his interests. On 14 June the committee for examinations ordered that he be discharged. During the interregnum he lived in Listin Green, Marylebone, and then from 1655 in Baldwins Gardens, St Andrew's, Holborn. In 1653 Swadlin preached a sermon to the Society of Astrologers, published that year as *Divinity No Enemy to Astrology*, but most of his published work in the period from 1653 to the Restoration was in defence of the protestant faith of the Church of England. He enquired, in the subtitle of one of them, *To all, paupertatis ergo ne pereant fame* (1658), 'whether it be better to turn Presbyterian, Romane, or to continue what I am, Catholique in matter of religion'.

In 1661, after the Restoration, Swadlin petitioned for restoration of his living, signalling his continued loyalty to the crown in *King Charles his Funeral* (1661). He was reinstated to St Botolph, Aldgate, and it was from there that, on 21 April 1662, Swadlin, as a widower, obtained a licence to marry Hester Harper, widow. He does not seem to have got along with his parishioners and resigned the living. He appears to have spent time in the early 1660s as curate of Marylebone, although in 1662 Archbishop William Juxon appointed Swadlin to the vicarage of St James, Dover, Kent, and a neighbouring rectory of Hougham. But the livings were poor, and Swadlin increasingly infirm. In 1664 the earl of Clarendon's influence gained for Swadlin the rectory of St Peter and the vicarage of All Saints in Stanford, Kent. He died on 9 February 1670 and was buried at Stanford. His wife Hester survived him.

GLENN BURGESS

Sources Foster, *Alum. Oxon.* • *Walker rev.*, 59 • Wood, *Ath. Oxon.*, new edn, 3.887–9 • IGI [parish register of St Botolph, Aldgate] • ESTC • JHL • JHC • catalogue of the Thomason Tracts • P. Curry, *Prophecy and power: astrology in early modern England* (Princeton, 1989), 42

Swæfbert (d. 738). *See under* East Saxons, kings of the (*act.* late 6th cent.–c.820).

Swæfred (fl. 693/4). *See under* East Saxons, kings of the (*act.* late 6th cent.–c.820).

Swaffer, Hannen (1879–1962), journalist, was born at Lindfield, Sussex, on 1 November 1879, the eldest of eight children, four boys and four girls, of a Folkestone draper, Henry Joseph Swaffer, and his wife, Kate Eugenie Hannen. He went to Stroud Green grammar school, Kent, and later, as he said, continued his education in Fleet Street. First he was appointed a reporter at Folkestone at 5*s.* a week. An often scornful critic, at the age of eighteen he was banned from the local theatre. A time came when he boasted of having been banned from twelve of forty-one theatres in the West End of London. He joined the *Daily Mail* in 1902 and worked for the future Lord Northcliffe for ten years. His employer, who because of his appearance liked to call Swaffer the Poet, made him editor for a while of the *Weekly Dispatch*. Swaffer's best work in his Northcliffe years helped to transform the *Daily Mirror*, after an unhappy start as a women's journal, into a mass-circulation picture paper.

In 1913 Swaffer, seeking fresh employment, invented 'Mr. Gossip' for the *Daily Sketch* as a new and bold kind of gossip feature. He then moved to the *Daily Graphic*, where he won even more praise for a gossip page signed 'Mr. London'. After contributing 'Plays and players' to the *Sunday Times* and being for a few months in 1924 editor of *The People*, he became in 1926 drama critic of the *Daily Express*. In this post he enjoyed full scope for his pungent candour. He campaigned against what he considered the over-Americanization of the stage and the press, and was smacked in the face by an American actress at the Savoy Hotel 'on behalf of America'. Affronts because of his critical trenchancy never perturbed this sharpest of critics. Someone slashed a portrait of him intended for the United States. Swaff, as he was now generally known, said: 'I heartily approve. I often feel like slashing my own face when I look in the mirror.'

Another phase of Swaffer's life opened in 1931 when he joined the *Daily Herald*. In this and other Odhams publications he not only exploited his wide acquaintance with the famous and the notorious but also championed many a cause. One was socialism, to which *Merrie England*, by Robert Blatchford, had won him over. He often wrote wisely, sometimes like a wiseacre, and always in a clear, homely style. His habit of pontificating on many subjects led him to be termed, to his deep satisfaction, the Pope of Fleet Street. He did not look the part, his appearance suggesting an actor of Sir Henry Irving's day: he wore a wide-brimmed black felt hat, black stock, high collar, dark flowing locks, and a melancholy expression. A kind and witty man, he was known by close friends to be shy under his mask of defiant self-confidence. In middle life he became a spiritualist, regularly attended séances, and was appointed honorary president of the Spiritualists' National Union, thus becoming titular head of the 500 churches devoted to his faith.

In his prime Swaffer was said to write nearly a million words a year. He was described at a gathering in his honour as the greatest reporter of the era and an immortal of his own time. Speaking in 1959 of his old employers he said: 'I know more about it than any of them. I had to fight the whole lot of them.' Earlier he had denounced a 'new kind of feudalism' among press magnates.

Swaffer resigned from the Labour Party in 1957 after a dispute arising out of a campaign to improve mental hospitals. Articles he and others wrote were said to use 'sick and helpless people to attract readers', a charge Swaffer deeply resented.

Swaffer's publications included *Northcliffe's Return*

Hannen Swaffer (1879–1962), by Karl Pollak, *c.*1948

(1925), *Really behind the Scenes* (1929), *Hannen Swaffer's Who's who* (1929), *Adventures with Inspiration* (1929), *When Men Talk Truth* (1934), *My Greatest Story* (1945), and *What would Nelson do?* (1946).

Swaffer married in 1904 Helen Hannah (*d.* 1956), daughter of John Sitton, a grocer living in Clapham; there were no children. Swaffer lived for many years in a flat overlooking Trafalgar Square in order, he said, to have a front seat when the revolution came. He died in University College Hospital, London, on 16 January 1962. In the week of his death he wrote, as usual, a commentary on current journalism for the *World's Press News*. The Hannen Swaffer journalistic awards announced every year are a memorial to a picturesque personality, who not only enlivened the popular journalism of his time but set an example of often candid gossip which continued to be followed.

LINTON ANDREWS, *rev.*

Sources *The Times* (17 Jan 1962) · private information (1981) · personal knowledge (1981) · *CGPLA Eng. & Wales* (1962)
Archives FILM BFI NFTVA, news footage
Likenesses K. Pollak, photograph, *c.*1948, NPG [*see illus.*] · D. Bisset, bust, Beaverbrook Art Gallery, Fredericton, New Brunswick, Canada · L. Bradshaw, bronze bust, Odhams Press, London · M. Heath, oils, NPG · J. Myers, portrait, *Psychic News* office, London · C. R. W. Nevinson, portrait, priv. coll. · M. Poncin, portrait, priv. coll. · M. Reid, bust, priv. coll. · A. Wolmark, portrait, Beaverbrook Art Gallery, Fredericton, New Brunswick, Canada · cigarette card, NPG
Wealth at death £13,047 3s. 5d.: probate, 11 May 1962, *CGPLA Eng. & Wales*

Swaffham, Robert of (*fl. c.*1250–1271), Benedictine monk, gave his name to and is the presumed author of the Peterborough Abbey cartulary which became the definitive reference point on the monastery's history and possessions up to his own time. He prefaced the work with the history of the house by Hugh Candidus, which he continued for the period 1177–1246. The Book of Robert of Swaffham contains surveys and some feudal records, but the bulk of a very bulky volume (of 392 folios) consists of charters. The main text dates from the 1250s. The only indication of personal taste may be found in the inclusion of the *Gesta Erwardi* ('The deeds of Hereward'), for if Robert came from Swaffham near Cambridge then he was a fenman by birth as well as by monastic profession. Almost no details survive about his life, but he is recorded as the abbey pittancer in 1269, when he lent the abbot 40s., and as its cellarer at Easter 1271. It is presumed that he died not long afterwards. His book narrowly escaped destruction by Cromwell's soldiery in 1643, being passed off as a Bible and then bought back: the receipt, for 10s., is copied on the flyleaf. It is appropriately first among the manuscripts of the dean and chapter of Peterborough.

EDMUND KING

Sources 'The book of Robert of Swaffham', CUL, Peterborough dean and chapter MS 1 · J. Sparke, ed., *Historiae Anglicanae scriptores varii*, 2 (1723), 97–122 · J. D. Martin, ed., *The cartularies and registers of Peterborough Abbey*, Northamptonshire RS, 28 (1978), 7–12 · E. King, 'Swaffham's cartulary', *Annual Report of the Friends of Peterborough Cathedral* (1972), 10–13
Archives CUL, Peterborough dean and chapter MS 1

Swain, Charles (1801–1874), poet and engraver, was born in Every Street, Manchester, on 4 January 1801 and baptized on 11 February 1801 at St Ann's, Manchester, the son of John Swain (*bap.* 1759?, *d.* 1806), a native of Knutsford, Cheshire, and Caroline Tavaré, a vivacious Parisienne. (Swain himself, his gravestone, and his early biographers claimed he was born in 1803.) He was educated at the private school of the Revd William Johns in Manchester and began work at the age of fifteen as a clerk in Tavaré and Horrocks's dye-works, of which his uncle Charles was part-owner. On 8 January 1827 Swain married Ann (1803–1878), the orphaned daughter of James Glover, a Liverpool merchant, and Alice Sedgwick. The Swains had six children, four of whom survived to adulthood; their only son died aged five.

From 1822 Swain regularly contributed poems to journals; in 1827 he issued *Metrical Essays on Subjects of History and Imagination*, dedicated to Charles Tavaré, and in 1831 *Beauties of the Mind: a Poetical Sketch with Lays Historical and Romantic*, dedicated to Robert Southey, the most notable of Swain's widening circle of literary friends. Southey wrote in a letter of 20 February 1832 that 'If ever man was born to be a poet, you are; and if Manchester is not proud of you yet, the time will certainly come when it will be so' (Manchester Central Library, MS FO91 S24, fol. 22). Swain's most ambitious poem, *The Mind* (1832), in nearly two hundred Spenserian stanzas, is a cumbrous sevenfold enlargement of the title-poem of his volume of 1831 and was frequently reissued with varying collections of shorter poems. The finely produced fourth edition (1841) was illustrated with vignettes from Thomas Stothard, Henry Liverseege, and others.

After fourteen years at the dye-works Swain began business as a bookseller, but gave up after two years, perhaps because of difficulties with a business partner obscurely hinted at in Swain's correspondence with Southey in July 1832. He joined Lockett & Co., engravers and lithographers of Manchester, and after some years bought and personally managed the engraving branch. Swain himself was an engraver 'for his own amusement, and in order that he might instruct his operatives in the method in which he desired them to work' (Bryan, 5.146). His artistic interests appeared in his *Memoir* (1835) of Liverseege, an artist whose reputation was based on paintings illustrating Scott's novels; in his own homage to Scott, *Dryburgh abbey, the burial place of Sir Walter Scott, a vision, forming a poetical catalogue of all the principal characters in the Waverley novels* (1832); and in *A Cabinet of Poetry and Romance: Female Portraits from the Writings of Byron and Scott* (1845).

Swain experimented with dialogue forms in *Dramatic Chapters* (1847), *Letters of Laura d'Auverne* (1853), and *Art and Fashion* (1863), each of which was the title-poem of more digestible collections of shorter poems. His most readable work is in *English Melodies* (1849), *Songs and Ballads* (1867), and the lyrics scattered through earlier volumes. Many of those lyrics, including 'When the heart is young', 'Tapping at the Window', and 'I waited in the twilight', were set to music, some by the poet himself. As Southey prophesied,

Swain was highly esteemed in Manchester; he was honorary professor of poetry at the Manchester Royal Institution, where in 1846 he lectured on modern poets. He was granted a civil-list pension of £50 on 1 December 1856. He died from an epileptic fit on 22 September 1874 at his home, Prestwich Park, Prestwich, a house near Manchester given to him by friends, and was buried in Prestwich churchyard; his widow followed on 7 April 1878. Their third daughter Clara Swain Dickins published four volumes of mostly religious verse between 1886 and 1908.

JAMES SAMBROOK

Sources C. Swain, autograph letters and MSS, Man. CL, MS FO91 S24 · C. Swain, biographical note with Swain's corrections, 1860, BL, Add. MS 28512, fols. 153–6 · *Manchester Examiner* (23 Sept 1874) · registers, St Ann's Church, Manchester · registers, Manchester Cathedral · *Selections from Charles Swain compiled by his third daughter*, ed. C. S. Dickins (1906) · Bryan, *Painters* (1930–34), 5.146 · W. E. A. Axon, ed., *The annals of Manchester: a chronological record from the earliest times to the end of 1885* (1886), 193–4, 344–5 · C. C. Smith, short life prefixed, in C. Swain, *Poems* (1864) · R. W. Procter, *Memorials of bygone Manchester* (1880), 151–4 · *IGI* · *Centenary edition of the works of Nathaniel Hawthorne*, ed. T. Woodson and others (1987), 17.148, 493, 551; 18.59 · *The letters of Mrs Gaskell*, ed. J. A. V. Chapple and A. Pollard (1966), 243, 1006 · J. Evans, *Lancashire authors and orators* (1850), 260–68 · M. A. Smith, 'The Charles Swain collection', *Manchester Review*, 9 (1962), 323–32 · *Manchester and Salford directory* (1841–72)
Archives JRL, letters · Man. CL, Manchester Archives and Local Studies, corresp. and papers · Mitchell L., Glas., letters · NL Scot., letters · Wordsworth Trust, Grasmere, Dove Cottage, letters | BL, letters to Royal Literary Fund, loan no. 96 · Bodl. Oxf., letters to W. Jerdan, MS Eng. lett. d.114, fols. 233–44 · U. Edin. L., letters to *Literary Gazette* and G. J. O. Allman, La.II.187–90
Likenesses W. Bradley, oils, c.1833, Man. CL · W. Bradley, oils, c.1833, Man. City Gall. · W. Bradley, oils, c.1833, Salford Art Gallery · E. G. Papworth, marble bust, 1860, Man. City Gall. · W. Bradley, drawing, Man. City Gall. · W. Bradley, miniature, Man. City Gall. · W. Bradley, print, Man. CL · F. J. Smyth, woodcut, BM · E. Walker, photograph, repro. in *Selections*, ed. Dickins, frontispiece · engraving (after photograph by D. W. Bentley), repro. in *Transactions of the Manchester literary club* (1875), 1.95
Wealth at death under £1500: probate, 11 Jan 1875, *CGPLA Eng. & Wales*

Swain, Francis (*bap.* 1719, *d.* 1782), marine painter and draughtsman, born probably in London and possibly the son of Francis Swain and his wife, Ann, was baptized on 22 June 1719 at St Botolph, Aldgate, London. His name appears as a messenger in a list of clerks and officers employed by the treasurer and commissioners of his majesty's navy in 1735. An imitator of Willem van de Velde the younger, his work was also influenced by those of his contemporaries Charles Brooking and Peter Monamy, with whom it is sometimes confused. On 27 June 1749 he married Mary Monamy at All Hallows, London Wall. They had a son, Monamy Swain, who was baptized on 27 February 1753 at St Dunstan and All Saints, Stepney. He became a painter of still life, genre, and marine subjects, and exhibited at the Free Society of Artists from 1769 to 1774.

Francis Swain enjoyed a considerable reputation, and was awarded premiums by the Society of Arts in 1764 and 1765. He exhibited largely with the Incorporated Society of Artists and the Free Society of Artists from 1762 until his death, sending chiefly studies of shipping in both calm and stormy seas, harbour views, and naval engagements, often on a small scale. He also took commissions for actions, and his paintings demonstrate an informed knowledge of British ships of the period. He was very partial to moonlight effects. Some of his works were engraved by P. C. Canot, P. P. Benazech, and others, and there is a set of plates of fights between English and French ships, several of which are from paintings by him. Much of his work, including many small wash drawings, was sold directly to dealers. Swain resided at Strutton Ground, Westminster, until near the end of his life, when he moved to Chelsea, Middlesex. He died in Chelsea in 1782, and seven works by him were included in the exhibition of the Incorporated Society of Artists in the following year. Two pictures by Swain are at Hampton Court, one is in the Glasgow Art Gallery and Museum, and seventeen are in the National Maritime Museum, Greenwich.

F. M. O'DONOGHUE, *rev.* ANNETTE PEACH

Sources *IGI* · E. H. H. Archibald, *Dictionary of sea painters* (1980) · S. Deuchar, 'Swaine, Francis', *The dictionary of art*, ed. J. Turner (1996) · Mallalieu, *Watercolour artists*, vols. 1–2

Swain, Joseph (1761–1796), Baptist minister and hymn writer, was born in Birmingham. Early left an orphan, he was apprenticed to an engraver of that town at a young age. He served the latter part of his apprenticeship in London with his brother. In 1782 he came under conviction of sin, and on 11 May 1783 he was baptized by John Rippon at Carter Lane, Southwark.

The registration of a meeting place in Garratt Lane, Wandsworth, dated 3 February 1788 makes reference to Joseph Swain as 'Teacher of God's Word' (Maryon, 17.135) and this would seem to refer to the subject of this entry, even though he was soon enlisted for other tasks. As early as 1779 a group of evangelical Christians in Walworth, most of whom were those who 'scruple the Baptizing of Infants, commonly called Baptists' (Philcox, 362), had secured a licence for worship and in 1780 opened a chapel. It was not until December 1791 that a church was formed, and Swain was ordained pastor on 8 February 1792. The new church was now founded on a specifically Baptist trust practising strict communion, whereas the previous work had embraced both Baptists and paedobaptists. The latter consequently harmoniously withdrew, with financial compensation, to form York Street Congregational Church. Increased numbers of hearers attracted by Swain's 'evangelical manner and style of preaching' (Ivimey, 4.400) caused the church to be extended three times in the course of his short but effective ministry, during which several young men were called into the Baptist ministry.

Swain combined his Walworth pastorate with a well-supported evening lectureship at Devonshire Square up to the time of his death at the age of thirty-five. This occurred on 16 April 1796 after a short illness involving violent fits and periods of delirium. He left a wife and four children and was buried at Bunhill Fields. Although no longer sung today, his hymns, many of which were collected in *Walworth Hymns* (1792), as also his devotional poetry, enjoyed considerable popularity in the Victorian period.

E. I. CARLYLE, *rev.* J. H. Y. BRIGGS

Sources J. Upton, *The sorrowful separation of the faithful pastor from his flock. A sermon occasioned by the death of Mr J. Swain* (1796) · 'Memoir', J. Swain, *Experimental essays on divine subjects* (1834) · J. Ivimey, *A history of the English Baptists*, 4 vols. (1811–30), vol. 4, pp. 400–03 · J. Julian, ed., *A dictionary of hymnology*, rev. edn (1907) · H. N. Philcox, 'Early days at East Street, Walworth', *Baptist Quarterly*, 9 (1938–9), 362–7 · H. Maryon, 'Late 18th century dissent in Surrey', *Transactions of the Congregational Historical Society*, 17 (1955), 128–35 · J. I. Jones and others, *The Baptist hymn book companion*, ed. H. Martin (1962), 286–7
Archives Harvard U., corresp.
Likenesses stipple, NPG; repro. in *Evangelical Magazine* (Dec 1795), 481

Swain, Joseph (1820–1909), wood-engraver, was born at Oxford on 29 February 1820, the second son of Ebenezer Swain, a printer, and his wife, Harriet, *née* James, and the grandson of Joseph *Swain, pastor of East Street Baptist Church, Walworth, and a religious poet. The family moved to London when he was nine, and in 1834 he was apprenticed to Nathaniel Whittock, a drawing-master and commercial artist with Oxford connections. Swain wanted to learn wood-engraving, in which Whittock was not expert, so he went to work for Thomas Williams, one of a family of wood-engravers who were among the leading practitioners of the craft in the generation after Bewick. With Williams, he moved away from Bewick's way of suggesting texture by means of various ingenious notations towards facsimile engraving—the precise reproduction of an artist's drawing.

Swain set up independently—at 18 Elder Street, Spitalfields—in 1842, and the following year he married Martha Cooper; they had three sons and a daughter. Swain's advancement resulted from a commission handed on to him by the engraver Orlando Jewitt in 1843. Bradbury and Evans, the publishers of *Punch* (begun 1841), were seeking new engravers and asked Jewitt to engrave a design by John Leech. Jewitt passed the job to Swain, whose efforts so pleased Leech that Swain was employed as manager of the engraving department of *Punch*. In due course, *Punch* agreed that Swain could expand his work in other directions, while still retaining responsibility for *Punch* engravings (which the firm continued to deal with until 1900). In 1855 Swain reappeared in trade directories as an independent engraver, at 58 Fleet Street, and from 1858 until almost the end of the century at 6 Bouverie Street, Fleet Street.

A member of Swain's staff (said to number six or eight in the early days) recalled that at first everyone—masters, journeymen, and apprentices—worked together in the same room around a large baize-covered table. In due course, hierarchy was asserted. The masters went to a room downstairs with 'No Admittance' posted over the door, while 'Mr. Swain removed to the first floor, had his room papered; put matting on the floor, and pictures on the walls, and was thus quite up to date' (Groves, 17). For a time the firm employed as manager W. H. Hooper, who later became better known when, after retirement, he engraved for William Morris at the Kelmscott Press.

The effectiveness of wood-engravings depends largely on the type of drawing provided. Those with tone need adaptation by the engraver, while those with clear lines can be exactly replicated. Engravers tended to specialize in either tint or facsimile. For the latter kind of work Swain's firm received many tributes:

> How is it you are able to preserve the character of each artist's drawing in the way you do? When I look over any engravings I can generally tell who the engraver is, but when I look at your work I can see at once who the artist is. (Ewart, 240–41)

'The proof is simply exquisite—I never had and never saw anything more perfectly engraved. It seems so strange to see anything like my own drawing on a proof that I am quite upset and unmanned' (Fred Barnard, letter to Swain, 11 Sept 1872, V&A). Swain used photography to assist in the engraving process as soon as this became possible. For instance, he wrote to Ford Madox Brown about a proposed design:

> Will you draw it on paper & have it photographed on to the wood or draw it on the wood direct? If you do it on paper I would advise that it be done larger than required so that it be reduced in the photograph. (letter, 18 March 1867, V&A)

This refers to transferring an image photographically to a woodblock for hand engraving; later it became possible for a photographed image to be mechanically engraved on zinc using acid, and Swain adopted this process.

Swain carried out a great variety of work, artistic and everyday, without becoming especially associated with any in particular. Unlike the Dalziel brothers, he did not try to act as artistic patron or originator of publications. But he had some artistic sensibility. He is credited with urging his workmen 'to search the drawing for the motive of the artist and work up to that' (Hartley, 10). Furthermore, he showed his firm's engravings at the Royal Academy, and went into print (apparently for the one and only time) with a series of short tributes to artists he had known who died before achieving fame (first in *Once a Week*, then reprinted in H. C. Ewart, *Toilers in Art*, 1891). Among the artistic achievements to which his firm contributed, one of the largest and most brilliant was Arthur Boyd Houghton's 'Graphic America' series in *The Graphic* (1870–73). The firm's engravings were signed 'SWAIN Sc'. Swain died at Ealing on 25 February 1909.

Swain's son, **Joseph Blomeley Swain** (b. 1844), was also a wood-engraver, at first working semi-independently (according to Engen) as John Swain, from 1860 at 266 Strand, an address shared by several wood-engravers. He took over the family firm on his father's retirement and expanded its activities into half-tone and colour printing.

ANTHONY BURTON

Sources M. H. Spielmann, *The history of 'Punch'* (1895) · J. B. Groves, 'Rambling recollections and modern thoughts by an old engraver', Punch library, London · R. K. Engen, *Dictionary of Victorian wood engravers* (1985) · E. de Maré, *The Victorian woodblock illustrators* (1980) · C. Fox, 'Wood engravers and the city', *Victorian artists and the city*, ed. I. B. Nadel and F. S. Schwarzbach (1980) · G. Beegan, 'The mechanization of the image: facsimile, photography, and fragmentation in nineteenth-century wood engraving', *Journal of Design History*, 8 (1995), 257–74 · G. Wakeman, *Victorian book illustration: the technical revolution* (1973) · H. C. Ewart, *Toilers in art* (1891) ·

Graves, *RA exhibitors* · *Book illustration of the sixties* (1923) [incl. introduction by H. Hartley; exhibition catalogue, National Gallery, London, 18 Jan – 31 Dec 1923]
Archives Harvard U., Houghton L., corresp.
Likenesses photograph, BM

Swain, Joseph Blomeley (*b.* 1844). *See under* Swain, Joseph (1820–1909).

Swaine, Ann Sykes (*bap.* 1821, *d.* 1883), suffragist and philanthropist, was baptized at Birstall, Yorkshire, on 15 September 1821, the eldest of the four daughters of Edward Swaine and his wife, Martha Sykes. She was a spinster, and lived in York for the last twenty-eight years of her life, nursing her ageing father until her own death at the age of sixty-one. A Unitarian, Swaine had a strong interest in social and educational questions, and was one of the first women in York to become involved in the women's suffrage movement. She supported the national campaigns for married women's right to hold property and for the extension of university education to women. Active in local education, Swaine was honorary secretary of the Yorkshire Ladies' Educational Association and a member of the Ladies' Council of Education of Yorkshire. She was also involved in Sunday school and cookery school work in York.

Swaine published a small number of texts, including a translation, *History of the Doctrine of the Deity of Jesus Christ* (1870), of the work by the French theologian Albert Réville, which ran to three editions. A year before her death she published a collection of short biographies for the Sunday School Association, entitled *Remarkable Women as Examples for Girls*. The volume included biographical sketches of Caroline Herschel, Harriet Martineau, Mary Carpenter, and Charlotte Brontë, among others. Ann Sykes Swaine was an active, clear-thinking woman who divided her time between philanthropy, feminism, publishing, translation, and domestic and familial duties. The *Englishwoman's Review* (1883) noted that her writings were characterized by her own common sense and pragmatism. She died unexpectedly from heart disease at 1 The Crescent, Micklegate, her home in York, on 21 June 1883, survived by her father.   HELOISE BROWN

Sources *Englishwoman's Review*, 14 (1883), 331–2 · *Yorkshire Gazette* (23 June 1883), 6 · d. cert. · IGI · CGPLA Eng. & Wales (1883)
Wealth at death £1693 14*s.* 9*d.*: administration, 10 Aug 1883, CGPLA Eng. & Wales

Swaine, John (1775–1860), draughtsman and printmaker, born on 26 June 1775 at Stanwell, Middlesex, was the son of John Swaine (*d.* *c.*1780) and his wife, Margaret. He became a pupil of Jacob Schnebbelie, draughtsman to the Society of Antiquaries, on whose death in 1791 he was transferred to Barak Longmate, and, following the latter's death in 1793, to his son Barak. On 31 December 1797 he married Elizabeth (*d.* 1822), the daughter of the elder Barak Longmate, at St Martin-in-the-Fields, London. He is best known for his facsimile prints after contemporary and old master works, particularly Marten Droeshout's portrait of William Shakespeare, William Faithorne's portrait of Thomas Stanley, and David Loggan's frontispiece

to the Book of Common Prayer. His painstaking and accurate workmanship was admired by many, notably William Pickering and William Ottley, to whose *History of Engraving* (1816) he contributed. He drew and engraved plates for many antiquarian and topographical works, such as William Marsden's *Oriental Coins, Ancient and Modern* (1823–5) and E. W. Brayley's *The History and Antiquities of the Abbey Church of St Peter, Westminster* (1822–3). His scientific illustrations include many for natural history books and for the transactions of the Linnean, Zoological, and Entomological societies. Swaine's few contemporary portraits include one of Marshal Blücher, after F. Rehberg. Some of his etched plates appeared in the publications of the Antiquarian Etching Club. From 1804 he contributed constantly to the *Gentleman's Magazine*. He died in Dean Street, Soho, London, on 25 November 1860, his wife having predeceased him in October 1822.

John Barak Swaine (1815–1838), printmaker and painter, his only son, studied in the schools of the Royal Academy, and while still a boy did some good antiquarian work. Drawings by him, illustrating papers by Alfred John Kempe, appeared in *Archaeologia* in 1832 and 1834. In 1833 he was awarded the Isis gold medal of the Society of Arts for an etching, and in that year he drew, etched, and published a large plate of the east window of St Margaret's, Westminster. Having taken up oil painting, he was employed in 1834 by an American named Jones to copy some of the best pictures at The Hague and in the Louvre, Paris. Among his travel sketches are some of the field of Waterloo (dated 8 October 1834), held in the British Museum. In Paris he tried his hand successfully at wood-engraving. He engraved in mezzotint Rembrandt's *Spanish Officer*, a picture by himself entitled *The Dutch Governess*, and a portrait of A. J. Kempe. In 1837 he etched a plate of the altar window at Hampton Lucy in Warwickshire. An experimental lithograph and etching, *Neapolia* (1820), is held in the Victoria and Albert Museum, London. Swaine was a versatile artist of great promise, but he died at the age of only twenty-three after a debilitating illness which affected his legs, at Queen Street, Golden Square, London, on 28 March 1838.

F. M. O'DONOGHUE, *rev.* JOANNA SELBORNE

Sources *GM*, 3rd ser., 10 (1861), 337 · Redgrave, *Artists*, 2nd edn · R. K. Engen, *Dictionary of Victorian wood engravers* (1985) · *Engraved Brit. ports.* · 'Biographical sketch of Mr J. B. Swaine', *GM*, 2nd ser., 9 (1838), 552 · *GM*, 1st ser., 103/2 (1833), 161, 545 · *GM*, 2nd ser., 8 (1837), 625 · I. Mackenzie, *British prints: dictionary and price guide* (1987) · Graves, *Brit. Inst.* · Graves, *Artists*, new edn · parish register (births), Stanwell, Middlesex · IGI · CGPLA Eng. & Wales (1860)
Archives BM · V&A
Wealth at death under £450: probate, 15 Dec 1860, CGPLA Eng. & Wales

Swaine, John Barak (1815–1838). *See under* Swaine, John (1775–1860).

Swainson, Charles Anthony (1820–1887), theologian, was born on 29 May 1820 in Liverpool, the second son of Anthony Swainson, a descendant of an old Lancashire family, and a merchant and alderman of Liverpool, and his wife, Mary, daughter of Thomas Clay. After passing some time at a private school at Christleton, near Chester, where he was an unusually studious boy, he entered the Liverpool Collegiate Institution. Joseph Barber Lightfoot, later bishop of Durham, joined the school a few years later, and was a lifelong friend. Swainson began residence at Trinity College, Cambridge, in October 1837, under the tuition of George Peacock (1791–1858), afterwards dean of Ely. He became scholar of Trinity in 1840, and in 1841 graduated as sixth wrangler. On 23 June 1841 he was elected to a fellowship at Christ's College and in 1847 he became one of the tutors. He was ordained by the bishop of Ely on his college title, deacon in 1843, and priest in the following year. In 1849 Bishop C. J. Blomfield appointed him Cambridge preacher at the Chapel Royal, Whitehall. In 1851 he resigned his tutorship, and after serving curacies at St George's, Hanover Square, London, and at Mortlake, he became principal of the theological college at Chichester in February 1854. In 1852 he married Elizabeth, daughter of Charles Inman of Liverpool and his wife, Jane, *née* Clay; she was the sister of Thomas and William *Inman.

In 1856 Swainson was appointed by Bishop Gilbert to a prebendal stall in the cathedral. In 1857 and 1858 he delivered the Hulsean lectures at Cambridge. Unwilling to relinquish altogether the practical work of the ministry, he undertook in 1861 the charge of two small parishes, St Bartholomew's and St Martin's, at Chichester. When, in 1861, the beautiful spire of Chichester Cathedral fell, he became secretary of the committee for its restoration. While this work was still in progress the dean and canons residentiary, exercising a privilege which probably they alone among the English chapters retained, co-opted Swainson as a residentiary. For several years he represented the chapter in convocation. In 1864, on the preferment of Professor Harold Browne to the see of Ely, Swainson succeeded him as Norrisian professor of divinity at Cambridge. Resigning his other appointments, he retained his canonry, and also became warden of St Mary's Hospital in Chichester, where he spent the whole of the income of his office in adding to the comforts of the aged inmates and restoring the chapel. In 1879 Swainson was chosen, without opposition, to succeed J. B. Lightfoot as Lady Margaret reader in divinity. In 1881 he was elected by the fellows of Christ's College to the mastership, and thereupon resigned his canonry. He was an active and genial master, inspecting the college estates—of critical importance in the years of agricultural depression—and giving great attention to the business occasioned by the introduction of the new code of statutes, which came into operation immediately after his accession to the mastership, and which required, among other things, a complete change in the method of keeping the accounts. He was vice-chancellor in 1885–6. His health declined from the time of his appointment, and he died in Cambridge on 15 September 1887.

In his theological opinions Swainson, though he was not untouched by the philosophy of Coleridge and by the Tractarian movement, was always in the main a disciple of Hooker and the older English divines. He had remarkable power of work, and was one of the most generous and unselfish of men. He exercised a beneficial influence on his pupils, and drew about him a large circle of attached friends.

In the course of a busy church and college life, he published quite frequently. His first publication, with Albert Henry Wratislaw (also fellow of Christ's College), was *Commonplaces Read in Christ's College Chapel* (1848). In 1856 he published *An Essay on the History of Article xxix*, a work of considerable research. His Hulsean lectures for 1857 were published in 1858 under the title *The creeds of the church in their relation to the word of God and the conscience of the Christian*, those for 1858 in 1859 as *The authority of the New Testament, the conviction of righteousness, and the ministry of reconciliation*. In 1871 he contributed to *Sussex Archaeological Collections* (vol. 24) an account of St Mary's Hospital at Chichester. In 1869 the interest which he took in the creeds, shown already in his Hulsean lectures, led him to join energetically in the controversy as to the use of the so-called Athanasian creed in divine service. Without in any way impugning its dogmas, he thought a confession of faith so full of technical terms of theology ill fitted for the use of ordinary congregations. On this subject he published a *Letter to the Dean of Chichester on the Original Object of the Athanasian Creed* (1870), and *A Plea for Time in Dealing with the Athanasian Creed* (1873). These were but preliminaries to a larger and more important work, *The Nicene and apostles' creed, their literary history, together with an account of the growth and reception of the sermon on the faith commonly called the creed of St Athanasius* (1875). This was the fruit of great labour and research, involving a long journey to various countries of Europe to visit the libraries where the principal ancient manuscripts of the Athanasian *Expositio fidei* were to be found. In 1875 he also published *The parliamentary history of the Act of Uniformity [of 1662], with documents not hitherto published*; in 1880 *The Advertisement of 1566: an Historical Enquiry*, and part one of *The constitution and history of a cathedral of the old foundation, illustrated by documents in the muniment-room at Chichester* (no more parts were published). His last substantial publication was *The Greek Liturgies, Chiefly from Original Sources* (1884). This book was based on considerable research, including photographs of manuscripts (subsequently deposited in the divinity school at Cambridge); parts of the book are still indispensable to the student of Greek liturgiology. Swainson also wrote elaborate articles on creeds and liturgies in Smith's and Cheetham's *Dictionary of Christian Antiquities*, and another article entitled 'Creeds considered historically' in Smith's and Wace's *Dictionary of Christian Biography*.

H. C. G. MATTHEW

Sources Venn, *Alum. Cant.* · *DNB* · *CGPLA Eng. & Wales* (1887)
Archives CUL, letters to Sir George Stokes · Durham Cath. CL, letters to J. B. Lightfoot
Likenesses E. Wilson, pencil and wash sketch, 1901, Christ's College, Cambridge · chalk drawing, U. Cam., Divinity School
Wealth at death £10,248 7s. 5d.: resworn probate, Jan 1888, *CGPLA Eng. & Wales* (1887)

Swainson, William (1789–1855), naturalist and artist, was born on 8 October 1789 at Newington Butts, London, the

William Swainson (1789–1855), by Edward Francis Finden, pubd 1840 (after Mosses)

son of John Timothy Swainson (1757–1824), customs collector, and his second wife, Frances Stanway (1769–1792). His father was a keen amateur zoologist, well informed and assiduous in his collection of shells, insects, and fossils; he was also a founder member of the Linnean Society of London. He remarried following the death of Swainson's mother and there were ten children from this, his third, marriage.

Little is known of Swainson's formal schooling. Although he was of delicate health and nervous temperament, his father's collections indoors (and the natural world outside) absorbed him utterly—at the cost of a disciplined attitude to spelling and grammar. He longed to travel abroad, but his father established him (at the age of fourteen) in the Port of London customs office where he worked as a clerk. Three years later he was transferred, again through his father's influence, to the office of the army's commissary-general and sent to General Fox's Mediterranean army (1808–15).

Swainson's official duties in the Mediterranean left him with ample time to botanize and zoologize. He spent the majority of his time in Sicily, but also visited or resided in Greece (1812), Malta (1812–14), and Italy (1810–14). Single-minded absorption in natural history blinded him to the risks he took in the matter of health and (more than once) life itself. However he lived to tell the tale, met other naturalists, notably Constantine Rafinesque-Schmalz, and in the autumn of 1815 returned to England laden with collections.

Swainson's next venture (1817–18) was a collecting foray into Brazil, where he witnessed horrifying scenes of revolution and violence. However, he returned with rewarding collections, and wrote an account of his travels for the *Edinburgh Philosophical Journal*, whose editor, Professor Robert Jameson, printed it without comment. Swainson took

this as a slight, and gave up the idea of a longer, more comprehensive, separate work. However, although his Brazil work never appeared in book form, the exquisite coloured lithographs in his collection of plates *Birds of Brazil* glow with all the shimmering colour of Charles Waterton's prose.

Before he left for Brazil, Swainson had been admitted to fellowship of the Linnean Society. On his return he was elected, on the nomination of Sir Joseph Banks, to fellowship of the Royal Society.

During the 1820s Swainson displayed his rich collection of shells, insects, and birds to many visitors. They included a young admirer called Mary Parkes (1794–1835); Swainson married this 'gentle friend' on 25 September 1823. They lived on his soldier's half pay from the Mediterranean campaign. Disappointed in his share of his father's legacy, he used his lithographic skills and zoological knowledge in a series of encyclopaedic works which occupied his time until 1840. To this end he visited Paris (a trip recorded in his wife's diaries and letters with great enjoyment). Here he met Baron Georges Cuvier and Auguste de St-Hilaire and had access to museums and zoological gardens.

In the 1820s Swainson also became interested in William Sharpe Macleay's circular system of classification, which elaborated a quinary system of his own. These proposals did not comply with the well-established Linnaean system and were not accepted by those engaged in biological work. As a result, Swainson's encyclopaedic productions were left relatively isolated. Anxious to obtain a post in the British Museum he was twice disappointed. However, the years with Mary and the five children were busy, productive, and tranquil, lived amid pleasant surroundings at Tittenhanger Green. Mary did hint in a letter to her parents that emigration was a remote possibility.

Emigration did come in 1841, but under tragic circumstances. By then Swainson's world had been shattered by the death of his beloved wife in 1835. In addition, he had worn himself down in the exacting and nerve-racking marathon of seeing his encyclopaedic works and illustrations into print while the British Museum doors remained firmly closed to him. He also had a young family to look after: William John (b. 1824), Mary Frederica (b. 1826), George Frederick (b. 1829), Henry Gabriel (b. 1830), and Edwin Newcombe (b. 1833). However, a Lieutenant Thomas Macdonnell had painted a glowing picture of prospects in the fledgeling colony of New Zealand—surely a land of opportunity for a zoologist and artist, who would be a respected figure and perhaps in time a well-to-do landowner? On 22 October 1840 Swainson married his children's governess, Ann Grasby (1807–1868), in haste (a marriage only to fulfil the requirements of emigration policy) and embarked the following year, with all but his youngest child, for pastures new.

Although Swainson's children saw their father's remarriage as a dreadful mistake, his new wife was a practical, good-hearted woman, who did her best as wife and stepmother. In time she was mother to Lucilla Frances (b. 1842), Edith Stanway (b. 1844), and Annette Elizabeth (b.

1851). However, the harsh realities of pioneer life, exacerbated by disputes with Maori claimants to territory, began to take their toll. Nevertheless Swainson began to develop his property in what became Lower Hutt near Wellington, and made some very good drawings of New Zealand bush trees. He was on board her majesty's steam survey ship *Acheron* during one of her Cook Strait tours of duty. He took up various other properties, but never became the man of substance he would have wished to be. Nor was the rest of the busy pioneering community at leisure to appreciate his talents.

Domestic difficulties culminating in the addition to the household of a trying sister-in-law sent Swainson off to Australia, where he hoped to be employed as a botanist. However, here again, expectation outran reality. He made some excellent drawings of eucalypts and casuarina species, but Australia already had its botanists, and he returned disappointed to New Zealand.

The final straw was the sudden death of his and Mary's only daughter, whom Swainson did not long survive. He died at Fern Grove, Lower Hutt, on 7 December 1855, and was buried on 9 December at St James's Church, Lower Hutt.

A sincere Christian believer in the literal truth of holy writ, Swainson had occupied a world created by a loving God; next came the angels, then man, and finally the lower orders, all conveniently arrangeable in groups of five. The quinary system was his big bang. It informs much of his writing in volumes he wrote for Jardine and Lardner's natural history cyclopedias. He himself admits to a propensity to seize upon and never let go of an idea— true for him simply because he saw with blinding clarity that it must be so. Among his enormous output of published works (more than forty publications between 1808 and 1855), it is his superb illustrations of cold, perfect shell, soft fur, and glowing sheen of feather that stay in the mind, so that his *Exotic Conchology* and *Birds of Brazil* recall his mentor Brodrip's words 'Your drawings are unrivalled'. The *Exotic Conchology* plates were issued in 1821–2 (first edition); the first three-volume version of *Zoological Illustrations* in 1821–3, and *The Birds of Brazil*, in five parts, in 1834. SHEILA NATUSCH

Sources S. Natusch and G. Swainson, *William Swainson of Fern Grove* (Wellington, New Zealand, 1987) · *William Swainson FRS FLS, naturalist and artist: diaries, 1808–1818*, ed. G. M. Swainson (1989) · *William Swainson FRS FLS, naturalist and artist: family letters and diaries, 1809–1855*, ed. G. M. Swainson (1992) · W. Swainson, *Taxidermy: bibliography and biography* (1840) · W. Swainson, *Exotic conchology* (1821) · W. Swainson, *A selection of the birds of Brazil and Mexico* (1841) · G. M. Swainson, 'A short biography of William Swainson', NL NZ, Turnbull L., QMS 1961 · R. J. Cleevely, letter to editor, 31 Oct 2000, on William Swainson, *The Linnean*, 17/2 (2000), 22–3
Archives Auckland Institute and Museum, New Zealand, drawings · Bodl. Oxf., Radcliffe Science Library, zoological corresp. · Linn. Soc., corresp.; drawings of New Zealand trees · Mitchell L., NSW, notes on Australian trees · National Gallery of New Zealand, drawings · National Museum of New Zealand, Wellington, archives, drawings · New Plymouth Public Library, New Zealand, travel journals · NL Aus., corresp. and papers · NL NZ, Turnbull L., scientific MSS · RBG Kew, drawings of Australasian trees · U. Cam., department of zoology, corresp. and papers · U. Cam., Museum of Zoology, papers | Oxf. U. Mus. NH, letters to F. W. Hope · Oxf. U. Mus. NH, letters to J. O. Westwood relating to his contribution to *Encyclopedia of Zoology* · RBG Kew, letters to Sir William Hooker
Likenesses E. F. Finden, stipple, pubd 1840 (after drawing by Mosses), NPG [*see illus.*] · G. H. Harrison, oils, RBG Kew · G. H. Harrison?, oils, NL NZ, Turnbull L. · T. C. Wageman, portrait, Taranaki Museum, New Plymouth, New Zealand; repro. in G. M. Swainson, ed., *William Swainson … diaries*

Swainson, William (1809–1883), lawyer and politician in New Zealand, born in Lancaster on 25 April 1809, was the eldest son of William Swainson, a merchant. He was educated at Lancaster grammar school, and, having entered the Middle Temple in 1835, was called to the bar in June 1838. He practised as a conveyancer, and rarely attended the Lancaster sessions.

In 1841 Swainson was appointed attorney-general of New Zealand, partly on the recommendation of his friend William Martin (1807–1880), who had just become chief justice. During the voyage out he assisted Martin to draft the measures required to set the new legal machinery in motion. He brought out with him the framework of the house in which he took up his residence, at Taurarua, Judges Bay, Auckland. The legislation which he carried through the council between December 1841 and March 1842 was comprehensive, lucid, and compact. In 1842 he advised the acting governor, Willoughby Shortland, that in his opinion the jurisdiction of the British crown did not *ipso facto* extend to the Maori, an opinion which drew a severe rebuke from Lord Stanley. In 1843 Swainson was sent to assess the Wairau affray in Marlborough, and found that the Maori were justified in repelling the invasion by arms: this attitude was unpopular with the settlers and the Colonial Office.

In 1854, on the introduction of an elective constitution, Swainson became the first speaker of the legislative council, and encountered rather a stormy political period. In 1855 he paid a visit to England, and took several opportunities, in London, Bristol, Lancaster, and elsewhere, of lecturing and publishing on the attractions and political situation in New Zealand. In May 1856, during his absence, he was pensioned off from his position as attorney-general; and, though he remained a member of the legislative council until 1867, he ceased to be active in politics after 1864. He devoted much of his energy to the furtherance of Bishop Selwyn's work in the foundation of the church in New Zealand, and was a member of the conference of June 1857 held to prepare the constitution, and of the first general synod; he took a large share in framing the organic measures introduced to the synod. He was also chancellor of the diocese of Auckland from 1866 until his death. As a radical and a humanitarian, he had been from the first concerned for the interests of the Maori, particularly with respect to land purchase policies. He opposed the New Zealand wars of the 1860s as impolitic, and arising from land questions he had foreseen.

After 1866 Swainson lived in comparative retirement, though his keen interest in the colony's welfare gave him much public influence; he was a member without portfolio of Sir George Grey's ministry from April to July 1879. Swainson died, unmarried, at Taurarua on 2 December 1883, and was buried in the cemetery there.

C. A. HARRIS, rev. JANE TUCKER

Sources G. Reid, 'Swainson, William', *DNZB*, vol. 1 · S. S. P. Hamilton, 'William Swainson, attorney-general of New Zealand, 1841–56', MA diss., University of Auckland, 1949 · A. H. McLintock, *Crown colony government in New Zealand* (1958) · J. O. Wilson, *New Zealand parliamentary record, 1840–1984* (1985) · *Lancaster Guardian* (17 Jan 1884)
Archives NL NZ, Turnbull L., letters to Mrs Lloyd
Likenesses photograph (after oil painting by Harrison?), NL NZ, Turnbull L.
Wealth at death £4141 6s. 2d.: testamentary records held at National Archives of New Zealand, 1884

Swale, Sir Richard (c.1545–1608), civil lawyer, was the son of Thomas Swale, landowner, of Askham Richard, Yorkshire. He was born in Yorkshire about 1545. His father belonged to a minor branch of an old Yorkshire family. Richard Swale matriculated as a sizar of Jesus College, Cambridge, in June 1566, graduated BA in 1569, became a fellow of his college in 1571, and proceeded MA in 1572. In 1576 he became a fellow and tutor of Gonville and Caius College, where his former tutor at Jesus College, Thomas Legge, was president. In 1581 the fellows of Gonville and Caius accused Swale and Legge of maintaining 'a covert faction in the college against the true religion received' and of corrupting the students with popery (*Memoirs of … Hatton*, 261). William Cecil, Baron Burghley, the chancellor of the university, authorized a visitation of the college, in which articles were presented against both men. Swale's opposition to the proceedings led Burghley to cancel his election as university proctor, but Swale none the less became president of his college over the protests of the fellows in 1582. As a fellow of Gonville and Caius, Swale studied civil law, and his legal education qualified him for his appointment as official of the archdeaconry of Ely in 1583. In July 1587 he received the degree of doctor of laws and on 9 October he was admitted as an advocate of the arches. In 1587 Sir Christopher Hatton, the lord chancellor, appointed Swale master in chancery. Swale was known as Hatton's 'creature', but the lord chancellor did not rely on his knowledge of civil law any more than on that of the other masters (Levack, 273). Early in 1588 John Whitgift, archbishop of Canterbury, appointed Swale as one of the commissaries for the archdeaconry of Ely. Later that year Swale became the chancellor of Ely diocese, a position he held until 1606. In June 1588 he received a dispensation to hold the rectory of Emneth, Norfolk, and in 1591 he became rector of Elm, on the Isle of Ely, upon the presentation of Elizabeth I. He was appointed JP for the Isle of Ely about 1591 and for Cambridge about 1592. He became JP for Oxford in 1604.

In 1589 Swale was elected MP for Higham Ferrers, Northamptonshire, presumably through the patronage of Hatton. About the same time he became the lay prebendary of Newbald in the diocese of York. He then resigned his college appointments, which included that of bursar,

and on 3 October 1590 gained admission to Doctors' Commons. This marked the beginning of a period of activity in the ecclesiastical and admiralty courts, including his appointment as judge of the court of audience by 1600. His knowledge of civil law led to his selection, together with Richard Bancroft, bishop of London, and Sir Christopher Perkins LLD, for a diplomatic mission to Emden to negotiate with Danish commissioners regarding commercial matters in April 1600. Swale expressed reluctance to accept this assignment but eventually yielded to pressure from Sir Robert Cecil, principal secretary, and the privy council. He was appointed a member of the court of high commission in 1602 and he served occasionally as a commissioner on the court of delegates, commissioner for admiralty criminal causes, and commissioner of piracy. Swale was knighted at Whitehall Palace on 23 July 1603. He attended the Hampton Court conference in 1604 and afterwards was one of four civilians included on a commission to regulate books printed without authority. In 1605 he served with two other civilians and one common law justice to decide a dispute between Portugal and the Netherlands. During the latter period of his career he resided both at Rotherhithe, Surrey, and in London with his wife, Susan, daughter of James Rolfe of St Albans, Hertfordshire. He held three manors in Yorkshire, including that of Askham Richard. He and his wife did not have any children, and when he died on 30 May 1608 he bequeathed his lands to his wife, whom he named as executor. She died in 1620, and his heir male, a distant cousin John Swale, may have benefited.

BRIAN P. LEVACK

Sources HoP, *Commons, 1558–1603* · B. P. Levack, *The civil lawyers in England, 1603–1641* (1973) · *DNB* · G. D. Squibb, *Doctors' Commons: a history of the College of Advocates and Doctors of Law* (1977) · Cooper, *Ath. Cantab.* · J. Heywood and J. Wright, *Cambridge University transactions*, 2 vols. (1854) · W. J. Jones, *The Elizabethan court of chancery* (1967) · *CSP dom.*, 1603–10, 216 · *Calendar of the manuscripts of the most hon. the marquis of Salisbury*, 24 vols., HMC, 9 (1883–1976), vol. 9, p. 129; vol. 17, pp. 182–3 · inquisition post mortem, PRO, C 142/302/115 · will, PRO, PROB 11/111, sig. 49 · *Memoirs of … Sir Christopher Hatton*, ed. N. H. Nicolas (1847)
Wealth at death lands: PRO C 142/320/115; will, PRO, PROB 11/111, sig. 49

Swallow, John Crossley (1923–1994), oceanographer, was born on 11 October 1923 at New Mill, near Huddersfield, Yorkshire, the second of the three children of Alfred Swallow (d. 1952), a timber merchant and wood turner, and his wife, Elizabeth Crossley (d. 1958), a teacher. He attended Hepworth council school (1928–34) and Honley grammar school (1934–41), and from there went to St John's College, Cambridge, with an exhibition in natural sciences and state and county major scholarships. At Cambridge he studied mathematics and physics. Electronics was a compulsory part of the two-year course, after which students left to contribute to the war effort. Following training in wireless installation and maintenance at the Admiralty signals establishment (ASE), then at Haslemere in Surrey, Swallow was stationed briefly at Scapa Flow before being posted to the naval base at Trincomalee, Ceylon, for the remainder of the war. When he returned to ASE in 1946,

Stefan de Walden encouraged him to go back to Cambridge, where he obtained a first-class honours degree in physics in 1948.

Swallow had thought of working in low temperature physics, but became a research student in the department of geodesy and geophysics, having attended stimulating lectures by E. C. Bullard during his final year. Maurice Hill and his team were pioneering the use of seismic methods to study the sea floor and developed a technique which could be operated by a single ship. Swallow and T. F. Gaskell took the equipment to sea in the survey vessel HMS *Challenger* during her circumnavigation of 1950–52. Observations from this voyage, and from later cruises in home waters, formed the basis of Swallow's PhD in 1954 and contained valuable new information on the structure and composition of oceanic crust.

Having made a significant contribution to a field that would shortly be at the centre of a revolution in earth science, Swallow went on to achieve a breakthrough which would fundamentally alter understanding of ocean circulation. His background and experience led to his being recruited in 1954 to the staff of the National Institute of Oceanography (NIO), which had recently moved to a former Admiralty building in Surrey (one where Swallow had trained during the war). Physical oceanographers were experiencing difficulty in measuring subsurface currents. Swallow suggested using neutrally buoyant floats, which, being slightly less compressible than sea water, could be precisely weighted to float at a given depth. The floats relayed sound signals which enabled their position to be tracked by a research ship, and were relatively inexpensive to build and operate. Early experiments attracted the attention of Henry Stommel, a leading American oceanographer, who needed observations to test his own mathematical theories of ocean circulation. Swallow floats were deployed in joint US/UK observations in the Gulf Stream and confirmed many of Stommel's predictions. However, in cruises off Bermuda in 1959–60, Swallow and his colleagues found that the floats were behaving erratically. It was the first indication that the deeper layers of the central area of the ocean are occupied by vigorous short-lived circulation events, shown by subsequent research to be highly variable mesoscale eddies, not unlike small-scale atmospheric weather systems. These findings, regarded as 'arguably the most significant discovery about the nature of the ocean made in the 20th century' (*The Independent*, 17 Dec 1994), added a new dimension to ocean circulation studies, in which descendants of the Swallow float continue to be an important research tool.

In 1958 Swallow married a widowed colleague, Mary Morgan, *née* Mackenzie (*b.* 1917), a geographer and NIO librarian. She and her young daughter, Lucy, to whom Swallow was a devoted stepfather, went with him to Bermuda in 1959–60. After their return, until her retirement in 1977, Mary Swallow was editor of the journal *Deep-Sea Research*. She gave her husband unstinting support both at home and in his scientific work.

In 1963 Swallow sailed in the new British oceanographic vessel RRS *Discovery* to take part in the international Indian Ocean expedition. Although he later made important contributions to understanding in other areas, notably the Mediterranean circulation and the north Atlantic (he spent a year in the USA as Rossby fellow at the Woods Hole Oceanographic Institution (WHOI), in 1973–4), it was the Indian Ocean, and adjacent bodies of water such as the Red Sea, which principally occupied Swallow for the rest of his life, both in his scientific work and in his seagoing. Professionally, it was the unique features of the area's atmospheric and ocean circulation and the close relationship between the two, expressed in their seasonal reversal during the monsoons, that interested him. Characteristically, however, his interest in the region was wide and included its geography, natural history, history, and food.

Swallow was elected a fellow of the Royal Society in 1968, having already received the Murchison grant of the Royal Geographical Society in 1965. However, his contribution was perhaps more widely recognized overseas. He had received the coveted albatross of the American Miscellaneous Society in 1960. Although ostensibly awarded as a joke, this was a prize given by oceanographers to colleagues who had made particularly significant new leaps in understanding. It was soon followed by more conventional honours, including the Bigelow medal of WHOI (1962), foreign honorary membership of the American Academy of Arts and Sciences, the Sverdrup gold medal of the American Meteorological Society (1978), and the Albert I of Monaco commemorative medal (the Manley-Bendall prize) from the Institut Océanographique (Paris and Monaco) (1984). In February 1994 Swallow became the first recipient of the Henry Stommel medal in oceanography, 'for fundamental and enduring contributions to observing and understanding ocean processes' and 'in recognition of his exemplary seagoing oceanographic studies of North Atlantic, Mediterranean, and Indian Ocean circulation'.

Swallow's career was interrupted by a severe heart attack in 1978, but he recovered well, and though he formally retired in 1983 he continued to be active in science. From 1983 the Swallows lived in the west country, where they continued their generous hospitality to friends and colleagues—which their mutual interest in gardening and good food, and his knowledge of wine, made additionally memorable. This quiet existence was punctuated by new voyages, in the French research vessel *Marion Dufresne* to the Indian Ocean, and in the German vessel *Meteor*. Swallow's capacity for physical hard work at sea was legendary, as was his meticulousness. He also had a rare capacity for entering into other people's interests, and conversations with him would lead to new perceptions on the most diverse of topics. All this, added to his own distinguished contribution, and his personality—he was a large, gentle, and genial Yorkshireman—made him a much liked and respected colleague. He was greatly affected by the untimely death in 1993 of his stepdaughter. He died suddenly at his home, Heath Cottage, Drakewalls, Gunnislake, Cornwall, of heart failure, on 3 December 1994 and was later cremated. He was survived by his widow.

MARGARET DEACON

Sources J. C. Swallow, interview, 1994, National Meteorological Library, Bracknell, Buckinghamshire · H. Charnock, *Memoirs FRS*, 43 (1997), 503–19 · P. J. Conquer, *Dr John Crossley Swallow, F.R.S.: a bibliography* (1995) · N. W. Rakestraw, *The life and activities of a physical oceanographer (John C. Swallow)* (1966) · W. J. Gould, 'Dr John Crossley Swallow FRS, physical oceanographer', *Ocean Challenge*, 5/2 (1995), 4–8 · *The Independent* (17 Dec 1994) · *The Times* (31 Dec 1994) · P. M. Saunders, *Quarterly Journal of the Royal Meteorological Society*, B121 (1995), 959 · J. Crease, 'John Swallow, 1923–1994', *IAPSO Proceedings*, 19 (1995), 490–91 · B. Molinari, 'John Swallow (1923–94)', *EOS: Transactions of the American Geophysical Union*, 76 (1995), 361–2 · J. Crease, W. J. Gould, and P. M. Saunders, 'An anniversary volume for John Swallow', *Progress in Oceanography*, 14 (1985), 1–5 · G. S. Ritchie, *Challenger* (1957)
Archives Southampton Oceanography Centre, National Oceanographic Library, scientific MSS | SOUND Meteorological Office, Bracknell, Berkshire, National Meteorological Library
Likenesses photograph, repro. in Charnock, *Memoirs FRS* · photograph, repro. in Conquer, *Dr John Crossley Swallow* · photograph, repro. in Gould, 'Dr John Crossley Swallow' · photograph, repro. in *The Independent* · photograph, repro. in *The Times* · photograph, repro. in Crease, Gould, and Saunders, 'An anniversary volume' · photograph (at date of election to Royal Society), RS
Wealth at death under £125,000: probate, 21 Feb 1995, *CGPLA Eng. & Wales*

Swalwell, Thomas (*d.* 1539), Benedictine monk and archivist, became a monk of Durham Cathedral priory about 1483. In 1486 he is recorded as a scholar at Durham College, Oxford, where he qualified as a doctor in theology in 1503. His notes for lectures on Peter Lombard's *Sentences* survive in the margins of one of the many early printed books that he owned and annotated in his distinctive handwriting. Some of these annotations were directed towards preaching and teaching, and they reveal Swalwell's very wide range of reading, from the Fathers through to contemporaries, and a conservative interest in such matters of current debate as the eucharist and papal authority, together with a great concern for decorum in the conduct of the liturgy. He provided many manuscripts in the community's collections with detailed lists of contents, so facilitating their use, and he catalogued the books at Durham's cell at Finchale.

Swalwell was entrusted with important offices in the monastery, as guest-master and chief land agent for ten years (1504–14), and then as almoner for over twenty, with responsibility for four hospitals and a school. It was perhaps the period between 1496 and 1500 when he was monastic chancellor that first stimulated his abiding concern for the monastic archives, where he broke new ground in important ways. He gathered up and arranged the series of annual accounts, presented by some twenty-five different monastic office-holders over a period of more than two centuries, and he devised a subject classification for a substantial proportion of the more miscellaneous material. These activities probably made a decisive contribution to the survival of very important sections of Durham Cathedral's muniments, which now form one of the most significant medieval archives in Britain. Swalwell died, probably in Durham, in the second half of 1539, shortly before the monastery where he had spent most of his long life was dissolved on the last day of the year.

A. J. PIPER

Sources A. J. Piper, 'Dr Thomas Swalwell: monk of Durham, archivist and bibliophile (*d.* 1539)', *Books and collectors, 1200–1700: essays presented to Andrew Watson*, ed. J. P. Carley and C. G. C. Tite (1997), 71–100 · Emden, *Oxf.*, 3.1828

Swan [*married name* Burnett Smith], **Annie Shepherd** [*pseud.* David Lyall] (**1859–1943**), novelist, was born on 8 July 1859 in Edinburgh, the daughter of Edward Swan (*d.* 1893), a farmer and potato merchant, and his first wife, Euphemia Brown (*d.* 1881). After the failure of her father's business in Berwickshire, Swan's life was divided between Mountskip Farm, near Gorebridge, Midlothian, and Maryfield, Easter Road, Edinburgh, where she attended a dame-school and later Queen Street Ladies' College. Her father was a member of Duke Street Chapel, an Evangelical Union congregation, but in adulthood Swan became a member of the Church of Scotland.

Swan's teenage persistence in writing fiction was rewarded when *Wrongs Righted* (1881) was published serially in the *People's Friend*, establishing her profitable association with the publisher John Leng. The success of *Aldersyde* (1883), the novel which made her reputation, was assured when William Gladstone wrote a letter in its praise to *The Scotsman* (his letter was published in facsimile in the second edition of the novel). She was throughout her life a pronounced Liberal and campaigner for Liberal causes.

On 27 December 1883 Swan married James Burnett Smith (1857–1927), a schoolteacher, and set up home in Star, Markinch, two years later moving to Morningside, Edinburgh, where Burnett Smith became a medical student at Edinburgh University, Swan paying his way through university. Swan confirmed her success with *The Gates of Eden* (1887) and *Maitland of Laurieston* (1891), novels modelled on the fiction of Margaret Oliphant but never rivalling Oliphant's literary complexity. It is estimated that during her career Swan 'wrote 162 novels under her own name and at least forty under the male pseudonym David Lyall' (Dickson, 329). Shortly after her husband's graduation, Swan achieved her ambition of moving to London, initially to 52 Camden Square, where her children were born: Effie on 10 January 1893 (*d.* 15 October 1973) and Eddie in 1896. Later the family moved to 252 Finchley Road, Hampstead.

Swan's prolific output was the result of rising at 6 a.m. and writing 3000 words which she never redrafted. She was much in demand for press interviews and because of her ability as a public speaker received invitations to speak for London city missions and, later in life, the Liberal Party, standing unsuccessfully as a candidate for Maryhill, Glasgow, in 1922.

William Robertson Nicoll, founder of the *British Weekly* made Swan chief contributor to *Annie Swan's Magazine* and its agony aunt in the feature 'Over the teacups'. Swan also wrote for the *British Weekly*, becoming acquainted with S. R. Crockett and J. M. Barrie whose fiction along with Swan's earned the lasting opprobrium of the Scottish literary establishment who damned it as 'kailyard', summing up their disgust with its parochialism and sentimentality.

Annie Shepherd Swan (1859–1943), by Elliott & Fry

In 1908, the Burnett Smiths moved to Hertford, where in September 1910 Eddie died after shooting himself accidentally. The family was devastated and Swan experimented briefly with spiritualism guided by W. T. Stead. During the First World War she went to France on a morale-boosting tour and also worked with Belgian refugees. Her home, the North House, was bombed in 1915. Invited by the Ministry of Information, Swan toured the United States in 1918 to explain the extent of British food shortages.

When Burnett Smith retired, the family moved to Bandrum, Fife, where Swan wrote *The Pendulum* (1926). Her success depended on her precise knowledge of the values of her mass readership, being regarded as an eminently 'safe' author who affirmed the values of the nonconformist conscience. *The Pendulum's* critique of these values provoked hostility among her readership demonstrating the extent to which the relation between writer and reader was one of consent rather than control. Swan never wrote another novel like it.

When James Burnett Smith died in 1927, Swan and her daughter moved to Gullane, East Lothian, where she was still in public demand: one journalist recorded that she was 'a charming woman, neat of foot, grey-haired, shingled, dressed in stylish mourning, with a quick smile'; another that she was 'plain, plump and motherly' (NL

Scot. accession 6003, box 2, folder 3a). She was made a CBE in 1930. Swan died of heart disease at Aldersyde, Gullane, on 17 June 1943 and was buried in Kinghorn, Fife.

B. DICKSON

Sources A. S. Swan, *My life* (1934) · B. Dickson, 'Annie S. Swan and O. Douglas: legacies of the kailyard', *A history of Scottish women's writing*, ed. D. Gifford and D. McMillan (1997), 329–46 · Gladstone, *Diaries* · NL Scot., Acc. 6003, box 2, folder 3a
Archives NL Scot., accession 6003
Likenesses Elliott & Fry, photograph, NPG [*see illus.*] · F. Inglis, photograph, repro. in Swan, *My life*, 282–3
Wealth at death £27,048 0s. 8d.: confirmation, 2 Aug 1943, CCI

Swan, John (*bap.* **1605**, *d.* **1671**), Church of England clergyman and encyclopaedist, was baptized at Ickleton, Cambridgeshire, on 26 September 1605, the eldest son of John Swan (*d.* 1639), vicar of nearby Sawston from 1600 to 1639, and his wife, Sarah, daughter of Thomas Adams of Wisbech. In 1622 Swan followed his father to Trinity College, Cambridge, graduating BA in 1626 and proceeding MA in 1629; he later described himself as BD. He was ordained deacon and priest at Peterborough in December 1629, and occurs as minister (probably curate) in Duxford St Peter, Cambridgeshire, in 1630. On 21 June 1634 at Sawston he married Frances Rudland (*d.* 1667).

In 1635 Swan published the first edition of his encyclopaedia, *Speculum mundi*. In dedicating it to the duke of Lennox, a contemporary at Trinity who shared the same tutor, he numbered himself among men 'of retired lives, and small-grown fortunes'. The work was loosely based on Guillaume de Saluste du Bartas, *Première semaine, ou, Création du monde* (1578), and subsequent editions, usually translated in English as *Divine Weeks*. He organized his material around the six days of creation, concentrating on cosmology, meteorology, mineralogy, zoology, and botany. Although essentially traditionalist, the work shows a critical spirit and a lively interest in recent discoveries and debates. On cosmology he generally followed Tycho Brahe, whose scheme he reproduced in diagrammatic form.

By the later 1630s Swan revealed himself as a pugnacious Laudian. It is not clear whether *A sermon pointing out the chiefe causes, and cure, of such unruly stirres, as are not seldom found in the church of God* (1639), preached at Sawston at the archdeacon's visitation on 19 September 1638, was delivered by Swan or by his father. However, the John Swan who wrote the violently anti-puritan *Profanomastix* (1639), which has stylistic similarities, was explicitly identified as the curate of Duxford St Peter. His *Redde debitum, or, A Discourse in Defence of the Three Chiefe Fatherhoods* (1640), written 'in confutation of all disobedient and factious kinde of people, who are enemies to both church and state', is in the same vein.

Yet Swan was not sequestered. In 1646 the county committee installed him briefly as interim following the ejection of the vicar of Duxford St Peter, George Chamberlaine. In 1647 Swan signed the Sawston registers for the first time as minister, and from the same year he was also rector of nearby Whittlesford, although both were poor livings, valued at £20 and £23 p.a. respectively in 1650.

Either he had modified his views or he had influential patrons; he certainly counted the militant parliamentarian astrologer, John Booker, among his friends. Swan himself was keenly interested in astrology, both natural and judicial, and vigorously defended it in *Signa coeli: the Signs of Heaven* (1652), a sermon preached the day before the notorious 'Black Monday', the solar eclipse of 29 March 1652. The following year he published a chronology of the ancient world, *Calumnus mensurans: the Measuring Reed, or, The Standard of Time*, dedicating it to councillor of state Bulstrode Whitelocke. He compiled a series of almanacs published annually in Cambridge from 1657, and may have been responsible too for other titles, such as those ostensibly by 'Swallow' and 'Dove'.

It is not entirely clear how Swan was affected by the Restoration. He did not sign the Whittlesford registers between 1659 and 1662, nor the Sawston registers between 1662 and 1664. Thereafter, however, his title seems to have been secure. Following the death of Frances Swan in 1667 he married Ellen or Helen Rudland (presumably from the same family) at Pampisford, Cambridgeshire, in September 1669. She was still alive when Swan made his will in 1670, as were three of his children. Swan died in 1671 and was buried at Sawston on 17 March.

BERNARD CAPP

Sources F. J. Bywaters, 'The clergy of Sawston, 1197 to 1948', *Proceedings of the Cambridge Antiquarian Society*, 42 (1948) · T. F. Teversham, *A history of Sawston* (1942–7) · *Walker rev.*, 78 · private information (1990; 2004) [D. M. Owen, J. M. Farrar] · B. S. Capp, *Astrology and the popular press: English almanacs, 1500–1800* (1979) · A. Milton, *Catholic and Reformed: the Roman and protestant churches in English protestant thought, 1600–1640* (1995) · *IGI*

Swan, John Macallan (1847–1910), painter and sculptor, was born on 9 December 1847 at Brentford in Middlesex. His parents, Robert Wemyss Swan, a civil engineer, and Elizabeth Macallan, were both Scottish. Swan's sister Alice Macallan Swan (1864–1939) was also a gifted artist and was trained by her much older brother John. Swan was brought up in Worcester, where his early abilities as an artist and interest in wild animals were nurtured by painting the animals of Wombwell's travelling menagerie. He studied at Worcester School of Art, then from 1872 at the Royal Academy Schools and a little later at Lambeth School of Art under John Sparkes. It was at this time that Swan became friends with the artist W. R. Symonds, who married another of his sisters, Margaret.

Dissatisfied with the teaching at the Royal Academy Schools, in 1874 Swan went to Paris where, at the École des Beaux-Arts, his drawings were deemed to be sufficiently good for him to paint from life immediately. There he studied under Jean-Léon Gérôme and learned much from his paintings. Jules Bastien-Lepage (1848–1884) and P. A. J. Dagnan-Bouveret (1852–1929) were fellow students and Swan found their realist paintings inspirational. Gérôme introduced Swan to the animal sculptor Emmanuel Frémiet (1824–1910), and the two subsequently studied together in the Jardin des Plantes. The animal sculptures of Antoine-Louis Barye (1796–1875) and Auguste-Nicolas

Cain (1821–1894) were also admired by Swan, who increasingly turned to modelling, until ultimately he divided his time fairly equally between painting and sculpture.

After five years in Paris, Swan returned to England, where he lived first at Abinger Mill, Wotton, Surrey, and then in Stanhope Street, London. Inspired by Gérôme's exotic lion pictures and by the sculptures of Barye and Frémiet, Swan spent many hours at the zoo in Regent's Park, sketching animals, particularly the wild cats. Although Swan could see these animals only in captivity, he was able to transpose his sketches of them into grand compositions, in which they were depicted in dramatic landscape settings, as in *Maternity* (Rijksmuseum, Amsterdam), *Leopards* (c.1907; Bradford Art Galleries and Museums), and *Adrift* (exh. RA, 1905; Aberdeen Art Gallery), in which three polar bears cling desperately to a piece of floating ice. This painting recalls the work of Sir Edwin Landseer, especially his famous *Man Proposes, God Disposes* of 1863–4 (Royal Holloway College, University of London). Swan, however, avoids Landseer's sentimentality and never gives his animals any anthropomorphic qualities—rather he emphasizes their power, beauty, and dignity. Swan is known to have used photographs of the polar regions to assist him when composing such paintings and also the photographs of Eadweard Muybridge, which captured animals in motion.

Swan did not restrict his subject matter to animals: the human form—and nudes in particular—were an important part of his *œuvre*. In Paris, at Frémiet's suggestion, he had studied the human form under the anatomists Gervais and Duval, and in London he continued to study at St Thomas's and St Bartholomew's hospitals. His first exhibited work, shown at the Royal Academy in 1878, combined both of his interests, having Dante and the leopard as its subject. Swan also exhibited at the Grosvenor Gallery, London, and in Paris, where both paintings and sculpture gained an honourable mention in 1885, a silver medal in 1889, and three gold medals in 1900 (at the Universal Exhibition).

Swan met his future wife, Mary Anne Rankin, in London. The eldest daughter of Hamilton Rankin of Carndonagh, co. Donegal, she was also an artist specializing in portraits, especially of children. They married in 1884, in Cork, where Swan's family was then living. They had two children, John Barye Rankin, a civil engineer, and Mary Alice, who followed her parents' profession.

Swan was one of the few English artists to achieve wide acceptance abroad at the outset of their careers. As well as the awards that he gained in Paris, he was awarded a gold medal in 1893 and the grand medal in 1897 at Munich, and two gold medals at the Chicago World Fair. He was a member of the secessions of Vienna and Munich, and in 1911, after his death, his work was awarded a memorial gold medal at Barcelona. Swan was elected a member of the Dutch Watercolour Society in 1885, four years before being elected a member of the London-based Royal Watercolour Society. He was elected an associate of the Royal Academy in 1894, and became a full member in 1905. In 1899 he was made full member of the Royal Institute of

Painters in Water Colours. He was also awarded an honorary LLD at Aberdeen University. Swan's work was admired by many notable collectors, including Alexander C. Ionides, whose portrait, and that of Mrs Ionides, he painted.

As well as working in oil, Swan excelled in producing pastel drawings, and in 1897 a special exhibition of his studies in this medium was held by the Fine Art Society, London. In his sculptures of animals Swan concentrated on underlying form rather than on surface colours and patterns. The sculptures are generally freer than his paintings, with bold use of the *cire perdu* technique, which allows the artist to work in malleable clay, then cast from this in bronze and silver. Among his works in sculpture are *The Walking Leopard* (Manchester City Galleries), *Indian Leopard and Tortoise* (Tate collection), and *A Lioness Drinking*, which was commissioned for the Jardin du Luxembourg in Paris. In his later years Swan was closely aligned with the New Sculpture movement, which influenced both his subject matter and the materials that he used. Thereafter he created a series of idealized statuettes in silver, such as *Orpheus* (a large bronze version of this work is in the collections of Manchester City Galleries) and *St John the Baptist* of 1899 (Perth Art Gallery). He was the author of a treatise on metalwork, which was delivered before the Royal Institute of British Architects in 1906, and of papers on technical artistic questions, some of which were printed in the *Proceedings of the Japanese Society*.

In 1907, on the advice of Sir Edward John Poynter, president of the Royal Academy, Herbert Baker selected Swan to model eight uniform lions for a planned memorial to Cecil Rhodes at Groote Schuur, Cape Town; later Swan also agreed to create a colossal bronze bust of Rhodes for the memorial. In October 1907 he journeyed to South Africa, where he stayed with Prime Minister Jameson. Swan completed the lion but collapsed in London while working on the bust of Rhodes. His wife took him to Thatches, their house at Niton on the Isle of Wight, where he died on 14 February 1910. He was buried at St John the Baptist Church, Niton. In June that year a number of academicians, including Lawrence Alma-Tadema and John Singer Sargent, sent a letter to *The Times* appealing for subscriptions to a special fund to acquire as many of Swan's drawings as possible, which were then to be distributed to galleries in Britain and the empire. Himself a generous subscriber, J. C. Drucker organized and administered the fund. That winter the original model for the Rhodes lion and the plaster bust of Rhodes were exhibited at the Royal Academy, along with nearly 100 other works by Swan. The lions and bust were cast and the entire monument dedicated on 5 July 1912.

WALTER ARMSTRONG, *rev.* JENNIFER MELVILLE

Sources R. A. M. Stevenson, 'J. M. Swan', *Art Journal*, new ser., 14 (1894), 17–22 · A. L. Baldry, *Drawings of John M. Swan R.A.* (1905) · A. L. Baldry, 'The work of J. M. Swan ARA', *The Studio*, 22 (1901), 74–80, 150–61 · G. M. Waters, *Dictionary of British artists, working 1900–1950* (1975) · S. Beattie, *The New Sculpture* (1983) · C. Monkhouse, 'John Macallan Swan', *Magazine of Art*, 17 (1893–4), 171–6 · personal knowledge (1912) · private information (1912, 2004) [Allan H. B. Swan, grandson] · *CGPLA Eng. & Wales* (1910)

Likenesses H. von Herkomer, group portrait, oils, 1908 (*The council of the Royal Academy*), Tate collection · W. G. John, bronze bust, c.1910, RA · London Stereoscopic Co., cabinet photograph, NPG · T. B. Wirgman, woodcut, BM

Wealth at death £4458 4s. 2d.: administration, 1 April 1910, *CGPLA Eng. & Wales*

Swan, Joseph (*bap.* 1791, *d.* 1874), anatomist, baptized on 30 September 1791, was the son of Henry Swan, a surgeon to the Lincoln County Hospital, and a general practitioner in that city; he was a member of an old medical family. After serving an apprenticeship to his father, Swan was sent in 1810 to the united hospitals of Guy's and St Thomas's in Southwark, London, where he became a pupil of Henry Cline the younger and gained the friendship of his master and of Astley Cooper. He was admitted a member of the Royal College of Surgeons on 1 October 1813, and then he went abroad for a short time, after which he settled at Lincoln, and was elected surgeon to the Lincoln County Hospital on 8 January 1814.

Swan won the Jacksonian prize at the Royal College of Surgeons in 1817 for his essay 'On deafness and diseases and injuries of the organ of hearing'. In 1819 he won the prize a second time with a dissertation 'On the treatment of morbid local affections of nerves'. This was published in 1820 and translated into German in 1824. He was awarded in 1822 the first college triennial prize for 'A minute dissection of the nerves of the medulla spinalis from their origin to their terminations and to their conjunctions with the cerebral and visceral nerves, authenticated by preparations of the dissected parts'. The triennial prize was again given to him in 1825 for 'A minute dissection of the cerebral nerves from their origin to their termination, and to their conjunction with the nerves of the medulla spinalis and viscera'. The college had so high an opinion of Swan's merits that he was voted its honorary gold medal in 1825.

In order to overcome the difficulty of obtaining subjects for dissection at Lincoln, Astley Cooper sent Swan every Christmas a large hamper labelled 'glass, with care', containing a well selected human subject. The example set by Cooper is said to have been followed by John Abernethy, and Swan was thus able to proceed uninterruptedly with his work.

Swan resigned his office of surgeon to the Lincoln County Hospital on 26 February 1827, moved to London, and took a house at 6 Tavistock Square, where he converted the billiard room into a dissecting room. Here he continued his research at leisure for the rest of his life, never attaining any practice as a surgeon, but doing much for the science of anatomy.

He was elected a life member of the Royal College of Surgeons in 1831, and in 1843 he was nominated a fellow of the college. He resigned his office of member of the council after a severe attack of illness in 1869, and died, unmarried, at Filey, Yorkshire, on 4 October 1874. He was buried in Filey churchyard four days later.

Swan was a born anatomist, practical rather than theoretical, and with a talent for dissection. Of a retiring and modest disposition, he remained personally almost unknown, and the value of his work was only later appreciated. His chief work was *A Demonstration of the Nerves of the Human Body* (in twenty-five plates, with explanations, 1830; republished, 1865). It is a clear exposition of the course and distribution of the cerebral, spinal, and sympathetic nerves of the human body. The plates are admirably drawn by E. West, and engraved by the Stewarts. The original copperplates and engravings on steel came into the possession of the Royal College of Surgeons of England, to whom they were presented in 1895 by Mrs Machin of Gateford Hill, Worksop, widow of the nephew and residuary legatee of Joseph Swan. A cheaper edition of this work was published in 1834, with plates engraved by Finden. It was also translated into French (Paris, 1838). Swan's *Illustrations of the Comparative Anatomy of the Nervous System* (1835) criticized the new approaches taken by French comparative anatomists.

D'A. POWER, *rev.* MICHAEL BEVAN

Sources *The Lancet* (7 Nov 1874) · private information (1898) · A. Desmond, *The politics of evolution: morphology, medicine and reform in radical London* (1989) · *Medical Times and Gazette* (17 Oct 1874), 459–60
Wealth at death under £12,000: resworn probate, Oct 1875, *CGPLA Eng. & Wales* (1874)

Swan, Sir Joseph Wilson (1828–1914), chemist and inventor, was born on 31 October 1828 at Pallion Hall, near Sunderland, co. Durham, the third of the eight children of John Swan (*b.* 1794/5) and his wife, Isabella, *née* Cameron. Both parents were of Scottish descent, their families having settled in co. Durham about the middle of the eighteenth century. John Swan was always ready to engage in new ventures, but his lack of business acumen led to a gradual decline in the family's circumstances. Joseph Swan's formal education was brief—a few years in a dame-school followed by a period at a boys' school near Sunderland, ending before his thirteenth birthday. From an early age he had learned much more by observing local craftsmen and the developing local industries.

In 1842 Swan was apprenticed to a Sunderland firm of druggists, Hudson and Osbaldiston. Both principals died within three years, freeing him from his articles, and in 1846 he joined his friend and future brother-in-law, John Mawson, in his business of chemist and druggist in Newcastle. Mawson was killed in a tragic accident in 1867 and Swan, by then a partner, took over the management of the business. He had married a school teacher, Frances (1829/30–1868), the daughter of a Liverpool merchant, William White, on 31 July 1862; three of their children survived to adulthood. In 1871 he married Hannah White, his deceased wife's sister; they had five children.

Swan was interested in photography, and made several significant contributions to its development, notably the production of collodion, the perfecting of the carbon or autotype process, the production of successful bromide dry plates, and the invention of bromide paper. F. S. Archer had described the collodion process for making photographic negatives in 1851. Swan began making collodion soon afterwards, and 'Mawson's collodion' became renowned. The basis of the carbon process for producing

Sir Joseph Wilson Swan (1828–1914), by Elliott & Fry

permanent prints had been known for some years before Swan patented a practicable process in 1864. It had far-reaching effects, leading to photogravure printing and to other printing processes. After patenting the carbon process Swan worked for many years on developing half-tone blocks for printing photographs. R. L. Maddox had proposed the use of silver bromide in gelatine to make dry photographic plates in 1871, but, despite its greater convenience, it was slow to replace the wet collodion process. Swan began supplying dry plates in 1877. Production problems led to the discovery that the sensitivity of the plates was highly temperature-dependent, and to improvements which made Mawson and Swan's bromide plates famous. Swan also, in 1879, invented bromide paper, which used the same methods of preparation, and which has remained in use ever since.

Swan's name is remembered chiefly for his invention of an incandescent electric lamp. His interest was aroused in 1845 when W. E. Staite demonstrated an incandescent filament at the Sunderland Athenaeum. Swan's first experiments, about 1860, came to naught. In the late 1870s there was great interest in electric lighting, and Swan took up his experiments again. The recently invented Sprengel vacuum pump, manipulated by Swan's collaborator C. H. Stern, a Liverpool bank clerk, made success possible. Swan demonstrated an experimental incandescent electric lamp at a private meeting in December 1878 and at a public lecture the following February. After a further eighteen months' development, Swan was able to demonstrate a technically and commercially viable lamp, with a filament of carbonized thread, at another public lecture in October 1880. A company was set up to produce the lamp, and was superseded by a larger company in 1882. At this point the company making Edison's electric lamp began legal action, claiming that Swan was infringing Edison's patents. The case did not come to trial, because the two companies agreed to merge. The question of priority was not resolved, and is misleading. Several men devised incandescent electric lamps. Edison and Swan achieved commercial success, and by combining they were able to suppress competition in Britain. The lamps sold in Britain, however, were almost entirely of Swan's design. Swan patented an improved filament made of extruded cellulose in 1883, but it was not used commercially for some years.

Swan had lived at Low Fell, Gateshead, since 1869, but the headquarters of the Edison and Swan company were in London, so in 1883 he moved south, to Lauriston, a house in Bromley, Kent, which he fitted out with a laboratory. With more numerous engagements in London, the family moved again in 1894, to 58 Holland Park, London. Swan had been made a chevalier of the Légion d'honneur after the Exposition Internationale d'Électricité in Paris in 1881. He was elected a fellow of the Royal Society in 1894, and was knighted in 1904. He received honorary degrees from the University of Durham, and medals from the Royal Photographic Society, the Society of Chemical Industry, the Royal Society, and the Society of Arts. Much of Swan's time was taken up with scientific societies, which he found more congenial than some of his business activities. At various times he was a visitor and a manager at the Royal Institution, served on the council of the Royal Society and on the general board of the National Physical Laboratory, was vice-president of Senate at University College, London, and a member of the royal commission for the St Louis Exhibition of 1904. Among other distinctions he was president of the Institution of Electrical Engineers in 1888–9, of the Society of Chemical Industry in 1900–01, and the first president of the Faraday Society, in 1904.

Swan's business interests were diverse. He continued experimenting throughout his life, and was responsible for several other innovations, such as the chrome tanning of leather, which developed from the carbon process, and the cellular lead plate for rechargeable batteries, patented in 1881.

By 1908 developing heart trouble made a quieter life necessary, and Swan moved to Overhill, Warlingham, Surrey, where he died on 27 May 1914, shortly before he was due to receive the freedom of the city of Newcastle. His son received the honour later, on his behalf. Swan was buried in Warlingham churchyard; his wife survived him.   C. N. BROWN

Sources M. E. Swan and K. R. Swan, Sir Joseph Wilson Swan: a memoir (1929) • C. N. Brown, J. W. Swan and the invention of the incandescent electric lamp (1978) • Photographic Journal, new ser., 38 (1914), 263–5 • Journal of the Institution of Electrical Engineers, 52 (1914), 794–5 • W. Garnett, PRS, 96A (1919–20), ix–xiv • The Times (28 May 1914) • Engineering (29 May 1914), 747–9 • The Engineer (29 May 1914), 597 • The Electrician (29 May 1914), 300 • 'The medal', Journal of the Society of Chemical Industry, 21 (1902), 900 [account of speech by E. K. Muspratt presenting the society's medal to Swan] • WWW, 1941–50

Archives CUL, corresp. with Lord Kelvin • ICL, letters to S. P. Thompson • Inst. EE • Tyne and Wear Archives Service, Newcastle upon Tyne, corresp. and papers

Likenesses M. A. Cohen, pencil drawing, 1894, NPG • W. Paget, oils, 1929 (posthumous), Inst. EE • Art Photogravure Co. Ltd, photogravure, repro. in Journal of the Society of Chemical Industry • Elliott & Fry, photograph, NPG [see illus.] • attrib., photograph, NPG • photographs, repro. in Swan and Swan, Sir Joseph Wilson Swan • photogravure, NPG • steel engraving, repro. in The Electrician (10 Nov 1893) • stipple and line engraving, NPG

Wealth at death £60,097 13s. 5d.: probate, 15 July 1914, CGPLA Eng. & Wales

Swan, William (d. after 1445), canon lawyer, probably came from Southfleet in Kent. A cleric of the diocese of Rochester, he may never have advanced beyond minor orders, thereby remaining free to marry. His wife, Joan, and at least two daughters lived at Southfleet, in a household which also included Swan's mother. In a surviving but undated letter, Joan Swan told her husband that she would be willing to join him at the curia but would not learn the vernacular, German, an indication perhaps that Swan was then with the papal curia at Constance. He had a sister, Agnes, and two brothers, John, a pewterer, and Richard, a skinner of London, who acted as Swan's agent.

Already an Oxford master of arts and *licentiatus* in canon law, Swan arrived at the papal curia in 1404 during the brief pontificate of Innocent VII (r. 1404–6). It was at this time that Swan was concerned in the intricate business of the marriage suit of John Arundel and Elizabeth Talbot, who after their marriage discovered that they were related within the forbidden degrees, yet wanted to remain married; Swan met the pope to discuss the fee for a new dispensation. He continued in curial employment under Gregory XII, when that pope was under pressure to resolve the stalemated schism. Swan travelled with the papal curia from place to place in Italy, as Pope Gregory flirted with the idea of a meeting with his Avignon rival, Benedict XIII, at Savona. While at Viterbo, Swan became stricken with dysentery and remained there for six weeks, being nursed by Alice Tudor, who had a suit at the curia. Tempted to leave the peripatetic papal entourage headed by an increasingly difficult pope, Swan was persuaded by the papal chamberlain to remain. His loyalty to Gregory survived that pope's deposition by the Council of Pisa in 1409. During the council Swan was with Gregory at Rimini, and he earned displeasure in England by continuing to sue bulls from the deposed Gregory. Clearly disillusioned, possibly stunned by this criticism, Swan returned about 1410 to England, where he continued his studies in canon law at Oxford. Yet when the fathers gathered at Constance in 1414, Swan was once again in the service of Pope Gregory, now as papal secretary, and, during the council (1414–18) was active in the matter of the disputed election of the abbot of Fountains Abbey (*Frank v. Rypon*).

After a brief stay in England, Swan returned to the papal curia in 1419 as a *scriptor* and *abbreviator* and became increasingly prominent in pursuing English interests, attracting a sizeable clientele of the famous and not-so-famous. He was involved in the difficult negotiations which led to the translation of John Kempe from London to the see of York in 1425 and also represented the interests of Henry Chichele, archbishop of Canterbury, in several matters brought before the papal curia. At an early stage of the Council of Basel (before 30 January 1433), Swan served as proctor for three English bishops: Worcester, Lincoln, and Bath and Wells. There is no evidence of his involvement in the council itself. Although Swan was said to have resigned his curial position by 1442, he seems to have acted as proctor for Christ Church Priory, Canterbury, in 1444. He is known to have rented a large house and garden from the English hospice of St Thomas in Rome. He died some time after 1445.

The letter-book of William Swan is a principal source for Anglo-papal relations in the first half of the fifteenth century. It exists in two somewhat overlapping versions. The Oxford version (Bodl. Oxf., MS Arch. Selden B.23), written at least in part in Swan's own hand, covers the years from 1406 to 1426 and is particularly rich for the years before the Council of Constance. The London version (BL, Cotton MS Cleopatra C.iv) contains nothing before the pontificate of Martin V (r. 1417–31) and extends to 1441. A letter in the Oxford collection describes Swan in this fashion: 'Master William Swan, bachelor in laws, proctor-general in the Roman curia, who, though young, is yet very wise and circumspect, faithful and diligent, and conducts himself with ability in all his doings' (Jacob, 68).

F. DONALD LOGAN

Sources Emden, Oxf. · E. F. Jacob, 'To and from the court of Rome in the early fifteenth century', Essays in later medieval history (1968), 58–78 · D. Wolff, 'William Swan's letter-book', Bodleian Quarterly Review, 6 (1929–31), 301–2 · F. Madan and H. H. E. Craster, A summary catalogue of Western manuscripts in the Bodleian Library at Oxford, 2/1 (1922), no. 3351 · M. Harvey, England, Rome, and the papacy, 1417–1464 (1993)
Archives BL, Cotton MS Cleopatra C.iv · Bodl. Oxf., Arch. Selden MS B.23

Swan, William (1818–1894), university teacher, was born in Edinburgh on 13 March 1818, the son and only child of David Swan (d. 1821), engineer, and his wife, Janet Smith, second daughter of Thomas *Smith (bap. 1752, d. 1815), the lighthouse engineer. Her sister Jane married Robert Stevenson (1772–1850), builder of the Bell Rock lighthouse. Swan's impoverished widowed mother took in the young Thomas Carlyle as a lodger, and, overprotective of her son, had him educated at home: 'My mother made a bungle of my education' (Galbraith, A Scotch Professor, 4), he later said, and evidently led a lonely and unhappy childhood, his only real friend being his first cousin and close contemporary, Thomas *Stevenson (1818–1887), also a lighthouse engineer.

Swan was sent to Edinburgh University at the age of seventeen to study divinity, but subsequently set up as a tutor of mathematics and physics. An evangelist in religion, he 'came out' at the Disruption of the Church of Scotland in 1843, and joined the Free Church. Between 1850 and 1852 he was mathematical master in the Free Church Normal School, Edinburgh. From 1853 he taught mathematics, natural philosophy, and navigation in the Scottish Naval and Military Academy, Edinburgh. In 1859, through the influence of Sir David Brewster, he was appointed professor of natural philosophy at St Andrews. Swan was at last in a financial position of enough security to marry Georgina Frances Downie (1809–1882), daughter of John Cullen, a Glasgow manufacturer, and his wife, Marion Downie. They had first met twenty-four years before; they married, in Edinburgh, on 2 June 1859. They had no children.

Throughout his teaching career, Swan published over twenty papers in scientific journals on various aspects of physics, including meteorology, lighthouse illumination, and the development of new instruments. On occasion he worked closely with the Adie firm of Edinburgh scientific instrument makers, particularly in developing prisms for spectroscopic work. Besides being elected a fellow of the Royal Society of Edinburgh in 1848, Swan received the honorary degree of LLD from Edinburgh University in 1869 and from St Andrews in 1886.

Swan was an extremely sociable man with a wide circle of friends in both Edinburgh and St Andrews. His wife, too, was a welcoming hostess, and they spent the non-academic half of the year at her home, Ardchapel, Shandon Row, Dunbartonshire, entertaining friends. In 1879 Swan was diagnosed with heart disease and went to live the entire year round at Ardchapel. He died there of heart disease on 1 March 1894.   A. D. MORRISON-LOW

Sources J. L. Galbraith, A Scotch professor of the old school: a sketch of the life of William Swan, LLD (1910) · J. L. Galbraith, The emeritus professor: a sketch of the last years of William Swan, LLD (1901) · R. L. Stevenson, Records of a family of engineers (1912) · E. M. Wray, ed., Swan's catalogue, 1880 (1984) · T. N. Clarke, A. D. Morrison-Low, and A. D. C. Simpson, Brass and glass: scientific instrument making workshops in Scotland (1989) · D. Thorburn Burns, 'Towards a definitive history of optical spectroscopy', pt 2, 'Introduction of slits and collinator lens, spectroscopes available before and just after Kirchoff and Bunsen's studies', Journal of Analytical and Atomic Spectroscopy, 3 (Jan 1988), 285–91 · m. cert. · d. cert. · parish register (baptism), Edinburgh parish, 15 March 1818
Archives U. St Andr. L., corresp. with George Forbes and J. D. Forbes
Likenesses photograph, c.1870, U. St Andr., department of Muniments

Swanborough. For this title name see Isaacs, Stella, marchioness of Reading and Baroness Swanborough (1894–1971).

Swanley, Richard (1594/5–1650), naval officer, was probably related to Richard Swanley, an East India captain whose family came from Framilode, Gloucestershire, and who was killed fighting the Portuguese in 1625. The future admiral first appears as a master's mate in the Jonas during the voyage to India of 1621–3. In the next voyage, of 1624–6, he was promoted master of the James and took a prominent part in the battle with the Portuguese off Gombroon. Both voyages were commanded by Captain John Weddell but in 1628 he was absent, serving the state in the Spanish war, and Swanley was promoted captain and commanded the expedition of 1628–31. Weddell returned after the end of the war to command the voyage of 1632–5 in which Swanley was captain of the *Jonas*. When Weddell quarrelled with the East India Company and left to serve in a new one financed by Sir William Courteen, Swanley went with him. His ship, the *Sun*, was the only one to survive the epic voyage to China. On the return journey he separated from Weddell to pick up a cargo of sugar at Achin in Sumatra and then sailed directly for England. The other two ships left Goa in January 1639 and were never heard of again.

When the first civil war broke out Swanley supported parliament. He was captain of the second-rate *Charles* in the summer fleet of 1642. While commanding the squadron blockading Portsmouth, he secured all the forts in the Isle of Wight for parliament and forced Southampton to surrender. In October 1642 he was appointed commander-in-chief of the fleet in the Irish Sea but in practice he seems to have alternated with another former Courteen captain, Robert Moulton, because the impossibility of securing victuals in an area dominated by the royalists and shortage of money frequently forced the parliamentary squadrons to return to Portsmouth. Despite the capture in Milford Haven of the valuable royalist vessel *Fellowship*, his first period in command from May to September 1643 was not very successful. He was too late to save Galway Fort from capture by the confederates and was powerless to prevent the fall of either Bristol or Tenby to the royalists. His next spell of duty between January and June 1644 brought better fortune. He took an active part in the recovery of Pembrokeshire, the conquest of Carmarthenshire and parts of Glamorgan. All these gains were lost during the summer and when he returned he had to do the job again which he executed with his customary vigour. When the main fleet arrived under Batten, all was prepared for the final dénouement, seamen playing an important part in the conclusive defeat of the royalists at Colby Moor. His ships were also instrumental in preserving the Munster ports of Cork, Youghal, and Kinsale when the earl of Inchiquin declared for the parliament. During 1645 and 1646 Swanley joined a group of Pembrokeshire gentry in a vendetta against John Poyer, the governor of Pembroke, which led in the summer of 1645 to his suspension from duty. He was eventually cleared, and restored to his command in October 1646, though the feud helped to push Poyer into supporting the royalists in 1648. Swanley continued to command parliamentary forces in the Irish Sea until 1647, the main event of his last period of command being the surrender of Dublin to parliament.

Swanley's name was missing from the winter fleet list of 1647–8 and he never served again. He is last mentioned attending a conference on 17 June 1648 called by the lord high admiral, the earl of Warwick, at the height of the second civil war. His surviving correspondence contains no expressions of religious fervour so his inactivity could indicate a distaste for the course parliamentary politics were taking; equally it could be due to ill health.

Though an excellent seaman and an able commander Swanley had a violent temper and was not above profiteering on the side. In 1628 he quarrelled with the company

factor over precedence and in 1631 struck his purser during a dispute. He was criticized for excessive private trading when in command in 1628–31. In June 1644 at the capture of Carmarthen he became the only known captain to carry out the parliamentary ordinance to throw any Irish prisoners into the sea. He was also one of a syndicate led by the earl of Warwick which financed the famous privateer the *Constant Warwick*. During his last years he lived at Limehouse, where he acted as churchwarden in 1649. He was buried at St Dunstan and All Saints, Stepney, on 4 September 1650. In his will dated 28 May 1649 and proved 11 September 1650 he mentions his second wife, Elizabeth, a daughter Mary and two sons, John and Richard, the last named a naval officer after the Restoration. He also had a son, George, by his first marriage.

MICHAEL BAUMBER

Sources W. Foster, ed., *The English factories in India*, 1 (1906) · J. R. Powell and E. K. Timings, eds., *Documents relating to the civil war, 1642–1648*, Navy RS, 105 (1963) · W. Ryley and H. Dethick, *The visitation of Middlesex begun in 1663* (1820) · *CSP col.*, vols. 6, 8 · *Swanley's journal, 1621–3*, vol. 24 of Marine Records of East India Company · E. B. Sainsbury, ed., *A calendar of the court minutes … of the East India Company*, [1]: *1635–1639* (1907) · 'Factories: Surat; Swanley's quarrel with purser', *The English factories in India*, ed. W. Foster, 4 (1910), 248–57 · *The travels of Peter Mundy in Europe and Asia, 1608–1667*, ed. R. C. Temple and L. M. Anstey, 5 vols. in 6, Hakluyt Society, 2nd ser., 17, 35, 45–6, 55, 78 (1907–36) · *Calendar of the manuscripts of the marquess of Ormonde*, new ser., 8 vols., HMC, 36 (1902–20), vol. 2 · *The manuscripts of his grace the duke of Portland*, 10 vols., HMC, 29 (1891–1931), vol. 1 · *JHL*, 7 (1644–5) · *JHL*, 10 (1647–8) · *CSP dom.*, 1644 · G. Penn, *Memorials of Sir William Penn*, 2 vols. (1833) · *History of the Irish confederation and the war in Ireland … by Richard Bellings*, ed. J. T. Gilbert, 7 vols. (1882–91) · A. L. Leach, *The history of the civil war (1642–1649) in Pembrokeshire and on its borders* (1937) · J. R. Phillips, *Memoirs of the civil war in Wales and the marches, 1642–1649*, 2nd edn (1878) · parish registers, St Dunstan and All Saints, Stepney, and St Olave, Hart Street · D. Lysons, *The environs of London*, 4 vols. (1792–6) · D. Lysons, *Supplement to the first edition of 'The environs of London'* (1811) · wills, Principal Registry of the Family Division, London [Pembroke] · PRO, HCA 13/61, fol. 385v · E. W. L. Keymer, 'Richard Swanley, the ancestor I wish I had met', *The Midland Ancestor, Journal of the Birmingham and Midland Society for Genealogy and Heraldry*, 12/4 (June 1999)

Swann, Donald Ibrahim (1923–1994), composer and pianist, was born on 30 September 1923 at 27 Coleshill Terrace, Llanelli, the elder of the two children of Herbert William Swann (1894–1969), a medical practitioner, and his wife, Naguimé Sultán, *née* Piszóva (1892–1935), a nurse. His forebears had emigrated to Russia in 1840; his father, having surmounted many difficulties to marry Naguimé, a Muslim of Azerbaijani parentage, in 1917, escaped to Britain with her in 1919. Swann grew up in a house as much Russian and transcaucasian as British, and the influences went deep into the music he was to compose. He was educated at Dulwich preparatory school and Westminster School, where he was a king's scholar, and also studied the piano with Angus Morrison and composition with Hugo Anson at the Royal College of Music. After a year at Christ Church, Oxford, in 1942–3, he registered as a conscientious objector. He joined the Friends' Ambulance Unit and saw service in Egypt, Palestine, and in Greece, a country which also entered deep into his life and music. In 1946 he returned to Christ Church, where he read modern Greek and Russian. He had already begun writing songs, and some of the most distinctive from this period were settings of John Betjeman, whom he met in Oxford. He graduated with a second-class degree in 1948.

Although Russia and Greece were to remain influences on his more personal compositions, Swann's fresh melodic gift also began turning him towards light music, especially when he encountered a friend from school days, Michael *Flanders, now confined by polio to a wheelchair. They collaborated in a number of revues for Laurier Lister, having particular success with some animal songs, including 'The Hippopotamus', much sung by Ian Wallace. Themselves popular performers at private parties, where many new numbers were tried out, they risked taking the New Lindsey Theatre, initially for a week, on the last day of 1956 for the evening show they called *At the Drop of a Hat*. Their following rapidly expanded, and they moved to the Fortune Theatre in the West End, where they remained for over two years. Recordings, publication, and worldwide tours ensued. A second show, *At the Drop of Another Hat*, followed at the Haymarket Theatre in 1963. By the time Swann decided to break off the partnership at the end of 1967, they had given 1700 performances in eleven years.

The shows were immensely popular. Flanders's witty, wry lyrics touched a vein of tunefulness in Swann, while their act also provided him with the opportunity for some more serious songs; and the combination of the bearded, urbane Flanders with Swann's bespectacled, innocent yet hectically committed presence at the piano had a wide appeal in the post-war years before the arrival of satire. But Swann found that the demands of touring bore heavily on him, and there was an inner unease about the material prosperity and artistic limitations that came with this way of life. New friendships with C. S. Lewis, whose *Perelandra* he made into an opera, and J. R. R. Tolkien, whose poems he set memorably, were based largely on his attraction to their fantasies of prelapsarian or utopian alternative worlds. Among his religious works were Anglican settings, a *Requiem for the Living*, to words by C. Day Lewis, and *The Five Scrolls*, to a text by Rabbi Albert Friedlander. There were other performing partnerships, including one with Lili Malandraki, who had been a courier in the Cretan resistance and sang songs of her island as well as his own Greek-inspired settings, and these provided outlets for the lyrically richer songs he was also writing. The latter were to embrace settings of Blake, Tennyson, Christina Rossetti, Hardy, Yeats, Emily Dickinson, Hermann Hesse, and others—music whose merit has been overshadowed by the more popular *Hat* numbers. They reveal Swann's melodic response to poetry of very different kinds, as well as a harmonic character influenced by Tchaikovsky and Rakhmaninov; his song style owes more to the Russian *romans* than to the German lied or any English tradition. His singing voice was untrained but distinctive and served his needs, and he was a fine pianist, with a unique manner which never translated easily to other performers. He himself referred to 'the serpentine way I play my songs, when every bar is just a little bit different and folds its way around the lyric' (*Swann's Way*, 233).

In person, Swann was short and compact, somewhat swarthy and with owl-like spectacles a-glint with friendliness. His gentleness, good nature, and cheerful response to the best in people endeared him to a wide circle of friends and to a closer group whose devotion to him was unswerving; but he was also acquainted with depression. Pacifism was one aspect of a nature that thought deeply and acted upon conviction; he caused misunderstanding by visiting South Africa four times during apartheid (twice at his own expense) in order to sing his songs of reconciliation to mixed racial audiences. His religious beliefs were strong but kept constantly under challenge, and some of these struggles were recorded in his books of memoirs. Baptized into the Church of England, at different times he considered various affiliations, among them Franciscan brotherhood, Judaism, and (after a visit to Mount Athos) Greek orthodoxy, but in the end made a return to the Quakerism that had inspired him during his time in the Friends' Ambulance Unit. He married Janet Mary Oxborrow (*b*. 1934), a teacher and potter, on 7 August 1955; they had two daughters. The marriage was dissolved in 1983, and on 19 August 1993, after some years of close companionship, he married the art historian Alison Smith (*b*. 1962). He died at Trinity Hospice, Clapham Common, London, on 23 March 1994, two years after cancer of the prostate was diagnosed. He was cremated at Lambeth crematorium, London, on 31 March.   JOHN WARRACK

Sources D. Swann, *Swann's way: a life in song*, ed. L. Smith, new edn (1993) · D. Swann, *The space between the bars* (1968) · *The Independent* (25 March 1994) · *The Times* (25 March 1994) · private information (2004) · personal knowledge (2004) · *WW* · *Who was who in America* · b. cert. · d. cert. · baptismal cert.
Archives priv. coll. | FILM BBC, partially complete film of one of the *At the drop of a hat* shows | SOUND Albert House Press, East Cheiley, Sussex, Alphabetaphon trilogy of cassettes · BL NSA, 'Flanders and Swann', V3294/2 · BL NSA, interview, H1486/02 · BL NSA, performance recordings · BL NSA, recorded talk · priv. coll.
Likenesses R. Westwood, photograph, 1957 (with Michael Flanders), NPG; *see illus. in* Flanders, Michael Henry (1922–1975) · G. Hoffnung, drawing, priv. coll. · B. Mathews, portrait, priv. coll. · photograph, repro. in *The Times* · photograph, repro. in *The Independent* · photograph, Hult. Arch.
Wealth at death £584,640: probate, 25 May 1994, *CGPLA Eng. & Wales*

Swann, Michael Meredith, Baron Swann (1920–1990), biologist and public servant, was born on 1 March 1920 in Cambridge, the elder son and eldest of three children of Meredith Blake Robson Swann, university demonstrator in pathology, and his wife, Marjorie Dykes. He was educated at Winchester College and as a scholar at Gonville and Caius College, Cambridge, of which his father was a fellow, and of which he himself became an honorary fellow in 1977. He left Cambridge at Easter 1940, after six terms, and as a result of a wartime dispensation was given a BA (zoology) in 1943 and an MA in 1946. In 1942 he married Tess Gleadowe, a keen musician, an associate of the

Royal College of Music and of the Royal College of Organists. She was the daughter of Reginald Morier Yorke Gleadowe, Slade professor of fine art at Oxford. They had two sons and two daughters.

During the Second World War Swann worked on radar at the War Office and on operational research in Normandy and Germany. He was mentioned in dispatches in 1944. In 1946, having registered as a research student at Cambridge, he was elected a fellow of his college. For the next six years he was a university demonstrator in zoology, and, during that period, was closely concerned with research on the structure during mitosis (the splitting of cell or nucleus) and with the process of fertilization of the eggs of sea urchins (sea urchins do not mate, but shed their eggs and sperm into the sea). His findings were recorded in a number of scientific papers which made Swann's reputation as a leading authority on cell biology. He obtained a PhD in 1950.

In 1952 Swann moved to Edinburgh University as professor of natural history. He continued his research but became increasingly involved in the administrative responsibilities of his post, and, by the time he was elected dean of the faculty of science in 1963, he had made his department one of the best centres for biological teaching and research in the United Kingdom. Having left his microscope for the instruments of academic business, he published his last scientific paper in 1962.

In 1965 Swann succeeded Sir Edward Appleton as principal and vice-chancellor of Edinburgh University, and was soon seen to be not only an able administrator within the university and the Committee of Vice-Chancellors and Principals, but also a notable authority on educational problems in wider fields beyond Edinburgh. He was a member of the Advisory Council on Education in Scotland (1957–61), the committee on manpower resources (1963–8), and the council for scientific policy (1965–9). However, his term of office as principal of the university coincided in the late 1960s with an upsurge of political activism among his students, and, although he dealt with the resultant problems with firmness and tact, he found the situation tedious and tiresome.

Meanwhile, relations between the chairman of the governors of the BBC, Baron Hill of Luton, and the director-general and his staff had not been running smoothly, and Edward Heath, the prime minister, was seeking as the new chairman somebody less assertive and blustering in carrying out the functions of that office. In 1973 Swann was offered and accepted the post. From the outset he made clear that he had no intention of trying to steer the ship, but would be prepared to help to hold her on course if rough weather were encountered. The next seven years were not without some rough weather. In 1977 the Central Policy Review Staff made recommendations regarding the external services of the BBC, which in the view of the corporation would have been disastrous if implemented. Swann took steps to ensure that the proposals were quietly shelved. In 1974 the committee on the future of broadcasting had been set up under Baron Annan. Its report, published in 1977, challenged the role of the governors. Having handled the committee with tact and good humour, Swann was able to ensure that the management of the corporation was not imperilled.

Throughout his term of office as chairman (1973–80) Swann earned not only the regard of the two directors-general with whom he worked, but also the respect and affection of all BBC staff. Sir Ian Trethowan paid tribute to him as 'an outstanding chairman steering the BBC through a number of political crises'.

Swann was knighted in 1972. In 1981 he was created a life peer, and in the House of Lords continued to defend the independence of the BBC. During that year (1980–81) he was provost of Oriel College, Oxford, but he was not happy there, and resigned after twelve months. He found it difficult to cope with the minutiae of college life after facing the demands of public life for so long, and the college itself was unprepared for the amount of time that his outside activities were to take up. He was a member of many organizations, in which he took an active part, including the Medical Research Council (1962–5), Council for Science and Society (1974–8), and the Wellcome Trust, of which he was a trustee from 1973 to 1990. From 1979 to 1990 he was chancellor of York University. From 1981 to 1985 he chaired the committee of inquiry into the education of children from ethnic minority groups, and the Swann report of March 1985 was radical. He was also chairman of the Royal Academy of Music from 1983 to 1990, an appointment which gave him special pleasure, and a trustee of the British Museum (Natural History), 1982–6. He received many academic honours, including honorary degrees from Aberdeen (1967), Leicester (1968), York (1968), and Heriot-Watt (1971). He was elected FRSE in 1952 and FRS in 1962.

Swann was a big, broad, heavy man, unathletic and with blond hair and a friendly manner. He never managed to look very smart, even when wearing his best clothes. He died on 22 September 1990 of a ruptured aorta, at his home, Tallat Steps, in Coln St Dennis, Gloucestershire. A memorial service was held in Westminster Abbey on 10 December 1990. H. F. OXBURY, rev.

Sources The Times (24 Sept 1990) • The Times (10 Oct 1990) • The Times (19 Oct 1990) • The Independent (24 Sept 1990) • J. M. Mitchison, Memoirs FRS, 37 (1991), 447–60
Archives U. Edin. L., corresp. and papers | CUL, corresp. with Peter Mitchell
Likenesses photograph, repro. in Mitchison, Memoirs FRS, 445 • photograph, repro. in The Times (24 Sept 1990) • photograph, repro. in The Independent
Wealth at death £206,351: probate, 5 March 1991, CGPLA Eng. & Wales

Swann [formerly Schwann], **Sir Oliver** (1878–1948), air force officer, was born in Wimbledon on 18 November 1878, the son of John Frederick Schwann, merchant, and his wife, Margaret Anne, formerly Holland. He was educated at a private school and then passed into the Britannia as a naval cadet; he was rated midshipman in 1895, and was commissioned in 1898. While carrying out the normal

439

SWANN, SAMUEL

duties of a naval officer he began to take an interest in flying; by the time he had reached the rank of commander he was selected, in 1910, to assist Captain Murray Sueter, arguably the father of naval aviation, in the construction and development of a naval airship, which had been ordered from Vickers Sons and Maxim in 1909. This airship was built at Barrow in Furness, but owing to structural weakness the vessel broke its back before it could be tested in flight. Meanwhile Schwann had changed his allegiance from the lighter- to the heavier-than-air vessel. From his own pocket, aided by subscriptions from friends, he bought an Avro landplane for £700, fitted floats to it, and, although he had not yet qualified as a pilot, succeeded in flying it off the water. Not surprisingly the aircraft crashed, but by Schwann's initiative and courage the seaplane—or hydro-aeroplane as it was then called—was born.

In 1912 Schwann took his international aviator's licence, no. 203, and became deputy to Murray Sueter, who was now director of the newly formed air department at the Admiralty. Over the next two years they oversaw the creation of the Royal Naval Air Service, which was ready for action by the outbreak of war in 1914. Schwann, by then promoted captain, was given command of one of the first seaplane carriers, the *Campania*, an old Cunard liner that had been fitted out to carry a dozen aircraft. Engine failures and missed communications denied the *Campania* a role in any important naval action, but on the formation of the Royal Air Force in 1918 Swann was transferred, with several other senior naval officers, to high appointments in the new service. He had by this time Anglicized the spelling of his name.

In the course of his successful career in the RAF Swann became, as air member for personnel (1922–3), a key member of the Air Council at a time when the future of the service was in balance. He was promoted air vice-marshal in 1923 and later that year was appointed air officer commanding in the Middle East (1923–6), where his administrative ability and his charm of manner made him an efficient and popular commander. It was somewhat ironical that one who was in the air department at the Admiralty when it was flouting the government's decision that there should be a unified air service (the Royal Flying Corps, naval and military wings) should end his career in the RAF. It is to his credit that once he had cast in his lot with the new service he gave it his undivided loyalty. He retired in 1929 but was re-employed during the Second World War, although past the normal age for recall. He served as air officer commanding Halton, and later as air liaison officer for the north midland region, and continued to devote himself to his country's service until he was sixty-five.

Swann married, on 2 December 1913, Elizabeth Adie, daughter of William Laidlaw-Purves, aural surgeon, of London; they had one son and two daughters. He was appointed CB and CBE in 1919 and KCB in 1924. He died at his home, Orange Grove, Littleton, Guildford, on 7 March 1948 and was cremated in Woking two days later.

P. B. JOUBERT, rev. MARK POTTLE

Sources *The Times* (8 March 1948) · *The Times* (10 March 1948) · personal knowledge (1959) · *CGPLA Eng. & Wales* (1948) **Archives** SOUND IWM SA, oral history interview **Wealth at death** £78,863 12s. 8d.: probate, 2 July 1948, *CGPLA Eng. & Wales*

Swann, Samuel (1704–1774), surveyor and politician in America, was born on 31 October 1704 in Perquimans precinct, North Carolina, the son of Samuel Swann (1653–1707) and his second wife, Elizabeth Lillington Fendall (1679–1725). His father, who moved from Virginia to North Carolina in 1694, was one of the wealthiest men in the colony, served on the council for many years, and held other high offices; his grandfather in Virginia was of like standing. His maternal grandfather, Alexander Lillington, was equally prominent. Young Swann was educated by Maurice Moore (who became his stepfather in 1713), Edward Moseley, and members of the Lillington family, as his father died before he was three. The elder Swann's plantation was left to his third wife, Jane Jones Swann (d. 1734), and at her death to his son Samuel.

Swann represented Perquimans county in the assembly during the years 1725–38, when he moved his family to his plantation, The Oaks, in Onslow county. He then represented that county as well as New Hanover county until 1762, for a total of thirty-seven years. In addition he was speaker of the assembly during the years 1742–62. There was no prohibition against multiple office-holding and, since each session of the assembly generally lasted only a matter of days, members were free to pursue other occupations. One of those in which Swann was active was land development, and in 1740 he advertised for sale one-half of Roanoke Island, about 6000 acres, owned by a resident of Massachusetts. He also was involved with the settlement of property held by himself and numerous relatives in and around the lower Cape Fear region, where several counties and the young port town of Wilmington were developing. He owned large tracts of productive agricultural land as well as pine forests which produced tar, pitch, timber, and masts for ships.

Always alert for a worthwhile activity, Swann in 1728 accepted appointment by Sir Richard Everard, governor of North Carolina, to a four-man joint commission created to survey and mark the boundary between his colony and Virginia. Since the 1665 charter of Carolina by Charles II to eight lords proprietors did not clearly identify the northern boundary, a strip of land about 30 miles wide had been in dispute for many years. To avoid further conflicts the crown, negotiating to acquire the Carolina region, ordered the commission to survey and mark the boundary. Work began on 28 March at Currituck inlet on the Atlantic Ocean, with each of the workmen accompanying the surveyors carrying between 40 and 70 pounds of supplies and equipment. They continued straight westward by the compass for six weeks, clearing a trail and marking it for 73 miles through largely unexplored territory. Because of the heat, insects, and rattlesnakes they suspended their work at that point. Resuming the course on 20 September, the surveyors and their retinue of tree cutters, load bearers, food gatherers, American Indian guides, and camp followers set off again. Some dropped out along the way, but by 4 October the line had been extended 50 miles farther than any known settler. Swann also noted that he was the first European to pass directly through the Great Dismal Swamp (a few previous explorers had seen it but gone around it).

The Virginian William Byrd assumed leadership of this expedition and kept an official journal, as well as a private or 'secret' one. In the latter he noted that Swann, after making his way through the swamp, was excused because he had recently married. The bride was Jane Jones (*b.* 1704), eldest daughter of Frederick, former chief justice of the colony.

Byrd's official journal was published in 1841, but the secret one was known to only a few people until it was published in 1929 by the North Carolina Historical Commission. Byrd used pseudonyms in writing of the surveyors and commissioners and called Swann Bo-otes, perhaps because he waded across the swamp wearing boots. The official account of the running of the dividing line came to be regarded as a classic in early American literature, and a valued description of early American life. When the University of North Carolina opened in 1795, it was given the instruments that had been used, but they disappeared when the university was closed during the years 1871–5.

Another significant role that Swann played in the colony came about after Governor Gabriel Johnston in 1746 secured legislative approval for the creation of another important commission. Since the laws of North Carolina had never been compiled and printed, they were only selectively known and therefore widely ignored; government functioned improperly as neither officials nor lawyers generally knew the law. Even the amanuensis who provided manuscript copies of new laws often made errors. To try to correct this unfortunate situation, four lawyers were named to collect the laws and have them printed. Of the commissioners, two seem never to have participated, while a third died early in the work. It was Swann on whom the task fell, and he saw the work to a successful conclusion. In 1749 the manuscript was laid before the North Carolina assembly, and portions of it were distributed among members for approval. Several months elapsed before the manuscript was released to be printed. It was left in New Bern with James Davis, North Carolina's recently designated printer, by whom it was published in 1751 as a 338 page book, the first to be issued in North Carolina. Bound in leather, probably inadequately tanned, it was a yellow colour and was promptly dubbed the Yellow Jacket. This long-anticipated work contained all of the laws then in force, as well as the titles of all the obsolete, expired, or repealed laws. The compiler of the laws was authorized payment of £60 and granted the right to sell copies for five years. There are eight known surviving copies of this edition; among the three in the North Carolina collection at the University of North Carolina in Chapel Hill is the one in the most perfect condition.

While such notable accomplishments as his role in the boundary survey and the compilation of the statutes surely lingered in Swann's memory for the remainder of his life, there were less notable roles to contribute to his satisfaction at having lived a useful life. As a veteran of many confrontations with colonial governors over the royal prerogative, for example, he played a most significant role in creating an atmosphere of revolution. He strove to make the lower house of the assembly in his colony very much like the House of Commons in parliament. Swann continued to practise law until 1770, maintaining his home in the town of Wilmington or on his plantation in rural New Hanover county. Survived by his wife and several children, to whom he left extensive property, he died in late February or early March 1774, and was buried in the family cemetery, still maintained at Onslow county, North Carolina.   WILLIAM S. POWELL

Sources M. E. E. Parker, 'Swann, Samuel', *Dictionary of North Carolina biography*, ed. W. S. Powell (1979–96) • T. F. Davis, ed., *A genealogical record of the Davis, Swann and Cabell families* (1934) • *Cyclopedia of eminent and representative men of the Carolinas in the nineteenth century* (1902), 302–3 • will, North Carolina State Archives, Raleigh • J. B. Grimes, ed., *Abstract of North Carolina wills* (1910) • W. L. Saunders and W. Clark, eds., *The colonial records of North Carolina*, 30 vols. (1886–1907), vols. 4–11; 22–23 • J. L. Cheney, ed., *North Carolina government, 1585–1979: a narrative and statistical history*, 2nd edn (1981) • W. K. Boyd, ed., *William Byrd's Histories of the dividing line betwixt Virginia and North Carolina* (1929) • *Sketches of church history in North Carolina* (1892) • B. Noyes, *To be sold, one moiety or half part of the island of Roanoke*, 1740, University of North Carolina Library, North Carolina collection [photocopy of broadside] • N. C. North, 'A study of William Byrd's journal, his secret history, and his history of the dividing line', MA diss., University of North Carolina, 1935 • S. B. Weeks, *The press of North Carolina in the eighteenth century* (1891) • D. C. McMurtrie, 'The first twelve years of printing in North Carolina, 1749–1760', *North Carolina Historical Review*, 10 (1933)

Archives North Carolina State Archives, Raleigh • University of North Carolina Library, Chapel Hill, Southern historical collection, family papers

Wealth at death land; livestock; personal possessions incl. books: will, Raleigh, North Carolina State Archives

Swansea. For this title name *see* Vivian, Henry Hussey, first Baron Swansea (1821–1894).

Swanston, Eyllaerdt (*d.* 1651), actor, was a member of the prestigious King's Men from about 1624 until the closure of the theatres in 1642. We do not know his parentage or when or where he was born. There are more than twenty variant spellings of his unusual forename, and at least ten of his surname. Our first record is of his marriage to Alice Ivieson (*d.* 1651) on 16 December 1619 in the parish of St Gregory by St Paul's, London. He and his wife lived in the parish of St Mary Aldermanbury, whose registers record the baptisms of ten of their children between 3 September 1620 and 21 January 1639.

Although Swanston spent most of his professional life with the King's Men, he was not one of those 'bred from Children in the kings service' ('Dramatic records', 371). He is to be found first with the Prince Charles's Players and with the Lady Elizabeth's Men. A list of the chief actors at the Phoenix made in 1622 includes Swanston, so he must by then have been an experienced actor. The Phoenix was a well-known theatre in Drury Lane. Swanston joined the King's Men some time before 20 December 1624, as on that date he and a number of other members of that company signed an apology to the master of the revels for performing *The Spanish Viceroy* without a licence. Almost ten years later Swanston again apologized to the authorities, this time for problems over censorship. 'Ellyart Swanstone' was one of fifteen King's players issued with black cloth for King James's funeral on 7 May 1625 ('Dramatic records', 325–6). The royal patent of 24 June the same year lists 'Elliart Swanston' as one of King Charles's well-beloved servants ('Royal patents', 282). Livery lists pertaining to the King's Men and dating from May 1629, April 1637, and March 1641 all include his name in diverse forms.

The King's Men performed an extensive and varied repertoire. Shakespeare's plays were revived regularly. An early theatrical chronicler, James Wright, tells us that Swanston played Othello but none of his other Shakespearian roles have been identified. Of his known roles three are in plays by Philip Massinger: Aretinus Clemens in *The Roman Actor* (performed in 1626), Ricardo in *The Picture* (performed in 1629), and Chrysalus in *Believe as you List* (performed in 1631). About the same time he also played Count Utrante in Lodowick Carlell's *The Deserving Favourite*, Alcidonus in Arthur Wilson's *The Swisser*, and Lugier in *The Wild Goose Chase*, a revival of a 'Beaumont and Fletcher' play. Other roles that can be assigned to him are Bussy D'Ambois, the hero of George Chapman's tragedy, and Philaster in Fletcher's tragicomedy. Swanston also appeared in John Ford's *The Lovers' Melancholy* (performed in 1628).

As a leading player and shareholder Swanston often acted for the company in financial matters. From 1632 to 1641 he, with his colleagues John Lowin and Joseph Taylor, regularly received the payments for the King's Men's frequent performances at court. In 1635 he and fellow King's Men Robert Benfield and Thomas Pollard petitioned the lord chamberlain for permission to purchase shares in the Globe and Blackfriars theatres. The surviving members of the Burbage family and John Shank, another colleague, objected, but the request was granted. However, no agreement could be reached, and eventually, as the 'Sharers' Papers' show, the matter was referred for arbitration to the master of the revels. Shank died in January 1636 with the matter unresolved. On 26 August 1639 Richard Benfield, Robert's kinsman, left bequests both to Swanston and to members of Shank's family.

During the civil war, perhaps surprisingly, Swanston seems not to have supported King Charles. According to James Wright, 'he profest himself a Presbyterian, took up the trade of a Jeweller, and liv'd in Aldermanbury' (Wright, 409). His alliance with the parliamentarians is confirmed by the statement in *A Key to the Parliament by their Remembrancer* (1648) that Swanston the player was one of them. During the interregnum a folio collection of the plays attributed to Francis Beaumont and John Fletcher was published. Swanston was one of the King's Men who signed the dedicatory epistle of the 1647 volume. He is also mentioned in one of its prefatory poems, Henry Vaughan's 'Upon Mr Fletcher's Playes, Published

1647'. Swanston made his will on 24 June 1651 and was buried, together with his wife, in St Mary Aldermanbury, London, on the 28th.

In a scene in Thomas Shadwell's *The Virtuoso* (performed in 1676) the theatre of 'the last Age' is compared unfavourably with the contemporary theatre. To Snarl, one of the participants in the debate, modern actors seem too tame when compared with the great King's Men of old: 'I, that have seen Joseph Taylor, and Lowin and Swanstead; Oh a brave roaring Fellow! Would make the house shake again' (Shadwell, *The Virtuoso*, 1691, 10). Although Swanston is scarcely known today, he was an important actor in his day and his reputation survived well into the Restoration period.

M. E. WILLIAMS

Sources parish register, St Mary Aldermanbury, GL, MS 3572/1 [burial] · parish register, St Gregory by St Paul's, GL, MS 10231 [marriage] · G. E. Bentley, *The Jacobean and Caroline stage*, 7 vols. (1941–68) · E. A. J. Honigmann and S. Brock, eds., *Playhouse wills, 1558–1642: an edition of wills by Shakespeare and his contemporaries in the London theatre* (1993) · M. Eccles, 'Elizabethan actors, IV: S to end', *N&Q*, 238 (1993), 165–76 · *The control and censorship of Caroline drama: the records of Sir Henry Herbert, master of the revels, 1623–73*, ed. N. W. Bawcutt (1996) · 'Dramatic records: the lord chamberlain's office', *Malone Society Collections*, 2 (1913–31), 321–416 · 'Royal patents for players', *Malone Society Collections*, 1/3 (1909) · A. Gurr, *The Shakespearian playing companies* (1996) · G. E. Bentley, *The profession of player in Shakespeare's time, 1590–1642* (1984) · D. George, 'Early cast lists for two Beaumont and Fletcher plays', *Theatre Notebook*, 28 (1974), 9–11 · T. J. King, *Casting Shakespeare's plays: London actors and their roles, 1590–1642* (1992) · E. Nungezer, *A dictionary of actors* (1929) · J. Wright, *Historia histrionica: an historical account of the English stage* (1699); repr. in *A select collection of old English plays originally published by Robert Dodsley*, 4th edn, 15 (1876)

Wealth at death no value given: Honigmann and Brock, *Playhouse wills*, 205–6

Swanton, Ernest William [Jim] (1907–2000), cricket commentator, was born on 11 February 1907 at 64 Vancouver Road, Forest Hill, on the southern outskirts of London, the only son and eldest of the three children of William (Bill) Swanton, stockbroker, and his wife, Lillian Emily, daughter of Hermut Wolters, a merchant from Dortmund. Being a chubby baby, he was called Jim, a derivation of Jumbo, from his earliest days. He was never heard to be called Ernest or William. He inherited his love of games from his father, for many years treasurer of Forest Hill cricket club. While still in his pram he was taken to a game of cricket in which W. G. Grace, then in his sixtieth year, scored 140 for London County against Forest Hill; but his first clear cricketing memory was of seeing Surrey collapse in their second innings against Hampshire at the Oval in June 1919. At the time Swanton was a weekly boarder at Brightlands preparatory school, later to become the boarding-house of Dulwich College Preparatory School. From Brightlands he went on to Cranleigh School, which he enjoyed but where he did not excel.

In 1924 Swanton went into Fleet Street, where he joined the Amalgamated Press, an arm of the Harmsworth publishing empire. He wrote a profile of Frank Woolley, the great Kent and England cricketer, after being granted an interview with him, for a magazine called *All Sports Weekly*, in 1926, the year in which he watched his first test match;

but it was not until he moved to the London *Evening Standard* in 1927 that he became a full-time writer on sport: cricket in the summer (sometimes in tandem with C. B. Fry) and rugby football in the winter. Broadcasting was added to this in 1934, first with the British Empire Service and then as a commentator on the MCC tour of South Africa in 1938–9, the first overseas cricket tour to be covered live by the BBC.

By the outbreak of the Second World War Swanton, then thirty-two, had gained a reputation as a well-informed and forceful critic. He had let slip the chance of covering the MCC tour of Australia and New Zealand in 1932–3 for the *Evening Standard* through missing an edition of the paper on the day in June 1932 when Herbert Sutcliffe and Percy Holmes set a new world record stand of 555, playing for Yorkshire against Essex at Leyton. This was an omission that left the world less knowledgeably briefed than it otherwise would have been on the topic of bodyline bowling, for in Swanton's place the *Evening Standard* sent Bruce Harris, a correspondent far better versed in tennis than cricket. But in 1938 it was Swanton whom H. S. Altham enlisted to update his *A History of Cricket*, first published by Allen and Unwin in 1926 and already the definitive work of its kind.

War service with the Bedfordshire yeomanry led to Swanton (by then an acting major) being captured at the fall of Singapore in February 1942, when he had an elbow nicked by a sniper's bullet. He spent the next three and a half years as a prisoner of the Japanese, much of it on the infamous Burma–Siam railway ('the railway of death', as it was sometimes called). While working on the railway his battery lost sixty-six of 202 men. He contracted polio but, as an officer, was relatively well treated: officers, he later noted, were 'engaged mostly in camp construction', and 'had the better of it' (Allen, 329). His copy of *Wisden Cricketers' Almanack* for 1939 (much rebound with remnants of gas cape held together with rice paste, and now on display in the museum at Lord's) did the rounds among his fellow prisoners, and his talks on cricket helped to remind them of what was at stake. He lost enough weight during his incarceration for his father to pass him by when he went to Waterloo Station to meet him on his return to Britain in 1945.

Barely a year later, amply renewed and course set, Swanton was re-crossing the Indian Ocean, this time on his way to Australia for the first of the seven tours he made there as cricket correspondent of the *Daily Telegraph*, the position which he held with uncommon influence and authority from 1946 until 1975. At the microphone, too, his summaries of a day's cricket were highly regarded, being judicious, comprehensive, and never scripted. On the air the burr and romanticism of John Arlott provided the ideal foil to Swanton's more stentorian style.

From being, in his own words, 'an instinctive but ignorant Christian' (Swanton, 137), Swanton became a deep and committed Anglo-Catholic, a conversion which took place during his years as a prisoner of war and led to his contemplating entering the priesthood. From 1946 until 1950 he had a set of rooms at Pusey House in Oxford at the invitation of its principal, Canon Frederic (Freddy) Hood. As Lord Runcie (the former archbishop of Canterbury) said in his address at Swanton's funeral, 'Jim loved the order, dignity and colour of Anglo-Catholic worship.' Neither, as Lord Runcie also said of him, was he a man plagued with self-doubt, a reality which, added to his physical dimensions (he was well over 6 feet tall and a good 15 stone in weight), some found distinctly overbearing. He always knew that he wanted, and when the war was over nothing much was allowed to stand in his way.

As a cricketer Swanton had failed to get into the Cranleigh eleven, but became a good enough opening batsman to be given three first-class matches for Middlesex in 1937 and 1938, albeit against Oxford and Cambridge. While sufficiently active he made it his business to play as much cricket as he could, and his own itinerant club, the Arabs, which he formed in 1935, soon became known for its cavalier style. In the 1950s and 1960s he took his own sides, a blend of legend, promise, and personableness, on tours of the Caribbean and the Far East, though a strong sybaritic tendency precluded his ever going to Pakistan in a professional capacity, and he reported on only one test match in India. As an increasingly outspoken critic of apartheid he refused to cover the MCC tour of South Africa in 1964–5, and in 1968 he staunchly supported Basil d'Oliveira when the South African authorities announced that they would not accept a team of which he was a member. Earlier that year he wrote a withering attack on Enoch Powell in *The Spectator*, after his 'rivers of blood' speech. It was to Swanton, in partnership with two cricketers of the highest renown, Richie Benaud and Sir Garfield Sobers, that the newly formed United Cricket Board of South Africa turned to speak at their inaugural dinner in Johannesburg in 1991. That, in its way, was as much of a compliment as being asked to give the address at Sir Frank Worrell's memorial service in Westminster Abbey, which Swanton did in April 1967.

In print Swanton was an expounder rather than a phrasemaker. John Warr, the Middlesex and England cricketer, and a man of famously nimble wit, described Swanton's literary style as being a cross between Enid Blyton and the ten commandments. In fact, he was always lucid, frequently trenchant, undoubtedly pontifical, and invariably accurate. His love of cricket, so long as it was decently conducted, never wavered. Although essentially a traditionalist, he adapted to change without necessarily welcoming it, and because he never lost his wits, or his wit, he became an inimitable source of reference and reminiscence. He wrote about his first test match at Lord's in 1930 and his last at the Oval in 1999, an unprecedented span. In all he penned some 8 million words on cricket alone. Of his numerous books, two were historical, one theological, and many anthological; he also published an autobiography, *Sort of a Cricket Person* (1972), and a collection of obituaries, *Cricketers of my Time* (1999). His correspondence with Sir Donald Bradman, a long-standing friend, would make an absorbing documentary, were it not specifically off the record.

Inevitably, Swanton had his critics, not to say his enemies, though the more benevolent and patriarchal he became the fewer they were. There were certainly three MCC tours—two to South Africa and one to Australia—when the England captain (Peter May on the first two and Raymond Illingworth on the other) took overt exception to the magisterial tone of his writing. Sometimes, those of whom he was critical put it down to class or county prejudice, but with insufficient cause. Charges of snobbery were not infrequently levelled at him, not without some justification, and he much regretted the passing of the amateur, but that was because of the independence of the amateur's contribution. 'The evolution of the game has been stimulated from its beginnings by the fusion of the two strains (the amateur and the professional), each of which has drawn strength and inspiration from the other,' he wrote (Swanton, 201). Another aversion was Kerry Packer's world series cricket, which he deplored for its aggression and flaunted commercialism. 'The modern evil of intimidation', he wrote, 'had its roots in the brutalising of cricket under Packer' (Allen, 303). The man himself he described as an anti-hero.

In the corridors of power at Lord's it came to be regretted that Swanton was never made president of MCC. In this, neither his perceived high-handedness nor his profession worked to his advantage. But the omission was redressed when his portrait, specially commissioned and painted by Andrew Festing, was hung in the Lord's pavilion. He was on the main committee from 1975 to 1984, chaired the arts and library subcommittee for many years, and did much to push through MCC's first indoor cricket school. He was also elected an honorary life vice-president of the club in 1989, a significantly rarer honour than the presidency itself.

Swanton married, on 11 February 1958, Ann Marion Carbutt (1911–1998), the widow of George Carbutt, chartered accountant, and the daughter of R. H. de Montmorency, an Eton housemaster and a noted games player. The Swantons, both keen golfers (Ann had been not far short of the top flight as a player), settled at Delf House, Sandwich, Kent, much attracted by the proximity of the famous links of Royal St George's. For forty years they spent time each winter in Barbados, where they built a house at Sandy Lane and became very much a part of the community. Swanton's affection for the Caribbean placed him in something of a dilemma in the 1980s, when the West Indies ruled the cricket world partly through the persistent use of intimidatory bowling, the method which he felt so damaged the game.

Even when Swanton was in his nineties, no day was wasted. He gave his time as zealously as ever to MCC, to Kent County Cricket Club, whose president he was in 1981, to *The Cricketer* magazine, whose fortunes he guided as editorial director from 1967 until his death, to the Cricket Society and the Forty Club, of both of which he was president, and to the parish church in Sandwich. He continued to be in demand as a speaker, remained an indefatigable letter writer, and his fortnightly columns for the *Daily Telegraph* during the summer months were still perceptive and widely read. His perspective was invaluable.

Swanton died of heart failure at the Chaucer Hospital, Canterbury, on 22 January 2000, six days after running short of breath while walking home from posting letters. The tributes paid to him were lavish. In *The Guardian* Matthew Engel, then the editor of *Wisden Cricketers' Almanack*, described Swanton's long innings as 'a breathtaking performance that will be remembered with awe' (*The Guardian*, 24 Jan 2000), while Ted Dexter, the former England captain, said: 'He was the standard by which other cricket commentators were judged' (*Sunday Telegraph*, 23 Jan 2000). One of Swanton's admirers, John Major, wrote in his autobiography, published when Swanton was alive, that 'Jonathan Aitken … once gave me a set of all the Swanton books I did not already possess and they are a proud part of my collection. I have often sat watching cricket with him and it is an education' (J. Major, *The Autobiography*, 1999, 23). For his services to cricket Swanton was appointed OBE in 1965, and advanced to CBE in 1994. His wife, an accomplished artist and pianist, predeceased him on 23 November 1998, the happiness of a marriage between two such positive personalities, both set in their ways, having come as something of a surprise to their many friends.   JOHN WOODCOCK

Sources E. W. Swanton, *Sort of a cricket person* (1972) · D. R. Allen, *E. W. Swanton: a celebration of his life and work* (2000) · *WWW* · *Sunday Telegraph* (23 Jan 2000) · *Daily Telegraph* (29 Jan 2000) · *The Times* (24 Jan 2000) · *The Independent* (24 Jan 2000) · *The Guardian* (24 Jan 2000) · private information (2004) · personal knowledge (2004) · b. cert. · m. cert.
Likenesses photograph, 1999, repro. in *Daily Telegraph* · A. Festing, portrait, probably Lord's cricket ground, London · photographs, repro. in Swanton, *Sort of a cricket person* · photographs, repro. in *Sunday Telegraph*
Wealth at death £1,114,531: probate, 2000, *CGPLA Eng. & Wales*

Swanwick, Ada Elizabeth Edith [Betty] (1915–1989), artist and art teacher, was born on 22 May 1915 at 2A Causton Villas, Upper Colfe Road, Forest Hill, London, the daughter of the marine painter Henry Gerard Swanwick (*d.* 1924/5) and his wife, Ethel Priscilla, *née* Bacon. Encouraged to draw by her father, when she was sixteen she entered Goldsmiths' School of Design, then after three years continued simultaneously at Goldsmiths', the Royal College of Art, and the Central School of Arts and Crafts (1934–6). She designed her first poster for London Transport at the age of nineteen and produced another eight for them between 1936 and 1954. In 1936 she joined the teaching staff at Goldsmiths', and she served as head of the design school from 1948 to 1969. She also taught occasionally at the Royal Academy Schools, the Royal College of Art, and the Central School. Considering that she spent most of her working life teaching, her output was considerable—book and magazine illustrations, designs for scarves and mugs, record covers, murals, and posters, as well as hundreds of paintings and large pencil and watercolour drawings.

Swanwick had a solo exhibition at the Little Gallery, London, in 1950, and sent work to mixed exhibitions of the Society of Industrial Artists, the Royal Watercolour

Society, and the Royal Academy summer exhibitions. She joined the Society of Mural Painters in 1937, the Society of Industrial Artists in 1960, and the Royal Watercolour Society in 1976, and was made a Royal Academician in 1979. She described herself as 'part of the small tradition of English painting that is a bit eccentric, a little odd and a little visionary' (Murphy, 5). Her favourite subjects, after the human figure, were the natural world and animals, and these played supporting roles in her fantastic, visionary figure compositions, which were inspired by poetry, mythology, music, a concern for the environment, and the parables of Jesus Christ. On her retirement from Goldsmiths' in 1969 she moved from London to Tunbridge Wells, where she lived and worked until her death, surrounded by her cats, her dogs, and an African grey parrot. Swanwick was not happy with the art movements of the 1960s and 1970s, and she reserved her fiercest criticism for abstraction and the abandonment of life-drawing in the art schools. Her earlier figurative work was described as jaunty and bold in design, while her paintings and watercolour drawings of later years became ever more luminous and ethereal, with their translucent layers of pale watercolour washes. A large watercolour drawing took up to 200 hours to execute and passed through several preparatory stages.

Swanwick painted several murals: first for the Rocket Restaurant at the Festival of Britain site on the South Bank, London, in 1951, then for the Lyric Theatre, Hammersmith, and two hospitals—the Evelina Children's Hospital in 1960 and the Great Ormond Street Children's Hospital. She wrote and illustrated her own novels, beginning with *The Cross Purposes* in 1945, in which animals masquerade as people. Nine further books followed, including *Hoodwinked* (1957) and *Beauty and the Burglar* (1958). John Betjeman called *Hoodwinked* 'strange, startling, funny, with a weird beauty' (Gardiner, 128), and all her novels may be described as social comedies with a surreal twist. Her paintings and watercolours are not found in public collections, with the exception of *Battle Scene* (1967), which is in the National Portrait Gallery. Her works were regular and distinctive features of Royal Academy summer exhibitions from 1965 onwards and they sold quickly to her devoted number of private collectors. Swanwick avoided publicity but was captured in print by Denton Welch, her old student friend from Goldsmiths' days; he set her as Betty in his novel *A Voice through the Clouds* (1950) and as Fat Bertha Swan in *A Party* (1951).

Swanwick died on 22 May 1989, her seventy-fourth birthday, in Tunbridge Wells. She suggested that money be given to the Friends of the Earth rather than spent on funeral flowers. JUDITH COLLINS

Sources B. Murphy, *The art of Betty Swanwick* (1989) • D. Gaze, *Dictionary of women artists* (1997) • C. Beetles, *The illustrators: the British art of illustration, 1800–1991* (1991) • S. Gardiner, 'Betty Swanwick: obituary', *Modern Painters*, 2/3 (autumn 1989), 128–9 • b. cert. • CGPLA Eng. & Wales (1989)
Wealth at death £197,016: probate, 31 Oct 1989, CGPLA Eng. & Wales

Swanwick, Anna (1813–1899), translator, writer, and social reformer, was born in Liverpool on 22 June 1813, the youngest of the three daughters of John Swanwick (d. 1837), a wealthy merchant, and Hannah Hilditch, of Trefflich Hall, Staffordshire. The Swanwicks were descended from Philip Henry, a seventeenth-century divine who was ejected from his living at Worthenbury, in north Wales, for his refusal to conform to the Act of Uniformity in 1662; and the family were subsequently Unitarian in religion and Liberal in politics. Anna was soundly grounded at home by her mother, and then indifferently educated at what was called 'the best girls' school in Liverpool' (Bruce, 19) until she was thirteen, and thereafter at home where, with some visiting tutors but largely by 'fighting her own way upward' (Knight, 276), she developed a remarkable facility in languages, particularly German and Italian. She yearned for the education accessible to boys ('I often longed to assume the costume of a boy in order to learn Latin, Greek, and mathematics'; Bruce, 19–20), and the breakthrough came when she was eighteen and James Martineau was appointed to the Paradise Street Unitarian Chapel in Liverpool. He taught her mathematics and philosophy, and a friendship was formed which lasted to the end of her life.

In 1838 Mrs Swanwick and her daughters moved to Tavistock Place, London, and shortly after Anna had the chance to spend eight months in Berlin in the home of Professor Karl Gottlob Zumpt and his family, where she not only perfected her German and mastered Greek but also became proficient in Hebrew. On her return she began her career as a translator and in 1843 published *Selections from the Dramas of Goethe and Schiller*, which so impressed Henry Bohn, the publisher, that he asked her to contribute to his Standard Library with a translation of Schiller's *Die Jungfrau von Orleans* and Goethe's *Egmont* and then the first part of *Faust*, and in 1850 her reputation was established. She published the second part of *Faust* in 1878, and the translation remains among the best.

It was at this time that Swanwick became keenly interested in the welfare and education of the poor in her part of London. The plight of girls especially attracted her sympathy, and in the early 1840s she established a school for working-class girls and then, with the encouragement of Martineau, one for boys. In 1848, as a result of Chartist agitation, Charles Kingsley and F. D. Maurice and others began the work of establishing working men's colleges and institutes, a movement in which Swanwick joined heartily, and when first Queen's College (1848) and then Bedford College (1850) were founded for the higher education of women she backed them from the start, enrolling as a student at Bedford. She followed the mathematics classes of F. W. Newman—and this was the beginning of another lifelong friendship. Her connections with Queen's and Bedford lasted fifty years—she presented the first graduates of Bedford in 1878, was its first woman visitor in 1884, presided at its jubilee, and was a trustee of the Pfeiffer bequest which bequeathed huge sums to both colleges in 1894.

and colleges in London, Oxford, Cambridge, Edinburgh, Aberystwyth, Cardiff, and Dublin.

Anna Swanwick lived latterly at 23 Cumberland Terrace, Regent's Park, London, and died, unmarried, at Summerhill House, Tunbridge Wells, Kent, on 2 November 1899. She was buried in Highgate cemetery, Middlesex.

BARBARA DENNIS

Sources M. L. Bruce, ed., *Anna Swanwick: a memoir and recollections* (1903) · W. Knight, *Retrospects* (1904) · *CGPLA Eng. & Wales* (1900) **Archives** BL, letters to W. E. Gladstone, Add. MSS 44403–44786, *passim* · Bodl. Oxf., letters to 'Michael Field' · DWL, letters to Henry Crabb Robinson · U. Reading L., letters to George Bell & Sons **Likenesses** K. Bruce, portrait, NPG [*see illus.*] **Wealth at death** £7648 7s. 1d.: probate, 4 April 1900, *CGPLA Eng. & Wales*

Swanwick [*née* Sickert], **Helena Maria Lucy** (1864–1939), suffragist, was born in Munich, Bavaria, in 1864, the only daughter of Oswald Adalbert Sickert (1828–1885), a commercial artist of Danish origin (who became a German by virtue of the Prussian invasion of Schleswig-Holstein), and his wife, Eleanor Louisa Moravia Henry (1830–1922), the illegitimate daughter of a professional dancer and a fellow of Trinity College, Cambridge. She had three brothers, of whom the eldest was Walter *Sickert, the artist. In 1868 the Sickerts moved to England and settled first in Bedford, and then in Notting Hill, London, where they were part of an artistic and literary circle that included the families of William Morris and Edward Burne-Jones, and later Oscar Wilde.

Helena was educated at a French boarding-school in Neuville, and then at Notting Hill high school. In 1882 she went to Girton College, Cambridge, where she studied with Henry Sidgwick, Alfred Marshall, and Neville Keynes. She gained second-class honours in the moral sciences tripos (1885). In 1885 she was appointed lecturer in psychology at Westfield College, London. In 1888 she married Frederick Tertius Swanwick (1851–1931), a Cambridge wrangler and lecturer in mathematics at Owens College, Manchester (later to become Manchester University). He was the son of Thomas Swanwick, a Manchester merchant from a Unitarian family. There were no children of the marriage. Helena Swanwick became a close friend of C. P. Scott and his wife, Rachel, and over the next eighteen years wrote and reviewed regularly for the *Manchester Guardian* on domestic and feminist subjects and gardening. Her first book, *The Small Town Garden*, was published in 1907.

Swanwick also did voluntary work in a girls' club, which brought her into contact with the local women's trade union council, the Women's Co-operative Guild, and ultimately the Labour Party. Through them she met Emmeline Pankhurst and her daughters, and became involved in the women's suffrage movement. However, she found the physical force tactics employed by the Pankhursts unacceptable, and in 1905 joined the North of England Suffrage Society, which was affiliated to Millicent Fawcett's National Union of Women's Suffrage Societies. In 1908 she addressed 150 mass meetings in all parts of

Anna Swanwick (1813–1899), by Katherine Bruce

Swanwick's literary life remained important to her. She had been elected as the first woman member of the Royal Institution in 1858; and, urged by Baron von Bunsen, she had completed a translation of the *Trilogy* of Aeschylus, published in 1865, and the whole of his dramas in 1873. These caused W. E. Gladstone to be added to the long list of her friends. With her considerable scholarship and her lively conversation, 'deep and earnest' but at the same time 'brilliant and witty' and full of 'flashes of fun and repartee' (Knight, 279), she was well known in a wide circle of those who formed the culture of the century. Her friends were thinkers and writers such as Thomas Carlyle, Henry Crabb Robinson, and Friedrich Max Müller, scientists such as W. B. Carpenter, Michael Faraday, John Tyndall, and T. H. Huxley, thinking clergy such as John William Colenso and Edward Stanley, eminent women such as Helen Faucit, Frederika Bremer, Frances Power Cobbe, and Josephine Butler, and the most notable poets of the day, Alfred, Lord Tennyson, and Robert Browning. Browning regarded her with particular warmth, perhaps because she reminded him of his wife—he remarked wistfully one day how much he would have liked the two to have known each other.

Swanwick's greatest contribution to society was the lead she took in women's affairs (she signed John Stuart Mill's petition to parliament in 1865 for a woman's right to vote, and made her first and only public speech on behalf of women's suffrage at the age of sixty) and in the education of women. In 1894 she was the joint trustee (with Sir Joshua Fitch and Anthony Mundella) of the Pfeiffer bequest of £60,000 for women's higher education: it benefited women all over the United Kingdom at the new halls

Britain, and in 1909–14 was editor of the suffragist newspaper, the *Common Cause*.

In 1914 Swanwick resigned from the paper because of differences with her colleagues over the issue of war, and became a member of the executive committee of the Union of Democratic Control, founded by E. D. Morel to campaign against secret diplomacy. From 1915 to 1922 she was chairman of the Women's International League for Peace, which aimed to harness feminism to the peace movement; and throughout the First World War she campaigned for a negotiated peace and the establishment of an international peace-keeping organization. She was highly critical, however, of the terms under which the League of Nations was set up in 1919, partly because the league was permitted the use of force and economic sanctions, and partly because it was committed to supporting the Versailles settlement, which she regarded from the start as an unjust and unstable peace. In 1920–21 she campaigned against the activities of the Black and Tans in Ireland, and in 1923–4 she campaigned against the French invasion of the Ruhr (the latter she saw as legitimizing renascent German nationalism).

Swanwick published a history of the Union of Democratic Control, *Builders of Peace* (1924), and from 1925 to 1928 was editor of the organization's journal, *Foreign Affairs*, which she aimed to make a more popular and widely read journal. Through its columns she continually attacked the 'war guilt' clause of the Versailles treaty, denounced the 'tragic-comedy' of the Locarno treaty, and argued that the new phenomenon of aerial bombardment had made any form of war an intolerable option, however just its cause. In 1924 and again in 1928–31 she was a member of the British empire delegation to the League of Nations assembly. In 1929 she visited Bavaria for the first time since her childhood: a visit that reinforced her sense of cultural sympathy with Germany, and of the injustice to the German people meted out by Versailles.

In 1930 Helena Swanwick was appointed CH for her services to 'peace and the enfranchisement of women'. Throughout the 1930s, however, she was an increasingly isolated figure. Her husband died in 1931; and she found herself increasingly estranged both from moderate members of the peace movement (who disliked her attacks on the League of Nations), and from its more extremist members (who disliked her refusal to countenance violent revolution). Her own stance in this period was one not of pure pacifism, but of non-interventionism and isolationism—a position that she defended on largely pragmatic grounds. She outlined her ideas and the rationale behind them in a very attractively written autobiography, *I have been Young* (1935). But her differences with other peace campaigners were reinforced by the rise of Nazism, and by her publication of *Collective Insecurity* (1937) and *The Roots of Peace* (1938). These books defended Adolf Hitler's foreign policies as no different from those of other imperialists, past and present, and claimed that nothing could be done about his uncivilized domestic policies (any more than the equally objectionable policies of Soviet Russia). Instead she argued for the development of a federal Europe, with communal control of all vital strategic areas, and for the cultivation of an 'international mind' among European citizens. In the context of the late 1930s such proposals confirmed her separation from all sections of British politics. She committed suicide on 16 November 1939 at her home, Satis, Boulters Lane, Maidenhead, Berkshire, after the outbreak of the Second World War.

JOSE HARRIS, *rev.*

Sources H. M. Swanwick, *I have been young* (1935) · H. M. Swanwick, *Builders of peace: being ten years' history of the Union of Democratic Control* (1924) · M. Caedel, *Pacifism in Britain, 1914–1945: the defining of a faith* (1980) · *DLB*, 4.168–71 · O. Banks, *The biographical dictionary of British feminists*, 1 (1985) · K. T. Butler and H. I. McMorran, eds., *Girton College register, 1869–1946* (1948) · *The Labour who's who* (1927)
Archives Bodl. Oxf., letters to Lord Ponsonby · JRL, letters to the *Manchester Guardian* · JRL, letters to Allan Monkhouse
Wealth at death £1184 1s. 1d.: probate, 24 Feb 1940, CGPLA Eng. & Wales

Swayne, John (d. 1439x42), archbishop of Armagh, was of English or Anglo-Irish origin. He first appears in the records in May 1399 when, as clerk of the diocese of Kildare, he was dispensed from the necessity of mentioning his illegitimate birth in future petitions. He was also permitted to hold pluralities, exchange benefices, and be promoted to episcopal or archiepiscopal dignities. At the same time he was made treasurer of the archdiocese of Dublin and was granted the canonry and prebend of Newcastle Lyons, Dublin. In April 1404 he was described as rector of Galtrim, Meath, apparently his earliest benefice, and was also a canon in the diocese of Ferns, holding the prebend of Taghmon. He was allowed to exchange Taghmon for Tacumshin (both in Wexford) but in May 1404 resigned his claim to the latter place. In July 1405 he resigned his treasurership in return for full possession of the canonry in Dublin and the prebend of Newcastle.

While collecting these Irish benefices Swayne was a law student in Italy, serving as a clerk at the papal court from the early 1400s. His stay was interrupted in 1407 when Henry IV ordered him and five others to return from Rome; but in a dispensation of 1408, in which he is described as *doctor utriusque iuris* he claimed the rectorship of the University of Siena. In 1409 he received leave of absence from Ireland, which was extended in 1414. In March of the former year he attended the Council of Pisa where Pope Gregory XII, under whom Swayne had worked for three years, was deposed and replaced by Alexander V. In August 1410 Nicholas Fleming, archbishop of Armagh, made Swayne one of his four proctors at Alexander's court. In 1412 he was papal secretary and in the following year Pope John XXIII awarded him the prebend of Swords, Dublin, and the archdeaconry of Meath. He was still at this point a simple clerk without major orders. He was dispensed from receiving orders for ten years despite holding Galtrim with cure of souls. He attended the Council of Constance in 1415–16 as legal adviser for various litigants and his notebook contains the most detailed contemporary narrative of the fracas, between the English delegates on the one hand and the French and Spanish on the other, which occurred at the council in November 1416.

By 1417 Swayne was working for the English nation at Constance. In September of that year Archbishop Fleming died and the chapter of Armagh elected Richard Talbot, brother of John Talbot, lieutenant of Ireland. The see remained vacant for a year in the absence of a pope and in the meantime Talbot opted for the archbishopric of Dublin which had also become available. The chapter of Armagh next chose Robert Fitzhugh, chancellor of St Patrick's Cathedral, Dublin, and rector of Finglas, Dublin, but by then the new pope, Martin V, had already chosen Swayne for the post. He was consecrated in February 1418 at Constance and by January 1419 was back in Ireland.

Swayne's time as archbishop was dominated by the struggle between Sir John Talbot, Lord Furnival, and James Butler, fourth earl of Ormond (1411–1452), for control of the Irish administration. The archbishop remained neutral in this quarrel but deplored its consequences, asserting that 'this debate between these two lords is the cause of the great harms that be done in this country' (Chart, 111). In 1428 he stated that £20,000 was owed by chief governors and soldiers in the country. He was particularly scathing about the use of purveyance to provision the king's forces, saying:

> soldiers live on the husbandmen, not paying for horse meat nor man meat, and the lieutenants' purveyors take up all manner of victuals, that is to say, corn, hay, beasts and poultry and all other things needful to their household, and pay nothing therefor to account but tallies … And all this the poor husbandry bears and pays for, and the war on the other side destroys them.   (Chart, 108)

One consequence of this which the archbishop bemoaned was emigration of the king's lieges in Ireland to England; and the overall result, according to him, was that the extent of the land obedient to the king's command in Ireland amounted to little more than one shire.

Swayne seems rarely if ever to have strayed from the English-controlled area of his province, and called for the Irish of Ulster to be destroyed by a force of archers provided from England. But he could also be pragmatic about relations with the Irish, as in 1426 when he petitioned the pope to allow the marriage between Roger Mac Mathghamhna and Alice White on the grounds that it would probably strengthen peace between the English and Irish. Swayne resigned in 1439 and was dead by October 1442. He died at Drogheda, where he was buried in St Peter's Church.   B. Smith

Sources D. A. Chart, ed., *The register of John Swayne, archbishop of Armagh and primate of Ireland, 1418–1439* (1935) · A. Gwynn, 'Ireland and the English nation at the Council of Constance', *Proceedings of the Royal Irish Academy*, 45C (1939–40), 183–233 · T. W. Moody and others, eds., *A new history of Ireland, 9: Maps, genealogies, lists* (1984)

Swayne, Joseph Griffiths (1819–1903), obstetric physician, born on 18 October 1819 at Bristol, was the second son of John Champeny Swayne, lecturer on midwifery in the Bristol medical school, whose father was for nearly sixty years vicar of Pucklechurch, Gloucestershire. His mother was the eldest daughter of Thomas Griffiths, an apothecary in Bristol. After education at the protestant but non-sectarian Bristol College, where one of his teachers was Francis William Newman, Swayne was apprenticed to his father and at the same time studied at the Bristol medical school and the Bristol Royal Infirmary. Later he went to Guy's Hospital and became MRCS and a licentiate of the Society of Apothecaries in 1841. He also studied in Paris, and in 1842 graduated MB of the University of London, obtaining the gold medal in obstetric medicine and sharing with Alfred Baring Garrod the gold medal in medicine. In 1845 he proceeded MD at London and joined his father as lecturer on midwifery in the Bristol medical school; he was sole lecturer from 1850 until 1895, during which time the school affiliated with and was then incorporated into Bristol University College. In 1895 he was appointed emeritus professor.

In 1853 Swayne was elected physician accoucheur to the Bristol General Hospital (founded in 1832), one of the first appointments of the kind outside London; he held this post until 1875, when he became consulting obstetric physician. Greatly esteemed as a consultant, he had a large practice in the west of England. He was an advocate of asepsis, and deprecated long hair or beards for those who practised surgery or midwifery. As early as 1843 he investigated cholera, and described a micro-organism which some suggested was the comma bacillus which Koch proved to be the cause of the disease in 1884. He married Georgina (d. 1865), daughter of the Revd G. Gunning, with whom he had one son and one daughter.

Swayne possessed much artistic and literary ability. He published, in addition to many papers in medical journals, *Obstetric Aphorisms for the Use of Students* (1856), which was translated into eight languages and which ran to many editions. Swayne died suddenly on 1 August 1903 at his home at Harewood House, 74 Pembroke Road, Clifton, Bristol, and was buried at Holy Souls cemetery, Arnos Vale, Bristol.

H. D. Rolleston, *rev.* Elizabeth Baigent

Sources *The Lancet* (15 Aug 1903), 503 · *BMJ* (8 Aug 1903), 338 · *BMJ* (1861), 232 · *Bristol Medico-Chirurgical Journal*, 21 (1903), 193–202 · G. Munro Smith, *A history of the Bristol Royal Infirmary* (1917) · J. O. Symes, *A short history of the Bristol General Hospital* (1932) · T. W. Sherborne, *University College, Bristol, 1879–1909* (1977) · CGPLA Eng. & Wales (1903) · P. J. Wallis and R. V. Wallis, *Eighteenth century medics*, 2nd edn (1988)
Likenesses photograph, repro. in *Bristol Medico-Chirurgical Journal*
Wealth at death £43,986 11s.: probate, 22 Oct 1903, CGPLA Eng. & Wales

Swaythling. For this title name *see* Montagu, Samuel, first Baron Swaythling (1832–1911); Montagu, David Charles Samuel, fourth Baron Swaythling (1928–1998).

Sweet, Henry (1845–1912), phonetician and comparative philologist, was born on 15 September 1845 at 11 Mecklenburgh Street, London, the eldest of the three sons of George Sweet (1814–1879), a barrister, and his wife, Alice Nicholson (d. in or after 1879). On his father's side the family had connections with the west country, and on his mother's, with Scotland. In adulthood Sweet was of medium height, with deep square shoulders, and blue eyes set in a long and broad face; in his youth his hair was golden-yellow in colour. From childhood on he suffered from severe myopia.

Linguist and phonetician From 1855 to 1861 Sweet was educated at Bruce Castle School, Tottenham, and from 1861 to 1863 at King's College School, London. It was possibly as a result of encouragement from his form master at the latter, Thomas Cockayne, that Sweet began to teach himself Old English and Old Icelandic. In 1863 he enrolled for a year at the University of Heidelberg, where he studied comparative and Germanic philology under Adolf Holtzmann, before returning to London to work in his uncle's law firm. The *Student's Dictionary of Anglo-Saxon*, first published in 1897, was begun about this time. Sweet also received lessons in phonetics in London from the Scottish phonetician Alexander Melville Bell. In 1868 his personal circumstances allowed him to move to Oxford to begin work on transcribing and editing the Hatton and Cotton manuscripts of King Alfred's Pastoral Care. The work was published in 1872 while Sweet was still an undergraduate.

In 1869 Sweet matriculated at Balliol College, Oxford, to read classics ('greats'). Benjamin Jowett was the master (from 1870), and Sweet's contemporaries included Herbert Asquith, Scott Holland, Arnold Toynbee, and Algernon Swinburne. Sweet was out of sympathy with 'greats', and he graduated BA in 1873 with a fourth class. He had spent almost all his undergraduate career working virtually alone in the Germanic languages. By the time he graduated, he had, among other things, published the *Pastoral Care*, critically reviewed nine works in the academic press, and read three papers to the Philological Society.

After Oxford, Sweet returned to London to live in the family home for the next few years. He had decided to make a career for himself in philological, particularly English, studies, and he became an active member of the Philological Society in London, also serving as its president from 1876 to 1878. He read papers on various subjects to the society, especially on the contemporary forms of languages, including German, Swedish, Danish, Icelandic, and Irish Gaelic. In later years his field of interest widened to include Welsh, Portuguese, Norwegian, Arabic, Chinese, and Sanskrit.

On 30 August 1887, in Long Ditton, Surrey, Sweet married Mary Aletheia Birch (1852–1935), a daughter of Samuel *Birch (1813–1885), the Egyptologist at the British Museum, and Charlotte F. Birch (née Gray). They chose to live at various places in the south and west of England from where Sweet could continue his work as a linguist and phonetician. He supported his wife and himself—there were no children—by means of a family legacy and the income from his books and from taking private pupils, especially non-native speakers of English who required specialist tuition in the language. In 1894 they moved to Oxford, where Sweet continued this *modus vivendi*.

After various attempts to obtain a university post, Sweet was finally appointed to the newly established readership in phonetics at Oxford in 1901 at the age of fifty-six. The only academic honour he otherwise received within Britain was an honorary LLD degree from the University of Glasgow in 1892. By contrast, Heidelberg awarded him an honorary PhD degree in 1875, and he was made a corresponding member of the Munich Academy of Sciences and of the Royal Prussian Academy of Sciences, and an ordinary member of the Royal Danish Academy. He was president of the International Phonetic Association from 1887 to his death. He declined offers of chairs from outside Britain on the ground that his life's work lay in implementing a scheme to alter radically the direction of linguistic studies in Britain, and more particularly in Oxford. Some of his feelings and frustrations can be sensed from the surviving outline of one of his unpublished novels (MacMahon, 1985). He was a solitary and fairly lonely man. His few recreations included fishing and skiing, but towards the end of his life he looked forward to flying. In matters of religion he veered towards the mystical, particularly Swedenborgianism.

Publications Sweet's career as an academic was relatively unconventional, in that for nearly thirty years he held no university teaching post: his reputation was built on his publications, especially on his books and his papers for the Philological Society. His academic interests ranged widely over topics such as phonetics, spelling reform, shorthand, grammar, the teaching and learning of languages, general linguistics, the history of the English language, other Germanic languages, and literature. His general strategy was to publish advanced material first of all, then simplify some of it in works targeted at the student learner.

In 1877 Sweet's *Handbook of Phonetics* appeared. This seminal work inspired a whole tradition of phonetic studies, especially in Britain and Europe. It presents a statement of general phonetic theory, illustrated by phonetic transcriptions of various languages, and an excursus on the nature of phonetic notational systems. In his discussion of Broad and Narrow Romic notations, Sweet was one of the earliest linguists to formulate the distinction between phonemic and allophonic transcriptions. Two later works on phonetics, the *Primer of Spoken English* (1890) and the *Primer of Phonetics* (1890), provide a less detailed account of phonetic theory. The text of the *Primer of Spoken English* is essentially a translation of his influential *Elementarbuch des gesprochenen Englisch* of 1885, written for German learners of English at a time when radical changes were under way in Europe in the teaching of modern languages. Towards the end of his life Sweet published a further exposition of English phonetics, the *Sounds of English* (1908).

During the late 1870s and early 1880s Sweet played a part in the academic discussions (particularly within the Philological Society) on the reform of English orthography. A further marker of his interest in the utilitarian application of linguistic principles is his *Manual of Current Shorthand* (1892).

The subject of grammar, especially the central question of how grammatical categories should be established, had interested Sweet in the 1870s. Twenty years later he set out his ideas in the *New English Grammar* (1892, 1898), in which he focused in turn on the contemporary and historical forms of the language. Two simplified accounts of grammar, based on the *New English Grammar*, are his *Short Historical English Grammar* (1892) and the *Primer of Historical Grammar* (1902).

Sweet became prominent in the movement which emerged in Europe in the mid-1880s to reform modern language teaching (MacMahon, 2001). His ideas are distilled in *The Practical Study of Languages* (1899), a large—and still influential—work, which discusses in detail the theories and practices of teaching and learning languages.

Two years after the publication of the *Pastoral Care*, and within a year of graduating from Oxford, Sweet published the *History of English Sounds* (1874), extensively revised in the light of further study and reissued in 1888. Both works provided the serious student of English philology, of whom there were few at this time—at least in Britain—with evidence of his palaeographical and editorial skills, as well as his ability to structure the presentation of large sets of sometimes ambiguous data.

The series of works designed for the student rather than the scholar began with his *Anglo-Saxon Reader* of 1876. Sweet knew how difficult it was to produce an introduction to Old English which also included texts of genuine intrinsic interest. The *Reader* has to be seen, then, not as an introductory textbook but as an intermediate one. His later decision to publish an easier book for beginners, namely the *Anglo-Saxon Primer*, in 1882 was, therefore, a wise one. Both books have remained in print, passing through several editions, for more than a century.

The edition of the *Epinal Glossary* (1883) was Sweet's next major research publication, despite his description of it as a mere 'introduction to the study of the MS'. Instead he envisaged a more critical account of it appearing, alongside other material from the corpus of Old English glosses, in a work in preparation, *The Oldest English Texts*. In the event the latter did not appear until 1886. Its preface makes interesting reading: not only for the charming honesty with which Sweet describes his labours and the development of his ideas, but also for his outspoken criticisms of what he regarded as the 'parasite philology' then current in Germany. The work as a whole provided scholars for the first time with the necessary tools for advancing the critical study of the earliest periods of Old English. Deliberately omitted from it, however, was the material he had published at the same time as the *Epinal Glossary*, namely *King Alfred's Orosius* (1883), based on a diplomatic reading of the Old English and Latin texts in the Lauderdale and Cotton manuscripts.

During the years between the publication of the *History of English Sounds* in 1874 and its revision in 1888, Sweet's own work, together with that of other scholars, revealed deficiencies in his original assessment of certain historical forms and their subsequent developments. Hence he undertook a full-scale revision of the entire text. The *History of English Sounds* (1888) was his last major scholarly study in the field of medieval English studies.

The *First Middle English Primer* (1884) was written for the benefit of those students needing a 'firm foundation' before they embarked on the study of dialect differentiations. The *Second Middle English Primer* (1886) deals solely with Chaucer.

It was during this period of intensive literary activity in the mid-1880s that Sweet published three further intermediate textbooks for students of Old English. His edition of *Ælfric's Homilies* (1885) was for those who, having mastered both the *Primer* and the *Reader*, were 'at a loss for further reading'. The *Extracts from Alfred's Orosius* (1885), based on his text of 1883, had a similar function. The *Second Anglo-Saxon Reader* (1887) introduces the reader to forms of the language other than West Saxon.

Sweet's central medieval interest, from both the research and teaching points of view, was Old English. He had a scholarly (and pedagogical) interest, however, in other Germanic languages, particularly the Scandinavian. His *Icelandic Primer* (1886) is an excellent example of his ability to present the essential facts of a medieval language in a form that is immediately attractive to students. There is a modicum of linguistic information, and this is described synchronically. There are no diachronic or cognate Germanic materials to distract the learner. It was Sweet's friendship with Guðbrandr Vigfússon and Frederick York Powell, both scholars of Old Norse at Oxford, and his reactions to their own introductory textbook on the language (1879), that played a part in his decision to write this particular primer. The *History of Language* (1900) is a necessarily condensed account, aimed at the general reader, of the principles that underlie comparative philology; the neo-grammarian thesis on language change informs much of the argument.

Achievements Sweet's major achievements were in phonetics and Old English studies. In his day no one doubted his prodigious learning, his ability to summarize and explain arguments succinctly and effectively, and his passionate attachment to the cause of reforming the learning and teaching of modern, medieval, and classical languages in Britain. Yet he made less progress as a practising academic than he achieved in print. Colleagues in Britain generally failed to recognize his considerable mastery of his subject area; by contrast, those in Europe were quick to do so, and from early on in his career Sweet was regarded as an authority. To many German scholars, for example, his achievements were simply 'trailblazing' ('bahnbrechend').

Sweet's personality was partly to blame for his lack of success in Britain. He was exceedingly sharp with his tongue (and pen) to colleagues with whose views he did not agree. Had he obtained an academic teaching post earlier, then the bitterness he felt about his treatment at the hands of men whom he regarded as his intellectual inferiors might have diminished—and a different style of linguistic scholarship and pedagogy might, conceivably, have evolved in Britain. Some insight into his personality is provided by George Bernard Shaw in *Pygmalion*, where the character of Henry Higgins is based to a limited extent on that of Sweet [*see* Jones, Daniel (1881–1967)].

Henry Sweet died at his home, 15 Rawlinson Road,

Oxford, of pernicious anaemia, on 30 April 1912, and was buried in Wolvercote cemetery. His wife died in Oxford on 2 July 1935.

Generations of students of English have benefited from the changes that Sweet wrought in the understanding of the historical and contemporary forms of the language. His structured introductions to many aspects of English—as well as to phonetics—reflect, on the one hand, his comprehensive knowledge of the subject matter, as well as, on the other, his pedagogical skills in selecting and explaining the essential features of that subject matter for the less advanced reader. His devotion to elucidating Old English manuscripts gave scholars access to certain texts far earlier than would otherwise have been the case. In language teaching, the intellectual and practical support that he gave to late nineteenth-century movements for curricular reform in the schools and universities, especially in Europe, was critical and timely.

M. K. C. MacMahon

Sources Athenaeum (4 May 1912), 504 • A. Brandl, 'Henry Sweet', Archiv für das Studium der Neueren Sprachen und Literatur, new ser., 30 (1913), 8–11 • A. Brandl, Zwischen Inn und Themse: Lebensbeobachtungen eines Anglisten: Alt-Tirol/England/Berlin (Berlin, 1936) • R. W. Chambers, 'Some great philologists of the past', Transactions of the Philological Society (1934), 100–02 • J. R. Firth, 'The English school of phonetics', Transactions of the Philological Society (1946), 92–132 • J. R. Firth, 'Philology in the Philological Society', Transactions of the Philological Society (1956), 1–25 • O. Jespersen, A linguist's life (Odense, 1995) • D. Jones, 'Henry Sweet', Maître Phonétique (June–Aug 1912), 97–9 • M. K. C. MacMahon, 'Henry Sweet's system of shorthand', Towards a history of phonetics, ed. R. E. Asher and E. J. A. Henderson (1981), 265–81 • M. K. C. MacMahon, 'Henry Sweet's linguistic scholarship: the German connection', Anglistik: Organ des Verbandes Deutscher Anglisten, 5/2 (1994), 91–101 • M. K. C. MacMahon, 'Henry Sweet', Medieval scholarship: biographical studies on the formation of a discipline, ed. H. Damico, D. Fennema, and K. Lenz, 2 (1998), 167–75 • C. T. Onions, 'Henry Sweet', DNB Supplement (1927), 519–20 • H. Raudnitzky, Die Bell-Sweetsche Schule: ein Beitrag zur Geschichte der englischen Phonetik, Marburger Studien zur englischen Philologie, 13 (Marburg, 1911) • J. A. S., 'Obituary: Henry Sweet, M.A., Ph.D., LL.D.', Oxford Magazine (9 May 1912) • D. L. Savory, 'Henry Sweet', Die Neueren Sprachen, 20/4 (June 1912), 193–200 • D. L. Savory, 'Oxford at the turn of the century', Contemporary Review, 190 (1956), 335–40 • The Times (1 May 1912), 11 • 'The debt to Henry Sweet', The Times (15 Sept 1945) • C. L. Wrenn, 'Henry Sweet', Transactions of the Philological Society (1946), 177–201 • P. A. Wright-Henderson, Glasgow & Balliol and other essays (1926) • H. C. Wyld, 'Henry Sweet', Modern Languages Quarterly, 4/2 (1901), 73–9 • H. C. Wyld, 'Henry Sweet', Archiv für das Studium der Neueren Sprachen und Literatur, new ser. 30 (1913), 1–8 • Collected papers of Henry Sweet, ed. H. C. Wyld (1913) • b. cert. • m. cert. • d. cert. • will • CGPLA Eng. & Wales (1912) • Boase, Mod. Eng. biog. • old parish registers, Edinburgh [Alice Nicholson] • burial records, Wolvercote cemetery, Oxford • M. K. C. MacMahon, 'Henry Sweet as a novelist', Revista Canaria de Estudias Ingleses, 10 (1985), 217–21 • M. K. C. MacMahon, 'Modern language instruction and phonetics in the later 19th century', History of the language sciences, ed. S. Auroux and others, 2 (Berlin and New York, 2001), 1585–95

Archives Balliol Oxf., Old English glossary | BL, corresp. with George Bernard Shaw, Add. MS 50549

Likenesses photograph, SOAS

Wealth at death £7355 4s. 3d.: probate, 8 July 1912, CGPLA Eng. & Wales

Sweet, Robert (1783–1835), horticulturist, was born at Cockington, near Torquay, the son of William Sweet and his wife, Mary. Nothing is known of his early education; at the age of sixteen he was placed under his half-brother, James Sweet, gardener to Richard Bright of Ham Green, near Bristol. Sweet remained there for nine years before moving to Woodlands, the residence of John Julius Angerstein, to take charge of a collection of plants.

In 1810 Sweet entered as a partner, with William Malcolm, in the Stockwell nursery, and when that was dissolved in 1815, became foreman at the nursery of Whitley, Brames, and Milne, of Fulham. In 1819, he entered the service of Messrs Colvill; while in their employ he was charged with having received a box of plants knowing them to have been stolen from the Royal Botanic Gardens, Kew, but was acquitted after trial at the Old Bailey on 24 February 1824. In 1826 he left the Colvills, and occupied himself until 1831 almost wholly in the production of botanical works, while still cultivating a limited number of plants in his garden at Parson's Green, Fulham. In 1830 he moved to Chelsea, where he had a larger garden and cultivated for sale to his friends.

In June 1831 Sweet suffered a complete nervous breakdown. He died on 20 January 1835, leaving a widow but no children. He had been elected a fellow of the Linnean Society on 14 February 1812. His works included Hortus suburbanus Londinensis (1818); Geraniaceae (5 vols., 1820–30); Sweet's hortus Britannicus (1826); Flora Australasica (1827–8); and an ornithological work, The British Warblers (1823). The botanical genus Sweetia was named in his honour by Candolle in 1825.

B. B. WOODWARD, rev. ALEXANDER GOLDBLOOM

Sources Desmond, Botanists, rev. edn, 667 • Gardener's Magazine, 9, 159 • Magazine of Natural History, 8, 410

Archives RBG Kew

Sweeting, Elizabeth Jane (1914–1999), arts administrator and theatre manager, was born on 19 November 1914 at 244 Ladbroke Grove, London, the only child of Frederick Sweeting (d. c.1931), a tobacconist's shop manager, and his wife, Ethel Guley (d. 1974). She was educated at Croydon High School for Girls, and acquired a love of the theatre by attending the Old Vic and Sadler's Wells. She won a scholarship to Royal Holloway College, University of London, where she took a first-class, BA (honours), and a distinction for her MA thesis published as Early Tudor Criticism: Linguistic and Literary (1940). She was president of the university drama society and produced plays. From 1938 she taught English at the King Edward Grammar School for Girls, Birmingham, and in the evenings and vacations gained a practical knowledge of backstage work at the amateur Crescent Theatre. From 1940 she lectured in English at University College, London, which spent the war in Aberystwyth. On its return to London she gained further experience working as assistant stage manager with Alec Clunes at the Arts Theatre.

This 'double life' (Sweeting, Beginners Please, chap. 1) in teaching and theatre ended when, in 1946, through George Rylands and 'Binkie' Beaumont, she became assistant stage manager of the Company of Four at the Lyric Theatre, Hammersmith. In 1947 she became an assistant manager with English Opera Group at Glyndebourne, 'a halcyon world' (ibid., 30), where Kathleen Ferrier sang in *Orfeo*, and Benjamin Britten premièred his *Albert Herring*. Britten appointed her to work with the Aldeburgh Festival of Music and the Arts, and as festival manager in its formative, creative period she was crucial to its success, settling in Aldeburgh from 1948 to 1955, and gaining wide experience of arts administration.

A sideways move to management training with Marks and Spencer brought valuable insights into industrial relations and personnel management, and as their social secretary Sweeting met international delegates when in 1956 she organized the duke of Edinburgh's conference on human relations in industry, held at Oxford. There she was introduced to Frank Hauser and his Meadow Players, and became general manager at the Oxford Playhouse from 1956 to 1961, when it became the Oxford University Theatre. Sweeting served as secretary to the curators and administrator until 1976. She organized extensive refurbishing of the playhouse in 1963, but despite problems over accommodation and finance, Meadow Players and the theatre prospered. Its productions included plays by Jean Anouilh, Jean Giradoux, and Ugo Betti. Theatregoers came up from London and she worked with distinguished actors, including Richard Burton and Elizabeth Taylor in their celebrated appearance in *Dr Faustus*. Susan Hampshire and Alan Ayckbourn began their careers there as assistant stage managers. Sweeting organized the transfer of fifteen productions to London, and tours to ten European festivals. This rich experience was captured in her compendious and useful *Theatre Administration* (1969), and in 1970 she was an examiner of the pioneering course on this subject at the Polytechnic of Central London. She recounted her personal story in the crisp and vivid *Beginners Please* (1971). She later wrote or edited several reports on arts conferences.

For thirty years Sweeting's base was Beaumont Buildings, Oxford, where she cared for her widowed mother, who died in 1974. She enjoyed teaching English literature as an occasional tutor at St Catherine's College. At various times she served on theatre boards: the Theatre Royal, Bury St Edmunds, the Watermill Theatre, Newbury, the Wyvern Theatre, Swindon, and the Theatre at Chipping Norton. She was a member of the drama panel of the Arts Council of Great Britain.

A visit to the Adelaide Festival in 1972, where Sweeting chaired a national conference, and a further spell in Adelaide in 1974 as visiting professor in English, led to her accepting an invitation from Don Dunstan, prime minister of South Australia, to direct the state's newly established Arts Council. She became his arts consultant, and instituted seminal postgraduate courses in arts management at the Elton Mayo School of Management, Adelaide (1976–81), and was appointed for a term to the Australia Council, the federal arts funding body. After her return to England in 1981 she retained these links with Australia.

Sweeting was an astute manager of people, sociable but firm, and always sensitive in her dealings with artists— 'human relations are the basic stuff of productivity', she wrote (Sweeting, *Beginners Please*, 78). When she retired to Ironbridge in 1985 she was co-opted by the Ironbridge Gorge Museum Trust. She continued her worldwide solo travels until 1998. In her last years a friend, Beris Hudson, cared for her in Sheffield, where she suffered a heart attack, and died in Henleigh Hall Nursing Home, 20 Abbey Lane Dell, on 7 December 1999. She never married.

JOHN D. HAIGH

Sources E. Sweeting, *Beginners please: working in the theatre* (1971) · private information (2004) [Don Chapman] · Oxford Playhouse celebration of Elizabeth Sweeting, 2001 · E. Sweeting, *Theatre administration* (1969), v–ix · *The Independent* (17 Feb 2000) · *The Australian* (29 Dec 1999) · *The Guardian* (11 Dec 1999) · *Oxford Times* (24 Dec 1999) · b. cert. · d. cert.
Likenesses photograph, repro. in *The Guardian* · photograph, repro. in *The Independent* · photograph, repro. in *The Australian*

Sweeting, Marjorie Mary (1920–1994), geomorphologist, was born on 28 February 1920, at 24 Radipole Road, Fulham, the only child of George Scotland Sweeting, geology lecturer at Imperial College, London, and Ellen Louisa Liddiard. She attended Mayfield School, Putney, London, before taking a first in geography at Newnham College, Cambridge, in 1941. She was awarded the degree of PhD in 1948 by the University of Cambridge for a thesis entitled 'The landforms of the Carboniferous limestone of the Ingleborough district, N. W. Yorkshire'. Between 1948 and 1951 she was a research fellow at Newnham, and in 1951 she moved to the University of Oxford bringing her expertise and enthusiasm for karst (Carboniferous limestone) studies. She remained at St Hugh's College where she was from 1951 a fellow and tutor, later dean and senior tutor, and was concurrently university lecturer in the school of geography (appointed 1953), reader (appointed 1977), and acting head of department (1983–4). She retired in 1987.

During her research career in Oxford, Marjorie Sweeting supervised over thirty graduate students including a significant number who became the major figures in karst research. The research fields and locations of her students reflected her broad interest in limestone studies around the world: Jamaica, Puerto Rico, Canada, Belize, Australia, China, Tibet, and Borneo. These areas were, however, but a few of the karst regions of the world that she visited. Perhaps the only major limestone areas which she did not visit were those of the Arab world.

The characteristic which Marjorie Sweeting showed in her research career was one of utilizing technical advances made in other sciences. Never shy of adapting to the current trend, she fashioned her approach to karst studies upon a variation of field location, laboratory innovations, and funded research topics for her students. Consequently her publications, over seventy in all, spanning 1943–95, including two major books (*Karst Landforms*, 1972, and *Karst in China: its Geomorphology and Environment*, 1995), represented a broad church of limestone enquiry.

In keeping with the academic environment of the time, Sweeting's early works concentrated upon the shape of karst landforms, upon the geological control (following the influence and co-research of her geologist father, G. S.

Sweeting), and, in the early 1960s, upon landscape denudation rates. This later interest in rates of process led her to experimental studies and laboratory measurement, activities which were innovative for the scientific climate of the time. Working with rather simple equipment she succeeded in noting the importance of mineralogy in controlling weathering rates. This work brought together the field study and analysis of her research students, particularly those working in Jamaica and Puerto Rico. This early research led her to publish her most important book, *Karst Landforms*, in 1972. The book was the synthesis of her extensive travels, her own and her research students' work, and of her collaboration and discussion with most if not all of the major researchers in the field of limestone studies. The influence of French and German ideologies in her book is obvious as is her discussion with Slavonic geomorphologists. The book is a benchmark of its time, classic and informative of the prevailing morphological (as opposed to process) orientation of karst studies in the 1950s and 1960s. The lack of speleological research in the book is surprising given her interest and influence with the British Cave Research Association, with whom she caved; on the basis of those experiences she often identified cave science as a necessary facet of limestone research. Nevertheless *Karst Landforms* remains a formative text and an essential primer for any serious student of karst studies.

After the publication of *Karst Landforms* China opened up as an accessible region for research. Present on the first cultural visit of British scientists to China in 1975, Sweeting formed close links with the Chinese Academy of Sciences in Beijing and with the Karst Institute in Guilin where she returned more than fifteen times over the next twenty years or so.

The Chinese limestone regions were little visited by foreign scientists but Sweeting managed to visit all of the important regions from Guilin in the south to Hubei, Outer Mongolia in the north; from Shanghai in the east to Chengdu in the west. Eventually she studied high-mountain karst in Tibet but although she retained her desire to travel, by the 1990s she inevitably took a more passive role in field research.

Armed with undoubtedly the greatest experience and field knowledge of Chinese limestone regions of any researcher, Sweeting set about her last major task, a book on the karst of China. In final manuscript form, edited by her, shortly before her death, the book was published in 1995, entitled *Karst in China: its Geomorphology and Environment*. The book documents a vast range of features in the most important limestone region of the world. She recognizes in the book the importance of understanding and managing limestone regions in one of the most densely populated areas of the world.

Ever the diplomat, Sweeting preferred to review rather too kindly idiosyncratic views held by differing scientific communities within China. As a result, the book fails to provide the incisive commentary that only she could have brought to bear, and which she was happy to acknowledge

in discussion but not prepared to publish. Notwithstanding this, the book remains the benchmark description of Chinese karst studies during the twentieth century.

Throughout her Chinese research, Sweeting maintained an interest in new lines of enquiry; research, by this date generally undertaken through her research students, broadened her interests into biogeomorphology (which she had highlighted as potentially important in *Karst Landforms* as early as 1972) and dating techniques.

Sweeting enjoyed watching sport of all kinds (and her students noted what great physical demands she made of herself in the field), opera, and entertaining, but she most enjoyed the travel and conviviality which fieldwork and conference-going brought.

Awarded honours from the Royal Geographical Society (notably the Busk medal in 1980) and from many foreign speleological and geomorphological societies, Sweeting was acknowledged as one of the twentieth century's most important figures in karst studies. She died on 31 December 1994 at the John Radcliffe Hospital, Oxford, after a protracted fight against cancer. She was buried at Enstone, Oxfordshire, the village where she lived, on 6 January 1995. Her estate, divided equally among St Hugh's College, Oxford, Newnham College, Cambridge, and the Royal Geographical Society, significantly increased funds available to assist travel for research purposes at each of these institutions and reveals her love of travel, her dedication to research and, in the absence of family, her loyalty to the institutions where she felt at home. PETER A. BULL

Sources H. A. Viles, 'A lifetime of landforms: Marjorie Sweeting's contribution to tropical and subtropical karst', *Zeitschrift für Geomorphologie*, suppl., 108 (1997), 1–4 · H. A. Viles, 'Marjorie Sweeting', *Transactions of the Institute of British Geographers*, new ser., 21 (1996) · B. A. Kennedy, 'Marjorie Sweeting', *The Independent* (18 Jan 1995) · personal knowledge (2004) · private information (2004) [H. Viles, E. Baigent] · epitome of the will and memorandum of Marjorie Mary Sweeting deceased, undated typescript, priv. coll. · A. S. Goudie, 'Marjorie Sweeting, 1920–1994', *GJ*, 161 (1995), 239–40 · b. cert. · m. cert.
Likenesses H. Rosotti, photograph, St Hugh's College, Oxford · H. Rosotti, photograph, U. Oxf., school of geography and the enviornment
Wealth at death £218,708: probate, 8 March 1995, *CGPLA Eng. & Wales*

Sweetman, John (1752–1826), Irish nationalist and brewer, was born in Dublin, the son of John Sweetman (*d.* 1784), brewer, and his wife, Mary, daughter of Patrick Sweetman, brewer. R. R. Madden described him as 'an eminent and opulent citizen of Dublin, of an old and highly respectable family' (Madden, 4.94). In 1784 he married Maryanne Atkinson, daughter of Edward Atkinson, also a brewer.

Sweetman was closely involved in the campaign for Catholic relief during the early 1790s and supported the radical element in the Catholic body, which led to a secession of many gentry and clergy from the Catholic Committee in 1791. He was also a member of the Catholic Convention that met in Dublin in December 1792. During 1792–3 the government used a letter connecting Sweetman to a person accused of Defenderism, to level charges of complicity in the widespread Defender disturbances against the Catholic lobby at large. Sweetman responded with *A refutation of the charges attempted to be made against the secretary to the subcommittee of the Catholics of Ireland [that is, Sweetman] particularly that of abetting the Defenders* (1793). He admitted to a lengthy correspondence with Thomas Patrick Coleman of Dundalk on the subject of Defenderism, but argued that this was merely to ascertain the actual situation. He had also supported a man who he believed had been mistakenly accused of Defender activities. Sweetman suggested that the purpose of the charges was to implicate Dublin Catholics in the disturbances, and denied all allegations made by the government.

During the later 1790s Sweetman became a high ranking, if often shadowy, member of the radical and militant United Irishmen. Madden characterized him as 'a man of high intelligence, sound judgement, and sober, well considered opinions, strongly attached to the rights and interests of his country' (Madden, 4.95). He was arrested at his brewery on Francis Street on 12 March 1798, at the same time as most of the Leinster delegates of the organization were arrested at Oliver Bond's house. Sweetman and the other state prisoners reached an agreement with the Cornwallis administration in July 1798. They agreed to provide information in return for their lives and voluntary exile. With his fellow prisoners Sweetman was transferred to Fort George, Scotland, in 1799, before being set at liberty in the Netherlands in 1802. He later moved to Lyons and in 1820 returned to Ireland where he died in May 1826. He was buried at Swords, co. Dublin.

LIAM CHAMBERS

Sources R. R. Madden, *The United Irishmen: their lives and times*, 2nd edn, 4 vols. (1857–60) · W. T. W. Tone, *Life of Theobald Wolfe Tone*, ed. T. Bartlett (1998) · Burke, *Gen. Ire.* (1976) · M. Elliott, *Partners in revolution: the United Irishmen and France* (1982) · *DNB*
Archives NA Ire., rebellion papers

Sweetman, Milo. *See* Sweteman, Milo (*d.* 1380).

Sweetnam [Swetnam], **John** (1579–1622), Jesuit, was born in Great Harrowden, Northamptonshire, a son of Francis Sweetnam, a baker for the Vaux family, and Alice Sweetnam. Born a Catholic, Sweetnam received his early education in his native village and, according to his own testimony, spent two years in Oxford where he studied rhetoric and logic. Fearful that he was wasting his time and convinced that further study there would result in bad morals rather than a good education, he consulted the Jesuit Henry Garnet, who advised him to leave England for Spain. On 21 June 1602 he was admitted to the English College in Valladolid; the marquesa de Montesclaros and Pedro de Toledo subsidized his formation. According to Jesuit catalogues he was ordained in 1604. Presumably he remained in the Iberian peninsula after ordination because he entered the Society of Jesus in Coimbra on 20 April 1608, where he remained until at least 1612. Thus it is unlikely that he is the Sweetnam referred to by Sir Charles Cornwallis's letter to the lord treasurer on 20 May 1609 (*Memorials of Affairs of State*, 3.43). By 1615 Sweetnam was at the English College at St Omer as preacher, confessor,

consultor, and prefect of the library. Before his transfer to Flanders he, according to Clancy, assisted Francisco Suarez in writing *Defensio fidei* (Clancy, 27).

Sent to England in either 1616 or 1617, Sweetnam was arrested some time thereafter. Through the intercession of Count Gondomar, Spanish ambassador, he was banished in June 1618 with eleven other secular priests and Jesuits. In a letter to Dudley Carleton from London on 3 December 1618 John Chamberlain complained that 'most of the eighteen [*sic*] priests and Jesuits whom the Spanish ambassador carried over are returned and four are taken. The king says "They shall truss for it"' (Foley, 4.592). Sweetnam may have been one of the priests who returned immediately: by 1621 he was working in Lancashire. He was neither recaptured nor trussed. In 1622 he was the English penitentiary in Loreto, Italy, where he died on 4 November 1622.

Of his three books two typify what Clancy calls Salesian spirituality because of a 'love of nature and created things, ... abundant imagery and love of stories' (Clancy, 26). Sweetnam treated favourite Salesian themes: the Blessed Virgin, Mary Magdalen, gardens, and Loreto in *S. Mary Magdalens Pilgrimage to Paradise* (St Omer, 1617) and *The Paradise of Delights, or, The B. Virgins Garden of Loreto* (St Omer, 1620).   THOMAS M. MCCOOG

Sources T. M. McCoog, *English and Welsh Jesuits, 1555–1650*, 2 vols., Catholic RS, 74–5 (1994–5) · T. M. McCoog, ed., *Monumenta Angliae*, 1–2 (1992) · H. Foley, ed., *Records of the English province of the Society of Jesus*, 7 vols. in 8 (1875–83) · G. Anstruther, *The seminary priests*, 2 (1975) · E. Henson, ed., *The registers of the English College at Valladolid, 1589–1862*, Catholic RS, 30 (1930) · A. F. Allison and D. M. Rogers, eds., *The contemporary printed literature of the English Counter-Reformation between 1558 and 1640*, 2 vols. (1989–94) · T. H. Clancy, *A literary history of the English Jesuits: a century of books, 1615–1714* (1996) · *Memorials of affairs of state in the reigns of Q. Elizabeth and K. James I, collected (chiefly) from the original papers of ... Sir Ralph Winwood*, ed. E. Sawyer, 3 vols. (1725)
Archives Archives of the British Province of the Society of Jesus, London · Archivum Romanum Societatis Iesu, Rome

Swein [Sveinn Haraldsson, Sveinn Tjúguskegg, Swein Forkbeard] (*d.* 1014), king of England and of Denmark, was the son of Harald Gormsson (Harald Bluetooth), king of Denmark; the name of his mother is not known. The earliest evidence for Swein's byname, Forkbeard, is in the Roskilde chronicle, compiled about 1140. Most accounts of Swein's career, both medieval and modern, have been largely based on the hostile comments of Adam of Bremen and the information, much of it demonstrably false, in the *Gesta Hammaburgensis ecclesiae pontificum* that he wrote in the 1070s. Adam denigrated Swein because the latter neither recognized the German emperor as his overlord nor acknowledged the ecclesiastical authority of the archbishop of Hamburg–Bremen, which in Adam's eyes was tantamount to paganism. Swein's contemporary, Thietmar, bishop of Merseburg, produced a chronicle in which he adopted much the same attitude to Swein as Adam, but he does provide valuable information about Swein's marriage to a Polish princess. More favourable, if equally partisan, comments on Swein are given in the *Encomium Emmae Reginae*, written in St Omer between 1040 and 1042. Swein is there described as a fortunate, generous, and religious king. Contemporary sources, in particular the Anglo-Saxon Chronicle and skaldic verse preserved in later Icelandic sagas, provide valuable clues, but much remains obscure and conjectural; most of the assertions in the following account should be qualified as 'probable'.

Harald Gormsson was deposed and driven into exile by a rebellion led by his son and successor Swein. Harald died soon afterwards in November 986 or 987. During his thirty-year reign Harald had radically changed the Danish kingdom. He had greatly enlarged it by bringing Sjælland and Skåne under direct royal rule, and after his conversion about 965 Christianity became the official Danish religion. He had also gained control of the lands flanking Oslofjord, and was recognized as overlord by the most powerful Norwegian chieftain, Hákon, earl (*jarl*) of Hlathir. In 983 his campaign in alliance with the Abodrites weakened German power north of the Elbe and so removed any immediate threat of German invasion.

When Swein seized power the Danish kingdom was, thanks to his father, more powerful and secure than it had been for over a century. He was free to lead viking raids himself, and was, indeed, the first reigning Scandinavian king known to have done so. His army was not a national militia; it comprised his own retainers and those of magnates who supported him. During his reign other bands of Scandinavian warriors were active in the Baltic and in western Europe. Some occasionally joined forces, but in combined operations with Swein, as king of the richest part of Scandinavia, he clearly had a leading role. The main target of the raiders at that time was England which was then rapidly becoming an exceptionally rich, if vulnerable, kingdom. Swein's ability to exact large sums of tribute from the English was an important factor in sustaining and extending his power in Scandinavia.

There are several indications that Swein first raided England in 991, and was the leader of the force that defeated the English at Maldon and forced them to pay £10,000 as tribute. The only Scandinavian leader of that raid named in the Anglo-Saxon Chronicle was Óláf Tryggvason, presumably because of the important role he played later in English efforts to counter Swein. Óláf was, however, in 991, a relatively unimportant Norwegian adventurer, while Swein was not only king of the Danes, but also overlord of Norway.

Within three years of that success Swein had greatly enlarged his Scandinavian empire by subordinating the Svear, who occupied what is now eastern Sweden. The Svear, for whom commerce with western Europe was an important source of wealth, resented Danish control of the route to the North Sea, and in 992 or 993 Erik, king of the Svear, supported by the Polish ruler Boleslav, whose sister he had married, attacked Denmark. According to Adam of Bremen, Erik was victorious and Swein was driven into exile until Erik died fourteen years later. He then returned only to be expelled once again by Erik's son Olof. This is a gross distortion of what happened. Erik was either killed in the campaign against Swein or died soon

after it. Swein took Erik's Polish widow as his wife, and was soon acknowledged as overlord by Erik's son and successor Olof, whose later byname was Skötkonung ('Tributary King').

Swein, accompanied by Óláf Tryggvason and other Scandinavian chieftains, returned to England in 994. They attacked London but after failing to take the city they ravaged extensively in the south-east until the English agreed to pay £16,000 tribute. The English king Æthelred II then persuaded Óláf to break with Swein and encouraged him to return to Norway in 995 to challenge Danish overlordship. This policy, which was clearly intended to distract Swein, confirms that the English perceived him as the main threat. The death of Earl Hákon at this time removed the main obstacle to Óláf's seizure of power and he was soon recognized as king by many Norwegians. This was not only a serious blow to Swein's prestige, it also threatened his security in Denmark. Swein did not return to England until he had regained control of Norway; to that extent the English were successful. Óláf did not, however, reign long. He was defeated and killed in 999 (a more probable date than the traditional 1000) in battle against Swein, who was supported by Olof, the Swedish king, and by the sons of Earl Hákon, who then became Swein's *jarls* in Norway.

It was during the reign of Óláf as king of Norway that a few coins were struck in Swein's name as king, apparently in response to an emission of similar coins by Óláf. Both issues were modelled on English coins struck between 991 and 997. A very much larger number of imitations of Æthelred's coins were struck somewhere in Denmark, probably in Lund, during Swein's reign, although he was not named in the blundered legends.

In 1003 Swein began a prolonged campaign in England that caused widespread destruction, but in 1005 a very severe famine forced him to return with his fleet to Denmark. The Anglo-Saxon Chronicle implies that Swein's fleet, with or without Swein as leader, returned in 1006 and exacted £36,000 as tribute. Swein is not named as a leader of a Danish army in England again until his campaign of conquest in 1013. Some, but not all, of the leaders of other Danish armies that operated in England during Æthelred's reign may have been Swein's men. The main exception was Thorkill, an independent Danish chieftain whose army overran a large part of England between 1009 and 1012 before the English bought peace by paying a tribute of £48,000. Thorkill then went over to the king with forty-five ships and served Æthelred loyally until the king died in 1016. Swein had reason to fear that Thorkill, with English support, could threaten his own position, as Óláf Tryggvason had done. This is probably the reason he decided to conquer England.

In the summer of 1013 Swein invaded England, and established his base at Gainsborough on the east bank of the River Trent. He soon received the submission of the whole area north of Watling Street that had been occupied by Danes in the ninth century. He then went south. The Anglo-Saxon Chronicle reports that when his army 'crossed Watling Street they did the greatest damage an army could do' (*ASC*, s.a. 1013). The implication is that Swein was able to restrain his warriors from plundering the friendly territory north of Watling Street. If that is true, he was certainly an exceptional commander. Oxford and Wallingford submitted to him, but when London resisted 'with full battle because King Æthelred was inside and Thorkill with him', Swein went to Bath where he received the submission of the south-west. The English then acknowledged defeat and 'all the nation accepted him as full king' (ibid.). London submitted and gave hostages to avoid destruction. After celebrating Christmas in the Isle of Wight, Æthelred crossed to Normandy. Swein did not live long to enjoy his triumph. He died at Gainsborough on 3 February 1014 and was buried initially at York but, according to Thietmar of Merseburg, an unnamed English woman, fearing that Æthelred would, on his return from exile, destroy the body, had it exhumed and sent to Denmark, where it was reburied in Roskilde.

The evidence, though slight, is sufficient to show that Swein was a remarkable, and a remarkably successful, king. His achievements outside Denmark are better documented than those in it, but there is no reason to suppose that his triumphs abroad were matched by failure at home. His external success, especially against the English, enabled him to retain the loyalty of the warriors on whom his power ultimately depended. The process of Christianization, begun by his father, continued in his reign. The names of three missionary bishops who worked in Denmark in his time are known; two were English and one was a Dane—there were probably others. At least two churches were built or completed while Swein was king: in Roskilde and, by 990 or earlier, in Lund.

Swein had three children with Erik's Polish widow, whose name is not known: Harald, who succeeded him as king of Denmark, *Cnut, and Estrid. He had at least two other daughters, one of whom, Gytha, must have been the result of an earlier, unrecorded liaison; she married Erik, son of Earl Hákon, during Óláf Tryggvason's reign as king of Norway, probably in 997. P. H. SAWYER

Sources *Magistri Adam Bremensis gesta Hammaburgensis ecclesiae pontificum*, ed. B. Schmeidler, 3rd edn, MGH Scriptores Rerum Germanicarum, [2] (Hanover, 1917) · A. Campbell, ed. and trans., *Encomium Emmae reginae*, CS, 3rd ser., 72 (1949) · *ASC*, s.a. 994, 1004, 1013–14 · *English historical documents*, 1, ed. D. Whitelock (1955), no. 27 · P. Sawyer, 'Swein Forkbeard and the historians', *Church and chronicle in the middle ages: essays presented to John Taylor*, ed. I. Wood and G. A. Loud (1991), 27–40 · P. H. Sawyer, 'The Scandinavian background', *The battle of Maldon: fiction and fact*, ed. J. Cooper (1993), 33–42 · L. Sobel, 'Ruler and society in early medieval western Pomerania', *Antemurale*, 25 (1981), 19–142 · L. Demidoff, 'The death of Sven Forkbeard—in reality and later tradition', *Medieval Scandinavia*, 11 (1978–9), 30–47

Swein [Sweyn], **earl** (*d.* 1052), magnate, was the eldest son of *Godwine, earl of Wessex (*d.* 1053), and his wife, *Gytha [*see under* Godwine]. He was the elder brother of *Tostig (*c.*1029–1066). In 1043 he was raised to an earldom which included Gloucestershire (once held by his maternal uncle Eilaf), Herefordshire, Oxfordshire, Berkshire, and Somerset. In 1046 he campaigned successfully against the south Welsh in alliance with Gruffudd ap Llywelyn of Gwynedd. On his return he abducted Eadgifu, abbess of Leominster, apparently intending to marry her and gain control of Leominster's vast estate in northern Herefordshire. The king withheld permission and Eadgifu returned to her abbey, which was subsequently disbanded. The ultimate beneficiary was Swein's sister, Queen *Edith, who held the manor of Leominster with all its appurtenances in 1066. Hemming, writing in the 1090s, claims that Swein was threatened with excommunication for this escapade by Eadsige, archbishop of Canterbury, and Lyfing, bishop of Worcester, but the chronology is impossible: Lyfing died on 23 March 1046, before Swein's Welsh campaign, and Eadsige, who died in 1050, was in retirement between 1044 and 1048. Swein may, however, have held the three Shropshire estates belonging to Worcester which he allegedly seized in revenge. These were Mærebroc (Testhill with Marlbrook), Cleobury North, and Hopton Wafers, all held in 1066 by Siward, son of Æthelgar, a grandson of Eadric Streona, ealdorman of Mercia. It may be that the estates were comital manors, once held by Earl Ranig (1016–42), Swein's predecessor in the west; indeed they might even be the unnamed Shropshire lands seized by Edwin (*d.* 1039), brother of Earl Leofric (*d.* 1057), who was probably Ranig's deputy.

Late in 1047 Swein left England to take refuge with Baldwin (V), count of Flanders, in Bruges. By the summer of 1048 he was in Denmark, where his cousin Swein Estrithson was trying to establish himself as king. The D text of the Anglo-Saxon Chronicle says that 'he ruined himself with the Danes' (*ASC*, s.a. 1049, text D), an assertion borne out by the later reputation of all Godwine's sons in Denmark. In 1049 he was back in England attempting to regain his lands and earldom, which in the interval had been divided between his brother Harold (later King *Harold II) and his cousin, *Beorn Estrithson. They were none too pleased to see him, though the D text of the chronicle (followed by John of Worcester) says that Beorn agreed to help him. At this time the exiled Osgod Clapa had gathered ships at Wulpe and King Edward turned out the English fleet, under the command of Beorn and his uncle Godwine, to repel any attempt at invasion. The English fleet was lying at Pevensey, while Swein's ships were at Bosham; both were places in Godwine's control. Swein asked Beorn to go with him to the king at Sandwich; but when they reached Bosham, he had his cousin dragged on shipboard and murdered. This act led to Swein's outlawry; even some of his own men deserted him and he fled back with only two ships to Bruges. In 1050, however, he was pardoned and reinstated through the mediation of his father's friend, Ealdred, bishop of Worcester.

By 1051, the tide was turning against Earl Godwine and his sons. The king's Norman followers (probably led by Osbern Pentecost) built a castle in Herefordshire, in Swein's sphere of authority, and 'inflicted every possible injury and insult on the king's men in those parts' (*ASC*, s.a. 1051, text E). A serious fracas at Dover, in Godwine's earldom, led to an open breach with the king; Godwine, Swein and Harold raised their forces and foregathered at

Beverstone, a berewick of the manor of Berkeley, Gloucestershire, which was under Godwine's control. The king's forces (for the moment) prevailed; Swein was outlawed for a second time and the whole family fled from England. Swein had a ship ready at Bristol, but in the event it was his brothers, Harold and *Leofwine, who used it, to seek help in Ireland. Swein went with the rest of his kindred to Bruges. It seems he had decided 'to look to the salvation of his soul' (Barlow, 120), for he set out from Bruges on the pilgrimage to Jerusalem. John of Worcester says that he walked barefoot all the way and that on the journey home he took cold and died in Lycia; text C of the Anglo-Saxon Chronicle places his death at Constantinople, at Michaelmas (29 September) 1052.

Swein seems very much the black sheep of Godwine's family. Hemming says that he claimed to be the son not of Godwine, but of Cnut himself, an allegation indignantly repudiated by his mother, with an oath supported by many West Saxon noblewomen. Eadmer records a son of Swein, Hakon, said to have been a hostage in Normandy until he was brought back by Harold in 1064, but nothing more is known of him.   ANN WILLIAMS

Sources ASC, s.a. 1046, 1047, 1049, 1050, 1051, 1052 [texts C, D, E] • Hemingi chartularium ecclesiæ Wigorniensis, ed. T. Hearne, 2 vols. (1723) • John of Worcester, Chron. • F. Barlow, ed. and trans., The life of King Edward who rests at Westminster (1962) • F. Barlow, Edward the Confessor (1970) • Adam of Bremen, History of the archbishops of Hamburg-Bremen, ed. and trans. F. J. Tschan (1959) • K. L. Maund, 'The Welsh alliances of Earl Ælfgar of Mercia and his family in the mid-eleventh century', Anglo-Norman Studies, 11 (1988), 181–90 • C. P. Lewis, 'An introduction to the Herefordshire Domesday', The Herefordshire Domesday, ed. A. Williams and R. W. H. Erskine (1988) • S. Keynes, An atlas of attestations in Anglo-Saxon charters, c.670–1066 (privately printed, Cambridge, 1993) • Guillaume de Poitiers [Gulielmus Pictaviensis], Histoire de Guillaume le Conquérant / Gesta Gulielmi ducis Normannorum et regis Anglorum, ed. R. Foreville (Paris, 1952) • Eadmeri Historia novorum in Anglia, ed. M. Rule, Rolls Series, 81 (1884) • A. Farley, ed., Domesday Book, 2 vols. (1783), vol. 1 • S. Keynes, 'Cnut's earls', The reign of Cnut, ed. A. R. Rumble (1994), 43–88 • A. Williams, The English and the Norman conquest (1995)

Swein Asleiffson (d. 1171?), pirate, was the son of Olaf Hrolfsson of Gairsay, chieftain on Orkney and steward of Caithness, and of Asleif, described as 'a wise woman, of good family and strongest character' (Orkneyinga Saga, trans. Taylor, 218). His exploits are known almost exclusively from Orkneyinga Saga. Some, such as the killing of Somerled of Argyll, are certainly fictitious, and the chronology of Swein's life must be treated as conjectural. Nevertheless, his existence is confirmed by the account of his great-grandson contained in Sturlunga saga. Moreover, Orkneyinga Saga was written soon after Swein's death and includes some information which can be corroborated.

Swein's youth was presumably spent on his father's estates, Gairsay in Orkney and Duncansby in Caithness. In late December 1135 his father, Olaf, was killed by an enemy of Earl Paul of Orkney and Caithness, and Swein's (perhaps elder) brother, Valthjof, was drowned while sailing from his estate on Stronsay. That Swein became known as Asleif's son may have been in reference to his mother's strong character, or to the fact that he was left fatherless at a young age. Soon after, Swein was outlawed

by Earl Paul for killing a member of the latter's bodyguard. He fled to the Hebrides, then joined Paul's halfsister Margaret and her Scottish husband, Maddad, earl of Atholl. In the spring of 1136 Swein returned to Orkney, kidnapped Paul, and took him to Atholl. The earldom immediately fell to a Norwegian claimant, Rognvald Kali Kolsson.

Paul was subsequently maimed or killed so that Harald, the young son of Margaret and Maddad, might become joint earl of Orkney with Rognvald. This plan may have been conceived with David I to enhance Scottish influence in the Scandinavian north. Orkneyinga Saga records that a Scottish bishop, John (possibly David's tutor, the bishop of Glasgow), travelled to Orkney in 1138 to formalize Harald's recognition. Hopes of influencing events in Caithness and Orkney would explain the assistance which King David and his successor, Malcolm IV, allegedly gave Swein on three later occasions.

By c.1139 Swein took over the lands of his father and brother; he became one of Rognvald's chieftains and (perhaps slightly later) was made his steward in Caithness. His sister, Ingigerd, married Thorbjorn, the young Earl Harald's councillor, and it may be at this time that Swein was briefly married to Ragnhild Ogmund's-Daughter, who bore Olaf, his first son. Swein wreaked vengeance on the faction responsible for his father's death, burning their house at Helmsdale in Sutherland. He then gave assistance to the Hebridean who had sheltered him while outlawed. This expedition, which raided Wales and Lundy island, led to his second marriage, to Ingirid Thorkel's-Daughter, a wealthy widow from the Isle of Man related to Earl Harald. They had a son, Andres (who married a sister of Bishop Bjarni of Orkney), and several unnamed daughters.

The couple were betrayed by Swein's Hebridean host and erstwhile ally, and returned to Orkney. After a retaliatory raid to the Hebrides, Swein angered several Orcadian chiefs, including his brother-in-law Thorbjorn, by claiming a disproportionate share of plunder. Earl Rognvald attempted to settle the dispute, until Margad (Swein's deputy in Caithness) killed one of the earl's supporters. Orkneyinga Saga claims that Swein refused to turn Margad, a companion since his youth, over to Rognvald and the slighted chiefs. After a siege near Freswick in Caithness, Swein and Margad escaped to David I, who arranged a settlement.

Swein's influence diminished after 1151, when Rognvald travelled to Jerusalem leaving Earl Harald and Thorbjorn in control. Feud arose when Swein's brother Gunnar was outlawed by Harald for having an affair with the latter's mother. Swein intercepted Harald's revenues, and subsequently retreated to the Scottish king to have his rights in Caithness recognized by a higher authority. He then joined Erlend, a new claimant to the earldoms, and took command of his campaign. However, after initial success, Erlend was killed during an attack by Harald and Rognvald (who returned in 1153) in December 1154.

Rognvald invited Swein to join him and arranged a

settlement. The chieftain gave up half his lands, his warship, and 2 gold marks, but warned that 'this settlement will hold best if I am not treated disrespectfully' (*Orkneyinga Saga*, trans. Taylor, 322). When Harald had Swein's house on Gairsay occupied, Swein was prepared to burn it, thinking that the earl was inside, but was persuaded that his own wife and daughters, who were within, would not be let out, and rather than burn them he disarmed Harald's men. The earl was not in fact there, and Swein's wife, Ingirid, would not betray the whereabouts of her kinsman Harald. Swein ran off Harald's ale and left with Ingirid and their daughters. A lasting settlement was arranged in 1155. Immediately afterwards, Rognvald returned his share of Swein's confiscated property, and Harald soon did the same. Swein later fostered Harald's son Haakon on Gairsay, and built a large drinking hall there.

Swein maintained a large retinue on the proceeds of piracy. According to *Orkneyinga Saga* he died when raiding in Ireland, one autumn between 1165 and 1180, through falling into a pit trap after securing Dublin's nominal surrender. His pious death-speech, out of character for this aggressively worldly figure, has been interpreted as a late addition to the saga. An unsuccessful Orcadian attack on Dublin is dated to 1171 by Gerald of Wales, the annals of Ulster, and other sources. In these accounts, however, the perpetrator is called John the Mad, and is described as assisting the ousted king of Dublin. Moreover, Gerald places these events around Whitsun (16 May) and states that John was killed in battle. The date of Swein's death thus remains, like most of the details of his life, conjectural. His exciting life is the subject of Eric Linklater's novel *The Ultimate Viking* (1955).   JAMES BARRETT

Sources A. B. Taylor, ed. and trans., *The Orkneyinga saga* (1938) · *Orkneyinga saga*, ed. F. Guðmundsson, Íslenzk Fornit, 34 (1965) · J. Anderson, ed., *The Orkneyinga saga*, trans. J. A. Hjaltalin and G. Goudie (1873) · *The Orkneyingers' saga*, trans. G. W. Dasent (1894) · H. Pálsson and P. Edwards, eds. and trans., *The Orkneyinga saga: the history of the earls of Orkney* (1978); repr. (1981) · R. Power, 'Scotland in the Norse sagas', *Scotland and Scandinavia, 800–1800*, ed. G. Simpson (1990), 13–24 · *Sturlunga saga*, ed. J. M. Johannesson, M. Finnbogason, and K. Eldjarn, 2 vols. (1946) · F. Guðmundsson, 'On the writing of *Orkeyinga saga*', *Caithness, Orkney and the North Atlantic in the viking age*, ed. C. E. Batey, J. Jesch, and C. D. Morris (1993), 204–11 · P. Foote, 'Observations on *Orkneyinga saga*', *St Magnus Cathedral and Orkney's twelfth century Renaissance*, ed. B. Crawford (1988), 183–91 · G. Storm, ed., *Islandske Annaler indtil 1578* (Oslo, 1888) · J. S. Clouston, *A history of Orkney* (1932) · M. Chesnutt, 'Local legendry in the saga of the Orkney islanders', *Copenhagen Folklore Notes*, 1–2/97 (1997), 6–12 · E. B. Fryde and others, eds., *Handbook of British chronology*, 3rd edn, Royal Historical Society Guides and Handbooks, 2 (1986) · B. E. Crawford, 'The earls of Orkney–Caithness and their relations with Norway and Scotland, 1158–1470', PhD diss., U. St Andr., 1971 · B. E. Crawford, 'The earldom of Caithness and the kingdom of Scotland, 1150–1266', *Essays on the nobility of medieval Scotland*, ed. K. J. Stringer (1984), 25–43 · P. Topping, 'Harald Maddadson, earl of Orkney and Caithness, 1139–1206', *SHR*, 62 (1983), 105–20 · W. P. L. Thomson, *History of Orkney* (1987) · C. D. Morris, C. E. Batey, and D. J. Rackham, *Freswick Links, Caithness: excavation and survey of a Norse settlement* (1995) · A. O. Anderson, ed. and trans., *Early sources of Scottish history, AD 500 to 1286*, 2 vols. (1922) · Giraldus Cambrensis, *Expugnatio Hibernica / The conquest of Ireland*, ed. and trans. A. B. Scott and F. X. Martin (1978) · W. M. Hennessy and B. MacCarthy, eds., *Annals of Ulster, otherwise, annals of Senat*, 4 vols. (1887–1901) · M. Ciklamini, 'Saint Rognvaldr and Sveinn Asleifarson, the viking', *Scandinavian Studies*, 42 (1970), 50–57 · E. J. Cowan, 'Caithness in the sagas', *Caithness: a cultural crossroads*, ed. J. R. Baldwin (1982), 25–44 · J. Jesch, 'Narrating Orkneyinga saga', *Scandinavian Studies*, 64 (1992), 336–55

Swerford, Alexander of (*b.* before 1180, *d.* 1246), administrator, was born probably not long before 1180, and took his name from the village of Swerford, in Oxfordshire near Chipping Norton, of which he became vicar and then rector in 1228 on the presentation of Osney Abbey, holding the church there until his death. It is possible that he was educated at Osney, but that honour could equally well belong to St Peter's Abbey, Gloucester, since in a deed he once styled himself as its 'devoted clerk', and he also had a nephew called Master Simon of Gloucester. An Emma of Swerford, who may possibly have been a relative, was a benefactor of Tewkesbury Abbey in Gloucestershire. Nothing is known of his father, except that he may have been called Henry. Swerford began as a clerk, and is likely to have been the treasury clerk called Alexander who was employed in conveying royal treasure to Normandy in the first few years of the reign of King John; the first mention of him is by a clerk of the usher, John of Wike. By November 1218 he had been appointed archdeacon of Shropshire, in the diocese of Hereford. Swerford's most senior ecclesiastical appointment was as treasurer of St Paul's Cathedral, a position he held from 15 January 1232 until his death; at the time of his appointment he was already a canon, having held the prebend of 'Consumpta per Mare' in Walton on the Naze since 1218. Some of his activities in that office are recorded in the St Paul's register known as the Liber Pilosus, and he witnessed many charters as treasurer. Despite his clerical orders, he was the father of at least one child, a daughter Agatha.

Swerford's main work, however, was not as a churchman but as a royal servant, principally at the exchequer. He is credited with the original compilation of the Red Book of the Exchequer, an important register or precedent book containing a collection of official documents, memoranda, charters, and writs, and information about knights' fees, to which other material continued to be added until the seventeenth century. The surviving version is not apparently the one he originally wrote, but a copy begun about 1230; it is not in his own hand. It is also thought that earlier, about 1206, he compiled the Black Book of the Exchequer with similar purposes in mind, and made some alterations and additions to it between then and about 1212. These volumes were important in preserving information about the early exchequer for posterity. Swerford himself recorded in the red book that he served at the exchequer in John's reign, during the treasurership of William of Ely, which lasted from 1196 to 1215. Among his other activities he seems to have continued to serve as a clerk, since in 1227 he was given an annual allowance of 20 marks at the exchequer to sustain him in the king's service, and he described himself in 1230 as still resident at the exchequer. On 6 July 1234 he was appointed a baron of the exchequer, the most senior of three new barons appointed that year, to judge by the fact that his salary of 40 marks was larger than that awarded to the other two, who received only 30 marks each. Swerford is thought to have been the first exchequer clerk to have been made a baron. The memoranda rolls give frequent references to his activities in the department, from the time of his appointment onwards until his death, and he has been credited with effectively reorganizing it during 1234 and 1235.

Swerford also served on diplomatic missions and on various royal commissions. In 1216 he acted as chaplain to the bishop of Coventry, with whom he went abroad; his connection with the diocese involved the tenure of a prebend at Lichfield, which he resigned in favour of his nephew in 1235. In 1221, he was sent on a diplomatic mission to Llywelyn, prince of north Wales (d. 1240), and in 1231–2 was active in settling border disputes in the marches at the king's command. In 1227 he was present at a council held in St John's Chapel, Westminster, to settle a dispute between the bishop of Hereford and the citizens of Hereford. Later in the same year he was dispatched to the papal curia, along with Master Walter de Cantilupe (d. 1266), as the king's proctor. In 1238 he acted as a principal papal judge-delegate in a dispute between the nuns of Lillechurch in Kent and their mother house. Other official activities included holding an inquiry into prises of wine in London in 1234, and into the liberties of the London mint in 1245. He was even, in April 1232, made sheriff of Berkshire, but held office for only a few weeks and never accounted at the exchequer.

It was probably Swerford's connection with St Paul's which led him, despite his western origins, to acquire property at Fobbing in Essex, Brent and Pelham Furneaux and Tewin (both annexed to the treasurer's office) in Hertfordshire, and Tolworth in Surrey; he is also known to have held land in Oxfordshire and Bedfordshire. Between 1206 and 1214 the abbot of Westminster granted him the abbey's houses in London between Ludgate and Fleet Bridge at an annual rent, describing him as 'our clerk'; it is unlikely that he was the Alexander, clerk of the exchequer, who held property in Westminster during John's reign. As treasurer of St Paul's he was, in 1235, granted for life the use of a turret in the wall of the city of London, by Ludgate. Another important mark of royal favour was the grant to him in 1243 of the reversion of any living in the king's gift worth 100 marks.

Swerford is last recorded as a baron of the exchequer on 14 July 1246, and according to the annals of Dunstable died between Michaelmas and Christmas. He probably died in October, and certainly before 1 November, when the bishop of Lincoln knew of his death. He was buried before the altar of St Ceadda (Chad), which he had built, at St Paul's, where he had endowed a chantry with one priest to celebrate mass daily for his soul. On his death he received a glowing obituary from Matthew Paris, whom he had evidently provided with some of the historical documents which were recorded in his chronicle: 'in elegance of form, in beauty of features, and a mind endowed with many forms of learning, he has not left his like in England' (Paris, 4.587–8).   DAVID CROOK

Sources H. Hall, ed., *The Red Book of the Exchequer*, 1, Rolls Series, 99 (1896) · N. Vincent, 'New light on Master Alexander of Swerford (d.1246): the career and connections of an Oxfordshire civil servant', *Oxoniensia*, 61 (1996), 297–309 · Paris, *Chron.*, 4.587–8 · *Chancery records* · *Pipe rolls* · H. E. Salter, ed., *Cartulary of Oseney Abbey*, 3, OHS, 91 (1931), 60–61 · *Ann. mon.*, 3.171 · W. H. Hart, ed., *Historia et cartularium monasterii Sancti Petri Gloucestriae*, 1, Rolls Series, 33 (1863), 257 · exchequer, king's remembrancer's memoranda rolls, PRO, E 159 · A. Hughes, *List of sheriffs for England and Wales: from the earliest times to AD 1831*, PRO (1898), 6 · BL, Cotton MS Vitellius E.xv, fol. 199 · M. Gibbs, ed., *Early charters of the cathedral church of St Paul, London*, CS, 3rd ser., 58 (1939), nos. 81, 85, 100, 153, 182, 197, 207, 270, 271, 277–8, 281, 294, 328, 331, 338 · E. Mason, J. Bray, and D. J. Murphy, eds., *Westminster Abbey charters, 1066–c.1214*, London RS, 25 (1988), nos. 335, 346, 413, 414, 423–4, 426, 439, 480 · R. C. Stacy, *Politics, policy, and finance under Henry III, 1216–1245* (1987), 41–2 · St Paul's register, Liber Pilosus

Swete, Henry Barclay (1835–1917), biblical scholar, was born on 14 March 1835 at Redlands, Bristol, the only child of the Revd John Swete (d. 1869), lecturer of St Mary Redcliffe, Bristol, and later rector of Blagdon, near Bristol, and his second wife, Caroline Ann Skinner Barclay (d. 1835). He was educated at Bishop's College, Bristol, King's College, London, and then as a scholar at Gonville and Caius College, Cambridge, where he was awarded the Carus Greek Testament prize, the first of the members' prizes, and a first class in the classical tripos; he graduated as seventh classic in 1858. He was then elected to a fellowship at Caius.

After his ordination in 1858 Swete spent some years in pastoral work as curate to his father at Blagdon. He returned to Cambridge in 1865 where he held the office of dean at Gonville and Caius College. During this period he was the first to recognize the authorship of his colleague J. R. Seeley in the anonymous work *Ecce homo* (1865). In 1868 he was beset by consumptive illness. He travelled to Palestine and Egypt. Once recovered he served as curate at Tormohun, Somerset, from 1869 until 1872. He then resumed academic office, acting as tutor until his resignation in 1875 and then as divinity lecturer until 1877.

These years were not successful at a professional level. Swete was 'too retiring and too sensitive to make him an effective college officer' (Chase, 110). During this period, however, he published his first serious theological work: two essays, in 1873 and 1876, on the history of the doctrine of the Holy Spirit. His views were later represented in his noted article, 'Holy Ghost', for the *Dictionary of Christian Biography* (vol. 3, 1882).

In 1877 Swete was offered the college living of Ashdon, Cambridgeshire, and this appointment, while appealing to his strong pastoral instinct, also afforded him leisure for study. He produced some significant textual critical work: the Latin version of the commentaries of Theodore of Mopsuestia on the minor epistles of St Paul (2 vols., 1880 and 1882) and an invaluable edition of the Septuagint version of the Old Testament, *The Old Testament in Greek According to the Septuagint* (3 vols., 1887, 1891, and 1894). This was later complemented by *An Introduction to the Testament in*

Greek (1900). In 1881 Swete was awarded the degree of doctor of divinity, and from 1882 to 1890 he held, with his living, the professorship of pastoral theology at King's College, London.

In 1890 Swete was elected regius professor of divinity at Cambridge. To succeed Brooke Foss Westcott presented a formidable challenge, and there was opposition to Swete's appointment from younger members of the faculty, who felt he did not have the charisma to represent the school during a time of biblical-critical and doctrinal controversy. His twenty-five years' tenure of the professorship, however, abundantly justified his selection. His commentaries on the Greek text of *The Gospel According to St Mark* (1898) and of *The Apocalypse of St John* (1906) furthered the tradition of textual criticism and exegesis pioneered by the 'Cambridge Three' or 'triumvirate' (Westcott, F. J. A. Hort, and J. B. Lightfoot). Aside from his literary work he developed unforeseen initiative and activity in stimulating and guiding theological study at Cambridge. He devised the divinity *testimonium* scheme, through which ordinands were encouraged to engage in serious biblical and theological study. He motivated students, setting them to work on individual fields of research. With his constant attention to the needs of ordinands, his lectures became the best-attended courses in the divinity faculty. Alongside his own writing, he was general editor of three volumes of essays dealing with contemporary theological and biblical questions and with early church history (*Cambridge Theological Essays*, 1905, 1909, and 1918). Swete also developed the series Cambridge Patristic Texts (from 1899), and the Cambridge Handbooks of Liturgical Study (from 1910). Through his initiative, a committee of scholars from Cambridge, Oxford, and Durham founded the *Journal of Theological Studies* in 1899. Swete was also the founder of the Cambridge Theological Society and of the Central Society of Sacred Study, in 1899.

Swete's literary output showed a wide range of theological interests: exegetical (in *The Appearances of Our Lord after the Passion*, 1907); doctrinal and patristic (in *The Apostles' Creed: its Relation to Primitive Christianity*, 1894); liturgical and textual (in *Two New Gospel Fragments*, 1908); and devotional (in *The Forgiveness of Sins*, 1917). All his work revealed precise and careful scholarship, and a singular delicacy and grace of style. His attitude towards historical critical interpretations of the Bible tended towards the conservative and his exposition of biblical texts was relatively traditional. He tended to avoid controversy. On fundamental questions of belief, such as the resurrection and the Virgin birth, he described himself as loyal to the 'vital truths' of the faith. (*Henry Barclay Swete*, 99).

Swete resigned his professorship in 1915 and retired to Hertfordshire, where he died suddenly at his home, 23 Old Park Road, Hitchin, on 10 May 1917. He was buried four days later at Hitchin cemetery. Swete was unmarried, a decision based on his belief that consumptive illness was hereditary. In recognition of his contribution to scholarship, Swete had been elected fellow of the newly founded British Academy in 1902. In 1911 he was made honorary DLitt of Oxford and also honorary chaplain to the king.

Although Swete could be 'provokingly diffident and retiring' (Chase, 111), this was none the less tempered by a gracious and winning personality. He was remembered as 'one who set the things of the Spirit above all else' (*Henry Barclay Swete*, 162).   JOANNA HAWKE

Sources M. B. K., H. G., and J. F. B.-B., *Henry Barclay Swete: a remembrance* (1918) • *WWW* • F. H. Chase, *Church Quarterly Review*, 85 (1917), 109–20 • Crockford (1860) • Crockford (1872) • Crockford (1878) • P. Schaff and S. M. Jackson, *Encyclopedia of living divines and Christian workers of all denominations in Europe and America: being a supplement to Schaff-Herzog encyclopedia of religious knowledge* (1887) • A. J. Mason, 'Henry Barclay Swete', *Journal of Theological Studies*, 18 (1916–17), 257–62 • J. H. Strawley, *The Caian*, 26 (1916–17), 101–12 • C. H. Turner, 'Bibliography of the published works of the late Henry Barclay Swete', *Journal of Theological Studies*, 19 (1917–18)
Likenesses H. Rivière, oils, 1906, Gon. & Caius Cam.
Wealth at death £1863 14s. 3d.: probate, 28 June 1917, *CGPLA Eng. & Wales*

Swete [*formerly* Tripe], **John** (1752–1821), antiquary and topographer, was born John Tripe on 1 July 1752 in Ashburton, Devon, the son of Nicholas Tripe, a surgeon, and his wife, Rebecca Yard (*d*. 1792). He was educated at Ashburton Free School and then, through the assistance of Sir Robert Palk, at Eton College (1767–70). In October 1770 he went to University College, Oxford, where he graduated BA in 1774 and proceeded MA in 1777. In 1775 he became curate at Highweek, Newton Abbot, and the following year, at Sir Robert Palk's request, he was appointed curate at Kenn, Exeter. He became a prebendary of Exeter Cathedral in 1781.

In 1780 by act of parliament Tripe changed his surname to Swete in order to inherit a considerable fortune from a relative of his father, Mrs Esther Swete, of Traine, Modbury, Devon. Following his appointment to Kenn, Swete had moved to Oxton House, near Exeter, which had been the home of his paternal grandmother's family, the Martyns. Swete's newly inherited wealth enabled him completely to rebuild the old Martyn family mansion. Over the next forty years he also redesigned and landscaped the extensive grounds and added a gatehouse and thatched Gothic hermitage (described in the *Gentleman's Magazine*, 1793).

Swete resigned his curacy at Kenn in April 1783 and set out on a tour of Wales, the Lake District, and Scotland, intending this to be a preparation for a continental tour. His plans came to nothing as he met Charlotte Beaumont (*d*. 1831) in Matlock, Derbyshire. They were married on 1 January 1784, and had twelve children, four of whom died in infancy. Between 1789 and 1800 he undertook a number of lengthy excursions around Devon, later recording his travels in a series of illustrated journals. These originally consisted of twenty volumes which contained over 670 watercolour illustrations. Three of the volumes were lost during the Second World War but the remaining seventeen, which cover most of the county, are an important source of topographical description for Devon. His comments are those of a man who defined the landscape in terms of its picturesque and Romantic qualities, noting particularly the seats of the gentry and their gardens. His observations on local industries and agricultural methods are especially valuable as these were made just before the changes brought about by the industrial revolution.

Swete composed at least six volumes of poems, and contributed seven poetical pieces to Richard Polwhele's *Poems Chiefly by Gentlemen of Devonshire and Cornwall* (1792). They were both members of the Exeter Literary Society and Swete provided Polwhele with material for the county history he was then engaged on. In 1796 three antiquarian articles by Swete appeared in *Essays by a Society of Gentlemen at Exeter*. The appearance of these furthered an already acrimonious and public feud between Polwhele and himself: Polwhele suggested in the *Gentleman's Magazine* and the *European Magazine* that Swete had misappropriated his research. Swete wrote several letters to the editor of the *Gentleman's Magazine* reproaching him for printing the comments and arguing that Polwhele's claim of plagiarism was baseless given that Polwhele's information was derived from Swete's own work. It was not until 1798 that relations between the two antiquaries were partially restored but in 1807 Swete severed their tie altogether. Nevertheless after Swete's death Polwhele composed an epistle to him. Swete also contributed to John Prince's *Worthies of Devon* (1810), to Tristram Risdon's *Survey of Devon* (1811), and to Richard Gough's edition of Camden's *Britannia* (1789). He also wrote the obituary of the Revd Christopher Beeke for the *Gentleman's Magazine* (1798).

In 1780 Swete excavated a number of barrows on the Haldon Ridge, west of the Exe estuary. The Haldon urn, which was discovered in a barrow known as the Great Stoneheap, is illustrated in volume 1 of his *Journals* (1997). There are glimpses of Swete in several of his own watercolours, and the Royal Albert Memorial Museum, Exeter, has what may be a self-portrait, possibly painted as a grotesque.

Swete died at Oxton House on 25 October 1821 after a long illness and was buried in Kenton churchyard. His eldest son, John Beaumont Swete, inherited his estate. His widow died at Camberwell, Surrey, on 10 December 1831 and was also buried at Kenton.   J. A. MARCHAND

Sources *Travels in Georgian Devon: the illustrated journals of the Reverend John Swete, 1789–1800*, ed. T. Gray and M. Rowe, 4 vols. (1997–2000) · J. Swete, 'A sketch of my own life', Devon RO, MS Z19/3/1 · T. Gray, *The garden history of Devon* (1995) · T. N. Brushfield, 'MS description of Devon: Rev. John Swete', *Western Antiquary*, 6 (1887), 269–70, 303 · D. Woolner, 'Picturesque sketches of Devon by the Rev. John Swete', *Report and Transactions of the Devonshire Association*, 93 (1961), 54–5 · *DNB* · *Trewman's Exeter Flying Post* (1 Nov 1821) · letter to the Revd Beeke, Devon RO, MS Z19/40 · will, proved, 20 Dec 1821

Archives Devon RO, autobiography · Devon RO, epitaph · Devon RO, essays · Devon RO, poetry · Devon RO, sketchbooks · Devon RO, topographical sketches of Devon · Devon RO, travel journals · Devon RO, watercolours of Oxton House and grounds · Royal Institution of Cornwall, Truro, 1780 tour in Cornwall

Likenesses J. Swete, self-portrait?, Royal Albert Memorial Museum, Exeter

Wealth at death bequeathed main estate to eldest son; bequeathed estates at Poltimone and Offwell and MS sermons to second son; bequeathed 100 guineas and £300 p.a. to wife; library divided between wife and children: will

Sweteman [Sweetman], **Milo** (*d.* 1380), archbishop of Armagh, was a member of the Sweteman family, which was prominent in the Kilkenny–Waterford area from the early fourteenth century and provided barons of Erley until the early seventeenth century. Milo Sweteman is first mentioned in 1341, when he was appointed by Richard Ledred, bishop of Ossory, as his attorney in Ireland. On Ledred's death in 1360, Sweteman, who was then treasurer of the diocese of Ossory, was elected to succeed him and travelled to Rome for confirmation of his appointment. Pope Innocent VI, however, had in the meantime quashed the election and appointed the English Dominican John Tatenhall. Sweteman was instead provided by the pope to the archbishopric of Armagh, vacant since the death of Richard Fitzralph in November 1360, was consecrated in November 1361, received the temporalities of the archdiocese in February 1362, and was in Armagh by August of the same year.

Sweteman's career as archbishop can be followed in some detail because of the survival of his register. This is the earliest in a series of surviving registers which ends with that of George Cromer, archbishop of Armagh from 1521 to 1543. Sweteman's register as it now stands is a small part of what was once a far larger record. Almost half of the entries contained within it concern the three years 1365–7 while documents for the years 1371–80 account for only a little over ten per cent of the total. Despite its incomplete nature, however, it offers an invaluable insight into the problems faced by the church in Ireland in the late fourteenth century. Much of Sweteman's energy was expended in his struggle with the archbishop of Dublin, Thomas Minot, about ecclesiastical primacy. Within his own province he had to discipline two of his suffragan bishops, Simon of Derry and Riocard Ó Raghallaigh of Kilmore, because of their failure to obey the injunction to clerical celibacy. He also faced opposition from his cathedral chapter at Armagh. In 1363 it elected the bishop of Raphoe, Pádraig Mac Maonghail, as archbishop on the grounds that Armagh was destitute of a pastor, but this was not put into effect.

The area covered by the diocese of Armagh was divided between the English and the Irish. Sweteman's relations with some of the powerful Irish rulers of the area were difficult and the Ó Néill and Ó hAnluain leaders regularly pillaged the archbishop's lands and tenants. In 1374 a Mág Aonghusa chief made a devastating raid into Louth during which the sheriff of the county was killed. Sweteman spent most of his time at his manors of Termonfeckin and Dromiskin, Louth, among the English but he visited his cathedral city of Armagh, which was in territory controlled by the Irish, on several occasions, and spent time in his capacity as metropolitan in the dioceses of Down and Kilmore. He worked hard to reconcile the English and the Irish and his immediate successors as archbishop repeated a command he had made to his suffragan bishops under pain of excommunication, 'to bring about, maintain and conserve the peace between the English and Irish … and preach peace between them and compel their subjects by all ecclesiastical censures to keep the peace' (Reeves, xvii). Sweteman advanced the career of his nephew, Maurice, whom he appointed in 1378 as his proctor in cases to be heard before the pope. Maurice was archdeacon of Armagh in 1381 and received custody of lands from the king in Meath and Kildare. Milo Sweteman died in his manor of Dromiskin on 11 August 1380, an event recorded by the Dublin annalist. B. SMITH

Sources H. J. Lawlor, ed., 'A calendar of the register of Archbishop Sweteman', *Proceedings of the Royal Irish Academy*, 29C (1911–12) · J. T. Gilbert, ed., *Chartularies of St Mary's Abbey, Dublin: with the register of its house at Dunbrody and annals of Ireland*, 2, Rolls Series, 80 (1884) · D. A. Chart, ed., *The register of John Swayne, archbishop of Armagh and primate of Ireland, 1418–1439* (1935) · E. St J. Brooks, *Knights' fees in counties Wexford, Carlow and Kilkenny, 13th–15th century*, IMC (1950) · W. Reeves, ed., *Acts of Archbishop Colton in his metropolitan visitation of the diocese of Derry, AD 1397*, Irish Archaeological Society (1850)
Archives PRO NIre., MS D104/2/1

Swetnam, Joseph (d. 1621), pamphleteer, had his roots in the west country. By his own admission he had no formal education. Nothing is known of his parents, or his wife, but he had a daughter called Elizabeth, who married one Rice Merricke in the church of St Augustine-the-Less in Bristol on 4 November 1613. It was Elizabeth's first marriage: she is described in the parish register as 'mayden'. She died in 1626, and the letter of administration drawn up after her death provides some information about her father's origins: he is here referred to as 'nuper de civit[ate] Bristoll' ('late of the city of Bristol').

That Swetnam was a west-country man is corroborated by his *The Schoole of the Noble and Worthy Science of Defence* (1617), one of the first English fencing manuals to appear in print. All contemporary references in this handbook relate to Devon and Cornwall. He also supplies a 'Farewell to Plimouth', recalling the times of war with Spain, when the city had prospered. He hints at having kept a fencing-school, although he does not specify the exact place; he also claims, in the dedication to Prince Charles, that he had once been a 'tutor in the skill of weapons' to Prince Henry, although there is no record of his employment in Henry's service. He claims Henry had read *The Schoole of Defence*, urging him to have it printed. The work also makes reference to a professional career which included periods abroad fighting in foreign wars as a soldier.

Swetnam's fame, or notoriety, rests on his having written *The Araignment of Lewd, Idle, Froward and Unconstant Women*, a poorly written, derivative, and incoherent misogynist pamphlet, first published under the pseudonym Thomas Tell-Troth in 1615. The pamphlet was reprinted in its first year of publication, this time under the author's real name. *The Araignment* was quite popular, with thirteen known reprints in the seventeenth century, another five editions in the early eighteenth century, and a reprint, by Joseph Smeeton, in 1807, presenting the work as being of antiquarian interest. Swetnam's work was translated into Dutch as *Recht-Banck tegen de Luye, Korzelighe, en Wispeltuyrighe Vrouwen* by the Leiden printer Willem

Christiaens van der Boxe, who brought out the work in 1641. This Dutch edition was reprinted four times in the seventeenth century, with two further editions in the early eighteenth.

The three chapters which make up *The Araignment* focus on the degeneracy of women, examples of female depravity, and remedies against love, but also offer marriage counsel and, surprisingly, a 'commendation of good women'. An appendix entitled 'The Bearebayting of Widdowes' ends the pamphlet. In all, it is a rambling diatribe against women, largely drawn from such diverse sources as courtesy books, 'wit books', and jest books. One demonstrable source is John Lyly's *Euphues*. Swetnam's prose style, when he does not borrow, is mainly characterized by proverbialism, a sign of his lack of education.

Within two years of its first publication Swetnam's attack on women was the subject of three scathing responses: Rachel Speght's *A Mouzell for Melastomus* (1617), Esther Sowernam's *Esther hath Hang'd Haman* (1617), and Constantia Munda's *A Soppe for Cerberus* (1617). Speght, not yet twenty years old when she wrote her response, is the only one to have published under her own name. A clergyman's daughter, she refers in her poem *Mortalities Memorandum* (1621) to having received adverse criticism following the publication of *A Mouzell*. Speght's response is obviously based on genuine indignation and in this respect is the most interesting of the three; the other two pseudonymous respondents throw themselves into the fray with amused scorn. The three responses make much of Swetnam's obvious ignorance, plagiarism, stylistic ineptitude and inconsistency: all three respond from a superior educational position.

While all three respondents comment with real or feigned concern on the enormous popularity of *The Araignment of Women* with the 'vulgar ignorant', the existence of the play *Swetnam the Woman-Hater, Arraigned by Women* (1620), in which Swetnam is presented merely as a comic figure, would seem to qualify the impact of Swetnam's diatribe among the common people. It was performed at the Red Bull Theatre in London, a theatre largely patronized by 'the man in the street'. As the play's title indicates, Swetnam's epithet, the Woman-Hater—an odium which he has not been able to shed—was already firmly established by 1620.

Swetnam died abroad in 1621, as confirmed by the letter of administration drawn up after his death. He left £21 to his daughter Elizabeth but he also left debts: one Francis Doughty of Hempsted in Gloucestershire, the administrator of Elizabeth's estate, is mentioned in the letter of administration drawn up after the latter's death in 1626 as one of his creditors. Although it is not known where Swetnam died, it might be inferred from his earlier references to active service that it was in one of the many 'foreign wars' which were being fought on the continent.

CIS VAN HEERTUM

Sources *A critical edition of Joseph Swetnam's 'The araignment of lewd, idle, froward and unconstant women'* (1615), ed. C. van Heertum (1989) · *Swetnam the woman-hater: the controversy and the play*, ed.

C. Crandall (1969) · *Swetnam the woman-hater*, ed. J. S. Farmer (1914) · *Swetnam the woman-hater arraigned by women*, ed. A. B. Grosart (1880) · PRO, PROB 6/10, fol. 140; PROB 6/12, fol. 96 · J. H. Morrison, *Prerogative court of Canterbury: letters of administration, 1620–1630* (1935)

Wealth at death £21: administration, PRO, PROB 6/10, fol. 140; PROB 6/12, fol. 96; Morrison, *Prerogative court*, 103

Swettenham, Sir Frank Athelstane (1850–1946), colonial administrator, was born on 28 March 1850 at 1 Gibfield Lane, Belper, Derbyshire, the youngest of five surviving children of James Oldham Swettenham, eccentric country solicitor, and his wife, Charlotte Elizabeth, daughter of Charles Carr, banker of London. Educated initially at home, he accompanied his mother when she left her husband in 1859 for Dollar, near Stirling, attending Dollar Academy until 1866. After his mother's death in 1861 he was brought up by an elder sister. From 1866 he boarded for two years at St Peter's School, York. His brother, Alexander (1846–1933), in the Ceylon civil service, and later governor of Jamaica, suggested that he apply for a cadetship in the Straits civil service. He passed second in the examination, reaching Singapore in January 1871.

Attached to the secretariat, Swettenham rapidly became fluent in colloquial Malay, a skill which stood him in good stead throughout his career. In 1872 he was posted to Penang and Province Wellesley to work in the land offices. The colonial government was under pressure from business interests to vary its policy of non-involvement in the affairs of the Malay states. The new governor, Sir Andrew Clarke, arrived with instructions to investigate this possibility. With Swettenham's assistance, he summoned representatives of the warring groups of Chinese tin-miners in Perak to meet him at Pangkor Island off the Perak coast, together with Raja Abdullah and his supporters, one of the several chiefs who aspired to the Perak throne. The miners agreed to submit their quarrels to decision by a three-man commission, which included Swettenham. Simultaneously, Clarke endorsed Raja Abdullah's claim to the title of sultan on the understanding that Abdullah would accept in his court a British resident, whose advice was to be followed on all matters except those of Malay custom and religion. These terms were incorporated in the Pangkor engagement of January 1874, drafted in both Malay and English, with Swettenham's help as interpreter. The precise translation from English into Malay of this key clause proved controversial. As one of the commissioners, over the next month Swettenham settled the miners' boundary disputes, dismantled stockades, and freed captive Chinese women, recording events in his semi-official diaries.

Swettenham's knowledge of the Malay language, tolerant cynicism, and tact resulted in a posting to Langat to give informal advice to the sultan of Selangor, who described him as 'very able; … very clever in the customs of Malay government and at gaining the hearts of Rajas with soft words, delicate and sweet, so that all men rejoice in him as in the perfume of an open flower' (PRO,

Sir Frank Athelstane Swettenham (1850–1946), by John Singer Sargent, 1904

CO273/76, fol. 300). Selangor consequently accepted a resident, Swettenham remaining as assistant resident.

In 1875 Swettenham made frequent visits to Perak to assist the first British resident there, James Wheeler Woodford Birch, whose dealings were marked by tactlessness and impetuosity. Birch was murdered by Malays on 4 November 1875 on the Perak River. Swettenham, who was upriver, managed during a hazardous overnight boat journey to evade the Malays waiting downstream to murder him. Birch's murder provoked the pacification of Perak by the British between November 1875 and April 1876. Swettenham distinguished himself in this campaign, as deputy commissioner for the forces advancing upriver, and was mentioned in dispatches. He played a major role in capturing the chiefs involved, and conducted the prosecution's case against them.

On his first leave Swettenham married, on 21 February 1878, Constance Sydney (1858/9–1947), 19-year-old daughter of Cecil Frederick Holmes, housemaster at Harrow School. Her inherited tendency towards manic depression was exacerbated by Swettenham's treatment of her; the marriage blighted his personal life for sixty years.

Meantime in March 1876 he was appointed assistant

colonial secretary in Singapore, with special responsibility for the affairs of the Native Malay States. His job involved frequent visits, chiefly to Selangor and Perak, to report on the state accounts and the residential system of government inaugurated by the Pangkor engagement. In Perak the experienced Hugh Low rapidly established peace and prosperity, including the abolition of slavery. Swettenham learnt much from this association. By contrast, in Selangor Swettenham became increasingly critical of the irascible, incompetent Bloomfield Douglas, whom he succeeded in October 1882.

As resident, Selangor, Swettenham energetically tackled major problems. Kuala Lumpur, a fire-prone slum, he replanned almost single-handedly, on modern lines, introducing sensible building regulations. He greatly strengthened local government by appointing as administrative headmen such dissident chiefs as survived, thus ensuring that potentially disruptive Malays were brought into the mainstream of British administration. While he recognized the importance of agriculture as a source of sustainable revenue, he was initially hostile to the planting of natural rubber, and his reservations over the value of higher education for any but the Malay élite retarded the development of Malay society along Western lines. He planned the first railway in the state to link Klang with Kuala Lumpur, and greatly extended the road system: the continuing construction of roads and railways on the west coast was to define his whole professional career.

In December 1883 Swettenham represented the Straits Settlements at the Indian and Colonial Exhibition in Calcutta, travelling widely in India. He acted as resident of Perak, 1884–6, completing the first Perak railway from Taiping to Port Weld. He also planned and built Taiping, the new state capital. At this time he accomplished the first journey on foot by a European over the main range, from Slim in Perak to Pahang, continuing by boat down the Pahang River to Pekan on the east coast. There his peremptory attitude in urging the appointment of a British resident for Pahang antagonized the sultan.

Swettenham became resident of Perak in 1889, a period marked by increasing rivalry with Sir William Edward Maxwell, motivated largely by professional jealousy. The controversy, focused on problems of land administration, showed Maxwell to be the better scholar, Swettenham the more practical administrator. Maxwell enlarged and embittered the controversy by initiating an investigation into private land dealings in Selangor by Swettenham and other government servants. Swettenham narrowly retained his post.

In 1894 Swettenham's wife returned to Perak from the most serious of several mental breakdowns, pregnant by another man. Swettenham dispatched her in semi-public ignominy to Britain, where her son was described as stillborn. Swettenham's own personal life was far from blameless; a misdemeanour formed the basis for blackmail, to which he was subjected from about 1890 until his retirement in 1904.

The increasing complexity of administering separate Malay states in the early 1890s led to a call for federation. Whether this was initiated by Swettenham, as he subsequently argued, is unclear. Certainly he swiftly recognized that the post of resident-general would be highly congenial. With the support of allies in the Colonial Office, he outmanoeuvred the opposition to both the concept and his appointment, led by Maxwell, whom he contrived to have posted to west Africa. Swettenham then visited the rulers of Perak, Pahang, Selangor, and Negeri Sembilan, and obtained their agreement to federation remarkably swiftly in mid-1895, on the fallacious argument that their sovereignty would not be diminished.

Appointed as first resident-general in 1896, Swettenham was deeply involved in the consequent administrative changes. Sultan Idris of Perak, rapidly realizing that his own powers, and those of his colleagues, had been diminished, registered discontent. The first durbar had to be postponed from 1896 to 1897, and the venue changed from Kuala Lumpur to Kuala Kangsar in Perak. At this time Swettenham planned and supervised the building of the resident-general's house, Carcosa, in Kuala Lumpur, and presided over the opening of the striking state secretariat buildings in central Kuala Lumpur. In 1900 he visited and reported on the naval station at Weihaiwei.

In 1901 Swettenham was appointed governor of Singapore, a post particularly agreeable to one so socially ambitious. Among his distinguished visitors was Gertrude Bell, who became a close friend for several years after his retirement. Much of his time as governor was spent in negotiations with the Siamese over the absorption of the states of Kelantan and Trengganu into the British sphere of influence. In this he failed, partly because of personal arrogance in his dealings with senior Siamese officials, and partly because he underestimated the importance for Franco-British relations of retaining Siam as an independent buffer state.

Increasingly public estrangement from the rulers, continuing blackmail, the prospect of a lucrative personal deal with the sultan of Johore over the routing of the railway through that state, combined with evidence received of his wife's adultery and the prospect of divorce, persuaded Swettenham to retire prematurely in 1904. His divorce proceedings failed, and the land in Johore proved less profitable than anticipated. In retirement Swettenham hastened to offer unsolicited advice to the Colonial Office, and endeavoured with only modest success to establish himself as the leading authority on colonial matters, chiefly through newspaper correspondence.

Tall, strikingly handsome even in old age, a witty raconteur, good shot, and keen hunting man, Swettenham achieved social heights in plutocratic Edwardian society seldom reached by retired colonial governors. His long retirement was financed by director's fees from rubber companies. Swettenham undertook two major tasks after retirement. In 1909 he chaired a royal commission to report on the finances of Mauritius. In 1914 he became an assistant director of the press bureau under F. E. Smith (later Lord Birkenhead), and in 1915 joint director. These posts he filled with distinction. He was appointed CMG in 1886, KCMG in 1897, GCMG in 1909, and CH in 1917.

In 1938 Swettenham divorced his wife under the Matrimonial Causes Act of 1937 on grounds of her incurable insanity. On 22 June 1939 he married Vera Seton (1890–1970), widow of Captain John Neil Guthrie and daughter of John Gordon. He had been living with her for several years. Months before his death at his home, 22 Mount Street, Hyde Park Gate, in London, on 11 June 1946, he made common cause with young Malay students in London, denouncing Colonial Office plans for Malayan union. He was buried on 19 June at Brookwood cemetery.

Swettenham was a better than average watercolour painter and a writer, initially of specialized papers on Malay subjects and Malay dictionaries. His early books, *Malay Sketches* (1895) and *The Real Malay* (1899), vividly depict nineteenth-century Malaya and evince a deep knowledge of Malay rural life. *Unaddressed Letters* (1898) was at the time his most popular work, with less Malay and a more personal emphasis, which equally marked *Also and Perhaps* in 1912. His personal interpretation of recent Malay history was established by *British Malaya*, first published in 1907. This, though marked by obsolete scholarship, remained through several editions the primary textbook on the subject until the 1950s. Finally, aged ninety-one, he published his autobiography, *Footprints in Malaya* (1942). H. S. BARLOW

Sources PRO, CO273/76 [fol. 300] · F. A. Swettenham, *Footprints in Malaya* (1942) · H. S. Barlow, *Swettenham* (1995) · F. Swettenham, *British Malaya: an account of the origin and progress of British influence in Malaya* (1907) · *Sir Frank Swettenham's Malayan journals, 1874–1876*, ed. P. L. Burns and C. D. Cowan (1975) · E. Chew, 'Sir Frank Swettenham's Malayan career up to 1896', MA diss., National University of Singapore, 1966 · J. de V. Allen, 'Two imperialists: a study of Sir Frank Swettenham and Sir Hugh Clifford', *Journal of the Malaysian Branch of the Royal Asiatic Society*, 37/1 (1964), 41–73 · J. de V. Allen, 'Johore, 1901–14, the railway concession: the Johore advisory board: Swettenham's resignation and the first general adviser', *Journal of the Malaysian Branch of the Royal Asiatic Society*, 45/2 (1972), 1–28 · Lim Chong Keat and H. S. Barlow, *Frank Swettenham and George Giles: watercolours and sketches of Malaya, 1880–1894* (1988) · m. cert. · d. cert. · *The Times* (13 June 1946) · *The Times* (20 June 1946)
Archives CUL, Royal Commonwealth Society collection, journal · National Archives of Malaysia, Kuala Lumpur, corresp. · National Archives of Malaysia, Kuala Lumpur, journals · National Archives of Malaysia, Kuala Lumpur, papers | U. Newcastle, Robinson L., letters to Gertrude Bell
Likenesses J. S. Sargent, oils, 1904, National Museum, Singapore · J. S. Sargent, oils, 1904, NPG [*see illus.*] · J. Cooke, oils, *c*.1905 (after J. S. Sargent); formerly in Kuala Lumpur, Malaysia · marble bust, *c*.1905, priv. coll. · W. Stoneman, photograph, 1917, NPG · C. L. Hartwell, bronze bust, 1919, behind Muzium Negara, Kuala Lumpur, Malaysia · charcoal drawing, repro. in *Institute of Medical Research commemorative volume, 1900–50* (Kuala Lumpur, 1951), frontispiece. · photographs, Arkib Negara, Malaysia; repro. in Barlow, *Swettenham* · photographs, CUL, library of Royal Commonwealth Society; repro. in Barlow, *Swettenham*
Wealth at death £27,117 7s. 2d.: probate, 1 Oct 1946, *CGPLA Eng. & Wales*

Sweyn. *See* Swein (*d.* 1014); Swein, earl (*d.* 1052).

Swift, Deane (1707–1783). *See under* Swift, Theophilus (1746–1815).

Swift, Edwin (1843–1904), brass-band conductor, was born at Spring Street, Upper Clough, Linthwaite, near Huddersfield, on 14 May 1843, the son of Joseph Swift, a handloom weaver, and his wife, Hannah, *née* Quarmby, the widow of a Mr Baxter. He was one of the three great brass-band conductors and trainers of the nineteenth century (the other two being John Gladney and Alexander Owen) who created the style and idiom of the British brass band.

Swift attended a local elementary school until he was nine years of age, when he left to work as a shuttler in a cotton mill. He had his first musical training in a drum and fife band in Huddersfield which was conducted by a publican named Joseph Thornton, and also received lessons in the rudiments of music from a Mr Quarmby (possibly a relative of his mother's), a local amateur clarinettist. At the age of ten he joined the Linthwaite Brass Band and took up the cornet. He showed a precocious talent and before his fourteenth birthday was made bandmaster and principal cornet player. While still in his teens he began arranging music for the band to play. The Linthwaite band was at this stage a village band, but under Swift's inspiration and leadership it became one of the most prominent contesting bands. It had several successes from the late 1860s, and under Swift won the British open championship in 1874.

Swift married Maria Mellor, of Upper Clough, Linthwaite, on 4 November 1864. Her father, Thomas Mellor, was also a brass-band player. They had five sons and three daughters. Two of the sons, Fred and Lawrence, died before their father, in 1899 and 1900 respectively.

On 14 May 1875—his thirty-second birthday—Swift resigned from his work as a handloom weaver to become a freelance professional band conductor, trainer, and arranger. He continued to live near Huddersfield but travelled widely. His most famous association, apart from that with Linthwaite, was with Wyke Temperance Band, which he conducted when they won the open contest in 1888, 1889, and 1898. However, he had many other successes and was famous for raising small village bands to championship standard.

Between 1873 and the end of the century all but one of the British open contests were won by bands conducted by Swift, Owen, or Gladney. The instrumentation used by these conductors, and the playing style they nurtured, defined the brass-band idiom. Unlike the other two men, Swift was effectively a self-taught musician. He studied classical music while working at his handloom and acquired deft skills and individuality as an arranger of classical music for brass band. His large-scale adaptations of the music of modern composers, including Wagner, were celebrated.

Swift died of cancer of the kidneys on 9 February 1904 at 59 Manchester Road, Milnsbridge, Huddersfield, and was buried on the 12th at the Wesleyan Chapel burial-ground, Hoylehouse. On the day of his funeral the engines in many of the local factories were stopped and the hundreds who formed his cortège were led by eighty men from six of the bands he had taught, who marched in their band uniforms with their drums muffled by black drapery which had been made in local mills. Swift was immensely popular in the brass-band community. A kind, dignified, modest and moderate man, he was widely regarded as a working-class hero.   TREVOR HERBERT

Sources *Life and career of the late Edwin Swift* (1904) · *British Bandsman* (13 Feb 1904), 1117 · *Huddersfield Weekly News* (13 Feb 1904) · b. cert.
Likenesses photograph, repro. in *Life and career of the late Edwin Swift* · photograph, repro. in *British Bandsman*, 1119 · photograph, repro. in A. R. Taylor, *Brass band* (1979), 104
Wealth at death £504 2s. 2d.: probate, 17 Jan 1905, *CGPLA Eng. & Wales*

Swift, Jonathan (1667–1745), writer and dean of St Patrick's Cathedral, Dublin, was born on 30 November 1667, probably at 7 Hoey's Court, St Werburgh's parish, Dublin, the second of two children of Jonathan Swift (1640–1667), steward of the King's Inns, Dublin, and his wife, Abigail Erick (1640–1710), whom he had met after arriving in Ireland. Swift minimized attention to the female line of his family, but it is known that his mother was the daughter of James Ericke, vicar of Thornton, Leicestershire, 1627–34. Accused of holding an unlawful nonconformist conventicle and of dereliction of duty in January 1634, Ericke was prosecuted in the court of high commission in May, and about October he left for Ireland. Abigail was born in Dublin.

Family background Swift's earliest known and direct male ancestor was William Swyfte of Canterbury (*c.*1500–1567), of unknown occupation, who married (*c.*1533) Agnes Barbett, also of Canterbury (*d.* 1569). Their eldest son, Thomas (*d.* 1592), was for forty years rector of St Andrew's, Canterbury. William, son of Thomas (1566–1624), succeeded him at St Andrew's, and William's son, also Thomas, the vicar of Goodrich in Herefordshire (1595–1658), was remembered as a staunch royalist noted for his loyalty in *Mercurius Rusticus* (1685) and for having been 'plundered by the roundheads six and thirty times' ('Family of Swift', 189). Of this Thomas's eleven children (Mary, Godwin, Dryden, Emily, Elizabeth, Thomas, Sarah, William, Katherine, Jonathan, and Adam) the eldest son, Godwin (1628–1695), was trained at Gray's Inn from 1650, was called to the English bar in July 1660, to the Irish bar in May 1663, and was attorney-general for Ormond's palatinate in Tipperary until June 1668. Godwin's brother Thomas married the eldest daughter of Sir William Davenant, leaving a son, also called Thomas, rector of Puttenham, Surrey. Godwin's youngest brother, Adam (1642–1704), reached Ireland last of all and lived in Bull Alley, near Godwin, practising as a solicitor. William was admitted a solicitor in Dublin in November 1661, and lived in nearby Bride Street. Thomas's fifth son, Swift's father, Jonathan, was probably the first of Godwin's brothers to migrate to Ireland and was named Jonathan after his mother's brother Jonathan Dryden. The satirist and the poet John Dryden (1631–1700) were second cousins once removed.

By 1660 Jonathan was working at the King's Inns, Dublin, the hall of the Irish lawyers' corporation, whose governing body included Sir John Temple, and in June 1664 he and Abigail married privately and by special licence issued

Jonathan Swift (1667–1745), by Isaac Whood, 1730

by the prerogative court of the archbishop of Armagh. In his autobiographical fragment Swift says simply that his father Jonathan 'had some employments, and agencyes' ('Family of Swift', 191): in fact he was an office-holder, having been appointed steward of the King's Inns, Dublin, on 25 January 1666, and attorney one day later. Two children were born of this marriage: Jane (*bap.* 1 May 1666, *d.* 1736) and Jonathan, born about seven months after the death of Jonathan senior, and probably at his uncle Godwin's house, 7 Hoey's Court (*Faulkner's Dublin Journal*). Jane probably remained in Ireland until her brother went to Kilkenny College in 1673, and thence went to England with her mother, but she was married from the Bride Street household of her uncle William, whom Swift described in November 1692 as 'the best of my relations' (*Correspondence*, ed. Woolley, 1.7). In spite of her brother's disapproval Jane married Joseph Fenton, a Dublin currier, in 1699, and although he never lost touch with her and met her several times after her marriage, he also provided her with an annuity of £15 for as long as she stayed out of Ireland. Her will is in Le Brocquy, *Cadenus* (Le Brocquy, pp. 149–51).

Education in Ireland The untimely death of Swift's father inevitably produced financial difficulties for his widow. Before he was a year old, and perhaps without his mother's knowledge or consent, the infant Swift was taken by his devoted nursemaid to Whitehaven, Cumberland. At some point after the event Abigail was informed, and consequently instructed the nurse to remain in

Whitehaven with the child until it was safe to attempt a return voyage. Swift remained with the nurse for three years, and was apparently able to spell and read the Bible by three years of age ('Family of Swift'). For reasons that cannot now be ascertained, but which may have included financial exigency, Abigail and her daughter, Jane, left Ireland and returned to her family in Leicestershire. There is no certainty that she saw her son again until his visits to her in spring 1689 and autumn 1692.

Swift's uncle Godwin is usually credited with the responsibility for taking charge of his education, but there is no reason for excluding William and Adam from sharing the cost. From the age of six and until fourteen Swift attended the best school available at the time, Kilkenny College, about 70 miles south-west of Dublin, where William Congreve was his younger contemporary, as were his cousin Thomas Swift (1665–1752) and Francis Stratford; the latter was to become a Hamburg merchant and director of the South Sea Company in 1711. Of his schooldays Swift later recalled 'the delicious Holidays, the Saterday afternoon, and the charming Custards in a blind Alley … the Confinement ten hours a day, to nouns and Verbs, the Terror of the Rod, the bloddy Noses, and broken Shins' (12 Nov 1708, *Correspondence*, ed. Woolley, 1.59). Both college masters during Swift's time, Edward Jones and Edward Ryder, were Cambridge trained and became bishops. Swift studied the humanist and scholastic curriculum, Latin and Greek composition and translation, oratory, and rhetoric, in a context of 'pious, royalist Anglicanism' (Ehrenpreis, 1.39).

On 24 April 1682 Swift and cousin Thomas were entered at Trinity College, Dublin, as pensioners, or fee-paying students. The undergraduate syllabus offered Latin, Greek, Hebrew, and Aristotelian philosophy. Aristotelian mathematics and politics were added for the MA. Narcissus Marsh was one of the provosts (1679–83) during Swift's time, and he produced a notable manual of logic specifically for the college, *Institutiones logicae*, which Swift was later to recall for the fourth voyage of *Gulliver's Travels*. His tutor was St George Ashe (later provost of Trinity College and bishop of Clogher), who remained a lifelong friend to Swift and also to Esther Johnson. Like Marsh he was a man deeply interested in the new sciences and mathematics in particular. Swift did 'passably well' in all subjects except abstract philosophy and formal rhetoric. As a student he was 'more than a drudge and less than an angel' (Ehrenpreis, 1.62, 70), but in his autobiographical fragment Swift claims that he was 'stopped of his Degree, for Dullness and Insufficiency' ('Family of Swift', 192). Swift was not a brilliant student, but he exaggerated his academic insufficiency: records indicate that, like four others out of thirty-eight students graduating with him, he was granted his BA *ex speciali gratia*, by what might be called a condoned pass grade.

According to his own account Swift experienced at this time the first symptoms of what was much later (1861) diagnosed as labyrinthine vertigo or Ménière's syndrome, a disease of the inner ear contracted 'before twenty years old', which Swift mistakenly attributed to 'a Surfeit of fruit' and which 'almost brought him to his Grave'. Symptoms began in his left ear and included vertigo, deafness, and 'coldness of Stomach' ('Family of Swift', 193), and in October 1724 he wrote of 'the Noise of seven Watermills in my Ears' (*Correspondence*, ed. Woolley, 2.626). In its acute form the disease is disabling.

England and Sir William Temple On 26 January 1689 Swift and his cousin Thomas left Trinity College, Dublin, in Jonathan's case two months short of the required seven-year period of residence required for the MA degree. Many Anglo-Irish protestants preferred exile in post-revolutionary England to continued residence in a prospectively rebellious and, under Richard Talbot, earl of Tyrconnell (appointed lord lieutenant in January 1687 and a supporter of James II), Roman Catholic oligarchy. Protestants in the army and the judiciary and privy councillors were systematically replaced, and in the first week of December 1688 rumour of a protestant massacre elicited no reassurance from the lord deputy, and a panic led to an exodus. During some months spent with his mother in Leicester, not demonstrably the first meeting since his infancy—since he may have visited her there either before or during his time at Trinity College—but perhaps only the second, there was a flirtation with Elizabeth Jones of Wanlip, Leicestershire. His 'Letters to Elisa' mentioned in his letter to John Winder were doubtless burnt (13 Jan 1699, *Correspondence*, ed. Woolley, 1.16).

Swift then entered upon a ten-year period of service (including two long breaks) with Sir William Temple, the son of the Swifts' benefactor Sir John Temple in Ireland. Sir William and his family had moved from Dublin to Sheen, Surrey, in 1665. His last surviving child, John, had drowned himself on 14 April 1689, and Swift arrived in the middle of the year. For the next ten years he was financially assisted in Temple's household by remittances from his uncle William and from first cousin Willoughby. He probably accompanied Temple when, early in the summer of 1689, he moved from Sheen to Moor Park, Surrey. In Temple's own words, 'his whole family having been long known to mee obliged mee thus farr to take care of Him' (29 May 1690, *Correspondence*, ed. Woolley, 1.1). Here, in a household run by Temple's sister, the widowed Martha, he first met Esther *Johnson (Stella) (1681–1728), the daughter of Temple's housekeeper, Bridget Johnson, and the widow of Edward Johnson. Swift later (1726) affirmed that he and Stella had been 'perfect Friends these 35 Years', then, five days later, 'thirty-three years' (ibid., 15 and 20 July 1726, 2.698, 700). Both were dependants, Stella as Lady Giffard's gentlewoman-in-waiting, and Swift as Temple's copyist, keeper of accounts, and his reader. Later on he was appointed editor of Temple's posthumous works.

It has been suggested, in Denis Johnston's *In Search of Swift* (pp. 111–12), that Stella may have been Temple's natural daughter by Bridget; that Swift's father died too soon to have been the writer's father, and that Swift may have been the natural son of Sir John Temple (1600–1677), master of the rolls, and Abigail Erick. If this were so Swift would have been the natural half-brother of Sir William

Temple, and Stella's uncle. Few have been convinced by this theory, although certainty is lacking in crucial details of the standard account, notably baptismal records. As his cousin Deane Swift was to say in the last year of Swift's life, 'A thousand stories have been invented of him within these two years and imposed upon the world' (4 April 1744, *Correspondence*, ed. Woolley, 4.1506). A somewhat tendentious genealogical table of the Temple and Swift families from 1600, angled to the theory that Swift was the son of Sir John Temple, is to be found in Johnston (pp. 232–3).

Swift was more than Temple's secretary and amanuensis. He was also employed as Temple's emissary to William III's court, and he claims to have met the king several times on the latter's visits to Moor Park. If Temple was a father figure for Swift, Temple regarded Swift not so much as a surrogate son but more as a valuable employee bound to him by obligations and duty. Recent scholarship (Elias, 46–7) has stressed Swift's awkward dependence upon the bounty of a vain and superficial cultural intelligence, with the ambitious young Swift rankling at his subordinate status in Temple's household. Even so, this must be set against the fact that at Moor Park he also came into contact with some whig grandees whose influence, though fading, would be useful to him in his own developing career. These included Charles Spencer, earl of Sunderland, future (and absentee) lord lieutenant of Ireland for ten months, and the earl of Portland, lord chamberlain. Over the king's opposition to the proposed bill for triennial parliaments, and through Portland, Swift made his first court appearance, carrying a historical explanation to the king of the grounds for the bill's introduction. It is not clear that Swift actually met the king, but when his venture failed to have its intended effect Swift took the experience as a salutary lesson in the ways of court intrigue. In May 1690, using the Temple sinecure as master of the rolls in Ireland, Temple offered him a post in that office worth 'about 120 ll a year'. Swift turned it down in favour of ordination, thereby indicating his disdain for merely materialistic self-advancement ('Family of Swift', 194; Ehrenpreis, 1.145–7). Temple further assisted Swift in the latter's application for the post of secretary to Sir Robert Southwell, secretary of state for Ireland in King William's expedition to reconquer Ireland after the rebellion. Swift was back in Ireland probably just after the battle of the Boyne was fought on 1 July 1690. No immediate benefit—not even the improvement in health promised by physicians—seems to have come from this early attempt to find a suitable Irish appointment, and he returned to England and reached Moor Park in December. By February 1692 Swift was weighing up his marriage prospects, beginning a career in the church, and knew enough about Leicester people to disparage them as 'a parcel of very wretched fools' (11 Feb 1692, *Correspondence*, ed. Woolley, 1.2) for their gossip about his conduct towards an unknown woman. On 5 July 1692, two days before Thomas, and less than a month after his incorporation from Hart Hall, Oxford (later Hertford College), he received the MA. He spent the autumn months with his mother.

First publications and an Irish parish Swift had been writing Pindaric odes in the elaborate style of Abraham Cowley since 1689, and his first published anonymous poem was 'Ode: to the King on his Irish Expedition' (Dublin, 1691), followed by 'Ode to the Athenian Society', published under his own name and with a rather embarrassing letter in praise of the non-existent society in the *Supplement to the Fifth Volume of the Athenian Gazette* (1692). With Temple's encouragement he also translated 200 lines of Virgil. In December 1693 he wrote his ode 'Occasioned by Sir William Temple's Late Illness and Recovery'. He left Temple's household for the second time in May 1694, apparently against the wishes of Temple himself, and with the stated intention of being ordained in Ireland in the following September. He felt that he had already spent too much time without settling into a profession. He was replaced as Temple's secretary for two years from 1694 by his parson cousin Thomas Swift. Before proceeding with the ordination, however, Archbishop Marsh insisted on the canonical requirement of testimonials to 'a good life and behaviour', and duly received a certificate relating to Swift's 'Morals and Learning' and his reasons for quitting Temple's household. Once this had been settled he was ordained deacon in Christ Church Cathedral, Dublin, on 28 October 1694, then priest on 13 January 1695, and both ceremonies were performed by William Moreton, bishop of Kildare. On 28 January he was appointed by the Irish government (through Lord Capel) to the prebend of Kilroot in the cathedral of Connor. Kilroot was effectively three parishes, worth about £100 a year, comprising the vicarages of Kilroot, on the north side of Belfast Lough, Templecorran, on the north and east boundary of Kilroot, and the rectory of Ballynure, north-west of Kilroot. In this sparsely populated, isolated, neglected, and overwhelmingly Scottish Presbyterian parish he was installed on 15 March.

Swift's sojourn at Kilroot was, materially speaking, comfortless at best, and theologically alarming at worst, given its poverty and its overwhelmingly nonconformist character. Weary of his new post after only a few months he accepted Temple's urging to return to Moor Park in May 1696, but not before pressing Jane Waring (1674–1720), daughter of the archdeacon of Dromore, to reconsider her earlier refusal of his marriage proposal; this had been based on doctors' advice about her own health and also on Swift's uncertain financial prospects. Swift gave her a latinized nickname, Varina, and she was thus the first of the 'three frail, fatherless, first-born young women to whom [Swift] attached himself' (Ehrenpreis, 1.165).

Moor Park again At Moor Park Swift returned to his earlier secretarial duties, but now with the special responsibility of preparing Temple's poems, essays, and three volumes of letters for the press. He also read very widely in Temple's library, especially in political and ecclesiastical history, the Greek and Roman classics, travel literature, French literature, and in the darker corners of esoteric religious works. Although there is no mention of its gestation this is the place and the period, in the second half of

1696, during which his first book, *A Tale of a Tub*, was conceived and written, notably the allegory of the three brothers representing Roman Catholicism (Peter), Calvinism (Jack), and Anglicanism (Martin), as well as the attacks on 'Moderns' in philosophy, science, and textual scholarship in the five 'digressions'. It is difficult to imagine Temple approving his secretary's satirical writing, no matter how brilliant, but there is one intriguing possibility suggesting that this was the case. Alone among biographical authorities Deane Swift claims that Temple not only read the *Tale*'s digressions but also that Swift submitted each of them 'to the judgment and correction of his learned friend' (D. Swift, 60; Elias, 155–206). Swift's *The Battle of the Books* is a defence of Temple's cultural opposition to certain branches of 'modern' learning such as accurate historical and textual scholarship and mathematics, as expressed in Temple's *Essay upon the Ancient and Modern Learning* (1690). This had been answered in the second version of William Wotton's *Reflections upon Ancient and Modern Learning* (1697), and by Richard Bentley, whose 'Dissertation upon the epistles of Phalaris' (June 1697) was designed to show up Temple's shaky scholarship. In 1705, and in response to the barbs in the anonymous *Tale of a Tub*, Wotton published a third and final version.

Swift did not formally resign from Kilroot until early in January 1698. Sir William Temple died on 27 January 1699, 'and with him all that was great and good among men', Swift remarked (Ehrenpreis, 1.257), leaving him a legacy of £100 and the obligation to prepare several unpublished works for the press. Swift petitioned the king through Temple's friend the earl of Romney for a prebend of Canterbury or Westminster, 'upon the Claym of a promise his Majesty had made to Sr W[illiam] T[emple]' ('Family of Swift', 195). Again nothing came of this and he returned to Ireland in August 1699, having accepted in June the invitation of the second earl of Berkeley, the new lord justice, to become his domestic chaplain and private secretary. Swift lost the secretarial position to the opportunist manoeuvrings of Arthur Bushe soon after arriving in Dublin, but remained Berkeley's chaplain for almost two years (to early April 1701), as well as gaining a lifelong friendship with Berkeley's second daughter, Lady Elizabeth Germain. On 30 November 1699 the first two volumes of his edition of Temple's letters were on sale, and these included his own translations from the French and Latin originals. On 16 February 1700 Swift was appointed to Laracor—the two vicarages of Laracor and Rathbeggan and the rectory of Agher, lying mostly to the south-east of Trim. With a combined value of about £230 annually this produced the bulk of Swift's income for the next twelve years. On 4 May and alleging her cooling ardour towards himself as well as 'untractable behaviour' (*Correspondence*, ed. Woolley, 1.18), Swift set out the conditions under which he would entertain marriage to Jane Waring. The full circumstances of this letter are not known, but it is hardly surprising, given its offputting demands and stern moral tone, that their relationship faded. Varina eventually died unmarried.

On 22 October Swift achieved his first substantial position in the church, and thereby the key to his eventual deanery, with his appointment to the prebend of Dunlavin in the cathedral of St Patrick. In 1701 (April to September) he was in England, having accompanied Berkeley when he was recalled, and published anonymously his first political work, on the balance of power in the state, *A Discourse of the Contests and Dissensions between the Nobles and Commons in Athens and Rome* (October 1701). The historian's art always compelled Swift's interest, and this is an example of parallel history, in which he defended the whig John, Lord Somers, under the name of Aristides, and also attacked his future patron Robert Harley and the Harleyites. Its allegorical technique foreshadows much of *Gulliver's Travels*.

Stella was also in London, now twenty, with a legacy from Temple made up of land leases in Ireland worth £1000, and half as much again in invested money. Swift persuaded her and her companion Rebecca Dingley (*c*.1666–1743) to move to Dublin. The latter had a small annuity of £14, both her parents had been first cousins to Temple, and she was fifteen years Stella's senior. Swift was to pay them an annual allowance of £44 (Ehrenpreis, 2.300).

In August 1701 Stella and Dingley, known by Swift in the *Journal to Stella* collectively as 'MD'—perhaps code for 'my dears'—moved from Moor Park to Dublin to live in William Street, between Trinity College and St Patrick's. Swift took the degree of doctor of divinity at Trinity College, granted on 16 February 1702, and then left for England in late April in the wake of the king's death on 8 March. There he arranged the publication of Temple's *Miscellanea, the Third Part* in July, including 'A defence of the essay on ancient and modern learning' for which Benjamin Tooke jun. paid him £30. The third volume of Temple's *Letters* (1703) earned him another £50 from the same source (2 September 1702). The key figures in the whig junto, Somers, Halifax, and Sunderland—the latter known to Swift from his Moor Park days—courted him when they learned that he was the author of the *Contests and Dissensions* and promised 'the greatest preferments'.

Swift was back in Ireland from October 1702 to November 1703. William King, bishop of Derry, became his formal ecclesiastical superior as archbishop of Dublin from March 1703: 'we generally differed in politicks', Swift recalled in 1717 (18 July 1717, *Correspondence*, ed. Woolley, 2.466), although each was whig in state politics and tory in church politics. He left Dublin for England on 11 December 1703, probably carrying the manuscript of *A Tale of a Tub* with him. The Lords' rejection in December of the bill designed to prevent occasional conformity elicited great political excitement and drew Swift into its factionalism: the Test Act was seen in Ireland as the crucial and primary defence of the Church of Ireland. Swift's views of the whigs and the danger in their moves to abolish the test this time may be seen in his later work *The Sentiments of a Church-of-England Man, with Respect to Religion and Government* (1708, published 1711). He was in England until May

1704, making another regular visit to his mother in Leicester, and in April he was discouraging by letter William Tisdall's suit for Esther Johnson without at the same time making such an offer to Stella himself.

The London publication of *A Tale of a Tub*, again issued anonymously, happened three weeks before Swift left the country (10 May). It was dedicated to Lord Somers by 'The Bookseller', and, like each of three subsequent reprints, was printed for John Nutt, even though Benjamin Tooke, who owned the copyright, paid Swift for it and employed John Nutt as the trade publisher. On 1 June 1704 Swift was back in Dublin; he remained there until November 1707, having completed his sixteenth crossing between Ireland and England (fourteen of which voyages may be identified). By February 1711 the total was nineteen.

England, 1707–1709 Swift attended the earl of Pembroke, lord lieutenant of Ireland, in London, from November 1707 to June 1709. At some point about December 1707, if not before, and in Dublin, Swift met the Van Homrighs. Hester, the widowed mother, two sons, and two daughters, Esther (1688–1723) and Mary, were newly arrived from Dublin and living in some style near St James's Square. Esther Van *Homrigh (Vanessa) was twenty-one years Swift's junior, and seven years younger than Stella. The only return visit to England made by Stella and Dingley coincided with Swift's time there, and they stayed for the summer months, returning to Dublin before November 1708. The two most important women in Swift's life were thus in London at the same time, and as far as is known each was kept unaware, then and later, of the other's true significance to him. Outside this very private circle his new friends included Pembroke's companion, the art collector and punster Sir Andrew Fountaine, and, by February 1708, Joseph Addison, Sunderland's under-secretary of state of the southern department, and also later appointed secretary to Thomas, earl of Wharton, lord lieutenant of Ireland. Swift's primary business was to represent Archbishop King and the Church of Ireland in negotiations for the remission to the Irish clergy of the first fruits and twentieth parts payable by them from the first year's ecclesiastical revenue of a benefice (effected in England in 1704 and converted into a fund known as Queen Anne's Bounty). Though *A Tale* and *Contests and Dissensions* had been published anonymously, he was soon making his mark on the world of the London wits. Addison described him in 1708 as 'The Truest Friend And the Greatest Genius of his Age' (Forster, 160) and both were on close terms with Somers.

In April the almanac maker and astrologer (or, in Swift's terms, 'Cobler, Starmonger, and Quack') John Partridge asserted in a letter to Isaac Manley, postmaster of Ireland, that reports of his own death had been much exaggerated. In a brilliant spoof of the almanac style, signed by 'Isaac Bickerstaff', Swift had predicted Partridge's death on 29 March in *Predictions for the Year 1708* (published January 1708). This was not only Swift's practical joke against vulgar superstition: it was also part of his moderate defence of the Church of England against 'the "low party" of the Dissenters, the freethinkers and the moneyed men, and

… the high Tories, who were either non-jurors or Jacobites' (*Prose Works*, 1.x). *The Tatler* (no. 9, April 1709) carried one of Swift's best poems, the urban georgic *A Description of the Morning*, and in June he had the first of two interviews with Sidney, earl of Godolphin, lord treasurer for the past six years and a strong supporter of the Occasional Conformity Bill. Godolphin made it clear that any hope Swift had for obtaining remission of the first fruits from the whig government would depend on using his influence to deliver the consent of the Irish clergy to the repeal of the Test Act in Ireland. Swift was deeply offended by this tactic, his second chastening experience of real court politics. And in what one of his commentators has called his winter of discontent (1708–9) prospects of preferment from whig politicians had seemed to shrink as his literary opportunities in a whig group blossomed. By July and in a letter to Ambrose Philips he was gleefully referring to himself, Addison, and Richard Steele as the 'Triumvirate' (a term he also applied eighteen years later to himself, Pope, and Bolingbroke) and enjoying London's coffee-house culture. Godolphin was dismissed by the queen on 8 October 1710 and Swift took his revenge with a lampoon, 'The Virtues of Sid Hamet the Magician's Rod'.

The years 1708–10 brought Swift's first extensive taste of life at the centre of English literary and political culture, and he revelled in it. He was occupied by his campaign against repealing the Test Act in Ireland, when he was 'writing [his] Speculations' (14 Sept 1708, *Correspondence*, ed. Woolley, 1.53) on church and state relations: the brilliantly perverse logic of *An Argument Against Abolishing Christianity* (written about April 1708, published 1711); the flatly didactic *A Project for the Advancement of Religion, and the Reformation of Manners* (written about August to September 1708, published 1709); *Remarks upon a Book [by Matthew Tindal], Intitled 'The Rights of the Christian Church Asserted'* (written at the end of 1707 and in early 1708, and not published until Faulkner's edition of Swift's *Works*, 1762); *A Letter from a Member of the House of Commons in Ireland to a Member of the House of Commons in England, Concerning the Sacramental Test* (published 1709); and *The Sentiments of a Church-of-England Man* (1708, possibly begun 1704, but not published until 1711 in *Miscellanies in Prose and Verse*). Swift met John Arbuthnot, physician-in-ordinary to the queen at this time, and to this period also belongs the first extant letter to his lifelong friend and confidant Charles Ford. A prose essay on the Act of Union (1707) and Ireland's relationship to England as a mistress cast off in favour of Scotland, *The Story of the Injured Lady*, was written between January and May 1710, but not published until 1746.

In April 1709 Benjamin Tooke jun. paid Swift £40 for the third part of Temple's *Memoirs* (published in June), the last pseudo-filial act of his literary executorship for Temple which over a period of ten years had earned him between £200 and £250 (£50 for the third volume of Temple's *Letters*, 1703; and perhaps the same for the two-volume 1699 *Letters* and 1701 *Miscellanea: the Third Part*). He set out for Ireland on 5 May, spending six weeks with his mother in Leicester—a visit that probably reflects her failing health, since she died on 29 April 1710—and probably completed the 'Apology' for the fifth edition of the *Tale* here also, since it is dated 'June 3, 1709'. On 19 June Edmund Curll's *Complete Key to the 'Tale of a Tub'* attributed Swift's *Tale* to Thomas and Jonathan Swift conjointly. The only direct evidence for this was Thomas's own suggestion, and it was roundly dismissed as an impertinence in Jonathan's letter from Dublin to Benjamin Tooke of 29 June. Lord Lieutenant Wharton, whom Swift disliked intensely, was coming to the end of his period of residence in Dublin, and Swift seems to have avoided Dublin and gone directly to his beloved country vicarage at Laracor, with visits to particular friends such as Ford, the Ashe brothers, and Lady Shelburne. In October–November he was embroiled in a dispute with Lady Giffard, who had been against publishing Temple's *Memoirs* and had accused him in print (*The Post-Man*, 6 Oct 1709) of publishing the 'Third part' against the author's stated intentions and from an unauthorized and 'unfaithfull' copy. Temple had written at the head of the text: 'Written for the satisfaction of my friends'. Swift refuted the charge (10 Nov 1709, *Correspondence*, ed. Woolley, 1.83), asserting that Temple himself had corrected the editor's copy.

Late in 1710 the fifth London edition of *A Tale of a Tub* appeared, printed for John Nutt and published anonymously by Benjamin Tooke jun., including the 1709 'Apology' containing important statements on his intentions and satiric techniques. Edmund Curll's *Key*, together with comments lifted from Wotton's observations on the *Tale*, were inserted beneath the text, the latter as if they were editorially from 'W. Wotton'. Swift's own (unsigned) comments were reproduced among these as notes. He remained in Ireland until August 1710. In London political power was inexorably slipping from the hands of Godolphin and the whig junto towards the outstretched arms of Robert Harley, tory moderate, and Swift was about to change his political loyalties.

London and tory propaganda Having been commissioned at the end of August 1710 by King and fellow Irish prelates to plead with the new government the cause of the Irish clergy, Swift left Dublin once more to seek remission of the first fruits. On his arrival in London on 7 September 1710, shortly before Godolphin's dismissal, he found himself 'caressed by both parties'. He was now a more experienced negotiator, sensitive to and prepared to deal with the wiles of political managers. Swift presented his arguments in person to Robert Harley, chancellor of the exchequer, on 4 October, and again in a four-hour meeting with Harley on the following Saturday at York Buildings, Buckingham Street, south of the Strand, perhaps the single most important meeting in Swift's political career. He decided thereafter to be less fond of the whiggish St James's Coffee House. Charles Jervas, the Irish portrait painter and Pope's teacher, was finishing his portrait at this time. On 21 October Swift learned that the queen had granted the request of the Irish church, a personal triumph for Swift. Harley had taken less than three weeks to effect something that Swift's whig friends had been unable or unwilling to do in three years. He also offered an introduction to Secretary Henry St John, a successful device to secure Swift's loyalty and propaganda services as unpaid editor of the tory weekly *The Examiner*, which had been running since August under the editorial control of Dr William King, assisted by Dr John Freind, Matthew Prior, Delarivier Manley, St John, and Francis Atterbury (whose state treason trial in 1723 was to provide the material for an episode dealing with espionage and secret codes in *Gulliver's Travels*, part 2, chap. 6). Its printer was John Barber, later appointed printer to the South Sea Company through Swift's influence (October 1711).

Swift's contributions to *The Examiner* comprise thirty-three essays written from a tory point of view 'to assert the principles, and justify the proceedings of the new ministers'. Published on Thursdays from 2 November 1710 (no. 14) to 14 June 1711 (no. 46, jointly written with Manley, the subsequent editor), Swift's essays were each answered in *The Medley* the following Monday by Addison's friend, the whig MP Arthur Mainwaring. As chief ministerial writer Swift dined at Harley's table, meeting Matthew Prior there on 10 October, and was in St John's company on several occasions before a formal meeting with him on 11 November. The go-between in forging these relationships was the Welshman Erasmus Lewis, Harley's undersecretary. On 17 February 1711 Swift was admitted to the first of Harley's Saturday Club dinners at his house in York Buildings, a kind of inner cabinet comprising Harley, St John, Sir Simon Harcourt, and Earl Rivers.

Harley took Swift to Windsor for the first time in July. St John and the British ministers had signed secret and public articles with the French by the end of September, and Swift was given the task of selling the policies and the peace to the English public. His most important and influential political publication came out on 27 November 1711 (predated 1712) and was a central element in the paper war between the whigs and tories. Aimed at winning over the 'country gentlemen', *The Conduct of the Allies* attacks the whigs for prolonging a war ruinously expensive for the nation but profitable to a monied clique driven by self-interest at the cost of the landed interest. It charged Queen Anne's general, the duke of Marlborough, with corruption and self-aggrandizement, and accused Godolphin and the whig junto of megalomania. It also described the inequitable financial burden carried by England on behalf of the allies. The pamphlet was read in proof and corrected by St John and others, and was purchased and distributed by the ministry. Harley made additions to both the second and fourth editions. The first edition of 1000 copies sold in two days, the second in five hours, the third in less than a week, and by the sixth edition in January a total of 11,000 copies had sold. A Dublin printing of the *Conduct* (also in 1712) by John Hyde incorporated authorial changes and later became Faulkner's copy text in 1738 (authorial changes ceased with the fourth London edition).

As the leading tory propagandist Swift could not have been nearer the centre of tory foreign policy in this specific example, yet this does not mean that he was privy to all ministerial policies. He had known nothing of the secretive Harley's peace negotiations with France begun in August 1710: Secretary of State St John himself did not learn of them until April 1711, and Swift four months later. Neither was he aware of the secret discussion about a second Stuart restoration, nor privy to Harley's connection with Daniel Defoe. His modern editor says: 'there is very little inside information in *The Examiner*' (Ellis, xxix–xxxi). Moreover Swift never met the queen or the duke and duchess of Marlborough (Ehrenpreis, 2.526). Two further works were instigated by and written for the tory ministers: *Some Remarks on the Barrier Treaty* (based on confidential papers and published on 22 February 1712), and *The Publick Spirit of the Whigs* (23 February 1714). On 27 February 1711 *Miscellanies in Prose and Verse* had appeared anonymously.

Antoine de Guiscard, a French double agent, attempted to assassinate Harley on 8 March 1711. The incident drove home to Swift how closely his own career was now bound up with Harley (elevated to the peerage as the earl of Oxford and of Mortimer on 24 May 1711), and a very deep affection and respect developed for Harley the man. Swift also dated the breach between Harley and St John from the time of this incident. On 26 April he took up residence in the riverside village of Chelsea, and he stayed there until 5 July, when he moved to Suffolk Street, near the Van Homrighs. Esther Van Homrigh's letters to Swift date from 1709, although his first extant letter to her is dated 18 December 1711. Her letters to him, with one exception (1 September 1712), are drafts retained by Vanessa, with many scorings and deletions.

A blow to Swift's chances of preferment was struck by his lampoon on the queen's favourite, the red-haired whig duchess of Somerset, *The Windsor Prophecy* (printed as a black letter broadside and in limited circulation on 24 December 1711, but with four printed editions before the end of the month). On 22 January he met Henry Sacheverell, the incendiary high-church tory preacher. Swift's close association with Harley's cultural interests is commemorated in the dedicatory remarks addressed to him in a project to found an English equivalent to that begun by the French Academy, *A Proposal for Correcting, Improving and Ascertaining the English Tongue* (written by 22 February and published over Swift's name on 17 May 1712). Its purpose was to establish 'a society or academy for correcting and settling our language, that we may not perpetually be changing as we do'. St John was raised to the peerage as Viscount Bolingbroke in July, and Swift moved further up the tory ladder. As evidence of his key political usefulness he was shown a draft of the queen's speech of 9 April 1713 and 'corrected [it] in sevrall Places' (*Journal to Stella*, 2.635), and he also had input into the queen's speech of 2 March 1714. In August and up to May 1713 he was working at a vindication of the queen and her last ministry by means of an account of the negotiations leading to the peace treaty of Utrecht. He was also incorporated into the Brothers' Club ('The Society') with John Arbuthnot (author of the five *John Bull* pamphlets, 1712), Matthew Prior, and others (originally twelve and eventually twenty-two members), which was founded by Bolingbroke as the tory answer to the

whig Kit-Cat Club. Yet in spite of his access to the ministers and to official correspondence, and largely because of the procrastination of both Oxford and Bolingbroke, Swift could not bring his *History of the Four Last Years of the Queen* (more precisely, a history of one sixteen-month period) to a satisfactory and timely completion. More positively he clearly savoured the recommendatory powers of a 'master of requests' (White Kennett's sardonic term: Ehrenpreis, 2.608), finding posts for Benjamin Tooke and John Barber as printers of the government *Gazette*, and introducing the Irish philosopher George Berkeley at court. Among the writers he helped were his fellow Irishman Thomas Parnell and the poets William Diaper and William Harrison, the latter a whig who edited and wrote most of the continuation of *The Tatler* in January–May 1711. But in May 1713 Swift fell out with Richard Steele, by now his political opposite number, over Steele's allusion in *The Examiner* to Swift's role.

In the middle of all this activity on behalf of others nothing seemed to be offering to satisfy Swift's own ambition 'to live in England, and with a competency to support me with honour' (4 May 1711, *Correspondence*, ed. Woolley, 1.126). His interest in the deanery of Wells, expressed in a letter to the earl of Oxford (5 January 1712), produced nothing. In April both Oxford and Bolingbroke dangled the prospect of his becoming a prebendary or canon of the royal free chapel of Windsor, but in the end it was Ireland that was to offer his best chance. On 21 April 1713, after terrible suspense and disappointments severe enough to induce him to quit London entirely, he heard that the deanery of St Patrick's was his. He received the news of his appointment as a sentence of exile.

From 2 September 1710 until 6 June 1713 a minutely detailed account of Swift's London years—the most hectic, influential, and satisfying period of his public life—is given in the *Journal to Stella*. This contains all sixty-five extant letters from Swift to 'MD' (or Stella) except three: an undated letter from some time in January 1698, another of 30 April 1721, and one dated 11 March 1727. With one or two exceptions Stella's own letters were destroyed, probably by Swift himself. There are many references to Mrs Van Homrigh's hospitality in the *Journal to Stella*, but Vanessa is never singled out for mention by name. The title *Journal to Stella* was invented by John Nichols in 1779, but it was Sheridan who first published the letters as a separate group under the title *Dr. Swift's Journal to Stella* in 1784 (the numbering is chaotic, the annotation sloppy, and the last letter is missing).

The golden years of toryism were now almost over, and although Swift did not yet know it Dublin would soon be his home, or 'what fortune hath made my home' (12 Oct 1727, *Correspondence*, ed. Woolley, 3.786) for the rest of his life. He arrived there via Holyhead on 10 June 1713, took the oaths, and three days later was formally installed dean, an appointment which also entailed an *ex officio* seat on the board of the Dublin workhouse and Foundling Hospital. He stayed for only two sickness-ridden weeks before shifting to his cottage at Laracor, hating 'the Thoughts of Dublin' and preferring 'a field-bed and an Earthen floor before the great House there, which they say is mine … I will never see England again … I am now fitter to look after Willows, and to cutt Hedges than meddle with Affairs of State' (ibid., 8 July 1713, 1.219). Even so he had not yet given up all hope of positions and preferment in England, and he was back in London on 9 September, only to find the tory leadership irredeemably split, with Bolingbroke distrusted, Oxford both intransigent and inert, and each capable only of subverting the other's position.

At Windsor in early October Swift composed *Cadenus and Vanessa*, a lengthy poetical history of his relationship with Esther Van Homrigh. He also spent time with Oxford, and the first extant letter from Alexander Pope to Swift (8 December 1713) is from this visit, although it suggests a friendship already well established—from Pope's point of view at least—since he alludes to a previous occasion on which Swift had offered him 20 guineas to change his religion. The House of Lords declared *The Publick Spirit of the Whigs* (23 February 1714) a seditious and scandalous libel (in particular for its remarks about Scottish peers), and within a month of publication a royal proclamation was issued offering a £300 reward for discovery of its author (20 March 1714). The work included an attack on Steele, the key remaining whig propagandist, editor of *The Englishman* and author of the recent *The Crisis* (19 January), for raising fears about the succession and of Catholic resurgence should the Hanoverian succession not be accepted, as well as for his attack on the tories' peace settlement. This was Swift's last defence of the Oxford–Bolingbroke ministry: its origin may not have been in a ministerial request but in what his biographer calls the 'bored disgust' of 'a truly independent citizen whose sense of justice has been outraged' (Ehrenpreis, 2.706).

In February 1714 Swift was elected a governor of Bethlem Hospital, and his licence for absence from Ireland was renewed. He thus spent more time in London with Pope, Arbuthnot, John Gay, and Parnell, in a literary fraternity known as the Scriblerus Club, hatching literary plots against the political and literary establishments. In time some of these would see the light of day as *Gulliver's Travels*, *The Beggar's Opera*, and *The Dunciad*. On 15 April he drafted an application for the vacant office of historiographer royal, but three months later the post went to Thomas Maddox. At the end of May the rift between Oxford and Bolingbroke, as well as his own failure to reconcile them, finally determined Swift to leave London in despair and for good. He stayed in Oxford for a week, and then (3 June) set off for Letcombe Bassett, 50 miles from London, in Berkshire, where he was visited by Pope. Swift's 'letter' to Pope dated 'Jan. 10, 1721' (more a pamphlet-apologia, not sent as a letter, and not published until 1741) is the best single account of his political credo and a direct explication of these crucial four years of Swift's political ascendancy. The 'letter' outlines his abiding principles in the current 'plot-discovering age' and explains his position in relation to the Hanoverian succession, to the 'Revolution-principle', to the maintenance of standing armies in peacetime, to annual parliaments, and to the rise of the monied interest and its opposition to the landed interest. He vents his anger 'at the End of a Pen' in *Some Free Thoughts upon the Present State of Affairs*, written in May–June 1714 at Upper Letcombe, near Letcombe Bassett. As causes of fatal tory weakness, it singled out Oxford's secretive and hesitant leadership (Swift gave him the ironic nickname 'The Dragon'); the turbulence of high-church tories (like Sacheverell) and dissenters; the ministry's inadequate defence of the established church; the ministry's failure to deal decisively with uncertainties over the Hanoverian succession; and the personal feuding of the two leaders. Swift's retirement to the country, 'weary to death of Courts and Ministers, and Business and Politicks' (11 June 1714, *Correspondence*, ed. Woolley, 1.278), was greeted by consternation among some of his friends.

Exile in Ireland and a new life On 27 July 1714 Oxford was dismissed by the queen. Bolingbroke enjoyed only four more days as secretary of state and was already engaged in secret negotiations with the Pretender. Oxford was imprisoned in the Tower, impeached for high treason and high crimes and misdemeanours. The Oxford–Bolingbroke ministry and all its plans were in tatters, and the political moment for Swift's *History* and *Some Free Thoughts upon the Present State of Affairs* had passed. The former was published posthumously in 1758, the latter in 1741. The queen's death on 1 August not only ended the prospect of a tory government; it also destroyed any remaining chances of Swift's preferment in England. Convinced that the future would be whig he returned to Ireland and arrived in Dublin on 24 August, having warned Vanessa on 12 August to be discreet about the few contacts he would permit her to have with him in Dublin. Before November she had followed him to Ireland and settled at Celbridge, a family property 11 miles west of Dublin. Tattle about their relationship began almost immediately. In exile he made new friends such as Knightley Chetwode, yet maintained his public melancholy in a poem 'In Sickness' (October 1714: 'My Life is now a Burthen grown / To others, e'er it be my own'). Arbuthnot kept him in touch with the Scriblerus Club in London, notably reporting the doings of Pope, Parnell, Gay, and others.

Rumours and relationships There is much to know about Swift's relationship with Vanessa and Stella, but it seems clear that Vanessa asked more from Swift than he was prepared to give. Her coercive letters to him are full of recriminations and the pain of deferred meeting: his to her are tense, replete with negatives, full of warnings about 'Decency' and the need for absolute discretion. There is an element of fear and sexual danger in his response to her assertiveness. His relationship with Stella, on the other hand, besides its much greater duration (from her childhood to her death at forty-seven) is more self-confident, playful, risk-free: his letters and poems to her read sometimes as though he is speaking to an extension of himself. A persistent tradition which, however unlikely it may seem, remains impossible to disprove or prove, dates a secret marriage between Swift and Stella somewhere between the end of July and 4 October 1716, at either Clogher or Dublin, performed by Swift's old tutor, St

George Ashe (Sheridan cites Mrs Sican as his authority for this event). If it took place at all it could not be consummated, the theory goes, because of their late discovered consanguinity either as uncle and niece or as first cousins (Johnston, 203). Apart from the three principals, the only person who could have settled these rumours, and who knew both women well enough, was Charles Ford, known as 'Glass heel' to Vanessa and as 'Don Carlos' to Stella. As Swift's most trusted emissary in all matters he never spoke about the issue. Whatever Swift's relationship with Stella may have been in private (apart from the fact of Swift being her mentor), their public one in verse and prose and in his letters to her in the *Journal to Stella* was that of an intimate and loving friendship between two people who understood each other perfectly and who each understood and indulged the other's mind games. Stella was far from the only woman in Swift's life, and for a time unwittingly competed for his attention with Vanessa, but she was undoubtedly the most important person in Swift's private life, the 'fairest Soul in the World' (27 July 1726, *Correspondence*, ed. Woolley, 3.702), and his deep and abiding attachment to her is beyond question. His love for her also transcends accurate chronology: on the night of her death, 28 January 1728, he writes that he had known Stella 'from six years old' (J. Swift, *On the Death of Mrs. Johnson*), yet she was born on 13 March 1681, and in 1687 he was still a student at Trinity College. A physical sexual relationship with Vanessa seems plausible even though the evidence is purely conjectural. It is too easy to assume that Vanessa represents the physical woman and Stella the companionable or maternal woman in this triangular relationship.

By the end of 1718 Swift had further consolidated his Irish friendships, notably with the Revd Patrick Delany, a junior fellow of Trinity College, a fellow churchman, and eventually author of the second biographical study, *Observations upon Lord Orrery's 'Remarks on … Swift'* (1754). Through him Swift met Dr Richard Helsham (senior fellow of Trinity) and Dr Thomas Sheridan (1687–1738), priest and schoolmaster, grandfather of Richard Brinsley Sheridan, and father of Swift's godson and future biographer Thomas (1719–1788). Stella's birthday on 13 March 1719 saw the first of Swift's graceful, lucid, gently ironic, and self-deprecating annual verse tributes to her. In a letter to Charles Ford there is the first mention of *Gulliver's Travels*. 'I am now writing a History of my Travells, which will be a large Volume, and gives Account of Countryes hitherto unknown; but they go on slowly for want of Health and Humour' (15 April 1721, *Correspondence*, ed. Woolley, 2.533). He was now rarely free for more than a month of attacks of deafness and dizziness, and adopted vigorous walking and horse-riding as a palliative measure. In June 1722 he was prescribing reading and exercise for Vanessa and urging that she might 'grow less Romantick, and talk and act like a Man of this World' (ibid., 1 June 1722, 2.563).

Irish life and writing Between Swift's return to Dublin in 1714 and the first of his Irish tracts lies a six-year period in which he learned that exile in Ireland would give him the greatest political and artistic challenge of his life. This was the period during which the patriotism of a would-be Englishman was refashioned into an anti-colonial humanitarianism that took Ireland as its point of reference. Unlike many writers of the time Swift forged a programme of political writing based on the evidence at his own doorstep: terrible human deprivation and social injustice. With exquisite timing his *Proposal for the Universal Use of Irish Manufacture* (May 1720) was published to coincide with the celebration of George I's sixtieth birthday. It signalled the end of Swift's retreat from public life, a return to the public world, and warned of much greater oppositional writing to come. He never romanticized the poor, and here, on the first of several occasions, he not only attacked the punitive trade laws which implemented England's crushing mercantilist domination of Ireland's economy but also targeted an exploitative Anglo-Irish gentry and landlord class, as well as a supine working population. Its printer, Edward Waters, was arrested, and at his trial was found not guilty. Chief Justice William Whitshed refused to accept the jury's verdict and sent them back nine times before the issue was finally resolved ten months later by the duke of Grafton, the new lord lieutenant. (Whitshed's betrayal of freedom and country at the abortive trial of another printer, John Harding, four years later was lampooned by Swift in 'Whitshed's motto on his coach … liberty and my native country').

For his 'Summer Rambles' in 1721 Swift chose co. Meath, and there wrote *The Journal*, a poetical account of a summer house party at the Rochforts' Gaulstown House. In the following year he speaks of travelling 400 miles in Ulster and sleeping in thirty different beds between May and October. He was at Clogher with Bishop Stearne, Loughgall with Robert Cope, and Quilca, co. Cavan, with Sheridan. On 2 June 1723 Vanessa died; she made no reference to him in her will but ensured that twenty-eight of his letters to her and seventeen of her drafts to him would survive. Swift set out on a four-month tour of southern Ireland. His apocalyptic mood is perhaps indicated by the melodramatically sublime imagery of his Latin poem 'Carberiae rupes', written at Skull, south-west Cork, in June 1723 (and later translated by Swift's protégé William Dunkin). He spent Christmas with Stella and Rebecca Dingley at Sheridan's Quilca and in January 1724 told Ford that he had 'left the Country of Horses, and am in the flying Island, where I shall not stay long, and my two last Journyes will be soon over'. In other words the fourth part of *Gulliver's Travels*, 'Voyage to the Houyhnhnms', had been written by the end of 1723 but before the third part, 'Voyage to Laputa', which belongs chiefly to 1724.

Swift was also about to intervene again in Anglo-Irish economics and politics, turning his attention to an iron-master called William Wood and his patent (granted on 12 July 1722 after a huge bribe had been paid to King George's mistress) to manufacture copper coins for Ireland. The 'Wood's ha'pence' controversy turned Swift into a popular hero and, borrowing the initials of the Roman tyrannicide patriot Marcus Brutus, his M. B. Drapier became a permanent figure in the history of Irish nationalism, whether Swift liked the status or not. Of the seven

Drapier's letters, the five printed by John Harding are: *A Letter to the Shop-keepers, Tradesmen, Farmers, and Common-people of Ireland … by M. B. Drapier* (March 1724); *A Letter to Mr Harding the Printer* (6 August); *Some Observations … Relating to Wood's Half-Pence* (5 September); *A Letter to the Whole People of Ireland* (22 October, the very day Carteret arrived in Dublin as lord lieutenant with specific instructions to soothe Irish feelings and facilitate the introduction of Wood's coinage); and *A Letter to … Viscount Molesworth* (31 December). His *A Letter to the Lord Chancellor Middleton* and *An Humble Address to both Houses of Parliament* (the former written by 26 October 1724) were not published until Faulkner's edition of Swift's *Works* of 1735. The former is notable for the way in which Swift dropped his pseudonym, flaunted his authorship, and paraded his address at the deanery. On 26 October Carteret offered a £300 reward, valid for six months, for the name of the author of the fourth *Letter*, but it was the printer, Harding, who was arrested, and who consequently died the following spring after his release from gaol. The Drapier's identity was public knowledge even to Carteret, but never officially revealed or received, and in April 1725 his creator was made a freeman of the city of Dublin. He was also appointed to the board of Dublin's charity school, the Blue Coat. In a gesture that reflects another aspect of his deepening Irish identity he had set about cultivating his 3 acre garden, Naboth's Vineyard, near the deanery, and built around it what he claimed to be the best wall in Ireland at the cost of £600. Still convinced that he was now 'out of the World' (19 June 1725, *Correspondence*, ed. Woolley, 2.646), he found that his Dublin friendships were also deepening, particularly those with Dr Patrick Delany at Delville, his villa outside Dublin, with the Grattans at nearby Belcamp, and with the Achesons at Market Hill. From April to October 1725 he, Stella, and Dingley stayed with Sheridan at Quilca, and it was during this visit that Swift completed *Gulliver's Travels*.

To England with Gulliver A full rough draft of Swift's masterpiece had been completed and was being transcribed by 14 August 1725. He told Ford: 'they are admirable Things, and will wonderfully mend the World' (14 Aug 1725, *Correspondence*, ed. Woolley, 2.662). The Irish parliament was formally told that Wood's patent had been cancelled on 7 September. There was no more need for the Drapier, and Swift was now free to prepare for the publication and reception of the *Travels*. He carefully informed his close friends about its purpose. His famous letters to Pope (29 September and 26 November 1725) explained its 'great foundation of Misanthropy (though not in Timon's manner)', and on 6 March he crossed St George's Channel with a fair copy of the manuscript. He spent two days with Pope in London, and during the next two weeks Arbuthnot accompanied him on visits to Lord Chesterfield, the earl of Pulteney, and Bolingbroke—who in April 1725 had returned from exile in France and was soon affecting to praise the life of Horatian retirement at his Dawley farm, near Uxbridge—and again with Pope at Twickenham. On 7 April Swift had an audience with the princess of Wales at Leicester House, and probably met Henrietta Howard,

mistress of the prince of Wales and, after 1724, Pope's neighbour at Marble Hill, Twickenham. He also learned that manuscript copies of 'Cadenus and Vanessa' (largely written at Windsor for Vanessa in 1713 and not intended for publication) were being circulated in Dublin. Along with friends he dined with Sir Robert Walpole at Chelsea and had a specially arranged formal interview with him on 27 April. Courageously, but again unsuccessfully, Swift pressed the case of Ireland's constitutional, economic, and educational inequalities under England's domination. He also stressed the abuses of church patronage by English appointees and the financial and social consequences of absentee landlords in language that strikingly anticipates *A Modest Proposal*. In May, along with Martha Blount and John Gay, he was Pope's guest at Twickenham, playing backgammon with Pope's mother and dining with Bolingbroke and Congreve. He visited Lord Bathurst, and was taken by Pope to Cobham's estate at Stowe. In May he received the news he most dreaded: Stella was seriously ill.

Before setting off for Dublin, where his return as 'the Drapier' was signalled by public acclamation (22 August 1726), Swift had composed a letter (written out by John Gay) to the publisher Benjamin Motte and using the pseudonym 'Richard Sympson', the name not only of Gulliver's cousin but also of one of the publishers of Temple's *Introduction to the History of England* (1695). The clandestine business of getting into print a pseudonymous and satirically explosive political satire entitled *Travels into Several Remote Nations of the World* (known from the start by its more popular title, *Gulliver's Travels*) was managed chiefly by Pope, with the assistance of John Gay and Erasmus Lewis. For speed, and to counter the risk of piracy, Motte used five printing houses (those of Edward Say, Henry Woodfall, James Bettenham, William Pearson, and, for the greatest share, that of Jane Ilive). The first edition appeared on 28 October 1726 in two octavo volumes at the price of 8s. 6d., but with unauthorized deletions and insertions by Andrew Tooke (the brother of Benjamin Tooke jun.), and sold out within a week. Gay wrote: 'From the highest to the lowest it is universally read, from the Cabinet-council to the Nursery' ([7] Nov 1726, *Correspondence*, ed. Woolley, 3.728). Motte followed up with two more octavo editions in 1726 and a duodecimo in 1727, and there was a serialized version which began in the *Penny Post* (25 November 1726). There were two Dublin editions before the end of 1726, each set up from Motte's first edition: the first, by John Hyde of Dame Street, containing Swift's corrections and revisions; the second for Risk, Ewing, and Smith, also of Dame Street, on 1–3 December. The book sold well in French: the first complete translation appeared at The Hague in January 1727, and an abridged adaptation by the Abbé Desfontaines in Paris in April. Swift never saw proofs of the *Travels*, so when he read the second volume he was dismayed by 'several passages which appear to be patched and altered … basely mangled, and abused, and added to, and blotted out by the printer' (ibid., [7] Nov 1726, 3.731). Swift provided Ford with a list of corrections for Motte (3 January 1727), all but two or three of which were adopted for his second edition of 1727. Ford's two copies of the interleaved first edition containing additions and corrections are extant (one in the Forster collection at the V&A, the other in the Pierpont Morgan Library, New York). Swift received from Motte £200 and possibly more from the sales of the book, largely due to Pope's effort at instilling into his friend the principles of 'prudent management' (ibid., 12 May 1735, 4.1156).

Gulliver's Travels is the book by which Swift is chiefly remembered, and it is the record of his own experience in politics under Queen Anne as an Irishman in what G. B. Shaw called 'John Bull's other island'. Its allegorical mode of satire constantly modulates between specific allusions and general types, reflecting characters and events traceable to prototypes in Stuart and Georgian court politics (in Lilliput and Brobdingnag), and to people and events in Swift's own personal life (the king of Brobdingnag as Temple, for example, or the Flying Island as an allegory of English imperialism in Ireland). It also includes moments of farcical low comedy in the Academy of Lagado (part 3) and elsewhere. It is in part 4 (the voyage to the land of the Houyhnhnms) that Swift reaches the supremely vexing point of his whole writing career, mixing comedy with the tragi-comic psychological collapse of Gulliver, the representative Englishman who turns his back on the whole human race because it has failed to live up to the ideal of reason.

Last visit to England Stella survived through 1727, though she remained seriously ill. Ireland itself was stricken by flooding rains, crops had failed for two successive years, the exchange rate had plunged, and there was widespread and acute rural poverty. One piece of good news was that Carteret, whom Swift had come to admire as lord lieutenant, returned to Dublin that November and Swift re-established contact with him. There was not much else to celebrate. For reasons which included his own health and a need to make arrangements for publication of two volumes of the Pope–Swift *Miscellanies* (1727) in prose and verse (designed by Pope to commemorate their friendship, with a title-page monogram combining the initials of their two names), Swift left for England on 9 April. He visited the family home at Goodrich, Herefordshire, and then proceeded to Oxford, to Twickenham by 22 April, and, with the intention of making his first visit to France, equipped himself with letters of introduction from Bolingbroke and Voltaire. News of the death of George I on the day he arrived in London stalled his plans, and he was eventually persuaded by Bolingbroke against the trip. Deafness and giddiness continued to plague him (at Twickenham, with Pope, 12 August), and since his licence of absence from Dublin expired in the first week of October he planned to return on 15 September. News of Stella's worsening illness and experience of his own poor health created an almost unbearable conflict within him. His travel plans were in jeopardy, but there was a possibility of convalescing either in France or at his cousin Patty Rolt's home in London. He eventually retreated to the latter at the end of August. On Monday 18 September he set off for

Ireland, reaching Holyhead six days later, and there was delayed for what seems to have been one of the most traumatic weeks of his life. Out of raging impatience, forced immobility, and the darkest foreboding, he wrote down an extraordinary and magnificently detailed record of this week in a stolen notebook, now known as *The Holyhead Journal*.

Stella died on 28 January 1728. Swift was desolate, too distraught even to attend her evening funeral service in St Patrick's, and moved to a corner of the deanery which screened him from all sight and sound coming from the cathedral.

Dublin literary life Gay's *The Beggar's Opera*, for which Swift had (apocryphally) provided the first hint of a 'Newgate [or Quaker] pastoral', opened triumphantly on 29 January 1728 at Lincoln's Inn Fields, with a record-breaking run of sixty-two performances: 'The Beggars Opera hath knockt down Gulliver, I hope to see Popes Dullness knock down the Beggars Opera, but not till it hath fully done its Jobb', Swift wrote on 28 March (*Correspondence*, ed. Woolley, 3.807). The third and last volume of the Pope–Swift *Miscellanies* appeared on 7 or 8 March 1728, and on 9 March Swift returned to the national tragedy with *A Short View of the State of Ireland*, a 'factual' listing of how the case of Ireland contradicted every one of fourteen received indicators of national prosperity. Pope's *Dunciad* appeared on 18 May, and the *Variorum Dunciad* of the following year was to be dedicated to Swift as 'Dean, Drapier, Bickerstaff, or Gulliver'. Dublin literary life was also enhanced by what Swift called a 'Triumfeminate' of bluestockings. He went out of his way to sponsor the poetical career of Mrs Mary Barber, wife of a Dublin woollen draper, and implausibly denominated her 'by far the best Poet of her Sex in England' (ibid., 2 Aug 1733, 3.1058). He permitted his commendatory letter about her to the earl of Orrery to stand as the preface to her *Poems on Several Occasions* (1734). He also encouraged Constantia Grierson, who was, until her early death on 2 December 1732 at the age of twenty-six, a classical scholar and editor of Terence and Tacitus, a minor poet, and wife of the printer George Grierson. The third member of the trio was Mrs E. Sican, a grocer's wife, a 'good reader and a judge' whose skills were rather more domestic than poetical.

With Thomas Sheridan Swift collaborated on a 'weekly' Dublin periodical, *The Intelligencer*. Printed by Sarah Harding (widow of the printer of *The Drapier's Letters*), it comprised twenty numbers running from 11 May 1728 to 10 May 1729. Swift wrote nos. 1 and 3 (the latter a defence of *The Beggar's Opera*), 5, 7, and 8 (the verse attack on Richard Tighe, 'Mad Mullinix and Timothy', is Swift's), 9 and 10 (Swift's contribution is 'Tim and the Fables', but not the last four lines), 15 (a reprint of *A Short View of the State of Ireland*, an analysis of the perilous Irish economy), 19 (on the shortage of silver coin in Ireland), and 20. From June 1728 to February 1729 he stayed at Market Hill, near Armagh, as the guest of Sir Arthur and Lady Acheson, as he did from June to October 1729, when his return to Dublin was celebrated with bellringing, bonfires, and illuminations, and yet again from the end of June to the end of September

1730. Here he wrote the 'Market Hill' poems, full of domestic and daily detail: 'I hate *Dublin*, and love the Retirement here, and the Civility of my Hosts', he remarked (2 Aug 1728, *Correspondence*, ed. Woolley, 3.819). In 1729 he went so far as to purchase land from Sir Arthur Acheson with the intention of building himself a house there. The scheme did not materialize, but the story of it remains in the poem called 'Drapier's Hill' (1729).

Swift returned to the vexed question of Ireland's manufacturing industries in 1729, in *A proposal that all the ladies and women in Ireland should appear constantly in Irish manufactures* (published 1765). In October 1729, against the background of the recent famine, in 1727, and Stella's death in January 1728, he wrote (as usual, anonymously) an icily rational fourteen pages of bleak and vertiginous irony describing the most appalling human suffering wrapped in the precise terms of a mathematical model: *A modest proposal for preventing the children of poor people from being a burthen to their parents, or the country, and for making them beneficial to the publick*. This, the most famous pamphlet in the English language and the finest example of Swift's transgressive irony, proposes infanticide and cannibalism as the solutions to Ireland's (apparent) problems of poverty, over-population, a crumbling economy, and food shortage. Here, the venerable economic adage that people are the riches of a nation is applied with a ruthless literal logic, so that babies raised in poor and Catholic families may be 'consumed' by the rich Anglo-Irish protestant class, just as the landlords have already 'consumed' their tenant-parents. The impartial narrator, whose wife is past childbearing age, expects that as a reward for his patriotism a statue will be set up for him in Dublin as a 'Preserver of the Nation' (*Prose Works*, 12.109).

In 1729 Swift met Matthew Pilkington and his wife, Laetitia, whose *Memoirs*, published in 1748–54, were to provide much garbled information on Swift's later years. In March 1731 he looked back on two years of more or less uninterrupted giddiness and periodic deafness. Bolingbroke informed him that efforts were still being made to get him an English preferment, and Drapier's clubs were set up in and around Dublin to celebrate Swift as the champion of Ireland. Notorious and notable poems from this period include 'The Lady's Dressing Room', 'A Beautiful Young Nymph Going to Bed', 'Strephon and Chloe', and 'Cassinus and Peter', dubbed misogynist by some and feminist by others. There is also the raging, levelling satire of 'The Place of the Damn'd' and 'The Day of Judgement'. He had by him two unfinished prose pieces dating back to 1704, *A Complete Collection of Genteel and Ingenious Conversation* (published 1738) and *Directions to Servants* (1745). About the end of the year he sent John Gay '3 acts [properly, scenes] of a play called the players rehearsal' (Elias, 71–2). This was *The Rehearsal at Goatham*, a ten-scene farce based on Master Peter's puppet show in *Don Quixote*. The final volume of the Pope–Swift *Miscellanies* appeared in October 1732, and Swift had by this date met his future biographer the earl of Orrery (14 October).

Swift's letters from this period are increasingly written about the past. When news of the death of John Gay on 4 December reached him Swift was unable to open the letter from Pope and Arbuthnot bearing the news for a full five days, 'by an impulse foreboding some misfortune' (Ehrenpreis, 3.734). As one of the governors of the city's hackney coaches, carts, and carriages, he enjoyed preferential treatment by the coachmen of Dublin, but this pleasure, along with his delight in evening walking, had to be curtailed because of dizziness. Swift nevertheless continued to regard the liberty of St Patrick's (a precinct independent of the archbishop's administration) as a little world under his own absolute control.

A month after its London publication in April, Swift denied writing *The Life and Character of Doctor Swift: Written by Himself*, possibly because he had intended the more detailed and libellous *Verses on the Death of Dr. Swift* (1739) to be published posthumously. It may also have been a ploy to focus public attention on the latter, the 'authentic' version, without doubt one of his best poems. The last stanza of the poem includes the lines

> He gave what little Wealth he had,
> To Build a House for Fools and Mad

—a signal of his intention to provide Dublin with a madhouse of its own. His will, he said, had 'settled my whole Fortune on the City, in trust for building and maintaining an hospital for Ideots and Lunaticks' (16–17 July 1735, *Correspondence*, ed. Woolley, 4.1176), and by the spring of 1736 he had £7500 out at interest, sufficient for both a site and for running costs. St Patrick's Hospital was not opened until 19 September 1757. It had a provision for fifty patients and was sited next to Dr Steevens's Hospital.

George Faulkner, the enterprising printer of the successful bi-weekly *Dublin Journal* from 1725 to 1775 (Swift's 'Prince of Dublin Printers'; 16 Feb 1734, *Correspondence*, ed. Woolley, 3.1080), proposed a subscription edition of Swift's works in four volumes. Swift indulged, he said, what he could not prevent, and although he would have preferred publication in England, he nevertheless actively assisted in Faulkner's project, particularly as it offered a chance to correct *Gulliver's Travels* from Ford's interleaved copy. Three volumes were published at the end of 1734, the fourth in January 1735, and these are collectively regarded by his modern editors (Davis and Williams) as the most accurate and most important authorized edition. Faulkner also acted as a trusted carrier of Swift's letters to Pope and John Barber in England. Lawfully recognized ownership of literary property did not exist in Ireland between 1670 and 1800, yet Swift condoned Faulkner's action in reprinting London publications because it triggered his sense of injustice (the operation of the English copyright law was yet another aspect of England's indifference to the interests and basic rights of its dependent colonies). Swift's own position in Dublin's print world was unassailable. When the Walpole administration discovered that he was the author of *An Epistle to a Lady*—which had included a sharp attack on both Walpole and his ministry from lines 133 onwards—the possibility of arresting Swift for libel was canvassed. The unlikelihood of extracting Swift peacefully from Ireland without deploying an army determined that the idea be dropped.

Nevertheless, the bookseller Motte was taken in charge. As another measure of Swift's symbiotic relationship with the world of print in Dublin, he supplied a preface for Shelton's and Blunt's 1733 translation of *Don Quixote*, published by Sarah Hyde (widow of John Hyde, the publisher of the first Irish *Travels*), J. Dobson, and R. Owen. This was also the period of the Anglo-Latin letters, joint letters, and occasional Anglo-Greek letters between Swift and Sheridan. Arbuthnot died on 27 February 1735, and in the same year Mrs Brent, Swift's faithful housekeeper since his days in Kilroot. She was succeeded by Mrs Ridgeway, although it is clear that his cousin, the recently widowed Martha Whiteway (1690–1768), the daughter of Swift's uncle Adam by his second wife, was assuming control in the deanery. She co-wrote with Swift a number of amusing and sharply expressed letters to and from Swift and others in the last ten years of his life, in which her own ironic wit echoes Swift's own. Increasingly, from 1740 to the end, it was Mrs Whiteway who wrote for Swift.

On 7 February 1736 Swift wrote to Pope: 'I have no body now left but you: Pray be so kind as to out-live me, and then die as soon as you please, but without pain, and let us meet in a better place, if my religion will permit' (*Correspondence*, ed. Woolley, 4.1239). And on 2 December to Pope he admitted: 'years and Infirmatyes have quite broke me. I mean that odious continual disorder in my Head. I neither read, nor write; nor remember, nor converse. All I have left is to walk, and ride' (ibid., 4.1304). He also continued the habit of reading Job 3: 3 on his birthday ('Let the day perish wherein I was born'). Nevertheless the volcano was still active. When landowners in the Irish House of Commons tried to deprive the clergy of their legal tithes of pasturage Swift turned on them with extraordinarily vitriolic energy in 'A character, panegyric, and description of the Legion Club' (in manuscript circulation in Dublin before London miscellany publication in June). His Irish patriotism was again recognized when he was made a freeman of the city of Cork in August 1737. The ageing Swift nevertheless maintained a lively interest in the younger generation of Swifts: there was his young cousin and future biographer Deane Swift, whom he introduced to Pope in a letter of 28 April 1739; and William Swift, fourth son of Swift's cousin Godwin, a student at Trinity College before being called to the Irish bar. He also began a correspondence with George Lyttelton. The fifth and sixth volumes of Faulkner's works of Swift appeared in April 1738. Another of his close friends, Thomas Sheridan, died on 10 October 1738. In January 1739 Dr William King, with Pope's active collaboration and Swift's consequent irritation, mangled the text of *Verses on the Death of Dr. Swift* for London publication, obliging him to publish the authentic text in Dublin; it was printed by Faulkner in February. Alderman John Barber presented the Jervas portrait of Swift to Oxford University in early 1739, and the St Patrick's chapter paid for Bindon's 1739 full-length portrait, now hanging in the deanery house. Swift thus lived long enough to savour fully the deserved rewards of his literary fame in Ireland.

Decline On 4 December 1739 Swift asked Faulkner if he knew the whereabouts of the manuscript of *Directions to Servants*, and towards the end of 1740 there were additional and increasing signs of Swift's distress and of a diminishing capacity to control his own affairs. There were disputes about his literary property and allegations by the earl of Orrery that Swift's letters (and Pope's to Swift) had been and were being stolen, possibly by the Revd Dr Francis Wilson, one of Swift's prebendaries then living at the deanery, and evidently a man capable of extraordinary brutality and cunning. Orrery also alleged that theft extended to some of those already printed in Faulkner's *Letters to and from Dr. J. Swift … 1714 to 1738* (13 June 1741). On 5 May 1740 Swift made his last will, superseding all earlier wills and including the now celebrated Latin inscription for his monument:

> *Hic* depositum est Corpus
> IONATHAN SWIFT S. T. D.
> Hujus Ecclesiæ Cathedralis
> Decani,
> *Ubi* sæva Indignatio
> Ulterius
> Cor lacerare nequit.
> Abi Viator
> Et imitare, si poteris,
> Strenuum pro virili
> Libertatis Vindicatorem.
> Obiit 19° Die Mensis Octobris
> A.D. 1745. Anno Ætatis 78°.
> (Here lies the body of Jonathan Swift, Doctor of Sacred Theology, Dean of this Cathedral, where savage indignation can no longer tear at his heart. Pass on, traveller, and, if you can, emulate his tireless efforts in defence of liberty. He died on the 19th day of the month of October, 1745, at the age of 78.)

A freely paraphrased English version was written by W. B. Yeats as 'Swift's Epitaph' (1931). Annuities were to be paid to Rebecca Dingley, land bought for his planned St Patrick's Hospital for 'Idiots, Lunaticks Incurables', and its financial future provided for. Bequests of land or money were provided for Martha Whiteway (who was to receive his repeating gold watch), his housekeeper Anne Ridgeway (daughter of Mrs Brent), Mary Harrison (Martha's daughter), and the Whiteway family. Memorial presents were to go to Pope (a miniature of Robert Harley, earl of Oxford), to Harley's son Edward (two gold medals), to the earl of Orrery, to his cousin Deane Swift, to Mrs Barber (a medal of Queen Anne), and to a group of Irish clergy including the Grattans and Delany; the Revd James Stopford was to receive Swift's portrait of Charles I by Van Dyck, and John Worrall his best beaver hat. In the summer of 1742 Swift's last decline began, so that by 22 November, according to Mrs Whiteway, his 'understanding was quite gone' (*Correspondence*, ed. Woolley, 4.1501). He lost weight, his memory was now permanently impaired, he was walking in his room obsessively for anything up to ten hours a day, and he was sleepless, suffering from boils, and in an agony of pain in one of his eyes, before becoming listless and generally inactive. After an investigation into the state of his body and mind (20 May 1742) guardians were appointed. A series of strokes meant that for the remaining three years of his life he spoke little. His last words were recorded by Deane Swift and included: 'I am what I am' and 'I am a fool' (ibid., 4 April 1744, 4.1506). Swift died aged nearly seventy-eight on 19 October 1745 and was buried three days later according to his wishes, on the south side of the middle aisle of St Patrick's. His death mask, taken just before the post-mortem and later presented by T. G. Wilson, is in Trinity College Library, Dublin (see Johnston, facing p. 186, for an illustration).

As a satirist Swift has no equal in English literature for range, subtlety, and power. His life and works continue to vex as well as instruct and amuse his readers. Those who printed and disseminated his work (Waters, Harding, Barber, Motte, Faulkner) fully recognized the incendiary nature of his writing and ran very severe risks: arrest and gaol were the common experiences, and one of them paid the ultimate price. A further sign of the controversial nature of both the man and the writing was the occasionally acrimonious flurry of critical biographies that appeared so promptly after his death: three full-length studies between 1752 and 1755 as well as the material included in Laetitia Pilkington's *Memoirs* of 1748–54. As early as 1726 Pope composed verse on Swift's ancestors and in a series of five 'Verses on *Gulliver's Travels*' (including one from Gulliver's wife, Mary), inaugurated a still flourishing genre of continuations in plays, poems, novels, and satirical imitations, the most notable of which has been Matthew Hodgart's *A new voyage to the country of the Houyhnhnms; being the fifth part of the 'Travels into several remote parts of the world' by Lemuel Gulliver* (1969)—close enough to the original to fool some unwary readers. Orrery, the first biographer, was quick to sense the public interest in his subject and had been compiling notes for a book during the last three years of Swift's life. Deane Swift's *Essay* was the last of the biographical essays (1755) that could claim any personal connection with its subject, but others of significance have appeared regularly in each generation: Samuel Johnson's in 1779, Thomas Sheridan's in 1784, Walter Scott's in 1814, Henry Craik's in 1882, John Middleton Murry's in 1954, and so on, until Irvin Ehrenpreis's three-volume Freudian critical biography of 1962–83.

Rumours and legends about Swift's parentage, alleged marriage, misanthropy, and madness started early and developed freely, not least during the Victorian period. In Swift's own century, and although fully sensitive to both his brilliance and his power, Dr Johnson, in *Lives of the Poets*, sharply criticized aspects of both Swift's writing and his personality, even managing to make his insistence upon personal hygiene sound eccentric. For his physical satire in the fourth part of *Gulliver's Travels* Swift was censured, notably in a lurid lecture by Thackeray published in 1853, in which he recommended his readers avoid reading it altogether ('the moral is horrible, shameful, unmanly; and giant and as great as this Dean is I say we should hoot him'), and in which Swift is demonized and Stella ('Who does not love her?') sentimentalized as the gloomy dean's innocent victim ('Swift', in *The English Humourists of the Eighteenth Century*). He has been commonly demonized for his poems on the body (both male and female), verse which still has the power to disturb, if no longer to shock. He was psychologized by Middleton Murry (who coined the famous phrase 'excremental vision' in 1954), savaged by both Aldous Huxley and D. H. Lawrence for an alleged dislike of what Huxley called 'the bowels', and more recently dubbed misogynist by some feminist critics. He has been commended for resisting the brutalities of colonialism in *A Modest Proposal* and in Gulliver's fourth voyage. As a member of the Anglo-Irish protestant ascendancy in an overwhelmingly Catholic country Swift sustained a powerful critique of what he called 'Fair LIBERTY' (*Verses on the Death of Dr. Swift*, 1731) as both a humane ideal for all and a means by which an oligarchy disguised its rapaciousness.

His satire is meant to bite. Coolly dispassionate readings of Swift are not common, and hardly possible. For a writer who described human life to Pope as 'a ridiculous tragedy, which is the worst kind of composition' (20 April 1731, *Correspondence*, ed. Woolley, 3.915), it is hardly surprising that paradoxes are characteristic of his writing and of responses to it. Of all the works of eighteenth-century English literature, it is probably *Gulliver's Travels* that is the best-known and most widely read today. Its printed and visual representations, always more or less censored, have been universally popular with younger readers. It was the subject of one of the first fully animated colour films ever made (director Dave Fleischer, Paramount, 1939), and there have been later film versions: in 1959 (*Three Worlds of Gulliver*); in 1976 (*Gulliver's Travels*: a live action and animation version aimed at children, and starring Richard Harris); and in 1995 as a television mini-series, not aimed at children.

Past and recent biographers have responded to a darker side of Swift. One has written of Swift and the modern imagination: 'He left us with the carefully cultivated image of a lonely misanthrope, chiselling his savage indignation on his tombstone, and leaving, as his benefactions to mankind, a privy and a madhouse' (Nokes, 413). Yet he is one of the very best letter-writers in English, and his correspondence speaks of a vivid and intensely sociable engagement with the public and private worlds about him. His poetry—raucous, acerbic, challenging, amusing, and occasionally moving—includes the most vivid representation of the human voice in any contemporary poetry. Together the letters and poems constitute an autobiography of the man. His work has provoked strong responses from each generation of readers, and he is one of those writers whose effect on our minds and imagination will not go away. In the words of a fellow Irishman, who also believed that Swift was the founding figure in Irish political nationalism, 'Swift haunts me; he is always just around the next corner' (W. B. Yeats, *The Words upon the Window-Pane*, 1934).   CLIVE PROBYN

Sources *The correspondence of Jonathan Swift*, ed. H. Williams, 5 vols. (1963–5) · *The correspondence of Jonathan Swift*, ed. D. Woolley, 4 vols. (1999–2004) · I. Ehrenpreis, *Swift: the man, his works and the age*, 3 vols. (1962–83) · *The poems of Jonathan Swift*, ed. H. Williams, 2nd edn, 3 vols. (1958) • D. Johnston, *In search of Swift* (1959) • L. A. Landa, *Swift and the Church of Ireland* (1954) • J. Swift, *Journal to Stella*, ed. H. Williams, 2 vols. (1948) • 'Family of Swift (1728–38)', *The prose works of Jonathan Swift, 5: Miscellaneous and autobiographical pieces, fragments and marginalia*, ed. H. Davis (1962), 187–95 • *The prose works of Jonathan Swift*, ed. H. Davis and others, 16 vols. (1939–74) • A. C. Elias, *Swift at Moor Park* (1982) • *A tale of a tub*, ed. A. C. Guthkelch and D. Nichol Smith (1958) • F. Ellis, ed., *Swift vs. Mainwaring: 'The Examiner' and 'The Medley'* (1985) • J. Woolley, ed., *Jonathan Swift and Thomas Sheridan, The Intelligencer* (1992) • C. Probyn, ed., *The art of Jonathan Swift* (1978) • H. Teerink, *A bibliography of the writings … of Jonathan Swift* (1937), rev. 2nd edn (1963) • J. Boyle, *Remarks on … Jonathan Swift* (1752) • C. M. P. G. N. S. T. N. S., 'Anecdotes of Dean Swift and Miss Johnson', *GM*, 1st ser., 27 (1757), 487–91 • P. Delany, *Observations on Lord Orrery's 'Remarks on … Swift'* (1754) • A. Downie, *Robert Harley and the press* (1979) • H. Craik, *The life of Jonathan Swift* (1882) • F. Falkiner, 'On the portraits, busts and engravings of Swift and their artists', in *Prose works of Jonathan Swift*, ed. T. Scott, 12 (1908), 3–18 • J. Lyon, 'Materials for a life of Dr. Swift', 1765 • D. Nokes, *Jonathan Swift: a hypocrite reversed* (1985) • *The letters of Jonathan Swift to Charles Ford*, ed. D. Nichol Smith (1935) • J. W. Phillips, *Printing and bookselling in Dublin, 1670–1800* (1998) • T. Sheridan, *Remarks on the life and writings of … Swift* (1784) • D. Swift, *An essay upon the life, writings and character of … Swift* (1755) • *Faulkner's Dublin Journal* (22 Oct 1745) • S. Le Brocquy, *Cadenus: a reassessment in the light of new evidence of the relationships between Swift, Stella, and Vanessa* (1962) • J. Forster, *The life of Jonathan Swift, 1: 1667–1711* (1875)

Archives BL, corresp., Add. MSS 4804–4806, 38671 • Bodl. Oxf., corresp., literary MSS, and papers • CUL, corresp. and literary MSS [transcripts and copies] • Harvard U., Houghton L., papers • Hunt. L., letters and literary MSS • JRL, corresp. and papers • King's Cam., catalogue of his library • King's Cam., letters and MSS • Longleat House, Wiltshire, letters • Morgan L., papers • NL Ire., letters [copies] • Trinity Cam., corresp., literary MSS, and papers • V&A NAL, diary, literary MSS, personal accounts, corresp., and letters [letters: copies] • Yale U., Beinecke L., personal records and receipts | BL, corresp. with Lord Hartley, MS loan 29 • BL, letters to first Lord Oxford, Add. MS 70292 • BL, letters to Rochfort family, Add. MS 38671 • BL, corresp. with countess of Suffolk, Add. MS 22625 • BL, corresp. with Esther Van Homrigh, Add. MS 39839 • Longleat House, Warminster, letters • NL Ire., corresp. with Thomas Sheridan • Yale U., Beinecke L., letters to Samuel Gerrard

Likenesses C. Jervas, oils, *c*.1710, Bodl. Oxf.; version, NPG • C. Jervas, oils, *c*.1718, NPG • F. Bindon, oils, *c*.1724, NG Ire. • I. Whood, drawing, 1730, NG Ire. [*see illus.*] • A. van Haecken, mezzotint, 1740 (after Markham), BM, NPG • death mask, 1745, TCD • attrib. F. Bindon, oils, NG Ire. • C. Jervas, oils, NG Ire. • J. van Nost, marble bust, NG Ire. • L. Roubiliac, marble bust, TCD • B. Wilson, etching (after T. Barber), BM, NPG; repro. in Lord Orrery, *Remarks on the life and writings of Swift* (1752)

Swift, Sir Rigby Philip Watson

Swift, Sir Rigby Philip Watson (1874–1937), judge, was born on 7 June 1874 at St Helens, Lancashire, the eighth child of Thomas Swift, solicitor, of St Helens, and the eldest child of his second marriage with Emily, daughter of Philip Daft, of Nottingham. Swift's father was called to the bar late in life and had a considerable practice on the northern circuit chiefly in criminal and licensing work in and around Liverpool, where he lived during his later years.

Swift was educated at Parkfield School, Liverpool, and later obtained the LLB degree of London University. His training in the law was unusual: he left school at seventeen and entered his father's chambers in Harrington Street, Liverpool; father and son remained together until the death of the former in 1899. Swift was called to the bar by Lincoln's Inn in 1895 within a month of reaching twenty-one. His proposer was Sir John Rigby, a cousin of his father. In due course he joined the northern circuit. At that time, and for the next twenty or thirty years, the circuit was probably stronger than at any other period in its history. Swift soon got work: he was faithful in his attendance in the crown court at assize time and was always ready to undertake a dock defence or to look after the interests of an accused at the request of the judge, and from this he gained invaluable experience in advocacy.

In the early years of the twentieth century Swift made rapid progress, and in 1910 he applied to the lord chancellor for silk and moved to London, taking chambers at 1 Garden Court in the Temple. His claims to silk were great: he had made for himself a very substantial practice and had held it; his work was varied; on the *nisi prius* side he had attained a position seldom reached by any junior on the circuit; he was recognized as an eminent advocate. He was still young, however, and probably for that reason had to wait two years for silk; it was not until 1912 that he was appointed in the same list as Gordon Hewart (afterwards lord chief justice) who had practised up to that time in Manchester. The appearance of these two new king's counsel meant a great change on the northern circuit. For a few years, until the claims of London called, they were opposed to each other in nearly all the work of importance. Swift's powers as an advocate grew and it would have been difficult to find a better jury advocate anywhere; and his practice was by no means confined to jury work.

Meanwhile, in 1902, Swift had married Beatrice, daughter of John Banks Walmsley, a Liverpool shipowner; they had no children. Having been defeated at the general election in January 1910, Swift was elected to parliament as Conservative member for St Helens at the general election of December 1910. He remained member until his defeat at the general election of 1918, but he was not active in debate. He was recorder of Wigan from 1915 to 1920.

For some years Swift had an extensive practice in London and his services were in great demand. It was no surprise, therefore, when, on the recommendation of Lord Birkenhead, he was appointed a judge of the King's Bench Division of the High Court in June 1920, and his appointment was welcomed. He was forty-six and for a time was the youngest judge on the bench. He certainly added strength to the judiciary: a sound knowledge of the law, wide experience of courts and of procedure, a quick brain, a great knowledge of human nature, and a keen sense of humour enabled him to fill the position in a way that made everything appear easy.

During his seventeen years on the bench Swift was frequently in the public eye and presided over many trials of general interest. His power over juries was soon apparent; this was chiefly due to his ability to marshal the facts of any case, however complicated, and to put them before the jury in an attractive way. He had not long been appointed when in 1921 there came before him a case in which seventeen members of the Irish Republican Army were charged with treason-felony at Manchester. It was no easy task, but in handling it he was at his best. In *Nunan* v. *Southern Railway Company* (1923) the widow of a workman sued the company for damages under Lord Campbell's act in respect of the death of her husband who had been killed in an accident on the railway. The husband was travelling on a workman's ticket on which was printed a condition to the effect that 'the liability of the Company is limited to a sum not exceeding £100'. Swift decided that, although the condition would have prevailed in an action by the husband, it did not avail in an action by the widow, and his judgment was upheld in the Court of Appeal. In *R.* v. *Woolmington* (1935) a young husband was tried at Bristol for the murder of his wife by shooting. At an earlier trial at Taunton before Sir William Finlay the jury had failed to arrive at an agreement. Swift told the jury:

> All homicide is presumed to be malicious, and murder, unless the contrary appears from circumstances of alleviation, excuse or justification. In every charge of murder the fact of killing being first proved, all the circumstances of accident, necessity, or infirmity, are to be satisfactorily proved by the prisoner unless they arise out of the evidence produced against him, for the law presumeth the fact to have been founded in malice until the contrary appeareth.   (Archbold, citing Foster)

Later he said:

> The Crown has to satisfy you that this woman died at the prisoner's hands. They must satisfy you beyond any reasonable doubt. If they satisfy you of that, then he has to show that there are circumstances to be found in the evidence which has been given from the witness box in this case, which alleviate his crime so that it is only manslaughter or which excuse the homicide altogether by showing that it was a pure accident.

The jury convicted the prisoner and he was sentenced to death. After an appeal to the court of criminal appeal had failed, the House of Lords quashed the conviction, holding that the direction to the jury was wrong, and that the onus of proof always remained on the prosecution in such a case. Although Swift was held to be wrong there was considerable authority in support of his view, and he had followed a principle laid down 150 years before. In 1935 Swift was one of four judges summoned to the House of Lords to advise on the 'trial by peers' of Lord de Clifford on a motor manslaughter charge.

Swift was a kindly man and gave away much of what he earned: seldom did he turn down an appeal for help, and many a member of the bar who fell on hard times had cause to be grateful to him. He liked above all things to see a young man doing his work well, and he never forgot one who showed promise. No one did more than he to encourage the young advocate: he often said that there ought to be something in the nature of a school of advocacy; it was just as necessary, he urged, to teach men how to speak and how to present a case as to teach them the law. He always retained a strong Lancastrian accent or dialect and a robust, blunt Lancastrian manner, which endeared him to the legal profession and beyond.

Happily married, Swift deplored divorce but also publicly deplored the 'cruel' contemporary divorce laws which did not recognize the fact of irretrievable breakdown. He lived just long enough to see the passing of A. P. Herbert's Matrimonial Causes Act of 1937, which provided some amelioration while seeking to bolster the institution of marriage.

Swift always liked to go his old circuit and until the end of his career he went to the far north at least every two years. From 1917 he lived at Crowborough in Sussex, where he took a keen interest in the golf club and in his farm. He was fond of meeting old friends; he enjoyed entertaining, and he lived well. This perhaps affected his health, and during the last few years of his life he showed signs of failing and was apt to become somewhat testy. Yet he remained all the time a personality, strong and fearless.

Swift was made a bencher of Lincoln's Inn in 1916 and would have been treasurer had he lived a little longer. In 1935 he received the honorary degree of LLD from Liverpool University. His wife's death in April 1937 was a blow from which he never really recovered, and he died at Crowborough on 19 October 1937.

J. E. SINGLETON, *rev.* ALEC SAMUELS

Sources E. S. Fay, *Life of Mr Justice Swift* (1939) · *The Times* (20 Oct 1937)
Wealth at death £25,201 5s. 5d.: probate, 13 Dec 1937, *CGPLA Eng. & Wales*

Swift, Robert (*c.*1534–1599), Church of England clergyman, was born at Rotherham into a family of Yorkshire gentry. The fact that in 1549 he was admitted to St John's College, Cambridge, where he was a pupil of James Pilkington, and graduated BA in early 1553, suggests he was born *c.*1534. Subsequently he became a fellow and appears to have been part of the advanced protestant circle which gathered around the master, Thomas *Lever. He may have followed Lever to the continent after the accession of Queen Mary. Certainly he married Lever's daughter Anne, and during this period of exile obtained the degree of LLB at Louvain, his studies apparently supported by some English merchants residing at Antwerp.

When Swift returned to England he obtained the patronage of James Pilkington, by now bishop of Durham, who appointed him his diocesan chancellor in 1561 and promoted him to a prebend in Durham Cathedral and the wealthy rectory of Sedgefield in the following year. Ordained deacon and priest in 1563, Swift became a loyal supporter of the bishop and brought his protestant convictions firmly to bear upon his work. In 1566 he was summoned before the high commission court at York accused of vestiarian offences, and in 1567 he caused consternation at Sedgefield by removing the communion table from the chancel, the churchwardens calling him 'a hinderer and no furtherer of God's service' (Raine, *Depositions*, 119). The extensive Catholic revivalism at Sedgefield recorded in 1569 was in part due to Swift's puritanical innovations.

Swift also played an active part in the administration of Durham Cathedral where he became a close ally of the dean, William Whittingham. He recovered his corpes land (the cathedral estate allocated for his maintenance as a prebendary) in a suit before the council of the north in

1566, and during 1572 and 1575 was a substantial beneficiary from the controversial 'lotteries' of leases distributed by the chapter. Swift was alleged to have received
£411 13s. 4d. from eleven leases granted in this way. During
the bitter controversies which beset the cathedral
between 1577 and 1579, following Pilkington's death,
Swift remained loyal to Dean Whittingham.

The new bishop, Richard Barnes, an implacable opponent of Pilkington and Whittingham, replaced Swift as
chancellor in 1577 and called into question 'all evil, cruel
and injurious dealing of the Chancellor of this diocese'
(Raine, *Ecclesiastical Proceedings*, 23). There is little independent evidence to support this charge. On the contrary,
Swift's surviving book of precedents suggests that he
attempted to reform the consistory and limit the fees
taken by its officers. During the 1580s Swift's energies
were directed principally towards Sedgefield and his cathedral duties. He prosecuted several suits to safeguard his
endowments and was never backward in confronting
even influential local gentry, such as Sir George Frevile.

Although he allowed the chapel at Fishburn to fall into
decay, other of Swift's actions were benevolent, especially
his endowment of Sedgefield School in 1596 for the education of 'all such poor men's children ... not deemed able to
pay their school hire' (Surtees, 3.419). He also intended to
leave money to St John's College, Cambridge, but his
death in 1599 intervened, and it was left to his widow to
make the gift under the terms of her will in 1607. He was
buried in Durham Cathedral under the organ loft on the
north side of the choir door. Two sketches in his book of
precedents dated 1574 may represent Swift in the dress of
a prebendary and chancellor respectively. The Swift family appears to have been close and supportive. Robert
Swift's only son, Robert, an attorney of Lincoln's Inn, died
in 1600 paying tribute to his 'most lovinge and kinde
parentes' (Hodgson, 176). A daughter, Anne, married
Stephen Hegge.   DAVID MARCOMBE

Sources D. Marcombe, 'The dean and chapter of Durham, 1558–
1603', PhD diss., U. Durham, 1973 • Venn, *Alum. Cant.*, 1/4 • C. H.
Garrett, *The Marian exiles: a study in the origins of Elizabethan puritanism* (1938) • *The registers of Cuthbert Tunstall ... and James Pilkington*, ed.
G. Hinde, SurtS, 161 (1952) • high commission act books, 3, 4, Borth.
Inst. • [J. Raine], ed., *Depositions and other ecclesiastical proceedings
from the courts of Durham, extending from 1311 to the reign of Elizabeth*,
SurtS, 21 (1845) • W. H. Longstaffe and J. Booth, eds., *Halmota
prioratus Dunelmensis*, SurtS, 82 (1889) • *The injunctions and other ecclesiastical proceedings of Richard Barnes, bishop of Durham*, ed. [J. Raine],
SurtS, 22 (1850) • W. Hutchinson, *The history and antiquities of the
county palatine of Durham*, [2nd edn], 2 (1823) • R. Surtees, *The history
and antiquities of the county palatine of Durham*, 3 (1823) • [J. C.
Hodgson], ed., *Wills and inventories from the registry at Durham*, 3,
SurtS, 112 (1906) • Durham Cath. CL, Hunter MS 18; Raine MS 124 •
U. Durham L., archives and special collections, register of wills 6,
fol. 253
Archives Durham Cath. CL, book of forms, Hunter MS 18 • Dur-
ham Cath. CL, book of forms, Raine MS 124
Likenesses sketches, 1574, Durham Cath. CL, Hunter MS 18

Swift, Dame Sarah Ann (1854–1937), nurse and a founder
of the Royal College of Nursing, was born on 22 November
1854 at Blossom Hall, Kirton Skeldyke, near Boston, Lincolnshire, the second of the three children of Robert

Dame Sarah Ann Swift (1854–1937), by Herbert James Draper

Swift, a landowner and independent farmer, and his wife,
Mary Ann Lamb. She attended Cowley School (1860?–1870)
at Donington, near Boston, and at the age of twenty-two
went to the Dundee Royal Infirmary to train as a nurse
(1877–80). The matron of the infirmary at the time was
Rebecca Strong, who had reorganized the nurses' training
in line with the latest developments. On completing her
training Swift's first job was as sister-in-charge of the
Home for Incurables in Dundee, where she remained for
six years. She then worked briefly at the City Hospital
North, Liverpool, and at the London Fever Hospital.

In 1889 Swift went to America to study nursing practices
in New York, and later travelled to Constantinople, where
she worked in the British Seamen's Hospital. On her
return to England, in 1890, she went to Guy's Hospital,
London, and after completing the one-year course for paying probationers she was appointed an assistant matron.
The following year she was appointed lady superintendent of the private staff, and in 1900 she was appointed
matron. Her years as matron (1900–09) were a period of
achievement both for herself and for the hospital. Her
administrative abilities and financial acumen served
Guy's well at a time of great development in medicine and
nursing, and when the hospital was expanding rapidly.
She believed that nursing was a profession with great
potential for women, and she worked to improve the status and working conditions of the nurses. One of her main
concerns was the lack of pensions for nurses, and she
became involved in several schemes to provide financial
relief and retirement homes for nurses, including the

Royal National Pension Fund for Nurses and the Nurses' Memorial to King Edward VII. She also established sports clubs and recreational facilities for the nurses and a Past and Present Nurses' League, which she used to develop professional awareness among Guy's nurses.

Although she retired in 1909, when the First World War started Swift offered her services and within a few months was appointed matron-in-chief of the joint war committee of the St John Ambulance Association and the British Red Cross Society (BRCS). During the war her department was responsible for over 6000 trained nurses, overseeing their selection and dispatch to hospitals at home and abroad, and also for interviewing VADs (members of voluntary aid detachments who were employed as assistant nurses). Swift personally inspected the 1500 auxiliary hospitals administered by the Red Cross and the hostels and hotels used by the nurses in transit. She was awarded the Royal Red Cross, first class, in 1916, and in 1919 she was created dame grand cross of the Order of the British Empire and made a lady of grace of the order of St John of Jerusalem.

Although Swift supported the professional associations that were founded before the war, she had not taken an active part in the campaign for state registration of nurses: her character avoided publicity. However, by the end of 1915 her war work had convinced her that something would have to be done about the chaotic state of nurses' training. Knowing that the leaders of the campaign for state registration, particularly Mrs Bedford Fenwick, would oppose any attempt to introduce a voluntary system of registration, she approached Arthur Stanley, chairman of the BRCS and treasurer of St Thomas's Hospital, and asked him to help her organize a college of nursing. Stanley agreed, and they enlisted the support of Sir Cooper Perry, medical superintendent of Guy's, and several matrons of leading London teaching hospitals. The founders of the college aimed to standardize the training of nurses, with a uniform curriculum, examination, and a register of the names of those nurses that had passed the examination. Despite the irreconcilable opposition of the ardent state registration campaigners, the new initiative was well received by the majority of matrons and managers of the large training schools and hospitals in the country, and the College of Nursing was established in April 1916.

In 1919 the Nurses' Registration Acts established three new statutory bodies which became responsible for the registration of trained nurses in England and Wales, Scotland, and Ireland. No longer responsible for the registration of nurses, and with a membership of over 17,000, the college was in a position to expand its role. Thanks to the foresight of its founders it became a successful professional organization, responding to the educational needs of nurses and providing leadership to the new profession. The achievements of the college were recognized in 1928 when it was granted a royal charter. However, it was not until two years after the death of Swift that it was given permission to use the prefix royal and became the Royal College of Nursing.

At the end of the war Swift stayed on at the joint war committee to help with the demobilization of nurses. The BRCS extended its charter to include peacetime health problems and Swift, a member of the council and executive committee, became very involved in this work. A League of Red Cross Societies was formed to carry out the peacetime work and she was appointed the nursing representative of the British society. She participated in numerous committees and international conferences throughout the 1920s and played an important part in setting up the first public-health nursing course in London for the league. This course attracted nurses from developing countries, who then worked as pioneers in public-health nursing in their home countries. The course was very successful and Swift took on the role of 'mother' to a generation of international students. In 1929 she was awarded the international Florence Nightingale medal for her distinguished contribution to international nursing. She also made significant contributions to developments that were taking place in nursing in Britain at the time, particularly in the care of the chronic sick and prison nursing.

Dame Sarah said that she was happiest when she was organizing and she never really retired from her work. In 1935, when she retired from the post of matron-in-chief of the BRCS, and was presented with a scroll acknowledging her years of service by the future George VI, she remained a member of the council of the society and on several of its committees. She was also a member of the council of the College of Nursing from 1916 until her death, was twice elected its president, then a vice-president, and an honorary treasurer. Her last public appearance was at the coronation of George VI. She died a few weeks later, after a short illness, on 27 June 1937, at her London home, 20 Melcombe Court, Dorset Square, Marylebone. Her funeral took place two days later at St Mark's, Marylebone Road, and was followed by a cremation service at Golders Green crematorium; a memorial service was held at Guy's Hospital chapel.

Swift was a very small, determined woman, about 4 feet 10 inches tall. Her whole life was devoted to nursing and her motivation was a genuine love of humanity. Her nurses knew her as a strict disciplinarian but were grateful to her for teaching them to accept responsibility. She was intensely private and disliked fuss. The many honours she received she accepted as tributes to her profession. She left instructions that on her death nothing was to be written about her.   SUSAN MCGANN

Sources Royal College of Nursing Archives, Edinburgh, Sarah Swift MSS · S. McGann, 'Sarah Swift: a supreme organiser', *The battle of the nurses: a study of eight women who influenced the development of professional nursing, 1880–1930* (1992), 160–89 · annual reports, 1898–1909, LMA, Records, Guy's Hospital, H9/GY/A94/2–4 · matron's journals, 1896–1911, LMA, Records, Guy's Hospital, H9/GY/C4/1–3 · matron's report books, 1899–1904, LMA, Records, Guy's Hospital, H9/GY/C5/3 · nursing certificates and prizes, LMA, Records, Guy's Hospital, H9/GY/C16 · nursing guide, 1911, LMA, Records, Guy's Hospital, H9/GY/C20/1 · *Guy's Hospital Gazette*, [3rd ser.], 8–23 (1894–1909) · joint war committee minutes, 1914–20, British Red Cross Archives, London, J/WC/1/1/1–3 · Sarah Swift, personnel records,

British Red Cross Archives, London • College of Nursing Ltd, 1916–28, Royal College of Nursing Archives, Edinburgh, RCN/01 • *Nursing Times* (3 July 1937) • b. cert. • d. cert.
Archives Royal College of Nursing Archives, Edinburgh | British Red Cross Archives, London • Guy's Hospital, London
Likenesses G. B. E., photograph, 1919, IWM • four photographs, 1925–9, Royal College of Nursing Archives, Edinburgh • H. J. Draper, oils, Guy's Hospital, London [*see illus.*]
Wealth at death £8479 0s. 11d.: probate, 16 Aug 1937, *CGPLA Eng. & Wales*

Swift, Theophilus (1746–1815), writer, was born at Goodrich Castle, Herefordshire, the third son of Deane Swift of Dublin and his wife, Mary Harrison. Both father and mother were cousins of Jonathan Swift (1667–1745).

The father, **Deane Swift** (1707–1783), was the son of Deane Swift (1674–1714) 'of Reper's Rest, near Dublin, Ireland, gent.', and grandson of Godwin Swift, the uncle of Jonathan Swift. He had entered Dublin University in 1723, but it is uncertain as to whether he took a degree. He matriculated from St Mary Hall, Oxford, on 10 October 1734, and graduated BA in 1736. The name Deane came from his great-grandfather Admiral Richard *Deane (*bap.* 1610, *d.* 1653). His cousin, the dean of St Patrick's, commended him to Pope in 1739, having been assured of his good name at Oxford by principal William King. In July 1739 he married Mary Harrison, the daughter of Martha Whiteway and her first husband, Theophilus Harrison. He enjoyed the small 'paternal estate' of the Swifts at Goodrich in Herefordshire, and died at Worcester on 12 July 1783. Deane Swift is chiefly remembered for his publication in 1755 of *An essay upon the life, writings, and character of Dr. Jonathan Swift, interspersed with some animadversions upon the remarks of a late critical author* [the earl of Orrery]. He was also responsible for five volumes of the large octavo edition of Swift's *Works* (edited by John Hawkesworth, 1769), containing the bulk of Swift's correspondence. He also rendered valuable aid to Nichols in his edition of Swift's *Works*. From his mother-in-law, Mrs Whiteway, Deane Swift obtained forty of the letters of the *Journal to Stella*, which he edited; the original manuscripts are now lost.

Theophilus Swift was educated at Oxford, matriculating at St Mary Hall on 24 March 1763, and graduating BA in 1767. He was called to the bar at the Middle Temple in 1774, and, after practising for a few years, settled in Ireland on inheriting some property in Limerick from his father in 1783. Some time before this he had married Charlotte Maria Pead, with whom he was to have two sons. He lived in Dublin, where his eccentricities attracted attention. After publishing three volumes of poems, *The Gamblers* (1777), *The Temple of Folly* (1787), and *The Female Parliament*, which were indifferently received, Swift came to public notice in 1789 with *A Letter to Sir William Brown, on the Duel of the Duke of York with Colonel Lenox*. He accused Lennox, later fourth duke of Richmond, of a treasonable attempt to assassinate 'the heir presumptive to the heir apparent', and cast aspersions on his parentage. Lennox challenged Swift to a duel, which took place in a field near the Uxbridge Road, London, on 3 July. Swift, who sustained a pistol wound, was undaunted and refused to retract his assertions. Later that year he published *A Letter to the King on the Conduct of Colonel Lennox*, which ran to three editions that year. In 1790 Swift's attentions were diverted from Colonel Lennox by a spate of highly publicized knife assaults on young London women by a figure known as 'the Monster'. Renwick Williams, a florist, was charged and imprisoned, but Swift was one of the few who maintained his innocence, and published *A Vindication of Renwick Williams, Commonly called the Monster* (1790). In 1794, enraged by the failure of his son Deane (1770?–1860?), 'the brightest lad in all Ireland', to gain distinctions in his examinations at Trinity College, Dublin, Swift published *Animadversions on the Fellows of Trinity College, Dublin*, a lurid account of how the fellows had broken their vows of celibacy. He was sued for libel, and received twelve months' imprisonment, while one of his adversaries, the Revd Dr Burrows, was jailed for six months for libelling him. Again, this did not subdue Swift, and from gaol he encouraged his son Deane to write and publish the satiric squib *The Monks of Trinity* which appeared in 1795.

In 1801 Swift's *Essay on Rime* appeared in the *Transactions of the Royal Irish Academy*, and during this decade he assisted Walter Scott in compiling his *Life of Swift*. By 1811 his contentious disposition had led him into another public dispute, articulated in *Mr Swift's Correspondence with the Rev Dr Dobbin and his Family*. He accused Emma, Dobbin's daughter who later became the mother of Sheridan Le Fanu, of jilting him with the encouragement of her family. Swift died in Dublin in 1815. His elder son, Deane, wrote for *The Press*, the organ of the United Irishmen, under the pseudonym Marcus, and his younger son, Edmund Lewis Lenthal (1777–1875), wrote plays and became keeper of the regalia in the Tower of London.

KATHERINE MULLIN

Sources R. Welch, ed., *The Oxford companion to Irish literature* (1996) • A. M. Brady and B. Cleeve, eds., *A biographical dictionary of Irish writers*, rev. edn (1985) • [J. Watkins and F. Shoberl], *A biographical dictionary of the living authors of Great Britain and Ireland* (1816) • J. Chambers, *Biographical illustrations of Worcestershire* (1820) • Watt, *Bibl. Brit.* • H. J. Rose, *A new general biographical dictionary*, ed. H. J. Rose and T. Wright, 12 vols. (1853) • C. Knight, ed., *The English cyclopaedia: biography*, 6 vols. (1856–8) • J. Hutchinson, ed., *A catalogue of notable Middle Templars: with brief biographical notices* (1902) • D. J. O'Donoghue, *The poets of Ireland: a biographical dictionary with bibliographical particulars*, 1 vol. in 3 pts (1892–3) • I. Ehrenpreis, *Swift: the man, his works and the age*, 3 vols. (1962–83) • *The correspondence of Jonathan Swift*, ed. H. Williams, 5 vols. (1963–5) • Burke, *Gen. Ire.* (1958) • *DNB*
Archives NL Scot., letters and notes on Dean Swift

Swinburne, Algernon Charles (1837–1909), poet and literary reviewer, was born on 5 April 1837 at 7 Chester Street, London, the second of six children of Admiral Charles Henry Swinburne (1797–1877) and his wife, Lady Jane Henrietta (1809–1896), daughter of George, third earl of Ashburnham (1760–1830), and his wife, Lady Charlotte Percy (*d.* 1862). Swinburne's father served in the Royal Navy from 1810 to 1836. He loved music and painting, practical activities such as carpentry, and experimented with photography. According to family friend William Sewell, the admiral 'ridiculed and discouraged' (Rooksby, 17) Swinburne's love of poetry when he was a boy. Swinburne

Algernon Charles Swinburne (1837–1909), by George Frederic
Watts, 1867

had a warm relationship with his mother, a cultured, maternal woman who had spent time in Italy and was able to teach her children French and Italian.

Early years In his book *Boswell's Clap and Other Essays: Medical Analyses of Literary Men's Afflictions* (1988), the American physician William B. Ober suggested that Swinburne was a premature baby with mild arrested hydroencephaly. This diagnosis sheds light on the nervous, involuntary movements of the feet and hands which Swinburne exhibited throughout life, as well as his strange, floating walk, difficulty with writing, his habit of covering one eye to read more easily, occasional epileptiform fits, and his masochism.

Swinburne's childhood was passed at East Dene, a large country house in the village of Bonchurch, near Ventnor, Isle of Wight. East Dene commands a fine view of the English Channel, with wooded slopes rising spectacularly to the downs above. The proximity of the sea fostered in Swinburne the intense love of the ocean which permeates his writing. One of his earliest memories was being thrown head first into the sea by his father.

As a child Swinburne was taken on annual visits to Ashburnham Place in Sussex and to his paternal grandfather's estate at Capheaton, Northumberland. Swinburne's uncle Bertram Ashburnham, the fourth earl, amassed an extraordinary library which Swinburne avidly explored when he was older. His beloved grandfather Sir John Edward Swinburne (1760–1860) was prominent in Northumbrian life, owning thousands of acres and heading such bodies as the Literary and Philosophical Society of Newcastle and the Society of Antiquaries of Newcastle. The Swinburnes' Northumbrian roots went back to the twelfth century and the poet was proud of his connection with the north of England. He composed and reconstructed 'border' ballads, and in later life was fond of calling himself a 'borderer'. Swinburne saw himself as descended from a line of Catholic and Jacobite exiles whom he romantically portrayed as martyrs in the cause of the Stuarts; he had a lifelong fascination with the figure of Mary Stuart.

William Sewell wrote of the young Swinburne:

> the moment he came into the room I saw that he was not a common boy. Very small, delicately formed, very small feet and hands, golden hair—it was not red exactly, pale eyes, freckled complexion, feminine features, a shy manner, but not awkward. And the moment you talked to him as if you respected him, he brightened up, and talked freely, especially of his passion for Shakespeare and Italian poetry. And he was then quite a boy. (Rooksby, 17)

Swinburne had four sisters, Alice (1838–1903), Edith (1840–1863), Charlotte (1842–1899), and Isabel (1846–1915), and one brother, Edward (1849–1890). Charlotte's twin brother, Charles John, died aged six months in 1843, when Swinburne was five, and this death may have influenced Swinburne's fond feelings for young children. The family was high-church Anglican. Swinburne wrote of his ecstatic participation in the mass as a child and youth but his later irrevocable rejection of Christianity caused some strain in family relationships.

Early education In 1848 Swinburne stayed at Brooke rectory in the west Wight with the Revd Foster Fenwick (1790–1858) who tutored him for Eton College. William Sewell suggested to the family that Swinburne would be better placed at Radley College, near Oxford, but on 24 April 1849 Swinburne entered Eton. His cousin Lord Redesdale described Swinburne as 'a fragile little creature',

> as he stood there between his father and mother, with his wondering eyes fixed upon me! Under his arm he hugged his Bowdler's Shakespeare … He was strangely tiny. His limbs were small and delicate; and his sloping shoulders looked far too weak to carry his great head, the size of which was exaggerated by the tousled mass of red hair standing almost at right angles to it … His features were small and beautiful, chiselled as daintily as those of some Greek sculptor's masterpieces. His skin was very white—not unhealthy, but a transparent tinted white, such as one sees in the petals of some roses … another characteristic which Algernon inherited from his mother was the … exquisitely soft voice with a rather sing-song intonation … His language, even at that age was beautiful, fanciful and richly varied. (Rooksby, 28)

Swinburne lived in the house of his tutor, James Leigh Joynes, and later spoke fondly of the kindness Mrs Joynes showed him at a difficult time when he felt vulnerable and cruelly deprived of East Dene and its environs. Eton stimulated Swinburne's passion for literature. Through its library he discovered writers who remained lifelong enthusiasms, such as Sappho, Catullus, Hugo, and Landor. He encountered Elizabethan and Jacobean drama in the plays of Marlowe and Webster, and Lamb's *Specimens of the English Dramatic Poets*, and proceeded to write imitations of them. Swinburne celebrated the visit of Queen Victoria and Prince Albert to Eton on 4 June 1851 with a poem entitled 'The Triumph of Gloriana'. He avidly read each novel of Dickens as it was published serially. His academic performance was generally good; in 1852 he won the prince consort's prize for modern languages. A family journey north in September 1849 led to the young Swinburne's meeting Wordsworth.

Eton also had a less fortunate influence on Swinburne's psychosexual development. Predictably, given his unusual appearance and manner, Swinburne was bullied by the other boys, and neither Joynes nor his parents took this seriously. There is evidence that he both witnessed and experienced Eton discipline through the customary mode of 'birching'. In adult life Swinburne enjoyed composing scenes in verse and prose in which schoolboys experience the terror and masochistic ecstasy of being beaten by figures of authority such as schoolmasters and fathers. No sexual acts are described, nor obscene words used, and the focus is obsessively on a few motifs. These compositions include 'Eton: another Ode', a flagellant counterpart to his official 'Eton: an Ode', a sequence of poems called 'The Flogging Block', 'The End of a Half', 'The Schoolboy's Tragedy', 'Redgie's Luck', 'Cuckoo Weir', and many others. A handful were published anonymously in Swinburne's lifetime, namely 'Arthur's Flogging', 'Reginald's Flogging', and (probably) 'A Boy's First Flogging' in *The Whippingham Papers* (1887), 'Charlie Collingwood's Flogging' in *The Pearl* (September 1879), and 'Frank Fane: a Ballad' in *The Pearl* (May 1880). It is not known whether this was with Swinburne's prior knowledge or consent. In addition to its presence in his poetry, numerous references to flogging in Swinburne's letters and fiction demonstrate the grip it exercised on his imagination. It is unlikely that Eton alone created this obsession in Swinburne but probable that the more brutal aspects of its regime stimulated a latent masochism, a psychological trait perhaps rooted in the physiological results of the arrested hydroencephaly which Ober has posited. Sadism and masochism feature in many of Swinburne's major works, including *Chastelard*, *Atalanta in Calydon* (both 1865), *Poems and Ballads*, and in the unfinished novel known as *Lesbia Brandon*.

Swinburne left Eton toward the end of his seventeenth year, either in late 1853 or early 1854. The exact reason for his departure is unknown. There may have been discipline problems, or the masters had recognized Swinburne's sexual temperament and were unsure how to handle a youth whose sensibility was so different. From Eton Swinburne went to Northumberland to be tutored by the Revd John Wilkinson, curate of Cambo, near Capheaton. It may have been at this time that he met Lady Pauline Trevelyan and her husband, Walter Trevelyan, whose home of Wallington was only a few miles from Capheaton Hall. The Trevelyans were the centre of an important artistic circle and Swinburne formed a respectful relationship with the cultured Lady Trevelyan who attempted to exert a restraining influence when the poet was about to publish the controversial *Poems and Ballads*.

Swinburne was also tutored by James Russell Woodford, later bishop of Ely, at Lower Easton, near Bristol. Swinburne's youthful imagination and reckless spirit were fired by news of the cavalry charge at Balaklava in 1854. He asked his parents if he could enlist and they refused. In an impulsive demonstration of a courage he thought *they* thought he lacked, Swinburne risked his life climbing the dangerous Culver cliff, a few miles north of Bonchurch. An account he wrote for his cousin Mary Gordon (1840–1926) claimed that he only just succeeded in reaching the top, and there narrowly avoided losing consciousness and falling off. Between July and August 1855 Swinburne made his first trip abroad in the company of a maternal uncle, Major-General Thomas Ashburnham. They visited France and Germany and Swinburne, ever ready to revel in the elements, was thrilled when they were caught in an unforgettable display of thunder and lightning during the return crossing over the channel. The experience inspired a lyric, 'A Channel Passage', some forty years later.

Oxford, 1856–1860 Swinburne matriculated from Balliol College, Oxford, on 24 January 1856. He did not take to Oxford particularly well. Neither what he described as its foggy damp weather nor its atmosphere of recent theological controversy appealed to him. At Balliol he came under the influence of Benjamin Jowett, classicist and later master of the college. The combination of the impulsive, iconoclastic poet and the even-tempered, reserved Jowett seems an unlikely one, but the two men eventually formed a bond which persisted (with much benefit to Swinburne) until Jowett's death in 1893, and was celebrated in a memorial essay, 'Recollections of Professor Jowett'. Academically, Swinburne did not please Balliol by failing the examination known as 'responsions' in his second term; he retook it on 10 December 1856. In the summer of 1856 Swinburne spent a few weeks visiting Radley College. The visit culminated with Sewell's banning him, fearing Swinburne would be a bad influence on the boys because of his 'sinister tenets' (James, 229).

Swinburne's rejection of Christianity was confirmed by his involvement with the Old Mortality Society and his friendship with its leading light John Nichol, later professor of English at Glasgow University, whom Swinburne described as the 'guide of my boyhood in the paths of my free thought and republican faith' (Lafourcade, *Jeunesse*, 1.122). The two men holidayed together in the western isles of Scotland in the summer of 1857 and in Guernsey in 1876. Old Mortality was convened in November 1856, though the second meeting was not held until May 1857. Over the next two years its term-time meetings were enlivened by Swinburne's papers on such figures as Emily Brontë, Christopher Marlowe, John Webster, Robert Browning, and William Morris. The society published three numbers of a journal, *Undergraduate Papers* (December 1857–April 1858), to which Swinburne contributed five pieces. Swinburne also had a short account of Congreve published in the *Imperial Dictionary of Universal Biography* (1857).

Swinburne's time at Oxford was chiefly important for bringing him into contact with the Pre-Raphaelite artists who painted the Oxford Union murals in the autumn of 1857. A mutual affinity was felt between Swinburne and Dante Gabriel Rossetti, Edward Burne-Jones, and William Morris, whose poetry Swinburne took up with much enthusiasm. Rossetti was delighted to have Swinburne as a model and protégé and introduced him to his brother William Michael Rossetti who became a lifelong friend. The Pre-Raphaelites' passion for all things medieval and Arthurian, coupled with the example of Morris's *The Defence of Guenevere* (1858), soon had Swinburne writing medievalist poems such as 'Queen Yseult'.

After a second-class pass in moderations Swinburne chose to read for honours in law and modern history. Despite his winning the Taylorian prize for Italian and French in June 1858, his academic studies were steadily eclipsed by other interests. In addition to his membership of Old Mortality, he attended political debates at the Oxford Union, and read widely in the Taylorian Library's holdings in French literature. Above all, Swinburne experimented with a number of poetic forms and voices, some medieval, but also imitating Browning, Shakespeare, Morris, and Keats. Early drafts of his first published works, the plays *The Queen Mother*, *Rosamond*, and *Chastelard*, originate from this period.

Swinburne's individualistic behaviour brought him inevitably into conflict with Balliol College. He was officially cautioned in June and December 1858, but matters came to a head in November 1859 when he was reprimanded for failing an examination and showing contempt for the authority of the college by being 'rusticated' (sent away from the university) for a term. He spent the first months of 1860 at Navestock in Essex studying law and medieval history with the Revd William Stubbs (1825–1901), later bishop of Oxford. On his return to Oxford he successfully resat his examination in April but his work for finals was interrupted by a fall from a horse at the end of May. He told his mother that if he felt unable to get a distinguished pass he would not sit the examinations. As a consequence, Swinburne left Oxford without a degree. In later years he embroidered this somewhat, describing his Oxford career as ending 'in complete and scandalous failure'.

The death of Swinburne's grandfather in September 1860 had the effect of closing Capheaton Hall to Swinburne, which had been an important home of his childhood and youth.

Early years as a writer in London, 1860–1865 Acceding to Swinburne's wishes, his father gave him an allowance of £400 p.a. on which to live in London. By the end of 1860 his first book, *The Queen-Mother, and Rosamond*, was published by Basil Montagu Pickering, the cost met by the author. It appears to have attracted only two brief, dismissive reviews. Although Swinburne published no more books until 1865, the quantity of his writing during these years is astonishing, and gradually from the imitative labours of the apprentice an individual voice and themes emerged. At no later period did he match the creativity of the six years between his leaving Oxford and the publication of *Poems and Ballads* (1866). Apart from scores of individual

poems (many lengthy), Swinburne wrote critical essays, a book on William Blake, several verse plays, at least six short stories for a collection provisionally titled the 'Triameron', and a longer narrative published posthumously as *Lucretia Borgia, or, The Chronicle of Tebaldeo Tebaldei* (1942). By 1862 he had finished the novel *A Year's Letters* (serialized in *The Tatler* in 1877, published in 1904 as *Love's Cross-Currents*) and by 1864 had started a second, *Lesbia Brandon*.

Through the Pre-Raphaelite set Swinburne met a number of important people in London's artistic society and impressed select gatherings with passionate or hilarious readings. In May 1861 he met Richard Monckton Milnes, Lord Houghton, who granted Swinburne access to his exotic library at Fryston in Yorkshire, and introduced him to the writings of the marquis de Sade in August 1862. Despite epistolary disclaimers, Swinburne became obsessed with de Sade and *La nouvelle Justine, ou, Les malheurs de la vertu*, frequently quoting or burlesquing this work in his letters. De Sade's example strengthened Swinburne's willingness to use sadistic images and to make explicit his own anti-theism. Another important friendship was with the explorer Richard Burton, whom Swinburne met in June 1861. Burton introduced Swinburne to the freethinking, progressive conversation of the Anthropological Society (which Swinburne formally joined in April 1864) and its wilder offshoot, the Cannibal Club. This relationship encouraged Swinburne's pagan and humanist views, and his drinking, which by 1866 reached alcoholic proportions.

In 1862 Swinburne published a border ballad, 'The Fratricide' (later retitled 'The Bloody Son'), and a short story, 'Dead Love', in George Meredith's *Once a Week*. In *The Spectator* Swinburne published a spirited and timely defence of Meredith's *Modern Love*, and also published the poems 'Before Parting', 'After Death', 'Faustine', 'A Song in Time of Revolution', 'A Song in Time of Order', 'The Sundew', and 'August', all later reprinted in *Poems and Ballads*. Swinburne also produced three critical articles on Victor Hugo for *The Spectator*, and championed Baudelaire's *Les fleurs du mal* within its pages. Swinburne's irrepressible sense of mischief also led him to submit reviews of two nonexistent French poets whose tone of moral outrage satirized that of so many contemporary reviews, a plan foiled only by the suspicion of the editor R. H. Hutton.

Georgiana Burne-Jones memorably described Swinburne at this period:

> His appearance was unusual and in some ways beautiful, for his hair was glorious in abundance and colour and his eyes indescribably fine. When repeating poetry he had a perfectly natural way of lifting them in a rapt, unconscious gaze, and their clear green colour softened by thick brow eyelashes was unforgettable … He was restless beyond words, scarcely standing still at all and almost dancing as he walked, while even in sitting he moved continually, seeming to keep time, by a swift movement of the hands at the wrists, and sometimes of the feet also, with some inner rhythm of excitement. He was courteous and affectionate and unsuspicious, and faithful beyond most people to those he really loved. (Hyder, 6)

One of the people Swinburne truly loved as a friend was Rossetti's wife, Elizabeth Siddal. He was one of the last people to see her alive and testified at the inquest held into her death in February 1862. Swinburne took rooms with Rossetti in Tudor House, Cheyne Walk, Chelsea, from October 1862 until some time in 1864. William Michael Rossetti and George Meredith also nominally participated in this scheme, though neither of them spent very much time at Tudor House, and Swinburne was often away. He suffered a further blow when in February 1863 his favourite sister, Edith, was taken severely ill at Bournemouth with the consumption first diagnosed in 1856. She was expected to die there but recovered sufficiently to be taken back to East Dene. Swinburne went to Paris in March with Whistler, where he met Fantin-Latour and Manet; a visit to the Louvre inspired the sonnet sequence 'Hermaphroditus'. He spent most of the summer at East Dene, where Edith died in September. His feelings about the hopelessness of his sister's death seem to colour certain chapters in *Lesbia Brandon*. Significantly, about this time he commenced the play that made him famous, *Atalanta in Calydon*, the central image of which is a person consumed as a brand thrust into a fire, a vivid symbol for the inner wasting fever of consumption.

While the rest of his family went to the continent to escape the painful associations of East Dene with Edith's death, Swinburne stayed at the Isle of Wight residence of the Gordon family, Northcourt. The Gordons were close friends and blood relatives of the Swinburnes. Originally intending to stay only a week Swinburne remained from October until the spring of 1864, the longest period that he and his cousin Mary Gordon had spent together since childhood. This stay marked the closest moment in their relationship. If there were strong feelings on his part for Mary this was probably the time when they were at their most intense, heightened by his loss of Edith. Mary delighted Swinburne when she played Handel on the Northcourt organ, the music filling his mind with new verses. He collaborated on her second book, *The Children of the Chapel* (1864), to which he contributed a morality play, 'The Pilgrimage of Pleasure'.

Swinburne's 'lost love' In his mid-twenties Swinburne suffered a disappointment in love which made him decide never to marry. The identity of the woman he loved and who inspired some of his finest lyrics remains the most important mystery of Swinburne's life. Swinburne told his first biographer, Edmund Gosse, of this disappointment and its relation to the poem 'The Triumph of Time'. In 1875 Swinburne congratulated Gosse on his impending marriage, adding:

> I suppose it must be the best thing that can befall a man to win and keep the woman that he loves while yet young; at any rate I can congratulate my friend on his good hap without any too jealous afterthought of the reverse experience which left my own young manhood 'a barren stock'—if I may cite that phrase without seeming to liken myself to a male Queen Elizabeth. (*Swinburne Letters*, 3.51)

'The Triumph of Time' clearly states that the woman in question is marrying someone else, and implies in its opening stanza that the speaker may not openly have declared his love. In 1959 Cecil Y. Lang published an article, 'Swinburne's Lost Love', in which he argued persuasively that the most likely candidate for this role was Swinburne's cousin Mary Gordon, who some time in 1863 or 1864 became engaged to Colonel Robert William Disney Leith, a distinguished soldier who returned home a local hero to Aberdeenshire (also the home of the Gordons) after serving in India. They married in June 1865. In her selection of Swinburne's correspondence, *The Boyhood of Algernon Charles Swinburne* (1917), Mrs Disney Leith denied that there had been any romance between them.

It is not known how or when Swinburne found out about this engagement. After leaving Northcourt in the spring of 1864 he went to France and Italy with Lord Houghton. In Italy he met one of his literary idols, Walter Savage Landor, and Seymour Kirkup, a friend of Blake's. After staying with Lord Houghton at Fryston in August, Swinburne joined his friend John William Inchbold, the Leeds-born painter, in Tintagel, north Cornwall, until November. While in Cornwall Swinburne finished *Atalanta in Calydon* and wrote an elegy for Landor when news reached him of Landor's death that September. During the stay in Cornwall Swinburne corresponded with Mary and he saw her in London when he returned. Given the lack of evidence, this seems the likeliest time for her to have told him of her decision to marry Colonel Disney Leith.

There has been a persistent ill-informed tendency to devalue Swinburne's writing by stating that it is founded on literature and does not have the authenticity of work which springs from deep, lived experience. In fact, his themes of disappointment in love, in love's transient or illusory nature, of death, sterility, and 'the mystery of the cruelty of things' ('Anactoria') can be seen to have a clear source in the emotional losses Swinburne suffered between 1860 and 1865, culminating in the marriage of the woman he loved from childhood. When Swinburne wrote in 'Dolores' that 'marriage and death and division / Make barren our lives', the sentiment came directly out of experience, not out of his reading.

Atalanta in Calydon (1865) and Poems and Ballads (1866) *Atalanta in Calydon* was published in March 1865 by Edward Moxon & Co. in an edition of at least 500 copies in a cream binding with a gold 'roundel' design by Dante Gabriel Rossetti. It drew on a story in Ovid and Apollodorus, and although there was disagreement as to whether as a tragedy *Atalanta* was truly Greek, reviews were favourable and some went as far as to hail Swinburne as a new poetic talent of the first magnitude. In November 1865 it was followed by a five-act play, *Chastelard*. Many reviews complained about the immoral nature of the passion of Chastelard for Mary, queen of Scots, and his wilful pursuit of romantic self-destruction. As if in imitation, Swinburne's personal life grew increasingly erratic after 1865. Among his newer friends were the artist Simeon Solomon, the Welsh anthologer George Powell (who appears to have shared to some degree Swinburne's preoccupation with flagellation), and Rossetti's friend Charles Augustus Howell.

In December 1865 there was an important exchange of letters between Swinburne and Lady Trevelyan, who was concerned that he should censor his own forthcoming poems so they could be enjoyed by the greatest number of readers. Swinburne chose largely to ignore this advice. Others whose opinion Swinburne respected, such as Ruskin, gave up trying to counsel the headstrong poet. In March 1866 Swinburne edited a selection of Byron's poems with an introduction that discussed the controversy that had greeted them. Ironically, this anticipated the furore over Swinburne's *Poems and Ballads* in August 1866.

Poems and Ballads sparked a controversy which has few rivals in English poetry. Even if he had never published anything else, Swinburne's fame was assured by this small green volume of 344 pages. *Poems and Ballads* contains such important poems as 'Anactoria', 'Hymn to Proserpine', 'Dolores', 'Hesperia', 'Itylus', 'The Garden of Proserpine', and 'Laus Veneris'. It was a dazzling collection. Swinburne had developed an original poetic voice, lyrical and possessed of an energy only matched in the period by Gerard Manley Hopkins, and written in a marvellous variety of stanza forms and metres. Much as Swinburne admired Tennyson, Browning, and Shelley, his work stood clear of theirs. His themes were guaranteed to be shocking to many Victorian readers. The poems espoused republicanism, fulminated against priests and kings, rejected the theology and consolations of Christianity, and celebrated decadent romantic and sexual feelings. The book was learned and cosmopolitan in outlook. It established Swinburne as not only the leading new poet of the day but an international icon for progressive thinkers. In the late 1860s and 1870s Swinburne's very name seemed a trumpet blast for those who wanted a more liberal, less puritanical society.

The first reviews, by Robert Buchanan in *The Athenaeum* and John Morley in the *Saturday Review* on 4 April, were very critical. The next day, frightened by rumours of imminent prosecution, James Bertrand Payne, head of Moxon, withdrew the book from sale. After seeking advice from friends, an irate Swinburne struck a deal with John Camden Hotten to reissue the book, despite the fact that Swinburne had that March rejected Hotten as a potential publisher of his work. *Poems and Ballads* appeared again in September 1866 and the debate over its merits resumed and persisted into 1867, but there was no prosecution. G. W. Carleton printed the book in America, where the controversy served to boost sales. In November Hotten brought out Swinburne's pamphlet *Notes on Poems and Reviews*. Witty and articulate, it is one of his best critical essays and a crucial document in the history of aestheticism and freedom of expression. Further commentary came from William Michael Rossetti who published *Swinburne's Poems and Ballads* at the same time.

From Christmas 1866 to February 1867 Swinburne stayed with his family at their new home of Holmwood, Shiplake, near Henley-on-Thames, where they had moved after quitting East Dene in 1865. There must have been some tensions between the poet and his parents, sisters, and brother, given the public outcry over his poems and their anti-Christian content. His sense of estrangement is alluded to in the original version of the lyric 'Pastiche', initially published as 'Regret'.

The political phase, 1867–1875   By 1867 Swinburne was consciously moving beyond the art for art's sake position that had underpinned his writing. His long-standing interest in French and Italian politics now inspired him to commence *A Song of Italy* in the autumn of 1866. This long lyric and the 'Ode on the Insurrection in Candia', both of which appeared in the spring of 1867, signalled this change of direction, which was based on the need to fill the void of belief dramatized in *Poems and Ballads*. The change was confirmed in March 1867 when Swinburne finally met his hero the Italian patriot Giuseppe Mazzini.

Early in 1868 Swinburne published his ground-breaking *Study of William Blake*, after five years' research, complete with hand-coloured facsimiles of Blake's illustrated writing. Swinburne's interpretation was a creative misreading that played down the significance of Blake's Christianity and developed some odd parallels with de Sade, but was important because Swinburne was the first critic to take Blake's work seriously. Swinburne's appreciation of the visual arts is evident in two essays published in 1868, 'Notes on some designs of the old masters of Florence' and *Notes on the Royal Academy Exhibition of 1868* (the latter with William Michael Rossetti).

During the winter of 1867–8 Swinburne had an affair with the American Adah Isaacs Menken, a highly paid popular entertainer who had also outraged public opinion, in her case with what were then judged to be indecorous theatre performances. Swinburne may have helped revise her verses, posthumously published as *Infelicia* (1868). Photographs of the poet with Menken were displayed in various London shop windows. Swinburne also found sexual diversion in a flagellant brothel in St John's Wood.

In 1868 while on holiday with his friend George Powell at Etretat, Normandy, Swinburne was carried out to sea by strong currents and was saved from drowning by French fishermen. By the late 1860s Swinburne's drinking was damaging his health and alienating his acquaintances. A pattern was established in which Swinburne's health would break down, messages would be conveyed back to his family, and his father would journey to London to take his son back to the calm and sobriety of Holmwood where Swinburne would recover, then return to London only to initiate another round of the cycle. By 1870 friends reported Swinburne exhibiting *delirium tremens*. His health was further disturbed by 'fits' that were reportedly not caused by drink. There were two such fits in July 1868, which led to Swinburne's being taken home by his father and remaining at Holmwood for several months. In 1869 Swinburne reviewed Hugo, published 'Notes on the text of Shelley', continued to scout disaster at the Arts Club by getting drunk and annoying the other members with his outbursts, and visited Vichy with Richard Burton, a holiday commemorated in late poems such as the 'Elegy 1869–91' written after Burton's death.

In 1870 Swinburne published the *Ode on the Proclamation of the French Republic* in pamphlet form and after many delays in 1871 a collection of philosophical and political verse, *Songs before Sunrise*. Swinburne's lyrical techniques and energetic metres are still in evidence, though there is a slight narrowing of imagery and vocabulary. The book had generally better reviews than *Poems and Ballads*, since Swinburne eschewed sexual themes for republican politics and a humanist positivism. *Songs before Sunrise* has often been judged as less personal than its predecessor, but it contains a personal animus directed at Christianity which Swinburne evidently felt failed him in his hour of need, during the tragedies of the early 1860s. *Songs before Sunrise* contains at least two of Swinburne's best poems, 'Hertha' and 'Before a Crucifix', as well as the rhetorically impressive 'Hymn of Man'.

Songs before Sunrise was published by F. S. Ellis because Swinburne had grown increasingly suspicious of Hotten, who he believed was reprinting *Poems and Ballads* without informing the author to avoid paying royalties. The 'Hotten question' is a continual theme in Swinburne's correspondence in the early 1870s, especially with William Michael Rossetti. Another publisher, D. White, brought out the pamphlet *Under the Microscope* (1872), which was composed of Swinburne's witty animadversions against the *Quarterly Review*, Alfred Austin, and Tennyson's *Idylls of the King*. This essay is a key document in the last controversy over the work of the Pre-Raphaelites. In October 1871 poet and critic Robert Buchanan had attacked Dante Gabriel Rossetti in an essay entitled 'The fleshly school of poetry', after Swinburne had published a laudatory review of Rossetti's *Ballads and Poems* in May 1870. The antipathy between Buchanan and the Pre-Raphaelites dated back at least to 1866, but the dispute proved the last straw for Rossetti's already strained nerves, precipitating a mental breakdown and suicide attempt in the summer of 1872. What first seemed a temporary hiatus in their communication became a permanent break. Some have suggested that Rossetti felt aggrieved at Swinburne for stoking the controversy, and when Rossetti died in 1882, Swinburne stayed away from the funeral.

By this time Swinburne had little contact with Burne-Jones, Morris, Burton (who was often abroad), or Lord Houghton. Simeon Solomon was *persona non grata* with Swinburne following Solomon's arrest and trial for soliciting in London in 1873. If there were losses, there were some gains. Swinburne remained on good terms with William Michael Rossetti, with whom he kept a learned and relatively sober correspondence. He made occasional trips to Oxford to see Jowett and went to Scotland with the master of Balliol on several reading parties in the early 1870s. In January 1874 the two men visited west Cornwall, staying at Penzance and exploring Kynance cove on the Lizard. Swinburne also befriended Edmund Gosse, his future biographer.

The most significant new relationship was with Theodore Watts, later Theodore Watts-*Dunton (1832–1914), a solicitor with literary ambitions, who was part of the Rossetti circle and met Swinburne in the autumn of 1872. Watts's first service to Swinburne was to take on the protracted negotiations with Hotten over Swinburne's publishing. An unexpected resolution came in 1873 when Hotten suddenly died. Control of Hotten's firm went to the more respectable Andrew Chatto who steered the imprint away from the murkier waters that Hotten had dredged, toward more salubrious tides. Eventually, after some fraught negotiations between Watts and Chatto, a deal was struck, and for the rest of his life Swinburne's books were published by Chatto.

The first was Swinburne's enormous *Bothwell* (1874), his second play to deal with events in the life of Mary Stuart. Six years in the writing, this herculean labour defeated Swinburne's dramatic vision, as his painstaking historical research demanded nothing be left out. The trilogy was completed with *Mary Stuart* (1881). Unexpectedly, the first edition of *Bothwell* sold out immediately and brought praise from many quarters, including his family and relations, no doubt relieved he had chosen an uncontroversial topic. The energies expended on *Bothwell* unfortunately diverted Swinburne from others more worthy, notably his novel *Lesbia Brandon*, where it was Swinburne's intention to mix prose and verse to create an original form, and his Arthurian poem *Tristram of Lyonesse* which, although started in 1869, did not appear until 1882.

More political poems were gathered in the vitriolic *Songs of Two Nations* (1875) which contained sonnets titled 'Dirae' that drew criticism because of their deployment of Christian allusions in a ferocious diatribe. However much he rejected Christian belief, Swinburne could not do without the resonance of its imagery and language. Swinburne ventured into Russian politics with the pamphlet *Notes of an English Republican on the Muscovite Crusade* (1876). Partly owing to Jowett's classical influence, *Erechtheus* (1876) returned to the Greek tragedy form of *Atalanta in Calydon*. *Erechtheus* has been admired by some but found too abstract and severe in outlook by others. Much of Swinburne's best criticism was collected in *Essays and Studies* (1875). Swinburne spent some months in the summer of 1874 on the Isle of Wight with Lady Mary Gordon at her house, The Orchard, Niton, only a few miles from East Dene. There he read Homer, swam frequently (almost drowning on one occasion), and worked on the innovative *George Chapman* (1875). *A Note on Charlotte Brontë* (1877) challenged the current estimation of George Eliot, by claiming that Charlotte and Emily Brontë were greater writers; Swinburne was a perceptive early admirer of *Wuthering Heights*. Swinburne's own novel *A Year's Letters* was serialized in *The Tatler* in 1877 under the pseudonym of Mrs Horace Manners.

Decline and recovery The quality of Swinburne's life steadily declined through the middle of the 1870s. In 1876 he spoke of 'the dull and monotonous puppet-show of my life, which often strikes me as too barren of action or enjoyment to be much worth holding on to' (Rooksby,

225). In March 1877 his father died and thereafter his mother was often not well enough personally to undertake the rescue missions to London which the admiral had carried out on many such occasions.

The poems written since 1866 which were elegiac and romantic rather than political were gathered in *Poems and Ballads Second Series* (1878), a worthy if less controversial successor to the 1866 miscellany. It contains the magnificent elegy for Baudelaire 'Ave atque vale', generally admired translations from Villon, as well as poems like 'At a Month's End', 'Relics', 'A Vision of Spring in Winter', and 'A Forsaken Garden', which spring from a contemplation of the romantic disappointment Swinburne suffered in his twenties. These lyrics have all the mellow yet intense colour of Tiffany stained glass, and, like *Songs before Sunrise*, represent an extension of his poetry, not a pale imitation of his earlier work.

Swinburne seems to have been very ill during the winter of 1878 (there is a significant gap in his correspondence) and friends such as William Michael Rossetti were concerned about his health. Now suffering from increasing deafness and a lack of money, Swinburne would probably have died within a short space of time of complications arising from alcoholism and self-neglect if Watts had not stepped in and invited the debilitated Swinburne to stay for a time at his sister's house in Putney. Watts was in the process of finding somewhere to live, and the two men reached an agreement to share a house. Swinburne rallied and spent much of the summer at Holmwood with his mother and sisters. In September 1879 Swinburne, Watts, and several other members of Watts's family moved to a house at the bottom of Putney Hill called The Pines. There Swinburne found the orderly life he had never known living on his own. Alcoholic excess became a thing of the past; Watts made sure that the poet drank only a bottle of beer at lunch. Swinburne found in Watts's extended family a partial cure for the loneliness he had experienced in the 1870s, forming an intense friendship with Bertie Mason, the young son of Watts's sister Miranda, which inspired fifty poems of little literary merit but some biographical interest. His life bedded down into domestic routine, if not quite as clockwork as many accounts have liked to state, under Watts's watchful, perhaps overprotective eye. There were yearly holidays, often to Watts's own East Anglia or the south coast.

This change in Swinburne's life also had negative features. Watts starved many of Swinburne's older friendships by not allowing people of whom he disapproved entry to The Pines. Watts coarsened Swinburne's critical judgement, a process aided by the creeping conservatism of age and Swinburne's own temperament which was always drawn to extremes of love or hate. The more comical aspects of this domestic arrangement have formed a literary legend which often substitutes for serious appraisal of Swinburne's later writing.

Last works The recovery of his health made Swinburne very productive as a writer, with twenty-three volumes appearing after 1879: ten volumes of poetry, six plays, six works of criticism, and his novel *A Year's Letters*, which found book publication in 1904 as *Love's Cross-Currents*. Swinburne's literary criticism declined in quality during this period. Genuine insights and discerning value judgements are partially hidden by the over-elaborate and sometimes shrill prose in which they are couched. The apparent recantations in the essays on Whitman (1887) and Whistler (1888) show the baleful influence of Watts's narrower opinions. Swinburne's criticism was published in *A Study of Shakespeare* (1880), *Miscellanies* (1886), *A Study of Victor Hugo* (1887), *A Study of Ben Jonson* (1889), *Studies in Prose and Poetry* (1894), and *The Age of Shakespeare* (1908).

The six plays of this period were *Mary Stuart* (1881), *Marino Faliero* (1885), *Locrine* (1887), *The Sisters* (1892), *Rosamund, Queen of the Lombards* (1899), and a fragment, *The Duke of Gandia* (1908). Although not without some fine writing and a growing compression in form, most of these are not truly dramatic entities. Archaic in form and style, they are damaged by Swinburne's habit of writing for an imagined Elizabethan audience. However, *The Sisters* is important for the glimpses it gives of Swinburne's early life, his passion for Northumberland, and the emotional loss he suffered as a young man.

Swinburne's later poetry comprises *Studies in Song* (1880), *Songs of the Springtides* (1880), *The Heptalogia* (1880, published anonymously), *Tristram of Lyonesse* (1882), *A Century of Roundels* (1883), *A Midsummer Holiday* (1884), *Poems and Ballads, Third Series* (1889), *Astrophel* (1894), *The Tale of Balen* (1896), and *A Channel Passage* (1904). Watts was largely responsible for the audaciously misrepresentative but frequently reprinted *Selections from Swinburne* (1887), where Swinburne allowed the bulk of his poetry prior to 1879 to be expunged in favour of more recent poems describing landscapes and the sea, subjects of which Watts approved.

Contrary to common belief, Swinburne did not 'die' as a poet in 1879. It is true that a large proportion of this later verse is unrewarding and mechanical, especially where the topics of choice were babies, Elizabethan and Jacobean plays, Shakespeare, Hugo, Landor, or queen and country. But the patient reader will find poems not only very good in their own right but that show Swinburne exploring new territory. These include 'By the North Sea', 'Evening on the Broads', 'On the Cliffs', 'Thalassius', 'In Memory of John William Inchbold', 'Loch Torridon', 'To a Sea-mew', 'The Lake of Gaube', 'In a Rosary', and 'A Nympholept', and pre-eminently *Tristram of Lyonesse* (1882).

Its nine cantos of lyrical heroic couplets retell the story of Tristram and Iseult in a manner that starkly contrasts with the versions by Arnold and Tennyson. Much of the success of *Tristram of Lyonesse* arises because the story had multiple personal resonances for Swinburne. He vivifies the legend by including landscape descriptions based on his knowledge of Northumberland, his visit to the Longships lighthouse in 1859, and to Cornwall in 1864 and 1874. The poem is a compendium of almost all his major themes and preoccupations, including romantic love, sexuality, death, time, and transience. Its hymning of the beauty and energy of the natural world, especially the sea, has an intensity which is almost mystical. Despite their tragic fate, the lovers enjoy a fully consummated love. If, as Swinburne wrote in 'Triumph of Time', 'Let come what will, there is one thing worth, / To have had fair love in the life upon earth', then for a while Tristram and Iseult do indeed possess 'the one thing worth'. In poetic terms at least *Tristram of Lyonesse* for its author reverses the 'reverse experience' of his lost love.

Swinburne's philosophical position develops from the atheistic 1866 poems through the humanism of *Songs before Sunrise* to an attempt to create a mythos in which Apollo as sun-god becomes god of poetry and life, as seen in a poem such as 'By the North Sea'. This in turn dissolves into an outlook arguably agnostic. In later poems such as 'Loch Torridon' or 'The Lake of Gaube' there is a fascinating tension between Swinburne's intellectual resistance to the notion of consciousness surviving death and an emotional desire to believe that it does. This tension is mirrored in the stylistic conflict between the prose organization of the poetry (what it says) and its lyricism (the way it says it). As with W. B. Yeats, Swinburne's later poetry exhibits a recurring engagement with death. He wrote many elegies in later years, some inspired by the deaths of relatives and close friends (Swinburne was survived only by his youngest sister, Isabel).

At the end of the 1880s Swinburne seems to have exchanged letters with his cousin Mrs Disney Leith. As Mary confessed, her marriage had caused 'something of a gap in our constant correspondence and intercourse' (Leith, 26–7), though Swinburne had kept in touch with her mother, Lady Mary Gordon. After Colonel Disney Leith died in 1892, Swinburne and Mary wrote more often, in a humorous cipher, and shared amused fantasies about schooldays and flagellation. She also visited him at The Pines. In the early 1890s Swinburne composed more flagellatory prose and poetry. He dedicated 'Eton: another Ode' to 'M. G.'. Some critics have seen in Mary's own novels and poetry an imaginative attempt to 'work out' the legacy of psychological conflict centred on her choice of marriage partner.

In 1892 Gladstone considered Swinburne as a possible candidate for poet laureateship on Tennyson's death but after correspondence with Lord Acton took his candidacy no further. A bout of pneumonia in 1903 left Swinburne a little weaker than he had been, although he continued to take his daily morning walk across Wimbledon common regardless of the weather, to sleep after lunch, and then work in the afternoon and after dinner in the evening. There were occasional visitors admitted to have lunch with the great poet and personally be shown some of the bibliographical treasures in his library. In 1904 his *Collected Poems* appeared in six volumes, followed by *Collected Plays* in five volumes a year later. He declined an honorary degree from Oxford in May 1907, and a civil-list pension in 1908. He was unsuccessfully short-listed for the Nobel prize for literature. Swinburne died peacefully at The Pines of pneumonia on 10 April 1909. His funeral at Bonchurch on the Isle of Wight on 15 April was not without controversy. His wish that the Church of England's burial rite should not be conducted over his grave was in some measure disregarded.

Posthumous reputation Following his death, Swinburne was the subject of books by Georgian poets Edward Thomas (1912) and John Drinkwater (1913). T. S. Eliot's 'Swinburne' as poet (*The Sacred Wood*, 1920) was less sympathetic, at once acknowledging Swinburne's achievement yet making it seem irrelevant to modern concerns. Edmund Gosse and T. J. Wise edited *Posthumous Poems* (1917), Swinburne's letters (1918), *Contemporaries of Shakespeare* (1919), and the twenty-volume *Bonchurch Collected Works* (1925–7) which included a revision of Gosse's 1912 biography, the first 'life'. Two studies with a specific focus were W. B. Drayton Henderson's *Swinburne and Landor* (1918) and William Rutland's *Swinburne: a Nineteenth Century Hellene* (1931). Georges Lafourcade's *La jeunesse de Swinburne* (1928), *Swinburne's Hyperion* (1927), and a biography in English in 1932 remain valuable.

Interest in Swinburne declined from about 1930 to 1960, owing in part to a general reaction against the Victorians, and the influence of Eliot, F. R. Leavis, and the new criticism. Despite this decline in critical currency, however, Swinburne figured in Mario Praz's *The Romantic Agony* (1933), Clyde K. Hyder published the excellent *Swinburne's Literary Career and Fame* (1937), and Randolph Hughes edited the hitherto unpublished *Lucretia Borgia: the Chronicle of Tebaldeo Tebaldei* (1942), *Pasiphae* (1950), and *Lesbia Brandon* (1952).

The iconoclastic 1960s and the rediscovery of the Pre-Raphaelites brought about a Swinburne revival. Cecil Y. Lang laid the foundation for modern Swinburne studies with his indispensable *The Swinburne Letters* (1959–62), some important articles (notably 'Swinburne's Lost Love', 1959), and *New Writings by Swinburne* (1964). Clyde K. Hyder edited *Swinburne Replies* (1966) and *Swinburne as Critic* (1972), and Francis J. Sypher provided a scholarly text of *A Year's Letters* (1974). John D. Rosenberg's preface to *Swinburne: Selected Poems and Prose* (1968) is an essential appraisal. There were biographies from Jean Overton Fuller (1968), Philip Henderson (1974), Donald Serrell Thomas (1979), and Rikky Rooksby (1997). Jerome McGann's *Swinburne: an Experiment in Criticism* (1972) set the bench-mark for sophisticated discussion of Swinburne as a major poet. Thomas Connolly (1964), Robert L. Peters (1965), David Riede (1978), Kerry McSweeney (1981), Anthony Harrison (1988), and Margot Louis (1990) have all written books on various aspects of Swinburne, while Terry L. Meyers has patiently assembled and annotated a collection of unpublished letters by and to Swinburne, which will supplement Lang's original compilation of the correspondence. By the close of the twentieth century Swinburne had been re-evaluated as a central figure in aestheticism, and there was also a renewed appreciation of his poetry, fiction, and criticism.

RIKKY ROOKSBY

Sources R. Rooksby, *A. C. Swinburne: a poet's life* (1997) · R. Rooksby and N. Shrimpton, eds., *The whole music of passion: new essays on Swinburne* (1993) · W. B. Ober, *Boswell's clap and other essays: medical analyses of literary men's afflictions* (1988) · *The Swinburne letters*, ed. C. Y. Lang, 6 vols. (1959–62) · Mrs D. Leith, *The boyhood of Algernon Charles*

Swinburne (1917) • E. W. Gosse, *The life of Swinburne* (1912) • G. Lafourcade, *La jeunesse de Swinburne* (1928) • G. Lafourcade, *Swinburne: a literary biography* (1932) • C. K. Hyder, *Swinburne: the critical heritage* (1970) • J. D. Rosenberg, 'Preface', *Swinburne: selected poems and prose* (1968) • D. S. Thomas, *Swinburne: the poet in his world* (1979) • L. James, *A forgotten genius: Sewell of St Columba's and Radley* (1945) • Gladstone, *Diaries*
Archives BL, Add. MSS 40887–40888, 45345, 60384, 60391, 60396, 60398, 60576, 62897, 71870 • BL, letters and papers, Add. MS 70628 • Boston PL, letters and literary MSS • Duke U., Perkins L., letters and literary MSS • Eton, MSS • Harvard U., Houghton L., letters and literary MSS • Hunt. L., letters and literary MSS • Mitchell L., NSW, letters and literary MSS • NL Scot., MSS • Ransom HRC, corresp. and papers, incl. literary MSS • Syracuse University, New York, corresp. • Yale U., Beinecke L., letters and literary MSS | Balliol Oxf., MSS and letters to T. Spencer Baynes • BL, letters to Karl Blind, Add. MSS 40125–40126 • BL, letters to Charles Augustus Howell, Ashley MS 5081 • BL, letters to Joseph Knight, Add. MS 62697 • BL, letters to William Morris, Add. MS 45345 • BL, corresp. with D. G. Rossetti, Ashley MSS 4995, 5074 • FM Cam., letters to Edward Burne-Jones; literary MSS, incl. proofs of *Atalanta in Calydon*; poems • Georgetown University, Washington, DC, Edith S. and John S. Mayfield collection • Mitchell L., Glas., corresp. with John Nichol [copies] • Ransom HRC, corresp. with Robert Browning • Rutgers University, New Brunswick, New Jersey, letters, mainly to William Michael Rossetti, and literary MSS • Trinity Cam., letters to Lord Houghton • U. Edin. L., corresp. with James Halliwell-Phillipps • U. Leeds, Brotherton L., letters to Sir Edmund Gosse • U. Newcastle, Robinson L., letters to Lady Trevelyan
Likenesses G. Richmond, group portrait, watercolour, 1843 (*Swinburne and his sisters*), NPG • albumen print, *c.*1851–1859, NPG • W. B. Scott, oils, 1860, Balliol Oxf. • E. Burne-Jones, group portrait, oils, 1861 (*The adoration of the magi*), Tate collection • D. G. Rossetti, watercolour, 1861, FM Cam. • Elliott & Fry, carte-de-visite, *c.*1865, priv. coll. • photograph, *c.*1865, Hult. Arch. • G. F. Watts, oils, 1867, NPG [*see illus.*] • Elliott & Fry, photograph, *c.*1890–1899, repro. in *The Bookman* (June 1909) • W. Rothenstein, chalk drawing, 1895, Hugh Lane Municipal Gallery of Modern Art, Dublin • R. P. Staples, chalk drawing, 1900, NPG • R. M. B. Paxton, oils, 1909, NPG • Ape [C. Pellegrini], caricature, watercolour study, NPG; repro. in *VF* (21 Nov 1874) • M. Beerbohm, drawing (posthumous), Tate collection • M. Beerbohm, drawing (posthumous), Merton Oxf. • M. Beerbohm, drawing (posthumous), AM Oxf. • A. Bryan, cartoon, sepia, NPG • H. Furniss, caricature, pen and ink sketch, NPG • H. M. King, group portrait, photograph, NPG • London Stereoscopic Co., cartes-de-visite, NPG • W. B. Scott, photograph, NPG
Wealth at death £24,282 10*s.* 8*d.*: probate, 14 May 1909, CGPLA Eng. & Wales

Swinburne, Henry

Swinburne, Henry (*c.*1551–1624), ecclesiastical lawyer, was born in Micklegate ward, York, the son of Thomas Swinburne and his wife, Alison Dalynson. He is believed to have been educated in Archbishop Holgate's school in York, and he started his career as a clerk in the office of the registrar of the consistory court at York, where he had become a notary public by 1571. Perhaps with the encouragement of Richard Percy, commissary of the York exchequer court, he went up to Oxford in 1576, and he studied at Hart Hall and Broadgates Hall, graduating as BCL in 1580. While in Oxford he married Ellen Lant, daughter of Bartholomew Lant of Oxford.

On returning to York Swinburne was admitted to practise as an advocate in the ecclesiastical courts of York in 1581, and he subsequently achieved a number of judicial positions. He was appointed auditor of the peculiar of the dean of York by 1593, and he was also custodian of the peculiar of Howden. In 1604 he became commissary of the exchequer court of York, which dealt largely with testamentary business, and he was commissary, or auditor, of the peculiar of the dean and chapter of York from 1613. He attended the high commission court between 1607 and 1622. By 1613 Swinburne's first wife had died and he had married Margaret Wentworth; a son was born to them in December 1613.

Swinburne's lasting claim to fame is as the author of two books on ecclesiastical law. The first of these, *A Briefe Treatise of Testaments and Last Wills*, was the first work of canon law to be published in English, rather than in Latin. It appeared in 1591 (date of colophon) and became a standard work. The second edition was published, under Swinburne's own supervision, in 1611, and the last of seven further editions was issued in 1803. His other published work, *A Treatise of Spousals, or Matrimonial Contracts*, appeared posthumously in 1686, with a further edition in 1711. This work on the law of matrimonial contracts was the first part of an uncompleted four-part work that was intended to include further sections on marriage, divorce, and bastardy. The two opening chapters of the section on marriage exist in a manuscript, believed to be in Swinburne's own hand (Durham University).

Swinburne's works display formidable learning in civil and canon law. Nevertheless, they were written with an eye to the needs of students, and are well-organized and lucid, with touches of homely wisdom. His writings present a personality of conservative views and conventional religious opinions, but not without sly touches of humour. Study of his sources reveals that he was familiar with nearly 300 legal works. He is likely to have owned copies of many of these himself, amounting to an impressive professional library by the standards of the time.

Swinburne died at the age of about seventy-three, between 17 January 1624, when he made a verbal codicil to his will, and 12 June that year, when probate was granted. A memorial inscription in York Minster described him as a friend to the widowed and fatherless, especially in having written in *Testaments* a work of considerable practical use to the bereaved. His will shows him to have been comfortably situated, but by no means rich. The principal beneficiaries were his wife, Margaret, who was still living in 1633, and their son, Toby (1613–1656), apparently his only child, who was the recipient of Swinburne's books and who eventually became a civil lawyer; there were also a number of charitable bequests.

In his own day Swinburne was greatly respected for his integrity and learning, while in later times his writings, although they emphasize theory rather than practice, have become important historical sources regarding the complex testamentary and matrimonial law of the sixteenth and seventeenth centuries, giving them enduring value. SHEILA DOYLE

Sources J. D. M. Derrett, *Henry Swinburne (?1551–1626): civil lawyer of York* (1973) • J. H. Baker, 'Henry Swinburne, B.C.L. (†1624)', *Ecclesiastical Law Journal*, 3 (1993), 5–9 • S. Doyle, 'An uncompleted work by Henry Swinburne on matrimony', *Journal of Legal History*, 19 (1998), 162–72 • R. A. Marchant, *The church under the law: justice, administration and discipline in the diocese of York, 1560–1640* (1969) • Wood, *Ath.*

Oxon., 1st edn, 1.386 · will, Borth. Inst., D and C v. 5 [Henry Swinburne], fols. 248v–249r · W. Paver, *Pedigrees of families of the city of York* (1842), 20

Archives Borth. Inst., papers relating to Swinburne in his official capacity · Durham Cath. CL, Raine MS 124, fols. 230–36 · U. Durham, Mickleton and Spearman MS 4

Likenesses memorial effigy, York Minster

Wealth at death £500 to his son; plus a sizeable house in Petergate, York; several small bequests to individuals and charitable causes: Derrett, *Henry Swinburne*, 9–10; R. Davies, 'A memoir of Sir Thomas Herbert', *Yorkshire Archaeological and Topographical Journal*, 1 (1870), 202

Swinburne, Henry (1743–1803), traveller, was born in Bristol on 8 July 1743, the fourth son of Sir John Swinburne, third baronet (*d.* 1745), of Capheaton, Northumberland, head of an old Roman Catholic family, and Mary (*d.* 1761), only daughter of Edward Bedingfeld, and granddaughter of Sir Henry Bedingfeld, of Oxburgh, Norfolk. Swinburne was educated at Scorton School, near Catterick, Yorkshire, the monastic seminary at Lacelle, France, the University of Paris, Bordeaux, and finally the Royal Academy in Turin, where he developed a keen interest in the arts.

By 1763 the deaths of his father, mother, and eldest brother left him financially independent. He undertook a tour of Italy, visiting the art treasures and antiquities of Turin, Genoa, and Florence, and learning Italian. On his return journey to England, he met in Paris Martha, daughter of John Baker, of Chichester, solicitor to the Leeward Islands. Martha was a wealthy heiress then being educated at a convent of Ursuline nuns. They were married at Aix-la-Chapelle on 24 March 1767.

The couple settled in Hamsterley, co. Durham, where Henry laid out the garden, combining 'the classic precision of the Italian style with the more wild and sylvan boldness of English park scenery' (H. Swinburne, *Courts of Europe*, ed. C. White, 2nd edn, 1895, xii), but they tired of English country life and went abroad again in 1774. They went together to France and in 1775 Swinburne went on without his wife, in the company of Sir Thomas Gascoigne, to Spain. Swinburne's account of their journey, *Travels through Spain in the Years 1775 and 1776* (1779), was illustrated with his drawings of Roman and Moorish architecture. A second edition (2 vols., 1787) and a French translation by J. B. de la Borde (1787) followed. Swinburne's *Views in Spain* (1794) was abridged in 1806 as *Picturesque Tour through Spain* (reprinted 1823).

After returning to Bayonne in June 1776 Swinburne departed with his family for Marseilles. An account of the journey entitled *Supplement to Mr. Swinburne's Travels through Spain* was published in 1787 (after the success of his travel accounts of Spain and southern Italy). From Marseilles they sailed to Naples and from 1777 until early 1779 toured the kingdom of the two Sicilies. They returned to England in July 1779 via Vienna, Frankfurt, and Brussels, but remained for only a few months before leaving once again for Italy. They spent 1780 in Italy and Vienna. As lovers of the arts and Roman Catholics, they mixed with the literati throughout their travels, and were favoured by Catholic sovereigns. In Vienna, Maria Theresa honoured Mrs Swinburne with the order of 'la croix étoilée', and the emperor Joseph stood godfather to their son Joseph. In 1781 they returned to England.

Swinburne's *Travels in the Two Sicilies, 1777–1780* (2 vols., 1783–5) is illustrated with his accomplished sketches. A second edition (4 vols., 1790) and French and German translations (both 1785) followed. An unexceptional—although unexceptionable—man, Swinburne met varying responses to his travel writing. In the preface to the first edition of *Travels in the Two Sicilies* he says that he pursues 'the dull plain track of truth' and claims as its 'merits' its 'truth, perspicuity, and common sense' (2nd edn, xvi). A contemporary reviewer, however, found the *Travels* 'dull and meagre' (*QR*, 159) but more recent commentators commend the simplicity and the lack of affectation in his travel accounts and point out that he was one of the first to relish travel for its own sake (Druène, 3).

By 1783 Swinburne's wife's property in the West Indies had been 'devastated and utterly laid waste by the French and Caribs' (H. Swinburne, *Courts of Europe*, xx). Swinburne went to the French court and, through the influence of Marie-Antoinette, was granted in compensation the uncultivated crown lands on the island of St Vincent, valued at £30,000. When Pitt imposed heavy taxation upon uncultivated lands throughout the West Indies in an effort to increase cultivation, many owners, including Swinburne, were forced to part with their property and Swinburne raised a mere £6500 for his. He declined to petition the House of Commons against this injustice, but retired to Hamsterley, where he devoted himself to educating his eldest son and daughter (he had four sons and six daughters in all). Still much favoured by the French queen, the family subsequently returned to Paris where Marie-Antoinette ordered that the eldest son be enrolled as a royal page.

In September 1796 Swinburne was again in Paris, having been sent by the government to negotiate the exchange of prisoners, a task complicated by the capture by the French of Admiral Sir (William) Sidney Smith on charges of spying. Swinburne's efforts were thwarted, and he was recalled to England in the following year. In November 1801 he accepted the post of vendue master in Trinidad, and also as commissioner, supervising the successful handover of the West Indian islands of St Croix, St John, and St Thomas to the Danes.

Swinburne died from the effects of sunstroke in San Juan, Trinidad, on 1 April 1803, and was buried in San Juan, where his friend Sir Ralph Woodford raised a monument to his memory. Swinburne's library had been sold on 10 January that same year by Leigh and Sotheby, the most interesting articles being bought by his brother.

In 1841 Swinburne's *The Courts of Europe at the Close of the Last Century* was published (2 vols.; 2nd edn, 1895). It consisted mainly of Henry Swinburne's letters from abroad, dating from March 1774, to his brother Sir Edward Swinburne. Edited incompetently by Charles White, it was criticized for its inaccuracies and triviality. Despite Swinburne's having witnessed events leading to the French Revolution and its aftermath, and having known members of the *ancien régime* and the future republican leaders, the *Quarterly Review* judged his account dull, and he was accused of sacrificing authenticity in order to amuse (*QR*, 147–54). Martha Swinburne, who knew Greek, Latin, and several modern languages, and was also a musician, revised and augmented her husband's manuscripts. The reviewer of *The Courts of Europe* considered a selection of her letters, written from France, shortly before the Revolution, to be 'the most interesting portion of the volumes' (*QR*, 164).

However, later critics (mostly French) claim the opposite. Chasles considered Swinburne's the most complete picture of Paris in this period, and claimed that his uniquely unaffected style 'laisse apercevoir à nu cette confusion étrange de la république mourante' ('allows us to take a fresh look at the strange confusion of a dying republic'; Chasles, 73).

Babeau considered Swinburne's account of France at this decisive moment 'assez complète' ('fairly comprehensive'; Babeau, *Les voyageurs*, 351) and Druène judged that he was 'bien informé' ('well-informed') and wrote about what he saw 'sans suspecte tendresse ou souci d'excuser' ('without suspect sensibilities or excuses'; Druène, 6). By concentrating on what he could write on with accuracy from his exceptional position, Swinburne's work is of minor but enduring worth.　　　　　J. E. THURGOOD

Sources B. Druène, *Le premier romantique? Swinburne aux Pyrénées* (Toulouse, 1953) [incl. Fr. trans. of *A journey from Bayonne to Marseilles*] · *QR*, 68 (1841), 145–76 · P. Chasles, *Études sur la littérature et les mœurs de l'Angleterre au XIXe siècle* (Paris, [1850]), 67–74 · A. Babeau, *Les voyageurs en France depuis la Renaissance jusqu'à la Révolution* (Paris, 1885), 351–6 · *European Magazine*, 8 (1785), 243 · *GM*, 1st ser., 54 (1784), 974 · *GM*, 1st ser., 63 (1793), 861 · *GM*, 1st ser., 73 (1803), 479 · *A catalogue of the extensive and very valuable library … of Henry Swinburne … which will be sold … by Leigh, Sotheby & Son … January 10, 1803* [1803] · Burke, *Peerage* · *La France et Paris sous le directoire: … des lettres de Swinburne, 1796–1797*, ed. and trans. A. Babeau (Paris, 1888) · Nichols, *Illustrations*, 3.759; 7.541 · Nichols, *Lit. anecdotes*, 8.640; 9.157 · R. Surtees, *The history and antiquities of the county palatine of Durham*, 2 (1820), 290

Archives Beds. & Luton ARS, corresp. with Lord Grantham

Likenesses H. D. Hamilton, pastel drawing, 1771, Fenman Castle, South Glamorgan · P. Batoni, oils, 1779, Laing Art Gallery, Newcastle upon Tyne · W. Angus, line engraving, BM, NPG; repro. in *European Magazine*, facing p. 243 · M. Bovi, stipple (after R. Cosway), BM, NPG; repro. in H. Swinburne, *Journey from Bayonne to Marseilles* (1787), frontispiece · C. Hewetson, bust, Leeds City Art Galleries, Lotherton Hall, Gascoigne collection

Swinburne, Sir James, ninth baronet (1858–1958), industrial chemist and electrical engineer, was born in Inverness on 28 February 1858, the third of the six sons of Lieutenant Thomas Anthony Swinburne RN and his wife, Mary Anne, daughter of Captain Edward Fraser of Gortuleg. A descendant of the second baronet, Swinburne succeeded a kinsman in 1934. Much of his childhood was spent in the lonely little island of Eilean Shona in Loch Moidart, where the servants and the children all spoke Gaelic. He was educated at Clifton College, Bristol, which was particularly strong in science, then apprenticed at a locomotive works in Manchester where he developed his remarkable inherent skill with his hands. Later he went to Black, Hawthorn & Co. at Gateshead. He was engaged for a time as a

Sir James Swinburne, ninth baronet (1858–1958), by Elliott & Fry

draughtsman with the South Shields Gas Company and in 1881 came first in the City and Guilds examination in gas manufacture. In the same year he joined Joseph Swan, who engaged him to establish lamp factories in Antwerp and Paris. Later he went to America on a similar activity for the Brush Company.

On 28 December 1886 Swinburne married Ellen (1863/4–1893), daughter of Robert Harrison Wilson, a doctor, of Gateshead. They had three sons, the second of whom, Spearman Charles (1893–1967), the survivor of twins, succeeded as tenth baronet. For some years after 1886 he worked as technical assistant and later manager in the dynamo works of R. E. B. Crompton and it was during this time that he invented a watt-hour meter and his well-known hedgehog transformer, leaving in 1894 to set up as a consultant in London, where he had his own beautifully equipped workshop and a chemical and physical laboratory.

During this period Swinburne developed the compound-wound dynamo and was a pioneer in the development of electrical instruments. It was he who coined the words 'rotor' and 'stator'. In 1898 he married Lilian Gilchrist (d. 1964), daughter of Sir Thomas Godfrey Carey, bailiff of Guernsey (1895–1902); they had two daughters. Swinburne was president of the Institution of Electrical Engineers (1902–3) and of the Faraday Society (1909–11), and was recognized as one of the leading authorities of the electrical industry. He was elected FRS in 1906.

Swinburne's professional interests were not confined to

electrical engineering. In 1904 he published a useful book, *Entropy, or, Thermodynamics from an Engineer's Standpoint*. Much of his research work was intimately connected with the application of physics and chemistry to industrial purposes and he was particularly susceptible to any suggestion for the development of new materials. It was he who suggested that lamp filaments and artificial silk might be made from viscose; he had a share in the syndicate manufacturing artificial silk which not long afterwards was taken over by Courtaulds. In the early years of the century, Luft, an Austrian chemist, showed him a piece of resin produced by the reaction of phenol on formaldehyde. He at once recognized its possibilities and in 1904 formed the Fireproof Celluloid Syndicate to investigate them. When he applied for a patent in 1907 he found that he had been anticipated by one day by the Belgian chemist L. H. Baekeland, working in the United States, who thus swept the solid plastic field. But Swinburne was successful in making a lacquer and in 1910 established the Damard Lacquer Company in Birmingham. In 1927 this company with two others was merged into Bakelite Ltd, in Great Britain, making Swinburne its first chairman, in which office he continued until 1953. He was president of the Plastics Institute in 1937–8.

On the occasion of Swinburne's 100th birthday Mr Justice Lloyd-Jacob in the Chancery Division paid tribute to the tremendous contribution which he had made to patent jurisprudence. Over a long period he was greatly in demand as an expert witness in fields which extended far beyond those of electrical engineering and included such diverse inventions as pneumatic tyres, soda syphons, and golf balls. Given with candour and humour, his evidence was unshakeable and completely honest. He himself filed 123 patents. His vigour was as remarkable as the range of his interests which included paper-bag machinery; naval gunnery; raising bullion from the *Egypt*; organ building (he was an accomplished musician) and the work of the Royal Musical Association; sociology; and horology, to which he returned as a hobby in his retirement. A man of great integrity, Swinburne was quite unimpressed by himself and never alluded to his own achievements. He was usually laconic in speech but could be a good talker and was an excellent listener. His sense of humour was acute; he could be scathing but rarely was, seldom lost his temper, and gave the impression of complete imperturbability. He neither smoked nor drank and had a lifelong sympathy with poor people deriving from his apprentice days when he had little money. He was of medium height, very good-looking, and had the courteous manners of a Victorian gentleman at his best.

Swinburne died at his home, Balholm Grange, Mornish Road, Branksome Park, Bournemouth, on 30 March 1958. He was the third fellow of the Royal Society to live to be over 100 years old.

F. A. FREETH, *rev.* ANITA McCONNELL

Sources 'Centogenarian', *Engineering* (28 Feb 1958), 267 · *Engineering* (4 April 1958), 420 · F. A. Freeth, *Memoirs FRS*, 5 (1959), 253–68 · private information (1971) · personal knowledge (1971) · 'Profile: Sir James Swinburne', *New Scientist* (27 Feb 1958) · W. H. E., *Journal of the Institution of Electrical Engineers*, new ser., 4 (1958), 269 · *Plastic Institute Transactions and Journal* (July 1958), J37–J40 · M. E. Swan and K. R. Swan, *Sir Joseph Wilson Swan: a memoir* (1929) · d. cert. · m. cert.
Likenesses T. C. Dugdale, portrait, priv. coll. · Elliott & Fry, photograph, NPG [*see illus.*] · photograph, repro. in *Engineering*
Wealth at death £43,367 14s. 6d.: probate, 5 Sept 1958, *CGPLA Eng. & Wales*

Swinden, Henry (1716–1772), antiquary, was a schoolmaster and subsequently became a land surveyor at Great Yarmouth, Norfolk, where he became a close friend of the herald John Ives. He spent twenty years collecting material for a history of Yarmouth, in which he was assisted both financially and with material by Ives. It was seen neither to be exhaustive nor to have any literary value. Swinden died in Yarmouth while the last sheet was in the press, on 11 January 1772, and the work, entitled *The History and Antiquities of the Ancient Burgh of Great Yarmouth*, was brought out in 1772 by Ives, with a short preface by him, for the benefit of Swinden's widow. Ives also erected a mural tablet to Swinden's memory in St Nicholas's Church, Yarmouth, where Swinden was buried. As well as this work, Swinden published in 1763 a broadsheet showing all the officers of Yarmouth at the time, and giving other topographical information. This was reprinted in 1863. A map or plan of the town by him was also published in 1779.   CHARLOTTE FELL-SMITH, *rev.* J. A. MARCHAND

Sources Nichols, *Lit. anecdotes*, 3.198 · F. Blomefield and C. Parkin, *An essay towards a topographical history of the county of Norfolk*, [2nd edn], 11 vols. (1805–10), vol. 11, p. 392 · *N&Q*, 4th ser., 5 (1870), 63, 175 · D. Turner, *Sepulchral reminiscences of a market town* (1848), 81 n. · J. G. Nall, *Great Yarmouth and Lowestoft* (1866), 9 · F. W. Steer and others, *Dictionary of land surveyors and local map-makers of Great Britain and Ireland, 1530–1850*, ed. P. Eden, 2nd edn, 2, ed. S. Bendall (1997), 498
Archives BL, collections for a history of Great Yarmouth, Add. MS 23012

Swinden, Tobias (1659–1719), Church of England clergyman, was born on 3 December 1659 in Nottinghamshire, probably the son of Tobias Swinden (1617/18–c.1661) of Worsborough, Yorkshire, appointed a prebendary of York in 1660. He entered Merchant Taylors' School in 1671, and was admitted to Jesus College, Cambridge, as a sizar, on 3 December 1674. He gained a Rustat scholarship, graduating BA in 1679 and proceeding MA in 1682. He was appointed rector of Cuxton, Kent, on 5 July 1688, and vicar of Shorne, Kent, on 13 April 1689. Swinden married Jean Whitticar (*bap.* 1668) of Ashwell, Hertfordshire, on 20 May 1689; they had two daughters. Following her death he married, on 14 February 1693, Susanna Collenvill, who survived him. They had at least eight children; at least three died before adulthood.

Swinden wrote *An Enquiry into the Nature and Place of Hell* (1714, second edition 1727), which maintained that hell was a place and its torments eternal, and conjectured that it was located in the sun. Drawing on classical, scriptural, and patristic authorities it applied traditional Christian teaching concerning hell to a Copernican universe. Swinden, a high-churchman, dedicated the book to Francis Atterbury. Translations were published in French

(Amsterdam, 1728, 1757; Leiden, 1733) and German (Leipzig, 1728, 1731; Cöthen, 1748). He published two sermons in 1713 and 1718 respectively: *The Usefulness of a General Standing Liturgy* and *The Divine Original and Authority of the Gospel*.

Swinden resigned his living in September 1719 in favour of his eldest son, Tobias. He died in 1719 and was buried on 2 December in Cuxton church near a monument to three of his sons.   ANDREW STARKIE

Sources *GM*, 1st ser., 59 (1789), 620 • will, PRO, PROB 11/572, sig. 42, fols. 341r–342r • Mrs E. P. Hart, ed., *Merchant Taylors' School register, 1561–1934*, 2 vols. (1936) • W. Cole, transcript of admissions to Jesus College, Cambridge, BL, Add. MS 5820, fol. 168 • 'Index ecclesiasticum', CUL, Foster MSS • J. Thorpe, ed., *Registrum Roffense, or, A collection of antient records, charters and instruments … illustrating the ecclesiastical history and antiquities of the diocese and cathedral church of Rochester* (1769), 770 • Shorne parish register, BL, Add. MS 33915, fols. 130ff. • J. L. Chester, ed., *The parish registers of St Mary Aldermary, London, containing the marriages, baptisms, and burials from 1558 to 1754*, Harleian Society, register section, 5 (1880), 34 • E. Freshfield, ed., *The register book of the parish of St Christopher le Stocks*, 3 vols. in 1 (1882), vol. 2, p. 12 • *Fasti Angl.* (Hardy), 3.226 • Foster, *Alum. Oxon.* • D. Church, *Cuxton: a Kentish village* (1976), 23 • W. Palin, *Stifford* (1871), 179

Swinderby, William (*fl.* 1382–1392), heretic, was a disciple of John Wyclif during the 1380s and 1390s. His origins, date of birth, and education are unknown. He is first recorded in Leicester in 1382, but was apparently not a native of the town; he was called a priest, but doubts about his ordination were later expressed. Late in his recorded career he described himself as 'only simply lettered' (Capes, 262), but his extensive citation of biblical, patristic, and canonistic authorities, in both Latin and English, suggests that he must have been familiar with academic sources.

Before his association with William Smith and other Lollards of Leicester, Swinderby had been a preacher and for a time a hermit, with varied reception, but some support, from the Augustinian canons at Leicester Abbey. He then began preaching Wycliffite views to enthusiastic congregations in and near the town. After an attempt to silence him failed, John Buckingham, bishop of Lincoln, in May 1382 ordered the investigation of sixteen articles brought by three friars; in July Swinderby abjured six heresies and five errors. Punishment was allegedly mitigated by the intercession of John of Gaunt, duke of Lancaster, and of his son. Swinderby was freed, but prohibited from further preaching without licence; he returned to Leicester briefly but soon left for Coventry. Little is known of his activities there, but he seems to have resumed the preaching of similar views, and to have been forced to leave the town.

Swinderby's next certain appearance was in the diocese of Hereford, where Bishop John Trefnant in 1390 obtained a transcript of the condemnation of 1382; evidently Swinderby's preaching was notorious along the Welsh border. In June 1391 Swinderby appeared before Trefnant, and produced a justification of his position on the articles in the Buckingham condemnation and other charges; because of a safe conduct he was allowed to depart unharmed. In the following months he was summoned to appear before Trefnant; this he repeatedly failed to do, although he sent a further document. In October Swinderby appeared and submitted another defence of a longer set of opinions; on these he was adjudged heretical, but he managed to escape from custody. He appealed in writing from Trefnant's condemnation to the king and parliament, but this went unheard, and by early March 1392 he was being sought in Wales. No more is known of his history.

The charges against Swinderby reveal him to have taught characteristic Wycliffite doctrines concerning the eucharist, absolution, tithes, preaching, and ecclesiastical temporalities; he seems to have gone further than some Wycliffites in urging the spiritual incompetence of clerics in mortal sin. It would seem that, despite the obscurity of much of his career, Swinderby was a considerable influence in the early spread of Lollardy.

ANNE HUDSON, *rev.*

Sources register of John Buckingham, Lincs. Arch., register XII, fols. 236–44 • W. W. Capes, ed., *Registrum Johannis Trefnant*, CYS, 20 (1916), 231–78, 408–9 • *Knighton's chronicle, 1337–1396*, ed. and trans. G. H. Martin, OMT (1995), 306–25 [Lat. orig., *Chronica de eventibus Angliae a tempore regis Edgari usque mortem regis Ricardi Secundi*, with parallel Eng. text] • K. B. McFarlane, *John Wycliffe and the beginnings of English nonconformity* (1952) • A. Hudson, *The premature reformation: Wycliffite texts and Lollard history* (1988)

Swindin, Norman (1880–1976), chemical engineer, was born at Silkstone Common, Silkstone, Yorkshire, on 16 December 1880, the eldest of three sons and a daughter of William Swindin, stationmaster at Silkstone, and his wife, Martha Normansell. The family moved in 1884 to Macclesfield, where Swindin attended St Paul's School, winning a scholarship to Macclesfield grammar school. His father died in 1892 and Swindin, aged fourteen, started work as a weigh-bridge clerk to help support his family. In 1895 they moved to his mother's home town of Barnsley, and Swindin found employment as a clerk at Rylands bottling plant. His interest in improving the operating systems in the plant brought home to him his lack of mathematical and scientific knowledge and he began to study at evening classes, a habit which continued throughout his working life.

In 1901 Swindin joined Davis Brothers, a firm of consulting chemical engineers in Manchester, as a draughtsman. He was given a good training and much responsibility, and as George Davis was the owner of the *Chemical Trade Journal*, Swindin found himself writing for this and for technical books published by the firm. He revelled in Manchester's cultural life, joined various social and radical groups, and exchanged his earlier orthodox belief for a respectful atheism. On 14 May 1910 he married Norah Beatrice Bayfield, the daughter of a shipper's clerk, and they set up house at Stockport. It was to be a long and happy, though childless, marriage.

George Davis's death in 1907 caused Swindin to seek work elsewhere. His next three years were spent at the Lennox foundry in south London where he designed chemical vessels to be cast in a non-corroding alloy invented by Lennox. Swindin did not enjoy his time there but learned much that was of use in later years. There was a brief episode with the Safety Celluloid Company, the first manufacturers of cellophane, before Swindin joined Edgar Ashcroft, a more generous inventor who gave him free rein. Around 1918 a change of management drove him out and he joined the staff of Beckton gasworks, spending two years there before moving to work for Frank Elmore designing apparatus for the extraction of zinc and lead from sulphide ores.

Swindin confessed in his autobiography that his whole career had consisted of interludes until he joined Elmore (Swindin, 122), but during his time at Elmore's Harlesden workshops he developed two techniques of fundamental importance for handling and processing corrosive chemicals, which also reduced the cost of plant construction. The first was the Swindin burner for submerged combustion, in which the flame was immersed within the liquor to be heated; the second was a method of bonding vulcanized rubber to mild steel so that corrosive liquors could safely be circulated through steel pipes, pumps, and holding tanks.

Elmore's lead-extraction process ended in failure and his company was taken over. Swindin decided that the time had come for him to set up his own consultancy; having recruited his brother Thomas, and a few friends from previous projects, he set up a laboratory at Wealdstone, trading under the name Nordac. The business flourished and Swindin was able to devote more time to professional activities. He was a member of the Institute of Mechanical Engineers and a founder member of the Institution of Chemical Engineers, in which he was too much of a maverick to reach high office, though he received its Osborne Reynolds medal. He took a keen interest in professional training for young engineers and developed a close association with Loughborough University, which awarded him an honorary degree in 1972. In 1946 and again in 1950 he and his wife crossed the Atlantic to visit chemical engineering plants in the USA and Canada, and in 1948 he was invited to lecture in Paris.

Reading was always Swindin's passion and his means of self-improvement. He retained a strong belief in social justice, without desiring to take part in politics. He was no stranger to the problems of management and administration, yet these had no appeal for him, and although a successful businessman, he never considered himself a capitalist. Swindin retired at the age of eighty, and moved to Bognor Regis, where he died at his home, 7 Parkway, on 25 August 1976.   ANITA MCCONNELL

Sources N. Swindin, *Engineering without wheels: an autobiography* (1962) · D. Freshwater, 'Famous men remembered: Norman Swindin', *Chemical Engineer* (Nov 1984), 68–9 · m. cert. · d. cert.
Archives Loughborough University of Technology Library, personal and business corresp. and papers
Likenesses photographs, repro. in Swindin, *Engineering without wheels*
Wealth at death £113,954: probate, 17 Nov 1976, *CGPLA Eng. & Wales*

Swineshead, Richard (*fl. c.*1340–1354), natural philosopher, has sometimes been confused with his presumably older contemporary Roger *Swineshead, who, like Richard, wrote on logic and natural philosophy and displayed some mathematizing tendencies. Both Swinesheads possibly originated from the Lincolnshire village of Swineshead and may even have been related. What is more certain is that Richard was educated at Oxford, and was a fellow of Merton College by 1344, and perhaps by 1340. To confuse matters further, there was also at Merton another Swineshead, this time called John, who devoted his later life to law, but is more clearly distinct from Roger and Richard than they are from each other.

In any case, although subsequent writers understandably got the names mixed up, it was the series of treatises known as the *Liber calculationum* that made Richard Swineshead the 'Calculator' *par excellence*. Two printed editions appeared before 1500 (Padua, *c.*1477, and Pavia, 1498) and a particularly widely diffused one came from Venice in 1520. Girolamo Cardano (*d.* 1576) counted him as one of the ten most outstanding intellects that the world had seen, and Robert Burton (*d.* 1640), in his *Anatomy of Melancholy*, wrote that he 'well nigh exceeded the bounds of human genius' (Burton, 63). Leibniz praised him as the person who 'introduced mathematics [*mathesis*] into scholastic philosophy' (*Opera omnia*, 5.567), and extolled the virtues of his *semi-mathematica* to the English mathematician John Wallis (*d.* 1703). But any modern reader who has approached Swineshead's work will not be surprised that it is more admired than read, and, especially if in jaundiced mood, will feel some sympathy with those Renaissance humanists who denounced such trifling *quisquiliae*. A fourteenth-century poet described Roger Swineshead as *subtilis*, but Richard came to be known as *subtilissimus*.

Part of the difficulty of the texts comes from their being written in an extremely elaborate scholastic mode with a multitude of positions, objections, counter-objections, distinctions, responses, and so on, so that it is often difficult to determine what Swineshead himself has concluded. And all this is laced with intricate mathematical niceties, expressed in a language which makes even the modern mathematically trained reader feel far more of a stranger than he or she would in the realms of ancient Greek geometry. It must be emphasized that Swineshead's *calculationes* had very little to do with any form of arithmetical reckoning, but they do share a concern with the quantitative, and particularly with how one may properly express the size of things that are not spatially extended, or at least not *only* spatially extended. For instance, in the first treatise of the work it is asked how the intensity and the contrary remissness of a quality are to be measured (or, more technically, 'attended'), whether (1) intensity by nearness to the highest degree and remissness by distance from it, or (2) intensity by distance from zero degree and remissness by distance from the highest degree, or (3) intensity by distance from zero degree and remissness by nearness to it. The general strategy is to represent the size of entities that are not spatially extended by lengths of lines, etc., even if Swineshead does not make much use of the geometrical diagrams that were later so characteristic of Nicole Oresme (d. 1382) and others. It should be stressed that there is precious little empirical reference to actual physical bodies in Swineshead's treatises. His discussions reek of the lecture hall, though it is difficult to imagine how any student would have had the intellectual nimbleness to absorb, much less combat, such intricate argumentation in a purely oral context.

Subsequent tracts of the *Liber calculationum* bring in further complications by, for instance, considering the distribution of intensities across an extended subject and the relation of the intensities of mixtures to those of the constituent elements. Similar treatments are meted out to such topics as rarity and density, action and reaction, intensities of light, maxima and minima, and, pervasively, motion. Throughout the work great use is made of a characteristically late-medieval and early-modern language of ratios, whose power may at first glance be disguised from the modern reader because of a syntactic change in mathematical language. For Swineshead and others of his time, the composition of ratios (what would now be regarded as the multiplication of fractions) was interpreted as addition. This had numerous important effects: for instance, it had allowed Thomas Bradwardine (d. 1349) to formulate a law of motion as, 'The ratio of speeds in motions follows the ratio of the power of the mover to the power of the thing moved' (*Tractatus de proportionibus*, 110); a simple statement, but one which, if translated into modern mathematical language, demands the use of a logarithmic or an exponential function. This law played an important role in Richard Swineshead's work but had been rejected in an earlier treatise by Roger Swineshead.

It would be as inappropriate as it would be impossible to attempt here anything like a full summary of the *Liber calculationum*, but it may be worth lingering a little over Treatise XI (modern edition by Hoskin and Molland, as 'Swineshead on falling bodies'), which has been described by Murdoch and Sylla as 'mathematically perhaps the most complicated and sophisticated section' of the work (Murdoch and Sylla, 198). It concerns a heavy body falling through the centre of the world, and it is asked whether the part that has already passed the centre (and so in a sense is falling upwards) resists the descent of the whole body, which would be completed when its centre coincided with the world's centre. Swineshead first assumes that it does, and then by very elaborate mathematical argumentation, and with use of Bradwardine's law of motion, he shows that, if this were the case, the body would continue to descend more and more slowly in such a way that its centre would never reach the centre of the world. This means for him that a natural desire on the body's part (in common with Aristotle, his physics had a strong teleological element) was incapable of natural fulfilment, which he regards as an absurd conclusion. He therefore adopts the alternative position that the body acted not as the sum of its parts but as a single whole, of which each part acted for the good of the whole. The discussion of this position is notably briefer and less mathematical than that of the rejected position, and it is difficult to see how it could have been otherwise. Thus there arises a paradoxical situation in which highly sophisticated mathematics has been used to undermine the possibility of a realistic mathematical treatment of the topic at issue. There has been much discussion concerning what influence Swineshead and those like him may have had on later developments in mathematical physics by such as Galileo. This treatise strongly suggests that, in the absence of greater, and perhaps inflated, confidence in the very possibility of the subject, fourteenth-century endeavours were all too liable to be self-defeating.

Besides the *Liber calculationum*, three other short treatises are generally attributed to Richard Swineshead which share much of the former's character. No printed edition has yet appeared, but the treatises are described, with information on location of manuscripts, by Murdoch and Sylla in their article in the *Dictionary of Scientific Biography*. The *Liber calculationum* is generally assigned to a date of about 1350. The intellectual vigour and subtlety displayed therein seem in 1349 to have been matched by physical vigour, if not subtlety, in the author's participation in the riotous election (or imposition) of his fellow Mertonian John Wylyot as chancellor of Oxford University. Deaths were reported to have occurred, and Swineshead was one of the named recipients of a royal command to return the university's seal and other things that had been forcibly carried off from the university chest. In 1354 he was ordained deacon to the title of his fellowship, and after that it is his works rather than his person that impinge on the historical record.   GEORGE MOLLAND

Sources J. E. Murdoch and E. D. Sylla, 'Swineshead (Swynesbed, Suicet, etc.), Richard', *DSB* · M. A. Hoskin and A. G. Molland, 'Swineshead on falling bodies: an example of fourteenth-century physics', *British Journal for the History of Science*, 3 (1966–7), 150–82 · A. G. Molland, 'The geometrical background to the "Merton School": an exploration into the application of mathematics to natural philosophy in the fourteenth century', *British Journal for the History of Science*, 4 (1968–9), 108–25 · A. G. Molland, 'Richard Swineshead and continuously varying quantities', *Actes du XIIe congrès international d'histoire des sciences* (1970–71), 4.127–30 · J. E. Murdoch, 'Mathesis in philosophiam scholasticam introducta: the rise and development of the application of mathematics in fourteenth century philosophy and theology', *Arts libéraux et philosophie au moyen âge: actes du quatrième congrès international de philosophie médiévale* (1969), 215–54 · Emden, *Oxf.*, 3.1836–7 · *CCIR, 1349–54*, 74 · A. G. Molland, 'Continuity and measure in medieval natural philosophy', *Miscellanea Mediaevalia*, 16/1 (1983), 132–44 · J. A. Weisheipl, 'Ockham and some Mertonians', *Mediaeval Studies*, 30 (1968), 163–213 · J. A. Weisheipl, 'Repertorium Mertonense', *Mediaeval Studies*, 31 (1969), 174–224 · M. Clagett, 'Richard Swineshead and late medieval physics', *Osiris*, 9 (1950), 131–61 · *Thomas of Bradwardine, his Tractatus de proportionibus: its significance for the development of mathematical physics*, ed. and trans. H. L. Crosby (1955) · R. Burton, *The anatomy of melancholy*, ed. F. Dell and P. Jordan-Smith (1927) · *Gothofredi Guillelmi Leibnitii … opera omnia*, ed. L. Dutens, 5 (1768), 567

Swineshead, Roger (d. 1365?), natural philosopher and Benedictine monk, is now, following the work of J. A. Weisheipl, generally assumed to have been a different person from Richard *Swineshead, an Oxford contemporary who wrote on similar themes. Roger's place of origin is unknown, but it might be conjectured that he came from the Lincolnshire village of Swineshead, and even that he was related, perhaps as older brother, to Richard Swineshead. His education was almost certainly at Oxford, but it would seem that, unlike Richard, he was never a fellow of Merton College. Nevertheless, the evidence strongly suggests an intellectual association with such Mertonians as Thomas Bradwardine, Richard Kilvington and William Heytesbury.

Roger Swineshead is chiefly known for two logical works, the *Insolubilia* and the *Obligationes*, both edited, with discussion, by P. V. Spade, and for a work on natural philosophy, known under various titles, but now usually referred to as *De motibus naturalibus*. A small part of this is edited in Sylla, 'Mathematical physics and imagination', and summary accounts of its contents are given in Weisheipl, 'Roger Swynesheed', and Sylla, *The Oxford Calculators and the Mathematics of Motion*; only two (rather unsatisfactory) manuscripts are known to be extant: Erfurt, Wissenschaftliche Bibliothek, MS Amplon. F135, and Paris, Bibliothèque Nationale, MS Lat. 16621.

The *Insolubilia* is mainly concerned with propositions of the 'liar paradox' type, in which, for instance, Socrates speaking of himself says, 'Socrates is uttering a falsehood'. Are we to think of him as speaking truly or falsely? Each assumption seems to lead to a contradiction, and, accordingly, the question aroused much medieval discussion. Swineshead's apparently novel solution involved demanding that for a sentence to be true it had *both* to tell it how it was *and* not to falsify itself; but this itself had some unwelcome conclusions. The solution was strongly criticized by William Heytesbury in his *Regulae solvendi sophismata* of 1335, but nevertheless exerted considerable subsequent influence, especially in the fifteenth century, both in England and on the continent; it was printed in two collections of logical texts, addressed respectively to students at Cambridge and at Oxford. Swineshead also seems to have been innovative in the rather obscure and puzzling logical theory of obligations, which Spade thinks should be seen as dealing with what in modern terms would be called counterfactual conditionals. Here Swineshead seems to have been building on work by Richard Kilvington, and the position that he adopted was soon regarded as one of the two principal ones then current in Oxford.

Swineshead's *De motibus naturalibus* is notable as a relatively early example of fourteenth-century attempts to give more mathematical accounts of motion, and not only of local motion (change of place), but of alteration (intensification and remission of qualities), and augmentation and diminution (change of size). Swineshead clearly made use of Thomas Bradwardine's *Tractatus de proportionibus* of 1328, but he rejected the now famous 'law of motion' to be found in part 3 of that work. This is in strong contrast to the later work of Richard Swineshead, where Bradwardine's law played an essential role. Besides its quantitative aspects, the *De motibus* also included ontological discussions of motion, time, elements, mixture, and so on, and made reference to burning mirrors, tides, meteorological phenomena, the generation of frogs and flies, and other such topics.

These three works belong in the context of Oxford University's arts faculty. But Swineshead also acquired a theological degree and at an unknown date became a Benedictine monk at Glastonbury. In this capacity he was praised in the course of a poem by the Franciscan Richard Trevytlam (probably written in the late 1360s) as:

Subtilis Swynyshed, proles Glastoniae,
Revera monachus bonae memoriae.
('Subtle Swineshead, son of Glastonbury, truly a monk of happy memory'; Furneaux, 204)

This was in contrast to another Glastonbury monk, John Sene, who was a *bête noire* for Trevytlam. In May 1365 the abbot of Glastonbury returned to Malmesbury Abbey two manuscript codices that Roger had borrowed, and so there is a strong possibility that he had recently died. One of the volumes contained a copy of the ninth-century philosopher John Scottus's *De divisione naturae*, which in 1225 had been condemned by Pope Honorius III and all copies ordered to be burnt.   GEORGE MOLLAND

Sources J. A. Weisheipl, 'Roger Swyneshed, OSB, logician, natural philosopher, and theologian', *Oxford studies presented to Daniel Callus*, OHS, new ser., 16 (1964), 231–52 · E. D. Sylla, 'Mathematical physics and imagination in the work of the Oxford calculators: Roger Swineshead's On natural motions', *Mathematics and its applications to science and natural philosophy in the middle ages: essays in honor of Marshall Clagett*, ed. E. Grant and J. E. Murdoch (1987), 69–101 · P. V. Spade, *Lies, language and logic in the late middle ages* (1988) · P. V. Spade, 'Roger Swyneshed's *Insolubilia*: edition and comments', *Archives d'Histoire Doctrinale et Littéraire du Moyen Âge*, 46 (1979), 177–220 · P. V. Spade, 'Roger Swyneshed's *Obligationes*: edition and comments', *Archives d'Histoire Doctrinale et Littéraire du Moyen Âge*, 44 (1977), 243–85 · Emden, *Oxf.*, 3.1837 · J. E. Murdoch and E. D. Sylla, 'Swineshead (Swyneshed, Suicet, etc.), Richard', *DSB* · N. Kretzmann, A. Kenny, and J. Pinborg, eds., *The Cambridge history of later medieval philosophy: from the rediscovery of Aristotle to the disintegration of scholasticism, 1100–1600* (1982) · E. D. Sylla, *The Oxford calculators and the mathematics of motion, 1320–1350: physics and measurement by latitudes* (1991) · E. D. Sylla, 'Medieval concepts of the latitude of forms: the Oxford calculators', *Archives d'Histoire Doctrinale et Littéraire du Moyen Âge*, 40 (1973), 223–83 · J. A. Weisheipl, 'Ockham and some Mertonians', *Mediaeval Studies*, 30 (1968), 163–213 · H. Furneaux, ed., 'Tryvytlam de laude universitatis Oxoniae', *Collectanea: third series*, ed. M. Burrows, OHS, 32 (1896), 188–209 · E. J. Ashworth and P. V. Spade, 'Logic in late medieval Oxford', *Hist. U. Oxf.* 2: *Late med. Oxf.*, 35–64
Archives Bibliothèque Nationale, Paris, MS Lat. 16621 · Wissenschaftliche Bibliothek, Erfurt, MS Amplon. F135

Swiney [née Biggs], (**Rosa**) **Frances Emily** (1847–1922), writer and women's rights activist, was born in Poona, India, on 21 April 1847, the daughter of Ensign John Biggs of HM 8th regiment, later to become a major in the 4th Royal Irish dragoon guards, and his wife, Frances Charlotte Malden. John Biggs's family claimed descent, through the Hesketh family, from Sir Isaac Newton. Frances Biggs spent most of her childhood in Ireland, returning to India apparently in early adulthood. Her first main interest was in painting. She studied under James Danby, son of Francis Danby RA, and specialized in pictures of

(Rosa) Frances Emily Swiney (1847–1922), by unknown photographer, c.1902

Indian scenery and life, exhibiting at Simla, Madras, and Birmingham. She had even intended taking up painting as a profession, but on 1 June 1871 she married Major John Swiney (1832–1918), of Donegal, who was fifteen years her senior, and became a full-time wife and mother. In 1877 Swiney returned to Britain and settled in Cheltenham, Gloucestershire, where her husband finally joined her ten years later (he retired in 1890). She soon became involved in political activity, first through the Primrose League, becoming a member of its executive council (although she later left the league) and writing pamphlets on Irish home rule of a generally Unionist character. She retained a keen interest in Irish affairs, towards the end of her life being a strong supporter of the 1921 treaty.

Despite her apparently conventional circumstances, Swiney held many ideas popular with the radical progressive intelligentsia of her day, and was an active member of such bodies as the Malthusian League, the Secular Education League, and the Eugenic Education Society. Her eugenic beliefs led her to write a series of leaflets entitled 'Racial Poisons', warning of the dangers of such things as alcohol, tobacco, and syphilis. However, her main political and philosophical interest was in feminism. She became involved with the Women's Emancipation Union, and in 1896 joined with Harriet McIlquham and others to form the Cheltenham Women's Suffrage Society, of

which she remained the president until it merged with the local Women Citizens' Association in 1920. Despite her long connection with Cheltenham, she seems to have found campaigning there hard, and described it on her retirement from the suffrage society as 'the town of no ideas'; on one occasion in 1913 she was mobbed while attempting to address a meeting on women's suffrage. Although her main official position linked her to the eventually non-militant National Union of Women's Suffrage Societies, she also joined the highly militant Women's Social and Political Union and the Women's Freedom League, and strongly defended militant action. In addition, from about 1907 she was the moving force behind the League of Isis, although she attributed its origin to Henry Ancketill of Durban, Natal. The object of the league was to promote the protection of maternity and more rational and humane sex relations generally. The league regularly met in the Eustace Miles Restaurant, London, and by 1911 it also had branches in New York, South Africa, and India.

At a time that saw a great flowering of feminist activity and theoretical writing, Frances Swiney stood out as a highly original feminist thinker. Her writing increasingly reflected her interest in a theosophical matriarchalism, and an evolutionary philosophy of feminism. As she put it in *Woman and Natural Law* (1912), she believed that '[t]he first male cell, and the first male organism, was an initial failure on the part of the maternal organism to reproduce its like, and was due to a chemical deficiency in the metabolism or physique of the mother'; much of her writing was concerned to redress the malign effects of that failure. A major feature of her work which has contributed to her popularity with more recent feminists was her view that women should have control over their own sexuality, expressed in terms similar to those of radical feminists such as Elizabeth Wolstenholme Elmy, as, for example, in her insistence that the female alone should have the right to regulate sexual intercourse.

Swiney's many feminist publications began with *The Plea of Disfranchised Women*, published in 1897 under the auspices of the Women's Emancipation Union, and continued regularly thereafter, including such titles as *The Awakening of Women* (2nd edn, 1905), *The Bar of Isis* (1907), and *The Cosmic Procession* (1906). She was a frequent contributor to periodicals. From 1902 to 1914 she wrote a regular column entitled 'Women among the nations' for Jaakoff Prelooker's monthly *The Anglo-Russian*, a paper which, as well as informing a British readership of the political situation in Russia, carried considerable information on feminist movements in Europe and the United States. In addition, from 1912 to 1914 she regularly wrote for *The Christian Commonwealth*, and at this time she also frequently contributed to the American feminist paper *The Woman's Tribune*. Above all, in 1913 and 1914 she wrote a series of major articles on sexuality for *The Awakener*, the journal of the Men's League for Women's Rights, a body campaigning against the traffic in women and for women's suffrage.

Swiney's last major work, and the culmination of her

philosophical beliefs, was *The Ancient Road, or, The Development of the Soul* (1918). However, that year also saw the death of General Swiney, at the age of eighty-six, and she herself did not long outlive him; she died of bronchial asthma on 3 May 1922 at her home, Sandford Lawn, Bath Road, Cheltenham, and was buried in Leckhampton churchyard three days later. She was survived by four sons and a daughter, all of whom had seen distinguished service in the First World War.
DAVID DOUGHAN

Sources *Gloucestershire Echo* (4 May 1922), 5 · A. J. R., ed., *The suffrage annual and women's who's who* (1913), 372–3 · *The Anglo-Russian* (1902–14) · *Cheltenham Chronicle* (13 May 1922), 6 · J. Prelooker, *Under the Russian and British flags* (1912) · *CGPLA Eng. & Wales* (1922) · *WWW* · m. cert. · d. cert. · Ecclesiastical returns of births, baptisms, marriages and burials (Bombay presidency), 1847 · will, proved, Gloucester, 1922
Archives Wellcome L., Stopes MSS
Likenesses photograph, c.1902, Mary Evans Picture Library, London [see illus.]
Wealth at death £879 5s. 9d.: probate, 23 June 1922, *CGPLA Eng. & Wales*

Swiney, George (1784–1868). *See under* Swiney, George (c.1786–1844).

Swiney, George (c.1786–1844), doctor and benefactor, was the son of William Swiney (1760–1820), Royal Navy lieutenant from January 1771, captain from May 1779, rear-admiral of the blue from February 1797, and admiral of the white from July 1810, a descendant of Major Matthew Swiney (1681–1766), who fought at Dettingen. Educated at Edinburgh University, he graduated MD in 1816 with a thesis entitled 'De insania'. After retiring from practice he settled in London and lived a secluded life, very seldom going out and acquiring a reputation as an eccentric. Latterly he spent much time revising his will and framing elaborate instructions for his funeral. He directed that it be on foot, that the coffin be covered with bright yellow cloth, and that the pall and the mourners' cloaks be the same material. In his last two years he did not shave, and his beard reached almost to his waist. Always exceptionally abstemious, in his last month he reportedly refused to eat.

Swiney died at Grove Street, Camden Town, London, on 21 January 1844, and his coffin was accompanied to St Martin's cemetery, Pratt Street, Camden Town, by an enormous crowd attracted by rumours and exaggerations in the newspapers concerning a parcel with mysterious instructions that Swiney had left at the Society of Arts, John Adam Street, London, about twelve years previously. The parcel contained a will in the society's favour, but as no trace could then be found of the testator it was regarded as a hoax. After Swiney's death, however, it was found in a codicil (dated 14 November 1835) to his will (dated 27 May 1831) that he had bequeathed £5000 to the Society of Arts to found a quinquennial prize for the best published work on jurisprudence (to be adjudicated jointly by the Society of Arts and the Royal College of Physicians); and £5000 to the British Museum to found a lectureship in geology, the lecturer to be an MD of Edinburgh. Swiney's will was proved on 6 February 1844.

Among the Swiney prize-winners since have been Sir Henry Maine, for his *Ancient Law* (1864), Leone Levi, and Sir Robert Joseph Phillimore. The prize, of £100 along with a cup then valued at £100 (designed by Daniel Maclise in 1849), is still awarded by the Royal Society of Arts.

A first cousin, **George Swiney** (1784–1868), army officer in the East India Company, son of John and Mary Swiney, was born at Tottenham High Cross, Middlesex, on 7 April 1784. Educated at the Royal Military Academy, Woolwich (February 1800 to January 1802), he went to India as an East India Company cadet in 1802 and served in the Bengal artillery. He was promoted lieutenant in August 1802, captain in October 1811, major in August 1819, lieutenant-colonel in May 1824, colonel in December 1834, colonel-commandant in December 1834, major-general in June 1838, lieutenant-general in November 1851, and general in May 1859. Swiney served in the Second Anglo-Maratha War (1804–5) including at the battle and capture of Dig (November and December 1804). He commanded the artillery in the three assaults on Bharatpur, in the last of which he was wounded, on 20 February 1805. He also commanded the artillery at the siege and capture of Emaum Ghur in 1810, and received the thanks of the vice-president in council and the commander-in-chief. He was principal commissary of ordnance from 1824 to 1835, and eventually became the senior officer of the Royal (Bengal) Artillery.

From March 1835 until his death Swiney was on furlough (sick certificate). He married in Bloomsbury, London, in October or November 1816 Julia Anne Catherine (1794/5–1818), only daughter of the Revd Hemsworth Ussher of Templeoran, co. Westmeath, rector of Clonfadforan. She died in Calcutta in April 1818. In Bengal, on 7 March 1823, Swiney married Maria Isabella (1800/01–1884), eldest daughter of Alexander Haig of the Bengal medical establishment. Swiney died at his residence, 5 Sandford Place, Bath Road, Cheltenham, Gloucestershire, on 10 December 1868. His nephew, Colonel George Clayton Swiney, entered the Bengal cavalry in October 1857, was transferred to the 6th dragoon guards, served in the Indian mutiny, and wrote *Historical Records of the 32nd (Duke of Cornwall's) Light Infantry* (1893).
THOMAS SECCOMBE, rev. ROGER T. STEARN

Sources *GM*, 2nd ser., 22 (1844), 100–01 · *ILN* (3 Feb 1844) · private information (1898, 2004) [Royal Society of Arts] · *Nomina eorum, qui gradum medicinae doctoris in academia Jacobi sexti Scotorum regis, quae Edinburgi est, adepti sunt, ab anno 1705 ad annum 1845*, University of Edinburgh (1846) · D. B. Smith and Royal Navy College, eds., *The commissioned sea officers of the Royal Navy, 1660–1815*, 3 vols. [n.d., c.1954] · V. C. P. Hodson, *List of officers of the Bengal army, 1758–1834*, 4 (1947) · Boase, *Mod. Eng. biog.*

Swiney, Owen. *See* Swiny, Owen (1676–1754).

Swinfen. For this title name *see* Eady, Charles Swinfen, first Baron Swinfen (1851–1919).

Swinfield, Richard (d. 1317), bishop of Hereford, came from Kent. His name suggests that his family originated from the parish of Swingfield near Folkestone, and he continued to hold land in the county, at Womenswold near Canterbury, while he was bishop. His date of birth is unrecorded and little is known about his family. His father, Stephen of Swinfield, died in 1282 and was buried near Ledbury in Herefordshire, and Richard had at least one brother, also called Stephen, who did not enter the church.

Swinfield attended university, obtaining the degree of doctor of divinity, although exactly where he took this, and when, is unknown. The record of his life becomes more detailed after 1264, when he entered the household of Thomas de Cantilupe, bishop of Hereford, whom he was to succeed in that office. According to at least one contemporary, Richard was to become the most important member of Bishop Cantilupe's *familia*. During the following years he gained extensive ecclesiastical preferment. He received two prebends at Hereford, one in 1277 and the second in May 1279. On 17 April 1280 Cantilupe also collated Swinfield to the archdeaconry of Shrewsbury in the expectation that James d'Aigueblanche was to be deprived of this post, but in the event this came to nothing. Swinfield had, however, risen to the position of archdeacon by September 1281 when he is first described as archdeacon of London; he had previously held the prebend of St Pancras at St Paul's Cathedral. He last appears as archdeacon in July 1282. Three months later, following the death of Cantilupe, he was elected bishop of Hereford. His election was confirmed by Archbishop Pecham on 31 December of the same year and he received the spiritualities of the see, followed swiftly by the temporalities on 8 January 1283. He was consecrated as bishop on 7 March 1283, beginning an episcopate of thirty-four years which was to be dominated by the memory of his immediate predecessor.

As bishop, Richard Swinfield rarely left his diocese and seems to have had little political interest. He had accompanied Cantilupe on the trip to Italy in 1282 during which the latter died, but throughout his attempts to secure Cantilupe's canonization he made no attempt to journey to Rome himself to plead his predecessor's case. In 1289 he acted as mediator between the bishop of Lincoln and the masters of Oxford in a dispute concerning presentation to the chancellorship of that university, and in 1296 he and the bishop of Norwich formed a deputation to Edward I, protesting against royal exactions on behalf of the prelates of the southern province. More often, however, he excused himself from attending parliaments and synods on the grounds of urgent business within the see or ill health. Indeed he used his London house so infrequently that in 1311 he let it to a prominent merchant and citizen of London, Hamo Chigwell (*d.* 1332).

It was true that Swinfield was greatly occupied within his see, not least with litigation. Conciliatory by nature, he was careful, for instance, to maintain good relations with Archbishop Pecham, with whom Bishop Cantilupe had been on such bad terms; nevertheless several quarrels, originating from before his episcopate, continued to trouble him. Thus it was he who had to bear the brunt of the lawsuit brought by one Peter Langon against Cantilupe, who had deprived him of his Hereford prebend, seeking the return of the prebend and the payment of

damages. This case was not resolved until 1290. Swinfield was also involved in a quarrel concerning the boundaries of the dioceses of St Asaph and Hereford; an agreement was made in 1288, but the bishop of St Asaph remained discontented. Hostility between the bishop of Hereford and the citizens of that city also had a long history, reaching back to the 1220s, and this too recurred during Swinfield's episcopate. As late as 1316 he had to threaten the people of Hereford with excommunication for usurping power in the bishop's fee.

Swinfield was greatly concerned with religious life within his diocese and zealous in carrying out visitations, at least in the early years of his episcopate. His surviving household roll, of 1289/90, provides a vivid picture of the strenuous nature of his careful diocesan administration. Thus 1 May 1290 found Swinfield and his retinue crossing mountainous territory to reach Pontesbury, but taking no rest before travelling on to Westbury near Caus where they spent two days, dining with Sir William Herbert. On 4 May the bishop moved once more, to Alberbury, where he consecrated the parish church. Two days later the entourage was travelling again, this time to Chirbury where Swinfield visited the parish church on the Saturday and dedicated it on the Sunday. Here he and his household were entertained under procuration by the house of Augustinian canons there, with whom the bishop seems to have parted on good terms, as he was presented with a colt by the prior as he left on 8 May. From here they travelled to Bishops Castle, where preparations for Ascension day took place: three days of fasting were to be followed by a celebratory feast, the great feature of which was to be venison, both fresh and salted. The next day the bishop set out again, for Clunbury. Meanwhile, payments recorded in the roll are a reminder that while the bishop was concerned with diocesan business, members of his household were attending to his other interests, at home and abroad.

Swinfield's concerns were expressed through practical action. Where irregularities and unrest were discovered in the monastic houses of the diocese, as at Leominster in 1283 and 1287, at Chirbury in 1287, and at Wigmore in 1289, he made strenuous efforts to have these errors corrected. Although appropriations to religious houses continued during his episcopate Swinfield did not give automatic consent to these, seeking to ascertain first whether or not they were necessary. Many of his charters concerning appropriations speak of the poverty of the appropriating houses, and he seems to have given genuine consideration to the financial state of the monasteries before approving such grants. In 1305 he proved extremely reluctant to approve the appropriation of Lindridge church to Worcester Priory, because of the latter's wealth.

Swinfield also demonstrated concern for the personnel of his diocese, although his adherence to ecclesiastical principles was tempered by realism. He acted swiftly when clerics were unjustly treated, as in the case of the chaplain of Hyssington, and refused the king's request to grant a prebend or benefice to Nicholas de Grenville, then just ten years old. However, he made no attempt to stop

John, dean of Hereford, remaining for long periods of time at the papal court, possibly feeling himself unequal to preventing this. Furthermore, he ensured that his own friends and family prospered. His nephew John was precentor of Hereford and held the prebend of Putson Minor, and another nephew, Gilbert, was chancellor of the same cathedral, while an unidentified Richard Swinfield held the prebend of Bartonsham until his death in 1311. Many Kentish place names also appear among his household, suggesting that he employed men already known to him. Highly educated himself, Swinfield retained an interest in education. He maintained a number of scholars at Oxford, particularly in the early and late years of his episcopate, and was closely associated with those friends of learning, the Franciscans, making frequent gifts to the order. Indeed, Robert of Leicester dedicated his work *De compoto hebreorum aptato ad Kalendarium* to Swinfield, as his patron.

Perhaps most important to Swinfield were his sustained attempts to have his former master, Thomas de Cantilupe, canonized. He had been present at Cantilupe's death, at Fiascone on 25 August 1282, and was responsible for returning the bishop's heart and bones to England, while in 1287 he directed the translation of these same bones from the lady chapel of Hereford Cathedral to a more prominent tomb in the north-west transept. When miracles started to be reported at this new tomb he began to seek the canonization of his predecessor. In April 1290 he wrote to Pope Nicholas IV (r. 1288–92), reporting these miracles and urging the canonization of a man so holy. The bishops of Durham, Ely, and Bath and Wells sent a similar letter, and in 1305 Edward I urged Clement V (r. 1305–14) to canonize the former bishop. In 1307 the pope did set up a commission to investigate these claims, including the bishops of London and Mende and Swinfield himself. But Swinfield was not to see his hopes realized, for Thomas de Cantilupe was not canonized until 1320, three years after Swinfield's death. This took place on 12 or 15 March 1317, at Bosbury, Swinfield's favourite episcopal manor. He was buried in his cathedral, where a monument, depicting the bishop in his episcopal costume and holding a small turreted building, can still be seen in the north wall of the transept.   PHILIPPA HOSKIN

Sources *The register of Richard de Swinfield, bishop of Hereford* (AD 1283–1317), ed. W. W. Capes, CYS, 6 (1909) • J. Webb, ed., *A roll of the household expenses of Richard de Swinfield, bishop of Hereford, during part of the years 1289 and 1290*, CS, 59, 62 (1853–5) • *Fasti Angl., 1066–1300*, [St Paul's, London; Monastic cathedrals; Lincoln; Salisbury] • W. Stubbs, ed., *Chronicles of the reigns of Edward I and Edward II*, 2 vols., Rolls Series, 76 (1882–3) • *Registrum epistolarum fratris Johannis Peckham, archiepiscopi Cantuariensis*, ed. C. T. Martin, 3 vols., Rolls Series, 77 (1882–5) • *Ann. mon.* • H. R. Luard, ed., *Flores historiarum*, 3 vols., Rolls Series, 95 (1890) • A. G. Little, *The Grey friars in Oxford*, OHS, 20 (1892) • *Acta sanctorum: October*, 1 (1643)
Likenesses effigy on tomb, 1317, Hereford Cathedral

Swing, Captain Francis (*fl.* **1830–1831**), mythical incendiarist, was the signatory of letters announcing incendiary raids in the agricultural areas of England, especially in the south, in the autumn and winter of 1830–31. The first 'Swing' letters were recorded in Kent by *The Times* on 21 October 1830. Initially, the letters supported rural incendiarism directed at farmers who were introducing machine threshing and had little overt political content. The movement rapidly broadened to include the demolishing of buildings, burglary, larceny, robbery, and riot of every kind. No person was identified as the original or the originator of Captain Swing, but many were arrested for acting or writing letters in his name as the whig government savagely restored order by hangings, imprisonment, and transportation. As a result of the last, Captain Swing also became a familiar figure in Australia. Although the disturbances were not directly linked to a political movement Captain Swing reminded the cabinet committee preparing the Reform Bill of the need for a bold measure. *The Genuine Life of Mr Francis Swing* (1831) purports to describe his life: he had good parents and education, but he took up poaching in bad company, and this led to rick burning. *The Life and History of Francis Swing, the Kent Rick-Burner, Written by Himself* (1830) is more political, mentioning the butchering of peaceful petitioners by the military and 'pluralist parsons taking a poor man's cow for tithe of his cabbage garden' as among his motives for violent protest.   H. C. G. MATTHEW

Sources 'An Inner Templar', *N&Q*, 3rd ser., 4 (1863), 398 • E. G. Wakefield, *Swing unmasked* (1831) • E. Hobsbawm and G. Rudé, *Captain Swing* (1969) • G. Rudé, '"Captain Swing" and Van Diemens Land', *Tasmanian Historical Research Papers and Proceedings*, 12 (1964) • J. R. M. Butler, *The passing of the great Reform Bill* (1914) • A. Charlesworth, *Social protest in rural society: the spatial diffusion of the Captain Swing disturbances of 1830–1831* (1979) • J. Thirsk, ed., *The agrarian history of England and Wales*, 6, ed. G. E. Mingay (1989)

Swingler, Randall Carline (**1909–1967**), writer, was born on 27 May 1909 at Glebe House, Church Lane, Aldershot, Hampshire, the fourth of the seven children of Humphrey Thomas Carline Swingler (1877–1938), assistant curate of Aldershot parish church, later vicar of Long Eaton in Nottinghamshire and Cranbrook in Kent, and his wife, Mabel Henrietta Davidson (1878–1962). His grandfather, Henry Swingler, was an ironmaster, railway builder, coal owner, and deputy lieutenant of Derbyshire. His maternal grandfather was Colonel Charles Elliott of the Seaforth Highlanders and the Madras artillery. His uncle and godfather was the archbishop of Canterbury Randall Thomas *Davidson (1848–1930). Stephen Swingler (1915–1969), his younger brother, became a junior minister in Harold Wilson's government.

Swingler was educated at home until he was ten, when he went to St Ronan's preparatory school in Worthing. He attended Winchester College from 1921 to 1928 and graduated from New College, Oxford, where he earned a reputation as a runner, flautist, and poet. In 1931 he met the concert pianist Geraldine Peppin (1913–1980), for whom he wrote *Poems* (1932). They married on 17 April 1933 and moved to the Cotswolds, where their daughter Judith was born in 1935. Swingler was a schoolteacher for a few years after leaving Oxford.

Like many of his generation Swingler believed that the

political and economic crises of the 1930s required revolutionary solutions, a conviction expressed in the poems of *Reconstruction* (1933) and the widely acclaimed *Difficult Morning* (1933). In 1934 the Swinglers joined the Communist Party and Randall gave away his inherited wealth to the party. With his Jean Gabin-like good looks and unworldly charm, Swingler was the best-known young writer then active in the party. He edited *Left Review* and published Nancy Cunard's *Authors Take Sides on the Spanish War* (1937). He wrote a new version of *Peer Gynt* for the Group Theatre (where he was assistant editor of the *Group Theatre Magazine*) and several plays for the Unity Theatre, including the mass declamation *Spain* (1936), and *Crisis*, about the Munich negotiations (1938). He wrote *Peace and Prosperity* (1937) for the London Choral Union, a new version of Handel's *Belshazzar* (1938) for the London Co-op Choirs, and the chorale finale of Alan Bush's *Piano Concerto* (1938). In 1938 he launched his own radical paperback publishing company, Fore Publications, selling half a million books in twelve months.

A flautist of professional standard (he played with the London Symphony Orchestra), he was active in the Workers' Music Association and in the Left Book Club, for whom he and Bush edited the *Left Song Book* (1938). Swingler and Bush also organized the 1939 Festival of Music and the People, which included an Albert Hall pageant written by Swingler and starring Paul Robeson, as well as the premier of Benjamin Britten's *Ballad of Heroes*, for whose libretto Swingler collaborated with W. H. Auden. Swingler published two well-received novels, *No Escape* (1937) and *To Town* (1939). In 1939 he was made literary editor of the *Daily Worker*.

During the first months of the Second World War Swingler worked as a staff reporter for the *Daily Worker*, writing anti-government blitz journalism until the paper was banned in 1941. He took over the journal *Poetry and the People*, relaunching it as *Our Time*, and brought the magazine *Seven* into the Fore Publications stable as a magazine of new writing from the forces. Called up at the end of 1941, he trained as a wireless operator before being posted overseas with the 56th divisional signals. Swingler took part in the Salerno landings in September 1943, and was in almost continuous action for the next twenty months. He was made a corporal at Anzio, and for his part in the battle of Lake Commachio (April 1945) was awarded the Military Medal for bravery.

Swingler returned to London in 1946 to edit *Our Time* with Edgell Rickword. He broadcast regularly for the BBC, taught adult education classes for the University of London, and collected his war poems in *The Years of Anger* (1946). A familiar figure in the London bars of Fitzrovia, he had a brief affair with the novelist Penelope Dimont [see Mortimer, Penelope Ruth (1918–1999)]; their daughter, Deborah, was born in 1948 after the affair ended earlier that year.

In cold war London Swingler found himself attacked from both sides. His adult education classes were investigated and he was blacklisted at the BBC; inside the Communist Party he was attacked for liberal sympathies and

forced to resign from *Our Time*. Its successors *Arena* and *Circus* both proved short-lived, too literary for the Communist Party and too political for the book trade. When in 1950 Fore Publications published a series of poetry books, including Swingler's *The God in the Cave*, they were ignored by literary London and denounced as 'bohemian' by the Communist Party. Visits to Czechoslovakia in 1953 and Romania in 1954 did nothing to persuade Swingler that communism was not in crisis, and he resigned from the Communist Party early in 1956, just prior to the Hungarian rising. The following year he helped found the journal *New Reasoner*.

Swingler spent the last decade of his life in the village of Pebmarsh in Essex. While Geraldine taught at the Guildhall School of Music, he stayed at home to look after their son Dan, born in 1951. He wrote a book about the Lidice massacre, in Czechoslovakia during the Second World War (unpublished), and several librettos for his friends Bernard Stevens and Alan Rawsthorne. By 1965 writer's block, political despair, financial worries, heavy drinking, and medication for a serious heart condition combined to cause a breakdown. He died of a heart attack on 19 June 1967, outside the York Minster pub in Soho, and was cremated at Golders Green crematorium, London.

Although Randall Swingler published only five books of poetry, he was a prolific playwright, novelist, librettist, critic, editor, and lyric poet, and a unique and unflinching witness to his times, from the idealistic communism of the early 1930s to the grim defeats of the cold war.

ANDY CROFT

Sources A. Croft, 'Comrade heart: a life of Randall Swingler', [forthcoming] · A. Croft, 'Politics and beauty: the poetry of Randall Swingler', *Re-writing the thirties*, ed. K. Williams and S. Matthews (1997) · A. Croft, 'The boys around the corner: the story of the fore pubs', *A weapon in the struggle: the cultural history of the communist party in Britain*, ed. A. Croft (1998) · A. Croft, 'The best of corporals: the Italian campaign in the poetry of Randall Swingler', *London Magazine, a Monthly Review of Literature*, new ser., 38/7–8 (1998), 23–39 · A. Croft, 'The achievement of Randall Swingler', *Critical Survey*, 10/3 (1998) · A. Rattenbury, 'Poems by Randall Swingler', *The 1930s: a challenge to orthodoxy*, ed. J. Lucas (1978), 161–81 · G. Thompson, ed., *The communist answer to the challenge of our time* (1947) · A. Croft, *Red letter days* (1990) · A. Croft, 'Authors take sides: writers and the communist party, 1920–56', *Opening the books: essays on the social and cultural history of British communism*, ed. G. Andrews, N. Fishman, and K. Morgan (1995), 83–100 · A. Croft, 'Writers, the communist party and the battle of ideas, 1945–50', *Socialist History*, 5 (summer 1995) · A. Croft, ed., *A weapon in the struggle: the cultural history of the communist party in Britain* (1998) · C. Hobday, *Edgell Rickword: a poet at war* (1989) · P. Hogarth, *Drawing on life* (1997) · J. Lindsay, *Meetings with poets* (1968) · A. Croft, 'The young men are moving together: the case of Randall Swingler', *Party people: communist lives*, ed. J. McIlroy and K. Morgan (2001) · A. Rattenbury, 'Total attainder and the helots', *The 1930s: a challenge to orthodoxy*, ed. J. Lucas (1978), 138–60 · A. Croft, 'Mapless in the wilderness: Randall Swingler in 1956', *Socialist History*, 19 (spring 2001)

Archives BBC WAC · BL, corresp. and literary papers, Add. MSS 62763–62766 · Marx Memorial Library, London · priv. coll. · Unity Theatre, London, archive · Workers' Musical Association, London, archive | People's History Museum, Manchester, communist party archive

Likenesses P. Hogarth, portrait, repro. in P. Hogarth, *Das Antlitz Europas* (1956)

Wealth at death £1577: administration, 8 Nov 1967, *CGPLA Eng. & Wales*

Swinhoe, Gilbert (*fl.* **1658–1671**), playwright, was the son of Gilbert Swinhoe (*c.*1594–1644x51) of Chatton, co. Durham, high sheriff of Northumberland in 1642, and Dorothy Guevara, daughter of Robert Clavering and Mary Collingwood who, after her husband's death in 1600, married Sir Henry Guevara. Swinhoe's parents married about 1620.

By the seventeenth century the Swinhoes had become a large family scattered throughout Northumberland and co. Durham; the several different branches, and several sons with the same forename, make confident identification difficult. What is known is that the surname derives from Swinhoe, a manor in the parish of Bamburgh. Swinhoe himself was a member of the Goswick branch (a cadet branch of the Rock side of the family), some of whom moved to Chatton. The manor of Chatton was part of the Percy estates; Swinhoe may have acted as bailiff to the earls of Northumberland in 1656. His immediate family was royalist. His younger brother, James, served as a lieutenant-colonel in 1643 and their father, charged with having raised the *posse comitatus* against parliament, was excluded from employment by a resolution of the House of Commons passed on 3 October 1644; in September of the following year, moreover, Gilbert senior was taken prisoner, shipped to London, and committed to the Tower, where it is likely that he died (by July 1651 his wife is described as a widow).

Much of what is known of Swinhoe's life has been adduced from the life—and death—of his brother James. That Gilbert Swinhoe of Chatton was the author of *The Tragedy of the Unhappy Fair Irene* (1658) has been inferred from the three commendatory verses written by his kinsmen which accompany the text of the play; the first of them, 'To his Dear Brother the Author', is subscribed 'Ja. Swinhoe' (sig. A1r). Each in its way emphasizes the youth of the playwright. The play itself is the first extant English drama to treat of Mahomet the Great's violently passionate, fatal love for Irene, a Greek woman of incomparable beauty, a tale which had first appeared in print in Bandello's novella (1554), which was rendered into English by William Painter (1566). Swinhoe is likely to have read the tale, however, in Richard Knolles's *The Generall Historie of the Turkes* (1603, 350–53). An uneven and haphazardly versified rendering, his play does not seem to have been performed publicly. His brother's intervention in a later incident helps to identify the protagonist as Gilbert Swinhoe the playwright. In February 1671 at Chillingham, a small village near Chatton, Swinhoe was provoked into striking Andrew Carr, who continued to exchange 'very hye and provoking words' with James Swinhoe for the rest of the evening (Raine, ed., *Depositions*, 188); the inference is that the company had been drinking for some time. After retiring, Carr sent Gilbert Swinhoe a note challenging him to a duel, but early the following morning Carr and James Swinhoe were found at swords drawn. They were parted. Later that afternoon they fought again, and James

Swinhoe was wounded in the arm, from which injury he bled to death. Carr was tried for manslaughter.

Raine states that Swinhoe married Susanna Rookebye (*bap.* 1637), the daughter of Francis Rookebye of Mortham, Yorkshire. In 1663 he settled at Crookhouse, a property high above Bowment Water which had been in the family for a century. It is not known when Swinhoe died.

JONATHAN PRITCHARD

Sources E. Bateson and others, eds., *A history of Northumberland*, 15 vols. (1893–1940), vol. 1, p. 334; vol. 2, pp. 124–7; vol. 5, pp. 456–8; vol. 7, p. 360; vol. 11, p. 210; vol. 14, pp. 208, 210, and the 'Clavering of Callaly' pedigree, tipped in between pp. 536–7 · J. Raine, *The history and antiquities of north Durham* (1852), 181–8, 235–7 · J. Raine, ed., *Depositions from the castle of York relating to offences committed in the northern counties in the seventeenth century*, SurtS, 40 (1861), 185, 187–9 · J. Swinhoe, 'To his dear brother, the author', in G. Swinhoe, *The tragedy of the unhappy fair Irene* (1658), sigs. A1r–v · E. Revett, 'To the hopeful youth of his much honoured kinsman, Gilbert Swinhoe, esq.', in G. Swinhoe, *The tragedy of the unhappy fair Irene* (1658), sigs. A1r–v · F. S., 'To the most ingenious author, his much honoured countreyman', in G. Swinhoe, *The tragedy of the unhappy fair Irene* (1658), sigs. A1r–v · D. N. Smith, 'Johnson's *Irene*', *Essays and Studies by Members of the English Association*, 14 (1929), [35]–53 · M. H. Dodds and H. Askew, *N&Q*, 166 (1934), 81, 160, 261–2, 322–3 · [W. Greenwell], ed., *Wills and inventories from the registry at Durham*, 2, SurtS, 38 (1860), 27, 56–60 · [R. Welford], ed., *Records of the committee for compounding, etc., with delinquent royalists in Durham and Northumberland during the civil war*, SurtS, 111 (1905), 155–7, 352–3 · *JHC*, 4 (1644–6), 291 · B. R. Alderson, ed., *The parish register of Rokeby, Yorks.*, 1598–1837 (1965), 13 [transcr. W. Oliver] · J. Hodgson, *A history of Northumberland*, 3 pts in 7 vols. (1820–58)

Swinhoe, Robert (**1836–1877**), diplomatist and naturalist, was born on 1 September 1836 in Calcutta. His family had served British interests in India for several generations; his father, Robert, was a lawyer in Calcutta. The Swinhoe family (variously spelt Swinho, Swinhow, Swindhoe or even Swynnow) originally came from Northumberland. Robert returned to England with his parents while still an infant. He studied at King's College, London, before matriculating at the University of London in 1853. In 1854 he was given a temporary position as interpreter in the foreign service in Hong Kong; he travelled out with his wife, Christina (*née* Lockie). In 1855 he was transferred to the British consulate at Amoy (Xiamen); he was promoted second assistant there in 1856 and he later worked in Shanghai.

In March 1856 Swinhoe visited Formosa (Taiwan) and, as well as performing his official duties, he amassed the first ornithological collection ever made there. With collections he made later in China and Formosa, it is of considerable scientific importance. His first scientific paper, 'Remarks on the fauna of Amoy', appeared in *The Zoologist* in 1858.

In 1858 HMS *Inflexible* sailed from Amoy to Formosa, with Swinhoe as interpreter. They explored the entire coast, and penetrated considerable distances inland. Swinhoe made important collections of animals and plants. In 1860 he was recalled from leave to act as staff interpreter for General Napier and the combined English and French forces during the north China campaign, of which he published a *Narrative* in 1861.

In December 1860, at the age of twenty-four, Swinhoe

was appointed vice-consul in Formosa, the first foreign diplomatist to be based there. He became ill in November 1861 and went back to Amoy for treatment, returning to Formosa a month later. For the next year the British consulate was based on the SS *Adventure*, moored in the Tamsui (Danshui) River, after which it was moved to San Domingo, the old Spanish fort in Tamsui.

Swinhoe returned to London in May 1862 due to illness. In Britain he was elected honorary member of the British Ornithologists' Union. His highly praised paper 'On the mammals of the island of Formosa' was published in 1862. In 1863 he compiled the first list of Chinese birds, updated in 1871, which increased the known species of that country from 474 to 675.

In 1863 Swinhoe returned to Tamsui to resume his duties. Here he built an aviary for captive breeding of the rare, endemic Swinhoe's pheasant. In spring 1864 he explored the Keeling and Suao areas, and later visited the Pescadores and the Kaohsiung–Hengchun coast. In August 1864 he was transferred to Kaohsiung, being promoted to consul in 1865. In 1866 he became consul at Amoy, then at Ningpo (Ningbo) in 1867. Here he began to suffer from paralysis, and was transferred to the healthier station of Chefoo (Yantai) in 1873. Ill health did not stop Swinhoe's ornithological studies, for he arranged to be carried about the countryside in an assortment of wheelbarrows and sedan chairs.

In October 1875 Swinhoe was retired on medical grounds and returned to London, where he was elected fellow of the Royal Society in 1876 and continued to work on his extensive natural history collections. He died at his home at 33 Carlyle Square, Chelsea, on 28 October 1877; his mortal paralysis is thought to have been caused by syphilis. Very little is known of his personal life, although he mentions a child in an official letter dated 1862. Swinhoe left his estate, valued at under £3000, to his widow. He had at least two younger brothers, Peter and Charles (1836–1923). The latter also became a famous naturalist; a colonel in the Indian army, he collected an important series of birds in Afghanistan between 1880 and 1881, and was a world expert on Indian lepidoptera.

Swinhoe's extensive travels in China, and particularly Formosa, resulted in the discovery of many new forms of animals and plants. He published over 120 articles on natural history, and left extensive collections (the birds alone numbering 3700), most of which are at the Natural History or Liverpool museums. Among the many forms named after him, probably the most famous are Swinhoe's pheasant *Hierophasis swinhoii*, Swinhoe's snipe *Gallinago megala*, and Swinhoe's storm petrel *Oceanodroma monorhis*—the last two of which Swinhoe himself scientifically described. CLEMENCY THORNE FISHER

Sources Y. Takahashi, *Biography of Robert Swinhoe, 1836–1877* (1935) · B. Mearns and R. Mearns, 'Robert Swinhoe', *Biographies for birdwatchers: the lives of those commemorated in western palearctic bird names* (1988) · *The Ibis*, 4th ser., 2 (1878), 126–8 · P. B. Hall, *Robert Swinhoe, a Victorian naturalist* (1987) · collecting labels, Liverpool Museum, bird skin collection · *CGPLA Eng. & Wales* (1879) · private information (2004) · *The Ibis*, 11th ser., 6 (1924), 362–3 [Charles Swinhoe]

Archives Liverpool Museum, collections · NHM, letters; collections
Wealth at death under £3000: probate, 13 Dec 1879, *CGPLA Eng. & Wales*

Swinnerton, Frank Arthur (1884–1982), writer and publisher's reader, was born on 12 August 1884 at Wood Green, London, the younger son and younger child of Charles Swinnerton, copperplate engraver, and his wife, Rose, a designer, daughter of Richard Pell Cottam, a craftsman printer. Swinnerton's stock, he claimed, derived from the midland English of his father and the Scottishness of his mother. The Swinnertons came from Hanley in Staffordshire, the Cottams from Edinburgh. 'They were all the most modest creatures in the world', claimed Swinnerton, 'but simultaneously they had the utmost indifference to the opinion of any person who was not a Swinnerton or a Cottam' (Swinnerton, *Autobiography*, 19). His education was perfunctory and spasmodic owing to poor health as a child and a lack of means. He attended various educational establishments in the neighbourhood of his home, where his childhood was happy and serene. There was little in his background to suggest that he would become a writer of distinction and be found at the intimate centre and in fraternal, almost conspiratorial, association with many of the literary giants of the age.

In his youth Swinnerton read avidly Henry James, Ibsen, and Louisa May Alcott, and was greatly influenced by E. Arnold Bennett, whose entry he later wrote for the *Dictionary of National Biography*, as he did that on J. T. (Frank) Harris. In his fifteenth year he arrived in Fleet Street and was briefly with the *Scottish Cyclist* at a wage of 6s. a week. It could be said that his 'literary life' began in 1901 when he joined the publishing firm of J. M. Dent as a clerk receptionist, in which capacity he assisted Hugh Dent in the 1906 launch of Everyman's Library. He had himself started writing at the age of ten, but it was not until 1909, after four abortive novels, that his first, *The Merry Heart*, was published mainly through the advocacy of Arnold Bennett.

As an author Swinnerton's industry and inventiveness never flagged. His calligraphy was exquisite if minute and his publisher was regularly informed that he might soon be receiving the typescript of a new book. There were in all some forty-two novels, fifteen other books of literary interest and purpose, a large output of reviews, comments, and articles, and talks and conversations with recording teams from all over the world from both sound and television.

Swinnerton enjoyed respect and affection as a writer, but great success, as today measured by sales, eluded him. His short novel *Nocturne* (1917) seems most likely to endure, and of his early novels *The Casement* (1911), *September* (1919), and *Young Felix* (1923) were highly regarded. Latterly *The Georgian House* (1922) and *The Two Wives* (1940) were thought to be among his best. His *The Georgian Literary Scene* (1935), *Swinnerton: an Autobiography* (1937), and *Arnold Bennett: a Last Word* (1978) together convey the essences of the era in which he occupied so uniquely observant a vantage point.

Frank Arthur Swinnerton (1884–1982), by Howard Coster, 1929

world of the mass media and communicative gadgetry. As often as not, and at least well into his nineties, their quarry might be found hedging and ditching the boundaries of his home, but immediately able to launch into vivid recollection and inimitable mimicry of such as Arnold Bennett, H. G. Wells, John Galsworthy, Sir Hugh Walpole, James Barrie, and others who formed a circle with its centre at the Reform Club, of which Swinnerton, in due time, was awarded honorary life membership.

Swinnerton was, above all, a great bookman. He cared deeply for writing and writers. He was the most trusted of men and of a lovable and generous nature. He never faltered for an apt word, a name, or a revealing anecdote. A small, neat figure with a trim beard, twinkling eyes, and small pince-nez glasses (which periodically dropped into his drink), he was a very private man. Once challenged by a friend, he admitted—with that little gruff grunt which was as distinctive as his chuckle—that he had declined to be made CBE. His own participation in life he rarely referred to, but by comment and anecdote about others could conjure up a vanished world. He was president of the Royal Literary Fund from 1962 to 1966. Swinnerton died on 6 November 1982 at Cranleigh Village Hospital.

ROBERT LUSTY, rev.

Sources F. Swinnerton, *Swinnerton: an autobiography* (1937) · personal knowledge (1990) · m. certs. · d. cert. · *CGPLA Eng. & Wales* (1983) · F. Swinnerton, *Figures in the foreground* (1963)
Archives University of Arkansas, Fayetteville, corresp., literary MSS, and papers | BBC WAC, corresp. with members of the BBC · BLPES, letters to A. G. Gardiner · Bodl. Oxf., corresp. with R. P. Eckert · Bodl. Oxf., corresp. with A. St John Adcock · Bodl. Oxf., corresp. with Sidgwick and Jackson · Brown University, Providence, Rhode Island, John Hay Library, corresp. with Alfred Gurney · CUL, letters to Morchard Bishop · JRL, letters to Allan Monkhouse · McMaster University, Hamilton, Ontario, William Ready division of archives and research collections, letters to Bertrand Russell · U. Reading L., letters to Wendell Argraves · U. Reading L., letters to Bodley Head Ltd, Chatto and Windus, Jonathan Cape | SOUND BL NSA, recordings (1964–6) of talks for Radio 4 series "Words words words"
Likenesses H. Coster, photograph, 1929, NPG [*see illus.*]
Wealth at death £100,263: probate, 13 Jan 1983, *CGPLA Eng. & Wales*

After six years with Messrs Dent, Swinnerton joined Chatto and Windus, reading for them busily and advising them through the next twenty-five years. Especially gratifying was his discovery of *The Young Visiters* (1919) by Daisy Ashford, to which he persuaded Sir J. M. Barrie to write a preface. Other acquisitions to a distinguished list were *Limbo* (1920) by Aldous Huxley, *Eminent Victorians* (1918) by G. Lytton Strachey, and *The Journal of a Disappointed Man* (1919) by W. N. P. Barbellion.

On 7 September 1920 Swinnerton married Helen Frances Olga Dicks (b. 1896/7). The marriage was unsuccessful, ending in divorce, and Swinnerton never spoke of it again to friends and family. While working for Chatto he met Mary Dorothy Bennett (1897/8–1980), and they were married on 15 March 1924. She was the daughter of George Bennett, a master tailor, and was unrelated to Swinnerton's lifelong friend Arnold Bennett. There were two daughters of the second marriage, but the elder died in infancy.

Swinny—to all his friends, with the exception of Arnold Bennett, his greatest, who called him Henry—encompassed uniquely an extraordinary era of English writing and authorship and became over his long life its most astute chronicler and the friend and intimate of nearly all the distinguished company which sustained it. Towards the end of his life a visit to his home, Old Tokefield in Cranleigh, Surrey, became almost a pilgrimage for students and literary researchers from all over the world, seeking firsthand knowledge and recollection of so different a scene from any they knew within their modern

Swinnerton, Henry Hurd (1875–1966), zoologist and geologist, was born at Bungay, Suffolk, on 17 September 1875, the son of the Revd George Frederick Swinnerton, a Wesleyan Methodist minister, and his wife, Mary (*née* Smith). The family moved about Britain because of the father's ministry, and Swinnerton acquired a good knowledge of the countryside. He matriculated in 1894, after attending Woodhouse Grove School, Airedale, Yorkshire, and Kingswood School, Bath.

Swinnerton became an assistant master at a boarding-school in Trowbridge (*c*.1894) but continued his studies through the university correspondence course and by regular visits to the Bristol City Museum. Encouraged by the curator, Edward Wilson, and by his course tutor, Dr Morley Davies, he was awarded a studentship at the Royal College of Science, University of London (1897). He graduated in zoology (1898) and then served as personal assistant to Professor G. B. Howes working on the New Zealand tuatara lizard *Sphenodon*. With typical ingenuity, he placed a dozen eggs in damp sand beneath the heating pipes of the laboratory and hatched the first *Sphenodon* in Europe. In 1902 Swinnerton was awarded a DSc following the completion of research on the cranium of the stickleback, which he had carried out while serving as a master at his old school in Bath. He married Florence Daisy Bennett, daughter of Joseph Bennett, postmaster, on 6 September 1906, and they had three daughters.

In 1901–2 Swinnerton was appointed lecturer in natural sciences at University College, Nottingham. During his subsequent forty-four years in the college he established the departments of natural science (1902) and geology and geography (1912), as well as laying the foundation for a department of archaeology. His interpretation of fossils as living organisms contributed to a better understanding of palaeoecology and evolution. He had enormous ability as a lecturer, was noted for his enthusiasm for field studies and also for his broad, philosophical attitude to science (Hawkins, 43), and was responsible for the introduction of visual aids into the lecture room (Marren, 265), but his real pleasure was to be 'out in the field with his hammer ... discovering the meaning of all things natural' (Evans, 1968, 344).

In 1942 Swinnerton was presented with the Murchison medal by the Geological Society in recognition of his extensive output in a wide range of zoological and geological subjects. He served as president of the Lincolnshire Naturalists' Union in 1936–7, of section C of the British Association in 1938, and of the Geological Society in 1939–40. In 1950 he was made a CBE for his services to university education. In addition to his professional and civic services in connection with young people, Swinnerton was an active member of the Methodist church. He retired as professor emeritus in 1946 and then briefly served as curator of the Margidinum collection of Roman antiquities before moving to Hertfordshire. He died at his residence, the headmaster's house, Haberdashers' Aske's School, Elstree, on 6 November 1966.   R. J. CLEEVELY

Sources W. D. E. [W. D. Evans], 'Henry Hurd Swinnerton (1875–1966)', *Proceedings of the Geological Society*, 1645 (1967–8), 343–4 · W. D. Evans, 'Professor H. H. Swinnerton', *Mercian Geologist*, 2 (1967–8), 123–31 [photograph, bibliography] · T. N. G. [T. N. George], 'Henry Hurd Swinnerton (1875–1966)', *Proceedings of the Geologists' Association*, 80 (1969), 124–6 · *The Times* (9 Nov 1966) · P. Marren, *The new naturalists* (1995), 133, 146, 149, 265 · H. L. Hawkins, 'Award of the Murchison medal', *Quarterly Journal of the Geological Society of London*, 98 (1942), xliii–xliv · *WWW, 1961–70* · *CGPLA Eng. & Wales* (1967) · m. cert. · b. cert.

Archives Lincs. Arch., notes and papers relating to Hogsthorpe **Likenesses** photograph, repro. in Evans, 'Professor H. H. Swinnerton', pl. 6 · portrait, U. Nott., department of manuscripts and special collections, 1928, ACC 253/4/24 [album of portraits of University College staff] · portrait, GS Lond.

Wealth at death £15,536: probate, 9 Jan 1967, *CGPLA Eng. & Wales*

Swinnerton, Thomas. *See* Swynnerton, Thomas (*d.* 1554).

Swinney, Sidney (1721–1783), Church of England clergyman and author, was born at Pontefract, Yorkshire, one of the five children of the Irish soldier Major Matthew Swinney (*b.* 1681) and Mary Kitchingham. Little is known of his family history and early life. He was educated at Eton College and at Clare College, Cambridge, where he received a BA in 1744, an MA in 1749, and a DD in 1763. Drawn towards a religious life, he was ordained a priest of the Church of England on 22 September 1745 and became curate of Swillington, Yorkshire, in the same year. Matthew Swinney had enjoyed a distinguished military career, and as a reward for his services his son Sidney was granted a chaplaincy in the British army. Swinney served as chaplain during the Seven Years' War (1756–63), participating in the British army's campaigns in Germany.

Swinney was an accomplished classical scholar, with a keen interest in ancient art and archaeology, which inspired him to travel widely in Europe and the Near East. He lived in Constantinople for several years, serving as chaplain to the British embassy. During his travels and residence in Constantinople, Swinney gathered an impressive collection of classical coins and other artefacts. In 1769 he published an account of an expedition through Asia Minor to examine the sites of the earliest Christian churches, *A Tour through some Parts of the Levant*, which combined his archaeological and religious interests. In recognition of his contribution to the study of classical culture, he was elected fellow of the Royal Society in 1764 and fellow of the Antiquarian Society in 1767.

During his lifetime Swinney acquired a respected reputation as a poet, publishing translations of classical poetry, occasional verse, songs, and epigrams in periodicals and newspapers. In 1767 he published an imitation of Horace's ninth satire. Many of Swinney's miscellaneous works were collected and reprinted as *Fugitive Pieces* (3rd edn, 1768). His most ambitious work was an epic poem celebrating the British victory over the French at the battle of Minden (1759) during the Seven Years' War. Although the first two books of the projected three-book epic were printed in 1769 and 1772 respectively, it appears that Swinney never finished the work. In the preface to the 1772 edition of *The Battle of Minden*, he explained that a four-year illness had delayed the composition of the second book, and perhaps recurring ill health prevented the poem's completion. Of little literary originality or merit, *The Battle of Minden* nevertheless represents a historically valuable firsthand account of the war in Germany written by an experienced, astute observer. Swinney was also a gifted preacher and published two sermons. He became rector of Barton-le-Street about 1775.

Swinney died at Scarborough, Yorkshire, on 12 November 1783. Reflecting upon his character and conscientiousness as a pastor, a correspondent in the *Gentleman's Magazine* praised him as a 'gentleman of uncommon generosity and benevolence'.   M. JOHN CARDWELL

Sources *GM*, 1st ser., 53 (1783), 982 · S. Swinney, *Fugitive pieces*, 3rd edn (1768), 4–12 · Venn, *Alum. Cant.* · election certificate, RS · Nichols, *Illustrations*, 1.144 · Allibone, *Dict.*

Swinnock, George (*c.*1627–1673), clergyman and ejected minister, was born at Maidstone in Kent, the son of George Swinnock of Maidstone. Following the early death of his father he was brought up in the house of his uncle Robert, a zealous puritan. On 28 May 1644 he was admitted to Emmanuel College, Cambridge, migrating on 7 October 1645 to Jesus College, where he graduated BA in 1648. He was back in Maidstone about April 1648, but soon sought preferment at Oxford. On 6 October 1649 he was made a fellow of Balliol College by the parliamentary visitors. He was incorporated BA on 29 November 1650 and proceeded MA the next day. Soon afterwards he resigned his fellowship; on 15 January 1651 the committee for the reformation of the universities ordered for his continued maintenance as vicar of Rickmansworth, 'the yearly sum of £27 and one boare reserved to the bishops of London' (Urwick, 309–10). This was later augmented by £30, though repeated orders in respect of these payments suggest a continuing struggle, over several years, to enforce them. Swinnock was ordained at St Andrew Undershaft, London, in October 1651.

Probably not long after this Swinnock married Joan (d. 1681/2); their first recorded child, Sarah, was born on 1 May 1654 and baptized at Rickmansworth on 8 June. In 1655 he was appointed to St Leonard's Chapel at Aston Clinton, Buckinghamshire, and on 29 September 1657 he was appointed an assistant to the commission into the ministry in Hertfordshire. He enjoyed the favour of the well connected with the influential Beresford family and dedicated *The Gods are Men, or, The Mortality of Persons in Places of Magistracy*, to John Beresford, sheriff of Hertfordshire. At the Restoration he was ejected from Rickmansworth following the reinstatement of the sequestered vicar, but on 10 January 1661 he was presented to the vicarage of Great Kimble, Buckinghamshire, by the influential local politician Richard Hampden (1631–1695), a friend of Richard Baxter, who had contributed a preface to Swinnock's *The Door of Salvation Opened* (1660). Not even Hampden could prevent Swinnock's ejection in 1662 from both St Leonard's and Great Kimble on the grounds of his nonconformity, but he was accommodated or supported by the family for some years. He became Hampden's chaplain, and the churchwardens complained on 14 October that he also preached at his own house. In 1665 he was described as living 'in great Kimbell of no profession by the maintenance of Richard Hampden Esq. patron of the said Vicaridge' (Bodl. Oxf., MS Willis 13). In that year there was issued a collection of his works with a dedication to Hampden. In 1669 Swinnock was reported preaching at Bledlow, High Wycombe, Thame, and Bicester. Under the declaration of indulgence he was licensed as a presbyterian teacher at High Wycombe on 12 April 1672 but he ended his days as pastor of a large congregation at his native Maidstone, where members of his family still lived. He died on 10 November 1673, aged about forty-six, and was buried in the parish church four days later. He was survived by his wife, who was still living in Maidstone on 4 February 1681, when she made her will (proved 15 November 1682), and by four sons and five daughters.

E. I. CARLYLE, *rev.* STEPHEN WRIGHT

Sources *Calamy rev.*, 473 · W. Urwick, *Nonconformity in Hertfordshire* (1884) · Venn, *Alum. Cant.* · J. T. Cliffe, *The puritan gentry besieged,*
1650–1700 (1993) · W. Newton, *History and antiquities of Maidstone* (1741) · G. Swinnock, *Life and death of Mr Thomas Wilson, minister of Maidstone* (1672) · G. Swinnock, *The fading of the flesh and the flourishing of faith* (1662), preface · PRO, PROB 11/371, sig. 139 [will of Joan Swinnock]

Swinton. For this title name *see* individual entries under Swinton; *see also* Lister, Philip Cunliffe-, first earl of Swinton (1884–1972).

Swinton, Alan Archibald Campbell (1863–1930), electrical engineer, born at 9 Albyn Place, Edinburgh, on 18 October 1863, was the third son of Archibald Campbell *Swinton (1812–1890), of Kimmerghame, Berwickshire, professor of civil law in the University of Edinburgh, 1842–62, and his wife, Georgiana Caroline (1823–1900), daughter of Sir George Sitwell, second baronet, of Renishaw, Derbyshire. As a child, Swinton showed a decided bent towards engineering, and developed considerable skill in photography, which remained a lifelong hobby. In 1878 he was sent to Fettes College, Edinburgh, where his hatred of games and dislike of orthodox methods of instruction seem to have made life very difficult for him. At the age of fifteen, two years after the invention of the telephone, he made, at school, an excellently working installation connecting two houses. In 1881 he went to Le Havre to study French and mathematics, and visited the Paris Exhibition, where he was deeply impressed by the electrical inventions that he saw.

In 1882 Swinton began a five years' apprenticeship in the engineering works of Sir William G. Armstrong at Elswick-on-Tyne. In 1883 his book, *The Principles and Practice of Electric Lighting*, was published by Longmans, and thereafter he became chiefly interested in the electrical side of Armstrong's business. He was the first to employ lead-covered wires and cables for electric wiring in ships, in place of the cumbersome methods then employed to prevent the penetration of moisture.

In 1887 Swinton went to London to work up an independent practice as electrical contractor and consulting engineer. He carried out electric lighting installations in many country houses, and was connected with several of the earliest electric supply companies, notably those which were the first to employ steam turbines—for example, the Scarborough Electric Supply Company and the Cambridge Electric Supply Company, of which latter he became managing director. His involvement with Messrs Crompton & Co. led to his becoming chairman, and he was consultant to Sir William Armstrong. He gave up the contracting side of his business in 1904.

His ability to estimate rapidly the value of new discoveries marked Swinton out as a pioneer in the application of electricity in Britain. The first photograph produced by X-rays in England was taken by him, and published in *Nature* (23 January 1896), within a month of the announcement of Röntgen's discovery. By 1897 doctors and surgeons were bringing him their patients for examination with the aid of X-rays. From this date onwards Swinton read many papers of fundamental importance before the Royal Society and other learned societies, dealing with his observations on X-rays and cathode rays. His writings were, in general, of a descriptive nature, his great skill as an experimenter and his extraordinarily wide scientific knowledge being his greatest assets. His discovery of the high temperatures obtainable by the focusing of cathode rays led to a study of the luminosity of rare earths, and was demonstrated by the conversion of a diamond into coke.

In association with Sir Charles Parsons, Swinton was intimately connected with the early development of the steam turbine and with the construction of the turbine ship *Turbinia*, a torpedo-boat destroyer, which at the naval review of 1897 attained the then astonishing speed of 33½ knots; he also served on the board of Parsons's company.

Swinton, who lived in London, in Chester Square, met nearly all the eminent men of science of his day, and received much encouragement in his work from Lord Kelvin, Lord Armstrong, and Sir William Crookes. In 1896 he introduced Guglielmo Marconi to William Preece, who was then engineer-in-chief to the Post Office; rapid developments in radio telegraphy ensued. Swinton was also responsible for investigating the papers left by the inventor David Edward Hughes, and proved that Hughes had made successful experiments in wireless telegraphy over short distances in 1879, some years before Hertz's discovery.

In the last decades of the nineteenth century, electricians were seeking a practical system of seeing at a distance, or television. The individual elements for such a system were known, but it was Swinton who achieved the breakthrough in ideas, proposing the use of cathode ray tubes for both the transmission of pictures and their reception or display. Swinton did not patent his arrangement, preferring to describe it in a letter to the journal *Nature*, written on 12 June 1908. He expanded on his scheme in a lecture to the Röntgen Society in 1911, and incorporated the technical advances which had taken place since the First World War in his paper in *Wireless World* in 1924. In the following years, much time and money was expended in Britain and elsewhere in developing mechanical systems of television, and when the Baird Company brought pressure on the British Broadcasting Corporation to adopt their crude equipment for use in a routine public television service, Swinton argued forcefully against it in his advice to the BBC engineers. He repeatedly pointed out the limitations of mechanical methods and urged the development of an all-electric system. Swinton did carry out his own experiments, but physical technique was still inadequate to deal with the problem, and he had no access to the large, well-equipped, and well-funded research facilities that were essential to solve it. In the flurry of later progress, his role was forgotten, and his obituaries in *The Times* and in the Royal Society's *Proceedings* barely touched on his achievements in this field.

Swinton was a member of the institutions of Civil, Mechanical, and Electrical Engineers, and was for four years vice-president of the IEE. In 1911 he was president of the Röntgen Society, and in 1913 of the Radio Society. For several years he was chairman of the Royal Society of Arts, and in 1915 was elected a fellow of the Royal Society. He gave his services freely to many scientific societies, which owed much to his philanthropy. His many letters to *The Times* on scientific subjects were generally written from the Athenaeum, of which he was a member for nearly thirty years. Swinton, who was unmarried, died of pneumonia at his house, 40 Chester Square, Westminster, London, on 19 February 1930. His cremation service at Golders Green on the 24th was attended by many of the eminent electricians of the day.

S. E. A. LANDALE, rev. ANITA McCONNELL

Sources A. A. C. Swinton, *Autobiographical and other writings* (1930) · *Nature*, 78 (1908), 151 [letter] · A. A. C. Swinton, presidential address, *Journal of the Röntgen Society*, 8 (1912), 7 · A. A. C. Swinton, *Wireless World*, 14 (1924), 51 · *Nature*, 125 (1930), 356, 385 · A. R., *PRS*, 130A (1930–31), xiii-xv · *The Times* (20 Feb 1930), 16b · J. D. McGee, 'The contribution of A. A. Campbell Swinton to television', *Notes and Records of the Royal Society*, 32 (1977–8), 91–105 · *The Times* (24 Feb 1930), 15d · d. cert. · CGPLA Eng. & Wales (1930)
Likenesses W. Stoneman, photograph, 1917, NPG · photograph, repro. in A. R., *PRS*
Wealth at death £99,785 8s. 2d.: probate, 25 March 1930, CGPLA Eng. & Wales

Swinton, Sir Alexander, Lord Mersington (1621x30?–1700), judge, was probably born between 1621 and 1630, the second son of Sir Alexander Swinton (c.1600–1652) of Swinton in Merse, Berwickshire, and his wife, Margaret, daughter of James Home of Framepath and St Bothans. John *Swinton (c.1620–1679), a leading figure in the Cromwellian administration in Scotland, was his elder brother. His father was sheriff of Berwickshire in 1641–5 and represented the county in parliament from 1644 to 1645. He was educated at the University of Edinburgh, graduating in 1651. In that year he was captured, and his brother Robert killed, fighting for Charles II at the battle of Worcester. The family were staunch presbyterians and their allegiance depended on the young king's signature to the solemn league and covenant. John Swinton's importance to Cromwell secured Alexander's release after a short period in prison. He settled into obscurity in the 1650s.

Preferment for Swinton was delayed after the Restoration, John Swinton's trial for treason in 1661 and subsequent forfeiture and imprisonment acting as a brake on Swinton fortunes, even though John, now a Quaker, was somewhat estranged from the family. John Swinton had received the property of John Maitland, earl of Lauderdale, from Cromwell, and the lands of Swinton in turn passed to Lauderdale on John's forfeiture, reducing the potential for political patronage. Alexander was able to turn to a career in the law, being admitted an advocate on 27 July 1671. His religious principles dictated the suspension of this career in 1681, officially at any rate, with his refusal to take the Test Act and oath. He found the notion of royal supremacy over religion completely unacceptable. However, he benefited from James VII and II's policy of presbyterian appeasement and was restored to his career by the king's letter of dispensation of 16 December 1686. He was admitted an ordinary lord of session on 23 June 1688, in place of John Wauchope of Edmonston. He took the title Lord Mersington after his property in Eccles, south Berwickshire, acquired in 1667.

At the revolution of 1688–9 Mersington revelled in his presbyterian enthusiasm. He famously led the attack on the palace of Holyroodhouse in December 1688, destroying property and arresting 'papists' with equal measure, including the Catholic printer Peter Bruce and his press. Subsequently he was re-appointed a lord of session in 1689 and fell under the patronage of George, earl of Melville, William and Mary's first secretary of state, helped by his nephew Sir John Swinton, parliamentary commissioner for Berwickshire from 1690 to 1707. He had the distinction of being the only judge of James VII and II to be continued in office by William and Mary.

Mersington was married twice, first, on 29 March 1653, to Eleanor (sometimes Helen or Helenor) Nisbit (d. 1666), with whom he had three sons and two daughters, then in 1666 to Alison Skene of Hallyards, with whom he had three sons and five daughters. In 1674 she was banished from Edinburgh by the privy council for demonstrating against Lauderdale's policies. Claims that he married a daughter of Sir Alexander Dalmahoy are unsupported by evidence, and may refer to his son Alexander. The Jacobite Lord Balcarres caricatures Mersington as a 'fanatical judge' and as 'drunk as ale and brandy could make him' (BL, Add. MS 33472) during the Holyrood riot. Given his distinguished career as a lord of session, the view of lord advocate Sir James Stewart, that Mersington was 'a good honest man', his death 'much regretted' (*State Papers and Letters*, 625), provides some balance. He died at Mersington in August 1700, leaving a modest estate, including debts owed to him by the Company of Scotland. Creditors disputed his estate for two decades.   A. J. MANN

Sources parish register, Edinburgh, NA Scot., OPR.685.1 [second marriage and children] · A. C. Swinton, *The Swintons of that ilk and their cadets* (1883), 55–62 · register of testaments, Lauder, NA Scot., CC 15/5, 5. 20/1/1653; 7. 15/4/1707, 30/6/1707; 8. 5/8/1718 · register of testaments, Edinburgh, NA Scot., CC 8/83, 19/3/1707 · H. Paton, ed., *Register of interments in the Greyfriars burying-ground, Edinburgh, 1658–1700*, Scottish RS, 26 (1902), 632 · H. Paton, ed., *The register of marriages for the parish of Edinburgh, 1595–1700*, Scottish RS, old ser., 27 (1905), 72 · BL, Add. MS 33472 · C. Lindsay [earl of Balcarres], *Memoirs touching the revolution in Scotland*, ed. A. W. C. Lindsay [earl of Crawford and Balcarres], Bannatyne Club (1841) · J. M. Thomson and others, eds., *Registrum magni sigilli regum Scotorum / The register of the great seal of Scotland*, 11 vols. (1882–1914), vol. 11, p. 519 · M. D. Young, ed., *The parliaments of Scotland: burgh and shire commissioners*, 2 (1993), 688–9 · NA Scot., Leven and Melville muniments, GD.26.13 · G. Brunton and D. Haig, *An historical account of the senators of the college of justice, from its institution in MDXXXII* (1832) · *State papers and letters addressed to William Carstares*, ed. J. M'Cormick (1774), 625 · D. Laing, ed., *A catalogue of the graduates … of the University of Edinburgh*, Bannatyne Club, 106 (1858), 71 · *DNB*
Wealth at death £6000 Scots, owed mostly by Company of Scotland: NA Scot., Edinburgh register of testaments, CC/8/83; CC/15/7; CC/15/8

Swinton, Archibald Campbell (1812–1890), advocate and jurist, was born on 15 July 1812 at Broadmeadows, Berwickshire, and baptized there; he was the elder son of John Swinton (1777–1867), then of Broadmeadows, later of Kimmerghame, Berwickshire, landed proprietor, and his wife, Catherine (d. 1821), only daughter of James Rannie,

merchant in Leith, and his wife, Catherine, daughter of William Mure of Caldwell. His younger brother was the portrait painter James Rannie *Swinton; he also had four sisters. On 29 July 1845 he married at Stichill his first wife, Katharine Margaret (1818–1846), third daughter of Sir John Pringle, bt (1784–1869), of Stichill, and his first wife, Emilia Ann Macleod (d. 1830). This marriage ended with his wife's death on 24 May 1846; they had one daughter. On 7 October 1856 Swinton married Georgiana Caroline (1823–1900), third daughter of Sir George Sitwell, bt (1797–1853), of Renishaw, and his wife, Susan Tait, sister of Archibald *Tait, archbishop of Canterbury. They had one daughter and three sons, the youngest of whom was the electrical engineer Alan *Swinton.

Swinton was educated at Edinburgh Academy and Edinburgh University, where he matriculated in arts in 1827, 1828, and 1830, and in law in 1831–4; he also studied at Glasgow University in 1829–30, and was a prizewinner in the logic class. He passed advocate on 23 November 1833. Glasgow University created him LLB in 1843, as an 'eminent man'; Edinburgh University made him LLD in 1860.

Swinton acquired a large practice and in July 1842 was also appointed professor of civil law in Edinburgh University in succession to Douglas Cheape. His lectures were appreciated but he did not publish anything on civil law and resigned the chair in May 1862, hoping to be appointed to the chair in public law, which went to James Lorimer. In 1850 his father had succeeded a maternal aunt, Mary Campbell, in the re-purchased family estate of Kimmerghame; he added Campbell to his surname and matriculated arms. Swinton succeeded him in 1867.

Swinton was also prominent in the general assembly of the Church of Scotland, as a representative elder. In addition he was an active Conservative, unsuccessfully contesting the seats for the Haddington burghs in July 1852 and for Edinburgh and St Andrews universities in December 1868. He took part in county business as JP and deputy lieutenant for Berwickshire, and was a member of certain royal commissions. He was on the 1876 commission on the Scottish universities, and also became involved in Edinburgh University affairs, being rector's assessor on the university court (1871–7), curator of patronage (1878–84), and chancellor's assessor (1881–7).

Swinton produced two volumes of *Justiciary Cases*, covering the period 1835–41 (published in 1838 and 1842), reports of individual trials in 1838 and 1839, and a digest of decisions from 1835 to 1843 in the Glasgow registration appeal court (1839, 1840, and 1844). He also published a family history, *The Swintons of that Ilk and their Cadets* (1883), originally in the *Proceedings of the Berwickshire Naturalists' Club* (1878), and a lecture, *Men of the Merse* (privately printed, 1858). Swinton died, after a five-year period of paralysis, at Kimmerghame, Berwickshire, on 27 November 1890.   W. M. GORDON

Sources A. C. Swinton, *The Swintons of that ilk and their cadets* (1883), 110–114 · minutes, NL Scot., Faculty of Advocates MSS FR7, FR8, FR9 · J. Lorimer, *History of the Lorimer family*, U. Edin. L., microfilm M1366 · U. Edin. L., special collections division, university archives · U. Glas., Archives and Business Records Centre · *The Times* (6

Dec 1890) • 'Swinton, James Rannie', *DNB* • S. P. Walker, *The Faculty of Advocates, 1800–1986* (1987) • *Alphabetical list of graduates of the University of Edinburgh from 1859 to 1888*, University of Edinburgh (1889) • W. I. Addison, *A roll of graduates of the University of Glasgow from 31st December 1727 to 31st December 1897* (1898) • W. I. Addison, ed., *The matriculation albums of the University of Glasgow from 1728 to 1858* (1913) • F. J. Grant, ed., *The Faculty of Advocates in Scotland, 1532–1943*, Scottish RS, 145 (1944) • parish register (birth), Edrom parish, Berwickshire, 15 July 1812

Archives NRA, priv. coll., corresp. | LPL, letters to A. C. Tait • U. St Andr., corresp. with James David Forbes

Sir Ernest Dunlop Swinton (1868–1951), by Eric Kennington

Swinton, Sir Ernest Dunlop (1868–1951), army officer and writer, was born on 21 October 1868 at Bangalore, India, the fourth of nine children of Robert Blair Swinton (*d.* 1912), judge in the Madras civil service, and his wife, Elizabeth Dorothy Rundall, daughter of a businessman in India. His early childhood was spent at Cuddalore, south of Pondicherry, until the family returned to England on his father's retirement. His education (from 1875) was disrupted by frequent transfers, on grounds of economy, but included spells at University College School, London, Rugby School, Cheltenham, and Blackheath proprietary school (1883–5). He then attended 'crammers' in Aldershot and Kensington in preparation for entry into the Royal Military Academy, Woolwich.

Swinton was commissioned into the Royal Engineers in February 1888, and completed the course in military engineering at Chatham two years later. He relished the opportunity to return to India for a five-year tour of duty. While on home leave in 1893 he visited Grace Louisa (*b.* 1868/9), daughter of his second cousin Major Edward Clayton, secretary to the Prison Commission. They were married in London on 28 January 1897. The couple had two sons, and a daughter who was killed in a road accident during the Second World War.

After 1896 Swinton drew on his experiences in surveying and improving military works and fortifications in India as assistant instructor in fortification at the school of military engineering, Chatham. Soon after the outbreak of the Second South African War he joined the military railway staff in Cape Town and helped to recruit an irregular force. As adjutant and, in 1900, commanding officer 1st battalion, Railway Pioneer regiment, he reconstructed wrecked bridges, established detached posts, and contemplated the use of bullet-proof plates on supply trains. He was appointed to the DSO in 1900. This experience of independent command formed the subject of an imaginative tactical manual for subalterns, presented in the form of a fantastical dream sequence. It was published in the *United Service Magazine* and reprinted in 1904 as *The Defence of Duffer's Drift*, under the pseudonym Backsight Forethought. Being an accessible exposition of the principles of defence, it was reprinted many times, and was still in widespread use in the Second World War.

Swinton was promoted major in 1906 and in the following year he was appointed chief instructor in fortification and geometrical drawing at the Royal Military Academy, Woolwich. He became an advocate of the use of new technology on the battlefield, for example, promoting the use

of kites for the observation of artillery fire. This idea came from a conversation with 'Buffalo Bill' Cody, and led Swinton to write a story, 'The Kite', for *Blackwood's Magazine* in 1907. It was republished with other stories on the subject of future warfare in *The Green Curve* (1909), under the pseudonym Ole Luk-Oie (a Danish term meaning, roughly, 'Shut-eye'). Swinton's lively literary facility and ability to demonstrate principles of action from acutely observed military experiences led to his appointment to the historical section of the committee of imperial defence (CID) in 1910. His contribution to the last two volumes of the naval and military history of the Russo-Japanese War resulted in the award of the Chesney gold medal by the Royal United Services Institution in 1913. In the course of this work he became aware of the devastating capacity of the machine-gun in modern war, and made enquiries into the production of this type of weapon in Germany. During 1913, as assistant secretary at the CID, he started to undertake wider responsibilities for the review of mobilization procedures.

On the outbreak of the First World War in August 1914 Swinton's expertise in fortifications and railways came to the fore. As deputy director of railways, British expeditionary force (BEF), he once again started to form additional railway units, but in September Lord Kitchener, the secretary of state for war, appointed him official war correspondent. This was part of a War Office plan to provide, as well as censor, news from the front, to counter public complaints about lack of information caused by Joffre's ban on press correspondents in the war zone. Swinton wrote 103 articles of a steadying official character under the name Eyewitness. But although his reporting was restricted, he observed with increasing concern the emergence of stalemate on the western front. It was in response to deadlock of entrenchment that Swinton had the idea for an armoured, gun-bearing caterpillar tractor to destroy barbed wire and gun emplacements. On 20 October 1914 he discussed this idea with his erstwhile chief, Maurice Hankey, secretary of the CID, who agreed that the idea should be pursued.

Swinton's claim to be the originator of the tank is problematic, however, as the relationship between his advocacy of machine-gun destroyers and the remarkable technical progress made on experimental vehicles by the Admiralty landships committee is by no means clear. First lord of the Admiralty Winston Churchill's energetic encouragement of landship design might well have been stimulated by ideas which Hankey gleaned from Swinton, but, to Swinton's chagrin, he stood outside the chain of causation in the development of tanks described by Churchill. Although Swinton made no contribution to overcoming technical problems in the development of the tank, he provided early plans for how caterpillar tractors might be employed, especially in his memorandum of 1 June 1915, 'The necessity for machine-gun destroyers'. He always had in mind the avoidance of costly infantry assaults and the restoration of surprise as an element of battle by the deployment of a large number of machines to break the German line. He chaired interdepartmental conferences on 28 August and 24 December 1915 and maintained the momentum of the Admiralty's pioneering work, ensuring that an order for fifty machines was placed with the Ministry of Munitions by the end of the year. To maintain secrecy, Swinton coined the euphemism 'tank', rather than cistern, reservoir, or quasi-rhomboidal, to describe the new weapon.

Swinton returned to London as secretary of the Dardanelles committee in July 1915; the press suggestion that he would succeed Hankey was quickly contradicted. Much of his persistent advocacy of tanks was pursued in addition to his general duties, but gradually his responsibility for the research, invention, and production of tanks was formalized. In February 1916 Hankey noted that the trial of a prototype tank at Hatfield Park had been 'a great triumph to Swinton and me as we have had to climb a mountain of apathy and passive resistance to reach this stage' (Roskill, 1.256). In the same month the tank detachment was formed. It was renamed heavy branch, machine-gun corps three months later, and in 1917 became the Royal Tank Corps. Swinton was given the task of recruiting and training the new unit, which, he noted regretfully, did not form part of the Royal Engineers. His lack of command experience, however, meant that he would not be chosen to lead the tank force in France. In great secrecy he created battle training conditions at Elveden, near Thetford, and despite mechanical and logistical problems, a small force of the heavy section, albeit with under-trained men, was available to participate in the renewal of the Somme offensive on 15 September 1916. Swinton had wanted to wait until sufficient tanks were available to make a substantial contribution, backed by the element of surprise, to the battle, but he was overruled. This premature deployment of the new weapon was to form a contentious element in his post-war writings.

Swinton's official connection with the new tank force ended in November 1916, and was not to be renewed until 1934. He returned to Whitehall, where his unusual experience of liaison duties between the War Office and the supply ministries led to his retention as assistant military secretary when the war cabinet secretariat was formed in December. In September 1917 he went to the United States as staff officer to Lord Reading's mission, and he accompanied Reading again in February 1918. This second visit expanded into a six-month speaking tour on behalf of the state department, in support of the third Liberty Loan. After the armistice he was employed at the Ministry of Labour, where he became controller of information and publicity. In the turbulent months after the ending of the war he sought to co-ordinate press statements on the vexed interdepartmental processes of demobilization. He retired from the army in 1919 with the rank of major-general, and until 1921 was controller of information in the civil aviation department of the Air Ministry, where he promoted air-mindedness. In 1922 he became a director of Citroen-Kegresse Cars Ltd, which had developed light half-track cars during the war. He followed their innovatory activities with great interest, and remained an active board member to the end of his life. In 1923 he was appointed KBE. Between 1921 and 1924 he also acted as a research assistant to Lloyd George, who was preparing his war memoirs; but Swinton refused to 'ghost' the memoirs, and retreated from the prospect of an intimate association with Lloyd George's vast civilian-centred project on his election to the Chichele chair of military history and a fellowship of All Souls College, Oxford, in 1925. His inaugural lecture in 1926 pointed towards a wholly contemporary engagement with the study of war. He held the chair until 1939.

In September 1936 Swinton, along with many other British public figures, attended Hitler's Nuremberg rally. He returned in a chastened mood, but his central preoccupation remained the First World War, not the one that was looming ahead. In *Eyewitness* (1932) he ruminated in a vast and sprawling memoir on the 'deeply rooted bias against novel ideas' in the army (p. 96), and asserted his own place in the genesis of the tank. He accepted the role of colonel-commandant of the Royal Tank Corps in 1934 and for four years thoroughly enjoyed the recognition which the position brought him. During the first year of the Second World War he broadcast a series of *War Commentaries* (published in 1940). Swinton died in Oxford on 15 January 1951, and was buried in Wolvercote cemetery on 19 January. He was survived by his wife. His autobiography was published later that year.   KEITH GRIEVES

Sources E. Swinton, *Eyewitness* (1932) · E. Swinton, *Over my shoulder* (1951) · E. Swinton, letters, HLRO, Lloyd George papers, G/216 · A. Stern, *Tanks 1914–18: the logbook of a pioneer* (1919) · J. F. C. Fuller, *Tanks in the Great War, 1914–1918* (1920) · CAC Cam., Hankey MSS, Swinton letters · G. W. Egerton, 'The Lloyd George *War memoirs*: a study in the politics of memory', *Journal of Modern History*, 60 (1988), 55–94 · K. Macksey, *The tank pioneers* (1981) · *The Times* (17 Jan 1951) · *The Times* (15 Feb 1951) · W. S. Churchill, *The world crisis*, 5 vols. (1923–9) · J. P. Harris, *Men, ideas and tanks: British military thought and amoured forces, 1903–1939* (1995) · B. H. Liddell Hart, *The memoirs of Captain Liddell Hart*, 1 (1965) · S. W. Roskill, *Hankey, man of secrets*, 3 vols. (1970–74) · T. Travers, *The killing ground: the British army, the* western front and the emergence of modern warfare, 1900–1918 (1987) · DNB · B. Bond, British military policy between the two world wars (1980) · m. cert. · CGPLA Eng. & Wales (1951) · The Times (20 Jan 1951)

Archives King's Lond., Liddell Hart C., papers relating to tank development · Tank Museum, Bovington, Dorset, MSS | BL OIOC, letters to Lord Reading, MSS Eur. E 238, F 118 · CAC Cam., Lord Hankey MSS · HLRO, David Lloyd George MSS, relating to Lloyd George's war memoirs · King's Lond., Liddell Hart C., corresp. with Sir J. E. Edmonds · King's Lond., Liddell Hart C., corresp. with Sir B. H. Liddell Hart · King's Lond., Liddell Hart C., Sir Albert Stern MSS · PRO, WO 32/5754 · U. Hull, Brynmor Jones L., letters and cards to O. A. Forsyth-Major | SOUND BBC WAC

Likenesses E. Kennington, pastel drawing, Tank Museum, Bovington, Dorset [see illus.]

Wealth at death £20,105 6s. 3d.: probate, 25 April 1951, CGPLA Eng. & Wales

Swinton, James Rannie (1816–1888), portrait painter, was born near Duns, Berwickshire, on 11 April 1816, the younger son of John Campbell Swinton (1777–1867) of Kimmerghame, Berwickshire, and his wife, Catherine Rannie (d. 1821). His grandfather was Archibald, fourth son of John Swinton of Swinton, Berwickshire, and his elder brother the jurist Archibald Campbell *Swinton. He was intended for the legal profession, but, having demonstrated a strong inclination for art, he was allowed in 1838 to pursue that profession. At Edinburgh, Sir William Allan and Sir John Watson-Gordon gave him much encouragement, and he was allowed to work in the latter's studio. He also studied at the city's Trustees' Academy. In April 1839 he went to London, where he was welcomed by Sir David Wilkie and Francis Grant. In 1840 he was admitted to the Royal Academy Schools, and in the same year went to Italy, where he remained for about three years, also visiting Spain. At Rome he found many sitters, and laid the foundation of his subsequent popularity as a portrayer of the fashionable beauties of his day; among those who sat to him at Rome were the Countess Grosvenor, Lady Canning, the countess of Dufferin, and Lady Charlotte Bury. His work possessed 'considerable skill and spirit', but in his portraits of ladies 'he surrendered exact likeness for an exaggerated sweetness and grace' (Bryan, Painters, 5.148).

On his return to London, Swinton settled in Berners Street, and soon became one of the most fashionable portrait painters of the day. Nearly every fashionable beauty sat to him. His portraits were chiefly life-sized, boldly executed but graceful crayon drawings, although many of them were completed subsequently in oils, and frequently at full length. A large portrait group of the three beautiful Sheridan sisters, the countess of Dufferin, the Hon. Mrs Norton, and the duchess of Somerset, was exhibited at the Royal Academy in 1852. Swinton also drew and painted the portraits of eminent men with great success, among them being Louis Napoleon (afterwards Napoleon III), Lord Stratford de Redcliffe, the duke of Argyll, Lord Canning, Bishop (afterwards Archbishop) Tait, Lord Dufferin, and others; a full length of Colonel Probyn was considered especially successful. Swinton exhibited for the first time at the Royal Academy in 1844, and his portraits were familiar there for thirty years. He was dependent on the vagaries of fashion for his vogue as a portrait

painter, and his portraits quickly lost their repute. He married, on 23 July 1865, Blanche Arthur Georgina, daughter of Lord Henry Fitzgerald de Ros and Baroness de Ros; they had no children. His sisters Catherine and Elizabeth were also artists. Swinton's health began to fail in 1869, causing a suspension in his painting, with a brief resumption in 1874. He died at his home, 49 Harrington Gardens, South Kensington, London, on 18 December 1888; his wife survived him.
L. H. CUST, rev. MARK POTTLE

Sources private information (1898) · P. J. M. McEwan, Dictionary of Scottish art and architecture (1994) · B. Stewart and M. Cutten, The dictionary of portrait painters in Britain up to 1920 (1997) · Wood, Vic. painters, 2nd edn · Bryan, Painters (1903–5) · CGPLA Eng. & Wales (1889)

Wealth at death £23,746 10s. 8d.—effects in United Kingdom: probate, 16 April 1889, CGPLA Eng. & Wales

Swinton, Sir John (c.1350–1402), landowner and soldier, is of Scottish origins. He is first recorded in 1370 on the English expedition to Brittany led by Sir Robert Knolles—an Anglo-Scottish truce had been agreed in 1369—and distinguished himself at the siege of Noyon. By 1372 he was retained by John of Gaunt, duke of Lancaster, as an esquire with an annuity of £20, an amount which was doubled in 1373, when Swinton is referred to as a knight. He served on Lancaster's campaign in France in the same year and on the expedition of Edmund Langley, earl of Cambridge, in 1374. Swinton remained closely tied to the Lancastrian affinity until 1384 and showed his devotion to it in displaying his badge of retinue, at considerable personal risk, in the face of a rioting anti-Lancastrian crowd in London in 1377. His English service seems to have enriched him considerably: his first wife, Joan, possessed valuable jewels at the time of her death in 1374 and he was later able to buy lands in Scotland with ready cash and silver vessels.

Perhaps because of the wealth and kudos attained in English service, Swinton forged powerful political connections within Scotland on his return in the mid-1380s, following the end of the Anglo-Scottish truce in 1384. He married Margaret, countess of Mar (d. before 22 Nov 1393), the widow of William, first earl of Douglas, by 27 July 1388, while his third wife, who survived him, was Margaret Stewart, daughter of Robert, earl of Fife and Menteith, later duke of Albany. His marriage to Margaret enabled Swinton to style himself lord of the earldom of Mar. Politically his attachments in Scotland were to the Douglases, and he had access to royal patronage, receiving annuities from both Robert II and Robert III. His landed base was in the east borders and he aggressively extended his influence there. In 1379, while visiting Scotland with a retinue of sixty men, he had contentiously acquired lands from the Durham priory of Coldingham when it had been temporarily seized into Scottish hands, and he was later prominently in receipt of lands from the earldom of March after the earl, George Dunbar had been forced to switch his allegiance to the English crown and flee across the border in 1400.

In 1386 and again in the 1390s Swinton took part in embassies to England, but his chief note is as a soldier. He served in the Otterburn campaign of 1388, and some chronicles accord him an important role in securing victory for the Scots. He died on 14 September 1402 at the battle of Homildon Hill, near Wooler, leading a quixotic charge by a segment of the Scottish army against the English archers. He had been at feud with Adam Gordon, with whom he was reconciled on the battlefield. Swinton knighted Gordon, and the two men fell together.

ALASTAIR J. MACDONALD

Sources A. C. Swinton, *The Swintons of that ilk and their cadets* (1883) · G. S. C. Swinton, 'John of Swinton: a border fighter of the middle ages', *SHR*, 16 (1918–19), 261–79 · NA Scot. · PRO · *John of Gaunt's register*, ed. S. Armitage-Smith, 2 vols., CS, 3rd ser., 20–21 (1911) · G. Burnett and others, eds., *The exchequer rolls of Scotland*, 23 vols. (1878–1908) · W. Bower, *Scotichronicon*, ed. D. E. R. Watt and others, new edn, 9 vols. (1987–98) · *Johannis de Fordun Scotichronicon, cum supplementis … Walteri Boweri*, ed. W. Goodall, 2 vols. (1759) · *RotS* · *Œuvres de Froissart: chroniques*, ed. K. de Lettenhove, 25 vols. (Brussels, 1867–77) · [T. Walsingham], *Chronicon Angliae, ab anno Domini 1328 usque ad annum 1388*, ed. E. M. Thompson, Rolls Series, 64 (1874) · *CDS* · S. I. Boardman, *The early Stewart kings: Robert II and Robert III, 1371–1406* (1996)
Likenesses seal, 1389, Drumlanrig Castle, Dumfriesshire, Buccleuch and Queensferry MSS
Wealth at death £20 crown annuity; plus lands in Berwickshire and East Lothian: NA Scot., Swinton charters; Swinton, *Swintons*, appx xiii

Swinton, John (*c.*1620–1679), politician, was the eldest son of Sir Alexander Swinton (*c.*1600–1652) of Swinton, and his wife, Margaret, daughter of James Home of Framepath, Berwickshire. His younger brother was Sir Alexander *Swinton, Lord Mersington. He was trained as a lawyer, and in 1645 he married Margaret (*d.* 1662), daughter of William Stewart, second Lord Blantyre. They had at least four children. As zealous supporters of the Scottish covenanters, Swinton and his father were on the committee of war for Berwickshire in 1646 and 1647, and in February 1649, after the defeat of the Engagers, who supported the king, he was appointed a lieutenant-colonel with the command of a troop of horse. In the same year, he was elected to parliament for the Merse.

Swinton was totally uncompromising in his hostility to royalist malignants, but unusually open towards the English Commonwealth. In recognition of his zeal for ideological purity, he was appointed a member of the Scottish parliament's committee for purging the army in January 1650. In the following February he opposed the sending of a covenanter deputation to negotiate with Charles II in the Netherlands, and when parliament passed an Act of Levy on 25 June 1650 in response to the threat of invasion from England, Swinton was one of only six MPs to vote against it. After the king arrived in Scotland at the end of June, Swinton worked with Sir John Cheisly and Sir John Hopetoun to disrupt the new covenanter royalism. Robert Baillie referred to:

> their strange affronting of the King at Leith; the putting of him to a new declaration; and, when he stucke but at some hard expressions concerning the persons of his Father, Mother, their procuring from the Kirk and State that terrible Act of disclaiming his interest, of the 13th of August; that same night, without the Kirk's knowledge, printed it, and sent to Cromwell with a trumpet. (Baillie, 3.114)

Following the covenanters' defeat at Dunbar and the subsequent defeat of the radical western remonstrance, which refused any support for Charles II unless he repented of his royalist associations, Swinton defected to the English in December 1650. According to Baillie, he was the 'agent' responsible for 'the randering of the Castle of Edinburgh' to the English (ibid., 3.125). Early in 1651 Swinton was condemned as a traitor by the Scottish parliament, and excommunicated by the kirk. He seems to have developed Independent sympathies, and in August Sir Archibald Johnston, Lord Wariston, heard of 'Swynton's strainge expressions, commending the sectaries to the skyes' (*Diary … 1650–54*, 119).

Swinton was present at the battle of Worcester on 3 September 1651, but took no part in the fighting, in which his younger brother, Robert, was killed attempting to capture the English standard. After the battle Swinton returned to Scotland and reported that 'many in Ingland was for declairing this a conquest, but the [General Cromwell] was for making it on nation' (*Diary … 1650–54*, 143). In April 1652 he was appointed a commissioner for the administration of justice, along with Sir John Hope of Craighall and William Lockhart. These three were the first Scotsmen to be appointed to high executive office by the English, and in the next few years Swinton was to be, in the words of Gilbert Burnet, 'the man of all Scotland that had been the most trusted and employed by Cromwell' (*Burnet's History*, 1.194).

In August 1652 Swinton was among twenty-one Scottish deputies elected to negotiate a treaty of union between England and Scotland. The deputies travelled to London in September, but despite months of negotiations the Bill of Union made little progress. From July to December he was one of only four Scots to sit in the nominated assembly, and in August 1654 he was elected to the first protectorate parliament as a member for Berwickshire. In May 1655 Swinton and Lockhart were the only Scots appointed as members of the new council of state in Scotland. Swinton was well rewarded for his loyal service to the regime. He received £600 per year as a member of the council, and £300 per year for his work as a judge, though he and Lockhart were removed from the commission of justice for 1656 partly because they resisted attempts to bring the Scottish legal system into line with the English system. In March 1656 Swinton's sentence of excommunication from the Church of Scotland was lifted after the lobbying of influential friends, though he himself had neither admitted any fault nor petitioned for readmission. Besides his duties in Scotland, he was also a member of the second protectorate parliament (September 1656–February 1658) and the third (January–April 1659). In May 1659 Swinton and Alexander Gibson (both deputies in the union negotiations of 1652–3) presented a petition to the restored Rump Parliament asking 'that the consideratioun of the union be resumed, prosequuted, and perfyted' (Terry, lxxxix). Although a Bill of Union was introduced, it never reached its third reading.

As one of the leading collaborators with the English, Swinton was deeply resented by his fellow Scots. Wariston recorded in his diary rumours of Swinton's corruption; he was said to be neglecting family worship, breaking the sabbath, playing cards, and spending lavishly. His wife was enjoying the trappings of power, riding around Edinburgh in a stately coach, and relishing her role as a political insider. An English satirist suggested that during the protectorate Swinton had rejected his earlier austerity, chosen 'notorious malignants for his intimate companions', engaged in a love affair with 'an English lady', and 'swaggered with the best of the Court in gallant apparel and powdred periwigs' (*A Lively Character of Sum Pretending Grandees of Scotland to the Good Old Cause*, 1659). In this context Swinton's conversion to Quakerism in the late 1650s came as something of a surprise.

Swinton's political downfall was as swift and complete as his rise to power. In January 1660 he was arrested and imprisoned at Leith, on suspicion of having plotted with General Lambert. He was soon released, but following the Restoration he was again arrested on 20 July 1660 at the house of a fellow Quaker in Westminster. In December he was transported to Edinburgh with the earl of Argyll to face charges of high treason, and was paraded through the city 'invironed with thousands of people, men and women' (Nicoll, 309). At his trial in February 1661, he spoke:

> with a sort of eloquence that moved the whole house, lay out all his own errors, and the ill spirit he was then in when he committed the things that were charged on him … he did so effectually prevail on them, that they recommended him to the King as a fit object for his mercy. This was the more easily consented to by the earl of Middleton, in hatred to the earl of Lauderdale, who had got the gift of his estate. (*Burnet's History*, 1.229)

Although he had avoided execution, Swinton was condemned to forfeiture and imprisoned in Edinburgh Castle for some years. His wife died in December 1662 shortly after giving birth. One of his fellow prisoners was David Barclay, father of the famous Quaker apologist Robert Barclay, and Swinton was instrumental in their conversions to Quakerism in 1665 and 1666 respectively. He also published a number of Quaker pamphlets, mostly in the period 1663–6. Swinton's imprisonment seems to have ended in 1667. In March he was allowed to leave prison until 1 June under penalty of £1000 sterling. George Fox reported that in 1667 Swinton had led a schismatic group of Scottish Quakers (apparently advocating the intense mysticism of John Perrot). But in 1668 'the Lord's power came over them so as they were made to condemn and tear all their papers of controversies to pieces' (Fox, 370, 435). In the same year Swinton briefly joined Fox on a tour of Quaker meetings in England, and in 1669 was described as a 'ringleader' of a conventicle of 100 people in Norton, co. Durham (Lyon-Turner, 3.758–9). He married Frances White of Newington Butts on 3 June 1671. In October 1672 he and Robert Barclay were arrested at Montrose while on a missionary tour of Scotland, and were imprisoned for several weeks. Swinton died at Borthwick, Lancashire, early in 1679.   JOHN COFFEY

Sources J. Nicoll, *A diary of public transactions and other occurrences, chiefly in Scotland, from January 1650 to June 1667*, ed. D. Laing, Bannatyne Club, 52 (1836) · *The letters and journals of Robert Baillie*, ed. D. Laing, 3 vols. (1841–2) · *Diary of Sir Archibald Johnston of Wariston*, 2, ed. D. H. Fleming, Scottish History Society, 2nd ser., 18 (1919) · *Diary of Sir Archibald Johnston of Wariston*, 3, ed. J. D. Ogilvie, Scottish History Society, 3rd ser., 34 (1940) · *Burnet's History of my own time*, ed. O. Airy, new edn, 2 vols. (1897–1900) · C. S. Terry, ed., *The Cromwellian union, 1651–2* (1902) · C. H. Firth, ed., *Scotland and the protectorate: letters and papers relating to the military government of Scotland from January 1654 to June 1659*, Scottish History Society, 31 (1899) · *Diary of Thomas Burton*, ed. J. T. Rutt, 4 vols. (1828) · *The diary of Alexander Brodie of Brodie … and of his son James Brodie*, ed. D. Laing, Spalding Club, 33 (1863) · F. D. Dow, *Cromwellian Scotland, 1651–1660* (1979) · W. C. Braithwaite, *The second period of Quakerism*, ed. H. J. Cadbury, 2nd edn (1961) · A. C. Swinton, *The Swintons of that ilk and their cadets* (1883) · G. L. Turner, ed., *Original records of early nonconformity under persecution and indulgence*, 3 vols. (1911–14) · G. Fox, *The Journal*, ed. N. Smith (1998)

Archives BL, letter to Byllynge, Add. MS 35125, fol. 136 · BL, letters to Quakers, Add. MS 36735, fols. 3b, 4, 8, 12, 15 · BL, petition to Rothes, Add. MS 23127, fol. 86

Swinton, John (1703–1777), Church of England clergyman and orientalist, was born in Cheshire, the son of John Swinton of Bexton, Cheshire. He entered Wadham College, Oxford, as a servitor, matriculating on 10 October 1719, and on 30 June 1723 was elected a scholar. He graduated BA on 1 December 1723 and MA on 1 December 1726. He was ordained deacon on 30 May 1725 and priest on 28 May 1727, and in February 1728 became rector of St Peter-le-Bailey, Oxford. On 30 June 1729 he was chosen a probationer-fellow of Wadham. Shortly afterwards he was appointed chaplain to the English factory at Leghorn. He travelled to Lisbon (1730–31), Genoa, and Pisa (1731). In July 1732 the British consul in Leghorn, Neil Brown, objected to having the chaplain living in his house. Swinton went to Florence (1733), claiming that the climate of Leghorn did not suit his health. He left Leghorn in February 1734 and returned to England, travelling via Venice, Vienna, and Pressburg in Hungary.

Swinton settled at Wadham College where he acted as subdean in 1734 and was the humanities lecturer from 1735 to 1737. There he became involved in a homosexual scandal that led to the resignation and flight abroad of the warden of Wadham, Robert Thistlethwayte, in February 1739. Swinton was also accused of sodomy by his pupil George Baker, but Baker signed a recantation that was published in the London newspapers. Later that year *A Faithful Narrative* gave full details of Swinton's homosexual relations with several college servants. In 1740 Baker successfully sued Swinton at the court of king's bench for defaming his character. Swinton became a prebendary of St Asaph on 11 October 1743, and vacated his fellowship; it may have been at this time that he married. In July 1745 he moved to Christ Church, becoming bachelor of divinity in 1759. He was elected keeper of the university archives in 1767, a post he held until his death.

Swinton published several scholarly works and was praised for his erudition as an oriental and Arabic scholar. On 16 October 1729 he was elected a fellow of the Royal

Society, and he wrote articles for their *Philosophical Transactions* on Parthian, Samnite, and Phoenician inscriptions. He contributed articles to the famous *Universal History* (1736–44, 1750) on several eastern and ancient cultures.

As the chaplain of Oxford gaol Swinton attended at the last days of Mary Blandy (convicted in 1752 for poisoning her father), and was praised as 'the worthy clergyman' in her very popular accounts of her case. An engraving in *The Malefactor's Register* (1779) shows him praying beside Blandy at the gallows. He became absent-minded, and Boswell in his *Life of Johnson* related that once when Swinton preached on repentance to several criminals to be executed on the following day, he told his audience that he would give them the remainder of his discourse on next Lord's day. When a colleague excused this gaffe by saying he had probably delivered the same sermon before the university, Johnson replied, 'Yes, Sir, but the university were not to be hanged the next morning' (Boswell, 193).

Swinton died in Oxford on 4 April 1777 and was buried in the antechapel of Wadham, where his wife was buried in 1784. He had no children. He has been confused with John Swinton who matriculated from Wadham in 1713, graduating BA in 1717 and MA in 1720; he came from Knutsford, Cheshire, and was probably a cousin.

E. I. Carlyle, rev. Rictor Norton

Sources R. B. Gardiner, ed., *The registers of Wadham College, Oxford*, 2 vols. (1889–95) • *A faithful narrative of the proceedings in the late affair between the Rev. Mr John Swinton, and Mr George Baker … to which is prefix'd a particular account of the proceedings against Robert Thistlethwayte* (1739) • Nichols, *Lit. anecdotes* • Nichols, *Illustrations* • *GM*, 1st ser., 54 (1784), 892 • A. Chalmers, ed., *The general biographical dictionary*, new edn, 32 vols. (1812–17) • R. Norton, *Mother Clap's molly house: the gay subculture in England, 1700–1830* (1992) • J. Boswell, *Life of Johnson*, ed. R. W. Chapman, rev. J. D. Fleeman, new edn (1970); repr. with introduction by P. Rogers (1980) • J. Black, *The British abroad* (1992) • *Hist. U. Oxf.* 5: *18th-cent. Oxf.* • *Fasti Angl.* (Hardy) • J. Ingamells, ed., *A dictionary of British and Irish travellers in Italy, 1701–1800* (1997)
Archives BL, travel journal, Add. MS 22978 • Bodl. Oxf., collections and papers • Wadham College, Oxford, diary | BL, corresp. with Thomas Birch, Add. MSS 4319, 4326, 4444, *passim*
Likenesses engraving (possibly imaginary), repro. in *The malefactor's register* (1779)

Swinton, John, Lord Swinton (1723–1799), judge, was born in Edinburgh on 5 March 1723, the eldest of twelve children of the advocate John Swinton (*d.* 1774) of Swinton, Berwickshire, and his wife, Mary (*d.* 1768), daughter of Samuel Semple, minister of Liberton. He was admitted advocate on 20 December 1743, and appointed sheriff-depute of Perthshire in June 1754. On 23 June 1758 he married Margaret (*d.* 1812), daughter of John Mitchelson of Middleton, with whom he had six sons and seven daughters. He was appointed solicitor for renewal of leases of the bishops' tithes, and solicitor and advocate to the commissioners for the plantation of kirks in Scotland in April 1766. He was elevated to the bench, as Lord Swinton, on 21 December 1782, and on the promotion of Robert Macqueen of Braxfield in 1788 was also made a lord of justiciary, continuing in these capacities until his death.

Swinton entered the contemporary debate on reform of the law relating to entails with a pamphlet *A Free Disquisition Concerning the Law of Entails in Scotland* (1765). His position was deeply hostile to the restrictions which entails imposed, particularly in respect of commerce. In another pamphlet, *A Proposal for Uniformity of Weights and Measures in Scotland* (1779), issued with extensive conversion tables, he argued for the effective implementation of existing laws in this area. He made the point that the seventeenth article of the treaty of union had provided for the adoption of English weights and measures, but that this provision had been entirely overlooked since then. Swinton's most serious proposals were contained in *Considerations concerning a proposal for dividing the court of session into classes or chambers and for limiting litigation in small causes and for the revival of jury trial in certain civil actions* (1789) which was indicative of a strong Anglicizing tendency on his part. The pamphlet, however, was reckoned to be such a significant contribution to the case for reform of the court of session that Henry Erskine had it republished in 1807.

Lord Cockburn esteemed Swinton as:

> a very excellent person; dull, mild, solid, and plodding; and in his person large and heavy. It is only a subsequent age that has discovered his having possessed a degree of sagacity, for which he did not get credit while he lived. (*Memorials … by Henry Cockburn*, 112)

Cockburn also remarked upon the unlikely friendship, given their contrasting temperaments and in spite of the latter's jokes upon him, between Swinton and Henry Erskine. Swinton died, after a short illness, at his home, Dean House, Edinburgh, on 5 January 1799, and was buried in Greyfriars churchyard, Edinburgh.

R. B. Swinton, rev. Lionel Alexander Ritchie

Sources A. C. Swinton, *The Swintons of that ilk and their cadets* (1883), 91–6 • A. C. Swinton and J. L. C. Swinton, *Concerning Swinton family records and portraits at Kimmerghame* (1908) • G. Brunton and D. Haig, *An historical account of the senators of the college of justice, from its institution in MDXXXII* (1832) • F. J. Grant, ed., *The Faculty of Advocates in Scotland, 1532–1943*, Scottish RS, 145 (1944), 204 • D. M. Walker, *A legal history of Scotland*, 5 (1998), 460–61 • Burke, *Gen. GB* (1972) • *Scots Magazine*, 61 (1799), 72 • N. Phillipson, *The Scottish whigs and the reform of the court of session, 1785–1830*, Stair Society, 37 (1990), 79–84 • N. T. Phillipson, 'Lawyers, landowners and the civil leadership of post-Union Scotland', *Juridical Review*, new ser., 21 (1976), 97–120 • *Memorials of his time, by Henry Cockburn* (1856), 112–13 • *IGI*
Archives NA Scot., MSS | NA Scot., corresp. with Henry Dundas

Swinton, William Elgin (1900–1994), palaeontologist and popularizer of natural science, was born on 30 September 1900 at 94 Dunnikier Road, Kirkaldy, Fife, the son of William Wilson Swinton, a clerk, and his wife, Rachel Hunter, formerly Cargill. He was educated at Morgan Academy, Dundee, Whitehill School, Glasgow, and Trinity College, Glenalmond, graduating from the University of Glasgow in 1922 with the equivalent of first-class honours. As a student he played rugby, took part in an expedition to Svalbard, and was successively secretary and president of the university's geological society. Swinton's first research was on some marsupials from south Australia, but the expedition to Svalbard propelled him into an investigation of Mesozoic bivalve molluscs. In 1924, after only two years of postgraduate research, he was fortunate in obtaining the post of curator of fossil amphibians, reptiles, and birds at what was then known as the British Museum (Natural History) in South Kensington, where he remained until 1961.

As a curator Swinton travelled widely, collecting fossils and undertaking lecture tours, visiting South Africa, Mexico, Canada, the USA, India, and the former USSR state of Georgia. He wrote over 200 papers, mostly in scientific journals, ranging from descriptions of new specimens of fossil tetrapods, reptiles, birds, and mammals, to philosophical discussions of the origins of flight and causes of extinction. He obtained his PhD from Glasgow in 1930. But Swinton became increasingly well known for his popular books, lectures, and broadcasts; he was an outstanding speaker, capable of talking for an hour without a single unwanted pause or broken line of thought. He could speak with authority on most subjects, but never pretentiously—his aim was to enlighten, not dazzle, and among the children whom he entertained and guided round the museum were the young princesses Elizabeth and Margaret Rose. He was also a co-founder of the museum's dramatic society and took the first lead in Shaw's *Fanny's First Play*, given at Cobb's Hall, Hammersmith.

In 1938 Swinton was commissioned into the Royal Naval Volunteer Reserve and during the Second World War he served with naval intelligence, reaching the rank of lieutenant-commander. He returned to South Kensington to enter on the subject which brought him the most fame and publicity, that of the dinosaurs. Swinton had written the first popular book on these little-known extinct creatures in 1934; *The Dinosaurs* was followed by a dozen more, most of them aimed at a wide readership. As the various genera and species of tetrapods were discovered and their relationship explored, Swinton was ideally placed to spread knowledge and understanding to an eager public. He was a frequent contributor on the subject of Darwin and evolution, and received the Darwin medal from the USSR Academy of Sciences on the centenary of the publication of *The Origin of Species*. He was an active participant in the British Association for the Advancement of Science, serving as president of the general science section in 1954 and as honorary general secretary from 1959 to 1961. A vocal advocate for museums and their role in education, Swinton was president of the Museums' Association in 1959–60 and served for many years as editor of the *Museums Journal*.

Swinton retired from the Natural History Museum in 1961 and joined the Royal Ontario Museum in Toronto—first as director of life sciences, and two years later as overall director. He also held a professorship of zoology at the University of Toronto. Swinton's stewardship brought a dramatic improvement; attendance soared, government funding increased, as did the museum's academic stature. 'I see museums as department stores of knowledge and the showcases as our shop window', he told *Globe Magazine* on 7 July 1962 (p. 8). He held a professorship at Massey College, University of Ontario, and on his retirement from

the Royal Ontario Museum in 1966 he was appointed centennial professor of the history of science at the University of Toronto. Always in demand for speaking engagements and for his sage advice, he became actively engaged in planning the Ontario Science Center, serving on the operating board after its opening in 1969.

Swinton was a man of great personal charm. He loved nothing better than a good chat and was himself an entertaining conversationalist. On the 150th anniversary of the naming of the first dinosaur, he spirited his audience from a lecture room in central Toronto to the drawing-rooms of pre-Victorian England. Retracing the footsteps of Gideon Mantell, an earlier popularizer of palaeontology, Swinton transported his audience back to the Sussex quarry where some teeth of *Iguanodon* had first been uncovered in February 1825.

Following a dinner given in celebration of his ninetieth birthday, Swinton was invited to talk about his long career in palaeontology. For a man of his advanced years to give a faultless presentation was an unrealistic expectation. But Swinton rose to his feet, and in his usual quiet and unassuming manner, delivered a word-perfect performance. He died, unmarried, on 12 June 1994 in Toronto, echoing in a sense what he had written of the demise of the dinosaurs in one of his books, their 'great race, entrenched on earth for so many million years … silently passed away … having no descendants of its own' (*The Dinosaurs*, 1970, 273).

CHRIS MCGOWAN and ANITA MCCONNELL

Sources *The Times* (21 June 1994) · *The Independent* (28 June 1994) · personal knowledge (2004) · b. cert. · R. Cocks, 'William Elgin Swinton, 1900–1994', *Museums Journal*, 94 (Aug 1994), 42 · *CGPLA Eng. & Wales* (1994)
Likenesses photograph, 1940–49, repro. in *The Times* · photograph, repro. in *The Independent*
Wealth at death £189,670—in England and Wales: probate, 1994, *CGPLA Eng. & Wales*

Swiny [McSwiny, Swiney, MacSwiny, MacSwinny], **Owen** (1676–1754), impresario, was born near Enniscorthy in Ireland, the son of the Revd Miles Swiny (d. 1690) of Ballyteige, co. Wexford. He entered Trinity College, Dublin, on 11 November 1694. By the spring of 1703 he was in London working with Christopher Rich at Drury Lane Theatre. His comedy *The Quacks* (after Molière's *L'amour médecin*) was performed there on 29 March 1705.

In August 1706 Swiny leased the Queen's Theatre in the Haymarket from Sir John Vanbrugh, and the theatre opened under his management on 15 October. He had been promised assistance by Rich, the patentee of Drury Lane, but in the following year a quarrel broke off the connection. Swiny wanted to obtain the services of Colley Cibber, whom Rich wished to retain in his own company. The affair was terminated by Cibber's deciding to throw in his lot with Swiny, and, owing to his assistance, the season of 1707 proved extremely successful. On 31 December 1707 the lord chamberlain, in the interest of Rich, ordered that the Queen's Theatre should be used for opera only. In 1708 Swiny engaged the castrato Nicolini for a period of three

Owen Swiny (1676–1754), by John Faber junior, 1752 (after Jean Baptiste van Loo, 1738)

years, and at first was so fortunate that in one winter, according to Cibber, he gained 'a moderate younger brother's fortune'. On Rich's eviction from Drury Lane by William Collier in 1709 Swiny was permitted to engage most of the Drury Lane actors and to perform plays as well as operas at the Queen's Theatre. But Collier in 1710, finding that this interfered with his own success, employed his influence at court to bring about a renewal of the former arrangement, by which the Queen's Theatre was reserved for opera. He took over the management of that theatre himself, and transferred Swiny, now in partnership with Cibber, Robert Wilks, and Thomas Doggett, to Drury Lane. In the next year Collier, having failed at the opera, brought his court influence into play once more, and transferred Swiny back to the Queen's Theatre for the season of 1711–12. He found the opera there in a sinking condition, and by January 1713 he was bankrupt and compelled to take refuge abroad. During his tenure as manager of the opera, Swiny signed the dedications of the librettos (and may have been responsible for the English translations) of Giovanni Bononcini's *Camilla* (first performed in London on 30 March 1706) and Alessandro Scarlatti's *Pirro e Demetrio* (14 December 1708).

After travelling in France and the Netherlands, Swiny was in Italy in 1715 and by 1721 had settled in Venice, where he acted as agent for the Italian opera in London, recruiting singers and recommending operas. He was also active commissioning Italian works of art, from painters such as Rosalba Carriera and the young Antonio Canaletto, for English collectors. It was Swiny's patronage that helped to establish the close connection between Canaletto and England. During the 1720s Swiny launched a series of twenty-four allegorical tomb paintings intended to commemorate great men of recent English history, with particular reference to the revolution of 1688. The subject matter of the paintings was devised by Swiny, who commissioned a team of Venetian and Bolognese artists including G. B. Piazzetta, Sebastiano and Marco Ricci, Canaletto, G. B. Pittoni, G. B. Cimaroli, Donato Creti, and Francesco Monti. Charles Lennox, second duke of Richmond, was an important patron of this project and acquired at least ten of the paintings. In the 1730s Swiny published a prospectus entitled *To the Ladies and Gentlemen of Taste of Great Britain and Ireland*, in which he invited subscriptions for a volume of engravings of these paintings, only nine of which eventually appeared in his *Tombeaux des princes, grands capitaines et autres hommes illustrés, qui ont fleuri dans la Grande-Bretagne vers la fin du XVII et le commencement du XVIII siècle* (1741). A second series of six paintings commemorating the achievements of the duke of Marlborough was planned but not completed.

Following some twenty years' residence abroad Swiny returned to England, where he obtained a place in the custom house and was appointed storekeeper at the king's mews. On 26 February 1735 he was given a benefit at Drury Lane, at which Cibber played; he had another benefit on 1 April 1736 at Covent Garden. In 1736 the directors of the Opera of the Nobility considered sending Swiny to Italy in search of singers. In 1746 Canaletto arrived in England with a letter of recommendation to Swiny, who introduced him to the duke of Richmond. About 1749 Swiny visited Paris on behalf of John Rich to arrange the visit in 1749–50 of a French troupe headed by Jean Monnet. He died on 2 October 1754 and was buried three days later at St Martin-in-the-Fields. He had made his will on 1 August 1752, leaving his estate in trust to Robert Maxwell, secretary to the duke of Dorset, lord lieutenant of Ireland, and Francis Andrews, a lawyer and fellow of Trinity College, Dublin, for the actress Margaret (Peg) Woffington. His substantial collection of pictures was sold in 1755 for her benefit.

Swiny's portrait was painted from life in 1737 by Peter van Bleeck, and an engraving of the original was made by van Bleeck in 1749; in 1752 another engraving, after Jean Baptiste van Loo's portrait of 1738, was executed by John Faber jun. in mezzotint.   ELIZABETH GIBSON

Sources C. Cibber, *An apology for the life of Mr. Colley Cibber* (1740) • *GM*, 1st ser., 24 (1754), 483 • J. Milhous and R. D. Hume, eds., *Vice Chamberlain Coke's theatrical papers, 1706–1715* (1982) • E. Gibson, *The Royal Academy of Music, 1719–1728: the institution and its directors* (1989) • G. Knox, '"The tombs of famous Englishmen" as described in the letters of Owen Swiny to the duke of Richmond', *Arte veneta*, 37 (1983), 228–35 • B. Mazza, 'La vicenda dei "Tombeaux des princes": matrici, storia e fortuna delle serie Swiny tra Bologna e Venezia', *Saggi e memorie di storia dell'arte*, 10 (1976), 80–102 • Swiny letters, W. Sussex RO, Goodwood MS 105 • J. G. Links, *Canaletto* (1982); rev. edn (1994) • G. Colman, *Posthumous letters from various celebrated men* (1820) • H. F. Finberg, 'Canaletto in England', *Walpole Society*, 9 (1920–21), 21–76 • Burtchaell & Sadleir, *Alum. Dubl.* • H. R. F. Brown, *Inglesi e scozzesi all'università di Padova dall'anno 1618 sino al*

1765 (Venice, 1922) • Highfill, Burnim & Langhans, *BDA* • J. Ingamells, ed., *A dictionary of British and Irish travellers in Italy, 1701–1800* (1997) • Society of Genealogists, Crookshank MSS, D. MS. 607

Archives Harvard TC, letters relating to his activities as a theatrical impresario | W. Sussex RO, letters to the second duke of Richmond, Goodwood MS 105

Likenesses G. Grisoni, drawing, *c*.1716, Hunt. L.; repro. in Highfill, Burnim & Langhans, *BDA* • B. Nazari, group portrait, oils, *c*.1730–1731 (Owen Swiny?; Lord Boyne in the cabin of his ship), repro. in I. Bignamini, *Grand tour: the lure of Italy in the eighteenth century*, ed. A. Wilton (1996), 105 [exhibition catalogue London and Rome, Oct 1996–April 1997]; copy, NMM • J. B. van Loo, oils, 1738, priv. coll.; repro. in *Old master paintings* (1987), 15 • P. van Bleeck, mezzotint, 1749 (after P. van Bleeck, 1737), BM • J. Faber junior, mezzotint, 1752 (after J. B. van Loo, 1738), NPG [*see illus.*] • oil copy (after oil painting by P. van Bleeck, 1737), NPG

Wealth at death land holdings in Ireland: will, PRO, PROB 11/811

Swire, John Kidston [Jock] (**1893–1983**), businessman, was born on 19 February 1893 in Kensingston Court, London, the elder son and second of four children of John Swire of Hillingdon House, Harlow, Essex, and his wife, Emily Kidston; he was the grandson of John Samuel *Swire (1825–1898), who moved the emphasis of the family's trading business from Liverpool to the Far East in the mid-1800s. Of Scottish descent, Jock Swire was educated at Eton College (1906–10) and University College, Oxford (1910–13), where he obtained a third class in jurisprudence.

Swire joined the family business, John Swire & Sons, in 1913, arriving in Hong Kong just before the First World War broke out. Having been commissioned in the Oxford OTC cavalry in 1912 and transferred to the Essex yeomanry in 1913, he served in the war with his regiment in France, rising to the rank of major. He was twice wounded and twice recommended for decorations; he remained partially deaf for the rest of his life. In 1920 Swire became the London-based director in charge of the company's overseas staff, and thereafter in a series of long, energetic, and often dangerous tours—the civil war in China was at its height—he regularly explored every nook and cranny of the company's Far Eastern empire. One of the suggestions, revolutionary at the time, which Swire put to his board in London, was that female clerks should work on an equal footing with men, and for the same pay; another was that Swire recruits earmarked for Eastern posts should be university graduates, and should also learn Chinese. His was also an important voice, together with that of his uncle G. Warren *Swire (1883–1949), in arguing that Chinese nationalism had to be accommodated by British firms, and that companies like Swires had, in effect, to 'Sinify' themselves, if they were to survive. On 18 July 1923 Swire married Juliet Richenda (1901–1981), daughter of Theodore Barclay, a Hertford stockbroker; they had two daughters and two sons.

In the Second World War, when German bombing destroyed the Swire head office in the City, Swire moved his entire staff to his mother's house in Harlow. He was high sheriff of Essex, 1941–2. As chairman of the port employers in London (1941–5), Swire was involved in organizing the loading of the myriad vessels needed to carry troops and stores for the invasion of Europe. Fortunately he had become friendly in the 1930s with Ernest Bevin, then a dock-union leader. Once, after a long negotiation, Swire invited Bevin for a drink and a sandwich at the City of London Club, where the chairman reprimanded him for having brought a working man into the club. Swire was delighted when Bevin subsequently became wartime minister of labour.

In 1946 Swire became chairman of the group, and he directed its operations until 1966. He succeeded his uncle, G. W. Swire, with whom he had seriously disagreed over the firm's direction. His finest hours came after VJ-day. His contribution, as chairman of John Swire & Sons, to the rebuilding of Hong Kong was inestimable. The colony had been devastated during the Japanese occupation. Swires' Taikoo dockyard was in ruins, Swires' ships sunk or dispersed. Hong Kong's great harbour, full of sunken vessels, was stagnant; the docks were at a standstill; so was public transport. Thanks to Swire's optimism, foresight, and dogged determination, the firm's operations were restored. The joint efforts of Swires, Jardine Matheson, and the Hongkong and Shanghai Bank (which provided unstinting financial support) enabled Hong Kong to rise from its rubble, and provided the foundations on which Chinese and foreign enterprise made it one of the commercial successes of the Eastern world. Swire was chairman of the China Association from 1951 to 1955.

Swire's other triumph was his creation of a worldwide airline. Before 1939 John Swire & Sons had tinkered with the idea: its large interests on passenger shipping made this a logical step forward. By 1947 it was obvious to John Swire that long-distance travel in the East, as elsewhere, would be by passenger aircraft. Despite the misgivings of his more conservative directors, he induced his company to acquire a small Hong Kong-based airline, Cathay Pacific Airways, recently founded by two wartime fliers. Though somewhat ramshackle, the airline had proved successful. Swire intended to develop a top-class regional airline serving cities in the East and Australia. With the jet age, however, Cathay was obliged to expand. Before he died in 1983, Swire, then honorary president of the company, had the exhilarating experience of watching one of his Cathay Pacific aircraft landing at Gatwick airport, the first of innumerable scheduled passenger flights from and to Hong Kong by the airline he had built up as an international enterprise.

Swire was very tall and good-looking, had a zest for life, and was a good horseman. He was warm, gregarious, crotchety, and humorous. His wife predeceased him in 1981; and he died on 22 February 1983 at his home, Hubbards Hall, Churchgate Street, Old Harlow, Essex. He was buried at St Mary's, Harlow, on 28 February.

GAVIN YOUNG, rev. ROBERT BICKERS

Sources C. Drage, *Taikoo* (1970) • G. Young, *Beyond Lion Rock: the story of Cathay Pacific Airways* (1988) • SOAS, John Swire & Sons MSS • John Swire & Sons Ltd, 59 Buckingham Gate, London, company archive • private information (2004) • d. cert.

Archives John Swire & Sons, 59 Buckingham Gate, London, company archive · SOAS, papers of John Swire & Sons Ltd
Likenesses D. Jagger, portrait, in or before 1957, priv. coll. · R. Swan, portrait (after D. Jagger), Swire House, 59 Buckingham Gate, London · photographs, Swire House, 59 Buckingham Gate, London
Wealth at death £954,653: probate, 1983, *CGPLA Eng. & Wales*

Swire, John Samuel [*called* the Senior] (**1825–1898**), merchant and shipowner, was born in Liverpool on 24 December 1825, the eldest son of John Swire (1793–1847), merchant, and Maria Louisa, *née* Roose (*c.*1794–1858). His father had founded the family import–export business in Liverpool about 1816, and it became John Swire & Sons in 1832. At his death in 1847 the elder Swire left equal shares in the firm, and capital to the value of £1000 each, to John Samuel and his younger brother, William Hudson Swire (1830–1884).

During his youth Swire sought physical adventure; in maturity he sought fulfilment in business. He spent five months in the American west in 1849, and in September 1854 he sailed for Australia to seek his fortune, working at diggings in New South Wales before founding a branch of the family firm in Melbourne. This episode exhibited two of his most salient personal characteristics: tenacity and commercial long-sightedness. A quick fortune eluded him, however, and he returned to resume his responsibilities in Liverpool; his brother, plagued by ill health, had been finding it difficult to cope with the business on his own.

One of Swire's first acts on returning to Britain was, on 15 November 1859, to marry Helen Abigail (*b. c.*1837), daughter of Adam Fairrie, a member of a notable sugar-refining family. She died at sea, however, on holiday in the Bay of Smyrna, on 5 May 1862, after only thirty months of marriage, leaving one child, John (Jack) Swire (1861–1933). Swire, shocked by the blow, retreated into the world of work. In the first two decades after the death of their father, the Swire brothers built up their business, establishing a solid presence in New York and Australia, and widening the range of goods they traded. Wine was imported from Le Havre, bottled Guinness was shipped to Australia, and raw cotton was acquired from the United States. By 1867, after twenty years of slow, steady growth, they had placed their enterprise on a secure foundation, sharply symbolized by their removal of the firm's head office to London that year. Swire bought out his brother's share of the company in 1876, but for many years before that the development and fortunes of the firm had been directed by the iron hand of the Senior (as he was nicknamed).

Swire is chiefly remembered as the great interloper among the foreign firms trading on the China coast, arriving late on the scene at the close of the decades of war and rebellion, and barging his way forcefully and quickly into a position of great prominence. The gentlemanly traders, Jardine Mathesons (the 'Princely Hong'), Dents, and Russell & Co., found their interests and ambitions sharply challenged by the upstart newcomer from the bourgeois English north-west. Unlike most firms already there, Swires was untarred by association with the illegal opium trade; it was also healthily interested in pursuing good relations with prospective Chinese customers. The sight of Swire employees entertaining Chinese merchants frankly appalled their foreign competitors.

Swires had initially sought new markets in China and Japan because of the disruption of the cotton trade after 1861 by the civil war in the United States. Ten years of extraordinary expansion of those business activities were quietly heralded by John Swire's arrival in Shanghai on 28 November 1866. Within a week of his landing Swire established a branch of the firm in a partnership (dissolved two years later) with Richard Shackleton Butterfield (*d.* 1879). Initially trading in tea, silk, and imports of cotton and piece-goods, the firm of Butterfield and Swire—Taikoo (from a local term meaning 'ancient and honourable')—became identified with interests as diverse as shipping, sugar, and insurance. After opening a second branch in Yokohama, Swire returned overland to Britain in mid-1867.

The key to Swire's success in China lay in his network of international contacts, and especially in his firm's close long-term association with the Ocean Steam Ship Company—the Blue Funnel Line—owned by fellow Liverpudlians Alfred and Philip Holt. Swire was an initial investor in the enterprise in 1865 and Taikoo first became Blue Funnel's Shanghai agents, in 1868, and then took on the Hong Kong agency, in 1870. Swire's influence on the Ocean Steam Ship Company's growth was great, and his loyalty solid; his was the broader vision which the Holts lacked; his too was the initiative behind the shipping conferences which regulated competition and unified Far Eastern shipping interests. The relationship was, of course, mutually beneficial: Blue Funnel ships were fed goods and passengers by the Swire-managed China Navigation Company (CNC), which operated on the Yangtze (Yangzi) River.

The story of CNC pointedly illustrates Swire's business approach. Close supervision of costs, tenacity, and patient long-term planning were combined with a willingness to take risks that others often considered foolish, and to drop schemes that went wrong. The capital for the firm was raised in London in 1872. Two existing ships were acquired for service on the Yangtze, and a further three ordered. By virtue, initially, of a fierce rates war, and latterly of rigid conference schemes, Swire built up the firm, forcing Russells to leave the river and holding his own against Jardines and other competitors. The company's progress illustrates the Senior's gritty idealism: CNC, he believed, deserved a fair share of an expanding trade that could easily support all the competing firms, and so Swire set out to seize that share. By 1883 CNC had twenty ships, and by 1894 it was the largest of the Yangtze shipping fleets with twenty-nine; by 1900 it boasted fifty ships and extensive shore properties, and the company had also established a successful presence in China's coastal trade. Unlike other companies John Swire & Sons kept out of treaty-port politics, and their voice was rarely heard in the special-pleading, China-lobbying groups; both activities diverted attention away from business, which remained the Senior's key passion.

While Swire's success depended partly on the quality of the men he employed and on the loyalty that his rigorously fair, but absolutely uncompromising, manner engendered, he also kept a close personal eye on activities and personalities in China and elsewhere. He travelled back out to Asia four more times and also revisited Australia twice, and built up the firm relentlessly. When not riding to hounds, or spying out possible horse purchases, he lived and talked business in the 1860s and 1870s. Wealth was not the spur, and he could have retired comfortably when his brother William chose to.

'I have always gone in for *glory*, and not £ & d', Swire wrote to his prospective second wife in 1881 (Swire to Warren, 24 July 1881, Swire Archives). Lonely since Helen's death it was with some trepidation and great reticence that he embarked on the courtship of Mary (*c*.1851–1918), the daughter of George Warren, a Liverpool shipowner. They married on 18 October 1881, and had one child, (George) Warren *Swire (1883–1949). In 1884 the couple moved to Leighton House, in Leighton Buzzard, where they were associated with various philanthropic ventures; apart from hunting, however, Swire played no active role in local public affairs.

The Senior never relinquished control over the company; and it was only some years after his death that his partners began to inaugurate projects he had previously opposed. In the last decade of his life rheumatoid arthritis caused him much pain, not least the tedium of spa visits to alleviate his suffering. Ill health failed to stop his frequent touring in Europe, but his beloved horse-riding came to an end in 1894. In November 1898 Swire was confined to bed for three weeks with a severe attack of arthritis. On 1 December he died of heart failure, at his London home, 31 Pembridge Square. He was buried at All Saints' Church, Leighton Buzzard, on 6 December 1898. He was survived by his second wife.   ROBERT BICKERS

Sources S. Marriner and F. E. Hyde, *The senior John Samuel Swire, 1825–98: management in Far Eastern shipping trades* (1967) · John Swire & Sons Archives, Swire House, London · SOAS, John Swire & Sons MSS · K. C. Liu, *Anglo-American steamship rivalry in China, 1862–1874* (1962) · *CGPLA Eng. & Wales* (1899) · *Leighton Buzzard Observer* (6 Dec 1898)

Archives John Swire & Sons, London, archives · SOAS | Merseyside Maritime Museum, Liverpool, Ocean Steam Ship Company/Alfred Holt Company MSS

Likenesses photograph, 1880–89, Swire House, London, Swire Archives · photograph, 1886, Swire House, London, Swire Archives · group photograph, 1895, Swire House, London, Swire Archives · double portrait, photograph, 1898 (with Mary Swire), Swire House, London, Swire Archives · H. von Herkomer, oils, 1901 (after photograph), John Swire & Sons, Swire House, London · E. Patry, oils, 1919 (after photograph), Luton House, Faversham, Kent

Wealth at death £220,194 14s. 0d.: probate, 27 Jan 1899, *CGPLA Eng. & Wales*

Swire, (George) Warren (1883–1949), merchant and businessman, was born on 27 May 1883 in Pembroke Gardens, London, the only child of John Samuel *Swire (1825–1898), and his second wife, Mary, *née* Warren (*c*.1851–1918). He was educated at Eton College from 1896 to 1901 (and

retained a lifelong affection for the school), and then in Weimar, Germany, from 1901 to 1902. He became a partner in the family firm, John Swire & Sons, leading China merchants, in 1904, and acceded to full managerial responsibility at its London headquarters in 1918.

Swire's early ambivalence about joining the firm was shared by his partners, who thought his character unsuited to business and who accordingly changed the firm to a limited liability company from 1 January 1914. However, Swire slowly settled in, and from 1912 he took a particular interest in the shipping side, especially the firm's China Navigation Company. This had for some years made a loss, and Swire undertook a scheme of new shipbuilding and other improvements which helped to bring it back into profitability. Swire's progress was only partially interrupted by the war. He joined a territorial regiment, the socially prestigious Royal Bucks hussars, in 1907, was mobilized in 1914, and was sent with the regiment to Egypt the following year. He was transferred back to Britain in 1916 to work in the control of shipping, in which he was patently of more use. His career in the army was far from happy: 'the head of JS&S is a bad place to learn subordination & obedience to incompetent fools, who aren't even gentlemen' he wrote at the time (Swire to C. C. Scott, 12 Dec 1915, Swire MSS, JSSI 3/5).

Swire was chairman of John Swire & Sons from 1927 to 1946, during one of the most traumatic periods of the firm's history. If he lacked the vision and flexibility of his nephew, John Kitson *Swire (1893–1983), who was to rehabilitate and expand the company after the Second World War, only he could have held it together through the inter-war period. After 1925 the company was threatened by civil war and revolution in China. The onset of the depression in 1928 badly affected its shipping operations, and the outbreak of the Sino-Japanese War caused further disruption to trade. The nationalistic economic policies and legislation introduced by the Guomindang government in China after 1927 also had an important impact on business. These undermined the treaty privileges enjoyed by Swires and other foreign companies, notably the inland navigation rights which enabled them to dominate China's domestic shipping trade. A man less interested in politics and diplomacy, and less confident in asserting his view of the necessity for adaptation by British companies, as well as the limits of compromise, would not have looked after the interests of the company so well. Swire believed that the firm was destined to stay in China, and was destined also to contribute to China's economic development, regardless of China's nationalist agenda and British government 'defeatism'. This strain of idealism was quite pronounced, and it contrasted sharply with his hard-nosed approach to practical business matters. Swire was an active member of the China Association, a frequent contributor to China discussions at the Royal Institute of International Affairs, and a compulsive writer of strong letters to prime ministers and lesser men.

Swire was feared by many of his staff, to whom he was often famously rude; equally he could be disarmingly kind. His periodic visits to the Far East were occasions for assessing his staff and for consulting diplomatic representatives. Such visits allowed him to keep a close eye on the minutiae of the firm's operations and its responses to London's policy decisions. While there, especially after 1929, Swire also eased relations with Chinese business and political leaders who had previously, as a class, been largely ignored by British firms. His was also an important voice in the shift of emphasis of the firm towards employing more Chinese staff, better targeting of Chinese customers, and the setting up of Sino-British subsidiary companies, such as the Taikoo Chinese Navigation Company. Swire recognized that nationalism in China was a permanent fixture of the post-1927 landscape, and that British firms had to adapt to its demands, or perish.

Swire nevertheless firmly believed that the company should be actively involved in furthering the interests of the British empire in China. In this, as in many other areas, he was influenced by his upbringing. He believed in the values of the Conservative Party, in hierarchy, and in race; he remained vocally pro-Nazi long after the Second World War began. In other ways he modelled himself on his father who had died when he was fifteen, and he saw himself more as a merchant adventurer than as a City businessman. Despite his difficult manner, however, he was widely respected by his colleagues and competitors.

Towards the end of the 1930s Swire began to disagree with his nephew over the direction the company was taking, starting a personal and professional rift that was never healed. After he retired as chairman in 1946 Swire busied himself with, among other projects, his work for the Port of London's Mission to Seamen and as a crown estate paving commissioner. He never married. His interests included music (especially Wagner), and photography. His country estate in Scotland, Glen Affric, and its deer hunting, formed another passion. Increasingly crippled by arthritis in his sixties which he refused to allow to restrict his life, Swire died suddenly on his feet, as he would have wished, of a heart attack, on 18 November 1949, at his home, 22 Chester Terrace, Regent's Park, London.   ROBERT BICKERS

Sources London, John Swire & Sons Archives, personal MSS · SOAS, John Swire & Sons MSS · S. L. Endicott, *Diplomacy and enterprise: British China policy, 1933–37* (1975) · C. Drage, *Taikoo* (1970) · S. Marriner and F. E. Hyde, *The senior John Samuel Swire, 1825–98: management in Far Eastern shipping trades* (1967)
Archives John Swire & Sons, London, archives · SOAS
Likenesses S. Tushingham, portrait, John Swire & Sons, London · photographs, John Swire & Sons, London
Wealth at death £179,210: probate, 30 Jan 1950, *CGPLA Eng. & Wales*

Swithberht [St Swithberht, Suidbert] (*d.* **713**), bishop and missionary, was one of the twelve companions of Willibrord in his mission to evangelize the Frisians. All that is known of him comes from the *Historia ecclesiastica gentis Anglorum* of Bede, who characterizes him as 'a meek-hearted man of sober ways' (Bede, *Hist. eccl.*, 5.11). He was probably one of those who had been sent to the continent with Willibrord by the ascetic and missionary patron Ecgberht in 690. On their arrival in Frisia, Willibrord immediately went on to Rome to obtain the permission of Pope Sergius I for the mission. In his absence, his companions chose Swithberht to be their bishop, and sent him, at some point between July 692 and August 693, to England for his consecration. Archbishop Berhtwald of Canterbury being absent, Swithberht was consecrated by the Northumbrian bishop Wilfrid, then in exile in Mercia. Soon after his return to the continent, Swithberht left his companions in order to missionize among a people whom Bede names the 'Boruhtware', that is, the Bructeri whom Roman writers located in southern Westphalia. He initially met with success, but the 'Boruhtware' were conquered by the still-pagan Saxons, and Swithberht's community of converts dispersed. Swithberht himself sought refuge with Pippin II, mayor of the palace of the Merovingian kings of the Franks and head of the Pippinid (later Carolingian) dynasty. Pippin and his wife, Plectrudis, gave Swithberht an island in the Rhine, Kaiserswerth, where he built a monastery. There, according to Bede, he lived out a life of great austerity. The report in the *Annales sancti Amandi*, of Carolingian date, that he died in March 713 is likely to be reliable.

Veneration of Swithberht as a saint followed swiftly. In the contemporary calendar of St Willibrord, he is entered at 1 March, still his feast day. Bede records that 'his heirs' still occupied Kaiserswerth when he was writing, *c.*730. In the section of the Frisian mission in his poem on the bishops, kings, and saints of York, Alcuin (*d.* 804) mentions Swithberht in the same verse as 'the priest Wira' Wiro. There is a sermon and poem on Swithberht by Radbod, bishop of Utrecht between 901 and 918, which add nothing to the stock of historical knowledge. The shrine preserving supposed relics of St Swithberht in the Stiftskirche at Kaiserswerth dates from the thirteenth century.   MARIOS COSTAMBEYS

Sources Bede, *Hist. eccl.*, 5.11 · J. M. Wallace-Hadrill, *Bede's Ecclesiastical history of the English people: a historical commentary*, OMT (1988) · W. Levison, *England and the continent in the eighth century* (1946) · H. A. Wilson, ed., *The calendar of St Willibrord from MS Paris Lat. 10837*, HBS, 55 (1918) · *Venerabilis Baedae opera historica*, ed. C. Plummer, 2 (1896) · 'Annales sancti Amandi', [*Annales et chronica aevi Carolini*], ed. G. H. Pertz, MGH Scriptores [folio], 1 (Stuttgart, 1826) · Alcuin, *The bishops, kings, and saints of York*, ed. and trans. P. Godman, OMT (1982) · Radbodus Trajectensis, 'Sermo S. Radbodi de S. Switberto', *Patrologia Latina*, 132 (1880), 547–50 · Radbodus Trajectensis, 'Carmen allegoricum pro S. Swiberto', *Patrologia Latina*, 132 (1853), 556–9

Swithhelm (*d.* 663). *See under* East Saxons, kings of the (*act.* late 6th cent.–*c.*820).

Swithred (*fl. c.*746). *See under* East Saxons, kings of the (*act.* late 6th cent.–*c.*820).

Swithun [St Swithun] (*d.* 863), bishop of Winchester, is better known for his activities as a miracle-working saint than for his tenure of episcopal office. He is said to have been ordained as a priest by his predecessor at Winchester, Helmstan, and follows him as deacon in the witness list of a Winchester charter, though this is of doubtful authenticity. His profession of obedience as bishop of Winchester to Archbishop Ceolnoth survives and the festival of his ordination was celebrated at Winchester from the late Anglo-Saxon period onwards. There is some uncertainty as to whether this fell on 30 October 852 or 29 October 853; his charter attestations as bishop begin in 854.

The earliest account of Swithun's life is that written probably in the late eleventh century in Winchester, though it was probably not the work of the Flemish hagiographer Goscelin, as has sometimes been claimed; it is lacking in circumstantial detail and bears out the claims of tenth-century writers that little survived in writing about the life of Swithun. Its main themes, besides the piety and humility of the bishop, are his close links with the royal house and his interest in the city of Winchester. Some of the claims, such as Swithun being entrusted with the education of Æthelwulf at Winchester, where the latter is said to have served as subdeacon, have no support and command little credence. However, both Ecgberht (r. 802–39) and Æthelwulf (r. 839–55) were believed to be generous patrons of Old Minster, Winchester, though many of their supposed charters are forgeries or seem to have been subject to interference. There is a hint of Swithun's possible importance to Æthelwulf's administration in a grant of land to him at Brightwell in what is now Berkshire, which is said to have been made to help defray the expense of entertaining foreign visitors. Both Ecgberht and Æthelwulf were buried in Winchester, which would have occupied a central position in the kingdom after it had been enlarged through Ecgberht's gains in the southeast. Excavations in the city suggest that there was expansion in the ninth century and it is perhaps in this context that Swithun's reputation as a builder should be placed. According to his life, he built and repaired churches and was also responsible for providing a stone bridge at East Gate. The only miracle recorded as having occurred during Swithun's lifetime was his restoration of the broken eggs of a poor woman who fell while she was crossing the bridge on her way to market. Swithun's erection of the bridge is dated to 859 in a Latin poem which purports to have been placed as an inscription on the bridge itself.

Swithun is recorded as dying on 2 July and although annalistic sources are divided over whether the year was 861, 862, or 863, the charter evidence supports 863. He was buried, as recounted in the late tenth century, beside a stone cross between the tower of St Martin and the west front of Old Minster. His life and the tenth-century accounts of his miracles claim that this choice of site was a sign of his humility as he wished people to trample over his grave; but such a prominent site is better interpreted as reflecting the importance of Swithun in Winchester, if not further afield. A similar ambiguity exists over how far the cult of St Swithun had developed before it was taken up during the Benedictine reform movement of the late tenth century. Writers of that time claim Swithun was neglected and his place of burial unknown before his cult was promoted by Bishop Æthelwold (d. 984) but this may be a hagiographical topos. The information they give about miracles performed immediately before the translation of his relics could be taken to imply that there was already a tradition of healing the sick by placing them between Swithun's tomb and the stone cross. Excavations have revealed high-status burials, which must date to before the late tenth century, clustered around the tomb; this may also indicate an established tradition that it was a holy site. Unless Swithun had already begun to establish a miracle-working reputation, he seems an unexpected choice for Æthelwold's promotion as there is no evidence that Swithun had ever been a monk; he was one of the secular clerks whom Æthelwold purported to despise. Æthelwold's patronage of Swithun provided a means of reconciliation with the secular clerks whom he had expelled from the Old Minster. In one of the manifestations that preceded the translation of his relics, Eadsige, one of the former clerks and a kinsman of Æthelwold, was chosen to convey the saint's wishes; Eadsige subsequently became a monk and a guardian of Swithun's shrine.

The translation of the body from its original burial site into the Old Minister was made on 15 July 971, apparently in pouring rain—the origin of the superstition that if it rains on St Swithun's day, it will rain also for the following forty days. On 22 October, probably in 974, part of the body was transferred to a gold, silver, and jewelled reliquary provided by King Edgar, which was placed on an altar in the shrine erected over the original burial site; other remains were kept on the high altar. The tomb shrine was incorporated into a magnificent westwork which was dedicated in 980. Accounts of the translations and miracles in prose by Lantfred and verse by Wulfstan Cantor record large numbers of miracles following the translation. Wulfstan remembered how his lessons as an oblate were repeatedly interrupted by the necessity of going to the church to celebrate yet another miracle, and Ælfric, who was also a monk at Old Minster, recorded the church 'hung around with crutches and stools of cripples from one end to the other on either wall' (Ælfric, 79); the blind and paralysed were particularly likely to be cured. People from all ranks of society came to Swithun to be healed, from the deaf nobleman who went to Rome and was told he would be cured if he visited Swithun's shrine to a manacled slave woman who was made invisible and miraculously transported inside the locked enclosure around the tomb. His feast days were widely observed in both England and France and some relics were transferred to other centres; Ælfheah (d. 1012) is said to have taken the head with him to Canterbury and Peterborough claimed to possess an arm. The cult remained important in Winchester after the Norman conquest and William of Malmesbury records that he witnessed a miracle through the saint's intercession. On 15 July 1093 the relics were transported from the Old Minster into the new cathedral where they were housed behind the high altar until they were transferred to a new site in the retrochoir in 1476. A chapel was maintained on the site of the burial with a tomb-shrine through which pilgrims could reach to touch the site of the grave. The cult was officially ended in 1538 when the shrine was destroyed. BARBARA YORKE

Sources 'Vita Sancti Swithuni … auctore Goscelino', ed. E. P. Sauvage, *Analecta Bollandiana*, 7 (1888), 373–80 • 'Sancti Swithuni …

translatio et miracula auctore Lantfredo', ed. E. P. Sauvage, *Analecta Bollandiana*, 4 (1885), 367–410 · *Wulfstani Cantoris narratio metrica de Sancto Swithuno*, ed. A. Campbell (1950) · Ælfric [abbot of Eynsham], *Lives of three English saints*, ed. G. I. Needham (1966) · *Willelmi Malmesbiriensis monachi de gestis pontificum Anglorum libri quinque*, ed. N. E. S. A. Hamilton, Rolls Series, 52 (1870), 160–62 · R. N. Quirk, 'Winchester Cathedral in the tenth century', *Archaeological Journal*, 114 (1957), 28–68 · D. J. Sheerin, 'The dedication of the Old Minster, Winchester, in 980', *Revue Bénédictine*, 88 (1978), 261–73 · B. A. E. Yorke, 'The bishops of Winchester, the kings of Wessex and the development of Winchester in the ninth and early tenth centuries', *Proceedings of the Hampshire Field Club and Archaeological Society*, 40 (1984), 61–70 · S. Keynes, 'The West Saxon charters of King Æthelwulf and his sons', *EngHR*, 109 (1994), 1109–49 · M. Biddle, 'Archaeology, architecture, and the cult of saints in Anglo-Saxon England', *The Anglo-Saxon church: papers on history, architecture, and archaeology in honour of Dr H. M. Taylor*, ed. L. A. S. Butler and R. K. Morris, Council for British Archaeology Research Report, 60 (1986), 1–31 · J. Crook, 'St Swithun of Winchester', *Winchester Cathedral: nine hundred years, 1093–1193*, ed. J. Crook (1993), 57–68

Switzer, Stephen (*bap.* 1682, *d.* 1745), landscape designer and author, was baptized on 25 February 1682 at Micheldever and Stratton parish church, Hampshire, the second of two sons of Thomas Switzer (*d.* 1697), farmer, and his wife, Mary, *née* Hapgood (*d.* 1682). The family, of long-standing Hampshire farming stock, spelled their surname variously, and it was pronounced Sweetsur during Switzer's lifetime. Nothing is known of any formal education; at his father's early death his elder brother took over the management of their farm in Micheldever and in 1699 Switzer was apprenticed to George London, senior partner of the remarkable enterprise known as the Brompton Park Nurseries, which was founded in the late 1680s by four gardeners to the greatest estates. London and his newly established partner, Henry Wise, were responsible for laying out many thousands of acres of landscape gardens throughout England in the early eighteenth century. Switzer rose to be lieutenant to the two men in their projects, and also formed a congenial relationship with the architects Vanbrugh and Hawksmoor. At Blenheim he lobbied the Treasury to be given its management, but was disappointed. His own first essays in what is now known as the English landscape garden began when he moved to Lincolnshire to work on the major property of the Berties, dukes of Ancaster. He transformed Grimsthorpe by encircling the existing gardens (which he remodelled and extended) with a broad, earthen-banked walk or terrace from which views of the adjacent, improved and tidy, landscape were a principal object and feature. The motif of wood–terrace–landscape first appeared in this form at Castle Howard (and he was probably responsible for the transformation there of Wray Wood), but once discovered it made the expansion of great gardens into landscape easy, agreeable, and exciting.

Switzer's experiences at Castle Howard, Grimsthorpe, and Blenheim, coupled with his extensive learning, appeared as *The Nobleman Gentleman and Gardeners Recreation* in 1715, followed three years later by second and third volumes—fully illustrated—under the general title *Ichnographia rustica*. Lord Bathurst, whose estate at Cirencester, Gloucestershire, extended 5 miles from the house

to its boundary on the Severn, followed Switzer's advice and the estate is the most intact survivor of his style and ideas: the terrace still encloses but long stretches of woodland with fruitful arable on one side and more pastoral parkland on the other lead from Cirencester House, past 'gardens' of vast size but conventional shape, to a great circle made up of forest plantation punctuated by estate buildings with avenues terminating on neighbouring parish churches. Some estate buildings were in the Gothic style, as recommended by Switzer for their beneficial and poetic association of ideas. He had conjured up an imaginary but potent place at Grimsthorpe by realizing in a secretive out-of-the-way spot (with, however, good views over rolling land) the exploits of King Grime of the Danelaw. At Cirencester it is Alfred's Hall which gives sense of place, history, and an agreeably gloomy resonance to the landscape.

The 1720s saw a wide but smaller-scale practice, marriage to Elizabeth (the date and her parentage are unknown), and the establishment of Switzer's very lucrative trade as a seedsman with premises at Westminster Hall. There he became a public figure from the mid-twenties, corresponding widely about improvements in the various aspects of landscape making—fertilizers, hydraulics, or beneficial legumes—and issuing a series of informative pamphlets. His great *Introduction to a General System of Hydraulicks and Hydrostaticks*, in two extensively illustrated volumes, appeared in 1729. It is his major and most scientific work, and was clearly of great importance to him; as a milestone in the development of industrial processes, especially the creation of the network of canals from mid-century, it deserves an honourable place. For his reputation as an artist, however, it became too intimately associated with a garden style which became first unfashionable, then anathema after 1745.

Sensing this change in the late twenties and early thirties, Switzer protested that he had begun the revolutionary changes, but his contributions were ignored by Horace Walpole whose version of events has been established since the 1750s. Although at Nostell Priory in the West Riding of Yorkshire, in the works of 1733, there are elements that form familiar aspects of the English landscape garden, for example a serpentine river and an informal park, there are also great geometric features, as essential for Switzer as the more naturalistic ones because they represented that emblem of Newtonian nature—an incomprehensible regularity.

Switzer died at his home in Millbank on 8 June 1745, a rich man, leaving a son at St John's College, Cambridge, and was buried five days later at St Margaret's, Westminster. He was 'well known for treatises on agriculture and husbandry' (*GM*) but his friend William Stukeley remarked in 1750 that people were 'ignorant that he had been the chief promoter of the present taste in gardening' (Lukis, 10).

W. A. BROGDEN

Sources DNB · W. A. Brogden, 'Stephen Switzer and garden design in early 18th century Britain', PhD diss., U. Edin., 1973 · D. D. C. Chalmers, *The planters of the English landscape garden* (1993) · *GM*, 1st ser., 15 (1745), 332 · *The family memoirs of the Rev. William*

Stukeley, ed. W. C. Lukis, 3, SurtS, 80 (1887), 10 · parish register (baptism), 25 Feb 1682, Micheldever and Stratton · private information (2004) [Miss Higginson, vestry clerk, St Margaret's, Westminster] **Archives** Hants. RO, wills | Bedford estate office, London, survey of his grace the duke of Bedford's estate in East and West Stratton (1730) [copy] · Berks. RO, articles of agreement between the earl of Cadogan and Stephen Switzer · BL, Add. MSS 19608, 19592 · Bodl. Oxf., letters to Stukeley · Gateshead Public Library, letters to Henry Ellison · Gateshead Public Library, letters to Thomas Sisson · Leics. RO, plan for Beau-Manor · Wilberforce Museum Library, Hull, corresp. with Thomas Broadley
Wealth at death average of bank account for 1743, £1241 7*s*. 6*d*.; 1744, £430 15*s*.; 1745, £545 0*s*. 6*d*.: C. Hoare & Co., Fleet Street, London

Sword, John Cuthill (1892–1960), road and air transport manager, was born on 17 April 1892 at Groveside Cottage, Alexander Street, Airdrie, Lanarkshire, the son of William Sword, baker, and his wife, Jeanie Russell Cuthill. He attended elementary school at Airdrie and then started work with his father at the age of fourteen, before setting up in a bakery business on his own account. However, the First World War provided him, like many others, with an opportunity to broaden his horizons and change his career. Service in the Royal Flying Corps developed in Sword a passionate interest in motor vehicles and aviation.

Returning to Airdrie after demobilization, Sword married Christina Gillespie Taylor in 1918, daughter of another master baker. He then went into road haulage using war-surplus vehicles, and subsequently expanded into running bus services around Glasgow. His Midland Bus Services Ltd, established in Airdrie during 1924, rapidly extended its operations throughout south-west Scotland, and pioneered express coach services from Glasgow to Blackpool and London.

Sword was involved in a complex series of mergers and take-overs from 1929 to 1932 with four other Scottish bus operators and the London Midland and Scottish (LMS) and London and North Eastern Railway (LNER) companies, out of which he emerged as managing director of Western SMT Ltd, a division of Scottish Motor Traction of Edinburgh, on the main board of which he also sat. From its base in Kilmarnock, Ayrshire, Western SMT operated chiefly in south-west Scotland, though it continued to develop long-distance coach services, in spite of the fact that these competed with the railway companies, which controlled both Western SMT and its Edinburgh parent.

While managing Western SMT during the 1930s, Sword also diversified into several other businesses on his own account. These included farming, perhaps inspired by his passion for horses, and also the manufacture of potato crisps in Airdrie, Manchester, and Reading. Sword became an active director of the Scottish Amicable Building Society of Edinburgh, and had other business interests in London and Liverpool. But his greatest efforts were directed towards the development of civil aviation in the early 1930s. His instrument was Midland and Scottish Air Ferries Ltd, a private company incorporated in March 1933 with a nominal capital of £20,000, held entirely by Sword and his wife. Based at Renfrew aerodrome near Glasgow, Sword's airline developed its first scheduled services in England, between Hooton in Cheshire, and Birmingham. This was followed by services linking Glasgow with Islay and Belfast, and Liverpool with Dublin. A London to Liverpool service was then set up, with onward connections to the Isle of Man and Belfast. Such was Sword's enthusiasm for the development of air travel that when a newly established rival lost the use of its sole aircraft as a result of an accident, Sword lent one of his to maintain its services. Sword also pioneered the air ambulance service between Renfrew and the Western Isles, and was a founder of the Scottish Flying Club.

The development of air services competing with their trunk routes was not popular with the railways, whose influence over Sword's core activity, Western SMT, was very powerful. They made determined efforts to stifle this competition. Travel agents who sold railway tickets were dissuaded from handling airline bookings; then the railways set up their own air services as a spoiling tactic. Eventually, the railway aviation interests and those of the pioneering private airlines were reconciled through a series of amalgamations, of which Sword's airline was an early casualty. His masters in LMS accused him of neglecting his responsibilities at Western SMT to run it, and they insisted he should sell it off. The airline was not profitable (nor were his farming or crisp manufacturing activities), whereas Western SMT provided Sword's main income, so he had no choice but to agree. Sword was compensated financially by SMT for sacrificing his airline, but seems to have resented the treatment he had received at the hands of the LMS, against which he appears to have borne a lasting grudge.

With the ending of his commercial aviation commitments in October 1934, Sword concentrated on running Western SMT, which was a very successful undertaking. His stewardship provided him with a handsome income, with which to subsidize his continuing unprofitable interests in farming and food-processing. With the nationalization of the railways by the Labour government in 1947, their subsidiary SMT metamorphosed into the state-owned Scottish Omnibuses group, of which Western SMT became a part. Sword ceased to be its general manager and became instead a director of Scottish Omnibuses.

As a business leader, Sword enjoyed the great gift of being able to delegate, while also following the course of the business. His early success was due in part to developing influential contacts with the air minister, Lord Londonderry. Both the air minister and the prime minister were guests at the launching of Sword's scheduled services between London and Belfast in April 1934.

After nationalization, Sword was able to devote more time to his family (he had four sons and a daughter) and to his private pursuits. As well as overseeing the work of his five Ayrshire dairy farms, he was also a noted horse breeder (at one time president of the British Hackney Horse Society) and collected paintings, clocks, railway models, and, above all, veteran and vintage cars. Some 250 such vehicles were housed at his farm, Balgray, near Irvine, Ayrshire, by the time of his death, and these were subsequently put on display in the Scottish Transport Museum in Glasgow. Sword died at Craigweil, Ayrshire, on 27 March 1960. His wife had predeceased him.

ALEX J. ROBERTSON

Sources J. King, 'Sword, John', DSBB • The Scotsman (28 March 1960), 3 • A. J. Robertson, 'The new road to the Isles: Highland Airways and Scottish Airways, 1933–39', Journal of Transport History, 3rd ser., 7 (1986), 48–60 • d. cert. • CCI (1960)
Archives Scottish Museum of Transport, Kelvin Hall, Glasgow, veteran and vintage motor vehicles
Wealth at death £112,512 3s. 6d.: confirmation, 18 Aug 1960, CCI

Swrdwal, Hywel (*fl. c.*1450), poet, derived his surname from Sourdeval, which is attested in the medieval lordship of Brecon and suggests descent from a Norman family. There is late evidence that Hywel was well versed in genealogy and that he was a man of some learning. His poems show clearly his connection with William Herbert, first earl of Pembroke, who continued and extended his family's tradition of patronizing the Welsh poets. Hywel celebrated the earl's lavish hospitality, and like his fellow poets, he lamented the earl's defeat and execution at Banbury in 1469, both as a catastrophe for the Welsh cause and as the result of the treachery of the English, giving an additional reason for hating them.

Ieuan ap Hywel Swrdwal (*d. c.*1470), Hywel's son, was also regarded as a man of learning. Indeed, he may have been at Oxford, and he may have been the author of a poem to God and the Virgin Mary, composed in English but according to the rules of Welsh *cynghanedd* (strict metres), and written in Welsh orthography. (It has also been attributed to Hywel Swrdwal and to Ieuan ap Rhydderch ab Ieuan Llwyd.) According to a rubric found in some copies it was composed in answer to a taunt that there was no Welsh poetry, and it has been hailed as the first Anglo-Welsh poem. On his death Ieuan was elegized and one of the two extant elegies evoked responses from other poets; together they throw valuable light on the state of Welsh poetry in south Wales in the late fifteenth century. Another of Swrdwal's sons, Dafydd ap thywel Swrdwal, is represented by the survival of a single poem, but it explains why he was also regarded as a proficient poet. The Swrdwal poets have not been well served by the Welsh manuscript tradition. Comparatively few of their poems have been preserved and some of the poems are attributed to both father and son as well as to other poets, but there are enough to show that they share the features characteristic of the poetry of the period.

J. E. CAERWYN WILLIAMS

Sources J. C. Morrice, Gwaith barddonol Howel Swrdwal a'i fab Ieuan (1908) • E. Rowlands, 'Un o gerddi Hywel Swrdwal', Ysgrifau Beirniadol, 6 (1971), 87–97 • W. G. Lewis, 'Herbertiad Rhaglan fel noddwyr y beirdd yn y bymthegfed ganrif a dechrau'r unfed ganrif ar bymtheg', Transactions of the Honourable Society of Cymmrodorion (1986), 33–60 • Mynegai i farddoniaeth gaeth y Llawysgrifau, University of Wales, Board of Celtic Studies, 12 vols. (1978), 1652–5, 1716–19 • E. J. Dobson, 'The hymn to the Virgin', Transactions of the Honourable Society of Cymmrodorion (1954), 70–122 • R. Garlick, Hymn to the Virgin (1985) • Gwaith Hywel Swrdwal a'i deulu, ed. D. F. Evans (2000)
Archives BL • NL Wales

Swynburne, Sir Thomas (*d.* 1412), mayor of Bordeaux, was the only son of Sir Robert Swynburne, lord of Little Horkesley, Essex, and his first wife, Agnes Felton, heir of lands in Northumberland from her uncle Sir William Felton. Thomas was described as a king's knight and served Richard II and Henry IV. He is best known as mayor of Bordeaux from 1405 until his death. His father held lands in East Mersea and Great and Little Horkesley, Essex, and from 1377 to 1390 was frequently summoned to parliament as one of two knights from Essex. Thomas Swynburne inherited from his mother her lands in Northumberland when she died, before February 1378. By 1380 he was already a knight. Before 1384 his father married Joan, granddaughter of Sir John Gernoun, and he died in August 1391.

Thomas Swynburne had begun to make his mark in the king's service before his father's death, having been named keeper of Roxburgh Castle in April 1386, and warden of Guînes Castle by 1391. Froissart included Swynburne among the knights at the jousts of St Inglevert in 1390, calling him a 'jeune chevalier ot de grande voulenté' ('a young knight of great determination'; *Œuvres*, 14.115). In August 1392 Swynburne left Guînes with a small retinue on a pilgrimage to the Holy Land. They left Venice on 2 September and landed in Alexandria on 20 October. They visited Cairo, Mount Sinai, Gaza, Bethlehem, and Jerusalem in just over two months. On 3 January 1393 they were already in Beirut seeking return passage, and by February 1393 Swynburne had returned to England and Guînes.

Swynburne was granted the lordship and castle of Hammes for life from its previous holder in March 1397. Within a month of Henry IV's accession he sought and obtained confirmation of this grant, paying 40 *s.* to the hanaper. Swynburne profited from Lancastrian rule. In 1401 he was appointed constable of Clare and steward of its lordship during the heir's minority, while continuing to hold Hammes. He served as sheriff of Essex in 1403 and 1404, and between May and October 1404 he appears as one of three English ambassadors to the duchess of Burgundy seeking settlement of the continuing quarrels between English and Flemish seamen.

King Henry had received pathetic pleas for help from Gascony, citing constant French attacks. In response, he appointed Thomas Swynburne, his experienced and trusted knight, mayor of Bordeaux in March 1405, with a complement of 50 men-at-arms and 100 archers. The privy council granted a voluntary loan to Gascony, to be sent over with Swynburne, whose departure was delayed until May by the need to gather the force assigned. On arrival in Bordeaux, Swynburne faced a powerful *jurade*, the ruling body of local bourgeois which, lacking English help, had taken the initiative in self-protection. Swynburne immediately took an active part in strengthening the defences of the city and its outlying towns to meet impending French attacks. In October 1406 the duke of Orléans's army laid siege to Bourg and Blaye, the keys to the Gironde. The mayor and *jurade's* decision to destroy the outlying abbey of St Romain at Blaye, whose abbot had conspired with Orléans, the defeat of a French fleet in mid-

December by the Gascon-English force led by Swynburne, and terrible winter weather encouraged the duke to abandon the siege in mid-January and withdraw to France. Swynburne returned to England in March 1408, seeking money and reinforcements, and was appointed captain of Fronsac, a key fortress for Bordeaux's protection. When he returned to Bordeaux, before 24 September 1409, he encouraged the city's purchase of the neighbouring county of Ornon, even loaning some of the needed money. He continued to act as mayor until at least February 1412, returning to England soon after.

Swynburne died on 9 August 1412 and was buried in the church of St Peter and St Paul, Little Horkesley, with his father. Their tomb had brasses of both father and son. Thomas is shown in full mail, wearing the Lancastrian collar of SS, and its inscription proudly proclaims him lord of Hammes, mayor of Bordeaux, and captain of Fronsac—a minor royal official, though a successful one.

MARGARET WADE LABARGE

Sources Chancery records · Archives municipales de Bordeaux, 3–4: Registres de la jurade (Bordeaux, 1873–83) · N. H. Nicolas, ed., Proceedings and ordinances of the privy council of England, 7 vols., RC, 26 (1834–7), vols. 1–2 · Rymer, Foedera, 3rd edn, 5.4 · F. C. Hingeston, ed., Royal and historical letters during the reign of Henry the Fourth, 1, Rolls Series, 18 (1860), 1 · 'Voyage en Terre Sainte d'un maire de Bordeaux au XIVe siècle', Archives d'Orient Latin, 2 (1884), 378–88 · Œuvres de Froissart: chroniques, ed. K. de Lettenhove, 25 vols. (Brussels, 1867–77) · J. H. Wylie, History of England under Henry the Fourth, 4 vols. (1884–98); repr. (New York, 1969), vol. 5, pp. 2–4 · X. Védère, 'Le tombeau des Swynburne, maires de Bordeaux', Revue Historique de Bordeaux et du département de la Gironde, ser. 2, no. 1 (1952), 113–16 · X. Védère, 'Les Swynburne, maires de Bordeaux', Revue Historique de Bordeaux et du département de la Gironde, 36 (1993)

Likenesses tomb brass (destroyed 1940), repro. in Védère, 'Le tombeau des Swynburne, maires de Bordeaux', 115; brass rubbing, 1901, V&A

Wealth at death owed considerable amount by king and city of Bordeaux: Archives municipales de Bordeaux, 4: Registres de la jurade

Swynfen [Swinfen], **John** (1613–1694), politician, was born at Swynfen Hall, Weeford, in south-east Staffordshire, on 19 March 1613 and was baptized there, at St Mary's, on 28 March, the eldest son of Richard Swynfen (bap. 1596, d. 1659), landowner, and his wife, Joan (bap. 1591, d. 1658), daughter of George Curitall, alias Harman, of Lichfield. Swynfen enrolled at Pembroke College, Cambridge, in autumn 1628 and obtained his BA four years later. He returned to the ancestral home in the tiny hamlet of Swynfen and in Weeford church on 26 July 1632 married Anne (bap. 1613, d. 1690), daughter of a neighbouring gentleman, John Brandreth. Anne proved 'an inestimable blessing to her husband' (Shaw, 2.25) in a union that lasted nearly fifty-eight years and produced six sons, all of whom died before their father, and four daughters.

In the 1640s Swynfen enthusiastically embraced the cause of parliament. He signed a radical petition in favour of parliamentary control of the militia and godly reformation in March 1642; took part in the defence of Lichfield Close against Prince Rupert's forces in April 1643; and was appointed a member of the Staffordshire parliamentary committee in June 1643. As a man who believed in the uncompromising prosecution of the war against the king,

Swynfen had a natural affinity with the leader of the militants on the Staffordshire committee, Sir William Brereton, with whom he developed a close partnership, supplying him with intelligence on military, political, and a host of other matters. Swynfen's support for Brereton involved him in the latter's bitter feud with Basil Feilding, second earl of Denbigh. In spring 1645 he furnished evidence against Denbigh in the House of Lords' investigation into the earl's conduct, accusing him of rank disaffection, pusillanimous leadership, and partiality in the treatment of royalist delinquents. Denbigh retaliated by berating Swynfen's own 'factious demeanour' (HLRO, House of Lords MSS, special depositions, 2 May 1645) as well as exposing the blatant favouritism which he had shown to sequestrated cavaliers such as Sir John Skeffington. Despite these allegations, in summer 1645 Swynfen was nominated a Staffordshire JP while in late October he secured election as a recruited MP for the borough of Stafford. His opponents called him 'Russet-coat, from his affected plainness and pretences to sincerity' (Shaw, 27), but Brereton, his parliamentary sponsor, declared that he was a 'very choice, able man' who would be 'very serviceable to the Kingdom' (Letter Books, 2.19), an accurate prediction as Swynfen turned out to be an outstanding MP.

From the outset Swynfen distinguished himself by his devotion to parliamentary business, serving on innumerable committees, and on 3 January 1648 he was rewarded with a prestigious appointment as member of the Derby House committee of both kingdoms. As 'a rigid Presbyterian' (Kidson, 29) who had subscribed to the solemn league and covenant and who had been appointed to a select committee for establishing classes and elderships in London peculiars in January 1646, Swynfen naturally opposed the radical religious and political stance of the New Model Army and on 3 August 1647 was one of the three MPs sent on the fruitless exercise of ordering it not to advance on London to intimidate parliament. Swynfen's alienation from the army became even more pronounced after the second civil war, when he threw his weight behind the Long Parliament's last-ditch attempt to reach a settlement with the king. During the negotiations Swynfen's fellow MP John Crewe, who was in direct communication with Charles I, constantly urged him to use his moderating influence in the Commons; 'you will do good service at London persuading the House to come nearer the King', he declared on 6 November 1648 (CSP dom., 1648–9, 319). To no avail, for one month later the army violently excluded all those MPs in favour of the Newport propositions, Swynfen among them.

Following Pride's Purge, in which he suffered arrest and imprisonment, Swynfen found himself in the political wilderness; and his sense of bitterness was compounded still further by the regicide, for 'he was always against the King's death' (Lacey, 446). Such was Swynfen's disaffection that on 27 March 1651 the Rump council of state ordered his confinement in Denbigh Castle; but this was rescinded a few days later after he had agreed 'to be of good behaviour' and provide a £1000 surety (CSP dom.,

1651, 114, 132). Swynfen then held aloof from national politics; and not even a personal invitation in June 1654 from one of the lord protector's leading counsellors, Sir Charles Wolseley, who had a high opinion of his 'abilityes for the management of publique affayres', to serve as an ambassador in the Netherlands to promote the 'Protestant interest', would win him back (William Salt Library, Salt MS 608). Swynfen busied himself in rebuilding his family's finances after the devastation of the civil wars when he reputedly 'lost his whole estate' (HLRO, House of Lords MSS, special depositions, 2 May 1645). He also secured employment as the steward to Lord Paget, for which he received a yearly allowance of £100. By the late 1650s Swynfen had overcome his scruples over holding office: he was nominated a Staffordshire assessment commissioner in June 1657; and returned to the national stage with his election as MP for Tamworth in January 1659. His resentment against 'swordsmen' had still not abated, as was evident by the part he played in drawing up articles of impeachment against Major-General Boteler and in drafting proposals in April 1659 to secure the protector and parliament from any further military coups.

With the fall of the protectorate and the restoration of the Rump Parliament, Swynfen, along with other MPs secluded in 1648, was first excluded then, on 1 February 1660, readmitted to Westminster. Swynfen sat on the council of state from 25 February to 31 May 1660, was returned for Stafford in the Convention Parliament, and enjoyed a reputation for being one of 'the old Parliament men', though Sir John Bramston thought he was a 'crafty' politician when he and others 'of that gang' outmanoeuvred the younger, inexperienced MPs in the choice of speaker (*The Autobiography of Sir John Bramston*, ed. [Lord Braybrooke], CS, 32, 1845, 116). While he clearly welcomed the Restoration, playing a pivotal role in the parliamentary arrangements for Charles II's reception in London on his return from exile, Swynfen fought a rearguard action to protect presbyterian ministers like his brother Richard from ejection from the newly restored Anglican church, arguing for a modified episcopacy and religious comprehension in accordance with the Worcester House declaration of 25 October 1660. He also pleaded for mercy for those regicides who had voluntarily surrendered themselves despite his abhorrence at their crime, showing a 'great moderation' (Lacey, 446) which was evident in all the subsequent parliaments in which he served after the Restoration.

Swynfen survived the royalist landslide in the elections to the Cavalier Parliament early in 1661, this time sitting for Tamworth. Though a somewhat isolated figure he continued to be an active member of the House of Commons 'with 200 committee appointments, seven tellerships and over a hundred recorded speeches' (Mimardière and Henning) to his credit. Samuel Pepys described him in November 1662 as the 'great Mr Swinfen, the parliament man' (Pepys, 3.254). As a leading light in the small party of 'old Presbyterians' in the house (J. R. Jones, *The First Whigs*, 1961, 10–11) Swynfen still espoused the cause of godly reform and sponsored bills for stricter sabbath day observance. Protestant unity was another issue championed by Swynfen, who vigorously opposed the penal legislation against protestant dissenters on the grounds that they were 'a people in communion with us in doctrine, though different in ceremonies' (Lacey, 444). Swynfen grew ever more critical of the court, and by the mid-1670s was becoming increasingly concerned with the pro-Catholic direction of Charles II's policies.

Having retained his seat in the new parliament of March 1679 Swynfen was determined to apportion blame for the current political crisis over the Popish Plot, an alleged Catholic plot to kill the king, and the possible exclusion of the Catholic James, duke of York, from the succession. In a debate on 27 April he accused the entire episcopal bench of negligence 'in the discovery of this horrible plot' (Grey, 8.156). 'Geneva, Geneva itself', expostulated the outraged MP Sir Thomas Clarges, 'could not more reflect upon the Holy Hierarchy than this gentleman' (DWL, R. Morrice, Ent'ring book, 1.164). Not content with this Swynfen also singled out the duke of York as the man who had given most 'encouragement to the whole Popish party' through his open conversion to Catholicism (Grey, 8.156); and he fully backed the campaign to debar him from the throne. He helped to draft the Exclusion Bill and when it was debated in the Commons on 11 May roundly declared: 'I take this case we are upon to be either the preservation or the ruin of the kingdom' (ibid., 248). Swynfen was now clearly identified with the whig interest, but despite his party's triumph in the elections to the second Exclusion Parliament in August 1679 he was defeated in his Tamworth constituency by a single vote. He secured re-election to the third Exclusion Parliament in March 1681 and once more made his position absolutely clear on the question of exclusion, saying 'I am for the Bill' (ibid., 313).

The subsequent tory reaction prevented Swynfen from standing for election to James II's parliament in 1685, though he was one of the royal nominees for Tamworth three years later. But parliamentary service under James was anathema to Swynfen, who 'absolutely declined to stand' and in any case his candidature was rejected by the king's electoral agents on the grounds that he was 'superannuated' (Mimardière and Henning). Swynfen's steadfast opposition to James won him the belated approval of the Anglican establishment, the dean and chapter of Lichfield Cathedral declaring in 1687 that they had been 'mistaken in him' and now considered him 'the fittest man to serve them' in a parliamentary capacity; but Swynfen himself remained deeply suspicious of 'the Churchmen', who, he was convinced, were 'not to be trusted' (Lacey, 466). After the revolution of 1688 Swynfen sat in one more parliament, that of 1690–95, representing Bere Alston as a court whig. He was now a sick man, having suffered a stroke in 1687, and he died on 12 April 1694 at Swynfen Hall, Weeford, Staffordshire. He was buried the following day at St Mary's Church, Weeford.

Swynfen died a rich man, with lands in Staffordshire and Warwickshire worth at least £2000 per annum. His deep religious faith is evident in the familial injunction in his will: 'I pray God guide and bless all my children and grandchildren that they may live in the fear of God and die in his favour' (will, PRO, PROB 11/89/109). Swynfen was highly regarded by friend and foe alike: the presbyterian minister Edmund Calamy thought him 'pious and judicious', while an anonymous cavalier described him as a 'very prudent and able man' (Lacey, 144). But the finest tribute to Swynfen occurs on his funerary monument in Weeford church which proclaims that the object of greatest pride in his life was his lengthy parliamentary service which 'he performed with singular honour and satisfaction to his country' (Shaw, 2.25).

Swynfen's fifth son, Francis (d. 1693), and his wife, Jane Doughty (d. 1716), were the parents of **Samuel Swynfen** (1679/80–1736), physician. Samuel matriculated at Pembroke College, Oxford, on 31 March 1696 aged sixteen, graduated BA in 1699, MA from New Inn Hall in 1703, MB in 1706, and MD in 1712. He was a lecturer in grammar at the university in 1705. At Weeford on 18 November 1710 he married Mabel (d. in or after 1736), daughter and coheir of Ralph Fretwell of Hellaby, Yorkshire. They had twelve children baptized at Lichfield, where Swynfen had established himself as a physician by 1715. While living in Lichfield he became godfather to Samuel Johnson, the lexicographer. He afterwards moved to Birmingham and died there on 10 May 1736. JOHN SUTTON

Sources S. Shaw, *The history and antiquities of Staffordshire* (1801), 2.25, 27, 29–30 · PRO, PROB 11/89/109 · JHC, 4–11 (1644–97) · *The letter books of Sir William Brereton*, ed. R. N. Dore, 2 vols., Lancashire and Cheshire RS, 123, 128 (1984–90), esp. 127.12–13, 18 · R. M. Kidson, 'The gentry of Staffordshire, 1662–1663', *Collections for a history of Staffordshire*, Staffordshire RS, 4th ser., 2 (1958), 1–41 · Swynfen letters, BL, Add. MSS 29910–29920, 30013 · Swynfen letters, William Salt Library, Salt MSS 254, 454 · A. Grey, ed., *Debates of the House of Commons, from the year 1667 to the year 1694*, 10 vols. (1763) · A. M. Mimardière and B. D. Henning, 'Swinfen, John', HoP, *Commons, 1660–90* · D. R. Lacey, *Dissent and parliamentary politics in England, 1661–1689* (1969) · H. R. Thomas, ed., *Weeford parish register*, Staffordshire Parish Register Society (1955) · J. C. Wedgwood, 'Staffordshire parliamentary history [2]', *Collections for a history of Staffordshire*, William Salt Archaeological Society, 3rd ser. (1920–22) · D. H. Pennington and I. A. Roots, eds., *The committee at Stafford, 1643–1645*, Staffordshire RS, 4th ser., 1 (1957), xxiii, 355 · DNB · Foster, *Alum. Oxon.* · Pepys, *Diary*, vol. 3 · Venn, *Alum. Cant.*

Archives BL, personal and family corresp., Add. MSS 29910–29920 · William Salt Library, Stafford, political corresp., Salt MSS 254, 454 | BL, letter-book of Sir William Brereton, Add. MSS 11331–11333 · Staffs. RO, corresp. with the fifth and sixth Barons Paget, Paget MSS D.603/K/2/2; K/2/4; K/3/2; K/3/4

Wealth at death lands valued at £2000 p.a.: anonymous compiler of a survey of the Staffordshire gentry, c.1662/3

Swynfen, Samuel (1679/80–1736). *See under* Swynfen, John (1613–1694).

Swynford, Katherine. *See* Katherine, duchess of Lancaster (1350?–1403).

Swynford, Sir Thomas (1368–1432). *See under* Katherine, duchess of Lancaster (1350?–1403).

Swynnerton [*née* Robinson], **Annie Louisa** (1844–1933), artist, was born on 26 February 1844 at 3 Vine Grove, Hulme, Manchester, one of the seven daughters of Francis Robinson, a lawyer, and his wife, Ann Sanderson. After training at the Manchester School of Art (from 1871), where she won a scholarship for watercolour and a gold medal for oil painting, she went to Paris; here she studied at the Académie Julian and admired the work of the naturalist painter Jules Bastien-Lepage. In 1874 she went to Rome with fellow Mancunian Susan (Isabel) Dacre for further artistic experience. She returned to her home town and in 1879 became co-founder with Dacre of the Manchester Society of Women Painters. This initiative was intended to supply the deficiencies of art training for women in the city.

With an introduction to Edward Burne-Jones, she made her début at the Royal Academy in 1879, which was followed by annual appearances there until 1886, and again from 1902 until 1934. Other appearances in exhibitions were at the Society of Women Artists (1887); the Grosvenor Gallery (1882–7) and its successor, the New Gallery (1890–1909); the International Society of Sculptors, Painters and Gravers; and the World's Columbian Exhibition in Chicago (1893). On 6 July 1883 she married the sculptor Joseph William Swynnerton (1848–1910), son of Charles Swynnerton, and they subsequently divided their time between Italy and England; their London studio was in Shepherd's Bush. After her husband died in 1910, her British base was a studio in Chelsea.

During her lifetime Swynnerton's professional distinctions included associateship of the Manchester Academy (1884), membership of the hanging committee of the autumn exhibition (1895), held at the Walker Art Gallery in Liverpool, and associateship of the Royal Academy (1922). In this last case she made history in so far as the RA had (controversially) elected no women to its membership since the founding academicians Angelica Kauffmann and Mary Moser in 1768.

Swynnerton became something of an 'artist's artist', counting G. F. Watts, George Clausen, and John Singer Sargent among her admirers and patrons. Her painting was noted by both admirers and critics for vigorous brushwork and bold subjects, often using the full-length nude figure (*Mater triumphalis*, 1892, Musée d'Orsay, Paris) and abstract or ideal themes (*The Sense of Sight*, 1895, Walker Art Gallery, Liverpool). An independent stylist, she incorporated aspects of Pre-Raphaelitism, neo-classicism, and impressionism into her work over the years. She also produced much successful portraiture of men, women, and children (*Henry James*, 1910; *Dame Millicent Fawcett*, 1930).

A retrospective of fifty-nine of Swynnerton's works was held at the Manchester City Art Gallery in 1923. She became well represented internationally within her lifetime, with paintings entering the collections of the Metropolitan Museum of Art in New York, the National Gallery of Victoria in Melbourne, the Johannesburg Art Gallery in South Africa, and the National Gallery of Canada in Ottawa; in addition, the Tate collection has six of her works. Acquiring a reputation in her older years as a 'character' because of her independent style in dress, her forthrightness and indifference to conventions, and her candid enthusiasm for her work, she led a reclusive life for her last few years as her sight began to fail. She continued to paint until a few months before her death on 24 October 1933 at her home, Sicilia, in Beach Road, Hayling Island, Hampshire. PAMELA GERRISH NUNN

Sources *The Times* (25 Oct 1933) · 'City Art Gallery', *Manchester Guardian* (4 April 1923) · L. Haward, *Paintings by Mrs Swynnerton* (1923) [exhibition catalogue, Man. City Gall.] · P. Dunford, *A biographical dictionary of women artists in Europe and America since 1850* (1990) · Thieme & Becker, *Allgemeines Lexikon*, vol. 32 · b. cert. · m. cert. · d. cert. · CGPLA Eng. & Wales (1934)
Likenesses photograph, 1922, repro. in *The Times* (25 Nov 1922)
Wealth at death £8984 19s. 8d.: probate, 11 Jan 1934, CGPLA Eng. & Wales

Swynnerton [Swinnerton], **Thomas** (d. 1554), evangelical preacher, first appears in history when he matriculated at Wittenberg University in 1526, one of the first Englishmen to study there. There is no evidence to substantiate later claims that he was educated at Oxford and Cambridge. Indeed Bishop John Longland of Lincoln wrote in 1536 that he 'never came in universitie', though his information would of course have been confined to the English universities. He was back in England by the early 1530s, when he was troubled in an obscure chancery case which revolved around his alleged abduction of a wealthy London merchant's serving-girl named Eleanor Wakefield. Interestingly, Swynnerton's version of events was that he and the girl were simply staying in Yorkshire at the house of her uncle, one William Wakefield, clerk (almost certainly the William Wakefield who a few years later became a chaplain to Thomas Cranmer). This case may explain John Bale's claim that Swynnerton adopted the alias John Roberts to avoid persecution at the hands of the lord chancellor, Sir Thomas More.

Bale also informs us that Swynnerton published two treatises in favour of the royal supremacy in 1534. One, the *Mustre of Schismatic Bishops of Rome*, appeared under his alias; the other, *A Litel Treatise Ageynste the Mutterynge of some Papistis in Corners*, anonymously. The *Litel Treatise* is a dull, though genuinely brief, piece of antipapal polemic. The *Mustre* is far superior. Forming a preface to a translation of a hostile life of Gregory VII by Cardinal Benno (a supporter of Emperor Heinrich IV), it is what its title suggests, a list of schisms between rival claimants to the papacy, with a racy commentary presenting the material as a refutation of the doctrine of papal infallibility, which Swynnerton calls 'a fonde folyshe fantasye ragynge in many mens heedes nowe a dayes' (sig. A2v). The following year he received a licence from the archbishop of Canterbury's faculty office to preach anywhere in the realm—doubtless in the interests of promoting the royal supremacy. He was among those who attempted (unsuccessfully) to win over the monks of the London Charterhouse to the king's cause in 1535. Over the next couple of years his preaching raised conservative hackles as far afield as Bedfordshire and Rye, as he used the vigorous assault on the papacy as a cover for disseminating evangelical doctrine. Bishop Longland lobbied Thomas Cromwell against him, but Swynnerton may have enjoyed Cromwell's patronage, as about this time he dedicated to

him a short work, *Tropes and Figures of Scripture*. This used a basic application to scripture of certain elements of Renaissance rhetoric to advance an evangelical agenda on such subjects as faith, purgatory, and monastic vows. The mixture of humanism and Reformation in the treatise is redolent of Wittenberg, although there are also signs that Swynnerton's theology was by now leaning more towards the Swiss school. Although it was clearly written for publication, the book was not printed.

By 1537 Swynnerton seems to have settled down to a curacy in the parish of Holy Trinity, Ipswich, and was soon reported to the bishop of Norwich for allegedly keeping a wife in Colchester. The charge raises the possibility that his alleged abduction of Eleanor Wakefield in 1531 was in fact a clandestine marriage, though formal proof is inevitably lacking. Although he was summoned to the consistory court, he never appeared (perhaps thanks to Cromwell's protection). His talents were not unappreciated in Ipswich. He was commissioned under the will of Robert Cutler (d. 1538) to preach three sermons (in place of the usual masses). The Cutlers, a local mercantile family, were to be prominent in the Reformation leadership of the town. The Ipswich wills in which Swynnerton figures as curate or witness are all distinctly evangelical in tone. He probably remained in Ipswich until 1541, when he was presented to the vicarage of St Clement's, Sandwich, by Edmund Cranmer, the archbishop's nephew. Together with the preaching licence and the earlier connection with William Wakefield, this suggests that Swynnerton's career enjoyed Cranmer's patronage as well as Cromwell's. He remained part of the archbishop's missionary effort in Kent until the accession of Queen Mary, upon which he fled to Emden, where he died in 1554. Although Swynnerton has not become as famous as many of the evangelical preachers of that first generation, his writings and the occasional records of his preaching (which, like that of many other evangelicals, often proved divisive and contested) show that he deserves a place among them. The vigorous and colloquial style he displays in his writings explains why he had such an impact from the pulpit. His life can be summed up in an exclamation uttered in his *Tropes and Figures*: 'Every man hath a Testament in his hande, wolde to God in his harte'. RICHARD REX

Sources *A Reformation rhetoric: Thomas Swynnerton's 'Tropes and figures of scripture'*, ed. R. Rex (1999) · Bale, *Cat.*, 2.76 · C. E. Foerstemann, ed., *Album academiae Vitebergensis ab A. Ch. MDII usque ad A. MDLX*, 3 vols. (1841–1905), 1.127 · D. S. Chambers, ed., *Faculty office registers, 1534–1549* (1966), 39 · *LP Henry VIII*, 10, nos. 804, 891 (PRO, SP1/103, fol. 274); 11, no. 1424 · act books, Norfolk RO, 5, fol. 212r · archeaconry of Suffolk probate registers, Suffolk RO, Ipswich, 12 (IC/AA2/12), fols. 230–31; 13 (IC/AA2/13), fols. 81–2; and 14 (IC/AA2/14), fol. 118 · Cranmer's register, LPL, fol. 390v · chancery, early chancery proceedings, PRO, C1/676/37

Sydall, Elias (1671/2–1733), bishop of Gloucester, was born in Norwich; his father was a glover but no further details of his parents are known. In 1688 he entered Corpus Christi College, Cambridge, as a bible clerk upon Archbishop Parker's foundation, and proceeded BA in 1691, MA in 1695, and DD, by royal mandate, in 1705. From 1696 to 1703 he was a fellow of Corpus Christi and in 1698 he served as university taxor. Having been ordained priest by John Moore, bishop of Norwich, in May 1697 he acted as priest-in-charge of St Benet's, Cambridge, from 1699 until 1702, when he was appointed chaplain to Thomas Tenison, archbishop of Canterbury and a former fellow of Corpus Christi. Tenison rapidly appointed Sydall to a succession of benefices in the diocese of Canterbury: Biddenden (held from 1702 to 1704), Ivychurch (held from 1704 to 1731), and Great Mongeham (held from 1707 to 1730). In 1707 Sydall also became prebendary of the fourth stall in Canterbury Cathedral, to which Tenison added the mastership of the hospitals of St John Northgate and St Nicholas, Harbledown, in 1711. On 29 June 1710, at St Mary Bredin, Canterbury, he married Mary Deedes (1688/9–1758), daughter of William Deedes, a Canterbury physician.

During the eventful convocation of 1710, held in the aftermath of Dr Henry Sacheverell's trial, Sydall served as proctor for the clergy of Canterbury diocese and was one of the joint committee of both houses of convocation working under the guidance of the prolocutor, Francis Atterbury, to prepare a 'Representation of the present State of religion'. However, Sydall did not share Atterbury's high-church convictions, and in the convocation of 1711 he attempted to prevent the passage of measures to censure the Arian opinions of William Whiston. Although it is recorded that Whiston had regarded him as one of the best candidates he had ever examined for orders Sydall seems to have felt no personal sympathy towards Arian doctrine: indeed in a subsequent diocesan proctorial election, in 1722, he enjoyed a decisive level of support from the orthodox clergy.

After the death of Queen Anne, in 1714, Sydall gave enthusiastic support to the new Hanoverian regime, publishing two sermons in 1715: *The Reasonableness of Rejoicing and Giving Thanks for his Majesty's Happy Accession* and a rhetorical piece preached at Canterbury on 5 November during the time of the Jacobite rising, *The insupportable yoke of popery, and the wickedness of bringing it in again upon these kingdoms, after so many deliverances from it; consider'd and apply'd, with regard to the present rebellion*. In this second performance Sydall denounced 'any kind of Tyranny, whether Ecclesiastical or Civil' (Todd, 207–8) and scorned assurances offered to the Church of England by James Francis Edward Stuart, the exiled Stuart 'pretender'. As a reward for such loyalty he was appointed a chaplain to George I in 1716, and held this office as well as that of chaplain to George II from 1727, until he was installed as dean of Canterbury, in succession to Dr George Stanhope, on 26 April 1728. Following the death of Archbishop Tenison in December 1715 Sydall was instrumental in ensuring that all due forms were observed by the Canterbury chapter during the election of Tenison's successor, William Wake, and was chosen to preach the sermon at the latter's primary visitation of the cathedral on 16 June 1716. He was one of the prebendaries trusted by Wake to keep him informed about chapter business, and was 'much respected' at Canterbury 'as a polite Scholar, and much beloved as a mild and diffident Man' (ibid., 204).

On 11 April 1731 Sydall was consecrated at Ely House in London to succeed Dr Smalbroke in the bishopric of St David's. The consecrating bishops were Edmund Gibson, bishop of London, Thomas Green, bishop of Ely, and Thomas Sherlock, bishop of Bangor. On 2 November 1731, on the translation of Joseph Wilcocks to the bishopric of Rochester, Sydall was advanced to the see of Gloucester, and retained this, together with the deanery of Canterbury, until his death, in London, on 24 December 1733 at the age of sixty-one. He was buried in the chancel of St James's, Piccadilly, on 31 December 1733; his wife, who died in 1758, aged sixty-nine, was buried near by. There were no children of the marriage. RICHARD SHARP

Sources H. J. Todd, *Some account of the deans of Canterbury* (1793), 200–10 · J. M. Cowper, *The lives of the deans of Canterbury* (1900) · Venn, *Alum. Cant.*, 1/4.194 · C. J. Abbey, *The English church and its bishops, 1700–1800*, 2 (1887), 76 · N. Sykes, *William Wake, archbishop of Canterbury*, 1 (1957), 205, 235–7; 2 (1957), 189–92 · J. Gregory, *Restoration, reformation and reform, 1660–1828* (2000), 32, 159
Likenesses oils (as dean of Canterbury), Canterbury Cathedral, deanery

Sydenham. For this title name *see* individual entries under Sydenham; *see also* Thomson, Charles Poulett, Baron Sydenham (1799–1841); Clarke, George Sydenham, Baron Sydenham of Combe (1848–1933).

Sydenham, Cuthbert (*bap.* 1623, *d.* 1654), Independent minister and political writer, was baptized at Truro, Cornwall, on 28 June 1623, the fourth son of Cuthbert Sydenham (1565/6–1630), a prominent local woollen draper who served as mayor in 1627, and his wife, Jane Gregor. Educated at Truro grammar school, Sydenham was admitted to St Alban Hall, Oxford, in 1639, although he left the university upon the outbreak of the civil war. By this stage he was clearly associating with puritans who had suffered under Archbishop Laud, such as Roger Quatermayne, for whose book Sydenham provided a preface in 1642. He subsequently worked with leading Independent ministers, such as the five dissenting brethren of the Westminster assembly, and married Frances, the daughter of one of them, Sidrach *Simpson. He also became friends with another figure, the politically Independent if religiously presbyterian Edward Bowles, probably after Sydenham settled in Newcastle, where he was later recalled as the minister who 'shined with the greatest lustre' (Longstaffe, 130). Sydenham served as lecturer at St John's parish until he was appointed alongside William Durant as lecturer at St Nicholas's Church (May 1645), with a stipend of £100 per annum. In July 1647 he became the sole lecturer at St Nicholas, and in April 1648 his stipend was raised to £140. Although he inclined towards religious Independency Sydenham was willing to co-operate with presbyterians. He later distanced himself from the beliefs of sectarian preachers in Newcastle, and defended infant baptism and the singing of psalms in a work called *A Christian Sober and Plain Exercitation*, published in 1653.

Sydenham's connections with leading Independents probably lay behind his employment as a polemicist by the republican regime. His first known commission was to write *An Anatomy of Lieut. Col. John Lilburns Spirit and Pamphlets* in October 1649, following the latter's trial at Guildhall, which was published with the assistance of Thomas May. That this was not his first work, however, is indicated by the fact that in January 1650 the council of state awarded Sydenham £50 for 'good services in writing several tracts upon various subjects' (*CSP dom.*, 1649–50, 476). Sydenham continued to write tracts for the new regime, producing *An English Declaration of the Scottish Declaration* (April 1650), and *The False Brother* (December 1650), the latter a history of Anglo-Scottish relations during the 1640s, an attack upon the demands for presbyterian church government, and a justification of English invasion of Scotland. This work was probably sponsored by the regime, which apparently issued the order for its publication. Sydenham may also have been responsible for *The True Portraiture of the Kings of England* (August 1650), guided through the press by another writer close to the government, Henry Parker, and once again financed by the council of state. In February 1651 Sydenham was awarded another £100 and an annual salary of the same sum, for 'good service in writing on behalf of the commonwealth' (*CSP dom.*, 1651, 42), which was paid until at least November 1653. His services were also rewarded with an official request, in March 1651, that he should be awarded an MA from Oxford.

Sydenham's services to the republic also extended to travelling to Scotland in the spring of 1652, along with other favoured preachers, from where he signed an epistle for a book by another English minister, Nicholas Lockyer. This visit was only brief, however, and Sydenham was back in Newcastle by July 1652, when he and other local ministers collaborated on *A False Jew*, the story of a Scottish Catholic in the town who was proclaimed as a converted Jew by local Baptists. Sydenham clearly sought to attack the local sectarians. In the following November, Sydenham was appointed master of the town's St Mary Magdalen Hospital, but ill health soon forced him to retire to London in September 1653, and when he published some of his sermons in 1654 as *The Greatness of the Mystery of Godlines* he was living in Axe Yard, off King Street in Westminster. Sydenham died in March 1654, leaving his widow, Frances, and two children. His widow was awarded a pension of £10 per annum by the authorities in Newcastle, and a further collection of sermons was published by his fellow preachers in Newcastle, as *Hypocrisie Discovered*. Edward Bowles apparently paid tribute to his friend by saying that 'there would not for many ages arise a prophet like this Moses' (Longstaffe, 131).

J. T. PEACEY

Sources *Memoirs of the life of Mr Ambrose Barnes*, ed. [W. H. D. Longstaffe], SurtS, 50 (1867) • *CSP dom.*, 1649–54 • R. Howell, *Newcastle upon Tyne and the puritan revolution: a study of the civil war in north England* (1967) • J. Polsue, *A complete parochial history of the county of Cornwall*, 4 vols. (1867–72) • M. H. Dodds, ed., *Extracts from the Newcastle upon Tyne minute book, 1639–1656*, Newcastle upon Tyne Records Committee, 1 (1920) • will, PRO, PROB 11/245, fol. 376v • Boase & Courtney, *Bibl. Corn.*, vol. 2 • R. Quatermayne, *Quatermayne's conquest* (1642) • IGI

Likenesses R. Gaywood, engraving, repro. in C. Sydenham, *Hypocrisie discovered* (1654) • R. Gaywood, etching, NPG, BM; repro. in C. Sydenham, *The greatness of the mystery of godlines* (1654)

Sydenham, Floyer (1710–1787), translator, was born in Devon, the third son of Humphrey Sydenham of Combe in Dulverton, Somerset, and his second wife, Katherine, daughter of William Floyer of Berne, Dorset. He was educated at Oxford; having matriculated from Wadham College on 31 May 1727, he graduated BA on 25 June 1731 and MA on 30 April 1734. He was elected a probationary fellow on 30 June 1733 and became a fellow, probably in the following year. He was admitted to the Inner Temple in 1729 and called to the bar at Lincoln's Inn on 12 April 1735. He held the rectory of Esher, Surrey, from 1744 to 1747.

Details of Sydenham's life during the next ten years are very vague. He is reported to have had 'strange travels' in the 'country of the blacks' (John Upton writing to James Harris; Yolton, Price, and Stephens), and by another source, to have joined the navy when he made no headway at the bar, and to have worked his passage back to England as a common sailor (Thomas Taylor; Dyce, 324). In 1757, persuaded by John Upton to begin a translation of Plato in order to earn some money, he devoted himself to the work, finding support, spiritual and financial, in his college contemporary James Harris (1709–1780), who had dedicated one of his *Three Treatises* to him (*Concerning Happiness*, 1741). One of Harris's earliest friends, Arthur Collier (1707–1777), worked in conjunction with Sydenham on the translation of six dialogues (Probyn, 50). Thomas Taylor (1758–1835), the Platonist, made his acquaintance at this time, and described how Sydenham was impoverished and partially insane. According to Taylor, Sydenham committed suicide the night before he was to be imprisoned for his debts, although other authorities say that he died in prison, on 1 April 1787. It was 'to expiate the grief and shame of the event, by a monument to his memory' that David Williams (1738–1816) founded the Literary Fund (Cross, 10). The varied scholarly interests which Sydenham cultivated all through his unfortunate life appear in the MS catalogue of his library, sold by auction in 1788 (Yale, Beinecke X348 571, 1788/2/28–3/1).

An excellent Greek scholar, Sydenham was the first in England to undertake a complete translation of Plato, publishing *A Synopsis or General View of the Works by Plato* along with *Proposals for Printing by Subscription* in 1759; but the public response failed to match the reviewers' enthusiasm. Due to difficulties with subscribers, by 1780 only nine translations with commentary were eventually published, first separately (*Io*, *Greater* and *Lesser Hippias*, *Banquet*, *Rivals*, *Meno*, *First* and *Second Alcibiades*, *Philebus*) and later collected in three volumes (*Dialogues of Plato*, 1767–80). Two complementary studies respectively illustrated Plato's rejection of relativism (*A Dissertation on the Doctrine of Heraclitus*, 1775) and theology (*Onomasticum theologicum, or, An Essay on the Divine Names According to the Platonic Philosophy*, 1784). An unfinished poem in blank verse entitled *Truth, or, The Nature of Things* and two philosophical poems in Latin hexameters remain unpublished (BL, Add. MSS 45181–45182).

Sydenham's Platonic scholarship, commended by Samuel Parr, was credited with 'just criticism and extensive learning, an elegant taste, and a genius naturally philosophic' by Thomas Taylor, who incorporated all nine translations (revised) in his first complete *Works of Plato* (1804, cvii).   E. I. CARLYLE, *rev.* ANNA CHAHOUD

Sources J. D. [J. Dybikowski], 'Sydenham, Floyer', *The dictionary of eighteenth-century British philosophers*, ed. J. W. Yolton, J. V. Price, and J. Stephens (1999) · Foster, *Alum. Oxon.* · F. A. Inderwick and R. A. Roberts, eds., *A calendar of the Inner Temple records*, 4 (1933), 209, 194, 395, 424 · W. P. Baildon, ed., *The records of the Honorable Society of Lincoln's Inn: admissions*, 1 (1896), 411 · W. Maltby, 'Porsoniana', in *Recollections of the table-talk of Samuel Rogers*, ed. A. Dyce (1856), 324–5 · N. Cross, *The Royal Literary Fund, 1790–1918: an introduction … with an index of applicants* (1984) · C. T. Probyn, *The sociable humanist: the life and works of James Harris, 1709–1780* (1991) · *GM*, 1st ser., 57 (1787), 366 · *Monthly Review*, 20 (1759), 284–8, 582–3 · *Monthly Review*, 21 (1759), 425–7 · *Monthly Review*, 25 (1761), 271–5 · *Monthly Review*, 26 (1762), 196 · *Monthly Review*, 36 (1767), 422–3 · F. B. Evans III, 'Platonic scholarship in eighteenth-century England', *Modern Philology*, 41 (1943–4), 103–10
Wealth at death £40 in debt: Maltby, 'Porsoniana', 328

Sydenham, Humphrey (1591–*c*.1650), Church of England clergyman and religious controversialist, was born at Dulverton, Somerset, the fifth of seven sons of Humphrey Sydenham of Combe and his first wife, Jane, daughter of John Champneys of Yarnscombe, also in Somerset. He matriculated from Exeter College, Oxford, in Lent term 1606 and graduated BA on 24 January 1611. In 1613 he became one of the fifteen founding fellows of Wadham College and on 3 December the first to graduate MA from Wadham. He was incorporated MA at Cambridge in 1625. Although in 1618 Sydenham 'incurred *scandalosam excommunicationem*, and was punished accordingly' (Gardiner, 1.9)—the nature of the offence is unknown—he was chosen Wadham's librarian (1623) and moderator of philosophy (1624). He was ordained a priest in 1621 by Lewis Bayly, bishop of Bangor. Charles I, possibly at the suggestion of William Laud, presented him to the vicarages of Ashbrittle (1627) and Puckington (1629) in his native county. By April 1634 Sydenham had married Mary Cox of Crewkerne, Somerset; they had two sons and a daughter. He served as a chaplain to Edward, Lord Howard of Escrick; John Walker suggested, with little evidence, that he also served Laud in this capacity.

According to Anthony Wood, Sydenham was 'a person of quaint and curious stile, better at practical, than school, divinity, and was so eloquent and fluent a preacher that he was commonly called *Silver-tongued Sydenham*' (Wood, *Ath. Oxon.*, 3.275). He preached at Paul's Cross, London, at Oxford, at the Somerset assizes, for episcopal visitations, and at the funerals of Sir John Sydenham and Sir Hugh Portman. These sermons and others he later published, together with *Moses and Aaron, or, The Affinitie of Civill and Ecclesiasticke Power* (1626), prepared for the opening of the second session of the 1625 parliament had Charles I not dissolved it. He dedicated many to members of the leading gentry families of Somerset. A Calvinist episcopalian, his earliest Paul's Cross sermon, on 4 March 1623, *Jacob and Esau* (1626), tackled the controversial topics of election and reprobation; 'grace', he stressed on this

occasion, 'is given to the faithfull, but it is first given that he should be faithfull … Here the Pelagian startles, and lately backt with a troope of Arminians, takes head against this truth' (H. Sydenham, *Five Sermons*, 1637, 53). By the time he delivered *Waters of Marah* (1630), he spoke of God's 'Children and Elect' while insisting that loyalty to the Caroline church and the monarch was indispensable to godliness (H. Sydenham, *Waters of Marah*, 1630, 42). In his *Sermons upon Solemne Occasions* (1637), he furiously criticized puritans, equating them with Catharists, Donatists, Anabaptists, and other schismatics and heretics whose true goal was personal aggrandizement. Unconvinced by their claim that the church's ceremonies injured their consciences, he said that 'their maine Ring-leaders and Seedes-men have bin such, as Universities have vomited … and Authority justly condemn'd to silence or suspension' (*Sermons upon Solemne Occasions*, 1637, 266–7). He praised the Laudian campaign for the beauty of holiness by denouncing the puritan who 'Pulls down an Organ, and advances an Houre-glasse', thereby making 'an House of Prayer, a fit den for Theeves' (ibid., 31). Sydenham delighted in the reassertion of clerical authority of the 1630s and urged that those who 'have a tongue for Geneva, and a heart for Amsterdam; their pretence of Old England, and their project for New' should have 'a hooke put in their Nostrils, and a bridle in their jaws' (ibid., 271). In dedicating the work to Laud himself Sydenham deftly compared attacks upon Laud by John Bastwick, Henry Burton, and William Prynne with his own situation. If 'bold men' such as they 'dare thus play with the very Beard of Aaron, what will they do to the Skirts of his Rayment … If Schismaticall hands be catching at the Mytre and the Rotchet, how will they rend the contemptible Hood and Surplesse' (ibid., sig. A3*r*, *v*).

On 19 May 1643 Sydenham gained a prebend at Wells Cathedral, and the following year the rectory of Odcombe, but he could not have been surprised when the parliamentary commissioners for Somerset seized his benefices in 1645. He died at Dulverton about 1650, and was buried there.   J. SEARS MCGEE

Sources Wood, *Ath. Oxon.*, new edn, 3.274 · J. Collinson, *The history and antiquities of the county of Somerset*, 3 vols. (1791) · D. Lloyd, *Memoires of the lives … of those … personages that suffered … for the protestant religion* (1668) · Foster, *Alum. Oxon.* · Venn, *Alum. Cant.* · R. B. Gardiner, ed., *The registers of Wadham College, Oxford*, 1 (1889) · *Walker rev.* · J. Walker, *An attempt towards recovering an account of the numbers and sufferings of the clergy of the Church of England*, 2 pts in 1 (1714) · T. G. Barnes, *Somerset, 1625–1640: a county's government during the personal rule* (1961) · A. Foster, 'The clerical estate revitalized', *The early Stuart church, 1603–1642*, ed. K. Fincham (1993), 139–60 · J. S. McGee, *The godly man in Stuart England* (1976) · F. Brown, ed., *Abstracts of Somersetshire wills*, 3 (privately printed, London, 1889), 56 · *Fasti Angl., 1541–1857*, [Bath and Wells] · *DNB*

Sydenham, John (1807–1846), antiquary, was born on 25 September 1807 at Poole, Dorset, the son of John Sydenham (1781/2–1866) of Poole, a bookseller and part-owner of the *Dorset Chronicle*, and his wife, Elizabeth. Sydenham apparently received a 'good general education' at a private academy in Poole, and was editor of the *Dorset Chronicle* from 1829 to 1842, during which time he wrote many articles of literary and antiquarian interest for the paper (*GM*, 211). In 1833 he married Anne Christina, daughter of William Zillwood, a schoolmaster of Dorchester, with whom he had five children.

Sydenham became involved in pamphleteering and local politics on the tory side after 1831, yet managed to complete his well-researched *History of the Town and County of Poole* (1839; republished in facsimile, 1986). Following his highly speculative *Baal Durotrigensis* (1841), about the giant figure at Cerne Abbas, he made a significant contribution to *Archaeologia* (30, 1844, 327–8) with 'An account of the opening of some barrows in south Dorsetshire', which gave details of twenty-five barrows, many of which he excavated in collaboration with Charles Warne. He was one of the first members of the British Archaeological Association. Editor of the Greenwich-based *West Kent Guardian* from 1843 to 1845, Sydenham returned to Poole in January 1846 to become the first editor and part proprietor of the *Poole and Dorsetshire Herald*. A lifelong sufferer from asthma, he fell ill of a pulmonary complaint and died at Poole, on 1 December 1846.

E. I. CARLYLE, *rev.* GLANVILLE J. DAVIES

Sources J. Hutchins, *The history and antiquities of the county of Dorset*, 3rd edn, ed. W. Shipp and J. W. Hodson, 1 (1861); facs. edn (1973), 67–8 · J. Sydenham, *The history of the town and county of Poole* (1839); repr. (1986) · J. G. Hillier, *Ebb-tide at Poole* (1985) · J. B. Calkin, 'Some records of barrow excavations re-examined', *Proceedings of the Dorset Natural History and Archaeological Society*, 88 (1966), 128–48 · C. H. Mayo, ed., *Bibliotheca Dorsetiensis: being a carefully compiled account of books and pamphlets relating to … Dorset* (1885), 127, 187 · *The Archaeologist* (May 1862), 115 · parish records, Poole, 1828–47, Dorset RO, PE/PL RE 4/2 [burial] · parish records, Poole, 1790–1863, Dorset RO, PE/PL RE 1/5 [baptisms] · *GM*, 2nd ser., 27 (1847), 211–12 · *Journal of the British Archaeological Association*, 3 (1848), 139 · parish records, Poole, 1847–73, Dorset RO, PE/PL RE 4/3 [burial]

Sydenham, Thomas (*bap.* 1624, *d.* 1689), physician, was baptized on 10 September 1624 at Wynford Eagle, Dorset, the third surviving son of William Sydenham (1593–1661), a gentleman, and Mary Jeffrey (*d.* 1644), of Wynford Eagle. His parents had nine sons (four died early) and five daughters. Little is known of his early life, though he must have had the equivalent of a Latin-school education.

Military service and study at Oxford At the rather late age of seventeen, on 1 July 1642, Sydenham matriculated at Oxford, residing at Magdalen Hall, one of the few surviving independent resident halls; it adjoined Magdalen College but had a quite different character. Under its principal, John Wilkinson, a presbyterian, Magdalen Hall had acquired a distinctly puritan cast. With the outbreak of civil war shortly after he had moved to Oxford, Sydenham left the hall to join his father and brothers in the parliamentary militia for Dorset. He held the rank of cornet, serving under his brother William *Sydenham (*bap.* 1615, *d.* 1661), a colonel and one of the leading anti-royalists in the south-west, and with his brothers Francis (a captain, then major) and John (lieutenant). He must have seen hard fighting. Dorset mainly supported the parliament, but following Prince Rupert's capture of Bristol on 27 July 1643, royalist forces entered in strength, taking Dorchester,

Thomas Sydenham (*bap.* 1624, *d.* 1689), by Mary Beale, 1688

Weymouth, and Portland (and exacting retribution from the inhabitants) before setting siege to Exeter, which was captured on 4 September 1643 (with Thomas's father among the prisoners). Many bitter skirmishes followed. In the summer of 1644 the earl of Essex's troops restored most of the towns and cities to parliamentary rule, William Sydenham being made the military governor of Weymouth. But bloody fighting continued, in which Sydenham's mother was killed in August 1644. Major Williams was blamed for it, and the brothers took revenge in a fight at Dorchester at the end of November, when William killed the major. Francis died defending Weymouth in February 1645, and Thomas himself may have been wounded in the skirmishing that followed the royalist take-over, which was reversed about three weeks later. In August, Cromwell and Fairfax captured the main royalist bastion of Sherborne, which lowered the level of fighting in Dorset until the end of the first civil war in June 1646.

With the fighting at arms over, Sydenham returned to Magdalen Hall (though exactly when is unknown) and helped parliament establish its power over the university. By an ordinance of 1 May 1647 parliament appointed visitors to purge Oxford of opposition; on 30 September the visitors in turn appointed delegates to the colleges and halls who were to investigate the behaviour and views of the members of the university. Sydenham was the sole delegate appointed on that date for Wadham College, apparently becoming a fellow-commoner of the college to pursue the business. During the second civil war of March to August 1648, he continued to combat royalist opposition within the university rather than return to the army. As the delegate for Wadham, Sydenham seems to have rooted out the opposition vigorously, for following the notorious convocation of 12–14 April 1648—when the chancellor, the earl of Pembroke, threatened force if the members of the university continued their obstruction, and required everyone both to submit to the parliament and to take the negative oath (not to support the king)—twenty-two people, including the master, were expelled from Wadham. On the last day of the same convocation, possibly as a reward for his loyalty and encouragement for his studies, Sydenham was granted a medical baccalaureate, as BM. (When on 4 May 1648 he was listed as a submitting member of Magdalen Hall, the letters MA followed his name; although there is no other official record of his having taken the master's degree, he later believed that he had been granted an MA, for which the records may be incomplete.) It is likely that he was the 'Syddenham' appointed a fellow of New College by the parliamentary visitors on 18 July 1648 (though these appointments seem never to have taken effect), while he was also 'intruded' on 3 October 1648 by the visitors in the place of an expelled fellow at All Souls (where twenty-seven of thirty-five did not submit). A few months later, on 29 March 1649, the visitors appointed him the senior bursar of All Souls, a position he held for the usual length of service of one year. All these appointments single him out as a particularly loyal servant of the parliamentary visitors. According to the extant bursar's accounts, Sydenham resided at All Souls from 13 October 1648 until he left again for military service in March 1651 (Meynell, 14).

The four years in residence at Oxford undoubtedly also gave Sydenham time to study while pursuing the political agenda. He had decided to study medicine at least by 1648 when he was created BM. The origin of this resolution is recounted by Sydenham in his dedication to Dr John Mapletoft for the third edition of *Observationes medicae* (1676), in which he states that at the end of the wars his brother William had been cared for during an illness by Dr Thomas Coxe, and Sydenham accompanied Coxe back to London.

> He, with his well-known kindness and courtesy, asked me what profession I was preparing to enter, now that I was resuming my interrupted studies, and was come to man's estate. I had at that time no fixed plans, and was not even dreaming of the profession of medicine; but moved by the recommendation and influence of so great a man, and in some way, I suppose, by my own destiny, I applied myself seriously to that pursuit. (Meynell, 68–9)

Sydenham is unlikely to have been a star pupil, however: according to William Stukeley, who heard it from Lord Pembroke, Sydenham was a 'chamber fellow' with Thomas Millington, who had also been appointed to a fellowship at All Souls by the visitors and who went on to become a very influential physician as well as intimate friend of Sydenham's. Millington reportedly said that Sydenham had been 'idle and never studied' during his first experience at Oxford, but after time in the army 'took a resolution to study Physick. By this time he had entirely forgot his Latin, but recover'd it again by obstinate reading of Cicero, translating it into English, and then into Latin, correcting it from the original' (Meynell, 64). Sydenham

later wrote of Cicero that he was 'the author I most admire, as the great teacher both in thought and language, the first genius of his own and perhaps of all ages'; and according to the report of Hans Sloane, Sydenham also kept a bust of Cicero in his library (Payne, 67, 213). Stukeley's report is in error at some points (such as his statements that Sydenham and Millington studied at Cambridge, that his army service was three years, and that his Latin works were written in that language by Sydenham himself), so it must be read with some care, but it is probable that Sydenham had much catching up to do as a student when returning from the field.

When the forces of the younger Charles Stuart presented a serious danger, Sydenham again left Oxford to join the military, accepting a commission on 21 April 1651 as captain in a cavalry regiment under the command of Colonel Robert Jermy. On 16 May his troop was put under the command of Colonel Rich, who was serving under Cromwell in the north of England and in Scotland. Evidence again points toward Sydenham's seeing heavy fighting: according to his later petition he had supplied money to his brother Major John Sydenham for horses and other necessities for his going to Scotland, and in the same petition he stated that he himself had 'lost much bloud, & thereby much disabled his body' in the campaign (Meynell, 61–3). Andrew Broun later claimed to have been told by Sydenham that he had been left for dead on the field (ibid., 63), and in the bursar's accounts at All Souls Sydenham apparently spent time there during the weeks of 29 August to 4 September and 19–25 September, perhaps suggesting that he was recuperating in Oxford after serious wounding in the fighting leading up to the battle of Worcester on 3 September, the last campaign of the war (Meynell, 14). His troop was disbanded around 20 October. Afterwards, he said, he was almost killed by a drunken soldier while in London, being awakened from his bed by the man, who grabbed his shirt and shot a pistol at him point-blank; fortunately his assailant shot his own hand, deflecting the ball and delivering Sydenham from injury (Meynell, 63). Such events must have reinforced his belief in providence.

After Oxford, development of Sydenham's medical thought

As an adult veteran Sydenham now sought new opportunities, though he did not immediately sever his ties to Oxford. Between the end of October 1651 and resigning his fellowship at All Souls four years later, according to the bursar's books he seldom resided at the college. Perhaps he continued to reside at the more congenial Magdalen Hall, but more probably he was living elsewhere. There is no evidence of his participation in the vigorous medical and natural philosophical investigations at Oxford during the 1650s conducted by men (many like Sydenham intruded by parliament) who later formed the Oxford Philosophical Society and powerfully contributed to the early Royal Society of London. He was clearly seeking means elsewhere to start an independent life. Sydenham's signature was among the many on a petition entered in the House of Commons on 27 August 1652 seeking reimbursement for the moneys spent in serving the parliament. According to the next petition he was to have been settled with land in Ireland, but was too far down the list to obtain any. About 3 March 1654 he requested from Cromwell the money he was due for equipping his brother, which Cromwell forwarded with his endorsement to the council of state; on 16 March the council recommended payment of £600 (received by Sydenham on 25 April) and further recommended that he be suitably employed. Sydenham subsequently took up the office of comptroller of the pipe, probably in January 1655, which he apparently held until the Restoration (Meynell, 10)—a position within the exchequer with responsibility for collecting and auditing receipts from the sheriffs. The new post meant that he could finally provide for a family; he resigned his fellowship at All Souls on 7 October and married Mary Gee in his home town of Wynford Eagle probably not long afterwards.

The French tradition that Sydenham travelled to Montpellier where he studied with the Calvinist Charles Barbeyrac (who became known as a superb clinician and private teacher) is not confirmed by documentation. The best evidence comes from Pierre Desault, who in a work of 1733 on venereal and other diseases reported that one of his former colleagues, M. Emeric the father, had met Thomas Sydenham in Montpellier and developed a strong friendship (*liaison*) with him (Meynell, 70–71; Payne, 89, 91–2). There is also a pass, dated 28 July 1659, to travel overseas issued to a 'Mr. Briggs and Sydenham' (*CSP dom.*, *1659–60*, 561), and it has been conjectured that this was Thomas Sydenham accompanying as a doctor the son of a wealthy MP from Norwich, Augustine Briggs, who died abroad (Payne, 91). But a William (Guilielmus) Sydenham matriculated in philosophy at the University of Leiden on 10 May 1649, and on 25 April 1650 enrolled in the medical faculty of Padua, where he was a pupil of the anatomy professor Antonio Molinetti (Innes Smith, 228); it is quite unlikely that this is either Thomas or his brother Colonel Sydenham. It is possible that the travels of yet another Sydenham were also for medical study: on 25 March 1650 the council of state issued a pass 'for John Sydenham and Clement Thin, his servant, to Leiden in Holland', and on 1 October 1652 it issued a pass 'for John Sydenham to foreign parts' (*CSP dom.*, *1650*, 531; *1651–2*, 575): again, however, this cannot have been Thomas's brother John, since he had been fatally wounded at the battle of Stirling in May 1651 (Meynell, 4). The Sydenham given a pass in 1659 is therefore most likely to have been one of the other two Sydenhams mentioned in earlier travel passes. If Thomas Sydenham did travel abroad, he never took a medical degree, since he did not enter evidence of one before the London College of Physicians, as he would have done upon entry. No further evidence of his possible travels has surfaced in the twentieth century. G. G. Meynell's recent attempts to pin down the matter have therefore led him to doubt the episode of foreign travel (Meynell, 70–71). Perhaps the story arose from confusing Sydenham with one of his later associates who studied in Montpellier, such as Hans Sloane.

In later writings Sydenham almost never referred to people and events before 1660, perhaps in an attempt to erase his ties to the Commonwealth—like Boyle he was publicly silent about the sources of his views and information—but it was in this period that his medical orientation probably took shape. The person whom Sydenham credited with encouraging his medical studies, Thomas Coxe, was associated with Samuel Hartlib's office of address and so with a group of parliamentarians actively involved in the reform of learning along the lines of Baconian empirical and utilitarian natural history (like many other contemporaries, Sydenham later referred to Bacon with the greatest regard). Mid-century medical reformers also tended to take inspiration from two lines of enquiry causing excitement at the time. One was neo-Hippocratic empiricism, which advocated giving keen and skilled observation priority over theory (or 'speculation'), pointing to environmental influences as among the most important causes of disease, supporting the actions of nature since it acted for the good, and applying medical knowledge to treating illness rather than emphasizing the search for its causes in human anatomy and physiology. A second line of investigation was stimulated by the potential benefits of alchemy and associated medical chemistry (iatrochemistry), particularly as advocated by Joan Baptista van Helmont. Helmontians generally thought that immaterial entities (in the form of archei—that is, 'physiological' powers) governed the actions of the natural world, including the organs of the body: when an alien archeus entered the body and interfered with the functioning of the local archeus, it caused disease. By using powerful essences made by chemical methods to counter particular archei, the physician could assist the forces of the body in expelling the alien archei and restoring patients to health. Whereas Hippocratism and Helmontianism can be distinguished from one another, in the minds of many mid-century writers they went together in supporting empirical and experimental clinical medicine. Almost every historical commentator has stressed that Sydenham later referred to Hippocrates with the greatest respect and took many of his basic themes from him. It should also be noted, however, that Sydenham also wrote about the importance of the blood as a carrier of the life force, therefore abhorring blood-letting in most instances (as the Helmontians did), felt free to advocate the use of medical specifics (including chemical remedies such as the Paracelsian laudanum and metallics such as steel), and referred favourably to Helmont's view of the archeus in his attack on medical anatomy (Dewhurst, 91). It may also have been that people at Magdalen Hall had stimulated an interest in Helmont on Sydenham's part, since the most important translator of Helmont into English was John Chandler, who had matriculated at Magdalen Hall just a year before Sydenham.

Move to London In his dedicatory letter to Mapletoft in 1676 and after writing of Coxe's encouragement to study medicine, Sydenham notes: 'After a few years spent in the arena of the University, I returned to London for the practice of medicine'. The reference to the 'few years' at Oxford undoubtedly relates to the period from about 1647 to 1651, but quite when he moved to London and began to practise medicine is unclear. He was definitely resident in London by later 1655. He may have lived first with his brother in government lodgings in Westminster, though on unknown authority Mackensie E. C. Walcott, writing in his *Westminster* (1849), said that Sydenham 'lived in a house upon the site of the *Ram's Mews*', on the west side of present-day Whitehall (Meynell, 19). Sydenham also later recorded (in his *Tractatus de hydrope*, 1683) having seen his first case of dropsy in a Mrs Saltmarsh of Westminster twenty-seven years before—that is, about 1656. Some time in the year before June 1658 he had moved to the eastern end of the new neighbourhood of Pall Mall, for he then appeared on the rate books as 'Docktor Syddonham': this is also the first clear evidence that he was publicly identifying himself as a medical practitioner, though he had not earned a doctorate, and he additionally appeared as a self-styled 'Dr.' in the record of 14 July 1659 on his appointment as comptroller of the pipe (*CSP dom.*, 1659–60, 29). His house in Pall Mall stood near that of Lady Rane-lagh, an important figure in the intellectual and social circles of the Commonwealth and sister of Robert Boyle, who lived with her for long periods; in June 1669 Syden-ham moved to the north side of Pall Mall. He still held out some hope of achieving political prominence in Dorset, for he stood for election to Richard Cromwell's parliament from Weymouth and Malcombe Regis, though he failed to gain the office on election day (6 June 1658).

With the Restoration of 1660 any remaining desires for political advancement Sydenham may have held must have disappeared, causing him to concentrate on his medical observations. When in 1663 the College of Physicians attempted to regain their regulatory authority to license all practitioners in London, Sydenham submitted himself for their three-part examination (on 24 April, 8 May, and 5 June). He was recorded for the first examination as master of arts of All Souls and bachelor of medicine; Richard Lower, however, reported to Boyle that he had asked the registrar of Oxford to search for a record of Sydenham's having taken an MA, but that the registrar had found only the evidence of his BM (Meynell, 69–70). At the quarterly meeting of the College of Physicians on 25 June, Syden-ham was voted a licentiate. During the plague epidemic of 1665 he left London, like many physicians partaking in the general exodus. According to a letter from John Beale to Boyle on 7 September 1665, Sydenham was one of the most wholehearted endorsers of the curing touch of Valentine Greatrakes, who was then causing a stir in London (Meynell, 74). Sydenham himself had become successful enough to have lent Lady Ranelagh £100 before September 1666 (Meynell, 79).

Publication of *Methodus* and relations with the London medical establishment It was probably while away from London during the plague that Sydenham composed the bulk of his first medical treatise, *Methodus curandi febres, propriis observationibus superstructa* ('Method of curing fevers based on original observations') of 1666 (with an Amsterdam edition of the same year following its publication in London). Dedicated to his friend and neighbour Boyle, who

sometimes visited patients with him, the book was reviewed in Henry Oldenburg's *Philosophical Transactions* for Monday 7 May 1666 (Latham, 1.xxvii–xxx). According to Henry Stubbe in his *Epistolary Discourse Concerning Phlebotomy* (1671, p. 180), the *Methodus* had been translated into proper Latin for publication by 'Mr. G. H.', identified by John Ward as Gilbert Havers (Dewhurst, 71), who also Latinized a number of works for Boyle in the early to mid-1660s (*Works of … Boyle*, 1.lxx). Sydenham divided his analysis into four topics: continued fevers, special symptoms accompanying continued fevers, intermittent fevers, and smallpox. The second edition of *Methodus* in 1668 contained additional observations on plague. The theme of both editions stems from Sydenham's neo-Hippocratic and Helmontian views: fever expressed the attempts of nature to rid the body of morbific particles, so that the main goal of treatment was to support and direct nature rather than fight it; and diseases were of particular species depending on the particulars of the morbific matter. (The view that particles of morbific matter caused disease suggests a corpuscularian view that was becoming common at the time among many, including Boyle, and was stimulated as much by Helmont and Gassendi as by Descartes). The most famous example of how Sydenham worked out the views exhibited in his work concerns smallpox, for which he advocated a new therapeutic regimen. Prevailing treatments tried to attack the disease by bed rest, heating, sweating, and bloodletting, whereas Sydenham strongly advised keeping the patient up and about in the early stages of the disease, after which bed rest was accompanied with open windows and no more bed-clothes or warmth than were ordinary for the time of year, while at the same time the patient's own inclinations toward drink directed the giving of fluids, particularly small beer. Most importantly, he turned away from bloodletting. According to the dedication to Sydenham's unpublished draft of a book on smallpox (c.1669), the first earl of Shaftesbury had allowed him to treat his family according to his method, which was successful (Dewhurst, 102).

Sydenham's views as expressed in the mid-1660s implicitly built on the reformist orientation of the Commonwealth, though they were presented as matter-of-fact. Indeed, Sydenham's later associate Richard Blackmore held that Sydenham developed his methods simply by acting in a way 'directly contrary in all Cases to the common Method then in Fashion among the most eminent Physicians' (Meynell, 71). But following the publication of the *Methodus*, Sydenham seems to have been thinking about joining in the more explicit contemporary attacks on academic physicians. In 1664–5 a group of enthusiasts were organizing the Society of Chemical Physicians in London, which briefly competed with the College of Physicians for royal patronage. Although the plague killed some of its key members and so destroyed its chances of success, the threat to academic physic from medical chemists and empirics continued, leading to a series of bitter pamphlet wars that spilled over into the early controversies about the Royal Society. Even Sydenham's friend and neighbour, the cautious Boyle, was linked to support for the anti-establishment party by the sharp controversialist Stubbe, and in his 1671 treatise *The Lord Bacons Relation of the Sweating-Sickness Examined*, Stubbe also explicitly associated Sydenham with the empirical chemist George Thomson and other critics of the College of Physicians. Stubbe drew attention to Sydenham's comment in the *Methodus* that people died from smallpox mainly because prideful physicians cared nothing for their patients and acted by the common procedures (Dewhurst, 35). The more conservative physicians must also have heard the rumour recorded by the Revd John Ward, who noted that 'Dr. Sydenham is writing a book which will bring physitians about his ears, to decri the usefullness of natural philosophie, and to maintain the necessitie of knowledg in anatomie in subordination to physick' (Meynell, 68). The explosive treatise being composed by Sydenham was never published, but partial sections of it from 1668 and 1669 survive in the hand of Sydenham's occasional amanuensis, John Locke, entitled 'De arte medica' and 'Anatomie'. The first manuscript attacks the disputes and 'speculative theorems' of learned physic while arguing instead for a new foundation of practice established on unbiased observations. The second argues that anatomy was not able 'to afford any great improvement to the practice of physick, or assist a man in the findeing out and establishing a true method' (Dewhurst, 85). Had either work been published, it would have been rightly viewed as lending support to the empirical chemists' attack on academic medicine. No wonder Ward could also record that Sydenham said that physic 'is not to be learned by going to Universities, but hee is for taking apprentices; and says one had as good send a man to Oxford to learn shoemaking as practising physick' (Dewhurst, 17).

Like Boyle, however, Sydenham held off publishing his most controversial views. He also kept his distance from the Society of Chemical Physicians, was never invited to join the Royal Society, and held only the lowly rank of licentiate in the College of Physicians. His former life probably precluded advancement at court. Years beforehand he had signed a petition (probably to the parliamentary visitors) against the 'ungodly habits' of people at All Souls that singled out Nicholas Greaves DD, whose younger brother Edward Greaves MD was now a fellow of the London College of Physicians and physician-in-ordinary to Charles II (Meynell, 16). Most of the patients Sydenham described in his works were in middling professions: chaplains, apothecaries, majors, physicians, booksellers, tradesmen and yeomen, and women of unspecified rank (Meynell, 24–5). Dr Robert Pitt also later reported that Sydenham received poor patients at his house every day, curing many of chronic disease by giving them preparations he made up himself (Meynell, 74). A few of his patients even had titles—Baron Annesley, the grandson of Lady Dacres, Lord Ossory, the earl of Salisbury, and the earl of Shaftesbury—but he never became an eminently fashionable doctor. He even deeply offended an associate of Boyle; a letter of Henry Oldenburg to Boyle dated 24 December 1667 complains that Sydenham was

the only man that I hear of, who, when I was shut up [in the Tower], thought fit (God knows without cause) to rail against me, and that was such a coward as afterwards to disown [his remarks], though undeniable. I confess that with so mean and immoral a spirit I cannnot well associate. (Latham, 1.33)

Sydenham's unpublished manuscript on smallpox speaks of 'how difficultly it has fared with me, who have under gone soe many rebukes and reproaches' for his medical recommendations (Dewhurst, 102). Still, his method of treating smallpox had gained him enough of a reputation as a particularly fine clinician for some other practitioners, at least, to seek his advice. For instance, Dr David Thomas wrote to Locke (19 October 1669): 'Pray let mee know whether the grypeing of the gutts of which soe many dy in London and are sicke in the country be Cholera morbus and what way of cure Sydnam useth. my humble service to him' (*Correspondence of John Locke*, 1.324–5). When Sydenham returned to the public eye in 1676 with the book that made him famous, he built on his previous work: what he called the 'third edition' of the *Methodus*, which was three or four times as large and bore a new title, *Observationes medicae*. Dedicated to (and Latinized by) a mere scholar, John Mapletoft (Meynell, 41–2), the work was registered with the Stationers' Company on 16 March 1676 and first advertised in the term catalogues in May, with an edition in Strassburg in the same year and imprints from both Geneva and Amsterdam in 1683. (The fourth edition, in 1685, contained no important changes from 1676.)

Observationes In the *Observationes*, Sydenham organized his findings according to the 'constitutions' dominant at different times: 1661–4, 1665–6, 1667–9, 1669–72, and 1673–5. The work also contained a concluding section on other fevers that had occurred but that did not fit the prevailing constitutions. Each of the periods is described in terms of the atmospheric conditions and acute epidemic diseases that expressed the nature of the time. Epidemic diseases were due to the exhalations of a particular atmosphere; other acute diseases (intercurrent ones) had their origin in the individual circumstances of particular bodies. It was on epidemic diseases and their origins in various natural constitutions that he concentrated. Diseases like smallpox might occur in each of the periods described, but slight variations between the periods in their symptoms revealed how they were affected by changes in the prevailing morbific material in the air. The periodic changes in the prevailing natural constitution were therefore not necessarily attached to seasons, but to hidden causes that altered the earth's constitution. Rather than speculate about the underlying causes (as he accused the learned physicians of doing), Sydenham preferred to sort the minute descriptive details and thereby to show the underlying consistencies among species of disease and also the subtle differences within species caused by variations in prevailing constitutions.

Sydenham's work on constitutions may be said to naturalize his views of providence. His opinions about God and nature are contained in an undated manuscript attributed to him, 'Theologia rationalis' (printed in Dewhurst, 145–59). He begins with the question 'how far the light of nature, if closely adverted to, may be extended towards the making us good men?' The answer draws on arguments from design and concludes with quotations from Cicero's *De divinatione*, which argued against Stoic fatalism. Sydenham held that nature demonstrated a 'perfect and exquisite' order so wondrous and profound as to require a wise and powerful creator, a 'Being' above nature 'which we call God'. Such a 'divine Architect or Maker', to whom we owe our own natures, requires adoration and thanks. Once the creator has set things in order, he cannot be expected to change natural law, but this does not mean that everything is pre-determined in human life: for example, one might be saved from shipwreck and drowning by having the 'Supream Being ... dispose the previous Circumstances of my Will and other things, as to prevent my going to Sea'. God thus allows for free will while also directing us providentially; Sydenham therefore argued against both determinism and chance in favour of 'some Superior direction' in our lives, though we cannot know the final causes to which our dispositions are directed. It is therefore reasonable and natural to pray for 'all that good, which is necessary for my mind and Body' and to pray 'for diverting' evil, especially to pray for virtue, while recognizing that the supreme being knows what is best. Sydenham goes on to derive other rules: one should strive to benefit 'mankind', to obey the laws of human society, and to preserve the dominion of mind over body, which includes a duty to speak truthfully, to think, speak and act decorously, and not to become dependent on worldly goods. To assist the mind in achieving these ends, it is reasonable to consider the soul—'the Principle of thinking'—to be immaterial and immortal: even the instincts of animals demonstrate an immaterial power over bodies, for 'we cannot conceive that matter should think'. Moreover, since this life did not make 'sufficient retribution' for the greatest virtues and vices, there has to be a future state in which the good and bad will be accounted for. This is why the natural laws outlined above 'are written upon our minds so clearly that he who hath not defaced them by sensuality may easily read them', the obeying or transgressing of which is known by 'Conscience'. These laws are embedded in our natures, and are universal to all humanity.

This is an early version of a genre that came to be called natural theology, moving Sydenham away from the Christian religion. There are no quotations from the Bible or religious literature, much less discussions of Christ, sin, and redemption. Sydenham allowed for free will and the power of prayer but stressed the providential direction of the supreme being and his natural laws, denying miracles. Like many other reformers of his period, perhaps, Sydenham believed that a moderate and widely shared providentialism could be shown to be derived from nature through reason, but he recognized no evidence about the world apart from the five senses, and no evidence about the soul apart from reason and conscience.

The fact that he concluded a work on 'theology' by quoting his favourite author, Cicero, shows how far his thinking was from ordinary Christian doctrine—but again, he did not publish these opinions. While publicly coy about the cause of the changing 'constitutions', then, Sydenham probably saw them as expressions of the living forces of the world governed by the creator, which exhibit themselves in different kinds of airs and diseases. In any case, his constitutionalism is perfectly in keeping with a providentialist naturalism.

Whether all Sydenham's readers recognized such arguments in his mature medical writings or not, his ability to make fine discriminations among diseases confirmed his reputation as a great clinician. Sydenham became well known for arguing that diseases could be distinguished one from another, just as botanical species could be identified; this helped to stimulate the development of nosology, or disease classification. Given his view about disease species which had accidental variations according to the prevailing constitution, he also promoted the importance of therapeutic specifics: remedies that helped nature attack the morbific matter causing the disease (which were still viewed with suspicion by many academic physicians). The best-known specific Sydenham recommended was cinchona bark, or 'Jesuits bark' (from which quinine was later derived), in certain kinds of intermittent fevers (agues). It had begun to be used in Europe in the 1640s, and Sydenham became one of its early advocates in England, recommending it with caution in his *Methodus* of 1655, and strongly asserting its virtues in the *Observationes*. Richard Talbor (or Tabor) received much of the credit, however, by publishing on agues and their specifics, including the bark, in a book of 1672, and cured Charles II of a bout of illness, which earned him a knighthood in 1678. In a letter to Locke of 3 August 1678, Sydenham expressed the view that he had been plagiarized by Talbor: 'I never gott £10 by it, he hath gott 5000. He was an Apothecary in Cambridg wher my booke of practise have much obteyned' (*Correspondence of John Locke*, 1.601–2). Sydenham nevertheless gave Locke and others instructions on how best to 'exhibit' the bark, and by 1679 had established his reputation among physicians as 'the much Celebrated, though Illegitimate [i.e., self-taught] Son of this Art' who had laid the basis for the only 'infallible Method' in the treatment of agues known to medicine (W. Harris, *A Farewell to Popery*, 1679, 20).

Final years On 18 May 1676, Sydenham finally graduated MD from Pembroke College, Cambridge, which his son was attending (Meynell, 18). He refined and expanded his earlier views by publishing two long letters in response to enquiries from Drs Robert Brady and Henry Paman as *Epistolae responsoriae duae* (1680): the letter to Brady dealt with epidemic constitutions up to 1679 and gave instructions on the treatment of specific diseases, including details on the use of the bark; the letter to Paman discussed the treatment of venereal disease, recommending salivation. Sydenham used the same form in 1682 (in the *Dissertatio epistolaris* to Dr William Cole) to publish further information on his treatments for smallpox and hysteria (in the latter case again recommending specifics in addition to vigorous exercise and a strengthening diet). Both were apparently translated into Latin by Mapletoft (Meynell, 41).

Since the wars Sydenham had seldom been in perfect health himself. As he passed into his fifties he suffered increasingly severe afflictions. In 1677 he was laid up with gout for twenty weeks, convalescing at the earl of Salisbury's Hatfield House. From the end of the 1670s he was continually ill with chronic diseases. Yet in addition to writing clinical pieces in the form of letters, he managed to produce the *Tractatus de podagra et hydrope* ('Treatise on gout and dropsy') of 1683, dedicated to Dr Thomas Short. Sydenham had intended a larger treatise on chronic diseases, but managed only these two substantial parts. It was quickly also published in English in 1684 by his friend John Drake. By this time he was becoming famous enough to see the appearance of editions of his collected *Opera*, one printed in Geneva from 1683 to 1689, another in Amsterdam in 1683, and finally a London edition in 1685 (with multiple editions following). Despite failing health Sydenham managed still another treatise in the form of a letter to Dr Charles Goodall, the *Schedula monitoria* (1686), describing the appearance of a new species of fever that had appeared in 1685. Sydenham had earlier written that Goodall, a keen advocate for the bark, had defended him against his critics like a son defending a father (Meynell, 23). In the same period, on the recommendation of Robert Boyle, he took the young doctor Hans Sloane under his wing, introducing and recommending him to patients, though discouraging him from travelling to Jamaica to pursue natural history (Meynell, 73). Sydenham had few known pupils aside from Thomas Dover and Bartholomew Beale, the son of his neighbour and portrait painter Mary Beale (who painted his likeness).

Influence At least one physician tried to follow Sydenham's analysis of constitutions: William Cole, in *A physico-medical essay concerning the late frequency of apoplexies: together with a general method of their prevention, and cure* (1689), in which he referred to his colleague as 'my Learned and Worthy Friend Dr. *Sydenham*' (p. 113). More generally, however, Sydenham's main impact was among other 'practical' doctors who stressed the importance of keen clinical observation and the development of new and successful methods of treatment. Walter Harris thanked Sydenham for encouraging him to discuss his work in finding new methods of treating children, and for using and endorsing his methods (W. Harris, *An Exact Inquiry into, and Cure of the Acute Diseases of Infants*, 1693). William Cockburn (who translated Harris into English) argued that ''Tis surely in Medicine as in all other Physical Knowledge, the more circumstances we know, the better judgment we are able to make', and thought that Sydenham had established the standard: 'our own Dr. Sydenham has writ in the most excellent and particular way' (W. Cockburn, *A Continuation of the Account of the Nature,*

Causes, Symptoms and Cure of the Distempers that are Incident to Seafaring People, 1697, sigs. A9v–A10). Abroad, a new generation of clinically inclined physicians applauded Sydenham: for instance, an eminent professor at Leiden University, Herman Boerhaave, always mentioned him with respect. Because of his reliance on detailed evidence derived from the senses alone, Sydenham's close associate John Locke mentioned him alongside Huygens and Newton in the preface to his *Essay Concerning Human Understanding*. Most notoriously, in two prefaces to his own works, Richard Blackmore recounted:

> When one day I asked him to advise me what Books I should read to qualify me for practice, he replied, 'Read Don Quixot, it is a very good Book, I read it still.' So low an Opinion had this celebrated Man of the Learning collected out of the Authors, his Predecessors. (Meynell, 71)

Sydenham himself put the same point to William Gould in a letter of 10 December 1687:

> I can only say this, that as I have bin very carefull to write nothing but what was ye product of faithfull observation soe when ye scandall of my person shall be layd aside and I in my grave it will appear that I neither suffered my selfe to be deceived by indulging to idle speculations nor have deceived others by obtruding any thing upon them but downright matter of fact. (Meynell, 64–5)

Death and posthumous publications That sentence can serve as his epitaph, for Sydenham's continued sufferings were brought to an end two years later, on 29 December 1689, when he died at his house in Pall Mall, having lived long enough to see another ambitious English king providentially overthrown. He was buried on 31 December at St James's Church, Piccadilly, and his will (printed in Meynell, 56–60) was proved on 4 January 1690; Mr Malthus, a former patient and Pall Mall apothecary (and great-grandfather of the cleric and political economist Robert Malthus) was his executor. Sydenham's wife had apparently died before him. The couple left behind two sons, William (c.1660–1738) and Henry (1668?–1741); another son, James, apparently died young. Nothing is known about Henry. William entered Pembroke College, Cambridge, as a pensioner, on 18 February 1675, and matriculated in 1677. He was admitted to Lincoln's Inn, London, on 13 November 1677, studied medicine, and took an MD at a university abroad; he obtained the licence of the London College of Physicians, like his father before him, on 29 November 1687, and in 1719 published *Compendium praxeos medicae Sydenhami*, a compendium of his father's medical receipts.

A work entitled *Processus integri*, which detailed Sydenham's treatments for particular diseases, appeared in 1693, and is said to have been compiled for the use of his son. It immediately appeared in a version translated into English by the prolific William Salmon, entitled *Dr. Sydenham's Practice of Physick* (1693), with other editions following. An English translation of many of his works had begun in 1686, when John Pechey initiated the serial publication of Sydenham's work together with some excerpts from a few other authors, gathered together behind one title-page as *Collections of Acute Diseases* in 1691. Pechey included these translations in *The Whole Works* of Sydenham which he brought out in 1696 (a second, enlarged edition appeared in 1706). John Swan's 1742 translation of Sydenham's *Works*, with a life of Sydenham by Samuel Johnson, became the main English source for Sydenham's thoughts until that of R. G. Latham in two volumes (1848–50) superseded it. In the nineteenth century, a Sydenham Society continued to make his and like-minded works available in up-to-date editions. Sydenham's work and reputation were such that he earned the epithet of 'the English Hippocrates'. HAROLD J. COOK

Sources G. G. Meynell, *Materials for a biography of Dr Thomas Sydenham* (1988) · K. Dewhurst, *Dr Thomas Sydenham (1624–1689): his life and original writings* (1966) · D. Bates, 'Thomas Sydenham: the development of his thought, 1666–1676', PhD diss., Johns Hopkins University, 1975 · J. F. Payne, *Thomas Sydenham* (1900) · J. D. Comrie, ed., *Selected works of Thomas Sydenham, M.D., with a short biography* (1922) · *CSP dom.*, 1650–52; 1659–60 · *The correspondence of John Locke*, ed. E. S. De Beer (1976–89) · *The works of Robert Boyle*, ed. M. Hunter and E. B. Davis (1999) · R. G. Latham, trans., *The works of Thomas Sydenham, M.D., with a life of the author*, 2 vols. (1848–50) · R. W. Innes Smith, *English-speaking students of medicine at the University of Leyden* (1932)
Archives Bodl. Oxf., notebook · CUL, *Theologia rationalis* · PRO, notes, PRO 30/24/47/2 · RCP Lond., medical observations | Bodl. Oxf., papers and letters to John Locke · PRO, Shaftesbury papers
Likenesses after M. Beale?, portrait, *c*.1672, RCP Lond. · oils, 1680?, RCP Lond. · M. Beale, oils, 1688, NPG [*see illus.*] · A. Blooteling, line engraving (after M. Beale), BM, NPG; repro. in T. Sydenham, *Observationes medicae* (1676) · J. Houbraken, line engraving (after P. Lely), BM, NPG; repro. in Birch, *Heads* (1747) · attrib. P. Lely, portrait, RCP Lond. · E. Sadler, oils, Hatfield House, Hertfordshire
Wealth at death see will, repr. in Meynell, *Materials*, 56–61

Sydenham, William, appointed Lord Sydenham under the protectorate (*bap.* 1615, *d.* 1661), parliamentarian army officer, was baptized at Wynford Eagle, Dorset, on 8 April 1615, the eldest son of William Sydenham (1593–1661) of Wynford Eagle and his wife, Mary (*d.* 1644), daughter of Sir John Jeffrey of Catherston, Dorset. It is claimed that he attended Trinity College, Oxford, but there is no evidence of his admission or graduation. In 1637 he married Grace (*d.* 1661), daughter of John Trenchard of Warmwell, Dorset.

When the civil war broke out Sydenham and his three younger brothers (among them the future physician Thomas *Sydenham) took up arms for parliament, and distinguished themselves by their activity in the local struggle. Sydenham was one of a knot of leading parliamentarian gentry—among them his father-in-law—who dominated the county committee. By April 1644 Sydenham had risen to the rank of colonel, and on 17 June 1644 the earl of Essex appointed him governor of Weymouth. In July, Sydenham defeated a plundering party from the garrison of Wareham at Dorchester, and hanged six or eight of his prisoners as 'Irish rogues' (Vicars, 286). This gave rise to equally cruel reprisals on the part of the royalists. In conjunction with Sir Anthony Ashley Cooper, Sydenham captured Wareham (10 August 1644) and Abbotsbury House. He also defeated Sir Lewis Dyve, the

commander-in-chief of the Dorset royalists, in various skirmishes, in one of which he killed, with his own hand, Major Williams, whom he accused of the murder of his mother. In February 1645 Sir Lewis Dyve surprised Weymouth, but Sydenham and the garrison of Melcombe Regis succeeded in regaining it a fortnight later. In November 1645 Sydenham was elected member for the seat of Melcombe Regis and Weymouth; and on 1 March 1648 the House of Lords ordered him £1000 towards his arrears of pay to be raised by discoveries of delinquents' lands. On 14 August 1649 he and Colonel Charles Fleetwood were appointed joint governors of the Isle of Wight.

Sydenham withdrew from parliament at Pride's Purge in December 1648. In February 1649 he appeared in the Commons to vote against the abolition of the House of Lords. Although he served on many committees of the Rump Parliament his political importance really began with its expulsion in 1653. He was a member of the council of thirteen appointed by the officers of the army (29 April 1653), was summoned to the nominated assembly (Barebone's Parliament), telling the votes in favour of designating it a parliament, and was re-elected by that assembly to the council of state on 9 July and 1 November 1653. His views, however, were too conservative for him to sympathize with the policy of Barebone's Parliament. On 10 December 1653 he counted the votes of the minority who supported the retention of an established church. Two days later Sydenham took the lead in proposing that the assembly should dissolve itself, and may therefore be considered one of the founders of the protectorate. Cromwell appointed Sydenham a member of his council, and made him also one of the commissioners of the treasury. His salary as councillor was £1000 a year, and he enjoyed a similar sum as commissioner. Sydenham sat for Dorset in the parliaments of 1654 and 1656, distinguishing himself during the debates of the latter by his opposition to the exorbitant punishment the house wished to inflict on James Nayler. When the protector's intervention on behalf of Nayler raised a complaint of breach of privilege, Sydenham recalled the house to the real question. 'We live as parliament men but for a time, but we live as Englishmen always. I would not have us be so tender of the privilege of parliament as to forget the liberties of Englishmen' (*Diary of Thomas Burton*, 1.274). He also spoke against anti-Quaker legislation, and during the discussion of the petition and advice against the imposition of oaths and engagements. Although he sided with the army officers in opposing the offer of the crown to Cromwell, in December 1657 Sydenham was summoned to Cromwell's House of Lords. A republican pamphlet remarked that, though 'he hath not been thorough-paced for tyranny in time of parliaments,' it was hoped he might yet be 'so redeemed as never to halt or stand off for the future against the Protector's interest'.

After the death of Oliver Cromwell, Sydenham became one of Richard Cromwell's council; but in April 1659 he acted with Charles Fleetwood, Desborough, and what was termed the Wallingford House party to force him to dissolve his parliament. According to Edmund Ludlow he was one of the chief agents in the negotiation between the army leaders and the republicans which led to Richard's fall.

On the restoration of the Long Parliament, Sydenham became a member of the committee of safety (7 May 1659) and of the council of state (16 May), though he had conscientious scruples against taking the oath required from members of the latter. He was also given the command of a regiment of foot. When John Lambert turned out the Long Parliament again Sydenham took part with the army, and was made a member of their committee of safety. He even attempted to justify the violence of the army to the council of state, 'undertaking to prove that they were necessitated to make use of this last remedy by a particular call of divine Providence' (*Memoirs of Edmund Ludlow*, 2.140). When the Long Parliament was again restored Sydenham was called to answer for his conduct, and, failing to give a satisfactory explanation, was expelled (17 January 1660). His regiment also was taken from him and given to John Lenthall, the speaker's son. At the Restoration the Act of Indemnity included him among the eighteen persons perpetually incapacitated from holding any office (29 August 1660), and he was also obliged to enter into a bond not to disturb the peace of the kingdom.

Sydenham died in July 1661 and was buried at Wynford Eagle on 1 August. His widow died about a week later and was buried eight days after her husband. His eldest son, William, had predeceased him, so the estate passed to the latter's son William.   C. H. FIRTH, *rev.* SEAN KELSEY

Sources D. Brunton and D. Pennington, *Members of the Long Parliament* (1954) • GEC, *Peerage* • D. Underdown, *Pride's Purge: politics in the puritan revolution* (1971) • A. Woolrych, *Commonwealth to protectorate* (1982) • A. R. Bayley, *The great civil war in Dorset, 1642–1660* (1910) • 'A second narrative of the late parliament (so called)', *The Harleian miscellany*, ed. W. Oldys and T. Park, 10 vols. (1808–13), vol. 3, pp. 470–89 • J. Hutchins, *The history and antiquities of the county of Dorset*, 4 vols. (1861–70), vol. 2 • J. Vicars, *God's arke over-topping the waves* (1646) • *CSP dom.*, 1644; 1649–50; 1658–61 • *The memoirs of Edmund Ludlow*, ed. C. H. Firth, 2 vols. (1894) • J. Rushworth, *Historical collections*, new edn, 5 (1721) • *JHL*, 7 (1644–5) • *JHC*, 7 (1651–9) • *Diary of Thomas Burton*, ed. J. T. Rutt, 4 vols. (1828) • W. B. Devereux, *Lives and letters of the Devereux, earls of Essex … 1540–1646*, 2 (1853), 418 • will, PRO, PROB 11/306, sig. 206 • G. Bankes, *The story of Corfe Castle* (1853)
Archives BL, Add. MS 29319, Egerton MS 2126, corresp. and papers as governor of Weymouth and Isle of Wight
Wealth at death made extensive gifts and bequests to friends and the local poor, and numerous legacies worth around £2,000 to various relatives: PRO, PROB 11/306, sig. 206

Sydney. For this title name *see* Townshend, Thomas, first Viscount Sydney (1733–1800).

Sydserff, Thomas (1581–1663), bishop of Orkney, was the eldest son of James Sydserff, an Edinburgh merchant. He graduated from the University of Edinburgh on 22 February 1602, and was enrolled as a student at the University of Heidelberg in 1609. He entered into the ministry, firstly at St Giles's, Edinburgh, to which he was admitted on 30 May 1611, before being translated to Trinity College Church as minister of the north-east quarter of Edinburgh on 26 January 1626. On 27 April 1614 he married Rachel, daughter of John Byers, an Edinburgh magistrate.

In 1617 Sydserff signed the protestation defending the liberties of the kirk. He was, however, present at the meeting of bishops and other ministers to discuss the introduction of a liturgy which took place during the king's visit to Scotland in 1633. In 1634 he was made dean of Edinburgh, a position which he held only briefly as, on the recommendation of Archbishop William Laud, he was promoted to the bishopric of Brechin and consecrated on 29 July 1634. His appointment to the see of Galloway was signed by Charles I on 30 August 1635, and he was installed the following November.

Sydserff was labelled, probably with some accuracy, as an Arminian by his presbyterian opponents, one of whom described him as 'a violent, virulent man, a great urger of conformity in Edinburgh' (Row, 375). Sydserff made active use of his episcopal powers against those who did not support his ecclesiastical viewpoint. In 1636 he summoned Samuel Rutherford, the minister of Anwoth, before the court of high commission and banished him to Aberdeen for publishing a treatise against Arminianism. He also sought to confine Alexander Gordon of Earlstoun to Wigtown for preventing the entry of an episcopal nominee into a parish. His most serious dispute was in 1636 with Kirkcudbright town council, which he attempted to force to accept the deposition of their parish minister, Robert Glendinning. It was during Sydserff's episcopate that the nave of Whithorn Priory was remodelled to accommodate the new styles of worship, including the raising of the east end as a platform for an altar.

As a prominent supporter of the religious policies of Charles I, Sydserff was a target for mob violence at the hand of those who opposed the introduction of the new service book in 1637. He was attacked at Falkirk, at Dalkeith, and, on 18 October 1637, by rioters in Edinburgh said to have been led by a group of women who 'after some quarrelling of him for his crucifix began to pluck at him and affray him' (*Letters and Journals of Robert Baillie*, 1.21). Sydserff was formally deposed by the general assembly on 13 December 1638 and retired first to England, where he was with Charles I at Newcastle in 1645, and later to the continent. He spent several years in Paris, where on at least one occasion (5 June 1651) he conducted ordinations at Sir Richard Browne's chapel. As the sole survivor of the pre-1638 episcopate at the Restoration, Sydserff was translated to the bishopric of Orkney in 1661. He lived in Edinburgh, however, where he died on 29 September 1663.   SHARON ADAMS

Sources *Fasti Scot.*, new edn • J. Row, *The history of the Kirk of Scotland, from the year 1558 to August 1637*, ed. D. Laing, Wodrow Society, 4 (1842) • W. Scot, *An apologetical narration of the state and government of the Kirk of Scotland since the Reformation*, ed. D. Laing, Wodrow Society, 19 (1846) • *The letters and journals of Robert Baillie*, ed. D. Laing, 3 vols. (1841–2) · John, earl of Rothes, *A relation of proceedings concerning the affairs of the Kirk of Scotland*, Bannatyne Club, 37 (1830) · Evelyn, *Diary*, 3.8–9

Syers [*née* Cave], **Florence Madeline** [Madge] (**1881/2–1917**), ice-skater, was one of fifteen children of Edward Jarvis Cave, a gentleman of independent means. Nothing more is known of her childhood. As a young woman, Madge's ability as a skater was revealed at the fashionable Prince's Club ice rink in Knightsbridge, where she quickly displayed more than a social interest in the sport, excelling at the relatively restrictive, formal style that was favoured by English skaters. In 1899, at eighteen, she won the challenge shield in a team event and shortly afterwards met her future husband, Edgar Morris Wood Syers (1863–1946), described as a gentleman of independent means, the son of Morris Robert Syers, merchant.

Edgar Syers was a skater eighteen years Madge's senior who, as an advocate of the more artistic and athletic international skating technique, considerably influenced the development of his wife's performance on the ice. He encouraged her to abandon English skating convention, placing emphasis instead upon aestheticism and ambitious, physically demanding movements. As pioneers in England of this international style, the couple won the first British pairs skating competition in Brighton in 1899, and in January 1900 distinguished themselves further in one of the first international pairs events in Berlin, where they came second to an Austrian couple. In the same year on 23 June, Madge and Edgar were married.

Two years later Madge Syers submitted her entry to compete in the figure-skating world championships held by the International Skating Union (ISU) in London against the Swedish defending champion, Ulrich Salchow, Martin Gordan of Berlin, and Horatio Torrome of Argentina. The event had been exclusively male and the ISU condemned Madge Syers's entry, but found that there was no provision in the rules of the contest for her exclusion. Cutting a striking figure in the contest, her slight frame clothed in an ankle-length wool skirt, satin blouse, doeskin gloves, and pearls, Syers quashed the ISU's outrage by winning second place, beaten only by Salchow; in addition, she won first place with Edgar in the pairs event. As a direct result of her successful participation in the competition, the ISU at its congress in Budapest in 1903 imposed a ban on women, preventing them from entering future championships. Madge Syers's reaction to the ban demonstrated her characteristic mettle; owing to a technicality the ruling could not be implemented immediately, and in 1903 she entered and won the first British singles championship, beating Torrome. In January 1904 she went on to win fourth place in the compulsory figures event in the European championships in Davos, Switzerland, and two months later she defended her title in the Swedish cup, defeating her husband to win it a second time. Her comprehensive series of victories over male skaters forced the ISU to admit that women skaters were as skilled and able as men, and in 1905 the ban on women was lifted. In 1906 a separate ladies' event was introduced at the world championships as a consequence of Syers's achievement.

Madge won the first ladies' championship in Davos in 1906 and again in Vienna in 1907, and the contest became an important international platform for women skaters, revealing existing and emerging talent.

By the time of the 1908 summer Olympics, held in London, Madge Syers was the world champion and home favourite. The figure-skating competition, held under the auspices of the International Olympic Committee and the National Skating Association of Great Britain, took place at the end of October, some weeks after the other events, at the Prince's Club, Knightsbridge, the rink where her career began. She was placed first by all five judges in the compulsory figures and free skating and became the first woman Olympic gold medallist in ice-skating. In the compulsory event it was reported that 'she has never given a better performance; its essential power was concealed by the ease of execution' (*The Times*, 29 Oct 1908, 10), while in the free skating her programme was described as being more difficult than that attempted by any of the other competitors, and was performed 'with her own particular dash and finish' (*The Times*, 30 Oct 1908, 5). In addition, she won a bronze medal with Edgar in the pairs event. These Olympic successes were to be her final appearances. Her health, which had caused her to withdraw from the British championships in February 1908, began to fade and she retired from skating. Shortly afterwards she fell ill with acute endocarditis, and on 9 September 1917 she died of heart failure at her home, Shaws, St George's Hill, Weybridge, Surrey, at the age of thirty-five.

Edgar Syers had been an active promoter of winter sports in Britain, and had helped to found a national figure skating club in 1901 and a ski club in 1903, but after Madge's death he became embittered with the National Skating Association, of which he was secretary. In 1921 he married Eva Victoria Critchel, aged twenty-four, and died in Maidenhead in 1946.   JUDITH WILSON

Sources I. Buchanan, *British Olympians: a hundred years of gold medallists* (1991) · D. L. Bird, *Our skating heritage: a centenary history of the National Skating Association of Great Britain, 1879–1979* (1979) · M. F. Heller, *The illustrated encyclopedia of ice skating* (1979) · S. Milton, *Skate: 100 years of figure skating* (1996) · L. Stephenson, *A history and annotated bibliography of skating costume* (1970) · m. cert. · d. cert.
Likenesses photograph, 1910, repro. in Bird, *Our skating heritage*
Wealth at death £975 7s. 9d.: probate, 1 March 1918, CGPLA Eng. & Wales

Syfret, Sir (Edward) Neville (1889–1972), naval officer, was born in Cape Town, Cape Colony, on 20 June 1889, the second child of five of Edward Ridge Syfret, a surgeon in Cape Town, and his wife, whose family name was Jones. His only brother was killed in the First World War. His early education was at the Diocesan College in South Africa and he passed into HMS *Britannia* at Dartmouth in 1904, becoming a chief cadet captain during his final year. In 1909, as a lieutenant, he specialized in gunnery and during the First World War was gunnery officer of the battle cruisers *Aurora*, *Centaur*, and *Curaçao*, all of which served for varying periods as flagship of Reginald Tyrwhitt commanding the Harwich force.

In 1913 Syfret married Hildegarde (d. 1976), daughter of

Sir (Edward) Neville Syfret (1889–1972), by Walter Stoneman, 1942

Herbert Warner, of Hyères, France; they had one son and one daughter.

Syfret was promoted commander in 1922 and captain in 1929 and on the outbreak of the Second World War was commanding the *Rodney* in the Home Fleet. Near the top of the captains' list and recognized in the navy as an 'intellectual', he was selected in November 1939 as naval secretary to the first lord, serving both Winston Churchill until he became prime minister in May 1940 and his successor, A. V. Alexander. He was promoted rear-admiral in 1940 and was appointed to command one of the Home Fleet cruiser squadrons, flying his flag in the *Edinburgh*. His first chance of showing his quality in command came a month later when his squadron was ordered to the Mediterranean as a temporary reinforcement for force H, based on Gibraltar, for an operation to pass a convoy of reinforcements and stores to Malta. Syfret was in charge of the last stages of the operation after the heavy ships of force H had turned back on reaching the Sicilian narrows, and, by taking the bold course of steering directly towards the enemy bases in Sicily, the attacking Italian aircraft were thrown off the scent. The success of the operation was complete, the convoy reaching Malta without the loss of a single ship. Syfret was appointed CB (1941) for his skill and daring in getting the convoy through.

In January 1942 Syfret succeeded Vice-Admiral Sir James Somerville in command of force H. His first major operation in this new command was the capture of Diego Suarez harbour in Madagascar to deny its use to Japanese

naval forces in the Indian Ocean. With force H, temporarily renamed force F and reinforced with units of the Home Fleet, an amphibious assault was planned on the harbour defences resolutely held by pro-Vichy French troops. To avoid the inevitable difficulties and casualties of a frontal attack on the harbour installations, Syfret directed his attack across the narrow isthmus at the rear of the harbour in spite of the navigational difficulties of approaching a rock-bound coast at night through narrow channels which had been mined. Complete surprise was achieved and the harbour was captured intact after only a few hours of hard fighting.

Syfret's next major operation was the passage of another convoy to Malta in August 1942. Known as operation Pedestal, it was probably the best-remembered and hardest fought of all the great convoy battles in the Mediterranean. For over two days the convoy and its escorting force were repeatedly attacked by day and night by heavy concentrations of German and Italian submarines and aircraft and by Italian motor-torpedo boats, and though several ships were sunk or damaged, five merchant ships were successfully brought to Malta with sufficient stores to maintain the island until its siege was lifted with the allied invasion of north Africa. Syfret was promoted KCB (1942) 'for bravery and dauntless resolution in fighting an important convoy through to Malta'.

In November 1942 an enlarged force H played a crucial part in covering the allied landings in north Africa from possible attacks by the Italian fleet, and later dominated the central Mediterranean to enable convoys to resupply and reinforce Malta without loss in preparation for the next offensives against Sicily and Italy. A serious illness forced Syfret to relinquish his command of force H in January 1943 but he was sufficiently recovered by June of that year to be appointed vice-chief of naval staff (VCNS), having been promoted vice-admiral in the meantime.

Syfret's undoubted qualities of quick decision making and intellectual approach to problems made him an ideal choice as VCNS and he proved an admirable partner for Admiral of the Fleet Sir Andrew Cunningham in the top direction of the war when Cunningham became first sea lord in October 1943. To Syfret as VCNS fell much of the overall direction of the allied landings in Normandy and the subsequent naval capture and clearance of French, Belgian, and Dutch ports as the armies advanced in Europe. To him also fell the organization and implementation of the British decision to send a major fleet into the Pacific to assist the United States in the naval war against Japan. At the end of his two years as VCNS in 1945 he was appointed KBE. He became admiral in 1946.

Shortly after the end of the war Syfret received his last appointment as commander-in-chief of the Home Fleet, a post he held for three difficult years. The run-down of the navy from a war to a peace establishment, accompanied by the problems of the demobilization of personnel, presented considerable difficulties in the maintenance of efficiency in the fleet, but throughout his three years of command he kept the Home Fleet in a state of high morale and readiness for any duty with which it might be faced. He was promoted GCB (1948) at the end of his tenure of this command and was placed on the retired list. Syfret died at his home in Highgate, London, on 10 December 1972. PETER KEMP, *rev.*

Sources *The Times* (11 Dec 1972) · S. W. Roskill, *The war at sea, 1939–1945*, 3 vols. in 4 (1954–61) · private information (1986) · *WWW*
Archives FILM BFI NFTVA, news footage · IWM FVA, news footage
Likenesses W. Stoneman, photograph, 1942, NPG [*see illus.*] · O. Birky, oils, *c.*1945–1948, Royal Naval College, Greenwich · W. Dring, pastel drawing, IWM

Sykes, Sir **Alan John** (1868–1950), industrialist and politician, was born on 11 April 1868 at Cringle House, Cheadle, Cheshire, the second son of Thomas Hardcastle Sykes (1833–1901), a bleacher, and his wife, Mary, the eldest daughter of John Platt, a machine manufacturer of Oldham and his wife, Alice. He was educated at Rugby School and Oriel College, Oxford, where he imbibed a strong sense of duty and a lasting attachment to freemasonry. Sykes served his apprenticeship in the long-established family bleachworks, Sykes & Co., at Stockport, but also occasionally visited Canada to oversee the family's farm there, the largest in Saskatchewan. He took over management of the bleachworks in 1900, when the firm joined the Bleachers' Association, one of the three large mergers which transformed the structure of the textile finishing industry. He acted as secretary of the formation committee of the Bleachers' Association and was a founder director, but in 1908 retired from the management of Sykes & Co.

Sir Alan John Sykes (1868–1950), by unknown photographer, *c.*1913

Increasingly Sykes's energies were absorbed in local political and social affairs, while he still undertook much foreign travel, including motoring to Russia. He was adopted as Conservative candidate for Knutsford in 1907 and became a leading Conservative organizer in the northwest, helping to rebuild the party in the face of the strong local challenges of Labour and the new Liberalism. A keen tariff-reformer, in January 1910 Sykes won Knutsford (ironically defeating a fellow director of the Bleachers' Association), which he retained in December 1910. In 1912 he had gained control of the Stockport-based Swain group of newspapers in order to create a reliable organ of toryism, a result secured for the next generation by the setting up of the Sir Alan Sykes Trust in 1943.

Within parliament, Sykes's main interest lay in his vigorous support of Britain's voluntary defence forces, both before and during the First World War. He was a member of the Officers' Training Corps at Oxford and commanded the 6th battalion, the Cheshire regiment from 1911 to 1914. Although he was unfit for active service in 1914, as an influential social leader he devoted himself enthusiastically to the volunteer movement during the war. He also acted as a government commissioner reviewing alien permits. He received a baronetcy in July 1917. In the House of Commons, however, Sykes had made little mark, and although he was re-elected in 1918 he resigned his seat in 1922 on grounds of ill health. Already holding 'more

offices than he can remember' (*Manchester Guardian Commercial*, 17 May 1923), he continued to play an important part in the networks of regional Conservatism, as *inter alia* chairman of the Cheshire division of the national union, treasurer of the North-West Provincial Conservative Association (1933–47), and chairman of the Knutsford Conservative Association (1922–46).

However, in 1916 Sykes's public stature as well as his industrial experience recommended him as chairman of the Bleachers' Association, which by 1914 had succeeded in gaining control of some two-thirds of the British market in cotton bleaching and employed some 13,000 operatives in what was now a reasonably profitable modern corporate enterprise. Having been heavily engaged in munitions production, the Bleachers' Association was well placed after the war to consolidate its market share and buy up competitors (between 1918 and 1927 twenty-one firms were acquired at a cost of some £1.99 million). This enabled it to maintain high prices, to an extent which, some believed, jeopardized British exports, now facing strong overseas competition. Sykes's own industrial philosophy was perhaps best seen in the enlightened welfare policy the firm adopted, with generous pensions provision, recreational facilities, and two model villages on garden city lines. The relative success of the Bleachers' Association was also well advertised by its showpiece headquarters, Blackfriars House, Manchester, opened in 1926.

From 1926 the firm's fortunes were steadily eroded, especially after 1929 as the market for British exports of bleached white goods plummeted. This required a new strategy for survival, which owed most to the firm's managing director Sir William Clare Lees. As chairman, however, Sykes supported within the firm the need for cost-cutting rationalization of production, technological modernization, overseas investment (in partnership with the Calico Printers and Bradford Dyers), and diversification beyond bleaching. Outside the firm he urged the importance of imperial trade and industrial protection, and was gradually won over to the need for governmental intervention in the cotton trade; he supported the Cotton Industry (Reorganization) Act of 1939. After 1945, while a critic of some aspects of planning, he welcomed the Labour government's export drive as the means to restore profits and dividends. Sykes remained chairman of the firm until his death, three weeks short of its fiftieth anniversary. He was also a director of Williams and Glyn's Bank (1918–48), an early supporter of the Federation of British Industries, and president for many years of the Lancashire and Cheshire Economic League.

Following family tradition, Sykes was a pre-eminent leader in the local community. He was a county magistrate from 1897 until 1950, the first chairman of the Cheshire police authority, and mayor of Stockport in 1910. He contributed largely to the success of Stockport grammar school as chairman of its governors (1921–50) and perhaps above all to Stockport Infirmary, the board of which he joined in 1897 and which he chaired between 1918 and 1948. Among other offices, he was chairman of the Manchester Northern Hospital (1928–48), of the Ephraim Hallam Trust in Stockport, and of the Oldham Blue Coat School. He thus well exemplified the voluntary ethic whose undermining he regretted with the growing welfare provision by the state after 1945.

Even so this public face concealed a shy, retiring man, whose main satisfaction, one suspects, may well have been derived from the hidden world of the freemasons. Here Sykes held a panoply of offices, ranging from grand deacon in the grand lodge of England in 1907 to that (in which he succeeded in 1948 the seventeenth earl of Derby) of grand superintendent of the Lancashire (east division) provincial grand chapter of the Royal Arch masons. Most at home in the mess, the boardroom, and the lodge, Sykes was a confirmed bachelor with a taste for yellow Rolls-Royces and annual gastronomic tours of France. At his home, South View, Cheadle, in suburban south Manchester, he lived with an excellent cook, a well-stocked cellar, and a number of loyal retainers. He died there on 21 May 1950.   A. C. HOWE

Sources A. C. Howe, 'Sykes, Sir Alan John', *DBB* · A. J. Sykes, *Concerning the bleaching industry* (1925) · *Manchester Guardian* (22 May 1950) · *The Times* (22 May 1950) · *Stockport Advertiser* (26 May 1950) · E. J. W. Disbrowe, *History of the volunteer movement: Cheshire, 1914–1920* (1920) · J. Christie-Miller, *Stockport and the Stockport Advertiser: a history* (1972) · D. J. Jeremy, 'Survival strategies in Lancashire textiles: Bleachers' Association to Whitecroft plc, 1900–1980s', *Textile History*, 24 (1993), 163–209 · d. cert.

Archives North-West Region Conservative Federation, Manchester, party archives · Quarry Bank Mill, Styal, Cheshire, Bleachers' Association business records · Whitecroft Holdings plc, Wilmslow, Cheshire, Bleachers' Association minutes, etc. · Knutsford, Cheshire, Tatton Conservative Association records

Likenesses photograph, c.1913, NPG [*see illus.*] · photograph, c.1914, repro. in Disbrowe, *History of the volunteer movement*, 6 · photograph, c.1950, repro. in Christie-Miller, *Stockport and the Stockport Advertiser* · photograph, repro. in Sykes, *Concerning the bleaching industry*, facing p. 31

Wealth at death £186,364 18s.: probate, 9 Aug 1950, CGPLA Eng. & Wales

Sykes, Arthur Ashley (c.1684–1756), Church of England clergyman and religious controversialist, was born in London, one of three sons of John Sykes (1622–1695), successively vicar of Ardeley and rector of Cottered in Hertfordshire. He was educated at St Paul's School, proceeding to Corpus Christi College, Cambridge, as an exhibitioner on 15 April 1701. He was elected to a scholarship on 4 February 1702 and graduated BA in 1705, MA in 1708, and DD in 1726. It seems he was briefly an assistant usher at St Paul's about 1705, and he kept up a connection with the school for the rest of his life. He was ordained deacon by the bishop of Norwich on 23 December 1705, and priest by the bishop of Ely on 21 December 1707. He was presented to the vicarage of Godmersham, Kent, on 7 February 1713 by Archbishop Tenison, a post he resigned on 12 April 1714 on presentation to the rectory of Dry Drayton by the dowager duchess of Bedford. This was near enough to Cambridge for him to observe events in the university and prepare a pamphlet in support of the disputatious master of Trinity, Richard Bentley. He remained there until presented by Robert Bristow MP, on 17 November 1718, to the rectory of Rayleigh, Essex, where he remained until his death, residing both there and in London. He married Elizabeth Williams (d. 1763), a widow and native of Bristol; they had no children.

Sykes's friendship with Samuel Clarke led to a connection with St James's, Westminster, and he became, on Clarke's nomination, afternoon preacher at its chapel of ease, King Street Chapel, Golden Square, from 22 December 1718, and successively morning preacher from 1721, and assistant preacher at St James's itself from 14 April 1725. Isaac Newton was a prominent member of his congregation, and Sykes was asked to prepare some of Newton's theological works for publication by Newton's niece, Catherine Conduitt, in her will, but nothing came of this proposal. He was presented to the deanery of St Buryan, Cornwall, on 28 February 1739, to prebendal stalls at Salisbury in 1724 and 1727, and at Winchester in 1740 by Benjamin Hoadley.

Sykes was a prolific controversialist, the author of about eighty pamphlets. In the first of these, a reply to the nonjuror Thomas Brett, Sykes defended the validity of baptism performed by dissenters. This work served as the prelude to his arguments, set out in *The Innocency of Error Asserted* (1715), which attempted to establish that scripture alone serves as the rule and testimony of truth, and consequently that no interpretation of the scriptures, 'where industry and honesty and diligence have been applied to find out truth', is culpable. He maintained that the church could not lay down absolute standards of doctrine, nor could any form of church government claim to be divinely ordained. He concluded, therefore, that claims to the contrary, whether from nonjurors or from high-church Anglicans, should be rejected, and as much latitude as possible should be allowed in the case of subscription to the Anglican articles. Sykes had already defended Samuel Clarke's Arian views of the Trinity in *A Modest Appeal for the Baptismal and Scriptural Notion of the Trinity* (1719) and anticipated Hoadley's views on the nature of the church, which he in turn defended, notably against Thomas Sherlock. Later he supported the dissenters in their attempts to have the Test and Corporation Acts repealed.

In 1721 Daniel Waterland, who had already attacked Clarke's views on the Trinity, took issue with Sykes in his *Case of Arian Subscription Considered*, arguing that scripture, interpreted in the light of the early fathers, was a certain authority in matters of both doctrine and church order. Sykes replied in the same year, reiterating his own views while questioning the propriety of Waterland's willingness to assent to supposedly Calvinist articles in an Arminian sense. He continued to oppose Waterland's views, not least his suppositions that participation in the sacrament was a positive ordinance and that ethical values were consequent on the benevolence of the divine will, to which Sykes counterposed Clarke's *a priori* view that good was necessarily good. Sykes's views were consolidated in his *Answer* (1730) to Waterland's attack on Clarke's posthumously published exposition of the catechism, and in his substantial book entitled *Principles and Connexion of Natural and Revealed Theology* (1740). He followed this up with an *Examination* (1744) of William Warburton's *Divine Legation*, in which he disputed Warburton's supposition that its lack of reference to any future state proved the divine origin of the Mosaic dispensation. Sykes further insisted that scripture had a single determinate meaning, and thereby avoided Warburton's allegorical and prophetic interpretations. He also disputed Warburton's account of Jewish theocracy, chronology, and the double meaning interpretation of ancient philosophy which recognized both exoteric and esoteric meanings. This led to an exchange of pamphlets between the two men during 1745 and 1746. Sykes also wrote interestingly on miracles; the gospel demoniacs, who he argued were merely insane; and on Phlegon, when he denied, contrary to William Whiston, that the eclipse described by Phlegon was that seen at the crucifixion. Overall Sykes's writings, especially his letters, show a wry wit, a detached interest in ecclesiastical politics and a bemused tolerance of his contemporaries.

Sykes was short, somewhat inclined to corpulency, and of a fresh complexion, though slightly marked with smallpox. After having suffered for many years from gout and the stone, he died of a stroke at his home in Cavendish Square, London, on 23 November 1756 and was buried in St James's on 30 November. His substantial estate was left successively to his wife, who died in January 1763, and his brother George.   JOHN STEPHENS

Sources J. Disney, *Memoirs of the life and writings of Arthur Ashley Sykes* (1785) [incl. complete listing of Sykes's writings] · M. McDonnell, ed., *The registers of St Paul's School, 1509–1748* (privately printed, London, 1977), 341, 350 · *Masters' History of the college of Corpus Christi and the Blessed Virgin Mary in the University of Cambridge*, ed. J. Lamb (1831), 282 · Venn, *Alum. Cant.* · *Fasti Angl., 1541–1857*, [Canterbury], 106 · *Fasti Angl., 1541–1857*, [Salisbury], 23 · *VCH Cambridgeshire and the Isle of Ely*, 6.76, 86 · J. P. Ferguson, *An eighteenth century heretic: Dr Samuel Clarke* (1976) · J. H. Colligan, *The Arian movement in England* (1913), 39–40 · I. Newton, *Theological manuscripts, selected and edited … by H. McLachlan* (1950), 3–4 · R. M. Holtby, *William Waterland* (1964) · A. W. Evans, *Warburton and the Warburtonians: a study in some eighteenth-century controversies* (1932) · R. M. Burns, *The great debate on miracles: from Joseph Glanvill to David Hume* (1981) · M. Wiles, *Archetypal heresy: Arianism through the centuries* (1996) · *DNB*
Archives Emory University, Georgia, Atlanta, Pitts Theology Library, corresp. and papers | BL, letters to Thomas Birch and biographical notes on him, Add MS 4319, fols. 70–91 · BL, letters to Cox Macro, Add MS 32556, fols. 154, 241
Likenesses J. Wills, portrait, priv. coll.; formerly in possession of Bristow family, 1785
Wealth at death substantial estate; legacies to Bristow family; also scholarships at Corpus Christi, Cambridge, and St Paul's: Disney, *Memoirs*

Sykes, Sir Charles (1905–1982), physicist and metallurgist, was born on 27 February 1905 in Clowne, Derbyshire, the only child of Sam Sykes, greengrocer, and his wife, Louisa Webster. With a county scholarship he went to the Staveley Netherthorpe grammar school, travelling 5 miles each way daily by train. He thereby became a bridge and chess expert, and indeed he could play chess without a board. He seemed to succeed without trying: he was good at all sports, gained three distinctions in the higher school certificate, and won scholarships to Leeds, Liverpool, and Sheffield universities. He chose Sheffield and gained a first-class honours BSc in physics in 1925.

Sykes was awarded a Department of Scientific and Industrial Research grant to do two years' research in physics but after one year the Metropolitan-Vickers Electrical Company of Trafford Park, Manchester, offered him a two-year research studentship to continue work on the alloys of zirconium which had been begun by one of their other scholars in the metallurgy department of the university. His professor generously allowed Sykes to change horses and thus he entered into a career in applied science in which he remained all his life. He published the work on zirconium with his collaborator and was awarded the degree of PhD in metallurgy in 1928 before being appointed to the staff of the research department of Metropolitan-Vickers. In 1930 he married Norah, daughter of Joseph Edward Staton, manager of the Clowne Mineral Water Company. They had a son and a daughter.

In Manchester, Sykes continued metallurgical work with a vacuum induction furnace similar to the one he had used in Sheffield, helped to design and construct larger versions, and produced great quantities of steels and other alloys. One aluminium/iron alloy greatly puzzled him: above a certain temperature its coefficient of expansion and its electrical resistivity suddenly changed. X-ray analysis showed that below that critical temperature the atoms were well ordered, while above that temperature the structure became disorganized, and thus Sykes began a new branch of physical metallurgy known as order/disorder. It was his work on this discovery that earned him the fellowship of the Royal Society in 1943. Sykes then studied metals harder than diamond, such as tungsten carbide, which were used for making cutting tools. He added other elements to increase hardness and toughness and developed a huge business. His hard metals were put into the tips of the armour piercing shells used so effectively at the battle of Alamein.

In 1940 Sykes was appointed superintendent of the metallurgy division at the National Physical Laboratory; he was shocked at the lax attitude of the staff in wartime, which was so different from the vigour prevailing in the laboratories in Trafford Park. He supervised the work on armour piercing shells, discovering ways of measuring the hardness inside the tips. The armaments research department at Fort Halstead asked him to take charge of their ballistics department while he continued his work at the National Physical Laboratory. He accepted the directorship of the Brown–Firth research department in Sheffield in 1944, contributing his great knowledge of armour piercing steels to the company's products and also to the special steels being developed for the novel high temperature gas turbines. These were steels which had very low creep so that the blades could run for 100,000 hours or more without failure. Sykes paid great attention to the growth of hair-line cracks, which have dominated metallurgical advances ever since, and he studied closely the part played by hydrogen in the failure of steel castings and forgings. In 1951 he became managing director of Thomas Firth and John Brown Ltd, in 1962 deputy chairman, and in 1964 chairman. He retired in 1967 but remained on the board for another six years.

Sykes was president of the Institute of Physics in 1952–4, chairman (1965–70) of the Advisory Council on Research and Development for Fuel and Power (Ministry of Power), a freeman of the Cutlers' Company of Hallamshire, a Sheffield magistrate, and pro-chancellor of Sheffield University (1967–71), which had given him the honorary degree of DMet in 1955. The Iron and Steel Institute awarded him the Bessemer gold medal (1956) and the Institute of Physics the Glazebrook medal (1967). He was appointed CBE in 1956 and knighted in 1964.

Sykes was one of very few graduates in pure physics who moved over to an applied science and reached the very top of their new profession; but he remained a dedicated scientist to the end, deceptively slow and careful of his words, critical, and constructive. In retirement he spent eleven years perfecting his gardening skills. Sykes died on 29 January 1982 at his home, Upholme, Blackamoor Crescent, Dore, Sheffield.   T. E. ALLIBONE, rev.

Sources T. E. Allibone, *Memoirs FRS*, 29 (1983), 553–83 · *WWW* · *The Times* (4 Feb 1982), 14g
Likenesses photograph, 1964, repro. in Allibone, *Memoirs FRS*

Wealth at death £102,814: probate, 5 March 1982, *CGPLA Eng. & Wales*

Sykes, Christopher (1831–1898). *See under* Sykes, Sir Tatton, fourth baronet (1772–1863).

Sykes, Christopher Hugh (1907–1986), writer and traveller, was born on 17 November 1907 in Sledmere, near Driffield, Yorkshire, the elder of twins and the second son and third child in the family of three sons and three daughters of Sir Mark *Sykes, sixth baronet (1879–1919), and his wife, Edith Violet (d. 1931), third daughter of Sir John Eldon *Gorst, solicitor-general. His father was first employed as honorary attaché to the British embassy in Constantinople, before helping to found the Arab Bureau with T. E. Lawrence and signing the Sykes–Picot agreement of 1916. Christopher followed an undistinguished academic career at Downside School and Christ Church, Oxford (which he left without a degree), by becoming honorary attaché at both the Berlin embassy (1928–9) and the British legation in Tehran (1930–31).

At Oxford, Sykes was thought of as a boisterous, if congenial, companion given to acts of bravado, rather like his early hero, and close friend of his father, Aubrey Herbert, the model for John Buchan's Greenmantle. Unlike Herbert or his father he was inhibited from embarking on a political career by a stutter, which grew more pronounced whenever the subject matter was such as might inspire disbelief. Since Sykes was chiefly interested in those areas of discussion which lie on the borders between personal experience, artistic embellishment, and fantasy, it was thought that a political career was closed to him. He took a course in Persian studies at the School of Oriental Studies, London, and in 1933 left for two years' travel in Persia and Afghanistan with Robert Byron. He wrote for *The Times*, *The Spectator*, and *The Observer*. In 1936 he married Camilla Georgiana (d. 1983), daughter of Sir Thomas Wentworth *Russell, pasha, chief of police in Cairo from 1917 to 1946, but this did little to improve the parlous financial situation of a younger son.

Of Sykes's writing before the war little survived after it: *Wassmus* (1936), a biography of the German Arabist, was followed by two light novels, one of them written under the puzzling pseudonym of Waughburton in collaboration with Robert Byron. The war itself saw him commissioned in the 7th battalion of the Green Howards. Later, as part of Special Operations Executive, he adorned general headquarters in Cairo when the presence of the Duff Coopers and other cronies made it the most elegant place to be, before being posted to Tehran as a spy attached to the British legation. Transferring to the 2nd battalion of the Special Air Service, he worked with the French resistance and was awarded the Croix de Guerre.

Many of these experiences came together in what will probably be seen as Sykes's masterpiece, *Four Studies in Loyalty* (1946), incorporating elements of biography and autobiography. It is memorable in particular for its study of a previous Christopher Sykes, his great-uncle. His *Two Studies in Virtue* (1953) was less successful in its treatment of Cardinal J. H. Newman and E. B. Pusey. Although Sykes was a cradle Catholic, intermittently devout and, like many Catholics of his class, enraged by the despoliation of the Roman liturgy after the second Vatican Council, his interest in the finer points of high Anglican conscience was limited.

After some foreign reporting, notably for the *Daily Mail* during the Azerbaijan campaign in Iran, Sykes joined the BBC in 1948. Following a short spell as deputy controller of the Third Programme he joined the features department (1949–68), where he was suspected of having formed a Catholic mafia.

Sykes's biography *Orde Wingate* (1959) may have described the sort of life he would have liked to live, but the life of Adam von Trott (*Troubled Loyalty*, 1968), the patriotic anti-Nazi, was closer to the world he eventually inhabited. After a life of Nancy Astor (*Nancy*, 1971), generally seen as a bit of a pot-boiler, he came, after some delay, to write the authorized biography of his old friend and boon companion, the novelist Evelyn *Waugh (1975). This might have been his best book. He was chosen because he was the only one of Waugh's obituarists who caught something of the gaiety as well as the recklessness of the man. Unfortunately, when he came to set pen to paper six years after his subject's death, the light had dimmed a little. Inhibited, as he said, by respect for Waugh's widow—she, in fact, had died two years before the book appeared—he had also suffered a decline in energy, a certain loss of optimism or hope. The book is marred not only by carelessness but also perhaps by a certain resentment at the dying of the light. Sykes's life had been a reasonably successful one, but not so successful as that of his *arriviste* friend.

Sykes was a most congenial man to meet, an excellent mimic, well mannered, and witty even in his cups, much loved by the young, to whom he was always pleasant and friendly. In appearance he was tall, with a dark, slightly saturnine countenance. He carried himself well, with a debonair and jaunty manner, which remained with him when age brought a certain heaviness, not to say majesty, to his gait. He spent his last years in a Kent nursing home. He died in the course of an agreeable house party at Sledmere, his childhood home, on 8 December 1986. He was survived by an only son, Mark, publisher and secondhand bookseller.   AUBERON WAUGH, *rev.*

Sources *The Times* (10 Dec 1986) · *The Independent* (11 Dec 1986) · personal knowledge (1996) · *CGPLA Eng. & Wales* (1987)
Archives BBC WAC, Caversham · Eton · Georgetown University, Washington, DC, corresp. and papers · Royal Society of Literature, London · Yale U., Beinecke L., literary papers and corresp. | Bodl. Oxf., letter to Frank Hardie · Georgetown University, Washington, DC, corresp. with Harman Grisewood · King's Cam., Hayward MSS · U. Reading, Bodley Head 'Adult Editorial' MSS
Wealth at death £11,317: probate, 24 July 1987, *CGPLA Eng. & Wales*

Sykes, Ella Constance (1863–1939), traveller and writer, was born on 11 November 1863 at 8 Acre Terrace, Stoke Damerel, Devon. She was the daughter of the Revd William Sykes (1829–1893), chaplain to the forces, and his wife, Mary (*d.* 1918), daughter of Captain the Honourable Anthony Oliver Molesworth RA (of the family viscounts Molesworth of Swords); the father had served at Sevastopol in 1855 and later at the Royal Military College, Sandhurst, and was also honorary chaplain to Queen Victoria. Ella and her younger sister Ethel Rosalie Sykes [*see below*] attended Plymouth high school and the Royal School for the Daughters of Officers, Lansdown, Bath. She was among the earliest students at Lady Margaret Hall, the Church of England foundation for women students at Oxford, studying there between 1881 and 1883 (her sister was there between 1881 and 1884). Following her father's death in 1893 her brother Percy Molesworth *Sykes invited her in October 1894 to accompany him to Persia, where he was being sent to establish consulates in the districts of Kerman and Baluchistan. She spent two years with him on his travels in the interior of Persia, and was the first European woman to visit these parts. After travelling along the Persian Gulf, visiting all the major coastal settlements on the way, they returned to Tehran before journeying home in February 1897. Her experiences were published in *Through Persia on a Side-Saddle* in 1898, which was considered a 'very readable narrative' delivered in a 'fresh and lively manner' (*The Times*, 28 April 1898, 7f). She followed this with a popular history, *Persia and its People*, in 1910 and several articles and lectures including 'Persian family life' in the *Journal of the Royal Central Asian Society* for 1914. She had been a founder member of the society in 1905 and was twice elected to its council, in 1916 and 1921. She was also elected a fellow of the Royal Geographical Society and was awarded a silver medal by the Royal Society of Arts.

Having established herself as a writer of travel literature, in 1911 Ella Sykes spent six months touring western Canada on behalf of the Colonial Intelligence League for Educated Women. The league was established in 1910 to promote employment opportunities in the colonies for educated women through the establishment of training settlements. Her task was to examine and report on current employment conditions for women in British Columbia, which she did in the guise of an inexperienced home-help in various employments. Her book, *A Home-Help in Canada*, published in 1912, was 'a frank corrective to the more effusive propaganda' (Hammerton, 172) being put out by the voluntary emigration societies. She described a life of hard drudgery where little account was taken of her social background or education and concluded that such work should be seen as a stepping-stone to better employment in the field of nursing, teaching, stenography, or farming. However, she was aware of the limited opportunities for educated and skilled women in the home country and asserted that 'if I were obliged to earn my living, were proficient in some useful art and knew what I know now, I should not hesitate for a moment between the wide free life of Canada, and my probable lot in overcrowded England' (p. ix).

This was not a counsel of despair or a radical political critique, for underpinning her interest in this question was a strong patriotic and imperialist outlook. In her conclusion she wrote:

> I consider that it is an Imperial work to help girls of high stamp to seek their fortunes beyond the seas—women who will care for our glorious flag and what it signifies … It is not too much to say that a British woman worthy of her great heritage can, in Mr Chamberlain's unforgettable words, be in very deed a 'Missionary for Empire'. (p. 304)

In 1912 Sykes was a member of the committee of the league, which continued its work until the outbreak of the First World War in 1914. On 5 March 1915 she set off on her third and final expedition, once again in the company of her brother, who was travelling to Kashgar, the capital of Chinese Turkestan, to act for the British consul, Sir George Macartney, who was taking leave. Her account of this adventure, *Through Deserts and Oases of Central Asia*, co-authored with her brother and not published until 1920, describes a journey through pre-revolutionary Russia to Tashkent in Russian Turkestan. From here they continued on ponies across the high passes to Kashgar. Describing the highest of these passes, which reached 12,000 feet, she wrote:

> I could hardly believe that it is possible to ride over these mountains, so steeply did they rise above us … the last pull to the crest is almost perpendicular, and is noted for accidents … but finally, caravan and all we reached the summit of the pass in safety. (p. 31)

On 10 April 1915, thirty-six days since their departure, 'we rode across the stony plain towards a long green line on the horizon that indicated the goal of our journey' (p. 37)—Kashgar oasis.

This was not the end of her adventures. In late May 1915 Ella and her brother set off on a tour of the Russian Pamirs, so recently the focal point of the 'great game'. She wrote, 'naturally my blood was stirred at the thought that I was about to start upon an adventure vouchsafed to very few women' (p. 105), and prided herself on being the first Englishwoman to negotiate the Katta Dawan, or great pass, at 13,000 feet. By the end of July they had returned to Kashgar, and in September they set off for Khotan, passing from oasis to oasis along the edge of the Takla-Makan Desert. Macartney returned in November and they retraced their route home, arriving about a month later, 'where the war, with its urgent claims upon every man and woman, took possession of our thoughts and energies' (p. 231).

During 1916 Sykes organized canteen work at Étaples behind the western front, and in 1917 she returned to the family home at Lyndhurst in Hampshire, where she was quartermaster of a small hospital and leader of a YMCA hut. Her mother died in 1918, and at some time afterwards she moved to London, residing for the rest of her life at 26 St George's Court, Gloucester Road, South Kensington. In addition to her long association with the Royal Central Asian Society, between 1920 and 1926 she was secretary of the Royal Asiatic Society. In 1926 she joined the committee of the Mary Curzon Hospital, and from 1927 until 1937 she was a member of the governing body of the Church of England Council of Empire Settlement.

Towards the end of her life Sykes, who did not marry or have children, gave much time to voluntary work with girls, primarily as honorary secretary of the Girls' Friendly Society in South Kensington. Her 'interest in "things Asian" never flagged and among her closest friends were men and women distinguished for exploration and wide travel in that continent' (*Journal of the Royal Asian Society*). She died at her home in London on 23 March 1939. The memorial service held at Christ Church, Victoria Road, Kensington, on 1 April was attended by representatives of all the societies with which she had been associated. She was regarded by her peers as 'one of the most remarkable women of her generation' (ibid.).

Her younger sister, **Ethel Rosalie Sykes** (1864–1945), born at 1 Collingwood Villas, Stoke Damerel, Devon, on 30 October 1864, was also single and childless, but, although like her sister she possessed independent means, she pursued a professional career. Between 1910 and 1912 she taught at Queen Mary's College, Lahore, under her friend Mary Western. In 1916 she was a clerk at the foreign trade department, and in that year she published in two volumes *Readings from Indian History for Boys and Girls*. Whether she travelled widely while teaching in India is unknown, but she, like her sister and brother, was a founder member of the Royal Central Asian Society in 1905.

In 1917 Ethel Sykes took up the post of supervisor of women in Lloyds Bank, London. This was a challenging post. Before the war the bank employed only a small number of women as telephonists or typists. By 1918 some 3300 women were employed as temporary clerks. With demobilization many of these women were replaced by former servicemen returning to their peacetime work. By 1920 the general recruitment of women as clerks had ended, although, in 1924, 1520 were employed in typing and filing work. During her time as supervisor the working regime was strict. Fraternization between the sexes during office hours was actively discouraged by a code of behaviour, and women who married had to leave their employment. She was the Lady Margaret Hall representative on the committee of the University Women's Club in South Audley Street, London, and undertook charitable work for the Pilgrims of Hope at St Mary Abbot's Hospital, Kensington. She died at Bankey Field Nursing Home, Hurstpierpoint, Sussex, on 8 March 1945, leaving a bequest of £500 to the Oxford Mission Sisterhood.

JONATHAN SPAIN

Sources *Lady Margaret Hall register 1879–1924* (1928), 3 • *WWW, 1941–50*, vol. 3 [1929–40] • E. C. Sykes, *Through Persia on a side-saddle*, 2nd edn (1901) • E. C. Sykes, *A home-help in Canada* (1912) • E. C. Sykes and P. Sykes, *Through deserts and oases of central Asia* • *Journal of the Royal Central Asian Society*, 26 (1939), 364–6 • *Journal of the Royal Asian Society* (1939), 508 • *The Times* (29 March 1939), 9a • *The Times* (1 April 1939), 17c • *The Times* (13 June 1939), 21b • C. M. R., 'Ella Constance Sykes', *Brown Book* (1939), 32–3 • *Brown Book* (1945) • b. cert. • d. cert. • census returns, 1881 • Foster, *Alum. Oxon.* • J. Robinson, *Wayward women: a guide to women travellers*, new edn (1991) • Burke, *Peerage* • Burke, *Gen. GB* (1952) • A. J. Hammerton, *Emigrant gentlewomen: genteel poverty and female emigration, 1830–1914* (1979) • J. R. Winton, *Lloyds Bank, 1918–1969* (1982) • *CGPLA Eng. & Wales* (1939) • b. cert. [Ethel Rosalie Sykes] • d. cert. [Ethel Rosalie Sykes]
Archives St Ant. Oxf., Percy Sykes MSS
Likenesses photograph, repro. in Sykes, *A home-help in Canada*

Wealth at death £9506 11s. 4d.: resworn probate, 7 June 1939, *CGPLA Eng. & Wales* · £25,585 8s. 7d.—Ethel Rosalie Sykes: probate, 1945, *CGPLA Eng. & Wales*

Sykes, Ethel Rosalie (1864–1945). *See under* Sykes, Ella Constance (1863–1939).

Sykes, Sir Francis, first baronet (*bap.* 1732, *d.* 1804), East India Company servant and politician, was baptized on 26 February 1732 in Thornhill, in the West Riding of Yorkshire, the youngest of the six children then living of Francis Sykes (*bap.* 1682, *d.* 1766), yeoman farmer, and his wife, Martha, *née* Fearnley (*d.* 1769). His family had been established in the immediate area of Thornhill since at least 1270. He was educated at John Randall's academy at Heath, West Riding, and was appointed writer to the East India Company on 19 December 1750. Arriving in Calcutta on 18 July 1751, he was appointed to the English trading factory at Cossimbazar, where Warren Hastings was already stationed. On 5 June 1756 the factory was captured by the nawab of Bengal, Siraj ud-Daula, but Sykes escaped to the French factory near by. From April to June 1757 he was with William Watts in Murshidabad in the vital negotiations with Siraj ud-Daula (and secretly with Mir Jafar) which preceded the battle of Plassey, escaping from there with Watts and Collet on 12 June 1757 to join Clive. In June and July 1758 he was acting resident in Hastings's absence at the nawab's court at Murshidabad and in 1760 was appointed chief of the Cossimbazar factory.

In January 1761 Sykes left Bengal for England with Warren Hastings's son George, whom he left in the care of Jane Austen's parents. On 18 February 1763 he purchased Ackworth Park, near Pontefract. Appointed as a member of Clive's select committee for Bengal, he sailed with Clive on the *Kent* on 4 June 1764, not arriving at Calcutta until 3 May 1765 due to contrary winds. Following the grant of the *diwani* by Shah Alam to the East India Company on 30 September 1765, he was appointed resident at Murshidabad and the first supervisor of the tax collections. Here he acted jointly with the nawab's chief minister in the direction of the nawab's government (his Mughal name was Intizam ud-Daula, the Administration of the State), the first time an English merchant became a member of the indigenous executive. He substantially reduced the number of internal customs posts, thus freeing up trade, and created the first courts of justice held on British lines outside Calcutta and having jurisdiction over the Indians. At the same time he was a member of Clive's Society of Trade (which had a monopoly of the trade in salt and betel nut) and engaged in substantial private trading, employing, on Hastings's recommendation, Krishna Kanta Nandy (Cantoo Babu) as his *banian* (trusted employee and agent but also *de facto* trading partner and contributor of capital and commercial expertise). On 31 January 1766 he was reappointed chief of Cossimbazar, which, together with his other posts, consolidated his already powerful position and in practice made him second only to Clive in Bengal.

On 7 February 1766 Sykes married Catherine Ridley (1746–1768), daughter of John Ridley, in Calcutta. There were two children of this marriage, Francis William (1767–1804) and John (1768–1786). Catherine Sykes died at Calcutta shortly before the family was due to embark for England and was buried in South Park Street cemetery.

Sykes returned to England in 1769 with one of the largest contemporary fortunes to come out of India, variously estimated at between £250,000 and £500,000. In 1770 he purchased the Gillingham Manor estate, Dorset (2200 acres), near the pocket borough of Shaftesbury. He was elected MP there four times although after the 1774 election he was unseated for corruption and was successfully sued for £11,000. In 1772 he was, with Clive, the object of parliamentary censure and public opprobrium, acquiring the sobriquet Squire Matoot after a tax levied by him in Bengal. He was a member of the Bengal Squad, a body of MPs who vigorously defended the interests of returned East India Company officials and later those of the company itself. In 1771 he purchased the Basildon estate, Berkshire (2500 acres), and in 1776 employed a fellow Yorkshireman, John Carr, to design a new house there in the Palladian style.

On 2 September 1774 Sykes married as his second wife Elizabeth Monckton (1754–1835), daughter of the second Viscount Galway, another Yorkshireman. They had one daughter, Eliza (1775–1822), who married a neighbouring landowner, Richard Benyon de Beauvoir of Englefield, Berkshire. On 8 June 1781 Sykes was created a baronet and in 1784 was elected MP for Wallingford, and was high steward from 1799, both of which positions he held for the rest of his life. His son Francis William was MP for Wallingford with him from 1794 to 1796. Sir Francis Sykes died at his house in Audley Square, London, on 11 January 1804, and was buried at St Bartholomew's Church, Lower Basildon, on 20 January. Hastings was one of his executors.

Sykes was regarded by the contemporary public as an archetypal nabob and was vilified accordingly. But he played an important role in the growth and consolidation of British power and influence in Bengal under Clive after the chaos of the early 1760s. Clive trusted him implicitly, as did Hastings, who credited him with having secured his appointment as governor of Bengal in 1771. He acted as Hastings's financial adviser and corresponded with him throughout his life. That he was shrewd and determined is manifest, both from his correspondence and from a portrait miniature of him painted in later life.

JOHN SYKES

Sources BL, Hastings MSS · East India Company records, BL OIOC · *Sykes: sometime of Thornhill county of York and of Basildon Berkshire*, privately printed (1862x6) · J. Cornforth, 'Basildon House', *Country Life*, 161 (1977), 1158–61, 1227–30, 1298–301 · S. C. Nandy, *Life and times of Cantoo Baboo (Krisna Kanta Nandy), the banian of Warren Hastings*, 2 vols. (1978–81) · P. J. Marshall, *East Indian fortunes: the British in Bengal in the eighteenth century* (1976) · M. E. Monckton Jones, *Warren Hastings in Bengal*, Oxford Historical and Literary Studies, 9 (1918) · A. M. Khan, *The transition in Bengal, 1756–1775: a study of Saiyid Muhammad Reza Khan* (1969) · M. Bence-Jones, *Clive of India* (1974) · L. S. Sutherland, *The East India Company in eighteenth century politics* (1952) · J. Hayes, *Gainsborough* (1975) · bank account records, Barclays Bank, Gosling's Branch, Fleet Street, London
Archives BL, corresp. with Warren Hastings, Add. MSS 29132–29194, *passim* · BL OIOC, East India Company records

Likenesses T. Richmond?, miniature on ivory, 1790–99 · H. Bone, miniature on card, 1804 (after T. Gainsborough) · J. Flaxman, marble effigy on a monument, 1804, St Bartholomew's Church, Lower Basildon, Berkshire · oils, *c*.1808 (after T. Gainsborough), Wallingford Town Hall

Wealth at death Ackworth Park estate, Basildon Park estate, Gillingham Manor estate, and house at Audley Square, London

Sykes, Sir Frederick Hugh (1877–1954), air force officer and colonial governor, was born in Croydon, Surrey, on 23 July 1877. His father, Henry Sykes, who died less than two years later, was a mechanical engineer; his mother, Margaret Sykes, was a distant cousin of her husband. Sykes had 'a somewhat chequered education': five years at a preparatory school on the south coast; then from the age of fifteen two years in Paris learning French in the hope of a diplomatic career. For a time he worked in a general store in order to save money. On returning to London he entered a shipping firm. He then spent some time working on tea plantations in Ceylon, eventually making a leisurely return to England via Burma, China, Japan, and the United States.

On the outbreak of the Second South African War, Sykes booked a passage to Cape Town and joined the imperial yeomanry scouts as a trooper. He was taken prisoner by C. R. De Wet at Roodevaal but was soon released, and was next commissioned in the bodyguard of Lord Roberts; he was wounded during a commando raid in 1901. Later in the year he joined the regular army and was gazetted second lieutenant in the 15th hussars.

Sykes served in India and west Africa, was promoted captain in 1908, and passed the Staff College in 1909. Very early on he was an enthusiast for ballooning. In 1910 he learned to fly, and he obtained his pilot's certificate (no. 96) in 1911. The following year he became commander of the military wing of the newly founded Royal Flying Corps. But on the outbreak of war in 1914, as still only an acting lieutenant-colonel, he was considered too junior to command the corps in action abroad. The command was given to Sir David Henderson, previously director-general of military aeronautics, and Sykes served as his chief of staff. He was succeeded as commander of the military wing by Major Hugh Trenchard. The two men were deeply antipathetic, and a bitter argument during the take-over set the keynote to their relationship for the rest of Sykes's military career.

Trenchard's hostility was soon displayed. In November 1914 Sykes was appointed to command the Royal Flying Corps in place of Henderson, who was promoted to command the 1st division. Meanwhile Trenchard had been posted to France to take charge of one of the new operational wings into which the Royal Flying Corps had been divided. As soon as he found that he was to be under Sykes he requested to be transferred to his original regiment. Lord Kitchener intervened to insist upon Henderson and Sykes reverting to their previous posts—an episode not calculated to improve relations.

During the next few months Henderson was on sick leave and Sykes acted as his deputy. According to Trenchard, Henderson came to the conclusion that Sykes was

intriguing to replace him. Whatever the truth of it, the upshot was that Henderson developed a deep distrust of Sykes, who was sent in May to Gallipoli to report on air requirements there and in July was given command of the Royal Naval Air Service in the eastern Mediterranean when the Gallipoli campaign was at its height. He remained there until the end, carrying out his task with conspicuous success, and was appointed CMG in recognition.

In March 1916 Sykes was made assistant adjutant and quartermaster-general of the 4th mounted division at Colchester. In June he became assistant adjutant-general at the War Office, with the task of organizing the machine-gun corps. In February 1917 he was promoted temporary brigadier-general and deputy director of organization at the War Office, and at the end of the year he joined the planning staff of the supreme war council under Sir Henry Wilson. Meanwhile the government, on the recommendation of J. C. Smuts, strongly backed by Henderson yet opposed by Trenchard, had decided to create an independent air force with its own ministry. Nevertheless Trenchard became the first chief of air staff, under Lord Rothermere, the first air minister; both were appointed on 3 January 1918. Henderson was made vice-president of the newly formed Air Council.

Trenchard and Rothermere soon quarrelled. Trenchard tendered his resignation on 19 March but was persuaded to defer it until after the official birth of the Royal Air Force on 1 April. On 13 April, Sykes, promoted major-general, succeeded him—a choice inevitably controversial in these circumstances; Henderson promptly resigned too. The confusion was increased by Rothermere's own resignation, which took effect on 25 April. He paid a high tribute to Sykes in his resignation letter as 'this brilliant officer with his singularly luminous mind … an ideal Chief of Staff of the Royal Air Force'.

Rothermere was succeeded by Sir William Weir, who retained the post until the end of the war. Sykes was chief of staff throughout this significant period and, as a convinced supporter of an independent air force, did much to establish the new service. His post-war plans, however, were regarded as too grandiose by Weir's successor, Winston Churchill, who from January 1919 held the posts of both war and air minister. He preferred those of Trenchard, whom he was consulting behind Sykes's back. In February 1919 Trenchard again became chief of air staff and Sykes was shunted into the post of controller of civil aviation. One of the conditions of this appointment was that he gave up his military commission, and thus he ended his career in the armed services.

On 3 June 1920 Sykes married Isabel Harrington (d. 1969), the elder daughter of Andrew Bonar *Law; they had one son. Sykes resigned from the Air Ministry in April 1922, dissatisfied with the financial treatment of civil aviation. He was offered but refused the governorship of South Australia, and decided to enter politics. At the general election of 1922 he was elected Unionist member for the Hallam division of Sheffield. In May 1923 he conveyed to George V his father-in-law's letter of resignation from the premiership. He retained his parliamentary seat until 1928, when he was appointed governor of Bombay.

Sykes's term of office in India covered a period of unprecedented financial difficulties and political and industrial unrest, which he faced with resolution and a patient determination to improve the lot of the common people. He would have wished for greater powers to deal more promptly and effectively with civil disobedience, but he was loyal in conforming to the central government's policy of conciliation. It was not until 1932 that emergency powers were granted; then, with civil disobedience on the decline, Sykes was able to give attention to the social and economic difficulties which he felt to be the real problem of India. When he left Bombay in 1933 he had the satisfaction of knowing that the outlook for the presidency was more hopeful than it had been five years earlier.

Sykes was again in parliament from 1940 to 1945 as Conservative member for the central division of Nottingham. He was appointed KCB and GBE in 1919, GCIE in 1928, and GCSI in 1934, and was sworn of the privy council in 1928. He was chairman of government committees on meteorological services (1920–22) and broadcasting (1923), of the broadcasting board (1923–7), of the Miners' Welfare Commission (1934–46), and of the Royal Empire Society (1938–41), and for many years he served as honorary treasurer of the British Sailors' Society. He was also a director of various public companies. His autobiography, *From Many Angles*, was published in 1942. He died at Beaumont House, Beaumont Street, London, on 30 September 1954.

Sykes was a person of high intelligence and much charm, although he did not thaw very easily. He was clearly a most capable administrator. However, his contribution to the formative period of the air force as an independent arm has been obscured by the hostility between him and some of his brother officers—Trenchard especially—whose opinions later became gospel in the Royal Air Force, thereby conditioning much of the service's historiography.   ROBERT BLAKE, *rev.*

Sources W. Raleigh and H. A. Jones, *The war in the air*, 6 vols. (1922–37) • F. Sykes, *From many angles* (1942) • R. Blake, *The unknown prime minister: the life and times of Andrew Bonar Law* (1955) • M. A. Beaverbrook, *Men and power, 1917–1918* (1956) • A. Boyle, *Trenchard* (1962) • P. Joubert de la Ferté, *The third service* (1955) • W. J. Reader, *Architect of air power: the life of the first Viscount Weir of Eastwood* (1968) • private information (1971) • personal knowledge (1971)

Archives BL OIOC, corresp. and papers, MSS Eur. F 150 | CUL, corresp. with Sir Samuel Hoare • IWM, corresp. relating to proposed biography of Field-Marshal Sir Henry Wilson | SOUND IWM SA, oral history interview

Likenesses W. Orpen, oils, *c*.1919, Conock Manor, near Devizes • W. Stoneman, photograph, 1919, NPG • L. F. Roslyn, bronze bust, 1920, IWM

Wealth at death £76,876 18*s.* 8*d.*: probate, 8 Nov 1954, *CGPLA Eng. & Wales*

Sykes, Godfrey (1824–1866), designer, was born in New Malton, Yorkshire, and baptized there at the Ebenezer Independent Chapel, Saville Street, on 28 December 1824 the son of George Sykes and Elizabeth Jagger (or Tagger). He was apprenticed to a Sheffield engraver and then worked for himself designing showcards and silverware, mostly for the firm of Edward Atkin in Sheffield. However,

when the Sheffield School of Design opened on 1 July 1843, he was one of the first pupils to enrol. These provincial schools were being established by the government to enable working craftsmen to learn the elements of design, especially for use in the local metal trades. Sykes's association with the Sheffield School of Design lasted sixteen years, first as a leading pupil, and then from 1856 as assistant master to the headmaster, Young Mitchell (1811–1865). He won many prizes between 1844 and 1854, and was given free studentship in 1848. In 1856 he designed a silver inkstand which was presented to Mitchell in 1857. Mitchell, the headmaster from 1846 to 1863, had been a pupil of the painter J. A. D. Ingres (1780–1867) in Paris, and of the sculptor and designer Alfred Stevens (1818–1875), who had spent nine years studying in Europe, at the Government School of Design, Somerset House. Mitchell persuaded Stevens to come to Sheffield in 1850 to work as a designer with Henry E. Hoole (*c*.1806–1891)—manufacturer of stoves, grates, and fenders—who wished to exhibit at the Great Exhibition in 1851. Stevens also spent time with the students at the school of design, and at Mitchell's home. Sykes worked three days a week, unpaid, at Hoole's, with access to Stevens's designs, drawings, and paintings, learning the technical skills of metalwork production. In his metalwork designs and decorative schemes, Sykes was influenced by Stevens's neoclassicism. His design for the telegraphic news room ceiling (1856; destr.) included allegorical figures and semi-abstract designs set in panels. He also produced domestic decorative schemes, for Richard Solly (1807–1869), an ironmaster (president of the school of design, 1847–9), in 1855, and for Sir John Brown (1816–1896), steel baron, at Endcliffe Hall (1863–5). It is possible that he also did some decorative work at Wortley Hall, the home of Lord Wharncliffe. In 1854 Sykes was commissioned to design a frieze, 60 feet long, for the Sheffield Mechanics Institute, showing a procession reminiscent of the Elgin marbles in which deities and allegorical figures combined with everyday subjects (steelworkers, miners, children). This frieze of thirteen panels is now in Sheffield City Art Galleries. Sykes also did paintings, watercolours, and drawings during his stay in Sheffield, many of which are in Sheffield City Art Galleries. They are of local characters, street scenes, Sheffield and Derbyshire landscapes, grinding hulls, tilt forges, and workshops.

In October 1859 Sykes left for London to work on the Horticultural Society's new buildings and later at the South Kensington Museum (now the Victoria and Albert Museum). For the latter he had been recruited by Henry Cole, who wanted designers with a thorough training and knowledge of Italian decorative art. In his history of the building of the Victoria and Albert Museum, John Physick noted that 'Sykes was so highly regarded that the Board decided that his "views on questions of decoration [were] to be adopted in future"' (Physick, 58). Sykes's team of assistants included two fellow students from Sheffield, Reuben Townroe (*c*.1883/1885–1911) and James Gamble (1835–1911), who carried out much of his design work in many media. They specialized in terracotta for external work with 'bold yet sensitive and spontaneous … model-ling' (ibid.). For the south court they produced decorative constructional ironwork, and in the refreshment rooms enamelled metalwork (restored *c*.1980). Sgraffito decor-ation in coloured cement covered walls, and ceramic mosaic was used on floors and in panels for wall decor-ation. They designed stained-glass windows, and patterns and pictures for tiles and majolica. Although he observed that the 'total effect of the decoration must have been one of incoherence', Physick stated that 'the work of Sykes and Gamble is of excellent quality' (ibid.). After his death Sykes's sketches continued to be used by Townroe and Gamble and other members of the design team until the end of the century. Queen Victoria and Prince Albert took a great interest in the museum and visited Sykes there and at his home.

In 1860 Sykes was asked by Thackeray to design the cover of the *Cornhill Magazine* which features a sower based on a drawing made in Heeley, Sheffield. He also designed the tomb of the artist William Mulready (1786–1863) in Kensal Green cemetery. Sykes died, aged forty-one, at his home, 2 Rich Terrace, Old Brompton, Middle-sex, on 28 February 1866, leaving a wife, Ellen, and was buried in Brompton cemetery beneath a stone designed by Gamble, who also used Sykes's designs as a basis for a memorial in Sheffield. Erected in 1875 in Weston Park, it consists of a stone base with panels containing inscrip-tions, reliefs of the artist's working tools, and a portrait of Sykes.　　　　　　　　　　　　　　　　　SUSAN GRAVES

Sources M. Diamond, *Art and industry in Sheffield: Alfred Stevens and his school, 1850–1875* (1975) · H. Armitage, *Cornhill Magazine*, [3rd] ser., 32 (1912), 464–73 · Sheffield and Rotherham Independent church registers · Sheffield School of Art, annual reports · census returns for Sheffield, 1841, 1851 · J. Physick, *The Victoria and Albert Museum: the history of its building* (1982) · *CGPLA Eng. & Wales* (1866) · *IGI*
Likenesses H. Gamble, memorial monument, 1875, Weston Park, Sheffield
Wealth at death under £2000: probate, 1866

Sykes, John Bradbury (1929–1993), physicist, lexicog-rapher, and crossword solver, was born in Folkestone, Kent, on 26 January 1929, the only child of Stanley Wil-liam Sykes, a borough treasurer, and his wife, Eleanor Sykes Sykes (*née* Bradbury). He was educated at Wallasey grammar school, Rochdale high school, and St Lawrence College, Ramsgate. He went up to Wadham College, Oxford, in 1947 as an open entrance scholar to read math-ematics, graduated with first-class honours in 1950, and went on, first as a Henry Skynner senior student at Balliol College (1950–52), and then as a Harmsworth senior scholar at Merton College (1952–3), to write a DPhil thesis entitled 'Some problems in radiative transfer'. While a postgraduate student he met his future wife, Avril Barbara Hart (they married in 1955), also an astrophysicist. His sub-sequent life can be divided into three stages and one absorbing hobby. After starting out as a theoretical physi-cist, he became a gifted translator and went on to become an expert lexicographer—all this while achieving

John Bradbury Sykes (1929–1993), by Peter Thevnor

national fame as consistently the most successful com-petitor in the *Times* national crossword championship.

After leaving Oxford in 1953 Sykes joined the theoretical physics division of the Atomic Energy Research Establish-ment at Harwell, as a senior scientific officer. In 1956–7 he gained further experience in astrophysics when he was seconded for nine months to the Yerkes Observatory in Williams Bay, Wisconsin. After his return he was appoin-ted head of the translations office in the Harwell Library. His remarkable facility for languages combined with his knowledge of astrophysics and mathematics made him an indispensable part of a unit that was being deluged with books and journals, especially in Russian and Ger-man, on matters to do with atomic physics. Harwell's records credit Sykes with reading six languages 'very well', four others 'fairly well', and another five (including Japanese and Hungarian) 'rather slowly'. Except for Ger-man and Dutch he could not speak these languages but in scientific works could read them with extraordinary facil-ity. In 1963 alone he translated over 500 scientific papers, specializing in Russian, besides editing translations made by others. His technique for learning a language was to acquire a knowledge of the vocabulary of physics and an outline knowledge of the grammar, while avoiding the spoken form of the language or its literary works. He was promoted to the grade of principal scientific officer in 1960, when he was also elected a fellow of the Institute of

Linguists, whose journal the *Incorporated Linguist* he edited from 1980 to 1986. Among the numerous works that he translated, some of them in collaboration with other translators, was the massive ten-volume *Course of Theoretical Physics* (1958–81) by the Russian authors L. Landau and E. Lifshitz.

About 1970 Sykes discovered a new challenge, after reading that the editor of the supplement to the *Oxford English Dictionary* was appealing for earlier printed evidence for a large number of modern words, including the astronomical term 'absolute magnitude'. He soon found himself immersed in the hunt for word origins, and it was not long before his obvious linguistic skills impressed the Oxford University Press. In 1971 he left Harwell to become editor of the *Concise Oxford Dictionary*. The *Concise* had fallen somewhat behind the times but its new editor transformed it in the sixth edition, published in 1976, in which the emphasis was very much on description rather than prescription. He went on to prepare a new edition of the *Pocket Oxford Dictionary* in 1978 and a seventh edition of the *Concise Oxford Dictionary* in 1982. He then became head of the press's newly constituted German dictionaries department. Again he was concerned to provide a practical tool rather than a prescriptive device, and he chose as his compilers professional translators rather than academic lexicographers. The *Oxford–Duden German Dictionary*, the product of collaboration between the Dudenverlag in Mannheim and the Oxford University Press, was duly published in 1990. Sykes then returned to English lexicography, as general editor in the final stages of the preparation of the *New Shorter Oxford English Dictionary* (published in 1993), and was at work on a new dictionary of word origins the day before he died.

Sykes's hobbies were, perhaps unsurprisingly, intellectual ones: chess, bridge, and the solving of cryptic crossword puzzles. He was the *Times* national crossword champion ten times, 'failing' only in years in which he resolved not to compete in order to give others a chance. His tall, imposing figure disguised a shy man whose life was devoted to the solving of problems in abstruse areas of mathematics and astrophysics and of translation and lexicography. There was one son of his marriage (which was dissolved in 1988). Sykes died of heart disease at his home, 68 Woodstock Close, Oxford, on 3 September 1993 and was cremated at Oxford crematorium a week later. He was survived by his son and former wife.

R. W. BURCHFIELD

Sources WW · *The Independent* (6 Sept 1993) · *The Times* (7 Sept 1993) · *The Guardian* (9 Sept 1993) · private information (2004) [PR manager, UKAEA, Harwell] · records, Wallasey grammar school · records, Rochdale high school · records, St Lawrence College, Ramsgate · archives, Wadham College, Oxford · Balliol Oxf., archives · archives, Merton Oxf. · Oxford University Press · personal knowledge (2004)
Likenesses P. Thevnor, photograph, News International Syndication, London [*see illus.*] · photographs, Oxford University Press, archives
Wealth at death £201,426: probate, 11 Jan 1994, *CGPLA Eng. & Wales*

Sykes, Marjorie (1905–1995), teacher and community worker, was born in the West Riding village of Mexborough on 11 May 1905, the first of the three children of Wilfrid Sykes (*d.* 1940) and his wife, Amelia Maxon. Both parents were teachers: her father was the headmaster of the local school. His training had included a year's study of the natural sciences in Dresden, an experience which fostered his international sympathies and, indirectly, his daughter's too. In 1919 Marjorie Sykes entered the Wakefield High School for Girls, and in 1923 she went to Newnham College, Cambridge. She took first-class honours in the second part of the English tripos in 1926. One element in her examination was a dissertation on William Blake, then an adventurous choice and an indication of her own vigorously independent religious interests. She responded warmly to the liberal and cosmopolitan spirit which prevailed in Cambridge in the 1920s, and particularly valued the ministry of Edward Woods, vicar of Holy Trinity Church, whose book *Everyday Religion* (1922) encouraged an egalitarianism congenial to someone brought up in a Yorkshire mining community.

Her father's example encouraged Sykes to stay on in Cambridge to take a teaching diploma. After a few months at a school near Liverpool, she looked for work overseas, and in May 1928 applied for and was appointed to the post of principal teacher of English at the Bentinck School for Girls in Madras. This was a missionary institution supported by the London Missionary Society, but the principal, Alice Varley, saw her task as befriending and appreciating rather than converting. Marjorie heartily sympathized with this approach, and entered with zest into the activities of the Madras International Fellowship, which was devoted to subverting the social barriers that kept Europeans and Indians apart. It was through the fellowship that she met Chakravarti Rajagopalachari, a prominent Indian politician and nationalist who succeeded Mountbatten as governor-general of India soon after independence. He introduced her to the ideas of Gandhi and his colleagues in the Indian National Congress, and these came to be reflected in her own work in the school.

In 1930 Alice Varley resigned as principal on her marriage to Ted Barnes, who worked at the Madras Christian College. Soon afterwards, Sykes was appointed in her place. She developed a regime in which co-operation was emphasized rather than competition, and all prizes were abolished. More controversially, everyone in the school, regardless of caste, was fed from the same kitchen and was expected to help with the cleaning and maintenance of the school premises. It was at this time that she first encountered members of the Society of Friends, and she joined them in 1936.

In 1939 she left the Bentinck School, having found her work increasingly hampered by the effects of the Government of India Act (1935), with its provision of separate electorates for religious minorities. Christian institutions found it difficult to avoid suspicion of political motives. She was relieved to have the opportunity of joining the staff of Rabindranath Tagore's Viswa-Bharati University at Santiniketan, in the countryside north of Calcutta. Here she came to know Gandhi's old friend Charles Freer Andrews well: he lived at Santiniketan from the autumn of 1939 until his death in April 1940. Tagore himself died sixteen months later, by which time she had helped him in translating three of his plays, and an account of his memories of childhood.

Sykes herself suffered a period of sickness after Tagore's death, and spent her convalescence with her former colleague Alice Barnes (now widowed) in Coimbatore in south India. Here she wrote her short biography of Tagore. In July 1942 she returned to Madras, this time to teach English at the Women's Christian College. She made her home in a poor area of the city, and established a nursery school there, so effectively that it continued to flourish for many years.

In the summer of 1944 Sykes returned to Santiniketan, where her main concern was to write, in collaboration with Benarsi Das Chaturvedi, a biography of C. F. Andrews, which was eventually published in 1949. Chaturvedi, a distinguished Hindi journalist, had been associated with Andrews since 1921, and shared his concern for the welfare of Indians working in east Africa. He had already written a biography of Andrews in Hindi. Marjorie Sykes herself visited Britain in 1946 to interview people who had known Andrews in his younger days. She returned in 1947 in time to witness the transfer of power of the two new dominions of India and Pakistan. She took Indian citizenship, to which her long residence in the subcontinent entitled her.

From 1949 to 1959 Sykes superintended the rigorously practical 'basic education' programme that Gandhi had established at his ashram community at Sevagram in central India. At this time she began to collaborate with Vinoba Bhave, who was carrying on Gandhi's 'constructive programme' to improve life in India's villages, and she joined with him in a project to train volunteers for a non-violent 'peace army'. This she continued to do after leaving Sevagram to rejoin Alice Barnes in the south. In 1964 she spent a few months in North America, undertaking the same kind of work there.

Sykes soon had an opportunity to apply her training in non-violence in the troubled north-eastern frontier region of Nagaland. The Nagas were a tribal people who had been converted to Christianity, and who hoped for recognition of their independence after British rule ended in 1947. This was rejected by the Indian government and violent resistance resulted, which was only suspended in 1964. The cease-fire required a team of observers to investigate incidents and to act as mediators, and Marjorie Sykes proved to be an invaluable recruit. Her handsome presence, her command of Indian languages, and her complete fearlessness were priceless assets in this difficult task.

After three years in Nagaland, Sykes returned again to the south, but Alice Barnes died, and thereafter Sykes spent more time travelling, visiting Quaker groups in many countries. In 1979 she again based herself in India,

this time at the Friends' rural centre at Rasulia, in Madhya Pradesh, where she supervised its work on organic farming. Here she found time to continue research which had long fascinated her into the history of Quaker contacts with India. Increasing ill health, however, led her to settle, in 1991, in the Quaker retirement home at Gerrards Cross, Buckinghamshire. A familiar figure in the library at Friends' House in London, frail and indomitable, she translated Vinoba Bhave's autobiography and wrote the history published posthumously as *A Quaker Tapestry*. She died at home at Swarthmore, Gerrards Cross, on 17 August 1995; her funeral took place a week later at Chilterns crematorium, Amersham.   GEOFFREY CARNALL

Sources M. Dart, *Marjorie Sykes: Quaker-Gandhian* (1993) [incl. bibliography] • M. Sykes, *An Indian tapestry*, ed. G. Carnall (1997) • H. Tennyson, 'India's faithful friend', *The Guardian* (20 Sept 1995) • personal knowledge (2004) • P. R. Brass, *The politics of India since independence* (1990) • private information (2004) [RS Friends, Lond.]
Archives RS Friends, Lond. | SOUND Newnham College, Cambridge
Likenesses M. Glover, drawing, c.1990, Friends' House, London • M. Glover, oils, c.1990, Woodbrooke College, Birmingham • photographs, repro. in Dart, *Marjorie Sykes*

Sykes, Sir Mark, sixth baronet (1879–1919), traveller and politician, was born on 17 March 1879 in London, the only son of Sir Tatton *Sykes, fifth baronet (1826–1913) [*see under* Sykes, Sir Tatton], of Sledmere, and his wife, (Christina Anne) Jessica (c.1856–1912), the third daughter of the Rt Hon. George Augustus Cavendish-Bentinck MP. Sir Tatton was a Yorkshire squire who owned 34,000 acres, followed the traditional sporting pursuits of his caste, and was addicted to foreign travel. Mark Sykes's education was random and eclectic. It was undertaken by a succession of tutors, with the exception of short spells at the Jesuit Beaumont College, the École des Jésuites at Monaco, where he found time to enjoy the principality's enticements, and at St Louis College, Brussels. He had been received into the Roman Catholic church at the age of three, alongside his mother, who subsequently took charge of his spiritual development. His faith was sincere, but never blinded him to the virtues of other religions, most notably Islam.

Travel in the company of his father formed the bedrock of Sykes's education. They travelled extensively across the Middle East, Egypt, and India, where their background gave them easy access to British pro-consuls and commanders. Naturally curious and open-minded, the young Sykes questioned, listened, and absorbed. During these and later wanderings he found much that was admirable in the societies and cultures he encountered, particularly in the Asian provinces of the Ottoman empire. He praised the spirit of 'fraternity and equality' which he detected among the Kurds (Leslie, 118) and sensed the powerful bonds which united Muslims, irrespective of their race or rulers. Unlike his contemporaries, Sykes was reluctant to judge the Turkish empire by contemporary European standards. While deploring the Armenian massacres, he commented in 1904, that 'it should be remembered that

Sir Mark Sykes, sixth baronet (1879–1919), by Leopold Pilichowski, 1915

massacre is still a recognised method of policy throughout the East and until lately in the West', adding a pointed reminder to recent events in China (ibid., 91).

This observation was made in *Dur ul-Islam* (1904), the second of Sykes's books about his Middle Eastern excursions. The first, *Through Five Turkish Provinces*, appeared in 1900; the third, *Five Mansions of the House of Othman*, in 1909; and the final, *The Caliphs' Last Heritage*, in 1915. Material for Sykes's first book had been gathered during leave from Cambridge, where he attended St John's College (1897–1900) and found the formal courses tiresome. He left without a degree, but with a reputation for a natural if wayward intelligence and a capacity to entertain as a cartoonist, mimic, and satirist. A tall, loosely and strongly built man with laughing eyes, Sykes retained those undergraduate talents which continued to provide amusement for his friends. Animated doodles decorated the scripts for his parliamentary speeches. Such indulgences and his light-hearted manner provided ammunition for his political enemies, who dismissed him as a dilettante and lightweight. One, T. E. Lawrence, wrote that: 'His instincts lay in parody: by choice he was a caricaturist rather than an artist, even in statesmanship' (Lawrence, 57).

In March 1900, holding the rank of captain, Sykes accompanied the militia battalion of the Yorkshire regiment to South Africa. There he remained for two years, performing routine lines-of-communication garrison duties in a blockhouse near a railway bridge at Barkly. Boredom was partially alleviated by reading and planning further expeditions to the Middle East and Asia. Military

customs also offered a chance for some ribbing, in the form of *Tactics and Military Training by Maj.-Gen. D'Ordel* (1902), a satire on the standard infantry drill manual which he compiled with Edmund Sandars.

On 28 October 1903 Sykes married Edith Violet (*d.* 1931), the third daughter of Sir John Eldon *Gorst, who accompanied him on some of his later travels. Their three sons, the second of whom was the writer Christopher Hugh *Sykes, and three daughters were born between 1904 and 1914. Soon after his marriage, Sykes began his political apprenticeship, acting as private secretary to George Wyndham, the Irish secretary (1904–5), and then as an honorary attaché at the Constantinople embassy (1907). On his return to Britain he was chosen as Unionist candidate for the East Riding constituency of Buckrose, where he was defeated in the two 1910 elections. In July 1911 he was returned as a Unionist for Kingston upon Hull, and thanks to the force of his personality retained the seat until his death.

Sykes was an unconventional Unionist. He belonged to the cavalier tendency within conservatism—a term which he disliked: 'it is impossible to be a Conservative when there is nothing left to Conserve' (Leslie, 206). Disraeli was his lodestar. Sykes would have been at home seventy years earlier among the Young England group, which he would like to have revived, and his principles were those of tory democracy, that theoretic alliance of the landed and working classes. Sykes's romantic toryism placed him on the fringes of his party, and some of his colleagues looked askance at his cleverness and enthusiasms. 'Too excitable' was Andrew Bonar Law's judgement (Ramsden, 104).

As a Catholic, Sykes was out of step with his party on home rule. During the passage of the Government of Ireland Bill in April 1914 he proposed a federal form of government for Ireland. He even suggested that 'general devolution' throughout the United Kingdom was better than a religious war in Ireland (*Saturday Review*, 28 March 1914). His principal preoccupations were military affairs and Britain's relations with the Ottoman empire. His maiden speech as an MP, delivered with careful preparation and characteristic fluency on 27 November 1911, drew heavily on his recent experiences in north Africa, as well as what he had seen and heard in various Ottoman provinces. 'A strong and united Turkish Empire' was as vital for Britain as it had been in Disraeli's time. If Britain entered a European war, he predicted that the inevitable reduction of garrisons in India, Egypt, and the Sudan would trigger widespread Muslim unrest, and that Mahdism still flourished (*Hansard 5C*, 33.99, 102–3).

On the outbreak of war in August 1914 Sykes raised a battalion from workers and tenants on his estates. He did not join them, but was attached to military intelligence. On account of his 'special knowledge of political and ethnological conditions in the Ottoman Empire' he was ordered to travel to Sofia, the Dardanelles, Egypt, Aden, and Mesopotamia to collect information on behalf of the recently formed de Bunsen committee (service record,

PRO, WO 374/66773). This inter-departmental body had been created by the cabinet to co-ordinate policy in the Middle East and, in particular, to lay plans for post-war policy towards former Turkish provinces. Although the focus of British power in the region had shifted from Constantinople to Cairo, Ottoman territory was still considered a vital glacis, defending India and its lifeline, the Suez Canal. If a vacuum was created, it was imperative that it should be filled by Britain, or its friends and clients. Sykes proceeded on his journey, collecting and collating the views of those on the spot about present and future policy. He faced difficulties at two levels. First, there were deep-rooted departmental jealousies; on his departure, Lord Hardinge, the viceroy of India, objected to his mission on the grounds that it would create 'friction and duplication of work' (ibid.). The former produced Sykes's second problem, reconciling policies adopted by individual departments. The civil and military authorities in Cairo favoured an alliance with Arab nationalists, one of whom Sykes interviewed, while the Indian government wished to establish direct British control over southern Iraq and populate it with Indian immigrants.

His Middle Eastern tour convinced Sykes that the existing administrative machinery was failing to meet wartime demands. In subsequent interventions in debates on the overall conduct of the war, he highlighted the lack of communication between the allies, heavy pressure on ministers, and the tendency of the government to lurch from one emergency decision to another. The only remedy was 'One master hand' directing the entire war effort (*Hansard 5C*, 80.41–6, 95.2188–95). Any post-war Middle Eastern settlement was bound to involve an accommodation with Russia, which was seeking control over the straits, and with France, which cherished territorial and political ambitions in Lebanon and Syria. If settled to French satisfaction, these would seriously compromise Cairo's negotiations with Arab dissidents, most notably Hussain, the sherif of Mecca, who had been a benevolent neutral since the beginning of the war. As Sykes had discovered in Cairo, the leading proponents of an Arab alliance (Sir Henry McMahon and Colonel Gilbert Clayton, of military intelligence) were also thinking in terms of a post-war disintegration of the Anglo-French entente and a return to the rivalry of the Fashoda era.

After reporting on the problems of policy-making, Sykes was chosen by the de Bunsen committee to negotiate the partition of Turkish Asia with the expansionist Charles Georges-Picot, the former consul-general in Beirut and the Quai d'Orsay's adviser on Middle Eastern affairs. Sykes's charm, francophilia, and sympathies with historic French Catholic interests in the Levant were his chief qualifications. Within a week and without rancour, an arrangement was agreed which was merged with the wider Sykes–Picot–Sazanov agreement for the division of the Ottoman empire in May 1916. Britain obtained direct control over the Tigris–Euphrates valley as far as Baghdad, a sphere of influence extending from the Persian Gulf across northern Arabia to what later became Jordan.

France was allocated a sphere encompassing much of modern Syria and northern Iraq, including Mosul, and direct rule over Lebanon and central Anatolia. Palestine would be an allied condominium. The compromise reflected political and military conditions at the end of 1915. Sir Edward Grey believed that Sykes had been too generous, but, and this was vital, he had forestalled any rift in the Franco-British alliance. Moreover, since Hussain had yet to declare for the allies, there was no reason for the treaty to take account of hypothetical Arab involvement in the war effort.

In April 1917, on the eve of General Allenby's Palestinian offensive, Sykes was sent as chief political officer to the Egyptian expeditionary force with responsibility for liaison with the Foreign Office. His position was fraught with difficulties created by the changing nature of the war. The treaty which carried his name had become an encumbrance; Curzon described it as a 'fancy sketch to suit a situation which had not then arisen' (Lloyd George, 2.663–5). The Arab revolt had begun in June 1916 and its leaders were aware of the implications, if not the exact details, of the treaty. These were explained to Hussain by Sykes and Georges-Picot in May 1917 during discussions in which key issues were fudged. Despite these new entanglements Sykes remained optimistic and was able to convince himself, if not those who worked with him, that everyone was being satisfied. None the less, in April 1918 he warned Georges-Picot that the agreement would have to be revised in the light of the new strategic situation.

A new complication had arisen with the Balfour declaration of December 1917. Sykes was an enthusiastic convert to Zionism; as a Romantic, he liked to see himself as a liberator of nations, a conceit which did not sit easily with his role as a power broker. As the Turkish fourth army disintegrated, Sykes suggested that Syria be placed under a temporary British administration headed by Allenby, who would be free to appoint French advisers. This would allow a breathing space in which the French and the Arabs could reach an accord. Sykes continued to enjoy the confidence of the Foreign Office, which ordered him to Syria in November 1918. He was instructed to advise on local Anglo-French co-operation, report on the requirements for political staff, and foster friendly relations between the Arabs and the French. After inconclusive talks in Beirut, Aleppo, and Damascus, he returned to the Paris peace conference on 4 February 1919, where he caught flu a week later. He died on 16 February at the Hotel Lotti. A few days later Lloyd George diagnosed the cause of Sykes's sudden collapse: 'He was a worried, anxious man. That was the cause of his death. He had no reserves of energy. He was responsible for the agreement which is causing us all the trouble with the French' (Riddell, 25). Not only was Sykes exhausted in mind and spirit, but, the prime minister believed, he had tormented himself with the belief that he alone had been responsible for an agreement which had turned out not to be in Britain's interests and had become a source of friction. In public, Lloyd George declared that Sykes's death had been a 'calamity' which had deprived the nation of a man with 'brilliant gifts' who would surely have 'attained great heights' (service record, PRO, 374/66773).   LAWRENCE JAMES

Sources R. Adelson, *Mark Sykes: portrait of an amateur* (1975) · S. Leslie, *Mark Sykes: his life and letters* (1923) · War Office record of services, PRO, WO 374/66773 · H. W. Sachak, *The emergence of the Middle East, 1914–1924* (1969) · B. C. Busch, *Britain, India and the Arabs, 1914–1921* (1971) · E. Kedourie, *In the Anglo-Arab labyrinth* (1976) · T. E. Lawrence, *Seven pillars of wisdom: a triumph*, new edn (1986) · *Real old tory politics: the political diaries of Robert Sanders, Lord Bayford, 1910–35*, ed. J. Ramsden (1984) · M. Sykes, 'An appeal to reason', *Saturday Review*, 117 (1914), 392–3 · *Hansard 5C* (1916), 80.41–6; (1917), 95.2188–95; 99.1411–15 · D. Lloyd George, *Memoirs of the peace conference*, 2 vols. (1939) · Lord Riddell, *Intimate diary of the peace conference and after, 1918–1923* (1933)

Archives East Riding of Yorkshire Archives Service, Beverley, MSS · PRO, FO 141, FO 371 · PRO, corresp., FO 800 · U. Hull, Brynmor Jones L., corresp. and papers · W. Yorks. AS, Leeds, letters relating to rebuilding of Sledmere Hall | CUL, corresp. with Lord Hardinge · NA Scot., corresp. with Philip Kerr · PRO, Arab bureau files, FO 882 · PRO, Jidda consulate files, FO 686 · Som. ARS, corresp. with Aubrey Herbert

Likenesses L. Pilichowski, oils, 1915, Sledmere House, Driffield, Yorkshire [*see illus.*] · B. Baker, bust, Sledmere House, Driffield, Yorkshire · W. Hester, caricature, mechanical repro., NPG; repro. in *VF* (26 June 1912) · memorial brass, Sledmere village, Yorkshire; repro. in Leslie, *Mark Sykes*

Wealth at death £20,000: will, PRO, WO 374/66773

Sykes, Sir Mark Masterman, third baronet (1771–1823), book collector, born on 20 August 1771, was the eldest son of Sir Christopher Sykes, second baronet (1749–1801), of Sledmere in the East Riding of Yorkshire, and his wife, Elizabeth (d. 1803), daughter of William Tatton of Withenshaw, Cheshire. He was at Westminster School (1784–5) and matriculated from Brasenose College, Oxford, on 10 May 1788, but did not take a degree. He was commissioned in the East Riding yeomanry in 1794 and in 1808–9, as lieutenant-colonel, he commanded the 2nd battalion of the East Riding militia. In 1795–6 he was high sheriff of Yorkshire, and on 17 September 1801 succeeded on the death of his father to the baronetcy and estates. Sykes was twice married: first, on 11 November 1795 to Henrietta, daughter and heir of Henry Masterman of Settrington, Yorkshire, on which occasion he took the additional name of Masterman. She died in July 1813, and on 2 August 1814 Sykes married Mary Elizabeth, daughter of William Egerton (formerly Tatton) and sister of Wilbraham Egerton of Tatton Park, Cheshire; she died in October 1846. There were no children by either marriage.

Sykes stood in the tory interest for the city of York, and on 14 May 1807 was returned for parliament against the Fitzwilliam candidate, Lawrence Dundas. Throughout his thirteen years in the House of Commons he is not known to have spoken, and he voted infrequently. He had a solid following in York, but his seat was contested in 1818, when he was again returned only to resign in 1820 on grounds of ill health which had necessitated prolonged absences abroad.

Sykes's reputation is rather that of agriculturalist and sportsman than parliamentarian, and of bibliophile above all these avocations. He assembled a fine private library at a time when opportunity was favourable and aristocratic competition keen. The Sykes library was strong in Elizabethan literature and in fifteenth-century editions of the classics, with the Mainz press of Fust and Schöffer and that in Rome of Sweynheym and Pannartz well represented. Sykes's marks of ownership usually add distinction to the provenance record of a rare book. He owned few manuscripts, but the later items in his collection included a report on Henry VIII's divorce convocation and Dugdale's heraldic visitation of Yorkshire for 1665–6. The chief treasure of his library was the vellum copy of the Rome Livy of 1469. Sykes had bought it at the Edwards sale in 1815 for £903; it was sold the year after his death for £472 10s., and three years later at the Dent sale of 1827 fetched only £262 10s. By then the 'bibliomania' which had quickly inflated the market had as rapidly turned to 'bibliophobia'; the 1469 Livy was acquired by Thomas Grenville (1755–1846), whose library was bequeathed to the British Museum. Sykes belonged to the Roxburghe Club, and presented to his fellow members in 1818 and 1822 well printed editions of two unique Caxton tracts then in York Minster Library. Sykes also collected pictures, bronzes, coins, medals, and engravings. The last included a complete set of Francesco Bartolozzi's work, with many proofs, which cost him nearly £5000.

Sykes died at Weymouth on 16 February 1823, and was succeeded by his brother Tatton *Sykes. All his collections were dispersed by auction in 1824, Evans disposing of the library in 3700 lots over twenty-five days in May and June, producing almost £18,000. His pictures fetched nearly £6000.   ALAN BELL

Sources HoP, *Commons* · B. Quaritch, ed., *Contributions towards a dictionary of English book-collectors*, 14 pts (1892–1921) · *GM*, 1st ser., 93/1 (1823), 375, 482 · *GM*, 1st ser., 93/2 (1823), 352, 451 · Burke, *Peerage*

Archives U. Hull, Brynmor Jones L., family and estate papers

Likenesses R. Grave, line engraving (after P. Rouw), BM, NPG

Sykes, Sir Percy Molesworth (1867–1945), diplomatist and author, was born on 28 February 1867 at Canterbury, the only son of Revd William Sykes (1829–1893), chaplain to the forces, and his wife, Mary (d. 1918), daughter of Anthony Oliver Molesworth, captain, Royal Artillery. He was educated at Rugby School (1882–6) and the Royal Military College, Sandhurst.

In 1888 Sykes was gazetted to the 16th lancers before transferring to the 2nd dragoon guards, an elite cavalry regiment he joined in India. He was promoted captain in 1897. During the Second South African War, Sykes served in the intelligence department and commanded the Montgomery imperial yeomanry. He was wounded, mentioned in dispatches, and awarded the queen's medal with three clasps. Sykes transferred to the Indian army in 1902, and was promoted major in 1906 and lieutenant-colonel in 1914. In 1902 he had married Evelyn, eldest daughter of Colonel Bruce Outram Seton RE; they had four sons and two daughters.

During the early part of the First World War, Sykes

Sir Percy Molesworth Sykes (1867–1945), by Walter Stoneman, 1919

worked in France as an interpreter for an Indian division before being sent in 1915 to Chinese Turkestan where he served as a substitute to Sir George Macartney, consul-general at Kashgar. In 1916, with the rank of brigadier-general, Sykes was sent to raise a force of 11,000 to replace the Persian gendarmerie, the greater part of which had either come under German influence or dispersed for lack of pay. Sykes arrived in Bandar-e-ʿAbbas in March 1916 with a handful of officers and a small escort, and at once began recruiting. In May he led his army, duly named the South Persian Rifles, inland towards Shiraz—an arduous march of over 1000 miles under a scorching summer sun—where he set up his headquarters. Although opposed by the Persian government who denounced his force as a threat to its sovereignty, and frustrated by the dual control exercised over him by the government of India and the Foreign Office, Sykes none the less restored some peace and security to the country—an achievement which has been credited to his unique knowledge of the country and his reputation and personal influence among the Persians.

In assessing this success over forty years later, Clarmont Skrine, who had firsthand experience of south Persia during the First World War, considered that Sykes 'cannot be denied the credit for exploiting British prestige, bluffing enemy agents and Persian hostiles alike, and thus, with quite inadequate resources, keeping south Persia comparatively quiet during a long and critical phase in the War' (C. P. Skrine, *World War in Iran*, 1962, xxiin.). When

the war ended Sykes left Persia, and in 1920 he retired from the army at the early age of fifty-two.

Except for the brief interludes during the Second South African War and the First World War, Sykes achieved greater renown as an administrator and author than as a soldier. He had become interested in Persia and the 'great game' at a young age, undertaking his first intelligence-gathering trip in 1892, to Samarkand on the recently opened Trans-Caspian railway, and he made his first Persian journey in 1893, travelling through on horseback for six months. He returned to Persia in October, entrusted with the task of building friendly relations with local leaders, and spent until June 1894 surveying and mapping, and climbing the extinct 12,500 foot volcano Kuh-e-Taftan. Later in the year Sykes was appointed the first British consul for Kerman and Persian Baluchistan, areas of growing political and economic interest to the government of India to whom he was primarily responsible and for whom he undertook a variety of assignments, usually in the company of his sister, Ella Constance *Sykes (1863–1939)—together they published *Through Deserts and Oases of Central Asia* in 1920. He and Colonel Thomas Holdich successfully demarcated 300 miles of the Perso-Baluch frontier in 1896 and over the course of the next year Sykes introduced polo to Tehran. In 1898 he founded the British consulate of Sistan and Kain, on the Afghan border, and he spent the next year mapping the area.

In 1902, following the Second South African War, Sykes returned to Kerman. He moved to Mashhad in 1905 and was appointed British consul-general and agent for the government of India in Khorasan. For the next eight years Sykes was responsible for producing annual trade reports, collecting intelligence about Russian activities across the border, and dealing with Shiʿi pilgrims from India. He continued to travel widely, earning his reputation as an authority on Persian history, geography, and customs.

Sykes's literary output is considerable. To the end of his life he remained interested in Persia and filled his years of retirement lecturing, reviewing, and providing introductions to other books, and writing his own books and articles on a variety of historical, geographical, and biographical subjects. In 1902 he published *Ten Thousand Miles in Persia*, a vivid account of his travels and discoveries. In 1914 he published the influential two-volume *History of Persia*, which reached a third revised edition in 1930. Although many of the ideas put forth in this work have passed into historical currency the volumes were intended in large part as a manual for British officers and ought to be viewed, it has been suggested, as the product more of 'the Victorian public school and the ideals of a soldier' than of a professional historian (Yapp, 355).

As honorary secretary of the Royal Central Asian Society from 1932 until his death, Sykes did great service in recruiting members and obtaining lecturers; in 1948 Lady Sykes and her family presented to the society the Sir Percy Molesworth Sykes memorial medal, to be awarded to those who make distinguished contributions promoting knowledge and understanding of Asian countries and their cultures. For his journeys in Persia he was awarded the Back grant (1899) and the Royal Geographical Society patron's gold medal (1902). He was appointed CMG in 1902, CIE in 1911, KCIE in 1915, and CB in 1919. He died in Charing Cross Hospital on 11 June 1945.

MARTIN BUNTON

Sources D. Wright, 'Sir Percy Sykes and Persia', *Central Asian Survey*, 12/2 (1993), 217–31 [includes complete list of works] · *DNB* · *The Times* (13 June 1945) · M. Yapp, 'Two British historians of Persia', *Historians of the Middle East*, ed. B. Lewis and P. M. Holt (1962), 343–56 · *CGPLA Eng. & Wales* (1945) · M. E. Yapp, *The Near East since the First World War* (1991)
Archives RGS, photograph collection · Royal Anthropological Institute, London, notes relating to Persia · St Ant. Oxf., papers | BL, corresp. with Macmillans, Add. MSS 55069–55070 · CUL, corresp. with Lord Hardinge
Likenesses W. Stoneman, photograph, 1919, NPG [*see illus.*]
Wealth at death £24,659 14s. 4d.: probate, 5 Dec 1945, *CGPLA Eng. & Wales*

Sykes, Sir Tatton, **fourth baronet** (1772–1863), landowner and racehorse breeder, was born at Wheldrake, near York, on 22 August 1772, the second son of Sir Christopher Sykes, second baronet (1749–1801), MP for Beverley, and his wife, Elizabeth Tatton (d. 1803). He was educated at Bishopthorpe, at Westminster School, and at Brasenose College, Oxford, where he was briefly in residence but did not take a degree. He was articled to Atkinson and Farrar, solicitors, of Lincoln's Inn Fields. While in London, he walked to Epsom to see the 1791 Derby, and he rode down to see the race the following year, but thereafter he never visited Epsom again. At this time he became an expert boxer, learning the sport from Gentleman Jackson and Jim Belcher.

Sykes worked for a bank in Hull for a short time, but in 1803 began sheep farming and breeding by purchasing ten pure Bakewells, and driving them on foot from Lincoln to his home at Barton, near Malton, Yorkshire. This was the start of a lifelong interest, and until nearly eighty he rode each year to sales of stock in the midlands. In 1861 he held his own fifty-eighth and last annual sale of sheep. It was said that he loved a good sheep almost, if not quite, as well as a good horse.

Sykes married on 19 June 1822 Mary Anne (d. 1861), second daughter of Sir William Foulis, bt. She was a cousin of his nephew Mark Foulis, and Sykes first suggested that the two cousins marry. When Mark Foulis rejected the idea Sykes replied 'If that is the case there is nothing for it but for me to wed' (Fairfax-Blakeborough, 67–8) and immediately proposed to her himself. They had two sons and six daughters. In the year after his marriage Sykes succeeded to the baronetcy following the death of his elder brother, Sir Mark Masterman *Sykes, on 16 February 1823, and moved to Sledmere, near Malton. Unlike his brother, he did not have parliamentary ambitions, and instead devoted his time to agriculture. He was keen on introducing new farming methods. His use of bone manure to enrich the land with phosphates enabled sheep to be fed and corn to be grown on previously infertile land and raised the agricultural value of his estates in the Wolds. He was also a master of foxhounds for forty years, hunting

the country from Coxwold to Spurn Head in the East Riding.

Sir Tatton was one of the largest breeders of bloodstock of his day, and at his death his stud numbered around 300 thoroughbreds. Such a number reveals that the emphasis was on quantity rather than quality, and it is remarkable that he never bred the winner of the Derby or St Leger, his best horses being Grey Momus, third in the Derby of 1837, and Black Tommy, second in 1857. He never sold any of his fillies and so lost the chance of seeing any of them compete in the fillies' classics.

Sir Tatton's connection with the turf as an owner was not extensive. The first horse he ran was Telemachus, at Middleton in 1803. For over twenty years after this he occasionally kept horses in training at Malton, and mainly rode them himself in races for gentleman riders. His last victory on one of his own horses was in 1829, when he won the Welham cup at Malton on All Heart and No Peel. He was a well-known patron of Doncaster races and saw seventy-seven runnings of the St Leger; in 1846 he had the honour of leading in the winner of the St Leger, which had been named Sir Tatton Sykes after him. During his visits to Doncaster he lodged, for forty years, with a cow-keeper whom he had once met by accident and who had offered him hospitality when he was unable to find lodgings in the town. This was typical of a man who made no distinction of classes; farmers, dealers, and stone breakers were welcome to his hospitality at Sledmere, when he would often serve them the famous Sledmere ale himself, and he treated poachers leniently, thereby preserving his own game. Sir Tatton died of pneumonia at Sledmere on 21 March 1863, and was buried there on 27 March. Three thousand people were present, and, as a mark of respect, there was no fox-hunting in Yorkshire that day. A memorial tower 120 feet high was erected at Garton Hill, near Sledmere, by public subscription. Like other sporting squires, he became a popular figure well beyond his native county and almost revered within it. He was mentioned in the sporting novels of Robert Smith Surtees, and was famous for his adherence to the fashions of the Regency. His family, however, knew him as a brutal figure, who ruled over them 'with the vicious rage of a stone-age tyrant' (Sykes, 'Behind the tablet', 13).

The eccentricities of his eldest son, **Sir Tatton Sykes**, fifth baronet (1826–1913), may be attributed to his barbaric upbringing. He was born on 13 March 1826, and on his father's death inherited both the baronetcy and the largest estate (some 34,000 acres) in the East Riding of Yorkshire. His wealth increased as he raised rents during the prosperity of the 1870s, but when depression took hold in the agricultural sector, he became a hated figure among his tenant farmers and received death threats. He re-established the Sledmere stud, which had been dispersed on his father's death. He was a more successful breeder than his father, and produced two Derby winners, Doncaster (1873) and Spearmint (1906), and Mimi, winner of the One Thousand Guineas and the Oaks in 1891.

Sykes's other great interest was church-building and

restoration: he reputedly spent £1.5 million in east York-shire on this object during his lifetime. In his early life, to escape his tyrannical father, he travelled widely in the Ori-ent, studying ecclesiastical architecture. Unlike his father, who had treated church-building as an aspect of estate management, he was deeply interested in high Anglican ecclesiology, and employed the Gothic revivalists G. E. Street and (later) Temple Moore to carry out his projects.

A shy and reserved figure, Sykes lived alone in Sledmere for over a decade before his marriage on 3 August 1874 to (Christina Anne) Jessica (c.1856–1912), daughter of George Augustus Cavendish-Bentinck MP. She was some thirty years her husband's junior and the marriage, which pro-duced only one child, was not a happy one. Lady Sykes, who was received into the Roman Catholic church in 1882, became increasingly estranged from her husband, who, it was alleged, failed to pay her marriage settlement. Their affairs, and her debts, were the subject of a legal dispute (*Sykes* v. *Sykes*) in 1897, when a judge described Sir Tatton as 'an obstinate and extremely whimsical old gentleman' (Sykes, 'Sir Tatton Sykes', 71). She subsequently published novels and an eyewitness account of the Second South African War, following a visit there in 1900.

The second Sir Tatton Sykes's oddities were marked by his belief that the body should be kept at a constant tem-perature. To achieve this, he would wear six overcoats or two pairs of trousers, discarding layers as necessary. Obsessive about diet, he had milk puddings specially pre-pared for him by his personal cook wherever he went. He hated seeing flowers in his farm and cottage gardens, believing they should be used for growing potatoes or other vegetables, and so strongly did he insist on his views that traditional country gardens largely disappeared from the Sledmere estate. He also disliked cottagers using their front doors, perhaps because he hated to see women gos-siping or children playing in the street, and as a result he built estate houses without front doors. A couple of years before his death he suffered the destruction by fire of his home, Sledmere House, on 23 May 1911. Sykes died of pneumonia in the Hotel Metropole, Northumberland Avenue, London on 4 May 1913 and was buried at Sled-mere. He was succeeded by his only son, Sir Mark *Sykes, sixth baronet.

Christopher Sykes (1831–1898), younger brother of the second Sir Tatton Sykes, reacted to his father's bullying by joining the 'swells' of London society in the 1850s. He was born at Sledmere on 10 January 1831, and was educated at Rugby School and at Trinity College, Cambridge, which he entered in 1848 but left without graduating. Never marry-ing, he became a man of fashion (and a snob), and was a connoisseur of books, china, and furniture. From 1865 to 1868 he was Conservative MP for Beverley, and represen-ted the East Riding of Yorkshire from 1868 to 1885, and the Buckrose constituency of the East Riding from 1886 to 1892. During his long parliamentary career he made only six speeches. His one intervention of note was his 1869 bill for the preservation of seabirds (which were being slaugh-tered by shooters off the east coast); this earned him the sobriquet the Gull's Friend.

Christopher Sykes fell in with the circle of the prince of Wales (the future Edward VII), whom he entertained lav-ishly at his seat at Brantingham Thorpe, Brough, York-shire, when they visited the Doncaster races, and at his London home, 11 Hill Street, Berkeley Square. He was one of the founders of the Marlborough club, promoted by the prince. Disraeli portrayed him in *Lothair* as Mr Brauncepath, the young man who knew the art of giving dinners supremely well. But the prince exploited his slav-ish loyalty, and subjected his courtier to a string of humili-ations; on one occasion he poured a glass of brandy over his head at a dinner, to which Sykes responded, 'As your royal highness pleases' (Sykes, 'Behind the tablet', 28). He was financially ruined by the prince's extravagance, and though his bankruptcy was narrowly averted in the early 1890s, he lost his country estate and his home in Berkeley Square. Sykes died at home (2 Chesterfield Street, Mayfair, London) on 15 December 1898 and was buried at Kensal Green cemetery. The prince erected a tablet to his mem-ory in Westminster Abbey. His life was the subject of a poignant memoir by his great-nephew Christopher Hugh *Sykes.   JOHN PINFOLD

Sources J. Fairfax-Blakeborough, *Sykes of Sledmere* (1929) • Thor-manby [W. W. Dixon], *Kings of the turf: memoirs and anecdotes* (1898) • *Baily's Magazine*, 2 (1860–61), 169–74 • *Bell's Life in London* (29 March 1863) • *ILN* (11 April 1863) • *The Times* (23 March 1863) • *Sporting Maga-zine*, 3rd ser., 41 (1863), 276–84 • The Druid [H. H. Dixon], *Scott and Sebright* (1862), 9–14, 131–43, 326 • The Druid [H. H. Dixon], *Saddle and sirloin, or, English farm and sporting worthies* (1870), 221–53 • C. S. Sykes, 'Sir Tatton Sykes: a helpless eccentric', in H. Bridgeman and E. Drury, *The British eccentric* (1975), 67–77 • B. English, 'On the eve of the great depression: the economy of the Sledmere estate, 1869–1878', *Business History*, 24 (1982), 24–47 • F. C. Burnand, ed., *The Cath-olic who's who and yearbook* (1910) • C. Sykes, 'Behind the tablet', *Four studies in loyalty* (1946), 11–39 • Boase, *Mod. Eng. biog.* [Christopher Sykes] • Venn, *Alum. Cant.* [Christopher Sykes] • P. Magnus, *King Edward the Seventh* (1964) • *CGPLA Eng. & Wales* (1898) [Christopher Sykes]

Archives U. Hull, Brynmor Jones L., estate papers, family, and personal | East Riding of Yorkshire Archives Service, Beverley, letters to Thomas Grimston

Likenesses T. Lawrence, oils, 1805, repro. in Fairfax-Blakeborough, *Sykes of Sledmere*, facing p. 46 • H. Hall, oils, c.1845–1850, Yale U. CBA • F. Grant, oils, 1847, Sledmere House, East Riding of Yorkshire • engraving, c.1860 (after photograph), repro. in *ILN* (11 April 1863), 413 • photograph, 1862, repro. in Fairfax-Blakeborough, *Sykes of Sledmere*, facing p. 148 • Corbold, caricature, 1879 (Christopher Sykes; *The Row in the season*), repro. in *ILN* (24 Dec 1898), 945 • Ape [C. Pellegrini], caricature (Christopher Sykes), repro. in *VF* (14 Nov 1874) • J. Brown, stipple, BM; repro. in *Baily's Magazine* • Spy [L. Ward], caricature (Tatton Sykes), repro. in *VF* (23 Aug 1879) • photograph (Tatton Sykes), repro. in Bridgeman and Drury, *British eccentric*, 72

Wealth at death under £140,000: resworn will, 16 May 1864, *CGPLA Eng. & Wales* • £289,446 17s. 0d.—Sir Tatton Sykes: probate, 10 July 1913, *CGPLA Eng. & Wales* • £6249 4s. 7d.—Christopher Sykes: resworn probate, May 1899, *CGPLA Eng. & Wales* (1898)

Sykes, Sir Tatton, fifth baronet (1826–1913). *See under* Sykes, Sir Tatton, fourth baronet (1772–1863).

Sykes, William Henry (1790–1872), army officer in the East India Company and naturalist, son of Samuel Sykes of Friezing Hall, Yorkshire, the descendant of the Drighlington branch of an old Yorkshire family, was born on 25 January 1790. He entered the military service of the East India Company as cadet in 1803, obtained a commission on 1 May 1804, and was promoted to a lieutenancy on 12 October 1805. He was present at the siege of Bharatpur under Lord Lake in 1805. In 1810 he passed as interpreter in Hindustani and Maratha. He served in the Deccan from 1817 to 1820, took part in the battles of Kirkee and Poona, and aided in the capture of the hill forts. He obtained a captaincy on 25 January 1819, returned to Europe in 1820, and spent four years travelling on the continent. In 1824 he married Elizabeth, youngest daughter of William Hay of Renistoun; they had children.

In October 1824 Sykes returned to India, receiving the appointment of statistical reporter to the Bombay government. For the next few years he was engaged in statistical and natural history researches, and completed a census of the population of the Deccan, two voluminous statistical reports, and a complete natural history report illustrated by drawings. On 8 September 1826 he was promoted major, and on 9 April 1831 lieutenant-colonel. As an economy measure the office of statistical reporter was abolished in December 1829; but he obtained leave to forgo his military duties and carry on the duties of his office unpaid until the work was completed. He finished in January 1831, receiving the thanks of the government, and left for Europe on furlough. In April 1833 and again in 1853 he gave evidence before a committee of the House of Commons on Indian affairs. He retired from active service with the rank of colonel on 18 June 1833.

In September 1835 Sykes became a royal commissioner in lunacy, and performed the duties unpaid until the reconstruction of the lunacy commission in 1845. He was elected in 1840 to the board of directors of the East India Company, of which he became deputy chairman in 1855 and chairman in 1856.

In 1847 Sykes stood unsuccessfully as a Liberal for one of the Aberdeen seats, but in 1857 was returned there as a Liberal and held the seat until his death. He had in the interval (March 1854) been elected lord rector of Marischal College. Sykes was elected a fellow of the Royal Society in 1834, and served more than once on its council; he was a member of the Royal Asiatic Society, and its president in 1858; he was one of the founders of the Statistical Society and president in 1863; he was also chairman of the Society of Arts. He died at his home, 47 Albion Street, Hyde Park, London, on 16 June 1872.

Sykes was a keen scientific observer, his favourite pursuits being zoology, palaeontology, and meteorology. He published papers in scientific journals and also *Vital Statistics of the East India Company's Armies in India, European and Native* (1845?) and the *Taeping Rebellion in China* (1863).

B. B. Woodward, *rev.* M. G. M. Jones

Sources J. Sykes, *Biographical notes of Colonel W. H. Sykes* (1857) [and MS appx] · *PRS*, 20 (1871–2), xxxiii · *Aberdeen Journal* (19 June 1872), 8 · *BL cat.* · *Catalogue of scientific papers*, Royal Society · Boase, *Mod. Eng. biog.* · *CGPLA Eng. & Wales* (1873)
Archives NHM, notes and sketches · RGS, papers · University of Western Ontario Library, sketches and MSS relating to Elloora caves | BL OIOC, report on statistics of the Deccan, MSS Eur. D 140–50 · Herts. ALS, letters to Lord Lytton, D/EK · NA Scot., corresp.

with Lord Dalhousie · RBG Kew, letters to Sir William Hooker · RS, corresp. with Sir John Herschel
Likenesses engraving, repro. in *ILN*, 30 (1857), 499 · engraving, repro. in *ILN*, 61 (1872), 60 · engraving, repro. in *The Graphic*, 6 (1872)
Wealth at death £7000: probate, 22 Feb 1873, *CGPLA Eng. & Wales*

Sykes, William Robert (1840–1917), railway signalling engineer, was born on 15 June 1840 at 11 Grosvenor Street, Westminster, London, the eldest in the family of two sons and one daughter of George Sykes, builder, and his wife, Mary Burden. His father died when he was thirteen. He was educated at the Blue Coat School, Westminster. In 1854 he began training in the workshops of the Electric Telegraph Company and four years later transferred to their central London headquarters. In 1860 he left this company and joined Charles Shepherd of Leadenhall Street, maker of chronometers and horological instruments and inventor of the electrical clocks used by the Royal Observatory.

In 1863 Sykes joined the London, Chatham, and Dover Railway, taking charge of maintenance of their telegraph instruments, clocks, and watches under the chief engineer for telegraphs and electric lighting. Within two years he had designed and installed electrical repeater devices, indicating to signalmen the position of semaphore signal arms which were outside their range of vision; an automatic device recording on tape the bell-code communications between signal boxes; and the first track circuiting in which the presence of a train on a section of track was indicated electrically in the signal cabin. In 1872 he introduced at Victoria on the Metropolitan District Railway an automatic train-protection system whereby a red lens positioned in front of a white signal light was raised above it on actuation from an electrical contact only when the track section ahead was clear. This system was also used later by the Métropolitain in Paris.

In 1875 Sykes achieved one of the greatest advances in safety in railway operation with his 'lock and block' system. In this the mechanical signals were interlocked with electrical block instruments in the signal cabins, by which a train was authorized to enter the succeeding section only when this was not occupied by another train. Thus the signalman was prevented from inadvertently releasing signals for a second train to enter the section before the first was clear. This system overcame the risks of human error which had been the cause of serious accidents. The Board of Trade repeatedly advocated the use of 'lock and block' in its accident reports. Sykes's system, which was also used for interlocking railway swing bridges across rivers, was applied widely in Britain and in the USA, Russia, and Japan. A later development was the combination of track circuiting, in which an electrical circuit is completed, detecting the presence of wheels of a train passing over a section of track, with 'lock and block' so that the electric-block instruments were controlled by the trains themselves and thus safety was doubly assured.

Electrically actuated signals worked by small switches and interlocked with the points they controlled were first introduced by Sykes at Penge in 1875 and were the fore-runner of large electro-mechanical signalling systems in which electrically actuated signals controlled by small slides were introduced, with lever-controlled points actuated by rodding. Sykes was also responsible for many other signalling and safety devices, including depression or fouling bars interlocked with signals, thus providing valuable protection against these inadvertently being set to allow the passage of a train if other trains were obstructing its path.

In 1899 the London, Chatham, and Dover and the South Eastern railways were brought under the operational control of a joint managing committee and Sykes was appointed consulting electrical engineer to the new organization, in which capacity he continued until his death, having served the same railway for fifty-four years. He also founded the W. R. Sykes Interlocking Signal Company, which was continued by his sons and eventually absorbed by Westinghouse Brake and Signal Company. Sykes obtained awards for his signalling and railway safety inventions at many international exhibitions, notably at Paris in 1881; Crystal Palace in 1882, 1892, and 1893; Antwerp in 1894; and Brussels in 1897.

Sykes married Eliza Church, from co. Cork. They had two daughters and four sons, one of whom (also an inventor) died relatively young, and three of whom became engineers. Sykes died on 2 October 1917 at his home, Roselands, Joy Lane, in Whitstable, Kent.

GEORGE W. CARPENTER, rev.

Sources *The Engineer* (12 Oct 1917) · *Railway Magazine*, 41 (Nov 1917) · *The electrical trades directory* (1898) · private information (1993) · *The Oxford companion to British railway history* (1979)

Wealth at death £16,815 4s. 2d.: probate, 23 Oct 1917, CGPLA Eng. & Wales

Syllas, Stelios Messinesos [Leo] **de** (1917–1964), architect, was born at Northbrook, Holmwood, Surrey, on 24 July 1917, the younger son of Stelios de Syllas, painter, and his wife, Vera Rose Palatiano. His mother came from a very conventional Greek family in Corfu, but had Anglo-Irish connections on her mother's side. Her parents disapproved of de Syllas, who came from a less respectable background, and as a result they eloped first to Munich, before moving to Britain in 1911. De Syllas's father had little success as a painter and turned to making toys. Leo was educated at Haberdashers' Aske's School, Hatcham, and Christ's College, Finchley, and proceeded to the Bartlett school of architecture at University College, London, in 1933. Here he rebelled against the classicism of Professor Albert Richardson by designing a modernist project, which was failed. He transferred in 1936 for his two final years to the Architectural Association, where the implications of modernism were being extended from the formal to their left-wing social, political, and intellectual dimensions by a lively group of students with whom de Syllas was associated as an editor of the magazine *Focus* (1938–9). Richard Llewelyn-Davies was a close friend and mentor, especially in political matters. In 1939 de Syllas, Anthony Cox (another *Focus* editor), and nine other recent Architectural Association graduates formed the Architects'

Co-operative Partnership with the intention of practising in the new collaborative and research-based manner for which they had campaigned as students.

Further progress was interrupted almost immediately by the war. De Syllas joined the research and experiments department of the ministry of home security. On 1 August 1942 he married Phoebe Helen (1913–1986), daughter of Ralph Lucas, engineering designer, and sister of the architect Colin Lucas, whose first husband, A. W. Nicol, an original Architects' Co-operative Partnership member, was killed in an accident. He had two stepsons and a son and daughter. In 1943 de Syllas went to the British West Indies as assistant architect to Robert J. Gardner-Medwin in the Colonial Development and Welfare Organisation to work on a programme of buildings for education, housing, and health. In 1946 he was appointed architect and planning officer to the government of Barbados, whose sugar production was valuable for the post-war British economy, and was responsible for the master plan of Bridgetown. De Syllas designed a training college in the grounds of Erdiston House (1947), which incorporated well-lit dormitories and classrooms, shaded with overhanging roofs, in local coral block masonry. On returning to Britain in 1947, de Syllas rejoined the pre-war partnership, which in 1951 was renamed Architects' Co-Partnership (ACP). Work was seldom attributed to individuals, but de Syllas was involved at this time in the design of Leesbrook School, a secondary modern, at Chaddesden in Derbyshire, completed in 1955.

The opportunities for building in developing countries continued to excite de Syllas, and in 1954 he opened a branch office of ACP in Lagos, Nigeria. Work included the Bristol Hotel, Lagos, completed in 1961, and a large housing development at Akosombo in Ghana to serve the upper Volta River project. He remained most fascinated by the technical and social aspects of architecture, describing himself on one occasion as 'only 99 per cent architect'. None the less, his rooftop extension to Simpson's, Piccadilly, London (1963), contributes by spirited contrast to Joseph Emberton's original building of 1935. In 1962 de Syllas was responsible for the winning ACP competition design for the St Paul's Cathedral choir school in New Change, which followed the materials of Wren's cathedral while breaking its own mass into separate units. Following his death this was built with only minor changes.

A man of enthusiastic energy, de Syllas pursued his overseas commitments without any diminution of his interest in architectural affairs at home. He was elected to the council of the Architectural Association in 1956 and was next in line for the presidency when he died. He strongly supported the merger, then being proposed, with Imperial College. He was active in the association's pioneering department of tropical studies and was largely responsible for establishing a link between the Architectural Association and the University of Science and Technology at Kumasi, Ghana. In 1963 he was chairman of the Royal Institute of British Architects Commonwealth Architects' Conference.

De Syllas was tall and striking in appearance. Although initially hampered by his non-English name and background, he came to recognize their exotic value. He was animated and fluent in movement, talking and gesticulating continuously. Warm-hearted and gregarious by nature, he showed a readiness to communicate in several languages uninhibited by an imperfect command of some of them, which was always compensated for by his genuine charm and sincerity. Full of stimulating ideas and with an infectious optimism, he got on notably well with young people, whose outlook he found refreshing. His early vision of modernism was modified by an increasing awareness of architectural context and tradition. He believed in combining practice with teaching and in the early 1950s joined other ACP partners in teaching the third year at the Architectural Association.

In 1951 de Syllas took his family to live in a Victorian house, St Julian's, near Sevenoaks, which was established as an experiment in communal living. Phoebe de Syllas, whose talents were overshadowed by her husband, was an interior designer and wrote on this subject. Leo de Syllas was killed in a road accident near Le Kef in Tunisia on 30 January 1964, while working on a project for new schools for the Tunisian government.

ANTHONY COX, rev. ALAN POWERS

Sources A. Cox, RIBA Journal, 71 (1964), 126 · Architects' Journal (12 Feb 1964), 350 · [L. de Syllas], 'Training college in Barbados', ArchR, 107 (1950), 154–64 · R. J. Gardner-Medwin, 'Development and welfare in the West Indies', Architects' Journal (22 Jan 1948), 83–9 · Architects Co-Partnership: the first fifty years (1989) · CGPLA Eng. & Wales (1964) · b. cert. · m. cert.
Archives Architects' Co-Partnership, Potters Bar · priv. coll., MSS
Wealth at death £14,485: probate, 26 Oct 1964, CGPLA Eng. & Wales

Sylvester, Albert James (1889–1989), political and private secretary, was born on 24 November 1889 in Harlaston, Staffordshire, the eldest of three children and only son of Albert Sylvester, a tenant farmer reduced to the role of farmworker by the agricultural depression, and his wife, Edith, daughter of James Redfern, also from Staffordshire but of no traceable address. He was educated at Guild Street School, Burton upon Trent, and while there studied Pitman's shorthand. After leaving school at fourteen to become a brewery clerk he devoted most of his leisure to perfecting his shorthand and typing, achieving the champion speeds of, respectively, 210 and 80 words a minute. As a young man he moved as a freelance typist to London, where his talents were soon in demand and he became a member, in 1911 and 1912, of the British international typewriting team, which competed (unsuccessfully) with the Americans.

In 1912, on the recommendation of a stranger whom he met on the underground after a concert at the Albert Hall, Sylvester was appointed to the secretarial staff of the royal commission on Indian public services. This took him to the subcontinent and introduced him to work in the official sphere. After the outbreak of war in 1914 he joined the staff of Colonel (later first Baron) M. P. A. Hankey, secretary of the committee of imperial defence. The following year he became the first shorthand writer to record the proceedings of a cabinet committee.

When, in December 1916, David Lloyd *George succeeded H. H. Asquith as prime minister, he at once established a war cabinet secretariat under Hankey, who chose Sylvester as his private secretary. In this capacity he showed such diligence, discretion, and efficiency that at the end of the war he was given the status of a higher-grade civil servant, without having to sit the examination. Immediately after the war he accompanied Hankey to the Paris peace conference, where he continued to work under intense pressure. In 1917 he married Evelyn Annie (d. 1962), daughter of William Welman, draper and Baptist lay preacher, of Norbiton. They had one daughter.

Sylvester's work for Hankey brought him into frequent contact with the prime minister, and in 1921 Lloyd George recruited him to the secretariat at 10 Downing Street. With Lloyd George he attended the Cannes and Genoa conferences, and he was also involved in the tortuous processes leading to the Anglo-Irish treaty in 1921. When, eleven months later, the Lloyd George coalition was brought down, Sylvester stayed on for a time under two Conservative prime ministers, Andrew Bonar Law and Stanley Baldwin. But in 1923 he left the civil service and rejoined Lloyd George.

Though Sylvester's chief motive for doing so was that he admired Lloyd George and found working for him exciting, Lloyd George facilitated the move by paying him a higher salary, and also a substantial sum to compensate him for the loss of civil service pension rights. He was given the title of principal private secretary, though in reality that role belonged to Lloyd George's mistress (later his second wife), Frances Stevenson (later Countess Lloyd George of Dwyfor).

Nevertheless, Sylvester accompanied Lloyd George on most of his travels abroad, including his controversial visit to Adolf Hitler in 1936, and at home ran the office at Thames House, Westminster, which at the height of Lloyd George's activity as an opposition politician had a staff of more than twenty. Sylvester dealt with his master's enormous correspondence and, when he was working on his War Memoirs (6 vols., 1933–6), carried out much archival research and interviewing of former colleagues on his behalf. His services were indispensable, and he stayed at his post until Lloyd George's death in 1945.

Any hopes Sylvester may have had that Lloyd George's widow would invite him to be, as it were, joint guardian of the shrine, and to collaborate in work based on the papers that had been left to her, were soon dashed. In 1947 he published a book of his own, The Real Lloyd George, which has its good points but is on the whole disappointing. In 1975 a selection from his diary appeared, edited by Colin Cross and entitled Life with Lloyd George, and this is a far more valuable publication. The diary, kept in shorthand, gives a vivid impression of Lloyd George and a detailed account of his life, though unfortunately it covers only the last phase, from 1931 to the end. The full text of the diary is now in the National Library of Wales.

Always at heart a countryman, Sylvester bought during the Second World War 150 acres of farmland in Wiltshire. In 1949 he moved from his London home in Putney to another Wiltshire property, Rudloe Cottage near Corsham, where he cultivated a small-holding, his larger holding being let to a tenant. He spent the rest of his life at Rudloe, becoming a JP (1953) and, in 1962, chairman of the local bench. In old age he took to ballroom dancing for which, at eighty-five, he received the top amateur award, thereby earning himself a place in *The Guinness Book of Records*.

Sylvester was well above medium height, clean-shaven, with a high forehead, longish nose, and fresh complexion. His vigorous and humorous temperament came across most effectively in the many radio and television interviews that he gave in his later years. Even when very old and infirm his resilience was remarkable. A visitor to Rudloe would find him slumped in an armchair before a fire that was nearly out, and his first words would be a plaintive 'I am very, very ill.' But soon he would be standing erect, throwing logs on the fire and reliving past experiences with strong voice and eloquent gesture. No doubt it was his personality as much as his great professional competence that appealed to Lloyd George.

Sylvester died at St Andrews Hospital, Chippenham, Wiltshire, on 27 October 1989, a month short of his 100th birthday. JOHN GRIGG, *rev.*

Sources A. J. Sylvester, *The real Lloyd George* (1947) · A. J. Sylvester, *Life with Lloyd George*, ed. C. Cross (1975) · *The Times* (28 Oct 1989) · *The Independent* (28 Oct 1989)
Archives NL Wales, diaries, notebooks, subject files, corresp., papers relating to his biography of David Lloyd George, papers | HLRO, corresp. with Lord Beaverbrook · King's Lond., Liddell Hart C., corresp. with Sir B. H. Liddell Hart
Wealth at death £302,425: probate, 18 Jan 1990, *CGPLA Eng. & Wales*

Sylvester, James Joseph (1814–1897), mathematician, was born on 3 September 1814 in London, the youngest son of five sons and four daughters of Abraham Joseph, merchant. Two of his older brothers emigrated to the United States and adopted the surname Sylvester, a convention which he and at least one other brother followed. Between the ages of six and twelve he studied at the boarding-school run by Neumegen in Highgate, where he so distinguished himself in mathematics that Olinthus Gregory, professor of mathematics at the Royal Military Academy, Woolwich, was asked to evaluate his mathematical abilities further. Gregory recognized real talent in the boy and urged that particular attention be paid to his subsequent mathematical training. Sylvester proceeded to Daniell's boarding-school in Islington before entering London University in its opening year of 1828.

London University presented the fourteen-year-old boy with prime opportunities: the school's non-sectarian policies allowed Sylvester, a Jew, not only to learn but also to take a degree, and its professor of mathematics was the

James Joseph Sylvester (1814–1897), by Alfred Edward Emslie, 1889

gifted Augustus De Morgan. Unfortunately, Sylvester studied there for only five months before his family withdrew him following an incident in the refectory in which he allegedly assaulted a fellow student with a table knife. In 1829 he was sent to live with aunts in Liverpool and to attend the Royal Institution School there. Although he once again distinguished himself in mathematics, winning the school's first prize in the subject, as well as a $500 prize from the contractors of lotteries of New York for the solution of a combinatorial problem, he was so unhappy in Liverpool that he ran away to Dublin. Quite by chance a member of the family discovered him there and returned him to England.

Sylvester was next entered as a sizar at St John's College, Cambridge, on 7 July 1831, matriculating officially four months later on 14 November. Illness interrupted his stay at Cambridge twice between June 1833 and 19 January 1836, when he was readmitted as a pensioner. In January 1837 he was second wrangler in the mathematical tripos, but, as a non-Anglican, he could not subscribe to the Thirty-Nine Articles of the Church of England and so could neither take his degree nor compete for further prizes or fellowships. (Cambridge would eventually award him the degrees of BA and MA *honoris causa* in 1872 following the repeal of the Test Acts, and made him an honorary ScD in 1890; Oxford made him a DCL in 1880.)

With Cambridge and Oxford closed to him at graduate level in the late 1830s, Sylvester won the professorship of natural philosophy at University College, London, in 1838. This should have been another prime opportunity for him, in light of the paucity of higher level teaching positions available in England for non-Anglicans, but he found the duties of the post uncongenial and resigned in 1841 to take the professorship of mathematics at the University of Virginia, founded in Charlottesville by Thomas Jefferson in 1819. His short tenure at University College had not been uneventful, however: his early papers on topics in mathematical physics had secured him a fellowship in the Royal Society in 1839; he had proven his first mathematical result in the algebraic theory of elimination (1840), a subject which would ultimately lead him to his seminal research in the theory of invariants; and he had officially earned both the BA and the MA from Trinity College, Dublin, in 1841.

In November 1841 the short, burly, and bespectacled Englishman with the cockney accent arrived in central Virginia, somewhat late for the academic term, to begin his duties teaching mathematics to young men from wealthy southern families. Although initially welcomed warmly into the university community, Sylvester soon found himself at odds with at least one disrespectful student in his classroom. At the end of February 1842 he called on the faculty senate to expel the student for insubordination. When the senate officially disciplined the student but did not expel him (perhaps fearing a recurrence of the student unrest that had, less than two years before, resulted in the murder of a member of the faculty), Sylvester protested at the decision and ultimately resigned his position in March 1842.

Sylvester left Charlottesville for his brother's home in New York city, and tried in vain to secure another academic position in the United States. He also met with the refusal—on religious grounds—of his proposal of marriage to a Miss Marston of New York. (He would never marry and had no children.) Thoroughly disheartened, he returned to England late in November 1843 to face uncertain prospects.

By December 1844 Sylvester had 'recovered [his] footing in the world's slippery path' (Sylvester to Joseph Henry, 12 April 1846, Smithsonian Institution, Henry MSS, M099, no. 8573) and had taken posts as secretary and actuary at the Equity and Law Life Assurance Company in London. Two years later, in 1846, he had also entered the Inner Temple to prepare himself for a career in law but, while he was called to the bar in 1850, he never practised. At some time during his four years of legal training, he met another misplaced mathematician studying for the bar, Arthur Cayley. This meeting developed into both a lifelong friendship and the sustained mathematical dialogue that would produce the field of invariant theory, an area of pure mathematics with deep applications in geometry as well as physics.

After publishing very little in the 1840s Sylvester truly came into his own as a mathematical researcher in the 1850s. Extending his work in elimination theory to an analysis of the determinants *per se* that arose in that research, he sought to develop what he termed in 1851 a 'general theory of associated forms'. This quickly led him to a study of the invariantive properties of such forms. In 1852 he began the process of creating a theory of invariants from numerous isolated results, in his massive paper 'On the principles of the calculus of forms' (*Cambridge and Dublin Mathematical Journal*, 7, 1852; 8, 1853). Among other things, this involved determining techniques for calculating explicitly the invariants of a given form and for exploring the interrelations between those invariants. His assault on the latter set of issues resulted in another mammoth paper the following year on the very sticky problem of detecting algebraic dependence relations, or 'syzygies' (the term he coined) among invariants. This paper also provided a dictionary of the evolving language of invariant theory that he gloried in creating out of his extensive knowledge of French, German, Italian, Latin, and classical Greek.

Concurrent with this mathematical research Sylvester carried out his actuarial work at Equity Law and Life with distinction, compiling a 'Table of whole life assurances with profits; annual premium for an assurance of 100 pounds' which was still in use by the society for ages twenty-five and older as late as 1923. He also founded the Law Reversionary Interest Society Ltd and served as its first actuary (1853–5). Despite these professional successes Sylvester had tired by the mid-1850s of his dual existence as actuary and research mathematician and tried, unsuccessfully, in 1854 for the vacant professorship of mathematics at the Royal Military Academy in Woolwich. When the new incumbent died shortly after assuming his duties, Sylvester reapplied, and this time won the post, which he held from 1855 to 1870.

Sylvester's first ten years at Woolwich proved fruitful and rewarding. He continued his research in invariant theory, made new breakthroughs in the not unrelated combinatorial field of partition theory (1859), and gave the first rigorous proof of Newton's rule for locating the imaginary roots of a polynomial equation (1864). His achievements also received significant recognition in the form of the Royal Society's royal medal in 1861 and the title of foreign correspondent to the French Académie des Sciences in 1863. Socially, he participated actively and regularly at the Athenaeum, the club of which he became a member in 1856. The last five Woolwich years, however, found him mathematically unfocused and increasingly at odds with the military authorities over his teaching load. Not even the second presidency, in 1866, of the new London Mathematical Society, nor the presidency of the mathematics and physics section of the British Association for the Advancement of Science at its 1869 meeting in Exeter served to soften the blow inflicted when a change in the regulations forced his premature retirement at the age of fifty-five and denied him a full pension.

The publication of Sylvester's only book, *The Laws of Verse* (1870), coincided with this bitter turn of events; indeed, it was not mathematics but poetry, a try for a seat on the London school board, and life at his club that largely occupied him from 1870 to 1875. These years saw the publication of only eight short and uninspired mathematical articles by the previously prolific and profound

Sylvester. In 1875, however, he found himself under serious consideration for the professorship of mathematics at the newly forming Johns Hopkins University in Baltimore, Maryland. Under the direction of its first president, Daniel Coit Gilman, Johns Hopkins was to be the first research-orientated university in the United States, one which emphasized both undergraduate and graduate teaching while it stressed original research and the active training of future researchers. Sylvester won the appointment, made yet another transatlantic move, and assumed his duties when the school opened in 1876.

The years at Johns Hopkins from 1876 to the end of 1883 marked a key phase in Sylvester's life and in the development of research-level mathematics in America. The opportunity to build a programme in mathematics, to teach talented advanced students, and to do his own research in a supportive institutional environment thoroughly re-energized Sylvester. This sense of revitalization comes out with characteristic exuberance and hyperbole in the address that he delivered in 1877 at the commemoration day celebration at Johns Hopkins. He proclaimed to his audience that:

> Mathematics is not a book confined within a cover and bound between brazen clasps, whose content it needs only patience to ransack … it is limitless as that space which it finds too narrow for its aspirations; its possibilities are as infinite as the worlds which are forever crowding in and multiplying upon the astronomer's gaze.

New research possibilities quickly opened before Sylvester's eyes at Johns Hopkins. He re-engaged in his invariant-theoretic research, spurred on by the students in his courses, and worked tirelessly to push and extend the methods of the British school of invariant theory that he and Cayley had animated. These efforts also led him back to partition theory, and he and his students made great strides in developing constructive—as opposed to analytic—methods for proving partition-theoretic results (1882). His lectures also stimulated him to branch off into the study of matrix algebras and to begin laying the foundations for a general theory of abstract algebras (1884). He published much of this new work on the pages of the *American Journal of Mathematics*, the research-orientated quarterly which he founded in 1878 and edited from 1878 until 1884. This journal is the oldest continuous mathematics research journal in the United States, and its success in Sylvester's hands marked America's entry into mathematics at the research level internationally.

The Johns Hopkins years also witnessed more official recognition for Sylvester from the broader scientific community. In 1880 he received the Copley medal of the Royal Society and in 1883 he was named foreign associate of both the Accademia dei Lincei in Rome and the National Academy of Sciences in the United States. He would later win the De Morgan gold medal from the London Mathematical Society in 1887. Despite such commendation, by the summer of 1883 Sylvester felt increasingly tired and overwhelmed by the pressures of 'the responsibility of directing and molding the mathematical education of 55 million of one of the most intellectual races of men upon

the face of the earth' (Sylvester to Felix Klein, 17 Jan 1884, Klein Nachlass XXII L, Niedersächsische Staats- und Universitätsbibliothek, Göttingen). He was also homesick for England and so had applied for the vacant Savilian professorship of geometry at Oxford. He tendered his resignation at Johns Hopkins in September 1883, effective 1 January 1884, despite the fact that the outcome at Oxford was then as yet unknown, was named to the Savilian chair in December, and sailed for England just before the end of the year. The autumn of 1884 found him settled in his rooms in New College, Oxford, and casting about in frustration for a topic for his inaugural lecture. After postponing the lecture due to the lack of a suitable theme, he gave it in December 1885 on a new topic in the theory of invariants—differential invariants, or reciprocants in his terminology—which he had begun to develop over the spring and summer of 1885. This would be his last major mathematical achievement, although he would continue to work intermittently on problems in invariant theory, in combinatorics, and on the Euler–Goldbach conjecture (1897) in number theory up until his death.

Sylvester's health began to fail in the early 1890s, with cataracts presenting the greatest difficulties. A deputy was appointed to perform the duties of his chair for him in 1892, and he officially resigned in 1894. He spent his final years living in and around London with the Athenaeum as his social focal point. He died at his home, 5 Hertford Street, Mayfair, on 15 March 1897 of cardiac failure, having suffered a stroke a fortnight earlier. He was buried on 19 March 1897 in the Jewish cemetery in Ball's Pond, Dalston. The Royal Society honoured his memory with the establishment of its Sylvester medal, an award 'for the encouragement of mathematical research irrespective of nationality, and not confined to pure mathematical research', given triennially from 1901 onward.

KAREN HUNGER PARSHALL

Sources R. C. Archibald, 'Material concerning James Joseph Sylvester', *Studies and essays in the history of science and learning offered in homage of George Sarton* (1947), 209–17 · R. C. Archibald, 'Unpublished letters of James Joseph Sylvester and other new information concerning his life', *Osiris*, 1 (1936), 85–154 · H. F. Baker, 'Biographical notice', in *The collected mathematical papers of James Joseph Sylvester*, ed. H. F. Baker, 4 vols. (1904–12); repr. with corrections [1973] · H. H. Bellot, *University College, London, 1826–1926* (1929) · L. Feuer, 'America's first Jewish professor: James Joseph Sylvester at the University of Virginia', *American Jewish Archives*, 36 (1984), 151–201 · P. A. MacMahon, 'James Joseph Sylvester', *Nature*, 55 (1896–7), 492–4 · K. H. Parshall, 'America's first school of mathematical research: James Joseph Sylvester at Johns Hopkins University', *Archive for History of Exact Sciences*, 38 (1988), 153–96 · K. H. Parshall, *James Joseph Sylvester: life and works in letters* (1998) · K. H. Parshall and D. E. Rowe, *The emergence of the American mathematical research community, 1876–1900: J. J. Sylvester, Felix Klein, and E. H. Moore* (1994) · I. Grattan-Guinness, 'The Sylvester medal: origins, and recipients, 1901–1949', *Notes and Records of the Royal Society*, 47 (1993), 105–8 · *Nature*, 55 (1896–7), 492–4

Archives Brown University, Providence, Rhode Island, John Hay Library, letters · St John Cam., corresp. and papers | BL, letters to Charles Babbage, Add. MSS 37189–37199, *passim* · Col. U., Rare Book and Manuscript Library, letters to W. J. C. Miller, etc. · CUL, corresp. with Lord Kelvin · CUL, letters to Sir George Stokes · Johns Hopkins University, Baltimore, Daniel Coit Gilman MSS · L. Cong., letters to S. Newcomb · Makarna Mittag-Lefflers Matematiska

Stiftelse, Djursholm, letters to M. G. Mittag-Leffler • Royal Institution of Great Britain, London, letters to John Tyndall • UCL, letters to Lord Brougham; letters to Edith Gigliucci; letters to Thomas Hirst • UCL, London Mathematical Society papers • University of Exeter Library, letters to Sir Joseph Lockyer • W. Sussex RO, letters to Sir Alfred Kempfe

Likenesses G. Patten, oils, 1841, priv. coll. • A. E. Emslie, oils, 1889, St John Cam. [see illus.] • A. E. Emslie, oils, second version, New College, Oxford • G. J. Stodart, stipple (after photograph by Messrs J. Stilliard & Co., Oxford), NPG; repro. in Nature, 39 (1889)

Wealth at death £2730 2s. 8d.: probate, 12 April 1897, CGPLA Eng. & Wales

Sylvester, Josuah [Joshua] (1562/3–1618), poet and translator, was born in Kent. His parentage is uncertain—his father may have been Thomas Silvester, a clothier of Burford, Oxfordshire, whose will of 1585 names a second son, Josua—but the major fostering figure in his early life was his uncle, William Plumbe, of Eltham and later Fulham, both near London. At nine Sylvester was enrolled in the Southampton grammar school, headed by Hadrianus Saravia, which specialized in the French language. While he later lamented leaving school after only three years, the grounding in French he received there enabled him to translate with little error the voluminous and often highly embellished writings of his literary hero, the Gascon Huguenot poet Guillaume de Saluste, sieur Du Bartas.

In 1576 Sylvester began a career in trade; since by 1590 he could style himself a merchant adventurer, probably much of the intervening time was spent as an apprentice to the Merchant Adventurers' Company, which controlled England's foreign trade in cloth. Perhaps part of his apprenticeship was served overseas: an autobiographical poem, 'The Woodman's Bear', locates him in his twenty-second year in East Friesland—probably at Emden, then the overseas centre of the Merchant Adventurers. His bent was not for trade, however; he later refers to his merchant years as 'lost' (Devine Weekes, 1.4, line 349), and he was soon devoting leisure time to his preferred work as poet, especially in translating French protestant works.

Translating the Devine Weekes Back in London, Sylvester began publishing his translations, beginning with the timely Canticle of the Victorie (1590), translated from Du Bartas's Cantique celebrating the victory of (then protestant) Henri of Navarre over the Catholic League at Ivry earlier that same year. If the Cantique was Sylvester's first introduction to Du Bartas, the impact was strong. He soon turned to the poet's main work, Les sepmaines, an epic of creation and biblical history. He published two sections in 1592—The Sacrifice of Isaac and The Shipwreck of Jonas, along with a shorter Bartasian work, The Triumph of Faith.

Sylvester continued translating La seconde sepmaine in the 1590s, but the work went slowly. In 1597 he sought a position that offered greater stability and more leisure to write, as secretary of the Merchant Adventurers. His petition failed, though the earl of Essex wrote two letters supporting him. Presumably Sylvester acquired this exalted if ineffectual patronage through Essex's associate Anthony Bacon (elder brother of Francis), who had known Du

Josuah Sylvester (1562/3–1618), by Cornelis van Dalen

Bartas in France, and among whose papers at Lambeth Palace the relevant letters are found. Of the six parts of The Second Week that Sylvester published in 1598, two each were dedicated to Essex and Bacon, and two to another Essex intimate, Lord Mountjoy. Nothing came of Sylvester's courting of Essex and his circle: by mid-1601 Essex and Bacon were both dead, and Mountjoy continued to prefer Samuel Daniel.

Help came from another Essex, however: in the early 1600s Sylvester went to live in Lambourn, Berkshire, with the family of William Essex, a wealthy country squire. An autobiographical passage inserted in the 1605 Devine Weekes (1.5, lines 957–64), which focuses on the Essex sons, implies that Sylvester was employed as their tutor. Certainly his duties left him more time for translating: before 1605 he was able to complete the next two books of La seconde sepmaine and revise the two fragments published in 1592 as well as translate the whole of La sepmaine, L'Uranie (a short work by Du Bartas), and the moral Quatrains of Guy du Faur, seigneur de Pibrac (1576). This increased productivity, along with affectionate dedications to Essex's wife and sister in the 1605 volume, suggests that William Essex (known as a lover of poetry) and his family encouraged Sylvester's endeavours.

With the completion of a substantial part of the epic

and the accession in 1603 of James I, an admirer of Du Bartas, Sylvester sought royal patronage. Since the printing business was disrupted in 1603–4 by plague, he offered a sample of his work to James in a presentation manuscript of 'The colonies' (*Devine Weekes*, 2.11, line 3) now in the British Library (BL, Royal MS 17 a.xli). Finally in 1605 Humfrey Lownes printed *Bartas his Devine Weekes and Workes*, comprising all of *Les sepmaines* published in Du Bartas's lifetime—the *First Week* and the first two days of the *Second Week*—as well as the *Urania*. An elaborate apparatus of sonnets in three languages dedicates the whole to King James. Commendatory verses were contributed not only by Sylvester's friends but by such major literary figures as Ben Jonson, Samuel Daniel, and John Davies of Hereford. The separately published translation of Pibrac (*Tetrastika*), also 1605, was dedicated to Prince Henry. In 1606 and 1607 followed translations of the remaining parts of *La seconde sepmaine* which had been published after the Huguenot poet's death: *I Posthumus Bartas* (the third day of the second week) and *II Posthumus Bartas* (the first two parts of the fourth day). One part of each was dedicated to James, and the second part of the 1607 volume to Henry. With the 1608 *Devine Weekes* Sylvester completed, with the remaining parts of the fourth day, his rendering of Du Bartas's massive though unfinished work (the fourth day of *La seconde sepmaine* ends with Nebuchadnezzar's conquest of Jerusalem (2 Kings); the last three days, which would have brought history up to the last judgment, were never written). By this time his appeals to Henry, if not those to James, had been successful, and the prince granted him a pension of £20 a year.

Now, if not before, Sylvester left William Essex's service and returned to London. His position as pensioner seems to have entailed some attendance on his young patron. Dedicatory and commendatory verses in Sylvester's and other volumes of this period link him with writers in Henry's circle, especially the prince's chaplain, Joseph Hall, and the military scholar Clement Edmondes. Probably around this time his improved prospects also allowed Sylvester to marry. Nothing certain is known about his wife, although Grosart proposed the name Mary Hill, based on a typographical singularity in an interpolated autobiographical passage in the *First Week* which looks forward to contentment in 'a Cottage on a lowly Hill', and a later reference to Mary Sylvester, a widow, in the parish records of St Bartholomew-the-Less for 1625. The same records earlier note the birth of a daughter, Ursula, to Sylvester in 1612 and the burial of his stillborn son in 1614.

Poverty in London By 1614 the bright prospects of 1608 and 1609 had darkened. King James had at last rewarded Sylvester with a grant of debts of £300, but in a letter to his friend Robert Nicholson, Sylvester complains that the death of 'Sir Caesar' (perhaps Sir Thomas Caesar, baron cursitor of the exchequer, who died in 1610) somehow—the mechanics are unclear—prevented him from collecting these moneys owed to the late Queen Elizabeth (Sylvester, 646). In 1612 the sudden death of his main patron, Prince Henry, cut off the pension as well as all hopes for further advancement there. In his elegy *Lachrimae*

lachrimarum (1612) Sylvester joined with special fervour in the outflow of public mourning. He perceived in this unexpected calamity a punishment for England's sins, but lamented as well his own personal loss

> that had no prop
> But Henry's hand, and, and, but in him, no hope.
> (ibid., 583)

With Henry dead and expectations of support from James dimmed by experience, Sylvester transferred his dedicatory attentions to Prince Charles. *The Parliament of Vertues Royal* (1614), translated from Jean Bertaut's *Panarete*, converts that work's high expectations for the French dauphin to the new English heir apparent. A desperate sonnet appended to the *Parliament* appeals for Charles's help to save from ruin not only himself but 'six that hang on me' (Sylvester, 445)—presumably his wife and five children. Charles and his sister Elizabeth, to whom Sylvester dedicated 'Little Bartas' in the *Parliament* volume, presumably responded with some assistance, since both are thanked in a personal passage at the end of *St Lewis the King*, published with some other short translated works in 1615. Sylvester also derived some income from clerical work he was doing for parliament, in what capacity is unclear. His address to the Lords and Commons as 'Your Under-Clerk' in the 1614 volume and later his self-characterization as a mote in the upper house's sun (*The Second Session of the Parliament of Vertues Reall*, 1616) suggest he served first in the Commons and then in the Lords under the clerk of the parliament. Since even the clerk himself usually needed additional revenue, his subordinate would not earn much. Sylvester continued his translating activity through these years with diligence but little reward. Even *Tobacco Battered* (1617), an original satiric poem that appealed to one of King James's favourite prejudices, brought no royal reward. In these years of poverty the Sylvesters may have lived at St Bartholomew's Hospital, an institution maintained for the poor. The parish record entries cited above point in that direction, as does Sylvester's own affectionate reference to the hospital in 'A Hymn of Alms' (Sylvester, 517).

Final years and death Sylvester was finally delivered from need by the same mercantile society that he had once been so glad to leave. By 1617 he was living in Zeeland, signing himself on a list of subscribers to John Minsheu's *Guide into Tongues* as secretary of the Merchant Adventurers at Middelburg. The following year Sylvester died, in Middelburg, on 28 September, aged fifty-five, as recorded in the memorial verses by John Vicars which appear in the 1621 and subsequent editions of Sylvester's work. After years of poverty and only a brief tenure back with the Merchant Adventurers, Sylvester probably had little to leave to his family. The great folio editions of his works in 1621, 1633, and 1641 which ratified—for the time at least—his high standing among contemporary poets and moralists, were of no benefit to his wife and children. When her daughter Bonadventure died in 1625, Mary Sylvester was living in the Proctor's House at St Bartholomew's. Of the surviving children nothing certain is known. Hunter found the 1657 will of one Peter Sylvester of London which lists several brothers—Nathaniel, Joshua, Giles, and Constant—and a 'Sister Cartwright' who might be the daughter Ursula born in 1612 (Hunter, 18–19). The name Joshua among Peter's siblings and his reference to his mother as Mary Sylvester, widow, of London, point to a connection with the poet. If so, the family fortunes had improved: Peter and Constant were both merchants, and Peter could anticipate leaving an estate of over £1000.

Another son apparently fared less well, in his early years at least. John Gee's *The Foot out of the Snare* (1624, sig. L4v) relates how one Henry Sylvester, son of the translator of Du Bartas, a scholar at Sutton's Hospital, fell under the influence of Catholic priests. They persuaded him to be sent overseas, presumably to train for the priesthood himself, though the plot was discovered before he left. At least part of the story seems true—a Henry Sylvester was indeed at Sutton's Hospital (the Charterhouse), an institution singled out for praise in Sylvester's 1615 'Hymn of Alms'. And surely one Sylvester son would be named Henry. If Gee had his facts right, it is ironic that this boy, son of one ultra-protestant and namesake of another, should have been tempted by Rome.

Literary afterlife Du Bartas's epic had a blazing but brief fame in France. The modern editors of the French original record forty-two editions of *La sepmaine* and twenty-nine of all or part of *La seconde sepmaine* in the closing years of the sixteenth century and the early years of the seventeenth. But with the rise of classical taste the Gascon's prolixity and his laboriously 'illustrated' language soon fell from favour. In England his reputation, more or less fused with that of Sylvester, was considerably longer in the ascendant and his influence on contemporary and later poets was far greater. The *Weekes* drew almost universal praise from contemporaries, including Edmund Spenser, Ben Jonson, Samuel Daniel, Michael Drayton, and Thomas Campion, as well as a host of lesser figures. Jonson later disparaged Sylvester's translation to Drummond of Hawthornden as inaccurate, but Drummond adds that his criticism was groundless since Jonson had no knowledge of French. In his collection of the best of modern poetry, his contemporary Robert Allott quotes Sylvester's Du Bartas 123 times: not much less than Daniel or Drayton and considerably more than Shakespeare. The work is cited extensively in John Bodenham's *Belvedere* (1600), John Swan's *Speculum mundi* (1635) and Edward Browne's *Sacred Poems* (1641), and incidentally in many others, from Peter Heylyn's *Microcosmos* (1621) to Isaac Walton's *Compleat Angler* (1655). Clearly everyone in pre-Restoration England who had received a literary education read the *Weekes* and almost all, including Jonson in the more celebratory mode of 1605, admired it.

In the latter part of the seventeenth century, Du Bartas / Sylvester fell out of fashion in a shift of taste parallel, though not identical, to the earlier one in France. John Dryden in his dedication of *The Spanish Fryar* to Lord

Haughton (1681) records the reversal in his own sensibility:

I remember, when I was a boy, I thought inimitable Spencer a mean Poet, in comparison of Sylvester's *Dubartas*: and was rapt into an ecstasie when I read these lines:

Now, when the Winter's keener breath began
To Chrystallize the Baltick Ocean;
To glaze the Lakes, to bridle up the Floods,
And periwig with Snow the bald-pate Woods:
I am much deceiv'd if this be not abominable fustian.

William Wordsworth in his turn felt the paradox of once-brilliant fame in total eclipse: 'Who is there that can now endure to read *The Creation* of Dubartas? Yet all of Europe once resounded with his praise' ('Essay supplementary to the preface', 1815).

The epic of Du Bartas and Sylvester, then, appealed only to its own moment in history. Part of that appeal in market terms was doubtless the encyclopaedic nature of the work; the *Weekes* is a compendium of traditional natural philosophy and human history. More centrally, contemporary valuation of the poem was based, in a way unfamiliar in modern criticism, on its lofty subject, which not only provided for the plenitude and variety so attractive to Renaissance taste but was actually felt to confer literary excellence in itself. Du Bartas's similitudes and correspondences had their parallels in early seventeenth-century English secular literature, especially drama and metaphysical poetry. But even as the *Weekes* simultaneously celebrated and enacted the universe as God's witty creation in which the most diverse things are interrelated and ultimately unified, it lost its value when that world view fell apart. Cut loose from its 'truth', the poem's baroque excesses seem at best quaint, at worst 'abominable fustian'.

Before that, *The Devine Weekes* found many imitators, both in the Christian-scientific mode of the *First Week* and in the biblical-heroic mode of the *Second Week*. Mostly they were lesser writers such as Thomas Moffett, Robert Aylett, Phineas Fletcher, and Francis Quarles, but even in those of greater ability such as Drayton (*Moses in a Map of his Miracles*, 1604; *Noah's Flood*, 1630) and Abraham Cowley (*Davideis*, 1656) the Bartasian influence was far from salutary. An exception is Giles Fletcher's original and highly wrought *Christ's Victory and Triumph* (1610).

Only in John Milton's *Paradise Lost* does the Bartasian divine model, totally absorbed and transmuted, contribute to superior poetry. In addition to the great theme of God's works in history, Du Bartas's influence is clearest in the invocations to Urania, the Christian muse; in the presentation of contradictory scientific hypotheses to be resolved in faith; and in the scriptural history recounted by Michael in the last two books. But Milton's way with the model sacred epic of his day was to heighten and perfect rather than merely imitate: where Du Bartas had directed his muse to the middle region (*Devine Weekes*, 1.1, line 136), Milton's voice will soar 'with no middle flight' (*Paradise Lost*, I. 14); God's judgement after the Fall is conveyed by the merciful Son, not the bad-tempered tyrant of the *Weekes*; Michael's prophecy summarizes, where *The Second*

Week endlessly elaborates, and brings human history through the incarnation of Christ to the end that the Gascon never reached. Above all, the large, controlled periods of *Paradise Lost*, highly wrought and rhythmically varied, owe nothing to Sylvester's smaller syntactic units with their often awkward formal patterning. In language Milton soon moved beyond the Sylvestrian style apparent in such early poems as his paraphrase on Psalm 114. Oddly enough, Sylvester's linguistic influence leapt over him to shape the standard poetic diction of natural description of the eighteenth century, with its feathered flocks, enamelled meadows, and scaly legions.   SUSAN SNYDER

Sources J. Sylvester, *Du Bartas his divine weekes and workes with a compleate collection of all the other … workes translated and written by that famous philomusus, Josuah Sylvester* (1633) · *The divine weeks and works of Guillaume de Saluste, sieur Du Bartas*, ed. S. Snyder, trans. J. Sylvester, 2 vols. (1979) · L. Parsons, 'Studies in the life and works of Joshua Sylvester, 1564–1618', MA diss., U. Lond., 1948 · J. Hunter, 'Joshua Sylvester', *Chorus vatum anglicanorum*, 11 [typed transcription of BL, MSS 24487–24492] · A. B. Grosart, 'Memorial introduction', in *The complete works of Joshuah Sylvester*, ed. A. B. Grosart, 1 (1880) · F. B. Williams, 'The bear facts about Joshua Sylvester the woodman', *English Language Notes*, 9 (1971), 90–98 · U. T. Holmes, J. L. Lyons, and R. W. Linker, eds., *The works of Guillaume de Salluste, sieur du Bartas*, 3 vols. (Chapel Hill, North Carolina, 1935–40) · J. Carscallen, 'English translators and admirers of Du Bartas', BLitt diss., U. Oxf., 1958
Likenesses C. van Dalen, line engraving, BM, NPG [*see illus.*]

Sylvester, Matthew

Sylvester, Matthew (1636/7–1708), ejected minister, was born at Southwell, Nottinghamshire, a son of Robert Sylvester, mercer, and his wife, Mary Lee. After attending Southwell grammar school he was admitted on 4 May 1654, at the age of seventeen, to St John's College, Cambridge. He graduated BA in 1658. About 1659 he became vicar of Great Gonerby, Lincolnshire. Unable to conform to the conditions laid down by the Act of Uniformity in 1662 he resigned his living, declining offers of preferment within the established church from his distant relative Robert Sanderson, bishop of Lincoln. In 1667 he was living at Mansfield, Nottinghamshire, with his 'dear and intimate Friend' Joseph Truman (Sylvester, sig. c3v). He served as domestic chaplain successively to Sir John Bright of Badsworth, Yorkshire, and to John White of Cotgrave, Nottinghamshire.

In 1671 Sylvester went to London and in 1672 was licensed as a presbyterian at Coleman Street. From a letter he wrote that summer to Richard Baxter (DWL, Baxter letters, i.176; Keeble and Nuttall, 2.135), it appears that in that year he succeeded John Chishul (*d.* June 1672), ejected rector of Tiverton, Devon, as minister of a congregation at Whitefriars. He may then have been living in Barnet, Hertfordshire, acting also as chaplain to a member of the Fiennes family. He afterwards became pastor of a congregation meeting in his 'own Dwelling-house', Rutland House, in Charterhouse Yard, Finsbury. He was on good terms with many of the Anglican clergy of London, particularly Benjamin Whichcote and John Tillotson. Through Truman, Sylvester came to know Richard Baxter, the pre-eminent minister among London nonconformists, who came to think very highly of Sylvester: indeed, 'no Man ever valu'd him more' (Calamy, *Abridgement*,

2.449). Baxter described Sylvester as 'a Man of excellent meekness … peaceable Principles, godly Life, and great ability in the ministerial Work' (*Reliquiae Baxterianae*, 3.96), and in a letter of 1684 to John Thornton he expressed his admiration for Sylvester's humility and pastoral dedication despite severe impoverishment, illness, and the constant threat of informers. Sylvester was a victim of the Hilton gang of anti-nonconformist informers, and in September 1682 he was fined £40 at the Middlesex sessions for preaching at a meeting-place in Westmorland Alley. In 1687 Baxter, then over seventy and newly released from prison, became Sylvester's unpaid assistant at Rutland House, styling 'himself (when somewhat pleasant) my Curate' (Sylvester, sig. c3v).

After Baxter's death in 1691 the congregation declined. Early in 1692 it removed to a building in Meeting House Court, Knightrider Street, Blackfriars. It appears that in 1693 Sylvester was living at Ealing, Middlesex. Edmund Calamy, who succeeded Baxter as Sylvester's assistant in 1692–5, described the congregation as 'not numerous' and Sylvester as 'a very meek-spirited, silent, and inactive man' in straitened circumstances (Calamy, *Own Life*, 1.318, 359). After Calamy left him, Sylvester continued his ministry unaided until his sudden death on 25 January 1708. He was buried at All Hallows, Bread Street, on 30 January, when Calamy preached the funeral sermon. Sylvester's first wife, Hannah, died, aged fifty-seven, on 12 April 1701 after thirty years of marriage. On 24 February 1704 he married Elizabeth (*bap.* 1670), daughter of Obadiah Hughes (*bap.* 1639, *d.* 1705), and his first wife, Elizabeth (*d.* 1672). After Sylvester's death she married his successor Samuel Wright. In his will Sylvester named three sons: Joshua, and Samuel (the eldest) and Matthew (the youngest), both of whom had 'obstinately' repudiated their father's authority.

Sylvester published a number of sermons (notably in the two volumes of *The Christian's Race*, 1702–8), but his chief claim to remembrance is as the editor of Baxter's autobiography. Baxter left all his manuscripts to Sylvester and from the autobiographical papers among them, upon which Baxter had worked since 1665, Sylvester, encouraged by Tillotson, edited, and in 1696 published, the 900 page folio *Reliquiae Baxterianae, or, Mr Richard Baxter's narrative of the most memorable passages of his life and times*; 'Elisha's Cry after Elijah's God', Sylvester's sermon on the occasion of Baxter's death, was included in an appendix. No one esteemed Baxter more highly than Sylvester; indeed, 'He desir'd to be known to Posterity by the Character of Mr. Baxter's Friend' (Calamy, *Own Life*, 2.450). For this very reason, however, no one could have been a more unhappy choice as literary executor. Regarding the manuscript as 'a sort of sacred thing', Sylvester 'was cramped by a sort of superstition' in his handling of it (ibid., 1.377). Weighed down by his responsibility—'My Heart akes exceedingly', he wrote in his preface, 'at every remembrance of my incumbent Trust'—and 'Deeply sensible of my inability for such Work; even to discouragement, and no small Consternation of Spirit', he was quite unable to take the drastic measures necessary to reduce Baxter's 'great quantity of loose Papers' to order. As a result, the chronology of the *Reliquiae*'s narrative is confused and its movement disjointed, overburdened with large blocks of documentations and disfigured by an inconsistent formal arrangement. A 'Rhapsody' Sylvester himself called it (Sylvester, sigs. b1, b3, b4v).

To Calamy, Sylvester's inadequacies as an editor had become apparent long before publication. He did prevail upon Sylvester to make some alterations but these changes did not satisfy him and he conceived the idea of rearranging and rewriting the *Reliquiae* as a third-person history of nonconformity. His *Abridgment of Mr. Baxter's History* (1702) and its two further revisions and enlargements take the reader far from Baxter's text: it is to Sylvester's credit that he did seek faithfully to present Baxter's own words. He planned, but did not effect, a selected edition of Baxter's letters.

ALEXANDER GORDON, *rev.* N. H. KEEBLE

Sources DWL, Baxter letters • M. Sylvester, preface, in *Reliquiae Baxterianae, or, Mr Richard Baxter's narrative of the most memorable passages of his life and times*, ed. M. Sylvester, 1 vol. in 3 pts (1696), sigs. b1–d1v • *Reliquiae Baxterianae, or, Mr Richard Baxter's narrative of the most memorable passages of his life and times*, ed. M. Sylvester, 1 vol. in 3 pts (1696), pt 3, p. 96 • E. Calamy, *An historical account of my own life, with some reflections on the times I have lived in, 1671–1731*, ed. J. T. Rutt, 1 (1829), 312, 359, 376–80; 2 (1829), 80–84 • E. Calamy, ed., *An abridgement of Mr. Baxter's history of his life and times, with an account of the ministers, &c., who were ejected after the Restauration of King Charles II*, 2nd edn, 2 vols. (1713), vol. 2, pp. 449–51 • E. Calamy, *A continuation of the account of the ministers ... who were ejected and silenced after the Restoration in 1660*, 2 vols. (1727), vol. 2, p. 603 • *Calamy rev.* • *Calendar of the correspondence of Richard Baxter*, ed. N. H. Keeble and G. F. Nuttall, 2 vols. (1991) • E. Calamy, *A funeral sermon, occasion'd by the sudden death of the Reverend Mr. Matthew Sylvester* (1708) • G. F. Nuttall, 'The MS of *Reliquiae Baxterianae* (1696)', *Journal of Ecclesiastical History*, 6 (1955), 72–9 • Venn, *Alum. Cant.* • G. L. Turner, ed., *Original records of early nonconformity under persecution and indulgence*, 2 (1912), 965 • W. Wilson, *The history and antiquities of the dissenting churches and meeting houses in London, Westminster and Southwark*, 4 vols. (1808–14), vol. 2, pp. 105–6, 108–11 • A. A. Rollason, 'Extract from the will of Richard Baxter referring to Sylvester and Morrice', *Transactions of the Congregational Historical Society*, 5 (1911–12), 370–71 • A. Peel, 'Richard Baxter, Roger Morrice, and Matthew Sylvester', *Transactions of the Congregational Historical Society*, 5 (1911–12), 298–300
Archives Bedford Office, London, Woburn Abbey MSS, iii.104 • Bodl. Oxf., sermon notes, MSS Rawl. D. 1120, E. 113, 123 • DWL, Baxter letters • DWL, Baxter treatises, extant portions of the original MS of the *Reliquiae* • LPL, letter to Tenison with presentation copy of the *Reliquiae*, Gibbon MS 24
Likenesses M. Vandergucht, line engraving (after I. Schivermans), NPG • oils, DWL

Syme, David (1827–1908), newspaper proprietor in Australia, was born on 2 October 1827 at North Berwick, Scotland, the youngest of the five sons of George Alexander Syme (1791–1845), a parish schoolmaster, and his wife, Jean, or Jane, *née* Mitchell, both from Forfarshire. Shy, awkward, but strong-willed, George was incapable of showing affection for his children and educated David tyrannically. On his father's death David broke away from 'extreme Calvinism' and studied theology for two years under the Revd James Morison at his academy in Kilmarnock, but following a *Wanderjahr* in Germany he abandoned the Christian faith and any native love for Scotland.

In mid-1851 Syme sailed for the Californian gold rush but after some unhappy months moved on to Victoria, Australia, and arrived in Melbourne late in 1852. Three turbulent years on the goldfields brought small success; in 1855 his rich claim was 'jumped' and his appeals to the authorities were futile. However, his digging experience developed grim self-reliance and he took up road construction and contracting for public works. Meanwhile in 1853 his brother Ebenezer *Syme (1826–1860) joined him with his family in Victoria. Their mother and sister followed. Ebenezer made his mark as a radical journalist, and when he purchased *The Age* in 1856, David contributed possibly a half share. However, Ebenezer was soon crippled by consumption, and in 1859 David took over as editor. He remained in charge for almost the next fifty years, though he was not the sole owner, for Ebenezer's widow, Jane, and her children each retained a share. David's remaining brother, George Alexander (1822–1894), migrated in 1863 and worked on *The Age* and its weekly *Leader*. On 17 August 1858 David had married Annabella Johnson (1838–1915) from Yorkshire at St James's Church of England, Melbourne.

Syme continued Ebenezer's radical policies in support of the unprivileged. Land selection, agricultural settlement, and breaking of the pastoral squatters' dominance were essential. Democratic movements and the attempts of the McCulloch–Higinbotham ministries in 1864–9 to gain fuller self-government and dominate over the upper house were supported. Syme was not 'the Father of Protection' (as he claimed) but after the 1864 election he made this his central policy in order to develop manufacturing. *The Age's* situation had been precarious, boycotted as it was by most government and business advertising. However, Syme's reduction of price to 2*d.* in 1862 and boldly to a penny in 1868 increased circulation to 15,000 and led to mastery over the conservative *Argus* and to long-term political power. Meanwhile he proceeded in the 1870s to freeze out Jane Syme and her children, except for Joseph, who retained a quarter share from 1878 until, after long conflict with David, he was bought out in 1890.

Syme ruthlessly imposed his policies on the public. *The Age* remained a journal of record, but its political content was inflammatory and recklessly partisan, with much distortion and suppression. His political allies were eulogized; they knew how dependent they were and that any backsliding would be fatal. His enemies, especially Irish Catholics and conservative free-traders, were vilified day after day. He created and destroyed politicians. In 1872 he found in A. L. Windsor an editor to carry much of the burden and worked intimately with him until 1900. He handsomely paid his protégés Alfred Deakin and C. H. Pearson to contribute regularly and bullied his lesser staff relentlessly: '*The Age* is not a newspaper; it's a political engine', one of his disillusioned journalists remarked (McKay, 10).

The formation of the strong National Reform and Protection League and the sweeping victory in 1877 of the high-protection liberals led by Graham Berry gave Syme the opportunity to put down, once and for all, the free-trading import merchants and bankers, the squatters, and, above all, the legislative council. Over four years of bitter conflict a limited land tax, payment of members, and other reforms were won; but Syme and Berry fell out, and as public enthusiasm waned the council managed to preserve its powers while conceding enlargement of its constituency. 'King David's' attack on the rich and powerful was thwarted. Although he supported the formation of the coalition ministries of 1883–90, he was unable to exercise close control.

The Age grew in circulation from 38,000 in 1880 to 100,000 about 1890 and 120,000 in 1899, when Syme was earning about £50,000 a year. He had invested widely in properties, and farmed seriously and experimentally as cultivator, grazier, dairy farmer, stock breeder, and fruit grower.

Syme was bewildered by the boom of the 1880s, especially the huge growth of the state railways, and by the colony's collapse in the early 1890s. He had little policy to offer except retrenchment and persecution of Richard Speight and the railways commissioners as scapegoats. He had earlier survived several libel actions, and twice in the 1860s, when called to the bar of parliament, had made grudging apologies and resumed abuse in the following day's paper. Now in 1892 Speight brought libel charges, which Syme fought over several months in court and, to public satisfaction, largely escaped, except for costs of about £50,000.

Yet the 1890s were Syme's greatest period of political dominance, when legend and fact approximate to tell of his dictating ministries and their members. Similarly the Victorians who were elected to the 1897 federal convention were the ten on the *Age* ticket. Syme had long doubted whether Victorian protectionist interests would be safeguarded under federation, and he provoked intercolonial hostility and behaved like a Victorian nationalist; but he was won over, and the Victorian vote was massively in favour. After 1900 *The Age's* power to make and unmake ministries fell away.

Syme published regularly and with some success on political economy. His *Outlines of an Industrial Science* (1876), arguing for protection and state socialism, was issued in German and American editions. *Representative Government in England* (1881) attacked the 'Westminster system', especially government by party; Syme supported popular election of ministries. Less well informed were his forays into debates on evolution, with *On the Modification of Organisms* (1890), and spiritualism, with *The Soul: a Study and an Argument* (1903).

'What is good for all', wrote Syme, 'and not merely for an individual or a class, should be undertaken by the state; what benefits only the few should be left to private enterprise' (D. Syme, *Outlines of an Industrial Science*, 1876, 185). As well as protection of local industry, he supported anti-sweating and factories and shops legislation, public works for the unemployed, trade unions (but not the new Labor Party), wages boards, a state bank, direct taxation to redistribute wealth, irrigation, and women's suffrage.

Grim and gaunt in appearance, Syme was 6 feet tall, with iron-grey hair and beard. In later life he often suffered from neuralgia and poor digestion. He had little social life; his wife was his prop and stay. His relations with his children to an extent reflected his own father's treatment of him. Emotionally violent, he could privately be an interesting talker, though he had few friends: the young Alfred Deakin had been exceptionally close and maintained a usually affectionate relationship after he had emancipated himself from Syme's dominance. Twentieth-century inheritors of the Victorian radical liberal tradition, which he did so much to create, have granted him little of the affectionate admiration accorded to George Higinbotham, Deakin, and H. B. Higgins.

Survived by his wife, five sons, and two daughters, Syme died at his home, Blythswood, Carson Street, Kew, Melbourne, on 14 February 1908 and was buried in the Boroondara cemetery there in a massive pavilion of his own design. His estate amounted to just short of £1 million. He had made substantial gifts to charities, was privately generous, and had endowed a major prize at the University of Melbourne for scientific research. His sons Herbert (1859–1939), Sir Geoffrey (1873–1942), and Oswald (1878–1967) carried on the business as a trust, which in 1948 was converted to a private company and in 1972 was sold to the Sydney-based Fairfax newspaper interests.

GEOFFREY SERLE

Sources S. Macintyre, *A colonial liberalism: the lost world of three Victorian visionaries* (1991) · C. E. Sayers, *David Syme: a life* (1965) · A. Pratt, *David Syme, the father of protection in Australia* (1908) · State Library of Victoria, Melbourne, La Trobe manuscript collection, Syme MSS · G. Serle, *The rush to be rich: a history of the colony of Victoria, 1883–1889* (1971) · *AusDB*, vols. 6, 12 · J. A. La Nauze, *Political economy in Australia* (1949) · J. A. La Nauze, *Alfred Deakin: a biography*, 2 vols. (1965) · *The Age* [Melbourne] (15 Feb 1908) · *The Argus* [Melbourne] (15 Feb 1908) · C. McKay, *This is the life* (1961)
Archives State Library of Victoria, Melbourne, La Trobe manuscript collection
Likenesses P. May, drawing, repro. in P. May, *Phil May in Australia* (1904), 12 · photograph, repro. in Sayers, *David Syme* · photographs, repro. in Pratt, *David Syme*
Wealth at death £880,000: *AusDB* · £972,300: Macintyre, *A colonial liberalism*

Syme, Ebenezer (1826–1860), journalist in Australia, the third son of George Alexander Syme (1791–1845), a schoolmaster at North Berwick state school, and his wife, Jean, or Jane, *née* Mitchell, was born at North Berwick, Scotland. He was educated at his father's school and from 1841 to 1845 at the University of St Andrews. His early inclination was to enter the ministry of the Church of Scotland, but he found himself unable to subscribe to any generally accepted creed. In August–September 1845 he attended classes at James Morison's liberal theological academy at Kilmarnock, and in October he began to travel through Scotland and northern England as an independent evangelist. But his doubts remained, and in May 1851 he wrote in his diary that he would 'leave the pulpit'. In July he moved to London and became assistant to John Chapman, a bookseller and the owner of the *Westminster Review*. Syme wrote for this and delivered public lectures, but in 1853, largely for reasons of health, he decided to emigrate to Victoria, Australia, with his wife, Jane Hilton, *née* Rowen (*b*. 1827/8), of Manchester, whom he had married on 21 April 1848, and his three young sons, the eldest, William, having been born in Glasgow on 25 January 1849.

After his arrival in July 1853 Syme was able to take advantage of the journalistic opportunity afforded by the rush to the diggings. He wrote first for the Melbourne *Argus*, then launched and edited the radical *Digger's Advocate*. However, he fell out with *The Argus* over his support for the Eureka rebels, and in December 1854 he joined its rival, the newly founded *The Age*. In June 1856 he bought the paper for £2000, when it was on the verge of collapse, and piloted it though its early struggles to become the colony's leading liberal organ. His work had a marked influence on colonial politics. He supported every radical movement of the day, both in his paper and as member of parliament for the Loddon from 1856 to 1859. That year, in failing health, he did not stand for re-election to parliament and relinquished the management and editorship of *The Age* to his brother David *Syme. He died on 13 March 1860 at Grey Street, St Kilda, Melbourne, from tuberculosis arising from his 'missions' in the late 1840s, and was buried in the Church of England section of Melbourne general cemetery. He was survived by his wife, who returned to England, and four sons and a daughter, who remained in Victoria. A. G. L. SHAW

Sources C. E. Sayers, *David Syme: a life* (1965) · C. E. Sayers, 'Syme, Ebenezer, 1826–1860', *AusDB*, vol. 6 · G. Serle, *The golden age: a history of the colony of Victoria, 1851–1861* (1963) · *Victorian parliamentary debates* (1856–9) · D. Elder, *Ebenezer Syme and the Westminster Review* (privately printed, Melbourne, 1967) · *The Age* [Melbourne] (15 March 1860) · P. Mennell, *The dictionary of Australasian biography* (1892) · m. cert. · private information (2004)

Archives State Library of Victoria, Melbourne, La Trobe manuscript collection

Wealth at death little wealth: Sayers, *David Syme*

Syme, James (1799–1870), surgeon, was born on 7 November 1799 at 56 Princes Street, Edinburgh, second son of John Syme (*d*. 1821), a lawyer, of Cartmore in Kinross and Lochore in Fife, and of Barbara Spottiswood (*d*. 1835), of Dunipace, Stirlingshire. He was educated in Edinburgh, first at Fulton and Knight's Private Grammar School and later at the high school. As a schoolboy he showed a strong interest in science, especially in natural history and chemistry. His father provided him with a chemical laboratory in the family home. When only eighteen, in the course of a series of experiments on the distillates of coal tar, he discovered the method, later patented by Charles Mackintosh, of dissolving rubber and using the solution to waterproof cloth. An account of this discovery provided his first scientific publication.

Syme began his studies at Edinburgh University in 1815, initially concentrating on botany and philosophy. In 1817 he took Thomas Hope's chemistry class and became a pupil of John Barclay, the eminent anatomist and extramural teacher. In Barclay's class he met Robert Liston, who was Barclay's demonstrator. In 1818 Liston set up his

own extramural teaching in anatomy and invited Syme to be his assistant. In 1820 Syme was appointed medical superintendent of the Edinburgh Fever Hospital, a post he shortly relinquished to become a house surgeon in the Edinburgh Royal Infirmary. In 1821 he became a member of the Royal College of Surgeons in London, and in 1822 he visited Paris, where he studied anatomy and operative surgery under Jacques Lisfranc and Guillaume Dupuytren.

Syme first came to notice as a surgical operator in 1823 when he successfully performed the first amputation at the hip joint to be undertaken in Scotland. The operation was performed according to his own modification of Lisfranc's technique. In the same year, Liston having decided to devote himself entirely to surgery, Syme took over the teaching of his anatomy class. He also became a fellow of the Royal College of Surgeons in Edinburgh, and the following year, 1824, he visited medical schools in Germany.

Syme was, by this time, developing a considerable surgical practice. Growing professional rivalry between him and Liston ended their friendship and he joined the Brown Square school of medicine, where he taught anatomy and practical surgery. In 1825 he enhanced his reputation by publishing an influential paper on wound management, in which he argued that blood and other discharges should be allowed free outlet. During a trip to Dublin in 1826 he was impressed by the operative advances being made by the Irish surgeons and he shortly resolved to devote himself entirely to the practice and teaching of surgery. He left the Brown Square school and set up an independent lecture course, which was soon the largest class in pure surgery in Edinburgh.

In 1829 Syme applied for a senior appointment to the Edinburgh Royal Infirmary, but he was not successful, the governors being apprehensive that he and Liston (who was already on the staff) would quarrel. In response Syme established a private surgical hospital at Minto House, Chambers Street, Edinburgh. Here he inaugurated a novel system of clinical instruction, in which the students were taught in the operating theatre rather than in the wards. In 1832 he published his magisterial textbook *Principles of Surgery*, and in 1833 he was appointed professor of clinical surgery in Edinburgh University, thereby securing wards in the Royal Infirmary. In the following year Liston accepted the chair of clinical surgery at the North London Hospital, leaving Syme unchallenged as Edinburgh's pre-eminent surgeon. In 1838 Syme was appointed surgeon-in-ordinary to the queen in Scotland. On Liston's death in 1847 Syme accepted the invitation to succeed him at University College Hospital, and he went to London in February 1848. Owing to misunderstandings regarding the extent of his duties, and to political intrigues within the college, he resigned in May and again took up his chair in Edinburgh. He wrote later:

> how the death of Liston led to my being invited to take his place at University College; how ambition made me sacrifice happiness; how I found such a spirit of dispeace in the College as to forbid any reasonable prospect of comfort. (Merrington, 37)

After his return to Edinburgh Syme was elected president of the Medico-Chirurgical Society, and in 1850 he became president of the Royal College of Surgeons of Edinburgh. Throughout the 1850s he played an active role in the politics of medical reform. For ten years he was the representative of Edinburgh and Aberdeen universities on the General Medical Council. He also played a part in changing the rules governing the presentation of medical evidence in the Scottish courts. Among many other honours, he received an honorary MD degree from Trinity College, Dublin, in 1867, and from Bonn in 1869, in which year he was also created DCL at Oxford.

Syme married twice: first, in 1829, to the daughter of Robert Willis, a Leith merchant. She died in 1840, survived by two daughters, the elder of whom, Agnes (1835–1903), married Joseph Lister (1827–1912), who succeeded his father-in-law in the chair of clinical surgery. Syme's second wife, Jemima Burn, whom he married in 1841, died in 1869, survived by a son, James. On 6 April 1869 Syme suffered a stroke which rendered him hemiplegic. He resigned his chair. He suffered a further stroke the following year and died at Millbank House, his home in the Grange suburb of Edinburgh, on 26 June 1870. He was buried four days later at St John's Episcopal Church, of which he had long been a member.

Syme was responsible for many advances in surgical technique. He introduced a number of procedures for saving limbs by excising diseased joints, notably the elbow, and parts of bones. His name was given to the operation of amputation just above the ankle joint, which he pioneered and which, in suitable cases, gave a more useful stump than the alternatives. Essentially a cautious and conservative surgeon, he could nevertheless be bold when circumstances required, as in his pioneering of the excision of the bones of the jaw and his heroic ligations of major aneurysms. He made improvements in the design of surgical instruments, in plastic surgery (notably in the repair of the lower lip), and in the surgical treatment of diseases of the urethra and the rectum.

Syme was involved in many disputes during his long career and developed a reputation as a determined polemicist. Many of these quarrels, for example with his fellow surgeons Robert Liston, James Miller, and John Lizars, had their basis in professional rivalry. He was prominent in the campaign mounted by the leaders of Edinburgh's orthodox medical profession against homoeopathy, and he vehemently opposed James Young Simpson's innovation of acupressure, which he resented as an unwarranted intrusion by an obstetrician into the surgical sphere. Surgical anaesthesia was introduced during Syme's tenure as professor of clinical surgery and, though initially cautious, he soon recognized it as a great benefit and became an authority on its application. At the end of his career he enthusiastically advocated the antiseptic technique of wound management pioneered by his son-in-law and former assistant, Joseph Lister. Renowned as a teacher of surgery and as a diagnostician, Syme was distinguished as an operator by his detailed anatomical knowledge and by his speed, dexterity, and simplicity of method. Given his pre-eminence and his combativeness, he was aptly dubbed, by one Edinburgh commentator, 'the Napoleon of surgery' (Miles, 174).

MALCOLM NICOLSON

Sources R. Paterson, *Memorials of the life of James Syme* (1874) · J. A. Shepherd, *Simpson and Syme of Edinburgh* (1969) · A. Miles, *The Edinburgh school of surgery before Lister* (1918) · *DNB* · W. R. Merrington, *University College Hospital and its medical school: a history* (1976)
Archives NRA, priv. coll., lecture notes · Royal College of Physicians of Edinburgh, lecture notes · Royal Medical Society, Edinburgh, dissertation · U. Edin. L., lecture and case notes
Likenesses G. Richmond, chalk drawing, 1857, Scot. NPG · J. Faed, engraving, 1865, repro. in Paterson, *Memorials* · G. R., oils, 1875, Royal College of Surgeons, Edinburgh · A. Brodie, marble bust, Edinburgh Royal Infirmary · J. Brown, engraving (after drawing by G. Richmond), repro. in Paterson, *Memorials* · J. Moffat, photograph, Wellcome L. · G. Richmond, oils, Scot. NPG · two photographs, Wellcome L.
Wealth at death £70,686 16s.: confirmation, 19 July 1870, NA Scot., SC 70/1/149/195–220

Syme, John (1755–1831), friend of Robert Burns, was born in Edinburgh, the son of John Syme (d. 1790), a writer to the signet, and his second wife, Mary Ravenscroft (d. 1779). He was educated in Edinburgh and trained as a lawyer, before serving for a short time in Ireland as an ensign in the 72nd regiment. On retiring from the army in 1774 he settled on his father's estate of Barncailzie, Kirkcudbrightshire, and devoted himself to gardening and agriculture. He was forced to give up this way of life when his father disposed of the estate following the collapse of the Douglas and Heron Bank in Ayr.

In 1791 Syme was appointed distributor of stamps at Dumfries, where he acquired a reputation for acuity in business and for providing lavish hospitality. Burns's first residence in Dumfries was over Syme's office; the poet was a frequent and honoured guest at Syme's home in Ryedale, and the two men became close friends. On one occasion Syme is said to have angered Burns by lecturing him on temperance, to a point where the latter drew (and promptly threw down) the sword that he carried as an excise officer ('the sword-cane incident').

In July 1793 Syme accompanied Burns on a tour of the stewartry of Kirkcudbright, and in 1794 went with him to Galloway. In his will Burns appointed Syme as one of his executors, and following the poet's death in 1796 Syme zealously defended his reputation, promoted a subscription raised on behalf of his family, and assisted in an edition of his *Works*. Syme died at Ryedale on 24 November 1831, and was buried in the parish churchyard.

T. W. BAYNE, *rev.* DOUGLAS BROWN

Sources Irving, *Scots.* · *The works of Robert Burns*, another edn, ed. W. S. Douglas, 6 vols. (1877–9) · *Register of the Society of Writers to Her Majesty's Signet* (1983) · *Dumfries Courier* (6 Dec 1831) · W. McDowall, *Burns in Dumfriesshire* (1870) · C. Rogers, *The book of Robert Burns: genealogical and historical memoirs of the poet, his associates and those celebrated in his writings*, 3 vols. (1889–91), vol. 2, p. 257 · *The life and works of Robert Burns*, ed. R. Chambers, rev. W. Wallace, [new edn], 4 vols. (1896), vol. 4, pp. 217–19 · M. Lindsay, *The Burns encyclopedia*, 2nd edn (1970) · *The letters of Robert Burns*, ed. J. de Lancey Ferguson, 2nd edn, ed. G. Ross Roy, 2 vols. (1985)

Syme, John (1795–1861), portrait painter, was born in Edinburgh. He was the nephew of Patrick *Syme (1774–1845). He studied at the Trustees' Academy and began his career as a flower painter working with his uncle Patrick. By the age of twenty he had become increasingly interested in portrait painting which dominated his *œuvre* for most of his working life. Syme worked throughout his career in his native city. He was an original member of the Scottish Academy, founded in 1826, and took an active share in its management.

Of his many excellent portraits, that of John Barclay, the anatomist, exhibited at the Royal Academy, London in 1819, and Robert Stevenson, the lighthouse engineer, exhibited at the Scottish Academy in 1833 (both Scot. NPG) are good examples. In 1827 Syme completed his portrait of the American bird artist J. J. Audubon (1826–7; White House, Washington), an uncharacteristically romantic portrayal which the sitter did not particularly like. Other important works were a commissioned portrait, *Sir James Baird* (1828) for the county hall of East Lothian, and *The Solicitor-General*, his diploma work (exh. Scottish Academy, 1833, subsequently in Parliament House, Edinburgh). All these portraits are painted in the manner of Sir Henry Raeburn.

Syme is known largely through his association with Raeburn whose pupil and assistant he was. After Raeburn's death in 1834 Syme completed his unfinished works. Two of his best portraits, *Alexander Henderson* and *Archibald Mackinley* (Merchant Company of Edinburgh), show how closely Syme approximated to Raeburn's style. Both are painted in simple half-length poses and the heads are keenly observed. The predominance of black, foiled by the touches of white and of red in a chair or curtain against a grey-green background, further recall Raeburn's manner. During his master's lifetime the two artists collaborated on an equestrian portrait of Raeburn, the horse being painted by Raeburn in 1834. Syme painted in the direct tradition established by Raeburn but without the latter's light, bold brushstrokes Syme's portraits are often dull in totality. Several were engraved by R. M. Hodgetts (*fl.* 1832–1837) and Thomas Hodgetts, including by the former a mezzotint of *Patrick Neill* (1837) and mezzotints of *John Broster* (1825) and *Andrew McKean* (1823) by Thomas Hodgetts. An aquatint by T. Hodgetts of his portrait of John Inglis, minister of Greyfriars Church, Edinburgh, is in the City of Edinburgh Art Collection. Syme's original was exhibited posthumously at the Royal Scottish Academy (1880).

From 1824 John Syme lived at 32 Abercromby Place, Edinburgh. Previously he had lived with his uncle Patrick in Queen Street. It seems that he married in the late 1820s, as a Mrs Syme is also listed in the Post Office annual directory at the same address from 1828 until 1832. After 1832 the name Mrs Syme no longer appears, perhaps indicating an early death. For the years 1836–8 a Miss Syme is listed as living at 32 Abercromby Place and offering drawing classes. She was probably the artist's sister. A portrait of his sister Maria Syme (1793–1868) by Syme (NG Scot.) depicts her fashionable and feminine appearance. Syme went on to live in Portobello before moving back into the city in 1851.

The Royal Scottish Academy has a bust portrait of the artist of probably *c.*1840; the two self-portraits in the Scottish National Portrait Gallery record the artist's appearance with the same unfussy, solid quality of his portraiture of others. John Syme died in Edinburgh on 3 August 1861. F. M. O'Donoghue, *rev.* Lucy Dixon

Sources D. Irwin and F. Irwin, *Scottish painters at home and abroad, 1700–1900* (1975) · J. Caw, *Scottish painting past and present, 1620–1908* (1908); repr. (1990) · D. Macmillan, *Painting in Scotland: the golden age* (1986) [exhibition catalogue, U. Edin., Talbot Rice Gallery, and Tate Gallery, London, 1986] · D. Macmillan, *Scottish art, 1460–1990* (1990) · [J. Lloyd Williams], *National Gallery of Scotland: concise catalogue of paintings* (1997) · H. Smailes, *The concise catalogue of the Scottish National Portrait Gallery* (1990) · W. D. McKay and F. Rinder, *The Royal Scottish Academy, 1826–1916* (1917) · Graves, *RA exhibitors* · P. J. M. McEwan, *Dictionary of Scottish art and architecture* (1994) · J. Halsby and P. Harris, *The dictionary of Scottish painters, 1600–1960* (1990) · *Summary catalogue of British oil paintings*, Glasgow Art Gallery and Museum (1971) · [E. Cumming], *Catalogue of the city of Edinburgh art collection*, 2 (1979)

Likenesses J. Syme, self-portrait, oils, *c.*1840–1849, Royal Scot. Acad. · J. Syme, two self-portraits, oils, Scot. NPG

Syme, Patrick (1774–1845), flower painter, was born in Edinburgh on 17 September 1774 and educated there. In 1803 he took up his brother's practice as a drawing-master and devoted his time to teaching the genteel art of drawing. He was one of a number of artists, including John Claude Nattes (*c.*1765–1839), Mrs Schetky (*d.* 1795), and the Nasmyth family, who provided classes for lady amateur artists. Such practices flourished in the late eighteenth and early nineteenth centuries, when tourists in search of the picturesque visited Scotland. With one of his pupils, Elizabeth (*b.* after 1783), daughter of the Scottish judge Claud Irvine *Boswell, Lord Balmuto, Syme eloped. Their subsequent marriage gave Elizabeth's parents lifelong displeasure. A tinted pencil drawing, *Elizabeth Boswell of Balmuto* (1817; priv. coll., Scotland), by William Douglas (1780–1832), illustrates the contemporary perception of the lady amateur artist: Elizabeth, in fashionable dress, holds a porte-crayon in her right hand and rests her portfolio on a rock. Their son was the botanist John Thomas Irvine *Boswell (1822–1888).

In Edinburgh in 1810 Syme published *Practical Directions for Learning Flower-Drawing*. This manual was intended as a 'useful guide to ladies in the country, who wish to learn flower-drawing' and is illustrated with rather timid drawings of single flowers. On 3 December 1811 Syme was appointed painter of fruits and flowers to the Caledonian Horticultural Society. He contributed drawings to the society's transactions and designed their letterhead; he may also have designed some of their medals—for example, their honorary medal (*c.*1820; National Museums of Scotland, Edinburgh). He also contributed botanical drawings (which were engraved by Weddell) to *Curtis's Botanical Magazine* between 1821 and 1823.

Syme was a student of botany and entomology, and made many excellent drawings of natural history. He was designated painter of objects in natural history to the

Wernerian Natural History Society in 1811 and in 1814 published with additions Werner's *Nomenclature of Colours*. This publication describes Werner's twenty-nine tints and how to make a particular colour; for example, to produce auricula purple mix 'plum purple with indigo blue and much carmine red'. In 1823 Syme issued *A Treatise on British Song Birds*, for which his wife hand-coloured the fifteen ornithological plates.

From 1808 Syme exhibited flower paintings at the Associated Society of Artists in Edinburgh, and from 1814 at the Edinburgh Exhibition Society. He occasionally painted portraits but is best-known for his flower painting. He was one of the associated artist members of the Royal Institution but took a leading part in the foundation of the Scottish Academy, occupying the chair at the first meeting in May 1826, and was one of the council of four then appointed to manage its affairs. He was art master at Dollar Institution (now Dollar Academy), from where, in 1831, he sent his diploma work, *Flowers*, to the Scottish Academy. The academy also holds Symes's *Fruit*. An album of sixty-seven watercolour sketches by Syme of flowers, birds, and insects is held in the National Gallery of Scotland, Edinburgh. Further examples of his work—for example, *Study of Mosses* (1817)—are held in a Scottish private collection, together with works by Elizabeth Syme. Patrick Syme died at Dollar, Clackmannanshire, in July 1845.   LUCY DIXON

Sources D. Irwin and F. Irwin, *Scottish painters at home and abroad, 1700–1900* (1975) · F. Irwin, 'Lady amateurs and their masters in Scott's Edinburgh', *The Connoisseur* (Dec 1974), 230–37 · P. Syme, *Practical directions for learning flower-drawing* (1810) · P. Syme, *A treatise on British song-birds* (1823) · *Werner's nomenclature of colours, with additions by P. Syme* (1814) · *Curtis's Botanical Magazine* (1821–3) · *Memoirs of the Caledonian Horticultural Society*, 1–4 (1810–26) · *Memoirs of the Wernerian Natural History Society*, 1–7 (1811–38) · C. Byrom and G. Dalgleish, 'All that glitters', *Caledonian Gardener* (2001) · Desmond, *Botanists*, rev. edn · K. Andrews and J. R. Brotchie, *Catalogue of Scottish drawings* (1960) · P. J. M. McEwan, *Dictionary of Scottish art and architecture* (1994) · Graves, *RA exhibitors* · J. Halsby and P. Harris, *The dictionary of Scottish painters, 1600–1960* (1990) · *The Post Office directory* · DNB

Syme, Sir Ronald (1903–1989), Roman historian, was born on 11 March 1903 in Eltham, a small market town in the province of Taranaki in the North Island of New Zealand. He was the elder son and eldest of three children of David Simpson Syme, solicitor, and his wife, Florence Mabel Selley. He was educated at Eltham primary school and Stratford district high school, where his interest in Latin was strongly encouraged by a first-class teacher, Miss Tooman. From 1918 to 1920 he attended New Plymouth Boys' High School, of which he was dux in 1919/20, winning a junior university scholarship. From 1921 to 1923 he was a student at Victoria University of Wellington, studying English, Latin, French, jurisprudence, and constitutional history. In the second year he added Greek; it is a very striking sign of his extraordinary linguistic aptitude, as demonstrated a few years later in Oxford, that it was only then that his formal study of Greek began. From 1922 to 1924, while still technically a student at Victoria, he was

Sir Ronald Syme (1903–1989), by Richard Foster, 1988

studying extramurally at the University of Auckland, to which he transferred formally in 1924. In 1923/4 he acted as assistant to the professor of classics, H. S. Dettmann. The story that in this role, after the professor took a headmastership, he set, sat, and marked his own papers for the BA in 1923 is unfortunately only a legend.

In 1924/5 Syme studied for an MA in classics at Auckland, winning first-class honours in Latin, a senior scholarship in Greek, Latin, and French, and a postgraduate scholarship in arts, which brought him in the autumn of 1925 to Oriel College, Oxford, to study *literae humaniores*, which then consisted of ancient history and philosophy. He was not to return to New Zealand until 1950, but remained profoundly attached to it, its mountain scenery, and memories of seeing Halley's comet in the clear New Zealand sky of 1910. His first and best-known book, *The Roman Revolution* (1939), was dedicated to his parents and his homeland ('parentibus optimis patriaeque'), and he kept his New Zealand citizenship throughout his life, speaking with unusual passion of the state-sponsored terrorism practised there by the French government in the matter of the sinking of a Greenpeace ship.

In Oxford Syme was deeply influenced by his tutor in ancient history, Marcus Niebuhr Tod, a specialist in the illumination of Greek history through the careful study of inscriptions, and famed for the delicacy and precision of his language, both spoken and written. Syme's own linguistic gifts were shown in the remarkable feat of his winning the Chancellor's prize for Latin prose and the Gaisford prize for Greek prose in 1926 (some five years after beginning Greek); these were followed by the Gaisford prize for Greek verse in 1927.

This quite outstanding talent had two consequences, the one merely of incidental interest, the other fundamental to his whole career. The former was a brilliant series of vignettes of Oxford life of the 1930s, in both Latin and Greek and in prose and verse, published in the *Oxford Magazine* ('de coniuratione Bodleiana'; or a memorable evocation in Homeric verse of a scene involving Provost L. R. Phelps at Oriel high table). More important was the fact that the areas of his attention, within Roman history, were always to be directed to those periods from which there survives contemporary literature in Latin. In his entire output Greek history is represented only by a single essay on Thucydides; and, with the exception of Strabo, the vast Greek historical literature of the Roman period did not engage his attention.

But first Syme had to take his degree, achieving a first (with rather modest marks in philosophy) in 1927; a typically elegant note from M. N. Tod informing him of the result is preserved in the extensive archive of Syme's papers which was at Wolfson College, Oxford, and is now held in the Bodleian Library. Tod continued to lend him his support, which led very quickly, in the fashion of the Oxford of those days, to his election as fellow and tutor in ancient history of Trinity College, Oxford, in 1929.

The decade which Syme spent at Trinity until the outbreak of the Second World War was his happiest and most creative period. Indeed it had already begun in 1928, a year after he took his finals, with an article on the legions under Domitian. That was a sign of one enduring preoccupation: military history, painstakingly reconstructed from literary sources and inscriptions, and set against the vast and varied landscapes of the Roman empire, from Spain to the Euphrates. With that went a deep engagement with European, especially German, scholarship. His command of both French and German was very considerable, but his knowledge of French was more typically deployed in an exhaustive acquaintance with modern novels. In German, however, there was not only a wide knowledge of literature, some of which—like parts of Goethe's *Faust*—he knew by heart, but also a profound relationship to the German scholarship of the previous few decades: not so much Theodor Mommsen, however, as W. Schulze's study of Roman names; the great article 'Legio' by E. Ritterling in Pauly-Wissowa's *Realencyclopaedie*; Friedrich Münzer on the history of Roman aristocratic families; perhaps (this is not so clear as might be supposed) Matthias Gelzer on the Roman nobility; and above all the two editions of the *Prosopographia imperii Romani* (1897 and 1933–). Reading in the library was supplemented by many visits to Germany and the Balkans, when he also walked long distances to gain a detailed understanding of the landscape.

Military history was perhaps the most obvious product of Syme's studies until the end of the 1930s, culminating in his still unsurpassed article entitled 'Flavian wars and frontiers' in the *Cambridge Ancient History*, vol. 10 (1936). But already other dominating themes of his work were developing. Among his papers later given to Wolfson College, there is a manuscript draft dated 1934 of a book entitled 'The provincial at Rome', to which he refers in the preface of his *Tacitus* (1958):

> It is suitable to confess in this place that the concluding section, 'The new Romans' (Chapters XLIII–XLV), owes something to a book begun many years ago, soon interrupted, and not yet terminated—'The provincial at Rome'.

It never was to be terminated, though *Colonial Elites* (1958) also owes much to it. But it is now clear how rapidly the main lines of his thought had developed, and how consistently he maintained them to the end of his life. The text of 'The provincial at Rome', scrupulously edited by Anthony Birley, has been published as *The Provincial at Rome* and *Rome and the Balkans, 80 BC–AD 14* (1999).

An interest in the 'provincial' coming to the centre from the periphery must, obviously, have owed much to Syme's background. But there are more general aspects to his use of prosopography, which he turned into a dominant mode in Roman history: the study of families over generations, the interplay of literary and epigraphical evidence; the structure of public careers; the possibility of filling the stage of Roman history not just with the Pompeys, Caesars, and Augustuses, but with a host of lesser mortals. All these themes came together, along with his reactions to the rise of the inter-war dictatorships and their gross misuse of language, to produce *The Roman Revolution*, finished in 1938 when he was thirty-five, and published in 1939. As a work of literature, and as an exercise in intellectual and stylistic control, it has no equal in the historiography of Rome, and few in that of any period or area.

The war then imposed a quite long hiatus, when Syme served in the Balkans, and was then professor of classical philology in Istanbul. He did indeed teach classics there; as to what other roles he played (as he certainly did), he never, to the end, gave the smallest hint. But one thing which he did was to give close attention to Strabo's account of Asia Minor. His work on this topic was published posthumously by Anthony Birley as *Anatolia: Studies in Strabo* (1995).

The post-war period saw Syme back in Oxford, where in 1949 he succeeded H. M. Last as Camden professor of ancient history, and fellow of Brasenose. It was very unfortunate that Last, a major figure but not to be compared with Syme in intellectual creativity, was there still as principal. Their profound disagreements, which the surviving correspondence shows to have been Last's fault, significantly soured his life at Brasenose and his attitude to it.

None the less it was in 1958 that Syme published the most original and creative of his works, the infinitely complex and fruitful two-volume work *Tacitus*, accompanied by *Colonial Elites*, and followed by his Sather lectures, *Sallust* (1964). A wider recognition came: in 1959 a knighthood, in 1976 the Order of Merit, as well as twenty honorary doctorates, and memberships of foreign academies. In 1956 (though no earlier) he made the first of many, ever more frequent, journeys across the Atlantic. All his life an extremely private person, Syme rarely developed close relations with colleagues, and tended to gain more pleasure from passing, if repeated, contacts with academic acquaintances made during his travels.

Before his retirement in 1970 Syme had developed a fascination, possibly excessive, with the late fourth-century collection of imperial biographies in Latin known as the *Historia Augusta*. In the same period, however, the generous initiative of the newly founded Wolfson College, Oxford, led to his election as a fellow and to his occupation of a fine penthouse apartment overlooking the River Cherwell, where he worked with great contentment, very productively, publishing *History in Ovid* (1978), *Some Arval Brethren* (1980), and a work of remarkable complexity, interest, and novelty, *The Augustan Aristocracy* (1986), at the age of eighty-three—not to speak of over fifty papers published in the 1980s.

Always extremely sociable, provided that his essential reserve was respected, Syme never married, something which was not in the least a sign of aversion from the opposite sex, or even of an inability to form a long and deeply affectionate relationship. Never inclined to superfluous expenditure, on clothes or anything else, he none the less maintained to very near the end a brisk and military appearance, walking wherever possible, and at a pace which only very late began to slow to that of ordinary mortals. His reserve also softened somewhat in later years, when he found the support of younger scholars and their families, who regarded him with affection, without rivalry, and with no thought of obtrusion beyond what he wished. The cheerful, multinational society of Wolfson also offered him both stimulus and a more comfortable environment than he had ever enjoyed before, while respecting his privacy.

Late in August 1989, when already suffering from cancer, he collapsed in his room in Wolfson, and never fully regained consciousness, dying only four days before a party, to be held by the college, which would have celebrated the fiftieth anniversary of the publication of *The Roman Revolution*. This book, together with *Tacitus*, remains the main memorial to his unique contribution to Roman history; he is universally acknowledged as its greatest practitioner in the twentieth century. His particular qualities are not easy to summarize, and the true importance of his work can hardly yet be assessed. But his qualities included sheer intelligence, and a memory of legendary accuracy; great sensitivity to language, and vast reading; an intense engagement with the individual lives and family histories which can be brought out from behind the surface of Latin inscriptions and Roman literature; and a sense of style, which could lapse into idiosyncrasy. That style is shown at its best in the last paragraph of his *Tacitus*, which may also serve as his own epitaph:

> The irony is restrained and impressive. When Tacitus wrote, colonials and provincials from the Latin West occupied the place of the Caesars. There was only one higher pinnacle: literary renown. To that also the epoch of Trajan and Hadrian

might confidently aspire. Men and dynasties pass, but style abides.

He died on 4 September 1989 in the John Radcliffe Hospital, Oxford. FERGUS MILLAR, *rev.*

Sources G. W. Bowersock, 'Ronald Syme, 1903–1989', *PBA*, 84 (1994), 538–63 · F. Millar, 'Style abides', *Journal of Roman Studies*, 71 (1981) · M. T. Griffin, *Journal of Roman Studies*, 80 (1990) · personal knowledge (1996) · private information (1996) [G. Gill]
Archives AM Oxf., corresp. and papers · Bodl. Oxf., papers
Likenesses R. Foster, drawing, 1988, Royal Collection [*see illus.*] · portrait, Trinity College, Oxford
Wealth at death £1,094,365: probate, 27 Feb 1990, *CGPLA Eng. & Wales*

Symeon of Durham (*fl.* *c*.1090–*c*.1128), Benedictine monk and historian, owes his reputation principally to a history of the church of Durham, written at some point between 1104 and 1109 on the orders of his superiors. Compiled from a variety of sources, Symeon's history deals with the fortunes of the bishopric from its foundation by St Áedán on Lindisfarne in 635 to the death of Bishop William of St Calais in 1096. It describes Bishop Eardulf's flight from Lindisfarne in 875 with the body of St Cuthbert, his settlement at Chester-le-Street, and the subsequent move of the see to Durham in 995. Approval is given to the events of 1083, when St Calais expelled a body of secular clerks from Durham in favour of twenty-three monks led by Aldwin of Winchcombe, who had settled in Jarrow ten years earlier under the patronage of St Calais's predecessor Bishop Walcher (*d.* 1080).

The earliest copies of the work, Durham University Library, MS Cosin V.ii.6, which has additions and alterations probably by the author, and the closely related BL, Cotton MS Faustina A.v, entitle it *Libellus de exordio atque procursu istius hoc est Dunhelmensis ecclesie* ('Tract on the origin and progress of the church of Durham'). The bald title *Historia Dunelmensis ecclesiae*, favoured by nineteenth-century editors, derives from Twysden's edition of 1652. Although no attribution of authorship is provided in the early manuscripts, rubrics in a late twelfth-century copy, CUL, MS Ff.1.27, credit the work to Symeon. Similar rubrics in a problematic, related manuscript of about the same date, Cambridge, Corpus Christi College, MS 139, attribute to Symeon a miscellaneous compilation of overlapping English historical material stretching between 616 and 1129.

The compilation has become known as the *Historia regum* from nineteenth-century editions, though the title has no manuscript authority. It comprises several distinct elements: 1 Kentish legends relating to the seventh and eighth centuries, particularly to the martyrs Æthelberht and Æthelred; 2 accounts of kings of Northumbria from the mid-sixth century to 737; 3 material derived mainly from Bede, particularly from the *Historia abbatum*; 4 annals from 732 to 802, taken from a lost Northumbrian source; 5 annals from 849 to 887, based mainly on Asser; 6 annals from 888 to 957; 7 extracts from William of Malmesbury's *Gesta regum*; 8 annals from 848 to 1118, based mainly on the chronicle of John of Worcester; 9 annals from 1119 to 1129.

Symeon's precise role in this compilation remains uncertain, especially as it is likely that texts 1–5 above were written by Byrhtferth of Ramsey in the late tenth or early eleventh century. Although internal inconsistencies make it improbable that the same author was responsible both for the *Libellus* on the church of Durham and for the *Historia regum*, it is possible that the latter represents an attempt by Symeon to gather together material for a more ambitious historical work which was not completed.

A brief account of archbishops of York from the seventh to the tenth centuries, concluding with a bare list of names after Oswald (972–92), can be assigned to Symeon with confidence, since he describes himself in the text as 'I Symeon, a poor servant of the servants of St Cuthbert' (Symeon of Durham, *Opera*, 1.226). Precisely when he wrote the piece is a matter of surmise, since he did so at the request of Dean Hugh of York, a name that occurs at intervals over a lengthy period from 1093 to 1135. Symeon also composed a letter to Holdebert—presumably Hildebert, successively bishop of Le Mans and archbishop of Tours (*d.* 1133)—extant in a mid-twelfth-century manuscript from Gloucester (Bodl. Oxf., MS Laud misc. 123) concerning uncertainties that Hildebert experienced on reading from Origen's homilies. John Bale's sixteenth-century index of British writers attributed to Symeon the composition of letters to Elmer, perhaps the prior of Christ Church, Canterbury, who died in 1137. The letters do not survive. Bale's additional attribution to Symeon of an account of a siege of Durham in 969 has no authority.

The sources provide a few glimpses of Symeon's life. Rud suggested in 1732 that Symeon was one of the twenty-three monks who came to Durham from Jarrow in 1083, but this is uncertain. Since his name occurs in thirty-eighth place in his own list of the monks of the house in Cosin V.ii.6, folio 7*v*, it may be deduced that he entered some time in the 1090s. His scribal work dates from this period until *c*.1128. It is known that he was present at the translation of St Cuthbert's incorrupt body to the new cathedral in 1104, thanks to the later twelfth-century writer Reginald of Durham, who provided a colourful account of Symeon's involvement in the occasion, albeit an imaginative one, as Reginald himself was not present. Holding a candle in his hand, and allowing his tears to flow freely, Symeon pressed kisses on the feet of the saint. Symeon subsequently became precentor at Durham, and his renown locally may be judged from the dedication to him of an account of a vision experienced by Orm, a fourteen-year-old youth, written shortly after 1126 by Sigar, the parish priest of Newbald in the East Riding of Yorkshire. By this date Symeon was probably at an advanced age. His death was commemorated by the Durham community on 14 October. BERNARD MEEHAN

Sources R. Twysden, ed., *Historiæ Anglicanæ scriptores X* (1652) · T. Rud, *Disquisitio de vero auctore hujus 'Historiae Dunelmensis ecclesiae', Symeonis monachi Dunelmensis libellus*, ed. T. Bedford (1732) · Symeon of Durham, *Symeonis Dunelmensis opera et collectanea*, ed. J. H. Hinde, SurtS, 51 (1868) · Symeon of Durham, *Opera* · *Reginaldi monachi Dunelmensis libellus de admirandis beati Cuthberti virtutibus*, ed. [J. Raine], SurtS, 1 (1835), 84 · H. Farmer, ed., 'The vision of Orm', *Analecta Bollandiana*, 75 (1957), 72–82 · Bale, *Index*, 408–9 · [J. Stevenson], ed., *Liber vitae ecclesiae Dunelmensis*, SurtS, 13 (1841), 146 · B. Meehan, 'A reconsideration of the historical works associated with Symeon of Durham: manuscripts, texts and influences', PhD diss., U. Edin., 1979 · M. Gullick, 'The scribes of the Durham cantor's book (Durham, Dean and Chapter Library, MS B.IV.24) and the Durham martyrology scribe', *Anglo-Norman Durham*, ed. D. Rollason, M. Harvey, and M. Prestwich (1994), 93–109 · D. Baker, 'Scissors and paste: Corpus Christi, Cambridge, MS 139 again', *The materials, sources, and methods of ecclesiastical history*, ed. D. Baker, SCH, 11 (1975), 83–123 · P. H. Blair, 'Some observations on the *Historia regum* attributed to Symeon of Durham', *Celt and Saxon: studies in the early British border*, ed. N. K. Chadwick (1963), 63–118 · D. W. Rollason, ed., *Symeon of Durham: historian of Durham and the north* [Durham 1995] (1998) · M. Lapidge, 'Byrhtferth of Ramsey and the early sections of the *Historia regum* attributed to Symeon of Durham', *Anglo-Saxon England*, 10 (1982), 97–122 · R. Sharpe, 'Symeon, Hildebert, and the errors of Origen', *Symeon of Durham: historian of Durham and the north* [Durham 1995], ed. D. W. Rollason (1998), 282–300 · H. S. Offler, *Medieval historians of Durham* (1958) · A. Gransden, *Historical writing in England*, 1 (1974), 114–21, 148–51

Archives BL, Cotton MS Faustina A.v · Bodl. Oxf., Laud misc. MS 123 · CCC Cam., MS 139 · CUL, MS Ff.1.27 · U. Durham L., MS Cosin V.ii.6

Symes, John Elliotson (1847–1921), college head, was born at 77 Grosvenor Street, London, on 31 December 1847, the second son of Edmond Sheppard Symes MD and his wife, Mary, formerly West. He was educated at University College School, London, before being admitted as a scholar at Downing College, Cambridge, in October 1867. He was president of the Cambridge Union and graduated in 1871 as tenth junior optime in the mathematical tripos; he proceeded MA in 1874. He taught at Lancing College, Sussex, from 1872 to 1875. In 1875 Symes was ordained priest and became a Cambridge extension lecturer, serving also as a curate in Stepney, London. Five years later he became second master at the Royal Grammar School, Newcastle upon Tyne.

In 1881 Symes was appointed professor of language and literature at the newly founded Nottingham University College. On 31 December 1884 in Gateshead he married Eleanor Sabina Baylee, daughter of W. C. P. Baylee, vicar of Alston, Cumberland. At Nottingham Symes lectured also on history and political economy (Henry, later Baron, Snell was one of his students). He introduced teacher training and commercial courses, and later created an engineering department. As principal from 1890 he had far-reaching ambitions for the college, proposing to the Bryce commission on secondary education of 1894–5 that it should become an educational centre to serve the whole of the east midlands. He also wanted to see each region of the country with its own university or college. However, Symes's three decades as professor and principal brought only relatively modest growth to the college. It relied almost wholly on funds from the municipality, and most councillors wished for little more than a technical college. Incapable of cajoling his paymasters into laying out funds as an act of civic pride, by his views and activities he unwittingly turned the worthies of Nottingham against him.

Although an acclaimed preacher in local churches, Symes shared platforms with such high-profile freethinkers as Charles Bradlaugh and with the unorthodox cleric Stewart Headlam. At the church congresses of 1877 and 1880 he helped to distribute humanist pamphlets, and at the latter congress commended the nobility of secularist principles. An executive member of the Guild of St Matthew, a pressure group for the promotion of Christian socialism, he regularly lectured to secularists in the hope of converting them.

For a while Symes enthusiastically supported Bradlaugh's Land Law Reform League, founded to publicize Henry George's proposals for a land tax. George Bernard Shaw later quipped that the radical Symes was 'the chaplain of a pirate ship' (*Bernard Shaw: Collected Letters, 1898– 1910*, ed. D. H. Lawrence, 1972, 489). However, Symes soon resigned from the league, and in *A Short Text Book of Political Economy* (1888) advocated a tax on the rental value of land, preferably topped up by a highly progressive income tax. He urged state action to relieve the widespread poverty and unemployment of the 1880s, advocating job-creating government workshops. He also protested at the low wages and poor working conditions of the Nottingham laceworkers. To assist the welfare of deprived children Symes was chairman of the committee of the Nottingham branch of the NSPCC and of the Children's Holidays in Country Cottages scheme.

In 1887 Symes caused further rumpuses by delivering some public lectures on the Irish question, and was condemned for using the college to spread political propaganda. Having in various ways incensed councillors, businessmen, and other influential local people, he gave them every excuse to withhold extra funds from the college, and this ruled out any move to its becoming a university during Symes's principalship.

Having fought off several attempts by the council to unseat him, Symes remained as principal until he retired in 1912, and was then made an emeritus professor. He thereafter intended to devote himself to work consistent with his strong sympathies; one part was the writing of *Broad Church* (1913), in which he maintained that a socialist programme must above all be a moral one, to improve human character, rather than a purely material one. He died at the Pension Suisse, via Monteleone, Palermo, Sicily, on 31 March 1921. He was survived by his wife and by two daughters, both teachers at independent schools.

T. A. B. CORLEY

Sources A. C. Wood, *A history of the University College, Nottingham, 1881–1948* (1953) · A. W. Coats, 'John Elliotson Symes, Henry George and academic freedom in Nottingham during the 1880s', *Renaissance and Modern Studies*, 7 (1963), 110–39 · B. H. Tolley, 'Technical education in the east midlands, 1869–1902', PhD diss., U. Nott., 1979 · 'Principal Symes' retirement', *The Trader* (17 Dec 1910) · J. Potter Briscoe, *Nottinghamshire and Derbyshire at the opening of the twentieth century: contemporary biographies*, ed. W. T. Pike (1901), 156 · *Nottingham Evening Post* (1 April 1921) · E. M. Beckett, *The history of University College, Nottingham* (1928), 45–8 · T. Peacock, 'The Guild of St Matthew', *DLB*, 8.97–103 · 'Royal commission on secondary education: minutes of evidence', *Parl. papers* (1895), 46.36ff., C. 7862-III · F. G. Bettany, *Stewart Headlam: a biography* (1926) · *WWW* · Venn, *Alum. Cant.* · b. cert. · m. cert.

Archives U. Nott., archives

Likenesses photograph, *c.*1901, repro. in Briscoe, *Nottinghamshire and Derbyshire* · photograph, *c.*1910, repro. in 'Principal Symes' retirement', *The Trader*

Wealth at death £248 16s. 8d.: probate, 26 May 1921, *CGPLA Eng. & Wales*

Symes, Michael (1761–1809), army officer in the East India Company and diplomatist, was born in co. Wicklow, the youngest of the five children of Richard Symes of Balletarth, and Eleanor, daughter of Loftus Cliffe of co. Wexford. He appears to have been well educated, for his later writings indicate that he was very familiar with many works in history, philosophy, and natural history. He went to India in 1780 as a cadet in the Bengal army of the East India Company. He was fortunate to arrive in India at a time when the army was very active and consequently promotion came quickly; Symes was made an ensign in 1780, and became lieutenant in 1781. He resigned his commission with the East India Company in 1788 and transferred as a lieutenant into the newly raised 76th regiment, royal army. He was made captain in 1793 and lieutenant-colonel in 1800.

In 1795 Symes was sent by the governor-general, John Shore, to the court of King Bodawpaya of Burma, to try to improve political and commercial relations, and also to confirm whether the French were actively courting the Burmese as they were rumoured to be doing elsewhere in Asia. Border tensions had recently escalated when Burmese troops had pursued Arakanese rebels into British territories and then refused to leave until the rebels were handed over. The embassy was counted a success, for Symes returned with signed documents which the British believed would open Burmese markets to British and Indian traders, and the French threat was shown to be largely illusory. These agreements, which fell short of what might properly be called a treaty, allowed British traders to purchase Burmese wood, instituted a procedure for addressing merchant grievances, and, provided import duties were paid, exempted British goods from inland customs and duties.

Symes wrote of his seven months in Burma—which took him from Rangoon to the capital at Amarapura—in *An Account of an Embassy to the Kingdom of Ava Sent by the Governor-General of India in 1795* (1800), one of the first detailed accounts of the country written in English. In just over 500 pages, it addressed the history, geography, culture, and economics of Burma, and the text was accompanied by illustrations and maps. It painted a generally favourable impression of Burma, emphasizing its civility, culture, and stability, while also hinting at the Burmese court's suspicions of the British.

In 1800 Symes went on furlough. While in Britain, on 18 February 1801, he married 29-year-old Jemima (1771–1835), daughter of Paul Pilcher of Rochester. They had several children. Symes rejoined his regiment at Cawnpore in 1801, but was soon after appointed to lead another embassy to the court of Ava. The treaty he had signed in 1795 had provided for the establishment of a British resident in Burma. Hiram Cox had accordingly been sent, but the Burmese court refused to grant him official recognition, and Cox returned to Calcutta. Cox blamed Symes for his failure, and for exaggerating Burmese good will and intentions. Yet few in Calcutta were at this point convinced by Cox, and Symes was still viewed as the authority on Burma. When hostilities along the Arakan frontier once again flared, Symes was the obvious choice to lead an embassy. This time he was instructed not only to try to improve relations, but also to seek Burmese agreement to a subsidiary alliance. Symes's second embassy to Burma was very different from the first: the Burmese court only reluctantly gave Symes an audience, and they avoided making any firm commitments on the political and commercial issues which Symes had been sent to discuss.

Most interpretations of Anglo-Burmese relations, when dealing with Symes, have tended to echo Hiram Cox, and dismiss Symes's reports as overly optimistic and uncritical. However, if these reports are read carefully, Symes does not appear as credulous as some have made him out to be. He was well aware of the court's insularity and suspicions of outsiders, and he reckoned that misunderstandings would frequently punctuate diplomatic relations. The setbacks of his second embassy led Symes to suggest that increased British intervention might be unavoidable. Yet his writings display a genuine fascination with Burmese society, and indicate that he was eager to seek some *rapprochement* with Burma.

Symes returned to Britain with the 76th regiment in 1806, and in 1808 joined Sir John Moore's army during the Peninsular War. Exhausted and injured during Moore's retreat from the battle of Corunna, Symes died *en route* for Britain on 22 January 1809, aboard the transport *Mary*. He was buried on 3 February 1809 in the churchyard of St Margaret's, Rochester. His widow later married Sir Joseph de Courcy Laffan.   DOUGLAS M. PEERS

Sir (George) Stewart Symes (1882–1962), by Bassano, 1938

Sources *Michael Symes: journal of his second embassy to the court of Ava in 1802*, ed. D. G. E. Hall (1955) · A. C. Banerjee, *The eastern frontier of British India, 1784–1826* (1966) · Dodwell [E. Dodwell] and Miles [J. S. Miles], eds., *Alphabetical list of the officers of the Indian army: with the dates of their respective promotion, retirement, resignation, or death … from the year 1760 to the year … 1837* (1838) · V. C. P. Hodson, *List of officers of the Bengal army, 1758–1834*, 4 vols. (1927–47) · *Hampshire Telegraph* (6 Feb 1809) · *GM*, 1st ser., 79 (1809) · G. P. Ramachandra, 'Captain Cox's mission to Burma, 1796–1798: a case of irrational behaviour in diplomacy', *Journal of Southeast Asian Studies*, 7 (1981), 433–51 · H. Cox, *Journal of a residence in the Burmhan empire* (1821) · D. M. Peers, *Between Mars and Mammon: colonial armies and the garrison state in India, 1819–1835* (1995) · W. J. Koenig, *The Burmese polity, 1752–1819: politics, administration and social organization in early Konbaung period* (1990) · *Calcutta Gazette* (21 Jan 1796) · Bengal army lists, BL OIOC, L/Mil/10/2 · M. Adas, 'Imperialist rhetoric and modern historiography: the case of Lower Burma before and after conquest', *Journal of Southeast Asian Studies*, 3 (1972), 175–92
Archives BL, instructions and corresp., Add. MSS 13871–13872

Symes, Sir (George) Stewart (1882–1962), army officer and colonial governor, was born at Wateringbury, Kent, on 29 July 1882, the only son and eldest of three children of Lieutenant-Colonel William Alexander Symes, of the 71st regiment (Highland light infantry), and his wife, Emily Catherine Shore, younger daughter of the second Lord Teignmouth. His father died when he was eight. Educated at Malvern College and the Royal Military College, Sandhurst, he was gazetted to a commission in the Hampshire regiment shortly after his eighteenth birthday.

In December 1900 Symes was posted to India to join the 1st battalion of his regiment, and in the next four years he saw service in India, South Africa, Aden, and the Somali coast. For operations in the Aden hinterland in 1903 to protect an Anglo-Turkish boundary commission from dissident tribesmen, Symes received the DSO (1904), and was mentioned in dispatches. His regiment returned to England and in 1905, dissatisfied with peacetime soldiering, he obtained a transfer to the Egyptian army. He was posted to the 1st battalion of Egyptian infantry at Berber in Sudan in January 1906 and in October of the same year became aide-de-camp to Sir Reginald Wingate, the sirdar and governor-general of Sudan. Symes was promoted captain in 1907 and served in the Blue Nile expedition of 1908. From 1909 to 1912 he was assistant director of intelligence at Khartoum and from 1913 to 1916 private secretary to the governor-general. During these years he travelled much throughout Sudan and so obtained a valuable knowledge of the country and its people. In 1913 Symes married Viola Colston (d. 1953), daughter of the late J. Felix Broun of the 71st regiment; they had one son (who was killed in the Second World War) and one daughter.

In 1917 Wingate became high commissioner in Egypt and took Symes to Cairo with him. There he became immersed in Egyptian and Arab politics with D. G. Hogarth, Gilbert Clayton, Ronald Storrs, and Kinahan Cornwallis as colleagues, and, as GSO1 for the Hedjaz operations, had much to do with the Arab advance on the eastern flank of Sir Edmund Allenby, under the leadership of T. E. Lawrence.

After the British victories in Palestine and the establishment of British administration there, Symes, who had been promoted major during the war, retired from the army with the rank of lieutenant-colonel and was appointed governor of the northern district; he held the post with such success from 1920 to 1925 that he was chosen to succeed Clayton as chief secretary to the government. In the difficult situation caused by Arab hatred of the Jewish national home and of Jewish immigration, Symes, supported by Lord Plumer, the high commissioner, steered a conciliatory course and maintained a high degree of law and order.

In 1928 Symes was appointed resident and commander-in-chief at Aden. In the three years of his tenure of this office, he promoted reorganization of the services, educational, medical, and economic; perhaps more importantly, he persuaded the tribal chiefs in the hinterland to co-operate mutually for the defence and better administration of the territory. In 1931 he succeeded Sir Donald Cameron as governor of Tanganyika, a territory severely hit by the worldwide economic crisis. Symes combined necessary retrenchment with administrative reform, and strongly supported his predecessor's policy in native administration or, as he preferred to call it, local government.

In 1934 Symes returned to Sudan as governor-general, where he put his ideas into practice. He did much to encourage economic advance, and to develop the role of departmental services in the administration. He deprecated the old-fashioned role of district officers as jacks of all trades, and considered that many of their duties should be transferred to specialist departments such as the police, the judiciary, and revenue services. He economized by amalgamating provinces and districts.

Symes's experience in Cairo and his acquaintance with many leading Egyptians were valuable during the negotiations for the Anglo-Egyptian treaty of 1936, and he maintained Sudan's constitutional position at the expense of relatively minor concessions to the Egyptians. In the two years before the outbreak of war in 1939 considerable preparations were made under his guidance: stores of all kinds and military supplies were accumulated which proved of the greatest value in the campaigns on Sudan's frontiers in 1940–41.

Until the Italians entered the war in June 1940 Symes was not allowed by the British government to expand the Sudan defence force or to let British civilians of military age leave Sudan to join the forces. For this he was much criticized locally, but it proved beneficial later when the Sudan defence force was expanded, and British civilians with Sudan experience were available for service in the new units and in occupied enemy territory administration.

The loyalty of the Sudanese people and their unswerving support for Britain and her allies in the darkest days of the war were a testimony to the policies of Symes and his predecessors in administering the country. An Arabic speaker, Symes had many contacts with the Sudanese, with both the educated élite and the country folk. Tall, slim, good-looking, he was forthcoming and easy with junior officers and in discussion his manner was friendly and open. He was critical of many long-held preconceived ideas and debunked many shibboleths, thereby effectively shaking up Sudan's administration. Towards the end of 1940 he left Sudan and settled in South Africa until the end of the war. During this period he wrote a book of reminiscences, *Tour of Duty* (1946). On his return to England he spent his retirement in voluntary work for several charitable causes.

Symes was appointed KBE in 1928 and GBE in 1939, CMG in 1917, and KCMG in 1932. He was also the recipient of Turkish, Egyptian, Ethiopian, and Hedjazi decorations. He died at Princes Hotel, Folkestone, on 5 December 1962.

J. W. ROBERTSON, *rev.*

Sources S. Symes, *Tour of duty* (1946) · personal knowledge (1981) · *The Times* (7 Dec 1962) · *WWW* · *CGPLA Eng. & Wales* (1963)
Archives NRA, priv. coll., corresp. and papers | U. Durham L., corresp. with Sir Reginald Wingate | FILM BFI NFTVA, news footage
Likenesses Bassano, photograph, 1938, NPG [*see illus.*]
Wealth at death £105,816 15s. 1d.: probate, 5 Feb 1963, *CGPLA Eng. & Wales*

Symington, Andrew (1785–1853), Reformed Presbyterian (Cameronian) minister, eldest son of a Paisley merchant, was born in that town on 26 June 1785. William *Symington was his brother. After attending Paisley grammar school for four years he entered Glasgow University, where he carried off first-class honours in mathematics, natural philosophy, and divinity, and graduated MA in 1803. He was destined for the ministry of the Reformed Presbyterian church, of which his father was a member, and to that end studied theology under the Revd John Macmillan. On being licensed to preach he accepted a call from his native town, and was ordained in 1809. With his wife, Jane Stevenson, of Crookedholm, Riccarton, Ayrshire, whom he married in 1811, he had fourteen children, of whom three sons and three daughters survived him. In 1820 he was appointed professor of theology in the Reformed Presbyterian church, as successor to John Macmillan, his former instructor. In 1831 he received the degree of DD from the Western University of Pennsylvania, and in 1840 he obtained the same degree from the University of Glasgow.

In addition to numerous tracts and sermons, Symington wrote *The Principles of the Second Reformation* (1841), *The Martyr's Monument* (1847), and *Elements of Divine Truth* (1854). He also contributed 'The unity of the heavenly church' and *Essays on Christian Union* (1845), wrote memoirs of Archibald Mason and Thomas Halliday, which are prefixed to the collected editions of their discourses, and wrote on the Reformed Presbyterian church for the *Cyclopaedia of Religious Denominations* (1853). Symington's balanced teaching on the Bible influenced a generation of Reformed Presbyterian ministers. He prepared formularies for his church which avoided emphasis on separativeness. He was active in the Bible Society and in the Evangelical Alliance. Contemporaries noted his 'benignity'. He died at Paisley on 22 September 1853.

E. I. CARLYLE, *rev.* H. C. G. MATTHEW

Sources W. Symington, *Departed worth and greatness lamented: a sermon on the death of the Rev. A. Symington* (1853) · A. Symington, *Elements of divine truth* (1854), preface · *DSCHT*

Symington, William (1764–1831), engineer, was born at Leadhills in Lanarkshire, in October 1764, where his father was an engineer with the Scots Mines Company. He was educated in the local school and was encouraged to consider a career in the ministry of the Church of Scotland, but he soon decided to enter his father's profession and went to work in the late 1770s in the nearby Wanlockhead mines. While there he assisted his brother George, the engineer at the mines, in constructing the new engine supplied by Boulton and Watt to drain the Margaret mine. The mine manager, Gilbert Meason, sent him in 1786 to take classes in anatomy, surgery, and chemistry at the University of Edinburgh, where he was taught by William Cullen, Joseph Black, and John Robinson. By this time Meason had fallen out with Boulton and Watt and was looking for another source of supply for pumping engines, and Symington seems to have spent some of his time at Edinburgh designing an improved steam engine, having already built an experimental model before he left for Edinburgh in the autumn of 1786.

In January 1787 Alexander Fergusson described Symington in a letter to Henry Dundas as 'one of the first rate mechanical geniuses this country ever produced' (Fergusson to Dundas, 30 Jan 1787, NA Scot., GD51/6/807). Helped by Meason, in June of that year Symington patented his designs, and during the autumn he modified one of the Watt engines at the mines using parts made by the Carron Company. Although seemingly successful it was never effectively put to the test. At the same time, like other inventors of the time, Symington, with his brother George and the mine overseer John Taylor, dabbled in the design of a steam carriage and made a working model that could be demonstrated to possible backers. This project was abandoned in the autumn of 1787 when the wealthy Edinburgh banker Patrick *Miller, of Dalswinton, invited Symington to design and build a steam engine to power one of his experimental paddle boats. Miller was introduced to Symington by James Taylor, John Taylor's brother, who was tutor to his sons and who had helped in the design of the original manual-mechanical propelling machinery.

Symington agreed to co-operate in Miller's work and the first trials of a steam-propelled vessel took place on Dalswinton Loch in October 1788, using a small engine made by an Edinburgh brass-founder. The 25 foot, doubled-hull boat, made of tinned iron plate, achieved a speed of 5 m.p.h. Encouraged, Symington took up the project with the Carron Company, who undertook in June 1789 to let him have as much money as he needed. He immediately started making a much larger set of engines, which dominated work at Carron during the autumn. This took much longer to build and was much more costly than Symington estimated, exasperating Miller. When finally completed the engines were mounted in a much bigger hull and trials in the presence of the partners in the Carron Company were carried out on the Forth and Clyde Canal

on 2 and 3 December 1789. To Miller's annoyance the paddle wheels broke. An infuriated Miller consulted James Watt, who considered that too much power was being lost in Symington's engines because of friction. Having seen Watt's rotary engine Miller was convinced and withdrew from further development, describing Symington as a 'vain extravagant fool' (J. Taylor, *Memorial and Original Correspondence*, 1857, 5). In 1789 Ann Miller of Wanlockhead bore Symington a son, James, who later became a tireless advocate of his father's claim to have invented steam propulsion. Symington married Elizabeth Benson of Carron, in 1790, and they had two sons and two daughters.

After his failure with Patrick Miller, Symington returned to Wanlockhead to install a pumping engine of his own design and using castings supplied by Carron at Whytescleuch. This was more successful than his first attempt and he began to receive orders for his engines from mines at Sanquhar and Leadhills. Following John Smeaton's retirement as engineer to the Carron Company in 1790, Symington took over some of his duties. He began by building engines for the Kinnaird estate, owned by James Bruce, who had recently returned from his adventures in Africa to find his mines neglected. Following Bruce's accidental death in 1794, Symington managed the Kinnaird mines, until 1802, and began to advise other coal owners. Carron supplied parts for almost thirty of Symington's engines between 1789 and 1806, including some for customers in London and elsewhere in England. However, the business south of the border was brought to a halt by Boulton and Watt in 1796, who accused Symington, probably justifiably, of infringing their patents. In 1804 Symington became a partner in the Callendar colliery, near Falkirk. This ended disastrously in a lengthy legal dispute which included accusations that he was drinking excessively.

Symington returned to his interest in steam navigation in 1792, making further experiments with rotary engines at Kinnaird. However it was not until 1800 that Thomas, Lord Dundas, a director of the Forth and Clyde Canal Company, asked him to supply the engines for a vessel designed by Captain John Schank. The new steamboat, named *Charlotte Dundas* after Dundas's eldest daughter, was tested at Carron in August 1801 and then on the canal. Proving to be underpowered and costly to operate, the experiment was abandoned and Symington concentrated on an improved vessel, the *Charlotte Dundas II*, paid for by himself and the Carron Company. As had happened before costs escalated and the canal company dissociated itself from the project. The duke of Bridgewater, the canal promoter, was more impressed and ordered eight boats of similar design if the *Charlotte Dundas II* met his expectations. Unfortunately for Symington the duke died before the first trial on 4 January 1803. Although Symington considered the trials to be successful, others had their doubts. James Lawson, Boulton and Watt's supervising engineer, wrote to Matthew Boulton on 5 February 1803:

> The Engine is made by Symington & turns a Wheel—which made so much *Splashing* that they were affraid of washing down the Canal Banks—tho' the boat only moved at 2

Miles—the papers say Lord Dundas is the great Patroniser of the scheme—which I rather think will Die without further noise. (Tann, 1.149)

Lawson's prediction was correct; without the patronage of Bridgewater or Dundas, further experiments were impossible and the hull was left to rot in the canal.

By his late forties Symington was drinking heavily, finding it harder to get business, and living in increasing poverty near Falkirk. Towards the end of his life he became caught up in the dispute about who was rightful inventor of steam navigation, fuelled by Henry Bell's inflated claims which a parliamentary committee confirmed in 1822. Symington and James Taylor protested, but Symington was only given a reward of £100, unlike Bell, who had been awarded a pension of £50 a year. James Watt, who had not always been on good terms with Symington, recognizing his contribution and the pitiful condition to which excessive whisky drinking had brought him, paid him in 1829 to write up his experiments, which were published in that year. Symington moved to London to live with his daughter during 1829 and died there on 22 March 1831; he was buried in St Botolph's, Aldgate.

T. H. BEARE, rev. MICHAEL S. MOSS

Sources W. S. Harvey and G. Downs-Rose, *William Symington: inventor and engine builder* (1980) · Birm. CL, James Watt MSS [amongst which a bundle of papers relating to William Symington] · J. Tann, ed., *The selected papers of Boulton and Watt*, 1 (1981)
Archives Birm. CA, James Watt MSS
Likenesses D. O. Hill, portrait, c.1830, Museum of Transport, Glasgow · Roffe, stipple, pubd 1834 (after bust), NPG · D. W. Stevenson, bust, 1890, Royal Scottish Museum, Edinburgh · T. O. Barlow, mixed-method engraving (after D. O. Hill), BM, NPG · J. F. Skill, J. Gilbert, W. Walker, and E. Walker, group portrait, pencil and wash (*Men of science living in 1807–08*), NPG

Symington, William (1795–1862), Reformed Presbyterian (Cameronian) minister, younger brother of Andrew *Symington, was born at Paisley on 2 June 1795, son of a merchant of that town. From an early age he intended to be ordained, and at the age of fifteen he entered the University of Glasgow. After the usual four years' course in arts, he attended for another four years the Theological Hall of the Reformed Presbyterian church, then under the charge of the Revd John Macmillan, the third of that name in the ministry at Stirling. He was licensed to preach on 30 June 1818. Called to Airdrie and Stranraer, he accepted the latter, and was ordained there on 18 August 1819. On 11 June 1820 he married Agnes Speirs. Symington was popular and successful; many people belonging to other denominations and from different parts of Galloway attended the services of the Cameronian meeting-house, and a new church was erected in 1824. He received the degree of DD from the University of Edinburgh on 20 November 1838.

On 5 March 1839 Symington was called to Great Hamilton Street Reformed Presbyterian Church, Glasgow, to succeed the Revd D. Armstrong, and was inducted on 11 July. Here also large audiences gathered to hear him, his Sunday evening lectures being especially popular. He took

a deep interest in Bible circulation, home and foreign missions, and other religious movements. One of his missionaries in Glasgow was John G. Paton DD, afterwards of the New Hebrides. On the death of his brother Andrew in 1853, William was chosen to succeed him as professor of theology in the Reformed Presbyterian church. He retained his pastorate in Glasgow, but in March 1859 his eldest son, William, then minister in Castle Douglas, was inducted as his colleague and successor in the ministry.

Among the Reformed Presbyterians Symington, like his brother, was a commanding influence. A noted evangelical in the covenanting tradition, he was none the less outward-looking and deeply involved in social issues such as slavery, illiteracy, and poor working conditions. Like Thomas Chalmers, whom he in part resembled, he advocated a Scotland cleansed and dedicated. Besides his published sermons, he recorded his views in *The Atonement and Intercession of Jesus Christ* (1834) and *Messiah the Prince* (1839; reissued 1881 with memoir). The latter was an important exposition of Cameronian ecclesiological thought. Symington died in Glasgow on 28 January 1862, and was buried in the Glasgow necropolis. His wife survived him.

T. B. JOHNSTONE, rev. H. C. G. MATTHEW

Sources R. Blackwood, *William Symington* (1985) · J. Smith, *Our Scottish clergy*, 1st ser. (1848) · *Reformed Presbyterian Magazine* (1862), 81–9 · J. M'Gill, *Funeral sermon on William Symington* (1862)
Likenesses J. G. Murray, mezzotint (after A. Craig), NPG · Schenck and McFarlane, lithograph, BM

Symmons, Charles (1749–1826), poet and biographer, was born at Cardigan, the younger son of John Symmons (1701–1764) of Llanstinan, MP for Cardigan in 1746–61, and his wife, Maria (d. 1763), daughter of Charles Phillips, of Sandyhaven, in the parish of St Ishmaels, Pembrokeshire. He was admitted at Westminster School on 14 January 1765 and showed early signs of his gift for writing poetry. Although he was made a member of Lincoln's Inn on 20 November 1765, Symmons did not pursue a legal career in adulthood. In 1766 he was at the University of Glasgow, where he began an enduring friendship with William Windham, the future politician. Symmons entered Cambridge University as a ten-year man on 14 February 1776, and graduated BD in 1786. He was ordained deacon by the bishop of St David's at Abergwili on 15 August 1773, and ordained priest on 14 August 1774. He was appointed to the rectory of Narberth with the chapelry of Robeston, Pembrokeshire, on 13 August 1778. In the following year he married Elizabeth, daughter of John Foley of Ridgeway, Pembrokeshire, and sister of the future Rear-Admiral Sir Thomas Foley. He was appointed to the prebendal stall of Clydey in St David's Cathedral on 11 October 1789.

Symmons went into residence at Cambridge in 1793 to take his DD soon after the trial of William Frend. This involved preaching two sermons, one in English, the other in Latin, before the members of the university at Great St Mary's Church. With loyalist feelings rising, Symmons's profession of moderate whig tenets in his English sermon was a risky strategy. One of his political opponents, Thomas Kipling, deputy regius professor of divinity and Boyle lecturer, borrowed the manuscript under some pretence and sent extracts, garbled and detached from the context, to Samuel Horsley, the bishop of St David's, Windham, and others. Symmons thereupon wrote Kipling a forceful letter of reproach (fifty copies were printed and distributed), and, persuaded that taking his higher degree had been rendered impossible, he was incorporated at Jesus College, Oxford, on 29 March 1794 and proceeded DD two days later. This whiggish sermon seemed briefly to compromise Symmons's hopes of further preferment, and it was with difficulty that Windham was able to secure him on 2 April 1794 the rectory of Lampeter Velfrey, Pembrokeshire, which adjoined Narberth. Symmons retained both these comfortable livings until his death.

Symmons was a good scholar and a man of undoubted literary skills, devoting most of his waking hours at his house in Chiswick to these studies. He appears as something of a depressive, warm-tempered and with a high expectation of others. Believing that Bishop Horsley had vetoed appointing him as his chaplain on translation to Rochester, he bombarded Windham with requests for preferment in the late 1790s, bemoaning his 'strange ill-luck' (letter of 21 May 1798, BL, Add. MS 37915, fol. 46) and his decayed fortune. Windham's inability to offer him anything—let alone the prebendal stall at Westminster Abbey that Symmons sought—for a time soured their amity. Symmons's earliest works include a volume of sermons dated 1787; *Inez*, an anonymous tragedy of 1796 dedicated to Windham before it was withdrawn when Burke and the French Revolution 'converted the object of my proud regard into the zealot of aristocratical and factious alarm' (Symmons, 215); and *Constantia*, a dramatic poem of 1800. Family losses thereafter retarded his output. Symmons was overwhelmed by grief after his daughter Caroline died of consumption on 1 June 1803, aged fourteen, followed by his son Charles, aged twenty-one, in May 1805. The loss of his daughter, by his own admission, left Symmons 'in sepulchral darkness'. *Poems for the Anniversary of the Literary Fund*, including poems by Caroline, appeared in tribute to her in 1813.

Symmons's mature works were a 'Life of Milton' prefixed to a seven-volume edition of Milton's works published in 1806 and reprinted in 1810 and 1822; a translation in rhyme of Virgil's *Aeneid* which first appeared in 1817; and a 'Life of Shakespeare, with some remarks upon his dramatic writings' prefixed to the edition of Shakespeare in 1826 by Samuel Weller Singer. Symmons also published several sermons, the most remarkable being that preached in Richmond-on-Thames church on 12 October 1806 on the death of Charles James Fox. He was a contributor to the *Monthly Review*, and was one of the triumvirate originally asked by Samuel Parr to compile his biography. Symmons died after a two-month illness at Bath on 27 April 1826. He left two sons and three daughters. Mrs Symmons died at Penglan Park, Carmarthenshire, in July 1830.

Charles Symmons's son **John Symmons** (1780/81–1842) went to Westminster School, and matriculated at Christ Church, Oxford, on 11 April 1799, aged eighteen, when he was elected to a studentship. He graduated BA in 1803 and MA in 1806, and was called to the bar at Lincoln's Inn on 24 November 1807, afterwards going on the Welsh circuit. He inherited many of his father's literary abilities, assisting the latter in his revised 1820 translation of Virgil, and publishing a translation in his own right of the *Agamemnon* (1824). Samuel Parr left mourning rings to both father and son, and lauded the son's retentive memory, extensive learning, and unassuming manners. John Symmons died in 1842, probably at Deal.　　　　　　NIGEL ASTON

Sources HoP, *Commons, 1715–54* · *Old Westminsters* · W. I. Addison, ed., *The matriculation albums of the University of Glasgow from 1728 to 1858* (1913), 80 · *DNB* · Venn, *Alum. Cant.*, 2/6.1380 · Foster, *Alum. Oxon.* · *GM*, 1st ser., 75 (1805), 584 · *GM*, 1st ser., 83/1 (1813), 25, 326 · *GM*, 1st ser., 96/1 (1826), 450, 552, 565–7 · *GM*, 1st ser., 100/2 (1830), 382 · *Fasti Angl.* (Hardy), 1.382 · H. Gunning, *Reminiscences of Cambridge* (1854), vol. 1, pp. 311–16 · F. Wrangham, *The raising of Jairus's daughter: a poem ... to which is annexed a short memoir ... of the late Caroline Symmons* (1804) · J. Taylor, *Records of my life*, 2 (1832), 367–70 · W. Field, *Memoirs of the life, writings and opinions of the Rev. Samuel Parr* (1828), vol. 2, pp. 298–301 · W. Derry, *Dr Parr: a portrait of the whig Dr Johnson* (1966), p. xiv · Pembrokeshire RO · C. Symmons, *Poems for the anniversary of the literary fund* (1813)
Archives BL, Add. MSS 37914, fol. 140; 37887, fol. 138; 37914, fols. 19, 23, 40, 47, 58, 60, 63, 73, 89, 97, 127,139, 233, 235; 37915, fols. 24, 45, 72, 78, 117, 233, 245, 322; 37916, fols. 13, 260; 39781, fol. 36 | BL, letters to William Windham, Add. MSS 37887, 37914–37916 · Lpool RO, corresp. with William Roscoe · NL Wales, St David's diocesan papers
Likenesses R. Graves, line engraving, BM, NPG

Symmons, Edward (*c*.1607–1649), Church of England clergyman and author, was born at Cottered in Hertfordshire. The names of his parents are not known, but he belonged to the junior branch of a family that owned land at Great Yeldham in Essex and was a distant cousin of the diarist Richard Symonds, a trooper in the Royal Life Guard. He matriculated as a sizar at Peterhouse, Cambridge, at Easter 1621, and graduated BA in 1624–5 and MA in 1628.

Ordained deacon on 4 June and priest on 24 September 1626, Symmons was appointed in 1630 as rector of Rayne in Essex, where he was 'very conscientious in discharging his calling' and 'profitable in his preaching, wherein he had a plain and piercing faculty' (Fuller, *Worthies*, 2.56). Four of his sermons were published in 1642, but thereafter his writing took a more polemical turn. Having fallen foul of the committee for scandalous ministers in 1642, he was voted a delinquent for speaking out in support of the royal prerogative and the common prayer book; and as a result of a sequestration order dated 3 March 1643 his wife, three children, and 'aged Father' were forcibly cast 'out of doores' by a troop of parliamentarian horse (*Mercurius Rusticus*, 27 May 1643, 16).

Symmons himself gives a vivid account of his sufferings and his principles in the introduction to *A Loyall Subjects Beliefe* (1643), an open letter to Stephen Marshall, minister of the neighbouring parish of Finchingfield, who was prominent in the movement for root-and-branch reform of the national church. Symmons's portrait of an ideal cavalier in *A Military Sermon* (1644), delivered in his capacity as chaplain to the Prince of Wales's life guards, has been said to epitomize 'grass-roots Anglican-Cavalierism' (G. E. Aylmer, *Transactions of the Royal Historical Society*, 5th ser., 37, 1987, 23). An encounter with some fanatical parliamentarian soldiers in the prison at Shrewsbury led him once again into dispute with Marshall in *Scripture Vindicated* (1645), this time over the wilful misinterpretation of God's word for political ends.

Symmons later played a major role in establishing the image of the royal martyr. *A Vindication of King Charles*—largely composed in Cornwall in the wake of the battle of Naseby, completed in France during 1646, and printed towards the end of 1647 after his return to England—contains a parallel between 'the sufferings of our Saviour and our Sovereign' (title-page); and it was Symmons who handed the manuscript of *Eikon basilike* to the printer in December 1648 and corrected the proofs, having earlier been instrumental in recruiting John Gauden to prepare a book from the king's own writings (Hollingworth, 9–11). According to his widow, he 'never joyed himself' after the execution of Charles I and died on 29 March 1649 at Gravesend, maintaining throughout his final illness that 'the Book was the Kings Book' (Hollingworth, 11; Madan, 133). He was buried in St Peter Paul's Wharf, London.

ROBERT WILCHER

Sources Fuller, *Worthies* (1840), 2.56 · Venn, *Alum. Cant.*, 1/4.76 · F. F. Madan, *A new bibliography of the Eikon basilike of King Charles the First* (1950) · E. Symmons, *A loyall subjects beliefe* (1643) · E. Symmons, *A vindication of King Charles, or, A loyal subjects duty* (1648) · R. Hollingworth, *Dr. Hollingworth's defence of King Charles the first's holy and divine book, called Eikon basilike* (1692), 9–16 · *Mercurius Rusticus* (27 May 1643), 12–16 · I. Roy, introduction, in *Richard Symonds' diary of the marches of the royal army*, ed. C. E. Long (1997), i–xi · *Diary of the marches of the royal army during the great civil war, kept by Richard Symonds*, ed. C. E. Long, CS, old ser., 74 (1859)
Wealth at death appears to have lost everything when sequestered

Symmons, John (1780/81–1842). *See under* Symmons, Charles (1749–1826).

Symon Simeonis [Symon Semeonis] (*fl.* **1322–1324**), Franciscan friar, traveller, and author, was from Ireland, probably of Anglo-Irish origin. In 1323–4 he undertook a journey from Ireland to the Holy Land which he describes in his *Itinerarium Symon Semeonis ab Hybernia ad Terram Sanctam*. The work survives in a firsthand copy written between 1335 and 1352, in which his second name, perhaps a patronym, is spelt Semeonis. This manuscript (now MS 407 in the library of Corpus Christi College, Cambridge) very soon came into the possession of, if it was not written for, Simon Bozoun, prior of Norwich from 1344 to 1352. Symon's work is an important source for European contacts with the Near East at the time, giving information on distances, prices, religion, the value of money, and the customs of the people through whose lands Symon's party passed. Throughout his journey Symon's greatest interest was aroused by the holy sites, especially shrines of saints, that he visited.

The *Itinerarium* tells how, having attended the Franciscan provincial chapter held at Clonmel on 4 October 1322,

Symon left Ireland in the company of Hugh Illuminator (le Luminour) on 16 March 1323, and landed in Anglesey. They journeyed through England to Dover, on to Paris and down the Rhône to Nice, by sea to Genoa, and thence to Venice, where they stayed for seven weeks. Sailing then through the Adriatic they arrived in Candia (Crete), where Symon encountered Gypsies—the earliest datable record of the people in Europe. With the arrival of the party in Egypt, at Alexandria, on 10 October 1323, Symon's field of observation widens as he describes the economic and social conditions of the mameluke sultanate. Having gained permission from the authorities, the party travelled to Cairo. Here Symon's companion Hugh contracted dysentery and died, much to Symon's distress. He was buried in the church of St Martin in Old Cairo. Despite his relatively close contact with Muslims during this period, Symon's account of their beliefs is often mistaken, and includes inaccurate citations from the Koran, probably drawn from one of the unreliable Latin translations then in circulation.

Symon obtained a passport from the sultan's officials, which authorized him to travel freely throughout Egypt and Palestine, and to visit the holy places without the payment of the ordinary dues. Symon and his party set out from Cairo across the desert to Gaza, and thence to Jerusalem, which they probably reached on 9 or 10 December 1323. They seem to have remained there for about seven weeks. The *Itinerarium* gives a detailed description of the church of the Holy Sepulchre, which closely resembles that in other pilgrim narratives, and of other landmarks in the city, before breaking off. From references in the text, it can be surmised that Symon was back in Cairo by 2 February 1324, had reached Alexandria by 4 March, and visited Rome on his way home. Any account of the homeward journey was, however, lost before the scribe of the surviving copy set to work. Of Symon, nothing more is known. His *Itinerarium* was first published by James Nasmith in 1778; a critical edition appeared in 1960.

MARIOS COSTAMBEYS

Sources *Itinerarium Symon Semeonis ab Hybernia ad Terram Sanctam*, ed. M. Esposito, Scriptores Latini Hiberniae, 4 (1960)
Archives CCC Cam., MS 407

Symon the Anker of London Wall. *See* Appulby, Simon (*d.* 1537).

Symon, Mary (1863–1938), poet, was born on 25 September 1863 in Dufftown, Banffshire, the elder of the two daughters of John Symon (1836–1908) and Isabella Duncan (1837–1924). Educated first at Mortlach public school, Mary Symon then attended the Edinburgh Institute for Young Ladies (later Edinburgh Ladies' College) where she came under the influence of the first English master, James Logie Robertson. As Hugh Haliburton, Robertson contributed to the revival of vernacular poetry, and also encouraged the 'renationalization' of Scottish life through his editorial work, journalism, and teaching. One of Mary Symon's near contemporaries said of him: 'We felt, young as we were, that his literature was life and our daily contact with the pioneer of the Scottish renaissance was an influence that struck deep root in our minds' (Skinner, 42). Mary Symon added to her knowledge of Scottish literature by attending David Masson's lectures at Edinburgh University. However, her knowledge of vernacular traditions did not come primarily from her formal education—her roots were in the class of energetic rural and small-town craftsmen and traders in which Scots was still spoken and Scots tradition maintained, even while a modern education and a command of standard English were encouraged. Her father, provost of Dufftown in the 1880s, continued the family saddlery business, diversified into farming, and helped to establish Pittyvaich Distillery.

Symon's first verses date from 1876, and as her range and skill developed, her work began to appear in the *Scots Magazine* and other periodicals under various pseudonyms—Mary Duff, Malcolm Forbes, and others. Like her contemporaries Violet Jacob and Marion Angus, Mary Symon is at her best in Scots, where she is more vigorous and original—even if she employs it mainly in conventional ways for lyric and comic verse. However, like many poets, she found that the First World War demanded a new kind of response. Symon's 'After Neuve Chapelle' (1915) is a call to arms, but it also depicts conditions at the front honestly, opening with a description of the terrible losses suffered by the Gordon Highlanders. 'The Glen's Muster-Roll', published in February 1916 before the Somme offensive, is a superbly idiomatic Scots monologue. An elegy for the war dead of a small community spoken by the dominie, the vernacular anchors it in the particular, while the schoolmaster's concern for the potential of the young underlines the waste of lives. In the ghostly 'class' which ends the poem, all justifications for the war are rejected, along with 'adult' political language, and the dominie's right to demand answers is turned on him:

Not mine but yours to question now! You lift unhappy eyes—
'Ah maister, tell's fat a' this means.' And I, ye thocht sae wise,
Maun answer wi' the bairn words ye said tae le langsyne:
'I dinna ken, I dinna ken. Fa does, oh Loons o'Mine?'

One of the finest Scots poems to come out of the war, 'The Glen's Muster-Roll' demonstrates that civilians were capable of understanding the suffering and loss it entailed.

Mary Symon's achievement is striking in that she spent much of her adult life at home in Dufftown in the caring role of the unmarried daughter. The regional basis of her work went against the direction taken by C. M. Grieve (Hugh MacDiarmid) and his allies in the post-war years, but her wartime reputation was significant enough for him to include six of her poems in *Northern Numbers* for 1921 and 1922. Her work was collected only towards the end of her life in *Deveron Days* (1933), which sold out immediately upon publication. She worked devotedly for Scots, but was also 'a woman of extraordinarily wide culture, familiar with several languages, and a keen and discerning student of literature, philosophy, and life' (*Dufftown*

News and Speyside Advertiser, 4 June 1938). Mary Symon died at her home, Pittyvaich House, Dufftown, Banffshire, on 27 May 1938, and was buried on 30 May alongside her parents in the cemetery at Mortlach Old Kirk, Dufftown.

COLIN MILTON

Sources *Dufftown News and Speyside Advertiser* (29 May 1938) • *Dufftown News and Speyside Advertiser* (4 June 1938) • M. Symon, *Deveron days* (1933) • L. W. Wheeler, ed., *Ten northeast poets* (1985) • C. Milton, 'A sough o'war: the Great War and the poetry of north-east Scotland', *Northern visions*, ed. D. Hewitt (1995), 1–38 • L. Skinner, *A family unbroken, 1694–1994: the Mary Erskine School tercentenary history* (1994) • private information (2004) [Banff RO]
Archives NL Scot., letters, poems, and lecture
Wealth at death £338 16s. 1d.: confirmation, 2 Sept 1938, *CCI*

Symonds, Sir Charles Putnam (1890–1978), neurologist, was born in London on 11 April 1890, the elder son (there were no daughters) of Sir Charters James *Symonds (1852–1932), surgeon to Guy's Hospital, and his wife, Fanny Marie (d. 1930), daughter of David Shaw, lieutenant-general in the Madras army. He was educated at Rugby School and won a classics scholarship to New College, Oxford. At Oxford he changed to medicine and in 1912 obtained a second-class degree in physiology and entered Guy's Hospital with a scholarship.

At the outbreak of the First World War, Symonds enlisted as a dispatch rider, served with the 1st division through the retreat from Mons and the battles of the Marne and Aisne, and was awarded the *médaille militaire*. He was wounded in September 1914 and returned to Guy's Hospital to complete his clinical studies, qualifying MRCS, LRCP, early the following year. He was then commissioned in the Royal Army Medical Corps and posted as medical officer to the Royal Flying Corps squadron at Farnborough. The post included duties at the Connaught Hospital, Aldershot, where the physiologist and neurologist E. D. Adrian was among his colleagues. It was at this point that Symonds decided to make his career in clinical neurology. In 1915 he married Janet Palmer (d. 1919), daughter of Sir Edward Bagnall *Poulton, Hope professor of zoology at Oxford. They had two sons. In 1920, in Baltimore, Maryland, USA, he married Edythe Eva, daughter of Frank Dorton, a tea planter, of Simla; they also had two sons.

Symonds took his MRCP in 1916 and returned to France to serve with 101 field ambulance and as medical officer of the 1st Middlesex regiment. After demobilization he qualified BM, BCh. in 1919 and proceeded to the MA and DM (Oxon.) in the same year. In 1919 he was resident medical officer at the National Hospital, Queen Square, London, and in 1920 was appointed assistant physician for nervous diseases at Guy's Hospital. He was awarded a Radcliffe travelling fellowship at Oxford in 1920 and at the insistence of Arthur Hurst, spent his time in the United States learning psychiatry and neurosurgery, under Adolf Meyer at the Johns Hopkins Hospital, Baltimore, and Harvey Cushing at Boston. At Boston he made his first important contribution to neurology when he diagnosed a cerebral aneurysm in a patient. When Symonds returned to London he joined the staff of the National Hospital, Queen

Square, in 1926, and was also appointed consultant in neurology to the Royal National Throat, Nose and Ear Hospital in Gray's Inn Road. He had been elected FRCP in 1924.

From his experience at these hospitals Symonds came to recognize a group of patients he described as suffering from otitic hydrocephalus. This proved to be a misnomer, but his clinical observations were accurate and his work resulted in an increased interest in cerebral venous thrombosis.

In 1934 Symonds became civilian consultant in neurology to the RAF and at the outbreak of the Second World War he was commissioned with the rank of group captain as a consultant in neurology and posted to the Central Medical Establishment at Halton to serve on medical boards. At first he spent much of his time in Oxford, organizing the Military Hospital for Head Injuries at St Hugh's College, with Hugh Cairns. As part of his duties with the RAF, Symonds had to deal with the condition known as 'flying stress'. With Denis Williams he analysed nearly 3000 cases of psychological disorder for a report entitled *Clinical and Statistical Study of Neurosis Precipitated by Flying Duties*, for which he received in 1949 the Raymond Longacre award for scientific contribution to aviation medicine. In 1944 Symonds was appointed CB. Early in 1945 he was promoted from air commodore to air vice-marshal, and retired later the same year. In 1946 he was appointed KBE.

Symonds returned to his hospital and private practice and continued to publish important papers and to teach. He was a fine teacher and was able to impart information clearly and concisely. By the time he retired from hospital practice in 1955 he was regarded as the greatest clinical neurologist of his time.

In 1953 Symonds visited Canada, Australia, and New Zealand as Sims travelling professor. Later he was visiting professor at San Francisco and at the Montreal Neurological Institute. He was visiting neurologist at the Johns Hopkins Hospital, an honorary member of the American Neurological Association and of the New York Neurological Association, and a corresponding member of the Société de Neurologie de Paris. He was also an honorary FRCP of Edinburgh. Symonds delivered many named lectures, including the Harveian oration in 1954. In 1956 he became president of the Association of British Neurologists. He had earlier been president of both the section of neurology and the section of psychiatry of the Royal Society of Medicine, and in 1964 he was elected an honorary fellow.

In 1963 Symonds retired from practice to a house he had built in Ham, Wiltshire, where he enjoyed bird-watching and fly-fishing. He had contributed the neurological section in Sir Frederick Taylor's *Practice of Medicine* (12th edn, 1922), and in 1970 he published a selection of his own papers as *Studies in Neurology*. Symonds died in the Ellern Mede Nursing Home, Totteridge, London, on 7 December 1978.   IAN MACKENZIE, rev.

Sources personal knowledge (1986) · private information (1986)
Archives Wellcome L., papers

Likenesses A. Freeth, drawings, 1963, priv. coll. · A. Freeth, drawings, 1963, Guy's Hospital, London · A. Freeth, drawings, 1963, National Hospital, Queen Square, London
Wealth at death £135,216: probate, 11 June 1979, *CGPLA Eng. & Wales*

Symonds, Sir Charters James (1852–1932), surgeon, was born in Dalhousie, New Brunswick, Canada, on 24 July 1852, the second son of Charles Symonds (*d.* 1860), barrister, and his wife, Margaret, eldest daughter of John Maltby of New Brunswick. Of pioneer stock established in Massachusetts in 1635, Symonds's great-grandfather settled at Saint John, New Brunswick, in 1764, and founded the school where Charters was educated. His father, tempted to the goldfields of California, died there in 1860; after further family tragedies his mother took Charters to London in 1869 where, with limited means, he studied at University College and at Guy's Hospital. At the London MB, BS examination in 1877 he gained first-class honours and gold medals in surgery, obstetrics, and forensic medicine. He graduated MD (1878) and MS (1880), and was elected FRCS (1881). At Guy's Hospital he held appointments as obstetric resident, house surgeon, house physician, senior anatomy demonstrator, and surgical registrar (1879). Always a keen microscopist, he acquired a profound knowledge of surgical pathology, which allied to excellence as a diagnostician contributed to his surgical success.

Assistant surgeon to Guy's Hospital in 1882 and surgeon in 1902, Symonds gained a reputation for inspired bedside teaching and also for courtesy and kindliness towards patients and students alike. It was said he had a natural love of teaching and delighted in watching the mind of a pupil develop under his influence. He had charge of the throat department at Guy's Hospital (from 1886 to 1902) and was also surgeon to the Evelina Hospital for Sick Children (from 1882 to 1888). On 10 July 1889 he married Fanny Marie (1869/70–1930), daughter of David Shaw, lieutenant-general in the Madras army. They had two sons, of whom Sir Charles *Symonds became physician for nervous diseases at Guy's Hospital.

Unlike certain contemporaries, Symonds accepted both Lister's antiseptic system and the additional benefits of aseptic surgery established between 1883 and 1893; to this revolution in operative techniques and instrumentation he made many contributions. After retiring in 1912, apart from during the war he taught clinical students fortnightly at Lambeth Hospital until shortly before his death twenty years later.

In 1915 Symonds joined the Mediterranean expeditionary force as consulting surgeon, and worked in Malta with the wounded from Gallipoli; invalided home with dysentery he continued to serve the southern army command until the end of the First World War.

From 1913 Symonds joined other enthusiasts in a crusade against venereal disease, as a result of which a royal commission was established; Symonds became a member of the National Council for Combating Venereal Disease.

In later years he was adviser to the home secretary on vivisection and chairman of the Invalid Children's Aid Association and the Children's Hospital, Hampstead; he proved a very dedicated treasurer of the Royal Medical Benevolent Fund.

Symonds is remembered for pioneering, in 1883, the extraperitoneal removal of a concretion from an appendix, after the subsidence of inflammation; soon this procedure was superseded by total appendectomy. Contemporaries remarked on Symonds's amazing manipulative skill in removing nasal polyps and laryngeal tumours, and in the passing of tubes and bougies through strictures. He introduced a classification of oesophageal neoplasms and initiated treatment for malignant obstruction by intubation with short gum-elastic catheters; Symonds's tubes continued to be employed for more than fifty years. Among the first to extirpate the larynx completely, he devised apparatus to help such patients speak. In medical literature 110 contributions stand to his credit.

At the Royal College of Surgeons, Symonds was vice-president (1916–18), Bradshaw lecturer (1916), and Hunterian orator (1921). He served as president of the Medical Society of London, the Hunterian Society, the Laryngological Society and the clinical section of the Royal Society of Medicine. His collection of pathological specimens and part of his library were donated to New Brunswick University, which in 1929 conferred on him an honorary LLD. For war services Symonds was mentioned in dispatches and made CB, and in 1919 was appointed KBE.

Symonds retired to Rowney, Mount Park, Harrow, Middlesex, where he died from a gastric carcinoma on 14 September 1932; he was buried three days later at Roxeth parish church, Harrow.   JOHN KIRKUP

Sources G. F. Stebbing, 'Sir Charters Symonds, KBE, MS, FRCS', *Guy's Hospital Reports*, 4th ser., 13 (1933), 258–72 · *BMJ* (24 Sept 1932), 611–2 · D'A. Power and W. R. Le Fanu, *Lives of the fellows of the Royal College of Surgeons of England, 1930–1951* (1953), 751–3 · *The Lancet* (24 Sept 1932), 709 · *DNB* · m. cert.
Archives University of New Brunswick, pathological specimens and other works
Likenesses photograph, 1896, RCS Eng., Council Club Album · W. Stoneman, photograph, 1918, NPG · Elliott & Fry, photograph, repro. in *BMJ*, 611
Wealth at death £88,341 0s. 4d.: resworn probate, 13 April 1933, *CGPLA Eng. & Wales*

Symonds, Emily Morse [pseud. George Paston] (1860–1936), novelist and playwright, was born on 4 September 1860 at St Mary in the Marsh, Norwich, Norfolk, the daughter of the Revd Henry Symonds, minor canon and precentor of Norwich Cathedral, and his wife, Emily Hannah Evans. Her first cousin was John Addington *Symonds; she did not admire his work. After her father's death she and her mother moved to London, where they lived at 7 Thurloe Square, Kensington, and travelled for several months each year.

Symonds's first published work—under the pseudonym of George Paston, which she used all her life—was a study of the Murray publishing house: *At John Murray's: Records of*

a Literary Circle (1892). She then turned to fiction, producing a number of novels with feminist themes. *A Modern Amazon* (1894) examines marriage, but it also looks at the position of working women:

> Of late years employers have made the startling discovery that women of birth and education may be adapted for other uses than those of household ornament and domestic pet; that they may be converted, in fact, into sober, industrious, and very useful drudges.   (p. 3)

A Study in Prejudices (1895) is a pointed examination of double sexual standards. The heroine of *The Career of Candida* (1896) is brought up as a boy and moves to London to teach gymnastics and fencing, the more interesting aspect of a novel which also shows her dutifully returning to her weak husband after he is disabled. *A Writer of Books* (1898), strong on women writers in Grub Street, firmly makes the point, in the final chapter, that 'In the life of the modern woman, blessed with an almost inexhaustible supply of strings, love is no less episodical than in the life of a man' (p. 341). *A Bread and Butter Miss* (1895) and *A Fair Deceiver* (1898) have more conventional romantic plots, though they still feature spirited women.

Arnold Bennett, who knew Symonds in the 1890s, claimed that she was 'on the whole the most advanced and intellectually-fearless woman I have met' (*Journals*, 17). But she thought little of most modern fiction and maintained a strong interest in previous centuries, turning to biography and writing lives of George Romney (1903), Benjamin Haydon (1905), Lady Mary Wortley Montagu (1907), and Pope (1909), in addition to other studies of the Georgian period. Her dramas, beginning with *The Pharisee's Wife* (Duke of York's Theatre, 1904), privileged women's roles above men's parts. In the subsequent decade some of her plays dealt with suffrage and feminist issues, including *Feed the Brute* (1909) and *Nobody's Daughter* (1910), which ran to 185 performances. Later dramatic works, such as *Double or Quits* (1919) and *Clothes and the Woman* (1922), were much more light-hearted, owing a good deal to the French comedies which she also translated.

In addition to book-length publications and plays, Symonds produced a good deal of literary journalism. She was extremely reticent about her own work: despite her productivity, she had what her *Times* obituarist termed 'an almost fanatical dislike of self-advertisement' (12 Sept 1936, 14). This obituary, a remarkably strong anti-feminist polemic, claims that her outmoded stress on women's issues was responsible for her rapid decline in popularity. Symonds died, unmarried, of heart failure at 7 Pelham Place, Kensington, London, on 11 September 1936.

KATE FLINT

Sources *The Times* (12 Sept 1936), 14 · *The journals of Arnold Bennett: 1896–1910*, ed. N. Flower (1932) · [A. Bennett], 'Some younger reputations: "George Paston"', *The Academy* (24 Dec 1898), 520 · Blain, Clements & Grundy, *Feminist comp.* · J. Sutherland, *The Longman companion to Victorian fiction* (1988) · *Who was who in the theatre, 1912–1976*, 4 vols. (1978) · D. Daims and J. Grimes, *Towards a feminist tradition* (1981) · D. Robinson, *Women novelists, 1891–1920* (1984) · b. cert. · d. cert.
Archives BL, Add MS 46655 fol. 249

Wealth at death £27,474 6s. 4d.: probate, 26 Oct 1936, *CGPLA Eng. & Wales*

Symonds, John (*bap.* 1728, *d.* 1807), historian, was baptized on 10 February 1728 at Horningsheath, Suffolk, the eldest son of John Symonds (1695/6–1757), rector of Horningsheath, and Mary (*d.* 1774), daughter of Sir Thomas Spring, bt, of Pakenham. Symonds was admitted to St John's College, Cambridge, on 11 July 1747 and graduated BA in 1752. In the following year he was elected a fellow of Peterhouse, and he proceeded MA in 1754. Between 1765 and 1769 he travelled in Italy. His nine-volume manuscript journal contains descriptions and watercolour illustrations of agricultural practices, a subject in which he maintained a lifelong interest.

In 1771 on the death of the poet Thomas Gray, Symonds was appointed regius professor of modern history at Cambridge University. In the following year he was created LLD by royal mandate and he moved to Trinity College. In 1778 Symonds published *Remarks on William Barron's Essay on the History of Colonisation*. His studies *The Expediency of Revising the Present Edition of the Gospels and Acts of the Apostles* and *The Expediency of Revising the Epistles* appeared in 1789 and 1794 respectively. He also contributed numerous articles to Arthur Young's periodical *Annals of Agriculture*. Symond's was later employed as the recorder for Bury St Edmunds where he died, unmarried, on 18 February 1807. He was buried at Pakenham, Suffolk.

E. I. CARLYLE, *rev.* PHILIP CARTER

Sources *GM*, 1st ser., 48 (1778), 421 · *GM*, 1st ser., 77 (1807), 281 · Nichols, *Lit. anecdotes* · Venn, *Alum. Cant.* · *IGI*
Archives Salisbury Cathedral, travel journals | BL, journals and letters to Arthur Young, Add. MSS 35126–35129 · CUL, letters on modern history (notes taken by James Plumptre)
Likenesses J. Singleton, stipple, pubd 1788 (after G. K. Ralph), BM, NPG

Symonds, John Addington (1807–1871), physician, was born on 10 April 1807 at Oxford, one of five sons and three daughters of John Symonds, a surgeon–apothecary proud of being the fifth generation of medical practitioners in Oxford and the sixth of Plymouth Brethren. Perhaps marriage to Mary Williams of an old Aston, Oxfordshire, family stimulated reaction against that narrow creed; John Symonds became a Latin scholar, studied philosophy, and held to less gloomy Calvinism. He never allowed the children to dance or enter a theatre; three sons became Anglican clergymen, and the daughters married clergymen.

His son, John Addington Symonds primus (as differentiated by contemporaries first from his brother, later from his son), like his ancestors, was debarred from Oxford by the Test Acts. Leaving Magdalen College School at sixteen in 1823 he worked as dresser in the Radcliffe Infirmary and attended the courses on anatomy given by Dr Kidd and on chemistry by Dr Daubeney. After three years in Edinburgh he graduated MD in 1828. Symonds then broke free of the family tradition of ancient, educated gentility willingly sacrificed to the suffocating preoccupation with spiritual interests. Although 'morally he held with them', he pursued remarkably diverse interests (Brown, 14). Indulging a lifelong passion for literature he invariably rose at six in order to study the arts for two hours.

From Edinburgh Symonds returned to Oxford, and for three years practised as assistant to his father. In 1831, on advice from his great-uncle Dr Addington of Bristol, Symonds primus removed there, leaving the practice to his brother Frederick Symonds (1813–1881) who, from 1853 to 1878, was surgeon to the Radcliffe Infirmary. Symonds primus was swiftly involved in the cholera epidemic of 1832. He served as secretary of the cholera committee, and was instrumental in founding the general hospital to meet the crisis. A pioneer of work in community medicine, until 1845 he lectured at the medical school. Meanwhile 'cautious in diagnosis, vigorous in treatment' (*BMJ*, 268), by skill, 'forceful personality and impressive intellectual gifts' he built up an enormous practice and became the mainstay of his numerous family (Grosskurth, 5).

In 1834 Symonds married Harriet (1808/9–1844), beautiful but delicate eldest daughter of James Sykes of Leatherhead and his wife, Henrietta, *née* Abdy, of Albyns, Essex. The loss of three infant sons, and the birth of three daughters and John Addington *Symonds secundus (1840–1893), weakened Harriet's constitution. She died of scarlet fever in 1844. Her formidable sister Mary Anne came to raise the four children. Symonds rarely spoke of his wife to the children, but regularly visited the tomb and 'took jealous care' that the railings were overgrown with ivy and flowers 'to withdraw the sacred spot from vulgar eyes' (Brown, 2).

Averse to hobbies or non-academic diversions to the extent of denying his son music lessons, Symonds was a leader of the Literary and Philosophical Society of Bristol. He bought the elegant Clifton Hill House in 1851. His reputation attracted prominent people to Bristol and Clifton. A man able to discuss Greek prosody with Gladstone and Tennyson, he frequently entertained Benjamin Jowett, Robert Louis Stevenson, Leslie Stephen, Holman Hunt, Professor James Forbes, Edmund Gosse, and Edward Lear among many friends.

Symonds served the hospital until 1848, and for many years was a council member of the Bristol branch of the British Medical Association. In 1853 elected an associate, and in 1857 the youngest fellow of the Royal College of Physicians, his dissertation, 'The headache', for the Goulstonian lectureship in 1858 was so detailed that it occupied six consecutive issues of *The Lancet*. In 1863 he was president of the British Medical Association. His numerous professional papers are noted in obituaries. His friendship with Dr James Cowles Prichard stimulated his own study of insanity, and an 1869 essay 'Criminal responsibility' supported Prichard's opinions as to the existence of 'moral insanity' as a disease. He studied all aspects of sleep and dreams, and analysed the interaction of memory, association, and imagination as their origin.

Kindly to the sick, affectionate to and loved by his family, Symonds was otherwise reserved, even humourless. Overworked, his health began to fail in 1868. Compelled to resign his practice early in 1870 he died at his home at Clifton on 25 February 1871, and was buried beside his wife in Clifton churchyard. His son felt the loss crushing. 'I have not only lost a father, but a best friend' (Brown, 280); he edited and published his father's literary remains. Revered by contemporaries as the most sympathetic and eminent physician in the west country, Symonds primus remains notable only as the parent and formative influence upon Symonds secundus, a man vastly dissimilar in physical and psychological constitution, who achieved wide reputation as a sparkling companion and major man of letters (Critchley, 40). Interest in Symonds secundus was revived by publication of his memoirs 'unique in the [autobiographical] genre during the nineteenth century' (Memoirs, 15). Symonds's death in 1871 and Oxford's new statute abolishing the celibacy qualification enabled his daughter Charlotte (1842–1929) [see Green, Charlotte Byron] to marry Thomas Hill Green (1836–1882), her brother's friend and then philosophy tutor at Balliol, who became Whyte professor of moral philosophy at Oxford. Her sister Edith married Sir Charles Cave of Bristol, and Mary Isabella had in 1857 become the second wife of Sir Edward Strachey, bt (1812–1901), of Somerset; she died in 1883 leaving three sons.　　　　ROGER HUTCHINS

Sources P. Grosskurth, John Addington Symonds: a biography (1964) · DNB · H. F. Brown, John Addington Symonds: a biography (1903) · M. Critchley, 'John Addington Symonds, primus and secundus', The citadel of the senses and other essays (1986), 40–50 · Munk, Roll, vol. 4 · BMJ (4 March 1871), 268 · The Lancet (4 March 1871), 324–5 · The memoirs of John Addington Symonds, ed. P. Grosskurth (1984), 15 · M. Symonds, Out of the past (1925), 6–9 · d. cert. [Harriet Symonds] · d. cert.
Archives JRL, letters to J. Kay-Shuttleworth, etc. · U. St Andr. L., corresp. with James David Forbes
Likenesses photograph, NPG
Wealth at death under £60,000: probate, 23 March 1871, CGPLA Eng. & Wales

John Addington Symonds (1840–1893), by Eveleen Myers

Symonds, John Addington

Symonds, John Addington (1840–1893), writer and advocate of sexual reform, was born on 5 October 1840 at 7 Berkeley Square, Bristol, the only surviving son (there were two older sisters and one younger) of Dr John Addington *Symonds (1807–1871), physician, and his wife, Harriet Sykes (1808/9–1844), eldest daughter of James Sykes of Leatherhead, Surrey, and Henrietta Abdy of Albyns, Essex.

Family and education The Symonds family descended from Adam Fitz Simon (d. before 1118), second son of Simon, lord of St Sever in Normandy, with land in Norfolk and Hertfordshire, specifically through the younger branch in Shropshire, eight generations of nonconformists who took up medicine as the main profession open to them. Symonds attributed his sense of duty to his sturdy puritan grandfather. His father was the most eminent physician in the west of England, and his social circle included eminent politicians, authors, scientists, historians, philosophers, and Christian socialists, among whom the young Symonds moved freely. From 1851 the family lived in the 1747 mansion of Clifton Hill House overlooking Bristol and the mouth of the Severn. Symonds's mother died in 1844, and her stern unimaginative sister raised the children. Strong bonds of sympathy developed between Symonds and his younger sister Charlotte, but

his father had a powerful influence on the formation of his character, including his enthusiasm for Greek and Italian art. Symonds acquired culture as diligently as his father, who studied art, literature, and history two hours daily.

After private tutelage at Clifton, Symonds in May 1854 went to Harrow School, remembered for its philistine discomforts; there he was disturbed by the boys' sexual rough-housing. The headmaster Charles Vaughan's affair with one of the boys appalled Symonds because of Vaughan's hypocrisy and because it threatened the idealization of homosexual love that Symonds was formulating with the help of Plato's Symposium and Phaedrus. Symonds dated the birth of his real self from spring 1858, when he fell in love with Willie Dyer, a chorister at Bristol Cathedral. He confessed his romantic affection to his father, who persuaded him gradually to end the affair. In 1859 Symonds revealed the story about Vaughan to a friend during an argument about 'Arcadian love', and was persuaded to tell his father, who forced Vaughan to resign his headmastership and hindered his subsequent career. Symonds was traumatically upset by these events, but concluded that his own role stemmed from carelessness rather than treachery.

Symonds went to Balliol College, Oxford, in autumn 1858, and began a lifelong friendship with its master, Benjamin Jowett; he became distinguished in classics and won the Newdigate prize for his poem 'The Escorial' (1860). He became a fellow at Magdalen College (1862–3), and received the chancellor's prize for his essay 'The

Renaissance'. Unsuccessful attempts to repress his forbidden desire for another cathedral chorister, Alfred Brooke, damaged his nervous constitution, and in 1863 his health collapsed, exacerbated by stress caused by the ensuing gossip. For three years a painful eye inflammation prevented serious work. Dr Spencer Wells, surgeon to the queen's household, diagnosed his disorders as resulting from sexual repression, and Symonds was advised to attempt the 'cure' of marriage. The role played by sexual repression and anxiety in a long series of physical and mental breakdowns should not be exaggerated, however, for nervous irritability and pulmonary disease were frequent on both sides of his mother's family: Symonds was to die of tuberculosis just as did his grandfather James Sykes, his sister Mary Isabella, and his own daughter Janet.

From 1860 to 1863 Symonds travelled in search of health to Belgium, Germany, Austria, France, Italy, and Switzerland, where in 1863 he met (Janet) Catherine North (1837–1913), second daughter of Frederick North, Liberal MP for Hastings, and Janet Marjoribanks of Ladykirk, Scotland. He and Catherine North married in St Clement's Church, Hastings, on 10 November 1864. Symonds could not alter his sexual orientation, and his haggard features in photographs from this period make painfully visible the strain of accommodating himself to conventional life. The couple settled in London, at 7 Half Moon Street in 1864, then at 47 Norfolk Square from January 1865. Symonds attempted to study law, but in 1865 his left lung was diagnosed as tubercular. In 1868, after another physical and nervous breakdown, they moved to 7 Victoria Square, Clifton. There he lectured on Greek art at Clifton College (1869) and at the Society for Higher Education for Women, and pursued a four-year affair with the Clifton schoolboy Norman Moor. Catherine and Symonds had four children, Janet (b. 1865), Charlotte (b. 1867), Margaret (b. 1869), and Katharine [see Furse, Dame Katharine], but in 1869 Catherine and Symonds agreed to a platonic marriage, while he would have male companions. Photographs of Symonds in Venice at this time demonstrate that he grew in health and vigour as he was freed from deceit and repression. Catherine and the children holidayed in Ilfracombe while Norman Moor and her husband spent much of each year together in Italy and Switzerland. Catherine initially expressed resentment, but grew to accept the arrangement; Margaret later said that her mother had possessed 'singular Sibylline fortitude' (M. Symonds, 163). Dr Symonds died in February 1871 and the Symonds family moved into Clifton Hill House in September.

Early writings During the 1860s Symonds contributed to various periodicals; bad health suggested writing as his best hope for a career, which he consolidated during the 1870s. His Clifton lectures produced his first two books, *An Introduction to the Study of Dante* (1872) and *Studies of the Greek Poets* (1873), followed by *Sketches in Italy and Greece* (1874), *Renaissance in Italy: the Age of the Despots* (1875), and *Studies of the Greek Poets, Second Series* (1876). He withdrew his nomination for the professorship of poetry at Oxford in 1876 when he was violently attacked for defending *paiderastia*

in the last chapter of *Studies of the Greek Poets*. The breadth and depth of his scholarship were acknowledged, but he was considered to be too bohemian and unconventional. Andrew Lang said that Symonds 'seems to us to be too fond of alluding to the unmentionable' (*The Examiner*, 23 June 1877). As his Italian studies progressed, critics rebuked him for unearthing 'scandals' and 'filth'; publication of his discovery in the Buonarroti archives that Michelangelo's poems and letters had been deliberately altered so as to obscure masculine love was deemed mischievous.

Symonds wrote popular rather than academic works; their extraordinary vividness sometimes becomes too picturesque. A gift for dramatized sketches enlivens his massive history of the *Renaissance in Italy* (*The Age of the Despots*, 1875; *The Revival of Learning*, 1877; *The Fine Arts*, 1877; *Italian Literature*, 2 vols., 1881; *Catholic Reaction*, 2 vols., 1886). Acknowledging his debt to Jacob Burckhardt, Hegel, and Darwin for 'evolutionary' history, Symonds celebrated paganism over Christian superstition, radically challenging Ruskin's Christian view of historical progress. He found within the Renaissance the roots of the modern perception that sexuality is in harmony with nature. The digressions and unevenness of this first *Kulturgeschichte* in English stem largely from Symonds's pursuit of references to homosexuality; his history of art embodies a theory of sexual liberation. Detection of 'the aura' similarly inspired most of his literary criticism.

In 1877 bronchitis brought on a violent haemorrhage, and Symonds dared not spend another winter in England. A journey aiming for Egypt was broken at Switzerland, at Davos Platz. He revisited Davos in 1878, and in 1880 settled there permanently, living first at Hotel Buol (Christian Buol became a companion). His own house (built in June–September 1881), called Am Hof after its meadow, became his home for the rest of his life. In Davos he helped many young men get a foothold in business, paid for the Davos *Gymnasium*, and took great pleasure in the physical life as president of the Winter Sports Club and Toboggan Club. Davos prospered as a winter resort through his magazine articles. Life at Am Hof was free from taboos, and Katharine knew the nature of her father's studies from the age of six. All topics were fully discussed, be they:

> the English Church, or the poems of Walt Whitman, or homosexuality, or the chimney sweep, or toboggan races … words like 'neurotic', 'neuropathic', and 'psychopathic', were in common parlance at Am Hof before they came into general use outside, even in medical circles. (Furse, 98–9)

Each spring and autumn the Symonds family rented the mezzanine floor of Ca' Torresella, 560 Zattere, overlooking the canal of the Guidecca, Venice, owned by Horatio Forbes Brown (1854–1926), Symonds's closest friend from 1872 (openly homosexual himself, though they were not lovers). Symonds played the *padrone* with scores of stevedores, gondoliers, hotel porters, and peasant mountaineers. In May 1881 he fell in love with Angelo Fusato (1857–1923), a handsome Venetian gondolier. With financial help from Symonds, Angelo was able to marry his mistress who had borne him two sons. Symonds hired Angelo as his gondolier and the two men openly lived and travelled together. Angelo remained Symonds's companion until Symonds's death, and Margaret and Katharine remembered him with affection.

Symonds's inheritance and regular income from investments were comfortable: he had increased his capital estate by £22,000 from 1877 to 1892, and had invested £2200 in 1892; most of his stocks were in land and railways; his earnings from literature that year were only £500, which he used to set up a gondolier in business (*Letters*, 3.762). He earned little from writing until his last few years, and scrupulously spent only his literary earnings on Angelo and other young men. Two Swiss farms provided security for the children.

Writings on homosexuality and literature The years at Am Hof were productive, though marked by Symonds's distress for Janet, who was diagnosed tubercular in 1883 and died in 1887. *A Problem in Greek Ethics* (written 1873, ten copies printed 1883), the first history of homosexuality in English, carefully argues that if homosexual relations were honourable in ancient Greece, they cannot be diagnosed as morbid in modern times. In 1889, inspired by the candour of *The Memoirs of Count Carlo Gozzi* which he translated (2 vols., 1890), Symonds began his own autobiography, not as a memoir of daily events but as a psychological study of 'self-effectuation', unique in its frankness. *A Problem in Modern Ethics* (1891, 50 copies) is the first 'scientific' psychological–sociological analysis of homosexuality in English, exposing vulgar errors by a well-judged mixture of sarcasm, science, and common sense. In June 1892 Symonds proposed that Havelock Ellis, editor of the Contemporary Science Series, publish a book on 'Sexual inversion' by him, because the subject 'is being fearfully mishandled by pathologists and psychiatrical professors, who know nothing whatsoever about its real nature' (*Letters*, 3.691). They decided to collaborate, but Symonds died before the project took final shape.

In addition to works already mentioned, Symonds wrote books on Boccaccio, pre-Shakespearian drama, and Walt Whitman (1893); critical introductions to works by Sir Thomas Browne, Marlowe, Heywood, Webster, and Tourneur, and the 'Uranian' poet Edward Cracroft Lefroy; evocative travel sketches and *Our Life in the Swiss Highlands* (1892, with his daughter Margaret); short biographies of Shelley (1878), Sir Philip Sidney (1886), and Ben Jonson (1886); masterly translations of *The Sonnets of Michael Angelo Buonarroti and Tommaso Campanella* (1878), and *The Life of Benvenuto Cellini* (2 vols., 1888). He also produced articles for the *Encyclopaedia Britannica* on Ficino, Filelfo, Guarini, Guicciardini, Machiavelli, Manutius, Metastasio, Petrarch, Poggio, Politian, Pontanus, the Renaissance, Tasso, and the history of Italy from 476 to 1796.

Writing poetry gave Symonds great joy, but his poetry is not successful. His unpublished and privately printed 'Uranian' verse is derivative of Marlowe's *Hero and Leander* ('Eudiades') and frankly masturbatory ('Phallus impudicus'); friends persuaded him to destroy some of it. He published many tightly knitted intellectual sonnets in the manner of the seventeenth-century metaphysical

poets. Though Symonds had been frankly sceptical of all religions since the mid-1860s—he did not believe in a personal God or in specifically Christian tenets—his Whitmanesque 'Cosmic Enthusiasm' pervades his poetry to an almost mystical degree. He disguised his homosexual sentiments with gnomic abstractions; 'unutterable things', 'valley of vain desire', 'l'amour de l'impossible', 'Chimaera', and 'Maya' are his codes for homosexual desire. Using this key, it can be appreciated how *Many Moods* (1878), *New and Old* (1880), *Animi figura* (1882), *Fragilia labilia* (1884), and *Vagabunduli libellus* (1884) trace Symonds's evolution from repression and self-loathing to self-realization and celebration. He felt 'very bitter' that homosexual poets had 'to eviscerate their offspring, for the sake of … an unnatural disnaturing respect for middleclass propriety' (*Letters*, 3.450–51). The sonnet sequence 'Stella Maris' (in *Vagabunduli libellus*), charts the progress of his affair with Angelo Fusato in 1881, though 'Many of these sonnets were mutilated in order to adapt them to the female sex' (*Memoirs*, 272).

Character and achievement Despite a naturally introspective temperament, Symonds was full of *joie de vivre*. Jowett declared that no one cherished friends more than he, and Robert Louis Stevenson (a fellow invalid at Davos) found him a delightful conversationalist. Affectionate and long-lasting friendships were established with women as well as men, such as Margot Tennant and Janet Ross, the latter of whom said that 'his talk was like fireworks, swift and dazzling, and he had a wonderful gift of sympathy' (Grosskurth, 304). Many photographs capture his slight build, frail but indomitable features, and apprehensive expression.

Symonds's lungs grew steadily weaker, while he worked at a killing pace in December 1892 on his monumental biography of Michelangelo (2 vols., 1893). During a lecture tour in April 1893 he caught influenza in Rome, and pneumonia engulfed both lungs; he died in his room at the Albergo d'Italia, via Quattro Fontane 12, Rome, on 19 April 1893, with Angelo at his side. The funeral was delayed until Catherine (who had fallen ill in Venice) and Charlotte arrived, and he was buried in the protestant cemetery on 22 April, a few steps below Shelley's grave; Jowett provided the epitaph.

Though a third of Symonds's waking life was spent recuperating from illness, his output was prodigious. In twenty years he wrote nearly forty books, plus uncollected reviews and unpublished poems, and more than 4000 letters, of which half survive especially to his friends Henry Graham Dakyns, Henry Sidgwick, Walt Whitman (whose work he popularized), Edmund Gosse, Robert Louis Stevenson and his wife, Samuel Richards, Vernon Lee (Violet Paget), Mary Robinson, and Arthur Symons. He told his sister Charlotte, 'I had hoped to make my work the means of saving my soul' (*Letters*, 2.310).

Symonds wrote to Catherine on the day he died, stressing that Brown, his literary executor, was to receive:

all Mss Diaries Letters & other matters found in my books cupboard … I do this because I have written things you could not like to read, but which I have always felt justified and useful for society. Brown will consult & publish nothing without your consent. (*Letters*, 3.839)

Catherine required that the autobiography be suppressed. Brown wrote his biography of Symonds, as Sir Charles Holmes recorded, 'exercis[ing] little more than ordinary discretion in cutting out the most intimate self-revelations. But a straiter critic had then to take a hand. The proofs, already bowdlerized, were completely emasculated' (Furse, 98)—probably by Edmund Gosse. With the homosexual backbone missing from Brown's biography (2 vols., 1895), readers were puzzled by the intensity of Symonds's quest for 'the Whole'.

The Ellis/Symonds material was published under both names first in Germany as *Das konträre Geschlechtsgefühl* (1896), then in London as *Sexual Inversion* (1897), with 'A problem in Greek ethics' as an appendix, and case histories collected by Symonds (Case XVIII, pp. 58–63, is his own). The English edition was bought up by Brown on the eve of publication to avoid scandal. Later in 1897 it was published as *Studies in the Psychology of Sex. Vol. I. Sexual Inversion. By Havelock Ellis*, with Symonds's name wholly expunged at Brown's insistence. Symonds's historical, cultural, and social material was omitted, and Ellis's medical model of homosexuality as a congenital neurosis prevailed. A bookseller was successfully prosecuted for selling this edition, which was suppressed as an 'obscene' work. The two revised *Problem* essays were surreptitiously printed by Leonard Smithers in 1896 and again in 1901 and Ellis's *Sexual Inversion* was published in Philadelphia (1901).

Brown died in 1926, bequeathing the autobiography and other Symonds papers to London Library, with instructions that nothing be published for fifty years. Charles Hagberg Wright, the librarian, and Edmund Gosse, chairman of the committee, burnt all these papers except the autobiography. The embargo expired in 1976, and in 1984 about four-fifths of the autobiography were published, edited by Phyllis Grosskurth, omitting many poems on youths, early descriptive writings, transcripts of letters sent to Symonds, letters sent by him to his wife, testimonials on several of his academic friends, and much material about Christian Buol.

Though Symonds's biography of Michelangelo and his translation of Michelangelo's sonnets and Cellini's autobiography were 'standard classics' for a century, and *The Renaissance* still provokes scholarly discussion, Symonds's studies of homosexuality and his autobiography are his most important contributions to modern ideas. The initial suppression of these writings has obscured his place as a pioneer in the sexual reform movement. Like many Victorian 'bourgeois radicals', Symonds felt a responsibility for reforming public opinion. He discreetly lobbied for the repeal of the laws against homosexuality, and rebuked friends and colleagues when they expressed anti-homosexual prejudice or ignorance. He was one of the first people openly to advocate homosexual emancipation in Britain, insisting that homosexuality was a natural 'minority' rather than an 'abnormality'.

RICTOR NORTON

Sources *The letters of John Addington Symonds*, ed. H. M. Schueller and R. L. Peters, 3 vols. (1967–9) • 'Memoirs of John Addington Symonds', MS, 2 vols., London Library [pt-pubd as *The memoirs of John Addington Symonds*, ed. P. Grosskurth (1984)] • P. Grosskurth, *John Addington Symonds: a biography* (1964) • J. A. Symonds, *On the English family of Symonds* (1894) • *Miscellanies by John Addington Symonds, M.D.* (1871) [with introductory memoir] • M. Symonds, *Out of the past* (1924) • K. Furse, *Hearts and pomegranates* (1940) • H. F. Brown, *John Addington Symonds: a biography*, 2 vols. (1895) • *Letters and papers of John Addington Symonds*, ed. H. F. Brown (1923) • J. G. Younger, 'Ten unpublished letters by John Addington Symonds [to Edmund Gosse] at Duke University', *Victorian Newsletter*, 95 (1999), 1–10 • P. L. Babington, *Bibliography of the writings of John Addington Symonds* (1925) • C. Markgraf, 'John Addington Symonds: an annotated bibliography of writings about him', *English Literature in Transition, 1880–1920*, 18 (1975), 79–138 • C. Markgraf, 'Update', *English Literature in Transition, 1880–1920*, 28 (1985), 59–78

Archives BL, notebook, RP2872 [copies] • BL, translation of life of Benvenuto Cellini, Add. MSS 40649–40652 • Bodl. Oxf., commonplace book • Bodl. Oxf., corresp. and papers • Bodl. Oxf., letters • Harvard U., Houghton L., *Miscellanies*, no. 3 • LUL, memoirs • LUL, memoirs and MS work on philosophy • University of Bristol, corresp., literary MSS, and papers • University of Bristol, family papers | BL, letters to Macmillans, Add. MSS 55253–55255, 55258 • BL, letters to R. L. Stevenson and Fanny Stevenson, Ashley MS 5764 • Bodl. Oxf., letters and typescript copies of letters to Margot Asquith • Bodl. Oxf., letters to Roden Noel • Dartmouth College, Hanover, New Hampshire, letters to Curtis family • JRL, letters to J. L. Warren • King's AC Cam., letters to Oscar Browning • priv. coll., letters to Henry Graham Dakyns and unpublished poetry • U. Birm. L., annotated copy of R. L. Stevenson's *Virginibus puerisque* • U. Leeds, Brotherton L., letters to Edmund Gosse

Likenesses Vigor, oils, 1853, University of Bristol • S. Richards, pen-and-ink drawing, 1890, Herron Museum of Art, Indianapolis; repro. in *Letters*, ed. Schueller and Peters, vol. 2, frontispiece • photograph, 1892, repro. in *Letters and papers*, ed. Brown, frontispiece • J. Brown, stipple (after drawing by E. Clifford), NPG • E. Myers, photograph, NPG [*see illus.*] • C. Orsi, chalk drawing, NPG • photographs, University of Bristol; repro. in Grosskurth, *John Addington Symonds*, facing p. 279

Wealth at death £75,666 2s. 1d.: resworn probate, Nov 1893, CGPLA Eng. & Wales

Symonds, Richard (*b.* 1609, *d.* in or after 1658), Independent minister, was born in Abergavenny, Monmouthshire, the son of Thomas Symonds. Members of his family were traders and burgesses in the town. After attending Exeter College, Oxford, from 1627 Symonds graduated BA on 5 February 1629. It is highly likely that he was ordained as a clergyman, perhaps in the diocese of St Asaph; at any rate it was after leaving a cure in north Wales, 'suspended' (*CSP dom.*, 1637–8, 249) for activities unacceptable to the church authorities, that Symonds removed to Shrewsbury to teach school there. It was during this period that he began an association with Walter Cradock which continued into the 1650s and which was based on a shared theological outlook and a commitment to evangelical preaching. Richard Baxter, a former pupil at Shrewsbury, noted the influence of the pair in the Shrewsbury area about 1635, and attributed not a little of his own spiritual development to their godly example.

By 1638 Symonds had secured an appointment as schoolmaster to the Harley family of Brampton Bryan, Herefordshire. It was while he was at Brampton under the patronage of Sir Robert and Brilliana, Lady Harley, that his separatist views became more pronounced. In February

1638 he, his patron, and the Brampton incumbent, Stanley Gower, were charged with nonconformity. However, Symonds's increasing involvement with Cradock's separatist group at Llanfair Waterdine revealed ecclesiological differences between him and the Harleys, and in November 1639 he moved on from the household, having declined to join with the family in a public fast. Where he settled after this move is unknown, but it was probably in Bristol, where he had preached on occasion during his time at Shrewsbury and Brampton. References in the great audit books of Bristol corporation suggest that he married Bridget, widow of George Hazzard of Bristol.

Before the outbreak of civil war Symonds had joined the general diaspora of puritan ministers from Wales and the marches towards the south-east. On 18 February 1642, at the behest of John Pym, Symonds was confirmed by a Commons order as lecturer at Andover, Hampshire, and he later preached in Sandwich, Kent. Before he left Monmouthshire a certificate from Symonds and other ministers denouncing the threat of popery in their county was presented in the Commons. Symonds's sponsor on this occasion was Oliver Cromwell, suggesting that he was well connected with the radicals in parliament. Thomas Edwards disapprovingly recorded his sermons in various London parishes. In London, Symonds preached liberty of conscience and sympathized with opponents of infant baptism. He celebrated the taking of Sherborne Castle on 17 August 1645 as a victory for the saints, evidence that he was an enthusiast for the alliance of the Independents and the New Model Army, and criticized the moves by the Westminster assembly and groups in parliament to restrict religious freedom.

Two days before Sherborne surrendered to the parliamentarian army Symonds, Walter Cradock, and Henry Walter were appointed by the House of Commons to preach itinerantly in south Wales, and were allocated funds from the sales of Llandaff Cathedral and diocesan lands. This order took the Commons over a year to confirm, and it was not until 13 November 1646 that it passed the Lords. Even then the Welsh preachers departed for Wales without the approval of the Westminster assembly, confirmation that what lay behind the delays was the political struggle between presbyterians and Independents at Westminster. Symonds preached before Lord General Sir Thomas Fairfax at Bath in the summer of 1646, and before the House of Commons on 30 September 1646 and 26 April 1648—periods when the radicals were in the ascendant. Nevertheless, Thomas Edwards's assessment of Symonds as an antinomian was well wide of the mark: he was, and remained, a high Calvinist in doctrine.

Symonds's association with Cradock and Walter as the favoured south Wales preachers of the Independents in the House of Commons was carried over into the rule of the Rump Parliament. In February 1650 the trio headed the list of clerical approvers appointed under the Act for the Propagation of the Gospel in Wales. Symonds seems only to have worked in Glamorgan, having in 1649 acquired for £557 4s. 2d. a fee farm rent of the bishop of Llandaff's estate worth £55 14s. 5d. a year. During this period, until the act lapsed in 1653, Symonds was reputed to have preached at Eglwysilan and Llanfabon, and a little after this, assisted Edmund Ellis, incumbent at St Fagans, in gathering in his tithes. Symonds is reported in the hostile and retrospective account of Francis Davies, a collaborator and informant of John Walker's, to have preached on Malachi 3: 10: 'Bring ye all the tithes into the storehouse'; if true, this is further evidence of his orthodoxy. Davies also attributes to Symonds the nickname the little Briton, presumably a comment on his height. Symonds was in reality a natural enemy of the Quakers; his appointment on 19 March 1657 as lecturer at Llandaff, as well as his episcopal estates and promotion of tithe paying, would doubtless have provided further fuel for conflict with them had he survived, but the silence of the record after 1658 suggests that he did not live to see the restoration of the monarchy.   STEPHEN K. ROBERTS

Sources *Letters of the Lady Brilliana Harley*, ed. T. T. Lewis, CS, 58 (1854) · T. Richards, *A history of the puritan movement in Wales* (1920) · *CSP dom.*, 1637–8; 1657–8 · *JHC*, 2 (1640–42); 4–5 (1644–8) · *JHL*, 7 (1644–5) · Foster, *Alum. Oxon.* · T. Edwards, *Gangraena, or, A catalogue and discovery of many of the errours, heresies, blasphemies and pernicious practices of the sectaries of this time*, 3 (1646) · Bodl. Oxf., MS J. Walker e. 4, c. 13 · J. Eales, *Puritans and roundheads: the Harleys of Brampton Bryan and the outbreak of the English civil war* (1990) · P. Jenkins, '"The sufferings of the clergy": the church in Glamorgan during the interregnum [pt 2]', *Journal of Welsh Ecclesiastical History*, 4 (1987), 9–41 · Bodl. Oxf., MS Rawl. B. 239 · A. F. Mitchell and J. Struthers, eds., *Minutes of the sessions of the Westminster assembly of divines* (1874) · F. Gawler, *A record of some persecutions … in south Wales* (1659) · J. A. Bradney, *A history of Monmouthshire*, 1/2 (1906) · R. Baxter, *Catholick communion defended*, 2 (1684) · W. H. Coates, A. Steele Young, and V. F. Snow, eds., *The private journals of the Long Parliament*, 3 vols. (1982–92), vol. 1, p. 411; vol. 2, p. 104 · great audit book, 1640–44, Bristol RO, 04026/22, pp. 166, 295; great audit book, 1644–9, 04026/23, pp. 90, 94

Symonds, Richard (*bap.* 1617, *d.* 1660), royalist soldier and antiquary, was baptized at Black Notley, near Braintree, Essex, on 12 June 1617, the eldest son of Edward Symonds (*d.* 1636) and his wife, Anne (*d.* 1641), the daughter of Joshua Draper of Braintree. The Symonds family originally came from Shropshire but had moved to Essex with Edward's father, and the senior branch of the family lived at Great Yeldham. Edward, the second son, lived at Black Notley on an estate largely brought into the family by his wife. Both branches produced a high proportion of men who entered the legal profession, including several who became cursitors in chancery. Richard Symonds was admitted a pensioner at Emmanuel College, Cambridge, on 10 October 1632. There is no record of his attendance at an inn of court. Like his father, uncles, and cousins he became a cursitor.

Left as head of the family at the age of about twenty-four upon his mother's death in 1641, Symonds found himself increasingly out of sympathy with political and religious developments in Essex on the eve of the civil war. He was probably a defender and patron of the Laudian rector of Black Notley, and even acted as parish clerk when the rest of the congregation turned against him. He was also the 'worthy good frend' of, and claimed kinship with, another local clergyman in trouble, Edward Symons. Symonds,

Richard Symonds (*bap.* 1617, *d.* 1660), by unknown engraver

who was unmarried, may have been lonely and introverted even before he became politically isolated. His family was divided. A first cousin, of the same name (1616–1645), fought for parliament and was killed at Naseby. By his own account Symonds was imprisoned by Miles Corbett MP, the later regicide, in March 1643, but escaped in October and fled to the king's forces at Oxford.

Symonds joined the mounted lifeguards of the king as an ordinary trooper. It was an élite and aristocratic corps, nicknamed, because of its splendid appearance, the 'Shew Troop', and he must have been among its least wealthy members. He saw action with the royalist forces from the spring of 1644 to the end of hostilities in early 1646. He was present at Cropredy Bridge, at the campaign in Cornwall when Essex's forces surrendered at Lostwithiel, at Newbury (October 1644), and in the following year at the decisive battle of Naseby, on 14 June 1645. He was with the king in his flight through Wales until the defeat at Rowton Heath, near Chester, in September, where the lifeguards were worsted and their colonel, the earl of Lichfield, killed. Disillusioned by these 'long and tedious' marches, Symonds left the troop to join Sir William Vaughan's mobile forces, which had been brought back from Ireland in 1643, and were now terrorizing north Wales and the marches (*Diary of the Marches*, 245). He ended the war in Lord Loughborough's headquarters at Ashby-de-la-Zouch: he was given a pass to return home with two servants by the governor of Leicester on 5 March 1646.

Symonds compounded for his small estate with a fine of one sixth its value, £295, in December 1646 (Green, 3.1610). The triumph of a hostile regime prompted him to go abroad. He settled his revenue on his sister (his next brother, Edward, an officer with the king, had died at Oxford in October 1644), borrowed money from his friend Edward Symons, and set off on the grand tour. His strong antiquarian, historical, and heraldic interests had no doubt been reinforced by his emotional and political ties to the old order in church and state during a destructive and (to his mind) sacrilegious war. He had seized every opportunity while on active service to see and record ancient monuments, stained glass, church furnishings, brasses, and inscriptions, in cathedrals, churches, Oxford colleges, and elsewhere. In early 1649 he went first to France, improved his French in Paris, and visited the sights. He moved on to Rome and stayed for nineteen months, observing and studying the artistic scene and learning the language. He visited Nicolas Poussin in his studio, bought books, prints, and pictures until his money ran out, and made a detailed record, such as on artists' workshop practice, in several small notebooks. Symonds's note, in one of these, written forty years after the painter's death, that Caravaggio's male model was also his lover, has influenced the modern view of the artist.

Symonds returned to London in December 1651, and thereafter lived in England, recording gossip in the capital about contemporary artists and current affairs, such as the dispersal of the Royal Collection of paintings. Many of these stories were reproduced in Horace Walpole's *Anecdotes of Painting*, including the tale of Cromwell's lifting the lid of King Charles's coffin. Symonds met again some of those who had participated in the civil war, and added material to his diary. Contact with old cavaliers may account for the order for his arrest, along with others in East Anglia, on rumours of an insurrection in 1655. He was released later the same year. He died intestate in 1660, perhaps in June, and was probably buried in London.

Symonds is important as a diarist and compiler. He kept, in four small leather-bound notebooks, a consecutive 'diary of the marches of the royal army', beginning on 10 April 1644 and ending in February 1646. Its value has been recognized in the edition of 1859 (ed. C. E. Long, Camden Society, vol. 74) and the new edition (ed. I. Roy, Camden classic reprints, 1997). To this can be added a book of musters, of the militia regiments of London in 1643 and of the royal forces in April 1644 at the rendezvous on Aldbourne Heath, Wiltshire (BL, Harley MS 986). In another volume he noted the contents of churches and colleges in the Oxford area (BL, Harley MS 964, part printed in 'Oxford church notes, 1643–44', *Collectanea*, 4, Oxford Historical Society, 1905, 95–134). The civil war diary is accurate and observant, supplying many details of the campaigns, personnel, and banners of the king's Oxford army not found elsewhere, and listing the garrisons, and their commanders, of the counties he passed through. It is, however, an impersonal, and at times spare and laconic, account of the war, in which his own contribution, and that of his unit, is seldom stated. His description of antiquities, even in the depths of the war, is fuller, and provides a valuable record of monuments, some later defaced or destroyed. Symonds is commemorated for this reason in a modern stained-glass panel in a house in the cathedral close at Exeter. His exact placing of the Eleanor cross outside Stamford was confirmed in the 1990s.

Symonds's books and papers were dispersed on his death. Gregory King obtained three volumes of Essex material, still in the College of Arms, which were used by Morant in his county history. Symonds's civil war diaries are in the British Library (Harley MSS 911, 939, and 944, and Add. MS 17062). His commonplace book, which reveals him as a solitary, taciturn, and sensitive man, is in private possession. The impression in wax of a portrait head carved on a signet ring, found among the genealogical papers in the library of the College of Arms, is assumed to be of Symonds, probably the work of the engraver Thomas Simon.   IAN ROY

Sources *Diary of the marches of the royal army during the great civil war, kept by Richard Symonds*, ed. C. E. Long, CS, old ser., 74 (1859); repr. with new introduction by I. Roy as *Richard Symonds' diary of the marches of the royal army* (1997) · P. Morant, *The history and antiquities of the county of Essex*, 2 (1768) · M. R. S. Beal, *A study of Richard Symonds: his Italian notebooks and their relevance to seventeenth-century painting techniques* (1984) · Venn, *Alum. Cant.* · J. Nichols, *The history and antiquities of the county of Leicester*, 3/2 (1804), appx 4, p. 67 · M. A. E. Green, ed., *Calendar of the proceedings of the committee for compounding … 1643–1660*, 3, PRO (1891), 1610 · *CSP dom.*, *1655*, 367–9 · C. Puglisi, *Caravaggio* (1998), 67, 221 · J. F. H. Smith, 'A fragment of the Stamford Eleanor Cross', *Antiquaries Journal*, 74 (1994), 301–11 · admin., PRO, PROB 6/36 and 11/305
Archives BL, civil war diaries, Harley MSS 911, 939, 944; Add. MS 17062 · BL, collections of anecdotes and memoranda, Harley MS 991 · BL, ensigns of the regiments of the City of London, Harley MS 986 · BL, memorandum book, Harley MS 943 · BL, notes on churches and monuments in Oxfordshire and Berkshire, Harley MSS 964, 965 · BL, notes on churches, public buildings and pictures of Paris and Rome, Harley MSS 924, 1278; Add. MSS 17062, 17919 · BL, notes on pictures and painting in Rome, Egerton MSS 1635–1636 · Coll. Arms, collections for the county of Essex · HLRO, alphabet of arms · priv. coll., commonplace book
Likenesses wax impression of seal, Coll. Arms, Richard Symonds papers [*see illus.*]
Wealth at death probably small; fine of £295 in 1646 might indicate an estate of c.£80 p.a.: will, PRO, PROB 11/305; Green, ed., *Calendar of the proceedings*, vol. 3, p. 1610

Symonds, Sir Thomas Matthew Charles (1813–1894), naval officer, second son of Sir William *Symonds (1782–1856) and his first wife, Elizabeth Saunders (d. 1813x15), daughter of Matthew Luscombe FRS of Plymouth, was born on 15 July 1813. He entered the navy on 25 April 1825, passed his examination in 1831, and was promoted lieutenant on 5 November 1832. In May 1833 he was appointed to the *Vestal*, from which he was removed in September to the *Endymion* on the Mediterranean station, and from her again to the *Britannia*. In December 1834 he joined the *Rattlesnake* (Captain William Hobson), ordered to the East Indies. On 21 October 1837 he was made commander and returned home; and from 27 August 1838 he commanded the sloop *Rover* (18 guns) on the North America and West Indies station until he was promoted captain on 22 February 1841. He married his first wife, Anna Maria, daughter of Captain Edmund Heywood RN, on 25 September 1845.

In May 1846 Symonds was appointed to the *Spartan* (26

guns) for the Mediterranean, where he remained until 1849. In January 1850 he commissioned the new 50-gun frigate *Arethusa*, which in 1852 went to the Mediterranean. In 1854 he served in the Black Sea, took part in the bombardment of Fort Constantine, Sevastopol, and early in 1855 returned home and was paid off. He was made a CB on 5 July 1855 and received the order of the Mejidiye (third class). In 1856 he married Prestwood Mary, daughter of Captain Thomas Wolrige RN. He became a rear-admiral on 1 November 1860 and a vice-admiral on 2 April 1866, and was made a KCB on 13 March 1867. From December 1868 to July 1870 he commanded the channel squadron and gained in the service a reputation as a tactician, being the originator of the group formation in the form of a scalene triangle, which replaced the older isosceles group. On 14 July 1871 he became admiral, and from 1 November 1875 until 1 November 1878 was commander-in-chief at Devonport. He became admiral of the fleet on 15 July 1879 and was made a GCB on 23 April 1880. During retirement he wrote pamphlets and letters to *The Times*, calling for a stronger navy and in support of his ideas on ship design. He died at his home, Sunny Hill, Higher Warberry, Torquay, on 14 November 1894; his second wife survived him.

Symonds's career was made by his father's post at the Admiralty, both his promotion to commander and, critically, that to captain being rewards for Sir William's services from his political friends. Like his father, he was a difficult man to work with—opinionated, argumentative, and obstinate.

J. K. LAUGHTON, *rev.* ANDREW LAMBERT

Sources A. J. Marder, *The anatomy of British sea power*, American edn (1940) · A. D. Lambert, *The last sailing battlefleet: maintaining naval mastery, 1815–1850* (1991) · S. M. Eardley-Wilmot, *Life of Vice-Admiral Edmund, Lord Lyons* (1898) · O'Byrne, *Naval biog. dict.* · *The Times* (15 Nov 1894) · *Army and Navy Gazette* (17 Nov 1894) · A. D. Lambert, *The Crimean War: British grand strategy, 1853–56* (1990) · Boase, *Mod. Eng. biog.* · Burke, *Peerage* · Kelly, *Handbk* · *CGPLA Eng. & Wales* (1895)
Archives BL, letters to Sir W. F. Martin, Add. MS 41413
Wealth at death £11,124 12s. od.: probate, 2 Jan 1895, *CGPLA Eng. & Wales*

Symonds, William (b. 1556, d. in or after 1616), Church of England clergyman and headmaster, was a native of Oxfordshire. He matriculated as a commoner of Magdalen College, Oxford, in 1571, and was a middle commoner from 1573 to 1578. On 1 February 1578 he graduated BA; he was a fellow from 1578 until 1582, taking his MA on 5 April 1581.

In 1583 Symonds became master of Magdalen School, Oxford, a tenure marked by mounting complaints which centred not only on the management of the school but on the egregious pluralism of the master. In 1585 the visitor was induced to intervene. One fellow reported:

> The School, … has been taught either by vice-gerents or very bad schoolmasters, about these ten years together, and by such a one now as hath two benefices, who only keeps the School until he can compass the twenty pounds in money which he gave for it. (Stanier, 110)

Another complained: 'He that is now schoolmaster had at

his coming a benefice in Lincolnshire, and now is said to have another' (ibid.). In this last matter the fellow was certainly correct. Ordained by the bishop of Lincoln on 11 June 1582, Symonds was instituted on 28 January 1583 to the rectory of Langton by Partney, Lincolnshire. It is not clear whether he was resident in Lincolnshire during the period of his mastership at Oxford, though two curates are listed for Langton Partney in 1585. There seems little doubt that, whether through corruption, inefficiency, or neglect, Magdalen School was in a very poor state during Symonds's mastership, which came to an end in 1586. In 1585 the visitor had 'rebuked the President and fellows for allowing the school to become an object of contempt' (ibid.).

In 1594 Symonds resigned from Langton Partney but acquired another Lincoln rectory at Theddlethorpe. In 1599 he was instituted to the rectory of Halton Holgate, also in Lincolnshire. He was selected to preach a sermon at Horncastle on 25 April 1603, at one of the services held to mark the first entry of King James I into the diocese of Lincoln. Following the promulgation of the new canons in 1604, however, his differences with the practice of the established church came to the notice of the authorities. Before and up to the bishop's visitation in August, Symonds had failed to wear the surplice—though the omission had not been reported—'but sithence he hath worn it', as the churchwardens later testified; Symonds appeared before the bishop on 3 October 1604, and afterwards subscribed (Foster, *State of the Church*, cxiv).

In 1600 Symonds had given up the vicarage of Well (acquired in 1597), and in 1605 he resigned from Theddlethorpe. Probably about this time he left Lincolnshire for London, and by August 1607 he had been replaced at Halton Holgate. In 1606 he and John Trundle, lecturers at Christ Church, Greyfriars, London, were instructed to show their conformity in 'reading public prayer and ministering the sacraments in the surplice according to the canon' (Seaver, 224). On 22 February Symonds was ordered to conform at St Saviour's, Southwark, where he had also acquired a lectureship, and he appears once more to have offered only token resistance.

At Halton Holgate, Symonds's patron had been Robert Bertie, Lord Willoughby. He had also become acquainted with William Crashaw, the preacher at the Temple. Either of these men may have helped or encouraged Symonds to come to London. Both were certainly involved with the effort to plant a colony in Virginia, and they enlisted Symonds in support of the enterprise. In *A sermon preached at White-chappel, on 25 April 1609, in the presence of the many worshipfull, the adventurers and planters for Virginia*, Symonds explained that it was 'God's purpose that the Gospel shall be preached through the world for a witness', and thus pretence of zeal could only be 'hypocrisy, when we rather choose to mind unprofitable questions at home, than gaining souls abroad' (preface). Symonds also saw the need for colonization as originating in material circumstances. English landlords, gentlemen, clothiers, rich shopkeepers, and engrossers were responsible for impoverishing many labourers, and for falsely telling them 'that

if the poor man were a good husband he might live well'. The poor woman with her small children 'worketh with her needle and laboureth with her fingers, her candle goeth not out by night'; she laments 'the bitterness of her life with sweet songs', but 'when all the week is ended, she can hardly earn salt for her water gruel to feed on upon the Sunday'. So it was that:

the strong old bees do beat out the younger, to swarm and hive themselves elsewhere. Take the opportunity, good honest labourers, which indeed bring all the honey to the hive; God may so bless you that the proverb may be true of you, that a May swarm is worth a king's ransom. (Anderson, 198–9)

Symonds's patron Bertie was also the patron of Captain John Smith. Obligation to Bertie, friendship with Crashaw, and his own sympathies with the Virginia enterprise, may each have drawn Symonds towards closer identification with it. At any rate, William Symonds played a major role in bringing to the press *A Map of Virginia*, issued in 1612 under Smith's name in two separate parts. The first, 'The description of Virginia' by Smith himself, was an account of the new land and its native inhabitants. In the second, 'The proceedings of the Englishe colonie in Virginia', edited by Symonds, several other colonists recalled their early tribulations. Although publicity was essential in the search for investors, the Virginia Company acted to block the publication of the book in London: it had quarrelled with Smith and sought to muzzle criticism of its own stewardship of the enterprise. But Smith and his friends were soon able to have their work issued at Oxford. After the main text Symonds appended a note:

Captain Smith, I return you the fruits of my labours, as Mr Croshaw requested me, which I bestowed in reading the discourses, and hearing the relations of such which have walked and observed the land of Virginia with you. The pains I took was great: yet did the nature of the argument, and hopes I conceived of the expedition give me great content … my prayer shall ever be, that so fair a land, may be inhabited by those that profess and love the gospel, Your friend, W. S. (Barbour, 464)

There is no evidence that Symonds travelled to America. He took his doctorate at Magdalen College in 1613, and may well have returned to Lincolnshire, since from 1612 to 1616 he held the rectory of Wyberton in that county. Nothing further is known of his life or death.

STEPHEN WRIGHT

Sources P. L. Barbour, *The three worlds of Captain John Smith* (1964) · C. W. Foster, ed., *The state of the church in the reigns of Elizabeth and James I*, Lincoln RS, 23 (1926) · R. S. Stanier, *Magdalen School: a history of Magdalen College School, Oxford*, OHS, new ser., 3 (1940); repr. (1958) · W. D. Macray, *A register of the members of St Mary Magdalen College, Oxford*, 8 vols. (1894–1915), vol. 3 · Foster, *Alum. Oxon.* · Wood, *Ath. Oxon.* · J. Anderson, *The history of the Church of England in the colonies* (1845–56), vol. 1 · R. Newcourt, *Repertorium ecclesiasticum parochiale Londinense*, 1 (1708) · W. Symonds, *A sermon preached at White-chappel* (1609) · P. S. Seaver, *The puritan lectureships: the politics of religious dissent, 1560–1662* (1970)

Symonds, Sir William (1782–1856), naval officer and naval architect, was born on 24 September 1782 at Bury St

Sir William Symonds (1782–1856), by Edward Morton, pubd 1850 (after Henry Wyndham Phillips)

Edmunds, the second son of Captain Thomas Symonds RN (*d.* 1793) and his second wife. He went to sea in September 1794, aboard the *London*, and served at Lord Bridport's action (23 June 1795) and the 1797 Spithead mutiny. Promoted lieutenant on 14 October 1801, he served afloat throughout the Napoleonic wars. Although widely acknowledged a fine seaman, he lacked interest and obtained no further promotion. On 21 April 1808 he married Elizabeth Saunders Luscombe, daughter of Matthew Luscombe of Plymouth; they had one daughter and four sons. Their second son was Sir Thomas Matthew Charles *Symonds. On 10 March 1818, after his first wife's death, Symonds married Elizabeth Mary, daughter of Rear-Admiral Philip Carteret, of Trinity Manor, Jersey. Between 1819 and 1825 he was captain of the port at Malta.

In 1821 Symonds used a small legacy from Admiral Sir William Cornwallis—who had left his estate to Symonds's sister, the widow of his best friend—to build an experimental yacht. George Vernon, a wealthy yachtsman, copied her, helped Symonds publish a pamphlet on naval architecture, and persuaded the Admiralty to build the corvette *Columbine*, by putting up a bond of £20,000 in case of failure. As a result, on 4 October 1825 Symonds was promoted commander. He was obsessed with speed under sail, and his wide-beamed, sharp-formed ships with their great spread of canvas were a response to the mortifying wartime experience of being out-sailed by French ships. His ships proved highly successful in skilled hands, but less satisfactory under hostile or clumsy commanders. In December 1826 Vernon introduced Symonds to William Cavendish-Scott-Bentinck, fourth duke of Portland, who

built two vessels to Symonds's design. In April 1827 Portland entered the cabinet under his brother-in-law George Canning, and began pushing Symonds's case with the duke of Clarence, the lord high admiral. Sailing trials in 1827 demonstrated the superiority of Symonds's entry. Clarence appointed Symonds to the royal yacht and promoted him captain on 5 December 1827.

The formation of Earl Grey's ministry in 1830, further successes during sailing trials in 1831, the support of Clarence (now King William IV), and the whigs' decision to abolish the Navy Board, provided Symonds with a new career. In 1831 he was ordered to design a large 50 gun frigate, named *Vernon*, for his original patron. He was appointed surveyor of the navy on 9 June 1832, following the abolition of the Navy Board. His patron Portland had been informed of the decision in February, in time to influence his vote in the reform crisis. The first lord of the Admiralty, Sir James Graham, intended Symonds to control the programme of shipbuilding and the dockyards, but the use of the title surveyor, which was linked to ship design, and weak drafting of the instructions, allowed Symonds to impose his own designs on the navy, despite widespread objections. The overtly political nature of the abolition of the Navy Board ensured that Symonds was the target for constant attacks by disappointed rivals, notably dockyard-raised shipwrights and the rising class of professional naval architects, who saw the appointment as an attack on their profession and their prospects. Naval architects, past and present, in criticizing his limited scientific knowledge and ignorance of practical shipbuilding, have failed to recognize the political and administrative issues.

Symonds relied on the talented assistant surveyor John Edye for the detailed design of his ships. Edye also introduced a new system of construction to facilitate even larger wooden warships. Symonds exploited the weak whig Admiralty boards of the 1830s to circumvent the flimsy controls Graham had placed on his work. He was a favourite with the king, who knighted him on 15 June 1836, without telling the Admiralty. Symonds also relied on Portland and the whig party. During the Peel administration (1841–6) he provided his whig friends with sensitive naval information, which both reflected and exacerbated the mistrust with which he was viewed by the first sea lord, Admiral Sir George Cockburn. He was elected FRS in June 1835.

The contemporary debate about Symonds's ships, conducted in newspapers and pamphlets, was heavily coloured by party politics and sectional interests. It resulted in a series of sailing trials, in which Symonds's great yachts, commanded by hand-picked captains, established their superiority in all but the most severe weather. Only in 1844 were the results sufficiently ambivalent to lend any credence to his critics. He responded by publishing the pamphlet *Facts versus Fiction* (1844), which rehearsed his case with more vigour than was welcome at the Admiralty.

Symonds, an autocrat in office, expected unquestioning

obedience from his subordinates, and unwavering support from his superiors. Sensitive to the slightest hint of criticism, he considered the adoption of any alternative design a personal attack. He has been accused of blindly opposing steamships and the screw propeller, but such generalizations, based on the memoirs of engineers attempting to sell their ideas to a sceptical Admiralty, do him little justice. Believing that steam was an auxiliary to the sailing navy, Symonds built some fine paddle-wheel steamships. He realized that the screw propeller would weaken the stern of ships and, so long as ships were built of wood, this was true. His sailing ships were built on larger dimensions than any previous ships, carried a heavier armament, had more space to fight their guns, and used their wide beam to provide support for a heavier rig. When in trim they were capable of outstanding performance, a feature that facilitated new tactics. Before 1830 the navy expected to win any battle at sea, but had to rely on the enemy providing the opportunity. Symonds's ships gave the fleet the chance to catch a fleeing enemy, and force him to give battle.

These ships, class for class the largest and most powerful sailing warships ever built, excited the envy and admiration of every other naval power. Symonds designed over 200 ships for the navy, although many large warships were completed after 1852 as steamships. In addition he travelled extensively, reporting on foreign navies and on British and overseas timber resources. His accounts of the Russian Baltic fleet in 1839, and the Black Sea Fleet in 1841, were the most accurate yet obtained, and demonstrated their inefficiency at a critical period in Anglo-Russian relations. His reports on the Forest of Dean, the New Forest, and the Apennine forests of Italy led to improved supplies of oak timber, although, as with so much of his work, the subject quickly lost its significance.

In 1846 the tory first lord, Lord Ellenborough, appointed a committee of reference to report on Symonds's designs. When the whigs returned to office in July 1846 they used the committee to pressure Symonds into retirement. The first lord, Lord Auckland, recognized that Symonds, whatever the merits of his ships, had become a political liability and an obstacle to the establishment of regular naval shipbuilding programmes; the controversy would end only when he left office. In April 1847 Symonds was ordered to make a radical alteration in the form of a new 90 gun ship. Aged sixty-five and ill, Symonds was not prepared to fight on. Despite the support of Portland he left the office in June, and took his pension (£500 p.a., in addition to his half pay as captain) in October 1847.

Within a few years Symonds's work, and the sailing navy, had passed into oblivion, his hull form having proved unsuited to screw propulsion. On 1 May 1848 he received a civil CB. In June 1853, prompted by Portland, Graham, again first lord, appointed him naval aide-de-camp to the queen. He became a retired rear-admiral in 1854. In 1851 he had married Susan Mary, daughter of the Revd John Briggs, and subsequently he lived abroad for his health, mostly in Italy and Malta. Travelling from Malta to Marseilles, Symonds died aboard the French steamship *Nil*

in the Strait of Bonifacio, off Sardinia, on 30 March 1856. He was buried in the protestant burial-ground at Marseilles. Under the terms of his will a valedictory biography was published, which repeated the arguments about his sailing ships long after the end of the sailing navy.

An obsessive monomaniac, Symonds used his intuitive genius for ship design to transform the dead-end career of a half-pay lieutenant into that of a senior naval administrator closely linked to the whig party and a clique of noblemen. Because the process by which he became surveyor, and the instructions under which he operated, were controversial and ill considered, he suffered a large degree of unwarranted obloquy. His designs, character, and attitudes contributed to the controversy, but they did not cause it. His sailing ships were outstanding, while his response to the advance of steam was conservative. In office he advanced the careers of several fine seamen, notably his successor Sir Baldwin Walker, and his second son, Sir Thomas Matthew Charles Symonds. His ships contributed to the maintenance of British naval mastery, while his term in office witnessed many significant developments in naval architecture, occasioned both by his efforts and by those of his critics. ANDREW LAMBERT

Sources A. D. Lambert, *The last sailing battlefleet: maintaining naval mastery, 1815–1850* (1991) · J. A. Sharp, *Memoirs of the life and services of Admiral Sir William Symonds* (1858) · A. S. Turberville, *A history of Welbeck Abbey and its owners*, 2 vols. (1938–9), vol. 2 · Cape Town University Library, Walker MSS · NMM, Minto MSS · PRO, Admiralty MSS · U. Nott. L., Portland MSS · BL, Martin MSS · D. K. Brown, *Before the ironclad* (1990) · PRO, Ellenborough MSS · BL, Peel MSS · C. J. Bartlett, *Great Britain and sea power, 1815–1853* (1963) · O'Byrne, *Naval biog. dict.* · Boase, *Mod. Eng. biog.*
Archives Royal Military College of Canada, Kingston, Ontario, Massey Library, bound plans relating to system of classifying ships | NMM, Minto MSS
Likenesses E. Morton, lithograph, pubd 1850 (after H. W. Phillips), BM, NPG [*see illus.*] · portrait, repro. in Lambert, *Last sailing battlefleet*, 68

Symonds, William Samuel (1818–1887), Church of England clergyman and geologist, was born at Hereford on 13 December 1818, the eldest child of William Symonds (*d.* 1840) and his wife, Mary Anne Beale (*d.* 1859). His father was lord of the manor of Elsdon in Herefordshire, and deputy lieutenant of the county. Symonds was educated in Cheltenham from where, after private coaching, he went up to Christ's College, Cambridge. While a student Symonds married, in 1840, Hyacinth Catherine (*d.* 1907), daughter of Samuel Kent of Upton upon Severn. They had a daughter and three sons, two of whom died young.

Symonds graduated in 1842 and was ordained the same year. In 1843, he was appointed curate at Offenham, near Evesham, Worcestershire, and in 1845 he became rector of Pendock, near Malvern. The living at Pendock was linked to the village manor, and Symonds was in fact lord of the manor, and justice of the peace. His clerical duties were not great, and this enabled him to devote himself to the study of local history, archaeology, and particularly geology.

Symonds's geological interests were first stimulated by

his seeing a parishioner's fossil collection at Offenham. There he also met Hugh Strickland (1811–1853), from whom he learned the elements of geology; they made numerous excursions together. Symonds soon gained the acquaintance and respect of eminent men of science such as Charles Lyell, Roderick Murchison, and Joseph Hooker. He studied the ancient rocks of the Malvern hills, particularly in the railway tunnel between Ledbury and Malvern, and made important discoveries of fossils in the adjacent strata. His home at Pendock, which overlooked the hills, was frequently opened to visiting men of science.

Symonds was exceptionally active in promoting local scientific studies. He co-founded the Malvern Naturalists' Field Club (1853), and was its president for eighteen years. He also took a prominent part in the proceedings of the Cotteswold Field Club, the Worcester Natural History Society, and the Woolhope Naturalists' Field Club. Symonds was elected a fellow of the Geological Society in 1853 and later served on its council. He regularly attended meetings of the British Association.

Symonds published forty-three scientific papers, mostly related to palaeontology. Though certainly not a leader in theoretical matters, he was willing to adopt unorthodox ideas. For example, he accepted the idea that the crystalline rocks of the Malvern hills were Precambrian. He also adopted Darwinism and the idea of a great antiquity of man, at a time when most of his fellow clergymen were battling against such ideas. He was much interested in glacial geology and cave excavations.

Symonds was important as a writer of popular geological and archaeological texts: *Old Stones* (1855), *Stones of the Valley* (1857), *Old Bones* (1860), *Records of the Rocks* (1872), and *Severn Straits* (1883). He also wrote two highly successful historical novels, *Malvern Chase* (1881) and *Hanley Castle* (1883), based on his knowledge of the long history of his family in the Malvern area. As a man of strong didactic tendency, Symonds took in private pupils, among whom was the gifted Alice Roberts, later wife of Edward Elgar. Symonds was writing to her familiarly in 1871 when Alice was twenty-three, and there is some hint in surviving correspondence of an emotional attachment. Keen on sport in his youth, Symonds enjoyed travelling in pursuit of his geological interests. He visited the Ardèche and Auvergne in 1874 (and in the two autumns following) to search for traces of ancient glaciers.

Symonds's health began to deteriorate in 1877, and for the next ten years his life 'hung by a thread'. He died at 6 Clarence Place, Cheltenham, on 15 September 1887, survived by his wife, and was buried in the graveyard of Pendock church three days later. His daughter, Hyacinth, married the ornithologist Sir William *Jardine, and, after his death, the botanist Joseph Dalton *Hooker.

DAVID OLDROYD

Sources J. W. Judd, *Proceedings of the Geological Society*, 44 (1888), 43–5 • P. M. Young, *Alice Elgar: enigma of a Victorian lady* (1978) • J. D. La Touche, *William S. Symonds rector of Pendock: a sketch of his life* [1914] • *CGPLA Eng. & Wales* (1887) • Burke, *Gen. GB* (1937) • Venn, *Alum. Cant.*

Archives GS Lond., letters to Sir R. I. Murchison • Malvern and Worcester Library, Worcestershire, Malvern Naturalists' Field Club corresp. • U. Edin. L., letters to Sir Charles Lyell
Likenesses photograph, Malvern Public Library, Worcestershire • photograph, repro. in Young, *Alice Elgar* • portrait, repro. in La Touche, *William S. Symonds*, frontispiece
Wealth at death £5121 18s. 8d.: probate, 20 Dec 1887, *CGPLA Eng. & Wales*

Symons, Alphonse James Albert (1900–1941), book collector and writer, was born on 16 August 1900 in Battersea, London, the eldest in the family of four sons and one daughter of Maurice (or Morris) Albert Symons (d. 1929), auctioneer, a Jewish immigrant from eastern Europe, and his wife, Minnie Louise, *née* Bull. Julian Gustave *Symons was his youngest brother. He was educated at Wix's Lane School, Battersea, and left at the age of fourteen to take up an apprenticeship to a firm of fur dealers for three years. Although declared unfit for military service, he joined the Artists' Rifles Officers' Training Corps and began an active social career. On 1 August 1924 he married Victoria Emily (Gladys) Weeks (b. 1897/8), the daughter of Arthur Weeks, a builder and decorator. The marriage ended in divorce in 1936; there were no children.

In 1922, supported initially by William Foyle, Symons had started the First Edition Club, a centre for bibliographical information and a dining club in Bloomsbury. Symons organized the selection of 'fifty books of the year' from 1926 on and, despite the end of his First Edition Club in 1931, became an important influence in the bibliographical world through the foundation, in 1930, of the *Book-Collector's Quarterly*. Symons specialized in the authors of the 1890s but, although he worked from 1925 to 1930 on compiling 'A select bibliography and history of the books of the nineties, with notes on their authors', his only separate bibliographical publication in this field was a check-list of W. B. Yeats (1924). His *Anthology of Nineties Verse* (1928) was followed by a biography of Emin Pasha in the same year, and then by a life of the explorer Sir Henry Martin Stanley (1933). In 1934 came Symons's best-known work, *The Quest for Corvo*, a brilliantly evocative account of how he established the facts surrounding the life and literary career of Baron Corvo (Frederick Rolfe), the eccentric homosexual writer. The book took the form of a detective fiction, in which the author's pursuit of the baron is intertwined with his account of the baron's own life. It was an immediate success, not only for its sexual interest and its association with the notorious Maundy Gregory, but also because it was seen as 'an experiment in biography' (Symons, *Life*, 132), revealing as much of the biographer and of his interest in his subject as it did of the subject himself. Writing did not come easily to Symons: 'the act of composition has always been accompanied by more pain than pleasure' (Symons and Holland, 200), and was often neglected in favour of social engagements.

Symons lived a financially precarious life to the full and, in his own phrase, 'no one so poor has lived so well' (Symons, *Life*, 268). He favoured suits of unusual colour and cloth with double-breasted waistcoats, and 'extravagant shirts and ties and pointed, hand-made shoes' (ibid., 60–61). He taught himself calligraphy by copying

Alphonse James Albert Symons (1900–1941), by Wyndham Lewis, 1932

out passages from the *Dictionary of National Biography* in a minute Gothic script. In 1931 he was associated with André L. Simon in the foundation of the Saintsbury Club and, in October 1933, with that of the Wine and Food Society, the aim of which was 'to raise standards of cooking throughout the country' and to provide 'practical demonstrations of the arts of the table' (ibid., 142). His many-sided aesthetic interests led him to surround himself with first editions, Bristol glass, mother-of-pearl knick-knacks, and, above all, his notable collection of musical boxes (later given to the Pitt Rivers Museum, Oxford). In reaction to his family, and possibly to their Jewish background, he sought an escape into social life and literary interests, his sensitivity to his first name leading him later to change it to Alroy, the name of a character in a novel by Benjamin Disraeli. His friends commonly called him AJ. He was possessed of an aggressive resolve for social success, coupled with an interest in (but not a taste for) the psychologically abnormal. An epitaph referred to 'kindness and culture, lovely things and mirth'. Symons died of cardiac failure in the Essex County Hospital, Colchester, on 25 August 1941.

GILES BARBER

Sources J. Symons, *A. J. A. Symons: his life and speculations* (1950) • *The Times* (29 Aug 1941) • J. Symons and V. Holland, 'A. J. A. Symons 1900–41, two personal notes', *Horizon*, 4/22 (1941), 258–71 • *Wine and Food*, 8 (1941), 196–202 • m. cert. • d. cert. • private information (2004) [J. Symons] • J. Symons, 'Autobiographical notes', in J. J. Walsdorf, *Julian Symons: a bibliography* (1996)
Likenesses W. Lewis, drawing, 1932, priv. coll. [*see illus.*]

Symons, Arthur William (1865–1945), literary scholar and author, was born in Milford Haven, Pembrokeshire, Wales (his family's temporary residence), on 28 February 1865, the second child and only son of the Revd Mark Symons (1824–1898), a Wesleyan Methodist minister, and his wife, Lydia Pascoe (1828–1896), the daughter of a wealthy farmer. Both parents were of ancient Cornish stock, in which Symons took pride. The Revd Symons's changes in clerical assignments every three years profoundly affected his son's sense of connection. In his autobiographical sketch 'A preface to life', in *Spiritual Adventures* (1905, 4), Symons wrote that he had never known what it was to have a home: 'If I have been a vagabond, and have never been able to root myself in any one place in the world, it is because I have no early memories of any one sky or soil'. Such an upbringing, which shaped his personality and art, contributed to his later bohemianism and restlessness. In his late teenage years he could no longer believe in God or Christianity.

Having attended various schools in Devon until he was seventeen, Symons, at that age, published his first article, a study of Robert Browning, which launched an extraordinarily prolific career as a writer. By the age of twenty-one he had published over thirty-five articles, reviews, and poems in addition to his first book, *An Introduction to the Study of Browning* (1886), dedicated to George Meredith, who praised the study, as did Walter Pater and Browning himself. In 1889 his first volume of poems, *Days and Nights*, displaying the influence of the French decadent poets, was dedicated 'in all gratitude and admiration' to Pater, who praised the work. With his friend Havelock Ellis he travelled to France in 1889 and in 1890, when he met such figures as Rodin, Mallarmé, Verlaine, and Huysmans.

In the 1890s Symons emerged as a leading figure espousing 'art for art's sake' by establishing himself as a noted critic and poet in avant-garde circles shaping *fin-de-siècle* literature. In 1890 he joined the Rhymers' Club and contributed to the club's two anthologies, but, most importantly, his consequent friendship with W. B. Yeats resulted in a mutually productive literary relationship. Symons's second volume of poems, *Silhouettes* (1892), reveals a more extensive immersion in French decadence and symbolism, particularly in the celebration of artifice and the dance. In 1893 his seminal article 'The decadent movement in literature' delineated the decadent/symbolist verse and prose of such writers as Mallarmé, Verlaine, Goncourt, Huysmans, and Maeterlinck.

During this time Symons (writing under the pseudonym Silhouette) was the regular reviewer of drama and music-hall entertainment in *The Star*. His poems now revealed his infatuation with ballet dancers, one of whom was Lydia (her last name unknown), their three-year turbulent relationship celebrated in such volumes of verse as *London Nights* (1895) and *Amoris victima* (1897).

In 1895, when Symons became editor of *The Savoy*, he enlisted, as his principal illustrator, Aubrey Beardsley, recently fired from the *Yellow Book* at the time of the Oscar Wilde trials because of his daring illustrations for *Salome*. Designed to surpass the *Yellow Book* as the principal avant-garde periodical of the 1890s, the first issue of *The Savoy* appeared in January 1896. With its eighth number in December, the periodical—which had contained the work of such contributors as Yeats, Ellis, Conrad, Shaw, Verlaine, Dowson, Max Beerbohm, and Symons—ceased publishing. Despite its sudden demise, the periodical had propelled Symons to the centre of London literary circles.

In the late 1890s Symons was engaged in writing and revising reviews and articles on various figures of the French symbolist movement, convinced by Yeats that the term 'symbolist movement' was a more accurate designation than the 'decadent movement' in characterizing the French avant-garde poets. In March 1900, after delays by the publisher, Symons's major work, *The Symbolist Movement in Literature*, dedicated to Yeats as 'the chief representative of that movement in our country', finally appeared. The essays evaluate the work of several writers originally discussed in 'The decadent movement in literature' (though Goncourt was now omitted). The additional writers were Villiers de l'Isle-Adam, Rimbaud, Laforgue, and Gérard de Nerval. The work's impact on early modernism may be gauged by the reaction of one reader, T. S. Eliot, who recalled that Symons's work, a 'revelation', had affected the course of his life.

In the early twentieth century Symons remained impressively productive: writing plays, working at translations in several languages, preparing a book on William Blake, and continuing as a reviewer for various publications. (During his career he published over 1300 articles and reviews.) His marriage on 19 January 1901 to Rhoda Bowser (1874–1936), whose father was a wealthy shipowner and shipbuilder, burdened him financially despite her later inheritance and her moderately successful career as an actress. Moreover, his failure to make his mark as a playwright contributed to his growing instability.

In late September 1908, while on a trip through Italy with his wife, Symons suffered a severe mental breakdown (most likely a manic-depressive psychosis) which required almost two years of confinement in mental institutions. Although he seemed to have recovered sufficiently by 1910 to resume his career, he published nothing further until 1911. For the remainder of his life, however, his intellectual functioning remained impaired. The publication of many articles and books, which usually consisted of revised articles previously published, too often revealed incoherence. Inevitably, his reputation as a noted critic and poet declined. In 1924 the publisher Martin Secker, having planned a sixteen-volume edition of Symons's works, terminated the contract when sales dwindled by the ninth volume. Symons's last notable work—though with evidence of incoherence—was the harrowing account of his breakdown in Italy, *Confessions: a Study in Pathology* (1930).

Increasingly Symons isolated himself at Island Cottage, his seventeenth-century cottage in Wittersham, Kent, only making occasional forays into London to see plays. After his wife died in 1936, his last years as a writer were of little significance. Arthur Symons died, childless, apparently of pneumonia, on 22 January 1945 in Wittersham, where he was buried with his wife's ashes.

KARL BECKSON

Sources K. Beckson, *Arthur Symons: a life* (1987) · A. Symons, *The memoirs of Arthur Symons: life and art in the 1890s*, ed. K. Beckson (1977) · *Arthur Symons: selected letters, 1880–1935*, ed. K. Beckson and J. M. Munro (1989) · K. Beckson and others, eds., *Arthur Symons: a bibliography* (1990)
Archives Bodl. Oxf., corresp. and literary MSS · Col. U., Butler Library · Harvard U., Houghton L., corresp. and papers · NRA, corresp. and literary papers | BL, letters to James Dykes Campbell, Add. MSS 49522–49523 · BL, corresp. with Macmillans, Add. MS 55011 · BL, letters to Ernest Rhys, Egerton MS 3248 · BL, letters to A. R. Waller, Add. MSS 43680–43681 · BL, letters to Theodore Watts-Dunton, Ashley A 4502 · Dorset County Museum, Dorchester, corresp. with Thomas Hardy · Harvard U., Houghton L., letters to Edward Hutton · LUL, letters to Austin Dobson · NRA, priv. coll., Walpole MSS · NYPL, Berg collection · Queen's University, Kingston, Ontario, letters to Henry Davray · Ransom HRC, corresp. with John Lane · U. Leeds, Brotherton L., letters to Sir Edmund Gosse · U. Lpool L., letters to John Sampson · U. Reading L., letters to Bodley Head Ltd; letters to Charles Elkin Mathews
Likenesses J.-E. Blanche, oils, 1895, Tate collection; repro. in T. E. Welby, *Arthur Symons: a critical study* (1925) · F. H. Evans, photograph, c.1900, NPG · A. L. Coburn, photogravure, 1906, NPG · A. John, two pencil drawings, c.1909, Tate collection · Elliott & Fry, photograph, c.1910 · R. H. Sauter, oils, 1935, NPG; version?, Gov. Art Coll. · A. John, oils, priv. coll.; repro. in A. W. Symons, *Cities and seacoasts and islands* (1918) · photographs, Princeton University, Symons MS, Box 28; repro. in Beckson, *Arthur Symons*
Wealth at death £486: Principal Registry of the Family Division, London

Symons, Benjamin Parsons (1785–1878), college head, was born on 28 January 1785, at Cheddar in Somerset, a younger son of John Symons, a prosperous gentleman tanner. His education before entering Wadham College, Oxford, as a commoner on 2 February 1802 is unknown. He was elected scholar on 25 October 1803, took the new honours BA in 1805 (classified as 'egregie'), and graduated MA in 1810, BD in 1819, and DD in 1831. He was ordained deacon in 1809, and priest in 1810. As fellow and tutor of Wadham (1811–31; also bursar 1814–23, sub-warden 1823–31) he helped establish the college as one where 'the tutors were of evangelical principles, and ... where some men worked' (*Life and Letters of Dean Church*, 10). He was elected warden in 1831, and married the 21-year-old Lydia (1809/10–1864), daughter of John Masterman (1781–1862), banker, later MP for the City of London. They had no children.

As one of a minority of evangelical 'heads', Symons clashed with the Tractarians. He especially abominated J. H. Newman's Tract 90 (1841), holding the Thirty-Nine Articles in their 'natural' (that is, protestant) sense as fundamental to the English church. In 1844 the Tractarians opposed in convocation the nomination of Symons as vice-chancellor but were heavily defeated. As vice-chancellor he presided over the degradation of W. G. Ward in 1845, although the proctors vetoed the accompanying condemnation of Tract 90. Later in 1845 he reported to the chancellor (Wellington) that Newman's

Benjamin Parsons Symons (1785–1878), by Henry William Pickersgill, exh. RA 1836

conversion to Rome had unsettled few except the 'young, inexperienced, and uninformed'. Symons was an equally fierce opponent of university reform. He was increasingly at odds with his own fellows over the admission of dissenters and the opening of fellowships to competition. He was induced to resign in 1871, aged eighty-six, amid allegations that he had run the college's estates irregularly, and, by implication, to his own advantage.

Symons was a large man, known as Big Ben or, when mounted, as the Elephant and Castle. A reputation for sternness is alleviated by glimpses of heavy-handed humour. There seems little sense of spiritual warmth about Symons's religion. It was left to his wife to initiate 'religious' conversation and to support the missions. In his prime he was a capable man of business, even serving (1834–43) as chairman of the Oxford Canal Company. Dean Church, an opponent in the battles over the Tracts, privately alleged fondness for the bottle. Symons died at his home, Burnham House, St Giles', Oxford on 12 April 1878 and was buried beside his wife in Holywell cemetery, Oxford, leaving £1000 to his college from an estate worth almost £180,000.   C. S. L. DAVIES

Sources R. B. Gardiner, ed., *The registers of Wadham College, Oxford*, 2 vols. (1889–95) · J. S. Reynolds, *The evangelicals at Oxford, 1735–1871: a record of an unchronicled movement*, [2nd edn] (1975) · P. A. Wright-Henderson, *Glasgow and Balliol and other essays* (1926) · J. Wells, *Wadham College* (1898) · W. R. Ward, *Victorian Oxford* (1965) · *Life and letters of Dean Church*, ed. M. C. Church (1894) · d. cert. · *CGPLA Eng. & Wales* (1878) · parish register (baptism), Cheddar, 28 March 1785 · *DNB*

Archives Bodl. Oxf., corresp. | U. Southampton L., letters to first duke of Wellington · Wadham College, Oxford, muniments
Likenesses H. W. Pickersgill, oils, exh. RA 1836, Wadham College, Oxford [*see illus.*] · W. Ward, mezzotint (after H. W. Pickersgill), AM Oxf.
Wealth at death under £180,000: probate, 10 May 1878, *CGPLA Eng. & Wales*

Symons, George James (1838–1900), meteorologist, was born at 28 Queen's Row, Pimlico, London, on 6 August 1838, the only child of Joseph Symons and his wife, Georgiana Moon. His education, begun at St Peter's Collegiate School, Eaton Square, was completed under two Irish private tutors at Thornton, in Leicestershire. He subsequently passed with distinction through Professor John Tyndall's course at the School of Mines, Jermyn Street. From boyhood he made observations on the weather with instruments of his own construction, and at the age of seventeen became a member of the British Meteorological Society.

In 1857 Symons became a meteorological observer to the registrar general. From 1860 to 1863 he held a junior post in the meteorological department of the Board of Trade. By this time Symons was increasingly involved with the establishment of a network of rainfall observations, and he resigned his post to devote himself completely to this task. He turned his gardens in his house at Camden Square into a menagerie of instruments, where he maintained an unbroken series of observations for forty-two years. He married, on 16 September 1866, Elizabeth (d. 1884), daughter of John Luke, gentleman, of Kensington. Their only child died in infancy and his wife assisted Symons in his work thereafter. The first of a series of 39 annual volumes containing statistics on the subject, entitled *British Rainfall*, was published by him in 1860; it included records from 168 stations in England and Wales. In 1898 the number of stations had grown to 3404, of which 436 were in Scotland and 186 in Ireland, and they were run by an army of over 3000 volunteer observers. This unique organization was kept by Symons under close personal supervision, and the upshot was the accumulation of a mass of data of standard value, unmatched in any other country. Concern with droughts and sanitation motivated the inquiry and Symons often served as consultant to water engineers. From 1863 he produced a monthly rain circular, which developed in 1866 into the *Monthly Meteorological Magazine*, and, after his death, into *Weather*. Symons also wrote a popular book on rain, *Rain: How, When, Where, Why it is Measured* (1867), a treatise on the *Floating Island of Derwentwater* (1888), and edited and reissued several old texts on meteorology.

Symons was a prominent member of the Meteorological Society for over forty years. He sat on the council from 1863, acted as secretary 1873–9 and 1882–9, and was elected president in 1880 and again in 1900, the year of his death. In his memory, the Meteorological Society founded a gold medal to be awarded for services to meteorological science. The honour recognized Symons's significant contributions to most, if not all, meteorological questions of his day, from the design of observation networks to the design of instruments, and from the impact of photography to seismology. His painstaking approach and caution in dealing with controversy were characteristic of the society's aims in his lifetime.

Symons's interests involved him in the work of many other scientific societies. He was member of the Royal Botanical Society from 1869 until 1890. He served on various committees appointed by the British Association, and as secretary to the conference on lightning rods in 1878 shared largely in the four years' task of compiling its report. Elected in 1878 a fellow of the Royal Society, he acted as chairman of the committee on the eruption of Krakatoa in 1883, and edited the voluminous report published in 1888. He sat on the council of the Social Science Association in 1878, and on the jury of the Health Exhibition in 1884; was registrar to the Sanitary Institute from 1880 to 1895, and drew up a report on the Essex earthquake of 22 April 1884 for the Mansion House committee. In 1876 he received the Telford premium of the Institution of Civil Engineers for a paper 'Floods and water economy', and in 1897 the Albert medal of the Society of Arts for the services rendered to the United Kingdom by his rainfall observations.

Symons was a member of the Scottish and Australasian Meteorological societies, and of many foreign learned associations. From 1872 he was active in the Société Météorologique de France, and was twice elected to its council. He was much respected internationally and became, in 1891, a knight of the Légion d'honneur. Symons was also a dedicated collector of books and pamphlets on meteorology and he left a library of 10,000 volumes. Struck with paralysis on 14 February 1900, he died at his home, 62 Camden Square, Camden Town, London, on 10 March, and was buried in Kensal Green cemetery.   A. M. CLERKE, rev. KATHARINE ANDERSON

Sources The Times (13 March 1900) • Nature, 61 (1899–1900), 475 • Quarterly Journal of the Royal Meteorological Society, 26 (1900), 154–9 • PRS, 75 (1905), 104–5 • H. S. Wallis, Symons's Monthly Meteorology Magazine (March 1900), 17–18 • E. G. Bilham, Quarterly Journal of the Royal Meteorological Society, 64 (1938), 593–9 • H. Mill, Meteorological Magazine, 73 (1938), 164–9 • J. Burton, 'Pen portraits of presidents: G. J. Symons', Weather, 48 (1993), 75–7 • b. cert. • m. cert. • d. cert.
Archives Meteorological Office, Bracknell, Berkshire, National Meteorological Library and Archives, corresp. | CUL, letters to Sir George Stokes • NHM, letters to Sowerby family
Likenesses photograph (in old age), repro. in Quarterly Journal of the Royal Meteorological Society, 154 • photograph (as young man), repro. in Mill, Meteorological Magazine, 164
Wealth at death £7004 14s. 8d.: resworn probate, May 1901, CGPLA Eng. & Wales (1900)

Symons, Jelinger Cookson (1809–1860), barrister and inspector of schools, was born on 27 August 1809 at West Ilsley, Berkshire, the son of the Revd Jelinger Symons (1778–1851) and his wife, Maria, eldest daughter of John Airey of Northumberland. Symons's father was vicar of Radnage, Buckinghamshire; he was an authority on botany and published Synopsis plantarum Insulis Britannicis indigenarum (1798).

Admitted at Trinity Hall, Cambridge, in 1827, Symons migrated to Corpus Christi College, where he graduated

BA in 1832. In the 1835 general election he finished last in the poll as one of three Liberal candidates who contested the two-seat Stroud constituency. Symons was called to the bar at the Middle Temple on 9 June 1843 and practised on the Oxford circuit. On 16 June 1845 he married Angelina, daughter of Edward Kendall of Austrey, Warwickshire.

In December 1837 Symons was appointed by the Home Office one of the nine assistant commissioners to the royal commission on the handloom weavers. Travelling extensively in France, Belgium, Switzerland, Austria, and Scotland, he gathered evidence of widespread depression in the native industry and warned of the effects of foreign competition. In November 1840 he was appointed one of the six sub-commissioners of the children's employment commission. He visited the Yorkshire coalfield, where he was appalled by the sexual immorality resulting from the intermixing of male and female labour underground. He also served as a tithe commissioner.

In 1847 Symons, R. R. W. Lingen, and Henry Robert Vaughan Johnson (1820–1899) were the three English commissioners responsible for the controversial Inquiry into the State of Popular Education in Wales which, based largely on one-sided evidence from Anglican landowners and clergy, denigrated the language, education, and morality of a country of predominantly Welsh dissenters. Symons's reports, dated March and September 1847, covered Brecknockshire, Cardiganshire, Radnorshire, and Monmouthshire.

On 11 February 1848 the marquess of Lansdowne, lord president of the council, appointed Symons as an inspector for poor-law schools, with responsibility for the west of England and Wales. To remove children from the contaminating influence of hereditary pauperism in workhouses, the inspectorate advocated the establishment of large separate residential district schools. Influenced by Pestalozzian ideas, Symons was heavily critical of contemporary rote learning. In his reports to the committee of the council on education, Symons was an indefatigable champion of agricultural training for pauper children. He constantly promoted the Quatt district school, started in Shropshire for that purpose by the Bridgnorth guardians' chairman, William Wolryche Whitmore (1787–1858). Symons was a hard-working and controversial inspector, often in acrimonious dispute with the central authorities and local boards of guardians. He had a particular interest in the education and moral reformation of young offenders. He visited numerous juvenile institutions, including the famous Mettray colony in France. As an expert witness to the 1852 select committee on criminal and destitute juveniles, he recommended the building of new reformatories funded by the state and parents.

In his best-known work, Tactics for the Times: as Regards the Condition and Treatment of the Dangerous Classes (1849), Symons articulated widespread contemporary fears in governing circles concerning an increase in criminal behaviour, owing to moral decline and disorder. He was critical of contemporary penal policy, but gave qualified support to capital punishment and transportation. As well as editing the *Law Magazine* (which amalgamated with the *Law Review* in 1856) and the *English Journal of Education*, Symons published more than twenty works on scientific and literary subjects. His paper at the British Association in 1856 on the revolution of the moon led to a celebrated dispute with William Whewell of Cambridge. Symons died unexpectedly of phthisis pulmonalis (a lung condition) at Great Malvern, Worcestershire, on 7 April 1860 and was survived by his wife and young family.

JOHN SHEPHERD

Sources J. E. Livingstone, 'Pauper education in Victorian England: organisation and administration within the new poor law, 1834–1880', PhD diss., London Guildhall University, 1993, U. Glas. L. · 'Select committee on criminal and destitute juveniles', *Parl. papers* (1852), 7.246–58, no. 515 · 'Royal commission on children's employment in mines and manufactories: first report', *Parl. papers* (1842), vol. 15, no. 380; vol. 16, no. 381 · 'Royal commission on handloom weavers', *Parl. papers* (1839), 42.511, no. 159 · M. J. Weiner, *Reconstructing the criminal: culture law and policy, 1834–1914* (1990) · *The Times* (12 April 1860) · D. Bythell, *The handloom weavers: a study in the English cotton industry during the industrial revolution* (1969) · Venn, *Alum. Cant.* · d. cert.
Archives priv. coll., William Wolryche Whitmore MSS · PRO, minutes of committee of council on education, ED 17 · PRO, government office corresp., MH 19 · PRO, corresp. between poor law commission and poor law unions, MH 12 · UCL, Chadwick MSS
Wealth at death under £800: probate, 7 May 1860, *CGPLA Eng. & Wales*

Julian Gustave Symons (1912–1994), by Wyndham Lewis, 1949

Symons, Julian Gustave (1912–1994), writer, was born on 30 May 1912 at Battersea, London, the youngest of five children of Morris Albert Symons (d. 1929), an auctioneer, and his wife, Minnie Louise, née Bull (d. 1964). Julian himself said he knew little about his father's family, who were Russian-Polish Jewish immigrants. Morris Symons was rarely affluent but had a taste for champagne and racehorses. Julian's brother Alphonse James Albert *Symons (1900–1941), twelve years his senior, was a celebrated aesthete and literary figure, whose best-known work is *The Quest for Corvo*.

Julian was educated at Wix's Lane School, Clapham, which he left at fourteen. After learning shorthand and typing, he worked as a clerk for an engineering firm. His real education came from reading—first Sherlock Holmes and Father Brown stories, then such ostensibly more sophisticated authors as Aldous Huxley, James Branch Cabell, Nietzsche, and Anatole France, borrowed from his brother's library. He subsequently repaid his brother's informal tutelage with a detached but affectionate biography, *A. J. A. Symons: his Life and Speculations* (1950).

Drawn into a fringe world of small highbrow journals and leftist splinter groups, Julian Symons wrote poems for the *Sunday Referee* and, as a rival to Geoffrey Grigson's *New Verse*, started a magazine, *Twentieth Century Verse*, with nine original subscribers. His poems, he recalled, were 'very political and romantic, full of young comrades scanning the horizon'. He considered himself a Trotskyist (and, even in mellower years, retained some regard for Trotsky as a failed genius) but afterwards, perhaps more accurately, 'a free-wheeling radical'. This early life among politicized intellectuals remained in his memory as an epitome

of the 1930s, which he said was 'not only a period in time but a way of thinking and feeling'.

On 25 October 1941 Symons married Kathleen Clark, whom he had met in the poet Roy Fuller's flat. They had two children: a daughter who predeceased him and a son. In the following year he was conscripted into the army, having failed to secure exemption as a conscientious objector to 'a capitalist war'. Service in the 57th tank regiment came to a premature end after a botched operation on his hand. While he was working as a copywriter for an advertising agency (a job he despised) Kathleen found an unpublished pre-war manuscript of his called *The Immaterial Murder Case*: it was really a joke, parodying various acquaintances and featuring an amateur detective named Teake Wood and a bland policeman called Bland. Although he never thought much of it ('slapdash', he said), they sent it to Gollancz, then one of the principal publishers of detective fiction. It appeared in 1945 to reviews sufficiently encouraging for Symons to feel that this was a vein worth pursuing.

Meanwhile Symons had succeeded George Orwell, on Orwell's recommendation, as a columnist for the *Manchester Evening News* at £9 a week. From then on, with Kathleen's support but to his mother's alarm, he decided to be a full-time writer. After producing two further lightweight detective stories, he realized that the crime novel could be used as a vehicle for social comment and psychological exploration, and wrote his first genuinely characteristic book, *The Thirty-First of February* (1950), about a man harried to death over a non-existent murder.

Although crime fiction rapidly became the staple of his bread-and-butter output, Symons continued throughout his life to write other kinds of books—biographies of Dickens, Carlyle, Poe, and Horatio Bottomley, accounts of the general strike and the Gordon relief expedition, a nostalgic evocation of his favourite period, *The Thirties: a Dream Revolved* (1960), and a brief autobiography, *Notes from another Country* (1972).

The mystery-writing world, however, occupied an increasing proportion of his energies. In 1972 Symons published a history of the genre, *Bloody Murder*, significantly subtitled 'From the detective story to the crime novel', a development which represented his own tastes and was exemplified in his novels. He was too good a craftsman not to take seriously the mystery element, with its concealments and revelations, but few of his books followed anything like the traditional pattern.

'The thing that absorbs me most', Symons said, 'is the violence behind respectable faces'. He was interested in ambiguous identities, weak personalities, pathological evil, preferably against a banal background of respectable suburbia or some pretentious housing estate, settings to which he brought a sharp descriptive eye and a caustic humour. Discernible too, though never emphasized, were traces of his youthful ideology. 'Up to 1943', he once said,

> almost all crime writers were right-wing. The story was about the removal of a piece of grit in the smooth running wheels of society … Things are very different today. The whole point of the story is the nature of those who are opposed to the social structure and show it by killing.

Symons's fiction had a wide range of forms and themes. *The Progress of a Crime* (1960) is a fairly straightforward puzzle. *The Man who Killed himself* (1967) is a black comedy about wife-murder. *The Players and the Game* (1972) is a trickily structured conundrum about serial killings. One of his last and best novels, *Death's Darkest Face* (1990), looks back to the 1930s, to a boy's first sexual disillusionment and half-understanding of the adult world, and to a disappearance which, in retrospect, was probably a murder.

Such variety may have limited Symons's popular appeal but it earned the respect of his peers. In 1958 he was elected chairman of the Crime Writers' Association, which he had helped, with John Creasey, to found, and from 1976 to 1985 was Agatha Christie's successor as president of the Detection Club. He won literary awards in Britain, America, and Sweden. In 1975–6 he enjoyed being a visiting professor at Amherst College, Massachusetts.

By now Symons was a genial, rather avuncular, impressively tall and bulky figure, sporting a grizzled goatee beard in memory of the crisp black beard he wore when young. Although a dedicated south Londoner, he lived latterly at Groton House, 330 Dover Road, Walmer, Deal, Kent, where he died of pancreatic cancer on 19 November 1994. He was cremated at Barham crematorium, Canterbury, on 30 November. He was survived by his wife.

ANTHONY LEJEUNE

Sources *The Times* (22 Nov 1994) · *The Independent* (23 Nov 1994) · personal knowledge (2004) · private information (2004) · J. Symons, *The thirties: a dream revolved* (1960) · J. Symons, *Bloody murder* (1972) · J. Symons, *Notes from another country* (1972) · J. M. Reilly, ed., *Twentieth-century crime and mystery writers* (1980)

Archives BL, literary papers and related material | Bodl. Oxf., letters to Jack Lambert and Catherine Lambert · Bodl. Oxf., corresp. with R. B. Montgomery · U. Leeds, Brotherton L., letters to *London Magazine* · U. Warwick Mod. RC, corresp. with Victor Gollancz

Likenesses W. Lewis, oils, 1949, priv. coll. [*see illus.*] · W. Lewis, three drawings (studies for portrait), priv. coll. · photographs, newspaper library

Wealth at death £83,013: probate, 1 May 1995, *CGPLA Eng. & Wales*

Symons, William Christian (1845–1911), decorative and fine artist, was the elder son of William Martyn Symons (*d.* in or after 1885) and his wife, Elizabeth White. His father, who came from Cornwall, ran a printing business in Vauxhall, Surrey, where Christian, his second child, was born in Bridge Street on 28 November 1845; there was one other son and two daughters. Symons was educated at a private school in Penzance and at Lambeth School of Art. In 1866 he studied for a short time at the Royal Academy Schools and was joint winner—with Walter William Ouless—of a silver medal for drawing from the antique. From the mid-1860s he exhibited at various London venues, including the Grosvenor Gallery, the Institute of Painters in Oil, and the Institute of Painters in Water Colours. In 1869 he exhibited for the first time at the Royal Academy, to which he contributed intermittently thereafter. In 1870 he became a Roman Catholic. In 1881 he joined the Society (from 1887 Royal Society) of British Artists, but seceded in 1888, with his friend James Abbott McNeill Whistler, and transferred his allegiance to the newly established New English Art Club. Symons's paintings included seascapes, landscapes, and genre subjects executed in a fluid, impressionistic style that suggests the influence of John Singer Sargent and may owe something to Whistler. For a time he worked at Newlyn, and though never a member of the so-called Newlyn school he wrote an account of it for the *Art Journal*. His flower paintings were seen by a contemporary as 'of particular excellence' (Robert Ross, *DNB*); he was also an accomplished portraitist.

Symons worked as an illustrator for journals that included *The Graphic*, *Strand Magazine*, and the *Magazine of Art*, and like many fine artists of his generation he had a parallel career as a decorative artist. He made designs for Doulton & Co., and in 1870 began a long association with the glass makers Lavers, Barraud, and Westlake, for whom he designed a number of stained-glass windows. He also established a long-standing association with the architect John Francis Bentley, for whom he painted—among other commissions—a frieze for a house in Sydenham and decorations for the church of St Luke, West Norwood, in 1885. He also designed and executed a number of decorations for John Francis Bentley's Westminster Cathedral, from 1899. This major project occupied him over several years; his contributions included mosaic decorations in the Holy Souls Chapel, mosaics of St Joan in the north transept and of St Edmund above the crypt altar, and a panel in the Sacred Heart Chapel. The mosaics were criticized for their over-emphasis of pictorial illusion, and the educationist and architect William Richard Lethaby complained about their sentimental vulgarity. But another contemporary critic noted that the 'unpleasant technique (*opus sectile*)' (*DNB*) used for some of the mosaics, on Bentley's instructions, did little justice to their 'fine design and courageous colour' (ibid.).

On 29 September 1885 Symons married Constance Cecilia (*b.* 1862/3), daughter of the late John Lancelot Davenport, a former manufacturer of Wildemlow, Derbyshire. Following his marriage he lived first in Hampstead but in 1890—perhaps because of his growing family—he moved to Sussex. His nine children—two daughters and seven sons—all survived him; the eldest, Mark Lancelot, also became a painter. Despite Ouless's view that Symons had 'more genius in his little finger than I have in my whole body' (Wood), Symons's success was uneven. Within artistic circles he was better known as a decorative artist and designer than as a painter, and he was little known to a wider public until the posthumous exhibition of his paintings and watercolours at the Goupil Gallery in 1912. He died at his home, Stocks House, Udimore, near Rye, on 4 September 1911, and was buried in Udimore; he was survived by his wife.

Symons's decorative work can be seen in a handful of public buildings; his paintings and graphic work can be found in several public collections, including those of Brighton Museum and Art Gallery; the British Museum, London; the Hugh Lane Municipal Gallery of Modern Art, Dublin; Leeds City Art Gallery; the Mappin Art Gallery, Sheffield; Manchester City Galleries; the National Portrait Gallery, London; Sunderland Museum and Art Gallery; Wolverhampton Art Gallery; and York City Art Gallery. An exhibition in Bath in 1994 brought his work as a fine artist to the attention of a new public; his work as a decorative artist and designer remains to be properly researched and evaluated.   CHARLOTTE BENTON

Sources *DNB* · C. Wood, *Life, light and colour: the rediscovery of William Christian Symons, 1845–1911* (1994) [exhibition catalogue, Victoria Art Gallery, Bath, 30 April – 25 June 1994] · **Archives** priv. coll. · **Wealth at death** £343 18s. 5d.: probate, 3 Nov 1911, *CGPLA Eng. & Wales*

Symons, Sir William Penn (1843–1899), army officer, was born at Hatt, east Cornwall, on 17 July 1843, the eldest son of William Symons (1818–1883) of Hatt and Caroline Anne Southwell, daughter of William Courtis of Plymouth. His father was recorder of Saltash (1846–71) and claimed descent from Simon, lord of St Sever, who came to England with William I. Educated privately, he was commissioned ensign in the 24th foot on 6 March 1863. He became lieutenant on 30 October 1866, and captain on 16 February 1878. On 13 February 1877 he married Jane Caroline (*d.* 16 March 1904), only daughter of Thomas Pinfold Hawkins of Edgbaston; they had no children.

Symons served with the 2nd battalion of his regiment in the operations against Sandile in Kaffraria in 1878, and in the Anglo-Zulu War of 1879. Owing to the destruction of the 1st battalion at Isandlwana, he obtained his majority on 1 July 1881. He went to India with his battalion in 1880, and on 30 September 1882 was appointed assistant adjutant-general for musketry in Madras. He served on the staff in the expedition to Burma in 1885, and afterwards organized a force of mounted infantry which won special praise from Lord Roberts. In 1889 he commanded the Burma column in the Chin-Lushai expedition, and was mentioned in dispatches. He was given the brevet rank of lieutenant-colonel (17 May 1886) and of colonel (1 July 1887), and the CB (14 November 1890).

On 31 January 1891 Symons was promoted regimental lieutenant-colonel, and commanded the 2nd battalion of the South Wales Borderers until 8 April 1893, when he became, by Lord Roberts's selection, assistant adjutant-general for musketry in Bengal. On 25 March 1895 he was appointed to command a second-class district in the Punjab as brigadier-general. He commanded a brigade in the Waziristan expedition of 1894–5, and in 1898 commanded a brigade in the Tochi field force, and afterwards the 1st division in the Tirah expedition. He was made KCB on 20 May 1898.

On 15 May 1899 Symons was appointed to the command of the troops in Natal, then numbering about 5000 men. War with the Transvaal republic was already anticipated, and in July Symons informed the governor that an increase of 1600 men was required to defend the colony against raids, and of 5600 men to defend it against an invasion. In the autumn reinforcements larger than he had asked for came from India and the Mediterranean, and on 20 September he was given the temporary rank of major-general. Symons, a 'fire-eater', rashly sent a brigade too far forward, to Dundee (70 miles north of Ladysmith), dangerously dividing the British forces. On 3 October Sir George White arrived and assumed the chief command in Natal. The Boer republics declared war on 10 October. The troops were organized as the 4th division of the South Africa field force, under Symons, who was made temporary lieutenant-general on 9 October. He was sent to Dundee, where four battalions, three batteries, and one cavalry regiment were encamped. There he was attacked on 20 October by about 4000 Boers with six guns under Lucas Meyer. These had come from the east, while two other bodies were approaching from the north and west, blocking the railway from Ladysmith. The guns of Meyer's force opened fire on the camp at daybreak from Talana Hill, 3 miles to the east of it. Symons decided to attack Meyer's force before Joubert's joined it. 'No genius—nor was he a fool' (Pakenham, 128), he used conventional battle tactics, including close-order infantry. He rashly sent his cavalry and mounted infantry away to cut off the enemy retreat: later, unsupported, they were forced to surrender. He led his infantry out to attack Talana Hill. Conspicuous with his red pennant carried by his aide-de-camp, Symons was shot in the stomach and mortally wounded. The hill was stormed and the Boers retreated. Two days later the British force, commanded by Major-General J. H. Yule, retreated towards Ladysmith, leaving behind at Dundee Symons and the other wounded men. Dying, Symons told the doctor, 'Tell everyone I died facing the enemy' (Pakenham, 147). He died at Dundee on 23 October 1899 and was buried on the 24th in the Anglican burial-ground there. A memorial window in Botusfleming church, near Saltash, Cornwall, was unveiled in October 1900.

E. M. LLOYD, rev. JAMES LUNT

Sources C. T. Atkinson, *The south Wales borderers, 24th foot, 1689–1937* (1937) • Lord Roberts [F. S. Roberts], *Forty-one years in India*, 2 vols. (1897) • H. D. Hutchinson, *The campaign in Tirah, 1897–1898: an account of the expedition against the Orakzais and Afridis* (1898) • L. S. Amery, ed., *The Times history of the war in South Africa*, 7 vols. (1900–09) • D. R. Morris, *The washing of the spears* (1966) • J. P. C. Laband, ed., *Lord Chelmsford's Zululand campaign, 1878–1879* (1994) • Burke, *Gen. GB* • G. Paton, F. Glennie, and W. P. Symons, eds., *Historical records of the 24th regiment, from its formation, in 1689* (1892) • *The Standard* (24 Oct 1899) • 'Correspondence relating to the defence of Natal', *Parl. papers* (1900), 56.49, Cd 44 • Boase, *Mod. Eng. biog.* • J. G. Bartholomew, ed., *The survey gazetteer of the British Isles* (1914) • T. Pakenham, *The Boer War* (1979)

Archives NAM, letters to Lord Roberts

Wealth at death £13,619 18s. 9d.: probate, 9 Jan 1900, CGPLA Eng. & Wales

Symson [Simson], **Andrew** (*c*.1638–1712), Church of Scotland minister and printer, was the youngest son of Andrew Symson (*b. c.*1601), author of a *Lexicon Anglo-Graeco-Latinum* (1658) and of several Biblical commentaries. Probably born in England, Symson attended the high school of Edinburgh and graduated MA from the University of Edinburgh on 19 July 1661. After teaching as Latin master at the high school of Stirling, he was licensed to preach by the bishop of Edinburgh on 23 January 1663 and dispatched to south-west Scotland to fill one of the numerous vacancies that had arisen following controversial legislation passed in 1662 obliging all established clergy to seek gentry patronage and episcopal collation.

Although Symson described his own entry to the parish of Kirkinner in Wigtownshire as 'so peaceable, so orderly & so generally assented to' that he encountered little initial opposition (Symson, *Tripatriarchicon*, preface, sig. A4r), Galloway remained the geographical focus for sectarian division and presbyterian nonconformist disaffection throughout the Restoration. In 1679, for example, when 'things were come to that hight, that the publick owning of us, was almost look'd on as a crime' (ibid., 6), Symson acknowledged his good fortune in receiving protection from one of his former fellow university students, Alexander Stewart, third earl of Galloway. As civil unrest continued, Symson was also obliged to supply the government with lists of the 'disorderly' in his parish, which in 1684 included the name of Margaret Lauchlinson, one of the notorious 'Wigtown Martyrs'. At the beginning of 1686 he left Kirkinner and was admitted to the parish of Douglas.

In response to Sir Robert Sibbald's appeal for assistance in the production of a Scottish atlas, Symson had earlier begun work on his 'Large description of Galloway'. Obliged to leave Douglas during the revolution of 1689, Symson settled at Dalclithick, in Glenartney, Perthshire, where he found 'time and leasure enough' in 1692 to revise the work (Symson, *Large Description*, preface), effectively producing a miniature statistical account of the region, recording, *inter alia*, supernatural phenomena alongside traditional farming methods. Although Sibbald

later acknowledged his satisfaction with Symson's 'full acount' (*Memoirs*, 76), it was not until 1823 that the work was first edited and published.

Relinquishing the ministry after the re-establishment of presbyterianism, Symson moved to Edinburgh where he set up a printing house in the Cowgate. Acknowledging that books were 'my delight, my heart, worth nectar and ambrosia', he claimed in 1696 that surrounded 'with walls of books on all sides, I dwell safe as in a fortress' (Symson, *Octupla*, preface). In 1699 he arranged the publication of the second edition of Sir George Mackenzie of Rosehaugh's *Laws and Customs of Scotland in Matters Criminal*, having formerly acted as Mackenzie's amanuensis when the work was first published in 1678. In addition to presenting books to the university libraries of Glasgow and Edinburgh, he welcomed the recent foundation of the Faculty of Advocates' library, promising that if he came across volumes of particular interest, he would 'have them transplanted from my obscure Nursery to your more publick and pleasant Garden' (Symson, 'Preface', sig. A2r). In 1705 Symson published his *Tripatriarchicon*, an epic poem of over 4000 lines which incorporated an allegorical account of his time in Galloway within its narrative of the lives of the three Jewish patriarchs. Together with the *Tripatriarchicon*, which he hoped would 'pass among the judicious for a tolerably good trotting poem' (Symson, *Tripatriarchicon*, sig. Av), Symson also published elegies on notable Galloway personages, including Mrs Janet Dalrymple, Lady Baldone, who later inspired the character of Lucy Ashton in Sir Walter Scott's novel, *The Bride of Lammermoor*, as well as on the murdered Archbishop Sharp, and on the vigorous anti-covenanter Sir George Mackenzie.

By his marriage to Jane Inglis, Symson had three sons, the second of whom, David, was appointed historiographer royal for Scotland in 1708, while the youngest, Matthias, worked with his father as a printer before becoming successively rector of Moorby and canon of Lincoln, as well as the author of several works on geographical, religious, and historical subjects. Symson died on 20 January 1712 in Edinburgh and was buried in Greyfriars churchyard. Following the publication of a catalogue entitled *Bibliotheca Symsoniana*, his collection of over 4000 books was sold by lottery and auction.

CLARE JACKSON

Sources W. J. Couper, 'Andrew Symson: preacher, printer and poet', *SHR*, 13 (1915–16), 47–67 • *Fasti Scot.*, new edn, vol. 3 • W. J. Couper, 'The Levitical family of Simson', *Records of the Scottish Church History Society*, 4 (1930–32), 119–37, 208–66 • A. Symson, *Tripatriarchicon, or, The lives of the three patriarchs, Abraham, Isaac and Jacob* (1705) • A. Symson, *A large description of Galloway*, ed. T. Maitland (1823) • *The memoirs of Sir Robert Sibbald (1641–1722)*, ed. F. Hett (1932) • A. Symson, 'Preface', in G. Mackenzie, *The laws and customs of Scotland in matters criminal*, 2nd edn (1699) • *Bibliotheca Symsoniana, or, Catalogue of the vast collection of books in the library of the late reverend and learned Mr. Andrew Symson* (1712) • 'Andrew Symson's Galloway', I. Donnachie and I. Macleod, *Old Galloway* (1974) • A. F. Hutchison, *History of the high school of Stirling* (1904) • A. Symson, ed., *Octupla: hoc est, octo paraphrases poeticae psalmi CIV authoribus totidem Scotis* (1696)

Archives NL Scot., 'A large description of Galloway'

Wealth at death extensive library: *Bibliotheca Symsoniana*

Synge, Charles (1789–1854), army officer, was born on 17 April 1789 in Rathmore, King's county, Ireland, the second son of George Synge of Rathmore and Mary, daughter of Charles McDonell of Newhall, co. Clare. He was commissioned cornet in the 10th hussars on 11 May 1809, becoming lieutenant on 8 February 1810 and captain on 12 August 1813. He served on the staff of General Ferguson and General Graham at Cadiz in 1810. He then became aide-de-camp to General Pack, and remained with him to the end of the war, being present at Busaco, Ciudad Rodrigo, Badajoz, Salamanca, Pyrenees, Nive, Nivelle, Orthez, and Toulouse. He distinguished himself especially at Salamanca, where he was severely wounded in the attack of the Arapiles. He exchanged to the 20th light dragoons on 12 November 1814, was made brevet major on 21 June 1817, and was placed on half pay in 1818. He was promoted lieutenant-colonel on 9 August 1821. In the latter part of his life he lived at Mount Callan, co. Clare, and was JP for that county. Synge was married to Caroline, daughter of P. Giles. He died in Dublin on 21 October 1854, leaving a son and three daughters.

E. M. LLOYD, *rev.* JAMES LUNT

Sources *GM*, 2nd ser., 43 (1855), 86 · Burke, *Gen. GB* · J. Paget, *Wellington's Peninsular War* (1990)

Synge, Edward (1614–1678), Church of Ireland bishop of Cork, Cloyne, and Ross, was born in Bridgnorth, Shropshire, on 14 August 1614, the eighth son of Richard Synge (*d.* 1631), tanner, a bailiff and alderman of Bridgnorth, and Alice (*bap.* 1574), a daughter of Richard Rowley of Rowley, Shropshire, and Anne, daughter of William King of Birmingham. His elder brother George *Synge, who had gone to Ireland in 1621 and became bishop of Cloyne, was probably responsible for arranging for Edward to be educated at Drogheda grammar school, which he entered about 1622. He entered Trinity College, Dublin, about 1624, but it is not known when he took his BA degree.

Synge was rector of Killary, diocese of Meath (where he succeeded his brother George) from 1638. In addition, from 1640 to 1661 he was prebendary of Aghadowey, co. Londonderry and from 1643 to 1661 rector of Drumachose and Tamlaghtfinlagen in the same county and diocese of Derry. In 1647 he became a minor canon of St Patrick's Cathedral, Dublin. In June 1647 commissioners appointed by the English parliament ordered that clergy of the Church of Ireland should cease to use the Book of Common Prayer. Synge, together with seventeen other Dublin clergymen, refused to use the liturgy of the *Directory for the Publique Worship of God* in its stead and in a petition on 9 July that year they pointed out that the Irish Act of Uniformity, upholding the prayer book, had not been repealed and that the Church of Ireland was independent of the Church of England and thus had the right to determine its own liturgical standards. Synge persuaded the auditor-general, Dr Gorges, to protect him from prosecution, and he retired to co. Cork, where in 1648 he secured the living of vicar of Inishannon, also holding those of vicar of Lustree, diocese of Dublin, and dean of Elphin.

Despite injunctions against him and complaints that he was in contempt of parliament he continued to use the Book of Common Prayer in co. Cork and was one of the episcopalian clergymen associated with the second earl of Cork.

After the Restoration, on 27 January 1661 Synge was consecrated bishop of Limerick and on 21 December 1663 was translated to the diocese of Cork, Cloyne, and Ross. His temporal estate, which had been seized during the Commonwealth, was restored to him on the same day. Maziere Brady described Synge as 'a learned and zealous preacher' who 'had one peculiar excellence … every one of his Congregation thought the Discourse particularly addressed to himself, and that the Preacher was privately instructing him in his Duty, and perswading him to the Practice of it' (Brady, 3.63).

Synge married Barbara (*d.* 1721), the eldest daughter of William Latham of New Place, co. Londonderry, and Barbara, daughter of Sir John Vaughan. They had seven children, five daughters and two sons. Of their sons, Samuel became dean of Kildare, and Edward *Synge (1659–1741) became bishop of Raphoe and archbishop of Tuam. The elder Edward Synge died on 22 December 1678, probably in Cork, where he was buried in Christ Church Cathedral.

MARIE-LOUISE LEGG

Sources W. M. Brady, *Clerical and parochial records of Cork, Cloyne, and Ross*, 3 vols. (1863–4) · J. B. Leslie, *Clogher clergy and parishes* (1929) · Burtchaell & Sadleir, *Alum. Dubl.* · K. C. S. Synge, *The family of Synge or Sing: pedigree tables of families bearing the above names* [1937] · T. C. Barnard, *Cromwellian Ireland: English government and reform in Ireland, 1649–1660* (1975)

Synge, Edward (1659–1741), Church of Ireland archbishop of Tuam, was born on 5 April 1659 at Inishannon, co. Cork, the second son of Edward *Synge (1614–1678), bishop of Cork, Cloyne, and Ross, and Barbara (*d.* 1721), the eldest daughter of William Latham of New Place, co. Londonderry, and Barbara, daughter of Sir John Vaughan. Edward's elder brother, Samuel Synge (*d.* 1708), became dean of Kildare. Edward Synge was educated at the diocesan school, Cork, and in July 1674 went to Christ Church, Oxford. At Oxford he met William Wake, later archbishop of Canterbury. Synge corresponded with Wake throughout his life, and wrote that he was 'one whose friendship I esteem above that of all other Men in the World' (Synge to Wake, 20 Aug 1703, Gilbert MS 28/5). He took his BA in 1677, although, possibly because his father was ill (he died in 1678), he did not take his MA at Oxford but returned to Trinity College, Dublin.

Synge's first preferment, from 1682 to 1686, was as rector of Laracor, Meath. In 1686 he became vicar of Holy Trinity, Cork, and prebendary of Christ Church, Cork, which he held until 1706. He was also, from 1691 to 1714, rector of Rathclarin, co. Cork, and held the parishes of Lackeen and Kilmaclenine and other parishes in Cloyne. In 1695 William King, archbishop of Dublin, put Synge's name forward for the diocese of Limerick. Synge expressed surprise that he had been considered, as he did

Edward Synge (1659–1741), by A. De L., 1738

not at that time know King well. However he did not get Limerick, and when he was offered the deanery of Derry in 1699 he refused it on the grounds that his elderly mother would not (or could not) accompany him. Shortly after, Ormond offered him the deanery of St Patrick's, Dublin, on behalf of the crown. However, there was a dispute between the crown and the chapter as to who had the right of presentation, and this was resolved only when King proposed that John Stearne should be dean and Edward Synge should become chancellor of St Patrick's and vicar of St Werburgh's. He was installed on 2 April 1705. As Archbishop King's vicar-general, Synge represented the chapter of St Patrick's at the convocation that met in 1713.

The following year, King recommended Synge for the diocese of Raphoe, describing him as a 'learned, prudent, pious and active man, the only objection against him was that he was a Whig' (*A Great Archbishop of Dublin, William King 1650–1729*, ed. C. S. King, 1906, 172). Synge was consecrated bishop in Dunboyne church on 7 November 1714 by William Palliser, archbishop of Cashel. In Raphoe he became involved in disputes about the legality of presbyterian marriages, and launched himself on a campaign of conversion through education. However he remained at Raphoe for only eighteen months. In 1715 his name had been put forward for the diocese of Meath, but George I was found to have nominated the bishop of Bangor. This greatly incensed the Irish bench of bishops, and the appointment of Edward Synge to the archbishopric of Tuam in June 1716 was in tacit atonement for what had been described as a public humiliation.

The see of Tuam needed a man who would provide leadership in what was a politically delicate situation. The previous incumbent, John Vesey, a tory who lived in co. Mayo, was thought to have been unsatisfactory. The appointment of a whig replacement was important because Dublin Castle was concerned at an apparent breakdown in municipal order in Galway and a possible taint of Jacobitism. Initially Synge resisted his removal from Raphoe, and he asked for time to consider. His reasons for hesitating were threefold: there was a great deal of work in Tuam (he was by then aged fifty-seven), a great deal of expense involved, and there was nowhere to live, as the archbishop's palace had been burnt during the civil war. Tuam had other drawbacks: there were few resident clergy and a number of parishes were impropriate. Further, there was a long-running problem about the *quarta pars episcopalis*, a quarter part of the tithes which had augmented the income of the archbishop and not that of the parish clergy. It had been proposed to abolish this custom in Tuam when Strafford was chief governor, but before the necessary legislation was enacted the documents were lost in the 1641 rising. The clergy had petitioned Archbishop Vesey for the money, but he had refused to accede. Synge was now advised to encourage the Tuam clergy to petition again for the abolition of the *quarta pars*, and to carry this through by act of parliament. Synge came to Tuam in January 1717 with good references: William King wrote to a Galway cleric: 'he is zealous to settle the *quarta pars* … he is a man of great knowledge, activity and honesty' (King to Fielding Shaw, 8 May 1716, TCD, MS 2533/228). It was proposed to spend the money released by the abolition of the *quarta pars* on supplementing the incomes of those clergy who were prepared to resign from plural livings. In this way Synge could provide for six parishes, four of which had not been served since the Reformation. He may have made some even more radical proposals, because King cautioned him, 'you have already parted with a great deal of what your archbishopric possessed which it haps your Successors will greatly grudge … I think it will be convenient to stop there at present' (King to Synge, 19 May 1719, TCD, MS 750/5/157–8). Synge built a new palace in Tuam, which was completed in 1723.

In the Irish House of Lords debates on the 1719 *Annesley* v. *Sherlock* case concerning supremacy of the English House of Lords as the final court of appeal for Ireland, Synge was said to have conducted himself 'with the greatest warmth and zeal for the Nation's Honour' (Nicholson to Wake, 11 July 1719, BL, Add. MS 6116). He told Wake that Ireland held 'all the courts, powers and jurisdictions' which England possessed (Synge to Wake, 17 Dec 1719, Gilbert MS 28/140). With Archbishop King, Synge was active in opposition to the Toleration Bill, introduced in the same year. In his speech on the bill he observed that although he had always believed in limited toleration for dissenters, he saw that religion was a continuing cause of strife, wars, and rebellions. He cited the existence of 180 sects in England which had flourished during the civil war, and warned that it should be not thought that these 'wild sects and parties' had gone. If the bill were passed, he said, not only the Church of Ireland but the civil state and even Christianity itself would be put at risk (Speech, BL, Add. MS 6117, 107–21). Both Synge and King were out of favour as a result of their opposition to the bill, and Synge feared that the career of his eldest son, also Edward *Synge (1691–1762), which he was anxiously fostering at that moment, would be jeopardized. Shortly afterwards, at the request of Archbishop King, Synge conducted a visitation on his behalf. King had recognized that, at that moment, advice from both himself and Synge on the state of religion in Ireland would offend his clergy, and he gave Synge careful instructions on the line to take. Even so, Synge's words were presented to the government as stirring up disaffection, though he gave a spirited account of himself to Dublin Castle.

Synge moved in an eclectic intellectual world: he met and wrote to Catholic priests and to theologians like Francis Martin of Louvain, with whom he corresponded about Christian unity. While acknowledging the difficulty that Catholics had in taking the oaths of allegiance and abjuration, which meant that they must be excluded from full rights in a civil society, the Synges, father and eldest son, believed that Catholics and dissenters should be prosecuted only if they posed a real danger to the state. Archbishop Synge attempted to draft a new oath of allegiance to meet the objections of both Roman Catholics and Quakers. During his life he published nearly sixty volumes of sermons and religious tracts. The appendix to his *Gentleman's Religion* (1698) is thought to have been written in answer to John Toland's *Christianity not Mysterious* (1696). To some extent Synge shared Toland's rationalism and deism, but he rebutted Toland's case that religion possessed no mysteries. He believed that mystery in religion must exist, even if we are unable to understand its nature. With William King, Berkeley, and Francis Hutcheson, Synge discussed the problem of innate perception, using the analogy of a blind man's understanding of shape and form. In October 1714 he preached a sermon at St Werburgh's which was attacked by the Catholic priest Cornelius Nary of Naas for advocating deism, and which resulted in a sharp exchange of pamphlets.

Synge married Anne (or Jane) Proude (d. 1723), daughter of Nicholas Proude, dean of Clonfert. They had five children: four sons, two of whom died about 1708, and one daughter. The two sons who survived were Edward *Synge (1691–1762), who became bishop of Elphin, and Nicholas, who became bishop of Killaloe and from whom the playwright John Millington Synge was descended. Anne Synge died in July 1723, just after the completion of the palace at Tuam. After her death, Synge told Wake that he proposed to 'remove to Tuam for good and all', and his son Edward later told Wake that his father had found great benefit from living there (E. Synge to Wake, 21 Oct 1723, TCD, MS 6201/1/208). Synge died in Tuam on 24 July 1741 and, although there was a family vault in Dublin, he was buried in the churchyard of the cathedral there. He spent the last months of his life relieving victims of the famine which had followed the hard winter of 1740–41, and on his death an elegy to his life and work was printed in *Faulkner's Dublin Journal*.   MARIE-LOUISE LEGG

Sources *Biographia Britannica, or, The lives of the most eminent persons who have flourished in Great Britain and Ireland*, 7 vols. (1747–66) · R. Mant, *History of the Church of Ireland*, 2 (1840) · J. Toland, *Christianity not mysterious*, ed. P. McGuinness, A. Harrison, and R. Keaney (1997) · D. Berman and A. Carpenter, eds., 'Eighteenth-century Irish philosophy', *The Field day anthology of Irish writing*, ed. S. Deane, A. Carpenter, and J. Williams, 1 (1991), 760–806 · P. Fagan, *Divided loyalties: the question of the oath for Catholics in the eighteenth century* (1997) · P. O'Regan, *Archbishop William King (1650–1729) and the constitution in church and state* (2000) · T. W. Moody and others, eds., *A new history of Ireland*, 9: *Maps, genealogies, lists* (1984) · K. C. S. Synge, *The family of Synge or Sing: pedigree tables of families bearing the above names* [1937] · Dublin corporation, Gilbert Library, Gilbert MSS · Nicholson to Wake, 11 July 1719, BL, Add. MS 6116 · E. Synge, speech, BL, Add. MS 6117

Archives Dublin City Archives, corresp. | BL, letters to William Wake, Add. MSS 6116, 6117, 6201 · Christ Church Oxf., letters to William Wake · Dublin corporation, Gilbert Library, Gilbert MSS · TCD, corresp. with William King · TCD, letters to William Wake **Likenesses** A. De L., oils, 1738, priv. coll. [*see illus.*]

Synge, Edward (1691–1762), Church of Ireland bishop of Elphin, was born in Cork on 18 October 1691, the eldest son of Edward *Synge (1659–1741), then vicar of Christ Church, Cork, and Jane (or Anne; d. 1723), daughter of the Revd Nicholas Proud (or Proude), also of Cork. His younger brother was Nicholas Synge, later bishop of Killaloe. He was educated in Cork by Mr Mulloy and entered Trinity College, Dublin, in 1706, and became BA in 1709; in 1710 he became a fellow of the college, and in the same year junior dean. His father became archbishop of Tuam in 1716, and the younger Synge was therefore well placed for advancement. In 1719 he was given the living of St Audoen's, Dublin, which carried with it a prebendal stall in St Patrick's Cathedral. In the following year he married Jane Curtis (d. 1737), daughter of Robert Curtis of Roscrea, co. Tipperary, MP for Duleek, and Sarah Curtis. Having been made provost of Tuam in 1726, he was consecrated by his father as bishop of Clonfert in 1730, and in 1731 was translated to Cloyne. In 1733 he was again translated, to Ferns and Leighlin, and in 1740 he went to Elphin where he remained until his death.

Like his father, Synge took a robust view of the penal laws, which he criticized on the grounds that they encouraged a 'furious and blind zeal for religion' which could disturb the civil state (E. Synge, *The Care of Toleration Considered*, 2nd edn, 1726, 2). In his sermon to the joint houses of parliament in 1725 on the text 'Compel them to come in', he made a clear distinction between legislation to ensure public order and laws controlling private worship. Rather than compelling Catholics to become protestants by law, he advocated the education of Catholic children in protestant schools. This sermon resulted in a pamphlet controversy with Stephen Radcliffe, vicar of Naas, in which Synge, in his response to Radcliffe, set out a form of oath of allegiance suitable for Catholics loyal to the crown.

In the 1720s Synge was a member of the group who were close to Lord Molesworth, a follower of Shaftesbury.

George Berkeley, whose lectures Synge had attended at college, was another member of this circle. It was probably here that Synge met the Presbyterian minister Francis Hutcheson, who had been invited to Dublin in 1720 to start a dissenting academy. Hutcheson acknowledges a deep debt to Synge's critique of the text in his *Inquiry into the Original of our Ideas of Beauty and Virtue* (1726), and, from Hutcheson's philosophical writing and Synge's correspondence, it is clear that they shared many attitudes.

Politically Synge was active: Chesterfield, as lord lieutenant in 1746, described him as one of the most able members of the Irish House of Lords. With Lord Roden he involved himself in the regulation of the linen trade. During the money bill dispute of 1753, he took the side of the speaker, Henry Boyle, in opposition to Primate Stone and the lord lieutenant, the duke of Bedford. Synge was intellectually lively and extremely well read, and had a considerable library. He was also musical and made a strong impression on Handel, who described him as 'a Nobleman very learned in Musick', when on his visit to Dublin in 1742 (Luckett, 132). Synge attended the first performance of *The Messiah* and wrote a warm appreciation of the work to Handel, suggesting a sequel, *The Penitent.*

Synge was wealthy through his marriage settlement and because of a life interest he inherited in the estate of his uncle, Samuel Synge, dean of Kildare. He himself acknowledged that he was also prosperous through his active management of his church estates. He was an improving farmer and, as a member of the linen board, he invested in flax seed, looms, and spinning-wheels to encourage the manufacture of cloth in co. Roscommon. Like his father before him he devoted part of his wealth to the improvement of the ministry of the Church of Ireland in his diocese. In Ferns and Leighlin he justified the collection of tithes on dry cattle (tithe agistment) by using the moneys raised to encourage a resident clergy. In Elphin he built a new palace (now in ruins) and new churches. However, his financial judgement was not always wise, and he became involved in a parliamentary enquiry into charitable funds in 1760 because of his rather lax management of a trust.

Synge and his wife suffered the loss in childhood or early youth of all their children, except the youngest, Alicia; Jane Synge died in December 1737 when Alicia was five years old. It is through Synge's letters to Alicia, written between 1746 and 1752, that we know him best. They show him as a loving father, anxious both for his daughter's health and for her education and manners as the only child of a rich man.

Synge died at his house in Kevin Street, Dublin, on 27 January 1762. He was buried in the Synge vault in St Patrick's Cathedral. MARIE-LOUISE LEGG

Sources *The Synge letters: bishop Edward Synge to his daughter Alicia,1746–52*, ed. M.-L. Legg (Dublin, 1996) • K. C. S. Synge, *The family of Synge or Sing: pedigree tables of families bearing the above names* [1937] • [C. Varley], *The modern farmer's guide by a real farmer* (1768) • *The autobiography and correspondence of Mary Granville, Mrs Delany*, ed. Lady Llanover, 1st ser., 3 vols. (1861); 2nd ser., 3 vols. (1862) • R. Luckett, *Handel's 'Messiah': a celebration* (1992) • F. Hutcheson, *An inquiry into the original of our ideas of beauty and virtue*, 2nd edn (1726) • T. W. Moody and others, eds., *A new history of Ireland*, 9: *Maps, genealogies, lists* (1984) • marriage settlement, NL Ire., PC 344(7) • *Register of St Patrick's* (1907) • W. Monck Mason, *The history of St Patrick's* (1820)
Archives Representative Church Body Library, Dublin, letters | NRA, priv. coll., letters to Lord Clanbrassil • PRO, letters to Lord Clanbrassil • TCD, letters to his daughter Alicia

Synge, George (1594–1652), Church of Ireland bishop of Cloyne, was born in Bridgnorth, Shropshire, the eldest son of Richard Synge (*d.* 1631), a Bridgnorth alderman and bailiff, and Alice (*bap.* 1574), daughter of Richard Rowley of Rowley, Shropshire, and Anne King of Birmingham. Edward *Synge (1614–1678) was a younger brother. George Synge was the first member of the family to live in Ireland, and the first of a dynasty of Church of Ireland clerics. He entered Balliol College, Oxford, as a commoner in February 1610, and took his BA on 21 October 1613 and MA on 12 June 1616. He subsequently took his DD at Oxford. About 1621 he went to Ireland, possibly at the invitation of Christopher Hampton, archbishop of Armagh, to whom he became chaplain and vicar-general. He was rector of Donoughmore and held the rectory of Killary, Meath, from 1621 to 1638. In 1622 he married Anne (*d.* 1641), daughter of Francis Edgeworth, clerk of the hanaper, in Dublin. From 1628 to 1635 he held successively the rectories of Loughgilly and Mansfieldtown, in the diocese of Armagh, and in 1635 became dean of Dromore, which he held together with the rectories of Dromballyrainey and Seapatrick.

Synge was involved in the controversy surrounding the Irish Jesuit William Malone, whose work *A Jesuit's Challenge* was published in 1623 and asserted the antiquity of the Roman Catholic church. Archbishop James Ussher responded in 1624 with *An Answer to a Challenge by a Jesuit in Ireland*, and Malone countered with *A Reply to Mr James Ussher his Answere …* (1627). Ussher was dissuaded from replying and left it to Synge, Roger Puttock, and Josiah Hoyle to respond on his behalf. Synge wrote *A Rejoynder to the Reply Published by the Jesuits* in 1632, dedicated to Lord Deputy Falkland, to whom he had been chaplain.

On 11 November 1638 Synge was consecrated bishop of Cloyne at Drogheda by Archbishop Ussher. With the outbreak of the 1641 rising, when Synge's property in Cloyne and elsewhere in Ireland was plundered, he fled to Dublin for protection. Before the rebellion he was a wealthy man; the value of his property taken from him in 1641 totalled over £5000. His family sailed to England, but Anne Synge, her mother, and five of the Synges' children were drowned at sea in their flight, among them their daughter Margaret, who had married Michael Boyle, dean of Cloyne and later archbishop of Armagh. In 1644 Synge and Boyle were employed by the lord lieutenant, the marquess of Ormond, in a failed bid to dissuade the earl of Inchiquin, protestant commander in Munster, from negotiating with the English parliament. In February 1644 Synge was sworn a member of the Irish privy council, and in the same year a commissioner for the lord lieutenant's accounts. In 1648 he once again negotiated with Inchiquin, who had now declared his support for the king.

Synge married his second wife, Elizabeth Stevens, about

1645. He was nominated to succeed John Maxwell as archbishop of Tuam on the latter's death in 1646, but because of the war was never instituted. He received no further preferment in Ireland, while his support for the royalist Ormond led to his personal and ecclesiastical possessions being sequestered by the English parliament. He kept up his links with Bridgnorth, having been made a burgess there in 1628. He had returned to Bridgnorth by the time of his death in 1652, and was buried there in St Mary Magdalene churchyard on 31 August. The inscription on his tomb recorded that he was 'A very grave and learned man, especially in controversial theology, and in the knowledge of each law. Moreover, of a rather tall stature, beautiful figure and well-bred manner of life' (Synge, xii). He was survived by his second wife. His eldest son, Francis, by his first marriage, became archdeacon of Ross; of the two sons of his second marriage, Richard became archdeacon of Cork while George became prebendary of Kilbrogan, Bandon, co. Cork.   MARIE-LOUISE LEGG

Sources K. C. S. Synge, *The family of Synge or Sing: pedigree tables of families bearing the above names* [1937] · R. B. Knox, *James Ussher archbishop of Armagh* (1967) · Foster, *Alum. Oxon.* · W. M. Brady, *Clerical and parochial records of Cork, Cloyne, and Ross*, 3 vols. (1863–4) · R. Mant, *History of the Church of Ireland*, 2 vols. (1840)

Synge, (Edmund) John Millington (1871–1909), playwright, was born on 16 April 1871 at Newtown Little, Rathfarnham, south of Dublin, the youngest child of John Hatch Synge (1823–1872) and Kathleen, *née* Traill (1838–1908). The pervasive religious gloom of the household was not lessened by the father's falling a victim of smallpox, and his burial on the youngest son's first birthday. The boy was sickly as an infant and, despite a rigorous and self-imposed regimen of hillwalking and other outdoor activities, Synge remained in poor health throughout his short life.

Family background and education John Hatch Synge's family were of English origin, but had been long established in Ireland, where they distinguished themselves as ministers and prelates of the established Church of Ireland. The Traills came from Orkney, through the east of Scotland into co. Antrim where they were settled in the late eighteenth century. Both sides of Synge's pedigree were stoutly evangelical: his grandfather John Synge (1788–1845) had participated in the fervent activities which led to the foundation (in Dublin city and nearby co. Wicklow) of the movement later known as the Plymouth Brethren. His uncle Alexander Hamilton Synge (1820–1872) served as a proselytizing minister on the Aran Islands in the 1850s and was a posthumous influence on his nephew's book, *The Aran Islands* (1907). J. M. Synge's maternal grandfather, the sternly anti-Catholic Robert Traill (1793–1847), died at Schull in west co. Cork (where he was rector) as a result of his valiant efforts to aid famine victims. His widow, Mrs Anne Traill, *née* Hayes (d. 1890), lived for the last two decades of her life in a double household which included her daughter Mrs Kathleen Synge and the young J. M. Synge (as he invariably signed himself).

With the death of J. H. Synge in April 1872, the widowed Mrs Synge moved closer to Dublin city, renting a house in

(Edmund) John Millington Synge (1871–1909), by John Butler Yeats, *c.*1905

Orwell Park, beside her mother. The two houses, soon linked by a communicating door, became the joint home first for an extended family of Traills and Synges and, after 1884 of Traills, Synges, and Stephenses. J. M. Synge's sister Annie (1863–1949) married Henry Francis Colcough Stephens (1856–1935) who came to exercise considerable influence in the family as Mrs Synge's—and subsequently J. M. Synge's—legal adviser. When, at Harry Stephens's instigation, the family moved to Kingstown (now Dún Laoghaire) in October 1890, the double home was reproduced in nos. 31/29 Crosthwaite Park East. A third move in July 1906 brought Synge and his mother to Glendalough House (a semi-detached property on nearby Adelaide Road) and the Stephens in-laws to Silchester House just up the hill.

Against the sustained compulsory intimacy of this domestic arrangement, the young Synge also experienced the steady disappearance of relatives, notably siblings. His eldest brother, Robert Anthony Synge (1858–1943), emigrated to the Argentine to join Traill kinsmen in ranching and other business activities. Edward Synge (1859–1939), though a comparative stay-at-home, worked for many years as a land agent in the Irish countryside, a profession of which J. M. Synge did not always approve. Samuel Synge (1867–1951), with whom J. M. Synge shared a room while they were growing up, became a medical missionary in China.

Synge's education was spasmodic, involving intermittent attendance at Mr Harrick's Classical and English School (Leeson Street, Dublin) and the Bray School (co. Wicklow). Private tutors were employed, again intermittently. The most salient factor of his education was his not being sent—for reasons either of health or expense—to the Rathmines School, an establishment run somewhat on the lines of Rugby School where all his brothers, his brother-in-law, and their friend the polymath John Joly (1857–1933) were pupils. At Rathmines in the 1860s and 1870s, a generation of Dublin protestant professional men were educated for lucrative survival in a changing society. Synge knew none of this camaraderie, instead he was taught by his mother and maternal grandmother, with occasional tutoring from members of the Rathmines staff who visited the Synge/Traill household.

The Synge family's prosperity had been steadily eroded throughout the nineteenth century. In 1797 Synge's great-great-grandfather the shadowy John Hatch (MP for Swords in 1769 and again in 1783) died. His son-in-law Francis Synge (1761–1831) had on marriage come into an extensive property in co. Wicklow, part of which had been acquired by Hatch in the course of various (and perhaps nefarious) business activities. Francis Synge left Glanmore Castle to his son John Synge (1788–1845; named after Hatch, for John was not a traditional name among the Synges), who died suddenly at the outbreak of the famine. The estate had been poorly managed and the generation which included J. M. Synge's father (a younger son, possibly the youngest by his father's first marriage) found themselves obliged to live as tenants of the encumbered estates court in what had come to be regarded as an ancestral home. The family's links with Glanmore were further stretched with the remarriage in 1879 of a recently widowed member (to a member of the exclusive wing of the Plymouth Brethren).

For the Synges, progressive dispossession of their Wicklow estates functioned as a slow-motion Edenic fall, with J. M. Synge the only one of his family who could not personally remember the age of ownership and the illusion of security. His mother's annual holidays at Greystones on the Wicklow coast, lasting until 1891 (when her youngest son reached the age of twenty), served to emphasize protestant exclusiveness while also encroaching on territory which could no longer be owned. The young Synge does not appear to have been much attracted by evangelicalism, though he did visit alienated Glanmore on several occasions: the result was a complex of desires and renunciations which eventually exploded in the prose works and plays for which he is remembered as a leading figure of the Irish literary revival.

Meanwhile at Trinity College, Dublin, where he pursued an undistinguished career between 1888 and 1892, his range of subjects (which included Gaelic and Hebrew) led some to think he might follow in the footsteps of his uncle Alec or other missioners to the general Irish populace. He graduated BA on 15 December 1892. In practice, his commitment during his undergraduate years had been to music, which he studied assiduously at the Royal Irish Academy of Music, socially and religiously a far more open institution than Trinity. His ambition to be a professional musician, encouraged by a prize (1892) in counterpoint and by the support of a cousin (Mary Synge), led to his travelling to Germany in 1893.

Early travels and early writings Between 1893 and 1903 Synge divided his time between Ireland and continental Europe, with Paris as his main exile station from January 1895 to March 1903. Germany, however, came first. Staying in a protestant guest house near Coblenz, and visiting Wurzburg, he gradually abandoned plans for a musical career principally because he was highly nervous of public performance. He read Ibsen, and began to write. His early continental writings were awkward exercises in sentimental decadence, though persistent attempts to mix lyric verse and romantic narrative (in imitation of Dante's *Vita nuova*) led to his appreciation of dramatic arrangement, transition, and other technical matters.

Among the early and immature writings, a play (known as *When the Moon has Set*, and difficult to date precisely) is remarkable for bringing together echoes of the best-forgotten Hatch side of the family history and pompous dialogue between a young woman of deep piety and a young man returned to Wicklow from Paris. Thematically, this had personal origins. The use of dialect by minor characters in the play anticipates *In the Shadow of the Glen* (1903), while the general movement of the plot is to reverse-write Ibsen's *Ghosts* (1881) by overcoming a guilty past through a quasi-pagan marriage.

Synge's late teens and early twenties were dominated by an infatuation with Cherie Marie Louise Matheson (1870–1940), known as Cherrie, daughter of a near neighbour in Kingstown who was a leader among Ireland's Plymouth Brethren. Cherrie Matheson was a more complex figure than the pious girl next door; she painted and exhibited watercolours, and featured at least once in the Paris salons. A sceptic from childhood in religious belief, Synge pursued a hopeless quest for married love, proposing to Cherrie on several occasions only to be repeatedly rejected, mainly on grounds of spiritual incompatibility. Synge's final rejection in the Matheson household occurred in early May 1898. Cherrie Matheson's short 1924 memoir ('John Synge as I knew him', *Irish Statesman*, 5 July 1924, 532–4), while discreet on their emotional or sexual relations, indicates that they shared intelligent interests in the theatre, and in the somewhat radical magazine *Dana* (1904–5). Although she married on 23 November 1902 and moved to South Africa, the latter reference establishes the survival of cordial relations after the final disappointment of Synge's hopes.

The Aran Islands Seeming to follow advice given him by W. B. Yeats two years earlier in Paris, Synge went to the Aran Islands for the first (10 May – 25 June 1898) of five annual visits between 1898 and 1902. Here his academic study of Gaelic bore fruit, and he quickly learned the colloquial language, living mainly with fishing families and spending his time listening to folklore, local history, and the calamities of seafaring life. In May–June 1898 he picked up the basic ingredients of three plays—the story of the father-killer protected by local people (*The Playboy of the Western World*, 1907), the legends of a miraculous well (ironically exploited in *The Well of the Saints*, 1905), and the stoical expressive grief of women robbed of their menfolk by Atlantic storms (*Riders to the Sea*, 1904). On his way back to Dublin he called (at Yeats's instigation) at Coole Park, Augusta Gregory's Galway mansion. On 12 May 1899 Synge attended a production by the Irish Literary Theatre of Yeats's *The Countess Cathleen*.

Always a keen if unsystematic note-taker, Synge had begun to write about island life even before he had moved out of the tiny hotel where he spent his first few days. *The Aran Islands* (completed by November 1901, but not published until April 1907) is the great prose manifesto of the Irish literary revival, celebrating a primitive but also transitional way of life, responding to a dying language, building friendship among ordinary people. It opens with a recollection of the Revd A. H. Synge, who had ministered there forty-five years earlier, but the book succeeds in implying a personal story also, an understated autobiography of spiritual regeneration. Behind the façade of Yeatsian Celticism, Synge was a reader of Nietzsche and Schopenhauer, Darwin, Marx, and Ibsen. While staying on Inis Meáin (the middle island of the group), on the night of Monday–Tuesday 25–26 September 1899 he dreamed of Alfred Dreyfus, the disgraced (but wholly innocent) French officer who had been a victim of rampant antisemitism.

Synge's Parisian circles included Irish political activists such as Maud Gonne, Arthur Lynch, Stephen MacKenna, and also—at some distance from these—the Celtic scholar Richard Best. Though he joined Gonne's *Association irlandaise* at the beginning of 1897, he distanced himself rapidly. According to MacKenna, Synge 'gently hated' Gonne, who was a rabid anti-Dreyfusard and a lifelong antisemite. MacKenna was transforming himself from journalist into Neoplatonic scholar, and it is in this frame of reference that the friendship of the two men (with the Celticist Richard Best also) should be regarded. Less easily classified are the women of Synge's acquaintance on the continent, though a striking proportion of them practised their religion diligently while he wavered but little from humanist scepticism.

Paris and Aran constituted the outer polarities of Synge's existence, though he also travelled in Italy (February–May 1896) and Brittany (April 1899).

But the centre of his career as a successful writer was to be Dublin and the place which recurred in both his writings and his recreations was Wicklow. From 1892 onwards his mother transferred her holiday base inland from Greystones to an area south of Glanmore Castle, on the edge of what had been the great Synge property. In a series of rented summer accommodations (of which Castle Kevin, a biggish house but not a castle, was the most notable), Synge returned annually to a society in which the vestiges of protestant landlord splendour survived amid more recent evidences of land war and Parnellite agitation.

The mature drama During summer 1902 Synge got to work on *In the Shadow of the Glen*, while staying with his mother and some Stephens relatives in Tomriland (a modest farmhouse, not far from Castle Kevin). By the second week of October he was able to show Yeats and Gregory versions of two one-act plays, *In the Shadow of the Glen* and *Riders to the Sea*. The following month he left the Aran Islands for the last time (having spent just over three weeks on Inis Oírr).

Drama virtually monopolized the rest of Synge's life. He abandoned his Parisian flat in the rue d'Assas in March 1903. On 8 October *In the Shadow of the Glen* was first produced by the Irish National Theatre Society at the Molesworth Hall in Dublin and *Riders to the Sea* at the same venue (a church hall) on 25 February 1904. What became known as the Abbey Theatre was formally established in 1904, with a revival of *In the Shadow* on the second night, 28 December 1904. The latter play excited opposition in Irish Catholic/nationalist circles, because it imported Parisian decadence by suggesting that a farmer's wife (believing herself a widow) might go off with a tramp. From 3 June to 3 July 1905 Synge toured the congested districts of the west of Ireland with the artist Jack Yeats, writing a series of articles for the *Manchester Guardian*.

The remainder of Synge's career was embittered by ideological conflict between the playwright and his public, which was not eased by the production of *The Well of the Saints* (his first three-act play) in February 1905 and was greatly exacerbated when *The Playboy of the Western World* was given its première in January 1907. A week of nightly rioting in the theatre did not deter the company from completing the advertised schedule of performances. While W. B. Yeats's defence of Synge and his new play was successful, the aesthetic reservations of some friendly commentators (notably the art curator Ellen Duncan) deserve respect. Two other plays—*The Tinker's Wedding* (two acts, 1903, but never produced in the author's lifetime) and *Deirdre of the Sorrows* (three acts, unfinished at his death)—complete a small but highly distinguished canon which gave the Abbey its first critical success and its general 'flavour' as Ireland's national theatre. On 22 September 1905 Synge had become a director (with Gregory and Yeats) of the limited liability company.

As a writer Synge brooked no interference. But he readily acknowledged the contribution of his fellow directors, of stage directors and producers, actors and actresses, even fellow writers (at a distance). 'All art is a collaboration', he wrote in the preface to *The Playboy* (1907). Despite various conflicts within the movement, he remained on friendly terms with William and Frank Fay, and Padraic Colum. In managerial matters he favoured 'democracy', at least in small matters, an attitude which made him more popular with the company than his haughtier fellow board members. His particular closeness was with Mary Allgood (1887–1952), known as Molly Allgood and acting as Máire O'Neill, who had a walk-on part in the first production of *The Well of the Saints*.

One side of their courtship can be traced in *Letters to Molly* (1971); her letters to Synge were evidently destroyed in one of the several domestic archival purgings which occurred after his death—and possibly as late as the 1920s. Differences of age, class, and religion (though neither was devout) made for a turbulent relationship. He was prone to jealousy, she possessed in full the skittishness of youth. On several occasions, wedding plans were seriously discussed, and the news even broken to Synge's mother, who reacted with unexpected sympathy. Synge's deteriorating health proved an insurmountable obstacle, though it can hardly be accepted as the only reason for their not marrying.

Illness and death Synge's childhood ailments had not abated as he entered puberty and advanced towards adulthood. His athleticism disguised an underlying frailty, and on 11 December 1897 he had undergone surgery to have swollen glands in his neck removed. This experience provided the basis for an uncharacteristically revealing essay, 'Under ether', first published in the posthumous *Works* of 1910. In August 1907, eight months after *The Playboy* riots, Synge was told peremptorily by a young medical man, Oliver St John Gogarty, to have these glands—once again swollen—removed without delay: further surgery took place in September. Gogarty's diagnosis (of Hodgkin's disease) has been generally accepted, though it may not have accorded with the patient's own opinion of the case. There is evidence (not least in his rewriting of Ibsen's *Ghosts*) to suggest that Synge feared he had either inherited or contracted syphilis.

The surgery of September 1907 was followed by a severe bout of asthma, which forced Synge to abandon a convalescent holiday in co. Kerry. His lesser writings were now appearing in print, journalism for the most part, but also *The Tinker's Wedding* (published under a new imprint, Maunsel & Co., December 1907). Inside the Abbey company, the conflicts first articulated at the time of *In the Shadow of the Glen* had intensified, principally concerning the theatre's relationship to nationalist sensibility. On 13 January 1908 the Fay brothers resigned, but Synge's response was to commit himself more fully to the programme of mixed productions, native and foreign, which characterized the management at this point. Despite his origins among the leisured classes, and his poor health, he was an active contributor to the theatre's ancillary business. In February 1908 he directed Augusta Gregory's translation of *Teja* by Hermann Sudermann, and in April *The Rogueries of Scapin*, her version of Molière's play. On 2 February he took rooms in Rathmines in preparation for marriage, but by the end of April he was once again in hospital. Between 30 April and 6 July he remained in Dublin's Elpis Nursing Home (in effect a private hospital) where on 5 May inoperable tumours in the abdomen were discovered. A revised version of *The Well of the Saints* was produced at the Abbey on 14 May with Molly Allgood now established in the role of the teasing Molly Byrne.

Synge was at work on a new play, to be known as *Deirdre of the Sorrows*. Drafts were presented to the Abbey in November 1907, and his serious meditation on the saga material had been well under way in 1900–01. Superficially it stands apart from all his other drama, most obviously in its mythic or proto-historical setting, its brocaded, heavy, sensuous cadences, and its highly self-referential mood of fatalistic tragedy. The title role was written for Molly Allgood, and the heroine's entrapment between an ageing king and an impetuous warrior clearly reflects Synge's personal concerns. Produced after his death in a version completed by Yeats, Gregory, and

Allgood, it has won a degree of respect but few critical plaudits.

After the unsuccessful surgery of May 1908, Synge spent two months in Elpis and six weeks further convalescence at his sister's home before departing for Germany on 6 October. His mother died on 26 October, but he was unable to undertake a rapid journey home for the funeral. On 2 February 1909 he re-entered Elpis for the last time. On 13 February he signed his last will and testament, establishing a trust to pay Molly Allgood £80 p.a. for life (reducing to £52 in the event of her marriage). His royalties he left to two nephews, Edward Stephens and Edward Hutchinson Synge. J. M. Synge died at Elpis, Lower Mount Street, Dublin, in the morning of 24 March 1909. He was buried in Mount Jerome general graveyard, Harold's Cross, Dublin.

The literary estate and posthumous reputation Synge's relative poverty gave to the question of copyright a particular urgency. In the United States, the lawyer and art patron John Quinn looked after his interests by arranging for limited edition publication to secure US rights. In Ireland, Maunsel & Co. (managed by the erratic George Roberts) had begun to move towards a collected *Works*. Disputes between Roberts and Yeats, with the Synge family occasionally contributing, delayed the appearance of a four-volume edition until late in 1910. The inclusion of Synge's 1905 articles for the *Manchester Guardian* was enforced against Yeats's advice: manuscript evidence also indicates that the very revealing essay, 'Under ether', may have been heavily edited for publication. Thus in various ways Synge's reputation was energetically shaped and reshaped within months of his death. Rumours also persisted about the cause of death: Yeats wrote to Augusta Gregory on 11 January 1912 that:

> one which seems to be believed as a matter of course is that Synge died of disease contracted by living an immoral life, I was told the other day that everybody knew that the story about cancer was invented to hide this.

After the First World War efforts (mainly by E. H. Synge) to tidy and expand Synge's canon were frustrated by the deteriorating political situation in Ireland. The gradual stabilization of the Irish free state saw slow recognition of his work as a classic contribution to a new canon. Daniel Corkery's ebullient *Synge and Anglo-Irish Literature* (1931) remains valuable as a memorial to this mode of thought. Alongside this, rumours concerning the playwright's death (and/or his moral condition) had persisted. In 1932 Samuel Synge (a qualified doctor) published a limpid memoir in the form of *Letters to my Daughter*, which sought to deny the diagnosis of cancer and yet failed to specify any other cause of death. Designed to integrate Synge into an adjusted family tradition incorporating approval of limited Irish independence, Edward Stephens's extensive biographical research was incorporated into D. H. Greene and E. M. Stephens, *J. M. Synge, 1871–1909* (first published 1959, revised edn 1989). A new and scholarly four-volume *Collected Works* (ed. Saddlemyer and Robin Skelton) was published in 1962–8, and a densely annotated two-volume *Collected Letters* (ed. Saddlemyer) in 1983–4.

Inclined to arrange his life in dramatic form—dialogue between opposing positions, movement between contrasting scenes—Synge avoided dramatic action or substance to a remarkable extent. In the kindly words of the poet James Stephens, 'his approach to knowledge was—to be silent'. Apart from his perpetual ill health, he remained in Yeats's words 'unsatisfied' and a virgin.

W. J. McCormack

Sources *The collected letters of John Millington Synge*, ed. A. Saddlemyer, 2 vols. (1983–4) · A. Carpenter, ed., *My uncle John: Edward Stephen's life of J. M. Synge* (1974) · W. J. McCormack, *Fool of the family: a life of J. M. Synge* (2000)
Archives Ransom HRC, corresp. and literary papers · TCD, corresp. and literary papers | NL Ire., letters, mainly to W. G. Fay · NL Ire., letters to Max Meyerfeld
Likenesses R. Gregory, chalk drawing, 1904, NG Ire. · H. Oakley, drawing, 1905, Hugh Lane Gallery, Dublin · J. B. Yeats, oils, c.1905, Hugh Lane Gallery, Dublin [*see illus.*] · J. B. Yeats, pencil drawing, 1905, NG Ire. · W. Orpen, caricature, 1907 (with Lady Gregory and Hugh Lane), NPG · J. B. Yeats, silhouette, Royal Collection · W. B. Yeats, caricature, ink drawing, NPG
Wealth at death £217 8s. 2d.—in England: probate, 7 Aug 1909, CGPLA Eng. & Wales

Synge [*formerly* Sing], **Richard Laurence Millington** (1914–1994), biochemist, was born in Liverpool on 28 October 1914, the only son and first of the two children of Laurence Millington Synge (1887–1962), stockbroker, who changed his name from Sing by deed poll in 1920, and his wife, Katherine Charlotte, *née* Swan (1885–1972). His grandfather A. M. Sing was resident of the Liverpool Athenaeum and a governor of the Liverpool collegiate school. Two generations further back he was related to William Roscoe MP (1753–1831), who helped to abolish slavery, founded the Liverpool Botanic Gardens in 1802, and donated his art collection to form the nucleus of the Walker Art Gallery.

Education As well as having a sharp intellect, the young Synge could be absent-minded. His mother later wrote to his close friend, the immunologist John Herbert Humphrey (1915–1987): 'I know I have an unusual son, when he was quite small he was so absent minded (really thinking of other things) that he was not safe to let walk the village street alone.' A visitor heard of this and commented: 'clever and absent minded, you've got a genius on your hands' (Gordon, 456). Synge was educated at home by his mother (who was much influenced by Charlotte Mason and the Parents' National Educational Union) until the age of nine, when he was sent to board at the Old Hall preparatory school, Wellington, Shropshire. From there he went to Winchester College, where he met Humphrey. Through the latter, whose father had been a founder of Imperial Chemical Industries, Synge came into contact with aspects of the industrial world in Britain.

It was also at Winchester that Synge's interest in proteins was first aroused. In 1932 he won an exhibition in classics to Trinity College, Cambridge, but he spent his final year catching up on science, to the extent that in 1933 he won the school science prize. When he entered Trinity later in the year he was allowed to transfer his exhibition. He read chemistry, physics, and physiology for part one of

Richard Laurence Millington Synge (1914–1994), by Elliott & Fry, 1952

his tripos—there was no part one course in biochemistry at that time and intending biochemists took the physiology course as this contained a substantial amount of physiological chemistry, taught by staff of the biochemistry department. He graduated with a double first in natural sciences in 1936.

Like many other students at the time, Synge was appalled at the evils of German Nazism and adopted a left-wing position similar to that of several Cambridge biochemists. Soon after he graduated the Spanish Civil War began and he joined the Communist Party. His interest in Russia and the work of Russian scientists led him to learn Russian, and later he became fluent in German and Swedish. Synge had no desire to bear arms but he did join the Cambridge Scientists' Anti-War Group in October 1936 and was a leading figure in their investigation of a government proposal for gas-proof rooms, as a measure of passive air defence. Their conclusion was that the main danger to the civilian population in wartime would be from high explosives, and that bomb-proof shelters should be built.

Protein analyses Synge remained in the biochemistry laboratory after he graduated, researching on protein analysis under Norman Wingate Pirie, in particular on the separation of acetyl acids. The known methods of analysing the complex mixture of amino acids obtainable by hydrolysis of proteins were still primitive, the main one being the slow procedure of crystallizing the derivatives.

Synge began considering other methods which might be suitable for the separation of small molecules, such as those derived by the partial breakdown of proteins. Because he was well aware of the use of fractional distillation, and knew that refluxing in a distillation column involved equilibration between the ascending vapour phase and the descending liquid phase, he paid special attention to the countercurrent principle that he had seen at the Solvay alkali plant at Winnington. He wrote, but did not publish, a historical review entitled 'Fractional distillation and the countercurrent principle', which covered contributions as far back as the sixteenth century.

Synge's ability in dealing with proteins was recognized by two Australian scientists, Sir Charles Martin, director of the Lister Institute, and Hedley Marston, who had analysed sheep's wool in relation to sulphur deficiency in certain soils and was in 1937 a guest worker in the biochemical laboratory. Both men felt that Synge might be able to progress this subject. Marston was an adviser for the International Wool Secretariat (IWS), a body funded by the wool growers of South Africa, Australia, and New Zealand for publicity and research. Because of the possibility that new synthetic fibres might displace wool, Marston urged the necessity for fundamental studies on the nature of wool to be financed by the IWS. The development of improved techniques for amino acid analysis was the first step. As at this time such methods were inadequate for studies on protein structure, their improvement by itself constituted a formidable challenge and Marston urged provision of a studentship for Synge to make this possible.

Amino acid chromatography In Cambridge in 1938 Synge had met Archer Martin, who was working at the Dunne Nutritional Laboratory, where he had devised apparatus for extracting vitamin E. Later that year Martin moved to the Wool Industries Research Association (WIRA) in Leeds, from where he collaborated with Synge to build an apparatus to work with the chloroform solvents which Synge was then using; together they built a steady state countercurrent machine which was capable of separating amino acids as their acetyl derivatives. Synge proceeded PhD in 1940; in 1941 he joined Martin at Leeds where he was appointed biochemist to WIRA. Continuing with their project, Synge later wrote:

> I remember that at about that time our chloroform water machine was playing up badly and we discussed changing it over so as to have only one phase on the move, and to put in the charge batchwise at the point of entry of the moving phase 'as if it were a chromatogram'. I am sure that it was this verbal twist that prompted us to go on to liquid–liquid chromatograms. (Gordon, 462)

In May that year Synge and Martin showed that, with a silica gel column partition, chromatography was a practical method of breaking down and analysing complex biological substances. It served to analyse the lower fatty acids and the penicillins, and was also used by Frederick Sanger to investigate the structure of insulin.

The crude chromatographic techniques for separating proteins which were available in the early 1940s were inadequate for the separation of individual amino acids. Following their trial of the silica gel column, Martin and Synge found that their procedure would work with porous filter paper. A mixture of free amino acids was spotted on the end of the paper, which was then dipped into a solvent, and hung up. This allowed the solution to pass down the paper; the various amino acids moved with it but at different rates. The filter paper was then dried and sprayed with a developer, such as ninhydrin solution. On heating, the portions of the amino acids are revealed as dark spots of various colours and can be identified by comparison with known substances. If, before developing, the paper is dried and turned through 90° and retreated, a finer resolution is obtained. It was also found that the method revealed not only the type but also the concentration of each amino acid. The simplicity and sensitivity of the method, which was announced in 1944, led to a transformation in protein chemistry. Its wide uses included the industrial purification of penicillin.

On 26 March 1943 Synge married Ann Davies, née Stephen, a medical practitioner. It was a happy marriage and brought them three sons and four daughters. They moved to London later in 1943 when Synge joined the Lister Institute. During the later stages of the war samples of Gramicidin-S, an antibiotic that had been isolated in the USSR, became available. Synge was able to show that it was composed of amino acids, and to obtain its intimate structure he prepared crystals for his colleague Dorothy Hodgkin to examine. Hodgkin was assisted by a fourth-year chemistry student named Margaret Roberts; when she later became eminent as Margaret Thatcher, Synge was able to claim her as his first student.

Research for agriculture After the war Synge spent a year in Uppsala working with the Swedish biochemist Arne Tiselius, who was also developing chromatographic methods for protein analysis. He returned to Britain having decided to work in a more practical area. From 1948 to 1967 he was head of the department of protein chemistry at the Rowett Institute, Aberdeen, where among his contributions was the study of the digestion of proteins and how to prevent their being wastefully fermented. He also investigated the nutritive value of by-products, including fish meal, from the herring industry. The growing family lived in a large house on the cliff edge at Muchalls where Ann, who became a councillor of Kincardineshire, had the opportunity to sail. In 1956 the family motored across Scandinavia, East Germany, and Poland to the USSR, and stayed in Moscow so that Synge could meet colleagues and attend a conference on the origin of life. His family also accompanied him in 1958–9 when he spent a year at the Ruakura Animal Research Station in New Zealand. He subsequently took on the deputy directorship at the Rowett. Synge and Martin were elected fellows of the Royal Society in 1950, and in 1952 they shared the Nobel prize for chemistry, an award unique in being given for a new method rather than for a new substance or a new relationship of substances.

Synge moved finally to the Agricultural Research Council's Food Research Institute at Norwich. He did further work on the reaction of polyphenols and quinones and with the bound forms of amino acids in plants, using high-resolution mass spectroscopy equipment. Thus in his last years he again entered a new field, to become a specialist on how best to format chemical information for storage on a computer. In 1972 he was made an honorary fellow of Trinity College, Cambridge. In 1977 he was one of those commemorated on a British postage stamp. He retired in 1976 and was appointed honorary professor of biology at the University of East Anglia, a post he held until 1984. This gave him access to the university's computers, and he continued his research until his death.

Throughout his life Synge was involved in peace matters, latterly with the Norwich Peace Council. He died at his home, 19 Meadow Rise Road, Norwich, on 18 August 1994, survived by his wife. HUGH GORDON

Sources H. Gordon, *Memoirs FRS*, 42 (1996), 455–79 · *WWW*, 1991–5 · *The Independent* (24 Aug 1994) · *The Times* (1 Sept 1994) · m. cert. · personal knowledge (2004) · private information (2004)
Archives Trinity Cam., corresp. and papers | Bodl. Oxf., corresp. with Dorothy Hodgkin
Likenesses Elliott & Fry, photograph, 1952, NPG [*see illus.*] · photograph, 1952, repro. in *The Independent* · Godfrey Argent studio, photograph, repro. in Gordon, *Memoirs FRS*, 454 · photograph, repro. in *The Times*
Wealth at death £82,785: probate, 21 March 1995, *CGPLA Eng. & Wales*

Synge, William Webb Follett (1826–1891), diplomatist and author, the son of the Revd Robert Synge (*d.* 1862), and his first wife, Anne (*d.* 1844), daughter of William Follett, was born on 25 August 1826. After being educated almost entirely abroad, on 26 June 1846 he entered the Foreign Office; from 15 September 1851 to 1 July 1853 he was attached to the British legation at Washington. There, on 27 January 1853, he married Henrietta Mary, youngest daughter of Robert Dewar, colonel in the United States army; they had four sons and a daughter. On their return to Britain later in 1853, Synge began to supplement his uncertain income by journalism, writing for *The Press* and *Punch*. At this time he became friendly with Thackeray (after whom he named one of his children), and with other literary figures. However, he resumed his diplomatic career, becoming secretary to Sir William Gore Ouseley's special mission to Central America (1856–9). During his absence he was appointed to a clerkship, at first temporary, in the Foreign Office in April 1857. He returned to Britain in 1860, probably by way of the USA. In Central America he met Anthony Trollope, who disapproved of his tory politics (see A. Trollope, *The West Indies and the Spanish Main*, 1860).

On 27 December 1861 Synge was appointed commissioner and consul-general for the Sandwich Islands, and in that capacity he stood proxy for the prince of Wales at the baptism of the prince of Hawaii. In 1865 he escorted Queen Emma of Hawaii to Britain. On 30 October 1865 he became consul-general and commissary judge in Cuba; but here his health, already impaired, gave way, and he retired from the service on 31 October 1868.

On settling first at Guildford, and then in 1883 at Eastbourne, Synge resumed his literary career. He wrote regularly for *The Standard* and, from 1883, for the *Saturday Review*. In 1875 he published his first novel, *Olivia Raleigh*, which was followed by *Tom Singleton, Dragoon and Dramatist* (1879), which he dramatized for the stage. He published many poems in periodicals, notably 'Sursum corda' (*Punch*, November 1854) and 'A Patriot Queen' (*Blackwood's Edinburgh Magazine*, 1878). He also wrote for children *Bumble Bee Bogo's Budget* (1888). He died at home at Lislee House, Eastbourne, on 29 May 1891. His son Richard Follett Synge also worked as a diplomatist and also served in the Pacific. C. A. HARRIS, *rev.* H. C. G. MATTHEW

Sources Allibone, *Dict.* · *FO List* (1890)
Archives Bodl. Oxf., letters to Sir John Fiennes Crampton · Notts. Arch., letters to John Saville
Wealth at death £7731 17*s.* 6*d.*: resworn probate, July 1892, *CGPLA Eng. & Wales* (1891)

Syrett, Janet [Netta] (1865–1943), writer and playwright, was born at 23 Harbour Street, Ramsgate, Kent, on 17 March 1865, the eldest of approximately eleven children born to Ernest Syrett (*d.* 1906), linen draper, and Mary Ann, *née* Stembridge (*d.* 1923). She was niece to the writer Grant Allen (1848–1899). Baptized Janet, she was always known as Netta. Until the age of eleven Netta Syrett was educated at home, but in 1877 she was sent to the North London Collegiate School for Girls with her sister Dora, where they boarded with the headmistress Frances Buss. Dora died of tuberculosis in 1881, and Netta left the school at the same time. She was not happy during her time there, and later in her memoir criticized Miss Buss for lacking sympathy with adolescents, and partially blamed her for her sister's death. Over the next few years Syrett learned German, completed the syllabus for the Cambridge higher local examination in one year, and in 1885 attended the Training College for Women Teachers at Cambridge. The family was comfortably off financially and her parents supported their daughters' choice of higher education and careers. When Syrett and four of her sisters were working or studying in London in the 1880s their father acquired a flat for them. Later, when Syrett was suffering from exhaustion and nerves, he funded an extended trip to Italy for her and her sister Nell. (After her father's death in 1906 the family's income was substantially reduced.)

In 1886 Syrett accepted a post as English mistress at Swansea high school, where she stayed for two years. Grant Allen, who influenced her thinking for many years, introduced her to many prominent writers during this period. Her first published story appeared in *Longman's* magazine (at Allen's instigation) while she was at Swansea. By 1890 she was the second mistress at the London Polytechnic School for Girls. Here she met Mabel Beardsley, who also taught at the school, and who introduced her to her brother Aubrey Beardsley's circle. Through these connections she contributed to the *Yellow Book*. She also started writing plays for children. Written in the 'new realist' style, her first novel, *Nobody's Fault* (1896), with a book jacket designed by Aubrey Beardsley, was published by John Lane in his Keynote series. She brought out a children's book, *Garden of Delight*, illustrated by her sister Nell (also a contributor to the *Yellow Book*) in 1898.

In 1902 Syrett's play *The Finding of Nancy* won a national competition organized by the Playgoers' Club, and was performed as a charity matinée for the Actors' Benevolent Fund. The critics' response was enthusiastic, but the subject matter of the play—a respectable single woman enters into a sexual relationship with a married man, whose wife is a dipsomaniac in an asylum—cost Syrett not only a commercial run, but also her job as a private schoolmistress. In the same year she published the novel *Roseanne*, in which the heroine destroys a friend's marriage. In 1905 she edited the single volume of a putative juvenile periodical, the *Dream Garden*. Contributors included fellow *Yellow Book* authors and artists. Her subsequent novels, *Women and Circumstance* (1906) and *Olivia L. Carew* (1910), continued to explore women's concerns. Syrett's children's books included several collections of plays, such as *Old Miracle Plays of England* (1911), also illustrated by her sister Nell. She had long been interested in establishing a children's theatre that would play during all the school holidays and offer a range of plays, not just the popular Christmas pantomimes. With her friend and fellow author Mabel Dearmer, she rented a theatre over the Christmas season of 1913. Unfortunately the expenses consumed any profit and the venture seems to have put the final seal on Syrett's bitterness about the theatre.

Syrett wrote thirty-eight novels in all, twenty books for young people, and numerous plays and short stories. Other than the *Yellow Book* she also contributed to many periodicals, including Charlotte M. Yonge's children's magazine, the *Monthly Packet*. Her later novels reflect many of her own experiences: her attendance at North London Collegiate School for Girls in *The Victorians* (1915), her career as a teacher in *The God of Chance* (1920), her years in the *Yellow Book* circle in *Strange Marriage* (1930), and her travels in Italy and France. One of her most popular novels was *Portrait of a Rebel* (1929), whose heroine was a leader in the women's suffrage movement (it was made into a film, *A Woman Rebels*, starring Katharine Hepburn, in 1936). Like other feminist authors of the New Woman fiction, Syrett rejected prescribed Victorian gender roles. Her heroines seek financial, psychological, and social independence, striving to combine personal aspirations with romance and domesticity. Her writing also addresses class issues, socialism and the labour movement, and educational reform. Having settled in Surrey, Netta Syrett died on 15 December 1943 of heart failure brought on by pneumonia at Roseacre Nursing Home, Priorsfield Road, Compton, Guildford; she was cremated at Woking on 20 December.

JILL SHEFRIN

Sources N. Syrett, *The sheltering tree* (1939) • J. O. Jones, 'Netta Syrett: a chronological annotated bibliography of her works, 1890–1940', *Bulletin of Bibliography*, 45 (March 1988), 8–14 • B. J. Robinson, 'Netta Syrett', *British short-fiction writers, 1880–1914: the realist tradition*, ed. W. B. Thesing, DLitB, 135 (1993) • J. T. Jones, 'Netta Syrett', *Late-Victorian and Edwardian British novelists: second series*, ed. G. M. Johnson, DLitB, 197 (1999) • K. L. Mix, *A study in yellow: the Yellow Book and its contributors* (1960) • A. L. Ardis, *New women, new novels: feminism and early modernism* (1990) • G. Krishnamurti, *Women writers of the 1890s* (1991) • M. S. Lasner and M. D. Stetz, *The Yellow Book: a centenary exhibition* (1994) [exhibition catalogue, Harvard U., Houghton L., Cambridge, Massachusetts] • *The Times* (18 Dec 1943) • Toronto Public Library, Osborne collection of early children's books • private information (2004) • b. cert. • d. cert.

Archives Bodl. Oxf. • Merton Oxf., MSS • NL Scot. | Toronto Public Library, Osborne collection of early children's books, agreements and corresp. with her agent and her publishers, juvenile MSS, and unpublished playscripts

Likenesses photograph, repro. in *London Magazine* (Oct 1906) • six photographs (with her sister Nell), Toronto Public Library, Osborne collection, Syrett archive

Wealth at death £1094 10s. 11d.: administration with will, 1944, CGPLA Eng. & Wales

Sysonby. For this title name *see* Ponsonby, Frederick Edward Grey, first Baron Sysonby (1867–1935).

Szabo [*née* Bushell], **Violette Reine Elizabeth** (1921–1945), secret operations officer, was born in Paris on 26 June 1921, the second child and only daughter in the family of five children of Charles George Bushell, a regular soldier, and his wife, Reine Blanche Leroy, a dressmaker from Pont-Rémy, Somme, France. He held various jobs in France and England before settling in 1932 in Brixton as a secondhand motor car dealer. From her mother's family Violette picked up fluent French, spoken with an English accent. She left the London county council school in Stockwell Road, Brixton, at fourteen to work as a shop assistant. She was under 5 feet 5 inches tall, but strikingly good-looking, with dark hair and eyes and vivacious manners.

Violette married in Aldershot, on 21 August 1940, Étienne Michel René Szabo, a thirty-year-old Frenchman of Hungarian descent from Marseilles, who had fought in Norway with the French Foreign Legion and elected to join General de Gaulle's nascent Free French forces. He was soon posted to north Africa, and never met their only child, Tania, a daughter born on 8 June 1941. He died on 27 October 1942 from wounds received the previous day in battle.

To avenge him, his widow joined the independent French section of the Special Operations Executive (SOE) in October 1943. During the usual paramilitary, parachute, and security training it emerged that Szabo was an admirable shot. She parachuted twice into occupied France, each time as courier to Philippe Liewer, an experienced agent. Her first mission began on 5–6 April 1944. They found that the Gestapo had broken up Liewer's former group of saboteur friends between Rouen and Le Havre; they returned to England by light aircraft on 30 April. Between her first and second missions she was commissioned an ensign in the First Aid Nursing Yeomanry.

Szabo and Liewer returned to France on 7–8 June 1944 to set up a new group of resisters between Limoges and Périgueux. On 10 June she and two companions, in a motor car, encountered a German road block at Salon-la-Tour, some 30 miles south-east of Limoges. Both sides opened fire. She was long thought, on the strength of her George Cross citation, to have covered her companions' retreat until she ran out of ammunition; in fact she tripped, fell,

Violette Reine Elizabeth Szabo (1921–1945), by unknown photographer

and was captured unarmed. Brutal interrogations got nothing out of her but contempt.

On 8 August, handcuffed to a neighbour on a train bound for Germany, Szabo crawled round offering water to her fellow prisoners while the train was under attack by the Royal Air Force. She was put in Ravensbrück concentration camp, whence she went with two SOE colleagues, Lilian Rolfe and Denise Bloch, on a working party at Torgau. They were then sent on a much fiercer one, some 60 miles eastward, at Klein Königsberg. Even her tremendously high spirits were lowered by its regime. Her companions returned from it hardly able to stand; she was not much sturdier. About 27 January 1945, shortly after their return to Ravensbrück, all three were shot dead. Szabo was awarded a French Croix de Guerre in 1944, and a posthumous George Cross. This was presented to the four-year-old Tania in 1946.

Violette Szabo's wartime exploits were immortalized in 1958 in a film, *Carve her Name with Pride* (from the book of that name by R. J. Minney). The role of Violette was taken by Virginia McKenna. Early in 2000 a museum about her was opened at Cartref, her uncle's home in Wormelow, near Hereford.   M. R. D. FOOT, *rev.*

Sources R. J. Minney, *Carve her name with pride* (1956) · M. R. D. Foot, *SOE in France: an account of the work of the British Special Operations Executive in France, 1940–1944*, 2nd edn (1968) · private information (1993) · *CGPLA Eng. & Wales* (1946) · m. cert. · P. Howarth, *Undercover: the men and women of the Special Operations Executive* (1980) · *The Guardian* (29 April 2000)
Archives PRO, HS, SOE files | FILM BFI NFTVA, 'Violette Szabo', BBC, 19 Sept 2002
Likenesses photograph, *c.*1945, Hult. Arch. · photograph, repro. in L. Jones, *A quiet courage* (1991) [*see illus.*] · photographs, repro. in Minney, *Carve her name with pride* · photographs, Special Forces Club, London
Wealth at death £332 1s. 11d.: probate, 20 July 1946, *CGPLA Eng. & Wales*

Szamuely, Tibor (1925–1972), historian and polemicist, was born in Moscow on 14 May 1925, the eldest of three children and elder son of György Szamuely and his wife, Elsa Szanto. Both Szamuely's parents came from Hungarian Jewish mercantile stock, his grandfather on his father's side being a corn merchant. In the Hungarian revolution of 1919 his uncle Tibor, as commissar for war, was held to have been responsible for the repression under the regime, and subsequently killed himself on being apprehended by Admiral Horthy's police while trying to flee across the Austrian border.

György Szamuely, who had worked as a journalist and had also taken part in the revolutionary government, secured passage to Moscow, where he obtained employment in the Soviet trade commissariat. In this capacity he went to London in 1932 with his family though he was also secretly working for the Comintern. The young Tibor Szamuely went to Beacon Hill School, near Petersfield, Hampshire, which was run by Bertrand Russell and his wife; he enjoyed the school, where he acquired an excellent knowledge of English. He also was sent briefly to the school at Summerhill near Leiston in Suffolk run by A. S. Neill, of which he thought less highly. In 1934 the Szamuelys returned to Moscow. Three years later György Szamuely was arrested and condemned to ten years of gaol 'without the right of correspondence'. He was never seen again.

The Szamuely family were evacuated to Tomsk in the Second World War, along with other Hungarians living in Moscow. Tibor Szamuely was eventually called up. In 1945 he found himself a member of the Allied Control Commission for Hungary, perhaps working for the NKVD, the Soviet secret service. He returned to Russia after a dispute in Budapest and attended the University of Moscow to study history. Szamuely next worked as a contributor to encyclopaedias. He also had imprudent connections with the United States embassy. On 2 December 1950, at dawn, he was arrested on a charge of being an American spy, for planning a terroristic attack on Georgy Malenkov, and for uttering anti-Soviet opinions. He denied the first two of these charges but admitted the third. He was sentenced to eight years' imprisonment. He discharged eighteen months of this sentence, at a lumber camp in a marshy region, but was released on the request of Mátyás Rákosi, then the secretary-general of the Hungarian Communist Party, still a family friend.

Szamuely then returned to Budapest as a lecturer in history at the university. He formed part of the so-called Petőfi Circle but, though already disillusioned about communism, played little part in the revolution of 1956 owing to his family connections with the old regime. As a result of this inactivity he was named vice-rector of the University of Budapest in 1957. He was, however, dismissed from this post, and from his teaching position, for refusing to lead an attack on the philosopher George Lukács.

After this Szamuely worked in the Hungarian Academy of Sciences. At that time, he produced most of his written work such as *Modern History, 1849–1945* (with György Ránki, 1959), *The Foundation of the Hungarian Communist Party* (1963), and *National Socialism* (1963). He afterwards accepted a teaching post offered to him at the Kwame Nkrumah Ideological Institute at Winneba in Ghana. He obtained this post through Kodwo Addison, whom he himself had taught in Hungary in the 1950s and who was at the time head of the institute. He profited from a holiday in Ghana in 1964 to go to England, where he remained, being in 1965 appointed lecturer in politics at the University of Reading, then expanding its activities. He became a British subject in 1969.

Szamuely swiftly established a reputation in Britain as a brilliant critic of the Soviet regime. He often wrote for *The Spectator*. His lectures at Reading were successful, though he lived in London, finally establishing himself at 17 Sutherland Place, Bayswater. He never, however, completed his long-planned history of the Soviet Union though his introduction to that work—a sparkling analysis of Soviet history—was published posthumously as *The Russian Tradition* (edited, with an introduction by Robert Conquest, 1974).

Szamuely was a warm-hearted conversationalist, always ready to recall his tragic experiences for those who cared to interest themselves. He died on 10 December 1972 of cancer in a London hospital. He was married in 1948 in Moscow to Nina Orlova (*d.* 1974), daughter of an expert in pestilence married to a doctor. Her grandfather, a merchant in old Russia, had been tortured and exiled in the first years of the Soviet regime. During the Szamuelys' London years she taught Russian at St Paul's Girls' School, and worked as a contributor to the *Concise Oxford English–Russian Dictionary*. There were two children of the marriage, a son, George, and a daughter, Helen.

THOMAS OF SWYNNERTON, *rev.*

Sources personal knowledge (1986) • private information (1986)
Wealth at death £37,605: probate, 17 April 1973, *CGPLA Eng. & Wales*

Szarvasy, Frederick Alexander (1875–1948), financier, was Hungarian by extraction, and was probably born in Hungary, the son of Alexander Szarvasy, a banker. Little is known of his early years. After spending some time in South America he went to London around 1901. There he joined a discount house, and later the stockbrokers Montagu Oppenheimer, where he became a close friend and colleague of Lord Charles Montagu (1860–1931) and Baron Springer of Vienna. He then decided to move into the new issue and company promotion business, first buying the Cornhill Contract Corporation, and in 1913 joining Springer on the board of the British Foreign and Colonial Corporation (BFCC), whose chairman he became in 1923. The BFCC was recognized as a major issuing house during the 1920s. H. C. Clifford-Turner, a London solicitor active in many company flotations, considered Szarvasy to be one of the leading financiers in the City between the wars.

One flotation with which Szarvasy's name was particularly linked was that of Imperial Airways in 1924. In 1920, through BFCC, he proposed the establishment of a monopoly airline to bring together several small carriers. There was opposition, but in 1923 the Air Ministry reached agreement with BFCC for a public flotation, Szarvasy having settled terms with the various companies and persuaded Sir Eric Geddes to become chairman. BFCC handled the flotation for out-of-pocket expenses only, 'in view

of the national importance of the business' (*The Times*, 5 June 1924).

Szarvasy knew Geddes well, as both had worked together at the Dunlop Rubber Company. In 1920 Dunlop had been brought to the brink of collapse by the speculative activities of the former chairman, Sir Arthur du Cros. Szarvasy was brought in as chairman in 1920 and cleared out many of the existing board members, introduced new capital to tide the company over its crisis, and put proper accounting procedures in place. By the time he handed over to Sir Eric Geddes in 1922 the immediate crisis was over; he remained on the Dunlop board until his death. Dunlop's accounts later became known as a model of information and clarity through the influence of Frederic de Paula, who joined the company in 1929.

During the 1920s Szarvasy was called in to several other companies where poor financial management threatened their survival. These included Marconi's Wireless Telegraph Company and William Beardmore & Co., among others. He was involved with Alfred Mond, Lord Melchett, in the restructuring of the south Wales anthracite industry, and on Mond's death succeeded to the chairmanship of Amalgamated Anthracite Collieries, which controlled around 80 per cent of Welsh anthracite production; he retained this post until his own death. In addition he was on the boards of several other finance houses, including the Anglo-French Banking Corporation, Martins Bank, Guardian Assurance, and the Daily Mail Trust. He was keen to develop opportunities for investment in European companies, and in 1931 he spoke out against impediments placed by governments in the way of free movement of goods, labour, and capital. In his financial dealings he was very secretive; when he died his safe was found to be empty of records.

In December 1921 Szarvasy married Kate Muriel Rhona (*d.* 1924), the daughter of Augusto Saavedra, who was in the French consular service; they had one daughter. Szarvasy was deeply interested in music and art. He was chairman of the Covent Garden opera syndicate and was a generous patron of young musicians; he played the violin well himself. He died at his London home, 74 Portland Place, on 3 July 1948.   FRANCIS GOODALL

Sources J. W. Scott and F. Goodall, 'Szarvasy, Frederick Alexander', *DBB* • J. Scott, *Legibus* (1980) • R. Higham, *Britain's imperial air routes, 1918 to 1939* (1960) • J. McMillan, *The Dunlop story: the life, death and rebirth of a multinational* (1989) • *The Times* (5 June 1924) • *The Times* (7 July 1948) • WWW
Archives HLRO, corresp. with Lord Beaverbrook
Likenesses A. Pan, portrait, repro. in Scott, *Legibus*
Wealth at death £71,491 15s. 0d.: probate, 13 Dec 1948, *CGPLA Eng. & Wales*

T. B. *See* Eachard, John (*bap.* 1637, *d.* 1697).

T. C. *See* Cokayne, Thomas (1587–1638).

T. V. *See* Vincent, Thomas (1634–1678).

Taaffe, Denis (*bap.* 1759, *d.* 1813), political writer, was baptized Dinish Taaffe on 3 February 1759 in the parish of Clogher, co. Louth, Ireland, the fourth of six children of Laurence Taaffe, farmer, and his wife, Mary Gallagher.

After being educated locally and in co. Westmeath he decided to enter the order of St Francis, and was then educated in the Franciscan colleges in Boulay, France, and Prague. He was ordained to the priesthood on 25 May 1782. He had returned to Ireland by 1786 and seemed a model member of his order, but he later showed that he had no vocation for the religious life, and had converted to the Church of Ireland by 8 November 1788. The reason for his conversion was apparently a violent quarrel with his superiors, the result of a volatile and stubborn temperament, combined with a drink problem.

As Taaffe soon quarrelled with his new superiors, he received no living as a minister of his new church; nor did he receive the yearly allowance of £40 allowed by law for Catholic priests who became protestants, which he still sought from the authorities in 1800. As a result he made a living as a translator, tutor, and pamphleteer, becoming sympathetic to the ideals of the French Revolution and of the United Irishmen. Due to his apostasy, Taaffe was ostracized by members of his old church, whose cause he advocated. His claims of poverty were genuine, although exacerbated by his drinking.

Taaffe claimed to have fought in the 1798 rebellion, claiming in particular that he had played a leading role in the battle of Ballyellis, a rebel victory, on 29 June. However, not only is the Ballyellis claim not supported by any government or rebel account, but Luke Cullen was told by some former rebels who had fought in the battle that the Wexford and Wicklow men were not 'such spiritless fools as to be commanded by a stranger' (Cullen, 44). Taaffe opposed the Act of Union in two pamphlets and in a newspaper, *The Shamroc*, the latter leading him and his publisher to be arrested for seditious libel on 14 March 1799. Subsequently released, he continued to live in poverty, later in lodgings in James's Street, subsisting, according to one account, on penny rolls and buttermilk (*Dublin and London Magazine*, 220). As well as *The Shamroc*, he wrote seven pamphlets, three under the pseudonym Julius Vindex. Also of interest among his other works are a *Sketch of the Geography, and of the History of Spain* (1808), *The Life of Saint Columb-Kille* (n.d.), and an unpublished Irish grammar (BL, Egerton MS 116). The most notable of his works, however, is his *An Impartial History of Ireland* (4 vols., 1809–11).

Taaffe was a good scholar, with a great proficiency in languages, including Hebrew, Greek, Latin, French, Italian, German, and Dutch. His mind was 'always in extremes, sometimes unusually vivacious, at other times absorbed in lethargic melancholy' (Cox, 'Memoirs', 7.515). Despite this, he firmly held to a radical and democratic Irish patriotism allied to a great Anglophobia, and his works are full of his defence of this patriotism and of the Catholic faith. He was a powerful writer with a vigorous, popular style and a good use of language; but he was careless with facts, and his lack of original research has meant that his works are almost forgotten. This is unfortunate, as they are very readable and present a useful view of an important period in Irish history.

Taaffe, a native Irish speaker, was an enthusiast of the Irish language and of Irish civilization before the coming of the Normans, defended in his works from claims that they were barbaric. He was also the first secretary of the Gaelic Society of Dublin, founded in 1806. He died in Dublin on 30 July 1813, reconciled to his old church, and was buried two days later in the churchyard of St James's Church, Dublin.   MURRAY SMITH

Sources W. Cox, 'Memoirs of the late Rev. Dennis Taaffe', *Irish Magazine*, 7 (June–Nov 1814), 286–7, 319–21, 408–9, 478–9, 514–16 • W. Cox, 'Memoirs of the late Rev. Dennis Taaffe', *Irish Magazine*, 8 (Feb–March 1815), 64–8, 115–18 • W. Cox, *Irish Magazine*, 6 (Aug 1813), 384 • L. Cullen, *Personal recollections of Wexford and Wicklow insurgents of 1798* (1959), 43–6 • *Milesian Magazine*, 5 (Oct 1813), 189–90 • J. Warburton, J. Whitelaw, and R. Walsh, *History of the city of Dublin*, 2 vols. (1818), 932–3 • W. J. Fitzpatrick, *Irish wits and worthies* (1873), 132–6 • NA Ire., Rebellion MSS, Taaffe MSS, 620/8/75 • NA Ire., Official MSS, vol. 1, p. 111, 74/4 • E. O'Byrne, ed., *The convert rolls*, IMC (1981) • T. O'Donnell, 'A Gaelic grammarian', *Franciscan College Annual* (1952), 141, 159–62 • *Dublin and London Magazine* (June 1828), 219–20 • C. Mooney, *Irish Franciscans and France* (1964), 70 • *Freeman's Journal* [Dublin] (2 Aug 1813) • parish registers (Roman Catholic), diocese of Armagh, parish of Clogher, 1744–99, NL Ire., p. 5599 • parish register, St James, Dublin, Representative Church Body Library [burial], 1 Aug 1813 • *DNB* • M. Hösler, 'Irishmen ordained at Prague 1629–1786', *Collectanea Hibernica*, 33 (1991), 7–53 • B. Millett, 'Some lists of Irish Franciscans in Prague, 1656–1791', *Collectanea Hibernica*, 36–7 (1994–5), 59–84

Archives BL, unpublished Irish grammar, Egerton MS 116 • NA Ire., letter to Charles James Fox, 20 January 1799, Rebellion MS 620/53/143 • NA Ire., Official MSS, petition of 19 Sept 1800, 74/4 • NA Ire., Rebellion MS, 620/8/75 | NA Ire., petition of Joseph Hill, printer of *The Shamroc*, 20 March 1799, Rebellion MS 620/8/85/11 • NA Ire., *Taaffe's National Shamroc*, nos. 5, 8, 11, Official MS 64/6

Taaffe, Francis, third earl of Carlingford (1639–1704), army officer and politician, was born at Ballymote, co. Sligo, the fourth of the seven children of Theobald *Taaffe, first earl of Carlingford (d. 1677), and his first wife, Mary, daughter of Sir Nicholas White of Leixlip, co. Kildare, and his wife, Ursula. The family was staunchly Roman Catholic. His father, a prominent Irish royalist soldier and diplomat, was a close companion in exile to Charles II. This connection ensured that at the Restoration he recovered his extensive estates in counties Louth and Sligo, which had been forfeited under the Commonwealth. In 1650 Ormond had sent him to Brussels, where he engaged in protracted negotiations to persuade Charles IV, duke of Lorraine, to intervene in Ireland. Lorraine was an ally of the Habsburgs, and the elder Taaffe's link to him may explain the decision to send Francis to study at the famed Jesuit college of Olmütz in Moravia, 'where by his faculties and talents he astonished the members of the university' (*Memoirs of the Family of Taaffe*, 16). In 1655, at the request of Charles II, he was made a page of honour at the imperial court, and in 1662 he received the title of Austrian hereditary territorial count; he was generally known as Count Taaffe for the remainder of his life.

Having chosen a military career, Taaffe joined the imperial army and served initially in Hungary as a captain in the regiment of Charles V, duke of Lorraine (1643–1690), with whom he established a lifelong friendship and close confidence. In 1673 he commanded Lorraine's regiment at the siege of Bonn, and in 1674 at the battles of Sinzheim and Mülhausen, where his bravery won favourable comment. In 1674 also he went to Poland during the royal election to deliver an eloquent, if fruitless, speech in favour of the candidacy of Lorraine. In 1675 he fought with distinction at the battle of Sasbach and was present at the subsequent engagements of Attenheim and Goldschier. He was then sent to the Palatinate to dissuade the elector from concluding a separate peace with France. In 1676 he was present at the siege of Philippsburg. In the same year he married Elizabeth Maximiliana Traudisch (*d.* 1700), widow successively of the cousins Wilhelm Heinrich Schlik and Franz Ernst Schlik, both counts of Bassano and Weisskirchen. Their only child, Anne, predeceased him.

In 1677 Lorraine, by now imperial commander-in-chief and soon to become the emperor Leopold's brother-in-law, resigned the proprietorship of his cavalry regiment to make a vacancy for Taaffe to be appointed in his place. In 1682 Taaffe became a major-general. In 1683, during the great war with the Turks, he courageously commanded a beleaguered rearguard of 400 horse at Petronell until relieved by Lorraine. He subsequently liaised between Lorraine and the emperor, who had retired to Passau. On 12 September he fought with the imperial cavalry on the left wing of John Sobieski's Christian army, which routed the immense Turkish army in the decisive battle on the Kahlenberg Ridge which relieved Vienna. He took part in the follow-up campaign against the Turks, distinguishing himself at the battles of Waizen and Gran and at the unsuccessful siege of Buda. His account of the campaign, described in letters to his brother Lord Carlingford, was published in London and remains an important primary source of information for the war, although it has little to say on his own role. In 1685 he sent booty, taken from the Turkish camp, to King James II in London, together with a tent of the grand vizier, which was erected for display in the garden of Somerset House.

The military events in central Europe attracted a number of English and Irish professional soldiers to temporary service with the imperial army. They included James II's illegitimate son, and favourite, James Fitzjames, duke of Berwick, who was entrusted by his father to Taaffe's care and served in his regiment. Berwick was not impressed by Taaffe's military ability, but otherwise found him 'one of the most agreeable noblemen in Europe, [a] thorough master of polite literature, and a very able statesman' (Petrie, 30). Elsewhere he was described as a man of martial appearance and elegant manners, who never campaigned without his favourite classical authors, Livy and Curtius, as his companions.

Taaffe played a prominent role in the capture of Buda in 1686, and the following year was promoted lieutenant-general of horse. In 1689, 1800 Irish soldiers sent by James II to reinforce the emperor were placed under his command. In 1694 he was appointed field marshal and had conferred upon him the order of the Golden Fleece. He inherited the title of earl of Carlingford, and two subsidiary titles, in 1690 in succession to his elder brother, a former English ambassador in Vienna, who was killed on the Jacobite side at the battle of the Boyne. His service with

the emperor, William III's most powerful ally, ensured that the family estates in Ireland were preserved from confiscation by both the English and Irish parliaments in 1697. At this time he was granted an audience with William at Loo, visited England, and possibly crossed to Ireland to secure his properties.

Charles V, duke of Lorraine, had died in 1690. In his will he named Taaffe as his best friend and commended his widow, the emperor's sister, and his heir, Leopold, to the Irishman's care. Taaffe had already been involved in Leopold's education, and he repaid Lorraine's trust by representing the young duke at the negotiations that led to the treaty of Ryswick in 1697. This resulted in the family's restoration to their dominion after a generation of French occupation. Taaffe became the young duke's chamberlain, prime minister, and finance minister, as well as governor of Nancy and colonel of his guards. He was also instrumental in the founding of an Irish Franciscan college at Boulay in 1698. He accompanied Lorraine to the French court in 1699 on his doing homage for the duchy of Bar and was presented to Louis XIV.

Having resided at Nancy since 1697, Taaffe died there in August 1704 and was buried in September in Nancy Cathedral, after his body had lain in state for a month. He was probably the most prominent Irishman of his generation on mainland Europe. His successor as fourth earl of Carlingford, and the residuary legatee of his estate, which included lands in Ireland, Lorraine, and Silesia (after bequests for wounded soldiers and towards the completion of Cologne Cathedral), was his nephew Theobald Taaffe, an officer in the imperial army. Taaffes continued to be prominent in the imperial service until the twentieth century, the best-known being Count Edward Taaffe (1833–1895), the eleventh viscount, who was Austrian prime minister from 1879 to 1893.

HARMAN MURTAGH

Sources *Memoirs of the family of Taaffe*, 4 vols. (privately printed, Vienna, 1856), 1–25, 225–47 · J. Lodge, *The peerage of Ireland*, rev. M. Archdall, rev. edn, 4 (1789), 296–7 · GEC, *Peerage*, new edn, vol. 3 · H. Murtagh, 'Two Irish officers and the campaign to relieve Vienna, 1683', *Irish Sword*, 15 (1982–3), 255–7 · C. Petrie, *The marshal duke of Berwick* (1953), 30 · J. G. Simms, *The Williamite confiscation in Ireland, 1690–1703* (1956), 80, 130–31 · T. Barker, *Army, aristocracy, monarchy: essays on war, society and government in Austria, 1618–1780* (1982), 56–8 · [W.] Cavenagh, 'Irish colonel proprietors of imperial regiments', *Royal Society of Antiquaries of Ireland Journal*, 57 (1927), 124
Archives Yale U., letters
Likenesses engraving, repro. in *Memoirs of the family of Taaffe*
Wealth at death estates in Ireland, Lorraine, and Silesia: Barker, *Army, aristocracy, monarchy*, 57; Simms, *Williamite confiscation*

Taaffe, John (*b.* 1646/7, *d.* after 1728), informer, claimed to be a Capuchin friar, Father Vincent, from the Irish friary at Bar-sur-Aube, Champagne; but surviving records of that house and the Irish Capuchin province have no trace of him. His age was given as forty-seven in May 1694. About 1688 he was allegedly acting as Catholic chaplain at Standish Hall, Lancashire. Involvement with a local Catholic girl, Mary Woodward (*fl.* 1688–1717), whom he later married, was presumably one cause of his apostasy. On 15 June

1688 Taaffe formally embraced Anglicanism in London before Thomas Tenison, though he continued to act as a priest (presumably to spy on Catholics) until exposed in March 1689. Thereafter he denounced alleged Jacobites and priests, and was the chief witness against Patrick Harding, the first man executed for treason under William III. From late 1690 he acted in Lord Bellomont's investigation to prove the prince of Wales supposititious and Irish: a £100 privy purse pension perhaps rewarded this. Destitute in mid-1689, he was letting lodgings in Westminster by May 1692, when he reported the Jacobite fantasies of his new (bigamous) brother-in-law, John Lunt.

Taaffe's main occupation from 1689 was as a false witness for the commission for superstitious lands (lands given to the Catholic church, so legally forfeit to the crown), a private body managed by disreputable whigs including Captain Henry Baker. The commission hired out the services of its perjurers, nicknamed the Friars, to any courtier able to obtain grants of the lands to which they made baseless claims. In 1693–4, now employing Lunt too, the commission prosecuted some leading Lancashire Catholics, not expecting them to resist and risk exposure of the Jacobite rising which Colonel John Parker was planning from Standish Hall. Instead, their victims prepared a prosecution for perjury.

To forestall this Lunt, backed by fresh perjurers, testified to a Lancashire plot resembling Parker's but implicating innocent rich Lancashire Catholics and Cheshire protestants. The whig secretary of state, the duke of Shrewsbury, took seriously news of the plot. In July 1694 Taaffe was involved in raids in Lancashire, which arrested mainly the innocent, before secretly changing sides. He had helped invent the plot, yet could not plausibly testify; and Lunt planned to spread it nationwide, superseding the commission. If, as opponents claimed, Taaffe (alone of the party) was prevented from plundering Catholic houses, this confirmed his decline. He also felt moral scruples at protestants being accused. That autumn, he enabled friends and a brother of the prisoner William Dicconson to witness Lunt boasting of his perjuries. At the first treason trial, at Manchester on 20 October 1694, Taaffe's testimony contributed to the collapse of the prosecution's case.

Taaffe wrote a 'Narrative' of the plot, portraying himself as an innocent and appealing to Anglican tory fears of dissenters. However, a parliamentary inquiry that winter exposed enough evidence of Parker's plot to convince both houses of parliament, and reconvince the government, that Lunt's story was true. Taaffe was briefly detained for receiving £100 from Dicconson, and was again arrested after the assassination plot of 1696. On returning to Lancashire, he obtained a £5 annuity from the former defendants. However, he secretly resumed priest-hunting in 1698, and his wife was a witness in outlawing Dicconson. During the Jacobite rising of 1715 Taaffe spied for Walpole. Afterwards he offered to capture the English Catholic bishops, and, then living at Chester with his wife and children, he revived his superstitious

lands allegations before the official forfeited estates commission, permanently polluting their records. He is last recorded after 1728 by Arthur Onslow, speaker of the Commons, as being very old and poor, still protestant, and still peddling his perjuries. PAUL HOPKINS

Sources *Report on the manuscripts of Allan George Finch*, 5 vols., HMC, 71 (1913–2003), vols. 2, 4 · *The manuscripts of Lord Kenyon*, HMC, 35 (1894) · *The manuscripts of the House of Lords*, new ser., 12 vols. (1900–77), vol. 1 · *Report on the manuscripts of the marquis of Downshire*, 6 vols. in 7, HMC, 75 (1924–95), vol. 1 · P. A. Hopkins, 'Aspects of Jacobite conspiracy in England in the reign of William III', PhD diss., U. Cam., 1981 · P. A. Hopkins, 'The commission for superstitious lands of the 1690s', *Recusant History*, 15 (1979–81), 265–82 · 'An exact catalogue of all the Irish Capuchins from … 1591 to … 1693, and their reception to the habit or profession', Bar-sur-Aube book of vestitions, 1649–75, Capuchin Friary, Church Street, Dublin, Capuchin Provincial Archives · LPL, Archbishop Tenison's MSS, MS 1029 · PRO, E133/151/50 [exchequer depositions] · *Bishop Burnet's History* · W. Beamont, ed., *The Jacobite trials at Manchester in 1694*, Chetham Society, 28 (1853) · *The trials at Manchester*, ed. W. Goss, Chetham Society (1864) · Northants. RO, Buccleuch papers, vol. 63 · 'Taff proposes Discovery's [*sic*]', [1717–19], BL, MS Stowe 247, 182–3 · PRO, Forfeited estates commission records, FEC 1 and 2 · W. Dicconson, Diary, 1694–9, Ampleforth Abbey, MS 88 · *Harding's case* (1690), 2 Ventris 315, 86 ER 461 · papers on prince of Wales, 1690–1702, Glos. RO, Lloyd-Baker MSS, D3549/2/4/12

Archives Birm. CA, version of his 'Narrative of plot to murder king' · LPL, MS 1029 | PRO, forfeited estates commission records, summary of his papers on 'findings' of Commission for Superstitious Lands

Taaffe, Nicholas, sixth Viscount Taaffe and Count von Taafe in the nobility of the Holy Roman empire (c.1685–1769),

army officer in the Austrian service, was the son of Francis Taaffe (the grandson of John, first Viscount Taaffe) and his wife, Anna Maria, the daughter of John Crean of O'Crean's Castle, co. Sligo. He was born at O'Crean's Castle about 1685, but, his family having attached themselves to James II, he was educated in Lorraine. He was made chancellor to Duke Leopold of Lorraine, whose son married Maria Theresa and became Holy Roman Emperor Francis I.

After passing into the Austrian service, in 1726 Taaffe held a commission as captain in command of a squadron of Count Hautois's regiment. In October 1729 he became its lieutenant-colonel and on 3 January 1732 he was made colonel of the Lanthieri cuirassiers. He served with this regiment against the French in the War of the Polish Succession (1734–5) and against the Turks in the war of 1736–9. He commanded the rearguard which covered the retreat of the army at Fort St Elizabeth in November 1737, and again in September 1738, at Pallesch. He was present at the battle of Semlin on 11 October 1738. On 11 February 1739 he was promoted major-general (General-Feldwachtmeister). He was given the command of a brigade in the main army under Wallis, and distinguished himself in the operations around Belgrade. On 2 July 1752 he was promoted lieutenant-general (Feldmarschall-Lieutenant).

On 30 October 1729 Taaffe had married Maria Anna (d. 1769), the daughter and heir of Johann Philipp, Baron and first Count Spindler of Lintz, and he was himself afterwards made a count of the Holy Roman empire. His wife was lady of the bedchamber to Empress Maria Theresa. By the death of his second cousin, Theobald, fourth earl of Carlingford, in 1738, he succeeded to the title of Viscount Taaffe in the peerage of Ireland. His claim to the Irish estates was disputed by Robert Sutton, who was descended from the only daughter of Theobald Taaffe, first earl of Carlingford, and who took advantage of the penal laws which enabled protestants to supersede Catholic heirs. It was ultimately agreed (and confirmed by 15 Geo. II, c. 49) that the estates should be sold, and that Taaffe should receive one-third and Sutton two-thirds of the purchase money. They were bought by John Petty Fitzmaurice (afterwards earl of Shelburne).

Taaffe distinguished himself at the battle of Kolin (18 June 1757), where he helped to rally the heavy cavalry of the Austrian right wing, though he was at that time seventy-two. In 1763, in response to the famine in Silesia, where he held a large estate, he introduced the potato, which was quickly established as the staple diet of the rural population. In 1766 he published (in Dublin and London) *Observations on Affairs in Ireland from the Settlement in 1691 to the Present Time*. This was a moderate and dignified plea against the penal laws, with which he contrasted the tolerant policy of William III and of the German sovereigns. He was chamberlain to Emperor Charles VI and to Empress Maria Theresa.

Taaffe died at the castle of Ellischau in Bohemia on 30 December 1769, aged eighty-four, and was buried at St Katherine's Church in Silberberg, Silesia, on 1 January 1770. He had two sons, of whom the elder, John (b. 1733 in London), was attached to the Austrian embassy in Madrid in 1755 and in 1764 was ambassador to Portugal. He died suddenly, in suspicious circumstances, on 11 December 1765 on his return from a mission to Naples. Thus it was his son, Rudolph (1762–1830), who served in several Austrian cavalry regiments, who succeeded to the title as seventh Viscount Taaffe. The Taaffe family continued in the Austrian service throughout the nineteenth century, holding both civil and military office. Successive heads of the family maintained their status as Irish viscounts until Henry Taaffe, twelfth Viscount Taaffe, was stripped of his peerage in 1919 under the terms of the Titles Deprivation Act (1917) for having borne arms against the United Kingdom during the First World War.

E. M. LLOYD, *rev.* JONATHAN SPAIN

Sources GEC, *Peerage* · *Memoirs of the Taaffe family* (1756) [privately printed] · J. Lodge, *The peerage of Ireland*, 4 (1754), 293–4 · 'Taaffe pedigree', *N&Q*, 5th ser., 2 (1874), 425 · W. E. H. Lecky, *A history of Ireland in the eighteenth century*, 1 (1892), 220–21
Likenesses J. Dixon, mezzotint, 1763 (after R. Hunter), BM, NPG · S. Harding, stipple, pubd 1801 (after R. Hunter), NG Ire. · E. Bocquet, stipple, pubd 1806, NPG · engraving, repro. in *Memoirs of the Taaffe family*, 302

Taaffe, Theobald, first earl of Carlingford (*d.* 1677), army officer and politician, was the son of John Taaffe, first Viscount Taaffe of Corren and baron of Ballymote (*d.* 1641/2), and his wife, Anne, daughter of Theobald Dillon, first Viscount Dillon of Costello-Gallen. Little is known of his early years. His first wife was Mary, daughter of Sir Nicholas White of Leixlip, co. Kildare, with whom he had seven children, of whom the third and fourth, Nicholas Taaffe and Francis *Taaffe (1639–1704), in turn succeeded him as earl of Carlingford. In 1639 Theobald was MP for Sligo.

Taaffe was one of the recruiting colonels licensed to transport veterans of Thomas Wentworth, earl of Strafford's disbanded army, and he may have been peripherally involved in planning the 1641 rising. At any rate two companies recruited for his regiment, in Sligo and Tyrone respectively, joined the insurgents while Phelim O'Neill, the insurgent leader, alleged that Taaffe's father was 'as deeply engaged in the business as he was' (Archdall, 4.293). Taaffe subsequently went to England to fight for Charles I. After the cessation (September 1643) between the confederate Catholics and Charles I Taaffe, along with Thomas Dillon, fourth Viscount Dillon of Costello-Gallen, his kinsman, and others, returned to Ireland and he attended the 1643 general assembly in Kilkenny. In the emergent split between clericalists, who demanded full religious freedom, and the *politique* Ormondist or Old English faction Taaffe was identified with the latter; he was, claimed a clericalist 'a seeming Catholicke' who 'would not suffer … but the privation of an acre of glebe land for the furtherance of religion' (Gilbert, *Contemporary history*, 1.76). The confederate Catholic supreme council appointed him commander of their army of Connaught in 1644, replacing John Bourke. He captured several parliamentarian garrisons, including the key outpost of Roscommon Castle. However, he neglected to place a reliable garrison in Roscommon Castle and it was subsequently surrendered to the parliamentarians. This reverse, and his failure to take the confederate oath of association, cast doubts on his loyalty and he was, in turn, replaced as commander of the Connaught army.

Taaffe returned to Kilkenny where, according to clericalist gibes, he passed on 'all the intelligence and secret intentions' (Gilbert, *Contemporary history*, 1.99) of the confederate Catholics to James Butler, marquess of Ormond, Charles I's deputy in Dublin. In 1646 he accompanied Ormond on what was intended to be a triumphal progress, proclaiming a definitive peace treaty between the royalists and the confederate Catholics. Later he was peripherally involved in attempts to suborn Thomas Preston's Leinster army from allegiance to the clericalist or rejectionist faction. Ormond's surrender of Dublin to the parliamentarians and departure from Ireland left Taaffe and the other Ormondists, including his kinsmen Viscount Dillon and Sir James Dillon with little option but that of *rapprochement* with the confederate Catholics.

In July 1647 Taaffe swore the confederate oath of association and, surprisingly, was appointed general of the Munster army. The latter had been rent by division between rival appointees, the nuncio Rinuccini's nominee, Edward Somerset, earl of Glamorgan, and the Ormondist Bonogh MacCarthy, Viscount Muskerry. Taaffe's appointment marked, effectively, Rinuccini's defeat; it is likely that Muskerry reasoned that he could best oppose the nuncio by taking a seat on the supreme council while Taaffe would be, politically, a safe pair of hands. At this point Taaffe may have been implicated in a plot by the royalist courtier George, Lord Digby, to recruit soldiers from the confederate Leinster and Munster armies for the French service. For this reason Digby pleaded with Taaffe not to risk his army in battle as his plans for French service 'depend on your preserving your army' (Ó Siochrú, 157). The Ormondists on the supreme council, led by Muskerry, shared Digby's fears that Taaffe would lose his army if he was allowed to give battle and wanted to keep it in being at all costs 'to countenance their faction' (McNeill, 277). However, the notorious sacking of Cashel in September 1647, and his raid on Callan (a town about 10 miles from Kilkenny, the confederate Catholic capital) finally goaded the confederates into confronting Murrough O'Brien, earl of Inchiquin. By the end of September the supreme council feared that Inchiquin, from east Munster, and Michael Jones, from north Leinster, might both advance towards Kilkenny and bisect confederate territory. The council now threatened to replace Taaffe if he did not fight Inchiquin.

Taaffe was thus shamed into giving battle, at Knocknanuss, near Mallow, in co. Cork, on 13 November 1647. Blaming the subsequent defeat on Taaffe's 'sheer incompetence' (Ó Siochrú, 158) is not too harsh a judgement. He enjoyed superiority of numbers and the advantage of higher ground but his army was unusually heterogeneous, comprising distinct infantry contingents from his native Connaught, Munster, and 'Redshanks' from western Scotland. He exacerbated this problem by deploying his 6000 infantry in separate Redshank/Connaught and Munster formations which 'by the interposition of a hill, had no sight the one of the other' (Irish Confederation, ed. Gilbert, 7.34). Alasdair MacColla MacDonald, recently returned from Scotland, commanded the Redshanks on the Irish right wing and charged, breaking the opposing wing and overrunning Inchiquin's artillery lines and baggage train. However, Taaffe did not support this local success and meanwhile the Munster contingent, commanded by Taaffe himself, after firing a single volley at their attackers, broke at the first charge 'wherein they lost not six men' (A Perfect Narrative of the Battell of Knocknones, 7). The allegation that Taaffe was bribed to leave MacColla to be overwhelmed was baseless; he tried ineffectually to rally his fleeing infantry and cavalry. However, the allegation conveys the depth of clericalist mistrust of Taaffe.

In all, Taaffe may have lost up to 4000 men in a battle where no quarter was given. This, together with the defeat at Dungan's Hill (August 1647), crippled the confederate Catholic military effort and made the Irish more amenable to hitherto unsatisfactory peace terms with the royalists. Taaffe held a relatively unimportant position as commander of the artillery in the reconstituted royalist–confederate Catholic alliance of 1649. He was present at the alliance's siege of Dublin (24 July – 2 August 1649) that concluded with the routing of the besiegers at the battle of Rathmines.

In autumn 1650 Ormond sent Taaffe to solicit money and supplies from Charles, duke of Lorraine, at Brussels.

In June 1651 he went to Paris to report to the English court in exile on the negotiations. Meanwhile, two other envoys arrived from Ireland and concluded a treaty with Lorraine (12 July 1652), acknowledging him as 'Protector Royal' of Ireland. Taaffe repudiated the treaty, ostensibly as an infringement of Charles II's sovereignty. Lorraine, in turn, lost interest and brusquely dismissed Charles II's invitation to renew negotiations.

After the Restoration Taaffe was created earl of Carlingford and, in 1665, Charles II sent him on a diplomatic mission to the Habsburg Emperor Leopold and the prince-bishop of Münster. In 1667 he was restored to all his own estates and, in addition, was granted the estates of Taaffe kinsmen in co. Louth and co. Tyrone who had been implicated in the 1641 rising. He died on 31 December 1677. He was survived by his second wife, Anne Pershall, daughter of Sir William Pershall of Suggenhall, Staffordshire. She married Randal Plunkett, Viscount Dunsany, in or before 1681 and died before May 1711.

Assessments of Taaffe's political activities vary, depending on the observer's perspective and political sympathies. He was 'bred for action' (Carte, 3.429) to the Ormondists but a 'common, cogging gamester' (Gilbert, Contemporary history, 1.145) to the clericalist faction. His military ineptitude, however, was indisputable.

PÁDRAIG LENIHAN

Sources J. T. Gilbert, ed., *A contemporary history of affairs in Ireland from 1641 to 1652*, 1 (1879), 76, 93, 99–100, 108, 125, 145, 153, 172–6 · M. Ó Siochrú, *Confederate Ireland, 1642–1649* (Dublin, 1999), 157–8 · B. O'Ferrall and D. O'Connell, *Commentarius Rinuccinianus de sedis apostolicae legatione ad foederatos Hiberniae Catholicos per annos 1645–1649*, ed. J. Kavanagh, IMC, 2 (1936), 265, 748 · *History of the Irish confederation and the war in Ireland … by Richard Bellings*, ed. J. T. Gilbert, 7 vols. (1882–91), vol. 5, p. 34; vol. 7, p. 35 · *A perfect narrative of the battell of Knocknones … by an officer of the parliament's army* (1647), 7 · C. McNeill, ed., *The Tanner letters*, IMC (1943), 269, 277 · GEC, *Peerage* · J. Lodge, *The peerage of Ireland*, rev. M. Archdall, rev. edn, 7 vols. (1789) · [T. Carte], *The life of James, duke of Ormond*, new edn, 6 vols. (1851), vol. 3, p. 429; vol. 6, pp. 262, 276 · C. O'Conor, *Columbanus ad Hibernos: an historical address*, 2 (1812), 447–60

Archives Yale U., Beinecke L., corresp. and papers

Taaffe, Sir William (d. 1631?), soldier and local official, was the second son of John Taaffe of Harristown and Ballybragan, co. Louth. He was a Catholic whose family were gentry landowners in co. Louth for more than two centuries and had been recipients of confiscated monastic property. In 1588 he was sub-sheriff of co. Sligo, and was included in complaints of oppression lodged against the administration of Lord President Richard Bingham. He was accused of extortion, seizure of property, and accepting bribes but he managed to survive the attack. Taaffe fought in the wars against Tyrone, serving under Henry Norris in 1596, and in 1597 was appointed constable of St Leger's Castle. He was promoted to a captaincy in 1598, and distinguished himself in the fighting which followed the landing of the Spaniards at Kinsale in 1601. In January 1603 he was sent to attack the MacCarthys at Carbery. He entered their stronghold and, in their absence, seized their herds. The MacCartheys pursued and charged him at Cladach and in the fight which followed 120 were killed or drowned in the Bandon. The former included Owen Mac-Egan, the recently arrived vicar apostolic. By this exploit Carbery submitted to the English government. Taaffe was knighted on 25 March 1605.

With the war's end Taaffe returned to co. Sligo, where he was again appointed sheriff. He also retained his links to the Old English Catholic community of the pale, and in 1606 he was nominated constable of Ardee, co. Louth, a post he resigned in 1611. Meanwhile he continued buying and selling property in co. Sligo to consolidate his estates, centred on Ballymote, but he was forced to defend his gains in costly legal cases. By the early seventeenth century his family were the largest resident landowners in the county. He also acted as local agent for the acquisitions of Richard Boyle, earl of Cork. He married twice. His first wife was Elizabeth, daughter of Sir William Brett of Tulloch in Fingal. They had no children. His second marriage was to Ismay (d. c.1631), daughter of Sir Christopher Bellew. They had at least one son and two daughters, both of the daughters marrying Taaffe kinsmen. About 1620 he returned to live in co. Louth, served as sheriff of that county, and died at Ardee, co. Louth, probably on 9 February 1631. He was buried at Ardee. He had left his Sligo property in the hands of his son John, who in 1628 was created Viscount Taaffe and Baron Ballymote. John married Anne Dillon, daughter of the first Viscount Dillon, and died shortly before 9 January 1642. He was buried in Ballymote. He was succeeded by his son Theobald *Taaffe, later earl of Carlingford. J. G. ALGER, *rev.* JUDITH HUDSON BARRY

Sources M. O'Dowd, *Power, politics and land* (1991), 94–8 · Burke, *Gen. Ire.* (1976) · C. Lennon, *Sixteenth-century Ireland: the incomplete conquest* (1994), 259 · 'Taafe of Corren', GEC, *Peerage* · *CSP Ire.*, 1603–6
Wealth at death extensive properties, particularly in Co. Sligo

Tabley, de. For this title name *see* Leicester, John Fleming, first Baron de Tabley (1762–1827); Warren, John Byrne Leicester, third Baron de Tabley (1835–1895).

Tabor [Talbor, Talbot], **Sir Robert** (*bap.* 1642, *d.* 1681), physician and apothecary, was baptized on 30 January 1642 at Holy Sepulchre Church, Cambridge, the son of John Tabor (1607–1645), registrar to the bishop of Ely, and his wife, Elizabeth Maltywade; they were married at St Clements, Cambridge, on 13 January 1631. Tabor's grandfather James Tabor (d. 1645) was registrary of Cambridge University and clerk of sewers. Tabor was educated at the Perse School, Cambridge, by a Mr Griffith or Griffin, and was apprenticed to Peter Dent, an apothecary in the town. On 19 May 1663 he was admitted as a sizar to St John's College, Cambridge.

There is no evidence that Tabor received a degree from Cambridge; within a few years he had moved to the Essex marshes, specifically to perfect a cure for the agues of the marsh. It is now known that most marsh ague was malaria, a parasitic disease transmitted in England by the *Anopheles atroparvus* mosquito and the cause of great sickness and mortality in the seventeenth century. As an apothecary's apprentice in Cambridge Tabor must have had access to a plant with febrifugal powers newly imported from South America and known as the Peruvian bark, quinquina, or the 'Jesuit's powder'. There was much controversy surrounding the use of this drug, but Tabor was quick to recognize its virtues if rightly prepared and corrected, and administered by a skilful hand. He carried out many different trials among ague sufferers in Essex, and by the late 1660s he was successfully curing patients in Essex and London. He published the results of his researches in 1672 in a work entitled *Pyretologia: a Rational Account of the Cause and Cure of Agues*. He was, however, very secretive about his exact remedy, declaring that he would not reveal his methods and medicines 'till I have made some little advantage my self, to repay that charge and trouble I have been at, in the search and study of so great and unheard of secrets'. A French nobleman related its virtues to Charles II while visiting Sheerness, one of 'the most fever-ridden places in the whole of England'. The king was so impressed with Tabor's remedy that on 27 July 1672, he appointed him one of the king's physicians-in-ordinary.

Tabor set up his sign next door to Gray's Inn Gate in Holborn and enjoyed a lucrative practice in London. His reputation advanced rapidly, though, according to Sir George Baker, 'in proportion as he gained the favour of the great world, he lost that of the physicians' (Baker, 207–8). On 3 May 1678 the crown informed the Royal College of Physicians that Tabor, who was not one of its members, should not be molested or disturbed in his practice. He was knighted in Whitehall on 27 July 1678. On 17 February 1679 he married Elizabeth Aylet, of Rivenhall, Essex, at St Matthew's, Friday Street, London. The ceremony was performed by his brother, Thomas, of Kelvedon in Essex. In the same year, Tabor was sent by Charles II to royal households in Europe, where he proceeded to cure the dauphin of France of his 'pernicious fever', and Louisa Maria, queen of Spain, of her intermittent fevers. With the new title of Chevalier Talbot, he travelled the courts of Europe with his secret remedy. While Tabor was abroad, Charles II lay dangerously ill of an ague at Windsor. His physicians were very reluctant to give him the bark, because it had been brought into vogue by Tabor, a mere apothecary, but after the intervention of Thomas Short, the bark was prescribed and the king recovered. At about the same time, Louis XIV paid a large sum of money—some 2000 louis d'or—to obtain the knowledge of Tabor's secret cure, promising that it would not be published until after Tabor's death.

Tabor returned to London a wealthy man, but died soon after in 1681. On 17 November 1681 he was buried in Holy Trinity Church, Cambridge, in the north chapel, in a handsome tomb which he had built there in memory of his family and his fame. In 1682 Tabor's 'secret remedy' was published in French and English by order of the king of France. The book, *The English remedy, or, Talbor's wonderful secret for curing of agues and feavers, sold by the author Sir Robert Talbor, to the most Christian king, and since his death, ordered by his majesty to be published in French, for the benefit of his subjects, and now translated into English for public good* revealed that the basis of Tabor's remedy was, indeed, the Peruvian bark, infused in wine and mixed with other natural plants, and given in larger doses and at more frequent intervals than was usual at the time. The bark came from the South American cinchona tree, which was later found to contain the alkaloid quinine: this remains in use today as an important anti-malarial drug. The significance of Tabor's role in popularizing a treatment for malaria was, however, quickly forgotten (or subsequently attributed to Thomas Sydenham and Richard Morton). As a result, Tabor has been regarded as little more than an undistinguished quack.   MARY J. DOBSON

Sources R. Talbor, *Pyretologia: a rational account of the cause and cure of agues* (1672) · N. de Blegney, *Le remède anglais pour la guérison des fièvres: publié par ordre du roy. Avec des observations de monsieur le premier médecin de sa majesté sur la composition, les vertus, et l'usage de ce remède* (1682) · G. Baker, 'Observations on late intermittent fevers; to which is added a short history of the Peruvian bark', *Medical Transactions*, 3 (1785), 141–216 · R. E. Siegel and F. N. L. Poynter, 'Robert Talbor, Charles II, and cinchona: a contemporary document', *Medical History*, 6 (1962), 82–5 · M. J. Dobson, 'Bitter-sweet solutions for malaria: exploring natural remedies from the past', *Parassitologia* (1997) · P. Sonnié-Moret, *La marquise de Sévigné: une amie de la médecine, ennemie des médecins, 1626–1926* (1926) · *Lettres de Madame de Sévigné de sa famille et de ses amis*, 8 vols. (1863), 7.128 · Evelyn, *Diary*, 2.197 [29/11/1694] · M. L. Duran-Reynals, *The fever bark tree: the pageant of quinine* (1947) · S. Jarcho, *Quinine's predecessor: Francesco Torti and the early history of cinchona* (1993) · monument, Holy Trinity church, Cambridge

Tabor, Robert Stammers (1819–1909), headmaster and Church of England clergyman, born in Colchester on 14 February 1819, was the son of Robert Tabor. He was educated at a private school in Essex, before matriculating as a sizar at Trinity College, Cambridge, in 1838, graduating BA in 1842 as twenty-fourth senior optime in the mathematical tripos, and proceeding MA in 1848. Ordained deacon in 1842 and priest in 1844, he was curate to Henry Montagu Villiers, later bishop of Carlisle, at St George's, Bloomsbury, from 1842 to 1844, before being presented in 1844 to the perpetual curacy of Christ Church, Enfield, by the patron, Robert Cooper Lee Bevan (1809–90). He married on 7 March 1845 Mary, second daughter of Francis Dollman, perpetual curate of St Mark's, Clerkenwell.

Villiers and Bevan, a wealthy banker who had built Christ Church, Cockfosters, had become interested in the fortunes of Cheam School, a private classical school which was in a low state and facing closure. They agreed that Bevan should buy out the sitting head, Henry Shepheard (c.1809–1878), a former fellow of Oriel College, and headmaster since 1846. Tabor, who had supplemented his stipend at Enfield by taking private pupils, was to be installed in Shepheard's place. On becoming headmaster of Cheam in 1855 Tabor set about converting it into a private preparatory school catering for boys up to the age of fourteen. This soon proved a success and numbers rapidly grew; by 1864 there were 100 pupils. Cheam School built up a reputation as a nursery for Eton College and attracted a fashionable clientele; pupils under Tabor included (Lord) Randolph Churchill. In 1874 Tabor was joined by his son Arthur Sydney Tabor (1851–1927), a Cambridge cricket blue, who succeeded his father as headmaster from 1891 to 1920. His eldest son, Robert Montagu Tabor (1845–1925),

educated at Eton and King's College, Cambridge, was assistant secretary to the Board of Education from 1903 to 1909. In all Tabor had seven sons and five daughters.

On 15 December 1887 Tabor married again; his second wife was Annie, daughter of J. Harvey, a barrister. After his retirement in 1890 he lived at 64 St George's Square, London, where he died on 14 January 1909.

DONALD P. LEINSTER-MACKAY

Sources E. Peel, *Cheam School from 1645* (1974) · *The Times* (18 Jan 1909) · *The Times* (20 Jan 1909) · Venn, *Alum. Cant.*
Wealth at death £37,820 17s. 7d.: probate, 23 Feb 1909, CGPLA Eng. & Wales

Taché, Alexandre Antonin (1823–1894), Roman Catholic archbishop of Manitoba, son of Charles Taché (1784–1826), a captain in the Canadian militia, and Henriette Boucher de la Broquerie, was born at Rivière du Loup, Lower Canada, on 23 July 1823. Being the third child, intellectual, and devout, he seems to have been destined for the church. Educated first at the Séminaire de Saint-Hyacinthe and then at the Grand Séminaire de Saint-Sulpice, both south of Montreal, he became a priest in 1842. His real enthusiasm was for missionary work and he joined the Oblate order two years later. The next year he departed on the 1400 mile journey to take up his work in the west.

St Boniface, the centre to which Taché reported, was part of the straggling Red River settlement situated near the site of what later became Winnipeg. Formally established by Lord Selkirk in 1811, the settlement was a heterogeneous mix of religious and ethnic groups in the middle of the vast Hudson's Bay territories. For Taché this presented both opportunities and problems. Under Sir George Simpson, the Hudson's Bay Company was suspicious of Catholic influence on the native population and tended to favour protestant efforts. Taché felt the missions were crucial to his calling. Over the next years he travelled across the west, preaching to native tribes and establishing missions. Through his diplomatic skills he avoided confrontation with the company and thereby established his importance to the church in the region.

Taché's ability and the scarcity of personnel in the north-west meant he was appointed bishop of Arath and coadjutor to Bishop Provencher in 1850 at the age of twenty-seven. In 1853, when Provencher died, Taché became bishop of St Boniface. Over the next decade he extended the missionary network among the Métis and American Indian populations. He proved effective at raising support both among orders such as the Grey nuns and among the populace in Lower Canada. By 1860 Roman Catholic missions stretched across the west, from Red River to the Rockies, and north into the subarctic.

The later 1850s marked the beginning of a distinct phase in both the history of the north-west and in Taché's life. Expansionists in the province of Canada (present-day Ontario and Quebec) had become interested in the north-west as a potentially rich agricultural hinterland. The region's isolation was ending as early settlers and adventurers from Canada moved to Red River in increasing numbers. The loud demands of the new arrivals for annexation to Canada upset the settlement's delicate social and political balance. Henceforth Taché directed much effort towards the support of the local French Catholic population, writing *Esquisse sur le nord-ouest de l'Amérique* (1869), an immigration tract aimed at drawing more Francophones to the region to counter English protestant immigration.

Taché's role on behalf of the Métis became more apparent later in 1869. Britain had agreed to transfer responsibility for the territories to Canada and Taché went to Ottawa to lobby the ruling Conservative Party on behalf of French Catholics in the region. At first he was treated casually, but when a group of Métis under Louis Riel established a provisional government and resisted the entry of Canadian officials Taché was called back from the First Vatican Council in Rome and appointed as an emissary for the federal government. By February 1870 he was back in Canada and on his way to Red River.

What happened next is controversial. When Taché arrived at Red River he promised that, among other things, there would be an amnesty for all those involved in the uprising. Those sympathetic to Taché argue that he was manipulated by the government into giving promises that were never intended to be honoured. Others argue that in the interval Riel had executed an Ontario protestant named Thomas Scott. Scott's execution made it impossible for the prime minister, John A. Macdonald, to continue on the course he had outlined to Taché; when Colonel Garnet Wolseley's expedition marched into Red River in late June, there was no amnesty and Riel fled into exile south of the border. Later efforts by Taché to obtain an amnesty were rebuffed by Macdonald.

Although the Red River resistance marked the height of his public profile, Taché was by no means inactive thereafter. In 1871 he became the first archbishop of Manitoba. Through the 1870s he continued his efforts to assert a French and Catholic institutional presence in the west. In spite of occasional efforts aimed at encouraging Catholic immigrants, he recognized that the majority of the population in the west was likely to be English and protestant. Legal buffers and constitutional protections were thus the best way of ensuring that a minority culture could survive. He continued in his efforts, concentrating in particular on the preservation of a distinct Roman Catholic educational system. The last great battle of his life was to resist the decision in Manitoba in 1890 to abolish the parallel system of protestant and Catholic education. In this he was unsuccessful, though a 'compromise' in 1897 did yield minor concessions for Roman Catholics.

Taché died on 22 June 1894 at Winnipeg, and was buried five days later at St Boniface. Less controversial than Riel, Taché's historical image is nevertheless strongly affected by similar currents, most importantly the transitional age in which he lived. Though born in Lower Canada (later Quebec), he had spent the majority of his life in the vast territories to the west of the Great Lakes that were, until 1870, under the control of the Hudson's Bay Company. He served not only as missionary to the native population but also as the diplomatic voice of Catholicism in discussions with the Hudson's Bay Company, as rival to protestant missionaries, and as primary interlocutor between local resistance and Canadian expansion. In his time the west changed from a native-based hunting and trapping economy with a powerful Catholic Métis presence to an agricultural frontier dominated by English protestants. Amid the shifts of population and power that this implied, Taché played a central role defending the interests of his religion and his language. He was ultimately overwhelmed by the sheer force of numbers. Yet the ongoing presence of a native Catholic tradition and of active Francophone communities indicate that Taché was not without influence upon the region. DOUG OWRAM

Sources G. Friesen, *The Canadian prairies: a history* (1984) · *DCB*, vol. 12 · W. L. Morton, 'Introduction', in *Alexander Begg's Red River journal* (1956) · W. L. Morton, *Manitoba: a history*, 2nd edn (1957) · D. Owram, *Promise of Eden: the Canadian expansionist movement and the idea of the west* (1992) · R. Painchaud, 'French Canadian historiography and the Franco-Catholic settlement in western Canada 1870–1915', *Canadian Historical Review*, 59 (1978), 446–66 · G. F. G. Stanley, *Louis Riel* (1985) · *Manitoba Free Press* (23 June 1894)
Archives Archives de l'Archevêché de Saint-Boniface · Archives des Oblats de Marie-Immaculée, Montreal, Quebec · Archives du Séminaire de Trois-Rivières, Trois-Rivières, Quebec

Taché, Sir Étienne-Pascal (1795–1865), politician in Canada, was born at St Thomas, Lower Canada (later Montmagny, Quebec), on 5 September 1795, the third son of Charles Taché, a trader, and Geneviève Michon, who altogether had ten children. His grandfather Jean Taché, a Paris merchant, migrated to Canada in 1739 and settled in Quebec. Alexandre Antonin *Taché was his nephew. The family had been very wealthy, and, although ruined in the Seven Years' War, kept its position of influence. Taché enrolled in the Roman Catholic Séminaire de Québec, but abandoned his studies to join the militia and fight against the United States in the Anglo-American War of 1812–14, latterly as a lieutenant in the Canadian *chasseurs*. After the war he studied medicine, first in Quebec and then in Philadelphia; he qualified in 1819. In 1820 he married Sophie Baucher of Beaumont, with whom he had fifteen children. He established an extensive medical practice in Montmagny and became an influential member of the Quebec medical establishment.

Like many of the French-Canadian professional class, Taché was a *patriote*, but he was a moderate who did not support armed rebellion, and, although he came under suspicion for complicity in the rebellions of 1837–8, he escaped arrest. In 1841 he abandoned medicine for politics and entered the new assembly of the united province of Canada as member for L'Islet and a follower of the moderate French-Canadian Reformers led by Louis-Hyppolyte LaFontaine and later by Augustin-Norbert Morin, whom Taché had sheltered during the rebellion. Although a minor politician in the struggle for responsible government, he gained a reputation for being a Conservative monarchist who abhorred the United States. In 1846, as a reward for his loyalty, he was appointed deputy adjutant-general of the militia for Lower Canada, and he gave up his assembly seat. In 1848 he was appointed for life to the legislative council and entered the LaFontaine–Baldwin ministry as commissioner of public works (1848–9). He strongly supported the Rebellion Losses Bill, which led to violent protest from the British minority in Lower Canada. It was widely believed but never proven that he killed William Mason, one of the rioters involved in an attack on LaFontaine's home.

During the 1850s a political realignment took place in the united province of Canada as the French-Canadian bloc led by Morin abandoned its historic alliance with the Reformers of Canada West and formed a new alliance with the Canada West Conservatives. Taché was one of the architects of this realignment and a central figure among the French-Canadian Conservatives (or *bleus*). He served as receiver-general (1849–56), speaker of the legislative council (1856–7), and commissioner of crown lands (1857), and was briefly one of the joint prime ministers of the united province (1856–7), first with Allan Napier MacNab and then with John A. Macdonald, thus sealing the Conservative–*bleu* alliance. As ethnic and sectional tensions in the united province worsened, Taché resigned in 1857. In 1860 he became president of the council of public instruction, a non-ministerial post. In 1858 he was knighted and in 1860 served as aide-de-camp to the prince of Wales during his Canadian tour. He was pressed back into politics during the political crisis of 1864, first as co-prime minister with Macdonald and then as the titular leader of the 'Great Coalition', which had confederation as its goal. Chosen as prime minister because he was an acceptable second choice to the leaders of the factions entering the coalition, he presided over the Quebec Conference in 1864. However, he suffered a slight paralysis in February 1865 and died on 30 July, and so played only a minor role in the debate over confederation in Lower Canada (Quebec after 1867). After a state funeral he was buried on 2 August at Montmagny.

Taché is largely a forgotten figure in modern Quebec, and he is often dismissed as a *vendu* because of his support for the British connection and confederation. Yet, in his transition from moderate Reformer to moderate Conservative after the establishment of responsible government, his growing fear of the United States, and his increasing sympathy for the imperial connection, he was typical of the majority of the French-Canadian élite in the aftermath of the failed rebellions of 1837–8.

PHILLIP BUCKNER

Sources *DCB*, vol. 9 · *Quebec Daily Mercury* (2 Nov 1864) · *Quebec Daily Mercury* (31 July 1865) · *Quebec Daily Mercury* (23 Aug 1865) · *DNB* · P. B. Waite, *The life and times of confederation, 1864–1867* (1962)

Taché, Joseph-Charles (1820–1894), journalist and civil servant, was born on 24 December 1820 at Kamouraska, Lower Canada, the first of five children of Charles Taché (1784–1826), notary, merchant, and militia captain, and his wife, Louise-Henriette, daughter of Joseph-Ignace Boucher de la Broquerie. The Tachés, a merchant and seigneurial family, had been established in Canada since 1730 and at Kamouraska since 1785. Taché entered le Petit Séminaire de Québec in 1832. He turned from classics to medicine in 1841, graduated from the Quebec Marine and Emigrant Hospital in 1844, settled at Rimouski, nearly 200 miles down the St Lawrence, and on 1 July 1847 married Françoise Lepage.

In 1848 Taché was elected to the Canadian legislative assembly, where he supported Louis-Hippolyte LaFontaine, who had just formed a ministry with the support of French Canada's increasingly ultramontane clergy. Taché helped to strengthen that support, gaining clerical admiration by his anti-liberal polemics.

In 1855 Taché was Canadian commissioner to the Paris Universal Exhibition. He contributed significantly to the success of Canada's exhibit but was accused of careerism by some English Canadians when the French government made him a chevalier of the Légion d'honneur. His own constituents had begun to repudiate him in 1854 when he had opposed a bill that abolished Lower Canada's feudal land tenure. Resigning his seat at the end of 1856 he accepted the editorship of *Le Courrier du Canada*, a newspaper being founded at Quebec to represent clerical opinion. Taché made it a model of ultramontane journalism, promoting a mix of French-Canadian nationalism and clerico-conservative social values.

Among his articles was an 1857 series advocating a federation of British North American provinces. Taché believed an effective central government could advance Canada's economic interests, yet he proposed a decentralized confederation in which federal powers were merely a 'limited concession from the different provinces', while provincial autonomy allowed 'the national and religious elements to develop their societies freely' (Taché, *Des Provinces*, 148, 151). Although the actual British North American confederation, devised seven years later, was more centralized than Taché's, several of its supporters insisted that his plan had been the blueprint.

Taché left the *Courrier* in 1859, entering government service as inspector of prisons, asylums, and public charities. He remained active in Quebec city's literary circle and took a leading part when they launched a journal, *Les Soirées Canadiennes*, in 1861. They wanted to create a French-Canadian national literature, and Taché thought they must seek its sources in the legends, traditions, and popular customs of the people. Despite the 1862 defection of most of his colleagues, Taché maintained the *Soirées* until the end of 1865. His own work, *Forestiers et voyageurs*, first published in 1863, reflected his ultramontane and romantic nationalism. It drew on folklore and his own forest experiences, mingling the picturesque, the adventurous, and a firm attachment to Catholicism.

In 1864 Taché became deputy minister of agriculture and statistics—a post he assumed in the federal administration after 1867. He supervised the censuses, doing innovative work on that of 1871; he represented Canada at the 1867 International Exhibition, and he was responsible for public health, introducing important reforms and creating facilities for the treatment of leprosy. Meanwhile, prompted by his brother, the archbishop of St Boniface (Manitoba), he helped obtain government assistance for French-Canadian settlement on the western prairies.

Injured in a fall in 1888, Taché was forced to retire from government service and take up residence in the Ottawa

General Hospital, where, crippled by arthritis, he continued to write both literary and medical works. He died on 16 April 1894 and was buried three days later at Ottawa. He was survived by his wife. Cabinet ministers and prelates mingled at the funeral in the Roman Catholic cathedral in homage to a pioneer of Canadian public service, French-Canadian literature, and ultramontane journalism.   A. I. SILVER

Sources E. Bossé, *Joseph-Charles Taché (1820–1894): un grand représentant de l'élite canadienne-française* (1971) · J.-G. Nadeau, 'Taché, Joseph-Charles', *DCB*, vol. 12 · J.-C. Taché, *Des provinces de l'Amérique du Nord et d'une union fédérale* (1858) · J.-C. Taché, *Forestiers et voyageurs* (1863); [another edn] (Montreal, 1981) · C. Piette-Samson, 'La représentation ultramontaine de la société à travers le Courrier du Canada', *Les idéologies au Canada Français, 1850–1900*, ed. F. Dumont and others (Quebec, 1971) · A. I. Silver, *The French-Canadian idea of confederation, 1864–1900* (1982) · E. Heaman, 'Commercial leviathan: central Canadian exhibitions at home and abroad during the 19th century', PhD diss., University of Toronto, 1996 · R. Robidoux, '"Les soirées canadiennes" et "Le foyer canadien" dans le mouvement littéraire Québécois de 1860', *Revue de l'Université d'Ottawa*, 28 (1958) · P. Sylvain, 'Les débuts du "Courrier du Canada" et les progrès de l'ultramontanisme canadien-français', *Les cahiers des dix* (1967) · *L'Evénement* [Quebec] (17 April 1894) · *L'Evénement* [Quebec] (18 April 1894) · *L'Evénement* [Quebec] (19 April 1894) · *La Presse* [Montreal] (19 April 1894) · *DCB*, vol. 12
Archives Archives Nationales du Québec, corresp., notes, poetry, lectures, family papers [collection covers the period 1730–1912] · Fonds Corporation Archiépiscopal Catholique Romaine de St-Boniface, Archives de la Société Historique de St-Boniface, letters | NA Canada, Department of Agriculture MSS · NA Canada, Dept of the Interior, dominion lands branch, file no. 165914
Likenesses photographs, NA Canada, reference no. C_081492

Tacitus (*b*. AD 56/7, *d*. in or after 113). *See under* Julius Agricola, Gnaeus (AD 40–93).

Tadema, Laura Theresa Alma- (1852–1909). *See under* Tadema, Sir Lawrence Alma- (1836–1912).

Tadema, Sir Lawrence Alma- (1836–1912), painter, was born Lorenz Alma Tadema on 8 January 1836 in the small village of Dronrijp, in Friesland, the sixth child of Pieter Jiltes Tadema (1797–1840) and Hinke Dirks Brouwer (c.1800–1863).

Education and early career Although his family had intended the young Lorenz Tadema to pursue a legal career, at fifteen he was diagnosed as consumptive, given only a short time to live, and allowed to spend his remaining days drawing and painting. At sixteen he began a formal art training at the Academy of Art in Antwerp. In 1857 he entered the studio of Louis Jan de Taeye (professor of archaeology at the academy, whose classes in history and historical costume he had attended), where he remained until November 1858. Influenced by his friendships with de Taeye and the Egyptologist Georg Ebers, he first produced work of a historical character on Merovingian and Egyptian subjects. In 1859 he joined the Antwerp studio of Baron Henri Leys, where he completed his first major painting, a Merovingian subject, *The Education of the Children of Clovis* (1861; priv. coll.). Although it was criticized by Leys, who compared its depiction of marble to cheese

Sir Lawrence Alma-Tadema (1836–1912), self-portrait, 1896

(Alma-Tadema, 204), it received excellent reviews and was acquired by King Leopold of the Belgians. The young artist soon established a reputation on the continent, and in 1864 *Pastimes in Ancient Egypt* (1863; Harris Museum and Art Gallery, Preston) was awarded a gold medal at the Paris Salon and a second-class medal in the Paris Universal Exhibition of 1867.

The years 1863 and 1864 marked a turning point in Alma-Tadema's life and career. On 24 September 1863 he married (Marie) Pauline (1837–1869), the daughter of Eugene Gressin, a French journalist living in Brussels, and that same year made his first trip to Italy. The couple's honeymoon visit to Pompeii coincided with the first systematic excavations of the site and Alma-Tadema, inspired by what he had witnessed, embarked on his first paintings depicting the classical world. From 1865 the representation of Roman life dominated his oeuvre. Set in Pompeian-type interiors characterized by vibrant red walls, these Roman pictures appropriate ancient architecture, decoration, and accessories, as well as Latin literature. A striking example of this type of painting is *Catullus at Lesbia's* (1865); set in a richly decorated Pompeian interior, it evokes the famous poem (Catullus 3) in which the Roman poet Catullus laments the death of his mistress Lesbia's pet sparrow.

Influenced by French néo-Grec painters such as Jean-Léon Gérôme, who significantly altered the treatment of ancient subjects by eschewing the depiction of well-known heroes in favour of scenes of everyday life, Alma-Tadema concentrated on historical genre subjects showing anonymous Romans engaged in ordinary activities.

Favoured subjects included courtship rituals (*A Silent Greeting*, 1889; Tate collection), bathing (*A Favourite Custom*, 1909; Tate collection), dining (*The Dinner*, 1873; William Morris Gallery, Walthamstow, London), and the performance of pagan rites (*A Dedication to Bacchus*, 1889; Hamburger Kunsthalle).

In 1864 Alma-Tadema secured a lucrative commission from the Belgian art dealer Ernest Gambart for twenty-four pictures; five years later he received a second contract for another forty-eight. Gambart exhibited Alma-Tadema's work at the French Gallery in London with the aim of enhancing the artist's reputation in Britain. By the time that Alma-Tadema exhibited his first works at the Royal Academy, in 1869—*A Roman Art Lover* (1868; Glasgow Museums and Art Galleries) and *A Pyrrhic Dance* (1869; Guildhall Art Gallery, London)—he was well known in European and British art circles.

Alma-Tadema and his wife, Pauline, had three children: two girls, Laurense and Anna, and a boy who died soon after his birth. In 1869 Pauline died, after years of ill heath. A year later, at the outbreak of the Franco-Prussian War, the family moved to London, where Alma-Tadema Anglicized his forename to Lawrence and, in 1873, was granted letters of denization from Queen Victoria. Meanwhile on 29 July 1871 he married his pupil Laura Theresa Epps, youngest daughter of the homoeopathic physician George Napoleon *Epps (1815–1874) and his wife, Anne Charlotte Bacon (1813–1890). **Laura Theresa Alma-Tadema** (1852–1909) became a painter in her own right. She concentrated on domestic and genre scenes, often in Dutch seventeenth-century settings. Following her death, on 15 August 1909, a memorial exhibition of her work was held at the Fine Art Society in 1910.

Success in London Shortly after moving to Britain Alma-Tadema established himself as a major figure in the Victorian art world, securing election as associate of the Royal Academy in 1876 and as academician only three years later. His first London residence—Townshend House, near Regent's Park—was decorated in an eclectic style incorporating Pompeian, Dutch, and Byzantine motifs. In 1886 he moved to a new house in Grove End Road, St John's Wood, an area fashionable among artists. Originally belonging to Jean-Jacques Tissot (also a former pupil of Baron Henri Leys) the house was extensively remodelled to Alma-Tadema's own design and once again incorporated eclectic motifs. A striking and original feature was the domed ceiling of the studio; covered with aluminium paint it cast a silvery light, allowing the artist to simulate a Mediterranean sunlight even in the winter months. Laura Alma-Tadema's studio, by contrast, was fitted with dark wood panelling in the image of a Dutch-style interior. The decoration of his studio had a profound effect on Alma-Tadema's work. The walls of his Antwerp studio were bright red, in Townshend House light green, and in Grove End Road silvery white. Accordingly by the 1880s the settings of his paintings had moved from Pompeian interiors of dark, rich tones to exteriors of glistening marble and bright Mediterranean sea and sky. For example the settings of *Coign of Vantage* (1895; priv. coll.) and *Silver Favourites* (1903; Manchester City Galleries), both completed in Grove End Road, with their marble terraces overlooking a clear blue sea, suggest the luxurious holiday villas built by wealthy Romans along the coastline of the Bay of Naples.

During the 1870s and 1880s Alma-Tadema turned to subjects illustrative of Roman history. However, rather than exemplifying high-minded ideals of moral courage and heroism these works depict inglorious moments in Roman history. *A Roman Emperor AD 41* (1871; Walters Art Gallery, Baltimore) shows the proclamation of Claudius as emperor after the murder of his infamous nephew Caligula; and *The Roses of Heliogabalus* (1888; priv. coll.), the artist's most glorious revel in Roman decadence, depicts a mad emperor in the act of suffocating his dinner guests under a deluge of rose petals.

Although mainly concerned with Roman subjects Alma-Tadema also turned briefly to Greece. Unlike Frederic Leighton, whose Greek paintings represented mythological or literary themes, or Albert Moore, who utilized Greek-type drapery styles and motifs essentially as embellishment of aesthetic paintings, Alma-Tadema's Greece is a historical world, as meticulously constructed as his Rome from ancient sources. Although depicting an imaginary event, *Phidias Showing the Frieze of the Parthenon to his Friends* (1868; Birmingham Art Gallery and Museum) shows the newly constructed Parthenon frieze and brings a tangibility to this most elevated symbol of Hellenism in the visual sphere. Alma-Tadema also painted a small number of portraits but avoided formal society commissions and concentrated on intimate depictions of family and friends. *94° in the Shade* (1876; FM Cam.), a portrait of Herbert Thompson, the son of Alma-Tadema's friend and doctor Sir Henry Thompson, evokes the balmy heat of a summer afternoon as a boy reads in the shaded corner of a hayfield. Furthermore it is one of the few examples to reveal the artist's skill as a *plein-air* landscapist. During the 1890s Alma-Tadema also played an important role in the visualization of the ancient world on the Victorian stage. He designed stage sets and costumes for major Shakespearian and modern dramatic productions, including Herbert Beerbohm Tree's *Hypatia* (1893)—based on Charles Kingsley's novel of the same name—*Julius Caesar* (1898), and Henry Irving's *Coriolanus* (1901).

Alma-Tadema's paintings are characterized by soft colour-harmonies, gorgeous textures, and settings of marbled interiors or sunny Mediterranean seascapes. Yet his works also reveal a remarkable knowledge of classical archaeology; it is salutary to note that he was awarded the gold medal of the Royal Institute of British Architects in 1906 in acknowledgement of the archaeological and architectural distinction of his reconstructions. Testimony to his knowledge of current archaeological developments is the accumulation of a vast library of over 4000 volumes, many of which were publications on ancient art and architecture by contemporary scholars and archaeologists. He also made numerous visits to sites in Italy and

Greece, where he was able to take his own measurements as well as make sketches. Many of his paintings present meticulous reconstructions of ancient buildings, including well-known Roman monuments, for example *The Coliseum* (1896; priv. coll.) and *Thermae Antoninianae* (*The Baths of Caracalla*) (1899; priv. coll.). He also depicted numerous sculptures, statuettes, and decorative objects based on Greek and Roman originals.

Photographs of ancient sculpture, architecture, and archaeological sites, along with a number of sketches by Alma-Tadema himself, formed part of an extensive reference collection (housed at the Heslop Library, University of Birmingham) of 167 portfolios. This collection assisted the artist in respect of both precision of archaeological detail and composition. Many of his works achieve an instantaneous impression, as found in photography, through the use of cut-off figures and buildings; a sense that the artist has caught a small part of a larger scene that continues beyond the confines of the canvas is conveyed. His method involved working directly on the canvas, from a quick initial sketch up to the final version. A perfectionist, he is known to have made alterations to paintings on the eve of exhibition and even after a work had already found a buyer.

Unlike other Victorian classical-subject painters, such as Frederic Leighton, Edward Poynter, and J. W. Waterhouse, whose repertoires included paintings of nudes and partially-clothed figures, Alma-Tadema produced few nudes. Those that he did paint are usually female figures set within the appropriate setting of the Roman bathhouse. The erotic potential of *Tepidarium* (1881; Lady Lever Art Gallery, Port Sunlight), depicting a flushed reclining nude, is diminished by its archaeologically-specific title and its tiny dimensions (24.2 cm x 33 cm). One of his few life-sized nudes, *A Sculptor's Model* (1877; priv. coll.), provoked the bishop of Carlisle to comment: 'for a living artist to exhibit a life-size, life-like, almost photographic representation of a beautiful naked woman strikes my inartistic mind as somewhat, if not very, mischievous' (A. M. W. Stirling, *The Richmond Papers*, 1926, 63). Alma-Tadema, however, was generally more interested in half-hidden suggestive allusions than in unashamed eroticism. For example *Spring* (1894; J. P. Getty Museum, Malibu) is a seemingly innocent and joyous scene showing a religious procession headed by a group of pretty flower girls. However, in the middle of the crowd a standard bears a Latin inscription, which can be recognized as a verse dedication (known as Catullus 18) to the fertility god, Priapus, while at the same time archaeological detail—silver statuettes of satyrs and decorative paintings of semi-nude frolicking couples—likewise points to another aspect of Roman religion; the initial, innocent reading of the painting is subverted.

Personality, death, and reputation Reminiscences from Alma-Tadema's contemporaries during the period are peppered with anecdotes relating to his jocular personality and lively sense of humour, though given the strong Dutch accent that he retained throughout his life his own stories and jokes often left his audience baffled. He was a notable member of the high cultural and social milieu of his day. His circle included the prince of Wales (later Edward VII) and the young Winston Churchill, while such illustrious guests as Tchaikovsky and Caruso attended his musical soirées. The painter Frederick Yeames and the critic F. G. Stephens described their meeting with him thus:

A short sturdily built man with twinkling eyes, cheery smile, hair parted in the middle of a broad forehead and small tawny beard, would hurry forward with an hospitable handshake, and bustling into his studio to look at pictures of Greek and Roman ladies reclining on the most marvellously painted marble, would talk rapid unfluent English telling stories quite outside his art, and beaming when he brought a smile to the lips of his guests. (Swanson, *Biography and Catalogue Raisonné*, 97)

From his time as an art student Alma-Tadema allocated each painting in his large oeuvre an opus number: *Portrait of my Sister, Artje* (1850), painted at the age of fifteen, is numbered 1, while two months before his death he completed *Preparations in the Coliseum* (1912; priv. coll.), numbered 408. During his lifetime he enjoyed both commercial success and a respected position in the art world. His patrons were international financiers who included Sir John Aird, the marqués de Santurce, and William Walters, and his works are now located in museums founded by such collectors: the Lady Lever Art Gallery, Port Sunlight, Cheshire; and the Walters Art Gallery, Baltimore. His standing in the British art world was acknowledged with a knighthood in 1899 and the Order of Merit in 1905. He died on 28 June 1912 at Kaiserhof Spa, Wiesbaden, Germany, where he was undergoing treatment for ulceration of the stomach, and was buried with full ceremony in St Paul's Cathedral, London, on 5 July.

A memorial exhibition held that year at the Royal Academy provoked unfavourable critical responses. The most scathing attack was by Roger Fry, who likened Alma-Tadema's figures and objects to 'highly-scented soap' (*The Nation*, 18 Jan 1913, 666–7). By the second decade of the twentieth century his brand of Victorian classicism was no longer fashionable. However, a renewed commercial and academic interest in Victorian painting during the late twentieth century revived his reputation, and his technical expertise, sensuous appeal, and subversive irony once again attracted a wide audience.

ROSEMARY BARROW

Sources V. G. Swanson, *The biography and catalogue raisonné of the paintings of Sir Lawrence Alma-Tadema* (1990) • *Sir Lawrence Alma-Tadema* (1996–7) [exhibition catalogue, Van Gogh Museum, Amsterdam, and Walker Art Gallery, Liverpool] • V. G. Swanson, *Sir Lawrence Alma-Tadema: the painter of the Victorian vision of the ancient world* (1997) • L. Lippincott, *Lawrence Alma Tadema: spring* (Malibu, 1990) • R. Barrow, 'The scent of roses: Alma-Tadema and the other side of Rome', *Bulletin of the Institute of Classical Studies*, 42 (1998), 183–202 • L. Alma-Tadema, 'Laurens Alma-Tadema, R.A.', *In the days of my youth*, ed. T. P. O'Conner (1901) • P. Cross Standing, *Sir Lawrence Alma-Tadema* (1905) • G. Ebers, *Lorenz Alma-Tadema: his life and work*, trans. M. J. Safford (1886) · A. Meynell, 'Laura Alma-Tadema', *Art Journal* (1883), 345–7 · R. Jenkyns, *Dignity and decadence: Victorian art and the classical inheritance* (1991) · b. cert. [Laura Theresa Epps] · m. cert. [Laura Theresa Epps] · d. cert. [Laura Alma-Tadema] · R. J. Barrow, *Lawrence Alma-Tadema* (2001)

Archives U. Birm. L., letters and portfolios containing photographs of his artwork | Bodl. Oxf., papers of his daughter, Laurense · Bodl. Oxf., letters to Sir George Lewis and Elizabeth, Lady Lewis · Bodl. Oxf., letters to F. G. Stephens · RA, letters to Royal Academy · RIBA BAL, corresp. with the Singtons · U. Birm. L., letters to Charles Deschamps · U. Glas. L., letters to D. S. MacColl · U. Leeds, Brotherton L., letters to Edmund Gosse

Likenesses L. Alma-Tadema, self-portrait, oils, 1852, Fries Museum, Leeuwarden · L. Alma-Tadema, self-portrait, 1859, Fries Museum, Leeuwarden · photograph, 1863, U. Birm. L. · double portrait, 1871 (with his wife), Fries Museum, Leeuwarden · L. Alma-Tadema, self-portrait, oils, 1883, Aberdeen Art Gallery · S. P. Hall, group portrait, chalk and wash, 1895 (*St John's Wood Art Club*), NPG · S. P. Hall, pencil drawing, 1895, NPG · E. Onslow Ford, bronze bust, 1895, RA · L. Alma-Tadema, self-portrait, oils, 1896, Uffizi Gallery, Florence [*see illus.*] · H. Furniss, pen-and-ink caricature, *c*.1900 (with H. Irving), Museum of London · L. Alma-Tadema, self-portrait, oils, 1908, Royal Accademia Romana di San Luca, Rome · W. Strang, chalk drawing, 1908, Royal Collection · F. Lion, pencil drawing, 1912, NPG · Ape [C. Pellegrini], caricature drawing, BM; repro. in *VF* · H. J. Brooks, group portrait, oils (*Private view of the Old Masters Exhibition, Royal Academy, 1888*), NPG · R. Cleaver, group portrait, pen and ink (*Hanging Committee, Royal Academy, 1892*), NPG · L. Connell, photograph, NPG · G. Grenville Manton, group portrait, watercolour (*Conversazione at the Royal Academy, 1891*), NPG · Lock & Whitfield, woodburytype photograph, NPG · London Stereoscopic Co., photograph, NPG · Walery, photograph, NPG

Wealth at death £58,834: administration with will, 27 July 1912, *CGPLA Eng. & Wales*

Tafawa Balewa, Sir Abubakar (1912–1966), prime minister of Nigeria, was born in December 1912 in the village of Tafawa Balewa (Black Rock) in the Lere district of Bauchi province, Northern Nigeria, the eldest son of Yakubu Dan Zala and his wife, Fatima Inna. From humble Islamicized and Hausa-speaking pagan stock and a Fulani mother, he was plucked from village school at Tafawa Balewa to attend Bauchi government provincial school. After studying at Katsina Higher College (1928–32), the 'Eton' for Northern Nigerian notables, where he had been sent on merit, he became a secondary school teacher. As a strict but kindly headmaster of Bauchi middle school from 1944, he was first exposed to corruption in public life. Sent to the University of London Institute of Education in 1946, he returned with an overseas teacher's certificate as Bauchi native authority (NA) educational assistant. A member of Emir Yakubu III's advisory council, Abubakar also became inspector of the province's schools.

The native authorities accepted their resident's hint that Abubakar should become Bauchi's representative to the northern house of assembly in 1947, and he was subsequently nominated to the central legislative council. He cautioned administrators and inexperienced legislators in Lagos House that a unitary Nigeria could never be moulded to the forms envisaged by south-western and south-eastern political parties stemming from minority tribal roots. Abubakar warned them that the north, lacking its own parties, put more into the budget than it

Sir Abubakar Tafawa Balewa (1912–1966), by Elliott & Fry, 1960

received, and that if the British 'quitted Nigeria', the northern people would continue their uninterrupted conquest to the sea. In 1949 the lack of 'senior service' northerners with university degrees was speciously answered by promoting four NA education assistants, including Abubakar, to the rank of education officer (NA). Abubakar in particular impressed the northern chief commissioner.

In the early 1950s the British governor, Sir John Macpherson, consulted widely on constitutional advance before introducing a system of electoral colleges, upwards to and through the regional assemblies. However, in 1951 northern urban election results, where progressive candidates won under southern-allied labels, alarmed many chiefs and traditionalist NA officials. The formerly 'cultural' Northern People's Congress (NPC) consequently established itself as a political party, of which Abubakar, although an NA official, became a prominent member. He went to Lagos in 1952 as a northern member of the central house of representatives, and became minister of works, overseeing a department controlled by an expatriate director, but able to travel widely throughout Nigeria. The leading politician in the north was Sir Ahmadu *Bello, sardauna of Sokoto. Initiatives were promptly taken to re-revise the constitution, accelerating ministerial control of services, in the wake of an unsuccessful motion by the western Action Group (AG) for self-government in 1956. That prospect left the country's politicians in turmoil amid northern threats of secession, to which Abubakar was not wholly averse. Following the establishment of the federal constitution in 1954, Abubakar was chosen as one of the three northern members of the council of ministers, and also served as minister of transport.

In 1954 the NPC elected a president-general. Abubakar was the popular choice, but the emirs and NA aristocrats backed the sardauna. Abubakar became first vice-president. In 1957 Abubakar's acceptability to the rivals of the NPC made it possible for him to be invited to form a government. He became Nigeria's first prime minister. The paradox followed that the country's political head was only the party deputy to the premier of the Northern Region. However, the extent to which Abubakar was under the sardauna's instructions has been exaggerated, as the prime minister was a strict constitutionalist, and the sardauna was only interested in the north and its place in the Muslim world.

Abubakar formed a government from all the leading parties. This federal coalition prepared for independence, accelerating localization of senior public services; economic development was led by railway extensions and oil exports. During the period from 1957 until Nigeria's independence on 1 October 1960, the British governor-general still presided over the council of ministers, and was responsible for the reserved subjects of defence, foreign affairs, and the civil service; but Abubakar was gradually introduced to the running of those departments so that when independence was achieved he had considerable experience of their problems.

The general election of 1959 gave the NPC a less than overall majority. The AG withdrew, and Abubakar's second administration was formed from only a coalition of the NPC and the National Council of Nigeria and the Cameroons (NCNC). The sardauna's wheeling and dealing with the mercurial Nnamdi Azikiwe, premier of the Eastern Region, resulted in the inflexible and humourless Chief Obafemi *Awolowo becoming AG leader of the opposition. It meant that the ambitious Azikiwe would preside over the senate before succeeding as governor-general a month after independence. To Abubakar's sorrow, the southern Cameroons, distrustful of its Igbo Ora neighbours, chose to join the new francophone state of Cameroon.

Internal troubles soon re-emerged to dispel the euphoria. The sardauna's efforts to become a leader in Islam strengthened southern fears of cultural as well as numerical domination. Schism in the Western Region in 1962 led to a suspension of its constitution and treason charges. The non-Yoruba parts of the west strengthened claims for a region of their own. A crisis over a corrupt census and its revision, confounding southern hopes of ever catching up with the north's numbers, widened the country's divisions and encouraged separatist thoughts in the non-Muslim areas of the north. Abubakar also recognized growing support for a republic. An election in 1964 under a further constitution provided for the institution of a president and a fourth region, the Mid-West Region. The NCNC boycotted this election, and Azikiwe, now constitutional president but believing in latent executive

powers, refused to invite Abubakar to form a government. He eventually conceded that he had no option. The boycotted constituencies duly elected the missing federal MPs. In 1965 a regional election in the truncated west resulted in virtual civil war. The sardauna's NPC in the north, having fallen out with the NCNC—which had been joining others to form the United Progressive Grand Alliance (UPGA)—had new ingratiating allies in the west and was itself regrouped with minority parties as the Nigerian National Alliance (NNA). This left the prime minister far less freedom to suspend the western government than in 1962. The federal cabinet faced stalemate.

Abubakar took refuge from internal tensions by presenting his country as Africa's international power. Abroad, except among the preachers of pan-Africanism, he was still seen as a prominent African statesman and as an icon of integrity. At independence he had committed the Nigerian army to the Congo. He impressed Nigeria's importance on the United Nations, on the Organization of African Unity, and on the Commonwealth. In January 1966 he hosted a meeting of Commonwealth heads of governments in Lagos, the first ever held outside the UK. The conference considered the problem of Rhodesia and was a success for Abubakar as chairman. However, he had failed to stem increasing disaffection within the army. In particular, three resentments grew: promotion blocks, with northerners holding many command appointments, dismay at corruption among ministers, and fear of religious and cultural domination by the sardauna's north. It was a fatal neglect, as after the Commonwealth conference a number of young, mostly Igbo, officers staged a *coup d'état*. On 15 January 1966 dissident soldiers murdered Abubakar, his finance minister, the sardauna, the western premier, and top northern army officers. The Nigerian general officer commanding imposed the first of a number of military governments.

Described by his *Times* obituarist as 'ascetic by nature, with a scholarly interest in Islam', Abubakar was an impressive, if reluctant leader. He was eloquent in English and known in Nigeria as the 'silver-voiced lion of the north'. He was 'calm and dignified where other politicians were flamboyant and florid' (*The Times*, 24 Jan 1966). Abubakar never sought to be prime minister: shrewd and commonsensical, he was a self-convinced patriot of a country that was artificial and far from united. He had many wives, the first of whom, Hafsatu, died in 1934, a year after their marriage. He was survived by four permanent wives and eighteen children. Appointed OBE in 1952, CBE in 1955, Abubakar was knighted in 1960 and was sworn of the privy council in 1961. He was buried on 22 January 1966 at Bauchi. A. TREVOR CLARK

Sources A. T. Clark, *A right honourable gentleman: Abubakar from the Black Rock* (1991) [full list of sources, oral and written, and bibliography] · *DNB* · *The Times* (24 Jan 1966) · personal knowledge (2004) · private information (2004)
Archives FILM IWM FVA, home footage | SOUND BL NSA
Likenesses C. Ware, photograph, 1959, Hult. Arch. · Elliott & Fry, photograph, 1960, NPG [*see illus.*] · Lady Cumming-Bruce, oils, Nigerian Institute of International Affairs, Lagos · portrait, repro.

in *Time Magazine* (5 Dec 1960), front cover · portrait, repro. on 5 naira Nigerian banknote
Wealth at death house in Bauchi; house in Kaduna; small number of personal effects; virtually no money

Taft [*née* Barritt], **Mary** (1772–1851), Wesleyan Methodist preacher, was born of farming stock at Hay, Colne, Lancashire, on 12 August 1772, the daughter of John Barritt, a non-believer, and his wife, Mary, a Methodist. She had one sister and five brothers, one of whom, John, a Wesleyan itinerant preacher, was very supportive of his sister's ministry. Converted at an early age she felt the importance of communicating her faith to others by taking part in prayer meetings and giving exhortations. In 1791 her superintendent minister threatened to expel her if she persisted in 'exhorting', but she felt she ought to obey God rather than men. When the minister saw the effect of her preaching, he encouraged her. She received many invitations, both from lay friends and itinerants, and travelled extensively throughout the north of England, including the Isle of Man and the north midlands, seeing many conversions in spite of much opposition. In several cases male preachers who were opposed to women preaching changed their minds when they realized that God 'owned' her work, and asked her to visit their circuits. A number of her converts became travelling preachers and missionaries. Mary attended the Methodist conferences in Manchester (1795) and Leeds (1801), chiefly to meet itinerants who were sympathetic to women's preaching. At the Bristol conference (1802), when the numbers for Grimsby were requested, George Sykes, the superintendent minister, replied, 'I left 530 members;—how many there are now I cannot tell,—for Mary Barritt is knocking them down like rotten sticks' (Taft, *Memoirs*, 2.39).

In June 1802 the possibility of marriage with Zechariah Taft (1772–1848), a Wesleyan itinerant, arose. Mary had worked happily with him previously and, although doubtful at first, eventually in July she became convinced that it was God's will and they were married at Horncastle, Lincolnshire, on 17 August. A supporter of women's preaching for its own sake and not simply because of his wife's talent, Zechariah encouraged her to preach, in the face of fierce controversy. After their marriage Zechariah was appointed to the Canterbury circuit and Mary preached there and in Dover. At first people were a little wary of female preaching, but were persuaded not only by her ministry but also by a letter from a respected former minister, John Pawson, in which he commended her, writing, 'if you do not hinder it, God will make Mrs Taft the instrument of great good to you' (pamphlet–letter from John Pawson, 25 Oct 1802, Methodist Archives). In June 1803 Mary travelled from London preaching *en route*, to Colne, while Zechariah went back to Dover, and on 26 June 1803 their daughter, also Mary, was born. Within a month Mary was preaching again, having been joined by her husband. Zechariah attended the conference in Manchester and, although the Dover circuit wished them to stay, conference sent them to Epworth in Lincolnshire, once the home of the Wesleys, where religion was at a very low ebb. This conference passed a resolution against women preaching, unless it was convinced there was a very extraordinary call, and even then there were a number of restrictions. However, it seems that Mary virtually ignored this dictum and continued with her ministry. Zechariah obviously agreed with her, as he wrote three pamphlets on the subject of women's preaching. Other preachers also endorsed her work, writing, 'Go on, never mind Conference! … do, and get all the good you can.'

In 1827 Mary published an account of her work as a revivalist and this, together with what is known of her subsequent work, shows that she was virtually another itinerant in her husband's circuits. Her preaching was attended by conversions and revivals. Mary Taft died at Sandiacre, Derbyshire, on 26 March 1851.

E. DOROTHY GRAHAM

Sources M. Taft, *Memoirs of the life of Mrs Mary Taft, formerly Miss Barritt*, 2 vols. (1827) · L. F. Church, *More about the early Methodist people* (1949) · *Wesleyan Methodist Magazine*, 74 (1851), 604 · JRL, Methodist Archives and Research Centre, Taft MSS · d. cert.
Archives Birm. CA, memoirs · JRL, Methodist Archives and Research Centre
Likenesses portrait, repro. in Taft, *Memoirs of the life of Mrs Mary Taft*, frontispiece

Tagart, Edward (1804–1858), Unitarian minister, was born in Bristol on 8 October 1804, the second son among seven children of William Tagart (1767?–1817) and his wife, Amy (1786?–1840), eldest daughter of Nicholas Lathy of Barnstaple. William Tagart was a wholesale dealer in cotton goods who, following business reverses, later settled in Bath as an accountant; after his death the family moved to London. Edward Tagart attended the school in Bristol belonging to the Revd John Evans (*d.* 1831) and the grammar school in Bath. Destined by family connection and personal desire to become a Unitarian minister, he entered Manchester College, York, in 1820.

Shortly before completing his college course, through the intervention of Thomas Belsham (1750–1829), Tagart was offered the pulpit of a new congregation in York Street, St James's, but declined in favour of the celebrated Octagon Chapel, Norwich, where he was ordained on 10 August 1825, succeeding Thomas Madge (1786–1870), who had taken Belsham's place at Essex Street, London. In 1828 Tagart married Helen, *née* Bourn (1797–1871); she had previously been engaged to another Unitarian minister, Thomas Biggin Broadbent (*d.* 1817), and was the widow of Thomas Martineau (1795–1824), a surgeon and the eldest brother of Harriet *Martineau (1802–1876) and James *Martineau (1805–1900). The Tagarts had one son and three daughters.

Open hostility between Tagart and the Martineaus, who had opposed the marriage, must have contributed to his leaving Norwich that year to accept a renewed invitation to York Street. The chapel was maintained by William Agar (1766?–1838), a well-known chancery barrister. The minister was in effect Agar's chaplain, but, as the number of subscribers grew, Tagart persuaded Agar to adopt a more usual form of organization. In 1833, the rented premises in York Street being no longer available, the congregation moved to a new chapel in Little Portland Street,

Marylebone, where Tagart, who was active in the Linnean and Geological societies and a member of the Society of Antiquaries, gathered an intellectual and fashionable congregation.

Like most of his fellow ministers Tagart usually avoided doctrinal topics to preach on scriptural and ethical subjects, though his admiration for Wordsworth's poetry and the eloquence of the American minister William Ellery Channing (1780–1842) may well have given his pulpit style a warmth lacking in preceding generations. Tagart's sermon on the death of Channing in 1842 attracted Charles Dickens, who regularly attended Little Portland Street for a number of years and became a good friend; another regular hearer was the geologist Sir Charles Lyell (1797–1875). The later years of Tagart's ministry were less successful. It has been suggested that awareness that he did not depend on his stipend made the congregation less zealous, while an insensitive side to his nature—no doubt related to the deep self-doubt he occasionally revealed—caused some hurt feelings.

Tagart was also distracted by wider denominational responsibilities. Shortly after his arrival in London, he joined the committee of the British and Foreign Unitarian Association and in 1832 succeeded John Bowring (1792–1872) as foreign secretary; on the resignation of Robert Aspland (1782–1845) in 1841 he became general secretary. Though sometimes neglectful of details, he was effective in the co-ordinating and propagandistic responsibilities of the office. With a strong interest in denominational history, he had a particular fascination with the old Unitarian communities in Transylvania.

Both at the British and Foreign Unitarian Association and in his writings—a catalogue, with commentary, is printed in the *Christian Reformer* of 1859—Tagart was a leading defender of the school of Unitarian thought descended from David Hartley (1705–1757), Joseph Priestley (1733–1804), and Belsham. He was certain that the attempt of James Martineau and John James Tayler (1794–1869) to ground religion inwardly, rather than in historical, biblical, and natural evidences, would mean the death of institutional Unitarianism. When Manchester College was transplanted from Manchester to London in 1853, as he had long advocated, he led a public protest against the appointments of Tayler and Martineau to professorships. His major published contribution in the conflict, reflecting his longstanding interest in metaphysical questions, was *Locke's writings and philosophy historically considered and vindicated from the charge of contributing to the scepticism of Hume* (1855), which is also a deeply felt defence of Hartley and Priestley.

While returning from an official visit to Hungary in 1858 Tagart died suddenly of a fever, possibly malaria, in Brussels on 12 October. He was buried in the family vault in the cemetery at Kensal Green on 20 October.   R. K. WEBB

Sources *Christian Reformer, or, Unitarian Magazine and Review*, new ser., 15 (1859), 65–85, 233–9 • *The Inquirer* (30 Oct 1858) • JRL, Unitarian College MSS, letters from E. Tagart to J. Gordon • H. Martineau, letters to J. Martineau, 27 Sept 1827, Harris Man. Oxf.; 22 Oct 1827, Harris Man. Oxf. [abstracts] • *Christian Reformer, or, Unitarian Magazine and Review*, 6 (1839), 56 • J. P. Frazee, 'Dickens and Unitarianism', *Dickens Studies Annual*, 18 (1989), 119–41 • *Christian Life* (5 Oct 1912) • *Life of Frances Power Cobbe: by herself*, 2 vols. (1894), vol. 2, p. 404 • *DNB*

Archives Boston PL, papers | JRL, Unitarian College MSS
Likenesses J. Linnell, watercolour, 1843; copy, Norwich Central Library • photograph, repro. in *Trustees Album*, DWL
Wealth at death under £14,000: administration, 2 Dec 1858, CGPLA Eng. & Wales

Taglioni, Marie (1804–1884), dancer, was born in Stockholm on 23 April 1804. She was the granddaughter of Salvatore Taglioni, a Neapolitan ballet master, and the daughter of Filippo Taglioni, who adopted his father's profession and migrated to Sweden, where he married in 1803 Marie Karsten, the daughter of a tragedian. Marie Taglioni's infancy was spent between Vienna and Kassel and her adolescence in Paris with her mother and brothers, one of whom, Paul, was also a noted dancer. Her father was a hard taskmaster, and for five months she was made to practise dancing for six hours a day, supervised by a colleague of her father named Coulon. She made her début in Vienna on 10 June 1822 in a ballet choreographed by her father to music by Rossini, *La réception d'une jeune nymphe à la cour de Terpsichore*. She appeared in 1824 in Paris and Monaco and in 1826 in Stuttgart and Munich. Her name was already well known when in Paris in July 1827 she made a great sensation in *Le Sicilien* and *Le carnaval de Venise*. Her triumph was confirmed in *Le dieu et la bayadère*, specially written for her by Scribe and Auber, and by her *pas de fascination* in Meyerbeer's *Robert le diable* on 21 November 1831, when she was already earning £1200 a year. Her dancing, especially her *ballon*—lightness of jump and elevation—was acclaimed from St Petersburg to Madrid as 'the poetry of motion'. She was first seen in London in 1829, and appeared on 3 June 1830 in a revival of *Flore et Zéphire*, which was acclaimed by the *Morning Herald*. For her benefit at Covent Garden on 26 July 1832 she appeared in *La sylphide*, which she had already performed at the Paris Opéra on 12 March and which was her most famous part. On 14 July 1832 she married, in a religious ceremony in London, Gilbert, comte des Voisins; the couple also underwent a civil ceremony in Paris on 20 September 1834.

Taglioni was the toast of many writers: Victor Hugo dedicated a book to her, Thackeray commemorated her in *Pendennis*, and Théophile Gautier referred to her as just as much a genius as Lord Byron and Lamartine. Chopin, also, was reported to have said that he derived inspiration more than once from Taglioni's dancing. The long skirt which she wore, the forerunner of the tutu, was given the name of 'a taglioni', and she introduced white in costume, which had not previously been widely used. In 1836, the year of the birth of her daughter Eugenia on 30 March, Alfred Bunn engaged her at the Italian Opera at a salary of £100 a night plus costly extras for other members of her family and benefits, bringing his expenses to £6000 overall. She appeared in St Petersburg every year from 1838 to 1842 in a variety of roles, but thereafter her appeal there began to wane. In 1839 her success was *Gitana*, at which bouquets were thrown on the stage. She and her husband divorced in Paris on 27 February 1844 after a number of years' separation, although a son born in Monaco on 5 October 1843 was named Georges des Voisins. In 1845 she was at Her Majesty's Theatre with Benjamin Lumley and was *première danseuse* in the celebrated *pas de quatre*, which was first performed in England by command of Queen Victoria, followed in 1846 by the *pas des déesses*. On 15 May 1847 she was presented at Her Majesty's with plate worth £300.

When the singer Jenny Lind came on the scene to challenge her position as diva, Taglioni preferred to retire than to compete, remarking at Lumley's annual garden party that 'La danse est comme la Turquie, bien malade'. Her last appearance was on 21 August 1847 in *The Judgment of Paris*. After this she spent much of her time in Italy, where she had a villetta, Mon Désir, at Belvio; she also inhabited the C'a d'Oro in Venice. From 1859 to 1870 she was at the Paris Opéra as a teacher and choreographer. One of the ballets she choreographed was *Papillon*, with St Georges and Offenbach, for her friend Emma Livery. Her husband died in 1863 and her finances declined through the Franco-Prussian War, incautious speculation, and the advice of her aged father. In 1874 she settled in London, at 6 Connaught Square, as a teacher of deportment when, it was said, it was sad to see her, white-haired, escorting a bevy of schoolgirls in Hyde Park or in Brighton. In 1882 she went to stay with her son Gilbert, comte des Voisins, at Château Ralli, Marseilles, where she died on 24 April 1884.

Taglioni excelled as much in national character dancing as in ballet. Her name was given to many things apart from the famous ballet skirt, a greatcoat, a stagecoach, caramels, nuts, and waltzes among them. Her mother suffered from a physical deformity, and she inherited a spider-like appearance with a somewhat shrunken chest and very long arms.   J. GILLILAND

Sources I. Guest, *The romantic ballet in England* (1954) · S. Lifar, *Histoire de la ballet russe* (1950) · D. Priddin, *The art of the dance in French literature* (1952) · S. D'Amico, ed., *Enciclopedia dello spettacolo*, 11 vols. (Rome, 1954–68) · Boase, *Mod. Eng. biog.* · L. C. Sanders, *Celebrities of the century: being a dictionary of men and women of the nineteenth century* (1887) · *The Times* (April 1884) · *The Era* (26 April 1884) · A. Bunn, *The stage: both before and behind the curtain*, 3 vols. (1840) · P. Larousse, ed., *Grand dictionnaire universel du XIXe siècle*, 17 vols. (Paris, 1866–90) · G. Vuillier, *A history of dancing from the earliest ages to our own times*, ed. and trans. J. Grego (1898) · Hall, *Dramatic ports.* · *DNB*
Archives Theatre Museum, London, letters
Likenesses A. E. Chalon, watercolour drawing, *c.*1831, NPG; repro. in A. E. Chalon, *Six sketches of Mademoiselle Taglioni* (1831) · Queen Victoria, three sketches, 1833–4, Royal Collection · G. LePaulle, oils, *c.*1835, Louvre, Paris · L. Haase & Co., carte-de-visite, NPG · C. Heath, print (*Beauties of the ballet*), Garr. Club · portrait, NPG · portrait, repro. in W. Ball and N. C. Bochsa, eds., *The musical gem*, 4 vols. (1829–33) · portrait, repro. in *Dublin University Magazine*, 93 (1879) · portrait, repro. in D'Amico, ed., *Enciclopedia dello spettacolo* · print, repro. in *Pall Mall Magazine*, 34 (1904), 172 · print, repro. in M. Alophe, *Theatres of London* · prints, BM · prints, repro. in *Smith's original letters* · prints, Harvard TC · prints, V&A

Tagore, Rabindranath (1861–1941), poet and educationist, was born on 7 May 1861 at 6 Dwarkanath Tagore Lane,

Rabindranath Tagore (1861–1941), by Sir William Rothenstein, 1912

Jorasanko, Calcutta, the fourteenth child and eighth son of Debendranath Tagore (1817–1905) and Sarada Devi (1826?–1875). The Tagores were one of the leading families of Calcutta, whose estates and assets were built up by the flamboyant entrepreneurial energy of Rabindranath's grandfather Dwarkanath Tagore (1794–1846) and consolidated by the high-minded frugality of his father, Debendranath (after paying off huge debts left behind by Dwarkanath). By the time Rabindranath came into his own inheritance, the estates had been divided between the many branches of the family; even so, estates in the Padma River region of north Bengal, and land that had been acquired by Debendranath near Bolpur, Bengal, gave him the property base he needed for the pioneering school and university at Santiniketan that he founded in 1901 and 1921 respectively.

Influences and early years Tagore's life and career were rooted in Bengal, and in the Bengali language he so enormously enriched and expanded. As a Bengali writer, he is known as Rabindranath; as an international and pan-Indian figure he was and still is known as Tagore (an Anglicization of his family's *padabi* or title: Thakur). His university, Visva Bharati, whose name means both 'universal [goddess of] learning' and 'all-India' and whose Sanskrit motto means 'where the whole world meets in one nest', was an attempt to bring these two identities together; but for most non-Bengalis they remained separate. Although he was the first Indian writer to become world-famous, the flowing hair, beard, and robes of his international image concealed rather than revealed his true nature and stature.

Most Western accounts of Rabindranath Tagore's

achievements have started with 'Tagore'; more than half a century after his death, and with a new wave of translations of his Bengali works into various languages available, it is time to put 'Rabindranath' first. To do this, it is necessary to have an understanding of the nineteenth-century Bengal Renaissance from which he stemmed, and of his main literary precursors. The Tagores, with their double mansion at Jorasanko in north Calcutta, occupied a central position in Calcutta's burgeoning literary, artistic, dramatic, musical, and journalistic culture; at the same time they were separated from many of its streams both by being Pirali Brahmans (a group of families not regarded as fully Brahmanical) and through being associated with the Brahmo Samaj, a Hindu reform movement headed by Debendranath Tagore. The luminaries of the Bengal Renaissance whom Tagore most admired (apart from his father) were Rammohan Roy (1772–1833), founder, with the support of Rabindranath's grandfather, of the Brahmo Sabha (later, Samaj), and Ishvarchandra Vidyasagar (1820–1891), principal of Sanskrit College. From Rammohan Roy, known as the Father of Modern India largely as a result of Tagore's essays and speeches, he derived his religious rationalism and determination to combine the best qualities of the East and the West; from the educationist and Sanskrit scholar Vidyasagar, he learned how important it was to breathe new, modern life into India's classical literary heritage. As a prose stylist, innovative though he constantly was, Tagore was indebted to Vidyasagar and the novelist Bankimchandra Chatterji (1838–1894); as a poet, the romantic lyrics of Biharilal Chakravarti (1834–1894) showed him the way; and the epic poetry of Michael Madhusudan Datta (1824–1873), though he initially disliked it, certainly indicated that Bengali poetry could be daring, modern, and international in its reach.

The unorthodox element in Tagore's background and upbringing was reflected in his lack of formal schooling. Short-lived attempts to send him to several different schools put him off conventional schooling for life, and were the basis of his own experiments as an educator. He acquired his knowledge of Sanskrit, English, and music as much from his talented older brothers Dwijendranath (1840–1926), Satyendranath (1842–1923), and Jyotirindranath (1849–1925) as from the private tutors who were procured for him. When he himself started to write, his sister-in-law Kadambari Devi was a great source of encouragement and friendly criticism, and her unexplained suicide when he was twenty-two was a shattering blow to him: it was the first of a series of bereavements so relentless that he was forced, as he put it, 'to make Death a friend'. Two years earlier, at Jyotirindranath and Kadambari's house, 6 Sudder Street, Calcutta, Tagore had had a sudden mystic vision of cosmic unity that was the source of his conviction that the spiritual and the poetic were essentially one. It released his natural poetic flow (in the poem 'Nirjharer svapnabhanga', 'The awakening of the fountain') and gave him what he later defined (in *My Reminiscences*, 1917) as 'the subject on which all my writings have dwelt—the joy of attaining the Infinite within the finite'.

Tagore was married in 1883, four months before Kadambari's death, to Bhabatarini, a ten-year-old Pirali Brahman girl from Jessore, the almost illiterate daughter of an employee on the Tagore estates. (After the wedding her name was changed to the more euphonious Mrinalini, influenced, perhaps, by a tradition in Indian poetry that the sun—*ravi*—and the lotus—*mrinalini*—are eternal lovers.) The gulf in education and sophistication between them was probably never wholly bridged, but she seems to have been intelligent, sensible, and loving, and under his guidance acquired enough education to write an abridged Bengali version of the *Ramayana*, and to act in his play *Raja o rani* (1889). Her death in 1902 aged thirty condemned Tagore to a loneliness exacerbated by the early deaths of three of their five children: their middle daughter, Renuka (Rani), in 1903, their youngest son, Samindranath, in 1907, and their eldest daughter, Madhurilata (Bela), in 1918.

Literary work As a Bengali writer, Tagore's output was prodigious and unceasing, from his first (anonymous) published poem 'Abhilash' ('Desire') in the Brahmo journal *Tattvabodhini Patrika* in 1874 when he was thirteen, right up to the poems dictated on his deathbed that were included in the posthumous collection *Shesh lekha* ('Last writings', 1941). One obstacle to the proper international appreciation of his Bengali œuvre is that he wrote no single *magnum opus*, no *Divina commedia* or *Faust*. Instead, he experimented ceaselessly in all the literary genres (except verse epic), composed about 2500 songs (words and music), and painted, towards the end of his life, nearly 3000 paintings. Only a fraction of his writings—maybe less than 5 per cent—have been translated well into English. Of his sixty-odd books of verse, the following are perhaps of particular significance (though none can be excluded from a complete assessment of his work): *Manasi* ('The Lady of the Mind', 1890, the book in which his adult voice was first heard); *Sonar tari* ('The golden boat', 1894, with its famous symbolic title poem); *Katha o kahini* ('Tales and Stories', 1900, in which he showed himself to be a master of narrative as well as lyric poetry); *Kshanika* ('The flitting one', 1900, characterized by breath-taking metrical innovations based on Bengali folk poetry); *Balaka* ('Wild geese', 1916, a return to poetic energy and Sanskritic richness after the austerity and introspection of the *Gitanjali* phase); *Purabi* (the name of an evening *raga* in Indian music, 1925, inspired partly by his friendship with Victoria Ocampo); *Mahua* (a flower from which an intoxicating liquor is made by the Santal tribespeople of Bengal and Bihar, 1929, an extraordinary burst of sensuous youthfulness in the 68-year-old poet); and the four books that he wrote in his last year of life. A distinctive rhythm and voice runs right through this vast corpus, but also a continuous modernization: in the *gadya-kabita* (free verse) of his later years, he often beat the 'post-Tagore' Bengali poets at their own game. As a short-story writer, Tagore achieved lyrical perfection in the mainly rural stories he wrote in the 1890s, which he spent managing his father's estates in the Padma River region; later stories—culminating in the trilogy *Tin sangi* ('Three companions', 1940)—extended his range of characters to intellectuals, scientists, and ever more self-reliant women. In his novels social and ideological conflicts are conveyed through human interactions, his most ambitious works being *Gora* (1910, steeped in late nineteenth-century religious and nationalist controversy) and *Ghare baire* ('The home and the world', 1916, in which the *swadeshi* movement against the partition of Bengal looms large). Many readers and critics, however, prefer the shorter novellas such as *Nashtanir* ('The Broken Nest', 1901, a domestic tragedy with roots, some say, in his love for his sister-in-law Kadambari), or *Chaturanga* ('Quartet', 1916, an exploration of the conflicting attractions of rationalist positivism and religious cultism, so avant-garde in technique that it counts as one of the world's first modernist novels). As a dramatist, Tagore was a constant rewriter and adaptor, converting the historical or mythological plays of his youth into experimental symbolic plays or operas or dance dramas, for performance by students and staff at Santiniketan. *Dak-ghar* ('The Post Office', 1912), written perhaps with his son Samindranath's death in mind, and flawless in language and conception, was the one play that he never reworked.

Politics and nationalism Partly because of the supremacy he so quickly achieved in Bengali letters (the first collected edition of his poems and dramas, *Kabyagranthabali*, was published in 1896 when he was thirty-five, and his frequent essays on social, political, aesthetic, religious, and philosophical topics put him at the centre of contemporary debate), Tagore attracted controversy, envy, and virulent criticism. Although this waned after the Nobel prize in 1913 gave him international standing, his political and moral interventions and pronouncements often attracted as much hostility from nationalist revolutionaries as his literary works and religious ideas had done earlier from conservative critics or neo-Hindus. Although one tendency in Tagore's nature regularly called him to withdraw from the fray into introspection or rural retirement, another—never fully quiescent even in old age—drew him to political and moral activism. The spirit of his poem 'Ebar phirao more' ('Turn me back now', 1896) was recurrent in him. Tagore the world citizen, the Great Sentinel (as Gandhi called him) of Indian nationalism, had already frequently occupied a public platform, adopting a strongly anti-imperialist stance that was later obscured by his emphasis on international harmony. In 1886 (aged twenty-five) he composed and sang the inaugural song at the second session of the Indian National Congress in Calcutta. In 1890 (aged twenty-nine) he read out a paper at a protest meeting in Calcutta against the policies of Lord Cross, secretary of state for India, calling for representatives of the people to be elected to the viceroy's council. In 1893, in a paper called *Ingrajer atanka* ('The Englishman's fear'), he warned Congress against neglecting the need for Hindu–Muslim unity (a theme he returned to constantly throughout his life). In 1897 he made the first of several attempts to persuade the Bengal provincial conference to

conduct its proceedings in Bengali. In 1905 he joined the forefront of the *swadeshi* campaign against Lord Curzon's decision to divide Bengal into two separate provinces, composing patriotic songs, calling for constructive non-co-operation, initiating the Rakhibandhan (Thread of Fraternity) ceremony as a symbol of Bengali unity, and leading a massive protest march through the streets of Calcutta. Two years later he withdrew from the campaign, disillusioned with its violence and indifference to the livelihood of ordinary shopkeepers and traders, and fearful of Hindu–Muslim conflict. This awareness of the dangers of demagogy and mass agitation also accounted for his phases of aloofness from Gandhi's non-co-operation campaigns in the 1920s and 1930s. For similarly moral reasons, he did his best to keep his distance from revolutionary terrorism in Bengal, though he frequently protested to the government about the treatment of political detainees.

Visit to Britain, and the Nobel prize The Tagore that the world beyond India came to know was catapulted into fame by the award of the Nobel prize for literature. In 1911 the English artist William Rothenstein and the German Indophile Count Hermann Keyserling (who was later to stage-manage Tagore's tours of Germany) had met him in the painter Abanindranath Tagore's part of the Jorasanko mansion. When Tagore decided to go to England in 1912, with the aim of acquainting the West with his educational work at Santiniketan, he gravitated towards Rothenstein's house in Hampstead. Before leaving Bengal, he had taken a break at Shelidah, his estate house by the Padma, to recuperate from an illness. To pass the time there, he experimentally translated some of his religious songs and lyrics into biblical English prose. He continued with this on the ship to England. The notebook containing the translations was temporarily lost on the London underground (enabling its lost property office to play a crucial role in Indian and Western literary history), but he had it with him when he visited Rothenstein—who was so impressed by the poems that he had copies typed and sent to, among others, W. B. Yeats. On 7 July 1912 the translations were read out by Yeats to a gathering at Rothenstein's house that included Evelyn Underhill, Ernest Rhys, Arthur Fox Strangways, and Alice Meynell, making a great impression. In November of that year *Gitanjali*, as the collection of 103 translations came to be called ('Song-offering'—the title of one of the several Bengali books from which Tagore had chosen the poems), was published in a limited edition of 750 copies by the India Society of London. In 1913 it was printed again by Macmillan, while Tagore was in America. His name was proposed to the Nobel prize committee by Thomas Sturge Moore. Mainly as a result of strong support from the Swedish poet Verner von Heidenstam (who was himself awarded the prize in 1916), Tagore was nominated. News of the award reached him by telegram at Santiniketan on 16 November 1913—the day on which Edward Thompson, Tagore's first serious foreign biographer and critic, happened to be visiting the school for the first time.

According to Thompson's journal account, Tagore's first comment was 'I shall get no peace now, Mr Thompson'.

Bengali anecdote also has it that he said that the prize money would pay for the drains. For better or worse, the prize totally altered his life. It turned him into the world's first intercontinental literary star, but based his reputation on false premises. As a Bengali writer, he undoubtedly deserved the prize. But his own English translations—from which numerous secondary translations were made into other languages—did not give a full or lasting impression of his range and power as a poet. Loved and admired for a while (for longer in Germany, Spain, and South America than in Britain or America), they have not stood the test of time. In 1932 Tagore wrote in a letter to Rothenstein:

> It was not at all necessary for my own reputation that I should find my place in the history of your literature. It was an accident for which you were also responsible and possibly most of all was Yeats. But yet sometimes I feel almost ashamed that I whose undoubted claim has been recognized by my countrymen to a sovereignty in our own world of letters should not have waited till it was discovered by the outside world in its own true majesty and environment. (26 Nov 1932; Lago, 346)

Because of the success of *Gitanjali*, successive volumes were rushed out, of decreasing quality. The stories were imperfectly translated by associates of Tagore at Santiniketan, and only cursorily checked by him. The plays reached a nadir of truncation and inaccuracy: *Bisarjan*, for example ('Sacrifice', 1890, a powerful five-act drama about the Kali cult), was reduced to twenty-nine obscure and formless pages in Tagore's own translation.

International tours Tagore's visit to England and America in 1912–13 was actually his third visit to the West. In 1878–9 he had visited England with his brother Satyendranath, the first Indian to qualify for the Indian Civil Service. He stayed in middle-class lodgings in London, Brighton, Tunbridge Wells, and Torquay, attended Henry Morley's English literature lectures at University College, London, with Loken Palit, son of a friend of Satyendranath, and heard W. E. Gladstone and John Bright speak about Irish home rule in parliament. His witty letters home were published in the journal *Bharati*. In 1890 he and Loken Palit again accompanied Satyendranath to England, visiting France and Italy on the way. His post-*Gitanjali* tours were quite different. He was treated not just as a literary celebrity but as a prophet and a guru, a role he himself encouraged by his long beard and robes, and oracular manner of speaking. The sculptor Jacob Epstein's description of his sitting for him in 1926 may be mischievous, but is also a rather shocking vignette of what fame did to the poet:

> He posed in silence and I worked well. On one occasion two American women came to visit him, and I remember how they left him, retiring backwards, with their hands raised in worship. At the finish of the sitting usually two or three disciples, who waited in the ante-room for him, took him back to his hotel. He carried no money and was conducted about like a holy man. (Kripalani, 304)

His nine foreign tours after 1912–13, in 1916–17, 1920–21, 1924, 1924–5, 1926, 1927, 1929, 1930–31, and 1932, covered Japan, America, England, France, Holland, China, Argentina, Italy, Austria, Norway, Sweden, Denmark, Germany, Czechoslovakia, Hungary, Bulgaria, Greece, Egypt, southeast Asia, Canada, Switzerland, Russia, Iran, and Iraq—some of these countries (especially Japan, America, and Germany) more than once. The practical motive for many of these arduous tours was to raise money for his school and university; but they were also an opportunity for Tagore to speak against war and nationalism (for example, in his lectures on nationalism in Japan and America, 1916–17), to promote pan-Asianism (in China, 1924), to expound India's spiritual heritage (*Sadhana: Realisation of Life*, 1913), his aesthetic and educational philosophy (*Personality*, 1917; *Creative Unity*, 1922), and his 'poet's religion' (*Religion of Man*, Hibbert lectures, 1930). On several occasions he got into hot water. He was threatened with assassination by revolutionary Indians in San Francisco in September–October 1916; falsely implicated in the trial of those same pro-German conspirators in 1918; and manipulated for propaganda purposes in Mussolini's Italy in 1926. With hindsight, one can say that like many others he was misled by Soviet Russia in 1930: but his favourable reaction to Soviet progress in education and agriculture (recorded in *Letters from Russia*, 1931) should be weighed against his doubts about the compulsion involved. As early as 1921, in his essay *Shikshar milan*, he had spoken about the Russian people being transferred from the dictatorship of the tsar to another type of dictatorship.

Controversies, and a knighthood returned Tagore also toured India extensively, and visited Ceylon three times, in 1922, 1928, and 1934. As with his foreign tours, fundraising was a major motive: at the age of seventy-five he risked his health by touring India with a dance troupe, until, at Gandhi's instigation, a cheque for Rs60,000 was (anonymously) presented to him by the industrialist G. D. Birla. Controversy attended many of his speeches, articles, and open letters to the press, particularly when he felt compelled to disagree with Gandhi (despite their strong mutual admiration) over non-co-operation, the cult of the spinning-wheel, 'basic education', birth control, or Gandhi's assertion (shockingly obscurantist to Tagore) that the Bihar earthquake of January 1934 was 'a divine chastisement' for the sin of untouchability. At times, however, Tagore was able to command the united support and sympathy of the Indian nation, notably when, as a protest against the Amritsar massacre in 1919, he returned the knighthood the British had conferred on him in 1915, writing to the viceroy, Lord Chelmsford, that 'I for my part wish to stand, shorn of all special distinctions, by the side of those of my countrymen who for their so-called insignificance are liable to suffer a degradation not fit for human beings' (Kripalani, 266).

At the very end of his life, with the Second World War raging, Tagore struck a similarly resonant note with his address *Sabhyatar samkat* ('Crisis in civilization'), read out at his eightieth birthday celebration at Santiniketan on 14 April 1941. No understanding of nationalist India's equivocal feelings towards Britain's war effort is complete without taking on board the eloquent agony of her greatest poet: torn between his earlier 'faith in the philanthropy of the English race', his bitter disillusionment with British imperialism, his continuing love for 'really large-hearted Englishmen' such as C. F. Andrews, his grief at India's poverty, his shame at her helplessness compared to self-reliant Russia or Japan, his horror at the 'demon of barbarity' let loose by war, and his abiding faith in 'unvanquished man' and hope of a new dawn 'from the East where the sun rises'.

Tagore as educationist Tagore's public career, for all its nobility and courage, was full of torment, and maybe his long and exhausting attempt to create a novel kind of school and university stemmed from the same burdensome ambition to do good in the world. In another letter to Rothenstein he wrote:

> The rich luxury of leisure is not for me while I am in Europe—I am doomed to be unrelentingly good to humanity and remain harnessed to a cause. The artist in me ever urges me to be naughty and natural—but it requires [a] good deal of courage to be what I truly am. (24 Aug 1930; Lago, 329)

His responsibilities at Santiniketan made a burden of his Bengali career, as well as his international one. As an educational theorist (for instance, in his moving essay 'A poet's school', 1926), his ideas about the cultivation of the child's imagination and avoidance of rote learning have contributed to modern pedagogy worldwide. Inevitably, however, the practical management of his school at Bolpur (Santiniketan), the rural development projects at Surul (Sriniketan) that extended the methods he had first attempted on the Padma River estates in the 1890s, and his university, Visva Bharati, caused him many frustrations. In its heyday Visva Bharati attracted famous Indian and also foreign scholars as teachers (Sylvain Lévi from Strasbourg, Moritz Winternitz and V. Lesny from Prague, and Gyula Germanus from Budapest among them); it also had devoted service from Tagore's English friends C. F. Andrews, W. W. Pearson, and L. K. Elmhirst. But it was always short of funds; Tagore had to appeal to Gandhi to 'accept this institution under your protection' when they met for the last time in February 1940; and it only achieved financial security when the government of independent India took it over in 1951. Tagore's hope that it would remain a 'meeting of East and West' has, since then, proved difficult to fulfil: but its national contribution—particularly that of the *kala bhavana* (art department) in the fields of art, craft, and design—has been extensive. And as guardian of the Tagore legacy—publications, archives, music, dance, and seasonal festivals—Visva Bharati has become indispensable to Bengali culture.

Death and reputation No thorough history of South Asia in the twentieth century can be written without taking Tagore's life and influence into account. The crowds that turned out in Calcutta for his funeral cortège and cremation, after he died on 7 August 1941 in the house where he was born, were of a size normally only seen for a head of state. His songs 'Jana-gana-mana' (written for the twenty-sixth session of the Indian National Congress in Calcutta in December 1911) and 'Amar sonar Bangla' ('My Golden Bengal') have entered deep into the polity of the subcontinent, through being adopted as the national anthems of India and Bangladesh. His compassionate wholeness of outlook, humanist, rationalist, as respectful of modern science as of India's spiritual heritage, has imparted a civilized ideal that has not been overturned. His huge *œuvre*—including the songs that have become the national music of Bengal (*Rabindra-sangit*), and the original, disturbing, spontaneous paintings that were his main escape from fame and anxiety in the last decade of his life—will remain an inexhaustible cultural resource. Tagore defined art in *The Religion of Man* (1931) as 'the response of man's creative soul to the call of the Real'. The 'Real' for him always meant the real world of human feeling and experience, as well as a spiritual reality beyond but always running through that world; hence his mastery of prose as well as poetry and song. For foreigners, too, his art, cosmic in its reach, minutely sensitive in its feeling, spectacular in its linguistic virtuosity, clear and cogent even when it is at its most romantic and rhapsodic, will, when revealed through full and exact translations, require no special pleading. Through the painstaking discovery of 'Rabindranath', 'Tagore' will in time be better understood. WILLIAM RADICE

Sources E. J. Thompson, *Rabindranath Tagore: poet and dramatist* (1948) · L. K. Elmhirst, *Rabindranath Tagore: pioneer in education* (1961) · S. Akademi, *A centenary volume: Rabindranath Tagore, 1861–1961* (1961) · K. Kripalani, *Rabindranath Tagore: a biography* (1962) · M. M. Lago, ed., *Imperfect encounter: letters of William Rothenstein and Rabindranath Tagore, 1911–1941* (1972) · M. Kämpchen, *Rabindranath Tagore and Germany: a documentation* (1991) · E. P. Thompson, *Alien homage: Edward Thompson and Rabindranath Tagore* (1993) · R. K. Dasgupta, *Our national anthem* (1993) · K. Dutta and A. Robinson, *Rabindranath Tagore: the myriad-minded man* (1995) · *The English writings of Rabindranath Tagore*, ed. S. K. Das, 1–3 (1994–6)
Archives BL OIOC, essays · Elmhirst Centre, Dartington · NRA, corresp. and literary papers · Rabindra Bhavan, Santiniketan | BL, corresp. with Macmillans, Add. MS 55004 · BL OIOC, Rothenstein MSS · BL OIOC, letters to Elizabeth Sharpe, MS Eur. B 280 · Bodl. Oxf., letters to E. J. Thompson · Harvard U., Houghton L., letters to Sir William Rothenstein · LUL, corresp. with T. S. Moore · NL Scot., corresp. with Sir Patrick Geddes · NYPL, Macmillan Company MSS | FILM BFI NFTVA, 'Rabindranath Tagore', Channel 4, 3 July 1986 · IWM FVA, documentary footage
Likenesses A. Tagore, pastel drawing, 1896, Bose Institute, Calcutta · W. Rothenstein, lithograph, 1912, Carlisle City Art Gallery · W. Rothenstein, pencil drawing, 1912, Man. City Gall. · W. Rothenstein, pencil drawing, 1912, Tate collection [*see illus.*] · M. Bone, drypoint, 1920?, Rabindra-Sadan, Santiniketan · E. Kapp, chalk drawing, 1921, Barber Institute of Fine Arts, Birmingham · J. Epstein, bronze bust, 1926, Birmingham Museums and Art Gallery · M. Bone, pencil drawing, *c.*1930, Airlie Castle, Tayside region · Ramkinkar, bust, 1941, Santiniketan

Tailboys, Gilbert, first Baron Tailboys (*c.*1500–1530). See *under* Tailboys, Sir William (*c.*1416–1464).

Tailboys, Sir William (*c.*1416–1464), landowner and gang leader, was the second son and eventual heir of Walter Tailboys of Goltho, Lincolnshire. His family had been prominent in the north of England and in Lincolnshire since the Norman conquest, and he had inherited extensive estates in the north and Lincolnshire from his great-grandmother Elizabeth, sister of Gilbert de Umfraville, earl of Angus (*d.* 1381) and lord of Kyme, and succeeded to South Kyme, Lincolnshire, and other estates on the death of his distant cousin, Sir Robert *Umfraville, in 1437. The identity of William's mother is unknown, but his father married in 1432 Alice, daughter of Sir Humphrey Stafford and widow of Sir Edmund Cheyne, which made him one of the wealthiest men in Lincolnshire, and he was also very active on local commissions. William inherited most of his estates in 1444 and the lands settled on his stepmother and brother's wife during the 1440s.

Nothing is known of William Tailboys's early life but he may have been 'the young layman by name Tailboys' who was living at Bardney Abbey in 1437 and 'did most foully browbeat and scold' one of the monks there (Virgoe, 462). By 1441 he was one of the king's household retainers, and remained so until at least 1448. His inheritance of his father's lands brought him election as knight of the shire for Lincolnshire in 1445 and appointment to the Northumberland and all three Lincolnshire commissions of the peace. But he rapidly became involved in a series of disputes which led to a great deal of violence. By 1448 he and his followers were accused of involvement in three homicides and many other crimes. Tailboys saw Lord Cromwell of Tattershall Castle as his greatest enemy and John, Viscount Beaumont, and William de la Pole, duke of Suffolk, as his patrons. When writs of exigent were issued against Tailboys and his followers in 1449 Suffolk persuaded the sheriff of Lincolnshire, Mauncer Marmyon, not to execute them, promising Marmyon a pardon—incidents that formed part of the charges against Suffolk in his impeachment in 1450. Near the beginning of the parliament of November 1449 Tailboys and his band of 'slaughterladdes' assaulted and allegedly tried to kill Lord Cromwell at a meeting of the king's council. The Commons, perhaps inspired by Lord Cromwell, brought an impeachment against Tailboys—the first for over half a century—demanding that he, 'named and noysed for a comon murderer, mansleer, riottour and contynuell breker of your peas', be put in the Tower of London, to stay there for twelve months while actions could be brought against him (RotP, 5.200). The king was forced to agree to the main clause and it is clear that this impeachment formed the model for the much more serious impeachment of the duke of Suffolk in January 1450, also perhaps inspired by Lord Cromwell.

Proceedings by bill of Middlesex, bringing him to trial at Westminster, allowed Cromwell to recover rapidly damages of £2000 from Tailboys, and a series of other civil and criminal actions were brought against him while in the Tower. His animus against Cromwell remained strong, however, and while in the Tower he continued to conspire against him, distributing critical verses over much of England linking him with the duke of Somerset as responsible for the disasters in France. Tailboys remained in the Tower for a year and then in the custody of the sheriffs of London for another four years. After the Yorkist victory of St Albans in 1455 Tailboys received a general pardon and was restored briefly to the peace commission in Kesteven. He was certainly much damaged by his years of imprisonment, even though in 1457 Lord Cromwell's executors forgave him much of the £2000 awarded seven years earlier. His activities over the next three years seem to have been equally violent and in the Coventry parliament of 1459 the Commons petitioned that he, then living at Enfield, and other criminals be imprisoned.

As the civil wars grew closer, however, Tailboys's influence in Lincolnshire, where he presumably remained friendly with Viscount Beaumont, became increasingly important to Henry VI. He served loyally on the Lancastrian side during the last four years of his life, being knighted in February 1461 at St Albans, where Lord Bonville, whose daughter, Elizabeth (d. 1491), he had married, was executed. He fought at Towton, defended, then surrendered Alnwick, and finally fought at the battle of Hexham in May 1464. After this battle he was discovered hiding in a coalmine near Newcastle with some 3000 marks intended for the Lancastrian forces. He was executed on 20 July 1464 at Newcastle and buried at the Greyfriars in Newcastle. He had been attainted in the parliament of 1461 and, though certain lands were left in trust for his widow, the rest had been distributed to Yorkist supporters. In the parliament of 1472 his son and heir, Robert (d. 1495), then MP for Lincolnshire, successfully petitioned for the restoration of his blood and over the next few years reacquired much of the Lincolnshire and Northumberland lands of his father.

Robert's grandson and William Tailboys's great-grandson, **Gilbert Tailboys**, first Baron Tailboys (c.1500–1530), landowner and administrator, was the son of Sir George Tailboys (1467–1538) and Elizabeth, daughter of Sir William Gascoigne. His father became insane and was placed under the custody of Cardinal Wolsey, whose servant Gilbert became by 1517. Wolsey may have been responsible for Gilbert's marriage by September 1519 to Elizabeth *Blount, mistress of Henry VIII and mother of Henry Fitzroy, duke of Richmond. Tailboys was a gentleman of the king's chamber by 1527 and active in Lincolnshire, where he sat on a number of commissions and was sheriff in 1526. To the Reformation Parliament in 1529 he was elected for Lincolnshire but was soon after promoted to the peerage, perhaps owing to his relationship with the king's son. He died on 15 April 1530 and was buried in South Kyme church. His two sons died before they were adult and his eventual heir was his daughter, Elizabeth, who married first Thomas Wimbush, who claimed unsuccessfully the title of Baron Tailboys, and afterwards Ambrose Dudley, earl of Warwick. Elizabeth died without heirs about 1560 and the barony came to an end.

ROGER VIRGOE

Sources R. Virgoe, 'William Tailboys and Lord Cromwell: crime and politics in Lancastrian England', *Bulletin of the John Rylands University Library*, 55 (1972–3), 459–82 · GEC, *Peerage* · PRO, expec. KB9, KB27, KB29 · PRO, C 140/15/49 · *Chancery records* · *RotP*, vols. 4–5 · HoP, *Commons, 1386–1421* · HoP, *Commons, 1509–58* · J. Gairdner, ed., *The historical collections of a citizen of London in the fifteenth century*, CS, new ser., 17 (1876) · *The Paston letters, AD 1422–1509*, ed. J. Gairdner, new edn, 6 vols. (1904) · *VCH Berkshire*, vol. 3 · *A year book of Edward IV*, fol. 20 · A. H. Thompson, ed., *Visitations of religious houses in the diocese of Lincoln*, 3 vols., Lincoln RS, 7, 14, 21 (1914–23)

Tailor, Robert (*fl.* 1613–1614), playwright, was the author of *The Hog hath Lost his Pearl*, a comedy more notable for the reaction it caused than for its content. On the surface the play is a burlesque in which a young gallant, Haddit, tricks the usurer, Hog, into thinking that his gold will be turned into pearl. On 23 February 1613 Sir Henry Wotton wrote to Sir Edmund Bacon that two days earlier sixteen apprentices, 'having secretly learnt a new Play without book, intituled, The Hog hath lost his Pearl', presented it at the Whitefriars Theatre until the authorities broke up the performance and arrested several of the players (McKenzie, iv). Wotton further noted that the public 'will needs have Sir John Swinnerton the Lord Maior be meant by the Hog, and the late Lord Treasurer [Robert Cecil, Lord Salisbury] by the Pearl'. Albright has shown that the play was probably satirizing Swinnerton's attempts to use his office to gain lucrative patents on sweet wines, and Clare notes that Salisbury had strenuously opposed these attempts (Clare, 227 n. 40). The pearl may have also mocked a pearl necklace which Swinnerton gave to Princess Elizabeth at her wedding, a week before the play's performance. The play was printed in 1614 with the title-page advertisement that it was 'divers times publickely acted, by certain London prentices' (sig. A2) and a prologue which slyly disavows any satirical intent.

Because the name is so common and the quarto gives no personal information it is difficult to identify the dramatist with any certainty among the many Robert Tailors living in London at the time. He may be the Ro[bin] Tailor who acted with the Lord Admiral's Men about 1598–1603, playing minor parts in 2 *Fortune's Tennis* and *The Battle of Alcazar* (Greg, 65). He is usually assumed to be the R. Tailor who wrote commendatory verses for John Taylor's *Nipping and Snipping of Abuses* (1614). He may also be the Robert Tailour who wrote *Sacred Hymns, Consisting of Fifti Select Psalms* (1615), a paraphrase of fifty psalms with twelve accompanying tunes for voice, viol, and lute. This man played the lute in Chapman's *Masque of the Middle Temple and Lincoln's Inn*, presented in February 1613 as part of Princess Elizabeth's marriage celebration, so he may well have witnessed Swinnerton's prominent role in the festivities (Ashbee, 4.39). He subsequently became a musician to Prince Charles, then a royal musician after Charles became king in 1625, and he was also a city wait of London from 1620. Upon his death in 1637 his position as a royal lutenist passed to his son John, who had been keeper of the royal music.   DAVID KATHMAN

Sources D. F. McKenzie, introduction, in R. Tailor, *The hogge hath lost his pearl* (1972), v–xvi • E. M. Albright, 'A stage cartoon of the lord mayor of London in 1613', *The Manly anniversary studies in language and literature* (1923), 113–26 • J. Clare, *Art made tongue-tied by authority* (1999) • W. W. Greg, *Dramatic documents from the Elizabethan playhouses* (1931) • D. Poulton, 'Tailour, Robert', *New Grove* • A. Ashbee, ed., *Records of English court music*, 9 vols. (1986–96)

Taine, Hippolyte Adolphe (1828–1893), philosopher, critic, and historian, was born on 12 April 1828 at Vouziers in the Ardennes, the only son and first of three children of Jean-Baptiste Taine (*d.* 1841), a lawyer, and his wife, Virginie, *née* Bezanson (1800–1880). He was educated in Paris at the Collège Bourbon (1841–8) and at the École Normale Supérieure (1848–51). His academic career was hampered by his heterodox opinions, and after a brief period as a provincial teacher he settled in Paris and made his living initially from private lessons and later from his pen. He is best known for his works of criticism (such as the four-volume *Histoire de la littérature anglaise*, 1863–4), for philosophical works that signalled his allegiance to a form of determinism (*Les philosophes français du XIXe siècle*, 1857, and *De l'intelligence*, 1870), and especially for his famous history of the French Revolution, *Les origines de la France contemporaine* (1873–93). He married Thérèse Denuelle on 6 June 1868; they had a daughter, Geneviève, and a son, Émile. Taine was elected to the Académie Française in 1878 and died at his Paris home, 23 rue Cassette, on 5 March 1893.

From boyhood, Taine was immersed in English culture, initially through the influence of an uncle who had worked in America. At the Collège Bourbon and at the École Normale Supérieure he read voraciously in English literature, especially of the seventeenth and eighteenth centuries; these were interests he shared with his friends Alexandre Prévost-Paradol, Cornélis de Witt, and Guillaume Guizot. But though he wrote extensively on English society and culture and became a noted Anglophile, Taine spent only short periods of time in Britain. A six-week visit from June to August 1860 largely confirmed the views he had already developed in articles on the relationship between national character and national literatures. During his visit he made extensive notes, which he recorded in small notebooks; these, together with similar notes made on subsequent visits, were to form the basis of his *Notes sur l'Angleterre*. In the autumn of 1860 and the spring of 1861 he published an important string of articles on Carlyle, Tennyson, and Mill, which were to form the substance of the final volume of his *Histoire de la littérature anglaise*. He made a second visit to England for about a fortnight between May and June 1862. By now it was clear that he was being seduced by what he considered to be the political superiority of the English, manifest in the quality of political discussion in the press.

Taine's third visit, which lasted for about three weeks in May and June 1871, was instigated by an invitation from Max Müller to give a series of lectures on seventeenth-century French theatre at the Taylor Institution in Oxford. On 8 June Taine was awarded an honorary DCL. The visit coincided with the suppression of the Paris commune, and the experience of civil war in Paris, together with defeat at the hands of Prussia, confirmed Taine in his despair at French political culture and his admiration for British political life. This is probably why, once returned to France, he set about completing and publishing his *Notes sur l'Angleterre*, which began to appear in serialized form in *Le Temps* in August 1871. The book appeared in December of the same year. It highlighted those aspects of life in which England seemed to Taine to possess a marked advantage over France: a representative system which was effective because it worked with the grain of social hierarchy; the habit of voluntary association; the educational system, with its happy emphasis upon a moral rather than a narrowly intellectual formation; and the Church of England, which Taine admired for its non-dogmatic emphasis upon moral instruction, and for its ability to nurture a learned clergy which harnessed religion and science together. Taine's knowledge of England, we should remember, was refracted by the circle of acquaintances to whom he was introduced by Guizot, and this circle was heavily weighted towards whig-Liberal politicians and liberal Anglican churchmen and scholars. The former included Richard Monckton Milnes, later Lord Houghton, Sir Mountstuart Grant Duff, and Odo Russell, and the latter, deans Stanley and Milman, and such Oxford luminaries as Benjamin Jowett and Mark Pattison. Their influence is rarely absent from his observations.

Taine's observations of England combined with the dual catastrophe that befell his homeland in 1870–71 to redirect his thinking and his energies towards politics. One aspect of this new direction was the role he played, both personally and through the influence exerted on French liberals by his *Notes sur l'Angleterre*, in launching the École Libre des Sciences Politiques, which was established in Paris in 1872 under the directorship of his friend and former pupil, Émile Boutmy. In the first place, the school aimed to nurture in France a class of 'natural leaders' such as Oxford and Cambridge supplied in England. In the second place, it sought to encourage the sort of comparative enquiry which Taine had pioneered. Boutmy himself was one of the earliest practitioners of this approach, which found its richest fulfilment in the work of one of his successors in the directorship, André Siegfried. Meanwhile Taine himself, having diagnosed some of the elements of English superiority, turned in the 1870s towards an investigation of the historical roots of France's political plight. The outcome was the work with which his name is most closely associated, *Les origines de la France contemporaine*.

Notes sur l'Angleterre was generally well received in Britain. It was translated into English by the journalist and former barrister William Fraser Rae, who had previously published a number of review articles in the *Westminster Review* in the 1860s. The translation first appeared, in abridged and serialized form, in the *Daily News* in 1872, and was published in book form the same year. Notable reviews appeared in *The Times*, *Blackwood's Magazine*, and *The Academy*. Taine's longer-term influence upon interpretations of Victorian England is harder to gauge. He continues to be much cited, especially by historians of education, the family, and religion, but should be read with some scepticism. When he published his *Notes sur l'Angleterre* he had spent only eleven weeks in Britain, and he made only two brief visits thereafter. His spoken English was poor. For the most part his views on England were inferred from his study of English literature and then reinforced by his observations and conversations. Furthermore, the authoritative claims of the *Notes* are perhaps vitiated by the inherent bias produced by the predominantly liberal Anglican circles in which he moved. The book was rather a diagnosis of France's political ills than a neutral comment on Victorian society.

H. S. JONES

Sources *H. Taine: sa vie et sa correspondance*, 4 vols. (Paris, 1902–8) · F. C. Roe, *Taine et l'Angleterre* (1923) · F. Leger, *Monsieur Taine* (1993)

Archives Bibliothèque Nationale, Paris
Likenesses R. D., drawing, *c*.1870, Bibliothèque Nationale, Paris · photographs, Bibliothèque Nationale, Paris

Tait, Alexander (*d.* 1781). *See under* Select Society (*act.* 1754–1764).

Tait, Andrew Wilson (1876–1930), accountant and industrialist, was born in Edinburgh on 16 January 1876, one of at least two sons of William Tait, a grocer and spirit dealer, and his wife, Eliza Wilson. He was educated at Daniel Stewart's College and at Edinburgh University and then became articled to the chartered accountant Alexander Thomas Niven, who had two decades earlier been principal to the chartered accountant George Alexander Touche. Tait was admitted a member of the Edinburgh Society of Accountants on 20 July 1899 and then moved to London, where he joined the recently formed firm of G. A. Touche. In 1910 he married Isabel May (*b.* 1882), the daughter of George White Allinson, a brewer of Greenbanks, Ellesmere, Shropshire, and his wife, Phoebe Sophia; they had a son and a daughter.

Tait was regarded by Touche as one of the outstanding accountants of his time. Like Touche himself, he was someone who 'thought big', with ambition, imagination, and drive. He is described in the firm's history as 'physically strong and a keen boxer' (Richards, *Touche Ross*, 16). Both partners had interests which extended far beyond their accounting firm. They were entrepreneurial in their outlook, and their fees, which were not treated as income of the firm, were thought to have been at least equal to their share of partnership profits. Andrew's brother James also joined the staff of G. A. Touche in 1911 and was admitted to partnership in 1917. James was regarded as a capable and steady worker but not of the same calibre as Andrew.

One of Tait's major achievements was the reconstruction of Ferranti. When the electronics firm neared bankruptcy in 1903, its bankers called in two accountants as receiver-managers. One of these, Arthur Whittaker, was from a local Manchester firm; the other was Tait, who became chairman. Following reconstruction, Sebastian Ziani de Ferranti, the firm's founder, was reduced to a relatively insignificant position within the company. Indeed, it appears that Tait ensured Ferranti was virtually excluded from the works after 1905 because of his alleged obstructive influence. According to the company's historian: 'Ferranti stands out as an excellent example of the growing importance of professionally trained businessmen, and especially accountants, in the management of manufacturing companies in the two decades preceding the First World War' (Wilson, 81).

Tait was active in the affairs of the British Electrical and Allied Manufacturers' Association. In this capacity he took a leading part in the formation of the Federation of British Industries (1916), and was appointed a member of its first executive council. In his role with the association he strove hard to organize the merger of British electrical manufacturers in order to help them compete with their

German and American counterparts. He was severely critical of excessive individualism among British industrialists, and while giving evidence to a committee on electrical industries in 1916 he argued that the government's failure to provide support for British industry 'twenty to twenty-five years ago' was the reason why it lagged behind the Germans, who 'used every effort, diplomatic and otherwise, to assist industry' (*DBB*). In 1918 Tait was appointed CBE for his work during the war on this and other committees.

Tait seemed destined to become one of the country's leading businessmen, and during the first two decades of the twentieth century he was heavily involved in the creation and management of investment trusts. He met with considerable successes, but the connection was to be the source of major set-backs, as well as managing to tarnish his professional reputation. He was director of the Edinburgh-based Electrical Securities Trust, formed in 1907, which failed, with the result that the ordinary shareholders lost all their capital. Much worse was to come as the result of Tait's work at Cedar Investment Trust, which he founded in 1918. He was the receiver and liquidator of the Magadi Soda Company, where plans were made for the sale of its assets to Brunner Mond. This led to a court case at the Chancery Division in February 1925, which proved extremely damaging to Tait. The case, brought by one of Magadi Soda's shareholders, revealed that Tait and his associates had made public statements designed to depress the value of the company's debentures, which were then purchased by the Cedar Investment Trust with the intention of resale to Brunner Mond at a substantial profit. Mr Justice Eve described Tait's part in this unsavoury adventure as discreditable and a breach of trust. Tait was subsequently removed from the boards of a number of companies, although he remained a partner in Touche and on the boards of many other companies right up to the date of his death.

Tait died after a long and wasting illness on 21 April 1930 at his home at 10 Holland Park, Notting Hill, London. The cause of death was chronic meningo-encephalitis, and it is thought that the disease may have been the explanation for his misconduct in the Magadi Soda affair. According to his obituary notice in *The Times*: 'Mr Tait had one of the shrewdest and sanest minds on financial matters which the City has known, and until his illness his advice was almost universally sought' (*The Times*, 22 April 1930).

JOHN RICHARD EDWARDS

Sources R. P. T. Davenport-Hines, 'Tait, Andrew Wilson', *DBB* · A. B. Richards, *Touche Ross & Co., 1899–1981: the origins and growth of the United Kingdom firm* (1981) · A. B. Richards, 'Touche, Sir George Alexander', *DBB* · *The Accountant* (26 April 1930), 550 · J. F. Wilson, *Ferranti and the British electrical industry, 1864–1930* (1988) · *WWW* · *The Times* (22 April 1930) · d. cert.

Wealth at death £529,206 1s. 4d.: probate, 4 July 1930, *CGPLA Eng. & Wales*

Tait, Archibald Campbell (1811–1882), archbishop of Canterbury, was born on 21 December 1811 in Park Place, Edinburgh, the ninth and last child of Craufurd Tait (*d.*

Archibald Campbell Tait (1811–1882), by James Sant, *c*.1865

1832), an improvident landowner, and his wife, Susan Campbell (*d.* 1814), daughter of Sir Ilay *Campbell, lord president of the court of session. He had three sisters and five brothers, two of whom died as youths.

Youth and Oxford From first to last, Tait's life was marked by physical suffering of his own and by the death of those closest to him. He was born with club feet—essentially healthy, so the doctors said, but bent double. They were straightened out successfully but painfully when he was eight, through encasing in tin boots which he had to wear night and day. A few years afterwards, he had barely begun to recover from scarlet fever when the same fever slew the brother, Ilay, who had accompanied him during the straightening out of his feet—a foretaste of the disease that would almost annihilate his own children thirty years later.

There was, however, little outward evidence of the fragility of Tait's life during his formal schooling. Although his father's enthusiastic efforts to improve his estate left the family in straitened financial circumstances, young Tait received an excellent education, first at Edinburgh high school (from 1821), then in the Edinburgh Academy (from 1824), where he was dux, and finally at the University of Glasgow (in 1827). Wherever he went, his powers of intellect and relentless self-discipline enabled him to capture most of the prizes, ultimately capped by the Snell exhibition, which sent him to Balliol College, Oxford, in 1829. His academic successes continued there unabated, carrying him to the senior tutorship of his college by the age of twenty-six.

A sturdy sense of religious vocation accompanied Tait's

ordination in 1836 into the ministry of the Church of England, necessitated by his tutorship. Though more interested in domestic and foreign politics than in ecclesiastical affairs, he had always envisaged a clerical career for himself. Even before he reached Balliol and was confirmed as a member of the Church of England, he had entertained clerical ambitions, including the archbishopric of Canterbury. Devotional dedication nevertheless undergirded his choice of profession. He added the arduous and financially unrewarding curacy of Baldon, outside Oxford, to his tutorial responsibilities as soon as he was ordained.

Tait's years in the senior common room of Balliol coincided with the first phase of the Oxford Movement, from Keble's assize sermon in 1833 through the publication of Newman's Tract 90 in 1841. The religious ferment embraced Balliol, where Newman's most unrestrained disciple, W. G. Ward, had been elected to a fellowship at the same time as Tait. Tait retained the friendship of Ward and other associates caught up in the Oxford Movement; but he was himself immune from its spell. He lacked the mystical sense to which it appealed, and it defied the political Liberalism that he embraced. When Newman attempted in Tract 90 to reconcile the expanding Catholicism of the Oxford Movement with the Thirty-Nine Articles of the Church of England, to which its clergy were required to subscribe, he violated Tait's sense of the intended and obvious meaning of those articles. Tait insisted on good sense in interpreting religious formularies, avoiding punitive elaboration but respecting the essential tenets they were designed to uphold. He had declined to be a candidate for the professorship of moral philosophy at Glasgow in 1838, when he found that it would require him to subscribe to the Westminster confession of faith with its emphatic Calvinism. He prized the latitude of interpretation which the articles and formularies of the Church of England allowed; but their whole point would, in his estimation, be destroyed if they were stretched to condone the precepts and practices they had been designed to condemn. He therefore drew up the protest that led the governing council of Oxford to condemn Tract 90 as incompatible with subscription to the statutes of the university.

Rugby and Carlisle   Tait's protest contributed to his appointment, on 28 July 1842, to succeed Thomas Arnold as headmaster of Rugby School; for Arnold had not only made Rugby the model public school of England, he had also put forward the most attractive alternative to the Oxford Movement for earnest members of the Church of England who sought a faith attuned to the progressive intellectual and political thought of the age. The trustees of Rugby looked instinctively to Oxford and particularly to Balliol, where Thomas Arnold's son Matthew had been one of Tait's pupils. Though just thirty years of age, Tait was not thought too young for the vacancy. Both as a serious educator and as a temperate but convinced critic of the Oxford Movement, he was a natural choice.

Yet the appointment did not prove felicitous; any successor to Arnold was bound to be a let-down. No one could replicate Arnold's pioneering application of his moral and intellectual appeal to the English public school; and the mystique of Rugby was soon enhanced by the biography A. P. Stanley wrote of Arnold. Tait had no prior experience of English public schools. He had a forceful personality but no charisma; he had a good mind but no taste for scholarship; and the masters who had been proud to serve under Arnold resented the intrusion of an outsider. Tait threw everything he had into his task, but he did not feel natural at it. He wrote out his sermons and lectures, rarely revealing his talent for extemporary speech. He was somewhat remote in manner, and restrained the schoolboy fervour Arnold had aroused.

Ever the institutional reformer, Tait curbed the excessive authority that the sixth form had acquired over the rest of the school. Enrolment at the school expanded under his administration, effectively capitalizing on Arnold's posthumous prestige. But Tait did not acquire a hold on the affections of the school until, six years after his appointment, in early 1848, rheumatic fever brought him to death's door. His brothers and sisters were summoned to take their leave of him, and his doctor prepared him for death. He survived, though with permanently damaged health. During the anxious days of waiting and then the slow weeks of recovery, the school was hushed. Concern for the health of the headmaster stopped an incipient rebellion by the junior school against the sixth. The boys greeted Tait's return to active duty with an outpouring of affection. The illness had a deepening effect on Tait himself; and he spoke afterwards with a depth of feeling which stirred those who had listened to him hitherto simply with respect. Physically the illness left him looking somewhat fragile but not weak, despite a stoop and collar-length wavy hair—an impression that persisted until he put on weight in his sixties.

Tait continued as headmaster for another two years, but his recovery was not equal to the demands of his position. In October 1849 he was offered and accepted what was regarded as a position of honourable retirement as dean of Carlisle and left Rugby in the summer of 1850. In Carlisle he recovered his strength beyond what had been anticipated. Happily married since 22 June 1843 to Catharine Spooner (1819–1878) [see Tait, Catharine], daughter of William Spooner, archdeacon of Coventry, Tait delighted in his expanding family, which eventually included six daughters and a son. Earnest in his commitment to his ministry wherever it took him, he attended immediately to the religious needs of the northern town to which he had been assigned, neglected as it had been by the clergy of the cathedral in its midst. Tait involved Carlisle in the transformation of English cathedrals from places of dignified retreat into centres of pastoral ministry and evangelism.

While at Carlisle, Tait also played a leading part in an improvement of national importance, reforming the University of Oxford. He had been alert to the need for reform there from his earliest days as a tutor at Balliol. As a Scot, he appreciated also what the English universities might learn from foreign models: in the summer of 1839 he had taken up residence in Bonn to familiarize himself with the organization and instructional methods of university education in Prussia, and he acquired sufficient command of the language to attend lectures and engage in discussion with German professors. That year he published a pamphlet on the reform of Oxford. Eleven years later, in 1850, when Lord John Russell contemplated appointing a commission to tackle the reform of Oxford, he sounded out Tait as a potential commissioner. Tait not only agreed but encouraged Russell to stick to his guns when the ecclesiastical interests of Oxford cried out in alarm at the prospect of reform. Once appointed, Tait threw himself into the work of the commission. He took a special interest in the admission of 'unattached' students, who might enjoy the benefits of education at Oxford without the costs associated with membership in its constituent colleges. His German experience fortified the commission's determination to make professors central to the lecturing at the university. Tait also encouraged the commission's efforts to reduce the restriction of teaching positions in the colleges and university to the clergy, believing that this reform would put the clergy in touch with the thinking of the laity and, so far as religious education was concerned, would only intensify commitment to it by making it voluntary. The whig leaders were delighted at their discovery in Tait of a friend to reform of the sort more often found in Scotland than Oxford.

But it was nothing welcome that drew the attention of Britain's governing élite to Tait in the spring of 1856. Within little more than a month, five of his seven children were carried away by scarlet fever. All five were little girls, from two years old to ten. The multiple tragedy drove what was left of the family, including the one son and a baby daughter, away from their home to a house lent them outside Carlisle. From the queen down, the country was moved at its tenderest point. Reeling from the succession of blows, Tait found deepened roots for the faith which he reaffirmed.

Bishop of London Within months of the tragedy Lord Palmerston offered Tait, and he immediately accepted, the most important bishopric in England: London. He had been encouraged to expect a bishopric from the whigs. He had largely recovered his health at Carlisle, and he had been a little disappointed that an offer had not come sooner. Still, his appointment to London was astonishing, for with a single exception over the past two centuries every bishop of London had served an apprenticeship in charge of a lesser diocese. Tait none the less accepted the appointment without hesitation or even preliminary prayer; he was consecrated at the Chapel Royal, Whitehall, on 22 November 1856.

Tait threw himself into the assignment with a burst of innovative energy. Though still higher office lay in store for him, it was at London that he made his greatest contribution to the ministry of the Church of England at its mid-Victorian height. Much had been done by his predecessor at London, C. J. Blomfield. One of the giants in that age of administrative reform, Blomfield had organized and funded a church building campaign that almost caught up

with the explosive population growth of the metropolis. But the expanding population did not pour into the new churches. Tait recognized this shortcoming, whether from its exposure in the religious census of 1851 or from personal observation during the sessions of the Oxford University commission in London. To fill the churches, he looked for more effective methods of evangelism. The methods he selected were not new, but their adoption by a prelate of the established church was startling. Obeying the command to the original apostles to take the gospel to the highways and byways, the new bishop set the example he wished his clergy to follow by preaching in the open air to those who fell outside the customary confines of parish churches: to immigrants in London's dockland, to bus drivers in the central London yard, to porters from a train platform, to fruit and vegetable sellers at Covent Garden. Loosening the liturgical shackles and social inhibitions of Sunday morning worship, he helped to design and then preached at popular afternoon services in large churches in the poorer parishes of his diocese. Shaking off the restraints he accepted at Rugby, he preached extemporaneously, another departure from the expected pattern of episcopal conduct. His methods proved successful, at any rate initially. He preached to churches packed with people whose clothing differed conspicuously from the well-dressed morning congregations. He sought to open the greatest churches within his diocese, Westminster Abbey and St Paul's Cathedral, for similar use: the abbey was quick to comply but the cathedral was slow.

It was primarily as an organizer that Tait increased the effectiveness of the mid-Victorian church. After initiating unfamiliar patterns of practice, he created new administrative institutions with special funding for all the methods of evangelism, old as well as new. All the while he encouraged independent initiatives among his clergy and laity, no matter whether they stretched the limits of accepted practice, so long as they did not violate the fundamental order and character of the English church. After barely one year in his see, Tait secured the co-operation of the clergy from the most densely populated parts of the metropolis in organizing a diocesan home mission for 'aggressive' evangelism in 1857. Six years later he won generous support in money and time from leading laymen to set up and run the Bishop of London's Fund. He designed it to pay mainly for personnel to advance the mission of the church: missionary clergy, additional curates, and laymen and -women to go into homes to read the Bible and minister to the people where they lived.

The immensity of the task for the church in the world's largest city led Tait to welcome innovations that he would not adopt himself. He refused to object when evangelical churchmen hired theatres for Sunday evening services comparable to those he promoted in the inner city churches and cathedrals. More controversial were the innovations of the advanced high church, for they threatened not just the accustomed dignity but also the protestant character of the established church. The disciples of the Oxford Movement in theology and the Cambridge movement in ritual revived a range of institutions and practices popularly identified with Roman Catholicism, including sisterhoods and monastic orders, auricular confession, and elaborate ceremonial at holy communion epitomized by the wearing of eucharistic vestments. These practices angered insistently protestant churchmen and enabled them to exploit the popular English prejudice against anything reminiscent of Rome and its continental and Irish clients. Tait feared that the inward-looking ecclesiasticism and exotic ritual of the advanced high church would repel soberly middle-class laymen, and he tried to persuade high-church zealots to avoid provocative conduct. Yet he knew that the church needed all the zeal that it could command to make headway against the spiritual destitution, blank secularism, and social misery prevalent in London. He was particularly impressed by the dedicated ministry in one of London's poorest corners of clergy who would be remembered by posterity as the founding saints of slum ritualism, C. F. Lowder and A. H. Mackonochie at St George-in-the-East. Tait never forgot the experience he and his wife had of working alongside these two men as, heedless of the threat to their health, they ministered to the victims of a cholera epidemic in 1866. So long as he was responsible for the diocese of London, Tait was more often a protector than the scourge of ritualism.

Tait was nevertheless obliged to uphold some law and order in his enormous diocese at a time when the Church of England was undergoing a far-reaching transformation. It had been a quintessentially national institution, a vital part of the established order in church and state. It was becoming primarily a church, less and less synonymous with the country as a whole, still central but in an international denomination which accompanied the diaspora of English-speaking people, and as Catholic as it was protestant. However much Tait recognized the church's need for zeal, he was fundamentally out of sympathy with this transformation. His objective, paradoxical in its liberalism, was to make the Church of England more effectively than ever the church of the nation.

The transformation was in an early, formative stage during Tait's dozen years at London. The advanced high-church party was feeling its way forward, not yet sure how far to take its reaffirmation of Catholic tradition, grateful for protection and deferential to episcopal authority. For a while Tait was able to secure acceptance of his guidance, more so indeed from the high church than from militant evangelicals. He gave his blessing to sisterhoods so long as they avoided lifelong vows and did not insist on frequent auricular confession, and some (though not all) of these new foundations accepted his terms. His ordination of Elizabeth Ferrard as a deaconess in 1861 and his subsequent support for the North London Deaconesses' Institute witnessed to his interest in a female religious community rooted in a strongly protestant tradition. It was harder to deal with the larger problem of ritualism, which provoked brawls at St George-in-the-East and angered powerful laymen led by the earl of Shaftesbury in the House of Lords. Tait managed to retard the escalation of ritualist ceremonial through judicious exercise of the few

legal powers at his command and outspoken condemnation of the most offensive practices, including insistence on confession to a priest, combined with undisguised gratitude for the pastoral ministry of ritualist clergy in the slums.

Tait's underlying fear of high-church ecclesiasticism remained none the less obvious. It made him suspicious of the movement to draw together the international Anglican communion, a movement symbolized in 1867 by the convening of all its bishops, however far from England, for the first Lambeth conference. In an anachronistic display of something more akin to the old imperialism than to the new, he sought to shore up the royal supremacy, the rule of English law, and the authority of the mother church against demands for ecclesiastical autonomy in the colonies. While Tait participated cordially in the proceedings of the conference, he prevented the bishop of Cape Town, as metropolitan of the ecclesiastical province of South Africa, from deposing and replacing the peculiarly unorthodox bishop of Natal, J. W. Colenso.

The same concern for middle-class laymen which made Tait critical of the Catholicizing high church made him uneasy about the efforts of liberal theologians. In the eyes of the reverent layman, the clergy in both groups were disloyal to the church they had been ordained to uphold. Tait shared the desire of liberal theologians to keep the teaching of the church and the thinking of its clergy attuned to the mind of the man in the pew. For Tait that meant concentrating on the central tenets and simple truths of the gospel. He was not shaken by the developments in natural science, historical criticism, and textual analysis of the Bible which drove men of more scholarly bent to re-examine their creed and religious teaching. Years earlier he had encouraged students at Oxford to undertake critical study of the Bible. But when they published conclusions which upset the faith of the man in the pew, Tait concluded that the liberals were 'deficient in religion'.

This divergence from his former students broke angrily into the open with the publication in 1860 of a volume entitled *Essays and Reviews*, written by an assortment of liberal theologians, including two of Tait's erstwhile pupils at Balliol who had since moved into posts he had formerly occupied: Benjamin Jowett, now tutor at Balliol, and Frederick Temple, headmaster of Rugby. Their contributions were the least offensive in the volume, as Tait acknowledged when Jowett and Temple came to see him after the book gave rise to a storm of controversy. They therefore felt betrayed when, along with the entire bench of bishops, Tait signed a statement declaring the more extreme assertions in the book to be incompatible with 'honest subscription to the formularies of our Church'. Yet subsequently, without quite appeasing his alienated friends, he infuriated the large orthodox majority, including high church and low, by agreeing as a member of the judicial committee of the privy council with its majority ruling that the statements from the offending volume which were brought before that tribunal did not plainly contradict the articles or formularies of the established church. The offence Tait gave to orthodox believers deepened when the other two episcopal members of the judicial committee, the archbishops of Canterbury and York, let it be known that they opposed the majority judgment.

Archbishop of Canterbury The unstinting way in which Tait met all the demands of his office took a toll on his health, which the quiet years at Carlisle had only partially restored. The strain, evident to himself from fainting spells and to the public from occasionally cancelled appointments, prompted Lord Palmerston in 1862 to offer him the more prestigious but less demanding archbishopric of York. Tait turned the offer down, anxious to put his work in London on a more secure basis, as he did the following year with the Bishop of London's Fund. He was repeatedly and more seriously sick in 1866; but nothing would stop him between bouts of illness from ministering personally to those who were stricken by the cholera epidemic of that year.

Appreciation of the leadership Tait offered the church prompted Queen Victoria to insist on his appointment to the archbishopric of Canterbury when it fell vacant in October 1868. Disraeli, who had recently become prime minister and faced a general election in which he needed to harvest votes from supporters of the established church, wanted to appoint a bishop whose doctrinal orthodoxy was above suspicion, and he gave way to the queen reluctantly. Tait accepted the offer without hesitation, and was enthroned as archbishop in February 1869.

Tait was immediately plunged into the most serious crisis of the relations between church and state in a generation. The Liberals won an overwhelming victory in the general election under the leadership of Gladstone, who had united his party by demanding the severance of the Irish branch of the established church from its privileged position in the state. Tait as a Liberal understood how anomalous the Irish church establishment was, commanding as it did the support of barely an eighth of the people of Ireland, but he dreaded the severance of any link between the kingdom and its church. He much preferred to extend the connection between church and state to include the majority Catholic church of the Irish, and he was anxious, if complete severance was unavoidable, to ensure that the separated Church of Ireland was so constituted under law as to protect it from domination by any one ecclesiastical party. The crisis tested all his political skills, for he had to gain the confidence of the church as its new leader while accepting some sacrifice of its treasured interests. Defiance of the huge Liberal majority in the new House of Commons on the prime issue that had pulled them together was likely only to damage the prospects for the church.

Amid this tangle, Tait pursued a controversial but ultimately creditable policy. Hoping for extensive amendment rather than rejection of the bill in the House of Lords, he negotiated on two fronts: with Conservative peers and his fellow bishops to allow the bill a second reading, and with the government to meet amendments with some sympathy. Neither side was readily compliant. The first hurdle was surmounted when the Lords carried the bill a second

time by a majority to which few of the bishops, but a crucial bloc of the Conservative lay lords, contributed, while Tait and the archbishop of York moved to the steps of the throne to abstain. Gladstone rejected most, though not all, of the amendments which the Lords then sent down. Tait fought on for his least popular demand, concurrent endowment of the Roman church in Ireland. But the threat of a constitutional deadlock between the two houses of parliament lasted for only a matter of hours. Tait and Gladstone plunged into negotiations along with Granville, the conciliatory Liberal leader in the upper house, and Hugh Cairns, the Ulsterman who had been lord chancellor in Disraeli's ministry. The bill as ultimately amended and enacted omitted concurrent endowment, but left the disposal of the surplus wealth of the Irish church to the future wisdom of parliament, and also improved the financial settlement for the disestablished institution.

Worn out by the months of intense work that preceded this outcome, Tait suffered a quick succession of convulsive strokes in late 1869 which looked likely to kill him. Gradually he recovered, but too slowly to contribute significantly to the legislative measure of 1870 which did more good for the Church of England than Irish disestablishment had done harm: the Elementary Education Act. Vindicating Tait's faith in the national church, that act not only incorporated the multitude of existing Church of England schools in the new national network but gave the church time to add to its schools before elected school boards could move to fill in the blanks with civic schools.

Ironically it was the continuing reform of higher education at Oxford that shook Tait's confidence that the interests of the church would not suffer from Liberal measures for improvement. He was not dismayed at the abolition early in Gladstone's ministry of the religious tests which fettered admission to Oxford, for Tait had long criticized reliance on oaths and subscriptions to protect religious interests. But he was worried by the parallel reduction in the restriction of college fellowships to the clergy of the established church, a reduction demanded by the rising generation of Oxford men who, as Tait had forewarned, were sick of the ecclesiastical preoccupations and pretensions of the Oxford Movement. This particular reform was applied ever more extensively through the 1870s, unrestrained by the Conservatives' return to office in 1874.

In other regards the return of the Conservatives facilitated a spurt of church reforming legislation for which Tait shared the credit. He welcomed the constitutional role of parliament as the legislature for the church because it obliged the church to defer to the wishes of the laity. He performed at his best in the House of Lords, where he commanded widespread respect. He much preferred that forum to the clerical assembly over which he presided as archbishop, the convocation of Canterbury. Still, in order to command the consent of the clergy and allay the uneasiness of the high church he did all he could to incorporate convocation in the process of legislation for the church. Even so it was hard to make headway under Gladstone and the Liberals. Gladstone had to reckon with the nonconformist critics of the church who bulked large among his political supporters, and as a devout high-churchman he wanted, more so than the archbishop, to promote the spiritual autonomy of the Church of England. Despite repeated efforts on Tait's part, his church-reforming legislative accomplishments during Gladstone's first ministry were very modest: one act in 1869 allowing disabled bishops to resign or secure episcopal assistants, and another in 1872 loosening a few of the rigidities in public worship mandated under the Act of Uniformity.

The return of the Conservatives to power under Disraeli in 1874 and the appointment of R. A. Cross to the Home Office gave Tait a rare opportunity for workmanlike legislative reform of the church's administrative structure, particularly the subdivision of overly large dioceses and creation of new ones. Cross, a sturdily middle-class lawyer and conscientious layman, saw to the creation of six new sees—more, he noted with uncharacteristic flourish, than anyone since Henry VIII.

Yet at the beginning of the Conservative ministry Tait's legislative initiatives placed the cohesion of the cabinet, and more seriously of the church, in jeopardy. He spent the rest of his archiepiscopate dealing with the damage inflicted on the church by the Public Worship Regulation Act of 1874. His response to ritualism had hardened since his removal from the pastoral demands of London. His appointment to Canterbury, with responsibility for the church as a whole, occurred just as Liberalism reached its height of ascendancy in the state. His appreciation of the church's need for all the spiritual resources it could command was, consequently, overtaken by his awareness of the dangers that Anglo-Catholicism posed to the unity of the church and its affiliation with the state. Initially Tait hoped to contain the various schools of churchmanship together within the confines of the law through judicial rulings arrived at in consultation between the leading judges and bishops of the country. Although this procedure disturbed high-churchmen concerned for the spiritual autonomy of the church, in a succession of judgments the judicial committee of the privy council upheld the right of the main schools of Anglican thought—first low, then broad, and finally high—to their legitimate place within the church. But the tolerance which the law thus displayed on matters of belief did not extend to the conduct of worship—nor did Tait wish it to. As the judicial committee explained in its judgment upholding the legality of the high-church doctrine of the real presence, public worship was meant to serve as 'common ground on which all Church people may meet, though they differ about some doctrines'. Catholic teaching might pass undetected, but everyone would notice innovations in Sunday worship. But reliance on the courts to regulate church ceremonial suffered from ultimately fatal drawbacks. The law on these matters was complicated, and rulings were quirky. When they came down against the

mainstream high-church practice of the eastward position as well as the more extreme use of eucharistic vestments, Tait sought to enforce the latter prohibition but not the former, and thus he undermined the impartiality of the law. Each ruling, furthermore, applied to the particular case in question and could not be enforced more broadly without further litigation.

To deal with these shortcomings Tait, at the urging of the queen, proposed legislation to Gladstone at the beginning of 1874. Abruptly, for unrelated reasons, Gladstone called a general election, which he lost, bringing the Conservatives to power. The cabinet which Disraeli put together was liable to the most acute internal divisions on religious matters, from which it therefore resolved to stand aside. Undeterred, Tait pushed ahead with his bill. It was designed to strengthen the ability of the bishops to enforce conformity of worship within moderate bounds in their dioceses. In the House of Commons the bill commanded such widespread respect that Lord Houghton remarked sardonically to Tait, 'You are as triumphant as Laud in his worst times', to which the archbishop replied, 'I hope that it will not end in the same way'. But in the House of Lords he lost control of his bill to the militantly protestant earl of Shaftesbury. Working in alliance with Lord Chancellor Cairns—a native of the north of Ireland—Shaftesbury transformed Tait's bill by placing lay courts in charge of enforcing the law on church services so long as the diocesan bishop did not veto proceedings. In that form, after dividing the Liberal as well as Conservative front benches, the bill was enacted. As the act took effect, the church lurched between embarrassment and frustration, barely escaping humiliation. Working in a manner unforeseen by its framers, the act turned conscientious ritualists into martyrs by sending them to gaol, from which they could be extricated only at Tait's manipulative contrivance.

Final years and death Personal tragedy saved Tait from discredit in these circumstances even in the eyes of the high church. He was already the queen's favourite archbishop. She packed off Prince Wilhelm of Prussia, the future Kaiser, to see him when the young man visited England. But the qualities that delighted the queen in her archbishop infuriated the high church. That anger was, however, subdued in 1878. Tait's son, the elder of the two children who survived the scarlet fever epidemic in 1856, had followed his father into the ministry. Modest in manner, he combined the piety of his mother with the liberal inclinations of his father, and he seemed set to become an exemplary parish priest. He won plaudits everywhere when he travelled to the United States to invite the bishops there to the second Lambeth conference. Towards the end of 1877, however, he showed signs of some previously undiagnosed illness; he lost strength over the winter and died at the end of May. The tragic tale was not yet over. The loss of the son was too great for his mother. Her health failed with her spirits, and she died within six months of him. The archbishop, aged beyond his sixty-six years, sought consolation in preparing a memoir of his wife and son for publication. It was accompanied with almost unbearable pathos by an account Mrs Tait had written twenty years earlier about the death of her five daughters. The book still stands like a great funerary sculpture on the literary landscape of Victorian England. The archbishop's terrible familiarity with death protected him from personal attack and curbed criticism of his policies.

Tait needed all the help he could get on other issues besides ritualism. The approach which he adopted towards one of the last remaining grievances of protestant nonconformists aroused more widespread opposition among the clergy than any policy of his for the church internally. Nonconformists were entitled to nothing more than silent burial in the graveyard of the parish in which they lived, treatment which reflected the tension between the conception of the established church as a national institution and as a distinctive denomination with its own religious requirements. Anxious to reaffirm the national character of the church, Tait sought to open parish churchyards to orderly burial observances by nonconformists. His action raised the professional and proprietary hackles of low- as well as high-church clergy. He reduced the intensity, though not the extent, of their opposition by offsetting the proposed concession to the nonconformists with one to the clergy, removing the obligation under which they laboured to read the burial service over everyone—except for suicides, the excommunicate, and the unbaptized—no matter how unrepentently reprobate when they died. The justice of his proposal persuaded the laity even in the House of Lords, and Conservative opposition began to crumble. When Gladstone returned to office after the general election of 1880, he moved quickly to settle the question along Tait's lines. By removing the last practical grievance of nonconformists, the Burials Act of 1880 served, as Tait hoped, to preserve the constitutional, but now largely symbolic, union of church and state.

Otherwise Tait's hopes failed him in the final years of his archiepiscopate. He joined forces with high-church and Conservative former opponents in the Lords to stem the anti-clerical tide among the dons at Oxford. The religious climate among the undergraduates there and at Cambridge was quite different, and in the 1880s recruitment to the ministry rose to an unprecedented height; but the spirituality that attracted most recruits was that of Tait's lifelong opponents, high rather than broad or national. The Public Worship Regulation Act subjected the church to ever deepening embarrassments, in face of which parliament retreated into indifference, making remedial legislation impossible. Tait used his deathbed to avert what threatened to be the most discreditable of all the scandals under the act, the imprisonment of his colleague from his finest London days, A. H. Mackonochie, the patriarch of slum ritualism. The archbishop died on 3 December 1882 at Addington, Surrey, his official country residence, and was buried in the churchyard there. He left three daughters, one of whom, Edith, was married to the later archbishop of Canterbury, Randall Davidson.

Conclusion The governing objective of Archibald Campbell Tait, whether as college tutor, headmaster, diocesan bishop, or primate, was to keep the Church of England in harmony with the concerns and progressing thought of the country at large, and thus to strengthen its moral foundation. His religious view was essentially national, and British more than English. The first Scot to become archbishop of Canterbury, Presbyterian by upbringing but with familial ties to the episcopal church in Scotland, he was repelled by the Oxford Movement's denial of ecclesiastical validity of the presbyterian denominations of his homeland, strongly though he personally rejected their Calvinism. None the less, at his death his policy of reliance on the courts to hold the church together within properly acceptable bounds—avoiding either of the religious extremes which he feared—had already been consigned to that refuge of the perplexed, a royal commission. The conclusions of the commission reflected esteem for the dead archbishop, but nevertheless represented an effort to repair the damage wrought by his initiative. Suspicious of anything poetical, Tait held the virtue of good sense, a virtue which he exemplified, in too much esteem fully to understand the pious enthusiasms of his contemporaries. He was inclined to deflate more than to utilize the excesses of religious fervour, except when confronted by the overwhelming needs of London. Tait's attempt throughout his leadership to bring the church abreast of the nation left the church bruised and intensified its preoccupations with its own well-being. Yet, ironically, he touched the religious sensibilities of his age as a result of his recurrent encounters with death, for Victorians the transcending human experience, which grounded and persistently deepened his own faith.

PETER T. MARSH

Sources W. Benham and R. T. Davidson, *Life of Archibald Campbell Tait*, 2 vols. (1891) · W. Benham, ed., *Catharine and Craufurd Tait, wife and son of Archibald Campbell, archbishop of Canterbury: a memoir* (1879) · P. T. Marsh, *The Victorian church in decline: Archbishop Tait and the Church of England, 1868–1882* (1969) · J. P. Parry, *Democracy and religion* (1986) · O. Chadwick, *The Victorian church*, 2 vols. (1966–70) · E. R. Norman, *Church and society in England, 1770–1970* (1976) · H. McLeod, *Class and religion in the late Victorian city* (1974) · Gladstone, *Diaries* · d. cert. · *DNB*

Archives Canterbury Cathedral, archives, corresp. · LPL, corresp. · LPL, corresp., diaries, and papers · NL Scot., address to Edinburgh Philosophical Institution | BL, corresp. with W. E. Gladstone, Add. MSS 44330–44331 · Bodl. Oxf., letters to Benjamin Disraeli · Bodl. Oxf., letters to first earl of Kimberley · Bodl. Oxf., letters mainly to Samuel Wilberforce · Durham Cath. CL, letters to J. B. Lightfoot · LPL, corresp. with Lady Burdett-Coutts · LPL, corresp. with Lord Selborne · LPL, corresp. with Frederick White · LUL, Loyd MSS · PRO, letters to Lord Cairns, PRO 30/59

Likenesses G. Zobel, mezzotint, pubd 1860 (after J. R. Swinton), BM, NPG · W. Behnes, marble bust, exh. RA 1861, LPL · J. Sant, oils, c.1865, NPG [*see illus.*] · L. C. Dickinson, chalk drawing, 1867, NPG · S. Hodges, oils, c.1869, Fulham Palace, London · G. Richmond, oils, 1879, LPL; replica, 1885, Balliol Oxf. · J. E. Boehm, marble bust, exh. RA 1883, Royal Collection; plaster cast, NPG · Bingham, carte-de-visite, NPG · Dalziel, woodcut, BM · Hill & Saunders, carte-de-visite, NPG · Lock & Whitfield, woodburytype photograph, NPG; repro. in T. Cooper and others, *Men of mark: a gallery of contemporary portraits* (1876) · Mayall, carte-de-visite, NPG · G. Pilotell, drypoint, BM · D. J. Pound, stipple and line engraving (after photograph by Mayall), NPG · J. J. Tissot, lithograph, NPG; repro. in *VF* (25 Dec 1869) · Walker & Sons, carte-de-visite, NPG · carte-de-visite, NPG ·

chromolithograph caricature, NPG; repro. in *VF* (25 Dec 1869) · marble medallion on panel, Balliol Oxf. · woodburytype photograph, NPG

Wealth at death £77,773 4s. 1d.: resworn probate, July 1884, *CGPLA Eng. & Wales* (1883)

Tait, Sir (William Eric) Campbell (1886–1946), naval officer and colonial governor, was born at Morice Town, Devonport, on 12 August 1886, the eldest son of Surgeon William Tait RN, and his wife, Emma, daughter of John Greenway, solicitor, of Ford Park, Compton Gifford, near Plymouth.

Having entered the Royal Naval College, Dartmouth, in 1902, Tait, always known as Campbell Tait, next served in the cruiser *Grafton* in the Pacific and then in the *Drake* in the Atlantic. He was promoted sub-lieutenant in August 1906 and after taking gunnery and navigation courses at Portsmouth, joined the battleship *Prince of Wales* in the Mediterranean in May 1907, but transferred to the cruiser *Flora* on the China station in August. He returned home in the autumn of 1909 having been promoted lieutenant in April. Between 1910 and 1912 he was watchkeeper successively in the battleship *Irresistible*, the cruiser *Furious*, the battleship *Hindustan*, and the destroyer *Staunch*, all in home waters. He went next to the *Collingwood*, in which he saw active service after the outbreak of war and was present at the battle of Jutland. In 1917 he was promoted lieutenant-commander, transferred to the *Malaya*, and during the last half of the year was acting equerry to Prince Albert, and was appointed MVO. In June 1919 he joined the royal yacht *Victoria and Albert* and in August 1921 was promoted commander. On 3 November 1919 he married Katie Cynthia, who survived him, daughter of Captain Hubert H. Grenfell RN, inventor of illuminated night sights for naval guns and one-time naval attaché for Europe. They had two daughters.

In January 1922 Tait took up an appointment for duty with naval officers under training at the University of Cambridge. Returning to sea in September 1922 he spent two years as executive officer of the light cruiser *Hawkins*, flagship of the commander-in-chief, China station. For the next two years he was training commander at Chatham and was promoted captain at the end of 1926.

After a senior officers' war course at Greenwich Tait returned to sea in February 1928 and commanded four cruisers in succession, an unusual occurrence in peacetime: the *Dragon* in the Mediterranean and the *Capetown*, *Delhi*, and *Despatch* on the America and West Indies station. Following a senior officers' course at Sheerness he became deputy director of the intelligence division of the naval staff at the Admiralty in April 1932. In November 1933 he joined the staff of the commander-in-chief, China station; and from 1934 to 1937 he commanded the cruiser *Shropshire* in the Mediterranean. In August 1937 he became commodore, and a year later rear-admiral, of the royal naval barracks, Portsmouth. There he played a major role in the smooth mobilization of the fleet in 1939 and was appointed CB in 1940. From May 1940 to his promotion to vice-admiral in October 1941 he was director of personnel services at the Admiralty and in January and February 1942

flew his flag in the *Resolution* as vice-admiral commanding 3rd battle squadron and second in command, Eastern Fleet. Then, until May 1944, he held the most important appointment of his naval career, that of commander-in-chief, south Atlantic, first at Freetown, Sierra Leone, and from March 1942 at Simonstown. In 1942, with Major-General I. P. de Villiers, general officer commanding, Coastal Command, in South Africa, he established a combined operations headquarters at Cape Town. This became one of the most successful examples of Commonwealth military co-operation. Through the closely co-ordinated operations of the Royal Navy and the South African army and air force the German U-boat threat to shipping in African waters was greatly reduced. Tait earned the 'respect and gratitude' of the South African forces for his important work in this time (Johnstone and Orpen, 761).

Tait was a well-built man of striking appearance, with a ruddy complexion, very pronounced bushy eyebrows, and red hair. His chief characteristics remembered by an obituarist were a 'strong common sense' and 'sympathy'; another referred to him as having a dry sense of humour, and with considerable reserve (*The Times*, 18 July 1946, 6). These qualities made him one of the most popular naval commanders. Tait was promoted KCB in 1943 and retired in December 1944 on his appointment as governor and commander-in-chief of Southern Rhodesia. He was promoted admiral in May 1945, but was able to make little contribution in his role in Rhodesia. He suffered ill health for some time and died, eighteen months into his term, at Government House, Salisbury, on 17 July 1946.

J. H. Lhoyd-Owen, rev. Marc Brodie

Sources *The Times* (18 July 1946) · I. J. Johnstone and N. D. Orpen, *DSAB* · M. Akers, *Encyclopedia of Rhodesia* (1973) · *WWW* · *CGPLA Eng. & Wales* (1947) · personal knowledge (1959) · private information (1959)

Archives NMM, logbooks and papers | SOUND IWM SA, oral history interview

Likenesses W. Stoneman, photograph, 1941, NPG · E. Rowarth, oils, c.1942–1944, NMM · photograph, repro. in Akers, *Encyclopedia of Rhodesia*, 351 · photograph, repro. in *The Times*, 6

Wealth at death £3127 10s. 5d.—in England: administration with will, 9 May 1947, *CGPLA Eng. & Wales*

Tait, Catharine (1819–1878), philanthropist, was born on 9 December 1819 at Elmdon, near Rugby, Warwickshire, the youngest daughter of Anna Maria and William Spooner (1778?–1857), rector of Elmdon and archdeacon of Coventry. Catharine Spooner was baptized by her father on 12 December 1819. Described as enthusiastic and earnest in her youth, she was brought up in the quiet surroundings of a country environment with few friends beyond her family circle. She was always to have a special love of the countryside. She read widely in English literature, history, and religion, and began to care for the sick and aged of the area. Evangelical by upbringing and religious habit, she was greatly influenced by her brother-in-law's Tractarianism, and retained a love of ceremonial and a sympathy for high-church devotion. In the first flush of her Tractarian commitment she heard that Archibald Campbell *Tait (1811–1882), one of the Oxford tutors who had protested

Catharine Tait (1819–1878), by Charles Henry Jeens, pubd 1879 (after Elliott & Fry, c.1869)

against Newman's Tract 90, had applied for the headmastership of Rugby School, and expressed the hope that he would not succeed.

Despite this apparent theological incompatibility, on 22 June 1843 Catharine Spooner married Tait, who had been appointed headmaster in 1842. Their relationship was extremely close and their religious life together mutually supportive. At Rugby Catharine Tait got to know the boys, helped her husband with his history lessons, learned German, ministered to the poor in the town, and established a school for girls. She also supervised the school accounts, demonstrating considerable business acumen in a role which she was to continue to fulfil in all her husband's subsequent posts, as well as in her own philanthropic work. Her life was very busy, but, according to her husband, 'She used to say that the Rugby time was the happiest of her life' (Benham, 30).

In 1849 Tait was appointed dean of Carlisle. In Carlisle Catharine Tait visited the local workhouse, taught in the school, and invited the poor to the deanery. The stay at Carlisle was marked by personal tragedy. In the spring of 1856 five daughters died from scarlet fever within six weeks; a son and daughter survived. (Two daughters were born later.) This was a devastating series of blows, but she found the strength to accept it as God's will even as she was going through the experience. She wrote a 139-page memorial account of the deaths of her daughters, intended originally for her family and friends. This was published at her request after her death. It was one of the most widely read Victorian books of consolation literature, and many bereaved parents wrote in gratitude to her widowed husband, one commenting on the way in which 'your sainted wife is fulfilling so precious a "ministry of consolation" still on earth' (W. H. Jellie to A. C. Tait, 27 Sept 1881; Jalland, 141–2).

On moving to London in late 1856, when Tait was appointed bishop, Catharine Tait adapted her philanthropic and church work to the metropolitan context. She was particularly involved in the parishes of St James's and Fulham, although she tried to meet as many as possible of the London clergy. A wide range of clergy, statesmen, literary figures, and charity workers, together with their children, attended her summer garden parties at Fulham Palace. She read to people at workhouses and visited almshouses and hospitals. She was instrumental in the erection of a penitentiary, St James's House, on part of the episcopal estate at Fulham. Recognizing the need to systematize the organization of women's charitable work, she established the Ladies' Diocesan Association to bring together women involved in Christian social work. The organization gave women, including those of status and influence, an opportunity to work among the sick, outcast, and lonely in hospitals, penitentiaries, and workhouses. During the 1866 cholera epidemic she visited hospitals and provided temporary shelter for the victims, and also worked with Catherine Gladstone (1812–1900) and Catherine Marsh (1818–1912) to set up homes for the orphans of the epidemic. She established St Peter's Orphanage for the girls, based for five years at Fulham and then in a larger house built by her on of the Isle of Thanet, raising all the necessary funds herself. To the latter she added a convalescent home for women and children. In order to secure the future of the orphanage, she set up a scheme of Children's Associates, an organization of upper-class women who each contributed towards the maintenance of an individual orphan while at the orphanage, thereafter continuing to be a personal mentor to the child in later life. She herself visited the orphanage as often as possible, and the sisters of St Peter's, Kilburn, helped to run it. The girls were taught by a qualified schoolteacher and were also trained in domestic service; some later went into nursing or schoolteaching. After 1869, when her husband became archbishop of Canterbury, Catharine Tait continued to work on these projects, as well as ministering to the poor in Lambeth: she sent them gifts of food, contributed funds to charities, and held a yearly garden party for them.

Another family tragedy struck in 1878, when the Taits' only son, the Revd Craufurd Tait, died on 29 May after a protracted illness. Catharine Tait never really recovered from the shock of losing her beloved son and companion, to whom she was especially devoted. She visited Scotland with her husband and three daughters to regain her health, but she suffered a bilious attack and died a week later, on 1 December 1878, in Great Stuart Street, Edinburgh, with her husband at her bedside. She was buried at Addington parish church, Surrey, on 7 December. Her husband pronounced the benediction. In his memoirs Archbishop Tait wrote, 'Thus ended her earthly life of fifty-nine years—refreshed from her childhood onwards, through the grace of God, by a wellspring of joy within, which poured forth in acts of kindliness to all whom she could reach' (Benham, 196).

Catharine Tait believed that wealth and influence carried responsibilities, and as the wife of a prominent churchman she used her position to support and to organize more effectively a traditional style of philanthropic work among the less fortunate and orphans. An attractive woman of great charm, she clearly inspired devotion, and was memorialized in reverential tones. Immediately following her death a resolution from the Society for Promoting Christian Knowledge praised her valuable contributions to the church, and she was later included in J. Johnson's *Noble Women of our Time* (1882).

RENE KOLLAR

Sources W. Benham, ed., *Catharine and Craufurd Tait, wife and son of Archibald Campbell, archbishop of Canterbury: a memoir* (1879) · J. Johnson, 'Catharine Tait among the orphans and in loving duty', *Noble women of our time* (1882) · W. Benham and R. T. Davidson, *Life of Archibald Campbell Tait*, 2 vols. (1891) · *The Times* (3 Dec 1878) · *The Times* (5 Dec 1878) · *The Times* (6 Dec 1878) · *The Times* (9 Dec 1878) · 'Tait, Archibald Campbell', *DNB* · P. T. Marsh, *The Victorian church in decline: Archbishop Tait and the Church of England, 1868–1882* (1969) · P. Jalland, *Death in the Victorian family* (1996) · m. cert.
Archives LPL, A. C. Tait MSS
Likenesses C. H. Jeens, stipple engraving, pubd 1879 (after photograph by Elliott & Fry, c.1869), BM; repro. in Benham, ed., *Catharine and Craufurd Tait* [see illus.] · O. G. Rejlander, photograph (late in life), LPL, MS 3181, fol. 6

Tait, Frederick Guthrie (1870–1900), golfer, was born at 17 Drummond Place, Edinburgh, on 11 January 1870, the third son of Peter Guthrie *Tait (1831–1901), professor of natural philosophy at Edinburgh University, and his wife, Margaret Archer Pörter (1839–1926). He was one of seven children in a games-playing family—his eldest brother, John Guthrie Tait (1861–1945), was a beaten semi-finalist in the amateur championship of 1887—and young Freddie initially learned his golf on the Musselburgh and St Andrews links. After preparatory school, he went to Edinburgh Academy in the winter of 1881 and subsequently to Sedbergh School in the May term of 1883. He had set his mind on an army career but, in 1887, after six months' cramming, he failed the Sandhurst entrance examination. In October 1887 he went to Edinburgh University and joined the university company of the Queen's Edinburgh volunteers and found time in 1889 to win the university gold medal for golf. In September 1889 he was finally accepted at Sandhurst. On 28 October 1890 he was gazetted to the 2nd battalion, the Leinster regiment (109th foot) and, while waiting to join his regiment, played rugby football for Edinburgh Wanderers. In June 1894, following an exchange with another officer, Tait joined the 2nd battalion, the Black Watch, with which he served for the rest of his life.

Tait's fame rests firmly on his abilities as a golfer. He is often credited with introducing golf to Sandhurst, and emerged, along with Harold Hilton and John Ball, as one of the dominant amateur golfers of the late Victorian era. He won the amateur championship twice: in 1896 at Sandwich, when he defeated Hilton easily in the final, and two years later, when he beat Mure Fergusson almost as easily in the final at Hoylake. But Tait's most celebrated final, and in Bernard Darwin's view one of the truly great matches in the history of the game, was one that he in fact lost, at Prestwick in 1899, losing to John Ball at the thirty-seventh hole after both had played remarkable recovery strokes from watery bunkers.

An aggressive competitor, with a putting stroke to match, Tait did not care greatly for medal play, although

Frederick Guthrie Tait (1870–1900), by John Henry Lorimer, 1901

his record in the Open championship was impressive, finishing third in 1896 and 1897, and as leading amateur on no fewer than six occasions. He also won the St George's challenge cup, then effectively the amateur stroke-play championship, on three occasions, and won no fewer than fifteen medals of the Royal and Ancient Golf Club, including the royal medal of 1894, the principal prize of the year, with a then record score of 78 strokes. He also broke numerous course records elsewhere, including Carnoustie and Luffness.

Blessed with a rare balance of power and a graceful, rhythmic swing, Tait was an extremely long hitter: on 11 January 1893, playing against Guy Grindlay at St Andrews on frozen ground, he drove a gutty ball which carried 250 yards and finished, after rolling, 341 yards from the tee. This disproved the scientific calculation of his distinguished father, Peter Tait, who had concluded that 190 yards was the maximum possible carry for the gutty ball. Some years earlier, on 31 July 1888, Tait was playing with Norman Playfair when he drove a ball right through a man's hat. When he grumbled to 'Old Tom' Morris about the 5s. it had cost him to replace the hat, Old Tom told him he was lucky that it was not the cost of an oak coffin.

Shortly after the start of the Second South African War,

Tait was posted to South Africa with his regiment to join the Highland brigade, and was wounded in the left thigh on 11 December at Magersfontein. After recuperation Tait rejoined his regiment but was killed in action at Koodoosberg on 7 February 1900, and on the following day was buried on the bank of the Riet River near Koodoosberg. Letters received by his family after his death showed the esteem in which he was held, both by his men and more generally by the golfing public at large. He was an exuberant, dashing personality, and Andrew Lang said of him that 'He played pibrochs around the drowsy town [St Andrews] at the midnight hour' (Low, *Tait*, 12–13). In 1928 his memory was honoured in South Africa by a party of touring British amateur golfers, and he is commemorated by the Freddie Tait cup, awarded annually to the leading amateur in the South African open championship.

R. A. DURRAN

Sources J. L. Low, *F. G. Tait: a record* (1900) • P. Ryde, ed., *Royal & Ancient championship records, 1860–1980* (1981) • J. L. Low, ed., *Nisbet's Golf Yearbook* (1909) • *Golfer's Handbook* (1924) • B. Darwin, 'Memories of Freddie Tait', *The American Golfer* (1933); selections repr. in *The American golfer*, ed. C. Price (1964)
Likenesses J. H. Lorimer, portrait, 1901, Royal and Ancient Golf Club, St Andrews [*see illus.*] • photographs, repro. in Low, *F. G. Tait*
Wealth at death £118 17s. 8d.: confirmation, 16 Aug 1900, *CCI*

Tait, James (1863–1944), historian, was born in Broughton, Salford, on 19 June 1863, the second son and third child among twelve children of Robert Ramsay Tait (*b.* 1831/2), seed merchant, and his wife, Annie Case (*b.* 1835). His father came from Jedburgh, his mother from a well-known academic family. After attending a private school he entered Owens College, Manchester, at sixteen, just before it became a college in the new Victoria University. Tait was one of the first history graduates of the new university (1883), and in 1884 he went, as an exhibitioner, to Balliol College, Oxford, where his tutor was Arthur Lionel Smith, and took a first-class degree in history in 1887.

Tait then returned to Manchester, where he spent the remainder of his career. He served successively as assistant lecturer in English history and literature (1887), as lecturer in ancient history (1896), and as professor of ancient and medieval history (1902–19). From 1890 to 1897 he held a non-resident prize fellowship at Pembroke College, Oxford. Having retired from the chair he lived quietly for more than twenty years in Fallowfield, south of Manchester, and later at Wilmslow, working indefatigably at his research yet keeping in close social touch with the university. During these years he served (1925–35) as chairman of the Manchester University Press. His closest friend was Edward Fiddes, the former registrar, and their wise counsel was of great service to the university.

The keynote of Tait's life was his consuming interest in historical research, which established his reputation as a scholar. None the less he was a successful and painstaking teacher, and played a great part in the development of the Manchester history school. The foundations had already been well laid by R. C. Christie and A. W. Ward when, in 1890, T. F. Tout succeeded Ward as professor of medieval and modern history, and thus began a thirty years' partnership that deeply influenced the development of historical studies in Great Britain. Alike in nothing but their shared devotion to research, Tout and Tait imparted to their school a new quality of exact scholarship, which gradually won for it an influence out of all proportion to its size. The introduction of an undergraduate thesis closely connected with the special subject was their chief pedagogic innovation, and the weight of the experiment was borne largely by Tait. The object was to make the undergraduate course a better bridge to advanced study, and in this aim they achieved considerable success. There was a new insistence upon research, which led in turn to the foundation of the Manchester University Press. Tait's *Mediaeval Manchester and the Beginnings of Lancashire* (1904), perhaps his best book, was the first volume in the historical series published by the press; it was reissued in 1972 and 1991. In addition to this focus on research the Manchester history course was almost alone in including the outlines of both ancient and European history. The continuous, obscure toil of undergraduate teaching that this ambitious scheme involved hampered, but never stopped, Tait's own steady output of learned work, and retirement, when it came, was simply an opportunity for further undistracted research.

Apart from his teaching, the events of Tait's life must be sought in his writings. A man of studied moderation in speech, reticent, and disliking any display of emotion, he did what was demanded in university politics and no more. His real life lay in his study. From 1891 to 1900 he contributed a great many articles to the *Dictionary of National Biography*. His subjects included Richard II, Wat Tyler, and Warwick the Kingmaker. His lucid prose and scholarly standards ensured that these articles stood the test of time rather better than many other entries on medieval subjects. In the same period he began a long connection with the *English Historical Review*, especially as a reviewer, a role for which his critical temper suited him to perfection. It was in fact a review (October 1897) of *Domesday Book and Beyond*, by F. W. Maitland, that first brought him to prominence and showed him to be as much a master of the early as of the later middle ages. Already he was drawn to municipal history, but the beginning made by his *Mediaeval Manchester* was not at once followed up. For the next fifteen years his energy was chiefly devoted to the Lancashire volumes of the *Victoria History of the Counties of England* and to the Chetham Society, which flourished anew under his presidency (1915–25). In his retirement he returned to the borough, on which, in addition to editing the second volume of Adolphus Ballard's unfinished *British Borough Charters, 1216–1307* (1923), he published *The Medieval English Borough* (1936). A definitive study that set the administrative history of English towns on a new footing, it was reprinted several times, most recently in 1999. Tait's last years showed no slackening of energy or loss of grip, and shortly before his death he completed an elaborate genealogical commentary on the Herefordshire Domesday.

The outstanding characteristics of Tait's work were its

immense range and the exacting standards of his scholarship. He saw his medieval history as a whole, but with a temperamental caution confined himself severely to what could be demonstrated by exact proof. His influence, exercised chiefly through his reviews and an extensive private correspondence, was very great and brought, although slowly, growing recognition. In 1920 he was made an honorary professor and received the honorary degree of LittD of Manchester University. In the following year he was elected a fellow of the British Academy, from which in 1943 he generously resigned in order to make way for a younger scholar. From 1923 to 1932 he was first president of the English Place-Name Society, to which he made notable contributions, and in 1933 he was elected an honorary fellow of Pembroke College, Oxford, and received the honorary degree of DLitt from the university. The presentation, on his seventieth birthday (1933), of *Historical Essays in Honour of James Tait* marked him out as the most revered figure in English medieval studies.

Tait's whole life was given to Manchester and to its university. He was unmarried, and his tastes were of the simplest. A traveller and a great walker, he ordered his life so as to achieve the maximum of continuous, unflagging study. A lover too of literature, music, and painting, he could find relaxation in reading novels and, more particularly, detective fiction. His friendships were firm if rarely intimate, and were lasting; and since he took children seriously he was a coveted visitor in the homes of his married friends. He died suddenly at 86 Altrincham Road, Wilmslow, on 4 July 1944.

V. H. GALBRAITH, *rev.* K. D. REYNOLDS

Sources F. M. Powicke, 'James Tait, 1863–1944', *PBA*, 30 (1944), 379–410 · V. H. Galbraith, 'James Tait', *EngHR*, 60 (1945), 129–35 · V. H. Galbraith, 'In memory of James Tait', *Chetham Miscellanies*, new ser., 8 (1945), 1–2 · personal knowledge (1959) · *WWW* · *Balliol College register* · census returns, 1881
Archives JRL, corresp. and papers | Man. CL, Manchester Archives and Local Studies, letters to William Farrer
Likenesses R. Allan, drawing, Manchester University Press · photograph, repro. in Powicke, 'James Tait'
Wealth at death £26,650 7s. 1d.: probate, 9 Oct 1944, *CGPLA Eng. & Wales*

Tait, James Haldane (1771–1845), naval officer, was born at Glasgow, the sixth son of William Tait, a Glasgow merchant, and his wife, Margaret, sister of Adam (afterwards Viscount Duncan). He entered the navy in April 1783 on the *Edgar*, commanded by his uncle, with whom he served also in the *Ganges*, guardship at Portsmouth. In 1787 he went into the service of the East India Company, in which he apparently remained six years, with the exception of a couple of months during the Spanish armament in autumn 1790, when he was a midshipman of the *Defence* with the Hon. George Murray. In October 1793 he joined the *Duke*, then carrying Murray's broad pennant, was with him again in the *Glory* in the channel, and in the *Resolution* on the coast of North America. After serving again on the home station he was promoted, on 6 July 1796, lieutenant of the frigate *Cleopatra* on the North American station, and he returned in her to England a few months later. Through 1797 the *Cleopatra* cruised successfully, and in November

of that year Tait was moved to the *Venerable*, his uncle's flagship, in the North Sea. In January 1799 he was appointed to the command of the hired lugger *Jane* for service in the North Sea, then infested with privateers. During the next twenty months there he captured fifty-six French and Dutch vessels, and, for the protection thus given to Scottish trade, was voted the freedom of Dundee and was specially recommended to the Admiralty by the magistrates and town council; in consequence he was promoted commander on 29 April 1802. Through 1803–4 he commanded the bomb-vessel *Volcano*, attached to the squadron in the Downs, under the orders of Lord Keith. Early in 1805 he was sent out to the East Indies, where he was appointed acting captain of the *Grampus* (50 guns). He was confirmed in the rank on 5 September 1806, and in 1807 was sent to the Cape of Good Hope, from where he returned to England, with convoy, in July 1809. In 1815 he went to the West Indies in command of the *Junon* (38 guns), was moved into the *Pique* (36 guns) in 1816, and was invalided home, from the effects of yellow fever, in March 1817. He had no further service, but was promoted rear-admiral on 23 November 1841 and died at Edinburgh on 7 August 1845.

Tait's career was built on his Scottish connections, which ranged from Duncan and Murray to Lord Keith.

J. K. LAUGHTON, *rev.* ANDREW LAMBERT

Sources D. Syrett and R. L. DiNardo, *The commissioned sea officers of the Royal Navy, 1660–1815*, rev. edn, Occasional Publications of the Navy RS, 1 (1994) · O'Byrne, *Naval biog. dict.* · service book, PRO · *GM*, 2nd ser., 24 (1845), 426
Archives NA Scot., papers relating to legal and family affairs

Tait, (Robert) Lawson (1845–1899), gynaecological surgeon, was born at 45 Frederick Street, Edinburgh, on 1 May 1845, the son of Isabella Stewart Lawson (1812–1882) and Archibald Campbell Tait. In adulthood, Tait dropped the name Robert. His father, a guild brother of Heriot's Hospital, was a butler and vintner. Tait began his education at George Heriot's School in 1852 and, rather than obtaining a trade apprenticeship, started attending lectures at Edinburgh University in 1859. His mentors at Heriot's intended that their promising scholar should earn a College of Surgeons' diploma. Hence instead of taking a medical degree, Tait attended the Extramural School where he was taught by several of the university's leading professors, including Alexander McKenzie Edwards (Sir William Ferguson's protégé) and Joseph Bell. Of all his teachers, James Young Simpson was most influential. Tait served as Simpson's assistant and embraced the obstetrician's conviction that ovariotomy was feasible.

In 1866 Tait became a licentiate of the Royal College of Surgeons and Royal College of Physicians of Edinburgh. The following year, he was appointed house surgeon to the Clayton Hospital in Wakefield, where in 1868 he performed his first ovariotomy—then a dangerous and controversial procedure for removing ovaries. In 1870 he became a member of the Royal College of Surgeons of England and a fellow of the Royal College of Surgeons of Edinburgh. In that same year Tait moved to Birmingham

(Robert) Lawson Tait (1845–1899), by John Collier, *c.*1887

where he purchased Thomas Partridge's practice and settled at the corner of Burbury Street, Lozell's Road. In Wakefield, he had become engaged to Sybil Anne, daughter of William Stewart, a solicitor; they married on 28 June 1871, but never had children.

Birmingham, a city reputed for enterprise and dissent, provided Tait with an environment conducive to promoting his practice and professional standing. He received support from prominent reformers such as the Unitarian minister George Dawson and politician Joseph Chamberlain. Dawson initially supplemented Tait's income by employing him as a writer for the radical *Birmingham Morning News.*

In 1871 Tait joined Dawson and Chamberlain at a meeting that launched a small hospital for the treatment of women's ailments. At twenty-six, Tait became junior surgeon at this institution, the Birmingham and Midland Hospital for Women. This specialized clinic provided him with the institutional affiliation and the professional relationships so essential for developing a lucrative private practice and for establishing himself as a gynaecologist. In 1878 the hospital was moved to larger premises. Tait purchased the old facility in 1882 for his own clinic in addition to his residence next door.

Tait's authority and autonomy gave him the power to make a number of innovations. He instigated a nurses' training programme, believing that good nursing was crucial when radical surgery was undertaken. Recognizing the benefits of hiring female practitioners to handle female complaints, he urged broadening education and professional positions for women as nurses and doctors.

Tait redefined surgical boundaries and was a pioneer in the field of abdominal surgery. Of all operations, however, his name is most closely linked with ovariotomy. This radical procedure had, until the mid-nineteenth century, been largely dismissed as tantamount to murder. The bold efforts of such renowned surgeons as Charles Clay and Thomas Spencer Wells had begun to draw attention to the possibility of performing ovariotomy, although their mortality rates remained extremely high. As a member of a younger generation of women's doctors who defined themselves as gynaecologists, Tait went further and eventually bitterly contradicted Wells, who considered that Tait sometimes operated unnecessarily. Tait strongly promoted ovariotomy sooner in cystic growth, arguing that patients' health was less compromised, and hence that recovery was swifter, and morbidity and mortality were lower. Tait greatly modified operative techniques, for instance in the management of ovarian pedicles (the tissue connecting some tumours to normal tissue). In 1873 he received the Hastings gold medal from the British Medical Association for his articles entitled 'Diseases of the ovaries'. Tait also undertook the salpingo-oöphorectomy ('Tait's operation') which involved the removal of the ovary and Fallopian tube. His most controversial practice was 'normal ovariotomy' for what he claimed were inflammatory conditions often caused by venereal disease. Tait was especially interested in tubal surgery. Surgical treatment for extrauterine gestation had been largely rejected until he presented cases evincing the possibility of saving lives. By the late 1880s he was an expert in this field. Indeed he became so confident that he advocated exploratory surgery when diagnoses were uncertain. Like numerous eminent surgeons, Tait devised some of his own surgical instruments, including a simple trocar for tapping ovarian cysts. By 1882 Tait had come to oppose the antiseptic surgery promoted by Lister, later characterizing it as a 'strange phase of medical eccentricity' (Moscucci, 155). Instead Tait was an advocate of aseptic surgery and performed one hundred ovariotomies without antisepsis, losing just three patients in the process. Tait ascribed his success to his increased experience in carrying out the procedure, 'the disciplinary regime to which he subjected both the nursing staff and the patient and the improvement of some of the techniques of ovariotomy' (ibid., 156).

Tait's ovariotomy experience led him to adopt similar techniques in other operations, for example in the management of uterine myoma (muscular tumours), for which he had performed his first hysterectomy in 1873. He promoted advances in peritoneal procedures and made important contributions to general abdominal surgery. He performed some of the earliest appendectomies and gall-bladder operations and was also a pioneer in liver and kidney surgery. In 1890 he was awarded the Cullen and Liston prize in Edinburgh for his medical contributions, especially those involving the gall-bladder.

These accomplishments established him as one of the world's leading surgeons. He was a founding member of the Birmingham Medical Society, where he was elected honorary secretary. From 1889 to 1893 he served as president of the Birmingham Medical Institute. Tait acted as consulting surgeon to hospitals in West Bromwich, Nottingham, and Southampton. In 1886 he became the second president of the British Gynaecological Society, and was an editor for the *British Gynaecological Journal*. He became professor of gynaecology at Queen's College in Birmingham in 1887.

Tait published regularly in the *Birmingham Medical Review* and two of his gynaecological texts were translated into French and published in Paris. Foreign students flocked to Birmingham to observe his work. He was particularly popular in the United States and Canada, where he toured in 1884, visiting hospitals and medical schools. In 1886 New York University awarded him an honorary MD as did the St Louis College of Physicians and Surgeons in 1889. In 1888 Union University, New York, made him an honorary LLD. On Tait's European excursions—some of which involved consultations and operations—he divided his time between professional encounters and his hobby of collecting curios. On other occasions he visited clinics and laboratories in Paris and Zürich, studying different styles of medical education and meeting several of Europe's leading doctors and scientists.

While seeking the status of a gentleman surgeon and scientist, Tait was adept at making himself unpopular. In religion, he abandoned his parents' Catholicism and in Birmingham aligned with the nonconformist sects. In politics he adopted radical-Liberalism. His vigorous antivivisectionism infuriated associates of the Royal College of Surgeons and the British Association for the Advancement of Science. Tait's ardent ambition was to gain Charles Darwin's respect, and he had published a pamphlet entitled *Has the Law of Natural Selection by Survival of the Fittest Failed in the Case of Man?* (1869). In 1871 Tait initiated a substantial sycophantic correspondence with Darwin. Darwin, however, was unimpressed with Tait's work as a natural historian and became annoyed when he realized that Tait was unwittingly replicating some of the work of the botanist Joseph Dalton Hooker. Tait hoped to be elected a fellow of the Royal Society, but in 1876 Darwin informed him of his rejection. Nevertheless, Tait continued his studies in the field and outraged some women at the Birmingham Health Lectures when he expounded on evolutionary theory as well as insisting that female sterility frequently resulted from venereal disease.

Tait and his wife belonged to the Birmingham Natural History Society (over which he presided in 1884–5) and the Birmingham Philosophical Society. These associations' journals gave Tait an avenue for publishing his work on the pitcher plant, his Darwinian views, his opposition to Herbert Spencer, and his support of broader education, public health, and anti-vivisectionism. From 1871 to 1879 Tait was a lecturer in physiology at the Midland Institute. He also served as a professor of anatomy at the Royal Society of Artists and Birmingham School of Design.

In 1866 Tait was elected to the city council representing Birmingham's Bordesley area. In that capacity, he was chairman of the health committee and a member of the asylums committee. He also sustained a busy social life, frequented cocoa-houses, enjoyed lavish meals, and chaired the Birmingham Dramatic and Literary Club. During his heyday, he owned several country houses, a yacht, and a houseboat.

Tait's final years, however, were marred by professional and physical decline. His belligerent unorthodoxy eventually alienated him from many of Britain's prominent surgeons, leading to a sharp decline in income from consultations. This was coupled with two lawsuits against him. In 1892 Dr Andrew Denholm near Manchester issued a libel suit claiming Tait had operated on a patient with uterine myoma, whom Denholm had treated with electrolysis. The patient died and Tait blamed Denholm. Ultimately charges were dropped but the publicity was damning when it was discovered that Tait had used funds from the Medical Defence Union, which he had helped establish, to cover his expenses. In addition to this, Caroline Burnell, one of Tait's former nurses, alleged that he had plied her with alcohol and sexually assaulted her, resulting in an illegitimate child for whom she demanded support. The case lasted two years before charges were withdrawn. But again the damage was done, and Tait's opponents such as Ernest Hart, editor of the *British Medical Journal*, had a field day.

In 1891 Tait was incapacitated with a septic hand from an infected surgical wound. Afterwards he suffered from chronic nephritis. Ill health and surgical squabbles drove him into almost complete retirement at his home at St Petrocks, Llandudno, where he died of nephritis on 13 June 1899. He was survived by his wife. His body was cremated in Liverpool, and his ashes were interred in Gogarth's Cave, an ancient burial place in the grounds of his Welsh home. Although his life ended on a sorry note, Tait was an outstanding abdominal surgeon and many of his innovations have been widely applied.

D'A. POWER, *rev.* JANE ELIOT SEWELL

Sources J. A. Shepherd, *Lawson Tait: the rebellious surgeon* (1845–1899) (1980) · W. J. S. McKay, *Lawson Tait: his life and work* · C. Martin, 'Lawson Tait: his life and work with personal reminiscences', *Birmingham Medical Review* (June 1931) · m. cert. · d. cert. · *DNB* · O. Moscucci, *The science of woman: gynaecology and gender in England, 1800–1929* (1990) · H. Marland, *Medicine and society in Wakefield and Huddersfield, 1780–1870* (1987) · G. C. Allen, *The industrial development of Birmingham and the Black Country, 1860–1927* (1929); repr. (1966) · J. Money, *Experience and identity: Birmingham and the west midlands, 1760–1800* (1977) · D. Fraser, ed., *Municipal reform and the industrial city* (1982) · V. Skipp, *The making of Victorian Birmingham* (1983) · *British Gynaecological Journal* (1876–99) · B. Gough, 'The Birmingham and Midland Hospital for Women, 1871–1972', Birmingham Medical Institute · *Wakefield Express* (23 Nov 1867)

Archives Birmingham Medical Institute, letters | CUL, corresp. with Charles Darwin

Likenesses J. Collier, cabinet photograph, *c*.1887, NPG [*see illus.*] · portrait, Birmingham Medical Institute

Wealth at death £9571 13s. 10d.: probate, 28 July 1899, *CGPLA Eng. & Wales*

Tait, Peter Guthrie (1831–1901), physicist and mathematician, was born on 28 April 1831 at Dalkeith, near Edinburgh, the only son among the three children of John Tait (*d. c*.1840), secretary to Walter Francis Scott, fifth duke of Buccleuch, and his wife, Mary Ronaldson. In his very early years Peter attended Dalkeith grammar school. On the death of her husband, Mary Tait and her children moved to Edinburgh where Peter spent about a year at Circus Place School prior to entering Edinburgh Academy in 1841. Eventually the children lived in Somerset Cottage, the home of their maternal uncle John Ronaldson. He was a banker with a keen interest in field sciences, and fostered Peter's scientific interests with geological rambles in summer, astronomical observations in winter, and experiments with the new art of photography. At the age of about thirteen, for example, Peter charted the positions of Jupiter's satellites on successive nights over a two-week period.

At the academy Tait spent his first four years studying classics under James Cumming, whose popularity inspired the formation in 1850 of the gentlemanly Cumming Club, consisting of the surviving members of the sixty-strong class of 1841. Throughout his six years at the academy, Tait headed his class as dux. In 1846 he competed against Lewis Campbell and James Clerk Maxwell (his seniors by one year) for the Edinburgh Academical Club prize; Campbell was first and Tait third overall but in mathematics the order was Tait, Campbell, Maxwell. The following year Maxwell was second and Tait third, while in mathematics Maxwell came first and Tait second. A culture of gentlemanly competition characterized the close friendship between Tait and Maxwell until the latter's death in 1879.

For his one session (1847–8) at Edinburgh University, Tait enrolled in the two highest of Philip Kelland's mathematical classes and entered himself in the highest of three divisions in James David Forbes's natural philosophy class, contrary to the advice of the professor to begin in the second division. Forbes afforded Tait an opportunity to combine mathematical and practical skills in the calculation of the sizes of wooden discs making up models of catenaries of various forms for the Natural Philosophy Museum.

Cambridge, 1848–1854 In 1848 Tait entered Peterhouse, Cambridge, where he and his fellow undergraduate William John Steele (a recent Glasgow University pupil of Professor William Thomson, also a Peterhouse graduate) were soon identified as likely high wranglers. They followed Thomson in having as their mathematical coach William Hopkins, the 'senior wrangler maker'. In the weeks leading up to the Senate House examinations Tait subjected himself to a rigorous programme of mathematical training and won the senior wranglership in January 1852, while the favourite, Steele, became second wrangler. Tait, only the second Scot to become senior wrangler, and the youngest on record, was also first Smith's prizeman.

Elected to a Peterhouse fellowship immediately after graduation, Tait spent a further two and a half years in

Peter Guthrie Tait (1831–1901), by Sir George Reid, *c*.1882

Cambridge. His attempt to establish himself as a mathematical coach met with limited results but his one pupil, previously written off by Hopkins, emerged ahead of Hopkins's best pupil, prompting Tait to remark: 'Oh, that's nothing—I could coach a coal scuttle to be senior wrangler' (Knott, 11). Tait collaborated with Steele on *A Treatise on Dynamics of a Particle*, a work shaped by a tradition of mathematical textbooks for prospective Cambridge wranglers. Tait commemorated Steele's early death by publishing the work under their joint names in 1856, with a second, revised edition in 1865 and the final and seventh edition, further revised, in 1900. In later years, however, Tait recalled without enthusiasm the role of the Cambridge coaches as those who 'spend their lives in discovering which pages of a textbook a man ought to read' (Knott, 11).

Belfast, 1854–1860 Appointed professor of mathematics in Queen's College Belfast from September 1854, Tait joined a dynamic group of academics that included the chemist Thomas Andrews, the engineer James Thomson (brother of William), and James McCosh (later president of Princeton). As well as conducting his own classes, Tait supplemented the natural philosophy professor's lectures with a voluntary class for honours students interested in the higher parts of dynamics. His teaching method involved not only a regular course of lectures but also tutorial instruction with set exercises and problems followed by individual guidance. As a result he gained a reputation as an admirable teacher, clear and systematic in his treatment of the various branches taught.

While teaching at Queen's College, Tait worked closely with Andrews, whose hallmark of experimental practice was extreme accuracy. Tait undertook calculations in support of the experimental work on the density of ozone and on the action of electric discharge on oxygen and other gases. He also helped in construction of the apparatus and developed his own skills in the art of glass-blowing. As he later told Andrews's widow:

I have always regarded it as one of the most important determining factors in my own life (private as well as scientific) and one for which I cannot be sufficiently thankful, that my appointment to the Queen's College at the age of twenty-three brought me for six years into almost daily association with such a friend. (Knott, 13)

During these Belfast years Tait also devoted himself to a thorough study of William Rowan Hamilton's *Lectures on Quaternions* (1853). Enthusiasm for this new algebra of complex numbers in more than two dimensions (a radical departure from Cartesian methods), combined with his conviction of its utility in solving physical problems, inspired Tait to begin work on his own *Elementary Treatise on Quaternions* (first published in 1867 but expanded in 1873 and 1890).

From Peterhouse days Tait had been well acquainted with the sons of a Belfast clergyman of very limited means, the Revd James Porter. The Porter brothers, William Archer and James, had been students at Glasgow under Professor James Thomson (father of James and William). Following William Thomson to Peterhouse, they graduated third and seventh wranglers in 1849 and 1851 respectively. James Porter later served as master of Peterhouse (1876–1901). Tait married one of their sisters, Margaret Archer (1839–1926), on 13 October 1857. Together with James Thomson's appointment to the Queen's College chair of engineering that year, these social networks prepared the ground for Tait's long association with the Glasgow professor of natural philosophy, William Thomson, a relationship later characterized by Thomson as one of continual creative engagement: 'We never agreed to differ, always fought it out. But it was almost as great a pleasure to fight with Tait as to agree with him' (Knott, 43).

Following Forbes's retirement from the Edinburgh University chair of natural philosophy seven candidates competed for the prestigious post, including four former Cambridge wranglers (Tait, Maxwell, E. J. Routh, and Frederick Fuller). The Edinburgh *Courant* reported in May 1860 that neither Fuller nor Routh had 'as yet acquired a reputation for powers of scientific investigation'. Yet despite Maxwell's recognized pre-eminence in this regard, the *Courant* admitted that it was the deficiency of 'the power of oral exposition' in 'Professor Maxwell principally that made the curators prefer Mr Tait … [who] has attained to great and solid scientific acquirements, and to very much of that habitual accuracy which his rival, Mr Maxwell, possesses by a sort of intuition' (Knott, 16–17). Tait had indeed a powerful presence in the lecture room, as J. M. Barrie described:

I have seen a man fall back in alarm under Tait's eyes, though there were a dozen benches between them. These eyes could be merry as a boy's, though, as when he turned a tube of water on students who would insist on crowding too near an experiment. (ibid., 17)

Energy physics During the 1850s James and William Thomson, James Prescott Joule, W. J. M. Rankine, and James Clerk Maxwell constructed a new physics centred on the doctrines of conservation and dissipation of energy. But their informal programme had been sketched and articulated only in papers scattered in the scientific and popular periodicals of the mid-Victorian period. A late convert to energy physics, Tait quickly made the science of energy into a crusade. By the close of 1861 he had joined forces with William Thomson at Glasgow to produce a complete, state-of-the-art *Treatise on Natural Philosophy* which would embody North British (as Scotland was then often known) energy physics in canonical form, capable of being translated around the world.

The *Treatise* (known popularly as Thomson and Tait, or 'T&T' in accordance with the style used by the authors to address each other) took Newton's *Principia* as the sacred text of the natural philosopher and proclaimed that the 'true' Newtonian gospel was founded on the doctrine of energy conservation. A strong preference for engineering and geometrical modes of expression characterized the work. In the end, however, only one of the projected four volumes was ever written. Much of the blame lay with Thomson whose other interests, combined with his dislike of writing, delayed publication of the first volume until 1867. A second edition, prepared by George Darwin, appeared as two parts, the first in 1879 and the second in 1883.

During the 1860s John Tyndall, professor of natural philosophy at the Royal Institution in London, allied himself with T. H. Huxley and other enthusiasts for Darwin's theory of evolution. Appropriating energy conservation, Tyndall attempted to place it alongside evolution as one of the foundations of the new creed of scientific naturalism. In so doing he tried to wrest control from the North Britons whose claims to scientific authority were largely founded on the experimental work of Joule. Tyndall therefore constructed an alternative hero in the figure of the German physician Julius Robert Mayer. Taking up the cause of Joule against Mayer, Tait quickly made himself the principal crusader for a North British science of energy in scientific and popular periodicals. Tait's *Thermodynamics* (1868; 2nd edn, 1877), the first textbook explicitly on the subject, performed the same crusading role for students. A later book, *Lectures on some Recent Advances in Physical Science* (1876), reiterated many of the claims made on behalf of his friends during the previous decade.

Although Tait's efforts to promote the science of energy as a natural philosophy in harmony with Christian belief were fully endorsed by North British allies, his publication (with Balfour Stewart) of the anonymous *Unseen Universe, or, Physical Speculation on a Future State* (1875) and its sequel, *Paradoxical Philosophy* (1878), was controversial. Ostensibly directed against the materialistic determinism of Tyndall's notorious Belfast address to the British Association for the Advancement of Science (1874), the *Unseen Universe*, consistent with Tait's political convictions, offered a conservative rather than a progressive vision. A visible universe in temporal decay formed part of an invisible whole in which the dissipation of energy did not appear to operate as a fundamental law. This unseen and eternal whole then provided the rationale for human immortality. It was a unified vision of things material and spiritual, human and divine, which suggested a self-renewing universe (like a perfectly reversible heat engine) rather at odds with Thomson's and Maxwell's decisive separation of the material (and transitory) from the spiritual (and eternal) worlds. *Unseen Universe* had reached its fourth edition within a year and its tenth by 1883.

In accordance with Forbes's earlier practice, Tait at first conducted his experimental researches in the classroom and professor's private room in the college. His loyal mechanical assistant, James Lindsay, had served Forbes's predecessor John Leslie as well as Forbes himself in that capacity since 1819. Tait's research programme included a continuation of work on the properties of ozone, investigation of the motion of iron filings on a vibrating plate in a magnetic field, and the production of electricity by evaporation and during effervescence. From 1866 he collaborated with Balfour Stewart, another former Forbes's student and laboratory assistant, on a series of investigations into the heating of a rapidly rotating disc *in vacuo*.

Practical teaching and research By 1867 Tait had successfully won financial support for the funding of laboratory facilities and within a year had secured accommodation for a formal laboratory through acquisition of the pathology professor's classroom, duly stripped of its benches. Opened in the autumn of 1868 and closely modelled on Thomson's well-established Glasgow physical laboratory, Tait's laboratory was open to all comers from the natural philosophy class for a voluntary course of practical physics upon payment of a fee of 2 guineas for the first session. Students, known as veterans, who chose to continue beyond the first session paid nothing more because their *raison d'être* was to assist the professor in his research. From 1868 until 1870 William Robertson Smith, later professor of Arabic in the University of Cambridge, served as Tait's laboratory assistant and provided students with systematic teaching in practical physics. Forbes's former private room became the centre of advanced investigation, especially into the thermoelectric properties of more than twenty metals over a considerable range of temperature.

These thermoelectric researches were closely allied to earlier work by Thomson on thermoelectricity as a branch of thermodynamics and especially to his claim that if a metal were subject to a temperature gradient then a source of electromotive power could exist between different parts of that metal (the Thomson effect). Again working closely to Thomson's agenda, for a circuit consisting of two metals Tait produced the first 'thermoelectric diagram', which represented the effects in terms of a straight-line graph (thermoelectric power plotted against temperature difference). He presented his results principally to the Royal Society of Edinburgh but also outlined his views in the 1873 Rede lecture delivered in the Senate House of the University of Cambridge at a time when Maxwell was preparing the ground for the introduction of experimental physics into an ancient university more accustomed to mathematical texts than laboratory practice.

Tait's other experimental work included investigation of the corrections needed for deep-sea temperature readings by self-recording thermometers aboard HMS *Challenger*, the development of a pressure-measuring instrument known as the Tait Gauge, and researches into golf-ball impact. Golf, indeed, combined Tait's love of experiment with his love of dynamics and in a series of articles published in *Nature* (1890–93) he revealed that underspin provided the great secret of long driving. At Edinburgh the removal of the anatomy department allowed a further expansion of the physical laboratory in 1880 by the conversion of the dissecting rooms into a junior laboratory and rooms for special magnetic and optical work. Tait's mathematical skills found their most powerful expression not only in his enthusiastic promotion of Hamilton's quaternions but also in the complexities of knots and knottiness (where he introduced a new vocabulary). Urged by Thomson, Tait devoted some years to an investigation of the foundations of the kinetic theory of gases.

Tait wrote, co-authored, and edited some twenty-two books (including two volumes of collected *Scientific Papers*) and published about 365 articles and reviews. He was made a fellow of the Royal Society of Edinburgh in 1860, a secretary in 1864, and general secretary from 1879 until his death. He was twice awarded the Royal Society of Edinburgh's Keith prize (1867–9 and 1871–3) and the Gunning Victoria jubilee prize (1887–90). He received a royal medal from the Royal Society of London (1886). He was fellow or member of the Danish, Dutch, Swedish, and Irish scientific academies, but never a fellow of the Royal Society. He was made an honorary ScD of the Catholic University of Ireland in 1875, an honorary fellow of Peterhouse in 1885, and an honorary LLD of Glasgow University in 1901.

His eldest son, John Guthrie, became principal of the Government Central College at Mysore. His third son, Frederick (Freddie) Guthrie *Tait was Scotland's champion golfer in 1896 and 1898; a soldier in the Black Watch, he served in South Africa from 1899, was wounded at Magersfontein, recovered, but was killed instantly at Koodoosberg on 7 February 1900 leading an assault on the Boers' position. Although Professor Tait continued for another year in the Edinburgh chair, he never recovered from the blow. Little more than three months after retirement, Tait died at Challenger Lodge, Wardie, Leith, on 4 July 1901. His funeral was at St John's Episcopal Church on 6 July, with burial in the churchyard to the east of the church.

CROSBIE SMITH

Sources C. G. Knott, *Life and scientific work of Peter Guthrie Tait* (1911) · C. Smith and M. N. Wise, *Energy and empire: a biographical study of Lord Kelvin* (1989) · D. B. Wilson, 'P. G. Tait and Edinburgh natural philosophy, 1860–1901', *Annals of Science*, 48 (1991), 267–87 • *DNB* • d. cert.

Archives NL Scot., corresp. • U. Edin. L., corresp. and lecture notes | Air Force Research Laboratories, Cambridge, Massachusetts, letters to Lord Rayleigh • CUL, corresp. with James Clerk-Maxwell • CUL, corresp. with Lord Kelvin • CUL, corresp. with Sir George Stokes • CUL, corresp. with William Thomson and G. G. Stokes • TCD, letters to Sir William Rowan Hamilton • U. Glas. L., corresp. with Lord Kelvin • U. St Andr. L., letters to James David Forbes

Likenesses G. Reid, oils, 1882, U. Edin. • G. Reid, portrait, c.1882, Scot. NPG [*see illus.*] • W. Hole, etching, 1884, NPG; repro. in W. Hole, *Quasi cursores: portraits of the high officers and professors of The University of Edinburgh at its tercentenary festival* (1884) • G. Reid, oils, 1891, Royal Society of Edinburgh; replicas, Scot. NPG, Peterhouse, Cambridge • T. Wageman, watercolour drawing, Trinity Cam.

Wealth at death £24,939 5s. 5d.: confirmation, 29 Aug 1901, CCI

Tait, Thomas Smith (1882–1954), architect, was born in Paisley, Renfrewshire, on 18 June 1882, the son of John Tait, master stonemason, and his wife, Elizabeth Smith. Educated at John Neilson's Institution, Paisley, and apprenticed to a local architect, John Donald, in 1896, he acquired a reputation as a brilliant draughtsman at Paisley Technical School, which led to his engagement in 1903 by Sir John Burnet as his personal assistant. In the same year a scholarship took him to Glasgow School of Art, where he fell under the influence of the Beaux-Arts professor Eugène Bourdon. Tait won three king's prizes, and on Burnet's advice undertook a continental study tour before rejoining him at his newly formed London office in 1905. There Tait acquired a leading role, and had a considerable hand in the design of the Kodak Building, Kingsway, London (1901–11), which developed ideas pioneered in American urban office buildings, particularly the Owen Building, Detroit, by Albert Kahn. Its austere pilastered elevations of metal-framed windows and spandrel panels set the pattern for much inter-war commercial building.

On 26 December 1910 Tait married Constance Winifred Blanche Hardy (c.1890–1961), the daughter of Albert Hardy, a station inspector. The financial pressures of setting up house induced him to assist the rival practice of Trehearne and Norman outside office hours, designing for them the elevations of a number of large commercial blocks connected with the Kingsway–Aldwych improvements of the London county council. These came to Burnet's notice, and caused serious differences with him late in 1913, compounding an earlier disagreement over a premiated but unauthorized entry (with James Mitchell Whitelaw) in an unofficial design competition for Regent Street. Tait sailed for New York early in 1914, leaving Constance and their son Gordon (b. 1912) at home, and secured a place with the Beaux-Arts modernist Donn Barber designing banks. There, briefly, he met Frank Lloyd Wright, whose work made a lasting impression on him.

Burnet almost immediately regretted Tait's departure and offered him a partnership if he would return, but Tait declined and instead took up a salaried post as chief draughtsman to Trehearne and Norman. He designed for them Shell Corner (designed 1914–15; completed 1919–20) and Adastral House on Kingsway, London, but the remaining war years had to be spent as a draughtsman at Woolwich arsenal. After the armistice Burnet was appointed architect to the Imperial War Graves Commission for the Middle East. He invited Tait to rejoin him as a partner for the second time and on this occasion Tait accepted. Major London commissions flowed in, notably the completion of Selfridges in conjunction with the American firm of Graham, Anderson, Probst, and White (1919–24), Vigo House, Regent Street, and the giant Adelaide House, London Bridge (both 1920–25). Adelaide House was the largest office block then built in London and certainly the most American, with its mullioned façades and deep Egyptian cornice, a by-product of Tait's voyage to Egypt for the war memorial at Port Taufiq. The more conservative elevations with high-level Corinthian colonnades which Tait had also sketched for this project subsequently found expression at Lloyds Bank, Cornhill (1925–7; with Campbell-Jones and Smithers), and the Thames-side landmark of Unilever House, Blackfriars (1929–32; with J. Lomax-Simpson), the curved frontage of which forms a setting for heroic sculptures by William Reid Dick.

Burnet's role gradually diminished throughout the 1920s. Tait was first acknowledged as an independent designer in 1923 at the second church of Christ Scientist, Notting Hill Gate, London, brick Early Christian and still very Burnetian; the earliest really large building unmistakably from Tait's hand was the Egyptianized classical *Daily Telegraph* building on Fleet Street, London, with stepped-back upper elevations to comply with the light regulations then required for tall buildings in City streets. More significant for the future was a fine and very early series of flat-roofed modernist houses for adventurous clients built from 1927 onwards; at Silver End village, Essex, for the window manufacturer W. F. Crittall, and at West Leaze, Aldbourne, Wiltshire, for Hugh Dalton. Associated with their design was Frederick MacManus (1903–1985), a Dubliner who had joined the firm from New York in 1927.

Major changes in the firm took place in 1930, the year Burnet retired. Tait took into partnership Francis Lorne (1889–1963), who had gained experience in the United States and Canada, in particular with the well-known New York architect Bertram Goodhue. He brought with him several other refugees from the Wall Street crash of 1929, most importantly his brother-in-law Gordon Farquhar, who had worked in New York for Raymond Hood. Lorne accelerated the changes Tait had already initiated, recruiting further staff with American (and in some cases Russian) experience, and reorganized the office on American lines. *The Information Book of Burnet Tait & Lorne* (1933), the architect's bible for the rest of the decade, spread their influence far and wide.

Tait had introduced something approaching the international style of the 1930s at Bechstein Hall, Brook Street, London (1929–30), but the transformation of the practice was nowhere more dramatically seen than at the Royal Masonic Hospital at Hammersmith (1930–33), where a neo-Georgian competition-winning scheme was dramatically redesigned in the brick style of the Dutch modernist architect W. M. Dudok. Lorne gained an entrée to the prince of Wales's circle and applied American job-getting techniques to the practice, securing the agreement of several adjoining properties to sell (sometimes without the others' knowledge), and then finding clients for the large site thus assembled. The major London works of those years were the big apartment blocks of Mount Royal, Oxford Street (1932), and Chelsea House, Lowndes Street (1934–5), the Burlington School, Hammersmith (1932), the Curzon Cinema, Mayfair (1933), Steel House, Tothill Street (1936–7), and the German Hospital, Dalston (1935–8). In similar vein were St Dunstan's Convalescent Hospital, Brighton, Sussex, the Infectious Diseases Hospital, Paisley (also both 1935–8), and Benenden Sanatorium, Kent (1937–8).

These buildings broke new ground in Britain but, as in America, a more monumental style was reserved for great public projects. These began with Limpopo Bridge, South Africa, designed in 1927–8. Further bridge commissions designed in consultation with civil engineers followed, notably at Bangkok, Kaar-el-Nil, Cairo, and Sydney Harbour (1932), the last being the finest of the series. At home Tait was selected to design the headquarters of the Scottish Office, St Andrew's House, Edinburgh (1934–9), which was skilfully composed to answer the profile of Calton Hill rising behind it. Its 'sculpturesque' style, with mullions rising into symbolic figures by William Reid Dick, had Dutch elements but was essentially American in composition. Equally monumental, but more austere, was the Anglo-American Corporation headquarters in Johannesburg (1935–40), which was overseen by Lorne. A fine scheme for the Colonial Office, Westminster, remained on paper because of the Second World War.

Tait's most famous work was the Glasgow Empire Exhibition of 1938, for which he received the commission as late as October 1936. He developed a standardized system of construction, and recruited a team of like-minded architects, mostly from the Burnet–Tait circle, to carry it out. Architecturally, if not financially, it was a success, making brilliant use of the hilltop site for water features, and with the whole being crowned by the gleaming landmark of Tait's Tower. Although the tower itself drew on ideas from Walter Gropius, the general concept developed themes invented by Raymond Hood for the 'Century of progress' exhibition, Chicago (1929–33), and, in certain respects, others from the Paris Exhibition of 1925, the Brussels Exhibition of 1934, and the Johannesburg Empire Exhibition of 1936.

Tait was offered a knighthood in 1938, but a breach of confidentiality that found its way from a bridge party to the gossip columns, and for which Tait was not responsible, resulted in its being withdrawn. Despite the importance of his wartime career as director of standardization at the Ministry of Works, 1940–42, no further honour came his way. Such things did not matter to him very much. Although robust in his opinions at times, he was rather shy of publicity, and took little interest in the affairs of the Royal Institute of British Architects beyond its golf club. Essentially he was a workaholic, happiest at the drawing-board in a haze of cigarette smoke. Although he lived in considerable style at Gate House, Wyldes Close, Hampstead, for which he designed spectacular art deco interiors and furniture in 1928, only late in life did he own a car, and then it was for Constance rather than himself. Tait went into semi-retirement in 1952 and died at his country house, Scotrea, Strathtay, on 18 July 1954. He was cremated at Golders Green, Middlesex, on 23 July. Of his three sons, Gordon continued the practice and Kenneth became an architectural photographer and set designer.

DAVID M. WALKER

Sources D. M. Walker, *St Andrews House: an Edinburgh controversy, 1912–1939* (1989) • C. A. McKean, *The Scottish thirties: an architectural introduction* (1987) • B. [R. A.] Crampsey, *The Empire Exhibition of 1938: the last durbar* (1988) • P. Kinchin and J. Kinchin, *Glasgow's great exhibitions, 1888, 1901, 1911, 1938, 1988* (1988) • private information (2004) [family and former staff] • *RIBA Journal*, 61 (1953–4), 427 • C. H. Reilly, 'T. S. Tait', *Building* (Oct 1931), 444–9 • *Glasgow Herald* (20 July 1954) • *The Times* (20 July 1954) • D. E. Caswell, 'Thomas Tait and St Andrews House', MPhil diss., U. Glas., 1997 • *Sir John Burnet, Tait and Partners: celebrating 150 years of excellence in architecture*, Burnet, Tait and Partners (1986) • b. cert. • m. cert. • T. N. Fox, 'Francis Lorne', *Thirties Society Journal*, 6 (1987) • S. Gold, 'The Royal Masonic Hospital', *Thirties Society Journal*, 2 (1982), 29–34 • J. N. Baxter, 'Thomas S. Tait and the Glasgow Empire Exhibition, 1938', *Thirties Society Journal*, 4 (1984)
Archives NA Scot., office of works files about St Andrews House
Likenesses W. R. Dick, bronze bust, 1925, priv. coll. • G. H. P., bronze bust, 1938, priv. coll. • photographs, priv. coll.
Wealth at death £17,837 1s. 5d.: English probate certified in Scotland, 16 Feb 1955, CCI

Tait, William (1793–1864), bookseller and publisher, was born at Edinburgh on 11 May 1793, the son of James Tait, a builder. He studied at Edinburgh University but did not graduate. He was briefly articled to a writer to the signet, but he soon abandoned law and set up business as a bookseller with his brother Charles. They were reasonably successful, publishing a number of works by distinguished Scottish writers, including Thomas Carlyle's *Specimens of the German Romance* and Patrick Fraser Tytler's *History of Scotland*. Charles eventually gave up the business, leaving William, as sole proprietor, to branch out into journalism and establish in 1832 the eponymous *Tait's Magazine*.

For the first two years of its run he edited it himself but, following a merger in 1834 with *Johnstone's Edinburgh Magazine*, Christian Isobel *Johnstone (1781–1857) took over as editor, so that *Tait's* was then the first major British periodical edited by a woman. The magazine was moderately popular from its inception; in the somewhat hyperbolic phrasing of one of Tait's apprentices, James Glass Bertram, 'William Tait and *Tait's Magazine* were, from the year 1832 to 1846, known over the length and breadth of the land' (Bertram, 29). *Tait's* offered a range of material, including articles on social, political, and cultural topics, book reviews, and short and serialized fiction. William Tait printed work by some of the most popular writers of the 1830s; his contributors included Catherine Gore, Mary Russell Mitford, John Galt, Harriet Martineau, Leigh Hunt, John Stuart Mill, and Thomas De Quincey. Aimed at a middle-class readership, the magazine, despite its eclecticism, also reflected Tait's politics, which were distinctly radical.

In 1833 Tait went to gaol (for four days) as a protest against church rates, and in 1844 he was actively involved in raising funds for a monument to mark the fiftieth anniversary of the transportation of Scottish radicals to Australia. He was also a friend of Lord Brougham, and, again in Bertram's words, had the 'happy knack of eliciting from Lord Brougham important statements of opinion' (Bertram, 29)—although Bertram concedes that Tait's enemies, rather less kindly, hinted that Brougham used Tait as his mouthpiece. De Quincey described Tait as 'a patrician gentleman of potential aspect and distinctly conservative build' (*DNB*). Tait retired from the publishing business in 1846, selling his magazine to a Glasgow firm managed by George Troup, and while it continued to appear until 1861, it was never again as successful.

William Tait died at his home, Prior Bank, near Melrose, Roxburghshire, on 4 October 1864.   PAM PERKINS

Sources J. G. Bertram, *Some memories of books, authors, and events* (1893) · *DNB* · *Wellesley index*, vol. 4
Archives NL Scot., corresp. | BL, corresp. with Richard Cobden, Add. MS 43665 · NL Scot., letters to John Burton · NL Scot., corresp. with Thomas De Quincey · U. Lpool L., corresp. with J. A. Roebuck · W. Sussex RO, corresp. with Richard Cobden · William Patrick Library, Kirkintilloch, letters to Peter Mackenzie

Tajfel, Henri [*formerly* Hersz Mordche] (1919–1982), social psychologist, was born in Włocławek, Poland, on 22 June 1919, the elder son of Icek Henyne Tajfel, a Jewish businessman, and his wife, Ruchla. Since university education was almost inaccessible for Jews, Tajfel went to France after completing his secondary schooling at the Jewish *Gymnasium* in 1937. His studies of chemistry at the University of Toulouse were cut short by the outbreak of war in 1939. He joined the French army, was captured in 1940, and was incarcerated as a prisoner of war until 1945. On his release he found that his parents, brother, and other family members had been exterminated. He went to work with international relief agencies for war victims, first in France and Belgium, and later in the British zone of West Germany. These experiences led him to turn to psychology, which he began to study part time at the University of Paris during 1946–7, continuing at the Université Libre de Bruxelles, where he qualified in 1949.

On 6 October 1948 Tajfel married Anna-Sophie Eber; they had two sons. He then moved to Britain, becoming a British citizen in 1957. On winning a state scholarship with an essay on prejudice, a topic that remained central to his work, Tajfel continued his studies and graduated in 1954 at Birkbeck College, London University. After two years as a research assistant at the University of Durham he completed a PhD at London and moved to Oxford to become lecturer in social psychology and fellow of Linacre College, Oxford, where he remained for ten years. Tajfel rejected the then prevailing mode of abstract psychologizing focused on the individual, stressing the importance of the social context. He demonstrated the key role of social categorization for the analysis of interactions between individuals and groups, initiating a new approach to the study of ethnocentrism, stereotyping, social influence, and inter-group relations that came to be adopted by the new generation of social psychologists. During the early 1960s Tajfel, with his enormous zest and cosmopolitanism, was prominent in helping to bring together a group of social psychologists from several European countries, which led to the foundation of the European Association of Experimental Social Psychology. He played a leading part in the creation of a distinctive European tradition in this sphere. During his period at Oxford Tajfel spent a year at the Center for Cognitive Studies at Harvard (1958–9) and another at the Center for Advanced Studies in the Behavioral Sciences at Stanford (1966–7). On his return to England from Stanford he was appointed to the first chair of social psychology at Bristol, where he stayed until 1982, retiring to Oxford shortly before his death.

At Bristol Tajfel assembled a talented group of researchers, many of whom became successful in their own right. His department became a place of pilgrimage for social scientists from all over the world. Not long after his arrival in Bristol Tajfel hit upon the minimal group paradigm, an idea that occurred to him as he walked in an Amsterdam street. It is a method for inducing an arbitrary differentiation between two groups, which, in spite of its artificiality (no actual contact), seems to affect the manner in which group members perceive 'the others'. It formed the basis of Tajfel's social identity theory, which holds that a critical element of groups is the fact that they build a defining identity into their members, which inevitably entails evaluation and comparison with other groups. The theory was extremely influential and gave rise to much debate as well as to a large volume of research on inter-group attitudes and behaviour. Although Tajfel wrote and edited several books, his main contributions are in journal articles and book chapters. An exception is his *Human Groups and Social Categories* (1981), which provides a condensed overview of his life's work.

Tajfel was not a religious person, but he had a deep sense of Jewish identity—so strong that even in a German prisoner-of-war camp he could not bring himself to conceal it, though he pretended to be a French Jew. Politically he was always a man of the left. As a student in France he belonged to a communist group until the Hitler–Stalin pact; in Britain he supported the Labour Party until he considered Liberals more radical. His interests were wide and varied. Apart from architecture, his tastes in the arts were for the moderns. It was typical that he used pictures by Kandinsky and Klee in some of his experiments, and he was fascinated by the history of the cinema. As regards music, he was particularly fond of such composers as Bartók and Schoenberg. Tajfel's character is admirably captured in a foreword to the above-mentioned book by the distinguished American psychologist Jerome Bruner:

> He is a man of huge hospitality in the broadest sense. He listens, reacts, brings you another drink, argues you down and sets you back up. He sets his guests at each other when he fears pseudo-agreement, thunders at them when he

thinks their differences finical. Add one further element to that. Tajfel is the canonical European, not only linguistically equipped with several languages deployed with breathtaking speed and fluency, but with a deep sense of European culture.   (Tajfel, xii/xiii)

Tajfel died of cancer at his home at 7 Polstead Road, Oxford, on 3 May 1982 and was buried at the Jewish cemetery, Wolvercote, in Oxford three days later.

GUSTAV JAHODA

Sources H. Tajfel, *Human groups and social categories* (1981) · W. P. Robinson, ed., *Social groups and identities* (1996) [incl. a list of Tajfel's works] · personal knowledge (2004) · private information (2004) · b. cert. · d. cert. · *CGPLA Eng. & Wales* (1982)
Archives University of Kent Library, Canterbury
Wealth at death £64,058: probate, 6 Oct 1982, *CGPLA Eng. & Wales*

Talbert, Bruce James (1838–1881), architect and designer, was born in Dundee, the son of a merchant, James Talbert. On leaving Dundee high school he was apprenticed first to a woodcarver called Millar and then to the architect Charles Edwards. His only known work in that area was heraldic decoration in the Kinnaird Hall, Dundee, now demolished. In 1856 Talbert moved to Glasgow, where he worked in two architectural practices: W. N. Tait of Govan and, from 1860, Campbell Douglas and Stevenson. During his time with the latter he was awarded two prizes: the Architectural Design medal and, in 1862, the Edinburgh Architectural Association medal, for a perspective drawing of a church belfry. In the same year he moved to Manchester to work for the cabinet-makers Doveston, Bird, and Hull. This proved a turning point in his career as a commercial designer, and within a short time his range of interests began to widen. Soon afterwards he took up a post in Coventry, designing silver and wrought-iron work for Francis Skidmore's Art Manufactures Company. He was employed as an 'architectural and perspective draughtsman and colourist' at 4 guineas a week (as advertised in *The Builder*, 18 Oct 1862) and his work included making detailed drawings from Sir George Gilbert Scott's designs for the gates of the Albert Memorial and the screen in Hereford Cathedral, one of the major exhibits of the 1862 International Exhibition (now in the V&A). This is likely to have been Talbert's last salaried position, as there is evidence that he had already begun to work on a freelance basis before leaving Coventry for London in 1865 or 1866.

Talbert's reputation as a gifted and versatile designer began to develop. He succeeded in winning the competition for a new masthead for the *Building News*, which also published a number of his designs. In 1867 the prestigious firm of cabinet-makers Holland & Co. commissioned him to design their stand at the Paris Exhibition, for which they were awarded the silver medal. At the time he was also supplying designs to the ecclesiastical firm of Cox & Sons and, possibly, to Gillows of Lancaster. In the same year he published the first volume of his book *Gothic Forms Applied to Furniture, Metal Work and Decoration for Domestic Purposes*. The second volume was published in 1868 at Dundee, where he had returned to recover from a period of ill

health. Dedicated to the architect G. E. Street, the publication was not the first book published to offer advice on the decoration of domestic interiors (C. L. Eastlake's *Hints on Household Taste* had appeared between 1864 and 1866) but proved more influential than its predecessors, as it was 'not so much addressed to the public as to the furniture trades' (Day, 194). It advised on the decor for each room in the house, including stained glass, furniture, carpeting, and drapery for decorating walls, ceilings, and floors. His overall aesthetic view even extended to the user, whose 'ever changing curves' he believed would provide adequate contrast to the horizontals and verticals of the static decoration.

The book became influential with cabinet-makers, furnishers, and interior designers in Britain and America, and Talbert's 'style became immediately the fashion' (Day, 194). His favoured style was based on medieval decoration of the twelfth and thirteenth centuries, as can be seen in his furniture designs of that time. He cautioned against copying medieval decoration, believing that it gave furniture an undesirable monumental character. Instead he rescaled gables, coves, columns, and trefoil arches, using angular brackets, trestles, and spindles, which he believed displayed honest construction regardless of functional form.

By 1870 Talbert had returned to London, and it was there that he set up a design studio with a number of assistants. Despite this he continued to list himself as an architect. He lived and worked from a number of different addresses, but in 1875 moved to 5 Euston Square, where he settled for the rest of his life with his wife, Amy Adkins, the daughter of a Birmingham maltster, whom he had married in the previous year. There he produced an enormous number of designs for many different manufacturers and shops. As well as for Holland & Sons and Gillows he also produced furniture designs for Marsh, Jones, and Cribb, of Leeds, and for the London shops Collinson and Lock, and Jackson and Graham, for whom he designed the 'Juno' cabinet (V&A), which was a prizewinner at Paris in 1878. Of framed construction, his later furniture was decorated with pierced work, low-relief carving, geometric inlays, and occasional small enamels. He disliked veneer and the glossy finishes produced by French polish and staining.

Throughout the 1870s Talbert designed for many forms of the decorative arts. He worked briefly with Daniel Cottier, an old friend from his Glasgow days whose business produced furniture, stained glass, and tiles, and he continued to design metalwork, including Cox & Sons' prizewinning Society of Arts entry in 1870, and cast iron for the Coalbrookdale Company.

In 1876 Talbert published his second book on interior design, *Examples of Ancient and Modern Furniture, Metalwork, Tapestries, Decoration etc*. This shows a marked change in the style advocated, from the Gothic of his earlier publication to a number of later historical influences, including 'Old English', Queen Anne, and Jacobean—his favourite. The book finally established Talbert as one of the major commercial designers of the nineteenth century, 'recognised as the first man in his profession and various firms in London and the provinces competed for designs from his pencil' (*Cabinet Maker and Art Furnisher*, 2, 1 July 1881, 5).

Talbert's interests were not restricted to three-dimensional objects, and he designed a wide range of repeating patterns for wallpapers and textiles. He was astute in recognizing potentially fashionable trends and produced some of the most characteristic aesthetic movement designs of the 1870s and 1880s. These included his sunflower wallpapers for Jeffrey & Co. (one of which won a gold medal in Paris in 1878) and a series of designs for woven silks. Though little is known today about Talbert's work for textile manufacturers this became a lucrative part of his studio's output. He sold designs for carpets to Brintons of Kidderminster, and for silk and woollen curtains and portières to Cowlishall, Nichol & Co. of Manchester, J. W. and C. Ward of Halifax, and Templetons of Glasgow. All reveal the harmony of pattern and colour advocated in his publications. The silks made by Warners of Spitalfields, London, are quite different, and, like his wallpapers, show the influence of Japanese design, but depicted in a particularly British way with natural background foliage such as willow. He also designed embossed leathers and flocked papers as well as velvets and stamped plushes, examples of which have survived as upholstery on dining chairs.

It is not known how much of his studio's output of textile designs was Talbert's own work. George C. Haité, George Charles, and Henry W. Batley were assistants who became popular and successful designers in their own right after they had left Talbert's employment. It is also doubtful that Talbert could have produced the bulk of designs credited to him in the later part of the 1870s, for on 28 January 1881 he died, of alcoholism, at his home in Euston Square. He was buried in Kensal Green cemetery on 1 February. He left his modest estate to his wife, Amy, who sold the house and contents in May of the same year. His artistic legacy proved far greater. His obituary in the *Building News* (reprinted in the *Cabinet Maker*) claimed that 'he made a name as a designer of furniture which has not been equalled in England since the days of Chippendale and Adams [*sic*]' (*Cabinet Maker and Art Furnisher*, 1 Aug 1881, 24–5). This reputation did not diminish with his death, especially within the trades that he worked for. Manufacturers continued to use his designs, and his publications proved essential reading for new designers. Examples of his designs, furniture, and textiles are in the Victoria and Albert Museum, London.   LINDA PARRY

Sources S. MacDonald, 'Gothic forms applied to furniture: the early work of Bruce James Talbert', *Furniture History*, 23 (1987), 39–66 • S. Jervis, 'Charles, Bevan and Talbert', *Decorative arts in the Victorian period*, ed. S. M. Wright, new ser., Society of Antiquaries, Occasional Papers, 12 (1989), 15–29 • *In pursuit of beauty*, Metropolitan Museum of Art (1986), 470–71 [exh. cat.] • S. Jervis, *The Penguin dictionary of design and designers* (1984) • B. J. Talbert, *Gothic forms applied to furniture, metal work and decoration for domestic purposes* (1867) • B. J. Talbert, *Examples of ancient and modern furniture, metalwork, tapestries, decoration etc* (1876) • E. Aslin, *The aesthetic movement* (1969) • *Victorian and Edwardian decorative arts*, V&A (1952) [exh. cat.] • d. cert. • L. F. Day, 'Victorian progress in applied arts', *Art Journal*, new ser., 7 (1887)
Likenesses engraving, repro. in *Cabinet Maker and Art Furnisher* (1 July 1881), 4
Wealth at death under £1200: probate, 1881, CGPLA Eng. & Wales

Talbot, Benjamin (1864–1947), steel company manager and metallurgist, was born on 19 September 1864 at Hadley, near Wellington, Shropshire, the second son of Benjamin Talbot, engine millwright, and his wife, Emma Isabella, *née* Todd. He attended Fulneck School, near Leeds, and served his apprenticeship at the Ebbw Vale works in south Wales. He then worked for his father, who owned the Castle ironworks at Wellington. When the family company ceased operating in 1890 Talbot emigrated to the USA, where he became superintendent of the Southern Iron and Steel Company at Chattanooga, Tennessee, and developed a basic lined gas-heated mixer for the preliminary refining of high-silicon pig iron. Three years later he was hired as superintendent by the Pencoyd Steelworks in Pennsylvania. There, in 1899, he applied the tilting furnace concept of Campbell and Wellman to develop a 'continuous' process for making basic open-hearth steel.

Talbot's process involved the sequential charging and tapping of a tilting vessel at frequent intervals. The furnace contained molten steel into which liquid iron was poured and which quickly decarburized on coming into contact with the highly oxidizing slag floating on top of the steel bath. Refining was completed in just four hours (in contrast to about twelve hours in a fixed furnace using cold metal practice) and 20–25 per cent of the finished steel was then tapped into ingot moulds and allowed to cool before rolling.

After Talbot returned to the UK in 1900, his new process played an important role in supporting the rapid growth of basic open-hearth steel making (which accounted for 18.2 per cent of output in the UK in 1906 and 36.7 per cent by 1914), primarily because the tilting furnace made it possible to handle the large amount of slag generated during the refining of highly phosphoric iron made from cheap, low-quality ore. However, his system promised other important advantages. The tilting furnace provided a more regular supply of steel to the rolling mills, increased both yield and output, and lowered labour, fuel, and repair costs. The use of a molten steel bath also made furnaces of much larger capacity (250 tons instead of 80–100 tons) economical. In cold metal open-hearth steel making, as furnace size increased, more time was needed to complete the refining process. How Talbot's system affected steel makers' capital costs is unclear: some contemporaries estimated a reduction of 25–30 per cent, while others believed the tilting vessel was more expensive to construct than a fixed furnace. However, his process lowered operating expenses by 20–25 per cent and was quickly adopted by firms with access to low-grade ores.

To license his process, Talbot formed the Talbot Continuous Steel Process Co. Ltd in association with Sir Christopher Furness. Though the Frodingham Iron and Steel

Company was the first to adopt the new system, three of Furness's steel firms—Cargo Fleet Iron, Palmer's Shipbuilding and Iron, and South Durham Steel and Iron—soon followed suit. In 1904 Talbot consulted for Cargo Fleet which had embarked on an ambitious reconstruction programme, and in 1907 he became managing director of this troubled firm. During the next seven years he transformed Cargo Fleet into a financially stable enterprise, but he could not overcome all the deficiencies arising from errors made in the initial planning of the new works prior to his arrival. He became a director of South Durham Steel in 1906, managing director in 1919, and chairman from 1940 to 1947. After the First World War South Durham adopted a hydrocarbon-lining process that Talbot invented for pipe making.

Although primarily a technical specialist, Talbot was a strong, all-round manager who exhibited sound organizational skills, pursued systematic methods, and developed effective sales and marketing plans. His talent for judging character was an asset when he strengthened Cargo Fleet's organization by hiring new staff, including several men who, like himself, had acquired experience abroad. His correspondence reveals a man who possessed strategic vision, yet retained absolute command of operational detail. He was also a very tough negotiator, especially when dealing with various steelmasters' associations. Indeed, from beneath his strong, broad brow, his eyes exuded determination.

Talbot was an adviser to the Ministry of Munitions during the First World War. As a member of the departmental committee formed to examine the position of the steel industry in 1918, he supported the majority opinion that Britain should impose tariffs to protect the trade from dumping. After 1945 he was an unrelenting critic of plans to nationalize the steel industry.

Talbot was awarded the Bessemer gold medal of the Iron and Steel Institute, the Elliott Cresson gold medal, and the John Scott medal of the Franklin Institute. In 1928 he was elected president of the Iron and Steel Institute and served as president of the National Federation of Iron and Steel Manufacturers. He was also a JP. His main hobby was hunting.

Talbot married Frances, daughter of J. P. Chapman of Siddington, Cheshire; they had three children. Benjamin Chetwynd Talbot, his only son, became deputy chairman of South Durham Steel in 1947 and served as chairman from 1950 to 1966. Benjamin Talbot died at his home, Solberge, Newby Wiske, Thirsk, Yorkshire, on 17 December 1947.   GORDON BOYCE

Sources W. G. Willis, *History of the South Durham Steel and Iron Co. Ltd* (1969) · J. C. Carr and W. Taplin, *History of the British steel industry* (1962) · G. Boyce, 'The development of the Cargo Fleet Iron Company, 1900–1914: entrepreneurship, costs, and structural rigidity in the north east coast steel industry', *Business History Review*, 63 (1989), 839–75 · 'Departmental committee appointed to consider the position of the iron and steel trades after the war', *Parl. papers* (1918), 13.423, Cd 9071 · b. cert. · d. cert. · WWW
Archives British Steel Records Centre, Middlesbrough, northern region, corresp.

Likenesses portrait, repro. in Willis, *History* · portrait, repro. in *Journal of the Iron and Steel Institute* (1947)
Wealth at death £201,784 5s. 1d.: probate, 11 March 1948, CGPLA Eng. & Wales

Talbot, Catherine (1721–1770), author and scholar, was born on 21 May 1721 in Berkshire, the posthumous and only child of Edward Talbot (1690/91–1720), archdeacon of Berkshire and preacher of the Rolls, and his wife, Mary (c.1691–1784), daughter of George Martin, prebendary of Lincoln. Although both parents came from ecclesiastical families, the Talbots were the more eminent. Catherine Talbot's grandfather, William *Talbot (1659–1730), was bishop of Durham. Her uncle, Charles *Talbot (*bap.* 1685, *d.* 1737), was lord chancellor. Five months before her birth, Catherine Talbot's father died of smallpox on 9 December 1720, at the age of twenty-nine. He left few resources, but Catherine was in a measure adopted by his close friend Thomas *Secker, a distinguished scholar and cleric, who had benefited from the Talbot family's preferment. In 1725 Secker married a friend of Mary Talbot, Catherine Benson (*d.* 1748), with whom Mary had lived since her husband's death; the Seckers offered their home at Houghton-le-Spring, Durham, to the mother and her four-year-old daughter. Mrs Talbot and Catherine remained with the Seckers, who were childless, until Thomas Secker died in 1768. From 1737 they resided in the summer in the bishop's palace in Cuddesdon, near Oxford, and in the winter at the deanery of St Paul's. In 1758, when Secker was made archbishop of Canterbury, they moved to Lambeth Palace. Secker provided the Talbots with an allowance, and they inherited £13,000 in the 3 per cent annuities from his estate.

Within the Secker household Talbot received a liberal education, learning classical, English, French, and Italian literatures, as well as history, scripture, drawing, painting, music, and astronomy, and she benefited from the intellectual preoccupations of Secker, his associates, and family friends. She was encouraged in her friendships, talents, and pleasures, and was indeed viewed as a delightful prodigy, whose letters and verses were circulated. In 1729 Thomas Rundle wrote a letter praising the eight-year-old girl, and anonymous poems celebrating her beauty and wit appeared when she visited Bath as a young adolescent in the 1730s. Even as late as 1753 the duchess of Somerset remarked on Talbot's childhood reputation. By the age of twenty-four, though, Talbot had come to abhor such praise and recognition, protesting her 'hatred to this detestable fame', and she dreaded being characterized as a pretentious literary lady—'a Phoebe Clinkett' (Beds. & Luton ARS, Lucas MSS, L 31/106). This fear of publicity no doubt contributed to her refusal to publish any but a few papers during her lifetime. At the same time she was gratified that her girlhood friends Jemima Campbell (later Marchioness Grey) and Mary Robinson encouraged and celebrated her scholarship and writings, just as she was bolstered by the admiration of other bluestocking friends such as Elizabeth Carter, her confidante and literary ally from 1741 until her death, and, in the early 1750s, by the literary patron and woman of letters, the duchess of Somerset.

Talbot was subject to a host of inhibitions and constraints that may also have contributed to her reluctance to publish. It would appear that she deferred to Secker's powerful personality and public stature. Moreover, celibacy was not her choice, but was determined by social convention as well as her relative poverty. In the early 1740s she pined for an unattainable and unidentified young man; in 1752 her family undertook unsuccessful negotiations to arrange a marriage with a man she never met; in 1758 she refused a proposal of marriage to George Berkeley on the grounds that the friends of neither would approve. When Berkeley married in 1761, she was deeply grieved, as her poetry of the subsequent period indicates. Meanwhile, for more than a decade before Secker's death in 1768, she carried out the quotidian business of being his housekeeper, personal secretary, and companion. Her journal and letters communicate a morbid anxiety about her usefulness, and record an arduous, self-imposed regime that included the duties of housekeeper and hostess, catechizer of servants, and supervisor of children, as well as the pursuit of scholarship. She engaged in agonizing introspection, and was afflicted with self-loathing. Occasionally, she voices a sardonic recognition of the narrow range of choices available to her.

Although Talbot could not after 1750 be persuaded to publish or even to circulate her work except among her closest friends, she herself generously advised authors and edited private and commercial works, most notably Samuel Richardson's *Sir Charles Grandison*. Richardson called her 'the Queen of all the ladies I venerate' (Eaves and Kimpel, 364). Talbot also urged, encouraged, and assisted Elizabeth Carter in her translation of *Epictetus*, and she herself never stopped writing. In the 1760s she even taught herself German, so as to be able to read Salomon Gessner's *The Death of Abel* in the original.

Talbot died from cancer on 9 January 1770 at her home in Lower Grosvenor Street, London. Catherine's mother bestowed on Elizabeth Carter her daughter's manuscripts, which included essays and occasional pieces recorded in 'the green book' often referred to in Catherine's correspondence (*Series of Letters*, 342). In the months following, Carter published her friend's *Reflections on the Seven Days of the Week*, a work of practical theology. Thirty-five separate editions and reprints were published between 1770 and 1861. Written as a series of homilies, the text is designed to help prepare the reader to take holy communion on Sunday morning. This work, together with her *Essays on Various Subjects* (1772; also published by Carter), which includes essays, dialogues, pastorals, allegories, occasional thoughts, prose poems, a children's story, and poetry, marks Talbot as an early rational moralist. Although new editions of her works continued to be published, aside from the posthumous praise of Susannah Duncombe's 'Sketch of the character of the author' (1772), Mary Scott's verses in *The Female Advocate: a Poem* (1774), and information included in biographies of Secker, little discussion of her life and works occurred until the

1790s. Talbot was then constructed as devout, self-effacing, and effortlessly, yet laudably, accomplished. This unproblematic identity was amplified and idealized over the following years when previously unpublished letters and occasional poems appeared within the context of biographies and anecdotes about various men of her acquaintance. By the end of the next decade, after Montagu Pennington's publication of the correspondence between Talbot and Carter, the significance of Talbot's female friendships was affirmed, but her standing as a woman to be revered as a model of femininity was diminished. Her formal literary work came to be viewed as an effect of Secker's paternal influence over her innate feminine characteristics. While subsequent nineteenth-century biographers and bibliographers merely repeated or emphasized aspects of Pennington's account, some twentieth-century commentators viewed Talbot's nineteenth-century reputation as justifying her eventual obscurity. Her work is criticized as insipid. Reynolds found 'Miss Talbot's moralizings pale and anemic' (Reynolds, 243). Similarly, critics after the mid-twentieth century have tended to read her letters with interest, but to dismiss her books as arid and conventional. Other literary historians ignore her writing altogether, to note her as only an extra among literary actors such as Richardson. Myers, however, examined both the context and the content of Talbot's work, and a feminist historicist reading of Talbot's life and work does indeed explain the popularity of her posthumous publications.

Talbot's early work of the 1740s in the *Athenian Letters* is presented in a sexless style, with a sober narrative voice. Nevertheless, by addressing matters of practical religious concern rather than abstract theological matters, and in seeking to direct the reformation of masculine conduct while arguing for the dignity of female celibacy, she constructs a specifically female voice within a male text and social universe. Later work similarly synthesizes learning, politeness, and morality. During the 1750s Talbot's promotion of piety in her *Reflections on the Seven Days of the Week*, in a paper contributed to *The Rambler*, and in essays and occasional writings, gains authority from their dispassionate tone and sense of immediate purposefulness.

A substantial proportion of Talbot's work is directed to women and their concerns about ethics, economy, manners, and learning. Personal letters to and about the young reveal the wit, charm, and care Talbot invested in the education of girls especially. Her essays, allegories, pastorals, imitations, and children's story reflect a keen sense of audience, as she seeks to educate and to persuade by means of direct language and use of character. By this means, she addresses the emerging role of middle-class women as teachers. Talbot's poems, like many of her letters to Carter and Berkeley, provide particular insights into the difficulty of achieving female dignity. The early poems typically welcome reconciliation with 'the real state of things' (C. Talbot, *Essays on Various Subjects*, 1772, 160). Employing classical allusion and conventional sentiment, the poetry attains formal resolution. By contrast, later poems, written after she had renounced her beloved, voice loss through a variety of forms and allusions, but each poem is a lament testifying to the cost of female honour. However, resignation to social codes does not, as her writings as a whole demonstrate, constitute compliance with an imposed identity. Talbot's work resists the notion of women's dependence and constraint and instead emphasizes the female capacity for individual development.   RHODA ZUK

Sources E. Berkeley, 'A singular tale of love in high life', *GM*, 1st ser., 66 (1796), 631–2 · S. Burder, *Memoirs of eminently pious women, of the British empire*, new edn, 3 (1815), 88–93 · W. Butler, 'Some account of Miss Catherine Talbot', *Memoirs of Mark Hildesley* (1799), 578, 583 · J. Campbell, later Marchioness Grey, Beds. & Luton ARS, Lucas MSS, L30/21/3–10; L30/21/3/12 · *A series of letters between Mrs. Elizabeth Carter and Miss Catherine Talbot … to which are added, letters from Mrs. Elizabeth Carter to Mrs. Vesey*, ed. M. Pennington, 2 vols. (1808), 342 · S. D. [S. Duncombe], 'A sketch of the character of the author of "Reflections on the seven days of the week" and "Essays on various subjects", by a lady', *GM*, 1st ser., 42 (1772), 257 · T. C. D. Eaves and B. D. Kimpel, *Samuel Richardson: a biography* (1971), 364 · A. K. Elwood, *Memoirs of the literary ladies of England* (1842), 127–43 · L. Faderman, *Surpassing the love of men: romantic friendship and love between women from the Renaissance to the present* (1981) · J. Hamilton, 'Advertisement', *Angelica's ladies library, or, Parents and guardians present* (1794) · M. Heathcote, Beds. & Luton ARS, Lucas MSS, L30/21/4/6 [photostat, LPL, Arch P/A Secker, bundle 25] · *The autobiography of Thomas Secker, archbishop of Canterbury*, ed. J. S. Macauley and R. W. Greaves (1988), 9, 26, 29, 32, 43 · S. Harcstark Myers, *The bluestocking circle: women, friendship, and the life of the mind in eighteenth-century England* (1990) · Nichols, *Lit. anecdotes*, 6.204–7 · 'Account of the life of Mrs. Catharine Talbot', *The works of the late Miss Catharine Talbot*, ed. M. Pennington, 7th edn (1809), vii–xxxvi · M. Pennington, *Memoirs of Mrs. Carter* (1808) · B. Porteous, 'A review of the life and character of Archbishop Secker', in T. Secker, *Sermons on several subjects*, ed. B. Porteous and G. Stinton, 1 (1770), i–xcvii · M. Reynolds, *The learned lady in England, 1650–1760* (1920), 243–6 · M. Scott, *The female advocate: a poem, occasioned by reading Mr. Duncombe's 'Feminiad'* (1774), lines 401–6 · duchess of Somerset, BL, Add. MS 19689, fols. 11–12 · journal at Wrest, Beds. & Luton ARS, Lucas MSS, L31/106 · journals, BL, Add. MS 46688, fols. 15–37; Add. MS 46690, fols. 1–107 · letters to Miss Campbell, later Marchioness Grey, and Lady Mary Grey, BL, Add. MS 4291 [copies] · letters to George, Anne, and Elizabeth Berkeley, BL, Berkeley MSS, Add. MSS 39311, 39312, 39316 · letters, LPL, MSS 1719 ff., 1349 · verses, BL, Add. MS 39316, fols. 41–56 · E. R. Wheeler, *Famous blue-stockings* (1910) · P. C. Yorke, *The life and correspondence of Philip Yorke, earl of Hardwicke*, 1 (1913), 207–8 · J. Todd, ed., *A dictionary of British and American women writers, 1660–1800* (1984)

Archives Beds. & Luton ARS, journal at Wrest, Lucas MSS, L31/106 · Beds. & Luton ARS, corresp., L30/21 · BL, corresp., verses, and journals, Add. MSS 4291, 46688–46690; 39311–39312 | BL, letters to George, Anne, and Elizabeth Berkeley, Add. MSS 39311, 39312, 39316 · BL, letters to Miss Campbell, and Lady Mary Grey, Add. MS 4291 [copies] · BL, 'Reflections on the seven days of the week', 1754, Add. MS 46689; [rev. copy] · LPL, letters, MSS 1719, 1349

Likenesses C. Heath, engraving, BM · C. Heath, stipple, BM, NPG; repro. in *The works of the late Miss Catherine Talbot* (1812)

Wealth at death negligible: Pennington, *Memoirs*, 281; 'Account of the life of Mrs. Catharine Talbot'; *Autobiography of Thomas Secker*, ed. Macauley and Greaves, 32; *GM*, 38 (Oct 1768), 452; photostat, LPL, Arch P/A Secker, bundle 25

Talbot, Charles, duke of Shrewsbury (1660–1718), politician, was born on 24 July 1660, and was the first godchild of Charles II following the Restoration. He was the first son

Charles Talbot, duke of Shrewsbury (1660–1718), by Sir Godfrey Kneller, *c.*1685–90

of Francis, eleventh earl of Shrewsbury (*c.*1623–1668), and his second wife, Anna Maria (1642–1702), the daughter of Robert, Baron Brudenell, afterwards second earl of Cardigan. Both parents were Roman Catholics. His two half-brothers from his father's first marriage died young, and his father died on 16 March 1668 from the wounds he had received in a duel which took place two months previously with his wife's lover, George Villiers, second duke of Buckingham, whereupon Charles became twelfth earl of Shrewsbury and *de jure* earl of Waterford in the Irish peerage.

Early life In his will of 10 March Shrewsbury's father placed his three children under the guardianship of four men: the earl of Cardigan (the new earl's grandfather); the Hon. Mervyn Tuchett, later earl of Castlehaven (*d.* 1686), his uncle through marriage to Mary Talbot, the daughter of the tenth earl of Shrewsbury; William Talbot (*d.* 1686) of Whittington (a kinsman: the uncle of Sir John Talbot of Lacock and father of the bishop of Oxford); and Gilbert Crouch (the family lawyer). Relations, however, were strained between the trustees and Shrewsbury's mother, even after she was forbidden by the House of Lords on 6

February 1673 to cohabit with Buckingham. She later married (before 24 June 1677) George Rodney Bridges, of Keynsham, Somerset.

At the age of fourteen Shrewsbury went abroad to study (pass dated 12 May 1674). He returned from Paris on 24 March 1676 at the request of his kinsman Sir John Talbot (presumably now one of his guardians, as his father's will allowed trustees to appoint new guardians following the decease of one of them) in order to pursue negotiations for a marriage with a daughter of James Compton, third earl of Northampton. When these (and other negotiations) failed Shrewsbury returned to the continent (pass dated 1 September 1676) to study at the academy in Paris. With war against France threatened in the spring of 1678, Shrewsbury was requested to attend his co-religionist James, duke of York, in command of the army in Flanders. He duly attended as a 'volunteer', but with no fighting actually breaking out he travelled back to England shortly after June 1678. In the midst of the furore surrounding the Popish Plot, and following extensive discussions with the Anglican divine John Tillotson, Shrewsbury converted to the Church of England, his first public acknowledgement of the fact being his attendance at a service conducted by Tillotson in Lincoln's Inn Chapel on 4 May 1679. Tillotson's continued influence on Shrewsbury may be seen in the rebuke issued by the prelate about the young man's dissolute lifestyle in October 1679.

At the beginning of 1680 it was reported by the dowager countess of Sunderland that Shrewsbury had 'a blemish on one eye, that 'tis offensive to look upon it', and by May it was 'out, and with great deformity yet, and the other in danger' (*Diary of the Times of Charles II by the Hon. Henry Sidney*, ed. R. W. Blencowe, 2 vols., 1843, 1.239; 2.62). Although his sight was saved, henceforth he wore an eyepatch over the wound. Shrewsbury's conversion to protestantism enabled him to avoid the provisions of the 1678 Test Act, which disabled papists from sitting in the House of Lords. He was summoned to the Lords on 19 October 1680 (before the attainment of his majority), subscribed to the Tests, and duly took his seat on the 21st, during the week-long Oxford parliament. Upon attaining his majority he began to accumulate local office as befitted his rank, starting on 2 September 1681 with the lord lieutenancy of Staffordshire. Nothing is known of his political views during the last years of Charles II's reign, but his appointment as a gentleman-extraordinary of the bedchamber on 3 April 1683 suggests that he was in favour at court.

James II and revolution With the death of Charles II, Shrewsbury's household post naturally lapsed. However, there can be no doubt about his initial loyalty to James II. In the wake of Monmouth's rebellion he was appointed captain and then colonel (July 1685) of a horse troop he had raised in Staffordshire. As a former Catholic he was an obvious target for James II's proselytizing, though upon refusing to comply with the king's wishes he resigned his commission in January 1687. He lost his lieutenancy of Staffordshire officially on 2 September 1687. By this date

Shrewsbury was noted as an opponent of the king's religious policies, and he had already made contact with William of Orange (having met Dijkvelt on the latter's mission to England on behalf of the prince in January 1687). Meetings of the opposition to James II were held at Shrewsbury's London home in May 1687, and he made a trip to The Hague in August bearing a letter of recommendation from the marquess of Halifax in which he was lauded as 'the most considerable man of quality that is coming up amongst us' (Somerville, 42). Shrewsbury was one of the seven signatories on 30 June 1688 to the letter inviting William to intervene in English politics. In September he reputedly borrowed £12,000 on his estate and then left England to join William. He returned with the invasion fleet in November and was one of the advance party which took possession of Exeter on 7 November. At the beginning of December he was dispatched to take control of Bristol with a small force designed to persuade the citizens of William's good intentions. As a trusted adviser of Prince William he was one of the negotiators sent to meet with James II's commissioners on 8 December. Upon James's return to London following his flight, Shrewsbury was one of those peers sent by William on 17 December to order the king out of London again, as a prelude to allowing him to escape to France, and then attended him, with great courtesy, on his departure. He was also present at the important meetings of peers held between 21 and 28 December 1688 to advise William on his future course of action.

With James II gone, Shrewsbury played an important role in consolidating the revolution. He was a firm supporter of bestowing the crown on William and Mary, supporting the motion that the crown was vacant and opposing plans for a regency. He received his reward from King William, regaining his regiment in January 1689 and then being named a privy councillor (14 February) and secretary of state for the southern department (19 February). Lieutenancies were also showered upon him, first Hertfordshire (during a minority) on 4 April 1689 (which he retained until 3 February 1692), then Worcestershire on 16 April (retained until his death).

William III's reign William III's first ministry was essentially a coalition of whigs and tories. Although Shrewsbury approved in theory of using 'the moderate and honest principled men of both factions' (*Private and Original Correspondence*, 15) he found the politics of a mixed ministry uncongenial, especially as his fellow secretary of state the earl of Nottingham was a tory. His unease was compounded by clear evidence that the king preferred the advice of the marquess of Carmarthen and Nottingham to his own, which he felt might have fatal consequences. As Shrewsbury told the king, while the tories might uphold the royal prerogative, 'I fear they have so unreasonable a veneration for monarchy, as not altogether to approve the foundation yours is built on' (ibid.). By August 1689 he was complaining of ill health, a characteristic of his period of office-holding, and beginning to talk about securing a release from the burdens of office. His failure to prevent the dissolution of parliament in February 1690, and the king's abandonment of the Abjuration Bill after initially signalling to Shrewsbury his support for the measure, led him to return the seals of office on 28 April 1690. However, the king would not accept them, and it was only on 3 June that Shrewsbury was able to resign. Almost immediately the naval defeat at Beachy Head (30 June) led him to offer his services to Queen Mary as titular commander of the fleet, in conjunction with an experienced seaman—a suggestion politely declined by the queen.

Out of office Shrewsbury joined in attacks in the Lords on the ministry. He also made contact with the exiled Jacobite court, and was implicated by Lord Preston in discussions held with William Penn over a possible Jacobite restoration in the winter of 1690–91. He was struck off the privy council by the queen following his decision in June 1692 to act as surety for the earl of Marlborough upon his release from the Tower. In January 1693 Shrewsbury backed a bill requiring annual parliaments, and after the veto by William III of the Triennial Bill in 1693 he may have contacted his kinsman the earl of Middleton, one of the leading 'compounders' at the Jacobite court. This may have been one of the reasons that James issued a conciliatory declaration aimed at public opinion in April 1693. The return to influence at court of the second earl of Sunderland saw Shrewsbury attend a meeting at the earl's seat at Althorp in August 1693. This presaged an increasing role in the ministry for the whigs. However, although Nottingham resigned in November 1693, Shrewsbury declined to succeed him in the secretary's office, reportedly because William would not promise to pass the Triennial Bill. But a deal may well have been struck, for in March 1694 Shrewsbury accepted the seals, being rewarded with the Garter (25 April), a dukedom (30th), and the lieutenancies of Herefordshire (31 May 1694 – 15 June 1704) and north Wales (31 May 1694 – 10 March 1696). Shrewsbury's key role in the ministry was to provide a link with the whig leaders, who provided the votes in the Commons which in turn passed the necessary financial legislation to fund the king's war policy, and as a proselytizer of country whig critics such as Robert Harley whom the ministry wished to win over. However, Shrewsbury disliked the tedium of office, and as before it seems to have had a deleterious effect upon his health. Ominously, he was ill in November and December 1694, at the very time when his fellow secretary Sir John Trenchard was dying. The death of Queen Mary in December 1694 also exaggerated the burdens on Shrewsbury, as in the years following he served as a lord justice while the king was abroad on campaign. The spring and summer of 1696 were particularly difficult, given the need to supply the troops in the field during an acute financial crisis, and Shrewsbury took the lead in trying to find a scheme which would raise the requisite sums of money.

The pressure on Shrewsbury increased when he was accused of Jacobite intrigue following the arrest of Sir John Fenwick in June 1696 for his role in the assassination plot. In an attempt to save himself, Fenwick implicated Shrewsbury, among others, in various of Lord Middleton's schemes. Although the king gave Shrewsbury his full support, the accusations were bound to be publicized, not least by Fenwick's friends in an attempt to save his life. Absent from London for a short sojourn into the countryside, in the first week of October Shrewsbury injured himself in a fall from his horse and was unable to travel up to town for the forthcoming parliamentary session. With, as Vernon put it, 'Shrewsbury spitting blood, while Sir John Fenwick is spitting venom' (*Bath MSS*, 3.93), and fearing that his absence gave the appearance of guilt, Shrewsbury offered to resign as secretary. The king refused, but Shrewsbury remained absent throughout the proceedings in both houses of parliament on the bill of attainder brought in to punish Fenwick. Shrewsbury finally returned to London in March 1697, with his alliance with Sunderland intact and a belief among commentators that together they would dominate the ministry. However, by late April a fresh bout of blood-spitting had forced Shrewsbury to retire again into the countryside. He returned to London in July, but he suffered a relapse in August and was faced with fresh allegations from assorted counterfeiters and coin clippers. Shrewsbury decided to resign again, but the political situation in the closing months of 1697, with the king unwilling to accept the whig Lord Wharton as secretary, saw all sides urging Shrewsbury to retain the office. So great was his perceived effectiveness as a mediator between the whigs and Sunderland that he was able to secure an undertaking that he would not actually attend to business. About this time he refused an offer of appointment as the governor of the duke of Gloucester, Princess Anne's only child. Shrewsbury was finally allowed to leave office on 14 December 1698. Almost immediately there were attempts to entice him back as lord chamberlain, William being desperate to employ either Sunderland or Shrewsbury, or preferably both, to act as intermediaries with the whig junto. Having been installed as chamberlain on 30 October 1699, Shrewsbury was ill again and left London on 21 November. By April 1700 he was pondering an offer to serve as groom of the stole and lord lieutenant of Ireland, but he had resigned as chamberlain by 24 June 1700 without accepting another office. Although Shrewsbury attended further meetings of the whig leaders and Sunderland, in the event he felt unable to influence them.

Sojourn abroad In response to continuing ill health, Shrewsbury left for the continent in November 1700, and following his arrival in Paris he was granted an audience with Louis XIV at Versailles. He settled at Montpellier in December, but fear of renewed hostilities between France and England led him to decamp for Geneva in March 1701. He left Geneva for Italy in August, and after travelling extensively he settled in Rome at the end of 1701. He was to stay there for nearly three and a half years. Meanwhile the accession of Queen Anne had brought to power Shrewsbury's long-time associates Sidney, Lord Godolphin, and John Churchill, earl and later duke of Marlborough. In April 1702 they offered him the post of master of the horse should he wish to return to England, but he declined the offer, owing to 'a certain incapacity both of body and mind ever to engage more in a court life' (BL, Add. MS 61131, fols. 1–2). While in Rome Shrewsbury eschewed politics, refusing to be drawn into the role as a mediator for French peace proposals in 1704, and reacting vigorously to refute rumours that he had again embraced the Catholic faith by means of a letter to a relative, Bishop Talbot of Oxford. Indeed, one theme of his letters to correspondents in England was criticism of the Roman Catholic church.

Shrewsbury eventually left Rome for Venice in April 1705. He then journeyed for Augsburg, where he was joined by his long-time acquaintance Countess Adelaide Roffeni (d. 1726), the widowed daughter of Marchese Paleotti, of Bologna, and his wife, Cristina, who claimed descent from Sir Robert Dudley. Shrewsbury married her on 9 September 1705, after she had agreed to accept the protestant faith. As early as July Marlborough had been alert to the possibility of recruiting Shrewsbury to the ministry should he return to England, but in the same letter to Marlborough in which Shrewsbury announced his marriage he disclaimed any desire for office. The two men met in Frankfurt in October, and at that point Shrewsbury apparently turned down an offer of employment. Shrewsbury continued his journey to England and landed at Deptford on 30 December.

Queen Anne Once he was in England Shrewsbury's first task was to procure an act of naturalization for his wife, and this followed rapidly upon his taking his seat in the Lords on 8 January 1706. The duchess duly attended the House of Lords on the 23rd to take the oaths preparatory to her naturalization. Her appearance and un-English manners were to fascinate observers for the remainder of her life: Sir William Simpson described her as 'extremely affected in her carriage, so full of gaiety and motion that it would not be borne with in a madamoiselle of 18 at Paris' (University of Kansas, Kenneth Spencer Research Library, MS C163, Simpson–Methuen correspondence, 8 Jan 1706). The duchess of Marlborough concurred, informing Lady Cowper of her behaviour at court, 'entertaining everybody aloud, thrusting out her disagreeable breasts with such strange motions' (The Diary of Sir David Hamilton, 1709–1714, ed. P. Roberts, 1975, 87 n. 145). Any hopes of an office for Shrewsbury appear to have been blunted by his old whig allies who still felt resentful over his departure from domestic politics in 1700, which they characterized as deserting them in their hour of need. Shrewsbury left London in the summer of 1706, later leaving his proxy for the Lords with Marlborough. His main preoccupation centred on his new estate at Heythrop, Oxfordshire, which he had purchased in 1697.

Shrewsbury had spent the years 1697–1700 looking for somewhere to reside. His previous house at Eyford he described as 'this cold melancholy cottage' (Private and Original Correspondence, 330), but Heythrop also needed extensive work. In February 1700 Shrewsbury described his dilemma: 'the wretchedness of the house I am now in [Heythrop], and my other house in Worcestershire [Grafton] being lately in part burned down, had put me upon fresh thoughts of building for want of a decent place to live' (Watney, 179). Shrewsbury investigated buying or leasing other property in Berkshire and Oxfordshire, including Cornbury Park, but left England before he could embark on a rebuilding programme. While in Italy he had Paolo Falconieri draw up plans for a house, and in England he commissioned Thomas Archer, an architect who had studied in Italy, to build a baroque palace. In late August 1706 Shrewsbury left his duchess in Bath while he toured his estates in Derbyshire and Staffordshire in order 'by fines and sale of some land to raise money to build, for I choose anything rather than run in debt' (BL, Add. MS 61131, fols. 37–8). Work appears to have started in earnest soon afterwards, because in October Marlborough wrote that 'you were at last resolved to build'. Heythrop's close proximity to Blenheim saw Marlborough take a keen interest in Shrewsbury's building plans, and by 1708 the new house was attracting favourable comment from the Marlboroughs.

While Shrewsbury's attention was focused on architectural matters he eschewed London society and did not appear at court, thinking 'it best to give no new jealousy to any in places, or in expectation of them' (Marlborough–Godolphin Correspondence, 2.873n.). Nevertheless, Shrewsbury was never far from the thoughts of the men in power, and when he visited London in the summer of 1707 there was talk that he 'had a mind to be employed' (ibid., 2.849). In December 1707 he was being considered by Marlborough, Godolphin, and Robert Harley as part of a scheme designed to reduce their dependence on the junto. Although nothing came of this scheme, Harley in particular continued to court Shrewsbury, especially following his own ejection from office in 1708. By the summer of 1709 Shrewsbury was showing an 'open dislike' of the whig junto, and was being regarded with suspicion in July 1709 when he appeared at court to speak to the queen, ostensibly concerning his relations. In mid-September 1709 Shrewsbury wrote to Harley asking if he should attend early in the next parliamentary session, and when he did arrive he voted with Harley and the tories against the impeachment of Henry Sacheverell in March 1710. It was precisely because of Shrewsbury's easy access to the queen that he was most useful to Harley in his attempts to persuade her that a change of ministry was feasible. Shrewsbury was also the ideal choice for Harley to make the first breach in the Godolphin ministry; his appointment as lord chamberlain in April 1710 was hard for Godolphin to oppose, even though he had not been consulted. It was a household post requiring close proximity to the queen, and Shrewsbury's whig credentials made it doubly difficult for the junto to take it ill, at least publicly.

Marlborough and Godolphin were surprised at Shrewsbury's resolution in entering the ministry, believing 'he must be very much altered since we knew him, if he holds it long' (Letters and Dispatches, 5.17–18). Indeed, both Godolphin and Marlborough hoped that he would become an ally, rather than an enemy, and Shrewsbury in fact affected friendship to all. However, as Shrewsbury knew the queen's views, it seems likely that he wished to follow the moderate course mapped out by Harley of an executive free from domination by party. He was also keen to see a negotiated peace, having seen as early as October 1706 the difficulties to which a long war was subjecting the landowners. The next stage in the ministerial revolution, the dismissal of the third earl of Sunderland from the secretaryship (14 June 1710), saw Shrewsbury dispatched to the imperial and Dutch envoys in London to assure them that no variation in foreign policy was intended by this change of personnel. When Harley was duly installed at the head of the ministry, Shrewsbury was one of his key managers in the Lords, where the government was at its weakest. At this time the need to be careful not to alienate supporters in the Lords was one of the persistent threads in his correspondence with Harley. Shrewsbury also retained his influence with the queen, who was charmed by his company and who was reputed to seek his advice on all matters (*Bath MSS*, 1.216).

Shrewsbury also played a vital role as a conciliator within the government, helping to smooth over the conflict engendered by the rivalry between Harley (from 1711 earl of Oxford) and Henry St John (Viscount Bolingbroke from 1712). He was involved from December 1710 in the initial contacts with the French for a peace, which led to the formal peace proposals from the French in April 1711. However, Shrewsbury was uneasy about Harley's intentions to hold separate negotiations with the French rather than hold talks in collaboration with the Dutch. This attitude probably explains his countenance, 'pensif et inflamé', when the French secret negotiator, Mesnager, met a full cabinet delegation for the first time on 20 September 1711. It also explains why, although nominated as a plenipotentiary, Shrewsbury did not sign the peace preliminaries. He took little further part in the subsequent negotiations with France, but his scruples over their conduct no doubt accounts for his insistence that James Stuart, the Pretender, would have to leave France before any treaty could be entered into, citing a Lords' resolution of May 1709. His concerns over the conduct of the negotiations probably also explain why he was conspicuously silent in the debate preceding the Lords' vote to accept the earl of Nottingham's 'No peace without Spain' motion of 7 December 1711.

As the rift in the ministry between Oxford and Bolingbroke grew wider, there were reports from September 1712 that Shrewsbury was beginning to side with St John and Lord Harcourt against the lord treasurer. In November Shrewsbury was appointed as ambassador to Paris in place of the duke of Hamilton, who had been killed in a duel. If this was a device conjured up by Oxford to remove Shrewsbury from the domestic political scene, it worked, for he was absent from January to August 1713. His main diplomatic tasks were to ensure that the French royal dukes renounced their claims to the Spanish succession and to resolve a dispute over French fishing rights in Newfoundland. He may also have been in contact with Jacobite agents as a means of bolstering support for the ministry among the parliamentary adherents of the exiled Stuarts. Having achieved his official diplomatic tasks, and made a

formal entry into Paris in June, Shrewsbury was able to take his leave of the French king and return to England. After arriving at Dover on 24 August he was much courted by Bolingbroke, and perhaps because of this he was soon on his travels again, leaving Windsor on 12 October *en route* for Dublin to take up his post as lord lieutenant. He faced a difficult situation in Ireland, exacerbated by a party dispute over the mayoralty of Dublin and by the tensions which derived from a tory majority in the Irish House of Lords and a whig majority in the Commons. His attempt to follow a moderate scheme was not a success, and he lost credibility in the eyes of many Irish politicians once his plans for compromise had been rejected by Westminster. Shrewsbury returned to England in June 1714 and again attempted to pursue a middle course. He opposed applying the Schism Bill to Ireland on 14 June, in company with Oxford, but then defended Bolingbroke from corruption charges arising out of the Anglo-Spanish treaty of commerce, apparently at the behest of the queen. Characteristically, at a dinner party on 5 July he sought to reconcile the two leading ministers, but when that failed he joined Bolingbroke and ensured that Marlborough was invited to return from exile.

Hanoverian succession Following the dismissal of Oxford, but before the ministerial position became clear, the queen collapsed and on her deathbed on 30 July appointed Shrewsbury as lord treasurer (the last person to hold this office). Shrewsbury's committed Hanoverianism ensured that he was acceptable to the whigs, and the tory ministers were anxious to avoid Oxford's return to power under the Regency Act. Following Anne's death Shrewsbury had the unique distinction of being the only serving minister also named by George I under the Regency Act. He was simultaneously lord treasurer, lord chamberlain, and lord lieutenant of Ireland. Having presided over the peaceful accession of George I, Shrewsbury did not retain these offices for long. Sunderland took over the lord lieutenancy of Ireland on 21 September, and Shrewsbury relinquished the Treasury on 13 October. Indeed, the new whig ministers were keen to see him removed from all positions of influence, especially as he opposed attacks on former tory ministers such as the earl of Strafford. He had resigned the lord chamberlaincy by 8 July 1715. He did, however, retain his post as George I's groom of the stole until his death.

In the Lords Shrewsbury continued to oppose the whigs' pursuit of the former tory ministers, supporting an amendment to the address in March 1715 which sought to defend the achievements of the previous ministry by replacing a reference to the new king's determination to 'recover' the reputation of the kingdom abroad with the word 'maintain'. He opposed the Septennial Act in April 1716, dismissing the argument that this reform would reduce expenditure: 'as to the saving of money, he could not see that, for he believed everybody knew that an annuity of seven years costs dearer than an annuity of three' (*Stuart Papers*, 2.123). Shrewsbury also helped to organize the supporters of the imprisoned earl of Oxford, although he felt that someone unconnected with the Oxford ministry should take the lead in any public move to petition for his freedom. Through his wife's post as a lady of the bedchamber to the princess of Wales, Shrewsbury was placed in an awkward position when the prince of Wales (later George II) fell out with his father in December 1717. However, by this date he had become completely disenchanted with whig attempts to monopolize office, and no doubt this led him to 'reinsure' himself with the Pretender, sending gifts of money through his aunt Lady Westmorland. It also explains why his name was linked to the Swedish Jacobite plot in 1717.

Death Shrewsbury died of inflammation of the lungs at Warwick House, Charing Cross, London, on 1 February 1718. He was buried on 23 February among his ancestors in Albrighton parish church, Shropshire. The Shrewsbury earldom was inherited by his cousin Gilbert Talbot, a Jesuit, who never claimed the title. In order to avoid the lands falling into the hands of the church, Shrewsbury settled them on Gilbert's younger brother George, also a Roman Catholic, but obtained a private act to ensure that the estate could not be alienated by a Catholic. He left the duchess his house in Warwick Street and £1200 per annum. She died on 29 June 1726 and was buried on 15 July.

Shrewsbury was seen by contemporaries as the embodiment of the courtly aristocrat. His grace and charm made him attractive to the monarchs he served. However, his prevailing character trait would appear to have been caution. This may have been instilled in him from an early age following the deaths in duels of his father and brother, and probably accounts for his contacts with the exiled Stuarts after the revolution. He was capable of firm action, especially in 1688–9, but the drudgery of office and his own ill health, particularly his aversion to London, made him unsuited to bureaucratic employment. Having gained office, his constant refrain was the need to retire. Perhaps Lord Dartmouth was correct when he opined that Shrewsbury 'had not resolution enough to be chief minister, but could not bear that another should be what he so often refused and could not help showing his dissatisfaction, even to invidiousness' (Burnet, 5.453). The duchess of Marlborough, too, felt that he played up his ill health, 'for upon every thing of consequence, that was to come out, he was frighted I believe, and pretended to be sick' (Gregg, 333). Perhaps the last word should be left to Prince Eugene who, on a visit in 1712, described Shrewsbury as 'a man of a great estate, very good part, and as sanguine as the Duke of Buckingham, yet not so resolute, but more easily brow beaten' (*Portland MSS*, 5.157). STUART HANDLEY

Sources D. H. Somerville, *The king of hearts: Charles Talbot, duke of Shrewsbury* (1962) • T. C. Nicholson and A. S. Turberville, *Charles Talbot, duke of Shrewsbury* (1930) • *The life and character of Charles, duke of Shrewsbury* (1718) • *Private and original correspondence of Charles Talbot, duke of Shrewsbury*, ed. W. Coxe (1821) • *Letters illustrative of the reign of William III from 1696 to 1708 addressed to the duke of Shrewsbury by James Vernon*, ed. G. P. R. James, 3 vols. (1841) • Vernon to Shrewsbury, Northants. RO, Montagu (Boughton) papers, 46–48 • *Report on the manuscripts of his grace the duke of Buccleuch and Queensberry ... preserved at Montagu House*, 3 vols. in 4, HMC, 45 (1899–1926), vol. 2 •

H. Horwitz, *Parliament, policy and politics in the reign of William III* (1977) • BL, Add. MS 61131 • E. Gregg, *Queen Anne* (1980) • B. W. Hill, 'Oxford, Bolingbroke, and the peace of Utrecht', *HJ*, 16 (1973), 242–62 • D. Szechi, 'The duke of Shrewsbury's contacts with the Jacobites in 1713', *BIHR*, 56 (1983), 229–32 • C. Jones, 'The impeachment of the earl of Oxford and the whig schism of 1717: four new lists', *Peers, politics and power: the House of Lords, 1603–1911*, ed. C. Jones and D. L. Jones (1986), 185–206 • *The Marlborough–Godolphin correspondence*, ed. H. L. Snyder, 3 vols. (1975) • *The letters and dispatches of John Churchill, first duke of Marlborough, from 1702 to 1712*, ed. G. Murray, 5 vols. (1845) • *Calendar of the manuscripts of the marquis of Bath preserved at Longleat, Wiltshire*, 5 vols., HMC, 58 (1904–80), vols. 1, 3 • V. J. Watney, *Cornbury Park and the Forest of Wychwood* (1910), 178–81 • *The manuscripts of his grace the duke of Portland*, 10 vols., HMC, 29 (1891–1931), vols. 2, 4–5 • M. A. Thomson, *The secretaries of state, 1681–1782* (1968) • will of Shrewsbury's father, PRO, PROB 11/327, sig. 80 • *Bishop Burnet's History* • *Calendar of the Stuart papers belonging to his majesty the king, preserved at Windsor Castle*, 7 vols., HMC, 56 (1902–23)

Archives BL, corresp. and papers, Add. MSS 9084–9090, 34519 • Harrowby Manuscript Trust, Sandon Hall, Staffordshire, corresp. from France and Italy • Leics. RO, corresp. and papers • Longleat House, Warminster, corresp. and related material • Northants. RO, corresp. and papers • TCD, Irish letter-books | BL, letters to first and second marquesses of Halifax, C9 • BL, corresp. with Lord Lexington, Add. MSS 46525, 46543, 46545 • BL, letters to Lady Longueville, Egerton MS 1695 • BL, corresp. with Sir William Trumbull, Downshire I • Bodl. Oxf., letters to Richard Hill • CKS, corresp. with Alexander Stanhope • Glos. RO, letters to Sir George Rooke • NA Scot., corresp. with Lord Melville • NL Scot., corresp. with first and second marquesses of Tweeddale • NRA, priv. coll., letters to Sir Robert Atkyns • NYPL, corresp. with Lord Bolingbroke • PRO, corresp. with George Stepney, SP105/54, 60, 82 • Surrey HC, letters from Lord Capell • TCD, letters from William King • U. Nott. L., letters to first earl of Portland

Likenesses G. Kneller, oils, c.1685, Boughton House, Northamptonshire • G. Kneller, oils, c.1685–1690, Eastnor Castle, Herefordshire [*see illus.*] • G. Kneller, oils, c.1685–1694, Charterhouse School, Godalming, Surrey • J. Smith, mezzotint, c.1695, NPG • P. Angelis, group portrait, oils, 1713 (*Queen Anne and the Knights of the Garter*), NPG • Lely, portrait, repro. in Nicholson and Turberville, *Charles Talbot, duke of Shrewsbury* • oils (after G. Kneller), NPG • portrait (as Lord Chamberlain), repro. in Somerville, *King of hearts* (1962)

Wealth at death £8000 p.a.: *Life and character*, 35–6

Talbot, Charles, first Baron Talbot of Hensol (*bap.* 1685, *d.* 1737), lord chancellor, was baptized on 22 December 1685 at Chipping Norton, Oxfordshire, the eldest son of William *Talbot (1659–1730), a Church of England clergyman, later bishop successively of Oxford, Salisbury, and Durham, and his wife, Catharine (*d.* 1702), daughter of Richard King, alderman of London. He matriculated from Oriel College, Oxford, on 25 March 1702. He was exempted from the requirement to keep terms on the grounds that he was the son of the bishop of Oxford, and graduated BA on 12 October 1704. In the same year he was elected a fellow of All Souls.

On 18 June 1707 Talbot was admitted to the Inner Temple. He is said to have been advised to study law by William Cowper, then lord chancellor. Probably in June 1708 he married Cecil (1692/3–1720), the daughter and heir of Charles Matthews of Castell-y-Mynach, Glamorgan, and also heir-presumptive of her uncle Richard Jenkins of Hensol, in the same county, a descendant of the royalist

Charles Talbot, first Baron Talbot of Hensol (*bap.* 1685, *d.* 1737), by Jacob Houbraken, 1739 (after John Vanderbank, *c.*1733–9)

judge David Jenkins (1582–1663). The marriage forced him to leave his All Souls fellowship. It may have been a love match—a contemporary remarked that 'Mr Talbot … is stolen by the Lady Matthew's daughter' (*Seventh Report*, HMC)—but given Talbot's circumstances it was fairly imprudent on Cecil's part, and Talbot did not remarry after her death. They had five sons: Charles (1709–1733); William (1710–1782), later second Baron and Earl Talbot; John (*c.*1712–1756), politician and lawyer; George (*d.* 1782), prebendary of York Minster; and Edward, who died young.

On 11 February 1711 Talbot was called to the bar, 'of grace', again without having completed the normal residence requirement. He did not establish himself in practice quickly. On 26 April 1714 he obtained the degree of LLB from the archbishop of Canterbury to qualify himself for his immediate appointment by his father (1 May) as chancellor of the diocese of Oxford. He retained this post until after he had become lord chancellor but its duties throughout were exercised by surrogates. By 1716 he was definitely in active practice at the bar, and on 31 May 1717 he was appointed solicitor-general to the prince of Wales, afterwards George II. The appointment suggests that at this time Talbot was connected to the opposition whigs led by Townshend and Walpole. On 15 March 1720 he was returned to the Commons at a by-election for the venal borough of Tregony, in Cornwall. He was immediately involved in mobilizing support for a private bill for the resettlement of the estates of his distant cousin Charles Talbot, duke of Shrewsbury; the bill narrowly passed the Commons with the help of Sarah Churchill, duchess of Marlborough, an opposition patron, to whom Talbot and his wife wrote to express their thanks. As a result of the bill, when Talbot's descendants inherited the earldom of Shrewsbury in 1858 they also inherited the estates. At the general election of 1722 Talbot was elected for the city of Durham on the interest of his father, who had been translated to that see in 1721. He continued to support the prince of Wales's interest.

By 1720 Talbot had become one of the leading chancery counsel. He was also steadily briefed in equity appeals to the House of Lords from 1719. He does not seem to have practised in the common-law courts at all before 1726, and appeared in one common-law appeal to the House of Lords in 1725, on a political matter. Lord Hervey commented on Talbot's eventual appointment as chancellor that he 'was an excellent Chancery lawyer and knew nothing of the common law' (Hervey, 1.284), and the law reports certainly bear this out. On the death of Sir Clement Wearg on 6 April 1726 Talbot was appointed (23 April) to succeed him as solicitor-general. He is fairly frequently reported as a parliamentary speaker on the ministry's side from 1726 onwards. He appeared for the crown in a few criminal and revenue cases but his main activity continued to be in chancery. He was later to claim that he had the enormous fee income of £7500 a year at this time.

On 19 November 1733 Lord Chancellor King was forced to retire by a stroke. Both Philip Yorke and Talbot sought the office; Yorke was senior, as attorney-general, but Talbot was slightly more eminent at the chancery bar and could only be promoted there, given his lack of common-law experience. He also lacked Yorke's problematic association with Macclesfield, who before his fall had been Yorke's patron, and so may have been a better choice on political grounds; Yorke was certainly of the opinion that Sir Robert Walpole wanted Talbot in the job. Walpole solved the problem by appointing Yorke to the chief justiceship of king's bench, made vacant by the death of Sir Robert Raymond in April, on the basis that Yorke would receive a peerage (as Baron Hardwicke) senior to Talbot's and an increase of £2000 in the salary, partly paid for by the lord chancellor. With this agreed Talbot could be given the great seal on 29 November; on 5 December he was raised to the peerage as Baron Talbot of Hensol.

Talbot was lord chancellor for only three years but his short tenure none the less had a substantial impact on chancery as it had been when he inherited it. King, as chancellor, had pursued a policy of deference to the common-law courts that had resulted in many cases being either sent for trial at common law or referred to the judges for their opinion. The result was that delays in chancery had become intolerable, and the rules in relation to the interpretation of wills had, through King's unwillingness to reject some common-law rules, become seriously incoherent. Talbot categorically abandoned King's policy in this field. He was generally 'unwilling to make any new unnecessary or refined distinctions, which would render the profession of the law a matter of memory rather than of reason and judgment' (*Cook v. Arnham*, 1734; 3 Peere Williams, 283 at 286) and insisted on construing the meaning of testators in the light of the will as a whole and the circumstances of the estate. His drive against delay, which is noticed by his obituaries, also found expression in explicit hostility to procedural and jurisdictional arguments that appeared to be merely dilatory. In some of these judgments he was later regarded as having exceeded his authority in overturning usually accepted precedents. However, where he considered a rule that he disagreed with to be clearly established he would not 'unsettle or alter it; because at that rate no counsel would know how to advise, his client' (*Fowler v. Fowler*, 1735; 3 Peere Williams, 353 at 354).

In spite of their competition for the office of chancellor Talbot and Yorke seem to have acted as a team in the House of Lords. It would appear that in February 1735 they co-ordinated procedural objections made by the ministry side to an opposition petition by Scots peers complaining of intimidation and corruption in the election of the representative Scots peers under the Act of Union. In May 1736 they joined with the bishops to kill the bill for relief of Quakers from vexatious suits for tithes on the ground that the procedure proposed threatened the structure of the legal system; in the same month they both deviated from their position as ministerialists by speaking for opposition amendments to the bill to protect excise officers, though they did not carry this so far as to join the opposition peers' protest. These divergences from ministerial policy perhaps account for the very favourable obituary that Talbot was given by the opposition paper *The Craftsman* on his death.

Talbot died suddenly, reportedly of either heart disease or a chest infection, at his house in Lincoln's Inn Fields, London, on 14 February 1737. He was buried on 23 February at Great Barrington, Gloucestershire. His contemporary obituarists gave him the panegyrics usual at the time, but it is perhaps noteworthy that no-one seems to have had a bad word to say of him except his former ally Sarah, duchess of Marlborough (whom he had offended by reopening the cause of the contractors at Blenheim Palace, who argued that they had been underpaid for their work by the Marlborough estate). Outside his professional and political career he appears as a normal country gentleman of the time; he was an enthusiast for field sports and is credited with rebuilding both Hensol Castle and his Gloucestershire home, Barrington Park. By later writers he is inevitably seen in the shadow of Philip Yorke, first earl of Hardwicke, who succeeded him as lord chancellor and remained in post for the exceptionally long period of nineteen years. However, Hardwicke and Talbot had worked together for several years before the latter's death. If Talbot's policy as chancellor can be seen as a precursor to Hardwicke's it might be equally proper to regard Hardwicke's policy as a continuation of Talbot's.

M. MACNAIR

Sources Foster, *Alum. Oxon., 1500–1714*, vol. 5 • T. Birch, *Heads of eminent persons deceased* (1743), 157 • BL, Add. MS 4224, fol. 1 • BL, Add. MS 35585, fol. 138 • J. Campbell, *Lives of the lord chancellors*, 8 vols. (1845–69), vol. 4, pp. 648–87 • [E. Curll], *The honour of the seals, or, Memoirs of the noble house of Talbot* (1737) • private information (2004) [B. Davies] • ER (1998–) • R. A. Austen-Leigh, ed., *The Eton College register, 1698–1752* (1927) • J. Hervey, *Memoirs of the reign of George the Second*, ed. J. W. Croker, 3 vols. (1884) • *Historical Register*, 22 (1737), 119–21 • *Seventh report*, HMC, 6 (1879), 507 • *Manuscripts of the earl of Egmont: diary of Viscount Percival, afterwards first earl of Egmont*, 3 vols., HMC, 63 (1920–23), vol. 1, pp. 13, 67–8, 247–8, 275–6, 358; vol. 2, pp. 23, 137, 148, 149, 151, 226–7, 272, 321, 348, 378 • *The manuscripts of the House of Lords*, new ser., 12 vols. (1900–77), vol. 12, pp. 250–51, 290–91, 413–14, 490–91, 500–02 • *The manuscripts of the earl of Carlisle*, HMC, 42 (1897), 112, 131, 135, 151–6, 161–2, 172 • *Calendar of the manuscripts of Major-General Lord Sackville*, 2 vols., HMC, 80 (1940–66), vol. 1, pp. 152–3 • D. Lemmings, *Professors of the law* (2000) • *The parliamentary diary of Sir Edward Knatchbull, 1722–1730*, ed. A. N. Newman, CS, 3rd ser., 94 (1963), 2, 17, 31, 44–5, 58, 124–9 • Oxford diocesan register, Oxon. RO, Oxford diocesan papers, c. 266, fols. 17v–18v, 33r • act book, 1701–1723/4, Oxon. RO, MS Archd. Oxon. c. 26 • act book, 1724–31, Oxon. RO, ODP c. 2134 • act book, 1731–4, Oxon. RO, ODP c. 2135 • Cobbett, *Parl. hist.*, 8.22, 467–8, 563–5, 566–7, 673–5, 680–82, 702–6, 1188–90, 1308n; 9.5, 10, 545, 725, 727, 870–82, 884–913, 1179–220, 1229–67 • R. S. Lea, 'Talbot, Charles', HoP, *Commons, 1715–54* • E. Cruickshanks, 'Tregony', HoP, *Commons, 1715–54*, 1.220 • *VCH Gloucestershire*, 6.19 • GEC, *Peerage* • Burke, *Peerage* (1999)

Archives V&A, letters to Lady Sundon

Likenesses oils, *c.*1733–1739 (after J. Vanderbank), NPG; version, Inner Temple, London • J. Houbraken, engraving, 1739 (after J. Vanderbank, *c.*1733–1739), NPG [*see illus.*] • J. Cheere, bronze bust, *c.*1749 (after J. Vanderbank), All Souls Oxf.

Talbot, Charles Chetwynd-, second Earl Talbot of Hensol (1777–1849), politician, born on 25 April 1777, was the elder son of John Chetwynd Talbot, first earl (1750–1793), and his wife, Charlotte (*d.* 1804), daughter of Wills Hill, first marquess of Downshire. Charles Talbot, lord chancellor, was his great-grandfather. Talbot succeeded to the peerage on the death of his father on 19 May 1793. He matriculated from Christ Church, Oxford, on 11 October 1794, and graduated MA on 28 June 1797. After leaving Oxford Talbot joined Lord Whitworth's embassy in Russia as a voluntary attaché, and formed a lasting friendship with his chief. On his return to England about 1800, he devoted himself to the improvement of his estates and to the general promotion of agriculture in England. Talbot married, on 28 August 1800, Frances Thomasine, eldest daughter of Charles Lambert of Beau Parc in co. Meath. They had ten sons and two daughters before she died, shortly after childbirth, on 30 December 1819, aged thirty-seven. Their younger daughter, Cecil [*see* Kerr, Cecil Chetwynd, marchioness of Lothian], married the seventh marquess of Lothian.

In 1803 Talbot took an active part in organizing a volunteer force in Staffordshire to oppose the invasion of England planned by Napoleon. In August 1812 he was sworn lord lieutenant of the county, and continued to hold the office until his death. On 9 October 1817 he took office as lord lieutenant of Ireland while Sir Robert Peel was Irish secretary (Peel was in Ireland until 1818). During his term of office he rendered considerable services to the agriculture of the country, in recognition of which he was presented with the freedom of Drogheda. In 1821, during his viceroyalty, George IV visited Ireland, and on that occasion Talbot was created a knight of the Order of St Patrick. Although Talbot steadily opposed Catholic emancipation, Daniel O'Connell gave him credit for impartiality, and Lord Cloncurry spoke of him as 'an honourable high-minded gentleman'. The discontent in Ireland, however, continued to grow during his administration, and in December 1821 Liverpool replaced him with Lord Wellesley. In 1833 he was encouraged to stand for the chancellorship of Oxford University, but withdrew in deference to Wellington.

In 1839 Talbot received in recognition of his services as lord lieutenant of Staffordshire a testimonial amounting to £1400, which he used to endow a new church at Salt. Talbot supported Peel's government and on 12 December 1844 was made a knight of the Garter on Peel's recommendation. Talbot subsequently supported the repeal of the corn laws, one of the first peers to do so.

Talbot died at his seat, Ingestre Hall, Staffordshire, on 10 January 1849 and was buried at Ingestre. He weighed 19 stone and was a jovial, unconventional man with a passion for shooting. He was succeeded, as third Earl Talbot, by his second son, Henry John Chetwynd, who on 10 August 1856 succeeded his distant cousin Bertram Arthur Talbot, as eighteenth earl of Shrewsbury.

E. I. CARLYLE, rev. H. C. G. MATTHEW

Sources The Times (12 Jan 1849) · GM, 2nd ser., 31 (1849), 313–15 · GEC, Peerage · N. Gash, Mr Secretary Peel: the life of Sir Robert Peel to 1830 (1961) · N. Gash, Sir Robert Peel: the life of Sir Robert Peel after 1830 (1972)
Archives Staffs. RO, corresp. and papers | BL, corresp. with earl of Liverpool, Add. MSS 38267–38291, 38572–38575, passim · BL, corresp. with Sir Robert Peel, Add. MSS 40194–40606, passim · PRO NIre., corresp. with William Gregory
Likenesses J. Bostock, portrait, 1837 · J. C. Bromley, engraving (after J. Bostock)

Talbot, Lord Edmund. See Howard, Edmund Bernard Fitzalan-, first Viscount FitzAlan of Derwent (1855–1947).

Talbot, Edward Keble (1877–1949), Church of England clergyman and religious superior, was born on 31 December 1877 in the Warden's House, Keble College, Oxford, the second child and eldest of the three sons of Edward Stuart *Talbot (1844–1934), first warden of Keble and afterwards bishop successively of Rochester, Southwark, and Winchester, and his wife, Lavinia *Talbot (1849–1939), daughter of George William Lyttelton, fourth Baron Lyttelton. He was educated at Winchester College (1891–6), and Christ Church, Oxford (1896–1900), where he took a second in Greats and formed a lifelong friendship with Edward Wood, afterwards earl of Halifax. Ordained in 1904 to a curacy at St Mary's, Woolwich, he joined the Anglican Community of the Resurrection at Mirfield in 1907, and was professed in 1910. There he remained for the rest of his life, apart from the First World War years of

1914–18, when he served with distinction as an army chaplain in France (in proximity to the Somme offensive) and Italy (where he was caught up in the retreat after Caporetto), and was awarded the MC. In 1922 he was elected superior, continuing in office until voted out in 1940; that this long tenure had taken its toll of his strength (in one who, unlike his predecessor W. H. Frere, was no natural administrator) became clear when he suffered a severe cardiac breakdown later that year. His health never fully recovered, though he resumed a programme of spiritual guidance, conducted retreats in various parts of the country, and contributed by his support, counsel, and influence to establishing St Catherine's, Cumberland Lodge, in Windsor Great Park.

Talbot could be said to have been cradled in the original ethos of Mirfield. Of the group which produced the symposium Lux mundi (1889), Edward Stuart Talbot was his father, Henry Scott Holland his godfather (and a major influence), and Charles Gore, the prime mover of the project, went on to found the Community of the Resurrection three years later. This undoubtedly created expectations of him in the eyes of others from which he had to learn to distance himself. Unlike those persons in his background he was a natural all-rounder rather than a pioneer or an original thinker. While he wrote well, it was significant that the most extended and most assured pieces that came from his pen were his memoirs of the pioneers of the tradition of his community—Gore, Frere, and J. N. Figgis in particular—which not only recalled them vividly as persons but captured the heart of their message in words that they could have endorsed. But as his years in office went on, that message became increasingly eclipsed in the minds of subsequent recruits by a less restrained and nuanced Anglo-Catholicism to which he had no immediately effective answer.

Another consequence of these expectations was that from very early on Talbot was invited to work outside his community in fields in which members of his family circle had distinguished themselves. Invitations included the posts of principal of Pusey House, which had been held by Gore at the time when he founded his community; chaplain fellow of Balliol (in succession to his younger brother Neville); and, after his war service, warden of Keble, whose first incumbent had been his father. By the first two offers at least he was strongly tempted, but his community decided otherwise. After he became superior, these conflicts apparently ceased; offers of preferment were answered promptly, tersely (often on a postcard), and in the negative. He now knew, among other things, that for him celibacy without life in community was not viable. He learned to work behind the scenes; his counsel was valued by many in church and state, among them two successive archbishops of York, and there is evidence that he used his influence, in places where it was most needed, to help secure William Temple's appointment as archbishop of Canterbury in 1942.

Both during and after his time as superior Talbot had an extensive ministry of personal spiritual direction and counsel. It included, unusually, members of his own immediate family. Those closest to him at this level have noted the profound influence on him of Friedrich von Hügel, at whose feet he was often able to sit during the latter's visits to his father at Farnham Castle.

Talbot's ability to lift the spirits of the company in which he found himself (despite an undercurrent of depression of which few were aware) was not confined to religious occasions. A gifted raconteur with a keen sense of the ludicrous, he was readily welcomed in the houses of his aristocratic relatives and friends, not least by the younger members of the families, into whose pursuits and games he entered with enthusiasm. A friend recalled 'the ridiculous games at Bishopthorpe where he and Archbishop Temple would keep an audience convulsed by their wit and mimicry' (Retreat Addresses, 11). Yet this was not switched off when he returned to his monastery; and, significantly, it was those at the junior end of the community who testified most vividly to the difference that his presence made: 'when he was there it was as though a light had come on', said Trevor Huddleston (Wilkinson, Community of the Resurrection, 156). Talbot's death on 21 October 1949 at Mirfield was sudden but not unanticipated. His funeral on 25 October was followed by interment in the cemetery of his community.

H. BENEDICT GREEN

Sources Edward Keble Talbot: his community and his friends, ed. G. P. H. Pawson (1954) · A. Wilkinson, The Community of the Resurrection: a centenary history (1992) · A. Wilkinson, The Church of England and the First World War (1978) · Retreat addresses of Edward Keble Talbot, ed. L. Menzies (1953) · G. Stephenson, Edward Stuart Talbot (1936) · E. Wood, earl of Halifax, Fulness of days (1957) · M. Jarrett-Kerr, 'In memoriam: Keble Talbot, C. R.', Christendom (1950), 160–62 · Borth. Inst., Talbot MSS, Mirfield deposit · private information (2004)

Archives Borth. Inst., corresp. and papers | BL, corresp. with Albert Mansbridge, Add. MS 65255A–B · St Catherine's, Cumberland Lodge, Windsor Great Park, Mirfield MSS

Likenesses photographs, Community of the Resurrection, Mirfield

Wealth at death £1531 19s. 11d.: probate, 16 Dec 1949, CGPLA Eng. & Wales

Talbot, Edward Stuart (1844–1934), bishop of Winchester, the younger son of John Chetwynd Talbot QC (1806–1852), fourth son of the second Earl Talbot and a leader of the parliamentary bar, and his wife, Caroline Jane (d. 1876), only daughter of James Archibald Stuart-*Wortley, first Baron Wharncliffe, was born at 10 Great George Street, London, on 19 February 1844. His father, who was a strong supporter of the Oxford Movement, died in 1852, and his widowed mother formed a close friendship with the two sisters Lady Lyttelton and Mrs Gladstone. Sent as a day boy in 1856 to Charterhouse, he was compelled by illness to leave in 1858. He went up to Christ Church, Oxford, in 1862, and obtained a first class in literae humaniores (1865) and in law and modern history (1866), in which year he was elected a senior student of Christ Church, where he remained for four years as modern history tutor. In 1869 he was appointed first warden of Keble College, Oxford (H. P. Liddon, the first choice, having declined), and was ordained deacon. In 1870 he was ordained priest and married Lavinia [see Talbot, Lavinia (1849–1939)], third

daughter of George William *Lyttelton, fourth Baron Lyttelton; her eldest sister, Meriel, was the wife of his brother J. G. Talbot. They had three sons and two daughters: Edward Keble *Talbot, who became superior of the Community of the Resurrection; Neville Talbot, bishop of Pretoria (1920–33) and subsequently vicar of St Mary's, Nottingham; Gilbert, killed in the Ypres salient in 1915; Mary, who married Lionel Ford, dean of York; and Lavinia. Toc H (Talbot House), often said to have been named after Gilbert, was in fact named originally after Neville, its chaplain.

In the autumn of 1870 Talbot went into residence at Keble. The university as a whole regarded the new foundation with contempt. To meet the situation no better warden than Talbot could have been found, and for eighteen years he presided successfully over the college. He aimed at giving it a sure foundation as a college in the university where men of limited means might lead a full common life under the influence of the Church of England. Frequent visits from W. E. Gladstone and his family gave prominence to the new college. Talbot was the college's first honorary fellow, elected in 1931.

A true son of the Oxford Movement, Talbot acknowledged the Tractarians as his spiritual fathers. He contributed to Lux mundi in 1889, but in contrast to that of Charles Gore his essay, 'The preparation in history for Christ', did not provoke controversy. Like all the Lux mundi school, Talbot endeavoured to bring Tractarian principles into relation with the thought of the later nineteenth century and to forward the social concern of the church. It was mainly due to his initiative that Lady Margaret Hall was founded at Oxford in 1878 as a definitely Church of England college for women. He was one of the earliest supporters of the Oxford Mission to Calcutta, and a major influence in the founding of Oxford House in Bethnal Green.

In 1888 Talbot was appointed vicar of Leeds, where he remained for six years (1889–95). There he found himself in contact with hard-headed business men, working-class culture, and with many members of the free churches. Once when asked to which political party he belonged, he replied: 'Conservative with a bad conscience'.

In 1890 Talbot declined the offer of the see of St Albans, but in 1895 was appointed bishop of Rochester. To the episcopate he brought academic distinction as well as educational and parochial experience. He completed the scheme inaugurated by his predecessors of dividing his unwieldy diocese, thus separating the more rural area round Rochester from the increasingly urbanized south London, where his bishop's house was located in Kennington. After protracted negotiations the work was accomplished, and Talbot was able to complete the other task which he had inherited, namely that of making the old church of St Saviour, Southwark, the cathedral of the new diocese. He was enthroned there in 1905. His relationship with his clergy was friendly, although breaches of prayerbook order by some of them placed him in a difficult position. The evangelical party suspected him as a Tractarian bishop, while high-churchmen resented his efforts to restore order. As time passed he was understood, and won the respect and love of all his clergy. By his own account he was not an original thinker, neither was he a ready speaker. At times he was hesitating, and in his anxiety to make his points clear could address his audience at too great a length. His son Neville characterized him as 'not mystical and deficient on the other-worldly side'. He showed that a high-churchman could work with evangelicals and liberals, and could understand free churchmen also.

In 1911 Talbot was translated to the bishopric of Winchester, which he held for twelve years at the end of a full and busy life. His prestige stood high and he spoke with great authority in the councils of the church. One of Archbishop Davidson's staunchest supporters and a member of his small group of close confidants, he was noted for his width of view and his great gift of fairness. The last ten years of his life were spent in retirement in Kensington, where he died on 30 January 1934 at 45 Lexham Gardens. He is buried in the cathedral graveyard at Winchester. As *The Times* obituary notice rightly says, 'he helped to create, as well as to maintain, a tradition essential both to religious and to national life'.

SANKEY, rev. GEOFFREY ROWELL

Sources G. Stephenson, *E. S. Talbot* (1936) • E. S. Talbot, *Memories of early life* (1924) • A. Mansbridge, *E. S. Talbot and Charles Gore* (1935) • G. L. Prestige, *Charles Gore* (1935) • *Life and letters of Dean Church*, ed. M. C. Church (1895) • Mrs Illingworth, *Life of J. R. Illingworth* (1917) • G. P. H. Pawson, *E. K. Talbot* (1954) • F. H. Brabant, *N. S. Talbot* (1949) • S. Paget and J. M. C. Crum, *F. Paget* (1913) • B. Askwith, *The Lytteltons: a family chronicle of the nineteenth century* (1975) • Gladstone, *Diaries* • *The Times* (31 Jan 1934)
Archives Balliol Oxf., letters to Sir John Conroy • BL, corresp. with Arthur James Balfour, Add. MS 49789, *passim* • BL, corresp. with Lord Gladstone, Add. MS 46047 • BL, letters to Mary Gladstone, Add. MS 46236 • BL, corresp. with W. E. Gladstone, Add. MSS 44400–44525, *passim* • BLPES, corresp. with E. D. Morel • Bodl. Oxf., corresp. with Lord Selborne • Borth. Inst., letters to Amy Buller • Hagley Hall, Worcestershire, Lavinia Talbot diary and papers • LPL, corresp. with Edward White Benson • LPL, letters from Edwin Palmer • LPL, corresp. with Athelstan Riley • LPL, corresp. with Tissington Tatlow • LPL, corresp. with Temple • Oxf. U. Mus. NH, letters to Sir E. B. Poulton • Pusey Oxf., corresp. with E. B. Pusey • U. St Andr. L., corresp. with Wilfrid Ward
Likenesses G. Richmond, oils, 1876, Keble College, Oxford • B. Stone, photograph, 1909, Birm. CL • O. Edis, autochrome, *c.*1912, NPG • H. Harris-Brown, oils, exh. RA 1912, Christ Church Oxf. • W. Stoneman, photograph, 1918, NPG • G. Henry, oils, 1924, Wolvesey, Winchester • O. Edis, photograph, NPG • Elliott & Fry, photograph, NPG • S. P. Hall, group portrait, watercolour (*The bench of bishops, 1902*) • RAY, chromolithograph caricature, NPG; repro. in *VF* (11 Oct 1911) • Spy [L. Ward], caricature, watercolour study, NPG; repro. in *VF* (21 April 1904) • C. Thomas, recumbent effigy, Southwark Cathedral • photograph, NPG
Wealth at death £3387 8s. 8d.: probate, 12 April 1934, *CGPLA Eng. & Wales*

Talbot, Elizabeth. *See* Mowbray, Elizabeth, duchess of Norfolk (*d.* 1506/7), *under* Mowbray, John (VII), fourth duke of Norfolk (1444–1476).

Talbot [*née* Hardwick], **Elizabeth** [Bess; *called* Bess of Hardwick], **countess of Shrewsbury** (1527?–1608), noblewoman, was one of four daughters and one son born to John Hardwick (*c.*1487–1528) of Hardwick, Derbyshire,

Elizabeth Talbot [Bess of Hardwick], **countess of Shrewsbury** (1527?–1608), by unknown artist, *c.*1590

and his wife, Elizabeth, daughter of Thomas Leake of Hasland, in the same county. Although the Hardwicks had for several generations been a moderately prosperous Derbyshire gentry family, Bess's early years were marked by hardship. When her father died in 1528, a significant portion of the 400 acres he had owned in and around Hardwick was seized by the crown, to be administered by the office of wards until his son and heir, James, came of age. It is unclear whether the modest manor house that had been in the Hardwick family for several generations—and on the site of which Bess later erected Hardwick Old Hall—was also seized in this manner. Few details are known of Bess's life in these years beyond the fact that her mother married Ralph Leche of Chatsworth, Derbyshire, probably in 1529. The marriage resulted in three additional children, all daughters. Leche, however, brought little land or money to the marriage, and he spent the period from 1538 to 1544 in a debtors' prison.

While still a young girl, Bess married Robert Barlow (or Barley) of Barlow, Derbyshire. Although the precise date of the marriage is unknown, it seems to have taken place before—or perhaps on—28 May 1543. The marriage produced no children, and it was later said that Barlow 'died before they were bedded together, they both being very young' (Margaret, duchess of Newcastle, 211). Upon Barlow's death on 24 December 1544 Bess received a modest inheritance.

Lady Cavendish On 20 August 1547 Bess married the twice-widowed Sir William *Cavendish (1508–1557), who had been appointed treasurer of the king's chamber the previous year. How Bess came to meet someone of Cavendish's standing is unclear, although it has been suggested that she was, at the time of her marriage, a lady-in-waiting to Frances Grey, marchioness of Dorset. While there is no real proof of this, it would help to explain not only how Bess met Cavendish, but also why the wedding took place in the Grey family chapel at Bradgate Manor, Leicestershire. Regardless of the marriage's origins, this was a brilliant match for Bess and one which was to change the course of her life. It was also by all accounts a happy union, not least because the couple shared a fierce ambition for social advancement. Between 1548 and 1557 Bess gave birth to eight children, six of whom survived into adulthood. Bess provided Cavendish with something neither of his first two marriages had produced: a healthy male heir. In fact they had three sons, all of whom survived, and two of whom founded dukedoms. Their eldest son was Henry *Cavendish. The dukes of Devonshire are descended from Bess's second son, William *Cavendish (1551–1626), and the dukes of Newcastle (and, indirectly, the dukes of Portland) are descended from her youngest son, Charles.

In selecting godparents for their children, Bess and Cavendish overwhelmingly chose prominent protestants. Among them were Princess Elizabeth, William Herbert, earl of Pembroke, John Dudley, duke of Northumberland, Lady Jane Grey, and numerous other members of the extended Grey family. It is difficult to say how far the choice of godparents reflected genuine religious belief, or a shrewd sense of self-preservation at a volatile court (in 1553, for example, Bess and Cavendish asked the new Queen Mary to be godmother to their son Charles). One point, however, is incontrovertible: Bess, as a result of her marriage to Cavendish, was now moving in aristocratic and royal circles.

In June 1549 Cavendish bought the estate of Chatsworth, which until 1547 had belonged to the Leches, to whom Bess was related by marriage. They almost immediately embarked on an ambitious project of rebuilding, and—as a household inventory of 1553 reveals—began to fill Chatsworth with the most splendid and luxurious furnishings. Although Chatsworth was the most glittering of the Cavendish properties in Derbyshire, it was by no means the only one: in 1550 Bess and Sir William had purchased the manor of Ashford and 8000 acres of land from the earl of Westmorland; in 1553 they bought 250 acres in Chatsworth and Baslow; and in 1554 they purchased an additional 70 acres near Chatsworth, as well as part of Edensor, the village which immediately bordered upon Chatsworth. It is difficult not to see these purchases as reflecting a desire on the part of Bess to return to her native Derbyshire in triumph, flaunting her new-found status as Lady Cavendish. As has been observed, her

> unrelenting acquisition of property and worldly goods, especially of property in the countryside of her birth, and if possible connected with her family and relatives, suggests the ambition of a local girl to demonstrate that the dim

squire's daughter had made good in a sensational way. (Girouard, *Hardwick Hall*, 6)

All the Derbyshire properties were held jointly in the names of both Bess and Sir William for both of their lives—a shrewd, if unusual, move designed to prevent the lands and property falling into wardship if, like Bess's father, Sir William should die before his eldest son attained his majority. As it happened, this proved a wise decision, for Sir William died in 1557, at which time his eldest son, Henry, was only seven years old. None the less, Bess found herself in a precarious financial situation in the wake of her husband's death, for Sir William died owing £5237 to the crown. This turn of events led Bess to lobby parliament in 1558 to protest against the proposed bill for the queen's debtors. It may also have had some bearing on the speed with which Bess married again, and on her choice of husband.

Lady St Loe At some point after Cavendish's death, but before Elizabeth I's accession, Bess married Sir William St Loe (*c.*1520–1565?). Like Cavendish, St Loe was a widower when he married Bess. Unlike Cavendish, however, St Loe hailed from an ancient and noble family. He was also considerably wealthier than Cavendish had been. Bess and St Loe spent much of their married life apart: Bess resided largely at Chatsworth, where she continued to oversee the on-going building works, while St Loe, owing to his duties at court, spent a great deal of his time in London. They had no children, and when St Loe died—probably in 1565—Bess, rather than St Loe's brother Edward, inherited the bulk of the estate. At the time the St Loe family accused Bess of exercising undue influence on her husband. Recent biographers, however, have suggested that Sir William may have had his own reasons for acting as he did.

If marriage to St Loe improved Bess's finances, it also brought her into Queen Elizabeth's inner circle. At the time of his marriage to Bess, St Loe was a member of the household of the then Princess Elizabeth. In 1559 he was named captain of the guard to the new queen. In the same year Bess was appointed a gentlewoman of the queen's privy chamber (and it is the fact that she is listed as 'Mrs St Loe' in privy chamber records that suggests that her third marriage must have taken place before Elizabeth I's accession). Bess and the queen fell out spectacularly over Bess's alleged involvement in the illicit marriage of Katherine Grey and Edward Seymour, earl of Hertford; as a result Bess was dismissed from the privy chamber. None the less, the relationship between the two women was more often than not amicable. In the late 1580s, when Bess's marriage to her fourth husband, the earl of Shrewsbury, had broken down, the queen intervened on Bess's behalf, asking Shrewsbury to permit his wife to see him.

Countess of Shrewsbury On 1 November 1567 Bess married George *Talbot, sixth earl of Shrewsbury (*c.*1522–1590), one of the richest and most powerful men in the north of England. At the time of their marriage Shrewsbury's property included the castles of Tutbury, Pontefract, and Sheffield, as well as a manor house at Sheffield and a lodge at Handsworth, hunting lodges at Tutbury and Worksop, and the converted monastic buildings at Rufford Abbey.

Shrewsbury's union with Bess, which brought together two great fortunes, was cemented—at Bess's insistence—by the arranged marriages of four of their children: Gilbert *Talbot, who became the seventh earl, wed Bess's daughter Mary, and Bess's eldest son, Henry Cavendish, wed Shrewsbury's daughter Grace.

In 1568 the queen designated Shrewsbury the keeper of Mary, queen of Scots, and the following year he and Bess received the Catholic queen at Tutbury. Mary remained in Talbot's custody until 1584, during which period she was moved on numerous occasions between Shrewsbury's various properties. In 1574 Margaret, countess of Lennox, and her son Charles Stuart came to visit the Scottish queen at Rufford, and Bess was on hand to entertain them. By the end of their five-day visit, the ever-resourceful Bess had engineered a match between Charles Stuart and her daughter Elizabeth Cavendish. They were married shortly thereafter, much to the fury of Shrewsbury and the queen, neither of whom had been consulted or informed of the marriage. A daughter, Arabella Stuart, was born in 1575. The child was frequently spoken of as a potential successor to the Virgin Queen, and Bess—who took charge of her granddaughter's upbringing after Arabella was orphaned in 1582—seems to have entertained great, if ultimately unrealized, ambitions for the young girl.

During the period of the Scottish queen's captivity, relations between the earl and countess steadily deteriorated. Bess repeatedly accused her husband of infidelities, including a probably unfounded charge that he had been intimate with Mary, queen of Scots. (This allegation may well have been designed primarily to damage Mary, with whom Bess—despite an initial period of friendship—had fallen out.) The earl, whose debts were mounting as a result of the expenses incurred as gaoler to the Scottish queen, chafed at the amount of time and money Bess devoted to the renovations at Chatsworth. In 1584 Bess separated from her husband and retired to Chatsworth.

At the time of their separation Shrewsbury attempted to claim Chatsworth as his under the terms of their marriage settlement. A legal battle ensued, which was finally resolved in 1587 when the courts awarded Bess both Chatsworth and a sizeable income from her husband. By this time, however, Bess had moved on to a new building project. In 1584, at which time Chatsworth's fate had been uncertain, Bess had purchased from her brother the family manor house at Hardwick. In 1587, armed with the financial means to realize her plans, she embarked on an ambitious plan for rebuilding, much as she and Cavendish had done earlier at Chatsworth. The majority of the renovations at Hardwick—comprising what is now called 'Hardwick Old Hall'—seem to have been completed by 1591.

As a result of her husband's death on 18 November 1590, Bess had inherited one third of the disposable lands that Talbot had owned at the time of their marriage. Almost immediately upon completing the building of Hardwick Old Hall, she turned her attention to building another Hardwick Hall, adjacent to the old one. Owing to the survival of extensive building accounts, a considerable amount is known regarding the construction of Hardwick

New Hall. The shell had been completed by the end of 1593, Bess took up residence on 4 October 1597, and the final building work was completed two years later. Bess occupied herself with furnishing and decorating the interior up until her death. This extraordinary house became the focal point of—as well as the enduring monument to—Bess's dynastic ambitions.

Probably the product of designs by Robert Smythson, Hardwick New Hall is remarkable in many respects. Like other houses designed by Smythson, it is an outward-facing, highly symmetrical structure, with an emphasis upon light and verticality (these two latter attributes achieved largely through the liberal use of bay windows). Other aspects of the design of Hardwick, however, are unique. It is the earliest surviving example of an English house with loggias but no internal courtyard. It is also unusual in that the hall, rather than running parallel to the long axis of the house, is instead placed at a right angle to it. The most distinctive feature of the house—and one which no one who has seen it can easily forget—is the emblazoning of the initials 'ES', surmounted by a countess's coronet, on the tops of each of the house's six towers.

The interior was, by all accounts, equally majestic and self-referential. An inventory of 1601 reveals that Bess filled Hardwick with a splendid collection of paintings, furniture, silver, tapestries, and embroidery. The public rooms, such as the long gallery and the high great chamber, were deliberately placed on the second storey rather than, as was customary at the time, on the first; the result was that all who came to Hardwick had the opportunity to process through the house, taking in its grandeur *en route* before being received by Bess. Even today the house reverberates with Bess's penchant for drama and self-presentation. Numerous extant features, including chimney-pieces, plaster friezes, and embroideries, integrate the initials 'ES'—along with the arms, crests, and attributes of the Hardwicks, Cavendishes, and Talbots—into their design.

Last years In 1601 Bess made her will, in which she bequeathed the contents of the two Hardwicks and also of Oldcotes (another Derbyshire property whose construction she had overseen) to her second and favourite son, William. The contents of Chatsworth she left to her eldest son, Henry. Bess also made provision for her other children, as well as for her grandchildren, her servants, and the residents of the almshouse that she had founded in Derby. On 20 March 1603 she altered her will, thereby disinheriting her son Henry and her granddaughter Arabella, with each of whom she had quarrelled bitterly for decades.

Bess died on 13 February 1608, and her body lay in state at Hardwick until her funeral, on or about 4 May 1608, in All Hallows (now All Saints' Cathedral), Derby. She was at the time of her death one of the richest people in England, and her tomb, designed by Robert Smythson, famously describes her as the 'aedificatrix' of Chatsworth, Hardwick, and Oldcotes. Although the intervening centuries have not always been kind to her—William Camden and Horace Walpole were just two of the many detractors who have cast her as a rapacious, social-climbing shrew—Bess is today viewed not only as the builder of perhaps the most magnificent of the Elizabethan 'prodigy houses', but also as the founder of a great dynasty.

ELIZABETH GOLDRING

Sources D. N. Durant, *Bess of Hardwick: portrait of an Elizabethan dynast*, rev. edn (1999) · M. Girouard, *Hardwick Hall* (1989) · M. Girouard, *Robert Smythson and the Elizabethan country house*, [new edn] (1983) · D. N. Durant and P. Riden, eds., *The building of Hardwick Hall*, 1: *The Old Hall, 1587–91*, Derbyshire RS, 4 (1980) · D. N. Durant and P. Riden, eds., *The building of Hardwick Hall*, 2: *The New Hall, 1591–98*, Derbyshire RS, 9 (1984) · L. Boynton, ed., *The Hardwick Hall inventories of 1601* (1971) · Margaret, duchess of Newcastle [M. Cavendish], *The life of William Cavendish, duke of Newcastle*, ed. C. H. Firth (1886) · A. Collins, *Historical collections of the noble families of Cavendishe, Holles, Vere, Harley and Ogle* (1752) · A. Wells-Cole, *Art and decoration in Elizabethan and Jacobean England* (1997) · *CSP dom.* · S. M. Levey, *An Elizabethan inheritance: the Hardwick Hall textiles* (1998) · E. Carleton Williams, *Bess of Hardwick* (1977) · M. Stepney Rawson, *Bess of Hardwick and her circle* (1910) · B. Stallybrass, 'Bess of Hardwick's buildings and building accounts', *Archaeologia*, 64 (1913) · J. Summerson, *Architecture in Britain, 1530 to 1830*, 9th edn (1993) · S. M. Levey and P. K. Thornton, *Of household stuff: the 1601 inventories of Bess of Hardwick* (2001)

Archives Chatsworth House, Derbyshire, account books · Chatsworth House, Derbyshire, Hardwick MSS · Coll. Arms, Shrewsbury and Talbot MSS · Folger, corresp. · LPL, corresp. and papers · Sheffield Central Library, corresp.

Likenesses oils, *c*.1560 (after H. Eworth), Hardwick Hall, Derbyshire · English school or R. Lockey?, oils, *c*.1580, Hardwick Hall, Derbyshire · oils, *c*.1590, Hardwick Hall, Derbyshire [*see illus.*] · tomb effigy, marble, *c*.1603, All Saints' Church, Derby · R. Lockey?, oils (second version), Montacute House, Somerset

Wealth at death very wealthy: will, Collins, *Historical Collections*

Talbot [*née* Jenyns; *other married name* Hamilton], **Frances**, **duchess of Tyrconnell** (1648–1731), courtier, was the second daughter of Richard Jenyns (*c*.1618–1668), MP, and Frances Thornhurst (1615–1693), and the elder sister of Sarah Jenyns [*see* Churchill, Sarah, duchess of Marlborough]. She was appointed a maid of honour to the duchess of York in 1664. A remarkably attractive and vivacious young woman, she was pursued in turn, but without success, by the duke of York, Charles II, and Richard Talbot. In February 1665 Pepys recorded that she went to the theatre disguised 'like an orange wench, and went up and down and cried oranges; till falling down, or by some such accident, though in the evening, her fine shoes were discovered, and she put to a great deal of shame' (Sergeant, 189).

Frances married, in the spring of 1666, an Irish Roman Catholic army officer, George Hamilton (*d*. 1676), the second son of Sir George Hamilton. At some time after the birth of her first child, in 1667, she converted to Catholicism and moved to Paris, where her husband joined the French army and in 1668 was created a count by Louis XIV. When Charles II heard that she had been left a widow with three daughters his sympathy was such that on 7 July 1676 he created her countess of Bantry. She was reunited in Paris with her one-time suitor Richard *Talbot (1630–1691), a Roman Catholic army officer and politician, and they married in November 1681. Although they had several children none survived infancy. They moved to Dublin in 1684. Talbot was created earl of Tyrconnell in 1685

and in 1687 he took over the government of Ireland as lord deputy.

On 10 June 1688 Frances was witness to the birth of the prince of Wales at St James's Palace, and at the time of the revolution she was in Ireland, where in March 1689 James II elevated Tyrconnell to a dukedom. At this time she wielded great influence in Dublin; she also developed a reputation for meanness, especially in her dealings with creditors. Lord Melfort suggested to the king that he send her to France to stop her meddling in matters of state, and William III was later told that during the war in Ireland she 'acted against Your Majesty, not with the duty of a wife to her husband, but with the malice of an open enemy, provoking him upon all occasions against the Protestants of this kingdom' (*CSP dom.*, 358). Though she met James when he rode into Dublin after the battle of the Boyne on 1 July 1690 there is no contemporary record of the celebrated exchange in which the king remarked 'Your countrymen, madam, can run well', and she replied 'Not quite so well as your majesty, for I see that you have won the race' (Simms, 153).

Frances sailed to France in August 1690 with her daughters and 40,000 gold coins. She was, wrote Melfort, 'robbing in a manner Irlande of so much money, and pretending it was the King's … But she is of the number of the fortunat may doe what they please' (Sergeant, 462). She was widowed for the second time on 14 August 1691. She was allowed to return to England in February 1692 to petition for the restoration of her Irish property. Against her it was argued that her success would 'tend to the great discouragement of the Protestant subjects … and to the strengthening of the Popish interest' (*CSP dom.*, 358). She was indicted in Ireland on 25 April 1693 but the charge of high treason was never proved and she was eventually allowed into possession in 1702. In the meantime she lived at St Germain-en-Laye as a lady of the bedchamber to Mary of Modena, and after 1699 she received a pension from James II. She was allowed to return to England and Ireland in 1702, following the restoration of her husband's estates in Queen Anne's first parliament (a measure engineered in large part by her sister Sarah), and in 1704 she settled in Delft.

Frances retired to Dublin in 1708; there she laid out money on the foundation of a convent of Poor Clares and settled in a house on Paradise Row, Arbour Hill, near Phoenix Park, where she died on 6 March 1731, in her eighty-third year. She was buried in St Patrick's Cathedral. Her three daughters, Elizabeth (*d*. 1724), Frances (*d*. 1751), and Mary (*d*. 1736), married respectively Richard Parsons, first Viscount Rosse, Henry Dillon, eighth Viscount Dillon, and Nicholas Barnewall, third Viscount Barnewall of Kingsland.

PIERS WAUCHOPE

Sources P. W. Sergeant, *Little Jennings and fighting Dick Talbot*, 2 vols. (1913) · S. Mulloy, ed., *Franco-Irish correspondence, December 1688 – February 1692*, 3 vols., IMC (1983–4) · A. Hamilton, *Memoirs of Count Grammont*, ed. G. Goodwin (1908) · J. G. Simms, *Jacobite Ireland, 1685–91* (1969) · *CSP dom., 1693* · G. S. Steinman, *Althorp memoirs* (1864) · F. Harris, *A passion for government: the life of Sarah, duchess of Marlborough* (1991) · GEC, *Peerage*

Likenesses S. Cooper, miniature, 1665, NPG · M. Beale, oils, Althorp, Northamptonshire; repro. in Sergeant, *Little Jennings*; version, Beaulieu, Hampshire · P. Lely, oils, Royal Collection; repro. in Sergeant, *Little Jennings* · Verelst, oils, repro. in Sergeant, *Little Jennings*

Talbot, Francis, fifth earl of Shrewsbury (1500–1560), magnate, was born at Sheffield Castle, the son and heir of George *Talbot, fourth earl of Shrewsbury (1468–1538), and his first wife, Anne Hastings. He inherited from his father a patrimony centred on Sheffield and including lands in south Yorkshire, Derbyshire, Nottinghamshire, and Shropshire; an undated *valor* gives them the clear value of £1518. During his father's lifetime Francis Talbot's involvement in national affairs was limited. He attended Henry VIII and Anne Boleyn at their meeting with François I in Calais in 1532, and a year later acted as his father's deputy in carrying Anne's crown at her coronation. In 1536 he assisted his father in resisting the Pilgrimage of Grace; after the duke of Norfolk's first meeting with the rebels at Doncaster on 27 October it was agreed that Francis Talbot should go with Norfolk and two of the pilgrims' spokesmen to court, where the latter should present the king with articles listing their grievances. As earl of Shrewsbury he served on the northern borders in 1544–5, directing a skilful holding campaign, organizing raids into Scotland, consolidating arrangements with individual Scots, and dealing with the consequences of the English defeat at Ancrum Moor on 27 February 1545. At the end of his tour of duty he was elected a knight of the Garter, after repeated failures in previous years.

But it was only after the death of Henry VIII that Shrewsbury became prominent in national affairs. He was involved in the ceremonial when Edward Seymour, earl of Hertford, was created duke of Somerset on 18 February 1547, and subsequently helped implement the duke's Scottish policy, in 1548 leading a large English army over the border to relieve the garrison besieged in Haddington. He now attended the House of Lords assiduously, and in January 1549 became a privy councillor. When he arrived in London in October 1549, at a time when the majority of councillors were protesting against Somerset's misgovernment, he was described by the imperial ambassador as 'one of the most powerful men in the kingdom' (*CSP Spain, 1547–9*, 457). Soon afterwards he was appointed lord president of the council in the north, replacing Robert Holgate, archbishop of York.

This may suggest that Shrewsbury was seen as a potential ally by John Dudley, earl of Warwick, but there are signs that by mid-1550 their relationship was strained, and that Shrewsbury's irritations with Warwick were linked with those of other noblemen, especially Edward Stanley, third earl of Derby. In September the imperial ambassador, referring to the refusal of the earl of Derby to obey a summons to appear at court until parliament met, noted the risk of disorder 'because the said lords Derby and Shrewsbury are powerful lords, of ancient lineage, faith and religion, and beloved of the people' (*CSP Spain, 1550–2*, 168–9): the two earls were reported to be intending to propose to the next parliament that Henry VIII's will—especially in matters of religion—should be observed until Edward VI came of age. In January 1551 the ambassador reported that councillors had decided that one form of religion should be strictly imposed and enforced: 'this will also provide a weapon to be used against certain great lords still holding the old religion like Derby and Shrewsbury' (ibid., 230).

In spring 1551 the discontents of Shrewsbury and Derby fused with those of the former protector, Somerset, who was seemingly modifying his own religious position. The religious and political ramifications of these dealings included the rumoured involvement of Princess Mary. One Benet of Ware, examined on 24 April, 'confessed that a certein talke ther was emonges them howe my ladie Marye wolde goo westwarde to th'erl of Shrewsburye' (*APC, 1550–52*, 264). But by the end of 1551 Shrewsbury was evidently reconciled to the government of John Dudley, now duke of Northumberland, even though he took no part in the trial of Somerset in December, despite a summons, and finally arrived in London on 28 January 1552, six days after the latter's execution. In spring 1553, stiffened by grants of lands which included Bolsover Castle, Derbyshire, the site of Pontefract Priory, and several London properties formerly belonging to the bishop of Durham, he acquiesced in Northumberland's attempt to divert the succession away from Mary. He signed the king's will, and after Edward's death was a signatory of letters on behalf of Lady Jane Grey.

Appearances may mislead, however. Shrewsbury was in effect something of a captive at court, and the imperial ambassador reported that he had been one of several noblemen who had demurred and made many difficulties before signing the king's will. Shrewsbury would not, however, run the risks of open rebellion, and he may well have believed that Northumberland's chances of success were high and that any open resistance would be futile. But the remark of one anxious supporter of the princess, 'the earl of Shrewburye beareth hymselfe equal: God kepe hym' (*The Copie of a Pistel*, sig. A viiv), hints that Shrewsbury's true sympathies lay with Mary, and that (with other councillors) he took such opportunities as presented themselves to turn the increasing difficulties of Northumberland's campaign to her advantage, especially in negotiations with the imperial ambassadors, who were actively seeking to build up support for Mary.

Shrewsbury was among those who proclaimed Mary as queen on 19 July, and on 2 August he and other councillors waited on her to beg her pardon. On 10 August she admitted him to her council, and then reappointed him president of the council in the north. He was one of a deputation from parliament that in November asked Mary to choose a husband in England. In spring 1554 Shrewsbury was named by Chancellor Stephen Gardiner as a 'heretic peer' for his part in the rejection by the House of Lords in May 1554 of a bill proposing capital punishment for heretics (*CSP Spain, 1554*, 251); but this was a tactical move, intended to protect his ownership of former monastic lands. In 1557 he was serving in the north again, with the task of watching out for a possible Franco-Scottish invasion: he shrewdly delayed mustering his troops until rumours of attack became compelling—and his timely mobilization was then a significant factor in deterring the Scots from launching their campaign.

On Elizabeth's accession Shrewsbury was reappointed a councillor. He did not agree with the following year's religious settlement, however, and on 18 March 1559 dissented in the Lords from the Uniformity Bill, though he was absent from the reading of a further revised bill on 22 March. Nevertheless he was again appointed president of the council in the north, and reported that the people under his governance received the English service daily and obediently. At his death he struck a last blow for his religious beliefs by requesting a requiem eucharist and communion. Shrewsbury had not been a leading player in the politics of the mid-Tudor reigns (it is hard to find any political issue on which he acted alone), and if his Catholicism became increasingly prominent, he was none the less always prepared to compromise and to go along with the government of the day. Perhaps he was fortunate that he was never compelled to decide irrevocably between loyalty to monarch and to religious principle.

Shrewsbury married twice. His first wife was Mary Dacre, daughter of Thomas, second Baron Dacre of Gilsland, who died in 1538. They had one surviving son, George *Talbot (c.1522–1590), the future sixth earl, and a daughter, Anne, whom Shrewsbury married to his ward John, second Baron Braye. After Mary's death he married Grace, née Shackerley, widow of Francis Carless: the expressions of condolence sent him on her death in 1558 by the fifth earl of Westmorland and Sir William Cordell suggest genuine affection. A year later Shrewsbury was unsuccessfully seeking the hand of Elizabeth, Lady Pope, widow of Sir Thomas Pope, founder of Trinity College, Oxford. In December 1559 she sent back a ring that Shrewsbury had sent to her and asked him no more to be a suitor to her, 'whyche yff it be so', Shrewsbury wrote, 'I must take as a punysment sent unto me from God' (LPL, Talbot papers, MS P, 355). Although negotiations continued into 1560, the financial bonds that Lady Pope demanded remained a sticking point: Shrewsbury saw himself as 'a faithless man altoguethers constrayned by bonde—whom I truste the worlde cannot chardge with juste cause of mystreating in any degre with any creature' (LPL, Talbot papers, MS E, 91). By now, however, Shrewsbury was increasingly ill, and he died at Sheffield on 28 September 1560, still a widower. His funeral took place in St Peter's Church, Sheffield (now Sheffield Cathedral), on 21 October.   G. W. BERNARD

Sources C. Jamison, G. R. Batho, and E. G. W. Bill, eds., A calendar of the Shrewsbury and Talbot papers in the Lambeth Palace Library and the College of Arms, 1, HMC, JP 6 (1966) · C. Jamison, G. R. Batho, and E. G. W. Bill, eds., A calendar of the Shrewsbury and Talbot papers in the Lambeth Palace Library and the College of Arms, 2, HMC, JP 7 (1971) · F. W. Steer, Arundel Castle archives, 1 (1968) · R. Meredith, Catalogue of the Arundel Castle manuscripts (1965) · N. Johnston, life of Francis Talbot, Sheffield Central Library · LP Henry VIII, vols. 5–21 · M. C. Hill, A guide to the Shropshire records (1952), 85–96 · CSP dom. · G. W. Bernard, 'The fourth and fifth earls of Shrewsbury: a study in the power of the early Tudor nobility', DPhil diss., U. Oxf., 1978 · G. W. Bernard, The power of the early Tudor nobility: a study of the fourth and fifth earls of Shrewsbury (1985) · GEC, Peerage, new edn, 11.710–12 · The copie of a pistel or letter sent to Gailbard Potter (1553) · CSP Spain, 1547–58
Archives Arundel Castle, corresp. · BL, corresp., Add. MS 32655 · Hunt. L., letter-book [copy] · LPL, corresp. and papers · Sheff. Arch., corresp. · Sheffield Central Library, collection · family papers, Add. MSS 46454–46464
Likenesses portrait, Ingestre Hall, Staffordshire
Wealth at death estates valued at £1518 9s. 6½d. late in life: Bernard, Power of the early Tudor nobility, 143

Talbot, George, fourth earl of Shrewsbury and fourth earl of Waterford (1468–1538), magnate, was born at Shifnal, Shropshire, the son and heir of John Talbot, third earl of Shrewsbury (1448–1473), and his wife, Katherine Stafford (d. 1476). He was a minor at his father's death, and his wardship was granted to Edward IV's favourite William, Baron Hastings, who married the young earl to his daughter Anne; the marriage was consummated when Shrewsbury was fifteen and a half. He served Henry VII in Yorkshire in 1486, at the battle of Stoke in 1487, after which he was made a knight of the Garter, and on the brief French campaign of 1492. He was frequently involved in court ceremonial, at royal weddings and at the creation of Prince Henry as duke of York in 1494 ('so well horssed an soo richely … that it was a tryhumphant sight'; Gairdner, 1.64–7), and in 1502 was appointed lord steward of the household with nominal responsibility for the royal household below stairs.

On 14 May 1509, following the accession of Henry VIII, Shrewsbury was appointed a chamberlain of the exchequer, but this office was simply a source of revenue (£52 3s. 4d. annually). He was also entrusted with diplomatic missions, being sent with the earl of Surrey to conclude the treaty of Westminster between Henry and Ferdinand of Aragon in 1511, conducting Queen Margaret of Scotland on her return to Scotland in 1517, and attending the Field of Cloth of Gold in 1520 and the meeting of Henry VIII and Emperor Charles V at Gravelines in 1521. His standing at court was sufficient to justify his receiving pensions from both Louis XII and François I of France. Shrewsbury served as lieutenant of the vanguard in the French campaign of 1513, raising 4437 men, the largest single contingent, and as lieutenant-general on the Scottish borders in 1522, when in Wolsey's words he was as 'active a captain as can be chosen within your realme, mete, convenable and necessary' (State Papers … Henry VIII, 1.30); in 1532, when invasion was again feared, he was once more appointed lieutenant-general on the Scottish borders.

Shrewsbury's most important service to the Tudor dynasty was his active loyalty during the risings of 1536. As soon as he heard of the disturbances in Lincolnshire, on 4 October, he mobilized his servants, tenants, and friends, raising 3654 men on horseback within a week. His action deterred Baron Hussey from joining the rebels. Moreover by sending the Lancaster herald with a proclamation commanding the rebels to disband under the threat of facing Shrewsbury's armed force (it was read out at Lincoln on the 11th), he contributed to the rebels' decision to disband. Then when the Pilgrimage of Grace broke out during that same month in Yorkshire, and the rebels captured York and Pontefract Castle and began to threaten the town of Doncaster, Shrewsbury fearlessly—rashly, in the opinion of the third duke of Norfolk, whom Henry VIII had sent north to join the earl—marched north to prevent its capture. Outnumbered, Shrewsbury and Norfolk were compelled twice to make a deal with the rebels, promising concessions if they disbanded and returned home, and then trying to win over rebel leaders. But Shrewsbury's actions halted the momentum of the rising, as Henry VIII recognized. If the rebels had been able to move south in large numbers, then they might have been able to exert overwhelming pressure on Henry VIII. That they moved no further south than Doncaster was not due to the attachment of the pilgrims to their own regions, but rather because their way was blocked by the area of influence of the earl of Shrewsbury, centred on Sheffield and extending southwards through Derbyshire to Nottinghamshire. The earl's loyalty to Henry VIII was ultimately crucial to the failure of the pilgrimage.

Shrewsbury's loyalty may have been maintained in spite of his own preferences, for he does not seem to have been very sympathetic to Anne Boleyn. In March 1531 the imperial ambassador Eustace Chapuys reported that Shrewsbury, referring to his privilege of holding the crown at the coronation of a queen, had said he would never place the crown on any other head than that of Queen Katherine, and in fact it was not he but his son Francis who performed that duty at Anne's coronation in 1533. He was also conservative in religion, providing in his will for 1000 masses for his soul and for an elaborate chantry chapel in what is now Sheffield Cathedral. But he and his family had owed a great deal to royal favour, he held many offices on crown lands (notably the stewardship of Tutbury, and of many other duchy of Lancaster estates in Staffordshire and Derbyshire, granted in 1509), and he displayed that instinctive loyalty to the crown that characterized the service nobility of late medieval and early modern England.

Shrewsbury's loyalty, firmly and boldly displayed, kept his own area free from rebellion. It also stiffened the commitment of other noblemen, notably Edward Stanley, third earl of Derby, in Lancashire, George Hastings, first earl of Huntingdon, and Thomas Manners, first earl of Rutland, in adjacent areas in the east midlands, as well as that of the duke of Norfolk. Furthermore, Shrewsbury's action deprived the pilgrims of the hope that they would receive support from great nobles and weakened their claim that such magnates were not being consulted by the government in the making of policy. Had the rebels resorted to military force, they would have found themselves fighting the very noblemen whose counsel they had been urging should be heeded by the king. Shrewsbury's role was thus crucial: 'which way he was inclined, it was thought verily the game were likely to go', as Holinshed later put it (*Holinshed's Chronicles*, 3.800). It is scarcely an exaggeration to say that in October 1536 the fate of Henry VIII lay in the hands of the fourth earl of Shrewsbury, or surprising that Thomas Cromwell should have assured the latter that he was the 'most woorthye erll that ever servyd a prince and suche a chefftayn as ys worthye eternall glorye' (LPL, Talbot papers, MS A, fol. 61).

Shrewsbury both added to and developed his estates. He enlarged—or possibly entirely rebuilt—Sheffield Manor, 'a goodly lodge or manor place on a hil top' in the midst of a deer park (Leland, 4.14). When Cardinal Wolsey stayed there under arrest in 1530, the earl 'would often requyer hyme to kyll a doo or ij ther in the parke' (Cavendish, 167). He was especially fond of South Wingfield Manor, Derbyshire, and when he died he was building a 'fair lodge' at Worksop Park, Nottinghamshire. He acquired the lands of the former monasteries of Rufford in October 1537, which included the manor of Worksop and the lordship of Rotherham, in exchange for his family's Irish estates, resumed to the crown a year earlier. Following his death his income was assessed at £1735.

Shrewsbury had several children from his marriage to Anne Hastings, whom he married to members of other leading noble families. Francis *Talbot, who succeeded as fifth earl, was his only surviving son (there may have been five more). Three daughters survived into adulthood: Margaret married Henry Clifford, later first earl of Cumberland; Mary was disastrously married in 1524 to Henry Percy, later sixth earl of Northumberland; and Elizabeth married William, third Baron Dacre of Gilsland. Anne having died, about 1512 Shrewsbury married Elizabeth, daughter and coheir of Sir Richard Walden of Erith, Kent. Their daughter, Anne (d. 1558), was married first to Peter Compton, son and heir of Sir William Compton, groom of the stool to Henry VIII, and then to William Herbert, first earl of Pembroke. Shrewsbury died at Wingfield on 26 July 1538; he was buried on 27 March 1539 at St Peter's Church, Sheffield, where his effigy survives on his tomb, along with one of his second wife. Elizabeth, who died in 1567, is also commemorated on her tomb in Erith church.

G. W. BERNARD

Sources C. Jamison, G. R. Batho, and E. G. W. Bill, eds., *A calendar of the Shrewsbury and Talbot papers in the Lambeth Palace Library and the College of Arms*, 1, HMC, JP 6 (1966) · C. Jamison, G. R. Batho, and E. G. W. Bill, eds., *A calendar of the Shrewsbury and Talbot papers in the Lambeth Palace Library and the College of Arms*, 2, HMC, JP 7 (1971) · F. W. Steer, *Arundel Castle archives*, 1 (1968) · R. Meredith, *Catalogue of the Arundel Castle manuscripts* (1965) · N. Johnston, life of George Talbot, Sheffield Central Library · chancery close rolls, PRO, C 54/412 · *LP Henry VIII*, vols. 1–13 · M. C. Hill, *A guide to the Shropshire records* (1952), 85–96 · G. W. Bernard, 'The fourth and fifth earls of Shrewsbury: a study in the power of the early Tudor nobility', DPhil diss., U. Oxf., 1978 · G. W. Bernard, *The power of the early Tudor nobility: a study of the fourth and fifth earls of Shrewsbury* (1985) · GEC, *Peerage*, new edn, 11.706–9 · *State papers published under ... Henry VIII*, 11 vols. (1830–52) · J. Gairdner, ed., *Letters and papers illustrative of the reigns of Richard III and Henry VII*, 2 vols., Rolls Series, 24 (1861–3) · *Holinshed's chronicles of England, Scotland and Ireland*, ed. H. Ellis, 6 vols. (1807–8) · *The itinerary of John Leland in or about the years 1535–1543*, ed. L. Toulmin Smith, 11 pts in 5 vols. (1906–10) · G. Cavendish, *The life and death of Cardinal Wolsey*, ed. R. S. Sylvester, EETS, original ser., 243 (1959)
Archives Arundel Castle, west Sussex · LPL · Sheffield Central Library

Likenesses tomb effigy, Sheffield Cathedral

Wealth at death total income inherited by son valued at £1735: 1538/9, PRO, chancery close rolls, C 54/412

Talbot, George, sixth earl of Shrewsbury (c.1522–1590),

nobleman, was the elder and only surviving son of Francis *Talbot, fifth earl of Shrewsbury (1500–1560), and his first wife, Mary (d. 1538), daughter of Thomas, second Lord Dacre of Gilsland. In 1538 he took the title of Lord Talbot, which he continued to use until he succeeded to the earldom twenty-two years later. On 28 April 1539, in London, he married Lady Gertrude (d. 1566/7), eldest daughter of Thomas Manners, first earl of Rutland, and his second wife, Eleanor, daughter of Sir William Paston of Paston, Norfolk. Talbot's early years were marked by the rapid acquisition of honours from the crown, many of which reflected his family's historic prominence in the north. On 20 February 1547, at the coronation of Edward VI, he was made a knight bachelor. In May 1549 he became a member of the council of the north, a position which he would continue to hold until his death. On 1 November 1549 he was named high steward of the honour of Pontefract and constable of Pontefract Castle. On 21 June 1553 he signed the instrument settling the crown on Lady Jane Grey, an act for which he was pardoned later that same year. On 30 May 1557 he was appointed captain-general of the footmen in the army in the north, and in 1561 he was elected a knight of the Garter. In July 1565 he was made joint lieutenant-general in the north, and the following month he was named lord lieutenant of the counties of Yorkshire, Nottinghamshire, and Derbyshire. The steep trajectory of these early years—in which one honour rapidly followed another—was not to be sustained. Although he continued to play a leading role in the politics of the north, he would never fully realize the promise of his early career at court.

Two events occurred in the late 1560s which had far-reaching and not altogether pleasant consequences for Shrewsbury. The first was his decision, in the wake of his wife Gertrude's death, to remarry. His second wife, whom he married in London on 1 November 1567, was the thrice-widowed Elizabeth, Lady St Loe [see Talbot, Elizabeth, countess of Shrewsbury (1527?–1608)], better known to posterity as Bess of Hardwick. At the time of their marriage Shrewsbury was one of the richest men in England; his property included the castles of Tutbury, Pontefract, and Sheffield, as well as a manor house at Sheffield and a lodge at Handsworth, hunting lodges at Tutbury and Worksop, and the converted monastic buildings at Rufford Abbey. Although cynics then and now have suggested that Bess's interest in him was purely—or at least primarily—motivated by a desire for financial and social gain, the marriage none the less seems to have begun happily enough: his early letters to Bess address her warmly as 'my owne sweet heart', 'my dear', or 'my jewel' (Collinson, 16). Relations between the earl and countess, however, deteriorated rapidly. By the late 1570s Shrewsbury was describing Bess as 'my wyked and malysyous wyfe' and 'so bad

George Talbot, sixth earl of Shrewsbury (c.1522–1590), by unknown artist, 1580?

and wicked a woman'. In the mid-1580s the couple endured an acrimonious and rather unprecedented separation, complete with a prolonged legal battle over their respective assets.

The other momentous event of the late 1560s was the queen's selection of Shrewsbury to be the custodian of Mary, queen of Scots. This post commenced in February 1569, when Mary was delivered to him at Tutbury. He remained Mary's keeper until September 1584, during which period the Scottish queen was moved on forty-six occasions between his many properties. The reasons behind Elizabeth's selection of Shrewsbury for this task were many and varied. That he owned numerous large houses made him one of a handful of aristocrats who could accommodate Mary and her extensive entourage of servants and guards. That these houses were located in the north—which is to say at some remove from the queen—no doubt added to their (and Shrewsbury's) appeal. That his properties were relatively remote from both Scotland and the sea—and thus posed comparatively few security risks—must also have been a factor. His religion was also in his favour. Although he was a protestant, he was not a militant, and was probably perceived as ideally placed ideologically to mediate between Elizabeth and Mary. Perhaps the most important point in his favour, however, was his enormous personal wealth. To feed, house, and guard Mary and her entourage was an undertaking which the famously parsimonious queen no doubt realized would best be executed by someone with deep pockets.

This last issue became a central theme in Shrewsbury's correspondence during his years as gaoler to Mary. In the beginning Elizabeth provided him with an allowance of £2700 per year for the cost of feeding, clothing, and guarding the Scottish queen, although he considered this sum insufficient. On 15 January 1570 he wrote to the marquess of Winchester and Sir Walter Mildmay complaining of the expenses incurred after just one year as Mary's keeper:

> The charges daily that I do now sustain, and have done all this year past, well known by reason of the Queen of Scots, are so great therein as I am compelled to be now a suitor unto you … my earnest trust and desire is that you will now consider me with such larger proportion in this case as shall seem good unto your friendly wisdoms.   (Lodge, 1.490)

Pleas such as these are frequent in Shrewsbury's correspondence both with the queen and with courtiers acting as intermediaries. His requests, however, seem to have fallen on deaf ears. Rather than increasing his allowance, the queen eventually reduced it to £1560 per annum and then to nothing at all. Even during the years in which he was meant to have received a royal allowance, the payment was often woefully overdue. He claimed that the expense of being the Scottish queen's custodian forced him into extensive borrowing. Increasingly, he came to despair both of his own financial situation and of the queen's estimation of him: 'the worlde must nedes thinke that eyther my desertes have ben very small, or else her Majestie doth make very small accompt of me' (Kershaw, 268). Yet this is difficult to reconcile with the evidence, which suggests that he was both 'the leading aristocratic industrialist of the Elizabethan period' and 'the most active entrepreneur' of the era (Stone, 328, 375). His wealth derived from a diversity of interests including farming, coal, lead, iron, steel, and shipping. It has been suggested by one historian that the salient fact to remember when assessing his finances is that 'he *felt* poor' (Kershaw, 269). In addition to providing for the Scottish queen and her entourage, he also had to contend with the increasing debts of his son Gilbert and the financial demands of his wife, Bess, the latter engaged in expensive building works at Chatsworth and Oldcotes.

If Shrewsbury's anxiety about his finances seems to have been ill founded, his sense that his status at court was slipping was rather more accurate. In marked contrast to his promising early career at court, his later years saw him increasingly marginalized. Although he was made a privy counsellor in 1571, the appointment was no springboard to greater things, largely because his duties as gaoler to Mary, queen of Scots, conflicted with his duties as a counsellor. Guardianship of the Scottish queen required Shrewsbury to supervise her every movement, with the result that he travelled south only once between 1571 and 1584, the year in which he was relieved of his duties with regard to the Scottish queen. This long absence from court had disastrous effects on his reputation and on any future chances of preferment. When he finally took up his seat on the privy council in 1584, he found that rumours were circulating to the effect that he had been disloyal to the English queen by taking up Mary's cause.

The notion that Shrewsbury had betrayed Elizabeth was not unrelated to the rumour circulated by his wife, Bess, that he had been inappropriately intimate with the Scottish queen. Whether this claim had any basis in fact is doubtful. In any event, it brought to a head the animosities that had long festered between the earl and countess of Shrewsbury. Although Queen Elizabeth attempted to enforce a reconciliation between the couple, they in effect lived separate lives from 1584 onwards. There was an ongoing dispute—settled in court in Bess's favour in 1587—regarding the ownership of Chatsworth, the Derbyshire house built by Bess and her second husband, Sir William Cavendish. The court ruling of 1587 also awarded Bess a substantial income from her husband. The financial squabbles that had plagued Shrewsbury in life did not cease with his death on 18 November 1590 at Sheffield Manor. His eldest surviving son and heir, Gilbert, alleged that his father's mistress, Elinor Bretton, had stolen considerable sums of cash from the bedside of the dying earl.

Of Shrewsbury the man we know that he was possessed of one of the more illegible hands in Elizabethan England, a result of his battles with both gout and arthritis. It also has been suggested, in the light of his persistent belief that nearly everyone in his life was at one time or another plotting against him, that he may have suffered from a form of paranoid dementia. As for his legacy to English history, it is probably fair to say, as Alan G. R. Smith has done, that he owes his fame primarily 'to his relationships with three remarkable women, his wife Bess of Hardwick, his sovereign Queen Elizabeth, and his involuntary "guest" Mary Queen of Scots' (Smith, 10). It is not, one suspects, the fame for which Shrewsbury himself would have wished.

Shrewsbury was buried on 13 January 1591 at St Peter's, Sheffield. He had seven children with his first wife: Francis, Lord Talbot, who in 1562 married Anne, daughter of William Herbert, first earl of Pembroke, but who predeceased his father; Gilbert *Talbot (d. 1616), who became the seventh earl; Henry; Edward, who succeeded his brother Gilbert as the eighth earl; Catherine, who in 1563 married Henry, Lord Herbert; Mary, who married Sir George Savile of Barrowby, Lincolnshire; and Grace, who married Henry, eldest son and heir of Sir William Cavendish of Chatsworth. Although Shrewsbury had no children with his second wife, his son Gilbert and daughter Grace married children of Bess's from her second marriage, to Sir William Cavendish.

ELIZABETH GOLDRING

Sources GEC, *Peerage*, new edn, vol. 11 · P. Collinson, *The English captivity of Mary, queen of Scots* (1987) · A. G. R. Smith, ed., *The last years of Mary queen of Scots: documents from the Cecil papers at Hatfield House* (1990) · E. Lodge, *Illustrations of British history, biography, and manners*, 2nd edn, 3 vols. (1838) · S. E. Kershaw, 'Power and duty in the Elizabethan aristocracy: George, earl of Shrewsbury, the Glossopdale dispute and the council', *The Tudor nobility*, ed. G. W. Bernard (1992), 266–96 · L. Stone, *The crisis of the aristocracy, 1558–*

1641 (1965) · *The state papers and letters of Sir Ralph Sadler*, ed. A. Clifford, 2 vols. (1809) · M. Girouard, *Robert Smythson and the Elizabethan country house*, [new edn] (1983) · *CSP dom., 1581–90* · E. G. W. Bill, ed., *A calendar of the Shrewsbury papers in the Lambeth Palace Library* (1966) · C. Jamison, G. R. Batho, and E. G. W. Bill, eds., *A calendar of the Shrewsbury and Talbot papers in the Lambeth Palace Library and the College of Arms*, 2, HMC, JP 7 (1971) · *A catalogue of the Arundel Castle manuscripts ... with an appendix of a calendar of Talbot letters* (1965)
Archives Arundel Castle, Sussex, corresp. · BL, Harley MSS, corresp. and papers · BL, Cotton MSS, corresp., etc. · BL, family papers, Add. MSS 46454–46464 · Bodl. Oxf., letter-book and corresp. · Coll. Arms, Shrewsbury and Talbot MSS · Hatfield House, Hertfordshire, letters and papers · Hunt. L., letter-book · LPL, corresp. · LPL, corresp. and papers · Sheff. Arch., corresp. | BL, corresp. and papers relating to Mary, queen of Scots, Add. MS 33594 · Folger, letters to Richard Bagot · Folger, letters to his wife, Bess of Hardwick · Sheffield Central Library, corresp. with B. Franks
Likenesses M. Gheeraerts senior, group portrait, etching, 1576 (*Procession of the Garter Knights*), BM · R. Lockey?, oils, c.1580, Hardwick Hall, Derbyshire · chalk drawing, 1580?, NPG [*see illus.*] · tomb effigy, c.1590, cathedral of St Peter and St Paul, Sheffield · British school, oils, 17th/18th cent., Tate collection · watercolour (after R. Lockey?, c.1580), NPG

Talbot, George

Talbot, George (1816–1886), papal official, was born at Evercreech, near Wells, the third son in the family of five sons and four daughters of James Talbot, a lawyer and third Baron Talbot of Malahide (c.1768–1850), and his wife, Anne Sarah (d. 1857), daughter of Samuel Rodbard of Evercreech in Somerset. After education at St Mary's Hall, Oxford (where he graduated BA in 1839 and MA in 1841), Talbot followed the familiar path of aristocratic younger sons to ordination in the Church of England, and in 1840 was appointed to a family living at Evercreech. He was received into the Roman Catholic church by Nicholas Wiseman in 1843 at St Mary's College, Oscott. He trained for the Catholic priesthood at Oscott alongside Edmund Stonor and Edward Howard. Both men were lifelong friends of his and also had influential careers in Rome. In June 1846 Talbot was ordained priest by Wiseman at Oscott. He applied to join the English Oratorian Congregation, newly formed by John Henry Newman, but was turned down in March 1847. Until 1849 he worked as a pastoral priest at the St George's Cathedral in Southwark, which he was reluctant to leave. However, through Wiseman's influence, he was appointed a canon of St Peter's, Rome, and a chamberlain to Pope Pius IX.

As a recent convert with only brief pastoral experience, Talbot's knowledge of the English Catholic scene was limited. Today he is best remembered for his view that the laity should be restricted to hunting, shooting, and entertaining (Purcell, 2.318). However, he gained the confidence and friendship of Pope Pius IX and exercised considerable influence for the next twenty years. Despite the fact that the rector of the English College in Rome acted as agent for the English bishops, Talbot became a self-appointed and unofficial agent, working assiduously for Wiseman and Henry Edward Manning, and strongly supporting their ultramontane line.

Many other English bishops resented Talbot, and his frank letters to his close confidant Manning caused the latter to describe him in later years as 'the most imprudent man who ever lived'. Manning's biographer, Edmund Sheridan Purcell, certainly made very free with Talbot's letters to Manning from Rome, thus providing Lytton Strachey with dubious ammunition for his hostile portrait of Manning in *Eminent Victorians* (1918). Talbot was implacably opposed to Newman, describing him as 'the most dangerous man in England'. In the jurisdictional dispute between Wiseman and his coadjutor George Errington, Talbot sided against Errington and did all he could to bring about the coadjutor's eventual resignation.

Talbot's presence and his influence in Rome undermined that of successive rectors of the English College. He exercised increasing influence over the college, and in 1860 was appointed delegate protector. In 1852 he was mainly responsible for establishing within the walls of the English College the Collegio Pio, reorganized in 1898 and now known as the Beda College, for the training of convert and older clergy. In 1866 he launched an ambitious plan to rebuild the college chapel and began fundraising with a donation of £100 from the pope himself. By 1867 his influence was such that he was able to force the resignation of the rector in office and persuade the pope to accept his nominee.

However, Talbot's days close to the papal throne were by then limited. Worry over the funding of the rebuilding of the chapel, possibly combined with his capacity for intrigue, spilled over into a genuine mental instability, and in 1869 he was removed from Rome to an asylum for the insane in Bon Secours convent at Passy, a suburb of Paris. For many years the pope kept Talbot's apartments in the Vatican ready in case he should return. He died at Passy on 16 October 1886, and was buried quietly in the cemetery of Père Lachaise.

JUDITH F. CHAMP, *rev.* MICHAEL PETERBURS

Sources S. Leslie, *Henry Edward Manning: his life and labours* (1921) · E. R. Norman, *The English Catholic church in the nineteenth century* (1984) · O. van der Heydt, 'Monsignor Talbot de Malahide', *The Wiseman Review*, 502 (1964), 290–308 · E. S. Purcell, *Life of Cardinal Manning*, 2 vols. (1896) · Burke, *Peerage* (1975) · Foster, *Alum. Oxon.*
Archives Archivio Vaticano, Vatican City, corresp. · English College, Rome, corresp. and diaries

Talbot, Sir George John

Talbot, Sir George John (1861–1938), judge, was born in London on 19 June 1861, the eldest son of John Gilbert Talbot (1835–1910), Conservative member of parliament for West Kent (1868–78) and for Oxford University (1878–1910), and his wife, Meriel Sarah, eldest daughter of G. W. *Lyttelton, fourth Baron Lyttelton, and sister of Arthur Temple *Lyttelton and Alfred *Lyttelton. He was a nephew of Edward Stuart *Talbot, bishop of Winchester. Talbot's father was at Charterhouse School, but his disapproval of the school's migration to Godalming caused him in 1873 to send his son to Winchester College, for which Talbot was ever grateful. In 1880 he gained a junior studentship at Christ Church, Oxford, obtained a first class in classical moderations (1882) and in *literae humaniores* (1884). In 1886 he was elected to a fellowship at All Souls, which he vacated in 1898 following his marriage in 1897 to Gertrude

Harriot, fourth daughter of Albemarle Cator, of Woodbastwick Hall, Norfolk. They were a happily devoted couple, who wrote to one another daily when parted. They had two sons and a daughter.

A career in the church or at the bar was obvious for Talbot. Perhaps the claims of heredity prevailed for the latter. On his father's side he was sixth in descent from Charles, Lord *Talbot, lord chancellor from 1733 to 1737; while on his mother's side he was thirteenth in descent from Sir Thomas *Littleton, judge of the common pleas (1466), and ninth in descent from Sir Thomas *Bromley, lord chancellor from 1579 to 1587. His grandfather John Chetwynd Talbot (a son of the second Earl Talbot), whose ample law library he inherited, had a highly successful career at the parliamentary bar in its busiest days of railway promotions. As all these ancestors were members of the Inner Temple, Talbot naturally followed them, and was there called to the bar in 1887. He took silk in 1906, became a bencher of his inn in 1914, and was its treasurer in 1936. Until late in his career at the bar his busy practice was mainly before parliamentary committees, and in work of a similar character—in the railway and canal commission court, for example. He was also a learned ecclesiastical lawyer, and was eventually chancellor of six dioceses. He was counsel to the University of Oxford from 1915 to 1923.

In October 1916 Lord Buckmaster, contemplating Talbot for a vacant judgeship of the King's Bench Division, consulted the prime minister, Asquith, who dissuaded him (to Buckmaster's subsequent regret) on the ground that promotion from the parliamentary bar would not be popular with the profession, and H. A. McCardie was appointed instead. This was a misfortune. If Talbot had been appointed at the age of fifty-five, instead of having to wait as he did until he was sixty-two, his judicial career would probably have ended in the House of Lords. At this time, and increasingly, Talbot's services were being sought in wider circles of the law, especially before the House of Lords, and the judicial committee of the privy council, in *Bowman v. The Secular Society* in 1917, for instance, and in Lady Rhondda's petition before the committee of privileges in 1922. In the latter, it was the opinion of Lord Greene, later master of the rolls, that Talbot's argument, before a troublesome and divided tribunal, was the finest effort of advocacy which he ever heard.

In November 1923, on the retirement of Mr Justice Darling, Lord Cave, as lord chancellor, redressed the mistake of 1916: Talbot became a judge of the King's Bench Division and was given the customary knighthood in 1924. It would be hard to decide whether he was in every way more different from McCardie, who had supplanted him, or from Darling, whom he succeeded. On the bench he displayed every quality of the ideal judge. He had learning, dignity, industry, patience, and courtesy; his decisions were almost invariably right, and on most occasions were thought to be so by the Court of Appeal. And (although he tried at least one sensational murder case) his name was unknown to the readers of the popular newspapers. Following his appointment to sit in the commercial court, he started there with a protest against one with so little

experience of that class of work being selected. That, however, was the fault of a very needless modesty—he did the work as well as he did everything else. In criminal trials on circuit, of which he had had little experience at the bar, he had no contemporary superior.

Towards the end of 1936 Talbot's powers, both physical and mental, began to fail. In June 1937 he resigned, and thereupon was sworn of the privy council. His resignation would probably have taken place earlier if he had not waited in order to be present at Winchester, on 29 May, when seven Wykehamist judges were received *ad portas*. Winchester College was, next to his wife and family, Talbot's greatest object of devotion. He was a fellow from 1930 until he resigned shortly before his death, and for a time was sub-warden. In 1935 he was elected an honorary student of Christ Church, and he served for thirty-five years on the council of Keble College, Oxford.

Talbot was a tall, handsome man with a fresh complexion. He was a tireless walker in the country, and his pleasure in walking was increased by his being an ardent and very learned botanist. He had a cold bath every morning, and was never known to wear an overcoat in town or country. His reading was widespread, and he remained a fine scholar throughout his life. When he left Oxford he set himself a great programme of Greek and Latin literature, and by the strict devotion of a fixed daily time he completed the task in upwards of thirty years. He was a great lover of music, especially of Handel, although he never played any instrument. Nature endowed him with a very hot temper, but his intense self-discipline concealed that fact. He was a very devout churchman, who went to the early communion every Sunday and on all major saints' days. Some foolish person allegedly once asked Charles Gore whether the law was a suitable career for a man of high ideals; the bishop answered: 'Do you know George Talbot?'

Talbot died on 11 July 1938 at Falconhurst, near Edenbridge, Kent, the pleasant estate created by his grandfather, and was buried at Markbeech near by. His wife survived him. Their elder son predeceased him in 1922; the younger son followed his father to the Inner Temple and the bar.   F. D. MACKINNON, *rev.* ALEC SAMUELS

Sources *The Times* (14 Oct 1936) · *The Times* (13 July 1938) · *The Wykehamist* (25 July 1938) · *Law Quarterly Review*, 61 (1945) · personal knowledge (1949) · private information (1949) · R. F. V. Heuston, *Lives of the lord chancellors, 1885–1940* (1964)

Archives HLRO, papers | All Souls Oxf., letters to Sir William Anson

Likenesses W. Stoneman, photograph, 1926, NPG · W. G. de Glehn, portrait, priv. coll. · photograph, All Souls Oxf.

Wealth at death £107,400 3s. 8d.: probate, 21 Sept 1938, CGPLA Eng. & Wales

Talbot, Gilbert, first Lord Talbot (1276–1346), landowner, was the eldest son and heir of Richard Talbot, a knight of Herefordshire and Gloucestershire, and Sarah, the daughter of William de Beauchamp of Elmley, Worcestershire, and the sister of William de *Beauchamp, earl of Warwick (d. 1298). Talbot, born on 18 October 1276, inherited property in Herefordshire and Gloucestershire on his father's death in 1306. His younger brother, Richard, became lord of Richards Castle and another brother, Thomas, became a priest. Talbot served against Edward I in Scotland in 1293 and on local commissions in Gloucestershire before 1312.

Talbot came to prominence during and after the contrariants' uprising against Edward II. He received a pardon in 1312 for the death of Gaveston, and may have been implicated in the execution either through his kinship with Guy de Beauchamp, earl of Warwick, whose first cousin he was, or through his association with Thomas, earl of Lancaster. The Talbots held a manor in Lydney, Gloucestershire, of the earls of Warwick and a manor in Longhope, Gloucestershire, of the earls of Lancaster. Gilbert Talbot received an annual rent of £40 for life from Thomas of Lancaster. His connection to Lancaster may explain his participation in the 1321–2 rebellion, although he was also called an adherent of Roger Mortimer. With his son Richard *Talbot he was among those accused of burning Bridgnorth in January 1322 and father and son were both captured at the battle of Boroughbridge on 16 March, Gilbert styled 'banneret' and Richard 'bachelor'. Talbot's lands were plundered, with losses of more than £60 from one estate at Credenhill, before they were taken into royal custody in December 1321.

Talbot, however, recovered quickly. Promising in July 1322 to pay a fine of £2000 and one tun of wine worth 40s. a year for life, he was released from prison and he retrieved his property. That October Edward commissioned him to arrest malefactors in Gloucestershire and on 1 November gave him custody of the castle and town of Gloucester. As another condition of his pardon Talbot served in Gascony in 1324–5. Described as one of Prince Edward's counsellors, he attended Edward's homage to the French king, Charles, on 24 September 1325, the first indication of a bond that lasted for the rest of Talbot's life.

Talbot returned to England with Edward, Mortimer, and Isabella to overthrow Edward II and so, at the age of fifty, stepped onto the stage of national politics. In August 1327 he was appointed chamberlain, the first since Hugh Despenser the younger fell from power, and accompanied Edward III to France to perform homage again in 1329. Four days after Mortimer's fall on 19 October 1330 Edward appointed Talbot justice of south Wales and renewed the grant for life in 1339. He became justiciar in the bishopric of St David's in October 1332, and stayed on as chamberlain until 1334. Edward assigned Talbot custody of Builth Castle in 1330, the castles of Blaenllyfni and Bwlchydinas for life in 1333, and Carmarthen Castle in 1340. His military career included serving in Scotland (1333–5), raising Welsh forces to fight in Scotland (1335–7), preparing for threatened French invasions (1337, 1345), and arraying troops in Herefordshire (1339).

Talbot had been sent as a county knight to a great council in 1324 and had been summoned to two councils in 1330, but he received his first summons to parliament in 1332, becoming Lord Talbot. He was a frequent witness to royal charters, received fees and robes as a knight of the royal household, and gained various other favours including several wardships. Edward gave him permission to alienate lands in mortmain to the family priory at Wormley, Herefordshire. Talbot was one of the trailbaston justices inquiring into official misconduct and local disorder in 1341, and served on other commissions until his death on 20 February 1346 at Eccleswall, when he was nearly seventy years old.

SCOTT L. WAUGH

Sources GEC, *Peerage*, new edn · F. Palgrave, ed., *The parliamentary writs and writs of military summons*, 2 vols. in 4 (1827–34) · *RotP* · *Chancery records* · Rymer, *Foedera*, new edn · *Chronicon Henrici Knighton, vel Cnitthon, monachi Leycestrensis*, ed. J. R. Lumby, 2 vols., Rolls Series, 92 (1889–95) · *Adae Murimuth continuatio chronicarum. Robertus de Avesbury de gestis mirabilibus regis Edwardi tertii*, ed. E. M. Thompson, Rolls Series, 93 (1889) · W. Stubbs, ed., *Chronicles of the reigns of Edward I and Edward II*, 2 vols., Rolls Series, 76 (1882–3), esp. *Annales Paulini, Gest Edwardi de Carnarvon, Vita et mors Edward II* · Justices Itinerant, PRO, Just1/1388m. 7d · Ancient Extents, PRO, E 142/26, 32 · N. Fryde, *The tyranny and fall of Edward II, 1321–1326* (1979) · G. A. Holmes, *The estates of the higher nobility in fourteenth-century England* (1957), p. 71, no. 5; p. 142 · S. Walker, *The Lancastrian affinity, 1361–1399* (1990), p. 28 and nos. 80–81 · N. Saul, *Knights and esquires: the Gloucestershire gentry in the fourteenth century* (1981), 42, 48, 79 · P. Chaplais, ed., *The War of Saint-Sardos (1323–1325): Gascon correspondence and diplomatic documents*, CS, 3rd ser., 87 (1954), no. 213 · R. A. Griffiths and R. S. Thomas, *The principality of Wales in the later middle ages: the structure and personnel of government*, 1: *South Wales, 1277–1536* (1972) · R. Nicholson, *Edward III and the Scots: the formative years of a military career, 1327–1335* (1965), 140, 176, 246, 248 · Tout, *Admin. hist.* · W. Rees, ed., *Calendar of ancient petitions relating to Wales* (1975), 51, 165, 319 · *CIPM*, 4, no. 377; 8, no. 714

Wealth at death each Gloucestershire manor valued at £10: *CIPM*, 8, no. 714

Talbot, Gilbert, seventh earl of Shrewsbury (1552–1616), landowner, was born on 20 November 1552, the second son of George *Talbot, sixth earl of Shrewsbury (c.1522–1590), politician, and Lady Gertrude Manners (d. 1566/7), daughter of Thomas *Manners, first earl of Rutland. As a younger son Gilbert was not destined to succeed. About 1566 he matriculated with his elder brother, Francis, from St John's College, Oxford; Gilbert later received an honorary MA from Cambridge, in 1595. Shrewsbury married Elizabeth Hardwick [see Talbot, Elizabeth, countess of Shrewsbury (1527?–1608)], on 1 November 1567 and Gilbert was still only fifteen at the double wedding at Sheffield on 9 February 1568, when he married his stepsister, Mary Cavendish (1557–1632), and his sister Grace married Henry Cavendish. This marriage, which made Bess of Hardwick his mother-in-law as well as his stepmother, served his parents' interests rather than his own, since it denied Gilbert the heiress who might have given him an independent future. Goodrich Castle, Monmouthshire, was assigned as their residence.

Having travelled through Europe and still under age Gilbert Talbot was elected to parliament for Derbyshire with his brother-in-law in 1572. From 1573 he attended court; Shrewsbury was rarely there because he was gaoler to Mary, queen of Scots. It was from close acquaintance that Elizabeth I thought Gilbert under his wife's thumb. Finance soured relations between father and son, Gilbert living so well above his allowance of £200 that he accrued debts of £5000. He alleged this was the result of the essential costs of court life but his father put it down to extravagance. Following Francis's death in 1582, Gilbert became

Gilbert Talbot, seventh earl of Shrewsbury (1552–1616), by unknown artist

Lord Talbot and attended the House of Lords in 1589, when he was appointed steward and constable of several castles and lordships.

Talbot succeeded as earl on 18 November 1590 and was immediately added to the commissions of the peace for Nottinghamshire, Shropshire, and Yorkshire. He became KG in 1592, but did not, however, succeed to his father's lord lieutenancies or his grandfather's presidency (or even membership) of the council of the north. Furthermore, he was banned from court, first in 1594 and again in 1595, for resisting royal intervention on behalf of his distressed tenants. His one diplomatic mission, to deliver the Garter to Henri IV at Rouen in 1596, was purely honorific. Shrewsbury's career was ruined by his notorious quarrels, often ill judged and always expensive, and by his long-lasting grudges. He was constantly litigating and, despite his enormous resources, he was often pressed for cash and in debt: throughout 1603–12 he can never have owed less than £600 to his friend Sir Michael Hickes. His feuds began with his father's quarrel with his stepmother, which he sought first to keep out of and then to reconcile, thus earning his father's enmity. Once his father was dead, dissension broke out over his will, with Bess of Hardwick prevailing in 1592. Bess was reconciled with her daughter shortly before her death in 1608 but never with the earl. He quarrelled also with his brother Edward, who declined to execute the will. Shrewsbury accused Edward of trying to murder him and challenged him in 1594 to a duel, which he refused. Edward sued Dr Wood, Shrewsbury's physician and instigator of the murder story, for slander in Star Chamber in 1595 and won, but was never forgiven.

Unable to prevent Edward from succeeding to his earldom, from his deathbed Shrewsbury secured privy council injunctions against him entering property to which his title had not been proved. This effectively disinherited him. Shrewsbury quarrelled also with his sister-in-law Lady Talbot, with his youngest brother, Henry, with his Manners cousins, with his neighbours the Wortleys, with his tenants, and with the Stanhopes of Shelford, Nottinghamshire.

In Professor Stone's words, Shrewsbury was an 'old-style grandee' (Stone, 555), who kept open house, entertained, hunted and hawked, and maintained several residences. Debt was but 'a moth in your garment' (ibid., 539). He was 'a prince (alone in effect) in two counties in the heart of England' (Kershaw, 276) and asserted himself in the old bastard feudal manner, sending 400 men to destroy the Stanhope fisheries at Shelford in 1593 and 120 to arrest Sir John Holles in 1598. His feud with Sir Thomas Stanhope was a *cause célèbre*. Focusing on Stanhope's weir at Shelford, Shrewsbury fomented agitation from his tenants, who petitioned the government, and then launched them against the weir, subsequently perverting the judicial system. Though such 'a mighty man of authority and power in these parts' on whose lordship 'all the country doth rely' (MacCaffrey, 77), the issue was not decided locally. Significantly, Stanhope's two brothers, John and Michael, were at court and furthered his cause there. Shrewsbury's traditional values were not shared by the government. 'When in the country you dwell in you will needs enter into a war with your inferiors there', Shrewsbury was told in 1592, 'we think it both justice, equity and wisdom to take care that the weaker part be not put down by the mightier' (Bernard, 15). Star Chamber found against Shrewsbury's men, who were fined, but not against the earl himself, who was however denied the victory, distinction, and preferment he expected.

Shrewsbury's political career recovered subsequently. A commissioner at the trial of Robert Devereux, earl of Essex, he became a privy councillor in 1601 and was confirmed by James I, whom he entertained on his progress southwards at Worksop, Nottinghamshire. Shrewsbury's rank brought ceremonial roles as cup-bearer at Elizabeth's funeral, as chief commissioner for claims at James's coronation, and as bearer of the crown at the investiture of Henry, prince of Wales. He was appointed chief justice of the forests beyond Trent in 1603 and to the northern ecclesiastical commission in 1605. He was selected, at last, as lord lieutenant of Derbyshire in 1605 and became constable and steward of Newark and forester of Sherwood in 1607. His influence over affairs concerning him in Derbyshire, Yorkshire, and Nottinghamshire was at its greatest. Such respect did not last. Years of litigation had made Shrewsbury many enemies and his wife's open Catholicism and support for her niece Arabella Stuart, who had a claim to the English throne, as well as rumours of his involvement in several plots, left him vulnerable. This, and ill health, made his last years difficult. The countess was put in the Tower in 1611. 'The good earl is found untainted with her faults', it was reported on

28 June, 'but forebears the Council table for her sake' (GEC, *Peerage*, 11.716n.). Although sometimes allowed out of the Tower to attend on her husband, the countess was more closely confined from 1613, and Shrewsbury secured her release only in 1615, six months before his death; her refusal to swear allegiance later brought a £20,000 fine. Shrewsbury died in his house at Broad Street, London, on 8 May 1616.

The earldom was separated from some of Shrewsbury's lands, which were at first partitioned between his three daughters, all countesses, and then reunited in the Howards, dukes of Norfolk. Both his sons, George and John, predeceased him. The third of his children, Elizabeth, married Henry Grey, earl of Kent [see Grey, Elizabeth, countess of Kent]. His will sought to keep his name alive in an almshouse and through lavish gold cups commissioned for members of the royal family, his descendants, and his friends. His last wish for burial among his forebears in the Talbot vault of Sheffield parish church 'in such sorte as befitted my Rancke and callinge' was interpreted on 12 August 1616 'with the greatest pomp ever seen in the kingdom' (PRO, PROB 11/127, sig. 51). He was the last Talbot earl of Shrewsbury to reside at Sheffield Castle.   MICHAEL HICKS

Sources *DNB* · GEC, *Peerage*, new edn, vol. 11 · A. G. R. Smith, *Servant of the Cecils: the life of Sir Michael Hickes, 1543–1612* (1977) · W. T. MacCaffrey, 'Talbot and Stanhope: an episode in Elizabethan politics', *BIHR*, 33 (1960), 73–85 · G. R. Batho, 'Gilbert Talbot, seventh earl of Shrewsbury (1553-1616): the "great and glorious earl"', *Derbyshire Archaeological Journal*, 93 (1973), 23–32 · D. N. Durant, 'A London visit', *History Today*, 24 (1974), 497–503 · L. Stone, *The crisis of the aristocracy, 1558–1641* (1965) · S. E. Kershaw, 'Power and duty in the Elizabethan aristocracy: George, earl of Shrewsbury, the Glossopdale dispute and the council', *The Tudor nobility*, ed. G. W. Bernard (1992), 266–95 · G. W. Bernard, ed., *The Tudor nobility* (1992) · PRO, PROB 11/127, sig. 51
Archives Arundel Castle, corresp. · BL, Additional Charter and Rolls, Egerton Charters and Rolls · BL, Shrewsbury (Talbot) Derbys, Add. Charter 72121–74194 · BL, misc. family papers, Add. MSS 46454–46464 · Hatfield House, letters and papers · LPL, Shrewsbury and Talbot Papers · Sheff. Arch., corresp. · Sheffield City Library, Arundel Castle MSS · Staffs. RO, executorship papers, incl. papers rel. to his estates | BL, additional charters · priv. coll., corresp. with Earl of Rutland · Sheff. Arch., letters to Sir William Wentworth · letters to his stepmother, Bess of Hardwick · letters to Richard Bagot
Likenesses G. P. Harding, wash drawing, AM Oxf., Sutherland collection · oils, Hardwick Hall, Derbyshire · oils, Rufford · oils, Worksop · oils, priv. coll. [*see illus.*]
Wealth at death £12,000 p.a.: Batho, 'Gilbert Talbot', 28

Talbot, Godfrey Walker (1908–2000), journalist and broadcaster, was born on 8 October 1908 at West Leigh, Walton, near Wakefield, Yorkshire, the fifth and last child of Frank Talbot, an agent for building materials, and his wife, Kate Bertha, *née* Walker, both ardent Methodists. The family moved to Leeds when Godfrey was four. From his early years he hankered to be a reporter, and left Leeds grammar school at sixteen to start as an office boy with the *Yorkshire Post*. To his dismay he was put in the commercial office, but after two years managed to transfer to the editorial side, where he soon shone. At twenty he was made assistant editor of the paper's weekly edition. Two

years later he moved to Manchester to join the *Manchester Guardian*'s equivalent, the struggling *City News*. He was made editor in 1932, but publication ceased in 1934. Talbot was switched to the middlebrow *Daily Dispatch*, as its Lancashire county reporter. He already had some acquaintance with this beat, having the previous year on 7 October married Bessie Owen (1906/7–1998), daughter of the borough engineer of Wigan. In 1937 he left newspapers altogether to join the BBC's north region as press officer.

As war loomed in September 1939, the corporation made a quick decision to increase its news staff. Talbot was summoned to London, noting as he drove there how empty was his side of the road, how crowded the other. Traffic was pouring out of the capital in expectation of air raids. The work was editing agency copy for the news bulletins. Until then the BBC had declined to have reporters of its own, for fear of accusations of partiality. Only Richard Dimbleby had persuaded the powers above to try him out as a 'news observer'. But in wartime there would clearly be a case for war correspondents equipped and trained to broadcast directly from the fronts, not excluding the home front. Talbot delivered his first reports during the London blitz, and it was obvious that he was a natural broadcaster. In 1942, when he had just had his call-up medical, he was sent to the Middle East to replace Dimbleby, who—not altogether deservedly—had fallen foul of the new army commander, General Montgomery. Talbot quickly won Montgomery's favour and, with Frank Gillard and Dennis Johnston, followed the Eighth Army on its epic advance from El Alamein to Tripoli.

Talbot's careful but vivid reports also impressed his superiors. As the BBC's editor-in-chief, William Haley, planned the coverage of the impending invasion of northern Europe, he complained that of all the correspondents at his disposal only Dimbleby and Talbot were up to standard. In the event, Talbot remained with the Eighth Army on the Italian front. He was mentioned in dispatches and made an OBE (military).

After the war, with the need for radio to have its own news-gathering team now unquestioned, Talbot was given the task of organizing it. One of his recommendations was that, like the newspapers, it should have specialist correspondents, including one accredited to Buckingham Palace. To his surprise he was given this job himself. He became the first BBC court reporter, and perhaps the last in the mould which the BBC had in mind. He was consulted about, and might sometimes pronounce discreetly upon, such delicate topics as Princess Margaret's marital upsets or the queen's relations with the duke and duchess of Windsor, but the public scandals of later years were still a long way off. Mostly he was heard as a commentator on state occasions or as a reporter delivering his daily tidings from a royal tour of distant parts. He was still a fluent and resourceful broadcaster—during Princess Elizabeth's 1951 Canadian tour, when the royal train stopped unexpectedly at a remote station, Talbot delivered his piece directly to London from a public telephone outside the gents' lavatory—but as television swept through Britain under the impetus of the coronation, it was the television commentator on ceremonial occasions who became identified in the public mind with royalty. This was, ironically, the colleague he had replaced in Cairo on the eve of El Alamein, Richard Dimbleby. Talbot was appointed LVO in 1960.

Talbot retired in 1969. He published a number of books about the royal family, some serious, others more fitted to the coffee table, and two volumes of memoirs, *Ten Seconds from now* (1973) and *Permission to Speak* (1976). He was president of the Queen's English Society from 1982, and though he sometimes let slip his concern at the way the BBC was changing he would, on special occasions, pick up a microphone again. On the fortieth anniversary of VE-day in 1985 he obtained an off-the-cuff interview with the queen, when she told him how on the day itself she had disguised herself and mingled with the crowds.

Talbot died on 3 September 2000 at Kenley, Surrey. His wife, Bessie, and one of their two sons predeceased him.

PHILIP PURSER

Sources G. Talbot, *Ten seconds from now* (1973) · G. Talbot, *Permission to speak* (1976) · J. Dimbleby, *Richard Dimbleby* (1975) · *The Independent* (5 Sept 2000) · *The Times* (5 Sept 2000) · *Daily Telegraph* (5 Sept 2000) · *The Guardian* (5 Sept 2000)
Archives FILM BBC Film and TV Archive, Ealing | SOUND BBC Sound Archives
Likenesses photograph, 1960, repro. in *The Independent* · photograph, 1986, repro. in *The Times* · photograph, repro. in *The Guardian*
Wealth at death £390,024—gross; £382,922—net: probate, 15 Jan 2001, *CGPLA Eng. & Wales*

Talbot, Howard [*real name* Richard Lansdale Munkittrick] (1865–1928), composer and songwriter, was born on 9 March 1865 in New York, USA, the son of an Irishman, Alexander Munkittrick, and his wife, Lillie. In 1869 the family returned to Britain, where their son later studied first medicine at King's College, London, and then music at the Royal College of Music. He married on 21 March 1895 the actress Amy Clare Betts (Ada Bellamy; 1871?–1895), who died eight months after their wedding, and later Dorothy Maud, the daughter of Arthur H. Cross of Sandringham, Norfolk. They had four daughters.

From early on he aimed at a career in the musical theatre, and his first stage pieces were produced by amateurs at Hunstanton, Oxford, and King's Lynn; he always used the pseudonym of Howard Talbot for his musical output. His first professionally staged piece, the comic opera *Wapping Old Stairs* (1894), had only a brief run, and although his next work, *Monte Carlo* (1896), did better, Talbot found his earliest niche in the theatre in the 1890s as a conductor, leading the orchestra for a number of shows in London and the provinces, where his 'cheery, goodnatured' character made him the 'most genial and easy of conductors' (*The Era*, 19 April 1902).

In 1899, however, Talbot provided the score for a little provincial musical comedy written by the popular librettist George Dance, and his fortunes turned. *A Chinese Honeymoon* soon proved itself a long-touring success, and when it was ultimately given a London run it turned into a record-breaker, becoming the first musical play anywhere

to run for more than 1000 consecutive metropolitan performances.

Over the following decade Talbot—while continuing to work as a theatre conductor—turned out a steady stream of musical comedy scores, and shows such as *The Blue Moon* (1904), *The White Chrysanthemum* (1905), *The Girl behind the Counter* (1906), and *The Belle of Brittany* (1908), for which he composed all or much of the music, were played with considerable success all around the English-speaking world. Then, in 1909, he topped all but his first huge hit when he combined with Lionel Monckton to write the score for Robert Courtneidge's production of the fantastical musical comedy *The Arcadians*. With *The Arcadians*, Talbot had his name at the billhead of the most successful musical comedy of the Edwardian era—just as he had a decade earlier with the most successful of the Victorian age.

In the years that followed Talbot continued to turn out light, tuneful songs and well-made but unpretentious concerted music for a whole series of musical shows. These included *The Mousmé* (1911) with its charming high soprano solos, moulded to the voice of the *Arcadians* star Florence Smithson, Courtneidge's up-to-date *The Pearl Girl* (1913), the interesting light opera *My Lady Frayle* (1915), which was full of good things but was dogged by bad luck, and the clever modern musical comedy *Mr Manhattan* (1916), written around the American musical-comedy star Raymond Hitchcock. Talbot also scored several short musical comedies for the music-hall stage.

At this point in time, many of the most important musical-theatre composers of the previous two decades were disappearing from the scene, unable or unwilling to adapt to the newly popular styles and rhythms in theatre music which had crossed the Atlantic in the years before the war. Talbot, whose educated but attractive and catchy writing was in no way bred to ragtime and the other rhythms of the American dance repertory, held his own, however, and at the height of the craze for what would become known as jazz he put his name to a third major hit. Teamed again with the equally 'old-fashioned' Monckton, he provided the score in 1917 for the musical comedy *The Boy*, a piece based on Sir Arthur Wing Pinero's play *The Magistrate*. With the comedian Bill Berry as star, *The Boy* took its place alongside *Chu Chin Chow* and *The Maid of the Mountains* as one of the trio of great hits of the British wartime years, before going on to further success on Broadway (as *Good Morning, Judge*) and the touring and colonial circuits. Talbot—paired this time with the young Ivor Novello—provided Berry with a second decided Pinero-based hit in *Who's Hooper* (1918), but a third attempt at adapting Pinero, *My Nieces* (1921), was a failure. It was also its writer's last West End score.

Talbot subsequently retired and, although he continued to compose, his last works were, like his first, for amateur companies. He died on 12 September 1928 at Reigate, Surrey, survived by his widow, Dorothy.

KURT GÄNZL

Sources K. Gänzl, *The encyclopedia of the musical theatre*, 2 vols. (1994) · K. Gänzl, *The British musical theatre*, 2 vols. (1986) · *The Era* (19

April 1902) • J. Parker, ed., *Who's who in the theatre*, 6th edn (1930) • *CGPLA Eng. & Wales* (1929) • will • *WWW*

Wealth at death £374 10s. 0d.: probate, 12 June 1929, *CGPLA Eng. & Wales*

Talbot, James, fourth Baron Talbot of Malahide in the peerage of Ireland, and first Baron Talbot de Malahide in the peerage of the United Kingdom (1805–1883), politician and archaeologist, was born at Tiverton, Devon, on 22 November 1805, the son of James Talbot, third Baron Talbot of Malahide in the Irish peerage (1767?–1850), and Anne Sarah (*d.* 1857), second daughter and coheir of Samuel Rodbard of Evercreech House, Somerset. His grandmother Margaret (*d.* 1834) was created *suo jure* Baroness Talbot of Malahide in 1831.

Talbot went to school in Hertford and entered Trinity College, Cambridge, in 1823. He was elected a scholar in 1826 and was tenth in the first class in the classical tripos in 1827. He graduated BA in 1827 and MA in 1830. After an extended tour in southern and eastern Europe, he settled in Ireland, where his family influence lay. He sat as a whig MP for Athlone from December 1832 until his defeat at the election in January 1835. On 9 August 1842 he married Maria Margaretta (*d.* 1873), youngest daughter and coheir (she owned 2645 acres of land in Scotland) of Patrick Murray, of Simprim, Forfarshire. They had seven children.

Talbot succeeded to the Irish peerage on his father's death in 1850, and on 19 November 1856, through the influence of Lord Palmerston, he was created a peer of the United Kingdom; he held the post of lord-in-waiting from 1863 to 1866. In the House of Lords he generally spoke on measures of social reform, such as the acts to prevent the adulteration of food (1855–60). In 1858 his archaeological interests led him to introduce a bill respecting treasure trove (based on a similar measure in force in Denmark). According to the provisions of this, any archaeological remains of substantial value discovered by an individual would be deposited before a justice of the peace and then valued so that they could be purchased, if desired, by the state for the national collections and the finder rewarded to their full value. But owing to the difficulties raised by the Treasury the bill was read only a first time on 5 July 1858.

Talbot was an active member of the Royal Archaeological Institute from 1845, and he filled the office of president with energy from 1851 to 1863 and from 1867 until his death. His special interest lay in Roman and Irish antiquities. He formed a collection of Irish gold ornaments and enamels, some specimens of which he presented to the Fitzwilliam Museum at Cambridge. Among his later memoirs were one on the circular temple of Baalbek, and another on the antiquities, and especially the epigraphy, of Algeria (1882). He gave help and encouragement to John O'Donovan in his Celtic studies, and he collected extensive materials for a monograph on the Talbots. His own estate and castle of Malahide, co. Dublin, had been in the family's hands since the Irish conquest; he owned 3573 acres in co. Dublin, co. Cavan, and co. Westmeath. His reputation as an archaeologist procured his election as FRS (18 February 1858) and FSA (19 January 1854). He was

also president of the Royal Irish Academy, from 1866 to 1869, and of the Anthropological Society, and a member of numerous other learned bodies. He died at Funchal, Madeira, on 13 April 1883.

THOMAS SECCOMBE, rev. RICHARD SMAIL

Sources *The Times* (17 April 1883) • Venn, *Alum. Cant.*, 2/6 • *N&Q*, 6th ser., 7 (1883), 320 • *Men of the time* (1868) • *GM*, 3rd ser., 2 (1857), 54 • GEC, *Peerage* • J. Bateman, *The great landowners of Great Britain and Ireland*, 4th edn (1883) • d. cert.
Archives Bodl. Oxf., corresp., journals, and papers
Likenesses G. Hayter, group portrait, oils (*The House of Commons, 1833*), NPG • Lock & Whitfield, woodburytype photograph, NPG; repro. in T. Cooper and others, *Men of mark: a gallery of contemporary portraits* (1876) • F. Sargent, pencil drawing, NPG
Wealth at death £23,354: probate, 10 July 1883, *CGPLA Eng. & Wales*

Talbot, James Robert (1726–1790), vicar apostolic of the London district, was born at Shrewsbury House, Isleworth, Middlesex, on 28 June 1726, the fourth son in a family of six sons and three daughters of the Hon. George Talbot (*d.* 1733) and Mary (*d.* 1752), daughter of Thomas, fourth Viscount FitzWilliam of Merrion. The younger brother of George, fourteenth earl of Shrewsbury, he was educated at Twyford School in Hampshire, a famous Catholic establishment run by the secular clergy, before being sent abroad in 1738 to the English College, Douai.

Ordained at Cambrai on 19 December 1750, Talbot joined the Douai teaching staff as professor of philosophy and later of theology. From his private income, he established a preparatory school at nearby Esquerchin and became its first president. In 1759 Richard Challoner, vicar apostolic of the London district, was taken seriously ill and requested Talbot as coadjutor, hoping that his aristocratic connections would make him an effective intermediary with the government and provide funds for impoverished Catholics. Talbot was consecrated by Challoner on 24 August 1759 as titular bishop of Birtha.

Challoner recovered, but thereafter stayed put, writing devotional and controversial works and ministering to his flock in London. Meanwhile, Talbot carried out episcopal visitations and confirmations throughout the district, covering all parishes every year and earning a reputation for eloquence as a preacher. He was very close to his younger brother, Thomas Joseph Talbot (1727–1795), who in 1766 was appointed coadjutor bishop in the midland district. While being conscientious and devout pastors, both brothers were diffident and fearful of the limelight.

Talbot's proneness to self-effacement was intensified when he became a target of informers, scheming to exploit for gain the widely disregarded penal laws against Catholics. In 1768 Talbot was indicted for the offence of saying mass as a priest, only to be acquitted on a technicality. This did not deter Talbot from founding a Catholic school and mission at Old Hall Green, Hertfordshire, in October 1769. Then in February 1771 he was brought to trial at the Old Bailey alongside John Fuller. The lord chief justice, William Murray, later first earl of Mansfield, threw out the case as no evidence was offered about ordination. Talbot and Fuller were the last Catholic priests in England to be tried for the offence; in 1775, after informers had reported his presence at St Edmund's College, Ware, officials unsuccessfully searched the lofts for him.

The task of lobbying the government to ease civil disabilities against Catholics was undertaken not by Talbot but, from 1778 onwards, by the Catholic Committee. The committee's efforts secured the passing that year of a limited Catholic Relief Act, depriving informers of their rewards; that led to the No Popery riots of 1780, instigated by Lord George Gordon. The aged Challoner died shortly afterwards, in 1781, and Talbot succeeded him as vicar apostolic; an inborn lack of decisiveness dogged him for the rest of his life.

Talbot corresponded regularly with the president of Douai, William Gibson, over whose regime he had jurisdiction. He took exception successively to the college's curriculum, discipline, and financial extravagance, but he lacked the strength of will to dismiss Gibson. Likewise, he omitted to control the Catholic Committee, which strove to disclaim certain religious tenets which protestants found objectionable and proposed an oath of allegiance to the crown. Unsettled by these moves, which in his view usurped the bishops' functions, in 1787 Talbot joined the committee in the fruitless hope of reining it in. He thought about having a coadjutor appointed, but failed to apply formally to Rome. He moved from London to reside quietly in a convent at Hammersmith; his mind began to fail, and he lost so many teeth that he could scarcely be understood.

Talbot died on 26 January 1790 at the convent, declaring on his deathbed that if he were to recover he would take stern measures against the committee. He was buried at St Paul's, Hammersmith (his remains were reinterred at St Edmund's College, Ware, in 1900). For his piety and his generosity to any number of charities from his inherited wealth he earned the name of the Good Bishop Talbot. His appearance is unknown, as he was too modest to sit for his portrait.
T. A. B. CORLEY

Sources B. Ward, The dawn of the Catholic revival in England, 1781–1803, 2 vols. (1909) • E. H. Burton, The life and times of Bishop Challoner, 1691–1781, 2 vols. (1909) • G. Anstruther, The seminary priests, 4 (1977), 268–9 • E. Duffy, 'Ecclesiastical democracy detected [pt 1]', Recusant History, 10 (1969–70), 193–209 • E. Duffy, 'Ecclesiastical democracy detected [pt 2]', Recusant History, 10 (1969–70), 309–31 • D. Milburn, 'William Gibson, president of Douai', Ushaw Magazine, 66 (1956), 69–79, 134–47; 67 (1957), 11–24 • E. Duffy, ed., Challoner and his church: a Catholic bishop in Georgian England (1981) • P. Hughes, The Catholic question, 1688–1829 (1929) • B. Ward, History of St Edmund's College, Old Hall (1893) • B. Ward, Catholic London a century ago (1905) • B. Plumb, Arundel to Zabi: a biographical dictionary of the Catholic bishops of England and Wales (deceased), 1623–1987 (privately printed, Warrington, [1987]) • C. G. Herbermann and others, eds., The Catholic encyclopedia, 17 vols. (1907–18), vol. 14 • New Catholic encyclopedia, 18 vols. (1967–89) • F. Blom and others, English Catholic books, 1701–1800: a bibliography (1996) • W. M. Brady, Annals of the Catholic hierarchy in England and Scotland, 3 (1877); repr. as The episcopal succession in England, Scotland and Ireland (1883)

Archives Birmingham Roman Catholic archdiocesan archives, Cathedral House, Birmingham, papers • Ushaw College, Durham • Westm. DA, corresp. and papers • Westm. DA, student notes

Wealth at death see will, PRO, PROB 11/1189/106

Talbot, John, first earl of Shrewsbury and first earl of Waterford (*c*.1387–1453), soldier, was the second son of Richard Talbot, fourth Baron Talbot, of Goodrich, Herefordshire, and of Ankaret, sole heir of Richard, Baron Lestrange of Blakemere, near Whitchurch, Shropshire. His father died in 1397, when he was about ten years old. Four years later his mother married Thomas Neville, Baron Furnival, a younger brother of Ralph *Neville, first earl of Westmorland, as part of a double contract which involved Talbot's own marriage to Furnival's sole daughter, Maud (*c*.1392–1422), heir to his estates and title. The alliance was propitious, for it brought together two families that had long been prominent in the service of the house of Lancaster, and linked Talbot with a man high in Henry IV's favour. Thomas Neville died in 1407; Talbot seems immediately to have entered his inheritance, based on the lordship of Sheffield, and to have been summoned as Lord Furnival to the next parliament, called in 1409.

Early career, 1404–1427 By the time his father-in-law died Talbot was already embarked on the military career that would occupy his life. It is possible that, despite his youth, he fought alongside Furnival at the battle of Shrewsbury, on 21 July 1403. He was soon fighting in the Welsh wars. His first command, in December 1404, was of the English garrisons at Montgomery and Bishop's Castle. More or less continuously in action thereafter, he participated in the sieges of Aberystwyth in 1407 and 1408, and Harlech in 1409, being appointed captain of Caernarfon that same year. Five years of military inactivity following the pacification of Wales were brought to an end by his appointment as lieutenant of Ireland in February 1414. His family had long-standing links with the lordship, kinsmen in the Talbots of Malahide, and a claim to the lordship of Wexford which he was subsequently to make good. He immediately proved himself a vigorous and belligerent viceroy, succeeding through a series of devastating raids into the lands of the Gaelic chieftains in improving the security of the English lordship. One Gaelic annalist remembered that 'from the time of Herod there came not anyone more wicked' (Curtis, 292); a view that the Welsh might have endorsed, and certainly the French soon would. But his longest-lasting legacy to the colony was the internal disarray into which it was plunged through his feud with the leading Anglo-Irish family, the Butlers, and its head the earl of Ormond. When he was recalled by Henry V in 1419 he left his brother Richard *Talbot, who had been provided archbishop of Dublin in 1417, to maintain the family cause.

Talbot's violent and quarrelsome reputation was already well established before he went to Ireland. Indeed it was a feud with the earl of Arundel, which seriously disrupted the peace of Shropshire in 1413, and led to a spell in the Tower of London, that had prompted Henry V to appoint him lieutenant in the first place. Later Talbot was to be at the centre of disturbances in Herefordshire in 1422–3, involved again in upheaval in Shropshire, entangled in a parliamentary precedence dispute with Lord Grey of Ruthin, and in 1425–7 implicated in Warwickshire in a feud with Joan, Lady Bergavenny, the earl of Ormond's mother-in-law, during which Talbot's brother William was killed. Given this record of disturbing the peace, it is not surprising that Henry V and subsequently the minority council of Henry VI directed Talbot's attention away from his fellow subjects against the king's enemies.

Talbot was first summoned to France by Henry V in 1419, although he was not mustered there until 1420. He took part in the siege of Melun (July–November) and then returned to England with the king. Having participated in the coronation of Queen Catherine he accompanied Henry V on his royal progress, before sailing once more to France and serving at the siege of Meaux which was to cost the king his life. He returned yet again to England before the town fell to deal with personal matters. He had inherited the barony of Talbot from his child niece in February 1421, and his own wife had died on 31 May 1422. In 1424 he was back in Ireland as the second in command to Edmund (V) Mortimer, earl of March. But the earl died in January 1425 and Talbot returned to England in May. He had already married, c.1424, Margaret Beauchamp [see below], eldest daughter of Richard *Beauchamp, earl of Warwick (1382–1439), and Elizabeth *Berkeley (c.1386–1422). In 1427 the duke of Bedford retained him to serve in France once more. He was already forty years old, and about to find his true vocation.

The war in France, 1427–1445 Talbot made his name as an independent commander in France in the recovery of Maine (1427–8), in which he showed the hallmarks of his generalship that were win him fame over the next twenty-five years: decisiveness and ruthlessness. He was the master of the punitive raid, the surprise assault, and, above all, the use of terror for military ends. He joined the earl of Salisbury on the march to the Loire in the summer of 1428, but was apparently not present in the force besieging Orléans when the earl was killed in October. He did, however, move up as joint commander of a second army in November and pressed the siege throughout the winter. He, and his fellow commanders, were unable to prevent the city's relief by Jeanne d'Arc and withdrew in May. The English army divided, and it was in command of one of its divisions that Talbot was surprised and overwhelmed at Patay on 18 June 1429. For the next four years he was a prisoner, and it was only after his father-in-law, the earl of Warwick, took Talbot's own captor prisoner that his release could be arranged. He was exchanged in July 1433.

Talbot returned at once to the wars, campaigning in eastern Normandy with the duke of Burgundy in 1433. In 1434, having returned to England to settle his affairs, he was made lieutenant-general for the conduct of the war on the eastern front, with special responsibility for the defence of Paris, now threatened on three sides. For eighteen months he operated out of Paris, clearing the lower Oise valley of French garrisons. In the summer of 1435 he was once more back in England, raising reinforcements. In that time St Denis had fallen; his immediate target therefore in the late summer was its recovery. But before St Denis was safely back in English hands Burgundy had made peace with France at Arras, and the duke of Bedford had died. In the autumn Talbot withdrew to Rouen, effectively abandoning Paris to its fate. His presence in Normandy was needed, for in the winter a popular rising in

the Pays de Caux, north of Rouen, rapidly reinforced by French troops, led to the loss of most of upper Normandy. But when Rouen itself was threatened, Talbot counterattacked, routing the French at Ry, 10 miles east of the city, and securing Caudebec downstream. While he could do nothing to save Paris in April 1436, a surprise attack on Gisors took further pressure off Normandy. In June the garrison was finally relieved by the duke of York with reinforcements from England. Talbot had saved Rouen.

For the next seven years Talbot saw almost unbroken action, summer and winter, in defending the frontiers of Normandy. His promotion to marshal of France in May 1436 made him the senior field commander, but as lieutenant-general of the land between the Seine, the Oise, and the sea he retained his particular responsibility for the eastern front. His daring recapture of Pontoise by surprise in February 1437, when his troops crossed the ice at dawn on Ash Wednesday before the garrison had recovered from the celebration of Mardi Gras, secured the Seine valley and opened up a possible threat to Paris. His main objectives were to prevent the remaining outlying posts of the conquest (Creil, Montargis, Meaux, and Le Crotoy) falling into enemy hands (despite frequent revictualling he could save neither Montargis nor Meaux); and to recover the principal towns downstream of Rouen that had fallen early in 1436, a task completed with the recovery of Harfleur in 1440. The drudgery of these sieges was relieved from time to time until 1439 by raids into the relatively untouched lands of the duke of Burgundy beyond the Somme. Nevertheless, the boundaries of Lancastrian Normandy were slowly pushed back; Dieppe was never recovered; and the French were able to establish a new salient south of the Seine. The last Herculean effort was the attempt to save Pontoise in the summer of 1441, during which Talbot narrowly failed to take Charles VII prisoner. In England in 1442 for the first time since 1435 to raise reinforcements, Talbot was created earl of Shrewsbury. But by now the war effort was petering out. A mutiny forced him to abandon a siege of Dieppe in 1443. In 1444 he welcomed the truce of Tours. To Shrewsbury, with his fellow generals, lords Fauconberg and Scales, should go much of the credit for preserving Normandy in Lancastrian hands after 1435.

The last years, 1445–1453 In March 1445 Talbot returned to England in the entourage of the new queen, Margaret of Anjou, and in the following June participated in the negotiations for peace at Westminster. He had already been reappointed lieutenant of Ireland. Leaving the government in the hands of his brother the archbishop of Dublin he delayed his journey to Ireland for over a year, arriving in the autumn of 1446. He stayed for barely a year, and apart from one campaign in the marches did little. By now his quarrel with the Butlers had been patched up. At the end of the year he was replaced by Richard, duke of York, and could return to Normandy with its new governor, his brother-in-law Edmund *Beaufort, now duke of Somerset, in 1448.

In the past three years the English administration and

military organization in Normandy had begun to disintegrate. Shrewsbury, who was given virtual independent command of Lower Normandy, attempted to restore discipline, but the garrison was not ready for a renewal of war. Nevertheless, Shrewsbury was fully involved in the attack on Brittany which precipitated an all-out French onslaught in the summer of 1449. Even Talbot seems to have been helpless in the face of overwhelming odds. Having avoided pitched battle he withdrew to Rouen, where he gave himself up as a hostage for the fulfilment of the terms of surrender. Treated honourably, he was not released until July 1450 when the whole of Normandy had been lost. Before returning home he went on pilgrimage to Rome.

The England to which Shrewsbury returned at the end of 1450 was in turmoil. He was immediately co-opted onto judicial commissions which toured Kent punishing rebels. Once released from this he took up his countess's cause against the Berkeleys. He was careful, however, not to become involved in the quarrel between York and Somerset. From York he received substantial annuities; with Somerset he was bound by family ties. At Dartford in 1452 he stood firmly beside the king—his presence perhaps a decisive deterrent to York. On the other hand he was acceptable to York as a mediator. He was no doubt relieved in the summer of 1452 to be preparing to go to war again. It is likely that the initial plan was for a raid on Normandy, but in September, in response to communication from Gascon dissidents, Shrewsbury set sail for Bordeaux as the king's lieutenant of Guyenne. With the help of collaborators, the city was easily taken and much of the Bordelais rose in the English cause. The real test was to defend in 1453 what had been recovered in 1452. The decisive engagement took place at Castillon on 17 July. The town, besieged by the French, appealed for help. Shrewsbury dashed to the rescue and threw his troops against a strongly fortified artillery park into which the besiegers had retreated. Underestimating the strength and preparedness of the defence, the assault faltered and fell back. The Anglo-Gascon army was cut down by artillery fire at close range. The veteran commander was himself killed endeavouring to rally his troops. His trampled and disfigured body was found and identified by his herald on the following day.

The 'Terror of the French' Talbot died heroically. The manner of his death, leading a charge against artillery, has come to symbolize the passing of the age of chivalrous warfare. He himself—'the Terror of the French', 'the English Achilles'—was long remembered in France and England as the last of the old chivalric breed, and was celebrated as such in Shakespeare's 'Talbot' play, 2 *Henry VI*. It is a reputation he deserved, both for his loyal service to the failing Lancastrian cause and for his prowess on the field of battle. He was not a 'great' general, but he was a soldier's soldier, whose finest hour was the saving of Normandy in 1436. He himself took the chivalric tradition seriously, as the collection of romances and treatises that he brought together and subsequently presented to Margaret of Anjou in 1445 reveals. A knight of the Garter since

1424, he accused Sir John Fastolf of dishonouring the order by his flight from the field of Patay. He donated ornaments decorated with the Garter to the altar of the church of the Sepulchre in Rouen, for use on St George's day. Shrewsbury was conventionally religious. Two small books of hours made for him and his countess have survived as Cambridge, Fitzwilliam Museum, MS 40–1950, and NL Scot., Blairs College, MS 1. He and his countess had licence for mass to be performed from a portable altar, at which perhaps the books of hours were designed to be used. The instruction in his will that a collegiate chapel dedicated to Our Lady and St George be established in the parish church at Whitchurch was not followed. He was a hard, ruthless, violent man, no doubt in need of as many prayers for his soul as could be mustered after his death as soldiers who had been mustered in his service during his life.

Shrewsbury spent relatively few of his sixty-six years in England. His closest attachment was to his native Shropshire, the county from which he took his title, and where his principal estates lay. With lands to the value of over £1500 per annum he was well able to support the dignity of an earl. He also traded on a significant scale, owning at least five ships at the time of his death. In 1446 he assumed the title of earl of Waterford; and, as his will indicates, he also believed that after the death of Anne Beauchamp in 1449 he had a right, through his countess, to the earldom of Warwick. During 1450–52 they contested, with some success, the settlement of the entire Beauchamp inheritance on Richard Neville. He was also generously rewarded in titles, lands, and offices in France, not all of which would have yielded an income in the later stages of the war. Nevertheless, it was calculated in 1447 that the marshalcy of France rendered over £800 per annum in wages and fees. Despite the heavy burden of his ransom, he was probably able to make a small net profit from the war which was invested in purchases of property mainly in Shropshire.

Family matters With his first wife, Maud Neville, Talbot had four children: John *Talbot, who succeeded him as earl; Thomas, who died young; Christopher, a renowned jouster, who was killed in suspicious circumstances in 1443; and Joan, who after her father's death married James, first Baron Berkeley. With his second wife, Margaret Beauchamp, he had five children: John, Viscount Lisle, who died beside him at Castillon, Humphrey, Lewis, Eleanor, and Elizabeth. Lady Eleanor [**Lady Eleanor Boteler** (d. 1468)], the elder of the two daughters, has attained a certain posthumous fame as the alleged object of the affections of Edward IV, whose supposed betrothal to her, as Lady Eleanor Boteler, was used in 1483 as justification for the illegitimization of his two sons and the usurpation of Richard III. Her date of birth is unknown, but she was married in 1450 to Sir Thomas Boteler, a son of Ralph *Boteler, first Baron Sudeley. Boteler died in 1461, and it may be that Eleanor's claims for dower brought her to the attention of the young king, a notorious womanizer and a bachelor at that time. But it is equally possible that the allegation derived from knowledge of discussions between Shrewsbury and York concerning a family alliance. In any case, the tendentious nature of the evidence makes it impossible to regard either the fact or the nature of the liaison as established. Eleanor died in 1468, and was buried in the Carmelite priory at Norwich.

Margaret Talbot [*née* Beauchamp], countess of Shrewsbury (1404–1467), was a formidable woman—well matched to her husband. John Rous later recalled that all who swore in her house, including her own children, she put on a diet of bread and water. Her life was dominated by her ambition to carve out a substantial inheritance for her eldest son. This involved both the partition of the Talbot inheritance and the seizing of the lordship of Berkeley to add to her own Lisle inheritance. The partition of the Talbot inheritance began in 1434, shortly after Talbot's release from captivity. It would seem that it was the price paid for Warwick's support. Eventually all the Shropshire estates and the manor of Painswick in Gloucestershire were earmarked for John the younger. But after the deaths of her husband and son at Castillon the countess was unable to enforce the partition, and had to be content with her dower alone. Her hopes were revived following the death of the second earl of Shrewsbury at Northampton in 1460. With the support of the new regime she occupied Blakemere and Painswick. However, she was forced to compromise in 1466, when she surrendered Blakemere to the third earl, who in exchange released all his claims to Painswick. In the event only Painswick passed into the Lisle inheritance.

The dispute over the Berkeley inheritance, between James, Lord Berkeley, and the three daughters of Elizabeth Berkeley and Richard Beauchamp, of whom Margaret was the eldest, was decidedly more violent. A division had been agreed upon in 1426, but James Berkeley reopened the issue when Warwick died in 1439. Further arbitration in 1448 failed to settle the dispute, which erupted into all-out war in 1450. In 1451 the Talbots seized Berkeley Castle, imprisoned Lord Berkeley in it, and forced him to accept the proposed settlement of 1448. In 1452 Margaret went a stage further and claimed the whole inheritance, but the deaths of Shrewsbury and Lisle at Castillon took the wind from her sails; by stages she abandoned her claims, an agreement with James Berkeley finally being reached in 1463, four years before her death. The death of her grandson Thomas *Talbot, Lord Lisle, in combat with the Berkeleys at Nibley Green in March 1470, signalled the final extinction of Margaret Talbot's ambitions.

It has been argued that the Devonshire tapestries, now in the Victoria and Albert Museum, were commissioned by John and Margaret Talbot, and contain contemporary portraits of them. Less controversial are the portraits of John Talbot, in profile, in the Shrewsbury book (BL, Royal MS 15 E.vi). He and his countess are also portrayed at prayer in their books of hours. A sixteenth-century portrait, or copy of an earlier portrait, of the earl hangs in the College of Arms; it supposedly hung above the memorial to the countess in Old St Paul's and was rescued from the fire in 1666.

John Talbot was first buried on the field of battle at Castillon. Forty years later his body was brought back to England by his grandson, Sir Gilbert, and interred, according to the terms of his will, in St Alkmund's, Whitchurch. Such was the respect with which he was regarded by his enemies that a chapel was built on the site of his death, dedicated to Our Lady. This was destroyed during the revolution, but a memorial still stands there. His tomb was opened in the late nineteenth century and his skull was found to have been fractured, thus seeming to endorse one early account of his death. A. J. POLLARD

Sources exchequer, king's remembrancer, accounts various, PRO, E 101 · eyre rolls, PRO, JUST 1 · court of king's bench plea rolls, PRO, KB27 · Trésor des Chartes, Archives Nationales, Paris · Manuscrits français, Bibliothèque Nationale, Paris, 25766–25778, 26044–26081 · Shrewsbury Book, BL, Royal MS 15 E.vi · Register Stafford and Kemp, LPL [Talbot's will: a transcript has been published with inaccuracies by G. H. F. Vane in *Trans. Shrop. Arch. Soc.*, 3rd ser., 4 (1904)] · *Chancery records* · C. L. Kingsford, ed., *Chronicles of London* (1905) · *La chronique d'Enguerran de Monstrelet*, ed. L. Douët-d'Arcq, 6 vols. (Paris, 1857–62), vols. 3–6 · *Chronique de Mathieu d'Escouchy*, ed. G. Du Fresne de Beaucourt, new edn, 3 vols. (Paris, 1863–4) · J. Stevenson, ed., *Letters and papers illustrative of the wars of the English in France during the reign of Henry VI, king of England*, 2 vols. in 3 pts, Rolls Series, 22 (1861–4) · A. J. Pollard, 'The family of Talbot, Lords Talbot and earls of Shrewsbury in the fifteenth century', PhD diss., University of Bristol, 1968 · A. J. Pollard, *John Talbot and the war in France, 1427–1453*, Royal Historical Society Studies in History, 35 (1983) · C. T. Allmand, *Lancastrian Normandy, 1415–1450* (1983) · M. G. A. Vale, *English Gascony, 1399–1453: a study of war, government and politics during the later stages of the Hundred Years' War* (1970) · R. A. Griffiths, *The reign of King Henry VI: the exercise of royal authority, 1422–1461* (1981) · E. Powell, *Kingship, law, and society: criminal justice in the reign of Henry V* (1989) · C. Reynolds, 'The Shrewsbury Book', *Medieval art, architecture and archaeology at Rouen*, ed. J. Stratford, British Archaeological Association, conference transactions, 12 (1993) · A. Claxton, 'The sign of the dog: an examination of the Devonshire hunting tapestries', *Journal of Medieval History*, 14 (1988), 127–79 · E. Curtis, *A history of medieval Ireland from 1086 to 1513*, 2nd edn (1938) · J. Weever, *Ancient funerall monuments* (1631)
Likenesses double portrait, 1500–99 (first earl and countess of Shrewsbury?; after portraits), Castle Ashby, Northamptonshire · G. Scharf ?, pencil drawing, NPG · Devonshire tapestries?, V&A · manuscript illustrations, repro. in BL, Royal MS 15 E.vi, fol. 1, 405 · oils, Compton Wyngates, Warwickshire · portrait, repro. in A. Thevet, *Les vrais pourtraits et vies des hommes illustres* (Paris, 1584) · portrait, Coll. Arms · portraits, Book of Hours?, FM Cam. · tomb effigy, St Alkmund's Church, Whitchurch, Shropshire
Wealth at death approx. £1500: Pollard, 'The family of Talbot', 314–35

Talbot, John, second earl of Shrewsbury and second earl of Waterford (*c.*1413–1460), magnate, was the eldest son and heir of John *Talbot, first earl of Shrewsbury (*c.*1387–1453), and his first wife, Maud Neville (*c.*1392–1422), sole daughter and heir of Thomas Neville, Lord Furnival. Little is known of the first forty years of his life. When only three he was contracted in marriage to Katherine, granddaughter and heir of Hugh, Lord Burnell, a match that in the event was not made. Talbot was knighted in 1426, in the general knighting of the young nobility of that year. Once he had reached adulthood, his father in 1435/6 granted Worksop and other properties from his mother's inheritance to him for his support. In the following years he also resided at Sheffield in Yorkshire, and it was there that he made his first will in 1446. Some time before March 1445 he married Elizabeth, daughter of James *Butler, fourth earl of Ormond, possibly as part of an attempted reconciliation between the two families who had been bitter enemies in Ireland for nearly twenty years.

Talbot's first major employment was as chancellor of Ireland, having been appointed by his father in March 1445. He went there with the latter in the autumn of 1446, possibly returning to England in the summer of 1447. In April 1448 he was replaced by Thomas Fitzgerald, earl of Kildare, on the nomination of the new lieutenant, Richard of York. But he successfully petitioned for restoration in the parliament of February 1449, for by November 1451, at the latest, his office was being exercised for him by deputy.

Relationships between the younger John Talbot and his father were strained. In 1424 John the elder had married as his second wife, Margaret, the eldest daughter and at that time joint heir of Richard Beauchamp, earl of Warwick. Ten years later, and shortly after being released from a spell of four years of captivity in France, Lord Talbot began the process of partitioning his estates between his two families. The Furnival inheritance, from his mother, was reserved for John himself; some of the Talbot and Lestrange inheritance was earmarked for Shrewsbury's eldest son from his marriage to Margaret. In 1434 the lordship of Blakemere in north Shropshire was conveyed to the junior line; in 1442 Painswick. By 1452, when Talbot senior drew up his will, he had granted further estates in Shropshire to the sons of his second marriage. Financially John stood to lose £500 by these measures; he would also be left with but one property, and that Tasley, which he had received in compensation for the broken Burnell marriage, in the county in which he was to inherit his title. Understandably he was not prepared to accept his partial disinheritance. He had already made his position clear, for in his will Shrewsbury enjoined his son 'in eschewing of my curse and as he will have my blessing' (LPL, Reg. Stafford, fols. 311–12), not to attempt to reverse his settlement, instructing his feoffees to sell any lands in their trust if he did.

In the event, circumstances in 1453 greatly assisted the second earl. First, his rival half-brother, John Talbot, Viscount Lisle, was killed alongside their father at Castillon; second, the one man who might have supported his stepmother, her brother-in-law Edmund Beaufort, duke of Somerset, fell from power not long afterwards. While the countess of Shrewsbury, at that time triumphant in her war with the Berkeleys in Gloucestershire, initially took control of Painswick, the new earl had no trouble in overturning his father's settlement in Shropshire. He was in possession of Blakemere by 20 September 1453; and on 10 November secured an order for the Shropshire escheator to give him full seisin of all the Shropshire estates. Moreover, early in 1454 he was able to oust the dowager countess from Painswick.

The threat to his inheritance goes some way towards explaining Shrewsbury's political alignment in 1453–4.

He was not a close associate of the duke of York. Indeed, in 1450 York had accused him of having 'layn in wayte to herkeyn upon me' (Griffiths, King and Country, 299), at Holt before he crossed to Ireland in June 1449, and in 1452 he was one of those at Shrewsbury indicting traitors, who may have been followers of York earlier that year at Dartford. Shrewsbury's antipathy to York undoubtedly had its roots in Irish politics, where he had clashed with the duke over the office of chancellor; itself probably linked with the quarrel between his brother-in-law James Butler, earl of Wiltshire, and the earl of Kildare. Wiltshire too quarrelled with York, whose retainer he had once been, and in May 1453 briefly replaced him as lieutenant of Ireland.

By the autumn of 1453, therefore, there was good reason for Shrewsbury to be wary of York, even though he was hardly likely to support Somerset. Yet he was also an ally of Ralph, Lord Cromwell, who had been nominated the sole supervisor of Shrewsbury's will in 1446, and who, like Wiltshire, was one of Shrewsbury's feoffees both before and after 1453. As an ally of Cromwell, he would be drawn towards the earl of Salisbury and against the duke of Exeter. And, because of the dispute over his own inheritance, he might well have felt some sympathy with the earl of Warwick, at odds with Somerset over the Despenser inheritance. Thus in the complex interplay of individual fears and hopes, rivalries and alliances that shaped factions during the early months of the king's incapacity, Shrewsbury at that time found himself, despite earlier antipathy, not without sympathy for York. The immediate benefit was that he was able to enter his full inheritance without serious opposition.

Shrewsbury was a frequent attender at council during the winter of 1453–4, supporting the establishment of the protectorate. He was one of the commissioners of oyer and terminer to sit in York to hear the indictment of the Percys in June 1454, and was appointed to keep the seas. In contrast he appears to have absented himself from court after the king's recovery at Christmas 1454, not welcoming, it may be supposed, the restoration of the duke of Somerset. He and Cromwell were reported to be marching towards St Albans when battle was joined there on 22 May 1455. The two lords, who found themselves caught between their loyalty to the crown and their fear of their enemies at court, may well have stood aside. But they joined the victorious party after the battle, Shrewsbury himself serving on the parliamentary committee for the defence of Berwick and Calais in July. Strains were soon to show, however, for a row flared between Cromwell and Warwick, which led to Cromwell's taking shelter with Shrewsbury. Neither lord attended the second session of the parliament in the autumn of 1455 that established York's second protectorate. After Cromwell's death on 4 January 1456, however, Shrewsbury put in an appearance at the third session, and was happy to associate himself with York, Warwick, and others, in a petition in favour of George Neville.

During 1456, with both Somerset and Cromwell dead, and himself securely established in his inheritance, Shrewsbury began to distance himself from York and the

Nevilles. Whether at this point he attached himself to Queen Margaret, who emerged at the beginning of the year as the focal point of opposition to York, is hard to determine. Certainly on 5 October he became treasurer of England in place of York's kinsman, Viscount Bourchier. This has been taken to indicate that he was the queen's man. But while it is true that the queen engineered the change of government in the autumn of 1456, it is apparent that she was unable subsequently to dominate affairs or the deliberations of council. It is perhaps significant that Shrewsbury and the new chancellor, Bishop William Waynflete, had both been active members of the council during the first protectorate. Waynflete was very much the king's man. Later his enemies picked out Shrewsbury as one who had been constantly about the king's person. Perhaps he was one of those courtiers, including the duke of Buckingham as well, who continued to see themselves as first and foremost the king's servants, endeavouring to execute his will, rather than partisans of the queen acting in her interest.

During the two years in which Shrewsbury was treasurer a policy of appeasement, culminating in the Loveday award of March 1458, was pursued. It is difficult to discern the authorship of this policy. It might have stemmed from the king himself, enjoying his last lucid spell; it might have been generated by the lords closest about him, by Shrewsbury as well as by Buckingham, who was also a significant figure at court; it might even have been initiated by the queen. Certainly these nobles were soon drawn into the queen's camp, Shrewsbury becoming a councillor of the prince of Wales in 1457, and contributing to the build-up of military power in the west midlands. His membership of this new curialist faction was sealed by the marriage of his heir, John, to Buckingham's daughter, Katherine, one of several marriages in the summer of 1458 that bound its members together. As treasurer Shrewsbury made a modest impact on the royal finances, not least as a personal lender to the crown without giving himself particular preference for obtaining repayment. The grant of the joint custody of most of the inheritance of Henry Tudor, earl of Richmond, at a nominal farm in 1458 may have been his chosen recompense. That he had not suffered financially is suggested by his purchase of Wingfield and Crich from the executors of Lord Cromwell. Other rewards that came his way included the Garter, and the offices of keeper of the royal mews, chief butler, and, in 1459, chief justice of Cheshire.

By the time of the last grant Shrewsbury was no longer treasurer. During a great council held at Westminster in October 1458 he was replaced by his brother-in-law, the earl of Wiltshire. These governmental changes marked the moment when Queen Margaret finally secured control of affairs; Shrewsbury was not, it would seem, sufficiently close to her person. He remained, however, unswervingly loyal, benefiting from, as well as participating in, the proscription of the Yorkists in the autumn of 1459. He was still in attendance on Henry VI, and with Buckingham and Viscount Beaumont led the outnumbered royal force that faced the Yorkists at Northampton

on 10 July 1460. All three leaders were killed defending the king.

Shrewsbury was buried at Worksop Priory, in accordance with his will. He had four sons: John, who succeeded him as earl; Gilbert, who became the head of the family after his elder brother's death in 1473, and fought alongside Henry Tudor at Bosworth; James; and Christopher; and two daughters: Anne, who married Sir Henry *Vernon of Haddon (the Talbot dog is emblazoned on the dining-room ceiling at Haddon Hall) [see under Vernon family]; and Margaret, who married Thomas Chaworth. His widow died on 8 September 1473. Shrewsbury's role as a loyal Lancastrian is enigmatic. In the last years of his life he was picked out by friend and foe alike as one of the key figures in the regime. To the queen's party he was 'the top mast of the ship of state, keeping it from harm' (GEC, *Peerage*, 11.705); to the Yorkists in 1460 he was 'one of oure mortaile and extreme enemyes, now and of long tyme past' (Davies, 88). Yet he seems never to have been the most dominant figure at court, nor, at least until 1459, was he the most virulently opposed to York. Perhaps it was his closeness to the king's person that marked him out for special notice. He does not appear to have been outstandingly able or assertive, giving rather the appearance of following where others led. But he was honourable and of unquestioned loyalty to his king, seeking until the eleventh hour to find some resolution and compromise between the competing factions. His efforts may have helped delay all-out civil war for two years. Unlike his cowardly brother-in-law, the earl of Wiltshire, Shrewsbury stood and fought at Northampton, dying for the failing Lancastrian cause in England, as had his estranged father for the same lost cause in France. A. J. POLLARD

Sources *Chancery records* · PRO, Chancery, inquisitions post mortem, C139–40 · [J. Raine], ed., *Testamenta Eboracensia*, 2, SurtS, 30 (1855) · N. Davis, ed., *Paston letters and papers of the fifteenth century*, 2 vols. (1971–6) · N. H. Nicolas, ed., *Proceedings and ordinances of the privy council of England*, 7 vols., RC, 26 (1834–7), vols. 5–6 · GEC, *Peerage*, new edn, 11.704–5 · J. S. Davies, ed., *An English chronicle of the reigns of Richard II, Henry IV, Henry V, and Henry VI*, CS, 64 (1856) · A. J. Pollard, 'The family of Talbot, Lords Talbot and earls of Shrewsbury in the fifteenth century', PhD diss., University of Bristol, 1968 · R. A. Griffiths, *The reign of King Henry VI: the exercise of royal authority, 1422–1461* (1981) · J. Watts, *Henry VI and the politics of kingship* (1996) · C. A. J. Armstrong, 'Politics and the battle of St Albans, 1455', *BIHR*, 33 (1960), 1–72 · R. A. Griffiths, *King and country: England and Wales in the fifteenth century* (1991)
Wealth at death approx. £1500: Pollard, 'The family of Talbot', 314–16 appendix II, 414–16

Talbot, Sir John (c.1769–1851), naval officer, was the third son of Richard Talbot (d. 24 Oct 1788) of Malahide Castle, co. Dublin, and his wife, Margaret (d. 27 Sept 1834), eldest daughter of James O'Reilly of Ballinlough, co. Westmeath. On 28 May 1831 his mother was created Baroness Talbot of Malahide. His elder brothers, Richard Wogan Talbot (c.1766–1849) and James Talbot (c.1767–1850), succeeded her as second and third barons respectively. Thomas *Talbot (1771–1853) was a younger brother.

John Talbot entered the navy in March 1784 on the *Boreas* with Captain Horatio Nelson, and served in her in the

West Indies. After she was paid off he was on the books of the *Barfleur* and the *Victory*, guardships at Portsmouth, and on 3 November 1790 he was promoted lieutenant of the *Triton* in the West Indies. In April 1793 he was appointed to the *Windsor Castle*, going to the Mediterranean with Lord Hood. He was afterwards in the *Alcide* in the Mediterranean, and in 1795 was first lieutenant of the *Astraea*, attached to the western squadron under Rear-Admiral Colpoys, and in sight of some of that squadron's ships when, on 10 April, she captured the more powerful French frigate *Gloire* after a sharp one hour's action. He was put in charge of the prize, which he took to Portsmouth, and on 17 April was promoted to command the sloop *Helena*, in the channel, from which on 27 August 1796 he was posted to the *Eurydice* (24 guns). He commanded her for upwards of four years in the West Indies and in the channel, capturing many prizes, and in May 1798 he assisted in the defence of the isles of St Marcouf. In 1801 he commanded the *Glenmore* on the Irish station.

In October 1804 Talbot was appointed to the *Leander* (50 guns) on the Halifax station, where on 23 February 1805 he captured the French frigate *Ville de Milan* and her prize, the *Cleopatra*; both were greatly disabled in the action in which the *Cleopatra* had been taken, and were incapable of offering any effective resistance. In December 1805 Talbot was moved into the *Centaur*, when, on leaving the *Leander*, he was presented by the officers with a sword valued at 100 guineas. In February 1806 he took command of the *Thunderer*, in the Mediterranean, and in the following year commanded one of the detachment under Sir John Thomas Duckworth, which in February forced the Dardanelles. He remained in the Mediterranean, and in October 1809 was moved into the *Victorious*, rated 74 guns but mounting 82. In February 1812 he was sent off Venice to keep watch on a new French ship, the *Rivoli* (74 guns), which had been built there and was reported ready for sea. In the afternoon of the 21st the *Rivoli* put to sea, but was seen and followed by the *Victorious* and brought to action on the morning of the 22nd. The *Victorious* captured her after a severe engagement lasting nearly five hours, during which the *Rivoli*, both in hull and rigging, was 'dreadfully shattered', and out of 810 men had upwards of 400 killed or wounded. Talbot, who was severely wounded in the head by a splinter, was awarded a gold medal. The *Victorious* was then sent home to be refitted, and, still commanded by Talbot, sailed for the West Indies in November 1812. From there she went, during the Anglo-American War, to the coast of North America, where she blockaded New London, Connecticut, and in summer 1814 was sent to Davis Strait in the Arctic to protect the whale fishery. She struck a rock and was so damaged that she had to return to England, and in August she was paid off.

Talbot had no further service. On 12 April 1815 he was made a KCB. He married, on 17 October 1815, Mary Julia (*d*. 9 Dec 1843), third daughter of James Everard, ninth Lord Arundell of Wardour; they had two sons and five daughters. Talbot became rear-admiral on 12 August 1819, vice-admiral on 22 July 1830, and admiral on 23 November 1841, and was made a GCB on 23 February 1842. A brave and skilful captain, he died at his seat, Rhode Hill, near Lyme Regis, Dorset, on 7 July 1851.

J. K. LAUGHTON, rev. ANDREW LAMBERT

Sources W. James, *The naval history of Great Britain, from the declaration of war by France, in February 1793, to the accession of George IV in January 1820*, 5 vols. (1822–4), vol. 3, p. 408; vol. 4, pp. 174, 263, 370, 385; vol. 5, pp. 245, 247 · D. Syrett and R. L. DiNardo, *The commissioned sea officers of the Royal Navy, 1660–1815*, rev. edn, Occasional Publications of the Navy RS, 1 (1994) · O'Byrne, *Naval biog. dict.* · P. Mackesy, *The war in the Mediterranean, 1803–1810* (1957) · Boase, *Mod. Eng. biog.* · *GM*, 2nd ser., 36 (1851), 319–20
Archives W. Yorks. AS, Leeds, papers | BL, corresp. with Sir H. Lowe, Add. MSS 20107, 20166, 20170, 20189, 20191, *passim*

Talbot, John, sixteenth earl of Shrewsbury and sixteenth earl of Waterford (1791–1852), Roman Catholic layman and patron of the Gothic revival, was born at Grafton Manor, Bromsgrove, on 18 March 1791, the eldest surviving child of John Joseph Talbot (1765–1815), who was the brother of Charles, the fifteenth earl of Shrewsbury, and his wife, Catherine (1768–1791), daughter of Thomas Clifton of Lytham, Lancashire. His mother died two months after his birth and on his father's remarriage he was entrusted to the care of his great-aunt, the dowager countess of Shrewsbury, at Lacock Abbey, Wiltshire. Born in the same year as the Catholic Relief Act was passed, Talbot was one of the first sons of the Catholic nobility to benefit from a Catholic education in Britain, being sent first to the Benedictines at Vernon Hall, Lancashire (the forerunner of Ampleforth College), then in 1802 to Stonyhurst, and finally in 1806 to St Edmund's College, near Ware. In 1812 he made a Mediterranean tour, accompanied by the Revd John Chetwode Eustace, and in Spain witnessed some of the action of the Peninsular War. In 1814 he married Maria Theresa (1794–1856), eldest daughter of William Talbot of Castle Talbot, co. Wexford; they had a son who died in infancy and two daughters.

In June 1827 Talbot succeeded to the earldom and estates of his uncle Charles. The Talbots were one of the oldest Catholic families in Britain, who had managed to retain most of their estates. They were the most important landowners in the midlands. The principal family seat at Heythrop, Oxfordshire, was burnt down in 1831, and the new earl took up residence at Alton Abbey, Staffordshire, a Gothic mansion erected by his predecessor. Reluctant to pursue the political career that was open to him following the Catholic Emancipation Act of 1829, he set about the realization at Alton of a Gothic dream, made possible by the artistic genius of A. W. Pugin, who had converted to Catholicism shortly after meeting him. Between 1839 and 1851 Pugin completed the mansion, now renamed Alton Towers, and built Alton Castle with its neo-medieval church, school, almshouse, and hospital, thereby embodying the spiritual ideals that Talbot shared with his close friend and collaborator Ambrose Phillipps De Lisle.

Shrewsbury sponsored the building of many of the churches designed by Pugin, notably that of St Giles's, Cheadle, Staffordshire, and provided financial support for

De Lisle's schemes for the reconversion of England. However, he took a far more realistic approach to the revival, and did not share De Lisle's conviction that the Oxford Movement would lead to the reunion of the Church of England with the Roman Catholic church. Although regarded by the leaders of the Catholic revival as their patron, 'the Good Earl John' (as he was known by them) retained something of the old Catholic suspicion of 'enthusiasm'. When the English Catholic hierarchy was restored in 1850, Shrewsbury defended the restoration in public and denounced the Catholic peers who distanced themselves from it; but he nevertheless felt that the triumphalism of Cardinal Nicholas Wiseman was imprudent and ill-advised. Politically he was a whig who nevertheless supported the union, and was distressed to find himself at odds with some of his fellow Catholics over Ireland. He deplored the support given to Daniel O'Connell by the Catholic periodical *The Tablet*.

By 1850 the earl was spending most of his time in Italy, closing Alton Towers for most of the year in order to save money for his schemes. In all, he is estimated to have spent some £500,000 on churches and charities. He died at Naples on 9 November 1852. His remains were taken to Alton, where his funeral on 14 December was the occasion for a solemn ritual worthy of its setting, and was attended by virtually all the leading Catholic churchmen and laity. Pugin died two months before his patron, in September 1852. Both Shrewsbury's daughters married Roman noblemen. The younger, Gwendalyn, Princess Borghese, died in 1840 at the age of twenty-two while ministering to the victims of an epidemic at Rome. The elder, Mary, born in 1815, married Prince Doria Pamphilji. Shrewsbury's will was the subject of a prolonged legal dispute between the family and the executors, Charles Scott Murray and Ambrose Phillipps De Lisle. He was succeeded by his cousin Bertram Arthur Talbot (1832–1856). On the death of the latter at the age of twenty-four the title passed out of Catholic hands and devolved upon Henry John Chetwynd, third Earl Talbot of Hensol.

E. B. STUART, *rev.* G. MARTIN MURPHY

Sources D. Gwynn, *Lord Shrewsbury, Pugin and the Catholic revival* (1946) · E. Price, 'Memoir of the late Earl of Shrewsbury', *Catholic Directory* (1854), 141–61 · M. J. Fisher, *Pugin-land: A. W. N. Pugin, Lord Shrewsbury, and the Gothic Revival in Staffordshire* (2002) · M. Pawley, *Faith and family: the life and circle of Ambrose Phillipps de Lisle* (1993) · M. J. Fisher, *Alton Towers: a Gothic wonderland* (1999) · *The Tablet* (16 Nov 1852) · *The Tablet* (30 Nov 1852) · Gillow, *Lit. biog. hist.*, 5.503–5 **Archives** Westm. DA, corresp. concerning St Edmund's | Birmingham Roman Catholic archdiocesan archives, letters to D. Rock · BL, letters to A. Panizzi, Add. MS 36716 · BL, corresp. with Sir Robert Peel, Add. MSS 40492–40609, *passim* · Brompton Oratory, London, corresp. with F. W. Faber · Ushaw College, Durham, corresp. with Thomas Walsh · Ushaw College, Durham, corresp. with Nicholas Wiseman **Likenesses** J. J. Hamburger, oils, 1832, Ingestre Hall, Staffordshire · double portrait, on reredos, figure, c.1840 (with the countess of Shrewsbury), St Peter's, Bromsgrove · C. Blaas, oils · J. F. A. Lynch, engraving (after oils by C. Blaas) · J. Morrison, engraving (after O. Oakley) · O. Oakley, oils · brass on monument, Alton Castle, Derbyshire **Wealth at death** £130,000: Pawley, *Faith and family*, 265

Talbot [*née* Lyttelton], **Lavinia** (1849–1939), promoter of women's education, was born on 4 January 1849 in London, the seventh of the twelve children of George William *Lyttelton, fourth Baron Lyttelton (1817–1876), and his first wife, Mary (1813–1857), daughter of Sir Stephen Glynne, bt, of Hawarden and his wife, Mary.

Lavinia Lyttelton grew up at Hagley Hall, the family seat in Worcestershire, governess-taught, but more deeply formed by her parents' Anglo-Catholic faith, and the happy family life that was threatened, but not broken, by her mother's death when she was eight. In 1864, aged fifteen, she succeeded her elder sisters in taking charge of the household at Hagley for her father, younger sister, and eight brothers. Lord Lyttelton remarried five years later; and in 1870, aged twenty-one, Lavinia married Edward Stuart *Talbot (1844–1934), a friend from childhood, who had just been appointed warden of the new Keble College, Oxford.

Lavinia Talbot plunged into a challenging married life. Edward's role as head of a college built in memory of John Keble made him at once a standard-bearer for the Anglo-Catholic wing of the church; the new college's religious bias was one reason why the old university snubbed it at every turn (though W. E. Gladstone frequently visited his niece by marriage in the warden's lodgings). But Edward went to war with a light heart, as he wrote later, and so did Lavinia. She identified thoroughly with his views and made the best of their cramped quarters, while her good looks, gaiety, and sympathetic interest softened the rawness of the place. She herself revelled in Oxford's beauty and took advantage of the ladies' lectures organized by a small committee on which she served with Louise Creighton, Mrs Humphry Ward, and other young dons' wives. (The university played no part.) Conscious of the defects of her own education, she took great pleasure in these lectures given by eminent Oxford men, and in writing such essays for their appraisal as 'The state of the papacy before Gregory VIII'.

Over the next years Lavinia and Edward were prominent among Oxford progressives who took the women's education question further. In 1878 an Association for the Promotion of the Education of Women was formed, to organize lectures for girls preparing for the Oxford local examinations. The Talbots saw a chance for the church to lead in providing a hall of residence for them, but other reformers were opposed to an overweening Anglican influence. Eventually the progressives split, the non-sectarian element laying down the non-denominational roots of Somerville, while the Talbot party launched Lady Margaret Hall. Edward took charge of its main committee, appointing a suitably high-church principal, while Lavinia worked on subcommittees to find and furnish a useful house and advise on domestic matters from gifts of furniture to servants' wages.

Both Edward and Lavinia served for many years on the council of Lady Margaret Hall, but they left Oxford in 1888 when Edward was appointed vicar of Leeds. In 1895 they moved to south London on his appointment as bishop of

Rochester; in 1911 his translation to Winchester established them grandly in Farnham Castle. In all these places Lavinia displayed the poise and competence she had shown as the fifteen-year-old 'housewife' at Hagley and the bride who, after a five-year courtship, had accepted the role of 'Mother Keble'. 'What cannot be endured *must* be cured' (apparently one of her favourite sayings) seems appropriate to Edward's work; and it was certainly with her backing that in 1913 he invited the Anglican feminist Maude Royden to address a male audience at the church congress on the subject of the white slave traffic. The initiative was characteristic. In the episcopate as at Keble he was one of those leading men who carried Anglo-Catholicism forward to develop a social gospel from its strong liturgical base.

The Talbots had three sons and two daughters, but their youngest son was killed in the First World War. In 1932 Edward consecrated the rising chapel at Lady Margaret Hall. He died in January 1934. Lavinia survived him, still good-looking but by then suffering from profound deafness. She died at The Blenheim, Wantage, Berkshire, on 10 October 1939, and was buried in Winchester Cathedral.

SHEILA FLETCHER

Sources L. Talbot, diary and letters, Hagley Hall, Worcestershire · G. Stephenson, *Edward Stuart Talbot* (1936) · E. Talbot, *Memories of early life* (1924) · Council minutes, Lady Margaret Hall, Oxford · *The Times* (16 Oct 1939) · A. M. A. H. Rogers, *Degrees by degrees* (1938) · S. Fletcher, *Victorian girls: Lord Lyttelton's daughters* (1997) · Gladstone, *Diaries* · *CGPLA Eng. & Wales* (1939) · Burke, *Peerage* · *DNB*
Archives Hagley Hall, Worcestershire, diary and letters
Likenesses F. Dicksee, crayon, 1920, Lady Margaret Hall, Oxford · photographs, priv. coll.
Wealth at death £1892 17s. 8d.: probate, 6 Dec 1939, *CGPLA Eng. & Wales*

Talbot, Margaret, countess of Shrewsbury (1404–1467). *See under* Talbot, John, first earl of Shrewsbury and first earl of Waterford (c.1387–1453).

Talbot, Mary Anne [*alias* John Taylor] (1778–1808), sailor and soldier, was born on 2 February 1778 at 62 Lincoln's Inn Fields, London, the youngest of her mother's sixteen children. Mary Anne was purportedly the illegitimate daughter of William Talbot, the first earl of Talbot (1710–1782), and her mother died while giving birth to her. Using the alias John Taylor, Talbot became one of Britain's most famous 'Amazons' of the eighteenth century, and joined the ranks of others such as Hannah Snell and Christian Davies who either chose or were forced to disguise themselves as men to join the military.

According to Talbot's autobiography in the 1804 edition of R. S. Kirby's *Wonderful … Museum*, her father died at the age of seventy-one, when she was four years old. She was raised in Worthen, Shropshire, by a wet-nurse from her birth until aged five, then attended Mrs Tapperly's boarding-school at Chester until she was fourteen. 'Here I remained nine years, unacquainted with the views of the world, and knew no happiness but that of seeing children more fortunate than myself receiving the embraces of their parents and friends' (Dowie, 140). Her misery was relieved only by an older sister, known as the Hon. Miss

Mary Anne Talbot [John Taylor] (1778–1808), by G. Scott, pubd 1804 (after James Green)

Dyer, whom she believed was her mother. But the sister died in childbirth when Talbot was nine.

From Miss Dyer, who was the first to tell Talbot about her parents, she inherited a fortune of £30,000 with an annual income of £1500. But her sister chose an unscrupulous guardian, a Mr Sucker, who placed Talbot under the care of Captain Essex Bowen of the 82nd regiment of foot. He took her to London where, instead of sending her to school as he had promised, he forced her to become his unwilling sexual partner.

Talbot then learned of Captain Bowen's plans:

> Conceiving me properly subjugated to his purpose and remarking my figure was extremely well calculated for the situation he had assigned me, he produced a complete suit of male attire and for the first time made me acquainted with the unmanly design he had formed of taking me with him to the West Indies, in the menial capacity of foot boy [personal servant]. (Dowie, 143)

Disguised as John Taylor, Talbot sailed aboard Captain Bishop's *Crown* from Falmouth for the Spanish colony of San Domingo. When a gale blew up *en route* Talbot was forced to man the pumps and received a crash course in nautical skills.

Talbot vividly evokes the hardships of life at sea and the difficulty of her situation, living in virtual servitude to Captain Bowen. Upon arrival in Port-au-Prince in June 1792, the ship's captain received orders to join the duke of York's troops in France. Captain Bowen threatened to have her sold into slavery unless she agreed to be enrolled as a drummer. In Flanders she was 'obliged to keep up a continual roll to drown the cries and confusion' on the battlefield. She was wounded at the capture of Valenciennes in north-eastern France, but took advantage of Captain Bowen's death to desert the regiment to avoid detection. In her sailor's clothes she travelled east through Luxembourg to the Rhine, avoiding towns, and sleeping under trees and hayracks. On 17 September 1793 she signed on with a French ship under Captain Le Sage without realizing that it was a privateer (an armed vessel with a government commission to capture the merchant vessels of an enemy nation) until a sea battle with a British ship four months later. Lord Howe's crew captured the French ship and she was taken aboard the *Queen Charlotte* for interrogation. Although she avoided mentioning her desertion from the duke of York's regiment, Lord Howe accepted her account and sent her to sail with Captain John Hervey's *Brunswick* (74 guns) as a powder monkey.

Captain Hervey noticed 'Taylor's' superior manner and education and so promoted her to principal cabin-boy. Three months after coming on board, while serving as an assistant to the gunners, the *Brunswick* fell into battle with the French on 1 June 1794. Talbot was badly wounded when a grapeshot shattered her left ankle and spent four months recuperating at the Haslar Royal Naval Hospital, Gosport, near Portsmouth. She then signed on with the *Vesuvius* bomb (a vessel armed with mortar for throwing bombs) as midshipman. The crew, however, was taken by two privateers along the Normandy coast and she languished in a Dunkirk prison for eighteen months. After her release she signed on with an American, Captain John Field of the *Ariel*, and set sail for New York in August 1796. After her return to London aboard the same ship in November, she was captured by a press-gang while ashore in Wapping and forced to reveal her true sex to avoid service. 'The officers upbraided each other with ignorance at not discovering before, my being a woman, and readily gave me a discharge' (Kirby, *Life and Surprising Adventures*, 186).

Talbot's retirement from sea marked the beginning of a precarious string of occupations which included jewellery making, acting on the London stage, and domestic service. Her ill health added to her financial troubles and she was frequently hospitalized for treatment of her left ankle. She confessed, however, that her frequent forays into the pubs in seaman's clothes to drink grog with her former mess-mates exacerbated her difficulties—'The reason of which, I imagine, proceeded from the wound breaking out afresh in consequence of my too free use of spirituous liquors' (Kirby, *Life and Surprising Adventures*, 189). Meanwhile she battled the navy pay-office in Somerset House for a pension (which she eventually was granted) and received 'presents' from Queen Caroline, the duke of Norfolk, and others who had heard of her naval exploits. Her final employment was with the publisher Robert S. Kirby, chronicler of her story, as a domestic at his house in St Paul's Churchyard. After three years her deteriorating health forced her to retire to a friend's home in Shropshire. She lived for only a few weeks, and died there on 4 February 1808.   JULIE WHEELWRIGHT

Sources *Kirby's wonderful … museum*, 6 vols. (1803–20), vol. 2, p. 160 · R. S. Kirby, *Life and surprising adventures of Mary Anne Talbot* (1809) [repr. in *Women adventurers*, 1893] · *European Magazine and London Review*, 53 (1808), 234 · *Chambers's Journal* (30 May 1863) · J. Wheelwright, *Amazons and military maids*, new edn (1994) · M. M. Dowie, ed., *Women adventurers* (1893) · *The Times* (4 Nov 1799) · S. J. Stark, *Female tars* (1996) · *DNB*
Likenesses G. Scott, two stipple engravings (after J. Green), BM, NPG; repro. in *Kirby's Wonderful … museum* (1804) [*see illus.*]

Talbot, Dame Meriel Lucy (1866–1956), women's welfare worker, was born on 16 June 1866 at 10 Great George Street, Westminster, London, the fifth child of John Gilbert Talbot (1835–1910), politician and temperance reformer, and his wife, Meriel Sarah (1840–1925), eldest daughter of the fourth Baron Lyttelton. Family links with the Lytteltons were further reinforced by the marriage of her mother's sister to her father's brother, Edward Stuart Talbot. Meriel grew up in a large, close-knit, extended family, and in later years recalled holidays spent with W. E. Gladstone and his wife, Catherine (her great-aunt). Her father's support for the temperance movement made him increasingly prominent as a public figure.

Educated initially at Kensington high school Meriel Talbot went on to undertake a wide variety of influential appointments in the period immediately before and during the First World War. She was for a short while secretary to Society, the Lambeth charity organization, before becoming secretary to the Victoria League in 1901—a position she held until 1916. In this capacity she travelled widely in the empire visiting Australia, New Zealand, and Canada, in 1910–11, and South Africa in 1912. Her knowledge and understanding of the Commonwealth was subsequently used to good effect when, after the war, she assisted in the settlement abroad of British women.

The First World War provided the opportunity for Talbot to utilize her extensive administrative and organizational talents in a wide variety of different ways. In 1915 she served on the official advisory committee for the repatriation of enemy aliens. In 1916 she was appointed the board of agriculture's first woman inspector. In the following year she became director of the women's branch of the board's food production department. Her duties effectively covered the mobilization and co-ordination of what was to become the Women's Land Army. Throughout the period she was very concerned that new recruits should uphold the high moral standards and good name of the land army. Indeed she was personally responsible for compiling several reports dealing specifically with this issue, the most influential of which was *The Women's Land Army: Need for More Effective Control* (June 1918). In this document she recognized the difficulties of imposing any kind of military discipline on women, because they were working for private employers. Her contribution to the development of the land army led to her appointment as OBE in 1917 and CBE in the following year. In 1920 she was made DBE.

During 1920 and 1921 Dame Meriel undertook an important role at the Ministry of Agriculture as their adviser on women's employment. In this role she was responsible for recommending suitable women to serve on the councils for agriculture in England and Wales and for recruiting women for the county committees. Her responsibilities also entailed co-ordinating the work of the Women's Institute and advising the ministry in the allocation of grants.

Dame Meriel was also for a number of years the intelligence officer of the overseas settlement department and a member of the relevant government committee. In 1929 she became a member of the royal commission on police powers and procedure. Two years later she accompanied the Headmistresses' Tour to Canada. She subsequently became chairman of the BBC central appeals advisory committee which assisted the corporation to select 'The week's good cause' and provided advice on its appeals policy in general. Between 1935 and 1951 she was also the chairman of the London Council for the Welfare of Women and Girls.

Widely regarded as a popular, enthusiastic person with exceptional powers to inspire others, Dame Meriel possessed an outstanding ability to transform the most mundane issues into matters of interest. Even in old age when her sight and hearing had deteriorated significantly she was still a persuasive communicator. In her eighties she proposed an elaborate plan to reduce road accidents. Dame Meriel never married, and died at her home, Newtimber Lodge, Newtimber, Hassocks, Sussex, on 15 December 1956. She was buried on the 18th at Markbeech parish church, near Edenbridge, Kent.   JOHN MARTIN

Sources *The Times* (17 Dec 1956) · *The Times* (19 Dec 1956) · *The Times* (22 Dec 1956) · *WWW* · P. Horn, *Rural life in England in the First World War* (1984) · CKS, Talbot papers · *The Countryman*, 34 (autumn 1946) · P. King, *Women rule the plot: the story of the 100 year fight to establish women's place in farm and garden* (1999) · d. cert. · b. cert. · *CGPLA Eng. & Wales* (1957)
Archives CKS, travel journals, incl. those recording visits to Australia, New Zealand, Canada, and South Africa · Victoria League of Commonwealth and Friendship Records
Wealth at death £13,518 12s. 2d.: probate, 5 Feb 1957, *CGPLA Eng. & Wales*

Talbot, Montague (*c.*1774–1831), actor and theatre manager, was born in Boston, Massachusetts, about 1774, the son of Captain John Talbot of the Irish branch of that family. His father drowned in 1782 when the East Indiaman *Grosvenor*, on which he was sailing, was sunk off the coast of Kaffraria, southern Africa. Educated at Exeter, Talbot was said to have been a student of law at the Temple, where he met William Henry *Ireland, and, finding him in the process of forging one of his 'Shakespearian' manuscripts, had connived at the 'discovery' of the documents in return for a share in the profits.

Talbot preferred the stage to the law, and took part in private theatricals, and is first mentioned as Douglas in the play of that name at Covent Garden on 13 January 1794. The performance was not well reviewed by the *European Magazine* of that month, and Talbot does not seem to have appeared again until 28 May, when he took the part of Cassander in *Alexander the Great*. His adoption of the stage cost him his share in the fortune of his uncle, a Dr Geech. The remainder of the season found him in Dublin at the Crow Street Theatre, performing under the name of Montague, where he enjoyed a measure of success in playing leading youthful roles. In September 1795 he appeared in Swansea as Othello and as Penruddock in Richard Cumberland's *The Wheel of Fortune*. By January 1796 he was back in Dublin, and he remained at Crow Street for the following two seasons. Still performing as Montague, he acted in August 1798 in Liverpool with Charles Mayne Young and met with a favourable reception.

The following year Talbot returned to the London stage, under his own name, playing Young Mirable in Farquhar's *The Inconstant* on 27 April 1799 at Drury Lane. In February 1800 he was Sir Charles Surface in *The School for Scandal*. He also appeared as Sir Charles Racket in Arthur Murphy's *Three Weeks after Marriage* and Roderigo in *Othello* and created the parts of Rezenvelt in Joanna Baillie's *De Montfort* and Algernon in Hoare's *Indiscretion*. Talbot was not particularly successful in London, and spent most of the rest of his career in Dublin. He was most appreciated in comedy roles such as Ranger in *The Suspicious Husband*, Monsieur Morbleu in *Monsieur Tonson*, and Lord Ogleby in *The Clandestine Marriage*. He also took the parts of Aufidius in *Coriolanus*, Romeo, and Lothario in *The Fair Penitent*. His youthful appearance was held to be a bar to his succeeding in tragedy.

In October 1800 it was reported that Talbot had 'lately' married Emily Coote Binden (*c.*1779–1832), an actress popular in Limerick and Cork; they had five children. In the summer of 1808 he bought Thomas Ludford Bellamy's interest in the Belfast, Newry, and Londonderry theatres. He opened the Belfast theatre on 23 January 1809 with *The Inconstant*, playing Young Mirable himself. But he faced constant difficulties in finding and retaining good actors, for whom America was often a more alluring prospect, and in 1820 he leased out his theatrical holdings to Mason of Glasgow. He continued to act, occasionally in Belfast, but usually as a member of the Crow Street company in Dublin, where he was highly popular. His audiences were loyal and refused to accept other actors in his roles, sometimes rioting when presented with another performer.

Talbot was a prominent freemason, and two of his benefits in Newry were attended by local masons in regalia. He died, after a lingering illness, at Belfast on 26 April 1831 and was buried in Friars Bush cemetery.

K. D. REYNOLDS

Sources Highfill, Burnim & Langhans, *BDA* · W. Donaldson, *Recollections of an actor* (1865) · Genest, *Eng. stage* · J. W. Cole, *The life and theatrical times of Charles Kean … including a summary of the English stage for the last fifty years*, 2nd edn, 2 vols. (1860) · Hall, *Dramatic ports.*
Likenesses S. Lover, watercolour (as M. Morbleu in *Monsieur Tonson*) · C. Maguire, engraving (as M. Morbleu in *Monsieur Tonson*) · engraving (as Colonel Cohenberg in *The siege of Belgrade*), NL Ire. · engraving (as M. Morbleu in *Monsieur Tonson*), repro. in *Dublin Theatrical Observer* (1821) · five prints, Harvard TC · portrait (as Young Mirable in *The Inconstant*), repro. in *Hibernian Magazine* (March 1805)

Talbot, Peter (1618/1620–1680), Roman Catholic archbishop of Dublin, was, according to different sources, born in early 1618 or on 29 June 1620, the second son of Sir William *Talbot (*d.* 1634), baronet, of Carton, and his wife,

Peter Talbot (1618/1620–1680), by unknown artist, c.1660

Alison Netterville of Castletown, co. Meath. The Talbots were one of the leading Old English families of the pale with sizeable land interests there.

Education and continental diplomacy Talbot entered the Jesuit house in Lisbon in May 1635 and studied philosophy in the college of Coimbra (1637–41) before teaching Latin there during 1642–5. After going to Rome in 1645 to study theology he was ordained in St John Lateran, Rome, on 6 April 1647. Apparently sent in disgrace to Florence for his tertianship, he returned to Portugal in 1649 to teach philosophy at Coimbra. Fluent in Latin, Italian, Spanish, Portuguese (presumably), and possibly Gaelic, by all accounts he was capable, intelligent, and a good priest. However, his immersion in the world of high politics led him to neglect his pastoral duties. Boundlessly ambitious, throughout his career he overreached himself pursuing chimerical schemes to advance the not always compatible causes of king, faith, fatherland, and family. While his erudite manner repeatedly won him the confidence of powerful figures, his quarrelsome nature and passion for intrigue alienated many.

In 1651 Talbot travelled to the Netherlands as an envoy of John IV of Portugal and then to Ireland to levy troops for the king in his war with Spain. There he remained until late 1652, before appearing at Madrid in spring 1653 appealing for Spanish aid for the Irish Catholics. Henceforth a vigorous partisan of Spain, he arrived in London in April with royal letters enjoining the Spanish ambassador to help him secure toleration for Catholicism in Ireland. In July he returned to Ireland to arrange the sending of Catholic agents to London.

Such hopes were soon dashed, and Talbot next appears

at Antwerp in July 1654. That autumn the exiled English king, Charles II, enlisted Talbot as a means of gaining Catholic aid, summoning him to his court at Spa, Germany. The Talbots had impressive royalist credentials: Peter's brother Sir Robert had strongly supported the leader of the Irish royalists, James Butler, marquess, later duke, of Ormond, from within the Catholic confederation during the 1640s. In 1656 Peter openly criticized the supporters of the former papal nuncio to Ireland, Giovanni Battista Rinuccini, who had thwarted an attempted alliance between the confederates and Ormond. While having little influence at Rome, Talbot was highly favoured by the Spanish, who were themselves at war with England from 1655. After February 1655 he was based in the Spanish Netherlands, where he was professor of theology at Antwerp, although he concentrated on building alliances between the king and various Catholic powers. More ambitiously in 1655 he repeatedly urged Charles's conversion to Catholicism to convince Spain and Rome of his good intentions. Historians have long believed that these arguments bore fruit, but all available evidence suggests otherwise—the king pointedly declined to even acknowledge these entreaties.

Mission to London During summer 1655 Talbot became acquainted with Edward Sexby, a very influential English Leveller and republican dissident who was seeking Spanish aid in overthrowing Oliver Cromwell. He acted as Sexby's intermediary with the Spanish and encouraged Charles II to co-ordinate his efforts with him. Although Sexby's schemes came to naught (he died in the Tower of London in 1658), through him Talbot developed links with discontented republican elements in England. The king and his two chief advisers, Sir Edward Hyde and Ormond, always regarded him warily. Talbot was clearly bent on rendering them dependent on the Catholic powers for the purposes of gaining toleration for Catholicism in Britain and the restitution of the dispossessed Irish landowners. His closeness to Sexby and his cohorts led Hyde to suspect he was in Cromwell's pay. Although he manoeuvred against Hyde he remained loyal to Charles, while being careful not to appear too royalist before his fellow clergy and compatriots.

From 1656 Talbot's youngest brother, Richard *Talbot, was the chief favourite of James, duke of York. The king had an uneasy relationship with York, and when the two quarrelled in January 1657 Peter was blamed for worsening matters. In summer 1658 Peter travelled to Madrid on York's behalf and successfully procured a rise in his pension. Suspecting Talbot's intentions, Charles opposed this mission. In late February 1659 Talbot went to England as an agent of Spain, apparently to secure peace with the republic. Many believed that during this crucial period he intrigued against the king in London. He was in close contact with the renegade royalist George Villiers, duke of Buckingham (whom he had befriended three years previously in Flanders), the Leveller John Wildman, and the republican double agent Joeseph Bampfield. Talbot was suspected of seeking either to ingratiate himself with the republicans or to put York on the restored throne. In

March the king complained to Talbot's Jesuit superiors, who had long viewed his meddling with disquiet. After ignoring orders to leave England immediately he was formally dismissed from the Jesuits in June.

The true purpose of Talbot's mission to London remains unclear; he subsequently claimed he was sent by Spain to divide the republicans, and according to one report only narrowly avoided execution while there. Confusingly, by the autumn the Spanish officials in Brussels also believed he had acted in bad faith. Trying to please many masters Talbot aroused the suspicion of all. He left England at the end of June, and appears in Paris on 11 July before heading to the Pyrenees for the peace negotiations at Fuenterabia between the Spanish, French, and English governments. There he convinced the king's representative in Spain, Sir Henry Bennet, of his loyalty. His meetings with royal ministers in France before and immediately after his mission to London suggest he sought a Franco-Spanish alliance against the republic. However, the war-weary powers were prepared only to pay this scheme lip service. Bennet's support and Talbot's influence with the chief Spanish minister in Madrid, Luis de Haro, led Charles to restore him to favour by October. On 2 December he left for Madrid on an ultimately successful mission to solicit money for Ormond, York, and the king.

Restoration Well rewarded after the Restoration, Talbot enjoyed an annual £200 pension by 1668 and became chaplain to the king's Portuguese queen in summer 1661. Ironically he had strongly opposed this marriage and the resulting alliance between England and Portugal against Spain. An attempt to undermine the match by informing the queen of her husband's unfaithfulness resulted in his dismissal and banishment from England in November 1662, though he was later permitted to return.

After 1660 Richard Talbot emerged as the main representative of the dispossessed Catholic landowners who bitterly resented the king's failure to restore most of them to their holdings. Ormond, lord lieutenant of Ireland from 1662, was the chief focus of hostility as the architect of the Restoration land settlement. His relationship with the Talbots, always uneasy, deteriorated markedly. In December 1664, after a dispute over a land case, Richard and Peter apparently threatened Ormond's life, for which they were briefly imprisoned.

None the less, the Talbots remained influential at court, enjoying the favour of York and the queen mother. Peter also had contacts with the opposition in England, being especially close to Buckingham. Both Catholic and dissenter had a common enemy in the resurgent Anglican party, which frustrated the king's plans to permit religious toleration. In 1667, with Clarendon in disgrace, Talbot's old acquaintance Arlington was for a time dominant at court. The new ministry displayed a preference for tolerating Catholicism. In 1669 Ormond was dismissed as lord lieutenant of Ireland. Talbot may have facilitated this by writing and clandestinely publishing two books accusing Ormond of the corrupt mishandling of Irish revenues and the land settlement. The works attributed to Talbot are *A Narrative of the Sale and Settlement of Ireland* and *Queries Relating to the Revenue of Ireland*.

Archbishop of Dublin Encouraged by the removal of Ormond, Rome decided to appoint a number of bishops to Ireland, and Talbot, who had lobbied for the archbishopric of Dublin in 1664, again put himself forward. This suit faced considerable opposition within the church, as he was held to be too close to a heretical monarch. However, the king discreetly put it about that he would not allow another archbishop to reside in Dublin; Talbot was duly consecrated at Antwerp on 9 May 1669 and was in Ireland by summer's end. The new lord lieutenant, John, Lord Robartes, generally clamped down on Catholicism, but Talbot was not molested, thanks to his connections. However John, Lord Berkeley, replaced Robartes in early 1670. Easy-going and tolerant, Berkeley had been associated with Talbot in the 1650s. Relations must since have soured, because Talbot reacted with dismay to this appointment, sending the governor a haughty letter upon his arrival in Dublin. Berkeley responded by conspicuously favouring the archbishop of Armagh, Oliver Plunkett, frequently summoning him from Drogheda to discuss matters concerning the Catholic church, ignoring Talbot who lived nearby. A resentful Talbot attempted to undermine the lord lieutenant, making common cause with hard-line protestant elements. In May 1670 he planned to travel to court to complain against Berkeley, but Plunkett refused permission.

Berkeley's goodwill towards Plunkett provoked a damaging rift between the latter and Talbot. During a national synod held in Dublin on 17 June 1670, Talbot disputed Plunkett's primacy and claimed, without providing proof, that he had royal licence to superintend the Catholic clergy in Ireland. He argued that Armagh's primacy was purely symbolic and contested Plunkett's rights of appeal and visitation in the province of Dublin. Both men appealed to Rome and wrote books upholding the claims of their respective archdioceses. In his dispatches to Rome Talbot persistently belittled and slandered Plunkett, variously accusing him of being too close to Berkeley, of being a crypto-protestant, and of having a mistress. He also encouraged opposition to him within the Ulster clergy, particularly among the Franciscans, and in 1672 used his influence to have a royal pension granted to Plunkett revoked. The two co-operated on occasion and were reconciled more than once, but their relationship always remained mercurial. Mild-mannered and diffident, Plunkett believed that if the clergy stayed out of politics they would be allowed to worship freely. The fiery Talbot was not content to rely on the government's sufferance and was set on restoring the socio-political power of Catholicism in Ireland, as well as advancing his own interests. If many of his actions were reckless and ultimately self-defeating, his courage and resolve deserve a measure of respect.

On assuming his archbishopric in 1669 Talbot was most immediately concerned with the restoration of hierarchical authority within the church. Discipline had broken down among many of the Irish clergy, who now resented efforts to bring them to account. This, combined with Talbot's tactlessness, inevitably led to dissension. Although hampered by Berkeley's hostility he made progress, holding provincial synods in 1670 and 1671. An equally pressing priority was the destruction of the remonstrant clergy within the Irish church. Led by Peter Walsh, this group swore allegiance to the king in a manner which denied the pope's temporal authority. Talbot strongly opposed the remonstrants, partly from animosity towards Ormond, who supported Walsh as a means of dividing the Catholic clergy. He deposed and banished any remonstrants in his archdiocese, excommunicating those who defied him. These were the opening shots in a four-year conflict between the Talbots and Ormond, the scope of which broadened beyond religious matters. In November 1670 Richard Talbot successfully petitioned the king to initiate an inquiry into the Irish land settlement on the grounds of bias against Catholics. Peter Talbot subsequently levied money on the Leinster clergy to further his brother's attempts to overturn the land settlement and discredit Ormond. Although out of office, the duke was not entirely out of favour and worked ceaselessly against the Talbots from London.

In early February 1671 Talbot was brought before the lord lieutenant and council in Dublin upon the accusations of the remonstrant clergy, but Berkeley ensured his acquittal. The lord lieutenant was an enemy of Ormond's and, regarding the remonstrants as his creatures, gave Talbot free rein against them. In January 1672 the king replaced Berkeley with Arthur Capal, earl of Essex. More formidable than his predecessor and on good terms with Ormond, Essex skilfully fomented the existing divisions within Irish Catholicism. Despite his precarious position Talbot continued to believe that the king's grace would preserve him, and in autumn 1672 claimed once again that he had a royal commission to oversee the Irish Catholic clergy.

Banishment and imprisonment On 8 September 1672 Talbot excommunicated John Byrne, a Dominican, over a disciplinary matter and laid his parish of Kilcock, co. Kildare, under interdict. Lord Dungan, Talbot's nephew and local JP, then imprisoned Byrne in February 1673. At Ormond's prompting on 19 March the English parliament petitioned against such proceedings. The result in May was an Irish government inquiry into Talbot's actions during which Plunkett, among others, testified against him. Charles always felt personally grateful to the Talbots for their support during his exile and was prepared to indulge them to an extent, but the findings of the inquiry were damning (from a protestant perspective). Moreover, his lenience towards Catholicism had provoked a backlash in England. Sensing a royal climb-down Talbot went to London in June and then to Paris in September. One month later a proclamation was issued banishing him from Ireland. In Paris he clashed with Sir William Throckmortin. Both men claimed to be representatives of York and presented rival schemes for gaining French support for Charles. Talbot also engaged in a bitter theological controversy with Dr

John Serjeant in 1675. By early 1676 he was back in England, living under York's protection at Poole Hall, Cheshire. In poor health and wishing to die in his native land he returned to Ireland in May 1678 with the government's tacit permission. On 11 October he was arrested at Lutrellstown for complicity in the Popish Plot. He was accused of planning to assassinate Ormond (once more lord lieutenant) and of abetting a planned French invasion of Ireland. His involvement in negotiations with France and his Machiavellian reputation lent these charges some credence. No evidence was found against him, but such was the prevailing anti-Catholic hysteria that Ormond dared not free him from incarceration in Dublin Castle. Apart from a few weeks in March–April 1680, when he was released for medical treatment, there he remained, suffering greatly through illness. Plunkett was imprisoned in an adjoining cell in December 1678, and the two prelates were reconciled soon afterwards. When Talbot nearly died in June 1680, Plunkett forced his way through the guards to administer the last rites. Talbot died at the castle about 15 November 1680.

A prolific author, in most of his works Talbot dealt with religious matters, although some were also of a political nature. His most interesting book is *A Treatise on Religion and Government*, published in 1670 at the high point of his career, in which he urges the king to grant religious toleration and to ally with Spain against France. He argues that Catholicism is the best upholder of monarchy and social order, whereas protestantism fosters anarchy. Anglicanism is critiqued as an unworkable compromise between the two. His theological writings demonstrate his continued affinity with the Jesuits, even after his dismissal from that order, in that they espouse an uncompromising Catholic orthodoxy and strongly uphold the theoretical powers of papal supremacy. During his career he fulminated against the Jansenists, the remonstrants, and what he saw as the Gallicanist tendencies of many of the English Catholic clergy.

TERRY CLAVIN

Sources *Calendar of the Clarendon state papers preserved in the Bodleian Library*, ed. O. Ogle and others, 5 vols. (1869–1970), esp. vols. 3–4 · D. Hawly, *The letters of Saint Oliver Plunkett* (1979) · P. Moran, *Spicilegum Ossoniense*, 1–3 (1874) · *Collectanea Hibernia*, vols. 1 and 3 · T. Carte, *Life of Ormond*, 4 (1854) · M. V. Ronan, *The Irish martyrs of the penal laws* (1935), 124–59 · J. L. O'Doherty, ed., *De praesulibus* (1944), 322–6 · *CSP dom.*, 1659–60; 1672–3; 1679–80; addenda, 1660–85 · M. V. Hay, *The Jesuits and the Popish Plot* (1934) · T. Carte, *An historical collection of letters*, 2 (1854) · P. Moran, *Memoirs of the Venerable Oliver Plunkett* (1895) · P. Talbot, *The friar disciplined* (Ghent, 1674) · J. Ardeskin, *Theologica tripartita* (Antwerp, 1686)
Likenesses oils, c.1660, NG Ire. [see illus.]

Talbot, Richard, second Lord Talbot (c.1306–1356), soldier and administrator, was the eldest son of Gilbert *Talbot, the first Lord Talbot (1276–1346), a knight-banneret from Gloucestershire and Herefordshire, and an unknown mother. One of that company of young knights and bannerets who surrounded Edward III during the years of his greatest victories, Talbot fought in Scotland and France, served in the king's household, and presided as a justice. Earlier, in 1321–2, he joined the contrariants' uprising against Edward II. Said to have been dispatched with his brother Gilbert by the bishop of Hereford, Adam Orleton, to bolster Roger Mortimer's forces, Talbot was captured at Boroughbridge with his father on 16 March, when he was styled 'bachelor'. Like his father he served in Gascony in 1324–5.

With the overthrow of Edward II in 1326–7, Talbot's fortunes dramatically improved. Some time before February 1327 he married Elizabeth Comyn, sister and coheir of John Comyn of Badenoch (d. 1314), the possessor of a plausible claim to the Scottish throne, and a daughter and coheir of Joan, sister of Aymer de Valence, earl of Pembroke. When Aymer died on 23 June 1324 his estate was to be divided among the descendants of his sisters, Joan and Isabel. Elizabeth was potentially a very wealthy woman and thus attracted the notice of the grasping Despensers. On Aymer's death they imprisoned her and then moved her from castle to castle, until, on 20 April 1325, she granted Hugh Despenser the elder the manor of Painswick, Gloucestershire, and Hugh the younger Castle Goodrich, Herefordshire. She was also forced to acknowledge a debt of £20,000 and was apparently kept imprisoned until the Despensers were executed in 1326. After their marriage Talbot and Elizabeth embarked on a successful campaign to recover her portion of the Pembroke and Comyn estates.

In 1330 Talbot and his father, Gilbert, were both summoned to royal councils, and in 1331–2 Talbot was named one of the keepers of Ireland, beginning two decades of intense service. Like his father he was summoned to parliament for the first time in January 1332 and, on 21 March, was named a keeper of the peace in Gloucestershire. Because of Elizabeth's claim to the Comyn lands in Scotland, which had been confiscated by Robert I for Comyn's support of England, Talbot counted himself among the disinherited who rallied to support Edward Balliol's claim to the throne of Scotland in 1332. In July Talbot joined the invasion of Scotland and was present at the battle of Dupplin Moor on 12 August; in recognition of his support Balliol named him lord of Mar and summoned him to a parliament at Edinburgh on 10 February 1334. That summer, however, the Scots rebelled against Balliol. Fleeing the insurrection, Talbot was captured on 8 September and ransomed a year later for about 2000 marks. In 1336 he was again named to a Gloucestershire peace commission, and in December 1337 became keeper of the town of Berwick and justiciar of the English lands in Scotland. He held that position until April 1340 but in February and March 1339 was keeper of Southampton, responsible for garrisoning the town. According to Froissart Talbot was at the unsuccessful siege of Tournai in September 1339.

During the 1340s Talbot continued to divide his time between military and domestic service, sometimes serving with his father. They were commissioned to make arrests in Wales in 1340, were appointed justices of oyer and terminer in Shropshire and Staffordshire in February 1341, and in 1344 sat as justices in Wales. In May 1341 Richard Talbot became the chief justice on a trailbaston commission for the counties of Gloucester, Worcester, and Hereford, which sat on and off through 1343, and presided

as a justice in Oxfordshire in 1344–5. In the summer of 1342, however, he fought as a captain of the English forces under William de Bohun at the battle of Morlaix in Brittany, where he captured Geoffroi de Charney. Recognizing his valuable services, Edward appointed Talbot steward of the household in May 1345, in which office he served for four years. In the spring of 1346 he was on another trailbaston commission in Worcestershire and, as steward, investigated accusations against the king's purveyors in several counties. That summer he embarked with Edward for France, where he was wounded during the campaign leading up to Crécy, although he was with the king at the battle and later at the siege of Calais.

Talbot continued this brisk pace of military and judicial service through the last decade of his life. He sat on several commissions of oyer and terminer, some dealing with trespasses in the royal households. Once again he served on local peace commissions: in the counties of Oxford and Worcester in 1348 and 1353 and in Gloucester and Hereford in 1351, which included enforcement of the Statute of Labourers. While still steward he was a member of the great council in 1348. Between 1348 and 1351 he had custody of Pembroke during the minority of the heir to the earldom. In 1349 he served on a commission to halt the smuggling of uncustomed wool from England into Flanders. As a result of his faithful service he reaped impressive awards, including wardships, marriages, cash, and pardons of debts. He also had some setbacks, losing the castles of Blaenllyfni and Bwlchydinas which he claimed had been granted to his father in fee. In 1343 the papacy gave him permission to found an Augustinian priory at Flanesford, Herefordshire.

Talbot died between 23 and 26 October 1356. His lands, most of which were of Elizabeth's inheritance and had been settled jointly on themselves or feoffees, passed to his son and heir, Gilbert, who was aged between twenty-five and thirty. Elizabeth remarried and survived until 1372.

SCOTT L. WAUGH

Sources GEC, Peerage · F. Palgrave, ed., The parliamentary writs and writs of military summons, 2 vols. in 4 (1827–34) · RotP · Chancery records · Rymer, Foedera · Chronicon Galfridi le Baker de Swynebroke, ed. E. M. Thompson (1889) · Œuvres de Froissart: chroniques, ed. K. de Lettenhove, 25 vols. (Brussels, 1867–77) · Scalacronica, by Sir Thomas Gray of Heton, knight: a chronicle of England and Scotland from AD MLXVI to AD MCCCLXII, ed. J. Stevenson, Maitland Club, 40 (1836) · Chronicon Henrici Knighton, vel Cnitthon, monachi Leycestrensis, ed. J. R. Lumby, 2 vols., Rolls Series, 92 (1889–95) · The 'Original chronicle' of Andrew of Wyntoun, ed. F. J. Amours, 6 vols., STS, 1st ser., 50, 53–4, 56–7, 63 (1903–14) · Adae Murimuth continuatio chronicarum. Robertus de Avesbury de gestis mirabilibus regis Edwardi tertii, ed. E. M. Thompson, Rolls Series, 93 (1889) · W. Stubbs, ed., Chronicles of the reigns of Edward I and Edward II, 2 vols., Rolls Series, 76 (1882–3), esp. Annales Paulini, Gesta Edwardi de Carnarvon, Vita et mors Edward II · Justices Itinerant, PRO, Just1/1388 · J. R. S. Phillips, Aymer de Valence, earl of Pembroke, 1307–1324: baronial politics in the reign of Edward II (1972), 2, 15, 24, 235 · N. Fryde, The tyranny and fall of Edward II, 1321–1326 (1979), 114–15, 230, 253 · N. Saul, Knights and esquires: the Gloucestershire gentry in the fourteenth century (1981), 79, 123, 173, 276, 281 · P. Chaplais, ed., The War of Saint-Sardos (1323–1325): Gascon correspondence and diplomatic documents, CS, 3rd ser., 87 (1954), 240, no. 1 · R. A. Griffiths and R. S. Thomas, The principality of Wales in the later middle ages: the structure and personnel of government, 1: South Wales,

1277–1536 (1972), 26 • R. Nicholson, *Edward III and the Scots: the formative years of a military career, 1327–1335* (1965), 66, 73, 80, 152, 158, 159–61, 163, 168–9, 172, 185 • Tout, *Admin. hist.* • W. Rees, ed., *Calendar of ancient petitions relating to Wales* (1975), 274–5, 493–4 • G. Wrottesley, *Crécy and Calais* (1897); repr. (1898) • *CIPM*, 8, no. 714; 10, no. 326 • *CPR, 1327–1330, 1350–54*

Talbot, Richard (*d.* 1449), archbishop of Dublin and administrator, was the third of five sons of Richard Talbot, fourth Lord Talbot (*c.*1361–1396), of Goodrich, Herefordshire, and Ankaret (1361?–1413), daughter and eventual heir of John Lestrange, Lord Strange, of Blakemere, Shropshire. The future archbishop was probably only a year or two younger than his second eldest brother, John *Talbot, first earl of Shrewsbury, who was born *c.*1387. His father's death in 1396, seven years before his eldest brother, Gilbert, fifth Lord Talbot, gained livery of his inheritance in 1403, proved no obstacle to Richard's early advancement. John Trefnant, bishop of Hereford, gave him the portion of Middlecourt in Bromyard on 22 October 1399 and the prebend of Putson Major on 6 June 1401. Talbot proceeded to Oxford. He was styled *magister* from January 1405. By January 1411 he was a bachelor of civil and canon law and in 1410–11 assisted the attempts of Archbishop Thomas Arundel to suppress Wycliffism within the university. Meanwhile Talbot had been ordained deacon at Hereford on 26 March 1407 and priest (by letters dimissory) at Lambeth on 22 December 1408. Among further benefices obtained were three by royal grant (including the rectory of Ludlow, held 1404–7) and two (including the precentorship of Hereford, 1407–12) in the gift of Trefnant's successor, Robert Mascall. By March 1414 Talbot was dean of Chichester. The opportunity for preferment in Ireland arose from the appointment of his brother John as king's lieutenant there the same year. When Archbishop Nicholas Fleming of Armagh died in June 1416, Richard Talbot was elected his successor. The election, however, was still unconfirmed when Archbishop Thomas Cranley of Dublin died in May 1417. Talbot withdrew his claim to Armagh and secured election to Dublin instead. Papal provision followed on 20 December, consecration between May and August 1418.

In Ireland, Talbot played a more prominent role in royal government than any other late-medieval archbishop of Dublin. He served as a justice and keeper of the peace for co. Dublin. He was chancellor of Ireland from 1423 to 1426 and from 1427 to 1431; and was appointed again (abortively) on 7 August 1442. He undertook three deputyships for absent lieutenants: two for his brother John (1419–20 and 1447–8) and one for Sir Thomas Stanley (1435–7). He served five times as justiciar, once by English-seal appointment in 1422–3 and otherwise by election by the Irish council (1420, 1430–31, 1437–8, and 1445–6).

As deputy and justiciar Talbot held at least five parliaments and three great councils, all of which met in Dublin. He shared enough of John Talbot's military prowess to relish the more strenuous demands of the chief governorship, mounting numerous campaigns and ordering other clerks into battle too. But his eagerness for political

office—and reluctance to relinquish it, shown in 1423 and 1431—were primarily due to his involvement in the Talbot–Ormond feud. His vigorous espousal of the quarrel that began *c.*1415–17 between John Talbot and James Butler, fourth earl of Ormond, played a crucial role in turning it into a long-running factional conflict in Ireland centred on a struggle to control or influence the power and patronage of the chief governorship. At least once Richard Talbot resorted to open violence against Ormond: in 1429 he was summoned to England to explain his involvement in various passages of arms and the imprisonment of the earl's son, John, in Dublin. But Talbot, who was elected to deliver a petition to the king from an Irish parliament of 1441, is best known for the blistering accusations he then made in England against Ormond following the latter's appointment to the lieutenancy in February 1442. It was apparently to these (BL, Cotton MS Titus B.xi, pt. i, 12; Graves, 273–6) that Ware referred in his identification of Talbot as the author of a work entitled *De abusu regiminis Jacobi comitis Ormondiae dum esset locum tenens Hiberniae* (*Whole Works*, 2/2, 323). Counter-charges were brought against Talbot in Ireland in November 1442. Nevertheless, in 1445 Talbot ousted Ormond's deputy lieutenant, Richard Nugent, Lord Delvin, and as justiciar ordered the confiscation of the earl's Irish lands. He abandoned the feud only when John Talbot, who had been reconciled with the earl in England in 1444–5, returned to Ireland as lieutenant in 1446–7.

As archbishop, Richard Talbot refused to allow any display of primatial jurisdiction in his province by the archbishops of Armagh. This did not prevent him from accepting election to Armagh again, briefly, in 1443, but his candidacy was superseded by the papal provision of John Mey. Talbot's rule apparently left his own see in poor financial shape: his successor, Michael Tregury, found the metropolitan cross in pawn and much of the archiepiscopal demesne alienated. However, more positive memorials in Dublin were provided by Talbot's foundation, with various associates, of a religious guild dedicated to St Anne in 1430 and his establishment in 1432 of minor canons and choristers in St Patrick's Cathedral. The latter appear beside him on the monument there (restored 1919) marking his burial-place in front of the altar steps. Talbot died on 15 August 1449.

ELIZABETH MATTHEW

Sources E. A. E. Matthew, 'The governing of the Lancastrian lordship of Ireland in the time of James Butler, fourth earl of Ormond, *c.*1420–1452', PhD diss., U. Durham, 1994 • J. H. Bernard, 'Richard Talbot, archbishop and chancellor (1418–1449)', *Proceedings of the Royal Irish Academy*, 35C (1918–20), 218–28 • Emden, *Oxf.* • Chancery records • E. Tresham, ed., *Rotulorum patentium et clausorum cancellariae Hiberniae calendarium*, Irish Record Commission (1828) • *CEPR letters*, vols. 7–10 • J. H. Parry, ed., *Registrum Roberti Mascall*, CYS, 21 (1917) • D. A. Chart, ed., *The register of John Swayne, archbishop of Armagh and primate of Ireland, 1418–1439* (1935) • J. Graves, ed., *A roll of the proceedings of the King's Council in Ireland… AD 1392–93*, Rolls Series, 69 (1877) • *The whole works of Sir James Ware concerning Ireland*, ed. and trans. W. Harris, 2 vols. in 3 (1739–45, [1746]) • N. H. Nicolas, ed., *Proceedings and ordinances of the privy council of England*, 7 vols., RC, 26 (1834–7), vols. 3–5 • A. J. Pollard, 'The family of Talbot, lords Talbot and earls of Shrewsbury in the fifteenth century', PhD diss.,

University of Bristol, 1968 · H. F. Berry and J. F. Morrissey, eds., *Statute rolls of the parliament of Ireland*, 4 vols. (1907–39), vol. 2 · W. W. Capes, ed., *Registrum Johannis Trefnant*, CYS, 20 (1916) · W. G. H. Quigley and E. F. D. Roberts, eds., *Registrum Iohannis Mey: the register of John Mey, archbishop of Armagh, 1443–1456* (1972) · R. Frame, ed. and trans., 'Commissions of the peace in Ireland, 1302–1461', *Analecta Hibernica*, 35 (1992), 1–43 · J. I. Catto, 'Wyclif and Wycliffism at Oxford, 1356–1430', *Hist. U. Oxf.* 2: *Late med. Oxf.*, 175–261 · *The episcopal register of Robert Rede*, ed. C. Deedes, 2, Sussex RS, 11 (1910) · A. J. Pollard, *John Talbot and the war in France, 1427–1453*, Royal Historical Society Studies in History, 35 (1983) · J. C. Crosthwaite, ed., *The book of obits and martyrology of the cathedral church … Dublin*, Irish Archaeological Society, 4 (1844) · H. J. Lawlor, 'The monuments of the pre-reformation archbishops of Dublin', *Medieval Dublin: the making of a metropolis*, ed. H. Clarke (1990) · LPL, Reg. Arundel, i, fol. 343

Archives BL, Cotton MS Titus B.xi, pt i, 12 | NL Ire., Harris collectanea, MS 4

Likenesses brass, 1919 (after seventeenth-century drawings; after fifteenth-century original on marble matrix), St Patrick's Cathedral, Dublin

Wealth at death successor complained in 1451 that profits of archiepiscopal *mensa* had been so greatly diminished by alienations of predecessor and by the effect of war that he received not more than £300 a year: *CEPR letters*, vol. 10, 99

Talbot, Richard, first earl of Tyrconnell and Jacobite duke of Tyrconnell (1630–1691), army officer and politician, was the eighth and youngest son of Sir William *Talbot, bt (d. 1634), of Carton, co. Kildare, and Alison (fl. 1595–1644), daughter of John Netterville of Castletown, co. Meath. As a youth Talbot served as a cornet of horse in General Thomas Preston's army and was captured by the parliamentarians at the battle of Dungan's Hill on 8 August 1647. He was with the royalist garrison defending Drogheda two years later. When the town fell on 11 September 1649, Cromwell ordered his men to give no quarter. Talbot 'received so many wounds that, although he did not die, he was left for dead and spent three days lying amongst the slain' (Anselme, 303). He was lucky enough to fall into the hands of Commissary-General John Reynolds and was allowed to escape disguised as a girl, an unlikely feat for a remarkably tall and well-built young man.

Spanish service and conspiracy By March 1653 Talbot was with his brother Peter *Talbot (1618/1620–1680) in Madrid, where he held the rank of captain in one of Ormond's Irish regiments serving in the Spanish army. In 1655 he put himself forward 'as one who was willing to assassinate Cromwell' (Sergeant, 41) and was brought by Colonel Daniel O'Neil to Cologne where the exiled Charles II was living. In July 1655 he and four other conspirators were sent to London. Talbot was arrested on his arrival, but was released so that his movements could be watched. On 17 November 1655 he was again arrested and on 25 November he was taken to Whitehall where Cromwell questioned him in person. Cromwell offered him 'great preferments' if he co-operated, and threatened him with the rack 'to spin the truth out of his bones' if he did not. Talbot replied: 'Spin me to a thread if you please, I have nothing to confess and can only invent lies' (ibid., 56). Knowing that he was to be taken to the Tower in the morning, he sent out for wine, got his guards drunk, 'slipped down to the Thames by a cord, where he had a boat prepared; and

Richard Talbot, first earl of Tyrconnell and Jacobite duke of Tyrconnell (1630–1691), by or after François de Troy, 1690

in that little thing was ten days at sea; landed at last at Calais still nailed and shut up between some boards of the boat' (ibid., 57).

In Flanders, Talbot returned to the Spanish service and in June 1656 served under Condé at the relief of Valenciennes. Following the treaty between Cromwell and Mazarin, James, duke of York, was forced to leave France for the Spanish Netherlands in September 1656 and through him Talbot had an extraordinary rise. According to Clarendon:

> He was a very handsome young man, wore good clothes, and was without a doubt of a clear, ready courage, which was virtue enough to recommend a man to the Duke's good opinion, which, with more expedition than could be expected, he got to that degree that he was made [a groom] of the bedchamber. (Sergeant, 84)

Three years older than the duke, he became the dominant partner in what proved to be a lifelong friendship.

While in Flanders, Talbot persuaded the duke to give him the command of his regiment. This was done in the face of opposition from the colonel of the regiment, Cormac MacCarthy, with whom he fought a duel. MacCarthy wanted a Munsterman appointed because the officers were all either his kinsmen or dependants, and the men all came from Munster. MacCarthy was supported by Ormond and Sir Edward Hyde, who both petitioned the king on his behalf, but Talbot's influence over the duke was such that he got his way. Talbot served in Flanders against the French and in December 1657 was with the duke in the siege of Mardyke. Although it is likely that he was present at the battle of the Dunes in June 1658, he did not serve with the duke of York's regiment as, with the exception of MacCarthy himself, every officer was killed or captured.

In August 1658 Talbot seconded Lord Taafe in a duel against Sir William Keith following an argument over 7 sovereigns won at tennis. Sir William was killed and Talbot wounded his second, Richard Hopton, in two places. Talbot was with the duke of York following the April 1659 treaty between France and Spain, and later that year was one of those waiting to embark at Étaples to join a royalist uprising in England. In the following year, when the monarchy was restored, Talbot returned with the duke to England.

Restoration courtier and 'agent-general' The notoriously unreliable *Memoirs of Count de Grammont*, written by Anthony Hamilton over forty years later, contain several colourful anecdotes of Talbot's behaviour at the Restoration court. Although some of these tales are demonstrably false, they have been seized upon by his detractors as evidence of his loose moral character. It is nevertheless clear that Talbot assisted the duke in organizing his private life. After the Restoration, and after his marriage to Anne Hyde, James had a number of secret mistresses and, according to Bishop Burnet, Talbot 'was looked on as the manager of these intrigues'. He 'had much cunning and had the secret of his master's pleasures for some years' (Sergeant, 113). This prompted Macaulay to refer to Talbot as the duke's 'chief pandar' (ibid.).

In Ireland the Catholics hoped that the restoration of the monarchy would bring about the restoration to them of the land confiscated by the parliamentarians during the interregnum. As Talbot was so close to the duke of York and spent so much time at court, he was in 1661 chosen by the Irish gentry to advance their proposals for a new land settlement. He proved a zealous if not initially a successful agent in their cause. So aggressive was he towards the duke of Ormond, the newly appointed lord lieutenant of Ireland, that the duke 'waiting upon his Majesty, desired to know if it was his pleasure that at this time of day he should put off his doublet to fight duels with Dick Talbot' (Sergeant, 126). Talbot was sent to the Tower, albeit for a short stay. Following his release, he was from January to April 1662 the envoy of the duke of York to Lisbon to make the final arrangements for the marriage of Catherine of Braganza to Charles II, which took place on 21 May.

The Act of Settlement which provided that land would be restored to those innocent of rebellion was passed in the summer of 1662, and Talbot returned to Ireland at a time when the dispossessed landowners were appearing before the court of claims to prove their innocence. Advertising his undoubted influence at court, he offered his services to those who entered into bonds to pay him large sums of money if he secured the restoration of confiscated land. He also took commissions in arranging compromises between reversioners of forfeited estates and those still in possession of the land. Over the next few years many Catholics owed the recovery of their estates to

Talbot, and he made a fortune. Following accusations that he had suborned witnesses and employed bribery to get satisfaction for one of his clients, Talbot made public threats against the duke of Ormond. This time his behaviour was of such violence that both the king and the duke of York were determined he be punished. In December 1664 he was again sent to the Tower for high misdemeanours, this time for about a month until his release in January 1665. Again, his disgrace was short-lived: he may well have been with the duke in the victory over the Dutch fleet off Lowestoft (3 June 1665), and was certainly with him when he left London for York to avoid the plague in August.

It was at this time that Talbot unsuccessfully wooed Frances Jenyns, the elder sister of Sarah Jenyns (later duchess of Marlborough) [see Talbot, Frances (1648–1731)]. She married Sir George Hamilton in 1666. Talbot married in the spring of 1669 Katherine Boynton (d. 1678), a maid of honour to the queen 'who had fainting fits at Tunbridge, at least twice a day, for love of him' (Hamilton, 2.114). His bride brought with her a dowry of £4000 paid by the king 'in remembrance of the services done by Colonel Boynton, the bride's father' (*CSP Ire.*, 1669–70, 139), who had died defending Scarborough Castle in 1651.

In 1670 Talbot led the attempt to get the Irish land settlement altered. In November he was commissioned by fifty Irish peers and gentlemen who had lost land to the Cromwellians to act as 'the agent-general for the Roman Catholics of Ireland' to petition the king and parliament. The petitioners protested their loyalty and complained that the strict terms of the Act of Settlement prevented them from recovering their lands. Talbot set out for England in belligerent fashion, threatening 'severe things against some who sting him in his business before the House of Lords' (*CSP Ire.*, 1669–70, 309) and presented the petition to the king in January 1671. Prince Rupert was appointed to preside over a government committee to inquire into the effects of the Irish land settlement.

Talbot's efforts were interrupted by the battle of Solebay on 28 May 1672 where he volunteered to serve in the *Royal Katherine* and was taken prisoner by the Dutch. His captivity was again short, and in October he was back in Ireland, where his influence had been enhanced by the appointment as viceroy of Lord Berkeley with whom he had successfully speculated in land in the previous decade. He purchased a captaincy in Lord Berkeley's horse, becoming the only Catholic officer in the Irish army.

Exile and imprisonment In England, Prince Rupert's committee and Talbot's efforts for his principals provoked increasing public hostility. In March 1673 parliament passed the Test Act to prevent Catholics from taking public office and petitioned the king to maintain the Act of Settlement, specifically demanding that Talbot 'might be immediately dismissed out of all commands, either civil or military, and forbid all access to court' (Sergeant, 252). Charles abandoned his attempts to adjust the Irish land settlement and recalled Prince Rupert's committee. The violence of feeling against Talbot was such that he kept out of public affairs and, after selling his commission in

Berkeley's horse for £1000, he for the next five years exiled himself, first to France and then to Yorkshire.

Talbot was back in Ireland in 1678 where in March his wife died, leaving him with two daughters. In that year he was the subject of an extravagant accusation by the perjurer Titus Oates of having accepted a commission from the pope to lead a military uprising. Although Ormond, the lord lieutenant, was content to allow him his liberty, orders were sent from London for his arrest and on 12 November 1678 Talbot was locked up in Dublin Castle where his brother Peter, a Roman Catholic archbishop, was already a prisoner. He petitioned the king for his release on the ground that his health was failing and was bailed on a bond of £10,000 in July 1679. He was given a pass to return to France to convalesce and by November was said to be 'as well at Paris as ever in his life' (Sergeant, 273). In November 1681 in Paris, Talbot married Frances Jenyns [see Talbot, Frances], now Lady Bantry, widow of Sir George Hamilton (comte de Hamilton), and with his new wife and family was allowed to return to Ireland in 1683. The political climate had much changed over the five years since his arrest and Talbot re-established contact with the duke of York. He restarted his political career by travelling to London to report to his patron on the reforms he felt necessary in the Irish privy council, magistracy, and army, reforms which could only be carried out if Ormond was replaced as viceroy.

Lord deputy of Ireland Within a month of James II's accession to the throne in February 1685 Ormond was recalled, his regiment given to Talbot 'and some talk as if there were a design for the papists regaining their estates in that kingdom' (Sergeant, 295). Talbot was sent to Ireland to report on the army, and on 20 June 1685 he was elevated to the Irish peerage as baron of Talbotstown, Viscount Baltinglass, and earl of Tyrconnell (the third creation of that title). He persuaded James that he could only rely upon Catholic troops, and received special instructions to remodel the Irish army so as to end its control by protestants. In March 1686 he was given the command of the army in Ireland, usurping one of the most important functions of the lord lieutenant, Lord Clarendon. Tyrconnell arrived in Ireland on 5 June 1686 to great popular reception and set about handing out commissions to Catholics and cancelling those of protestant officers. He issued orders that only Catholics were to be recruited into the army, although when questioned by Clarendon he denied having done so: 'God damn me', said Tyrconnell, 'I could not give such orders' (ibid., 329). By the end of 1686, two-thirds of the hitherto all protestant army was Catholic. 'He was', according to his secretary and bitter enemy Thomas Sheridan 'so false that a most impudent notorious lie was called at Whitehall and St James's one of Dick Talbot's ordinary truths' (Stuart Papers, 6.47). He was, according to William King, commonly known as 'Lying Dick Talbot' (King, 112).

On his return to London in September 1686 Tyrconnell engineered Clarendon's recall and, with the help of Sunderland, his own appointment as viceroy. Although his formal appointment as lord deputy was made on 8 January 1687, and he was sworn in on 12 February, the only Catholic viceroy since the Reformation, it was clear that he had dominated Irish policy for the year beforehand. In early 1686 he had persuaded James to appoint Catholic judges, and by further appointments he ensured Catholic domination of the courts by 1687.

Tyrconnell's consistent objectives were to reverse the Act of Settlement so as to restore Catholics to their confiscated lands, to place the civil administration in Catholic hands, and to prevent any armed opposition to this by purging the army of protestants and by disarming the protestant militia. The principal beneficiaries of these policies were to be the Old English, the Catholic gentry who had lost the most during the Cromwellian settlement. His dislike of 'the O's and the Macs, and in particular the Ulster men' (Stuart Papers, 6.17) was known even to James, and it was through the extraordinary influence he had over James that he was able to give effect to these policies. His hold over the king was so strong that he boasted that he was responsible for James's conversion to Roman Catholicism.

In June 1687 Tyrconnell was issued, at his own instigation, with a royal warrant empowering him to grant new charters to cities and corporations. This gave him the means to control representation in a future parliament that would be dominated by Catholics eager to repeal the Act of Settlement. In August he was summoned to meet the king at Chester, where the two discussed the act. Although it was rumoured that the act was to be repealed, Tyrconnell's proposals were actually a compromise designed to leave the Cromwellians in possession of half of their holdings, the remaining half going to the former proprietors. However, his plans were foiled by William of Orange's invasion of England on 5 November 1688 and the subsequent flight to France of James.

Preparing for war With civil war imminent, Tyrconnell intended to forestall a northern revolt by replacing the garrison of Londonderry with a new Catholic regiment, but his instructions were carried out with the utmost incompetence. Instead of a simultaneous handover, the city was left ungarrisoned for two weeks, so that when the replacement garrison arrived on 7 December 1688 the gates were shut against it by an armed mob, an action which in time provided the rebels with a fortified stronghold which would prove instrumental in determining the course of the war. His brigadier-general, the protestant Lord Mountjoy, managed to negotiate the return of two companies of protestant troops into the city, and then travelled to Dublin to seek a general pardon for the Londonderry rebels. Tyrconnell feared that in the event of a general rising in the north, Mountjoy would be the natural leader. He made a show of appearing sympathetic to Mountjoy's views and agreed that King James should keep out of Ireland rather than provoke a civil war. In mid-January 1689 he allowed Mountjoy to travel to France so that he could speak to James in person, but sent with him Sir Stephen Rice with instructions to ensure that Mountjoy did not return.

By the end of January, Tyrconnell was determined to fight. He wrote to James: 'Sir, I beg of you to consider whither you can with honour continue where you are when you may possess a Kingdom of your own' and promised that 'I shall very soone make a bolde stroke for your service' (Sergeant, 653). The 'bolde stroke' involved dispatching Richard Hamilton at the head of a small army to crush the northern rebellion. Once assured that James was coming to Ireland, he issued a proclamation offering a pardon to all who lay down their arms, except for ten named as 'principal actors in the rebellion' who were 'not deserving of His Majesty's mercy or favour' (Leslie, 22). Above Dublin Castle he flew a flag emblazoned with the words: 'Now or Never, Now and Forever'.

Pressed by Tyrconnell's letters, James set sail from France on 10 March 1689 with his secretary of state, Lord Melfort, and a flotilla of ships laden with supplies and 200 experienced officers. Tyrconnell wrote optimistically to the duke of Hamilton, not knowing that the duke had already declared for William: 'I hope before the end of July to have the honour to embrace you in Scotland' (Sergeant, 436). Tyrconnell welcomed the king to Dublin on 24 March 1689, and on 30 March he was created marquess and duke of Tyrconnell (some three months after James's flight from England, but while he was still *de facto* king of Ireland).

The war of the two kings The war in the north began well for Tyrconnell's men, who confined the protestant rebels to Londonderry and the unfortified town of Enniskillen. Tyrconnell busied himself in building an army and in the preparations for a loyal parliament. He nominated the members and left it to the sheriffs to make the returns, which they obediently did. Tyrconnell did not want James to join the army in the north, not least because he needed to ensure the king's presence in Dublin to give his assent to the legislation which would break the Act of Settlement. James nevertheless did travel to Londonderry, where the rebels fired at him, but to Tyrconnell's relief he was back in Dublin in time to open parliament on 7 May 1689. Later that month, in accordance with Tyrconnell's long-term plan, the Act of Settlement was repealed and all land was restored to the owners of 1641.

Tyrconnell did not attend the session as he was struck down by ill health. From early April until late August he was confined either to his own house at Talbotstown or to Chapelizod at the official viceregal residence, suffering from heart palpitations and leg ulcers. King Louis's special ambassador Count d'Avaux thought his illness 'is depression as much as anything else; he is upset that Lord Melfort has too much influence over the king and that he governs almost everything in this country' (D'Avaux, *Négociations de M. le Comte d'Avaux en Irlande, 1689–90*, 1860, 148). Tyrconnell charmed d'Avaux and convinced him that he was as good a servant of Louis as he was of James, and that he was willing to use his influence to get James to stay in Ireland until it was properly subdued rather than take an army to Scotland as James and Melfort wanted. He even told d'Avaux that he could arrange the transfer of the best ports in the country to the French. He wrote to Mary of Modena of d'Avaux:

> Wee have need of every body's good word. Let us make as many friends and as few enemies as wee can. It's a dissembling age. I must confesse I doe not love it, and care not to practice it, but noething is lost by being civill to all. (Tate, 121)

He enlisted d'Avaux as an ally against Melfort, and between them they forced James to send him back to France in August 1689. Affairs in Ireland thereafter were run by a council of three, Tyrconnell, the king, and d'Avaux.

By the time Tyrconnell was off his sickbed at the end of August the military situation had worsened. MacCarthy had been captured at Newtownbutler, Londonderry had been relieved, and an English army led by the duke of Schomberg had landed at Bangor and occupied Belfast and Carrickfergus. After months of inactivity, but invigorated by his victory over Melfort, Tyrconnell raced 20,000 reinforcements to Drogheda to block Schomberg's route to the capital. Unwilling to risk a battle, Schomberg halted at Dundalk and waited until it was safe to break camp and move into winter quarters.

French reinforcements arrived in Ireland on 14 March 1690 commanded by d'Avaux's replacement, Count Lauzun, whom Tyrconnell made a point of winning over: 'I love him extreamly and doe make it my studdy to make all things as easy to him as I can' (Tate, 128). But the two did not get on, not least because Lauzun's instructions were to confine the war to Ireland, whereas James wanted to invade England, a policy supported by Tyrconnell since he had succeeded in repealing the Act of Settlement. Although Tyrconnell was now as diplomatic and scheming as ever, the energy that he had exhibited after his long illness in the previous year had deserted him. He had over the years grown heavy, 'of a size to fill a porch' (Sergeant, 271), and was now 'an old and infirm man' (ibid., 526).

Preparations for the campaign of 1690 started late as both sides waited for provisions and for the grass to grow to support the cavalry. The first move came in May when Schomberg took the fort at Charlemont. In that month Tyrconnell wrote to Mary of Modena in France, urging her to persuade the French to send a fleet to take the king to England with most of the army. Even if Ireland were left at William's mercy, 'I am sure I could keep up the bustle here and give him work enough' (Tate, 127) until the king had secured England and sent help back to Ireland.

William arrived in Ireland on 14 June 1690, and a week later Tyrconnell was still advising against facing him in battle, hoping to play out the war until an opportunity arose to invade England. Not even the loss of Dublin was important, so long as 'you can preserve the small army from being beaten, you have an hundred chances for you' (Tate, 133). At the battle of the Boyne (1 July 1690) he did nevertheless behave with great valour in what proved to be a rearguard action at Oldbridge. By sending Count Meinhart Schomberg to cross upstream, William drew the main part of the Jacobite army 4 miles inland. Tyrconnell was left at Oldbridge commanding the 8000 men who faced what proved to be the greater part of the Williamite army, and it is there that the battle took place. The resistance was fierce but Tyrconnell's troops, locally outnumbered by almost three to one, were beaten.

After the battle Tyrconnell and Lauzun persuaded James to return to France, which he did. The Irish army, the greater part of which had not been engaged in the fighting, reformed on the road to Limerick. Nevertheless, Tyrconnell, who had little faith in his army's ability to hold Limerick, was concerned to see if he could negotiate a treaty. He presented a council of war with a declaration signed by most of the senior French officers to the effect that the city's defences were so weak that they would not be able to withstand King William's army for more than three days. In doing this he greatly misjudged the mood of his officers. His apparent willingness to negotiate rather than to gamble everything allowed those in the 'war party', notably Sarsfield and Henry Luttrell, to represent him as a defeatist. Seeing that his suggestion had no support, Tyrconnell changed his stance, resolved to fight, made preparations to defend Limerick, and thwarted a coup planned by Sarsfield's supporters. Rather than stay under siege in Limerick he, with Lauzun and his French brigade, travelled to Galway from where he authorized Sarsfield's celebrated raid on the Williamite artillery train.

William's failure to storm Limerick and the retreat of his army on 30 August 1690 did not lessen the opposition to Tyrconnell within his own army. To Sarsfield's party, the Irish army's defence of Limerick had been made possible despite rather than because of the viceroy. The French noted that his popularity had waned: 'The Irish cannot stand Lord Tyrconnell since his illness and since he sent his wife, daughters and 40,000 gold coins to France' (Mulloy, 920).

Mission to France Once the immediate danger was over, Tyrconnell determined to go to France to report to James. He aimed first to ensure that French aid was sent in time for the spring campaign, and second to secure his position against the inevitable representations that would be made in France by his now numerous political enemies. In mid-September he sailed from Galway accompanied by Lauzun, leaving Berwick as his deputy with particular instructions not to allow anyone to follow him. According to O'Kelly, he duped Lauzun into going on to Paris ahead of him to sing his praises, arriving himself a few days later where he 'outwitted, or rather betrayed, the French courtier' (O'Kelly, 40). He reported to James and Louis that the Irish would fight, and that they had been let down by Lauzun. He got from James the assurances he needed concerning his own position and from Louis the promise of more French officers, supplies, and money to continue the war.

While Tyrconnell was in France, Sarsfield persuaded Berwick to send a deputation to the king to demand that he dismiss Tyrconnell. It was hoped to persuade James:

> that My Lord Tyrconnell was not qualified for such a superintendance as he had hitherto exercised, that his age and infirmitys made him require more sleep than was consistent with so much business, that his want of experience in military affairs rendered him exceedingly slow in his resolves and incapable of laying projects; which no depending General officers would do for him, first by takeing a great deal of pains to make him conceive it; and then either have it rejected, or he to have the honour of it, if successful. (J. S. Clarke, ed., *The Life of James the Second, King of England*, 1816, 2.423)

Should Tyrconnell return 'with the same authority again, it would utterly dishearten the body of the nation' (ibid.).

In December 1690 Tyrconnell set out for Ireland, but was delayed by illness. While bed-bound in Brittany, he discovered that Sarsfield's deputation, which included Henry Luttrell, had arrived in France. He wrote to James to urge him to keep the delegation in France as they would otherwise interfere with his attempts to conciliate Sarsfield. Although James treated the delegation with some coldness, and refused their demands to dismiss Tyrconnell, he did agree to have a French general sent to Ireland.

The final campaign Tyrconnell arrived in Limerick on 14 January 1691, but was soon confined to bed with a swollen foot and was thereafter dogged by ill health throughout the spring. Sarsfield, despite being repeatedly ordered to Limerick, did not arrive until the end of February, and Tyrconnell was nevertheless determined to placate him. He received him with great charm, presented him with patent of the earldom of Lucan, and gave him the task of reforming the army in readiness for the coming campaign. Sarsfield, disappointed at the failure of his deputation, was not won over and continued to plot against the viceroy. Tyrconnell's interference in military matters proved to be a continuing source of discontent among Sarsfield's party and when the promised French general, St Ruth, arrived in Ireland on 9 May 1691, accompanied by Henry Luttrell, it was not clear whether he or Tyrconnell was the supreme commander of the army. This ambiguity emboldened Sarsfield and his supporters. Tyrconnell wrote that when he joined the camp at Athlone: 'I was shocked to discover that while the enemy was within cannon shot of us, these men: Lord Lucan, Purcell and Luttrell; were spending their time and effort taking round a petition calling for my resignation' (Mulloy, 1484). One officer felt confident enough to threaten to cut his tent ropes unless he left. 'Here Tyrconnell made a noble conquest of himself' (Gilbert, 132) and, rather than inflame matters, he travelled back to Limerick. Before leaving he advised St Ruth to demolish the eastern walls of the town so that if Athlone fell, the English would not be able to hold it. His advice was ignored and in his absence St Ruth lost Athlone (30 June 1691), and then disastrously faced Ginckel in a pitched battle at Aughrim (12 July 1691) in which the Irish army was routed and St Ruth killed.

Tyrconnell was back in charge, but the situation was now desperate. He wrote to France demanding help without which he would be forced to make terms. Ginckel marched first on Galway, which surrendered after two days, but nevertheless gave Tyrconnell time to reform the army outside Limerick and concentrate his efforts on completing the city's defences. The fortification of Limerick had been directed by French engineers since the raising of the siege of 1690, and the walls had been screened by massive earthworks. In order to strengthen the resolve of his troops, Tyrconnell made every soldier take an oath not to surrender without King James's consent.

Nevertheless, the débâcle at Aughrim had demoralized and divided the opposition to Tyrconnell. On 2 August 1691 Sarsfield had Henry Luttrell arrested for corresponding with the enemy. Tyrconnell, although unable to bully a court martial into having his opponent found guilty and executed, was at least now able to have him imprisoned.

> Tyrconnell, after putting everything in good order for a vigorous defence, was, on a Monday, the tenth of August, invited to dinner by Monsieur d'Usson, the first lieutenant-general. He and the company were very merry; but at night, upon his preparing to go to bed, he found himself indisposed.   (Gilbert, 155)

He had suffered a stroke. He was able to settle his affairs and appoint three lords justices to succeed him, but by the Thursday was speechless. He died in Limerick on the afternoon of Friday 14 August 1691. 'Thus this great man fell who, in his fall, pulled down a mighty edifice, videlicet, a considerable Catholic nation, for there was no other subject left able to support the national cause' (ibid.). He was buried on the night of Sunday 16th in Limerick Cathedral 'not with that pomp his merits exacted, but with that decency which the present state of affairs admitted' (ibid., 157). No monument was erected over his grave. On 25 August, Ginckel's army arrived outside Limerick. The war ended fifty days after Tyrconnell's death. Limerick surrendered on 3 October 1691. 'If the Duke of Tyrconnell were then alive (I utter it with certainty)', wrote his anonymous champion, 'he would not hearken to any offer of surrender' (ibid., 175).

Tyrconnell's widow lived at St Germain-en-Laye until 1704, where she was a lady-in-waiting to Mary of Modena, and afterwards at Delft. In 1708 she returned to Dublin where she lived until her death in 1731. Tyrconnell's title passed to his brother, William Talbot of Haggardstown. His only legitimate child to reach maturity, Charlotte, married his nephew Richard Talbot, the third earl. The title became extinct in 1752. Among his illegitimate children were Brigadier Richard Talbot who died in the French service in 1702, and Colonel Mark Talbot, a signatory to the treaty of Limerick.   PIERS WAUCHOPE

Sources P. W. Sergeant, *Little Jennings and fighting Dick Talbot* (1913) · J. Miller, 'The earl of Tyrconnell and James II's Irish policy, 1685–1688', *HJ*, 20 (1977), 803–23 · J. McGuire, 'Richard Talbot, earl of Tyrconnell and the Catholic counter-revolution', *Worsted in the game, losers in Irish history*, ed. C. Brady (1989), 73–83 · Sir C. Petrie, *The great Tyrconnel* (1972) · S. Mulloy, ed., *Franco-Irish correspondence, December 1688–February 1692*, 2 vols. (1983–4) · A. Hamilton, *Memoirs of Count Grammont*, ed. G. Goodwin (1908) · 'Letter-book of Richard Talbot', ed. L. Tate, *Analecta Hibernica*, 4 (1932), 99–138 · *Calendar of the Stuart papers belonging to his majesty the king, preserved at Windsor Castle*, 7 vols., HMC, 56 (1902–23), vol. 6 · *CSP Ire.*, 1669–70 · T. Gilbert, ed., *A Jacobite narrative of the war in Ireland, 1688–1691* (1971) · W. King, *The state of the protestants of Ireland under the late King James* (1692) · C. Leslie, *An answer to a book intituled 'The state of the protestants in Ireland'* (1692) · C. O'Kelly, *Macariae Excidium, or, The destruction of Cyprus* (1846) · GEC, *Peerage*, new edn, 12/2.116–23 · M. A. Anselme, 'Oraison Funebre de Milord Richard Talbot, duc de Tyrconnel … 22 Aoust 1692', *Recueil des Diverses Oraisons Funebres* (1712), 4.287–337 · *DNB*

Archives BL, letter-book, Add. MS 38145 · Bodl. Oxf., papers | CKS, letters to Alexander Stanhope

Likenesses J. Bulfinch, ink and wash on paper, c.1670 (after Kneller), NG Ire. · H. Rigaud, oils, c.1685, NPG · by or after F. de Troy, oils, 1690, NPG [*see illus.*] · oils, c.1690, NPG · W. N. Gardiner, stipple, BM, NPG; repro. in S. Harding, *Biographical mirrour* (1794) · portrait, priv. coll.

Wealth at death little in Ireland as everything confiscated; but shipped out 40,000 gold coins to France in year before death

Talbot, Robert (1505/6–1558), antiquary, was born in Thorpe Malsor, Northamptonshire, in 1505 or 1506, the son of John Talbot. He was admitted to Winchester College in 1517, aged eleven. In 1521 he entered New College, Oxford, where he was admitted BA in 1525 and supplicated for his MA degree on 10 December 1529. He was a schoolmaster at Brentwood ('Borned Wodde'), Essex, by 1531, and may have acted as tutor to the children of Sir Thomas Wriothesley. He held a number of ecclesiastical benefices in Essex, Kent, Somerset (where he was a canon and prebendary at Wells Cathedral), Northamptonshire, Norfolk, and Buckinghamshire, and was one of Cranmer's chaplains. In 1547 he was made a prebendary and canon of Norwich Cathedral, a position he retained until his death in August or September 1558; he also acted as treasurer. He died at Norwich and was buried in the cathedral. His will, dated 20 August 1558, was proved on 12 February 1561.

Praised for his love of learning by John Bale, and the subject of a verse encomium by John Leland, Talbot was a pioneer in the field of antiquarian studies. His principal work was his topographical analysis of the Antonine Itineraries, *Annotationes in eam partem Itinerarii Antonini quae ad Britanniam spectat*, which laid the groundwork for future studies of Roman Britain. William Camden, among others, took extracts, and Thomas Hearne published it in his edition of John Leland's *Itinerary* (Oxford, 1710–12, 3.128–48). Talbot's unpublished *Aurum ex stercore, sive, Veterum aenigmatum et prophetiarum collectio* survives only in a seventeenth-century copy contained in Oxford, Corpus Christi College, MS 258.

The notebook containing Talbot's autograph copy of the *Annotationes Itinerarii Antonini* (now Cambridge, Corpus Christi College, MS 379) passed to Matthew Parker after Talbot's death, as did his transcripts of Anglo-Saxon charters (now part of Cambridge, Corpus Christi College, MS 111). The charters were of interest to Talbot because they contained place names and terms for topographical features in Old English. His annotations to Cambridge, Corpus Christi College, MS 383, a twelfth-century compilation of Old English laws, indicate the same sort of linguistic and topographical concerns. In his notebook Talbot also made a list of Old English words and their Latin equivalents, and this list, the earliest of its kind in the sixteenth century, represents the beginning of modern Anglo-Saxon lexicographical studies. He examined runic alphabets in several manuscripts, and made an attempt, not altogether successful, to understand the differing forms of runes.

As Talbot's annotations establish, some ten manuscripts containing Old English passed through his hands; their varying medieval provenances suggest that he made a genuine effort to track down Old English materials rather than just happening on manuscripts. He was part of a circle of collectors and exchanged materials with John Leland, to whom he lent Byrhtferth's 'computistical miscellany' from Thorney (now Oxford, St John's College, MS 17) and the Old English Orosius and Anglo-Saxon Chronicle (now British Library, MS Cotton Tiberius B.i). He lent Robert Recorde Tiberius B.i, and probably also Cambridge University Library, MS Kk.3.18 (a Worcester copy of the Old English Bede). Talbot made notes in more than twenty medieval manuscripts associated with Norwich Cathedral, although he probably did not take personal possession of them. In the *Index Britanniae scriptorum* John Bale lists twenty-two titles of works, not all from the Anglo-Saxon period, which he saw in Talbot's library.

In his will Talbot left his choice manuscripts to New College, Oxford, but requested that they be delivered first to Henry Cole, dean of St Paul's Cathedral, London, and John Harpsfield, dean of Norwich Cathedral, both of whom had been fellows at New College. It seems highly unlikely that any of the books got to New College, however, probably because Cole and Harpsfield, both Catholics, were arrested early in Elizabeth's reign. Writing to Matthew Parker on 30 July 1560, Bale observed that Talbot's executors—his nephew Robert Quince and Dr John Barret, prebendary of Norwich—had 'many noble antiquytees' (Graham and Watson, 25), and books owned or annotated by Talbot ended up in a variety of other locations.

JAMES P. CARLEY

Sources Emden, *Oxf.*, 4.555, 739 · N. R. Ker, ed., *Catalogue of manuscripts containing Anglo-Saxon* (1957) · N. R. Ker, 'Medieval manuscripts from Norwich Cathedral Library', *Transactions of the Cambridge Bibliographical Society*, 1 (1949–53), 1–28; repr. in *Books, collectors and libraries*, ed. A. G. Watson (1985), 243–72 · Bale, *Index* · *The recovery of the past in early Elizabethan England: documents by John Bale and John Joscelyn from the circle of Matthew Parker*, ed. T. Graham and A. G. Watson (1998) · T. Graham, 'Robert Talbot's "Old Saxonice Bede": Cambridge University Library, MS Kk.3.18 and the "Alphabeticum Norwagiaum" of British Library, Cotton MSS, Domitian A. IX', *Books and collectors, 1200–1700: essays presented to Andrew Watson*, ed. J. P. Carley and C. G. C. Tite (1997), 295–316 · T. Graham, 'The earliest Old English word-list from Tudor England', *Medieval English Studies Newsletter*, 35 (Dec 1996), 4–7 · T. Graham, 'Early modern users of Claudius B. IV: Robert Talbot and William L'Isle', *The Old English Hexateuch: aspects and approaches*, ed. R. Barnhouse and B. C. Withers (Kalamazoo, MI, 2000), 271–316 · *DNB*

Archives BL, Ct Vit D vii · CCC Cam., collection of transcripts | Gon. & Caius Cam., MS copy of *Annotationes in eam partem Itinerarii Antonini quae ad Britanniam spectat* with MS additions by John Caius

Talbot [*née* Bonnell], **Sara** [Sadie] **(1888–1993)**, volunteer ambulance driver and member of the FANY, was born Sara Bonnell at 26 Mortlake Road, Kew, Surrey, on 4 June 1888, the daughter of Bentley Jay Bonnell, a dentist who was born in Philadelphia, Pennsylvania, USA, and his wife, Harriet Powell (*née* Coffin). She was educated at Bedales

School, Petersfield, Hampshire, which had been recently founded as a co-educational experiment. After leaving school she returned home and, as she later recalled, 'looked after the servants, that kind of thing' (*The Independent*, 9 Nov 1988). She learned to drive and in 1915, when the Zeppelin raids began on London 'I asked [the authorities] if I could drive an ambulance, but it wasn't considered the right thing for a woman to do' (ibid.). Her experience was similar to those of Vera Laughton Mathews who, applying to the Admiralty for any job, however humble, was dismissed curtly with, 'We don't want any petticoats here', and Dr Elsie Inglis, who was informed, 'My good lady, go home and sit still' (Popham, 15). Instead Bonnell took a job driving an ambulance in London for the Canadian Army Service Corps.

In December 1917 Bonnell joined the First Aid Nursing Yeomanry (FANY) which had been founded by Sergeant-Major Edward Charles Baker in 1907 as a corps of nurses on horseback 'tending Britain's soldiers on the field' (Terry, 25). Together with other members of the FANY she crossed the channel to serve as a driver with the Canadian Army Service Corps in France and Belgium. At first she drove field kitchens, mobile bathing facilities, and supply lorries, but as the casualties mounted the job resolved itself into driving ambulances ferrying the constant stream of wounded soldiers from advanced dressing stations to field hospitals and channel ports. It was a nightmare situation for the ambulance drivers, transporting the wounded over poor roads and across bumpy railway lines. The vehicles had rudimentary windscreens, inefficient springs, unreliable engines, no self-starters, and tyres which punctured easily. Sometimes the men in the back were quiet. It was worse when someone screamed, 'Sister, I can't stand much more of this, drive fast and get it over!' (Popham, 28). Maintaining the vehicles was part of the job and, during the winter, it became almost impossible. At hourly intervals throughout the night the duty drivers had to crank the engines and warm them up. Often the engine would backfire, causing the handle to kick and either break an arm or throw the driver over the mudguard. When, at the age of 100, Talbot was asked by an interviewer whether it took courage to drive often twenty-four hours without a break, on thin tyres which punctured easily, to the background of men's cries of pain, her forthright reply was: 'If I may say so, you do ask awfully silly questions. It wasn't a matter of courage. I was there to do something useful.' She went on to recall that on one occasion she was handed a single severed arm. 'Really, I didn't know quite what I was expected to do. I mean the arm had already lost its body' (*The Independent*, 9 Nov 1988).

On the night of 18–19 May 1918 Bonnell won the Military Medal for her coolness and courage in collecting wounded men from an advanced dressing station near St Omer while under bombardment for five hours. She and four other women drove throughout the air raids. For that night's work sixteen military medals and two croix de guerre were awarded to the FANY and voluntary aid detachments crews. 'All the decorations were questioned', noted Beryl Hutchinson, a member of the FANY, in her personal memoir, 'as there were far too many for one small unit, but each one was so strongly supported for their cool example that in the end all 18 [decorations] were allowed' (Popham, 41). General Sir Herbert Plumer, general officer commanding Second Army, presented the military medals in the field. Bonnell's citation read as follows:

> For gallantry and conspicuous devotion to duty, when an ammunition dump had been set on fire by enemy bombs and the only available ambulance for the removal of wounded had been destroyed. [Bonnell] subsequently arrived with three ambulances, and, despite the danger arising from various explosions, succeeded in removing all the wounded. [Her] conduct throughout was splendid. (*London Gazette*, 8 July 1918)

When asked how she had coped during those hectic days, Sadie's blunt reply again illustrated an unequivocal attitude towards her interviewer: 'What another very silly question. Of course I didn't cope. Who did? But there was a job we had to get done' (*The Independent*, 9 Nov 1988). 'I was not frightened during those drives', she said. 'I did not think about it. I enjoyed being out in France and, if it was dangerous, that did not seem to matter at the time' (*The Independent*, 11 Sept 1993).

Bonnell returned to England after the war, in April 1919, and thereafter continued to be associated with nursing and undertook voluntary work in hospitals. On 1 September 1919 she married Major Herbert Marriott (1892/3–1921), the son of Herbert Marriott, railway manager. They had met in France, where he had been a gas victim. He died in 1921 in the influenza pandemic. After his death his widow built herself a cottage, Thrushling, Upper Hartfield, Sussex, where she lived with her second husband, Charles Leslie Talbot (d. 1967), a sales manager and son of the Revd Walter Charles Talbot, Congregational minister. They married on 8 August 1948. There were no children of either marriage.

Talbot was a tall and very pretty woman with a lovely smile who, in later life, was described as having the features of a Victorian porcelain doll and a very direct manner. She was described as a tomboy who loved sport and who seized the opportunities offered by the war to break out of the conventional Edwardian mould. She loved fast cars and between the two world wars drove a six-cylinder AC, similar to the model which became the first British car to win the Monte Carlo rally in 1926. Her car had a red fish mascot on the bonnet, a reminder of a senior British army officer's description of the FANYs in France: 'Neither fish, flesh nor fowl but damned good red herring' (Popham, xii). She was deeply attached to her family, her only sister, Phoebe Weber (1886–1979), and the latter's three children, Irene Sweny, John Weber, and Rosemary Foster, who described their famous aunt as 'autocratic, a bit of a disciplinarian, but as brave as a lion in words and deeds, very loving and devoted to her family'. On her ninety-fifth birthday her one regret was that she could 'no longer drive fast cars' (*The Independent*, 11 Sept 1993). She died at the age of 105 on 2 September 1993 at Dorset House, Blackfriars Avenue, Droitwich, Worcester, where she had lived for a number of years.

Talbot was an outstanding member of a body of volunteers who, disregarding official hostility, ignoring the hazards of warfare, and defying conventions, undertook essential humanitarian tasks for the British army in France and Belgium during the First World War. They set an exceptional example which earned them plaudits from royalty as well as from senior military officers. Field Marshal Earl Wavell's comment was typical of the esteem which the FANYs earned during their wartime work. 'The FANY corps has the oldest traditions and the proudest record of all women's corps in this country', he said, 'and therefore the greatest spirit' (Popham, 121). The tally of decorations awarded to members of the corps during the First World War speaks for itself—seventeen military medals, twenty-seven croix de guerre, one appointment to the Légion d'honneur, one to the order of the Crown (Belgium), two to the order of Leopold, two OBEs, two MBEs, and eleven mentioned in dispatches.

ROY TERRY

Sources H. Popham, *FANY: the story of the women's transport service, 1907–1984* (1984) · I. Ward, *FANY invicta* (1955) · R. Terry, *Women in khaki* (1988) · *The Independent* (9 Nov 1988) · *The Independent* (11 Sept 1993) · private information (2004) [J. H. E. Weber] · *Daily Telegraph* (13 Sept 1993) · b. cert. · m. certs. · *The Times* (9 Sept 1993)
Archives Women's Transport Service (FANY), Duke of York Headquarters, London, FANY archives
Likenesses photograph, repro. in *The Times* · photograph, repro. in *Daily Telegraph* · photographs, FANY, London
Wealth at death under £125,000: probate, 19 Oct 1993, *CGPLA Eng. & Wales*

Talbot, Thomas, second Viscount Lisle (c.1449–1470), magnate, was the son of John Talbot, first Viscount Lisle (d. 1453), and Joan Chedder, and the grandson of John *Talbot, first earl of Shrewsbury (d. 1453), and his second wife, Margaret *Talbot née Beauchamp [see under Talbot, John, first earl of Shrewsbury]. He inherited his lands, titles, and claims from his paternal great-grandmother, Elizabeth *Berkeley, countess of Warwick. His inherited lands, including Kingston Lisle in Berkshire, which he entered on coming of age in 1469, were worth approximately £200 p.a. His father died on the field of Castillon when he was just five and Talbot became the ward of his grandmother. On her death in 1467 he became the heir to two claims: lands settled on his father from the Talbot inheritance, and the lordship of Berkeley. She had been in possession of Painswick from the Talbot inheritance and the other Gloucestershire manors of Wotton under Edge, Cowley, and Simondshall from Berkeley.

Lisle immediately faced a challenge from William, Lord Berkeley. Both parties resorted to violence; Berkeley attacked Wotton and Lisle attempted to seize Berkeley Castle. In March 1470, taking advantage of the Lincolnshire rebellion and the collapse of royal authority, Lisle challenged Berkeley to battle. Marching down to confront Berkeley at the head of a band of armed tenants and retainers, he was ambushed on 19 March on Nibley Green, between Berkeley and Wotton. Wounded in the face by an arrow, he was finished off by a dagger-thrust. The skirmish on Nibley Green is supposedly the last 'private' battle fought in England; it was certainly symptomatic of the manner in which the participants in private feuds took advantage of the dynastic conflicts of the Wars of the Roses to settle their own differences.

Nibley Green brought half a century of local conflict to an end. In 1466 Lisle had married Margaret (d. before 1503), youngest daughter of William Herbert, earl of Pembroke. He died childless; and she reputedly miscarried when Wotton manor was sacked after the skirmish. His title, inheritance, and claims passed to his sister Elizabeth, who in 1475 married Edward Grey, younger son of Edward Grey, Lord Ferrers, and brother of Queen Elizabeth Woodville's first husband. He made a formal release of all his claims on the Berkeley inheritance in 1482, but retained possession of Painswick. A. J. POLLARD

Sources Chancery records · J. Smyth, The Berkeley manuscripts: the lives of the Berkeleys ... 1066 to 1618, ed. J. Maclean, 3 vols. (1883–5) · GEC, Peerage, 8.57–8 · A. J. Pollard, 'The family of Talbot, Lords Talbot and earls of Shrewsbury in the fifteenth century', PhD diss., University of Bristol, 1968
Archives Glos. RO
Wealth at death approx. £200: receiver-general's account of Lord Lisle, c.1475–1483, PRO, SC 6/1119/6

Talbot, Thomas (c.1535–1595×9), antiquary, was born about 1535 at Salesbury Hall, Lancashire, the second son of John Talbot (1501–1551), gentleman, and the eldest son of the six sons and three daughters born to him and his second wife, Anne, daughter of Richard Bannester of Altham. His father was lord of the manor of Salesbury, which his family had owned since the early fifteenth century. The date of Thomas's birth is not recorded, but the 1533 Visitation of Lancashire notes that there were then no children of John Talbot's recent second marriage, and it may be assumed that he was born not much later. Although he was probably educated at Cambridge (matriculating from Trinity College 1553; scholar, 1554; fellow, 1555; BA, 1557/8) rather than Oxford, Wood includes him in his Athenae Oxonienses, and calls him Limping Talbot on account of his lameness, adding that he did, 'by the help of a good memory, become a most excellent genealogist, and a man of singular skill in our antiquities' (Wood, Ath. Oxon., 1.265). In 1566 he transcribed the 'Encomium Emmae reginae' and he was probably working on the records in the Tower of London by 1573. Certainly in 1578 he was writing to his brother-in-law with the results of genealogical searches, probably in the Tower, and before 1580 he had become a clerk of the records there. He became a member of the Elizabethan Society of Antiquaries and is recorded in 1591 as taking part in a discussion of the antiquity of the English shires.

It is principally for his archival work that Talbot deserves notice. Although he published nothing, he was as assiduous as his friend Robert Glover in collecting and making available evidence from original records, both private and public. John Philpot and Thomas Abingdon were both indebted to his work, he was on friendly terms with John Stow, and Camden wrote: 'Not to conceal my

obligations to any, I must acknowledge myself under very great ones to Thomas Talbot, a diligent examiner of records and a perfect master of our antiquities' (Camden, 1.cxlviii). A volume of his antiquarian gatherings survives in the National Library of Wales, Aberystwyth (MS 21744E), and there are also genealogical and historical collections made by him, along with manuscript lists of office-holders, among the Cottonian, Harleian, Lansdowne, and Additional manuscripts in the British Library, London, and among the Ashmolean and Dodsworth manuscripts in the Bodleian Library, Oxford.

The exact date of Talbot's death is unknown. He was certainly still alive in 1593, and the fact that Francis Tate's list of members of the Society of Antiquaries of c.1590 carries later annotations marking four deceased members, who included William Fleetwood and James Strangman, dead in 1594 and 1595–6 respectively, but not Talbot himself, suggests that the latter lived into the second half of the decade. But he was not one of the members recorded in the year 41 Elizabeth, which ran from 17 November 1598 to 16 November 1599, and so it seems likely that he died between 1595 and 1599. IAN MORTIMER

Sources Wood, Ath. Oxon., new edn, 1.265–6; 2.108 · VCH Lancashire, vol. 6 · C. E. Wright, 'The Elizabethan Society of Antiquaries and the formation of the Cottonian Library', The English library before 1700, ed. F. Wormwald and C. E. Wright (1958), 176–212 · W. H. Black, A descriptive, analytical and critical catalogue of the manuscripts bequeathed unto the University of Oxford by Elias Ashmole, 2 vols. (1845–66) · W. A. Abram, A history of Blackburn, town and parish (1877); repr. (1990) · W. Flower, A visitation of the county palatine of Lancaster, made in the year 1567, ed. F. R. Raines, Chetham Society, 81 (1870) · W. Langton, ed., The visitation of Lancashire and a part of Cheshire ... AD 1533, 1, Chetham Society, 98 (1876) · DNB · C. J. Wright, Sir Robert Cotton as collector (1997) · M. McKisack, Medieval history in the Tudor age (1971) · W. Camden, Britannia, or, A chorographical description of the flourishing kingdoms of England, Scotland, and Ireland, ed. and trans. R. Gough, 2nd edn, 1 (1806) · Venn, Alum. Cant., 1/4.198 · Foster, Alum. Oxon.
Archives BL, account of the court claims at the coronations of Richard II, Henry IV, and Henry V, Lansdowne MS 279 · BL, collection of monastic records and chronicles, bound together by Sir Robert Cotton, Ct Vesp D xvii 12b · BL, folio entitled 'Talbot's extracts of records', Harleian MS 6723 · BL, collection ... for the use of Sir Robert Cotton (1 vol), Harleian MS 2223 · BL, collectanea de familiis Angliae ex chartis et literis patentibus regum Angliae, Harley MS 4010 · BL, collection relating to Yorkshire, Add. MSS 26717 ff [copies] · BL, custodes rotulorum cancellariae Angliae, 1294–1588; summi Angliae justiciarii et capitales justiciarii ad placita coram rege; capitales justiciarii de banco ..., Harleian MS 6082 · Bodl. Oxf., archicamerarii Angliae · Bodl. Oxf., collectanea, e rotuli in Turri Londinensi servatis · Bodl. Oxf., collection of monastic records and chronicles now in the BL [copies] · Bodl. Oxf., pedigrees derived from public records with occasional references to Talbot's collections · Bodl. Oxf., copies of his pedigrees by Robert Glover, incl. some in Talbot's own hand · Bodl. Oxf., genealogical scraps in his own hand · Bodl. Oxf., genealogy of the Montacute, Neville, and Brown families · Coll. Arms, extracts from inquisition post mortems relating to Yorkshire and from other records · NL Wales, antiquarian collection

Talbot, Thomas (1771–1853), army officer and settler in Canada, was born at Malahide Castle, co. Dublin, on 19 July 1771, the fourth son of Richard Talbot (d. 1788) of Malahide Castle and his wife, Margaret (d. 1834), the daughter of James O'Reilly of Ballinlough, co. Westmeath. His

Thomas Talbot (1771–1853), attrib. James Buckingham
Wandesford

younger brother was Admiral Sir John *Talbot. He entered
the army on 24 May 1783 as an ensign in the 66th foot,
became lieutenant on 27 September 1783, and was on half
pay from 1784 to 1787, when he was gazetted to the 24th
foot and attending Manchester Free Public School. He
served as an aide-de-camp to the marquess of Buckingham, the lord lieutenant of Ireland. In 1790 he accompanied his regiment to Quebec, and in February 1792 became
the acting private secretary of Upper Canada's first
lieutenant-governor, John Graves Simcoe. On 6 March
1794 he was promoted to major of the 85th foot. In June of
that year he left his position with Simcoe and went to England, and later served in the Netherlands and Gibraltar.
On 12 January 1796 he purchased a lieutenant-colonelcy in
the 5th foot, but on 25 December 1800 he sold his commission and left for Upper Canada.

In May 1803 Talbot obtained a field officer's grant of
5000 acres on the northern shore of Lake Ontario, about
150 miles from Simcoe's new capital, York (later Toronto),
and settled at Port Talbot. He was to allot his 5000 acres to
settlers in 50 acre parcels, with each allotment securing
him an additional 200 acres. In 1807 he began ignoring
these provisions, keeping his original grant as a demesne,
settling families outside of it, and acquiring new lands for
himself. He also ignored normal procedures for register-
ing the lands of his settlers. The provincial government,
eager for growth, acquiesced in all this. To improve access
to his settlement, Talbot pushed for the right to build a

road to the Niagara frontier. Having been successful in
this, in 1811 he secured permission to extend it all the way
to the Detroit River in the west. He reported in 1817 that he
had settled a total of 804 families. But by this time he had
won a number of enemies, notably many of the highland
Scots settlers of his original area, who objected to their
tiny 50 acre allotments, and members of the provincial
government, who knew that his disregard of normal procedures denied officials and the province needed fees and
revenues. In 1818 Talbot travelled to England, where the
colonial secretary, Lord Bathurst, sanctioned his unusual
practices. Consequently his settlement continued to
expand, and by 1828 ranged over 130 miles. In 1829 he estimated that it had 50,000 inhabitants. His autocratic ways
continued to earn him enemies, however, and in 1838
Lieutenant-Governor Sir Francis Bond Head, supported by
Lord Glenelg, the colonial secretary, asked him to relinquish his settlement. Glenelg congratulated him on having discharged his duties 'with so much honor to yourself
and advantage to the Public' (Governor General's Office
Letter Books, vol. 45, J. Macaulay to Col. Talbot, Toronto, 23
June 1838, National Archives of Canada). Talbot dallied in
divesting himself of his responsibilities. An eccentric and
a recluse, he lived on at Port Talbot, though in his last year
he moved with his servant, confidant, and heir, George
Macbeth, and his wife, to nearby London, Canada West,
where he died unmarried on 5 February 1853. He was buried at Tyrconnel, near Port Talbot, on 9 February.

Talbot was, and is, a controversial figure. He was sufficiently popular that for a quarter of a century 21 May was
celebrated in his neighbourhood as founder's day, yet he
was particularly disliked by some of his highlanders. He
reciprocated the feeling, advising others not to settle
north-country Scots. He also fell foul of politicians, government officials, and, later, historians. Some of the last
have argued that he actually retarded, not helped, settlement. Impartial judgement, however, would allow that
his road-building activities facilitated development. Despite his Britishness and his love for Britain (he returned
there six times after settling in Upper Canada), and his suspicion of Americans (he commanded the London district
militia in the Anglo-American War of 1812–14 and lost a
mill to marauders), he ignored those in government who
wished to exclude Americans from the province. In this,
he did signal service.   COLIN FREDERICK READ

Sources F. C. Hamil, *Lake Erie baron: the story of Colonel Thomas Talbot* (1955) • A. G. Brunger, 'Talbot, Thomas', *DCB*, vol. 8 • C. O.
Ermatinger, *The Talbot regime, or, The first half century of the Talbot
settlement* (1904) • E. Ermatinger, *Life of Colonel Talbot, and the Talbot
settlement. Its rise and progress, with sketches of the public characters, and
career of some of the most conspicuous men in Upper Canada, who were
either friends or acquaintances of the subject of these memoirs* (1859) • J. H.
Coyne, ed., 'The Talbot papers—edited with preface, introduction
and some annotations (portrait)', *Proceedings and Transactions of the
Royal Society of Canada*, 3rd ser., 1 (1907), section 2, pp. 15–210 • J. H.
Coyne, ed., 'The Talbot papers—part 2', *Proceedings and Transactions
of the Royal Society of Canada*, 3rd ser., 3 (1909), section 2, pp. 67–196 •
J. M. S. Careless, ed., 'Letters from Thomas Talbot to John Beverley
Robinson', *Ontario Historical Society Papers and Records*, 49 (1957), 25–
41 • P. Baldwin, 'The political career of Colonel Thomas Talbot',
Ontario History, 61 (1969), 9–18 • W. Paddon, *The story of the Talbot*

settlement, 1803–1840: a frontier history of south-western Ontario (1976) • *St Thomas Weekly Dispatch* (15 Feb 1853) • R. S. Harris and T. G. Harris, eds., *The Eldon House diaries: five women's views of the 19th century* (1994) • Governor General's Office Letter Books, NA Canada, vol. 45 [microfilm]

Archives University of Western Ontario, London, Ontario | Herefs. RO, corresp. with Lord Airey • NA Canada, state papers, E.3, vol. 87 • Public Archives of Ontario, Toronto, Robinson MSS • Toronto Public Library, Simcoe MSS

Likenesses watercolour, *c*.1830, University of Western Ontario, London, Ontario • J. E. Alexander, pen and ink, *c*.1840, NA Canada • J. B. Wandesford, lithograph, 1849 (after his earlier work), priv. coll. • attrib. J. B. Wandesford, watercolour, University of Western Ontario, London, Ontario, McIntosh Gallery [*see illus.*] • silhouette, University of Western Ontario, London, Ontario

Wealth at death approx. £50,000—almost all left to servant and confidant, George Macbeth: Ermatinger, *The Talbot regime*, 299; Hamil, *Lake Erie baron*, 289

Talbot, Sir William, first baronet (*d.* 1634), politician, was the son of Robert Talbot of Carton, co. Kildare, and grandson of Sir Thomas Talbot of Malahide, co. Dublin. He was educated for the law in Dublin, and subsequently attained a leading position as a lawyer in the city. About 1603 he was appointed recorder of Dublin, but, being a staunch Roman Catholic, he was soon afterwards removed for recusancy. At an unknown date he married Alison (*fl.* 1595–1644), daughter of John Netterville of Castleton, co. Meath. They had eight sons and eight daughters.

On 13 April 1613 Talbot was returned to the Irish parliament for co. Kildare, and he at once became the 'legal oracle' of the Catholic party in the Irish House of Commons (Gardiner, 290). Thomas Ryves complained to the home government that Talbot had abetted the return to parliament for Dublin 'of two of the most Spanish and seditious schismatiques in all the city'. During the disorderly scenes which marked the election of a speaker in the Irish House of Commons, Talbot urged that the house should first purge itself of such protestant 'New English' members as had been elected illegally. On 30 May he was appointed by the house as one of the deputies to represent to James I the corrupt practices employed in the elections to secure a protestant majority, and the arbitrary treatment of the Anglo-Irish Catholics. He crossed to England in July, and was examined by the privy council on his conduct in the Irish House of Commons. During the discussion of this question Archbishop Abbot demanded Talbot's opinion on a book (probably the *Defensio fidei catholicae*) in which the Jesuit Suarez openly maintained the right of Catholics to kill a heretical king. Talbot hesitated to express abhorrence of this doctrine, but was ready to acknowledge James I as lawful king. The council was not satisfied, and on 17 July Talbot was committed to the Tower. On 13 November the Star Chamber sentenced him to a fine of £10,000. Early in the next year, however, Talbot was allowed to return to Ireland, and probably the fine was remitted. James I, on releasing him, disclaimed any intention of forcing the Irish Catholics to change their religion. From this time Talbot became a supporter of the government, but took little part in politics. On 4 February 1623 he was created a baronet, and he subsequently received various grants of land.

In 1628 Talbot was one of the commissioners sent to England to represent the interests of the Catholic 'Old English' in negotiations with Charles I which eventually gave rise to the famous 'graces'. Described as 'the apex of Old English political achievement', they secured no more than an 'inferior' status within the system of privilege in Ireland (Clarke, 'Selling royal favours', 238). Nevertheless, they became the touchstone of political right and freedom for a generation of Catholic politicians in Ireland, a set of concessions which Lord Deputy Wentworth forcibly rebuffed during his tenure at Dublin Castle.

Talbot died on 16 March 1634 and was buried on 1 April at Maynooth, co. Kildare. He was survived by his wife. Their eldest son, Robert, succeeded as second baronet; from his daughter Frances, who married Richard Talbot of Malahide, descended the barons Talbot of Malahide. Their second son was Peter *Talbot, Roman Catholic archbishop of Dublin, and the eighth was Richard *Talbot, duke of Tyrconnell.   A. F. POLLARD, *rev.* SEAN KELSEY

Sources GEC, *Baronetage* • S. R. Gardiner, *History of England from the accession of James I to the outbreak of the civil war, 1603–1642*, 10 vols. (1901–7), vol. 2, pp. 290, 294–5 • A. Clarke, *The Old English in Ireland, 1625–1642* (1966) • A. Clarke, 'Selling royal favours, 1624–32', *A new history of Ireland*, ed. T. W. Moody and others, 3: *Early modern Ireland, 1534–1691* (1976), 233–42 • A. Clarke, 'Pacification, plantation, and the Catholic question, 1603–23', *A new history of Ireland*, ed. T. W. Moody and others, 3: *Early modern Ireland, 1534–1691* (1976), 187–232 • A. Clarke, 'The government of Wentworth', *A new history of Ireland*, ed. T. W. Moody and others, 3: *Early modern Ireland, 1534–1691* (1976), 243–69

Archives NL Ire., corresp. | PRO NIre., letters to earl of Kildare

Talbot, William [*name in religion* William of the Holy Spirit] (*b. c.*1580), Roman Catholic priest, was born near Navan, co. Meath. He belonged to a branch of one of the most prestigious Catholic Old English families in Ireland. He began studying at the Irish College in Lisbon about 1600 and passed from there to the Dominican order (one of sixteen students to do so between 1593 and 1615). Thereafter he was known as William of the Holy Spirit and was educated at Salamanca University and in one or more of the flourishing Iberian Dominican *studia generalia* until 1610.

In 1613, while procurator in Madrid of the fledgeling Irish Dominican congregation, Talbot was charged by Seraphinus Secchi, master-general, with the task of obtaining a college exclusively for Irish Dominicans from Philip III of Spain. On 27 January 1615 Talbot reported to Ross MacGeoghegan, vicar of the Irish congregation, that he had been in Seville for three months in pursuit of his objective, outlining the personal difficulties he had encountered. On 3 February he wrote of his optimistic vision for political and religious development for Ireland. He had learned that negotiations were in progress for a royal marriage between England and Spain from which it was hoped that liberty of conscience for Catholics might follow. With colleges and houses established abroad, Irish religious orders would be able to send members to Britain and Ireland to promote the recovery of the orders and the Catholic faith. In Talbot's eyes, the foundation of an Irish Dominican college in Spain was doubly important, both for the political interests of Spain, and for the revival of the order in Ireland; should the English revoke liberty of conscience, Spain would have many friends and sympathizers and it would then prove possible to remove Ireland from English control. These personally stated views were later robustly contested by his opponents.

There is ample evidence that Talbot was employed throughout the 1620s as an agent of the Spanish crown. He may also have been at times a double agent, working for English crown officials, notably John Bathe, his Irish cousin, and George Villiers, duke of Buckingham. It would appear that English instructions and indeed misinformation were passed on to him, chiefly by Bathe, a known spy, who feigned to be a loyal agent of the Spanish king. It was this same John Bathe who assassinated Donal O'Sullivan Beare in Madrid on 16 July 1618.

In September 1627 Spanish officials carried out a secret investigation into Talbot's activities, in the course of which they consulted John Falvey, a prominent Irish exile, and Florence Conry, the Franciscan archbishop of Tuam. Falvey alleged that Talbot was in regular communication with all the English ambassadors and spies in Spain, that he professed to know what went on at meetings of the Spanish council of state, and that he had been in hiding for some time when sought by the inquisitor-general and had escaped by accompanying Count Gondomar, ambassador in London, on his journey to Flanders. In conclusion, Falvey advised his correspondent, the marqués de Montesclaros, to discuss the matter with Conry and his Franciscan companion Hugh Burke, the Dominican Richard de la Peña Caron, Richard Gould of the Trinitarian order, and other Irish residents in Madrid. Conry described Talbot as 'an absurd person' (Flynn, 117), who was not Irish at heart, but an Englishman hostile to those Irish who served the interests of Spain. He asserted that when the prince of Wales was in Madrid in 1628, Talbot had sought to ingratiate himself. In a memorial Talbot reviled the exiled Irish and threatened to denounce the baron of Louth to the English privy council for alleged dealings with prominent Irish exiles. Conry also accused Talbot of communicating Spanish state secrets to John Bathe. For this and other similar reasons, Talbot had been exiled from court several times and was badly thought of among those of his own order. Conry hoped that the Spanish king's ministers were not deceived by Talbot and his fellow spies and that they would manipulate them in favour of Spain. Spanish officials were adept at checking the credentials and real intentions of their agents, Gaelic Irish and Old English alike. Their declared policy on William Talbot was that he should be shown approval, given reasonable travel expenses, and asked to continue supplying information. In September 1628 Talbot and Sir Endymion Porter left England on secret diplomatic business to the court of Madrid.

After 1631 the enigmatic William Talbot abruptly disappeared from the Anglo-Hispanic political and diplomatic theatre, and from the continental world of the Irish Dominicans. The date and place of his death are unknown.

THOMAS S. R. O'FLYNN

Sources Archivum Romanum Societatis Jesu, Rome, Lusitania 44 • Biblioteca Nacional, Madrid, Gayangos MS 18420 • Archivo General de Simancas (Valladolid), Simancas, Estado, leg. 2041, 2758, 2783, 2785, 2787 • T. S. Flynn, *The Irish Dominicans, 1536–1641* (1993) • M. Gonçalves da Costa, ed., *Fontes inéditas Portuguesas para a história de Irlanda* (Braga, 1981) • M. Kerney Walsh, *Destruction by peace: Hugh O'Neill after Kinsale* (Monaghan, 1986) • B. Jennings, ed., *Wadding papers, 1614–38* (1953)
Archives Archivo General, Simancas, Spain | Biblioteca Nacional, Madrid, Gayangos MS 18420

Talbot, William (1659–1730), bishop of Durham, was born at Stourton Castle, Staffordshire, the only son of William Talbot (d. 1686) of Lichfield and Stourton Castle, Staffordshire, and Mary (d. 1661), daughter of Thomas Doughty of Whittington, Worcestershire. He entered Oriel College, Oxford, as a gentleman commoner and matriculated on 28 March 1674, aged fifteen. The next year he performed remarkably well in a speech in the encaenia. He graduated BA on 16 October 1677, and MA on 23 June 1680. According to Thomas Hearne, Talbot was 'a very great Rake all the Time he liv'd in the University; and afterwards when in orders was very much addicted to Gaming' (*Remarks*, 1.106). Following ordination he became rector of Burghfield, Berkshire, in 1682. That year he married Katherine (d. 1702), daughter of Richard King of Upham, Wiltshire, alderman of London, and his wife, Mary. Katherine's mother had married secondly John Crispe, attorney-at-law of Chipping Norton, Oxfordshire, leading Hearne and others to describe her as Crispe's daughter. Talbot and his wife had eight sons and two daughters.

Through the influence of his kinsman, Charles Talbot, twelfth earl and subsequently duke of Shrewsbury, Talbot obtained the deanery of Worcester on 23 April 1691 following the ejection of George Hickes as a nonjuror, and on 8 June he received a Lambeth DD from John Tillotson, archbishop of Canterbury. Distinguished as a preacher he preached before Mary II in 1692 and 1694 at Whitehall. Oxford conferred upon him a DD by diploma on 8 August 1699. He was consecrated bishop of Oxford on 24 September 1699, with leave to hold his deanery *in commendam*. His promotion has been ascribed to the preference of the whig ministers for 'moderate or latitudinarian divines' (Holmes, 46). Following the death of his first wife he married Agnes (d. 1730), daughter of Sir William Hartopp, of Rotherby, Leicestershire, on 3 September 1703, at Worcester Cathedral. As a whig bishop in the Lords he did not always oppose high-church measures and at first sympathized with supporters of occasional conformity bills, but his decision to oppose the Occasional Conformity Bill of December 1703 ensured that the measure was lost. He spoke in favour of the union with Scotland in the House of Lords in 1707, a measure regarded with suspicion by many bishops as presbyterianism would be established in one part of the new state of Great Britain. On 16 March 1710, in the Lords debate on the impeachment of Henry Sacheverell, he was one of four bishops recommending his condemnation, and of two (with Gilbert Burnet) who spoke against passive obedience. He published charges in 1712 and 1717, the former maintaining the validity of lay baptism.

William Talbot (1659–1730), by Sir Godfrey Kneller, 1718

Following the accession of George I, Talbot was appointed dean of the Chapel Royal. He preached the sermon at the king's coronation on 20 October 1714. Hearne dismissed him on the occasion as a 'republican' (*Remarks*, 4.422) but the sermon has been interpreted as a statement of the whig argument that the protestant succession and whig political ascendancy was specially favoured by providence. He was translated to Salisbury on 23 April 1715, when he resigned his deanery at Worcester. There, in 1716, he published a circular to his clergy directing a collection for the persecuted Moravian brethren from central Europe. During his period as bishop of Salisbury he began to gather around him a distinguished circle of younger men. Early protégés included John Bampton; when Talbot's second son, Edward, archdeacon of Berkshire from 1717 and treasurer of Salisbury from 1718, died in 1720, he recommended to his father Joseph Butler, Martin Benson, and Thomas Secker. Other protégés were Thomas Sharp and Thomas Rundle. Talbot was appointed a governor of the Charterhouse in 1721.

Talbot was translated to the see of Durham on 7 November 1721, when he resigned from the Chapel Royal. A document in the collection of a Newcastle lawyer called Gray, consulted by the eighteenth-century writer William Hutchinson, suggested that he obtained the see by a douceur of £5000–£6000. On the death of Richard Lumley, first earl of Scarbrough, George I appointed him lord lieutenant and *custos rotulorum* of the county palatine of Durham. He made his public entry into Durham diocese on 12 July 1722. He preferred living at Auckland Castle rather than at Durham.

Talbot inherited a wealthy diocese and his episcopate at Durham would be remembered more for his zeal to maximize the wealth of the diocese than for his spiritual example. His freehold and copyhold rental lists 1694 tenants and properties widely dispersed through co. Durham without the grand lease of Gateshead and Whickham, but including, besides small freeholders and copyholders, most of the local gentry. His agents added other colliery leases. He became very unpopular in the diocese by introducing two measures in parliament. The first, in February 1722, was intended to enable bishops and other holders of spiritual preferment to lease mines under their unenclosed lands or wastes, not previously demised, without consent of their chapters. Its opponents realized that this would deprive ancient leaseholders and copyholders of their mines. The bill passed the Lords, but through the strenuous opposition of Sir John Eden, MP for co. Durham, the bill was altered greatly in the House of Commons and was dropped altogether. Eden's return to Durham was greeted by a cavalcade of gentry, clergy, and others, with about thirty coaches.

Talbot already had great wealth from the mines in his own manors. He suggested now to the dean and chapter, who were lenient landlords, that there was room for increase of the fines payable on their renewals of leases. Many of the older prebendaries died at this time and by appointing his favourites he attempted to get the chapter to increase its revenues, adding to his unpopularity. Talbot's son-in-law, Exton Sayer, whom he had appointed chancellor of the diocese, held leases of rich coal mines, and his steward, Stonehewer, accepted bribes in respect of the disposal of other profitable leases. Talbot, whose expenses exceeded his income, was seen as a grasping and worldly man; his opulence and extravagance led to financial embarrassments from which his lawyer son Charles *Talbot, later first Baron Talbot of Hensol and lord chancellor, had to extricate him.

Talbot died in Hanover Square, London, on 10 October 1730 and was buried on 14 October in St James's, Westminster. His widow, Agnes, died on 24 November 1730.

MARGOT JOHNSON

Sources Wood, *Ath. Oxon.*, new edn, vol. 3 • Foster, *Alum. Oxon.* • W. Hutchinson, *The history and antiquities of the county palatine of Durham*, 1 (1785), 566–74 • W. Fordyce, *The history and antiquities of the county palatine of Durham*, 1 (1857), 80–81 • R. Surtees, *The history and antiquities of the county palatine of Durham*, 1 (1816), cxx–cxxi • J. L. Lowe, *Durham*, Diocesan Histories (1881), 295–6 • *Remarks and collections of Thomas Hearne*, ed. C. E. Doble and others, 11 vols., OHS, 2, 7, 13, 34, 42–3, 48, 50, 65, 67, 72 (1885–1921), vol. 1, p. 106; vol. 2, pp. 19, 72, 362; vol. 3, pp. 5, 11, 140; vol. 4, p. 422 • J. C. Shuler, 'The pastoral and ecclesiastical administration of the diocese of Durham, 1721–1771: with particular reference to the archdeaconry of Northumberland', PhD diss., U. Durham, 1975, 87–8, 92 • E. Hughes, *North country life in the eighteenth century: the north-east, 1700–1750* (1952), 261–2, 298, 301, 304–5, 308, 313–17, 329 • J. Spearman, *An enquiry into the ancient and present state of the county palatine of Durham: wherein are shewn the oppressions which attend the subjects* (1729) [with MS notes] • J. Ingamells, *The English episcopal portrait, 1559–1835: a catalogue* (1984), 374 [privately published for the Paul Mellon Centre for Studies in British Art] • E. Marshall, *Oxford*, Diocesan Histories (1882), 164 • T. Bartlett, *Memoirs of the life, character and writings of*

Joseph Butler, late lord bishop of Durham (1839), 14 · W. H. Jones, *Salisbury*, Diocesan Histories (1880), 265 · G. Holmes, *The trial of Doctor Sacheverell* (1973) · GEC, *Peerage*, new edn, 12/1.621–2 · Burke, *Peerage* (1999)

Archives U. Durham L.

Likenesses G. Kneller, portrait, 1715, Cathedral School, Salisbury · G. Kneller, oils, 1718, priv. coll. [*see illus.*] · G. Vertue, line engraving, 1720, BM, NPG · J. Faber junior, mezzotint (as chancellor of the Garter; after G. Kneller), BM, NPG · oils (after G. Kneller), Bishop Auckland Palace, Durham · oils (after G. Kneller), Raby Castle, Durham · portrait (as bishop of Durham), Auckland Castle, Durham

Talbot, William Henry Fox (1800–1877), pioneer of photography, was born on 11 February 1800 at Melbury, Dorset, the only child of William Davenport Talbot (1764–1800), army officer, of Lacock Abbey, Wiltshire, and Elisabeth Theresa (1773–1846), eldest child of Henry Thomas Fox-Strangways, second earl of Ilchester (1747–1802), and his wife, Mary Theresa (*d.* 1790). The father died when his son was five months old, leaving an estate in ruinous condition and forcing the boy and his mother to live in a succession of family homes. Then, in 1804, Lady Elisabeth married Captain (later Rear-Admiral) Charles Feilding (1780–1837) and the boy effectively gained a real father. Two half-sisters, Caroline Augusta Feilding (1808–1881; later Lady Mount Edgcumbe) and Henrietta Horatia Maria Feilding (1810–1851; later Horatia Gaisford), became close and both exerted artistic influence on him. His extensive family connections provided him access to élite circles in science and politics, and Caroline's later position as lady-in-waiting to the queen strengthened his royal contacts. Although referred to as Fox Talbot by some of his contemporaries and many later writers, Talbot strongly disliked this use of the family name, almost always signing Henry F. Talbot or H. F. Talbot.

William Henry Fox Talbot (1800–1877), by Antoine Claudet, 1846

The brilliant student Lady Elisabeth's firm management restored the Lacock Abbey estate before Talbot attained his majority. He was a brilliant student and eager to learn, but was painfully shy and reclusive by nature. His mother's facility with foreign languages was reflected in his later philological and translation work. Her propensity for travel abroad diversified his education and contacts, and the intense interest in botanical studies and gardening throughout her family inspired his lifelong involvement in botany. Following his initial tutoring at home and in Sussex, he was accepted at Harrow School in 1811. He entered Trinity College, Cambridge, in 1817, becoming a scholar in 1819. In 1820 he won the Porson university prize in Greek verse. In 1821 he became twelfth wrangler and won the second chancellor's classical medal before securing his BA. He proceeded MA in 1825. On 20 December 1832 Talbot married Constance Mundy (1811–1880) of Markeaton in Derbyshire. Almost simultaneously, he was elected to parliament as the reform candidate for Chippenham.

By the time he met John Herschel in Munich in 1824, Talbot had already published six papers in mathematics. This chance meeting established a friendship and a scientific collaboration crucial to Talbot's later success, and probably influenced Talbot's turn towards research into light

and optical phenomena. In 1826 Herschel introduced him to the Scottish natural philosopher David Brewster; Brewster's and Talbot's researches on light frequently overlapped, Brewster began publishing Talbot's scientific articles in his journal, and the two men forged an unusually close and lifelong friendship. In 1831 Talbot was elected a fellow of the Royal Society.

The concept of photography Talbot had his most famous intellectual breakthrough in October 1833, on the Italian shores of Lake Como, when he found himself in the frustrating position of being unable to sketch the scenery. As he stated in the introduction to his 1844 *The Pencil of Nature*, the camera lucida (a drawing instrument unrelated to photography) was no help, 'for when the eye was removed from the prism—in which all had looked beautiful—I found that the faithless pencil had only left traces on the paper melancholy to behold'. A decade before, also in Italy, he had tried to sketch using the common artist's tool, the camera obscura, but with no better success. This led him to:

> reflect on the inimitable beauty of the pictures of nature's painting which the glass lens of the Camera throws upon the paper in its focus—fairy pictures, creations of a moment, and destined as rapidly to fade away … the idea occurred to me … how charming it would be if it were possible to cause these natural images to imprint themselves durably, and remain fixed upon the paper.

Thus was the concept of photography born.

Talbot possessed no facilities for experimenting while travelling and was immediately plunged back into parliamentary duties on his return to England. At Lacock Abbey, some time later in spring 1834, he began to turn his dream into reality. By coating ordinary writing paper with alternate washes of table salt and silver nitrate, he embedded a light-sensitive silver chloride in the fibres of the paper. Placed in the sun under an opaque object such as a leaf, the paper would darken where not defended from light, producing a photographic silhouette. He called the resulting negatives (a term devised later, by Sir John Herschel) 'sciagraphs'—drawings of shadows. He continued his researches in Geneva during the autumn. Unable at this stage to use his paper in the camera, he asked an unidentified artist friend to scratch a landscape design into opaque varnish coated on glass. Using this as a negative, he then made multiple copies on his photographic paper, originating the artistic technique later known as *cliché-verre*. It was also in Geneva that Talbot first mentioned stabilizing his images against the further action of light by washing them with potassium iodide—a process now called fixing (again, Herschel's term). Another method of fixing, probably noticed by Talbot even before Geneva, was based on his observation that the edges of his paper sometimes darkened at a different rate than the centre. Tracing this to different proportions of salt and silver, he concluded that a strong solution of table salt defended the image against further action of light.

Encouraged by the 'brilliant summer' of 1835, Talbot laboured to increase the sensitivity of his coatings sufficiently to make camera negatives practical. He realized that his negatives could themselves be printed on sensitive paper, reversing the tones back to normal, and allowing the production of multiple prints from one negative. While his cameras at this stage were small, crude, wooden boxes, left about the grounds of Lacock Abbey for long exposures (leading Constance to christen them 'mousetraps'), the fundamental concepts of permanent negative–positive photography were all within Talbot's grasp two years after his initial frustration at Lake Como. By the end of 1835, although he had already achieved a high degree of success, he desired to improve matters further before publication, and the knowledge of his discovery remained within his family. During the following three years, he was fully engaged in other optical studies and in refining his mathematical works.

Although Talbot had little taste for politics, attending parliament faithfully but speaking infrequently, his 1835 retirement had not stopped his political life. In 1838, when the 'Royal vegetable patch' known as Kew Gardens was threatened with closure, he challenged the chancellor of the exchequer. He then galvanized the council of the Linnean Society to petition the Commons. Although carried through by others, it was largely Talbot's initiative, born of strong personal convictions, that firmly established this treasure as a national collection. In 1836, because of his investigations of crystals, he was invited to give the Bakerian lecture to the Royal Society. In 1838 he received the society's royal medal for his work in mathematics. By the start of 1839 he had published nearly thirty scientific papers and two books, with two more to follow within the year.

Competition with Daguerre During November 1838 Talbot finally returned to his photographic experiments and started drawing up a paper for presentation to the Royal Society. In a brutal shock just weeks later, word came from Paris in January 1839 that Louis Jacques Mandé Daguerre had frozen the images of the camera obscura. With no details disclosed, Talbot was faced with the possible loss of his discovery if Daguerre's method proved identical to his. In the gloomy light of an English winter, he could not demonstrate his own process, but on 25 January, Michael Faraday displayed some of Talbot's still-preserved 1835 examples at the Royal Institution. On 31 January, Talbot's 'Some account of the art of photogenic drawing' was read before the Royal Society. This hastily written but wide-ranging paper gave a new name to his process and explored many of its implications. Three weeks later, he detailed his working procedures before the Royal Society.

Daguerre's method, disclosed seven months later, proved to be totally different from Talbot's, but the damage was already done. Fervent support by the French government and singularly impressive early results gave the Frenchman an early lead. The year 1839 was unremittingly gloomy for the English inventor, both in the weather and in his own spirits. The Royal Society gave him little support, refusing to publish his work on photography in its *Transactions* (it was partially to atone for this with the 1842 award of the prestigious Rumford medal). Fortunately for Talbot the sun acquired unusual vigour early in 1840. Spurred on by the active experimenting of Herschel and the enthusiastic support of Brewster, Talbot succeeded by summer in producing a significant body of hauntingly beautiful photographs. The very process that he had invented also taught him to see, giving him for the first time the ability rapidly to translate the complex scenes of nature into monochrome renderings on paper. He was the first artist to be tutored by photography and, in turn, he became its first artist.

The image captured: the calotype Talbot's 'photogenic drawings' had been achieved by the direct action of light. When the negative was removed from the camera, the image was fully visible, but this required enormous solar energy and thus very long exposures. His continuing researches paid off in a series of brilliant observations in September 1840. He discovered that a very short exposure triggered an invisible effect in his silver paper. By employing a chemical developer he could build this latent image into a full-strength negative. Exposure times, previously measured in minutes or even hours, plunged to seconds. Publicly announcing this new process the following spring, Talbot called it 'calotype photogenic drawing'; it was soon known as the calotype, or among his friends, the 'Talbotype'. Responding to the urgings of his mother and of Brewster, he patented this process: it was a move that was to bring him endless trouble.

In June 1844 Talbot began selling his serial *The Pencil of Nature*, illustrated with original photographic prints and designed to demonstrate the potential of photographic publication. In 1845 he issued by subscription *Sun Pictures in Scotland*, illustrated with twenty-three original photographic prints. Another 6000 original prints were supplied to the *Art-Union* for inclusion in its 1846 volume. However, this all went wrong; when put to the test of mass production the difficulties of photographic publishing were brought to the fore. Each hand-coated sheet of paper was exposed under fickle sunlight, then fixed and washed, often with inadequate or contaminated water supplies. With so many variables affecting the quality of the print, insuring the stability of silver-based photographs proved impossible. Many of the plates began to fade, often to the derision of artists who had felt threatened by the new invention. When his mother died in 1846, Talbot lost both a demanding friend and the inspiration for many of these pioneering projects. *The Pencil of Nature*, a bold effort ahead of its time that had drawn praise from contemporary critics, was discontinued after twenty-four prints in six fascicles had been issued.

Other complications ensued. Of Talbot's various patents, four were for motive power, two dealt with metallurgy, and six were concerned with aspects of photography. None of his patents was lucrative and the ones for photography began to cause him great anxiety. His motivations for patenting photography were complex, but arose in part from the tense competitive circumstances of 1839. Whereas Daguerre received lavish French government support and public recognition, Talbot was all but ignored by his own government. He had freely published photogenic drawing, but received little recognition. While the terms he set for the calotype patent were generous, it undoubtedly limited the spread of photography on paper in the 1840s, at a time when resentment against patents in general was widespread. Scott Archer's 1851 wet collodion process produced a glass negative by bringing out a latent image in a chemical developer, but Talbot felt that its conceptual basis lay in his original invention, and should be covered by his patent. Meanwhile, wealthy amateurs, interested in forming a photographic society, viewed Talbot's patent as an impediment. He was persuaded by 1852 to relinquish all coverage save for the commercial production of portraits, but still this proved insufficient: he was savagely (and generally unfairly) attacked in print. Even Talbot's priority of invention was contested, with implications that he had appropriated others' work. When tested in court in December 1854, in spite of affidavits by Sir John Herschel and Sir David Brewster, Talbot's patent was disallowed. The court recognized him as the true inventor of photography but ruled that newer processes were outside his patent. The acrimonious proceedings had stained Talbot's reputation so severely that the prejudices raised continue to surface in historical literature.

The image made permanent: 'photographic engraving' This ruling came as a great personal blow to Talbot, adding to the chronic ill health that dogged him in the closing years of the 1840s. Removed from further experimenting, he ceased to take original photographs. However, as his health began to recover in the 1850s, Talbot proved far from discouraged, as he began building on experiments dating from the very beginnings of his photographic researches. Finally accepting that silver images could never be made truly permanent, he sought a way to realize his photographic images in time-proven printers' methods. In 1852 he patented his 'photographic engraving' process, which produced an intaglio plate that could be printed by conventional methods—the final rendering of the photographic image was in stable printer's ink. Spending more time resident in Edinburgh, he was able to draw on its innovative printing industry. By 1858 he had evolved a much improved process which he called 'photoglyphic engraving' and a second patent was granted. These were direct ancestors of the modern photogravure process, and while they did not succeed commercially within his lifetime, Talbot was on absolutely the right track in this pursuit. Into the twentieth century, far more photographs were seen rendered in ink than in silver. He continued to perfect these processes until the end of his life, finally spending more time on photomechanical printing than he ever had on photography. The 1862 International Exhibition in London awarded him a prize medal for photoglyphic engraving.

Talbot remained intellectually active throughout his life. In later years, in addition to his work on photoglyphic engraving, he turned increasingly to studies of the Assyrian cuneiform, publishing many important translations. After many years of heart disease he died in his study at Lacock Abbey on 17 September 1877; he was buried at Lacock. In a manuscript biography preserved at Lacock Abbey, Talbot's son concluded that his father's 'mind was essentially original ... he disliked laborious application in beaten paths'. In 1863 Edinburgh University celebrated this intellectual diversity by awarding Talbot an honorary doctor of laws degree 'because of his pre-eminence in literature and science, and the benefits his discoveries have conferred upon society'. (In the same ceremony Lord Palmerston, in whose reform parliament Talbot had served, was honoured). The inventor's name is preserved in various scientific fields: in mathematics, there is Talbot's curve; in physics Talbot's law and the Talbot (a unit of luminous energy); in botany two species are named after him; in astronomy a crater of the moon is named after him; and there is the persistent testimony of an art that has become so pervasive in society that its products are sometimes as invisible to us as are his latent images.

In his lifetime, Talbot had published seven books and nearly sixty scientific and mathematical articles. He left extensive archives of photographs, correspondence, manuscripts, and research notes, which his son, Charles Henry, inherited along with Lacock Abbey. On his death, he gave the abbey and its contents to his niece, Matilda Gilchrist-Clark (1871–1958), the daughter of Talbot's third daughter, Matilda Caroline. The niece changed her surname to Talbot and actively managed the abbey and the village. In the 1930s she made extensive efforts to ensure that her grandfather's work (especially that in photography) would be preserved, and generously distributed examples worldwide. In 1944 she presented Lacock Abbey to the National Trust. LARRY J. SCHAAF

Sources H. J. P. Arnold, *William Henry Fox Talbot: pioneer of photography and man of science* (1977) · L. J. Schaaf, *Out of the shadows: Herschel, Talbot and the invention of photography* (1992) · M. Weaver, *Henry Fox Talbot, selected texts and bibliography* (1992) · L. J. Schaaf, *Records of the dawn of photography: Talbot's notebooks P and Q* (1996) · G. Buckland, *Fox Talbot and the invention of photography* (1980) · L. J. Schaaf, *The photographic art of William Henry Fox Talbot* (2000) · Fox Talbot Museum, Lacock Abbey, Wiltshire, Talbot MSS · d. cert.
Archives Fox Talbot Museum, Lacock Abbey, Wiltshire, corresp. and papers · J. Paul Getty Museum, California · National Museum of Photography, Film and Television, Bradford, prints and negatives · National Museum of Photography, Film and Television, Bradford, Royal Photographic Society collection · NL Wales, botanical notes · NRA, corresp. · Sci. Mus., corresp. and papers · Smithsonian Institution, Washington, DC | BL, letters to Charles Babbage, Add. MSS 37186–37201, *passim* · Bodl. Oxf., corresp. with Sir Thomas Phillipps · RBG Kew, library, letters to Sir William Hooker · Royal Institution of Great Britain, London, letters to Sir William Grove · RS, corresp. with Sir John Herschel; letters to Sir John Lubbock · U. Newcastle, Robinson L., letters to Sir Walter Trevelyan · U. St Andr. L., corresp. with James David Forbes
Likenesses daguerreotype, *c*.1840–1849, Fox Talbot Museum, Lacock Abbey, Wiltshire · R. Beard, daguerreotype, *c*.1842, Fox Talbot Museum, Lacock Abbey, Wiltshire · C. R. Jones, daguerreotype, *c*.1845, Fox Talbot Museum, Lacock Abbey, Wiltshire · A. Claudet, daguerreotype, 1846, Fox Talbot Museum, Lacock Abbey, Wiltshire [*see illus.*] · J. Moffat, photograph, 1864, Sci. Mus. · daguerreotype, Sci. Mus. · silhouette (as a child), H. P. Kraus Junior, New York
Wealth at death under £12,000: probate, 8 Nov 1877, *CGPLA Eng. & Wales*

Talboys, David Alphonso (1789/90–1840), publisher and translator, was the son of Thomas Talboys, a bookseller in St Aldates, Oxford, and his wife, Elizabeth. Little is known of his early life, but in later years he described himself as self-educated and in 1811–13 he is recorded as paying rates on a property in Bedford High Street. On 15 May 1811 he married seventeen-year-old Jemima Miller (1794–1817), daughter of Joseph and Ann Miller of St Mary's, Bedford.

In 1814 Talboys moved to the St Clements suburb of Oxford and began printing, publishing, and selling books from his premises there. By that time he had two daughters. On 23 December 1817 Jemima Talboys died following the birth of a third daughter six days previously. As she lay dying in an upstairs room, her eldest daughter's clothes caught fire downstairs, and the child also died. On 24 June 1818 Talboys married Eliza Hurdis (1799/1800–1823), the eighteen-year-old daughter of Richard Hurdis, an Oxford shoemaker; they had two daughters, in 1819 and 1820, but both died in infancy. In 1823 Eliza also died and was buried at St Clement's Church on 1 February. On 29 April 1823 Talboys was married again; his third wife was Mary Wheeler, 'only daughter of Mrs Wheeler' (*Jackson's Oxford Journal*, 23 May 1840), and the sister of his partner in the printing business, J. L. Wheeler. They had nine children (five sons and four daughters), two of whom died in infancy. The two daughters from his first marriage also predeceased him.

Meanwhile Talboys was becoming known for his intimate knowledge of books and the book trade. His *Catalogue of Old and New Books, for the Year 1822–3* ends with a list of sixteen books published by him. In 1827 he dissolved the partnership with Wheeler, and moved to a shop in Oxford High Street, where he remained until his death. In that year he was matriculated by the university as a privileged person. Between 1830 and 1836 he was printing in partnership with G. Browne. His *Catalogue* of 1837 listed over seventy works published by him and gave a London address at 6 Waterloo Place. The *Chronological Tables of the History of the Middle Ages … and of Modern History* which he compiled and published in 1838, 1839, and 1840 gave his London address as 113 Fleet Street.

Talboys had considerable intellectual and linguistic ability, publishing his own translation of A. H. L. Heeren's *Manual of Ancient History* (1829; 2nd edn, 1833), *Historical Researches into the Politics, Intercourse and Trade of the Carthaginians, Ethiopians, and Egyptians* (1832), and *A Manual of the History of the Political System of Europe and its Colonies* (1834). These translations materially aided the study of history in England. He travelled regularly to the continent, notably to the Leipzig book fair to select the German editions of the classics for sale.

In 1830 Talboys had published *The Pursuit of Literature and Science Compatible with the Habits of Business*, a prize essay which he had read before the Oxford Mechanics' Institution, and the views expressed in it recur in the preface to his translation of Friedrich von Adelung, *Historical Sketch of Sanskrit Literature* (1832), a work undertaken following the appointment of the first Boden professor of Sanskrit at Oxford. In this work Talboys argued that it was 'very natural that a bookseller, who aims at being something more than the mere go-between of author and reader, should desire to gain some information respecting a subject now likely to form a new department of his calling'.

The publisher's device present on the title-page of many works published by Talboys depicts an axe laid to a treetrunk from which is suspended the city of Oxford's coat of arms. On either side of the trunk are the initials D. A., and on a scroll round it the words TAILLE BOIS. This recalls the device of the humanist printer Étienne Dolet, burnt at the stake in Paris in 1546, and may be seen as symbolic of his reforming outlook in local Oxford affairs. In 1826, as an ex-churchwarden, he had published *A Brief Account of the Charities Belonging to St. Clement's Parish* with the aim of showing how they had been badly managed in the past; and in 1835, following the reforms of the Municipal Corporations Act, he was elected one of the councillors for the east ward of the city and acted as the leader of the radicals, though he objected to this term, maintaining that he held 'moderate liberal opinions' (*The Times*, 4 Sept 1835). He was made sheriff in 1836 despite opposition from the conservatives on the grounds that he was not a freeman, and in that year in *A Letter to the Burgesses of the East Ward of the City of Oxford* he attacked 'the extravagance, the faults, the abuses, and the fopperies' of the old corporation in an attempt to establish the council's finances on an entirely new basis. This, and other pronouncements, led him into conflict with the staunchly tory *Oxford University, City, and County Herald*, which was part-owned and edited by Philip Bliss, the university registrar and an arch-conservative. Bliss ran a vitriolic campaign against him, implying that members of the university should boycott his bookshop. It was this attack which was said to have ruined both his business and his health. He died aged fifty on 23 May 1840 at 86–7 High Street, Oxford, and was buried in St Clement's churchyard, Oxford, on 30 May; his wife survived him. His will, proved in the prerogative court of Canterbury on 4 December 1840, named as one of his executors the London publisher William Pickering, with whom he had collaborated on the Oxford English Classics. His stock was sold in three sales in May, October, and December 1842 by L. A. Lewis of Fleet Street, London. He was replaced on Oxford council by a conservative. Talboys was the initiator of a major publishing enterprise but his death prevented him reaping its benefits. In 1834, shortly after the death of Franz Passow, Talboys had proposed to Robert Scott that Scott should translate and revise Passow's *Greek–German Lexicon*, and Scott had agreed provided that he could take on Henry Liddell as his collaborator. The first edition of Liddell and Scott was published by the Clarendon Press in 1843, three years after Talboys's death. DAVID VAISEY

Sources *Jackson's Oxford Journal* (27 June 1818) · *Jackson's Oxford Journal* (1 Feb 1823) · *Jackson's Oxford Journal* (27 Oct 1827) · *Jackson's Oxford Journal* (23 May 1840) · *Oxford University, City, and County Herald* · *GM*, 1st ser., 87/2 (1817), 633 · *GM*, 2nd ser., 14 (1840), 220 · *Oxford Protestant Magazine*, 1 (1847), 301–2 · [S. Quelch], *Early recollections of Oxford, etc., in twelve letters … by an old freeman* (1900) · Foster, *Alum. Oxon.* · *List of catalogues of English book sales 1676–1900 now in the British Museum* (1915) · F. G. Emmison, ed., *Bedford St Mary parish register*, Bedfordshire Parish Registers, 35 (1947) · transcripts of parish register, Oxford, St Clement and St Peter-in-the-East, 2 Feb 1818 [baptism]; 1 Feb 1823 [burial, Eliza Hurdis]; 29 April 1823 [marriage, Mary Wheeler]; 23 May 1840 [death]; 30 May 1840 [burial], Bodl. Oxf., MSS Top. Oxon. c. 876–7, 919–21 · H. Paintin, collections concerning St Clements, Oxford, Bodl. Oxf., MSS Top. Oxon. d. 284–6 · rate books, St Paul's, Bedford, Beds. & Luton ARS, P1/4/1 and P1/11 · marriage licence, 13 May 1811, Beds. & Luton ARS, ABM 65 · will, PROB, PROB 11/1938, fols. 226r–227v
Archives Bodl. Oxf., group of catalogues issued by him

Talboys, Sir William. *See* Tailboys, Sir William (c.1416–1464).

Talcott, Joseph (1669–1741), colonial governor, was born on 11 November 1669 in Hartford, Connecticut, eighth of the nine children of John Tallcott (c.1626–1688), magistrate, and his wife, Helena Wakeman (d. 1674), daughter of John and Elizabeth Wakeman of Fairfield, Connecticut. His parents were born in England and taken to Connecticut as young children by their parents. His father and paternal grandfather were both large landowners in Hartford and members of the governor's council. Talcott (who adopted a different spelling of his surname from his father) was the first governor of Connecticut to be born in the colony.

Although he was the fourth son of his parents, Talcott was the eldest one to survive childhood and from an early age seemed destined for political leadership. Elected a member of the selectmen's board, Hartford's highest office, at the age of twenty-three, Talcott was the youngest selectman in Hartford's colonial history. He may have gained some early local experience because, unlike the sons of most prominent families, he did not attend college. Although biographical sketches written in the nineteenth century by family members identify him as a lawyer, Talcott neither formally trained in nor practised law. He did, however, serve as a justice of the peace and as a judge of the superior court of Connecticut: this probably accounts for the biographical error.

Talcott's rise in Connecticut public life followed a path trod by many patricians. He saw active duty in the militia, and rose to the rank of major in 1710; he was a member of numerous town committees; and beginning in 1708 he served as a deputy from Hartford to the general assembly, which named him speaker of the assembly in 1710. The following year the freemen elected him to the governor's council, where he served from 1711 until he was elected deputy governor in 1723 to replace Nathan Gold, who died in office. Less than a year later, when Governor Gurdon Saltonstall died in the late summer of 1724, Talcott was appointed to finish the term and was elected governor in his own right in 1725. Re-elected until his death in 1741, his seventeen-year tenure was the longest in eighteenth-century Connecticut, and was characterized by stability and tranquillity. Talcott inherited a relatively peaceful ship of state from his predecessor, Saltonstall, and kept a steady hand on the tiller.

Known neither for brilliance nor bold leadership, Talcott was a capable administrator who presided over the orderly settlement of Litchfield county, the last of Connecticut's lands not populated by British colonists. He also successfully settled vexatious boundary disputes with the neighbouring colonies of Massachusetts, New York, and Rhode Island. At the end of his governorship the outline of the map of Connecticut looked substantially as it does today. Much of his correspondence as governor dealt with military matters, and royal officials regarded him as competent and co-operative. A cautious, conservative man, who built up one of Connecticut's largest estates through land investments, Talcott also exhibited common sense in his private affairs. He attended church in Hartford's First Society all of his life, but never expressed himself publicly on theological matters. Talcott lived and served in the generation caught between the golden age of the zealous, intellectual puritan founders and the enthusiastic, disputatious era of evangelicals and revolutionaries. No great causes seized his person or his governorship. He quietly guided Connecticut through its final evolution as a colony and efficiently co-ordinated its functioning within the British empire.

Talcott married twice: first in 1693 Abigail Clarke (1670–1705) of Milford, with whom he had three sons, and second on 26 June 1706 Eunice Wakeman, *née* Howell (1678–1738), of Fairfield, widow of Jabez Wakeman, with whom he had six children. He died on 11 October 1741 (not December, as a replacement headstone states), just as bitter divisions over religion, currency, and western land speculation were about to plunge Connecticut into turmoil. He was buried in the burial-ground of the First Church, Hartford, and left an estate worth £10,262, the largest of any Connecticut colonial governor.

BRUCE C. DANIELS

Sources M. K. Talcott, ed., *The Talcott papers: correspondence and documents during Joseph Talcott's governorship*, 2 vols. (1892–6) · R. M. Hooker, 'Talcott, Joseph', *DAB*, 18.282–3 · J. H. Trumbull and C. J. Hoadly, eds., *The public records of the colony of Connecticut*, 15 vols. (1850–90), vols. 4–6 · S. U. Talcott, *Talcott pedigree in England and America* (1876) · R. F. Gould, *Ezra Thompson Clark's ancestors and descendants* (1975)
Archives Connecticut Historical Society, Hartford, Connecticut, letters · Mass. Hist. Soc., Belcher MSS, letters
Wealth at death £10,262: Connecticut State Library, Hartford, probate inventory, Hartford District, file 5376, 1741

Talfourd, Francis [Frank] **(1828–1862)**, playwright, was the only surviving son of the family of three sons and two daughters of Sir Thomas Noon *Talfourd (1795–1854), writer, judge, and politician, and his wife, Rachel, eldest daughter of John Towill *Rutt (1760–1841). He was educated at Eton College from 1841 to 1845 and on 15 May 1845 matriculated at Christ Church, Oxford. He was called to the bar at the Middle Temple, London, on 17 November 1852 and occasionally went on circuit, but was chiefly known as the writer of a series of burlesques and extravaganzas.

While Talfourd was at Oxford he and W. C. Bedford, an undergraduate from Brasenose College, had founded the Oxford Dramatic Amateurs, and Talfourd's first piece, *Macbeth Travestie*, was originally presented at Henley-on-Thames during the regatta on 17 June 1847, and opened afterwards at the Strand Theatre on 10 January 1848, and at the Olympic on 25 April 1853. He wrote for many of the theatres, and his pieces, though light and ephemeral, were very popular in their day. Among his best-known were *Alcestis, the Original Strong-Minded Woman*, a burlesque (4 July 1850); *The Rule of Three*, a comedietta (20 December 1858); and *Tell and the Strike of the Cantons* (26 December 1859). All these works were produced at the Strand Theatre. Talfourd continued to produce plays for the London stage throughout the 1850s, including *Shylock, or, The Merchant of Venice Preserv'd* (4 July 1853) and *Electra, in a New Electric Light* (25 April 1859). He collaborated with Henry James Byron on his last piece, *The Miller and his Men*, which opened at the Strand Theatre on 9 April 1860.

On 5 November 1861 Talfourd married Frances Louisa Morgan, second daughter of Josiah Towne, a solicitor of Margate, Kent. He died at Menton, France on 9 March 1862. His obituary in *The Athenaeum* noted that 'Talfourd … has left the world with little or no adequate witness of his powers—the travestie and burlesque in which he revelled showing but one, and that the poorer, side of his gay and brilliant intellect' (*The Athenaeum*, 365).

MEGAN A. STEPHAN

Sources *GM*, 3rd ser., 12 (1862), 520 · *The Athenaeum* (15 March 1862), 365 · H. E. C. Stapylton, *The Eton school lists, from 1791 to 1850*, 2nd edn (1864), 190 · Allibone, *Dict.*
Likenesses H. Watkins, albumen print, c.1855–1859, NPG

Talfourd, Sir Thomas Noon (1795–1854), writer, judge, and politician, was born at Reading, Berkshire, on 26 May 1795, the son of Edward Talfourd, a brewer, and his wife, Ann, the daughter of the Revd Thomas Noon. Both Talfourd's father and his paternal grandfather, a dissenting minister in Reading, were deeply religious; Talfourd himself as an adult became a practising Anglican. After studying with private tutors he was educated at the recently founded protestant dissenters' grammar school in Mill Hill, Middlesex (1808–10), before transferring to the grammar school at Reading (1810–12), where he became head boy. He was profoundly influenced there by the headmaster, Dr Richard Valpy. Valpy nurtured his pupil's enthusiasms for literature and for good causes, expressed in the precocious publication of Talfourd's *Poems on Various Subjects* (1811), including 'The education of the poor', and a tragedy, 'The Offering of Isaac', which was influenced by Hannah More's *Sacred Dramas*. As a schoolboy Talfourd became inspired by the theatre after watching Sarah Siddons and John Philip Kemble, and he discovered the love of Greek drama which was to inform his later play-writing.

Prevented by his family's poverty from attending university, Talfourd visited Henry Crabb Robinson on 23 February 1813 to discuss his future. On the advice of Lord Brougham he decided on a legal career. He spent the years between 1813 and 1817 in the chambers of Joseph Chitty in the Inner Temple, London, and took what business he could as a pleader between 1817 and his call to the bar in 1821. But during this period he also developed his interest in literature. In 1813 he published in *The Pamphleteer*, which was edited by Valpy's brother, 'An attempt to estimate the poetical talent of the present age', in which his appreciation of Shakespeare and Wordsworth is particularly apparent. In 1815 his farce, *Freemasonry, or, More Secrets than One*, was performed at the old theatre in Friar Street, Reading, and he made the acquaintance of Charles Lamb, whose letters he later edited in two separate volumes (1837, 1848). But he was simultaneously becoming involved with philanthropic causes, publishing a plea for the abolition of the pillory in *The Pamphleteer* (1815). He inaugurated his political career on 19 October 1819, when to thunderous applause at a meeting held at the town hall in Reading, he addressed a speech in defence of the right of public assembly, in protest against the Peterloo massacre.

In 1821 Talfourd was called to the bar by the Society of the Middle Temple, and he joined the Oxford circuit and Berkshire sessions. In 1822 he contracted a happy marriage to Rachel, eldest daughter of John Towill *Rutt, a nonconformist minister. She was fiercely unfashionable and regarded as a lovable eccentric. They had several children; Talfourd was heartbroken in 1824 by the death in infancy of their first child, a son, and by the death of another son, Charles (named after Lamb), in 1837. But he was devoted to Mary and Kate, their daughters, and especially to Francis (Frank) *Talfourd (1828–1862), their surviving son. After his marriage, being unwilling to ask his father for financial support, he supplemented his income through journalistic work until the early 1830s. He reported on legal cases for *The Times* and contributed essays to the *Law Magazine*, including a graphic portrait of Lord Tenterden (February 1833). He also published prolifically on drama and literature in the *Edinburgh Review*, the *New Monthly Magazine* (for which he was drama critic from 1820 to 1831), the *Retrospective Review*, and the *London Magazine*. He contributed articles to the *Encyclopædia Metropolitana* on Homer, Greek history, the Greek lyric poets, and the Greek tragedians.

For unknown reasons Talfourd's application to become QC in 1832 was turned down. But in 1833 he accepted the rank of serjeant-at-law and was soon to become the most respected member of the Oxford circuit and a popular figure in London society. In the early 1830s he became famous for the dinner parties which he and his wife gave in their home at 56 Russell Square, London. His dinners were remembered for their informality, conviviality, swarming children, and numerous cats. Regular guests included Douglas William Jerrold, William Makepeace Thackeray, William Charles Macready, Daniel Maclise, John Forster, and Talfourd's old friend from Reading, Mary Russell Mitford. He was particularly loved by Charles Dickens and provided the archetype of the idealistic Tommy Traddles in *David Copperfield*; his children Frank and Kate gave their names to two youngsters in Dickens's *Nicholas Nickleby*. Dickens later wrote of him:

> If there ever was a house … where every art was honoured for its own sake, and where every visitor was received for his own claims and merits, that house was his … Rendering all legitimate deference to rank and riches, there never was a man more composedly, unaffectedly, quietly, immovable by such considerations … On the other hand, nothing would have astonished him so much as the suggestion that he was anyone's patron.   (Dickens, 117)

Talfourd's personal popularity was the result of outstanding charm and kindness, combined with winning humour and scintillating conversation, which he displayed at his favourite haunt, the Garrick Club. His sophisticated friends were disarmed by the confusing impression he gave of being simultaneously an idealist cosmopolitan and a provincial patriot: he was unashamed of being able to speak no foreign languages, was an enthusiast for English food and drink, and besides a brief visit on legal business to Lisbon in 1818, did not visit Europe until he was forty-six.

Talfourd's family's local background helped him to win his first election to parliament at Reading on 7 January 1835. He was on the radical wing of the Liberals, supported universal male suffrage, and campaigned ardently for black emancipation. As member of parliament his rise in London society was rapid. Henry Crabb Robinson observed with surprised approval in his diary in 1836 that this provincial brewer's impoverished son was now dining with Lord Melbourne. Talfourd was re-elected on the accession of Queen Victoria in 1837 but kept out of parliament between 1841 and 1847, alienated by the factionalism of the Reading radicals, and in particular by his distrust of Chartism: he spoke in the prosecution of the Chartist Thomas Cooper at Stafford in 1842. But he was returned to parliament at the 1847 election and kept the seat until he became a judge in 1848.

As member of parliament Talfourd was responsible for two pieces of important legislation. The Infant Custody Act (1839) modified in mothers' favour the previously unlimited power fathers had exercised over their children, giving the court discretion to award custody of children under seven years of age to the mother in cases of separation or divorce, provided she was not guilty of adultery. In 1837, encouraged by Wordsworth, Talfourd delivered a brilliant speech introducing the Copyright Act. This was designed to enable the dependants of authors to profit from the sales of their writings after their deaths. Although it did not become law until 1842, when he was not in parliament, it was known as Talfourd's Act. Dickens applauded this initiative in the touching dedication to Talfourd of *The Pickwick Papers* (1837). Talfourd also campaigned for the repeal of the Theatrical Patents Act (1843).

Yet Talfourd's most important legacy was his poetic tragedy *Ion*, written after he was elected to parliament. *Ion* was an extraordinary success when first performed at Covent Garden Theatre, London, on his birthday, 26 May 1836. He had circulated the play privately to influential individuals, including Wordsworth, Robert Southey, and Gladstone, which ensured that the theatre was packed with the most distinguished audience contemporary reviewers could remember, including Dickens, Robert Browning, Walter Savage Landor, Pitt, Melbourne, Lord Chief Justice Denman, Lord Grey, and Lady Blessington. *Ion* caused a sensation and remained popular for many years. Written in blank verse, it is an idiosyncratic combination of Romantic utopian Hellenism derived from Shelley with nonconformist religiosity, especially articulated in the hero Ion's extreme altruism. Talfourd's advocacy of social reform was grounded in religious principles and presupposed moral and spiritual reform.

Ion was important to the regeneration of serious theatre in the early Victorian period because it directly inspired plays such as Browning's *Strafford* and Bulwer-Lytton's *The Lady of Lyons* (1839), the latter of which was dedicated to Talfourd. But *Ion* was also politically significant. Talfourd was united in opposing the lord chamberlain's prerogative of theatrical censorship with his friend Bulwer, on whose 1836 edition of Hazlitt he collaborated. They both believed that literature needed a reformist and propagandist voice. In *Ion*, Talfourd used Greek models to legitimize contemporary political developments, especially the Great Reform Act (1832), the abolition of slavery (1833), and the democratizing acts following the municipal corporations commission (1835). *Ion* imitates the tragedy of the same name by Euripides, and Sophocles' *Oedipus tyrannus*, in both of which a foundling discovers that he is the hereditary monarch of his country. But unlike his classical archetypes, Talfourd's Ion responds by reforming the judiciary and disbanding the army. He then makes his people promise never again to tolerate monarchy, and commits suicide. This conclusion was particularly politically charged, since the ancient Greek democracies were in

1836 still viewed by many with suspicion, and were associated with the dangerous radicalism of Thomas Paine and William Cobbett. The political impact of *Ion* was increased by the known republican sympathies of the actor in the leading role, William Charles Macready.

Ion was seen as a stage play of lasting stature. It was performed continuously for over a year and consistently revived in London until at least 1861. It was even more popular in the United States, where the transvestite actress Ellen Tree performed in it repeatedly. In the *North American Review* (1837) Cornelius C. Felton, professor of Greek literature at Harvard University, declared it a masterpiece, and it was often revived in the American commercial theatre until at least 1881. In his day Talfourd had the reputation of being a foremost dramatist; in *A New Spirit of the Age* (1844) Richard Hengist Horne included an extended discussion of Talfourd, thus implicitly equating him with Dickens, Wordsworth, Tennyson, and Carlyle. *Ion* was so popular among the reading public that it ran through two private editions and four public ones by 1837 (many more subsequently), in addition to German and American editions.

In *The Athenian Captive*, in which Macready starred at the Haymarket Theatre in 1838, Talfourd attacked slavery and once again portrayed an ancient Greek people's uprising against a tyrannical autocrat. But the republican tenor of *Ion* was replaced by a less constitutionally specific appeal for 'liberty', for in *The Athenian Captive* a corrupt old monarch is replaced by a virtuous young one, as if to echo the hopes of the British middle classes in respect to their youthful new Queen Victoria, who had ascended the throne in 1837.

These theatrical productions represent a remarkable moment in the history of British Hellenism's manifestation in the theatre because they constitute the last significant uses of Greek tragedy on the professional stage for a radical political purpose until Gilbert Murray's stagings of Euripides in the Edwardian era. Although Talfourd later produced two further tragedies, *Glencoe* (1840), set in Scotland, and *The Castilian* (a Spanish tragedy published posthumously in 1853), neither was to prove as successful as his plays on Greek themes. He diversified into travel writing, including *Recollection of a First Visit to the Alps in August and September 1841* (1842), and *Vacation Rambles* (1845). As a literary celebrity he was also engaged in public speaking, delivering a famous oration, *The Importance of Literature to Men of Business* (1852) to a meeting of the Manchester Athenaeum in October 1845.

But in his last fifteen years Talfourd focused on his legal career. There is no record of most of his forensic speeches because he often extemporized with such rapidity that reporters and shorthand writers could preserve only the outline. He had an intuitive and unshakeable sense of right and wrong, and spoke with conviction and passion if not always to the point. On 23 June 1841 he defended Edward Moxon, a bookseller who had been prosecuted for blasphemously publishing works of Shelley. The speech, which Talfourd published in 1841, is a rhapsodical appreciation of poetry and defence of poetic freedom. In July 1849 he was raised to the bench of the common pleas and received the customary honour of the knighthood. Although not an outstanding judge, he is said to have exercised his responsibilities and duties with good humour, sound judgement, and unimpeachable integrity. His later life was blighted by anxieties caused by his son Frank's debts, failure to take his degree at Christ Church, Oxford, and half-hearted attempts to make a career in law. But Frank later redeemed himself by writing successful extravaganzas for the popular theatre, beginning in 1850 with a burlesque of Euripides' *Alcestis*, which brought his father great pleasure.

Talfourd was struck by an apoplectic seizure as he was addressing the grand jury, on the issue of the regrettable estrangement of the social classes, from his judge's seat at Stafford on 13 March 1854. He died a few hours later at his lodgings in that town. The moment of the seizure, when his son Frank rushed to attend him, was represented in a life-size plaster cast donated to the Reading Museum by his daughter Mary. Talfourd was buried in Norwood cemetery, Surrey.   EDITH HALL

Sources 'A memoir of Mr Justice Talfourd', *Law Magazine*, 51 (1854), 298–326 · 'Life and writings of the late Mr Justice Talfourd', *North British Review*, 25 (1856) · R. S. Newdick, 'Sir Thomas Noon Talfourd', Reading Public Library · R. S. Newdick, 'Talfourd as dramatist', Reading Public Library · T. N. Talfourd, preface, *Tragedies: to which are added a few sonnets and verses* (1844) · J. Brain, 'An evening with Thomas Noon Talfourd', *Berkshire ballads* (1904) · *ILN* (28 July 1849), 52 · *Diary, reminiscences, and correspondence of Henry Crabb Robinson*, ed. T. Sadler, 3rd edn, 2 vols. (1872) · *The diaries of William Charles Macready, 1833–1851*, ed. W. Toynbee, 2 vols. (1912) · W. Maginn and D. Maclise, *A gallery of illustrious literary characters, 1830–1838*, ed. W. Bates (1873), pp. 194–7, no. 73 · C. Clark, *Dickens and Talfourd* (1919) · *The modern British essayists*, 7 (1850) · [C. Dickens], 'The late Mr Justice Talfourd', *Household Words* (25 March 1854), 117 · *DNB* · *IGI*

Archives Berks. RO, legal and personal papers incl. calendar of cases · Essex RO, Chelmsford, family papers · Hunt. L., corresp.; literary MSS · Reading Central Library, corresp., diaries, and papers | BL, letters to Leigh Hunt and Marianne Hunt, Add. MSS 38109–38111 · BL, letters to Royal Literary Fund, loan 96 · BL, letters to T. J. Serle, MS 52476 · JRL, corresp. with Mary Russell Mitford · NL Scot., corresp. with Robert Cadell

Likenesses W. Holl, stipple, 1840 (after K. Meadows), BM, NPG; repro. in Saunders, *Political reformers* (1840) · engraving, 1849, repro. in *ILN*, 15 (1849), 52 · J. G. Lough, bust, 1855, crown court, Stafford · D. Maclise, caricature, 1873, repro. in W. Bates, ed., *Gallery of illustrious literary characters*, no. 73 · J. C. Armytage, stipple, NPG · J. Lucas, oils, Garr. Club · H. W. Pickersgill, oils, NPG; on loan to Law Courts · H. W. Pickersgill, oils, Middle Temple, London · Roffe, stipple (after B. R. Haydon), BM, NPG · drawing, repro. in Toynbee, ed., *Diaries of William Charles Macready*, vol. 1, p. 328 · oils, Harvard U., law school · portrait, council chamber, Reading

Taliesin (*fl.* **6th cent.**), poet, was one of five early British vernacular poets commemorated in the *Historia Brittonum* as contemporaries of Ida, first Anglian king of Bernicia. This section of the *Historia Brittonum*, sometimes called the 'northern history', consists of a Northumbrian regnal list, of late eighth-century date, to which notes have been added on events in particular reigns. The part of the text pertaining solely to the sixth century, before the reign of Æthelfrith, father of Oswald and Oswiu, has three such notes, attached respectively to the reigns of Ida (*r.* 547/548–559/560), Frithuwald (*r.* 579–85), and Hussa (*r.*

585–92). The first note, attached to the reign of Ida, is itself complex, consisting, first, of a statement about Ida, namely that he joined Din Guayroi (Bamburgh) to Bernicia; second, that Eudeyrn was the principal British enemy of the English during his reign; third, moving away from direct reference to Ida, the note about the five poets; and, finally, a note on Maelgwn Gwynedd and his descent from Cunedda. The sentence on the five poets belongs to a type familiar from historical texts: '[X] was famous [in some way or other] at that time'. So the *Historia Brittonum* itself says about the reign of the emperor Maximus, 'Martin, bishop of Tours, was (then) famous for his miracles' (*Historia Brittonum*, chap. 29). The sentence includes a phrase, *poema Britannicum*, which probably means 'poetry in the British language' rather than simply 'poetry among the Britons' since the corresponding suffix in Welsh ('-eg' as in 'Brythoneg') is used for the names of languages. For the *Historia Brittonum*, it seems, Taliesin was one of a group of early vernacular British poets whose floruits overlapped with the reign of Ida. Problems arise, however, as soon as the *Historia Brittonum* is compared with the surviving corpus of poetry ascribed to Taliesin.

An early fourteenth-century manuscript, now in the National Library of Wales, has long been known as the Book of Taliesin. The poems in the manuscript claiming to be by Taliesin have been divided by modern scholars into two categories: those in praise of known sixth-century kings, principally Urien Rheged and his son Owain, and those that use a traditional poetic persona, to which the name of Taliesin had been attached. Several of these latter poems contain claims to recondite knowledge enjoyed by the poet; and the claims are sometimes so phrased as to imply rivalry with scholars working in the ordinary Latin tradition. Poets, it is suggested, command the same learning as Latin-based scholars, but also have something more. These poems have links with the treatment of the character of Taliesin found in the *Ystoria Taliesin*, even though the latter is first preserved as a part of a world chronicle composed by the early sixteenth-century Welsh soldier and scholar, Elis Gruffydd. In this tradition, Taliesin was the poet, not of Urien or of Maelgwn Gwynedd, but of Elffin ap Gwyddno.

Leaving aside the second category of poems, there are still problems arising from those which have been seen as authentic sixth-century compositions and thus, perhaps, genuinely the work of Taliesin. The majority are in praise of Urien, king of Rheged (probably around Carlisle), and his son Owain. Urien, however, was the most prominent of the northern British kings mentioned in the notes on northern history contained within the *Historia Brittonum*; yet the note on his career is attached to the reign of Hussa (r. 585–92), who is said to have been the enemy of four British kings, the first-named of whom was Urien. Hence, the *Historia Brittonum* attaches the poet to the reign of Ida (r. 547/548–559/560) but his patron to the reign of Hussa (r. 585–92). That is not all: Urien's final campaign and death are recorded after a sentence on hostilities between himself and Theodric; and the latter is most naturally taken as the Theodric who reigned from 572 to 579. The internal

evidence of the text suggests that the author of the *Historia Brittonum* may well have had little evidence to enable him to date either Taliesin or Urien.

T. M. CHARLES-EDWARDS

Sources *Canu Taliesin*, ed. I. Williams (1960) · *The poetry of Taliesin*, ed. J. E. Coerwyn Williams (1968) · Nennius, *'British history' and 'The Welsh annals'*, ed. and trans. J. Morris (1980) · *Ystorya Taliesin*, ed. P. K. Ford (1992) · M. Haycock, '"Preiddeu Annwn" and the figure of Taliesin', *Studia Celtica*, 18–19 (1983–4), 52–78 · M. Haycock, 'Llyfr Taliesin', *National Library of Wales Journal*, 25 (1987–8), 357–86 · K. H. Jackson, 'On the northern British section in Nennius', *Celt and Saxon: studies in the early British border*, ed. N. K. Chadwick (1963), 20–62 · J. Morris-Jones, 'Taliesin', *Y Cymmrodor*, 28 (1918) [whole issue] · P. Sims-Williams, 'Gildas and vernacular poetry', *Gildas: new approaches*, ed. M. Lapidge and D. N. Dumville (1984), 169–92 · P. H. Blair, *Anglo-Saxon Northumbria*, ed. M. Lapidge and P. H. Blair (1984) · D. N. Dumville, 'On the northern British section of the *Historia Brittonum*', *Welsh History Review / Cylchgrawn Hanes Cymru*, 8 (1976–7), 345–54 · D. P. Kirby, 'Bede and Northumbrian chronology', *EngHR*, 78 (1963), 514–27 · I. Williams, *Chwedl Taliesin* (1957) · J. E. C. Williams, 'Gildas, Maelgwn and the bards', *Welsh society and nationhood: historical essays presented to Glanmor Williams*, ed. R. R. Davies and others (1984), 19–34
Archives NL Wales, 'Book of Taliesin'

Taliesin ab Iolo. *See* Williams, Taliesin (1787–1847), *under* Williams, Edward (1747–1826).

Tallack, William (1831–1908), penal reformer, was born on 15 June 1831 at St Austell, Cornwall, the son of Thomas Tallack (1801–1865) and his wife, Hannah (1800–1876), daughter of Samuel Bowden. Both parents were Quakers, and Tallack himself was a lifelong member of the Society of Friends. He attended the Quaker school at Sidcot and became a pupil teacher there; subsequently he became a student at Founder's College, York (1852–4), and was a teacher in Croydon and Ackworth between 1852 and 1857. He married Augusta Mary Catlin (1844–1904) at Stoke Newington on 18 July 1867; they had several children.

In 1857 Tallack travelled abroad as tutor to a fellow Quaker's delicate son; the boy died but Tallack continued his journey to the United States, where he stayed for four months. He visited the model prison at Philadelphia where penal reformers had influenced the state authorities to establish the 'separate system' of prison administration in the early nineteenth century. It was believed that prisoners held in cellular isolation would be overwhelmed by reflection and repentance and would turn with gratitude to the teachings of chaplains, educators, trade trainers, and other officers who would visit and reform them. Tallack returned to England filled with enthusiasm for this system and devoted the rest of his life to penal reform. He always claimed that he was also influenced by Peter Bedford (1780–1864) and Thomas Barwick Baker (1807–1886), two important nineteenth-century penal reformers, but the foundation-stone of his approach was his faith as a Quaker in the inherent potential of each human spirit to find atonement, forgiveness, and salvation. On that ground he espoused abolition of the death penalty, because he believed that capital punishment denied the offender the chance to turn from wickedness and find salvation.

In 1863 Tallack became secretary to the Society for the

Abolition of the Death Penalty. He gave extensive evidence to the 1866 royal commission on capital punishment, arguing that abolition in other countries had not led to any increase in murder or serious crime. But a subsequent bill to introduce degrees of murder (and therefore at least reduce executions) failed to pass: not until the 1920s was abolitionism to make much headway again.

In 1866 Tallack became founding secretary of the Howard Association at £150 per year, a post he held until his retirement in 1901. The association, named after the famous late eighteenth-century prison reformer, existed to collect and disseminate information regarding the most effective methods of crime prevention and penal treatment and to promote those methods. Tallack brought immense energy to this project: under his influence the Howard Association campaigned for the principle that repression of crime could be accomplished only by a system of punishment which combined moral reformation with retribution and deterrence, and by a system of social policy which was educative and preventive. Tallack therefore advocated systematized organization of charity to prevent pauperization and to provide improved sanitation, better housing, strict control of alcohol, and sound schooling.

Supported by the chair of the association, Francis Peek, Tallack publicized his message that all intervention must strengthen personal responsibility and morality among offenders and the poor in general, and that a crusading philanthropy among the established orders should be the foundation of a united and Christian society. Although a discursive and at times self-contradictory writer, his basic view was that all policy and practice should have as its vision the stimulation of self-help and independent, honest living. Consequently he deplored promiscuous charity or comfortable reformatories because he felt that they stimulated the appetite for easy and idle dependence. He advocated severe punishment, holding that, within this deterrent ethos, true benevolence lay in helping prisoners to maintain themselves by moral reform and by learning new skills in prison. Severity meted out retribution on earth, with the accompanying possibility of atonement and divine forgiveness; it combined hope and fear, reward and punishment.

Tallack's view of the causes of crime was progressive: he argued that neglectful parents and overcrowded homes with no respect for religion or education led impressionable young people to admire local examples of intemperance and vice; their unchecked passions would then lead them into crime. Essentially, therefore, the criminogenic environment drew the offender further and further from God. Tallack urged the adoption of a host of new penal schemes: cumulative sentencing for habituals, schemes of restitution, systems of conditional liberty under the supervision of moral exemplars as an alternative to custody, reduction of the number of children sent to prison, rescue schemes for those drifting into crime, and fines graduated to income. He never wavered in his faith in severely moralistic separate confinement for prisoners and, indeed, believed in corporal punishment for cruel offenders.

Tallack's relationship with Sir Edmund Du Cane (1830–1903), the formidable and autocratic chairman of the Prison Commission, was variable. While both agreed as to the need for unmanipulable severity, Tallack's criticisms of the prisons were public and serious. He exposed the high levels of self-mutilation among convicts and brutality by some warders in his evidence (which he subsequently published) to the royal commission on penal servitude of 1878–9. He also complained that the centralization of local prison government restricted his access to prisons. Yet the two men respected one another despite Du Cane's periodic rages with Tallack (in one of which he referred to the Howard Association as a 'piddling little association'). When Du Cane was brought down by his many enemies in 1895, Tallack was one of the few who spoke of him with respect.

In the early 1890s Tallack's vision of penality was looking increasingly outdated with the rise of the New Liberalism, which placed its faith in collective effort based on understanding of the new social science and emphasized methods of reformatory intervention calibrated to the individual offender's character type. He was under attack from the Humanitarian League, set up in 1891, which was fiercely critical of old-fashioned penal methods. In his evidence to the Home Office departmental Gladstone committee of 1895, which set a new agenda for prisons, he nevertheless robustly advocated his solutions.

Tallack had always propagated his views on penality in a prolific output of pamphlets, articles, letters to the press (notably *The Times*), and books: his best known works were *Defects of Criminal Administration* (1872) and *Penological and Preventive Principles* (1889). However, he also wrote on wider social issues, such as pauperism, as well as publishing books and articles about Quaker theology and personalities. In addition he wrote books about places he had visited overseas, such as Malta and California: Tallack had travelled extensively in North America, Australasia, and the Middle East, visiting penal establishments and addressing the numerous international congresses on crime and punishment. He played an important role in the success of the 1872 International Congress on the Prevention and Repression of Crime, held in London, to which twenty-two nations sent delegates. Tallack died at his home, 61 Clapton Common, Clapton, London, on 25 September 1908, having an international and enduring reputation as a most effective founding figure of a major British penal reform group. He was buried at the Quaker burial-ground at Winchmore Hill, London, on 30 September.   BILL FORSYTHE

Sources *The Times* (28 Sept 1908), 11c · G. Rose, *The struggle for penal reform* (1961) · 'Royal commission to inquire into … penal servitude', *Parl. papers* (1878–9), 37.1, C. 2368; 37.67, C. 2368-I · 'Departmental committee on prisons', *Parl. papers* (1895), 56.1, C. 7702; 56.55, C. 7702-I · 'Royal commission on capital punishment', *Parl. papers* (1866), vol. 21, no. 3590 · S. McConville, *English local prisons, 1860–1900: next only to death* (1995) · L. Radzinowicz and R. Hood, *A history of English criminal law and its administration from 1750*, rev. edn, 5: *The emergence of penal policy in Victorian and Edwardian England*

(1990) • W. Forsythe, *Penal discipline and reformatory projects, 1895–1939* (1991) • PRO, HO 45 - 9707 - A50752 • *CGPLA Eng. & Wales* (1908) **Archives** U. Warwick Mod. RC, notebooks and papers | Howard League, archives **Likenesses** two portraits, repro. in W. Tallack, *Howard letters and memories* (1905) **Wealth at death** £8598 12s. 2d.: probate, 10 Oct 1908, *CGPLA Eng. & Wales*

Tallaght, Óengus of. *See* Óengus of Tallaght (*fl. c.*830).

Tallents, Francis (1619–1708), clergyman and ejected minister, was born in November 1619 at Pilsley, North Wingfield, Derbyshire, the son of Philip Tallents (*d.* 1633/4). Francis was fourteen when his father died and his uncle, also called Francis Tallents, vicar of Tibshelf, Derbyshire, sent the boy to the free schools of Mansfield and Newark, both in Nottinghamshire. On 14 May 1636 Tallents was admitted sizar at Peterhouse, Cambridge, but later migrated to Magdalene College; he graduated BA in 1641 and proceeded MA in 1645. About 1642 he travelled to France as tutor to the sons of the earls of Suffolk and on his return he became a fellow of Magdalene. He received presbyterian ordination by the third London classis at St Mary Woolnoth Church on 29 November 1648.

In the summer of 1652 the parish of St Mary's, Shrewsbury, invited Tallents to become its minister. A little later Richard Baxter wrote to him urging him to accept the invitation; Tallents did so, and became curate of St Mary's in November. He received the stipend of £150 per annum, to which the committee for plundered ministers added another £50. Baxter described Tallents as 'A good Scholar, a godly, blameless Divine, most eminent for extraordinary Prudence and moderation, and peaceableness towards all' (*Reliquiae Baxterianae*, 3.94).

Tallents was a man of wide-ranging intellectual interests. In a letter of January 1650 he advised on works on mathematics and by Gassendi and Kepler on astronomy, reporting that he had seen Jonas Moore's *Arithmetick*, which 'seems to be a handsome piece, short, useful and not very difficult … Gassendi his *Institutio astronomica, sec*[*undum*] *hypotheses veterum et recentiorum* may be had, and so may Kepplar' (*Egmont MSS*, 1.492). Most intriguing are Tallents's links with Robert Boyle, who may have met him in Cambridge in December 1645, presumably coming to know him through Boyle's Irish and kin links with pupils of Tallents. Through Boyle, Tallents was from late 1646 informed about the activities of the fraternity of correspondents sharing a common utopian and utilitarian scientific outlook known as the 'Invisible College', of which he became a 'peripheral adherent' (Webster, *Great Instauration*, 62). Boyle wrote to Tallents on 20 February 1647 of how those of the Invisible College 'take the whole body of mankind for their care' (ibid., 381). Tallents's own universalist concerns would be demonstrated in his *View of Universal History*, published in 1685.

In 1654 Tallents became an assistant to the Shropshire ejectors, and he received a yearly fee of £130 from the town council of Shrewsbury as his fee for being the town's public preacher. At the Restoration he 'made some advances towards a compliance in ecclesiastical matters' but in the end chose to be ejected from his living rather than conform to the restored Church of England and receive Anglican reordination. Matthew Henry recorded:

> He hath sometimes observ'd … that before the Wars the Puritans generally made a shift to conform and come into the Church, notwithstanding the hard usage they foresaw (by the trouble frequently given to those of that character) they were likely to meet with in it. To prevent which for the future … new barriers were erected by the Act of Uniformity to keep them out.   (Henry, *A Sermon*, 50)

In 1662 Tallents was several times imprisoned in Shrewsbury Castle for illegal preaching. In his will he described himself as 'formerly Publick preacher of the Gospel from the year 1652 till 24 August 1662', and for the rest of his life he observed St Bartholomew's day as a day of humiliation and fasting (*Calamy rev.*, 474).

Tallents attended St Mary's Church as a layman, 'as a token of charity towards those whom we stately cannot join with' (Palmer, 3.155). He and John Bryan junior, the ejected vicar of St Chad's, were the acknowledged leaders of the Shrewsbury nonconformists until Bryan's death in 1699. In 1663–5 he was frequently in London collecting money for ejected ministers. After the Five Mile Act of 1665 he spent some time at the house of John Gell at Hopton in his native county.

From February 1671 to July 1673 Tallents was travelling in Europe with two pupils, one of whom was the future whig politician John Hampden, and spent some time at Auteuil near Paris. Tallents, the grandson of a Huguenot, spoke French fluently. When the Popish Plot agitation began in 1678 rumours began to circulate that he was a French Jesuit. The rumours persisted and were fuelled by the fact that Bryan and other nonconformists presented an address to the Catholic king James II when he paid a visit to Shrewsbury in August 1687. The history of this 'notorious lye' is set out in a letter from Tallents to Baxter in February 1690. Tallents gives as one reason for the rumour a general slur against nonconformist preachers as Jesuits, as another 'because I have 2 or 3 times been in France' (Keeble and Nuttall, 2.303). Rather, as Calamy recalled, Tallents 'often said, that what he saw abroad of the Popish religion, and what conference he had with its advocates, added much to his conviction of the falshood and wickedness of it, and confirmed him in protestantism' (Palmer, 3.153). While at Paris, according to Matthew Henry, Tallents had written a 'Description of the Roman Catholick religion', a lengthy work in which Tallents provided a detailed account of popish practices and beliefs as a warning of the dangers of Romanism. In 1693 he prosecuted a man who alleged that he was a Jesuit; the man was fined 50s.

Francis Tallents married four times. On 9 June 1653 he married Anne Lomax, the niece of another future ejected minister, Samuel Hildersham, rector of West Felton, Shropshire (where they were married) and granddaughter of the famous puritan minister Arthur Hildersham. Together they had at least two children: Hildersham, who lived less than a fortnight in the spring of 1655, and Francis, who was born on 7 September 1656 and died in early adulthood. Anne died in Shrewsbury in March 1658. Three and a half years later, on 27 November 1661, Tallents married Martha Clive, the daughter of Thomas Clive of Walford, Shropshire; she was buried in St Mary's, Shrewsbury, on 21 July 1663. Ten years later in December 1673 Tallents married again; his third wife was a widow, Mary Greenhill (*b. c.*1633) of Harrow on the Hill, Middlesex, who died in 1685. About 1687 Tallents married his fourth wife, a woman called Elizabeth, whose surname is unknown; and for a fourth time he attended the funeral of a wife when she was buried at St Mary's on 11 March 1702.

The nonconformist congregation in Shrewsbury had to endure persecution in the years after 1662. In 1683, Matthew Henry recorded, 'the meetings in Shrewsbury [were] suppressed, and he [Tallents] was forced into obscurity and durst not be seen there' (Henry, *A Sermon*, 56). In 1685 Tallents was arrested at the time of Monmouth's rebellion when he came to town to pay his last respects to his third wife, who had died while on business there; he was imprisoned in Chester Castle. Moreover, the nonconformists had no permanent place of worship. At one time they met in the house of Mrs Elizabeth Hunt and after her death in 1690 Tallents's own house on Claremont Hill was licensed for nonconformist worship under the Toleration Act of 1689. A purpose-built meeting-house in the high street was opened in October 1691. On its walls Tallents had written, 'That it was built not for a faction or a party, but for promoting repentance and faith, in communion with all that love our Lord Jesus Christ, in sincerity', and in a memory of his Huguenot ancestry, 'added that scripture with which the French churches usually begin their worship: "Our Help stands in the Name of the Lord, who made heaven and earth"' (Henry, *A Sermon*, 58). In 1703 Tallents annulled the trust deed of 1691 and vested the ownership of the building in Thomas Hunt, a London merchant, to be leased to the dissenters at a peppercorn rent.

Tallents wrote several works. His *Universal History* (1685) was a series of chronological tables, which he had engraved on sixteen copper plates in his own house. Another work of his, *A History of Schism* (1705), led to a lengthy controversy with the Anglican Samuel Grascombe, in which, Calamy notes, Tallents challenged the latter's 'new and bold assertion, that there can be no Church or salvation, in any ordinary way, without a canonical bishop' (Calamy, *Continuation*, 2.722). Tallents also wrote *A Sure and Large Foundation* (1689?), of which there is a copy in Shrewsbury School Library. He died in Shrewsbury on 11 April 1708, aged eighty-eight, and was buried alongside his first wife at St Mary's, Shrewsbury, four days later. In his will of July 1706, proved on 30 April 1708, he left the bulk of his estate to a Shrewsbury distiller, John Dutton, to be disposed for charitable purposes. He also gave a legacy of £60 to the presbyterian church in Shrewsbury.

Francis Tallents was a gifted teacher who could have followed an academic career. Instead he chose to become a minister in Shrewsbury. He could in 1662 have accepted reordination and retained his £330 a year, or gone on to preferment in the Church of England. Instead he chose the hazardous life of an ejected minister. Seventeenth-century dissent owed an incalculable debt to such men.

C. D. Gilbert

Sources *Reliquiae Baxterianae, or, Mr Richard Baxter's narrative of the most memorable passages of his life and times*, ed. M. Sylvester, 1 vol. in 3 pts (1696) · *Calendar of the correspondence of Richard Baxter*, ed. N. H. Keeble and G. F. Nuttall, 2 vols. (1991) · E. Calamy, *A continuation of the account of the ministers … who were ejected and silenced after the Restoration in 1660*, 2 vols. (1727) · *The nonconformist's memorial … originally written by … Edmund Calamy*, ed. S. Palmer, [3rd edn], 3 (1803) · *Calamy rev.* · A. Beresford, *The story of Unitarianism in Shrewsbury* (1962) · H. Owen and J. B. Blakeway, *A history of Shrewsbury*, 2 vols. (1825) · C. Webster, *The great instauration: science, medicine and reform, 1626–1660* (1975) · M. Henry, *A sermon, preached at the funeral of the Reverend F. Tallents … With a short account of his life and death* (1709) · Venn, *Alum. Cant.* · private information (2004) [Janice Cox, Shrewsbury] · C. Webster, 'Benjamin Worsley: engineering for universal reform from the Invisible College to the Navigation Act', *Samuel Hartlib and universal reformation: studies in intellectual communication*, ed. M. Greengrass, M. Leslie, and T. Raylor (1994), 213–35 · A. S. Langley, 'Correspondence of Sir Edward Harley, K. B. and Rev. Francis Tallents', *Transactions of the Congregational Historical Society*, 8 (1920–23), 267–77, 306–17 · M. Henry, *An account of the life and death of Mr Philip Henry* (1698) · *Report on the manuscripts of the earl of Egmont*, 2 vols. in 3, HMC, 63 (1905–9), vol. 1, pp. 474–5, 491–2 · R. E. W. Maddison, *The life of the Honourable Robert Boyle, FRS* (1969), 70 · J. E. Auden, 'Ecclesiastical history of Shropshire during the civil war, Commonwealth and Restoration', *Transactions of the Shropshire Archaeological and Natural History Society*, 3rd ser., 7 (1907), 241–307 · W. Phillips and J. E. Auden, eds., 'The Ottley papers (2nd series): the Commonwealth and Restoration', *Transactions of the Shropshire Archaeological and Natural History Society*, 4th ser., 1 (1911), 233–318 · W. G. D. Fletcher, 'Shropshire clergy who contributed to the free and voluntary present to his majesty in 1662', *Transactions of the Shropshire Archaeological and Natural History Society*, 4th ser., 2 (1912), 209–14 · PRO, C213/214 [association oath] · Shrewsbury council minutes, 1652–1708, Shrops. RRC · nonconformist records, Shrops. RRC · J. L. Chester and J. Foster, eds., *London marriage licences, 1521–1869* (1887), 1313 · parish register, West Felton, Shropshire, 9 June 1653 [first marriage] · parish register, Shrewsbury, St Mary's [marriages, burial]
Archives Bodl. Oxf., travel journal [copy] · Shrops. RRC, travel journal and notes for sermons | BL, Stowe MSS, letter to John Hampden · DWL, Blackmore MSS
Likenesses J. Caldwall, line engraving, NPG · J. Hopwood, stipple, BM, NPG
Wealth at death see will, Lichfield RO

Tallents, Sir Stephen George (1884–1958), civil servant and public relations expert, was born on 20 October 1884 in London, the eldest son of George William Tallents, a conveyancing barrister, and his wife, Mildred Sophia Cubitt, daughter of the first Baron Ashcombe. He had two brothers and two sisters. On his father's side he was descended from a line of midland- and then London-based lawyers. His descent on his mother's side was historically the more distinguished and for Tallents personally the more influential. His maternal great-grandfather had been Thomas Cubitt (1788–1855), a highly successful and ultimately very wealthy architect and builder, patronized by Queen Victoria. As a child, Tallents frequently holidayed at Denbies, near Dorking in Surrey, a country house designed by Cubitt, set in extensive estates, and the home of Tallents's maternal grandparents. Country living made a lasting impression upon his personality and private

Sir Stephen George Tallents (1884–1958), by Bassano, 1947

enthusiasms. He expressed all his life a delight in the countryside, although largely as a place of beauty and recreation rather than as a site of production and employment.

Education and early career Tallents's education, with its emphasis upon literature and classical learning, was conventional for one of his class and abilities. Following initial instruction by governesses at home in Knightsbridge, he progressed in 1894 to a preparatory school and then in 1897 to Harrow School, like his father before and his brothers later. From there, in 1903 he went to Balliol College, Oxford. His university career did not mark him out as a high-flyer. He obtained a second class both in classical moderations in 1905 and in *literae humaniores* in 1907. Thereafter the important decision was to follow his father's advice and seek entry not into his father's profession of the law but into the civil service. However, he was too poorly placed in the competitive entrance examinations to be sure of any post except in the Indian Civil Service, which, again on his father's advice, he declined. He was determined to try again, and the setback had the positive effect of providing Tallents with a more varied education and less orthodox experiences than routine entrants to the civil service. Dispatched to the University of Grenoble for three months, he came back fluent in French and a francophile. After his return, like a few other young men from privileged backgrounds, he volunteered to work in the East End settlement at Toynbee Hall and was brought face-to-face with social deprivation. The experience may have been additionally useful because shared by

William Beveridge and Hubert Llewellyn Smith, under whom in the civil service Tallents subsequently and profitably served. Renewed study at a 'crammer' eventually secured his entry to the civil service; but still lowly placed in the list of examinees he had to wait in reserve until a vacancy at last arose as an upper-division clerk in the marine department of the Board of Trade in April 1909.

Among his humdrum duties, Tallents began to show initiative. For example, following a chance encounter with a medical scientist, he discovered the board's official ignorance of the probable causes of beriberi among Lascar seamen. His recommendations to tackle the problem met with approval and were implemented with beneficial results. On many future occasions Tallents showed a respect for scientists which was then uncommon among civil servants. Shortly thereafter he made the first of the several high-risk transfers—some successful, some not—which distinguished his career. Against the cautionary advice of colleagues, in January 1911 he moved, as a staff divisional officer, to that branch of the Board of Trade which was charged under Beveridge with establishing a nationwide network of labour exchanges. Tallents's skills in office management, and his role in setting up the juvenile advisory committees, led Beveridge to rely further on him when the unemployment insurance scheme was being inaugurated in 1912. His administrative talent was again put to the test when with the outbreak of war he was involved in the rapid recruitment of the dockyard labour needed for the war effort. By then Tallents was married to Bridget (1890/91–1968), the wealthy heir of Samuel Hugh Franklin Hole, a barrister. Their earlier engagement, and even wedding plans, had been disrupted, but they were married on 19 May 1914. This was a secure and happy marriage; there were two sons and two daughters.

Wartime service Tallents could perhaps have remained a civil servant throughout the war. But reflecting the qualities of his class, culture, and age, he went to fight. He had become a member of the volunteer Surrey yeomanry in 1903, but when mobilized they had a full complement of officers, and so in September 1914, aged nearly thirty, he joined the Irish Guards. It was another risky change of career. By January 1915 he was in France; and in May he was severely wounded, with a bullet through his right thigh which put his life and not just his leg in danger. The legacies of his war experience included a trim military bearing, a limp, the short stories and autobiographical essays largely about the war which he had written mainly for the *Manchester Guardian* while recuperating, and his 'Notes for the guidance of platoon commanders in the trenches', which the War Office adopted.

Meanwhile, another new government department needed administrative ability, and late in 1915, while Tallents was still mending, Llewellyn Smith and Beveridge, his seniors at the Board of Trade, got him appointed to the Ministry of Munitions. This too carried career risks. His efforts to secure exemption from military service for munitions workers brought him into conflict with the

War Office, and even, on one occasion, with Lord Kitchener himself. However, Tallents's abilities and achievements were such that when in August 1916 he was judged fit once more for military service, his patrons refused to let him go. Instead, he was transferred to another controversial new government department, the Ministry of Food; there, as a principal assistant secretary, he worked again with Beveridge in introducing food rationing and as chairman of the Milk Control Board.

The armistice brought with it doubts about the future of the Ministry of Food. In any case, feeling exhausted by routine civil service work, and once more rejecting the advice of career-minded colleagues, Tallents took another chance: he volunteered to work for the European recovery programme set up by the allies. In January 1919 he was appointed chief British delegate for the relief and supply of Poland, which was just re-emerging in battered condition following the collapse in eastern Europe of the Russian and German empires. This appointment was followed by further instructions in February to report on the condition of adjacent new states, and this initiated a remarkable period in the life of a civil servant, as British commissioner for the Baltic provinces. Equipped with the temporary status of lieutenant-colonel, a limited staff, the occasional presence of members of a British military mission, and in the background the Royal Navy, Tallents provided robust support to the new governments of Estonia, Latvia, and Lithuania in their efforts to secure internal stability and external security. It was a time of severe material shortages, conditions made more difficult by frontier disputes between the new states and military activity by German, Bolshevik, and Polish armed forces. He took upon himself considerable diplomatic and administrative responsibilities as well as an advisory role, and even acted for a few days as governor of Riga.

Finally replaced by a career diplomat in October 1920, and somewhat distanced from his earlier civil service connections, Tallents's next move brought him to another unstable post-war political environment. Early in 1921 he became private secretary to Lord FitzAlan, the last lord lieutenant of Ireland. Republicanism in Ireland led to military conflict and eventually partition and the Anglo-Irish treaty in December 1921. Thereafter, from 1922 to 1926, Tallents served in Northern Ireland as imperial secretary, acting as liaison officer with the Northern Ireland government and administering the services reserved to the British government by the Government of Ireland Act of 1920. He was perhaps in a career backwater.

Developing public relations Tallents's success in tackling these post-war challenges brought him to the attention of L. S. Amery, secretary of state for the dominions, and in 1926 he was recalled to England. He was first required to serve as secretary to the cabinet committee which handled the general strike, before Amery could secure him as secretary of the Empire Marketing Board (EMB). This appointment, taken up in May 1926 at the age of forty-one, represented another high-risk step for Tallents. He was to head a government operation whose funding, powers,

composition, and purposes were unconventional. Consequently, inside and outside Whitehall it aroused curiosity and even hostility. But the move was a turning point for Tallents, and launched him into the culture of public relations. The EMB was intended by Amery to secure closer imperial economic integration by increasing British consumption of empire-produced foods and raw materials. It aimed to do this by improving the quantity and quality of empire supplies through scientific research into problems of production and distribution, through financing market research and the provision of market intelligence, and through increasing the appeal to consumers of empire products by advertising and other publicity campaigns. Tallents directed operations, helped devise strategies, brought in or liaised with outside experts, and defended the work of the board against critics. Of lasting importance for Tallents were the board's experiments in the use of modern publicity methods. He learned a lot from working with private-sector pioneers such as Frank Pick, managing director of the London underground, and Sir William Crawford, head of one of the country's largest advertising companies; from the employment of talented poster artists such as McKnight Kauffer and film-makers such as John Grierson; and from contacts between the EMB and the BBC.

These experiences prompted Tallents to reflect on the proper role of official information services in a modern democracy. He developed a concept of public relations, a phrase he may even have coined, which in the public sector he visualized as the creation among its employees of a sense of pride and purpose and among the general public of an intelligent awareness of the services which government departments were providing. Some of his other ideas were distilled in a widely noticed pamphlet published in 1932, *The Projection of Britain*, which argued for the use of the modern media to promote British products and values overseas as an extension of normal diplomatic activities.

Before this time very few government departments in peacetime had attempted even to keep the public informed about their activities. Moreover, government's use of propaganda during the First World War had aroused distaste. The board was therefore subject to much hostility, especially from the Treasury, and by 1930 its funding was being cut. Tallents's own career could have been brought down with the board. However, in 1931, impressed by Tallents and the publicity operations of the EMB, Clement Attlee, then postmaster-general in the second Labour government, invited Tallents to join the publicity advisory committee of the General Post Office (GPO). This connection proved valuable. Attlee's successor as postmaster-general in the National Government, Kingsley Wood, picked Tallents out of the wreck of the EMB when it finally folded in 1933 and appointed him to a new position as public relations officer at the GPO. He brought with him what became the GPO film unit plus a conviction that public relations in the public service was important.

The BBC and after The GPO, with its tradition of marketing and its dependence on public use, was a more secure base for Tallents's career than a disputed offshoot of a government department. But it is understandable why he left the GPO in 1935 to join the BBC as controller of public relations. John Reith, as director-general, was committed to a concept of public-service broadcasting which cohered with Tallents's own beliefs. However, Tallents's career thereafter suffered setbacks. Understandably, he hoped to succeed Reith as director-general, but in July 1938 the appointment went elsewhere. Moreover, with war looming, Tallents had been acting from July 1936 as director-general designate of a shadow Ministry of Information, but his plans to centralize publicity and increase staffing were rejected and he was dismissed in January 1939. Later, in May 1940, he was made responsible for the overseas services of the BBC, but he could not protect his patch in the dark days of the war when tougher characters were brought in to run more aggressive external broadcasting operations. He was forced to resign in September 1941. Perhaps in his career he had taken one step too many. Still only fifty-six, he spent the next year or so writing his memoirs. Only in 1943 was he to regain a public appointment, when until 1946 he served as public relations officer in yet another new government department, the Ministry of Town and Country Planning.

Tallents had collected conventional honours during his official career: a CB in 1918 as a reward for his war work, a CBE in 1920 on his return from eastern Europe, and a CMG in 1929 followed by a KCMG in 1932 during his time at the EMB. But the respect which he attracted in the private sector was more distinctive. Since he greatly helped to define and promote the public relations profession, it is fitting that in 1935 he should be the first civil servant to be awarded the cup of the Publicity Club of London, then the highest honour in the advertising world; that he should be made the first president of the Institute of Public Relations (IPR) in 1948–9, which he had also helped to establish; that he should be asked to serve again as president in 1952–3; and that the IPR should continue to remember him by establishing in 1984 the Stephen Tallents medal for exceptional contributions to the development of public relations.

In his retirement Tallents was also made an honorary associate of the Royal Institute of British Architects in 1946, an honorary fellow of the Society of Industrial Artists in 1949, a member of the council of the Royal Society of Arts in 1953, and president of the Design and Industries Association in 1955–6. He also maintained various business connections. Otherwise, he saw out his retirement with a variety of countryside pursuits, mainly centred on his home—St John's Jerusalem at Sutton-at-Hone, near Dartford in Kent—and with more writing. He had already published two collections of short stories and sketches, *The Starry Pool and other Tales* (1918) and *The Dancer and other Tales* (1922), several essays on publicity and the work of the EMB, and the first volume of his autobiography, the years to 1920, called *Man and Boy* (1943), and he followed these up with further reflections on public relations, articles in the *Sunday Times*, and a collection of short pieces on country life called *Green Thoughts* (1952). 'Empire experiment',

his account of the work of the Empire Marketing Board, failed after the war to find a publisher and survives only in manuscript. He died at the Royal Marsden Hospital, Chelsea, aged seventy-three, on 11 September 1958. *The Times* headed its obituary 'An imaginative civil servant'.

STEPHEN CONSTANTINE

Sources S. Tallents, *Man and boy* (1943) • *The Times* (13 Sept 1958) • S. Constantine, 'Bringing the empire alive: the empire marketing board and imperial propaganda, 1926–1933', *Imperialism and popular culture*, ed. J. M. MacKenzie (1986) • J. Harris, *William Beveridge* (1977) • M. Grant, *Propaganda and the role of the state in inter-war Britain* (1994) • A. Briggs, *The history of broadcasting in the United Kingdom*, 2–3 (1965–70) • P. M. Taylor, *The projection of Britain: British overseas publicity and propaganda, 1919–1939* (1981) • T. Willcox, 'Projection or publicity: rival concepts of the pre-war planning of the ministry of information', *Journal of Contemporary History*, 18 (1983), 97–116 • I. McLaine, *Ministry of morale: home front morale and the ministry of information in World War II* (1979) • M. Ogilvy-Webb, *The government explains: a study of the information services* (1965) • L. S. Amery, *My political life*, 2: *War and peace* (1954) • *DNB* • *CGPLA Eng. & Wales* (1958) • m. cert. • d. cert. [Lady Tallents] • *WWW*, 1951–60
Archives BLPES, family corresp. • U. Lond., Institute of Commonwealth Studies, MSS | BL, corresp. with Sir Sydney Cockerell, Add. MS 52755 • BLPES, Beveridge MSS • BLPES, Markham MSS • U. Lond., Institute of Commonwealth Studies, Empire Marketing Board papers and corresp. • University of East Anglia, Institute of Public Relations MSS • University of Stirling, corresp. with John Grierson
Likenesses W. Stoneman, photographs, 1932, NPG • H. Coster, photograph, 1940–49, NPG • W. Stoneman, photograph, 1942, NPG • Bassano, photograph, 1947, NPG [*see illus.*]
Wealth at death £15,106: probate, 22 Dec 1958, *CGPLA Eng. & Wales*

Tallents, William Edward (*bap.* 1780, *d.* 1837), political agent and lawyer, was baptized at Newark-on-Trent, Nottinghamshire, on 31 August 1780, the youngest of the eight children (five sons and three daughters) of Philip Tallents (1741–1789), attorney, and Elizabeth Webster (1740–1827). He was articled to Samuel Allen, a solicitor in Newark, on 5 January 1796, and entered the firm of Godfrey and Tallents (established by his father with the influential Newark banker Edward Smith Godfrey) in 1801.

Tallents married Elizabeth Tomlinson (1787–1850), one of the fourteen children of William Tomlinson and Elizabeth Broadhurst of Newark, on 13 October 1806. The couple established a family home at Cartergate in Newark and had seven children (three sons and four daughters). The eldest, Elizabeth (1807–1858), married into the Godfrey family. The youngest daughter, Mary Ann (1817–1839), married, on 24 January 1837, John Hartpole Lecky of Cullenwood House in Dublin. They had one child, William Edward Hartpole *Lecky (1838–1903), the historian.

Obituarists and admirers have often referred to Tallents as 'indefatigable' (see Heron, 234) in the range and capacity of his work. His leading place in Nottinghamshire (especially Newark) politics and society for over thirty years was secured by his association with Godfrey, personal capabilities, and, as critics put it, the 'possession of every … public appointment which this Town and District have the disposal of' (*Nottingham Journal*). Chief among these were Tallents's period as town clerk of Newark from

15 April 1806 to 3 May 1833 and his subsequent appointment as alderman; he also served as councillor (east ward) from 1 January 1836. He was deputy clerk of the peace for Nottinghamshire from February 1834. Many of Tallents's positions were assumed on his death by his eldest son, Godfrey Tallents (1812–1877).

Tallents's services as a political agent were in continual demand from aristocrats and candidates; his appointment as land steward and political agent to the fourth duke of Newcastle on 26 April 1826 is the principal example. His role as superintendent of the family's substantial estate and electoral influence in the Newark constituency and (after 1832) south Nottinghamshire brought him into close working contact with successive MPs in the Newcastle interest, and in particular, from 1832 to 1837, with W. E. Gladstone. Tallents acted as Gladstone's counsellor and mentor in maintaining his often fragile relations with Godfrey and other leading Conservatives, represented in the Red Club at Newark. In the dispute over the publicans' bills arising from the 1832 election, Tallents sided with Gladstone against many of his colleagues: 'notwithstanding my near connection with some of the Parties … I cannot avoid seeing & deeply regretting the course they pursue' (Tallents to Lord Lincoln, 13 May 1835, Nottingham University, MS Ne C 11825). Gladstone himself found Tallents to be 'a cultivated & very agreeable man' (Gladstone, *Diaries*, 3 Oct 1832) and, together with Newcastle, presented him with a pair of silver wine coolers for his dedicated service. On Tallents's death Newcastle stated that he had 'lost a real & valuable friend as well as a man upon whose judgment & ability I could confidently rely' (Nottingham University, MS Ne 2 F5, 24 Dec 1837).

Although Tallents was most closely associated with defending Newcastle's power and influence in the period when it was threatened by a whig government (1830–34), his services were not confined by partisanship. He maintained a long-standing connection with the whig Yarborough family and superintended their electoral influence in Lincolnshire and at Great Grimsby (among whose members was Sir Robert Heron). Despite his local allegiance to Newcastle, he assisted Serjeant Thomas Wilde (Gladstone's opponent at Newark) in prosecuting the Swing rioters at Salisbury in December 1830, and worked with Wilde's agent, Charles Pearson, on electoral matters at Great Grimsby. Tallents was Brougham's choice in August 1831 as boundary commissioner for the Reform Bill, and Lord John Russell consulted him on municipal corporation reform in June 1835 (G. Tallents, diary, 2 June 1835). Despite Newcastle's chagrin, Tallents stated that he had 'always thought it better to take the helm out of the hands of those who would steer an evil course and man the Decks with those who can and will direct it for the good of Society' (Tallents to Newcastle, 27 July 1836, Nottinghamshire Archives, MS 3937).

On 11 November 1835 Tallents purchased a London home at 26 Great George Street, Westminster, as a preparation for cultivating his national connections. It was there, on 22 December 1837, that he died from complaints associated with asthma, from which he had suffered for many years. He was buried in the family vault in the parish church at Newark-on-Trent (St Mary Magdalene) on 30 December. A tablet on the wall of the north chancel aisle records a tribute to Tallents's 'ability … integrity and … industry', qualities which are well reflected in his portrait by Thomas Barber.

RICHARD A. GAUNT and PETER O'MALLEY

Sources Notts. Arch., Tallents papers • G. Tallents, diary, 1828–41, Notts. Arch. [microfilm] • correspondence and diaries of the fourth and fifth dukes of Newcastle, U. Nott., Newcastle MSS, Ne C, Ne 2F • priv. coll., Tallents MSS [family and genealogical papers] • G. S. Hemingway, 'The Tallents of Newark', Notts. Arch., 6–14 • Gladstone, *Diaries* • R. Heron, *Notes*, 2nd edn (1851), 234 • R. A. Preston, 'The structure of government and politics in Nottinghamshire, 1824–35', DPhil diss., U. Oxf., 1978, 282–3 • *Nottingham Journal* (13 Nov 1824) • R. A. Gaunt, 'The political activities and opinions of the 4th duke of Newcastle (1785–1851)', PhD diss., U. Nott., 2000 • R. A. Gaunt, 'A stern unbending tory and the rising young hope: Gladstone, Newark and the fourth duke of Newcastle, 1832–1846', *The Gladstone umbrella*, ed. P. Francis (2001), 14–34
Archives Notts. Arch., Tallents, acc. 3937 • priv. coll., MSS | BL, Gladstone MSS • U. Nott., Newcastle MSS, corresp. and diaries of the fourth and fifth dukes of Newcastle, NeC, Ne 2F, 8 vols.
Likenesses T. Barber, portrait, 1829, priv. coll. • T. Lupton, engraving, pubd 1838, priv. coll. • T. Bedford, family vault and memorial, 1840, Newark parish church
Wealth at death under £12,000: probate, 1838

Tallis, Thomas (*c*.1505–1585), musician and composer, was born probably about 1505. Nothing is known about his parents, place of birth, or early education, and the date of his birth can be conjectured only from the fact that one of his works was copied into a music manuscript (BL, MS Harley 1709) apparently in the later 1520s. Eight years before his death, in a petition to Queen Elizabeth dated June 1577, Tallis described himself as 'verie aged'.

Early career to *c*.1543 Like most professional church musicians, Tallis almost certainly began his career as a choirboy. In that capacity he would have learned the rudiments of music and been taught how to compose and play the organ. The fact that the Marian antiphon *Salve intemerata*, his earliest known work, is substantial and ornate implies that his chorister years were spent at a major choral foundation where elaborate music was performed. It is possible that he had an early connection with Kent and the south-east of England. Tallis's first known position was as organist of the Benedictine priory of Dover in the years 1530–33; he was later a lay clerk at Canterbury Cathedral; it was of Kentish properties that he received valuable, grants of crown leases; and as his wife's will makes plain, in later life he maintained strong personal contacts with a prominent Kentish family.

Tallis probably stayed at Dover Priory until its dissolution in 1535. His next recorded appointment (1537–8) was in London, as a singing-man of the choir of St Mary-at-Hill, a parish church with a particularly strong musical tradition. Possibly he also served as organist there. In 1538 he moved to the Augustinian abbey of Waltham Cross in Essex, presumably through contact with the abbot, whose London residence was close to St Mary-at-Hill. This position too was short-lived; Waltham Abbey was dissolved in March 1540, and as one of its lay employees Tallis was paid off with a gratuity. One of the abbey manuscripts, a book of music theory (BL, MS Lansdowne 763), bears his signature, and may have passed into his hands at the dispersal of the library. By the summer of 1540 Tallis had moved to Canterbury Cathedral, where his name heads the list of singing-men in the newly expanded choir. His two-year stint at Canterbury marks the end of his early career. By 1543–4 he had joined the choir of the Chapel Royal, and he remained a member of that institution until his death.

Salve intemerata apart, very few works by Tallis can be firmly attributed to these early years. A Canterbury connection has been suggested for some of the pieces copied into a set of music books (now CUL, MSS Peterhouse 471–4), copied about 1540–41, which includes two further works by Tallis. One of them is a mass partly derived from the music of *Salve intemerata*, a form of musical cross-reference that English composers learned from their counterparts in France and the Low Countries. Also likely to date from these early years is an organ alleluia based on a plainchant melody, copied probably in the 1530s into Oxford, Christ Church, MS Mus. 1034A. To judge from these and other conjecturally early works, Tallis's musical voice at the beginning of his career was confident and competent but not yet strongly characterized, and there is evidence of influence from established figures such as Robert Fayrfax and John Taverner.

Earlier Chapel Royal years, 1543–1558 The choir of the Chapel Royal, which had been developed significantly by Henry VIII during the first two decades of his reign, retained its high standards throughout the sixteenth century, despite the general decline in English church music evident after 1559. All three of Henry's children (Edward VI, Mary I, and Elizabeth I) were given training in music as part of their education, and as his heirs they maintained their father's concern for musical excellence within their households. Tallis was a beneficiary of this. Throughout his mature years he performed with and could compose for a team of exceptionally talented singers, and his post was comfortably remunerated, both in wages and (from 1557) in grants of leases containing substantial potential for the generation of clear income. By the time of his death, more than forty years after joining the Chapel Royal, Tallis had risen through the ranks to become the choir's most senior member. Officially designated a 'gentleman' (lay singer) of the chapel throughout that period, in a publication of 1575 he also styled himself organist (jointly with his younger colleague William Byrd), and he may have served in that capacity for many years. During Mary's reign Tallis married, apparently for the first time. His wife, Joan, was widow of Thomas Bury (d. 1554), who too had been a gentleman of the Chapel Royal. Like many other members of the royal household choir, they lived in Greenwich.

In addition to performing at special occasions of state such as coronations, weddings, and funerals, the choir of the Chapel Royal sang the normal round of daily liturgical services, and Tallis would have contributed to this on a rota basis. The musical repertory changed according to the prevailing political and religious climate. At the time of his appointment it was still firmly rooted in tradition; the break with Rome did not mean a break with the Sarum rite, and it was for this liturgy that Tallis initially wrote choral settings of hymns and office responsories, based on traditional plainchant melodies. That repertory would have been set aside soon after the accession of Edward VI in 1547, and certainly after publication of the Book of Common Prayer in 1549. In response to the reformed liturgy, a totally new repertory of canticles and anthems to English texts was introduced, and Tallis contributed significantly to it. With Edward's death in 1553 and the accession of Mary, the pendulum swung sharply in the opposite direction, and the Roman Catholic liturgy was restored. For five years the choir of the Chapel Royal must again have sounded much as it did in the later years of Henry VIII's reign.

No music books used by the Chapel Royal survive from Tallis's lifetime, and a large number of his works written for the choir have almost certainly been lost. Nevertheless, pieces both major and minor by him are found in other sources. Towering above them all is *Gaude gloriosa Dei mater*, a vast and virtuosic antiphon for six-part choir in praise of the Virgin Mary. As with the majority of Tallis's works, its composition cannot be linked to any specific event, nor can it be precisely dated. Almost certainly it would have been sung during Mary I's reign, when the Marian theme of its text would have been doubly appropriate; but the piece may actually have been written before Henry VIII's death, since an adaptation of the piece to (unrelated) English words also exists, apparently made during the reign of Edward VI. Tallis's large-scale setting of an English version of the Te Deum, imperfectly preserved, was probably written for important occasions of state, when the hymn was traditionally sung. According to some authorities, the grand seven-part mass based on the plainchant melody *Puer natus est nobis*, although ostensibly a Christmastide work, may be linked to Queen Mary's announced (but illusory) pregnancy in 1554. The theory is problematic, but on the basis of style a date in the 1550s seems right for this work.

Less easily dated are the settings of hymns and responsories. On grounds of style it is tempting to place the four-voice responsories (including *Audivi vocem* and *In pace in idipsum*) in the 1540s, and the more elaborate settings (such as the six-voice *Videte miraculum* and seven-voice *Loquebantur variis linguis*) in Mary's reign, but there is no concrete evidence to support that view. Uncertainty also surrounds the Latin Magnificat and Nunc dimittis, a paired setting that has long been linked with Walter Haddon's Latin translation of the prayer book (1560) but may in fact derive from the version by Alexander Ales published in 1549, and may therefore have been used in Edward VI's Chapel Royal. Like the majority of Tallis's compositions, these works survive only in Elizabethan manuscripts copied by amateur collectors for their own use, and therefore can be dated only tentatively.

As far as continuity of use is concerned, the most enduring of Tallis's compositions from these central years are the anthems and canticles he wrote during the formative years of the protestant rite (1549–53). Although simpler and shorter than the works to Latin texts, these pieces are rhetorically effective and exquisitely crafted. Some of them, including the anthems 'If ye love me' and 'Hear the voice and prayer', and the short (or 'Dorian') service, have become firmly lodged in the Anglican repertory. In the later sixteenth century they served as models for a younger generation of composers. It is precisely because of Tallis's position as one of the founding fathers of protestant church music that his name has remained so visible in English cathedral worship from the sixteenth century right up to the present day.

Later Chapel Royal years, 1558–1585 Tallis served at the funeral of Queen Mary (13 December 1558) and at the coronation of Elizabeth (15 January 1559). The latter event marked the beginning of the most stable part of his career. For the next twenty-seven years he remained an important figure in Elizabeth's household chapel, even if (as seems likely) age eventually prevented him from taking a full and active part in its daily activities. Very few surviving vocal works by him can be linked with certainty to the Elizabethan Chapel Royal repertory, and it is unclear whether his notated keyboard music (such as the two magnificent pieces based on the plainchant melody *Felix namque*) were written for chapel use or for other purposes.

Early in Elizabeth's reign Tallis's financial situation was secure; but steep inflation apparently changed his circumstances, and in 1573 he and William Byrd jointly petitioned the queen for additional income. In January 1575 the two men were granted a royal privilege for twenty-one years to print music and music paper, and to control the market for importing foreign printed music. The enterprise did not work to their advantage; in June 1577 the patentees petitioned the crown for a lease in reversion, claiming to have 'fallen out to our great loss and hinderance to the value of two hundred marks at least' (Fellowes, 9–10). Only one book of music was printed according to the terms of their licence, a collection of Latin motets by Tallis and Byrd called *Cantiones quae ab argumento sacrae vocantur* (London, 1575). Its erudite contents and musical demands cannot have recommended it to a wide readership in England, where the market for printed music (other than metrical psalms) was still very small, and it hardly surprises if the book was published at a financial loss. Nevertheless, its historical and musicological interest is considerable.

The collection is dedicated to the queen, and it contains seventeen works by each composer, appropriate for a book published in the seventeenth year of her reign. Verses by Richard Mulcaster and Ferdinand Richardson preface it; they celebrate English music, but remark (correctly) that it is little known outside the country. Through this publication, England's music now 'boldly advances where no voice has sung' ('Audacter quo non ore canenda venit'); export of copies of the book may have been envisaged. The contents are a showpiece of the two composers'

achievements. Byrd, still at the start of his career, contributed largely new music, but for Tallis it was an opportunity to bring together a wide cross-section of his music, and recent compositions rub shoulders with pieces composed in Mary's reign, or even written before the death of Henry VIII. In this publication Tallis effectively looks back over his own composing career. It was his only substantial monument in print. Eight years earlier a group of nine harmonized psalm tunes by him had been included in Archbishop Matthew Parker's *The Whole Psalter Translated into English Metre*, but these are insubstantial compared with the elegant and erudite motets of the *Cantiones sacrae*.

The survival of so many Elizabethan motets by Tallis, some of which set texts that can be construed as being sympathetic towards Roman Catholicism, raises questions about their intended audience. One of them, the dramatic *In ieiunio et fletu* (published in the 1575 *Cantiones sacrae*), speaks of priests 'fasting and weeping [and praying]: Spare thy people'; its words are taken from the Catholic liturgy. Tallis's two celebrated settings of verses from the Lamentations of Jeremiah, *Incipit lamentatio* and *De lamentatione*, which survive only in manuscript, refer to the destruction of Jerusalem, a theme commonly interpreted as a metaphor for the suppression of the Catholic faith. One of the *Cantiones sacrae* motets, *Derelinquit impius*, sets a liturgical text that appears to have been favoured by one of England's prominent Catholics, Henry Fitzalan, twelfth earl of Arundel; music books owned by Arundel include three settings of that text by the foreign composer Derrick Gerarde, who appears to have been in the earl's service. Arundel is also implicated in the story of Tallis's most spectacular motet, the forty-voice *Spem in alium*. Although various attempts have been made to link this massive work with Queen Elizabeth, and specifically with her fortieth birthday celebrations in 1573, an anecdote preserved in an early seventeenth-century notebook (CUL, MS Dd.5.14) connects it instead to Thomas Howard, fourth duke of Norfolk, who is said to have commissioned the motet about 1571. A copy of *Spem in alium* is included in a 1596 inventory of Arundel's books, and according to the anecdote the work was first performed at Arundel House in the Strand in London. This motet also draws its text from the Roman Catholic liturgy.

Although there is no direct evidence to suggest that outwardly Tallis was anything other than a conforming member of Elizabeth's Church of England, his closest friends and patrons included some principled recusants. His friendship with William Byrd was close. Although they belonged to different generations—Byrd was born probably in 1542 or 1543—the two men worked closely together and were clearly intimates. Tallis was godfather to Byrd's son Thomas; Byrd witnessed Tallis's will. After the older man's death Byrd wrote a lament, 'Ye Sacred Muses', that closes with the words 'Tallis is dead, and music dies'. Unlike Tallis, Byrd moved in prominent Catholic circles; he was first cited for recusancy in 1585, and later in life openly published Roman Catholic liturgical music. Shared religious views, no less than musical interests, may have helped forge a strong bond between the two men. Further evidence of Tallis's links with Roman Catholic circles is posthumous. The will of Joan Tallis, his widow and heir (12 June 1587), opens with a bequest of a gilt bowl to 'Anthony Roper esquire … in respect of his good favours showed to my late husband and me'. The recipient is credibly identified as the lawyer Anthony Roper (*c*.1535–1597), a grandson of Sir Thomas More, who appears among the 'Catholics in England' in a 1574 list of Kentish gentry, and who was mentioned in 1577 as a recusant member of Lincoln's Inn.

Thomas Tallis died on 23 November 1585. He was buried in the chancel of the parish church of St Alfege, Greenwich. The place was marked by a brass memorial, set up after the death of his wife, Joan, but before the death of Queen Elizabeth. It was destroyed during the Second World War, but the text was recorded by Strype. It included the following lines:

He serv'd long Tyme in Chapp[ell] with grete prayse,
Fower sovereygnes reignes (a thing not often scene),
I mean King Henry and Prince Edward's Dayes,
Quene Mary, and Elizabeth our Quene.
He maryed was, though Children had he none,
And lyv'd in Love full thre and thirty Yeres …
As he did Lyve, so also did he dy,
In myld and quyet Sort (O! happy Man).

Reputation Tallis's English anthems and settings of the canticles have enjoyed an almost unbroken tradition of liturgical use through the centuries, partly on account of their intrinsic merit, partly because of Tallis's chronological position as one of the first composers of English protestant church music. His Latin works, conversely, were largely forgotten by the mid-seventeenth century. A few were adapted to English words for protestant use; *O sacrum convivium*, for instance, circulated with the contrafact text 'I call and cry to thee' even in Tallis's own lifetime, and others were adapted by later antiquarians such as Henry Aldrich (*d*. 1710), dean of Christ Church, Oxford. However, it was not until the later eighteenth century that they began to attract attention with their original Latin words. The modern assessment of Tallis began with the historian Charles Burney (1726–1814), who characterized him as 'profound' and judged him to be 'one of the greatest musicians, not only of [England], but of Europe, during the sixteenth century' (Burney, *Hist. mus.*, 2.65). His opinion, based on personal if necessarily selective enquiry into the forgotten repertories of 'ancient' music, set the tone for all subsequent evaluation.

Even so, interest in Tallis's works has often centred on the curious rather than the characteristic. *Spem in alium* in particular has won him fame as the composer of a 'monster motet'. Several of the tunes he provided for Matthew Parker's psalter—a book evidently published for private circulation—have become very famous; they include the canonic 'Eighth Tune', now widely known in adapted form as 'Tallis's Canon' to the words 'Glory to thee, my God, this night', and the strongly modal 'Third Tune', on which Ralph Vaughan Williams based his *Fantasia on a Theme by Thomas Tallis* (1910). Only with the publication in 1928 of Tallis's collected works to Latin texts in the series Tudor Church Music did easy access to the music become possible for all. Today Tallis ranks among the most performed, recorded, researched, and respected composers of Tudor England, and in popular estimation is placed second only to his friend and colleague William Byrd.

JOHN MILSOM

Sources P. Doe, 'Tallis, Thomas', rev. D. Allinson, *New Grove*, 2nd edn (2000) · A. Ashbee and D. Lasocki, eds., *A biographical dictionary of English court musicians, 1485–1714*, 2 vols. (1998) · P. Doe, *Tallis*, 2nd edn (1976) · N. Sandon, 'The manuscript London, British Library Harley 1709', *Music in the Medieval English liturgy*, ed. S. Rankin and D. Hiley (1993), 355–80 · J. Bennett, 'A Tallis patron?', *Royal Musical Association Research Chronicle*, 21 (1988), 41–4 · E. Fellowes, *William Byrd* (1948) · Burney, *Hist. mus.*, new edn · will, 20 Aug 1583, PRO, PROB 11/68, sig. 52 · will of Joan Bury, wife, 12 June 1587, PRO, PROB 11/74, sig. 54
Likenesses print reproduction (after rare Italian engraving), BM
Wealth at death see will, PRO, PROB 11/68, sig. 52 · will of Joan Bury, wife, PRO, PROB 11/74, sig. 54

Talman, John (1677–1726), antiquary and art collector, was born in King Street, Westminster, in July 1677 and baptized in St Margaret's Church, Westminster, on 19 July, the eldest son of the architect William *Talman (*bap.* 1650, *d.* 1719) and his wife, Hannah. He was educated at Eton College; there is no record of attendance at Oxford or Cambridge universities. He probably trained as an architect with his father, for numerous accomplished designs in his hand exist; however, as far as is known, none of his designs resulted in a finished building. In 1697 he went abroad; he lived in the Netherlands for two years and studied at Leiden University. In 1699 he went to Italy via Germany, and spent nearly two years there, based in Rome, making architectural drawings and studying the churches. By 1702 he was back in Britain. During the next few years, moving between London and his father's estate at Ranworth in Norfolk, John Talman developed his skills as an ecclesiastical antiquary, making many drawings of church interiors and monuments. He was a founder member of an antiquaries' club that began to meet in December 1707, and that would eventually develop into the Society of Antiquaries; fellow members of this group included Humfrey Wanley, Thomas Madox, George Holmes, and Peter le Neve.

In August 1709 Talman set off for Italy, where he remained until 1717; his travelling companions were the virtuoso Daniel Lock and the young William Kent, who was going to Rome to train as a painter. Talman was being funded by his father to stay in Italy, to make or commission drawings of architectural details and all aspects of Italianate interior design. These would be added to the great collection of prints and drawings that William Talman was accumulating as a reference archive of the arts of design that would be of service to English practitioners. This 'Musaeum Talmanicum' never found a suitable location for its display, but the concept shaped John Talman's collecting habits throughout his life. Once settled in Italy, first in Florence (November 1709–April 1710) and thereafter in Rome, he became the leading English observer of the Italian art scene, able to act as an agent for English collectors. Patrons with whom he had dealings included Lord Somers, the earl of Pembroke, the duke of Devonshire, and Richard Topham. His greatest coup was the purchase of the superlative collection of old master drawings known as the Resta collection, which he secured for Lord Somers in 1711, most of which eventually passed into the Devonshire collection at Chatsworth.

John Talman was a covert Catholic, as his personal letters reveal. Although he was confirmed in the Church of England in April 1704, he seems privately to have practised as a Roman Catholic, and his time in Italy allowed him the free exercise of his religion. He became an admiring recorder of the ceremonies of the Roman church, and also of its ecclesiastical treasures, of which he made many hundreds of drawings. He became acquainted with Pope Clement XI, himself an antiquary, who granted him the rare privilege of access to the Vatican treasures, recognizing that Talman might have a role to play in advertising the glories of the Roman church to an English audience. Talman also established friendly relations with Cardinal Ottoboni, the principal artistic patron of Clementine Rome. In 1710 Talman became a member of the Accademia dell' Arcadia, a society which attracted the leading cognoscenti in Rome. The high point of his social career was the lavish entertainment he offered to his Arcadian associates in May 1711, the theme of which was the rise of the arts in Britain; its success secured for Talman a reputation as the outstanding English virtuoso in Rome.

Talman travelled widely in Italy, mostly in search of ecclesiastical rarities. He visited Ravenna at least five times, and Venice on several occasions; his drawings of these places show an interest, unusual for the time, in Byzantine art forms. A partial record of his stay in Italy is preserved in his letter-book in the Bodleian Library: these letters give the impression of an intense, sociable, somewhat gauche figure, passionate about the splendours of the Roman Catholic church.

Talman returned to Britain in the spring of 1717, in time to participate in the founding of the Society of Antiquaries at the Mitre tavern in Fleet Street in July, when he was elected the first director; his role was 'to superintend and regulate all the Drawings, Prints, Plates and Books of the Society and all their works of printing, drawing or engraving' (Evans, 59). In 1718 he married Frances Cockayne of Hinxworth in Hertfordshire, to which place he now moved. The National Portrait Gallery owns an engaging baroque picture which commemorates his marriage, and the second marriage of his father in 1717, showing the two Talmans with their wives and some of their choicest artistic treasures under the approving gaze of the gods. The artist was Giuseppe Grisoni, whom Talman had brought back from Italy. In November 1719 William Talman died, leaving John in sole possession of the largest collection of prints and drawings in the country: one estimate suggests it contained 26,000 prints and 7000 drawings. Talman may have made further visits to Italy: dated drawings suggest that he was there in 1719, 1721, and 1723. He died in London on 3 November 1726, and was buried at Hinxworth

church. Four of his six children survived him: Frances (*b.* 1720), Mary (*b.* 1722), John (*b.* 1725), and Elizabeth (*b.* 1726). His collections were sold at auction in 1727 and 1728, and dispersed, but important components are preserved in the British Museum, the Ashmolean, and the Victoria and Albert Museum.   GRAHAM PARRY

Sources G. Parry, 'The John Talman letter-book', *Walpole Society*, 59 (1997), 3–179 · J. Ingamells, ed., *A dictionary of British and Irish travellers in Italy, 1701–1800* (1997) · Colvin, *Archs.* · J. Evans, *A history of the Society of Antiquaries* (1956) · Beds. & Luton ARS, MSS HY 939, HY 940/1–3, HY 941, HY 943 · IGI
Archives AM Oxf., collection of drawings · Beds. & Luton ARS · BM · Bodl. Oxf., letters, mainly from Italy [copies] · LPL, accounts and letters from Italy · S. Antiquaries, Lond., albums · V&A
Likenesses G. Grisoni, group portrait, oils, *c.*1718–1719, NPG; *see illus. in* Talman, William (*bap.* 1650, *d.* 1719)

Talman, William (*bap.* **1650**, *d.* **1719**), architect and collector, was baptized on 1 December 1650 at St Margaret's Church, Westminster. He was the second son of William Talman (*d.* 1663) and his wife, Elizabeth, of Eastcott Manor House, near West Lavington in Wiltshire. When his father died in 1663, his elder brother, Christopher, inherited the family estate and William received the leases on three houses in King Street, Westminster. Nothing is known about his early life or training as an architect.

Early career In 1678 Talman obtained the office of king's waiter in the port of London, probably through the patronage of Henry Hyde, second earl of Clarendon. He shared this office with Thomas Apprice, and surrendered it in favour of his brother-in-law James Tate in 1711. In May 1689 he was appointed comptroller of the king's works, a post he retained until the death of William III in 1702, when in May of that year he was dismissed and John Vanbrugh was appointed in his place. Also in 1689, when Hans Willem Bentinck, first earl of Portland, was appointed superintendent of the royal gardens, Talman was appointed as his deputy with George London. In these two official capacities Talman was largely responsible for the interior decoration of Hampton Court Palace and probably also to some extent for the extensive new gardens.

Talman acquired a property at Thames Ditton in Surrey about 1696, on the opposite side of the River Thames from Hampton Court Palace. Here he began to build himself an elaborate new house and garden. The house was incomplete when Talman lost his place as controller and he sold the property to George London, who completed a much smaller house for himself, probably also to Talman's designs. He went on to purchase property at Ranworth in Norfolk, and in 1718 he purchased the estate of Felmingham in the same county. His marriage to Hannah produced three sons and a daughter. Talman often sent his eldest son, John *Talman (1677–1726), to the continent on various occasions to purchase material for his burgeoning collection of architectural books, drawings, and prints, which he described in 1713 as 'the most valuable Collection of Books, Prints, Drawings &c, as is in any one person's hands in Europe, as all the artists in Towne well know' (J. Harris, 19, n. 2). The probate inventory drawn up after Talman's death in 1719 also records his collection of

William Talman (*bap.* 1650, *d.* 1719), by Giuseppe Grisoni, *c.*1718–19 [*The Talman Family Group*: Talman, left, with (left to right) his son John Talman, his daughter Frances Cokayne, and his wife, Hannah Talman]

marbles, antique sculptures, and chimney-pieces, which has led Howard Colvin to suggest that he may have been commercially involved in their supply (Colvin, 'The Problem', 121–2).

Talman was the leading country house architect of the late seventeenth century, responsible for some of the most innovative and influential designs of the period. But the lack of direct documentary evidence about his career has made it very difficult to prove beyond doubt the extent of his work. Recent research into country house archives has now produced hard evidence for Talman's involvement in over thirty houses, though in many cases it is still unclear exactly to which architectural works this evidence refers. Among the earliest works associated with Talman's name are a group of relatively plain Renaissance-style houses. These include: Holywell House, St Albans, built about 1686 for John and Sarah Churchill; Stanstead Park in Sussex, built 1686–90 for Richard Lumley, first earl of Scarbrough; Uppark in Sussex, built about 1690 for Ford Grey, third Lord Grey of Warke and later first earl of Tankerville; and Swallowfield House in Berkshire, built 1689–91 for his early patron, the second earl of Clarendon. Although all these houses were somewhat old-fashioned in style, the only survivor, Uppark, is a magnificent example of its type, which shows great sophistication in its composition and design detail. And the only

surviving interior by Talman, in any of these houses, is a small oval vestibule at the centre of the garden front at Swallowfield, which suggests that they may not have been quite so plain or old-fashioned in their original plan form or decoration. Talman later designed two even plainer three-storey houses, Kimberley Park in Norfolk for Sir John Wodehouse and Fetcham Park in Surrey for Arthur Moore. Both have projecting three-window centrepieces topped with pediments, though the former was designed with corner towers and the latter was built with single-storey wings.

Major commissions By far the most important group of documented commissions by Talman is on an altogether grander scale. At Burghley House in Northamptonshire he had a hand in the important internal remodelling begun for John Cecil, fifth earl of Exeter, in 1682. Talman, who visited in 1688 and was finally paid £200 by the earl's trustees in 1704, was probably responsible for its magnificent new suite of staterooms, including those painted by Antonio Verrio. At Chatsworth House in Derbyshire he designed for William Cavendish, first duke of Devonshire, perhaps his most important work, the grand south front, the first truly baroque façade in England. He also designed the east façade and the unique suite of staterooms approached from the painted great hall and stone staircase. He also added important architectural embellishments to the new gardens laid out by George London, including the Temple of Flora and the west terrace with its elaborate staircase. At Dyrham Park in Gloucestershire, Talman designed the new stables and completed the house for William Blathwayt by the addition of a grand new three-storey façade with a suite of panelled rooms behind. He also designed a magnificent new conservatory, and possibly other architectural elements in the elaborate new water gardens, also laid out by George London between 1691 and 1704. Finally, and distinctly Roman baroque in style, Talman designed the inner courtyard façade at Drayton House in Northamptonshire for Sir John Germain in 1702. Here his alterations included the addition of cupolas to the towers, and probably the side colonnades completed in 1706, plus, internally, the remodelling of the medieval great hall and the insertion of a new stone staircase.

Talman was an arrogant and argumentative man with an inflated idea of his own worth, according to the sparse surviving contemporary references to his character. He openly criticized Christopher Wren's competence as surveyor after the collapse of work at Hampton Court Palace. Eventually his overcharging lost him what might have been his greatest architectural opportunity, when both he and John Vanbrugh were consulted by Charles Howard, third earl of Carlisle, about designs for his new house at Castle Howard in Yorkshire. Though Talman lost the commission, it seems likely that some of the most important new ideas incorporated into Vanbrugh's final design were introduced by him. This rivalry between Talman and Vanbrugh continued over the proposed new house for John Holles, third duke of Newcastle, at Welbeck Abbey in Nottinghamshire. Though this commission was abandoned, it produced a letter from Vanbrugh to the duke of Newcastle in which he names a number of clients who suffered 'vexation' at Talman's hands (Whistler, 1648–52). This list includes three patrons whose employment of him can be substantiated by other documentary evidence (the first duke of Devonshire, the third earl of Carlisle, and Sir John Germain), and leaves five further names who may have commissioned him. The inclusion on this list of Edmund Sheffield, third earl of Mulgrave and marquess of Normanby, could either refer to his new house in London, Buckingham House, designed according to Colen Campbell by William Winde, though possibly altered in execution by Talman, or to his country seat at Normanby Park in Lincolnshire, where additions were also made about 1700. The reference to Lady Falkland probably relates to Knebworth House in Hertfordshire, where the surviving great hall was remodelled about 1700. Lord Coningsby's inclusion presumably relates to Hampton Court in Herefordshire, where the house was remodelled from about 1680 and where elaborate gardens were laid out between 1706 and 1710 by George London. The reference to Lord Portmore relates to possible additions to Dorchester House in Surrey. Finally, the reference to Lord Kingston refers to the additions made by Evelyn Pierrepont, fifth earl of Kingston upon Hull, to West Dean House in Wiltshire, where Talman carried out alterations and added a great garden terrace with central steps and flanking conservatories (Smith, 86–106).

Houses associated with Talman The surviving evidence of Talman's involvement in the design of other country houses is tantalizingly unclear. His name has long been associated with Thoresby House in Nottinghamshire, a seminally important country house in the development of the baroque style in England. The surviving accounts show that the house was remodelled for William Pierrepont, fourth earl of Kingston upon Hull, between 1685 and 1687, but Nicholas Hawksmoor records that it was burnt out as soon as it was completed and an attic storey added when it was refitted, before 1690. The only clue to the designer of this house was thought to be contained in Colen Campbell's statement in *Vitruvius Britannicus* that Thoresby was 'performed by the same hand that afterwards built Chatsworth', but it now seems more likely that this refers to Benjamin Jackson as the builder, rather than Talman as the architect. The only other known link between Talman and Thoresby is Vanbrugh's reference to Lord Kingston, but since it now seems that this refers to the fifth earl's additions to West Dean House, there is no conclusive evidence to confirm or deny Talman's involvement at Thoresby.

Talman probably provided designs for Charles Powlett, later first duke of Bolton, but it is not clear whether these designs relate to Hackwood Park in Hampshire, built 1683–8, or to Abbotstone in the same county, rebuilt about 1685, or to both. At Milton House in Northamptonshire, Talman is known to have given advice to Baron Fitzwilliam of Lifford in 1688 about designs for a new house, but the only architectural work carried out was the new stables, which were built 'according to Mr. Sturges his

draught' in 1690 (Colvin, *Archs.*, 943). While at Lowther Hall in Westmorland, Talman supplied a design for a new house for Sir James Lowther, which was built 1692–5, but probably altered in execution. William Talman is known to have provided an estimate for remodelling Castle Ashby in Northamptonshire, for George Compton, thirteenth earl of Northampton, in 1695, and though nothing came of this he may have been responsible for designing the now demolished greenhouse built that same year. Talman's involvement in the design of Kiveton Park in Yorkshire, built between 1698 and 1704 for Thomas Osborne, first duke of Leeds, is based on a single surviving plan, which does not match the house as built. Similarly drawings by Talman for Raynham Hall in Norfolk prove that he was consulted about its remodelling by Charles, second Viscount Townshend, about 1703, but they do not prove that the subsequent alterations were carried out to his designs. At Witham Park in Somerset, Talman made designs for Sir William Wyndham about 1702, but these were definitely not carried out. Talman may have provided designs for Herriard Park in Hampshire for Thomas Jervoise, but no designs by him have been identified among the many surviving drawings, and the house built about 1703 was probably designed by John James. At Bulstrode Park in Buckinghamshire, seat of the former superintendent of the royal gardens, the first earl of Portland, significant alterations were made to the house and garden in 1706–7, though the only evidence of Talman's involvement are payments made to him by Henry or William Henry Bentinck, second earl, in 1715. Most tantalizing of all is Cannons House in Middlesex, where Talman provided designs for a new house and also designed and supervised the building of the offices for James Brydges, Baron Chandos of Sudeley and later first duke of Chandos, in 1713–14. Unfortunately the appearance of these buildings was not recorded before they were demolished in 1747. While at Panton Hall in Lincolnshire, built for Joseph Gace about 1719, Talman's claim to involvement in the design of the house is based on a set of drawings now lost.

Talman was an original and eclectic designer who produced designs in a range of styles. He gathered ideas from his wide-ranging collection of architectural books, which included not only the latest designs of continental baroque architects but also the designs of earlier English architects, such as Inigo Jones. His use of these diverse sources is most clearly illustrated by the varied designs he produced for the duke of Newcastle's proposed new house at Welbeck Abbey in Nottinghamshire. The only country house for which a truly complete set of Talman's drawings survive is the one he designed for himself at Thames Ditton, where he shows a distinct personal preference for contemporary French architecture. His broad range of styles, or lack of stylistic consistency, has led to many stylistic attributions being made to Talman's *œuvre*. John Harris, the leading authority on the architecture of William Talman, has attributed a number of other houses to him on such stylistic evidence, including Bretby Hall in Derbyshire for Philip Stanhope, second earl of Chesterfield,

Waldershare Park in Kent for Sir Robert Furness, Blyth Hall in Nottinghamshire for Edward Mellish, Whitton House in Middlesex for Sir Godfrey Kneller, and Appuldurcombe House on the Isle of Wight for Sir Richard Worsley. All of these have architectural features which might suggest Talman's hand, but as yet no reliable documentary evidence has come to light to confirm or deny these attributions.

Talman's involvement at the royal gardens suggests that he had a particular interest in gardens and their architectural embellishment. This is confirmed by his work at Chatsworth and by the recent discovery that Talman designed and built the magnificent 300 foot long terrace for Lord Kingston's new gardens at West Dean House. Talman and the gardener George London worked together not only at Hampton Court Palace but also at Chatsworth, Dyrham, Cannons, and probably Hampton Court in Herefordshire, where some of the most elaborate gardens of the day were created. Harris has again suggested that Talman's close working relationship with George London may well have extended to other gardens where London is known to have worked. From this he has attributed to Talman some of the important buildings found in other gardens known to be by George London, such as the greenhouse and bowling pavilion at Wanstead House in Essex, built for Sir Richard Child.

Death and reputation Knowledge about Talman's architectural career is still fragmentary, but those buildings and designs which are known to be by him suggest an architect of stylistic range and adaptability. Many of his better documented commissions show that he was able to provide appropriate architectural solutions to difficult architectural problems, so long as he did not fall out with his patron first. At Drayton he produced a dramatic and original solution to the designing of a new façade within a castellated courtyard house. At Dyrham he produced a plain but grand new range, which provided an appropriate setting for Blathwayt's increased status, and also an excellent backdrop for his magnificent new garden. At Chatsworth, Talman produced, within the strictures of an older house, a bold and radical baroque design for the south front, the perfect counterpoint to the splendid great parterre laid out before it. The fact that many of his commissions involved altering older houses might suggest that Talman specialized in solving these often difficult planning problems. The statement of his arch-rival Vanbrugh that he caused many of his clients 'vexation' should be treated with caution, especially since it now seems likely that Talman produced important works for most of the clients cited. Talman died on 22 November 1719 at Felmingham and he was buried in the churchyard there, under a black marble slab inscribed with his triple-T monogram.   PETER SMITH

Sources J. Harris, *William Talman, maverick architect* (1982) · H. Colvin, 'The problem of William Talman', *Baroque and Palladian: the early 18th century great house*, ed. M. Airs (1996) · R. G. M. Baker, 'William Talman and a supposed project to improve Hampton Court, Surrey', *Archaeological Collections*, 75 (1984), 177–83 · F. Harris, 'Holywell House, St Albans: an early work by William Talman',

Architectural History, 28 (1985), 32–9 · L. Whistler, 'Talman and Vanbrugh: episodes in an architectural rivalry', *Country Life*, 112 (1952), 1648–52 · P. Smith, 'West Dean House, Wiltshire', *Georgian Group Journal*, 9 (1999), 26–32 · Colvin, *Archs.* · G. Worsley, 'William Talman: some stylistic suggestions', *Georgian Group Journal*, [2] (1992), 6–18 · S. Jeffery, 'John James and George London at Herriard', *Architectural History*, 28 (1985), 40–70 · M. D. Whinney, 'William Talman', *Journal of the Warburg and Courtauld Institutes*, 18 (1955), 123–39 · H. M. Colvin and others, eds., *The history of the king's works*, 5 (1976), 33–7, 133–5, 157–9, 162–7 · J. Lever, ed., *Catalogue of the drawings collection of the Royal Institute of British Architects: T–Z* (1984), 9–12 · will, PRO, PROB 11/572, sig. 44 · 22 Dec 1719, PRO, PROB 3/19/45 (inventory)
Archives Castle Ashby, Northampton, estimate for Castle Ashby
Likenesses G. Grisoni, group portrait, oils, *c*.1718–1719, NPG [*see illus.*] · attrib. W. Sonmans, oils, Freemasons' Hall, London
Wealth at death £1500 to son John; annuities to wife and three young children: will, PRO, PROB 11/572, sig. 44; inventory, PRO, PROB 3/19/45

Talorg mac Congus (*d.* 734). *See under* Picts, kings of the (*act. c*.300–*c*.900).

Talorgan mac Drostan (*d.* 739). *See under* Picts, kings of the (*act. c*.300–*c*.900).

Talorgen (*d.* 657). *See under* Picts, kings of the (*act. c*.300–*c*.900).

Tambimuttu, Meary James Thurairajah (1915–1983), writer and journal editor, was born on 15 August 1915 at Atchuveli in the Jaffna peninsula of Ceylon (Sri Lanka), second child of the five sons and one daughter of Henry Tambithurai Tambimuttu (1887–1971), of the Government Printing Press, Colombo, and his first wife, Mary Ponnammah Santiapillai. The scholar Ananda Coomaraswamy was his uncle and he claimed descent from the kings of Jaffna. Mary James, as he was originally named, attended St Mary's Convent and the Catholic St Joseph's College, Trincomalee, where he was educated in English. After further schooling at St Joseph's College, Colombo, he won an exhibition in botany to Ceylon University College but left before completing his degree, taking up employment in the Ratnapura Kachcheri and public works department, Colombo. By the time he left Ceylon, Tambimuttu's literary ambitions were clear: he had issued three volumes of poetry—the first set and printed by himself—composed several songs, and produced a jazz musical.

Tambimuttu arrived in England in January 1938, known only for a popular record sold in Woolworths. His confidence, generosity, strikingly handsome appearance, and literary intuition gained him immediate entry to London's bohemian set. Following a discussion with Dylan Thomas and Keidrych Rhys, he and Anthony Dickins, a young musician and writer, issued a prospectus offering subscription to *Poetry*, a magazine whose first number appeared in February 1939. After the second number Dickins's close involvement ceased, the title became *Poetry* (*London*), and Tambi, as he was always known, asserted his chaotic yet inspired style of editorship.

Poetry (*London*), whose first number declared that 'every man has poetry within him', introduced many important new writers, while gaining the support of established figures. George Barker, Louis MacNeice, Lawrence Durrell,

Meary James Thurairajah Tambimuttu (1915–1983), by Edward Lucie-Smith

and Dylan Thomas, among the first published, became regular contributors. Editorial roles given to Tambimuttu by T. S. Eliot for *Poetry in Wartime* (1942) and Reginald Moore for *Selected Writing One* (1942) encouraged the publisher Nicholson and Watson to sponsor *Poetry (London)* and an additional series of books, Editions Poetry London, which promoted both authors and artists. Paired collaborations for the series included Kathleen Raine and Barbara Hepworth; David Gascoyne and Graham Sutherland; and Nicholas Moore and Lucian Freud, while Henry Moore's acclaimed *Shelter Sketch Book* appeared in 1945. Tambimuttu's encouragement of Keith Douglas led to the publication of *Alamein to Zem Zem* (1946), and, eventually, to a posthumous edition of his collected poems. In 1947 Richard March became Tambimuttu's principal financial backer and early in 1949, after an acrimonious dispute, assumed control of an operation which had issued some fourteen numbers of *Poetry (London)*, six pamphlets, and over fifty books.

Tambimuttu's devotion to poetry was matched by his passion for the area in London he named Fitzrovia. His extraordinary dynamism beguiled those whom he led from pub to pub through London's nocturnal streets (spending money borrowed for more strictly literary purposes). Hard living eventually took its toll on happiness, security, and companionship; a marriage on 2 March 1940

to Jacqueline Stanley lasted little more than a year before the couple separated (an annulment being granted in 1947). Tambimuttu sailed for Ceylon, arriving back on 7 December 1949. After a year of writing and broadcasting (a skill learned with the BBC in London) he travelled to Bombay, where he met Safia Tyabjee, whom he married on 15 July 1951. They embarked for New York in 1952, arriving in November with $600 and no return ticket.

The stories which Tambimuttu contributed to the *New Yorker* and *The Reporter* were tenderly written and more accessible than the long poems he had published in London: *Out of this War* (1941) and *Natarajah* (1949). His small income was supplemented by lectures given at institutions such as the Poetry Center and New York University. In 1956, backed by a wealthy patron, he started *Poetry London (New York)*, awarding himself $80 a week. Despite initial success, only four numbers appeared, the last in 1960. Times again became difficult, and Safia returned to India in May 1958, a prelude to divorce. Another marriage, in 1961, to Esta Smith (*b.* 25 Oct 1937), resulted in the birth in 1962 of his only daughter, Shakuntala. After the collapse of this marriage, Tambimuttu joined Timothy Leary at his League for Spiritual Discovery until 1968. His failure in that year to obtain a post running the Poetry Room at Harvard resulted in a period of restlessness, during part of which he stayed at Shakespeare & Co. in Paris.

Tambimuttu finally settled in London, where moments of success and vision punctuated an otherwise precarious existence. The Lyrebird Press was launched on 21 June 1972, with Katharine Falley Bennett, while other ventures included a limited edition of Indian love poems illustrated by John Piper (1977), two issues of *Poetry London/ Apple Magazine* (1979 and 1983), originally to have been backed by the Beatles, and a handmade anthology delivered to Buckingham Palace as a wedding gift for Prince Charles and Lady Diana Spencer. In 1982 he visited India and Sri Lanka, meeting Indira Gandhi, who supported his foundation of the Indian Arts Council in London, and J. R. Jayawardene, with whom he discussed publishing a library of Sri Lankan classics (as part of the programme of the Sri Lankan Arts Council for which he had made initial plans).

On 22 June 1983 Tambimuttu died of heart failure in University College Hospital, London, where he had been taken after a serious fall in his office in Bloomsbury's October Gallery. He was cremated on 30 June and his remains sent to his childhood home. A memorial concert at the Bhavan Centre in London was held on 17 March 1984. A portrait by Augustus John is reproduced in *Out of this War*.

CHRISTOPHER FLETCHER

Sources J. Williams, ed., *Tambimuttu: bridge between two worlds* (1989) · P. Poologasingham, *Poet Tambimuttu: a profile* (1993) · S. J. Rajah, *A life-sketch of Mr S. Tambimuttu Pillay*, trans. A. L. V. Victoria (1988) · A. Dickins, 'Tambimuttu and Poetry London', *London Magazine, a Monthly Review of Literature*, new ser., 5/9 (1965), 53–7 · G. Ewart, 'Tambi the Great', *London Magazine, a Monthly Review of Literature*, new ser., 5/9 (1965), 57–60 · A. T. Tolley, *The poetry of the forties* (1985) · *The Times* (24 June 1983) · *New York Times* (24 June 1983) · 'New magazine in Manhattan', *Time Magazine* (14 May 1956) · BL,

Reginald Moore MSS • M. J. Tambimuttu, 'Fitzrovia', *Harpers and Queen* (Feb 1975) • D. Nadkarni, 'Tambimuttu: patron of young writers', *Times of India* (26 April 1982) • private information (2004) • Pooter, *The Times* (5 July 1969)

Archives BBC WAC • Northwestern University, Illinois | BL, Keith Douglas MSS, Add. MSS 53773–53776, 56355–56360, 60585–60586, 61938–61939 • BL, Reginald Moore MSS
Likenesses F. Topolski, charcoal sketch, *c.*1972, repro. in Williams, ed., *Tambimuttu* • A. John, pencil, repro. in M. J. T. Tambimuttu, *Out of this war* (1941) • E. Lucie-Smith, photograph, NPG [*see illus.*] • photographs, repro. in Williams, ed., *Tambimuttu*
Wealth at death circumstantial evidence suggests none; cremation paid for partly by Royal Literary Fund grant

Tancarville. For this title name *see* Grey, Sir John, count of Tancarville (1384x91–1421).

Tancred, Christopher (1689–1754), benefactor, was born on 11 November 1689 at Whixley, Yorkshire, the second son of Christopher Tancred (*d.* 1705) of Whixley, and his second wife, Catherine, daughter of Sir John Armytage of Kirklees. His father was in 1685–6 high sheriff of Yorkshire, and was master of the harriers to William III; his great-grandfather, Sir Richard Tancred, had as a royalist compounded for his estates under the Commonwealth, and was knighted by Charles II for his services and sufferings during the civil war.

Although there is no record of his having been admitted to an inn of court, Tancred claimed some training as a lawyer, and after his father's death on 21 November 1705 spent most of his time at Whixley, performing the duties of a county justice. In addition to a short pamphlet, *A scheme for an act of parliament for the better regulating servants, and ascertaining their wages* (1724), he published *An essay for the general regulation of the law, in which the great corruptions and expenses of law controversies are exposed, and effectual methods proposed to redress such great national grievances* (1727), a substantial tract of some 240 pages addressed to Lord King, in which he elaborated extensive plans for law reform. He called for the simplification of special pleading and the more intricate forms of writs; the shortening of interlocutory orders in chancery; the establishment of a salaried legal bureaucracy in the Westminster courts; the abolition of special bail in civil proceedings and the relief of debtors from perpetual imprisonment; the simplification of conveyancing; the establishment of a general register for property transactions; and the lessening of the fees and limiting of the numbers of 'those upright dealers and worthy patriots called attorneys-at-law'. While the surviving evidence is circumstantial, Tancred's connections with the West Riding, the nature of his proposals, and his assertion that the language of the law was generally unknown to the 'vulgar Sort of People', suggest that he may have had a role in the presentation in 1728 of petitions to parliament from JPs and 'other gentlemen' assembled at meetings of quarter sessions in Yorkshire which called for reforms to make it easier for ordinary people to gain access to the courts. Although most of Tancred's proposals had to wait more than a century to come near to realization, the Yorkshire petitions appear

to have had some impact on several contemporary law reforms, including the 1729 Attorney Act (2 Geo. II, c. 23) and the act of 1731 which abolished Latin and law French as the legal languages of record (4 Geo. II, c. 26).

With his character of law reformer Tancred combined that of racing man and horse dealer. He spent part of his time at Newmarket, where he possessed a small property, which he ultimately left to Christ's College, Cambridge, for the purpose of endowing an exhibition, and in 1734 he served the minister of the duke of Mecklenburg—then resident in London—as 'gentleman of the horse and domestick', and was employed to buy horses for him.

Tancred died at Whixley, unmarried, on 21 August 1754. His unusual instruction that his body should not be put underground was literally obeyed, as his coffin hung in chains in the hall of the house for many years, before being removed to a cellar, and then finally coming to rest in a sarcophagus in the chapel attached to the house. His will of 1746 left an annuity of £60 p.a. to his housekeeper, Mrs Elizabeth Tottingham, widow, and made her sole executor. Evidently because of a long-standing family quarrel he was determined to disinherit his five sisters, to whom he left 1 shilling each. In 1721 he had settled his property in trust, in default of male heirs, to the use of the masters of Christ's and Gonville and Caius colleges, Cambridge, the president of the College of Physicians, the treasurer of Lincoln's Inn, the master of the Charterhouse, and the governors of Chelsea Hospital and the Royal Hospital, Greenwich, and their successors, for the foundation of twelve Tancred studentships, for which purpose £50 apiece was to be paid to twelve young persons of 'such low abilities as not to be capable of obtaining the education' (Yorkshire Archaeological Society, Leeds, DD160). Four were to be educated in the study of divinity at Christ's College, four in the study of physic at Gonville and Caius, and four in the study of the common law at Lincoln's Inn. In return for this support, one of the students was obliged every year to give a lecture in Latin in the hall of either Christ's College or Lincoln's Inn. In addition, another trust of £20 apiece was established for twelve 'decayed and necessitated' (Yorkshire Archaeological Society, Leeds, DD160/2) gentlemen, clergymen, commissioned land or sea officers of fifty years of age or more. They were to live in the manor house, which was to be called Tancred's Hospital and its inmates Tancred's pensioners.

Although no record of his admission to either Lincoln's Inn or a Cambridge college has been found, a number of his relatives had been educated at these institutions, and his connection with Christ's was sufficiently close for him to request that his body should rest there for ten days if he were to die away from home. His will of 1746 confirmed the earlier settlement, but the charities were not established until after his plans had successfully weathered a challenge in chancery from his sisters in 1757 and his trustees had secured a private act of parliament (2 Geo. III, c. 15), which authorized them to act. Although the records of the trust give little detail about how either the students or the pensioners were selected, the charities appear to have been competently administered for most of the nineteenth century. There was more concern about the behaviour and sobriety of the pensioners than about the conduct of the students. Partly because of this indiscipline the charity commissioners, on the application of the governors, in 1872 approved a scheme whereby the hospital was closed and annuities given to the existing pensioners. Henceforth, £80 per annum was to be paid to outpensioners. Despite the unusually long tenure (seven years) of the studentships, and an increase in the value of each to £100 per annum, by the mid-1920s the trustees were evidently finding it difficult to secure enough candidates. Later in the twentieth century, besides continuing to provide studentships, surplus income from the trust was used to support the fellows and scholars of the colleges.

WILLIAM CARR, rev. CHRISTOPHER W. BROOKS

Sources records of Tancred Foundation, W. Yorks. AS, Leeds, Yorkshire Archaeological Society, DD160 · J. Foster, ed., *Pedigrees of the county families of Yorkshire*, 1–2 (1874) [West Riding] · C. Tancred, *An essay for the general regulation of the law* (1727) · *N&Q*, 3rd ser., 10 (1866), 155, 450, 522 · E. Hargrove, *The history of the castle, town, and forest of Knaresborough*, 5th edn (1798) · *The manuscripts of the House of Lords*, 4 vols., HMC, 17 (1887–94), vol. 4, p. 166 · *JHC*, 21 (1727–32), 274, 236–7, 313, 622–3 · A. Shipley, *The Times* (21 April 1925) · A. Shipley, *Christopher Tancred: a neglected benefactor* (privately printed, Cambridge, 1925)

Archives BL, MSS relating to Christ's College and Gonville and Caius College benefactions, Add. MS 5820, fols. 150–54 · W. Yorks. AS, Leeds, Yorkshire Archaeological Society, records of Tancred's foundation, DD160

Likenesses oils, Christ's College, Cambridge · portrait, Gon. & Caius Cam.

Tandy, James Napper (1737–1803), Irish nationalist, was born in Dublin, the eldest son of James Tandy (1706–1790), ironmonger, and Maria Bella Jenkins. The testimony given by his son in October 1802 that he was then sixty-five years old makes his birth date 1737 rather than 1740 as traditionally stated. He was descended from the Tandys of Drewstown, co. Meath, and from the Nappers of Loughcrew, co. Meath, from whom he derived the distinctive patronymic, Napper. As a younger son his father had to make his own way and he chose trade when he was admitted in 1730 to the Holy Trinity Guild of Merchants. Twenty years later he was running his own ironmonger's business in Cornmarket, Dublin. James Napper Tandy seemed destined to follow in his father's footsteps after receiving 'a suitable education' (*Walker's Hibernian Magazine*, 14.553) at the popular school run by the Quaker Abraham Shackleton at Ballitore, co. Kildare, which he entered in April 1749. Though described in 1766 as an ironmonger Tandy was too restless to confine himself to such a conventional and time-consuming occupation. His marriage in February 1765 to Ann Jones (1747–1820) of Platton, co. Meath, who was described as 'an agreeable lady with a large fortune' (*Freeman's Journal*, 2 March 1765), may not have been as financially liberating as contemporaries assumed, but it allowed Tandy to exchange the iron trade for the more socially acceptable role of land agent and rent collector by 1770. The couple had one son, also named James, but the marriage was not mutually agreeable and James and Ann

James Napper Tandy (1737–1803), by unknown artist

had effectively, if not formally, separated by the late 1790s.

Municipal activist Since his grandfather and great-grandfather had been 'proscribed for opposing the civil and religious tyranny' exercised by James II, Tandy's admirers liked to suggest that he was driven by an inherited 'love for our constitutional establishment' as well as by his desire to promote 'just ideas' (*Walker's Hibernian Magazine*, 14.553–4). Tandy's initiation into political activism in the 1760s is ill documented, but it was evidently connected with the return from exile of Dr Charles Lucas, the champion of the Dublin Protestant populace, who was widely admired in the city for upholding the rights of the common council in the late 1740s. Tandy was a committed supporter of Lucas, from whom he was 'informed of the undoubted rights of the Irish subject' (ibid., 554). He was particularly disturbed by what he regarded as the regressive agenda of the lord lieutenancy of the first Marquess Townshend (1767–72), but it was not until after Townshend's departure and Lucas's death that Tandy emerged from the political shadows. He joined forces with Sir Edward Newenham, who shared his vision of a reformed Irish constitution, and became a leading figure in the influential political club, the Society of Free Citizens. Tandy helped to advance Newenham's electoral ambitions in the constituency of co. Dublin by promoting the principle that an MP's role was to receive and to respond to the instructions of his constituents. Tandy's efforts to persuade the freemen and freeholders of Dublin city and county in 1775 to adopt a test whereby parliamentary candidates undertook to disavow electoral and parliamentary corruption was also important. However, it took the outbreak of hostilities between the colonists and the crown in North America to create an environment where Tandy's brand of earthy radicalism could flourish.

Tandy and other critics of the existing political establishment regarded the American colonists as their fellow subjects and connected the colonists' efforts to secure their liberties and properties to their own resistance to what they saw as creeping despotism in Ireland. In keeping with his sympathy to the American cause, Tandy later observed that he would 'have joined her standard if not prevented' (National Archives of Ireland, Rebellion papers, 620/12/144). He instead publicly expressed his support for the colonists and was satisfied that this defence of public liberty was popular: in 1777, on the first of five consecutive occasions, he was elected to the common council of Dublin corporation as a representative of the merchants' guild.

Tandy's election encouraged his populist instincts and appropriately he was among the earliest recruits of the duke of Leinster's corps of Dublin volunteers. Volunteering epitomized his whig vision of the subject as citizen soldier. So when it emerged in 1778 that the British parliament was unwilling to cede Irish merchants the legal right to trade on the same terms as their British equivalents, he had no hesitation in appealing to the volunteers to bring pressure on the British government to secure this concession. Imitating the American colonists, he advocated non-importation and non-consumption campaigns targeted at British goods. He secured the backing of the citizens of Dublin in summer 1779 and, following the opening of parliament in October, increased the pressure further by encouraging the volunteers to demonstrate their commitment to the concession of free trade. The most spectacular protest occurred on 4 November (the anniversary of William III's birthday and the principal commemorative occasion of Protestant Ireland) when the Dublin volunteers, including Tandy, assembled before the parliament on College Green and attached free-trade slogans to the pedestal of the equestrian statue of William they had come to salute. Conscious that they had lost the battle for public opinion and that any attempt to resist Irish demand would only endanger the Anglo-Irish connection, ministers backed down and agreed to concede free trade in spring 1780.

Buoyed up with this success, Tandy perceived that the logical next step for the volunteers was to remove the legislative fetters—Poynings' law and the Declaratory Act—that limited the legislative autonomy of the Irish parliament. Acknowledged as the leading municipal political activist, he did not see any limit to what could be achieved by the *ad hoc* coalition of volunteers, parliamentary patriots, and the public, that he had helped to forge. To this end he persuaded the freemen and freeholders of Dublin city and county to issue declarations in spring 1780 in favour of 'such a modification of *Poynings' Law* as should effectually prevent all usurped, improper and unconstitutional interference between the King, Lords and Commons of Ireland' (*Hibernian Journal*, 1 March 1780). He also encouraged the volunteers to stand forward with similar

declarations but the opposition of his commanding officer, the duke of Leinster, to 'constitutional points being forced with the bayonet' (Coughlan, 33) resulted in his expulsion from the corps. Tandy was too resilient for this to be anything other than a temporary setback and he was quickly readmitted to a prominent place in another corps. However, his actions had exposed damaging differences within the hitherto united ranks of the volunteers between moderates, who were anxious to uphold the primacy of parliament, and radicals, who were palpably less deferential. In the short term this division did not work to Tandy's advantage as the initiative in respect of legislative independence remained with the moderates. None the less, his continued involvement with the volunteers ensured that he retained a high public profile, demonstrated when his corps was sent to guard the approaches to the House of Commons on 27 May 1782 as MPs gathered to learn that legislative independence had been secured.

Parliamentary reformer Tandy now directed his energies towards a campaign to reform the representative system. Absent from the grand national convention of volunteer delegates that met in Dublin in November 1783, his influence at the outset was modest. However, he warmly endorsed the moderate programme of reform that ensued and, following the second rejection in April 1784 of a scheme of moderate reform founded on Protestant principles, he and a number of allies initiated a campaign for more radical reform. They drew support from the outraged response of Dublin's population to the rejection of a series of popular measures, including reform and protective duties. Support was also forthcoming from Dublin corporation and Tandy was now the leading radical voice on the common council. His high profile subjected him to vilification from the government-controlled press, where he and his allies were caricatured as 'America bitten Patriots' (*Volunteer Evening Post*, 24 April 1784). In point of fact Tandy aspired neither to emulate the American colonists nor, as was also suspected, to engage in a treasonable intrigue with France, for parliamentary reform, not political independence, was his object. However, his readiness at this point to advocate a plan of reform that approved the admission of Catholic males to the franchise on the same terms as Protestants was too radical a departure for many of his colleagues, most notably Edward Newenham. This was one reason why the planned reform congress never generated the required public momentum that would have overcome the opposition of parliamentary opinion.

Tandy's efforts to overcome vested aristocratic interests in the Irish parliament earned for him a national profile that consolidated his reputation as the leading popular politician. He also incurred the severe disapproval of the political establishment, who refused to accept him as their social equal. This was vividly highlighted in 1784 when the irascible attorney-general, John FitzGibbon, let it be known that he would not accept a challenge to a duel from Tandy because Tandy was not a gentleman. Since FitzGibbon had publicly questioned his creditworthiness,

Tandy attempted to provoke the attorney-general to present a challenge in a bid to sustain his reputation. Tandy's failure not only revealed the political establishment's antipathy towards him, but also reinforced his social marginality.

Though the rumours of Tandy's financial problems were exaggerated, his continued residence in lodgings in Abbey Street suggests that his circumstances, personal as well as financial, were far from ideal at this point. His inability to stop Dublin corporation from awarding the freedom of the city to the lord lieutenant, the duke of Rutland, in October 1784 indicated that his influence in that quarter had diminished. However, he retained public confidence and was able to play a key role in securing public approval for a petition against William Pitt's proposal for a commercial union between Britain and Ireland in 1785. He was also an effective critic of the new police introduced in the city of Dublin in 1786. He earned further praise during the regency crisis of 1788–9 for his popular stand in favour of the prince of Wales, and in 1790 for upholding the rights of the common council in an acrimonious dispute with the board of aldermen over the nomination of a lord mayor.

Tandy concluded the 1780s with his reputation restored. His continuing popularity was highlighted by his election as master of the Guild of Merchants in 1788 and by his nomination as sheriff of the city on eight successive occasions from 1785. He was cited as 'a proper person to represent the metropolis in parliament' (Hibernian Journal, 8 Oct 1788), and admitted to the Whig Club in 1789, but the perception of him as a popular demagogue continued to tell against him. His exertions on behalf of Henry Grattan and Lord Henry Fitzgerald helped to elect them MPs for Dublin city, but did nothing to overcome the condescension of those higher in the social firmament.

United Irishman The suspicions surrounding Tandy were reinforced by the enthusiasm with which he greeted the French Revolution. On 14 July 1791 200 volunteers under his command marched at nightfall through the streets of Dublin, preceded by an illumination bearing the slogan 'we do not rejoice because we are slaves; but we rejoice because of the French being free' (Hibernian Journal, 15 July 1791). Though he played no part in the formation of the Society of United Irishmen in Belfast in October, he was asked to convene the group of eighteen radicals on 9 November that formed the Dublin Society of United Irishmen, of which he was the first secretary. His vision of the society as a 'citizen club' was more populist and radical than was favoured by the professional men who came to dominate its ranks. Yet, ironically, the greatest threat to his position arose out of his ill-considered response to slighting words uttered by the solicitor-general, John Toler, at his expense in the Commons on 20 February 1792. Ever sensitive where his personal reputation was at stake, Tandy contrived to manoeuvre Toler into a duel but he misjudged his antagonist and went into hiding rather than face a spell in prison. It was precisely the wrong thing to do. Widely suspected of cowardice, he was perceived by friends and enemies alike as having 'lost his reputation as

a gentleman' (Agnew, 1.398) and his ill-considered attempt to redeem himself in the courts exacerbated the situation. To compound matters, his preparedness to stand forward in favour of Catholic enfranchisement in winter 1792–3 alienated many of his traditional supporters among the Protestant freemen of Dublin. He resigned from the corporation in 1795.

Tandy responded by spearheading the attempt to found a national guard, inspired both by the French organization of the same name and by the volunteers. He intended to re-create the circumstances that had helped achieve commercial and constitutional reform in the early 1780s. The privy council directed magistrates to prevent meetings of 'ill affected persons' under the 'colour of laudable associations' and threatened to prosecute Tandy for distributing 'inflammatory handbills' (Agnew, 1.448). His timidity, allied to his 'irregular' lifestyle (ibid., 1.474), led him to back down. The hopes of the Dublin society were dealt a further blow in March 1793 when Tandy was prosecuted at the co. Louth assizes for distributing a 'seditious' address entitled Common Sense. Tandy was not particularly concerned at first. Yet when it emerged that the co. Louth grand jury was preparing 'other bills of indictment, containing charges of a much more dangerous kind' (Anthologia Hibernica, 1.240–41), that had arisen out of his overtures to the Defenders, a politicized Catholic peasant movement, he quickly appreciated the gravity of his situation. If, as reported, it could be shown that he had taken the Defender's oath he could receive the death penalty. Unwilling to run this risk or that of a long term in prison, Tandy took flight.

Tandy spent the next two years in 'concealment' in England (Bartlett, 114). His wish was to return to Ireland but when this proved impossible he joined the small network of United Irish exiles, including Theobald Wolfe Tone, in Philadelphia in July 1795. There he remained for two years before accepting an invitation 'in the name of the government' to travel to France in 1797 'to assist in the formation of an expedition to Ireland' (Coughlan, 113). While the French were understandably eager to secure the participation of Ireland's best-known and still most popular radical politician, Tandy's vanity and indiscretion meant that he was a doubtful asset. His conspicuous and boorish behaviour en route for Paris, reinforced by information gleaned from intercepted correspondence, provided the Irish and British authorities with important insights into United Irish activities. More significantly, his unwarranted assumption that he was the natural leader of the Irish in France as well as of any invading French force in Ireland soon had him at odds with Tone, who pursued a more secretive strategy. Tandy's age and reputation encouraged some to excuse his vainglorious posturing, but the debilitating flow of information on the activities of the United Irishmen in France that found its way to London could not be stemmed.

Tandy was provided with an opportunity both to redeem his reputation and to sustain the claim made on his behalf that he could draw '30,000 United Irishmen' to his standard in Ireland (Bartlett, 827) following the outbreak of rebellion in Ireland in May 1798. Appointed a general in the French service and commander of the ship *Anacreon*, he was dispatched in July to Dunkirk to lead the first of three expeditions to Ireland. Though his continuing lack of discretion suggested that he believed the expedition could not fail, his heavy drinking in the weeks before and during the course of the voyage indicated that he was racked by anxiety. Such self-indulgence also sapped the confidence of those under his command. It was not surprising, therefore, that when the *Anacreon* reached Rutland Island off the co. Donegal coast on 16 September the ship's officers, on learning of the defeat of the rebels in Ireland, decided to re-embark and head for home. A damaging encounter with a number of British vessels forced the ship to port at Bergen from where Tandy set out to return, via Copenhagen and Hamburg, to France. Detained shortly after his arrival in Hamburg on 22 November at the request of the British minister, Sir James Crauford, Tandy was the subject of a long diplomatic tussle as the representatives of France and Britain argued over his future. Tandy was handed over to the British and brought to England in October 1799, from where he was transferred to Ireland the following month. Tried for high treason at the court of king's bench in February 1800, he was acquitted on a technicality. A subsequent trial at Lifford assizes for his part in the invasion of Rutland Island resulted in a capital sentence, but this was not carried out. The Irish executive was happy with banishment. Botany Bay was suggested, but the intervention of the first consul of France and the conclusion of the peace of Amiens ensured that France would be his destination. Tandy was accorded a hero's welcome on his arrival in Bordeaux on 14 March 1802. He spent the last year of his life in the city, where he fathered a child with Marie Barrière, his housekeeper. He died there of dysentery on 24 August 1803 and was buried at the foreigners' cemetery.

The large military and civilian crowd that attended Tandy's funeral in Bordeaux on 25 August vividly illustrates the remarkable reputation he enjoyed during his lifetime as the leader of Irish radicalism at home and abroad. Ironically, though his activities as a United Irishman have attracted most notice, he was not an effective revolutionary. He possessed little of the resolve, discipline, or tactical skill necessary to succeed at this ruthless game. It is significant that, other than his contribution in forming the Dublin Society of United Irishmen, he achieved remarkably little in that capacity. This contrasts with his efforts as a political activist in the 1770s and 1780s when he successfully bound the patriot connection in the Irish Commons, the volunteers, and the municipal political activists in a potent alliance that ensured the concession of free trade and legislative independence. Had parliamentary reform followed he, like many others active in the ranks of the United Irishmen in the early 1790s, might not have felt it necessary to embrace republicanism, though the condescension of the political establishment may have pushed him in this direction in any event. What

is irrefutable is that his efforts on behalf of the politicized public over twenty years generated a bond of affection and respect that survived his mistakes and misjudgements in later life. This has contributed also to the positive reputation he enjoys within the Irish nationalist tradition to the present, though few who know the words of the ballad 'The Wearing of the Green', in which his name is most commonly evoked, appreciate that it is as a political radical rather than as a republican that he made his most important contribution.   JAMES KELLY

Sources 'Memoirs of James Napper Tandy', *Walker's Hibernian Magazine*, 14 (1784), 553–5, 622 · J. Kelly, 'Napper Tandy: radical and republican', *Dublin and Dubliners*, ed. J. Kelly and U. MacGearailt (1990), 1–24 · R. Coughlan, *Napper Tandy* (1976) · W. T. W. Tone, *Life of Theobald Wolfe Tone*, ed. T. Bartlett (1998) · M. Elliott, *Partners in revolution: the United Irishmen and France* (1982) · *The Drennan–McTier letters*, ed. J. Agnew, 3 vols. (1998–9) · M. Elliott, *Wolfe Tone: prophet of Irish independence* (1989) · P. Weber, *The United Irishmen and Hamburg, 1796–1803* (1997) · *Anthologia Hibernica*, 4 vols. (1793–4) · DNB · J. Kelly, *That damn'd thing called honour: duelling in Ireland, 1570–1860* (1995) · J. Kelly, *A passion for Protestant liberty: the life and politics of Sir Edward Newenham* (2003) · J. Hill, *From patriots to unionists: Dublin civic politics and Irish Protestant patriotism, 1660–1840* (1997) · E. J. McAuliffe, *The roll of the Quaker school at Ballitore, county Kildare* (Dublin, 1984), 6

Archives NA Ire., Rebellion papers, intercepts and reports, 620/12 | PRO, Chatam papers, intercepted corresp., PRO 30/8/330 · Suffolk RO, Ipswich, Pretyman papers, intercepted corresp., HA 119/T108/34 · TCD, Corbet papers, account of time in Hamburg, MS 5967

Likenesses J. Gillray, caricature, etching, 1799, NG Ire., NPG; repro. in D. Dickson and others, eds., *The United Irishmen* (1993) · J. Heath, stipple (after J. Petrie), BM, NPG; repro. in J. Barrington, *Historic memoirs* (1815) · F. Wheatley, group portrait, oils (*The volunteers in College Green, 1779*), NG Ire.; version, watercolour, V&A · engraving (after J. Petrie), repro. in R. R. Madden, *The United Irishmen: their lives and times* (1846) · group portrait, coloured lithograph (*The United Irish patriots of 1798*), NPG · oils, NG Ire. [*see illus.*] · portrait, repro. in Coughlan, *Napper Tandy*, jacket

Wealth at death £2000: son's estimate but this is not compatible with his will · will, repr. in Coughlan, *Napper Tandy*, 252

Tandy, Jessie Alice [Jessica] **(1909–1994)**, actress, was born on 7 June 1909 at 58A Geldeston Road, Upper Clapton, London, the third child of Henry Tandy (*d. c.*1921), a commercial traveller for a rope manufacturer, and his wife, Jessie Helen (*née* Horspool), the head of a school for mentally handicapped children. Her father died when she was twelve and her mother began teaching evening classes to supplement her income. Frequent bouts of tuberculosis blighted her education at Dame Alice Owen's Girls' School, although she regularly accompanied her mother to night school and became an enthusiastic student of poetry, dance, calisthenics, and drama. In 1924 she enrolled at Sir Ben Greet's Academy of Acting, under the tutelage of Lillian E. Simpson, and, on 22 November 1927, made her stage début in *The Manderson Girls*, at London's Playhouse Six.

Following a spell with Birmingham repertory, she made her West End bow on 21 February 1928 in C. K. Monroe's *The Rumour*, at the Court Theatre. She graduated to Broadway on 18 March 1930 in G. B. Stern's *The Matriarch*, which also marked her first appearance as Jessica Tandy, a change suggested by the famous producer Lee Shubert.

Jessie Alice [Jessica] **Tandy** (1909–1994), by Gordon Anthony, *c*.1950

After returning to London, she worked steadily on stage, entered films with a walk-on part as a maid in the musical *The Indiscretion of Fear* (1931), and on 22 October 1932, married actor Jack *Hawkins (1910–1973), with whom she would have a daughter, Susan.

After making her reputation as Manuela in Crista Winsloe's *Children in Uniform* at the Duchess Theatre in October 1932, she began alternating between classical and popular roles, most notably playing Ophelia opposite John Gielgud in *Hamlet* at the New Theatre (November 1934) and Viola and Sebastian alongside Laurence Olivier and Alec Guinness in the Old Vic's *Twelfth Night* in February 1937. She also spent much time in the United States and, having played Cordelia in Gielgud's *King Lear* at the Old Vic in April 1940, decided to emigrate to further her film career.

Despite signing a five-year deal with MGM, Tandy was considered insufficiently beautiful for screen stardom. Moreover, Broadway restrictions meant that alien actors had to wait six months between engagements, and she had to resort to playing Princess Nada in the radio show *Mandrake the Magician*. As she later lamented, 'I am just sitting here perfecting cooking recipes—and getting worse and worse at it all the time' (*The Playmakers*, 1996).

Salvation came in the form of Hume Cronyn (1911–2003), a Canadian actor and writer, whom she met while appearing in A. J. Cronin's *Jupiter Laughs* at the Biltmore Theater. After divorcing Hawkins in 1942, she married Cronyn on 27 September that year. They had two children, Christopher and Tandy, and formed one of show-business's most enduring partnerships. As she later told

the *Washington Post*, 'The reason we can live and work together is that in no way do we threaten each other. We're safe. I can't play him and he can't play me' (23 Dec 1982).

Tandy finally made her Hollywood début when she teamed with Cronyn and Spencer Tracy for *The Seventh Cross* (1944) and then, despite being his senior, played Cronyn's daughter in *The Green Years* (1946). A loan-out to Twentieth Century Fox for *Dragonwyck* (1946) was followed by her first screen lead, as Janet Spence in *A Woman's Vengeance* (1947). Yet still film fame eluded her, despite director Joseph L. Mankiewicz's avowal in a 1947 memo to Fox boss Darryl F. Zanuck, 'I have rarely seen acting the equal to hers … Tandy has it over Bette Davis as an actress, and is certainly more attractive' (Cronyn, p. 189).

It was Tandy's stage performance in Tennessee Williams's *Portrait of a Madonna* (January 1946) at the Las Palmas Theater, Hollywood, that transformed her fortunes, as it persuaded the playwright to offer her the role of Blanche DuBois in *A Streetcar Named Desire*. Directed by Elia Kazan, *Streetcar* opened at the Ethel Barrymore Theater on 3 December 1947 and earned Tandy a Tony award and the best reviews of an illustrious career. Even Brooks Atkinson, the feared *New York Times* critic, opined, 'Miss Tandy acts a magnificent part magnificently' (14 Dec 1947). She finally left the company after 600 performances, but was the only member of the original cast—who included Marlon Brando, Karl Malden, and Kim Hunter—to be overlooked for Kazan's screen version, for which Vivien Leigh won an Oscar. Tandy had to settle instead for Frau Rommel in *The Desert Fox* (1951).

Tandy became a US citizen in 1952 and spent much of the ensuing decade collaborating with Cronyn. In addition to ten stage productions, they also appeared together in seven plays for television's *Omnibus* series. They scored notable successes in Jan de Hartog's *The Fourposter* (1951–2) and Peter Shaffer's *Five Finger Exercise* (1959–60), pioneering the practice of first-run stars taking Broadway hits on tour. Yet, they also endured their share of misfires, including a television sitcom, *The Marriage* (1953–4), which was cancelled after just seven episodes. Consequently the couple had to auction their art collection in January 1958 to pay off mounting debts.

Acclaimed in Edward Albee's *A Delicate Balance* at the Martin Beck Theater (September 1966) and Williams's *Camino Real* at the Lincoln Center (January 1970), Tandy began converting accolades into awards in her later years. She won a Drama Desk award for *Happy Days* and an Obie for *Not I* at the Lincoln Center's 1972 Samuel Beckett festival. A further Drama Desk and a Tony followed for D. J. Coburn's *The Gin Game* at the John Golden Theater in October 1977. She even added an Emmy to the same double scoop as Annie Nations in Susan Cooper's *Foxfire* at the Ethel Barrymore (November 1982), as well as drawing another Tony nomination for Andrew Davies's *Rose* at the Court Theater (March 1981). No wonder the *New York Times*'s Frank Rich averred 'Everything this actress does is so pure and right that only poets, not theater critics, should be allowed to write about her' (12 Nov 1982). Yet she still found time to earn a law degree from the University of Western Ontario in 1974.

Tandy co-starred with Cronyn for the final time on stage in Brian Clark's *The Petition* at the John Golden in 1986. However, by then they were in great demand in Hollywood. Previously, there had been long gaps between screen assignments—seven years between *The Desert Fox* and *The Light of the Forest* (1958), a decade between Alfred Hitchcock's *The Birds* (1963) and the British-made *Butley* (1973), and nearly another one before *Honky Tonk Freeway* (1981). But suddenly a slew of supporting roles came her way, including solo outings in *The World According to Garp* (1982) and *The Bostonians* (1984), and *Cocoon* (1985), *batteries not included* (1987), and *Cocoon: the Return* (1988), which she made with Cronyn.

The pinnacle, however, was becoming, at eighty years and eight months, the oldest winner in Academy award history for her superbly testy performance as a southern matriarch in *Driving Miss Daisy* (1989). Yet, she still managed to secure another nomination, this time for best supporting actress, for *Fried Green Tomatoes* (1991), before bowing out with *Camilla* and *Nobody's Fool* (both 1994). Despite the celebrity cinema brought her, she told the *New York Times Magazine* 'My parts are never big in films, but that's all right … Films aren't as satisfying to me as the theater' (26 Dec 1982). She died of ovarian cancer in Easton, Connecticut, on 11 September 1994, and was cremated. She was survived by her husband. DAVID PARKINSON

Sources M. S. Barranger, *Jessica Tandy: a bio-bibliography* (Westport, CT, 1991) • H. Cronyn, *A terrible liar: a memoir* (New York, 1991) • www.uk.imdb.com, 8 Dec 2001 • b. cert. • m. cert. • *The Times* (13 Sept 1994) • *The Independent* (13 Sept 1994)

Likenesses G. Anthony, photograph, c.1950, Hult. Arch. [see illus.] • photographs, 135 Salisbury Road, London, Kobal collection • photographs, 78 Mildmay Park, London, Huntley archive • photographs, 2 Dugard Way, London, Ronald Grant archive

Tanfield, Elizabeth. *See* Cary, Elizabeth, Viscountess Falkland (1585–1639).

Tanfield, John. *See* Radford, John (c.1562–1630).

Tanfield, Sir Lawrence (c.1551–1625), lawyer, was probably born in Stanley, Huntingdonshire, the son of Robert Tanfield (d. 1575) and his wife, Wilgeford Fitzherbert, and the grandson of William Tanfield of Gayton, Northamptonshire. He was admitted to the Inner Temple in 1569, aged about eighteen; the date of his call to the bar is not recorded. In 1579 he came to prominence as an advocate in a family dispute, arguing that an arrangement between his mother and his aunt had been effective in depriving his cousin of his inheritance. His argument was unsuccessful, but it is said that Edmund Plowden, the opposing counsel, was much impressed by Tanfield and his career advanced rapidly. On 26 October 1584 Tanfield was returned to parliament as MP for New Woodstock, Oxfordshire, and he continued to sit for that borough during the remainder of Elizabeth's reign. By 1585 he had married Elizabeth (d. 1629), daughter of Giles Symonds of Claye, Norfolk, and niece of Sir Henry Lee, high steward of New Woodstock; their only child, Elizabeth, later Elizabeth

*Cary (1585–1639), was born that year. In Lent 1595 Tanfield became reader at the Inner Temple, and in Easter 1603 he was created a serjeant-at-law. On 9 September 1603 King James, during his journey from Scotland, visited Tanfield at Burford Priory, where Tanfield had lived since at least 1600; the king stayed for three nights.

On 7 March 1604 Tanfield was returned for the county of Oxford in the king's first parliament and on 14 March he was knighted at the Tower of London. He was appointed a puisne judge of king's bench on 13 January 1606 and was advanced on 25 June 1607 to the office of chief baron of the exchequer, which he returned for the rest of his life. He amassed great wealth and was a member of the Newfoundland Company, which was founded in 1614.

As a lawyer Tanfield had a good reputation among his contemporaries: his judicial colleague Richard Hutton described him as a resolute and reserved man of great learning and the property in the Temple formerly known as Bradshaw's Rents was renamed Tanfield Court in his honour. Others were less positive. Insinuations of corruption are not wanting against him. His near-kinsman Sir Antony Maine accused him of fraud in diverting property to himself while acting as Maine's lawyer; the inhabitants of Great Tew in Oxfordshire, where he had an estate, complained bitterly of oppression by both Tanfield and his wife, who 'saith that we are more worthy to be ground to powder than to have any favour showed to us, and that she will play the very devil among us' (*Third Report*, HMC, 31–3). He is said to have impoverished the vicarage of Burford by entering into a collusive settlement with the vicar for the time being, and to have initiated litigation in his own court to deprive the burgesses of the town of their privileges. He was assiduous in the enforcement of his own rights, so much so that in one dispute his tenants complained that they were being prevented from getting a lawyer to represent them. So bad was his reputation that the evils of the wicked 'Lord Tanfield' remained an active part of Oxfordshire folk-tradition into the twentieth century. Tanfield died in Burford on 30 April 1625 and was buried on 1 May in Burford church. He had disinherited his daughter—perhaps on the grounds of her Roman Catholicism, perhaps because of her husband's profligacy—and, after a life interest in favour of his widow (who died in 1629), his estate passed to his grandson Lucius *Cary, second Viscount Falkland (1609/10–1643).

E. I. CARLYLE, *rev.* DAVID IBBETSON

Sources M. S. Gretton, *Burford past and present* (1920), 55–6, 73–81 • R. S., *The Lady Falkland, her life* (1861), 1–7 • A. Harding, 'Tanfield, Lawrence', HoP, *Commons, 1558–1603*, 3.475–6 • J. Fisher, *A history of the town of Burford, Oxfordshire* (1861) • R. H. Gretton, *The Burford records* (1920), *passim* • *Folk-lore*, 40 (1929), 374–6 • *Third report*, HMC, 2 (1872), 31–3 • *Les commentaries, ou, Les reportes de Edmunde Plowden* (1571), 539 • W. J. Monk, *History of Burford* (1891), 33–4 • A. W. Hughes Clarke and A. Campling, eds., *The visitation of Norfolk … 1664, made by Sir Edward Bysshe*, 2 vols., Harleian Society, 85–6 (1933–4) • E. K. Chambers, *Sir Henry Lee: an Elizabethan portrait* (1936), 206–7 • W. H. Cooke, ed., *Students admitted to the Inner Temple, 1547–1660* [1878], 67 • F. A. Inderwick and R. A. Roberts, eds., *A calendar of the Inner Temple records*, 1 (1896), 378, 397 • *VCH Oxfordshire*, 11.231 • will, PRO,

PROB 11/145, fol. 361 • inquisition post-mortem, PRO, C142/417/44 • PRO, PROB6/2, fol. 75v [letters of administration of father's estate] • G. Baker, *The history and antiquities of the county of Northampton*, 2 vols. (1822–41) • Baker, *Serjeants*, 539 • Sainty, *Judges*, 31, 95
Likenesses attrib. G. Christmas, effigy on monument, 1628, Burford church, Oxfordshire • T. Athow, wash drawing (in robes), AM Oxf.
Wealth at death lands assessed at £26: PRO, C142/417/44; will, PRO, PROB 11/145, fol. 361

Tang, Abraham ben Naphtali [Abraham Abrahams] (*d.* 1792), theologian and historian, was probably born in London. He was the grandson of Abraham ben Moses Taussig Neungreschel (thus the acronym Tang), a Prague rabbi who died in 1699. His son Naphtali left Prague and settled in London where he married the daughter of R. Nathan Apta of Opatow in Poland, rabbi of the Hambro Synagogue. Naphtali composed several rabbinic works which were never published, including an expansive commentary on the ethics of the fathers. That Abraham his son later chose to compose his own commentary on this rabbinical collection of ethical maxims might be more than coincidental. Like many other Jewish writers of this period, there are few personal details of Tang's life; we do not know, for example, whether he was married.

Tang's teacher in London was Moses Minsk, preacher of a small congregation that existed in London about 1770 called Hevrat Sha'are Zion (The Society of the Gates of Zion). The only information about its membership is gleaned from a collection of Minsk's sermons published in London in 1772 and from those of his successor Phineas ben Samuel published in 1795. From the lists of subscribers to both volumes, it is possible to gain some sense of the community with which Tang was probably affiliated. Among the subscribers was a certain Leib ben Naphtali Tang, probably Abraham's brother.

Among the many texts Minsk discussed in his published sermons was the enigmatic rabbinic story of the first-century Palestinian rabbi Joshua ben Hananiah and his strange encounter with the sages of Athens, where he had been sent by the Roman emperor. That Tang actually heard this sermon or studied the text with Minsk is suggested by an original composition Tang penned in honour of Minsk on the very same story. In Tang's hands, however, the text served no moral or homiletical purpose; rather, it offered a lesson in political science about how the rabbis worked surreptitiously on behalf of the Roman government to undermine a political faction in Athens that threatened the stability of Roman rule.

Tang's other Hebrew writings were considerable, although most were neither completed nor printed. His largest work, *Behinat Adam* (*Examination of Man*), relied on the vast taxonomies of Samuel Bochart, Edward Stillingfleet, and others to demonstrate how pagan philosophers and native Africans and Americans all acknowledged the one God. To underscore his deist and anti-clerical message, he translated into Hebrew two long sections from Voltaire's dictionary: his 'Chinese catechism' and his entry on 'God'. In a discussion heavily influenced by

Locke, Tang asserted that faith without reason was meaningless. He criticized Talmudists who dealt with the minutiae of the law and cabbalists who falsely followed the irrationality of their imagination.

Tang evinced considerable interest in the life sciences as testimony to the divine hand of creation. He was also fascinated by ancient history and mythology and used the latter to explore the mentality of the rabbis and ancient Judaism. For Tang, it was important for Jews to know mythology because he believed that Moses and the rabbis were familiar with it; because the myths could be correlated with the Bible and understood to reveal the one God; and because of the poetic and literary value of these heroic stories.

Tang's commitment to recovering a fundamental belief in one God in all cultures and in correlating that belief with the Jewish one diminished the singularity of the Jewish tradition to the vanishing point. Despite his plentiful use of Jewish sources, there is no compelling message in his writings that distinguishes Judaism from other religions. He was clearly a deist by belief and a Jew by cultural inclination. He may also have been a freemason.

Tang's other Hebrew writings included an incomplete commentary on the book of Ecclesiastes, which contains a unique handbook of classical mythology for students of rabbinic literature, offering texts in the original Latin or Greek with Hebrew and English translations. He also translated William Congreve's *Mourning Bride* into Hebrew, and wrote an unfinished commentary on the meaning of the commandments. Tang also had some artistic pretensions. His manuscripts were copied in a clear penmanship that emulated the perfection of the printed page. He occasionally included colourful charts and diagrams and, as on the printed page, often used footnotes to expand points made in the body of the text.

Tang's only published works were in English: his aforementioned commentary and translation entitled *The Sentences and Proverbs of the Ancient Fathers in Six Chapters called Abouth* (1772) and a pamphlet entitled *A Discourse Addressed to the Minority* (1770). In both cases, he signed the works as penned 'by a primitive ebrew'. Tang's translation represented the first undertaken in the English language. In his commentary he attempted to correlate the teachings of the rabbis with deism, underscoring Judaism's rationality and sound philosophy, the pre-eminence it gave to moral precepts over 'indefatiguable ceremonies', and its lack of enthusiam and stress on inward duties. The second work represents Tang's remarkable defence of the English radical John Wilkes and his critique of the undemocratic nature of the way he had been removed from office. In publicly identifying himself with the radical Wilkites, in articulating a deistic faith that safeguarded the rights and opinions of even 'primitive ebrews', and in demonstrating an authentic emotional attachment to his British homeland, this work stands out as Tang's most unusual composition. It is hard to conceive of a similar work written by any Jew at the end of the eighteenth century. Tang died in 1792; the exact dates and places of his death and burial are unknown.   DAVID B. RUDERMAN

Sources D. B. Ruderman, *Jewish enlightenment in an English key: Anglo-Jewry's construction of modern Jewish thought* (2000) · D. Ruderman, 'Was there an English parallel to the German Haskalah?', *Two nations: British and German Jews in comparative perspective*, ed. M. Brenner, R. Liedtke, and D. Rechter (1999), 15–44 · S. Leperer, 'Abraham ben Naphtali Tang: a precursor of the Anglo-Jewish Haskalah', *Transactions of the Jewish Historical Society of England*, 24 (1970–73), 82–88 · S. Leperer, 'The first publication of *Pirkei Avot* in English', *L'Eylah: a Journal of Judaism*, 26 (1988), 41–6 · C. Roth, 'The Haskalah in England', *Essays presented to … Israel Brodie*, ed. J. Zimmels, J. Rabbinowitz, and I. Finestein, 1 (1967), 368–72 · J. Schirmann, 'The first Hebrew translation from English literature: Congreve's *Mourning bride*', *Scripta Hierosolymitana*, 19 (1967), 3–15
Archives Cincinnati HUC, MS of *Behinat Adam*, 728/1 · Jews' College, London, MSS no. 7, no. 35 · St Petersburg RNL, MS of *Behinat Adam*, Heb. II A22 · Frankfurt am Main, MS of *Behinat Adam*, 8*59

Tangley. For this title name *see* Herbert, Edwin Savory, Baron Tangley (1899–1973).

Tangye, Sir Richard (1833–1906), machine tool manufacturer and engineer, born at Broad Lane, Illogan, Cornwall, on 24 November 1833, was the fifth son in a family of six sons and three daughters of Joseph Tangye, a Quaker Cornish miner of Redruth (who afterwards became a small shopkeeper and farmer there), and his wife, Anne (d. 1851), daughter of Edward Bullock, a small farmer and engine driver. Until the age of eight he attended a local school and helped on the farm, but when he broke his right arm it was supposed he would be unable to earn a living by manual work. His parents were advised to extend his education, and he spent three years (1844–7) at a school at Redruth kept by William Lamb Bellows, father of the printer and lexicographer John Bellows; thence he went in February 1847 to the Friends' school, Sidcot, Somerset, where he formed a lifelong friendship with William Tallack, the prison reformer. He remained there as pupil teacher and assistant until 1851.

Tangye was under 5 feet tall and the butt of children's jokes. He disliked teaching, and at the end of 1852 moved to Birmingham to work as a clerk for Thomas Worsdell, tool manufacturer. His younger brother George soon joined him as junior clerk; they were followed by two other brothers, James and Joseph, mechanical experts who had worked under Brunel for William Brunton, engineer to the West Cornwall Railway, and had made a hydraulic press, which favourably impressed Brunel.

James Tangye set up as a machine tool manufacturer. Richard left Worsdell's employment and began a general hardware business in 1856, but he soon joined his brother, being joined also by George and Joseph. They rented a room at 40 Mount Street, Birmingham, for 4s. a week. In 1856 Brunel, mindful of James and Joseph's earlier efforts, commissioned the brothers at Birmingham to supply him with hydraulic lifting jacks to launch the *Great Eastern* steamship. The successful performance of this commission proved the first step in the firm's prosperity. 'We launched the *Great Eastern*, the *Great Eastern* launched us' was Richard Tangye's successful advertisement. In 1858 the brothers bought the sole right to manufacture differential pulley blocks, recently invented by J. A. Weston; but rival claims to the patent rights involved them in 1858 in a long and costly, though successful, lawsuit. On 24 January 1859 Richard Tangye married Caroline, daughter of Thomas Jesper of Birmingham, a corn merchant. They had four sons and two daughters.

The firm, joined by a fifth brother, Edward, now devoted itself solely to the manufacture of machinery and every kind of power machine. The growth of the industry led to their removal in 1859 to new premises in Clement Street, Birmingham; three years later the firm acquired 3 acres of land at Soho, 3 miles from Birmingham, and built there the Cornwall works in 1864. Ultimately this factory absorbed 30 acres of surrounding land and employed 3000 workers. Richard Tangye gradually took over the duties of the other brothers. He was an exceptional organizer of large-scale production (unusual in the Birmingham area) and a very successful marketer of his products. He expanded into Europe—unsuccessfully initially in a Belgian branch opened in 1863—and in the empire, with branches in Sydney, Melbourne, and Johannesburg. There were also branches in Newcastle, Manchester, and London. One of the engineering successes of the firm was the use of their hydraulic jacks in placing Cleopatra's Needle (weighing over 186 tons) on its site on the Thames Embankment on 12 September 1878. The firm became a limited liability company, Tangyes Limited, on 1 January 1882, Richard Tangye continuing as chairman until his death.

Tangye was a paternalistic and philanthropic employer. He introduced Saturday half-holidays in 1872, and a nine-hour day in 1878, thus averting a strike. His Birmingham works had a large dining-hall, and offered educational classes, concerts, and lectures. Trade unions were accepted, if not encouraged.

Tangye was active in Birmingham religious, municipal, and political life. In his early days there he helped Joseph Sturge at the Friends' Sunday schools. A staunch Liberal in politics, he supported John Bright in every election at Birmingham, but refused many invitations to stand for parliament himself. He was a firm free-trader, and, unlike Bright, remained loyal to Gladstone after the home-rule split of 1886, keeping alive the principles of Liberalism in the *Daily Argus*, which he founded in 1891 with Sir Hugh Gilzean Reid. He was knighted in 1894 on Lord Rosebery's recommendation. A member of the Birmingham town council from 1878 to 1882 as a progressive Liberal, and of the Smethwick school board, Tangye and his brothers were generous benefactors to the town. The firm gave £10,000 to Birmingham art gallery for buildings and acquisitions. Tangye also loaned his fine collection of Wedgwood ware, of which a handbook was published in 1885. The School of Art (founded in 1843), to which the Tangyes in 1881 contributed £12,000, was rebuilt in 1884.

Tangye was fascinated by the history of English dissent. From 1875 he accumulated a large collection of printed materials and artefacts about Oliver Cromwell and in 1889 he bought the fine Cromwellian collection of J. de Kewer Williams, Congregational minister, to which he made many additions. He published *The Two Protectors, Oliver and*

Richard Cromwell (1899) and several pamphlets. A catalogue of his Cromwellian collection of manuscripts, miniatures, and medals, by W. Downing, was published in 1905.

Between 1876 and 1904 Tangye made eight extended voyages, visiting Australia, America, South Africa (where his firm had business branches), and Egypt. He published accounts of these travels, and also wrote his autobiography, *One and All* (1890, revised in 1905 as *The Rise of a Great Industry*).

Tangye lived in Birmingham until 1894, spending his summers from 1882 at Glendorgal, his house near Newquay, Cornwall. In 1894 he moved to Kingston upon Thames. He died at his home, Coombe Bank, Kingston Hill, on 14 October 1906, and was buried in Putney Vale cemetery. He was survived by his wife, three of his sons, and his two daughters. His eldest son, Harold Lincoln Tangye (1866–1935), was created baronet in 1912.

W. B. OWEN, *rev.* H. C. G. MATTHEW

Sources R. Tangye, *The rise of a great industry*, rev. edn (1905) · S. J. Reid, *Sir Richard Tangye* (1908) · *The Times* (15 Oct 1906) · *Biograph and Review*, 2 (1879), 266 · L. Jones, 'Tangye, Sir Richard', *DBB* · R. E. Waterhouse, *A hundred years of engineering craftsmanship: a short history of Tangyes Ltd., 1857–1957* (1957) · *CGPLA Eng. & Wales* (1906)
Archives Bishopsgate Institute, London, letters to George Howell · BL, corresp. with John Bright and his daughters, Add. MS 44877
Likenesses W. R. Colton, bronze memorial plate with relief portrait, exh. RA 1916, Birmingham Museums and Art Gallery · E. R. Taylor, oils, Birmingham School of Art
Wealth at death £226,319 6*s.* 2*d.*: probate, 17 Dec 1906, *CGPLA Eng. & Wales*

Tani, Yukio (1881–1950), judo master, was almost certainly born in Tokyo. It is known that his father and grandfather were both teachers of ju-jitsu, but there are no further details of his early life in Japan.

On 26 September 1900 Yukio Tani and his elder brother K. Tani, the first two true ju-jitsu experts to arrive in Europe, disembarked from the SS *Wakasu Maru* in the port of London, brought over by Edward William Barton-Wright (1860–1951) to be instructors in ju-jitsu at the Bartitsu Club, a school of arms he had opened in Shaftesbury Avenue in 1898. Barton-Wright, a consultant engineer fascinated by all forms of fighting, had spent three years in Japan learning ju-jitsu which, on his return to London, he taught under the name Bartitsu. A month later, in October 1900, a third expert, S. Yamamoto, reached London, having also embarked in Kobe, Japan. He, too, was sponsored by Barton-Wright.

Wrestling and strongman acts were immensely popular in the music-halls at the time, and it soon became apparent that Barton-Wright had plans for the Japanese to follow this lucrative career. But Yamamoto and K. Tani refused to debase their art in front of a paying public and returned to Japan. In 1901 a replacement, Sadokazu Uyenishi (who performed under the name Raku), arrived from Japan, also sponsored by Barton-Wright. He and Yukio Tani had no scruples about public performances, and in August 1901 they appeared at the Tivoli Music Hall in the Strand, London, demonstrating and inviting members of the audience to participate.

At first the public had doubts about the two performers. For instance, Tani, the smaller, was 5 feet 3 inches and barely 9 stone, so how could such a small man defeat massive wrestlers sometimes double his weight? When it was realized that the defeats of the many challengers were genuine, the two became a sensational success, with reports appearing in all the major newspapers, sometimes at length. Eventually they broke with Barton-Wright and went their own ways: Raku, though still doing some stage work, opened a school in Golden Square, Soho, and continued there until about 1907 or 1908, when he left Britain; Tani elected to pursue a stage career, appearing in the music-halls throughout Britain, industriously carving his way through all the leading wrestlers of the day, including those from abroad, often several in the same evening, and becoming in the process a household name throughout Britain.

Tani's exploits were not confined to Britain. For instance, in November 1905 Katsukuma Higashi, based in America and calling himself ju-jitsu champion of the world, appeared at the Hippodrome in Paris, where he issued the usual challenge to the audience. Tani took up the challenge, leaving Higashi hospitalized in a much-publicized event that was reported by Arnold Bennett among others. His manager, the strong man William Bankier (1870–1949), reckoned that Tani earned a quarter of a million pounds during the years 1901 to 1909. But Tani had no head for money affairs, and his financial innocence was not helped by gambling and living the life of an Edwardian man about town, at times hiring a Thames steamer and inviting the whole company of a theatre for a trip with supper. In 1906 Tani and a compatriot, Taro Miyake, wrote *The Game of Ju-Jitsu: for the Use of Schools and Colleges*, which received excellent reviews.

Tani denied his reputation that he was unbeatable, confessing on several occasions that he was no champion by Japanese standards, and stating that he was second- or third-rate compared with the top men in Japan, but adding that he was unsurpassed in dealing with wrestlers, boxers, and street fighters. He was top of the bill wherever he went, but his glory days and the great days of the halls came to an end shortly before the First World War. Even so, he was famous enough to be welcomed at theatres round the country. About this time he met his wife, Mary Alice Fearon (1878/9–1947); they had one daughter, Moya (*b.* 1920).

In 1918, when Gunji Koizumi founded the Budokwai Club in London, Tani became its professional judo master. He continued at the Budokwai until smitten by a stroke in February 1937, though he eventually recovered sufficiently to coach from the edge of the mat. On 24 January 1950, at the age of sixty-nine, he died in the St Charles Hospital, London, of cerebral thrombosis. He was cremated at Golders Green crematorium, and his ashes were scattered in the cemetery there. One of his pupils recalled, 'I can hear once again one of Mr Tani's oldest friends, himself a great wrestler and one who went down before Tani's shattering attack, who, putting his arm around this glorious little man, called him "old tiger heart"' (Mossom).

RICHARD BOWEN

Sources private information (2004) [daughter] · archives on the history of judo in Britain, priv. coll. · d. cert. · K. Itoh, *The Japanese community in pre-war Britain* (2001) · E. H. Mossom, *Budokwai Quarterly Bulletin* (April 1950) · *Britain and Japan: biographical portraits*, 5 [forthcoming]
Likenesses G. Lambourne, oils, 1939, Budokwai Club, London · portrait, repro. in *Japanese in Britain, 1863–2001: a photographic exhibition* [exhibition catalogue]

Tankerville. For this title name *see* Grey, Ford, earl of Tankerville (*bap.* 1655, *d.* 1701); Bennett, Charles, fourth earl of Tankerville (1743–1822) [*see under* White Conduit cricket club (*act. c.*1785–1788)].

Tannahill, Robert (1774–1810), songwriter, was born in Paisley on 3 June 1774, the fifth child of the seven sons and one daughter of James Tannahill, silk gauze weaver from Kilmarnock, and his wife, Janet Pollock, daughter of a farmer near Beith. Tannahill began to write verses while still at school, and at about the age of twelve was apprenticed as a cotton weaver. He worked in Lochwinnoch, and from 1800 to 1802 in Bolton, until he returned home on hearing of his father's approaching death. Thereafter he lived with his widowed mother in Paisley, and remained unmarried.

Tannahill composed at the loom, jotting down ideas at a desk attached to the frame. His first published piece was a poem in praise of Ferguslie Wood, where he would ramble on summer evenings playing his flute. Other early material appeared in the *Glasgow Courier*. In January 1805 he became founding secretary of the Paisley Burns Club, and later that year his own volume of poems, *The soldier's return: a Scottish interlude in two acts, with other poems and songs, chiefly in the Scottish dialect* (1805) was published by subscription. The 900 copies were quickly disposed of, but the author was anxious that he had published too hastily, and almost immediately began work on a revised and expanded edition intended for the open market.

Soon after returning to Paisley, Tannahill met Robert Archibald Smith, a fellow weaver (and later the leading church musician of his generation in Scotland), who was to compose the airs and published arrangements of some of his best-known songs. James Barr of Kilbarchan and John Ross of Aberdeen seem also to have supplied tunes and arrangements. Tannahill was influenced by Burns and to a lesser extent by James Thomson and William Shenstone. His themes were often conventional, the registers including formal literary English, stage Irish, and vernacular Scots of varying densities. Like Burns he 'mended' folk-songs, but his reputation was to rest upon a handful of beautiful original songs including 'Jessie, the flower o' Dunblane', 'Oh, are ye sleeping, Maggie', 'Thou bonnie wood o' Craigielea', and 'Gloomy winter's now awa'', the latter set to an exquisite new air by Alexander Campbell:

Gloomy winter's now awa',
Saft the westlan' breezes blaw;
'Mang the birks o' Stanley shaw

The mavis sings fu' cheery, O;
Sweet the crawflower's early bell
Decks Gleniffer's dewy dell,
Blooming like thy bonnie sel',
My young, my artless deary, O.
(Tannahill, ed. Semple, *Poems*, 160–62)

Technically, his songs were deceptively simple, reflecting a single mood and based as a rule on a simple contrast—between summer and winter, town and country, age and youth, worldly show and honest worth. Yet they possessed a rich and sensuous natural imagery, and while Tannahill was quite realistic about his powers, hoping, at best, 'to be reckoned respectable among the minor Bards of his country' (Tannahill, ed. Semple, *Poems*, xvii), his stress on the naïvety of his work was misleading. He was addressing, with considerable skill and sophistication, the burgeoning new early nineteenth-century drawing-room market, whose demand for Scottish popular art-songs, arranged for one or more voices with accompaniment for the piano and other instruments, was beginning to become commercially significant. Since the consumers were predominantly genteel and female, the requirement for chastely worded texts was important, and the 'delicacy' of his verses was to win frequent and favourable contrast with those of Burns. Tannahill's influence in this area was very great. 'Jessie the flower o' Dunblane', for example, inspired innumerable 'X the flower o' Y' imitations, in song-sheets and slips, newspaper 'poetry corners', and little volumes of local verse throughout the nineteenth century.

Although swiftly accommodated to the myth that poverty was the true nursemaid of genius, and that 'Scotland's sweetest bards were bred beneath a roof o' strae' ('The star o' Rabbie Burns'), Tannahill was secure financially and died with money in the bank. Yet the growing secular cult of pilgrimage and devotion focusing on important plebeian poets like Burns and himself not only affected his reputation when dead but disturbed his peace while alive. The weaver–poet William Thom declared that 'Church bells rang not for us. Poets were indeed our Priests' (Findlay, 360) and the major creators of popular art-song could find themselves exposed to an overwhelming—sometimes even fatal—celebrity. Tannahill was sought out by literary lion-hunters, which distracted him from composition and presented a constant irritant. He began to suffer bouts of depression, and came to believe that he was developing consumption and being persecuted by his friends. When James Hogg, 'the Ettrick Shepherd', went to see him in the spring of 1810, Tannahill declared, on parting, 'Farewell! We shall never meet again' (Tannahill, ed. Semple, *Poems*, xxxvi).

The second edition upon which Tannahill had pinned so much hope was rejected by Constable the publisher—possibly because of the author's reluctance to pursue the normal channels of patronage—and in a fit of despondency he recalled his correspondence and destroyed his papers. He ended his life following a serious nervous breakdown. Friends found him on the morning of 17 May 1810 drowned in a culvert of the Maxwellton Burn under the

Glasgow, Paisley, and Johnstone Canal, near Paisley. The body was recovered by Peter Burnet—Black Peter—an African-American friend of the family. Tannahill was buried in the West Relief church, Paisley.

WILLIAM DONALDSON

Sources R. Tannahill, *The works of Robert Tannahill: with life of the author and a memoir of Robert A. Smith the musical composer*, ed. P. A. Ramsay (1851) · R. Tannahill, *The poems and songs of Robert Tannahill*, ed. D. Semple (1874) · bap. reg. Scot. · R. L. Crawford, 'New light on Robert Tannahill, the weaver–poet of Paisley', *N&Q*, 211 (1966), 184–9 · R. Tannahill, *Centenary edition: complete songs and poems of Robert Tannahill with life and notes, also, a history of the Tannahill club, with an account of the centenary celebration on 3rd June 1874* (1874) · Chambers, *Scots.* (1855) · [W. Motherwell], ed., *The harp of Renfrewshire: a collection of songs and other poetical pieces* (1872) · C. Rodgers, ed., *The Scottish minstrel: the songs of Scotland subsequent to Burns* (1873) · D. Cook, 'Not Tannahill's: spurious songs included in his works', *Scots Magazine*, 34 (1941), 393–6 · W. Findlay, 'Reclaiming local literature: William Thom and Janet Hamilton', *The history of Scottish literature*, ed. C. Craig, 3: *Nineteenth century*, ed. D. Gifford (1988), 353–76 · R. Ford, *Song histories* (1900) · H. G. Farmer, *A history of music in Scotland* (1947)

Archives NL Scot., poems and letters, MS 10335, fol. 147 · NL Scot., letter, MS 2524, fol. 84 · NL Scot., letter, MS 582, no. 681 · NL Scot., facsimile of poem, song, and letter, MS 807, fol. 35 · U. Glas. L., corresp., papers, and commonplace book

Likenesses S. Freeman, stipple, pubd 1835 (after A. Blair), BM, NPG; repro. in Chambers, *Scots.*, 1st edn · engraving (after pencil drawing by J. Morton, 1810?), repro. in Tannahill, *Poems*, ed. Semple

Tanner, David (*bap.* **1743**, *d.* in or after **1805**), ironmaster, was baptized on 27 December 1743 at St Mary's parish church, Monmouth. He was the fourth child of David Tanner (1702–1754), ironmaster, and Mary (*d.* 1797), the daughter of Walter Davis of Mitcheltroy, Monmouthshire. The three eldest children died at an early age and David's birth was followed by that of three other children. The youngest, William (1754–1806), became a junior partner in some of David's enterprises. Their grandfather was a cooper and then a timber merchant. Tanner's father died when he was eleven and he was brought up by his mother and her brother, the Revd Dr John Davis (1721–1798), vicar of Monmouth. As a young adult Tanner became involved in local politics. He became a burgessman and a member of the common council of Monmouth. Elected mayor in 1782, in 1792 he was appointed sheriff of Monmouthshire. Monmouth, situated on the navigable River Wye, was just upriver from the charcoal furnaces at Redbrook and Tintern and was in close proximity to long-established charcoal ironmaking centres in south Wales, the Forest of Dean, and Herefordshire. It was from around Monmouth in 1769 that Tanner, at the age of twenty-six, obtained the right to extract iron cinder which could be sold to local ironworks for resmelting. This was the start of a self-made industrial career that was to earn him the reputation of being the last of the great charcoal ironmasters.

In south Wales large amounts of money were being spent on mineral leases and on the construction of large coke-fired furnaces. Tanner did not have this level of finance. Initially he and his mother obtained money by acquiring land and then mortgaging it. This was a strategy that he continued to employ by himself throughout his career. He concentrated on obtaining leases of charcoal furnaces that could be had relatively cheaply and required very little capital investment. Although they were smaller and less than half as productive as the average newly erected coke-fired furnaces in south Wales, Tanner was able to partly compensate for this by importing large amounts of haematite from Cumberland to some of his furnaces. The haematite contained up to twice the content of iron as local ores and produced iron that he could sell at a premium. Because the quality of local outcrop coal to be found in the Forest of Dean was too poor to use in coke-fuelled furnaces, and the supply of wood from the forest was readily available, there was little incentive for Tanner to invest in coke-fuelled furnaces. Tanner leased his first furnace at Tintern in 1772. A few months later, he leased the Ynysgedwyn Furnace, situated 60 miles away, at the head of the Swansea valley. He also worked in the Forest of Dean and at various times leased Lydney Furnace and its two forges, Rowley, Clanna, and Barnedge forges, Redbrook Furnace, and Lydbrook Upper and Middle forges.

In 1784 Tanner leased a foundry at Cyfarthfa, Merthyr Tudful, which he relinquished to Richard Crawshay in 1786 to concentrate on his acquisitions from Jane, the widow of John Hanbury of Pontypool. This was composed of the lease of the furnace, tinworks, and forges at Pontypool, the furnace at Llanelli (Brecknockshire), and a forge at Caerleon. The lease was to run from 2 February 1786 to 2 February 1797, during the minority of her oldest son. Tanner paid the first instalment of the lease but refused to pay further instalments until he could finance them from profits. Jane Hanbury retaliated by denying that a formal lease had ever existed and tried to recover her property. A long case ensued in chancery that was effectively won by Tanner. During his period at Pontypool, Tanner erected two coke-fired blast furnaces on freehold land at Blaendare, partly to pressurize Jane Hanbury into dropping her case against him. In addition to iron, tin, and wire, Tanner manufactured cannon for a period of at least ten years. This chiefly took place at Tintern, as well as for a short period at Cyfarthfa; but most of his cannon failed Board of Ordnance quality standards.

By 1796 Tanner was experiencing serious financial difficulties. He was tricked by two local solicitors into appearing to commit an act of bankruptcy and was declared bankrupt in November 1798. He and his brother William were committed to the king's bench prison. Tanner's proven debts of £85,000 may well have actually exceeded £100,000, which would have made him one of the largest known bankrupts outside London up to that time. In December 1799, before Lord Kenyon and a special jury, Tanner was found not to have committed an act of bankruptcy but the bankruptcy commission was not rescinded. This was probably because many of his assets had already been disposed of and, since he had lost his manufacturing base, he would have been financially incapable of continuing his operations. In August 1801 Tanner left to join his friend Harford Jones (later Sir Harford Jones Brydges), the East India Company's resident at Baghdad. He was accompanied by his son John, who remained at Basrah. Tanner set out for India in March 1803 and proceeded to Bengal in May. No report of Tanner's death has been found in India and it is not known when he died. He seems to have returned, as it was reported at Bath in 1805 that he had been found wandering shoeless and starving.

J. A. H. EVANS

Sources J. A. H. Evans, 'David Tanner, 1743–c.1806', MA diss., U. Wales, Cardiff, 1993 · PRO, E144/38 · parish registers, St Mary's, Monmouth, Gwent RO, D/PA. 58 · Herefs. RO, Kentchurch MSS · J. Hoppit, *Risk and failure in English business, 1700–1800* (1987)
Archives Gwent RO, Evans and Evill MSS · Herefs. RO, Kentchurch MSS · NL Wales, Bedford MSS · NL Wales, Leonard Twiston Davies MSS

Tanner, Edmund (d. **1579**), Jesuit and Roman Catholic bishop of Cork and Cloyne, is said to have been born in the province of Dublin in 1526, although there is some uncertainty about this. On 14 June 1565 he entered the Jesuit noviciate at Sant' Andrea, Rome, and wrote in the book of the novices his age, thirty-nine years, indicating 1526 or 1527 as his year of birth, but the papal letter of his appointment as bishop of Cork and Cloyne, dated 5 November 1574, states that he was then fifty, indicating 1523 or 1524. The same letter implies that Tanner came from somewhere in the Dublin archdiocese, although it has also been claimed that he came either from a village in co. Cork or from Cork city. Given Tanner's connection with Viscount Baltinglass and the Eustaces, it is also possible that he was born in co. Kildare. Walter, the brother of the 1580 rebel James Eustace, third Viscount Baltinglass, was instructed in the faith by Tanner.

Nothing certain is known about Tanner's life before he, already a priest, joined the Jesuits in 1565, except that he had left Ireland by 1559 and had been in Spain before going to Italy. On 5 January 1566 he began attending the Collegium Romanum, and on 1 September 1567 he set out for Germany with an Irish confrère, Robert Rochford, and attended the university at Dillingen. In 1568–9 he was spiritual prefect at Würzburg, and in 1570 was sent to the Jesuit province of Lower Germany, despite his pleas to be sent to Ireland. For reasons of health, and with the blessing of his superiors, he had to leave the society in 1571.

Having been to Louvain, Tanner returned to Rome, where he wrote to Cardinal Giovanni Morone, protector of Ireland, on 26 October 1571, offering himself for the Irish mission. For his qualifications he referred Morone to some prominent British ecclesiastics in Rome and two eminent Jesuits. Through Morone he received a doctorate in theology, and a canonry in Milan from Charles Borromeo, who required him to teach moral theology, but Tanner sought an appointment in Ireland. On 5 November 1574 he was appointed bishop of Cork and Cloyne. Consecrated in Rome on 6 February 1575, he received on 10 April special permission to perform episcopal functions throughout Leinster and Munster in the absence of local bishops, and to settle the question of the revenues of the monastery of Baltinglass taken by the viscount and others. He set out for Ireland with a letter of commendation from the pope dated 12 May 1575. In Paris in June he

ordained a future Jesuit, Florence O'Moore. He then went to Madrid, and the nuncio there recommended him to the nuncio in Portugal, who got him a berth on a Venetian ship going to England.

On 21 June 1576 Tanner arrived at the port of Galway as a commissary of Pope Gregory XIII. Going south he was captured with a companion priest on 27 August and thrown into prison in Clonmel. While there he was visited by a bishop, probably Patrick Walsh of Waterford and Lismore, who entered into controversy with him but had to change his own mind. Tanner was set free, possibly through the influence of Lord Barrymore, who kept him in his house for a long time. For about three years the bishop tried to carry out his duties in secret, helped by the Jesuits Richard Rochford and Charles Lee (with whom he had journeyed to Ireland), and by Nicholas Eustace, who was his vicar; he was in Cork in 1577 and 1579. A zealous, early Counter-Reformation bishop in Ireland, Tanner may have been restricted in his ministry, even though John Howlin, writing c.1596, said he covered most of 'the kingdom'. He was forced to leave his diocese about April 1579. Worn out, he died at Cullahill in the parish of Durrow, diocese of Ossory, on 4 June 1579 in the house of the lord of Upper Ossory, Baron Fitzpatrick. Bruodin, strangely, placed him in a prison in Dublin for 18 months before his death. Some correspondence of his has survived, and lecture notes on theology (including the *Summa* of Thomas Aquinas) from c.1568–70.

IGNATIUS FENNESSY

Sources E. Hogan, ed., *Ibernia Ignatiana, seu, Ibernorum Societatis Jesu patrum monumenta* (1880), 16–26 · E. Hogan, *Distinguished Irishmen of the sixteenth century* (1894), 18–23, 122–3 · P. F. Moran, ed., *Spicilegium Ossoriense*, 1 (1874), 83–4 · E. Bolster, *A history of the diocese of Cork*, 2: *From the Reformation to the penal era* (1982), 73–9 · T. M. McCoog, *The Society of Jesus in Ireland, Scotland, and England, 1541–1588* (1996) · P. Ó Fionnagáin, *The Jesuit missions to Ireland in the sixteenth century* (privately printed, Dublin, [n.d., c.1975]) · W. P. Burke, *History of Clonmel* (1907), 37 · J. Linchaeo [J. Lynch], *De praesulibus Hiberniae*, ed. J. F. O'Doherty, IMC, 2 (1944), 145 · A. Bruodinus, *Propugnaculum Catholicae veritatis* (Prague, 1669), 432–3 · C. McNeill, 'Tanner, Edmund', *The Catholic encyclopedia*, ed. C. G. Herbermann and others, 14 (1912) · CSP Rome, 1558–71, 467–8; 1572–8, 204, 236 · A. de Backer and others, *Bibliothèque de la Compagnie de Jésus*, new edn, 7, ed. C. Sommervogel (Brussels, 1896), col. 1855 · P. B. Gams, *Series episcoporum ecclesiae Catholicae*, 1 (1873), 214 · W. Carrigan, *The history and antiquities of the diocese of Ossory*, 2 (1905), 241 · MacErlean transcripts, Irish Jesuit Archives, Dublin, MACE/MTYR/art 79
Archives Archivio Vaticano, Vatican City, Minuti dei Brevi, CC, 17947; CCXCIX, 17930 · Archivio Vaticano, Vatican City, Nunziatura di Portogallo, ii, 161; iii, fol. 41 · Archivio Vaticano, Vatican City, Sec. Brevium, xxxv, fols. 210r–213v, 258v; xxxvi, fol. 496

Tanner, Dame Emmeline Mary (1876–1955), headmistress and educational reformer, was born on 28 December 1876 at 1 Locksbrook Place, Weston, Bath, the eldest of the seven children of Samuel Thomas Tanner JP (1849–1929), coal merchant, and his wife, Jeanetta Jane, daughter of George Fry of Lynton and his second wife. She was born into a lower-middle-class family, and her parents valued education as a necessary means to the employment of their children. Financial pressures, however, meant that Emmeline's schooling was very limited: from a small private establishment she went on, at the age of thirteen, to

Dame Emmeline Mary Tanner (1876–1955), by Lafayette, 1931

become a student teacher, then taught in private schools in Birmingham and Southampton before taking up an appointment in 1897 at the Ladies' College, Halifax, where she gained a valuable social education and training. From an early age she had had an ambition to succeed, and she continued her studies while working, taking the examinations of the College of Preceptors when thirteen and the Cambridge senior locals at fifteen. Unable to attend university as an internal student, she studied for an external degree of the University of London, graduating with first-class honours in history in 1904. Despite these inauspicious beginnings, she was appointed as history mistress to Sherborne School for Girls from the beginning of 1905. While there she wrote her only book (1908), a widely used text on the Renaissance and the Reformation.

Emmeline Tanner's five years at Sherborne formed the introduction to what was to become a remarkable career. In 1910 she became the first headmistress of the new Nuneaton high school. There she was fortunate to have the encouragement and practical assistance of the county director of education, Bolton King, whose advice she valued throughout her life. She stayed there for ten years before moving to Bedford high school, a school desperately needing the change and reform that she was able to bring. In 1924 she reluctantly moved to Roedean, having been determinedly headhunted by Penelope Lawrence. She proved an able successor to the Lawrence sisters, and remained at Roedean for the rest of her teaching career.

Tall, erect, dignified, neatly and simply dressed, with blue eyes behind pince-nez, Emmeline Tanner had a compelling physical presence. Magnanimous and caring, with a sense of humour and fun, she was said to be always smiling. She had a lasting memory for names, and a phenomenal grasp of detail, which was the root of her outstanding administrative ability. She put her stamp on all her schools, and earned a lifelong love and respect from both pupils and staff. By the 1920s her many gifts increasingly meant that she was holding office in regional and national organizations. She served on the education committees at Nuneaton, Bedford, and Brighton. A member for nearly thirty years of the executive committee of the Association of Headmistresses, she became first chair of committee (1923–5) and later president (1937–9), proving herself an

able negotiator and policymaker; she then became chair of the Joint Committee of Four Secondary Associations (1940–42). In 1920 she was invited to become one of four women members of the consultative committee of the Board of Education, and in 1924 was reappointed for another six years. She was a signatory to several reports, notably the Hadow report of 1926. By the 1930s she was recognized as the leading representative and spokeswoman for girls' education, and was regularly called upon regarding educational matters. A member of the Board of Education (Fleming) committee on public schools from 1942 to 1944, she helped draft new educational policy and played an important role in the discussions leading up to the 1944 Education Act. Unlike many of her fellow headmistresses in this period, Emmeline had not only national interests but was actively involved in international causes. A dedicated supporter of the League of Nations, she served on many committees with international purposes, and listed travel as her sole recreation in Who's Who. She was not afraid to become involved in politics—as an independent Liberal—nor to speak on political platforms. Though brought up as a member of the Swedenborgians, she became a member of the Church of England in 1913.

One major plank of Emmeline Tanner's educational philosophy, mirroring her own experience, was that no one should be held back from education for want of money, and she strove to make this part of her practice and policy making. Her hope was to enable girls to develop their differing gifts through a varied curriculum which allowed for flexibility. Her philosophy, however, extended beyond classroom and curriculum to the individual child's relationship with the whole world outside: girls should learn to be members of a community and gain a sense of the corporate life, enabling them better to play their part in the world outside school. She believed in training her girls for useful work in the world, in the professions and other careers, including motherhood, and she encouraged them to become responsible citizens, using their votes in both local and national elections.

Emmeline Tanner was a woman of courage, wisdom, and integrity, a great headmistress, an outstanding teacher and administrator, and an influential committee member. At a normal retirement age she was demonstrating her planning genius in the move of Roedean to Keswick at the beginning of the Second World War. She was not allowed to retire until 1947, when she was seventy-two. In that year she was created DBE for services to education and given an honorary MA from the University of London. Unwilling to face settling down, she set off for South Africa and India; on her return, in 1950 and 1952, she took on acting headships at Southwold and Harrogate respectively. After a long journey to southern Africa she moved at last into her retirement home in December 1954. Three weeks later she had a fall, which led to her death. She died on 7 January 1955 in Savernake Hospital, Marlborough, and was cremated at Oxford on 13 January. A memorial service at St Martin-in-the-Fields, London, on 24 January was attended by a large congregation.

SYLVIA HARROP

Sources S. Major, *Doors of possibility: the life of Dame Emmeline Tanner, 1876–1955* (1995) · *The Roedean School Magazine* (Nov 1947) · K. M. Westaway, ed., *Seventy-five years: the story of Bedford high school, 1882–1957* (1957) · D. E. de Zouche, *Roedean School, 1885–1955* (privately printed, Brighton, 1955) · *A history of Roedean School, 1885–1985* (privately printed, 1985) · *The Times* (8 Jan 1955) · *The Times* (14 Jan 1955) · *The Times* (24 Jan 1955) · *The women's who's who, 1934–5: an annual record of the careers and activities of the leading women of the day* (1934) · *WWW* · b. cert. · d. cert. · *CGPLA Eng. & Wales* (1955)
Archives priv. coll.
Likenesses Lafayette, photograph, 1931, NPG [*see illus.*] · T. C. Dugdale, oils, 1947, Roedean School, Brighton; repro. in De Zouche, *Roedean School*, 119 · photographs, repro. in Major, *Doors of possibility* · portraits, repro. in *A history of Roedean School*, 23, 39, 40
Wealth at death £7374 1s. 3d.: probate, 4 March 1955, *CGPLA Eng. & Wales*

Tanner, Frederick Arthur [Robin] (1904–1988), etcher and educationist, was born on 17 April 1904 at 5 Ryde Road, Knowle, Bristol, the third son of six children of Sydney Albert Tanner, journeyman carpenter, and Emily Annie, formerly Baker, a housemaid from Kington Langley, Wiltshire. On leaving Chippenham grammar school (1915–21) Robin Tanner, as he was known, became a student primary school teacher at Ivy Lane School, Chippenham, and then moved to London to study teaching at Goldsmiths' College (1922–4). Subsequently he taught at Blackheath Road Boys' School, Greenwich, London, attending evening classes in life drawing and etching at Goldsmiths' School of Art under Clive Gardiner and Stanley Anderson.

Inspired by exhibitions of work by F. L. Griggs and Samuel Palmer, Tanner produced his first etching, *A Tithe Barn*, in 1926, followed by *Alington in Wiltshire* (1927). Devoting himself to etching full time, he produced prints firmly rooted in the Wiltshire countryside, including *Martin's Hovel* (1928) and *Christmas* (1929). That year he returned to teach at Ivy Lane School as the overseas market for English prints began to fail. However, despite being appointed an inspector of schools in 1935, necessitating a move to Leeds (1935–7), this decade saw some of his most enduring images, including *Harvest Festival* (1930), *Autumn* (1933), and *Wren and Primroses* (1935). In 1937 he was made an inspector of schools for Gloucestershire and subsequently for Oxfordshire (1956–64). Owing to these commitments, *June* (1946) was the last print he was to do until he resumed etching in retirement and produced *Meadow Stile* (1970), the first of an abundant second flowering.

Elected an associate of the Royal Society of Painter-Etchers and Engravers in 1936, Tanner was made a senior fellow in 1973. He was also elected a member of the Royal West of England Academy in 1952. Of his work he wrote: 'My etched world is also an ideal world—a world of pastoral beauty that could be ours if we did but desire it passionately enough' (Tanner, *Etcher's Craft*, 18).

On 4 April 1931 Tanner married his childhood sweetheart Heather Muriel Spackman (1903–1993), a teacher, at Corsham church, Wiltshire. She was the second of three daughters of Herbert Spackman and Daisy Goold who owned grocery and drapery stores in Corsham. The Tanners enjoyed a long and happy marriage living in Old Chapel Field, the characterful home they built and made together in Kington Langley, Wiltshire. Designed in the style of Voysey, the house was largely furnished with pieces by many of the best contemporary craftspeople and surrounded by a burgeoning garden. The couple were childless but in 1938 they gave asylum to Dietrich Anselm Hanff (1920–1992), a Jewish boy fleeing Nazi Germany; he lived with them for the rest of his life.

Robin and Heather shared many interests and were always generous hosts to their numerous friends. Both were committed Quakers and pacifists and staunch supporters of the Campaign for Nuclear Disarmament. Their love and understanding of the English countryside, its customs and traditions, is reflected in their joint publications such as *Wiltshire Village* (1939), *A Country Alphabet* (1984), and *A Country Book of Days* (1986). *Woodland Plants* (1981) reveals both the depth of their botanical knowledge and their strong preoccupation with ecology and conservation. Another joint concern was to establish the Crafts Study Centre in 1970, and, together with friends and colleagues, they succeeded in creating a unique collection and archive of leading British craftspeople of the twentieth century. It first opened to the public within the Holburne of Menstrie Museum, Bath, in 1977 and subsequently moved to the Surrey Institute of Art and Design, University College, Farnham, in 2000. In 1987 Robin Tanner's autobiography was published. The following year he died at Old Chapel Field, on 19 May 1988, and was cremated five days later at Haycombe cemetery and crematorium, Bath. Sets of his etchings may be seen at the Ashmolean Museum, Oxford, and the City of Bristol Museum and Art Gallery.

BARLEY ROSCOE

Sources *Robin Tanner: the etchings*, Garton & Co. (1988) · *Double harness: an autobiography by Robin Tanner, teacher and etcher* (1987) · *From Old Chapel Field: selected letters of Robin Tanner*, ed. T. Fenn (1991) · R. Tanner, *The etcher's craft* (1980) · *Robin Tanner, RE, RWA: paintings, drawings and etchings* (1980) [exhibition catalogue, City of Bristol Museum and Art Gallery, 1980] · *After many a summer … an exhibition of English pastoral etchings* (1974) [exhibition catalogue, Penn Print Room] · *The more angels shall I paint: a selection from the sketchbooks, writings and common place books of Robin Tanner* (Old Stile Press, 1991) · *Robin Tanner and the Old Stile Press: being printed examples of twenty original patterned paper designs*, Old Stile Press (1994) · *What I believe: lectures and other writings by Robin Tanner*, Crafts Study Centre (1989) · *Tributes to Robin Tanner, 1904–1988*, Crafts Study Centre (1990) · *The Guardian* (30 June 1993) · b. cert. · m. cert. · d. cert. · private information (2004) [Heather Tanner]
Archives U. Lond., Institute of Education, corresp. and papers · University College, Farnham, MSS, papers, prints, and collection · University of Bristol Library, letters and MS of autobiography |SOUND University College, Farnham, Crafts Study Centre, Surrey Institute of Art and Design
Likenesses photographs, 1920–80, Crafts Study Centre, Surrey Institute of Art and Design, University College, Farnham · P. Drury, drawing, 1924?–1928, AM Oxf. · D. Thorpe, photographs, 1981, repro. in *The Guardian*

Tanner, Frederick John Shirley [Jack] (1889–1965), trade unionist, was born at Kitchenham Place, Whitstable, Kent, on 28 April 1889, the son of John Silvanus Tanner, described as 'of independent means', and his wife, Regina Florence de la Porte. Jack, as he was always known, was the second of three brothers. The family moved to London, where his father was sports organizer at Alexandra

Palace. His mother was the daughter of a musician. He attended board schools in Hampstead and Camberwell, and was apprenticed at fourteen as a fitter and turner in a Southwark engineering works.

With his elder brother, Tanner joined the Marxist Social Democratic Federation. They then became friends with a Hammersmith tailor who had known William Morris and passed on his anarcho-socialism to them. Tanner joined the Amalgamated Society of Engineers in 1912, which merged with other unions to become the Amalgamated Engineering Union (AEU) in 1920. He recalled in an AEU election address in 1930: 'From the beginning of my membership I have been identified with the more advanced sections of the industrial movement through its various phases of development' (Tanner).

Like Tom Mann, Tanner was drawn to syndicalism while retaining strong socialist beliefs. He served on the Industrial Syndicalist Education League executive, and chaired the first International Syndicalist Congress held in London in 1913. He also helped to establish the National Federation of Women Workers, early evidence of his abiding feminism.

In 1913 Tanner walked from Ostend, through France, to Barcelona in company of a young Scottish journalist. Upon his return to England he married in 1914, and he and his wife, Grace Elizabeth, set up home in Hammersmith near the river. He returned to France in 1915 and worked in engineering. He joined the French union, the CGT, and worked with Alfred Rosmer's syndicalist group within it.

Back in London in 1917, Tanner was caught up in industrial unrest in west London. At the beginning of 1918, he and other militants formed a shop stewards' organization. Tanner edited its paper, the *West London Metal Workers' Record*. The organization became the West London Engineering Workers' Committee; Tanner became its chairman and edited its new organ, *Solidarity*, until 1921. As a leading 'revolutionary' shop steward, he visited Russia in 1920 to attend the Second Congress of the Communist International. Lenin questioned him with keen interest about the British shop stewards' movement. On his return from Russia, Tanner, who obtained work at the *Evening Standard*, where he organized the men who maintained the presses, chaired the founding conference of the British Communist Party in January 1921. He joined the Communist Party, but left after only eight months without, however, breaking with either his revolutionary convictions or his communist colleagues. This initial commitment to the party and subsequent swift exit on friendly terms was not unique. A. J. Cook followed the same course. Both men played leading roles in the engineering and mining 'rank-and-file' movements in the mid-1920s, remaining on intimate terms with leading communist union activists, notably Harry Pollitt and Arthur Horner.

Cook had serious political differences with the communists from late 1928 over their new oppositional line towards the Labour Party and support for breakaway unions. Tanner evidently had no reason to break with the communist militants in the AEU, notably because they refused to follow the Comintern's line of splitting 'reformist' unions. Indeed, it was the powerful militant network inside the AEU in north London which ensured Tanner's election in 1930 as full-time AEU divisional organizer. Tanner and his communist comrades operated a policy of involving rank-and-file members in union business at every opportunity. Their syndicalist beliefs were doubtless reinforced by the need to secure members' support in the frequent elections which ambitious AEU full-time officials had to fight. Tanner was an energetic official and progressed up the AEU hierarchy, loyally assisted by communist networks. He was elected executive councillor in 1935, and president of the AEU in 1939. Militants viewed his success as a decisive victory for rank-and-file principles.

Tanner's home was destroyed in the 1940 blitz, and the family moved to East Dulwich. When his only child, a daughter, died in 1942 of gastric jaundice, both he and his wife felt the loss deeply.

During the war Tanner supported shop-floor organization and joint production committees in order to maximize war production. In 1940 he pressurized the government to appoint a committee on 'skilled men in the services', which led directly to the formation of the regiment of electrical and mechanical engineers. In the union he manoeuvred energetically to persuade craftsmen to admit women into the AEU. Tanner joined the TUC general council in 1943 and tirelessly promoted engineering planning, earning the nickname Tanner the Planner. Invariably good-humoured and a highly entertaining speaker, he was well liked throughout the movement, and widely known as Handsome Jack.

Tanner's standing was high in 1945. He was tipped as a possible ambassador to Washington, though foreign secretary Bevin adopted a policy of making traditional appointments from the diplomatic service. There was a general expectation that Tanner would play a leading role on the TUC general council. However, he failed to fulfil the promise of his wartime years. The onset of the cold war affected him profoundly. After the communist coup in Czechoslovakia in the summer of 1948, he publicly distanced himself from his communist allies in the union and from his own earlier left-wing views. However, despite the hopes of right-wing union leaders, he never became either an enthusiastic or effective social democrat. Unlike Will Lawther, another notable left-wing 'fellow traveller' who moved rightwards in the cold war, Tanner refrained from strident denunciations of his former political associates on the left, and remained on good personal terms with them.

Nevertheless, the communist caucus in the AEU did not grant him any political quarter. AEU rules provided for regular re-election, and Tanner had won three presidential election contests (the third held in January 1948) decisively on the first ballot, with strong communist support. In his final contest in 1951 he faced Claude Berridge, a leading London communist. Berridge waged a vigorous, bitter campaign, gaining sufficient votes to force a second ballot before Tanner won by a comparatively narrow margin.

Tanner served as TUC president in 1954, the year of his retirement from the AEU presidency. He and his wife then lived quietly on their smallholding in Heathfield, Sussex. In 1956 he lent his name and support to the formation of Industrial and Research Information Services, an anti-communist organization aimed at influencing union elections, notably in the AEU. Tanner's motive was his belief that trade unions must be revitalized by genuine shopfloor democracy. He died at Roundels Nursing Home, near Heathfield, on 3 March 1965.   NINA FISHMAN

Sources The Times (4 March 1965) · Evening Standard (5 May 1952) · W. Carron, AEU Journal (April 1965) · Daily Express (4 March 1965) · b. cert. · d. cert. · The Labour who's who (1927) · H. A. Clegg, A. Fox, and A. F. Thompson, A history of British trade unions since 1889, 3 (1994) · J. Tanner, AEU Annual Report (1930) [election address for organizing divisional delegate, interleaved into report] · E. Frow and R. Frow, Engineering struggles (1982), 456 · J. B. Jefferys, The story of the engineers, 1800–1945 [1946], 233, 249, 251, 253, 257, 263–4 · R. Croucher, Engineers at war, 1939–1945 (1982), 65, 105, 225 · N. Fishman, 'Tanner, Frederick John Shirley', DLB · TUC biography, London Metropolitan University, Trade Union Congress collection · Trade Union Congress reports and congress proceedings, 1926 · Trade Union Congress reports and congress proceedings, 1927 · AEU election addresses (1935, 1939, 1951) [interleaved with AEU Annual Reports] · private information (2004) [John Boyd]

Archives Nuffield Oxf., papers
Likenesses D. Low, pencil caricature, NPG
Wealth at death £7667: probate, 4 June 1965, CGPLA Eng. & Wales

Tanner, Sir Henry (1849–1935), architect, was born in St Pancras, London, in 1849 and baptized there on 14 December 1849 the son of Robert Tanner (fl. c.1820–1853), master carpenter, and his wife, Elizabeth Selby (b. c.1820, d. after 1891). He attended the Royal Academy Schools, and obtained practical experience on building sites in Wiltshire and Surrey before entering the architectural office of Anthony Salvin. He also attended the Architectural Association's classes, winning a sessional prize for the best series of papers on construction. In March 1871 he was appointed by competitive examination as clerk in the country district B (post and telegraph services) of HM office of works on a salary of £100 p.a. 'Diligent, intelligent and thoroughly conversant with the duties of his profession' (PRO, WORK 22/9/7, fol. 11), he was promoted first assistant in April 1873 at £210 p.a. He was twice married: in 1872 to Lucy (1848–1889), daughter of William Gardner, with whom he had five sons and three daughters; and in 1894 to Emily Sophia, daughter of Josiah Leal.

In 1877 Tanner moved across to the London district of the office of works under John Taylor. The department's ever growing workload brought his promotion in 1882 to surveyor, second class, stationed at Leeds. In August 1884 he returned to London as first-class surveyor on an increased salary of £800 p.a., with general responsibility for the post and telegraph services. Tanner reorganized his sector on a more systematic basis, with more regular and local supervision, achieving large reductions in maintenance costs. Applying for fellowship of the RIBA in 1891, Tanner stated that he had designed the York probate registry and post offices at York (1885; his first major postal building), Bradford, Halifax, Liverpool, Barrow in Furness, Leicester, Birmingham, and many other towns, as well as major Post Office buildings in London—which included the savings bank in Carter Lane (1890–94). His designs were often in a classical style, frequently of French Renaissance derivation, but sometimes in a formal Tudor or Jacobean. In 1892 he was engaged on designs for new post offices at Liverpool, Nottingham, and Cardiff. There was also much extending and remodelling of existing buildings. On the completion of the 'commodious and imposing' General Post Office (north), St Martin's-le-Grand, London (cost £220,000), the postmaster-general praised its design and arrangement as 'admirably adapted to the requirements of the Public Service' (PRO, WORK 22/9/7, fol. 44, 14 Nov 1895).

When Sir John Taylor retired in 1898, Tanner succeeded as principal surveyor of the office of works (£1200 p.a.), responsible for final approval of all major designs before they were submitted to the minister. He undertook the vast Post Office Savings Bank at Hammersmith (1899–1903) and the massive Jacobean Land Registry (1900–06) in Lincoln's Inn Fields. For his realization that 'a building should be designed for the work for which it is intended' he was regarded as 'a first-rate planner' (RIBA Journal, 3rd ser., 18, 1910–11, 170). Taylor remained however as consultant architect—not altogether to Tanner's delight—for the great wave of building new public offices, work initially allotted to private architects by competition. But Brydon, architect of the Great George Street offices (now the Treasury), died in 1901, his plans just completed: Tanner executed them, effecting drastic economies; his primary contribution was structural, employing steel framing, but he made some changes in the external design; he also executed the St James's Park extension in 1908–15, introducing further modern construction methods. At the same time he designed and executed the west extension (1908–12) of the law courts in the Strand, a work closely in sympathy with G. E. Street's adjoining main block. By 1910 the department's work had so increased that Tanner was almost breaking down under the burden; additional staff enabled him to concentrate on supervising design.

Tanner's interest in construction made him quick to appreciate the merits of reinforced-concrete framing. In 1907 he chaired a major committee on reinforced concrete, declaring that 'reinforced concrete would have to be used' (RIBA Journal, 3rd ser., 12, 1904–5, 503). As the office of works was free of the building controls hindering use of the new technique, he seized on its economies of space and money for his crowning achievement, the King Edward Building of the General Post Office (1907–10; £323,000), 'the largest Post Office in the world ... [and] the largest building ... carried out in ferro-concrete' (ibid., 172). Employing Hennebique's patented system which provided shear reinforcement in concrete beams, thereby establishing full reinforced-concrete framing for buildings, he saved £60,000 compared with a steel-frame construction. Tanner's lead was 'of great value' (The Builder, 1160), though the short street façades were of stone, and the constructional framework was expressed only in the loading bay. Tanner served as president of the Concrete Institute, and was a fellow of the Institution of

Structural Engineers that developed from it; he was also sometime chairman of the Royal Sanitary Institute.

Tanner had been elected an associate of the RIBA in 1876 and a fellow in 1891. He won the RIBA's Tate prize for a classical architectural design in 1878, and throughout his career stressed his design role; in 1901 his title was changed from 'principal surveyor' to 'principal architect and surveyor' as more accurate terminology. But although he received gratuities at the rate of about three-quarters of one per cent on major new works, rewards were much greater in private practice. He was knighted in 1904. After retiring from the office of works at the end of 1913 (though he continued to supervise the Great George Street offices), this indefatigable man joined his son's architectural firm, which he attended daily until his death.

Frank-looking, with upturned nose, Tanner wore a full but trimmed beard and moustache; he was known for his extraordinary memory. He died on the doorstep of his house, 31 Rosslyn Hill, Hampstead, London, 'when returning home from business' on 2 September 1935 (*The Times*, 4 Sept 1935), and was buried three days later at Elmers End cemetery, Beckenham, Kent, near his home of the 1880s and 1890s. He left an estate valued at under £14,000. He was survived by his widow and his eldest son, Henry (1876–1947). Assisted by his brothers Hugh and Edwin, and, as mentioned above, by his father from 1914, the younger Henry Tanner maintained an important commercial architectural practice, including large blocks in Regent Street (Sir Henry had served on the Plymouth committee of 1913 to determine their general character), hotels for John Lyons & Co., Park Lane Hotel (1928; attributed to Sir Henry), and National House in Moorgate.

M. H. PORT

Sources PRO, WORK 22/9/7 and 22/9/6 • M. H. Port, *Imperial London: civil government building in London, 1850–1915* (1995) • *IGI* • biographical file, RIBA BAL • *RIBA Journal*, 42 (1934–5), 934–5 • *RIBA Journal*, 12 (1904–5), 502–3, 513–41 • H. Tanner, 'The new General Post Office, London', *RIBA Journal*, 18 (1910–11), 149–77 • *WWW* • *The Builder*, 149 (1935), 394 • census returns, 1851, PRO, HO 107/1493, fol. 225; 1881, RG 11/209, fols. 58–63, 1891, RG 12/627, fol. 97 • London Post Office directories • *Debrett's Peerage* • *CGPLA Eng. & Wales* (1935) • *The Times* (4 Sept 1935) • *The Times* (6 Sept 1935)
Archives PRO, minutes and drawings, Work 30
Likenesses A. Lewis, photograph, repro. in *Building News* (16 May 1890) • sketch, repro. in *Architects' Journal* (12 Jan 1922)
Wealth at death £13,640 8s. 10d.: probate, 18 Nov 1935, *CGPLA Eng. & Wales*

Tanner, John Sigismund (*c.*1704–1775), engraver and medallist, was born in Saxe-Gotha. Early in his life he was an engraver of snuff-boxes and gun locks. He moved to England in 1728 and in January 1729 was appointed probationer engraver by John Conduitt, master of the Royal Mint from 1727 to 1737. Tanner succeeded Johann Croker as chief engraver in 1741.

Tanner engraved the dies for the gold coins from 1739, the silver from 1743, and the copper from 1740. He also engraved dies for a number of medals, including one in commemoration of Conduitt (1737). His most spectacular portrait work was arguably on the reverse die of the royal family medal of 1732, which depicted the seven children of George II. The obverse, showing the busts of George II and Caroline of Ansbach face to face, was by Croker. This medal was issued in reply to one produced in 1731 by Ottone Hamerani, the papal engraver, which portrayed the two sons of the *de jure* James III, Prince Charles and Prince Henry, on the occasion of the eleventh birthday of Prince Charles. The message conveyed by the reply on behalf of George II was that he was the *de facto* king, he had more children, and he could afford a bigger medal.

In addition to these activities, and at the request of Richard Arundell, master of the mint from 1737 to 1744, Tanner engraved dies to provide replicas of the coins of Oliver Cromwell by Thomas Simon of 1658, using some of the original punches. The rarity of the sixpence by Simon and the availability of Tanner's restrikes led to the sixpence being known in common parlance as a 'tanner'. Tanner's name therefore lived on until the sixpence was demonetized soon after decimal coinage was introduced in 1971.

Tanner's sight failed about 1760, and Richard Yeo took over his duties. He was retired on full pay in 1768 and died in David Street, London, on 14 March 1775. Tanner's signature was 'TANNER', 'TANNER.LONDONI', or 'T'. His puncheons and dies for medals were auctioned with Croker's by Gerard in Soho, London, on 18 June 1783.

W. W. WROTH, *rev.* MICHAEL SHARP

Sources C. E. Challis, ed., *A new history of the royal mint* (1992) • L. Forrer, *Biographical dictionary of medallists*, 8 vols. (1904–30) • E. Hawkins, *Medallic illustrations of the history of Great Britain and Ireland to the death of George II*, ed. A. W. Franks and H. A. Grueber, 2 vols. (1885) • N. Woolf, *The medallic record of the Jacobite movement* (1988)

Tanner, Joseph Robson (1860–1931), historian, was born at Frome, Somerset, on 28 July 1860, the eldest of the three sons and one daughter of Joseph Tanner, printer, and his wife, Fanny Robson. His father was a JP and head of the firm of Butler and Tanner, of Frome. Tanner was educated at Mill Hill School, London, and in 1879 entered St John's College, Cambridge, where he spent his career. He became a scholar of the college in 1881, took a first class in the historical tripos in 1882, and was president of the union in the following year. He was successively lecturer at St John's (1883–1921), fellow (1886–1931), tutor (1900–12), and tutorial fellow (1900–21); he was also the Indian Civil Service teacher of Indian history from 1885 to 1893. On 4 April 1888 he married Charlotte Maria, second daughter of George James Larkman, JP, of Belton, Suffolk. They had no children.

Tanner had a natural aptitude for administration, and his skills were much in demand by the university—as a member of the council of the senate, as chairman of the special board for history and archaeology, and as a syndic of the university press. For the press he edited the *Historical Register of the University of Cambridge* (1917) and, for some years, the *University Calendar* and the *Student's Handbook of the University*. He was also treasurer of the union (1902–15). In the teaching and administration of the history school he played a considerable part at a time when it was rising to be one of the largest undergraduate courses of study in Cambridge. As a chairman he was effective, conciliatory, and constructive. The best energy of his life was given to his college and his pupils, who remembered him for his sympathy, humour, and inspiration. His lectures, always read, were enlivened with happy quotations, and for generations attracted large classes. It was Tanner who devised the course of reading about the workings of the constitution pursued by the future King George V in 1894. He retired from teaching and administrative work at the end of the First World War, and in 1921 moved with his wife to Aldeburgh in Suffolk, where he had leisure for historical work. For recreation he played golf; he was a happy raconteur and was considered good company. In 1926 and 1927 he was pleased to be recalled to Cambridge to act as deputy for J. B. Bury, the regius professor of modern history, remarking that 'It is like being taken down off the shelf and dusted'.

As a historian Tanner's interests lay primarily in seventeenth-century English naval history, and Tudor and Stuart constitutional history. In 1896 he edited *Two Discourses of the Navy*, by John Hollond, for the Navy Records Society, and in 1903 he brought out the first volume of his *Descriptive catalogue of the naval manuscripts in the Pepysian Library at Magdalene College, Cambridge*, which eventually ran to four volumes and was completed in 1923. He delivered the Lees Knowles lectures at Trinity College in 1919, which were published in 1920 as *Samuel Pepys and the Royal Navy*. His interest in Pepys was unabated, and he went on to publish *Mr Pepys: an Introduction to the Diary together with a Sketch of his Later Life* (1925) and to edit *Samuel Pepys's Naval Minutes* (for the Navy Records Society, 1926), the *Private Correspondence of Samuel Pepys, 1679–1703* (2 vols., 1926), and *Further Correspondence of Samuel Pepys, 1662–1679* (1929), which remain the standard editions.

Tanner lectured principally on constitutional history and he published three books in the field: *Tudor Constitutional Documents* (1922), *English Constitutional Conflicts of the Seventeenth Century* (1928), and *Constitutional Documents of the Reign of James I* (1930). The latter volumes were largely superseded by J. P. Kenyon's *The Stuart Constitution* (1966) but Tanner's volume of Tudor documents, which was an advance on G. W. Prothero's *Select Statutes and other Constitutional Documents* (1894) for the reigns of Elizabeth and James, continues to be used. Cambridge University Press and G. R. Elton intended *The Tudor Constitution* (1960) to replace Tanner's volume, correcting mistranscriptions and embracing a wider range of themes, but Tanner remains the published source for several documents not included by Elton.

In 1918 Tanner became one of the editors of the *Cambridge Medieval History*, with two of his former pupils, C. W. Previté-Orton and Zachary Nugent Brooke. The project had run aground during the war, under the editorship of J. P. Whitney, and the appointment of Tanner, who was no medievalist, was clearly in tribute to his administrative expertise. He played a large part in the thankless editorial tasks of chivvying recalcitrant authors and smoothing the relationship between his co-editors (to whom the actual editing of the texts fell). The decision, taken in 1916, to jettison all 'enemy aliens' from the list of authors for the

Medieval History damaged the enterprise intellectually; the eight volumes were finally completed in 1936.

Tanner died at his home—Woodside, Aldeburgh, Suffolk—on 16 January 1931, and was survived by his wife. He was buried in Cambridge. He was a generous benefactor to St John's College.   E. A. BENIANS, *rev.* K. D. REYNOLDS

Sources *The Eagle*, 56 (1931), 184–7 [magazine of St John Cam.] · *The Times* (17 Jan 1931) · *Cambridge Review* (30 Jan 1931) · personal knowledge (1949) · *WWW* · Venn, *Alum. Cant.* · P. A. Lineham, 'The making of the *Cambridge Medieval History*', *Speculum*, 57/3 (1982), 463–94 · G. R. Elton, *The Tudor constitution* (1960), preface · P. Smith Fussner, *Tudor history and the historians* (1970)
Archives St John Cam., papers | CUL, letters to Lord Acton · King's AC Cam., letters to Oscar Browning
Likenesses Mrs L. E. Shore, portrait, priv. coll.
Wealth at death £14,125 18s. 7d.: probate, 8 April 1931, *CGPLA Eng. & Wales*

Tanner [*née* Priestman], **Margaret** (1817–1905), social reformer, was born on 25 October 1817 at Summerhill, Newcastle upon Tyne, the second of the nine children of Jonathan Priestman (1787–1863), a tanner, and Rachel Priestman, *née* Bragg (1791–1854). Two of the children died in infancy and a third in her late teens. Both her parents were Quakers, and their meeting had recorded its unity with their vocal ministry. They were active in the anti-slavery movement and early became total abstainers.

The Reform Bill agitation was among the family's early political interests, and friendship with John Bright, who in 1839 married Margaret's elder sister, Elizabeth (1815–1841), brought them into a more vigorous and reforming circle, and in particular into the anti-corn law struggle. Quakers of that time were chary of the excitement of political involvement and Rachel Priestman's letters to her son-in-law expressed some degree of unease.

Margaret Priestman married on 1 July 1846 Daniel Wheeler (1812–1848), a Bristol cotton spinner, son of Daniel *Wheeler (1771–1840), the agriculturist, who with his family had spent many years in Russia. She continued to live at Montpelier, Bristol, until 1855, when she moved to Sidcot, Winscombe, Somerset, on her marriage to Arthur Tanner (1817–1869) on 28 March of that year. There were no children from either marriage.

After their father's death in 1863 Margaret's younger sisters Anna Maria (1828–1914) and Mary (1830–1914) moved to Clifton, Bristol, and in 1866 her niece Helen Priestman Bright (1840–1927) married William Stephens Clark (1839–1925) of the shoe manufacturing firm C. and J. Clark of Street. There thus developed a Somerset-based family conclave, united in reforming interests.

With her sisters Margaret Tanner was actively and devotedly involved in the campaign of Josephine Butler for the repeal of the Contagious Diseases Acts: indeed, Josephine Butler described the three sisters as her 'body guard, a *corps délite* on whose prompt aid, singleness of purpose, prudence and unwearying industry I could … rely upon at all times' (Walkowitz, 121–2). Margaret Tanner was treasurer of the Ladies' National Association from its foundation in 1869 until her death. William and Helen Bright Clark were active in the campaign and also supported their aunts' concern for the higher education of women and for women's suffrage. Margaret Tanner was also a temperance advocate, an active Liberal, and concerned for peace issues.

Conversation at Margaret's home, Oakridge, Sidcot (where John Bright was a visitor), ranged widely and she had the ability to draw out others, including shy scholars at the nearby Quaker school. Though conversation was kept at a high level, the atmosphere was not always serious and the house could resound to the singing of Gilbert and Sullivan or to imaginative party games.

Quakers in Britain, though always giving to women an equal share with men of the vocal ministry in meetings for worship, had not extended the like equality in administration—meetings for church affairs being separately conducted, with those of women Friends subordinate to those of the men. During the later nineteenth century joint sittings increased, and it was Margaret Tanner in the yearly meeting of 1896 who led (with success) the plea for complete equality in joint business meetings. Margaret died at the home of her sisters, 37 Durdham Park, Bristol, on 17 March 1905; her body was interred in Sidcot Friends' burial-ground.   EDWARD H. MILLIGAN

Sources *The Friend*, new ser., 45 (1905), 199–200 · *Annual Monitor* (1906), 138–42 · *The Friend*, new ser., 54 (1914), 817 · J. R. Walkowitz, *Prostitution and Victorian society: women, class and the state* (1980) · P. McHugh, *Prostitution and Victorian social reform* (1980) · 'Dictionary of Quaker biography', RS Friends, Lond. [card index] · Durham quarterly meeting births digest, RS Friends, Lond.

Likenesses group photograph, 1897 (with her sisters), repro. in P. Lovell, *Quaker inheritance* (1970), facing p. 32

Wealth at death £7337 8s. 6d.: resworn probate, 7 Aug 1905, *CGPLA Eng. & Wales*

Tanner, Paul Antony [Tony] (**1935–1998**), university teacher and literary scholar, was born on 18 March 1935 at East Sheen, Richmond, Surrey, the younger of the two sons of Arthur Bertram Tanner, a civil servant, and his wife, Susan (*née* Williamson), a schoolteacher. He attended Raynes Park County Grammar School, Wimbledon, from 1945 to 1953, and did national service in the intelligence corps, based mainly in Germany, from 1953 to 1955. In October 1955 he went to Jesus College, Cambridge, to read English. He graduated with a double first in 1958 and took up a Harkness fellowship at the University of California, Berkeley. When he left Berkeley two years later, one of his teachers there, the great Americanist Henry Nash Smith, rightly predicted 'a distinguished career in American Studies' (letter of reference, Tanner student records). On his return to Cambridge in 1960 Tanner was elected fellow of King's College and began a thesis, 'The use of wonder and naivety in American literature'. He was appointed assistant lecturer in 1964 and obtained his PhD degree in 1965.

Tanner's was the English faculty's first PhD dissertation on an American topic, and his major achievement in Cambridge was to develop the study of American literature. Under his impetus and guidance, it was established as a fundamental to the faculty's undergraduate and graduate teaching. His influence in this respect, however, extended well beyond Cambridge. He was ready to lecture, examine, and advise wherever he was asked, and this, together

with his publications in the field, made him a key figure in shaping the study of American literature in Britain and elsewhere. Those publications bear witness to what he described as his 'uninterrupted interest and pleasure in the distinguishing features and singular achievements of American writers and writing' (A. Tanner, preface, *Scenes of Nature, Signs of Men*, 1987, x). *The Reign of Wonder: Naivety and Reality in American Literature* (1965) was described by Frank Kermode as being, save for only D. H. Lawrence's *Studies in Classic American Literature*, 'the most impressive contribution hitherto made by an Englishman to the study of American literature' (Tony Tanner in conversation with Alison Carter). *City of Words: American Fiction, 1950–70*, which introduced a generation of readers to the vitality of the contemporary American novel, was published in 1970. On 21 August 1965 Tanner married Marcia Verne Albright, *née* Koenigsberg (*b.* 1940/41), and in 1966 he was appointed lecturer in the Cambridge English faculty.

Tanner made his only break with Cambridge in 1976 when he left to take up a chair at Johns Hopkins University, a move he quickly regretted. The following year saw him reappointed to his Cambridge lectureship and re-elected to his King's fellowship. Having been divorced from Marcia Albright in 1977, he married Nadia Fusini (*b.* 1946), a distinguished critic and Italian translator of Virginia Woolf, on 4 July 1979. Tanner's ambitious *Adultery in the Novel* was published in 1979. In 1980 he was made reader, and the first of two books on Henry James, *Henry James: the Writer and his Work*, was published in 1985. His *Jane Austen* (1986) became a standard critical work and demonstrated that his teaching and writing were not confined to American literature. He also wrote significant articles on a number of other writers, notably Conrad. Tanner's numerous essays on American literary topics were collected in *Scenes of Nature, Signs of Men* in 1987, and in 1989 he was appointed professor of English and American literature. *Venice Desired*, a rich exploration of literary imaginings of Venice, was published in 1992. A substantial accomplishment towards the end of his life was his set of prefaces to the individual plays in the new Everyman edition of Shakespeare (1992–6). *Henry James and the Art of Non-Fiction* was published in 1995.

Tanner was a literary critic rather than a scholar, his strength lying in his ability to produce deep understanding of literary works through close reading that drew freely and illuminatingly on ideas derived from other disciplines. It lay too in his response to literature as a source of pleasure and in the enthusiasm with which he wrote about and taught it—an enthusiasm evident in his twelve books and large number of articles.

Tanner was a fellow of King's for almost forty years and for much of that time resident there. King's was his special place, 'the most civilized corner of the world', and he prized the opportunity he saw it as offering for tolerant, civil exchange across disciplinary boundaries: his ideal of a true education. A handsome man, with thick dark hair and eyebrows, expressive grey-blue eyes, an infectious smile, and a voice of convivial richness, Tanner had great warmth of presence. His enjoyment of the company of others was intense and he excelled at conversation, for him the supreme fulfilment of the pleasure of human fellowship (talking was one of the two recreations he listed in his *Who's Who* entry; travelling was the other). In his late forties and early fifties he knew periods of severe depression and physical collapse; from these he recovered, but with impaired mobility. His teaching and writing, however, were not affected, and he continued to give lectures across the world, retaining to the last his humanely ironic sense of humour and his intellectual generosity. His marriage to Nadia Fusini was dissolved in 1998.

Tony Tanner died of cancer in King's College on 5 December 1998. He was cremated at Cambridge crematorium on 11 December 1998, and his ashes were placed in the crypt of King's College chapel in March 1999. *The American Mystery: American Literature from Emerson to DeLillo*, a further collection of his essays, which Tanner had been planning, was posthumously published in 2000.

STEPHEN HEATH

Sources King's Cam., Tanner MSS · Jesus College, Cambridge, Tanner student records · 'Tony Tanner: bibliography', *Critical Quarterly*, 41/2 (summer 1999), 100–104 · T. Tanner, 'My life in American literature', *Tri Quarterly*, 30 (spring 1974), 83–108 · personal knowledge (2004) · Tony Tanner in conversation with Alison Carter, King's Cam. [cassette/CD recording]
Archives Jesus College, Cambridge, student records · King's AC Cam., corresp. and papers | King's AC Cam., letters and postcards to G. H. W. Rylands
Likenesses photographs, King's Cam., Tanner papers
Wealth at death under £200,000—gross; under £100,000—net: probate, 25 Jan 1999, *CGPLA Eng. & Wales*

Tanner [*née* Young], **Rosalind Cecilia Hildegard** [Cecily] **(1900–1992)**, mathematician and historian of mathematics, was born in Göttingen, Germany, on 6 February 1900 and named Rosalinde Cäcilie Hildegard, the oldest of three daughters and second of six children of the first husband-and-wife team of creative research mathematicians, William Henry *Young (1863–1942) and Grace Emily *Young (*née* Chisholm) (1868–1944). A younger brother, Laurence Chisholm Young, and a niece, Sylvia M. Wiegand, daughter of Laurence, were also well-known professional mathematicians. The family lived in Göttingen until 1908, then in Geneva until 1915, and then in Lausanne until 1925. Cecily Young studied in Lausanne to her *licence* in mathematics and physics, and then, from 1925, like her mother, as a postgraduate student in Cambridge and, also like her mother, as a member of Girton College. Her PhD thesis of 1929, supervised by E. W. Hobson, earned her only the title of the degree, as women did not receive Cambridge degrees until after the Second World War. However, Girton College awarded her a fellowship until 1932. At that time during the depression appointments were very difficult to get and Cecily did not find one for a year, but in 1933 she joined the department of mathematics of the Imperial College of Science and Technology, University of London, where she remained until her retirement in 1967.

Cecily Young's research interests were mainly close to her parents' interests in mathematical analysis. Perhaps her most significant research was published in the

Mathematische Annalen in 1931 ('The algebra of many-valued quantities') and the *Proceedings of the Cambridge Philosophical Society*, also in 1931 ('On many-valued Riemann-Stieltjes integration I, II'). She also translated mathematical texts from French and German into English. The most significant was her translation of a book by Konrad Knopp, *Theorie und Anwendung der unendlichen Reihen*, published as *Theory and Application of Infinite Series* (1925; 2nd edn, 1951). She collaborated with Sydney Chapman while he was at Imperial College on a textbook which was never finished. In 1939 she won the Gamble prize of Girton College with an essentially mathematics-historical essay. After the death of her parents she maintained their papers. On 3 September 1953 she married, in the Holy Trinity Church in Wallington, Surrey, Bernard William Tanner (1881–1954), an electrical engineer who had been the chief maintenance engineer at Imperial College, and who was nineteen years her senior, and widowed. He died only nine months after the marriage.

From 1953 onwards Cecily published under the name of Tanner, mostly in the history of mathematics, especially the history of inequalities. In the mid-1960s and to the end of her life her interest concentrated on Thomas Harriot, who had invented the symbols > and < to denote inequalities. About one-third of her published papers were in French, and a few were in German. From childhood she suffered from impaired hearing, which became more severe over the years and restricted her contacts outside her family, though she learned to lip-read and had many friends, especially among fellow mathematicians. She was a talented violinist, wrote poetry, and was intermittently a churchgoing Christian. She donated generously to a number of organizations, especially those concerned with her historical interests, at Oxford, Durham, and Cambridge. She died in the Mayday Hospital, Croydon, from bronchopneumonia, acute myeloid leukaemia, and congestive heart failure on 24 November 1992, and was cremated in Croydon.

B. H. NEUMANN

Sources I. Grattan-Guinness, *British Journal for the History of Science*, 26 (1993), 229–31 · I. Grattan-Guinness, 'Cecily Tanner', *British Society for the History of Mathematics Newsletter*, 23 (1993), 10–15 · m. cert. · d. cert. · private information (2004) [P. M. Neumann; I. Grattan-Guinness; Laurence Chisholm Young; Angela Young; Sylvia M. Wiegand; J. G. Fauvel; H. A. Priestley] · personal knowledge (2004)
Archives U. Lpool L., William Henry Young and Grace Chisholm Young MSS
Wealth at death £166,755: probate, 19 Feb 1993, *CGPLA Eng. & Wales*

Tanner, Thomas (1630–1682), historian, son of Daniel Tanner, citizen of London, was born in the parish of St Matthew's, Friday Street, London. He was educated at St Paul's School and entered Pembroke College, Cambridge, in 1646, graduating BA in 1649. He was incorporated at Oxford on 4 February 1651 and became a fellow of New College in the same year. He graduated MA at Edinburgh while travelling in Scotland and at Oxford in 1652. In 1657 he wrote *The Entrance of Mazzarini, or, Some Memorials of the State of France*. As some doubt was expressed concerning his authorship of this work, he wrote a sequel, *The*

Entrance of Mazzarini Continued, the following year to prove he was indeed the author, although he acknowledged an Italian source. In 1660 he was elected senior proctor of Oxford University, but soon afterwards was ejected from his fellowship by the royal commissioners and left the university. He entered Gray's Inn and was called to the bar in 1663. After travelling in Italy and Flanders he took holy orders and in 1666 became vicar of Colyton in Derbyshire. He subsequently became chaplain to George Morley, bishop of Winchester, who presented him to the rectory of Brixton on the Isle of Wight in 1676. Tanner transferred to Winchfield, Hampshire, in 1679 and exchanged Brixton for North Waltham. He wrote several minor works and sermons, some against popery, of which *Primordia, or, The Rise and Growth of the First Church of God Described* was published posthumously, but he was a mediocre writer and his works were not in great demand. He died at Winchfield in October 1682 and was buried in the church there. According to Wood he was survived by a wife, Elizabeth, about whom no further details are known.

T. F. HENDERSON, rev. MARJA SMOLENAARS

Sources Wood, *Ath. Oxon.*, 2nd edn · Foster, *Alum. Oxon.*

Tanner, Thomas (1674–1735), bishop of St Asaph and antiquary, was born at Market Lavington, Wiltshire, on 25 January 1674, the eldest child of Thomas Tanner (1640?–1719), vicar of that parish from 1671, and of his first wife, Sarah Willoughby (d. 1711). After education at home and at Shrewsbury Free School, Tanner matriculated, on 17 December 1689, at Queen's College, Oxford. Through the favour of Archbishop Thomas Lamplugh (1615–1691), sometime fellow of Queen's and a friend of Tanner's father, he became a Bible clerk of the college in 1690. He proceeded BA in 1693, MA in 1696, and BD and DD in 1710.

Tanner was soon noted as a young scholar of exceptional promise and it was natural that his talents should flourish at Queen's, a pioneering centre of antiquarian and Anglo-Saxon studies. Edward Thwaites and Edmund Gibson were among his contemporaries, and the latter became a lifelong friend. Tanner assisted Gibson with editions of Camden's *Britannia* (1695) and the *Reliquiae Spelmannianae* (1698), and it was appropriate that Tanner's posthumously published edition (1748) of John Leland's collected *Bibliotheca Britannico-Hibernica, sive, De scriptoribus* should be dedicated to Gibson, who in 1693 had first encouraged his interest in this text. Although it provided material for later, inferior catalogues, by John Bale (1548) and by John Pits (1619), Leland's original compilation of 1546 had never been published, and by the late seventeenth century the need for an accessible edition, incorporating the new material indicated by William Cave's *Scriptorum ecclesiasticorum historia literaria* (1688), had become acute. Tanner 'exactly envisaged the problem' (Douglas, 157). His original scheme, for 'the bare printing of Leland and Boston of Bury and supplying what was wanting by wholesale out of Bale and Pits within a twelvemonth' (Davies) was rapidly superseded. Finding that Leland 'had entirely omitted above 2000 British Writers'

Thomas Tanner (1674–1735), by unknown artist

and 'of those he does mention he had given a very imperfect account', Tanner resolved 'to add such new Authors and writings as later searches of Libraries have discovered, interweaving his Writers with my own' (Douglas, 162).

At about the same time Tanner also began work to improve on Robert Hegge's edition of *The Legend of St Cuthbert, with the Antiquities of the Church of Durham* (1663). In 1694 he issued a prospectus for a projected history of Wiltshire, a task inspired by the pioneering local studies of Sir William Dugdale. Although the work was never published Tanner worked energetically at collecting material for what 'may have been one of the great unwritten county histories' (Douglas, 160) and these important manuscript collections were included with his other papers, which were given to the Bodleian Library after his death. However, *Notitia monastica, or, A Short History of the Religious Houses in England and Wales*, proposed in 1693 as a necessary updating of Dugdale's *Monasticon Anglicanum* (1655–73), was published in 1695.

Tanner's ability soon secured him valuable contacts. His interest in the history of Wiltshire brought him to the notice of John Aubrey, who offered him the use of his own papers, and won the support of another Wiltshire man, Arthur Charlett, the influential master of University College, Oxford. Charlett recommended Tanner to Anthony Wood, the Oxford antiquary, who in November 1695, shortly before his death, placed his general manuscripts in the joint care of Tanner and of James Bisse of Wadham College, under Charlett's supervision, directing that some be burnt and that others should not be opened for seven years. On 28 November 1695, the day before he died, Wood committed his remaining collections, for the continuation of his *Athenae Oxonienses*, with great ceremony to Tanner for his sole use, without any restrictions.

In December 1694 Tanner was examined for deacon's orders by the bishop of London, Dr Henry Compton, and the chapter of St Paul's, and passed 'very well' (Bodl. Oxf., MS Ballard 5, fol. 81, Gibson to Charlett, 22 Dec 1694). On 27 January 1695 he was appointed by the warden, Leopold William Finch, to the chaplaincy of All Souls, Oxford. Tanner acknowledged his obligation in his dedication to Finch of the first edition of *Notitia monastica* (1695), where he admitted that, but for this assistance, 'he must have left [Oxford] and his studies'. On 2 November 1696 he was elected a fellow of All Souls, and while still resident in Oxford he pursued his scholarly career with vigour. In 1697 he compiled, for Edward Bernard's *Catalogue of Manuscripts* (1697, 1.249–63, 268–71), particulars of the collections of Francis Junius and of Richard James, and of Gerard Langbaine's *adversaria*, all of which are preserved in the Bodleian Library, but most of his time was devoted to Leland. Having exhausted sources in Oxford by April 1698 he pursued the work in Cambridge, Norwich, and London. However, he continued to collaborate with other scholars, encouraging the young Humfrey Wanley, from 1695, and assisting William Wake against Francis Atterbury during the convocation controversy, for which he was insulted in the streets of Oxford by high-church dons. He also contributed material to George Hickes's monumental *Linguarum veterum septentrionalium thesaurus grammatico-criticus et archaeologicus* (2 vols., 1703–5).

In 1698 Tanner was appointed chaplain to John Moore, bishop of Norwich, a whig and a low-churchman but a noted bibliophile and manuscript collector. On 6 March 1701 he was collated, by the gift of the bishop, to the chancellorship of Norwich diocese. Moore also made him commissary in the archdeaconry of Norfolk, on 24 November 1703, and, on 1 January 1707, commissary of the archdeaconry of Sudbury and the town of Bury St Edmunds. In June 1706 he was presented by Duncan Dee, common sergeant of London, who later appeared for the defence at the trial of Dr Sacheverell (1710), to the rectory of Thorpe Bishop's, near Norwich. In 1707 Bishop Moore was translated to the see of Ely and, in 1713, he bestowed a canonry in that cathedral upon Tanner, who continued to be involved in the main with Norwich diocese. On 26 December 1721 Tanner was raised to the archdeaconry of Norfolk; he vacated his stall at Ely on 15 February 1724, when he was installed as a canon of Christ Church, Oxford, in succession to Henry Egerton, who had been consecrated bishop of Hereford. Tanner subsequently became treasurer of Christ Church, and in 1727 he was elected to the largely symbolic office of prolocutor of the lower house of convocation.

Tanner's departure from Oxford to Norwich disrupted his scholarly career. The new pressures of ecclesiastical and domestic duty left little time for study and research. In 1701 he married Rose, eldest daughter of Bishop Moore; her death, on 15 March 1707, at the age of twenty-five, was alleged to have resulted from excessive brandy drinking

(*Remarks*, 8.171). Their one child, a daughter, Dorothy, died on 17 February 1704, aged fourteen months. Tanner married, next, Frances, daughter of Jacob Preston, a citizen of London but descended from Norfolk gentry. She was described as 'discreet and excellent' (Nichols, *Illustrations*, 3.404) and the marriage was singularly happy but she died on 11 June 1718, aged forty, and was buried, like Tanner's first wife, in the bishop's chapel in Norwich Cathedral, under a white marble monument. The iron palisade door to this chapel was erected at Tanner's expense, and his arms, with those of his first two wives, are on it. Tanner had two daughters with Frances, both of whom died young, and a son, Thomas Tanner (*d*. 1786), a canon of Canterbury and rector of Hadleigh and Monk's Eleigh in Suffolk, who married Mary, third daughter of Archbishop Potter.

Despite such distractions Tanner continued with important antiquarian work throughout his time at Norwich and assisted many other scholars, including Samuel Knight in his lives of Colet (1724) and of Erasmus (1726), and Robert Hawes (*d*. 1731) in his compilation on Framlingham. His research on Norfolk sources secured him the posthumous honour of the dedication, in warm terms, of the county history compiled by his protégé, Francis Blomefield (*b*. 1705) and it has been said that 'few scholars, themselves distinguished, have ever had a larger anonymous share in the books of other men' (Douglas, 159). Tanner maintained regular correspondence with Peter Le Neve, president of the Society of Antiquaries, until the latter's death in 1729 (Nichols, *Illustrations*, 3.401–35) and also with the nonjuring antiquary Thomas Baker of St John's College, Cambridge. He was one of those most concerned in the preparation of the *Concilia magnae Britanniae et Hiberniae, a synodo Verulamensi, AD 446 ad Londinensem AD 1717*, published in four folio volumes by David Wilkins in 1737 and 'perhaps the greatest single accomplishment in medieval scholarship made by the Anglican Church in this period' (Douglas, 159). In addition he continued to labour on Leland's *De scriptoribus*, on a revision of his *Notitia*, and on the *Athenae Oxonienses*, but progress was fitful. For a short period after the death of his first wife Tanner was able to work rapidly and it was expected that 'Leland … will be ready for the Press in a little time' (*Remarks*, 2.25) but nothing materialized. Instead a rival edition was published in 1709 by a fellow of Queen's, Anthony Hall, with the support of Edward Thwaites. Taking heart from the weakness of Hall's edition and ignoring the rebuff Tanner resolved to continue 'in the public good' (Davies). Despite his hopes at this time, in September 1709, 'to finish the work of our English writers by the end of winter' (*Remarks*, 2.254n.), the task was still unfinished in 1725, when Hearne saw Tanner with 'about six Folios before him which he said were what he had done for his Scriptores Britannici which I understand from him he still prosecutes with as much Industry and Application as his Affairs will permit' (ibid., 9.31). The work was eventually completed and published by David Wilkins in 1748; more than a century later, in 1861, it was said to be 'still the highest authority to which the inquirer can refer' (Douglas, 164).

The revision of the *Notitia* went on in a similar manner, hampered by Tanner's official duties and, latterly, by his infirmities. At his death much remained unfinished but the work was eventually completed by his brother John Tanner, vicar of Lowestoft and precentor of St Asaph Cathedral. It was printed in 1744 by William Bowyer with assistance from the Society for the Encouragement of Learning, and reprinted, with many additions, by James Nasmith in 1787. Progress with *Athenae Oxonienses* had been almost equally slow. On 7 March 1706 Thomas Hearne complained that 'This wife and preferment together with his intimacy wth the low Church Party have put a stop (as 'tis believed) to the Publication of the 3d Volume of Mr Wood's Athenae, wch Mr Tanner has' (*Remarks*, 1.200). However there were other reasons for delay since Tanner feared, very understandably, that the publication of material referring to persons still living might provoke retaliation. Nevertheless, he was widely blamed for his caution, and when an edition prompted by Jacob Tonson's purchase of copyright in the previously published portion of the work eventually appeared in 1721, many suspected that the 500 biographical notices added by Tanner had been altered drastically from Wood's more robust original version. The work was coolly received and Hearne dismissed it as 'the spurious edition' (*Remarks*, 8.171).

Like many antiquaries Tanner was an energetic collector. He assembled a very important collection of books and manuscripts, much of which suffered badly when the barge transporting it from Norwich to Oxford sank near Wallingford on 11 December 1731 (*Remarks*, 11.9). By his will, dated 22 November 1733, Tanner bequeathed this material to the Bodleian Library, where it was received in 1736. The manuscript collection, in 473 volumes, contains much valuable material, including part of John Nalson's collection of civil war documents and the papers of Archbishop Sancroft, for which Tanner paid £90. It was said that 'Mr Carte was about purchasing these MSS before Dr Tanner, but the very day he was to have had them the Proclamation came out for his Apprehension' (*Remarks*, 10.473). He also had a substantial collection of English coins and medals, some of which he lost by theft in 1732 (ibid., 11.111). These distractions happened at about the time that Tanner became bishop of St Asaph. He was consecrated at Lambeth Palace on 23 January 1732 but retained his canonry at Christ Church *in commendam*. Having been dangerously ill in 1730 Tanner was by this time extremely corpulent but he endeavoured to be a conscientious bishop and visited his diocese as soon as possible, despite his poor health. From 1733 he supplemented the revenues of his poor diocese with income from the sinecure rectory of Llandrillo, Merioneth. A further accession of wealth came when, on 12 May 1733, he married, as his third wife, Elizabeth Scottowe of Thorpe by Norwich, an heiress with a fortune of some £20,000, but it was soon reported that, although his scholarly generosity continued, he was 'grown miserably covetous' (*Remarks*, 11.317). His wife, having outlived him, married the elderly

Robert Britiffe, sometime whig MP for Norwich (d. 1749), and died at the age of seventy-seven in 1771.

Tanner died at Christ Church, Oxford on 14 December 1735, 'of a bloody flux' said to have been aggravated by taking Ward's pills (Nichols, *Illustrations*, 3.401); on 26 December he was buried near the pulpit in Christ Church Cathedral, where his handsome monument and epitaph may still be seen on the first pillar of the south side of the nave. A funeral address was delivered by Dr Fyfield Allen. In a partisan age Tanner had been generally respected; even Thomas Hearne admitted that 'tho' a little low Church, [he] is so extraordinary a good-humoured Person & so communicate that every body admires him' (*Remarks*, 5.63n.). A more recent appraisal recognizes 'the immense industry which made him in due course one of the most erudite members of a learned Church' and also the 'general benevolence which enabled him, though sincerely devoted to the Low Church Party in the Establishment, to avoid the acrimonies of contemporary politics and so to infuse a friendly forbearance into his relations with his fellows' (Douglas, 158). Among several charitable bequests he left the sum of £200 towards the provision of education and for the relief of the poor in his birthplace, Market Lavington.
RICHARD SHARP

Sources *Remarks and collections of Thomas Hearne*, ed. C. E. Doble and others, 11 vols., OHS, 2, 7, 13, 34, 42–3, 48, 50, 65, 67, 72 (1885–1921) · Nichols, *Illustrations*, 3.402–35 · D. C. Douglas, *English scholars, 1660–1730*, 2nd edn (1951), 156–64 · W. T. Davies, 'Thomas Tanner and his *Bibliotheca*: a bicentenary rediscovery', *TLS* (14 Dec 1935), 856 · T. Tanner, *Notitia monastica, or, An account of all the abbies, priories, and houses of friers … in England and Wales, and of all the colleges and hospitals founded before AD MDXL* (1744) · Nichols, *Lit. anecdotes*, 2.161–3 · *DNB* · Foster, *Alum. Oxon.*

Archives BL, copy of *Notitia monastica* with his MS notes and additions · Bodl. Oxf., corresp. and papers; notebook · CUL, Cambridgeshire collections, MS Add. 3824 · CUL, list of additions to Bishop Moore's MS library, nos. 831–1025 · Norfolk RO, transcripts by him of collections relating to the diocese of Norwich; act book of consistory court of Norwich · Suffolk RO, Ipswich, transcripts of his Suffolk collections | BL, memorandum books for the *Bibliotheca Britannica*, Add. MSS 6261–6262 · BL, letters to John Anstis, Stowe MS 749 · Bodl. Oxf., letters to John Aubrey · Norfolk RO, letter to Peter Le Neve

Likenesses G. Vertue, line engraving, pubd 1736, BM, NPG; repro. in Tanner, *Notitia monastica*, frontispiece · H. Cheere, bronze head, c.1756, All Souls Oxf. · oils, Christ Church Oxf. [*see illus.*] · oils, copy, All Souls Oxf. · painting, All Souls Oxf.

Tanner, Thomas Hawkes (1824–1871), physician, son of Thomas Tanner, who between 1783 and 1847 was secretary to the army medical board, was born in London on 9 July 1824. He was educated mostly at the Charterhouse School, where he suffered a serious accident, which impaired his health for many years. He began his medical studies at King's College, London, in 1843, and graduated DM at St Andrews University in 1847. He then began general practice at 10 Charlotte Street, Bedford Square, London, and was shortly afterwards elected physician to the Farringdon General Dispensary. He was enrolled a member of the Royal College of Surgeons in 1847 and of Physicians in 1850, and began a consulting practice. From 1851 to 1857 he was physician to the hospital for women in Soho Square, and from about 1851 specialized in gynaecology, though he was lecturer on forensic medicine at the medical school attached to the Westminster Hospital until about 1853. He was a fellow of the Linnean, Zoological, Royal Medical and Chirurgical, and many other societies.

In 1859 Tanner, with William Tyler Smith, Edward Rigby, and C. Hewitt, was instrumental in founding the Obstetrical Society of London. He was its secretary from 1859 to 1863 and much of its success was due to his energy and perseverance. In 1860 King's College Hospital, London, appointed him one of two assistant physicians for the diseases of women and children, but he resigned under the pressure of work in 1863. Tanner acquired a large practice, which he moved in 1862 from Charlotte Street to 9 Henrietta Street, but it overtaxed his strength. He was forced to leave London, and he died at 12 Royal Crescent, Brighton, on 7 July 1871, leaving a widow, Mary Willes Tanner.

Tanner was a voluminous and lucid medical writer. His chief work was *A Manual of the Practice of Medicine* (1854), which in its numerous editions sold successfully in England and America, being valued for its careful observation of disease and sound views on treatment. The 7th edition was revised by W. H. Broadbent.

Tanner's other works, which were generally well reviewed and often ran to several editions, ranged from a general *Manual of Clinical Medicine* (1855) to more specialized works such as *A Practical Treatise on the Diseases of Infancy and Childhood* (1858) and *On the Signs and Diseases of Pregnancy* (1860).

D'A. POWER, rev. ELIZABETH BAIGENT

Sources *Proceedings of the Royal Medical and Chirurgical Society*, 7 (1871–5), 36 · Boase, *Mod. Eng. biog.* · *CGPLA Eng. & Wales* (1871) · *Medical Times and Gazette* (15 July 1871), 87 · *Medical Times and Gazette* (21 July 1871), 115 · book review, *BMJ*, 1 (1861), 118–19 · Allibone, *Dict.* · *Men of the time* (1885) · O. Moscucci, *The science of woman: gynaecology and gender in England, 1800–1929* (1990)
Likenesses E. Edwards, photograph, 1868, Wellcome L. · photograph, Wellcome L. · photograph, repro. in T. H. Barker, ed., *Photographs of eminent medical men*, 2 vols. (1867–8)
Wealth at death under £14,000: probate, 1 Aug 1871, *CGPLA Eng. & Wales*

Tannock, James (1783–1863), portrait painter, was born in Kilmarnock, Ayrshire, on 13 July 1783, and was baptized there on 20 July the second child of Adam Tannock, a shoemaker, and Agnes Rankine. He spent his childhood in the town and was apprenticed to his father. His interest in art led him to move to Edinburgh in 1803 where he studied under the landscape painter Alexander Nasmyth. Tannock worked in Paisley, Greenock, Irvine, and Stirling before moving to London in 1810, where he enrolled in the Royal Academy Schools, and attended Sir Charles Bell's anatomical lectures.

From 1813 until 1841 Tannock exhibited portraits annually at the Royal Academy including one of Sir James Shaw, bt (1817; East Ayrshire council), the lord mayor of London, also from Kilmarnock, which the artist presented to his home town. Shaw introduced Tannock to a number of notable people, some of whom commissioned him to paint their portraits. These included the novelist John Galt; Elizabeth Benger, who wrote *Memoirs of Mary Queen of*

Scots (1823); and George Chalmers, the author of *Caledonia*, whose portrait he painted in 1824 (Scot. NPG) and whose friendship and patronage he also enjoyed.

Tannock painted portraits of a number of Scottish figures, including the writer Mrs Grant of Laggan (Scot. NPG) and Henry Bell the marine engineer (versions in Scot. NPG and Glasgow Museums). Bell's portrait was engraved by J. Scott as the frontispiece to Edward Morris's *The Life of Henry Bell* (1844). In his lifetime Tannock was renowned for his portraits of Robert Burns, one of which was based on Alexander Nasmyth's famous work. Those he painted for Kilmarnock corporation (East Ayrshire council) and the Kilmarnock Burns Club were included in the Burns exhibition in Glasgow in 1896. The song-writer Robert Tannahill highly praised the version he painted for the Kilbarchan Burns's Anniversary Society.

Although Tannock spent most of his life in London, he regularly returned to the house on Grange Street in Kilmarnock where his brother William Tannock (c.1793–1877), who was also an artist, lived. The property, which has a carving on the exterior of an artist and easel, provided a studio and a gallery for the Dutch and Flemish old-master paintings Tannock acquired in London. James Tannock died, apparently unmarried, on 6 May 1863 at his house in Kilmarnock. Archibald McKay wrote that as 'an artist he was modest and unassuming, and as a man amiable and intelligent' (McKay, 281). He has been a neglected artist whose works are characterized by a pure execution and accurate delineation of likeness. James Caw claimed that Tannock alongside other Scottish portrait painters, including Thomas Fraser (*d.* 1851) and W. Smellie Watson RSA (1796–1874) 'wrought in the manner of their time, but, for the most part, were tradesmen rather than artists' (Caw, 90). On seeing one of his paintings, however, Benjamin West, president of the Royal Academy when Tannock was studying there, subsequently responded: 'It is nature itself; it is the man sitting before you; he [Mr Tannock] is a man of genius' (McKay, 280).

GEORGE FAIRFULL SMITH

Sources A. McKay, *The history of Kilmarnock*, 4th edn (1880) · private information (2004) [Dick Institute, Kilmarnock, East Ayrshire Council] · Graves, *RA exhibitors* · *North British Daily Mail* (7 May 1863), 4b · H. Smailes, *The concise catalogue of the Scottish National Portrait Gallery* (1990) · Irving, *Scots.* · R. Walker and others, *Memorial catalogue of the Burns exhibition* (1898) [exhibition catalogue, Royal Glasgow Institute of the Fine Arts, 15 July – 31 Oct 1896] · E. Kilmurray, *Dictionary of British portraiture*, 2 (1979) · D. Foskett, *Miniatures: dictionary and guide* (1987) · P. J. M. McEwan, *Dictionary of Scottish art and architecture* (1994) · J. L. Caw, *Scottish painting past and present, 1620–1908* (1908) · bap. reg. Scot.
Wealth at death £142 2s. 5d.: confirmation, 18 Aug 1864, NA Scot., SC 6/44/31 p. 274–6

Tansley, Sir Arthur George (1871–1955), plant ecologist, was born in central London on 15 August 1871, the only son and younger child of George Tansley and his wife, Amelia Lawrence. George Tansley conducted a profitable business providing for society functions, but his real interest lay with the Working Men's College, where he studied, then taught. From his father Arthur Tansley inherited a liberal outlook and from another instructor at the college he received early encouragement in field botany. He attended Westbury House preparatory school, Worthing, from 1883 to 1886, then entered Highgate School, Middlesex, where he stayed for only seven terms. Finding Highgate's teaching of science 'farcically inadequate' (Godwin, 1977, 3) and 'perfunctory and inferior' (Godwin, 1958, 1) he left to attend classes at University College, London, in 1889. In 1890 he entered Trinity College, Cambridge. Even before completing his first-class degree in the natural sciences tripos, he returned to University College as a Quain student, from 1893 to 1895, and remained there, now as a colleague rather than a pupil of the professor of botany, F. W. Oliver, returning only briefly to Cambridge to take his final examinations in 1894. Oliver's interest in fern-like plants was echoed by Tansley's earliest published investigations, in which one of his student collaborators was Edith Chick. The daughter of a lace merchant, Samuel Chick, she became Tansley's wife in 1903. They had three daughters.

Tansley became influential in the development of botany through his single-handed launching in 1902 of The New Phytologist, which he edited for thirty years. But it was ecology that was becoming his chief interest. In 1904 a dozen British botanists, with Tansley at their centre, formed the British vegetation committee to further the description of British plant communities. Despite returning to Cambridge in 1907 to lecture in botany, Tansley remained central to the committee's work, editing and largely writing Types of British Vegetation (1911), the first systematic account of its kind. In 1913, the committee matured into the British Ecological Society (BES), and Tansley became its first president. He was elected FRS in 1915. In 1917, while holding a clerical position with the Ministry of Munitions, he became editor of the Journal of Ecology, a position he held for twenty-one years. It was a periodical which enhanced both the society's reputation and his own. In 1923 Tansley published Practical Plant Ecology (rewritten in 1946 as Introduction to Plant Ecology) which, more than any other book, helped to introduce ecology into schools. Tansley's successful book, The New Psychology and its Relation to Life (1920), reflected his interest in philosophy and psychology, particularly as expounded by Freud. In 1923–4, resigning his university post, he studied under Freud in Vienna while continuing to write influential botanical works.

In 1927 Tansley was appointed Sherardian professor of botany at Oxford, where he raised the standing of Oxford botany by his own teaching and prestige and by gaining very able staff. Enforced retirement in 1937 on grounds of age disappointed but did not disenchant Tansley. He became professor emeritus at Cambridge and served a second spell as president of the BES. His largest, celebrated book, The British Islands and their Vegetation, appeared in 1939 and secured him the gold medal of the Linnean Society in 1941. The same year, concerted planning began for post-war statutory conservation of nature in Britain. Tansley fought with resolution and much courage to avert totalitarianism in science while promoting the popular case for conservation with works such as Our Heritage of Wild Nature (1945). His role was vital in the foundation of the Nature Conservancy in 1949. Aged seventy-seven, he became its first chairman and held office until increasing deafness forced his resignation in 1953. In 1944, he had been elected an honorary fellow of Trinity College, Cambridge; in 1947, he became an honorary member of BES, and his knighthood came in 1950.

After middle age Tansley's silvering hair, tallish, spare figure, and somewhat unathletic movements suited his unassuming distinction. On relaxed occasions he was jovial and humorous. He overlooked faults in others, thinking virtues more important. To his close friends, whether distinguished or not, 'A. G.' made it clear that he valued their friendship. He died at his home of forty-eight years, Grove Cottage, Grantchester, Cambridgeshire, on 25 November 1955.

Tansley confessed to having no facility for experimentation and an inability to recognize plant species in the field. But he could recognize an organizational need with perfect timing and fulfil it by galvanizing others with similar interests. He displayed an 'incisively critical and logical mind … an extreme lucidity and economy' with words, the 'zeal of a reformer … skill and shrewdness in pursuing his … convictions [and] considerable financial astuteness' (Godwin, 'Sir Arthur Tansley', 22–3). At Kingley Vale national nature reserve on the Sussex downs, a place beloved by Tansley, an inscribed stone commemorates the father of ecology 'who during a long lifetime strove with success to widen the knowledge, to deepen the love, and to safeguard the heritage of nature in the British Isles'.

J. F. HOPE-SIMPSON, rev. DAVID E. EVANS

Sources H. Godwin, 'Sir Arthur Tansley: the man and the subject', Journal of Ecology, 65 (March 1977), 1–26 · H. Godwin, 'Sir Arthur George Tansley, F.R.S.', Journal of Ecology, 46 (March 1958), 1–8 · H. Godwin, Memoirs FRS, 3 (1957), 227–46 · J. Sheail, Seventy-five years in ecology: the British Ecological Society (1987) · J. Robertson, 'Sir Arthur Tansley', 1990 · CGPLA Eng. & Wales (1956)
Archives NHM, corresp. and papers · RS, corresp. and papers · U. Cam., department of plant sciences, papers | BL, corresp. with Marie Stopes, Add. MS 58468 · Bodl. Oxf., letters to O. G. S. Crawford · U. Glas., Archives and Business Records Centre, corresp. with Bowes
Likenesses D. G. Lillie, caricature, 1908, NPG · L. J. Watson, oils, 1949? (The Naturalists), U. Cam., department of plant sciences · Mrs de Glehn, two portraits, crayon, priv. coll. · W. G. de Glehn, oils · L. J. Watson, oils, English Nature, Peterborough
Wealth at death £30,912 7s. 10d.: probate, 14 April 1956, CGPLA Eng. & Wales

Tans'ur, William (bap. 1706, d. 1783), psalmodist, was baptized at Dunchurch, Warwickshire, on 6 November 1706, the son of Edward Tanzer (d. 1712), labourer, and his wife, Joan Alibone (1660/61–1712). On 20 May 1730 he married, at Ware, Elizabeth Butler (d. 1767); they had at least two sons. He seems to have become a teacher of psalmody at an early date, and published his first collection, The Compleat Melody, or, The Harmony of Sion, in 1734. Together with his second volume, The Melody of the Heart (1737), this was republished as The Works of Mr William Tans'ur and ran to several editions. Several later collections also appeared, published at Cambridge (1754 and 1776), Stamford (1756), and Boston (1761). The Royal Melody Compleat (1754–5) reached an eighth edition in 1830 and was printed in revised form as *The American Harmony* (1771). Tans'ur was 'one of the most successful exponents of the elaborate hymn tune of the time' (*New Grove*), and several of his tunes (including 'Bangor') continued in use in the twentieth century, although his style has been criticized as 'pretentious' and 'grandiose' (ibid.). His theoretical work, *A New Musical Grammar* (1746), designed for the country church musician, was in widespread use into the nineteenth century. Tans'ur lived in St Neots for the last forty years of his life, where he was a stationer, bookseller, and teacher of music. He died there on 7 January 1783.

F. G. EDWARDS, rev. K. D. REYNOLDS

Sources Grove, *Dict. mus.* (1927) · *New Grove* · J. Love, *Scottish church music* (1891) · IGI
Likenesses line engraving, 1760, NPG · B. Cole, line engraving, BM; repro. in W. Tans'ur, *The royal psalmodist compleat* (1748) · E. Newton, line engraving, BM; repro. in W. Tans'ur, *Melodia sacra*, 2nd edn (1772) · woodcut, BM; repro. in W. Tans'ur, *Heaven on earth* (1738)

Tanswell [*formerly* Cock], **John** (1800–1864), lawyer and antiquary, was born at Bedford Square, London, on 3 September 1800, the sixth son of Stephen Cock and his wife, Ann Tanswell (or Taswell), a relative of the Revd William Taswell (*d.* 1731), rector of St Mary's, Newington, Surrey. He trained as a lawyer and, having qualified as a solicitor in Michaelmas term 1834, took offices at 5 King's Bench Walk, Inner Temple, London. Tanswell was a keen antiquary and published *The History and Antiquities of Lambeth* in 1858. In the same year, in the *Proceedings of the Somersetshire Archaeological Society*, he published a paper on the rectory and manor of Limington, Somerset, where the Tanswell family had once lived. He was also an occasional contributor to *Notes and Queries*. After an apoplectic seizure, he died unmarried at his home, Temple House, Nunhead, London, on 18 October 1864. He was buried in Nunhead cemetery and his property passed to his nephew Thomas Pitt Taswell-Langmead.

W. P. COURTNEY, rev. NILANJANA BANERJI

Sources GM, 3rd ser., 17 (1864), 793–4 · *Law List* (1864)
Wealth at death under £3000: probate, 27 Oct 1864, CGPLA Eng. & Wales

Tany, Sir Luke de (*d.* 1282), soldier and administrator, was an important landowner in Yorkshire and Northumberland, and served as constable of Tickhill and Knaresborough at the end of the barons' wars of Henry III's reign. A thoroughgoing royalist, he was responsible for beheading some of those he captured, though apparently after some form of trial. He went with the future Edward I on crusade in 1270, serving as his admiral.

On return from the crusade Tany was appointed seneschal of Gascony. He already had an interest there, as he had been granted the town of Lalinde by Edward in 1267. After Edward's departure for England in 1274 Tany's powers and authority as seneschal were carefully defined, but his rule does not appear to have been successful. He was involved in the prolonged dispute between Edward I and

Gaston, count of Béarn. A succession of other legal disputes went unresolved, and appeals were made to the *parlement* of Paris. There was trouble at Bazas, and a major dispute in Dax, where the bishopric had been taken into Edward's hands in 1272, and the townspeople resisted Tany by force. In 1278 Otto Grandson (*d.* 1328) and Robert Burnell (*d.* 1292), the two men on whom the king perhaps most relied, went to Gascony to investigate. Luke de Tany was removed from office, but was not disgraced. His failure was the result of attempting to rule with too firm a hand, and there was no charge of incompetence or corruption to be laid at his door.

In Edward I's second Welsh war Tany was appointed on 18 August 1282 to command the English troops on the island of Anglesey. An ambitious plan was formed for a bridge of boats to be constructed so that an attack on the mainland could be mounted. In the second half of October Tany, along with Roger Clifford, William Audley, and others, sailed for Anglesey. On 6 November Tany and his men, acting prematurely, crossed the bridge to attack the Welsh on the mainland. The move was conceivably intended to thwart peace negotiations conducted by the archbishop of Canterbury. Precisely what happened is not clear, as chronicle accounts vary, but it seems that Tany and his men advanced inland some distance, and then returned to the bridge of boats. One version is that the route was cut off by the rising tide; the Welsh swooped, and drove the English into the sea. An alternative suggests that as the English made the return crossing, the bridge became overloaded, and as the pontoons sank many were drowned. Whatever the truth of the matter, Tany was one of the main casualties in a rare disaster.

MICHAEL PRESTWICH, rev.

Sources *The chronicle of Walter of Guisborough*, ed. H. Rothwell, CS, 3rd ser., 89 (1957) · *The chronicle of Pierre de Langtoft*, ed. T. Wright, 2, Rolls Series, 47 (1868) · J. P. Trabut-Cussac, *L'Administration anglaise en Gascogne sous Henry III et Édouard I de 1254 à 1307* (Geneva, 1972) · M. Prestwich, *Edward I* (1988) · S. D. Lloyd, *English society and the crusade, 1216–1307* (1988) · J. B. Smith, *Llywelyn ap Gruffudd, prince of Wales* (1998)

Tany, Theaurau John. *See* Totney, Thomas (*bap.* 1608, *d.* 1659?).

Tapp, John (*c.*1575–1631), writer on navigation and publisher, was entered as an apprentice to the Drapers' Company in 1589 and was discharged in 1596. In the same year, while living near the Bulwark gate on Tower Hill, he re-edited the English translation by Richard Eden of Cortes's *Arte de navegar* for the bookseller Hugh Astley. Tapp omitted Cortes's and Eden's prefaces and added a declination table. According to Tapp this book was 'my first Tutor into my marine practices' (Taylor, 193). By 1600 Tapp was teaching navigation and acting as an adviser and instructor to the seamen, and in the same year he transferred to the Stationers' Company and inherited Astley's business. He began to publish nautical and mathematical books for sailors and in 1602 he made his most original contribution to the art of navigation as he compiled and published the first edition of the nautical almanac for which he is best known, the *Seaman's Kalendar*. The book proved a great success and was frequently brought up to date, with a new edition appearing every three years; by 1615 it was into a fifth edition and had been enlarged. Captain John Smith commended it highly in his *Sea Grammar*, while the book influenced Edward Gunter, the mathematician.

In 1608 Tapp was chosen as auditor of the yeomanry by the Stationers' Company and in the same year paid £3s. 4d. to the company 'in respect thother half of the art of navigation is entered to him' (Jackson, 34); he also published Smith's account of Virginia, *A True Relation*. In 1613 Tapp published *The Pathway to Knowledge Containing the Whole Art of Arithmetic* which he dedicated to Sir Thomas Smyth, the governor of the Muscovy and East India companies. In his dedication he states that there had been a lectureship in navigation which had lapsed and called for it to be re-established, though his pleas fell on deaf ears. In the same year he published Edward Wright's *The Description of a Sphere*. The following year, in 1614, Tapp published both Ralph Handson's *Trigonometry* and Borough's *Variation of the Compass*, to which he probably added mathematical additions. His short explanation of arithmetical navigation in his reprint of Norman's *Newe Attractive* was 'the clearest introduction to its subject' (Waters, 401). In 1621 Tapp was among the members of the Stationers' Company who petitioned against the patent granted to Boisloré, Wood, and Symcock 'for things printed on one side of the paper only' (Greg, 168). Tapp was again appointed as an auditor by the Stationers' Company in 1625.

Captain Luke Fox, a friend and possibly a pupil of Tapp, consulted him in 1631 about his proposed expedition to find the north-west passage. Tapp was described as 'of St Magnus the Martyr' when he composed his will on 19 March 1631, 'praying the lord of his mercy to bring us all to eternal glory'. Having bequeathed his soul to God and his body to earth, and some small monetary bequests to his cousins, he named his wife, Elizabeth, as sole executor 'and in regard the settling in order my Shop wares and copies will be somewhat troublesome to her' he appointed 'my good friend John Clarke' to help her (PRO, PROB 11/159 fol. 503). His burial took place on 10 May 1631 at St Magnus the Martyr. Through the mathematical additions he made to the books he printed on navigation Tapp 'ranks high amongst the men who … went far towards transforming the art of navigation into a science by bringing into use the methods of arithmetical navigation' (Waters, 401).   PETER LE FEVRE

Sources E. G. R. Taylor, *The mathematical practitioners of Tudor and Stuart England* (1954), 193 • D. W. Waters, *The art of navigation in England in Elizabethan and early Stuart times* (1958), 195n., 215, 239, 320, 400–401 • PRO, PROB 11/159, fol. 503 • W. A. Jackson, ed., *Records of the court of the Stationers' Company, 1602 to 1640* (1957), 34, 91, 107, 111, 174 • W. W. Greg, ed., *A companion to Arber* (1967), 168 • parish register, St Magnus the Martyr, London, 10 May 1631 [burial]

Tappenden, James (*bap.* 1742, *d.* 1841), lawyer, banker, and ironmaster, was baptized on 13 October 1742 at St Mary's Church, Faversham, Kent, the only surviving child of James Tappenden (1707–1745), hoyman and mayor of Faversham (1743), and his wife, Mary Jones, daughter of Captain Isaac Jones, of the same town. He was articled to Faversham attorney Thomas Buck in 1757, and took over his practice when Buck died in 1779. In 1765 he married Mary Frances Beckwith (1745–1771), with whom he had three children, one of whom died in infancy. In 1780 he married his cousin Margaret Tappenden, with whom he had four sons and four daughters, one of whom married George Giles Vincent, son of the dean of Westminster. Tappenden had four separate but overlapping careers, in local government, law, banking, and industry. He was an excellent example of a general type of eighteenth-century men of affairs.

In local government Tappenden took all the important posts: he was appointed town clerk of Faversham and clerk to the wardmote (borough) court in 1779; he was clerk to the justices of the upper division of the lathe of Scray, giving him influence beyond the ancient borough. His regional influence was reinforced by his stewardship of the manor and hundred of Faversham and of the manors of Leysdown and Chilham and, by 1812, his chairmanship of the key audit committee of the Cinque Ports. He was, not surprisingly, also clerk to the vestry.

Tappenden was Faversham's leading attorney. In 1814 a judge in Doctors' Commons thought Tappenden 'a considerable guarantee of the fairness of the transaction' (*The Times*, 4 May 1814). The town's nineteenth-century historian E. Crow noted that 'few men stood higher in legal knowledge, or was consulted upon more various subjects' (Crow). He was also a scrivener—a specialist in property conveyancing and mortgages—a skill he put to his own advantage as he acquired considerable property in east Kent with his increasing wealth.

In 1789 Tappenden brought together his close knowledge of other people's affairs, and built on the confidence people had in him, by establishing the Faversham Bank. His choice of partner, William Bennett, a well-known local merchant, was wise, as it brought a valuable London trade dimension to the town's first bank. It survived twenty-five turbulent years, supported by its London agent, Williams & Co., and was held in high esteem by individuals and institutions in the area.

In 1801 Tappenden and his relatives invested £40,000 in a co-partnership in a new ironworks in Aber-nant, in Glamorgan, which was to lead to his financial collapse and disgrace. In 1807, when the investment had risen to £70,000 for no financial return, his Welsh partners (Jeremiah Homfray and James Birch) withdrew. Tappenden's ambitious attempt to build an integrated and competitive business included the construction of three furnaces, 8 miles of tramroad from Aber-nant to the head of the Neath Canal, and a 100-ton-per-week rolling mill at Pontypridd, the latter undoubtedly a stimulus to the development of that place. Tappenden's son called the Welsh enterprise a 'gigantic concern' (Centre for Kentish Studies, U1823/17 C1 T16–21). But just as the company's operating costs increased, aggravated by the loss of a protracted lawsuit against the Neath Canal Company, so the price of pig and bar iron weakened. This put intolerable strain on a business by then too reliant on credit.

Williams & Co. petitioned for the bankruptcy of the Abernant Iron Company in December 1814, at the same time stopping the Faversham Bank. Creditors of the Welsh business claimed debts of £270,000. These claims were in addition to the claims on the Faversham Bank, and to the £130,000 invested by Tappenden, suggesting that total claims were upwards of £500,000. Thus Tappenden ranked among the largest business failures of the period; embarrassing questions as to where such large sums had gone went unanswered.

The people of Faversham were shocked by the downfall of their leading citizen and, in an immediate gesture of support, elected his son Charles to all his public offices; here, too, their trust was misplaced, for Charles was imprisoned for felony in 1818. Tappenden died, insolvent, at Milbank Street, Westminster, on 5 April 1841.

PETER TANN

Sources CKS, Faversham town records · Canterbury Cathedral Archives, Faversham town records · J. Lloyd, *The early history of the old south Wales ironworks, 1760–1840* (1906), 116–26 · NL Wales, Maybery papers · P. L. Tann, 'James Tappenden: town clerk of Faversham, attorney, baker, industrialist and bankrupt, 1742–1841', *Archaeologia Cantiana*, 115 (1995), 213–29 · P. L. Tann, 'The Tappenden tramroad', *Journal of the Railway and Canal Historical Society*, 32/2 (July 1996) · P. L. Tann, 'The Abernant ironworks', *Morgannwg*, 40 (1996) · CKS, U1823/17 C1 T16–21 ['Gigantic concern' in Wales citation] · *The Times* (4 May 1814), 3, 5 · E. Crow, 'Historical gleanings relative to the town of Faversham', 1855, CKS, MSS vol. 2, Fa/Z/41/2 · records of the upper division of the lathe of Scray (petty sessions), CKS, P/S · F. Hull, ed., *A calendar of the white and black books of the Cinque Ports, 1432–1955*, Kent Archaeological Society Records Branch, 19 (1966) · J. Hoppit, *Risk and failure in English business, 1700–1800* (1987), 136 · BL, Add. MS 5520, piece 75 [pedigree of Tappenden family] · parish register (baptism), Faversham, St Mary, Canterbury Cathedral Archives, U3/146/1/2, 13 Oct 1742 · register of affidavits, 1749–1784, PRO, INO 1 4568 · parish register (second marriage), West Ham, All Saints, 1780 · death duty register, PRO, IR 26/1755

Wealth at death under £20: PRO, death duty registers, IR 26/1755

Tapping, Mrs Alfred B. *See* Cowell, Florence (1852–1926), *under* Cowell, Samuel Houghton (1820–1864).

Tara. For this title name *see* Preston, Thomas, first Viscount Tara (*b.* in or after 1585, *d.* 1655).

Tarawali, Ibrahim (*c.*1785–1880), political leader and educationist, was born in the town of Forecariah, Moriah kingdom, in Guinea, west Africa. Ibrahim Tarawali was a son of Ibrahim Konditu Fofana, a leading entrepreneur and Muslim religious leader. The Fofana trace themselves back several centuries to Jakha in the Mali empire and are members of the Jakhanka, composed of five notable Muslim clerical clans in western Africa. The Fofana also are renowned specialists in long-distance trade. Because of missionary and trade activities the Fofana travelled widely in west Africa, and Tarawali's kinsmen entered the coastal region of Guinea before 1700 and played a very significant part in creating political, economic, and religious institutions in the area. Owing to their great religious authority the Fofana had the responsibility of crowning the *alimami* (king) of Moriah. Tarawali's grandfather, Yusufu, and his father were important merchants and scholars. His older brother, Konditu Modu Fofana, who founded Konditoya in Port Loko, Sierra Leone, before 1820, was a wealthy trader and powerful political figure.

Ibrahim Tarawali received his primary and secondary education from local Muslim scholars in Forecariah from about 1790 to 1805. Then he was sent to the Islamic university in Tuba, Guinea, for advanced education in law and theology. The university was directed by members of the Suwaré family, another of the Jakhanka clans. There he received the title *fodé*, one who specializes in Koranic studies, and he was superbly prepared for a career in diplomacy and in religious education. He probably spent more than fifteen years in Tuba as was customary for specialists in law and theology. He returned to Forecariah after 1820, and not long after that the Muslim ruler of Tawiya, Dura Tumani Sankoh, asked the king of Moriah, Alimami Ali Gberika Ture, to send Fodé Tarawali to establish an educational centre in his region, in what is now Sierra Leone. Fodé Tarawali agreed to come, and Dura Tumani granted him land for his religious establishment. He founded the town of Gbilé in 1830 or earlier, and he developed a renowned Islamic university there.

Between 1830 and 1860 Fodé Tarawali acquired additional land, expanded the university, and produced a very large family of scholars and merchants. Among his sons were Hafiyu, Luseni (al-Husain), Bokari (Abu Bakr), Fodé Sheikhu, Baimba Dee, Sheikhu Baimba, Maju, Konditu, al-Hajj Salim, and Muhammad Sharif, all of whom were prominent in regional affairs. Two grandsons, in particular, Fodé Sheikhu Muhammad Sanusi (son of al-Hajj Salim) and Sheikhu Luseni (son of Fodé Sheikhu), became important leaders in northern Sierra Leone after the establishment of the British protectorate in 1896.

The British became interested in the northern hinterland of Sierra Leone in the late eighteenth century and, after the proclamation of the crown colony of Sierra Leone in 1808, British agents made many trips to the region to collect information and establish good relations. By 1860 Great Britain was deeply involved in the political, economic, and military affairs of the northern region, and the government interpreter, Thomas George Lawson, was frequently dispatched to negotiate with African rulers about matters of trade and warfare. He reported that Fodé Tarawali was among the most important leaders in the northern territories. In a long memorandum to the colonial governor of Sierra Leone, Lawson described Tarawali as the 'high Priest' of Moriah, who was assisted by two of his sons as 'sub-priests'. Tarawali was the principal mediator in a long series of civil wars between various factions for control of the northern territories and was often consulted about these matters by the colonial government. Some of this correspondence has been preserved in the Sierra Leone Archives at Fourah Bay College, Freetown.

In 1872 Edward Wilmot Blyden, who became the director of Muslim education for the colony and protectorate of Sierra Leone, visited Fodé Tarawali in Gbilé. In a letter dated 19 January 1872, from Blyden to Henry Venn of the

Church Missionary Society in London, he described what he learned:

> Billeh [is] a sort of University town—the Oxford of this region—where are collected over five hundred young men studying Arabic and Koranic literature. … The president of this institution is Fodé Tarawally, celebrated throughout the country for his learning. He was educated at Tuba a town in the Fulah country of great literary repute. … His father before him, all of his brothers, and all of his sons have been distinguished for their learning.   (CMS MSS, Birmingham University)

It was the most prestigious Islamic educational institution in the Sierra Leone hinterland, with more than a thousand scholars at various levels of learning, and a library of hundreds of Arabic texts on law, theology, and philosophy. It was responsible for educating many of the sons and grandsons of African rulers, some of whom were not Muslims. In addition to directing the university, Tarawali supervised the construction of many town mosques in the region. Thus, he was instrumental in not only enhancing Islamic culture but spreading its influence throughout the northern territories.

In one of the series of civil wars in the region the university and most of its books were destroyed by fire in 1875. War continued to ravage the region for several more years, and Fodé Tarawali's skill as a mediator and his influence as a Muslim leader did not lead to an end of the warfare, which continued for five years after his death in 1880. Alimami Bukhari of Moriah reported that Fodé Tarawali was attacked and killed while conducting prayers at the mosque in Famoria, but Tarawali family informants claim that he died peacefully of old age in Gbilé. He left extensive farm lands and a large Islamic library when he died, and his descendants continued to play prominent roles in political, economic, and religious affairs in northern Sierra Leone. His grandson, Sheikhu Luseni, was the principal scholar and political leader at Gbilé until 1980.

DAVID E. SKINNER

Sources D. E. Skinner, *Thomas George Lawson* (1980) · D. E. Skinner, 'Mande settlement and the development of Islamic institutions in Sierra Leone', *The International Journal of African Historical Studies*, 11 (1978), 32–62 · private information (2004) [Sheikhu Luseni, grandson] · Arabic letter books, Fourah Bay College, Freetown, Sierra Leone archives · U. Birm. L., special collections department, Church Missionary Society archive
Archives U. Birm. L., Church Missionary Society MSS · University of Sierra Leone, Freetown, Sierra Leone archives, government interpreter's records
Wealth at death homes, extensive farmlands, and large collection of Arabic/Islamic texts: Native Affairs Department minute papers 570/Dec 1895, enclosure B, Sierra Leone Archives, Freetown

Tarbotton, Marriott Ogle (1834–1887), civil engineer, was born on 6 December 1834 at Brunswick Terrace, Leeds, the second of five children of Samuel Tarbotton (1799/1800–1850), druggist and later oil merchant, and his wife, Grace (*bap.* 1803), daughter of Robert Ogle. He was educated at Leeds grammar school and became articled to Charles Clapham of Wakefield, civil engineer. After Clapham's death Tarbotton practised on his own for a number of

years. In 1855 he was appointed borough engineer and surveyor to Wakefield corporation. On 8 September 1857 he married Emma Maria Stanfield, daughter of John Stanfield, bookseller, of Wakefield. They had four children, two boys and two girls.

In 1859 Tarbotton was appointed borough surveyor to Nottingham corporation, being selected from fifty-two applicants. He was the first full-time surveyor to the corporation. He came at an important time in Nottingham's development, when the corporation was beginning to tackle the insanitary and overcrowded conditions which had been severely criticized by the health of towns commission in 1845. This situation had arisen partly from the refusal of the burgesses to allow building on the common lands surrounding the town. This had started to become possible after an Enclosure Act had been obtained. Progress to implement the act had been slow and was to be one of Tarbotton's concerns. Another factor he had to face was the situation caused by a small stream, the River Leen, which ran through several parishes adjoining the borough. The use of this river for industry and as a sewer caused health problems when the river entered the borough, and also affected the Nottingham Canal.

One of Tarbotton's first briefs from the town's sanitary committee was to report on this problem, for which the committee had already received a report from Thomas Hawksley (1807–1893). Hawksley had been the engineer to Nottingham Waterworks Company but in 1852 had moved to London, where he had an engineering practice which became influential. Tarbotton no doubt soon became acquainted with Hawksley, who was president of the Institution of Civil Engineers from 1871 to 1873, and who proposed Tarbotton for membership of the institute. Another of Tarbotton's supporters in his application for membership was J. W. Bazalgette, the distinguished London engineer who was knighted in 1874. (Tarbotton was successful in his application, and was also a fellow of the Geological Society and of the Meteorological Society.) Tarbotton's efforts to deal with the drainage and sewage problems were hampered by the difficulties caused by lack of co-ordination with the adjoining parishes. This was partly resolved in 1877 when the Borough Extension Act brought them within the borough. Tarbotton prepared the first detailed plan of the borough and the adjoining parishes. Other activities during his period as borough engineer included acting as official referee under the 1845 Enclosure Act, designing a new bridge over the River Trent, drawing up plans and specifications for a university college, and from 1874 serving as gas engineer.

Tarbotton resigned as borough engineer in 1880 and was appointed engineer to the water, gas, and sewage disposal committees. A major work he supervised in this period was the building of a new water pumping station at Papplewick, 7 miles north of the town. His work for the sewage disposal committee included a new farm and disposal works, but he did not live to see the completion of these. He was taken ill at a meeting of the committee and died two days later at his home, Castledene, The Park, Nottingham, on 6 March 1887. His death was said to be the result of overwork, and colleagues said he never had sufficient rest or recreation. The official cause of death was inflammation of the brain, diarrhoea, and exhaustion. He was buried in the Church cemetery, Nottingham, on 9 March, the service being conducted by the Anglican clergyman of St Mary, Nottingham. Tarbotton does not appear to have had any recognized religious affiliation. His obituary in the *Proceedings of the Institution of Civil Engineers* ended as follows:

> Few engineers have left behind them such artistic memorials for Mr. Tarbotton took care that all his structures should be fitly and gracefully decorated. He was by nature both artist and engineer and felt deeply the sentiment of any work on which he was engaged. He was an accomplished scholar, full of classical lore, and a refined gentleman kindly and genial in the last degree.

He was survived by his wife and four children.

GEOFFREY OLDFIELD

Sources records of the borough of Nottingham: vol. 9, 1956 · D. Gray, *Nottingham through 500 years* (1960) · D. Gray, *Nottingham: settlement to city* (1953) · J. Beckett and others, eds., *A centenary history of Nottingham* (1997) · J. Beckett and K. Brand, *Nottingham: an illustrated history* (1997) · G. Oldfield, 'The construction of Papplewick pumping station', *Transactions of the Thoroton Society*, 99 (1995), 81–7 · *PICE*, 91 (1887–8), 426–9 · *Nottingham Journal* (8 March 1887) · *Nottingham Daily Express* (8 March 1887) · *Nottingham Daily Guardian* (8 March 1887) · K. D. G. Brand, ed., *Nottingham Civic Society Newsletter* [forthcoming] · *Wakefield Echo* (11 March 1887) · m. cert. · d. cert. · parish register, Leeds, 2 April 1835 [baptism]
Archives Inst. CE · Local Studies Library, Angel Row, Nottingham · Notts. Arch.
Likenesses portrait, repro. in M. O. Tarbotton, *History of Old Trent Bridge, Nottingham* (1875)
Wealth at death £25,651: 1887

Tarleton, Sir Banastre, baronet (1754–1833), army officer and politician, was the second son of John Tarleton (1719–1773) of Aigburth, Liverpool, merchant and shipowner in the sugar and slave trades, and mayor of Liverpool in 1764, and his wife, Jane (*d.* 1797), daughter of Banastre Parker of Cuerden, Lancashire. Banastre Tarleton was born at his father's house in Water Street, in Liverpool on 21 August 1754. Educated in Liverpool, he was admitted to the Middle Temple in April 1770 and matriculated at University College, Oxford, in November 1771. When his father died he inherited £5000, most of which he gambled away. His fortune fast disappearing, in April 1775 he purchased, with his mother's help, a commission in the 1st dragoon guards.

Tarleton volunteered for service in America and took part in the ill-fated expedition against Charles Town, South Carolina, in the spring and early summer of 1776. With the rest of the troops on the expedition, he subsequently served in the much more successful campaign in New York. At the end of 1776 Tarleton, attached to the 16th light dragoons, was one of the party that captured the American General Charles Lee. Over the next three years Tarleton took part in all the major engagements of the American War of Independence, in New Jersey, Pennsylvania, and New York. He became a captain in the newly raised 79th foot, or Liverpool regiment, in January 1778, but continued to act as a cavalry officer and won the

Sir Banastre Tarleton, baronet (1754–1833), by Sir Joshua Reynolds, 1782

admiration of many of his colleagues for his vigour and daring. He also acquired a reputation for ruthlessness towards civilians whom he believed were involved in the uprising. He urged a more full-blooded prosecution of the war with the characteristic claim that 'Coolness Apathy & Civil Law will never supply Hussars with Horses' (Tarleton to Captain John André, 19 Feb 1779, Clinton papers).

Tarleton's fame and notoriety reached their peaks in the southern campaigns of 1780 and 1781, by which time he was lieutenant-colonel commanding the British Legion, a mixed infantry and cavalry unit of American loyalists. He played an important part in the successful siege of Charles Town. On 13 April 1780 his fast-moving legion cavalry seized Monck's Corner, a strategically important post on the Cooper River, and so effectively closed the final escape route for the Charles Town garrison. Two weeks after the surrender of Charles Town, Tarleton's cavalry caught and comprehensively defeated a Virginian force that had been marching to relieve Charles Town but which had begun to retreat northwards when they learned of its capitulation. This victory at the Waxhaws was to be a mixed blessing, however, for in its aftermath American prisoners were killed and, although Tarleton denied instigating this, the affair was subsequently used to justify similar outrages by the Americans.

Tarleton played an important part in the decisive British victory over Horatio Gates's army at Camden on 16 August 1780, and two days later he destroyed a numerically superior force under General Sumpter at Catawba Fords: 'the public prints', he proudly told his brother on 21 August, 'will announce two Glorious Actions for Britain' (Lpool RO, Tarleton papers, 920 TAR 4/1). But despite initial appearances to the contrary these triumphs did not pacify South Carolina. Tarleton's British Legion, effective though it was as a light cavalry force, seems through its harsh and undisciplined treatment of the local population to have contributed significantly to reigniting the rebellion. When his men's ill conduct was brought to his attention Tarleton denied any knowledge of such behaviour, but his corps was criticized bitterly by colleagues as well as opponents, which suggests that there may have been substance to the complaints. Tarleton did punish some of the worst excesses of his troops, yet his well-known preference for severe methods may well have led his subordinates to believe that he regarded pillage and plunder as an acceptable weapon against insurgents: 'Nothing will secure these People but Fire & Sword', he reported to his commanding officer and mentor, Earl Cornwallis (Cornwallis papers, 30/11/4, fol. 63).

So far Tarleton's career as a cavalry commander had been one of almost uninterrupted success. In November 1780 he again defeated Sumpter, adding to Cornwallis's high opinion of his abilities. At the end of the year, as British troops were preparing for the invasion of North Carolina, he hoped that 'my good Genius still smiles' (letter to his brother, 18 Dec 1780, Tarleton papers, Lpool RO, 920 TAR 4/2). However, a month later his fortunes changed dramatically. Cornwallis began his march into North Carolina and detached Tarleton with a force of regular infantry and his own legion troops to attack an American force under Daniel Morgan. Tarleton caught up with Morgan at Hannah's Cowpens on 17 January 1781. The American commander, however, was more than a match for the impetuous Tarleton, who was accused by an American loyalist of 'dreadful bad management' (journal of Alexander Chesney, BL, Add. MS 32627, fol. 21). Over 800 of Tarleton's 1100 men were either killed or captured. Tarleton was never again to be trusted with such an independent command during the war. Injured while leading his troops in Cornwallis's pyrrhic victory at the battle of Guilford Court House on 15 March 1781, Tarleton was part of Cornwallis's army that surrendered at Yorktown, Virginia, in October 1781.

On his return to England in January 1782, Tarleton was feted as a hero, his reputation as a dashing cavalry officer reinforced by the story that he had been prepared to break out of the Yorktown defences to lead an attack on Philadelphia (Peter Johnston to James Murray, 25 Jan 1782, Scottish RO, Broughton and Cally Muniments, GD 10/1421/7/344). During the war he had lost two fingers: this was to prove an electoral asset. He became a friend of the prince of Wales, and it was at this time that the famous

full-length picture of Tarleton in the distinctive green uniform of his legion cavalry was painted by Reynolds, and another, less well known, by Gainsborough.

Tarleton's obsession with gambling and a long-running affair, from May 1782 to May 1797, with Mrs Mary (Perdita) *Robinson (1756/1758?–1800), the actress, poet, and former mistress of the prince of Wales, were the subject of much gossip. They lived extravagantly, reportedly spending £2500 a year. In 1797, according to the diarist Joseph Farington, Mrs Robinson 'separated from Tarleton on account of his designs on her daughter who is now 21' (Farington, *Diary*, 3.832). In 1786 letters were published in the press criticizing Tarleton's conduct at Cowpens. Stung by these he published his *History of the Campaigns of 1780 and 1781, in the Southern Provinces of North America* (1787), which was self-justificatory and criticized Cornwallis. The piece provoked a hostile response from a fellow officer, Roderick Mackenzie—*Strictures on Lt. Col. Tarleton's History* (1787)—and then a defence from a former colleague, George Hanger, *An Address to the Army in Reply to Strictures, by Roderick Mackenzie* (1789).

Tarleton's *History* might also have owed something to his political ambitions. In the 1784 general election, he was narrowly defeated at Liverpool, where his family was still influential. He succeeded there in 1790. Through his connection with the prince he had become an associate of Charles James Fox—a somewhat curious alliance, given Tarleton's role in the war and Fox's opposition to the coercion of the Americans. Defeated in 1806 but re-elected in 1807, Tarleton left the Commons in 1812. A Foxite, in parliament he spoke often and on a variety of subjects, but principally on military matters, and in defence of the slave trade, in which Liverpool had a special interest. Apart from a brief period when he supported the Portland ministry between 1807 and 1809—rewarded with the governorship of Berwick and Holy Island—he generally voted with the opposition.

Meanwhile Tarleton remained in the army, becoming major-general in 1794, lieutenant-general in 1801, and full general in 1812. He held an independent command for a short time in Portugal from the end of 1798, but did not see truly active service after the American war, the most important phase of his life. He was colonel of the 21st dragoons from 1802, then of the 8th light dragoons from 1818. He married, on 17 December 1798, Priscilla Susan Bertie, illegitimate daughter of Robert Bertie, fourth duke of Ancaster; they had one daughter. Tarleton requested, through the duke of York, a baronetcy, and was made a baronet on 23 January 1816; he was created GCB on 16 May 1820. Allegedly 'vanity' was his 'prevailing foible' (HoP, *Commons, 1790–1820*, 5.336). He died at Leintwardine, Herefordshire, on 23 January 1833, survived by his wife.

STEPHEN CONWAY

Sources DNB · HoP, *Commons, 1790–1820*, 5.332–6 · *GM*, 1st ser., 103/1 (1833), 273–4 · R. D. Bass, *The green dragoon: the lives of Banastre Tarleton and Mary Robinson* (New York, 1957) · Lpool RO, Tarleton papers · priv. coll., Tarleton papers · U. Mich., Clements L., Sir Henry Clinton papers · PRO, Cornwallis papers · Farington, *Diary*, vol. 3 · H. A. C. Sturgess, ed., *Register of admissions to the Honourable Society of the Middle Temple, from the fifteenth century to the year 1944*, 1

(1949), 371 • J. Hutchinson, ed., *A catalogue of notable Middle Templars: with brief biographical notices* (1902), 239
Archives NRA, priv. coll., corresp. and papers
Likenesses T. Gainsborough, oils, *c.*1782 • J. Reynolds, oils, 1782, National Gallery, London [*see illus.*] • C. Townley, stipple (after R. Cosway), BM

Tarleton, John (1755–1841), merchant and politician, was born at Liverpool, the third of the seven children of John Tarleton (1719–1773), a merchant, and Jane Parker (1726–1797), daughter and coheir of Banastre Parker of Cuerden, Lancashire. At his death the elder John Tarleton left an estate worth some £80,000, of which £5000 went to his son. Where the younger John was educated is unknown, but three of his brothers—Thomas, Banastre *Tarleton, and Clayton—went to Oxford University.

Tarleton became a freeman of Liverpool in January 1777 and went on to become a leading West Indian and African trader. By 1785 he had an office in Duke Street and was a partner in the firm of Tarleton and Backhouse; the other partners included his brothers Thomas and Clayton, and Daniel Backhouse. Through Tarleton and Backhouse his standing in Liverpool rose substantially, and in 1788 he was one of the delegation of Liverpool merchants who attended parliament to give evidence on the state of the African slave trade. In the same year he had a meeting with the prime minister, William Pitt the younger, but failed to persuade him to abandon his support for the abolitionist cause. Recounting this meeting to Clayton Tarleton, he expressed his fears for the future of the trade, 'except we can prove that it is not carried on with that shocking inhumanity that is imagined by all ranks of mankind out of doors' (Tarleton MS 920 TAR 4/5).

Despite failing to prevent parliament from regulating the slave trade in 1788, Tarleton and Backhouse remained a prominent investor in slaving voyages. Between 1786 and 1804 the firm backed forty ships, many intended for the African trade. In March 1790, with monetary interests of some £85,000, Tarleton and Backhouse was the third largest investor at Liverpool in slaving voyages. Throughout the 1790s Tarleton seems to have been a regular partner in the firm, though he left it temporarily in 1792 after a 'very violent quarrel' (Tarleton MS 920 TAR 4/26) with Backhouse. The earnings it achieved are difficult to calculate, but one writer, referring to Thomas Tarleton, claimed that 'two scions of the Old Stile House', a former residence of Edward Tarleton (1620–1690), 'formed a partnership with a third individual, in July 1776, each advancing £5000', and in 'the course of less than twenty-seven years, their gains amounted to £233,633' (Herdman, 16). In 1792 alone £68,406 was said to have 'appeared to their credit' (ibid.). However, one cannot be sure that these claims are accurate or that they relate to Tarleton and Backhouse. Surviving accounts for the firm suggest, nevertheless, that it had a healthy balance sheet during its life.

While remaining active in trade, Tarleton's interests shifted towards politics and real estate during the 1790s. Having joined the Whig Club in 1787, he stood for the Cinque Ports parliamentary seat of Seaford in 1790 as a Pelhamite whig. Beaten in the election, he was seated on petition on 19 March 1792. In parliament he remained a staunch opponent of abolition and also opposed the Liverpool Corporation Loan Bill in 1793, though he did not vote against the government on any major issue in 1792–6. Declaring himself a 'decided supporter of the general measures of the present administration' (Port and Thorne), he stood at Liverpool in the 1796 parliamentary elections, thereby challenging his brother Banastre, who was one of the two sitting members for the constituency. His campaign was tarnished by accusations that he had failed to pay debts of £3000 arising from the Seaford election and charges of 'unbrotherly' conduct. Unsupported by any of his close family, he finished bottom of the poll. This crushing defeat ended his political ambitions and may, temporarily at least, have caused a rift with his family; his mother and brother Clayton died in 1797 and, of their close relatives, only John was denied a bequest in their wills.

His political hopes thwarted, Tarleton devoted the rest of his life to his family and his real estate interests. On 26 October 1790 he married Isabella (*c.*1770–*c.*1850), daughter and heir of Alexander Collingwood of Unthank and Little Ryle, near Alnham, Northumberland. They had four children, all born in Liverpool between 1792 and 1806. On marrying, he began to seek a country residence outside Liverpool, and by 1796 was described as a gentleman living at Finch House, West Derby, Lancashire. One authority claims that he 'failed in business and went to Holland' (Stewart-Brown, 63), but this has not been verified. In later years, however, he inherited the Collingwood estates in Northumberland and also acquired property in Gloucester Place, London.

John Tarleton died on 20 September 1841 at 14 Grove Terrace, London, and was buried at St Pancras. He was survived by his wife. DAVID RICHARDSON

Sources D. Richardson, ed., *The Tarleton papers: an introduction* (1974) • R. Stewart-Brown, 'Tarleton of Bolesworth Castle, co. Chester', *Cheshire Sheaf*, 3rd ser., 27 (1930), 50–52, 55–7, 59–64 • 'Minutes of evidence taken before a committee … against the abolition of the slave trade', *British Sessional Papers: Accounts and Papers*, 29 (1790), 500, no. 698 • W. G. Herdman, *Pictorial relics of ancient Liverpool* (1843) • Lpool RO, Tarleton papers, 920 TAR • M. H. Port and D. R. Fisher, 'Tarleton, John', HoP, *Commons* • M. H. Port and R. G. Thorne, 'Liverpool', HoP, *Commons* • poll for the election of 1796, Liverpool, Lpool RO • R. Craig and R. Jarvis, *Liverpool registry of merchant ships*, Chetham Society, 3rd ser., 15 (1967) • F. E. Hyde, B. B. Parkinson, and S. Mariner, 'The port of Liverpool and the crisis of 1793', *Economica*, new ser., 18 (1951), 368–9
Archives Lpool RO | PRO, letters to William Pitt, PRO 30/8

Tarlo, (Lambert) Beverly. See Halstead, (Lambert) Beverly (1933–1991).

Tarlton, Richard (d. **1588**), actor and clown, became a legend in his own lifetime and was constantly reinvented for two decades after his death. As a result, fictions about his life have become inextricably tangled with its facts. Thomas Fuller, who was at some pains to verify the facts that informed his *History of the Worthies of England*, says that he was born at Condover in Shropshire, where his father was a pig farmer, but Fuller was making his enquiries over

Richard Tarlton (*d.* 1588), by John Scottowe

a century after Tarlton's birth (*The History of the Worthies* was published in 1662, a year after Fuller's death), and the authenticity of his claim cannot be guaranteed. We know from Tarlton's will, proved on 6 September 1588, that his mother was called Katherine, and, from subsequent litigation, that he had a married sister called Helen.

Fuller's claim that Tarlton's father moved from Shropshire to Ilford is credible, not least because his contemporaries associated him with the county of Essex, but there is a decidedly fictional air about his further assertion that, while still in Condover, Tarlton:

> was in the field, keeping his Father's Swine, when a servant of Robert Earl of Leicester ... was so pleased with his *happy unhappy* answers, that he brought him to Court, where he became the most famous Jester to Queen Elizabeth. (Fuller, 2.311)

There is greater likelihood in the story casually told by Simplicity in Robert Wilson's play *The Three Lords and Three Ladies of London*, that Tarlton in his youth was a water-carrier. Wilson was, after all, a close colleague of Tarlton's during their years with the Queen's Men.

What is not in dispute is that Tarlton arrived in London as a provincial immigrant. It was as a rustic clown, dressed in a russet suit and buttoned cap, that he stamped his enduring image on the city. The role enabled him to speak to and for the uprooted countrymen struggling to come to terms with urban living, and the effectiveness of his comic improvisations owed much to his natural ability to observe the customs of the city from the outside.

Tarlton was either still alive, or very recently dead, when Wilson's play was first performed (*The Three Lords* is variously dated between 1584 and 1589). Even so, we should be wary of trusting too far the authenticity of the water-carrier story. By the 1580s Tarlton's association with

ale, beer, and taverns was so well established that the suggestion that he once made money out of water may have been intended to excite hilarity in the playhouse. He was a freeman of the Company of Vintners, gaining his freedom by redemption in late 1584. He bound his first and only apprentice ten days later. There are references to his keeping an inn in Colchester, the Saba tavern in Gracechurch Street, and an ordinary in Paternoster Row. It must have been in such places, before his formal entry into the theatrical profession, that he inaugurated his 'themes', those extemporized (often rhymed) responses to subjects suggested by drinkers to challenge his ingenuity that first brought him to public attention. Robert Wilson was the only contemporary to rival Tarlton as an improvising comedian, but Wilson was neither as abrasive nor as obscenely outspoken as Tarlton. There is a strong probability that the transference of his tavern style to the public theatres was Tarlton's peculiar innovation as an actor and the basis of his extraordinary popularity.

The likelihood is that Tarlton joined the acting company of Thomas Radcliffe, third earl of Sussex and the queen's lord chamberlain, in the latter half of the 1570s. In the surviving fragment of *Tarleton's Tragical Treatises* (1578) he describes himself as 'Servaunt to the right Honourable the Lorde Chamberlaine Earle of Sussex', and the dedication is to Lady Frances Mildmay, Radcliffe's sister. By 1583 he was prominent enough to be appointed a founder member of the revived Queen's Men, and he remained with the company until his death, thus earning the right to describe himself in his will as 'one of the Groomes of the Queenes maiesties chamber' (Honigmann and Brock, 57). The only part that can be confidently assigned to him is that of Dericke in *The Famous Victories of Henry the Fifth*. The role was one in which what was done must generally have had greater impact on the audience than what was said, but what also characterizes this raw text is the parade of opportunities it offers to Tarlton as Dericke to indulge his metatheatrical talent as a maker of exits and entrances. On the open stages of Elizabethan London it was impossible to enter or leave the platform unobtrusively. Actors coming on to open a scene had first to locate themselves in order to place the narrative; actors leaving had to have a reason to go. Either way, they had a distance to cover from or to the stage door. That distance was Tarlton's playground, and *The Famous Victories* furnishes it richly.

It was in the interest of playwrights to the Queen's Men to provide suitable opportunities for the leading clown, but Tarlton's real chance to shine came more consistently in the post-play jigs. These jigs, though they included music and dancing, were essentially vehicles for clowns. A handful of jigs, though none of Tarlton's, survive in manuscript. They rely on song and allow for patterned dancing, but they were essentially raucous afterpieces: framed as short farces, they feature sexual misdemeanour and cross-dressing, and can easily accommodate the defamatory mockery characteristic of Elizabethan libels. Tarlton was the master clown of the jig. He had successors, of whom William Kemp is the best known, but never a superior. Almost certainly he wrote some, if not all, of the jigs in which he starred. Like many comedians through history, he made capital out of his own peculiar appearance. Claims that surviving images of Tarlton, even the much-reproduced drawing by John Scottowe, have any status as likenesses have been largely discredited, but we can accept verbal accounts of his rough ugliness. The impression is insistently plebeian—Robert Weimann has called Tarlton 'the first plebeian artist to achieve national recognition in England' (Weimann, 186). It may have been curiosity value that endeared him to the queen and her courtiers.

The historical Tarlton can no longer be distinguished from the hero of the posthumously published jest book. *Tarlton's Jests* was first published in full in 1611, but the first part at least was in circulation during the 1590s, and the second part was entered in the Stationers' register in 1600. All three parts belong to a literary subgenre, and the anecdotes (few of them jests in a modern sense) of which they consist admit a limited responsibility to historical truth. Even so, Tarlton was too recently dead for the unknown compiler to risk utter falsification. The character recorded, or created, in the *Jests* is a prodigious plebeian, hard-drinking, provocative, often forced to improvise himself out of ignominy, outstandingly short-tempered, a misogynist, an adversary of radical protestantism, anti-Catholic too, inclined to draw attention to the functions and appurtenances of the human body's lower half, verbally as well as physically agile, not infrequently violent, and almost always combative. The arrival of this Tarlton, whether in a room, a tavern, a street, or onto the stage, put the timid on their guard and the assertive on their mettle. People in search of a reputation for wit sought to outface him, only to end up outfaced. This is a persuasive aspect of the jest-book portrait, not least because it hints at a comic style subsequently exploited by Elizabethan playwrights and by later generations of stand-up comedians: threatened with what looks like inevitable humiliation, the fool/clown suddenly turns the tables on his humiliators. It may be that there are echoes of Tarlton in Shakespeare's Falstaff.

The image of the strong-bodied clown, emanating aggression and provocation, lingered after Tarlton's death. George Wilson, in his *Commendation of Cockes, and Cock-Fighting* (1607), alludes to a Norwich cock called Tarlton 'because he alwayes came to the fight like a drummer, making a thundering noyse with his winges ... which cocke fought many battels, with mighty and fierce aduersaries' (Nungezer, 356). The historical Tarlton was certainly capable of looking after himself. He was sufficiently skilled as a swordsman to be awarded the accolade of master of fence in 1587. In one of the few authenticated anecdotes, however, he appeared in the role of peacemaker. The occasion was a visit of the Queen's Men to Norwich in June 1583. A scuffle broke out when a Norwich citizen called Wynsdon tried to get in to see the play without paying, and Tarlton was one of the three members of the company to rush to the scene. When Wynsdon ran away,

Tarlton tried to prevent the actor John Bentley from following him, but Bentley escaped his clutches and may have inflicted on Wynsdon the sword wound from which he later died.

Any attempt to reconstruct Tarlton's life is bedevilled by contradiction, partly because no other Elizabethan actor was so much spoken and written about after his death. In the minds of many Elizabethans he represented more than the theatre. In the mind of the compiler of *Tarlton's Jests* he represented sturdy individualism opposed to petty authority, and he did so from the standpoint of the common man.

The separate titles of the three parts of the *Jests* indicate the range of Tarlton's appeal: his 'Court Witty Jests' display him among aristocrats and their ladies, and carry him into the company of the queen herself; his 'Sound City Jests' take him out and about in London; his 'Country Pretty Jests' suggest the kind of impact he made during the provincial tours of the Queen's Men. He earned, or had thrust upon him, privileged access to the masses as well as to their masters. Whatever his private preferences may have been, the masses claimed him as theirs. There is an indicative marginal entry in John Stow's *Annales*: 'Tarleton so beloued that men vse his picture for their signes' (Stow, 698). The reference is to the use of his familiar face to advertise alehouses. According to the historian of Shoreditch, 'His portrait, with tabor and pipe, still serves as a sign to an alehouse in the Borough' in 1798 (Ellis, 209). There is also a possibility, gratifying to those who look to Tarlton for carnival scurrility, that his portrait sometimes adorned the doors of privies.

There is nothing new about the commercial exploitation of popular heroes. Publishers and printers made use not of his face but simply of his name in the effort to increase sales, and this makes it difficult to determine what Tarlton actually wrote. His jigs, if they were ever printed, have been lost. So has the text of the two-part comedy *The Seven Deadly Sins*, which he wrote for the Queen's Men about 1585. What has survived from that play, a precious but enigmatic document in theatre history preserved in the Dulwich College collection, is 'The Platt of the Secound Parte of The Seven Deadlie Sins'. It is, in effect, a synopsis of the twenty-four scenes of an episodic moral narrative containing three separate stories, each bearing on a single sin. The story of Gorboduc illustrates envy, of Sardanapalus sloth, and of Tereus and Philomel lechery. It is possible to recover from the 'platt' (plot) the bare outline of the action, but the real interest of the document is in the information it provides about the distribution of parts to named actors. Beyond that, the actual purpose originally served by the 'platt' remains unclear.

Tarlton's name first appears in print at the end of a ballad, written in 1570, lamenting the havoc wreaked in Bedfordshire and Lincolnshire by the October floods. It is an undistinguished piece of the kind Autolycus purveys in *The Winter's Tale*. Since his was not yet a household name, Tarlton might well have been the author. None of the other publications ascribed to him is certainly his, and their contribution to the Tarlton legend is unreliable. Tarlton belonged primarily to an oral tradition, and it is in the interplay of orality and literature in street ballads and prose pamphlets that his literary influence is preserved. Tarlton's contemporary Gabriel Harvey went so far as to accuse the gifted pamphleteer Thomas Nashe of plagiarizing Tarlton when he wrote accusingly that Nashe's ideas were 'right-formally conueied, according to the stile and tenour of Tarltons president, his famous play of the seauen Deadly sinnes … now pleasantlie interlaced with diuers new-founde phrases of the Tauerne' (Weimann, 207). Few people were better equipped than Tarlton to redirect the dialect of the tavern into satirical channels, and Harvey was not the only Elizabethan who heard the voice of Tarlton when reading the pamphlet literature of controversy.

If the details of Tarlton's public life are overlaid by legend, the details of his private life remain obscure. The Sarah who married Abraham Rogers, son of the archdeacon of Chester, may have been a second sister, and, if we accept the possibility that he preferred to identify himself by his trade rather than his profession, 'Thamsyn the wief of Richard Tarlton vintener', who was buried at St Martin Ludgate on 23 December 1585, may have been Tarlton's partner. There is a record of a marriage between Richard Tarlton and Thomasyn Dann in Chelmsford, Essex, on 11 February 1577, and the known association between Tarlton and Lady Frances Mildmay, whose home was in Chelmsford, lends plausibility to the identification. The quarrelsome, abused wife mentioned in the *Jests* is there called Kate, but that is probably a transference from the known name of the mother who survived him.

Legend has it that Tarlton's will was written in the house of Emma Ball, a Shoreditch prostitute, where the destitute clown had taken refuge, but the image of poverty is contradicted by the dispute over £700 in property between two of the executors, Tarlton's mother and a lawyer called Robert Adams. It is to be hoped that the bitterness of the altercation did not lead them to neglect the care of Tarlton's six-year-old son, Philip. The boy had been named after his godfather Sir Philip Sidney, and the extraordinary stretch of Tarlton's life is nicely exemplified by the distance between this elegant nobleman and Emma Ball. Tarlton died in Shoreditch on 3 or 5 September 1588, and was buried, evidently on the same day, in St Leonard, Shoreditch. Nothing is known of the life of the son whose future welfare is the exclusive concern of Tarlton's will.

PETER THOMSON

Sources E. Nungezer, *A dictionary of actors* (1929) · E. A. J. Honigmann and S. Brock, eds., *Playhouse wills, 1558–1642: an edition of wills by Shakespeare and his contemporaries in the London theatre* (1993) · Fuller, *Worthies* (1811) · R. Weimann, *Shakespeare and the popular tradition in the theatre* (1978) · J. Stow and E. Howes, *Annales, or, A generall chronicle of England … unto the end of this present yeere, 1631* (1631) · H. Ellis, *The history and antiquities of the parish of St Leonard, Shoreditch, and liberty of Norton Folgate* (1798) · D. Wiles, *Shakespeare's clown* (1987) · *Tarlton's jests*, ed. J. O. Halliwell (1844) · C. J. Sisson, *Lost plays of Shakespeare's age* (1936) · J. H. Astington, 'Illustrations of the English stage', *Shakespeare Survey*, 50 (1997) · J. H. Astington, 'Tarlton and the sanguine temperament', *Theatre Notebook*, 53 (1999), 2–7 · M. Eccles, 'Elizabethan actors, IV: S to end', *N&Q*, 238 (1993), 165–76 · *DNB* · parish register, Chelmsford, Essex, 11 Feb 1577 [marriage]

Likenesses J. Scottowe, manuscript drawing, BL, Harley MS 3885, fol. 19 [*see illus.*] · line engraving (facsimile of woodcut), BM; repro. in *Tarlton's jests* (1611) · portrait, Magd. Cam.

Wealth at death approx. £700 in property: Nungezer, *Dictionary of actors*

Tarn, Sir William Woodthorpe (1869–1957), ancient historian, was born in London on 26 February 1869, the eldest of the two sons and one daughter of William Tarn (*b.* 1841/2), silk merchant, and his wife, Frances Arthy (*b.* 1843/4). His was a privileged childhood: in 1881 the family kept eight servants at their London house, at 21 Lancaster Gate. He was educated at Eton College (1882–8), where he was a king's scholar and captain of the school. He entered Trinity College, Cambridge, in 1888, and took a first in part one of the classical tripos in 1891 and a first in part two in 1892, having studied with Henry Jackson, to whom he owed a lifelong interest in Greek philosophy. In accordance with his father's wishes he then studied for the bar at the Inner Temple under the leading chancery barrister Spencer Perceval Butler. He was called to the bar in June 1894 and began to make a name for himself as a chancery barrister. In 1896 he married Flora Macdonald (*d.* 1937), daughter of John Robertson, a landowner of Orbost, Skye. They had one daughter, Otta, for whom Tarn wrote a fairy story, *The Treasure of the Isle of Mist* (1919), which became a classic of its kind and was regularly reprinted until 1959.

The long and dangerous illness of Tarn's wife undermined his own health, and in 1905 he had a serious breakdown and retired from legal practice. He left London for Scotland, where he made his home first at Mountgerald, near Dingwall, and later at Muirtown House, near Inverness. As his health recovered he found intellectual stimulation in the leisurely study of Hellenistic culture and political history. His interest in Greek philosophy reappeared in his first book, *Antigonos Gonatas* (1913); a biography on the grand scale, he sought to bring his subject, whom he admired, to life. Despite technical advances and changed interpretations Tarn's book continued to dominate the subject at the end of the twentieth century.

In 1914 Tarn was refused by the army because of his sight, but he spent the next four years in intelligence work at the War Office in London. The war over, he returned to Scotland and his scholarly pursuits; he had neither need nor desire for academic employment. He became one of the most eminent among the diminishing number of gentleman-scholars in the twentieth century. He was at his most productive between the wars. He contributed many chapters to the *Cambridge Ancient History*—on the rise of the Hellenistic world, on Alexander the Great, and on Parthia—and parts of the chapters between the death of Caesar and the death of Cleopatra. His account of Alexander, which was published separately in 1948 as *Alexander the Great* with a companion volume, *Alexander the Great: Sources and Studies*, showed an admiration verging on hero-worship. Tarn depicted Alexander as the originator of the idea of the unity of mankind, and his conquests as part of a mission to bring civilization to the barbarians. This interpretation, though it was propagated in antiquity, notably by Plutarch, bears the imprint of a late-Victorian British ideal of gentlemanly imperialism. It has subsequently been challenged, rejected, and overturned but it has proved impossible to ignore. The work was reprinted in 1979. In 1927 Tarn published *Hellenistic Civilisation*, a survey of the field, which he revised for the third edition in 1952 and which remained in print in the 1970s.

Tarn published in learned journals, especially on ancient military and naval history. A forceful if courteous controversialist, he trenchantly rejected J. S. Morrison's early argument about the construction of triremes. His Lees Knowles lectures at Trinity College, published as *Hellenistic Military and Naval Developments* (1930), have remained in print ever since. He then spent several years working on the pioneering *The Greeks in Bactria and India* (1938); marshalling and combining evidence for the first time, it became a classic in the field. Tarn was elected FBA in 1928 and took a Cambridge LittD in 1931. He was a member of several learned societies and academies in Britain and abroad, and was made an honorary LLD by Edinburgh University in 1933. In 1939 he was made an honorary fellow of Trinity College, Cambridge, an honour that he prized above all others. In 1952 he was knighted.

As he grew older Tarn rarely met other scholars, but his advice was often sought and never refused; he had a wide correspondence. He enjoyed country pursuits and was a good shot. His home was the centre of much hospitality to his English friends and highland neighbours and connections. In old age his health deteriorated and he could no longer travel far but he derived much happiness from the company of his daughter and grandchildren at their home in Skye, which he visited every summer. He died at his own home—Muirtown House, near Inverness—on 7 November 1957.   F. E. ADCOCK, rev. K. D. REYNOLDS

Sources F. Adcock, 'Sir William Tarn', *PBA*, 54 (1958), 253–62 · *The Times* (8 Nov 1957) · *WWW* · Venn, *Alum. Cant.* · *The Eton register*, 5 (privately printed, Eton, 1908) · private information (1971) · personal knowledge (1971) · census returns, 1881 · A. B. Bosworth, *Alexander and the East* (1996)
Archives Bodl. Oxf., corresp. with Sir Auriel Stein
Likenesses S. Macdonald, portrait, priv. coll. · A. Paterson, photograph, repro. in Adcock, 'Sir William Tarn'
Wealth at death £48,472 14s. 1d.: probate, 24 Jan 1958, *CGPLA Eng. & Wales*

Tarrant, Dorothy (1885–1973), classical scholar, was born on 7 May 1885 at 6 Craven Terrace, Wandsworth, London, the only daughter (there were two sons) of the Revd William George Tarrant (1853–1928), Unitarian minister and journalist, and his wife, Alice, daughter of Henry Stanley of Manchester. She was educated at home until 1895, then at Wandsworth high school (1895–8) and the Girls' Public Day School Company's Clapham high school (1898–1904). While still at school she was placed in the first class of the examination for a London University external pass degree in classics. In 1904 she won a scholarship to Girton College, Cambridge, where she achieved firsts in the classical tripos, part one (1907) and part two, ancient philosophy (1908). While at Girton she won the Agnata Butler and

Therese Montefiore prizes and was awarded the Gilchrist fellowship for research, 1908–9. Cambridge did not then award degrees to women, but as a student of Bedford College, London, she was awarded the University of London BA with first-class honours in classics (1906), followed by an MA in 1909 with a thesis entitled 'The genesis of Plato's theory of ideas'. She took a London PhD in 1930.

Tarrant became assistant lecturer in classics, Bedford College, University of London, in 1909, and in Greek in 1915. She was also acting head of Latin (1913–14) and was promoted to lecturer in 1921 and to university reader in 1929. In 1936 she became university professor of Greek and head of the department of Greek. Her inaugural lecture was 'Plato and the Greek genius'. She was the first female professor of Greek in Britain and after retiring in 1950 held the title of professor emeritus. She became an honorary fellow of Girton College in 1955 and of Bedford College and of Manchester College, Oxford, in 1969. She was president of the Hellenic Society in 1953–6 and president of the Classical Association in 1957–8.

Tarrant's academic publications centre on Plato and on Greek conceptions of the soul and their applications to ethics. Her major work, *The Hippias Major Attributed to Plato* (1928), includes a substantial introduction and commentary. She related the disputed authorship of the dialogue to study of Plato's early metaphysical theory, arguing from her analysis of content, style, and vocabulary that the work belonged to the Platonic period but was not written by Plato. This work together with her 'Imagery in Plato's *Republic*' (*Classical Quarterly*, 1946) and her later article 'Plato as dramatist' (*Journal of Hellenic Studies*, 75, 1955) pioneered the analysis of Plato's style. Other significant academic publications by Tarrant include articles, notes, and reviews, mostly on Plato, and 'Early Greek ideas of the soul: Homer to Anaxagoras' (*Transactions of the Society for Promoting the Study of Religion*, 1932). Her presidential address to the Classical Association, published in 1958 as 'The long line of torch-bearers', discussed authors and other aspects of the classical tradition. Within this field she included copyists and translators. Her address analysed and compared versions of the *Odyssey* by Pope, Samuel Butcher and Andrew Lang, and E. V. Rieu, with special attention to the challenges to the translator who wished both to convey the language and ideas of the past and also to relate them to contemporary concerns.

This interest in the relationship between ancient and modern also infused Tarrant's lectures and publications on Unitarian topics. She explored Plato's contribution to free religious thought, while her writings on temperance, of which she was an advocate, examined biblical and classical sources for evidence of social attitudes to alcohol and to the practical and ethical shortcomings of policies of moderate drinking.

Tarrant's father had been editor of *The Inquirer* as well as a major contributor to several hymnals. She followed in this tradition as a contributor to the *Hibbert Journal* and *The Inquirer*, and to *A Golden Treasury of the Bible* (1934). She undertook extensive administration and committee work for the Unitarians, and was president of the National Unitarian and Free Christian Association from 1948 to 1951. Her Essex Hall lecture in 1949 was published as *The Contribution of Plato to Free Religious Thought*. As president of the Unitarian Assembly in 1952–3, her presidential address, 'The visible witness of free religion', which was published in *The Inquirer* (19 April 1952, 123–4), examined the parallels between religious and personal freedom ('diversity of views is the inevitable concomitant of our freedom'). Her Sims Woodhead memorial lecture (1951) is a valuable document for the social history of Unitarianism in which she commented on her upbringing as a minister's daughter and on changes in the temperance tradition among nonconformists. Alongside her discussion of the drunken Heracles episode in Euripides' *Alcestis* and the passage in *Odyssey*, xiv on wine ('a crazy thing. It sets the wisest man singing and giggling like a girl'; line 463), she also meditated on the impact of advertising in setting role models for young people. She was visitor to the Unitarian College, Manchester, from 1955 to 1958, its president from 1961 to 1963, and the first woman trustee of Dr Williams's Trust from 1945 to 1973. From 1924 to 1971 she compiled the prayers and readings for the bi-monthly newsletter of the Unitarian Women's League.

Tarrant was notable as one of the first women to develop a full academic career and also as an example of the links between Unitarianism, women's education, and classical scholarship (particularly in the context of Bedford College). Her published work shows her at the interface between the nineteenth-century tradition of using classical sources as quasi-biblical models for ethical insight and a modern awareness of social change. She lectured on classical subjects to women's groups and to inmates in Holloway prison. Published works and formal photographs represent her as socially conservative and morally earnest. However, friends and colleagues testified to her sense of fun and disarming humour (obituary in *The Inquirer*, 29 September 1973). Her unpublished handwritten lecture notes and some photographs also suggest a rounded personality. As early as 1926 she was lecturing to passengers on a Mediterranean cruise. Her wartime lecture on the history of Bedford College affirms the humanism and international values of scholarship and ruminates on 'what our College stands for and what it can and should achieve'. In the same period of evacuation to Cambridge she lectured, humorously, in May 1941 on a manuscript, 'Socrates and a Friend', supposedly recently discovered. The fragmented document revealed that most of the members of the ancient Academy were women, evacuated from the city to cold and windswept conditions, instituting previously unknown rituals such as 'the hour for making black' and relieved only by the symposia to which they were invited by male sophists (in this connection she inferred that the term 'maidens' in the document might refer merely to the youth of the women).

In retirement Tarrant lived in Wandsworth, London, lecturing at least until her late seventies and continuing to proof-read for the Lindsey Press. In the year before her death she addressed envelopes for an appeal for *The Inquirer*. She died of pneumonia and old age at St James's Hospital, Balham, London, on 4 September 1973. She never married.   LORNA HARDWICK

Sources *The Inquirer* (29 Sept 1973) · K. T. Butler and H. I. McMorran, eds., *Girton College register, 1869–1946* (1948) · Royal Holloway College, Egham, Surrey, Bedford College archives, private MSS of Dorothy Tarrant [incl. MSS with classical connotations], GB 0505 PP17 · cuttings of items by and about Dorothy Tarrant, Royal Holloway College, Egham, Surrey, Bedford College archive, RF 141/8 · M. Tuke, *A history of Bedford College, 1849–1934* (1939) [incl. photograph of Tarrant] · b. cert. · d. cert. · WWW

Archives Royal Holloway College, Egham, Surrey, archives of Bedford College, cuttings of items, RF 141/8 · Royal Holloway College, Egham, Surrey, archives of Bedford College, unpublished lectures, GB 0505 PP 17

Likenesses Elliott & Fry, photograph, *c*.1938, Girton Cam. · photograph, *c*.1950–1959, Royal Holloway and Bedford New College, Bedford College Archive · photograph, Royal Holloway and Bedford New College, Bedford College Archive; repro. in Tuke, *History of Bedford College* · photograph, repro. in 'Dorothy Tarrant, Professor of Greek 1936–50', *Bedford College, University of London: memories of 150 years*, ed. J. Mordaunt Crook (2001) · photograph, repro. in Tarrant's presidential address, *The Inquirer* (19 April 1952), following p. 123 · photograph, repro. in *The Inquirer*

Wealth at death £12,172: probate, 16 Nov 1973, *CGPLA Eng. & Wales*

Tarrant, Margaret Winifred (1888–1959), artist and illustrator, was born on 19 August 1888 at 1 Stanley Villas, St James's Road, Battersea, London, the only child of the artist Percy Tarrant (*d*. 1934) and his wife, Sarah Wyatt (*d*. 1934). Encouraged by her father, she excelled at drawing and painting from an early age, and while attending Clapham high school won several awards which encouraged her to become an art teacher. However, concerned about her ability to instruct, she decided that teaching was not for her and, after discussion with her father, became a full-time artist and illustrator.

In 1907 the family moved to Gomshall, in Surrey, and in 1908—at the age of nineteen—Margaret Tarrant undertook her first commission, to illustrate Charles Kingsley's *The Water Babies* for J. M. Dent & Sons. Other commissions followed, including *Alice in Wonderland* (1916), *Hans Anderson* (1917), and *Nursery Rhymes* (1914 and 1923) for Ward Lock & Co., and two sets of postcards for the Oxford University Press. She also illustrated some twenty books for the publisher George G. Harrap between 1915 and 1929. Always concerned with improving her techniques, she attended several courses at Heatherley's Art School during this period.

In 1920 Tarrant began working regularly for the Medici Society, a long and fruitful association which led to her being made a shareholder in the company in 1938. During the 1920s she illustrated a highly successful series of fairy books for the company. These were first published at the same time as the rather better known series of Flower Fairy illustrations by her friend and sketching partner Cicely Mary Barker, who was later to become an executor of Margaret's will.

In 1934 both of Tarrant's parents died within three months of each other. Her father had always been an inspiration to her, and she had written to the Medici Society during his final illness: 'I miss his ever ready criticism and help with my work so much … I may say that I have no other relatives' (priv. coll.). Shortly after this, Tarrant moved to Peaslake in Surrey, and she soon became a well-known figure in the community there. Although she never married, she made many loyal and long-lasting friends, both through her painting and her membership of the local church. Her friends described her as full of energy, travelling around the area on an ancient bicycle to save petrol, despite not always being in the best of health herself. Many neighbours were used as models for her pictures. She was well known for her love of animals and for her formidable cat companion, Bobby.

A deeply religious individual, Margaret Tarrant was inspired to paint many spiritual and scripture-based paintings, which the Medici Society published as prints and postcards. She was her own harshest critic, and later regretted the sentimentality of some of these paintings, such as *All Things Wise and Wonderful*, first published in 1925. Ironically, it is probably for these pictures that she is best remembered.

While her paintings and illustrations were often of fairies or religious subjects, Tarrant believed fervently in sketching from life, though her finished works often exhibit a much romanticized style. Many of her paintings were bordered with leaves and flowers characteristic of the arts and crafts movement and the art nouveau style which she much admired. Her true love lay in painting wild flowers, of which she had an extensive knowledge, and she considered the illustrations for a series of wild flower postcards published by the Medici Society between 1937 and 1952 to be among her best works.

Shortly before the Second World War Tarrant was finding it hard to be inspired in her work, so in 1936 the Medici Society financed a six-week trip to Palestine. It was hoped that she would produce more paintings in the same vein as *All Things Wise and Wonderful*. Bravely travelling only with a female artist friend, Margaret said of her visit to the Middle East: 'I think they [the Medici Society] expected some more of my children's cards but with an Israeli flavour, but they didn't get them—Israel wasn't like that' (priv. coll.).

During the early 1950s Tarrant's eyesight began to deteriorate, a source of great frustration to her. Her health in general was not so good, although she still made the effort to go into the countryside and sketch from life whenever she could. Eventually multiple myeloma (a type of cancer causing gradual deterioration of the bones) was diagnosed, and Tarrant spent some months in hospital bearing her illness with characteristic good humour and inner strength. She died at her home, Troon, Wonham Way, Peaslake, on 28 July 1959, leaving some pictures to friends and the rest of her estate to twelve charities. Her work is still popular and much of it remains in print as greetings cards, postcards, and prints.

CLAIRE HOUGHTON

Sources J. Gurney, *Margaret Tarrant and her pictures* (1982) · M. Tarrant, *A journey to the Holy Land* (1988) · correspondence between Margaret Tarrant and the Medici Society, 1920–59, priv. coll. · correspondence between friends and neighbours of Margaret Tarrant and the Medici Society, 1977–80, priv. coll. · b. cert. · d. cert. · private information (2004)
Archives priv. coll., corresp. with Medici Society
Wealth at death £17,413: probate, 20 Sept 1959, *CGPLA Eng. & Wales*

Tarras. For this title name *see* Scott, Walter, earl of Tarras (1644–1693).

Tarring, John (*bap.* 1805?, *d.* 1875), architect, was probably baptized at Holbeton, near Plymouth, Devon, on 11 August 1805, the son of Nicholas Tarring and his wife, Ann. He worked there as a carpenter or plasterer until he moved to London in May 1828 to take up architecture. On 23 September 1830 he married Ellen Pearse, with whom he had two sons. He studied drawing with the architect and surveyor Richard Brown at Brown's academy in Wells Street, which he later bought, possibly working in a builder's yard in Paddington at the same time. Brown, who called himself 'Architect and Professor of Perspective' and in 1815 published *The Principles of Practical Perspective and Scenographic Projection* (which ran to a second edition), practised in London but appears to have had connections with Devon, and it is possibly through these that Tarring came to him. Tarring received a Royal Academy silver medal for a measured drawing and had eight drawings exhibited at the Royal Academy between 1838 and 1876. He became a fellow of the Institute of British Architects on 27 January 1845.

Between 1867 and his death in 1875 Tarring worked in partnership with his younger son, Frederick William Tarring (1847–1925), who succeeded him (and was to become surveyor to the Worshipful Company of Cooks). He designed and restored many private residences, notably Combermere Abbey, Cheshire (*c.*1850–54), for the earl of Combermere, and Thornton Hall, Buckinghamshire (*c.*1854), seat of the Hon. Richard Cavendish; but he was best-known for his numerous chapels for nonconformist bodies in London and the provinces, which led him to be styled 'the Gilbert Scott of the Dissenters'. These included, in 1849, Bethnal Green Chapel, 'the first dissenting place of worship built in London with a spire' (Britton, 30). Between 1848 and 1852 he built for the Wesleyans churches at Wandsworth, Brixton, and Clapham in London, and at Malvern, Worcestershire, and Rochester, Kent; for the Presbyterians churches in Cork, Ireland, and at Lewisham and in the Edgware Road, London; for the Baptists he built a church at Victoria Road, Leicester; he also built Congregational churches at Luton, Bedfordshire; at Rochester, Kent; at Blackburn, Lancashire; and at Exeter and Tavistock in Devon, the latter with schools. For the Congregationalists he also built a memorial hall in Farringdon Street (1859–60). He also submitted plans to the government for concentrating the government offices in a single block of buildings on Parliament Street, and submitted a respected entry in the ensuing competition. Other later works included houses, shops, and warehouses, a gas meter manufactory, and the City Bank, Ludgate Hill branch. He died at home at St Audries in Torquay,

Devon, on 27 December 1875, aged seventy. Tarring's numerous works were listed by John Britton in his obituary of Tarring in *The Builder*. HELENE FURJAŃ

Sources [J. Britton], 'The late Mr John Tarring, architect', *The Builder*, 34 (1876), 30 · *Dir. Brit. archs.* · Boase, *Mod. Eng. biog.* · [W. Papworth], ed., *The dictionary of architecture*, 11 vols. (1853–92) · Graves, *RA exhibitors* · 'Tromer Lodge, Down, Kent', *Civil Engineer and Architect's Journal*, 17 (1854), 296 · *Civil Engineer and Architect's Journal*, 19 (1856), 141 · *The Builder*, 10 (1852), 414 · *The Builder*, 30 (1872), 366–7 · *The Builder*, 34 (1876), 30 · *DNB* · *IGI* · *CGPLA Eng. & Wales* (1876)
Archives RIBA, nomination MSS · RIBA BAL, biography file
Wealth at death under £2000: probate, 31 Jan 1876, *CGPLA Eng. & Wales*

Tarsus, Theodore of. *See* Theodore of Tarsus (602–690).

Tarte, Joseph-Israël (1848–1907), journalist and politician in Canada, was born on 11 January 1848 at Lanoraie, Canada, the eldest of the three children of Joseph Tarte (*d.* 1851), a farmer, and his wife, Louise Robillard. He studied at the Collège de l'Assomption (1860–67), then became articled to a local notary, Louis Archambault, and was admitted to the notariate in 1871. Influenced by Archambault, who was a prominent Conservative politician, he began to write for Conservative newspapers and soon attracted the attention of party leaders. In 1874 he was invited to edit Quebec City's *Le Canadien*, the organ of Sir Hector-Louis Langevin, minister of public works in the late federal government of Sir John A. Macdonald.

At Quebec, Tarte supported the party's ultramontane wing, arguing that the clergy ought to guide voters in the exercise of their franchise. However, as Langevin's chief organizer in an 1876 federal by-election, he pushed those ideas too far. Langevin won the election, but it was annulled by the courts, which ruled that the clergy had interfered unduly.

Tarte himself was elected to the Quebec legislature in 1877. He abandoned ultramontanism after a warning from the Vatican in 1881 against clerical excesses, and by 1883 he was supporting the Conservative Party's moderates and even discussing a possible coalition with moderate Liberals. That year he became editor of a second Quebec newspaper, *L'Événement*.

Tarte's loyalty to the Conservative Party was shaken in 1885, when Macdonald's government allowed Louis Riel to be hanged for leading a rebellion in the north-west. Like most French Canadians, Tarte believed Riel would not have been executed had he not been French and Roman Catholic; yet he returned to the fold after a brief protest.

In 1890 Tarte's newspapers published reports of serious corruption involving a Conservative businessman, Thomas McGreevy, and the federal department of public works, again presided over by Sir Hector Langevin. When McGreevy sued for libel, Tarte engaged as his lawyer the leader of the federal Liberal Party, Wilfrid Laurier. The following year Tarte was elected to the federal parliament, officially as an independent, but with Liberal support. When he raised the McGreevy scandal in the Commons, Langevin was forced to resign from the cabinet and his career was effectively ended. Tarte himself was financially ruined by the affair. Estranged from the Conservative Party, he moved to Montreal with *Le Canadien* and threw his support behind Wilfrid Laurier's Liberals.

Tarte's attention was now drawn by the struggle of Manitoba Roman Catholics against an 1890 provincial law that ended public funding of Catholic schools. Although education was normally under provincial jurisdiction, the imperial privy council ruled in 1895 that the federal government could intervene to protect the religious minority. Yet the Conservative government still hesitated: most English Canadians opposed intervention; French Canadians demanded remedial action.

While the Conservatives delayed and tried to evade the issue, Tarte appealed to Quebec opinion by demanding action on behalf of Manitoba's Catholics (about half of whom were French Canadian). During the 1896 general elections he managed the Liberal campaign in Quebec, making this the main issue. Despite the traditional suspicion with which the Catholic church viewed the Liberals, Tarte convinced Quebec voters that Laurier, a French Quebecker and a Catholic, would do a better job than the Conservatives of restoring Catholic school rights. The Liberals won the elections, doing especially well in Quebec, though Tarte himself was returned to parliament only in a by-election two months later. Laurier gave him Langevin's old portfolio, public works, and sent him to Winnipeg to help negotiate a settlement of the school question. The compromise announced in November 1896 disappointed the clergy but was accepted by most voters.

Tarte was an energetic minister but not an easy colleague to work with. In 1899 he opposed Canadian participation in the Second South African War, so outraging pro-imperial opinion in English Canada that demonstrators burned him in effigy, badly embarrassing Laurier's government. In 1902 he began to campaign for higher tariffs—a contradiction of traditional Liberal ideas. His colleagues protested, and he was forced to leave the cabinet. He crossed over to the Conservatives, but many of them resented what they considered his former betrayals. The leader of their Quebec wing refused to appear in public with him, and Hector Langevin's son-in-law Thomas Chapais published a book-length attack entitled *Judas Iscariote Tarte* (1903).

Tarte continued to advocate high tariffs, calling also for imperial preferences and even joining the British Empire League to promote them. His articles now appeared in *La Patrie*, a Montreal newspaper he had bought in 1897 and given to his sons Louis-Joseph and Eugène. (He had closed down *Le Canadien* and lost control of *L'Événement* in 1893.)

On 20 June 1904 Tarte's wife, Georgiana, *née* Sylvestre, died. (They had been married at L'Assomption on 23 November 1868 and had had six children.) On 23 March 1905 he married his longtime secretary, Emma, *née* Laurencelle, the widow of Dr Narcisse Turcot. A daughter was born to them in 1907, but Tarte died shortly afterwards, on 18 December 1907, at Montreal, and was buried at the city's Côte des Neiges cemetery on 21 December.

A conservative at heart, he had been instrumental in securing the Liberal Party's triumph in Quebec, where it would remain dominant through most of the twentieth century. Yet his real vocation had been the newspaper, and he was considered the most brilliant French-Canadian journalist of his time.   A. I. SILVER

Sources M. Brassard and J. Hamelin, 'Tarte, Joseph-Israël', *DCB*, vol. 13 · L. LaPierre, 'Politics, race and religion in French Canada: Joseph Israel Tarte', PhD diss., University of Toronto, 1962 · H. B. Neatby, *Laurier and a liberal Quebec* (1973) · R. Rumilly, *Honoré Mercier et son temps*, 2 vols. (1975) · A. Perrault, 'Joseph-Israel Tarte', *Revue Canadienne*, 54 (1908) · A. Beaulieu and J. Hamelin, *La presse Québécoise des origines à nos jours*, 2 vols. (1973–5) · *La Patrie* (18 Dec 1907) · *La Patrie* (19 Dec 1907) · *La Patrie* (23 Dec 1907) · H. J. Morgan, ed., *The Canadian men and women of the time* (1898) · L. LaPierre, 'Joseph Israel Tarte: relations between the French Canadian episcopacy and a French Canadian politician', *Report of the Canadian Catholic Historical Association* (1958) · *Judas Iscariote Tarte* (1903) [T. Chapais]
Archives NA Canada, MSS
Likenesses photograph, repro. in *La Patrie* (18 Dec 1907), front page · photograph, repro. in Perrault, 'Joseph-Israel Tarte', 105 · photograph (as younger man), repro. in Rumilly, *Honoré Mercier*, vol 2, p. 127; priv. coll.
Wealth at death 'a life insurance policy for $50,000 (paid for by his sons), a house at Montreal and a country house at Boucherville': Brassard and Hamelin, 'Tarte, Joseph-Israël'; LaPierre, 'Politics, race and religion'

Tarver, Edward John (1841–1891). *See under* Tarver, John Charles (1790–1851).

Tarver, John Charles (1790–1851), lexicographer, was born on 27 March 1790 at Dieppe, the son of John Tarver of London and his wife, Sarah Fox. When war broke out between Britain and France in 1793 the Tarvers were imprisoned, together with the other British residents. John was then staying in the house of M Féral, a friend of his mother, and chief engineer of the *ponts et chaussées* for Seine-Inférieure. Subsequently his parents escaped to England, leaving him in France, where M Féral brought him up as his own son, educating him himself and at the government school at Pont Audemer. In 1805 Féral employed him in the service of the *ponts et chaussées*, and three years later got him a job in the *administration de la marine*, in which service he remained, first as secretary to the admiral of the fleet at Toulon, and afterwards at Leghorn, La Spezia, Genoa, and Brest.

In March 1814, when the war had ended, Tarver joined his mother and his brother and sister in England. He went to Paris during the 'hundred days' immediately after the flight of Louis XVIII, but his prospects appeared to be poor, so he went back to England. He became a French master at Macclesfield Free School. There he was struck by the lack of guidance afforded by existing dictionaries on the right French or English word to choose when a number of equivalents were given. As a result he prepared his *Dictionnaire des verbes français* (1818); this was later followed by the more comprehensive *Royal Phraseological English–French and French–English Dictionary* (2 vols., 1845).

In 1819 Tarver married his cousin, Mary Cristall. Soon afterwards he was appointed French tutor to Prince George, duke of Cambridge, and lived at Windsor. In 1826 he was appointed French master at Eton College, where he stayed for the remainder of his life. He also published *Familiar Conversational French Exercises, Introduction à la langue usuelle* (1836), and *The Eton French Grammar*. He revised several historical abridgements, French grammars, manuals, and dictionaries. His only other work of importance in addition to the phraseological dictionary was a prose translation from Dante, *L'inferno, en français* (1824), with a volume of notes.

Tarver died at Windsor on 16 April 1851, having been a master at Eton for twenty-five years. He had five sons, among them Francis Batten Cristall Tarver, a postmaster of Merton College (1848–52); Charles Féral, the eldest son, who was a fellow of King's College, Cambridge, tutor to the prince of Wales, canon of Chester, and rector of Stisted, where he died on 19 August 1886; Joseph Tarver, the third son, graduated from Worcester College, Oxford, in 1849, and in 1850 became rector of Tyringham with Filgrave, Buckinghamshire.

The youngest son, **Edward John Tarver** (1841–1891), was educated at Eton and at Bruce Castle, Tottenham, and was then articled in 1858 to Benjamin Ferrey, architect. He commenced work as an architect on his own account in 1863 and married Edith Harriet Wornum (*b. c.*1843) on 25 January 1869. His chief ecclesiastical work was the large octagonal All Souls Church at Harlesden Green (1875, partly demolished), and his other works include a country house for the Murrieta family at Wadhurst, Sussex, the rectory at Broadstairs (1870), and the Brixton orphanage. He was president of the Architectural Association in 1874, and in 1888 published *A Guide to the Study of the History of Architecture*, which was based on his lectures on the subject to the Architectural Association. Tarver was a fellow of the Society of Antiquaries and of the Royal Institute of British Architects. He died of pneumonia at his home, 11 Crossfield Road, Hampstead, London, on 7 June 1891, and was buried at Hampstead cemetery on 10 June. He was survived by his wife.

THOMAS SECCOMBE, *rev.* JOHN ELLIOTT

Sources Allibone, *Dict.* · *Journal of Proceedings of the Royal Institute of British Architects*, new ser., 7 (1890–91), 90—91, 338, 349, 356–7, 360 · Foster, *Alum. Oxon.* · H. E. C. Stapylton, *The Eton school lists, from 1791 to 1850*, 2nd edn (1864) · *GM*, 2nd ser., 33 (1850), 658 · *GM*, 2nd ser., 34 (1850), 649 · *GM*, 2nd ser., 35 (1851), 681 · *The Builder*, 60 (1891), 470, 476 · *Building News* (11 July 1890), 40 · *Building News* (12 June 1891), 828 · *IGI* · census returns for Crossfield Road, Marylebone, 1881 · m. cert. [Edward John Tarver]
Likenesses photograph (E. J. Tarver), RIBA BAL; repro. in *Building News* (11 July 1890), 42
Wealth at death £1321 16s. 4d.—Edward John Tarver: administration with will, 15 Aug 1891, *CGPLA Eng. & Wales*

Tasburgh [*née* Kitson], **Dorothy** [*other married name* Dorothy Pakington, Lady Pakington] (**1531–1577**), landowner, was born in London, one of four daughters of the wealthy London mercer and sheriff Sir Thomas *Kitson (1485–1540) and his second wife, Margaret Donnington of Stoke Newington, Middlesex. In November 1540 Dorothy's widowed mother married Sir Richard Long (*d.* 1546), a gentleman of the privy chamber, and in 1548 she took as her third husband John Bourchier, second earl of Bath. On 20 September 1546, only days before her stepfather's death, Dorothy was granted a dispensation to marry Sir

Thomas Pakington (c.1530–1571) of Hampton, Worcestershire, son of the evangelical London merchant Robert Pakington (who was murdered in 1536). Thomas and Dorothy had three sons and three daughters; their eldest son, Sir John *Pakington (1549–1625), known as Lusty Pakington, was a courtier and favourite of Elizabeth I. Following Thomas Pakington's death in June 1571, Dorothy remained a widow for at least a year before taking as her second husband the young Buckinghamshire lawyer and future exchequer teller Thomas Tasburgh (c.1554–1602) of Hawridge.

Dorothy's celebrity derives from her role as a parliamentary patron. Shortly before their marriage Dorothy's first husband, Thomas Pakington, had inherited the lordship of Aylesbury in Buckinghamshire from Chief Justice John Baldwin, his maternal grandfather and guardian, and in 1554 Aylesbury was incorporated as a borough under the control of the Pakington family, who usually returned their friends as MPs. As a widow Dorothy Pakington exercised the full powers of lordship herself, including returning the writ for the 1572 parliament. On 4 May 1572 she nominated Thomas Lichfield and George Burden as the borough's two MPs; Lichfield, a family friend, was to marry Dorothy's eldest daughter, Margaret, the following year. Although Lady Pakington's 1572 return was not unique, returns of MPs by widows were extremely rare in early modern England. They presented the authorities with a dilemma, for in 1586 the privy council expressed concern at a woman nominating burgesses, yet at the same time there was a powerful reluctance to restrict any property rights, even when exercised by widows. With her husband's consent, Dorothy made her will on 30 April 1577, requesting burial in the parish church at Hawridge, Buckinghamshire. The will, which has a protestant preamble, was proved on 21 June 1577. 　　P. R. N. CARTER

Sources J. E. Neale, The Elizabethan House of Commons, rev. edn (1963) · HoP, Commons, 1558–1603 · VCH Buckinghamshire, vol. 3 · M. A. Kishlansky, Parliamentary selection (1986) · S. Mendelson and P. Crawford, Women in early modern England, 1550–1720 (1998) · HoP, Commons, 1509–58 · D. S. Chambers, ed., Faculty office registers, 1534–1549 (1966) · PRO, PROB 11/53, fol. 238 [Sir Thomas Pakington's will] · PRO, PROB 11/59, fol. 186v [Dorothy Tasburgh's will]

Taschereau, Elzéar-Alexandre (1820–1898), Roman Catholic archbishop of Quebec and cardinal, was born at the manor house, Ste Marie de la Beauce, in the province of Quebec, on 17 February 1820. He came of an old family from Touraine in France. Thomas Jacques Taschereau, the son of Christophe Taschereau, emigrated to Canada from Touraine about 1715. His grandson, Judge Jean Thomas Taschereau (d. 1832), married Marie (d. 1866), daughter of Jean Antoine Panet, first president of the legislative assembly, and their son was the future cardinal. The family was devout but with liberal inclinations.

Taschereau entered the Quebec seminary on 1 October 1828. Thence, having visited New York and Britain, he went to Rome, where he received the tonsure on 20 May 1837. He was persuaded to abandon his intention of remaining in Rome. From 1837 to 1842 he studied theology in Quebec, and then became a teacher in the seminary. In

1847, as an English speaker, Taschereau was called to minister to the unfortunate Irish emigrants who were stricken with typhus fever on Grosse Island; he caught the fever and narrowly escaped death. On 17 July 1856 the degree of doctor of canon law was conferred upon him at Rome. In 1860 he was appointed superior of the Quebec seminary, which he had served in various capacities since 1842. The appointment carried with it the rectorship of Laval University, of which Taschereau had been one of the founders and whose development he nurtured, greatly adding to its library. He attended the ecumenical council at Rome in 1870, and on 19 March 1871 Monsignor Lynch consecrated him archbishop of Quebec, in succession to Baillargeon, an elevation promoted by the diplomatic efforts of Sir John Macdonald, the governor-general, and others. He ran the diocese without the usual coadjutor and introduced what some called the 'reign of order', greatly increasing diocesan efficiency. His moderate liberalism was the target of the ultramontane press.

Fifteen years later Taschereau became the first Canadian cardinal. The announcement of his elevation was formally received at Quebec on 8 May 1886 and was a notable anti-ultramontane victory. During June the legislative assembly presented an address of congratulation, and the dignitaries of the Anglican church took a prominent part in the demonstration sparked by the popularity of the promotion. The installation was performed at the basilica on 21 July 1886, the day being observed as a general holiday in Quebec, where 25,000 strangers gathered from all parts of the dominion. At public ceremonies Cardinal Taschereau was accorded a place next to the lieutenant-governor. In 1891, illness required him to hand over his day-to-day responsibilities to a coadjutor, Bishop Bégin. He died at Quebec on 12 April 1898. His funeral was attended by Cardinal Gibbons, who had been elevated by Leo XIII along with Taschereau. Taschereau was a person of rigorous personal devotion, a brilliant administrator, an outstanding educationist, and an effective frustrater of ultramontanist ambitions.

THOMAS SECCOMBE, rev. H. C. G. MATTHEW

Sources DCB, vol. 12 · H. Têtu, Notices biographiques: les évêques de Québec (1889) · D. Gosselin, 'Le cardinal Taschereau', La Semaine Religieuse de Québec, 10 (1897–8), 531–6 · D. C. Lyne, 'Sir John A. Macdonald and the appointment of the first cardinal', Journal of Canadian Studies, 2 (1967), 58–69
Archives Archives de l'Archidiocèse de Québec · Sacra Congregazione di Propaganda Fide, Rome

Taschereau, Sir Henri-Elzéar (1836–1911), judge in Canada, born at Ste Marie de la Beauce, province of Quebec, on 7 October 1836, was the eldest son of Pierre-Elzéar Taschereau, a member of the Canadian legislative assembly, and Catherine Hénédine, the daughter of the Hon. Amable Dionne, a member of the legislative council. The Taschereau family went from Touraine to Canada in the seventeenth century, and Taschereau was a co-proprietor of the Quebec seigniory of Ste Marie de la Beauce, which had been ceded to his great-grandfather in

1746. The Taschereaus had been for two generations distinguished in the judicial and ecclesiastical life of Canada. Cardinal Elzéar-Alexandre Taschereau was Henri's uncle.

Taschereau was educated at the Quebec seminary, was called to the Quebec bar in 1857, and practised in the city of Quebec. On 1 May 1857 he married Marie Antoinette (*d.* June 1896), the daughter of R. U. Harwood, a member of the legislative council of Quebec; they had five sons and three daughters. Taschereau became a QC in 1867, and in 1868 was appointed clerk of the peace for the district of Quebec, but soon resigned. From 1861 to 1867 he represented Beauce county as a Conservative in the Canadian legislative assembly, and supported Sir John Alexander Macdonald and Sir George Cartier on the question of federation. On 12 January 1871 he became a puisne judge of the superior court of the province of Quebec, on 7 October 1878 a judge of the supreme court of Canada, and in 1902 chief justice of Canada in succession to Sir Samuel Henry Strong. He was knighted in 1902 and became in 1904 a member of the judicial committee of the privy council. In 1906 he resigned the chief justiceship and was succeeded by Sir Charles Fitzpatrick. Twice in that capacity he administered the government as deputy to the governor-general.

Taschereau was an LLD of both Ottawa and Laval universities. When a law faculty was established at Ottawa University he was appointed to a chair, and in 1895 became dean of the faculty in succession to Sir John Sparrow Thompson.

Taschereau's extensive knowledge of Roman and French civil law, as well as of the English statute and common law, enabled him to render important service to Canadian jurisprudence. As a legal writer he made his reputation by publishing the *Criminal Law Consolidation and Amendment Acts of 1869 for the Dominion of Canada* (2 vols., 1874–5), *The Criminal Statute Law of Canada* (1888), and *Le code de procédure civile du Bas-Canada* (1876). As an expert in Canadian criminal law, he played an influential role in the development of the Canadian criminal code of 1892. He further published in 1896 a *Notice généalogique sur la famille Taschereau*. Tall in stature, he was a scholar and a cultured man. In March 1897 he married Marie Louise, the daughter of Charles Panet of Ottawa. Taschereau died at Ottawa on 14 April 1911.

Sir Henri-Thomas Taschereau (1841–1909), judge in Canada, a first cousin of Henri-Elzéar Taschereau, was born in Quebec on 6 October 1841, the son of Jean-Thomas Taschereau, a judge of the supreme court of Canada, and his first wife, Louise-Adèle, the daughter of the Hon. Amable Dionne, a member of the legislative council. After education at the Petit Séminaire de Québec (1851–9) and at Laval University, where he graduated BL in 1861 and BCL in 1862—and received the honorary degree of LLD in 1890—he was called to the Quebec bar in 1863 and established a very successful practice there. While an undergraduate he edited in 1862 a journal, *Les Débats*, in which he first reported verbatim in French the parliamentary debates. He was also one of the editors in 1863 of the Liberal journal *La Tribune*. On 22 June 1864 he married Séverine

Pacaud, the daughter of Edouard-Louis Pacaud, a lawyer, in Princeville, Lower Canada. They had ten children.

From 1871 to 1873 Taschereau was a member of the city council of Quebec. He actively promoted the North Shore Railway, and served on its board for four years. After unsuccessfully standing in the 1863 election, he sat as a Liberal in the dominion parliament for Montmagny from 1872 to 1878, where he supported Sir Antoine Aimé Dorion and Alexander Mackenzie. On 7 October 1878 he was appointed a puisne judge of the superior court of the province of Quebec. On 15 April 1885 he married Coralie Globensky, the widow of Henri Masson, in Montreal. In 1901 Taschereau led a federal inquiry into paper manufacture and found that a cartel was pushing prices up. In 1905 he led a second inquiry, into prostitution, which he discovered was widespread and tolerated by the police, a situation which he denounced. On 29 January 1907, on the resignation of Sir Alexander Lacoste, he was made chief justice of the king's bench for Quebec, and the following year (on 26 June) he was knighted. Taschereau left Canada in May 1909 for a tour of England and France; he died suddenly at the residence of his daughter, Mrs J. N. Lyon, at Montmorency, near Paris, on 11 October 1909.

C. P. LUCAS, *rev.* JAMES G. SNELL

Sources *Canada Law Journal*, 47 (1911), 284–5 · D. H. Brown, *The genesis of the Canadian criminal code of 1892* (1989) · J. G. Snell and F. Vaughan, *The supreme court of Canada: history of the institution* (1985) · *Toronto Daily Mail* (15 April 1911) · *Montreal Daily Star* (15 April 1911) · L. Dechêne, 'Dozer, Christian Henry', *DCB*, vol. 12 · G. Bale and E. B. Mallett, 'Ritchie, Sir William Johnston', *DCB*, vol. 12 · A. Désilets, 'Mousseau, Joseph-Alfred', *DCB*, vol. 13 · *Canadian Law Times*, 29 (1909), 1045–6 · *Quebec Daily Telegraph* (12 Oct 1909)
Likenesses portrait, repro. in *Canadian Magazine*, 20, 291

Taschereau, Sir Henri-Thomas (1841–1909). *See under* Taschereau, Sir Henri-Elzéar (1836–1911).

Tasciovanus (*d. c.*AD 10). *See under* Cunobelinus (*d. c.*AD 40).

Tasker, Thomas Joseph (1948–1982). *See under* Boardman, Peter David (1950–1982).

Tasker, William (1740–1800), poet and antiquary, was the only son of William Tasker (1708–1772), rector of Iddesleigh, Devon, and his wife, Jane (1711/12–1795), 'the last branch of the ancient family of the Vickries'. Tasker was educated at Barnstaple, and matriculated from Exeter College, Oxford, on 20 February 1758. He remained there as sojourner until 10 March 1762, and graduated BA on 2 February 1762. On 24 June 1764 he was ordained deacon, and on the next day was licensed to the curacy of Monk Okehampton, near his father's parish. He was ordained priest on 12 July 1767.

At his father's death Tasker was instituted (on 6 November 1772), on his mother's presentation, to the vacant rectory of Iddesleigh. He began to publish poetry after he took up this post; his first work was 'Ode to the Warlike Genius of Great Britain', published anonymously in 1778 (2nd edn, 1779), and reprinted with other poems in a volume in 1779. He also translated into English the 'Carmen seculare of Horace', in 1779, and published several other odes and elegies, including an 'Elegy on the Death of

David Garrick' (1779). His *Select Odes of Pindar and Horace Translated* appeared in 1780 (2nd edn, 3 vols., 1790–93).

The description of Tasker's interview with Samuel Johnson on 16 March 1779 is one of the most lifelike passages in Boswell. James Boswell found Tasker submitting his poems to the judgement of the 'great critick'.

> The bard was a lank, bony figure, with short black hair; he was writhing himself in agitation while Johnson read, and, showing his teeth in a grin of earnestness, exclaimed in broken sentences and in a keen, sharp tone, 'Is that poetry, sir—is it Pindar?'

Tasker's romantic and poetic temperament led to a more general imprudence, however, and on 23 March 1780 the revenues of his benefice were placed under sequestration. His own complaint was that the sequestration was obtained in an 'illegal mode', by his 'unletter'd brother-in-law', arising out of 'merciless and severe persecutions and litigations'. This controversy raged on, until the death of his opponent in 1790. In the meantime, Tasker had continued to write, producing such works as *Annus mirabilis, or, The Eventful Year, 1782* (1783); *A Series of Letters* (1794, chiefly on the wounds and deaths in the *Iliad*); and *Arviragus: a Tragedy* (1796; 2nd edn, 1798), which was performed twice in March 1797 at the Exeter Theatre.

Tasker was a friend of Dr William Hunter, attended his lectures, and studied botany in the gardens at Kew. He was also interested in physiognomy and anatomy, and was an outstanding Greek scholar. Tasker was employed at the time of his death on a history of physiognomy from Aristotle to Lavater, and many letters by him on this subject appeared in the *Gentleman's Magazine* (vols. 67–9). After a long struggle, Tasker died in agony at Iddesleigh rectory on 4 February 1800. He was buried close by the chancel, near his father's tomb, a mural tablet being erected to his memory on the north side of the tower (*The Genealogist*, 263–4). His widow, Eleonora, died at Exbourne on 2 January 1801, aged fifty-six, and was buried in the same grave as her husband. They had no children.

W. P. COURTNEY, rev. REBECCA MILLS

Sources J. Watkins, *The universal biographical dictionary*, new edn (1821), 983 · *Boswell's Life of Johnson*, ed. G. B. Hill, 3 (1887), 373–4 · Foster, *Alum. Oxon.* · R. Cole, 'William Tasker revisited', *N&Q*, 244 (1999), 365–8 · *GM*, 1st ser., 51 (1781), 277–8 · *GM*, 1st ser., 61 (1791), 161–2 · *GM*, 1st ser., 65 (1795), 616 · *GM*, 1st ser., 70 (1800), 283–4 · G. C. Easton, 'Monumental inscriptions at Hyslegh, N. Devon', *The Genealogist*, 7 (1883), 262–4 · J. Gorton, *A general biographical dictionary*, new edn, 4 (1851), 450 · S. Halkett and J. Laing, *A dictionary of the anonymous and pseudonymous literature of Great Britain*, 4 vols. (1882–8) · Allibone, *Dict.* · Watt, *Bibl. Brit.* · Nichols, *Lit. anecdotes*, 206–8
Wealth at death financial problems through most of life: *DNB*

Tasma. *See* Couvreur, Jessie Catherine (1848–1897).

Tassie, James (1735–1799), modeller and portrait medallionist, was born on 15 July 1735 in Pollokshaws, a village in the parish of Eastwood, near Glasgow, into which city the parish had been absorbed by the end of the nineteenth century. He was the fourth child and eldest son of William Tassie (1697–1758), a mason, and his wife, Margaret McGhie, from the nearby parish of Govan, who were married in 1728.

Tassie probably trained initially as a mason with his father, but he recalled in later life that he had been 'first brought up in work-man-ship of Sculpture the size of life' (Tassie to Mrs Alexander Wilson, 16 July 1792, City of Glasgow Archive, TD/68/1, 57). This suggests that he quickly moved from decorative stonework to training with a more sophisticated master, who may well have been responsible for sending him as a student to the academy of art which the Glasgow printers Robert and Andrew Foulis had set up in the city's college in 1754. The emphasis here was both practical and liberal, furnishing skills in drawing for military draughtsmen and designers of manufactures as well as forming taste in the fine arts. The academy contained art collections for imitation, and two Italian craftsmen were employed specifically to teach skills in modelling. The Foulis brothers were (and remain) noted for the quality of their editions of classical authors, and there must have been a strong emphasis on the ancient world, which would be of great importance to Tassie in future years. It was here also that he struck up a friendship with the painter David Allan, who later provided illustrations for the two-volume catalogue of Tassie's gemstone reproductions published in 1791.

At some time in 1763 Tassie left Glasgow for Dublin, where he established contact with that city's most eminent physician, Dr Henry Quin. Quin was a keen amateur of classical cameos and intaglios and was experimenting with vitreous materials which could be used to reproduce them. It is not clear what part Tassie played in the formulation of the material which has become associated with his name, but Quin found him useful and congenial. In due course he appears to have encouraged Tassie to apply the results of their work together to the jewellery trade in London, and Tassie moved there at some time in 1766.

Tassie's commercial success was almost immediate, and he must be the 'ingenious modeller' the 'perfection' of whose work (Dossie) was noticed by the Society for the Encouragement of Arts, Manufactures, and Commerce shortly after the society had ceased awarding premiums for such reproductive work. It was certainly reproductive work that concerned him most at this stage, and he sought out collections of engraved gemstones, both classical and modern, from which to make casts. His work in glass, both cameo and intaglio, in a variety of colours and degrees of opacity, and sometimes with complex striations, was used mainly by the jewellery trade, while complete collections in plaster, sulphur wax (coloured by red lead), and, of course, glass were acquired by connoisseurs. In the last case the individual items were usually wrapped round with thick gold-edged paper, numbered on the outside to correspond with the catalogue, and mounted within shallow drawers, the bottom of which might be coloured. The height of Tassie's success came when a complete collection in this form, in cabinets designed by the architect James Wyatt, was ordered by Catherine the Great of Russia in 1781.

Tassie's fuelling of this neo-classical rage, which took him as far as Paris in early 1785 to seek new collections, was paralleled by a series of portraits of contemporaries, and it is on these that his artistic reputation now rests.

Usually modelled from life, they are a modest but intensely observed vision of a whole society. Many, though not all, were, in Tassie's words, of 'the first people in the Kingdom', including such figures as Robert Adam, Hugh Blair, James Hutton, admirals Keppel and Duncan, Lord Mansfield, and Adam Smith—this last, modelled in 1787, being the only authentic portrait of the great economist.

Much technical information on the production of these portraits, as well as information on his business generally, may be found in the largest body of Tassie's surviving correspondence, a group of sixty-nine letters sent to the Glasgow bookseller and stationer Alexander Wilson. The first stage, nearly always of the head and shoulders in profile, and about 3 inches in height, was modelled in red wax. This was followed by concave and convex plaster casts, from the latter of which a vitreous paste mould was made, the final step before the cameo portrait was cast in the same material. These portraits were also neo-classical in essence, and their intended resemblance to marble might finally be enhanced by grinding the surface or treating it with hydrofluoric acid. The image was then mounted on a sheet of oval glass, clear or translucent, behind which was placed a piece of blue or greenish paper. From about 1773, however, having enlarged his furnace, Tassie was able to cast image and background in one piece, though always with difficulty. Despite the technical problems associated with size, Tassie's enamel (the word he tended to use) had the great quality of not shrinking, unlike Wedgwood's ceramic material, as Tassie himself pointed out with some glee.

It remains unclear how large the 'editions' of these portraits were, though they seem to have been small in number unless the subject, such as Viscount Duncan, was of immediate public interest. If commissioned, a fee of 5 guineas was charged for the initial sitting (there were usually three sittings), and the final cost of the portrait in the 1780s ranged from 10s. 6d. to 1 guinea. Tassie was always willing to travel to his sitters, and late in 1791 he was modelling portraits in Edinburgh and Glasgow. During this expedition he must have met the painter Henry Raeburn, for there is a medallion self-portrait of Raeburn in Tassie's enamel, dated 1792, which Tassie must have cast on the painter's behalf when he had returned to London.

Tassie's premises when he first moved to London were in Great Newport Street, where he appears to have lodged from 1767 to 1772 with a Mr Lewis. This was followed by a period in Old Compton Street (1772–8), but the greater part of his activities were at 20 Leicester Fields (later Square), where he moved in 1778 and remained for the rest of his life. Among his recorded assistants were his nephew William Tassie, who took over the business on his uncle's death, his younger brother John, and a Henry Laing, whose origins were in Strathmiglo in Fife.

Little is known of Tassie's family life. Although he married twice, he was childless, and William became his heir. His first wife may have been Agnes King, who married a James Tassie in Renfrewshire on 5 April 1761. On 25 December 1775, when described as a widower, Tassie married Ann Harker (bap. 1730, d. 1790) of St Clement Danes. The portrait Mrs Tassie by Tassie's fellow student David Allan (NG Scot.) must be of this second wife. She died shortly before 29 September 1790, when Tassie refers in his correspondence to the distress he had lately experienced while attending his 'late poor sick & Dieing [sic] spouse' (Tassie to Alexander Wilson, 29 September 1790, City of Glasgow Archive, TD/68/1, 46).

The crown on Tassie's commercial success was probably the publication in 1791 of the lavish two-volume catalogue of his stock, which at this date stood at 15,800 items. This catalogue also enumerates some 111 of his larger-scale portraits, mostly from life. It was compiled for Tassie by the odd German émigré, archaeologist, and mineralogist Rudolph Eric Raspe, now better known as the author of Baron Munchausen's Marvellous Travels. It was an enlargement of the manuscript catalogue Raspe had prepared earlier for Catherine the Great, and was in both English and French. In addition to Raspe's lengthy essay on the history of engraved gemstones, it contained fifty-seven plates of etched illustrations by David Allan. The subscribers, headed by the King of Sweden, included many eminent people, among them, rather touchingly, Henry Quin ('2 copies'), who had set Tassie on his way nearly thirty years before.

Tassie remained active—even experimental—until the very end. There are records of him casting glass stereotype printing plates on behalf of the Glasgow professor Patrick Wilson (brother of Tassie's long-time correspondent), who successfully showed that such plates, suitably reinforced, could be passed through a press and might be used for printing banknotes with greater security. In a letter describing their work, Wilson refers to his colleague as 'the justly celebrated Mr Tassie of London', which this Scot assuredly was.

Tassie died on 1 June 1799 and was buried in a graveyard attached to a meeting-house near Angel Place in Southwark, known as Colliers' Rents. A headstone 'recording his virtues and his artistic skill' and bearing a portrait of Tassie is said to have been erected, but all traces had vanished before the end of the nineteenth century.

DUNCAN THOMSON

Sources J. M. Gray, James and William Tassie: a biographical and critical sketch with a catalogue of their portrait medallions of modern personages (1894) • D. Thomson, 'Two medallionists in Georgian London: the letters of James and William Tassie', Country Life, 151 (1972), 214–19 • J. Holloway, James Tassie, 1735–1799 (1986) • R. E. Raspe, A descriptive catalogue of a general collection of ancient and modern engraved gems, cameos as well as intaglios (1791) • letters to A. Wilson, Mitchell L., Glas., Glasgow City Archives, TD/68/1 • R. Dossie, Memoirs of agriculture, and other oeconomical arts (1768), vol. 1, pp. 34–5
Archives Mitchell L., Glas., Glasgow City Archives, letters to Alexander Wilson, TD 68 • NA Ire., letters to Henry Quin
Likenesses J. Paxton, oils, c.1775, Scot. NPG • silhouette, 1776, Scot. NPG • D. Allan, oils, c.1781, Scot. NPG • W. Tassie, paste medallion, c.1795, Scot. NPG • W. Tassie, paste medallions, Scot. NPG
Wealth at death left thriving business to his nephew, William Tassie

Tassie, William (1777–1860), modeller, born in London, was probably the son of David Tassie (bap. 1750), youngest brother of James *Tassie (1735–1799), the modeller whom he assisted in the production of portrait medallions and casts of antique jewels. Aged twenty-one he produced a copy of his uncle's medallion of Lord Duncan to exhibit at the Royal Academy. Following his uncle's death in 1799 he took over the business at 20 Leicester Square. The change was advertised in Edinburgh, where Tassie 'respectfully informs the Pupils and Friends of his late uncle' that he has:

> executed Medals of several of the Scotch Kings [of which] he has sent specimens, in paste enamel, to Marshall & Sons, High Street, Edinburgh, where they may be seen; who will receive orders for them and also for portraits modelled by the late Mr Tassie. (*Edinburgh Evening Courant*, 27 July 1799)

Later he was assisted by William Hardy Vernon (1795–1880), son of his sister Anne Tassie and James Vernon, who modelled intaglios of Milton and of Byron. Vernon matriculated at Magdalen College, Oxford, in 1824 and died vicar of Wootton, Bedfordshire.

Tassie's shop had a counter running its full length, behind which were rows of drawers containing antique gem casts; in the window, covered by a glass dome, stood his uncle's replica of the Portland vase. The studio was a salon for artists and literary men, including Moore and Byron. Tassie was a kindly, cultivated man who loved to feed birds at the back of his house, until developers built over the ground and shot them. Out of kindness he bought a £1 ticket for the Boydell lottery from a struggling artist; on 28 January 1805 he won the chief prize—the Shakspeare Gallery in Pall Mall, pictures, and estate. Tassie made a present to the artist and sold the whole property by auction in May 1805, when the works of art realized more than £6180.

Tassie added to his uncle's collection of reproductions of gems and medals; he supplied additional casts to the imperial collection of Russia. His most popular products were seals and gems in composition paste, inscribed with original mottoes and devices, of which he published a descriptive catalogue in 1816 (2nd edn, 1820) and 1830. His collection of intaglio and cameo impressions in enamel, sulphur, or paste finally consisted of more than 20,000 specimens; among them were many originals of contemporary notables, including Napoleon, Nelson, and Lady Hamilton, by artists employed by him. In 1822 Shelley instructed Thomas Love Peacock to procure for him 'two pounds worth of Tassie's gems' (*DNB*). Tassie also modelled portrait medallions in wax and cast them in the white enamel paste used by James Tassie, but his work did not have the ease and precision of his uncle's. He executed a set of twelve medallions of the passions, signed 'W. T.'.

In 1840 Tassie retired from his prosperous business, which was continued by his partner John Wilson, an artist who had entered his employment about 1827 and exhibited at the Royal Academy from 1824 to 1856. Tassie moved to 8 Upper Phillimore Place, Kensington, where he died, unmarried, on 26 October 1860; he was buried in Brompton cemetery. He left most of his estate to his nephew the Revd William Hardy Vernon and his great-nephew the Revd William Tassie Vernon. In two codicils he left a detailed bequest to the National Galleries of Scotland of portraits of his uncle and aunt by David Allan, a landscape by Nicholas Poussin, and an extensive collection of portrait medallions and casts of gems, giving as complete a collection as possible of the work of his uncle and himself. Those gems that he felt were 'licentious' were omitted, and these he destroyed. A portion of the collection was left to his nephew, and part of this was sold at Wootton in February 1881, the remainder at Christies in April 1882; many of the large Tassie medallions were included in the Shadford Walker sale in 1889. JOHN MALDEN

Sources J. M. Gray, *James and William Tassie* (1894) · J. Holloway, *James Tassie* (1986) · J. P. Smith, *James Tassie, modeller in glass* (1995) · J. S. Tassie, 'The Tassies', *Proceedings of the 13th Wedgwood International seminar, 25–27 April 1968* · J. S. Tassie, 'The Tassie family', *Canadian Collector*, 14 (March×April 1979) · 'The letters of James and William Tassie', ed. D. Thomson, *Country Life*, 151 (1972) · W. T. Vernon, 'The Tassie gems', *Leisure Hour* (Dec 1886), 836–9 · *CGPLA Eng. & Wales* (1860) · W. H. Vernon, correspondence to W. Tassie, NA Scot., RG14 · H. B. Wheatley, *London past and present: its history, associations and traditions … based upon the 'Handbook of London' by the late Peter Cunningham*, 3 vols. (1891) · *IGI*
Archives Mitchell L., Glas., Glasgow City Archives, letters to Alexander Wilson, TD 68
Likenesses J. Hagbolt, wax medallion, c.1833, priv. coll.; repro. in Gray, *James and William Tassie*
Wealth at death under £35,000: probate, 1860

Tata, Sir Dorabji Jamshed (1859–1932), industrial magnate and philanthropist, was born at Bombay on 27 August 1859, the elder son of Jamshed Nasarwanji *Tata (1839–1904), pioneer of Indian industries, and his wife, Berabai (1847/8–1904), daughter of Kharsetji Daboo. The politician Shapurji *Saklatvala was his first cousin. In 1875, after attending the Bombay proprietary school, he was sent to England to a private tutor in Kent, and in 1877 he entered Gonville and Caius College, Cambridge, where he obtained his colours for cricket and football. He returned to Bombay in 1879, studied further at St Xavier's College, and obtained the BA degree of Bombay University in 1882. His father then placed him as an apprentice in the office of the *Bombay Gazette* in order that he might gain experience of men and affairs. Two years later he was sent first to Pondicherry and then to the Empress cotton mills, Nagpur, for training, and in 1887, together with his cousin R. D. Tata, was taken into partnership in the newly formed company of Tata & Sons. Under his father's wise guidance he gained greatly in knowledge and understanding of Indian industry and finance, and on J. N. Tata's death in 1904 was well fitted to become the head of the firm. During the next twenty-five years the firm (reconstituted in 1907 as Tata Sons & Co., and again in 1917 as Tata Sons Ltd) expanded and became the largest industrial concern in India, with aggregate funds estimated in 1945 at £54,000,000 and giving employment to 120,000 men and women.

Tata's great contributions to Indian progress were the successful completion of the three bold and far-sighted projects planned and initiated by his father, in which he was assisted by his brother, Sir Ratan Tata (*d.* 1918), and other members of his family, and his munificent public benefactions. Through his keen personal interest in the

Sir Dorabji Jamshed Tata (1859–1932), by Manchershaw Pithawalla

early work and his energy and drive in finding the capital, construction of the first project, the Tata iron and steel works, commenced in 1908 and the first iron was produced in 1911. As the number of employees grew, the town of Jamshedpur came into being. He brought the same energy and resource to his father's bold plan for harnessing the heavy monsoon rainfall of the western ghats, and by 1919 three companies were in being. The endowment and establishment in 1911 of the Indian Institute of Science at Bangalore at an initial cost of £200,000 was a work of filial devotion for the two sons of J. N. Tata. Their father died before he could make the bequest, and his sons after protracted negotiations entered into a tripartite agreement with the government of India and the government of Mysore whereby, as he had intended, young Indians could receive scientific training at a high level in India, and by the practical applications of science advance the industrial development of their country.

In recognition of his services Tata was knighted in 1910. He was president of the Indian Industrial Conference in 1915 and a member of the Indian Industrial Commission from 1916 to 1918. From early manhood he took a keen interest in Indian cricket and athletics and did much to bring about India's participation in the Olympic Games. He was a patron of learning as well as of sport. He endowed a chair of Sanskrit at the Bhandarkar Institute, and helped many deserving scholars in their researches. About 1920 he gave £25,000 to the University of Cambridge for the equipment of the laboratories in the school

of engineering, and in 1922 he was elected an honorary fellow of his old college. His private charities were said to have totalled £150,000.

In 1898 Tata married Meherbai, daughter of a distinguished educationist, Hormasji Jehangir Bhabha, inspector-general of education in Mysore. There were no children of the marriage. After his wife's death in 1931 he set apart a sum of nearly £200,000 for the Lady Tata Memorial Trust, the object being to provide prizes and scholarships for research in any part of the world on diseases of the blood, and for work in India on subjects related to the alleviation of human suffering. In the last year of his life he created the trust which bears his name and endowed it with the whole of his private fortune. In accordance with his wishes it has rendered help without distinction of caste or creed. The endowment, estimated at £2,000,000 in 1945, had by then expended £800,000 in a wide range of charities including the endowment and maintenance of the Tata Memorial Hospital for Cancer, the Tata Institute of Social Sciences, and the Tata Institute of Fundamental Research (the last-named being jointly established by the government of Bombay and the trust).

After executing the trust deed Tata left India in April 1932. He was taken seriously ill in Europe and died at 1 Ringstrasse, Bad Kissingen, Bavaria, on 3 June 1932. His remains were taken to England and laid beside those of his wife in the Parsi cemetery at Brookwood, Woking.

R. CHOKSI, rev.

Sources *The Times* (4 June 1932) · *Times of India* (4 June 1932) · F. R. Harris, *Jamsetji Nusserwanji Tata: a chronicle of his life* (1925) · Records of the Sir Dorabji Tata Trust · private information (1949) · *CGPLA Eng. & Wales* (1933)
Likenesses M. Pithawalla, portrait, Tata Central Archives, Bombay [*see illus.*]
Wealth at death £13,298 12s. 7d. effects in England: administration with will, 26 Jan 1933, *CGPLA Eng. & Wales*

Tata, Jamshed Nasarwanji (1839–1904), entrepreneur and industrialist in India, born on 3 March 1839 at Navsari, in Gujarat, was the only son of five children of Nasarwanji Ratanji Tata, a Parsi of priestly family, and his wife (and cousin), Jiverbai Cowasjee Tata. He went to Bombay at the age of thirteen to work in the office of his father's new business enterprise, and then attended Elphinstone College, graduating after three years in 1858. Early marriages among the Parsi community were general at that time, and in 1858 he married a ten-year-old girl, Berabai (d. 1904), daughter of Kharsetji Daboo. They had a daughter, who died in infancy, and two sons.

In 1859 Tata visited China and began a successful export business, which expanded by forming branches in Japan, China, Paris, and New York, and agencies in London and elsewhere. Having returned from China in 1863, Tata visited England, mainly to float an Indian bank in London. This scheme was frustrated by the severe financial crisis and stock market crash in Bombay that followed the ending of the cotton boom caused by the American Civil War. The family firm was threatened with bankruptcy as a result of these events, but Tata revived its fortunes in 1868 by founding a new private trading company, which

Jamshed Nasarwanji Tata (1839–1904), by unknown photographer, 1885

obtained contracts to supply the Indian army expeditionary force to Abyssinia (Ethiopia).

Tata began his industrial career in 1874, when he floated the Central India Spinning, Weaving, and Manufacturing Company to develop a cotton mill in Nagpur. This plant began production in 1877, and was named the Empress mills since it was opened on 1 January, the day on which Queen Victoria was proclaimed empress of India. In 1886 he established a second cotton manufacturing centre near Bombay, naming this the Swadeshi ('own country') mills to take advantage of rising nationalist sentiment in favour of Indian-owned and Indian-run manufacturing industry. After an unpromising start, and despite initial scepticism displayed by both the banks and the investing public, the Swadeshi mills became established as one of the best Indian-owned cotton mills of their day, both in terms of productivity and of employee welfare. One significant innovation in the management of the mills was that the Tata managing agency took a commission only on the profits of the manufacturing companies that it ran and not, as was common elsewhere, on the volume of production or sales.

Indian cotton mills in the nineteenth century concentrated, in the main, on the manufacture of coarse yarn (and later cloth) that could be produced from the native, short-staple, raw cotton using relatively cheap capital equipment imported from England. Tata broke away from this pattern by importing longer-stapled cotton from Egypt and installing more complex ring-spindle machinery from the United States to spin finer yarn that could

compete with imports from Lancashire. In 1896 he published a pamphlet, entitled 'Growth of Egyptian cotton in India', setting out a scheme (already rejected by the government's agricultural advisers) to acclimatize Egyptian cotton in India. He attempted to implement the scheme in Sind, but without lasting success. Another pamphlet in 1893 discussed ways of increasing the supply of skilled labour to the mills. In 1893 he also began a campaign to reduce the heavy freight charges between Bombay and the Far East by helping to promote the NYK (Nippon Yusen Kaisha—Japanese Steam Navigation Company) and his own Tata Shipping Line to break the hold of three oligopolist steamship companies—P. & O., the Austrian-Lloyd, and the Rubinatto. A freight war followed, to which Tata contributed a popular pamphlet attacking the use made by P. & O. of its subsidized government mail contract to maintain a monopoly that damaged India's trade. In June 1896 he helped to negotiate an agreement that established a permanent reduction in freights on a reasonably competitive basis. Tata also vigorously opposed the excise duty on Indian cotton production that was imposed to offset the protective effect of modest import duties imposed on cotton goods in 1894 and 1896, and he directed an elaborate statistical inquiry into the hampering effects of the duty on the industry.

In the 1890s and early 1900s Tata became increasingly involved in ambitious plans to lay the foundations of a heavy industrial sector in India. These schemes required careful and meticulous planning, as well as long-term and risky investment. They reached fruition only after his death in the Tata Iron and Steel Company (TISCO; 1907), the Tata Hydro-Electric Power Supply Company (1910), and the Indian Institute of Science at Bangalore (1911). TISCO, which opened its plant at Jamshedpur in Bihar in 1908, was the leading iron and steel producer in India before independence, and became a symbol of Indian technical skill, managerial competence, and entrepreneurial flair. Tata also provided a number of urban amenities in Bombay, notably the Taj Mahal Hotel, which opened in 1903 as the first building in the city to be illuminated by electricity. He was taken ill suddenly while in Germany in the spring of 1904, and died at Nauheim on 19 May 1904. He was buried in England at the Parsi cemetery, Brookwood, Woking, Surrey. His extensive business interests were carried on after his death by his sons, Sir Dorabji Jamshed *Tata (1859–1932) and Ratan Jamshed Tata, and other family members.

F. H. BROWN, *rev.* B. R. TOMLINSON

Sources F. R. Harris, *Jamsetji Nusserwanji Tata: a chronicle of his life*, 2nd edn (1958) · R. M. Lula, *The creation of wealth* (1981)
Likenesses photograph, 1885, Tata Central Archives, Bombay [*see illus.*] · W. R. Colton, bronze statue, 1912, Bombay

Tate, Christopher Thomas (1811–1841), sculptor, born on 16 August 1811 in Drury Lane, Newcastle upon Tyne, Northumberland, and baptized on 9 September at the nonconformist church of St Nicholas (later the cathedral) in the same city, was the third son of John Tate, hairdresser, of Drury Lane, and Elizabeth, daughter of William Penny, keelman, of North Shields, Northumberland.

His name was Christopher Thomas Tate and not Christopher J. A. Tate, as sometimes stated (*Dictionary of British Sculptors*, 380). He was first apprenticed to the sculptor R. G. Davies (*fl.* 1820–1857) and afterwards worked for David Dunbar the younger (*d.* 1866). Leaving Dunbar to establish himself as an independent artist, Tate achieved some recognition with a *Dying Christ* (suitable for Catholic chapels) and a statue of Blind Willie. He then obtained a number of commissions for portrait busts, among them those of the duke of Northumberland, David Urquhart, Sheridan Knowles, Lord Byron, and Miss Elphinstone. The *Gentleman's Magazine*, in his obituary, remarked: 'His busts, for execution, precision, and arrangement, can scarcely be surpassed' (p. 102). He afterwards produced a *Judgment of Paris* and a *Musidora*, praised in the same obituary for the skill with which so young an artist had tackled 'such difficult subjects' (ibid.), evidencing in such work 'an original and vigorous mind' (ibid.).

Tate suffered from consumption, and in 1840, while engaged on a statue of the duke of Northumberland for the Master Mariners' Asylum at Tynemouth, he became seriously ill. Although he had evidently finished the most important parts, his former master, Davies, had to complete the work. In an attempt to regain his health, Tate went on a voyage to the Mediterranean. He stayed some weeks in Malta but, realizing that he was close to death, he sailed for home. He got as far as London and died there on 22 March 1841, aged twenty-nine; he was buried in London.

Tate had made very little money from his work and left a wife and two children unprovided for (although a relief fund was evidently started up soon after his death). There are a large number of tombs by him in the churches and churchyards of Newcastle upon Tyne and the surrounding area, for example his monument to the Revd Robert Wasney (1836) in St Thomas's, Barras Bridge. For his native city he carved the royal coat of arms (1838) for the pediment of the Theatre Royal, considered by both the obituarist in the *Gentleman's Magazine* and a later writer, Rupert Gunnis, to be a particularly fine piece of work. According to his obituarist, 'his store of information was inexhaustible. Whatever the subject under discussion, Mr Tate was always able to take a prominent part' (*GM*, 102).

CAMPBELL DODGSON, rev. TERRY CAVANAGH

Sources *GM*, 2nd ser., 16 (1841), 102 • R. Gunnis, *Dictionary of British sculptors, 1660–1851*, new edn (1964) • Graves, *RA exhibitors* • Redgrave, *Artists* • *Tyne Mercury* (30 March 1841) • IGI • private information (2004)

Tate, Francis (1560–1616), judge and antiquary, was born at Gayton, the eldest son of Bartholomew Tate (*d.* 1601) of Delapré, Northamptonshire, and his wife, Dorothy, daughter of Francis Tanfield of Gayton. He was raised with two brothers and four sisters at nearby Hardingstone, on monastic lands bought by his father. He matriculated as a commoner to Magdalen College, Oxford, on 20 December 1577, but left without a degree. Admitted to Staple Inn by 1579 he entered the Middle Temple with his brother William on 2 June 1579, and was called to the bar on 30 June 1587. An active member, he was never fined for missing a

duty or report, and preferred for admission many young men from east midlands families, several of whom became judges. He was patronized in his legal career by the Tanfield family, his sister's having married Sir Laurence Tanfield, chief baron of the exchequer.

A noted scholar at Magdalen, Tate became a famous legal antiquary at the Temple, where he was renowned for his knowledge of Anglo-Saxon and medieval laws and customs. He was elected bencher and Lent reader in 1607, and assisted in drafting the inn's new perpetual charter of 13 August 1608. Active in its parliament he sat on many committees including treasury, library, surveyors, discipline, and house rules and orders, becoming treasurer on 24 November 1615. He constructed a three-storey brick building over the cloisters between the Middle and Inner temples in Vine Court in 1612 at his own expense, keeping three chambers for his library and use. As a resident he was active in moots and readings. Numerous copies exist of his notes on lecturers, and his own reading on tithes was erudite in canon, civil, and common law, history and philology.

Tate was returned to parliament for Northampton in 1601, and served as its legal counsel by 1602. He sat for Shrewsbury 1604–11 even though the borough ordered that it should not elect a non-resident. A scholar of parliamentary history he believed that the three parts of king, Lords, and Commons always had an equal role. He also placed great store in the statutes of the thirteenth century, especially Magna Carta. Providing Sir Edward Coke with a volume of abstracts from the rolls of parliament, his views supported the later arguments of Coke on the 'high court of parliament' (Fussner, 83–4) and its antiquity. An active speaker, he sat on several committees including impositions and grievances. For example, in the debate on scutage on 4 December 1606 he gave a history of the divisions of feudal tenures. He gave similar lengthy lectures on the history of impositions. He had observed that privy councillors took the initiative in guiding and controlling the Commons in Elizabeth's reign, and were most effective when they worked through unconnected MPs, using flattery and friendly persuasion.

A judicial career paralleled Tate's time as scholar and parliamentarian. He was a JP in the counties of Brecknockshire, Glamorgan, and Radnor, and a justice of assize for Brecon 1604–16. He also practised in the court of wards, and in king's bench 1610–12. An original member of the Society of Antiquaries he was for some time its secretary. He maintained a collection of the society's papers, including a journal of its activities 1590–1601. Tate was an inveterate collector. He spent many hours in London's Guildhall Library copying legal manuscripts, and took many of them, which were not returned and ended up in Sir Robert Cotton's library with some of his notebooks. He also researched state archives such as the exchequer, where he also borrowed original papers. Working with Cotton, William Lambarde, John Stowe, and John Jones of Gallilyfdy, he acquired the largest private collection of legal manuscripts of his time.

Approximately sixteen original works stemmed from

his pen, none of which was printed in his lifetime, although ten were published later by either Thomas Hearne or John Gutch. They dealt with the antiquity and precedents concerning arms, cities and towns, combats, and funerals; with parliament and Star Chamber; with the offices of knights, doctors of civil law, serjeants, high steward, and lord chancellor; with words and names in Domesday Book and Northamptonshire; and with the ancient Britons. None of these was substantial apart from his tract on parliament. He was also the translator and / or editor of fourteen works, only one of which has been published. These were primarily medieval, ranging from household and wardrobe accounts to charters, statutes, and legal treatises.

Tate's career might never have blossomed had he not recovered from an illness in 1602 and left Northamptonshire that year for Wales, the ancestral homeland of his grandfather John Tate (d. 1514), mercer, and sheriff of London in 1495. On giving up his post as recorder of Northampton he made his will, on 22 June 1603. He gave praise to his sister Jane in caring for his 'illness' (PROB 11/129), and to his brother-in-law William, Lord Zouche of Harringworth. He had returned, however, by 1604, when he was elected MP for Shrewsbury. There is a significant omission of his name in the *Middle Temple Records* from June 1601 to February 1605. Tate died, probably at Middle Temple, on 15 November 1616. He gave most of his books to his nephew Robert Tanfield and many of his manuscripts landed in the Stowe collections, now in the British Library.   LOUIS A. KNAFLA

Sources *Reg. Oxf.*, 2/2.76 · Wood, *Ath. Oxon.*, 1st edn, 2.179 · C. H. Hopwood, ed., *Middle Temple records*, 4 vols. (1904–5), vols. 1–3 · A. R. Ingpen, ed., *The Middle Temple bench books* (1912), 67–8, 93, 172 · J. Hutchinson, ed., *Notable Middle Templars* (1902), 239–40 · HoP, *Commons, 1558–1603*, 3.479 · will, PRO, PROB 11/129, sig. 46 · J. H. Baker, *Readers and readings in the inns of court and chancery*, SeldS, suppl. ser., 13 (2000), 175, 235n., 346, 407–8, 438, 481 · W. R. Prest, *The rise of the barristers: a social history of the English bar, 1590–1640* (1981), 200–01, 250, 394 · D. H. Willson, *The privy councillors in the House of Commons, 1604–1629* (1971), 9–12, 118, 206, 219, 226 · J. Bridges and P. Whalley, *The history and antiquities of Northamptonshire*, rev. edn, 2 vols. (1812) · J. C. Cox, ed., *The records of the borough of Northampton* (1898), 72, 495 · H. Townshend, *Historical collections, or, An exact account of the proceedings of the four last parliaments of Queen Elizabeth of famous memory* (1680) · S. d'Ewes, *The journals of all the parliaments during the reign of Queen Elizabeth* (1682) · F. S. Fussner, *The historical revolution: English historical writing and thought, 1580–1640* (1962), 83–4, 145 · T. Hearne, *A collection of curious discourses*, rev. edn (1771)
Archives BL, antiquarian collections and notes, St MSS 1045, 298, 568, 414–415, 541 · BL, further papers, notes, corresp., etc., Ct Julius C iii 97b, 103b, F vi 288; Hg 249, 32; Harley 305, 253; Lands ccccxci 7; Sl 1786 · BL, papers, notes, corresp., etc., Add. MSS 12453, 12514, 25247, 22587, 22591, 36901, 45144 · Bodl. Oxf., notes on hard words in Domesday and copy of a treatise · CUL, brief notes on the antiquity, use, and privilege of cities, boroughs, and towns

Tate, George (1746–1821), naval officer in the Russian service, was born on 14 June 1746 near London. He was the third son of George Tate (1700–1794) and his wife, Mary (d. 1770). His father had served in the Russian fleet in the era of Peter the Great and later acted as a British Admiralty agent for securing mast timber, first in Russia and then in New England. Tate grew up on the Maine coast and pursued a career at sea. After the tragic accidental death of his mother in 1770 his father helped him gain a commission in the Russian navy.

In the *Count Orlov* Tate saw action in the Russo-Turkish War of 1768–74 at the great battle of Chesma in the Mediterranean (1770). He remained in the Black Sea Fleet until the mid-1770s, when he was promoted captain. He then commanded ships based in Kronstadt and Archangel, before returning to the Black Sea for Catherine the Great's Russo-Turkish War of 1787–92. Tate was wounded at the siege of Izmail and returned to the north again to take part in the war against Sweden (1788–90) in the Baltic Sea battles of Åland, Högland, and Reval. After his capture of an enemy warship at Viborg he was presented with a miniature of the empress set in diamonds. A seasoned combat commander, Tate was promoted rear-admiral in 1793.

In 1798 he was made vice-admiral in the Baltic fleet and won the order of St Anne. During the War of the Second Coalition, Tate took part in the combined Anglo-Russian fleet operations off the Netherlands; but when Emperor Paul reversed his alliances and broke diplomatic relations with England, Tate, with other officers of British origin, was removed from his post and was obliged to spend the winter of 1800–1 in Moscow.

In a letter to his brother Robert, Tate wrote that 'the death of the late Emperor put affairs on the old footing' (Holden, 36). Tsar Alexander re-established relations with England and in 1802 rewarded Tate with a promotion to admiral and an order of St George for his participation in eighteen naval campaigns. After the peace treaty of Tilsit in 1807 Tate was kept ashore again for over two years and wrote to his brother Samuel, '… my income is greatly curtailed' (ibid., 36). Despite his advanced age Tate returned to service during the crisis of 1812. In the victory the admiral was accorded an honour seldom bestowed upon foreigners, an appointment to the Russian senate, and he was again showered with decorations, including the orders of Alexander Nevsky and St Vladimir.

Admiral Tate died in St Petersburg on 17 February 1821. He never married but had kept contact with his relatives in England and New England. Brothers Robert and Samuel, both merchant captains, did not survive him. His estate was divided among his brother William, who had settled in England, his nieces and nephews in Maine, and two godsons in Russia, Edward Simpson and James Booker.   RICHARD H. WARNER

Sources C. Holden, 'Serving tsar and king: George Tate, admiral in the Russian imperial navy', *American Neptune*, 51 (1991), 33–44 · W. D. Barry, 'Maine's one and only Russian admiral', *Down East*, 30/5 (1983), 39, 66–9 · R. C. Anderson, 'British and American officers in the Russian navy', *Mariner's Mirror*, 33 (1947), 17–27 · R. C. Anderson, 'Great Britain and the rise of the Russian fleet in the eighteenth century', *Mariner's Mirror*, 42 (1956), 132–46 · R. C. Anderson, *Naval wars in the Levant, 1559–1853* (1952) · R. C. Anderson, *Naval wars in the Baltic during the sailing-ship epoch, 1522–1850* (1910); repr. as *Naval wars in the Baltic, 1522–1850* (1969) · *Obshchii morskoi spisok* [General naval list] (1885–1907) · V. N. Berkh, *Zhizneopisaniia pervikh rosisskikh admiralov* [Descriptions of the lives of the first Russian admirals] (St Petersburg, 1843) · F. F. Veselago, *Kratkaia istoriia russkogo flota* [A short history of the Russian fleet] (1939) · V. A.

Divin and others, eds., *Boevaia letopis' russkogo flota* [Chronicle of the battles of the Russian fleet] (Moscow, 1948) · F. Peabody, *Tate House: crown of the Maine mast trade* (1982) · E. V. Tarle, 'Chesmenskii boi i pervaia ekspeditsiia v arkhipelag' [The battle of Chesme and the first expedition to the archipelago], *Tri ekspeditsii russkogo flota* [Three expeditions of the Russian fleet] (Moscow, 1956)
Archives Tate House, Portland, Maine, personal MSS
Wealth at death considerable property, money, and personal effects, incl. gold sword given to him by George III: will, Barry, 'Maine's one and only', 39, 66–9

Tate, George (1805–1871), topographer and naturalist, born on 21 May 1805 in Alnwick, was the son of Ralph Tate (1781–1827), builder and draper, and brother of Thomas *Tate the educationist. He was a freeman of Alnwick by patrimony, and attended the borough and grammar schools there. Subsequently he worked as a linen draper, and in 1848 he was appointed postmaster, an office he held until a fortnight before his death. Tate was active in all public movements in the town, and helped to organize the work of the Alnwick Mechanics' Scientific Institution, of which he acted as secretary for thirty years. This inspired him to study geology. He was clerk of Alnwick council from 1850 to 1858, and used the opportunity to study the borough records. The result was his authoritative *History of Alnwick*, which appeared between 1865 and 1869, and was his chief publication. It included the history of Alnwick Castle and the Percy family, with accounts of old customs, sports, public movements, local nomenclature, the botany, zoology, and geology of the district, and biographies of the notabilities of the town. He was also secretary of the Berwickshire Naturalists' Club from 1858 until his death.

Tate chiefly interested himself in the archaeology and natural history of his town and district and especially distinguished himself by his geological explorations, being the first to record marks of glaciation on rocks in Northumberland. He published in 1865 *Sculptured Rocks of Northumberland and the Eastern Borders*. He examined and wrote papers on other ancient British remains for the proceedings of the Berwickshire Naturalists' Club. Of these, the most important were 'The old Celtic town of Greaves Ash' and 'The hut-circles and forts on Yevering Bell'. His account of his journey along the Roman wall, with his examination of its geology, was published as a part of John Collingwood Bruce's *The Roman Wall* (2nd edn, 1853). His account of the fossil flora of the eastern border was incorporated in George Johnston's *The Natural History of the Eastern Borders* (1854), and that of the geology of Northumberland in J. G. Baker and Tate's *New Flora of Northumberland and Durham*. Tate formed a museum which was especially rich in fossils collected in the course of his investigations in the carboniferous and mountain limestone formations, and his name was given by T. Rupert Jones to three species: *Estheria striata tateana*, *Candona tateana*, and *Beyrichia tatei*.

Tate married in 1832 Ann Horsley, also of Alnwick, who died on 21 December 1847. Two sons and three daughters survived him. His eldest son, George Ralph Tate MD FLS, was a notable plant collector, whose Chinese specimens

are now at Kew. Tate died in Alnwick on 7 June 1871, and was buried on 9 June in Alnwick churchyard, on the south side of the church.   SARAH WILSON, *rev.* C. M. FRASER

Sources R. Middlemas, 'Memoir of the late George Tate', *Proceedings of the Berwickshire Naturalists' Club*, 6 (1869–72), 269–79 · R. Welford, *Men of mark 'twixt Tyne and Tweed*, 3 (1895), 488–93 · J. C. Hodgson, 'George Tate the historian of Alnwick', *Archaeologia Aeliana*, 3rd ser., 15 (1918), 100–08 · P. Davis and C. Brewer, eds., *A catalogue of natural science collections in north-east England* (1986), 252
Archives Northumbd RO, Newcastle upon Tyne, local history collection, incl. corresp. and photographs
Likenesses pen-and-ink sketch, repro. in Welford, *Men of mark*, 489
Wealth at death see probate, 1871, CGPLA Eng. & Wales

Tate, Harry [*real name* Ronald McDonald Hutchison] (1872–1940), music-hall artist and comedian, was born at 47 Osborne Terrace, Clapham Road, Kennington, London, on 4 July 1872, the son of Robert Henry Hutchison, a mercantile clerk, and his wife, Mary Elizabeth Delauney. He reputedly took his stage surname from the company of sugar-refiners for whom he had once worked, and first appeared under it at the Oxford Music-Hall on 13 April 1895. His early act consisted of sketches in which he mimicked music-hall stars of the day, utilizing ingenious clip-on paper costumes to allow as many as forty-two changes in one act. He married Julia Maude Kerslake Baker in 1898.

In the first decade of the twentieth century Tate developed the comic persona and sketch style on which his reputation would be made, gathering around him a cast of six oddly-assorted performers with whom he toured extensively until the 1930s. The sketches in which this small, riotous troupe appeared revolved around Tate's good-humoured, though occasionally testy, ineptitude. His stage persona was that of a larger-than-life, genial bourgeois, inexpertly fascinated with the latest gadgets and fads. Dressed in loud checks and a gaudy waistcoat, and sporting a large false moustache, he would in a typical sketch veer between a self-delighting hobbyist enthusiasm and bluster and bluff as he worked hard to remain, in his own words, 'master of the situation', in the face of a combination of cussed technology and the antics of his stooges—comedy enhanced by his rich, fruity roar and the elaborate see-sawing of his moustache.

Tate's greatest success with this format came before the First World War with 'Motoring', which began a series of sketches that reflected Tate's preoccupation with the typical enthusiasms and crazes of the burgeoning lower-middle classes, among them 'Gardening', 'Fishing', 'Selling the Car', 'Flying', 'Golfing', 'Billiards', 'Wireless', and 'Going Round the World'. In 'Motoring', which would be extended and filmed as a six-reeler in 1927, Tate's unsuccessful attempts to start his car were variously disrupted by his inept chauffeur, passing drunks and urchins, and a policeman intent on arresting him on a charge of 'furious driving'. His precarious mastery of the situation was further tested by the exasperating falsetto comments of his stage son, Tommy Tweedly, perched high on the car's back seat in top hat and Eton suit. The regular calls of 'Good-

Harry Tate (1872–1940), by Houston Rogers

been taken literally by many commentators. Others have seen it as the irrepressible and enduring last laugh of a humorous and highly talented wag.   DAVID GOLDIE

Sources J. Fisher, *Funny way to be a hero* (1976) · R. Wilmut, *Kindly leave the stage!* (1989) · W. MacQueen-Pope, *The melodies linger on* (1950) · 'Motoring', 'Fishing', H. Tate and others, *The old time stars' book of comedy sketches* (1971) · 'Fishing', *The old time stars' book of comedy sketches* (1971) · *The Times* (15 Feb 1940) · J. Agate, *Ego 4: yet more of the autobiography of James Agate* (1940) · G. J. Mellor, *They made us laugh* (1982) · R. Busby, *British music hall: an illustrated who's who from 1850 to the present day* (1976) · J. R. Nash and S. R. Ross, *The motion picture guide*, 12 vols. (1987) · b. cert. · *WWW* · microfiche, General Register Office for England

Archives FILM BFI NFTVA, documentary footage · BFI NFTVA, performance footage |SOUND BL NSA, documentary recordings · BL NSA, performance recordings

Likenesses H. Rogers, photograph, Theatre Museum, London [*see illus.*]

bye-ee' as the car made to set off and then didn't move, became a much-used catch-phrase and would be made the basis of a popular song of the First World War. Other catch-phrases that Tate popularized included 'I don't think' (as in the disparagement, 'He's a nice chap, I don't think') and 'How's your father?', which Tate would employ as a device to change the subject when the conversation threatened to take him out of his depth.

Tate's status as one of the nation's best-loved entertainers was enhanced by his reputation as a favourite comedian of royalty, having famously amused George V with his motoring sketch during the first royal variety performance in 1912; in all he appeared four times in royal shows. His appeal across class boundaries was one reason for the longevity and popularity of his career as a sketch-based comic: he was one of the few performers who was able to extend a reputation made in music-hall to the newer modes of variety, revue, and the broadcast media.

Tate was widely admired also as a gifted comic actor and revue comedian. He featured as chief comedian in several revues, starting with *Hullo, Tango!* at the London Hippodrome in 1913. According to a *Times* obituary, his performance as a dogged suburban householder 'Fortifying the home' against enemy spies in *Razzle-Dazzle* in 1915, 'remains in many elderly memories, as one of the joys of the dreary years of the last war' (*The Times*, 15 Feb 1940). Tate was one of the first entertainers to be broadcast on radio, and later played a substantial number of supporting roles in films, beginning with *Her First Affaire* in 1932 and including an appearance in the first British technicolor film, *Wings of the Morning* in 1937. He continued, in spite of rumours of his heavy drinking, to be held in high esteem throughout the thirties, touring with his son, Ronnie Tate, until his final performance in *All Clear* at the Theatre Royal, Brighton, in December 1939.

Harry Tate died on 14 February 1940 at Sutton, Surrey, having suffered a series of illnesses including partial blindness and a heart attack. His claim to journalists that these were consequences of his having been injured during one of the first air raids of the Second World War has

Tate, Sir Henry, first baronet (1819–1899), sugar refiner and benefactor, was born at Chorley in Lancashire on 11 March 1819, the eleventh child of the Revd William Tate (1773–1836), and his wife, Agnes, daughter of Nathaniel Booth of Gildestone, Yorkshire. Tate's parents had twelve children in all, four having died before Henry's birth. To eke out a living as a Unitarian minister, William Tate opened a private school for poor children. It was here that Henry received his only formal education. At the age of thirteen he was apprenticed to one of his older brothers, Caleb Ashworth Tate (d. 1846), who was a grocer in Liverpool. Seven years later Henry set up on his own, by buying the business of Aaron Wedgwood in Old Haymarket, Liverpool. By the time he was thirty-six, Henry Tate had six shops—four in Liverpool, one in Birkenhead, and one in Ormskirk. He also expanded into the wholesale trade in 1857.

Tate began a more significant commercial diversification in 1859, when he went into partnership with John Wright, a cane sugar refiner of Manesty Lane, Liverpool. This proved sufficiently successful for Tate to sell the six shops in 1861, and for the partners to establish their own refinery in the following year. A second refinery was built in 1864. Five years later Wright withdrew, and the company changed its name to Henry Tate & Sons. The subsequent years were difficult for British refiners, as imports of refined beet sugar, supported by state subsidies, entered the market from continental Europe, particularly Germany. Several businesses in Britain went bankrupt. Tate and other cane sugar refiners argued for some form of protection from such subsidized imports, but the chief response of his and other successful companies was to innovate and expand to meet competition.

In 1870 Tate built a new refinery in Love Lane, Liverpool. Here he incorporated the so-called 'Greenock method' of refining (Greenock then being one of the centres of refining), which included boiling the sugar in a partial vacuum, and at a low temperature, to reduce caramelizing. The refinery began operating in 1872, but before it did so Tate was introduced to another new method, developed in France by Bovin and Loiseau, using lime and carbonic acid to purify the sugar. Tate bought the rights to this, and

Sir Henry Tate, first baronet (1819–1899), by Sir Hubert von Herkomer, 1897

introduced it to Love Lane. Much of Tate's commercial success was based on his ability to recognize an opportunity, and to his judgement in introducing new technologies from elsewhere. This was illustrated again in 1874–5, when he bought a derelict shipyard on the Thames at Silvertown. It was to be the site of his largest refinery, which began operating in 1878, under the control of his son, Edwin. The construction of a new refinery represented a significant risk for the company; the costs were such that Tate was forced to withdraw his daughter, Isolina, from boarding-school.

At the time of the move to London, Tate learned of a process for making sugar into small cubes, patented by Eugen Langen of Cologne. Hitherto sugar had been sold in blocks or 'loaves', which needed to be broken or chopped into smaller usable pieces. Tate (jointly with another refiner in Liverpool, David Martineau) bought the rights to the Langen cube-making process in 1875, with an agreement not to pay royalties until his refinery was producing them successfully. In 1892 Tate bought outright, for £12,000, the exclusive British rights to a superior cube-making process, which had been patented by Gustav Adant of Brussels. Tate's refinery began to use this process in 1894. The family firm became a private limited company two years later, when Henry retired and his eldest son, William Henry, was made its first chairman.

It was said by some contemporaries that Tate was much guided by his first wife, Jane. She was the daughter of John Wignall of Aughton, Lancashire. They married on 1 March 1841 and had seven sons (one of whom died in infancy) and three daughters. Tate outlived his first wife and married

for a second time, on 8 October 1885; his new wife was Jane Amy Fanny, daughter of Charles Hislop of Brixton Hill. Tate's family life was always private—indeed, he was a very private man. He was guided by the religious beliefs and values of his Unitarian upbringing, though he was attracted to the Congregational church at the time of his second marriage. His public activities and benefactions were, however, invariably apolitical and non-sectarian. He enjoyed a good reputation as an employer. He never sought public or political office except for serving briefly on Liverpool city council in the 1860s as a Liberal. He was also a JP in Liverpool and Surrey. He fought shy of public acclaim and nearly always avoided public speaking, a task he hated, and at which he was said to be very poor.

Tate in some respects typified the Victorian nonconformist bourgeois, with a somewhat ascetic lifestyle of modesty and discretion. Yet he took a great interest in art, sought to encourage young artists, and built up an extensive collection of contemporary paintings at his home in Park Hill, Streatham Common, London. He was a close friend of Sir John Everett Millais, director of the Royal Academy. It had been Tate's intention to donate his collection to the National Gallery, but the trustees were prepared to accept only a sample. Thus, after some difficulty in finding a site, he endowed a new gallery at Millbank in London. This became the National Gallery of British Art, but has always been far better known as the Tate Gallery. He donated sixty-five of his own pictures, and three sculptures to the gallery. They included many which reflected his conservative taste, such as Orchardson's *Her First Dance* and *The First Cloud*; Waterhouse's *Lady of Shallot*; Millais' *Ophelia*, *Vale of Rest*, and *North-West Passage*; and several by Tindeman, Reid, and—Queen Victoria's own favourite—Sir Edwin Landseer.

The building for the new gallery was designed by Sydney R. J. Smith, and opened by the prince of Wales on 21 July 1897. On this occasion Tate broke his self-imposed public silence and made a speech presenting the gallery to the people. The initial cost of the gallery had been £190,000 but later additions brought the total close to half a million pounds. In recognition of this, and other benefactions, Tate was made a baronet in 1898. He had twice declined this honour, but was eventually persuaded to accept by Lord Salisbury, who told him that a refusal would be a snub to the royal family. For twenty years the new gallery was administered by the National Gallery, of which Tate had been made a trustee.

Tate made many other donations, often anonymously, and always discreetly. They included £42,500 for Liverpool University, £3500 for Bedford College for Women, and £5000 for building a free library in Streatham; additional provisions were made for libraries in Balham, Lambeth, and Brixton. There was £10,000 for the library of Manchester College, Oxford, and, also to Manchester College, £5000 to promote the 'theory and art of preaching'. In addition he gave £20,000 to the (homoeopathic) Hahnemann Hospital in Liverpool in 1885, £8000 to the Liverpool Royal Infirmary, and £5000 to the Queen Victoria Jubilee Institute, which became the Queen's Institute for District

Nurses. In 1887 he gave £5000 to the Tate Institute in Silvertown, to serve as a non-sectarian, and apolitical meeting-place for working people. It had a large hall and several meeting rooms, a reading room, billiard room, and nine bathrooms.

Sir Henry Tate died at his home in Streatham, Park Hill, on 5 December 1899, after a long illness, and was buried at Norwood cemetery. He was survived by his second wife and succeeded in the baronetcy by his eldest son, William Henry.   ROGER MUNTING

Sources P. Chalmin, *The making of a sugar giant: Tate and Lyle, 1859–1989*, trans. E. Long-Michalke (1990) [Fr. orig., *Tate and Lyle, géant du sucre* (1983)] · T. Jones, *Henry Tate, 1819–1899*, rev. edn (1960) · J. A. Watson, *A hundred years of sugar refining: the story of Love Lane refinery, 1872–1972* (privately printed, Liverpool, 1973) · A. Hugill, *Sugar and all that: a history of Tate and Lyle* (1978) · *The Times* (28 Nov 1899) · *The Times* (6 Dec 1899) · *DNB* · J. Rothenstein, *The Tate Gallery* (1962) · J. G. Millais, *The life and letters of Sir John Everett Millais*, 2 vols. (1899) · H. O. Gray, *The life of Sir William Quiller Orchardson* (1930) · D. J. Jeremy, 'Tate, Sir Henry', *DBB*
Archives Leics. RO, hunting journals · Tate collection, corresp. and papers relating to the founding of the Tate Gallery | Bodl. Oxf., letters to Sir William Harcourt and corresp. relating to Tate Gallery
Likenesses H. von Herkomer, oils, 1897, Tate collection [*see illus.*] · T. Brock, bronze bust, exh. RA 1898, Tate collection · T. Brock, bronze bust, *c*.1905, Library Garden, Brixton Road, London · bust, U. Lpool L. · photograph, repro. in *Year's Art* (1898), frontispiece
Wealth at death £1,264,215 5*s*. 5*d*.: resworn probate, Oct 1900, CGPLA Eng. & Wales

Tate, James (1771–1843), headmaster, was born at Richmond in Yorkshire on 11 June 1771, the only surviving son of Thomas Tate, a working maltster originally from Berwick, and his wife, Dinah Cumstone, who came from a family of small farmers in Swaledale. In May 1779, after attending two private schools, James entered the grammar school at Richmond, where his ability was recognized by the master, the Revd Anthony Temple. On Temple's recommendation, Tate became in 1784 amanuensis to Francis Blackburne, rector of Richmond and latitudinarian controversialist. Enjoying access to Blackburne's library, Tate owed much to the stimulus of this early influence and, with Temple's help, he obtained a sizarship at Sidney Sussex College, Cambridge, where he matriculated in 1790, graduating BA in 1794 as sixth senior optime and proceeding MA in 1797. He was from 1795 to 1796 a fellow of his college before, on 27 September 1796, he was appointed master of Richmond School, the fulfilment, it was said, of a childhood ambition. Two days later he married, at Kensington parish church in London, Margaret, second daughter of Feilding Wallis, the actor. He was ordained deacon in 1795 and priest in 1800, held the perpetual curacy of Bellerby, Yorkshire, from 1800 to 1808, and was in October 1808 appointed rector of Marske, near Richmond, a living which he held until his death.

Tate transformed Richmond School (of which he was master until January 1833), into one of the leading classical schools of his day, attracting boys from throughout the country. Between 1812 and 1833 six pupils a year on average proceeded to the universities. Their successes at Cambridge earned them the title of 'Tate's invincibles' (Wenham, 68); thirteen were elected to fellowships at Trinity College. At his instigation the school buildings were considerably enlarged in 1815. Rejecting corporal punishment and refusing to rule by fear, Tate succeeded instead in inspiring his pupils, as one of them recalled, 'with that passion for learning by which he was himself animated' (*GM*, 1843), encouraging the most promising boys during walks with them in the Yorkshire dales. Himself trained in mathematics, he applied the same precise methods to classical teaching, instilling habits of rigid accuracy. He was a widely respected classical scholar. Robert Surtees, the Durham antiquary, recalled that on the occasion of their first meeting they spent the night in quoting the *Iliad* (G. Taylor, *Memoir of Surtees*, 1852, 128), and Sydney Smith, who by chance travelled in the same coach as the master of Richmond, declared to a friend that he had fallen in with 'a man dripping with Greek'. Most of Tate's published works were schoolbooks: they included an edition of James Moor's *Elementa linguae Gracae* (1824) and *An Introduction to the Principal Greek Tragic and Comic Metres* (1827; 4th edn, 1834). With George Dunbar, professor of Greek at Edinburgh University, he added to Andrew Dalzell's *Collectanea Gracea majora* (1805–20). His most important work was *Horatius restitutus* (1832), an attempt to arrange the books of Horace in chronological order, applying the method of Richard Bentley. Reaching a third edition, it was favourably noticed by H. H. Milman in the *Quarterly Review* (62, Oct 1838), and later by W. B. Donne in the *Edinburgh Review* (92, Oct 1850).

Like his father, Tate was a strong whig, advocating Catholic emancipation in an assize sermon delivered in 1825. During the long period of tory ascendancy, his politics debarred him from the preferment which he sought to relieve the burden of his large family (seven sons and four daughters); he was among the unsuccessful candidates at the time of Thomas Arnold's appointment as headmaster of Rugby School in 1827. His fortunes improved on the return of a whig administration. In January 1833 Lord Grey appointed him canon of St Paul's, and by virtue of his canonry he became incumbent of the parish church of Edmonton in Middlesex. Tate died at Clifton, Bristol, on 2 September 1843 and was buried in St Paul's Cathedral. When, in 1850, Richmond School moved to a new site, the building, paid for by 140 subscribers, was a Tate memorial. His eldest son, James Tate (1801–1863) succeeded him as master of the school.

WILLIAM CARR, *rev.* M. C. CURTHOYS

Sources *The Times* (8 Sept 1843) · *GM*, 2nd ser., 20 (1843), 437–9 · Venn, *Alum. Cant.* · L. P. Wenham, *The history of Richmond School, Yorkshire* (1958) · *Letters of James Tate*, ed. L. P. Wenham, Yorkshire Archaeological Society Record Series, 128 (1965)
Archives N. Yorks. CRO, corresp. and papers · Richmond School, Yorkshire | BL, corresp. with Bishop Butler, Add. MSS 34583–35892, *passim* · LPL, letters to Charles Wordsworth · U. Durham L., letters to Earl Grey · York Minster Library, letters to Francis Wrangham
Likenesses H. W. Pickersgill, portrait, 1834, Sidney Sussex College, Cambridge · S. Cousins, mezzotint (after H. Pickersgill), BM,

NPG · plaster bust; known to be at Richmond Science Library, 1889

Tate, James William (1875–1922), composer and songwriter, was born on 30 July 1875 at 12 Compton Road, Wolverhampton, the eldest of the nine children (six boys and three girls) of Jacob James Tate (c.1849–1902), wine and spirit merchant, and his wife, Maria Doughty (1858/9–1916). Both his parents were musical, and his youngest sister, almost thirteen years his junior, was the soprano Dame Margaret (Maggie) *Teyte (1888–1976).

Tate was educated at St Wilfrid's College, Cheadle, Staffordshire, with the Roman Catholic priesthood in mind. However, in his youth he went to America, where he was a church organist, worked on a cattle train, and appeared as an actor. After returning to Britain, he became a musical director with the Carl Rosa Opera Company before orientating himself towards the popular musical theatre. In 1898 he was on tour as conductor of the musical comedy *The White Blackbird*, in which the leading lady was the singer and dancer Charlotte Louisa Collins, known as Lottie *Collins (1865–1910), celebrated for her performance of the song 'Ta-ra-ra-boom-de-ay'. They married on 16 August 1902, in which year he went into management to stage her in the musical *The Dressmaker*, adapted from a popular French play. In 1903 they had a daughter, Marie.

Also in 1903 Tate made a further tour as a musical director; but increasingly thereafter he concentrated on composing popular songs. He contributed songs to Liza Lehmann's music for the play *Sergeant Brue* by Owen Hall (1904) at the Prince of Wales's Theatre in 1904, and two particular variety theatre successes were 'If I should plant a tiny seed of love' and 'Come over the garden wall', both composed in 1908 to lyrics by Ballard Macdonald. Tate was a brilliant improviser at the piano, and in 1906 he began a variety theatre act as on-stage accompanist to Clarice Mabel Dulley (1886–1966), who appeared under the stage name Clarice Mayne. The pair came to be billed as 'Clarice Mayne and "That"', the latter name being the description by which his partner somewhat dismissively referred to the monocled Tate. After the death of Lottie Collins, the couple married on 19 March 1912.

Tate had set up a songwriting operation from an office initially in Green Street, Leicester Square, London, from where he moved later to Lisle Street. With remarkable fluency, he was able to turn out a rapid succession of songs, mainly in partnership with the lyricist Frank Clifford Harris (1875–1949), who was joined in 1914 by 'Valentine' (Archibald Thomas Pechey (1876–1961), father of the future television chef Fanny Craddock). The best of Tate's songs were performed by his wife, who provided welcome wartime relief with such light-hearted numbers as 'I was a good little girl till I met you' (1914), 'Broken doll' (1916), and 'Ev'ry little while' (1916). The latter two songs were also heard respectively in *Samples* (Playhouse, 1915) and *Some* (Vaudeville, 1916), two of a series of theatrical revues that became popular just before the First World War. Both were written by Harry Grattan (1867–1951), their titles demonstrating their piecemeal nature.

Through his marriage to Lottie Collins, Tate had acquired as stepdaughter the singer José *Collins (1887–1958), who in December 1916 opened at the Prince's Theatre, Manchester, in the pre-London try-out of Frederick Lonsdale's musical play *The Maid of the Mountains*. When it was felt that Harold Fraser-Simson's score lacked hit-number appeal, José Collins realized she knew just the man in her stepfather James W. Tate, who happened to be in Manchester at the time. Tate wired his lyricist partners Clifford Harris and Valentine to join him in Manchester, and together they added four songs. Three of them ('My life is love', 'A bachelor gay', and 'A paradise for two')— written in a romantic style quite different from Tate's normal idiom—became outstanding hits of the show.

Later in 1917 Tate provided the music for *Lads of the Village*, a wartime piece for the Oxford Theatre, London, and *The Beauty Spot*, adapted from the French by Arthur Anderson and starring Régine Flory at the Gaiety Theatre. Clarice Mayne also had a further major success with his song 'Give me a little cosy corner' (1918). However, Tate was by now increasingly involved with the composition and musical supervision of the touring revues and provincial pantomimes for which he had formed a partnership in 1913 with the producer Julian Wylie (1878–1934). Each Christmas the pair would produce as many as nine or ten provincial pantomimes, and it was while visiting one such work at the Theatre Royal, Hanley, in wintry weather that Tate was taken ill with pneumonia, which led to heart failure. He died in Longton Cottage Hospital, Stoke-on-Trent, on 5 February 1922, aged forty-six, remembered as a man of genial good nature, with an unerring ability to know what the public wanted. Tate was buried on 8 February 1922 in Hampstead cemetery, Fortune Green.

ANDREW LAMB

Sources *The Era* (8 Feb 1922) · *The Era* (15 Feb 1922) · Valentine [A. T. Pechey], *Leaves of memory* (1939) · W. Macqueen-Pope, *Shirtfronts and sables* (1953) · G. O'Connor, *The pursuit of perfection* (1979) · K. Gänzl, *The British musical theatre*, 2 vols. (1986) · b. cert.
Likenesses photograph, repro. in *The stage year book, 1914–1915*
Wealth at death £8802 15s. 8d.: admon (limited), 1922, *CGPLA, Eng. & Wales* (1922)

Tate, John (c.1448–1507/8), merchant and paper maker, was probably the eldest son of John Tate (c.1409–1478), mercer and sometime mayor of London, and his wife, Elizabeth, whose maiden name was probably Marshall. He was apprenticed to the Mercers' Company and was made free in 1474. It was probably in this year that he married Elizabeth, with whom he had three sons, John, Robert, and Thomas. Elizabeth outlived her husband by at least fifteen years and remarried. In his will, Tate described himself as 'of Mincing Lane … Citizen and Mercer of London' (Blewett, 'John Tate … further observations', 258–63). Tate must have inherited his father's house in Mincing Lane where he also owned another at the time of his death as well as estates near Hertford, in Essex, and elsewhere, so he possessed considerable wealth.

Tate traded as a mercer and therefore principally in fine cloth but possibly in other goods too. The Tate family was influential in the city of London for its members held the offices of alderman, sheriff, and mayor at various times. His father was also a member of the staple at Calais. They would have had trading links with Italy as well. Whether it was these connections or the return from the continent in 1475 of another mercer, William Caxton, who established the first printing press in Britain in London, that turned Tate's attention to paper making will never be known.

The first paper that was used in England came from Italy and France, and by this period had become of sufficient quality and cheap enough to rival parchment. The colophon in the *De proprietatibus rerum* printed by Wynkyn de Worde in 1495 reveals that John Tate had established a paper mill in England and had made the paper for this book. The paper has Tate's unique watermark, an eight-pointed star or petals of a flower set in a double circle, and de Worde used this paper in some of his other books. This watermark appears also in the printed version of a papal bull recognizing the marriage of Henry VII to his distant cousin Elizabeth of York, issued in 1494. This is the earliest definite surviving evidence of Tate's paper, although earlier dates of 1476, 1485, and 1491 have been suggested. To have produced paper ready for printing in 1494 must have required an earlier production date but when is not known. The quality of Tate's paper is good and stands comparison with contemporary sheets.

The moulds Tate used to produce the paper were probably Italian and a study of the watermarks shows that he made at least two different sizes of sheet on various moulds. This suggests that the mill was quite a large establishment. Tate adapted the water-powered Sele mill, a little upstream from Hertford and its royal castle. No details of the machinery have survived. Henry VII visited the mill in May 1498 when Tate probably had special watermarks of Tudor roses attached to his moulds. Publications and manuscripts with Tate's watermarks have been found as late as 1510 or even 1512 but it is very doubtful whether production continued as long as this. Tate instructed in his will, made on 10 October 1507, that his paper mill be sold, which suggests that it was not functioning by then. However, Thomas Bolle of Hertford was to receive some 'whit or other paper' which must indicate that the Sele mill was in use at least as a warehouse (Blewett, 'John Tate … further observations', 258–63). The reasons for Tate's ceasing production are unknown. He died in London in 1507 or 1508, and was buried at St Dunstan-in-the-East. It would be another fifty years before a second paper mill was established in Britain and then only for brown paper.

RICHARD L. HILLS

Sources R. L. Hills, *John Tate, England's first papermaker* (1993) · P. Blewett, 'John Tate, mercer and papermaker', *International Association of Paper Historians Year Book*, 7 (1988), 3–9 · P. Blewett, 'John Tate, mercer and papermaker: further observations', *International Association of Paper Historians Year Book*, 7 (1988), 252–65 · R. L. Hills, 'John Tate and his mill', *International Association of Paper Historians Year Book*, 7 (1988), 59–72 · A. H. Shorter, *Paper mills and paper makers in England, 1495–1800* (1957) · D. C. Coleman, *The British paper industry, 1495–1860* (1958) · A. H. Shorter, *Paper making in the British Isles: an historical and geographical study* (1971) · A. Stevenson, 'Tudor roses from John Tate', *Studies in Bibliography*, 20 (1967), 17–33
Wealth at death see will, PRO, PROB 11/16, sig. 24 (1507)

Tate, Maurice William (1895–1956), cricketer, was born at 28 Warleigh Road, Preston, Brighton, on 30 May 1895. He was the eldest in the family of three sons and seven daughters of Frederick William Tate (1867–1943), professional cricketer, and his wife, Gertrude Beach. One of his younger brothers, Cecil Frederick Tate, played a few first-class games for Derbyshire and Warwickshire between 1928 and 1933. Maurice Tate was educated at Belvedere School, Haywards Heath, but was not good enough to play for the school eleven, and aspired rather to become a farmer. However, encouraged by his father, he had a trial for Sussex County Cricket Club when he was fifteen and made his début when he was seventeen. Fond legend has it that his father, following his own somewhat traumatic part in the 1902 test against Australia at Old Trafford when his dropped catch contributed substantially to defeat in a close-run contest, consoled himself with the anticipation that his son, then but a seven-year-old, would compensate in effective kind. He lived to enjoy that pleasure.

Tate played for Sussex from 1912 to 1937, with an interruption of four seasons during the First World War when he served in France as a signaller in the Royal Artillery. During his Sussex career, embracing 525 matches, he took 2211 wickets for the county at an average cost of 17.41 runs. No mean bat, he also scored just over 17,000 runs for Sussex, and he did the double of 100 wickets and 1000 runs seven times for Sussex alone. Counting all first-class cricket he completed the much-cherished double in eight domestic seasons and once overseas. Three times he took 200 wickets and scored over 1000 runs in a season, while his best bowling performance was nine for 71 for Sussex v. Middlesex at Lord's in 1926. In all first-class cricket he had 2784 victims, at an average of 18.16, and he took 100 wickets in each of fourteen seasons. With his hard-hitting and combative style he scored 21,717 runs (average 25) in all first-class cricket, his highest score being 203—one of his twenty-three centuries—for Sussex against Northamptonshire at Hove in 1921. Earlier in that year, on 20 January 1921, he had married Kathleen Miriam, the 21-year-old daughter of Alfred Charles Freeman, artist, with whom he had twin daughters and two sons.

Although Tate made his considerable name as a bowler, it is proper to acknowledge that, as one of only nine cricketers to have accomplished the substantial feat of scoring 20,000 runs and taking 2000 wickets, he should be recognized as one of cricket's leading all-rounders. It was as a bowler that he was first chosen to play for England; he made his début in 1924 and thereafter won thirty-nine caps, including appearances in twenty consecutive test matches against Australia, and nineteen against South Africa, India, and the West Indies. He took 155 wickets, at an average of 26.16, for England, quite a haul for the period, his best series being during the MCC tour of Australia in 1924–5, when he took thirty-eight wickets, a record for England versus Australia until broken by J. C. Laker in 1956, just after Tate's death. He is still regarded as second only to the great S. F. Barnes as the scourge of Australian batsmen on their own soil.

Under the influence of the Sussex and England captain

Maurice William Tate (1895–1956), by unknown photographer

A. E. R. Gilligan, who converted him from the slower mode he had inherited from his father, Tate developed into a fast medium bowler from 1922. He was able to control deceptive swerve and telling accuracy over exacting periods. His briskness of pace off the pitch became legendary and he is said to have been the first bowler deliberately to have deployed the ball's seam in his technique. He is generally regarded as one of the best two or three fast medium bowlers in cricket's annals, with only notables such as Sir Alec Bedser or George Lohmann, both of Surrey, thought of as worthy of comparison. As C. B. Fry, cited in Tate's *Wisden* obituary, said, Maurice Tate 'could make the ball rear off the pitch like a snake striking' (Green, 877).

'Chubby' Tate was the most whole-hearted and cheerful of competitors. He was a large, strong man of genuinely and pleasantly rustic character. He constantly bore a huge grin and this, together with his massively booted feet, made him the darling of the sports cartoonists of his day, notably Tom Webster of the *Daily Mail*. That greater press coverage, coupled with the social efforts of colleagues such as Herbert Sutcliffe and Walter Hammond, marked the transition in the status of professional cricketers from the old-style 'feudal' position to something more akin to a well-respected technician. Maurice Tate was the first 'pro' to captain Sussex; he was made an honorary life member of the county club, where memorial gates commemorate him, and he was one of twenty-six former professionals made MCC life members in 1949. He published his memoirs in 1934, and in the early 1930s sponsored commercial products including Hovis bread and Shredded Wheat breakfast cereal.

Tate's decline was abrupt—he was no longer a lethal bowler—and his first-class career ended in 1937, when he was 'paid off' by the county in circumstances that left him aggrieved. He played professional league cricket for Walsall for a spell, and undertook occasional journalism. During service in the Second World War he was commissioned as a billeting officer, a further sign of the cricket professional making good. In 1950 he was appointed cricket coach at Tonbridge School. The amiable host of several Sussex hostelries, Tate died suddenly from a blood clot at the Greyhound Hotel, Wadhurst, Sussex, where he was landlord, on 18 May 1956. He was buried in Wadhurst churchyard, survived by his wife.   ERIC MIDWINTER

Sources G. Brodribb, *Maurice Tate: a biography* (1976) · J. Arlott, *Maurice Tate* (1951) · B. Green, ed., *The Wisden book of obituaries* (1986), 876–7 · P. Bailey, P. Thorn, and P. Wynne-Thomas, *Who's who of cricketers* (1984) · J. Marshall, *Sussex cricket: a history* (1959) · R. Sissons, *The players* (1988) · b. cert. · m. cert. · *CGPLA Eng. & Wales* (1956)

Archives FILM BFI NFTVA, news footage · BFI NFTVA, sports footage |SOUND BL NSA, 'A piece about fast bowler Maurice Tate', 29E BBC REC86H 32BD2

Likenesses T. Webster, cartoon, 1935, repro. in Brodribb, *Maurice Tate*, 164 · photograph, repro. in Marshall, *Sussex cricket*, facing p. 135 · photograph, NPG [*see illus.*] · photographs, repro. in Brodribb, *Maurice Tate*, following p. 120 · photographs, MCC Library · photographs, Sussex County Cricket Club · photographs, Roger Mann Collection · three photographs, repro. in Arlott, *Maurice Tate*

Wealth at death £824 13s. 4d.: administration, 21 Aug 1956, *CGPLA Eng. & Wales*

Tate [*née* Hogg; *other married name* Gott], **Mavis Constance** (1893–1947), politician and feminist, was born Maybird Constance on 17 August 1893, the daughter (there was also a son) of Guy Weir Hogg (1861–1943), sheriff of St Helena and managing director of Solomon, Hogg & Co., and his wife, Constance Piercy Marsden (d. 1920). She was educated privately and at St Paul's Girls' School, London. She married, on 9 August 1915, Gerald Ewart Gott (1892/3–1966), a captain in the Bedfordshire regiment, son of George Arthur Gott of Will Hall, Alton, Hampshire. This wartime marriage, of which there were no children, ended in divorce in 1925. That year (22 August 1925) she made a second marriage, to Henry Burton Tate (b. 1883/4), also a divorcee, of independent means, the son of Henry Tate, also of independent means. His previous marriage to Ida Guendolen Legge had ended in divorce in 1925. In 1930 she rejected her original first name, Maybird, and adopted Mavis by deed poll.

Like many women of her class and generation Mavis Tate was not originally a feminist, but during the 1920s she took advantage of the many changes in British society and politics to extend her interests beyond the purely conventional. At this time her recreations included not only gardening and reading but also flying, a subject on which she later became a political authority. She served as a JP for Middlesex. In March 1931 she contested a London county council seat at Islington, and then stood for the West Willesden parliamentary constituency as a National Conservative at the general election in October 1931. Though this was not a Conservative constituency, the landslide victory won by the National Government swept her into parliament.

As a back-bencher Tate spoke frequently on a wide range of subjects, refusing to be confined to the domestic topics then considered appropriate for female politicians. For example, she took an interest in overseas trade, which led her to criticize the government for failing to gain preference for manufacturers of sugar refining machinery in the Ottawa agreements in 1932. Above all, she made well-informed speeches on civil aviation, and she anticipated the failure of the disarmament convention by urging an acceleration of air force rearmament in 1934. By the mid- and late 1930s she found herself taking an increasingly feminist stance on such issues as maternal mortality rates, birth control clinics, women's nationality, and equal pay. In 1935 she presented a petition designed to allow married women to enjoy independent nationality, just as married men and single women did. In the same year, in a debate on women's pay, she attacked the view that the state had the right to push women into marriage and out of employment. Tate had found her vocation at last, but as her Willesden seat seemed likely to revert to Labour, her career was in jeopardy. Decisive as ever, she switched to a slightly safer constituency at Frome, in Somerset, for the 1935 election; her narrow victory there kept her in parliament until 1945.

It was the Second World War that brought Tate's career to its peak, though at the price of a breakdown from overwork in 1940. By working closely with the women Labour and Liberal members, she harassed the coalition government for its neglect of women's interests, helping in the process to create what, in effect, was a women's party for the duration of the war. Tate's major achievement was to demand that female civilians be awarded equal compensation with men rather than the two-thirds the authorities considered appropriate. She presented several petitions in support of this claim, and persuaded ninety-five members to vote against the government in a debate in November 1942. As a result the government established a select committee, and in April 1943 accepted its recommendation for equal compensation. From 1943 onwards Tate became a leading figure in the Equal Pay Campaign Committee, whose object was to pressurize the government into conceding equal pay in the civil service and teaching. After a narrow defeat over teachers' pay in 1943 the government resorted to a royal commission as a delaying tactic.

In spite of her growing political role, however, Tate's life began to deteriorate rapidly by the closing stages of the war. Separated since 1938, she was divorced from Henry Tate in 1944. Her defeat at the general election in 1945 at least left her with more time to campaign for equal pay; but she became angry as the report of the royal commission was delayed until 1946. Meanwhile she maintained pressure on the Labour members, but was frustrated by the new government's insistence that no resources could be found to meet the costs of equal pay for women. After her visit to the German concentration camps with other

MPs in 1945 her health deteriorated. She had several operations for gallstones and suffered acute pain for lengthy periods. The culmination came on 5 June 1947 when she was found dead from carbon monoxide poisoning at 6 Bloomfield Terrace, her Westminster home. In a note to her brother, Colonel K. W. Hogg, Tate explained the reasons for her suicide:

> As I have no one dependent on me it seems to me the wiser thing to do to end my life. An invalid is only a national liability today, and I cannot endure the extensive and constant pain in my head and practically no sleep at all week after week.   (*The Times*, 11 June 1947)

The coroner recorded that she had taken her life while the balance of her mind was disturbed by ill health. Though only fifty-three, she doubtless realized that her chances of returning to parliament were poor, and the prospect of continual physical pain made the situation unendurable.

Mavis Tate had emerged from a background within the British establishment to make a mark as a radical in public life, and during the 1930s and the Second World War she became a prominent advocate of women's causes. Her vivacious personality, ready wit on the platform, and striking appearance (*The Times*, 6 June 1947) gave her an advantage as a public figure. However, her life was punctuated by unhappiness and tragedy, which reflected her decisive temperament and a tendency to overwork.

MARTIN PUGH

Sources *The Times* (6 June 1947) · *The Times* (11 June 1947) · *Hansard 5C* (1931–45) · M. Pugh, *Women and the women's movement in Britain, 1914–1959* (1992) · A. Potter, 'The equal pay campaign committee: a case study of a pressure group', *Political Studies*, 5 (1957) · *WWW* · Burke, *Peerage* (1967) [Hogg] · m. certs. · d. cert.
Archives Women's Library, London, the equal pay campaign committee minutes | FILM IWM FVA, actuality footage · IWM FVA, news footage
Likenesses photograph, 1936, Hult. Arch. · photograph, 1945, Hult. Arch.
Wealth at death £35,482 8s. 8d.: administration, 29 July 1947, *CGPLA Eng. & Wales*

Tate, Nahum (*c.*1652–1715), poet, playwright, and translator, probably born in Ireland, was the second of the four sons of Faithful Teate (*c.*1627–1665/6), and his wife, Katherine. The couple also had three daughters. Tate's father and grandfather (also called Faithful, (*d.* 1660)) were clergymen of puritan sympathies who had both attended Trinity College, Dublin, and had both held livings in Ireland and England. Tate's grandfather and his family were ill-treated, and his valuable property destroyed, in the Irish Catholic uprising of 1641. Tate's father was the author of seven published works, most notably *Ter tria* (1658), a long stanzaic poem in the metaphysical manner on the nature of the Trinity.

Nahum Tate and his brother (another Faithful) registered as students at Trinity College in June 1668. They had received their schooling under Henry Savage of Belfast, a Trinity contemporary of their grandfather. In his last undergraduate year Nahum was elected a scholar of Trinity, and graduated BA in 1672. By 1676 he had moved to London, where he soon established himself in literary circles. He lived there as a professional writer (with perhaps a brief period as a schoolmaster between 1687 and 1692) for the rest of his life. During the early 1680s Tate wrote committedly in support of Charles II, and initially welcomed James II's succession in 1685. But he seems to have become rapidly disenchanted with James's extreme pro-Catholic policies, and at the revolution of 1688–9 transferred his allegiance to William III, whom he hailed as a pious peacemaker and defender of English liberty. After the death of Thomas Shadwell in 1692, on 8 December Tate was appointed to the poet laureateship, a position which he held for life.

Tate's poetic career began with a set of complimentary verses to the second edition (1676) of the *Poems* of Thomas Flatman. In 1677 he published his own collection of *Poems*: sixty-nine short pieces, including love lyrics, melancholy Flatmanesque reflections, and one poem ('On the Present Corrupted State of Poetry') which provides early evidence of his pious tendencies. An expanded and revised edition of the collection, with many metrical and stylistic improvements, appeared in 1684. About 1680 Tate had made the acquaintance of two contemporaries who were to influence his career significantly: Charles Sackville, earl of Dorset, who soon became his patron, and who later, as lord chancellor, was to recommend his appointment to the laureateship, and John Dryden, with whom he soon became involved in several poetic projects. Tate wrote three versions from Ovid's *Heroides* for *Ovid's Epistles* (1680), a collaborative venture to which Dryden also contributed translations and a critical 'Preface'. In 1682 he published complimentary poems to Henry Dickinson's *Critical History of the Old Testament* translated from the French of Richard Simon (the occasion for Dryden's *Religio laici*), to the third edition of Dryden's *Absalom and Achitophel*, and to Dryden's *The Medall*. In the same year, Tate and Dryden collaborated directly on *The Second Part of Absalom and Achitophel*, with Dryden supplying the portraits of 'Doeg' (Elkanah Settle), 'Og' (Thomas Shadwell), and 'Ben-Jochanan' (Revd Samuel Johnson), and Tate writing most of the remainder, in close imitation of Dryden's original poem. Tate pursued his interest in translation with versions from book 7 of Ovid's *Metamorphoses* (in the 1684 *Poems*) and a rendering of books 4 and 5 of Abraham Cowley's *Six Books of Plants* (1689). His apparent plans for further Ovidian translations in the early 1690s, which eventually bore fruit in versions of book 4 of the *Metamorphoses* (1697) and *The Speeches of Ajax and Ulysses* from book 13 (with Aaron Hill, 1708), seem to have provoked the rivalry of Dryden, who in a letter to his publisher Jacob Tonson of 3 October 1692, wrote of his intention to 'spoyl Tate's undertakings' by speedily bringing out his own translation of 'The first book of Ovid's *Metamorphoses*'. But relations between Tate and Dryden remained sufficiently cordial to allow Tate to contribute versions of satires 2 and 15 to the Dryden–Tonson *Satires of Juvenal and Persius* (published November 1692; dated 1693), and to write, probably about the same time, the version of Ovid's *Remedia amoris* eventually included in *Ovid's Art of Love* (1709). Tate's translation *Syphilis, or, A Poetical History of the French Disease*, (1686), from

the Italian of Girolamo Fracastoro, was reprinted in the third Dryden–Tonson miscellany, *Examen poeticum* (1693).

As well as satire and translations Tate published a substantial amount of occasional and complimentary verse, including poems on Thomas Creech's *Lucretius* (1683) and John Oldham's *Remains* (1684), and celebrations of Sir Godfrey Kneller (1692), Henry Purcell (1698), and the grammarian Lewis Maidwell (1707). The bulk of his output from 1692, however, took the form of official laureate verse, mostly in the form of pindaric odes, often designed for musical setting, which celebrated monarchical achievements and anniversaries, lamented royal deaths, commemorated military victories, and applauded prominent public figures and events. The pressures of royal patronage and public duty were temporarily in abeyance during Tate's composition of *Panacea* (1700; revised, 1702), a relaxed mock-heroic poem on the origins and virtues of tea-drinking.

Tate's religious commitment became increasingly evident in his later years. He compiled an anthology, *Miscellanea sacra, or, Poems on Divine and Moral Subjects* (1696; revised, 1698, 1705), wrote to the bishop of London (6 February 1699) with proposals 'for Regulating of the Stage & Stage-Plays', and published, from 1694, *A New Version of the Psalms of David, Fitted to the Tunes used in Churches* (first complete edition, 1696; revised version, 1698; supplement, 1700). The last, written in collaboration with Nicholas Brady, was intended to replace the Elizabethan versified psalter by Sternhold and Hopkins (1562), used regularly in Anglican worship as the equivalent of a hymnbook. The *New Version* was designed to achieve a modernity and elegance of idiom, while remaining compatible with the traditional psalm tunes. The Tate–Brady *Psalms* were attacked for their inaccuracy and for 'light and airy' modishness by Bishop William Beveridge in *A Defence of the Book of Psalms* (1710). Their poetical variety and liturgical practicality were immediately and vigorously defended by Tate in *An Essay for Promoting of Psalmody* (1710). Some of the *Psalms* and their associated hymns (including the celebrated 'While shepherds watch'd their flocks by night') survive in hymnals to this day. In 1713 Tate acted as co-editor of a short-lived periodical *The Monitor*, 'Intended for the Promoting of Religion and Virtue, and Suppressing of Vice and Immorality'.

Tate published a substantial quantity of prose throughout his career, including translations from Heliodorus (1686) and Lucian (1711), an edition of Quintus Curtius Rufus's *Life of Alexander the Great* (1690; with a dedication comparing William III with Alexander), and *A Present for the Ladies: being an Historical Vindication of the Female Sex* (1692). He was also active, particularly in the earlier part of his career, as a dramatist and librettist. His first play *Brutus of Alba* (performed in 1677–8; published in 1678), a tragedy in blank verse based on Book 4 of Virgil's *Aeneid* and heavily influenced by Dryden's *All for Love*, was soon followed by a second tragedy, *The Loyal General* (published 1680). Tate's tactless decision to mount this adaptation of Shakespeare's *Richard II* at the politically sensitive moment of the exclusion crisis resulted in performances being twice forbidden (December 1680; January 1681). In *The Ingratitude of a Commonwealth* (1682), an adaptation of *Coriolanus*, he signalled his royalist commitment in less ambiguous terms. During the mid-1680s Tate wrote the farces *A Duke and No Duke* (performed in 1684; published in 1685; based on a play by Aston Cokain), and *The Cuckolds-Haven* (1685; based on the Jonson, Chapman and Marston *Eastward Ho!*), and an adaptation from Fletcher, *The Island Princess* (1687). He later adapted Webster's *The White Devil* as *Injur'd Love* (1707). Tate's two most famous dramatic works are his adaptation of Shakespeare's *King Lear* (1681), and his libretto for Henry Purcell's *Dido and Aeneas*. The former survived as the standard stage version of Shakespeare's play until well into the nineteenth century. The latter was performed at Josias Priest's School for Young Gentlewomen in Chelsea in 1689, but may have previously received a private performance at court (possibly about 1684).

Tate's later years were marred by ill health and financial difficulties, including imprisonment for debt. He died in the Mint on 30 July 1715 and was buried on 1 August in St George's Church, Southwark. Though it has been assumed that Tate never married (Spencer, 37), a commission granted to his principal creditor Henry Whiteing for the administration of his assets after his death (PRO, PROB 6/92, fol. 157v) describes him as a widower. Nothing further, however, seems to be known about his marriage.

Tate seems to have had an agreeable personality. According to contemporary accounts, he was learned, courteous, modest, and moral, but also, according to the antiquary William Oldys, 'a free, good-natured fuddling companion' (Baker, 1.443). His work, however, has had a consistently bad press. Though admired by some contemporaries, it was soon pilloried by Pope, Parnell, and Swift, and has subsequently been subjected to almost universal contempt. The *Dictionary of National Biography* gives Tate's occupation, without further qualification, as 'poetaster', and his changes to the plot of *King Lear*—which include the introduction of a love interest between Edgar and Cordelia, the omission of the Fool, and the contrivance of a happy ending in which Lear, Gloucester, and Cordelia all survive—have been regularly regarded as risible examples of Restoration obtuseness and poor taste. However, while much of Tate's large output is now of only historical interest, some of his couplet verse attains genuine distinction; several of his religious poems still retain their currency after three centuries; and his version of *King Lear* is arguably an intelligent response to features of Shakespeare's original which distinguished critics such as Dr Johnson have found equally perplexing and problematic.

DAVID HOPKINS

Sources C. Spencer, *Nahum Tate* (1972) [incl. full bibliography of primary and secondary material] • S. A. Golden, 'Nahum Tate', PhD diss., TCD, 1954 • H. F. Scott-Thomas, 'The life and works of Nahum Tate', PhD diss., Johns Hopkins University, 1932 • H. F. Scott-Thomas, 'The date of Nahum Tate's death', *Modern Language Notes*, 49 (1934), 169–71 • H. F. Scott-Thomas, 'Nahum Tate, laureate: two biographical notes', *Modern Language Notes*, 56 (1941), 611–12 • B. Wood and A. Pinnock, '"Unscarr'd by turning times"? The dating of Purcell's *Dido and Aeneas*', *Early Music*, 20 (1992), 372–90 • S. A. Golden, 'The late seventeenth century writer and the laureateship: Nahum Tate's tenure', *Hermathena*, 89 (1957), 30–38 • S. A. Golden, 'The three Faithful Teates', *N&Q*, 200 (1955), 374–80 • S. A. Golden, 'Variations in the name of Nahum Tate', *N&Q*, 201 (1956), 72 • St J. D. Seymour, 'Faithful Teate', *Journal of the Royal Society of Antiquaries of Ireland*, 6 ser., 10 (1920), 39–45 • D. E. Baker, *Biographia dramatica, or, A companion to the playhouse*, rev. I. Reed, new edn, rev. S. Jones, 3 vols. in 4 (1812)

Wealth at death see will, PRO, PROB 6/92, fol. 157v

Tate, (Alexander) Norman (1837–1892), analytical chemist and teacher of science, was born on 24 February 1837 at Wells, Somerset, the son of James Tate, an alderman, and his wife, Emma Norman. He was educated at the cathedral grammar school and in 1857, after practising pharmacy for a time, he began studying chemistry in the laboratory of James Sheridan Muspratt's Royal College of Chemistry in Duke Street, Liverpool. In 1860 he was engaged as an analyst by John Hutchinson & Co., alkali manufacturers of Widnes, but in 1863 he and his brother, Frank, established their own analytical and consulting practice in Newstead Road, Windsor South, Liverpool.

Tate, in several analytical papers (published by the Chemical Society of London), paid particular attention to the study of American petroleum which was then being brought onto the market as an illuminant. Following the publication of his *Petroleum and its Products* (1863), which was translated into French and German, he temporarily gave up his Liverpool practice in order to erect oil refineries processing coal and shale on the Isle of Man and in Flintshire. In 1869 he married Elizabeth Millicent Faulkes of Claughton, Lancashire; the couple had two daughters. On his marriage Tate rejoined his brother in consultancy, at the same time establishing a School of Technical Chemistry in Old Hall Street, Liverpool. In 1873 the school became the Liverpool College of Science and Technology in new premises in Hackins Hey. Classes were conducted in a basement hall fitted with benches, the students having to provide their own apparatus. Here, besides teaching chemistry, Tate gained a considerable reputation as a specialist in the analysis of oils, fats, and waxes for W. H. Lever and other soap and food manufacturers.

Tate was an original member of the Society of Chemical Industry on its foundation in 1881, and was at various times president and vice-president of its Liverpool section. He also took a prominent part in furthering scientific education in Liverpool. In partnership with James Samuelson in 1871, and under the aegis of the Department of Science and Art, he founded operatives' evening classes. Tate taught chemistry, botany, physiology, and general biology in these classes and founded both the Liverpool Science Students' Association and the Liverpool Science and Art Teachers' Association. In addition, he was active in local geological and microscopical associations, being particularly interested in the chemical geology of the Merseyside boulder clay. In 1880, at Liverpool town hall, he was awarded a public testimonial for his educational work. In 1888 he founded a monthly magazine, *Research*, which was devoted to the popularization of science, but editing proved too time-consuming and it was discontinued at the close of its second year. A man of tremendous energy and enthusiasm, Tate died from cancer, at his home, Benarth, 27 Shrewsbury Road, Orton, Birkenhead, on 22 July 1892, leaving 'a void in the intellectual life of Liverpool' (*Geological Society Proceedings*). The firm of Norman Tate & Co., consulting chemists, continued. W. H. BROCK

Sources W. Jeffs, 'In memoriam: Alexander Norman Tate', *The Naturalist* (Oct 1892), 305–8 · *Nature*, 46 (1892), 298 · G. W. Roderick and M. D. Stephens, 'Private enterprise and chemical training in nineteenth century Liverpool', *Annals of Science*, 27 (1971), 85–93 · *Geological Society Proceedings*, 49 (1893), 60–61 · D. W. Broad, *Centennial history of the Liverpool section, Society of Chemical Industry* (1981) · *Research: a Monthly Illustrated Journal of Science*, 2 vols. (1888–90) · d. cert. · *CGPLA Eng. & Wales* (1892)

Likenesses photograph, repro. in *The Naturalist*, 305

Wealth at death £3797 14s. 5d.: probate, 24 Aug 1892, *CGPLA Eng. & Wales*

Tate [*married name* Frank], **Phyllis Margaret Duncan** (1911–1987), composer, was born on 6 April 1911 at Lexden Ovalway, Gerrards Cross, Buckinghamshire, the only child of the architect John Duncan Tate (*d.* before 1932) and his wife, Annie Stewart Holt. The family moved to London after the First World War, and Tate attended a small private school until she was expelled at ten for singing a bawdy music-hall song (taught to her by her father). She had no further formal schooling, but took up the ukelele, started composing foxtrots and blues, and joined a group of musicians who gave concerts for charity as well as playing in hospitals and old people's homes. The composer Harry Farjeon heard her performing and encouraged her to undertake a more formal musical education.

Tate studied from 1928 to 1932 at the Royal Academy of Music, London, where her principal study was composition (with Farjeon) but where she also took lessons in conducting and the timpani. Several of her works were played at the academy while she was a student, including a symphony and an operetta, *The Policeman's Serenade* (with a libretto by A. J. Herbert). After leaving the academy she achieved more performances of her work: her cello concerto was given a prestigious première by the Bournemouth Symphony Orchestra under Dan Godfrey in 1934, and four songs for tenor and piano and a string quartet in A (1936) were played at the Macnaghten–Lemare concerts in London.

Oxford University Press started publishing Tate's music in 1935. In that year she married Alan Clifford Frank (1910–1994), a clarinettist. Her husband was a music editor, and served as head of music at OUP (1954–75). The couple had two children: a son, Colin, in 1940 and a daughter, Celia, in 1952. During the 1930s Tate published commercial light music under various pseudonyms such as Max Morelle and Janos. An accomplished arranger, she later published numerous arrangements of a wide variety of traditional songs. Always extremely self-critical, Tate felt dissatisfied with her early concert works and after the Second World War destroyed almost all of them. The first work she was prepared to acknowledge was her concerto for alto saxophone and strings (1944), commissioned by the BBC. This was followed by two works which firmly established her reputation as an inventive and imaginative composer: the chamber cantata *Nocturne for Four Voices* (1945) to a text by

Sidney Keyes, for four singers accompanied by string quartet, double bass, bass clarinet, and celesta, and a sonata for clarinet and cello (1947). In 1947 she was featured in a BBC Third Programme series entitled *Contemporary British Composers*.

Tate delighted in creating unusual sounds and textures, always presented within a clearly defined structure. She believed that music should entertain and give pleasure, an approach that can be clearly seen in her interest in composing for children and amateurs. But in all her works she was concerned to be directly communicative, while never compromising her very individual musical language and sound-world.

Tate was apparently not interested in writing large-scale instrumental works, and from the 1950s onwards she turned increasingly to vocal and choral music while continuing to explore the world of chamber music. Her striking cantata to Tennyson's famous poem *The Lady of Shallott* (1956), for tenor, viola, two pianos, and percussion, was commissioned by the BBC Third Programme as part of its tenth anniversary celebrations. Her opera *The Lodger*, based on the story of Jack the Ripper, was premièred at the Royal Academy of Music in 1960 and broadcast on the Third Programme four years later. Other stage works included the television opera *Dark Pilgrimage* (1963), *The What d'ye Call it* (1966), after the play by John Gay, and several works for children. She later expressed interest, unfortunately never realized, in writing a musical based on the life of Mrs Beeton, in which she would set the recipes from her *Household Management* as songs.

From 1954 Tate lived in Hampstead, north London, and became involved with local musical groups such as the Hampstead Music Club and the Barnet and District Choral Society. She was president of the latter, for which she wrote the cantata *St Martha and the Dragon* (1977) for narrator, soloists, chorus, children's chorus, and chamber orchestra. She was also involved in national musical organizations, serving on the executive committee of the Composers' Guild and the management committee of the Performing Right Society's members' fund. She died at the Royal Free Hospital, Camden, London, on 29 May 1987. SOPHIE FULLER

Sources S. Fuller, 'Phyllis Tate', *The Pandora guide to women composers: Britain and the United States, 1629 – present* (1994), 307–10 · P. Tate, 'Briefly speaking: a potted autobiography (1979)', *Phyllis Tate, 1911–1987*, British Music Information Centre, 10, Stratford Place, London WC1 [memorial booklet] · *Daily Telegraph* (1 June 1987) · *The Guardian* (2 June 1987) · *The Independent* (3 June 1987) · *The Times* (1 June 1987) · N. Kay, *MT*, 116 (1975), 429–30 · H. Searle, 'Phyllis Tate', *MT*, 96 (1955), 244–7 · M. Carner, 'Phyllis Tate', *MT*, 105 (1964), 20–21 · M. Carner, 'The music of Phyllis Tate', *Music and Letters*, 35 (1954), 128–33 · H. Carpenter, *The envy of the world: fifty years of the BBC Third Programme and Radio 3, 1946–1996* (1996) · b. cert. · d. cert. · *CGPLA Eng. & Wales* (1987)

Archives SOUND BL NSA, *Composer's portrait*, BBC, 12 Oct 1966, M968W C1 · BL NSA, *Composer's portrait*, BBC Radio 3, 29 June 1973, T595BW C1 · BL NSA, *Music weekly*, B764/1 · BL NSA, 'Phyllis Tate', BBC Radio 3, 8 April 1986, B643/2

Wealth at death £95,474: probate, 30 Sept 1987, *CGPLA Eng. & Wales*

Tate, Thomas (1807–1888), scientist and educationist, was born at Alnwick, Northumberland, on 28 February 1807, the son of Ralph Tate, a builder. Along with his elder brother George *Tate he attended the borough school in Alnwick, but unlike George he does not appear to have proceeded to the Dukes (Grammar) School. It is likely that he studied in Edinburgh for a short time with an architect, though J. P. Kay-Shuttleworth later referred to him as self-taught. His brother George ascribed his interest in mathematics and science to membership of the Alnwick Scientific and Mechanical Institution (founded 1825).

Tate's first experiences of teaching came from giving evening classes in Alnwick and Newcastle. In 1835 he was appointed lecturer in chemistry at the recently established York medical school. There, besides providing innovative evening classes on science, he also edited a weekly mathematical problem column in the *York Courant*. In 1840 he joined the staff of Battersea Teacher Training College and in 1849 he moved to the newly established Kneller Hall Training College in Twickenham as first master, with a salary of £250, under Frederick Temple as principal. In 1851 he was elected a fellow of the Royal Astronomical Society.

It was as an educator that Tate was most noted. He wrote more than twenty popular texts on various aspects of mathematics and science, including the *First Principles of Arithmetic, after the Method of Pestalozzi* (1845), which in various editions sold over 100,000 copies; a popular introductory text on the calculus (a topic that he introduced into the curriculum at Battersea); and the first volume of what was intended to be a multi-part *Mathematics for Working Men* (1856). His textbooks displayed his strong desire to demonstrate the usefulness of mathematical and scientific knowledge. He fought hard to establish teaching as a profession and to acquire status for it. To these ends he founded in 1853 the *Educational Expositor*, a periodical for teachers and all interested in education, and also became president of the newly created United Association of Teachers. His *Philosophy of Education* (1854) reached a third edition by 1860 and was also published in the USA. This book attempted to provide a balance of theory and practice in education. It shows Tate's debt to Francis Bacon, Johann Heinrich Pestalozzi (1746–1827), and, above all, John Locke, and also his acceptance of the then fashionable faculty psychology, by which the various cognitive faculties could be cultivated by being exercised on appropriate subjects within the curriculum. Its original contributions relate to the debate on 'method' in education, to an understanding of children's cognitive development, and to discussion of the qualifications of schoolteachers in relation to their professional duties.

Tate also did valuable work as a mathematician and scientist. He collaborated much with the noted engineer Sir William Fairbairn, for example in performing mathematical calculations required in the planning of the Britannia and Conwy bridges. Together they published several joint papers on topics related to engineering problems, and presented these to the Royal Society and the British Association for the Advancement of Science. In addition Tate developed several of his own instruments and mechanisms, including 'Tate's double-piston air pump'.

In 1855 Frederick Temple resigned his position at Kneller Hall after much criticism and inadequate government support, and the college was closed. In the following year Temple wrote to the committee of council on education to request a pension for Tate, whose health was in a poor state, and told it that:

> as an author and teacher he must be considered to stand quite at the head of his profession … It would be difficult to find any man who in proportion to his opportunities has done so much for education in this country.   (*Minutes*, 32–3)

Within three weeks Tate was awarded a pension of £120 per annum, and effectively his career as an educator was at an end.

Tate married twice but the last thirty years of his life are shrouded in obscurity. He died at his home, 51 Catherine Street, Liverpool, at the age of nearly eighty-one, on 18 February 1888, and was buried in Highgate cemetery, Middlesex. He was survived by his second wife, Lavinia, and three children, one of whom, George Tate, was an analytical chemist.   GEOFFREY HOWSON

Sources G. Howson, *A history of mathematics education in England* (1982) · *Minutes of the committee of council on education* (1856–7), 32–3 [letter by F. Temple] · J. Kay-Shuttleworth, *Four periods of public education* (1862) · G. Tate, *A history of Alnwick* (1866–9) · W. Pole, ed., *The life of Sir William Fairbairn, bart.* (1877) · E. G. Sandford, *Frederick Temple* (1907) · M. P. Black and A. G. Howson, 'A source of much rational entertainment', *Mathematical Gazette*, 63 (1979), 90–98 · J. H. Wetherill, 'The York medical school', *Medical History*, 5 (1961), 253–69 · D. Layton, *Science for the people* (1973) · d. cert. · *DNB*
Wealth at death £1947 2s. 10d.: probate, 31 May 1888, *CGPLA Eng. & Wales*

Tate, William (1748–1806), portrait painter, was born in Liverpool in September 1748, and was the brother of the Liverpool merchant and amateur painter Richard Tate. He attended a school at Woolton, near Liverpool. The painter Joseph Wright lodged with Richard Tate in 1769 and shortly thereafter William became his pupil. He was in London c.1771–2 and exhibited at the Society of Artists between 1771 and 1791; he was elected a fellow in 1773. Tate was in Manchester in 1773 but had returned to Liverpool by 1774, when he exhibited at the first art exhibition organized by the Society of Artists in Liverpool and where he showed two portraits and two studies in black chalk of Venus. He seems to have remained in Liverpool for the next couple of years, as he exhibited at the Royal Academy from Liverpool in 1776, but in the following year from 1 Red Lion Square, London.

On 31 March 1777 Tate entered the Royal Academy Schools, where he gave his age as twenty-eight last September. From 1778 until 1782 he gave his address as 11 Craven Street, Wright's London address when exhibiting. However, like Wright, Tate seems to have quarrelled with the academy, for in April 1787 Wright wrote to a mutual acquaintance:

> My ingenious & very worthy friend Tate, whom you know, has not for several years past, owing to some ill treatment he met wth at The Academy exhibited any pictures, by wch omission he finds himself lost to the world and neglected. (Nicolson, 138)

Although Tate exhibited only intermittently at the academy, he showed at both the Society of Artists and at the exhibitions held by the various Liverpool societies in Liverpool in 1784 and 1787.

Tate was evidently well regarded in Liverpool, to where he seems to have returned, as one of the seven portraits he showed in 1784 was hung in a prestigious position next to a portrait by Reynolds. He received commissions from prominent Liverpool families including Daniel Daulby, a member of a brewing family. Daulby sat to Tate, as did both his first and second wives, Elizabeth Knowles and Margaret, sister of the collector William Roscoe (all Walker Art Gallery, Liverpool). Tate evidently fared better in the north, possibly owing to his brother's connections, as by 1787 Wright was able to say of his friend's situation 'he is now advantagiously fixed at Manchester where he is encouraged & respected equal to his wishes' (Nicolson, 138). Tate's relationship with Wright was both professional and personal. After Wright's death in 1797 Tate completed a number of his portraits that had been left unfinished; he also owned a number of oil paintings and watercolour studies by Wright, which he bequeathed to members of his family.

Tate moved to the fashionable spa resort of Bath in January 1804, where he died on 2 June 1806, leaving a widow Ann. The Walker Art Gallery, Liverpool, has a number of his portraits.   DEBORAH GRAHAM-VERNON

Sources M. Bennett, ed., *Merseyside painters, people and places* (1978) [exhibition catalogue, Walker Art Gallery, Liverpool] · Waterhouse, *18c painters* · E. R. Dibdin, 'Liverpool art and artists in the eighteenth century', *Walpole Society*, 6 (1917–18), 12–91 · B. Nicolson, *Joseph Wright of Derby: painter of light*, 2 vols. (1968) · E. Morris and E. Roberts, *The Liverpool Academy and other exhibitions of contemporary art in Liverpool, 1774–1867* (1998) · Graves, *RA exhibitors* · S. C. Hutchison, 'The Royal Academy Schools, 1768–1830', *Walpole Society*, 38 (1960–62), 123–91 · will, PRO, PROB 11/1448, fols. 194v–198v

Tate, William Edward (1902–1968), teacher and historian, was born on 28 March 1902 in Retford, Nottinghamshire, the only son of three children. His parents were John William Tate (1870–1933), a railway clerk and Methodist preacher, and his wife, Mary, *née* Woodhead (1869–1947), a schoolmistress. The Tate family had come from a farming background in Yorkshire. W. E. Tate was educated at Grove Street School and King Edward VI Grammar School at Retford, where he was a scholar. In 1917 he left school, aged fifteen, to work for two years in war service as a laboratory assistant analysing steels in Sheffield. He qualified as an elementary schoolteacher at Westminster Teacher Training College (1920–22).

Tate taught scientific subjects at various elementary schools between 1922 and 1945, and became headmaster of Sutton Bonington village school, Nottinghamshire, in 1925, where he insisted upon higher-quality village education. Active in local politics, he was a founder and chairman of the Sutton Bonington Labour Party and of the Sutton Bonington and Normanton branch of the National Union of Agricultural Workers. His Labour Party membership was continuous from 1923. He was brought up a Methodist and joined the Church of England in 1933. His interests in agricultural history and parliamentary enclosure developed from the late 1920s at Sutton Bonington. He became a fellow of the Royal Historical Society in 1927 and of the Society of Antiquaries in 1947. In 1935 he became headmaster of the Sneyd Holy Trinity School in Burslem, Staffordshire. By all accounts he was extremely good with children and a very fine teacher. He was also a very enthusiastic Workers' Educational Association member and tutor from 1935 to 1962.

In 1945 Tate left schoolteaching to go to Oxford University (Ruskin and Balliol colleges). He was awarded a BLitt in 1947. At Oxford he was Houblon-Norman research fellow in agrarian history (1945–7) and the G. W. Medley senior research scholar at All Souls (1948–50). From 1947 to 1950 he was senior programme assistant in the history unit of the schools department of the BBC.

In 1950 Tate became a lecturer in the education department at Leeds University, and in 1959 he was promoted to a readership there. From 1956 he was also curator of the Museum of the History of Education, University of Leeds, which he started. In these capacities he produced many publications, particularly on the history of education and the charity schools of Yorkshire. He wrote in a 1959 curriculum vitae that 'I am a teacher with an interest in scholarship rather than a scholar with a taste for teaching, and I find myself happy, and I hope useful, in the atmosphere of a Department of Education' ('Summary of particulars', Tate MS 1093). Much of his best academic work on agricultural history was pursued as a leisure-time activity. He retired from Leeds University in 1966, and went to Clare Hall, Cambridge, as a visiting fellow.

Tate's most famous publication was *The Parish Chest: a Study of the Records of Parochial Administration in England* (1946), an erudite and wide-ranging survey of local records. This book retains much interest and is still widely read. He also published *The English Village Community and the Enclosure Movements* (1967). In addition he published very many county handlists of enclosure acts and awards, often in the historical and archaeological journals of local record societies. An example is *Nottinghamshire Parliamentary Enclosures, 1743–1868* (Thoroton Society record series, 5, 1935). These came together after his death in *A Domesday of English Enclosure Acts and Awards* (1978), a magisterial and widely consulted reference work which was completed, co-authored, and introduced by Michael E. Turner. Tate wrote many articles in scholarly journals. His publications stretched to such subjects as child welfare, the history of education, Yorkshire local history and topography, inn signs, travellers in Yorkshire, and a number of school texts. Among his lesser-known books were *His Worship the Mayor: a Handbook of Citizenship for Children who are to Grow up in a Democracy* (1944), *English Inns and Inn-Signs* (1951), *British Institutions* (1955), and *A History of Yorkshire* (1960, with F. Singleton).

Tate married in 1925 Ethel Markham (1902–1941), a schoolteacher, with whom he had a son and two daughters. Following her death he married in 1942 Margery Whitfield (1912–1991), another schoolteacher. This marriage produced a daughter. The couple divorced in 1953.

Tate married a third time in 1958, to Margery Kerr (c.1911–1973). He died in Bristol from a heart attack on 22 March 1968, and was buried at Westbury-on-Trym.

Tate is best remembered as a pioneer in agricultural history—researching local enclosures on a county-by-county basis, laying the foundation of a complete 'Domesday' of these, advancing academic study of rural history—and as a historian who introduced many others to the broad spectrum of local and administrative records. His work has greatly assisted countless researchers in local and agrarian history.

K. D. M. SNELL

Sources U. Reading, Tate MSS, 1093 [incl. an almost entire bibliography of Tate] · private information (2004) [Mrs Pat Hunter, Mrs Ann Best, Alan Everitt, Dennis R. Mills, Joan Thirsk, and Michael E. Turner] · W. E. Tate, *The English village community and the enclosure movements* (1967), 13–19 · W. E. Tate and M. E. Turner, *A Domesday of English enclosure acts and awards* (1978), 3 · I. Elliott, ed., *The Balliol College register, 1900–1950*, 3rd edn (privately printed, Oxford, 1953) · *CGPLA Eng. & Wales* (1968)
Archives Surrey HC, MS notebook 'English enclosure acts and awards vol. 34 Surrey' · U. Reading L., corresp. and papers, MSS 1093, 1234 · U. Reading L., holding includes bibliography, CV, corresp., and many other papers · University of Leicester, Centre for English Local History · York Minster Library, notes relating to Thomas Gent and Yorks schools
Wealth at death £2134: probate, 15 July 1968, *CGPLA Eng. & Wales*

Tate, Zouch (1606–1650), politician, was born in March 1606 at Delapre, Northamptonshire, the eldest son of Sir William Tate (b. before 1560, d. 1617) and his wife, Elizabeth Zouch (d. 1617), daughter of Edward, eleventh Baron Zouche of Harringworth, Northamptonshire, president of the council of Wales, warden of the Cinque Ports, and a director of the Virginia Company. Like his father and uncle, the antiquary Francis Tate, he studied at Oxford, matriculating from Trinity College in 1621, and like them entered the Middle Temple, in 1625; in 1623 he had studied French during a tour of France. Like his father, and his grandfather Bartholomew Tate, he served as justice of the peace in Northamptonshire. In addition to the family estate at Delapre, just south of Northampton, granted to his grandfather in 1590 by Elizabeth I and valued at £1500 per annum, he owned several other properties including two manors in Northamptonshire and one in Warwickshire, and was coheir to three manors in Hampshire.

Tate was elected MP for Northampton in April 1640 and in November 1640, again emulating his father (MP for the county in 1614, and for Corfe Castle in 1593) and uncle Francis (MP in 1601). With the outbreak of civil war he appears to have been among those parliamentarians more committed to pursuing military victory against the king, and supported the creation of the Anglo-Scottish executive committee of both kingdoms in 1644. In March 1644 he favoured the appointment of the earl of Manchester as lieutenant-general and Lord Robartes as field marshal, and that same year chaired a committee concerned with the composition of parliament's principal field army, under the earl of Essex. By November his committee had been allocated the unenviable task of investigating the charges and counter-charges of misconduct between the earl of Manchester, general of the eastern

association, and Oliver Cromwell, his lieutenant-general. As the Commons braced itself to debate the issue on 9 December, however, Tate opened with a speech which sought to avoid laying blame, asserted that the 'chief causes of our division are pride and covetousness' (Kaplan, 87), and urged that quarrels be sunk in a general ban on the wartime holding of offices in parliament's gift by members of either house. Appealing to his colleagues' sense of the righteousness of a cause greater than factional differences, his call was generally welcomed and soon embodied in the self-denying ordinance. The measure coincided with the reorganization of parliament's armies associated with the birth of the New Model Army, and Tate's committee took on the assessment of officers for the new force.

While serving as a peacemaker for political and military unity, however, Tate held divisive views on religion. A lay member of the Westminster assembly, at some point he joined its grand committee, and was recognized by the Scottish minister Robert Baillie as one of the more inflexible supporters of strict presbyterian settlement for the Church of England. He vigorously opposed an October 1644 proposal by Henry Vane the younger and Oliver St John to extend toleration to Independents and co-operated with Baillie in 1646 in an unsuccessful bid to block the imposition of lay commissioners upon the English church, a move which Baillie and his allies saw as a dilution of plans for a full presbyterian system. In early 1647 he supported efforts to promote conformity to the planned national church, not least within the parliamentary armies, and on 7 April 1647 was appointed to the Derby House committee, effectively a parliamentarian executive, dominated by political presbyterians, and set for collision with the New Model Army. Tate's presbyterian intolerance, combined with his vocal opposition to the army's 'remonstrance' of November 1648 made him an obvious candidate for exclusion from the Long Parliament at Pride's Purge in December 1648.

Tate had married Catherine (c.1607–1700), daughter of Sir Giles Allington of Horseheath, Cambridgeshire, and granddaughter of Thomas Cecil, earl of Exeter, making him a relative by marriage of the MPs Sir Robert Crane and Sir Thomas Fanshawe. The Tates had three sons: William (d. 1695), heir to Delapre, who married Mary (d. 1699), daughter of James Stedman, MP for Chippenham, in 1656; Sir John Tate (d. 1692), who became recorder of London; and Zouch (d. 1683), a soldier who died defending Tangier. The Tates' daughters were Elizabeth, and Catherine who married John Carew of Somerset. Zouch Tate died in December 1650 and was buried at Hardingstone church, near Delapre, beside his parents.

DANIEL WEBSTER HOLLIS, III

Sources Keeler, *Long Parliament* · A. N. B. Cotton, 'Cromwell and the self-denying ordinance', *History*, new ser., 62 (1977), 211–31 · L. Kaplan, *Politics and religion during the English revolution* (1976) · *CSP dom., 1623–5; 1635–7; 1644–5* · Foster, *Alum. Oxon.* · *The writings and speeches of Oliver Cromwell*, ed. W. C. Abbott and C. D. Crane, 4 vols. (1937–47) · S. R. Gardiner, *History of the great civil war, 1642–1649*, new

edn, 2 (1893) · *JHC*, 3–4 (1642–6) · Burke, *Gen. GB* (1833–8) · J. H. Gleason, *The justices of the peace in England, 1558 to 1640* (1969) · *VCH Northamptonshire* · K. B. Sommers, 'Court, country and parliament: electoral influences in five English counties, 1586–1640', PhD diss., Yale U., 1978 · M. A. Kishlansky, *The rise of the New Model Army* (1979) · R. S. Paul, *The assembly of the Lord: politics and religion in the Westminster assembly and the 'Grand debate'* (1985) · D. Underdown, *Pride's Purge: politics in the puritan revolution* (1971)
Archives Beds. & Luton ARS, letter to R. St John, no. 88
Wealth at death approx. £2000 p.a.: Keeler, *Long parliament*

Tatersal, Robert (*fl.* **1734–1735**), poet and bricklayer, is an obscure figure. Nothing is known of his origins or life beyond the publication in 1734 and 1735 of a two-part collection of poems entitled *The Bricklayer's Miscellany*. The work is described as 'in allusion to Stephen Duck' and is both heavily indebted to the successful thresher poet and aspiring to similar recognition.

The preface to *The Bricklayer's Miscellany* reveals Tatersal to be 'A poor country bricklayer of Kingston upon Thames'. The poems have been written during the winter,

> wherein I had not the employment to exercise the more material business of my calling … For the gentlemen of our profession I may not improperly compare to cuckoos who are brisk and gay … so long as the summer endures, but when winter approaches retire to their respective cells.
> (Tatersal, *Bricklayer's Miscellany, Second Part*)

Tatersal's minor collection of verses is significant for the light it casts on the nine-days-wonder phenomenon of Stephen Duck, and on the working life of a jobbing bricklayer in the 1730s. Tatersal is engagingly candid about his calling, especially on its seasonal ups and downs—in winter 'you may behold him, with an empty purse, forlorn and dirty' contenting himself with 'a few boil'd sprats and a dram of gin (which are a dish of great repute among bricklayers in the winter season'. In the summer, by contrast, when the sun 'begins to dart his oblique rays over Hampstead Hill; then we begin to look as sharp after a job, as a hound after a hare' (Tatersal, *Bricklayer's Miscellany, Second Part*, i–iii).

The title poem of Tatersal's collection 'The Bricklayer's Labour' is a competently written, lively, and informative descriptive poem of the daily work of a bricklayer:

> 'A line, a line,' the foreman cries, 'my boys',
> When tuck and pat with Flemish bond they run,
> Till the whole course is struck complete and done.

The echoes of Duck are very strong, and Tatersal is clearly hoping to attract something of the thresher's fame.

> Since rustick Threshers entertain the Muse
> Why may not bricklayers their subjects chuse?

proclaims the title page, and he adds: 'O happy Stephen! Were my life like thine' (Tatersal, *Bricklayer's Miscellany, Second Part*, 1). He uses an apposite conceit in invoking the 'trowel' of Ben Jonson to validate his claim as a literary bricklayer, despite the modern preference for the 'stupendous flail'.

In an advertisement in the endpapers of *The Second Part* Tatersal offers his services not only as bricklayer and surveyor, but also as tutor in 'writing, arithmetick, geometry and dialling'. The advertisement refers to one William Tatersal—presumably a close relative—as a writing-master of Kingston.

As a poet Tatersal, like his envied rival Duck, is effective when he is depicting his working day, and trite when addressing topics such as 'temperance' or in complimentary verses on Richard Onslow, lord lieutenant of Surrey and the dedicatee of the collection. He does, however, display a sense of humour, some awareness of literary works and styles, and a pleasing ability to poke gentle fun at his solitary artisan life.   WILLIAM R. JONES

Sources R. Tatersal, *The bricklayer's miscellany*, 2nd edn (1734) · R. Tatersal, *The bricklayer's miscellany: the second part* (1735) · R. Lonsdale, ed., *The new Oxford book of eighteenth-century verse* (1984)

Tatham, Charles Heathcote (1772–1842), architect and designer, was born on 8 February 1772 in Duke Street, Westminster, the youngest of the five surviving sons of the thirteen children of Ralph Tatham (1732–1779) of Stockton-on-Tees, co. Durham, and Elizabeth Bloxham (1739–1809), daughter of Jabez Bloxham, a wealthy wholesale hosier and property owner in Cateaton Street, Cheapside. On her marriage on 14 March 1761 Elizabeth brought her husband a considerable dowry with which, from 1772, he farmed and bred horses, unsuccessfully, at Havering Park, Havering atte Bower, Essex. He then became private secretary to Captain (later Admiral Lord) Rodney, a family friend, but died suddenly in London, of cholera, aged forty-seven, while on his way to join ship at Portsmouth.

Early years Tatham was educated at Louth grammar school, Lincolnshire, under Revd John Emeris, where his proficiency in the classics led to persuasion by his uncle the Anglican divine Dr Richard *Shepherd to adopt the church as a vocation. Tatham was averse to the idea, and developed instead an interest in the fine arts, particularly drawing. On returning to London in 1788, at the age of sixteen, Tatham was unsettled; he worked briefly in a timber merchant's counting house, learned drawing under John Landseer, made drawings for his mother's uncle Mr Butler, a coach-maker who built the state coach (designed by Sir William Chambers and S. Cipriani in 1760), and learned mathematics near Fleet Street. At the instance of another relation of his mother's, John Linnell, the furniture maker and interior designer, Tatham became a clerk to Samuel Pepys Cockerell (1753–1827), architect and surveyor, in Stratton Street, Piccadilly. Set to menial tasks without wages or proper accommodation, his training comprised copying leases for the Pulteney estate. Although articled initially for three years, Tatham's unbearable situation caused him to escape after one year, his flight precipitated by the humiliation of having to wait at dinner upon Warren Hastings. After returning to his mother's home at Bridge Street, Westminster, he spent a year copying the architectural orders from Sir William Chambers's *Treatise* (1759; rev. 3rd edn, 1791) and French ornament from Jean Le Pautre's *Oeuvres d'architecture* (1652). Linnell showed Tatham's drawings to Henry Holland, architect to the prince of Wales, whereupon Holland immediately took Tatham, aged almost nineteen, into his office as a trainee draughtsman. Holland was then

Charles Heathcote Tatham (1772–1842), by Benjamin Robert Haydon, 1823

engaged on additions and alterations to Carlton House, Pall Mall, for the prince of Wales, and to Woburn Abbey, Bedfordshire, for Francis, fifth duke of Bedford. Assisting Holland's draughtsmen, including Dominique Daguerre, Jean Pierre Théodore Trécourt, John Jagger, and David Hartley, Tatham contributed to both these commissions. In 1791–4, for Richard Brinsley Sheridan, Holland rebuilt the Theatre Royal, Drury Lane, where Tatham designed and drew at large all the ornamental decorations for the royal boxes and the proscenium, his cartoons being pricked off and painted in fresco by Charles Catton the younger.

Visit to Italy The declaration of war by France on 1 February 1793 made the exchange of ideas and the supply of French furnishings, so admired by the prince of Wales, increasingly difficult to organize. Despite Tatham's growing value in his office, Holland encouraged his resolve to go to Italy, to their mutual benefit. Knowing his master's requirements and to mitigate the indefinite loss of French sources, Tatham agreed to act as Holland's direct agent in Rome by supplying designs, casts of antiquities, and original pieces, simultaneously advancing his architectural studies at the source of neo-classical activity and increasing his own prospects of patronage. Linnell's offer of £100, later withdrawn, was replaced by £100 from John Birch, surgeon-extraordinary to George III and brother to Ann Birch, his mother's closest friend. To this Holland added an allowance of £60 a year for two years.

Tatham sailed for Leghorn in May 1794, with the architect and painter Joseph Gandy. After travelling via Siena, they arrived in Rome in July. Through the offices of the wealthy dealer and painter in Rome, Thomas Jenkins, Tatham moved into apartments in the via Barberini, which he was to occupy throughout his two-year stay. While sketching at the Villa Borghese, he met Mario Asprucci the younger, architect to Prince Marcantonio Borghese, and Don Isodoro Velásquez, an exhibitioner from the academy at Madrid; all three exchanged drawings and tracings and became firm friends. Tatham's letters of introduction included one from the architect Joseph Bonomi to his brother Giovanni Carlo Bonomi (1743–1801), professor of theology at the college of *propaganda fide*, Rome, who almost succeeded in converting Tatham to Roman Catholicism and for whom Tatham retained a lifelong admiration. At the home near Trinità dei Monti of the historical painter Angelica Kauffmann (aunt of Mrs Joseph Bonomi) and her husband, Antonio Zucchi, Tatham was introduced by the Venetian painter Giuseppe Bossi to the celebrated sculptor Antonio Canova, with whom he also became close friends.

By his elder brother John, who spent much time in Italy on account of his health, Tatham was introduced to Prince Ernest, duke of Cumberland, and Prince Augustus, duke of Sussex, thereby gaining an entrée into the highest social circles and the latest archaeological excavations. In partnership with the Irish painter Robert Fagan and others, Prince Augustus had opened several sites outside Rome, notably at Laurentium, of which Tatham subsequently published details of finds. Visiting museums (particularly the Vatican), villas (notably Hadrian's), baths, gardens, and churches both in the capital and its vicinity, Tatham made drawings, many in the linear style which later characterized his publications. During one of his many visits to Rome, Tatham met the eccentric and wealthy collector Frederick Hervey, fourth earl of Bristol and bishop of Derry (1730–1803), who intended building at his family seat, Ickworth, Suffolk, a neo-classical version of his Irish house, Ballyscullion, co. Londonderry, to house his immense art collections. Late in 1794 he invited Tatham to draw up plans and gave every indication of awarding him the commission. His designs were not accepted, however, and the building was executed by Francis Sandys to a design, unmentioned by Tatham, by Asprucci. Although the project drew attention to his name (and Holland exhorted him continually to make the most of his connections), the experience left Tatham with an ambivalence towards aristocratic patronage and architectural competitions which he was never to lose.

In his studies of furniture, Tatham considered the Italian bronze manufacturers superior to the French, and supervised the casting of candlesticks and other pieces, many destined for Carlton House, mostly to his own designs. He became an honorary member of the Accademia Clementina at Bologna on 29 March 1795 and a month later presented a design for a sculpture gallery, whose interiors prefigured that at Castle Howard. In 1796 he became a member of the Accademia di San Luca at Rome, where he submitted a design for a hunting-lodge.

By November 1795 Tatham's projected two-year visit was more than half over. Hoping to visit Athens, he set off for Naples and visited *en route* Cardinal Borgia's museum, where, as at the Vatican, he was impressed by the unrestored Egyptian antiquities. In Naples he was entertained by the British minister, Sir William Hamilton, who obtained for him a licence to view antiquities, and Lady Hamilton, whose post-prandial performance of her 'Attitudes' sealed Tatham's opinion of her moral character, and he was introduced to the German artist Wilhelm Tischbein, Goethe's companion. Diminishing funds prevented Tatham's continuing to Athens and, having seen the Farnese *Hercules* and all the museums, including the Portici, and climbed Vesuvius, he returned, in January 1796, to Rome.

In mid-1796 Tatham learned from Holland of the deaths of Jagger and Linnell, Trécourt's terminal illness, and his master's reduced activity owing to increasing ill health. In the face of the advancing French, potential patrons had returned to Britain and the acquisition of fragments was impossible, and Tatham left Rome on 9 July 1796. He reached Venice by 13 July and then travelled, drawing all the way, via Prague, Dresden, and Berlin and Potsdam, before arriving back in England in September.

Early career and marriage Tatham first exhibited at the Royal Academy in 1797, the earliest of fifty-three designs he was to exhibit there up to 1836. Except for a brief encounter in Italy with Frederick Howard, fifth earl of Carlisle, which was to prove fruitful, he had been singularly unsuccessful on his tour in attracting patronage, preferring to await what 'time and convenience may bring about' (V&A, D.1479-1551-1898, fol. 18). Recognizing 'that accurate Drawings upon the spot, might turn to good account in a publication' (ibid.), he spent two years working on the 102 plates showing the best examples from Holland's collection, and published in 1799 *Etchings of ancient ornamental architecture drawn from the originals in Rome and other parts of Italy during the years 1795 and 1796*. Of the 210 subscribers, almost a third were architects and craftsmen. The linear style which in Italy had been an expedient of time now became one of cost to ensure wide availability: his use of 'chaste outline' reflected the simplicity he advocated in providing 'a true picture of the original' (ibid., fol. 8).

Tatham aimed to make accessible 'an accurate delineation of the best approved specimens' of antique ornament, 'a map to the study of Nature', enabling designers to exercise their genius and imagination, but 'an imagination corrected by judgement' (*Etchings of Ancient Ornamental Architecture*, 3, 6). More polemically, he criticized the otherwise 'matchless' Piranesi and, by implication, Robert Adam as undiscriminating classicists for having used decoration in a highly subjective way that showed a dangerous indifference to the integrity of classical sources. A second edition of *Etchings* also appeared in a German translation in Weimar, Goethe's city, in 1805, and a third in London in 1810. Some remaining pieces were published as *Fragments of Grecian and Roman Architectural Ornaments* in 1806, by which time the title had significantly been altered, and both works were republished in a single volume in 1826. Tatham's drawings had first informed Holland's work at Southill House, Bedfordshire, remodelled 1796-1800 for Samuel Whitbread (1764-1816), but the published plates soon influenced the work of others, notably the firm in which Tatham's brother Thomas was a partner, Marsh and Tatham (later Marsh, Tatham and Bailey), and the firm of Vuillamy.

Tatham's first independent commission was for an interior at Stoke Edith, Herefordshire, for the Hon. Edward Foley MP, together with a cottage and park gate. In an unusual exploded drawing dated September 1800 Tatham placed sofas facing each other and at right angles to the fireplace, providing one of the earliest instances of such an informal arrangement in England. For Foley he also made a survey of Great Malvern priory church, Worcestershire, and gave an estimate for repairs in 1802. After Foley's death in 1803 ended hopes of further patronage, Tatham designed a monument to him, executed by Robert Bloor, in Stoke Edith church, Herefordshire. A more significant commission, for the earl of Carlisle at Castle Howard, Yorkshire, was the fitting up in 1800-01 of Sir Thomas Robinson's palladian west wing of 1753-9 as a sculpture gallery and museum. Other galleries were completed in 1811-12. The groined coving, continuous arch mouldings, and rooms, alternately cubes and double cubes, were influential on gallery design, notably on John Soane's Dulwich Picture Gallery, London (1811-14). Tatham published *The Gallery at Castle Howard* and *Representations of a Greek Vase* in 1811 and also *The Mausoleum at Castle Howard* (designed 1729-36 by Nicholas Hawksmoor) in 1812. He also carried out work for the earl at Naworth Castle, Cumberland.

On 23 October 1801 Tatham married Harriet (1780-1834), daughter of William Williams, a button-maker, of 103 St Martin's Lane, London, at the church of St Martin-in-the-Fields (Harriet's elder sister had died in 1799 after only a year of marriage to Tatham's elder brother Henry). They moved soon afterwards to a house designed by Tatham at 35 Alpha Road, St John's Wood, then still in the country. The house became a focus of artistic activity: visitors included William Blake, Benjamin Robert Haydon, and Samuel Palmer. Charles and Harriet had four sons and six daughters: Caroline (1804-1842); Frederick (1805-1878), who became a painter and sculptor and a close friend of Blake; Arthur (1808-1874), for over forty years rector of Broadoak and Boconoc, Cornwall, and prebendary of Exeter Cathedral; Julia (1811-1881), who married George Richmond, the portrait painter; Edmund (*b.* 1822) and Robert-Bristow (1824-1881), both of whom emigrated to Natal in 1850; Harriet; and Maria, Augusta, and Georgiana, all three of whom married in the 1840s.

In 1799 Tatham submitted designs to the Treasury for a national monument in commemoration of recent naval victories. Having heard nothing by 1802, he published the designs that year, dedicating them to the earl of Carlisle. In his only known excursions into designing medals Tatham was responsible for the Rumford medal of the Royal Society of 1802 and the board of agriculture medal for Francis, fifth duke of Bedford (1765–1802), struck between 1803 and 1805. In *Designs for Ornamental Plate* (1806) he decried the prevalence in metalwork of 'light and insignificant forms' devoid of 'good Ornament' and recommended instead 'Massiveness' as 'the principal characteristic of good Plate' (*Designs for Ornamental Plate*, preface). From Tatham's drawing of the Barberini candelabrum (the basis of pl. 16 to the *Designs*) William Pitts made an attenuated silver-gilt candelabrum for the second Earl Spencer at Althorp in 1800, which, together with the mahogany candelabrum for Carlton House (Kenwood House, London) and a pair of candelabra cast in bronze (Basildon Park, Berkshire), demonstrate precisely those transpositions of scale, medium, and form advocated by Tatham.

Architectural works Tatham's architectural work to 1820, much of which has been either radically altered or destroyed, comprised mainly alterations, both internal and external, and additions, such as cottages, garden buildings, park gates, and entrance lodges, at Cheshunt nunnery, Hertfordshire (*c*.1802), for William Butt; Wilton Park, Wiltshire (1803–5; dem. 1967), characterized by severe, sharp-edged, almost abstract geometrical blocks, with minimal decoration, for James Dupré, and Dropmore, Buckinghamshire (*c*.1806–9), equally uncompromising for Lady Greville; Balgowan (*c*.1806), for Colonel Thomas Graham (later Lord Lynedoch), and Ochtertyre, Perthshire, including a Gothic mausoleum (1809), for Sir Patrick Murray; Trentham Park, Staffordshire (1807–8), for the second marquess of Stafford; Althorp, Northamptonshire (1809), for Earl Spencer; and Cowsfield Wiltshire (1814; dem.), for Sir Arthur Paget. Houses for which he was entirely responsible seem few: Cowdray Lodge (now Cowdray Park), Sussex (*c*.1800; rebuilt 1876), for W. S. Poyntz; Roche Court (*c*.1805) for Francis T. Egerton and Broxmore House (*c*.1810; dem.), Wiltshire, for R. Bristow; Lynedoch Lodge, Perthshire (1807–9; dem.), for Colonel Thomas Graham; and Hennerton House, Berkshire (*c*.1817; partly dem.; later additions), in which elliptical arches are the principal motif, for C. F. Johnson. In London he added to Cleveland House a new, top-lit west picture gallery, the west front to St James's Park, and a tetrastyle Doric portico (1803–6; dem. 1840) for the second marquess of Stafford. For the earl of Carlisle he designed a library (*c*.1805) at 12 Grosvenor Place. He designed a picture gallery (1807) for the first Lord Yarborough at Brocklesby Park, Lincolnshire, and published *The Gallery at Brocklesby* in 1811. His grim mausoleum (1807–8) at Trentham, combining Egyptian pylon and stepped pyramid from Halicarnassus, remains his most extreme statement of severe primitivism and austere monumentalism.

In 1819 Tatham was accused of negligence concerning repairs at Castle Howard, and although the arbitrator found in his favour, he incurred great expense. On several other occasions he was involved in litigation, and the consequent desertion by his wealthy and noble patrons and his refusal to work for builders led ultimately to the ruin of his practice. Between 1820 and 1836, when his architectural career ended, Tatham's work comprised interior decorations in a sumptuous neo-classical style for the fourth earl of Albemarle at Quidenham Hall, Norfolk (*c*.1820), and in Hampshire a porticoed house, Rookesbury (1821–5), which was adversely criticized by C. R. Cockerell as severe and idiosyncratic, for the Revd W. Garnier, alterations and additions for William Sloane-Stanley at Paultons (1826–8; dem. 1955), and a rectory at Morestead (1835–6). He also wrote the letterpress for John Coney's *Ancient Cathedrals* (1829–31). Of his many unexecuted designs one, dated 1827, for the Fitzwilliam Museum, Cambridge, and another for *A Mansion for the Duke of Wellington* demonstrate the extent of Tatham's talent and aspirations.

On 13 January 1834 Tatham's wife Harriet died, aged fifty-four; she was buried in Brompton cemetery. His house and valuable collection were sold; much of the latter went to Sir John Soane's Museum, where it has since remained. His final submission to the Royal Academy, in 1836, was an earlier design for a picture gallery at Bridgewater House, St James's. The following year the duchess of Sutherland, the Rt Hon. Thomas Grenville, and other friends secured for Tatham, then sixty-five, the post of warden of Trinity Hospital, Greenwich. That year he drew up plans to renovate the hospital's garden and chapel, and made a drawing of what he conjectured to have been the original appearance of the tomb of Henry Howard, first earl of Northampton, the hospital's founder. Visitors were 'much struck by the pleasing tranquillity' which pervaded the hospital under Tatham's wardenship (Mercers' Company, C. H. Tatham MS 1/116, 8). He published two addresses 'given to the aged poor men' of Trinity Hospital in 1837 and 1841. Tatham died there, probably from the dyspepsia from which he suffered all his life, on 10 April 1842, aged seventy-one, having ended his days happily and usefully, and was buried in the hospital chapel. 'To him', wrote Joseph Gwilt in 1853, 'perhaps more than any other person, may be attributed the rise of the Anglo-Greek style which still prevails' (Papworth, 3.104).

RICHARD RIDDELL

Sources Colvin, *Archs.* · H. J. Curtis, *Notes for a pedigree of the Tathams of co. Durham, England* (1928) · C. Tatham, 'Reminiscences', unpublished autobiographical fragments, priv. coll. · Holland–Tatham correspondence and drawings, V&A, D.1479–1551–1898 · C. Proudfoot, 'C. H. Tatham, architect, 1772–1842', BA diss., U. Cam., 1970 · C. Proudfoot and D. Watkin, 'A pioneer of English neo-classicism: C. H. Tatham', *Country Life*, 151 (1972), 918–21, 1322 · C. Proudfoot and D. Watkin, 'The furniture of C. H. Tatham', *Country Life*, 151 (1972), 1481–6 · D. Udy, 'The neo-classicism of Charles Heathcote Tatham', *The Connoisseur*, 177 (1971), 269–76 · J. Harris, 'Precedents and various designs collected by C. H. Tatham', *In search of modern architecture: a tribute to Henry-Russell Hitchcock*, ed. H. Staring (1982), 52–63 · R. Riddell, 'Neo-classical designs for medals by C. H. Tatham', *Apollo*, 123 (1986), 116–22 · R. Riddell, 'Tatham, C(harles) H(eathcote)', *The dictionary of art*, ed. J. Turner (1996) · H. Hayward, 'The drawings of John Linnell in the Victoria and Albert Museum', *Furniture History*, 5 (1969), 1–6 · Graves, *RA exhibitors* · A. M. W. Stirling, *The Richmond papers* (1926), 24, 32, 98–9 · J. Jacob, 'A candelabrum to a design by C. H. Tatham', *The Connoisseur*, 174 (1970), 116–19 · A. G. Grimwade, 'Silver at Althorp [pt 2]', *The Connoisseur*, 152 (1963), 159–65, esp. 163–5 · D. Udy, *Neo-classical works of art* [n.d.] · F. Herrmann, ed., *The English as collectors: a documentary chrestomathy* (1972), 163–7 · C. Wainwright, 'The furnishing of the Royal Library, Windsor', *The Connoisseur*, 195 (1977),

104–9 · S. Zamboni, 'Leopaldo Pollach e Charles HeathcoteTatham: due progetti inediti', *Atti e memorie dell'Accademia Clementina di Bologna*, 13 (1978), 69–72 · J. Harris, *Regency furniture designs, 1803–1826* (1961) · S. Jervis, *The Penguin dictionary of design and designers* (1984) · [W. Papworth], ed., *The dictionary of architecture*, 11 vols. (1853–92), vol. 3, p. 104; vol. 8, p. 11 · R. Riddell, 'The early career and publications of C. H. Tatham', MA diss., Royal College of Art, 1984

Archives V&A, Tatham–Holland corresp. and drawings | BL, conjectural reconstruction of Northampton tomb, Add. MS 32364 · BL, letters to Lord Grenville, Add. MS 58997 · Castle Howard, Yorkshire, J14/1/592; 599; 601; J14/18/50 · Mercers' Company, London, archives, Misc MSS · Mercers' Hall, London, Mercers' Company archives, C. H. Tatham MSS · priv. coll., 'Reminiscences' [transcript of fragment of MS autobiography written 1826] · Sir John Soane's Museum, London, V&A MSS; sculpture collection; designs for the naval monument [copies]

Likenesses B. R. Haydon, pastel drawing, 1823, BM [*see illus.*] · B. R. Haydon, crayon, 1826, priv. coll. · F. Tatham, marble bust, 1837, Trinity Hospital, Greenwich · T. Kearsley, oils

Tatham, Edward (*bap.* 1749, *d.* 1834), college head, was born at Milbeck, Dent, in the parish of Sedbergh, West Riding of Yorkshire, and baptized at Dent on 1 October 1749. When he went up to Oxford in 1769 his father, James Tatham of Sedbergh, was described as a plebeian, but when he dedicated his first theological book to him in 1780 Edward described him as a gentleman and explained he sought not an illustrious name but 'a more humble patron; yet one whom I esteem the highest honour to address' (E. Tatham, *Twelve Discourses*). He was educated at Sedbergh School by Dr Bateman, whose Greek scholarship he later praised highly. Although admitted to Magdalene College, Cambridge, on 11 May 1767, he did not take up residence and matriculated at Queen's College, Oxford, on 21 June 1769. He graduated BA in 1772, and proceeded MA in 1776, BD in 1783, and DD in 1787. He was made a deacon in 1776 and ordained priest in 1778.

After a first curacy served at Banbury and an early publication proposing architectural improvements in Oxford, Tatham was elected on 27 December 1781 to one of the Yorkshire fellowships at Lincoln College, Oxford; he became rector of the college on 15 March 1792, and remained so until his death forty-two years later, enjoying during this period the rectory of Twyford, Buckinghamshire, and the right of residence at the rectory house at Combe, Oxfordshire, which went with the job. In 1801 he married Elizabeth Cook (*d.* 1847), the wealthy daughter of a Cheltenham builder, John Cook. Both her financial acumen and her temper matched Tatham's and public arguments between them were common; they had no children. They kept separate bank accounts and, when she died in 1847, Mrs Tatham left a large fortune to her sister. In 1829 Tatham was appointed rector of Whitchurch, Shropshire, but he continued to reside in Oxfordshire.

In 1789 Tatham gave the Bampton lectures and their publication as *The Chart and Scale of Truth by which to Find the Cause of Error*, (2 vols., 1790) constitutes his major work. This is the great exposition of the philosophy which informed his whole academic life and underlay the position he took in a series of controversies with his academic colleagues. In the lectures he mounted a major critique on Aristotelian logic, denouncing 'the falsehood and absurdity of the Aristotelian Dialectic' (*Chart and Scale of Truth*, 1.338). In its place he advocated the modern, inductive logic of Francis Bacon, whom he venerated as 'this great man, who has been justly styled the "Father of Philosophers"' (*A Letter to the … Dean of Christ Church*, 1807, 21). Aristotle he characterized as 'that uncircumcized and unbaptised Philistine of the Schools' (Tatham, *An Address to the Members of Convocation at Large, on the Proposed Statute on Examination*, 1807). When Cyril Jackson, dean of Christ Church, introduced a series of reforms at Oxford leading to a new public examination, Tatham was a fierce critic of the centrality of Aristotelian logic in the scheme and the neglect of modern, scientific studies: 'the youth of this University are still to bow the head and to bend the knee to the Old Pagan Idol of the Schools!!!' (*A Second Address to Convocation*, 1807, 4). He accused Oxford of neglecting the study of mathematics and natural science because Bacon and Newton had been Cambridge men, and he dared to suggest that in many respects Cambridge was the superior university. The Oxford syllabus set out in the new statute was 'radically and *fundamentally* bad; because the Discipline and Studies which it enjoins are not adapted to the Advancement of sound and useful science in the present age' (*A Fifth Address*, 1808, 3).

Politically Tatham was a keen ally of Burke. His *Letters to the Right Honourable Edmund Burke on Politics* are dated 2 April 1791 and welcomed Burke's *Reflections* before it was fashionable to do so. He mounted a staunch defence of the established constitution in church and state and the social hierarchy. He denounced dissenters in general and Joseph Priestley in particular, taking a side-swipe at William Paley as 'that unauthorized compiler' along the way (*Letters to Burke*, 47). When invited to join a celebration of the second anniversary of the French Revolution he published his acerbic refusal in a letter *To the Stewards of the Anniversary of the French Revolution*, of 23 June 1791. In the same year in his *Letters to Dissenters* Tatham defended the 'Church and King' mob who wrecked Priestley's house in Birmingham. In 1810 he explained 'I like the Papists, I confess, better than the Dissenters … because they are friends to kingly government and because I think them less dangerous to the Constitution' (*A New Address to the Free and Independent Members of Convocation*, 1810, 25). But, like Burke, though an enemy to revolution, Tatham was not a complete reactionary: 'I am neither a Democrat, nor Aristocrat, but a friend of Monarchy under just restraint: a Representation in Parliament according to the Property of the Nation, and … a new regulation of the Poor Laws … might produce such a salutary change and renovation in the political economy and government of these kingdoms, without the shock of a Revolution' (*An Address to … Lord Grenville*, 1811, 34).

As an advocate of modern studies, Tatham took a keen interest in economics and wrote a number of tracts on war finances, the national debt, currency, and taxation. He strongly advocated the printing of more paper money to help the economy expand and, in 1820, supported Thomas Attwood's ideas on currency reform. He argued that money 'is become the most critical and important engine in every state' and that lack of it had led to the French Revolution (*On the Scarcity of Money*, 1819, 46). In 1811 he claimed to have been the inventor of income tax, having advocated such a tax on property in his *Third Letter to William Pitt* of 9 December 1797.

The positions which Tatham adopted were firmly based on consistent and clearly argued principles, but there is little doubt that he was a cantankerous man who enjoyed controversy. A Yorkshireman of humble origins who never lost his northern accent, he was disputing with the other fellows of Lincoln long before he was elected rector. As rector he engaged in quarrels with the other heads of houses, the Hebdomadal board and convocation. On a national level he entered fully into economic debates on taxation, currency, and the reform of the poor law. At home he argued with his wife and, after 1815 when he largely withdrew from Oxford to live at the rectory house at Combe as a pig farmer, he became embroiled in disputes with curates and parishioners. As he informed convocation in 1807, 'I am a plain man, blunt in my manner, and abrupt in my expression; incapable of disguising my sentiments, and apt to give them just as they arise upon every subject, whatever they may be' (*Address to the Members of Convocation*, 17).

Tatham died at Combe rectory on 24 April 1834 after suffering a paralytic stroke. He was buried in the vestry of All Saints' Church, Oxford. He had told Timothy Miller, parish clerk of All Saints', head porter of Lincoln, and one of his few friends, that he wished his tomb to be used as the vestry table and bread for the poor to be distributed from it each Sunday.   ROBERT HOLE

Sources V. Green, *The commonwealth of Lincoln College, 1427–1977* (1979), 360–86 • E. Tatham, *Twelve discourses introductory to the study of divinity* (1780) • Lincoln College, Oxford, COR/34, CVI/1–4, CFE/15 Tatham • Venn, *Alum. Cant.* • Foster, *Alum. Oxon.* • *GM*, 2nd ser., 2 (1834), 549 • *GM*, 2nd ser., 35 (1851), 444 • *DNB* • *Hist. U. Oxf.* 5: 18th-cent. Oxf.
Archives Lincoln College, Oxford
Likenesses H. Weekes, marble effigy on a monument, 1843, Lincoln College, Oxford • oils, Lincoln College, Oxford; repro. in Green, *Commonwealth of Lincoln College*, facing p. 436

Tatham, John (*fl.* 1632–1664), playwright, was probably born about 1612, though nothing is known about his place of birth or parentage. His first play, a pastoral drama called *Love Crowns the End*, was published in 1640 in his volume of verse entitled *The Fancies Theater* (reissued as *The Mirrour of Fancies* in 1657), but it had been 'acted by the scholars of Bingham, in the county of Nottingham in 1632' (*Dramatic Works*, 3). He probably saw military service on the royalist side during the civil war under Lord Carnarvon, and his writings show a staunch devotion to the king's cause. (They also show an immoderate dislike of Scotland and the Scots.) A second play, called *The Distracted State*, was published in 1650 (dated 1651). According to the title-page it was written in 1641, but this may well be a ruse to distract attention from the evident contemporary relevance of its royalist story. The Sicilian King Evander has been deposed in a civil war; a series of usurpers contend for power until the supposedly dead king reappears. It

seems that neither *The Distracted State* nor Tatham's subsequent satirical comedy *The Scots Figgaries* (1652) was ever performed. But his play *The Rump, or, The Mirrour of the Late Times* achieved widespread notoriety with its satire of actual republican politicians. 'Acted Many Times with Great Applause, at the Private House in Dorset-Court' (title-page), it was first staged in June 1660, a month after the king's return, and repeated at Oxford in July 1661. Printed in autumn 1660 it was expanded and went through three further editions in 1661. Tatham's political satire was given a new lease of life in the exclusion crisis when *The Rump* was plagiarized by Aphra Behn in 1681 for her play *The Roundheads*. Also attributed to Tatham, though doubtfully, is a brief play called *Knavery in All Trades, or, The Coffee-House* (1664), which was 'Acted in the Christmas Holidays by several Apprentices with great Applause' (title-page). Besides these plays Tatham published a volume principally consisting of love poems, *Ostella, or, The Faction of Love and Beauty Reconcil'd* (1650). *Daphnes, a Pastorall* was printed in 1651, but only the title-page survives.

Tatham found his widest and most appreciative audience with the pageants which he wrote annually from 1657 to 1664 for the lord mayor of London. Staged partly on land and partly on the river most were celebrations of the good government and commercial success of the City: the 1659 pageant staged by the Grocers' Company includes appreciative speeches from a European, an Egyptian, and a Persian, while the 1661 celebration features the allegorical figures of Justice and Mercy. In July 1660 the City welcomed the return of Charles II with Tatham's spectacular pageant called *Londons Glory Represented by Time, Truth, and Fame*. The disappearance of Tatham from view after 1664 has prompted speculation that he died in the plague of 1665 or in the great fire of 1666.

ERIC SALMON

Sources *DNB* • *The dramatic works of John Tatham, with introduction and notes* [by J. Maidment and W. H. Logan] (1879); repr. (1967) • D. B. J. Randall, *Winter fruit: English drama, 1642–1660* (1995) • [D. E. Baker], *The companion to the play-house*, 2 vols. (1764)
Likenesses R. Vaughan, line engraving, NPG • line engraving, BM, NPG

Tatham, William (1752–1819), geographer and engineer, was born on 13 April 1752 at Hutton in the Forest, Cumberland, the eldest son of Sandford Tatham (1721/2–1777), rector of Hutton and vicar of Appleby, and his wife, daughter of Henry Marsden of Gisborne Hall, Yorkshire. He had one sister and three brothers, one of whom, Charlie, was to help him in his schemes in adult life. William was brought up in Lancaster in the house of his maternal grandmother until her death in 1760. His family was wealthy and well connected, being related to the earl of Lonsdale; but Tatham seems to have had a rift with his family, as in 1769 he was sent to America to seek his fortune. He became a clerk with Carter and Trent, merchants on the James River, Virginia. Early in 1776 he moved to the Watauga settlement in the Tennessee country, where he became involved in politics and from 1776 to 1781 fought intermittently in the War of Independence on the American side, further estranging himself from his family. He saw action in several parts of the country, including the south-west frontier where he was involved in several campaigns against the Cherokee and Creek peoples, who were allies of the British in the war. Between campaigns he continued his civilian activities: in 1778 he was trading in Virginia, and in 1780 he and Colonel John Todd of Kentucky prepared a 'History of the western country' of which the manuscript has been lost.

By 1781 Tatham had returned to civilian life and, after trading as a merchant in Philadelphia and visiting Havana, he began to study law, being called to the bar of Virginia on 24 March 1784. In 1786 he helped establish the settlement of Lamberton, near Fayetteville, North Carolina. In 1787 he was elected to represent Robeson county in the state legislature of North Carolina, which body elected him lieutenant-colonel of militia. In 1788 he visited England, having been reconciled with his family, but returned to Virginia in 1789 where he was employed by the state government to furnish the war office with information about the south-west frontier. He was given accommodation at the public expense and had free access to the archives of state. In 1791 he published *A Topographical Analysis of the Commonwealth of Virginia* and that year he was authorized by the legislature of Virginia to raise by lottery money to complete his geographical survey of the state, which was to be part of a general topographical survey of the whole of America. In 1792 he returned to the Tennessee country where he practised law, mapped the region, and gathered material for its history. In 1796 he went to Spain as American envoy, hoping to use the geographical information and historic maps which he had collected to settle disputes which had arisen on the frontiers of Florida; but the Spanish authorities ordered him to leave, angered by his interference in the country's internal affairs.

Tatham arrived in England on 16 August 1796 and shortly afterwards began to publish in periodicals and pamphlets on agriculture, the construction of canals, and other engineering projects. In 1801 he was appointed superintendent of the London docks at Wapping, where he took charge of the office of works, but he left in July that year, 'somewhat mortified by the idea of checking his own ideas in favour of those of others' (*Annual Biography*, 157). While in England he had numerous contacts with the Society of Arts, and his relationship with the society epitomizes his character. He joined in 1802 after corresponding earlier with the society on the subject of the growing of hemp in Canada. A self-proclaimed authority on the matter, despite never having been to Canada, he successfully reshaped the system of bounties offered by the society to foster hemp growing. He became very active on committees and had grand schemes for admitting American members; but his enthusiasm and his schemes fizzled out, and by 1804 he had contacted his old friend James Munroe, who happened to be in London, with a view to obtaining a position in the US and returned there in 1805 with a letter of recommendation to James Madison.

Tatham was appointed commissioner for surveying the coast of North Carolina and his map of the state (1807) survives in the Library of Congress. After this he spent about five years as draughtsman and geographer in the department of state, Washington, and in 1817 Munroe secured him employment as military storekeeper at the New United States Arsenal at Richmond, Virginia. He had amassed an important collection of military models, maps, topographical descriptions, and other documents, which he offered to the United States congress, and in his offers he anticipated the importance of amassing a national library collection. At the time of his first offer in 1806 his collection contained nearly all the surveys known to have been made in America by topographical surveyors of England, France, and Spain, and he continued to collect geographical material as he moved about the country. At Richmond he turned to drink which worsened the poverty to which his restless life, estrangement from his family, and grandiose ambitions had always left him prone. He committed suicide on 22 February 1819 by stepping in front of a cannon as it was fired. He was unmarried.

Although well enough known in Britain to warrant long death notices, Tatham rapidly fell into almost complete obscurity there, although in the United States he remained better known, not least because of his contacts with political figures of the importance of Jefferson, Madison, and Munroe. He has been hailed as the founder of the US topographical and coast surveys, because of his own maps, charts, and plans, and schemes to extend them throughout the country; of conservation in the US, because of his concern to safeguard the natural resources of the western part of the continent; and of the idea of a Library of Congress for the benefit of the nation, amassing documents and artefacts recording the nation's history. He was short of neither ideas nor energy, but it is as an 'adventurer' (Boyd, 241), rather than a 'versatile' (Herndon, *William Tatham ... American Versatile*), that he is remembered because of his failure to sustain solid achievement in any of his many fields of activity.

ELIZABETH BAIGENT

Sources G. M. Herndon, *William Tatham, 1752–1819: American versatile* (1973) • G. M. Herndon, *William Tatham and the culture of tobacco* (1969) • W. Tatham, *The defence of Norfolk in 1807* (1970) • S. C. Williams, *William Tatham, Watangan* (1947) • E. E. McPherson, 'Letters of William Tatham', *William and Mary College Quarterly*, 2nd ser., 16 (1936), 162–91, 362–98 • *Annual Biography and Obituary*, 4 (1820) • D. G. C. Allan, 'Colonel William Tatham: an Anglo-American member of the society', *Journal of the Royal Society of Arts*, 108 (1959–60), 229–33 • *GM*, 1st ser., 89/1 (1819), 376 • A. Nicholas, *Beginning of conservation in America* (1910) • *The papers of Thomas Jefferson*, ed. J. P. Boyd, 6 (1952)

Archives RSA | L. Cong., Jefferson MSS • L. Cong., Madison MSS

Tatlock, Eleanor (*fl.* 1799–1811), poet, was the daughter of Richard Tatlock, a naval surgeon (*d.* before 1797), and his wife, Elizabeth Smith (*d.* 1797). She might have been born in Sandwich, Kent, where she spent her youth and where her mother died; she later lived in two Buckinghamshire villages, Wooburn and Great Marlow, having left Kent at some time before 1811. Tatlock was a deeply religious woman who described herself as a dissenter (although not a 'bigoted' one), but she was baptized in the Church of England, and continued to attend its services, at least on occasion. In one of her poems she praised Church of England worship at Wooburn and she addressed another to the Reverend George Edwards, whose congregation she joined when she lived in Great Marlow.

Tatlock began to publish her poems in religious periodicals, including *The Evangelical*, during the final years of the eighteenth century; in 1811 she reported that she had been contributing to those magazines for 'more than a dozen years' (Tatlock, 1.iii). Her most important work—and her only publication except for the poetry which appeared in religious magazines—was a two-volume collection, called simply *Poems*, which she published under her own name in 1811. The collection is dominated by 'Thoughts in solitude', a meditative and digressive blank verse poem in six books, which she wrote to comfort herself during a 'gloomy winter' after she moved away from her friends in Kent (ibid., 1.iii–iv). 'Thoughts in solitude' gives evidence of the range of her interests, which included theology, history, natural history, and social issues such as the problem of fallen women (notes refer to a female penitentiary). Despite the range of topics touched on in this work, Tatlock claims to have worried about leaving herself open to charges of 'female pedantry' and so avoided full documentation of her reading (ibid., 1.211). Almost everything that is known about her life and opinions comes from information which she included in these volumes, and a number of the shorter pieces, which include hymns and poems based on biblical tales, give further evidence of Tatlock's religious convictions. Like most evangelicals, Tatlock supported abolition; she was also interested in missionary work, which she writes about in poems such as her 'Plea for the Jews'. Part of her interest apparently arose from her admiration for the work being done by the ladies affiliated with the missionary societies, whom she praises in her notes on that poem, suggesting that like some other women dissenters of her generation, she might have been willing to explore, however tentatively, the possibility of public (if necessarily secondary) roles for women in religious movements. Tatlock seems not to have married, and there is no certain information about her life after 1811, although Virginia Blain suggests that she might have been the Ellen Tatlock who died in Battersea in 1818, at the age of fifty-five (Blain, Clements & Grundy, *Feminist comp.*, 1055).   PAM PERKINS

Sources E. Tatlock, *Poems*, 2 vols. (1811) · Blain, Clements & Grundy, *Feminist comp.* · J. R. de J. Jackson, *Romantic poetry by women: a bibliography* (1993)

Tatlow, Tissington (1876–1957), general secretary of the Student Christian Movement, was born in Crossdoney, co. Cavan, Ireland, on 11 January 1876, the eldest son of Tissington W. G. Tatlow, land agent to Lord Kingston's estate, and his wife, Blanche, daughter of Thomas Steuart Townsend, who was bishop of Meath in 1850–52. Tatlow was educated at St Columba's College, Rathfarnham, and in the engineering school of Trinity College, Dublin. He decided to become a foreign missionary and on graduating in 1897 at the age of twenty-one became travelling secretary of

the recently formed Student Volunteer Missionary Union. A year later he was appointed secretary of its associated body, the British College Christian Union. Founded in 1893, it was subsequently renamed the Student Christian Movement (SCM). In 1900 he returned to Trinity College, this time to the divinity school, and he was ordained deacon in 1902 and priest in 1904. In 1902 he became curate at St Barnabas, Kensington, and in the following year married Emily, daughter of Richard Scott, a Dublin insurance manager. The couple had three daughters.

Called back to the general secretaryship of the SCM in 1903, Tatlow held the office until 1929. Although not its founder, it was owing to him more than to any other one man that the movement came to exercise its great influence over the life of the church. Tatlow was the vital centre of its committee and secretarial group, its spiritual leader and brilliant organizer. Not content to remain in his office chair he travelled widely to visit the colleges and universities not only of this country but also of Europe and America, and took a leading part in the life of the World's Student Christian Federation. When Edinburgh University made him an honorary DD in 1925, W. P. Paterson deservedly hailed him as 'the apostle of the student world'.

In 1926 Tatlow was appointed rector of All Hallows, Lombard Street, and in 1937, on the amalgamation of a number of City parishes, rector of St Edmund, King and Martyr. In addition to the normal work of a City parish he made his church a centre for students and teachers. He held the living until his death. In 1926 he was appointed honorary canon of Canterbury. He was honorary fellow and treasurer of Sion College and president in 1940–41. In 1925 Edinburgh University made him an honorary DD.

Tatlow was a man of many interests. In 1936 he launched the Institute of Christian Education and as its honorary director for over twenty years gave outstanding leadership in its work of promoting the cause of Christian education in this country and overseas. His name soon became as well known among the schools as it had been for years in the universities. He was founder in 1912 of the influential Anglican Fellowship, its first secretary, and in 1913–17 its chairman. He was associated with William Temple and others in the gallant attempt to launch a new kind of Anglican weekly, *The Challenge*, and was chairman of its board (1915–22). Under his leadership the SCM had a way of initiating other enterprises in such realms as religious education, foreign missions, literature, social responsibility, care for foreign students, theological education, and Christian unity, which after a while were deliberately detached from the movement so that often they became unaware of the source of their initial impulse. He brought a most creative mind to the service of the whole church and touched its life for good at many points. His achievement was not less because normally he was content to remain in the background, not caring who got the credit so long as the job was done.

Next to students and teachers, nearest to Tatlow's heart was the cause of Christian unity. He had a large share in securing the success in 1910 of the world missionary conference at Edinburgh which was by common consent the starting point of the modern ecumenical movement. The archbishops made him honorary secretary of their committee to prepare for the world conference on faith and order in Lausanne (1927), and Tatlow became the European treasurer of the resulting Faith and Order Movement, which was to become a constituent part of the World Council of Churches. So closely was he associated with a number of the organizations involved that he must be reckoned one of the chief architects of the British Council of Churches and of the ecumenical movement as a whole. At a luncheon in Tatlow's honour on his eightieth birthday, Archbishop Geoffrey Fisher, who presided, paid tribute to his far-reaching influence, and spoke of the debt which he and his three immediate predecessors felt they owed him.

Perhaps Tatlow's most profound mark on the church was made through his training of generations of SCM secretaries. Many thousands of students came under his influence at the annual conferences and in other ways, but closely associated with him were young colleagues, twenty to thirty at a time, who served the movement for two or three years before going on to their life work. Tatlow knew how to pick men and women and how to get the best out of them, and many who later occupied positions of leadership in different walks of life have testified to what they owed to his pastoral care and inspiring guidance. A man who got things done with efficiency, 'T', as everybody called him, was also a strong and sympathetic personality.

Tatlow died at his home, 31 Templars Avenue, Golders Green, Middlesex, on 3 October 1957 and was cremated on 8 October. An obituary in the Trinity College magazine noted that when he first took office in the SCM in 1898 'it was scarcely known: when he relinquished the secretaryship thirty-one years later it was a force in every college and university throughout the kingdom' (Trinity, 50).

HUGH MARTIN, rev.

Sources T. Tatlow, *The story of the Student Christian Movement* (1933) · *Trinity*, 10 (1958), 50 · *The Times* (5 Oct 1957) · *WWW* · R. Lloyd, *The Church of England, 1900–1965* (1966) · A. Hastings, *A history of English Christianity, 1920–1990*, 3rd edn (1991) · *CGPLA Eng. & Wales* (1958)
Archives LPL, papers relating to work as secretary of Faith and Order conferences
Likenesses D. Banner, oils, Student Christian Movement Headquarters, Birmingham
Wealth at death £40,417 19s. 2d.: probate, 15 Jan 1958, *CGPLA Eng. & Wales*

Tattam, Henry (1788–1868), Church of England clergyman and Coptic scholar, was born on 28 December 1788 at Church Farm, North Marston, Buckinghamshire, the youngest child of John Tattam (*b.* 1740?), a yeoman farmer, and his wife, Jane, née Gurney (*b.* 1743?). He was tutored privately, by the Revd William Pinnock, incumbent of North Marston, who eventually encouraged him to enter the priesthood. After ordination as priest on 27 June 1819 he held curacies at Hinderclay in Suffolk (1819–21) and at Waddesdon, Buckinghamshire, before taking up an appointment as chaplain to the Episcopal church in Amsterdam. Through the influence of his elder brother, an inspector-general of customs, he was presented to the rectory of St Cuthbert's, Bedford, by the lord chancellor on 13 August 1822. He was admitted as a sizar of Christ's College, Cambridge, on 18 March 1823, but never graduated. He married Eliza Ann Platt, née Nash (*d.* in or before 1855), widow of William Platt, at St Cuthbert's on 18 October 1830; they had no children.

On 12 August 1831 Tattam was presented to the rectory of Great Woolstone, Buckinghamshire, by his friend and patron the eccentric miser John Camden Neild, about whom he published a memoir in 1852. He held his benefices until 1849, during which time both churches were rebuilt—Great Woolstone in 1832–3 and St Cuthbert's in 1847—and a new parsonage was built at Bedford in 1843. From 1845 to 1866 Tattam was archdeacon of Bedford, but he was non-resident for much of this time as in 1849 he was presented by the crown to the living of Stanford Rivers, Essex, where he spent the rest of his life. From 1853 to 1868 he was also a chaplain-in-ordinary to the queen. In later life he took a greater interest in his studies than in his ecclesiastical duties, and as a non-resident archdeacon he lacked the commitment needed at a time of major change in the church. He also became involved in a public controversy over the dismissal of a curate, the Revd Montagu Sparrow, at Stanford Rivers, in 1858.

Tattam's circle of friends included Dr John Lee of Hartwell, Joseph Bosworth, and George Lipscomb. He was a founder member of the Bedfordshire and Buckinghamshire archaeological societies. His theological and philological interests led to an extensive *oeuvre* of published works, beginning with his *Helps for Devotion* (1825, reissued in 1862). He was the author of several works in Coptic and English, Latin, or Arabic, including editions of the gospels (1829), the book of Job (1846), the New Testament (1847), and the apostolic constitutions (1848). His *Compendious Grammar of the Egyptian Language* was published in three parts in 1830. A second edition appeared in 1863. In 1835 he compiled a lexicon of Egyptian and Latin. Accompanied by his stepdaughter, Eliza Platt, who wrote an account of their tour, Tattam first visited Egypt and the Holy Land in 1838–9; he returned in 1842. On these visits he met the patriarch and secured a number of important Coptic and Syriac manuscripts for the British Library. He also published *A Defence of the Church of England Against the Attacks of a Roman Catholic Priest* (1843) and left manuscript histories of the parishes of St Cuthbert's, Bedford, and of Biddenham.

A diffident and modest man who was reluctant to take credit for his works, Tattam was held in high regard both for his pastoral work and preaching and for his scholarly achievements. His academic accomplishments were recognized in later life by numerous honours. He was elected a fellow of the Royal Society in 1835, and he received the degree of DD from the archbishop of Canterbury. He was also given the honorary degrees of LLD from Trinity College, Dublin, DD from Göttingen, and DPhil from Leiden. He died on 8 January 1868 at the rectory, Stanford Rivers, and was buried on the 14th in Stanford Rivers, where he is commemorated by a small brass plate in the church chancel.   THOMPSON COOPER, *rev.* CHRIS PICKFORD

Sources *Bedford Times and Bedfordshire Independent* (14 Jan 1868) · *GM*, 4th ser., 5 (1868), 263 · ordination papers, 1818–19, Norfolk RO, DN/ORR 4/1, DN/ORD 21 · *BL cat.* · parish register (marriage), Bedford, St Cuthbert's, 18 Oct 1830 · m. cert. · census returns for Bedford St Cuthbert, rectory, 1841 · L. R. Conisbee, 'Some Bedfordshire clergy of the past: scholars and pedants', *Northamptonshire and Bedfordshire Life*, 4/39 (1974), 42–4 · *ILN* (18 Jan 1868) · Venn, *Alum. Cant.* · Boase, *Mod. Eng. biog.* · letters to the bishop of Lincoln (John Kaye), Lincs. Arch., Diocesan records, Cor. B5/7/4/1–24 [re Rev. T. R. Matthews] · J. Varley, 'A Bedfordshire clergyman of the reform era and his bishop', *Worthington George Smith and other studies, presented to Joyce Godber*, Bedfordshire Historical RS, 57 (1978), 113–40 · *Men of the time* (1868), 768 · *Essex County Chronicle* (14 Jan 1868), 5 · *A scholar of a past generation: a memoir of Professor S. Lee*, ed. A. M. Lee (1896), 103 · *The Guardian* (15 Jan 1868), 63
Archives BL, Coptic and Syriac MSS, Add. MSS 31, 289 | Beds. & Luton ARS, archdeacon's letters, ABA 6/37–95, and orders, ABC v 132/1 · BL, corresp. with Sir A. H. Layard, Add. MS 39101 · BL, corresp. with John Lee, Add. MSS 47490–47491a · Woburn Abbey, Woburn, letters to duke of Bedford
Likenesses photograph, *c.*1865, Beds. & Luton ARS, Z 50/141/175
Wealth at death under £6000: resworn probate, April 1868, *CGPLA Eng. & Wales*

Tattersall family (*per. c.*1765–*c.*1940), bloodstock auctioneers, created one of Britain's greatest bloodstock auction houses, which, still existent after more than two centuries, remained in family control for more than 175 years.

Richard [i] **Tattersall** (*bap.* 1725, *d.* 1795), founder of the firm, was the second son of Edmund [i] Tattersall (1686–1764), a Lancastrian farmer, and his wife, Ann Varley of Laund. He was born in the hamlet of Hurstwood, near Burnley and baptized at Burnley on 5 June 1725. Between 1730 and 1740 he was educated at Burnley grammar school, before being apprenticed to a wool-stapling friend of his father. In 1745 he opted to go to London, where he became head ostler at Beevor's Repository in St Martin's Lane. From there he moved to become stud-groom, and later possibly master of horse, for Evelyn Pierrepoint, second duke of Kingston.

By 1766 Richard had accumulated sufficient funds to purchase a ninety-nine-year lease of property at Hyde Park Corner from Lord Grosvenor, where he set up as a horse and hound auctioneer. The business boomed, partly because of his reputation for integrity but also through his cultivation of potential clients with dinners and other hospitality; clients included members of the Jockey Club and the French royal family. In 1780 he added subscription rooms which became the site for the making and settling of bets by the higher echelons of the racing fraternity. He also ventured into thoroughbred horse ownership, most spectacularly in 1779 with the purchase for £2500 from Lord Bolingbroke of the unbeaten Highflyer, whose successful career at stud–he was champion sire twelve times–earned Richard far more than the outlay from both stud fees and commission on the sales of his offspring. Some of this money went towards the purchase and redevelopment of New Barns, a country house near Ely which he renamed Highflyer Hall. There he entertained Charles Fox, William Windham, and the prince of Wales, whose

stud Tattersall sold in July 1786. Apart from a loss-making move into proprietorship of the *Morning Post* between 1783 and 1792, Richard or Old Tatt as he was known in later years, proved to be an astute businessman and took Tattersalls to a commanding position among British bloodstock auctioneers.

In 1756 Richard married Catherine Somerville, a granddaughter of the twelfth earl of Somerville, who in 1758 gave birth to their only son, Edmund [ii]. By 1784 the firm was advertising itself as Tattersall & son, and two years before his death, at his Hyde Park home on 21 February 1795, Richard had begun the process of transferring the control of the firm to Edmund [ii]. Most of his wealth was left to the younger Edmund, but 200 guineas and an annuity of £50 went to Richard's servant Sarah Povey as well as sums of between £500 and £2000 to her five children. The size of these legacies has led to a suspicion that some of the children, particular the one named Richard [ii] Tattersall, were fathered by Old Tatt himself; Richard [i] was buried in St George's, Hanover Square, London. Far more cultured than his father, thanks to extensive continental tours, Edmund [ii] (1758–1810), a man of good looks and charming manner, was more interested in hunting than auctioneering, though he had a solid grounding in, and understanding of, the family business. Perhaps his wisest decision was to bring his own son, Richard [iii] [*see below*] into partnership in 1806. Although he did not share his father's appetite for money making, the death of Edmund [ii], diagnosed as being from brain fever, on 23 January 1810, left his wife, Elizabeth Wilshin (*d.* 1843), a wealthy widow; she survived him by thirty-three years.

Of Edmund and Elizabeth's children, little is known of the daughter, Elizabeth; the youngest son, George [i] (1792–1853), managed the firm's stud farm at Dawley, near Uxbridge, after getting into financial difficulties as a farmer in Norfolk. He married Eliza Reeve of Wighton, Norfolk; they had three children, including Edmund [iv] (1816–1898). The second son, Edmund [iii] (1789–1851), a lifelong bachelor, was a partner in the family firm for over forty years but never played a prominent role. The eldest son, **Richard** [iii] **Tattersall** (1785–1859), took command on his father's death and under his direction within a decade the firm became a leader in the world of bloodstock auctioneering, with sales to the continent increasing and the development of annual yearling sales for some of the major studs. Old Dick, as he was known to distinguish himself from his son Richard [iv], was responsible for the expansion of the firm's activities to include sales at Doncaster and Hampton Court. Although he disapproved of heavy gambling—a deeply religious man, he never bet himself—in 1815 he opened new subscription rooms at The Corner where gambling debts could be settled. He was married to Mary Grace Robson, though the date of marriage is unknown. Following complaints of drowsiness and constant headaches, Old Dick died when on holiday at Dover on 22 July 1859.

The business was taken over by Old Dick's elder son, Richard [iv] Tattersall (1812–1870), known as Richard the younger, who had been a partner since 1840. Under his stewardship the firm moved to Albert Gate at Knightsbridge following the expiration of the Hyde Park Corner lease in 1865. At the end of the 1860s he was instrumental in bringing in the first non-family partner, Thomas Pain, who developed a market for hunters and hounds in the midland shires. His last four years of life were painful, with heart problems and swellings in his legs—he had been lamed as a child—and he died on 3 May 1870. Old Dick's younger son, **George** [ii] **Tattersall** (1817–1849), artist and architect, better known under the pseudonym Wildrake, was born at Hyde Park Corner on 13 June 1817 and baptized on 9 July at St James's, Westminster. He did not enter the family business, instead achieving moderate fame as an artist, publishing engravings of racehorses and illustrating Nimrod's *Hunting Reminiscences*. As an architect based at 52 Pall Mall, London, he specialized in stables, kennels, and other sporting buildings, and was responsible for rebuilding the stables at Willesden, Essex, the new location of the Tattersalls stud farm. For a brief period in the mid-1840s he also edited the *Sporting Magazine* and the *New Sporting Almanack*. Shortly after a visit to the United States he married, in 1837, Helen Pritchard; they had four children. He died of brain fever at his home in Cadogan Place, London, in 1849.

Richard Tattersall the younger's marriage was childless and control of the firm fell to his cousin Edmund [iv], son of George [i] Tattersall and Eliza Reeve. Born at his father's farm at Sculthorpe, Norfolk, Edmund was educated at Henley and Guildford grammar schools. He set himself up as an independent horse auctioneer at Newmarket before being offered a partnership in the family firm in 1851. On 3 September 1862 he married Emily Elizabeth Byers; they had at least four sons including Edmund Somerville Tattersall [*see below*]. Following attendance at a cold and wet Houghton meeting at Newmarket, Edmund took ill and never again left his home at Coleherne Court, South Kensington, in the eighteen months before his death on 5 March 1898.

Edmund Somerville Tattersall (1863–1942), eldest son of Edmund [iv], then became the last Tattersall to direct the firm, in a year when Tattersalls was responsible for 72 per cent of all blood stock sold at auction in England. Born on 12 August 1863, Sommy, as he was known, was educated at Eton College and later at an academy at Vevey on Lake Geneva. Fluent in French and German, as a young man he pursued skiing and mountaineering, but his passion was music, so much so that in 1904 he took a flat at 34 Rutland Gate so as to be nearer the Albert Hall. He became a partner in Tattersalls in 1885 and was later assisted by his younger brothers, Harry George (partner 1891) and Rupert Reeve (partner 1901). The former, fond of drink and careless with money, resigned from the firm in 1905 after a quarrel with Edmund Somerville, a man with a strict sense of decorum; Rupert lost a leg in the First World War and retired from the firm in 1919. A third brother, Richard Brooke, was not taken into partnership but sent to America to establish a branch of the business there, but he proved ineffective and died in comparative poverty in New Orleans. By the outbreak of the Second World War much of the auctioneering and direction of the firm had passed to non-family members and when the unmarried Edmund Somerville died on 26 October 1942, after a series of small strokes, dynastic control of the great auction house ended. During the second half of the century and into the twenty-first, Tattersalls has remained one of Britain's, and Europe's, leading firms of bloodstock auctioneers. The name Tattersalls also continues to be used at most British racecourses for the enclosure next to the members' enclosure. It is also widely applied to a check material used primarily as shirting in men's and women's 'country' clothes.   WRAY VAMPLEW

Sources V. Orchard, *Tattersalls: two hundred years of sporting history* (1953) · P. Willett, *The story of Tattersalls* (1987) · *DNB* · *Bailey's Magazine* (1 Jan 1888) · 'Under the hammer', *All the Year Round*, new ser., 339 (29 May 1875), 207–12 · 'At Tattersall's', *All the Year Round*, new ser., 865 (27 June 1885), 345–8 · IGI
Archives W. Sussex RO, letters from Richard Tattersall to duke of Richmond
Likenesses T. Beach, portrait (Richard Tattersall) · crayon (Richard Tattersall)

Tattersall, Edmund Somerville (1863–1942). *See under* Tattersall family (*per. c.*1765–*c.*1940).

Tattersall, George (1817–1849). *See under* Tattersall family (*per. c.*1765–*c.*1940).

Tattersall, John Brown (1845–1925), cotton spinner, was born on 30 September 1845 at Sandy Lane, Royton, Oldham, Lancashire, one of the nine children of Stanley Tattersall, a master tailor, and his wife, Nancy, *née* Kershaw. Having started work at the age of ten as a half-time little piecer in the Sandy Lane cotton mill, he graduated to become a minder of cotton mules and became actively involved in the spinners' union. He was elected to the executive committee of the Oldham Operative Cotton Spinners' Union in April 1870, participated over the years 1870–73 in the shorter working hours campaign, served on the Oldham Trades Council in 1872, and became a key figure in the Factory Acts Reform Association. On 18 December 1867 he married Mary Ann Cocker (*b.* 1843/4), a weaver, the daughter of Matthew Cocker, a draper, at Prestwich parish church.

Meanwhile, Tattersall had accumulated funds which he invested in the Royton Spinning Company. In November 1873 he made the transition from manual to white-collar worker when he was appointed secretary of the Royton mill. Thereafter he moved through various jobs—he was in Manchester for a spell as yarn salesman for Royton—and into company management. He served successively as general manager (1891–1903), managing director (1903–6), and chairman of the Royton company (1906–23). The survival of the company through the slump in the 1920s is testimony to the firm foundations which he laid. His opposition to mill recapitalization in 1919–20 played an important part in this. Tattersall used the Royton company as a base from which he invested in and promoted other limited liability cotton manufacturing companies in the region. By the 1900s his directorships included twelve mills, and he controlled almost half of the spinning capacity of the Royton area.

It was perhaps inevitable that Tattersall, as a prominent and gregarious employer, should become embroiled in the politics of the industry. He was an active member of the Limited Liability Association in the 1870s and 1880s (acting as secretary for a while) and in February 1890 was elected to the executive committee of the Oldham Master Cotton Spinners' Association, of which he became president a year later. One of his earliest confrontations with the Oldham Spinners' Union concerned his opposition to proposed new factory legislation (1891), the irony of which was not overlooked by his former trade union colleagues.

In the early 1890s Tattersall worked to promote more representative and powerful employer combinations in cotton spinning, and he played a key part in the formation of the Federation of Master Cotton Spinners' Associations (FMCSA) in 1892; later he became federation vice-president. He was one of a handful of mill owners (including Macara, Andrew, and Reyner) who led the industry-wide Brooklands lock-out and the negotiations thereafter. During this pivotal confrontation Tattersall gained a reputation as an uncompromising hardliner and champion of managerial prerogatives: 'We cannot allow the operatives', he commented, 'to dictate as to the conditions upon which we shall work our concerns—it won't do at all!' (*Cotton Factory Times*, 13 Jan 1893).

For almost thirty years Tattersall devoted his energies to industry politics and the advancement of mill owners' interests; he remained president of the Oldham Master Cotton Spinners' Association until 1919, and was vice-president of the FMCSA until 1914 and president from 1914 to 1918. He was an active Liberal in politics, one-time president of the Royton Liberal Association, and a staunch supporter of free trade. He co-ordinated the FMCSA's parliamentary monitoring and pressure group activities (serving on the cotton employers' parliamentary committee, 1893–1910), became involved in cotton trade regulation (through the federation cotton committee and the British Cotton Growing Association), and served as a committee member of the International Cotton Spinners' Association (1903–14). Through active involvement in the organization committee, Tattersall bears some credit for the increasing power of the FMCSA, which grew from representing around 40 per cent (17 million spindles) of the capacity of the spinning industry in 1892 to nearly 75 per cent (46 million spindles) in 1918.

As far as industrial relations policy making was concerned, Tattersall was involved at the highest levels of the federation, representing the employers in the conciliation board, the emergency committee, the various wage-list committees, and the joint disputes committees which met under the Brooklands procedure. He developed a reputation as a defender of managerial rights, an astute and tough negotiator who promulgated, on a number of occasions, the use of the industry-wide lock-out as a tactic. Over time, however, he came to realize the potential within the formalized disputes procedure for containing and defusing trade union militancy and became adept at exploiting the system to protect employers' interests. In

one dispute over a mill owner's alleged use of shoddy raw cotton in 1901, for example, he entered the mill (J. Mayall's, Ashton) as part of a joint inspection team, immediately held up a wet finger, and declared that an east wind was blowing off the Pennines and that the spinning could not be inspected properly until it had stopped! The inspection took place several days later, giving the mill owner time to purchase better cotton and get it through the mules.

Mainly because of the paucity of extant source material, Tattersall's role has been overshadowed by that of Charles Macara, FMCSA president from 1894 to 1914. What appears evident from the records of the mill owners' associations, however, is that Tattersall's contribution to cotton industry politics was far more significant than Macara's autobiography and biography were willing to concede.

Tattersall presided over the FMCSA, after Macara resigned in 1914, during the difficult wartime years. He retired from his associational activities in 1918–19 and from his directorships in 1923. He was reported to have been in failing health for some time, and died on 3 September 1925, at his home, Ash Grove, Oriel Road, Didsbury, Manchester, leaving £71,661 gross.

ARTHUR MCIVOR

Sources Oldham Master Cotton Spinners' Association, minutes and reports · Federation of Master Cotton Spinners' Associations, minutes 1891–2, reports 1892–1918 · Cotton Employers' Parliamentary Association, minutes 1899–1911 · *Textile Mercury* (4 Sept 1925) · *Cotton Factory Times* (11 Sept 1925) · *Cotton Factory Times* (5 Aug 1892) · *Cotton Factory Times* (13 Jan 1893) · *Oldham Chronicle* (3 Sept 1925) · J. Longworth, *The Oldham Master Cotton Spinners' Association Ltd, 1866–1966* (1966) · *Oldham Standard* (9 Nov 1907) · *Oldham Standard* (16 Dec 1919) · *Eightieth anniversary, 1871–1951*, Royton Spinning Company (1951) · H. A. Turner, *Trade union growth, structure, and policy: a comparative study of the cotton unions* (1962) · A. Fowler and T. Wyke, eds., *The barefoot aristocrats: a history of the Amalgamated Association of Operative Cotton Spinners* (1987) · A. J. McIvor, 'Employers' organisations and industrial relations in Lancashire, 1890–1939', PhD diss., University of Manchester, 1983 · m. cert. · d. cert. · *CGPLA Eng. & Wales* (1926)

Likenesses photograph, *c.*1900, Oldham and Rochdale Cotton Employers' Association

Wealth at death £71,660 19s. 0d.: probate, 23 Jan 1926, *CGPLA Eng. & Wales*

Tattersall, Richard (*bap.* **1725**, *d.* **1795**). *See under* Tattersall family (*per. c.*1765–*c.*1940).

Tattersall, Richard (**1785–1859**). *See under* Tattersall family (*per. c.*1765–*c.*1940).

Tattersall, William de Chair (*bap.* **1751**, *d.* **1829**), Church of England clergyman and musician, was baptized on 11 September 1751 at Charing, Kent, the second son of James Tattersall (*d.* 1784), and his first wife, Dorothy, daughter of the Revd William de Chair and sister of the Revd Dr John de Chair, rector of Little Rissington, Gloucestershire, and a chaplain to George II. His father was successively rector of Blatchington, Sussex (1742–6), and of Charing, Kent (1746–55); curate of Egerton, also in Kent (1749–55); and rector of Streatham, Surrey (1755), and of St Paul's, Covent Garden, until his death.

William Tattersall was admitted to Westminster School as a king's scholar in 1765; there, as an actor, his performance of Phormio in Terence's play of that name is said to have elicited David Garrick's praise. He was elected to Christ Church, Oxford, in June 1770, as head of the list of king's scholars, and having graduated BA in 1774 and MA in 1777 he was presented by his college in 1778 to the rectory of Wotton under Edge, Gloucestershire. About this time his father presented him to the sinecure rectory of Westbourne, Sussex, where he appears to have spent the remainder of his life. On 16 February 1779, at St Paul's, Covent Garden, he married Mary (d. 1852), eldest daughter of George Ward of Wandsworth, Surrey.

Tattersall officiated as chaplain to Sir Francis Buller, and in 1803 was appointed a chaplain to George III. However, his most durable contribution was musical, and consisted of new, more accessible psalm settings, which effectively united music and worship in the lives of the 'lower orders'. This formed part of 'an attempt to reform English parish church music' (Holman), which Tattersall achieved by introducing idioms of a dissenting nature into the Church of England. He adapted the 'refined and "poetic" version of the psalms' (ibid.) by James Merrick for the use of his own congregation and then published, complete with preface, *A version or paraphrase of the Psalms by J. Merrick, adapted to the purposes of public or private devotion* (1789), set in three parts to new and existing melodies. Encouraged by George Horne (bishop of Norwich), Richard Beadon (bishop of Gloucester), and others, Tattersall divided the psalms into stanzas and republished the work, which appeared as late as 1822. The next volume, entitled *Improved Psalmody* (1794), also enjoyed several editions and contained tunes adapted from Handel and the old masters, as well as many new ones contributed by leading composers and organists of the day. Among these were 'his intimate friend' (*GM*) Sir William Parsons and Haydn, who produced six masterful settings. Many of the contributors, including Haydn, were members of the Musical Graduates Club. The collection had a very impressive list of subscribers, including royalty; there were, after all, long-standing family connections with the highest echelon of society. A third volume, dedicated to the king, was published in 1802 and 'in deference to the tastes of George III' (Temperley), used settings based solely on Handel's sacred works. These works were a popular and influential, if not lucrative, enterprise. Only three volumes of twenty-five psalms each were issued (rather than all 150 in 6 volumes), though they were conceived with use in the home as well as the church in mind and could incorporate a range of instrumental accompaniment if an organ was not available.

Tattersall, who was 'of a most hospitable disposition' (*GM*), died at Rectorial House, Westbourne, on 26 March 1829 (*GM*; Temperley gives Wotton under Edge on 26 May). He was survived by his wife, their two sons, James and John, and two daughters, Mary-Anne and Jane. Another son, George, had predeceased his father, leaving a son and a daughter of his own. The eldest son, James, fellow of the Royal College of Physicians and physician to the Surrey dispensary, died on 8 May 1855.

CHARLOTTE FELL-SMITH, rev. DAVID J. GOLBY

Sources GM, 1st ser., 99/2 (1829), 88 · P. Holman, disc notes to 'Haydn and his English friends' [CD recording, Hyperion, CDA67150, 2000] · N. Temperley, 'Tattersall, William Dechair', *New Grove*, 2nd edn · J. Holland, *The psalmists of Britain* (1843) · Foster, *Alum. Oxon.* · *Old Westminsters* · J. Welch, *The list of the queen's scholars of St Peter's College, Westminster*, ed. [C. B. Phillimore], new edn (1852), 383, 391–2, 440, 449, 452, 549 · Nichols, *Illustrations*, 5.853, 8.651 · Allibone, *Dict.* · O. Manning and W. Bray, *The history and antiquities of the county of Surrey*, 3 vols. (1804–14), vol. 2, pp. 237, 248, 250; vol. 3, p. 295 · E. Hasted, *The history and topographical survey of the county of Kent*, 2nd edn, 3 (1797), 220, 223 · J. Dallaway, *A history of the western division of the county of Sussex*, 2 vols. in 3 pts (1815–32), 1.105 · Munk, *Roll* · J. D. Reuss, *Alphabetical register of authors, 1790–1803*, 2 vols. (1804), 2.374 · D. Rivers, *Literary memoirs of living authors of Great Britain* (1798) · BL, Add. MS 5697, fol. 339 · IGI · will, PRO, PROB 11/1760, sig. 508

Tattersfield, Frederick (1881–1959), agricultural chemist, was born on 23 April 1881 at Kilpin Hill near Dewsbury, Yorkshire, the third son of Frederick Tattersfield, woollen manufacturer, and his wife, Frances Mary Walker. He was educated at the Wheelwright Grammar School, Dewsbury, and the University of Leeds, taking first-class honours in chemistry at London University (1908) as an external student. He was awarded a DSc in 1927.

Tattersfield's first job was in association with the Leeds city analyst, where his work ranged over all the typical activities in such a department, from food and drug analysis to post-mortems. In 1908 he went to Newcastle to join the International Paint and Antifouling Company Ltd, where for five years his work was chiefly concerned with research on antifouling paints. On the outbreak of war in 1914 he went to France as a founder member of the Friends' Ambulance Unit. In 1917 he was invalided back to England and early in 1918 went to the Rothamsted Experimental Station to work with A. W. Rymer Roberts on soil insecticides. He remained at Rothamsted for the rest of his working life. He originally had a temporary appointment in the chemistry department, but he soon founded the department of insecticides and fungicides of which he was the head for twenty-nine years.

Tattersfield's earliest work was concerned with the control of soil pests, and he carried out some research on the structure–toxicity relationships of chemicals to wireworms. He also studied factors influencing the decomposition of naphthalene in the soil and the effect of different rates of decomposition on its insecticidal action. He then proceeded to study the effect of a wide range of chemicals on insects which attack the aerial parts of plants, again attempting to relate toxicity with structure in some systematic way. In the course of this work he discovered the outstanding ovicidal properties of dinitro-2-methyl phenol, a substance that found application in winter washes for fruit trees.

Due to the shortage of funds for the development of effective synthetic organic chemicals for pest control, Tattersfield, in his search for highly biologically active chemicals, turned his attention to plant sources. He examined a wide variety of plants for insecticidal activity and his contributions on the isolation of the active principles of plant products, the assessment of their insecticidal activity, and their chemical estimation were quite outstanding. He studied many phases of the production and assay of pyrethrum as an insecticide and played a large part in the founding of the Kenya pyrethrum industry, which became valuable to the country's economy. Tattersfield evolved precise methods of administering doses of chemicals to insects and introduced statistical procedures for the quantitative assessment of results.

A catalogue of Tattersfield's contributions to knowledge on insecticides, substantial though they were, gives only an inadequate idea of what the subject owes to his widely felt influence at home and abroad. He is sometimes regarded as the founder of modern research in this field. When he started his research, seldom was any serious attempt made to obtain reproducible quantitative results of known significance. He insisted on the importance of precise quantitative data in which factors known to influence results were, as far as possible, standardized, and in which both the design of the experiment and the results would satisfy accepted statistical criteria. The standards he set have, over the course of years, been accepted, to the benefit of the subject.

Tattersfield was a source of inspiration to his colleagues, to whom he was unfailingly kind and helpful. His justly acquired reputation never changed his modest and unassuming manner, or affected the uncompromising integrity which was perhaps his most notable quality, combined with great gentleness and a delightful sense of fun. He retired in 1947 and was appointed OBE.

In 1931 Tattersfield married Janie, elder daughter of Archibald Campbell, a farmer of Ennerdale, Cumberland; they had one son. In his youth he had been a very good cricketer and he remained keenly interested throughout his life. He was also a man of wide cultural interests. He was at one time an active member of the Literary and Philosophical Society of Newcastle and he had a fine appreciation of poetry. He collected etchings, engravings, and mezzotints. He was keenly interested in archaeology and was a member of the Pre-Historical Society. Tattersfield was a member of the Society of Friends, of which he became a much respected elder. He died at his home, Westholme, 5 Maple Road, Harpenden, on 1 May 1959.

CHARLES POTTER, rev. K. D. WATSON

Sources *Nature*, 183 (1959), 1778 · *The Times* (4 May 1959), 15f · *The Times* (7 May 1959), 18c · private information (1971) · personal knowledge (1971) · *CGPLA Eng. & Wales* (1959)
Likenesses H. Perry, drawing, priv. coll.
Wealth at death £51,152 4s. 2d.: probate, 19 Aug 1959, *CGPLA Eng. & Wales*

Tatwine [Tatwin] (d. **734**), scholar and archbishop of Canterbury, is known almost entirely from Bede, who in his *Historia ecclesiastica gentis Anglorum* (Bede, *Hist. eccl.*, 5.23) notes that before his election to Canterbury, Tatwine had been a priest at the monastery of Briudun (Breedon on the Hill, Leicestershire), and that he was 'renowned for his devotion and wisdom and excellently instructed in the Scriptures'. Breedon, which had been founded in the 680s, was one of the great minster-churches of central Mercia, sited in a commanding position in an Iron Age hill fort, and (at a time after Tatwine's death, perhaps c.800) embellished with a spectacular collection of carved friezes; the prestige of the church is reflected in the fact that one of its priests could be elected to the archiepiscopacy. Tatwine was consecrated by four bishops at Canterbury on Sunday 10 June 731. Two years later, having received his pallium from Rome, he himself ordained bishops for Lindsey and Selsey. He died on 30 July 734 and was buried at Canterbury.

The quality of Tatwine's scholarship is clearly seen in the two works which have survived in his name: a grammar and a collection of forty metrical *enigmata*. The grammar, properly entitled the *Ars de partibus orationis*, is an example of what has been termed an 'elementary' grammar; that is to say, its structure is modelled on the earlier grammatical treatises (*Ars maior*, *Ars minor*) of Donatus in that it treats the parts of speech—noun, pronoun, verb, adverb, participle, conjunction, preposition, and interjection—in sequence, illustrating the inflecting parts with series of paradigms, especially of verbs (to which he also devoted an additional appendix). In compiling his grammar Tatwine drew principally on the earlier grammatical treatises of Priscian and Consentius, as well as on the late antique commentators on Donatus, such as Pompeius and Servius; the heavy use of these sources, as well as occasional use of a number of others, implies that Tatwine had at his disposal a well-stocked library. On occasion Tatwine supplemented the examples found in his sources by means of biblical quotations, especially from the psalms. The most striking feature of Tatwine's grammar is its clear exposition of grammatical categories, a feature which made it especially useful for English-speaking beginners for whom Latin was not a native language.

The surviving manuscripts of Tatwine's *Ars de partibus orationis* (three complete manuscripts of the late eighth century and a fragmentary one of the late ninth) were all written on the continent; but although no English manuscript of the work survives, there is no doubt that it was studied intensively in Anglo-Saxon schools, because in all four continental manuscripts Tatwine's lists of nouns are frequently accompanied by glosses in Old English, which the Carolingian scribes evidently took over from their (English) exemplars. But whatever its utility for beginners, the fact that no Carolingian grammarian shows any debt to Tatwine's grammar indicates that this utility had been superseded by the ninth century.

Tatwine's other surviving work is a collection of forty *enigmata* (literally 'mysteries', a term used by early Anglo-Latin authors to describe metrical riddles). These forty *enigmata* are framed by a vast acrostic with two legends; the first letter of the first line of each of the forty poems participates in the first acrostic (SVB DENO QVATER HAEC DIVERSE ENIGMATA TORQVENS), and the last letter of each first line participates in the second (STAMINE METRORVM EXSTRVCTOR CONSERTA RETEXIT). The poems themselves, which vary from four to twelve lines in length, are concerned with both the physical aspects of Christian life (many of the *enigmata* describe objects such as 'parchment', 'pen', 'bell', 'altar', 'paten', 'lectern') and the spiritual ('love', 'evil', 'humility', 'pride'), as well as the ways in which its profound message must be interpreted (the opening sequence of *enigmata* treats such subjects as 'wisdom', 'faith, hope, and charity', 'the four ways of interpreting scripture', 'literature'). A few of the *enigmata* reflect Tatwine's occupation as schoolmaster (for example, one *enigma* treats 'prepositions which take two cases'). The diction of the poems is highly compressed, sometimes to the point of incomprehensibility, and reveals substantial familiarity with classical Latin poets, especially Virgil and Horace, as well as with the techniques of composing quantitative verse (though there are occasional infelicities in the placement of caesurae).

It is not possible to determine when or where Tatwine composed these two literary works. According to a metrical epitaph which (presumably) adorned his tomb in Canterbury, he was at the time of his death 'worn down with the burden of old age' (Lapidge, 370–71). These words possibly imply that he was in his sixties or seventies when he died (hence that he was born *c*.670, and was thus contemporary with Bede). It is reasonable to infer that his scholarly production belongs to an earlier phase of his life, certainly to that before his elevation to Canterbury, and may be roughly dated to the years around 700; in other words, that Tatwine's scholarship belongs to the first period of florescence of Anglo-Latin literature in late seventh-century Southumbria.   MICHAEL LAPIDGE

Sources Bede, *Hist. eccl.*, 5.23–4 · *Tatuini opera omnia*, ed. M. de Marco (Turnhout, 1968), 1–208 · V. Law, *Grammar and grammarians in the early middle ages* (1997), 105–6, 109–13 · V. Law, 'The Latin and Old English glosses in the *Ars Tatuini*', *Anglo-Saxon England*, 6 (1977), 77–89 · V. Law, 'The transmission of the *Ars Bonifacii* and the *Ars Tatuini*', *Revue d'Histoire des Textes*, 9 (1979), 281–8 · M. Lapidge, *Anglo-Latin literature, 600–899* (1996), 370–71 · Symeon of Durham, *Opera*, vol. 2

Tauber [*formerly* Denemy], **Richard** (1891–1948), singer, was born on 16 May 1891 in Linz, Austria. He was illegitimate and was baptized Richard Denemy after his mother's maiden name. His father, (Anton) Richard Tauber, was an actor, and his mother, Elisabeth Denemy (later Seiffert), played musical comedy roles. He studied at the conservatory in Frankfurt (1909–11) and with Carl Beines in Freiburg, and made a youthful début in 1913 as Tamino in *The Magic Flute* at the Neues Stadt-Theater in Chemnitz, of which his father was director, with instant success. He was soon engaged on a five-year contract with the Dresden Opera, where he sang all the leading lyrical tenor parts. In 1915 he made his first appearance at the German Opera House, Berlin. From 1922 his career centred on Vienna, where he sang the classical repertory at the Staatsoper and operetta at the Theater an der Wien.

During the Mozart festivals in both Munich and Salzburg, Tauber became enormously popular as Tamino, Belmonte, and Don Ottavio. The famous Swedish Don Giovanni, John Forsell, declared that the young Tauber was the greatest Ottavio he had ever heard, and he was noted for the intense conviction with which he declaimed to his Donna Anna (in the German text then still generally in use, even at festivals) the solemn oath, 'Ich schwöre'. Among his non-Mozartian roles those of Max in Weber's *Der Freischütz* and of Hans in the German version of Smetana's *The Bartered Bride* were especially successful.

Tauber's name and achievements became better known to the general public, however, in the sphere of lighter music: in operetta rather than in opera, and above all in the stage works of Franz Lehár, in which he charmed thousands by his sympathic tenor quality and by the grace and variety of his vocal inflections. The song 'You are my heart's delight' from Lehér's operetta *The Land of Smiles* (1929) was one of his most famous, and it was in this work that he first came to England in 1931. He also showed marked ability as a conductor with the London Philharmonic Orchestra and as a composer. His operetta *The Singing Dream* (1934) was a great success in Vienna, and his other works included the operetta *Old Chelsea* (1943) and an orchestral piece, *Sunshine Suite*. Except for a film version of Leoncavallo's *Pagliacci*, his film career was mainly an extension of his operetta activities.

It would not be quite true to claim that Tauber's wide experience of light music, and the strain of singing long parts, with numerous encores, throughout the week left no mark on either his style or his vocal chords, but he can be justly likened to two other similarly popular tenors, John McCormack and Tito Schipa, in his ability to return successfully to serious music until the end of his career. In 1938 and 1939 he appeared under Sir Thomas Beecham at Covent Garden in his three greatest Mozartian roles and in a German-language *Bartered Bride*, and after the war he insisted on taking part, with his old colleagues, the visiting Vienna State Opera, as Don Ottavio in a *Don Giovanni* at Covent Garden—his final stage appearance in September 1947.

In appearance Tauber was not handsome, but genial. His first marriage, in 1927, to the operetta singer Carlotta Vanconti, was unsuccessful and led to protracted divorce proceedings, which were not finalized until 1936; in that year he married his second wife, the English stage and film actress, Diana Napier, and settled in England. He was naturalized British in 1940. After his death Diana Napier wrote (or collaborated in) three volumes of biography or memoirs. There were no children of either marriage. Tauber died from lung cancer on 8 January 1948 at the London Clinic, 20 Devonshire Place, London.

DESMOND SHAWE-TAYLOR, *rev.*

Sources D. N. Tauber, *Richard Tauber* (1949) · D. N. Tauber, *My heart and I* (1959) · D. N. Tauber and C. Castle, *This was Richard Tauber* (1971) · W. Korb, *Richard Tauber* (1966) · *CGPLA Eng. & Wales* (1948) · D. Shawe-Taylor, 'Tauber, Richard', *New Grove*
Archives FILM BFI NFTVA, advertising film footage · BFI NFTVA, documentary footage · BFI NFTVA, home footage · BFI NFTVA, performance footage |SOUND BL NSA, documentary recordings · BL NSA, performance recordings · BL NSA, 'Richard Tauber', B8333/05 · BL NSA, 'Richard Tauber – a golden voice, a generous heart' (parts 1–3), H44/01, H44/02, H44/03 · BL NSA, *Talking about music*, 113, 1LP0152935 S1 BD2 BBC TRANSC

Likenesses P. Vézelay, oils, 1925, NPG · photograph, repro. in
Shawe-Taylor, 'Tauber, Richard', 594
Wealth at death £2472 4s. 7d.: administration, 20 April 1948,
CGPLA Eng. & Wales

Taubman, Matthew (d. 1690?), poet and satirist, of whose
early life nothing is known, worked as laureate for the
lord mayor of London's inauguration from 1685 until
1690. His earliest printed texts, *The Courtier's Health* (1682?)
and *An heroick poem to his royal highness the duke of York on his
return from Scotland … with some choice songs and medleyes on
the times* (1682), betray a close observation of recent political events. The latter sought to legitimize the royal succession with repeated references to the duke's heritage
and achievements:

> You, Sir, are both the heavn's and Oceans care,
> Whose Gods in your protection claim a share;
> Who from devouring Deeps, as him before,
> Did in your life, our lives and hopes restore.
> (ll. 5–8)

Written in the fragile aftermath of the Popish Plot when
the stability of social order was threatened by the actions
of dissenters and cabals, Taubman's collection of *Loyal
Poems and Satyrs upon the Times, since the Beginning of the Salamanca Plot* (1685) is punctuated by familiar themes of parentage and inheritance. Acting as an editor, he dedicates
the verses to the gentlemen of the 'Loyal Club at the Dog
in Drury Lane', implying that his earlier works had
received an unenthusiastic literary reception (sig. A2v).

Following the death of Thomas Jordan later in the same
year, Taubman became responsible for producing a series
of annual civic festivities to mark the mayoralities of Sir
Robert Jefferys (*London's Annual Triumph*, 1685, for which
he received a payment of £10 out of a total budget of
expenditure of £473), Sir John Peake (*London's Yearly Jubilee*,
1686), Sir John Shorter (*London's Triumph, or, The Goldsmiths
Jubilee*, 1687), Sir John Chapman (*London's Anniversary Festival*, 1688), and Sir Thomas Pilkington (*London's Great Jubilee*,
1689). J. G. Nichols speculated that Taubman's apprenticeship for this post could be traced back to a broadside dated
1659 and initialled 'M. T.' (*The Cities New Poet's Mock Show*,
now held in the British Library), which attacked the previous year's pageant conceived in honour of Sir John Ireton
(Nichols, 107–8, 115). Heralded by the *London Gazette* as created 'to express the benefits the city enjoys of peace and
plenty under his Majesties happy government', the entertainments represented a sequence of visually stunning
ratifications of the capital's wealth, status, and influence,
while providing simultaneous opportunities for the valid-
ation of sovereignty and for London's governing factions
to promote the triumph of popular will. Full textual
descriptions, introduced by two panegyrical dedications
to the monarch and to the sponsoring company, were
printed to perpetuate these effects: 'Nor is the Book the
least Addition to the Luster of this Day, which is read by
those who see not the Pageantry; and when all the rest is
over, remains a lasting and visible Monument to Posterity'
(M. Taubman, 'Preface' to *London's Yearly Jubilee*, 1686).
Within the pageants themselves, themes of loyalty,

peace, harmony, obedience, industry, sanctioned authority, and watchfulness reverberate, culminating in 1689,
when Sir Thomas Pilkington, a 'leading Presbyterian' and
whig dissenter who had twice been imprisoned for his
actions in protecting London's privileges, was installed as
lord mayor. Taubman's civic rituals were shot through in
this year with strong libertarian, populist references:

> When Arbitrary Force, and the Lawless Usurpation had
> Unreasonably Imposed upon us New Lords, and New Laws,
> contrary to the Practice, and known Customs, of this City.
> Then did You, in Defence of our Just Rights and Liberties,
> stand in the Gap, and Bravely Oppos'd the Violence of the
> Impetuous Torrent. (M. Taubman, *London's Great Jubilee*, sig.
> A2r)

This pageant was revived on 9 November 1761. It is
assumed that Taubman died in 1690. There were no civic
festivities that year, and Elkanah Settle inherited his post
in 1691.

Taubman's son **Nathaniel Taubman** (d. 1716) took
orders and became a chaplain in the Royal Navy, accompanying the British squadron in Mediterranean campaigns in 1708–9. His experiences formed the basis of
*Memoirs of the British fleets and squadrons in the Mediteranean,
anno 1708 and 1709 … to which is annexed, a cursory view of
Naples* (1710), which was dedicated to Edward, earl of
Orford, and to Sir Edward Whitaker 'for his Generous and
Kind Regard to Chaplains serving at Sea in general, and for
Favours to the Author in particular' (p. 121). In 1710 he was
appointed on a five-year contract as chaplain to the English factory at Leghorn (although the opposition from the
Inquisition prevented Taubman from leaving England
until October 1711) and on 14 November he obtained the
degree of MA from Pembroke College, Oxford. In 1716 he
printed *A funeral sermon [on Ecclesiastes 7: 1] preach'd in the
chapel belonging to the British Society of Merchants at Leghorn;
… occasion'd by the death of … B. Kennet, D.D., some time their
minister*, as a delayed tribute to his predecessor. Taubman
also produced a volume of verse, *Virtue in Distress, or, The
History of Mindana*, 'a faint Imitation of Dryden's Knight's
Tale from Chaucer' (sig. [A1r]) in 1706. Latin and English
verses were also appended to *Memoirs of the British Fleets and
Squadrons* (pp. 131, 190–94). He died in 1716.

ELIZABETH HARESNAPE

Sources BL cat. · H. Ellis and F. Douce, *A catalogue of the Lansdowne
manuscripts in the British Museum*, 2 vols. (1812–19) · *Index of manuscripts in the British Library*, 10 vols. (1984–6) · Wing, *STC* · M. Taubman, *An heroick poem to his royal highness the duke of York on his return
from Scotland* (1682) · M. Taubman, *London's anniversary festival…for
Sr. John Chapman* (1688) · M. Taubman, *London's annual triumph*
(1685) · M. Taubman, *London's great jubilee restor'd* (1689) · M. Taubman, *A description of the several pageants, exhibited on the 29th day of
October, 1689, being the day on which the late Sir Thomas Pilkington, knt.
entered for a second time on his mayoralty* (1761) · M. Taubman, *London's
triumph, or, The Goldsmiths jubilee* (1687) · M. Taubman, *London's yearly
jubilee* (1686) · M. Taubman, *Loyal poems and satyrs upon the times, since
the beginning of the Salamanca plot, written by several hands* (1685) ·
N. Taubman, *A funeral sermon [on Ecclesiastes 7:1] preach'd in the chapel
belonging to the British Society of Merchants at Leghorn…occasion'd by the
death of…B. Kennet, D. D., some time their minister* (1716) · N. Taubman,
*Memoirs of the British fleets and squadrons in the Mediteranean, anno
1708 and 1709…to which is annexed, a cursory view of Naples* (1710) ·

N. Taubman, *Virtue in distress, or, The history of Mindana* (1706) • Foster, *Alum. Oxon.* • HoP, *Commons, 1660–90* • J. G. Nichols, *London's pageants: 1, Accounts of fifty five royal processions and entertainments in the City of London, 2, A bibliographical list of lord mayors pageants* (1831) • W. Hone, *The every day-book, or, The guide to the year*, 1 [1859], 671 • J. P. Malcolm, *Londinium redivivum, or, An antient history and modern description of London*, 2 vols. (1802–7), 2.45–7 • K. Sharpe, '"So hard a text?": images of Charles I, 1612–1700', *HJ*, 43 (2000), 383–406 • G. S. De Krey, 'Political radicalism in London after the Glorious Revolution', *Journal of Modern History*, 55 (1983), 585–617 • J. K. Wood, '"A flowing harmony": music on the Thames in Restoration London', *Early Music*, 23 (1995), 553 • M. Burden, '"For the lustre of the subject": music for the lord mayor's day in the Restoration', *Early Music*, 23 (1995), 586–91 • *DNB*

Taubman, Nathaniel (d. 1716). *See under* Taubman, Matthew (d. 1690?).

Taunt, Henry William (1842–1922), photographer, was born in Penson's Gardens, St Ebbe's, Oxford, on 14 June 1842, the only son of Henry Taunt (c.1821–1882), a plumber and glazier, and his wife, Martha Darter (c.1813–1886). He was educated at Penson's Gardens Sunday school and St Ebbe's national school and also at the church school in West Ilsley, Berkshire, his mother's home village. After leaving school about 1852, he worked with his father and in several shops in Oxford before joining Edward Bracher, an early Oxford photographer, in 1856. He started as a basic utility hand and took his first photograph, a group in Exeter College quad, about 1858. When Bracher sold his business to Wheeler and Day, the High Street stationers, in 1863, Taunt became their photographic manager. On 17 September 1863 he married Miriam Jeffrey (1837/8–1929), an Oxford dressmaker, the daughter of Stephen Jeffrey, a gardener; the couple had no children.

In 1868 Taunt set up as a photographer on his own account, opening a small but central shop at 33 Cornmarket Street in 1869. His photographs of the Oxford area and the River Thames soon attracted praise and he publicized them through magic-lantern lectures and in his book, *A New Map of the River Thames* (1872), which included pastedown prints and his own survey of the river between Oxford and London. In 1874 he moved to larger premises at 9–10 Broad Street and he had a branch at Easton Street in High Wycombe, Buckinghamshire, between about 1875 and 1889. In 1889 Taunt leased Canterbury House in Cowley Road, renamed it Rivera after the River Thames, and established his main photographic and printing works in the grounds. A dispute over renewal of the lease of his Broad Street shop forced Taunt into bankruptcy in 1895 with debts which he estimated at over £3000. He moved his central premises to 41 High Street and later to no. 34 but, from 1906, he operated solely from Rivera. By 1922 he had amassed over 60,000 negatives, though his assistants, notably Randolph Adams, took many of the later photographs. In his later years he became a prolific author of local histories and guidebooks, publishing over fifty titles; he also diversified into printing and became a major publisher of picture postcards. Between 1893 and 1906 he was a fellow of the Royal Geographical Society.

Taunt was a tall, distinguished-looking man with a full beard, almost invariably seen wearing nautical garb and a yachting cap. He was a competent musician and was at one time organist and choir leader at St Mary Magdalen Church in Oxford; his sense of fun was demonstrated by humorous poetic jingles and annual children's entertainments but he was also a fierce campaigner, battling for clean city water in 1880 and against electric tramways in 1906. A Conservative nationally, he deplored local party politics and stood unsuccessfully as an independent candidate for the city council's west ward in 1880 and 1881. He never suffered fools gladly and was convicted of assault in 1878 after a fight with an apprentice. Henry Taunt died at Rivera on 4 November 1922 and was buried on 9 November in Rose Hill cemetery, Church Cowley Road, Cowley; his wife survived him. Like many other nineteenth-century photographers, Taunt documented the local urban and

Henry William Taunt (1842–1922), by unknown photographer

rural scene but his artistic temperament and historian's eye raised his work on to a higher plane and gave it an enduring appeal.   MALCOLM GRAHAM

Sources M. Graham, *Henry Taunt of Oxford: Victorian photographer* (1973) · M. Graham, 'Oxford in the 1850s: reminiscences of Henry Taunt', *Top. Oxon.*, 18 (1972), 11–17 · B. Brown, *The England of Henry Taunt: Victorian photographer* (1973) · *Oxford Times* (28 Oct 1882) · *Oxford Journal Illustrated* (8–15 Nov 1922) · electoral rolls, 1866–1922, Oxford City Archives · St Mary Magdalen, Oxford, parish magazine, 1875, Centre for Oxfordshire Studies, Oxford · parish register (marriage), Oxford, St Paul, 1841, Oxfordshire Archives · parish register (burial), Oxford, St Ebbe's, 1886, Oxfordshire Archives · census returns for St Ebbe's, 1851 · m. cert. · d. cert. [Miriam Taunt]
Archives Centre for Oxfordshire Studies, Oxford, research papers relating to local history; photographic collection, incl. Henry Taunt prints; works | English Heritage, Swindon, National Monuments Record, Henry Taunt glass plate negatives · http://viewfinder.english_heritage.org.uk, 14,000 Taunt images from Centre for Oxfordshire Studies and EHNMR, 21 Jan 2003
Likenesses photograph, Centre for Oxfordshire Studies, Oxford [*see illus.*] · photographs, Centre for Oxfordshire Studies, Oxford

Taunton. For this title name *see* Labouchere, Henry, Baron Taunton (1798–1869).

Taunton, Ethelred Luke (1857–1907), ecclesiastical historian, born at Rugeley, Staffordshire, on 17 October 1857, was the youngest son of Thomas Taunton (*b. c.*1808), of Rugeley, and his wife, Mary Clarke. In 1868 he was sent to the Benedictine college at Downside, near Bath, where his father had been a fellow pupil of W. B. Ullathorne. Though he was withdrawn from the school in 1871 because of delicate health, he retained a lifelong devotion to the Downside community. In 1874 he joined the Institute of St Andrew founded by Father Bampfield at Barnet, then transferred in 1880 to the Oblates of St Charles Borromeo at their house in Bayswater established by Cardinal Manning. He was ordained priest at St Thomas's seminary, Hammersmith, on 17 February 1883. On leaving the Oblates in 1886 he was appointed by Manning to take charge of a new mission at Stoke Newington, but his already precarious health was broken by an accident in the church, and he now retired from pastoral work to devote himself to historical research. By 1896 he was in debt to the sum of £1269, but worked his way back to solvency by journalism, and became a frequent contributor to the Catholic press in the USA.

Taunton's first major work, *The English Black Monks of St Benedict* (2 vols., 1897), covering the periods both before and after the Reformation, was written under the close supervision of Edmund Bishop, who supplied him with his own transcripts of manuscripts in the British Museum. In dealing with the defection to the Benedictines of English students from Jesuit seminaries in early seventeenth-century Spain, Taunton was highly critical of Robert Persons, whom he represented as having aimed at the total control of the English Catholic community by the Society of Jesus. A critical review of the work by the Jesuit J. H. Pollen in *The Month* (December 1897) led to a reopening of old wounds, and a controversy ensued in the correspondence columns of *The Tablet*. Taunton provoked further controversy by his *History of the Jesuits in England* (1901), which was

again challenged by Pollen in *The Month*. Taunton was also a composer of motets and other pieces. Some of his hymn settings were printed.

Taunton died suddenly of heart failure, in Bloomsbury, on 9 May 1907, and was buried six days later at Kensal Green cemetery. His posthumous article on the Jesuits for the eleventh edition of the *Encyclopaedia Britannica* (1911), while moderating the tone of the text written for the ninth edition (1880) by F. W. Littledale, produced a final riposte from Pollen (*The Month*, 117, 1911, 561–74). Taunton left unfinished a life of Cardinal Pole. In an unpublished manuscript, 'A key to Jesuit politics', preserved at Downside, he indicted Francisco Suárez as the 'theological miscreant' who, by his teaching on the papal deposing power and on tyrannicide, 'set the fuse from Rome and Coimbra which exploded in England'.   G. MARTIN MURPHY

Sources *Downside Review*, 26 (1907), 223–4 · N. J. Abercrombie, *The life and work of Edmund Bishop* (1959) · *The Tablet* (18 May 1907), 785 · *The Times* (20 May 1907) · *The Month*, 97 (1901), 512–18 · *The Month*, 98 (1901), 315–18 · *The Month*, 117 (1911), 561–74 · *DNB*
Archives Downside Abbey, near Bath, papers and corresp., EB tracts 295

Taunton, John (*bap.* 1769, *d.* 1821), surgeon, son of Charles Taunton, a farmer, was born at Pye Mill in Paxford, a hamlet of Blockley in Gloucestershire. He was baptized on 21 May 1769 in the parish church of Chipping Campden, Gloucestershire, and was brought up as a farmer; but a study of anatomy drew him to London. Being a stranger to London he asked at a shop in Holborn for the name of the best surgeon and anatomical instructor, and was advised that it was Andrew Marshal, whose anatomical school was in Thavies Inn, Holborn. Taunton immediately called upon Marshal, but he did not attend his classes, and he eventually became a pupil of Henry Cline at St Thomas's Hospital.

In 1801 Taunton was appointed demonstrator of anatomy at Guy's Hospital, in temporary charge during the illness of John Cunningham Saunders, and he subsequently became principal lecturer at the London Anatomical Society. He was surgeon to the City Dispensary in 1801, at a time when the charity was almost bankrupt; but under his able guidance it quickly became a flourishing establishment. His position as surgeon to the City Dispensary led him to treat large numbers of poor weavers in Spitalfields who suffered from *prolapsus ani*, hernia, and other diseases common to their occupation. Curing these conditions required expensive medical equipment, and this led to the establishment of the City of London Truss Society in 1807, when Taunton, with the assistance of a young bell-hanger, began to manufacture trusses for distribution among the poor of the neighbourhood. Taunton had also become surgeon to the Finsbury Dispensary some time about 1800, and reformed its whole constitution.

Taunton took an active part at the Medical Society of London, which he nearly wrecked in 1812 by proposing as secretary, and carrying against all opposition, Thomas Joseph Pettigrew, his former apprentice, then newly admitted a member of the Royal College of Surgeons, instead of Dr Birkbeck, whose position as a senior member of the profession should have won him the contest. Taunton had a very large dispensary practice and visited the sick poor at their own homes, which were distributed over large areas. He performed his duties conscientiously, yet he still found time to carry out innumerable post-mortem examinations and to make many pathological preparations. He also established a private medical school, at which he sought to supplement the poor training given to medical students at the various hospitals in London. Married, with three sons, Taunton died at his house in Hatton Garden, London, on Monday morning, 5 March 1821. D'A. POWER, rev. RICHARD HANKINS

Sources *London Medical Repository*, 15 (1821), 344 · private information (1898) · 'Marshal, Andrew', *DNB*
Likenesses oils, Truss Society Offices, Finsbury Square, London · photograph, Wellcome L.

Taunton, Sir William Elias (1773–1835), judge, was born at Oxford, the eldest son of Sir William Elias Taunton, town clerk of Oxford and clerk of the peace for the county, and his wife, Frances, daughter of Stephen Grosvenor, subtreasurer of Christ Church, Oxford. He was admitted as king's scholar at Westminster School on 15 January 1785, and was elected to Christ Church, Oxford, matriculating from there on 12 June 1789. He graduated BA in 1793 and MA in 1796. In 1793 he gained the chancellor's prize for the English essay. He was admitted student of Lincoln's Inn in 1794, was called to the bar in Easter term 1799, and joined the Oxford circuit. In 1801 he became a commissioner of bankrupts, and in 1806 succeeded Charles Abbot as recorder of Oxford. On 10 October 1814 Taunton married Maria, youngest daughter of Henry William Atkinson, provost of the Company of Moneyers. He was created king's counsel in 1821 and elected a bencher of his inn in 1822. On 12 November 1830 he was appointed a justice of the king's bench, and was knighted five days later. Taunton soon in his career acquired the reputation of a black-letter lawyer (Foss, *Judges*, 9.96); as an advocate he was a somewhat dull and slow speaker who, however, 'made the monotony of his voice impressive and used his sluggishness as a power' (*Law Magazine*, 13, 1835, 168). He died somewhat suddenly in his house in Russell Square on 11 January 1835. He was survived by two sons and four daughters. WILLIAM CARR, rev. ERIC METCALFE

Sources Foster, *Alum. Oxon.* · *The Times* (13 Jan 1835) · *The Times* (15 Jan 1835) · *GM*, 2nd ser., 3 (1835), 431–2 · G. F. R. Barker and A. H. Stenning, eds., *The Westminster School register from 1764 to 1883* (1892) · *Law Magazine*, 13 (1835), 165–9
Likenesses oils, *c.*1795, Oxford town hall · R. Dighton, caricature, etching, pubd 1807, NPG · H. P. Briggs, oils, *c.*1833, Christ Church Oxf.

Tautphoeus [née Montgomery], **Jemima von**, Baroness **von Tautphoeus** (1807–1893), novelist, was born on 23 October 1807 at Seaview, co. Donegal, Ireland, the daughter of James Montgomery, a local landowner, and his wife, Jemima, daughter of James Glasgow of Aughadenvarn, co. Leitrim. She was the niece of Sir Henry Conyngham Montgomery, first baronet, and a cousin of Maria Edgeworth, whom she labelled 'one of the most interesting people it

was possible to know' (Thompson, 115). Educated at home, she was married on 29 January 1838 to Cajetan Josef Friedrich, Baron von Tautphoeus of Marquartstein in the Bavarian nobility (1805–1885), chamberlain to the king of Bavaria; the remainder of her life was principally spent in Bavaria, where she was equally at home in court circles and, as her works demonstrate, with the peasantry and the middle classes.

Although Jemima von Tautphoeus's novels have now fallen into obscurity, during her lifetime they ran through numerous editions in Britain, the US, and Germany, and were ranked as 'English classics' (*The Critic*, 12). Her first novel, *The Initials* (1850), became immensely popular, despite modest critical attention. A 1901 study claimed that 'not to have read *The Initials* was … to have left one's self out of the range of intellectual conversation and almost of human sympathy' (Howells, 303). Her four novels are entertaining combinations of romance and travelogue: often set in the Bavarian alps, they drew on her knowledge of English and German manners, customs, and scenery, and their central romances often involve cultural or class conflicts. They are also notable for their lively, intellectually curious heroines like the passionate Hildegarde, of *The Initials*, who speaks four languages at the age of seventeen and prefers reading to housework, or Leonora, in *Quits* (1857), whose development of the life of the mind protects her from the lures of fashionable (that is, frivolous) society. *Cyrilla* (1853) is a tragic romance based on a real-life incident, the German murder trial of Assessor Zahn, and this deviation from the happy denouements of her earlier novels resulted in mixed reviews. Her last novel, *At Odds* (1863), was written during an extended period of ill health and was, in her own opinion, the least successful of her works.

Baron von Tautphoeus died on 14 November 1885, a few days after his only son, Rudolf Edgeworth Josef (1838–1885), who had become the Bavarian ambassador to Rome. Jemima von Tautphoeus died in Munich on 12 November 1893 and was interred in the family vault at Marquartstein Castle in the Bavarian highlands near Salzburg on 15 November of that year.

RICHARD GARNETT, rev. ALICIA GRIBBEN

Sources *DNB* · *The Times* (17 Nov 1893) · 'The Baroness Tautphoeus', *The Critic* [New York, NY] (6 Jan 1894), 12 · M. L. Thompson, 'Baroness Tautphoeus', *Atlantic Monthly*, 74 (July 1894), 114–19 · W. D. Howells, 'The heroine of *The initials*', *Harper's Bazaar*, 35 (Aug 1901), 303–09 · Blain, Clements & Grundy, *Feminist comp.* · 'Quits', *New Quarterly Review*, 6 (1857), 440–45 [review] · 'Cyrilla, a tale', *New Quarterly Review*, 2 (1853), 389–91 [review] · *The Athenaeum* (25 Nov 1893), 736 · J. Foster, *The peerage, baronetage, and knightage of the British empire* [1880–83] · *Gothaisches genealogisches Taschenbuch der freiherrlichen Häuser* (1889), 884–6

Taverner, John (*c.*1490–1545), composer, is of unknown parentage. He was probably a native of Lincolnshire. In 1525/6 2*s.* 4*d.* sufficed to hire a man to escort him from Boston to visit his 'country', indicating family settlement in south Lincolnshire within one or two days' ride of Boston.

Education and early career, c.1490–1526 It appears likely that Taverner was educated as a chorister of a major church choir. Those of Holy Trinity collegiate church, Tattershall, Lincolnshire, and of Boston parish church (St Botolph's) were close to home and sufficiently illustrious to offer him suitable training and experience; nevertheless, he was not so recorded at either, and it was not uncommon for choirboys of unusual talent to be engaged far from home. The composer cannot be identified with the John Tavernar who in 1514–15 was admitted an associated member (*secularis*) of the London guild of parish clerks and professional musicians (the Confraternity of St Nicholas), and indeed nothing is known of him before late 1524 when, as a singing-man of the choir of Tattershall College, he received a substantial gratuity at St Botolph's, Boston, as a guest singer in its choir. His designation as Master Taverner indicates his achievement already of significant eminence in his profession by the mid-1520s.

The Tattershall College choir, of sixteen men and ten boys, had long enjoyed a vigorous and productive musical tradition; by the time he left in 1526 Taverner was probably some thirty-five years old, and a fair proportion of his surviving music may already have been composed. Pieces attributable to his Tattershall years or even earlier appear likely to include the Marian antiphon *Ave Dei patris filia* and the mass *O Michael*, which display many features symptomatic of composition by an inexperienced but highly talented and ambitious hand; also likely to be early is the antiphon *Gaude plurimum*. Meanwhile, suitable for use on Tattershall's patronal festival was the monumental and marvellously accomplished mass *Gloria tibi trinitas*; if composed at Tattershall, as seems probable, this shows the extent to which Taverner had already achieved maturity as a composer well before his departure for Oxford.

Cardinal College, Oxford, 1526–1530 Taverner was present at Tattershall on 17 May 1525, but by now his celebrity was such that in the autumn of that year he was commissioned to become the inaugural master of the choristers of the choir of Cardinal College, Oxford, newly founded by Cardinal Thomas Wolsey, archbishop of York. Wolsey's agent considered Taverner 'very meet' for the job; he, however, evidently knowing his worth, was loath to co-operate, alleging his satisfaction with both his work and his remuneration at Tattershall, and 'that he is in way of a gud mariage, whiche he shuld loose if he dydd reamove frome thens' (PRO, SP 1/139, fol. 239*r*). Nevertheless, he was prevailed upon to relent. From 25 March 1526 he was on the college payroll; by May he was using Wolsey's royal commission to recruit singers for his new choir (from Boston, among other places), and his work in Oxford began in earnest with the opening of Cardinal College on 19 October. His stipend was a generous £15 per year.

The college statutes required the master of the choir to be 'exceptionally skilled in music' (*musices peritissimus*) and made correspondingly elaborate provision for the musical refinement of the services. Its membership of twenty-six men and sixteen boys ranked the choir as among the greatest in the land. However, there appears to be no substance in the assertion that the Forrest–Heyther partbooks of c.1528–30 were compiled at Cardinal College or assembled under Taverner's direction or used there by his choir.

The statutes laid special emphasis on the performance with polyphony of the daily Lady mass, and within the Gyffard partbooks of c.1555–8 one section devoted to music for this observance preserves works by Taverner possibly dating from his Oxford years, including both the *Leroy* Kyrie and the mass *Western Wynd*. The Kyrie takes as *cantus firmus* one of a body of pre-existing abstract melodies known as 'squares', and in the mass Taverner pursued this compositional principle to an unprecedented but logical conclusion. On thirty-six almost unvaried statements of what may well have been a newly composed melody of his own creation he based an entire mass, distinguished by a flow of contrapuntal invention as seemingly inexhaustible as it is melodious and memorable. Taverner's melody was later seen to bear a superficial similarity to a courtly song 'Western wind, when wilt thou blow', which misleadingly led the name 'Western Wynd' to become attached to this mass. Other works for Lady mass composed by this time included a mass for boys' voices (now lost) and Kyries and sequences (fragments survive) sung in 1529 at King's College, Cambridge.

At Cardinal College the feasts of St Nicholas and St William of York enjoyed an elevated status. Taverner's setting of *Sospitati dedit aegros* was proper to the first, while for the daily votive antiphon to St William prescribed in Wolsey's statutes he composed a concise and elegant setting of words which probably originally began 'O Wilhelme, pastor bone' and included a prayer for the good estate of Wolsey as founder. Also specified in the college statutes was the daily performance of the antiphons *Ave Maria* and *Sancte Deus*, for each of which Taverner composed succinct but clearly articulated settings for five-voice choir.

Probably contemporary is Taverner's five-voice mass deriving some of its music from *O Wilhelme, pastor bone*, possibly composed for the tercentenary of the canonization of St William (21 March 1527). Eschewing floridity of expression, this seems concise and direct, and earned itself the descriptive (and by no means pejorative) nickname 'Small devotion'. Possibly contemporary is the mass *Mater Christi*, derived in a similar manner from Taverner's hybrid Marian–Jesus antiphon *Mater Christi sanctissima*. The composition of a paired mass and votive antiphon for use together on a great feast was by no means new in England; Taverner was developing a particular mode of pairing, importing into the mass by 'parody' whole sections of pre-existing music first created for the antiphon.

Taverner's four years at Oxford were not uneventful. Since about 1526 there had developed there a covert cell of religious dissidents, primarily clerics and students, attracted to Lutheranism; its members were serviced by one Thomas Garrard, a clandestine purveyor of heretical books. Between 19 and 29 February 1528 the cell was exposed, and Garrard's associates were rounded up for questioning; among them were John Radley and Thomas Lawney, respectively lay clerk and chaplain of Cardinal

College choir, and Taverner himself. Doubtless Lawney and Radley had encountered Garrard at Boston, where until 1526 they had been members of St Botolph's choir and he had been schoolmaster (1524–6). Taverner had recruited Lawney and Radley from Boston to Oxford, unwittingly facilitating thereby Garrard's introduction to his Oxford clientèle. Six members of Cardinal College, all clerics, were imprisoned for interrogation. Taverner and Radley, being laymen, and therefore theologically unlearned, were more lightly treated. Radley confessed to being Garrard's clandestine host during his Oxford visits. Taverner was associated more with one of the clerics, John Clerk, a senior canon of Cardinal College, whose suspect books Taverner confessed to having hidden under the floorboards of the choirboys' practice-room, and to a little of whose compromising correspondence with Garrard he was privy.

Their confessions were reported to Wolsey; to him, however, only clerical Lutheranism appeared at this time to be actually dangerous. He dismissed both Taverner and Radley as 'unlerned and nott to be regarded' (PRO, SP 1/47, fol. 111r), and beyond the frightening experience of arrest, interrogation, and confession neither was imprisoned or otherwise punished. Such leniency was well judged. Although apparently he was led into at least evangelical heterodoxy by superiors and colleagues, Taverner's association with these covert Lutherans cannot be lightly dismissed; no one flirted with heresy merely to oblige his friends. The death in custody of four of the suspects, including Taverner's friend Clerk, seems to have sufficed to remind him of the virtues of orthodoxy, and there is no sign that ever again was he tempted to dabble in any form of heterodox belief.

In April 1528 Thomas Cromwell reported enthusiastically to Wolsey on the standard of the liturgical service in Cardinal College chapel, 'so devout, solemn and full of harmony that in mine opinion it hath few peers' (Ellis, *Original Letters*, 2nd ser., 2.139), and by July Taverner stood as high as ever in Wolsey's favour, attending upon him at Hampton Court with four of his ablest choirboys. However, soon after Wolsey's dismissal from royal service in November 1529 the choir of Cardinal College began to be run down, and by April 1530 provision for the conduct of the choral service was becoming sufficiently threatened for Taverner to take his departure.

Boston, 1530–1545 It appears that Taverner now returned to Boston; certainly it was as 'Taverner of Boston' that he was commonly known to his immediate posterity, including John Foxe, Thomas Whythorne, and John Baldwin. It is likely that he was recruited to the choir maintained in St Botolph's parish church by and at the expense of the Guild of St Mary established therein. Certainly in 1538–9 he was recorded as recently a tenant of one of the guild's domestic properties, the record of whose tenancy shows it to have been reserved for occupation by members of its choral staff. It is not unlikely that Taverner now served the Boston choir as master of the choristers, enjoying employment there (at not less than its established salary of £17 6s. 8d.) from 1530 until probably 1536 or 1537.

Within this magnificent church the Guild of St Mary maintained a choir of (until about 1536) some eighteen to twenty men and eight to ten boys. To John Leland the church was 'servid so with singging, and that of cunning men, as no paroche is in al England' (*The Itinerary of John Leland, in or about the Years 1535–1543*, ed. L. T. Smith, 5 vols., 1906–10, 5.33). Possibly it was for Boston that Taverner wrote his masterpiece, the festal mass *Corona spinea*. The crown which to the Guild of St Mary was of significance so great that it was displayed as a badge on the livery of its almsmen may very well have been the crown of thorns, so rendering this a piece appropriate for high mass on any of the guild's greatest feasts. The unidentified *cantus firmus* may be a chant from the use of Lincoln.

Simultaneously Taverner was also exploring a style increasingly animated by systematic use of imitation, as in the Jesus antiphon *O splendor gloriae*. Moreover, it was probably at this time that he developed the genre of choral office responsory composed on a monorhythmic *cantus firmus*. Aurally *Dum transisset sabbatum* is a work of the greatest refinement; yet within the apparently effortless flow of its polyphony lies embedded and concealed the *cantus firmus* disposed in severe and unyielding semibreves. This technique permitted participation by choir chaplains unlearned in polyphonic notation, who were unlikely to have been employed at Cardinal College, but very likely—in the guise of, for example, the six 'choir priests' maintained by the Guild of St George—to have been encountered at St Botolph's.

About 1536–7 Taverner's employment by the Guild of St Mary ended. The prodigious spiritual privileges available to subscribing members, including plenary remission of sins and the 'Scala coeli' indulgence for the delivery of souls from purgatory, were of papal origin. Consequently the gathering of membership funds, the source of the guild's enormous income, became illegal on the break with Rome in 1534, and the 'Scala coeli' indulgence was outlawed altogether under the ten articles of 1536. Probably the guild hereupon became unable to continue Taverner's remuneration, and certainly by May 1538 he had chosen to retire altogether from employment in church music. It appears that, either through accumulated personal means or through advantage arising from marriage (or both), by this time he was a wealthy man, able to choose not to seek another job, but to spend the last years of his life as a prosperous and respected burgher, and composer, of his adopted town. Much later, John Foxe, knowing of Taverner's brush with Lutheranism at Oxford and anxious to portray him as an enduring stalwart for evangelical truth, remarked that 'This Taverner repented him very muche that he had made Songes to Popish Ditties in the time of his blindnes' (*Acts and Monuments*, 5.50). It seems that Foxe, himself born and partly brought up in Boston, had heard correctly of a final withdrawal by Taverner from an active career in church music, but was merely guessing at, and succeeding only in entirely misrepresenting, Taverner's actual motivation.

The date of Taverner's marriage to Rose (d. 1553; a widow with two daughters, who sprang originally from one of Boston's leading families, the Parrowes) is not known. However, already by May 1538 he had lately been leasing a large family mansion on Wormgate, Boston, at a substantial annual rent of 40s. By 1541 he was styled 'gentleman' and was beginning to appear as one of the town's leading worthies. In 1537 he was admitted to membership of Boston's select Guild of Corpus Christi, whose objectives were the veneration of the transubstantiated sacrament and the provision of masses for the souls of members deceased. Taverner's commitment to such pillars of Catholic orthodoxy located him in not only the religious but also the social mainstream, and this encouraged him to cultivate the favour of Thomas Cromwell, now the king's principal secretary, with whom it is likely that he had become acquainted when both were employed within Wolsey's circle. On 11 September 1538 Taverner reported that the town had complied with an order from Cromwell for the demolition and incineration of the rood screen and figures from St Botolph's Church. His report included no observation that he had himself been present or had participated in any way. Meanwhile, he endeavoured to capitalize on Cromwell's favour by seeking the opportunity to purchase a local wardship, and on another occasion by petitioning for Cromwell's favourable intervention in a kinsman's lawsuit.

Evidently Taverner was known locally as a kindly individual, and it was to him that in 1537–8 the friars of Boston came to lament their loss of public support and consequent utter indigence. He assured them of his personal goodwill and generosity, and obliged them by writing to Cromwell urging a speedy determination of the fate of the local friaries. His benevolent intervention paid him good dividends; following the surrender of the houses he and one other Boston businessman were granted the opportunity to purchase the sites from the crown.

Taverner also took much self-sacrificing trouble as an executor of the will of one Roger Meres. Indeed, another Boston businessman, Anthony Robertson, recollecting how he had undertaken complete repayment to Taverner of a loan of £20 despite the latter's inability to cancel the paperwork through its temporary misplacement, credited him as 'a verye honest man' in whose word and promise he placed 'an especyall trust and confidens' (PRO, C1/1259, nos. 14, 17). Taverner's stature in Boston appears steadily to have grown in the last years of his life. He served as treasurer of the Corpus Christi guild in 1541, 1542, and 1543, and upon the grant to Boston of its first municipal charter in May 1545 his prominence was sealed by his appointment as one of the twelve aldermen of its inaugural governing council.

Although no longer employed in church music, Taverner may very well have continued after 1536 to compose for St Botolph's choir, which—albeit with much reduced forces on much reduced pay—remained in existence right up until 1548. During these years of hardship it is likely that its boys' section was disbanded (in 1538 Leland had noted the presence only of singing-men), so creating the circumstances satisfied by Taverner's late compositions, all of which are for men's voices alone; they include the Magnificat for four voices, the five-voice Te Deum, the fine four-voice arrangement of *Dum transisset sabbatum*, and the *Meane mass*. These exhibit an increasing concern for directness of expression assimilated into a disposition of imitation now sufficiently systematic to stand beside free invention as the prime melodic generator.

Early in August 1545 Taverner's health appears suddenly to have collapsed, an associate perceiving that 'the said Taverner did greatly decay' (PRO, C1/1164, no. 44). Such was his affliction that when on 18 October 1545 he died, probably in Boston, he had made no will. Rose Taverner, who had busily settled his affairs at the beginning of August, was granted the administration of his effects; his property included tenements in Boston and agricultural land in the vicinity. He was buried within St Botolph's Church, beneath the great west tower. He had no children and was survived only by his widow, who died between 1 and 18 May 1553, and by a younger brother, William.

Reputation Taverner's pre-eminence among contemporary English composers was complete, not least for his mastery of stylistic diversity and range of genre, extending even to four secular songs and to the untexted and strangely scored *Quemadmodum*. Indeed, irrespective of their different stylistic heritages, his work emerges impressively from comparison with that of Adrian Willaert, Nicolas Gombert, or Cristóbal de Morales, the most illustrious of his continental contemporaries. During a composing life of only some thirty-five years he took to its culmination the prevailing English style of expansive, virtuosic, and sonically luxuriant polyphony, and exhibited in particular a sure-footed degree of control over the most grandly conceived designs. He also forged a successor style more concise in its expression, terse in its thought, and economical in its deployment of melodic material, animated in part by the working of successive imitative points capable of generating on their own the characteristics of entire musical phrases. This style could either supersede entirely the former melismatic luxuriance (as in the *Meane mass*) or be combined with it (as in the four-voice Magnificat).

Though similar to features found somewhat earlier in continental Catholic composition, these initiatives seem likely to have arisen simply because like circumstances were giving rise independently to like developments, rather than as a consequence of some putative acquaintance on Taverner's part directly with continental music. Certainly the devotionally very limited substance of the Henrician Reformation up to 1545 was not such as to create on its own account any local stimulus towards modifying the prevailing manner of musical composition for the church services. And irrespective of surface stylistic trends, there remain underlying all Taverner's finest works his abiding 'gift of incisive melodic invention, his capacity to create a sense of coherent discourse by generating extended lines out of small motifs, and his purposeful sense of progress expressed through control of harmonic rhythm and direction' (private information).

Taverner's influence on his younger colleagues and successors was extensive. Christopher Tye and John Sheppard wrote masses both on Taverner's 'Western Wynd' *cantus firmus* and in emulation of his *Meane mass*. The suave elegance of the four-voice 'In nomine [Domini]' passage of the Benedictus of the mass *Gloria tibi trinitas* proved amenable for performance by viols, and spawned a whole genre of instrumental composition that lasted as far as Henry Purcell. In 1547–9 the enduring value of Taverner's music was recognized in the adaptation of two of his masses to the words of the new vernacular communion service, and later in the fitting of English words to two of his votive antiphons and to the original 'In nomine'. Influences emanating from the *Meane mass* have been discerned in William Byrd's four-voice mass.

Taverner's pre-eminence was evident not only to the creators of repertory manuscripts of his own day, but also to the nostalgic anthologizers who in Elizabeth I's reign strove to preserve the treasures of the pre-Reformation past. In their collections are now to be found the majority of Taverner's surviving works. Never entirely unknown to music historians, these were systematically recovered and published in the 1920s, and since the 1960s have been extensively performed and recorded.

ROGER BOWERS

Sources *LP Henry VIII*, vol. 4 · PRO, SP/1/136; SP1/1/142; SP/1/156; SP/1/159 · *The acts and monuments of John Foxe*, ed. S. R. Cattley, 8 vols. (1837–41), vol. 5 · *John Taverner*, ed. H. Benham, 5 vols., Early English Church Music, 20, 25, 30, 35–6 (1978–86) [1: *Six-part masses*; 2: *Votive antiphons*; 3: *Ritual music and secular songs*; 4: *Four- and five-part masses*; 5: *Five-part masses*] · D. S. Josephson, *John Taverner: Tudor composer* (1979) · *John Taverner, c.1495–1545*, ed. P. Buck and others, 2 vols., Tudor Church Music, 1, 3 (1923–4) · R. Bowers, 'The cultivation and promotion of music in the household and orbit of Thomas Wolsey', *Cardinal Wolsey: church, state, and art*, ed. S. J. Gunn and P. G. Lindley (1991), 178–218, esp. 196–202 · R. Bowers and P. Doe, 'Taverner, John', *New Grove*, 2nd edn · D. Josephson, 'In search of the historical Taverner', *Tempo*, 101 (1972), 40–52 · P. Thompson, *The history and antiquities of Boston* (1856) · H. Benham, 'The formal design and construction of Taverner's works', *Musica Disciplina*, 26 (1972), 189–209 · H. Benham, 'The music of Taverner: a liturgical study', *Music Review*, 33 (1972), 251–74 · J. Bergsagel, 'The date and provenance of the Forrest–Heyther collection of Tudor masses', *Music and Letters*, 44 (1963), 245–8 · N. Davison, 'The Western Wind masses', *Musical Quarterly*, 57 (1971), 427–43 · P. Doe, 'Latin polyphony under Henry VIII', *Proceedings of the Royal Musical Association*, 95 (1968–9), 81–96 · N. Morgan, 'The Scala coeli, indulgence and the royal chapels', *The reign of Henry VII* [Harlaxton 1993], ed. B. Thompson (1995), 82–103 · H. Ellis, ed., *Original letters illustrative of English history*, 2nd ser., 4 vols. (1827) · PRO, E150/580/18 · PRO, C142/74/130 · private information (2004) [Professor Nick Sandon]

Taverner, John (1584–1638). *See under* Taverner, Richard (1505?–1575).

Taverner, Richard (1505?–1575), translator and evangelical reformer, was probably born at Brisley, Norfolk, the eldest of the four sons of John Taverner (1457?–1545) of North Elmham, Norfolk, and his first wife, Alice, daughter and heir of Robert Sylvester of Brisley. Educated initially at Corpus Christi College, Cambridge, Richard transferred to the newly founded Cardinal College, Oxford, where he graduated on 21 June 1527 and was among those accused of heresy in 1529. His move to Oxford may partly reflect the influence of his kinsman the composer John Taverner, who was master of the choristers at Cardinal College and was also charged with heresy. Returning to Cambridge, where he was incorporated BA in 1529, Richard Taverner proceeded MA the following year, but was then persuaded to go abroad to study. But the friend who had been supporting him died, and late in 1530 Taverner wrote to Thomas Cromwell appealing for help from the king. Cromwell persuaded the duke of Norfolk to provide an annuity and Taverner returned to Cambridge, remaining there until 1534, probably as a fellow of Gonville Hall.

In 1532 Taverner sent Cromwell his translation of Erasmus's *Encomium matrimoni*, presented as an attack on clerical celibacy, which inaugurated his work as 'the most prolific populariser of Erasmus whom England produced' (McConica, 117), as well as anticipating the assault on religious houses. For Taverner, Erasmus was 'the incomparable lerned man' (Wooding, 29). Within the year he was contributing to official apologetic for the royal divorce, and had come to be identified as Cromwell's publicist. In a letter to Cromwell on 2 July 1533, Martin Tyndall, a fellow of King's College, offered a translation of Erasmus's life of Colet: 'Let Master Taverner, last year master of Greek in Cambridge, now your client, oversee it' (*LP Henry VIII*, vol. 6, no. 751). Taverner also studied law at Stroud Inn, one of the inns of chancery, proceeding thence to the Inner Temple, 'where his humour was to quote the law in Greek, when he read any thing thereof' (Wood, *Ath. Oxon.*, 3rd edn, 1.420). He was at court by 1534, while in 1536 or 1537 Cromwell secured his appointment as one of the clerks of the signet, though he maintained close contact with the minister. In August 1537, when investigating the advowson of Brisley church in Norfolk, he reported that he was preparing to marry. His wife was Margaret, daughter of Walter Lambert of Chertsey, and they had four sons and three daughters. In January 1539 Taverner was granted the lease of Alvingham Priory and two rectories in Lincolnshire, making him financially independent.

Taverner became Cromwell's principal propagandist for religious reform. As well as putting a protestant face on Erasmus in translation, he produced 'at the commaundement of his Master' English versions of the Augsburg confession with the *Apologie of Melanchthon* in 1536. Christoff Mont, Cromwell's German specialist, had introduced Henry VIII to Sarcerius's *Loci communes* (1528), which Taverner translated in 1538, with a prefatory epistle to Henry VIII explaining why it was to be preferred to Melanchthon's *Loci*, itself dedicated to the king: 'this tempreth his penne also to the capacitie of younge students of scripture'. Taverner expressed the moderation in doctrinal controversies of continental protestant humanists, who 'have denied freewyl onely in spirituall mocyons and that also in such persons as be not yet regenerate and renued by the holy ghost' (sig. A5). Nevertheless, his promotion of *sola scriptura* as the solution to doctrinal conflict was combined with the anti-papal polemic of the supremacy to urge that 'we all togither with one accorde, followynge your highnes as our heed and myghty shepherde maye utterly vomyt out of us all papysticall venym, and hertely at last imbrase the pure and syncere verite of gods moost holy worde' (sigs. A4r–v). In 1539 he translated Capito's psalm paraphrases as the *Summe or Pith of the 150 Psalmes of David*. The conservative Act of Six Articles (1539) prohibited the printing of unorthodox religious books, which may account for the removal of reference to Capito in the second edition of the *Summe*, the *Epitome of the Psalmes*, printed later that year. Between 1538 and 1540 he directed the operations of Richard Bankes's press, which published his works at this time.

Taverner's activity as a biblical translator stemmed from the need to revise the controversial 1537 Matthew Bible, itself a revision of Tyndale by John Rogers:

> Rogers's attacks on clerical celibacy, on purgatory, and on fasting were all eliminated, as was the comparison of the Pope to Anti-Christ, with a consequent change in tone from a distinctly Protestant work to a moderate and characteristically Erasmian compromise.   (McConica, 165)

The 1539 Taverner Bible was itself replaced later that year by the Great Bible, a far more thorough revision. Although a Greek scholar, Taverner was no Hebraist, and he employed the Latin Vulgate and the recent Latin translation by Pagninus for his Old Testament revisions. However, his New Testament revisions bring the text closer to the original Greek, anticipating the Rheims Bible.

Taverner retreated from Lutheran translation after Cromwell's fall in 1540; the act of attainder against the minister included a charge of having circulated heretical works. Having been briefly in Stephen Gardiner's custody, Taverner turned to Erasmus's humanist works as sources for a series of proverb collections, probably unsponsored. He was the first English translator of the *Apophthegmata*, upon which he drew heavily for *The Garden of Wysdom* (1539), and also included select *Adagia* in the 'thyrde boke': 'these works form one of the greatest repositories of Erasmian adages and classical wisdom made available to the sixteenth-century English reader' (McConica, 184). Taverner also drew on the *Opuscula aliquot* for subsequent expansions of his collection, often adding his own glosses in order to support the royal supremacy and the Henrician settlement, blending protestantism and humanism in his comments on contemporary affairs. The *Epistles and Gospelles* (1540), partly written and overseen by Taverner, was intended to supply the want of 'plentie of sobre modeste and sincere teachers' to feed the Christian flock 'not with rash erronyouse, hereticall or fabulous sermons, but sobre, discret, catholike, and godly instructions'. Substantial sections of these postils for each Sunday mass, which Cranmer edited, were later included verbatim in the Elizabethan *Book of Homilies*.

On 2 December 1541 Taverner once more found himself in Gardiner's custody, this time for failing to report the rumour that Anne of Cleves was pregnant by Henry VIII:

> This abominable slander was told to Taverner, of the Signet, by his mother-in-law, wife of Lambert, the goldsmith, and by his own wife, who said they had it of Lilgrave's wife and old ladye Carowe. Taverner kept it secret till Sunday, when he told Dr. Cox, who informed the Lord Privy Seal.   (*LP Henry VIII*, vol. 16, no. 1414)

The others were also imprisoned, as was a brother of

Taverner, who was not released until March 1542. Richard himself was soon released, however. In 1544 he served in the army in France, and in April of that year acquired the manor of Woodeaton, Oxfordshire, along with former monastic lands there, and began building. In 1544 or 1545 the king gave him the site of the dissolved Franciscan priory at Northampton; in the following year he received 'Nun's acres', part of the lands of Stamford Priory, and in 1546 other lands in Horningtoft, Norfolk.

In 1545 translations of Erasmian works advocating reform began to make a tentative reappearance, among them Taverner's version of *De amabili ecclesiae concordia*, now lost, in support of the king's appeal to parliament for mutual toleration within the English church. Taverner may have been involved in the compilation of the *King's Primer*, published in the same year, which included some of his translations of Capito. Nevertheless his translations of Melanchthon and Sarcerius were burnt at Paul's Cross in 1546.

In 1547 Taverner was returned to parliament as MP for Liverpool. He probably owed his seat to evangelical patronage, perhaps that of Sir William Paget, who became chancellor of the duchy of Lancaster in the same year. After parliament was dissolved in 1552 he received a licence to preach, even though not ordained. He is said to have preached at court before Edward VI, and in public both during his reign and that of Elizabeth, 'wearing a velvet bonnet or round cap, a damask gown and a chain of gold about his neck' (Wood, *Ath. Oxon.*, 3rd edn, 1.420). At Mary's accession he lost his position as clerk of the signet, but lived unmolested at Norbiton Hall, Surrey—his chosen residence while building work proceeded at Woodeaton. In 1558 he addressed a congratulatory Latin epistle to Elizabeth. He declined the offer of a knighthood, but served as a JP for Oxfordshire, and was high sheriff of the county in 1569.

In January 1562 Margaret Taverner died. Richard subsequently married Mary, daughter of Sir John Harcourt of Stanton Harcourt. They had a son, Harcourt, and a daughter, Penelope; she was the maternal grandmother of the Oxford antiquary Anthony Wood, who preserved valuable family reminiscences of Richard Taverner. The latter died at Woodeaton on 14 July 1575 and was buried beside Margaret in the parish church there on 29 July. In his brief will (PRO, PROB 11/57, fol. 242r–v), drawn up on 15 June, he divided his lands into three parts and bequeathed a third each to his sons Peter and Edmond. The last third, not disposed of in the will, may have been intended for the eldest son, Richard, who, however, was only specifically left a gold chain, and was not made an executor—perhaps the two men had quarrelled. Two daughters were left sums of money, and a fourth son, John, was to have 'all my Lattin and Greek books'. Along with Peter and Edmund, John was both an executor and a residuary legatee.

The Taverners were a talented family. The eldest of Richard's younger brothers, **Roger Taverner** (d. 1572), surveyor and writer, is said by Wood to have studied at Cambridge, albeit without graduating. But this is not confirmed by university records. Probably in the 1540s he was made a surveyor for the court of augmentations, becoming Sir Francis Jobson's deputy, and was later employed in the same capacity by the exchequer until 1573. A number of his reports on crown woods survive (in BL, Lansdowne MSS 43, 56, 62). It may have been Jobson who secured Taverner's election to parliament in 1555 as a member for Newport iuxta Launceston, Cornwall. He wrote several tracts on economic issues, for instance 'Remedies … of derth of victualles' (Corpus Christi College, Cambridge, MS 376), whose dedication to Queen Elizabeth mentions a similar work sent to her two years previously. More influential, though unprinted, was his 'Arte of surveyinge' of 1565. He made his will on 6 January 1578, but it was not proved until 5 February 1582. With his wife, a member of the Hulcote family, he had three sons, one of whom, John, is reported by Wood to have also become a surveyor.

Another **John Taverner** (1584–1638), Church of England clergyman, was the second son of Richard's second son, Peter, who had established himself at Hexton, Hertfordshire. He was educated first at Westminster School and then at Trinity College, Cambridge, where he matriculated c.1597, became a scholar in 1599, graduated BA in 1602, and proceeded MA in 1605. He was incorporated at Oxford on 10 March 1606. He was secretary for nine years to John King, bishop of London between 1611 and 1621, and was also professor of music at Gresham College from 1610 to 1638; drafts of some of his lectures survive (as BL, Sloane MS 2329). Ordained deacon in London on 24 December 1620 and priest on 13 March 1625, in 1624 he became vicar of Tillingham, Essex, resigning that benefice in 1629 to become vicar of Hexton and rector of Stoke Newington. Still holding both livings he died between 26 and 29 August 1638 and was buried at Stoke Newington.

ANDREW W. TAYLOR

Sources Wood, *Ath. Oxon.*, new edn, 1.419–24 · Venn, *Alum. Cant.*, 1/4.202 · J. K. Yost, 'Taverner's use of Erasmus and the protestantization of English humanism', *Renaissance Quarterly*, 23 (1970), 266–76 · H. H. Hutson and H. R. Willoughby, 'The ignored Taverner Bible of 1539', *The Crozier Quarterly* (1939), 161–76 · E. J. Devereux, *Renaissance English translations of Erasmus* (1983) · G. R. Elton, *Reform and renewal* (1973) · J. K. McConica, *English humanists and reformation politics* (1965) · V. Westbrook, 'Richard Taverner revising Tyndale', *Reformation*, 2 (1997), 191–205 · R. Masters, *The history of the College of Corpus Christi and the B. Virgin Mary … in the University of Cambridge* (1753) · *DNB* · J. E. Mozley, *Coverdale and his bibles* (1953), appx 1 · C. C. Butterworth, *The English primers (1529–1545)* (1953) · L. E. C. Wooding, *Rethinking Catholicism in Reformation England* (2000) · *LP Henry VIII*, vols. 5–21 · HoP, *Commons, 1509–58*, 3.424–6 · will, PRO, PROB 11/57, fol. 242r–v

Archives BL, Lansdowne MS 43, 56 62, Roger Taverner's reports on crown woods [Roger Taverner] · BL, Sloane MS 2329, drafts of John Taverner's music lectures at Gresham College [John Taverner]

Wealth at death £300 to daughter Martha and £200 to daughter Penelope on their marriages: will, PRO, PROB 11/57, fol. 242r–v

Taverner, Roger (d. 1572). *See under* Taverner, Richard (1505?–1575).

Taverner, William (c.1677–1731), playwright, born in London, was descended from the Taverners of Hexton in Hertfordshire. His father was Jeremiah Taverner (b. 1651), a successful portrait painter in the late seventeenth and early eighteenth centuries, who was probably the same Jeremiah Taverner who married Elizabeth Needham in April 1676. Little is known of Taverner's early life except that he trained for a legal career in Doctors' Commons, where he became a proctor of the court of arches of Canterbury. Baker records that Taverner inherited his father's 'genius for painting, but never exercised it with a view to profit' (Baker, 1.704). Instead, while continuing to practise as a lawyer, Taverner began to write for the stage. His first work, a masque entitled *Ixion* (1697), was performed as part of Edward Ravenscroft's *The Italian Husband* at Lincoln's Inn Fields during the winter of 1697–8. Several years later Taverner produced his first full-length play, *The Faithful Bride of Granada*, which was staged at Drury Lane in the winter of 1703–4. This may have been followed by a comedy entitled *The Lunatick* (1705), which is sometimes attributed to Taverner on account of its similarity to his later work *The Female Advocates* (1713). *The Lunatick* was rejected by the actors at Lincoln's Inn Fields and consequently failed to reach the stage. Taverner's next comedy, *The Maid the Mistress*, met with a half-empty house at Drury Lane in June 1708, a failure which prompted the playwright to promise 'never … to bring again on the Stage any more of my Scribling' (Taverner, *Maid the Mistress*, 1708, sig. A3r).

After a gap of several years Taverner began work on *The Female Advocates, or, The Frantic Stock-Jobber*, recycling a number of incidents from *The Lunatick*. The finished comedy was staged at Drury Lane on 6 January 1713. In March 1716 Taverner produced a three-act farce entitled *Every Body Mistaken*, based on Shakespeare's *Comedy of Errors*. To this he affixed a masque, *Presumptuous Love*, set to music by William Turner. A third-night benefit performance of the two pieces at Lincoln's Inn Fields on 13 March 1716 earned Taverner over £75. As a result of this success, John Rich, the theatre manager at Lincoln's Inn Fields, afforded Taverner the luxury of new costumes for his next work, *The Artful Husband*, which premièred on 11 February 1717. The central episode of *The Artful Husband*, in which the heroine disguises herself as a man, then marries her guardian's widow in order to reclaim her stolen inheritance, is taken from *The Counterfeit Bridegroom* (1677), a comedy sometimes attributed to Thomas Betterton. Further incidents in Taverner's play are lifted from Shirley's *The Lady of Pleasure* (1635). Despite the extensive borrowing, *The Artful Husband* was a success. Taverner made over £84 from ticket sales on the third and sixth days of performance, but was denied a third benefit night by Rich. In the preface to the printed edition of *The Artful Husband* (1717), Taverner praises the actors but rails at what he terms 'a private Injustice from the Master of the House' (Taverner, *Artful Husband*, 1717, sig. A3v). On 3 December 1717 Taverner produced a sequel to his comedy, entitled *The Artful Wife*, which ran for three nights. A further comedy, *'Tis Well if it Takes*, was staged on 28 February 1719, and ran for five nights. Neither play matched the success of *The Artful Husband*, which was revived during the 1718–19 season, and again in 1721, when Taverner finally received the benefit night owing to him. Long after Taverner's death,

The Artful Husband was adapted by the elder George Colman and retitled *The Female Chevalier* (1778). Taverner's comedy also served as the basis for William Macready's *The Bank Note* (1795).

Aside from his work as a dramatist, little is known of Taverner's life. He continued to practise as a lawyer until his death on 8 January 1731 at his house in Doctors' Commons. A short obituary notice in the *Gentleman's Magazine* describes Taverner as a man 'remarkably honest in his business' (*GM*, 33). His widow, Alathea Taverner, whom he had married about 1702, took out letters of administration at the prerogative court of Canterbury on 6 February 1731. Their son, William *Taverner, inherited the family talent for painting and subsequently pursued a career as an artist. CHARLES BRAYNE

Sources D. E. Baker, *Biographia dramatica, or, A companion to the playhouse*, rev. I. Reed, new edn, rev. S. Jones, 1 (1812) • E. L. Avery, ed., *The London stage, 1660–1800*, pt 2: *1700–1729* (1960) • R. Clutterbuck, ed., *The history and antiquities of the county of Hertford*, 3 (1827) • J. E. Cussans, *History of Hertfordshire*, 2/1 (1874); facs. repr. (1972) • R. M. Glencross, ed., *A calendar of the marriage licence allegations in the registry of the bishop of London*, 2, British RS, 66 (1940) • E. W. White, *A register of first performances of English operas and semi-operas from the 16th century to 1980* (1983) • *GM*, 1st ser., 1 (1731), 33 • administration, PRO, PROB 6/107, fol. 40v

Wealth at death see will, PRO, PROB 6/107

Taverner, William (1700–1772), lawyer and landscape painter, was born on 25 November 1700 in London, and baptized the same day at St Martin Ludgate, the son of William *Taverner (*d.* 1731), lawyer and dramatist, and his wife, Alathea Taverner, and grandson of Jeremiah Taverner, portrait painter. He followed his father into the specialized profession of ecclesiastical law, becoming a public notary in 1737 and in 1739 proctor of the court of arches, the archbishop of Canterbury's court of appeal for the province of Canterbury. This court was based in Bow church, London, and Taverner appears to have spent the whole of his life in and near the capital. By 1733 he was already well known as a painter and was described by George Vertue as possessing 'a wonderfull genius to drawing of Landskap in an excellent manner adornd with figures in a stile above the common & paints in oil in a very commendable & masterly manner' (Vertue, *Note books*, 3.68).

Since he was not, like most professional landscape painters of the period, obliged to paint country house or estate views in order to earn a living, Taverner seems to have been free to experiment more widely than his contemporaries with subject matter and technique. Martin Hardie considered him to be 'our first regular and systematic painter of free landscape in watercolour' (Hardie, 1.69). It is not known who taught him the rudiments of painting, but the open, airy atmosphere and panoramic composition of some of his watercolours strongly suggest the influence of Peter Tillemans (*c*.1684–1734), who moved to London from Antwerp in 1708. It is also clear that Taverner's choice of landscape subjects (typically sandpits and woodland ponds in the vicinity of London), and their compositional structure, owe much to the Italianate paintings of Gaspard Dughet (1615–1675), whose work was widely collected in England throughout the eighteenth century. Taverner is unusual among early English watercolourists in his frequent introduction to his landscapes of groups of classically inspired figures. An example is the highly accomplished chalk, ink wash, and watercolour drawing *Diana and her Nymphs by a Woodland Pool* (with Agnews, London, 2003), one of several drawings of this subject, which belonged to the print dealer John Thane (1748–1818); it was engraved in 1780, after Taverner's death, by Thomas Gaugain (1748–1812). Taverner's Diana drawings may have been one source of inspiration for Thomas Gainsborough's notable series of drawings on the theme of Diana and Actaeon executed in the 1780s. In broader terms, Taverner's use of various combinations of chalks, ink, watercolour washes, and bodycolour to produce a generalized but imaginative form of landscape appears to have had an effect on Gainsborough's approach to the depiction of nature. Paul Sandby (1725–1809), who owned a number of drawings by Taverner, also owed a great deal to his example.

Taverner did not contribute to the public exhibitions organized by the Incorporated Society of Artists and the Society of Arts in the 1760s, or the Royal Academy exhibitions, inaugurated in 1769. He was also peculiarly reluctant to show his work to visitors to his own house. Despite (or perhaps in a perverse way, because of) this diffidence, his work was widely known and admired—the diarist Joseph Farington noted 'Taverner had much quaking abt. shewing his pictures, which raised their reputation' (Farington, *Diary*, 3.765).

Taverner the watercolourist is now reasonably well represented in public collections, his *Italian Composition: the Outskirts of a Town* (Tate collection), *Landscape with Nymphs Bathing* (Yale Center for British Art, New Haven), and *Country Road Leading to a Church* (British Museum, prints and drawings), for example, illustrating the range of his style and technique. His oils are rare: a *Wooded Landscape with Nymphs and Satyrs* (University of Liverpool) is close in style to the work of George Lambert; *Jonah and the Whale* (Stourhead) is after Gaspard Dughet. Other examples were evidently familiar to Colonel Maurice Grant, who described them as 'dignified canvases relieved from gloom by touches of smart and peculiar colour introduced here and there over the work' (Grant, 191). The sale held after Taverner's death (Langfords, Covent Garden, 21 February 1774) included oil studies of 'histories', heads, dogs, plants, and even 'hares, lions etc', showing him to have been a more diverse artist than the one we now know. The sale catalogue also reveals the breadth of his collection, which included prints after Marco Ricci, Raphael, Poussin, Claude, Domenichino, and Vouet, as well as a large number of engravings after Rubens—this enthusiasm being reflected in the eight landscape watercolours 'in the style of Rubens' by Taverner himself, which were also included in the sale. He is not known to have married. He left a bequest and all his personal effects to his servant Sarah Davis and died in London on 20 October 1772.

ANDREW WYLD and SUSAN SLOMAN

Sources Vertue, *Note books*, 3.68 • Farington, *Diary*, 3.765–6 • *Catalogue of the valuable collection of prints, drawings, and books of prints, of the late William Taverner, esq. … Mess. Langford's … Great Piazza, Covent Garden, 21 February 1774 and 4 following evenings* (1774) [copy in dept of prints and drawings, BM] • [A. French], *Gaspard Dughet called Gaspar Poussin, 1615–75* (1980) [exhibition catalogue, Kenwood House, London] • E. Einberg, *George Lambert* (1970) [exhibition catalogue, Iveagh Bequest, Kenwood, London] • A. Lyles and R. Hamlyn, *British watercolours from the Oppé collection* (1997) [exhibition catalogue, Tate Gallery, London, 10 Sept – 30 Nov 1997, and elsewhere] • M. Hardie, *The eighteenth century* (1966), vol. 1 of *Water-colour painting in Britain* • M. H. Grant, *A dictionary of British landscape painters, from the 16th century to the early 20th century* (1952) • A. Wilton, *British watercolours, 1750 to 1850* (1977) • artist's file, archive material, Courtauld Inst., Witt Library • *The art of Paul Sandby* (1985) [exhibition catalogue, Yale U. CBA, 10 April – 23 June 1985] • *GM*, 1st ser., 42 (1772), 496 • will, PRO, PROB 11/983, fols. 52r–52v

Wealth at death £2900 bank 3 per cent consolidated, annuities, collection of prints to be sold; left £2900 in trust for servant Sarah Davis to provide interest and income during her life, after her death the funds to be sold and monies arising to be paid to Amabella (or Annabella?) Taverner: will, PRO, PROB 11/983, fols. 52r–52v; *Catalogue*

Tawney, Richard Henry (1880–1962), historian and political thinker, was born on 30 November 1880 in Calcutta, the son of Charles Henry Tawney (1837–1922) and his wife, Constance Catherine Fox (*d.* 1920). His father was a notable Sanskrit scholar in the Indian education service and head of Presidency College in Calcutta. The family returned to England when Tawney was a young boy, settling in Weybridge, Surrey. Tawney was educated at Rugby School (1894–9) and Balliol College, Oxford (1899–1903). Though he became a noted critic of private education in later life and referred comparatively rarely to his formal schooling, there can be little doubt that these institutions were important in his development. His mature philosophy and commitments owed much to Rugby's distinctive traditions of broad-church Anglicanism, social activism, and high-mindedness. On his first day at school, waiting on the platform at Rugby railway station, he met his lifelong friend and coadjutor, William Temple, later archbishop of Canterbury. Tawney's headmaster, the Revd. John Percival, had been involved in establishing extramural education in the University of Oxford; Michael Sadler, another product of Rugby and Oxford, had turned university extension into a national educational movement. Tawney followed this path, linking the universities with the working class as a tutor for the Workers' Educational Association a generation later. At Balliol, Tawney read Greats and graduated with a second-class degree, much to the dismay of his father who described it as a disgrace. Edward Caird, the master of the college, suggested more charitably that, though Tawney's mind was chaotic, the examiners 'ought to have seen that it was the chaos of a great mind' (Ashton, 461–2).

Adult education Tawney was educated in the remarkable atmosphere that Benjamin Jowett and T. H. Green had created in Balliol and which Caird perpetuated. Philosophical idealism, the distinctive intellectual position that marked many Balliol men of this era, encouraged progressive Liberal politics and the determination to serve the community. It was said that some Balliol men 'went out east' in the service of the empire while others went to the East End of London. Tawney chose the latter course, leaving Oxford for Toynbee Hall, the university's settlement in Whitechapel, founded in the 1880s as a pioneering centre of civic leadership, Christian activism, and education in the slums of the capital. Tawney lived there for three years

Richard Henry Tawney (1880–1962), by John Mansbridge, 1953

with a close friend from Balliol, William Beveridge, whose research into the London labour market during this period laid the basis for his own career in the civil service and as architect of the welfare state. Tawney took a position as secretary of the Children's Country Holiday Fund which had been established by the warden of Toynbee Hall, the Revd Samuel Barnett, to take children out of the courts and alleys of the city. He began teaching adult education classes and, in 1905, joined the executive committee of the Workers' Educational Association (WEA), which had recently been established by Albert Mansbridge. Tawney discovered that education was more to his taste than good works: as he wrote to Beveridge in 1906, 'teaching economics in an industrial town is just what I want ultimately to do' (Tawney to Beveridge, 20 Sept 1906, BLPES, Beveridge papers).

After a two-year interlude (1906–8) as assistant lecturer in economics at Glasgow University, during which he also wrote editorials for the *Glasgow Herald*, Tawney was enabled to do just this when engaged jointly by the WEA and University of Oxford to teach the first adult tutorial classes. It was as a full-time tutor in university adult education between 1908 and 1914 that Tawney laid down many of the bases of his subsequent career: his focus on economic history, attachment to working people, commitment to socialism, and advocacy of universal education. Tutorial classes were designed to take working-class men and women whose income and circumstances prevented them from studying at a university through a rigorous course of study over three years. Tutors were suggested by the universities but chosen by the classes themselves, and class members also advised on the subjects to be studied. Tawney later referred to these arrangements as 'an experiment in democratic education' (*Political Quarterly*, May 1914) and he was instinctively suited to the type of collaborative learning that the WEA promoted.

Tawney's first classes at Rochdale in Lancashire and Longton in the Potteries of north Staffordshire, starting in early 1908, set the pattern and quickly assumed an almost legendary status. They were on the economic history of the eighteenth century and he set out to explain to his students how the industries in which they worked and the communities in which they lived had emerged. He inspired his students, keeping them up to the rigorous academic standards he expected, and his natural capacity for fellowship won him many admirers and wider recognition in the communities in which he taught. E. S. Cartwright, the class secretary at Longton, and A. P. Wadsworth, the youngest member of the class in Rochdale and later an editor of the *Manchester Guardian*, became Tawney's lifelong friends. He went on to teach in other locations including Chesterfield, Littleborough, and Wrexham, before scaling back his teaching commitments on his appointment in 1912 as director of the Ratan Tata Foundation, established in association with the London School of Economics (LSE) by an Indian businessman, to 'promote the study and further the knowledge of methods of preventing and relieving poverty and destitution'. Tawney recruited other WEA tutors to help in this research; he himself published in 1914 and 1915 two important studies on the establishment of minimum rates in the chain-making and tailoring industries under the terms of the 1909 Trade Boards Act.

On 28 June 1909 Tawney married Annette Jeanie (Jeannette) Beveridge (*d*. 1958), William Beveridge's younger sister and the daughter of Henry Beveridge, a judge in the Indian Civil Service, and his second wife, Annette Susannah Ackroyd. Their wedding at Shottermill, near Haslemere, Surrey, was a WEA occasion. William Temple, the organization's president, and Samuel Barnett officiated; the treasurer, Tawney's friend from Toynbee Hall, T. Edmund Harvey, was best man; and Albert Mansbridge looked on.

Evolution of a socialist In the years immediately preceding the First World War, Tawney kept an occasional diary, published posthumously as his *Commonplace Book*, which illuminates the development of his social thought in this formative period. Alongside details of his students' wages, piece-rates, and household budgets, Tawney focused on two issues: the nature of social equality and the means by which to achieve a socialist transformation. Though he had joined the Fabian Society in 1906, Tawney here took issue with the characteristic Fabian strategy of permeating the institutions of the state and using them as instruments in the construction of a socialist society. Though he later advocated wholesale nationalization of the most important sectors of British industry as a vital preliminary step towards socialism, at this stage Tawney placed a higher value on moral and spiritual transformation: only by recognizing 'the industrial problem' as a 'moral problem' and working to instil a 'moral ideal' in society by education among other means, could a better society be created (*Tawney's Commonplace Book*, 9, 12, 46, 66, 76). Fabianism might promote social legislation or the refinement of public administration, intending thereby to establish collectivist policies through control of the central state. But without popular understanding of and commitment to the principles of reform, legislation and bureaucracy were likely to be hollow and ineffective. Laws had to embody the moral inspiration of society. True socialism, to Tawney, depended on changing human hearts and the collective consciousness. Tawney was no sentimentalist: he never recoiled from the difficult and tedious business of institutional analysis and reform, nor preached a philosophy limited to purely personal conduct. Nevertheless, throughout his life he believed that socialism depended on ethical behaviour: he set an example of righteous conduct and strove through public actions and writing to instil the values of a just and fair society.

Equality was such a value, and in the *Commonplace Book* Tawney explained his commitment to it as a corollary of his Christian faith: if men and women were equal in the sight of God, so they must be treated as of equal worth in their dealings with each other. Any social system which discriminated against some of its members, or which allowed some people to be used as a means to others' ends, or which obscured common humanity by emphasizing the differences between people, was immoral (*Tawney's Commonplace Book*, 53-4, 67-8). Tawney found many further reasons to justify social equality, but his fundamental premise was a Christian one. Indeed, Christianity was the most powerful source for his social philosophy at every stage of his life. He thought and wrote little about theology—his faith was essentially simple and profound—but he held to a social Christianity which mandated, in his view, that the churches involve themselves powerfully and constantly in economic and social affairs. He termed modern capitalism 'anti-Christian'; to explain, as a historian, how this had come to pass and to change economic behaviour so that it might once more embody Christian teaching were dual aims of his academic and political careers. In light of his Christian inspiration, distrust of the state, and emphasis on individual morality, it is not difficult to appreciate why Tawney was untouched by Marxism or other varieties of theoretical socialism. Socialism, in his view, would be the willed creation of men and women rather than the product of historical necessity ('British socialism today', in R. H. Tawney, *The Radical Tradition*, ed. R. Hinden, 1964, 170). Marxism may have influenced a younger generation of intellectuals in the 1930s but Tawney was formed in an Edwardian labour movement with purely indigenous roots that was distant from and often suspicious of continental socialism.

Wartime soldiering and post-war reconstruction Aged thirty-four, Tawney volunteered in November 1914 for the army. He declined a commission and joined the 22nd Manchester regiment: he had lived in the city since his marriage in 1909. He believed sincerely that 'Prussianism' had to be fought, but he was probably also impelled to enlist from a sense of solidarity with the working-class men whom he had come to know and who formed the mass of the British army. He rose to the rank of sergeant. Though his fellow soldiers did not share the intellectual tastes and aspirations of his former students, and showed him a quite different aspect of working-class life and attitudes, he never wavered in his respect for their decency. Tawney was wounded severely in the chest and abdomen by machine-gun bullets at Fricourt on 1 July 1916, the first day of the Somme offensive. He lay in no man's land for many hours until carried back to British lines. He lived with pain and discomfort for the rest of his life. Out of 820 men in Tawney's company who attacked that morning, there were 450 casualties on the first day alone, and only 54 were left unscathed several days later. While convalescing in a temporary military hospital in Oxford, and later at the home of his mentor and friend Bishop Charles Gore, Tawney published an account of these events under the title 'The attack' in the *Westminster Gazette*, all the more shocking for its understatement. Subsequent 'Reflections of a soldier' published a few weeks later in *The Nation* were more acerbic, developing two themes made famous by the poets of the First World War: that the soldiers sympathized with their German adversaries and that they resented bitterly the false images of the war fed to non-combatants at home. Yet, paradoxically, the war altered little for him: his faith in God and man remained intact.

Once recovered, Tawney threw himself into political and educational work. He argued that the war could be won only if the energies of the people were unlocked by a true democratization of British politics and society. He also worked to ensure that the sacrifices of the war might be offset by lasting social advance. He was a member of the Ministry of Reconstruction's adult education committee, and largely wrote its compendious report on the future development of adult education, known to the movement itself as the '1918 report'. The committee's interim report, which he also wrote, was a remarkable assault on the physical, moral, and spiritual deprivation of working people caused by the nature of the economic system. He also contributed to the Church of England's report 'Christianity and industrial problems' (1918). And he was active in the movement for general educational advance that encouraged passage of the Education Act of 1918. Indeed, Tawney had a role in all the great educational legislation of the subsequent period. As a member of the Board of Education consultative committee from 1912 to 1931 he contributed to its report *The Education of the Adolescent* (1926)—the Hadow report—which laid down the principles later embodied in the Education Act of 1944. He was consulted by the minister for education, R. A. Butler, when that measure was being framed. As a member of the Labour Party's advisory committee on education from its creation in 1918 Tawney wrote its famous pamphlet *Secondary Education for All* (1922). For four decades he also contributed dozens of articles and editorials on education to the *Manchester Guardian* and other newspapers and journals.

At the end of the First World War, Tawney was briefly employed by the WEA as a resident tutor in north Staffordshire, teaching and organizing classes there. But two events at this time—his membership of the royal (Sankey) commission of inquiry into the coalmining industry in 1919 and his appointment to the staff of the London School of Economics (LSE) in 1920 established his new position in society. His sharp questioning of witnesses before the commission, especially the mine owners, and his mastery of the details of the industry brought him to national attention and consolidated his position within the labour movement. He had already contested Rochdale for the Labour Party in the 'coupon election' of 1918. Unsuccessful there, he was also defeated when he stood at Tottenham South (1922) and at Swindon (1924) as a Labour candidate. His services to the party were thus of a more intellectual kind as an adviser, draftsman, and propagandist. He wrote the important 1928 policy statement *Labour and the Nation*, and the 1934 document *For Socialism and Peace*. He also published one of the most effective criticisms of the party's failings in government in his essay 'The choice before the Labour Party' (1934). Here, and in other statements and actions, he made his distaste for Ramsay MacDonald's leadership of the party and betrayal in 1931 abundantly clear. His curt, written response when MacDonald offered him a peerage in 1933—'What harm have I ever done to the Labour Party?'—has passed into Labour legend. He remained a Labour loyalist throughout, as prepared to attend ward meetings of his local party as to advise on national policy.

The Acquisitive Society and Equality At the London School of Economics, where he became a reader in 1923 and professor of economic history in 1931, Tawney built a reputation as the leading economic historian of his generation. He was a founder of the Economic History Society in 1926 and of its journal the *Economic History Review*, which he co-edited between 1927 and 1934. His postgraduate seminar 'Economic and social England, 1558–1640' attracted and trained some of the best historians of the future. His collaboration with Eileen Power, another pioneering economic historian with whom he edited a volume of *Tudor Economic Documents* in 1924, was especially creative.

Tawney was at his most productive and effective in the 1920s. The three books he wrote in this decade, *The Acquisitive Society* (1921), *Religion and the Rise of Capitalism* (1926)—perhaps the most popular and influential history book published between the wars—and *Equality* (1931) are generally considered to be his most important publications, though an equal case could be made for some of his social and political essays, collected in two volumes entitled *The Attack and other Papers* (1953) and *The Radical Tradition* (1964), whose immediacy and directness have not faded over time.

Tawney's assault on the acquisitive society probably owed something to his confrontation with the coal owners, a particularly unattractive group of capitalists, on the Sankey commission. The book focused on two ideas, economic function and economic purpose. Tawney argued that any and every economic enterprise should function for the benefit of the community and fulfil a socially useful purpose. By these tests, however, contemporary capitalist society was failing: too many of its enterprises were designed for the acquisition of wealth for its own sake or for the sake of an owning class at the expense of the majority. Tawney called for a reordering of the economy to meet collective needs and for a reordering of human values that would make economic activity a means to life rather than an end in itself. He also called for a resurrection of 'the peculiar and distinctive Christian standard of social conduct' (*The Acquisitive Society*, 228). The book's conclusion, criticizing the reluctance of the church to engage in discussion of the morality of economic and social behaviour, thus pointed forward to Tawney's subsequent historical study of the church's abdication 'of one whole department of life' in *Religion and the Rise of Capitalism*.

Equality, published a decade later, and based on his Halley Stewart lectures of 1929, was a more contextualized study in which details of the social conditions and arrangements of inter-war Britain were deployed by Tawney in making a case for wholesale social reform. An unequal society misapplied resources to the comfort and privileges of the few when the many required better homes, schools, and hospitals. It failed to develop the talents and skills of the population: thus inequality limited the productive capacity of society. It protected powerful vested interests, whose perpetuation was an affront to a true democracy; and it encouraged social and class divisions, limiting what might be achieved in a society and economy organized on the principle of co-operative effort. Tawney was less interested in achieving an equality of income than in ending the advantages and privileges of a social élite. His aim was an equality of 'environment, and circumstance, and opportunity' (4th edn, 1952, 56) and his primary concern was to make a case for institutional reform. A civilized society was marked by its determination to eliminate inequalities arising from its own organization. As desirable in themselves and as the means to the elimination of privilege, Tawney called for progressive taxation to fund communal services in health, education, and welfare. Private schools should be opened up to all children; a national investment board would plan and direct the British economy; the major industries and services would be transferred to public ownership; and in the new nationalized enterprises the workers themselves would play a managerial role. Tawney even discussed the form of bureaucracy required for directing a centralized and socialized state.

As this may suggest, *Equality* was an important milestone in the development of socialist thinking in Britain and a prescient guide to the intentions and achievements of the Labour governments after 1945. But Tawney's focus on the particular weakened the book as a more general, philosophical discussion of equality, and as a lasting contribution in the history of political thought. There is relatively little discussion of equality itself: Tawney largely ignored the categories of civil and legal equality which had been so central to the history of the preceding liberal age. He wrote for an audience in agreement with his programme for social equality and did not attempt to present counter-arguments to this as fully and fairly as might be expected if *Equality* was to have been something more than the presentation of a single case related to a specific society at a particular moment. Tawney's passionate moralism and his emphasis on selfless fellowship cannot fail to move and inspire readers. But some of his prescriptions, including, for example, his opposition to the practice of inheritance, whether of small or large fortunes, betrayed a blindness to aspects of human psychology whether in the rich or the humble. The great political thinkers have generally started from a theory of human behaviour and a realistic appreciation of human motives, needs, and frailties, and have built their models on this basis. As the later critic Raymond Williams, who came from the same educational and political traditions as Tawney, pointed out, he assumed that men and women could be persuaded to see the world through his eyes and would comply with his principles for moral reformation. The assumption, as Williams noted, was an indication of Tawney's limitations as a political thinker.

Economic history: the rise of capitalism Tawney asked questions of history in order to understand the present. As he explained in his inaugural lecture at the LSE, he had 'found the world surprising' and 'turned to history to interpret it' ('The study of economic history' in *History and Society: Essays by R. H. Tawney*, ed. J. M. Winter, 1978, 48). In particular he turned to the so-called 'transition from feudalism to capitalism' in the early modern period and made the decades between the Reformation and the English civil war into 'Tawney's century' as he sought to explain how modern capitalism emerged in Britain. He made three signal contributions to the study of this subject: an early analysis of the commercialization of agriculture; a study of the relation between capitalism and religious thought; and a structural analysis of social change before the civil war, focusing on the rise of the gentry.

Tawney's first history book was written as a text for his WEA classes. *The Agrarian Problem in the Sixteenth Century* (1912) was the first detailed discussion of changes on the land and to social relations as agriculture shifted from subsistence farming on open fields to commercial farming based on enclosures, and as rural social structure changed in turn from a society of peasants and landlords to the pattern of landholders, tenant farmers, and landless labourers which had emerged by the eighteenth century. There can be little doubt that he disapproved of these changes. He explained them by reference to the growth of a market economy impelled by urbanization; the effects of inflation, which caused landlords to alter traditional forms of landholding; and the more aggressive exploitation of estates, particularly by a new class of landowner created by the sale of church property at the Reformation. Local magnates stood to gain from these changes and encouraged them; Tudor and Stuart monarchs, seeking social stability, tried to mitigate their effects. But during the 1640s, with the monarchy gone, the peasantry were subjected to the full rigour of capitalist transformation; evictions and enclosures followed and the material basis was laid for a subsequent age dominated by great landholders. Much of this interpretation is open to question; subsequent research has pointed to factors such as population growth which Tawney largely ignored. Nevertheless, he raised a set of issues linking together economic, social, and political change which have remained current to this day.

Having described and explained what occurred, in his next great study, *Religion and the Rise of Capitalism*, which grew out of the Holland memorial lectures which he delivered in 1922, Tawney set out to explain the great shifts in attitude towards economic behaviour in this period which not only made these changes possible but also legitimated them. Tawney's book is often set beside Weber's classic essay *The Protestant Ethic and the Spirit of Capitalism* in something known as the 'Weber–Tawney thesis' on the origins of capitalism. But they were investigating quite different things. Weber wished to understand the effects of reformed religion on the inner life, motives, and economic behaviour of individuals—to explain the role of religious ideas in the formation of a capitalistic personality—whereas Tawney wanted to study a broad transformation in social ethics, the slow retreat over centuries of a Christian social tradition. Medieval Christianity had never doubted its obligation to define appropriate economic morality; why, then, did modern Christianity ignore the question entirely, as Tawney saw it? According

to Tawney, 'the capitalist spirit' was 'as old as history' and was not the product of the Reformation (pp. 226–7). Rather, protestantism, and Calvinism in particular, had replaced social solidarity with individualism, and encouraged the separation of economic from ethical interests. The quest for material gain thus became the central and sanctioned mission of life, rather than one aspect of wider obligations and responsibilities. However, if Christian social ethics had changed for the worse at the Reformation, they might be reinvigorated and applied effectively in the twentieth century. Tawney's historical study of attitudinal change was designed to show that things were not always thus: there was no reason why the modern church should not take a stand on economic morality and social organization.

Tawney's third contribution to early modern history was to set out a theory of social change in two essays of the early 1940s, 'Harrington's interpretation of his age' and 'The rise of the gentry', on which generations of undergraduates have since cut their teeth, for they gave rise to a spirited, indeed virulent, post-war academic controversy. These essays explained political conflict, indeed the civil war itself, in terms of the changing distribution of property and power in the preceding century. They were linked directly to Tawney's earlier work for they proposed that an emergent gentry class, who bought up church lands in the 1530s and 1540s and who took advantage of the profits of commercial agriculture, rose to challenge the social pre-eminence of a less dynamic aristocracy. Tawney offered a new interpretation of the origins of the English revolution based on this conflict of classes. But he owed little to Marxism in this. He had never subscribed to Marxist theory or politics, and if other socialist intellectuals of the age saw the Soviet Union as an example to applaud and emulate, Tawney was unimpressed. These structural theories of social change emerged naturally from his own work and thought. Some of Tawney's critics developed wholly legitimate counter-arguments based on historical evidence; but others seem to have challenged his conclusions because they appeared close in spirit to a strictly materialist theory of history. Tawney offered a brief 'postscript' to his views in 1954 but largely ignored the controversy. Believing that historians should stimulate debate by developing new and challenging theories, he saw little need to defend original ideas offered in the true spirit of open enquiry.

Tawney's final historical work, published close to the end of his life in 1958, was a study of the Jacobean trader, financier, and politician Lionel Cranfield, earl of Middlesex and lord high treasurer. In so far as this monograph, entitled *Business and Politics under James I*, drew on many of the themes Tawney had already developed in his work and offered a detailed example of an individual career set within the new capitalist economy, it was some sort of ending to his historical interests. But it was not the great work that Tawney had hoped to produce in his retirement and his friends and colleagues had encouraged him to write: a grand synthesis of the seventeenth century, based on his lectures at the LSE, was never completed. Nevertheless, the close relation of the different parts to the whole is a very evident aspect of Tawney's historical writing. And this historical corpus was intimately related to Tawney's social and religious commitments. Few public intellectuals have produced a body of work focused so effectively on a range of interlocking issues and questions as Tawney—and few have written in a comparable style. Tawney's writing was aphoristic, pungent, and ironic, redolent with biblical quotations and classical allusions. He could sweep the reader up in his impassioned sentences, though dense and complex syntax could also obscure and confuse.

Later interests and honours Tawney's historical interest in agrarian economic and social structure led to an interest in China in the early 1930s. He made two visits there, the second, lasting for several months, as an educational adviser to the League of Nations. The trips resulted in Tawney's neglected classic *Land and Labour in China* (1932), focusing on the crucial issue that the nationalist regime failed to address: land reform. After the enormous creativity of the 1920s, the 1930s were for Tawney, as for so many others, a decade of disillusion: it was impossible to ignore the failings and divisions of the Labour Party in the early years and the growing international crisis at the decade's end. But he became a mentor to the next generation of Labour leaders, among them Hugh Gaitskell and Evan Durbin, who were encouraged by Tawney to think afresh about the party's direction and policies.

When the Second World War came, Tawney made several contributions including joining the Home Guard. His famous essay 'Why we fight', published in the summer of 1940 in the *New York Times* and articulating the stoical convictions of the British people at that moment, deserves to be anthologized in every volume of war literature. As in 1917–18, Tawney was alive to the opportunity for social renewal in wartime and alongside his promotion of educational advance he articulated an agenda of social reforms for the Labour Party, captured in his essay 'We mean freedom' (1944). He also spent a year in the British embassy in Washington, DC, in 1941–2 as labour attaché. Britain's dependence on American war production made it advisable to send over someone who might win the trust of American workers and advise on American labour questions. Tawney had visited America already: he was invited on several occasions through his career to teach and lecture at the University of Chicago. Though he never warmed to such a material civilization, he nevertheless knew enough about the United States to be useful. Working from a hut in the embassy grounds, he wrote several briefing papers, one of which, published posthumously as *The American Labour Movement* (1979), was an insightful history of the institutions of the American working class. Tawney was also on hand to assist the British ambassador, Lord Halifax, in calming diplomatic waters when a fraternal visit by the general secretary of the Trades Union Congress, Walter Citrine, led to friction between the two American trade union conglomerations, the American

Federation of Labor and the Congress of Industrial Organizations. The irony of Tawney's collaboration with a leading Conservative politician and arch 'appeaser' in silencing the voice of British trade unionism was not lost on him.

Tawney retired as president of the WEA in 1943 after fifteen years in the position. There followed five years as a member of the University Grants Committee, charged with distributing public funds to British universities. He retired from the LSE in 1949 but, being Tawney, remained active in many different political and scholarly organizations, all the time compiling the material for his final book on Cranfield. He also began research for a biography of his friend Sidney Webb at the request of the Webb trustees. But he gave up the project in understandable anger and frustration in summer 1949 on learning that Margaret Cole, herself a member of the trust, was already at work on a study of the Webbs, later published as *The Webbs and their Work* (Terrill, 77–8). He was honoured by several universities including, in chronological order, Manchester, Chicago, Paris, Oxford, Birmingham, London, Sheffield, Melbourne, and Glasgow, and several learned societies including the British Academy. He was briefly a fellow of Balliol at the end of the First World War (1918–21) and was elected an honorary fellow of the college in 1938.

Tawney and his legacy Tawney was known to some intimates as Harry but to the rest of the world he was just Tawney. He was of above average height. His 'massive, magnificent head on top of a clumsy body' gave him, in the description of the Labour minister Richard Crossman, 'the look of a great benign sea lion' (Crossman, 'Passionate prophet'). He lost his hair in early middle age and is characteristically remembered leaning back in his chair with spectacles pushed up and perching precariously on his great bald skull. He wore a moustache throughout his life. He was notoriously untidy—his desk was always awash with papers, books, and the paraphernalia of a habitual pipe-smoker—and comically shabby; many a respectable interlocutor was caught out because of that shabbiness. Tawney used to pad around his home in Mecklenburgh Square in Bloomsbury, London, in carpet slippers and his old khaki sergeant's tunic from the First World War. He described himself as 'a displaced peasant' and in middle and later life spent considerable periods at his home, Rose Cottage, in Elcombe, near Stroud, Gloucestershire, where he enjoyed fishing, walking, and drinking with the locals.

Though it is difficult to be precise, Tawney's marriage does not seem to have fulfilled him. There were no children; Jeannette was often ill; her behaviour could be eccentric; and her disorganization coupled to Tawney's untidiness rendered home life chaotic. Tawney was always generous with money, writing cheques and remitting fees to the WEA whenever he could; Jeannette, meanwhile, was profligate in her many purchases of expensive trifles. In consequence the couple were often short of money and Tawney lived in straitened circumstances at the end of his life. The one woman whom he evidently admired and possibly loved was the clever and beautiful Eileen Power—

though their relationship, if very close, was never more than that between colleagues. Her early and sudden death in 1940 affected him deeply.

Tawney's wife died in 1958. On the occasion of his eightieth birthday, in 1960, his many friends and admirers organized a dinner in his honour at the House of Commons and, for the occasion, produced a brief and affectionate biography, *R. H. Tawney: a Portrait by Several Hands* (the most active of which belonged to Richard Titmuss, his younger colleague at the LSE). In 1961 a Festschrift appeared, *Essays in the Economic and Social History of Tudor and Stuart England*, edited by F. J. Fisher and including pieces by former pupils and academic admirers including Christopher Hill, Joan Thirsk, Lawrence Stone, and Gerald Aylmer. Tawney was now in physical decline. Early in 1962 he was moved to a nursing home at 16 Fitzroy Square, Bloomsbury, and he died there a few days later on 16 January 1962. He was buried beside his wife at Highgate. The address at his memorial service, in St Martin-in-the-Fields on 8 February following, was delivered by the then leader of the Labour Party, Hugh Gaitskell, who described Tawney as 'the best man I have ever known'. In his will, after a few personal gifts and the bequest of his papers to the LSE, Tawney left the balance of his estate, a comparatively modest £7000 or so, to his beloved WEA, which had always had the first claim on his time and affections.

The influence of other socialist thinkers of this era like Harold Laski, G. D. H. Cole, and Sidney and Beatrice Webb has faded since their deaths. But Tawney remains a living presence. So important is he to socialist and progressive politics in Britain that the formation of the Social Democratic Party as a centrist breakaway from the Labour Party in 1981–2 led to a public debate on his political legacy when the new party chose to call its policy forum the Tawney Society. Participants included the former Labour minister Shirley Williams and the author of Labour's election manifesto of 1945, Michael Young, against the socialist historian and polemicist Raphael Samuel and the then leader of the Labour Party, Michael Foot. Tawney reflexively sided with working people and the trade union movement throughout his life and the attempt to appropriate him by moderate Social Democrats was doomed to fail. Without doubt he was a socialist and Labour man to his core, though one who believed in a party and movement that encouraged democratic participation and open debate. For this reason, though references to Tawney's impact and influence are common in the contemporary Labour Party, it is not evident that the party's centralized discipline and consistent resort to legislative and bureaucratic action in the 1990s and beyond would have met with his favour.

Tawney was the most representative of Labour's twentieth-century intellectuals. His life spanned the origins, rise, and consolidation of the Labour Party almost exactly. He was educated in late Victorian idealist ethics which provided a philosophical basis for the transition from individualism to collectivism. His religious faith linked him to earlier and continuing traditions of Christian socialism in Britain. His democratic spirit evoked the nineteenth-century struggles of working people to secure the franchise. His experience in workers' education gave him intimate knowledge of the working class so that, unlike other intellectuals, he knew the people he spoke for and led. His aversion to the spiritual void in industrial capitalism echoed the formative influence of Ruskin over the British labour movement. His love of fellowship and his faith in the fundamental decency of men and women is reminiscent of William Morris. He takes his place with the many historians, from Thomas Carlyle to E. P. Thompson, who have had such influence over the imagination and political commitment of the British left, a movement whose inspiration has generally come from the past. Tawney synthesized all these elements into an ethical socialism that should be accounted the distinctive British contribution to the wider history of socialism itself.

LAWRENCE GOLDMAN

Sources R. Terrill, *R. H. Tawney and his times: socialism as fellowship* (Cambridge, MA, 1973) · A. Wright, *R. H. Tawney* (1987) · J. M. Winter, 'R. H. Tawney as historian', *History and society: essays by R. H. Tawney*, ed. J. M. Winter (1978) [ed. with an introduction by J. M. Winter] · J. M. Winter, 'R. H. Tawney's early political thought', *Past and Present*, 47 (1970), 71–96 · J. M. Winter, 'A bibliography of the published writings of R. H. Tawney', *Economic History Review*, 2nd ser., 25 (1972) · [J. R. Williams, R. M. Titmuss, and F. J. Fisher], *R. H. Tawney: a portrait by several hands* (privately printed, London, 1960) · T. S. Ashton, 'Richard Henry Tawney, 1880–1962', *PBA*, 48 (1962) · *R. H. Tawney's commonplace book*, ed. J. M. Winter and D. M. Joslin (1972) · M. Berg, *A woman in history: Eileen Power, 1889–1940* (1996) · R. Williams, *Culture and society, 1780–1950* (1961) · L. Goldman, *Dons and workers: Oxford and adult education since 1850* (1995) · F. J. Fisher, ed., *Essays in the economic and social history of Tudor and Stuart England: in honour of R. H. Tawney* (1961) · A. H. Halsey and N. Dennis, *English ethical socialism: Thomas More to R. H. Tawney* (1988) · D. Ormrod, 'R. H. Tawney and the origins of capitalism', *History Workshop Journal*, 18 (autumn 1984), 138–59 · S. Williams, *Politics is for people* (1981) · M. Foot, 'My kind of socialism', *The Observer* (10 Jan 1982) · R. Samuel, 'The SDP's escape from the Christian heritage of socialism', *The Guardian* (29 March 1982); (5 April 1982) · M. Young, 'Why the SDP are the true inheritors of Tawney's libertarian legacy', *The Guardian* (10 May 1982) · R . Crossman, 'An anthology of Tawney', *New Statesman* (26 Nov 1960) · R. Crossman, 'Passionate prophet', *Daily Herald* (30 Nov 1960) · D. Marquand, 'R. H. Tawney: prophet of equality', *The Guardian* (26 Nov 1960) · 'The caravan', *Highway*, 1 (1909), 164

Archives BLPES, corresp. and papers · U. Lond., Institute of Education, papers relating to educational reform, DC/TY · University of York, corresp. and papers | BL, corresp. with Albert Mansbridge, Add. MSS 65257A, 65258 · BL OIOC, letters to Sir Richard Denman, MS Eur. C 176 · BLPES, Beveridge papers, corresp. with Beveridge family · BLPES, collections relating to the coal industry · BLPES, letters to Brian Pearce · Bodl. Oxf., letters to John Hammond · Bodl. Oxf., corresp. with Gilbert Murray · Bodl. RH, Creech Jones collection · JRL, letters to *Manchester Guardian* · London Metropolitan University, TUC collections, papers relating to the Workers' Education Association · NL Wales, corresp. with Thomas Jones · U. Cam., Marshall Library of Economics, letters to John Maynard Keynes · U. Warwick Mod. RC, notes and comments relating to *A new statement of socialist principles* | SOUND BL NSA, 'A portrait of R. H. Tawney', BBC Third Programme, 1963, NP789R

Likenesses J. Mansbridge, drawing, 1953, NPG [see illus.] · C. Rogers, oils (on his seventieth birthday), London School of Economics · Vicky, sketch drawing, London School of Economics; repro. in Crossman, 'An anthology of Tawney'

Wealth at death £7096 19s. 10d.: probate, 6 April 1962, CGPLA Eng. & Wales

Taxster [Tayster], **John of** (*fl.* **1244**–*c.***1270**), Benedictine monk and chronicler, took the habit at Bury St Edmunds, Suffolk, on the feast of St Edmund (20 November), 1244—a fact recorded in the chronicle composed at Bury *c.*1265. This chronicle, which covers the period from the creation of the world to 1265, survives in two fair copies, BL, Cotton MS Julius AI, written *c.*1270, and London, College of Arms, Arundel MS 6, written in the last half of the fourteenth century. (Since Arundel 6 almost certainly descends directly from Julius AI, it cannot be regarded as an independent authority.) In the annal for 1244 the Cotton manuscript of the chronicle records 'hoc anno scriptor presentis voluminis habitum suscepit monachicum dictus I. de Taxst' [Tayster in Arundel 6] die sancti Edmundi'. Taxster, therefore, was the scribe of Julius AI, and the fact that he made several marginal additions (that is, of the names of ten of the popes and five passages, one of nearly a hundred words), all of which are in the text of Arundel 6, justifies the common assumption that Taxster, as well as being the scribe of Julius AI, himself composed the chronicle.

Taxster was a man of some learning. The chronicle includes allusions to, and citations from, a number of late Roman writers (Apuleius's *De Deo Socratis*, Aulus Gellius's *Noctes Atticae*, Justin's epitome of Trogus Pompeius, and Eutropius's *Historia miscella*), while its early Christian sources include St Jerome's translation of Eusebius's chronicle, St Augustine's *Confessions* and *City of God*, Orosius's *Historia* and Boethius's *De consolatione philosophiae*. For the medieval period Taxster used a wide variety of standard histories and chronicles, most of them of English provenance. However, his main source to 1131 was the chronicle of John of Worcester. He probably used the Bury copy of the latter, now Bodl. Oxf., MS Bodley 297. It was owing to the influence of John's chronicle that he adopted the practice of giving each annal alternative dates, according to the evangelists and according to Dionysius. Taxster's next main source was Ralph de Diceto, and then, for King John's reign, a chronicle compiled at Bury, the so-called *Annales sancti Edmundi*. Since the only known copy of the *Annales* (BL, Harley MS 447) ends incomplete in the annal for 1212, it is impossible to be certain when Taxster stopped using them.

From 1212 Taxster's chronicle is independent of all known chronicles. Until 1264 the annals are brief and mainly of value for the entries concerning the abbey's history, but the annals for 1264 and 1265 are detailed, and a valuable source for the barons' war. Taxster's sympathies, like those of nearly all chroniclers of the period, are with the baronial opposition to Henry III. For example, he records that after the death of the baronial leader, Simon de Montfort, at the battle of Evesham (1265) his body worked miracles. This notice is in Arundel 6, but has been erased from Julius AI, possibly in response to the dictum of Kenilworth (1266), chapter 8, which prohibited Montfort's cult. Taxster's chronicle has historiographic importance because a revised version formed the starting point for two continuations, to 1296 and 1301 respectively, both valuable sources for Edward I's reign. The revised version of Taxster's chronicle and its continuation to 1296, used to be attributed to John Everden, and was borrowed from by chroniclers in a number of other monasteries, most of them in East Anglia. It was this revised version and not, as Luard supposed, Taxster's chronicle itself, which was used at Norwich by Bartholomew Cotton (*d.* 1321/2) for the annals 1258–63 in his chronicle.

ANTONIA GRANSDEN

Sources A. Gransden, ed. and trans., *The chronicle of Bury St Edmunds, 1212–1301* [1964], xvi–xx, xxiii, xxxv, xxxviii, 13n. • R. Pauli and F. Liebermann, eds., [*Ex rerum Anglicarum scriptoribus*], MGH Scriptores [folio], 28 (Stuttgart, 1888), 584ff. • F. Liebermann, ed., *Ungedruckte anglo-normannische Geschichtsquellen* (1879), 102–7 • E. Clarke, *Bury chroniclers in the thirteenth century* (1905), 4–5, 8 • A. Gransden, 'A critical edition of the Bury St. Edmund Chronicle in Arundel MS 30 (College of Arms)', PhD diss., U. Lond., 1956 • *Bartholomaei de Cotton … Historia Anglicana*, ed. H. R. Luard, Rolls Series, 16 (1859), lii–liv • A. G. Watson, *Catalogue of dated and datable manuscripts, c.700–1600, in the department of manuscripts, the British Library*, 2 vols. (1979), vol. 1, p. 103; vol. 2, pl. 158 • A. Gransden, *Historical writing in England*, 1 (1974), 1.395–6, 401, 407 (n. 24), pl. XIa • BL, Cotton MS Julius A.I
Archives BL, Cotton MS Julius A.I • Coll. Arms, chronicle, Arundel MS 6

Tayler, Charles Benjamin (1797–1875), Church of England clergyman and writer for the young, son of John Tayler, was born at Leytonstone, Essex. He was educated at Guildford under the Revd William Hodgson Cole, and entered Trinity College, Cambridge, as a fellow commoner on 23 October 1815, graduating BA in 1819 and MA in 1822. After taking holy orders he was licensed to a curacy at Hadleigh in Suffolk in 1821, where he adopted strong protestant views and a rooted antipathy to Roman Catholicism. He left Hadleigh in 1826, and successively served, each for a short time, curacies in Kent, Surrey, and Hampshire. From 1831 to 1836 he had the sole charge of the parish of Hodnet in Shropshire. In 1836 John Bird Sumner, bishop of Chester, presented him to the living of St Peter's in Chester, where he was also evening lecturer at St Mary's, a large church in which he usually preached to about 1200 people. While at Chester he published from 1838 a series entitled Tracts for the Rich. In 1846 he was appointed by the earl of Abergavenny rector of Otley in Suffolk, which he resigned shortly before his death. Here he specially laboured among the young. He married, while at Otley, Adine Louisa Lewis, daughter of A. D. Lewis Agassiz of Finsbury Square, London, who survived him.

Tayler's numerous books and tracts, which were published on both sides on the Atlantic, were either warnings against the errors of the Catholics or relentlessly moralizing manuals of religious instruction for the young. They included *The Child of the Church of England* (1834; new edn, 1852), *Facts in a Clergyman's Life* (1849), *Sermons for All Seasons*, (1850), *Memorials of the English Martyrs* (1853), *Legends and Records, Chiefly Historical* (1854), *The Tongue of the Swearer: a Suffolk Story* (1861), *The Race Course and its Accompaniments* (1867), *Found at Eventide: the True Story of a Young Village Infidel* (1870), and *Sacred Records in Verse* (1872). Tayler died at his home, Chapel House, Worthing, Sussex, on 16 October 1875.

G. C. BOASE, *rev.* TRIONA ADAMS

Sources C. B. Tayler, *Personal recollections* (1876) · Venn, *Alum. Cant.* · C. B. Tayler, *Facts in a clergyman's life* (1849) · Add. MSS 19168, fols. 194–194, 19174, fol. 697 · Allibone, *Dict.* · Boase, *Mod. Eng. biog.* · *CGPLA Eng. & Wales* (1876)
Likenesses T. G. Lupton, engraving (after portrait by Boaden), repro. in C. B. Tayler, *The records of a good man's life*, 2 vols. (1832) · portrait, repro. in Tayler, *Personal recollections*
Wealth at death under £1000: probate, 15 Aug 1876, *CGPLA Eng. & Wales*

Tayler, (John) Frederick (1806–1889), watercolour painter and etcher, was born on 30 April 1806 at Borehamwood in Hertfordshire, one of seventeen children of Archdale Wilson Tayler, a country landowner until forced to go into the army, having been ruined by his agent; he died when Tayler was still a child. A younger brother, William *Tayler, became commissioner of Patna in India, and an uncle, Charles Henry Hall, was dean of Christ Church, Oxford. Intended by his family for the church Tayler was educated at both Eton College and Harrow School. He determined to become an artist, however, and attended Henry Sass's school in Bloomsbury and the Royal Academy Schools. In Paris the animal paintings of Theodore Géricault inspired Tayler to take lessons from the equestrian artist Horace Vernet, and he bought parts of horses from butchers in order to study their anatomy. He also shared a studio with Richard Parkes Bonington, who must have encouraged his preference for watercolour; he sketched on the French coast with John Skinner Prout, and he visited Rome.

In 1830 Tayler exhibited an oil painting, *The Band of the 2nd Regiment of Life Guards*, at the Royal Academy. In 1831 he was elected an associate of the Society of Painters in Water Colours, and became a full member three years later. In all he exhibited 500 pictures with the society, including twelve drawn with George Barret. Queen Victoria, who first saw Tayler's work in 1834, became an important patron and purchased work for Windsor Castle. Thereafter aristocratic taste and Tayler's considerable social connections enabled him to sell his work for high prices; *Return from Hawking*, for instance, was purchased for £465 3s. in 1864. He signed himself F. Tayler. Tayler's work can be divided into three groups: sporting scenes, often in costume and with horses; pastoral scenes, mostly Scottish; and historical illustrations, frequently inspired by the Waverley novels. Henry Walker, in *Our Living Painters* (1859), commented:

> His paintings have great dash, and evince power of a sketchy kind, albeit they are somewhat washy and blotty in execution, and, at a day when care and finish are becoming almost universal, are works not wholly up to our time. (244–5)

Tayler was a member of the Etching Club and made prints throughout his career, from *Frederick Tayler's Portfolio*, a series of lithotints published in 1844 and 1845, to *Studies in Animal Painting*, in 1884.

On the death of Copley Fielding, in 1855, Tayler became for eight months acting president of the Society of Painters in Water Colours. During that year a dispute at the Paris Universal Exhibition over the hanging of drawings, particularly those of John Frederick Lewis, made Tayler seriously ill from stress; yet when Lewis resigned as president, in February 1858, Tayler was unanimously elected to replace him. He remained in office until 1870 but was not considered very effective: 'Amiable and generous in his nature, he was not one who loved to thrust himself into the forefront as an advocate' (Roget, 2.215). A less generous critic, William Evans 'of Eton', said that Tayler's 'lukewarmness' was positively harmful (Royal Watercolour Society MSS, J30/18). Art brought Tayler other worldly honours. He received the Légion d'honneur of France, and other awards from Belgium, Bavaria, and Austria; he was also elected a member of the Pennsylvanian and the Royal Cambrian academies, and of the Société des Aquerellistes of Belgium.

A photograph of about 1863 portrays Tayler as a rather prim figure; he has a high forehead, side whiskers, a long nose, small, deep-set eyes, and hair which curls at the ears. In 1837 he married Jane Parratt, with whom he had three surviving sons and two daughters. Tayler lived in London for most of his life; the catalogues give various addresses around London, and two for periods, in 1838 and in 1887, when he lived in Brighton. Late in his life he lost heavily through unfortunate investments. Frederick Tayler died at his home, 63 Gascony Avenue, West Hampstead, on 20 June 1889 and was buried in Hampstead cemetery. His remaining works were sold by Christies on 27 January and 17 February 1890. He was a prolific artist; the Victoria and Albert Museum, the British Museum, and many other galleries have drawings by Tayler, but his work has never recovered its once great popularity. A daughter, Kate Tayler (*fl.* 1870–1908), exhibited with the Society of Women Artists and with the Dudley Gallery. Norman Tayler (1843–1915), Tayler's second son, was elected an associate of the Society of Painters in Water Colours in 1878; his watercolours were primarily genre scenes.

SIMON FENWICK

Sources J. L. Roget, *A history of the 'Old Water-Colour' Society*, 2 vols. (1891) · J. Jordan, 'Landseer of watercolour', *Watercolours, drawings & prints*, 9 (winter 1994), 16–19 · Bankside Gallery, London, Royal Watercolour Society MSS · H. Walker, *Our living painters* (1859), 244–5 · *DNB*
Archives Bankside Gallery, London, Royal Watercolour Society MSS, Jenkins papers
Likenesses photograph, *c.*1863, Bankside Gallery, London · wood-engraving (after photograph by J. Watkins), repro. in *ILN* (6 July 1889)

Tayler, Herbert (1912–2000), architect, was born in Parapattan, Batavia, on 28 July 1912, the only son of Thomas Jack Tayler, a sugar exporter of Scottish descent, and Louise Dorothea Obertop, who was Dutch. His family returned to Britain in 1919, and Herbert went to Shrewsbury School, where his talent for drawing led to his entry to the Architectural Association School in 1929. Tayler was an exceptional student, as the complete archive of his surviving student drawings demonstrates, although his love of music (he was a good pianist) diverted his attention and he had to be summoned by the director to explain which career he most wanted to follow. Friends in the ballet enabled Tayler to spend many evenings in the wings of the Old Vic theatre, and his final-year design was for a national opera house in Regent's Park. After graduating he made a special journey to Glasgow to see the buildings of Charles Rennie Mackintosh, still little known at the time. Tayler knew the artist John Piper and contributed an article to the final issue of *Axis* magazine, edited by Myfanwy Piper, in 1937, as well as beginning a writing career in the *Architectural Review*. His occasional writings were exceptionally witty and perceptive in commenting on the contemporary architectural scene, frequently comparing the puritanism and philistinism of England unfavourably with continental Europe, to which he felt strong family links.

In his final year at the Architectural Association in 1933–4 Tayler got to know a student contemporary, **David John Green** (1912–1998), born on 11 September 1912, the son of a well-established Lowestoft architect. Tayler and Green became professional and domestic partners from 1938 onwards. Their first joint project was The Studio, Duke's Head Yard, Highgate (1937–40), a modern building elegant in its planning, colours, and textures, whose construction was researched by Green in great detail, leading to a careful mixture of modern and traditional materials and techniques. It was widely published, as was a flat conversion they did for themselves in Earl's Terrace, Kensington, on the top floor of Mrs Tayler's house. Both schemes show close attention to interior details and furnishings with a Scandinavian leaning towards patterns and indoor plants.

In 1941 Green's father died suddenly and Tayler and Green moved to the bomb-scarred seaside town of Lowestoft to work on war-damage repairs, taking over the practice. Tayler was caught under a falling building and Green nursed him back to health, living in a converted caravan in the grounds of Ditchingham Hall as guests of Lilias Rider-Haggard. In 1943 Tayler and Green built two small developments of council housing in local villages under a special government scheme, rationalizing the standard house plans and making the most of scarce materials. The shallow-pitched roofs with deep overhangs were a precursor of the 700 council houses Tayler and Green built for Loddon district council between 1945 and their retirement in 1973. This was their main professional work and the results, mostly terraces of between six and ten houses as close as possible to existing village centres, were soon recognized as the best council housing in post-war Britain. A larger concentration of housing is found in Loddon itself, where they hoped to build new council offices.

Tayler was the designer, with a sure sense of spacing and rhythm in elevations and a gift for composing forms in the gentle Norfolk landscape. Green was the enabler, who dealt with drains, cost controls, and clients, who were too easily put off by Tayler's sardonic manner. Both men shared a genuine desire to improve the quality of life for village people without losing the feeling of familiar building forms such as individually colour-washed house fronts, patterned brick gable ends, and barge boards. The result was not strictly modern architecture, but neither was it neo-traditional, being closer to Swedish or Swiss housing of the time than anything else in England. Their particular planning innovation was a 'through store' between the front and back of the house which enabled the residents to run a wheelbarrow through to the back garden without breaking the line of the terrace. Every house had a front garden with a white-painted wicket gate, to which residents responded by 'gardening like gods', in Tayler's words, while their back gardens were screened from public view and allowed them to do what they liked.

Outside Loddon, Tayler and Green designed a house at Kingston, a showroom in London, and a factory at Uxbridge for Godfrey Imhof, a successful electronics engineer who was an ideal client. A few other jobs came in, including housing in Hatfield New Town and Basildon, a few individual houses, shops, and banks. Their competition design for Churchill College, Cambridge, 1959, was a thoughtful project, more austere than their housing. Tayler was appointed OBE in 1965. An exhibition entitled 'Tayler and Green, architects, 1938–1973' was held at the Prince of Wales Institute of Architecture, London, in May 1998. Five of their buildings have been added to the list of buildings of special architectural or historic interest.

Tayler and Green retired to Spain in 1973 and built themselves a house at 53 San Chuchim, Altea, on the Costa Blanca, from which they continued to travel in Europe to attend music festivals. David Green died in Altea on 3 October 1998. Tayler died at their home on 3 February 2000.   ALAN POWERS

Sources E. Harwood and A. Powers, *Tayler and Green, architects, 1938–1973* (1998) [exhibition catalogue, Prince of Wales Institute of Architecture, London] · Tayler and Green drawings and office files, Suffolk RO · S. Cantacuzino, 'The work of Tayler & Green', *Architecture & Building*, 25/1 (Jan 1960), 2–23 · I. Nairn, 'Rural housing: the post-war work of Tayler & Green', *ArchR*, 124 (1958), 226–36 · *The Independent* (7 March 2000), 6 · *The Guardian* (13 March 2000) · b. cert. · *The Independent* (9 Oct 1998) [obituary of David Green] · *The Times* (3 Nov 1998) [obit. of David Green]
Archives Suffolk RO, Tayler and Green drawings and office files | FILM *One foot in the past*, BBC2, July 1996 | SOUND BL NSA, Architects' Lives series
Likenesses photograph, c.1956, priv. coll.

Tayler, John James (1797–1869), Unitarian minister and college head, was born on 15 August 1797 at Church Row, Newington Butts, in Surrey, the elder son of John Tayler (1765–1831), a nonconformist minister, and Elizabeth, the daughter of John Kenning of Walthamstow. When John James Tayler was five years old the family moved from London to Nottingham, where his father took the prestigious post of minister of High Pavement Chapel. In addition to his ministerial work John Tayler started a school in his own home, where his son was a pupil until the age of seventeen. It was here that John James acquired his command of the English language as well as a comprehensive knowledge of Latin and German.

In 1814 John James Tayler was sent to train for the Unitarian ministry at Manchester College, York, under the principalship of Charles Wellbeloved (1769–1858). A letter written by Tayler at this time records that he was studying Greek, Hebrew, Arabic, and mathematics, all in the same week. His days at Manchester College were happy ones, but at the close of his second year he left York and spent the following two years at the University of Glasgow reading for a BA degree. After gaining the degree in 1819 he returned straight away to Manchester College as a temporary assistant tutor in classics, while his former tutor John Kenrick (1788–1877) was in Germany studying with Schleiermacher.

The year spent as a tutor changed the course of Tayler's life. He had previously hoped to study medicine and combine the duties of a minister with those of a doctor. However, the financial difficulties of a long medical training, combined with his increasing interest in theology, caused him to abandon the idea. Thus in 1820, at the age of twenty-three, he accepted an invitation to become the minister of Mosley Street Chapel (later Upper Brook Street), Manchester. On 16 January 1825 he married Hannah, the daughter of Timothy Smith of Icknield; none of their children survived him.

Like his contemporaries, the members of the Oxford Movement, Tayler was also influenced by Romanticism. From his published correspondence, which is a little cameo of Victorian intellectual life, it can be seen that as a student of Glasgow he was avidly reading Scott, and on one of his early visits to the Lake District he joined Wordsworth for tea and the two men went for a long walk together later in the week. Further influence of the Romantic movement on Tayler can be seen by the fact that in 1839 Sir Charles Barry, the architect of the new houses of parliament, was commissioned, amid controversy, but with Tayler's approval, to build the new Upper Brook Street Chapel in a splendid Gothic style. This move away from the rectangular and octagonal chapels which were light, airy, and conducive to rationalism, towards Gothic-style churches with stained-glass windows, choir pews, and high altars which were never used, was a reflection of the moving of Unitarian thought from an excessive reliance upon rationalism, as propounded by Joseph Priestley, towards a more spiritual and romantic religion in which devotion to Christ was central. Tayler achieved this revolution within Unitarianism partly through his joint editorship of the influential *Prospective Review* and partly through his control of Manchester College, which was the sole institution for the training of Unitarian ministers.

During the year 1834–5, as D. F. Strauss was publishing his *Life of Jesus*, Tayler, who had suffered from nervous exhaustion, spent a year in Germany to recover, and used the opportunity to study continental theology. Thereafter he remained a keen student of German religious thought and was always an admirer of the German way of life. He was greatly impressed by the works of F. D. E. Schleiermacher and at Göttingen attended, at eight o'clock every morning, the lectures of Professor J. K. L. Gieseler on church history. Gieseler's systematic approach to his subject influenced Tayler's own study of church history. Contact between English and German religious thought in the nineteenth century was wider than is sometimes portrayed, but Tayler was one of the more interesting links in this chain. He spoke German and regularly conducted services in German while he was in London. After visiting Germany for the first time in 1834 he corresponded with several leading German professors. Tayler also formed a close friendship with Baron Christian Bunsen, and studied his works several years before they were made famous by Rowland Williams in *Essays and Reviews* (1860).

In 1840 Manchester College moved back to Manchester from York, with an enlarged staff and with a determination to become a small university. Tayler was appointed professor of ecclesiastical history, with James Martineau (1805–1900) as professor of philosophy and Francis Newman (1805–1897) as professor of classics. Tayler continued his ministry at Upper Brook Street, holding the two posts in tandem until 1853, when the college moved to London and he was appointed principal of the new institution, a post he held until his death in 1869. Tayler fought vigorously for church unity within a wider state church, on the grounds that such a unity would not duplicate resources but would encourage a highly trained ministry, strengthen the parochial system, and enable Christians to unite in social action. He strongly advocated this position in his publication *A Catholic Christian Church, the Want of our Time* (1867).

In London, Tayler took his place in the intellectual society of the capital. He was a close friend of Henry Crabb Robinson (1775–1867), and was the most regular attender at Crabb Robinson's famous dinner parties. Charles Lyell (1769–1849), the geologist, corresponded with him and called to consult him concerning his own research. Tayler's literary output in this period numbered some fifty major books and papers, including *A Retrospective of Religious Life of England* (1845) and *English Nonconformity: its Principle and Justification* (1859), as well as a large number of written sermons and an extensive private correspondence.

Tayler died at his home, The Limes, Rosslyn, Hampstead, on 28 May 1869. A quiet, thoughtful, and good man, his portraits in the senior common room and the library at Manchester College portray him with a kindly face. In his tribute to Tayler, his old friend James Martineau called him 'the English Schleiermacher' and added, 'No one could look at him and say that the power of Christianity is spent' (Martineau and Beard).   RALPH WALLER

Sources J. H. Thom, *Letters embracing the life of John James Tayler*, 2 vols. (1872) · *The Inquirer* (29 May 1869) · *The Inquirer* (5 June 1869) · W. H. Herford, *Recollections of the late Rev. John James Tayler* (1869) · A. Gordon, *The blessing of the pure in heart: in memory of Rev. John James Tayler* (1869) · J. Martineau and C. Beard, *Obituary notices of the late John James Tayler* [1869] · V. D. Davies, *A history of Manchester College* (1932) · *DNB* · J. E. Carpenter, *James Martineau* (1905) · C. G. Bolam and others, *The English presbyterians: from Elizabethan puritanism to modern Unitarianism* (1968)
Archives Harris Man. Oxf., papers | DWL, letters to Richard Tayler
Likenesses G. Patten, oils, 1848, Harris Man. Oxf. · J. P. Knight, oils, c.1862, Harris Man. Oxf.
Wealth at death under £10,000: probate, 13 July 1869, *CGPLA Eng. & Wales*

Tayler, Joseph Needham (1785–1864), naval officer, born at Devizes, Wiltshire, was the son of Samuel Tayler, five times mayor of Devizes and commandant of local volunteers, and his wife, Sally, daughter of Joseph Needham MD, and niece of Henry Needham, a partner in Child's Bank. An elder brother, Samuel Tayler, a lieutenant in the 13th light dragoons, was killed in the Peninsula; another, Thomas Tayler, major of the 9th Bengal native infantry, died in India.

Joseph entered the navy in July 1796 in the *Royal George*, flagship of Lord Bridport, and witnessed the Spithead mutiny in April and May 1797. In 1799 he was moved to the *Anson* with Captain Philip Durham, whom he followed in February 1801 to the *Endymion*. He was promoted lieutenant on 29 April 1802, and in October 1803 was appointed to the *Leopard*, one of the squadron with Lord Keith in the Downs and off Boulogne. In March 1806 the *Leopard* was sent to convoy six East Indiamen to the southward of the Cape Verde Islands, off the coast of west Africa; when one of them struck a reef near St Iago and became a total wreck, Tayler succeeded in saving thirty of the crew, though more were lost. In March 1807 he was moved to the *Maida*, one of the ships in the attack on Copenhagen, and landed in command of a party of seamen for one of the batteries. In 1808 he was in the *Spencer*, flagship of Rear Admiral Robert Stopford, on the coast of France. In 1809 he was in the *Heroine*, and in 1810 in the *Goldfinch* on the north coast of Spain. On 27 August 1810 he was promoted commander of the *Sparrow* (16 guns), then in the West Indies, but did not join her until the following February. He then cruised in the Mona passage for several months to suppress piracy. He returned to England with a convoy, and in 1812 was employed on the north coast of Spain, co-operating with the army. He carried home the dispatches after the battle of Vitoria and returned to take part in the siege of San Sebastian, where, on 24 July in the sailors' battery, he was almost torn to pieces by an exploding shell—his head was cut open, he had a severe wound in the groin, and his left leg was smashed. He was sent home and, on 9 August 1813, to the Haslar Royal Naval Hospital, where he was confined to bed for twenty-eight weeks. It was upwards of two years before his wounds were healed. In November 1814 he was awarded a pension of £200 a year, which in 1815 was increased to £250. He was also made a CB on 8 December 1815 and received £100 from the Patriotic Fund and the freedom of Devizes.

From July 1838 to August 1841 Tayler was captain of the Ordinary at Plymouth; but, with this exception, the greater part of his life was passed at Devizes, which he devoted his energy and money to improving. He pulled down and rebuilt shops and houses, and stopped only when his funds were exhausted, for the improvements did not seem to have been a paying investment. He made various inventions, including a transporting carriage for ships' guns for field service ashore. In 1838 he took out a patent for 'a certain method of abating or lessening the shock or force of the waves … preventing the injury done to, and increasing the durability of, places exposed to the violent action of the waves', and improvements upon his original plan were suggested by him in 1840, 1843, and 1846. In 1840 he published *Plans for the Formation of Harbours of Refuge*, and in 1848 *The Defence of the Coast of Great Britain*. A model of his floating breakwater was seen at the Great Exhibition of 1851, but it appears to have had only a modified success in practice. In 1852 he submitted to Trinity House a proposal to erect a 'shipwreck asylum' on the Goodwin Sands off the coast of Kent. Nothing came of this proposal, but a harbour of refuge seems to have been erected at Le Havre in 1855 in accordance with his suggestions. Tayler accepted the rank of rear-admiral on the retired list on 10 October 1846. During his later life he resided at Brixton, Devon, where he died, unmarried, on 18 March 1864.   J. K. LAUGHTON, rev. ANDREW LAMBERT

Sources private information (1898) · D. Syrett and R. L. DiNardo, *The commissioned sea officers of the Royal Navy, 1660–1815*, rev. edn, Occasional Publications of the Navy RS, 1 (1994) · O'Byrne, *Naval biog. dict.* · *The Times* (23 March 1864) · *Devizes and Wiltshire Gazette* (23 Nov 1893) · *GM*, 3rd ser., 16 (1864), 672

Tayler, Roger John (1929–1997), astrophysicist and plasma physicist, was born on 25 October 1929 in Birmingham, the elder child of Richard Henry Tayler (1899–1963), a commercial traveller, and his wife, Frances Florence Bessie, *née* Redrup (1901–1979), an elementary school teacher. Both Roger and his brother (Harold) Clive (later a circuit court judge) received strong parental encouragement to develop their respective academic talents. From Solihull School, Roger went up in 1947 to Clare College, Cambridge, with a state scholarship and a major open scholarship in mathematics; in 1949 he became a wrangler and in 1950 passed part three of the mathematical tripos with distinction, sharing the prestigious Mayhew prize.

During 1950–53 Tayler was Hermann Bondi's research student. His PhD thesis yielded three pioneering papers on the structure of stars which remain unmixed, developing a gradient in the helium abundance and so in the mean molecular weight as they evolve through thermonuclear processing of hydrogen in the hot convective core. For stars of moderately high mass, and using just an electrically driven mechanical desk calculator, Tayler tracked the beginning of their evolution in the Hertzsprung–Russell (luminosity–colour) diagram from the main sequence towards the red giant domain, pointing out how the curves could be used to estimate the ages of star clusters. Similar studies of very massive stars led to his independent discovery of the phenomenon of 'semiconvection'.

After a year in the United States at Caltech and Princeton, as a Commonwealth Fund (Harkness) fellow, during which he suffered a serious automobile accident which left him with a permanently weakened ankle, Tayler returned to the UK to marry his Cambridge fiancée, Moya Elizabeth Fry (b. 1933), a graduate of Girton College in French and German. For most of their married life Moya was a secondary school teacher; they had no children. They settled first near Abingdon, close to Harwell where Roger began work with the thermonuclear group in the UK Atomic Energy Authority, first as senior research fellow, followed by successive promotions through the scientific grades. His work there on the stability problems of model plasmas is now a classic, including important results derived independently by Marshall Rosenbluth in the USA and Victor Shafranov in the USSR. The most notable is on the potential stabilizing effect of an axial magnetic field, imposed on a perfectly conducting, pinched cylindrical current with its circular magnetic field, the whole system surrounded by a conducting cylinder.

In 1961 Tayler returned to Cambridge as Department of Scientific and Industrial Research senior research fellow, to work with Fred Hoyle on cosmical nucleosynthesis, simultaneously becoming a fellow of Corpus Christi College and director of studies in mathematics. In 1964 he became university lecturer in applied mathematics. This period yielded a short but famous paper, 'The mystery of the cosmic helium abundance' (Nature, 203, 1964, 1108–10), in which Hoyle and Tayler drew attention to observational evidence suggesting a likely universal primordial helium abundance. Their calculation of the expected helium generation during the initial phases of a 'hot big bang' model of the expanding universe (done with the assistance of John Faulkner) generalized the earlier treatments by taking account of the existence of the μ-neutrino as well as the electron neutrino. In their first draft they also commented on the theoretical prediction of a cosmical microwave background, but this somehow got lost in the published version. There remained a tantalizing disagreement with observation, and in fact their paper allowed the possibility that the helium could have been produced in a fairly uniform manner in supermassive stellar objects rather than in a smooth cosmical background. In 1968 and subsequently, Tayler pointed out that a precise estimate of the cosmical helium generation is sensitive to the actual half-life of the neutron: a prophetic remark, for the improved measurements made some twenty years later reduced the half-life to just under 10.3 minutes, yielding predictions from the simplest Big Bang nucleosynthesis theory of both primordial helium and also of deuterium and of ^{7}Li, in excellent agreement with the latest observational estimates. The work also pointed out the sensitivity of the cosmic helium abundance to the number of different types of neutrino that actually exist. A further paper ('Helium production in an anisotropic Big-Bang cosmology', Nature, 209, 1966, 1278–9), co-authored with Stephen Hawking, showed how the predicted abundance would change if the expansion of the universe in its early phases deviated from spherical symmetry.

In 1965 the newly founded University of Sussex invited Professor William McCrea to become research professor of astronomy, supported by the Science Research Council, and in 1967 Tayler was appointed the first professor funded by the University Grants Committee, along with supporting staff. Together with the visiting faculty from the neighbouring Royal Greenwich Observatory at Herstmonceaux, Tayler and McCrea were instrumental in putting the University of Sussex on the world astronomical map as a centre of teaching and research. Tayler was a superb teacher, admirably clear without being prolix, and adept at setting out his arguments. For five years he held the exacting position of dean of the school of mathematical and physical sciences. His administrative and diplomatic skills and his patent honesty made him a highly respected member of senate. In addition, his public services to astronomy were unrivalled. Over two decades he was successively secretary, treasurer, and finally president of the Royal Astronomical Society, and was also the managing editor of its Monthly Notices. From 1969 to 1975 he served as Gresham professor of astronomy at the City University. Meanwhile his research activity continued, being directed first to the problems of magnetism, convection, and rotation in stars, where he applied the expertise acquired at Harwell, and later to the chemical evolution of galaxies.

During this period Tayler wrote three undergraduate texts which have been appreciated worldwide for their balance and lucidity: The Stars: their Structure and Evolution (1970), The Origin of the Chemical Elements (1972), and Galaxies: Structure and Evolution (1978). As a committed Christian he served for many years as churchwarden at St Anne's Church, Lewes, and on the parochial church council. Recognition of his overall services to astronomy came with appointment as OBE in 1990, and for his academic work with election to the Royal Society in 1995.

In 1989 Tayler was diagnosed as suffering from myeloma. The technical expertise and dedication of the staff at the Royal Marsden Hospital in Sutton, Surrey, and the devoted support of Moya, gave him a 6½ year period of remission. With characteristically quiet courage and dignity he carried on with teaching and research, writing two more books: The Hidden Universe (1991) and The Sun as a Star (1997). While emeritus professor his research was supported by the Leverhulme Foundation, and in particular he carried on his fruitful collaboration with Eric Pitts. The myeloma recurred during 1996, and he finally succumbed at the Royal Marsden on 23 January 1997, peacefully and in full control of his faculties; on 7 February he was cremated at Woodvale crematorium, Brighton. He was survived by his wife.   LEON MESTEL

Sources L. Mestel and B. E. J. Pagel, Memoirs FRS, 44 (1998), 403–16 · L. Mestel, Towards the understanding of the entire universe [forthcoming] [first Tayler memorial lecture, 1999] · Daily Telegraph (8 Feb 1997) · private information (2004) [Moya Tayler]
Archives U. Sussex, books, MSS, papers
Likenesses photograph, RAS · photograph, repro. in Mestel and Pagel, Memoirs FRS, 403

Tayler, William (1808–1892), East India Company servant, youngest of the seventeen children of Archdale Wilson Tayler of Boreham Wood, Elstree, Hertfordshire, and his wife, Frances Eliza, sister of Charles Henry *Hall, was born at Boreham Wood on 31 March 1808. John Frederick *Tayler was his elder brother. William was educated at Charterhouse School and in early 1829 had just spent a term at Christ Church, Oxford, when he was unexpectedly offered a writership in the Bengal civil service.

Tayler arrived in Bengal in October 1829 and in June 1830 was appointed assistant to the commissioner of Cuttack. On 17 July 1830, in Calcutta, he married Charlotte Brydges, daughter of John Palmer, a merchant. Of their seven children, two daughters died in infancy. Tayler held various posts in Bengal, including that of postmaster-general, before becoming in 1855 commissioner of Patna. He was competent in Hindustani and Persian; like many district officers, he prided himself on knowing the country and her people and, furthermore, knowing them better than his superiors did. He was a keen amateur dramatist and skilful caricaturist, but while his witty portraits of Anglo-Indian notables won him some influential friends in Calcutta, the light-hearted nature of his artistic pursuits earned for him a reputation as a somewhat flighty, unserious officer. Moreover, in spite of his pen's readiness to deflate other people's vanities, he was himself remarkably thin-skinned and saw behind every hitch in his career cabals of intriguers and pompous, incompetent superiors.

Some months before the uprising of 1857 Tayler warned the Bengal government that there were signs of disaffection among the people of Bihar, in particular the Muslims. In response the lieutenant-governor, Frederick Halliday, suggested that this was partly Tayler's own fault and singled out for criticism his over-enthusiastic collection of 'voluntary' subscriptions from local gentry for an industrial school he wanted to establish. It was a slight Tayler never forgave. In May 1857, when the Indian mutiny did finally break out up-country, Tayler, having long feared such a calamity, was quick to implement defensive measures in his own division, so quick in fact that the authorities in Calcutta worried that he was goading Bihar's still relatively peaceable population into rebellion. On 19 June he invited the leading Indians of Patna to his house, ostensibly for friendly discussions, and then arrested three of them, all prominent Muslim divines, whom he was convinced were plotting against the British. Halliday was appalled at such an act of bad faith. On 25 July the sepoys at Dinapore mutinied and laid siege to the station of Arrah. This was exactly what Tayler had feared most, and on 31 July, giving up Arrah and indeed all of the Bihar countryside as a hopeless case, he ordered the civil officers of his division to abandon their posts and fall back on Dinapore. To the authorities in Calcutta this smacked of panic, and on 4 August Halliday suspended Tayler from the commissionership.

Tayler's reading of the military situation had been determined by his unshakeable conviction that the Muslims of Bihar had masterminded a province-wide rebellion; he had expected therefore only to be able to hold the city of Patna, if indeed he could hold that. In part, of course, he was unlucky. Had Arrah fallen, as it could so easily have done, his insistence on defending Patna would have been deemed far-sighted. But in a war in which accounts of desperate last stands and acts of derring-do were instantly becoming part of imperial legend, his Cassandra-like defeatism was doomed to be seen as cowardice.

Tayler was aghast at his suspension and, convinced that he was a victim of Halliday's malice and envy, embarked upon an appeal process which was so vitriolic and intemperate that it inexorably led to his exit from the civil service. In 1858 he was appointed judge of Mymensingh, but in January of the following year was again suspended, on the grounds of his 'insufferably offensive conduct', and resigned the service in March. He appealed for redress to every secretary of state in succession from 1857 to 1888 and in 1888 also managed to have his case heard before the House of Commons. In spite of the fact that he had many influential supporters, among them two prominent historians of the uprising—J. W. Kaye and Colonel G. B. Malleson—and Sir Henry Havelock and *The Times*, his appeals were all rejected outright, not least because of his refusal to modify his intensely personal criticism of Halliday.

For eight years after his resignation Tayler practised successfully as an advocate in Calcutta before returning to London in 1867. In addition to numerous pamphlets connected with his case, he published in 1881–2 a two-volume autobiography, *Thirty-Eight Years in India*, profusely illustrated with his own sketches. He died at his home, 19 Markwich Terrace, St Leonards, Sussex, on 5 March 1892; he was survived by his wife. Both of their sons, Skipwith Henry Churchill and Henry Vansittart, had careers in the Indian Civil Service.

STEPHEN WHEELER, rev. KATHERINE PRIOR

Sources W. Tayler, *Thirty-eight years in India from Juganath to the Himalaya mountains*, 2 vols. (1881–2) · C. E. Buckland, *Bengal under the lieutenant-governors*, 2 vols. (1901) · L. J. Trotter, *William Tayler of Patna: a brief account of his splendid services, his cruel wrongs and his thirty years' struggle for justice* [1887] · R. L. Arrowsmith, ed., *Charterhouse register, 1769–1872* (1974) · BL OIOC, Haileybury MSS · Foster, *Alum. Oxon.* · *The Times* (12 March 1892), 7 · H. A. C. Sturgess, ed., *Register of admissions to the Honourable Society of the Middle Temple, from the fifteenth century to the year 1944*, 2 (1949) · CGPLA Eng. & Wales (1892)

Archives BL OIOC, public and judicial department of India office files

Likenesses photograph, repro. in Tayler, *Thirty-eight years in India*, vol. 2, frontispiece

Wealth at death £308 15s. 10d.: probate, 12 April 1892, CGPLA Eng. & Wales

Taylor. *See also* Tailor, Tayler.

Taylor, Abraham (*fl.* 1726–1740), Independent minister and tutor, was the son of Richard Taylor (*d.* 1717), Independent minister of Little Moorfields, London. He was a classical scholar and trenchant defender of Calvinist orthodoxy. His first (anonymous) publication, *The Scripture Doctrine of the Trinity Vindicated* (1726; 2nd edn, 1728) was directed at Isaac Watts, and shows his strict adherence to orthodoxy, against Watts's more reconciling spirit. At about the same time (though not published until 1732) he wrote a two-volume defence of the Trinity 'in opposition to the Arian scheme'. In 1730 he published a dismissive *Letter to the author* (Strickland Gough) *of an enquiry into the causes of the decay of the dissenting interest*; Gough, a dissenting minister, had taken orders in the Church of England.

This work brought Taylor to the notice of William Coward, who appointed him one of nine preachers of a weekly lecture in defence of Calvinism at Paved Alley, Lime

Street. The lectures, including four by Taylor, were delivered in 1730–31 and published in 1732. While the lectures were proceeding, the King's Head Society (founded 1730) selected Taylor as divinity tutor. After a two-year classical course under Samuel Parsons at Clerkenwell, the students were sent to Taylor for four years at Deptford, where he had been minister since 1728, and had been ordained in 1731. Though he had a harsh temperament, revealed in 1732 in an angry controversy with John Gill, one of the Lime Street lecturers, in point of attainment Taylor was well fitted for the post. Alexander Cruden, commending Taylor to Marischal College, Aberdeen, for the award of DD wrote: 'he exceeds all the Dissenting ministers of my acquaintance for Learning' (P. J. Anderson, *Fasti academiae Aberdonensis*, 1897, 2.82). The doctorate was awarded in 1736.

Taylor preached and published several exhortations and funeral sermons, most notably that for his close friend and former pastor John Hurrion, minister of Hare-court, Aldersgate (1733). Such was his influence that Philip Doddridge's friends feared the academy which Coward proposed to endow after his death would be put under Taylor rather than Doddridge; and later that the settlement of Coward's will would favour Taylor, and 'Bigotry [be] intailed on the rising Generation' (*Calendar*, ed. Nuttall, 85 [no. 467]). These fears proved unfounded, but Coward's trustees, who included Watts, withdrew financial support from the seven of Taylor's students whom Coward had been funding personally until his death in April 1738, and resolved to place no more with him. To what extent these decisions contributed to Taylor's financial difficulties is only conjecture, but in 1740, after enquiry into his circumstances, the King's Head Society dismissed Taylor, who disappears from the public record and is thought to have died in penury.   JOHN HANDBY THOMPSON

Sources W. Wilson, *The history and antiquities of the dissenting churches and meeting houses in London, Westminster and Southwark*, 4 vols. (1808–14), vol. 1, p. 212; vol. 2, p. 530; vol. 4, p. 218 · H. McLachlan, *English education under the Test Acts: being the history of the nonconformist academies, 1662–1820* (1931), 175–6, 276, 287 · T. Timpson, *Church history of Kent* (1859), 348 · D. Bogue and J. Bennett, *History of dissenters, from the revolution in 1688, to … 1808*, 2nd edn, 2 (1833), 218 · J. Waddington, *Congregational history*, 3 (1876), 265–8 · *Calendar of the correspondence of Philip Doddridge*, ed. G. F. Nuttall, HMC, JP 26 (1979), nos. 405, 407, 465, 467 · J. H. Thompson, *A history of the Coward Trust: the first two hundred and fifty years, 1738–1988* (1998), 12–13 · *Fasti academiae Mariscallanae Aberdonensis: selections from the records of the Marischal College and University, MDXCIII–MDCCCLX*, 3, ed. J. F. K. Johnstone, New Spalding Club, 19 (1898), 82 · T. S. James, *The history of the litigation and legislation respecting Presbyterian chapels and charities in England and Ireland between 1816 and 1849* (1867), 712, 715 · A. Taylor, *A letter giving some account of the late John Hurrion addressed to his sons John and Samuel, December 31, 1731* (1733) · DNB

Archives DWL, MS lecture, 'An introduction to logic' · DWL, MS lecture, 'Natural and revealed theology'

Taylor, Alan John Percivale (1906–1990), historian, was born on 25 March 1906 in Birkdale, Lancashire, the only son (and sole surviving child) of Percy Lees Taylor, Preston cotton merchant, and his wife, Constance Sumner

Alan John Percivale Taylor (1906–1990), by Maggi Hambling, 1988

Thompson, schoolmistress. His well-to-do Edwardian Liberal parents subsequently became ardent Labour supporters, which shaped Taylor's lifelong commitment to left-wing causes, notably the first Campaign for Nuclear Disarmament. Precocious, learned, and spoilt, he was educated at Bootham School in York and Oriel College, Oxford, where, as something of a gilded youth who flirted with the Communist Party, he took a first class in modern history as a medievalist in 1927.

Abandoning his intention of becoming a labour lawyer, Taylor went to Vienna in 1928 as a Rockefeller fellow to work on modern diplomatic history. Appointed a lecturer at Manchester University in 1930, he came under the influence, which he later denied, of his professor, Lewis Namier, and wrote the first of his more than thirty books, *The Italian Problem in European Diplomacy, 1847–1849* (1934) and *Germany's First Bid for Colonies, 1884–1885* (1938), both mischievous products of hard work, rarely repeated thereafter, in the archives. He schooled himself to lecture (and speak publicly) without notes, a craft he later brought to perfection; contributed regularly as reviewer and leader writer on the *Manchester Guardian* under A. P. Wadsworth; travelled widely; and cultivated his vegetable garden at Disley in the High Peak.

With Namier's crucial support, Taylor returned to Oxford in 1938 as a fellow of Magdalen College, to which he remained devoted until his retirement in 1976. Soon established as an outstanding tutor of responsive undergraduates and a charismatic, early-morning lecturer, he began to make a wider name for himself as an incisive speaker on current affairs, in person and on the radio.

Throughout the Second World War his house at Holywell Ford was a centre for writers young and old, wayward musicians, and the grander Slav refugees clustered in north Oxford as well as his pupils coming on leave. In 1941 he published the most elegant of his books, the elegiac first version of *The Habsburg Monarchy*, and this was followed in 1945 by his initial best-seller, *The Course of German History*, a graphic, opinionated *pièce d'occasion* and the clue to much of his later work in its anti-German assumptions.

Notorious as an early critic of the cold war, Taylor emerged as a national figure with the advent of television. On *In the News* and *Free Speech* he caught the viewers' fancy as a quick-witted debater, a Cobbett-like scourge of the 'establishment', and, quite simply, something of a card, much appreciated by the 'man on the Clapham omnibus', in the phrase of his exemplar, Lord Macaulay. First of the television dons, he retained this primacy into old age as he delivered unscripted lectures direct to the camera on historical themes to a vast audience. Meanwhile he was taken up by Lord Beaverbrook, a lover of maverick left-wingers, as the charms of Oxford faded. A highly paid, sometimes outrageous columnist on the *Sunday Express*, and the first (and last) director of the Beaverbrook Library, Taylor paid uneasy tribute to an improbable but close friend in *Beaverbrook* (1972), the last of his substantial works and dedicated to the only man who ever persuaded him to cross the Atlantic.

Long before, Taylor had consolidated his academic reputation. In 1954 *The Struggle for Mastery in Europe, 1848–1918* was at once recognized as a model analysis, with its careful attention to the published records. This massive work, with the brief but perceptive *Bismarck* (1955) and the self-indulgent Ford lectures, *The Trouble Makers* (1957), fully justified his election to the British Academy in 1956. (Perversely, he resigned on libertarian grounds in 1980 when Anthony Blunt relinquished his fellowship.) Contrary to many expectations, however, Taylor was not appointed regius professor at Oxford in 1957. This failure, in which Namier played some part, remains a subject of uncertain legend, but it did not prevent an embittered man denigrating the university he loved. Thereafter he was consoled by honorary doctorates at Bristol, Manchester, New Brunswick, Warwick, and York, as well as honorary fellowships of both Magdalen (1976) and Oriel (1980).

Superficially, Taylor was an old-fashioned historian, holding that 'politics express the activities of man in society', with the addendum that economic and social circumstances must be taken into modest account. A master of narrative but essentially an analyst, he founded no school, despite his influence upon younger historians, and his methods could be a dangerous model. In his heyday Taylor came to rely upon assiduous reading in five languages and sheer intuition—'green fingers', in Namier's envious phrase. There was no elaborate filing system, but a prodigious memory could usually supply some evidence for the thousand words tapped out each well-organized morning. Despite his commitment to popular journalism, he was also a superb and creative essayist, and published several volumes based upon serious reviews in the learned journals and *The Observer*.

Ultimately, Taylor's scholarly standing depends upon three major achievements. *The Struggle for Mastery* remains unrivalled as a totally authoritative study of international relations in a complicated period. *English History, 1914–1945* (1965) is an enthralling, highly idiosyncratic account of his own times, regarded by some as his best book. *The Origins of the Second World War* (1961) was a dazzling exercise in revisionism, which earned him a mixture of international obloquy and acclaim. Whatever its flaws, this treatment of Hitler as a product of German tradition summed up Taylor's paradoxical, provocative, and inventive approach to historical explanation. A pragmatic loner, suspicious of philosophies of history and a brilliant stylist, he was admired even by his many critics for the range of his erudition, his clarity of presentation, and the fertility of his hypotheses.

Though he enjoyed portraying himself as a simple, true-born Englishman, Taylor was a cosmopolitan intellectual, with an expert knowledge of European architecture, music, and wine. An admirable but frugal host, his table talk was inimitable; a shrewd if nervous man of business, he was soothed by domestic chores; and in old age he became an indefatigable walker in town and country. Short, stocky, and bespectacled, he was vain about his appearance, but always happiest in a crumpled tweed or, more often, corduroy suit, invariably accompanied by a flamboyant bow-tie.

An emotional man, despite the brash exterior, Taylor was three times married and devoted to his six children. In 1931 he married a musician, Margaret, the daughter of Harold Adams, an English merchant trading in India; they had two sons and two daughters. Margaret was later an over-indulgent patron of Dylan Thomas. This marriage was dissolved in 1951 and in the same year he married Eve, daughter of Joseph Beardsel Crosland, under-secretary at the War Office, and sister of Tony Crosland, Labour politician. There were two sons of this marriage, which was dissolved in 1974. In 1976 he married the Hungarian historian Eva Haraszti, daughter of Mitse Herczke, an ironmonger in east Hungary. Taylor's last years were clouded by Parkinson's disease and he died at a nursing home in Barnet on 7 September 1990. His remains were cremated at Golders Green on 17 September.   A. F. THOMPSON, *rev.*

Sources A. J. P. Taylor, *A personal history* (1983) · A. J. P. Taylor, *Letters to Eva* (1991) · A. Sisman, *A. J. P. Taylor* (1994) · K. Burk, *Troublemaker* (2000) · C. J. Wrigley, 'Alan John Percival Taylor, 1906–1990', *PBA*, 82 (1993), 493–524 · personal knowledge (2004) · *CGPLA Eng. & Wales* (1991)

Archives Ransom HRC, corresp., research notes, and papers · U. Warwick Mod. RC, notes relating to his views on the Campaign for Nuclear Disarmament | HLRO, Aitken MSS · HLRO, corresp. with Lord Beaverbrook · HLRO, letters to Eva Haraszti Taylor · JRL, letters to the *Manchester Guardian* · King's Lond., Liddell Hart C., corresp. with Sir B. H. Liddell Hart · U. Sussex Library, corresp. with *New Statesman* magazine

Likenesses M. Hambling, oils, 1988, NPG [*see illus.*]

Wealth at death £307,083: probate, 5 April 1991, *CGPLA Eng. & Wales*

Taylor, Alec Clifton- (1907–1985), architectural historian and lecturer, was born on 2 August 1907 at Sutton, Surrey, the eldest of three children and the only son of Stanley Edgar Taylor (*fl.* 1870–1935), corn merchant, and his wife, Ethel Elizabeth Clifton Hills (*fl.* 1875–1960). He adopted the hyphenated form of his surname by deed poll in the 1930s. He was educated at Bishop's Stortford College, Queen's College, Oxford, where he read modern history (he obtained third-class honours in 1928), and the Sorbonne. Taylor's father was a good photographer, but his mother provided his main cultural and intellectual stimulus. It was his father's expectation that one day he would run the family business. He therefore joined Lloyds, but the commercial world proved so uncongenial that when the Courtauld Institute of Art opened in 1931 he persuaded his father to allow him to give up insurance and pursue aesthetics.

Clifton-Taylor graduated from the Courtauld with first-class honours in 1934 and went to live in South Kensington, London, where he remained until the time of his death. He began lecturing for the Institute of Education at London University, and learned to paint. In the war years he served in the Admiralty, first in Bath and in 1943–6 in London as private secretary to the parliamentary secretary.

Clifton-Taylor resumed lecturing extramurally for London University in 1946. Much of the conventional art-historical teaching he considered arid and unexciting, and he persuaded the authorities to institute a new diploma course of his devising, 'The aesthetic approach to the visual arts'. In this he pioneered a fresh approach, looking at works of art less in terms of their provenance than in the ways in which they were composed in colour, texture, and material, considering above all whether they were great works and why. He was reputedly among the first in England to use colour slides in his lectures, which caused some stir at the time within the art establishment.

In 1956 Clifton-Taylor went freelance, writing articles and reviews for *The Connoisseur* and *The Listener*, with an occasional broadcast. Over the next twenty years he was much in demand as a lecturer, notably for the National Trust, British Council, and English-Speaking Union. He lectured in every continent and in thirty-two American states. He now concentrated his visual approach towards architecture and the traditional building materials. In 1962 he published his masterwork *The Pattern of English Building*, revised twice by himself and published again with his posthumous amendments edited by Jack Simmons, in 1987. This is the fullest work in the English language on the history of building materials, considered comprehensively in terms of their history, use, and aesthetic qualities. Six books followed, notably *The Cathedrals of England* (1967), and *English Parish Churches as Works of Art* (1974, reissued 1986). Despite Clifton-Taylor's love of church architecture he was not religious. He contributed essays to eighteen volumes of *The Buildings of England* edited by Sir Nikolaus Pevsner, whose close friend he was for forty years. Much of the material for all this output was readily available; everything he saw he noted in tiny, neat handwriting in diaries and jottings carefully indexed.

At the age of sixty-eight Clifton-Taylor made his television début. His immediate success led to three series of programmes about English small towns for BBC television. He was president of the Kensington Society from 1979, a vice-president of the Men of the Stones, and a trustee of the Historic Churches Preservation Trust. He became FSA in 1963, honorary fellow of the Royal Institute of British Architects in 1979, and OBE in 1982.

Clifton-Taylor expressed his likes and dislikes forcefully, yet his opinions were always reasoned and informed by a lifetime's keen observation. For example, he held that glazing bars should always be in place in a Georgian façade, and creepers never allowed to obscure good craftsmanship. He disliked Victorian building in machine-made materials, and he was unsympathetic to the modern movement, particularly with high-rise and naked concrete. His aim was to convey learning by looking; even his most cogent criticism was tempered with humour and sincerity.

An incessant worker and indefatigable traveller, in his late fifties Clifton-Taylor walked the formidable strada degli Alpini and he returned from a strenuous tour of southern India only six weeks before his death. His lifestyle was modest, yet he was generous in his friendships, in many public causes, and with help to private individuals. The residue of his substantial estate he left to the National Trust. His life was happy and fulfilled; he died, unmarried, on 1 April 1985, in St Stephen's Hospital, London. His remains were cremated about a week later at Mortlake, London.   DENIS MORIARTY

Sources personal knowledge (2004) · private information (1990) [Philip Burkett, Jack Simmons, Peter Crawley, Mervyn Blatch] · *WWW* · b. cert.

Archives RIBA BAL, architectural notebooks | priv. coll., diaries · priv. coll., travel MSS | FILM BBC Film and Video Archive, 3 series on English Towns, (1978, 1981, 1984) | SOUND BBC Sound Archive

Likenesses photographs, priv. coll. · photographs, priv. coll.

Wealth at death £1,022,074: administration, 23 Aug 1985, *CGPLA Eng. & Wales*

Taylor, Alfred Edward (1869–1945), philosopher, was born at Oundle on 22 December 1869, the elder son of the Revd Alfred Taylor, a Wesleyan minister, and formerly a missionary on the Gold Coast, and his wife, Caroline Esther Fax. He was educated at Kingswood School, Bath, and at New College, Oxford, of which he was elected a scholar and, in 1931, an honorary fellow. He obtained first classes in honour moderations (1889) and *literae humaniores* (1891).

Taylor's career was entirely academic, beginning with a prize fellowship at Merton College, Oxford (1891–8), and after service as assistant lecturer in Greek and philosophy at the University of Manchester (1896–1903), as Frothingham professor of philosophy at McGill University, Montreal (1903–8), and as professor of moral philosophy in the University of St Andrews (1908–24). It ended with the professorship of moral philosophy at the University of Edinburgh, from which he retired in 1941, while continuing to

Alfred Edward Taylor (1869–1945), by Drummond Young, *c*.1935

do the work of the chair until 1944. He married in 1900 Lydia Jutsum (*d.* 1938), an author, second daughter of Edmund Passmore, of Ruggs, Somerset. They had one son.

Taylor was a man of very remarkable learning. On Plato he was an authority of international repute. With John Burnet, who was his colleague at St Andrews, he adhered steadfastly to the theory that most of what Plato in his dialogues attributes to Socrates comes from Socrates' own teaching; but this did not prevent him from learning from other Platonic scholars who did not share his views in this matter, notably in his later years from Professor Werner W. Jaeger, whose *Paideia* he wholeheartedly admired.

It was said that Taylor was too learned ever to be a real philosopher, and that his knowledge, classical, historical, literary, scientific, and mathematical, interfered with sustained metaphysical analysis and construction. Certainly his scholarly work occupied much of his time, and he was incapable of writing without a wealth of learned allusion. Yet in the end he was a philosopher, and his contribution to the subject was threefold.

Taylor was close to F. H. Bradley when he was at Merton, and his early work on conduct and metaphysical issues showed the influence of the Oxford brand of Hegelian idealism. In *Elements of Metaphysics* (1903), Taylor presented Bradleian idealism in textbook style. Yet his first published work, *The Problem of Conduct* (1901), maintains that ethics is independent of metaphysics and its study can only take an empirical form. *Contra* Hegel, Taylor argues that the self and society are at odds with one another and that no resolution is possible between them, only compromise.

Taylor moved on from British idealism, partly as a result of a study of the writings of Ernst Mach, partly as a result of association with Samuel Alexander at Manchester, and with G. F. Stout at St Andrews, partly as a result of sustained study of Galileo, Leibniz, and Descartes. Gradually a revised conception of the task of metaphysical philosophy formed in his mind, and the fruits of it may be seen not only in his Gifford lectures delivered at St Andrews in 1926–8 (published in 1930) as *The Faith of a Moralist* but in the earlier study, 'Theism', contributed to Hastings's *Encyclopaedia of Religion and Ethics*. This latter work is one of the most valuable introductions to theistic metaphysics in the English language, and is a noteworthy combination of scholarly and analytical acumen. It is perhaps of more lasting worth than his last book, *Does God Exist?* (1945), where possibly too much weight is placed on the argument from design.

Secondly, Taylor's deep interest in the problems of religion drove him inevitably to a study of the medieval schoolmen. The fruits of this are to be seen in all the writings of his post-Bradleian period, and he is always remarkable for the discriminating freedom with which he handles scholastic concepts. His contribution to the development of neo-scholasticism is important because it is indirect.

But, thirdly, Taylor's work as a moralist is perhaps most important. In scattered articles on such problems as freedom, the nature of goodness, the relation of the right and the good, he showed something of the depth of his reflection. He was of course a profound student of Plato and Aristotle, as his works, including *Plato: the Man and his Work* (1926) and *A Commentary on Plato's 'Timaeus'* (1927), show; but he had also mastered Kant's ethics, considering them of far greater importance than their author's theory of knowledge. To his students he conveyed the sense of standing in a great tradition of reflection on the problems of conduct, which he was concerned to expound and develop. With many of the moderns (for example, the Oxford deontological school) he was impatient; and by the time one had heard him out, the grounds of his impatience were clear.

Taylor was a strong Anglo-Catholic and on occasion spoke at Anglo-Catholic congresses as well as contributing to the well-known symposium *Essays Catholic and Critical* (edited by the Revd Edward Gordon Selwyn, 1926). None who heard him speak on religion easily forgot the depth of his faith; none who knew him at all forgot the great kindness and generosity of which he was capable, shown not least to his assistants and to the very weakest members of his classes.

Taylor received many honours, including the fellowship of the British Academy (1911) and several honorary degrees. He died at his home, Mornscott, 20 Ross Road, Edinburgh, on 31 October 1945.

DONALD M. MACKINNON, *rev.* MARK J. SCHOFIELD

Sources W. D. Ross, *PBA*, 31 (1945), 407–24 · *Manchester Guardian* (16 Nov 1945) · A. Quinton, 'Alfred Edward Taylor', *Biographical dictionary of twentieth-century philosophers*, ed. S. Brown, D. Collinson, and R. Wilkinson (1996) · *CGPLA Eng. & Wales* (1946)

Archives BL, corresp. with Macmillans, Add. MS 55166 · CUL, letters to E. H. Blakeney · JRL, letters to Samuel Alexander
Likenesses D. Foggie, pencil drawing, 1934, Scot. NPG · D. Young, photograph, c.1935, NPG [*see illus.*]
Wealth at death no value given: confirmation, 25 Jan 1946, *CGPLA Eng. & Wales*

Taylor, Alfred Swaine (1806–1880), medical jurist and toxicologist, born at Northfleet, Kent, on 11 December 1806, was the eldest son of Thomas Taylor, a captain in the East India Company's maritime service, and his first wife, Susan Mary, daughter of Charles Badger, manufacturer of gun flints, a member of an old Kentish family. Taylor was privately educated at Dr Benson's school, Albemarle House, Hounslow, and in June 1822 he was apprenticed to Mr D. Macrae, a medical practitioner at Lenham, near Maidstone, Kent. In October 1823 he was entered as a student at the united hospitals of Guy's and St Thomas's, London where he took a particular interest in chemistry taught by William Allen and Arthur Aikin. He spent the summer of 1825 in Paris, and on his return to London received the anatomical prize at St Thomas's. On the separation of the two hospitals he attached himself to Guy's studying under Sir Astley Cooper and Joseph Henry Green, gaining a reputation for his knowledge of physiology.

Taylor became a licentiate of the Society of Apothecaries of London in 1828 and then embarked upon a tour of the medical schools of Europe. In Paris he attended the lectures of the toxicologist Matthieu Joseph Bonaventura Orfila, the surgeon Guillaume Dupuytren and the chemist Joseph Louis Gay-Lussac. Taylor spent time in the Auvergne, where he prepared a note on the geology of the Puy de Dôme which was published in the *London Medical and Physical Journal*. He visited the medical school at Montpellier before boarding a ship for Naples, which he reached after a stormy and perilous voyage. At one stage of his journey Taylor was arrested for having dangerous books in his possession and he was to be arrested again on his homeward journey, this time as a suspected spy, after sketching the fortifications near Brescia.

Taylor stayed in Naples for nine months and wrote two articles on physiology which were published in the *Giornale Medico Napolitano*. His account of the Grotta de' Cani, notorious for its suffocating fumes, was later published in the *London Medical and Physical Journal*. The overland journey home, much of it on foot, began in February 1829. He travelled through Italy, Switzerland, the Tyrol, Germany, and the Low Countries visiting medical schools in Rome, Florence, Bologna, Milan, Heidelberg, Leiden, Amsterdam, and Brussels. He spent the winter of 1829–1830 at Guy's Hospital and became a member of the Royal College of Surgeons in March 1830. A third visit to Paris was made in the summer of 1830 at the time of the revolution and Taylor was able to study gunshot wounds and their treatment by the surgeons Jacques Manec and Jacques Lisfranc at La Pitié.

The visits to Paris had aroused Taylor's interest in forensic medicine at the time when the Society of Apothecaries made the subject a requirement for its licentiate diploma.

In 1831 Taylor was appointed to the newly created post of lecturer of medical jurisprudence at Guy's Hospital, and he held the post as professor until 1877. His inaugural course of lectures was attended by some leading members of the bar and some judges. Taylor was particularly interested in the application of chemistry to medicine and in 1832 he was appointed joint lecturer in chemistry at Guy's with Arthur Aikin: from 1851 until his resignation in 1870 he held the chair in chemistry alone. In July 1834 he married Caroline, only daughter of John Cancellor, a London stockbroker; they had one child, a daughter, Edith.

In 1836 Taylor published the first volume of *Elements of Medical Jurisprudence*, but finding that the scale of the work would require four volumes he rearranged the subject matter to provide a more convenient and practical guide for the medical jurist. The revised work, *A Manual of Medical Jurisprudence*, was published in 1844 and went through ten editions in Taylor's lifetime. In 1848 he published *Poisons in Relation to Medical Jurisprudence and Medicine* which like the earlier *Manual* presented codified legal precedents and rulings together with relevant, anatomical, clinical, and chemical data. Taylor's *Principles and Practice of Medical Jurisprudence* appeared in 1865; a second edition in two volumes followed in 1873. These books became standard works and established Taylor as the major contributor to the professional establishment of medical jurisprudence. He contributed a regular series of articles on medico-legal cases to the *British Medical Journal* and to the *London Medical Gazette*, acting as editor of the latter between 1844 and 1851. Taylor became FRS (1845), MRCP (1848), and FRCP (1853). In 1852 he received the honorary degree of MD from the University of St Andrews, and in 1859, in recognition of his writings on medical jurisprudence, he was awarded the Swiney prize by the Society of Arts.

By the mid-1850s Taylor had been consulted on about five hundred medico-legal cases and was recognized as a leading medical jurist. His public reputation was built upon his appearances as an expert witness in a number of highly publicized murder trials. As a toxicologist Taylor's experience was equalled only by Robert Christison, and he appeared as a witness for the prosecution in a number of trials for suspected murder by poisoning, becoming in time adviser to the Treasury in cases of particular difficulty. By combining legal precedent and judicial ruling with chemical and anatomical evidence he established forensic toxicology as a medical specialism. The most notable trial in which he appeared was that of William Palmer, who was accused of murdering John Parsons Cook with strychnine. Taylor's evidence, and the criticism of it by Sergeant Robert Shee for the defence, were widely reported. After Palmer's execution Taylor published an assessment of the evidence in *On poisoning by strychnia, with comments on the medical evidence at the trial of William Palmer for the murder of John Parsons Cook* (1856).

The controversial trials of Palmer in 1856 and Dr Thomas Smethurst in 1859 did much to influence Taylor's opinions concerning the nature and use of medical evidence in murder trials. Early in his career Taylor had been aware of problems posed by medical evidence. In the first edition of his *Manual* he laid down the principle that it was the task of the jury to decide the verdict and that the medical jurist must, in doubtful cases, refrain from devoting his energies to only one side of the question. His subsequent experience in poisoning cases led him to conclude that analytical results, obtained by the imperfect methods of his time, provided only a certain degree of probability and where admitted as evidence should be used only to supplement the medical observations. The uncertainties were such that he opposed the system of engaging medical witnesses for prosecution and defence and he advocated instead a system of assessments by independent medical experts.

Taylor was also a pioneer of photography and devised improvements in the fixing and printing processes used by William Henry Fox Talbot. He described his methods in his *On the Art of Photogenic Drawing* (1840). He also had an interest in thermometry and published two works on the subject, *A thermometric table on the scales of fahrenheit, centigrade and Reaumur, compressing the most remarkable phenomena connected with temperature* (1845) and *On the Temperature of the Earth and Sea in Reference to the Theory of Central Heat* (1846). He revised and edited *A New Treatise of the Use of Globes* by Thomas Keith (1848), and in 1853 assisted George Owen Rees in editing the final part of *The Elements of Materia medica and Therapeutics*, which was left incomplete by the death of Jonathan Pereira. In 1863 he and George Brande published *Chemistry* and in 1876 he published an edited version of *Elements of Physics* by Neil Arnott.

Taylor was described as a man of commanding stature who was calm and earnest in his manner. He was an accomplished amateur artist, had a knowledge of Latin and Greek, and was fluent in French, Italian, and German. He was said to be a man of quiet domestic traits and rarely to be seen at medical social events. Taylor lived in almost complete retirement in his last years and died of heart disease on 27 May 1880 at his home, 15 St James's Terrace, Regent's Park, London.   M. P. EARLES

Sources *BMJ* (12 June 1880), 905–6 · *Medical Times and Gazette* (12 June 1880), 642–3 · N. G. Coley, 'Alfred Swaine Taylor (1806–80), forensic toxicologist', *Medical History*, 35 (1991), 409–27 · A. Besson, 'The medico-legal tracts collection of Dr A. S. Taylor, FRCP', *Journal of the Royal College of Physicians of London*, 17 (1983), 147–9 · Munk, *Roll* · *Annual Register* (1845) · *Annual Register* (1856) · *DNB*
Archives BL · NHM, autobiographical notes · RCP Lond., report of analyses in case of suspected poisoning
Likenesses E. Edwards, photograph, 1868, Wellcome L. · Barraud & Jerrard, photograph, 1873, Wellcome L. · Horne & Thornwaite, photograph, V&A · miniature, RCP Lond. · photograph, Wellcome L.
Wealth at death under £60,000: probate, 5 July 1880, *CGPLA Eng. & Wales*

Taylor [*née* Martin], **Ann** (1757–1830), writer, was born on 20 June 1757 in London, the daughter of Thomas Martin (1734/5–1764), a disciple of George Whitefield, and his wife, Mary Plaxton (*d.* 1798?), daughter of a clergyman's son (or grandson) from Yorkshire. Her childhood was not happy. Her father, whom she adored despite his being a religious fundamentalist whose beliefs bordered on the deranged, died when she was six; her mother married

Ann Taylor (1757–1830), by Isaac Taylor, *c.*1790

again twice and Ann was neglected by her stepfather, a Mr Hewitt, and treated contemptuously by her half-siblings. At her day school in London, however, an enquiring mind and a flair for writing quickly marked her out; her 'poetic and often satirical effusions soon gained her a local celebrity' (*Autobiography*, 1.15).

On 18 April 1781 at St Andrew's, Holborn, Ann married Isaac *Taylor (1759–1829), a young engraver and committed dissenter whom she had known since childhood. He had initiated his courtship by secreting a poem in a teapot of hers that he had been commissioned to engrave. She responded indignantly in kind and there ensued a 'paper war, which, for a time, made the gossip of the little circle' (*Autobiography*, 1.16), but which ended in their engagement. Isaac and Ann were singularly well matched—in intelligence, in outlook, and in talents—and remained deeply in love throughout their life together. There were eleven children, six of whom survived to adulthood: three girls (Ann, Jane, and Jemima) and three boys (Isaac, Martin, and Jefferys). Four became writers: Ann *Gilbert (1782–1866) [*see under* Taylor, Jane], Jane *Taylor (1783–1824), Isaac *Taylor (1787–1865), and Jefferys *Taylor (1792–1853).

Ann Taylor found the early years of her marriage hard; money was short and the responsibilities of motherhood were exacerbated by the frail health of her children. Constitutionally a worrier, she became so weighed down with cares that a friend was moved to warn her to take action to retain her husband's interest and affection. Since she had no other time to spare, her response was to institute a practice of reading aloud to him at mealtimes, thereby keeping her own mind active and providing material for subsequent discussion. This practice continued for over forty years and in due course made an important contribution to her children's education too—though her daughter Ann believed that it also played havoc with her mother's digestion and hindered the children's acquiring the art of conversation.

Ann Taylor participated fully in her children's remarkable education, which was carried out almost exclusively at home. Her influence upon the characters and mental habits of her talented children was very considerable and gratefully acknowledged. However, despite her own early predilections she did not encourage her daughters Ann and Jane to write, being wont to declare that female authors 'would have done better to employ themselves in mending the family stockings' (Taylor, 'Memoirs', 1.28). It was a nice irony that she later became the first female member of the family to publish in her own name.

Ann Taylor's health was never strong and she suffered from deafness from quite an early age. The strain of nursing her husband through a near fatal illness in 1793 further undermined her constitution and she contended with frailty, and perhaps with migraines, for the rest of her life. Her character was not overshadowed by these infirmities. As her youngest child, Jemima, remembered in a letter of 26 January 1869, 'though an anxious temper, [she] had much native sprightliness, which sparkled beautifully sometimes' (Taylor collection, HD 588/6/107). Her daughter Ann annotated a portrait of her mother thus: 'She always wore a turban … The face and features generally give the idea of a larger woman than she was, but they retain the impression of constant pain, almost extreme deafness, and deep retired thought and feeling' (*Ann Taylor Gilbert's Album*, 81).

Ann Taylor was a prolific and lively correspondent, writing regularly to her children whenever they were apart. The texts of many of these letters survive; in them the spirit of the youthful satirist gleams through the pages of sound maternal advice, together with an eye for detail and a striking gift for narrative. About 1811 she composed for Jemima, then thirteen, a manual of instruction—a blend of spiritual, behavioural, and practical advice. The method was apparently chosen because Ann's increasing deafness made conversation difficult. She had originally no thought of its being published but was later persuaded that it would benefit a wider readership; in 1814 it was published as *Maternal Solicitude for a Daughter's Best Interests*. It sold extremely well, going into fifteen editions (two of them American) over the next sixteen years. There followed other works in the same vein: *Practical Hints to Young Females* (1815); *The Present of a Mistress to a Young Servant* (1816); *Reciprocal Duties of Parents and Children* (1818); and, in collaboration with her daughter Jane, *Correspondence between a Mother and her Daughter at School* (1817). Most proved equally popular and influential. Their tone was moral but lacking in sanctimony, and the advice on parenthood and education strikingly permissive for its time. Ann also published two moralistic novellas, or 'tales', for the young—*The Family Mansion* (1819) and *Retrospection: a Tale* (1821)—and a collection of moral essays, *The Itinerary of*

a Traveller in the Wilderness (1825), a work much preoccupied with death and the afterlife.

In her own eyes, however, Ann Taylor's true monument was her family, to whom, after God, her life was devoted. An unidentified visitor to the Taylor household in 1824 declared, 'I never met with a person so truly great and yet so affectionately tender as Mrs Taylor' (Armitage, 85). Yet the tenderness was spiced with an acerbic wit. Her husband's death on 12 December 1829 apparently deprived her of the will to live; having survived him by less than six months she died at her home in Ongar on 27 May 1830. She was buried at the Independent burial-ground in Ongar on 4 June; her grave, beside that of her husband, now lies under the vestry floor of the United Reformed church in Ongar. ROBIN TAYLOR GILBERT

Sources *Autobiography and other memorials of Mrs Gilbert (formerly Ann Taylor)*, ed. J. Gilbert, 2 vols. (1874) • I. Taylor, 'Memoirs and correspondence of Jane Taylor', *The family pen: memorials biographical and literary, of the Taylor family of Ongar*, ed. I. Taylor, 1 (1867) • C. D. Stewart, *The Taylors of Ongar: an analytical bio-bibliography*, 2 vols. (1975) • R. Gilbert, 'The Taylors of Ongar and their houses there', *Aspects of the history of Ongar*, ed. M. Leach (1999) • St Andrew's, Holborn, registers • Ongar, United Reformed church, records • *Ann Taylor Gilbert's album*, ed. C. D. Stewart (1978) • Suffolk RO, Bury St Edmunds, Taylor collection, HD 588/4/14; HD 588/1/147; HD 588/4/7; HD 588/6/107 • D. Armitage, *The Taylors of Ongar* (1939) • letters, Toronto Public Library, Osborne Collection of Children's Books, Taylor collection • private information (2004)
Archives Suffolk RO, Bury St Edmunds, MSS | Toronto Public Library, Osborne collection of children's books, MSS
Likenesses I. Taylor, crayon drawing, c.1790, Suffolk RO, Bury St Edmunds, Taylor collection, sketchbook of Taylor, HD 588/4/30 [*see illus.*] • I. Taylor, oils, c.1790, Guildhall, Lavenham, Taylor Room • J. Gilbert, pencil drawing, 1830 (in old age), Toronto Public Library, Osborne collection of children's books, Taylor collection, family album of Ann Gilbert • J. Gilbert, pencil drawing (in late middle age; after I. Taylor), Toronto Public Library, Osborne collection of children's books, Taylor collection, family album of Ann Gilbert • I. Taylor, miniature (in late middle age), Guildhall, Lavenham, Taylor Room • I. Taylor, portrait, photograph, Suffolk RO, Bury St Edmunds, Taylor collection, HD 588/12/1
Wealth at death in comfortable financial circumstance, but hardly wealthy: will, PRO, PROB 11/1773, sig. 415; will, PRO, PROB 11/1764 [Isaac Taylor]

Taylor, Annie Royle (*b*. 1855, *d*. after 1908), traveller and missionary, was born on 17 October 1855 at Egremont, Cheshire, the second of the ten children of John Taylor, director of the Black Ball Line of sailing ships, and his wife, Carolina Francisca, daughter of Peter Foulkes, merchant. She came of a family aware of far horizons. Her father had travelled widely in his youth and her mother was born in Brazil. Annie was a delicate child, overindulged and under-employed, who grew up restless and discontented until conversion to evangelical Christianity at the age of thirteen gave her a purpose in life by making her determined to become a missionary. Although she was strongly opposed by her father, her iron will prevailed, and, after spending the intervening years working in the slums of Brighton and London and studying medicine in London, she sailed for Shanghai on 12 September 1884, in the service of the China Inland Mission.

In 1886 Annie Taylor was posted to Lanzhou in northwest China, close to the frontier with Tibet. She had

Annie Royle Taylor (*b.* 1855, *d.* 1908), by Thomas Charles Turner, pubd 1893

always been interested in the 'forbidden land', closed to strangers by the Buddhist priesthood backed by neighbouring China, tenacious of its commercial and political interests. 'Poor things,' mused missionary Taylor, 'They know no better. No one has told them of Jesus' (A. R. Taylor, 159) and she became convinced that God called her to claim the forbidden land in his name. Her recall from Lanzhou because of ill health brought to an end her work for the China Inland Mission, though she remained on their books until 1893. She regained her health on a holiday in Australia with her parents, returning determined to answer God's call to Tibet. While studying the language in a Sikkim monastery, she encountered Pontso, a young Tibetan whom she converted to Christianity and who was to accompany her on her travels.

In March 1891 Annie returned to Shanghai accompanied by Pontso and together they took the long road across China to the Tibetan frontier. Their plan was simple: to ride through Tibet to Lhasa and on over the Indian frontier to Darjeeling, claiming the country in some unspecified way for 'the Master'. They began their journey with ten horses, two months' supply of food, a few pieces of silver and some Chinese cloth to pay their way, and a box of presents for chiefs. They set off in September 1892 on a journey of unimaginable hardship and danger, climbing mountain passes, fording rivers, attacked by bandits, weakened by fatigue and exposure, their horses dying by the wayside. They might yet have made it but for Noga, the only survivor of the three men hired for the journey, who became increasingly aware of the danger to himself of escorting strangers to Lhasa and was to betray them to the authorities as they neared the forbidden city.

Annie Taylor was sustained throughout by her conviction that she was under God's protection. 'He will undertake for me,' runs her diary, 'He has sent me on this journey and I am His little woman' (A. R. Taylor, 223). There were pleasant interludes: they had been joined by Penting, a friendly young Tibetan, and, giving Noga the slip, Annie and her two men enjoyed 'a nice Christmas Day, sun shining brightly … quite safe here with Jesus' (A. R. Taylor, 240), for which she contrived a Christmas pudding.

Early in the new year they were within a few days' march of Lhasa, to find that Noga had been before them and reported them to the local authority. Arrested and required to appear before local representatives, Annie was not intimidated though she knew they were in deadly peril. The day before the hearing she spent in 'washing my sleeves, so as to look presentable' (A. R. Taylor, 255) and in cheering Penting and Pontso (the latter in tears); the night was spent in prayer. Confronted next day by a 'big Chief' and a crowd of spectators, she utterly refused to return to China with exhausted horses and few provisions by the long route of their arrival. She demanded good horses, sufficient provisions, and safe conduct for herself and her two men by the shortest route out of Tibet. She got her way and in April she and Pontso arrived safely in China, having said goodbye to Penting at his home. They had been in Tibet for seven months and covered some 1300 miles.

Annie returned to England to much acclaim, in which Pontso shared. She failed, however, to establish a 'Tibetan pioneer band' on the Sikkim–Tibet border and in May 1894 she and Pontso moved to Yatung in this border area, from where there was a view of Tibet down a narrow valley. Here the British had set up a market to promote trade with Tibet, and here Annie opened a little store. She was visited at Yatung by William Carey, who in 1902 published her edited diary. In time she tired, and, leaving Pontso to run the store, she stayed in Yatung until some time between 1907 and 1909 when she returned to Britain; it is not known where or when she died. Annie's sister Susette Martha Taylor was born on 20 September 1860 at Egremont Villa, Norwood, Surrey. She was educated abroad and at King's College, London, before reading modern languages at Lady Margaret Hall, Oxford, in 1884–6. She obtained a baccalaureate from the University of Barcelona in 1890. A fellow of the Royal Geographical Society, she shared the family interest in travel and visited her sister in 1903 in Yatung where she reported her to be comfortably installed and quite a local character. Back in

Britain, Susette was involved in teaching and in censorship and intelligence work in the First World War, when her command of languages proved useful. She published several works, mainly translations from Spanish and Russian. She died unmarried on 28 January 1920 of pleurisy at 22 Cromwell Crescent, Kensington, London. The Susette Taylor travelling fellowship at Lady Margaret Hall, Oxford, was founded in her memory by her sister Mrs Bethell.

DOROTHY MIDDLETON

Sources A. R. Taylor, 'My diary in Tibet', ed. W. Carey, in W. Carey, *Travel and adventure in Tibet* (1902), 173–285 · D. Middleton, *Victorian lady travellers* (1965) · I. S. Robson, *Two lady missionaries in Tibet* (1909) · J. H. Taylor and Mrs H. Taylor, *Life of Hudson Taylor*, 2 vols. (1911) · C. Avent and H. Pipe, eds., *Lady Margaret Hall register, 1879–1990* (1990) · M. Bell and C. McEwan, 'The admission of women fellows to the Royal Geographical Society, 1892–1914: the controversy and the outcome', *GJ*, 162 (1996), 295–312 · *GJ*, 57 (1921), 238 [obit. of Susette Taylor] · b. cert. [Susette Taylor] · A. R. Taylor, 'My adventures in Tibet', *Scottish Geographical Magazine*, 10 (1894), 1–8
Likenesses T. C. Turner, photograph, pubd 1893, NPG [*see illus.*] · two photographs, repro. in Middleton, *Victorian lady travellers*, 130–31

Taylor, Brook (1685–1731), mathematician, was born on 18 August 1685 in Edmonton, Middlesex, the eldest son of John Taylor (1655–1729), merchant, and his wife, Olivia (*d.* 1716), daughter of Sir Nicholas Tempest, baronet, of Durham. John's puritan father, Nathaniel Taylor (*d.* 1684), was a barrister who had been selected by Cromwell in 1653 to represent the county of Bedford in parliament. In 1694 John Taylor purchased the estate of Bifrons within a large park in the parish of Patrixbourne, near Canterbury. Here he ran his household with an autocratic hand, his austere nature succumbing to one domestic pleasure, music. Among its celebrated practitioners, Lully, Couperon, Babel, and Geminiani were invited to perform at his home. In a painting by Closterman of the eight children of John Taylor about 1698 the young Brook is shown seated with recorder in hand while two of his older sisters prepare to crown him with a laurel wreath.

During his adolescence Taylor became an accomplished musician and artist, talents which would find mathematical expression in later years in his pioneering study of the vibrating string, and in his treatise on linear perspective. A portrait by Goupy depicts the adult Taylor beside his harpsichord, pointing to an open copy of this treatise, with a landscape on the wall behind him, presumably executed by his own hand. After being tutored at home Taylor was admitted as a fellow-commoner to St John's College, Cambridge, on 3 April 1701; he graduated LLB in 1709 and LLD in 1714. He was admitted an advocate in the court of arches in 1714, but no mention of any legal activity on his part has been found.

During his years at Cambridge, Taylor became proficient in mathematics and physics, and he was elected fellow of the Royal Society on 3 April 1712. Two weeks later he was chosen, along with Abraham De Moivre and Francis Aston, to serve on the Royal Society committee charged with adjudicating the priority controversy between Newton and Leibniz over the invention of the calculus. Although the committee's task was completed one week

Brook Taylor (1685–1731), by Louis Goupy?, 1720

later, allowing Taylor only limited participation, this was his first public act as a partisan of Newton and paved the way for his subsequent activity as a proponent of Newtonian mechanics and the fluxional calculus. John Keill, Savilian professor of astronomy at Oxford and Newton's most outspoken advocate, became Taylor's mentor and friend. In his correspondence with Keill in 1712 and 1713 Taylor discussed many of his important discoveries, which appeared later in his book *Methodus incrementorum*. Two results on the centre of oscillation, composed in 1708, and on the vibrating string, were first published in the *Philosophical Transactions of the Royal Society* (1713).

In response to the Royal Society's interest in experiments that would advance Newtonian physics, Taylor worked on his own and with curators Francis Hauksbee and J. T. Desaguliers to try to determine the laws of capillarity, magnetic force, and thermometry. On 13 January 1715 he was elected secretary of the Royal Society after the death of Richard Waller. His book *Linear Perspective* appeared later that year, written in formal mathematical style with axioms and theorems. Although the abstruse and concise nature of the text made it inaccessible to most artists, the work influenced later writers on the subject and holds a prominent place in the history of perspective. Not only did it contain contributions to the theory of inverse problems and direct construction, but it was the first to call attention to the importance of vanishing points and lines. Taylor published an expanded version, *New Principles of Linear Perspective*, in 1719.

During the year in which his first treatise on perspective appeared Taylor also published his chief mathematical work, *Methodus incrementorum directa et inversa* (1715; 2nd edn, 1717). He felt that his new method of increments, which came to be known as finite differences, would furnish a stronger and more consistent basis for the Newtonian fluxional calculus than Newton himself had given. The first part of the text concerns the fundamental principles of the method and the transformation and solution of finite difference and differential equations. The second part contains applications of both his method and the calculus to problems in mathematics and mechanics. Several of these, including the formulae for the derivatives of the inverse function, the recognition of a singular solution to a differential equation, a comprehensive discussion of the number and type of boundary conditions to be adjoined to finite difference and differential equations, the equation of motion and fundamental period of the vibrating string, and the differential equation for the path of a ray of light in the atmosphere, were first treated by Taylor. Others, like the catenary, isoperimetric problems, and the centres of oscillation and percussion, had been treated by continental mathematicians, especially Huygens, Leibniz, and the brothers Jacob and Johann Bernoulli.

The celebrated series known as the Taylor series occurs in proposition 7, corollary 2 of *Methodus incrementorum*. Taylor proved it using finite differences and the Gregory–Newton interpolation formula and invoked a passage to the limit that modern mathematicians would not consider rigorous. There is no discussion of a remainder term or convergence. Although Taylor was not the first to find the form of the series—he was anticipated by James Gregory, Newton, Leibniz, Johann Bernoulli, and De Moivre—he can be credited with publishing it first, along with a proof based on his theory of finite increments. Moreover he was the first to appreciate its importance and to demonstrate its applicability as an analytical tool: he employed it to generate series solutions to differential equations of all orders, to obtain series representations for integrals, and to find approximations to the roots of ordinary equations. Although the Taylor series about zero came to be associated with Colin MacLaurin, when MacLaurin published his own derivation using the method of undetermined coefficients, he acknowledged his predecessor: 'This theorem was given by Dr Taylor method. increm.' (C. MacLaurin, *A Treatise of Fluxions*, 2, 1742, 611).

Despite praiseworthy comments about Taylor's achievements from Euler, Lagrange, and others, his *Methodus* was not without its detractors. By citing no one but Newton in the text, Taylor incurred the wrath of Leibniz and Johann Bernoulli, both of whom accused him of deliberate obscurity and lack of originality. Bernoulli went further and charged Taylor with plagiarism. Most would agree that Taylor's style is excessively terse and obscure and that he was negligent in failing to acknowledge the work of his continental predecessors, but Taylor's unpublished papers in London (RS, MS 82) and Cambridge (Taylor MSS, St John's College) show the charge of plagiarism to be unfounded. Nevertheless, the controversy between Taylor and Bernoulli escalated, with accusations from each side

appearing publicly in the journals and in their private correspondence with others.

Taylor's most frequent correspondent and confidant was the French probabilist Pierre Rémond de Monmort (1678–1719), whom he met on a visit to Paris in 1715. A disciple of Malebranche, Monmort engaged Taylor in an amicable public debate concerning the merits of Newton's gravitational theory over the vortex theory adhered to by many French Cartesians. Realizing later that Taylor could not be swayed, Monmort vowed, 'I shall love you without loving your attractions, and you shall love me without loving our little vortices' (Monmort to Taylor, 5 Nov 1718, St John's College, Taylor MSS). According to Taylor's grandson, in Paris, Taylor 'was eagerly courted by all who had temper to enjoy, or talents to improve, the charms of social intercourse' (Young, 23–4). Among those seeking his society, in addition to the savants of the Académie Royale des Sciences, were the Abbé Conti, the comte de Caylus, Bishop Bossuet, and Lord Bolingbroke, who became his close friend. It was through the Abbé Conti that Leibniz and Bernoulli sent a challenge problem to the English mathematicians, on orthogonal trajectories for families of curves. Newton was in his seventies by then, and it was left to his younger colleague Taylor to salvage the pride of the English. His solution appeared in the *Philosophical Transactions* (30, 1717). Through Monmort, Taylor sent the Leibnizians two more challenges, on the motion of a projectile in a resisting medium and on the integration of rational fractions. Both problems provoked more bitterness, attacks, and recriminations between Taylor and Bernoulli. Having declared himself neutral in the dispute between Newton and Leibniz, Monmort agreed to play the role of intermediary between Taylor and Bernoulli, but to no avail. The feud ended without resolution after Taylor decided to remain silent in the face of further attacks.

Other events in Taylor's life came to occupy his attention during this time. On 21 October 1718 he resigned as secretary of the Royal Society, informing his fellow secretary Edmond Halley that personal matters would keep him away from London. His health deteriorated and he was sent to recuperate in the spa of Aix-la-Chapelle. Indeed the last decade of his life was marked by failing health and severe emotional strain. In 1721 he married Sarah Elizabeth Brydges, of Wallington, Surrey. The marriage caused an estrangement with his father, since she was 'of good family, but of small fortune' (Young, 33) and his father's consent had not been obtained. In 1723 she died in childbirth, along with the child, but the tragic event had a positive consequence, namely reconciliation between father and son. With his father's approval in 1725 Taylor married Elizabeth (Sabetta), daughter of John Sawbridge of Olantigh, Kent. In July 1729 on the death of his father, Brook inherited the family estate of Bifrons, which was to remain in the Taylor family for close to a century. In March of the next year he lost his second wife in childbirth. This time the child, Elizabeth, survived. (In Taylor's will a second daughter, Olive, is mentioned, but it is not known whether she survived to adulthood.) Years later

Elizabeth's son, Sir William *Young, second baronet, at the request of some members of the Académie Française, composed a short biography of his grandfather and had it printed, along with some of Taylor's correspondence and an unfinished essay entitled *Contemplatio philosophica*. After the death of his second wife, burdened by grief and beset by ill health, Taylor died 'of a decline' (Young, 40) on 30 November 1731 in Somerset House, London. He was buried in London on 2 December 1731, near his first wife, in the churchyard of St Anne's, Soho.

LENORE FEIGENBAUM

Sources W. Young, *Contemplatio philosophica: a posthumous work of the late Brook Taylor … to which is prefixed a life of the author, by his grandson* (privately printed, London, 1793) • L. Feigenbaum, 'Brook Taylor and the method of increments', *Archive for History of Exact Sciences*, 34 (1985), 1–40 • Venn, *Alum. Cant.* • RS, MS 82 • St John Cam., Taylor MSS • K. Andersen, *Brook Taylor's work on linear perspective* (1992) • J. L. Heilbron, *Physics at the Royal Society during Newton's presidency* (1983) • *GM*, 1st ser., 1 (1731), 501 • will, PRO • W. A. Scott Robertson, 'Patricksbourne church, and Bifrons', *Archaeologia Cantiana*, 14 (1882), 169–84 • E. Hasted, 'Patrixborne', *The history and topographical survey of the county of Kent*, 2nd edn, 9 (1800), 277–86 • L. Feigenbaum, 'Happy tercentenary, Brook Taylor!', *Mathematical Intelligencer*, 8 (1986), 53–6 • J. E. B. Mayor, ed., *Admissions to the College of St John the Evangelist in the University of Cambridge*, pts 1–2: *Jan 1629/30 – July 1715* (1882–93), 156 • Burke, *Gen. GB* (1834–8)

Archives RS, letters • St John Cam. | CUL, papers relating to Lucasian professorship

Likenesses J. Closterman, group portrait, oils, 1696? (*The children of John Taylor of Bifrons Park*), NPG • oils, *c*.1715, RS; repro. in Feigenbaum, 'Happy tercentenary, Brook Taylor!' • L. Goupy?, gouache miniature, 1720, NPG [*see illus.*] • R. Earlom, mezzotint (after B. Taylor), BM; repro. in W. Young, *Contemplatio philosophica: a posthumous work of the late Brook Taylor … to which is prefixed a life of the author, by his grandson* (privately printed, London, 1793)

Wealth at death inherited extensive family estate and neighbouring properties

Taylor, Sir Brook (1776–1846). *See under* Taylor, Sir Herbert (1775–1839).

Taylor, Cecil Philip (1929–1981), playwright, was born on 6 November 1929 at 10 Burnbank Terrace, Glasgow, the only son of Max Taylor (*b*. 20 March 1898), a commercial traveller, and Fay, *née* Leventhal (*b*. 1901). Both parents were Jewish and born in Russia. Max, who was born Max Girschovitz, became a naturalized British citizen in February 1920. Cecil Taylor left Queen's Park secondary school, Glasgow, in 1943 at the age of fourteen and had no other formal education. He began a succession of jobs, including electrician, television engineer, and record salesman, while writing stories and poems in his spare time. In 1954 he won a prize from the Jewish Congress for his play *Mister David*, which eventually received its première production at the Jewish State Theatre, Warsaw, thirteen years later. On 8 March 1956 C. P. Taylor, as he was known professionally, married his first wife, Irene Rebecca Diamond (*b*. 30 April 1931), with whom he had two children, Avram and Clare. In 1957 he left Glasgow for Northumberland, where he lived for the rest of his life.

In 1962 Taylor's first professional production, *Aa Went to Blaydon Races*, was staged in Newcastle upon Tyne. He started his long association with the newly formed Traverse Theatre Club in Edinburgh in 1965 with *Happy Days are Here Again*, which played to packed houses. At this time Taylor met Elizabeth Anne Screen (*b*. 6 Dec 1945), with whom he lived from 1966 and had two children, David and Cathryn. His divorce from Irene was achieved in February 1973 and he married Liz on 9 April 1973.

Meanwhile, Taylor had become, and was to remain until the end of his life, among the most prolific dramatists of his, or any other, generation. He battered out an extraordinary profusion of scripts for stage and television, and for amateur and professional performance, on a series of manual typewriters in a wooden shed in his garden. Since there is no precise audit of his lifetime's work, it is difficult to put a final figure on the number of plays he wrote. His conviction that playwrights should contribute usefully to the community in which they lived compelled him to write prolifically for youth theatres, especially the Northumberland Experimental Youth Theatre at Backworth Drama Centre, and for schools, including Northgate special school, near Morpeth, where he worked regularly with disabled children. At the same time Taylor was literary adviser to the Tyneside Theatre Company in Newcastle upon Tyne and the Liverpool Everyman Theatre. He was also a willing mentor to every aspiring playwright who sought his support and advice, and was a founding member of both the Scottish Society of Playwrights and the Northern Playwrights' Society.

Taylor's small Northumberland homes, first at Capheaton and later in Longhorsley, were always full of children and animals (he was an enthusiastic naturalist) and marked by the sound of the constantly ringing telephone. In the relative peace of his garden shed he worked at white heat, knowing that he would edit or discard most of what he wrote. At a time before word processing, he would always reckon to produce at least ten drafts of every play. While producing scripts did not seem to be a problem to him, shaping and structuring what he wrote certainly was. He needed to work with actors and a director he could trust, and produced his performing drafts out of the experience of the rehearsal room. For this reason his working relationships with the Traverse Theatre in Edinburgh, the Live Theatre Company in Newcastle upon Tyne, and, towards the end of his life, with the Royal Shakespeare Company (RSC), were especially productive. The eccentricity of his method was demonstrated while he was working on his two full-length Walter plays, *Getting By* and *Going Home* (Traverse, 1977), in which a dying Glaswegian music hall comedian reviews his complicated domestic and sexual relationships and his lifelong commitment to revolutionary socialism. The two plays were to be performed on consecutive evenings, and Taylor astounded the company after the first read-through by withdrawing the second play in its entirety, returning two days later with a new second script. His hyperactive working method, coupled with his inability to file his various drafts in any sort of order, continue to make the jobs of publisher and producer especially difficult. Typically, the success of *Good* (RSC, 1981), which tells the story of how an apparently good man ends up running a Nazi extermination camp, owes a great deal to the work of the original director, Howard Davies, and to the RSC actors.

At the outset of his career Taylor was convinced that his plays would inspire the working classes to demand social justice, taking to the streets if necessary. Experience caused him to scale down this headstrong ambition and one of the resultant dilemmas faced throughout his work is seen in the idealist's attempt to affect the course of history contrasted with his seeming inability to control his own private and personal life. In addition to *Good*, essential reading in Taylor's *œuvre* includes *Allergy* (Traverse Theatre Club, 1966; published by Penguin, 1966), in which Jim, the editor of *Socialist Reflection* (circulation 150 copies) erupts in a skin rash every time he seeks sex and political enlightenment from Barbara; *Bread and Butter* (Traverse Theatre Club, 1966; published by Penguin, 1967), which traces the lives of two Scottish-Jewish couples from 1931 to 1965 and examines the way in which the great events of history affect their domestic relationships and political views; and *Lies about Vietnam* (Traverse Theatre Club, 1969; published in Methuen Gay Plays, 2, 1985), in which two gay anti-Vietnam War activists are harassed by a homophobic hotel manager.

Taylor's death was sudden and unexpected. He returned home from London after the opening of *Good* on 9 December 1981 in a state of exhaustion and was eventually taken to Morpeth General Hospital, where he died hours later from heart failure. With cruel irony *The Guardian* had announced his new play thus: 'Goodbye, C. P. Taylor'. He left no will and his estate was shared between his widow and his four children. He was buried on 15 December in St Helen's churchyard, Longhorsley, Northumberland.

MICHAEL WILCOX

Sources personal knowledge (2004) · private information (2004) · C. P. Taylor, *Scotland on Sunday Edinburgh International Festival study guide* (1992) · J. Elsom, 'Taylor, C. P.', *Contemporary dramatists*, ed. J. Vinson (1973) · d. cert.
Archives Newcastle Central Library · NL Scot.
Wealth at death £8660: probate, 4 June 1982, *CGPLA Eng. & Wales*

Taylor, (May Doris) Charity, Lady Taylor (1914–1998), prison administrator, was born on 16 September 1914 at West Lea, York Road, Woking, Surrey, the third daughter and youngest of four children of (Wron) George Clifford, journalist, and his wife, Emma Ada, formerly Cundy. Her father wrote on snooker and angling for the *News of the World*. Brought up in Huntingdon, Charity excelled at Huntingdon grammar school and trained in London as a doctor at the London (Royal Free Hospital) School of Medicine for Women. In the late 1930s Dr Clifford was a house surgeon at the Royal Free Hospital and the Elizabeth Garrett Anderson Hospital. She married Stephen James Lake Taylor (1910–1988), also a doctor, on 3 October 1939; two sons and a daughter were born between 1940 and 1950. Resolved to continue working, Charity Taylor in 1942 became an assistant medical officer at HM prison Holloway, the largest women's gaol in Britain. Conditions were bad there during the war, as internment of Nazi

sympathizers caused overcrowding. Despite soap shortages, Dr Taylor improved hygiene and won promotion to medical officer.

Charity Taylor became the first ever female governor of Holloway prison in 1945. Though reluctant to abandon medicine, she wanted to show that a woman could run a major gaol as well as a man (if not better). Portraits of Elizabeth I, Joan of Arc, and Florence Nightingale adorned her office walls. Women's magazines liked to interview the pretty young brunette who combined motherhood with a career commonly associated with severe spinsters. The governor explained that she virtually worked from home, since the Taylors lived in the big battlemented governor's house within the prison complex. Having children may have given her greater insight into certain problems: her study of women gaoled for child neglect in 1948–9 concluded that their offences were due to inadequacy and ignorance rather than to conscious cruelty.

The Criminal Justice Act 1948 allowed some liberalization of the prison regime. More letters and visits were permitted. Access to libraries and recreation improved. Dr Taylor had an open mind on the value of psychiatry. Everyone must stand on their own two feet, she believed, but she could be a good listener as well as a great talker. To boost prisoners' self-esteem, she let them use make-up and choose the colour of their uniforms. The range of educational opportunities widened, though a special pre-release course failed to attract many participants. More successful was the jam factory founded in 1951.

The governorship of Holloway was the toughest job in the women's prison system. With the start of 'open' prisons at Askham Grange and Hill Hall, the population of Holloway dropped to about three hundred after 1952— less than half full—yet the proportion of 'unreformables' grew. Alcoholism and self-harm were common, and tension mounted at the time of executions: Styllou Christofi in 1954 and Ruth Ellis in 1955. Dr Taylor arranged separate blocks for remand prisoners, first-time offenders, and younger inmates. She deemed the work of a governor easy so far as prisoners were concerned: a written code determined their respective roles.

Holloway was a traditional radial prison, opened in 1852, and now grimly antiquated. The governor blamed her own chronic rheumatism on the damp. Its closure, promised in 1938, was postponed in 1939 and 1950; redecoration in brighter colours failed to disguise the pervading gloom, against which Charity Taylor struggled to create a calm and domestic atmosphere. She was certain that cleanliness, orderliness, and discipline had a good effect. Visitors compared her to a firm and efficient headmistress.

Lady Taylor acquired her title in August 1958 when her husband, Labour MP for Barnet (1945–50), became Baron Taylor of Harlow on receipt of a life peerage. In 1959 she took charge of the whole structure of female prisons and borstals in England and Wales as assistant commissioner and inspector of prisons (women)—a post renamed assistant director when the Prison Commission was turned into a department of the Home Office in 1963. Of a total prison roll of 26,000 in 1959, fewer than one thousand were women, but the very smallness of the service presented difficulties, as it could render specialized programmes uneconomic. Lady Taylor was a proficient administrator who assimilated information and made decisions with extraordinary rapidity. She put much effort into training staff and opened a women's prison at Styal, Manchester, in 1963. Plans for another in Essex foundered in 1965, however: the long-awaited redevelopment of Holloway could not begin until 1970. Lady Taylor was a member of the General Advisory Council of the BBC (1964–7).

When Lord Taylor accepted the vice-chancellorship of the Memorial University of Newfoundland in 1967, Charity took early retirement and accompanied him to Canada, where she became president of the Newfoundland and Labrador Social Welfare Council (1968–71). They returned to Britain in 1973 to live near Llangollen. Widowed in 1988, Lady Taylor died at the Princess Royal Hospital, Haywards Heath, Sussex, on 4 January 1998. Her fourteen years at HM prison Holloway had banished any doubt about women governing women's prisons.

JASON TOMES

Sources The Independent (7 Jan 1998) · The Times (14 Jan 1998) · S. J. L. Taylor, A natural history of everyday life (1988) · S. Stokes, Come to prison (1957) · Ann D. Smith, Women in prison (1962) · J. Camp, Holloway prison (1974) · WWW · b. cert. · m. cert. · d. cert.
Likenesses photograph, repro. in The Times

Taylor, Charles (1756–1823), engraver and biblical scholar, was born on 1 February 1756 near Brentwood, Essex, the eldest of the five children of Isaac *Taylor (1730–1807), engraver, and his wife, Sarah Hackshaw Jefferys (1733–1809). Evidence about his schooling is unclear, but he probably spent time at Sir Anthony Browne's school, Brentwood, before briefly attending a school in the City of London. At the age of sixteen he was articled to his father as an engraver and is believed to have studied under Francesco Bartolozzi. On 27 May 1777 he married Mary Forrest (b. 1754), daughter of Edward and Mary Forrest of Isleworth, Middlesex, and Carmarthen; they had one son and two daughters. Taylor spent the following twelve months in Paris, still then regarded as the principal school of engraving. The precise nature and scope of his studies in Paris are obscure, but he appears to have frequented the king's library. As a scholar he appears to have been largely self-taught, mastering not only Latin and Greek, but also Hebrew and 'two or three modern languages' (Taylor, 'The family pen', 2–3).

On his return to London in 1778 Taylor set up home and business at 114 High Holborn, producing engravings after pictures by Robert Smirke and Angelica Kauffmann. Early in 1780 he moved to 8 Dyers Buildings, Holborn, but was briefly forced to flee with his family when Landell's distillery near by was set on fire during the Gordon riots. At this time he was involved, with his brother Isaac *Taylor (1759–1829), whom he briefly employed, in the engraving and publishing of illustrations to the plays of Shakespeare (The Picturesque Beauties of Shakespeare, 1783–7), which attracted favourable notice from John Boydell. In 1785 he moved to 10 Holborn and finally, in 1796, to 108

Hatton Garden. In the late 1780s he began to publish, under the pseudonym Francis Fitzgerald, volumes also containing the work of other engravers, including The Cabinet of Genius (1787) and The Elegant Repository and New Print Magazine (1791–2).

Although Taylor's income came from engraving and later also from publishing, in both of these fields he was surpassed, respectively, by his brothers Isaac and Josiah (1761–1834). In his brother Isaac's opinion, 'he had some artistic feeling, but no delicacy of touch' (Taylor MSS, HD 588/4/14). Charles Taylor's renown was founded upon a quite different accomplishment. In his seventeenth year he had by chance come upon a copy of Calmet's Dictionnaire historique et critique de la Bible (1734). This massive work of scholarship fired his imagination, and he determined then and there that he would produce a new edition of it, in English, with a commentary of his own. It was a further twenty-six years before, in 1797, he felt ready to begin to publish the results of his labours. There is evidence that he at first sought sponsorship for the project in his own name. The rebuff that he received, at least from the bishop of London, was perhaps what persuaded him to publish anonymously, and thereafter, as further instalments and then further editions appeared, to refuse to acknowledge any connection with the work, beyond those of publisher and engraver. In the judgement of his nephew, Isaac Taylor, the work itself was too important to Charles Taylor to allow him to risk its being discounted by the academic establishment through association with himself—'a layman, a Nonconformist, a member of the university' (Taylor, 'The family pen', 9–10). The reception by the learned world of the first sample of his revision and commentary (in the form of dissertations entitled 'Fragments'), illustrated by himself, was enthusiastic, enhanced no doubt by the mystery then surrounding the identity of the author. Even the archbishop of Canterbury enquired diligently who he might be. Taylor's edition of Calmet, which drew upon a wide range of new sources, especially in Jewish and oriental literature, became for many years a model for biblical scholarship.

Eventually the edition of Calmet was a financial, as well as a scholarly, success. However, in January 1798, shortly after its publication, Taylor was in sufficiently straitened circumstances to be briefly imprisoned for debt at the suit of one Robert Wright, a carpenter. He later inherited the bulk of his father's fortune, including properties in London and Essex, but this seems not at all to have altered his frugal and industrious way of life. Taylor also edited two periodicals, the Literary Annual Register and its successor, the Literary Panorama—to which he contributed well-received articles on political economy and state policy. For some years he served as honorary librarian to the London Library Society, founded in 1785. Indeed, in 1801 the library itself was moved to his premises at 108 Hatton Garden, where it remained for several years. He wrote several other books and pamphlets on art and on religious topics, including Facts and Evidences on the Subject of Baptism (1815) and A Familiar Treatise on Perspective (1816).

Charles Taylor was, like his brother Isaac and like his

forebears on his mother's side, a dissenter, and a regular worshipper at the Old Meeting-House in Fetter Lane, Holborn. He was, however, by temperament a deeply conservative man and, despite an early flirtation with the ideas of the Arian theologian William Whiston, as orthodox in his theological opinions as he was extraordinary and even eccentric in his intellectual range and habits. He was, in apparent contrast to his father, who had supported Wilkes, a 'thorough-going Tory' (Taylor, 'The family pen', 9). In appearance he was, according to his nephew Isaac:

> a man—then just past mid-life—powerful in bony and muscular framework—singularly hirsute—well limbed, well filled out, erect in walk, prominent and aquiline in feature— teeming, as one should say, with repressed energy.   (ibid., 4)

His niece, Ann Gilbert's, picture is of a:

> tall figure, slightly bending, or appearing to do so, from the habit of constantly walking with his left arm under his coat behind, his full grey hair turned loosely back, a plain, shrewdly good-natured countenance, with always a welcome, a queer speech or a pun, on his lips.   (Gilbert, 153–4)

Charles Taylor's brother Isaac, by no means an envious or ungenerous man, 'never regarded him as learned' (Taylor MSS, HD 588/4/14) and attributed his achievements to a facility for epigraphy, acquired through a natural shrewdness supplemented by practice, and to a quite extraordinary memory, which gave him almost total recall of anything he read even many years afterwards.

Charles Taylor died of asthma on 13 November 1823, at his home, 108 Hatton Garden, London, and was buried with several of his maternal forebears in the family vault in the Bunhill Fields burial-ground, Finsbury, London.

ROBIN TAYLOR GILBERT

Sources I. Taylor, 'The family pen', *The family pen: memorials, biographical and literary, of the Taylor family of Ongar*, ed. I. Taylor, 1 (1867) · I. Taylor, 'Memoir of the late Mr. Charles Taylor', *Calmet's dictionary of the Bible*, ed. C. Taylor, 6th edn (1837) · *Autobiography and other memorials of Mrs Gilbert* (formerly Ann Taylor), ed. J. Gilbert, 1 (1874) · Suffolk RO, Bury St Edmunds, Taylor MSS, HD 588/1/36, HD 588/1/49, HD 588/1/51, HD 588/1/103, HD 588/1/144, HD 588/4/14 · A. Tuer, *Bartolozzi and his works* (1882) · will · uncatalogued MS letter, bishop of London to Charles Taylor, 27 Dec 1797, Suffolk RO, HD 2559 · uncatalogued MS, signed instruction 26 Jan 1798, Charles Taylor to attorneys of the king's bench, Suffolk RO, HD 2559
Archives Suffolk RO, Bury St Edmunds, papers and related material, HD 588/1, HD/588/3
Likenesses C. Taylor, self-portrait, 1774, priv. coll.; photograph, Taylor collection, Suffolk RO, Bury St Edmunds (HD 588/12/4)
Wealth at death inherited in 1809 the greater part of his late father's property (including a house at 41 Lombard Street): Suffolk RO, HD 588/1/36, HD 588/1/103

Taylor, Charles (1840–1908), college head, born in Westminster, London on 27 May 1840, was the son of William Taylor, tea dealer, and Catherine his wife. The family had formerly been settled near Woburn in Bedfordshire. His grandfather, who acquired considerable property in Regent Street, then in course of construction, is said to have been the first jobmaster in London. Taylor lost his father at the age of five, and his mother, with her three young sons, went to live near Hampstead. He attended the grammar school of St Marylebone and All Souls (in union with King's College), London, and, afterwards, King's College School itself, winning prizes at both schools. At King's College School he began his lifelong friendship with Ingram Bywater, afterwards regius professor of Greek at Oxford.

In October 1858 Taylor entered St John's College, Cambridge, where at first he devoted himself mainly to mathematics. In 1860 he was elected to one of the new foundation scholarships, and in 1862, when St John's had six wranglers out of the first ten, he was ninth wrangler. In the same year he was placed in the second class of the classical tripos; in 1863 he obtained a first class in the theological examination; and in 1864 the Crosse scholarship and the first Tyrwhitt scholarship, while in his college he vacated the Naden divinity studentship for a fellowship.

In 1863 Taylor published *Geometrical Conics, Including Anharmonic Ratio and Projection*. This was followed, in 1872, by a textbook entitled *The Elementary Geometry of Conics*, which passed through several editions, and, in 1881, by a larger treatise, *An Introduction to the Ancient and Modern Geometry of Conics*, including a brief but masterly sketch of the early history of geometry. He stressed the principle of geometrical continuity, usually associated with the name of Poncelet, and traced this principle back to Kepler. He returned to the subject in the memoir on *The Geometry of Kepler and Newton*, which he contributed to the *Transactions of the Cambridge Philosophical Society*. He was one of the founders of the *Oxford, Cambridge, and Dublin Messenger of Mathematics*, and continued to be an editor from 1862 to 1884. He joined the London Mathematical Society in 1872, and was president of the Mathematical Association in 1892. His mathematical writings include some thirty or forty papers, mostly on geometry. They are 'marked by elegance, conciseness, a rare knowledge of the history of the subject, and a veneration for the great geometers of the past' (A. E. H. Love, 'Note on Weierstrass' E-function in the calculus of variations', *Proceedings of the London Mathematical Society*, [2nd ser.], 6, 1907–8, 205–9).

Taylor was ordained deacon in 1866 and priest in 1867, the year in which he obtained the Kaye university prize for an essay published in an expanded form under the title of *The Gospel in the Law*. He had given a course of sermons on the subject as one of the curates at St Andrew's the Great. In 1873 he was appointed college lecturer in theology. He soon made his mark as a Hebrew scholar. In 1874 he issued *The Dirge of Coheleth in Ecclesiastes xii. Discussed and Literally Interpreted*. This was followed in 1877 by his edition of the *Sayings of the Jewish Fathers, in Hebrew and English, with Critical and Illustrative Notes* (2nd edn, 1897; appendix, 1900), which was authoritatively pronounced to be 'the most important contribution to these studies made by any Christian scholar since the time of Buxtorf' (J. H. A. Hart, in *The Eagle*, 30, 1909, 71).

In 1877–8, during the Cambridge University commission, Taylor took an active part in the discussions on the revision of the statutes of the college. In 1879 he was chosen one of three commissioners to represent the college in conferring with the university commission. Before the new statutes came into force the master (W. H. Bateson) died, and on 12 April 1881 Taylor was chosen as his successor. On 14 June he was presented by the public orator for the complete degree of DD *jure dignitatis*. As master, Taylor left details of administration to others, but he was not inactive. His college sermons, delivered in a quiet, level tone, with no rhetorical display, were marked by a solid grasp of fact and a patient elaboration of detail. His commemoration sermons of 1903 and 1907 mainly dealt with three college worthies, William Gilbert, Thomas Clarkson, and William Wilberforce. While master, Taylor published: *The Teaching of the Twelve Apostles* (1886); *An Essay on the Theology of the Didache* (1889); *The Witness of Hermas to the Four Gospels* (1892); and *The Oxyrhynchus Logia, and the Apocryphal Gospels* (1899).

From November 1880 Taylor was a member of the council of the university. Between 1885 and 1888 he presented the university with £200 in each year, to increase the stipend of the reader in Talmudic. He represented the university at the commemoration of the 250th anniversary of the founding of Harvard, Cambridge, USA, where he received an honorary degree on 8 November 1886. From new year's day, 1887, to the corresponding date in 1889 he served as vice-chancellor. On 18 July 1888 the vice-chancellor invited more than eighty bishops attending the Lambeth conference, and nearly seventy other guests, to a memorable banquet in the hall of St John's. At the end of the year he presented to the university his stipend of £400 as vice-chancellor for the year, and the money was spent in providing nine statues for the new buildings of the university library. Taylor was one of the two university aldermen first chosen in 1889 as members of the borough council; he held the office until 1895. To the university library he generously gave the Taylor–Schechter collection of Hebrew manuscripts, which, by the energy of Dr Solomon Schechter, the university reader in Talmudic, and by the generosity of Taylor, had been obtained from the genizah of Old Cairo, with the consent of the heads of the local Jewish community. Taylor and Schechter published in 1899, under the title of *The Wisdom of Ben Sira*, portions of Ecclesiasticus from Hebrew manuscripts in this collection. Taylor was friendlily disposed to British Jewry and its aspirations. In 1907 he presented to the university library a fine copy of the *Kandjur*, which 'at once secured for Cambridge a first place among the repositories of Buddhist texts'. In his own college he supported the mission in Walworth, south London, and the Lady Margaret boat club, while his gifts to the general funds were constant and lavish.

Taylor was fond of sculling, and he also rowed in the college boat races from 1863 to 1866. He was always a great walker. From 1870 to 1878 he was an energetic mountaineer, in spite of his bulky physique. He wrote for the *Alpine Journal* (6.232–43) a record of a notable ascent of Monte Rosa from Macugnaga in 1872 (see also T. G. Bonney, in *The Eagle*, 30, 1909, 73–7). He was a member of the Alpine Club from 1873 until his death.

On 19 October 1907, at St Luke's Church, Chelsea, Taylor married Margaret Sophia (1877–1962), daughter of the Hon. Conrad Adderly Dillon and his wife, Ellen. He died suddenly on 12 August 1908, at the Goldner Adler, Nuremberg, Germany, while on a foreign tour. After a funeral service in St John's College, his body was buried in St Giles's cemetery, Cambridge, on the 17th. He was commemorated by a stained-glass window placed in the college chapel by his widow.

According to his obituary in *The Eagle*:

> He had an intense church feeling, without the slightest appearance of ecclesiasticism, … and his moderation, which was no part of a policy, but was natural to the man, was an invaluable quality in the head of a large college containing many varieties of religious opinion.

The obituarist noted also that although reserved and stiff in manner, Taylor was endeared to his friends by 'his practical wisdom, sense of humour, detachment of view, and absolute freedom from petty enmities'.

J. E. SANDYS, *rev.* JOHN D. PICKLES

Sources *The Guardian* (20 Aug 1908) · *Cambridge Review* (15 Oct 1908) · *The Eagle*, 30 (1908–9), 34–85, 196–204 · *Alpine Journal*, 24 (1908), 396 · *Catalogue of scientific papers*, Royal Society, 8 (1879); 11 (1896); 19 (1925) · CGPLA Eng. & Wales (1908) · WWW · Burke, *Peerage*
Archives St John Cam., papers | King's Cam., letters to Oscar Browning · LPL, letters to *Church Quarterly Review* and papers · St John Cam., letters to Sir J. Larmor
Likenesses C. Brock, oils, 1896, St John Cam. · F. Newman, bronze medallion, 1908, St John Cam. · Elliott & Fry, photograph, repro. in *The Eagle*, facing p. 64
Wealth at death £39,910 8s. 7d.: resworn administration, 14 Oct 1908, CGPLA Eng. & Wales

Taylor, Charles Bell (1829–1909), ophthalmic surgeon, was born at Nottingham on 2 September 1829, the son of Charles Taylor and his wife, Elizabeth Ann Galloway. His father and brother were veterinary surgeons in the town. After working for a short time in the lace warehouse of his uncle, William Galloway, he apprenticed himself to Thomas Godfrey, a surgeon at Mansfield. He was admitted a member of the Royal College of Surgeons in 1852, and as licentiate of the Society of Apothecaries in 1855. He graduated MD at the University of Edinburgh in 1854, and in 1867 obtained the fellowship of the Royal College of Surgeons, Edinburgh. In 1854 Taylor was pursuing his medical studies in Paris, where he was president of the English Medical Society of Paris. He acted for some time as medical superintendent at the Walton Lodge Asylum, Liverpool. In 1859 he joined the staff of the newly established Nottingham and Midland Eye Infirmary, continuing to live and practise in Nottingham for the rest of his life.

A consummate and imperturbable operator, especially for cataract, Taylor soon enjoyed a practice that extended beyond Great Britain. He always operated by artificial light, held chloroform in abhorrence (preferring ether), used only his manservant, Walter, as an assistant, and had a poor opinion of trained nurses. He published *Lectures on Diseases of the Eye* (1888) as well as numerous lectures and papers on the eye.

An uncompromising individualist, Taylor took a prominent, and professionally unpopular, part in securing the repeal of the Contagious Diseases Act, corresponding with Daniel Cooper, of the Rescue Society of London, and helping to organize public opposition to the extension of the act in 1869. Unlike Josephine Butler, Taylor distinguished between the voluntary internal examination of private patients and the compulsory examination of registered prostitutes. He was a determined opponent of vivisection and of compulsory vaccination. He held strong views on diet, was an abstainer not merely from alcohol and tobacco but even from tea and coffee, and took only two meals a day. He lived about 4 miles from his consulting rooms in Nottingham, and rode to work each day on one of his collection of some thirty tricycles and bicycles. He continued to operate even up to his death at the age of eighty.

Taylor was unmarried. He died of influenza at his home, Beechwood Hall, Mapperly Park, Nottingham, on 13 April 1909, and was buried at the Nottingham general cemetery. Most of his estate of £116,000 he left to the British Union for the Abolition of Vivisection; the London Anti-Vivisection Society; the British committee of the International Federation for the Abolition of the State Regulation of Vice; the National Anti-Vaccination League; and the Royal Society for the Prevention of Cruelty to Animals.　　　　D'A. POWER, *rev.* HUGH SERIES

Sources *BMJ* (24 April 1909), 1033–4 · *The Lancet* (1 May 1909), 1287 · *WWW* · *Ophthalmoscope*, 7 (1909), 376 · *Ophthalmic Review*, 28 (1909), 133 · *The Times* (1 July 1909) · A. Thomson, *Eighty years' reminiscences*, 2 vols. (1904), 2.235 · J. R. Walkowitz, *Prostitution and Victorian society: women, class and the state* (1980) · *CGPLA Eng. & Wales* (1909)
Likenesses photograph, repro. in *Ophthalmoscope*, 376 · photograph, repro. in *Ophthalmic Review*, 133
Wealth at death £116,163 13s. 10d.: probate, 18 June 1909, *CGPLA Eng. & Wales*

Taylor, Christopher (1614/15–1686), religious writer and schoolmaster, was born in north Yorkshire, near the Westmorland border, possibly near Skipton, and was probably the son of Thomas Taylor, described as of Ravenstonedale, Westmorland. He matriculated at Magdalen College, Oxford, aged eighteen, on 22 March 1633 and graduated BA on 28 May 1636. According to John Whiting's *Persecution Exposed*, he served as a preaching minister until his conversion to Quakerism in 1652 by George Fox. Another source describes how in 1652 or 1653 William Dewsbury and Christopher's brother Thomas *Taylor came to him, 'a Priest of a Chappell, called Chappell in the Bryers, betwixt Brighouse and Hallifax, who was convinced of the Truth, & bore Testimony to it, and was Instrumental in Settling a Meeting at Bradford' (Penney, 291–2). In 1654 he was injured in an assault on his way to a Quaker meeting and between 1654 and 1656 underwent harsh treatment in Appleby gaol. His *The Whirl-Wind of the Lord* (1655) was a warning to the north in general and to Westmorland in particular. *A Warning from the Lord to this Nation* and *Certain Papers which is the Word of the Lord* are undated. In 1659 he was stabbed by a youth whom he had rebuked for vice. On 11 August 1661 he was imprisoned following his arrest at a Friends' meeting.

Taylor ran a school for Friends' children in Hertford, and when Fox opened a Quaker school in Waltham Abbey in Essex in 1668 he took over the headship, perhaps assisted by his wife, Frances (d. 1685). On 1 July 1670 he appeared at the sessions in Chelmsford, charged with teaching school without a licence; in 1674 he was indicted for absence from parish worship. Taylor published *A Faithful and True Witness to the Light of Jesus Christ* and *An Epistle to Friends in the Truth* in 1675. In 1676, when he was enumerated among the Quaker 'First Publishers of Truth' and also listed as of the Quaker meeting at Plaistow in Essex, he issued *The Counterfeit Convert Discovered*, as well as his Latin translation of a primer for Quaker children by George Fox and Ellis Hookes, *Institutiones pietatis*. In 1678 he was in Bristol. In 1679, the year that he was committed to prison for absence from parish worship, Taylor collaborated in producing a key to Latin, Greek, and Hebrew, *Compendium trium linguarum*, which used passages only from the Bible and not from classical texts, and published an account of a religious ecstasy that had gripped the children of his school, *A Testimony to the Lord's Power*. He moved with the school a few miles to Edmonton in Middlesex the same year. *A Testimony for Isaac Pennington and an Epistle of Caution to Friends* both followed in 1681, and *Something in Answer to Two Late Malitious Libels* in 1682.

Taylor left England for Pennsylvania in 1682, leaving the school in the charge of George Keith. Taylor represented Bucks county in the province's first assembly, was a member of the council of state until his death, registrar-general of the colony, and apparently a source of criticism of Penn. With his wife, a minister, Taylor became an architect of the structures of American Quakerism. He died and was buried in Philadelphia in 1686 and his 'Testimony concerning Thomas Taylor', his brother, was issued in a compilation in 1697.　　　MICHAEL MULLETT

Sources J. Besse, *A collection of the sufferings of the people called Quakers*, 2 vols. (1753) · J. Whiting, *Persecution exposed: in some memoirs relating to the sufferings of John Whiting and many others of the people called Quakers*, 2nd edn (1791) · J. Smith, ed., *A descriptive catalogue of Friends' books*, 1 (1867) · W. C. Braithwaite, *The second period of Quakerism*, ed. H. J. Cadbury, 2nd edn (1961) · W. C. Braithwaite, *The beginnings of Quakerism* (1912) · E. E. Taylor, *The valiant sixty* (1947) · *A collection of memorials concerning divers deceased ministers … of the … Quakers in Pennsylvania, New Jersey* (1824) · Foster, *Alum. Oxon.* · *The manuscripts of the duke of Leeds*, HMC, 22 (1888) · Greaves & Zaller, *BDBR*, 225–6 · 'Dictionary of Quaker biography', RS Friends, Lond. [card index] · H. L. Ingle, *First among Friends: George Fox and the creation of Quakerism* (1994) · *DNB* · N. Penney, ed., 'The first publishers of truth': being early records, now first printed, of the introduction of Quakerism into the counties of England and Wales* (1907)
Archives RS Friends, Lond., Swarthmore collection, i, 14

Taylor, Claude Crosland (1889–1935). *See under* Taylor, George Crosland (1858–1923).

Taylor [*née* Doughty], **Clementia** (1810–1908), women's activist, was born on 17 December 1810 at Brockdish, Norfolk, one of twelve children of John Doughty (d. 1837), a farmer and tanner, and his wife, Mary (*née* Simons). The family's faith was Unitarian and it was probably through a Unitarian connection that Clementia (known to her friends and family as Mentia) was employed as governess to the daughters of a Unitarian minister, J. P. Malleson (1796–1869), who ran a boys' boarding-school in Hove. On

27 September 1842 at West Gate Chapel, Lewes, she married Peter Alfred *Taylor (1819–1891), a cousin of her pupils. Her obituarist was to describe her as:

> somewhat tall as well as slight; the features were refined and regular—the head well formed and carried, the hair bright blonde, the brow broad, the speaking grey eyes rather deep set, the nose slightly acquiline [sic], a certain firmness about the mouth, a delicately pointed chin. (*Englishwoman's Review*, 157)

P. A. Taylor was a partner in the family firm, Courtaulds, a wealthy man and radical Liberal MP for Leicester (1862–84). After their marriage, which was childless, the couple were involved in the main social and political movements of the day. Clementia Taylor was, from 1845, a close friend of Mazzini, helping him by organizing concerts and bazaars for the benefit of the school for poor Italian children which he had established, and by finding employment for Italian exiles. The Taylors were both concerned that slavery should be abolished: Clementia took under her wing, and into her home, Sarah Parker Remond (1824–1894), a young black woman who toured Britain lecturing on the slavery issue. On the outbreak of the American Civil War she formed the Freedmen's Aid Association and in 1863 founded and became honorary secretary of the newly formed Ladies' London Emancipation Society, the first national female anti-slavery society.

In 1860 the Taylors had rented Aubrey House in Kensington, and in 1863 bought its freehold. This early eighteenth-century house, once the country home of Lady Mary Coke, became a centre for mid-nineteenth-century radical movements. Elizabeth Malleson, the daughter-in-law of J. P. Malleson, wrote:

> Those monthly [other sources say fortnightly] parties during the London season were unique and very enjoyable, for Mentia and her husband ... were admirably free of class prejudice in persons and opinions, so that all kinds of literary people—refugees from several countries—artists and humble lovers of social enjoyment, mingled with supporters of 'causes' of all kinds. (*Elizabeth Malleson*, 98)

The American author Louisa May Alcott also described the charm of Clementia Taylor's salon:

> I consider her a model Englishwoman—simple, sincere and accomplished, full of good sense, intelligence and energy. Her house is open to all, friend and stranger, black and white, rich and poor. Great men and earnest women meet there. ... Though wealthy and living in an historical mansion ... the hostess [is] the simplest dressed lady. (Alcott, 281–2)

In 1846 Clementia Taylor had been on the committee of the Whittington Club, a radical Unitarian venture launched in 1846 which offered working people rational recreation and amusement, while providing libraries, reading-rooms, and lecture halls. Following this initiative, and that of Elizabeth and Frank Malleson in founding the Working Women's College in 1864, the Taylors opened in 1869, in the grounds of Aubrey House, the Aubrey Institute, to give young men and women the opportunity of rectifying a deficient education. Mary Grant, wife of P. A. Taylor's secretary, was employed as a teacher and the Taylors equipped a lending library and reading-room with over 500 books. Their friends, many eminent, were volunteer lecturers at the institute, which continued successfully until the Taylors were forced, by P. A.'s ill health, to sell Aubrey House and move to Brighton. Clementia carried on her philanthropic work by establishing in 1875 a Home for Young Women Servants in Pimlico.

Clementia Taylor was on the organizing committee of the 1866 petition in favour of women's suffrage that J. S. Mill presented to parliament; the 1499 signatures were collated in Aubrey House. She was treasurer of the London Provisional Petition Committee set up in 1866 to capitalize on the momentum created by the Mill petition. It was in Aubrey House that this committee's successor, the Committee of the London National Society for Women's Suffrage, held its first meeting on 5 July 1867. Clementia Taylor took the chair in July 1869 at the first public women's suffrage meeting ever held in London. She was joint secretary of the London Society for Women's Suffrage until 1871, when she resigned from the society with other radical members, after a conflict with Mill. At this time George Eliot, a good friend, wrote 'Welcome back from your absorption in the franchise! Somebody else ought to have your share of work now, and you ought to rest' (*George Eliot Letters*, 5.150). However, she carried on supporting the cause, chairing meetings and in 1878 rejoining the executive committee of the central committee of the National Society.

In addition, in the 1870s Clementia Taylor was on the executive committee of the Married Women's Property Committee (1876–82); a member of the committee of the Ladies' National Association for the Repeal of the Contagious Diseases Acts; treasurer of the Personal Rights Association; and on the general committee of Dr Garrett Anderson's newly founded Woman's Hospital in London. She was a member of the council of the Women's Franchise League when it was formed in 1889, and later joined the Women's Emancipation Union, still being a member in 1897. In all her associations Clementia Taylor demonstrated a commitment to a radical interpretation of women's rights. She died at the age of ninety-eight, on 11 April 1908, at her home, 16 Eaton Place, Brighton, after some years of failing health and memory.

ELIZABETH CRAWFORD

Sources *Englishwoman's Review*, 39 (1908), 145–58 • F. M. Gladstone, ed., *Aubrey House, Kensington, 1698–1920* (1922) • *Elizabeth Malleson, 1828–1916, autobiographical notes and letters, with a memoir by Hope Malleson*, ed. H. Malleson (privately printed, 1926) • *Mazzini's letters to an English family*, ed. E. F. Richards, 3 vols. (1920–22) • *The George Eliot letters*, ed. G. S. Haight, 9 vols. (1954–78) • L. M. Alcott, *Shawl-straps* (1873) • R. V. Holt, *The Unitarian contribution to social progress in England*, 2nd edn (1952) • A. Ruston, 'Clementia Taylor', *Transactions of the Unitarian Historical Society*, 20/1 (1991–4), 62–8 • P. A. Taylor, ed., *Some account of the Taylor family, originally Taylard* (privately printed, London, 1875) • *Auld lang syne: selections from the papers of the Pen and Pencil club*, Pen and Pencil Club (privately printed, London, 1877) • E. C. Stanton, S. B. Antony, and M. J. Gage, eds., *History of woman suffrage*, 3 (1886) • S. S. Holton, *Suffrage days: stories from the women's suffrage movement* (1996) • C. Midgley, *Women against slavery: the British campaigns, 1780–1870* (1992) • m. cert. • d. cert.

Archives BL, family MSS, Add. MSS 37682–37686, Add. Ch. 54653–54700

Likenesses photograph, repro. in Gladstone, ed., *Aubrey House, Kensington*, facing p. 46 • photograph, repro. in Stanton, Anthony, Gage, and Harper, eds., *History of woman's suffrage*, facing p. 833
Wealth at death £749 3*s*. 5*d*.: probate, 28 May 1908, *CGPLA Eng. & Wales*

Taylor, Dan (1738–1816), General Baptist minister and founder of the New Connexion of General Baptists, was born on 21 December 1738 at Sourmilk Hall, Northowram, Yorkshire, the elder son of Azor Taylor and his second wife, Mary Willey; his younger brother was John *Taylor (1743–1818), Baptist minister. As Azor was a coalminer, he took his young son underground to work with him before his sixth birthday. Though he received no formal education, Dan Taylor took his books with him down the mine. He walked many miles to listen to the Wesleys and Whitefield and threw in his lot with the Methodists; at the age of twenty-three he preached his first sermon for them at Hipperholme. The local Methodists were so impressed with him that they wanted him to talk to John Wesley about being trained as one of Wesley's preachers. However, Taylor disagreed with certain aspects of Wesley's practices, so did not pursue that end. In fact, during the summer of 1762 he left the Methodists, becoming leader of a group of seceders from the Wadsworth Methodists.

Taylor's doubts about the validity of infant baptism led him to make a study of W. Wall's *History of Infant Baptism*, which convinced him of the Baptist case. He applied to several Particular Baptist ministers in the West Riding of Yorkshire for baptism, only to be refused because of his Arminian views. Taking John Slater with him he set out for Lincolnshire, where he believed there were Arminian Baptists. One night they found themselves surrounded completely by water, so they slept on a haystack. Next day they discovered that they had passed through Gamston, Nottinghamshire, where there was a General Baptist church. Retracing their steps they found the church and Taylor was baptized by the minister, Joseph Jeffery, in the River Idle, on 16 February 1763.

On his return to Wadsworth, Taylor baptized Slater and several others, who formed themselves into a Baptist church and joined the Lincolnshire association. That autumn Taylor was ordained by Gilbert Boyce of Coningsby. Soon the meeting-house where they met became too small. A new chapel was built at Birchcliffe, where Taylor ministered for the next nine years. He travelled extensively beyond the association and came into contact with the Leicestershire churches which had been formed as a result of an evangelical revival. He noticed that throughout the country churches were at a very low ebb, morally and theologically, and many had dwindled numerically. 'They degraded Jesus Christ, and he degraded them' (A. C. Underwood, 152), he wrote. To remedy this situation, he proposed a union of the Leicestershire churches with those General Baptist churches elsewhere that remained evangelical in a New Connexion. The New Connexion held its first assembly in Church Lane, Whitechapel, from 6 to 8 June 1770. It was led by Taylor, who was usually in the chair; he presided over its academy from 1798 to 1813 and edited the first issues of the *General Baptist Magazine* from

1798 to 1800. He did not formally leave the old general assembly, where he represented the Leicestershire association, until 1802. The New Connexion continued until in 1891 it joined the Baptist Union.

In 1782 a church was formed in Halifax to which Taylor was invited as pastor. The association hit on an experiment: for one of the Birchcliffe members to fill the pulpit for six months, while Taylor ministered at Halifax. He settled as pastor of Halifax in October 1783. Two years later, when he was invited to become the colleague of the venerable John Brittain at Church Lane, Whitechapel, the association voted for him to go to London, where he could do more 'to the glory of God' (Taylor, *New Connection*, 2.207) than if he remained in Yorkshire. He assisted Brittain for some nine years before taking sole charge in 1794. Brittain seldom preached after Taylor's arrival. They disagreed over the practice of laying hands on the newly baptized as a prerequisite of participation in the Lord's supper, although Taylor raised no objection provided that he did not perform the ceremony; after Brittains's death the church left the matter to individual choice. Taylor had long deplored the poor education of the ministry. When the denomination decided to start an academy, it was Taylor whom they appointed as its tutor at Mile End in 1798. There he remained until 1813, when the academy moved to Wisbech.

Taylor was a phenomenally robust leader of the New Connexion: he travelled 25,000 miles, preached nearly 20,000 sermons, and wrote more than 50 books and pamphlets. He stridently opposed Arian, unitarian, and universalist views, and debated theological differences with Andrew Fuller, a leading Particular Baptist, while retaining his friendship.

Taylor was four times married. His first wife, Elizabeth Saltonstall, whom he married on 10 November 1764 at Heptonstall, Yorkshire, died on 22 October 1793; on 12 August 1794 he married Elizabeth Newton, who died on 14 October 1809. His third wife was Mary Toplis, a widow whom he married on 24 March 1811 and who died on 18 December 1812. About a month before his death he married, on 21 October 1816 at St Dunstan and All Saints, Stepney, Mrs Sarah Saunders. He retained his powers of body and mind until he was seventy. Thereafter, he grew gradually weaker, until on 26 November 1816 he collapsed and died in London. He was buried in Bunhill Fields.

E. F. CLIPSHAM

Sources W. Underwood, *The life of the Rev. Dan Taylor* (1870) • A. Taylor, *Memoirs of Dan Taylor … with extracts from his diaries, correspondence, and unpublished manuscripts* (1820) • A. Taylor, *History of the English General Baptists*, 2: *The new connection of General Baptists* (1818) • A. C. Underwood, *A history of the English Baptists* (1947), 149–59 • W. E. Blomfield, 'Baptist churches of Yorkshire in the 17th and 18th centuries', *The Baptists of Yorkshire, being the centenary memorial volume of the Yorkshire Baptist Association*, ed. C. E. Shipley (1912), 98–115 • C. E. Welch, 'The origins of the New Connexion of General Baptists in Leicestershire', *Leicestershire Archaeological and Historical Society Transactions*, 69 (1995), 59–70 • E. F. Clipsham, 'Taylor, Dan', *The Blackwell dictionary of evangelical biography, 1730–1860*, ed. D. M. Lewis (1995) • W. J. Avery, 'The late Midland College: principals and tutors [pt 3]', *Baptist Quarterly*, 1 (1922–3), 263–9 • *DNB*

Likenesses composite engraving, repro. in Underwood, *History of the English Baptists*, facing p. 168

Taylor, David (1715–1783), evangelist and preacher, was born on 28 April 1715 in Wymeswold, near Loughborough, the son of Joseph Taylor and his wife, Dorothy. He is said to have had a 'tolerable education' (Seymour, 1.43) and was employed in domestic service with Lady Huntingdon's family, though in the 1750s he was described as a husband-man. It is often stated that he was converted by Benjamin Ingham or the Moravians in 1741 and that in the same year Lady Huntingdon encouraged him to preach in Leicester-shire. There is, however, some evidence that he was at least 'awakened' as early as 1735, and was preaching and founding societies in the Sheffield area before 1740. Here he probably encountered Ingham and the Moravians, and certainly John Bennet and John Nelson, who later became Methodist preachers.

Taylor's preaching in Leicestershire for Lady Hunting-don from early 1741 led to the development of religious societies which, however, developed Baptist principles. In 1770 they joined with Dan Taylor's societies to form the General Baptists of the New Connexion. In October 1741 David Taylor was invited by John Bennet to visit Derby-shire, where he influenced some members of the Chinley Presbyterian Chapel and precipitated Bennet's evangel-ical conversion in January 1742. In 1743 Taylor settled in Mobberley, Cheshire, and preached chiefly in that county, Derbyshire, and Lancashire. Some of his religious soci-eties in these areas were later taken over by the Mora-vians, others by John Bennet, and through Bennet became part of John Wesley's Methodist Connexion.

In 1742 Wesley and Lady Huntingdon were already alarmed at Taylor's apparent intention to create an inde-pendent organization. His reputation was also damaged by contracting an irregular marriage. He apparently dis-approved of the Anglican clergy and Anglican marriage and instead made vows with his partner, Mary (1717–1770), before witnesses after the Quaker manner. He also offended some by his alleged antinomianism. The exact status of his marriage remains unclear. Moravian sources record that he was married in Wrexham in 1745, but also that his first son, David, was born on 13 January 1744, though his baptism is recorded in the Mobberley parish register on 2 January 1743 (NS?). The couple had nine other children (five sons and four daughters), two dying in infancy. Those born before 1751 were baptized as Anglicans, the rest as Moravians. The eldest son, David, later became a Moravian worker in Jamaica.

Continuing an irregular preacher, Taylor had contacts with the Moravians and Methodists during the rest of the 1740s. In 1747 Bennet said he had left off preaching, but in 1749 he supported Bennet and John Wesley against the mob in Bolton, Lancashire. The parish register of Mobber-ley in 1749–50 described Taylor as a Methodist 'teacher' (that is, a preacher). However, on 11 January 1751 he was received as a member of the Moravian church, though recorded as a 'backsliding member' by 1755. His letters between 1750 and 1760 suggest that he was in a state of spiritual confusion, with his temporal affairs often in dis-order, though he still wanted to preach and perhaps become a Moravian minister. He and his wife were finally expelled by the Moravians on 15 April 1765 for assisting a clandestine marriage. His wife died in 1770 and in 1772 in Manchester, Taylor attempted to convince a Moravian woman that he was guided by God to marry her. In his last years he seems to have vacillated in allegiance between the Moravians, Methodists, and Quakers, and to have lost his preaching gift.

In appearance Taylor is described as of moderate height, rather stoutly made, grey-headed in later life, and in one place called 'the little beauty' (Tyerman MSS, 3, fol. 500). His career illustrates certain features of the early years of the evangelical revival. Like other local and regional evan-gelists he pioneered work later taken over by more sys-tematic organizers. His irregularities and changeable alle-giances were not due simply to personal weaknesses, but were characteristic of the doctrinal and moral uncertain-ties created by the experience of revival. Taylor died in Jackson's Row, Manchester, on 8 July 1783 and was buried in the town's Quaker burial-ground.   HENRY D. RACK

Sources List of Dukinfield members, 1745–90, Fairfield Moravian Archives, Manchester, 1755–1782 · Dukinfield congregation diary, Fairfield Moravian Archives, Manchester, 15 April 1765 · elders' conference, Fairfield Moravian Archives, Manchester, 14 April 1765 · JRL, Tyerman MSS, 3, fols. 301–2, 500–501, 522 · J. Everett, *Historical sketches of Wesleyan Methodism in Sheffield* (1823) · A. Taylor, *History of the General Baptists*, 2 vols. (1818), 2.3–4, 7, 15 · *The letters of John Pawson*, ed. J. C. Bowmer and J. A. Vickers, 3 vols. (1994–5), vol. 3, p. 142 · diary of John Bennet, JRL · *Wesleyan Methodist Maga-zine*, 58 (1835), 606 · parish register, Mobberley, 1749–50, Man. CL, Manchester Archives and Local Studies · *The diary of James Clegg of Chapel en le Frith, 1708–1755*, ed. V. S. Doe, 1, Derbyshire RS, 2 (1978) · *The works of John Wesley*, [another edn], 26, ed. F. Baker and others (1982), 74–6 · J. Everett's Manchester notebook, JRL, fol. 424 · C. Atmore, *The Methodist memorial* (1801) · [A. C. H. Seymour], *The life and times of Selina, countess of Huntingdon*, 1 (1840), 43 · parish regis-ter (baptism), 28/4/1715, Wymeswold, Leicestershire
Archives Fairfield Moravian Archives, Manchester, MS letters

Taylor, Desmond Christopher Shawe- (1907–1995), music critic, was born at 92 Lower Leeson Street, Dublin, on 29 May 1907, the elder of the two sons of Francis Man-ley (Frank) Shawe-Taylor (1869–1920), of Castle Lambert, co. Galway, magistrate and high sheriff for co. Galway, and his wife, Agnes Mary Eleanor (1874–1939), eldest of the three daughters of Christopher Ussher, of Eastwell, co. Galway. He was a great-nephew of (Isabella) Augusta, Lady Galway, playwright and literary patron, and a cousin of the art collector Sir Hugh Lane. A happy childhood was violently interrupted by his father's murder at the hands of the IRA, and he was taken to England and sent to Shrewsbury School. He went up to Oriel College, Oxford, where he graduated with a first in English in 1930, and then spent some time in Germany and Austria before beginning in 1933 to contribute musical, literary, and (as Peter Galway) film reviews to various London journals, including the *New Statesman*. During the war he served in the Royal Artillery, and on demobilization in 1945 he returned to the *New Statesman* as music critic, with a distin-guished group of writers who included his old friend

Desmond Christopher Shawe-Taylor (1907–1995), by unknown photographer

Edward Sackville-*West. Together and with another friend, the painter (Edward) Eardley Knollys, they bought a Queen Anne rectory at Long Crichel, near Wimborne in Dorset, where they were later joined by Raymond Mortimer. There Shawe-Taylor wrote a slim but perceptive history, *Covent Garden* (1948).

Long Crichel became a house of warmth and delight, dispensing hospitality, music, and enlivening conversation to a stream of visitors chiefly from the literary and musical worlds. It was also the base for *The Record Guide* (1951, with revisions and supplements), an anthology by Sackville-West and Shawe-Taylor recommending preferred recordings, but valuable long after its immediate purpose for the comments on composers and their works. David Cairns, later his colleague on the *Sunday Times*, was responding to something avian in Shawe-Taylor when he described the book's 'great bird's eye survey which combined the sweeping vision of an eagle with a kingfisher's brilliance and the darting sensibility of a humming-bird' (Cairns, address at memorial service).

The record collection begun by Shawe-Taylor as a boy was constantly expanded over the years into the CD era, and was a resource for his enduring devotion to the human voice. He became the most perceptive critic of singing among his colleagues, delighting in voices from an age preserved on his oldest records but quick to welcome new artists, and was also a friend to singers including Emma Eames, Lotte Lehmann, and, a Long Crichel guest, Elisabeth Schumann. His quarterly articles for *The Gramophone*, 'The gramophone and the voice' (1951–73), and seventeen occasional articles for *Opera*, 'A gallery of great singers' (1955–88), deeply pondered and carefully

constructed, were among those journals' most distinguished contributions.

In 1958 Shawe-Taylor succeeded Ernest Newman as chief music critic of the *Sunday Times*. Though he had anxieties about taking over from so distinguished and long-established a predecessor, readers kindled to his enthusiasm, his lightly worn learning, his quick response to music of many kinds, and his truthfulness to his own reactions, all expressed in elegant, engaging prose. He took immense trouble with his articles, worrying away at niceties of style, sparing neither himself nor, by postcard, colleagues who he felt had sinned. Composers he championed included, at early stages of their careers, Britten and Tippett; in the 1950s he was also more responsible than any other critic for winning English recognition of Janáček as a great opera composer. He was appointed CBE in 1965.

Apart from a year's break writing for the *New Yorker* in 1973–4, Shawe-Taylor remained at the *Sunday Times* until semi-retirement in 1983. He continued to write occasional articles, but spent more time at Long Crichel. The original quartet had by now long dispersed or died, but with the added presence of the ophthalmic surgeon Patrick Trevor-Roper the house maintained much of its original character. Domestically, Shawe-Taylor could be as exacting over details of life as he could over a misplaced comma, and sometimes as irritable, but his charm and the evident goodness of his nature set such matters near the surface where they belonged. He was rare in being as excellent a host as he was a guest, always quicker to take pleasure than umbrage. Frances Partridge, a frequent Crichel visitor and at one point nearly a member of the ensemble, wrote of his 'boundless high spirits, optimism, volatility and interest in everything that comes his way' (*The Independent*). Though an encroaching confusion of his short-term memory from about 1993 constrained his activities, he was still writing and preparing broadcasts at the time of his death, which took place peacefully at Long Crichel House on 1 November 1995 as a result of heart failure, after a country walk near Crichel. He was unmarried. A memorial service was held at St Martin-in-the-Fields, London, on 26 March 1996, and he was buried at Long Crichel church.

JOHN WARRACK

Sources *The Times* (3 Nov 1995) · *The Independent* (4 Nov 1995) · D. Cairns, address at memorial service, St Martin-in-the-Fields, London, 26 March 1996 · *WWW*, 1991–5 · Burke, *Gen. Ire.* · personal knowledge (2004) · private information (2004) [family, friends] · b. cert.

Archives Royal College of Music, London | Bodl. Oxf., letters to Jack and Catherine Lambert · King's Cam., letters to G. H. W. Rylands

Likenesses D. Grant, portrait, *c*.1960, priv. coll. · group portrait, Long Crichel House, Wimborne, Dorset · photograph, News International Syndication, London [*see illus.*] · photograph, repro. in *The Independent*

Wealth at death £1,304,202: probate, 12 June 1996, *CGPLA Eng. & Wales*

Taylor, Edgar (1793–1839), lawyer and author, the fifth son of Samuel Taylor, and great-grandson of the dissenting divine and Hebrew scholar John Taylor (1694–1761), was born at Banham, Norfolk, on 28 January 1793. He was at school at Palgrave, Suffolk, under the Presbyterian schoolmaster Charles Lloyd (1766–1829) who trained him as classical scholar. In 1809 he was articled to his uncle, Meadows Taylor, solicitor, of Diss, Norfolk. He had mastered Italian and Spanish before going to London in 1814; subsequently he learned German and French. In 1817, in conjunction with Robert Roscoe, a son of William Roscoe, the historian, he inaugurated the firm of Taylor and Roscoe, solicitors, in King's Bench Walk, Temple. He was an original member of the 'Noncon Club', founded in July 1817. His legal career, chiefly in equity practice, was prosperous. He married, in 1823, Ann, daughter of John Christie of Hackney. Between 1824 and 1826 his anonymous translations from the *Kinder und Haus-Märchen* of J. L. and C. G. Grimm were published under the title *German Popular Stories*, with illustrations by George Cruikshank. A second edition, entitled *Gammer Grethel*, appeared in 1839. In 1827 Taylor became incurably ill and from 1832 he was compelled to relinquish much of his professional work. He found literature a solace amid pain.

Taylor's interest in the legal recognition of the rights of nonconformists was keen and untiring. As a dissenting deputy he took an active part in the movement for repeal of the Test and Corporation Acts; in 1837 he was appointed a commissioner (unpaid) for carrying out the Dissenters' Marriage Act. In ecclesiastical politics he co-operated with Robert Aspland. His personal charm and strength of character were described as very great. After long suffering, he died at Bedford Row on 19 August 1839, and was buried in Highgate cemetery. He was survived by his wife and an only daughter.

Among his publications were works concerning constitutional law, the Norman conquest, a revision of the Authorized Version of the New Testament (edited by William Hincks), and *The Suffolk Bartholomeans: a Memoir of John Meadows* published in 1840, edited by Emily Taylor [*see below*]. He wrote in *The Jurist*, *Legal Observer*, *Retrospective Review*, *Westminster Review*, and *Morning Chronicle*. Among his contributions to the *Monthly Repository* were a memoir of John James Wetstein, the biblical critic; and 'Observations on Mahometanism'.

His sister, **Emily Taylor** (1795–1872), schoolmistress and author, was also born in Banham, Norfolk. Partially deaf as a result of contracting scarlet fever at the age of seven, she had no formal education but was allowed free access to her father's library. When she moved with her father to nearby New Buckenham she established a school there for about thirty boys and girls. Partly thanks to her friendship with Sarah Glover, improver of the tonic sol-fa system of musical notation, the school successfully emphasized the teaching of singing. Many girls from Buckenham School became music teachers in schools and choirs. In 1842 Emily Taylor moved to London to live with a widowed sister. After some years spent superintending Lady Noel Byron's Schools in Ealing and elsewhere, she established a small middle-class school for girls in her neighbourhood of London. Her publications reflect her career as a schoolteacher. She wrote *England and its People* (1860), a school

history, numerous historical tales, and a popular biography of Sir Thomas More. She was also the writer of many hymns. Originally a Unitarian, she joined the Church of England, before middle age, under the influence of Frederick Denison Maurice, though it was said that she was not interested in matters of religious doctrine. She died in London on 11 March 1872.

ALEXANDER GORDON, rev. ERIC METCALFE

Sources *Field's memoir of Edgar Taylor* (1839) • *Christian Reformer, or, Unitarian Magazine and Review*, 6 (1839), 739–40 • E. Taylor, *Suffolk Bartholomeans: a memoir of John Meadows* (1840) • R. B. Aspland, *Memoir of the life, works and correspondence of the Rev. Robert Aspland* (1850), 404 • W. James, *Memoir of Thomas Madge* (1871), 153 • P. W. Clayden, *Samuel Sharpe* (1883), 40, 79 • J. Julian, ed., *A dictionary of hymnology* (1892) [Emily Taylor] • *Sketch of Emily Taylor* • CGPLA Eng. & Wales (1872) [Emily Taylor]
Likenesses C. Turner, mezzotint, pubd 1841 (after E. U. Eddis), BM, NPG • H. Crabb Robinson, sketch, repro. in *Christian Reformer*, 739
Wealth at death under £5000—Emily Taylor: will, 1872

Taylor, Edward (*c.*1642–1729), minister in America and poet, was born in Sketchley, Leicestershire, the son of William Taylor, a yeoman farmer, and his wife, Margaret. Taylor's extant correspondence shows that he had at least two siblings: a brother, Richard, and another brother, Joseph, whose wife was named Alice. While his infancy was punctuated by the vicissitudes of the civil war, after 1650 Taylor's childhood and teenage years passed in relatively undisturbed comfort on his parents' productive farm. According to his obituary, printed in the *Boston Weekly News-Letter* in August 1729, the young Taylor attended the local grammar school, where he was so proficient a scholar that he became himself 'qualified to keep a School' and did so for a portion of a year at Bagworth, Leicestershire.

Ezra Stiles, a grandson of Taylor and one of Yale University's early presidents, wrote that his grandfather 'was a vigorous Advocate of Oliver Cromwell' (Stanford, 'Edward Taylor', 320). Upon the Restoration, however, Taylor's good fortunes began to shift. When in 1662 Charles II issued the Act of Uniformity, compelling schoolmasters, like the clergy, to accept the Book of Common Prayer in its entirety and abjure the solemn league and covenant, Taylor became restive, but it was the Conventicle Act of 1664, which made it illegal for Taylor and other nonconformists to practise their faith in 'conventicles', or groups of more than five, that forced him to consider another venue where he might worship in peace. By the middle to late 1660s Taylor had set his eyes on emigration to the Massachusetts Bay colony.

Taylor set sail for Boston on 26 April 1668. In his diary, begun on the voyage, Taylor was scrupulous to record his unpleasant bouts of seasickness and was careful to note that sabbath exercises for the duration of the journey fell to him, predicting his later vocation. In a particularly diverting passage the young man remarks that, just before going to sleep one evening, he read 'the fourth chapter of John in Greek' ('Diary', 12), indicating that his knowledge far exceeded that taught at New England's Latin grammar schools of this period. Despite his sessions of seasickness Taylor devoted a great portion of the diary to close observations of birds, fish, and debris encountered by the vessel, suggesting the keen interest in nature he would later display in his poetry.

Upon arrival in Boston, Taylor declared his intentions to become 'settled in the college' of Harvard ('Diary', 15), and he recorded his admission to the college on 23 July 1668. He graduated BA in 1671, and proceeded MA in 1674. After receiving his first degree Taylor at first hoped to continue at the college as one of its tutors, but he soon took the opportunity to serve as minister to Westfield, Massachusetts, where he delivered his first sermon on 3 December 1671.

By 1673 Taylor had been given a parsonage and a meeting-house, which doubled as a fort for protection against native Americans. He then turned his attention towards the prospect of marriage. His desires were realized soon after he met Elizabeth Fitch (d. 1689) from Norwich, Massachusetts, whom he married in 1674. Taylor's sincere and moving courtship of Elizabeth is recorded in a letter and an elaborate acrostic poem dated 8 July 1674 and in another poem of 27 August 1674; the acrostic poem is particularly noteworthy as it is as ingenious in its complex architecture (a heart surrounded by a 'ring of love', encased in a triangle celebrating the Trinity, with the words of the poem entwined about these figures) as it is touching in its sentiment.

Taylor was not ordained until 27 August 1679 because of the distractions provoked by the conflict known as King Philip's War. Not long after his ordination he composed one of his major poems, *Gods Determinations Touching his Elect*. Taylor apparently wrote this long, often dramatic, tract as an aide to his parishioners wishing instruction in the church's catechism; while he may have had plans to publish *Gods Determinations*, he almost certainly allowed it to be circulated in manuscript among his parishioners.

Many of his occasional poems, such as the well-known 'Upon the sweeping flood Aug: 13.14, 1683', 'Upon a wasp child with cold', 'Huswifery', and 'Upon a spider catching a fly', were composed during this same period, and Taylor allowed Cotton Mather to publish two stanzas from 'Upon wedlock, and death of children' in his *Right Thoughts in Sad Hours* (1689). Having written thousands of lines of poetry, from his adolescence until his last years, Taylor permitted only these two stanzas to appear during his lifetime. The wonder is that Taylor, whose busy schedule demanded he serve his parish as physician as well as pastor and spiritual adviser, could have found the time to construct such a large poetic opus.

Taylor's reputation as a poet rests primarily on his *Preparatory Meditations, First and Second Series*, a collection of poems numbering nearly 220, many of which were composed in preparation for the administration of the eucharist. Like the sermons Taylor's poems, with the exception of the two stanzas which appeared in 1689, only began appearing in print in the 1930s.

Taylor's poetry is marked by his positive application of classical knowledge, in contrast to the hostility towards the ancient world and mythology conventionally expected from puritan writers. While Taylor's homilies include negative anecdotes and examples from the ancient classical world, his *Preparatory Meditations*, which should be understood as his private colloquies with his idea of God, contain many classical references employed in the positive contexts one might expect from a recipient of the typical Renaissance college education that Taylor obtained at Harvard. In the *Preparatory Meditations* he faithfully practised the *meditatio*, deriving from the classical rhetorical exercise of memory (imagination and the senses), understanding (reason), and will (resolve to act upon instruction from the understanding), a rhetorical praxis early adapted to Christian rhetoric by such church fathers as Augustine.

The classicism which characterizes his best poetry yields to Taylor's orthodox theology expressed in the plain, unadorned style of his sermons. This same orthodoxy characterized his public service to his community. In 1688, for example, Solomon Stoddard, who had been librarian at Harvard during Taylor's college days, established in his own parish the controversial half-way covenant, by which unregenerate sinners were allowed to participate in the performance of the eucharist. This practice so offended the orthodox Taylor that he denounced both Stoddard and the half-way covenant from his pulpit on many occasions. During this same period, moreover, tragedy struck the Taylor family with stubborn persistence. Elizabeth Taylor dutifully bore eight children: Samuel, Elizabeth, James, Abigail, Bathsheba, Elizabeth (the first Elizabeth had died), Mary, and Hezekiah. She died on 7 July 1689 soon after the birth of Hezekiah. Taylor memorialized his intense grief for Elizabeth in one of the most moving of his many elegies wherein he declares his 'Onely Dove' (*Poems*, 473) has now his 'harp ... turned to mourning' (ibid., 472); 'Not Proud ... [but] Grave, Courteous, ever good', Elizabeth Taylor was one who 'I'th' golden mean did goe' (ibid., 474)—that is, her life displayed the principal classical virtue, moderation.

Three years passed before Taylor married again. His second wife was Ruth Wyllys (d. 1729/1730), from Hartford, Connecticut, whom he married at Westfield on 2 June 1692, and who survived her husband by about six months. With her Taylor had six more children: Ruth, Naomi, Anna, Mekitabel, Keziah, and Eldad. During Taylor's second marriage he renewed his friendship with the colonial merchant and diarist Samuel Sewall, with whom he had shared a room at Harvard. In 1705 Taylor wrote a poem of 190 verses about the discovery of huge bones (probably those of a mastodon) that had been unearthed at Claverack not far from Albany, New York. It is a testament to Taylor's reputation for learning that at least two teeth from this 'monster' were brought to him at Westfield for his investigation. Towards the end of his life, Taylor embarked upon the construction of a long poem of over 20,000 lines. He left this substantial tract untitled, although his twentieth-century editor, Donald E. Stanford, gave it the title *A Metrical History of Christianity*; again, Taylor probably shared this work with his parishioners for purposes of instruction.

Taylor died on 24 June 1729 at Westfield, Massachusetts, where he was buried. He left his parish the solid legacy of his orthodox, puritan theology, a tradition of thorough medical care (Taylor's personal library included many books on surgery and pharmacology), and a sizeable body of sensitive and intellectually challenging poetry. While most of his poetic *œuvre* remained unknown to Westfield's denizens, this extensive and learned collection constitutes some of the best poetry written in America before 1800. Of this collection, it is the *Preparatory Meditations*, the elegies, and the several occasional pieces which establish Edward Taylor's place among the best of British American colonial poets. Thomas H. Johnson initiated the recovery of Taylor's poems and prose works when in 1937 he published selections from the 400-page manuscript of the poems left by Taylor and housed in the Yale University Library since 1883. A more complete edition of the poems appeared in 1960 as *The Poems of Edward Taylor*, edited by D. E. Stanford.   JOHN C. SHIELDS

Sources N. S. Grabo, *Edward Taylor*, rev. edn (1988) · T. M. Davis, *A reading of Edward Taylor* (1992) · J. A. Hammond, *Sinful self, saintly self: the puritan experience of poetry* (1993) · K. Keller, *The example of Edward Taylor* (1972) · K. Rowe, *Saint and singer: Edward Taylor's typology and the poetics of meditation* (1986) · J. C. Shields, 'Edward Taylor's classicism', *The American Aeneas: classical origins of the American self* (2001), chap. 2 · 'Diary of Edward Taylor', *Proceedings of the Massachusetts Historical Society*, 18 (1880–81), 4–18 · D. E. Stanford, 'Edward Taylor', *American colonial writers, 1606–1734*, ed. E. Elliott, DLitB, 24 (1984), 310–32 · *The poems of Edward Taylor*, ed. D. E. Stanford (1960) · *Edward Taylor's Christographia*, ed. N. S. Grabo (1962) · *Edward Taylor's minor poetry*, ed. T. M. Davis and V. I. Davis (1981) · *Upon the types of the Old Testament*, ed. C. W. Mignon, 2 vols. (1989)
Archives Boston PL · Mass. Hist. Soc. · Redwood Library and Athenaeum, Newport, Rhode Island · University of Nebraska, Lincoln, Love Library · Westfield Athenaeum, Massachusetts · Yale U., Beinecke L.
Wealth at death left MSS

Taylor, Edward (1784–1863), lecturer and writer on music, the son of John *Taylor (1750–1826), a hymn writer and nonconformist minister, and his wife, Susanna *Taylor (1755–1823) [*see under* Taylor, John (1750–1826)], a literary hostess, was born in Norwich on 22 January 1784. He came from an old Unitarian family, and his great-grandfather was the dissenting divine and Hebrew scholar John Taylor (1694–1761) of Norwich. His brothers included John *Taylor (1779–1863), Richard *Taylor, and Arthur Taylor (*b.* 1790). Sarah *Austin was his sister.

From 1808 to 1815 Taylor was in business at the corner of Rampant Horse Street, Norwich, and in 1819 he was sheriff of Norwich. His early musical education was somewhat irregular. He took lessons from John Christmas Beckwith, organist of Norwich Cathedral, and on the flute and oboe from William Fish, a well-known local musician. For the first triennial Norwich music festival of 1824 he trained the chorus, fixed the band and singers, and arranged the entire programme. He achieved some success as a singer, thanks to a fine rich bass voice and commanding presence. In 1825 he moved to London and joined his brother Philip *Taylor and a cousin, John Martineau, as civil engineers at York Place, City Road. Lack of success in the business led Taylor to enter the music profession in 1827, at the age of forty-three, as a professional singer, teacher, and music journalist. That year he sang at the Norwich festival, and he conducted there in 1839 and 1842. For the festival of 1830 he translated Spohr's *Die letzen Dinge* as *The Last Judgement*, which was then performed for the first time in England. He was a great personal friend of Spohr, who was his guest at 3 Regent Square, King's Cross, in 1839 and 1847. He also visited Spohr at Kassel in 1840. In addition to *The Last Judgement*, he translated Spohr's *The Crucifixion, or, Calvary* (1836), *The Fall of Babylon* (1842), and *The Christian's Prayer* (c.1860), all of which were produced at Norwich festivals. His friendship with Spohr seems to have aroused animosity among other journalists, and Taylor was viewed by some as an enemy of young English composers.

On 24 October 1837, following the death of Richard John Samuel Stevens, Taylor was appointed professor of music at Gresham College, in the City, a post which he held until his death. In January 1838 he gave his first three lectures, which were published in the same year. He gave frequent lectures with great success in different parts of the country, and one on 'Madrigals' which he delivered at Bristol in 1837 resulted in the formation of the Bristol Madrigal Society. His lectures did much to raise the profile of music among the general public, and he prepared the way for the sight-singing movement of the 1840s. He was the founder of the Purcell Club and Vocal Society, and from 1829 to 1843 he was music critic of *The Spectator*. In addition to the translations already mentioned, his works included a few songs, words for songs, and adaptations. He translated Friedrich Schneider's *The Deluge*, Mozart's Requiem under the title *Redemption* (1845), and Haydn's *The Seasons*. *The Vocal School of Italy in the Sixteenth Century* (1839, reissued in 1868) consisted of a selection of madrigals and anthems by Italian masters, adapted to English words. 'The cathedral service, its glory, its decline, and its designed extinction' appeared anonymously (in two articles) in the *British and Foreign Review* for 1844, and was republished (again anonymously) in 1845. In 1843 Taylor edited Purcell's *King Arthur* for the Musical Antiquarian Society (which he founded with William Chappell and Edward Rimbault) and, in conjunction with James Turle, he edited *The People's Music Book* (1844) and *The Singing-Book* (1846). Some manuscripts by him were placed in the library of the Royal College of Music, including several lectures on music 'written and delivered by Edward Taylor at Gresham College and elsewhere', *Musical Illustrations to Several Courses of Lectures* (24 vols. and separate parts), mostly in Taylor's autograph, and his *Ode for the Opening of Gresham College* (2 November 1843), in score.

Taylor died at his house, Gresham Cottage, Cornlands Road, Brentwood, Essex, on 12 March 1863, and was buried in the old dissenting burial-ground, King's Road, Brentwood. He left a son, John Edward Taylor, a printer of Weybridge, Surrey, whose output appears to have included some of his father's works.

F. G. EDWARDS, *rev.* DAVID J. GOLBY

Sources J. C. A. Brown, 'The popularity and influence of Spohr in England', DPhil diss., U. Oxf., 1980, 321–8 · J. C. A. Brown, *Louis*

Spohr - a critical biography (1984), 278 • B. Rainbow, 'Taylor, Edward', *New Grove* • *Louis Spohr's autobiography: translated from the German* (1865), 215–88 • private information (1898) • *CGPLA Eng. & Wales* (1864)

Archives Norfolk RO, lecture notes and papers • Royal College of Music, London • UCL, Spink MSS | UCL, letters to Society for the Diffusion of Useful Knowledge

Likenesses H. E. Dawe, mezzotint (after T. S. Tait), BM • G. H. White, ink and pencil drawing, NPG

Wealth at death under £8000: resworn will with codicil, July 1864, *CGPLA Eng. & Wales*

Taylor [*née* Coles], **Elizabeth** (1912–1975), writer, was born on 3 July 1912 at Reading, Berkshire, the daughter of Oliver Coles, an insurance inspector, and his wife, Elsie May Fewtrell. She was educated at the Abbey School in Reading, where Jane Austen—the writer Elizabeth Taylor most admired, and to whom she was often compared—was a former pupil. After leaving school Elizabeth worked as a governess, and then in a library. She joined the Communist Party in her early twenties and delivered leaflets from door to door in various London boroughs. She later transferred her allegiance to the Labour Party, which she supported for the rest of her life. In 1936 she married John William Kendall Taylor (*b.* 1908/9), the owner of a confectionery business, and settled with him at Penn in Buckinghamshire. Their children—a son, René, and a daughter, Jo—were born in the late 1930s.

Elizabeth Taylor's first novel, *At Mrs Lippincote's*, was published in 1945. It was followed a year later by *Palladian*, which—more than any other of her works—displays the influence of Jane Austen. There are several sly references to *Northanger Abbey* and *Mansfield Park*, and the principal female character is named Cassandra Dashwood. Despite her political sympathies, Taylor gives no indication in this curious novel of an England ravaged by war: the bombed sites, bread queues, and ration books are all notably absent. The man who woos Cassandra is an aesthete called Marion Vanbrugh, who lives in a decaying country house and reads the Greek classics in the original. *Palladian* is rescued from bookishness, from literary parody, by the vividly drawn people on the periphery of Cassandra's and Marion's courtship—the vengeful nanny (encountered, perhaps, during Taylor's time as a governess) who 'feigned eccentricity as Hamlet feigned part of his madness', and the alcoholic Tom, who 'could not bear stoicism in those he hurt, could not bear the guilt of forcing them into such courage'. This last observation is typical of the shrewd analyst of the human heart Elizabeth Taylor was to become in the fiction of her maturity.

The world Elizabeth Taylor describes in her twelve novels and four collections of short stories is confined, in the main, to the English home counties. The majority of her men and women have outwardly comfortable lives. They patronize tearooms and antique shops, attend gymkhanas and church fêtes, and seldom discuss the burning issues of the day. Her prose is clear, almost to the point of transparency, and thus an immediate pleasure to read. This clarity of expression is the product of deep and careful consideration, for Taylor believed that the best art

Elizabeth Taylor (1912–1975), by Lotte Meitner-Graf, 1957?

always gives the appearance of effortlessness. She is a stylist in the Evelyn Waugh mode, using the right word in the right place to maximum effect. In the late story 'Sisters', from *The Devastating Boys* (1972), the protagonist, Mrs Mason, is described as 'made for widowhood' and the widow's complacency is conveyed in a few deft phrases: 'Mrs Mason pottered in her garden, played patience in the winter, or read historical romances from the library. "Something light", she would tell the assistant, as if seeking suggestions from a waiter'. Elizabeth Taylor is one of those writers who concern themselves with seeming domestic trivia, with the unimportant quotidian. When she creates a 'comic turn', usually in the form of a charwoman, she takes discreet pains to show that the performance is a form of self-protection, put on for the employer's amusement. In what is probably her finest novel, *Mrs Palfrey at the Claremont* (1971), which is set in a genteel Kensington hotel occupied entirely by the elderly, the sadness of Mrs Palfrey's plight is offset with many exquisite humorous touches. The other, more famous Elizabeth Taylor, the film actress, is alluded to when the 'blowsy Mrs Burton' comes to stay, and an unpleasant old bigot, Lady Swayne, prefaces her most repellent pronouncements with 'I'm afraid': 'I'm afraid I'd like to see the Prime Minister hanged, drawn and quartered.'

Elizabeth Taylor was much admired by Elizabeth Bowen and Angus Wilson, who were also distinguished practitioners of the short story. The short form was her métier, in which—as Wilson once observed—her 'warm heart, sharp claws and exceptional powers of formal balance' were joined together in perfect artistic harmony. She is, essentially, a miniaturist, as her stories continue to demonstrate, never more persuasively than in the mordant 'A

Dedicated Man' in the collection with that title (1965). This is one of Taylor's masterpieces, and in it two frustrated, fraudulent lives—lives replete with snobbery and duplicity—are examined and exposed in satisfying detail.

Elizabeth Taylor was shy by nature and genuinely modest, given to blushing when praised to her face. She was also, as the poet and critic D. J. Enright noted in an obituary that appeared in *The Bookseller*, extremely pretty. Enright had been her editor at Chatto and Windus, but her work needed very little editing since she was scrupulous in matters of style and punctuation.

For many years Taylor maintained a correspondence with the novelist, critic, and biographer Robert Liddell. He lived in Greece and Italy and welcomed her news from England. They had one great friend in common, the novelist Ivy Compton-Burnett, and Elizabeth Taylor recounted every visit she made to Ivy's flat in Kensington. Very few of these letters survive, though to judge by the two or three quotations from them in Hilary Spurling's *Secrets of a Woman's Heart: the Later Life of I. Compton-Burnett, 1920–1969* (1984), they must have been vivid and brilliantly detailed. Taylor describes this friendship by post in the story 'The Letter Writers' (in the collection *The Blush*, published in 1951). She and Liddell made a pact that the letters would be destroyed at their deaths, and alas they kept that pact.

One of the reasons why Elizabeth Taylor's friendship with Ivy Compton-Burnett lasted so well was that the latter was fond of chocolates. Whenever she went to London, Elizabeth Taylor never forgot to bring a box of the most expensive chocolates from her husband's factory. These were accepted with gratitude, though Compton-Burnett deplored their cost, wondering why Mr Taylor could not manufacture cheaper sweets.

In 1974 Elizabeth Taylor was diagnosed as having an inoperable cancer. 'Try to keep me alive until I have finished my novel', she urged the doctors who examined her. That novel, *Blaming*, was published posthumously, in 1976. She died at her home, Grove's Barn, Penn, on 19 November 1975. A selection of her best stories, with the apposite title *Dangerous Calm*, appeared in 1995. It confirmed her steadily growing reputation as one of the most assured English short-story writers of the twentieth century.

PAUL BAILEY

Sources private information (2004) · *The Times* (21 Nov 1975) · *CGPLA Eng. & Wales* (1975) · b. cert. · d. cert. · m. cert.
Archives NRA, papers | Bodl. Oxf., letters to Barbara Pym
Likenesses A. McBean, photograph, *c*.1949, NPG · L. Meitner-Graf, photograph, 1957?, NPG [*see illus.*]
Wealth at death £74,452: probate, 23 Dec 1975, *CGPLA Eng. & Wales*

Taylor, Emily (1795–1872). *See under* Taylor, Edgar (1793–1839).

Taylor, Eva Germaine Rimington (1879–1966), geographer and historian of science, was born at Southwood Lane, Highgate, Middlesex, on 22 June 1879, the third child and second daughter of Charles Richard Taylor, a solicitor, and his first wife, Emily Jane Nelson. Her mother ran away when Eva was about three years of age, an event which seems to have marred her young life—for the 'sin' of the mother was visited upon her children, who were allowed neither toys nor domestic pets. Eva's sturdy nature turned to hedgerow flowers, birds, and wild animals, and throughout her long life she showed a keen enjoyment of natural history and of gardening. She was educated at home, at the Camden School for Girls, and at the North London Collegiate School for Girls. A scholarship took her to Royal Holloway College and in 1903 she obtained her University of London BSc with first-class honours in chemistry.

Taylor's first appointments were as a teacher of chemistry at the Burton upon Trent School for Girls and at a convent school in Oxford. In 1906 she became a student at the University of Oxford and subsequently obtained the certificate of regional geography and the diploma of geography, both with a mark of distinction. From 1908 to 1910 she was a private research assistant to A. J. Herbertson, head of the School of Geography at Oxford. She spent the next six years in London writing highly successful geography textbooks for schools and drafting wall maps (mainly in collaboration with J. F. Unstead). She continued to combine work with bringing up a young family, and from 1916 to 1918 she lectured at Clapham Training College for Teachers and at the Froebel Institute. In 1920 she became a part-time lecturer at the East London College (later Queen Mary College), and a year later she moved to a similar post at Birkbeck College, again in collaboration with Unstead. In 1929 she proceeded to her DSc in geography (London), and in 1930 she was appointed (in open competition) to the chair of geography at Birkbeck College, a post which she retained until her retirement in 1944.

Taylor was not only a brilliant lecturer, she was also a great scholar. Before retirement she published two outstanding works—*Tudor Geography, 1485–1583* (1930) and *Late Tudor and Early Stuart Geography, 1583–1650* (1934). Until a stroke in 1964 damaged an optic nerve, impairing her vision and her mobility, she maintained after her retirement an active interest in geographical and related studies, contributing numerous articles both to learned and to popular journals. Between the ages of seventy-five and eighty-seven she published three remarkable volumes: *The Mathematical Practitioners of Tudor and Stuart England* (1954); *The Haven-Finding Art: a History of Navigation from Odysseus to Captain Cook* (1956); and *The Mathematical Practitioners of Hanoverian England* (1966).

In 1938 Taylor chaired the committee appointed by the Royal Geographical Society to prepare a memorandum for the Barlow commission on the distribution of the industrial population. She was also a keen advocate of a national atlas of Britain as a basis for national and regional planning. During and immediately after the Second World War she helped the Association for Planning and Regional Reconstruction prepare evidence to the committee on land utilization in rural areas and to the Schuster committee on the qualifications of planners. Birkbeck College remained in London during the war, and in the 'phoney war' period she instructed officers of the eastern command in map-reading and interpretation.

Taylor was twice president of section E of the British Association for the Advancement of Science. The Royal Geographical Society awarded her the Victoria medal in 1947 and honorary fellowship in 1965. She was a vice-president of the Hakluyt Society, an honorary member of the Institute of Navigation (in 1959 she delivered the first duke of Edinburgh lecture), and an honorary vice-president of the Society for Nautical Research. In 1949 the University of Aberdeen conferred on her the honorary degree of LLD, and in 1960 she was elected one of the first fellows of Birkbeck College. To mark her eightieth birthday the societies with which she had been closely involved initiated an endowed annual lecture to be given in a branch of knowledge to which she had contributed; these lectures have proved a considerable intellectual and social success.

Taylor's was a masterful personality. Beneath her rather formidable manner there was a warm-hearted affection, loyalty, and an unfailing kindness. She was a brilliant talker and raconteur. Eila Campbell, who followed in her wake at Birkbeck and in several learned societies, took particular care of her in her years of retirement. Campbell's papers reveal their warm personal relationship and Campbell's role in seeing Taylor's last book through the press, in setting up the Taylor lecture, and in ensuring that Taylor's reputation did not suffer through the publication of articles—for instance on the Vinland map, written when Taylor's judgement had deteriorated.

Taylor was for some time the partner of the pipe manufacturer Herbert Edward Dunhill, and he was father to at least one of her three sons (*b.* 1912, 1915, and 1919). The second died in infancy, but Taylor proved a devoted mother to the other two.

Taylor died at St Anne's Nursing Home, Wokingham, Berkshire, of heart failure on 5 July 1966. Thirty years later her published work and her memory continue to command respect.

EILA M. J. CAMPBELL, *rev.* ELIZABETH BAIGENT

Sources personal knowledge (1981) · private information (1981) · b. cert. · d. cert. · *CGPLA Eng. & Wales* (1967) · b. cert. [Spenser Dunhill] · *The Times* (7 July 1966) · P. Barber, 'The Eila Campbell papers', *Imago Mundi*, 47 (1995), 10–11 · WWW
Archives BL, corresp. and papers, Add. MSS 69466–49490
Likenesses Elliott & Fry, photograph, 1947, RGS · photograph, repro. in *The Times* · photograph, U. Lond., department of Geography, Birkbeck College
Wealth at death £25,095: administration with will, 6 Feb 1967, *CGPLA Eng. & Wales*

Taylor, Frances Margaret [*name in religion* Mary Magdalen] (1832–1900), journalist and Roman Catholic nun, was born on 20 January 1832 in Stoke Rochford, Lincolnshire, and baptized an Anglican at the rectory there. She was the last of the ten children of Henry Taylor (1777–1842), an Anglican clergyman, and Louisa, *née* Jones (1793–1869). She was educated at home, moving to London with the rest of the family after her father's death in 1842. While in London she, along with three of her sisters, became attracted to Tractarianism. At the age of sixteen she followed her sister Emma into Priscilla Seddon's Anglican sisterhood at Plymouth, working in Devonport during the 1849 cholera outbreak. She returned home after six months, taking up charity work.

Although under the prescribed age of twenty-four Taylor volunteered in 1854 to nurse British soldiers wounded in the Crimean War, and after training at St George's Hospital, London, went to Turkey with Mary Stanley's group, with whom she worked in Scutari and Koulali hospitals. On 14 April 1855 she was received into the Roman Catholic church by Father Sidney Woollett, army chaplain. She always stressed the importance of her fellow nurses, who were Irish Sisters of Mercy, and the faith of the Irish Catholic soldiers she nursed in leading her to Catholicism. One of the many Irish sisters in the Poor Servants of the Mother of God later noted, 'Her love and esteem for the Irish would more than satisfy the most enthusiastic of Erin's children' (Troughton, 121). On returning to England in November 1855 she resumed charitable work, now guided by the convert to Catholicism Henry Manning. Her family's financial position became precarious and she contributed income by writing and publishing *Eastern Hospitals and Eastern Nurses* (1856). Its success led on to *Tyborne and Who Went Thither* (1857), a novel about Elizabethan Catholic martyrs.

From 1862 to 1871 Taylor was proprietor and editor of *The Lamp*, a Catholic periodical for the middle and lower classes. In 1864, at the request of the Jesuit fathers, she helped to establish a new Catholic newspaper, *The Month*. As editor during its first year she worked with leading Catholic writers and clergy, including J. H. Newman. Her writing drew to her another Catholic convert writer, Lady Georgiana Fullerton. They became close friends, Lady Georgiana, who was older, married, and socially her superior, taking the part of mentor and guide. They shared an interest in the new female religious congregations of the time and in 1861 Taylor spent a short time in the noviciate of the Sisters of Charity in Paris. Both believed that there was a place for a welfare congregation in England which did not divide members into choir and lay sisters and could accept women unable to afford dowries. In October 1868 they rented rooms off Fleet Street and Taylor started a small community. Favourably impressed by the rule of a Polish congregation, the Little Servants of the Mother of God, she visited Poland with the thought of opening a branch of the order in England, but later resolved to found a new congregation. After her mother's death in 1869 she moved in with the community permanently, making her religious vows on 12 February 1872 and, as Mother Magdalen, founding the Congregation of the Poor Servants of the Mother of God. The question of financial support for a poor congregation undertaking welfare work was resolved by establishing it in the commercial laundry business. The congregation was well received, spreading beyond London to Lancashire and Ireland in the 1870s and 1880s. By 1900 it had women's refuges in Streatham, Soho, Brentford, and Liverpool; orphanages in Roehampton and Brentford; homes for the elderly in Dublin and Rathdown Union; a hostel in Paris;

schools in Rome and Cork; and, its most ambitious undertaking, Providence Hospital, a free industrial hospital in St Helens, Lancashire. Afterwards, the congregation spread to the USA, Venezuela, and Kenya. As Mother Magdalen she continued to write and edit throughout her life. She died of diabetes in the Soho Square convent on 9 June 1900 and was buried in Maryfield convent, Roehampton.

SUSAN O'BRIEN

Sources F. C. Devas, *Mother Mary Magdalen (Fanny Margaret Taylor): foundress of the Poor Servants of the Mother of God* (1927) · R. G. Wells, *A woman of her time and ours: Mary Magdalen Taylor, SMG* (1988) · M. Geraldine, *Born to love* (1970) · M. C. Troughton, *Life of Mother Magdalen Taylor* (privately printed, 1972)
Archives Archives of the Congregation of the Poor Servants of the Mother of God, Brentford · Maryfield Convent, Roehampton, London
Likenesses photograph, repro. in Devas, *Mother Mary Magdalen*

Taylor, Frank Sherwood (1897–1956), chemist and historian of science, was born on 26 November 1897 at Bickley, Bromley, Kent, the son of Seaton Frank Taylor (1844–1930), a prosperous solicitor, and his wife, Helen Sennerth Davidson. He was educated at Sherborne School and won a classical scholarship at Lincoln College, Oxford. However, the First World War kept him from taking this up and he instead served as a private in the Honourable Artillery Company. In October 1917 he was seriously wounded at Passchendaele, and underwent some fourteen operations in the space of nine months. By the time he arrived in Oxford in 1919 he had decided to change his intellectual course from classics to chemistry. While still an undergraduate, on 21 April 1920, he married Dorothy Gertrude Workman (b. 1887/8). She was the daughter of Captain William Herbert Nash, of the Army Service Corps, and had been twice married: first to Herbert David Corgill, and then to Eric Woodside Workman.

In 1921 Taylor obtained his first degree and became a chemistry teacher in several schools including Gresham's (Holt) and Repton. In 1923 he registered as a part-time student at University College, London. Work on Greek alchemy had gained him an Oxford BSc in that year, and he gained his London PhD in 1931. This remained his life interest. An important paper in the *Journal of Hellenic Studies* and a later translation of the alchemical writings of Stephanos of Alexandria established him as a specialist in this field, leading eventually to his most influential book *The Alchemists* (1951).

Taylor was never hard up: he had additional income from a legacy (including several small shops) and the profits of several textbooks; his *Inorganic and Theoretical Chemistry* (1931) ran to nine editions. He aimed at enlightening the adult as well as the schoolchild, and in 1936 he published *The World of Science* which remained in print with revisions for more than thirty years. In 1933 Taylor moved to university teaching at East London College (later Queen Mary College). He left in 1938 for full-time writing, seeking at the same time an academic post in what was still a limited field of scholarship: the history of science. In 1938 he defined his own position with his *Galileo and the Freedom of Thought*. He was received into the Roman Catholic

church in 1940. He declared his views on the relation between faith and science in *The Fourfold Vision* (1945).

Taylor's later books covered broad fields of scientific development without claiming to offer any new research, except, that is, for *The Alchemists*, which remained for many years a leading work in its field. He helped in the formation of the Society for the History of Alchemy and Early Chemistry, and promoted the subject by editing the society's journal *Ambix* from its launch in 1937 until his death in 1956. He also helped to found the British Society for the History of Science and was its president from 1951 to 1953.

Taylor also held two important museum posts, the first with enduring success, the second with sad frustration. In Oxford some enthusiasts for the history of science, led by R. T. Gunther, began to collect scientific instruments of historic significance. These had been given a home in the Old Ashmolean Museum (subsequently the Museum of the History of Science) on Broad Street. Taylor was appointed curator of this collection in 1940. He developed its organization (renovation of the building was completed in 1949) and campaigned for the establishment of a diploma in the history of science. In 1950 the director of the South Kensington Science Museum died suddenly and Taylor was appointed to succeed him. Although welcomed by the younger curatorial staff he was resented by some of the older heads of departments as an interloper. Some also took exception to his open religious standpoint. Taylor was also faced with operations on a far bigger scale than any he had met before, notably the involvement of the South Kensington complex of museums in the Festival of Britain. His individualism had to be adapted to work with civil servants and a powerful advisory council.

Taylor was prepared to learn new techniques of communication and took part in radio and television programmes. His Royal Institution Christmas lectures to children (December 1952–January 1953) survive as *An Illustrated History of Science* (1955). He continued to contribute to journals in his field, always impressing by clarity and substance. He responded well to exposure to the history of applied science. He had nearly completed a *History of Industrial Chemistry* when he died, at his home, St Denis, The Avenue, Crowthorne, Berkshire, on 5 January 1956. This work was completed and seen through the press by one of the younger Science Museum curators whom he had encouraged. In his will, dated 4 December 1955, he left all his property to his wife, Margaret Annie Taylor, *née* Sturt. The couple had a son, Albert Sherwood Taylor.

Taylor was of medium height but impressive without arrogance, concerned for his appearance but without vanity, a good listener and an impressive speaker. If he can be said to have had a leading aim it was to aid the unification of science and religion.

FRANK GREENAWAY

Sources MHS Oxf., MSS Taylor 1–300; MS Museum 104 · A. V. Simcock, 'Alchemy and the world of science: an intellectual biography of Frank Sherwood Taylor', *Ambix*, 34 (1987), 121–39 · E. F. Caldin, *Proceedings of the Chemical Society* (1957), 151–2 · *The Times* (7 Jan

1956) • m. cert. [Dorothy Gertrude Workman] • personal knowledge (2004) • will, probate registry, Principal Registry of the Family Division, London • *WWW*

Archives MHS Oxf., corresp. and papers

Likenesses photographs, MH Oxf.

Wealth at death £12,273 13s. 2d.: probate, 25 May 1956, *CGPLA Eng. & Wales*

Taylor, Sir Geoffrey Ingram (1886–1975), physicist and engineer, was born on 7 March 1886 at 10 Blenheim Villas, St John's Wood, London, the elder son (there were no daughters) of Edward Ingram Taylor, artist, of St John's Wood, and his wife, Margaret (1858–1935), daughter of George *Boole, professor of mathematics at Queen's College, Cork, and Mary *Boole *née* Everest. He was educated at University College School (1899–1905) where already he was strongly attracted to physical science. At Trinity College, Cambridge, he read first mathematics (part one, 1907, twenty-second wrangler) and then natural sciences, in which he obtained first-class honours in part two (1908). The award of a major scholarship by Trinity College in 1908, followed by a prize fellowship two years later, enabled him to stay on in the Cavendish Laboratory.

Taylor's first research project, suggested to him by Sir Joseph Thomson, was a simple test of the compatibility of the new idea of quantization of energy with the wave character of light when the intensity of the light is extremely small. But tangible macroscopic physics had a greater appeal for Taylor, and virtually all his subsequent investigations were concerned with the mechanics of fluid and solid materials and their applications in geophysics and engineering. He was actively engaged in research from the time of his graduation in 1908 to 1972 when he suffered a severe stroke, during which time he wrote over 200 scientific papers and articles, nearly all of which were later republished by Cambridge University Press in four volumes. His research was profoundly original. In his ability to combine incisive mathematical analysis and simple imaginative experiments to illuminate a fundamental mechanical process or phenomenon he had few equals, yet he was modest, unassuming, gentle, and boyish in manner, and much loved by those who knew him.

Taylor's first major investigation concerned the turbulent transfer processes in the friction layer of the earth's atmosphere, and was undertaken on his appointment in 1911 to the Schuster readership in dynamical meteorology at Cambridge. A year or so later he was invited to serve as the meteorologist on an expedition to observe the path of icebergs in the north Atlantic following the sinking of the *Titanic*, and this gave him an opportunity of observing the distributions of mean wind velocity, temperature, and water vapour content at different heights above the sea. This early work was the beginning of a preoccupation with the nature of turbulent motion of fluids and led to a remarkable series of pioneering papers which extended over twenty-seven years and transformed the understanding of turbulence.

Early in the First World War, Taylor was recruited to the Royal Aircraft Factory at Farnborough with several other

Sir Geoffrey Ingram Taylor (1886–1975), by Howard Coster, 1944

able young scientists to help put the design and military operation of aeroplanes on a scientific basis. This experience led directly to some useful investigations in aerodynamics and in the strength of materials, and it was also the origin of a continuing interest in aeronautics and many important research developments in later years, for example in supersonic flow. He also gained a pilot's certificate in 1915.

Taylor returned to Cambridge in 1919 as a fellow and lecturer in mathematics at Trinity College and was given the use of experimental facilities in the Cavendish Laboratory. He was elected FRS in 1919, and in 1923 was appointed to the Royal Society Yarrow research professorship, which he chose to hold at the Cavendish Laboratory. On 15 August 1925 Taylor married Grace Stephanie Frances (1884/5–1967), known as Stephanie, a schoolmistress, who was daughter of Thomas Holmes Ravenhill, a general practitioner in Birmingham. There were no children. In the period up to the outbreak of the Second World War, Taylor brought to fruition two great research themes, one on the deformation of crystalline materials and dislocation theory and the other on the statistical theory of turbulence, as well as a host of other novel investigations in fluid and solid mechanics.

During the Second World War Taylor was much in demand as a consultant and adviser to civil and military authorities faced with new technical problems. The detonation of high explosives, propagation of blast waves, effects of blast waves on structures, and undersea explosions represented the main areas of his work. In 1944–5 he visited Los Alamos, New Mexico, and worked with the group making the first nuclear explosion. Many of these wartime problems suggested basic research investigations in new areas of mechanics to which he turned later.

In 1952 Taylor retired formally from his research professorship, but he continued working in the Cavendish Laboratory with undiminished enthusiasm and fertility and for twenty years explored a remarkable range of novel and unconventional problems in fluid mechanics. In this last phase of his research life he was the international great man of mechanics, welcome at every conference, and he enjoyed the opportunities for travel and the honours that came to him. Sailing was an interest shared with his wife, and they made a number of notable voyages together, in one case to the Lofoten islands, Norway. These voyages provided part of the stimulus for Taylor to produce a startlingly original design of anchor which had a much better holding power than conventional designs and became popular with owners of small boats.

Taylor was knighted in 1944 and admitted to the Order of Merit in 1969. He was awarded many honorary degrees by universities at home and abroad (including Oxford, 1938, and Cambridge, 1957), was elected to honorary membership of a large number of learned societies, and received many prizes and medals, among which were the Copley medal of the Royal Society in 1944 and the US medal for merit in 1946.

Taylor's greatness as a scientist lay in his ability to foresee those narrow and unpromising problems in mechanical science which would turn out to be of significant value, and to pursue these in preference to more fashionable themes. Taylor died on 27 June 1975 at his home, Farmfield, Huntingdon Road, Cambridge, soon after a second stroke. G. K. BATCHELOR, *rev.*

Sources G. Batchelor, *The life and legacy of G. I. Taylor* (1997) · personal knowledge (1986) · G. K. Batchelor, 'Geoffrey Ingram Taylor, 7 March 1886–27 June 1975', *Journal of Fluid Mechanics*, 173 (1986), 1–14 · G. K. Batchelor, *Memoirs FRS*, 22 (1976), 565–633 · b. cert. · m. cert. · d. cert.
Archives NMM, papers relating to naval designs · Trinity Cam., corresp. and papers | IWM, corresp. with Sir Henry Tizard · Nuffield Oxf., corresp. with Lord Cherwell · Trinity Cam., letters to Rosenthal family · University of Bristol, corresp. with H. E. Hinton
Likenesses W. Stoneman, two photographs, 1933–58, NPG · H. Coster, photographs, *c.*1940–1959, NPG [*see illus.*] · T. C. Dugdale, pencil drawing, 1949, Trinity Cam. · photograph, repro. in Batchelor, *Memoirs FRS* · photograph, repro. in Batchelor, 'Geoffrey Ingram Taylor'
Wealth at death £137,390: probate, 4 Sept 1975, *CGPLA Eng. & Wales*

Taylor, George (*c.*1710–1758), pugilist and showman, made his first appearances as a combatant in his teens in the early days of the sport when boxing was only just separating itself from swordplay and cudgelling. He fought at the amphitheatre, half great fairground booth and half theatre, which had been opened by James Figg on the Oxford Road, London, in 1719. Taylor joined its band of well-

George Taylor (*c.*1710–1758), by Andrew Miller

known boxers, which included the Gypsy 'Prince' Boswell, Tom Smallwood, and John Smith, unflatteringly known as 'Buckhorse' from his appearance. Above all there was Jack Broughton, already famous for one athletic feat in winning the annual Doggett's Coat and Badge rowing race for watermen, and soon to be celebrated as pugilism's first rule maker and earliest undisputed champion.

George Taylor, a strong, shifty fighter with a powerful wrestling throw, was still prepared to begin contests in the old-fashioned way with a spell of swordplay. In 1734, shortly after Figg's death and while still in his early twenties, he took over the management of the amphitheatre. As a manager and showman he enjoyed considerable success. His advertisements for the amphitheatre were always lurid with the promise of blood and he used the press to put out heated challenges and counter-challenges from supposedly enraged fighters. The crowds flocked in and, as Taylor charged an expensive 2*s.* 6*d.* for entrance, a day's takings of £150 was not uncommon. He was, moreover, calling himself the 'champion', conveniently ignoring the fact that Jack Broughton had beaten him just before he took over the running of the amphitheatre and had also been victorious over all comers. At the start of the 1740s everything appeared to be set fair for Taylor; he won plaudits for a successful fight against Boswell and his business was flourishing, but Broughton split with him in 1742 and a year later, with powerful backing led by the duke of Cumberland, opened a new amphitheatre of his own, much more comfortable than Taylor's spartan establishment and furnished with boxes and a viewing gallery. Moreover, it was virtually adjacent to Taylor's premises and Broughton timed its opening to clash with a contest between Taylor and James Field, adding insult to injury by undercutting his rival's prices and charging no more than 1*s.* for entry.

The new venture was an immediate success. There was a bitter war of words in the press with Taylor at length falsely accusing Broughton of taking more than the proprietor's usual one-third share of the takings, a charge that was quickly shown to be false. There was little left for Taylor but to close his own theatre and cross over to Broughton's, taking his fighters with him. It was a great setback from which he never recovered and after a few years he left the amphitheatre to become landlord of The Fountain inn, Deptford. Like too many of his successors in the ring, however, he decided to fight again, taking up the challenge of Tom Faulkner whom he had beaten twice in the past but who now sensed a chance for revenge. They fought on 5 August 1758 near St Albans for 200 guineas and the gate money. It was a long, hard struggle which ended with defeat for the ageing Taylor. Both of his eyes were closed from bruising. His pride was finally shattered and he died a few months later in December.

DENNIS BRAILSFORD

Sources *Pancratia, or, A history of pugilism*, 2nd edn (1815) · H. D. Miles, *Pugilistica: the history of British boxing*, 3 vols. (1906) · D. Brailsford, *Bareknuckles: a social history of prize fighting* (1988) · F. Henning, *Fights for the championship*, 2 vols. (1902)
Likenesses A. Miller, engraving, NPG [*see illus.*] · drawing, repro. in Henning, *Fights for the championship*, 21 · pencil drawing, Yale U. CBA, Paul Mellon collection; repro. in T. Sawyer, *Noble Art* (1989), 136

Taylor, Sir George (1904–1993), botanist, was born in Edinburgh on 15 February 1904, the only son and youngest of four children of George William Taylor, a painter and decorator specializing in gilding, and his wife, Jane, *née* Sloan, a domestic servant. The family struggled financially and from an early age George took on a number of delivery rounds and was also sent to live with an aunt and grandmother at various periods during his childhood. These early experiences of hardship no doubt helped to develop the tough, formidable, and financially conscious character that was to emerge in later life. He started his primary education at Bruntsfield public school and from there progressed to Boroughmuir secondary school. There, his enthusiasm and interest, particularly in science and biology, were noticed by the science master, Mr Ogilvie, who took a particular interest in fostering his ability. Eventually, feeling that the school could not fully develop his talents Ogilvie persuaded George's parents to send him to the much more prestigious George Heriot's School, a well-established public school in Edinburgh. The fees were met by one of his three older sisters and George flourished under the guidance of the science master, George Scott. He passed all his examinations with ease and was accepted by the University of Edinburgh in 1922 as a student of biology.

At the time that Taylor was a student at Edinburgh the university department of botany was housed at the Royal Botanic Garden, and Sir William Wright Smith was both professor of botany and regius keeper of the garden. During the latter part of the nineteenth century and the early part of the twentieth century the Royal Botanic Garden was the major centre in the United Kingdom for the study and introduction of Sino-Himalayan plants and included staff such as George Forrest, who had already made eight collecting trips to China and had brought back numerous plants, both as seed and herbarium specimens, many new to science. The proximity of the department and the garden ensured close collaboration between their staff, and students were able to observe and discuss the management of living collections and the organization of the herbarium and library. There is no doubt that this was to stand Taylor in good stead later in life. During his time as a student Taylor took on extra work, such as acting as a demonstrator of botany to medical students, earning him £5 per term. As part of his degree work he undertook small research projects such as surveying the vegetation of Duddingston Loch (a small loch on the south-east side of Arthur's Seat in the centre of Edinburgh) and anatomical and developmental studies. As a result of his hard work and natural ability he graduated with first-class honours in botany in 1926. He was also presented with Edinburgh's most prestigious biology award, the Vans Dunlop scholarship, which provided the recipient with £100 per annum for three years to undertake research for the degree of PhD.

Following discussions with Wright Smith and Dr J. R. Matthews, a lecturer who had taken a particular interest in Taylor, he took up the study of the classification of the genus *Meconopsis* (the Himalayan and Welsh poppies). The richness of the genus in the Himalayas and China was only just being revealed thanks to collections made by Forrest and others. Not only were their herbarium specimens extensive but they collected seed also, giving Taylor the chance to work on both dried and living material, an interest that was to develop to a greater extent in later life. During the second year of his PhD Taylor was invited to take part in a plant collecting expedition to South Africa organized by a group of eminent horticulturists. This was his first venture abroad and it gave him good experience in the organization and routine of an expedition. Taylor had letters of introduction to General Smuts, a keen gardener and amateur botanist. The general and the young Taylor got on well and the two went plant collecting on Table Mountain more than once. Taylor completed his work on *Meconopsis* by 1928 but did not obtain his PhD until 1934. Soon afterwards he published his research as a book and, despite much subsequent collecting of new plants, it remained the standard work on the genus. On 26 August 1929 he married his first wife, Alice Helen (*d.* 1977), daughter of Thomas William Pendrich of Edinburgh; they had two sons, William (*b.* 1936) and Andrew (*b.* 1940).

In 1928 Taylor was appointed to the post of assistant in the general herbarium of the British Museum (Natural History) in London. There he worked on various plant groups, making determinations and publishing revisions.

In 1934 he acted as leader of the British Museum expedition to the mountains of east Africa. A colleague at the museum, Frank Ludlow, had a great interest in plants from the Himalayas and had already made four expeditions to Tibet and Bhutan with George Sherriff, the British consul at Lhasa in Tibet. He invited Taylor to join their next expedition, planned for the Tsangpo Gorge in eastern Tibet in the summer and autumn of 1938. This expedition made a deep impact on Taylor and he retained an interest in plants from the area until his death. Meanwhile, his work at the museum continued and he developed a particular interest in aquatic plants, especially the genus *Potamogeton*, publishing eighteen papers jointly with James Dandy, and in so doing solving most of the outstanding taxonomic problems presented by the genus in Britain, and forming the basis of all accounts of the genus since.

During the war Taylor was seconded to the Air Ministry as a principal and spent most of his time in Harrogate. At the end of the war he returned to the museum, being made deputy keeper of botany in 1945. Promotion meant increased administrative work, with less time being devoted to research. However, his interest in cultivated plants developed, stimulated by the flowering in gardens of many of the plants collected on the 1938 expedition. With this interest came more and more involvement with the Royal Horticultural Society, and he was elected to its council in 1951. In 1950 he was appointed keeper of botany at the museum and his efforts turned more to management and the wider world of taxonomic botany.

In 1956 Taylor was appointed director of the Royal Botanic Gardens, Kew, a post he held until his retirement in 1971. At this time Kew was still recovering from the effects of the war and was in something of a decline. Taylor needed all his energy, intelligence, and enthusiasm to reorganize and revitalize the management and administration. One of his early achievements was to persuade the Ministry of Agriculture, which funded the gardens, to set up a committee to look into the running of Kew and to make recommendations for the future. Under the chairmanship of Sir Eric Ashby the committee not only endorsed proposals made by Taylor but also recommended increasing staff numbers by 15 to 20 per cent.

As well as overhauling the management of the gardens Taylor was responsible for making improvements to both horticulture and science at Kew. He reorganized many parts of the garden and was responsible for the addition of a new wing to the herbarium and library, and for a complete rebuilding and restructuring of the Jodrell Laboratory. In 1965 he negotiated with the National Trust a 99 year lease on Wakehurst Place, a large estate in west Sussex. Here, owing to the cooler, moister climate, and larger space, it was possible to grow large numbers of temperate plants in a more naturalistic way than was possible at Kew. An important horticultural development at Kew was the Queen's Garden, a formal historic garden containing many medicinal plants. This was funded jointly by the ministry and the Australian philanthropist and plant lover Stanley Smith, which was a novel funding approach at the time. Smith helped Taylor again, this time in rescuing the historic but financially burdensome journal *Curtis's Botanical Magazine*. Started by William Curtis in 1787 and noted for descriptions and high-quality colour illustrations of plants coming into horticulture, the magazine had a complex history, was expensive to produce, and sold poorly. With Smith's financial help Taylor was able to put the magazine on a sounder financial footing.

Taylor's years at Kew were happy, positive, and full of achievement. He had an ability to spot talent among his staff and he supported and promoted those he believed to have real ability into positions where they could have influence. He made numerous beneficial changes at Kew which formed the basis of the organization's subsequent successful development. Public recognition came in 1962, when he was knighted. He and his first wife were divorced in 1965, and later the same year he married Norah, daughter of William Christopher English, of Carrycoat's Hall, Northumberland. She died in 1967 and in 1969 he married Beryl, daughter of Harvey Walker of Heathgates House, Heathgates, Shropshire. She was the divorcee of Edward Chorley Cookson and the widow of Mortimer Philip Reddington and of Frederick John Vivian Smith, second Baron Colwyn.

Taylor retired from Kew in 1971 aged sixty-seven. During the last few years of the 1960s he had held discussions with Stanley Smith about the possibility of setting up a worldwide horticultural trust. Smith died in 1968 and never saw the trust launched, but his plans were fully implemented by his wife, May, and his daughter, Barbara Fane (later De Brye), who founded in his memory the twin Stanley Smith horticultural trusts, one in the USA, the other in the UK. On his retirement Taylor became director of both trusts and moved to Belhaven House, Dunbar, East Lothian, from where he administered the trusts for the next eighteen years. The directorship of the trusts allowed Taylor to develop a wonderful garden at Belhaven, using many of his favourite Chinese and Himalayan plants (despite the unsuitable climate and soil), and to keep in touch with taxonomists and horticulturists throughout the world. He was able to support numerous worthwhile projects such as garden restorations, botanical expeditions, and taxonomic research. Belhaven became a mecca for gardeners and botanists from around the world, and Taylor delighted in hearing of news, projects, and developments in the horticultural and botanical world. During this time Taylor also became chairman of Haddington Garden Trust, a trust established by himself and the duke of Hamilton to recreate a seventeenth-century Scottish garden in the historic area of Haddington adjacent to St Mary's Church. Many of the ideas for this garden were taken from the Queen's Garden he had created at Kew.

By 1986 ill health, mainly problems of arthritis, had forced Taylor to take to a wheelchair, and he finally decided that he would have to give up work for the trust in 1989. In the same year he married his fourth wife, June Maitland, his third wife having died in 1987. With the help of June he was able to remain for some time longer at Belhaven House, where he enjoyed the garden and the constant stream of visitors, but in 1991 he was finally forced to move to a smaller house in Dunbar, better adapted to a wheelchair user. He died at Old Harbour House, Dunbar, on 12 November 1993, survived by his fourth wife and the two sons from his first marriage. He was buried on 19 November at Dunbar parish church.

During his lifetime Taylor served on many national and international committees and organizations. He was particularly involved with the Royal Horticultural Society. Having been elected to its council in 1951 he served until 1973; in 1974 he became vice-president and honorary professor of botany. He was awarded its major award, the Victoria medal of honour, in 1956. He contributed to many other organizations, including the gardens committee of the National Trust (chairman, 1961–72); the Commonwealth War Graves Commissions (botanical adviser, 1956–89); the Botanical Society of the British Isles (president, 1955); the Linnean Society (botanical secretary, 1950–56); the British Association for the Advancement of Science (general secretary, 1951–8); and the Royal Geographical Society (1957–61, vice-president, 1964). He was awarded many honours and prizes, and was elected a fellow of the Royal Society of Edinburgh in 1933, and of the Royal Society in 1968. His career in taxonomic research was relatively short, as his abilities and ambition inevitably pushed him up the managerial ladder. Nevertheless the work that he did do was accurate and pragmatic, and much of what he achieved either remained widely accepted or underlay subsequent work. His greatest achievement was undoubtedly at Kew, which he reinvigorated after the war.

Taylor did not suffer fools gladly and he could sometimes be intimidating and forthright. However, to those who knew him well and to those he trusted he was warm, friendly, and encouraging. He was a wonderful raconteur, with a great memory for detail and a mischievous sense of humour, which was often directed at those for whom he had little time. He enjoyed helping young people and gave good advice. He had enormous energy, drive, ambition, and charm, and these served him well as a committee man and administrator. In his spare time he was a keen fisherman and all his life he was interested in music.

DAVID RAE

Sources J. Cullen, *Memoirs FRS*, 41 (1995), 457–69 · WWW · *The Times* (16 Nov 1993) · *The Independent* (16 Nov 1993) · *The Scotsman* (16 Nov 1993) · D. Meikle, 'Sir George Taylor', *Kew Bulletin*, 27 (1971–2), 1–2 · WW (1994)
Archives NL Scot., corresp. and MSS · RBG Kew, corresp. and papers · University of Dundee, corresp. and papers | BL OIOC, corresp. with Reginald Schomberg · Commonwealth War Graves Commission, personnel file for Imperial War Graves Commission
Likenesses G. Argent, photograph, 1969?, repro. in Cullen, *Memoirs FRS*, 458 · double portrait, photograph, 1973 (with the queen mother), repro. in *The Times* · photograph, repro. in *The Independent*
Wealth at death £203,033.95: confirmation, 22 Feb 1994, Scotland

Taylor, George Crosland (1858–1923), bus company operator, was born on 31 January 1858 at Greenhead Lane, Huddersfield, Yorkshire, son of Henry Dyson Taylor, woollen manufacturer of Huddersfield, and his wife, Sarah, née Crosland. George Taylor and his sons all took Crosland as part of their surname. At the age of sixteen George went to work at his father's mill, and in his early twenties travelled to Australia on his father's business. With his brother James he formed the British Insulated and Helsby Cable Company in 1882. On 8 October 1884 he married Mary, daughter of William Radford, at Kirk Langley in Derbyshire.

By the turn of the century Crosland Taylor, who was essentially an electrical engineer, was taking an interest in motor cars. At the Paris motor show of 1905 he met Georges Ville, and on his return he started to assemble and sell cars of Ville's design, hence his adoption of the trading name Crosville for his company. Only five Crosville cars were ever made, but the company, registered in 1906 at Crane Wharf, Chester, went in for car hire, sales, driving tuition, and a range of automotive activities. In 1910 it acquired an Albion charabanc, with which it started a bus service between Chester and Ellesmere Port.

Crosland Taylor's eldest son, Edward, played only a small part in company affairs before emigrating to America in 1911. Edward's brother **Claude Crosland Taylor** (1889–1935), who was born on 28 September 1889 at Ravenscar, Helsby, Cheshire, did not complete his engineering course at Liverpool University, perhaps due to Edward's departure; he took over the running of the company, and by 1914 had brought it into profit. Some expansion took place during the war years, centred on the munitions factory at Queensferry, while by 1915 a service to Crewe justified opening a depot at Nantwich. The company also undertook haulage and tractor-drawn ploughing at that time.

George Crosland Taylor's youngest son, **Winthrop James Crosland Taylor** (1894–1967) (always known in the industry as W. J. Crosland-Taylor), was born at Ravenscar in 1894. He embarked on an engineering course at Liverpool University but did not return from military service to complete his degree. He served in the Royal Navy and the Royal Marines and was awarded the Military Cross, a very rare achievement for a sailor. He joined Crosville in 1919 to help his brother and father run the company in a period of rapid expansion that continued throughout the 1920s, including numerous acquisitions—an unusual policy at that time.

George Crosland Taylor suffered a heart attack and died at his home, 20 Castle Street, Chester, on 12 January 1923. His wife survived him. Claude succeeded him as chairman of the company, devoting his long working hours to its development. It was to his efforts that Crosville Motor Services owed its success, as the memoirs of his younger brother make plain. It remained a family business, with George's widow and his brother on the board, until the four main line railway companies in 1928 obtained powers to run buses, and early the next year the London, Midland, and Scottish Railway (LMSR) made an offer for the company's share capital. Despite other offers, the two brothers advised the board to accept the sum of 27s. 6d. per share, and from 1 May 1929 the company became L.M.S. (Crosville).

The shareholders made a good profit on the deal, and Claude and his brother, with all the staff, were kept on by the new owners. Railway money was used for the purchase of other businesses, 'out of all proportion to their value', according to W. J. Crosland Taylor. Then, as a result of the settlement reached between the Tillings and British Electric Traction interests and the railway companies, from 1 May 1930 the company reverted to its original name, but was jointly owned by the LMSR and Tillings and British Automobile Traction. Claude remained as managing director, the board being chaired by W. S. Wreathall.

The Crosland Taylor family did not limit its activities to buses: George had been a magistrate from 1899 until his death, and was a fellow of the Royal Geographical Society; Claude was mayor of Chester in 1925. Both were men who pushed themselves to the limit. Claude died on 31 March 1935 at the Westminster Nursing Home, Liverpool Road, Chester, having succumbed to peritonitis, after an appendix operation. He was survived by his wife, Hilda Nancy. His memorial service was held in Chester Cathedral.

With route licensing now in place, Crosville was established as the dominant bus company in much of Cheshire, throughout north Wales, and down the coast as far as Cardigan, as well as on the Wirral and in south Lancashire. Express coach services complemented the bus operations. W. J. Crosland Taylor inherited this as general manager, remaining in office until 31 December 1959. He died of heart failure at Twyford Abbey, Ealing, London, on 4 October 1967. His period of office saw control of the business pass to Thomas Tillings in 1942, and then to the British Transport Commission in 1948. Yet it is true to say that Crosville Motor Services, based at Chester, was one of the great territorial bus companies. It remained in some sense a family business, so long as members of the Crosland Taylor family were in charge—even when the chairmanship was in the hands of men such as John Spencer Wills (1904–1991) and Sir Frederick Heaton (1880–1949).

JOHN HIBBS

Sources W. J. Crossland-Taylor, *Crosville—the sowing and the harvest* (1948) · W. J. Crossland-Taylor, *Crosville: state owned without tears, 1948–1953* (1954) · *Bus and Coach* (May 1962) · *Modern Transport* (21 March 1953) · b. cert. [George Crosland Taylor] · m. cert. [George Crosland Taylor] · d. cert. [George Crosland Taylor] · b. cert. [Claude Crosland Taylor] · d. cert. [Claude Crosland Taylor] · b. cert. [Winthrop James Crosland Taylor] · d. cert. [Winthrop James Crosland Taylor] · *CGPLA Eng. & Wales* (1935) · *CGPLA Eng. & Wales* (1923)
Archives Kithead Archive, Droitwich Spa, Crosville company records

Likenesses portraits, repro. in Crosland-Taylor, *Crosville—the sowing and the harvest*
Wealth at death £45,187 3s. 7d.: probate, 1923 · £45,797 14s. 6d.—Claude Crosland Taylor: probate, 1935

Taylor, George Francis (1903–1979), intelligence officer and banker, was born on 13 January 1903 in Windsor, Melbourne, Australia, the son of George Arthur Taylor, a merchant, and his wife, Annie Mary Ryan, both of whom hailed from Melbourne. Taylor attended Xavier College, Melbourne (1917–21), where he was 'dux of school' in his final year and excelled in debating. He read history, philosophy, and law at the University of Melbourne, taking a BA, an MA, and an LLB between 1925 and 1928. He continued to win prizes for debating and took up student journalism. By the time he left university Taylor's interest had shifted from law to international relations, and he aspired to a career in journalism. He wrote occasionally on foreign affairs for the Melbourne press between 1927 and 1929, but freelance journalism did not pay, and in 1930 he joined Shell Oil.

Both the oil business and his ambition to write a book on British foreign policy brought Taylor to London in the mid-1930s. He married Vivian Judith Elizabeth Rose Price (b. 1915), the daughter of Vivian Franklin Lyon Rose Price, a Royal Navy officer, on 17 June 1937; they had three children. In March 1939 Taylor wrote to Rex Leeper, head of the Foreign Office news department, offering his services in the event of war. Later in the spring he was introduced by the mining magnate Chester Beatty to Colonel Laurence Grand, the founder of section D (for 'destruction') of the Secret Intelligence Service. Grand hired Taylor in July and made him head of D's Balkan network.

Section D, the principal predecessor of the Special Operations Executive (SOE), had been established in 1938 to investigate 'every possibility of attacking potential enemies by means other than the operations of military forces' (SOE headquarters file 63). This meant sabotage and subversion, and south-east Europe was a prime target because of the importance then attached to interdicting the flow of Romanian oil to Germany. Taylor's contribution, however, lay as much in defining section D's (and later SOE's) strategy and tactics as it did in conducting operations from London or in the field. Before the fall of France, Taylor pressed for continuous, widespread, but small-scale sabotage of communications by local patriots under British direction. After June 1940 he was an architect of the 'secret army' strategy which led to the formation of SOE in July, and by which it was imagined that Britain might yet win the war through fomenting massive and co-ordinated uprisings by the peoples of occupied Europe when strategic bombing and blockade had prepared the way. This hope held sway until first Russia, and then America, entered the war.

Hugh Dalton, the minister in charge of SOE, dismissed Grand but embraced both his ethos and his deputy. Taylor became chief of staff to Sir Frank Nelson, the first executive head (known as CD) of SOE, in the autumn. Having discovered that the only functional asset inherited by SOE from section D was Taylor's Balkan organization, Nelson and Dalton sent him to the region in January 1941 to take charge of preparations for countering the expected German offensive. According to Taylor, Churchill had told Dalton in December that the Balkan situation 'was the acid test for SOE' (Stafford, 52–3), which must make good its claim to represent a vital new instrument of warfare. After conferring at general headquarters in Cairo about help for the Greeks, Taylor set up shop in Belgrade, for without Yugoslav co-belligerency the defence of Greece would be hopeless. SOE agents worked both to stir up popular opposition to accession to the axis pact and to organize the overthrow of the government if it did accede. The Yugoslav government succumbed to German pressure on 25 March, but was toppled by a military coup two days later. Although SOE's links had been with the cheerleaders rather than the ringleaders of this putsch, its success redounded to SOE's credit. The acid test had been passed, notwithstanding the failure of the Balkan campaign which followed.

Taylor returned to London as Nelson's chief of staff after two months' internment in Italy with most of Britain's Belgrade-based diplomats and agents. In March 1942 he was appointed director of overseas groups and missions. Although never relegated from SOE's first division, Taylor's status waned after Nelson's retirement in May 1942 and his replacement by Sir Charles Hambro. Embarrassment over a concordat on operational spheres which he negotiated in Washington in the summer of 1942 with SOE's American clone and rival, the office of strategic services, but which his headquarters repudiated in favour of a better deal struck in London, was followed in early 1943 by implication in a botched operation to seize axis ships in the harbour of the Portuguese colony of Goa which the Foreign Office had forbidden. Taylor returned as Hambro's chief of staff in mid-1943, but it was to professional soldiers rather than to civilians that the top jobs now went. Taylor served out the war as director of SOE's Far East group, enjoying the rank of local brigadier on his far-flung travels and being appointed (civil) CBE in 1943.

Taylor was a short, dark man with sharp features and methodical habits. Julian Amery recalled how Taylor ordered identical meals when they dined together on three successive evenings at the same restaurant in the autumn of 1940. Asked why, Taylor explained that he always ate the same dishes until he grew bored with them, at which point he would choose something else from the menu for the same treatment (Amery, 211–12). Taylor was invariably described by both admirers and detractors as utterly ruthless. His friends added 'but brilliant'. He wrote vastly long memoranda and signals which brooked no opposition. The last CD under whom he served, Major-General Colin Gubbins, described him as 'a very able, quick-thinking officer, of great energy and persistence, who at times presses his points too hard' (SOE personal file of G. F. Taylor).

Taylor joined the Bank of London and South America after the war, becoming a director in 1950, deputy chairman in 1966, and transitional chairman in 1970–71. He implemented the previously agreed merger with Lloyds

Bank Europe and the formation of what was to be known (albeit briefly) as Lloyds and BOLSA International Bank. He returned with his wife to Australia in 1975 and they settled in Perth, where he died of heart failure at Shenton Park on 17 January 1979 and was buried two days later in Karrakatta Roman Catholic Lawn cemetery, Perth.

MARK C. WHEELER

Sources PRO, SOE papers · G. Taylor's personal file, courtesy of SOE adviser, Foreign and Commonwealth Office, London, PF22661A · 'Recommendations with regard to the control of "extra-departmental" and "para-military" activities', G. Taylor's personal file, courtesy of SOE adviser, 5 June 1939, Foreign and Commonwealth Office, London, SOE/HQ63 · B. Sweet-Escott, *Baker Street irregular* (1965) · D. Stafford, *Britain and European resistance, 1940–1945: a survey of the special operations executive* (1980) · P. Wilkinson and J. B. Astley, *Gubbins and SOE* (1993) · M. R. D. Foot, *SOE: an outline history of the Special Operations Executive, 1940–46* (1984) · C. Cruickshank, *SOE in the Far East* (1983) · J. Amery, *Approach march: a venture in autobiography* (1973) · *The Xaverian* [Melbourne, yearbooks] (1921–2) · *The Xaverian* [Melbourne, yearbooks] (1925–9) · G. Taylor's Melbourne University student record · *Report of the directors and statement of accounts for the year ended 31st December 1970,* Bank of London and South America · N. West [R. Allason], *Secret war: the story of SOE, Britain's wartime sabotage organisation* (1992) · P. Auty and R. Clogg, eds., *British policy towards wartime resistance in Yugoslavia and Greece* (1975) · CGPLA Eng. & Wales (1979) · m. cert.
Archives St Ant. Oxf.
Likenesses photograph, repro. in *The Xaverian* (1921–2) · photograph, Foreign and Commonwealth Office, London, SOE personal file · photograph, Lloyds TSB Archive
Wealth at death £2493: Australian probate sealed in England, 15 Aug 1979, CGPLA Eng. & Wales

Taylor, George Ledwell (1788–1873), architect, was born on 31 March 1788 in London, the son of Henry Taylor and his wife, Elizabeth. He was educated at Rawes's academy, Bromley. In 1804 his uncle General George *Harris (afterwards first Baron Harris) introduced him to James Burton. This architect, being about to retire, transferred his pupil to Joseph T. Parkinson (1783–1855) of Ely Place, London, who was district surveyor of Westminster, and then engaged in laying out the Portman estate. Taylor, while articled to Parkinson, superintended the building of Montagu Square and Bryanston Square (both 1811) and the neighbouring streets. His fellow pupil, both at Rawes's academy and under Parkinson, was Edward Cresy (1792–1858), with whom he maintained an uninterrupted friendship for more than fifty years. In 1816 he took two walking tours with Cresy to study English architecture—the first in the south-western counties, the second, a tour of forty days, from York to Lincoln, Peterborough and Ely. On 23 June 1817 he started with Cresy on a grand tour, at his mother's expense, which lasted two years. In 1817 they travelled, mostly on foot, through France, Switzerland, and Italy, spending the winter at Rome and Naples. On 1 May 1818 they left Naples for Bari and Corfu, and spent the summer in Greece, in company with John Sanders and William Purser. Their one discovery of importance, found by Taylor himself when his horse stumbled over the buried remains, was that of the famous Theban lion at Chaeronea on 3 June 1818. Taylor was later to be compelled to write an account of the find (*The Builder*, 20, 1862, 908) to counter claims then being made that attributed the find elsewhere. After a second winter spent at Rome, Taylor returned to Britain on 12 May 1819. Of a journey of 7200 miles, 4000 miles had been performed on foot. His sketchbook of this tour is in the Victoria and Albert Museum collection, with additional drawings at the Brighton Art Gallery.

Taylor now took an office with Cresy in Furnival's Inn, London. He lived at 52 Bedford Square, and afterwards in Spring Gardens, until he built a house for himself at Lee, Kent. On 8 June 1820 he married Bella Neufville, with whom he had eleven children. Taylor was married three (according to some accounts four) times. Between 1820 and 1822 he exhibited thirteen drawings at the Royal Academy. On 3 February 1824 he was appointed surveyor of buildings to the naval department, the successor to Edward Holl. In this capacity he superintended important works in the dockyards at Chatham, Woolwich, and Sheerness, and in 1828–32 alterations in the Clarence victualling yard, Gosport. A survey he made of the naval dockyards is in the National Maritime Museum. He built the Melville Hospital, Chatham, Kent (1827); the Woolwich River wall (1831); a custom house, Glasgow (c.1840); and various schools, rectories, and private houses. His most remarkable building was the 170 foot high Gothic tower of Hadlow Castle, Kent (c.1840), an early Victorian folly. (A lithograph by Taylor of his 'projected tower' appears in C. Greenwood, An Epitome of County History: County of Kent 1838.) He received some attention from William IV, and claimed credit for inducing the king in 1830 to accept 'Trafalgar Square' instead of 'King William IV Square', the name originally proposed for the site. In 1837 a scheme for retrenchment at the Admiralty involved Taylor's dismissal. He was obliged to take up general practice, and qualified as a district surveyor. In 1843–8 he laid out considerable portions of the bishop of London's estate in Paddington, including Westbourne Terrace (where he built a house for himself), Chester Place, and parts of Hyde Park Square and Gloucester Square. In 1848 he succeeded his former teacher Joseph Parkinson to the post of district surveyor of Westminster. In 1849 he undertook the continuation of the north Kent Railway from Stroud, through Chatham and Canterbury to Dover, but the negotiation fell through, at a considerable financial loss to Taylor. He seems after this to have abandoned active professional work for archaeology.

In 1856 Taylor revisited Italy with his wife, and stayed at Rome from 20 November 1857 to 22 March 1858, collecting materials for The Stones of Etruria and Marbles of Antient Rome, which he published in 1859. He finally returned to Britain in 1868. During 1870–72, while residing at Broadstairs, Kent, he published a collection of sketches and descriptions of buildings which he had visited in his travels, under the misleading title The Autobiography of an Octogenarian Architect (2 vols., 1870–72). He also published several pamphlets on technical and professional subjects, and published jointly with Edward Cresy The Architectural Antiquities of Rome (2 vols., 1821–2; new edn, 1874), Revived Architecture of Italy: Palaces of Genoa (1822), and Architecture of the Middle Ages in Italy: Pisa (1829).

Taylor was a member of several clubs and societies: he belonged to the Architects' Club (founded in 1819) and was its president between 1822 and 1823; he was a fellow of the Institution of Civil Engineers, the Society of Antiquaries, and the Royal Institute of British Architects, becoming an honorary member of the latter institution shortly before his death at his home, The Maisonette, Broadstairs, on 1 May 1873.   CAMPBELL DODGSON, rev. HELENE FURJAŃ

Sources Colvin, Archs. [incl. complete work list] • [W. Papworth], ed., The dictionary of architecture, 11 vols. (1853–92) • Dir. Brit. archs. • Graves, RA exhibitors • D. Ware, A short dictionary of British architects (1967) • Boase, Mod. Eng. biog. • Mirror [Journal], iii, 88 • The Builder, 20 (1862), 908 • IGI • CGPLA Eng. & Wales (1873)
Archives Brighton Art Gallery, collection of drawings • NMM, survey of naval dockyards • RIBA BAL • V&A, sketchbook | RIBA BAL, Edward Cresy MSS
Wealth at death under £1500: probate, 11 June 1873, CGPLA Eng. & Wales

Taylor, Sir Gordon Gordon- [formerly William Gordon Taylor] **(1878–1960)**, surgeon, was born at Streatham Hill, London, on 18 March 1878, the elder of two children of John Taylor, wine merchant, and his wife, Alice Miller, daughter of William Gordon, stockbroker, of Aberdeen. In 1885 John Taylor died and his widow moved with her son and daughter to Aberdeen where Taylor gained a scholarship at Robert Gordon's College. He was happy at school, a hard worker, and fond of walking, climbing, and cricket; summer holidays were spent at Ballater on Deeside. He was brought up in the Presbyterian church.

William Gordon Taylor, his name until he changed it in 1920 to Gordon Gordon-Taylor, held a bursary at Aberdeen University where in 1898 he obtained third-class honours in classics. He then entered the Middlesex Hospital with a scholarship, took the gold medal in anatomy in the intermediate MB examination, and qualified MRCS, LRCP on 29 October 1903; an intensive course of anatomical study was rewarded with first-class honours (1904) in the newly instituted BSc in anatomy of the University of London. He obtained his FRCS in 1906, and a year later at the early age of twenty-nine he was appointed assistant surgeon to the Middlesex Hospital. He was consulting surgeon to the Fourth Army in France during the First World War, after making a name for himself as a casualty clearing surgeon.

Gordon-Taylor married in 1920 Florence Mary (d. 1949), daughter of John Pegrume; there were no children. In the same year he became full surgeon to the Middlesex Hospital and in the next twenty years he built up a great reputation as a fearless, but obsessively careful surgeon, whose results were excellent. His approach to surgery was characterized by a fierce desire to help his patients, an unquenchable optimism, and a superb knowledge of anatomy. This allowed him to perform massive resections of tissue, such as in hindquarter amputations (lower limb plus half the pelvic bone) which most of his colleagues could not contemplate. He was equally at home operating everywhere in the body, except perhaps within the skull. He was also more aware of the importance of physiology than many of his contemporaries: his understanding of the importance of replacing lost blood stemmed from his

First World War experiences and he was a strong advocate and practitioner of blood transfusion. His patients adored him. To them he was—Edwardian attire, carnation in buttonhole, and all—guide and friend as well as healer.

Gordon-Taylor was consultant to the Royal Navy in the Second World War, with the rank of surgeon rear-admiral, and travelled to Russia, America, and India in the course of his duties. He was appointed CB in 1942, and KBE and commander of the United States Legion of Merit in 1946.

At the Royal College of Surgeons, Gordon-Taylor served on the council (1932–48) and was vice-president (1941–3). He was a Hunterian professor on several occasions; delivered the Bradshaw lecture in 1942 on the abdominal injuries resulting from modern warfare; and twice gave the Thomas Vicary lecture. In this he demonstrated both his knowledge of surgical history and his abiding Scottish patriotism, speaking in 1945 about the medical and surgical aspects of the Jacobite rising of 1745, and recounting in 1954 the life and work of the great surgeon and anatomist, Sir Charles Bell. With E. W. Walls he enlarged the lecture on Bell into a full-length biography in 1958. His heart remained in the Scottish highlands: he frequently took his whole surgical team for a weekend of walking in the Cairngorms.

Gordon-Taylor was an honorary fellow of the Irish, Australasian, Canadian, and American colleges of surgeons; an honorary foreign member of the Académie de Chirurgie in Paris; and the recipient of honorary degrees from Cambridge, Toronto, Melbourne, and Athens. His links with Australasian surgery were particularly strong. Young Australians visiting the UK to further their surgical education found in him a willing and enthusiastic mentor. Gordon-Taylor was president of the Association of Surgeons of Great Britain and Ireland, of the Medical Society of London (1941–2), and of the Royal Society of Medicine (1944–6), which also awarded him in 1956 its rarely bestowed gold medal. The many ceremonial addresses which he was invited to deliver and the other honours he was awarded are listed in the *Journal of Medical Biography* (Hobsley, 'Biography', 83–9). He was a frequent contributor to medical and surgical journals and his books included *The Dramatic in Surgery* (1930) and *The Abdominal Injuries of Warfare* (1939).

Gordon-Taylor died in London, on 3 September 1960, in his beloved Middlesex Hospital: he had been knocked down by a vehicle as he left Lord's cricket ground. He left the bulk of his fortune to the Royal College of Surgeons for its library and to the Middlesex Hospital for its nurses.

CECIL WAKELEY, *rev.* MICHAEL HOBSLEY

Sources R. H. O. B. Robinson and W. R. Le Fanu, *Lives of the fellows of the Royal College of Surgeons of England, 1952–1964* (1970) • Colleagues at Middlesex Hospital Medical School, *In memoriam. Sir Gordon Gordon-Taylor, 1878–1960* (1961) • *The Times* (5 Sept 1960) • *BMJ* (24 Sept 1960), 947–8 • *Annals of the Royal College of Surgeons of England*, 27 (1960), 292–6 • M. Hobsley, 'Sir Gordon Gordon-Taylor: two themes illustrated by the surgery of the parotid salivary gland', *Annals of the Royal College of Surgeons of England*, 63 (1980), 264–9 • M. Hobsley, 'Sir Gordon Gordon-Taylor: a biography and an appreciation', *Journal of Medical Biography*, 1 (1993), 83–9 • E. W. Riches, 'Recollections of an apprentice', *British Journal of Surgery*, 45 (1957–8), 414–16 • R. Vaughan Hudson, 'The late Sir Gordon Gordon-Taylor', *Middlesex Hospital Journal*, 60 (1960), 264–9 • personal knowledge (1971, 1996) • private information (1971, 1996)

Archives Central Middlesex Hospital, London • RCS Eng., notes on carnivora and ungulata

Likenesses W. Stoneman, photograph, 1947, NPG • black and white photograph, *c.*1950, priv. coll.; repro. in Hobsley, 'Sir Gordon Gordon-Taylor' • A. Zinkeisen, oils, 1958, Central Middlesex Hospital, London • J. Gunn, oils, 1960, Royal Australasian College of Surgeons, Melbourne • J. Gunn, sketch, oil study, 1960, RCS Eng. • H. Coster, photographs, NPG

Wealth at death £40,130 4s. 10d.: probate, 1960, CGPLA Eng. & Wales

Taylor, (Thomas) Griffith (1880–1963), geographer and explorer, was born on 1 December 1880 at 9 Greenleaf Lane, Walthamstow, Essex, the first of the five children of James Taylor (1849–1927), metallurgical chemist, and his wife, Lily Agnes, daughter of Thomas Griffiths, accountant, and his wife, Elizabeth. Taylor's parents were devout Unitarians, but he pronounced himself either agnostic or atheistic. After a spell in Serbia where the father's work took the family between 1881 and 1884, Taylor returned to England, attended modest private schools, and in 1893 the family went to Sydney, New South Wales, where his father took up an appointment as government metallurgist. Taylor continued in private education at Sydney grammar school and the King's School, Parramatta, subsequently completing degrees in science (BSc, 1904) and mining and metallurgy (BE, 1905) at Sydney University. Under the guidance of the geologist and later Antarctic explorer Edgeworth David, Taylor developed a research interest in palaeontology, a passion for strenuous fieldwork, and a belief in the civic value of a geographical education. Thanks in part to David's personal example and sponsorship, he was awarded an 1851 Exhibition scholarship to Emmanuel College, Cambridge, where he completed a BA (research) in 1909, and obtained employment as physiographer to Australia's commonwealth weather service. He joined Robert Falcon Scott's *Terra nova* expedition to the Antarctic (1911–12) and led the highly regarded western geological party. This party was distinct from the ill-fated pole party led by Scott himself. Taylor returned to write *With Scott: the Silver Living* (1916), one of a number of accounts of the expedition which was broadly sympathetic to Scott. The powerful mystique associated with this expedition undoubtedly promoted Taylor's early career in Australia. Grif (also Griff) married Doris Marjorie Priestley, sister of his Antarctic colleague, Raymond Edward *Priestley, and daughter of Joseph Edward Priestley, headmaster of Tewkesbury grammar school, and his wife, Henrietta Rice, on 8 July 1914, at Queen's College, University of Melbourne; they had two sons who survived them and a daughter who died in infancy.

Until 1920, increasingly confident and ambitious in his liberally defined weather service employment, Taylor consolidated his international reputation in physical geography and related fields, successfully submitted his Antarctic work for a Sydney doctorate (1916), and produced some of his most enduring statements on the severe environmental limits to the expansion of agriculture and settlement in Australia. This brought him into fiery conflict with nationalist–imperialist boosters who were promising that 'Australia unlimited' could support hundreds of millions of contented antipodean Britons: as early as 1911, in *Australia in its Physiographic and Economic Aspects* Taylor had predicted a total population of approximately 19 million for the year 2000. He stepped up his campaign on his return to Sydney University in 1920, as foundation head of Australia's first independent department of geography. Lithe, tall, and with gaunt, chiselled features which softened briefly in middle age, Taylor was alert, pugnacious, extrovert, and at times mischievously philistine. He presented himself as the resolute and very public champion of environmentally rational development. Most of his influential opponents skirted his straightforward analyses, preferring instead to label him a pessimist, a traitor, or just another 'environmental determinist' who ignored the growing ability of people to harness nature.

Taylor's early publications included *The Australian Environment* (1918) and *Australian Meteorology* (1920), essays on climate and settlement, on obstacles to white settlement in the tropics, and on the evolution and distributional characteristics of race, culture, and language. Some of his strongest opinions received a prior airing in the Australian press since he thought 'experts' morally obliged to engage openly with the leading issues of their day. Taylor's speculative work on the development of tropical Australia occasionally suggested the utility of Asian peasant settlement in the Australian north and his broader studies of racial origins and dispersions, brought together in *Environment and Race* (1927), pointed to a type of Asian evolutionary supremacy which infuriated supporters of the white Australia policy. One of his geography texts was officially banned in Western Australia because of its insistence on the predominating handicap of aridity.

Reviled in the daily press, rebuked by his campus peers, and repeatedly denied a full professorial chair, Taylor finally decided to continue his academic career in North America. At the universities of Chicago (1929–35), and Toronto (1935–51), where he was the foundation professor of geography, he was increasingly inclined towards orthodox academic discourse. Seldom at ease with mid-western society, he never ventured disputatious predictions on the relationship between environment and development in the United States. More at home in Canada he once again applied his idiosyncratic approaches to a primary national issue, the limitations imposed by the cold deserts: in this case, however, he opposed pessimistic governmental and popular perceptions. *Environment and Nation* (1936), and *Urban Geography* (1949), expanded old interests and enhanced his academic reputation. He relaxed his deterministic stance and offered a substitute which he called 'stop-and-go' determinism, using the traffic lights analogy. Under Taylor's editorship, *Geography in the Twentieth Century* (1957) provided a valuable international perspective on the subject and gave him the opportunity to reply to his critics in some robust footnotes.

President of the geography section of the British Association for the Advancement of Science in 1938, Taylor was the first non-American president of the Association of American Geographers in 1940, and became a fellow of the Royal Society of Canada in 1942. Returning briefly to Australia in 1948 as a consultant on specialized research schools at the newly founded Australian National University, Taylor delighted in his warm reception. He retired to Sydney in 1951 shortly after being elected president of the new Canadian Association of Geographers. His final geographical writings addressed questions of environmental awareness and the subject's contribution to global peace. In 1954 he was made a fellow of the Australian Academy of Science and five years later became the first president of the Institute of Australian Geographers.

Griffith Taylor died in the Sydney suburb of Manly on 5 November 1963, survived by his wife and sons, and was cremated. His achievements are commemorated in the naming of topographical features in Antarctica and in the Canberra district, in the issue of a special Australian postage stamp, and in the dedication of university buildings.

Taylor's post-war reception in Australia was an acknowledgement of his earlier travails and a partial acceptance that his bold arguments might be credible. Among geographers he is remembered throughout the Anglophone world as a doughty pioneer and as a proponent of the undervalued civic purpose of research and scholarship, but is criticized for his tendency to over-generalization and hasty judgement and especially for his use of allegedly scientific data and methods to offer strongly worded and very public statements on the capacities of regional environments to sustain increasing populations. His eccentric sorties into anthropological and cultural issues had restricted academic currency, but demographers, ecologists, and historians alike have noted his prescient stand on environmental limitations in times and places in which the development imperative might have been allowed even freer rein.   J. M. POWELL

Sources NL Aus., Taylor MSS · G. Taylor, *Journeyman Taylor*, ed. A. A. McGregor (1958) · M. Sanderson, *Griffith Taylor: Antarctic scientist and pioneer geographer* (1988) · J. M. Powell, *Griffith Taylor and Australia unlimited* (1993) · J. M. Powell, *An historical geography of modern Australia* (1991) · *Sydney Morning Herald* (6 Nov 1963) · *Geographical Review*, 53 (1964), 427–9 · *Annals, Association of American Geographers*, 54 (1964), 622–9 · *Canadian Geographer*, 17 (1963), 197–200 · *Australian Geographical Studies*, 2 (1964), 1–9 · *GJ*, 130 (1964), 189–91 · D. N. Livingstone, *The geographical tradition* (1992) · *The Times* (7 Nov 1963) · b. cert.
Archives NL Aus. · Scott Polar RI, corresp. and papers · University of Sydney, papers · University of Toronto, papers | University of New England, Armidale, New South Wales, former department of geography and planning, Antarctic MSS | FILM BFI NFTVA, documentary footage
Likenesses D. Toovey, portrait, University of Sydney

Taylor, Harold Dennis (1862–1943), designer of optical instruments, was born at Lockwood House, Lockwood, Yorkshire, on 10 July 1862, the son of Joseph Walter Taylor, a wool manufacturer, and Annie Victoria Taylor, (*née* Bainbridge), and was educated at St Peter's School in York. He started to train as an architect, but his strong scientific interest led him to take up a post with Thomas Cooke &

Sons of Bishophill, York, a highly respected manufacturer of astronomical and optical instruments. Despite his lack of formal training, Taylor rapidly made his mark, rising to the position of optical manager: whereas Thomas Cooke had blended good mechanical practice with artistic intuition, Taylor was to put lens making onto a firm quantitative basis while at the same time retaining an aesthetic simplicity in his approach. On 24 July 1888 he married Charlotte Fernandez (b. 1856/7), daughter of William Barff, wool merchant, of Liverpool. They raised a daughter, Nina Dennis Taylor, and two sons, one of whom, Wilfred [see below], followed in his father's professional footsteps.

Taylor's design of the Cooke triplet lens, originally in 1893, removed all aberrations; that is, all effects which caused parallel light not to be focused to a point were consistently corrected. With three lenses, each with two distinct curvatures, and two lens spacings, there were just enough degrees of freedom to achieve his purpose via what was for the late nineteenth century an algebraic extravaganza. In addition, by combining lenses of low and high refractive index, he achieved an impressive flatness of field. This revived an analytic approach to lens design in the British optical industry, which had failed to build on earlier work of Airy, Hamilton, and in particular Coddington.

As well as contrasting sharply with the empiricism of his industry, Taylor's work was distinct from the more complex theoretical approaches of German opticians of the period—his was a kind of minimalist approach to the aberration problem. The manufacture of Cooke triplet lenses for photography was licensed to Taylor, Taylor, and Hobson of Leicester (they were not related): the patents were drawn up in such a detailed way that it was relatively easy for others to copy the principle, but nevertheless the Cooke triplet philosophy dominated lens design for inexpensive cameras until computers began to be used for the task.

Taylor's approach to optics was enshrined in his classic *A System of Applied Optics* (1906), while his short guide, *The Adjustment and Testing of Telescopic Objectives* (1901), described novel autocollimation techniques for the alignment of telescopes. The latter proved an invaluable manual for amateur and professional alike, and was still being reprinted in the 1980s. In addition Taylor made important advances in lenses for refracting telescopes, first with the achromatic triplet using an innovative glass developed at the Schott glassworks at Jena, and in the Franklin–Adams telescope which was responsible for producing star maps of outstanding quality for both the northern and southern hemispheres early in the twentieth century. He also discovered that light was transmitted through a lens when there was a thin corrosion layer on it, and patented a coating technique which was the forerunner of later 'blooming' technology. In all close to fifty patents carry his name.

Taylor was a modest man, fiercely loyal to his employers, and it was not until after his premature retirement in 1915 that the impact of his lens research was fully appreciated and recognized in the awards of the Royal Photographic Society medal (1933) and the Duddell medal of the Physical Society (1934). He continued to act as consultant to Taylor, Taylor, and Hobson, and moved to Coxwold in the foothills of the North York Moors, where he pursued his hobbies of gardening, astronomy, photography, and natural history. In 1924 he received the Traill–Taylor medal for services to photography, and gave the memorial lecture to the Royal Photographic Society, at the end of which he caused some astonishment by declaring that he had been a member of the Society for Psychic Research for more than eighteen years, and was inclined to believe that photography could reveal supernatural beings invisible to the unaided human eye. Although he acknowledged that some such photographs were fakes, he nevertheless found others convincing. Taylor died at The Hall, Stillington, on 26 February 1943, survived by his wife and children.

Taylor is perhaps best summed up by his son Wilfred, who followed his father into Thomas Cooke & Sons:

> My father was a man of encyclopaedic knowledge, who seemed always to be working out some new optical invention or formula. He could, none-the-less, put all this to one side and derive great pleasure from a country walk, cycle ride or climb. His tastes were simple and he was very self-sufficient. My mother understood him well and knew how to order the household so as to give his genius full scope. (Payne, 563–4)

(Edward) Wilfred Taylor (1891–1980), was born at Bootham Terrace, York, on 29 April 1891, and went from Oundle School into an apprenticeship at Thomas Cooke & Sons, rising to optical manager, technical director, and joint managing director along with James Simms Wilson, a post which he held from 1937 until their retirement in 1956. He played a key role in the development of the Tavistock theodolite, the first double-reading optical theodolite manufactured in Great Britain, and in the Second World War presided over a huge expansion of Cooke, Troughton, and Simms in York to meet demand for rangefinders and optical measuring tools, for which he was made CBE in 1946. In the post-war period, his key papers in phase-contrast microscopy earned him fellowship of the Royal Society in 1952. He died at Cookridge Hospital, Leeds, on 1 November 1980, and was survived by a son, Julian, and two grandchildren; his wife Winifred Mary (née Hunter) died in 1964.   J. A. D. MATTHEW

Sources A. McConnell, *Instrument makers to the world: a history of Cooke, Troughton & Simms* (1992) • T. Smith, *Nature*, 151 (1943), 442–3 • T. Smith, *Proceedings of the Physics Society of London*, 55 (1943), 508–11 • B. O. Payne, *Memoirs FRS*, 27 (1981), 563–77 • *Photographic Journal*, 83 (1943), 160 • H. D. Taylor, 'The future of the cinema projector; and photography as an extension of vision', *The Photographic Journal*, new ser., 48 (1924), 63–90 • b. cert. • m. cert. • d. cert. • b. cert. [(Edward) Wilfred Taylor] • d. cert. [(Edward) Wilfred Taylor]

Archives Borth. Inst., Vickers Instrument archive • University of York, department of physics, Vickers Collection Museum, artefacts | FILM Borth. Inst., Vickers Instruments archive, footage from Cooke, Troughton & Simms [(Edward) Wilfred Taylor]

Likenesses photograph, repro. in Payne, *Memoirs FRS*

Wealth at death £87 13s. 11d.: probate, 19 July 1943, *CGPLA Eng. & Wales* · £96,071—(Edward) Wilfred Taylor: probate, 3 March 1981, *CGPLA Eng. & Wales*

Taylor, Harold McCarter (1907–1995), physicist and architectural historian, was born on 13 May 1907 in Dunedin, New Zealand, the younger son of James Taylor (1873–1958), merchant, and his wife, Louisa Urquhart, *née* McCarter (1875–1932), daughter of George Alfred McCarter and his wife, Matilda Mary, *née* Urquhart. His father's family had migrated to the Scots settled city of Dunedin from Aberdeen, and his mother's from Coleraine, co. Londonderry.

Taylor was educated at Otago Boys' High School, and the University of Otago, graduating MSc with double first-class honours in 1928. From there he won a scholarship to Clare College, Cambridge, where he took the second part of the mathematics tripos in 1930, achieving senior wrangler with distinction in section B. Subsequently he joined the Cambridge Cavendish Laboratory when Sir Ernest Rutherford and his team of physicists were making spectacular advances in atomic research. He worked with mathematicians and theorists, headed by Ralph W. Fowler and including H. R. Hulme, who formed a productive partnership with the experimental physicists. Initially he conducted his research under Fowler and Nevill Mott, and between 1931 and 1936 he wrote or collaborated in writing important papers treating the anomalous scattering of alpha particles and the internal conversion of gamma rays. In 1933 he gained his PhD, was appointed university lecturer in mathematics, and elected fellow of Clare College. On 8 April the same year he married Joan Sills (1903–1965), biologist and teacher, and daughter of George Reginald Sills, of Lincoln. They had two sons and two daughters.

Taylor distinguished himself as scientist, teacher, and administrator not only in university service, but also in military service. His training in artillery began with a New Zealand territorials commission in 1925. He transferred to the British territorials, and was adjutant of the Cambridge area Officers' Training Corps from 1936. In 1941 he joined the School of Artillery, Larkhill, rising to senior instructor and lieutenant-colonel. In 1943 John Cockcroft and Nevill Mott invited him to join in atomic research, but he believed that he would contribute more to the war effort by remaining in gunnery. He went to Europe to solve problems of communication and rangefinding between British and American gunners, and in 1946 was awarded the J. H. Lefroy medal of the Royal Artillery for his distinguished work in artillery science.

In 1945 Taylor decided not to return to mathematics and took the post of Cambridge University treasurer. He moved from financial to academic administration eight years later when he became secretary-general of the faculties. He was appointed principal of the University College of North Staffordshire in 1961 and in the following year, when the college became the University of Keele, Taylor became its founding vice-chancellor. Keele embodied the boldest experiment in university education then being made in Britain. Its approach had been spearheaded by Alexander Lindsay, first Baron Lindsay of Birker, the first principal of the University College of North Staffordshire. Lindsay had advocated broad based education, developed at Keele in a four-year degree programme initiated by a foundation year of studies in both arts and sciences. Taylor, who at Cambridge had advocated joint courses in arts and sciences, espoused Lindsay's philosophy, and also showed his progressive outlook in establishing the first comprehensive university counselling service, covering educational, vocational, and personal needs. Taylor came to Keele when it was poised for expansion, but lack of funding hindered progress. He was highly regarded as vice-chancellor and took a leading role in issues of university funding after the Robbins report.

Taylor's interest in Anglo-Saxon architecture had evolved soon after his arrival in England, and by 1936 he and his wife, Joan—who shared his interest—had shaped plans for a comprehensive survey of surviving pre-conquest fabric in English churches. In thirty years they visited more than 400 churches to record Anglo-Saxon work, either intact, or preserved fragmentarily in later rebuildings. In addition to site work they searched out published discussions, antiquarian accounts, and other records of supposed Anglo-Saxon structures. Volumes 1 and 2 of *Anglo-Saxon Architecture* (1965) gave new impetus to research, providing a comprehensive, detailed, and accurate catalogue of surviving structures. Joan died suddenly only weeks before their publication.

This change in personal circumstance prompted Taylor to retire from Keele in order to have time to complete the final volume of *Anglo-Saxon Architecture* and in 1967 he returned to Cambridge, having, on 21 March 1966, married his former personal assistant Dorothy Judith Samuel (b. 1931), daughter of Charles Samuel of Liverpool. She provided further assistance in research. Volume 3 of *Anglo-Saxon Architecture* (1978) concentrated upon a well-defined group of churches, analysing their features in some detail. Harold and Joan Taylor had originally hoped that typological analysis of architectural features in England and on the continent might make it possible to date them more precisely, but Taylor concluded that to establish a chronology would be premature.

After 1965 Taylor published more than sixty papers, including some arising from new collaborations with archaeologists. Between 1971 and 1984 he worked with Philip Rahtz and L. A. S. Butler in a detailed investigation of St Mary's Church, Deerhurst, Gloucestershire. Excavations and the stripping of modern plaster from walls uncovered hitherto concealed evidence for the phases of Anglo-Saxon construction. Between 1974 and 1988 he worked with Martin Biddle and Birthe Kjølbye-Biddle at St Wystan's, Repton, revealing new details about the evolution of the church and its crypt mausoleum.

Taylor was a modest, mannered man of acuteness and precision, with a deep Christian faith. His energy was remarkable. Much of his research was conducted in his spare time, while holding onerous administrative positions. At Keele he and his wife Joan were known to rise before dawn to conduct research before his punctual arrival at the vice-chancellor's office each morning. Other leisure activities included walking and alpine skiing. Ill health ended his research in his last years. He died of pneumonia in St Neots, Cambridgeshire, on 23 October 1995, and was survived by his wife and the four children of his first marriage. He was cremated on 30 October and his ashes were interred at All Souls' cemetery, Cambridge, on 3 December.   GREG WAITE

Sources *The Times* (1 Nov 1995), 21 · *British Archaeology*, 10 (Dec 1995) · *New Scientist* (4 May 1961), 244–5 · J. Hendry, *Cambridge physics in the thirties* (1984) · J. M. Kolbert, *Keele: the first fifty years* (2000) · L. A. S. Butler and R. K. Morris, eds., *The Anglo-Saxon church: papers on history, architecture, and archaeology in honour of Dr H. M. Taylor*, Council for British Archaeology Research Report, 60 (1986) · M. Biddle and others, 'Anglo-Saxon architecture and Anglo-Saxon studies: a review', *Anglo-Saxon England*, 14 (1985), 293–317 · *Nature*, 189 (1961), 710 · *The Times* (8 Feb 1961), 15 · private information (2004) [Judith Taylor, widow; John Kolbert] · J. G. Crowther, *The Cavendish Laboratory, 1874–1974* (1974) · ministry of defence service records · Otago University, student records · *WWW* · *CGPLA Eng. & Wales* (1996)
Archives English Heritage, Swindon, National Monuments Record, notebooks, files, and photographs relating to Anglo-Saxon architecture · S. Antiquaries, Lond., papers and records relating to excavations at Deerhurst, MS 952
Likenesses R. Dean, bronze sculpture, 1965, Keele University · I. Henderson, oils, 1967, Keele University · P. Rahtz, photograph, repro. in Butler and Morris, eds., *The Anglo-Saxon Church*, frontispiece · photograph, repro. in *The Times* · photograph, repro. in *New Scientist*, 244
Wealth at death £220,499: probate, 15 Feb 1996, *CGPLA Eng. & Wales*

Taylor, Harriet. *See* Mill, Harriet (1807–1858).

Taylor, Helen (1818–1885), children's writer, was the only child of Martin Taylor (1788–1867), of Ongar, Essex, and his first wife, Elizabeth Venn. Martin Taylor was the second surviving son of the nonconformist preacher Isaac *Taylor (1759–1829), of Ongar, whose family were well known for their skill at engraving and their writing; Isaac *Taylor (1787–1865) and Jefferys *Taylor were Martin's brothers. Martin was regarded as the least talented of the Taylor children; in 1809 he was sent to London to work in a publishing house in Paternoster Row. Thereafter he and his family are little noticed in any account of the Taylor family.

Helen was presumably born in London. Her immediate family, like that of her uncle Isaac Taylor of Stanford Rivers, apparently became members of the Church of England. Her publications indicate involvement in religious education for children. Two, *Sabbath Bells: a Series of Simple Lays for Christian Children* (1844) and *Missionary Hymns, for the Use of Children* (1846), emulate the children's verses of her aunts Jane *Taylor and Ann *Gilbert [*see under* Taylor, Jane]. Helen also wrote *The Child's Book of Homilies, by a Member of the Church of England* (1844), and she contributed to *The Teacher's Treasury*. Her works have been generally obscured by the great outpouring of Sunday school literature in the middle of the nineteenth century as well as the fame of her aunts. Helen Taylor never married. She died on 25 June 1885 at Mayfield, Parkstone, Dorset, and was buried at Parkstone.

                                    BARBARA BRANDON SCHNORRENBERG

Sources *DNB* · C. D. Stewart, *The Taylors of Ongar: an analytical bio-bibliography*, 2 vols. (1975) · *Autobiography and other memorials of Mrs Gilbert (formerly Ann Taylor)*, ed. J. Gilbert, 3rd edn (1878) · D. M. Armitage, *The Taylors of Ongar* (1939) · M. N. Cutt, *Ministering angels: a study of nineteenth-century evangelical writing for children* (1979) · Boase, *Mod. Eng. biog.* · d. cert.
Archives BLPES, diary

Taylor, Helen (1831–1907), promoter of women's rights, was born on 27 July 1831 at Kent Terrace, London, the youngest of three children and the only daughter of John Taylor (d. 1849), partner in the wholesale drug firm of David Taylor & Sons, and his wife, Harriet Taylor (1807–1858) [*see* Mill, Harriet (1807–1858)], daughter of surgeon Thomas Hardy. The family resided in London, though Harriet Hardy's family was from Birksgate, near Kirkburton, Yorkshire. Her brothers were Herbert (b. 1827) and Algernon (b. 1830), who was known in the family by the name of Haji. Helen herself was known by family members as Lily. Like her mother, she was a striking presence, slender and apparently beautiful.

Helen Taylor received little formal education, instead travelling widely with her mother in Europe during her girlhood. From an early age, her passion in life was the theatre and she nursed a desire to enter the acting profession, a desire which her mother long resisted. Finally, in the autumn of 1856 Harriet Taylor relented, on the condition that the family's name was not made public in this enterprise. Helen secured a place with a provincial theatre company working primarily in the north-east of England. Accompanied by the younger of her brothers, and with the help and encouragement of a friend, the actress Fanny Stirling, she assumed a variety of roles under the stage name Miss Trevor. After working for two years in northern England and in Scotland, Taylor was called away by her mother's death and never returned to the stage.

Harriet Taylor had married the philosopher and writer John Stuart *Mill almost two years after the death of her first husband, Helen's father, John. Mill and Taylor were married on 21 April 1851, the marriage formally witnessed by Helen Taylor and her brother Algernon. Harriet Taylor died after an acute attack of bronchitis in Avignon, France, on 3 November 1858, after which Helen lived continually with, and acted as amanuensis for, her stepfather until his death fifteen years later in 1873. They divided their time between Blackheath Park in Kent and St Véran, Avignon, where Mill had purchased a house to be near his wife's grave. Taylor retained the Avignon property until 1905.

In the years before Mill's death, Helen Taylor was deeply involved alongside her stepfather in the women's suffrage cause and acted, too, as his letter writer on many issues. Indeed, in his letters Mill is candid about those issues on which he bowed to his stepdaughter's superior knowledge. Their shared belief that there should be no distinction made in suffrage eligibility between married and single women was not wholeheartedly shared by the activists of the women's suffrage movement. It was a division which led to serious and long-term rifts in the suffrage societies of the 1860s. Taylor played an important role in organizing the Ladies' Petition on the suffrage which her stepfather presented to the House of Commons on 7 June 1866. Though the architect of the petition was Barbara Bodichon, Taylor was influential in its wording, organization, and presentation, and was the main conduit of correspondence and contact between Mill and the women petition organizers. Her article 'The claim of Englishwomen to the suffrage constitutionally considered' appeared in the *Westminster Review* shortly after the presentation of the petition in parliament. In the following year, Taylor donated £20 towards the appeal of Mrs Philippine Kyllmann, a widow who unsuccessfully claimed her right to vote as a freeholder.

Despite her outspoken opinions and apparent lack of tact, Taylor was valued within feminist circles. In 1865 Emily Davies, founder of Girton College, Cambridge, invited her to become a member of the London women's debating circle, the Kensington Society. Taylor was also a close friend of Katharine, Viscountess Amberley, and was godmother to Lady Amberley's third child, Bertrand Russell, born in 1872. Millicent Garrett Fawcett, later leader of the constitutional suffrage movement, regarded it as a great honour to be invited to dine with Taylor and Mill.

Taylor, along with her stepfather, opposed the controversial Contagious Diseases Acts passed in the 1860s, which regulated prostitution in military areas. They both regarded the movement for the repeal of these acts, which gathered steam in the 1870s, as firm evidence of the urgent need for women's representation in parliament. Both, however, feared the impact of too close an association between suffrage and the issue of prostitution. They sought consistently to separate the two issues publicly in order not to taint the cause of the suffrage, which for Taylor remained paramount.

Much of the 1870s were taken up for Taylor with editing tasks. Mill had turned over to her, at the time of his election to parliament in 1865, his editorship of the works of his friend and disciple the late Henry Thomas Buckle, historian and philosopher. Her three-volume edition of Buckle's writings appeared in 1872. When her stepfather died the following year, she devoted herself to the editing of his works for publication. By 1879 she had successfully completed and published editions of his *Autobiography*, the *Three Essays on Religion: Nature, the Utility of Religion and Theism*, *Chapters on Socialism*, and the fourth and final volume of *Dissertations and Discussions*. In the late 1890s she was to oversee an Italian edition of his work on socialism, *Il socialismo* (1899), for which she provided an introduction in Italian.

After Mill's death, Taylor's financial security was assured, for she had been left money by her mother and both money and property by Mill. She devoted her life to a swathe of political causes, including but not limited to the feminist issues with which she had earlier been associated. In 1876 she stood as school board candidate for the London constituency of Southwark at the invitation of the local radical association, which had extended the same invitation to her stepfather in the autumn of 1870. Mill had declined to stand, but his stepdaughter now won her election with the largest majority ever counted in a school board election. She was elected again in 1879 and in 1882, and remained a member of the board until her resignation, on grounds of ill health, in 1884. During that time she campaigned tirelessly for free and universal education, for the abolition of corporal punishment, for the community's right to the use of school facilities outside of school hours, and for the provision of free meals and clothing for needy children. When fellow woman board member Florence Fenwick Miller was prevented from standing for re-election for financial reasons, Taylor was among those who offered to fund her campaign, though Miller accepted money, in the event, from other quarters. Taylor was also instrumental in the appointment of working-class parents as school managers.

Taylor's personal generosity and her uncompromisingly radical demands as a board member made her popular with the Southwark electors. She was, however, sued by the chairman of the industrial schools subcommittee for libel in 1882. A scandal had erupted in that same year when eight boys attending the St Paul's Industrial School had, as a protest against the poor conditions they claimed they endured, tried to set fire to the school buildings. There was, at the same time, an allegation of financial irregularity in the management of the school. Taylor, in an attempt to ensure that the subsequent inquiry set up by the home secretary was fairly conducted, wrote to a member of the school board accusing Thomas Scrutton, chair of the industrial schools subcommittee and the school's manager, of accepting money on false pretences and for culpability in the earlier deaths of boys at his school. The case against her came to court in June 1882 and, though the judge exonerated Taylor from personal malice, none the less found against her, and ordered her to pay £1000 in costs and damages. Her action succeeded, however, in bringing about changes in the running of industrial schools in London.

In other political arenas, Taylor became a champion of Irish home rule and of land reform in particular. She was an outspoken opponent of the coercive Irish policy of the Liberal government of the early 1880s. She was a member of the Irish Ladies' Land League, the Land Reform Union, and the League for Taxing Land Values, through which she came to know the American land reformer and author Henry George. She was the only woman to serve on the executive of the Land Nationalisation League, of which she was a vice-president. She gave eight lectures for the society in the winter of 1891–2, and was the most active of the league's lecturers. She called in these lectures for a system of state tenancy and tied the issue, too, to the absolute necessity of women's suffrage. She published two tracts under the imprint of the Land Nationalisation League. She was on the first executive committee of the Marxist-inspired Democratic Federation, founded in 1881, and had been a vocal supporter even before then of labour representation in parliament.

Taylor had strong views on morality. She was an avowed enemy of fox-hunting throughout her life, and in January 1870 published an attack on the sport, and on Anthony

Trollope's defence of it, in the *Fortnightly Review*. She was a member of both the Moral Reform Union and the National Vigilance Association, and though she and Mill had requested their views be kept in the background she was also a member, albeit not active, of the Ladies' National Association for the Repeal of the Contagious Diseases Acts. In 1885 she attempted to stand for parliament as a candidate for the London constituency of North Camberwell, infuriated by the decision of the local Liberal Association to set aside the nomination of William Alexander Coote, the secretary of the Vigilance Association and a prominent social purity campaigner. Taylor sought to replace him in the contest. Her stand was a radical one: she campaigned on the issues of universal suffrage without a property qualification, a fair day's pay for a fair day's work, co-operative labour, a graduated direct income tax, free education, the outlawing of wars unless waged with the consent of the people, and home rule and legislative independence for Ireland. Though the returning officer refused to accept her nomination or election deposit, Taylor's campaign had attracted considerable and lively attention.

Taylor was never prominently involved in the movement for the expansion of women's education, and, indeed, her early friendship with pioneer educationist Emily Davies was increasingly strained by political differences. None the less, she was a strong believer in women's higher education and twice offered, though without success, to pay the fees for her nieces, daughters of her brother Algernon, to attend Newnham College, Cambridge. In 1904 she donated her stepfather's library to Somerville College, Oxford, where it was used as a working library by the women students. She also sat on the council of the South London Working Men's College in the early 1880s.

Though she travelled frequently between continental Europe and England, Taylor refused three invitations to attend women's meetings in the United States in the 1880s and 1890s. On one occasion she withdrew from an American conference where she was to speak before the US senate committee on women's suffrage because another of the delegates was a woman of whose morals she did not approve. Late in the 1880s she withdrew from public life, spending most of her time in the cottage at St Véran which Mill had purchased at the time of Harriet Taylor's death. Failing health brought her back to England in the winter of 1904–5, where she was cared for by her niece, Mary Taylor. Helen Taylor lived in Torquay, Devon, where she died on 29 January 1907. She was buried in Torquay cemetery.

Taylor was a woman of strong opinions, and was seldom shy in expressing them. Though at times her relations with other women activists were strained, her principles and her radicalism played an important role in carving out a space for political women. In particular, her humanitarian principles as a member of the early London school board were an important contribution to the changing politics of the later nineteenth century. Though close to her stepfather throughout his life, Taylor developed her own political personality and opinions early on, and was an independent and highly original thinker.

PHILIPPA LEVINE

Sources J. Kamm, *John Stuart Mill in love* (1977) · *John Stuart Mill and Harriet Taylor: their correspondence and subsequent marriage*, ed. F. A. Hayek (1951) · M. G. Fawcett, *What I remember* (1924) · J. Purvis, *Hard lessons: the lives and education of working-class women in nineteenth-century England* (1989) · D. Rubenstein, *A different world for women: the life of Millicent Garrett Fawcett* (1991) · P. Levine, *Feminist lives in Victorian England: private roles and public commitment* (1990) · F. E. Mineka and D. N. Lindley, *The later letters of John Stuart Mill, 1849–73* (1972) · P. Hollis, *Ladies elect: women in English local government, 1865–1914* (1987) · A. Robson, 'Taylor, Helen', *BDMBR*, vol. 3, pt 2 · B. McCrimmon, 'Helen Taylor, suffragist', *Manuscripts* (spring 1978) · *The Times* (31 Jan 1907) · *DNB* · *Wellesley index*
Archives BLPES, corresp. and papers · JRL, letters and papers · priv. coll., letters · Women's Library, London, letters
Wealth at death £18,909 4s. 6d.: probate, 21 Feb 1907, *CGPLA Eng. & Wales*

Taylor, Henry (1711–1785), religious controversialist, was born at South Weald, Essex, in May 1711 and baptized there on 17 June 1711, the second son of William Taylor (1673–1750), and his wife, Anne Crisp (1680–1739), daughter of Edward and Ann Crisp. His father was a London merchant with property in Essex and enjoyed some reputation as a wit. Taylor was sent to school in Hackney, where John Hoadly, the youngest son of Benjamin Hoadly, was a contemporary, and from there he matriculated at Queens' College, Cambridge, in 1729. He took his BA in 1731, and was elected a fellow in 1734 before proceeding MA the next year.

Taylor was ordained deacon in 1733, then priest in 1735 by the bishop of Winchester, Benjamin Hoadly, 'that great defender of civil & religious liberty', and his major patron (H. Taylor to the third duke of Richmond, 3 Oct 1774, CUL Add. MS 7901/4/14). In 1736 he became curate of Rivenhall, Essex, and in 1737 he was instituted to the rectory of Wheatfield, Oxfordshire, which he held for a minor. On 16 June 1740 he married Christian (Kitty) Fox (*bap.* 1715, *d.* 1769), fourth daughter of the Revd Francis Fox, vicar of St Mary's, Reading, and his wife, Susannah. Her fortune relieved his indebtedness and they had a family of eight surviving children. Taylor was meanwhile enhancing his preferment. On 1 February 1744 Hoadly collated him to the rectory of Baughurst, Hampshire, which he held with Wheatfield. On 12 December 1745 he was instituted to the vicarage of Portsmouth by Winchester College and thereupon resigned Baughurst. In 1748 he was appointed chaplain to James Dalrymple, third earl of Stair. On 3 August 1753 he was collated to the rectory of Ovington, also in the bishop's gift, resigning Wheatfield. In early 1755 he was instituted to the rectory of Crawley with the chapel of Hunton, Hampshire, which he held with Portsmouth, resigning Ovington. From this date Crawley became his main residence and he employed curates at Portsmouth parish church.

Unlike his patron Bishop Hoadly, Taylor openly espoused the restrained Arianism of Samuel Clarke, and this held him back from the highest offices, especially after he went a step further and embraced the Apollinarian heresy which questioned the human nature of Christ's person. This he did in a series of letters addressed to Elisha Levi (1771–7) purporting to be the 'apology' of Benjamin Ben Mordecai for embracing Christianity. Though anonymous, the work was known as Taylor's, and was so acknowledged in the second enlarged edition of 1784. It abounds in learning and argument, but is very discursive. In 1772 Taylor was one of the clergy petitioning for relief from subscription; Mrs Taylor's nephew, Francis Stone, was chairman of the Feathers tavern petitioners. He was disappointed by the unsuccessful outcome, as would be expected from one who habitually omitted the Athanasian creed in his services. 'How', he complained of his Winchester colleague, Archdeacon Thomas Balguy, 'can a man have the face to tell us, that the doctrine of three coequal persons is plainly revealed in scripture?' (H. Taylor to Mrs Jebb, CUL Add. MS 7901/3/9, n.d., c.1774). His *Considerations on Ancient and Modern Creeds* appeared posthumously in 1788, edited by his son William.

Taylor was an ambitious controversialist who used a number of pseudonyms. He appeared as Indignatio in a tract directed against Bishop William Warburton called *Confusion Worse Confounded* (1772), and as Khalid E'bn Abdallah with *An Enquiry into the Opinions of the Learned Christians* (1777). In that year he engaged anonymously against Soane Jenyns with his *A Full Answer to a … Late View of the Internal Evidence of Christian Religion*, and then replied to Gibbon (within a broad millenary context) on his five causes favouring the progress of Christianity in *Thoughts on the Nature of the Grand Apostacy, with Reflections on … Gibbon's History* (1781). In this, as in most of Taylor's writings, there was a sharp anti-Roman Catholic flavour. He published *Farther Thoughts on the Nature of the Grand Apostacy of the Christian Churches* two years later. Here, *inter alia*, he contended that the Bible was the unique test of faith and not made-up articles of human framing. Taylor was an entertaining, sometimes idiosyncratic letter writer who inherited his father's wit and epigrammatic skills. His verses on marriage, 'Paradise Regain'd', are in Dodsley's *Collection of Poems by Several Hands* (1758, 6.126). In politics, he was staunchly whig and an opponent of the American War of Independence. The Cambridge antiquary William Cole called him 'a cheerful, lively, and sensible little man, very thin, and of no promising appearance' (Nichols, *Lit. anecdotes*, 8.428).

Taylor was respected as a controversialist, but inclined to prolixity. He was a copious correspondent and on good terms with non-Anglican Arians such as Richard Price. He died at Titchfield, Hampshire, on 27 April 1785 (the residence of his son, the Revd Peter Taylor), and was buried on 3 May in the chancel of Crawley church. His wife had died earlier, on 23 July 1769.   NIGEL ASTON

Sources P. A. Taylor, ed., *Some account of the Taylor family, originally Taylard* (privately printed, London, 1875) · Venn, *Alum. Cant.* · F. Stone, 'Brief account', *Monthly Repository*, 8 (1813), 285–7 · *Monthly Repository*, 12 (1817), 625 · 'List of the petitioning clergy', *Monthly Repository*, 13 (1818), 15–18, esp. 16 · D. B. Price, 'Memoir of the late Rev. Henry Taylor', *Christian Reformer, or, Unitarian Magazine and Review*, new ser., 5 (1849), 65–78 · B. Mardon, 'The late Rev. Henry Taylor', *Christian Reformer, or, Unitarian Magazine and Review*, new ser., 5 (1849), 235–6 · Nichols, *Lit. anecdotes*, 1.663; 3.124; 8.428, 590 · *GM*, 1st ser., 55 (1785), 402–3 · *GM*, 1st ser., 92/1 (1822), 286 · *The theological and miscellaneous works of Joseph Priestley*, ed. J. T. Rutt, 25 vols. in 26 [1817–32], vol. 8, p. 472 · R. Wallace, *Antitrinitarian biography*, 3 (1850), 604 · H. T. Lilley and A. T. Everitt, *Portsmouth parish church* (1921) · H. Taylor, letter to the third duke of Richmond, 3 Oct 1774, CUL, Add. MS 7901/4/14 · H. Taylor, letter to Mrs Jebb, c.1774, CUL, Add. MS 7901/3/9 · *DNB* · parish register, South Weald [baptism]

Archives Hants. RO, diocesan act books, 35M48/6/546 | BL, Cole MS Athenae Cantab. · CUL, corresp., literary and family papers, Add. MSS 7901–7905

Taylor, Sir Henry (1800–1886), poet and public servant, was born on 18 October 1800 at Bishop Middleham, co. Durham, the youngest of three sons of George Taylor (1772–1851), gentleman farmer and classicist, and his first wife, Eleanor Ashworth (d. 1801?), the daughter of a Durham ironmonger who shared her husband's literary interests. Shortly before his wife's death, George Taylor had resettled his family at St Helen Auckland, where he farmed and pursued his classical studies for the next eighteen years, publishing an occasional essay in the *Quarterly Review*. Although preferring a quiet, retired life, George Taylor served briefly as secretary to the commission on the poor laws in the early 1830s before family concerns forced his resignation. In 1818 he married Jane Mills (1770–1853), long-time family friend; she became a devoted companion and adviser to the young Henry, though unfortunately she was as emotionally reserved as his father. On his marriage George Taylor moved to the village of Witton-le-Wear, where he lived until his death thirty-two years later.

In his *Autobiography* Henry Taylor describes his childhood home as sombre, marked by his father's melancholy following the death of his first wife. George Taylor educated his three sons at home, and Henry confessed that by comparison with his talented, older brothers he proved an indifferent scholar, acquiring, literally, little Latin and less Greek. In 1814 his father permitted him to follow his desire to go to sea. In April he went aboard the *Elephant* as a midshipman, later being transferred to a troopship and finally a frigate; between them these postings took him to Canada and near the United States at the end of the Anglo-American War of 1812–14. In December he was discharged, finding life aboard ship suited neither his character nor his health. He returned home where he read widely in his father's library. When he was sixteen, he obtained, through the offices of Charles Arbuthnot, then secretary of the Treasury and a family friend, a clerkship with the storekeeper-general. At first he lived in London with his brothers until, in 1818, they contracted typhus and died shortly after within the same month. Following their deaths, Henry continued for a short while in London on his own before being transferred to Barbados. His duties came to an end in 1820 when his department was consolidated with another branch of the Treasury, and he returned a second time to his father's house.

For the next three years Taylor lived quietly at home. Looking back, he called this time 'dull, almost to disease' (*Autobiography*, 1.43). He filled his days with miscellaneous

Sir Henry Taylor (1800–1886), by Julia Margaret Cameron, 1865

reading, ranging from Machiavelli and Hume to the Koran and Milner's *Church History*. He also improved his Latin and Greek and taught himself Italian, translating Ariosto and reading widely in Italian poetry. At night he devoted himself to writing his own poetry. He had read the popular poets and novelists of the day—Scott, Byron, Moore, and Campbell—and composed long narrative poems on exotic topics in the manner of Byron. He also wrote his first verse drama, a tragedy on the story of Don Carlos. Apart from these Byronic juvenilia, he began his literary career in earnest. In 1822 he made his publishing début, submitting an essay on Moore's *Irish Melodies* for the *Quarterly Review*. The *Quarterly* editor William Gifford invited his new contributor to submit another essay, which he soon did. He also found his articles welcome at the *London Magazine*. The success of these first attempts at journalism encouraged him to venture to London in 1823 to earn his living by his pen. These early literary efforts were encouraged by his stepmother and her cousin Isabella Fenwick, a woman of independent means who was for many years a close friend and neighbour of Wordsworth and, while Taylor's senior by some years, one of his most intimate literary confidantes until her death in 1856.

During the early 1820s Taylor began to form friendships with important literary contemporaries as well. He met and corresponded with Wordsworth, visited Coleridge often at Highgate, and developed an especially close bond with Southey, despite differences of age, temperament, and politics. The two toured Holland, France, and Belgium in 1825 and again in 1826, and Southey wrote the only favourable review of Taylor's first published drama, *Isaac*

Comnenus (1827). In London, Taylor also became a frequent guest at Samuel Rogers's literary breakfasts, and he joined the debate society frequented by John Stuart Mill, Charles Austin, and other 'radical, Benthamite, *doctrinaires*' (*Autobiography*, 1.77) where he spoke against Benthamite principles and for pragmatic reform.

Taylor's need to earn a living by writing was permanently altered in 1824 when Sir Henry Holland recommended him for a clerkship in the Colonial Office, based on his prior colonial experience as well as his literary abilities. Taylor immediately distinguished himself and in January 1825, despite his youth, was appointed senior clerk for the Caribbean colonies (initially at £600 per annum, later £900), a post he held until his retirement in 1872. In the Colonial Office at that time his status as a senior clerk gave him certain privileges. Colonial secretaries and under-secretaries allowed a large part of the administrative load to devolve on the senior clerks. Taylor even had direct access to the colonial secretary, especially during the period (1846–52) when his friend Henry George, the third Earl Grey, held the post.

Taylor dealt with the West Indian colonies during the agitation that led to the end of slavery in 1834, the brief but troubled apprenticeship period that followed, and the subsequent difficulties of a post-slavery society. Taylor supported emancipation, but distrusted the ability of black West Indians to be self-governing. As a result, he favoured an apprenticeship plan to effect a transition from slavery to freedom as well as safeguards against what he foresaw as abuses by the planters who remained in control of local assemblies, except in crown colonies. When abuses led to a premature end of the apprenticeship period in 1838, Taylor argued that West Indian assemblies needed to come more directly under crown control or he predicted disaster would follow. For Taylor, the 1865 Gordon riots in Jamaica were exactly that disaster, and resulted in the Jamaican assembly relinquishing sovereignty to the crown, a move he had argued for in 1838 and that he claimed would have prevented such riots. While he supported Governor Eyre's controversial restoration of order following the Gordon uprising, the uprising itself was in his mind the inevitable result of failed policies.

Taylor took little part in the political questions of the day, except on two notable occasions: first, when he came to the defence of his close friend Charles Eliot, British plenipotentiary in China, who in 1840 was attacked in both parliament and the press for 'gunboat' diplomacy to protect British merchants, an action which precipitated the First Opium War; and, second, when he published a pamphlet, *Crime Considered* (1869), addressed to Gladstone, then prime minister, on certain proposed reforms in the penal code, especially as they applied to the colonies, including his controversial support for corporal punishment.

Taylor was an astute observer of the day-to-day workings of government bureaucracy, and he published a frank yet ironic look at those operations in *The Statesman* (1836), a work composed of maxims and practical advice based on his career in the civil service. The manuscript was reviewed by his Colonial Office colleagues and friends, Edward Villiers, James Spedding, editor of Francis Bacon, and Gladstone. Contemporaries regarded the work as too cynical, even Machiavellian, but it has since become something of a minor classic, remaining in print throughout the twentieth century. Taylor's superiors offered him advancement, including the under-secretaryship, but various reasons always kept him from taking advantage of proffered promotion. In 1859, when a severe asthmatic attack nearly forced his retirement, he was allowed to work at home rather than in the Downing Street offices.

Working in the Colonial Office brought Taylor friendships with a number of the leading statesmen of the time. One particular friendship with Thomas Spring Rice, secretary for war and colonies in Melbourne's first cabinet, eventually led to his marriage to the secretary's daughter Theodosia Alice Spring Rice (1818–1891) on 17 October 1839, following a three-year courtship marked by a break in relations owing to Taylor's religious diffidence. Despite their differences in age (he was nearly twenty years her senior), their home life was by all accounts happy and affectionate, full of the pleasure of company and friends and the complete opposite of the sombre home of his youth. The couple settled first in London, in Blandford Square, moving in 1845 to Ladon House at Mortlake on the Thames. In 1853 they built a house designed by Alice abutting Sheen Common where they lived until Taylor's retirement. They had five children. The eldest son, Aubrey, died on 16 May 1876, and a daughter, Una, wrote *Guests and Memories* (1924), a memoir about her parents, their Bournemouth summer home purchased in 1861, and the notable guests they entertained there, in particular, Aubrey De Vere, James Spedding, Benjamin Jowett, Robert Louis Stevenson, and Mary Shelley and her son Sir Percy. Their eldest daughter was the biographer Ida Alice Ashworth *Taylor.

Despite his appointment in the Colonial Office and the often long hours required of him there, Taylor pursued his career as a poet, publishing five novel-length verse dramas and a volume of lyric poems. Following the failure of *Isaac Comnenus*, Taylor worked for seven years on his next historical drama and produced his greatest success in 1834 with the publication of *Philip Van Artevelde*, a tale drawn from Froissart and Barante in which he blends political conflict with domestic drama in an Elizabethan style but with a modern emphasis on psychological states more than dramatic action. In *Van Artevelde* Taylor also championed a more restrained poetic style against what he regarded as the excesses of the school of Byron and Shelley. Aware of going against popular taste, he provided *Van Artevelde* with a preface that set forth at length his critique of Byron and Shelley whose poetry, despite its powerful feeling and beautiful imagery, lacked, in his view, moral reflection and the balance of passion with reason. For his contemporaries, the 'Preface' to *Philip Van Artevelde* signalled a significant shift in poetic taste, corresponding to Carlyle's call to set aside Byron for Goethe.

The publication of *Van Artevelde* was widely and extensively reviewed, including in the *Revue des Deux Mondes*. It brought Taylor immediate fame, and he was briefly lionized by Lady Holland and other London hostesses, and was ever afterwards referred to by close friends as Philip Van Artevelde Taylor. His contemporaries compared the accomplishment to Shakespeare's, and William Macready was so taken by the work that he staged an abridged version which, however, ran for only six nights. But Taylor never again achieved the popular success of *Philip Van Artevelde*. In 1842 he published *Edwin the Fair*, a work even he came to regard as deficient in dramatic interest. For his next play Taylor attempted an Elizabethan romantic comedy, *The Virgin Widow* (1850). He published only one other drama, *St Clement's Eve* (1862), a return to Barante as a source and his most successful work since *Van Artevelde*. Although his work is uneven, he did win the regard of contemporaries, including admirers as different as Macaulay and Swinburne, the latter being so genuinely impressed by the historical dramas he sought out the elderly poet's company and friendship in the 1870s. A collected edition of his work in five volumes appeared in 1877–8, but following his death his poetry quickly sank into obscurity and has not been reprinted since.

In his later years Taylor received a number of honours. Oxford University awarded him the DCL in 1862 and he was made KCMG in 1869 for his contributions in the Colonial Office. Although he stopped writing poetry, he did revise his plays for the collected edition, and continued to see close friends, such as De Vere, Tennyson, and his irrepressible Freshwater neighbour Julia Margaret Cameron, who found his features extremely handsome and used him frequently as a model for her photographs. He died at his home, The Roost, Bournemouth, on 27 March 1886, survived by his wife, who died on 1 January 1891, and his youngest son Harry and three daughters.

Taylor sought fame as a poet, yet, ironically, it is his prose which has remained significant. His *Autobiography* has proved invaluable to historians of the Colonial Office and West Indian affairs. Likewise, *The Statesman* provides a portrait of the Colonial Office and civil service in the years preceding the Northcote–Trevelyan report. Even of his historical dramas, only the 'Preface' to *Philip Van Artevelde* is still read and then as a classic statement of the shift in taste from Romantic to Victorian, even though the play itself, among all Taylor's work, is most deserving of being remembered. In her photographs Julia Margaret Cameron appears to have given Taylor a fame more lasting than any of his writings, as she has immortalized the calm face, pensive eyes, and magnificent flowing beard he grew after the 1859 asthmatic attack left him unable to shave.

MARK REGER

Sources H. Taylor, *Autobiography, 1800–1875*, 2 vols. (1885) · U. Taylor, *Guests and memories: annals of a seaside villa* (1924) · *Correspondence of Henry Taylor*, ed. E. Dowden (1888) · W. Ward, *Aubrey de Vere: a memoir* (1904) · D. M. Young, *The colonial office in the early nineteenth century* (1961) · D. J. Murray, *The West Indies and the development of colonial government, 1801–1834* (1965) · W. L. Burn, *Emancipation and apprenticeship in the British West Indies* (1937); repr. (1970) · DNB · H. G. Merriam, *Edward Moxon: publisher of poets* (1939) · M. Weaver, *Julia Margaret Cameron, 1815–1879* (1984) · *The Times* (30 March 1886), 10

Archives BL, MS autobiography, Add. MS 39179 · Bodl. Oxf., corresp., papers, diaries, and literary MSS · Bodl. Oxf., letters · Hunt. L., letters · U. Durham L., papers concerning slavery | BL, corresp. with W. E. Gladstone, Add. MSS 44355–44490, *passim* · BL, letters to Lord Stanmore, Add. MSS 49199, 49236, 49240 · Bodl. Oxf., corresp. with James Ingram; corresp. with Lord Kimberley · CUL, corresp. with Sir James Stephen · NA Canada, letters from Sir Thomas Frederick Elliot · NL Scot., corresp. with A. R. D. Elliot; corresp. with Sir T. F. Elliot · NL Scot., letters to Sir Alexander Hope · NL Scot., corresp. with Lady Minto · TCD, letters to W. E. H. Lecky and Elizabeth Lecky · U. Durham L., corresp. with third Earl Grey · Wordsworth Trust, Dove Cottage, Grasmere, letters to Wordsworth family

Likenesses L. Macdonald, marble bust, 1843, NPG · J. M. Cameron, photographs, 1864–7 · J. M. Cameron, photograph, 1865, NPG [*see illus.*] · O. Rejlander, carte-de-visite, NPG · G. F. Watts, oils, NPG · photographs, Bodl. Oxf., Sir H. Taylor album of Cameron photographs

Wealth at death £7719 6s. 4d.: probate, 13 May 1886, *CGPLA Eng. & Wales*

Taylor, Henry (1885–1951), swimmer, was born at 27 Maple Street, Oldham, Lancashire, on 17 March 1885, the second son and second child of James Taylor, a coalminer, and his wife, Elizabeth Morris. His parents, both English, died while he was young and he was brought up by his elder brother William. His formal education was quite patchy. He left school unable to write effectively, and found work in a local cotton mill.

Taylor learned to swim in the Hollinwood Canal at Chadderton and also swam at the central baths, Oldham, on 'dirty water' day (when admission charges were reduced). There, aged seven, he won a silver medal for winning a two-length race. Captivated by the thrill of competition, he went on to join Chadderton swimming club, based at the more conveniently sited Chadderton baths, built in 1894. He also spent a lot of time training alone in open water—during his lunch break in Hollinwood Canal and in the evening in Alexandra Park boating lake in Oldham.

Taylor was a stocky man (5 feet 5 inches and 10 stone 6 pounds at the age of twenty-three). Many regarded him as the finest exponent of the trudgen stroke, a double over-arm stroke requiring considerable upper body strength and stamina. In particular, he generated tremendous drive from a very effective scissor kick, giving him a reputation as a tireless distance swimmer. His greatest successes came in 1906 and 1908. At the 1906 intercalated Olympic games in Athens the swimming events were held in the open sea at Phalerum Bay, where conditions were rough. Taylor was the surprise of the games, particularly as he was a travelling reserve. He thrived in the difficult conditions, and won three medals—a gold (1 mile), a silver (400 metres), and a bronze (4x250 metres team race). Taylor won three gold medals at the fourth Olympiad in London in 1908. He won the 400 metres, setting the first official world record of 5 min. 36.8 sec. Similarly, he won the 1500 metres, establishing the first official world record of 22 min. 48.4 sec. Finally, he helped the 4x200 metres freestyle team to an unexpected win. Taylor, swimming the anchor leg, entered the water third, 3 yards down on the American Rich and 10 yards behind the Hungarian

Halmay. Taylor caught Rich 50 metres from home and went on to pass Halmay, winning by 3 yards. He returned home to a hero's welcome in Lancashire with admirers calling him Britain's greatest amateur swimmer. American swimmers using a new front crawl stroke broke Britain's domination of Olympic middle-distance swimming at the following Olympiad in Stockholm in 1912. Taylor did not progress beyond the semi-finals in the 400 metres and the 1500 metres but won a bronze medal in the 4x200 metres team race. Similarly, Taylor won an eighth medal (bronze) at the seventh Olympiad in Antwerp in 1920 as a member of the 4x200 metres relay team. Taylor won eight Olympic medals between 1906 and 1920, a record for a British Olympian in any sport. He also won fifteen national titles from 440 yards to long distance between 1906 and 1920. He also won fifteen northern titles from 100 yards to 1 mile between 1906 and 1923 and gained twelve international water polo caps. He retired from swimming in 1926.

Taylor remained a bachelor. Although 'he was a handsome figure of a man … he was never allowed near the ladies because his brother felt it would interfere with his training' (*Oldham Evening Chronicle*). He found his lack of formal education a considerable handicap. His one excursion into business as a publican was a failure. He mortgaged his thirty-five trophies and over 300 medals and prizes to purchase the Nudger Inn at Dobcross, Saddleworth. He never redeemed them. On leaving the Nudger, he worked on various ships before returning to Chadderton to lodge for eighteen years with Mr Jimmy Wells and his family in Burnley Lane. He was unemployed for a considerable time until the local council found him a post as an attendant at Chadderton swimming baths, where he had done so much of his swimming. He held the post until a few months before his death on 28 February 1951 at 68 Brierley Street, Chadderton, Oldham.

PETER BILSBOROUGH

Sources I. Buchanan, *British Olympians: a hundred years of gold medallists* (1991) · P. Besford, *Encyclopaedia of swimming* (1971) · J. Bancroft, *Olympic champions in Manchester* (1993) · R. D. Binfield, *The story of the Olympics* (1948) · British Olympic Council, *Official report of the Olympic games of 1908* (1909) · R. J. H. Kiphuth, *Swimming* (1949) · *Amateur Swimming Association Handbook* (1924) · *Oldham Evening Chronicle* (16 Nov 1968) · b. cert. · d. cert.

Likenesses photograph, repro. in British Olympic Council, *Official report* · photograph, repro. in *Olympic Games of London, 1908: a complete record with photographs of winners* (1908) · two photographs, repro. in C. M. Daniels, H. Johansson, and A. Sinclair, *How to swim and save life* (1907)

Wealth at death £259 8s. 7d.: administration, 28 May 1952, *CGPLA Eng. & Wales*

Taylor, Henry Martyn (1842–1927), mathematician, was born at Bristol on 6 June 1842, the second son of the Revd James Taylor, who afterwards became headmaster of Wakefield grammar school, and his wife, Eliza Johnson. Both his brothers became schoolmasters, and later, private tutors. He was educated at Wakefield and at Trinity College, Cambridge, which he entered as a minor scholar in 1861. He graduated BA as third wrangler in 1865, and was awarded the second Smith's prize in 1866.

Taylor cherished for a time the intention of going to the bar, and was in fact called by Lincoln's Inn in November 1869, but soon relinquished the plan. After holding the post of vice-principal of the School of Naval Architecture and Marine Engineering at Kensington (1865–9), he returned to Cambridge in 1869 as assistant tutor on the mathematical staff of Trinity College. He had been elected a fellow, under the old competitive system, in 1866. Thereafter his life was spent in the service of the college and university until his retirement in 1894. He became tutor of the college in 1874, and held the position for the usual period of ten years.

Taylor's mathematical leanings were mainly towards geometry, in its intuitive aspect, as is indicated by the papers which he contributed to the London Mathematical Society (of which he was one of the earliest members), to the *Philosophical Transactions*, and the *Cambridge Transactions*, for example, on inversion, plane curves, and solid geometry. He had a rigid standard of verbal and logical accuracy, and was often consulted by friends, including Lord Rayleigh, on stylistic and other matters.

When released from tutorial duties at the early age of fifty-two, Taylor might reasonably have looked forward to some years of useful mathematical research; however, he soon suffered an attack of influenza which was followed by partial, and later by complete, blindness. He reacted with what contemporaries considered admirable courage. He continued for a time to interest himself in mathematical questions, and indeed his two most original papers, requiring a high degree of constructive imagination, were those which he contributed, after his blindness, to the *Philosophical Transactions* and to the volume commemorating the jubilee of Sir G. Gabriel Stokes (1900).

Taylor's most notable work, however, arose from consideration of how, with his own special training and personal achievement, he could most usefully help other blind people. He found that although a certain amount of literature was accessible to blind readers through the medium of the Braille script, there was no provision of a scientific kind. Taylor set out to remedy this. He soon made himself expert on the Braille typing machine, and transcribed a series of elementary books on mathematics and various branches of natural science. He was faced with the problem that the Braille system had no provision for mathematical notation, and diagrams posed a special difficulty. Taylor therefore gave much thought to the invention of suitable symbols and contrivances. Reproduction and multiplication of the bulky volumes was costly and, in order to meet this, Taylor, with the assistance of friends, started an Embossed Scientific Books Fund, which was, to his great satisfaction, accepted as a trust by the Royal Society and came to be administered by a committee of the fellows. (Taylor had himself been elected a fellow in June 1898.)

In addition to his scientific and educational interests Taylor had a strong practical sense which found an outlet in the administrative business of his college and, later, in municipal affairs. He was one of the university representatives on the Cambridge town council, was an alderman (1898–1925), and was mayor in 1904.

Taylor was described as 'singularly modest and devoid of personal ambition … a loyal and generous friend, and a scrupulously fair opponent' (*PRS*). Before his blindness, he had been fond of sporting recreations, foreign travel, and mountain excursions. His last few years were clouded by increasing infirmity. He died at his home, The Yews, Newnham, Cambridge, on 16 October 1927. He never married, and left most of his estate to Trinity College.

HORACE LAMB, *rev.* ALAN YOSHIOKA

Sources H. Lamb, *PRS*, 117A (1928), xxix–xxxi · Venn, *Alum. Cant.* · *The Times* (16 Dec 1927)
Archives King's Cam., letters to Oscar Browning
Likenesses G. Spencer, pencil drawing, 1927, Trinity Cam. · photograph, repro. in Lamb, *PRS*
Wealth at death £9737 2s.: resworn probate, 18 Nov 1927, *CGPLA Eng. & Wales*

Taylor, Sir Herbert (1775–1839), courtier and army officer, second son of the Revd Edward Taylor (1734–1798), of Bifrons, Kent, rector of Patrixbourne, and his wife, Margaret (d. 1780?), daughter of Thomas Payler of Ileden, Kent, was born on 29 September 1775 at Bifrons. He was educated privately on the continent between 1780 and 1790, and became a good linguist. Through Lord Camelford and Lord Grenville, he was employed in the Foreign Office under James Bland Burgess. His knowledge of foreign languages made him very useful, and Lord Grenville occasionally employed him on confidential work at his own house. In December 1792 Taylor accompanied Sir James Murray (afterwards Murray-Pulteney) on a special mission to the Prussian headquarters at Frankfurt. After a few weeks Murray left Frankfurt to take up his military duties as adjutant-general to the duke of York's army at Antwerp, and Taylor remained behind for a short time in charge of the mission. In April 1793, he joined the army headquarters where Murray presented him to the duke of York, to whom he became greatly attached. He was employed as Murray's secretary, and was present as a volunteer at the action of St Amand (8 May), the battle of Famars (23 May), and the sieges of Valenciennes and Dunkirk.

On 25 March 1794 Taylor was given a commission as cornet in the 2nd dragoon guards, and in July was promoted to be lieutenant. On Murray's return to England, Taylor remained with the duke of York as assistant secretary. He generally joined his regiment when in the field, and was present at the April actions near Cateau Cambrésis, those near Tournai in May, and at other operations of the campaign, including the retreat into the Netherlands. In May 1795 he was promoted to be captain in the 2nd dragoon guards. When the duke of York returned to England, Taylor remained with the army as assistant secretary to the commander-in-chief of the British forces on the continent, and served in that capacity successively with Lieutenant-General Harcourt and Sir David Dundas.

On 16 September 1795 Taylor returned to England, having been appointed aide-de-camp to the duke of York. He was soon afterwards nominated assistant military secretary in the commander-in-chief's office. In July 1798 he accompanied Lord Cornwallis to Ireland on the latter's appointment as lord lieutenant, in the threefold capacity of aide-de-camp, military secretary, and private secretary. Cornwallis described him as 'indefatigable in business; and in honesty, fidelity and goodness of heart he has no superior' (*Taylor Papers*, 56). He returned to England in February 1799 to take over the duties of private secretary to the duke of York. He went to the Netherlands as aide-de-camp to the duke in the expedition to The Helder in September, and was present at several battles.

In January 1801 Taylor was promoted to be major in the 2nd dragoon guards, and in December of the same year to be lieutenant-colonel in the 9th West India regiment. On 25 June 1802 he was placed on half pay, and on 25 May was brought into the Coldstream Guards, of which the duke of York was colonel. He rose to the rank of lieutenant-general in 1825. He continued in the appointment of private secretary and aide-de-camp to the duke until 13 June 1805, when he was appointed private secretary to the king. The king placed every confidence in him, so that his position was one of great delicacy, but his straightforwardness secured the good opinion of all. On the establishment of the regency he continued in the same office to the queen, who was appointed by act of parliament guardian of the king's person. By the same act Taylor was appointed one of the three commissioners of the king's real and personal estate.

In November 1813 Taylor was appointed to command a brigade in the army of Sir Thomas Graham (afterwards Lord Lynedoch), which was besieging Antwerp. He returned to England in March 1814, when he was sent on special military missions to Bernadotte, crown prince of Sweden (then commanding the Swedish force in Germany), and to The Hague. During these absences from the court his place was taken by his brother Brook Taylor [*see below*]. He resumed the duties of private secretary to Queen Charlotte on his return, and continued in this office until her death in November 1818. In 1819 he was made a knight of the Royal Guelphic Order, and on 5 October of the same year he married Charlotte Albinia, daughter of Edward Disbrowe of Walton Hall, Derbyshire, vice-chamberlain to Queen Charlotte, and granddaughter of the third earl of Buckingham; they had two daughters.

From 1820 to 1823 Taylor represented Windsor in parliament, resigning his seat because he found he could not satisfactorily fulfil both his parliamentary and his other duties. On 25 March 1820 he was appointed military secretary at the Horse Guards, and in 1824 he was made a knight grand cross of the Royal Guelphic Order. In January 1827 he was appointed military secretary to the new commander-in-chief, the duke of Wellington; but on the duke resigning in July 1827, Taylor was nominated by Lord Palmerston to be a deputy secretary at war in the military branch of the War Office; the king had already made him his first and principal aide-de-camp.

On 19 March 1828 Taylor was appointed master surveyor and surveyor-general of the ordnance of the United Kingdom. On 25 August of the same year he became adjutant-general of the forces, an appointment which he held until the accession of William IV, to whom he became private secretary, and continued in that office during the whole of the reign. He played a significant part as mediator between the king and the government during the Reform Bill crisis.

On 16 April 1834 Taylor was awarded the grand cross in the Order of the Bath. On the death of William IV in 1837 he retired into private life, but remained first and principal aide-de-camp to Queen Victoria. He had already received from George III a pension of £1000 a year on the civil list, with remainder to his widow. In the spring of 1838 he went to Italy, and he died at Rome on 20 March 1839. His body was embalmed for conveyance to England, but was buried in the protestant cemetery at Rome. In the middle of April his remains were exhumed and sent to England, and on 13 June were deposited in a vault of the chapel of St Katherine's Hospital, Regent's Park, London, to the mastership of which he had been appointed in 1818 by Queen Charlotte.

Taylor, who was a confidential friend of the duke of York, his go-between in the financial negotiations with Mary Anne Clarke, and one of his executors, wrote the *Memoirs of the Last Illness and Decease of HRH the Duke of York* (1827).

Taylor's younger brother, **Sir Brook Taylor** (1776–1846), joined the diplomatic service under the patronage of Lord Grenville, and was British minister to Cologne and Hesse-Cassel in 1801–6, to Denmark in 1807, to Württemberg in 1814–20 and to Bavaria in 1820–28. He was minister at Berlin in 1828–31, and was created GCH in 1822 and sworn of the privy council in 1828. He died, unmarried, at Eaton Place, London, on 15 October 1846.

R. H. VETCH, *rev.* K. D. REYNOLDS

Sources *The Taylor papers, being a record of certain reminiscences, letters and journals in the life of Lieut.-Gen. Sir Herbert Taylor*, ed. E. Taylor (1913) · *The later correspondence of George III*, ed. A. Aspinall, 5 vols. (1962–70) · *The correspondence of George, prince of Wales, 1770–1812*, ed. A. Aspinall, 8 vols. (1963–71) · *The letters of King George IV, 1812–1830*, ed. A. Aspinall, 3 vols. (1938) · *The Reform Act, 1832: the correspondence of the late Earl Grey with His Majesty King William IV and with Sir Herbert Taylor*, ed. Henry, Earl Grey, 2 vols. (1867) · *GM*, 2nd ser., 11 (1839), 654–5 · *GM*, 2nd ser., 12 (1839), 669–70 · *GM*, 2nd ser., 27 (1847), 82 [obit. of Sir Brook Taylor] · Ward, *Men of the reign* [Brook Taylor]
Archives Harrowby Manuscript Trust, Sandon Hall, Staffordshire, account of last days of duke of York · Royal Arch., papers relating to his work as private secretary to George III and William IV | Balliol Oxf., letters relating to Turkish commercial treaty · Beds. & Luton ARS, corresp. with second Earl de Grey · BL, corresp. with Lord Aberdeen, Add. MS 43030 · BL, corresp. with Sir James Willoughby Gordon, Add. MSS 49471, 49512D, *passim* · BL, corresp. mainly with Lord Liverpool, Add. MSS 38241–38380, 38474, 38573, *passim* · BL, corresp. with Sir Hudson Lowe, Add. MSS 20130–20139, *passim* · BL, letters to Sir T. B. Martin, Add. MSS 41367–41368 · BL, corresp. with Sir Robert Peel, Add. MSS 40301–40607 · BL, corresp. with Lord Ripon, Add. MS 40862 · BL, corresp. with his brother Sir Brook Taylor, Add. MSS 62953–62954 · BL, letters to Lord Wellesley, Add. MS 37311 · Chatsworth House, Derbyshire, letters to sixth duke of Devonshire · CUL, corresp. with Spencer Perceval · Derbys. RO, corresp. with Sir R. J. Wilmot-Horton · Durham RO,

corresp. with Lord Londonderry · Lpool RO, letters to Lord Stanley · Morgan L., letters to Sir James Murray-Pulteney · NA Scot., corresp. with Lord Dalhousie; letters to Sir John Dalrymple, eighth earl of Stair · NL Scot., corresp. with Sir George Brown; corresp. with Edward Ellice; corresp. with Lord Lynedoch · NMM, corresp. with Lord Minto · NRA, priv. coll., corresp. with Henry Duncan · PRO, corresp. with Sir George Murray, WO 80 · Royal Military College, Sandhurst, letters to General Le Marchant · U. Durham L., corresp. with second and third earls de Grey; letters to Viscount Ponsonby · U. Southampton L., letters to Lord Palmerston · U. Southampton L., letters to Lord John Russell · U. Southampton L., letters to first duke of Wellington · W. Sussex RO, letters to duke of Richmond · Woburn Abbey, Woburn, letters to George William Russell

Likenesses W. Ward, mezzotint, pubd 1836 (after W. J. Newton), BM · W. J. Newton, portrait, repro. in *Taylor papers*, ed. Taylor · oils, NPG · portraits, repro. in *Taylor papers*, ed. Taylor (1913)

Wealth at death under £12,000—bequeathed annuities of £20 to two stewards; residue to wife and daughters: will, 1834, PRO · £12,000 mostly in various policies effected on his life: *GM*, 2nd ser., 12 (1839), 669–70

Taylor, (James) Hudson (1832–1905), missionary, was born in Barnsley, Yorkshire, on 21 May 1832, the eldest of the five children (two sons and three daughters, one son and one daughter dying in childhood) of James Taylor, chemist and Wesleyan local preacher, and his wife Amelia, daughter of the Revd Benjamin Brook Hudson, Wesleyan minister. Taylor was educated at home and at a private day school, and as apprentice to his father. At fifteen he worked in a bank to learn accountancy, until his eyesight gave trouble. In June 1849, aged seventeen, he underwent an evangelical conversion and determined to bring the Christian gospel to the Chinese, although inland China was closed to foreigners. He began medical training, first in the slums of Hull, and then at the London Hospital, but sailed unqualified as first agent of the new Chinese Evangelization Society. He landed in Shanghai on 1 March 1854.

In 1855, to the disgust of established missionaries, Taylor adopted Chinese dress and a pigtail. Inland travel and preaching became easier at once, though he had hair-raising adventures and was not naturally brave. Meanwhile his society's inefficiency left him destitute. He severed connections. Following the example of the preacher and philanthropist George Müller and applying his own highly original survival training in Hull, he lived by the principles of faith and prayer on which he later built his mission: never appealing for funds except to God, and administering all gifts with scrupulous stewardship. In 1858, at Ningbo, he married Maria Jane (*d.* 1870), orphaned daughter of the Revd Samuel Dyer, missionary in Singapore. They had five sons and three daughters. Ill health drove Taylor back to England in 1860 and in 1862 he qualified MRCS and in midwifery.

The treaty of Nanjing had opened the interior of China, but no existing mission had accepted the challenge. Taylor therefore published a pamphlet, *China: its Spiritual Need and Claims*, and founded the undenominational China Inland Mission in 1865, praying for twenty-four 'willing, skilful labourers', two symbolically for each province. In 1866 the Taylors took their children and most of their

twenty-four workers to Shanghai. The China Inland Mission's early years inland were hazardous, with riots, some internal dissension, and opposition from established missionaries, who especially objected to the use of Chinese dress. Despite sickness and discouragement Taylor persevered and every province was penetrated. Maria Hudson died in childbirth at Zhenjiang in July 1870. On 14 November 1871, in London, Taylor married her best friend and fellow missionary, Jane Elizabeth (Jennie; 1842/3–1904), daughter of Joseph William F. Faulding, fret-cutter and piano-frame maker of St Pancras. They had one son and one daughter.

At home, Taylor's writings and dramatic appeals stirred the churches: among volunteers who responded was the celebrated C. T. Studd in 1885. Taylor promoted all missions, and believed that the surest way to help the East was to deepen spirituality in the West. The mission now grew rapidly until by 1895 Taylor was directing nearly half the protestant force in China. He was ahead of his time in identification with the people, working towards indigenous leadership. He also took a strong part in famine relief and the campaign to abolish the British opium trade to China. In the Boxer uprising (1899–1901) a total of seventy-nine China Inland Mission missionaries and children were killed. Taylor refused compensation, to the amazement of the mandarins, who issued proclamations applauding the spirit of the Christians. He retired as general director of the mission in 1902.

Taylor, who had a strong sense of humour, was small, sandy-haired, musical, and affectionate. His example and strategies, his integrity, saintliness, courage, and originality had a lasting influence on Christian missions worldwide. The fast-growing, and later wholly indigenous, protestant church in China owed more to him than to any other foreigner. He died on 3 June 1905 at Changsha, Hunan, China. JOHN POLLOCK, *rev.*

Sources A. J. Broomhall, *Hudson Taylor and China's open century*, 7 vols. (1981–90) · G. Taylor and H. Taylor, *Hudson Taylor*, 2 vols. (1911–18) · J. C. Pollock, *Hudson Taylor and Maria, pioneers in China* (1962) · m. cert. · *CGPLA Eng. & Wales* (1905)

Archives SOAS, diaries, corresp., and papers

Wealth at death £212 4s. 10d.: administration with will, 22 Sept 1905, *CGPLA Eng. & Wales*

Taylor, Hugh (1789–1868), land agent and estate commissioner, was born on 22 November 1789 at Shilbottle Lodge, Newburn, Northumberland, the fourth, but third surviving, son of Thomas Taylor (*d.* 1810) of Newburn, farmer and mineral agent to Hugh Percy, duke of Northumberland, and his wife, Mary Nixon. His father established the Taylor family interest in the north-eastern coal trade, and looked to his three sons to consolidate this. The eldest son, Thomas Taylor, of Whitehill Point and later of Cramlington, Northumberland, became a leading coal owner in the newly opened and fast-expanding Tyne basin or eastern coal district on the north bank of the lower Tyne, where best-quality Wallsend house coal was found at great depth. The second son, John Taylor, of Shilbottle, became a noted mining engineer, and Hugh Taylor himself was apprenticed to a colliery owner to learn the art of winning and working coal in the deep.

When his father died in 1810 Hugh Taylor, though no more than twenty-one years old, succeeded him as mineral agent to the second duke of Northumberland. Under the third duke, who succeeded in 1817, he quickly advanced to a more senior position in the ducal administration. At that time the Percy estates were managed by three commissioners, each of whom managed a separate territorial district, and under each commissioner were a number of bailiffs, who held farms at low rents in return for looking after a number of fellow tenants. Taylor was promoted to one of these commissionerships, while retaining the colliery agency. Experience made him highly critical of this system of divided managerial responsibilities, which tended to upset the tenantry because policies and practices varied from one commissioner's district to another; but the third duke disliked the idea of change. On his death in 1847 Taylor persuaded the fourth duke to make a clean sweep of the whole system, and a reformed and hierarchical management structure was set up, with himself as chief commissioner. He was entrusted with sole and undivided authority over all the Northumberland estates and controlled a staff of salaried agents for territorial subdistricts and specialized functions such as colliery matters, building works, and land drainage. This centralized and authoritarian regime for managing a vast estate—over 180,000 acres in Northumberland—may well have owed much to the example of James Loch's administration of the Sutherland estates, which undoubtedly would have been known to Taylor.

The fourth duke, known as Algernon the Good and Algernon the Benevolent, was resolved to spend his large income liberally, but it was Taylor who acted as the channel for the duke's munificence. Much of the expenditure which he supervised was of a benevolent or philanthropic character: national schools were supported, churches were built, fishing villages were provided with barometers, and, with the example of Grace Darling on the doorstep, lifeboats were placed along the coast. Most of the expenditure, however, was designed to promote the prosperity of the estate and was to the mutual advantage of the duke and his tenantry. The agricultural expenditure was immense—£0.5 million on field drainage and farm buildings between 1847 and 1865—and the estate was in the van in trying out steam ploughing and town sewage irrigation. By the 1860s it had the reputation of being one of the best-run estates in the country, much visited by agricultural tourists. But it was in industrial affairs that Taylor excelled, and his most important services to the Percy fortunes were in the protection and promotion of the duke's colliery and wayleave interests in the manor of Tynemouth; he had a major role in securing the establishment of the Tyne commissioners and the building of the Northumberland Dock. He was himself a colliery owner at Earsdon in the manor of Tynemouth, where he purchased a farm in 1824 and built himself a house, paying both royalty and wayleave rents to the duke, but apparently feeling no conflict of interests. He was a respected authority on the coal trade, an important witness before the 1829 select committee of the House of Lords on the coal trade, and for many years chairman of the Coal Trade Association of Northumberland and Durham.

Hugh Taylor was much helped in colliery matters by his nephew, **Thomas John Taylor** (1810–1861), eldest of the four sons of John Taylor of Shilbottle, the mining engineer, and his wife, Margaret Darling of Ford, Northumberland. Thomas John was educated at Ponteland School and Edinburgh University, and he then trained as a colliery viewer and soon became manager of Haswell colliery, in which his uncle Hugh was a partner. In 1847 he was appointed colliery agent to the fourth duke of Northumberland, and with the professional support of John Buddle, the leading colliery viewer of the previous generation, he rose to eminence as a mining engineer and was one of the founders of the North of England Institute of Mining Engineers in 1852, and its first vice-president. He was one of the expert witnesses consulted by the select committee on the rating of mines in 1857. He devised a scheme for rescuing the sixteen to eighteen waterlogged collieries of the Tyne basin, on both banks of the river, which had been abandoned through flooding, leaving the seams below the High Main unwrought; however, the common drainage company which he suggested was only set up after his death. He investigated the behaviour of tidal rivers and estuaries, and in 1851 published a pamphlet on the improvement of the River Tyne, which enunciated the principles on which the improvement of several other tidal harbours was based. He was involved in the planning and construction of the Border Counties Railway, farther up the north Tyne from Hexham, which was intended originally to open out a small field of inferior coal at Plashetts but which became a pawn in high-level railway politics as a key section of the 'Waverley route' to Edinburgh avoiding use of both north British and North Eastern rails. In 1839 he married his first cousin Eliza Taylor, who died in 1840, presumably in giving birth to their only child, Eliza Anne. Thomas John Taylor died on 2 April 1861 while preparing for a meeting of Border Counties directors, at Bellingham, on the north Tyne. His youngest brother, John Taylor (1820–1879), of Earsdon, was also a leading mining engineer, specializing in the lead mines of Northumberland and Durham, while his second brother, Charles Taylor (1812–1856), of Sunderland, was also in the coal trade. The most successful of all the family, in worldly terms, was his third brother, another Hugh Taylor (1817–1900), coal owner and partner in several collieries in Durham as well as in Northumberland, MP for Tynemouth (1852–4 and 1859–61), who purchased Chipchase Castle and its estate, on the north Tyne, in 1862, from another coal owner, R. W. Grey, and there established a landed family.

Hugh Taylor senior purchased a second farm in Earsdon in 1852 to add to the one he had bought in 1824, and when the duke's business did not keep him in Alnwick Castle he lived in Earsdon and was much attached to the village. He never married, and on his death on 30 August 1868 at Earsdon he left £1600 to endow a charity—one third of the income to go to the aged poor of Earsdon, and the rest to the local voluntary school; his land went to his nephew John Taylor for life, and then to another nephew, Hugh Taylor, rector of Wark, Northumberland.

F. M. L. THOMPSON

Sources R. Welford, *Men of mark 'twixt Tyne and Tweed*, 3 (1895), 494–501 · Alnwick Castle, Northumberland, Alnwick MSS [especially 40 vols. of business minutes covering the period 1847–67] · F. M. L. Thompson, 'The economic and social background of the English landed interest, 1840–70', DPhil diss., U. Oxf., 1956 · *A history of Northumberland*, Northumberland County History Committee, 15 vols. (1893–1940), vol. 9, pp. 8–10, 22 · 'Select committee … on the state of the coal trade', *Parl. papers* (1830), 8.404, no. 9; (1836), 11.169, no. 522 · 'Select committee to inquire into … the rating of mines', *Parl. papers* (1856), vol. 16, no. 346; (1857), session 2, 11.533, no. 241 · T. J. Taylor, *Inquiry into the operations of running streams and tidal waters* (1851)

Archives Alnwick Castle, Northumberland, Alnwick MSS

Wealth at death under £90,000: resworn probate, Sept 1871, *CGPLA Eng. & Wales* (1868) · under £7000—Thomas John Taylor: administration, 10 Oct 1861, *CGPLA Eng. & Wales*

Taylor, Ida Alice Ashworth (1847–1929), biographer, was the eldest daughter and second child of the five children of Theodosia Alice Spring-Rice Taylor (1818–1891) and Sir Henry *Taylor (1800–1886). She was born at East Sheen, Surrey, and spent her childhood there and at the family's seaside villa at Bournemouth. Her father's dual career as poet and Colonial Office administrator brought his children into contact with many of the leading political and literary figures of the Victorian age. 'Politicians, philosophers, theologians, priests of many and divers churches and poets of the world' gathered at the Taylors' Bournemouth home, and included among Sir Henry's associates were Carlyle, Tennyson, J. S. Mill, Southey, and the poet Aubrey De Vere, who was a cousin of Mrs Taylor (V. A. Taylor, 19). While there is no record of Ida's formal education, the intellectual and cultured atmosphere that pervaded the Taylor home no doubt influenced her thinking and stimulated her interest in a literary career.

After their mother's death in 1891, Ida and her younger sister Una left the Taylor home and took a small house in Montpelier Square, London, where they conducted a popular literary salon. Neither sister married, and they apparently supported themselves primarily through their writing. Ida Ashworth Taylor was a prolific biographer, whose works reflect the expanding historicism and pervasive interest in the past which characterized the Victorian period. Taylor contributed historical pieces regularly to *Longman's Magazine*, *Nineteenth Century*, and *Temple Bar*, and her works were frequently reprinted in *Littell's Living Age*. Although she wrote several novels (*Venus' Doves*, 1884; *Allegiance*, 1886) and biographies of divers historical figures (*Revolutionary Types*, 1904; *The Making of a King*, 1910), Taylor is most strongly identified with her studies of prominent women. *Queen Hortense and her Friends* (1907), *Lady Jane Grey and her Times* (1908), and *The Life of Madame Roland* (1911) are

crammed with factual details, demonstrating a typical Victorian emphasis on historical accuracy and a strong dependence on the evidence of letters, journals, and diaries. Her works on women not only follow in the tradition of Agnes and Elizabeth Strickland's famous histories of female royalty, but reflect the growing movement, largely undertaken by women writers, to call attention to women's historical presence and contributions.

Taylor's works generally enjoyed both popular and critical favour and were often noted for their clear style and focused attention to narrative detail. But it appears that the Victorian fascination with 'great men' led to her omission from the canon of Victorian biographers. With the general trend to study past lives she fully complied; however, the female subjects that she examined in many of her works were deemed insignificant by some critics, and hence unworthy of study. Though acknowledging that Taylor's work on Queen Hortense was 'the best complete account of her in any language', the *American Historical Review* (1907–8) dismissed the queen as having 'slight importance' and deserving 'scant mention' in the history of the Napoleonic era. Commenting on *Christina of Sweden* (1909), another reviewer allowed that the biography was 'excellently written', but concluded that the book focused on a 'silly ass', whose life was scarcely worth mention (*New York Times*). The devaluation of scholarship concerning women's historical significance was not uncommon in Taylor's time, with the *American Historical Review* often relegating narrative histories of women to the 'Minor notices' section. In addition to such prejudice against her subject matter, the advancing specialization of biography writing in the late Victorian period served to undermine and eventually to edge out the 'amateur' biographers, such as Taylor, who also wrote other types of works and who generally stood outside academic and professional circles.

The last member of her family, Ida Ashworth Taylor died on 13 October 1929 at her home at Wootton Wood, New Milton, Hampshire. Her obituary in *The Times* stated that Taylor's biographies of women were 'most characteristic of the authoress', and that her work was marked by 'a sincere and womanly sympathy with its subject'. Such a characterization indicates the contemporary categorization of women writers and their works which led to Taylor's subsequent obscurity.

CHRISTINE PALUMBO-DE SIMONE

Sources *The Times* (22 Oct 1929) · U. Taylor, *Guests and memories: annals of a seaside villa* (1924) · [H. Taylor], *Autobiography of Henry Taylor*, 2 vols. (1885) · G. M. Dutcher, *American Historical Review*, 13 (1907–8), 137–8 [review] · *New York Times* (16 April 1910), 214 · B. Smith, 'The contributions of women to modern historiography in Great Britain, France, and the United States, 1750–1940', *American Historical Review*, 89 (1984), 709–32 · *CGPLA Eng. & Wales* (1930)

Wealth at death £12,553 16s.: probate, 4 Jan 1930, *CGPLA Eng. & Wales*

Taylor, Isaac (1730–1807), engraver, was born on 13 December 1730 in the parish of St Michael in Bedwardine, Worcester, the third of the seven known children of William Taylor (*fl.* 1710–1753), brass-founder, and his wife, Anne (*fl.* 1710–1740). In 1739 he was apprenticed to his father and he soon made a speciality of engraving book-plates and silverware. By the late 1740s his father's business interests included the production of engraved prints commemorating local events. At some point, perhaps in 1753, Taylor became a freeman of the city of Worcester, but the evidence for the date is confused. Early in 1752, after a quarrel with his father, he set off for London, walking 'by the side of the waggon' (C. Taylor, 593) and 'fired with the ambition of distinguishing himself as an artist' (I. Taylor, 'Jane Taylor', 81). Soon after his arrival in London he found work with Thomas Jefferys, the topographer and map engraver, and in due course was entrusted with the engraving of a number of plates for the *Gentleman's Magazine* and for *Owen's Dictionary*.

It was through this connection that Taylor met his future wife, Sarah Hackshaw Jefferys (1733–1809), the niece and housekeeper of Thomas Jefferys and the daughter of Josiah Jefferys (1709?–1770), a successful cutler, and his wife, Jane (*née* Hackshaw). They were married on 9 May 1754 at Shenfield, Essex, where Taylor's father-in-law had property. For a short time after his marriage Taylor practised unsuccessfully as a land surveyor at Shenfield, before returning to London to resume the profession of engraver. There were five children: Charles *Taylor (1756–1823); Isaac *Taylor (1759–1829); Josiah (1761–1834), a successful bookseller and publisher; Sarah (1763–1845), who married Daniel Hooper; and Ann (1765–1832), who married James Hinton (1761–1823) and was the mother of the Baptist minister John Howard Hinton (1791–1873). Isaac Taylor appears to have been more conscientious than loving as a father: he ensured that his sons were scrupulously well trained as engravers, but 'though a strictly moral man … he exhibited towards his family an austere reserve which was little calculated to awaken the domestic affections to genial life' (Gilbert, 1.5–6).

Isaac Taylor undoubtedly fulfilled his ambition to distinguish himself as an artist and in particular as an engraver. Before about 1750 superior examples of the engraver's art had been virtually a monopoly of French and other continental engravers, but during Taylor's working lifetime, and owing in part to his own achievements, that preeminence passed decisively to England, albeit with the help of immigrants such as Francesco Bartolozzi, of whom Isaac Taylor's sons possibly became pupils. Taylor did, as was common practice, produce full-scale engravings of other artists' paintings—his engraving for John Boydell, *A Flemish Collation* (1765), after Van Harp was an early example—and between 1765 and 1780 he exhibited them and other works regularly at the Incorporated Society of Artists, of which he was a director in 1772–3 and secretary from 1775 probably until his death.

However, Taylor's speciality was book illustration. In this field he almost always engraved to his own designs. After the death of Anthony Walker in 1765 he could lay claim to be the pre-eminent living illustrator. Among his finest works were the vignettes to the *Poetical Works* of John Langhorne (1766) and to Oliver Goldsmith's *Deserted Village* (1770) and the illustrations for Samuel Richardson's *Sir Charles Grandison* (1778). Towards the end of his active career Taylor also engraved a number of county maps. Plates engraved by him were said to wear better at the press than those of any other engraver of his time.

In 1770 Taylor bought the business, and premises at the Bible and Crown, Holborn, of the booksellers and publishers A. and Henry Webley, with whom he had worked as an engraver since 1767. Architectural works were already prominent in Webley's catalogues, and Taylor concentrated almost exclusively upon such publications. The business, which became known as the Architectural Library in 1787, later achieved, under Taylor's son Josiah, a virtual monopoly in this field. Taylor appears to have been a shrewd businessman and initially gave priority to the practical manuals required to support the building boom of the late eighteenth century, such as *The Practical Builder* (1774) by William Pain and *The Builder's Price Book* (1776). However, he also had an eye for emerging talent and was quick to secure the young John Soane for his list.

Engraving and publishing made Taylor's reputation and his fortune, but painting was perhaps nearer to his heart. He retired early when he was little more than fifty and moved from London to the village of Edmonton, Middlesex. There he amused himself by painting in oils.

Although Taylor's sons became prominent dissenters, there is no reason to suppose that Isaac Taylor was of that persuasion. According to his granddaughter Ann *Gilbert (1782–1866) [*see under* Taylor, Jane], he was, though 'a man of sense and ability', not 'under the influence of Christian principle' (Gilbert, 1.5). He was a supporter of John Wilkes and lost the astonishingly large sum of 'considerably more than £1000' (ibid., 1.184) as a result. He had many friends in the literary and artistic world, including Oliver Goldsmith, Francesco Bartolozzi, Robert Smirke, Henry Fuseli, and, probably, David Garrick. Thomas Bewick was his protégé and mentions him in his autobiography with affection and respect, despite the fact that Taylor had reacted ungraciously when the young Bewick decided to abandon a promising career in London.

Shortly after his marriage in 1754 Taylor painted a fine pair of portraits in oils of his wife and of himself, outdoor subjects in the manner of Gainsborough. Another surviving portrait, a pencil drawing of Taylor in late middle age, probably by his son Isaac, brings out the austere side of Taylor's nature. Isaac Taylor died at his home in Church Street, Edmonton, on 17 October 1807 and was buried on 24 October in the churchyard of the parish church of All Saints, Edmonton.

James Taylor (1737/8–1790), engraver, was a younger brother of Isaac Taylor. He was born in 1737 or 1738 and it is a reasonable supposition that he was born in Worcester. He worked for some years as a china painter in Worcester, before following his brother to London, where he practised engraving, first in association with his brother and then independently. He exhibited at the Society of Artists between 1770 and 1776. Anker Smith was one of his pupils. He died, according to an obituary by his nephew Charles in the *Literary Panorama* of 1808, on 21 December 1790, aged fifty-two.   ROBIN TAYLOR GILBERT

Sources [C. Taylor], 'A biographical memoir of the late Isaac Taylor, engraver, F.S.A. Sec etc', a part of 'Recollections of circumstances connected with the art of engraving, chiefly that part of it which is directed to the embellishment of books', *Literary Panorama*, 3 (1808), 588–94 and 4 (1808), 809–16 · *Autobiography and other memorials of Mrs Gilbert (formerly Ann Taylor)*, ed. J. Gilbert, 1 (1874) · I. Taylor, 'Memoirs and correspondence of Jane Taylor', *The family pen: memorials biographical and literary, of the Taylor family of Ongar*, ed. I. Taylor, 1 (1867) · minutes and rough minutes of the Incorporated Society of Artists of Great Britain, RA, SA/4, SA/8, SA/9/1 · exhibition catalogues of the Incorporated Society of Artists of Great Britain (1765–80) · I. Taylor, 'Memoir of the late Mr. Charles Taylor', *Calmet's dictionary of the Bible*, ed. C. Taylor, 6th edn (1837) · E. Harris and N. Savage, *British architectural books and writers, 1556–1785* (1990) · A. Macdonald, 'Two 18th century parliamentary elections in Worcester', *Transactions of the Worcestershire Archaeological Society*, new ser., 22 (1945), 55–68 · parish registers, St Michael in Bedwardine, Worcester, Worcs. RO · parish register, St Mary's, Shenfield, and All Saints, Edmonton, Suffolk RO, Bury St Edmunds, HD 588/1/51, HD 588/2/2 [transcripts in Suffolk RO] · freemen's book, 1753–4, 1780, Worcs. RO [incl. other records of the city of Worcester] · Bryan, *Painters* (1886–9) · *Worcester Journal*, 2074 (20 April 1749) · Suffolk RO, Bury St Edmunds, Taylor MSS, esp. HD 588/2/1–2 · T. Bewick, *A memoir of Thomas Bewick*, ed. I. Bain (1975/81) · A. Tuer, *Bartolozzi and his works* (1882) · S. C. Hutchinson, *The history of the Royal Academy, 1768–1986* (1986)
Archives Suffolk RO, Bury St Edmunds, papers and related material, HD 588/1, HD 588/2 | BM · RA, records of Incorporated Society of Artists of Great Britain, 1–45
Likenesses I. Taylor, self-portrait, oils, c.1755, Guildhall, Lavenham, Suffolk · I. Taylor, pencil drawing, c.1785, priv. coll.
Wealth at death possessed freehold lands: Suffolk RO, Bury St Edmunds, HD 588/1/36, HD 588/1/103

Taylor, Isaac (1759–1829), engraver and educationist, was born in London on 30 January 1759, the second son of Isaac *Taylor (1730–1807), engraver, and his wife, Sarah Hackshaw, née Jefferys (1733–1809). He spent his early years at Shenfield, Essex, and was first educated locally, probably at Sir Anthony Browne's School in Brentwood, before briefly attending a school in the City of London. Like his brother Charles *Taylor (1756–1823) he was apprenticed to his father as an engraver and may later have become a pupil of Francesco Bartolozzi.

One of Taylor's first commissions was to oversee the preparation of the plates for Abraham Rees's revised edition of the *Cyclopaedia* of Ephraim Chambers. This work and Taylor's many discussions with Rees were, by his own account, what first filled him with a thirst for knowledge. In 1777 and in 1780 he exhibited landscapes and drawings at the Incorporated Society of Artists, of which his father was secretary. From an early age Taylor became a committed member of the Fetter Lane Independent congregation in London and was prevented from seeking ordination as a young man only by severe illness. Throughout his life he rose early and spent the first hour of every day, and usually the last also, in prayer.

On 18 April 1781 Taylor married Ann Martin (1757–1830) [see Taylor, Ann]; three sons and three daughters of the marriage survived to adulthood. The couple first set up house in Islington. Taylor's capital was £30, supplemented by Ann's dowry from her grandfather of £100 and his own income of half a guinea a week for three days' work for his brother Charles, together with whatever he could earn for himself in the other three days.

Taylor used Ann's dowry to commission Robert Smirke to produce four circular paintings representing morning, noon, evening, and night, which he then engraved and sold. Between 1783 and 1787 he was engaged with his brothers and with several painters, including Smirke, in an enterprise to produce illustrations to Shakespeare's plays, *The Picturesque Beauties of Shakespeare* (1783–7). The success of this enterprise prefigured the later, larger project of John Boydell, in which Taylor was a leading participant (he received 500 guineas for an engraving of *Henry VIII's First Sight of Anne Boleyn*, 1802, after Thomas Stothard). It certainly drew Taylor to the attention of Boydell and won him the lucrative commission (250 guineas) to engrave *The Assassination of Rizzio* by John Opie; this work was awarded the gold palette of the Society of Arts for the best engraving of the year in 1790.

Taylor's success as an engraver lay in his great technical skill combined with a flair for design, qualities which he also demonstrated as a painter of portraits and landscapes. One of his finest achievements was *Specimens of Gothic Ornament* (1796), a series of engravings illustrating architectural details of the parish church of St Peter and St Paul in Lavenham, Suffolk. Later in his career he engraved the illustrations for Josiah Boydell's *Illustrations of Holy Writ* (1813–15), the designs for which were accounted the finest artistic work of his son Isaac *Taylor (1787–1865). Thereafter his published engraving was confined to illustrations of books by members of the family.

In 1783 the Taylors moved to Holborn but the annual rent of £20 was high and the environment injurious to the health of a growing family, almost all of whom were prone to illness. In 1786 Taylor made the decision to move to the country and, after characteristically diligent enquiry about prices and amenities, rented for £6 per annum a large house, Cooke's House, in Shilling Street, Lavenham, Suffolk. There his two eldest children, Ann and Jane, and his business, flourished.

Taylor's sketchbooks from his time in Lavenham contain many fine drawings and watercolour portraits of family members and of local acquaintances. The garden at Lavenham also provided the setting for his best-known portrait in oils (1792; NPG), that of his daughters Ann *Gilbert (1782–1866) [see under Taylor, Jane] and Jane *Taylor (1783–1824). In 1792, however, the Taylors' landlord gave them notice to quit and Taylor bought, for £250, the house next door, which was then in a ruinous condition. Its renovation (interrupted by Taylor's contracting typhoid, which nearly killed him) cost a further £250, but his careful and imaginative planning transformed house and garden from dereliction to delight.

Taylor had become a deacon of the Independent congregation in Lavenham and was closely involved in the founding of a Sunday school there. In 1794 he might have become minister, had the congregation not shrunk from the appointment of one of its own number. In late 1795 Taylor, who was gaining a reputation as a preacher, was invited to become minister of the Bucklersbury Lane Independent congregation in Colchester. In January 1796, having accepted the call, Taylor and his family moved to Colchester, where they rented a house in Angel Lane (now West Stockwell Street). On 21 April 1796 Isaac Taylor was ordained.

The move to Colchester coincided with a period of high inflation and the collapse of the art market in the wake of the war with France. Taylor suffered 'a grievous reverse of fortune' (*Autobiography*, ed. Gilbert, 1.100) and was reduced to engraving dog collars. Taylor wanted his daughters to be able to earn their own living; as soon as they were old enough all the children were employed to assist in the engraving business. The boys, Isaac (1787–1865), Martin (1788–1867), and Jefferys *Taylor (1792–1853), were formally apprenticed, but his daughters, who were both to become published writers, were tolerated, rather than encouraged, in their literary vocation.

In Lavenham, Taylor's successive workrooms had doubled as schoolrooms for his own children and later for those of neighbours too, Taylor giving instruction from his engraving stool as he worked. This practice continued in Colchester, providing a welcome supplementary source of income. Taylor's object was 'to give them a taste for every branch of knowledge that [could] well be made the subject of early instruction' (*Family Pen*, 126) and he believed that 'a principal object of education [is] to prevent the formation of a narrow and exclusive taste for particular pursuits, by exciting very early a lively interest in subjects of every kind' (ibid., 113). His teaching methods were original and he made much use of carefully drawn visual aids, in the preparation of which his older children assisted. In late 1798 he began a series of monthly lectures for young people, delivered free of charge in the parlour of his own house; these proved extremely popular and the programme continued for several years.

Later in life Taylor wrote, and illustrated with engravings, a large number of very successful educational books, including the *Scenes* series ('for the Amusement and Instruction of Little Tarry-at-Home Travellers'), and two volumes, *The Mine* (1829) and *The Ship* (1830), for the popular Little Library series published by John Harris. He also produced a number of books for the young, of a religious and improving nature, including *The Child's Birthday* (1811), possibly originally written for his youngest child, Jemima (1798–1886), *Advice to the Teens* (1818)—the first recorded use of the word to denote young people—and *Bunyan Explained to a Child* (2 vols., 1824–5). The preface to this last book is revealing of Taylor's approach to education and to religion, warning parents against expecting their children to read 'all the many hours a wet Sabbath presents', lest they 'make that day hated, which ought to be loved' (p. iv).

In June 1810 Taylor, exasperated by the apparently ineradicable antinomian tendencies of many in his congregation, announced his resignation from his pastorate in Colchester. A year later he accepted a call from the congregation at Ongar, where he remained for the rest of his life, rejuvenating and expanding the congregation, stimulating the intellectual life of the small town, and earning the respect even of the Anglican clergy. He instituted weekly lectures and prayer meetings, restarted the Sunday school, and played a leading part in a thriving book society—the while continuing to exercise his profession as an engraver and producing more than twenty books. He rented, first, Castle House and then New House Farm, just outside the town, and finally, in 1822, he bought a house at what is now 10 Castle Street.

Taylor, who had a stocky frame and an appearance usually of rude health, was described as 'a genial portly figure … his cheek ruddy with apple tints' (*Autobiography*, ed. Gilbert, 2.94). However, his life was punctuated by serious illnesses, including a three-year period in his late fifties, during which he almost succumbed to successive bouts of rheumatic fever. For almost a decade thereafter he maintained a pace of life that eventually proved too much for his constitution. On 12 December 1829, after a short illness, he died at his home. He was buried on the 19th in the Independent chapel's burial-ground; his grave now lies under the vestry floor of the United Reformed church, beside those of his wife and of his daughter Jane.

ROBIN TAYLOR GILBERT

Sources *Autobiography and other memorials of Mrs Gilbert (formerly Ann Taylor)*, ed. J. Gilbert, 2 vols. (1874) · I. Taylor, *The family pen: memorials, biographical and literary, of the Taylor family of Ongar*, 1 (1867) · 'Memoir of the late Rev. Isaac Taylor of Chipping Ongar, Essex', *Congregational Magazine* (March 1832), 129–35 · C. D. Stewart, *The Taylors of Ongar: an analytical bio-bibliography*, 2 vols. (1975) · R. Gilbert, 'The Taylors of Ongar and their houses there', *Aspects of the history of Ongar*, ed. M. Leach (1999), 50–103 · records of the United Reformed Church, Ongar · *Ann Taylor Gilbert's album*, ed. C. D. Stewart (1978) · I. Taylor, notes on family history, Suffolk RO, Taylor papers, HD 588/4/14 [copied by Euphemia Taylor, 1913] · I. Taylor, genealogical notes, Suffolk RO, Taylor papers, HD 588/1/147 [copied by Euphemia Taylor] · I. Taylor, 'Memoir of the late Mr. Charles Taylor', *Calmet's dictionary of the Bible*, ed. C. Taylor, 6th edn (1837) · A. Tuer, *Bartolozzi and his works*, 2nd edn, 2 (1885) · private information (2004) · I. Taylor, *Bunyan explained to a child*, 2 vols. (1824–5) · will, PRO, PROB 11/1764 · I. Taylor, 'Minutes of the affairs of the Church of Christ at Ongar whilst under my cognisance', priv. coll. [in possession of R. T. Gilbert]
Archives Guildhall, Lavenham, Suffolk, MSS · Suffolk RO, Bury St Edmunds, papers and related works | Colchester Museum Resource Centre, Gertrude Taylor collection
Likenesses I. Taylor, miniature, 1799, Colchester Museum Resource Centre · J. Andrews, stipple, pubd 1832, NPG; copy, Suffolk RO, Bury St Edmunds · J. Gilbert, chalk drawing, 1862, NPG · T. Blood, stipple (after I. Taylor), BM, NPG; repro. in *Evangelical Magazine* (June 1818) · attrib. I. Taylor, miniature, oils, priv. coll. · attrib. I. Taylor, oils (late middle age) · attrib. I. Taylor, silhouette, black-washed paper on white mount, Suffolk RO, Bury St Edmunds · I. Taylor, watercolour miniature (aged about forty), Guildhall, Lavenham, Suffolk · photograph (of I. Taylor, oils), Suffolk RO, Bury St Edmunds, Taylor collection · wood-engraving, NPG; repro. in *ILN* (1865)
Wealth at death comfortably off

Taylor, Isaac [*known as* Isaac Taylor of Stanford Rivers] (1787–1865), writer on theology, artist, and inventor, was born at Lavenham, Suffolk, on 17 August 1787. He was the fourth child and eldest surviving son of Isaac *Taylor of

Ongar (1759–1829), artist, engraver, and dissenting minister, and his wife, Ann Martin (1757–1830) [see Taylor, Ann], author of several advice and conduct books. The family moved to Colchester in 1796 when the senior Taylor was called as pastor of an independent congregation; in 1810 they moved to another Essex pastorate in Ongar.

The three sons and three daughters of the Taylor family were educated together at home. All were taught drawing and engraving by their father; both parents shared in directing reading, discussions, and religious instruction. While living in Colchester, Isaac and his brother Martin went to a neighbour for some instruction and attended lectures by visiting speakers. All the children were encouraged to write and to make drawings and engravings, first for the family circle and then for publication. By the turn of the century the elder daughters, Ann and Jane [see Taylor, Jane], were beginning to publish verses and stories for children in periodicals and in book form. These works were illustrated by various family members including Isaac; most probably the entire family also contributed to the stories. After the move to Ongar, Isaac the younger executed engraving and drawing commissions and worked with his father on several projects. In 1810 he joined Martin in London, where they worked as engravers for a publishing house in Paternoster Row.

London air did not agree with Isaac; by 1812 he had developed a pulmonary or bronchial complaint which responded favourably to the milder climate of the west of England. He spent the next three or four winters at Ilfracombe, Devon, and Marazion, Cornwall. His sister Jane was his primary companion during this period; they became close friends and confidants. Isaac encouraged Jane in her writing, and she listened to his ideas and plans. In the summers they returned to Essex and made visits to London. Taylor's time was spent in reading, writing, and discussions with friends made in the west. It was probably during this period that he became attracted to the Church of England, although he may not have become a member until after Jane's death. Taylor also began his lifelong interest in the early church and patristic studies in this period. He is said to have coined the word patristic.

In 1818 Josiah Conder, editor of the *Eclectic Review*, invited Taylor to join his staff as a regular contributor. Conder was a family friend who had been publishing the work of Ann Taylor Gilbert and Jane Taylor for several years. While continuing his study of the writers of the early church Taylor also became interested in the philosophy of Francis Bacon. His first independently published work, *Elements of Thought* (1822), was an introduction to the study of moral philosophy for young people. His second work, a new translation of the *Characters of Theophrastus* (1824), appeared pseudonymously under the name Francis Howell. The first edition included the Greek text and illustrations by Taylor. He continued to live at Ongar, making visits when necessary to London. The death of Jane in 1824 precipitated several changes in her brother's life.

Taylor was his sister's literary executor. In 1825 he published *Memoirs and Poetical Remains of the Late Jane Taylor*. A revised memoir, correspondence, and other family sketches were published by Isaac's son, also Isaac Taylor, as *The Family Pen: Memorials, Biographical and Literary, of the Taylor Family of Ongar* (2 vols., 1867). Taylor moved to Stanford Rivers, about 2 miles from Ongar, in 1825. According to his son, the 'rambling old-fashioned farmhouse, standing in a large garden', provided seclusion and space for the 'literary labours' and 'silent meditations' of a 'literary recluse' (Taylor, 1.65). On 17 August 1825 he married Elizabeth (1804–1861), second daughter of James Medland of Newington; she had been a friend and correspondent of Jane Taylor. For the remainder of his life Taylor lived at Stanford Rivers with his wife and large family. Six daughters (Jane, Phoebe, Rose, Catherine, Jessie, Euphemia) and three sons (Isaac, James Medland, Henry) survived their father; two daughters predeceased their parents. The children were educated at home: in *Home Education* (1838) his method and plan for training children from infancy to the late teens were outlined. He encouraged flexibility and attention to the varying talents and abilities of children. He was opposed to schools for girls and compulsory public education.

Although Taylor always maintained that because he was a layman he was not a theologian, most of his publications were concerned with Christianity, its doctrines and history, and the various manifestations of church organization and teachings. He argued in favour of the historical validity of the Bible in *History of the Transmission of Ancient Books to Modern Times* (1827) and *The Process of Historical Proof* (1828), urging that the same methods be applied to scripture as to pagan Greek histories. His interest in textual studies of the classics and the Bible continued throughout his life. In 1829 Taylor published his abridged translation of Herodotus; he edited a new translation of *The Jewish Wars of Flavius Josephus* (2 vols., 1849–51). At the end of his life *The Spirit of Hebrew Poetry* (1861) and *Considerations on the Pentateuch* (1863) reflected this aspect of his studies. He was not, however, trained in modern critical methods, so that his arguments in the end rested primarily on moral grounds. The Bible must be true because it was pure, beautiful, and morally right.

The work which made Taylor's reputation was *The Natural History of Enthusiasm* (1829). Responding to the social, political, and religious ferment of his own day, he set out the dangers inherent in all sorts of excessive enthusiasm. His path was the Anglican middle way; the belief that the study of scripture and moderation would mean the victory of protestant Christianity. Many of his later works continued this theme. *Fanaticism* (1833), *Spiritual Despotism* (1835), and *Four Lectures on Spiritual Christianity* (1841) all stressed the need to return to scripture and the advantages of Anglican polity. Two studies of religious leaders, *Loyola* (1849) and *Wesley and Methodism* (1851), continued Taylor's arguments that the best kind of religious establishment was to be found in the Anglican model.

The Oxford Movement's use of the early church to support its proposals for reforming the Church of England took Taylor back to his patristic studies. His vehement and lengthy attack on the Tractarians, *Ancient Christianity, and the Doctrines of the Oxford 'Tracts for the Times'* (2 vols., 1839–

40) attempted to prove that Puseyite doctrine was already permeated with all the errors and superstitions of the middle ages. His views were attacked or praised according to the convictions of the reader.

By the mid-1830s Taylor's works were highly regarded by many serious students of theology and philosophy. In 1836 he was urged to stand for election to the chair of logic at the University of Edinburgh. This seems to have been the only time he was tempted to leave his retreat at Stanford Rivers. He allowed his name to be put forward, but he was narrowly defeated by Sir William Hamilton. According to his son he was asked to stand for other Scottish chairs, but he never again considered such a post.

Taylor seldom left Stanford Rivers except to give lectures or to make an occasional visit to a family member. As a change from reading and writing he took long solitary walks and worked in his shop. In 1824 he patented a widely used beer tap. He also developed a machine for engraving on copper, patented in 1848. Although he lost considerable sums on this invention, it was ultimately adapted for engraving patterns on copper cylinders used in printing calicos. In 1862 he received a civil-list pension of £200 a year. He died at Stanford Rivers on 28 June 1865 and was buried in the churchyard there.

A liberal Anglican of an old-fashioned type, Taylor's ideas about religion, education, and society were grounded in the eighteenth century and showed little awareness of the changes taking place in his own day. None the less his works were popular in both Britain and the United States; his straightforward style and lack of sectarianism commended him to many protestants. But advances in scholarship, science, and economics made many of his views seem irrelevant and outdated by the latter part of the nineteenth century. His rural seclusion allowed him to cultivate 'the breadth and catholicity of his religious feelings, and the calm judicial tone of his literary temper' (Taylor, 1.76), but it also sheltered him from many contemporary realities. He was, however, the most prolific and best-known member of a remarkable family.

BARBARA BRANDON SCHNORRENBERG

Sources DNB · I. Taylor, ed., The family pen: memorials biographical and literary, of the Taylor family of Ongar, 2 vols. (1867) · Autobiography and other memorials of Mrs Gilbert (formerly Ann Taylor), ed. J. Gilbert, 3rd edn (1878) · C. D. Stewart, The Taylors of Ongar: an analytical bio-bibliography, 2 vols. (1975) · D. M. Armitage, The Taylors of Ongar (1939) · B. Hilton, The age of atonement: the influence of evangelicalism on social and economic thought, 1795–1865 (1988)
Archives Suffolk RO, Bury St Edmunds, papers and related material | NL Scot., letters to Alexander Campbell Fraser
Likenesses J. Gilbert, drawing, 1865, NPG · print, 1865, NPG

Taylor, Isaac (1829–1901), philologist and historian of writing, was born on 2 May 1829 at Stanford Rivers, Essex, the eldest son and second child in the family of eight daughters and three sons of Isaac *Taylor (1787–1865), author and engraver, and his wife, Elizabeth (1804–1861), daughter of James Medland of Newington. His grandfather Isaac *Taylor (1759–1829) and great-grandfather Isaac *Taylor (1730–1807) were both engravers and writers. His aunts Ann *Gilbert (1782–1866) [see under Taylor, Jane] and Jane

*Taylor (1783–1824) and his uncle Jefferys *Taylor (1792–1853) were also authors. Taylor, who assisted his father in his writing from an early age, himself wrote a lively picture of this talented family entitled The Family Pen (1867), more an account of shared literary enterprise than genealogical memoir.

Taylor was educated at private schools, and was from 1847 to 1849 at King's College, London. In 1849 he was admitted to Trinity College, Cambridge, where he carried off many college prizes, including the silver oration cup. He graduated BA in 1853 as nineteenth wrangler, and in the following year he published Charicles: Illustrations of the Private Life of the Ancient Greeks, a translation of W. A. Becker's version of Charicles with additional notes and excursuses of his own. On leaving Cambridge he went as a master to Cheam School until 1857, when he proceeded MA and was ordained to the curacy of Trottiscliffe, Kent. It was there that he wrote his pamphlet The Liturgy and the Dissenters (1860), which aroused controversy by advocating a revision of the prayer book 'as an act of justice to the Dissenters'. He was curate of St Mary Abbots, Church Street, Kensington, London, in 1860–61, and of St Mark's, North Audley Street, from 1861 to 1865, when he became vicar of St Matthew's Bethnal Green. The same year saw the death of his father and, on 31 July, his marriage to Georgiana Anne (1825–1907), youngest daughter of the Reverend and Honourable Henry Cockayne Cust, canon of Windsor.

Taylor's new parish had a population of 7000, drawn from the poorest class, and the difficulties of ministering to it without funds or helpers were intensified by the outbreak of cholera in 1866. After a year he estimated that his own annual expenses were about £350, of which the great bulk was in salaries for those engaged in poor relief. In December 1866, at Highgate, Taylor preached a sermon on behalf of east London charities. It was published, at the expense of one who heard it, as The Burden of the Poor (1867), and made a deep impression on the public. Taylor's vivid account of the Spitalfields silk weavers (some of whom he hoped to encourage to emigrate to the weaving districts of the north) and the child workers in and about his parish brought him subscriptions of over £4000. But the strain of administration and an attack of typhoid fever finally compelled his retirement. In 1869 he was nominated vicar of Holy Trinity, Twickenham, and in 1875 he was presented by Earl Brownlow (his wife's cousin) to the living of Settrington, Yorkshire, which he held until his death. In 1885 he was made canon of York and prebendary of Kirk Fenton.

Before going to Bethnal Green, Taylor had developed an interest in the etymological study of place names, resulting in his Words and Places (1864). This successful work was an early application of the nascent science of comparative philology exclusively to toponyms. Later, a winter in Italy led him to join the growing numbers engaged in interpreting the Etruscan language. His Etruscan Researches (1874) argued that it was not an Indo-European tongue but a member of the same family as the Altaic and Finno-Ugrian languages, which (like other scholars of his day) he believed to be related. Although some passages in this book relied on the reputed physical characteristics of different language groups, in 1889 he published *The Origin of the Aryans*, in which he attacked Max Müller's theory of a central Asian cradle for the Aryans and argued that kinship of race cannot be postulated from kinship of speech.

Taylor's most impressive scholarship, however, was in the history of writing, sometimes known as grammatology. After *Greeks and Goths* (1879), arguing that the runic alphabet was derived from the Greek one, and a paper on Glagolitic printed in German in 1881, he moved on to a wider plane, and in 1883 published *The Alphabet* (2 vols., 2nd edn, 1899), which in a more recent history of the subject was adjudged the 'first book on writing from a scientific perspective' (P. T. Daniels and W. Bright, *The World's Writing Systems*, 1996, 6). It is especially strong on Indian scripts, containing certain factual material that does not appear to survive elsewhere. It is also the earliest work to classify writing systems as logographic, syllabic, or alphabetic, introducing thereby a tripartite distinction that has since dominated the subject. Less successfully, he sought to apply a principle of selection, which he called the law of least effort, to the evolution of written symbols.

Taylor was prominent in the Domesday celebration of 1886, and contributed three essays to the memorial volume (1888). One of these, 'The ploughland and the plough', proposed a theory regarding the geldable carucate of Domesday Book which was described by Horace Round as 'probably the most notable contribution to our knowledge that the Domesday Commemoration produced' (*Feudal England*, 1895, 87–8). Notes for a revised and enlarged version of *Words and Places*, which his health disabled him from completing, appeared as a dictionary of place names entitled *Names and their Histories* (1896; 2nd edn, 1897, with a supplementary essay on village names in England). He wrote many articles for *Chambers's Encyclopaedia* and often contributed to *The Academy*, *The Athenaeum*, and *Notes and Queries*. In 1879 the University of Edinburgh conferred on him the honorary degree of LLD, and in 1885 he was made doctor of letters by his own University of Cambridge.

Taylor's scholarly activities did not distract him from religious debate. He was a member of the Curates' Clerical Club (CCC), and counted F. D. Maurice, A. P. Stanley, F. W. Farrar, Stopford Brooke (a fellow curate at Kensington), Hugh Haweis, and J. R. Green among his friends in London. His paper on Islam at the 1887 Wolverhampton Church Congress, pleading for a more tolerant comprehension of what he called 'the second greatest religion in history', was greeted with some indignation in the press, while his more developed views in *Leaves from an Egyptian Note-Book* (1888) and his stringent criticisms of the methods of missionary societies in the *Fortnightly Review* (November and December 1888) compounded the fault in his critics' eyes. His less controversial pursuits included the practice of photography and the study of botany, entomology, geology, and archaeology. He was an original

member of the Alpine Club, joining in 1858 and retiring in 1891.

Taylor died on 18 October 1901 at Settrington, and was buried there. His only child, Elizabeth Eleanor, married in 1903 Ernest Davies, son of the vicar of Chelsea Old Church.   [Anon.], *rev.* C. E. A. Cheesman

Sources *The Times* (19 Oct 1901), p. 6, col. A; (19 Jan 1903) [E. E. Taylor]; (15 March 1907) [G. A. Cust] • *The Biograph and Review* (April 1881) • *Athenaeum and Literature* (Dec 1901) • *York Diocesan Magazine* (Dec 1901) • Venn, *Alum. Cant.* • census returns, 1881
Archives Suffolk RO, Bury St Edmunds, corresp., papers, and related material | NL Scot., letters to Alexander Campbell Fraser
Likenesses photograph, NPG
Wealth at death £13,497 12s. 8d.: resworn probate, June 1902, *CGPLA Eng. & Wales* (1901)

Taylor, James (1737/8–1790). *See under* Taylor, Isaac (1730–1807).

Taylor, James (1753–1825), naval engineer and potter, was born on 3 May 1753 at Leadhills, Lanarkshire, the son of John Taylor, the overseer of the earl of Hopetoun's mines there. He was educated at Wallacehall School, Closeburn, Dumfriesshire, and then at Edinburgh University where he was a student from 1775 to 1781, studying medicine, mathematics, and natural philosophy. Sponsored by Hopetoun, he was destined for the ministry or medicine, but while in Edinburgh he became interested in a career 'where his love of chemistry, mechanics, and mineralogy could be put to good use' (*Ayr Advertiser*, 22 Sept 1825). After he left Edinburgh he seems to have set up a foundry and engineering works in Ayr in partnership with his brother John. Through his friendship with Alexander Fegusson of Craigendarroch, also in Dumfriesshire, Taylor was appointed tutor in 1785 to the children of Patrick Miller, who had newly acquired the Dalswinton estate. At the time Miller was devoting much of his time to experiments with the mechanical propulsion of ships on the Forth and almost certainly recruited Taylor to assist him as well as to teach his children. Taylor quickly suggested that the obvious solution was to replace hand-turned windlasses with a James Watt steam engine modified to drive paddle wheels. Through his father he introduced Miller to the engineer William Symington, and this led to the famous trials of a steamboat at Dalswinton in 1788 and on the Forth in 1789.

By this time Taylor had come to the notice of Margaret, countess of Dumfries, who was full of misplaced enthusiasm for introducing industrial practices to the family's Ayrshire estates, leaving behind a trail of half-completed projects and disappointed artisans. The countess, convinced that coal mining and iron-working were the road to wealth, commissioned Taylor in 1790 to carry out a mineral survey of the estate. In the following year the earl appointed him manager 'of the lime works, coal works, black lead or wadd works, ironstone, clays, leads and whole works or operations regarding every kind that are discovered or should be thereafter discovered' (Quail, 9). This was an ambitious prospectus which was never to be realized. Taylor's first project was to reopen the flooded black lead Craigman mine. When it was found that the quality was not good enough for pencils the countess turned her attention to making foundry crucibles and then to establishing a pottery. Her imagination quickly ran away with her and she conceived a sizeable venture with no consideration of whether her china would survive a journey across the bumpy roads of Ayrshire. It was James Taylor's misfortune to be given the task of supervising the establishment of the pottery at Cumnock, the nearest village to Dumfries House, in 1794. Nothing went well; the Glasgow potters, who were responsible for the day-to-day management, left within two years without producing a pot and debts mounted. In order to avoid bankruptcy Taylor, who was a partner in the business, had no alternative but to begin production. For almost twenty years he struggled to keep it going, making an attractive domestic creamware from local clays along with crucibles. In some years the pottery remained closed due to lack of demand, adding to Taylor's difficulties. Although Taylor managed the earl's coal mines efficiently the price of coal was depressed and local competition intense. He resigned in 1815, but continued to operate the pottery with rising debts which could be largely attributed to the terms of his lease.

In 1822 Taylor looked for some relief from the campaign to reward those who had been involved with the development of the steamboat. At first he took issue with the now dissolute William Symington about his role in this, and then after a meeting they came, as he thought, to an understanding. Early in 1823 he took out a patent (no. 4751) for the construction of ships' bottoms and the positioning of pumps to prevent damage to the cargo, and declared that he was engaged in other important developments. At the end of his tether, he petitioned parliament for a pension in April 1824. He died at Cumnock on 18 September 1825 before a decision was reached. Soon after his death Symington and his supporters attacked the accuracy of Taylor's claim to have contributed to the development of the steamboat and dismissed him simply as a schoolteacher. After a long struggle against the continuing attacks from Symington (himself desperate for money), Taylor's widow was granted a pension of £50 p.a. and his surviving daughters were awarded a bounty of £50 apiece. Taylor was included in the *Dictionary of National Biography* along with all those who had been associated with the beginnings of steam propulsion; but in reality he deserved inclusion as a representative of all those men and women who nurtured small enterprise often at considerable cost to themselves during the first phase of industrialization and by so doing laid the foundation of Britain's later prosperity.   MICHAEL S. MOSS

Sources matriculation records, U. Edin. L., special collections division, university archives · Mount Stuart Trust, Isle of Bute, Bute MSS · Hopetoun House, Linlithgow MSS · G. Quail, *The Cumnock pottery* (1993) · J. Rankine and W. H. Rankine, *Biography of William Symington, civil engineer: inventor of steam navigation by sea and land* (1862)
Archives Mitchell L., Glas., Glasgow City Archives, 'Narrative of steam boats', account of his experiments in steam navigation ·

U. Edin., papers | Hopetoun House, Linlithgow MSS · Mount Stuart, Bute MSS
Likenesses W. Tassie, paste medallion, 1801, Scot. NPG

Taylor, James (1788–1863). *See under* Taylor, John (1781–1864).

Taylor, James (1813–1892), minister of the United Presbyterian church, civil servant, and historian, was born in Greenlaw, Berwickshire, on 18 March 1813, the son of Alexander Taylor, farmer, and his wife Violet, *née* Pringle. From the parochial school of his native district he passed to the University of Edinburgh, and afterwards to the Divinity Hall of the United Secession church with a view to ordination. On 29 May 1839 he was ordained minister of the United Secession church in St Andrews. He graduated MA at Edinburgh University on 20 April 1843. His marriage to Mary Munro brought them at least two sons and a daughter, born between 1840 and 1845.

On 26 February 1846 Taylor was translated to Regent Place Church, Glasgow, and on 11 July 1848, with the greater portion of the members, he left for the new church erected in Renfield Street, Glasgow, where he ministered until 1872. From 1872 until 1885 he was secretary to the new education board for Scotland set up by the Liberal government in that year (the United Presbyterian church had been active in safeguarding its interests during the passing of the bill). Taylor oversaw the establishment of a national system of school boards for all except Episcopalians and Roman Catholics, a smoother and more comprehensive system than its English equivalent.

The rest of Taylor's days were spent in Edinburgh in literary work. Besides numerous articles in the *Encyclopaedia Britannica, Imperial Dictionary of Biography, United Presbyterian Magazine*, and individual sermons and pamphlets, Taylor published several works on Scotland, including *The Pictorial History of Scotland* (2 vols., 1852–9; enlarged edn, 6 vols., 1884–8), *The Scottish Covenanters* (1881), *Curling, the Ancient Scottish Game* (1884), *The Great Historic Families of Scotland* (2 vols., 1887), and *Lord Jeffrey and Craigcrook Castle* (1892). He also enlarged and continued Tytler's *History of Scotland* (1845, 1851, 1863), abridged Kitto's *Cyclopaedia of Biblical Literature* (1849), and edited *The Family History of England* (6 vols., 1870–5). His *The Victorian Empire* (3 vols., 1897–8) was published posthumously.

Taylor received the degrees of DD from St Andrews University in 1849 and of LLD from Edinburgh University in 1892. He was an effective preacher, a forcible debater, and a clear and accurate historian. Lord Beaconsfield, in his humorous mention in *Lothair* of the United Presbyterian church of Scotland as being founded in recent times by two Jesuits, made sarcastic reference to Taylor as one who had a wide knowledge of the statesmen and statecraft of his time and who urged his views on members of parliament and other leaders in church and state with unflagging pertinacity. Taylor died of heart disease at St John's, Corstorphine, Edinburgh, on 16 March 1892.

      T. B. JOHNSTONE, *rev.* H. C. G. MATTHEW

Sources personal knowledge (1898) · Boase, *Mod. Eng. biog.* · R. D. Anderson, *Education and opportunity in Victorian Scotland: schools and universities* (1983) · *CCI* (1892) · d. cert.

Taylor, Sir James (1902–1994), mathematician and physicist, was born at 11 Brunton Terrace, Sunderland, on 16 August 1902, the son of James Taylor, a stonemason, and his wife, Alice, *née* Hunter. Left an orphan at an early age he benefited from a cosmopolitan education, attending Bede College, Sunderland, Rutherford College, Newcastle upon Tyne (part of Durham University), and Cambridge, from where he graduated in 1923 with a first-class degree in physics followed by a PhD in 1925. In 1927 he gained a doctorate in physics and maths at Utrecht, followed in 1931 by a DSc at Durham. At the Cavendish laboratories, Cambridge, under J. J. Thomson and Lord Rutherford, and later at the University of Paris (the Sorbonne), he acquired a taste for research which was developed further when in 1928 he joined the Nobel division of ICI in Aberdeen. On 16 November 1929 he married Margaret Lennox Stewart (1904/5–1990); they had two sons and a daughter.

During the 1930s Taylor became a leading authority on explosives. With the outbreak of war he joined the Royal Naval Volunteer Reserve and was posted to the Admiralty where, under Sir Charles Dennistoun Burney, he worked on the development of rockets and airborne torpedoes for the navy. At the end of the war he was appointed MBE, resuming his work at the Nobel division as research director. He became joint managing director in 1951 and joined ICI's main executive board in the following year, a position he retained until 1964. Between 1958 and 1964 he was responsible for decentralizing ICI metal interests and establishing three separate but co-ordinated subsidiary companies of which he was the chairman: Imperial Aluminium Company, Yorkshire Imperial Metals, and the Imperial Metal Industry Company. In 1959 Taylor's experience of explosives led to his appointment as the deputy chairman of the Royal Ordnance factories board, a position he retained until 1972. Between 1961 and 1964 he was also a member of the board of Nuclear Developments Ltd.

In 1962 Taylor joined the Royal Society of Arts (RSA) after presenting a series of three Cantor lectures, 'The modern chemical industry in Great Britain'. Two years later he was elected a member of the RSA council, becoming its chairman in 1969–71. During this period he contributed six major lectures which ranged from 'Arts, crafts, and technology' to 'The seventies and society'. They reflected his industrial and commercial experience together with his deep interest in the arts.

Taylor relinquished his close association with executive management in 1965 to become a member of the Ministry of Defence advisory committee on scientific research, and in the following year he joined the Advisory Council on Calibration and Measurement. In 1974 he was appointed chairman of Chloride Silent Power, which had the remit of developing a new form of battery for electric cars and vans. A prolific writer, he contributed to the *Proceedings of the Royal Society*, the *Philosophical Magazine*, the *Transactions of the Institution of Mining Engineers*, the *British Association for the Advancement of Science Reports*, and *ICI Magazine*.

Throughout his working life, which encompassed the period 1928 to 1985, Taylor's activities covered a wide variety of areas. He became a leading authority on explosives, mining techniques, metallurgical developments, and the nuclear industries. He made significant contributions in a variety of spheres ranging from explosives and rocket projectiles to improved metals for industry, nuclear research, electric propulsion, and the chemical industry. In all these activities he remained a leading exponent of the need for closer co-operation between the science and the arts. In addition to his appointment as MBE for his wartime work he was awarded a knighthood in 1966 for his services to the Royal Ordnance. He was also an honorary member of the Institution of Mining Engineers and was awarded the silver medal of the Chemical Society.

Taylor's hallmark characteristics were a sober enthusiasm and an agile mind. As a young man he had been a skilled rock climber, and in later years his interests turned to cooking and gardening. He was widely regarded as an energetic, approachable, and stimulating person who gave his time generously to many causes. Following his formal retirement he became a director of the Surrey Independent Hospital near his home at Seale. He and his wife celebrated their diamond wedding in 1989 shortly before Lady Taylor's death in the following year. He died of heart disease on 4 October 1994 at his home, Culvers, Littleworth Road, Seale, Farnham, Surrey.

JOHN MARTIN

Sources *The Times* (7 Nov 1994) · WWW · *Daily Telegraph* (26 Oct 1994) · b. cert. · m. cert. · d. cert. · CGPLA Eng. & Wales (1995)
Archives FILM BFI NFTVA | SOUND BL NSA
Likenesses photograph, repro. in *The Times*, 21A
Wealth at death £1,307,923: probate, 12 Jan 1995, CGPLA Eng. & Wales

Taylor, James Frater (1873–1960), business manager, was born on 23 March 1873 at South College Street, Aberdeen, one of the six children of Alexander Taylor (d. 1887), a ship's mate, and his wife, Mary Lowe, *née* Frater. He attended Aberdeen grammar school (1886–8) and by 1891 was an apprentice clerk in Aberdeen. In 1897 he married Frances Alice, the daughter of Joseph Hill of West Hartlepool; they had one son and two daughters.

In 1891 Taylor went out to India as assistant general manager of Madras Electric Tramways, a British company in difficulties. He returned home later that year, and then worked for Samuel Allsopp & Sons Ltd, the brewing giants of Burton upon Trent, also in acute difficulties. Taylor rapidly rose through its ranks; by 1907 he was general manager and director, but in December 1908 he resigned. He was then recruited by a fellow Scot, Robert Fleming, to represent his interest in the Lake Superior Corporation of Canada, owners, *inter alia*, of Algoma Steel. Taylor, who became Algoma's president, reconstructed the company and made it a sector leader. In 1918 he moved on to manage businesses in which the Bank of Montreal was a large creditor, and eventually set up in Montreal as an independent financial agent.

During the 1920s many very large British industrial concerns faced collapse, with grave implications for the manufacturing economy, employment, and the stability of the banking system. The Bank of England's preferred policy was one of industrial rationalization, and Montagu Norman, the governor of the bank, sought a manager to reorganize Sir W. G. Armstrong Whitworth & Co. Ltd, one of the largest engineering businesses at risk. Sir Frederick Williams-Taylor of the Bank of Montreal recommended Taylor for the job, describing him as 'unimportant in appearance with a clear, keen, sparkling eye, not much given to talking but always very much to the point'. Although not noted for his diplomacy, 'he would probably get along with people who are simple, direct and straightforward as himself'. Above all,

> he gets to the bottom of things. Having decided that a certain course is in the interest of those he has undertaken to serve, he would not easily be moved by opposition nor influenced by considerations of what he proposes would be popular or unpopular. (Barings archives, PF 39, f.108)

In July 1925 Taylor became a member of Armstrong Whitworth's board at an annual retainer of £5000 from the Bank of England; he remained a director until 1929. He dismembered the business, eventually converting it into a holding company, merged some parts with competitors, wound up others, and wrote down capital. In 1929 this was described as the 'greatest achievement of financial salvage ever attempted' (*The Economist*, 16 Feb 1929), and Taylor emerged as a leading architect of rationalization.

Taylor's success at Armstrong Whitworth underlined his ruthlessness and facility for correcting the business mistakes of others. When in 1926 he joined the Pressed Steel Co. Ltd as a director, he outlined his management methods learned in North America. These involved the production of half-yearly budgets, monthly sales and costs forecasts, monthly balance sheets, and profit and loss accounts; the installation of largely executive boards and local management committees; the appointment of commercially minded engineers; the creation of local cost and profit centres, if need be through the conversion of departments into subsidiary companies; and 'a firm grip on the purse strings' (*DBB*). By the late 1920s he had a deserved reputation at the Bank of England as an excellent manager of big manufacturing business, and he was a natural choice in 1929 as first managing director of Securities Management Trust, a Bank of England vehicle to promote rationalization. In the same year Montagu Norman also arranged for his appointment to the Macmillan committee on finance and industry. Another important appointment in 1929 was as chairman of William Beardmore & Co. Ltd, one of Armstrong Whitworth's tottering competitors. Taylor refused initially, but 'reluctantly agreed' after Norman 'earnestly begged' him to do so, such was Taylor's standing and Norman's need (Barings archives, PF 407, f.55). Suffering from recurrent ill health due to overwork, Taylor resigned in December.

After his recovery in 1931, Taylor was appointed chairman of Pease & Partners Ltd, the important Darlington firm with iron and coal interests, which was in grave difficulties. As management expert and Bank of England nominee, Taylor played a key role in industrial reorganization

in Britain during the difficult inter-war years. He continued to care for certain Bank of England interests in Newfoundland, and early in 1940 he departed to live in Canada, where he became a self-appointed 'general purposes man' for the bank and undertook other commissions for his old contacts. He died at 508 Hycroft Tower, Vancouver, on 23 February 1960.   JOHN ORBELL

Sources J. Orbell, 'Taylor, James Frater', *DBB* · J. F. Taylor, *Economics of every day life* (1932) · *The Times* (1 March 1960) · *The Times* (3 March 1960) · *The Economist* (16 Feb 1929) · ING Barings, London, Barings archives, PF 39, f.108; PF 407, f.55 · K. H. Hawkins, *A history of Bass Charrington* (1978) · J. R. Hume and M. S. Moss, *Beardmore: the history of a Scottish industrial giant* (1979) · 'Report of the committee on finance and industry', *Parl. papers* (1930–31), 13.219, Cmd 3897 · R. S. Sayers, *The Bank of England, 1891–1944*, 3 vols. (1976) · J. D. Scott, *Vickers: a history* (1962) · W. J. Reader, *Bowater: a history* (1981) · birth registers, General Register Office for Scotland, Edinburgh

Archives Bank of England Archives, London, files | ING Barings, London, Barings archives, W. G. Armstrong and Pressed Steel Co. files

Taylor, James Haward (1909–1968), geologist, was born at Esher, Surrey, on 24 February 1909, the only child of James Taylor of Milngavie, Dunbartonshire, a partner in Balmer, Lawrie & Co., Indian merchants, and his wife, Lilian Dudley Ward Haward, of Spalding, Lincolnshire. His paternal grandfather and great-grandfather were both ministers of the Church of Scotland and his maternal grandfather served with the surveyor-general of India. Taylor spent his early childhood in India. At his preparatory school in Surbiton and at Clifton College, which he entered in 1923, he gained an abiding interest in the classics, but when he went up to King's College, London, in 1926, it was to read for a pure science degree, and he eventually specialized in geology.

Taylor graduated BSc with first-class honours (1931), became an associate of King's College, was awarded the Tennant and Jelf medals in 1931, and embarked on research in petrology under A. K. Wells. In 1933 he was elected to a Henry fellowship which took him to Harvard to work with R. A. Daly and E. S. Larsen jun. and which enabled him to travel widely in the western states. He returned to England with an MA degree in 1934. A financially difficult year followed, but in the autumn of 1935 he gained one of the four vacancies on the staff of the Geological Survey of Great Britain. His London PhD was awarded in 1936 and he remained on the staff of the Geological Survey until 1948.

Taylor's early work was directed to the use of the accessory minerals in British granites as an aid to correlation (establishing correspondence between stratigraphic units). His American studies dealt with the metamorphism of limestone adjacent to intrusive monzonite. However, when he joined the geological survey he was assigned to the midlands unit for work in collaboration with Sydney Ewart Hollingworth on the Droitwich 1 inch sheet. Here he was concerned with the sedimentary rocks of the Old Red Sandstone and Trias, with only one small igneous intrusion, the Brockhill Dyke. Taylor was a first-rate field man, and he was elected a fellow of the Geological Society in 1938. With the coming of the war normal geological work was interrupted and Taylor was assigned to a team led by T. H. Whitehead which was to aid the ironstone mining industry working in the belt running from Scunthorpe through Corby to Banbury. This belt represented Britain's almost sole domestic source of iron ore, and in a short time production was raised to over 20 million tons annually. Taylor was particularly concerned with the Northamptonshire area, where, in addition to much detailed surveying, he was assigned the task of investigating the petrography and mineralogy of the ironstones. His memoir on the subject (1949) firmly established him as one of the leaders in this field in Europe. An important result of the team's work was a new understanding of the superficial processes of movement in the ironstone belt, a subject of considerable significance in developing the large open pits necessary to get the required output.

In 1949 Taylor returned to King's as professor of geology. His interest in his geological survey work continued until the important memoir of the stratigraphy, structure, and reserves of the Northampton Sands ironstone was produced in 1951. From about 1953 he extended his activities to Northern Rhodesia, where he investigated the remarkable lead ore deposits at Broken Hill. Taylor's tall, distinguished figure now began to be seen in professional circles. He was geological adviser to the Iron and Steel Board from 1954 onwards, and he served on industrial committees. His work took him to Portugal, Nigeria, Ghana, Northern Rhodesia, and Newfoundland. He was a council member of the Institution of Mining and Metallurgy and was president of the Mineralogical Society (1963–5). He was also a member of the Natural Environment Research Council at the time it was involved in merging the home and Overseas Geological Surveys into the Institute of Geological Sciences.

Taylor was elected fellow of the Royal Society in 1960. He was a member of its council (1963–4), and was its representative to the International Union of Geological Sciences meeting at New Delhi in 1964. In the same year he became chairman of the British National Committee for Geology. He was awarded the fellowship of King's College, London, in 1962. He was president of section C of the British Association for the Advancement of Science at its Aberdeen meeting in 1963, and at the time of his death was president of the International Association of Sedimentologists. An active career of teaching, research, and administration brought him to the front rank of British geologists, but this was prematurely terminated when he was drowned while observing underwater the processes of limestone formation off the Seychelles on 25 January 1968. British geology could ill afford to lose his unassuming but wise guidance. He was not married.

KINGSLEY DUNHAM, rev.

Sources K. C. Dunham, *Memoirs FRS*, 14 (1968), 443–8 · *Transactions of the Institution of Mining and Metallurgy*, 5/77 · personal knowledge (1981) · *CGPLA Eng. & Wales* (1968) · WWW
Likenesses portrait, repro. in Dunham, *Memoirs FRS*

Wealth at death £50,889: probate, 5 Aug 1968, *CGPLA Eng. & Wales*

Taylor, Jane (1783–1824), children's writer, was born on 23 September 1783 in Islington, London, the second of the eleven children (six of whom survived infancy) of the Revd Isaac *Taylor (1759–1829), engraver, writer, and nonconformist minister, and Ann *Taylor, *née* Martin (1757–1830), children's writer. Jane Taylor's sister, Ann [**Ann Gilbert** (1782–1866)], with whom she was later to collaborate, was born on 30 January 1782, also in Islington. In 1786, for financial reasons, the family left London and settled in Lavenham, Suffolk, when Ann and Jane were four and three, respectively. The parents devised an innovative, if strict, regimen of home instruction in which no time was wasted: during mealtimes the mother read aloud, and during picnics the father taught the children to draw picturesque landscapes. As very young girls, Jane and Ann began to collaborate in inventing and acting out little fictions; they frequently impersonated not only royal princesses, but also 'two poor women making a hard shift to live' (Gilbert, 29). In their make-believe poverty, they gathered little plants for their winter food and stored them, with cheeses, in the reclaimed pigsty they used as their playhouse. In a painting by their father, now in the National Portrait Gallery, the two girls are depicted holding hands in their Lavenham garden. From early childhood, Jane's disposition combined a pensive seriousness with a witty turn of mind. She was a lover of nature and solitude, but when she was lifted onto the kneading board at the house of the local baker, she showed a brilliant talent for entertaining the neighbours with her stories and songs.

In 1796, when Jane Taylor was thirteen, the family moved to Colchester, Essex, where her father presided over a nonconformist church. The engraving business fell on hard times, so he let his apprentices go and trained his eldest children, including Jane and Ann, as engravers. In 1798, with other adolescent girls of Colchester, Jane and Ann formed a literary circle, known as the Umbelliferous Society, which required them to produce an original piece of poetry or prose each month. The circle was called umbelliferous to indicate that many buds and blossoms might flourish from the one productive stem. The sisters had so little leisure to write that they would scribble down poems in their spare moments on the margins of their engraving projects. In 1798 Ann published a rhymed answer to a riddle in the *Minor's Pocket Book* and, for the next thirteen years, continued to make contributions to the same periodical, including her poem 'Crippled Child's Complaint', which was prompted by the lameness of her brother Jefferys *Taylor (1792–1853), also a writer for children. Following Ann's lead, in 1804, Jane published her first poem, 'The Beggar Boy'. The publishers Darton and Harvey next invited the sisters to contribute to *Original Poems* (1804–5), which achieved immediate and enduring success, and was translated into Dutch, French, German, and Russian. Although the book had other contributors, most of the poems were by Jane and Ann, whose

Jane Taylor (1783–1824), by unknown artist

'My Mother' was much loved, imitated, and parodied in the nineteenth century.

The Taylor sisters' talent for capturing the child's voice is again evident in *Rhymes for the Nursery* (1806), especially in Jane's classic 'Twinkle, twinkle little star', and in Ann's 'The Baby Dance', which imitates the pleasurable rhythms of baby-talk:

> Dance little baby, dance up high,
> Never mind baby, mother is by;
> Crow and caper, caper and crow,
> There little baby, there you go.

From *Limed Twigs to Catch Young Birds* (1808) and *The Associate Minstrels* (1810) to *The Linnet's Life* (1822), the Taylor sisters' books were often composite productions including poems and engravings by other family members. Jane herself engraved the frontispiece for *Hymns for Infant Minds* (1810), an enormously popular book written in the tradition of Isaac Watts and Mrs Barbauld. According to family legend, their great-grandmother had sat on the knee of Watts and been given a precious copy of his *Divine Songs for the Use of Children* (1715). Ann Taylor describes the thrill of meeting Mrs Barbauld in 1807: 'a small, plain, lively, elderly lady made her appearance; but it was Mrs. Barbauld, and that was enough!' (Gilbert, 133).

In the winter of 1812–13, when their brother Isaac *Taylor (1787–1865) was forced by bad health to move to Ilfracombe in Devon, Ann and Jane accompanied him. The daily collaboration of the sisters ended when Ann moved to Yorkshire on her marriage on 24 December 1813 to Joseph *Gilbert (1779–1852), a Congregational minister, who courted Ann after falling in love with her poetry. Mrs Gilbert found it difficult to achieve the high standard of her early writings while raising eight children, but her autobiography (written during the last decades of her life) is a memorable account of her girlhood struggle to

become a writer and of her mixed feelings regarding the superior celebrity of her sister.

During the years 1813–16, while living in Devon and Cornwall with Isaac, Jane Taylor revelled in wandering on the wild coastline. She completed *Display: a Tale for Young People* (1815) and *Essays in Rhyme* (1816), in which she began to write openly as a dissenter. In response to a letter criticizing her for impropriety, she rejected the idea that women should be silent on controversial topics. After all, she quipped, 'Who ever blamed Mrs. [Hannah] More for poking the steeple into almost every page of her writings?' (*Memoirs* 1.154). In 1816, when a crowd assembled to welcome her to Sheffield, the shy writer became uneasy. Yet, upon being asked 'What do you consider the principal defect in the Quaker system?', she retorted with ready wit, 'Expecting women to speak in public, sir' (Gilbert, 227). Early in 1817 Jane confided to Ann, as the only married woman not too 'blunted' to understand her literary ambitions, that she rejoiced in her 'increasing capability of intellectual pleasure' (*Memoirs*, 1.162–3).

Tragically, that spring Jane Taylor detected a lump in her breast; her health began a slow decline. In the autumn she made a public profession of faith and put herself under the pastoral charge of her father, who had since 1811 presided over the meeting-house in Ongar. Jane's final essays, written periodically for the *Youth's Magazine* (1816–22), are shrewdly designed to appeal to the intellectual and ethical interests of teenagers; they are collected in *The Contributions of Q. Q.* (1824). Jane died of breast cancer on 13 April 1824 in her parents' house, New House, Ongar, and was buried beside her father's church in Ongar. Ann died at her home in College Street, Nottingham, on 20 December 1866, and was buried in Nottingham.

SYLVIA BOWERBANK

Sources *Memoirs and poetical remains of the late Jane Taylor: with extracts from her correspondence*, ed. I. Taylor, 2nd edn, 2 vols. (1826) · *Autobiography and other memorials of Mrs Gilbert (formerly Ann Taylor)*, ed. J. Gilbert, 3rd edn (1878) · C. D. Stewart, *The Taylors of Ongar: an analytical bio-bibliography*, 2 vols. (1975) · C. D. Stewart, 'Notes', in *Ann Taylor Gilbert's album*, ed. C. D. Stewart (1978) · D. M. Armitage, *The Taylors of Ongar* (1939) · I. Taylor, ed., *The family pen: memorials biographical and literary, of the Taylor family of Ongar*, 2 vols. (1867) · F. V. Barry, 'Introduction', in *Jane Taylor: prose and poetry* (1925) · H. C. Knight, *Jane Taylor: her life and letters* (1880) · *CGPLA Eng. & Wales* (1866) [Ann Taylor]
Archives Notts. Arch., letters · Suffolk RO, Bury St Edmunds, corresp. and papers, related material | Suffolk RO, Bury St Edmunds, Ann Gilbert MSS
Likenesses I. Taylor, double portrait, oils (with Ann Gilbert), NPG · charcoal and coloured chalk drawing, NPG [*see illus.*]
Wealth at death under £800—Ann Gilbert: will, 1867

Taylor [née Ionn], **Janet** (1804–1870), teacher of navigation and supplier of nautical instruments, was born on 13 May 1804 at Wolsingham, co. Durham, the sixth of eight children of the Revd Peter Ionn (1762–1821), master of Wolsingham Free Grammar School, and his wife, Jane Deighton. She attributed her knowledge of navigation to the fact that it was taught by her father and her education probably began at his school. She then attended a small school in London under the patronage of Queen Charlotte, who is said personally to have waived the minimum entry age for her. In 1829 she was in London; on 30 January 1830, at the British ambassador's residence at The Hague, she married George Taylor Jane (1792–1853), a widower with three children. The couple adopted the surname Taylor. She had a small inheritance from her father and spent 'several thousand pounds' on the publication of her early books. The first of these, *Luni-Solar and Horary Tables*, published in 1833, was hastily prepared and critically reviewed. However, in 1835 she earned recognition for her simplified lunar distance method, with pecuniary rewards from the Admiralty, Trinity House, and later the East India Company, and gold medals from the kings of Holland and Prussia. Her principal works were *Lunar Tables* (1834), with seven editions to 1854, and *An Epitome of Navigation* (1842), a general textbook, with twelve editions to 1859. Her 'mariner's calculator' for solving navigational problems mechanically, patented in 1834, was unsuccessful and soon abandoned.

From 1833 to 1835 the Taylors lived at 6 East Street, Red Lion Square, in Holborn, London, and Janet almost certainly already had pupils for instruction in navigation. In early 1835 she was teaching navigation at 1 Fen Court, Fenchurch Street, and later that year opened a nautical academy and navigation warehouse selling charts and instruments, at 103 Minories. Although the business was listed under her husband's name she took the lead in it. She had the sole agency for Dent's chronometers and offered instrument repairs, and, from 1843, compass adjustment. In 1845 the business, now under her own name, moved to 104 Minories and she hired instrument makers and began manufacturing instruments on the premises. Octants, a sextant, compass, barometers, and a telescope with her name are known and she exhibited at the Great Exhibition of 1851 and International Exhibition of 1862. The navigation school expanded steadily as nautical education was gradually formalized.

Janet Taylor had eight children of whom six survived infancy. Her husband died in 1853. He had supported her activities and published some of her books, but he had no settled career and she claimed to be the family breadwinner. She found life difficult without him and in 1860, in recognition of this and her work for seafarers, she was awarded a civil-list pension of £50 per annum. About the same time she gave up sole control of her business and by 1868 had retired completely. As a woman Janet Taylor was unique in reaching such prominence in the nautical world. This was achieved not only by competence but also by exceptional determination, particularly in the bold promotion of her work in the highest quarters. She died of bronchitis on 26 January 1870 at her sister's house in St Helen's, Auckland, co. Durham, where she was buried.

SUSANNA FISHER

Sources K. R. Alger, *Mrs Janet Taylor 'authoress and instructress in navigation and nautical astronomy'* (1804–1870), Fawcett Library Papers, 6 (1982) · private information (2004) · parish registers for Wolsingham, co. Durham, St Katherine Coleman, London · trade directories, London, 1833–70 · rate assessment books for City of London and Holborn · 'Incoming Letters' and 'Letterbooks', MOD, hydrographic department · reports of the Juries, Exhibition 1851,

and International Exhibition 1852, 1862, and 1863 · *Nautical Magazine*, 4 (1835) [review and correspondence] · J. Taylor, *The principles of navigation simplified, with luni-solar and horary tables, and their application to nautical astronomy*, 2nd edn (1834); 3rd edn (1837) · d. cert.

Archives Ministry of Defence, hydrographic department, letter-books · NMM, instruments

Wealth at death possibly little or none; lived last years in rented accommodation then with sister

Taylor, Jefferys (1792–1853), children's writer, was born on 30 October 1792 in Cooke's House, Shilling Street, Lavenham, Suffolk, the ninth child of Isaac *Taylor (1759–1829), engraver, and his wife, Ann *Taylor, *née* Martin (1757–1830), also a children's writer. He was named for the family of his paternal grandmother, who was born Sarah Jefferys, the niece of Thomas Jefferys the geographer. Taylor was born lame, a misfortune commemorated in an early poem by his sister Ann (Ann *Gilbert (1782–1866) [see under Taylor, Jane (1783–1824)]). Like all his siblings he was educated at home, benefiting from a remarkably broad curriculum devised by his father and aimed principally at exciting intellectual curiosity. He was trained by his father as an engraver and, like his older brothers, Isaac *Taylor (1787–1865) and Martin, formally apprenticed to him.

Until Taylor's marriage on 20 June 1826 to Sophia Mabbs of Mount Nessing, Essex, he appears to have lived at home, successively in Lavenham, in Colchester, and in Ongar, and it was at New House Farm just outside Ongar, during a painful illness, that he wrote his first book, *Harry's Holiday*, which was published in 1818. It ran to several editions and was followed over the next ten years by a string of other successful books for the young, including *Aesop in Rhyme* (1820), *The Little Historians* (1824), and *Parlour Commentaries on the Constitution and Laws of England* (1825). Most of his books were overtly educational in purpose, but often supplied with a superficial fictional context; in a few, such as *Harry's Holiday* and *Ralph Richards the Miser* (1821), this emphasis was reversed and the fictional element predominated. Most were illustrated with engravings; those not signed by others were probably his own work.

Throughout his life, Jefferys Taylor was fascinated by machinery and, in his ramshackle attic under the leads at New House Farm, he invented a machine for ruling straight and close lines for engravings, which was a considerable financial success. On the death of his father in 1829, he seems to have taken on his commitments to the popular Little Library series published by John Harris, for which he wrote *The Forest* (1831), *The Farm* (1832), and *The Ocean* (1833). There is then a gap of nearly ten years before the publication of his next book, *The Young Islanders* (1842), an early Robinsonnade, in which an entire boys' school is cast away on a desert island; it was particularly successful in America, where it ran to eight editions over the next forty years. *Incidents of the Apostolic Age of Britain* (1844) was an early historical novel for children and probably the first of the genre to deal with very remote events. *A Glance at the Globe and at the Worlds Around Us* (1848), an introduction to cosmology and world history, is interesting in that it anticipates Charles Kingsley in avowedly attempting to reconcile for children belief in a divine creator with recent discoveries in geology and palaeontology.

Jefferys Taylor's first married home was grand, a large Jacobean house (now the Dower House) at Forty Hill, Enfield, Middlesex. Later, for over ten years, he lived at Pilgrim's Hatch, Essex, then a common abutting extensive woodland, until in 1846 financial difficulties forced him to sell up and move to Broadstairs St Peter's, Kent. Here, in July 1852, in a house in the High Street, he suffered a paralytic stroke from which he never recovered. Nursed at the end by his recently widowed sister Ann—his own wife lay bedridden in an adjacent room—he died on 8 August 1853. Although brought up a dissenter, like his brothers he had joined the established church in later life, and he was buried in the churchyard of St Peter's, Broadstairs. His tombstone, sketched by a relative in 1895, has not survived.

Jefferys Taylor was by all accounts an avuncular and genial man, much given to jokes and puns, but had also a penchant for the ghostly and the macabre, a combination likely to appeal to children then as now. (It was his tragedy that the only child of his own marriage, Edward, had died young.) His appearance and character are described by his nephew Josiah Gilbert:

> Indeed, his massive head and sparkling grey eye seemed to indicate more of power than the delicate features of his brother Isaac, but it was a power untrained, and fitfully exerted, and the whole aspect of the man, the halting gait, supported by a stick, the burly form, the quizzical features, bespoke the wayward genius he too truly was.   (Gilbert, 2.141)

ROBIN TAYLOR GILBERT

Sources *Autobiography and other memorials of Mrs Gilbert (formerly Ann Taylor)*, ed. J. Gilbert, 2 vols. (1874) · C. D. Stewart, *The Taylors of Ongar: an analytical bio-bibliography*, 2 vols. (1975) · *Ann Taylor Gilbert's album*, ed. C. D. Stewart (1978) · I. Taylor [1787–1865], 'Preface', in J. Taylor, *The family Bible newly opened* (1853) · I. Taylor [1759–1829], genealogical notes transcribed by Henry Taylor [1837–1916], Suffolk RO, Bury St Edmunds, Taylor Collection, HD 588/1/147 · d. cert. · Suffolk RO, Bury St Edmunds, Taylor Collection [for example HD 588/8/4] · H. Taylor, 'An annotated catalogue of books written by the Taylors of Ongar' [duplicated typescript, 1895] · I. Taylor [1787–1865], 'Memoirs and correspondence of Jane Taylor', *The family pen: memorials biographical and literary, of the Taylor family of Ongar*, ed. I. Taylor [1829–1901], 1 (1867)

Archives Suffolk RO, Bury St Edmunds, papers, artwork, and related material, HD 588

Likenesses I. Taylor (1759–1829), miniature, pencil sketch on card, 1798, Colchester Museum Resource Centre · I. Taylor (1787–1865), outline pencil sketch, Suffolk RO, Bury St Edmunds · I. Taylor (1787–1865), silhouette, Suffolk RO, Bury St Edmunds · photograph of portrait (in middle age; after J. Gilbert?), Suffolk RO, Bury St Edmunds

Taylor, Jeremy (*bap.* 1613, *d.* 1667), Church of Ireland bishop of Down and Connor and religious writer, was born at Cambridge, where he was baptized at Trinity Church on 15 August 1613. He was the third son of Nathaniel Taylor, a barber, and Mary Dean. The Taylors were a well-established Cambridge family: Nathaniel and his father, Edmond (*d.* 1607), were both churchwardens of Trinity Church; at the time of Jeremy's birth the family was probably living at a house known as the Black Bear, opposite Trinity Church, but at some date after 1621 they moved to the Wrestlers' Inn in Petty Cury, in the parish of St Andrew the Great. Jeremy was instructed in grammar

Jeremy Taylor (*bap.* 1613, *d.* 1667), by Pierre Lombart, pubd 1660

and mathematics by his father, and later educated at the Perse School under its master Thomas Lovering. He entered Gonville and Caius College as a sizar, or poor scholar, on 18 August 1626 and matriculated on 17 March 1627. His tutor was Thomas Bachcroft, who later became master of the college. Taylor was elected a scholar on the Perse foundation at Michaelmas 1628 and took his BA in 1631. In 1633 he was elected to a Perse fellowship of the college and was ordained, although still under twenty-one years old. He proceeded to an MA in 1634 and was appointed a praelector in rhetoric by the master of Caius.

Early career Apparently Taylor came to the attention of Archbishop William Laud when he stood in for Thomas Risden, his university friend, as a lecturer at St Paul's Cathedral. According to George Rust's sermon at Taylor's funeral, Laud had Taylor preach before him and was impressed, especially by his quick-witted response to the remark that he was very young: Taylor 'humbly begged his grace to pardon that fault, and promised, if he lived, he would mend it' (*Works*, 1.17). Laud organized his preferment within the University of Oxford. On 20 October 1635 Taylor was admitted MA from University College. A few days later Laud recommended him for a vacant fellowship at All Souls, and when Gilbert Sheldon, the warden, objected to his election on a technicality, Laud used the authority which devolved to him as college visitor to ensure that Taylor was admitted—first as a probationary and then, on 14 January 1636, as a permanent fellow. Soon afterwards Taylor was appointed chaplain to Laud and a chaplain-in-ordinary to Charles I.

Taylor was a rising star and inevitably attracted adverse as well as positive comment. There were rumours of crypto-popery. In 1641 he was to be accused of 'teaching that a man cannot be saved without confession to a priest' (Milton, 74n.). His friendship with the Franciscan Christopher Davenport gave rise to suspicions. Perhaps these rumours were allayed by the Gunpowder Plot sermon Taylor preached at the university church of St Marys, Oxford, on 5 November 1638. Dedicated to Laud, the published sermon was a virulent and historically detailed attack on the treachery of Roman Catholics. Although Davenport told Anthony Wood that Taylor had 'expressed some sorrow for those things he had said against them' (Wood, *Ath. Oxon.*, 3.782), Taylor remained a fierce critic of 'popery' throughout his life. In a letter from the late 1650s published as part of *A Dissuasive from Popery* (1664) he described Rome as 'a church that protects itself by arts of subtilty [*sic*] and arms, by violence and persecuting', and states that its erroneous doctrines pandered to evil inclinations: the Church of England was a far safer path, yet Taylor could not bring himself to say that all Catholics were damned (*Works*, 11.187, 197). Taylor was a combative preacher, and even his admirers voiced the occasional reservation: William Chillingworth told a mutual friend that, for all his qualities, Taylor:

> wants much of the ethicall part of a discourser, and slights too much many times the arguments of those he discourses with; but this is a fault he would quickly leave, if he had a friend that would discreetly tell him of it. (*Holy Living*, xvii)

In 1638 Bishop Juxon preferred Taylor to the rectory of Uppingham in Rutland. Taylor was instituted into the living on 23 March 1638 and took up residence in his parish; the parish registers attest to his concern for his flock and his church, and his pulpit and paten survive in the parish church. It was at Uppingham on 27 May 1639 that he married Phoebe Langsdale (*d.* 1651), daughter of Gervase Langsdale of Holborn, London, and sister to Edward Langsdale (1619–1684), who had been one of Taylor's pupils at Cambridge in 1633. Taylor and Phoebe had several children: William, who was buried at Uppingham on 28 May 1642; two other sons (George? and Richard), who succumbed to smallpox in the winter of 1656–7; Charles, who survived to adulthood only to die a few days after his father; and two daughters, Phoebe, who never married, and Mary, who in 1662 married Francis *Marsh, dean of Armagh and later archbishop of Dublin. When John Evelyn met Mary in 1680, 'she seemed to be a knowing woman beyond the ordinary talent of her sex' (*Diary of John Evelyn*, 4.19).

Civil war and interregnum Jeremy Taylor was not able to enjoy the life of a parish priest for long. The outbreak of the civil war impelled him to join Charles I. Although details of his movements are not entirely clear, and depend heavily upon Wood's account, it seems that he joined the king at Nottingham and then accompanied the court to Oxford. On 1 November 1642 Taylor received a DD from the University of Oxford by royal mandate, probably in recognition of his recently completed book *The Sacred Order and Offices of Episcopacy* (Oxford, 1642). After Charles I had allegedly declined the honour, this outspoken book was dedicated to Christopher Hatton, later Lord Hatton, royalist courtier and politician, and a stalwart patron of Taylor for several years to come. In 1644 there appeared from the university printer at Oxford *The Psalter of David*, an anonymous work that was frequently attributed to Hatton and yet which bears Taylor's literary hallmark. Wood writes of Taylor as preaching frequently before the court at Oxford in the early 1640s and accompanying the royal army as a chaplain. There are no more entries by Taylor in the register at Uppingham after the summer of 1642, but it was not until May 1644 that his living was finally sequestered and the royalist *Mercurius Aulicus* could luridly report his house plundered, his estate seized, and his family put out. Since the living of Uppingham was effectively lost to him in 1642, his institution to the rectory of Overstone, Northamptonshire, in 1643 may have been intended as some form of compensation, but there is no evidence of his residence there, and his successor was in possession by May 1647. Meanwhile the fortunes of war had gone against Taylor. In January or February 1645 he was taken prisoner after the defeat of the royalist force under Colonel Charles Gerard outside Cardigan Castle in Wales. His prominence was such that the parliamentary propagandists crowed at the capture of this 'most spruce neat formalist, a very ginger-bread Idoll, an Arminian in print' (*Walker rev.*, 302).

Taylor was probably free again by April and able to resume his scholarly and clerical life. Whether his role as a military chaplain had brought him to south-west Wales or he had retired there looking for peace, he found refuge as a teacher at a school in the grandly named Newton Hall in the parish of Llanfihangel Aberbythych, Carmarthenshire. Set up by William Nicholson, the ejected vicar of nearby Llandeilo, with the assistance of William Wyatt, this school prepared the sons of local gentlemen for university. In 1646 Taylor and Wyatt wrote and published *A New and Easie Institution of Grammar* (Oxford, 1646), and the same year Taylor's *Discourse Concerning Prayer ex tempore* also appeared at Oxford. It is uncertain whether Taylor's presence at the school brought him into the orbit of Richard Vaughan, second earl of Carbery, or the school owed its location and even existence to the proximity of Carbery's mansion. Whichever it was, Taylor soon became chaplain to the Carbery household and a resident at Golden Grove (Gelli-aur), a few miles south-west of Llandeilo and to the east of Carmarthen. Carbery's early Elizabethan house was palatial. It was taxed at thirty hearths in 1670, and if, as has been suggested, the engraved frontispiece to Taylor's book *Golden Grove* includes a depiction of the house in an idealization of the Tywi valley, it was a delightful retreat (Gathorne-Hardy and Williams, 63–5). Carbery had retired here from politics in 1644 after a less than distinguished military career as a royalist general. He enjoyed a parliamentary pardon and the protection of the earl of Essex. Taylor savoured a congenial atmosphere of piety—especially with Frances, countess of Carbery—and bookishness.

During the next few years Taylor produced a series of important works. *The Liberty of Prophesying* (1647) was the first and perhaps most uncharacteristic, as it argued for religious toleration. Then 'weary and toiled with rowing up and down in the seas of questions' (*Works*, 2.xiii), Taylor turned his mind to winning people over to Christianity rather than to a party, and produced a series of devotional works, *The Great Exemplar* (1649), *Holy Living* (1650), and *Holy Dying* (1651). The last two were dedicated to Carbery. Poignantly *Holy Dying* was intended as tribute to the countess of Carbery, but before Taylor could finish it, she died in childbirth on 9 October 1650. Taylor preached and later published a funeral sermon for the 'dear departed Saint'. When he came to dedicate *Holy Dying* (which was entered in the Stationers' register on 23 June 1651, while Thomason dated his copy 3 September 1651), Taylor added a personal note by remarking on his own sad experience of grief. Apparently his wife, Phoebe, had died in the first half of 1651.

To judge by his publications, Taylor spent the next year or two assiduously preaching at Golden Grove and preparing two volumes of sermons 'for all the Sundays of the year', which were published as *Eniautos* in 1651 and 1653. Yet even in the fastnesses of Carmarthenshire, religious controversy was alive. Taylor found himself at odds with a Jesuit, John Sarjeant, over the doctrine of the eucharist. By April 1653 Taylor had completed *The real presence and spirituall of Christ in the blessed sacrament, proved against the doctrine of transubstantiation* and sent the manuscript to Brian Duppa, the deprived bishop of Salisbury. By November Duppa had received a copy of the printed book and recommended it to Sir Justinian Isham:

> You will find it to be a discourse occasioned by a conference he had with a Jesuit, against whom he hath argued with so much sharpness as if all his study had been in controversies, and yet hath framed his bookes of devotion so as if he understood nothing of them. (*Correspondence of ... Duppa and ... Isham*, 75)

There were many calls on Taylor's time and energy, as can be glimpsed from another of Duppa's letters. On 9 May 1654 he wrote that Taylor

> hath been lately at London with an intention to make use of some books for the perfecting of a very good work which he hath now in hand. But being here, the labours of the pulpit took him off from the care of the press: for he was not suffer'd to be in quiet. Preach he must, both in season and out of season, till at last being wearied out with it, he is retired back to the Golden Grove. (*Correspondence of ... Duppa and ... Isham*, 88)

Taylor had conceived a grand project, a work of casuistry or 'cases of conscience', which would be his *magnum opus* and a complete protestant answer to the many Roman Catholic manuals of casuistry. His correspondence of the 1650s contains frequent references to his progress on the book: part one was complete late in 1654; in April 1656 the book, entitled *Ductor dubitantium*, was entered in the Stationers' register; parts of the text were being set up on the printing presses in the winter of 1656–7; he was still hard at work in 1659, by which time he was in Ireland; and the huge tome finally appeared in 1660. Throughout these years Taylor's life was precarious. Money was always a problem. He depended on the generosity of sympathizers and patrons, some of whom had fallen on hard times themselves or even, like Hatton, gone into exile. Through Duppa he received at least one donation from Sir Justinian Isham; John Evelyn would be another benefactor, and there was some rather tense financial arrangement with Gilbert Sheldon. Taylor's personal liberty was far from assured. A letter to Taylor from John Evelyn, dated 9 February 1655, appears to refer to some recent restraint or imprisonment that Taylor had undergone in Wales. There is no other evidence of this, and yet some scholars have supposed a connection between this putative imprisonment and possible offence given to the authorities by the outspoken episcopalianism of the preface to *Golden Grove*, his devotional manual which appeared in December 1654 (despite a title-page date of 1655). Tradition and over-enthusiastic scholarship may have exaggerated the number of occasions on which Taylor was imprisoned, but the fear and insecurity were all too real.

In March 1655 Taylor was once again in London. He preached at St Gregory by Paul's, where he was heard by Evelyn. He no doubt also took this opportunity to deliver the manuscript of *Unum necessarium* to Richard Royston, the Anglican royalist bookseller who printed most of Taylor's works. This title was entered in the Stationers' register on 3 May, and Thomason dated his copy July 1655. At some stage Royston, either on his own initiative or at the behest of the author, sent several of the printed sheets of this work to Duppa. This was a wise precaution because Taylor had denied the doctrine of original sin. Yet when Duppa returned 'his exceptions and arguments with some severity' and Bishop John Warner of Rochester wrote in protest, Taylor simply included their complaints and his reply in the preface. He

> thereby tells everybody of it, before they read so farr into the booke, & by that meanes, it is universally spoken of, and by every single person that I heare of, disliked, and by the B[isho]ps disclaimd. I wish with you, hee would advise before he runs these hazards[.] But I feare, it will not bee. Poor man is in affliction close at Chepstow Castle. (Hammond? to Sheldon?, 14 September [1655], BL, Harley MS 6942, fol. 124)

The unrepentant Taylor was confined in Chepstow Castle between May and October 1655, possibly as a consequence of the crackdown prompted by the royalist rising in Wiltshire in March 1655. His gaolers were, however, 'civil to my person' and allowed him unimpeded correspondence and the facilities to write (*Works*, 9.365). Taylor was free and back in Carmarthenshire by November, but he was now living at Mandinam, near Llangadog, on the estate of his second wife, Joanna Bridges. The date of their marriage is unknown. Mandinam was close to Golden Grove, but Taylor may no longer have been officiating there in view of the recent ordinance prohibiting the employment of Anglican clergymen as domestic chaplains.

Controversy In the winter of 1655–6 Taylor was busy defending his position on original sin both in private letters and in works intended for the press. *A Further Explication of the Doctrine of Original Sin* was published in November 1655 and was subsequently incorporated in later editions of *Unum necessarium* as chapter 7. He visited London in the following spring: on 12 April he dined with Evelyn at Sayes Court in the company of Robert Boyle, John Wilkins, and George Berkeley; and in May Evelyn visited Taylor in London and successfully sought his help in gaining episcopal ordination for Jacques Le Franc, minister of the Walloon church in Norwich. In July Taylor was back in Wales, but keen to settle in London; he was also looking forward to the imminent publication of *Deus justificatus* and his *Answer to a Letter*, both further defences of his teaching on original sin. It is sometimes suggested that Taylor was imprisoned in Wales in the winter of 1656–7, but this claim seems to rest on a letter to Evelyn dated 21 November 1656. Internal evidence indicates that this letter has been misdated and was sent in November 1655. Certainly the winter of 1656–7 was not kind to Taylor. In February 1657 he wrote to Evelyn of the death from smallpox of two of his sons:

> I have now but one son left, whom I intend (if it please God) to bring up to London before Easter; and then I hope to wait upon you, and by your sweet conversation and other divertissements, if not to alleviate my sorrows, yet, at least, to entertain myself and keep me from too much intense and actual thinkings of my troubles. (*Diary and Correspondence*, 578)

That summer Taylor seems to have finally moved to London: he was to be found baptizing Evelyn's newborn child in June, preaching the funeral sermon for Sir George Dalston, a pious supporter of the church, in September, and frequently preaching in one or more private houses to a circle of pious Anglicans. He was befriended by Lord and Lady Conway and visited them at Kensington and Ragley in Worcestershire. He collected his controversial works, going back to his 1642 defence of episcopacy and including some of his works on original sin, in one folio volume, *Simbolon ethiko-polemikon, or, A Collection of Polemic and Moral Discourses*, and produced *A Collection of Offices, or Forms of Prayer* (appeared December 1657), which was explicitly designed to fill the gap left by the ban on the Book of Common Prayer. Yet, characteristically, Taylor remained unsettled:

> I have some thoughts of retiring from noise and company, and going to my studies in a far distant solitude, but not to Wales. This place [London] is expensive of my no money and my little time, concerning both which I am constrained to take some more care. (19 December 1657, BL, Tanner MS 52, fol. 216)

The last clause was a reference to his wife's current pregnancy, which was mentioned in Lady Conway's letters and the outcome of which is unclear. Taylor and Joanna Bridges had at least two children: Edward, who was buried at Lisburn, co. Antrim, on 10 March 1661, and Joanna,

upon whom her mother's estate was settled in reversion as part of her marriage settlement of 1668 with Edward Harrison (1644–1700) of Magheralin, MP for Lisburn.

In London during the winter of 1657–8 Taylor continued to preach, to write, and to offer spiritual guidance and moral support to a mainly Anglican group. A story that he was imprisoned in the Tower of London seems based on a misreading of a letter from Evelyn to the lieutenant of the Tower: Evelyn alludes to suspicions of Taylor as popishly affected and suggests a meeting, and this in turn suggests that the letter may properly belong to January 1658 rather than its apparent date of 1657. If that is the case this allusion may be connected to the council of state's recommendation of 22 December 1657 that Peter Gunning and Taylor be summoned for 'an account of the frequent meetings of multitudes of people held with them' and that the ban on the prayer book be enforced (*CSP dom.*, 1657–8, 226). One fruit of this was the raids on various congregations using the prayer book on Christmas day 1657, but there is nothing to confirm that Taylor was caught up in these events (*Diary of John Evelyn*, 3.203–5).

Taylor's desire to retire from London was noted by his friends. In May 1658 he refused Conway's offer of a lectureship at Lisburn (Lisnagarvey), co. Antrim, in which he would have alternated with another lecturer and been dependent on the whim of the subscribers and the local ecclesiastical authorities. Moreover the stipend was insufficient to cover even the costs and trouble of moving his family to Ulster. Nor were the authorities any keener to let him go to Ulster. On 10 June the council of state had refused a pass for Taylor to travel to Ireland. Edward Conway was not to be thwarted, however. He dragooned his friends to cajole Taylor with offers of land in Ireland and help from local patrons, and he even got a pass for Taylor and his family from Lord Protector Cromwell himself. So later that summer Taylor and his family arrived in Ireland.

Ireland Taylor was based on Conway's estate at Portmore, in the parish of Ballinderry, 8 miles from Lisburn. The religious situation in Antrim, as in the whole of Ireland, was complex. The majority of the population was Roman Catholic, while the protestant governing élite was divided. The episcopalian Church of Ireland had suffered like the Church of England, yet it had maintained an identity and a presence. The aged Bishop Leslie of Down and Connor had not lost contact with his diocese. He had been sheltered in Arthur Hill's house at Hillsborough, where 'the publick liturgy of the church is greatly valued, and diligently us'd' (Barnard, 151). The presbyterians who had occupied many of the livings of the Irish church were a strong group, closely linked to the Scottish presbyterians but also royalist. The Cromwellian army of occupation had brought religious radicals, Baptists and Independents, to political dominance in Ireland in the early 1650s. However, since the arrival of Henry Cromwell in 1655 there had been a steady transfer of local power back to the protestant landed class and a weakening of religious radicalism. Presumably the arrival of Taylor was intended to bolster this process in the corner of Antrim where Conway had his large estates. Despite the displeasure of the local presbyterians at his presence, Taylor quickly set to work. He preached; he served as chaplain in the Conway household and that of Conway's brother-in-law, George Rawdon, commander of the Lisburn garrison; and tradition has it that he officiated in the ruined church of Ballinderry in the marshes west of Lough Beg. He was involved in the uniting of parishes and in the building of a new parish church. And in his study he polished the final chapters of *Ductor dubitantium*.

A minor irritation arose in June 1659 when Philip Tandy, a local Independent preacher, complained to Henry Cromwell that Taylor had baptized a child with the sign of the cross. There may have been an element of pique in this: Lord Conway had heard that the quarrel was because Tandy 'thinks Dr Taylor more welcome to Hillsborough than himself' (*Works*, 1.cccxxxviii). Tandy's complaint was overtaken by events. The following month Henry Cromwell lost power and left office; following the collapse of the protectorate, radical republican elements assumed authority. On 11 August it was ordered that Taylor be brought to Dublin to answer charges, but nothing was done: on 3 November Taylor confessed himself baffled by events. Then, in December, he was summoned to Dublin only to find, after a painful journey, that the radical regime had fallen apart. He was soon back in his study at Portmore watching events unfold and waiting for the end of winter and a safe passage to England.

April 1660 was an opportune moment to arrive in London: Taylor signed a 'loyal' or royalist address to General Monk on 24 April; and he dedicated his *Ductor dubitantium*, which appeared in June, to Charles II. On 6 August Taylor was nominated as bishop of Down and Connor. His preferment in Ireland is explicable in several ways. He was a well-known and respected devotional and controversial writer, and an undisputed 'sufferer' for the Anglican and royalist cause, but he was also an uncompromising episcopalian and heterodox in his teaching on original sin: in short, Taylor was not the kind of churchman to suit the inclusive English church under consideration in 1660. In Ireland, however, with John Bramhall designated for the primacy and the duke of Ormond a powerful ally at court, the strident Taylor was a natural choice.

In Ireland a power struggle was in full swing. After nominating the Irish bishops, Charles II had not rushed to have them consecrated or translated to their new posts for fear that the sight of zealous Irish prelates acting against local presbyterians would damage the delicate English negotiations. Taylor, still only a nominee, was wise to tread carefully in Down. In the course of 1660 many presbyterian clergy had regained the livings that they had lost to Independents in the Cromwellian years. In December Taylor heard that the presbyterian ministers 'have lately bought my books, and appointed a committee of Scotch spiders to see if they can gather or make poison out of them' and that they were now planning to charge him before the Irish privy council as an Arminian, Socinian, and 'a heretic in grain' (Seymour, 196–7; *CSP Ire., 1660–62*, 115). They

had refused his invitations to confer, saying they would 'speak with no bishop'. For his part, he told Ormond, he would prefer to be a village curate 'than a bishop over such intolerable persons' (*Holy Living*, xxxi). But Taylor was not one to shrink from a fight. He wrote to Lord Conway in January 1661 from Dublin, hoping that his business would be done speedily so 'that I may go into the North and take care of my friends and my enemies' (Stranks, 225). The consecration of Taylor and eleven other prelates took place on 27 January 1661 in St Patrick's Cathedral, Dublin. Taylor himself preached the sermon and did not mince his words: 'without bishops there can be no priests, and consequently no sacraments' and no church; the presbyterians were simply schismatic (*Works*, 6.349). In Rawdon's view he 'taught them the office of a Bishop' (*CSP Ire., 1660–62*, 199). He had now been sworn in as vice-chancellor of Trinity College, Dublin, an institution which he proceeded to reform energetically. In February he gained his wish to become a member of the Irish privy council. Disappointed of his hopes for the bishopric of Meath, he was given the additional responsibility of administering the diocese of Dromore. On 8 May he preached at the opening of the Irish parliament and was vitriolic about the 'criminally disobedient' dissenters. He castigated the presbyterians for not conforming to the protestant episcopal church and denounced the notion of liberty for tender consciences. A few days later parliament issued a declaration that all subjects conform to episcopal church government and the liturgy as established by law.

Steps were now taken to bring the presbyterian clergy to heel. Bishop Taylor was undeniably belligerent. His visitation at Lisburn was probably held in March or April 1661, in other words before parliament's declaration, but this made no difference to his attitude or that of the presbyterians. Only two presbyterian ministers attended, and Taylor immediately declared thirty-six livings vacant. One hostile witness claimed that he did so because their ministers did not have episcopal ordination. No doubt Taylor did not believe them properly ordained (although there was no explicit legal requirement for episcopal ordination in Ireland until 1667), but more obviously he would not brook opposition to his own authority as bishop.

Taylor was now 'full of public concerns and the troubles of business in my diocese' (*Diary and Correspondence*, 599, Dublin, 16 November 1661). His duties took him to Dublin often: he preached there on 4 May and 10 August 1662, and on 15 February and 16 July 1663. In the summer of 1663 he planned 'to visit the churches in Antrim up as farre as Colerane and so about to Glenarme and Caricfergus; to put all perfectly right' (Gathorne-Hardy and Williams, 110–11). In 1662–3 he investigated local ghost sightings, and this information eventually found its way into Joseph Glanvill's *Saducismus triumphatus* (1682). In 1664 he published a *Dissuasive from Popery*, which linked false Catholic doctrines such as purgatory and transubstantiation to the credulity and folk beliefs of the Irish-speaking natives, and revealed his own increasing pessimism about the success of the Church of Ireland. Taylor's was a strenuous and troubled episcopate, and he dreamed of a return to England, if only for the winter; 'and I hear is preparing court sermons already' reported Rawdon in 1665 (*CSP Ire.*, 1663–5, 551). Although his health was indifferent, he was still working hard as bishop and controversialist: in July 1665 he 'is so close at his study replying to [the] answers to his book against Popery that he is hardly got out of his closet' (ibid., 603). In 1660–61 he had lived at Hillsborough and then Portmore, but after 1664 he lived mainly in Castle Street, Lisburn, although he owned other houses and a farm at Megharalin. It was at Castle Street, Lisburn, after suffering ten days of fever, apparently contracted while visiting the sick, that Taylor died at about 3 p.m. on 13 August 1667. According to George Rawdon, who was present, Taylor had to be reminded to write his will, and contrary to expectations he left little save £1500 in the hands of the earl of Donegal and £600 held by Lord Conway (*CSP Ire.*, 1666–9, 425, 429). It was Taylor's wish to be buried either in the church he had built at Dromore or at Ballinderry if that church was consecrated before his death. He was buried in a vault in the chancel of the cathedral church at Dromore.

Writings Taylor's difficult years in Ireland and his early death around the age of fifty-four cannot overshadow his literary achievements, which are all the more impressive in view of the hand-to-mouth existence he was leading for much of the 1640s and 1650s. His published writings were the basis of his fame during his lifetime and since. Although many of his works defy easy classification, there are three areas in which he made his mark.

Taylor enjoys a reputation as a proponent of religious toleration. This is entirely due to his early work *The Liberty of Prophesying*, which is an extended essay, in a plainer prose than he later used, on the need for religious liberty. This liberty was defined as freedom from persecution and the freedom to profess and teach all religions so long as they did not promote impiety or disturb the public peace. Taylor was prepared to include Anabaptists and Roman Catholics within such a liberty. Although the influence of William Chillingworth and John Hales is discernible, Taylor was undoubtedly far in advance of most protestant thought on the subject, and yet there is an apparent absence of rigour in his position. His central tenet was that there is no more certain and universal rule of faith than the apostles' creed, and so this must become the measure of Christian unity of faith; he proposed that it should serve as the basis of church communion, with all other theological, liturgical, and ecclesiological teachings dismissed as non-fundamentals. Taylor assumed that all individuals had to judge for themselves, and that the honest error of an innocent person would incur no punishment:

> it concerns all persons to see that they do the best to find out the truth; and if they do, it is certain that, let the error be ever so damnable, they shall escape the error, or the misery of being damned for it. (*Works*, 8.231)

Beyond this, the tract is merely an exhortation to prudence, charity, and humility and a denunciation of pride, violence, and schism, all made, of course, at least in part

on behalf of a proscribed and persecuted Anglican church. Even during his own lifetime, this tract began to haunt him. Taylor added more than twenty-three folio pages to the 1657 edition to show why Anabaptism was an error. It hardly needs to be said that his own episcopate demonstrated scant tolerance of those who disagreed with the episcopalian church.

The achievement of which Taylor was most proud was his contribution to the creation of an English casuistry. *Ductor dubitantium, or, The Rule of Conscience* (1660) was designed as a comprehensive manual of cases of conscience which would form a capstone to the English protestant edifice already created by Robert Sanderson, Joseph Hall, and William Perkins. No longer would English clergy need to consult Roman Catholic casuists and run the risk of being misled by their 'probabilism' (the teaching that a course of action was allowed if *some*, rather than a majority of, moral theologians permitted it). Taylor promised general rules from which every particular case could be resolved. Unfortunately, in the opinion of many readers, his huge work lost sight of this goal and became lost in its own digressions: K. E. Kirk described it as 'erudite, tortuous and garrulous' (Kirk, 205); Cardinal Newman marvelled 'how weak a thread of thoughts' connected the book's quotations and references (Miller, 132–3). In common with his fellow protestant casuists, Taylor inclined towards 'probabiliorism' and was often severe in his conclusions; for example, he denied the distinction of mortal and venial sins. In effect, Taylor believed that there is always a right answer in moral dilemmas, even if human reason cannot fathom it; and while offering the conventional teaching on the obligation of an 'erroneous conscience', he placed an overwhelming emphasis on the duty of human reason to discern the good act where 'good' is defined by rational nature and divine commands.

Among his contemporaries Taylor's devotional works were far more popular than his 1100-page casuistical tome. His devotional writings ranged from liturgical collections to sermons, from arguably the first English life of Christ, *The Great Exemplar*, a mixture of narrative and prayer, to two great manuals of practical piety, *Holy Living* and *Holy Dying*. The popularity of Taylor's writings in this vein was overwhelming: they were among the best and steadiest sellers of the century; *Holy Living* and *Holy Dying* had both reached their nineteenth edition by 1695. These pious books were treasured by devout Anglicans like John Evelyn, who used Taylor's meditations and prayers as inspirations for his own private devotions. In a letter of 1654 Dorothy Osborne described herself as a devotee of Taylor's works and paraphrased *Holy Living* on the duty of submission. Clandestine Anglican congregations may have used his various liturgical works in place of the prohibited prayer book.

Significance Taylor's success owes as much to his literary talent as his intellect. He was notable for his eloquence, his almost poetical imagination, and his wide biblical and classical learning: even his opponents recognized his 'admirable wit, great parts, quick and elegant pen, his abilities in critical learning, and his profound skill in antiquities' (Wood, *Ath. Oxon.*, 3.784). His sonorous prose has been criticized as over-elaborate; some have suggested that Taylor exemplifies an ornate and copious prose style, occasionally described as Ciceronian, which depends upon extended similes and self-conscious flights of fancy to achieve its powerful emotional effects. He certainly builds up long sentences of linked clauses, often using figurative language and embellished with classical and biblical parallels, but rarely does so without a clear rhetorical purpose in mind. And when necessary, brevity is employed.

Taylor was not a systematic, nor even a particularly consistent, thinker or theologian; the confusion of his sacramental doctrine, for instance, has often been noted by commentators. Taylor's churchmanship, as is to be expected in a protégé of the Laudians, included a preference for such things as private confession to the priest, confirmation, vestments, and ritual, and a single-minded devotion to the Book of Common Prayer. In theology he was uncompromisingly Arminian: he described the works of the Arminian systematizer Episcopius as 'excellent' and containing 'the whole body of orthodox religion'; Hugo Grotius was also among his influences. Taylor's assertion of episcopacy in 1642 took a Cyprianic line on the necessity of bishops to the being of a church, and he may have been the first to deny categorically the validity of the clerical orders of the European Reformed churches. He was a central figure in what is sometimes called the 'holy living' school of mid-seventeenth-century Anglicanism. This severe outlook required a rigorous commitment from the individual Christian. In Taylor's writings, repentance was a once-and-for-all event. So convinced was he of this that he took his view to its logical, and controversial, conclusions: in *Holy Living* and elsewhere, Taylor dismissed deathbed repentance as utterly inadequate and ineffective. When preparing his manual on repentance, *Unum necessarium*, he 'found the usual doctrines of original sin to be one' of the 'principles of evil life', and so without compunction he repudiated the doctrine (Bodl. Oxf., MS Tanner 52, fol. 101). In chapter 6 of *Unum necessarium*, he argued from Romans 5 that Adam's sin was imputed to humankind: 'the effect of one sin, and the cause of many; a stain, but no sin' (*Works*, 9.94). In other words, human beings do not inherit original sin, so sin can neither destroy our liberty nor make us sin of necessity. For Taylor, God does not damn anyone solely on the grounds of an inherited sin, but for the actual sin they voluntarily commit. Taylor was adamant that humans enjoyed free will, and would not retract his teaching on original sin even in the face of a barrage of criticism from fellow Anglicans such as Sheldon, Sanderson, and Duppa, and from puritans such as Henry Jeanes, John Gaule, and Nathaniel Stephens. He consoled himself that his teaching was on 'that side where God's justice and goodness stand apparently'; the 'precepts of holiness might as well be preached to a wolf as to a man, if men were naturally and inevitably wicked' (Bodl. Oxf., MS Tanner 52, fol. 101; *Works*, 9.46). In all this, Taylor stood so far outside the Augustinian assumptions of the majority of English protestant theologians that he was widely perceived as 'semi-Pelagian'. Modern readers, however, may find Taylor's work remarkable for its emotional power, acute sense of human capabilities and responsibilities, and emphasis on the practical duties of a Christian profession.

Taylor was stubborn and surprisingly pugnacious for one so famed for his piety. Those who knew him remarked on his polemical tendencies. 'I am glad he left no more trouble behind him', remarked Archbishop Sheldon on news of his death. 'He was of a dangerous temper apt to break out into extravagancies, and I have had, till of late years, much to do with him to keep him in order, and to find diversions for him' (Bodl. Oxf., MS Carte 45, fol. 222). In 1664, when asking for translation to an English see, Taylor told Sheldon that he had heard on good authority 'that your grace was pleased once to say, that I myself was the only hindrance to myself of being removed to an English bishopric'. It was obtuse of Taylor not to appreciate what Sheldon really meant and tactless (or brazen) to repeat it to him. Others, however, saw Taylor as a saintly figure: for John Evelyn he was a spiritual guide, his 'ghostly father'. Taylor's circle of friends was diverse, including Henry More and Herbert of Cherbury, and several notable women, such as the poet Katherine Philips, Lady Conway, and the countess of Carbery. Above all it was his literary legacy, admired by Wesley, Coleridge, Lamb, Arnold, Heber, and Gosse, that was most significant. For once, even the acerbic Anthony Wood has only praise to offer: Taylor's writings 'will be famous to all succeeding generations for the exactness of wit, profoundness of judgement, richness of fancy, clearness of expression, copiousness of invention, and general usefulness to all the purposes of a Christian' (Wood, *Ath. Oxon.*, 3.783).

JOHN SPURR

Sources The whole works of the Right Reverend Jeremy Taylor, ed. R. Heber, 15 vols. (1828); rev. and corrected, ed. C. P. Eden, 10 vols. (1850–54) · Holy living and holy dying, ed. P. G. Stanwood, 2 vols. (1989) · R. Gathorne-Hardy and W. P. Williams, eds., Bibliography of the writings of Jeremy Taylor to 1700 (DeKalb, Illinois, 1971) · Wood, Ath. Oxon., new edn · Wood, Ath. Oxon.: Fasti, new edn · Evelyn, Diary · Diary and correspondence of John Evelyn, ed. H. B. Wheatley and W. Bray (1906) · The correspondence of Bishop Brian Duppa and Sir Justinian Isham, 1650–1660, ed. G. Isham, Northamptonshire RS, 17 (1951) · Walker rev. · E. Gosse, Jeremy Taylor (1904) · M. H. Nicholson, ed., Conway papers (1930) · E. Berwick, ed., Rawdon papers (1819) · CSP Ire. · CSP dom. · H. T. Hughes, The piety of Jeremy Taylor (1960) · H. R. McAdoo, Jeremy Taylor: Anglican theologian, Church of Ireland Historical Society (1997) · H. R. McAdoo, The spirit of Anglicanism (1965) · H. B. Porter, Jeremy Taylor — Liturgist (1979) · C. J. Stranks, The life and writings of Jeremy Taylor (1952) · T. Wood, English casuistical divinity during the seventeenth century, with special reference to Jeremy Taylor (1952) · A. Milton, Catholic and Reformed: the Roman and protestant churches in English protestant thought, 1600–1640 (1995) · K. E. Kirk, Conscience and its problems (1927) · R. B. Miller, 'Moral sources, ordinary life and truth-telling in Jeremy Taylor's casuistry', The context of casuistry, ed. J. F. Keenan and T. A. Shannon (Washington, 1995) · I. Green, Print and Protestantism in early modern England (2000) · St. J. D. Seymour, The puritans of Ireland, 1647–1661 (1921) · T. Barnard, Cromwellian Ireland (1975) · Bodl. Oxf., MSS Tanner 52, fols. 101, 216; 58, fol. 468 · Bodl. Oxf., MS Carte 45, fol. 222 · BL, Add. MS 4274, fols. 140, 142; Add. MS 29851, fol. 5; Add. MS 29584, fols. 6, 8; Add. MS 78298, fols. 60v, 66v, 69, 70v, 71v, 78, 80, 81, 110 · BL, Harley MS

6942, fol. 124 · BL, Harley MS 541, fol. 111 · BL, Sloane MS 4274, fol. 125

Likenesses W. Faithorne, line engraving, BM, NPG, NG Ire.; repro. in J. Taylor, *The rule and exercises of holy living* (1663) · P. Lombart, line engraving, BM, NPG; repro. in J. Taylor, *The rule and exercises of holy dying* (1650) · P. Lombart, line engraving, BM, NPG; repro. in J. Taylor, *Ductor dubitantium* (1660) [*see illus.*] · oils, All Souls Oxf.

Wealth at death see *CSP Ire., 1666–9*, 425, 429; Nicholson, ed., *Conway papers*, 287

Taylor, John (*d.* 1534), Catholic priest and diplomat, was born into a poor family at Barton under Needwood in the parish of Tatenhill, Staffordshire, the eldest of male triplets. According to tradition, the boys were presented to Henry VII, who undertook to pay for their education. In 1500 Taylor was a student in the law faculty at Ferrara, where he received the degree of DCnL. By the time he was ordained a priest in April 1503 Taylor had already begun to accumulate benefices in England, beginning with the rectory of Shottesbrooke, Berkshire, followed by that of Bishop's Hatfield, Hertfordshire, in December 1500, and a prebend at Wells in April 1505. His advancement was aided by papal dispensations for plurality granted in 1501 and 1504. In August 1504 he was sent on his first diplomatic mission, in the company of John Yonge, master of the rolls and a fellow student at Ferrara, to negotiate a commercial treaty with the duke of Burgundy. His efforts were rewarded with the rectory of Sutton Coldfield, Warwickshire, in January 1505, and he was soon appointed a royal chaplain to Henry VII.

With the accession of Henry VIII, Taylor's career prospered, and he soon added the rectory of All Hallows-the-Great in London and Coldingham in Northamptonshire to his portfolio of livings, together with the prebend of Eccleshall at Lichfield. Despite his lack of chancery experience, Taylor was appointed clerk of parliaments on 20 October 1509, and by 1515 his reforms of record keeping had produced the first proper Lords' journal. He accompanied the English army invading France in the summer of 1513, composing a detailed account of the campaign for his patron John Yonge (BL, MS Cotton Cleopatra C.v 64). His diplomatic work continued: he regularly replied to foreign ambassadors' orations at court, and in early 1515 he was included in an aborted embassy to Rome. Taylor also served as prolocutor of the 1515 Canterbury convocation, in which capacity he addressed the bishops on behalf of the lower clergy, rejecting royal tax demands. Closely associated with Cardinal Wolsey, by late 1516 he was employed in chancery as deputy to the master of the rolls, Cuthbert Tunstall. These services to crown and cardinal continued to bring rich rewards, with appointments as archdeacon of Derby (March 1516) and archdeacon of Buckingham (December 1516) followed by a canonry of St Stephen's, Westminster (March 1518). As a royal chaplain Taylor was present both at the Field of Cloth of Gold in the summer of 1520, and shortly afterwards when Henry VIII met the emperor Charles V at Gravelines.

Taylor's first major diplomatic assignment came in the autumn of 1525, when he was dispatched as an ambassador to France following the battle of Pavia. He was present at the release of François I at Bayonne in March 1526, and spent several months travelling with the itinerant French court; the Venetian ambassador credited Taylor with persuading François I not to ratify the treaty to which he had agreed while a prisoner of the Habsburgs. As in 1513, Taylor kept a diary of his travels, recording his impressions of French churches and the many fraudulent relics they contained (BL, Cotton MS Caligula D.ix 107). Throughout the summer of 1526 he worked under Wolsey's direction to arrange a league between England, France, and the papacy, but in mid-August he was replaced by John Clerk, like himself a clerical diplomat. Returning via Paris (where he attended some Greek lectures), Taylor reached Dover in late November.

On 27 June 1527 Taylor was named master of the rolls, but four months later returned to France to invest François I with the Garter, and then remained in Paris as ambassador. By the summer of 1528 he was occupied in making arrangements for the journey of the papal legate Campeggi to England, and dealing with one of his servants under investigation for Lutheranism. Taylor's second French embassy lasted until Easter 1529, when the imminent legatine court in England necessitated his recall. He was present at the opening session on 18 June 1529 and was soon occupied in taking depositions from witnesses. The failure of the legates to resolve the king's Great Matter led to the fall of Wolsey; as master of the rolls Taylor took custody of the great seal, surrendered by his former patron on 7 October 1529, and delivered it to the king three days later.

In September 1531 the veteran diplomat led a third embassy to France, designed to strengthen the Anglo-French alliance in order to pressure Pope Clement VII to grant Henry VIII an annulment. Having successfully concluded a treaty and arranged a meeting between Henry and François at Calais, by November 1532 Taylor had returned to his duties as master of the rolls at Westminster. He resigned the archdeaconry of Derby in early 1533, but rumours that he might be elevated to the episcopate (perhaps to the vacant see of Coventry and Lichfield) proved unfounded. However, another John *Taylor (*d.* 1554), bishop of Lincoln from 1552, is thought to have been his nephew or illegitimate son. In May 1534 it was believed that Taylor would soon resign as master of the rolls (probably due to illness); on 21 September Stow reported that he had been discharged from office. Five days earlier Taylor had made his will, which was revised on 1 October and proved on 24 November 1534. He died during October and was buried in the chapel of the former hospital of St Anthony, in Threadneedle Street, London, but his enduring monument is the church which he erected during the 1520s, on the site of the humble Staffordshire cottage where he was born.

P. R. N. CARTER

Sources *LP Henry VIII*, vols. 1–7 · C. G. Cruickshank, *Army royal: Henry VIII's invasion of France, 1513* (1969) · Emden, *Oxf.*, 4.559–60 · G. R. Elton, 'The early journals of the House of Lords', *EngHR*, 89

(1974), 481–512 · *Staffordshire*, Pevsner (1974) · *CEPR letters*, vols. 17–18 · J. Stow, *A survey of London*, rev. edn (1603); repr. with introduction by C. L. Kingsford as *A survey of London*, 2 vols. (1908); repr. with addns (1971) · C. L. Kingsford, ed., 'Two London chronicles from the collection of John Stow', *Camden miscellany, XII*, CS, 3rd ser., 18 (1910) · Cooper, *Ath. Cantab.*, vol. 1 · prerogative court of Canterbury, wills, PRO, PROB 11/25, fol. 142r–v
Archives BL, Cotton MSS, corresp. with Thomas Wolsey

Taylor, John (*d.* 1554), bishop of Lincoln, was probably born at the beginning of the sixteenth century, either a nephew or an illegitimate son of John *Taylor (*d.* 1534) of Barton, Staffordshire, who was extensively used by Henry VIII on diplomatic missions. The two Taylors had similar coats of arms. The younger was educated at Cambridge and eventually became DTh in 1538, but had spent some of his time as fellow of Queens' College (1523–37) and proctor for the university (1532–3). He was clearly known at court. He received his first living, that of St Peter Cornhill, London, from the king's physician, William Butts, and was appointed master of St John's in July 1538 by Henry VIII himself. He subsequently said that he owed everything to the king, 'he looked for nothing of the gift of any of the bishops' (Baker, 1.123). In the event, he was to need all the help that the king could give him. He quarrelled with the fellows of St John's, and the bishop of Ely was required to adjudicate as visitor between master and fellows in 1542. It was by grant of the king, to whom by 1543 he was a chaplain, rather than at the gift of John Longland, bishop of Lincoln, that Taylor was made dean of Lincoln early in 1539. Longland had wanted a conservative candidate who would be resident, and had expected the king to agree to his suggestion. He was outwitted. Taylor was inducted by proxy to the deanery on 29 March that year, but was not installed in person until August, and he did not reside in the close or preside at chapter until 1546.

While still master of St John's, Taylor began to make a name for himself as a preacher, though not without unsettling effect. When preaching in London in 1538 in his own church, he was questioned about his views on the sacrament by John Lambert, who had a history of heresy behind him. Taylor asked Lambert to put his views in writing. The result was that Lambert's views were referred successively to Robert Barnes, Cranmer, and Henry VIII, and Taylor was appointed with others to dispute them formally. Lambert was burnt. Taylor in this incident revealed his sympathy with the evangelicals of Lutheran persuasion, but he was clearly prepared to hand over to the stake a man like Lambert, whose sympathies lay with south German and Swiss protestantism. This was not time-serving, because in the following year he was one of two who had the courage in the lower house of convocation to oppose the decision to allow the king and bishops to answer the questions of faith which were ultimately enforced in the six articles; no doubt Taylor took the temperature of the king and house of bishops correctly.

In March 1547, after the death of Henry VIII, Taylor's conscientious dilemmas were to be resolved and his fortunes were to advance notably. He resigned the mastership of St John's, and on 3 March 1549 was presented to the lucrative prebend of Corringham to support his residence at Lincoln. What lay behind his resignation is not wholly clear. It may have been that he was compromised both in the college and at court by the outspoken opinions of a former fellow, Thomas Dobbe, who took issue with clerical celibacy and interrupted a sermon in St Paul's, so giving reforming evangelicals cause to fall out among themselves and a bad name. But it is also apparent that by the time Taylor protested major residence at Lincoln on 13 August 1546, and resided sufficiently to take chapter meetings, his relationship with Dobbe, if not Dobbe's memories of him, were a thing of the past. There was a need for strong leadership among the evangelicals to advance reform. This may have been easier for Taylor to undertake from Lincoln than from an acrimonious and somewhat conservative college in Cambridge. In any event he was well placed to promote change after the king's death, and in 1547 he was appointed a royal visitor for the dioceses of Peterborough, Lincoln, Oxford, and Coventry and Lichfield.

Taylor made no contribution as dean of Lincoln until he took up residence. Thereafter his tenure was marked by very generous grants of decanal property to his friends. The manor of Little Chester was granted to Thomas Smith, secretary to Protector Somerset, in whose house Taylor was eventually to die. The grant was for eighty years, and envisaged an increase in rent after the first five of £1 6*s*. 8*d*. Another grant of the lands of the rectory of Chesterfield was made, to commence in 1587 for fifty-nine years, when neither Taylor himself nor the other members of the chapter would be alive to face the consequences. In effect, the rectory had been granted away well into the next century at the same rent. He gave advowson grants, not just for one term, but always for two. But he was more careful in religious matters. His injunctions to his cathedral church in 1548 required of the chapter that they make sure that scripture was read daily and in the houses of the vicars and choristers, and that a rota for preaching was introduced. He also ordered that the library be checked for its holdings in the early fathers. He required that all anthems be sung in English, and this made his cathedral an obvious testing place for their eventual use. He was among the small group of reformers who helped Cranmer draw up the prayer book of 1549, and then defended *The Supper of the Lorde and the Holy Communion, Commonly called the Masse* during the debates about it in convocation and the House of Lords. He was also on commissions to examine Anabaptists, and he seems to have served for a time on the commission to reform the canon law.

Taylor had strong views against the celibacy of the clergy. He is reported when attending convocation in November 1547 to have said 'that the prystes of Englande are not votoryes, nor bounde with any vowe of single life, but that they maye frely and with good conscience marry' (Bailey, 57). It is not certain that Taylor married: he is one of many whose deprivation under Queen Mary was thought to have been due to his marital status, but actually seems to have had more to do with his appointment by letters patent on 13 May 1552 to be bishop of Lincoln, as well as with his views on the sacrament; these had impelled him to walk out of the House of Lords when mass was celebrated in the first year of Mary's reign. In the event he was imprisoned in the Tower on 5 October 1553, and although he was pardoned on 5 January 1554, he was deprived of his see on 20 March on the grounds of the nullity of his consecration and defect of his title.

Taylor's appointment as bishop of Lincoln, and his subsequent consecration on 26 June 1552, preceded the death of Edward VI by a single year, so his reforming zeal as bishop can only be inferred from sparse but significant details such as his appointment of Matthew Parker as dean. His diocesan register does not survive. He was clearly a friend of Thomas Cranmer as well as of his predecessor at Lincoln, Henry Holbeach. Fuller said that he had 'the merriest and pleasantest wit' (Fuller, 2.399); true, maybe, but not for those like Lambert who aroused his antagonism. He died in December 1554 at Ankerwick.

MARGARET BOWKER

Sources private information (2004) [D. MacCulloch] · *DNB* · R. E. G. Cole, ed., *Chapter acts of the cathedral church of St Mary of Lincoln*, 2–3, Lincoln RS, 13, 15 (1917–20) · D. MacCulloch, *Thomas Cranmer: a life* (1996) · T. Baker, *History of the college of St John the Evangelist, Cambridge*, ed. J. E. B. Mayor, 2 vols. (1869) · *The acts and monuments of John Foxe*, ed. S. R. Cattley, 8 vols. (1837–41), vol. 5 · Venn, *Alum. Cant.*, 1/4.205 · T. Fuller, *The church history of Britain*, ed. [J. Nichols], 2 (1837) · D. MacCulloch, *Tudor church militant: Edward VI and the protestant Reformation* (1999) · *Fasti Angl., 1541–1857*, [Lincoln] · C. Wriothesley, *A chronicle of England during the reigns of the Tudors from AD 1485 to 1559*, ed. W. D. Hamilton, 2 vols., CS, new ser., 11, 20 (1875–7) · D. S. Bailey, *Thomas Becon and the reformation of the church in England* (1952)
Archives CCC Cam., Parker Library, drafts of his visitation injunctions of 1548 · St John Cam., letters written as master

Taylor, John [*called* the Water Poet] (**1578–1653**), poet, was born in the parish of St Ewen's, Gloucester, on 24 August 1578. His parents are unknown, though a stray comment he made many years later suggests that his father was a barber–surgeon. The family was prosperous enough for Taylor to be sent to an elementary school in Gloucester and then on to a grammar school, perhaps the Crypt School, but he found Latin grammar impenetrable and soon left. In the early 1590s he moved to London, and was apprenticed to a waterman, probably in Southwark. He became a proud Londoner; his life was to be bound up with the watermen's affairs for the next fifty years, and in publications he styled himself 'John Taylor the Water-poet'.

Early career There are only fleeting glimpses of Taylor's early years in the capital. The Watermen's Company supplied men for the navy in times of war, and Taylor later boasted of having served Elizabeth at sea on seven occasions. He took part in 1596 in the expedition to Cadiz led by Essex and Lord Howard of Effingham, and sailed in the *Rainbow* on the voyage to the Azores in 1597. On one occasion, he later recalled, he and some friends went ashore to explore the small island of Flores, and were stranded for five days without food by bad weather. Taylor also hints at an early visit to Ostend, possibly during the siege of 1601–4. After completing his apprenticeship, about 1597, Taylor

John Taylor (1578–1653), by Thomas Cockson, 1630

plied his trade as a waterman. He also married at some point before 1612; his wife's identity is unknown, though her first name was probably Abigail and her maiden name possibly Miles. The couple settled on the Bankside in Southwark, and remained there until 1643. About 1605 Taylor was appointed 'bottleman' at the Tower, under its lieutenant, Sir William Waad. The post involved rowing out to ships bringing in cargoes of wine, and demanding two large bottles as a perquisite due to the lieutenant. Taylor served very happily until Waad was removed from office in 1613 and his successors demanded large fees for Taylor's continuation in office. He was eventually turned out on refusing to pay a further exorbitant increase, but was so stung by rumours that he had been sacked for dishonesty that he bought it back in 1616 for an annual fee of £72, which, rather perversely, he recouped by selling some of the wines collected for the lieutenant for his own profit. Late in 1617 a rival offered a higher bid for the post, and Taylor was ousted again, this time for ever. In *Taylors Farewell to the Tower Bottles* (1622) he presented an account of his experience.

Native wit, an affable personality, and good manners made Taylor stand out from the start among the rough breed of Thames watermen, and attracted the notice of some of the courtiers he ferried. In 1613 he was recommended by Viscount Haddington to be one of the King's Watermen, a select and liveried group who served the crown on ceremonial occasions. He also became a spokesman for the Watermen's Company on official business, and in 1614 was chosen to press its suit to the king against the new theatres erected north of the river. The watermen had enjoyed a huge trade ferrying visitors to the Globe and other theatres on the Bankside, and the move to the northern suburbs was a serious blow. Despite sympathetic words from Francis Bacon and Somerset, the king's favourite, nothing was achieved.

Taylor's links with the Bankside theatres included

actors, writers, and spectators with court connections. These contacts, and those he made through his post at the Tower, triggered a new interest in books and learning. He began to read voraciously, and before long started to write himself. In 1612 he brought his verses together and published them as *The Sculler, Rowing from Tiber to Thames*, with a simple woodcut of the author rowing his boat and a Latin version of the waterman's cry as an epigram. The title-page encapsulated the strategy he was to pursue throughout his literary career, playing on the novelty and incongruity of a lowly waterman aspiring to poetry and rubbing shoulders with men of letters and power. There were complimentary verses by Samuel Rowlands and Nicholas Breton, and though Ben Jonson offered nothing, Taylor pointedly claimed Jonson as a dear friend.

One of Taylor's verses made a derisive reference to the humorous writer and traveller Thomas Coryate, and this sparked a heated pamphlet war which he relished as a further opportunity for self-publicity. Both Coryate and Taylor petitioned the king, and one of Taylor's pamphlets was ordered to be burnt by the public hangman, providing still more publicity. In 1614 he became embroiled in conflict with another writer and entertainer, William Fennor. They arranged a joint appearance at the Hope theatre to stage a contest by performing dramatic impressions of contemporary characters. Taylor's flair for publicity ensured that the theatre was full, and Fennor's failure to turn up left him facing a near riot by his audience. He published a damning account as *Taylors Revenge* (1614), and though Fennor replied, Taylor fired a second salvo and claimed victory.

During these years Taylor was also busy turning out publications of many other kinds. There were verses on the death of Prince Henry in 1612, and the marriage of Princess Elizabeth the following year. A miniature 'thumb-bible', a verse summary of scripture published in 64mo, appeared as a toy for courtiers in 1614, with a dedication to the queen and Prince Charles. A similar version of John Foxe's *Acts and Monuments* appeared the following year. *The Nipping and Snipping of Abuses* (1614) offered satirical comments on the manners and vices of the age, while *Taylors Urania* (1615) presented his religious reflections in verse. He published verse essays, mock encomia, and nonsense writings too. His influences, as diverse as the genres, included Thomas Nashe, George Wither, and Thomas Heywood, while he also expressed his admiration for Philip Sidney, Christopher Marlowe, and Jonson. He could number many of the writers of the age among his friends and acquaintances, among them Samuel Daniel, Thomas Dekker, Breton, Rowlands, Philemon Holland, Heywood, and Wither.

Travels and adventures Taylor was to continue producing verse throughout his life. He never achieved the recognition or material rewards he felt he deserved, notwithstanding his frequent self-deprecating allusions to his modest talents and lack of education. Many better and better-connected writers found it equally hard to make a living by their pens, or to win substantial patronage. Taylor had an unusually entrepreneurial spirit, however, and found his own solution, by promoting his image as a 'personality' and turning it to financial account. His greatest success lay in designing a series of exotic journeys, publicizing them in advance, and persuading large numbers of acquaintances to sponsor him in return for a copy of a published account of his adventures following his return. The destination was usually of little importance; the point lay in the mode of travel, and the mock-heroic account of his adventures on the way. There were several models for such ventures, including Coryate and Will Kempe, but none matched Taylor in the publicity they achieved or the rewards they obtained. The first of these journeys was to Hamburg, in the summer of 1617, which Taylor used to publish a jocularly xenophobic account of German customs and society, in the popular style of the grotesque. The adventure was sufficiently successful to encourage Taylor to plan more adventurous schemes.

Taylor's next, and most successful, adventure was described in *The Pennyles Pilgrimage* (1618), an account of his visit to Scotland in the summer and early autumn that year. He travelled on foot, pledging to take no money, and not to beg any food, drink, or lodging on the way, a handicap sufficient to persuade 1650 sponsors (among them Edward Alleyn the actor–manager) to pledge to pay for an account of his adventures if he survived to publish them. Given his huge circle of acquaintances and invincible bonhomie, Taylor was unlikely to die of starvation. Friends old and new provided him with food and shelter, and the later stages of his journey to Edinburgh took on something of the character of a progress. He enjoyed the sights of Edinburgh, and later joined the earl of Mar on a lavish hunting party in the highlands at Braemar. Some alleged that Taylor's visit was designed to parody or steal the thunder from Ben Jonson's own trip to Scotland that year, a charge he repudiated; he paid a friendly call on Jonson at Leith on 25 September before returning to London. By now a consummate showman, he orchestrated his return to London in impressive style, arranging a grand supper for his friends at Islington, with entertainment by the earl of Derby's players, who performed 'The life and death of Guy of Warwick'—a jocular device, perhaps, to celebrate a new 'hero' by recalling the adventures of an old one. Taylor's humorous account of his travels was finished within a fortnight of his return, and published with a dedication to Buckingham, the king's new favourite.

Several further 'travels' followed in quick succession. The first and most bizarre was in July 1619, when Taylor and a friend sailed down the Thames to Quinborough in a boat he had fashioned, for a wager, out of brown paper, kept half afloat by inflated animal bladders attached to the sides. In August 1620 he set out on a much longer and less frivolous journey, to Prague. Taylor was a fervent protestant and patriot, and deeply disturbed by news of the Catholic Habsburg armies massing to crush the Bohemian revolt and drive out the new king, Frederick, and his British wife, Elizabeth. He had welcomed the marriage of Frederick and Elizabeth in 1613 as an important building block in an anti-Habsburg alliance, and was appalled that Frederick's election to the Bohemian crown was now under threat. In *An English-Mans Love to Bohemia* (1620) he urged English readers to enlist in the volunteer forces being raised to defend the Bohemian protestants, offering stirring reminders of English heroism in earlier campaigns from Crécy to the Armada. His journey to Prague, which he began on 4 August 1620, was designed to boost public interest further and feed the huge appetite for fresh and reliable news. Taylor can be plausibly seen as a forerunner of the modern war correspondent. He and his friend Tilbury Strange travelled via Amsterdam and Leipzig, joined along the way by his brother, who lived at Bückeburg, the seat of Count Ernst von Schomberg, and may have been able to act as interpreter. They found a warm welcome at the royal court in Prague, where they remained for several weeks before returning in an epic boat-trip 600 miles down the Elbe to Hamburg. Taylor's published account had to tread carefully in handling the political issues, but its partisan spirit would have been obvious to all. The battle of the White Mountain crushed the Bohemian revolt only a few weeks after Taylor's return, however, and signalled the collapse of his dreams. Some of the short pamphlets he published in the last years of James's reign made it clear that he was dismayed by the government's failure to intervene in the continental struggle, and that he shared the national relief at Prince Charles's safe return from his quixotic mission to Spain in search of a royal, Catholic bride.

The next two journeys were ambitious 'voyages' in a waterman's wherry. In July 1622 Taylor and some friends rowed a wherry down the Thames into the North Sea, and then along the east coast to the Humber, and so to York. At Hull he was fêted by the mayor, and at Cawood he dined with Toby Matthew, the archbishop of York, though to his chagrin the mayor of York declined to buy the battered wherry as a souvenir. In July 1623 he set off on a similar 'voyage' to Salisbury, through the English Channel and up the Wiltshire Avon. This trip capitalized on the king's own recent progress to the west, and had the more serious goal of promoting a scheme to investigate whether Salisbury's struggling economy could be rescued by making the Avon navigable to the sea. In the event Taylor and his companions were lucky to survive, for their boat was repeatedly battered by high seas and came close to foundering; when they were driven ashore one day their misery was compounded by a suspicious constable who thought they were pirates and tried to detain them. There were compensations too, however; at Portsmouth they were welcomed aboard the flagship of the fleet waiting to fetch Prince Charles home from Spain, and during his stay at Salisbury, Taylor found an opportunity to go sightseeing at Wilton House, seat of the earls of Pembroke. But despite the jocular tone of his published narrative, Taylor was so chastened by his narrow escape from drowning that he never again went to sea in a small boat.

The middle years The more sober court of Charles I was a less auspicious milieu for comic eccentrics, and from choice or necessity Taylor now began to present himself in a slightly more dignified manner. In 1625 he was among the royal watermen to escort the new queen, Henrietta

Maria, to Oxford to escape the plague; he occupied lodgings in Oriel College during the court's residence there, and wrote a vivid pamphlet on the epidemic. In 1630 he published his collected *Workes*, an extraordinary decision for a popular rhymer who was placing himself in the company of Shakespeare, Jonson, and Daniel (a friend). It was an act of defiance and self-assertion, however, rather than triumph or celebration. Taylor had no grand patrons, and pointedly dedicated his volume to 'the world', with dispirited comments on his failure to win recognition. It is typical that the same year that saw this bid for literary respectability also saw him devising a project to bring Nicholas Wood, 'the Great Eater of Kent', to London and turn his gargantuan appetite into a money-raising venture by holding public 'performances' at the Bear Garden.

For much of the ensuing decade Taylor was employed on official business. In 1631 he accompanied an expedition sponsored by the crown to survey the upper Thames, from Staines to Oxford, and report on the obstacles to navigation and opportunities for improvement. This was a project close to his heart, and he published an account of his personal observations on the trip, noting hazards and the appropriate remedies. During the 1630s he was frequently preoccupied with the affairs of the Watermen's Company, one of the largest and most turbulent of the city's companies. He served as one of its rulers, or overseers, in 1630–32 and again in 1638–40, and later as its clerk. Probably the most polished and well-connected of the ruling group, he was the obvious choice to lead the company's campaign to defend the watermen against competition from the hackney coaches, which were stealing much of their trade. From April 1634 Taylor was busy pleading their cause to government officials, and his efforts bore some fruit in a royal proclamation in January 1636 which banned hackney coachmen from carrying fares on journeys of under 3 miles. This fell short of the watermen's aspirations, however, and deepened the resentment and distrust of rank-and-file watermen which was to explode only a few years later.

Taylor's literary output during the 1630s was more journalistic than in earlier years. One of his most successful pieces was a humorous verse-biography of the centenarian Thomas Parr, who was brought to London in 1635 as a prodigy at the alleged age of 152; Taylor's account passed through three quick editions and was reprinted at Amsterdam in a Flemish translation. Other offerings included two consumers' guides to taverns in London and the home counties, a characteristic combination of business and pleasure, and *The Carrier's Cosmographie* (1637), a valuable handbook which set out information on the times and departure points of carriers and wagons leaving London for destinations in the provinces, and similar information on packet-boats. In 1639 Taylor took advantage of one of the periodic revivals of the 'woman question', which his friend Heywood had stirred up once more, and published two jocularly misogynist collections (*Divers Crab-Tree Lectures*, 1639, and *A Juniper Lecture*, 1640). They were quickly followed by a spirited and sometimes perceptive counterblast giving the woman's view, *The Womens Sharpe Revenge* (1640), which was published anonymously but bears clear signs of Taylor's own hand. At the very end of the decade Taylor revived his old practice of making a summer jaunt to the provinces. In July 1639 he embarked on a lengthy and convivial tour of the midlands, East Anglia, and Yorkshire, travelling this time by horse. Following his return to London in September he published an account which gave no hint of the gathering storm clouds.

The civil wars The collapse of Charles I's personal rule marked a decisive turning point in Taylor's life as well as in the affairs of the country. He played a characteristically combative role in the upheavals that followed. There were some aspects of the new order he could welcome in the months after parliament met in November 1640. He rejoiced at the attack on monopolies with a powerful broadside, *The Complaint of M Tenter-Hooke* (1641), illustrated with a woodcut of a monster whose fierce claws and grotesque costume showed how the consumer had been exploited and devoured by greedy monopolists. Taylor also praised the crackdown on Catholics, and identified parliament and the Scots as crucial defences against the threat of popery. He readily took the protestation (against Catholicism) twice. But in most respects the new order appalled him. In *Differing Worships* (1640), written before the Short Parliament met, he mounted a strong defence of the established church, including controversial practices such as bowing at the name of Jesus, against presbyterian and separatist critics. As a traditionalist, Taylor had always strongly disliked religious radicals, and he was deeply alarmed by their new prominence and confidence. When rioters smashed the altar-rails which had long stood in St Saviour's, Southwark, his parish church, in June 1641 he joined in petitioning the House of Lords, successfully, for their arrest and punishment. He is also found interrupting a radical preacher at Rotherhithe. More importantly, he poured out a flood of polemical pamphlets, some of them appearing anonymously, defending the episcopal church, lamenting that the prayer book was being abandoned in parish worship, and ridiculing the radicals. *A Swarme of Sectaries* (1641) sparked a ferocious and obscene pamphlet war with the parliamentarian preacher Henry Walker, which continued into 1642, and included an inspired burlesque sermon published as *A Seasonable Lecture* (1642), soon famous as 'Toby's Dog'.

The political upheavals also triggered a crisis in the Watermen's Company. Like many other London companies it faced strong pressure for reform from rank-and-file members who accused the ruling oligarchy of corruption and demanded a more democratic system in which the 'rulers' would be directly elected by every waterman. The ruling group viewed this demand as anarchic, and sought to tighten its own grip. In March 1641 the two sides presented rival petitions to parliament, and in May a Commons committee considering a bill to strengthen the overseers' authority was ordered to consider the radicals' complaints too. Taylor was one of the inner circle now accused of corruption, and he played a leading role in the bitter and sometimes violent exchanges. When the reformers changed tactics and took their case to the mayor and aldermen in February 1642, it was Taylor who was chosen to present the overseers' case. The eventual outcome, perhaps inevitably, favoured the reformers. A new system of choosing officers was introduced, though based on indirect rather than direct elections, and the company's elections in March 1642 swept away the old guard. It was the end of Taylor's association with the company, which had lasted over half a century.

Taylor continued to cling on to other aspects of his old life for as long as he was able. In the summer of 1641 he had made another of his epic wherry-voyages, sailing up the Thames as far as Cirencester, carting the boat across to a tributary of the Severn, and then navigating the Severn, Avon, and Wye. The voyage lasted twenty days, during which he calculated his party had rowed and sailed 1200 miles. The published narrative offered a familiar blend of humorous anecdote and passionate advocacy for the cause of inland navigation, including the value of a canal to link the Thames and Severn river systems, and detailed assessments of the problems and opportunities for commercial traffic on each of the rivers they had explored.

The king's enforced flight from London early in 1642 filled Taylor with dismay, and the ensuing slide to civil war left him in a highly exposed position. His devotion to the crown and the Book of Common Prayer was widely known, and no one doubted where his allegiance lay. But he was too old to fight and lacked the means to retire to a place of safety. In November 1642 he was arrested and interrogated by the radical MP Miles Corbet and the lord mayor over seditious remarks he was alleged to have made about the five members. In December he called for a compromise between royal prerogative and parliamentary privilege that would restore peace and enable the two parties to unite to crush the Irish uprising. But committed parliamentarians saw Taylor as an enemy, and rumours of death threats crystallized in an alarming attack by a mob while he was drinking in a tavern near the Guildhall, when he was lucky to escape with his life. He faced new dangers after refusing to pay a parliamentary tax early in 1643, and decided that flight was his only remaining option. Taking a boat to Windsor, where some parliamentary soldiers recognized him and accused him of planning treachery, he made his way on foot to Henley and arrived safely at Abingdon, in royalist territory, after a series of adventures. From there he made his way to Oxford, where the king gave him a friendly welcome and, more important, a livelihood. Taylor was appointed a yeoman of the guard and joint water bailiff, with responsibility for taking up boats to transport ammunition and supplies, and for keeping the waterways clear. His wife, whom he had been forced to leave behind in Southwark, died shortly after his departure, and can probably be identified with the Abigail Taylor buried at St Saviour's, Southwark, on 18 September 1643. Their modest estate was seized by parliament.

Taylor's most important contribution to the royalist cause lay in the stream of political squibs he produced during his time in Oxford. Polemical and satirical, they were designed to boost morale rather than convince the uncommitted, and the tone was jaunty and confident. Taylor was more concerned to establish appropriate images for the king and his enemies than plunge into the details of the issues at stake, largely beyond him and many of his readers. He presented the king's war as a defensive struggle, with Charles a good protestant upholding the established church and his traditional prerogatives against hypocritical and aggressive parliamentary enemies. According to the parliamentarian John Booker, Taylor also collaborated with George Wharton and John Berkenhead on the royalist newspaper, *Mercurius Aulicus*. He remained in Oxford until its surrender in July 1646. Under the terms of surrender, the king's former household servants were allowed to apply for a competent allowance from the committee for the king's revenue, and Taylor became a zealous campaigner on his own and their behalf, forwarding some two hundred petitions to the committee. But it was no secret that he had been a political activist rather than a mere household attendant, and he can hardly have been surprised that he was awarded nothing.

The last years Taylor's final years were spent in poverty. There was no longer a royal court, the Watermen's Company was in the hands of his enemies, and most likely patrons were living in poverty or exile. Taylor settled in Westminster, and by 1647 was running the Crown alehouse near Covent Garden. About 1647 he married again, though his wife's identity is unknown except that her first name was Alice. After the king's death he changed the alehouse's name to the Mourning Crown, and then, when this aroused disapproval, to the Poet's Head, with a sign bearing his own portrait.

As the alehouse afforded only a modest living, Taylor continued to supplement it by his pen. He never abandoned his support for the royalist cause, though circumstances now obliged him to support it with more circumspection. When the king was held captive in the Isle of Wight in 1648, Taylor decided to visit him, acknowledging frankly that he was moved by the need to make money as well as by a genuine longing to see his sovereign once more. His published account of the visit mixed comedy and pathos, describing his misadventures on the road before going on to stress the king's unshakeable piety and patience, and the miraculous cures he had wrought on the island by the royal touch. Although Taylor was still clinging to hopes of a settlement, his portrayal of the king was already that of a royal martyr. In the books of nonsense he published in his last years, he made it clear that the absurdly fractured language and jumble of ideas and images were intended to reflect the madness of the age.

In his last few years Taylor made four more of his traditional travels, designed to relieve his poverty. For his journey to the west in the summer of 1649 he found almost 3000 subscribers, testimony to his remarkable enduring popularity as well as his energy. He wrote a vivid account of the war-torn land he passed through on a long and sometimes dangerous journey that took him all the way to Land's End, where he carved his name on the shore. The journey brought him little profit, however, for on 15 August, shortly after his return, he was arrested on suspicion of espionage, and his papers were seized. Among them were the names and addresses of his sponsors, and their loss dealt a crippling blow to his marketing plans.

Despite this setback Taylor made another journey in the summer of 1650, this time sailing to Ipswich, travelling through East Anglia, and returning via Cambridge. This was a less demanding expedition, and he enjoyed the warm welcome he found from Sir William Paston at Oxnead and many other hosts. The Scottish invasion of 1651 ruled out any travels that year, but in 1652 Taylor embarked on an ambitious journey that took him to Chester and then on a tour round the Welsh coast. He was greeted warmly by the cavalier gentry, but viewed with suspicion by the parliamentary garrisons, and was afraid of being arrested as a spy once more. The summer of 1653 saw his final journey: a much shorter trip to Sussex, where he enjoyed the rich food and drink lavished on him by his various hosts.

Taylor's later pamphlets contain numerous references to his failing health, and he did not long survive this last journey. He was buried on 5 December 1653 in St Martin-in-the-Fields. His widow, Alice, died in January 1658.

Like most writers, Taylor never achieved the recognition he thought his due. Having successfully constructed a comic persona as the rhyming waterman, it was an impossible challenge to be accepted as a serious poet. His achievement was none the less impressive. As a literary entrepreneur and showman he was far more prosperous in his heyday than most writers; few watermen or struggling poets were also subsidy men or had to pay ship money. Taylor pursued a successful literary career for over fifty years, demonstrating a remarkable range, facility, and inventiveness. He played a pioneering role in the development of nonsense verse, popular political journalism, and travel writing. His travel pamphlets offer a distinctive veneration for antiquity combined with a ringing endorsement of innovation: he admired the public amenities of well-ordered towns, and championed signs of economic progress, whether manifested by coal mines or developments in inland navigation. Taylor anticipated Daniel Defoe more than he echoed John Leland. The travel writings, like almost everything he published in both verse and prose, had a strongly autobiographical dimension, and they provide a vivid picture of a bluff, shrewd, convivial man, with an appetite for life that won him friends across the political spectrum. William Winstanley and Anthony Wood paid tribute to his natural gifts as a writer. The portrait in Watermen's Hall and those contained in his publications reinforce the surviving pen portraits from Taylor himself and his friends.

BERNARD CAPP

Sources B. Capp, *The world of John Taylor the Water-Poet, 1578–1653* (1994) • F. Dow, 'The life and times of John Taylor the Water Poet', PhD diss., Harvard U., 1930 • W. Notestein, *Four worthies* (1956) • J. Taylor, *All the workes of John Taylor* (1630); facs. repr. (1973) • *Works of John Taylor the Water Poet not included in the folio volume of 1630*, Spenser Society (1870–78); repr. (New York, 1967) • N. Malcolm, *The origins of English nonsense* (1997) • J. Chandler, ed., *Travels through Stuart*

Britain: the adventures of John Taylor, the Water Poet (1999) · C. O'Riordan, 'The democratic revolution in the company of Thames watermen, 1641–2', *East London Record*, 6 (1983)

Archives Bodl. Oxf., misc. literary MSS

Likenesses T. Cockson, engraving, 1630, BM, NPG; repro. in Taylor, *All the workes* [*see illus.*] · J. Taylor, oils, 1655, Bodl. Oxf. · engraving, repro. in J. Taylor, *Taylor's motto* (1621) · line engraving, NPG; repro. in J. Taylor, *A memorial of all the English monarchs* (1622) · oils, Watermen's Company, London; repro. in Capp, *World of John Taylor*

Taylor [*alias* Grimston], **John** (1597–1655), diplomat, was born in Yorkshire, the eldest of five children (three sons and two daughters) of Stephen Taylor (*d.* 1618) of Bickerton, steward of the earl of Cumberland, and his wife, Dowsabell (*fl.* 1597–1620), daughter of William Grimston of Newport, Isle of Wight. His parents were both Roman Catholics and saw to it that he was brought up and educated in the Catholic faith. In 1612 he was enrolled in the English College, St Omer, in Flanders, where he studied for seven years. On 19 October 1619 he was admitted as a convictor at the English College, Rome. However, he decided to forgo a religious career and left in the late spring of 1621, after less than two years of study.

Taylor's whereabouts and activities during the following seven years are unclear, though it may have been during this time that he married Jane Gibbs; they had three children by 1639. Taylor settled upon a career in government service, and by 1628 he had secured his first government employment, probably on the strength of his language skills and contacts made through the earl of Cumberland. By 1630 he had begun serving as a diplomatic agent at foreign courts, particularly those of the Habsburgs in Vienna, Brussels, and Madrid. In his dealings abroad Taylor served the interests of the court party which supported peace with the Habsburgs. This was often a difficult task, for the emperor had deprived Charles I's brother-in-law, Frederick V of the Palatinate, of his hereditary lands and titles and parcelled them out to Spain and Bavaria. On his first known assignment Taylor gathered news in Brussels, where he was present in April 1630. He was soon sent to the empire in an unofficial capacity to promote a peaceful settlement of the Palatinate question, first at the electoral meeting at Regensburg in October and November 1630, and afterwards at the imperial court in Vienna. Despite his efforts and those of Sir Robert Anstruther, the accredited English ambassador to the emperor, no agreement was reached, and Taylor departed Vienna in August 1632. He returned to Brussels in October and resumed his news-gathering activities there for a time, but soon returned to England, where he was investigating a scheme to promote trade between Ireland and Spain for Wentworth in the summer of 1633.

Taylor quickly became more directly involved in Spanish affairs: from July 1634 to May 1635 he was employed on a diplomatic mission to Madrid to expedite negotiations for an Anglo-Spanish maritime treaty underway in England. In the estimation of Hopton, the English resident agent at Madrid, Taylor was 'a very honest and careful man' who acquitted his duties there satisfactorily (MS

Clarendon 5, fol. 324). Soon after Taylor's return to England he secured an important post as resident agent to the imperial court in Vienna, where he arrived on 22 November 1635. He was instructed to remonstrate against the peace of Prague and offer the emperor a provisional alliance with England in return for satisfaction regarding the Palatinate. Taylor, ever hopeful of an agreement between England and the Habsburgs, allowed himself to be convinced that the emperor was willing to grant full restitution and sent home optimistic reports to this effect. On the basis of these reports Charles I sent the earl of Arundel as ambassador-extraordinary in 1636 to conclude the final settlement; however, he was soon disappointed in his mission and returned to England in disgust. Taylor remained at the imperial court to continue the negotiations, but his role was limited after the death of Ferdinand II in February 1637, since Charles I refused to recognize the new emperor, Ferdinand III, or to send Taylor fresh credentials. During the following two years Taylor continued to represent English interests at the imperial court. He was periodically reprimanded for indiscretions in his conduct of the negotiations, and was finally recalled in early 1639.

In April that year Taylor reached England and was soon called to account for promoting a conference with the Habsburgs at Brussels without the commission to do so. The real cause of his disgrace, however, was not his undertakings with the Habsburgs (which were covertly encouraged by the crown), but rather that their exposure prejudiced English negotiations for a French treaty underway at Hamburg. Taylor was committed to the Tower in September, where he remained for at least seven months. In dire financial straits, he repeatedly petitioned Windebank for his release, which was probably granted before the outbreak of the civil war.

Despite this bad treatment, Taylor remained a staunch royalist, and at some point he left England for the continent, eventually returning to Vienna. Although he was lightly esteemed by Sir Edward Hyde, who regarded him as a 'fool', he was employed on the strength of his loyalty and good reputation with the emperor to muster support for Charles II's cause from various Catholic princes and the imperial diet during the interregnum (*Clarendon State Papers*, 3.97; *Diary of John Evelyn*, 4.257). He may have acted as an agent to the emperor for some weeks in the autumn of 1649. In September 1652 he was accredited as agent to the electors of Cologne and Mainz and the emperor in Vienna, where his brother Francis was court chaplain. This was the final mission of Taylor's career; he died, presumably in Vienna, in the autumn of 1655, probably in November.   T. L. LINDQUIST

Sources Bodl. Oxf., MSS Clarendon 5–18, 43–50 · R. Scrope and T. Monkhouse, eds., *State papers collected by Edward, earl of Clarendon*, 3 vols. (1767–86), vol. 2, p. 71 · *Calendar of the Clarendon state papers preserved in the Bodleian Library*, 3: *1655–1657*, ed. W. D. Macray (1876), 67 · state papers, foreign, German empire, and Hungary, PRO, vols. 7–10 · state papers, foreign, Spain, PRO, vol. 37 · state papers, foreign, Flanders, PRO, vol. 19, fol. 335; vol. 22 · state papers, domestic, Charles I, PRO, vol. 189, fol. 145; vol. 423, fol. 20; vol. 273, fol. 151; vol. 289, fol. 145; vol. 433, fol. 102; vol. 446, fol. 52; vol. 448,

fol. 112; vol. 470, fols. 164–5 · *Report on the manuscripts of the earl of Denbigh, part V*, HMC, 68 (1911) · *CSP dom., 1625–49* · *CSP Venice* · G. Holt, *St Omers and Bruges colleges, 1593–1773: a biographical dictionary*, Catholic RS, 69 (1979) · H. Foley, ed., *Records of the English province of the Society of Jesus*, 6 (1880), 290 · M. R. Trappes-Lomax, 'Who was John Taylor the diplomatist?', *Recusant History*, 7 (1963–4), 43–5 · Thurloe, *State papers*, 1.238, 467; 2.469; 4.103, 169 · *The Nicholas papers*, ed. G. F. Warner, 1, CS, new ser., 40 (1886), 307–8; 2, CS, new ser., 50 (1892), 5–6 · *The diary of John Evelyn*, ed. W. Bray, new edn, 4, ed. J. B. Wheatley (1906), 256–7 · G. Radcliffe, *The earl of Strafforde's letters and dispatches, with an essay towards his life*, ed. W. Knowler, 1 (1739), 95–6, 104–5 · archdiocese of York, archiepiscopal visitation court books, Borth. Inst., 1604, fol. 26; 1615, fols. 31–2; 1619, fols. 23–4 · W. Dugdale, *The visitation of the county of Yorke*, ed. R. Davies and G. J. Armytage, SurtS, 36 (1859), 214 · BL, Add. MS 18827, fols. 15–6 · 'The parish registers of Bilton in Ainsty co. York, 1571–1812', transcribed by W. Brigg, Family History Library, Salt Lake City · A. Kenny, ed., *The responsa scholarum of the English College, Rome*, 1, Catholic RS, 54 (1962), 327 · W. Kelly, ed., *Liber ruber venerabilis collegii Anglorum de urbe*, 1, Catholic RS, 37 (1940), 191 · R. T. Spence, 'The pacification of the Cumberland borders, 1593–1628', *Northern History*, 13 (1977), 59–160 · E. A. Beller, 'The diplomatic relations between England and Germany during the Thirty Years' War', DPhil diss., U. Oxf., 1924?, 348–78 · P. Haskell, 'Sir Francis Windebank and the personal rule of Charles I', PhD diss., U. Southampton, 1978, 208–19 · L. J. Reeve, 'Quiroga's paper of 1631: a missing link in Anglo-Spanish diplomacy during the Thirty Years' War', *EngHR*, 101 (1986), 913–26
Archives Bodl. Oxf., Clarendon MSS

Taylor, John (1694–1761), Presbyterian minister and tutor, was born at Scotforth, Lancaster, the son of an Anglican timber merchant and his wife, a dissenter. Destined for the Christian ministry, he entered Thomas Dixon's dissenting academy at Whitehaven in 1709, where Caleb Rotheram, afterwards of Kendal, was among his contemporaries. During the course of his studies (1712) he devised his own Hebrew grammar, which ran to 100 pages, thereby laying the foundation for his scholarly eminence in that field. Three years of further instruction followed at Findern Academy under the capable classicist Thomas Hill. In his funeral oration for Taylor, Edward Harwood pronounced his classical scholarship 'almost unrivalled', though Samuel Parr queried his competence in Latin. Taylor left Findern on 25 March 1716. On 7 April he took charge of the extra-parochial chapel at Kirkstead, Lincolnshire, which was used for dissenting worship under the patronage of the Disney family, and was ordained by Derbyshire ministers on 11 April, no formal doctrinal subscription being sought. He undertook to 'maintain the truths of the Gospel, especially such as are beyond controversy determined in the Holy Scriptures' (James, 804). On 13 August 1717 he married a widow, Elizabeth Jenkinson (d. 1761) of Boston. Their two surviving children were Richard (d. 1762), father of Philip (1747–1831), minister at Kay Street, Liverpool (1767), and at Eustace Street, Dublin (1771), and of John (1750–1826), the hymn writer; and Sarah (d. 1773), who married John Rigby of Chowbent, and whose son was the physician Edward Rigby (1747–1821).

Life was hard at Kirkstead. Taylor eked out his annual stipend of £33 by conducting a boarding-school. Even so he was not always able to heat his study—to which cause he later attributed the rheumatism in his knees; neither could he afford to complete the abridgement of Matthew Henry's commentaries on which he had embarked. Though invited to the Pudsey church in 1726, Taylor continued at Kirkstead until 1733, when he became Peter Finch's colleague at Norwich. Finch, the son of the ejected Henry Finch (1633–1704), had been maintaining orthodox Calvinism and expounding the Westminster catechisms at Norwich since 1691, and did so until his death in 1754. On his arrival, Taylor selected Samuel Clarke's *The Scripture-Doctrine of the Trinity* for congregational study, and was himself influenced by it in the direction of Arianism. As Harwood later remarked, 'if ever he expressed an uncommon warmth and honest indignation against anything, it was against *Athanasianism*, which he thought one of the greatest corruptions of pure and genuine Christianity, as this doctrine entirely subverts the unity of God' (Harwood, 40).

In 1735, under the influence of Samuel Clarke, Taylor finished writing *The Scripture-Doctrine of Original Sin*, but it was not published until 1740, with a second edition in the following year. It is widely reported that an unnamed Irish Calvinist minister warned his flock, 'I desire that none of you will read it, for it is a bad book, and a dangerous book; and, what is worse than all, the book is unanswerable' (Davis, 36). Influenced by Limborch, Taylor sought to rebut the Calvinist view of original sin on scriptural grounds, larding his case with moral repugnance. The Calvinist doctrine turns God into a monster: 'pray consider seriously what a God He must be who can be displeased with and curse His innocent creatures even before they have a being' (*Scripture-Doctrine of Original Sin*, 151). Among respondents to Taylor were John Wesley, who in *The Doctrine of Original Sin* (1757) charged Taylor with overthrowing the foundations of primitive, scriptural Christianity; Samuel Hebden who, standing foursquare on the Westminster confession, upheld the sole agency of the Holy Spirit in regeneration against Taylor's view that virtue and holiness result from the free and right choices of human beings; and Jonathan Edwards who, in *The Great Christian Doctrine of Original Sin Defended*, argued that if we do not posit universal depravity we cannot explain how every individual does, in fact, freely choose what is evil. Nevertheless, with hindsight it was observed that Taylor's *Original Sin* 'did more than any other [book] to emancipate the English Presbyterian Dissenters from Calvinism' ('British and Foreign Unitarian Association Centenary Exhibition', *Transactions of the Unitarian Historical Society*, 3, 1923–6, 228).

In the meantime Taylor had, in 1737, earned the favour of some and the disapprobation of others for his defence of the layman Joseph Rawson, who had been accused of embracing Arianism, and had accordingly been removed from the membership roll of Castle Gate Church, Nottingham, at the instigation of the minister, James Sloss, a former pupil, though clearly not a clone, of the liberal John Simson of Glasgow, who had himself been threatened with a heresy trial. Taylor was utterly opposed to what he took to be unwarrantable tests of church membership, and in *A Further Defence of the Common Rights of Christians* (1738) he thundered, 'A popish, anti-christian Spirit, I will ever oppose, as God shall enable me' (*Further Defence*, 78). In 1745 he published his *Paraphrase with Notes on … Romans*, which prompted John Barker's expostulation to Philip Doddridge in a letter of 26 March 1745: 'What an Audacious theolougue is that Taylor! Unhappy Norwich! Poor Mr. Finch!' (Nuttall, no. 1048). Taylor prefixed a 'Key to the apostolic writings' to his *Paraphrase*, concerning which, and with reference to Taylor's indebtedness to Locke, Doddridge, in a letter to Samuel Wood of 19 April 1745, declared that 'a certain Key … seems broke in the Lock' (ibid., no. 1055).

In 1750 Taylor published *A Collection of Tunes in Various Airs*, to which is prefixed an introduction to the art of singing. He used the book when training his choir of young people at Norwich. *The Scripture-Doctrine of the Atonement* appeared in 1751, followed by the two volumes of Taylor's *The Hebrew Concordance Adapted to the English Bible* (1754, 1757). In the former work, which drew a reply from the high-Calvinist Baptist John Brine, Taylor insists (unlike later liberal exponents of exemplarist views of the atonement) that Christ died to take away sin, but he does not accept that the Son had to die in order to make the Father merciful. The first volume of the latter work, dedicated to the archbishops and bishops of England and Ireland, contains a subscription list including twenty-two English bishops, fifteen Irish bishops, and such prominent nonconformists as Job Orton, Joseph Priestley, and Taylor's college contemporary Caleb Rotheram. For his biblical work Taylor was, on 20 January 1756, awarded the degree of DD by the University of Glasgow, his promoters including William Leechman and Adam Smith. Looking back, the Congregationalist John Stoughton judged that 'The Independents had no Hebrew scholar to be compared with Taylor of Warrington' (J. Stoughton, *History of Religion in England, from the Opening of the Long Parliament to the End of the Eighteenth Century*, 1881, 6.322).

On 12 May 1756 Taylor preached at the opening of the Octagon Chapel in Norwich, the foundation-stone of which he had laid on 25 February 1754. When John Wesley visited the building, designed by Thomas Ivory, on 23 December 1757 he described its elegant interior, ruefully wondering, 'How can it be thought that the old coarse gospel should find admission here?' (J. Wesley, *The Works of the Rev. John Wesley, A.M.*, 1872, 2.431). In 1756 Taylor published *The Lord's Supper Explained upon Scripture Principles*, and in 1757 there appeared *The Covenant of Grace, and Baptism the Token of it*, in which he drew an analogy between paedobaptism in the church and circumcision in the Old Testament. The Baptist Grantham Killingworth published a rebuttal in the following year.

By the end of 1757 Taylor had, in response to insistent appeals, moved to Warrington to become the first tutor in divinity and moral philosophy at the academy which had opened on 20 October. The secretary of the trustees and inspiration of the entire project, John Seddon, received a letter from his friend Philip Holland concerning the proposal to extend an invitation to Taylor:

> There can be no doubt, I think, but he will undertake the care of the Academy, when invited to it, but I wish there will not be some little difficulty in finding him a colleague that he will approve of, and that he may not aim at too much in the business of lecturing. (McLachlan, *Warrington Academy*, 18)

In the event, Taylor was not happy at Warrington: 'My condition ever since I came to Warrington has been very uneasy, and I may say, wretched' (Harwood, 49). A variety of factors conspired against him. For a start, he was not in good health, and rheumatism now required his use of two sticks, and he was concerned for his wife's frailty. His relations with Seddon deteriorated for he was incensed when Seddon took it upon himself to offer some theological lectures, and complained that Seddon refused to purchase library books recommended by the tutors. He opposed Seddon and those Liverpool ministers who were urging set forms of worship, and in his posthumous work *The Scripture Account of Prayer* (1761) he made out a strong case for free prayer in worship, though 'only so far as it is rational; not any extravagant effusions' (*Scripture Account of Prayer*, 5). Although in his annual address to the students Taylor advocated the impartial weighting of evidence and the according of conscientious rights of judgement to others, it is suggested that he waxed dictatorial when students adopted opinions other than his own. In particular, and despite his associations with Glasgow, he is said to have been displeased when the students inclined more towards Hutcheson's moral sense theory of ethics (of which Taylor published an *Examination* in 1759) than towards that of William Wollaston, to whose book *The Religion of Nature Delineated* Taylor's *A Sketch of Moral Philosophy* (1760) was intended as a guide and endorsement. However there is no evidence of friction on this score between Taylor and Hutcheson's pupil and disciple Samuel Bourn during the latter's assistantship to Taylor from 1754 to 1757. The rightness of an action, Taylor argues, does not depend upon the agent's will, or upon teleological considerations, but solely upon the nature of the action as such, this being determined by reason—that is, by conscience. Taylor's divinity class notes, *A Scheme of Scripture Divinity*, first printed for the use of students by the Warrington trustees in 1761, were posthumously published in 1763.

Taylor died in his sleep, a disappointed man, in Warrington on 5 March 1761. A number of subscribers to Warrington Academy invoked the ungracious treatment of Taylor as the ground (or the pretext) of their discontinued support, but other more deep-rooted problems brought about its closure twelve years later. Taylor and his wife, who died three months later, on 2 June 1761, were buried at Chowbent Chapel graveyard, Atherton, Lancashire. A tablet in the vestibule at Chowbent commemorates them both, and in the Octagon Chapel, Norwich, there is a memorial tablet to Taylor.   ALAN P. F. SELL

Sources E. Harwood, *A sermon occasioned by the death of the Rev John Taylor, DD* (1761) • J. Taylor and E. Taylor, *History of the Octagon Chapel, Norwich* (1848) • W. Turner, *Lives of eminent Unitarians*, 1 (1840), 299ff. • A. P. F. Sell, *Dissenting thought and the life of the churches: studies* *in an English tradition* (1990), chap. 7 • E. Taylor, *Monthly Repository*, 21 (1826), 482–94 • *DNB* • H. McLachlan, *English education under the Test Acts: being the history of the nonconformist academies, 1662–1820* (1931) • H. McLachlan, *Warrington Academy: its history and influence*, Chetham Society, 107, new ser. (1943) • W. Turner, *The Warrington Academy* (1957) • P. O'Brien, *Warrington Academy, 1757–86: its predecessors and successors* (1989) • V. D. Davis, *A history of Manchester College* (1932) • T. S. James, *The history of the litigation and legislation respecting Presbyterian chapels and charities in England and Ireland between 1816 and 1849* (1867) • *Calendar of the correspondence of Philip Doddridge*, ed. G. F. Nuttall, HMC, JP 26 (1979)

Archives Lancaster District Library, letters mainly to Dr Benson **Likenesses** Houbraken, line engraving, 1746 (after D. Heins), BM, NPG; repro. in J. Taylor, *The Hebrew concordance* (1754), frontispiece • crayon drawing, Harris Man. Oxf.

Taylor, John (1703–1772), itinerant oculist, the elder son of John Taylor (d. c.1709), a Norwich surgeon and apothecary, was born in Norwich on 16 August 1703. He came from a family which produced medical men for at least five generations. In 1722 he became an apothecary's assistant in London, where he also studied surgery under William Cheselden at St Thomas's Hospital and developed a special interest in eye diseases. He practised for some time in Norwich as a surgeon and oculist but encountered opposition, and in 1727 he began travelling around Britain as an itinerant eye-doctor.

In 1733 Taylor obtained an MD degree from Basel, where he was made a fellow of the College of Physicians; in 1734 he was granted further MD degrees from the universities of Liège and Cologne. In the same year he made a tour through France and the Netherlands, and visited Paris. Taylor returned to London in November 1735, and was appointed oculist to George II in the following year. For more than thirty years he continued his itinerant method of practice, with London as his headquarters. He visited in turn nearly every court in Europe, with a tour through Spain and Portugal from 1737 to 1742; an appearance in Rouen in 1743; another tour of the British Isles from 1744 to 1746; the Netherlands and Flanders in 1747; Germany and Austria in 1750; Rostock in 1751, at the invitation of the duke of Mecklenburg-Schwerin, followed by visits to Hamburg and Denmark; Sweden in 1752; a return visit to northern Europe and Russia in 1753 to 1754; Germany and Bohemia in 1755; a visit to Italy in 1756; Vienna and Ghent in 1757; and another tour of the British Isles in 1759 to 1760, living for a while at Gravel Street, Hatton Garden, London. Taylor went around in style, travelling with two coaches and many liveried servants, and presenting the appearance of a grand seigneur. The ostentatious narration of his wanderings in his three-volume autobiography, *History of the Travels and Adventures of the Chevalier John Taylor* (1761–2), with its endless name-dropping of eminent people treated and grand ladies flirted with at masked balls, must be taken with a pinch of salt, but he was clearly a tireless traveller in pursuit of glory in his craft.

Taylor possessed considerable skill as an operator. His early book *Mechanism of the Eye* (1727) is an able compendium of contemporary science; his *Nosographia*

John Taylor (1703–1772), by John Faber junior (after Paul Ryche)

ophthalmica (1746) was the first attempt at an atlas of diseases of the external eye, containing an accurate description of conical cornea and dealing in a competent fashion with lesions of the eyelids, lacrimal passages, conjunctiva, and cornea. Taylor's main claim to priority lies in his views on strabismus. He kept up with the discoveries of the day, made original contributions to the treatment of squint, and was expert at couching for cataract. Works such as *An Exact Account of 243 Diseases to which the Eye and its Coverings are Exposed* (1759) show the range of his knowledge. No less a figure than Albrecht von Haller judged him 'a skilful man, but too liberal of promises' (Coats, 152).

One of the principal medical entrepreneurs of his day, Taylor was a shameless self-advertiser, continually dropping the names of princes and savants. Styling himself 'Chevalier' and 'ophthalmiator pontifical imperial and royal', he stated in his autobiography that he was 'the most public man under the sun, being personally known not only in every Town in Europe, but in every part of the globe' (Taylor, 2.100). His vanity and range of boasted cures knew no bounds: he claimed to have restored Bach's sight (in truth he may have been remotely responsible for the composer's death). He also treated Handel in 1758, diagnosing a paralytic disorder in the near-blind composer. Taylor finally quit England about 1767, and, after visiting Paris, he died in a convent at Prague on 6 June 1772. He is said to have become blind before his death. With his wife, Ann King, he had an only son, John Taylor [*see below*], but little is known of his family life.

Taylor's methods of self-promotion were those of a charlatan, which caused him to become the subject of many satires and pasquinades, including *The Operator: a Ballad Opera* (1740) and *The English imposter detected, or, The life and fumigation of the renown'd Mr. J—— T——* (1732). He was accustomed to make bombastic orations before performing his cures, expressing himself in what he called the true Ciceronian style; its idiosyncrasy consisted in commencing each sentence with the genitive case and concluding with the verb. He skilfully played upon the fascination with light and sight that was so strong in the age of enlightenment, and stressed before Johann Kaspar Lavater how the eye was the index of the mind—hence the oculist was also a kind of psychologist. Johnson declared him 'an instance of how far impudence could carry ignorance' (Boswell, 1022), and doubtless his ostentatious behaviour betrays personal vanity; but it also says much about the need for self-promotion at that time in the precarious world of those pioneering the new medical specialities.

His son, **John Taylor** (*c*.1724–1787), oculist, was born in London and educated at the Collège du Plessis in Paris. About 1739 he moved to London, and, after studying under his father, he practised independently as an oculist. On the death of the Baron de Wenzel, Taylor succeeded as oculist to George III in 1772. In 1761 *A Life and Extraordinary History of the Chevalier John Taylor* was published in his name. Exceedingly scurrilous, it represented his father as a libertine and his alleged cures as mere frauds. No serious attempt to disown the book was made at the time by the younger Taylor, but according to John Taylor, the chevalier's grandson, the biography was really the production of Henry Jones (1721–1770), who, after being entrusted with the materials, had betrayed his trust. Taylor died at Hatton Garden, London, on 17 September 1787, and was buried six days later in the new burying-ground of St Andrew's. Taylor and his wife, Ann Price, had three sons, of whom the eldest, John *Taylor (1757–1832), was afterwards oculist to George III and George IV.

ROY PORTER

Sources G. Coats, 'The Chevalier Taylor', *Studies in the history of ophthalmology in England prior to the year 1800*, ed. R. R. James (1933), 132–219 · W. B. Ober, 'Bach, Handel and "Chevalier" John Taylor, MD, ophthalmiator', *New York State Journal of Medicine*, 69 (1969), 1797–1807 · D. M. Jackson, 'Bach, Handel and the Chevalier Taylor', *Medical History*, 12 (1968), 385–93 · F. Berg, 'The Chevalier Taylor and his strabismus operation', *British Journal of Ophthalmology*, 51 (1967), 667–73 · P. Trevor-Roper, 'Chevalier Taylor – ophthalmiator royal, 1703–1772', *Documenta Ophthalmologica*, 71 (1989), 113–22 · J. Boswell, *Life of Johnson*, ed. R. W. Chapman, rev. J. D. Fleeman, new edn (1970); repr. with introduction by P. Rogers (1980), 1022 · *DNB* · J. Taylor, *The history of the travels and adventures of the Chevalier John Taylor, Opthalmiator*, 3 vols. (1761–2) · A. Jessop, 'Notes on the history of Breccles Hall, Norfolk', *Norfolk Archaeology*, 8 (1879), 303–18, esp. 317
Likenesses P. Endlich, engraving, 1735 (after his portrait), Wellcome L. · W. Hogarth, group portrait, etching, 1736 (*The company of undertakers*; after his portrait), Wellcome L. · R. Cooper, engraving (after W. de Nune), Wellcome L. · J. Faber junior, mezzotint (after P. Ryche), NPG, Wellcome L. [*see illus.*] · J. B. Scotin, engraving (after P. Ryche), Wellcome L. · line engraving (after P. Ryche), Wellcome L. · stipple (after P. Ryche), Wellcome L.

Taylor, John (*bap.* **1704**, *d.* **1766**), classical scholar and Church of England clergyman, was baptized on 22 June 1704 at St Alkmund's Church in Shrewsbury, where his father, John Taylor, was a barber. He was educated under Richard Lloyd at Shrewsbury School, where his grandfather John Taylor (*bap.* 1629, *d.* 1688) had been third master from 1659 to 1688. A bookish boy, he was noticed by one of his father's customers, Edward Owen of Condover, who decided to fund his education at university. On 7 June 1721 he was admitted a sizar at his grandfather's college—St John's, Cambridge—whence he graduated BA in 1725 and proceeded MA in 1728. He became a fellow and tutor of his college in 1726. In 1730 he delivered the Latin oration in Great St Mary's Church on the anniversary of Charles I's execution, and the music speech at the public commencement in July; both were published. In March 1732 he was appointed university librarian, an office that he exchanged for that of registrar in 1734.

Taylor, who shared his family's tory allegiance, had found himself increasingly at odds with his patron's Jacobitism, and broke with Owen when he refused to join in a Jacobite toast, thus dashing his hopes of benefiting from the considerable church preferment at Owen's disposal. Taylor therefore concentrated on establishing his reputation as a classicist. In 1732 he issued the prospectus for a new edition of Lysias, which appeared in 1739. In the following year he took the degree of LLD, and in 1741 he published an edition of *Demosthenes contra Leptinem*, which he intended as a specimen of a projected complete edition of Demosthenes and Aeschines. He published the third volume of the work in 1748 and the second in 1757, but he failed to complete the first volume, which is represented only by the notes that Anthony Askew gave to Johann Jacob Reiske. He henceforth was known as Demosthenes Taylor.

A scholar not only of Greek oratory but also of Greek law, it is unsurprising that Taylor turned to the law as an alternative career to the church. He was admitted to Doctors' Commons in 1741 and transferred to the court of arches as an advocate later in that year. About this time he gained the favour of a valuable patron, Lord Carteret (later Lord Granville), who in 1742 seems to have considered making Taylor his under-secretary of state. Instead Taylor was appointed chancellor of the diocese of Lincoln in 1744, having been introduced to the bishop, Dr John Thomas, by Carteret. He remained in office until 1766.

Taylor returned to his first choice of career—the church—when he was ordained deacon and priest in September 1747 at Lincoln. He received the college living of Lawford, Essex, in April 1751 and became archdeacon of Buckingham in January 1753; he resigned as registrar of Cambridge University in 1751. In 1752–3 he tutored Granville's grandsons the third Viscount Weymouth (1734–1796) and Henry Frederick Thynne (1735–1796) while they were undergraduates at St John's College, Cambridge. In response to Granville's request that his grandsons received a thorough grounding in the principles of civil law Taylor drew up extensive notes on the subject, amply illustrated by quotations from classical texts. These notes were published as *Elements of the Civil Law* (1755; 2nd edn,

1769) and in an abridged version as *Summary of the Roman Law* (1773). His account of the persecution of the early Christians was severely attacked by William Warburton, who took great offence when Taylor reportedly declared that Warburton was 'no scholar'. Taylor also contributed to the second edition of John Foster's *Essay on the Different Nature of Accent and Quantity* (1763) and began an appendix to Suidas.

In July 1757 Taylor was appointed a canon residentiary of St Paul's Cathedral, once again thanks to the good offices of Granville. He moved to London, where he took part in the learned societies; elected fellow of the Royal Society and of the Society of Antiquaries, he contributed to the transactions of the former and served as director and vice-president of the latter. He died at his house in Amen Corner, Paternoster Row, on 4 April 1766 and was buried in the vault under St Paul's Cathedral. He bequeathed his extensive library to his old school, which could then boast of having the best school library after Eton College, and a fund to found an exhibition at St John's. His manuscripts and annotated books were left to Anthony Askew, his executor, most of which are now in the Bodleian Library, Cambridge University Library, and the British Library.

E. C. MARCHANT, *rev.* S. J. SKEDD

Sources GM, 1st ser., 48 (1778), 456–7; 74 (1804), 646–7 · A. Chalmers, ed., *The general biographical dictionary*, new edn, 29 (1816), 179–87 · T. Baker, *History of the college of St John the Evangelist, Cambridge*, ed. J. E. B. Mayor, 2 vols. (1869) · C. Leach, *A school at Shrewsbury: the four foundations* (1990)

Archives Bodl. Oxf., letters, commonplace book, and notes

Taylor, John (1710/11–1775), button manufacturer, is thought to have been born of humble parentage. Although little is known of his early years, William Hutton stated in his *History of Birmingham* in 1782 that Taylor began his working life as an artisan. Taylor was married to Mary Baker (1710/11–1784).

In July 1755 two Londoners wrote of a visit to 'Mr Taylor, the most considerable Maker of Gilt-metal Buttons and enamell'd snuff-boxes' at his workshops, possibly in Crooked Lane, off Dale End (*Four Topographical Letters*, 55). Four years later Taylor was one of two manufacturers explaining to a House of Commons committee the importance of the metal toy trade in Birmingham. They claimed that the town had increased by roughly a half since the industry began, employing at least 20,000 people in Birmingham and the neighbouring towns and having a trade value of about £600,000 per year, of which the greater proportion was exported. They also stressed the use of machines or engines, invented by the people of Birmingham, which 'lessens the manual labour, and enables boys to do men's work' (Hopkins, 7).

In 1766 Lord Shelburne was impressed by Taylor's use of an alloy, by the heavy reliance on machinery, and his division of labour to speed the production process. 'Thus a button passes through fifty hands, and each hand perhaps passes a thousand a day; ... by this means the work becomes so simple that ... children of six to eight years old

do it as well as men, and earn from ten pence to eight shillings a week' (Fitzmaurice, 403). The value of Taylor's weekly output of buttons was estimated as at least £800.

Three processes were used in the finishing and decorating of Taylor's wares: gilt plating, japanning or enamelling, and painting. One employee is recorded as regularly earning £3 10s. by painting 3360 snuff-boxes weekly. Taylor was credited with the production of the unique and fashionable wavy tinted patterns on one line of snuff-boxes, on which, using his thumb on a second coat of colour while it was still wet, 'he wove, in endless variety, the patterns he desired' (S. Lloyd, 41).

Taylor's business acumen and flair for organization led to the founding of Birmingham's first bank in 1765, in partnership with Sampson *Lloyd (1699–1779). Taylor and Lloyd expanded to London, becoming Lloyds Bank in 1852. The capital of £8000 was raised equally between the partners, but Lloyd family correspondence indicates that Taylor may well have been the force behind the venture.

Beginning the trend for wealthy industrialists to live outside town, Taylor bought land and began rebuilding Bordesley Hall at an eventual cost of £10,000. His rent books from 1754 show properties in Bishops Itchington, Coleshill, Yardley, Bordesley, and Sheldon, with rents from 30s. to £290 annually. By 1765, when he wrote his will, he had forty-three properties including houses, farms, and land, producing an annual income of £872.

Taylor was held in high esteem by his fellow townsmen and he was one of fifty commissioners named in the local Improvement Act of 1769 for the betterment of Birmingham streets. His participation in a venture was thought to guarantee success. Boulton called him 'our great manufacturer' (Hopkins, 84); he was eulogized by Hutton as 'the Shakespeare or Newton of his day' (ibid.); he was one of the 'valuable acquaintances' made by Samuel Johnson; and Boswell noted that Taylor had acquired a fortune 'by his ingenuity in mechanical inventions, and success in trade' (Sayers, 7).

John Taylor died in Bath on 27 March 1775; he was interred in the family vault in St Philip's Church, Birmingham, on 2 April. In his will he bequeathed an annuity of £1600 to his wife; £10,000 and a harpsichord to his daughter Mary; and £8000 each to his younger sons, William and Charles. His properties were left to his eldest son, John, and after various bequests the residue of his estate, reputed to total £200,000, was to be divided equally between the sons. *Aris's Birmingham Gazette* described him on 3 April 1775 as 'a man to whose extraordinary Ingenuity and indefatigable Diligence, the Trade and Manufactures of this Town are much indebted for their Increase and Estimacion'. POLLY HAMILTON

Sources V. Skipp, *A history of Greater Birmingham, down to 1830* (privately printed, Birmingham, 1980) · E. Hopkins, *Birmingham, the first marketing town in the world, 1760–1840* (1989) · W. Hutton, *An history of Birmingham*, 2nd edn (1783) · H. Lloyd, *The Quaker Lloyds in the industrial revolution* (1975) · R. P. [Resta Patching], *Four topographical letters written in July, 1755 ... from a gentleman of London to his brother and sister in town* (1757), 55 · *Life of William, earl of Shelburne ... with extracts from his papers and correspondence*, ed. E. G. P. Fitzmaurice, 1

(1875), 403 • S. Lloyd, *The Lloyds of Birmingham* (1907) • C. Gill, *Manor and borough to 1865* (1952), vol. 1 of *History of Birmingham* (1952–74) • R. S. Sayers, *Lloyds Bank in the history of English banking* (1957) • *Aris's Birmingham Gazette* (3 April 1775) • *JHC*, 28 (1757–61) • will, PRO, PROB 11/1008, sig. 208

Archives Birm. CL, burial index and transcription of monuments of St Philip's Church, Birmingham • Birm. CL • Birmingham RO, MS rent books, IIR 20 435798–435800

Wealth at death approx. £200,000; plus property and monetary bequests of over £27,150: Hutton, *History of Birmingham*; will, PRO, PROB 11/1008, sig. 208

Taylor, John (*bap.* **1711**, *d.* **1788**), friend of Samuel Johnson, baptized at Ashbourne, Derbyshire, on 18 March 1711, was the son of Thomas Taylor (1671–1730?) of Ashbourne and his wife, Mary, daughter of Thomas Wood. He was educated with Samuel Johnson by the Revd John Hunter at Lichfield grammar school, and he and Edmund Hector were the last survivors of Johnson's schoolfriends. Taylor would have followed Johnson to Pembroke College, but was dissuaded by his friend's report of the ignorance of William Jorden, the tutor, and on the same advice matriculated from Christ Church, Oxford, on 10 March 1729, with a view to studying the law and becoming an attorney. He left without taking a degree, and apparently for some years practised as an attorney. On 9 April 1732 he married at Croxall, Derbyshire, Elizabeth, daughter of William Webb of that parish. She was buried at Ashbourne on 13 January 1746. His second wife was Mary, daughter of Roger Tuckfield of Fulford, Devon. They were not happy, and in August 1763 she left him.

At some time after 1736 Taylor was ordained in the Church of England, and in July 1740 he was presented, on the nomination of the family of Dixie, and, as it is believed, by purchase from them, to the valuable rectory of Market Bosworth in Leicestershire. This preferment he retained until death, although he was unpopular with his parishioners. As a whig in politics and a political power in Derbyshire, Taylor was made chaplain to the duke of Devonshire, lord lieutenant of Ireland from 1737 to 1745. He returned to Oxford and graduated BA and MA in 1742. In 1752, as a grand-compounder, he proceeded LLB and LLD.

On 11 July 1746 Taylor obtained, no doubt through the influence of the duke of Devonshire, a prebendal stall at Westminster, which he retained for life. By the appointment of the chapter he held in succession a series of preferments, all of which were tenable with his stall and with his living of Market Bosworth. These were the post of minister of the chapel in the Broadway, Westminster (1748); the perpetual curacy of St Botolph, Aldersgate (1769); and the place of minister of St Margaret's, Westminster, which he held from April 1784 to his death. Johnson remarked of this position: 'It is of no great value, and its income consists much of voluntary contributions' (*Letters of Samuel Johnson*, 2.397). Although Taylor was possessed of large resources, both official and private—amounting in all, so it was rumoured, to £7000 per annum—and never voluntarily paid a debt, he always hankered after better preferments.

Taylor spent much time at his family residence at Ashbourne. He became JP for Derbyshire on 6 October 1761, and thenceforth was known as 'the King of Ashbourne'. Through life he maintained his friendship with Johnson. Johnson was at Ashbourne in 1737 and 1740, and in the thirteen years from 1767 to 1779 only thrice failed to visit Taylor. He acted in 1749 as mediator in the quarrel of Garrick and Johnson over the play *Irene*. He read the service at Johnson's funeral.

Johnson said of Taylor that he was 'a very sensible, acute man', that he had 'a strong mind', and that 'he had great activity in some respects, and yet such a sort of indolence, that if you should put a pebble upon his chimney-piece, you would find it there, in the same state, a year afterwards' (Boswell, 827). Boswell and Johnson arrived at Ashbourne on 26 March 1776, driving from Lichfield in Taylor's 'large roomy postchaise, drawn by four stout plump horses, and driven by two steady jolly postilions'. The house and establishment accorded with this description, and their host's 'size and figure and countenance and manner were that of a hearty English squire, with the parson superinduced' (Boswell, 716). Boswell thought that Taylor 'praised everything of his own to great excess' (Boswell, 867) and wondered how Johnson and Taylor could be friends. Joshua Reynolds had speculated that Johnson was to be Taylor's heir. However, Johnson had said of Taylor:

> I love him; but I do not love him more; my regard for him does not increase. As it is said in the Apocrypha, 'his talk is of bullocks': I do not suppose he is very fond of my company. His habits are by no means sufficiently clerical: this he knows that I see; and no man likes to live under the eye of perpetual disapprobation. (Boswell, 861)

Taylor died at Ashbourne on 29 February 1788, and was buried in Ashbourne church, tradition says in the nave, on 3 March. He had no surviving child and disappointed his nieces by leaving all his property—£1200 a year besides personalty—to a boy, William Brunt (*b.* 1772), who had been engaged as a page. It was stipulated that the legatee should take the name of Webster, which had long been connected with this family of Taylor.

Taylor published in 1787 *A Letter to Samuel Johnson, LL.D., on the Subject of a Future State*, which was inscribed to the duke of Devonshire, at whose command it was issued. It is said to have been drawn up at Johnson's request, and with reference to his remark that 'he would prefer a state of torment to that of annihilation'. Appended to it were three letters by Dr Johnson. After Taylor's death there came out—volume 1 in 1788, and volume 2 in 1789—*Sermons on Different Subjects, Left for Publication by John Taylor, LL.D.*, which were edited by the Revd Samuel Hayes. They were often reprinted, and are believed to have been in the main the composition of Johnson, in whose 'Prayers and meditations' is the entry, on 21 September 1777, 'Concio pro Tayloro' ('A sermon for Taylor'). Boswell wrote down in Taylor's presence, and incorporated in the *Life*, 'a good deal of what he could tell' about Johnson. Many letters from Johnson to him were printed in *Notes and Queries* (6th ser., 5.303–482). Three of them were known to Boswell, and about twelve were printed by Sir John Simeon, their owner in 1861, for the Philobiblon Society. These communications, with others, are included in Hill's edition of Johnson's letters. Further letters are in the same editor's *Johnsonian Miscellanies* (2.447, 452).

W. P. COURTNEY, *rev.* MICHAEL BEVAN

Sources J. Boswell, *Life of Johnson*, ed. R. W. Chapman, rev. J. D. Fleeman, new edn (1970); repr. with introduction by P. Rogers (1980) · *Johnsonian miscellanies*, ed. G. B. Hill, 2 vols. (1897) · *Letters of Samuel Johnson*, ed. G. B. Hill, 2 vols. (1892) · D. Macleane, *A history of Pembroke College, Oxford*, OHS, 33 (1897) · Foster, *Alum. Oxon.* · *GM*, 1st ser., 19 (1749), 45 · *GM*, 1st ser., 39 (1769), 511 · *GM*, 1st ser., 58 (1788), 274 · private information (1898) [Revd F. Jourdain, vicar of Ashbourne] · *Fasti Angl.* (Hardy), 3.366, 368
Likenesses J. Opie, oils, Johnson Birthplace Museum, Lichfield
Wealth at death left £1200 p.a. plus personalty: *DNB*

Taylor, John (*c*.1724–1787). *See under* Taylor, John (1703–1772).

Taylor, John (1739–1838), portrait painter, was born in Bishopsgate, London, the son of a customs official. He may have been the John Taylor baptized on 24 February 1739 at St Ethelburga, Bishopsgate, the son of John Taylor and his wife, Mary. He studied art at the drawing academy in St Martin's Lane, London, and also under Francis Hayman. He was with Hayman by the mid 1760s, 'by which time he had produced a drawing of Hayman's *Triumph of Britannia* for S. F. Ravenet to work up into a large engraving published by Boydell in 1765' (Allen, 506). In 1766 he was one of the original members of the Incorporated Society of Artists. In 1772 he gave his address as 'At Mr Hayman's, Dean Street, Soho', suggesting that he was with his master for some years. His lengthy anecdotal poem *Frank Hayman: a Tale* contains many witty reminiscences of those years. Although few of his early works (which were painted in a variety of media) survive, a large number of highly finished pencil portraits (his speciality), dating from 1767 to 1771, are in the Ashmolean Museum, Oxford. *A Young Scholar and his Tutor*, signed and dated 1772, is a typical example and shows the influence of his master in the treatment of the eyes and lips. As he only obtained between 7*s.* 6*d.* and 1 guinea for his drawings he became, with the assistance of his friends Paul Sandby and J. A. Gresse, a drawing-master in London. Between about 1788 and 1791 he was in Rome, where he made miniature copies after the old masters. By March 1788 Lord Gardenstone had bought his miniature after Correggio's *Mystic Marriage of St Catherine* (*c*.1520s) and commissioned several others. In 1790 he was recorded as a miniature painter living by the Quartiere dei Avignonesi.

Taylor's teaching enabled him to accumulate a sum which he invested in annuities to last him to the age of 100. This he nearly attained (thereby gaining the distinguishing title Old Taylor), as he died in Cirencester Place, Marylebone, Middlesex, on 21 November 1838 in his ninety-ninth year. He exhibited a variety of historical, literary, and mythological works at the Society of Artists (1764–77), the Royal Academy (1778–1824), and the British Institution (1808–38). He was a friend of the eccentric sculptor Joseph Nollekens, who made a bust of him, and left him a legacy in his will.

Another **John Taylor** (1745?–1806), landscape painter, was born in Bath. He painted marine landscapes with figures and cattle, and was also an etcher. He died at Bath on 8 November 1806.   L. H. CUST, *rev.* ANNETTE PEACH

Sources B. Allen, 'Francis Hayman and the English Rococo', PhD diss., Courtauld Inst., 1984, 494, 506–7 · *GM*, 2nd ser., 11 (1839), 100 · *IGI* · J. Ingamells, ed., *A dictionary of British and Irish travellers in Italy, 1701–1800* (1997) · Redgrave, *Artists*

Taylor, John (1743–1818), minister of the New Connexion of General Baptists, was born on 16 June 1743 at Fold in the township of Northowram in the parish of Halifax, the fourth of eight children of Azor Taylor, coalminer, and his second wife, Mary, daughter of Robert Willey of Fold. His elder brother was Dan *Taylor (1738–1816), the founder of the New Connexion of General Baptists. John was put to work in a coalmine in 1749. Such education as he had came from his mother and brother Dan. The home was not particularly religious although his parents attended the parish church. It was his brother Dan who stimulated his spiritual interests. By the time John was eleven he and his brother were reading the Bible and praying together. He met for worship with the local Methodists for a number of years but never joined a class or became a member of the society. He was drawn to the Particular Baptist cause in Halifax, and this resulted in discussion and debate with his brother Dan who, as a consequence of his Methodist background and Arminian theology, was strongly opposed to Calvinism. Doctrinal differences between the brothers were resolved, and when his brother started an Independent church at Wadsworth John became a member, was baptized on 7 March 1770, and subsequently started preaching. On 22 April 1764 he had married Betty Whitely (*d.* 1806) at Halifax.

When a church was formed at Queenshead, near Halifax, John Taylor was ordained its first pastor on 30 September 1773. The ordination took place in the context of personal tragedy: his three-year-old daughter died on the evening of the ordination and his son at the end of the week on the Friday; both died from smallpox. The infant church had a troubled early history: internal problems, together with poverty and a heavy debt on the church building, resulted in little progress. For most of his ministry John Taylor worked either as a miner or wool-comber. Although he received invitations to more prosperous churches he complied with the request of the New Connexion's assembly to continue his ministry at Queenshead. He had a thirst for knowledge, was self-taught, and read widely. Theologically a General Baptist he was much influenced by the evangelical revival, 'I preach experience', he said (Taylor, *Memoirs*, 63). He wrote a manuscript autobiography and two 'Association letters', 'Family worship' in 1790 and 'The religious education of children' in 1810.

In the early stages of the development of the New Connexion, formed in 1770, John assisted his brother Dan, thereby giving him more time to travel the county on connexion business. His own ministry involved a considerable amount of travel, preaching and meeting the pastoral needs of the churches of the connexion: 'For two years I was not one Lord's day more than half my time at home' (Taylor, *Memoirs*, 37). In 1795 he lost sight in one eye; his son Adam attributed this to the 'fatigues of so many journeys, during the winter season' (ibid., 63). The effect was to curtail his travels. Although he was assisted by a number of young preachers their tenure was short, usually as a result of being called to minister elsewhere.

The area around Queenshead suffered badly during the depression at the turn of the century. In January 1801 Taylor described the distress this caused as 'inexpressible' (Taylor, *Memoirs*, 74). Following his wife's death in March 1806 he married 'a poor but worthy widow' in November of that year. The final years of his life were marked by increasing debility. He died at Queenshead on 26 December 1818. A man whose ministry was exercised in adverse circumstances, Taylor had a reputation for piety and devotion. His two sons, Adam and James, also became ministers in the connexion, and the elder, Adam, wrote an early history of the connexion.   FRANK W. RINALDI

Sources A. Taylor, *Memoirs of the Rev. John Taylor, late pastor of the General Baptist church Queenshead, near Halifax Yorkshire, chiefly compiled from a manuscript written by himself* (1821) • A. Taylor, *History of the English General Baptists*, 2: *The new connection of General Baptists* (1818) • J. H. Wood, *A condensed history of the General Baptists of the New Connexion* (1847) • DNB • IGI

Taylor, John (1745?–1806). *See under* Taylor, John (1739–1838).

Taylor, John (*d.* 1808), writer, entered the service of the East India Company in 1776 as a cadet in the Bombay army. He was promoted lieutenant on 1 May 1780, captain in December 1789, major on 20 March 1797, and lieutenant-colonel on 6 March 1800. At some time before 22 August 1789 he married. On that date he set out from London with his wife, two male companions, and two servants for an overland journey to India. Personal matters demanded his attention in India and, there being no prospect of his travelling by the normal sea voyage, he resolved to make an overland journey. He later described it in *Travels from England to India in 1789 by way of the Tyrol, Venice, Scandaroon, Aleppo and over the Great Desart to Bussora* (2 vols., 1799). This work is an odd mixture of a travel journal, a compendium of useful information for travellers, a discussion of the strategic importance of the Middle East as a meeting place of East and West, an analysis of the contemporary strategic and political situations in the Middle East and India, and a detailed account of why the overland route to India is preferable to the normal sea route. Taylor had no eye for landscape, little interest in the individuals he met, and no pretensions to a pleasing style. While seeking to show that the overland route was perfectly feasible for ordinary travellers, Taylor did not attempt to boast its attractions. Instead he relentlessly described the delays he experienced in Europe, where he bemoaned the shortage of horses as a continual problem, his descriptions of the places he passed through being largely confined to practical details concerning accommodation and provisions which the traveller might need to know.

After successfully making the overland journey to India, Taylor became a firm advocate of the route. In 1795, after having made his journey but before having published his *Travels*, he published *Considerations on the practicability and advantages of a more speedy communication between Great Britain and her possessions in India*. This work was based on James Capper's *Observations on the Passage to India* (1783) but Taylor particularly recommended the use of the overland route for letters through Egypt, he having found the delay in receiving news in India particularly frustrating and having successfully taken with him several important papers on his own overland voyage. Taylor published two more works on India before his death at Poona on 10 October 1808. Under the terms of his will his wife, Joanna, was his sole executor and residuary legatee. She was described as his 'present wife' and thus may or may not have been the wife who accompanied him on his voyage. Joanna had entrusted to her the care of his natural daughter.

The John Taylor described above should not be confused with **John Taylor** (*d.* 1821), translator, who was born in Edinburgh and graduated MD from the university in 1804. He entered the Bombay service and was appointed assistant surgeon on 26 March 1808, and promoted surgeon in 1821. He was the author of several translations from Sanskrit and was a member of the Asiatic Society of Bombay and of the Literary Society of Bombay. He died on 6 December 1821 at Shiraz, Persia, leaving a son, John (1804–1856), who became a member of the Royal College of Physicians of Edinburgh, and died in that city on 14 July 1856.

E. I. CARLYLE, *rev.* ELIZABETH BAIGENT

Sources Dodwell [E. Dodwell] and Miles [J. S. Miles], eds., *Alphabetical list of the officers of the Indian army: with the dates of their respective promotion, retirement, resignation, or death … from the year 1760 to the year … 1837* (1838) • E. Dodwell and J. S. Miles, *An alphabetical list of the medical officers of the Indian army, from 1764 to 1838* (1839) • will, PRO, PROB 11/1508, fols. 385r–385v • *European Magazine*, 38 (Dec 1800), 431–5 [review of Lieutenant-Colonel Taylor, *Letters on India* by M (Joseph Moser)] • *N&Q*, 2nd ser., 6 (1858), 464

Taylor, John (1750–1826), hymn writer, was born at Norwich on 30 July 1750, the second son of the eight children of Richard Taylor (*d.* 1762), a manufacturer, of Colegate, Norwich, and was grandson of John *Taylor (1694–1761). His mother was Margaret (*d.* 1781), daughter of Philip Meadows, mayor of Norwich in 1734, and granddaughter of John Meadows, the ejected divine. Her only sister, Sarah, was the grandmother of Harriet Martineau.

Taylor was educated under Mr Akers at Hindolveston, Norfolk, but upon the death of his father he left to assist his mother in the family business. Three years later he was apprenticed to Martin and Wingfield, a firm of manufacturers in Norwich, after which he spent two years as a clerk to a banking firm in London. He there began to contribute verses to the *Morning Chronicle*. In 1773 he returned to Norwich, and started a yarn factory in partnership with his younger brother, Richard. On 24 April 1777 John Taylor married Susanna (1755–1823), *née* Cook [*see below*]; they had seven children.

Taylor was active in municipal and social affairs at Norwich, and was a prominent member of the Octagon Presbyterian Unitarian Chapel, of which he acted as deacon for nearly fifty years. He devoted his leisure to literary pursuits, and his verse and hymns were held in wide repute. He was a member of the Norwich Anacreontic Society, and sang in more than one of the festivals. His stirring song 'The trumpet of liberty', with the refrain 'Fall, tyrants, fall', was first published in the *Norfolk Chronicle* of 16 July 1791; it has been ascribed in error to William Taylor (1765–1836).

Taylor was the author of several hymn tunes, but his musical composition was inferior to that of his elder brother, Philip Taylor of Eustace Street Presbyterian Chapel, Dublin, grandfather of Colonel Philip Meadows Taylor. On the other hand, his hymns and verses were everywhere used in Unitarian services. He edited *Hymns Intended to be used at the Commencement of Social Worship* (1802), in which ten by himself are included, and published a collection of forty-three of his own compositions in 1818. These, with additions, were reprinted in *Hymns and Miscellaneous Poems* (1863), with a memoir reprinted from the *Monthly Repository* (September 1826) and edited by his son, Edward Taylor. Many of these hymns are to be found in Robert Aspland's *Psalms and Hymns for Unitarian Worship* (1810; 2nd edn, 1825), the *Norwich Collection* (1814; 2nd edn, 1826), James Martineau's *Hymns of Praise and Prayer* (1874), *Hymns for the Christian Church and Home* (1840), and W. Garrett Horder's various collections. Perhaps the best-known are those beginning 'Like shadows gliding o'er the plain', 'At the portals of Thy house', and 'Supreme o'er all Jehovah reigns'.

Taylor contributed anonymously to the *Cabinet* (3 vols., 1795) verses in the style and orthography of the seventeenth century, of which those on Richard Corbet were included in Gilchrist's edition of the bishop's poems, and others on 'Martinmasse day' were cited in *Time's Telescope* (1814) as an ancient authority for the way in which that day is kept. Taylor's *History of the Octagon Chapel, Norwich* was completed by his son Edward, and published in 1848. John Taylor died after a fall from a gig near his son Philip's house at Halesowen in Shropshire on 23 July 1826, and was buried in the Unitarian burial-ground at Birmingham.

John Taylor's wife, **Susanna Taylor** [*née* Cook] (1755–1823), born in Norwich on 29 March 1755, was the daughter of John Cook and Aramathea Maria Phillips. She was a woman of much force of character, who shared the liberal opinions of her husband, and is said to have danced 'round the tree of liberty at Norwich on the receipt of news of the taking of the Bastille'. Sir James Mackintosh corresponded with her on many subjects, and Anna Letitia Barbauld was her devoted friend, speaking of her 'strong sense, her feeling, her energy, her principle, her patriot feelings, her piety, rational, yet ardent' as marking 'a character of no uncommon sort' (*Monthly Repository*, 20, 1825, 487). Her other friends included Sir James Edward Smith, Henry Crabb Robinson, John Alderson, Amelia Opie, William Enfield, Frank Sayers, William Taylor (who was no relation), Basil Montagu, the Gurneys of Earlham, and the Sewards. A political element was added to her literary gatherings by Sir Thomas Beevor, Lord Albemarle, and Thomas William Coke (afterwards earl of Leicester),

member for Norfolk (1790–1818). Her intimate friends called her Madame Roland, from the resemblance she bore to the French champion of liberty. She also contributed essays and verse to the budget read at periodic meetings of the Taylor and Martineau families, for which many of her husband's verses were composed.

Susanna Taylor took charge of her daughters' education, instructing them in philosophy, Latin, and political economy. Susan Taylor (1788–1853) was later to marry Henry *Reeve (1780–1814), and Sarah Taylor was to achieve fame as Sarah *Austin (1793–1867), translator and literary hostess, the wife of John *Austin (1790–1859), jurist. Susanna Taylor's sons were also gifted: John *Taylor (1779–1863) was a successful mining engineer; Richard *Taylor (1781–1858) became a printer and naturalist; Edward *Taylor (1784–1863) became Gresham professor of music; Philip *Taylor (1786–1870) was a civil engineer; and Arthur Taylor (*b.* 1790) was a printer and author of historical works.

Susanna Taylor died in June 1823. A monument to her and her husband was erected by their children in the Octagon Chapel, Norwich.

CHARLOTTE FELL-SMITH, *rev.* M. CLARE LOUGHLIN-CHOW

Sources E. Taylor, *Monthly Repository*, 21 (1826), 482–94 • review of *The works of Anna Laetitia Barbauld*, *Monthly Repository*, 20 (1825), 486–7 • E. Taylor, 'Memoir', in J. Taylor, *Hymns and miscellaneous poems*, ed. [E. Taylor] (1863), ix–xlii • J. A. Ross, *Three generations of Englishwomen: memoirs and correspondence of Mrs John Taylor, Mrs Sarah Austin and Lady Duff Gordon*, 2 vols. (1888) • W. Turner, *Lives of eminent Unitarians*, 1 (1840), 341–2 • J. Julian, ed., *A dictionary of hymnology*, rev. edn (1907) • *Christian Reformer, or, New Evangelical Miscellany*, 12 (1826), 288 • *Memoir and correspondence of the late Sir James Edward Smith*, ed. Lady Smith, 1 (1832), 170; 2 (1832), 99, 315 • L. Aikin, 'Memoir', in *The works of Anna Lætitia Barbauld*, ed. L. Aikin, 1 (1825), viii–lxxii, esp. lv • P. H. Le Breton, *Memoirs, miscellanies, and letters of the late Lucy Aikin* (1864), 124–49 • A. J. C. Hare, *The Gurneys of Earlham*, 1 (1895), 79 • J. W. Robberds, *A memoir of the life and writings of the late William Taylor of Norwich*, 1 (1843), 46 • *Memoirs of the life of the Right Honourable Sir James Mackintosh*, ed. R. J. Mackintosh, 2 vols. (1835), vol. 1, pp. 147, 215, 439 • E. Taylor, *The Suffolk Bartholomeans* (1840) • M. Taylor, *The story of my life*, ed. A. M. Taylor, another edn, 3 vols. (1878) • IGI
Archives Harris Man. Oxf., papers

Taylor, John (1757–1832), writer and journal editor, was born in Highgate on 9 August 1757, the eldest son of Ann Price and John *Taylor (*c.*1724–1787) [*see under* Taylor, John (1703–1772)]. His grandfather was the Chevalier John *Taylor (1703–1772), well-known oculist to George II, and his father followed the same profession with equal success, becoming oculist to George III. John Taylor received a basic education under Dr Crawford in Hatton Garden and at a school at Ponder's End, Middlesex. At first he followed the family profession, and with his brother, Jeremiah Taylor MRCS, was appointed oculist to George III. His love of the theatre, combined with an ability to write verse, however, gradually attracted him to journalism. For some time he was drama critic to the *Morning Post* before succeeding William Jackson as the paper's editor about 1787. He purchased the *True Briton*, and in 1813 went on to become editor and proprietor of *The Sun*, a violent tory paper. The existing editor, William Jerdan, owned a share in *The Sun*, and there was a bitter quarrel followed by two or three years' litigation before Jerdan was bought out by Taylor in 1817. In 1825 Taylor sold the paper to Murdo Young, who changed its politics.

As a writer Taylor is best known for 'Monsieur Tonson', a poem suggested by a prank of Thomas King, the actor. A dramatic version of the poem was read or rehearsed by William Thomas Moncrieff on 8 September 1821, but never publicly performed. When it was recited by John Fawcett at the Freemasons' Tavern, however, it drew large crowds. In a later publication (1830) it was illustrated by Richard Cruikshank.

At the Turk's Head Coffee House and the 'Keep the Line' Club, Taylor mingled with the celebrities of his day. He wrote numerous addresses, prologues, and epilogues for the stage and was totally captivated by the theatrical world. Jerdan vividly describes him as 'a being of the artificial stage, not of the actual living world ... looking for surprises and dénouements; as if the game of life were a comedy or a farce' (Jerdan, 73). According to his own account he gave advice to Boswell on the eve of his publication of the *Life of Johnson*. He entered into brief correspondence with Wordsworth who sent him a copy of the *Lyrical Ballads*, wanting to know 'what impression his poems, written by an author living in rural retirement, had made upon a man living in the bustle of active life' (De Selincourt, 1.325). In his later years Taylor wrote *Records of my Life* (1832), a work full of gossip and discreditable stories.

Taylor was married twice and wrote a number of moving sonnets about his first wife, who died young. He died in Great Russell Street, Bloomsbury, London, in May 1832. Other works by Taylor include: *Statement of Transactions Respecting the King's Theatre at the Haymarket* (1791); *Verses on Various Occasions*, including 'The stage' (1795); *The Caledonian Comet* (1810); *Poems on Several Occasions* (1811); and *Poems on Various Subjects* (1827).

CHARLOTTE FELL-SMITH, *rev.* S. C. BUSHELL

Sources W. Jerdan, *The autobiography of William Jerdan: with his literary, political, and social reminiscences and correspondence during the last fifty years*, 4 vols. (1852–3), vol. 2, pp. 52, 66–80, 96–109, 137–60 · J. Taylor, *Records of my life*, 1 (1832), 1–23 · *GM*, 1st ser., 102/2 (1832), 89–90, 542–6 · H. R. Fox Bourne, *English newspapers: chapters in the history of journalism*, 1 (1887), 224, 368; 2 (1887), 26 · *The letters of William and Dorothy Wordsworth*, ed. E. De Selincourt, 2nd edn, rev. C. L. Shaver, M. Moorman, and A. G. Hill, 8 vols. (1967–93), vol. 1, pp. 325–6 · H. J. Rose, *A new general biographical dictionary*, ed. H. J. Rose and T. Wright, 12 vols. (1853) · Allibone, *Dict.* · Genest, *Eng. stage*, 9.96
Archives RA, corresp. | BL, letters to Thomas Hill, Add. MS 20082 · BL, letters to Lord Liverpool and others, index of MSS, IX, 1985 · Sir John Soane's Museum, London, letters to Sir John Soane
Likenesses Dance, portrait · Daniell, engraving (after painting by Dance) · A. J. Oliver, portrait · stipple, BM; repro. in Taylor, *Records*

Taylor, John (d. 1821). *See under* Taylor, John (d. 1808).

Taylor, Sir John (1771–1843), army officer, was born on 29 September 1771, the son of Walter Taylor of Castle Taylor, co. Galway, and his second wife, Hester, daughter of Richard Trench, and sister of William Power Keating Trench, earl of Clancarty. He entered the army in November 1794 as ensign in the 105th foot, became lieutenant in the 118th on 6 December, and captain in the 102nd on 9 September 1795. He was brigade major and aide-de-camp to Major-General Trench during the 1798 Irish uprising, and was aide-de-camp to General Hutchinson during the 1799 campaign in the Netherlands and that of Egypt in 1801. He had been transferred to the 26th foot on 30 October 1799, but was soon afterwards placed on half pay. He was made a brevet major on 2 September 1801, and a lieutenant-colonel on 28 February 1805.

On 18 May 1809 Taylor was made lieutenant-colonel in the 88th (Connaught Rangers), and went to Cadiz in command of the 2nd battalion in 1810. In the following winter it joined Wellington's army within the lines of Torres Vedras. It was attached to the light division, and after Masséna's retreat it took part in the combat of Sabugal (3 April 1811). A year afterwards it was sent home, having been reduced by a large draft to the 1st battalion to make up for its losses at Badajoz. On 4 June 1813 Taylor was made brevet colonel. He returned to Spain soon afterwards, and on 9 September took command of the 1st battalion, which formed part of the 3rd division. He commanded it until the end of the war, and received the gold medal with two clasps for Nivelle, Orthez, and Toulouse. At Orthez he was severely wounded.

Taylor was made CB for his Peninsular services and afterwards KCB (17 October 1834). He was promoted major-general on 12 August 1819, and lieutenant-general on 10 January 1837. On 15 March 1837 he was made colonel of the 80th foot.

Taylor married Albinia Frances, daughter of St John Jeffreys of Blarney Castle, co. Cork, and widow of Lieutenant-Colonel Freemantle; they had two daughters. Taylor died in London on 8 December 1843.

E. M. LLOYD, *rev.* DAVID GATES

Sources Burke, *Gen. GB* · R. Cannon, *Records of the 88th foot or Connaught rangers* (1838) · J. Philippart, ed., *The royal military calendar*, 3rd edn, 5 vols. (1820)

Taylor, John. *See* Talbot, Mary Anne (1778–1808).

Taylor, John (1779–1863), mining manager and entrepreneur, was born on 22 August 1779 at 75 Gildengate, Colegate, Norwich, the eldest of the seven children of John *Taylor (1750–1826), yarn manufacturer and dissenting minister, and his wife, Susannah *Taylor (1755–1823) [*see under* Taylor, John (1750–1826)]. The many activities of his father included being a Hebrew scholar, as well as a hymn writer and founding the Octagon Chapel, Norwich. Taylor was apprenticed as a land surveyor and civil engineer. In 1798, at the age of nineteen, he was appointed manager of the Wheal Friendship copper mine near Mary Tavy, Devon, as a result of his family's connection by marriage with the Martineau family, who owned shares in the mine. At his instigation major improvements were made to the mine, including the introduction of advanced methods for dressing copper ore and the construction of the Tavistock Canal, which provided water transport between the mine and the port of Morwellham. At this time he also took a direct financial interest in the reopening of the neighbouring Wheal Crowndale mine. In these early years he developed a reputation for being an innovator of the latest mining technology and for developing mines by the heavy investment of capital, which was contrary to normal practice within the industry. On 14 October 1805 he married Ann Rowe Pring of Awliscombe, Devon, the adopted daughter of Dr Thomas Burnaford, who was a surgeon to many of the mines in the Tavistock area. They had two sons, John (b. 1808) and Richard (b. 1810).

In 1812 Taylor established a chemical works for the manufacture of vitriol in Stratford, Essex, with his brother, Philip, and with the financial backing of the Martineau family. This company later diversified into mechanical engineering and it manufactured printing equipment for Marc Isambard Brunel. The Taylor brothers also formed a separate company for producing gas from oil. John Taylor withdrew from these businesses in the 1820s as he increased his involvement in metal mining. The expansion of his mining activities led him in turn to go into partnership with his sons in 1837.

Taylor became involved in all the major metal-mining areas of the British Isles, either by himself or through the firm of John Taylor & Sons. This included acting as mineral agent to a number of great estates, including those of the duke of Devonshire and the duchy of Cornwall. He also served as secretary of the Wheal Friendship mine in Devon; as inspector of the Greenwich Hospital mines; and as adviser to the commissioners of woods and forests regarding their mineral property. John Taylor & Sons also owned the Charlestown tin-smelting works in Cornwall, owned shares in numerous mining companies, and leased and managed mines throughout Britain and Ireland. Under Taylor's influence and through his extensive business operations, efficient mining equipment was introduced in all the major metal-mining areas. Similarly his distinctive management and employment practices were widely adopted, including the extensive use of the tribute system of paying miners in proportion to the quantity and quality of ore mined (a system admired by Charles Babbage and John Stuart Mill).

Taylor's activities were also international. In 1824 he became involved in the South American mining boom, and was instrumental in founding the British Real del Monte Mining Company and the Bolanos Mining Company in Mexico. These proved relatively unsuccessful, and the London-based management was criticized for failing to appreciate the difficult local conditions. Taylor was later involved in the Nouveau Mond Gold Mining Company, which operated in California and Spain, the Spanish mines of the Linares Lead Mining Company, and other mining activities in France, Germany, Italy, and Australia.

Taylor developed an interest in science and education and the dissemination of scientific knowledge, to which he applied his administrative skills. He was an early member of the Geological Society of London and later became its vice-president; he was also its treasurer from 1816 to 1847. He was elected a fellow of the Royal Society in 1825 and was an early member of the Institution of Civil Engineers. He was one of the founders of the University of London (later University College, London) in 1826 and served on its council and committee of management; he was treasurer from 1842 to 1860. He was also involved in the founding of the British Association for the Advancement of Science, and was its treasurer from 1831 until 1861. Through his involvement in the British Association, he was instrumental in the founding of the Museum of Economic Geology in 1839 for the collection of mining data. He was the author of *Statements Concerning the Profits of Mining in England* (1825); he edited *Records of Mining* (1829), in which he advocated the establishment of a mining school in Cornwall; and he contributed numerous articles to scientific journals.

Taylor maintained a reputation for honesty and trustworthiness in his business dealings, as well as for managerial and financial expertise. Towards the end of his life, when affected by ill health, he withdrew from mining to devote himself to his other interests. He died at his home, 31 Chester Terrace, Regent's Park, London, on Easter day, 5 April 1863, aged eighty-four. The family business continued in operation as an international mining concern until 1969.

EDMUND NEWELL

Sources R. Burt, *John Taylor: mining entrepreneur and engineer, 1779–1863* (1977) · R. W. Randall, *Real del Monte: a British mining venture in Mexico* (1972) · *Mining and Smelting Magazine*, 3 (1863), 269–70 · *PRS*, 13 (1863–4), v–vi · R. Shambrook, 'John Taylor and Anne Rowe Pring – later Mrs John Taylor', *Journal of the Trevithick Society*, 15 (1988), 82–6 · d. cert.

Archives BL, letters to Charles Babbage, Add. MSS 37186–37193, 37201, *passim* · Pachuca, Hildalgo, Mexico, Real del Monte MSS

Likenesses T. Lawrence, portrait, 1825, Athenaeum Club, London · C. Turner, mezzotint, pubd 1831 (after T. Lawrence), BM, NPG

Wealth at death under £40,000: probate, 29 July 1863, *CGPLA Eng. & Wales*

Taylor, John (1781–1864), publisher and writer, was born on 31 July 1781 at Market Square, East Retford, Nottinghamshire, the third of the nine children of James Taylor (1752–1823), bookseller and printer, and his wife, Sarah, *née* Drury (b. 1760). Following his education at Lincoln and Retford grammar schools he assisted in his father's business at East Retford before moving to London in 1803. There, over the next three years, he worked for various publishers and booksellers. In 1806 Taylor, along with his close friend James Augustus Hessey (1785–1870), set up the firm of Taylor and Hessey, publishers and booksellers, at 93 Fleet Street, London, with Taylor assuming responsibility for publishing matters (this side of the business moved to 13 Waterloo Place in 1823).

The partnership, never economically sound, was dissolved in 1825. Until then the staple publishing fare of the house had been 'sermons, domestic homilies, and moral tracts [...] books which firmly reflected the interests of the reading public' (Chilcott, 12, 67). Taylor, however, is best-known for publishing and supporting a number of predominantly second-generation Romantic writers, especially the poets Keats and John Clare. Publishing such writers often proved a high-risk, low-profit venture; outstandingly so in the cases of William Hazlitt and Keats, where the ideologically liberal Taylor attracted considerable personal critical hostility from many tory periodicals by his advocacy of supposedly anti-establishment writing. In an age of increasing commercial detachment he none the less developed unusually close personal, artistic, and financial associations with many of his writers—Keats and Clare particularly—even if several later complained of his extensive, usually unauthorized, copy-editing.

From 1821 to 1825 Taylor was joint owner with Hessey of the *London Magazine*. He always remained the main power behind the venture and, with varying degrees of editorial assistance, acted as managing editor until late 1824. Under Taylor, the magazine cost 2s. 6d. until December 1824, when the price increased to 3s. 6d. During the first two years of his editorship the magazine, with its brilliant and critically perceptive if temperamentally brittle group of contributors, came to exemplify the artistic spirit of its age. The famous monthly *London* dinners of the early 1820s, hosted by Taylor for his writers, who included Lamb, De Quincey, and Hazlitt, became a paradigm for editor–contributor harmony, short-lived though this was in most cases.

Operating under his own name only, Taylor became publisher and bookseller to the new University of London in 1827. Among the books he published were *A System of Popular Algebra* (1827), *Familiar Astronomy* (1830) by George Darley, and *Lectures on the Steam Engine* (1828) by Dionysius Lardner. In 1836 he formed a new publishing partnership with a Mr Walton. Until 1853, when he retired from business, he published mostly ephemeral works of 'useful knowledge'.

Erudite, depressive, deeply Christian with a moderate dissenting bent, and possessing a liking for litigation over copyright matters, Taylor was also a prolific writer. He published four of his own works on the identity of Junius in the 1810s and went on to write over forty scholarly, usually well-received, books, pamphlets, tracts, and magazine articles on a disparate range of subjects. Many of these concerned politico-economical matters (most often the vexed question of the relative importance and value of bullion and paper money); others handled religious, scientific, antiquarian, geographical, and philological themes. Additionally he contributed two dozen or so miscellaneous articles and poems to the *London* as well as compiling many of the editorial 'Lion's Head' columns for the magazine.

Having spent the whole of his publishing life in London, Taylor died there, a bachelor, at 7 Leonard Place, Kensington, on 5 July 1864. He was buried in the village churchyard in Gamston, near East Retford.

James Taylor (1788–1863), brother of John Taylor, was born in East Retford on 28 February 1788. In 1802, after receiving a local education, he moved to Bakewell, Derbyshire, home for the rest of his life, to help his sister Ann and her husband in their linen drapery business, later establishing himself as a successful and influential banker there and marrying in 1811. James Taylor was the lifelong intimate of his publisher brother, and kept the latter's business ventures solvent with numerous sizeable loans. A polymath like his brother, he published about a dozen (firmly identifiable) works, mostly on political economy, specifically currency matters, and on theological subjects. He died on 27 August 1863 at Bakewell, where he had been chairman of the local Wesleyan Missionary Society for nearly forty years. He was buried there on 9 September.   BARRY SYMONDS

Sources T. Chilcott, *A publisher and his circle: the life and work of John Taylor, Keats's publisher* (1972) · E. Blunden, *Keats's publisher: a memoir of John Taylor (1781–1864)* (1936) · O. M. Taylor, 'John Taylor, author and publisher, 1781–1864', *London Mercury*, 12 (1925), 158–66, 258–67 · H. E. Rollins, ed., *The Keats circle*, 2 vols. (1965) · J. Bauer, *The London magazine, 1820–29* (1953) · T. De Quincey, 'Sketches of life and manners', *Tait's Edinburgh Magazine*, new ser., 7 (1840), 765–71 · *DNB* · C. A. Prance, *Peppercorn papers* (1964) · F. P. Riga and C. A. Prance, *Index to The London Magazine* (1975)
Archives Derbys. RO, literary coresp. and family papers · Hunt. L., letters · NYPL, commonplace books and letters · priv. coll. | BL, Egerton MSS 2245–2249 · UCL, letters to the Society for the Diffusion of Useful Knowledge
Likenesses drawing (probably in his twenties or thirties), priv. coll.; repro. in Blunden, *Keats's publisher* · paste medallion (in later life), NPG; repro. in Blunden, *Keats's publisher*
Wealth at death under £450: administration with will, 7 Jan 1865, *CGPLA Eng. & Wales* · under £25,000—James Taylor: will, 15 Jan 1864, *CGPLA Eng. & Wales*

Taylor, John (1805–1842), surgeon and Chartist, was born on 16 September 1805 at Newark Castle, Ayrshire, the eldest son of Captain John Taylor of Blackhouse, Ayrshire, who had served in India and married an Indian lady. His family was connected with the Ayr Coal Company and owned considerable property in Ayrshire. Taylor was, in his own words, 'born to immense affluence' and 'educated in the most splendid fashion' (*True Scotsman*, 27 April 1839), with poetry, Byron, and political reform as his chief interests from youth. He was trained in medicine, probably at Edinburgh University, and was for a time a naval surgeon.

Taylor spent a substantial part of a £30,000 legacy fitting out a ship which he took to the aid of the Greeks in their war of independence. Much of the remainder disappeared in legal costs defending his libel of Thomas Kennedy, who had defeated him in the 1832 parliamentary election for Ayr burghs. That cost him control of the *Ayrshire and Kilmarnock Gazette*. His next two years were spent trying to make a commercial success of the Ayr Chemical Company. Then he used the remaining funds to purchase the Glasgow trade-union-supported newspaper *The Liberator*, which survived until May 1838. His obsession with Byronic heroics led him into several jousts with the law, especially in the first year of the Chartist movement, but initially in France in 1826 for plotting sedition with French republicans, and again in September 1833 for challenging Kennedy—now a lord of the Treasury—to a duel (*Case of Duel and Statement of Conduct of T. F. Kennedy M.P., 1833*).

By the end of 1836 Taylor had contested two parliamentary elections, become a leader of the Anti-Corn Law Association and chairman of the West of Scotland Radical Association. His handsome appearance, with dark flashing eyes and flowing locks of curled hair—'he carried ladies' hearts by storm', Harney later commented (*Newcastle Weekly Chronicle*, 5 Jan 1889)—together with his impassioned eloquence helped to establish his widening reputation as a radical reformer. He became popular in the north of England in the winter of 1837–8 with his campaign to support the Glasgow cotton spinners against their sentence of transportation. His main claim to fame and notoriety came with the blossoming of the Chartist movement, in which Taylor quickly became identified as one of the 'physical force' wing, tempted to move beyond the mere threat and demonstration of popular strength.

Taylor's initially moderate behaviour in the general convention earned him the sobriquet of Mirabeau of the Chartists, but this was displaced after May 1839 by periodic declarations promising liberty or death. After his arrest and brief imprisonment, following the Bull Ring riots, he denounced most of the convention as spies, cowards, and traitors, and engaged himself in plotting insurrection in Cumberland and Northumberland. This was intended to be part of what proved to be a badly co-ordinated plot for synchronized uprisings in Yorkshire and south Wales, along with Taylor's 'men of the north', which resulted in partial outbreaks at Newport in November, and later at Sheffield, Dewsbury, and Bradford. By that time Taylor had been arrested in Newcastle, bailed for £400 sureties in Carlisle, and plagued by chronic illness, lack of money, and shattered dreams of heroic rescues. By February 1840 even the authorities decided they need no longer take him seriously and the charges of sedition were dropped. In March he left Hull for Germany, before returning to Larne, Northern Ireland, where he spent the rest of his life at the manse of his brother-in-law the rector of Island Magee. There he devoted himself to writing religious verse and to religious study with a view to entering the church. Taylor, who never married, died of consumption at the rectory on Island Magee on 4 December 1842, and was buried two or three days later in Island Magee churchyard, where a statue was erected over his grave. Commemoration dinners were held by the Chartists of Ayr, Prestwick, and Greenock. A statue in 'Taylor's cemetery' at Wallacetown, Ayr, was erected by public subscription in Ayr and Kilmarnock in 1858. Apart from his editorial writings of the 1833–8 period, Taylor's publications include *Letters on the Ballot* (1838), *The Coming Revolution* (1840), *Christian Lyrics* (1851), and other verses in *Modern Scottish Poets* (vol. 15, 1893). ALEXANDER WILSON

Sources A. Wilson, *Scottish chartist portraits* (1965) · A. Wilson, *The chartist movement in Scotland* (1970) · Birmingham Public Library, Lovett collection, vol. 2 · D. Urquhart, *The chartist correspondence* (1855) · BL, Place Collection, Add. MSS 27820–27822, 34245 · R. M. W. Cowan, *The newspaper in Scotland: a study of its first expansion, 1815–1860* (1946) · *Northern Star* (1838–45) · *True Scotsman* (1838–40) · *Ayr Advertiser* (1834–42) · D. H. Edwards, *Modern Scottish poets, with biographical and critical notices*, 15 (1893) · *Newcastle Weekly Chronicle* (5 Jan 1889)

Likenesses statue, Wallacetown cemetery, Ayr · statue, Island Magee churchyard

Wealth at death depended on hospitality of brother for two years until death

Taylor, John (1808–1887), leader of the Church of Jesus Christ of Latter-Day Saints, was born on 1 November 1808 in Milnthorpe, Westmorland, the second of the ten children of James Taylor (1773–1870), excise officer and farmer, and his wife, Agnes Taylor (1787–1868), daughter of John Taylor of Pooley, Barton, Westmorland, and his wife, Agnes Whittington. John was christened at the Heversham parish church on 4 December 1808. After formal schooling at Liverpool, then at Beetham, near Hale, Westmorland, where his family moved on to a small farm in 1819, he became a skilled wood-turner and cabinet-maker. After his apprenticeship in Penrith, Cumberland, he established his trade in Hale.

Experiencing a strong religious awakening, Taylor joined the Methodist church at the age of sixteen and shortly thereafter became an exhorter, then a local preacher. He later recalled having a 'strong impression to go to America to preach the gospel' (Taylor, 267). He followed his parents to Toronto in Upper Canada in 1832, set up his trade, and continued his preaching for Methodism. While so engaged he met the gentle and refined Leonora Cannon, whom he married on 28 January 1833. Leonora was born on 6 October 1796 in Peel, Isle of Man, the oldest child of Captain George Cannon (1766–1811) and Leonora Callister (1775–1822). She had emigrated to Canada in 1832. John and Leonora were to have four children.

In 1836 a Latter-Day Saint apostle named Parley P. Pratt preached the message of the restored gospel to the Taylors in Toronto. After thorough investigation, John became convinced of the truth of the message and was baptized a member of the Church of Jesus Christ of Latter-Day Saints. Shortly thereafter he was appointed to preside over several branches in Canada. This was the beginning of a half-century of devoted and valiant service in his newly found faith.

In 1837 the Taylors moved to Far West, Missouri, where John was ordained as one of the church's twelve apostles on 19 December 1838. He was to hold this high office for over forty years. He played a prominent role in assisting the Saints as they fled mob persecutions to a new gathering place at Commerce (later Nauvoo), Illinois.

In 1839 Taylor accepted a call to return to his native England as a missionary. He was based in Liverpool and preached the restored gospel here and in surrounding cities, including Manchester and Preston. He introduced the same message into Ireland and the Isle of Man, and extended his labours into Scotland. He gained a reputation as a powerful speaker, debater, and writer, and his work resulted in the conversion of many to Mormonism. He was to return again on a short-term mission to England in 1846–7, at which time he also ministered for a brief period in Wales.

In 1841 Taylor rejoined his family and the Saints in Nauvoo, where he began a career of considerable community service as he continued his spiritual ministry. He was appointed as a city councilman, regent of the Nauvoo University, and judge-advocate in the Nauvoo Legion. In recognition of his literary talents he was appointed editor of the *Times and Seasons* (1839–46), a Latter-Day Saint periodical, and he published a weekly, the *Nauvoo Neighbor* (1843–5).

In June 1844 Taylor was invited to accompany Joseph and Hyrum Smith to Carthage gaol, Illinois, where the Smiths were detained while awaiting a hearing involving the destruction of an anti-Mormon newspaper. Taylor was to assist with the legal proceedings. An angry mob attacked the gaol and murdered both Joseph and Hyrum Smith. Severely wounded himself, Taylor survived to continue his ministry in the church.

Under intense persecution, the Latter-Day Saints left Nauvoo in the winter of 1846 and headed westward under the leadership of Brigham Young. Taylor's vigorous opposition to the tyranny of persecution during this and later periods gained him the title Champion of Liberty. 'I am God's free man,' he said; 'I cannot, will not be a slave' (Roberts, 424). Later, in 1847, he led one of the companies of pioneers to the Great Salt Lake valley and the free exercise of their religion.

In 1849 Taylor was called to open France to the preaching of the restored gospel. He preached and published extensively both in Paris and, later, in Hamburg, Germany, overseeing the production of the *Book of Mormon* in both French and German. After nearly three years he returned to the Salt Lake valley. In the summer of 1854 Taylor responded to yet another mission call, this time to the eastern states of America, with his headquarters in New York city. Here he published *The Mormon* (1855–7), a periodical which did much to allay harsh feelings against the church. Upon his return to Utah he was appointed speaker of the house of representatives in the Utah territorial legislature for five successive sessions and remained a member until 1876. He was also elected as territorial superintendent of schools in 1877.

In his private life Taylor was a kind and loving husband and father. He accepted the ancient biblical order of plural marriage when it was a revealed and authorized practice among Latter-Day Saints, and married several additional women. By seven of his wives—Leonora Cannon (1796–1868), Elizabeth Kaighin (1811–1895), Jane Ballantyne (1813–1900), Mary Ann Oakley (1826–1911), Sophia Whitaker (1825–1887), Harriet Whitaker (1825–1882), and Margaret Young (1837–1919)—he fathered thirty-five children. He went to great lengths to be fair and impartial while caring for each of his families.

With the passing of Brigham Young in 1877, the mantle of church leadership fell upon John Taylor. In October 1880 he was sustained as the prophet and president of the church, the only president to this day born outside America. His ministry is notable for pushing forward with increased zeal work on temples; the further definition of priesthood responsibilities, such as holding of local weekly priesthood meetings and of monthly priesthood meetings in larger areas (stakes); further development of children and youth programmes; increase in missionary effort; assistance to the poor and those in debt; and his bold defence of the restored gospel in a time of intense government prosecution.

Besides scores of articles and pamphlets on Mormonism, Taylor wrote *The Government of God* (1852), in which he compared and contrasted the governmental systems of God and man; *Items on Priesthood* (1881), a treatise on priesthood and especially the duties of a bishop; and *Mediation and Atonement of our Lord and Savior Jesus Christ* (1882), an assembling of scriptural passages with his own personal witness relating to the pre-eminent role of Christ in the salvation of humankind. A number of his talks and sermons are preserved in the *Journal of Discourses* (1854–86), especially volumes 5–26, and a compilation of many of his writings and discourses is found in *The Gospel Kingdom* (1943).

John Taylor was nearly 6 feet tall, weighing 180 pounds, with high forehead, deep-set grey eyes, firm chin, and silvery white hair. He seemed an English gentleman, of affable and kindly manner and noble bearing, deeply resolute, an ardent lover of liberty, and possessed of great courage and determination. He was a bold advocate and defender of the faith he espoused.

During Taylor's administration anti-polygamy legislation and prosecution increased. For what he felt was the public good, in the interests of peace, and out of his deep-felt conviction to abide by his religious principles rather than be subject to legalized persecution, Taylor went into self-imposed exile in 1885 to continue to lead the church. The strain took a great toll on his health. On 25 July 1887, after two and a half years in exile, he died in Kaysville, Utah, of congestive heart failure. He was eulogized as a 'double martyr' for his near-fatal wounds in Carthage gaol and for his sacrifice for religious principles. He was buried on 29 July 1887 in the Salt Lake City cemetery.

J. LEWIS TAYLOR

Sources J. Taylor, 'History of John Taylor. By himself', *Manuscript history of the Church*, bk G, 265–75 • B. H. Roberts, *The life of John Taylor* (1892) • D. H. Ludlow, ed., *Encyclopedia of Mormonism*, 3 (1992), 1438–41 • A. Jenson, *Latter-Day Saint biographical encyclopedia*, 1 (1901), 14–19 • R. L. Jensen, 'The John Taylor family', *Ensign* (Feb 1980), 50–56 • P. Nibley, 'John Taylor', *The presidents of the church* (1959), 69–100 • F. M. Gibbons, *John Taylor: Mormon philosopher, prophet of God* (1985) • S. W. Taylor and R. W. Taylor, *The John Taylor papers: records of the last Utah pioneer*, [2 vols.] (1984–) • G. H. Durham, ed., *The gospel kingdom* (1943) • parish register, Westmorland, Heversham, 4 Dec 1808, Cumbria AS, Kendal [baptism] • *Deseret News*, 26 July 1887, LDS Archives, film 026,922 • *Deseret News*, 29 July 1887, LDS Archives, film 026,922

Archives Church of Jesus Christ of Latter-Day Saints, Salt Lake City, Utah, historical department • U. Cal., Berkeley, Bancroft Library | FILM Brigham Young University Production, Provo, Utah, 'Prophets of the Restored Church' [video production]

Taylor, John (1829–1893), author and librarian, born on 12 September 1829 at 15 (later 32) Berkeley Place, Clifton, Bristol, was the eldest son of John Taylor, ironmonger, and his wife, Ann Ackland. After leaving school he assisted his father in his business, but found time for much private study. During 1858–9 he contributed to the *Bristol Times* several pieces, chiefly translations from the early Latin poets of the church. His attainments attracted notice, and he was appointed, on 26 March 1860, under-librarian to the Bristol Library Society, the largest subscription library in the west of England. He was elected librarian on 30 March 1863 and under him the number of subscribers, previously in decline, steadily increased. The Bristol Library and the Bristol Institution having united, in 1871 he became librarian of the Bristol Museum and Library, as the joint association was designated.

In 1874 Taylor proposed the formation of an archaeological society in Bristol and Gloucestershire and began to gather signatures in support of the idea. His scheme bore fruit in 1876, when the Bristol and Gloucestershire Archaeological Society held its first meeting. Spurning dilettantism, the society set itself high standards, which it substantially attained. Between 1876 and 1886 Taylor contributed antiquarian articles to the *Saturday Review*. His connection with the *Athenaeum*, which began in 1876, continued until his death.

On 16 October 1883 Taylor was elected city librarian of Bristol, which then had four free libraries. He kept this office until his death. In June 1885 a branch for Redland and West Clifton was opened, and in January 1888 one for Hotwells. This extension of branch libraries into middle-class suburbs, as well as into poorer districts, was actively supported by Taylor, who sent regular reports to the local press to argue that public libraries were not just philanthropic institutions for the poor, but an essential part of urban life.

Taylor wrote on the history and antiquities of Bristol and the west country. He was author of *Tintern Abbey and its Founders* (1867), *Guide to Clifton and its Neighbourhood* (1868), *A Book about Bristol … from Original Research* (1872), which was part guidebook, part antiquarian work, and *Bristol and Clifton, Old and New* (1877). His most important work was the *Ecclesiastical History* [of Bristol] (1881), which forms the second volume of *Bristol Past and Present* and is the most valuable part of a generally useful book. Some of his *Antiquarian Essays Contributed to the 'Saturday Review'*, were collected and published in 1895. Taylor died at Wordsworth Villa, Redland, Bristol, on 9 April 1893. He left a widow, three sons, and three daughters. His eldest son, Lancelot Acland Taylor, became librarian of the Museum Reference Library, Bristol.

WILLIAM GEORGE, rev. ELIZABETH BAIGENT

Sources W. George, 'Memoir', in J. Taylor, *Antiquarian essays* (1895) • C. R. J. Currie and C. P. Lewis, eds., *English county histories: a guide* (1994) • 'The inaugural meeting', *Transactions of the Bristol and Gloucestershire Archaeological Society*, 1 (1876), 7–9 • H. E. Meller, *Leisure and the changing city, 1870–1914* (1976) • I. Gray, *Antiquaries of Gloucestershire and Bristol*, Bristol and Gloucestershire Archaeological Society Records Section, 12 (1981) • E. Ralph, 'The Society, 1876–1976', *Essays in Bristol and Gloucestershire history* (1976), 1–49 • *Transactions of the Bristol and Gloucestershire Archaeological Society*, 17 (1892–3), 324 • *Transactions of the Bristol and Gloucestershire Archaeological Society*, 18 (1893–4), 7 • *Public libraries in Bristol, 1613–1974*, City and County of Bristol Arts and Leisure Committee (1974)
Archives Bristol Reference Library, corresp. and notes
Likenesses portrait, repro. in Taylor, *Antiquarian essays*

Taylor, Sir John (1833–1912), architect, was born at Warkworth, Northumberland, on 15 November 1833, the son of William Taylor, joiner, and his wife, Elizabeth Bolton. He married in 1860 Emma Hamilton, daughter of Henry Hadland; they had three daughters. After technical training under Anthony Salvin, Taylor served with the contractors George Smith & Co., by whom he was strongly recommended in 1859 as first assistant to the office of works' assistant surveyor for London at £600 p.a.

In July 1866 Taylor himself became assistant surveyor for London, employed chiefly as an architect superintending works costing about £50,000 p.a. The scope of his duties rapidly expanded to include county and police courts and in 1871 the buildings of the Department of Science and Art. As the new government offices were completed they came under his care. He extended the Thames Embankment alongside Millbank (essentially an engineering work); made additions to Marlborough House, the chief being a new storey (1886); and designed the new Bow Street police court and station (1879), and additions (including the central staircase) to the National Gallery and the sculpture gallery and White wing at the British Museum in the 1880s. He carried out the reconstruction of Hyde Park Corner in 1883–4. He also made considerable savings on the architect's estimate by executing the display fittings of the new Natural History Museum (£125,000). His minister praised the 'zeal, industry and the tact with which [his] varied duties are always carried out', and in recommending him for a salary of £1200 p.a. told the Treasury that 'in adopting an official … career … Mr Taylor has closed to himself those opportunities of fame and profit which are at the command of men certainly not his superiors in his profession' (20 Nov 1884, PRO, WORK 22/9/6, fol. 22). In 1883–4 he played a crucial role in the assessing of the competition for a new Admiralty and War Office building. In the 1890s came the bankruptcy buildings in Carey Street, the Chancery Lane front of the Public Record Office (£80,000), and the Patent Office library, besides many smaller official buildings, including police courts and park lodges. He was responsible for the general maintenance of the house of parliament, in which many alterations were made from time to time. He also conducted the structural arrangements for several important public functions, such as the thanksgiving services held at St Paul's Cathedral for the recovery of the prince of Wales (1872), and at Westminster Abbey for Queen Victoria's jubilee (1887).

With a vast programme of public works commencing as Taylor's retirement approached, the office was keen to retain the services of its 'most able and experienced technical expert' (20 Nov 1884, PRO WORK 22/9/6, fol. 60), so it was agreed that after March 1898 he should not only complete the works he had in hand, but also arrange for purchasing the necessary sites for the new buildings. When in late 1900 the architect appointed to design the new War Office, William Young, died, Taylor was entrusted jointly with Young's son with its construction; but his age was telling: 'Dear old Taylor … hasn't the physical *push* in him to get things forward', complained a colleague (Esher MSS, 5/13, 162–3). On the completion of the War Office in 1906 he resigned his position as consulting architect but remained a member of the advisory committee on the new public buildings.

Taylor was regarded by the many first commissioners of works under whom he served as a sound and cautious adviser, and was much appreciated and esteemed by all those with whom he came in contact in the course of his public service. In planning, his buildings were regarded as admirably suitable for their purpose, but his elevations were pedestrian. In recognition of his services he was made CB in 1895 and KCB in 1897. He was elected a fellow of the Royal Institute of British Architects in 1881, and served on the council (1899–1900), as a vice-president (1905–6), and as a member of the art standing committee. A member of the Civil Service rifle volunteers, he won many cups in the competitions of the National Rifle Association, until his official duties prevented further attendance. A keen golfer, he was at one time captain of the Royal Wimbledon Club, and a founder member of the Royal St George's Club at Sandwich. He died on 30 April 1912 at his residence, Moorfield, Langley Road, Surbiton Hill, Surrey.   HENRY TANNER, rev. M. H. PORT

Sources PRO, WORK 22/9/6 • M. H. Port, *Imperial London: civil government building in London, 1850–1915* (1995) • *The Times* (2 May 1912) • *RIBA Journal*, 19 (1911–12), 491 • *Building News* (16 May 1890), 706 • Burke, *Peerage* (1898) • CAC Cam., Esher MSS • *WWW* • *CGPLA Eng. & Wales* (1912)
Likenesses Deneulain, photograph, repro. in *Building News*
Wealth at death £23,566 16s. 1d.: probate, 5 July 1912, *CGPLA Eng. & Wales*

Taylor, John Edward (1791–1844), newspaper editor, was born at Ilminster, Somerset, on 11 September 1791. His father was the Revd John Taylor (1753–1817), who came of a Lancashire farming family and was educated at Stand grammar school, near Manchester; his mother was born Mary *Scott (1751/2–1793), daughter of a linen manufacturer of Milborne Port, Dorset. He had one elder sister. Taylor senior was one of two ministers sharing dissenting chapels at Ilminster and South Petherton who were decisively influenced by the French Revolution but in different directions: Taylor to become a Quaker and his colleague, the Revd John Noon, to enter extreme radical (Jacobin) politics. Mrs Taylor, a friend and correspondent of the poet Anna Seward, wrote feminist essays, religious verse, and an epic entitled *The Messiah*. The parents' marriage (May 1788) took place after an engagement of eleven years, protracted by Miss Scott's attentions to her aged mother. It was described (McLachlan, 30) as unhappy, deeply so for the mother, who was unable to reconcile her adherence to the Unitarian faith with the evident harshness of her husband's Quakerism. She died on 4 June 1793, when John Edward was not yet two.

After a short appointment in Bristol, Taylor senior moved to Manchester where, under Quaker patronage, he set up a classical academy in the rural suburb of Hulme. John Edward received all his formal education, apart from some instruction in mathematics by the scientist John Dalton, at his father's school, which he left at the age of fourteen. Against his father's wishes he decided as a young man to follow his mother's religious persuasion,

and became an active member, from 1840 a trustee, of the Cross Street Chapel, the home of Unitarianism in Manchester.

Taylor was originally intended for medicine, but his father apprenticed him instead to a cotton manufacturer, Benjamin Oakden, with whom, before he was twenty-one, he became a partner. On parting from Oakden he became a partner in the mercantile business of John Shuttleworth. He plunged into public life in Manchester as a founder of the Junior Literary and Philosophical Society and secretary, about 1810, of the Lancasterian school in the town.

During Taylor's boyhood popular opinion in Manchester was almost as much opposed to the early reformers, most of them middle class, as were the magistracy and the moneyed inhabitants of the town. ('The people', Haslam Mills wrote, 'voted steadily for Barabbas'.) With the economic crisis towards and at the end of the war with France, sentiment shifted. Strikes became frequent. Machine smashing disturbed the Lancashire cotton towns. It was then that Taylor, alongside a successful business career, involved himself in liberal politics. He went to London occasionally and was much impressed by, among others, Leigh Hunt, whom he visited in gaol. In 1812–13 he began to write regularly for the town's newspapers, principally William Cowdroy's *Manchester Gazette*, which among the several, mostly short-lived, papers of the time was the only representative of liberal opinion. Taylor's contributions were given credit for much of the paper's success in circulation. In a time of social turbulence he found himself constantly balancing his keen desire for political reform against inflammatory outbursts in the streets. Judicious comment, where friends and colleagues would have preferred more vigorous opposition to the perceived abuses of the time, was to be characteristic of his later career.

Also in 1812 a meeting called to support Lord Sidmouth's appointment as home secretary led to a riotous counter-demonstration in which the Royal Exchange was burned down. Rumours attributed to Taylor a handbill headed 'Now or never' which was posted in the town and was held to have provoked the arson. Six years later, in 1818, a conservative manufacturer, John Greenwood, at a meeting of commissioners of police called to appoint assessors, caused Taylor's name to be rejected on the specific ground that he was indeed the author of the manifesto. Taylor demanded withdrawal of the charge and, failing to secure it, published a letter calling Greenwood 'a liar, a slanderer, and a scoundrel'. A grand jury at Salford quarter sessions found an indictment against him for criminal libel. At his trial at Lancaster assizes on 29 March 1819, in which he conducted his own defence, Taylor made legal history in being allowed by the judge, Baron Wood (who was otherwise hostile), to plead the truth of his statement, a defence not previously admitted in a libel case. Counsel for the prosecution, James Scarlett (later Lord Abinger), surprisingly acquiesced in that decision. In his address to the jury Taylor asserted that he, not Greenwood, was the injured party. After conferring well into the night, under the persuasive foremanship of John Rylands, the jury went to the judge's lodgings and delivered to him, in bed, its verdict of not guilty.

This episode was quickly followed by a graver one. On 16 August 1819 a huge but apparently peaceful crowd gathered in St Peter's Fields, Manchester, to hear the popular orator Henry Hunt. The magistrates ordered Hunt to be arrested by the Manchester yeomanry, who were largely recruited from young members of the tory families in the town, supported by six troops of the 15th hussars. The mounted yeomanry quickly found themselves immersed in the crowd, and turned their swords on those around them. In the bloodshed which became known as the Peterloo massacre eleven people were killed and some hundreds wounded. *The Times*'s correspondent, John Tyas, having been arrested along with Hunt, Taylor sent a report of the event to a London newspaper so that the magistrates' own report should not by default become the received version. Archibald Prentice, his colleague on the *Gazette* and neighbour in Islington Street, Salford, did likewise, and their reports were corroborated by the *Liverpool Mercury* and *Leeds Mercury*. Sidmouth wrote to thank the magistrates for their 'prompt, decisive, and efficient' measures and placed the government's own account before parliament. Taylor responded with a substantial pamphlet, *Notes and Observations Critical and Explanatory* (1820), which, though anonymous, was known to be from his hand, in eloquent rebuttal of the government's account of the disturbance. Here again his cautious use of language was evident. He referred to the 'tragedy' rather than the 'massacre', differentiated between good and bad magistrates, and attributed the attack upon the crowd to a minority in the yeomanry's ranks 'whose political rancour approaches to absolute insanity'. He devoted much time to the committee set up to relieve the sufferers.

Largely on the strength of these events Taylor became the obvious choice among leaders of the moderate reform movement, most of them Unitarians, as the man to control a new newspaper catering for their interests. Twelve men together subscribed £1000, although Taylor was sole proprietor from the start. These men were mostly engaged in the textile trade, and included George Philips MP as well as the leading Manchester Liberals Thomas and Richard Potter. The *Manchester Guardian* was launched on 5 May 1821.

Until then Taylor had enjoyed the friendship and support of Prentice, who was influential among the radicals of the town, but Prentice soon found the *Guardian* insufficiently outspoken for his taste. In later years his criticism developed into animosity, more especially after Prentice, supported by some of Taylor's original backers who were disillusioned by the line taken by the *Guardian*, had himself taken over one rival newspaper and started another. Taylor joined the Anti-Corn Law League on its foundation in 1838, but was prepared to accept a reduction in the levy on imported grain if abolition was not forthcoming. His detractors alleged that his opposition to the grain duty owed more to his wish to keep wages down than to his consideration for the poor, but the ethical underpinning of his career suggests that was a calumny.

Taylor's *Manchester Guardian*, which he conducted in collaboration with Jeremiah Garnett, established a personality which endured for many years. It combined reformist editorial policies with a much more thorough news service than the town had previously been given. It thus became the required reading of manufacturers and merchants who valued its reporting and overlooked its politics; its price at 7*d*., including 4*d*. stamp duty, in any case restricted a wider sale.

Taylor's credit with the business community was augmented in 1823 by another libel action which this time he lost. He had denounced a local lawyer, John Dicas (though not by name), for putting out worthless currency notes. Dicas sued, was technically successful, but was awarded only £10 in damages against the £5000 he demanded. The action cost Taylor £483, of which businessmen contributed £307. The balance was in effect Taylor's purchase price for much favourable publicity. He was able to repay the initial subscribers and assume the sole ownership.

Taylor took on the business and civic responsibilities expected of one in his position. He frequently attended deputations to London to promote parliamentary legislation in the interests of his town and for several years he was deputy chairman of the improvement committee of the commissioners of police. He was a small man of louring mien and a priggish temperament. 'Moral indignation came easily to him and he could be infuriatingly patronising' (Ayerst, 87). On 4 May 1824, after a five-year engagement, he married his cousin, Sophia Russell Scott, daughter of Russell Scott, Unitarian minister, and C. P. Scott's aunt. The fourth of their children, also named John Edward *Taylor, succeeded to the headship of the newspaper. Sophia died in 1832; on 1 June 1836 Taylor married Harriet Acland (1802–1844), youngest daughter of Edward Boyce of Tiverton, who had joined his household the previous year as governess. Of the three daughters of this marriage, Harriet Ann Taylor married the economist William Stanley *Jevons. Taylor died of a chronic inflammation of the throat at his home, Beech Hill, Cheetham, on 6 January 1844, and was buried on 13 January.

GEOFFREY TAYLOR

Sources W. H. Mills, *The Manchester Guardian: a century of history* (1921) • A. Prentice, *Historical sketches and personal recollections of Manchester intended to illustrate the progress of public opinion from 1792 to 1832*, 3rd edn (1970) • H. McLachlan, 'The Taylors and Scotts of the Manchester Guardian', *Transactions of the Unitarian Historical Society*, 4/1 (1927–30) • [J. R. Beard], *Christian Reformer, or, Unitarian Magazine and Review*, 11 (1844), 158–73 • D. Ayerst, *Guardian: biography of a newspaper* (1971) • *Manchester Guardian* (10 Jan 1844) • *Manchester Guardian* (17 Jan 1844) • DNB

Archives JRL, Manchester Guardian archive

Likenesses drawing, repro. in Ayerst, *Guardian* • drawing, repro. in Mills, *The Manchester Guardian*

Taylor, John Edward (1830–1905), newspaper proprietor and art collector, was born on 2 February 1830 at Woodland Terrace, Higher Broughton, a suburb of Manchester, the younger son of John Edward *Taylor (1791–1844), founder of the *Manchester Guardian*, and his first wife,

John Edward Taylor (1830–1905), by unknown artist, c.1849

Sophia Russell Scott (d. 1832). He had one sister, Sophia Russell Taylor (1826–1868). His upbringing reflected the life of a well-to-do Unitarian family. After early education under tutors, including a Dr Heldenmeyer at Worksop, who practised Pestalozzi methods and encouraged conversational French and German, Taylor went to University College School, London. In 1847–8 he learned some rudimentary journalism at the *Guardian* office, and attended James Martineau's lectures on philosophy and William Gaskell's on history and literature at Manchester New College, before spending several months in Germany. As a student at the University of Bonn in 1848 he attended political occasions in Berlin and the national assembly at Frankfurt. He then travelled extensively in Europe, making himself familiar with many of the principal galleries, and also visited the Holy Land.

On his return to England in 1849, Taylor began to assemble his art collection. At the same time he studied law; he was called to the bar at the Inner Temple on 6 June 1853 but did not practise. While Taylor was in Germany, his elder brother, Russell Scott Taylor, with whom he had been joint proprietor of the *Manchester Guardian* since the death of their father in 1844, died suddenly, leaving him effectively the sole owner. By 1855 the slim, handsome young man with a shock of red hair was conducting the

paper in partnership with Jeremiah Garnett, who had been editor alongside his father and continued in that post until 1861. In 1855 the abolition of the remaining stamp duty on newspapers enabled the two men to transform the paper from a bi-weekly at 5*d*. to a daily at 2*d*. Two years later a price reduction to 1*d*. strengthened the company, so that during the 1860s it was making an average annual profit of £16,000; Taylor paid himself between £700 and £800 a year as editor and took thirteen-sixteenths of the profits.

In the combined role of editor and proprietor after Garnett's retirement, Taylor's main interest was managerial. Under his vigorous chairmanship, a group of provincial newspapers undertook a long agitation against the three telegraph companies that held a monopoly in the distribution of news. The result was the formation in 1868 of the Press Association, a newspaper co-operative, which sent out its first dispatch in 1870. The year 1868 was eventful in other ways: Taylor opened an office for the paper in London, rented a private wire to Manchester, and gained entry for staff writers into the House of Commons press gallery. He acquired the *Manchester Evening News* from Mitchell Henry, who had founded it to support his candidature (withdrawn at the last minute) in the general election of that year.

By the late 1860s Taylor had begun to withdraw from editorial functions, in favour of his youthful cousin C. P. *Scott, whom he appointed editor in January 1872. He had already moved his home to London, spending the winters in Paris or on the Riviera; he had a country house, The Coppins, at Iver, Buckinghamshire. He returned to Manchester briefly during the general election of 1874 to stand (unsuccessfully) as a Liberal, along with Peter Rylands, for Lancashire South-East. From a distance Taylor continued to take a detailed interest in the performance of his morning newspaper; he greatly encouraged Scott in some controversial causes, including support for Irish home rule and opposition to the Second South African War (during which the paper lost a seventh of its circulation), but asked him not to pursue others, including the Female Suffrage Bill of 1892, and proportional representation. During 1873 he announced without explanation that no further racing tips were to appear (the rule held, with only minor breaches, for more than ninety years). He adhered to several of the social conventions of his time. Regretting that his newspaper had not reported the trial of Oscar Wilde in 1895 he wrote to his editor saying that, if other papers had acted similarly, 'where would have been one half the punishment of the guilty and where the warning to others, which—between ourselves—is sadly needed I fear?'

Taylor was a generous contributor to the Liberal Party, and refused a baronetcy offered by Lord Rosebery in 1895. He became a trustee of Owens College (later the University of Manchester) in 1864 and a life governor in 1870; on his death he left the college a legacy of £20,000 which was used to endow a chair of English literature in his name at Manchester University. The first appointment to the chair was made in 1921. From 1854 until his death he was a trustee of Manchester New College, a Unitarian foundation, which ultimately became Manchester College of the University of Oxford. He engaged in educational charities, was a strong advocate of temperance and free trade, and encouraged the work of the British and Foreign Bible Society.

Taylor's enduring interest was his important collection of watercolours and other *objets d'art*, including Limoges enamels and ancient cloisonné. As early as 1857 he was a guarantor of the Manchester Art Treasures Exhibition; he lent works to the Manchester Exhibition of 1887, and to the Burlington Fine Arts Club, of which he was a member. In 1892–3 he gave 154 watercolours and four oil paintings to the new Whitworth Art Gallery, Manchester. Among the collection were twenty-four works by J. M. W. Turner, and seven by Blake. He gave more than sixty watercolours to the Victoria and Albert Museum, and to the British Museum a complete set of Turner's *Liber Studiorum*.

Taylor was married on 3 August 1861, in Marylebone, to Martha Elizabeth (1828–1912), youngest daughter of Robert William Warner, a shipowner of Thetford, Norfolk; there were no children. Their home in Manchester was in Bury Old Road; from the late 1880s they lived at 20 Kensington Palace Gardens, London, which Mrs Taylor continued to occupy after her husband's death. Taylor died at the Chatsworth Hotel, Eastbourne, on 5 October 1905. He was buried at Kensal Green cemetery. After the death of his widow in 1912 the sale of his art collection occupied twelve days at Christies in July of that year, realizing £358,500.　　　GEOFFREY TAYLOR

Sources *Manchester Guardian* (6 Oct 1905) • D. Ayerst, *Guardian: biography of a newspaper* (1971) • W. H. Mills, *The Manchester Guardian: a century of history* (1921) • DNB • *British watercolours from the John Edward Taylor collection in the Whitworth Art Gallery, University of Manchester* (1973)
Archives JRL, corresp. with C. P. Scott
Likenesses portrait, *c*.1849, repro. in Ayerst, *Guardian*, following p. 65 [*see illus.*] • portrait, repro. in Mills, *The Manchester Guardian*, following p. 138
Wealth at death £367,484 18*s*. 8*d*.: probate, 6 Dec 1905, CGPLA Eng. & Wales

Taylor, John Ellor (1837–1895), curator and popularizer of science, was born on 21 September 1837 at Levenshulme, near Manchester, the eldest son of William Taylor (*d*. 1864), a Lancashire cotton-factory foreman, and his wife, Maria Ellor (*b*. *c*.1806, *d*. after 1895). He received minimal education, and was first employed at a locomotive works at Longsight, Manchester, about 1850. About 1852 he was bound apprentice there as a fitter and turner. Encouraged to private study in classical languages and natural history, he attended classes at Manchester Mechanics' Institution when seventeen, and a year later became a Wesleyan lay preacher.

Taylor's opinions obliged him to choose between a religious and a scientific career; geological studies led him to Norwich, where he began popular lecturing about 1858. He commenced sub-editing on the *Norwich Mercury* for Richard Noverra Bacon in 1863, and soon gained success as editor of its offshoot, the *People's Weekly Journal*, which he made a vehicle for his popular scientific effusions. He was

scarred by smallpox while investigating social conditions attending a severe outbreak of the disease in Norwich. He married on 22 January 1867 Sarah Harriet (*b*. 1846/7), youngest daughter of William Bellamy, headmaster of the Boys' Model School, Norwich. They later had four daughters.

Together with John Gunn, Taylor established the Norwich Geological Society in 1864, and his original researches in Pliocene and Pleistocene deposits led to his election as fellow of the Geological Society of London in 1869. In 1870 he founded the Norwich Science-Gossip Club and by invitation catalogued the displays at Ipswich Corporation Museum, where he was appointed curator in 1872. Between 1872 and 1892 he delivered annual free lecture series in natural sciences in Ipswich (the material was later reworked as popular books), frequently commanding attendances of more than 450, meeting all expenses, and winning widespread affection. Robert Hardwicke appointed him editor of *Hardwicke's Science-Gossip Magazine* in 1872 (where he gained a national readership), and the following year introduced him to fellowship of the Linnean Society. He may have obtained a doctorate about 1874—from about this date he identifies himself in book titles as a PhD. Taylor lectured in many parts of England, and through the Ipswich Scientific Society he guided a young intellectual circle towards industrial and technological innovation, so promoting enlightened governance of that town in the forthcoming generation. He helped assemble the founding group of the *East Anglian Daily Times* (1874), through which his lectures were widely disseminated.

Taylor was a companionable man of liberal and humane sympathies, and his teaching reconciled orthodox science with reverence for the divine principle in creation; his gifts of popular exposition were particularly admired by Professor Ray Lankester. Having enlisted Richard Wallace's patronage, he masterminded the creation of the new museum at Ipswich in 1881, soon afterwards receiving a testimonial of £733 raised from public subscription in recognition of his public service and modest salary. R. S. Smythe promoted his successful lecture tour of Australia in 1885. Weakening health compelled him to resign his editorial duties and curatorship in 1893, and in September 1893 he was declared bankrupt, owing £735. Taylor continued to lecture until two weeks before his death at his home, 3 Little Colman Street, Ipswich, on 28 September 1895. He was buried at Ipswich cemetery two days later. He was survived by his wife and four daughters.

STEVEN J. PLUNKETT

Sources DNB • F. W. Wilson, 'Death of Dr. J. E. Taylor at Ipswich', *East Anglian Daily Times* (30 Sept 1895) • 'Presentation of a testimonial to Dr. J. E. Taylor, F.G.S., F.L.S.', *Ipswich Journal* (6 Dec 1881) • H. B. Woodward, 'memoir of John Gunn', *Memorials of John Gunn*, ed. H. B. Woodward and E. T. Newton (1891), 4–29 • [J. E. Taylor], 'Ipswich Museum lectures', *Suffolk Chronicle* (1872–92) • [H. Miller], Ipswich Scientific Society, minute books, 1872–95, Suffolk RO, Ipswich, GH 444 • [J. E. Taylor], ed., *Hardwicke's Science-Gossip Magazine* (1872–92) • J. E. Taylor, *Our island continent: a naturalist's holiday in Australia* (1886) • R. A. D. Markham, *A rhino in high street: Ipswich Museum,* *the early years* (privately printed, Ipswich, 1990) · certificate of election as fellow of Linnean Society, 1873, Linn. Soc. · biography files, Suffolk RO, Ipswich · m. cert. · d. cert.

Archives Ipswich Museums, collections and minute books · Suffolk RO, Ipswich, scrapbook of museum lectures, etc., qS 92
Likenesses W. Vick and others, photographs, 1872–89, Ipswich Borough Museums, Ipswich Scientific Society Album · W. Vick, photograph, *c*.1880, repro. in Markham, *Rhino in high street* · E. Aldis, oils?, *c*.1881 · W. Griffith, oils, *c*.1890, Ipswich Borough Museums · engraving, repro. in *Hardwicke's Science-Gossip*, new ser., 2 (1896), 210
Wealth at death bankrupt owing £755 in Sept 1893: Suffolk RO, Ipswich

Taylor, John Henry (1871–1963), golfer, was born at Northam, north Devon, on 19 March 1871, the second son in the family of four sons and one daughter of Joshua Taylor, a labourer of that village, and his wife, Susannah Heard, midwife, of Barnstaple. Having reached the sixth standard at the local school, Taylor left school at the age of eleven, but took great pains to further his education. He was a frequent reader of Dickens and Boswell, and wrote without any help his own autobiography, *Golf: my Life's Work* (1943). His early life was bound up with Westward Ho!, formed in 1864 and one of the first golf clubs in England. From school he became a caddie at the club, and after a spell working as a gardener's boy, and a labourer on the construction of Bideford quay, returned to Westward Ho! as a groundsman in 1888, after the army and navy had turned him down because of his poor eyesight.

Taylor's sense of justice and powers of oratory might have fitted him for the role of an early trade union leader. If so, his talents were not wasted for as a young man he became the spokesman for a group of club professionals trying to protect the trading interest of their shops. From this movement sprang the Professional Golfers' Association, of which in 1901 he became the first president. Taylor was appointed greenkeeper-cum-professional to the Burnham club in Somerset in 1891 and from there came his big chance. A match was arranged between him and a renowned Scottish golfer, Andrew Kirkaldy, who was employed at Royal Winchester. Taylor won and Kirkaldy's praise of the young Englishman was such that Taylor succeeded him at Winchester. In 1893 Taylor was emboldened to try his luck in the open championship at Prestwick, hitherto a purely Scottish preserve. The astonishing accuracy of his long shots to the hole, hit flat-footed with a firm punch and often a little grunt, spread consternation among the Scots.

When the championship crossed the border for the first time in 1894, at Sandwich, Taylor became the first English professional to win. He won again at St Andrews in 1895, after coming with a great rush through the rain. In 1896 Harry Vardon beat him in a play-off, depriving him of a hat-trick. It was the first of the six times Taylor finished second in the championship, in addition to his five victories. He won handsomely in 1900 at St Andrews after leading all the way, as he liked to do. His fourth victory was in 1909 at Deal and his last in a gale at Hoylake in 1913. Those who watched him there described it as the finest golf they had ever seen.

Among Taylor's other achievements in the game were victory in the French open and the matchplay championship, twice each, in the German open, and, a feat which is often overlooked, second place in the United States open in 1900. Even when he was fifty-three he finished fifth in the British open of 1924, and his score over six rounds, including the two qualifying ones, was lower than that of anyone else. Highly strung and emotional though he was, Taylor managed to master his feelings and when he had done so, he was, in the estimation of Bernard Darwin, perhaps the most clearly inspired player of his age. Resolute to the point of obstinacy, on the golf course he was a true fighter. Together with James Braid and Harry Vardon, he formed the great 'triumvirate' of golf at the turn of the century.

Taylor retired from the Royal Mid-Surrey club in 1946 after forty-seven years' service there, and the honours began to roll in, for one who had done so much to raise the status of his fellow professionals. In 1950 he was elected an honorary member of the Royal and Ancient Golf Club, a gesture made to two other golfers only up to that time, and later he was given a silver salver signed by all living captains of the club. More than fifty American professionals paid him a similar compliment in 1955, and in 1957 Westward Ho!, later Royal North Devon, paid him the great honour of electing him president of the club where he had started as a caddie.

In 1896 Taylor married Clara Fulford, a teacher. He lost his wife shortly after celebrating their diamond wedding in 1956. He died on 10 February 1963 at the village of his birth, and was survived by six of his family of three sons and six daughters. PETER RYDE, *rev.*

Sources D. Steel and P. Ryde, eds., *The Shell international encyclopaedia of golf* (1975) · B. Darwin, *Playing the like* (1934) · P. Lawless, *The golfer's companion* (1937) · J. H. Taylor, *Golf: my life's work* (1943) · *The Times* (11 Feb 1963) · *Country Life*, 99 (19 April 1946) · CGPLA Eng. & Wales (1963)
Archives FILM BFI NFTVA, sports footage |SOUND BL NSA, current affairs recordings · BL NSA, oral history interview
Likenesses C. Flower, group portrait, 1913, Royal and Ancient Golf Club, St Andrews; *see illus. in* Vardon, Henry William (1870–1937) · Spy [L. Ward], pencil and colour wash
Wealth at death £27,901 9*s*. 2*d*.: probate, 3 May 1963, *CGPLA Eng. & Wales*

Taylor, John Sydney (1795–1841), journalist, was born in Dublin, the second son of John M'Kinley, a goldsmith. His father (who assumed the name of Taylor) was descended from Captain David M'Kinley, who led the advance of King William's troops at the Boyne, while his mother was a descendant of Patrick Sarsfield, titular earl of Lucan. Taylor was educated at Samuel White's academy in Dublin, the school of Richard Sheridan and Thomas Moore, and at Trinity College, Dublin, which he entered in 1809. He obtained a scholarship in 1812, graduated in 1814, and was a prominent member of the College Historical Society.

In 1815 Taylor was admitted to the Middle Temple, and was called to the English bar in 1822. As a student in London in 1820 he edited a weekly paper with Thomas Crofton Croker called *The Talisman*. Shortly after his call he began writing for the *Morning Chronicle*. In 1827 he married a Miss Hull, niece of James Perry, who had been a proprietor of the *Morning Chronicle*. He also began writing for the *Morning Herald*, of which he was for a time the editor. Under his management the newspaper became the voice of the Anti-Slavery Society, and was particularly associated with Thomas Clarkson.

Taylor resigned as editor in order to return to the bar, where he made his name in the Roscommon peerage case in 1828, when he established the claim of Michael James Robert Dillon to the dormant peerage. He also proved the madness of Edward Oxford who was charged with shooting at the queen. Taylor was a close college intimate of Charles Wolfe, the author of the lines on the death of Sir John Moore, and in a letter addressed to the *Morning Chronicle* (27 October 1824) first established Wolfe's claim to the authorship of the poem. In 1823 he was a member of a committee, led by Lord Brougham, which promoted the founding of the London Mechanics' Institute, later Birkbeck College. He also spoke in the defence of a number of London church buildings threatened by inappropriate restoration, and was successful in protecting the screen of York Minster. Taylor died on 10 December 1841 and was buried at Kensal Green.

C. L. FALKINER, *rev.* MARIE-LOUISE LEGG

Sources *Selections from the writings of J. Sydney Taylor with a brief sketch of his life* (1843) · Burtchaell & Sadlier, *Alum. Dubl.* · H. A. C. Sturgess, ed., *Register of admissions to the Honourable Society of the Middle Temple, from the fifteenth century to the year 1944*, 3 vols. (1949) · *The Dublin University Magazine* (Feb 1842)
Likenesses J. Thomson, stipple (after C. Moore), BM

Taylor, John William (1851–1910), gynaecologist, was born at Canonhold, Melksham, Wiltshire, on 27 February 1851, the third son of James Taylor, a Wesleyan minister, and his wife, Mary Matcham. After education at Kingswood School, Taylor entered Charing Cross Hospital medical school, where he held resident posts on both the medical and the surgical sides. In 1877 he qualified FRCS and graduated MD (Brussels). The following year he moved to Birmingham and was appointed medical officer to the Provident Dispensary at Camp Hill, where he also set up in private practice. However, he soon became dissatisfied with the mundane nature of much of his work and gave up private practice to devote himself to gynaecology, in which he believed his training and abilities could find a wider scope. In May 1884 he was appointed honorary surgeon to the Birmingham and Midland Hospital for Women, and a month later he became chief assistant to Lawson Tait, the renowned gynaecological surgeon. On 29 June 1889 Taylor married Florence Maberly Buxton, daughter of Joseph Holmes Buxton, a surgeon; they had two sons and three daughters.

Taylor undoubtedly benefited from his association with Tait, who was one of the most original and innovative gynaecologists of his generation, with a vast private practice. When Tait died in 1899, Taylor succeeded him in the post of professor of gynaecology at Queen's College, Birmingham; a year later the University of Birmingham was opened and Taylor was elected professor of gynaecology. Taylor was president of the Midland Medical Society in

1897–8, and vice-president of the Obstetrical Society of London in 1904. He was a founder member of the British Gynaecological Society (1884), of which he became president in 1904, and in 1902 he was appointed governor of Charing Cross Hospital, London. He was also consulting surgeon to the Wolverhampton Hospital for Women, and consulting gynaecological surgeon to the Birmingham and Midland Skin and Lock Hospital.

A bold and skilful operator, Taylor introduced many improvements in technique and methods of treatment: especially important were those arising from his investigations into the prolonged use of small doses of mercuric iodide in the treatment of gonorrhoeal salpingitis. He was also an original thinker who made many valuable contributions to the literature of gynaecology. Jointly with Frederick Edge he published in 1895 *A Manual of Gynaecology and Obstetrics*, a translation of the original by Dührssen. In 1898 he delivered the Ingleby lectures at Birmingham on extra-uterine pregnancy, and the following year he published *Extra-Uterine Pregnancy: a Clinical and Operative Study*, a work which at once established his reputation as a leading authority on the subject. He was the author of the article entitled 'Disorders and diseases of pregnancy' in Quain's *Dictionary of Medicine* (1902 edn) and contributed many papers on allied subjects to the *British Journal of Gynaecology* and the *Birmingham Medical Review*, as well as *The Lancet* and the *British Medical Journal*. Taylor took a keen interest in the question of the falling birth-rate: he considered this to be a grave national danger, and in his inaugural address as president of the British Gynaecological Society he discussed at length the moral issues which, he believed, lay at the root of the problem.

Taylor's achievements were not confined to medical matters. An accomplished musician, he composed several hymns which revealed the depth of his Anglo-Catholic belief, as well as the anthem 'Gaudeamus', a humorous piece that was sung annually by the Birmingham University students. As a result of various holidays spent in the south of France and western England, in 1906 he published *The Coming of the Saints: Imaginations and Studies in Early Church History and Traditions*, in which he discussed the legends surrounding the journeys of Mary, Martha, Lazarus, and Joseph of Arimathea in France and England.

In his late fifties Taylor began to suffer from heart disease and in 1909 he was forced to resign his post at the Midland Hospital for Women; soon after he also gave up his professorship in the hope that his condition might improve with more rest and care. However, his health continued to deteriorate, and he died at his home, 22 Newhall Street, Birmingham, on 26 February 1910, of chronic heart disease, and was buried at Northfield church, Worcestershire, on 2 March. He was survived by his wife. Taylor's *The Doorkeeper, and other Poems* (1910) was published posthumously.

ORNELLA MOSCUCCI

Sources *The Lancet* (5 March 1910), 687–8 · *BMJ* (5 March 1910), 607 · b. cert. · m. cert.
Likenesses H. J. Whitlock & Sons Ltd, photograph, repro. in *BMJ*

Taylor, Jonas Dearnley (1829–1902), building society manager, was born on 19 January 1829 at Skircoat, Halifax, the son of William Taylor, woollen manufacturer. Apart from his nonconformist upbringing, which had a formative influence upon his life, other aspects of his childhood and youth remain obscure. He attended King Cross Wesleyan Methodist Sunday School, Halifax, but later became associated with Sion Congregational Church and then Park Congregational Church, of which he became a founder member in 1869, deacon, and secretary. After leaving school he became a solicitor's clerk with the Halifax attorneys E. M. Wavell and later Stocks and Franklin, before founding his own firm of chartered accountants. At the time of his death he was the oldest chartered accountant in Halifax. He married first, at the age of nineteen, on 21 April 1848 at Halifax parish church, Martha Ann Eastwood (1824/5–1893), the daughter of Thomas Eastwood, a cloth dresser, and soon after her death he married at St Paul's Church, South Kensington, London, on 7 September 1894, his second wife, Ellen Sarah Hill (1857/8–1935), the daughter of John Hill, a butcher, whom he had met returning to England from the United States of America. He loved the company of children, and his first wife 'bore him a numerous family'.

Taylor is principally remembered for his pioneering role in the foundation and development of the Halifax Permanent Benefit Building Society, of which he was secretary for almost half a century from its foundation in February 1853 until his death in September 1902. He was a member of the deputation which secured from the chairman of the Board of Inland Revenue exemption for the society from income tax in 1864. He evidently possessed a genius for organization and a talent for bookkeeping, patenting several labour-saving devices in that connection. He urged the development of a strong branch network, and during his term of office the society acquired some fifty branches, mostly in Yorkshire, including major branches at Huddersfield, Hull, Leeds, and Bradford. He also maintained strict controls on expenditure. During his lifetime the number of head office staff never rose above ten, and staff salaries and office running costs were kept as low as possible, for example by drafting letters on reused envelopes. At the time of his death the society had acquired assets of £1.5 million sterling. Taylor was respected for his integrity and for his 'foremost thought' that 'should a person bring money to the society, he should receive it back again' (Home Owner, 5). He was a Liberal by conviction but took no active part in politics; when approached to contest a seat in the local municipal elections, he suddenly withdrew at the last moment. However, he served briefly in 1848 to 1849 as secretary of the Halifax Co-operative Trading Society and in 1857 he became a leading campaigner for public baths in the town. He also helped to promote a major model housing development of some 300 dwellings at West Hill Park, Halifax, to 'encourage thrifty artisans, clerks and others to obtain freehold dwellings for themselves', for which the Halifax Permanent advanced loans amounting to nearly £45,000 (J. Hole, The Homes of the Working Classes with Suggestions for their Improvement, 1866, 75).

Photographs and a portrait in oils commissioned by the Halifax Permanent Benefit Building Society from the artist Ernest Moore shortly before Taylor's death reveal a man of medium height and portly build with silvery white hair and neatly trimmed beard and moustache. A former colleague later recalled that he usually 'came to business attired in a dark morning coat and striped trousers' sporting a top hat and umbrella and 'always commanded much attention', particularly when 'slowly picking his way through the crowds', escorted by a junior clerk laden with heavy bags of cash on his regular journeys to the Halifax Joint Stock Bank to bank the receipts from the society's branches (Hobson, 57–61). In business, he was 'autocratic, but kind and with a sense of humour' (ibid., 61), 'of quick temper, but readily conciliated' (History of the Halifax Permanent Benefit Building Society, 137), and had 'a brisk and energetic manner' (Hobson, 57). He was 'a strict disciplinarian in the office' and a stickler for punctuality. The mainspring of his character was 'a strong and rather simple kind of faith', and in private life 'nothing pleased him better than to spend an evening at home in the company of some of his friends, especially men associated with him in church activities' (ibid., 537–61).

Shortly after presenting his forty-ninth annual report to the society's annual general meeting, Taylor's health began to fail, and he died on 3 September 1902 at Bute House, 6 The Crescent, Bridlington, Yorkshire, from diabetic gangrene. He was survived by his second wife, but by only two sons and one daughter from his first marriage. After an impressive funeral service at Park Congregational Church, Halifax, Taylor was buried at the Halifax general cemetery, Lister Lane, Halifax, on 6 September. His funeral procession was headed by the directors of the Halifax Permanent Benefit Building Society, bankers and solicitors, surveyors and auditors, staff at the society's head office, branch secretaries, and agents. In his eulogy, the Revd G. S. Smith described him as 'a man of minute detail' who was 'straight as an arrow in all his dealings and righteously indignant with all who deviated from the right course' (Halifax Guardian, 13 Sept 1902). One local newspaper in its obituary maintained that he had 'probably done more to encourage thrift than any other single individual' in the town of Halifax, where an extraordinarily large proportion of householders were owner-occupiers (Halifax Courier). His tombstone inscription recorded simply that he had been a founder and for fifty years secretary of the Halifax Permanent Benefit Building Society.   JOHN A. HARGREAVES

Sources The history of the Halifax Permanent Benefit Building Society (1903) • J. A. Hargreaves, Halifax (1999), 126–7, 176 • O. R. Hobson, A hundred years of the Halifax (1953) • P. Pugh, The strength to change (1998) • Halifax Guardian (19 Feb 1853) • Halifax Guardian (6 Sept 1902) • Halifax Guardian (13 Sept 1902) • Calderdale MBC grave survey, 1984, Halifax general cemetery, Lister Lane, Halifax • The Home Owner [centenary issue] (1953) • Halifax Courier (6 Sept 1902) • J. A. Jowitt, ed., Model industrial communities in mid-nineteenth century Yorkshire (1986) • M. H. Yeadell, 'Building societies in the West Riding of Yorkshire and their contribution to housing provision in the nineteenth century', Building the industrial city, ed. M. Doughty (1986), 58–103 • m. certs. • d. cert. • d. cert. [William Taylor] • B. Wilson,

'The struggles of an old chartist', *Testaments of radicalism*, ed. D. Vincent (1977), 193–242, esp. 212

Archives W. Yorks. AS, Calderdale, Halifax Permanent Benefit Building Society records, HXB: 29–352

Likenesses E. Moore, oils, 1902 · photograph, repro. in *The history of the Halifax*

Wealth at death £7377 3s. 5d.: probate, 17 Oct 1902, CGPLA Eng. & Wales

Taylor, Joseph (*bap.* 1586?, *d.* 1652), actor, was probably (although his name was far from uncommon) the child who was baptized under that name at the church of St Andrew by the Wardrobe, London, on 6 February 1586. He is first recorded as a player in 1610, when he became a founding member of the Duke of York's Men, a company formed under the patronage of the ten-year-old Prince Charles. A patent of 30 March 1610 names seven players, including 'John Garland Willyam Rowley' and 'Joseph Taylor … already sworne servauntes to our deere sonne the Duke of york and Rothesay' (Chambers and Greg, 273). Garland was the leader of the group. Will Rowley was the playwright and comic actor who later collaborated with Thomas Middleton in his greatest plays.

The King's Men, the acting company that performed Shakespeare's plays in London up to 1642, acquired Joseph Taylor in 1619, when Richard Burbage died. Burbage had been the company's leading player for the first twenty-five years of its existence. He was the first player of Hamlet and all the other leading roles in Shakespeare, most of which Taylor inherited. Taylor must therefore have been a highly skilled and versatile player. Even before he joined the King's Men, who worked, and most of whom lived, in Southwark, parish records appear to locate Taylor as living in the parish of St Saviour's, Southwark. He married Elizabeth Ingle there in 1610, and between 1612 and 1623 eight of his children were baptized there, and one buried. Taylor must have known some of Shakespeare's company long before he began to work with them.

One of the King's Men whom Taylor knew was very likely John Heminges. In 1610 five of York's players in the new venture bought their company's first costumes from Heminges, a purchase which later gave Taylor some trouble. At Easter 1611 he left the company 'by the licence and leave of his said Master the Duke upon some speciall reason' (Chambers, 2.243). The reason was to help form the Lady Elizabeth's Men, who came into existence with a patent just after Easter 1611. Heminges brought a lawsuit for non-payment of the York's company's bill against Taylor, who alleged that the other four signatories had contrived to lay the blame on him. His 1611 departure was to join the last of the five companies formed in King James's time to be given royal patronage. James had made himself patron of the leading company in 1603, and given the next two best to his elder son and wife. In 1608 a new company was established for his younger son, Charles, then aged eight, and his daughter Elizabeth acquired hers in 1611. The Lady Elizabeth's Men was formed, like York's before it, with a core of six experienced adult players and several youths from a company of boy players, now grown into their early teens. Taylor led this group until 1615, a difficult time for players, when more playing companies were struggling to stay in London than there were playhouses to perform in. His company then amalgamated with the Prince Charles, the former Duke of York's, his original company. He was not a man to hold grudges, and was to prove a sturdy team player and leader. For the next three years the merged company divided its time between playing at the Curtain Theatre, the oldest and poorest in London, and the new dual-purpose theatre also used for bear-baiting, the Hope. Its leader player was a graduate of the Blackfriars boy company, Nathan Field, who led the company with Taylor for several years, until Field preceded him into the King's Men.

Under Field and Taylor the company did not lack ambitions. The King's Men were pre-eminent, abandoning their traditional open-air Globe each winter for the roofed hall playhouse, the Blackfriars. With Edward Alleyn's support the Taylor company tried to get themselves a hall too, the abortive Porter's Hall project. When the privy council banned it, they reverted to the new Hope, playing Jonson's *Bartholomew Fair* there in 1614. But that proved not to be a desirable venue. On 20 March 1616 Alleyn and Henslowe's old partner in the royal bear business, Jacob Meade, signed an agreement with a group of the leading Prince Charles's and Lady Elizabeth's players, one of whom was Taylor. An undated letter to Alleyn from Taylor, Rowley, and five others, which probably belongs to 1616, is an apology for leaving the Hope on Bankside, not because of the intemperate weather but because of the 'more intemperate Mr. Meade', the controller of the bears, who were also players at the Hope (*Henslowe Papers*, 93). The letter asks Alleyn to find them another playhouse, and to give them a loan to tide them over. The last record of his work for the merged Lady Elizabeth's–Prince's Men is when he performed in the Inner Temple masque of January or February 1619.

While in the Lady Elizabeth's, Taylor played in such hits as Jonson's play and two Beaumont and Fletcher plays, *The Coxcomb* and *The Honest Man's Fortune*. Once he joined the King's Men, about April 1619, he played Hamlet, and Iago in *Othello*, Truewit in *Epicene*, Face in *The Alchemist* and Mosca in *Volpone*, Philaster in the Beaumont and Fletcher play of that name, Amintor in their *Maid's Tragedy* and Arbaces in *A King and No King*, Ferdinand in Webster's *Duchess of Malfi*, Mathias in Massinger's *The Picture*, Paris in his *The Roman Actor*, and Rollo in *The Bloody Brother*. These were not all roles he inherited from Burbage, since Burbage played Othello and Subtle. On some evidence that has not survived, Edmond Malone also thought that he might have painted the Chandos portrait of Shakespeare.

Once John Heminges retired from working as a King's Men's player and their financial manager in the mid-1620s, a role he performed for thirty years, Taylor became one of the two leaders of the company. Traditionally at least two of the leading players, or 'sharers' in a London-based company's costs and profits, had the authority to sign papers and collect payments on behalf of the whole company. From about 1625 until 1642, when all the companies were dissolved, Taylor served with John Lowin, and sometimes Eliart Swanston, as the King's

Men's chief agent and co-leader. After Heminges died in 1629 Taylor acquired a share in the company's two playhouses, the Blackfriars and the Globe, a source of revenue at least equal to his income as an actor. His status as the King's Men's manager also gained him a royal appointment in 1639 as yeoman of the revels, a post which gave Taylor access to the wardrobe of costumes and properties used for court performances and paid him 6*d*. per day, about half the daily wage of a skilled artisan. Five years earlier, on twelfth night 1634, Taylor had presented a revival of Fletcher's *The Faithful Shepherdess* before the king and queen at Whitehall, with costumes given to Taylor by Henrietta Maria from 'the year before of her owne pastorall' (Bentley, 2.595).

After the theatres closed in September 1642 Taylor's occupation was gone, but he stayed loyal to it. He was one of the ten King's Men who signed the dedication to the 1647 Beaumont and Fletcher folio, and he was captured at the Cockpit in 1648 during an illegal performance of *Rollo, Duke of Normandy, or, The Bloody Brother*. He died in 1652 in Richmond, Surrey, and was buried there on 4 November. After the Restoration he was remembered nostalgically as the most distinguished player in the great company which kept the plays of Shakespeare and Jonson on stage up to 1642.   ANDREW GURR

Sources G. E. Bentley, *The Jacobean and Caroline stage*, 7 vols. (1941–68), vol. 2, pp. 592–8 · E. K. Chambers, *The Elizabethan stage*, 4 vols. (1923), vol. 2, pp. 243–4 · M. Eccles, 'Elizabethan actors, IV: S to end', *N&Q*, 238 (1993), 165–76 · W. W. Greg, *Henslowe papers: being documents supplementary to Henslowe's diary* (1907), 90–91, 93 · E. K. Chambers and W. W. Greg, eds., 'Dramatic records from the patent rolls', *Malone Society Collections*, 1/3 (1909), 260–84

Taylor, Joseph (1833–1910), folk-singer, was born on 10 December 1833 at Binbrook, Lincolnshire, the eldest of nine children born to James Taylor (*b. c.*1806), an agricultural labourer, and his wife, Mary (*b. c.*1810). From the evidence of his later career, Taylor must have received some education, but it is not known how or when. By the age of seventeen he was working as a farm labourer.

In 1856 Taylor married Elizabeth Hill (1827–1909) from Huttoft, Lincolnshire, and over the next fifteen years they had seven children, six of whom survived into adult life. In 1862 the family moved to Saxby All Saints, also in Lincolnshire, and Taylor's material conditions improved. He specialized as an estate woodman and carpenter, and by 1891 he had risen to become the local agent of the landowner J. Hope Barton and was a well-known and respected local figure. He was parish clerk of Saxby from 1875 to 1906 and sang in the church choir for more than forty years.

In 1905 a class for folk songs was instituted at the north Lincolnshire musical competitions held at Brigg. Taylor entered and won first prize for 'Creeping Jane', a song about a horse race. One of the folk song collectors eagerly listening and awaiting the chance to interview the singers was the young Australian pianist and composer Percy Grainger. The singing of Taylor and the other competitors made an immediate and deep impression on him and over the next four years he returned to Lincolnshire again and

again, with Taylor as his main source. In 1906 Grainger began to use the phonograph for folk song collecting and in 1908 he arranged for the Gramophone Company (later HMV) to make recordings of Taylor's singing. These were not a commercial success, but through Grainger's interest and initiative Taylor's songs and vocal style can be studied in a way that is impossible with most other traditional singers from the pre-1914 period. His is, truly and almost uniquely, a voice from a lost and unimaginable past.

Taylor appears to have learned most of his songs as a boy at Binbrook. He had a poor memory for song words, but, as Grainger wrote of him, 'his mind is a seemingly unlimited storehouse of melodies, which he swiftly recalls at the merest mention of their titles; and his versions are generally distinguished by the beauty of their melodic curves and the symmetry of their construction' (Grainger, 164). Taylor relied more on vocal effects than any other singer Grainger met: he wrote of Taylor's 'effortless high notes, sturdy rhythms, clean unmistakeable intervals, and his twiddles and "bleating" ornaments (invariably executed with unfailing grace and neatness' (ibid., 164). The gramophone recordings made in 1908 were eventually edited and re-released as *Unto Brigg Fair* in 1972, and Taylor's performance style has been a powerful influence on modern folk-singers. The song which will always be associated with his name is 'Brigg Fair', whose tune was made the basis of an orchestral rhapsody by Frederick Delius.

Joseph and Elizabeth Taylor celebrated their golden wedding in November 1906. By then, their two elder sons also held responsible positions as estate woodmen and their youngest daughter had become a schoolteacher. The family were mainstays of the local choir and choral society. Elizabeth Taylor died in November 1909. Joseph Taylor was still hale and hearty and had the appearance of a much younger man, but on 3 May 1910 he was driving a horse trap on estate business when the horse kicked over the traces and he was thrown out. Taylor was able to drive on, complete his business, and return home, but he collapsed and died the following day. He is buried in Saxby churchyard, where a tombstone can be seen.

C. J. BEARMAN

Sources R. W. Pacey, 'Folk music in Lincolnshire', DPhil diss., U. Oxf., 1978 · P. Grainger, 'Collecting with the phonograph', *Journal of the Folk Song Society*, 12 (1908), 164 · *Hull Daily Mail* (5 May 1910) · *Hull and Lincolnshire Times* (24 Nov 1906) · *Lincolnshire Star* (7 May 1910) · census returns for Binbrook, 1841, PRO, HO 107/627/22/23; 1851, HO 107/2112/146/13, 107/2112/153/26; 1861, RG 9/2384/47/2 · census returns for Saxby All Saints, 1871, PRO, RG 10/3438/89/3; 1881, RG 11/3291/109/5; 1891, RG 12/1539/79/11 · *CGPLA Eng. & Wales* (1910)
Archives SOUND Grainger Museum, Melbourne, Australia, 1906–8 phonograph recordings · Vaughan Williams Memorial Library, Cecil Sharp House, London, Sound Library, 1908 Gramophone Company master discs
Likenesses photograph, repro. in J. Bird, *Percy Grainger*, 3rd edn (1999), pl. 14
Wealth at death £181 18s. 8d.: administration, 18 July 1910, *CGPLA Eng. & Wales*

Taylor, Maria Susanna (1837–1904). *See under* Ternan, Ellen Lawless (1839–1914).

Taylor, Mary (1817–1893), advocate of women's rights, was born on 26 February 1817, probably at the Red House, Gomersal, near Leeds, Yorkshire, the fourth of the six children of Joshua Taylor (1766–1840), cloth manufacturer, and his wife, Anne Tickell (1781?–1856). Her father, a well-travelled, highly cultivated man, was a radical and New Connexion Methodist; bankrupted in 1826, he dedicated the rest of his life to repaying his creditors, a task that was completed by his sons. His wife's 'unhappy disposition' (*Letters of Charlotte Brontë*, 438) alienated all her family and from 1845 she lived alone.

All their children were 'restless, active spirits', but it was Mary who was most like her father. Lively, impulsive, and clever, she shared his independence of mind, was tenacious in her opinions and forthright in her expression of them, and, throughout her long and active life, defied custom and propriety to practise what she preached. 'It is vain to limit a character like hers within ordinary boundaries—', wrote Charlotte Brontë in 1841; 'she will overstep them—I am morally certain Mary will establish her own landmarks' (*Letters of Charlotte Brontë*, 242–3).

They first met in January 1831, when Charlotte joined Mary and her younger sister Martha (1819–1842) at Roe Head School, Mirfield. Their friendship was stimulated by their diametrically opposed political and religious views: 'we used to astonish each other at every sentence' (*Letters*, 162), Mary confessed, while Charlotte found 'the society of the Taylors … one of the most rousing pleasures I have ever known' (*Letters of Charlotte Brontë*, 190). Even at school, Mary, nicknamed Polly and Pag, was defiant of authority. Set what she considered a futile rote-learning task, she refused to do it and bore the punishment of going to bed supperless for a month cheerfully and without complaint. 'Her rebellion was never outspoken', recalled a schoolfriend. 'She was always quiet in demeanour' (Shorter, 235).

After the death of her father in December 1840 Mary took a European tour, then joined her sister as a pupil at the Château de Koekelberg, Brussels. Her letters describing the pictures and cathedrals she had seen inspired Charlotte with 'the wish for wings' which took her to Brussels in 1842. When Martha died of cholera in October 1842, Mary went to Hagen, Germany, where she flouted convention by teaching young men ('nice *dull* ones') and learning algebra 'because it is odd in a woman to learn it, and I like to establish my right to be doing odd things' (*Letters*, 45, 50).

In March 1845 she fulfilled another 'outrageously odd' (*Letters of Charlotte Brontë*, 251) ambition and followed her youngest brother, Waring (1820?–1903), to Wellington, New Zealand. Parting from Charlotte for what was to be the last time, she urged her to leave home too: 'Think of what you'll be five years hence!' (*Letters*, 161). Determined to find an effective way of earning money, Mary took the bold step of setting up shop in Wellington with her cousin Ellen Taylor (1826–1851), and was so successful that by 1859 she could afford to retire. A payment of £3000 from her father's estate, now debt-free, ensured her future financial security. She returned to Gomersal, where she

Mary Taylor (1817–1893), by unknown engraver, pubd 1893

built a house, High Royd, which was to be her home for the rest of her life.

Far from settling into quiet retirement, Mary took annual climbing holidays in the Swiss Alps and, at the age of almost sixty, led a party of five women on a ten-week expedition which culminated in an ascent of Mont Blanc. Their account of the adventure was privately published as *Swiss Notes by Five Ladies* (1875). A passionate advocate of women's suffrage and property rights, Mary contributed twenty-eight powerful polemical essays on feminist issues to Emily Faithfull's *Victoria Magazine*, a journal edited and printed by women. Reprinting fourteen of her articles as *The First Duty of Women* (1870), she added a characteristically blunt preface: 'The object of most of the following pages is to inculcate the duty of earning money' (Taylor, *First Duty*, iii). Women would be happier, she argued, 'if they had not been taught, or if they could unlearn, that money-getting is a depraved taste or a bad habit … the really degrading idea [is] that it is some one else's duty to do this business for them'; the mere effort to earn a living, even if unsuccessful, 'would have a much better effect than quietism in keeping their minds strong, straight, equable, and self-controlled' (ibid., 246).

This message was also the central theme of Mary's only novel, *Miss Miles, or, A Tale of Yorkshire Life Sixty Years Ago* (1890), which she began in the 1840s and worked on intermittently for forty years. Though her authorship has been questioned—the book has even been attributed to Charlotte Brontë—it is undoubtedly Mary's own work, reflecting opinions and ideas she had frequently advanced in *Victoria Magazine*. It describes the struggle of four young women to earn their livings; true to the doctrine Mary had always preached, the one who is denied the chance to work dies, a heart-broken victim of her own inertia. Of little literary merit, it is chiefly interesting as a companion piece to Charlotte Brontë's *Shirley* (1849), in which the Taylor family served as models for the Yorkes. Though amused by her own portrait—'What a little lump of perfection you have made me!' (*Letters*, 97)—Mary was outraged by Charlotte's treatment of women working:

this first duty, this great necessity you seem to think that *some* women may indulge in—if they give up marriage and don't make themselves too disagreeable to the other sex. You are a coward and a traitor. A woman who works is by that alone better than one who does not.   (ibid., 94)

As a schoolgirl, Mary had apparently been considered 'too pretty to live' (Shorter, 234); her only surviving photograph, taken in late middle age, bears out her own description of herself as 'a stout personage with few words, grey hair, and decidedly well-worn garments' (Taylor, 'Notes of a Swiss tour', 304). Mary provided Mrs Gaskell with some telling anecdotes for *The Life of Charlotte Brontë* (1857), but refused all later attempts to interview her about her friend. She died of a stroke on 1 March 1893 at High Royd and was buried in Gomersal parish churchyard three days later.   JULIET BARKER

Sources *Mary Taylor, friend of Charlotte Brontë: letters from New Zealand and elsewhere*, ed. J. Stevens (1972) · *The letters of Charlotte Brontë*, ed. M. Smith, 2 vols. (1995–2000), vol. 1 · M. Taylor, *Miss Miles, or, A tale of Yorkshire life sixty years ago* (1890) · M. Taylor, *The first duty of women: a series of articles reprinted from the Victoria Magazine, 1865–70* (1870) · M. Taylor, 'Notes of a Swiss tour', ed. [E. Faithful], *Victoria Magazine*, 17 (1871), 289–307 · M. Taylor, G. Hirst, F. M. Richardson, M. Nielson, and M. Ross, *Swiss notes by five ladies* (privately printed, 1875) · C. K. Shorter, *Charlotte Brontë and her circle* (1896) · J. H. Murray, 'The first duty of women: Mary Taylor's writings in *Victoria Magazine*', *Victorian Periodicals Review*, 22 (1989), 141–7 · J. Bellamy, 'Mary Taylor, Ellen Nussey, and Brontë biography', *Brontë Society Transactions*, 21/7 (1996), 275–83 · *ILN* (18 March 1893) · S. M. Taylor, 'Notes on her meeting with Grace Hirst', 1931, Brontë Parsonage Museum, Haworth, Yorkshire, MS BS.IX, T
Archives Morgan L., MS MA 2696 · U. Texas | BL, Ashley collection · Brontë Parsonage Museum, Haworth, Yorkshire, Bonnell collection · NYPL, Berg collection
Likenesses E. Walker, photograph, 1880?, repro. in Shorter, *Charlotte Brontë* · engraving, pubd 1893, NPG [*see illus.*]
Wealth at death £109 6s.: administration, 15 May 1893, CGPLA Eng. & Wales

Taylor, Michael Angelo (1756/7–1834), politician, was the only child of Sir Robert *Taylor (1714–1788), architect, and his wife (1722/3–1803). He entered Westminster School in January 1766 and then, destined for the law, he was admitted to the Inner Temple in 1769, transferring to Lincoln's Inn in 1770. He was called to the bar in November 1774, three weeks after admission to Corpus Christi College, Oxford, where he graduated BA in 1778, proceeding MA from St John's College in 1781. Endowed by his father with £20,000 and £2000 a year, he subordinated his professional to political ambitions, at first supporting Pitt the younger's administration. His initial bid to enter the House of Commons in 1784, as MP for Preston, was thwarted by an unfavourable decision on the electoral franchise, but he found another constituency, Poole, where he was newly appointed recorder during the same election. A diminutive figure, disingenuous and pompous by turns, although not malicious, he excited ridicule after describing himself in debate on 9 February 1785 as 'but a chicken' in his profession: in that guise he was lampooned by Sheridan and often caricatured by Gillray and others. He first differed from Pitt over parliamentary reform, to which he was opposed from 1784 to 1785. In 1787, too, he became one of the managers' committee for the impeachment of Warren Hastings, which was espoused by the whig opposition leaders.

The death of his father in 1788 provided Taylor with a life interest in £100,000, the residue of which was reserved for founding the Taylor Institution at Oxford. On 7 August 1789 he married Frances Anne Vane (*d*. 1835), the attractive daughter and heir of the Revd Sir Henry Vane, first baronet (1729–1794), of Long Newton, co. Durham, and his first wife, Frances Tempest. They had one daughter. His marriage procured him a whig electoral interest. He joined Brooks's Club in 1789 and the Whig Club in 1791. Despite defeat at Poole in 1790, he regained the seat on petition on 25 February 1791, after sitting by substitution for Heytesbury, Wiltshire, since 22 December previous. He became a regular whig spokesman and teller on many issues, publicly converting to parliamentary reform on 30 April 1792 as a member of the Society of Friends of the People. His bid on 28 March 1792 to abolish the national lottery on moral grounds failed. Critical of the hostilities with revolutionary France, he opposed repression and growing state power at home and subsidies to continental allies. He also espoused the cause of George, prince of Wales. His electoral interest at Poole was undermined by his agent, and he was defeated in 1796. Despite talk of his switching to Southwark, it was as MP for Aldeburgh that he was returned to parliament. After joining Fox in arguing for the dismissal of the ministry and in favour of parliamentary reform, in May 1797 he seceded from parliament with the Foxites until June 1798. Subsequently he opposed Pitt on all major measures. On 17 March 1800 he succeeded his brother-in-law as member for Durham City. In 1801 he was mentioned as a plausible candidate for the speakership. He lost his Durham seat in 1802.

Taylor remained out of parliament until 1806, when his friends took office. He had taken up residence in Yorkshire, first at Park Hill, Bawtry, then at Ledstone Hall, where he entertained the prince of Wales, and later at Cantley. In 1806, refusing other offers, he was returned for Rye as a Treasury nominee. Illness curtailed his attendance, but he voted against his friends' dismissal by George III on 9 April 1807. At the ensuing election he came in for Ilchester on the prince of Wales's interest, becoming in 1808 a member of the prince's duchy council. He acted with the whig opposition unless the prince objected, and served as amanuensis for the prince when he wrote his acceptance of the regency on 11 January 1811. In 1812 he was one of two MPs who took evidence from witnesses to Spencer Perceval's assassination. The regent's abandonment of the whigs embarrassed him, particularly as his return for Poole in 1812 received Treasury support. He still leaned to opposition on some questions, such as legal reform and Catholic relief; but he had no wish to quarrel with the regent, who professed 'he loved no man so well' (*Creevey Papers*, 1.211). Frances Taylor was a vivacious hostess and their dinner table at Privy Gardens, Whitehall, was at her connivance a frequent resort of whig politicians. It was there that the regent's daughter Princess Caroline fled in June 1814. Taylor's break with the regent, foreshadowed by his vote against renewed hostilities with Napoleon in 1815, became complete after Sheridan's death in 1816, Taylor's hopes of succeeding to his duchy office being dashed. He turned increasingly to opposition, and his recapture of Durham in 1818 enabled him to join the whigs with impunity: he held the seat until 1831. In 1827 he claimed, 'I have supported the Whigs for eight and thirty years at an expense of above £30,000' (ibid., 2.116).

Whatever his political difficulties, Taylor was untrammelled in his pursuit of one aim in parliament: the reform of the chancery court, which under Eldon's chancellorship had become a byword for delay. From 1810 he regularly sought a remedy. The creation of the vice-chancellorship in 1813 helped, but he was unable to obtain sufficient support, nor was he severely critical of Eldon: by 1823 the whigs counted on another reformer, John Williams. Taylor continued to play his part: on 12 February 1828 he told the house the history of his campaign, and in his last speech, on 31 July 1833, claimed that the court operated to the ruin of all property. Aspects of criminal law reform also interested him. In 1815 he secured the abolition of the pillory, and he opposed capital punishment for forgery. Another interest was improvement of public environmental amenities: his Metropolitan Paving Act of 1817 legislated for the removal of nuisances and obstructions from London streets: he also promoted their gas lighting. In 1820–21 he sought to curb pollution from steam engines and furnaces and to reduce the speed of stagecoach drivers, and in 1825 he exposed faults in London's water supply. He advocated poor law relief, and humane treatment of ailing prisoners (1823) and lunatics (1827).

Disappointed in hopes of office in 1827, Taylor had to be satisfied with a privy councillorship, granted on 23 February 1831 following the whigs' return to power. That month he presented a Durham parliamentary reform petition, even though he was critical of strident reformers. In the reformed house of 1832 he sat for Sudbury, Suffolk. Sometimes styled 'Father of the House', he appeared in Sir George Hayter's oil painting of the Commons of 1833. He died on 16 July 1834 at his town house, in Privy Gardens, Whitehall, and was buried on 23 July in the family vault in St Martin-in-the-Fields, London. His wife died on 14 January 1835.   ROLAND THORNE

Sources HoP, Commons, 1790–1820 · J. Almon, ed., The debates and proceedings of the British House of Commons, 11 vols. (1766–75) · J. Stockdale, ed., The debates and proceedings of the House of Commons: during the sixteenth parliament of Great Britain, 19 vols. (1785–90) · Cobbett, Parl. hist. · The Creevey papers, ed. H. Maxwell, 2nd edn, 2 vols. (1904) · S. Romilly, Memoirs of the life of Sir Samuel Romilly, 3 vols. (1840), vol. 2, pp. 374, 392, 397; vol. 3, pp. 13, 31, 166 · A portion of the journal kept by Thomas Raikes from 1831–1847: comprising reminiscences of social and political life in London and Paris during that period, 1 (1856), 266 · GM, 1st ser., 58 (1788), 903 · GM, 1st ser., 73 (1803), 1261 · GM, 2nd ser., 1 (1834), 430 · H. M. Colvin, A biographical dictionary of British architects, 1600–1840, new edn (1978), 854 · The correspondence of George, prince of Wales, 1770–1812, ed. A. Aspinall, 5: 1804–1806 (1968), pp. 345–6, n.2 · F. G. Stephens and M. D. George, eds., Catalogue of political and personal satires preserved … in the British Museum, 6–7 (1938–42) · Creevey's life and times: a further selection from the correspondence of Thomas Creevey, ed. J. Gore (1934), 334, 337 · DNB · GM, 2nd ser., 3 (1835), 220 · Old Westminsters, 2.907 · register, Inner Temple, London · W. P. Baildon, ed., The records of the Honorable Society of Lincoln's Inn [incl. Admissions, 2 vols. (1896), and Black books, 6 vols. (1897–2001)] · register, CCC Oxf.

Archives Northumbd RO, Newcastle upon Tyne, letters to Thomas Creevey · U. Durham L., letters to Lord Grey · UCL, Creevey MSS

Likenesses J. Gillray and others, caricatures, 1785–1810, repro. in Stephens and George, eds., Catalogue of political and personal satires, 5–8 (1935–47) · J. Gillray, caricature, etching, pubd 1797, NPG · S. W. Reynolds, mezzotint, pubd 1822 (after J. Lonsdale), BM, NPG · G. Hayter, group portrait, oils (The House of Commons 1833), NPG

Wealth at death £100,000: PRO, death duty registers, IR 26/1400; will, 1831

Taylor, Michael Waistell (1824–1892), physician and antiquary, son of Michael Taylor, an Edinburgh merchant, was born at Portobello in Midlothian on 29 January 1824. He was educated at Portsmouth and matriculated at Edinburgh University in 1840, and he graduated MD in 1843. In the following year he obtained a diploma from the Royal College of Physicians of Edinburgh. While at Edinburgh University he made a special study of botany, and was appointed assistant to Professor John Hutton Balfour. Taylor was also one of the founders and early presidents of the Hunterian Medical Society. In 1844 he studied surgery at Paris for nine months, and afterwards he visited various foreign cities collecting botanical specimens.

In 1845 Taylor settled in Penrith in Cumberland, and soon after succeeded to the practice of Dr John Taylor. In 1858 he achieved distinction by ascertaining that scarlet fever might be caused by contamination of the milk supply. In the same year he married Mary, a daughter of J. H. Rayner of Liverpool. In 1868 he played a large part in founding the border counties' branch of the British Medical Association, and he was the second to hold the office of president. He was the author of many treatises on medical subjects, and in 1881 wrote an important article on the fungoid nature of diphtheria. He was a member of the Epidemiological Society.

Taylor was a member of the 1st battalion of the Cumberland volunteer corps, and he served as its staff surgeon. He also played an important part in the founding of the Penrith Literary and Scientific Society. Professionally he was no less known as an antiquary than as a physician. He was elected a fellow of the Society of Antiquaries of London on 27 May 1886, and was a fellow of the Scottish Society of Antiquaries and a member of the council of the Royal Archaeological Institute. He joined the Cumberland and Westmorland Antiquarian and Archaeological Society soon after its formation in 1866. Taylor made several important local discoveries, particularly of the vestiges of Celtic occupation on Ullswater, the starfish cairns of Moor Divock, the prehistoric remains at Clifton, and the Croglin moulds for casting spearheads in bronze. By the time of his death he had completed a very elaborate work, Old Manorial Halls of Cumberland and Westmorland (1892).

Taylor retired from medical practice in 1884. He died at his home, 202 Earls Court Road, London, on 24 November 1892, and was buried at Penrith in the Christ Church burial-ground. He left a widow, three sons, and three daughters.   E. I. CARLYLE, rev. MICHAEL BEVAN

Sources BMJ (10 Dec 1892), 1315 · The Times (2 Dec 1892) · Carlisle Journal (29 Nov 1892) · Nomina eorum, qui gradum medicinae doctoris in academia Jacobi sexti Scotorum regis, quae Edinburgi est, adepti sunt, ab *anno 1705 ad annum 1845*, University of Edinburgh (1846) • M. W. Taylor, 'Memoir', *Old manorial halls of Cumberland and Westmorland* (1892)

Likenesses portrait, repro. in Taylor, *Old manorial halls of Cumberland and Westmorland*

Wealth at death £22,587 15s. 1d.: probate, 4 Jan 1893, *CGPLA Eng. & Wales*

Taylor, Peter (*bap.* **1756**, *d.* **1788**), decorative artist and painter, was baptized at South Leith on 21 January 1756, the son of Peter Taylor and his wife, Katherine Carfrae. On 21 March 1786 he married Elizabeth Low and resided in West Register Street, Edinburgh, where he worked as a coach painter and interior decorator. He is said to have painted portraits of his friends, but his seated, half-length portrait, executed in oils on a small wooden panel, of Burns is the only work definitely attributed to him.

Burns and Taylor met in December 1786, shortly after the poet's arrival in Edinburgh, at a dinner party which extended into the small hours. Burns agreed on the spur of the moment to sit for his portrait the very next morning. He gave three sittings, taking breakfast with Taylor before each session. Mrs Taylor was present at the last and by far the longest session shortly before Burns left Edinburgh on 5 May 1787.

The existence of this portrait was unknown until 1812 when James Hogg and two friends paid a visit to Taylor's widow. Mrs Taylor opened a clothes-press and removed the small wooden panel from a little box. Hogg commented, 'It is particularly like Robert in the form and air; with regard to venial faults I care not' (J. Hogg, letter of 27 Nov 1829 cited in *Burns Chronicle*, 1, 1892, 86). Several of the poet's contemporaries, when shown the Taylor portrait, failed to recognize Burns and thought that it might be his brother Gilbert; but both Burns's widow, Jean, and his confidante Mrs Agnes McLehose (Clarinda), as well as Sir Walter Scott and Mrs Dunlop of Dunlop, considered it a good likeness. Mrs Taylor's account was confirmed by the engraver John Burnet who stated that a friend of his, at one time in Taylor's employment, recalled him working on the painting. The panel has the inscription 'T. 1786' on the reverse, although that could have been added at a later date. This painting was used as the basis of J. Horsburgh's engraving, executed in December 1829, and a stone statue-group carved by John Greenshields in 1830. The panel portrait was bequeathed to the Scottish National Portrait Gallery, Edinburgh, in 1927 by the artist's great-grand-nephew. Taylor also produced a larger version of the portrait, in oils on canvas. Its existence did not come to light until 1893 and was first publicly exhibited in 1895. It was purchased by Captain Wardlaw Ramsay of Whitehill and acquired by the Scottish National Portrait Gallery in 1938.

Taylor was also interested in industrial developments and introduced the manufacture of painted waxcloth, 'the figuring of linen floorcloth for carpeting', into Scotland, for which he was awarded a premium of £100 on 13 February 1788 by the board of manufactures 'towards the expense incurred by him in erecting the necessary building, machinery, and apparatus for carrying on the work'

(*Edinburgh Literary Journal*, 5 Dec 1829). Taylor suffered from pulmonary tuberculosis and retired to the south of France where he died at Marseilles on 20 December 1788, leaving his widow and an infant daughter, Elizabeth.

J. L. CAW, *rev.* JAMES A. MACKAY

Sources 'Unpublished remains of Robert Burns … Account of a lately-discovered portrait, with letters concerning it', *Edinburgh Literary Journal*, 2 (21 Nov 1829), 352 • 'More information concerning Robert Burns – The New Portrait &c.', *Edinburgh Literary Journal* (5 Dec 1829), 384–5 • H. Smailes, *The concise catalogue of the Scottish National Portrait Gallery* (1990) • Records of the board of manufactures, NA Scot. • B. Skinner, *Burns: authentic likenesses* (1963) • J. Mackay, *Burnsiana* (1988) • registers of births and marriages, Edinburgh and Leith • P. Williamson, *Williamson's directory for the city of Edinburgh, Canongate, Leith and suburbs* (1787–8)

Taylor, Peter Alfred [PAT] (**1819–1891**), politician and radical, was born in London on 30 July 1819, the eldest of the five children of Peter Alfred Taylor (1790–1850), silk merchant, and his wife and first cousin, Catherine (*b.* 1795, *d.* in or after 1875), daughter of George Courtauld of Braintree, Essex. His uncle Samuel *Courtauld instigated the celebrated Braintree case against church rates. He was educated at the school in West Hove, Sussex, run by the Revd J. P. Malleson, his cousin and the Unitarian minister at Brighton. It was through this connection that he met Clementia Doughty, who became governess to the Taylor family [see Taylor, Clementia (1810–1908)]. They married on 27 September 1842 and jointly undertook many activities in support of radical causes.

Taylor entered the family firm of Samuel Courtauld & Co. in the late 1830s. He later became a partner, and it was the wealth from this family connection that enabled him to develop his radical interests and to support them financially. He grew up in the Unitarian circle centred on South Place Chapel, Finsbury, of which his father was a leading member. His father helped to bring PAT, as he was widely known, into a leading position in the Anti-Corn Law League, where he met the leading radicals of the day.

In 1845 the Taylors met Giuseppi Mazzini, the Italian patriot, who made an indelible impression on them, and they became his close friends and supporters. A secret hiding place was prepared for Mazzini in the Taylors' home, in case his life should be threatened. In the late 1840s Taylor helped to found the Society of Friends of Italy, and as its first treasurer was its primary fund-raiser. The Taylors kept open house for leading radicals from Britain, Europe, and America, first, from the early 1850s, in Powis Place, Great Ormond Street, London, and then from 1861 at Aubrey House, Notting Hill Gate.

Taylor advocated a democracy in Britain, and was an early member of the Northern Reform Union, founded in 1858 to promote manhood suffrage. After unsuccessful candidatures at Newcastle upon Tyne (1858) and Leicester (1861), he was elected unopposed as an advanced Liberal MP for Leicester in February 1862. At his election, when his programme included abolition of church rates and separation of church and state, he was attacked as 'anti-everything'. He was a member of the Emancipation Society, founded in 1862 to promote the cause of the northern states in the American Civil War, he supported Polish independence (1863), and he was a member of the Garibaldi committee, set up in 1864 to welcome the Italian patriot to Britain. He was a vice-president and one of the few middle-class supporters of the Reform League, constituted early in 1865 to campaign for manhood suffrage and the ballot, and appeared on league platforms during the parliamentary reform crisis of 1866–7. He attempted to achieve unity with the National Reform Union, which sought the more limited aim of household suffrage. With J. S. Mill he was a parliamentary spokesman for the Jamaica Committee, formed in response to Governor Eyre's brutal suppression of riots in Jamaica in 1865.

After 1868 Taylor championed all the leading radical causes: women's suffrage, opposition to the Contagious Diseases Acts, payments for MPs, disestablishment of the church, land tenure reform, abolition of the game laws, the abolition of flogging in the army and navy, opening of museums on Sundays, opposition to compulsory vaccination, and press freedom. Critics saw his many causes as 'the very embodiment of faddism' (*Leicester Daily Post*). He attracted notoriety in 1871 by his identification with the republican cause; he supported Charles Dilke's motion opposing the dowry and annuity to Princess Louise. He was proprietor of the radical newspaper *The Examiner*, edited by William Minto, from 1873 to 1878.

In 1873 ill health forced Taylor to retire from London to Brighton, where he founded clubs for working men, notably the Nineteenth Century Club, a forum for advanced radical and secularist views. He stood down from parliament in June 1884. During his twenty-two years as MP for Leicester he had 'refused, though a wealthy and generous man, to subscribe to a single public object in Leicester, that it might be perfectly clear he was not buying his seat in the Commons' (*The Times*, 21 Dec 1891). In retirement he cut himself off from other radicals in 1886 by refusing to support Irish home rule. In 1875 he published an opulently bound history of the Taylor family. Taylor died at his home, 18 Eaton Place, Brighton, on 20 December 1891 and was buried at the extramural cemetery in Brighton on the 23rd. Clementia Taylor, his widow, survived him; there were no children. His funeral service was conducted by Dr Stanton Coit of South Place, thus maintaining a long family connection with that Unitarian congregation.

ALAN RUSTON

Sources N. J. Gossman, 'Taylor, Peter Alfred', BDMBR, vol. 2 · *The Times* (21 Dec 1891) · *The Times* (24 Dec 1891) · *Leicester Daily Mercury* (21 Dec 1891) · *Leicester Daily Post* (22 Dec 1891) · *Leicester Chronicle* (26 Dec 1891) · *Christian Life* (26 Dec 1891) · *Brighton Herald* (26 Dec 1891) · *Brighton Herald* (18 April 1908) [obit. of Clementia Taylor] · *The Times* (13 April 1908) [obit. of Clementia Taylor] · P. A. Taylor, ed., *Some account of the Taylor family, originally Taylard* (privately printed, London, 1875) · A. Ruston, 'Clementia Taylor', *Transactions of the Unitarian Historical Society*, 20/1 (1991–4), 62–8 · F. M. Gladstone, ed., *Aubrey House, Kensington, 1698–1920* (1922) · *Mazzini's letters to an English family*, ed. E. F. Richards, 1, 3 (1920–22) · *Englishwoman's Review*, 23 (1892), 65–6 · *Englishwoman's Review*, 39 (1908), 145–58 [obit. of Clementia Taylor] · d. cert.

Archives BL, family collections, Add. MSS 37682–37686, Add. Ch. 54653–54700 | Bishopsgate Institute, London, Howell collection · Co-operative Union, Holyoake House, Manchester, letters to George Holyoake · Durham RO, Cowen collection

Likenesses Bellin, mixed engraving, pubd 1850 (after *Council of the Anti-Corn Law League* by J. R. Herbert), BM, NPG · Dalziel, woodcut, BM · photograph, repro. in Taylor, ed., *Some account of the Taylor family*, frontispiece · photographs, repro. in Gladstone, ed., *Aubrey House* · portrait, repro. in *Illustrated News of the World*, 9 (1862), 137 · portrait, repro. in *Black and White* (2 Jan 1892)

Wealth at death £4840 12s. 6d.: probate, 29 Feb 1892, CGPLA Eng. & Wales

Taylor, Peter Murray, Lord Taylor of Gosforth (1930–1997), judge, was born on 1 May 1930 at 242 Westgate Road, Newcastle upon Tyne, the son of Herman Louis Taylor, a doctor, and his wife, Raie Helena, *née* Shockett. His father had been born in Leeds in 1891: the family name had originally been Teiger or Teicher, reflecting either Lithuanian or German origins. His mother was born in Marimpol, Lithuania, in 1890 into a distinguished rabbinical family called Palterovitch (from whom the actress Gwyneth Paltrow is also descended). She, her parents, and grandfather arrived in Leeds in 1895. His parents met either at school or Hebrew school, or both. As a wartime evacuee, Peter Taylor lived between 1942 and 1944 in Penrith in Cumberland in a house with no bathroom and no electricity, an experience which he cited, in later years, as vindicating his claim to be a judge in the mainstream of the nation's life.

Early career Taylor was educated at the Royal Grammar School, Newcastle upon Tyne and in 1951 won an exhibition to Pembroke College, Cambridge, where he obtained an upper second in both parts of the law tripos, graduating in 1953. In 1954 he was called to the bar by the Inner Temple; he joined the Westgate Road Newcastle chambers of Norman Harper as pupil of John Harvey Robson and practised on the north-eastern circuit. On 8 August 1956 he married Irene Shirley Harris (1932/3–1995), daughter of Lionel Montague Harris, a company director; they had three daughters and a son.

Taylor took silk at the early age of thirty-six in 1967, and then joined the chambers founded by George Waller, a fellow Geordie, at 11 King's Bench Walk. He was leader of his circuit from 1975 until 1980. Taylor soon found that one of the advantages that a traditional circuiteer enjoys over a metropolitan specialist is exposure to a wide range of practice. In this he had more in common with his predecessor as 'Chief', Lord Lane, than with his successor, Lord Bingham of Cornhill. From his first days at the bar Peter Taylor encountered common-law litigation in its various manifestations. He was not, however, a jack of all trades, but rather a master of all, and a grand master of crime.

Two of his most celebrated cases were the prosecutions in 1974 of the architect John Poulson and civil servant George Pottinger (as second silk to John Cobb QC) at the Leeds crown court for corruption, and in 1979 of the former leader of the Liberal Party Jeremy Thorpe at the Old Bailey for conspiracy to murder. But he was no less potent a counsel for the defence: Mr Justice Melford Stevenson, a trial judge of unrivalled experience in the post-war era, considered him for that reason a threat to the administration of justice.

As an advocate Taylor was fluent, formidable, and concise. (As lord chief justice he later sought to ensure that long-winded barristers did not profit at the expense of the legal aid fund from their excessive oratory.) His opening in the Thorpe trial, all the more powerful for its absence of rhetorical flourish, is rightly quoted in textbooks. His quip about Pottinger, 'Some are born with great coats, some acquire great coats: and others have great coats thrust upon them' (*Daily Telegraph*, 30 April 1997), also deserves a place in the anthologies. It showed another facet of his forensic skills, his fondness for adapting literary quotations.

Taylor acquired wide experience as a recorder, initially in Huddersfield from 1969 to 1970 and then in Teesside from 1970 to 1971. He became deputy chairman of the Northumberland quarter sessions in the same year, and in the wake of the post-Beeching abolition of the assizes, and the Courts Act of 1971, a recorder of the crown court. In 1979–80 he served for a year as chairman of the bar council; he was knighted in 1980. It was then—as it is no longer—the convention that, save exceptionally, the holder of such a post is offered a High Court judgeship, and he was duly appointed to the Queen's Bench Division in 1981. From 1984 until 1988 he was a presiding judge on the north-east circuit, and in 1988 was promoted to the Court of Appeal.

In 1989 Taylor chaired an inquiry into the Hillsborough football disaster in which ninety-five football supporters died after being crushed against fencing in an FA Cup semi-final between Liverpool and Nottingham Forest. The response to his report (published in 1990 and known as the Hillsborough report) changed the face of British football. A regular, while a schoolboy, on the terraces at Newcastle United, he can justly be described as the 'onlie begetter' of the all-seater stadium.

Lord chief justice The justified enhancement of Taylor's image as a judge with a keen sense of the possible and a broad humanity made him, despite his brief service in the Court of Appeal, one of the favourites among the *cognoscenti* to succeed Lord Lane as lord chief justice, and, which is not always the case with favourites, he duly did so in 1992. At the same time he was created a life peer, becoming Lord Taylor of Gosforth.

Taylor's post-war predecessors in his office, lords Goddard, Parker, Widgery, and Lane, had been in the eyes of the public at large and the majority of the profession, remote, even awesome figures. Although he lacked nothing in terms of authority or character in comparison with that quartet, approachability was the defining factor of Lord Taylor's judicial style. He marked his appointment as lord chief justice by holding a press conference; such a conference, without precedent, became an annual event. Taylor wished to abolish wigs in court and was both surprised and disappointed to be defeated by the combined forces of traditionalists, including circuit judges and (as was alleged) criminals; he was more successful in allowing women barristers to wear trousers in court. He was the first judge to appear on BBC television's *Question Time* and to be the castaway on BBC Radio 4's *Desert Island Discs*,

where his choice of music was as eclectic as his barrister's practice—it included opera, Sidney Bechet, and string quintets. In 1992 he delivered the Dimbleby Lecture for the BBC entitled 'The judiciary in the nineties'—another judicial first.

As lord chief justice Taylor concentrated on criminal appeals. There was a considerable backlog to break and he needed to strengthen the staff of his office, so when the deputy chief justice Tasker Watkins retired, although he did not reconfer the unique title on anyone else, he put equivalent deputies in post. More compellingly, there was a need to restore public confidence in the criminal justice system after a series of miscarriages of justice, mainly arising out of IRA terrorist atrocities on the mainland. Taylor had himself been part of the prosecuting team in the trial of Judith Ward for murder of the passengers who died in 1974 when the IRA left a bomb in a coach travelling on the M62 motorway. He also prosecuted Stefan Kiszko for the murder of an eleven-year-old girl (though evidence later emerged that would have cleared Kiszko). Though he himself was blameless in each instance, the belated revelation of the flaws in the evidence in each sharpened still further Taylor's awareness (born of experience at bar and on bench) that criticism of the trial process could not always be dismissed as the imaginings of malcontents.

In Lord Lane's time the tradition of the lord chief justice as presider over the divisional court in crown office—that is, public law work—had atrophied. Lord Taylor did not revive it, although both as a puisne and as an appellate judge he had been involved in judicial review matters—the fastest developing area of English law of the time. Notably, in one case he took a robust attitude to executive use of telephone tapping: 'I do not accept', he stated, 'that the court should never inquire into a complaint against a Minister if he says his policy is to maintain silence in the interests of national security' (*R. v. Secretary of State for the Home Department ex parte Ruddock*, 1987). In another, where the subject matter was a complaint of racial discrimination in the army, he held that since the army board of the defence council was dealing with fundamental statutory rights, it should achieve a high standard of fairness. But it was left to his successors to divide their judicial time more evenly between criminal appeal, civil appeal, and public law hearings.

In an interview in *The Independent* shortly after his appointment Lord Taylor listed various desirable qualities which should lead to 'good judgment and a safe pair of hands' (*The Independent*, 30 April 1997); he had both in full measure. But while he was for those reasons a great judge he delivered few great judgments (partly because of the very speed of his ascent to the pinnacle of legal office and his choice of priorities once he attained it). He was a sound lawyer without being a profound scholar. Compared again to his successors Taylor wrote little, and his speeches were more significant for their authorship than for their content. None the less, he fashioned defences of provocation and diminished responsibility for battered wives. He extended the concept of murder so as to provide protection to the unborn child while in the mother's womb. On one of only three occasions that he sat as a member of the appellate committee in the House of Lords, he gave a resounding speech on the importance of legal professional privilege, which he described as being 'a fundamental condition on which the administration of justice as a whole depends' (*R.* v. *Derby Magistrates Court ex parte B*, 1996).

Taylor was in favour of stiff sentences for drivers who killed while under the influence of alcohol, but wished for an end to mandatory life sentences for murder. He called for disclosure of defence evidence before the trial. A supporter of the rights of criminal suspects to elect for trial by jury, he nevertheless upheld the rights of judges to direct juries as to the significance of the accused's silence. He favoured a change in the law to allow defendants in rape cases to remain anonymous unless convicted. Along with many other leading judges of his era, Taylor proposed the incorporation into domestic laws of the European Convention of Human Rights (which happened, three years after his death, with the coming into force of the Human Rights Act of 1998). His views on crime and punishment were the product of humane pragmatism not of prescriptive philosophy, but they were never concealed. 'There is a need', he once said, 'for the judiciary to be more open with the media and the public by explaining what they do and how they do it' (private information).

Where Lord Taylor deviated from normal judicial habit was in his vocal expression of opinion, even on matters of political controversy. He believed that judges should not only murmur, but speak out on issues within their sphere of experience and knowledge. In an address to Scottish solicitors at Gleneagles in spring 1993, he attacked two provisions of the Criminal Justice Act of 1991 (restricting the power of a judge to imprison offenders) which, he said 'defied common sense' (*The Times*, 30 April 1997). By May 1996 government policy had changed and so had the direction of his assault. In his final speech in the House of Lords before retirement (distributed in advance in case—as did not happen—he lacked the strength to deliver it in the chamber), Taylor savaged the proposal of Michael Howard, then home secretary, for minimum sentences for persistent burglars and drug dealers, and automatic life sentences on second convictions of certain violent and sex offences. 'Never in the history of our criminal law', he said, 'have such far-reaching proposals been put forward on the strength of such flimsy evidence. Quite simply minimum sentences must involve a denial of justice' (*The Times*, 30 April 1997).

At various junctures Lord Taylor challenged too the Conservative government's asylum legislation and its proposals to reduce legal aid. A childhood friend who met him shortly before he died quoted him as saying: 'Party politics never interested me. Perhaps that reflects my general failure to be excited about causes, ideologies or theories' (private information); none the less he ruffled political feathers. A distinguished legal commentator described the relationship of judiciary and executive in his time as 'a Trial of Strength'. If so, Lord Taylor was a prominent gladiator in the arena. Constitutional purists

indeed wondered whether his combative approach was properly faithful to the doctrine of separation of powers. For him, however, the issues at stake were ones of principle; on such issues he declined to hold his peace.

In the context of practice, procedure, and the profession, by contrast, Lord Taylor was something of a traditionalist. He was opposed both to trial by television and to trial on television. He was a supporter of the circuit system and of the division of the legal profession into barristers and solicitors. Proud to have been a barrister, he would not easily concede that true forensic virtue could ever reside in the other branch of the profession. He strongly opposed the grant of rights of audience in the higher courts to solicitors or crown prosecutors, and warned against any infusion of political correctness into the system of judicial appointments. He argued for more judges to diminish the law's delays, and won the argument.

Character and assessment   Peter Taylor was a man of many talents. A fine prop forward, he played rugby for Northumberland. He narrowly missed a blue in the same sport at Cambridge but did play many times for the university and was a member of the LX club. In addition he was a sufficiently gifted musician to contemplate a career as a concert pianist. Favouring Schubert, Liszt, and Chopin, he performed solely at charity events so that, as he put it, 'if something goes wrong nobody can demand their money back' (*The Times*, 30 April 1997).

Taylor's religion was not demonstrative: he described himself once as 'out on a long leash from Judaism'. In another of his phrases, he was not a Jewish chief justice but a chief justice who happened to be Jewish. Taylor was indeed at least as much a Geordie as a Jew; but he was not wholly detached from his origins. He led delegations of Jewish lawyers on visits to Israel, and he and his wife were commemorated by a music therapy project in that country. Consistently with mainstream Anglo-Jewish thinking, he spoke out strongly against race discrimination, but was not in favour of affirmative action. He had certainly needed none himself.

Taylor had the robust build of a sportsman; his aquiline profile suggested a Roman emperor. The bronze head in the foyer of the Royal Court of Justice does not wholly capture his forceful personality. He is better portrayed by Andrew Festing in portraits at the Royal Grammar School, Newcastle upon Tyne, and the Inner Temple, attired in full chief-justice fig. He was also depicted posthumously in a group portrait by Julia Mendoza (hung in the Inner Temple Hall), painted at a time when the five other senior judicial offices were all held by members of his inn. Off the bench Taylor was a famously dapper dresser, distinguished in the summer months by his combination of Panama hat and Garrick tie. While conscious of the dignity of his office, he was the least stuffy of men, clubbable and convivial. Parties he enjoyed; people he understood. He had boundless energy, wit, and charm. Lady Taylor was integral to his public achievement, ensuring that the judge did not become detached from the man. Irene died of cancer in 1995, to his palpable distress. It was a bitter irony that so soon after he himself fell victim to the same malady.

Taylor's last year was marked by an inevitable erosion of his powers, which saddened his many friends, but he displayed an extraordinary stoicism in the face of this fate, calmly and sequentially surrendering the functions of his office. In his last case in April 1996 Taylor dismissed Rosemary West's application for leave to appeal against her murder convictions. Thereafter and until the appointment of his successor he undertook only administrative duties.

In 1997 Lord Taylor was due, in recognition of his achievements, to have conferred on him, unusually, honorary degrees by both the universities of Oxford and of Cambridge. However, his death occurred before either ceremony could take place. He died of a brain tumour on 28 April 1997, a few days before his sixty-seventh birthday, at his home, Wancom Edge, Puttenham Heath Road, Puttenham, Surrey. Described by a long-standing friend as 'totally in touch with his time' (private information), he changed fundamentally the public perception of the judiciary. One obituary said, epigrammatically, 'Good judges die young' (G. Robertson, *Guardian*, 30 April 1997). It is not always so, but in his case it surely was.

MICHAEL BELOFF

Sources *The Times* (30 April 1997) · *The Independent* (30 April 1997) · *Daily Telegraph* (30 April 1997) · *The Guardian* (30 April 1997) · private information (2004) · J. Rozenberg, *Trial of strength: the battle between ministers and judges over the law* (1997) · *The historical register of the University of Cambridge: supplement, 1951–55* (1956) · *Inner Temple Yearbook* (1997–8) · *Pembroke Annual Gazette* (1997) · b. cert. · m. cert. · d. cert. · *Inner Temple Yearbook* (1997–8) · *Annual Gazette* [Pembroke College] (1997)
Likenesses N. Sinclair, bromide print, 1993, NPG · A. Festing, oils, Royal Grammar School, Newcastle upon Tyne · A. Festing, oils, Inner Temple, London · J. Mendoza, group portrait, Inner Temple, London
Wealth at death £662,320: probate, 5 Aug 1997, *CGPLA Eng. & Wales*

Taylor, Philip (1786–1870), civil engineer, was the fourth son of John *Taylor (1750–1826), hymn writer of Norwich, and his wife, Susanna *Taylor (1755–1823) [*see under* Taylor, John (1750–1826)], essayist and daughter of John Cook of Norwich. He was the brother of Richard *Taylor (1781–1858), Edward *Taylor (1784–1863), and the better-known John *Taylor (1779–1863), a mining engineer. Philip was educated at Dr Houghton's school in Norwich, and at fifteen was sent to live with his brother John and to study surgery under Dr Harness, a relative of John's wife, at Tavistock. However, having a horror of witnessing or causing pain, he returned to Norwich, where he joined a Mr Fitch in business as a chemist and druggist, and set up a factory for making wooden pillboxes by machine. In 1812 he and his brother John started a chemical works at Stratford, east London.

In 1813 Taylor married Sarah, daughter of Robert Fitch, surgeon, of Ipswich. They settled at Bromley by Bow, adjoining Stratford, where the brothers' visitors included many of the famous engineers and chemists of the day, both English and French. In 1816 and 1818 Taylor patented the application of high-pressure steam to evaporation, a process which was taken up in Whitbread's brewery and by various sugar refiners. He then devised a method of making gas from oil (that is, naphtha) and was able to light public and private buildings by naphtha, which was at first cheaper and more efficient than coal gas. Covent Garden Theatre, Mile End Road, the Imperial Library at St Petersburg, and the city of Bristol were lighted by his process; but when the gas companies lowered their prices, Taylor was driven out of business.

Between 1816 and 1825 Taylor's inventive nature led him to apply for several engineering patents, and in 1822 he made his first visit to Paris. He assisted Marc Isambard Brunel in 1821 in his debt crisis, and he was a director of the Thames Tunnel Company. In 1824 he moved his family to south Wales when he became connected with the British Iron Company and took out a patent for making iron. Involved in the company's ruin, and with his chemical works rendered unprofitable by the bad management of his partners, he went in 1828 to Paris, founded engineering works, and patented the hot-blast process in the manufacture of iron, which two other engineers simultaneously patented in London. The validity of the French patent was disputed, and was not established until 1839, just before its expiration. In 1834 Taylor submitted to King Louis-Philippe a scheme for supplying Paris with water by a tunnel from the Marne to a hill at Ivry, just as he had previously proposed for London a 9 mile tunnel to Hampstead Hill; but the expense was too great and nothing came of it.

In 1834, moving south for the benefit of his wife's health, Taylor erected machinery for a flour mill at Marseilles and became a partner in the business, which, however, under protectionist pressure, was soon deprived of the privilege of grinding in bond. Taylor thereupon, with his sons Philip Meadows and Robert, founded in 1836 engineering works at Marseilles, and in 1845 he bought a shipbuilding yard at La Seyne, near Toulon, which became a large and flourishing concern employing 2000 men. Papa Taylor, as he was called, was very popular with his workmen. From 1847 to 1852 he resided at San Pier d'Arena, near Genoa, where the Sardinian government had invited him to establish engineering works; but the political troubles induced him to return to Marseilles. The sudden loss of four of his eight children having affected his health, he disposed of his business in 1855 to the Compagnie des Forges et Chantiers de la Méditerranée.

Taylor prided himself on having taken part in the first steamboat trip at sea, on having seen the start of the first steam engine, and on having witnessed Sir Charles Wheatstone's first electric telegraph experiments, at Somerset House. He was made a knight of the French Légion d'honneur in 1846 and was awarded the Sardinian order of St Maurice and St Lazarus. He died at his home at St Marguerite, near Marseilles, on 1 July 1870.

J. G. ALGER, *rev.* ANITA MCCONNELL

Sources P. M. Taylor, *A memoir of the family of Taylor of Norwich* (privately printed, London, 1886)

Taylor, Philip Meadows (1808–1876), army officer and official in the Hyderabad service and novelist, was born in Liverpool on 25 September 1808. His father, Philip Meadows Taylor, was a merchant in Liverpool, and was descended from John Taylor (1694–1761) of Norwich; his mother was Jane Honoria Alicia, daughter of Bertram Mitford of Mitford Castle, Northumberland. At the age of fifteen, Taylor was sent out to India to enter the house of Mr Baxter, a Bombay merchant, with the promise of being made a partner when he should come of age. On arriving, however, he found that the condition of Baxter's affairs had been much misrepresented, and took up the offer of a commission in the service of the nizam of Hyderabad which was procured for him in November 1824 by Mr Newnham, chief secretary to the Bombay government, a relative of his mother's. After a short period of military service he obtained civil employment and taught himself surveying, engineering, Indian and English law, botany, and geology. Before long, however, he was obliged to return to the army, and was promoted adjutant in the nizam's service in 1830. At about this time he appears to have married. His autobiography inaccurately gave 1840 as the date of his marriage, but is otherwise reticent of details.

Independently of Colonel William Henry Sleeman, Taylor became interested in the detection and suppression of thuggee, and turned his inquiries to account in his first novel, *The Confessions of a Thug*, which was published in 1839 on his return to England on furlough and proved a great success. After his return to India he acted as a correspondent for *The Times* (1840–43). In 1841 he was commissioned by the resident of Hyderabad to pacify the rebellious state of Shorapur, which he continued to administer during the minority of the raja, until 1853. Taylor was then transferred to Berar, recently ceded by the nizam, where he organized surveying operations and road building. On the outbreak of the Indian mutiny in 1857 Taylor was dispatched to the district of Buldana in north Berar, which he kept in order until British forces reappeared. He was also able to supply General Whitlock's Madras division with the means of transport which enabled it to capture the Karwi treasure, subsequently the object of much litigation, and out of which Taylor himself never received a rupee. In the same year (1858) he was appointed commissioner of his old district of Shorapur, which his former pupil the raja had forfeited by rising against the British government.

In 1860 Taylor's health failed, and he returned to England, where he wrote five more Indian novels. He also wrote an autobiography, published in 1877, after his death, the letterpress for several illustrated works on India, and a students' manual of Indian history. He was made a companion in the Order of the Star of India in 1869. In 1875 his sight failed, and on the advice of physicians he decided to spend the winter in India, where, however, he was further debilitated by an attack of jungle

Philip Meadows Taylor (1808–1876), by Charles Grey, 1840

fever. He died at Menton, France, on his way home, on 13 May 1876.

Meadows Taylor's modest background and work in the service of an Indian prince guaranteed that he would not leave a large mark on the annals of British Indian history. However, as a man of letters, he occupied a unique position among Anglo-Indian writers. His *Confessions of a Thug* is a classic adventure novel, which inspired the young of several imperial generations and was much imitated by other colonial fiction writers for over a century.

RICHARD GARNETT, *rev.* DAVID WASHBROOK

Sources M. Taylor, *The story of my life*, ed. A. M. Taylor, 2 vols. (1877) · M. Taylor, *Confessions of a thug*, 3 vols. (1839) · Burke, *Peerage*
Archives BL, agreements, accounts, and corresp. with Richard Bentley, Add. MSS 46613, 46650–46551 · BL, Layard MSS · NL Scot., corresp. with Blackwoods · NL Scot., letters to J. S. S. Stuart
Likenesses C. Grey, pen sketch, 1840, NG Ire. [*see illus.*] · J. Kirkwood, etching (after C. Grey), BM, NPG; repro. in *Dublin University Magazine*, 18 (1841) · W. Taylor, lithograph (after his portrait), NG Ire.

Taylor, Polycarpus (*d.* **1780**), naval officer, whose parentage and upbringing are unknown, was promoted second lieutenant in the *Augusta* with Sir Chaloner Ogle on 21 June 1739. He appears to have gone out with Ogle to the West Indies, and in June 1741 was moved by Edward Vernon in to the *Boyne*, his own flagship. On 2 May 1743 he was promoted captain of the frigate *Fowey* on the Jamaica station and he continued in her until 1747 when he was moved by Rear-Admiral Charles Knowles to the *Elizabeth* (64 guns). Later, following the abortive attempt on Santiago de Cuba, he moved to Knowles's flagship, the *Cornwall*.

As flag captain Taylor took part in the engagement off Havana on 1 October 1748 and his conduct was clearly well regarded by his commanding officer. Writing to Lord Anson on 25 January 1749, Knowles included Taylor among several seamen who 'are good' (BL, Add. MS 15956, fol. 169). He was then appointed commander of the *Ripon* and senior officer on the station at Knowles's return to England. He was recalled soon afterwards, arriving at Spithead early in January 1750. In 1756 he was appointed to the *Marlborough* but then moved (7 June) to the *Culloden* with orders to take Sir Edward Hawke and join her new ship at Gibraltar.

Taylor appears to have brought the *Culloden* to England in 1757 and to have had no further active service. He is wrongly credited with the command of the *Ramillies* in 1758—in fact held by Wittewronge Taylor, who also served on the *Cornwall* with Knowles on the Jamaica station. Taylor was superannuated with the rank of rear-admiral five years after his retirement, and passed the rest of his life in retirement at his home in Durham. Details of his family life are scant, though a son, also Polycarpus, was baptized at Norton, Durham, on 20 July 1753. The elder Taylor died at Durham in 1780.

J. K. LAUGHTON, *rev.* PHILIP CARTER

Sources J. Charnock, ed., *Biographia navalis*, 5 (1797), 261 • BL, Add MS 15956, fol. 169 • IGI

Taylor, (Cara) Prunella Clough- [*known as* Prunella Clough] (**1919–1999**), artist, was born on 14 November 1919 at 39 Parkside, Knightsbridge, London, the only child of Edward Lorne Frederick (Eric) Clough-Taylor, a Board of Trade official and poet, and his wife, Thora Grace Zelma, *née* Gray (formerly Smith). The Grays traced their roots back to the fifteenth century, Thora Gray and her sister Eileen Moray Gray [*see* Gray, (Kathleen) Eileen Moray], later well known as a designer, growing up among the Anglo-Irish landed gentry at Brownswood, co. Wexford. Their father, James Maclaren Gray (formerly Smith), was an amateur painter who travelled in Switzerland and Italy; he changed his name from Smith to Gray following his wife's inheritance in 1893. The Clough-Taylors came from Yorkshire, and there were Scottish elements to match the Irish in Clough's ancestry.

Little is known of Clough's education. In later years she was famously reticent and became skilful at circumventing questions about all aspects of her life. It seems most probable that she was initially privately educated and

(Cara) **Prunella Clough-Taylor (1919–1999)**, by Snowdon, *c.*1959

then sent briefly to various schools. Her father died when she was young and she was brought up by a mother preoccupied with spiritualism, who had little sympathy or understanding of her daughter's growing interest in art. Nevertheless, she managed to pursue her studies at Chelsea School of Art (*c.*1937–1939), where she was taught by Ceri Richards, Robert Medley, and Henry Moore. She spent a year with Moore in the sculpture studio, modelling from life in clay. She also took a course in commercial graphic design, studying the principles of layout and fabric printing. This early training was to stand her in good stead in later years. During the Second World War she worked for the office of war information (USA) in Grosvenor Square, drawing charts and maps, and later took various odd jobs in design and typography. She continued to study part-time after the war at Camberwell School of Arts and Crafts under Victor Pasmore, and held her first solo show at the Leger Galleries in 1947. This consisted mostly of beach and sea paintings, for Clough had been drawn into the neo-Romantic group, counting Graham Sutherland a mentor, and John Minton and Keith Vaughan as friends. (She was later to be Vaughan's executor.)

Clough herself dated the emergence of her mature style to 1949. The work of these years was figurative though austere in a semi-cubist manner, the palette grouped around browns, greys, and ochres. The fishermen and their boats and nets gave way to lorry drivers and scenes from the London docks. Clough's vision became increasingly urban as she was drawn to the unpeopled chaos of industrial wastelands. It was a logical development therefore that her art in the 1960s began a journey towards abstraction, a journey which touched upon all the developments of the day (for example, abstract expressionism, colour field, and hard-edge abstraction), while maintaining a thoughtful distance which guaranteed her independence and freedom of expression. Growing up with surrealism, she always retained an interest in the vegetal forms of Max Ernst, but her enthusiasms never rigidified, and she remained open and experimental to the end. She was intensely aware of what went on around her, as equally interested in an exhibition of the pop artist Claes Oldenberg, for instance, as in late Braque, and no doubt bringing something from both to bear upon her own work.

In the 1940s Clough began to experiment with printmaking and taught herself lithography from books. Prints were to become a crucially important aspect of her artistic activity. For a time she owned her own press, but she preferred working with different master printers, enjoying the process of collaboration. She was as innovative in printmaking as in paint, stretching techniques and focusing on the unexpected eloquence of detritus. She had a genius for capturing the trace of things, rather than simply describing their presence.

When out and about, perhaps on a foray around the backstreets of an out-of-season seaside resort, Clough tended to take photographs rather than make drawings. These might be of bundles of wire, reflections in shop windows, or rubbish in the gutter. They were source material in a sense, though back in the studio she rarely referred to them, preferring to rely on memory and imagination. Her art was informed by her fascination for the marginal and the generally overlooked, the slightly shabby and the commonplace. She avoided obvious subjects, but on the other hand nothing was too lowly for her, whether a packet of plastic toys or a carrier bag blown against a wall. Even such apparently unpromising material she was able to transform into art of rare beauty.

Clough was expert at the structuring of images, inventive in her fluid juggling and exact placement of details. (This attention to detail may have been because she was short-sighted and peered at things.) She gave access to a world of generally unregarded objects, vast or microscopic, the unseen components of daily life. She looked at the world, as it were, out of the corner of her eye, finding poetry in worn surfaces and silhouettes. For all its subtlety and allusiveness, her work was characterized by its boldness and clarity and its assuredness (although prolific, she destroyed the pictures not up to her high standards), as well as its light, witty touch. The light touch was literal as well: Clough applied her paint in thin membranes, printing a pattern or motif onto the picture's ground, using stencil, spray, chalk, or collage as and when the image demanded. Although she could use the brightest of hues on occasion, her colours tended to be muffled, moving towards the putty and buff of her early post-cubist work.

She was perhaps less interested in colour than in texture, and the range of texture she achieved in her paintings and prints has rarely been equalled.

Clough was intensely private. She was a woman of originality and integrity, with a gift for friendship. A succinct conversationalist, she wrote diaries, letters, and postcards. Her discretion was such, however, that in her last years she burnt most of her writing. She was an inspiring teacher, working part-time initially at Chelsea School of Art (1956–69) and then at Wimbledon School of Art (1966–97). She was a person of great loyalty, both to friends and family, and moved into her own home only after the death of her mother. Her aunt, Eileen Gray, had been a role model for her, and in the 1970s she went to Paris every weekend to look after the ailing woman. After Gray's death, Clough was appointed trustee of her estate. It was she who licensed the reproductions of Gray's furniture and who passed on all the annual royalties to art schools as bursaries and equipment grants. The first computers in the design departments of many art schools came from Clough's generosity—though no one would have known this, as her donations were strictly anonymous—while many impoverished fellow artists likewise benefited from her philanthropy. She was frugal in her own life, and insisted on keeping the prices of her prints and paintings relatively low, so that buying her work would not become solely the preserve of the wealthy. When she won the prestigious Jerwood prize for painting in 1999, although delighted by the honour, with characteristic generosity she gave away the prize money. Her unfailing modesty ensured that she remained little known to a wider public, though she did permit her work to be shown from time to time, notably at the Whitechapel Gallery (1960), the Serpentine Gallery (1976), Camden Arts Centre (1996), and Kettle's Yard, Cambridge (1999). She died at the Chelsea and Westminster Hospital, London, on 26 December 1999, of cancer of the liver, and was cremated at Putney Vale crematorium on 13 January 2000. She was unmarried.

ANDREW LAMBIRTH

Sources *Prunella Clough: the late paintings and selected early paintings* (2000) [exhibition catalogue, Annely Juda Fine Art, London, 1 Nov – 16 Dec 2000] · *Prunella Clough* (1999) [exhibition catalogue, Kettle's Yard Gallery, Cambridge, 7 Aug – 26 Sept 1999, and Graves Art Gallery, Sheffield, 4 Dec – 22 Jan 2000] · *Prunella Clough, David Carr: works, 1945–1964* (1997) [exhibition catalogue, Austin Desmond Fine Art, London] · J. Collins and others, *Prunella Clough* (1996) [exhibition catalogue, Camden Arts Centre, London, 17 May – 30 June 1996, and Oriel 31 Gallery, Newtown, Powys, 14 Sept – 30 Oct 1996] · *The Guardian* (28 Dec 1999) · *Daily Telegraph* (28 Dec 1999) · *The Times* (29 Dec 1999) · *The Independent* (29 Dec 1999) · *WWW* · personal knowledge (2004) · private information [Robin Banks] (2004) · b. cert. · d. cert.
Archives priv. coll.
Likenesses Snowdon, bromide print, c.1959, NPG [see illus.] · G. Hermes, bronze, 1962, repro. in *The Independent* · photograph, repro. in *The Times* · photograph, repro. in *The Guardian* · photograph, repro. in *Daily Telegraph*
Wealth at death £4,816,417: probate, 2000, *CGPLA Eng. & Wales*

Taylor, Rachel Annand [*née* Rachel Annand] (1876–1960), poet and literary scholar, was born on 3 April 1876 at 51 Queen Street, Aberdeen, the second of the five children of

John Wilson Annand, mason and socialist pioneer, and Clarinda Dinnie of the Deeside highlands. She was influenced by her father's passionate intellect and her mother's knowledge of highland mythology. She had a robust 'disregard for the more bourgeois virtues of prudence and respectability' (Grierson, 153) and her awareness of the effects of poverty mingled with pride in what could be achieved under its constraints is evident in one of her most often anthologized poems, 'The Princess of Scotland'.

Rachel Annand trained as a teacher at Aberdeen Training Centre (1894–7), where she was eligible to attend university classes. Although she did not graduate, she was one of the first women to take arts classes after the admission of women to the university, and in 1943 was awarded an honorary doctor of laws degree by Aberdeen University. She studied philosophy and English literature with Herbert J. C. Grierson, who remembered her as 'a young woman with a startling shock of red hair whom, when an essay came to be read, I placed alone in the first class' (Grierson, 152). She continued to excel in her studies and some early poetry was published in the *British Weekly*. Rachel Annand taught at the High School for Girls in Aberdeen before marrying Alexander Cameron Taylor (1875–1943), an Aberdeen graduate, on 15 July 1901. Alexander Taylor was a classics teacher in Dundee, where the couple settled at 9 Balgon Avenue.

Taylor's first volume of poetry, *Poems*, which clearly demonstrates her links with aestheticism, was published in 1904. Sir Patrick Geddes, with whom Taylor became acquainted in Dundee, raised a subscription to bring out her second collection, *Rose and Vine* (1909). She wrote two further volumes, *The Hours of Fiammetta* (1910), a sonnet sequence, and *The End of Fiammetta* (1923). Fiammetta, the muse of Boccaccio, is used as a symbol of the feminine 'behind all the processes of art' (*The Hours of Fiammetta*, preface).

When her husband's mental health collapsed and he was institutionalized, Taylor embarked on a precarious writing career in London, describing the trauma of the previous period to Geddes as, 'the dim nightmare called Dundee' (NL Scot., MS 10572, fol. 25). Her niece, the Glasgow artist Louise Annand, believes Taylor supported herself by reviewing. She stayed at 17 Jenner House, Hunter's Street, Bloomsbury, within easy reach of the British Museum reading room, where she conducted research into medieval and Renaissance literature. At the request of Gilbert Murray, Taylor produced *Aspects of the Italian Renaissance* (1923) which, together with *Leonardo the Florentine* (1927), contained 'a vividly imaginative interpretation and recreation of the picturesque past' bringing the aims of Pater, Symonds, and Wilde to their apotheosis (Aldington, 6). Taylor's scholarly work, though largely disregarded by subsequent commentators, also contains evidence of attitudes towards contemporary cultural debates. Her chapter 'Women of the Renaissance' in *Aspects* is an important early twentieth-century reflection on the significance of female gender. This theme is

revisited in the preface to *Hours*, where she describes herself as 'equally inimical ... to the opposing camps of hausfrau and suffragist' (*Hours*, 5–6); and in *The End of Fiammetta*, where Taylor writes regretfully about not having had children because of her devotion to writing (*End*, 100–01).

Taylor's poetic style was criticized by C. M. Grieve (Hugh MacDiarmid) because its aesthetic embellishment and non-Scottish focus was, by his modernist analysis, merely effete, 'It is mostly very preciose, very far-fetched, very mannered, very unreal' (MacDiarmid, 326). In 1931 Taylor published a monograph, *Dunbar: the Poet and his Period* (1931) on the medieval poet, her contribution to the renewed interest in Scottish literature encapsulated in MacDiarmid's phrase 'Not Burns, Dunbar!'

Louise Annand remembers her aunt as a somewhat 'formidable' woman whose 'dress could only be described as "Celtic"!' (Forrest, 28). Towards the end of 1959 Taylor sustained a fall in her home. She died of non-alcoholic cirrhosis of the liver and heart failure on 15 August 1960 at the Elizabeth Garrett Hospital, St Pancras, London, and was cremated at Golders Green crematorium on 18 August.

B. DICKSON

Sources 'Descriptive list of poems by Rachel Annand Taylor (1876–1960) and related papers, 1899–1908', 1970, U. Aberdeen, 2742/1–6, introduction, 1–2 · H. J. C. Grierson, 'Rachel Annand Taylor', *Aberdeen University Review*, 30 (1942–4), 152–6 · V. Forrest, 'Opening doors to the ladies of letters', *Leopard* (Feb 1989), 28–9 · *The Scotsman* (10 Dec 1960) · *Press and Journal* (18 Aug 1960) · NL Scot., Acc. 10572, fols. 1–39, 106–7, 109–21 · *WW* · *Roll of graduates 1860–1900*, ed. W. Johnston, Aberdeen University Studies, 18 (1906), 541 · R. Aldington, ed., *The religion of beauty: selections from the aesthetes* (1950) · H. MacDiarmid, *Contemporary Scottish studies*, ed. A. Riach (1995)
Archives NL Scot., papers, incl. some literary MSS · U. Aberdeen L., special libraries and archives, literary MSS and related papers | Bodl. Oxf., letters to Gilbert Murray · NL Scot., letters to Patrick Geddes · NL Scot., papers and letters to Sir Herbert Grierson
Likenesses photograph, repro. in *The Scotsman*

Taylor, Reynell George (1822–1886), army officer, was the youngest son of Thomas William Taylor of Ogwell, Devon, who served with the 10th hussars at Waterloo. Taylor was born at Brighton on 25 January 1822. From Sandhurst, where his father was lieutenant-general, he was gazetted cornet in the Indian cavalry on 26 February 1840. He first saw service with the 11th light cavalry (Bengal) in the Gwalior War of 1843, and at the close of the war was appointed to the bodyguard. In the First Anglo-Sikh War he was severely wounded in the cavalry charge at Mudki on 18 December 1845, and on his recovery was appointed assistant to the agent at Ajmer. Thence, in 1847, he was sent to Lahore, and became one of that famous group of men who worked under Henry Lawrence, and subsequently John Lawrence, in the Punjab. The same year, and when only twenty-five years of age, he was left, at a critical period, *hakim-i-wukt* (ruler) of Peshawar, in charge of 10,000 Sikh troops and the whole district. His firmness and his justice in criminal cases earned him the love of the people, ensured discipline, and gained the praise of his superiors. When it was decided to occupy the province of Bannu, Taylor organized the column from Peshawar, and led 4000 men in safety through the Kohat Pass (November and December 1847). The outbreak of the Second Anglo-Sikh War found Taylor in charge of Bannu. On hearing of the murders of Patrick Alexander Vans Agnew and W. A. Anderson at Multan on 20 April 1848, he at once dispatched all his most trustworthy troops to the assistance of Sir Herbert Benjamin Edwardes, and remained alone at his post. In July he was ordered to proceed to Multan, which was besieged, and thence he set out as a volunteer to rescue the English captives at Peshawar. His efforts being frustrated by treachery, he endeavoured to help Herbert, who was besieged at Attock. With this end in view, he gathered an irregular force of 1021 foot, 650 horse, and 3 doubtful guns, and laid siege to the fort of Lakki, the key to the Derajat, on 11 December 1848. Though far removed from all possibility of support, and unaided by a single fellow-countryman, he captured the fort on 11 January 1849. For his services he was promoted captain on 15 December 1851, and major the next day. On 11 December 1854 he married Ann, daughter of Arthur Holdsworth of Widdicombe, Devon. They had a large family and she survived him.

In 1855, after his prolonged visit to England, Taylor was appointed commandant of the corps of guides. During the Indian mutiny he was in charge of the Kangra district, and in 1859 he was appointed commissioner of the Derajat. He was promoted lieutenant-colonel on 21 December 1859 and in 1860 he took part, as chief political officer, in the Waziri expedition. Before retiring from the Derajat, in order to become commissioner of Peshawar in the spring of 1862, he induced the Church Missionary Society to establish a station in the district at considerable cost to himself. In 1863 he served throughout the Ambela war, was gazetted colonel on 3 April 1863, and CE the following month; but it was not until June 1866 that he was made CSI. After a short visit to England in 1865 he returned for the last time to India, to become commissioner of the Ambala division, and in 1870 of the Amritsar division. He retired in 1877 as major-general, becoming lieutenant-general that year, and general on 15 December 1880. He died at his home, Malston House, Newton Abbot, Devon, on 28 February 1886, and was buried at East Ogwell church, Devon, on 5 March. His bravery in the field had won him the title of 'the Bayard of the Punjab'; the Indians called him always their *ferishta* (good angel), and his charity had made him a poor man.

E. G. Parry, rev. M. G. M. Jones

Sources E. G. Parry, *Reynell Taylor, CB, CSI* (1888) · *East-India Register* · Boase, *Mod. Eng. biog.* · *CGPLA Eng. & Wales* (1886)
Archives BL OIOC, corresp. with Henry Lawrence, MS Eur. F 85 · BL OIOC, letters to General Pearse, MS Eur. E 205 · NAM, department of archives, letters to David Wilkie
Likenesses Annan & Swan, photograph, repro. in Parry, *Reynell Taylor*
Wealth at death £3214 9s. 3d.: probate, 25 June 1886, *CGPLA Eng. & Wales*

Taylor, Richard (1781–1858), printer and naturalist, was born at Norwich, Norfolk, on 18 May 1781, the second son of John *Taylor (1750–1826), wool factor, and his wife,

Susannah *Taylor, *née* Cook (1755–1823) [*see under* Taylor, John], and the great-grandson of the Presbyterian divine John *Taylor (1694–1761). He was educated at a Norwich dissenting day school run by the Revd John Houghton, where he acquired a good knowledge of the classics and the stimulus to acquire proficiency in French, Italian, Flemish, Old English, and their literatures. He remained a practising Unitarian throughout his life. In March 1797, on the recommendation of the botanist Sir James Edward Smith, he was apprenticed to the Unitarian printer Jonas Davis, in Chancery Lane, London. It was through the happy accident that Davis printed the Linnean Society's *Transactions* and, from 1798, the independent *Philosophical Magazine*, that Taylor became a printer and publisher of scientific books and periodicals.

In 1800 Davis abandoned printing, selling the business to John Taylor and Richard Wilks on the understanding that Richard Taylor would become a partner on reaching his majority. The partnership was dissolved in 1803 after violent quarrelling between Wilks and Richard Taylor, the firm becoming R. Taylor & Co. A younger brother, Arthur (1790–1870), was a partner from 1814 to 1823, and a nephew, John Edward Taylor (1809–1866), from 1837 to 1851, by which time the firm was housed in Red Lion Court, Fleet Street. Its printing device, a roman lamp, and motto, *Alere flammam*, were first adopted in 1815.

Taylor was at the forefront of new printing technology and between 1809 and 1818 he partnered Richard Bensley, George Woodfall, and Friedrich Koenig in the development of Koenig's mechanized printing press. Taylor lost money in this venture. Although John Walter, the owner of *The Times*, bought two machines in 1814, Taylor had to deal with financial discord between Walter and the partners, devious behaviour by Bensley, insuperable technical problems, and the appearance of cheaper machines from competitors such as Augustus Applegarth. Only after 1828, when Taylor contracted to print the *Weekly Dispatch* on his own cylindrical press, did his firm become financially secure.

On 7 April 1807 Taylor married Hannah Corke of St Paul's, Covent Garden. Their only daughter, Sarah, was born in 1808. It was not a successful marriage, and Taylor fell in love with Sarah Taylor's governess, Frances Marshall Francis (1797–1854), described at her death as the 'widow of Richard Francis, printer'. There were two illegitimate children, William (1817–1904) and Rachel Francis (1820–1913). Despite Hannah's likely death in the 1830s, Taylor never legitimized Frances's position, his real relationship with their children being kept a closely guarded family secret that scandalized his distinguished brothers John (1779–1863) and Edward (1784–1863) in 1852, when William Francis, who had studied chemistry and biology in Germany at Giessen and Berlin, was taken into partnership, the firm becoming Taylor and Francis.

From the beginning Taylor acquired a reputation for careful printing that ranged across poetry, fine editions of Old English classics, newspapers, textbooks, and examination papers. His chief interest, however, was science. In 1807 he became a fellow of the Linnean Society, and its under-secretary from 1810 to 1857. He was also a fellow of the Society of Antiquaries, the Royal Astronomical Society, and the Philological Society, as well as a regular supporter of the British Association from 1831. In 1822 he joined Alexander Tilloch as editor of the *Philosophical Magazine*, and he was a founder editor of the *Annals of Natural History* in 1838. He also sponsored and edited five important volumes of translations, *Scientific Memoirs*, between 1837 and 1852. For thirty-five years he represented the ward of Farringdon Without on the common council of the City of London, where he played a particularly active role in educational matters such as the founding of the City of London School and the Guildhall Library.

On suffering a nervous breakdown in 1852, Taylor retired to Richmond, Surrey, where he died from bronchitis at his home, Alton Lodge, on 1 December 1858. He was buried in St Peter's churchyard, Petersham, Surrey. The printing and publishing house was continued by William Francis.   W. H. BROCK

Sources *Annals of Natural History*, 3/3 (1859), 58 · W. H. Brock and A. J. Meadows, *The lamp of learning: Taylor and Francis and the development of science publishing*, 2nd edn (1998) · R. Taylor, 'On the invention and first introduction of Mr Koenig's printing machine', *London, Edinburgh, and Dublin Philosophical Magazine*, 3rd ser., 31 (1847), 297–301 · St Bride Printing Library, London, Taylor MSS · S. Sheets-Pyenson, 'From the north to Red Lion Court: the creation and early years of the *Annals of Natural History*', *Archives of Natural History*, 10 (1981–2), 221–49 · J. A. Ross, *Three generations of Englishwomen: memoirs and correspondence of Mrs John Taylor, Mrs Sarah Austin and Lady Duff Gordon*, 2 vols. (1888)
Archives St Bride Printing Library, London, corresp. and papers | NHM, letters to Sowerby family · Royal Museum, Edinburgh, letters to Sir William Jardine
Likenesses A. Craig, sketch, 1839, BM, NPG · R. Hicks, stipple, 1845 (after E. U. Eddis), NPG · T. H. Maguire, lithograph, 1851 (after drawing by G. Ransome), Linn. Soc.; repro. in *Ipswich Museum Portraits* · T. H. Maguire, lithograph, BM, NPG; repro. in *Ipswich Museum Portraits*
Wealth at death under £30,000: probate, 7 Jan 1859, CGPLA Eng. & Wales

Taylor, Richard Cowling (1789–1851), surveyor and geologist, the third son of Samuel Taylor, farmer, and Jane Cowling, was born at Hinton, Suffolk, on 18 January 1789. He was educated at Halesworth, Suffolk, and articled to Edward Webb, land surveyor at Stow on the Wold, Gloucestershire, in July 1805. He received further instruction from the geologist William Smith, who had also been a pupil of Webb, and finally became a land surveyor at Norwich in 1813. In 1820 he married Emily, daughter of George Errington of Great Yarmouth, with whom he had four daughters. He moved to London in October 1826. In the early part of his career he was engaged on the Ordnance Survey of England. Subsequently he reported on mining properties, including that of the British Iron Company in south Wales, his plaster model of which received the Isis medal of the Society of Arts. In July 1830, after the spectacular failure of the British Iron Company, he went to the United States of America. He first surveyed the Blossburg coal region in Pennsylvania, producing a report in 1833 (microfilm edn, 1991) on its geology and a possible

railway connection to it. He then spent three years exploring the coal and iron veins of the Dauphin and Susquehanna Coal Company in Dauphin county, Pennsylvania, and published two elaborate reports with maps (1840). He also surveyed and reported on copper mining in Cuba (1836) and asphalt mining in Halifax, New Brunswick.

Taylor's knowledge of theoretical geology led him to assign the Old Red Sandstone that underlies the Pennsylvania coalfields to the Old Red Sandstone of Europe. He was elected a fellow of the Geological Society of London and was a founder member in 1840 of the Association of American Geologists and Naturalists, from which developed the American Association for the Advancement of Science. His published works included early writings on the archaeology and geology of East Anglia and works on coal. As well as general works published in 1848 and 1861, he wrote numerous specialist reports, mostly published in the United States, about coal in places as far away as China. His crowning work was *Statistics of Coal* (1845), a long, authoritative, and compendious work. He also wrote on Native American archaeology. He died at Philadelphia on 26 October 1851.

G. C. BOASE, *rev.* ELIZABETH BAIGENT

Sources H. S. Torrens, 'Taylor, Richard Cowling', *ANB* · I. Lea, 'Memoir', *Proceedings of the Academy of Natural Sciences of Philadelphia*, 5 (1850–51), 290–96 · *GM*, 2nd ser., 37 (1852), 201–5, 218 · Allibone, *Dict.* · J. G. Wilson and J. Fiske, eds., *Appleton's cyclopaedia of American biography*, 7 vols. (1887–1900)

Taylor, Robert (1710–1762), physician, was born in Newark, Nottinghamshire, in April 1710, the son of John Taylor, twice mayor of the town. He was educated at Newark grammar school before going on to St John's College, Cambridge, where he was admitted on 23 June 1727. However, on 27 October 1727 he moved to Trinity College. It was there that he became a scholar in 1729, and there that he took the degree of bachelor of medicine in 1732, followed by that of doctor of medicine on 7 July 1737.

Immediately after taking his first degree Taylor entered medical practice in Newark, where he filled the vacancy that had been left unoccupied since the death of Mordecai Hunton in 1723. He quickly won the esteem of his fellow townsfolk, for his polished manners, professional assiduity, and general erudition. It was while practising at Newark that the event occurred which laid the foundation for his professional success in London. Richard Boyle, third earl of Burlington, was on a visit to Belvoir Castle, some 25 miles from Newark, when he was taken dangerously ill. Taylor was summoned and managed to save his patient, despite the gravest apprehensions, by the bold administration of opium. Thereafter, Lord and Lady Burlington persuaded Taylor to move to London, where, owing especially to the efforts of Lady Burlington, he quickly built a large practice and obtained the patronage of Edward Hulse, physician to the king—the position which Taylor was in time to hold himself.

Taylor became a fellow of the Royal Society on 23 June 1737. He was admitted a candidate of the Royal College of Physicians on 4 April 1738, being elected a fellow on 20 March 1739. The following year he gave the Goulstonian lecture and in 1755 the Harveian oration, making clear the college's then favourable views on the recently introduced practice of inoculation. A collection of his writings was published as *Miscellanea medica* in 1761.

Taylor was married twice: first to Anne (*d.* 1757), the youngest daughter of John Heron, and then, on 9 November 1759, to Elizabeth Mainwaring of Lincoln, who had a fortune of £10,000 and who died on 10 May 1812, aged eighty-six. With Elizabeth he had a son, Robert, who died an infant, and a daughter, Elizabeth, who survived both parents and in 1781 married Charles Chaplin (1759–1816) of Blankney Hall, Lincolnshire, who was later MP for that county.

Taylor died on 15 May 1762 and his body was interred in South Audley Street Chapel, London. However, in 1778 it was moved to Winthorpe, near Newark, where his widow had constructed a small private vault and where she and their infant son were also laid to rest. A monument to their memory was erected by their daughter.

W. W. Webb, *rev.* Giles Hudson

Sources Munk, *Roll* · Venn, *Alum. Cant.* · *The record of the Royal Society of London*, 3rd edn (1912) · Burke, *Gen. GB* · HoP, *Commons*
Likenesses portrait; in possession of Henry Chaplin at Blankney Hall, Lincolnshire, in 1898

Taylor, Sir Robert (1714–1788), architect, was the son of Robert Taylor (*d.* 1742), master mason and master of the London Masons' Company in 1733, who 'built himself a villa at Woodford in Essex and lived beyond his means' (Colvin, *Archs.*, 962). Horace Walpole states that Taylor got nothing from his father, 'excepting some common schooling, a fee, when he went pupil to the sculptor Sir Henry Cheere, and just enough money to travel on a plan of frugal study in Rome' (*Anecdotes of Painting*, 5.192). The future Sir Robert was apprenticed in 1732 to Cheere, whose rococo style, especially in chimney-pieces, later greatly influenced his architecture. His father's death in 1742, the year he left for Rome, required his immediate return; he discovered that his father was bankrupt. This crisis undoubtedly persuaded Taylor to adopt a hard-working regime. His pupil George Byfield told the landscape painter and diarist Joseph Farington that 'Sir Robert Taylor had three rules for growing rich, viz: rising early, keeping appointments and regular accounts' (Farington, *Diary*, 4.841). Walpole comments that 'he never slept after four in the morning' (*Anecdotes of Painting*, 5.195).

Sculptural commissions Having been apprenticed to Henry Cheere, Taylor was working for him still in 1736–7, when payments to him were recorded in Cheere's account at Hoare's Bank. He was admitted to the freedom of the Masons' Company by patrimony on 4 August 1744 and his emergence as an independent sculptor occurred in the same year, when, in competition with Roubiliac, Rysbrack, and others, he received the commission for the pediment relief on the newly built Mansion House. The choice of Taylor was made largely because of his City connections and the executed composition is certainly less accomplished in design than those proposed by Roubiliac and Rysbrack, as well as being carved with less finesse than works by his rivals. Later views of Taylor as a sculptor

have, however, made too much of hostile remarks by contemporaries, and his later work shows him to have been an inventive artist whose designs were original and distinctive, even if their execution is often somewhat crude. His next major commission was that given by parliament for the monument to Captain Cornewall; this followed a Commons vote in 1747 after a debate in which the only figure to have emerged with any credit after the battle of Toulon was used as a focus for opposition to the government. Completed in 1755, the monument was then one of the largest in Westminster Abbey and was given a very prominent position at the west end, being moved in a truncated form to the cloisters only in the 1930s. Notwithstanding its later neglect, the monument attracted much comment as an 'illustrious instance of national gratitude' (*GM*, 25, 1755, 90). With its rocky base, battle relief, and figures of Fame and Britannia flanking a palm tree, it recalled the French *pompes funèbres* mentioned by P. A. Grosley, who thought that the 'pomp and magnificence displayed around it seem rather to suit a funeral decoration, than a standing monument' (Grosley, 2.67). Of all native-born sculptors until Wilton, Taylor showed the deepest familiarity with continental sculpture and his smaller monuments, such as that to General Guest (erected 1761) in the abbey—praised by Vertue (*Note Books*, 3.161) for its 'ornaments to the bust and beautyes of the Marble'—make intelligent use of the rococo motifs of Oppenord and Meissonier. (Given these French interests, perhaps the later bequest of his fortune to found an institute for the study of modern languages is not so surprising.) The French and Italian qualities of his sculpture are most evident in the book containing both his own designs—some sketches as well as more finished drawings—and drawings made in Rome after works by sculptors such as Pierre Legros the younger; this, along with his library, is housed in the Taylor Institution, Oxford. While Taylor was beaten by Peter Scheemakers in his bid to secure the commission for the Shelburne monument at High Wycombe in 1751, he successfully contended with the same rival sculptor for the unusual monument to Lord Somers at North Mimms, Hertfordshire. During the 1750s his workshop continued to produce modestly sized monuments such as those to Daniel Adey at Wotton under Edge, Gloucestershire, and Edward Manning in Kingston, Surrey; many of them are recognizable from their distinctive decorative features, recalling Taylor's chimney-piece designs.

Architecture It is uncertain when Taylor turned to architecture. He was wealthy enough to build himself a house at 66 Charing Cross after 1745. His first recorded architectural work is for interiors at 14 St James's Square (1748–50) for Peter du Cane. By *c.*1750 he had designed 112 Bishopsgate Street for John Gore. In making the transition from sculptor to architect he must surely have made a study tour of the neo-Palladian architecture of Lord Burlington, William Kent, and Roger Morris. William Chambers later did the same when he established himself in London in 1755. As Taylor grew in stature, so does the pattern of his patronage become clear. His commissions came principally from the newly wealthy, principally bankers and directors of the East India Company, West Indian merchants and traders, lawyers and judges, and also soldiers and sailors who became wealthy through their exploits. In the course of his hard-earned career he was involved in a dozen public buildings, probably more than fifty country houses, and a very large number of town houses, in addition to groups or terraces of urban building.

The villa Like Chambers, Taylor drew out of his Palladian observations ideas for the making of a Taylorian style applicable to the design of an evolving sequence of villas: Harleyford, Buckinghamshire (1755); Copfold Hall, Essex (1755); Barlaston Hall, Staffordshire (1756); Asgill House, Richmond (1761); Danson Hill, Kent (1762); Chute Lodge, Wiltshire (1768); Sharpham House, Devon (1770); Mount Clare, Surrey (1771); and Thorncroft, Surrey (1772). He clearly admired Roger Morris's astylar 'cubist' villas of the 1730s, notably Combe Bank, Kent, Whitton House, Middlesex, and Westcombe House, Greenwich. Similarly, all Taylor's villas are astylar, without porticoes or orders. Volumetric movement is provided by the projection of canted or semicircular bays of varying height to the elevations. He favoured the use of rustication or vermiculation, as might a sculptor, to enliven the surrounds of windows and entrances, as at Chute Lodge, or the ground floor of Ely House, London, or later at the Guildhall, Salisbury (1788). His plans are compact, the rooms sometimes arranged around a stairwell, as in Campbell's Stourhead. In contrast to the neo-classical conformity outside and in of Chambers's villas, at first Taylor was influenced by his training under the arch-rococo Cheere, evident in the decorative trophies in the saloon at Harleyford, or the ornaments in the dining-room at Trewithen, Cornwall (1763). Among the few surviving designs by Taylor, those for chimney-pieces (Taylor Institution, Oxford) are in a rococo style commonly associated with Cheere as a sculptor. A parallel can be made with John Linnell the cabinet-maker, who was equally proficient in both the rococo and neo-classical styles.

By the 1770s Taylor had abandoned the rococo and was competing with Adam and Chambers. The ceilings of the octagonal saloon at Chute (1768), or the hall at Purbrook, Hampshire (1770), could be mistaken for something by Chambers. There can be little doubt that Taylor admired Chambers's Gower House, Whitehall (1765). As a colleague of Chambers, Taylor would have examined his works with care. Indeed, at Danson almost identical rooms by Taylor and Chambers (c.1770) are located cheek by jowl. Purbrook is a departure from the cubist villa model and reverts to the compact Palladian (tower) house theme of Morris's Combe Bank. However, the hall may claim to be the first columnar Roman atrium in domestic planning. Here Taylor has discovered his true métier based on his revived ideas of ancient Roman architecture, using the ornamental vocabulary of Palladio's fourth book of the *Quattro libri*. This is a result of the challenge to design new apartments for the Bank of England from 1765. In 1777 at Gorhambury, Hertfordshire, the hall was based upon the Pantheon via the Bank Stock Room, and its façade with a noble hexastyle Corinthian portico is Roman in spirit. If Taylor departed from the villa or enlarged villa norm at Gorhambury, so did he at the same time at Heveningham Hall, Suffolk, in an unusual palace or palazzo style that has been likened to a piece of urban architecture prefiguring John Nash's Regent's Park Terraces, and owing something to Chambers's Strand front of Somerset House.

The town house Urban, not the least speculative, building in London was Taylor's principal source of wealth. He was involved in more than forty houses, and probably many more, including eighteen in John Street and Theobalds Road (1759–61) and fourteen in Grafton Street (1768–75). He eschewed the use of orders, preferring plain brick façades, as did Chambers. An exception was the stone façade of the astylar Ely House, Dover Street (1772), 'a masterpiece of street architecture … a narrow front that shall at once be self-contained and yet part of the street's elevation' (Hussey, 26). The interiors of his town houses cannot be dissociated from those in the country. His early rococo trade marks are octagonal glazing, rococo plasterwork and chimney panels, serpentine inset panels to doors, and chinoiserie fret balustrades to stairs. Busts on brackets or set in roundels owe much to the décor of James Paine, who was likewise a child of the rococo, and one whom Taylor regarded with respect. Always the staircases are spatially ingenious, influenced by those by Paine and Chambers. By the mid- to later 1760s, the period of the bank designs, Taylor was drawing on the ornament of ancient Rome, but would also have been aware that that was the case with Burlington and Kent. He favoured cross-vaulted passages and corridors. The walls of the ballrooms of 4 Grafton Street (c.1768) and The Oaks, Epsom (c.1770), have a columnar articulation based on an arched recess motif and combined with circular bas-reliefs, a style that could be by no other than Taylor.

The Bank of England This was the great public work of Taylor's career, as was Somerset House for Chambers. Walpole wrote of the bank rooms, that when 'M. de Calonne saw them, he pronounced them, with no exception but St Paul's the first architecture in London' (*Anecdotes of Painting*, 5.194). This cannot be disputed. His first essay, the bank buildings of 1764, was outside the main older complex, on the site of the present Royal Exchange. To the *Civil Engineer and Architect's Journal* (vol. 10, 1847, 340) it was 'a masterpiece of street architecture, not surpassed by any in Europe'. It has never received its proper modern due. The following year Taylor tackled the problem of enlarging the bank proper. He did this by creating two blocks of offices extending the accommodation to east and west, tying them altogether behind a noble elevation of porticoes and attached columns, in its total elevation looking like the later Heveningham, which it may well have influenced. The eastern block contained his Roman Rotunda, a mini-Pantheon enclosed on three sides by vaulted columnar bank or transfer offices, and entered by a noble oval vestibule. Within the west block was a Garden Court or

West Quadrangle, with the Court Room on its north side and the reduced annuity office in the south-west corner. What is remarkable about the transfer offices and the reduced annuity office is their evolutionary method of top-lighting, which later provided Sir John Soane with inspiration when he, too, was appointed bank architect following Taylor's death. Were it not for the destruction of Taylor's bank halls, he would undoubtedly be judged with Chambers, Adam, and Wyatt as one of the outstanding English architects of the second half of the eighteenth century.

In the course of Taylor's career, appointments and honours flowed in. He had been appointed surveyor to the Bank of England in 1764; in March 1769 he joined the office of works, succeeding Chambers in the post of one of the two architects of the works; in 1777 he became a member of the board of works with the title of master carpenter; in 1780 he was promoted master mason and deputy surveyor, again to Chambers; in 1788 he became surveyor to Greenwich Hospital, and he was also surveyor to Lincoln's Inn and the Foundling Hospital. In all these appointments he was exceptionally conscientious, a fact that would have pleased Chambers. His architectural practice was notable as he was the first English architect to take pupils, as opposed to apprentices. Among the better-known of these were Charles Beazley, George Byfield, S. P. Cockerell, John Nash, and William Pilkington. In 1782, following his public service as a magistrate, first in Westminster, then the City, on his election as sheriff of London he was knighted. He died at his house at 34 Spring Gardens, Westminster, on 27 September 1788 and was buried with extravagant pomp in St Martin-in-the-Fields.

The study of Taylor's works has been made more difficult by the almost total loss of the paper contents of his office. His will of 4 January 1788 is extraordinary for its tiresome length of more than sixty pages. His executors were long-suffering. Of his fortune said to be more than £180,000, he left bequests totalling about £85,000, including £50,000 to his only son, Michael Angelo *Taylor, who in 1792 commissioned for private distribution a set of thirty-two aquatint plates by Thomas Malton of his father's principal works. The beautiful drawings for these are in the Ashmolean Museum, Oxford. He generously rewarded the pupils in his office with £5000 each. Surprisingly, his most famous bequest, to the University of Oxford, 'for erecting a proper Edifice … for establishing a Foundation for the teaching & improving the European Languages' (the Taylor Institution) took the form of a codicil which he failed to sign (PRO, DEL 9/9, fol. 13). After a long dispute with Taylor's son the university eventually accepted a settlement of £65,000 in 1835. The Taylor Institution is by C. R. Cockerell, the son and pupil of S. P. Cockerell, who was himself a pupil of Sir Robert Taylor.

JOHN HARRIS and MALCOLM BAKER

Sources M. Binney, *Sir Robert Taylor: from rococo to neo-classicism* (1984) • M. Binney, 'The villas of Sir Robert Taylor', *Country Life*, 6 (13 July 1967) • M. Binney, *Country Life*, 13 (20 Nov 1967) • M. Binney, 'Sir Robert Taylor's Grafton Street', *Country Life*, 12 (19 Nov 1981) • Colvin, *Archs.* • *Anecdotes of painting in England, 1760–1795 … collected by Horace Walpole*, ed. F. W. Hilles and P. B. Daghlian (1937) • C. Hussey, *The story of Ely House* (1953) • will, PRO, DEL 9/8; and DEL 9/9, fols. 1r–14v • limited admon pending suit, PRO, PROB 6/164, fols. 26v–27v • G. Barber, 'The Taylor Institution', *Hist. U. Oxf.* 6: 19th-cent. Oxf.*, 631–40 • K. A. Esdaile, 'Sir Robert Taylor as sculptor', *ArchR*, 103 (1948), 63–6 • D. J. Gilson, *Books from the library of Sir Robert Taylor* (1973) • M. Baker, 'Rococo styles in English sculpture', *Rococo: art and design in Hogarth's England*, ed. M. Snodin (1984), 278–309 and cat. nos. S21–4, S50–51, S53 [exh. cat.] • M. Baker, 'Lord Shelburne's "costly fabrick": Scheemakers, Roubiliac and Taylor as rivals', *Burlington Magazine*, 132 (1990), 841–8 • London Masons' Company court minutes, GL, MS 5304/3 • Vertue, *Note books*, vol. 3 • *GM*, 1st ser., 25 (1755), 90 • P. A. Grosley, *A tour to England* (1772)
Likenesses E. Scott, stipple, pubd 1789 (after W. Miller), BM • attrib. W. Miller, oils, U. Oxf., Taylor Institution • oils (after Reynolds), RIBA • watercolour drawing, NPG
Wealth at death £180,000: *Anecdotes of painting*, 5.198

Taylor, Robert (1784–1844), deist, the sixth son of John Taylor (d. 1791), ironmonger, and his wife and cousin, née Elizabeth Jasper, was born at Walnut Tree House, Edmonton, Middlesex, on 18 August 1784. Following his father's death, he was placed in the guardianship of his uncle, Edward Farmer Taylor of Chicken Hall, Bridgnorth, Shropshire. He attended the Revd Morgan Davis's boarding-school at Edmonton, and in 1801 he was articled to Samuel Partridge, then house surgeon at Birmingham General Hospital. He underwent a conversion experience in Birmingham, having heard the Calvinist preacher Edward Burn. In 1805 he walked Guy's and St Thomas's hospitals under Sir Astley Paston Cooper and Henry Cline; he was admitted an MRCS in 1807.

The influence of Thomas Cotterill, perpetual curate of Lane End, Staffordshire, led Taylor to study for the church, and in October 1809 he matriculated at St John's College, Cambridge, as Queen Margaret's foundation scholar. He came under the influence of Charles Simeon, the evangelical preacher, who, following Taylor's graduation and ordination in 1813, secured for him the position of curate-in-charge at Midhurst, Sussex. He preached his first sermon on the day of his ordination to the diaconate, 14 March 1813, at St Dunstan-in-the-West, Fleet Street, London. Ordained priest in October, he remained at Midhurst until the summer of 1818, holding also the neighbouring perpetual curacy of Easebourne. A Midhurst tradesman gave him the use of his library, and, from reading Gibbon, Paine, and Voltaire, sceptical doubts were raised in Taylor's mind. He announced his conversion to deism in January 1818, and resigned his curacy the following July after preaching a contentious sermon on Jonah. He recanted in December, placing an advertisement in *The Times* on 11 December in which he ascribed his lapse to a mental aberration. He was invited by George Gaskin, rector of Stoke Newington, to officiate at Edmonton, Tottenham, and Newington, but his views (which had not, in fact, changed) made it difficult for him to obtain preferment until a friend gave him the curacy of Yardley, near Birmingham, where he hoped to rehabilitate his clerical reputation. But the bishop of Worcester insisted on his dismissal, and Taylor, under notice to quit, openly preached deism in the parish church.

Taylor's brothers offered him a monthly allowance on condition that he leave England. He went to the Isle of Man; when his allowance was stopped, he wrote for local newspapers. An article justifying suicide brought him before the bishop, George Murray. Making off to Whitehaven, he got £10 from his old master, Partridge, and sailed for Dublin, where he became assistant master in Jones's school in Nutgrove; he also assisted the rector of Rathfarnham, co. Dublin, until his presence was discovered by Archbishop Magee, and he was again dismissed. He began a series of attacks on the church under the title *The Clerical Review*, and was noticed by Archibald Hamilton Rowan and Henry Augustus Dillon-Lee, thirteenth Viscount Dillon, under whose auspices he formed in 1824 the Society of Universal Benevolence. He hired the Fishamble Street theatre for Sunday morning lectures, but a riot at the second lecture (28 March 1824) closed the experiment.

Having returned to London, Taylor drew up a petition for permission to preach 'natural religion' which was presented to the House of Commons by Joseph Hume on 18 June. He taught classics, formed a Christian Evidence Society, and gave lectures, followed by discussions, at various public rooms. In the summer of 1826 he hired an old independent chapel at Founders' Hall, Lothbury, and conducted (from 30 July) Sunday morning services with a liturgy, unusual for advocating a sitting position during prayer, and more remarkable for directing that no word or phrase was ever to be altered, added, or omitted. Richard Carlile, the radical publisher, whose attention had originally been drawn by Taylor's activities in Dublin, and who was otherwise sympathetic to Taylor, commented that 'Such trash as this new liturgy is not instructive, is hypocritical ... and is a disgrace to the pretensions of Mr Taylor and his flock' (Royle, *Radical Politics*). His preaching, none the less, drew large congregations, and their subscriptions enabled him to purchase Salters' Hall Chapel, Cannon Street, London. On 1 January 1827 it was reopened by Taylor as his Areopagus. In the same month he was arrested and indicted for blasphemy. He was sued simultaneously for the recovery of £100, a bill he had accepted from a Bristol man named May, and was imprisoned for debt. He went through the bankruptcy court to obtain his release, and the Salters' Hall Chapel was resold at a loss.

Taylor was tried in full canonicals for blasphemy on 24 October 1827 before Charles Abbott, first Lord Tenterden, and found guilty. (Other charges, of conspiracy to overthrow the Christian religion, were dropped.) He was sentenced to a year's imprisonment in Oakham gaol and to find securities (amounting to £1000 in all) for good behaviour for five years. Richard Carlile raised a subscription for him and published a weekly letter from Taylor in his paper, *The Lion*. In Oakham gaol Taylor wrote his *Syntagma of the Evidences of the Christian Religion* (1828) and *The Diegesis* (1829), his two most important works. On his release in February 1829 he lectured occasionally at Carlile's shop in Fleet Street, and at the Universalist Chapel, Windmill Street, Finsbury Square. In May he and Carlile set out on an 'infidel mission' to the midlands and north, challenging ministers to debate. They began their campaign in Cambridge, where Taylor fastened the challenge to the door of the divinity schools. No debate was forthcoming, and the two men moved on through Nottingham to Yorkshire, Lancashire, and Cheshire before returning to London.

In May 1830 Taylor took the Rotunda, Blackfriars Road, London, and preached in episcopal garb to large audiences. His services were theatrical affairs, and his sermons full of 'coarse remarks' and 'excremental jokes', which mocked through imitation the rites of the Anglican church: in 1834 he was reported to have drunk gin and water, 'which he says is as good as the blood of Jesus Christ' (McCalman, 203). Two sermons on the devil (6 and 13 June) gained him the title of the Devil's Chaplain from Henry Hunt; the Rotunda became known as the Devil's Pulpit. The latter name was seized on by Taylor for the serial publication of his sermons in 1831. He was tried at the Surrey sessions in July 1831 for preaching blasphemy the previous Easter, found guilty, and sentenced to two years' imprisonment in Horsemonger Lane gaol, a fine of £200, and recognizances for good behaviour as before. Released from prison in 1833, Taylor retired from public view, although he again held infidel services at Theobold's Road Chapel in 1834. In 1833 he married an elderly woman of some property; the marriage was a happy one, but it exposed Taylor to an action for breach of promise of marriage on the part of Georgiana Richards, caretaker at the Rotunda, to whom the jury awarded damages of £250. To escape paying, Taylor and his wife fled to France, where he practised as a surgeon at Tours until his death there on 5 June 1844.

The Diegesis, a critical examination of the origins of Christianity through comparative mythology and philology, in which Christianity was expounded as a scheme of solar myths, was described in the nineteenth century as 'ill-arranged writings ... of no original or scientific value' (*DNB*); a twentieth-century re-evaluation called it 'a major contribution to popular English freethought' (Royle, *BDMBR*, 469). Taylor's intellectual influence on Carlile was perhaps his most lasting contribution to freethought.

ALEXANDER GORDON, rev. K. D. REYNOLDS

Sources E. Royle, 'Taylor, Robert', *BDMBR*, vol. 1 · E. Royle, *Radical politics, 1790–1900: religion and unbelief* (1971) · Venn, *Alum. Cant.* · J. M. Wheeler, *A biographical dictionary of freethinkers of all ages and nations* (1889) · *GM*, 2nd ser., 22 (1844), 550 · I. McCalman, *Radical underworld: prophets, revolutionaries, and pornographers in London, 1795–1840* (1988)
Archives Hunt. L., letters to Richard Carlile
Likenesses engraving, 1827 (after drawing by W. Hunt)

Taylor, Rowland (*d.* 1555), clergyman and protestant martyr, was born at Rothbury, Northumberland. Nothing is known of his parents or early years. He studied civil law at Cambridge, possibly at Pembroke College, where he proceeded to the degree of BCL in 1530 and DCL in 1534. He was principal of Borden Hostel, a hostel for law students, from 1531 until 1538, and also gave poorly attended lectures on Justinian's *Institutes*. He was ordained exorcist and acolyte in 1528, but went no further until 1539, serving instead as an official of the archdeacon of Ely. In 1554 he said that he and his wife, Margaret (whose surname is unknown), had married in John Tyndale's London residence. W. H. Frere wrote that this had occurred twenty-nine years earlier, but this is inconceivable, since in 1525 Taylor would have been a nineteen-year-old undergraduate. The marriage probably took place after 1534, which would explain Taylor's move to Borden Hostel instead of into a fellowship. The Taylors had nine children. Susan, George, Ellen, Robert, and Zachary predeceased him, and there were at least three others, Thomas, Mary, and Anne. The ninth may have been the orphan Elizabeth, whom Foxe reports they adopted.

In a letter to John Foxe, William Turner claimed to have been instrumental in Taylor's conversion to 'the evangelical doctrine' at Cambridge (Craig, 'Marginalia', 411). Hugh Latimer's sermons, which Turner persuaded Taylor to attend, were particularly influential, and Taylor soon attached himself to Latimer. During Latimer's brief term as bishop of Worcester, Taylor was his commissary-general and one of his chaplains. All of Latimer's chaplains preached in the diocese as part of his aggressive campaign to blanket it with reformist preaching. During a preaching tour in 1538 Taylor preached in Kidderminster, where a disgruntled tailor called his effort 'a folysshe sermonde of the new lernynge' and wished that the horse from which he preached 'had wynsyd and broken his necke' (PRO, SP 1/134, fols. 298r–300r). In March 1539 Latimer collated him to the parish of Hanbury, which he retained until his death, although he never served it personally. In the same year he was ordained deacon and admitted to St Swithin's in Worcester, with a dispensation for pluralism, which he held until 1544. After Latimer's resignation in July 1539 Taylor moved into Cranmer's service as a chaplain, and was ultimately ordained priest. In 1543 he investigated the prebendaries' plot, and in April 1544 Cranmer presented him to Hadleigh in Suffolk.

Foxe depicts Taylor as the ideal pastor in Hadleigh. Until recently historians accepted that account. However, it is now clear that Hadleigh was served by curates, and Taylor was not active in borough affairs. His denunciation of 'nobl ritch gentlemens' as 'prowd, enviowis, slothfull, covetowis, glotenewis, letcherus, carnall and worldly, bestly, epycuyrs, oppressors, diffeyners, receyvers, tyrandes, hypochrytes, idolatars' (Craig, 'Marginalia', 415) may indicate his feelings about some of Hadleigh's merchants, and suggests tense relations with them. Taylor's many duties and appointments often kept him from Hadleigh. He preached in several dioceses for the 1547 royal visitation and, at the lord mayor's request, in London at Whitsuntide 1548. He was made a canon of Rochester Cathedral in August 1547, archdeacon of Bury St Edmunds in May 1548, one of the six preachers of Canterbury and a commissioner to reform the ecclesiastical laws in 1551, and archdeacon of Cornwall in May 1552. He was also employed in the *sede vacante* administration of Norwich and Worcester in the early 1550s. In general Taylor served

as Cranmer's troubleshooter and it is as that, not as Foxe's ideal pastor, that he is best regarded.

Taylor was implicated in Northumberland's plot to secure the throne for Lady Jane Grey, and the council ordered his arrest on 25 July 1553. He was released on 9 November, but his reformist views and contempt for the Roman church, which he called 'the purpld spirituall hore, the gowldin giltd harrand drab' (Craig, 'Marginalia', 415–16), made a subsequent arrest inevitable. He refused to flee, writing later that '*verbum Dei* made us goo to London' (ibid., 414) when the council ordered his arrest on 26 March 1554. He was held in the king's bench prison for several months, during which time Gardiner examined him at St Mary Overie, Southwark. These examinations were dominated by spirited but inconclusive debates over transubstantiation and clerical celibacy. His views also appear in his prison letters, in which he rejected transubstantiation, affirmed that the pope was Antichrist and the Bible was sufficient in all matters of doctrine and salvation, and supported the oath of supremacy. Writing to his wife he defended justification by faith, attacked the mass as 'spiritual whoredom', and denounced transubstantiation for contradicting scripture and the creed on the location of Christ's body and for making Christ a 'cake-god' (Brown, 87–92).

Taylor once wrote in his bible that 'preachars must be bowld and not mylk mowthed' (Craig, 'Marginalia', 420) and he was certainly that. But although he had a reputation for learning Taylor did not publish. His views are known from accounts of his examinations (BL, Harleian MS 590, fols. 64r–68r), marginalia in a Latin Bible that he annotated from the late 1540s until his death, and a handful of letters—one to Cranmer, Ridley, and Latimer in his own hand (BL, Add. MS 19400, fol. 29) and copies of four written from prison (published by Bickersteth in 1837). He was also probably the author of the anonymous letter from 'the faithfull in Suffolke' to Nicholas Shaxton following Shaxton's 1546 recantation (Crowley). No contemporary paintings or drawings survive, but a favourable eyewitness to his examinations described Taylor as 'a man of comely personage, and good stature, his color good, his berd grate and somewhat short cut' (BL, Harleian MS 590, fol. 64r).

On 22 January 1555 Taylor was condemned to death, and on 4 February was degraded by Bonner. He was executed on 9 February on Aldham Common, north of Hadleigh. Foxe's vivid description of Taylor's progress to his execution includes his humorous remarks about the worms of Hadleigh churchyard being cheated of the opportunity to feast on his large carcass. He also distributed alms to the local poor. Before his death many lamented while others treated him roughly. Foxe's account suggests that Taylor was killed by a blow to the head, after which his body was burnt. The place is marked by a rough-hewn stone bearing the inscription '1555 D. Tayler in defending that was good at this plas left his blode' (Brown, 1), as well as by an obelisk erected by public subscription in 1819.

ERIC JOSEF CARLSON

Sources J. Craig, 'Reformers, conflict, and revisionism: the Reformation in sixteenth-century Hadleigh', *HJ*, 42 (1999), 1–23 · J. S. Craig, 'The marginalia of Dr Rowland Taylor', *Historical Research*, 64 (1991), 411–20 · W. J. Brown, *The life of Rowland Taylor LL. D.* (1959) · *The acts and monuments of John Foxe*, ed. S. R. Cattley, 8 vols. (1837–41), vol. 6, pp. 676–703 · S. Wabuda, '"Fruitful preaching" in the diocese of Worcester: Bishop Hugh Latimer and his influence, 1535–1539', *Religion and the English people, 1500–1640*, ed. E. J. Carlson (1998), 49–74 · *DNB* · W. H. Frere, *The Marian reaction in its relation to the English clergy: a study of the episcopal registers* (1896) · E. Bickersteth, *The letters of the martyrs* (1837) · [R. Crowley], *The confutation of. xiii, articles, whereunto Nicholas Shaxton … subscribed and caused to be set forth in print* [1548] · BL, Harleian MS 590, fols. 64r–68r · BL, Add. MS 19400, fol. 29 · PRO, state papers, general series, Henry VIII, SP 1/134, fols. 298r–300r

Taylor, Samuel (1748/9–1811),

stenographer and angler, was born probably at or near Shrewsbury, Shropshire. In his treatise *Angling in All its Branches, Reduced to a Complete Science* (1800), Taylor stated that the Severn, particularly the Terne brook, was the scene of his earliest fishing exploits. When a boy he was permitted by the owner of those waters

> to angle in any part of it, where I have often taken so many of these noble *Perch*, that I have gone a mile or two round rather than pass by that gentleman's hall, as if conscious that I had made too shameful a slaughter.   (*Angling*, 35)

Taylor was apparently married and had two children. Nothing else is known of his life until late 1781 when, as the originator and teacher of a shorthand system more simplified and practical than those of his predecessors, he launched an extensive teaching tour of England, Scotland, and Ireland, which ended in the summer of 1784. Taylor taught his then unpublished system at Edinburgh, Aberdeen, and at least seven other cities and towns in Scotland. Among the testimonials to the excellence of his method and his teaching was that of the poet James Beattie, then professor of moral philosophy and logic at Marischal College, Aberdeen, to whose son Taylor gave six lessons for the fee of 1 guinea and 1 shilling. Taylor spent about a year in Ireland, and recorded on 29 October 1783 a speech in the Irish parliament by John Foster.

Taylor's system, as modified and refined during the course of his tour, was published on 1 January 1786 as *An Essay Intended to Establish a Standard for an Universal System of Stenography, or Short Hand Writing*, its author being described as 'many years professor, & teacher of the science at Oxford, & the universities of Scotland & Ireland'. Dedicated to Frederick, Lord North, chancellor of the University of Oxford, the work had 312 subscribers, including Sir Thomas Dundas, to whom *Angling* was later dedicated.

Taylor's system, which was indebted to William Williamson's *Stenography* (1775), was arguably the best shorthand system before that of Sir Isaac Pitman, whose early work was based on Taylor's. Taylor's system presented a simplified alphabet that admitted of less ambiguity when characters were joined, indication of vowels only when sounded in initial or final position, use of only three terminations, no arbitraries, and a high degree of legibility.

Taylor did more than any of his predecessors to establish the art and use of shorthand in Great Britain, and his influence extended quickly throughout Europe. A petition promoting the adoption of Taylor's system was introduced in the Assemblée Nationale Legislative on 25 June 1792. His system was adapted and translated into French, Italian, Spanish, Portuguese, German, Swedish, and Hungarian. Adapted and improved in English by some forty authors, most notably William Harding, George Odell, and John Henry Cooke, it remained in use throughout the nineteenth century.

In 1800 *Taylor notarius* yielded the field to *Taylor piscator* (Wright, 1.34) with the publication of *Angling in All its Branches*. Although some confusion arose in the nineteenth century concerning the authorship of this work, and it was often assigned to another writer of the same name (including in the British Library catalogue), evidence such as the wording of the dedication and other stylistic similarities indicates that Taylor wrote both on stenography and on angling (see A. T. Wright). *Angling in All its Branches* represented the culmination of Taylor's more than forty years' experience as an angler: the work lists alphabetically the counties of Great Britain and describes the fishing waters of each, an arrangement borrowed by the Revd William Barker Daniel in his popular *Rural Sports* (2 vols., 1801–2). It also describes various fish, and discusses the merits of different types of bait and artificial flies, with instructions for their creation and use.

Allowing even for the rhetorical conventions of the time, Taylor's works suggest a man deferential to patrons and sometimes patronizing to others. Taylor died on or about 4 August 1811 at his home in Palace Street, Pimlico, London, and was buried on 10 August 1811 in St Margaret's Chapel yard, Westminster. His obituary (*Sun*, 2 Sept 1811) claims he was an eccentric, secretive man of 'strange and rough' manners, who none the less held a high reputation as a teacher.   PAGE LIFE

Sources A. T. Wright, *Samuel Taylor, angler and stenographer … to which is appended a facsimile reprint of the first American edition of Taylor's system*, 2 vols., Willis-Byrom Club Series, 2–3 (1904–5) · M. Levy, 'Samuel Taylor', *N&Q*, 7th ser., 2 (1886), 308, 377, 457–8 · M. Levy, 'Samuel Taylor, shorthand writer', *N&Q*, 9th ser., 9 (1902), 410, 471 · *The Sun* (24 Aug 1811) · *The Sun* (2 Sept 1811) · A. Paterson, 'Some early shorthand systems: no. 10, Samuel Taylor's "universal stenography"', *Phonetic Journal*, 47 (1888), 398–400 · K. Brown and D. C. Haskell, *The shorthand collection in the New York Public Library* (1935); repr. (1971) · *DNB* · *The Times* (10 April 1902), 6f. · *James Beattie's day-book, 1773–1798*, ed. R. S. Walker (1948) · J. Westby-Gibson, *The bibliography of shorthand* (1887) · M. Levy, *The history of short-hand writing* (1862)

Archives NYPL, shorthand collection holograph MS, 'Taylor's essay on stenography'

Wealth at death always in debt: *Sun* (2 Sept 1811)

Taylor, Samuel Coleridge- (1875–1912),

composer, was born on 15 August 1875 at 15 Theobalds Road, Holborn, London. His parents were registered as Daniel Hugh Taylor, surgeon, and Alice Taylor, *née* Holmans. His father was in fact Dr Daniel Peter Hughes Taylor (*c*.1848–1904), who returned to his native Sierra Leone after studying at Taunton and King's College, London, probably unaware that Alice Hare Martin (1856–1953) was pregnant. There is no record of their marriage. Alice raised her son in Croydon, aided by her mother, Emily Ann Martin, and by Sarah and

Samuel Coleridge-Taylor (1875–1912), by French & Co.

Benjamin Holman or Holmans. This latter may have been Alice Martin's father; he gave Samuel Coleridge Taylor a violin in 1880 and his first violin lessons. Holman's son Benjamin (1839–c.1915) was a professional musician living near Folkestone from the 1870s and had three musical children. The family expanded after Alice Martin married George Evans (c.1837–c.1908), a railway storeman. Their three children also had music lessons, and their son, Victor, also became a professional musician, without achieving the fame of his half-brother.

Coleridge-Taylor (he adopted the hyphen in the 1890s) was a small man, with tiny fingers that would have made a successful instrumental career unlikely. His obvious African descent attracted attention (W. Wallis, a local artist, painted his portrait in 1881), and he was noticed by a silk merchant and army volunteer, Colonel Herbert Walters, who encouraged him in church choral music and in 1890 sponsored him at the Royal College of Music. This patronage (the first biography of the composer was dedicated to Walters, 'to whom the world owes the discovery of Coleridge-Taylor') led commentators to ignore the early music lessons and drew attention away from his unorthodox family. His family had little of the respectability so important in Victorian society, and this, along with his African descent, profoundly affected Coleridge-Taylor. He won a violin scholarship to the Royal College of Music for four years, but changed to study composition under Charles Villiers Stanford. His works were presented at college concerts, attracting the attention of August Jaeger, whose employer, Novello, published Coleridge-Taylor's five anthems in 1892. Jaeger reported his progress in the press, and became a formative influence. Jaeger and Edward Elgar recommended the Three Choirs festival to commission the ballade in A minor, which was performed in September 1898. Two months later 'Hiawatha's Wedding Feast' was premièred in London; these early successes encouraged Coleridge-Taylor to become a professional composer. On 30 December 1899 he married Jessie Sarah Fleetwood Walmisley (1869–1962), daughter of Walter Milbanke Walmisley, stockbroker, and a distant relative of the composer Thomas Attwood Walmisley. They had a son, Hiawatha (1900–1980), and a daughter, Gwendolen (later Avril; 1903–1998), who were both to have musical careers.

'The Death of Minnehaha' (October 1899) and 'Hiawatha's Departure' (March 1900), with an overture, completed the cantata *The Song of Hiawatha*; which for decades was a much beloved and performed staple of choral societies. Having sold the copyright to *Hiawatha*, Coleridge-Taylor derived no lasting financial benefit from the popularity of the work, and financial pressures help explain the volume of his compositions: he poured out incidental music for the theatre (much commissioned by Beerbohm Tree for His Majesty's Theatre), sacred and secular choral works (of which *A Tale of Old Japan*, 1911, is perhaps the best), pieces for strings and for piano, orchestral works, and an unpublished grand opera (*Thelma*, 1907–9). His capacity for melodic line was strong: Jaeger observed 'Here is a real melodist at last' and that 'He has a quite Schubertian facility of invention' (Brewer, 94); Elgar wrote 'I have Taylor's theme jogging in the vacuities of my head … the theme remains' (Young, 12). However, apparent haste in orchestration can be heard in some of his instrumental works. *Hiawatha*'s popular success came in part from its secular theme, which meant that performances were not restricted to the church calendar, but also from its musical repetitions and simple developments, which suited its amateur performers. In the 1920s and 1930s thousands attended colourful performances of *Hiawatha* at the Royal Albert Hall, London. Generations of piano students played 'Demande et réponse' from his *Petite suite de concert*.

Invited by the Coleridge-Taylor Choral Society of Washington, DC (founded in 1901 by black choral singers), Coleridge-Taylor three times visited the United States (in 1904, 1906, and 1910). His identity as a black composer was important to him, and provided inspiration for a number of his works: he used themes from spirituals in the overture to *Hiawatha*; the symphonic poem *Toussaint l'ouverture* (1901) was concerned with Haiti; and he wrote the operatic romance *Dream Lovers* (1898) in co-operation with the African-American poet Paul Dunbar, who had also inspired the songs in his *African Romances* (1897) and the keyboard *African Suite* (1898). Seeking melodies in folk music was widespread in the 1890s, and Coleridge-Taylor used African, Caribbean, and American themes in his *24 Negro Melodies* (1905) which was published only in America, with a preface by a leading African-American citizen. He was visited in Britain by leading musical African-

Americans, including the baritone Harry Burleigh and violinist Clarence Cameron White, who worked with Coleridge-Taylor in Britain. Back in the United States they encouraged performances of his works in black colleges, developing his identity in that country.

Coleridge-Taylor taught composition (at Trinity College of Music, London, from 1903, and at the Guildhall School of Music from 1910), judged competitions, and conducted orchestras around Britain. He was improving his German, in anticipation of visiting that country, when he died from pneumonia at his home, Aldwick, St Leonard's Road, Croydon, on 1 September 1912, at the age of thirty-seven. Thousands attended his funeral and interment at Bandon Hill cemetery near Croydon.

Coleridge-Taylor's music fell out of favour with the decline of the amateur choral societies after the Second World War, and even *Hiawatha* and *A Tale of Old Japan* have been seldom performed since the 1960s. A revival of interest in the composer, as a symbol of the achievements of black Britons, took place towards the end of the century. The mixed responses and inconsistencies of his obituarists reveal something of the prejudices against which his work was judged: one paper thought he had brought 'an exotic raciality into English music' (*Manchester Guardian*, 2 Sept 1912), while another wrote 'Of African rhythms or folk-music pure and simple there is here no trace' (*Daily Telegraph* 2 Sept 1912). *The Times* declared that the original features in his music were 'racial characteristics' (2 Sept 1912), and two years later, the African-American composer and conductor James Reese Europe declared that Coleridge-Taylor's was 'not real Negro work' (Badger, 126). Coleridge-Taylor was a man of gentle disposition and great personal dignity; his works enjoyed enormous popularity, and although his significance has come to be seen primarily as that of an icon of black success, his achievements as a composer of light orchestral and choral music were noteworthy. JEFFREY GREEN

Sources W. C. B. Sayers, *Samuel Coleridge-Taylor, musician: his life and letters* (1915) · G. Self, *The Hiawatha man* (1995) · P. McGilchrist and J. Green, 'Some recent findings on Samuel Coleridge-Taylor', *Black Perspective in Music*, 13/2 (1985), 151–78 · J. Green, '"The foremost musician of his race"—Samuel Coleridge-Taylor of England, 1875–1912', *Black Music Research Journal*, 10/2 (1990), 233–52 · J. Coleridge-Taylor, *A memory sketch, or, Personal reminiscences of my husband, genius and musician* (1943) · A. Coleridge-Taylor, *The heritage of Samuel Coleridge-Taylor* (1979) · J. Green, 'Perceptions of Samuel Coleridge-Taylor on his death (September 1912)', *New Community*, 12/2 (1985), 321–5 · P. Richards, 'Africa in the music of Samuel Coleridge-Taylor', *Africa*, 57/4 (1987), 566–71 · *MT*, 50 (1909), 153–8 · b. cert. · m. cert. · d. cert. · A. H. Brewer, *Memories of choirs and cloisters* (1931) · P. Young, *Letters to Nimrod: Edward Elgar to August Jaeger, 1897–1908* (1965) · R. Badger, *A life in ragtime: a biography of James Reese Europe* (1995) · *New Grove*

Archives BL, scores and music, Add. MSS 50763–50765, 54370–54372, 62519–62521, 63798–63813 · Black Cultural Archives, London, scores · Royal College of Music, London, papers | Howard University, Washington, DC, Moorland-Spingarn collection, Hilyer MSS | SOUND BL NSA, 'The African Mahler', BBC Radio 3, 3 Aug 1997, H9105/3 · BL NSA, documentary recording · BL NSA, performance recording

Likenesses photographs, 1876–1904, repro. in McGilchrist and Green, 'Some recent findings on Samuel Coleridge-Taylor' · W. Wallis, oils, 1881, NPG · carte-de-visite, c.1888, Royal College of Music, London · photograph, c.1896, Royal College of Music, London · Debenham & Gould, photograph, c.1900, Royal College of Music, London · photographs, 1900–04, repro. in J. Green, *Black Edwardians: black people in Britain, 1901–1914* (1998), 184–5, 191 · Breitkopf & Härtel, photograph on postcard, 1900–12, Royal College of Music, London · J. Redfern, photograph, c.1902, Royal College of Music, London · French & Co., photograph, NPG [*see illus.*] · photographs, repro. in Sayers, *Samuel Coleridge-Taylor, musician*

Wealth at death £874 5s. 7d.: administration, 16 Oct 1912, *CGPLA Eng. & Wales*

Taylor, Sarah. *See* Austin, Sarah (1793–1867).

Taylor, Sedley (1834–1920), music scholar and benefactor, was born on 29 November 1834 at Kingston upon Thames, Surrey, the son of George Taylor, a surgeon. He was educated at University College School, London, and he matriculated at Trinity College, Cambridge, in Michaelmas 1855; he became a scholar in 1857, graduated BA (sixteenth wrangler) in 1859, and proceeded MA in 1862. He was junior bursar of Trinity from 1866 to 1869. Elected a fellow in 1861, and obliged as Trinity statutes then stood to proceed to ordination, he took deacon's orders and served as curate of St Michael's, Handsworth, Birmingham, in 1863–4. In 1869, however, he wrote that 'a course of inquiry … carried on for several years, has led me to form convictions very seriously at variance with the formularies which bind the conscience of the English clergy' (*The System of Clerical Subscription*, 1869, 25). In 1897 Taylor declared that his loss of faith had 'dislocated and in great measure crippled' his life (*Cambridge Review*, 25 Feb 1897, xliii–xlv).

Since he did not take priest's orders Taylor's fellowship lapsed when he ceased to be bursar in 1869. Thereafter, he resided in Trinity until his death without a post in college or university, apart from serving as librarian of Trinity in 1870–71: he was of a type that subsequently became rare in Cambridge, dependent for his status as a don on personal activity rather than formal office. He remained unmarried. Conviviality was a way of life, and he took obvious and infectious pleasure in telling jokes and rendering comic songs, although a certain reserve suggested subtlety of character. Distinctive in appearance, his thick and spreading black beard is said to have provoked Alfred Marshall to refer to him as 'that owl in the ivy bush' (Knight, 85).

Enjoying a private income, Taylor devoted himself to a variety of pursuits and good causes: he gave to many charities and privately to needy students. He was a constant supporter of Addenbrooke's Hospital and in 1907 began, with a crucial gift of funds, the Cambridge Dental Institute for the treatment of children's teeth, the first such agency in England. In 1911 he was given the freedom of the city of Cambridge because of his services. He was Liberal in his politics, and his long-continued advocacy of profit-sharing in industry, on which he became a British expert, should be seen as his sensitive response to current denunciations by Ruskin and others of unbridled capitalism. His essays on the subject were published as *Profit-Sharing between Capital and Labour* (1884). On the main university contention of the day Taylor was an enthusiast for women's education. In the 1860s he helped to lead the group of dons planning the college that became Girton; he took a far-sighted view of its future, and opposed Emily Davies herself in his judgement that the college should move from Hitchin to Cambridge: 'the moral objections seem to be imaginary. There has never been the slightest difficulty with the ladies' lectures [at Cambridge], though many of those who attend are young girls' (Stephen, 246). Taylor was a member of Girton from 1872 until his death, and a generous benefactor.

Music was an abiding pleasure and scholarly concern. Absorbed by the physics of music, Taylor carried out experiments on sound in the Cavendish Laboratory, and argued with scientific detail for the superiority of the tonic sol-fa notation over the staff system. He brought to his researches fluency in French and German, and his *Sound and Music* (1873) transmitted to English readers the revolutionary acoustical theories of Hermann Helmholtz; it enjoyed two later editions, and was a standard textbook until the twentieth century. Other writings, on J. S. Bach and Handel, also exploited continental scholarship, but Taylor too modestly disclaimed his own creative talent, notably in clearly assembling the evidence for Handel's extensive borrowings and his genius in transforming them. Ahead of his time in his devotion to J. S. Bach, he translated and published some cantata choruses as anthems. He also composed some short pieces of music, although these attracted little popularity outside Cambridge, and he was a talented pianist and organist. While never having a stipendiary post, he was a luminary of the Cambridge faculty of music during its golden age under Sterndale Bennett and Stanford. Taylor was president of the Cambridge University Musical Society as an undergraduate, and again for many years as a don. He was also a leading figure in the Cambridge University Musical Club, founded in 1889 to promote chamber music; at its 500th concert in 1912 he was acclaimed in a celebration ode as 'chief elder brother of our brotherhood … loving pilot of our music's Odyssey' (Knight, 96).

Taylor died at Fallowfield, Manchester, on 14 March 1920, and was buried in Weston Colville, Cambridgeshire, on 18 March after a funeral service in Trinity College chapel.   PETER SEARBY

Sources *Cambridge Review* (14 May 1920) · *The Times* (16 March 1920) · Venn, *Alum. Cant.* · B. Stephen, *Emily Davies and Girton College* (1927) · F. Knight, *Cambridge music from the middle ages to modern times* (1980) · account with Novello, 1912–15, CUL, MS Add. 6255/151
Archives CUL, corresp. and papers, Add. MSS 6254–6260, 6263, 6290 · Trinity Cam., letters | King's Cam., letters to Oscar Browning
Likenesses three photographs, *c.*1870–1900, Trinity Cam. · photograph (after portrait), Trinity Cam.
Wealth at death £37,829 10*s.* 10*d.*: probate, 5 July 1920, *CGPLA Eng. & Wales*

Taylor, Silas (1624–1678), parliamentarian army officer and antiquary, was born on 16 July 1624 at Harley, near Much Wenlock, Shropshire, the eldest son of Silvanus Taylor, a 'grand Oliverian' (Wood, *Ath. Oxon.*, 1st edn, 1691–2, 464). Wood says that Taylor's surname was Domville, but that he rarely used this alternative name. Nothing is

known about the subject's mother but his father was a 'busie man against the King's party' (ibid.). Silvanus Taylor was a member of the high court of justice in 1650, lieutenant of the Tower (1649–50), and a regular member during the 1650s of various committees and commissions in the counties of Herefordshire, Shropshire, Radnorshire, and Middlesex. He appears to have lived in the parish of St Clement Danes, Westminster.

Early years Silas Taylor entered Shrewsbury School in September 1637; Wood's statement that he was also at Westminster School is unconfirmed. He entered New Inn Hall, Oxford, at the beginning of 1641. On the outbreak of the civil war he joined the parliamentary army, becoming a captain under Colonel Edward Massey, the garrison commander of Gloucester, whose command also included Herefordshire and Monmouthshire. Virtually nothing is known of Taylor's exploits during the war, nor of his marriage, but he was in Hereford in 1645 when his wife was buried in the cathedral (Hereford Cathedral archives, fabric accounts). According to John Aubrey, Taylor's 'eldest sonne, wife and children were all burnt in their beds in … near Lothbury' (*Brief Lives*, 310) presumably the street of this name, near the Guildhall in the City of London. Taylor never remarried. In August 1647, along with Massey and other officers loyal to the Presbyterian parliament, Taylor was in arms in Hyde Park, intending to defend London against the New Model Army.

Taylor's father was active in the Herefordshire land market and purchased for £728 the manor of Bosbury when the lands belonging to the cathedral church of Hereford were auctioned in 1649. Some of this land, according to Wood, was settled upon his son who added to it other church properties including Litley Court in the parish of Hampton Bishop, close to Hereford; the disused 'almshall' of the hospital of St Ethelbert, adjoining the cathedral close; and in 1655 the major portion of the bishop's palace at Hereford, which he shared with Colonel John Birch. On the last 'he lay'd out much money in building and altering' (*Brief Lives*, 309).

High office in Herefordshire Early in the 1650s Taylor was appointed joint sequestration commissioner for Herefordshire with Captain Ben Mason. His pragmatic approach to this powerful office made him 'beloved by all the King's party' in Herefordshire (*Brief Lives*, 308) but created friction with his fellow commissioner who was more dogmatic but less scrupulous in accounting for the moneys which passed through his hands. A bitter dispute ensued. Taylor's letters to his masters in London suggest that by means of prevarication he certainly allowed many 'papists and delinquents' to enjoy their estates longer than the parliamentary administrators expected, and thus lost them income, as Mason was quick to point out. He drew up a series of articles against Taylor in 1653 who responded with a similar list of Mason's irregularities. After an inquiry held in Gloucestershire in August, Taylor was acquitted and eventually became the sole sequestration officer for Herefordshire. At the root of the dispute with Mason lay Taylor's increasing tendency to become identified with the county community of Herefordshire. During disputed elections in 1656 Taylor is noticed as one of those prominent in supporting the candidature of Colonel Edward Harley and John Scudamore—two members of the most prominent families in Herefordshire and both alienated from the parliamentary regime at this date.

Taylor's religious views, like those of his father, appear to have been Erastian and Presbyterian, favouring the survival of a state church, under lay control. His vicious attack upon the cathedral minister Richard Delamaine, published anonymously as *Imposter magnus* (1654), was a response to the latter's apparent radicalism. Taylor says that with his father, Silvanus, and the celebrated divine John Tombes, he witnessed one of Delamaine's sermons, with which he inflamed his congregations. His exploitation of women in his congregations, and his 'strange applications' of the scripture, said 'farewell to that very genuine sense of the word *Religion*, and to all civil society' (Taylor, *Imposter magnus*, 9). Taylor, an educated man, also distrusted a minister who lacked a university education, whose Latin was weak, and who could not even make a scale drawing of an ancient monument! There may have been a hint of intellectual arrogance here, for Wood records that Taylor was especially skilled in 'Mathematics and Tongues' (Wood, *Ath. Oxon.*, 1st edn, 1691–2, 466). Moreover, Delamaine was an ally of Mason and of the governor of Hereford Castle, Colonel Wroth Rogers, and thus represented a threat to Taylor's ascendancy in Herefordshire. They viewed Taylor's new acquaintances with suspicion and when he held a music meeting in January 1652— a few months after Charles II's descent upon Worcester— the presence of many royalists made the garrison of the castle 'keep to their arms' (Taylor, *Imposter magnus*, 26). The music was also conducted by Taylor's friend Matthew Locke, 'a papist that was in armes amongst the Rebels in Ireland' (*The Close Hypocrite Discovered*, 18).

Issues concerning Hereford Cathedral Library According to Aubrey, Taylor found the cathedral library at Hereford in disorder, the books and archives 'lay uncouth and unkiss' (*Brief Lives*, 309). Rawlinson, writing soon after the Restoration, said the library had been 'plunder'd and several valuable MANUSCRIPTS taken away, but preserv'd by Silas Taylor' (Rawlinson, vii). Thus, though Aubrey and Wood insist that Taylor 'ransacked' the library, modern commentators have found it difficult to prove this imputation. According to the scrupulous late twentieth-century catalogue of the cathedral library (Mynors), the only manuscript for which evidence exists for Taylor's misappropriation is 'De brevis relatio de glorioso Rege Willelmo' bound with Lanfranc's 'Constitutiones', which Taylor may have found unbound, and in this state gave it to the Bodleian Library in 1658, after transcribing it for publication as an appendix to *Gavelkind* (1663).

Taylor's antiquarian collections for the history of Herefordshire, contained in BL, Harley MS 6726, show that far from looting the cathedral library he exploited its contents thoroughly, especially the bishop's registers, which are all present in the library at the beginning of the twenty-first century. The 'History of the county of Hereford' was prepared for publication and even includes a crude title-page with Celtic, Roman, Saxon, and Norman figures ranged around a canopied opening. There is a general introduction on the 'Island of Great Britain' with much sympathy displayed for the indigenous population such as the 'stout Silures' while, in keeping with seventeenth-century radical thinking, the Normans are regarded as oppressive usurpers, 'outlandish inmates … strangers (to) the comons of England'. The focus is very much upon Herefordshire and the marches and there are tantalizing references to sources in Taylor's possession, including 'a ms chronicle in my custody' relating to Arthur's battles (Harley MS 6726). A major part of the manuscript is devoted to the topography of the county combining local and national archive material, with published histories and personal observations made by the author between 1655 and 1657. The manuscript seems to have been left for safe keeping in the hands of Colonel Harley at Brampton Bryan in Herefordshire and the spare quire of paper purchased by Taylor for the 'History' was later used for recording the militia assessment for Herefordshire of 1663. In 1672 he hoped to persuade John Olgilby to publish his collections in the third volume of 'Britannia' only to find that he 'desired mee to epitomize my collections into 9 or 10 sheets of paper for Herefordshire, & he would put it into what stile of English he thought fit' (BL, Egerton MS 2231, fol. 259). It seems likely that the manuscript remained at Brampton Bryan until it found its way into the Harleian collection. It was one of the sources rediscovered and exploited by John Duncumb for his *Collections towards the History and Antiquities of the County of Hereford*, vol. 1 (1804).

London and Dunkirk, 1659–1663 From the evidence of Harley MS 6726 Taylor remained resident in Herefordshire until 1659 when 'upon the rising of George Booth in Cheshire … he received a Commission to be Captain of a Troop of Horse for the Militia of the City of Westminster, and showe'd himself very active in that employment' (Wood, *Ath. Oxon.*, 1st edn, 1691–2, 463). Along with his father he was also commissioner for the Westminster militia and in this role he makes an appearance in the diary of Samuel Pepys on 21 February 1660. While Pepys was listening to 'a canon of 8 voices composed by Mr Lock', Captain Taylor (probably Silas, though Pepys also has another seagoing colleague called Captain Taylor) reported amid the bonfires celebrating the passing of the Rump, that the gates of the city (recently destroyed on the orders of the Rump) were 'to be made up again' and those members of the city in prison 'were to be set at liberty' (Pepys, 1.63).

Aubrey says that after the king's return Taylor was 'faine to disgorge all he had gott, and was ruined' (*Brief Lives*, 309). But following a brief period in Scotland he found employment as the keeper of armaments at Dunkirk where Colonel Harley (now Sir Edward) was governor between 1660 and 1661. Taylor's practical turn of mind is demonstrated in a brief letter to Harley written in April 1661 reminding him of 'those engines that are made to quench fire by casting water' (*Portland MSS*, 3.251). During this time he took refuge from his 'daily Turmoyl' (Taylor, *Gavelkind*, preface) in writing *The History of Gavelkind* (1663) which was dedicated to Harley. The book explores the tradition that in certain regions of England land tenure was pre-feudal. It was a response to an essay in the same field by M. William Somner of Canterbury, which simply explored 'the common Etymologistical notion thereof' (ibid., 1–2). Taylor, however, set out to prove that the custom of gavelkind was a 'British original' (ibid., preface, 2), which had survived the Roman, Saxon, and Norman invasions of England. He corresponded with John Aubrey about the book and eventually sent him a copy.

Final years and appointments In November 1664, through the offices of Sir Paul Neile, an active member of the Royal Society and a friend of Pepys, Taylor was appointed by royal warrant commissioner of the king's storehouse at Harwich for the annual fee of £1000. Pepys notes that some of those close to the king felt the choice of an old 'fanatique' for such a post was ill-considered. On becoming a member of the corporation in 1672 he had access to the books and records of the borough, and carried out a search among the records of the Tower of London. Another book was prepared for publication but 'the Thread of his Life being not long after cut off' (Dale, i) the manuscript was seized by his creditors. Eventually it found its way into the hands of the antiquarian Samuel Dale who used it as a palimpsest for his own researches, and published Taylor's original text, combined with his own in the form of notes, as *The History and Antiquities of Harwich and Dovercourt* (1730).

Pepys was regularly in touch with Taylor, and even read a draft of his play—'The Serenade, or, Disappointment'—sent to him in 1669. He was embarrassed in June 1666 when Taylor sent him misleading news of an English victory over the Dutch at Dunkirk. Nevertheless he regarded Taylor as 'a good schollar, and among other things a great antiquary' (Pepys, 6.81) and in 1665 was shown Taylor's copy of the charter of King Edgar, in which the king refers to himself as *Rex marium Britanniae*. This, according to Aubrey, had been 'garbled' from the library at Worcester Cathedral and was offered to the king for £120. After Taylor's death Aubrey tried to interest the secretary of state in the document, since the prebends of Worcester 'cared not for such things' (*Brief Lives*, 309). Taylor also tried to sell the king a manuscript on the philosopher's stone, but again with no success.

Pepys, Aubrey, and Taylor also shared a common interest in music. Aubrey noted that he had composed for the king and that in 'those unmusicall dayes' after the civil war he possessed a fine chamber organ (*Brief Lives*, 347). Wood remembered that Taylor had played in the music faculty at Oxford before 1660 while Pepys also commented on his skill as a composer. He was, however, less flattering about an anthem played at the Chapel Royal in June 1668, which he declared was

a dull, old-fashioned thing, of six and seven parts, that nobody could understand: and the duke of York, when he

came out, told me that he was a better store-keeper than anthem-maker, and that was bad enough too   (Pepys, 9.251)

Two of his compositions were published in John Playford's *Court Ayres* (1655) and several other pieces are known to have existed in manuscript. His younger brother, Sylvanus (*d.* 1672 in Dublin), also composed and performed music.

Taylor died in straitened circumstances—'his papers lying with him' but some already pawned (Wood, *Ath. Oxon.*, 1st edn, 1691–2, 464)—at Harwich on 4 November 1678. He was buried in the chancel of the parish church of St Nicholas and, according to Dale, 'without either Grave Stone or Inscription to preserve his Memory to Posterity' (Dale, 37).   DAVID WHITEHEAD

Sources John Aubrey: 'Brief lives', ed. J. Buchanan-Brown (2000) • Pepys, *Diary* • Wood, *Ath. Oxon.*, 1st edn • M. A. E. Green, ed., *Calendar of the proceedings of the committee for compounding … 1643–1660*, 1, PRO (1889); 3 (1891); 4 (1892) • G. E. Aylmer, 'Who was ruling in Herefordshire from 1645–61?', *Transactions of Woolhope Natural Field Club*, 40 (1970–72), 373–87 • S. Dale, *The history and antiquities of Harwich and Dovercourt* (1730) • BL, Harley MS 6726 • J. Webb, *Memorials of the civil war … as it affected Herefordshire*, ed. T. W. Webb, 2 vols. (1879) • [S. Taylor], *Imposter magnus* (1654) • [R. Delamaine?], *The close hypocrite discovered* (1654) [copies in Hereford City Library] • *The manuscripts of his grace the duke of Portland*, 10 vols., HMC, 29 (1891–1931), vol. 3 • G. Aylmer and J. Tiller, eds., *Hereford Cathedral: a history* (2000) • *New Grove* • R. Rawlinson, *The history and antiquities of the city and cathedral-church of Hereford* (1717) • C. H. Firth and R. S. Rait, eds., *Acts and ordinances of the interregnum, 1642–1660*, 3 vols. (1911)
Archives BL, Herefordshire collections, Harley MSS 4046, 4174, 6726, 6766, 6856, 6868 • Hereford Cathedral Library
Wealth at death in debt: Wood, *Ath. Oxon.*; John Aubrey: 'Brief lives', ed. Buchanan-Brown

Taylor, Simon (1742–1772/1796), botanical artist, was born in October 1742 and trained in the drawing-school of William Shipley in London. About 1760 he was engaged by Lord Bute to paint the rare plants in the Royal Botanic Gardens at Kew. John Ellis wrote to Carl Linnaeus on 28 December 1770: 'We have a young man, one Taylor, who draws all the rare plants of Kew Garden for Lord Bute; he does it tolerably well: I shall employ him very soon' (*Correspondence of Linnæus*, 1, 1821, 255). He was also employed by the physician and botanist John Fothergill. He died in 1772 (or possibly 1796). After Lord Bute's death in 1792, a large collection of paintings of plants on vellum by Taylor was sold by auction in 1794. The paintings he executed for Fothergill were sold on Fothergill's death in 1780 to Catherine the Great, empress of Russia, for £2000, not a high price considering that Taylor usually charged 3 guineas for each of his paintings. Examples of his work are in the British Museum, London, and the Royal Botanic Gardens at Kew.   G. S. BOULGER, *rev.* ANNETTE PEACH

Sources Desmond, *Botanists*, rev. edn

Taylor, Susanna (1755–1823). *See under* Taylor, John (1750–1826).

Taylor, Theodore Cooke (1850–1952), woollen manufacturer and politician, was born at New Hall, Carlinghow, Batley, West Riding of Yorkshire, on 3 August 1850, the eldest son of Joshua Taylor (1821–1879), cloth manufacturer, and his wife, Alice (*d.* 1860), daughter of Samuel Cooke, carpet manufacturer of Liversedge, West Riding of Yorkshire. He was educated at a preparatory school in Batley and at Batley grammar school. At the age of thirteen he moved to the northern Congregational school at Silcoates near Wakefield, a school for nonconformist ministers and laymen. He left at the age of sixteen and entered the family woollen business, with which he was to be connected until his death eighty-six years later. His grandparents had been clothiers in the Batley district. In 1845 his father had founded a cloth manufacturing firm at Blakeridge, Batley, as the junior partner of two older brothers, John (1816–1884) and Thomas (1818–1891); Joshua Taylor worked at Blakeridge Mill as a cloth finisher. Theodore, on entry to the business, gained experience in all its departments, as was common practice at the time. In 1874 he married Sara Jane, his first cousin and daughter of W. J. P. Ingraham of Philadelphia, USA. She had been born in England and Theodore met and courted her on her visits as a girl to her English relations. They had three children, Evelyn Sarah, Lilian Gertrude, and Laurie.

The heavy woollen district of Yorkshire, within which the Taylors' firm was situated, was benefiting from its success in spinning yarn and weaving cloth using a mixture of new wool and shoddy, wool reclaimed from rags. Strength to the cloth was often provided by the use of cotton yarn as a warp to make 'union cloths'. The firm used shoddy from an early date and the subsequent success of the business was built on the competitive advantages this fibre allowed. The rise of the ready-made clothes trade, notably in Leeds, provided business. In 1879 Theodore Taylor took over his father's role in the business, acting partly as designer and partly as salesman, as well as buyer and as blender, the most important function for a firm of its nature. He was joined in the business by his younger brother, Arthur, in 1871, a cousin, John Taylor, in 1872, and another cousin, Thomas Frederick, in 1883. On 26 January 1892 he agreed with the other partners that he should take complete control of the business, which at that time employed 600 people. The firm made an increasing variety of union cloths, at a time when that was the most successful, and profitable, section of the British wool textile industry. By 1900 the workforce had increased to 1000 in three large mills. Control allowed Taylor to start putting into practice an idea which he had long considered and of which he was a great advocate—profit-sharing in industry. He set up a successful scheme whereby workers received payment in shares as a 'bonus', according to their proportion of the pay bill. By 1918, when 1800 were employed, the issue of bonus shares amounted to half the company's capital. By 1952 the proportion was over four-fifths. Taylor maintained control of the business, however, by keeping voting rights firmly in his own hands. It has been estimated that the profit-sharing scheme transferred a total of £3 million to Taylor's employees in shares and bonuses.

Taylor's wife and first daughter died within two days of one another in the influenza epidemic of 1919. The following year, on 16 March, he married Mary Isabella (b. 1873/4), daughter of Colin Alexander McVean, a highland laird of Kilfinichen in the Isle of Mull, Scotland, and Mary Wood, née Cowan. With her he moved from his home in Batley to Grassington in the Yorkshire dales. He remained a devout Congregationalist, supporting financially the local Congregational Union and Silcoates School. He was a teetotaller and disapproved of smoking and gambling. He was described as a man of resolute will and deep conviction who 'liked neither fools nor knaves', and was reluctant to compromise. He had a reputation of being somewhat humourless, but to celebrate his hundredth birthday he took his employees to Blackpool, where he was pictured doing the palais glide with mill girls.

In 1889 Taylor started his political career when he was elected, for three years, to the new West Riding county council. In 1900 he was invited by Herbert Gladstone, son of the Liberal leader, to stand for parliament. He successfully fought the constituency of Radcliffe-cum-Farnworth, which he represented for eighteen years. He supported old-age pensions in his maiden speech at the budget debate of April 1901, and worked behind the scenes in the Liberal government supporting the principle of pensions. In spite of the difficulties of his industry, he was a strong advocate of free trade. His major political contribution, however, was in the anti-opium crusade. He opposed the majority report of the opium commission set up in 1893 and successfully moved a private member's ballot opposing the trade. He visited China in 1907 to see its effects at first hand, and continued his campaign to 1917, when the government finally released China from its treaty obligations to admit Indian opium.

Taylor was an inveterate traveller, for pleasure and for business, visiting many of the markets to which his cloth was sent. He toured Europe at the age of seventeen. In his late nineties he made an extensive tour of North America to sell cloth, the last of his twenty-four crossings of the Atlantic. He died at the age of 102, on 19 October 1952, from the after-effects of a heavy cold, at his home, The Moraine, Grassington; he was buried at Batley.

D. T. JENKINS

Sources G. A. Greenwood, *Taylor of Batley: the story of 102 years* (1957) · T. C. Taylor, *One hundred years: records, recollections and reflections* (1946) · D. Boothroyd, 'Taylor, Theodore Cooke', *DBB* · S. Pollard and R. Turner, 'Profit sharing and autocracy: the case of J. T. and J. Taylor of Batley, woollen manufacturers, 1892–1966', *Business History*, 18 (1976), 4–34 · *CGPLA Eng. & Wales* (1953)

Archives Sheffield University, business records of J. T. and J. Taylor

Likenesses photograph, repro. in Greenwood, *Taylor of Batley*, jacket

Wealth at death £185,233 0s. 5d.: probate, 9 Feb 1953, *CGPLA Eng. & Wales*

Taylor, Thomas (1576–1632), Church of England clergyman, was born at Richmond, Yorkshire, where, according to the account of his life in the 1653 edition of his works, his father was the recorder; both his parents were zealous supporters of the puritan cause. In 1592 he matriculated from Christ's College, Cambridge, where he graduated BA in 1595, proceeded MA in 1598, and was a fellow from 1599 to 1604 and Wentworth Hebrew lecturer from 1601 to 1604. For a time he was probably chaplain to William, Lord

Russell of Thornhaugh, to whom in 1606 he dedicated his edition of William Perkins's *Exposition upon … Jude*. Taylor was a prominent member of the group of Perkins's disciples who came to embody the mainstream of moderate puritan divinity in early Stuart Britain. He had entered the pulpit at the age of twenty-one and preached at Paul's Cross before Elizabeth I and James I, but he soon clashed with the emerging anti-Calvinist wing of churchman. At the university church in Cambridge he sharply attacked Archbishop Bancroft's campaign against puritan ministers. Samuel Harsnett, conducting Bancroft's metropolitan visitation in 1608, silenced Taylor and threatened him with degradation.

Taylor left Cambridge, but it is not clear what benefices, if any, he held for the next seventeen years. By 1612 he was preaching at Watford, Hertfordshire, and he also preached frequently at Reading, where from 1616 his younger brother Theophilus was pastor at St Laurence's, and where Taylor himself directed a puritan seminary, 'a little nursery of young Preachers' ('Life', sig. B2v). He was evidently not without patrons and used what he called his 'silent time' for writing, notably his massive *A Commentarie upon … Titus* (1612), published in a second, enlarged edition in 1619. His *Davids Learning* (1617) was dedicated to William Knollys, Viscount Wallingford, then master of the court of wards. The dedication, in which Taylor refers to himself as 'one who you pleased to favour as a soules Physician' (sig. A1r), reads like an effort to urge Wallingford back to the protestant cause upheld by his father, the Elizabethan courtier Sir Francis Knollys. Taylor's *Christ's Combat* (1618) was dedicated to the courtier's younger son and namesake.

At some point Taylor served as chaplain to Edward Conway, secretary of state from 1623 and later first Viscount Conway. Sharing Conway's anti-Spanish outlook, Taylor spoke out firmly against James I's plans for a Spanish marriage for his heir. Reminding his readers in *A Mappe of Rome* (1620) of 'how insatiable [Rome] hath alwaies been … of English Blood', he could not 'thinke we can be so inconsiderate as to dreame of any toleration' for English Catholics (p. 2). In two sermons, published in 1624 with a bold preface to MPs then in session, he roundly denounced anyone who proposed allying England and Spain, reconciling protestants and Roman Catholics, or advocating moderation towards Catholics anywhere. Their religion consisted of 'filthy and formall Idolatry', and he warned that 'whosoever communicates in the sinne of this Westerne Babel' would certainly 'drinke of the wine-presse of the wrath of God' (*Two Sermons*, 1624, sigs. E3r, E4r).

In 1625 Taylor accepted a call made on 22 January to be lecturer and curate at St Mary Aldermanbury, London, one of the few city parishes in which the vestry owned the advowson and a rare but potent model 'of a congregational polity within the Established Church' (Seaver, 138). His parishioners there included Conway's son-in-law, Sir Robert Harley, to whom Taylor dedicated his 1630 treatise, *The Progresse of Saints*. As in Reading, he kept a puritan seminary, and he continued to be active in the protestant cause. In 1627 Taylor joined William Gouge, Richard

Sibbes, and John Davenport in an effort to raise funds to relieve the Palatinate's Calvinist preachers. In 1628 they were reprimanded by the court of high commission and the new bishop of London, William Laud, for this meddling in affairs of state. However, the same year efforts by the anti-Calvinist Bishop Matthew Wren of Ely to block the grant of Taylor's Cambridge DD were defeated, probably with help from Conway.

Although in his many published works Taylor was indeed 'an iron pillar and a brazen wall against Popery and Arminianisme' ('Life', sig. B3r), his opposition to separatism and antinomianism was no less vigorous. Admitting that the Church of England was not 'free from all blemish and spotte', he nevertheless insisted that whoever doubted that 'in our assemblies wee have God present teaching his people' is 'as blinde as a Mole, and palpably deluded' (T. Taylor, *The Beawties of Beth-El*, 1609, 80–81). His much admired *Regula vitae* (1635) opposed 'our new audacious Antinomists, and Libertines, and Familists' because he found some members of his own flock 'looking that way' (sigs. A4v–A5r). Wood called Taylor 'an illuminated doctor' for his skill at 'opening an allegory' (Wood, *Ath. Oxon.: Fasti*, 1.457): his *Christ Revealed* (1635)—republished in 1653 as *Moses and Aaron*—was an early manual of typology that influenced many English and North American theologians in the seventeenth century. Taylor was liberal with charitable gifts 'without sounding of the Trumpet' ('True relation', sig. A4r); in 1629 he had given £15 to the aldermen and burgesses of his birthplace 'to be laid out yearly in coals for the use of the poor people' (C. Clarkson, *The History of Richmond*, 1814, 208). His will, made on 8 February 1631 when he was in good health, made careful provision for his wife, Anne, for his sons, Francis and Samuel, for his four daughters, for several siblings, and for the poor of St Mary Aldermanbury. He died of pleurisy in 1632 (his will was proved by his widow on 15 May) but went to his grave 'much cheered in his spirits for the great successes' of Gustavus Adolphus of Sweden against the Habsburgs ('Life', sig. B3v). He was buried at St Mary Aldermanbury after a funeral sermon preached by William Jemmat, Taylor's former assistant at Reading and the editor of several of his works, including *Christ's Victorie over the Dragon* (1633) and *Christ Revealed, or, The Old Testament Explained* (1635). In 1653 Edmund Calamy and eleven other leading puritan ministers brought out the first of several collections of Taylor's works (including previously unpublished ones), noting that 'the iniquity of the former times' had denied 'such births … a kindly delivery' (ibid., sig. B1v).

J. SEARS MCGEE

Sources 'The life of Dr. Taylor', *The works of … Dr. Thom. Taylor* (1653) · 'The true relation … of Doctor Thomas Taylor', *The works of … Thomas Taylor* (1659), vol. 2 · S. Clarke, *The lives of thirty two English divines*, in *A general martyrologie*, 3rd edn (1677) · Venn, *Alum. Cant.* · J. Peile, *Biographical register of Christ's College, 1505–1905, and of the earlier foundation, God's House, 1448–1505*, ed. [J. A. Venn], 1 (1910) · Foster, *Alum. Oxon.* · P. S. Seaver, *The puritan lectureships: the politics of religious dissent, 1560–1662* (1970) · R. Newcourt, *Repertorium ecclesiasticum parochiale Londinense*, 1 (1708) · G. Hennessy, *Novum repertorium ecclesiasticum parochiale Londinense, or, London diocesan clergy succession from the earliest time to the year 1898* (1898) · Wood,

Ath. Oxon.: Fasti (1815), 457 • J. B. Mullinger, *The University of Cambridge*, 2 (1884) • C. Coates, *The history and antiquities of Reading* (1802) • will, PRO, PROB 11/161, fols. 464v, 465r • B. Brook, *The lives of the puritans*, 2 (1813) • T. Cogswell, *The blessed revolution: English politics and the coming of war, 1621–1624* (1989) • A. Milton, *Catholic and Reformed: the Roman and protestant churches in English protestant thought, 1600–1640* (1995) • K. Fincham, *Prelate as pastor: the episcopate of James I* (1990) • T. Webster, *Godly clergy in early Stuart England: the Caroline puritan movement, c.1620–1643* (1997)

Likenesses W. Marshall, line engraving, c.1632, BM, NPG • engraving, repro. in Clarke, *The lives of thirty two English divines*, 125 • line engraving, NPG; repro. in T. Taylor, *The Parable of the Sower and the Seed* (1634)

Wealth at death significant: will, PRO, PROB 11/161, fols. 464v, 465r

Taylor, Thomas (1617/18–1682), Quaker minister and writer, was born at Carlton near Skipton in Craven, on the borders of Yorkshire and Westmorland, probably the son of Thomas Taylor of Ravenstonedale, Westmorland. Like his brother Christopher *Taylor he was educated at Oxford and became a clergyman before eventually moving to Quakerism. He was licensed to preach and became lecturer at Richmond, Yorkshire, after which he was curate of the chapel of Preston Patrick in Westmorland, and preached in neighbouring places. A strong puritan, he moved well beyond godly orthodoxy and refused to baptize his own children, and in 1650 held a conference or disputation on baptism with three neighbouring ministers in Kendal church. He also refused to receive maintenance from tithes and gradually came to minister to separatists at Preston Patrick, taking only what they were willing to provide. The chapel there became the focus of a Seeker community.

In 1652 Taylor went at Judge Fell's invitation to meet George Fox at Swarthmoor Hall. In reply to Fox's questioning he owned that he had never been called to preach as the apostles had been. Fox noted in his journal that Taylor was convinced about this time and accompanied him into Westmorland, where at Crosscrake chapel he was moved to speak of his state prior to conversion. Although he had a wife, Elizabeth (d. 1682), and five or six children, Taylor resigned his benefice and 'travelled up and down in many parts of England, preaching the word of the Lord, and his gospel freely' (Fox, 'Testimony'). His itinerant work took him to south Lancashire, the midlands, and Yorkshire. Once when returning to Richmond:

> he was made to go there, and turn his back to the priest, and put his hands to both his ears and stop them, as a sign, how God had stopped his ears unto their sacrifice, and service, and offering. (ibid.)

In September 1653 Taylor was taken prisoner at Appleby for speaking in the church. He was released in 1655 but was again in Appleby gaol, possibly in 1656 (though this may well be confused with an earlier or later imprisonment) and certainly from August 1657 to August 1658 after he refused to pay the fine of 5 marks imposed on him for abusing Francis Higginson, the fiercely anti-Quaker vicar of Kirkby Stephen, when the latter was preaching at Appleby. Taylor had shouted at him, 'Come down, lyar, for thou speakes contrary to the doctrin of Christ, for Christ hath said, sweare not at all' (Raine, 79). He was also imprisoned at York, Richmond, Leicester, Worcester, and Coventry. At the Stafford assizes in 1662 he incurred a sentence of *praemunire* for refusing to swear the oaths of allegiance, and was imprisoned for more than ten years. His wife hired a house nearby where he was sometimes allowed to go to be with his family. He was also permitted to write books and teach children, but was not released until the general pardon granted by Charles II in March 1672. In 1679 he was fined £20 for preaching to two or three friends in a house in Keele and was again imprisoned in Stafford gaol. He died from a 'distemper' at Stafford on 18 March 1682 in his sixty-fifth year; his wife, Elizabeth, died the following December. He was buried in Stafford on 21 March.

Taylor was a man of some learning and a great admirer of Jakob Boehme. He wrote prolifically and his collected works, entitled *Truth's Innocency and Simplicity* (1697), contains numerous addresses, warnings, and exhortations. Many of these are short testimonies against sports and amusements such as bear- and bull-baiting, maypoles, bells, bonfires, and lotteries, which Taylor believed to be cruel, or a waste of valuable time, and heathen in origin. Some of his longer tracts are also of interest, such as *Ignorance and Error Refuted* (1662) which is an answer to the arguments of the ejected minister of Wolverhampton, John Reynolds, and outlines the Quaker position on various issues, for example the sufficiency of the inner light and the role of scripture in Friends' thought. He attacked Richard Baxter's *The Cure of Church-Divisions*, describing the author as 'a Man who (through a shew of Learning and Religion) had gotten in Oliver Cromwell's Days, a great Esteem in the Minds of the Ignorantly zealous professors of Religion in this Nation' (Taylor, *Truth's Innocency*, 201). Taylor in turn drew upon himself the fire of Lodowick Muggleton, who both attacked him in print and pronounced a curse upon him for the critical marginalia he had written in a Muggletonian book which he had been lent by a convert from Quakerism.

Taylor's collected works contain numerous valuable testimonies to his life, including those from his son Thomas and daughter Hannah, and that from his brother Christopher, who wrote of him, 'the course of his life was eminently exemplary, so grave, tender and humble he was, and self-denying' (C. Taylor, 'Testimony'). A further testimony, from Robert Barrow, describes Thomas Taylor as 'comely … fair and ruddy' (Barrow, 'Testimony').

CHARLOTTE FELL-SMITH, *rev.* CAROLINE L. LEACHMAN

Sources G. Fox, 'A testimony concerning Thomas Taylor', in *Truth's innocency and simplicity shining through the conversion … of … Thomas Taylor* (1697) • R. Barrow, 'Testimony concerning Thomas Taylor', in *Truth's innocency and simplicity shining through the conversion … of … Thomas Taylor* (1697) • *The journal of George Fox*, ed. N. Penney, 2 vols. (1911) • W. C. Braithwaite, *The beginnings of Quakerism*, ed. H. J. Cadbury, 2nd edn (1955); repr. (1981) • W. C. Braithwaite, *The second period of Quakerism*, ed. H. J. Cadbury, 2nd edn (1961); repr. (1979) • J. Besse, *A collection of the sufferings of the people called Quakers*, 1 (1753) • J. Smith, ed., *A descriptive catalogue of Friends' books*, 2 (1867) • C. Taylor, 'Testimony concerning Thomas Taylor', in *Truth's innocency and simplicity shining through the conversion … of … Thomas Taylor* (1697) • T. Taylor, 'Testimony concerning his father', in *Truth's innocency and simplicity shining through the conversion … of … Thomas Taylor*

(1697) · W. Fallowfield, 'Testimony concerning Thomas Taylor', in *Truth's innocency and simplicity shining through the conversion … of … Thomas Taylor* (1697) · digest registers of births, marriages, and burials, RS Friends, Lond. · L. Muggleton, *A letter sent to Thomas Taylor, Quaker, in the year 1664* (1665) · *DNB* · J. Raine, ed., *Depositions from the castle of York relating to offences committed in the northern counties in the seventeenth century*, SurtS, 40 (1861), 79, 87 · *CSP dom., 1658–9* · Foster, *Alum. Oxon., 1500–1714* [Christopher Taylor]

Archives RS Friends, Lond., Swarthmore MSS, vol. 1: 8, 15, 16, 17, 18, 19, 20, 21 (MS vol. 351); vol. 3: 27, 28, 29, 30, 31, 32, 140a (MS vol. 354); vol. 4: 43 (MS vols. 355–6)

Taylor, Thomas (1738–1816), Methodist preacher, son of Thomas Taylor, a tanner, was born on 11 November 1738 at Rothwell, Yorkshire, and raised as a Presbyterian. His parents died before he was six years old, and he proved careless and headstrong as a youth. At seventeen he was impressed by George Whitefield's preaching, but soon reverted to his old lifestyle. Three years later he was 'convinced of sin', joined the Methodists, and began to preach. Wesley met him at Birstall in 1761 and invited him to attend that year's conference in London, where he was appointed the first itinerant preacher of the connexion in Wales. During his fifty-five years as a travelling preacher he saw hard service, with privations and persecution in Wales, England, Ireland, and Scotland (where he pioneered Methodist work in Glasgow). He was one of the inner circle of preachers on whom Wesley relied in the last decade of his life. He was president of the conference in 1796, when Alexander Kilham, founder of the Methodist New Connexion, was expelled from the society, and again in 1816.

In 1767 Taylor had married, at Chester, Nancy, the granddaughter of a Huguenot refugee. James Everett described him as:

> Large in person; ordinary features. Good understanding; a useful preacher; matter, manner, and style homely, though not coarse … voice a little husky, and natural temper short and peevish, but subdued by divine grace … with few drawbacks, a fine specimen of the old school. (Everett, 1.345–6)

A man of little formal education, Taylor had by hard study mastered Latin, Greek, and Hebrew. He published numerous sermons, controversial tracts, including *An Answer to Paine's 'Age of Reason'* (1796), and a detailed *History of the Waldenses and Albigenses* (1793). He died at Birch House, near Bolton, Lancashire, on 13 October 1816. His desire, expressed in his last sermon shortly before his death, 'to die, like an old soldier, sword in hand', was granted, and James Montgomery's poem ('The Christian Soldier's Death') conveys his indomitable spirit:

> Servant of God! well done,
> Rest from thy lov'd employ.
> (*Methodist Magazine*, 474)

JOHN A. NEWTON

Sources T. Jackson, ed., *The lives of early Methodist preachers, chiefly written by themselves*, 3rd edn, 6 vols. (1865–6) · J. Everett, *Wesleyan takings*, 2 vols. (1841) · L. Tyerman, *The life and times of the Rev. John Wesley*, 3 vols. (1870–71) · *Methodist Magazine*, 39 (1816), 474–6

Archives JRL, Methodist Archives and Research Centre, corresp. and papers; letters

Likenesses W. Ridley, stipple (aged fifty-eight), BM; repro. in *Arminian Magazine* (1797) · engraving, repro. in *Wesley and his successors: a centenary memorial* (1891), 77

Taylor, Thomas (1753–1806). *See under* White Conduit cricket club (*act. c.*1785–1788).

Taylor, Thomas (1758–1835), philosopher and translator, was born on 15 May 1758 near Bunhill Fields, London, the son of Joseph Taylor, staymaker, of Round Court, St Martin's-le-Grand; details of his mother are unknown. He was sickly as a child and spent some years in Staffordshire, but on 10 April 1767 he was admitted to St Paul's School, his parents intending him for the dissenting ministry. There he evinced an aptitude for philosophical studies, and began his acquaintance with classical languages, but his dissatisfaction with the teaching at the school, together with his disinclination for the Christian ministry, led to his withdrawal from the school after a few years. At about this time he fell in love with Mary Morton (d. 1809), whom he later married. During this period at home he began his study of mathematics. When he was fifteen Taylor was sent to work for an uncle at the dockyard at Sheerness, which he left after three years. The next two years were spent as a pupil of Mr Worthington of Salters' Hall meeting-house, where he revived his knowledge of Greek and Latin, while at the same time paying court to his future wife, and deepening his knowledge of mathematics. The time came for him to go to the University of Aberdeen, but the discovery by their parents of his precipitate marriage to Mary Morton required him to seek employment, first as a boarding-school usher, and later as a bank clerk at Lubbock's Bank. At that time they moved south of the Thames to 9 Manor Place, Walworth.

During this period Taylor in his spare moments embarked on his study of philosophy, beginning with Aristotle and then moving to Plato, both of whom he studied in the original, seeking guidance from ancient commentaries, mainly of Neoplatonic inspiration. After six years as a bank clerk Taylor sought escape by drawing on his studies to devise a perpetual lamp. The demonstration at the Freemasons' Tavern was disastrous, but brought him to the attention of potential patrons and thus enabled him to devote his time to the study of ancient philosophy. His next public enterprise was a series of twelve lectures on Platonic philosophy at the house of the sculptor John Flaxman. In Flaxman's circle he may very well have met William Blake, though there is no positive evidence of their personal acquaintance. In 1787 he began to publish translations of works of ancient philosophy, beginning with the earliest of Plotinus's *Enneads* (i.6), on the 'beautiful', and the 'Orphic hymns', this latter with a lengthy preface on the life and theology of Orpheus. Various of these translations were subsidized by patrons, for instance his translation of Aristotle's *Metaphysics* (1801) by the brothers William and George Meredith. However, his most notable early patron was Charles Howard, eleventh duke of Norfolk, who made it possible for Taylor to publish the first English translation of the complete works of Plato (1804), revising and completing the work begun by

Floyer Sydenham (1710–1787), whom he had known in his latter years.

In 1797 Taylor obtained the post of assistant secretary to the Society of Arts, which he resigned in 1806 to devote himself more completely to translation. While working on his translation of Plato, Taylor visited Oxford, where he was graciously received, though he felt himself the object of condescension on the part of the dons and was depressed by the 'monkish gloom' and 'black melancholy' of the university (letter dated 20 June 1802, Raine, 20n.). These translations were followed by many others, including the works of the later Neoplatonists, such as Plotinus, his disciple Porphyry, Iamblichus, Julian the Apostate, Synesius the Christian bishop, but especially Proclus, as well as the religious sources of their philosophy, for example, the Chaldaean oracles.

Taylor's approach to this philosophy was determined by his initial encounter with it, through reading Aristotle and Plato together with the Neoplatonic commentaries, which encouraged an understanding of the essential unity of Aristotle and Plato, provided by their Neoplatonic interpretation. His approach then flew in the face of what understanding there was of classical philosophy; even someone like Samuel Taylor Coleridge, more sympathetic than most to later Neoplatonism, was profoundly convinced of the fundamental contrast between Plato and Aristotle. Taylor's translations were received with almost uniform derision, which focused on his awkward English and his evident enthusiasm for late Neoplatonism (not least its defence of paganism). Even Coleridge said that with Taylor 'difficult Greek is transmuted into incomprehensible English' (*Notebooks*, n. 1740), and when Stephen MacKenna undertook his acclaimed translation of Plotinus's *Enneads* he confessed 'for reasons mainly literary, that the work of this devoted pioneer would not be helpful' (Plotinus, 1.114). It was to be many years before Taylor's enthusiasm for later Neoplatonism would find any kind of echo in the world of scholarship.

Taylor was also lampooned as 'the modern Platonist' in Isaac Disraeli's novel *Vaurien* (1797), and is perhaps the model for Sipsop the Pythagorean in Blake's *An Island in the Moon*; in both cases fun is made of his fondness for animals, especially cats. (An earlier publication had been his *Vindication of the Rights of Brutes* (1792), written in response to Mary Wollstonecraft's *Vindication … of Men* (1790), in which he asserted the rationality of animals.) Other nicknames included the Platonist, and the (English) Pagan. It was said of Taylor that there was 'nothing remarkable in his exterior', and that he was of 'middle size […] regular, open and benevolent' of countenance (Welsh, 133). However, his surviving portrait, by Sir Thomas Lawrence, with his large eyes and thick eyebrows, makes him look rather hawkish.

It was through Taylor's translations that the Romantic poets had access to Platonism: they are probably one of the sources of Blake's mythology, as well as his repudiation of the natural science of Bacon and Newton, and his late tempera painting *The Arlington Court Picture* was almost certainly inspired by Taylor's translation of Porphyry's *On the Cave of the Nymphs*; there is no doubt that Coleridge's acquaintance with Proclus was assisted by Taylor's translation and commentary, though Coleridge's appreciation of Taylor is invariably laced with acid criticism. Taylor's immediate influence in England was short-lived; only at the end of the century did those with an enthusiasm for ancient Gnosticism, such as G. R. S. Mead, revive his memory. His fate in America was very different. R. W. Emerson read Taylor's translations enthusiastically, and Taylor's influence was felt among Emerson's disciples, adepts of 'transcendental philosophy' such as Amos Bronson Alcott, William T. Harris, Thomas M. Johnson, Hiram K. Jones, and Thomas Wentworth Higginson, though that influence had waned by the end of the century. Emily Dickinson, who was a friend of Higginson, therefore probably owed her Platonism ultimately to Thomas Taylor.

Taylor's marriage to his childhood sweetheart ended with her death on 1 April 1809; they had two daughters and four sons, the youngest of whom was called Thomas Proclus. Taylor married again, and had more children; his second wife died on 23 April 1823. He died of a disease of the bladder at Walworth on 1 November 1835, and was buried on 6 November in the graveyard of St Mary's, Newington Butts, London.   ANDREW LOUTH

Sources DNB · *Thomas Taylor the Platonist: selected writings*, ed. K. Raine and G. M. Harper (1969) · K. Raine, 'Thomas Taylor in England', in *Thomas Taylor the Platonist: selected writings*, ed. K. Raine and G. M. Harper (1969), 3–48 · G. M. Harper, 'Thomas Taylor in America', in *Thomas Taylor the Platonist: selected writings*, ed. K. Raine and G. M. Harper (1969), 49–102 · 'Mr Taylor the Platonist', *Public Characters of 1798* (1798–9); repr. in *Thomas Taylor the Platonist: selected writings*, ed. K. Raine and G. M. Harper (1969), 105–21 · J. J. W. [J. J. Welsh], 'A brief notice of Mr. Thomas Taylor the celebrated Platonist', in *Thomas Taylor the Platonist: selected writings*, ed. K. Raine and G. M. Harper (1969), 131–2 · W. E. A. Axon, 'Thomas Taylor the Platonist: a biographical and bibliographical sketch', *The Library*, 2 (1890), 245–50, 292–300; repr. in *Thomas Taylor the Platonist: selected writings*, ed. K. Raine and G. M. Harper (1969), 122–32 · *The notebooks of Samuel Taylor Coleridge*, ed. K. Coburn, 1: *1794–1804* (1957), notes · Plotinus, *The ethical treatises*, trans. S. MacKenna, 1 (1926)

Archives BL, working page of one of subject's works · Hist. Soc. Penn., letter · RSA, letter

Likenesses T. Lawrence, oils, exh. RA 1812, National Gallery of Canada, Ottawa · R. Evans, oils (after Lawrence), NPG · bust (after photograph)

Taylor, Thomas (1786–1848), botanist and physician, was born on 10 May 1786 in a boat on the Ganges River in India, the eldest in the family of at least six children of Joseph Irwin Taylor (1765–1811), a wealthy major in the Bengal artillery of the East India Company, and his wife, an Indian woman known as Poor Begum. The Taylor family, freethinking Unitarians, had settled near Kenmare in co. Kerry in 1650 and Taylor's grandfather had inherited the townland of Dunkerron. About 1793 Taylor was sent back to Ireland for schooling—he attended the French School at Cork. He proceeded to Trinity College, Dublin, graduating BA, in 1807, MB, and MD in 1814. He married his cousin Harriet, daughter of Colonel Thomas Taylor, on 6 September 1809. She had also been born in India and educated in Ireland; they later had two sons and a daughter.

Taylor remained in Dublin after his graduation; he was physician-in-ordinary to Sir Patrick Dun's Hospital until 1820, when he was appointed professor of natural history in the Royal Cork Scientific Institution. In 1830 he retired to the family property at Dunkerron where he lived in increasingly declining circumstances as physician, magistrate, and farmer. During the 1840s he was physician to the union workhouse at Kenmare until he contracted the 'fever' and died at his home on 4 February 1848. He was buried in the protestant cemetery at Neddeen.

Taylor was a member of the Royal Irish Academy, and became a fellow of the Linnean Society in 1813. His chief interests were botanical, especially bryophytes (both mosses and liverworts) and lichens, on which he published thirty-four papers or books, some of which were collaborative works with either William Jackson Hooker or Joseph Dalton Hooker. His major works included *Muscologia Britannica* (with W. J. Hooker) in 1818; 'Lichenes' in Mackay's *Flora Hibernica* of 1836 (the first major Irish lichen flora); and significant contributions, with J. D. Hooker, on southern hemisphere hepatics and lichens collected by Hooker on his Antarctic voyage of 1839–43. Taylor's herbarium, purchased in 1849 by the wealthy Bostonian, John Amory Lovell, passed to the Boston Society of Natural History, and then to the Farlow Herbarium of Cryptogamic Botany at Harvard. Taylor, either alone or in collaboration with the Hookers described more than 800 new cryptogamic species. His name is commemorated in the moss genus *Tayloria*, named by W. J. Hooker in 1816.

D. J. GALLOWAY

Sources G. Sayre, 'Biographical sketch of Thomas Taylor', *Journal of Bryology*, 14 (1987), 415–27 · G. Sayre, 'A Thomas Taylor bibliography', *Journal of Bryology*, 12 (1983), 461–70 · D. L. Hawksworth and M. R. D. Seaward, *Lichenology in the British Isles, 1568–1975* (1977) · W. J. Hooker, 'Death of Doctor Thomas Taylor', *Journal of Botany*, 7 (1848), 162–3 · Burke, *Gen. GB* (1858)

Archives Harvard U., Farlow Herbarium, herbarium | NHM, cryptogamic herbarium

Likenesses silhouette, priv. coll.; repro. in Sayre, 'Biographical sketch', 415

Wealth at death owned estate of Dunkerron, near Kenmare, co. Kerry: Sayre, 'Biographical sketch', 415–27

Taylor, Thomas (1932–1958). *See under* Busby Babes (*act.* 1953–1958).

Taylor, Thomas Edward (1811–1883), politician, was born at Ardgillan Castle, Dublin, on 25 March 1811, eldest son of the Revd Henry Edward Taylor (1768–1852), fifth son of Thomas Taylor, first earl of Bective and first marquess of Headfort, and his wife, Marianne (*d.* 1859), daughter of the Hon. Richard St Leger. He was educated at Eton College and commissioned in 1829 in the 6th dragoon guards, from which he retired as captain in 1846. From 1847 to 1874 he was lieutenant-colonel of the Royal Meath militia and subsequently honorary colonel. On 11 November 1862 he married Louisa (*d.* 1928), second daughter of Hugh Francis Tollemache, rector of Harrington, and granddaughter of Louisa Tollemache, countess of Dysart. They had three sons and two daughters.

In 1841 Taylor was elected as a Conservative MP for Dublin county and represented it until his death. From 1853 he was an assistant whip for the protectionist tories under Sir William Jolliffe, whom he succeeded as chief whip in 1860. He was a lord of the Treasury in the second Derby ministry in 1858–9 and became parliamentary secretary of the Treasury in the Conservative ministry formed in July 1866. In November 1868 he became briefly chancellor of the duchy of Lancaster. In 1873 he was recalled as whip, during the illness of the chief whip, Gerard Noel. He resumed the post of chancellor of the duchy of Lancaster in the second Disraeli ministry. In the by-election caused by his appointment he was opposed by Charles Stewart Parnell, but his vote was nearly twice Parnell's. He was bitter when he failed to get a peerage in 1880.

Taylor was given credit for the defeat of the Palmerston government on Thomas Milner Gibson's vote of censure in February 1858, and, by Disraeli himself, for his work during the Reform Bill debates of 1867. He promoted party organization in the constituencies, and his responsibility for the party's central fund led to his citation in election petitions. In the 1850s he held that a revival of tory fortunes depended on the adoption of distinctive policies. He warned, when Derby was trying to form a cabinet in February 1855, that the adhesion of Gladstone would offend many protestant tories. He encouraged Disraeli's protestant strategy in the 1868 election. He helped the tory revival in Ireland in the 1850s, and in 1871 recommended home rule as a means of raising Irish support. In 1874 he expected tory gains, but thought they would be greater with the fifteenth earl of Derby as leader. Taylor died on 3 February 1883 at his sister's house at 15 Fitzwilliam Place, Dublin, and was buried in the family vault at Balbriggan, co. Dublin.

E. J. FEUCHTWANGER

Sources Boase, *Mod. Eng. biog.* · *DNB* · Burke, *Peerage* · *Disraeli, Derby and the conservative party: journals and memoirs of Edward Henry, Lord Stanley, 1849–1869*, ed. J. R. Vincent (1978) · R. Stewart, *The foundation of the conservative party, 1830–1867* (1978) · E. J. Feuchtwanger, *Disraeli, democracy and the tory party: conservative leadership and organization after the second Reform Bill* (1968) · Bodl. Oxf., Dep. Hughenden · W. White, *The inner life of the House of Commons*, ed. J. McCarthy, 2 vols. (1897)

Archives BL, letters mainly to Lord Hardwicke, index of MSS IX, 1985 · Bodl. Oxf., Hughenden MSS · Som. ARS, Hylton MSS · Som. ARS, letters to Sir William Jolliffe · W. Yorks. AS, Leeds, letters to Rowland Winn

Likenesses Ape [C. Pellegrini], chromolithograph caricature, NPG; repro. in *VF* (4 July 1874) · W. & D. Downey, carte-de-visite, NPG

Wealth at death £11,078 8s. 8d.—in England: Irish probate resealed in England, 23 May 1883, *CGPLA Eng. & Wales*

Taylor, Thomas Glanville (1804–1848), astronomer, was born at Ashburton, Devon, on 22 November 1804, the son of Thomas Taylor (*b.* 1772) and his wife, Susannah, *née* Glanville. In 1807 his father was employed as an assistant at the Royal Greenwich Observatory, and was persuaded by the astronomer royal, John Pond, to divert his son from an intended career in medicine to one in astronomy. The young Taylor joined the observatory in 1820 and in August 1822 was given responsibility for making the nightly transit observations. His skill and reliability as an observer was such that Sir Edward Sabine recruited him as an assistant in his pendulum observations. Meanwhile, Taylor devoted his spare time to calculations for Groombridge's star catalogue, and also compiled and published ephemerides for some of the asteroids and minor planets.

Taylor's reward for these labours was his appointment as director of the East India Company's observatory at Madras, founded in 1819. He arrived there on 15 September 1830, with a set of apparatus by Dollond consisting of a 5 foot transit, a 4 foot mural circle, and a small equatorial telescope. Early in 1831 he began work with four Indian assistants, whom he trained to maintain the programme of observations during his obligatory absences on the trigonometrical survey of India. He married on 4 July 1832 Eliza Baratty, the daughter of Colonel Eley CSI; they had three sons and a daughter.

In 1837 Taylor began a magnetic survey of southern India with John Caldecott, the astronomer at Trivandrum observatory, with Caldecott taking the western coast and Taylor the eastern; they went south from Madras, taking magnetic observations every 25 miles, crossing the magnetic equator and thence to Trivandrum. By this time they realized that their instruments were defective and, after having repairs effected locally, they took fresh observations on their northward passage, obtaining the first detailed picture of this magnetically important region.

During the years 1831–9 Taylor published five volumes of astronomical observations, and in 1844 issued the *Madras General Catalogue* of 11,015 stars for the epoch 1 January 1835, a production later praised by Sir George Airy as the greatest catalogue of modern times for the number of observations, the number and distribution of stars, and for the fact that the work had been entirely carried out in one place, under Taylor's supervision. His determination of the longitude of Madras was of value to navigators, though in need of further correction when submarine telegraphy made this possible. He also observed Halley's and Wilmot's comets. His observations were generally regarded as the first of satisfactory accuracy from this region.

Taylor visited England in 1840 to restore his health and returned to Madras in 1841. Already a fellow of the Royal Astronomical Society, on 10 February 1842 he was elected fellow of the Royal Society. In the following year, while staying at Trivandrum observatory, his poor sight led to an accident from which he never fully recovered. About 1845 the East India Company dispatched a set of meteorological instruments to him, but it was not until late 1846, when he was convalescing in the Nilgiri hills, that he was able to organize a meteorological station there, at 8640 feet above sea level, with a bungalow for an observer.

Taylor returned to England on 4 April 1848 to see his daughter, who was gravely ill; she died the following day. Taylor himself was suffering from a wasting disease, and he died at 11 Hanover Buildings, All Saints, Southampton, on 4 May 1848. His widow, bereft of support for herself and her young family pending the probate of Taylor's will and the return of his possessions from India, appealed to the East India Company for assistance. She was granted £50 temporary relief, but the company declined further payment.   A. M. CLERKE, *rev.* ANITA MCCONNELL

Sources *Monthly Notices of the Royal Astronomical Society*, 9 (1848–9), 62–3 · C. L. F. André and G. A. P. Rayet, *L' astronomie pratique et les observatoires en Europe et en Amérique*, 2: *Écosse, Irlande et colonies anglaises* (Paris, 1874), 82–4 · T. G. Taylor and J. Caldecott, *Observations on the direction and intensity of the terrestrial magnetic force in southern India* (1839), 1–2 · [T. G. Taylor], *Meteorological observations made at the meteorological bungalow on Dodabetta … in the years 1847–8* (1848), i · E. Mailly, 'Tableau de l'astronomie dans l'hemisphère austral et dans l'Inde', *Mémoires couronnés, l'Académie Royale des Sciences, des Lettres et des Beaux-Arts de Belgique*, coll. in octavo/23 (1873), 124–9 · BL OIOC, B/216, 614, 698–9 · BL OIOC, B/217, 238–9, 292 · BL OIOC, B/271, 84 · will of Thomas Glanville Taylor, BL OIOC · d. cert. · BL OIOC, N/2/15, p. 196

Taylor, Thomas John (1810–1861). *See under* Taylor, Hugh (1789–1868).

Taylor, Sir Thomas Murray (1897–1962), lawyer and university principal, was born at Keith, Banffshire, on 27 May 1897, the only son of John Taylor, farmer and head of a firm of cattle dealers, and his wife, Jenny Nichol Murray. From Keith grammar school he proceeded to the University of Aberdeen as third bursar in 1915. He was rejected from military service owing to a heart condition. He took a first class in classics in 1919 and won the Ferguson scholarship, open to the four Scottish universities. With a political career in mind, he then studied law in Aberdeen, and graduated LLB in 1922 with special distinction in jurisprudence and constitutional law. He read for the bar in Edinburgh, was called in 1924, and took silk in 1945. Passionately concerned for social improvements, he identified himself with the Labour Party and spoke in its interest from 1928. He became prospective Labour candidate for Cathcart in 1930 but resigned in 1931 when he thought it his duty to support the 'national' government. His resignation from the crown office, where he had been junior advocate depute since 1929, was not accepted and in 1934 he was appointed home advocate depute. In 1935, however, he left Edinburgh and was delighted to return to Aberdeen and occupy the chair of law in the university. This office, together with the sheriffdom of Argyll (held from 1945) and Renfrew (from 1946), he resigned in 1948 on his appointment as principal of the university.

In background, career, ability, character, and personality Taylor was ideally fitted to be the principal, and, as their leader, he quickly commanded and never lost the confidence and affection of his colleagues. Throughout his tenure of his chair Taylor had been dean of the faculty of law and he was now at last able to be the means of making his faculty, as he had always wished, a school of study and not merely a legal apprenticeship. The last decade of his principalship was a period of university expansion. He was not a man to shirk the challenge presented by a national need, and he did acquire sites and superintend a large building programme, but he resisted, beyond certain limits, an expansion which might conflict with the traditions of his university and jeopardize the excellence of its work. He cemented the good relations between town and gown in Aberdeen, and one project, ever dear to his heart, the restoration and preservation of Old Aberdeen as a mixed community, he saw coming to fulfilment shortly before his death.

Taylor was a highly respected member of the Committee of Vice-Chancellors and Principals, and might have become its chairman had he been prepared to make constant journeys to London. He was the architect and builder of an alliance between the Scottish and the Scandinavian universities, and this work was recognized in 1954 by the conferment of the Swedish order of the North Star. In the same year he was knighted. He was appointed CBE in 1944. He was an honorary DD of Edinburgh (1952) and an honorary LLD of St Andrews (1950) and Glasgow (1960). He frequently served as chairman of committees on wages questions and other matters of social concern, but what most excited his imagination was his chairmanship of the Crofters' Commission (1951–4), for he had long wanted to do something to preserve the crofting way of life. Always liberal at heart, he came more and more to put the welfare of Scotland above the narrower issues of party politics.

In 1939 Taylor married an Aberdeen graduate in medicine, whom he had known since their student days together: Helen Margaret, daughter of David Little Jardine, minister of Durisdeer. They adopted a son in 1944 and a daughter in 1945. The happiness of his home was one of the two rocks on which Taylor's life was built. The other was his religion. As he said in one of his sermons (published in *Where One Man Stands*, 1960), he was 'intellectually convinced of the truth of the Christian faith'. He learned that faith in boyhood, joined the United Free Church in Keith, and there was ordained an elder in the Church of Scotland in 1936. Loyal to his own church, and a frequent attender and speaker at its general assembly, he yet had wide sympathies, especially with other protestant churches. He was a member of the executive committee of the World Council of Churches (1948–54); from 1955 he chaired its commission on the prevention of war in an atomic age and was one of the two authors of its report (1961). His ecumenical work had taken him to Amsterdam, Geneva, and even to India, but he often enjoyed continental holidays, especially in north Italy. His faith found expression in sermons delivered, mainly to undergraduates, in King's College chapel, Aberdeen, and elsewhere. No one who heard him preach could fail to be moved by his rigorous argument and the ringing tone of his profound conviction. The same conviction, together with his reflections on law and government, comes out in *The Discipline of Virtue* (1954), his Riddell lectures in the University of Durham.

Tom Taylor (as his friends knew him) had a lovely smile and a beautiful voice; he was a fine singer, whether of hymns in the college choir or of songs at parties in his ever hospitable home; and he loved playing golf. Tall and handsome, he was gay and humorous too when he relaxed with his friends. He could be severe, especially with culprits who tried to shuffle off responsibility for their actions; deceit could not look him in the face. He was free of pomposity, warm-hearted, and loved his fellow men, because,

as he would have said, he loved God first. He himself was much loved not only by his intimates but by countless Scots in every walk of life.

Taylor died in Aberdeen on 19 July 1962. His wife survived him. T. M. KNOX, *rev.*

Sources A. M. Hunter and W. Lillie, *Speaking to graduates* (1965) · private information (1981) · personal knowledge (1981) · *The Times* (20 July 1962) · *WWW* · *CCI* (1963)
Archives U. Aberdeen, corresp. and papers
Likenesses G. Barron, bronze bust, c.1958, U. Aberdeen
Wealth at death £29,812 11s. 8d.: confirmation, 15 Jan 1963, *CCI*

Taylor, Sir Thomas Weston Johns (1895–1953), chemist and university administrator, was born in Little Ilford, Essex, on 2 October 1895, the only son of Thomas George Taylor, accountant, and his wife, Alice Bessie Aston Johns. He was educated at the City of London School and at Brasenose College, Oxford. His studies were interrupted by the First World War, during which he served in the Essex regiment, in France and at Gallipoli, and was twice wounded. He obtained a first-class degree in chemistry and was elected fellow of his college in 1920, and became university lecturer in organic chemistry in 1927. In 1931 he was a Rhodes travelling fellow. In 1922 he married Rosamund Georgina, younger daughter of Colonel Thomas Edward John Lloyd, of Plas Tregaean, Anglesey, and a junior commander in the ATS, who shared his wide interests and introduced him to some new ones, including painting and botany. They had no children.

Taylor was an able and versatile, if not a remarkably original, scientist. In conjunction with W. Baker he edited a new edition (1937) of Sidgwick's *Organic Chemistry of Nitrogen*, and with A. F. Millidge he edited the second volume of Richter–Anschütz, *The Chemistry of the Carbon Compounds* (1939). He contributed a number of papers to the *Journal of the Chemical Society*, and served on its council from 1936 to 1939. His greatest ability, however, lay in teaching. He had a genius for communicating enthusiasm as well as knowledge, both at undergraduate and postgraduate levels. Indeed, some of his research students subsequently achieved great distinction.

Although Taylor sometimes expressed regret that he had not himself reached the highest academic honours, the range of his interests was simply too wide to have allowed it. He was a capable field naturalist, with an encyclopaedic knowledge of the flora and fauna of many parts of the world; he took part in two important ecological investigations, in Spitsbergen in 1936 and in the Galápagos Islands in 1938–9, and on each occasion his skill in improvising field techniques contributed much to the success of the expedition. Outside the range of the natural sciences, he was a competent amateur in watercolours, a capable amateur musician, a voracious reader, with an open book on every flat surface in his home, and an ardent Francophile—between the wars, he spent most of his long vacations in France.

When war broke out in 1939 Taylor joined the chemical branch of the Royal Engineers. He served for three years in the Middle East and was mentioned in dispatches. In 1943 he was appointed director of the British Central

Scientific Office in Washington, a post for which his wide interests made him well fitted. In Washington the range of his concerns included such unconnected topics as insecticides, the design of paper parachutes for dropping small packages, the prevention of metal corrosion, and the composition of shark repellents. In 1944 he was transferred to south-east Asia command as head of the operational research division. He was appointed CBE in 1946.

Taylor's war experience revealed in him an unsuspected talent for organization, and gave him a taste for life in the tropics. In 1946 he was appointed principal of the proposed University College (later the University) of the West Indies, which was to be sited in Jamaica but to serve all the countries of the British Caribbean. The task posed many difficulties, both political and financial. Taylor assembled a gifted and—under his leadership—closely united senior team. He quickly infected both colleagues and community leaders with his own energy and enthusiasm, and his prodigious capacity for work and talent for improvisation overcame, at least in part, financial stringency. Following the devastating hurricane in 1951, he was instrumental in rebuilding morale and re-invigorating the efforts of staff and students. As a result, the university became a success, a sturdy, growing institution with high academic standards in teaching and research. Taylor was knighted in 1952, the year in which he left Jamaica to become principal of the University College of the South West, later the University of Exeter. However, in the following year he died suddenly on 29 August at the Hotel Rosa, Milan, while on holiday in Italy. His wife survived him.

'T' was a slight, bird-like man, who seemed to irradiate ideas and restless energy. He had a quick, irreverent wit, and was often impatient of people slower than himself. With friends and colleagues he was direct and plain in speech, sometimes to the point of rudeness, but any offence he might have given was quickly removed by his evident warmth and friendliness, and by a quick smile of singular sweetness and charm. His colleagues were said to be devoted to him.   J. H. PARRY, *rev.* PETER OSBORNE

Sources *Nature*, 172 (1953), 652–3 · *The Times* (1 Sept 1953) · *WWW* · private information (1971) · personal knowledge (1971) · *CGPLA Eng. & Wales* (1954)
Likenesses H. Whistler, oils, University of the West Indies
Wealth at death £14,557 9s. 4d.: probate, 6 Jan 1954, *CGPLA Eng. & Wales*

Taylor, Tom (1817–1880), playwright and comic writer, was born on 19 October 1817 in Bishopwearmouth, Sunderland, Durham, the second son of Thomas Taylor (1769–1843) and his wife, Maria Josephina, *née* Arnold (1784–1858). His father rose from farm labourer in Cumberland to partner in a brewery, and his mother was of German ancestry. After attending Sunderland Grange School, Taylor proceeded in 1832 to the University of Glasgow, where he received numerous awards. He entered Trinity College, Cambridge, in 1837, was elected to a scholarship in 1838, and graduated BA in 1840 as junior optime in mathematics, being in the first class in the classical tripos. According to John Sheehan, Taylor was 'the life of his College, and at

Tom Taylor (1817–1880), by London Stereoscopic Co.

the head of the intellectual fun of Trinity' (Sheehan, 148). A member of the University Reform Club, and one of the Apostles, Taylor organized theatricals, and wrote for the Liberal *Cambridge Independent*, and for the short-lived *Cambridge University Magazine*. Elected a fellow of Trinity College in 1842, he proceeded MA in 1843.

Taylor moved to London in 1844, where he served as professor of English at the University of London in 1845 and 1846, kept his terms at the Inner Temple, was called to the bar on 20 November 1846, and established himself as a dramatist and writer. Between 1844 and 1846, the Lyceum Theatre staged at least seven Taylor plays, including burlesques written with Albert Smith and with Charles Kenney, and his first major success, the 1846 comedy *To Parents and Guardians*. He was also composing leaders for the *Morning Chronicle* and the *Daily News*, and writing for *Douglas Jerrold's Illuminated Magazine* and for the comic publication *Puck*. With his first contribution to *Punch* on 19 October 1844, he began a thirty-six year association with the magazine, which ended only with his death.

Taylor made the northern circuit until 1850 when he became assistant secretary of the Board of Health. On its reorganization in 1854, he was appointed secretary, and when its functions were transferred to the local government act office in 1858, Taylor moved too. (He would retire in 1872.) During the 1850s he wrote or co-wrote over thirty comedies, extravaganzas, burlesques, farces, and pantomimes. Most notable were the comedies written with Charles Reade, including *Masks and Faces* in 1852, *Two Loves and a Life* and *The King's Rival* in 1854, and *The First Printer* in 1856. *Still Waters Run Deep*, his 1855 adaptation of a Charles Bernard novelette, was a success for the Olympic Theatre, and his Haymarket comedies included *Victims* in 1857 and *The Contested Election* in 1859. *Our American Cousin*, the play Abraham Lincoln was watching when assassinated in 1865, was a transatlantic success in 1858, largely owing to Edward Askew Southern's performance as Lord Dundreary.

According to Winton Tolles, Taylor in 1860 was 'England's leading and most versatile living dramatist' (Tolles, 188). Despite twenty new productions in the following decade, however, his reputation would decline. *The Overland Route* was a success in 1860, and his 1863 melodrama *The Ticket of Leave Man* was Taylor's most popular play. The melodrama *Mary Warner* and the comedy *New Men and Old Acres* both pleased audiences in 1869, but his dramas do seem to be the work of the 'popular and transient Victorian playwright' Tolles describes (ibid., 220). In later years Taylor wrote a number of verse dramas on historical subjects, including *Twixt Axe and Crown* in 1870, *Jeanne Darc* in 1871, and *Anne Boleyn* in 1876.

Taylor was famous for drawing his plots from other plays and fictions, often French. Ellen Terry fondly called him 'Tom the Adapter' (Terry, 114), and his friend John Coleman admitted that the 'most successful works were not of native growth' (Coleman, 118). Others were less tolerant, and a lengthy public exchange occurred in 1871, when a profile in *The Athenaeum* suggested that Taylor was virtually a plagiarist. Whether new or borrowed, though, his were some of Victorian England's most successful farces, sentimental comedies, melodramas, and historical plays.

The other great constant in Taylor's literary life was *Punch*. During the 1840s he averaged roughly three columns a month; in the 1850s and 1860s this output doubled. His contributions were generally humorous commentary or comic verses on politics, civic news, and the manners of the day. When the first editor of *Punch*, Mark Lemon, died in 1870, Taylor became an unofficial assistant editor to Shirley Brooks, and when Brooks himself died in 1874, Taylor succeeded him. Though according to M. H. Spielmann, the nineteenth-century historian of *Punch*, 'It cannot be said that his editorship was a success' (Spielmann, 340), R. G. G. Price finds it 'surprising to look at the paper he produced and see how much of it lives' (Price, 111). Sir John Tenniel and Gerald Du Maurier were still holding up the artistic side, and Francis Cowley Burnand, who would succeed Taylor as editor, was contributing to the textual side, though, especially during the summer, Taylor and Percival Leigh would find themselves writing almost the entire issue between them. What can perhaps be said is that while *Punch* easily survived Taylor's editorship, under him it became rather sombre and pompous.

As *The Times* art critic from 1857, and *The Graphic* art critic during the 1870s, Taylor was second only to John Ruskin in prominence. Many artists considered Taylor a kind-hearted philistine, fond of modest and sentimental pictures, and unsympathetic to innovation. When he testified during James Whistler's libel proceedings against Ruskin, for instance, Taylor described Whistler's paintings as only one step above delicately tinted wallpaper, earning him a place in that artist's *Gentle Art of Making Enemies*. Taylor edited the posthumous autobiographies of two artists: a rather unsympathetic *Life of Benjamin Robert Haydon* in 1853, and the highly favourable *Autobiographical Recollections by the Late Charles Robert Leslie* in 1860. In 1865 Taylor also completed and published Leslie's manuscript on the *Life and Times of Sir Joshua Reynolds*.

Taylor was of middle height, bearded, with what John Coleman called 'a pugilistic jaw' and 'eyes which glittered like steel' (Coleman, 2.117). Though Ellen Terry praised his 'generous, kindly nature' (Terry, 116), friends like Coleman remembered him as 'bumptious and dictatorial' (Coleman, 2.120). He was 'quick spoken and fidgety', Burnand recalled, 'mighty obstinate and not ordinarily ready to forgive and forget' (Burnand, 2.6, 228). Taylor's energy was legendary. An avid swimmer and rower, a talented amateur actor, and one of the Whitehall Civil Service rifle volunteers, he rose each day at 5 or 6 and wrote for three hours before taking an hour's brisk walk to his Whitehall office from the home he and his wife had built on Lavender Sweep, near Clapham Common, Wandsworth. He had married Laura Wilson Barker (*d*. 1905), the daughter of a Yorkshire clergyman, on 19 June 1855. She wrote music for Taylor's lyrics and plays, and composed her own orchestral works as well. The Taylors' two children, Laura Lucy Arnold and John Wycliffe, inherited their parents' artistic interests.

Lavender Sweep became a gathering place for politicians and artists, with Taylor serving as 'showman, stage manager, chief tumbler, leader of all the revels', as his friend Thomas Hughes put it (Hughes, 299). Taylor's own politics were those of many *Punch* men. A strong Liberal and social reformer, he was nevertheless sceptical and dismissive of working-class movements. And while Spielmann finds 'a decidedly Radical, anti-Beaconsfield, anti-Imperial turn' in the Taylor-edited *Punch* (Spielmann, 99), Price claims that Taylor consciously strove to be more of a 'great Victorian' than his *Punch* peers: 'As the record of his charitable enterprises and public functions extends, one feels he is turning into marble before one's eyes' (Price, 61).

Taylor's literary reputation has always been mixed. Tolles describes him as 'an industrious and sound workman who aimed not at greatness or permanency for himself or his work, but rather at satisfying the demands of the public he so well understood' (Tolles, 273). His *Punch* work, which Price describes as the 'result of long hours and grim determination' (Price, 69), is undistinguished. While admitting his 'punctuality, kindness of heart, open-handed charity, and thorough respectability', Edmund Yates, no friend of *Punch*, remarked that possessing 'such virtues does not qualify a man to be a contributor to a satirical journal' (Yates, 322). Arthur Adrian accurately claims that Taylor 'had a facile pen and could knock off a poem in an hour or two' (Adrian, 39), but Shirley Brooks's diary records an occasion when he asked Taylor 'for a *good* poem' and was pleased to get back 'one better than usual' (Layard, 408–9). Even Taylor's *Punch* obituary praised his industry and kindness, rather than his talent or wit.

Taylor died suddenly at his home, Lavender Sweep, Wandsworth, on 12 July 1880; he was buried in Brompton cemetery three days later.   CRAIG HOWES

Sources W. Tolles, *Tom Taylor and the Victorian drama* (1940) · M. H. Spielmann, *The history of 'Punch'* (1895) · R. G. G. Price, *A history of Punch* (1957) · J. Sheehan, 'Our portrait gallery, second series no. 43: Tom Taylor', *Dublin University Magazine*, 90 (1877), 142–58 · J. Coleman, 'Tom Taylor', *Players and playwrights I have known: a review of the English stage from 1840 to 1880*, 2nd edn, 2 (1890), 117–39 · T. Hughes, 'In memoriam', *Macmillan's Magazine*, 42 (1880), 298–301 · Venn, *Alum. Cant.* · F. C. Burnand, *Records and reminiscences, personal and general*, 2 vols. (1904) · M. Banham, 'Introduction', in [T. Taylor], *Plays by Tom Taylor* (1985) · E. H. Yates, *Fifty years of London life: memoirs of a man of the world* (1885) · E. Terry, *The story of my life* (1908) · A. À Beckett, *The À Becketts of Punch: memories of father and sons* (1903) · A. A. Adrian, *Mark Lemon: first editor of 'Punch'* (1966) · G. S. Layard, *A great Punch editor: being the life, letters, and diaries of Shirley Brooks* (1907) · [T. Purnell], 'Mr Tom Taylor', *The Athenaeum* (3 March 1871), 679; (22 April 1871), 505–6 [see also exchange with Taylor] · *The Times* (13 July 1880) · *Punch*, 79 (1880), 25 · *DNB* · *IGI*

Archives Hunt. L., letters · Theatre Museum, London, MSS of plays · University of Kent, Canterbury, MSS of plays [copies] | *Punch* Archive, London, Henry Silver diary, etc. · BL, letters to Sir A. H. Layard, Add. MSS 38982–38983, 38985–38986 · BL, letters to Lord Ripon, Add. MSS 43547, 43621–43622 · BL, letters to Royal Literary Fund, loan 96 · Bodl. Oxf., letters to the Aclands · NL Scot., letters to J. S. Blackie

Likenesses attrib. A. C. Sterling, photograph, 1853, NPG · R. Lehmann, crayon drawing, 1872, BM · Elliott & Fry, cartes-de-visite, NPG · Elliott & Fry, photograph, repro. in Burnand, *Records and reminiscences*, 2.224 · Leech and Doyle, caricatures, repro. in Spielmann, *History of Punch* · Lock & Whitfield, woodburytype photograph, NPG; repro. in T. Cooper and others, *Men of mark: a gallery of contemporary portraits* (1881) · London Stereoscopic Co., photograph, priv. coll. [*see illus.*] · Maull & Polyblank, cartes-de-visite, NPG · D. J. Pound, stipple and line print (after photograph by J. and C. Watkins), BM, NPG; repro. in D. J. Pound, ed., *The Drawing Room Portrait Gallery of Eminent Personages* (1860) · G. Reid, portrait; formerly lent to the Victorian Exhibition, 1898 · Southwell Bros., cartes-de-visite, NPG · Spy [L. Ward], caricature, chromolithograph, NPG; repro. in *VF* (11 March 1876) · J. & C. Watkins, cartes-de-visite, NPG · woodcut (after photograph by J. Watkins), NPG; repro. in *Illustrated London Review* (8 May 1873)

Wealth at death under £16,000: probate, 21 Aug 1880, *CGPLA Eng. & Wales*

Taylor, Vincent (1887–1968), biblical scholar and theologian, was born on 1 January 1887 at 148 Market Street, Edenfield, Lancashire, the son of Benjamin Taylor (*d. c.*1910), grocer, and his wife, Margaret Emmett (*d. c.*1925). The family moved in 1890 to Accrington, where he attended Accrington grammar school and passed the northern universities' matriculation examination. His heart was set on becoming a Wesleyan Methodist minister, but first he became a pupil teacher. One of his fellow pupils was Elizabeth Alice Harrison (1887–1978), who on 3 January 1914 became his wife. After a brief career as a teacher, he was in 1906 accepted as a candidate for the ministry and served as a supply minister in Leeds before entering Richmond College, London, in 1907 to be trained. He wished to take a divinity degree, but because his matriculation was not recognized by London University he had to spend part of his time obtaining the London matriculation, and so left college in 1910 with only the intermediate BD examination to his credit, but with an insatiable thirst for learning and a single-minded determination to equip himself as a biblical scholar.

As an external student throughout the early years of his busy ministerial life, Taylor obtained in turn the London degrees of BD, BD honours (then a postgraduate degree), PhD, and DD. The distinction and scholarly importance of his two doctoral dissertations is evidenced by the fact that both were accepted for publication by the Oxford University Press: *The Historical Evidence for the Virgin Birth* (1920) and *Behind the Third Gospel: a Study of the Proto-Luke Hypothesis* (1926). These remarkable achievements established Taylor's reputation in the world of New Testament scholarship. He remained to the end of his life—in the face of widespread opposition—a firm believer in the substantial truth of the Proto-Luke hypothesis (that the basis of Luke's gospel was a non-Marcan compilation of traditional material which Luke, after discovering Mark's gospel, expanded by inserting blocks of Marcan material before publishing his own gospel in its canonical form). His last scholarly work, published posthumously as *The Passion Narrative of St Luke: a Critical and Historical Investigation* (1972), provided a weighty contribution to the ongoing debate on the subject.

After three years' ministry in Aberdeen (where his long association—as regular contributor and unofficial editorial consultant—with the *Expository Times*, founded there by James Hastings in 1889, was cemented), Taylor in 1930 became New Testament tutor at Wesley College, Headingley, the Methodist theological college at Leeds. There he remained, with a brief interlude as minister at St Anne's while the college was temporarily closed during the Second World War, until his retirement in 1953. His onerous duties as a theological college tutor—particularly after his appointment as principal and resident tutor in 1936—did nothing to stem the flow from his pen of major contributions to the criticism, exegesis, and theology of the New Testament. His outstanding gifts as a teacher were reflected in *The Gospels: a Short Introduction* (1930), which became a standard textbook for generations of biblical students in many countries, and in *The Formation of the Gospel Tradition* (1933), which provided for English-speaking students an admirably clear and judicious introduction to *Formgeschichte* (form criticism).

The works for which the name of Vincent Taylor will chiefly be remembered, however, occupied the years of his maturity, between the mid-1930s and the late 1950s. Central to these is that which must rank as his *magnum opus*, his magisterial commentary *The Gospel According to St Mark: the Greek Text with Introduction, Notes and Indexes* (1952), which quickly won its place among the great biblical commentaries of the century. On either side of this mammoth task there appeared two trilogies which established his reputation not merely as a New Testament scholar of the first order, but also as a biblical theologian of outstanding importance and influence. The former presents an exhaustive study of the New Testament doctrine of the atonement: *Jesus and his Sacrifice: a Study of the Passion-Sayings in the Gospels* (1937); *The Atonement in New Testament Teaching* (1940); *Forgiveness and Reconciliation: a Study in New Testament Theology* (1941). In the later trilogy (based on the speaker's lectures delivered in the University of Oxford) the author turned his attention to Christology: *The Names of Jesus* (1953); *The Life and Ministry of Jesus* (1954); *The Person of Christ in New Testament Teaching* (1958).

By temperament Vincent Taylor was gentle and reserved—though in theological or ecclesiastical debate, and in dealing with lazy or unruly students, he could be trenchant and formidable. The first impression he gave was one of austerity, but his students found that as they got to know him (and he them) better, the austerity gave way to warm sympathy and friendliness, and their respect for him to genuine affection. He was a man of deep faith and of unfailing loyalty to his vocation as a minister of the gospel. He was president of the international Studiorum Novi Testamenti Societas in 1954–5 and visiting professor in New Testament studies at Drew University, New Jersey, in 1955–6, a special series of lectures delivered there being published under the title *The Cross of Christ* (1956). He was awarded honorary doctorates of divinity by the universities of Glasgow, Leeds, and Dublin, was elected fellow of the British Academy in 1954, and was awarded the Burkitt medal for biblical studies in 1960. He died at Otterbourne, Hampshire, on 28 November 1968 and was cremated there on 3 December. OWEN E. EVANS

Sources O. E. Evans, 'Vincent Taylor', *Theologians of our time*, ed. A. W. Hastings and E. Hastings (1966), 47–56 · C. L. Mitton, 'Vincent Taylor: New Testament scholar', in V. Taylor, *New Testament essays* (1970), 5–30 · O. E. Evans, 'A list of the published writings of Vincent Taylor', in V. Taylor, *New Testament essays* (1970), 141–6 · A. R. George, 'Vincent Taylor: memorial service address', in V. Taylor, *New Testament essays* (1970), 1–4 · C. K. Barrett, 'Vincent Taylor, 1887–1968', *PBA*, 56 (1970), 283–92 · *Minutes and Yearbook of the Methodist Conference, 1969* (1969), 193–4 · *CGPLA Eng. & Wales* (1969) · b. cert. · private information (2004) [daughter]
Archives JRL, Methodist Archives and Research Centre, corresp. and papers · JRL, Methodist Archives and Research Centre, corresp., record book | NL Scot., corresp. with publishers
Likenesses photograph, *c.*1940, repro. in Taylor, *New Testament essays*
Wealth at death £16,028: probate, 5 Aug 1969, *CGPLA Eng. & Wales*

Taylor, Walter Ross (1838–1907), Free Church of Scotland minister, born on 11 April 1838 in the manse of Thurso, was the only son in a family of five children of Walter Ross Taylor DD, minister of the parish; at the Disruption of the Church of Scotland in 1843 Taylor's father joined the Free Church and became moderator of its general assembly in 1884. Taylor's mother was Isabella, daughter of William Murray of Geanies, Ross-shire. Educated at the Free Church school at Thurso, he in 1853 entered Edinburgh University, where he won prizes in Greek and natural philosophy, the medal in moral philosophy, and the Stratton scholarship. Leaving without a degree, he entered the ministry of the Free Church, studying theology at New College, Edinburgh. In 1861 he was licensed to preach by the presbytery of Caithness. In the following year he

became minister of the Free Church at East Kilbride, and in 1868 was translated to Kelvinside Free Church, Glasgow, where he ministered until his death. His collected addresses, *Religious Thought and Scottish Church Life in the Nineteenth Century*, were published in 1900. In 1876 he married Margaret Innes, daughter of Dr Joshua Paterson of Glasgow.

Taylor played a leading part in the affairs of his church. As convener of the sustentation fund (1890–1900) and joint-convener of the sustentation and augmentation funds (1900–07), he sought to raise ministerial stipends within his church to a minimum of £200. A powerful advocate and practical organizer of the union of the Free and United Presbyterian churches of 1900, he was elected, in May 1900, moderator of the last general assembly of the Free Church, and in October he constituted the first general assembly of the United Free Church. Taylor was fairly liberal in his theology (he proposed Marcus Dods, the pronounced liberal theologian, for his chair in 1889) and steadily favoured a conciliatory attitude towards those who were opposed to the creation of the United Free Church. With Robert *Rainy he shared the burden of the work connected with the crisis of 1904, when a judgment of the House of Lords handed over the whole property of the undivided Free Church to a small minority who resisted the union. At meetings throughout the country he eloquently defended the amalgamation, and was largely responsible for the passing of the act of parliament of 1905, which aimed at an equitable division of the property of the Free Church between the majority and the dissentient minority.

Taylor received an honorary DD from Glasgow University in 1891. He died, after a protracted illness, at his residence in Glasgow, 1 Marchmont Terrace, Kelvinside, on 6 December 1907, and was buried in Glasgow necropolis three days later. His wife survived him, with three sons and two daughters.

W. F. GRAY, rev. H. C. G. MATTHEW

Sources *Glasgow Herald* (7 Dec 1907) · 'The Late Rev. Dr Ross Taylor: a biographical sketch', *Scottish Review* (12 Dec 1907), 587–9 · A. I. Robertson, 'The Rev. Dr Walter Ross Taylor', *British Monthly*, 4 (Dec 1903–Nov 1904), 347–52 · P. C. Simpson, *The life of Principal Rainy*, 2 vols. (1909) · *CCI* (1908)
Archives U. Edin., New College, letters to A. R. MacEwen
Likenesses Annan, photograph, repro. in *Scottish Review*, cover · photographs, repro. in Robertson, 'The Rev. Dr Walter Ross Taylor' · portrait; known to be at United Free Church assembly building, Edinburgh, 1912
Wealth at death £10,117 5s. 3d.: probate, 14 Jan 1908, *CCI*

Taylor, (Edward) Wilfred (1891–1980). *See under* Taylor, Harold Dennis (1862–1943).

Taylor, William (d. 1423), Lollard heretic, was born in Worcestershire, to unknown parents, and studied at Oxford. He was a master of arts by 1405–6, when he is recorded as principal of St Edmund Hall. He and his successor, Peter Payne, were probably responsible for making the hall a centre of Wycliffite teaching at Oxford. Taylor incurred official hostility when he preached a sermon at Paul's Cross in 1406, criticizing clerical rights of dominion, and supporting the power of the laity to withdraw ecclesiastical temporalities. The surviving text of this shows that he was a man of considerable learning. After failing to respond to a citation by Archbishop Thomas Arundel (*d.* 1414) he was excommunicated for contumacy, the citation being renewed without success in 1410. At some unidentified date during this period he was replaced as principal of the hall, and probably left Oxford.

Taylor presumably did not participate in Sir John Oldcastle's rebellion of 1414, for he is next noted as an offender in 1417, when twelve jurors in a secular court presented him for preaching against the honouring of images and speaking against the anti-Lollard statute of the Leicester parliament in 1414. He may initially have faced investigations before the bishop of Worcester, but in February 1420 was tried before Archbishop Henry Chichele (*d.* 1443) and admitted that he had remained excommunicated for fourteen years after Arundel's sentence. He submitted, was absolved, and granted letters of purgation, but later in the year was arrested for heretical preaching, along with Thomas Drayton, a Lollard priest who had been prominent in the rising of 1414, but had been pardoned and received a benefice in Bristol. Drayton was tried in the Worcester episcopal court, but Taylor's case was reserved to convocation in the following May, when he was found guilty of teaching heresy and was condemned to life imprisonment. He was again pardoned, and gave pledges in chancery not to preach heresy in future. He relapsed, however, and in February 1423 was charged with communicating heretical ideas to another Bristol priest, Thomas Smith. The principal charges concerned veneration of images, but in none of the proceedings was he ever accused of denying transubstantiation. (Significantly in his sermon of 1406 he seems deliberately to have avoided this issue.) As this had been Wyclif's most radical heresy, Taylor probably did not share his master's views. Two men later accused of heresy who admitted association with him, John Walcote in 1425 and William Emayn in 1429, were also not accused of this belief. As in 1406 he was critical of priests exercising temporal dominion and was hostile to the mendicancy of the friars, declaring that his views were approved by Christ's law, despite their condemnation by the Council of Constance. After being found guilty he refused to recant, and was sentenced to death as a relapsed heretic. He was degraded from his orders, handed over to the secular arm, and burnt at Smithfield on 2 March 1423.

JOHN A. F. THOMSON

Sources T. Walsingham, *The St Albans chronicle, 1406–1420*, ed. V. H. Galbraith (1937) · E. F. Jacob, ed., *The register of Henry Chichele, archbishop of Canterbury, 1414–1443*, 4 vols., CYS, 42, 45–7 (1937–47), esp. vol. 3, pp. 67–9, 158–73 · A. Hudson, ed., *Two Wycliffite texts*, EETS, 301 (1993) · A. Hudson, *The premature reformation: Wycliffite texts and Lollard history* (1988) · A. B. Emden, *An Oxford hall in medieval times: being the early history of St Edmund Hall*, rev. edn (1968) · J. A. F. Thomson, *The later Lollards* (1965)

Taylor, William (1765–1836), reviewer and translator, was born on 7 November 1765 in Surrey Street, Norwich, the only child of William Taylor (1731/2–1819), merchant, and

William Taylor (1765–1836), by Thomas Goff Lupton, 1833 (after John Barwell, exh. Norwich Society of Artists 1832)

his wife, Sarah (1735/6–1812), daughter of John Wright of Debenham, Suffolk, and later Diss. Intended for a mercantile career, he was tutored in languages from an early age by John Bruckner, pastor of the French and Dutch protestant churches in Norwich. In 1774 he was sent to the recently opened school at Palgrave, near Diss, run by Rochemont and Anna Letitia Barbauld. The latter made a profound impact on Taylor, who subsequently described her as 'the mother of his mind' (Robberds, 2.570). Removed from the school in 1779, he was taken on a business tour of the Netherlands, France, and Italy by his father's trading partner, Casanave. After briefly returning to Norwich in 1781, Taylor was sent away again, this time to Germany, where he spent a year mastering German in Detmold. There he was befriended by Lorenz Benzler (1747–1827), a minor literary figure who nurtured Taylor's interest in contemporary German writing and confirmed his literary proclivities. Taylor returned to Norwich at the end of 1782 and immediately entered the family business; a *Norwich Directory* for 1783 lists 'Taylor Wm. Son and Casanave, *Merchants*'. In his leisure hours he immersed himself in literary pursuits and read widely in heterodox literature. He resumed an important friendship with Frank Sayers, begun at the Barbaulds' school; it is possible the two men were lovers, and probable, in any case, that Taylor was homosexual.

Ostensibly a Unitarian like his parents, in the late 1780s Taylor became increasingly prominent in the whiggish and dissenting intellectual circles in Norwich. He actively supported such liberal causes as the abolition of the slave trade and repeal of the Test and Corporation Acts. He gained a reputation as a formidable conversationalist with a passion for argument. His literary efforts became more ambitious and increasingly reflected his other concerns: about 1789 he made an accomplished translation of Goethe's *Iphigenie auf Tauris*, then in 1790 proceeded to translate Lessing's *Nathan der Weise* and make a startling free adaptation of Bürger's 'Lenore'. Of these works, *Nathan*, which he felt encouraged 'mutual indulgence between religious sects' (preface to 1805 edn), meant the most to Taylor, and he had his translation printed for distribution among his acquaintances. The other translations circulated in manuscript for several years, that of 'Lenore' gaining considerable celebrity. In 1789–90, excited by the French Revolution, Taylor experienced the feelings of ebullience common to young radicals of his generation. He helped found the Norwich Revolution Society in November 1789 and subsequently conducted the society's correspondence. In May 1790 he made an enthusiastic visit to Paris, on his return publishing a series of pro-revolutionary articles in the *Cambridge Chronicle* over the signature 'A Friend to Liberty'. There was something innately sceptical in Taylor's thinking, however, and it is the relativity of 'truth' which these letters finally seem to celebrate.

Taylor's ambiguous stance towards religious and political 'progress' became more marked in 1791. After the Birmingham riots which destroyed the house of Joseph Priestley, he responded, rather surprisingly, with an adaptation of Samuel Butler's *Hudibras* that presented Priestley as the mystical nonconformist Ralpho. A former admirer, he now felt, apparently, that Priestley's bigoted claims for Unitarianism had harmed the dissenting interest. In the 1790s Hume, whom Priestley had attacked on more than one occasion, became, and remained, the major influence on Taylor's thinking. Religion, he increasingly felt, should be judged according to its utility, not its 'truth'. Dialogue became Taylor's preferred mode for expressing ideas, and he appropriately embarked on a translation of several of Wieland's Lucianic *Göttergespräche*, a genre he imitated in one of his finest original works. The success of his friend Sayers's *Dramatic Sketches of the Ancient Northern Mythology* (1790) had seemingly inspired Taylor with the idea that he too might attempt a literary career. In 1791–2 he was able to use the threat to the Norwich trade posed by disturbance on the continent to persuade his father that they should give up the family business. By 1795 the Taylors' withdrawal from commerce was complete, but already, in 1793, Taylor had become a regular, salaried reviewer for the best-selling *Monthly Review*. His talents were perfectly suited to reviewing: he was exceptionally widely read, and his dialogic method engaged skilfully with a book's arguments and assumptions. Although he always took the 'liberal' side on political and religious questions, his underlying position remained the relativity of truth. He should almost certainly be considered the outstanding British reviewer of the 1790s; Hazlitt later credited Taylor with pioneering 'philosophical criticism' (*The Spirit of the Age*, 1825, 308). Confirming his new status as a professional man of letters, Taylor now published his major translations: *Iphigenia in Tauris* (1793), *Dialogues of the Gods* (1795),

Ellenore (1796), and *Nathan the Wise* (1805). In this period he was undoubtedly England's foremost Germanist.

Taylor was closely involved with the immensely successful *Monthly Magazine* from its foundation in 1796. It provided him with a suitable forum for articles on all manner of subjects, as well as short translations and original poems. His articles are of a peculiar originality. He often presented facts, ideas, and opinions culled from his vast reading as though they were the results of his own research: in this respect it would be easy to dismiss him as a compulsive plagiarist. But he had a talent for placing information in a fresh and provocative light, often by drawing out contradictions inherent in the material, or introducing contradictory facts from other sources. Moreover Taylor was the channel by which a great deal of knowledge of the intellectual scene on the continent, especially Germany, reached the English-speaking world. He was particularly attracted to the 'higher criticism', not only promoting Eichhorn's ideas, but making some bold sallies into biblical scholarship himself. His most notorious theory, published as *A Letter Concerning the Two First Chapters of Luke* (1810), argued that 'Zacharius [*sic*], who wrote those chapters, meant to hold himself out as the father of Jesus Christ' (Robberds, 2.281–2). Many copies were destroyed by incensed readers. Another book-length work which developed out of his periodical writing was *English Synonyms Discriminated* (1813).

From the mid-1790s Taylor's life assumed a regular routine. He continued to live with his parents, working in the morning, exercising in the early afternoon, socializing in the evening. From this date his biography is a relatively straightforward account of involvement with various periodicals and increasing disrepute in Norwich. He left the *Monthly Review* in 1799, having quarrelled with the editor, George Edward Griffiths; he did not write for it again until 1808. Between 1802 and 1808 he reviewed prolifically for the *Annual Review*. In 1803–4 he edited a whiggish Norwich paper, *The Iris*, and in the same years wrote for the *Critical Review*, which he rejoined briefly in 1809. In 1807 he started writing for *The Athenaeum*, the periodical John Aikin had established in opposition to the *Monthly Magazine*. After 1810 his writing commitments simplified, and he wrote mainly for the *Monthly Review* and *Monthly Magazine*. The total volume of Taylor's periodical writing is enormous, yet his Norwich contemporaries took less interest in his literary industry than his social habits. He became notorious for frequent drunkenness and spreading extremely unorthodox opinions among the young men he liked to surround himself with, the most famous of whom was George Borrow.

Most of Taylor's best writing was done in the 1790s. In the early 1800s he wrote too much to maintain such standards, and by 1807 there were pressing financial reasons for him to privilege quantity. Though rich when he retired from business, Taylor's father had made a series of risky investments, which by this date were causing Taylor considerable anxiety. A long-developing financial crisis finally descended on the Taylors in 1811, and they were forced to move to a smaller house in King Street. It was to be a decade of constant attrition, with the death of both his parents, and the onset of Taylor's own long struggle with illness. His writing steadily deteriorated, and he lost faith in his ability to produce the sort of large-scale work his friends expected from him. About 1820, however, possibly inspired by Borrow, Taylor did start working towards what eventually became the three-volume *Historic Survey of German Poetry* (1828–30). This gathered together four decades' worth of translations and critical writing on German literature, but was out of date, and accordingly condemned by Carlyle in the *Edinburgh Review*. Taylor, who had already abandoned periodical writing, was past caring; his health had declined alarmingly and by 1830 he was given to 'sit[ting] for hours absorbed in a dull lethargic silence' (Robberds, 2.254). He clung on for another six years, died at his home on 5 March 1836, and was buried in the Octagon Chapel, Norwich.   DAVID CHANDLER

Sources J. W. Robberds, *A memoir of the life and writings of the late William Taylor of Norwich*, 2 vols. (1843) · D. Chandler, 'The foundation of "philosophical criticism": William Taylor's initial connection with the *Monthly Review*, 1792–3', *Studies in Bibliography*, 50 (1997), 359–71 · D. Chandler, 'William Taylor of Norwich', *George Borrow Bulletin*, 7 and 8 (1994), 8–16, 10–15; 9 (1995), 4–10; 12 (1996), 4–22 · D. Chandler, 'William Taylor's pluralist project: the major translations, 1789–91', *European Romantic Review*, 11 (2000), 259–76 · *Norfolk Chronicle and Norwich Gazette* (2 May 1812) · *Norfolk Chronicle and Norwich Gazette* (28 Aug 1819) · *Norwich Mercury* (2 May 1812) · *Norwich Mercury* (28 Aug 1819) · *Norwich Directory* (1783) · IGI
Archives DWL, letters | UCL, corresp. with G. C. Robertson
Likenesses T. G. Lupton, mezzotint, 1833 (aged sixty-nine; after J. Barwell, exh. Norwich Society of Artists 1832), BM, NPG [*see illus.*] · J. Barwell, oils · engraving (after J. Barwell), repro. in Robberds, *Memoir of … William Taylor of Norwich*

Taylor, William (1813/14–1854). *See under* Rochdale Pioneers (*act.* 1844).

Taylor, William (1865–1937), designer of optical instruments, was born at 4 Norfolk Place, Hackney, on 11 June 1865, the second son of Richard Taylor, hosier, and his wife, Mary Ann Smithies, the daughter of a York draper. He and his brother were interested in mechanics from an early age. They learned the elements of turning with a small lathe made by themselves and studied science from the *Edinburgh Encyclopaedia*. Their knowledge was widened at the Cowper Street School, Finsbury, under Richard Wormald, a pioneer of the teaching of science in schools. There they studied turning, joinery, and cabinet making, and in the school workshops produced two of the first telephones ever made in England, and one of the first copies of Edison's tin foil phonograph. They also built a workshop at home.

In his last term at school Taylor became interested in the design of lenses. He therefore learned as much as he could about optics and the use of logarithms. He became one of the first students at the Finsbury Technical College under H. E. Armstrong, W. E. Ayrton, and John Perry before being apprenticed to Messrs Paterson and Cooper. While with the company he made an ammeter for Ayrton and Perry; it was later housed in the Science Museum, South Kensington. In 1885 the family moved to Leicester. On 23 July 1892 Taylor married Esther Margaret, daughter of John Coy of

William Taylor (1865–1937), by Walter Stoneman, 1935

Leicester; she survived him with their son and four daughters.

In 1886 the brothers founded the firm of T. S. and W. Taylor (afterwards Taylor, Taylor, and Hobson). From the beginning William Taylor did most of the designing, and it was his remarkable talent in this field which determined the character of the products of the firm and their mode of production. He was much impressed by the degree to which standardization had been developed in America, and he invented a method which ensured interchangeability of screws for the mountings of lenses. But it was not until the ideas of the British lens makers had been empirically proved wrong that the trade accepted the specification embodying Taylor's suggestions, published in 1901 by the Royal Photographic Society.

Although Taylor did much work for the government and for various committees, the example set by the firm under his direction did much to raise the standard of mechanical and optical manufacture in Great Britain. Under his direction the firm produced the anastigmatic camera lens designed by Harold Dennis Taylor, and adopted methods of mass production. These made it possible to manufacture very large numbers of camera lenses of such high quality that they acquired a commanding position all over the world. Taylor's study of factory organization and skill in design, coupled with the novel range of machines for grinding and polishing lenses which he devised and patented, were all essential factors in this achievement.

In addition, Taylor's interest in the game of golf led him

to study the form and flight of the golf ball, and he designed the 'dimple' ball and a mechanical driving machine for testing it. He also produced an engraving machine which achieved worldwide sales. The distinguishing features of Taylor's ability were a comprehensive knowledge of engineering practice, an authoritative grasp of the desired result, and, most marked of all, untiring patience and inexhaustible stamina in persevering to reach his objective.

Taylor was made OBE in 1918 and elected FRS in 1934. He died in a snowdrift at Laughton Hills, Leicestershire, on 28 February 1937.   F. TWYMAN, rev. S. BRADBURY

Sources F. Twyman, *Obits. FRS*, 2 (1936–8), 363–5 · H. W. L., *Nature*, 139 (1937), 537–8 · *The Times* (2 March 1937) · personal knowledge (1949) · b. cert. · m. cert. · d. cert.
Likenesses W. Stoneman, photograph, 1935, NPG [*see illus.*] · portrait, repro. in Twyman, *Obits. FRS*
Wealth at death £4543 4s. 10d.: probate, 6 Nov 1937, *CGPLA Eng. & Wales*

Taylor, William Benjamin Sarsfield (1781–1850), painter of landscapes and military subjects and writer, was born in Dublin, the son of John McKinley Taylor (*fl.* 1765–1819), a map and seal engraver. John McKinley Taylor had assumed the name Taylor on inheriting property from his maternal grandfather. J. M. Taylor was descended from David McKinley, a captain of the Inniskilling dragoons, who fought at the battle of the Boyne. Through his mother, William Taylor was descended from Patrick Sarsfield, titular earl of Lucan. The barrister and journalist John Sydney *Taylor was his younger brother. He became a pupil in the Dublin Society Schools in 1800 and in 1801 won the prize for the second best landscape. He exhibited at the society's exhibitions in various years from 1802 to 1817, although by 1804 he had left the schools and was supporting himself as a teacher of drawing.

Taylor spent some time in the army, serving in the commissariat in the Peninsular War. He was present at the siege of San Sebastian, and would later exhibit sketches of the engagement.

After returning to Dublin, Taylor exhibited there in 1815, 1816, and 1817. He became a member of the committee responsible for the foundation of the Royal Hibernian Academy in 1823. Afterwards he moved to London, although his work was exhibited at the Royal Hibernian Academy from 1827 to 1829. He exhibited landscapes, seapieces, and military subjects at the Royal Academy, the British Institution, the New Society of Painters in Water Colours, and the Society of British Artists between 1829 and 1847. He became better known as an art critic and writer, contributing critical essays to the *Morning Chronicle*, and he published in 1841 *The Origin, Progress, and Present Conditions of the Fine Arts in Great Britain and Ireland*. Other publications included *A Manual of Fresco and Encaustic Painting* (1843); a translation of J. F. L. Mérimée's *Art of Painting in Oil and Fresco* (1839); an abridged translation of the *Origin and Outline of the Penitentiary System in the United States of North America* (1833), from the report of G. de Beaumont and A. de Tocqueville; and his best-known work, a *History*

of the University of Dublin (1845), which contains biographical notices of alumni, and is illustrated with coloured plates drawn and etched by Taylor himself.

Towards the end of his life Taylor was curator of the St Martin's Lane Academy. He died at his home, 46 Robert Street, Hampstead Road, London, on 23 December 1850. A *Seascape* by Taylor is in the Williamson Art Gallery and Museum, Birkenhead.   PAUL A. COX

Sources W. G. Strickland, *A dictionary of Irish artists*, 2 vols. (1913) · Graves, *Artists* · Graves, *RA exhibitors* · Graves, *Brit. Inst.* · J. Johnson, ed., *Works exhibited at the Royal Society of British Artists, 1824–1893, and the New English Art Club, 1888–1917*, 2 vols. (1975) · A. M. Stewart and C. de Courcy, *Royal Hibernian Academy of Arts: index of exhibitors and their works, 1826–1979*, 3 vols. (1985–7) · A. J. Webb, *A compendium of Irish biography* (1878)

Taylor, William Cooke (1800–1849), historian and journalist, born at Youghal, co. Cork, on 16 April 1800, was the son of Richard Taylor, a manufacturer, and a member of a family resident at Youghal from the time of the settlement by Oliver Cromwell. His mother was Mary Cooke, a descendant of John Cook, the regicide. He was educated by Robert Bell DD, at a school in Youghal, and then went to Trinity College, Dublin, which he entered on 13 January 1817. At the beginning of 1820 he removed his name from the lists, but replaced it in June 1821 to stand for a scholarship. He was unsuccessful in the competition, and returned to Youghal as an assistant at his old school.

After a short time Taylor returned to the university, and graduated BA in 1825. While at college he won prizes for compositions in prose and poetry, and in 1825 and 1826 he won several of the primate's prizes for Hebrew. His first essays in print were some contributions, carefully concealed in later years, to a newspaper in Cork. His first book was *A Classical Geography for Use of Youghal School*. He then edited several of the catechisms of William Pinnock and the various histories that had been compiled by Oliver Goldsmith.

In 1829 Taylor settled in Camden Town, London, and set up as a writer. His considerable energy and wide knowledge equipped him well for his role, and he was much more than the mere journeyman author that his list of publications at first glance suggests.

Taylor, unusually for his time, combined the writing of substantial histories with astute social and economic observation of the contemporary scene, which remains of interest and importance. Unfortunately, the sharp analytical approach of his observation of factory life in Manchester is largely absent from his histories, in which analytical intentions are blurred by narrative.

Between 1829 and his death Taylor wrote sixteen historical works, many of them in several volumes. Although holding a generally whiggish view of progress, he was especially interested in interruptions to it, as is shown in his *History of the Civil Wars in Ireland* (2 vols., 1831; Taylor believed that civil war was the constant feature of Irish history until 1800, when, he thought, the union abolished it) and *The Revolutions, Insurrections, and Conspiracies of Europe* (2 vols., 1843). His work often discussed what he considered to be the disruptive force of Islam, and his *History of Mohammedanism* (1834) went into several editions and was translated into German in 1837. His manuals for students on ancient history (1836) and modern history (1838) were standard works, the latter revised by C. D. Yonge and G. W. Cox and still used at the end of the century. Taylor stressed the historical significance of geography: *The World as it is* (3 vols., 1849–53), whose compilation Charles Mackay assisted, was an attempt at a new and comprehensive system of modern geography. Taylor supplemented this sturdy output with works on India (1842), the fall of the Roman empire (1836), *Memoirs of the House of Orleans* (3 vols., 1849)—a work that irritated Louis-Philippe—and many editions of classical and modern texts, including Homer, Cicero, Plutarch, Swift, and Bacon. Among many other works, Taylor published *The National Portrait Gallery* (4 vols., 1846–8).

Taylor wrote for *The Athenaeum* from 1829 until his death. On the foundation of the British Association in 1831, he became one of its leading members and was often on its statistical committee. He was interested in inventions and wrote *An Account of the Electro-Magnet Engine* (1841). He quite frequently returned to Ireland and became friendly with Richard Whately, archbishop of Dublin, to whom several of his works are dedicated and who often quoted them, especially Taylor's anonymous letters published as *The Bishop* (1841). Having toured a number of French schools in 1846, he supported Whately's educational policy in his *Notes of a Visit to the Model Schools in Dublin* (1847).

Taylor was a strong free-trader. Prompted by Richard Cobden, he travelled in the industrial north and concluded that great industrial cities were the pattern of the future, not a passing aberration. He strongly opposed factory regulation and believed urban destitution was the result not of low wages but of rural incompetents who over-optimistically came to the towns. An early member of the Anti-Corn Law League, he edited its newspaper, *The League*, from its move to London in 1843. His articles gave the paper a historical dimension, with comments, for example, on the Roman corn laws. He published several pamphlets which are important accounts of the 'factory system' (as he called it). His book *Notes on a Tour in the Manufacturing Districts of Lancashire: Letters to the Archbishop of Dublin* (1842) was secretly financed by the league. Taylor's *Life and Times of Sir Robert Peel* (3 vols., 1846–8) is an interesting presentation of Peel from the league's point of view and the first of the various substantial studies of that prime minister.

Some expected Taylor to be the first president of Queen's College, Cork, but he was not. After the repeal of the corn laws in 1846, C. P. Villiers, the prominent free-trader, got his brother Lord Clarendon, lord lieutenant of Ireland in the whig government, to give Taylor a post as statistical writer to the Irish government. He also wrote for the government's Dublin paper, the *Evening Post*, and wrote pseudonymous tracts, including *Reminiscences of Daniel O'Connell. By a Munster Farmer*. In the late 1840s he was involved in agitating for the further extension of the franchise.

Taylor's ability was recognized in his LLD from Trinity College, Dublin, conferred on 7 July 1835. In September 1836 he married, at Cork, Marianne, only daughter of John Taylor of Youghal. He died of cholera at 20 Herbert Street, Dublin, on 12 September 1849 and was buried at Mount Jerome cemetery. He was survived by his wife, three daughters, and a son, Richard Whately Cooke-Taylor of Glasgow.   H. C. G. MATTHEW

Sources *GM*, 2nd ser., 33 (1850), 94–6 · *DNB* · N. McCord, *The Anti-Corn Law League, 1838–1846* (1958) · J. Morley, *The life of Richard Cobden*, 2 vols. (1881) · B. Hilton, *Corn, cash, commerce: the economic policies of the tory governments, 1815–1830* (1977)
Archives W. Sussex RO, letters to Richard Cobden

Taylor, William Ernest (1856–1927), Swahili scholar and missionary, was born on 25 January 1856 at 26 The Cross, St Nicholas, Worcester, the eldest child in the family of at least four sons and two daughters of Samuel Taylor (1822–1884), perfumer, and his wife, Harriette Fussell (1827–1907). From King's School, Worcester, he won a scholarship in 1873 to Hertford College, Oxford, and obtained a third class in classical honour moderations in 1876. He studied at the medical school of Edinburgh University in 1879.

In July 1880 Taylor was made deacon by the bishop of Mauritius for the bishop of London, and in the same month he sailed for east Africa, to the Nyanza mission, under the auspices of the Church Missionary Society (CMS). The greater part of this first tour was spent in or near Mombasa, when the Swahili-speaking people still formed the overwhelming majority of the island's population. Taylor quickly began to acquire that complete command of the Swahili language and that intimacy with its literature on which his fame would rest. He was fortunate in having as his teachers two of Mombasa's foremost scholars, Mu'allim Sikujua bin Abdallah al-Batawi and Bwana Hemedi bin Muhammad al-Mambasi.

Taylor returned to east Africa for a second tour at the end of 1884, and was ordained priest by Bishop James Hannington in Frere Town, Mombasa, on 31 May 1885. In 1891 came the publication of *African Aphorisms, or, Saws from Swahili-Land*, an annotated collection of some 600 proverbs: the work (reissued in 1924) provided an outlet for his immense erudition, and became recognized as a classic in the domain of Swahili studies. In the same year the British Museum acquired its first Swahili manuscript (BL, MS Or. 4534), the vendor being Taylor.

On 21 April 1892 Taylor married Catherine Tesseyman (1864–1959); they had five sons and a daughter. Following his marriage he left England on his third and final east African tour. In 1895 he became examining chaplain to the bishop of eastern equatorial Africa, Alfred Tucker. In 1896 the CMS requested Taylor to continue his translation work in Swahili in Cairo, not Mombasa. After a brief visit to Omdurman in 1900, he returned to England. In 1903 he was a CMS missionary in Khartoum and acting chaplain to the forces, but on medical grounds he was compelled to retire to England later that year. Taylor then held a succession of clerical appointments, the last of which was the benefice of Halton Holgate, Lincolnshire, in 1921.

Zaburi za Davidi (1904), the Psalms of David, is probably

Taylor's finest Bible translation—it may reasonably be compared with the Coverdale psalter. In 1910 Taylor's fellow missionary Alice Burt published her *Swahili Grammar and Vocabulary*; the standard of Swahili adopted was that set by Taylor. At the end of the twentieth century, this work remained the unrivalled grammatical introduction to the Swahili of Mombasa. In 1915 Taylor published the Mombasa version of a much-loved poem *al-Inkishafi*; the poetic rendering that accompanied the recension was the first printed English translation of a major Swahili poem.

Taylor was the first to realize that, on linguistic grounds, Swahililand should be studied as three regions; he was the first to study in depth the phenomenon of aspiration in Swahili; he was the first and (with the exception of H. E. Lambert) the only European to compose and publish Swahili poetry; and he was the only European to have caused a new genre to be introduced to Swahili poetry, 'mahadhi ya Tela' ('Taylor's tune'). With his teachers he salvaged from oblivion many of the Swahili poets, notably the Mombasa poet Bwana Muyaka. Only two other Englishmen approached Taylor's achievement—H. E. Lambert (1893–1967) and J. W. T. Allen (1904–1979): all three were amateurs.

Taylor was a non-smoker and a teetotaller. The evidence suggests that he did not relate well to other people—the literati of Swahili Mombasa being the exception. Taylor died of a heart attack at Manvers Hall, Bath, on 2 October 1927, and was buried five days later at Lyncombe, Widcombe, and St James's cemetery, Bath. He bequeathed his linguistic books and papers to the British Museum, but the bequest was turned down. Much of his invaluable collection went to the library of the School of Oriental and African Studies in London, and other items were acquired by the University of Hamburg. P. J. L. FRANKL

Sources P. J. L. Frankl, 'William Ernest Taylor (1856–1927): England's greatest Swahili scholar', *Afrikanische Arbeitspapiere*, 60 (1999), 161–74 [Swahili Forum], · Y. A. Omar and P. J. L. Frankl, '14th / 19th century Swahili letters from the Taylor papers', *South African Journal of African Languages*, 15, suppl. 1 (2001), 17–24 · *The Times* (5 Oct 1927) · *Bulletin of the School of Oriental and African Studies*, 4 (1926–8) · *Zeitschrift für Eingeborenen-Sprachen* [Hamburg], 19 (1928–9) · P. J. L. Frankl, 'Mombasa under the Bu S'aidi: a leaf from the Taylor papers', *Zeitschrift der Deutschen Morgenländischen Gesellschaft*, 141 (1991), 131–8 · b. cert. · Foster, *Alum. Oxon.* · m. cert. · Crockford (1927) · d. cert. · Church Missionary Society, 'Register of missionaries from 1804 to 1904', list 1, item 905 · register of Lyncombe, Widcombe, and St James's cemetery, Bath

Archives SOAS, papers relating to East African languages | BL, MS Or. 4534 · U. Birm. L., Church Missionary Society Archives · Universität Hamburg, Institut für Afrikanistik und Äthiopistik, MSS 3552–3556 inclusive

Likenesses photograph, RGS

Wealth at death £3403 11*s.* 3*d.*: probate, 2 Jan 1928, *CGPLA Eng. & Wales*

Taylor, Winthrop James Crosland (1894–1967). *See under* Taylor, George Crosland (1858–1923).

Taylor, Wittewronge (*b.* before **1719**, *d.* **1760**), naval officer, details of whose parentage and upbringing are unknown, entered the Royal Navy as a volunteer per order or king's letter-boy in the *Kingston* about 1727; he was subsequently listed as being on seven other ships in just

seventeen months. His first seagoing experience appears to have been in 1736 on the *Windsor*. He remained in her, together with the *Ipswich* and *Anglesea* (in which he took part in the failed attack on Cartegena in April 1741), for five years. On 3 September 1741 he passed his lieutenant's examination, at which date he was judged more than twenty-two years old, having been at sea for more than ten years.

On 7 September Taylor was promoted lieutenant of the *Duke* on the home station. During 1743 and 1744 he held the same rank in the *St George* from which in October 1744 he was chosen to accompany Vice-Admiral Davers to the West Indies in the *Cornwall* in the rating of midshipman extra. In August of the following year Davers gave him a commission as fifth lieutenant of the *Cornwall* and in November he appointed him to command the *Vainqueur* tender. Taylor returned to the *Cornwall* eighteen months later, was present at the action off Havana on 1 October 1748, and was subsequently promoted by Sir Charles Knowles to command the sloop *Weasel*. Sent home, the ship was paid off in May 1749. In March 1755 he commanded the *Seaford* and afterwards the *Raven* in the channel and then with the western squadron until posted to the *Monarch* on 2 December.

Taylor held a number of commands over the next couple of years. In early 1758 he was appointed to the *Ramillies* (90 guns), the flagship of Sir Edward Hawke with whom he served continuously until the blockade of Brest in 1759. He remained in her when Hawke struck his flag and moved to the *Royal George* (14 November), taking command of the *Ramillies* on her return to Plymouth for refitting. In February 1760 she sailed as part of a squadron of three-deckers under the command of Admiral Edward Boscawen. On 15 February a severe westerly gale divided the ships and forced the *Ramillies* onto the rocks at Bolt Head with the death, including that of Taylor, of all but 26 of the 734 crew. Taylor was survived by his wife, about whom further details are unknown; shocked by the loss of the *Ramillies* and so many of his former crew, Admiral Hawke soon afterwards sought to guarantee Taylor's widow's security. J. K. LAUGHTON, *rev.* PHILIP CARTER

Sources J. Charnock, ed., *Biographia navalis*, 6 (1798), 151 · R. F. Mackay, *Admiral Hawke* (1965) · PRO, Adm 1/90, fols. 147–57

Taylor, Zachary (1653–1705), Church of England clergyman, the son of Zachary Taylor (1618/19–1692) and Abigail Ward, was born at Bolton, Lancashire, on 20 April 1653 and was baptized at the parish church four days later. His father, a graduate of Trinity College, Dublin, served as a chaplain in the royalist army during the 1640s, but in the following decade he joined Lancashire's second presbyterian classis and served a number of cures in both Cheshire and Lancashire. At the time of the Restoration Taylor senior was acting as assistant to the vicar of Rochdale and parish schoolmaster, and although ejected from the first post under the terms of the 1662 Act of Uniformity he retained the second until 1666. In 1672 Taylor took out a licence, under the terms of Charles II's declaration of indulgence, for a presbyterian meeting at Rochdale, but following the revocation of this declaration he returned to teaching, assuming the post of schoolmaster of Kirkham, which he was to hold until his death, aged seventy-three, in 1692.

Zachary Taylor junior was admitted at Jesus College, Cambridge, in 1671, where his tutor was the Lancashire native Richard Wroe, and graduated BA in 1675 and MA three years later. On 13 July 1678 he was incorporated at Oxford. No doubt aided by the support of his former tutor Wroe, who had left Cambridge in 1674 to take up a position as chaplain to the bishop of Chester, Taylor chose to make his career in the restored Church of England to which his father had found it impossible fully to conform. In 1677 Taylor was appointed one of Lancashire's six king's preachers, an office established in 1599 with the intention of furthering the Reformation in those parts of the county most resistant to protestantism, and it seems likely that during the late 1670s he also served as curate of Wigan, before being appointed on 9 March 1680 vicar of Ormskirk. Five years later, on 12 July 1685, Taylor married Barbara Stanley (1666–1689), the daughter of Sir Edward Stanley, third baronet, of Bickerstaffe, Lancashire. In 1692 Taylor resigned his cure at Ormskirk and returned to the post of curate of Wigan, in which he was to remain, apart from a brief spell between 1695 and 1696 as rector of Croston, Lancashire, until his death on 20 May 1705. He was survived by his second wife, Anne, and seven children.

Though he never reached the higher echelons of the Anglican church, Taylor attained some contemporary notoriety through a number of pamphlets. His first surviving work, published in 1682, was *A Dissuasive from Contention*, in which he argued that the breach between Anglicans and protestant dissenters had been occasioned by disagreements concerning ceremonies rather than the more serious matter of doctrine, but that having created this schism dissenters had been drawn into activities which threatened to undermine both the church and state. Taylor's prescription was not, however, an accommodation with dissenters but a demand that they subject themselves to the discipline of the national church. Such sentiments were in keeping with the prevailing political sentiments of the early 1680s, but his next published work contributed to, rather than merely followed, national political developments. In 1689 Archbishop Sancroft had published, in response to the events of the revolution of 1688, the Anglican canons which had been drawn up in 1606, Sancroft pointing to the canons' denial of the subject's right of resistance. However, in *Obedience and Submission to the Present Government*, published between April and October 1690, Taylor emphasized the twenty-eighth of the canons, which stated that once a usurper had achieved stable government then allegiance was due to a regime which governed *de facto* if not *de jure*. For those tories and Anglican clergymen suffering a crisis of conscience caused by the conflict between the requirement to take the oaths to William and Mary, and their belief in the binding nature of their oaths to James II, Taylor's argument offered a justification for acquiescing to the demands of the new regime. His interpretation prefigured that of William Sherlock, the dean of Christ Church, whose pamphlet *The Case of Allegiance due to Soveraigne Powers*, published in 1691, expanded Taylor's arguments and prompted a long and fierce pamphlet debate.

Taylor never again wrote on national matters, but he remained a controversial figure within the context of the political and religious divisions of Lancashire. In 1696 he published *The Devil Turn'd Casuist*, a critique of the claims made by local Catholics to have effected a successful exorcism, and two years later he attacked, in *The Surey Impostor*, the claims of a group of Lancashire's dissenting ministers to have exorcised Richard Dugdale. Taylor dismissed the episode as a fraud perpetrated upon the nonconformist ministers by local Catholics, and his attack upon Lancashire dissent led to his being criticized in two pamphlets for his hostility towards fellow protestants. Both were called *The Lancashire Levite Rebuk'd* (1698), drawing a comparison between the story of the Good Samaritan, where the Levite had bemoaned the protagonist's misfortune but failed to offer any assistance, and Taylor's alleged indifference to the fate of Richard Dugdale. Taylor responded, in two pieces entitled *Popery, Superstition, Ignorance and Knavery* (1698–9), with a vituperative attack upon dissenters, labelling them as schismatics whose division from the established church was both unwarranted and damaging to the protestant cause. Though retiring from political and religious pamphleteering after producing the second of these pamphlets, Taylor remained a staunch tory until the end of his life.   RICHARD D. HARRISON

Sources Calamy rev., 479–80 · VCH Lancashire, 3.245; 6.89 · J. Brownbill, ed., 'List of clergymen … in the diocese of Chester, 1691', *Chetham miscellanies*, new ser., 3, Chetham Society, 73 (1915) · E. Axon, 'The king's preachers in Lancashire, 1599–1845', *Transactions of the Lancashire and Cheshire Antiquarian Society*, 56 (1941–2), 67–104, esp. 96–9 · Venn, *Alum. Cant.*, 1/4.211 · DNB · IGI · H. Fishwick, *The history of the parish of Kirkham in the county of Lancaster*, Chetham Society, 92 (1874), 147 · will, Lancs. RO, WCW · *The diary of Henry Prescott, LLB, deputy registrar of Chester diocese*, ed. J. Addy and others, 2, Lancashire and Cheshire RS, 132 (1994), 49 · M. F. Snape, '"The Surey impostor": demonic possession and religious conflict in seventeenth-century Lancashire', *Transactions of the Lancashire and Cheshire Antiquarian Society*, 90 (1994), 93–114 · J. Westaway and R. D. Harrison, '"The Surey Demoniack": defining protestantism in 1690s Lancashire', *Unity and diversity in the church*, ed. R. N. Swanson, SCH, 32 (1996), 263–82

PICTURE CREDITS

Strang, William, first Baron Strang (1893-1978)—© National Portrait Gallery, London

Strange, Sir Robert (1725-1792)—National Museums of Scotland

Strangways, Giles Stephen Holland Fox-, sixth earl of Ilchester (1874-1959)—© National Portrait Gallery, London

Stratford, John (c.1275-1348)—by kind permission of the Dean and Chapter of Canterbury; photographer: Mrs Mary Tucker

Stratford, Nicholas (bap. 1633, d. 1707)—© The Bishopric of Chester

Straub, Marianne (1909-1994)—© Geoffrey Ireland; collection National Portrait Gallery, London

Streat, Sir (Edward) Raymond (1897-1979)—© National Portrait Gallery, London

Streatfeild, (Mary) Noel (1895-1986)—by permission of The Noel Streatfeild Estate; collection National Portrait Gallery, London

Street, George Edmund (1824-1881)—© National Portrait Gallery, London

Strickland, Agnes (1796-1874)—© National Portrait Gallery, London

Strickland, Hugh Edwin (1811-1853)—© National Portrait Gallery, London

Strode, Sir George (1583-1663)—© National Portrait Gallery, London

Strong, Leonard Alfred George (1896-1958)—© National Portrait Gallery, London

Strong, Thomas Banks (1861-1944)—Christ Church, Oxford

Struthers, Sir John (1823-1899)—in the collection of the Royal College of Surgeons of Edinburgh; photograph courtesy the Scottish National Portrait Gallery

Struthers, Sir John (1857-1925)—© National Portrait Gallery, London

Strutt, John William, third baron Rayleigh (1842-1919)—V&A Images, The Victoria and Albert Museum

Strype, John (1643-1737)—© National Portrait Gallery, London

Strzelecki, Sir Paul Edmund de (1797-1873)—location of original unknown; copy from a version in the Mitchell Library, Sydney

Stuart, Lady Arabella (1575-1615)—© National Portrait Gallery, London

Stuart, Charles, Baron Stuart de Rothesay (1779-1845)—© Crown copyright in photograph: UK Government Art Collection

Stuart, Frances, duchess of Lennox and Richmond (1578-1639)—© National Portrait Gallery, London

Stuart, Frances Teresa, duchess of Lennox and Richmond (1647-1702)—The Royal Collection © 2004 HM Queen Elizabeth II

Stuart, Gilbert Charles (1755-1828)—Redwood Library and Athenaeum, Newport, Rhode Island

Stuart, James, fourth duke of Lennox and first duke of Richmond (1612-1655)—The Metropolitan Museum of Art, Marquand Collection, Gift of Henry G. Marquand, 1889. (89.15.16) Photograph © The Metropolitan Museum of Art

Stuart, James (1713-1788)—RIBA Library Photographs Collection

Stuart, James Gray, first Viscount Stuart of Findhorn (1897-1971)—© National Portrait Gallery, London

Stuart, John, third earl of Bute (1713-1792)—© National Portrait Gallery, London

Stuart, John Crichton-, second marquess of Bute (1793-1848)—private collection

Stuart, John Patrick Crichton-, third marquess of Bute (1847-1900)—© National Portrait Gallery, London

Stuart, Katherine, Lady Aubigny (d. 1650)—Widener Collection, Photograph © 2004 Board of Trustees, National Gallery of Art, Washington

Stuart, Ludovick, second duke of Lennox and duke of Richmond (1574-1624)—© National Portrait Gallery, London

Stubblefield, Sir (Cyril) James (1901-1999)—© National Portrait Gallery, London

Stubbs, George (1724-1806)—© National Portrait Gallery, London

Stubbs, Philip (1665-1738)—© National Portrait Gallery, London

Stubbs, William (1825-1901)—© Bodleian Library, University of Oxford

Stuckey family (per. c.1770-1845) [Stuckey, Vincent (1771-1845)]—© National Portrait Gallery, London

Studd, Charles Thomas (1860-1931)—© National Portrait Gallery, London

Stukeley, William (1687-1765)—© National Portrait Gallery, London

Sturge, Emily (1847-1892)—The Women's Library, London Metropolitan University

Sturge, Joseph (1793-1859)—Birmingham Museums & Art Gallery

Sturgeon, William (1783-1850)—© National Portrait Gallery, London

Sturt, Charles (1795-1869)—© National Portrait Gallery, London

Stutchbury, Samuel (1798-1859)—© National Portrait Gallery, London

Style, William (c.1599-1679)—© Tate, London, 2004

Suckling, Sir John (bap. 1609, d. 1641?)—© The Frick Collection, New York

Sudbury, Simon (c.1316-1381)—The British Library

Suett, Richard (bap. 1755, d. 1805)—Garrick Club / the art archive

Sugden, Edward Burtenshaw, Baron St Leonards (1781-1875)—The Honourable Society of Lincoln's Inn. Photograph: Photographic Survey, Courtauld Institute of Art, London

Sugden, Samuel (1892-1950)—© National Portrait Gallery, London

Sulivan, Sir Bartholomew James (1810-1890)—© National Portrait Gallery, London

Sullivan, Sir Arthur Seymour (1842-1900)—© National Portrait Gallery, London

Sullivan, (Thomas) Barry (1821-1891)—Howarth-Loomes Collection; photograph National Portrait Gallery, London

Summerskill, Edith Clara, Baroness Summerskill (1901-1980)—© National Portrait Gallery, London

Summerson, Sir John Newenham (1904-1992)—© Stephen Hyde; collection National Portrait Gallery, London

Sumner, Charles Richard (1790-1874)—by kind permission of the Bishop of Winchester and the Church Commissioners

Sumner, John Bird (1780-1862)—by kind permission of the Provost and Fellows of King's College, Cambridge

Sumner, Mary Elizabeth (1828-1921)—© National Portrait Gallery, London

Sumter, Thomas (1734-1832)—Independence National Historical Park

Surtees, Robert Smith (1805-1864)—© reserved

Sutch, David Edward (1940-1999)—Getty Images - Hulton Archive

Sutcliff, Rosemary (1920-1992)—© News International Newspapers Ltd

Sutcliffe, Francis Meadow (1853-1941)—© The Sutcliffe Gallery, Whitby. www.sutcliffe-gallery.co.uk

Sutcliffe, Herbert William (1894-1978)—© National Portrait Gallery, London

Sutcliffe, Reginald Cockcroft (1904-1991)—Godfrey Argent Studios / Royal Society

Sutherland, Angus (1848-1922)—© National Portrait Gallery, London

Sutherland, Graham Vivian (1903-1980)—© National Portrait Gallery, London

Sutherland, Helen Christian (1881-1965)—© reserved / print supplied by Tate Gallery Archive

Sutherland, Mary Elizabeth (1895-1972)—Labour Party / People's History Museum

Sutherland, Robert Garioch (1909-1981)—© Alexander Moffat; photograph courtesy the Scottish National Portrait Gallery

Sutherland, Sir Thomas (1834-1922)—© National Portrait Gallery, London

Sutton (bap. 1777, d. 1863)—Suttons Consumer Products, Paignton, Devon

Sutton, Sir John Bland-, first baronet (1855-1936)—© National Portrait Gallery, London

Sutton, Martin John (1850-1913)—© National Portrait Gallery, London

Sutton, Thomas (1532-1611)—© National Portrait Gallery, London

Sutton Hoo burial (early 7th cent.)—© Copyright The British Museum

Swaffer, Hannen (1879-1962)—© reserved; collection National Portrait Gallery, London

Swainson, William (1789-1855)—© National Portrait Gallery, London

Swan, Annie Shepherd (1859-1943)—© National Portrait Gallery, London

Swan, Sir Joseph Wilson (1828-1914)—© National Portrait Gallery, London

Swanwick, Anna (1813-1899)—© National Portrait Gallery, London

Swettenham, Sir Frank Athelstane (1850-1946)—© National Portrait Gallery, London

Swift, Jonathan (1667-1745)—by courtesy of the National Gallery of Ireland

Swift, Dame Sarah Ann (1854-1937)—Guy's and St Thomas' Charitable Foundation

Swinburne, Algernon Charles (1837-1909)—© National Portrait Gallery, London

Swinburne, Sir James, ninth baronet (1858-1958)—© National Portrait Gallery, London

Swiney, (Rosa) Frances Emily (1847-1922)—Mary Evans / The Women's Library

Swinnerton, Frank Arthur (1884-1982)—© National Portrait Gallery, London

Swinton, Sir Ernest Dunlop (1868-1951)—Tank Museum, Dorset

Swiny, Owen (1676-1754)—© National Portrait Gallery, London

Sydenham, Thomas (bap. 1624, d. 1689)—© National Portrait Gallery, London

Syfret, Sir (Edward) Neville (1889-1972)—© National Portrait Gallery, London

Sykes, Sir Alan John (1868-1950)—© reserved

Sykes, John Bradbury (1929-1993)—© News International Newspapers Ltd

Sykes, Sir Mark, sixth baronet (1879-1919)—private collection. Photograph: Photographic Survey, Courtauld Institute of Art, London

Sykes, Sir Percy Molesworth (1867-1945)—© National Portrait Gallery, London

Sylvester, James Joseph (1814-1897)—© National Portrait Gallery, London

Sylvester, Josuah (1562/3-1618)—© National Portrait Gallery, London

Syme, Sir Ronald (1903-1989)—© courtesy the Artist's Estate / Bridgeman Art Library; The Royal Collection © 2004 HM Queen Elizabeth II

Symes, Sir (George) Stewart (1882-1962)—© National Portrait Gallery, London

Symonds, John Addington (1840-1893)—© National Portrait Gallery, London

Symonds, Richard (bap. 1617, d. 1660)—The College of Arms

Symonds, Sir William (1782-1856)—© National Portrait Gallery, London

Symons, Alphonse James Albert (1900-1941)—© Wyndham Lewis Memorial